HOLT
ELEMENTS OF
LITERATURE

Third Course

HOLT, RINEHART AND WINSTON

A Harcourt Education Company

Orlando • Austin • New York • San Diego • Toronto • London

EDITORIAL
Editorial Vice President: Laura Wood
Project Directors: Kathleen Daniel, Mescal Evler
Executive Editors: Kristine E. Marshall, Laura Mongello
Senior Editors: John Haffner Layden, Susan Lynch, Kathryn Rogers, Jennifer Tench, Hester Weeden
Managing Editor: Marie Price
Senior Product Manager: Don Wulbrecht
Editorial Staff: Abraham Chang, Steven Fechter, Christine Han, Jennifer Schwan, Crystal Wirth, Michael Zakhar
Copyediting Manager: Michael Neibergall
Copyediting Supervisor: Mary Malone
Copyeditors: Christine Altgelt, Elizabeth Dickson, Emily Force, Leora Harris, Anne Heausler, Julia Thomas Hu, Kathleen Scheiner, Nancy Shore
Associate Managing Editors: Lori De La Garza, Elizabeth LaManna
Editorial Support: Christine Degollado, Danielle Greer, Erik Netcher
Editorial Permissions: Carrie Jones, Susan Lowrance, Erik Netcher

ART, DESIGN, AND PRODUCTION
Director: Athena Blackorby
Senior Design Director: Betty Mintz
Design and Composition: Preface, Inc.
Prepress: H&S Graphics, Inc.
Production Manager: Carol Trammel

COVER
Photo Credits: (Inset) *Fisherman at Sea* (ca. 1913) by Henry Ossawa Tanner. Oil on canvas. Copyright Smithsonian American Art Museum, Washington, D.C./Art Resource, NY. (Background) Lightning. © Steve Bloom/Getty Images.

	Collection 1	Collection 2	Collection 3	Collection 4	Collection 5	Collection 6
Literary Response	Analyze plot structure and development of time and sequence. Analyze setting and how it affects character, mood, and tone.	Analyze characterization. Analyze character traits, internal and external conflicts, and motivation.	Analyze narrators, or points of view (omniscient, first person, and third-person limited), tone, and voice.	Analyze theme. Compare universal themes. Compare and contrast themes across genres.	Analyze irony (verbal, situational, and dramatic), ambiguity, contradictions, and the surprise ending.	Analyze symbolism and allegory.
Reading Informational Text	Generate research questions. Use research sources, including print sources and the Internet.	Use primary and secondary sources.	Synthesize information from several sources on a single topic.	Synthesize information from several sources on a single topic. Analyze characteristics of news features. Distinguish between fact and opinion.	Evaluate an author's argument and evidence.	Synthesize information from several sources (by one author) on a single topic.
Vocabulary	Use prefixes to understand word meanings. Understand connotations of synonyms. Understand word derivations. Identify words from myths. Create a vocabulary resource file. Understand multiple-meaning words.	Understand shades of meanings of synonyms. Create semantic maps. Understand word derivations. Understand word analogies. Understand figures of speech. Use context clues.	Use context clues. Identify degrees of intensity among synonyms. Create word maps showing etymology, meaning, and context. Understand Greek and Latin roots. Understand synonyms.	Understand word origins. Understand word analogies. Create semantic charts. Use a thesaurus to find synonyms. Identify denotations and connotations. Understand multiple-meaning words.	Understand diction. Use context clues. Understand synonyms.	Identify and interpret similes. Identify denotations and connotations. Understand word origins. Create semantic maps. Use context clues.
Writing, Listening, and Speaking	Write an autobiographical narrative. Present an oral narrative.	Write a short story.	Write an expository essay analyzing a biography.	Write an essay comparing and contrasting news media.	Write a persuasive essay. Debate an issue.	Write a descriptive essay. Present a description.

Third Course Program Organization

	Collection 7	Collection 8	Collection 9	Collection 10	Collection 11	Collection 12
Literary Response	Analyze and interpret characteristics and types of poetry.	Analyze elements of style, including figurative language, imagery, mood, tone, diction, and sentence structure.	Analyze a literary work using biographical and historical approaches. Analyze historical setting.	Analyze characteristics of epic poetry. Analyze characteristics of myths. Analyze how a work of literature is related to its historical period.	Analyze and interpret drama.	
Reading Informational Text		Evaluate the credibility of opposing arguments.	Use primary and secondary sources.	Evaluate an author's argument and evidence.	Synthesize information from several sources on a single topic.	Analyze elements of consumer documents. Analyze technical directions. Analyze the structure, format, and logic of workplace documents.
Vocabulary	Create a word bank. Understand multiple meanings of words.	Understand Greek and Latin prefixes and root words. Create semantic maps. Understand denotations and connotations. Use context clues.	Complete word analogies. Create semantic maps. Understand jargon, or technical vocabulary.	Create semantic maps. Understand Homeric (epic) similes. Understand synonyms. Understand epithets. Understand words from Greek and Roman myths. Use context clues. Understand idioms. Understand words from Norse myths.	Create semantic maps. Understand word origins. Understand figures of speech. Understand the history of the English language. Understand denotations and connotations. Understand multiple-meaning words.	
Writing, Listening, and Speaking	Write an analysis of a poem. Present an oral interpretation of a poem.	Write an analysis of a short story.	Write a research paper. Present a research report.	Write a persuasive cause-and-effect essay.	Write an essay comparing a play and a film.	Write a business letter and the minutes of a meeting.

LITERARY SKILLS	Grade 6	Grade 7	Grade 8	Grade 9	Grade 10	Grade 11	Grade 12
Alexandrine							■
Allegory				■	■	■	■
Alliteration	■	■	■	■	■	■	■
Allusion	■	■	■	■	■	■	■
Ambiguity				■	■	■	
American Indian oratory						■	
Analogy		■	■	■	■	■	■
Anecdote	■	■	■			■	■
Antagonist			■	■	■	■	■
Anticlimax							■
Antithesis							■
Aphorism						■	■
Apostrophe							■
Approximate rhyme			■	■	■	■	
Archetype						■	■
Argument					■	■	
Arthurian legend		■			■		■
Aside				■	■		
Assonance			■	■		■	■
Atmosphere		■	■	■	■	■	■
Autobiography	■	■	■	■	■	■	■
Ballad			■	■	■	■	■
Biography	■	■	■	■	■	■	■
Blank Verse				■	■	■	■
Cadence						■	
Caesura							■
Carpe Diem							■
Catalog poem				■		■	■
Character	■	■	■	■	■	■	■

Program Scope and Sequence

LITERARY SKILLS	Grade 6	Grade 7	Grade 8	Grade 9	Grade 10	Grade 11	Grade 12
Character interactions		■		■	■		
Character traits	■	■	■	■	■		
Characterization	■	■	■	■	■	■	■
Chronological order	■	■	■	■	■	■	
Classicism							■
Climax	■	■	■	■	■	■	■
Comedy			■	■	■	■	■
Comic devices			■			■	
Comparing texts	■	■	■	■	■	■	■
Conceit							■
Conflict	■	■	■	■	■	■	■
Connotation	■	■	■	■	■	■	■
Contradiction				■	■		
Couplet		■	■	■	■	■	■
Deism						■	■
Denotation	■	■	■	■	■	■	■
Denouement				■	■	■	■
Description	■	■	■	■	■	■	■
Dialect	■	■	■	■	■	■	■
Dialogue	■	■	■	■	■	■	■
Diction			■	■	■	■	■
Didactic literature	■	■	■				■
Direct characterization	■	■	■	■	■		
Drama	■	■	■	■	■		■
Dramatic irony			■	■	■	■	■
Dramatic monologue				■	■	■	■
Elegy		■	■			■	■
End rhyme	■	■	■	■	■		
Epic			■	■			■

LITERARY SKILLS	Grade 6	Grade 7	Grade 8	Grade 9	Grade 10	Grade 11	Grade 12
Epic conventions							■
Epic hero			■	■			■
Epic simile							■
Epigram							■
Epiphany							■
Epitaph							■
Essay	■	■	■	■	■	■	■
Exposition		■	■	■	■	■	■
Extended metaphor	■	■	■	■	■	■	■
External conflict	■	■	■	■	■	■	■
Fable	■	■	■	■	■		■
Farce					■		
Fiction	■	■	■				
Figurative language	■	■	■	■	■	■	■
First-person narrator	■	■		■	■	■	■
First-person point of view	■	■	■	■	■	■	■
Flashback	■	■	■	■	■	■	■
Flash-forward		■		■	■		
Flat character				■	■		
Foil				■	■		
Folk tale	■	■	■	■			
Foreshadowing	■	■	■	■	■	■	■
Frame story						■	■
Free verse	■	■	■	■	■	■	■
Gothic tale						■	■
Haiku	■				■		■
Harlem Renaissance	■		■			■	
Historical context	■			■	■	■	■
Historical fiction		■	■				

LITERARY SKILLS	Grade 6	Grade 7	Grade 8	Grade 9	Grade 10	Grade 11	Grade 12
Humanism							■
Hyperbole	■					■	■
Iambic pentameter		■	■	■	■	■	■
Idiom	■	■	■	■	■	■	
Imagery	■	■	■	■	■	■	■
Implied metaphor			■	■	■	■	
Indirect characterization		■	■	■	■		
Interior monologue						■	
Internal conflict	■	■	■	■	■	■	■
Internal rhyme	■	■	■	■	■	■	
Inversion			■		■	■	
Irony	■	■	■		■	■	■
Kenning							■
Legend	■	■	■		■		
Literary criticism	■	■	■	■	■	■	■
Lyric poetry		■	■	■	■	■	■
Magic realism					■	■	■
Main idea	■	■	■	■	■	■	■
Memoir	■	■				■	■
Metamorphosis	■	■	■			■	
Metaphor	■	■	■	■	■	■	■
Metaphysical poetry							■
Meter	■	■	■	■	■	■	■
Metonymy							■
Mock epic			■				■
Modernism						■	■
Mood	■	■	■	■	■	■	■
Motif	■	■	■				■
Motivation	■	■	■	■	■	■	■

LITERARY SKILLS	Grade 6	Grade 7	Grade 8	Grade 9	Grade 10	Grade 11	Grade 12
Myth	■	■	■	■	■	■	■
Narration	■	■	■	■	■	■	■
Narrative	■	■	■			■	
Narrative poem	■	■	■	■	■	■	
Narrator	■	■	■	■	■	■	■
Naturalism						■	
Neoclassicism							■
Nonfiction	■	■	■	■	■	■	■
Objective writing		■	■		■	■	
Ode	■	■	■		■		■
Omniscient narrator		■		■	■	■	■
Omniscient point of view		■	■	■	■	■	■
Onomatopoeia	■	■	■	■	■	■	■
Ottava rima							■
Oxymoron							■
Parable					■	■	■
Paradox						■	■
Parallelism				■	■	■	■
Parody						■	■
Pastoral							■
Persona				■	■		
Personification	■	■	■	■	■	■	■
Persuasion	■	■		■	■	■	■
Plain style						■	
Plot	■	■	■	■	■		■
Poetry	■	■	■	■	■	■	■
Point of view	■	■	■	■	■	■	■
Postmodernism						■	■
Protagonist	■	■	■	■	■	■	■

LITERARY SKILLS	Grade 6	Grade 7	Grade 8	Grade 9	Grade 10	Grade 11	Grade 12
Proverb						■	■
Rationalism						■	■
Realism						■	■
Refrain	■	■	■	■	■	■	■
Regionalism						■	
Renaissance							■
Repetition	■	■	■	■	■	■	
Resolution	■	■	■	■	■	■	■
Rhyme	■	■	■	■	■	■	■
Rhyme scheme	■	■	■	■	■	■	■
Rhythm	■	■	■	■	■	■	■
Romance					■	■	■
Romanticism						■	■
Round character				■	■		
Satire			■	■	■	■	■
Scene design			■	■	■		
Setting	■	■	■	■		■	■
Short story	■	■	■	■	■	■	■
Simile	■	■	■	■	■	■	■
Situational irony			■	■	■	■	■
Slant rhyme		■				■	
Soliloquy			■	■	■		■
Sonnet		■	■	■	■	■	■
Sound effects	■	■		■	■	■	
Speaker	■	■	■	■	■	■	■
Speech		■	■	■	■	■	■
Spenserian stanza							■
Stanza	■	■	■				
Static character		■	■	■	■		

LITERARY SKILLS	Grade 6	Grade 7	Grade 8	Grade 9	Grade 10	Grade 11	Grade 12
Stereotype						■	
Stock character					■	■	
Stream of consciousness						■	■
Style			■	■	■	■	■
Subjective writing		■	■		■	■	
Subplots			■				
Surprise ending	■			■			
Suspense	■	■	■	■	■		
Symbol	■	■	■	■		■	■
Synesthesia						■	■
Tall tale	■	■	■			■	
Tanka					■		■
Teleplay	■	■	■				
Terza rima							■
Theme	■	■	■	■	■	■	■
Third-person limited point of view	■	■		■	■		
Title	■	■	■	■	■	■	
Tone	■	■	■	■	■	■	■
Tragedy			■	■	■		■
Tragic hero				■			
Transcendentalism						■	
Understatement			■			■	■
Universal themes			■	■	■		
Unreliable narrator			■	■	■		
Verbal irony			■	■	■	■	
Vernacular						■	■
Villanelle						■	■
Voice				■	■		

READING SKILLS	Grade 6	Grade 7	Grade 8	Grade 9	Grade 10	Grade 11	Grade 12
Anachronism					■		
Analogy		■	■	■	■	■	■
Application forms	■	■					
Argument		■		■	■	■	■
Assertions	■					■	
Author's opinion				■	■	■	■
Author's purpose	■	■	■	■	■	■	■
Bias		■		■	■		■
Cause and effect	■	■	■	■	■	■	
Chronological order	■	■	■	■	■	■	■
Claim				■	■	■	■
Coherence			■	■	■	■	■
Comparing texts	■	■	■	■	■	■	■
Comparison and contrast	■	■	■	■	■	■	■
Connotation	■	■	■	■	■	■	■
Consumer documents		■	■	■	■		
Context clues	■	■	■	■	■	■	■
Credibility				■	■	■	■
Denotation	■	■	■	■	■	■	■
Drawing conclusions	■	■	■	■	■	■	■
Emotional appeals	■	■		■	■	■	■
Evaluating evidence	■	■	■	■	■	■	■
Evaluating historical accuracy			■				
Evidence	■	■	■	■	■	■	■
Fact	■	■	■	■	■		
Fallacious reasoning	■	■	■	■	■	■	■
Generalizations	■	■	■	■	■	■	■
Generating research questions				■	■		
Graphic features	■	■	■	■	■	■	■

READING SKILLS	Grade 6	Grade 7	Grade 8	Grade 9	Grade 10	Grade 11	Grade 12
Graphic organizers	■	■	■	■	■	■	■
Graphs	■	■	■	■	■	■	■
Historical context	■	■	■	■	■	■	■
Idiom	■	■	■	■	■		
Inferences	■	■	■	■	■	■	■
Informative texts	■	■	■	■	■	■	■
Internet sources	■	■	■	■	■	■	■
Inversion				■		■	
Judgments			■				
Logic	■	■	■	■	■	■	■
Logical appeals	■	■		■	■	■	■
Logical order			■	■	■	■	■
Main idea	■	■	■	■	■	■	■
Maps	■	■	■	■	■	■	■
Monitor reading	■	■	■	■	■	■	■
Note taking	■	■	■	■	■	■	■
Objective writing		■	■		■	■	
Opinion	■	■	■	■	■	■	■
Outlining	■	■	■	■	■	■	■
Paraphrasing	■	■	■	■	■	■	
Persuasion	■	■	■	■	■	■	■
Predictions	■	■	■	■	■	■	■
Previewing			■				
Primary sources				■	■	■	■
Prior knowledge	■	■	■			■	
Propaganda	■	■					
Proposition and support			■				
Public documents		■	■	■	■	■	■
Purpose of texts	■	■	■				

READING SKILLS	Grade 6	Grade 7	Grade 8	Grade 9	Grade 10	Grade 11	Grade 12
Questioning			■				
Reading for details	■	■	■	■	■	■	■
Reading for information	■	■	■	■	■	■	■
Reading poetry	■	■	■	■	■	■	■
Reading rate	■	■		■	■	■	■
Researching information	■				■	■	
Retelling	■	■	■			■	
Rhetorical devices						■	■
Secondary sources				■	■	■	
Stereotyping		■	■				
Subjective writing		■			■	■	
Summarizing	■	■	■	■	■	■	■
Syntax				■	■		
Synthesizing sources				■	■		
Text structures	■	■	■	■	■	■	■
Vernacular						■	
Visualizing	■		■	■	■		
Workplace documents		■	■	■	■		
Writer's perspective		■		■	■	■	■

VOCABULARY SKILLS	Grade 6	Grade 7	Grade 8	Grade 9	Grade 10	Grade 11	Grade 12
Affixes	■	■	■	■	■	■	■
Analogies		■	■	■	■	■	■
Anglo–Saxon roots and affixes	■	■	■	■	■	■	■
Antonyms	■		■	■	■	■	■
Archaic words					■		
Borrowed words	■	■	■	■	■		
Connotations	■	■	■	■	■	■	■

VOCABULARY SKILLS	Grade 6	Grade 7	Grade 8	Grade 9	Grade 10	Grade 11	Grade 12
Context clues	■	■	■	■	■	■	■
Definition	■	■	■				
Denotations	■	■	■	■	■	■	■
Dialect	■	■	■	■	■	■	■
Diction			■	■			
Dictionary	■	■		■	■		
Epithets				■		■	■
Etymology	■	■	■	■	■	■	■
Figurative language	■	■	■	■	■	■	■
Foreign words used in English	■	■	■	■	■		
Greek roots and affixes	■	■		■	■	■	■
History of English language			■	■			
Homographs			■				
Homophones			■				
Idioms	■	■	■	■	■	■	
Indo-European roots			■	■			
Informal words			■	■	■		
Jargon				■	■		
Latin roots and affixes	■	■	■	■	■	■	■
Metaphor	■	■	■	■	■	■	■
Multiple-meaning words	■	■	■	■	■	■	■
Personification	■	■	■	■	■	■	■
Prefixes	■	■			■	■	■
Puns			■		■		
Restatement		■	■				
Root words	■	■	■	■	■	■	■
Semantic maps	■			■	■		■
Simile	■	■	■	■	■	■	■
Suffixes	■	■		■	■	■	■

VOCABULARY SKILLS	Grade 6	Grade 7	Grade 8	Grade 9	Grade 10	Grade 11	Grade 12
Synonyms	■	■	■	■	■	■	■
Technical vocabulary				■	■		
Thesaurus	■	■	■	■	■		■
Word derivations	■	■	■	■	■	■	■
Word knowledge	■	■	■	■	■	■	■
Word maps	■	■	■	■	■	■	■
Word origins	■	■	■	■	■	■	■
Word trees	■	■					

WRITING SKILLS	Grade 6	Grade 7	Grade 8	Grade 9	Grade 10	Grade 11	Grade 12
WRITING MODE							
Analyze a biography				■			
Analyze a character			■				
Analyze a novel						■	
Analyze a poem				■			■
Analyze a short story				■	■	■	
Analyze nonfiction						■	■
Analyze works of literature							■
Autobiographical narrative				■	■	■	
Biographical narrative					■	■	
Business letter				■	■		
Compare and contrast media genres				■	■		
Compare and contrast two literary works							■
Comparison–contrast essay	■	■	■				
Descriptive essay	■	■		■	■	■	■
Editorial						■	
Historical research report						■	
Informative report		■	■				
Literary research paper							■
Minutes of a meeting				■			

WRITING SKILLS	Grade 6	Grade 7	Grade 8	Grade 9	Grade 10	Grade 11	Grade 12
Personal narrative	■	■	■				
Persuasive cause-and-effect essay				■			
Persuasive essay	■	■	■	■	■		■
Problem-solution essay	■	■	■		■		
Reflective essay						■	■
Report	■						
Research paper				■	■		
Short story	■	■	■	■	■	■	■
Technical documents					■		
WRITING PROCESS							
Prewriting							
Choose topic	■	■	■	■	■	■	■
Identify purpose	■	■	■	■	■	■	■
Identify audience	■	■	■	■	■	■	■
Generate ideas	■	■	■	■	■	■	■
Gather information	■	■	■	■	■	■	■
Organize information	■	■	■	■	■	■	■
Draft thesis statement	■	■	■	■	■	■	■
Writing a draft							
State main point	■	■	■	■	■	■	■
Include relevant support	■	■	■	■	■	■	■
Include elaboration	■	■	■	■	■	■	■
Follow plan of elaboration	■	■	■	■	■	■	■
Revising							
Revise for content	■	■	■	■	■	■	■
Revise for style	■	■	■	■	■	■	■
Publishing							
Proofread for grammar, usage, and mechanics	■	■	■	■	■	■	■
Publish or share writing	■	■	■	■	■	■	■
Reflect on the writing experience	■	■	■	■	■	■	■

Program Scope and Sequence

LISTENING and SPEAKING SKILLS	Grade 6	Grade 7	Grade 8	Grade 9	Grade 10	Grade 11	Grade 12
LISTENING AND SPEAKING MODE							
Debate an issue				■	■	■	■
Informative speech	■	■	■				
Multimedia presentation	■			■	■		
Oral autobiographical narrative				■	■		■
Oral descriptive essay				■		■	■
Oral interpretation of a poem				■		■	
Oral narrative	■	■	■	■		■	
Oral problem-solution essay	■						
Oral recitation of literature		■	■	■	■	■	■
Oral reflective essay						■	■
Oral research report				■	■	■	■
Oral response to a literary work	■		■	■	■	■	■
Persuasive speech	■	■	■	■	■	■	■
LISTENING AND SPEAKING PROCESS							
Analyze a documentary		■					
Analyze and evaluate a speech	■	■	■	■	■	■	■
Analyze content	■	■	■	■	■	■	■
Analyze delivery	■	■	■	■	■	■	■
Analyze electronic journalism		■					
Analyze organization	■	■	■	■	■	■	■
Analyze strategies used by media	■		■	■	■	■	■
Plan and organize speech or presentation	■	■	■	■	■	■	■
Rehearse and deliver speech or presentation	■	■	■	■	■	■	■
Understand and identify logical fallacies				■		■	■
Understand and identify propaganda techniques	■			■		■	■
Use rhetorical techniques				■		■	■
Use verbal and nonverbal techniques	■	■	■	■	■	■	■

MEDIA SKILLS	Grade 6	Grade 7	Grade 8	Grade 9	Grade 10	Grade 11	Grade 12
Analyze and use media	■	■	■	■	■	■	■
Analyze a documentary		■					
Analyze electronic journalism		■					
Analyze strategies used by media	■		■	■	■	■	■
Compare and contrast media genres				■	■		
Create graphics for technical documents			■				
Multimedia presentation	■			■	■	■	■
Use electronic texts to locate information	■						

MINIMUM COURSE OF STUDY

	Literature	Informational Text	Writing Workshop	Listening and Speaking Workshop
COLLECTION 1	• "The Most Dangerous Game"	• "Can Animals Think?"	• Writing an Autobiographical Narrative	
COLLECTION 2	• "Thank You, M'am"	• "Teaching Chess, and Life" • "Community Service & You" • "Feeding Frenzy"		
COLLECTION 3	• "The Interlopers" • "The Cask of Amontillado"	• "Poe's Final Days" • "Poe's Death Is Rewritten as Case of Rabies, Not Telltale Alcohol" • "If Only Poe Had Succeeded When He Said Nevermore to Drink" • "Rabies Death Theory"		
COLLECTION 4	• "The Sniper" • "Cranes"	• "A Country Divided" • "Lives in Crossfire" • "Internment" • "Peace Isn't Possible"		
COLLECTION 5	• "The Gift of the Magi" • "The Lady, or the Tiger?"	• "A Defense of the Jury System"	• Writing a Persuasive Essay	
COLLECTION 6	• "The Scarlet Ibis" • "The Golden Kite, the Silver Wind"			
COLLECTION 7	• "A Blessing" • "The Seven Ages of Man" • "Women" • "I Wandered Lonely as a Cloud" • "Legal Alien / Extranjera legal"			
COLLECTION 8	• "A Sound of Thunder"	• "Rising Tides" • "An Arctic Floe of Climate Questions"	• Analyzing a Short Story	
COLLECTION 9	• "American History"		• Writing a Research Paper	
COLLECTION 10	• from the *Odyssey*, Part One			• Giving a Persuasive Speech
COLLECTION 11	• *The Tragedy of Romeo and Juliet*, The Prologue, Acts I and II			• Analyzing and Evaluating Speeches
COLLECTION 12		• Reading Consumer Documents • Following Technical Directions	• Writing Business Letters	

Program Authors

Kylene Beers established the reading pedagogy for *Elements of Literature*. A former middle-school teacher, Dr. Beers has turned her commitment to helping readers having difficulty into the major focus of her research, writing, speaking, and teaching. Dr. Beers is currently Senior Reading Researcher at the Child Study Center of the School Development Program at Yale University and was formerly a Research Associate Professor at the University of Houston. Dr. Beers is also currently the editor of the National Council of Teachers of English journal *Voices from the Middle*. She is the author of *When Kids Can't Read: What Teachers Can Do* and the co-editor of *Into Focus: Understanding and Creating Middle School Readers*. Dr. Beers is the 2001 recipient of the Richard Halle Award from the NCTE for outstanding contributions to middle-level literacy education. She has served on the review boards of the *English Journal* and *The Alan Review*. Dr. Beers currently serves on the board of directors of the International Reading Association's Special Interest Group on Adolescent Literature.

Lee Odell helped establish the pedagogical framework for writing, listening, and speaking for *Elements of Literature*. Dr. Odell is Professor of Composition Theory and Research and, since 1996, Director of the Writing Program at Rensselaer Polytechnic Institute. He began his career teaching English in middle and high schools. More recently he has worked with teachers in grades K–12 to establish a program that involves students from all disciplines in writing across the curriculum and for communities outside their classrooms. Dr. Odell's most recent book (with Charles R. Cooper) is *Evaluating Writing: The Role of Teachers' Knowledge About Text, Learning, and Culture*. He is past chair of the Conference on College Composition and Communication and of NCTE's Assembly for Research. Dr. Odell is currently working on a college-level writing textbook.

Writers

Robert Anderson is a playwright, novelist, screenwriter, and teacher. His plays include *Tea and Sympathy; Silent Night, Lonely Night; You Know I Can't Hear You When the Water's Running;* and *I Never Sang for My Father*. His screenplays include *The Nun's Story* and *The Sand Pebbles*. Mr. Anderson has taught at the Writers' Workshop at the University of Iowa, the American Theater Wing Professional Training Program, and the Salzburg Seminar in American Studies. He is a past president of the Dramatists Guild of America, a past vice president of the Authors League of America, and a member of the Theater Hall of Fame.

John Malcolm Brinnin, author of six volumes of poetry that have received many prizes and awards, was a member of the American Academy and Institute of Arts and Letters. He was a critic of poetry, a biographer of poets, and for a number of years the director of New York's famous Poetry Center. His teaching career included terms at Vassar College, the University of Connecticut, and Boston University, where he succeeded Robert Lowell as Professor of Creative Writing and Contemporary Letters. Mr. Brinnin wrote *Dylan Thomas in America:*

Flo Ota De Lange and **Sheri Henderson**

Flo Ota De Lange is a former teacher with a thirty-year second career in psychotherapy, during which she studied learning processes in children and adults. Those careers led to her third career, as a writer.

Sheri Henderson brings to the program twenty years of experience as a California middle-school research practitioner and full-time reading and language arts teacher at La Paz International School in Saddleback Valley Unified School District. She regularly speaks at statewide and national conferences.

Since 1991, DeLangeHenderson LLC has published forty-three titles designed to integrate the teaching of literature with standards requirements and state and national tests.

Madeline Travers Hovland, who taught language arts for several years, is a writer of educational materials. She studied English at Bates College and received a master's degree in education from Harvard University.

John Leggett is a novelist, biographer, and former teacher. He went to the Writers' Workshop at the University of Iowa in the spring of 1969.

In 1970, he assumed temporary charge of the program, and for the next seventeen years he was its director. Mr. Leggett's novels include *Wilder Stone, The Gloucester Branch, Who Took the Gold Away?, Gulliver House,* and *Making Believe.* He is also the author of the highly acclaimed biography *Ross and Tom: Two American Tragedies* and of a biography of William Saroyan, *A Daring Young Man.* Mr. Leggett lives in Napa Valley, California.

David Adams Leeming was for many years a Professor of English and Comparative Literature at the University of Connecticut. He is the author of several books on mythology, including *Mythology: The Voyage of the Hero; The World of Myth;* and *Encyclopedia of Creation Myths.* For several years, Dr. Leeming taught English at Robert College in Istanbul, Turkey. He also served as secretary and assistant to the writer James Baldwin in New York and Istanbul. He has published the biographies *James Baldwin* and *Amazing Grace: A Life of Beauford Delaney.*

Mara Rockliff is a writer and editor with a degree in American civilization from Brown University. She has written dramatizations of classic stories, collected in a book called *Stories for Performance.* She has also published feature stories in national newspapers and is currently writing a novel for young adults.

Diane Tasca, a graduate of Temple University, earned a doctorate in English from the University of Illinois. Over the past thirty years, Dr. Tasca has taught various college courses in composition, literature, and performance and has developed, written, and edited instructional materials for high school and college language arts textbooks. A member of the San Francisco Bay Area theater community, she has performed in numerous plays and assisted playwrights with the development of new dramatic works. She currently teaches drama at Foothill College in Los Altos Hills, California.

Senior Program Consultant

Carol Jago is the editor of CATE's quarterly journal, *California English*. She teaches English at Santa Monica High School, in Santa Monica, and directs the California Reading and Literature Project at UCLA. She writes a weekly education column for the *Los Angeles Times*. She is the author of several books, including three in a series on contemporary writers in the classroom: *Alice Walker in the Classroom*; *Nikki Giovanni in the Classroom*; and *Sandra Cisneros in the Classroom*. She is also the author of *With Rigor for All: Teaching the Classics to Contemporary Students; Beyond Standards: Excellence in the High School English Classroom*; and *Cohesive Writing: Why Concept Is Not Enough.*

ADVISORS

Cynthia A. Arceneaux
Administrative Coordinator
Office of Deputy Superintendent,
    Instructional Services
Los Angeles Unified School District
Los Angeles, California

Dr. Julie M. T. Chan
Director of Literacy Instruction
Newport-Mesa Unified School
    District
Costa Mesa, California

Al Desmarais
English Department Chair and
    Curriculum Specialist in
    Language Arts
El Toro High School
Saddleback Valley Unified School
    District
Lake Forest, California

José M. Ibarra-Tiznado
ELL Program Coordinator
Bassett Unified School District
La Puente, California

Dr. Ronald Klemp
Instructor
California State University,
    Northridge
Northridge, California

Fern M. Sheldon
K–12 Curriculum and Instruction
    Specialist
Rowland Unified School District
Rowland Heights, California

Jim Shields
Instructor
El Toro High School
Saddleback Valley Unified School
    District
Lake Forest, California

CRITICAL REVIEWERS

Paulette Dewey
Toledo Public School
Toledo, Ohio

R. E. Fisher
Westlake High School
Atlanta, Georgia

Janice Gauthier
Everett High School
Everett, Massachusetts

Kimberly Hoelterhoff
Temple City High School
Temple City, California

Victor Jaccarino
Herricks High School
New Hyde Park, New York

Barbara Kimbrough
Kane Area High School
Kane, Pennsylvania

Dr. Louisa Kramer-Vida
Oyster Bay-East Norwich SD
Oyster Bay, New York

Cynthia Marr
Arlington High School
Riverside, California

Faith Nitschke
Hoover High School
Fresno, California

Toni Lee Olson
Nogales High School
La Puente, California

Norm Rush
Chaffey High School
Ontario, California

Mary Ellen Snodgrass
Hickory High School
Hickory, North Carolina

David Trimble
Norwin High School
N. Huntingdon, Pennsylvania

Donna Walthour
Greensburg Salem High School
Greensburg, Pennsylvania

John Williamson
Ft. Thomas Schools
Ft. Thomas, Kentucky

FIELD-TEST PARTICIPANTS

Sandra J. Gilligan
Passaic High School
Passaic, New Jersey

Lee Lowery
Highlands High School
Fort Thomas, Kentucky

Pamela Rockich
Barberton High School
Barberton, Ohio

Ellen Schunks
North County High School
Bonne Terre, Missouri

Casey Williams
Highlands High School
Fort Thomas, Kentucky

CONTENTS IN BRIEF

Collection 1

PLOT AND SETTING

INFORMATIONAL READING FOCUS

GENERATING RESEARCH QUESTIONS

Collection 2

CHARACTER

INFORMATIONAL READING FOCUS

USING PRIMARY AND SECONDARY SOURCES

Collection 3

Narrator and Voice

INFORMATIONAL READING FOCUS

SYNTHESIZING
SOURCES

Collection 4

COMPARING THEMES

INFORMATIONAL READING FOCUS

SYNTHESIZING
SOURCES

Collection 5

IRONY and AMBIGUITY

INFORMATIONAL READING FOCUS

EVALUATING AN
ARGUMENT

Collection 6

Symbolism and Allegory

INFORMATIONAL READING FOCUS

SYNTHESIZING
SOURCES

Collection 7

Poetry

FIGURES OF SPEECH

Elements of Literature

■ **Figures of Speech: Seeing Connections**

THE SOUNDS OF POETRY

Elements of Literature

■ **The Sounds of Poetry: Rhyme, Rhythm, and More**

Collection 8

LITERARY CRITICISM

Evaluating Style

INFORMATIONAL READING FOCUS

EVALUATING ARGUMENTS:
PRO AND CON

Collection 9

LITERARY CRITICISM

BIOGRAPHICAL AND HISTORICAL APPROACH

INFORMATIONAL READING FOCUS

USING PRIMARY AND SECONDARY SOURCES

Collection 10

Epic and Myth

INFORMATIONAL READING FOCUS

EVALUATING AN
ARGUMENT

COLLECTION 10: SKILLS REVIEW

Collection 11

DRAMA

INFORMATIONAL READING FOCUS

SYNTHESIZING SOURCES

Collection 12

CONSUMER AND WORKPLACE DOCUMENTS

THE WORLD OF COMPUTER GAME DEVELOPMENT

by Flo Ota De Lange *and*
Sheri Henderson

Resource Center

SKILLS, WORKSHOPS, AND FEATURES

SKILLS

ELEMENTS OF LITERATURE ESSAYS

LITERARY SKILLS

READING SKILLS
FOR LITERARY TEXTS

READING MATTERS

READING SKILLS
FOR INFORMATIONAL TEXTS

VOCABULARY SKILLS

WORKSHOPS

WRITING WORKSHOPS

LISTENING AND SPEAKING WORKSHOPS

FEATURES

A CLOSER LOOK

GRAMMAR LINK

LANGUAGE HANDBOOK

SKILLS REVIEW

TEST SMARTS

WRITER'S HANDBOOK

SELECTIONS BY GENRE

FICTION

DRAMA

COMEDY

TRAGEDY

POETRY

EPIC

SONG

NONFICTION AND INFORMATIONAL TEXT

AUTOBIOGRAPHY

BIOGRAPHY

ENCYCLOPEDIA ARTICLE

HISTORY BOOK

INTERVIEW

Elements of Literature on the Internet

TO THE STUDENT

At the *Elements of Literature* Internet site, you can read texts by professional writers and learn the inside stories behind your favorite authors. You can also build your word power and analyze messages in the media. As you move through *Elements of Literature*, you will find the best online resources at **go.hrw.com**.

Here's how to log on:

1. Start your Web browser, and enter **go.hrw.com** in the Address or Location field.

2. Note the keyword in your textbook.

INTERNET

More About Plot

Keyword: LE5 9-1

3. Enter the keyword and click "go."

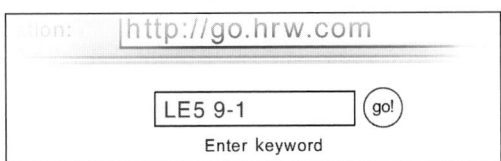

FEATURES OF THE SITE

More About the Writer
Author biographies provide the inside stories behind the lives and works of great writers.

More About the Literary Element
Graphic organizers present visual representations of literary concepts.

Interactive Reading Model
Interactive Reading Workshops guide you through high-interest informational articles and allow you to share your opinions through pop-up questions and polls.

More Writer's Models
Interactive Writer's Models present annotations and reading tips to help you with your own writing. Printable Professional Models and Student Models provide you with quality writing by real writers and students from across the country.

Vocabulary Practice
Interactive vocabulary-building activities help you build your word power.

Projects and Activities
Projects and activities help you extend your study of literature through writing, research, art, and public speaking.

Speeches
Video clips from historical speeches provide you with the tools you need to analyze elements of great speechmaking.

Media Tutorials
Media tutorials help you dissect messages in the media and learn to create your own multimedia presentations.

A Walk Through
Elements of Literature

The *Elements of Literature* program is logically organized and sequenced so that students build literary, reading, writing, vocabulary, and listening and speaking skills. The *Elements of Literature Student Edition* is the primary tool for building knowledge and understanding of these skills. Opportunities for practice and remediation, reteaching, and assessing are offered throughout the program.

Collections

The collections in *Elements of Literature* are organized to cover grade-level skills in literary response and analysis, reading comprehension, writing, vocabulary, and listening and speaking. Each collection has a literary and informational reading focus that appears on the first page of the collection. Each collection also includes a variety of informational texts related to the literary selections, multiple opportunities for students to master each skill, and a review section.

Elements of Literature

An **Elements of Literature** feature illustrates **one key literary element** that is developed in the collection. Examples, excerpts from selections, and diagrams are often used in this feature.

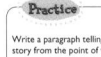

Before You Read

Before You Read precedes every selection, giving students adequate prereading information, motivation, and a purpose for reading. The skills focus is listed on the page so students know what skills they will be learning.

Make the Connection asks students to think or write about issues they will encounter in the literature they are about to read.

Literary Focus enables students to learn about or review a key literary element in the selection.

Reading Skills introduces a skill that will help students' reading comprehension, such as making inferences, summarizing, or making predictions.

Background provides students with necessary information that will help them understand the context of the literature.

Vocabulary Development lists the key vocabulary words from the selection and their definitions.

Directed-Reading questions appear throughout many of the selections. They model the thinking and questioning strategies students need to build strong reading skills.

Before You Read

The Cask of Amontillado

Make the Connection
Quickwrite ✎

Poe was a master at writing stories of revenge. What experiences could lead someone to seek revenge? How could an obsession with vengeance lead to tragedy? Jot down your responses, and include examples from stories or movies.

Literary Focus
Unreliable Narrator

Writers sometimes assume a **persona**, which is a mask or a voice for a first-person narrator. When you read a story told by a **first-person narrator**, you need to ask yourself if you can trust the narrator. Sometimes a writer will purposely use an unreliable narrator to tell a story.

An **unreliable narrator** may not always know the whole truth or may purposely choose to deceive us. A narrator's actions, statements, and **voice**—his or her style of speaking, **diction** (word choice), and **tone** (attitude)—will provide you with clues about his or her reliability.

Reading Skills
Drawing Conclusions

When you read, you act like a detective. You gather evidence and draw **conclusions**, or make judgments, based on that evidence. To decide if the narrator of Poe's story is unreliable, look closely at all the narrator says and does. Then, examine what his enemy, Fortunato, says. What details could support a charge of unreliability—even insanity? The questions at the open-book signs will help you.

go.hrw.com

INTERNET

Vocabulary Practice
•
Cross-Curricular Connection
•
More About Edgar Allan Poe
•
Keyword: LE5 9-3

SKILLS FOCUS

Literary Skills
Understand the first-person narrator and the unreliable narrator.

Reading Skills
Draw conclusions.

Background

Centuries ago Christians in Italy buried their dead in catacombs—long, winding underground tunnels. Later wealthy families built private catacombs beneath their homes. Dark and cool, these chambers were suitable not only for burial but also for the storage of fine wines, such as amontillado (ə·män'tə·lä'dō). Poe's story is set during carnival, which is celebrated before the start of Lent, the season during which Christians give up various pleasures. During carnival, many people wear costumes and dance in the streets.

Vocabulary Development

precluded (prē·klōōd'id) v.: made impossible in advance; prevented.

impunity (im·pyōō'ni·tē) n.: freedom from punishment or harm.

retribution (re'trə·byōō'shən) n.: punishment.

immolation (im'ə·lā'shən) n.: destruction.

connoisseurship (kän'ə·sur'ship) n.: expert knowledge.

impose (im·pōz') v. (used with upon): take advantage of.

recoiling (ri·koil'iŋ) v. used as adj.: moving backward, as in fear.

endeavored (en·dev'ərd) v.: tried.

obstinate (äb'stə·nət) adj.: stubborn.

succession (sək·sesh'ən) n.: series.

172   Collection 3   Narrator and Voice • Synthesizing Sources

---

The thousand in[juries of Fortunato I had] borne as best I [could, but when he ven]tured upon insult, I vowed revenge. You, who so well know the nature of my soul, will not suppose, however, that I gave utterance to a threat. At length I would be avenged; this was a point definitively settled—but the very definitiveness with which it was resolved <u>precluded</u> the idea of risk. I must not only punish, but punish with <u>impunity</u>. A wrong is unredressed[1] when <u>retribution</u> overtakes its redresser. It is equally unredressed when the avenger fails to make himself felt as such to him who has done the wrong.

It must be understood that neither by word nor deed had I given Fortunato cause to doubt my goodwill. I continued, as was my wont, to smile in his face, and he did not perceive that my smile *now* was at the thought of his <u>immolation</u>. 📖

DRAWING CONCLUSIONS

1. What does the narrator's smiling at the thought of Fortunato's death tell you about his character?

He had a weak point—this Fortunato—although in other regards he was a man to be respected and even feared. He prided himself on his <u>connoisseurship</u> in wine. Few Italians have the true virtuoso spirit. For the most part their enthusiasm is adopted to suit the time and opportunity—to practice imposture upon the British and Austrian millionaires. In painting and gemmary, Fortunato, like his countrymen, was a quack—but in the matter of old wines he was sincere. In this respect I did not differ from him materially: I was skillful in the Italian vintages myself and bought largely whenever I could.

It was about dusk, one evening during the supreme madness of the carnival season, that I encountered my friend. He accosted me with excessive warmth, for he had been drinking

---

1. **unredressed** (un'ri·drest') v. used as adj.: not set right or not made up for.

dress, and his head was surmounted by the conical cap and bells. I was so pleased to see him that I thought I should never have done wringing his hand.

I said to him, "My dear Fortunato, you are luckily met. How remarkably well you are looking today! But I have received a pipe[3] of what passes for amontillado, and I have my doubts."

"How?" said he. "Amontillado? A pipe? Impossible! And in the middle of the carnival!"

"I have my doubts," I replied; "and I was silly enough to pay the full amontillado price without consulting you in the matter. You were not to be found, and I was fearful of losing a bargain."

"Amontillado!"

"I have my doubts."

"Amontillado!"

"And I must satisfy them."

"Amontillado!"

"As you are engaged, I am on my way to Luchesi. If anyone has a critical turn, it is he. He will tell me—"

"Luchesi cannot tell amontillado from sherry."

---

2. **motley** (mät'lē) n.: multicolored costume worn by a clown or jester.
3. **pipe** n.: barrel.

Vocabulary

precluded (prē·klōōd'id) v.: made impossible in advance; prevented.

impunity (im·pyōō'ni·tē) n.: freedom from punishment or harm.

retribution (re'trə·byōō'shən) n.: punishment.

immolation (im'ə·lā'shən) n.: destruction.

connoisseurship (kän'ə·sur'ship) n.: expert knowledge.

174   Collection 3   Narrator and Voice • Synthesizing Sources

Meet the Writer

Edgar Allan Poe

A Haunted Life

Edgar Allan Poe (1809–1849) was the son of traveling actors. His father deserted the family, and his beautiful young mother died in a theatrical rooming house in Richmond, Virginia, before Edgar was three years old. The little boy was taken in as a foster child by the wealthy and childless Allan family of Richmond.

At first, Edgar's foster parents were pleased with his brilliant scholarship and athletic ability. But later they became angry at his moodiness and irresponsibility with money. Poe went to the University of Virginia but dropped out with heavy gambling debts. (John Allan apparently refused to support him any longer.) Eventually Poe and his foster father split up completely, and Poe was left penniless. After several failed courtships, Poe married a thirteen-year-old cousin, Virginia Clemm, and moved to New York City. There, in 1837, they set up house, together with Virginia's mother, whom Poe fondly called Muddy.

Poe drank excessively at times, and he was always in need of money. He wrote regularly, however, and had increasing success, although his unusual poems and stories were mocked by conservative critics. "The Cask of Amontillado" was published in 1846, during a time when Poe was enduring vicious insults from critics. The story might have been Poe's way of getting even not only with hostile critics but also with his foster father. The Montresor motto is the motto of Scotland; John Allan was Scottish and, like the hated Fortunato, a businessman and a Mason.

Poe's one refuge in life was threatened when Virginia became ill with tuberculosis. (Almost 25 percent of Americans in the nineteenth century died from tuberculosis.) When she died, Poe broke down completely. Two years later he was found delirious in a tavern in Baltimore on a rainy election day. The great master of horror died a few days later.

For Independent Reading

For more tales of terror by Poe, read "The Pit and the Pendulum," in which the narrator faces heart-stopping threats to his life, and "The Tell-Tale Heart," in which a haunted man tries to convince us he's not mad. Mystery lovers will enjoy "The Gold Bug," one of Poe's tales that set the stage for the modern detective story.

180   Collection 3   Narrator and Voice • Synthesizing Sources

---

Meet the Writer

Meet the Writer appears after each literature selection, providing students with background on the author, including **quotations from the author** about personal life experiences reflected in the selection.

Response and Analysis

A **Response and Analysis** page guides comprehension of the selection. **Questions** clearly assess the skills focus and reading skills taught with the selection.

Reading Check questions tap students' basic comprehension of the selection.

Thinking Critically offers interpretive and analytical discussion questions that explore the students' deeper understanding of the selection.

Extending and Evaluating offers questions that encourage students to find real-world applications for key concepts they have discovered in their reading.

Writing Assignments give students the opportunity to use the selection as a springboard for imaginative assignments. They also provide opportunities for analysis, comparison and contrast, and other higher-level thinking skills.

Response and Analysis

Reading Check

1. What does Montresor admit is his **motive** for this crime?

2. According to Montresor, what makes a perfect crime?

3. According to Montresor, what kind of person is Fortunato?

4. How does Montresor lure Fortunato farther and farther into the catacombs?

5. What evidence suggests that Montresor has committed the perfect crime?

Thinking Critically

6. How would you describe the **persona** that Poe has created for Montresor? Why might Poe have chosen someone like Montresor to tell his story?

7. What **character traits** in Fortunato make him fall prey to Montresor?

8. In your opinion, what is Montresor thinking when he says, "*In pace requiescat*"? Explain your interpretation.

9. To whom could Montresor be talking, fifty years after the murder, and for what reasons?

10. Montresor's **voice**—the way he speaks and his **tone**—is frequently **ironic**. Which of Montresor's comments to the unsuspecting Fortunato mean something different from what they seem to mean?

11. Think about whether or not Montresor is an **unreliable narrator.** Do any details suggest that he might have imagined "the thousand injuries" and the insult—or even the whole story? Can you find evidence in the story to support Montresor's claim that Fortunato *did* in fact injure and insult him? To support your answers, consider Montresor's actions, statements, and **voice.**

12. Think about Poe's decision to set his story during carnival. What is **ironic** about the **setting**? In what ways does the setting suit the plot of the story?

Extending and Evaluating

13. Is this just a gripping horror story told only for entertainment, or do you think it reveals some truth about people who are consumed by a desire for revenge? Give reasons for your opinions. (Be sure to check your Quickwrite notes.)

WRITING

Fortunato's Version

Suppose this story were told from Fortunato's **first-person point of view.** Write a **new beginning.** Start at the point where the two men meet at dusk, and end when they begin their journey underground. Let the reader know what Fortunato thinks of Montresor. Is he guilty of the thousand injuries and the insult that Montresor refers to? Create an individual **voice** for Fortunato (one that is different from Montresor's) by giving him a distinct tone and style of speaking. For example, is he frank, confused, or overconfident?

Crime and Punishment

Suppose the person to whom Montresor is telling his story has turned him over to the police. Montresor's lawyer will argue that he is insane. The prosecution will argue that Montresor knew exactly what he was doing and that he even planned the murder in advance. Write a **speech** for either lawyer, and argue your case before your classmates.

INTERNET
Projects and Activities
Keyword: LE5 9-3

SKILLS FOCUS

Literary Skills
Analyze the unreliable narrator.

Writing Skills
Write a new beginning for a short story.
Write a speech.

The Cask of Amontillado   181

Vocabulary Development

Vocabulary Development focuses on the skills students need to build strong vocabularies, with exposition and practice exercises.

Grammar Links

Grammar Links provide instruction and practice on common errors in usage, mechanics, and style.

Vocabulary Development

Word Maps
PRACTICE

A word map can supply several different kinds of information. It can give the word's **etymology**, or origin, by listing **root words** and **prefixes**. It can also give a definition and a sample sentence. Use a dictionary to make a word map for each word in the Word Bank. (A map of *precluded* appears below.)

Word Bank
precluded
impunity
retribution
immolation
connoisseurship
impose
recoiling
endeavored
obstinate
succession

precluded

Etymology	Meaning	Sample sentence
< Latin prae–, "before" < Latin claudere, "to close"	made impossible in advance; prevented	Cara's injury precluded her entering the gymnastics meet.

Grammar Link

Dialogue—Who's Talking?

Dialogue in a story can advance the plot, reveal the thoughts of a character, or present important information to a reader. In American usage, **dialogue** is enclosed in double quotation marks (" "). Usually a new paragraph lets us know when a different person begins to speak, as in this example from "The Cask of Amontillado":

SKILLS FOCUS

Vocabulary Skills
Create word maps showing etymology, meaning, and context.

"You do not comprehend?" he said.
"Not I," I replied.
"Then you are not of the brotherhood."

Most writers use **tag lines** (such as *he said* and *I replied*) to identify the speakers in a dialogue. Some writers do not always use tag lines, however. Poe, for example, has written long passages of conversation between Montresor and Fortunato in which ... is directly identified. Re-... lines should not be ...ation marks.

PRACTICE

Look back at the dialogue beginning "Amontillado!" on page 174 and at the dialogue beginning "You do not comprehend?" on page 177.

1. Get together with a partner, and read the dialogues aloud. Use your voices to distinguish one speaker from another.

2. Now, add tag lines to Poe's dialogue. (Be sure to punctuate them correctly.) Compare your edited versions of Poe's dialogue in class.

3. Finally, look at what Poe's dialogue accomplished. What did you learn about the characters or plot from this exchange?

▶ **For more help, see Quotation Marks, 13c–j, in the Language Handbook.**

...or and Voice • Synthesizing Sources

Informational Text
LINK TO "THE CASK OF AMONTILLADO"

Four Readings About Poe's Death

Synthesizing Sources: Seeing the Big Picture

When you research a subject, you read many different sources carefully. Then you need to **synthesize** the information, putting all the pieces together to see the big picture. Follow these steps:

• **Find the main idea.** Look for each writer's main idea, and take notes about it. To work your way through a difficult passage, **paraphrase** it—re-state the passage in your own words.

• **Look for supporting evidence.** Ask yourself, "Does the writer support his or her ideas with facts, statistics, examples, anecdotes (brief real-life stories), or quotations? Does the writer use logic and reasoning to prove a point?" For help identifying the writer's main ideas and support, try making a chart.

Main Idea 1	Main Idea 2
Support 1 Support 2	Support 1 Support 2

• **Compare and contrast.** Look for similarities and differences between your sources. In particular, compare and contrast the main ideas and the types of support the authors use.

• **Make connections.** Does the information in your sources remind you of ideas that you've read about in the past—perhaps in other articles or books or even in a story or poem?

• **Put it all together.** Once you've completed these steps, you're ready to put all the pieces together. To **synthesize** what you've learned, you may want to write a research report, an editorial, a speech, or a letter.

Vocabulary Development

insensible (in·sen′sə·bəl) *adj.*: not fully conscious or aware.

imposing (im·pō′zin) *adj.*: large and impressive looking.

stupor (stoo′pər) *n.*: dull, half-conscious state.

spectral (spek′trəl) *adj.*: ghostly; unreal.

expired (ek·spīrd′) *v.*: died.

maligned (mə·līnd′) *v.* used as *adj.*: falsely accused of bad conduct; slandered.

belligerent (bə·lij′ər·ənt) *adj.*: angry and aggressive or ready to start a fight.

conspicuous (kən·spik′yoo·əs) *adj.*: obvious; noticeable; notable.

ascribe (ə·skrīb′) *v.*: assign or attribute something to a cause.

chronic (krän′ik) *adj.*: frequently occurring.

transmitted (trans·mit′id) *v.*: passed on.

Connecting to the Literature

The life of Edgar Allan Poe, author of "The Cask of Amontillado," is shrouded in mystery. Most scholars believe that Poe died as a result of drinking too much alcohol. According to another theory, Poe died of rabies, a disease people can get when they are bitten or scratched by an animal infected with the rabies virus. The following four selections present a debate about what killed this tragic genius.

SKILLS FOCUS

Reading Skills
Synthesize information from several sources on a single topic.

Four Readings About Poe's Death **183**

Informational Text

Preceding every informational selection is a page linking the informational text to the preceding literary selection. This **Informational text** page explains in detail the main reading skill students will focus on in the selection.

Vocabulary Development introduces students to unfamiliar words from the selection.

Connecting to the Literature explains how the informational selection is related to the literature selection students have just read.

The **Skills Focus** is listed on the page so students know what they are expected to accomplish.

Analyzing Informational Text

Reading Check

1. Make a time line of Poe's last days, based on the information in the biography "Poe's Final Days."

2. Summarize the **evidence** cited to support Dr. Benitez's theory in the article ("Poe's Death Is Rewritten as Case of Rabies, Not Telltale Alcohol").

3. According to Burton R. Pollin and Robert E. Benedetto, what is the major weakness of Dr. Benitez's theory?

SKILLS FOCUS

Reading Skills
Synthesize information from several sources on a single topic.

Test Practice

1. What is the **main idea** of the letter by Pollin and Benedetto?

   A Poe has been unjustly accused of being an alcoholic.

   B There is a great deal of evidence that Poe's death was due to alcoholism.

   C Poe's cat could not have bitten him and given him rabies.

   D Poe was a great writer, but he had human faults.

2. What is the *strongest* **evidence** Dr. Benitez presents in his letter to defend his theory?

   F Rabies has a long incubation period, and many victims do not remember being attacked by an animal.

   G There was no available vaccine for pets at the time of Poe's death.

   H During Poe's lifetime, doctors knew how rabies was passed on.

   J Louis Pasteur first used a rabies vaccine in 1885.

3. What information in the biography could support Dr. Benitez's theory that rabies caused Poe's death?

   A It had been raining, and Poe may have suffered from exposure.

   B Dr. Moran stated that Poe sweated and addressed "imaginary objects on the walls."

   C Poe was so ill that he was taken to the hospital.

   D No one knows where Poe was the week before he appeared at the tavern.

4. Which of the following statements that **contrast** the biography with Pollin and Benedetto's letter is *not* true?

   F The biography states that Dr. Moran eventually claimed Poe didn't die from drinking too much, but the letter states that Dr. Moran provided evidence for this theory.

   G Pollin and Benedetto refer to Poe's letters as evidence, but the biography does not.

   H The biography does not discuss the rabies death theory, but the letter does.

   J The letter does not refer to Joseph Walker's description of Poe, but the biography does.

   (continued)

5. Which statement is the *most* important **similarity** between the article and Dr. Benitez's letter?

   A Both inform the reader that Dr. Benitez is an assistant professor of medicine.

   B Both use statistics as support.

   C Both point out that the lack of a bite or scratch does not weaken the rabies death theory.

   D Both state that only highly skilled doctors can diagnose rabies.

6. Which of the following statements is the *best* **synthesis** of the information in these four sources?

   F Poe was a tortured genius.

   G Poe's symptoms could point to several different causes of death.

   H All theories should take into account that Poe died drunk.

   J Poe's illness would have been correctly diagnosed by modern doctors.

Application

Imagine that you are writing a biography of Poe. Write the last few paragraphs of your book, in which you tell about Poe's death. In your discussion, **synthesize** the information from the four sources by **paraphrasing** the ideas and **comparing and contrasting** the points. End your account by drawing your own **conclusions** from the information.

▶ Use "Analyzing Nonfiction," pages 194–201, for help with this assignment.

Vocabulary Development

Understanding Word Derivations: Useful Roots

PRACTICE

A **root** is the part of a word that establishes its core meaning. Knowing what some common roots mean will help you figure out the definitions of new words. Match each root in the chart below with a word from the Word Bank. (Note that two words share a root.) Then, define the word, and write another word with the same root.

Word Bank
insensible
imposing
stupor
spectral
expired
maligned
belligerent
conspicuous
ascribe
chronic
transmitted

SKILLS FOCUS

Vocabulary Skills
Understand Greek and Latin word roots.

Word Roots	
Latin Roots	
–bel–, "war"	–spec–, "look"
–mal–, "ill"	–spir–, "breathe"
–mit–, "send"	–stup–, "be stunned or amazed"
–pon–, "place"	
–scrib–, "write"	**Greek Root**
–sent–, "feel"	–chron–, "time"

Analyzing Informational Text

An **Analyzing Informational Text** page immediately follows every informational selection.

Reading Skills introduced on the link to the informational text page are followed up here. Students are provided with a variety of questions that test their understanding of the selection. These questions include multiple-choice questions and a longer application question that clearly assess the skills focus.

Connection

A number of selections are followed by a **Connection** feature: an additional work, often in a different genre, that makes a pertinent literary connection to the main selection. Newspaper articles, poems, and essays appear as Connection features, enabling students to compare and contrast different treatments of a theme and make relevant personal connections.

Meet the Writer

Saki

An Exotic Imagination

Hector Hugh Munro (1870–1916) wrote stories with snappy endings that were either wickedly funny or terrifying. Munro was born in Burma, where his father was an officer in the military police. When his mother died suddenly, he went to live with his grandmother and two stern aunts in a house in England whose windows were never opened. The aunts considered Hector sickly; he played with few children and was not sent to school until he was ten.

When he began writing stories, Munro took a foreign pen name, Saki, after the character who served wine to the gods in the then-popular poem the *Rubáiyát of Omar Khayyám*. (Omar Khayyám was a Persian poet.)

For Independent Reading

If you enjoyed "The Interlopers," try Saki's story "The Open Window," about a young girl with an unusual imagination.

The Granger Collection, New York.

CONNECTION / FABLE

The Trapper Trapped

Vai (African) traditional, retold by Roger D. Abrahams

Goat and Fox were quarreling, and Goat told Fox that he intended to get him into trouble so bad he would never be able to get out. Fox said, "All right; you do that, and I will return the favor to you."

Goat went for a walk and saw Leopard. Being frightened, Goat asked, "Auntie, what are you doing here?" "My little one is sick," said Leopard. Then Goat, thinking quickly, said, "Fox has medicine that will make your little one well." Leopard said to call Fox, so Goat went to Fox and said, "They are calling you."

"Who is calling me?" replied Fox. "I don't know," said Goat; "I think it is your friend. Go this way and you will run into him." Fox went down the path and at length came upon Leopard. Fox was frightened, and inquired: "Did you call me?" "Yes, my son. Goat came just a while ago and told me you had medicine that would make my little one well." "Yes," said Fox, "I have medicine that will cure your little one, but I must have a little goat horn to put it in. If you get me a goat horn, I will let you have the medicine." "Which way did Goat go?" asked Leopard. "I left him up there," replied Fox. "You wait here with my little one, and I will bring you the horn," said Leopard, and away she ran. Soon after, Leopard killed Goat and returned with his horns to Fox.

Beware, lest you fall into the trap you set for someone else.

READ ON: FOR INDEPENDENT READING

FICTION
Crisis in a Small Town

Harper Lee's *To Kill a Mockingbird* is a riveting story of race relations as viewed by a wise, plucky child. Eight-year-old Scout and her brother, Jem, learn an unforgettable lesson about courage, justice, and compassion when their father takes part in a shocking trial that will change their hometown forever. You're not likely to forget this Pulitzer Prize–winning novel.

FICTION
California Dreams

When Panchito lived in Mexico, the most excitement he ever had was hunting for chicken eggs and going to church on Sundays. Then Panchito's father moves the family to California, where jobs for migrant workers abound and the promise of an American education awaits. In Francisco Jiménez's *The Circuit*, Panchito describes his family's odyssey from one labor camp to another as they pursue the American dream.

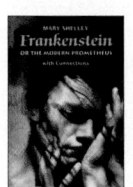

FICTION
The Monster's Revenge

Mary Shelley's classic novel, *Frankenstein,* has two narrators: Dr. Frankenstein, an obsessed scientist who creates a monster in the image of a man (and later comes to fear his creation); and the monster himself, a huge, misshapen creature who fights the men who have hurt him. Who is the real monster in this story? The answer just might surprise you.

This title is available in the HRW Library.

NONFICTION
On the Outside Looking In

Adeline Yen Mah, a young girl living in Shanghai, was a family outcast. Her father had trouble remembering her name, and her stepmother treated her no better than a servant. However, her memoir, *Chinese Cinderella*, is not about hardship alone: It also describes her friends, her aunt and grand-father, and the teachers who encouraged her talent as a writer that would one day lead Adeline into a whole new world.

Read On   193

Read On

At the end of each collection, a **Read On** provides students with suggestions for independent reading of fiction and nonfiction. The recommended books have themes or subjects similar to those in the collection.

Writing Workshops

Writing Workshops at the end of each collection guide students through the writing process. Each workshop covers a different mode of writing, such as narration, persuasion, description, or exposition, and is a logical extension of the literary and informational selections covered in the collection.

Prewriting provides step-by-step instruction to help students get started and think about the audience they want to reach.

Writer's Framework shows students how to structure their papers.

Writer's Model demonstrates the workshop assignment with annotations to help students understand the structure and development of an essay.

Editor in Charge offers a three-step process with specific actions for students to take to locate and correct weaknesses in their papers.

Style Guidelines encourage students to revise their papers a second time for precise and effective language.

Writing Workshop

Writing a Persuasive Essay

Writing Assignment
Write a persuasive essay on a topic about which you have a strong opinion.

As you read in his essay "A Defense of the Jury System," Thomas M. Ross has strong feelings about the jury system. What issue do you care about, and how can you get others to care about the issue, too? One way to share your views and convince others to accept them is to write persuasively. In a **persuasive essay** your goal will be to state your opinion clearly and support it with reasons and evidence.

Prewriting

Choose an Issue

A Powerful Issue For your persuasive essay, consider **issues** that stir up strong feelings in you and in others. What situations make you and other people angry, sad, or enthusiastic? List a few issues that you really care about. Then, pick the one you have the strongest views about and the one about which you can gather enough evidence to defend your position. Keep in mind that your essay should be at least 1,500 words, so choose an issue that is interesting enough to hold readers' interest in a paper of that length.

Write an Opinion Statement

Get on Your Soapbox You probably already know where you stand on your issue. Share your clear and well-defined **perspective** with readers by drafting an opinion statement (also known as a thesis statement). Your **opinion statement** should clearly state both the issue and your position on it. One student brainstormed the following issues and positions as she developed an opinion statement.

Issue	Position
Recycling	helps to protect our natural resources.
People who ride motorcycles	should be required to wear helmets.
Banning bicycles on sidewalks	would force riders onto unsafe streets.

SKILLS FOCUS

Writing Skills
Write a persuasive essay.

Keep your own opinion statement in mind to help you focus your ideas as you plan and draft your essay.

Listening & Speaking Workshop

Giving a Persuasive Speech

Speaking Assignment
Adapt your persuasive cause-and-effect essay for a persuasive speech, and deliver it to your class.

A persuasive speech, like an essay that uses cause and effect to persuade, may change the audience members' beliefs, unite them behind a common cause, or inspire them to take action to solve a problem. A speech and an essay share the basic techniques of persuasion. In this workshop you will learn how to take advantage of those techniques and some additional strategies.

Adapt Your Essay

Tailor-Made To adapt your cause-effect essay for a speech, first think about your **audience.** Because a listening audience can't rehear a word, phrase, or sentence, be sure that your vocabulary is simple and easily understood. For a formal speech, however, maintain the same formal **tone** as you used in your essay.

Beginnings The art of verbal persuasion begins with the first words that you speak to your audience. Adapt the **introduction** of your essay so that you can make a dramatic impact from the very beginning. For example, use an intriguing literary quotation, an interesting anecdote, or a reference to an authority on the subject of your speech. Sometimes repeating your opinion statement to your audience reinforces the importance of your ideas.

Endings Conclude your speech by summarizing the effects of your situation. Restate your opinion in a memorable fashion. Then, make a lasting impression by saying your final sentence slowly enough that the audience can feel its impact. A great last line usually is rewarded by the audience's applause.

In the Middle, Make Your Case You will spend the majority of your time explaining why your audience should agree with your opinion statement. How will you formulate your arguments for your listeners? Keep the following suggestions in mind as you review the body paragraphs of your essay.

- Remember that you have a limited amount of time to present your material. You may need to evaluate your description of the situation's cause, the explanation of its effects, and the supporting evidence you have used. Present only the information that will be most compelling to your audience, but make sure your evidence is both valid and credible. Each piece of evidence, as well as the logi[c] you use, should be relevant to your explanations o[f] and its effects.

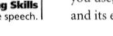

INTERNET
Speeches
Keyword: LE5 9-10

SKILLS FOCUS
Listening and
Speaking Skills
Deliver a persuasive speech.

742 Collection 10 Epic and Myth • Evaluating an Argument

Listening and Speaking Workshop

Some collections feature a **Listening and Speaking Workshop** that guides students in delivering focused, coherent presentations and in evaluating a variety of oral and media communications. Each **Listening and Speaking Workshop** is tied to a **Writing Workshop** and focuses on a different kind of presentation, such as narration, exposition, persuasion, research, and response to literature.

Practice and Apply encourages students to follow easy steps to help them construct, deliver, and evaluate a presentation.

Skills Review

A **Skills Review** at the end of each collection provides **standardized-test practice** and a review of the collection skills in reading, writing, and vocabulary.

Collection 3: Skills Review
Literary Skills

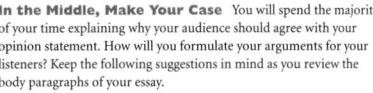

Narrator and Voice

DIRECTIONS: Read the following selection. Then, read and respond to the questions that follow.

Snow

Julia Alvarez

Our first year in New York we rented a small apartment with a Catholic school nearby, taught by the Sisters of Charity, hefty women in long black gowns and bonnets that made them look peculiar, like dolls in mourning. I liked them a lot, especially my grandmotherly fourth-grade teacher, Sister Zoe. I had a lovely name, she said, and she had me teach the whole class how to pronounce it. *Yo-lan-da.* As the only immigrant in my class, I was put in a special seat in the first row by the window, apart from the other children, so that Sister Zoe could tutor me without disturbing them. Slowly, she enunciated the new words I was to repeat: *laundromat, cornflakes, subway, snow.*

Soon I picked up enough English to understand holocaust[1] was in the air. Sister Zoe explained to a wide-eyed classroom what was happening in Cuba. Russian missiles were being assembled, trained supposedly on New York City. President Kennedy, looking worried too, was on the television at home, explaining we might have to go to war against the Communists. At school, we had air-raid drills: An ominous bell would go off and we'd file into the hall, fall to the floor, cover our heads with our coats, and imagine our hair falling out, the bones in our

arms going soft. At home, Mami and my sisters and I said a rosary[2] for world peace. I heard new vocabulary: *nuclear bomb, radioactive fallout, bomb shelter.* Sister Zoe explained how it would happen. She drew a picture of a mushroom on the blackboard and dotted a flurry of chalk marks for the dusty fallout that would kill us all.

The months grew cold, November, December. It was dark when I got up in the morning, frosty when I followed my breath to school. One morning, as I sat at my desk daydreaming out the window, I saw dots in the air like the ones Sister Zoe had drawn—random at first, then lots and lots. I shrieked, "Bomb! Bomb!" Sister Zoe jerked around, her full black skirt ballooning as she hurried to my side. A few girls began to cry.

But then Sister Zoe's shocked look faded. "Why, Yolanda dear, that's snow!" She laughed. "Snow."

"Snow," I repeated. I looked out the window warily. All my life I had heard about the white crystals that fell out of American skies in the winter. From my desk I watched the fine powder dust the sidewalk and parked cars below. Each flake was different, Sister Zoe had said, like a person, irreplaceable and beautiful.

---

1. **holocaust** (hä′lə·kåst′) *n.*: great or total destruction of life.

2. **rosary** (rō′zər·ē) *n.*: in the Roman Catholic religion, series of prayers counted off on a special set of beads.

Pages 202–203
cover
Literary Skills
Analyze narrator
(or point of
view) and voice.

202 Collection 3 Narrator and Voice • Synthesizing Sources

T70

Reading Matters

Reading Matters is a handbook that offers students strategies designed to improve their reading skills. It focuses on issues such as reading comprehension and reading rate.

When the Text Is Tough

Remember the reading you did back in first, second, and third grades? Big print. Short texts. Easy words. Now in high school, however, the texts you read are often filled with small print, long chapters, and complicated plots or topics. Also, you now find yourself reading a variety of material—from your driver's-ed handbook to college applications, from job applications to income-tax forms, from e-mail to e-zines, from classics to comics, from textbooks to checkbooks.

Doing something every day that you find difficult and tedious isn't much fun—and that includes reading. So, this section of this book is designed for you, to show you what to do when the text gets tough. Let's begin by looking at some *reading* matters.

READING UP CLOSE: HOW TO USE THIS SECTION

- **This section is for you.** Turn to it whenever you need to remind yourself about what to do when the text gets tough. Don't wait for your teacher to assign this section for you to read. It's your handbook. Use it.

- **Read the sections that you need.** You don't have to read every word. Skim the headings, and find the information you need.

- **Use this information for help with reading for other classes,** not just for the reading you do in this book.

- **Don't be afraid to re-read the information you find in Reading Matters.** The best readers constantly re-read information.

- **If you need more help, then check the index.** The index will direct you to other pages in this book with information on reading skills and strategies.

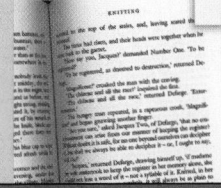

Test Smarts

Test Smarts is a handbook that gives students strategies for taking multiple-choice tests and writing tests. It includes questions for reading comprehension, vocabulary, and analogies.

Test Smarts

by **Flo Ota De Lange** *and* **Sheri Henderson**

Strategies for Taking Multiple-Choice Tests

Whatever you choose to do in the future, a high school diploma can open doors for you. It is a basic requirement for many, many jobs as well as for getting into college. But to get that diploma, you'll have to pass a lot of tests—pop quizzes in class, midterm exams, finals, your state's standardized tests required for graduation, and the SAT or ACT if you are thinking about college.

Taking tests doesn't have to be the scary nightmare many students make it out to be. With some preparation you'll do just fine. The first thing you have to do, of course, is study. Read all your assignments at least once, and make sure you have mastered the skills being taught.

Even when you know all the material, however, you might not do well on a test if you get nervous or are not familiar with the kinds of questions being asked. This section will give you some strategies that will help you approach your tests with confidence and let your abilities shine through.

Stay Calm

It's test time. You have studied the material, and you know your stuff, but you're still nervous. That's OK. A little nervousness will help you focus, but so will a calm body. Take a few deep breaths—five slow counts in, five slow counts out. Now you're ready to begin the test.

Track Your Time

First, estimate how much time you have for each question. Then, set checkpoints for yourself—how many questions should be completed at a quarter of the time, half of the time, and so on. That way you can **pace yourself** throughout the test. If you're behind, you can speed up. If you're ahead, you can—and should—slow down.

Master the Directions

Read the directions carefully to be sure you know exactly what to do and how to do it. If you are supposed to fill in an oval, fill it in cleanly and carefully. Be careful also to match the number of the question to the number on the answer sheet. Do just what the directions say to do.

Study the Questions

Read each question once, twice, three times—until you are certain you know what the question is asking. Watch out for words like *not* and *except;* they tell you to look for choices that are false, different, or opposite in some way.

Anticipate Answers

Once you are sure you understand the question, **anticipate the answer.** Then, read the choices. If the answer you gave is there, it is probably correct. To be sure, though, check out each choice. If you don't know the answer, eliminate any choices you think are wrong. Then, make an educated—not a wild—guess about the choices that remain. Be careful to **avoid distracters,** answers that are true but don't fit the question.

Don't Give Up

If you are having a hard time with a test, take a deep breath and **keep on going.** On most tests the questions do not get more difficult as you go, and an easier question is probably coming soon. The last question on a test is worth just as many points as the first, so give it your all—all the way to the end.

Types of Test Questions

You will feel a lot more confident taking a test if you are familiar with the kinds of questions given. The following pages describe and give examples of the different types of multiple-choice questions

Language Handbook

The **Language Handbook** is a quick reference guide that gives students an overview of important issues in grammar, usage, and mechanics.

Language Handbook

I THE PARTS OF SPEECH

PART OF SPEECH	DEFINITION	EXAMPLES
NOUN	Names person, place, thing, or idea	captain, swimmers, Maria Tallchief, team, Stratford-on-Avon, stories, "The Scarlet Ibis," justice, honesty
PRONOUN	Takes place of one or more nouns or pronouns	
Personal	Refers to one(s) speaking (first person), spoken to (second person), spoken about (third person)	I, me, my, mine, we, us, our, ours you, your, yours he, him, his, she, her, hers, it, its, they, them, their, theirs
Reflexive	Refers to subject and directs action of verb back to subject	myself, ourselves, yourself, yourselves, himself, herself, itself, themselves
Intensive	Refers to and emphasizes noun or another pronoun	(See Reflexive.)
Demonstrative	Refers to specific one(s) of group	this, that, these, those
Interrogative	Introduces question	what, which, who, whom, whose
Relative	Introduces subordinate clause and refers to noun or pronoun outside clause	that, which, who, whom, whose
Indefinite	Refers to one(s) not specifically named	all, any, anyone, both, each, either, everybody, many, none, nothing
ADJECTIVE	Modifies noun or pronoun by telling *what kind, which one, how many,* or *how much*	**an old, flea-bitten** dog, **a Sioux** custom, **that** one, **the twelve red** roses, **more** water
VERB	Shows action or state of being	
Action	Expresses physical or mental activity	paint, jump, write, know, imagine
Linking	Connects subject with word identifying or describing it	appear, be, seem, become, feel, look, smell, sound, taste
Helping (Auxiliary)	Combines with another verb to form a verb phrase	be, have, may, can, shall, will, would
ADVERB	Modifies verb, adjective, or adverb by telling *how, when, where,* or *to what extent*	drives **carefully, quite** dangerous, **shortly afterward,** arrived **there late**
	Relates noun or pronoun to another word	across, between, into, near, of, on, with, aside from, instead of, next to
	Joins words or word groups	
	Joins words or word groups used in same way	and, but, for, nor, or, so, yet

(continued)

Language Handbook **1045**

Handbook of Literary Terms

For more information about a topic, turn to the page(s) in this book that are indicated on a separate line at the end of the entry. For example, to learn more about *alliteration,* turn to page 456.

On another line are cross-references to entries in this handbook that provide closely related information. For instance, at the end of *Alliteration* is a cross-reference to *Assonance.*

ALLEGORY A narrative in which characters and settings stand for abstract ideas or moral qualities. In addition to the literal meaning of the story, an allegory contains a symbolic, or **allegorical,** meaning. Characters and places in allegories often have names that indicate the abstract ideas they stand for: Justice, Deceit, Vanity. George Orwell's novel *Animal Farm* is a well-known modern allegory.

See pages 341, 364.

"I think I'll wait for the next elevator."

Drawing by Chas. Addams; © 1988 The New Yorker Magazine, Inc.

ALLITERATION Repetition of the same or very similar consonant sounds usually at the beginnings of words that are close together in a poem. In this example the sound "fl" is repeated in line 1, and the "s" sound is repeated in line 2:

> Open here I flung the shutter, when with many a
>   flirt and flutter,
> In there stepped a stately Raven of the saintly days
>   of yore.
>
>   —Edgar Allan Poe, from "The Raven"

See pages 456, 475.
See also *Assonance, Onomatopoeia, Rhyme.*

ALLUSION Reference to a statement, a person, a place, or an event from literature, history, religion, mythology, politics, sports, science, or pop culture. In calling one of his stories "The Gift of the Magi" (page 287), O. Henry uses an allusion to the wise men from the East called the Magi, who presented the infant Jesus with the first Christmas gifts.

AMBIGUITY An element of uncertainty in a text, in which something can be interpreted in a number of different ways. Ambiguity adds a layer of complexity to a story, for it presents us with a variety of possible interpretations, all of which are valid. Edgar Allan Poe's "The Cask of Amontillado" (page 173) is ambiguous because we don't know if we should trust the narrator's claims. **Subtleties,** or fine distinctions in meaning, in a text help create ambiguity. The significance of these subtleties is open to question.

See pages 284–285, 297.

ANALOGY Comparison made between two things to show how they are alike in some respects. During the Revolutionary War the writer Thomas Paine drew an analogy between a thief breaking into a house and the king of England interfering in the affairs of the American Colonies (*The Crisis,* No. 1). Similes are a kind of analogy. However, an analogy usually clarifies something, while a simile shows imaginatively how two different things are alike in some unusual way.

See page 308.

Handbook of Literary Terms **1019**

Handbook of Literary Terms

The **Handbook of Literary Terms** serves as a reference guide to the important literary terms and concepts students will encounter throughout the text.

Program Resources

Planning

Annotated Teacher's Edition

This planning and teaching tool offers

- Specific questions to help reinforce and evaluate reading and literary skills for each selection
- Special approaches for learners having difficulty, English-language learners, and advanced learners
- Planning charts in the interleaf pages for each collection that provide information about the collection's scope and sequence of skills, core content, and resources
- Specific sequencing suggestions to ensure coverage of grade-level skills, effective testing, and remediation and reteaching opportunities

One-Stop Planner CD-ROM with ExamView Test Generator

This time-saving planning software contains print-based teaching resources, clips from the video program, and valuable assessment tools. The *One-Stop Planner* also

- Simplifies lesson planning and management
- Includes all the teaching resources for *Elements of Literature*
- Includes printable program resources and an easy-to-use test generator
- Offers previews of all teaching resources, including assessments and worksheets linked to the **Student Edition**
- Launches directly to the **go.hrw.com** Web site

PowerNotes for Literature and Reading

- Contains fully editable instructional PowerPoint® presentations that teach literary elements and reading skills and that introduce literary periods
- Includes teacher's notes with discussion questions and student note-taking worksheets with graphic organizers for each presentation

Professional Development

Web-Based Professional Development

Teaching Literacy to All Students, Grades 6–12, is a 9-module online professional development program that is ideal for all subject areas. *Teaching Reading to All Students, Grades 6–8,* is a 16-module online professional development program designed for middle school language arts teachers. Each module provides video demonstrations of best teaching practices tied to web-based content that includes explanations and examples, interactive applications to the teacher's own classroom, graphic organizers and lesson-planning templates, printable classroom handouts, and assessment instruments. The modules cover topics such as

- Planning schoolwide literacy programs
- Using assessment data to drive instruction
- Modifying instruction for English language learners
- Helping struggling readers with comprehension and fluency
- Integrating standards-based instruction

Face-to-Face Professional Development

Holt, Rinehart and Winston provides customized, comprehensive teacher training to assist school districts and individual teachers in the effective implementation of *Elements of Literature*.

- The training is facilitated by highly qualified professional development providers with language arts and reading expertise.
- Training institute and workshop topics include effective teaching practices, evidence-based research, and standards-based instruction.

Differentiating Instruction

The Holt Reader

This worktext includes alternative direct instruction and additional practice for the skills taught in each collection of *Elements of Literature*. The consumable format offers students' an interactive, hands-on approach to building reading, vocabulary, and literary analysis skills. Students circle, underline, and write responses in the margins of the selections.

- **Part 1** contains key literary selections from *Elements of Literature* and additional literary selections that extend student's practice. Instruction is focused on vocabulary, literary elements, and reading skills.
- **Part 2** contains informational texts such as magazine and newpaper articles, editorials, and essays. Also offered are vocabulary exercises and standardized-test practice.

Holt Adapted Reader

This consumable worktext contains the literary and informational adaptations found in **Holt Reading Solutions**. With scaffolded instruction that provides guided support, the **Holt Adapted Reader** can be used with struggling readers while other students in the class read the same selection in **The Holt Reader** or the **Student Edition**.

- Adaptations are within the reading range of English-language learners, special education students, and reluctant readers
- "Here's How" annotations model vocabulary, literary analysis, and reading comprehension skills; "Your Turn" annotations ask students to answer a question using the skill just modeled
- Graphic organizers help students review and consolidate what they've learned

Holt Reading Solutions

This book pulls together all of the reading resources in the *Elements of Literature* program to create a powerful tool for intervention and whole-class instruction. It includes

- Diagnostic assessment tools
- Lesson plans for English-language learners and special education students
- Adaptations of selected reading selections
- Vocabulary and comprehension worksheets
- Information on phonics and decoding
- Additional instruction and practice in remedial reading skills and strategies

Supporting Instruction in Spanish

Provides the following Spanish-language materials as extra support for students who are making the transition from Spanish to English:

- Summaries of selections in *Elements of Literature*
- Criteria for major writing modes
- Definitions and examples of key grammar terms and concepts
- Introductions and summaries of Visual Connections segments

Audio CD Library

- Includes dramatic readings by professional actors that bring to life nearly every reading selection in *Elements of Literature*

Audio CD Library, Selections and Summaries in Spanish

- Includes Spanish translations of key selections in *Elements of Literature* that assist students in reading and developing their own sense of a selection
- Includes recordings of summaries in Spanish of virtually every selection in *Elements of Literature* that serve as a valuable tool for English-language learners

Workshop Resources: Writing, Listening, and Speaking

Supports instruction and assignments in the **Student Edition**

- Includes worksheets for each Writing Workshop and each Listening and Speaking Workshop
- Includes exercises and lesson plans with alternative teaching strategies for English-language learners and special education students

Family Involvement Activities in English and Spanish

- Offers a selection of letters written for the parents or guardians of students using *Elements of Literature*
- Suggests activities that can be completed at home to extend the material in the **Student Editions**
- Allows parents or guardians to participate in students' education and helps foster an atmosphere in the home that encourages academic success

Reading/Literature/Vocabulary

The Holt Reader

This worktext includes alternative direct instruction and additional practice for the skills taught in each collection of *Elements of Literature*. The consumable format offers students' an interactive, hands-on approach to building reading, vocabulary, and literary analysis skills. Students circle, underline, and write responses in the margins of the selections.

- **Part 1** contains key literary selections from *Elements of Literature* and additional literary selections that extend student's practice. Instruction is focused on vocabulary, literary elements, and reading skills.
- **Part 2** contains informational texts such as magazine and newspaper articles, editorials, and essays. Also offered are vocabulary exercises and standardized-test practice.

Holt Adapted Reader

This consumable worktext contains the literary and informational adaptations found in *Holt Reading Solutions*. With scaffolded instruction that provides guided support, the *Holt Adapted Reader* can be used with struggling readers while other students in the class read the same selection in **The Holt Reader** or the **Student Edition.**

- Adaptations are within the reading range of English-language learners, special education students, and reluctant readers
- "Here's How" annotations model vocabulary, literary analysis, and reading comprehension skills; "Your Turn" annotations ask students to answer a question using the skill just modeled
- Graphic organizers help students review and consolidate what they've learned

Holt Reading Solutions

This book pulls together all of the reading resources in the *Elements of Literature* program to create a powerful tool for intervention and whole-class instruction. It includes

- Diagnostic assessment tools
- Lesson plans for English-language learners and special education students
- Adaptations of selected reading selections
- Vocabulary and comprehension worksheets
- Information on phonics and decoding
- Additional instruction and practice in remedial reading skills and strategies

Vocabulary Development

- Includes copying master worksheets that expand on students' ability to define and use the Vocabulary words identified in the **Student Edition**
- Includes cumulative reviews that reinforce students' mastery of the Vocabulary words

HRW Library

- Offers a comprehensive selection of the best novels, works of nonfiction, anthologies, and connected readings, with selections drawn from a variety of cultures
- Includes Study Guides that help motivate students and enhance their appreciation and understanding of classic and contemporary literature

Writing/Grammar and Language/Listening and Speaking

Workshop Resources: Writing, Listening, and Speaking

Supports instruction and assignments in the **Student Edition**

- Includes worksheets for each Writing Workshop and each Listening and Speaking Workshop
- Includes exercises and lesson plans with alternative teaching strategies for English-language learners and special education students

Language Handbook Worksheets

- Includes practice and reinforcement worksheets that cover the material presented in the Language Handbook section of **Elements of Literature**
- Includes tests at the end of each section of the booklet that can be used either for assessment or as end-of-section reviews

Daily Language Activities

A notebook of transparencies that reinforce skills in reading, writing, grammar, usage, and mechanics that are covered in **Elements of Literature**. Transparencies are grouped into the following categories:

- Proofreading Warm-ups
- Vocabulary
- Analogies
- Sentence Combining
- Critical Reading

Assessment

Holt Assessment: Literature, Reading, and Vocabulary

Contains diagnostic, progress, and summative assessment tests, as follows:

- An Entry-Level Test and diagnostic tests for each collection assess students' level of preparation
- Tests for every reading selection provide ongoing evaluation of students' skill development
- Summative tests for each collection and an End-of-Year Test then offer cumulative assessment opportunities

Holt Assessment: Writing, Listening, and Speaking

- Includes assessment of writing, listening, and speaking skills in a variety of test formats, including standardized tests
- Provides scales and rubrics for each workshop assignment

Holt Online Assessment

- Includes entry-level and summative assessments
- Provides tools to monitor student progress through tracking student mastery and recording and analyzing scores

One-Stop Planner CD-ROM with ExamView Test Generator

Time-saving planning software that includes a printable version of all the tests from **Holt Assessment: Reading, Literature, and Vocabulary** and **Holt Assessment: Writing, Listening, and Speaking** as well as an easy-to-use test generator.

Holt Online Essay Scoring

- Provides writing prompts for the types of writing most common in state assessments
- Instantly scores and gives holistic and analytic feedback on student essays
- Provides writing tips, activities, and model essays geared to students' results

Technology
Internet

Elements of Literature Basic Online Edition

A Web-based version of the print edition of **Elements of Literature**, this "digital textbook"

- Delivers the content of the textbook in an online format that lightens the load students carry in their backpacks
- Enables students to complete homework online
- Includes access to an online notebook for storing student work, taking notes, and responding to the same questions and activities that appear in the student book

Elements of Literature Enhanced Online Edition

In addition to all the features of the Basic Online Edition described above, the Enhanced Online Edition includes a number of selections from the student text that are enhanced with various interactive features. The Enhanced Online Edition

- Provides point-of-use interactive critical thinking and literary response questions that pop up in the Notebook, where students can type responses, edit, save, and print their work
- Includes audio excerpts from the selection in both English and Spanish
- Features vocabulary links in English and Spanish, with accompanying audio
- Delivers links to high-interest video clips that enhance students' understanding of selections and build their prior knowledge

- Provides Spanish summaries of selections, in audio
- Includes highlighting and annotation tools for use by both students and teachers
- Features an Image Gallery where students can click to see art and graphics from their textbook

AuthorSpace

A Web environment available on *Elements of Literature* **Enhanced Online Edition** that provides students opportunities to dig deeper into the lives and works of various authors

- Uses a variety of interactive features such as timelines, maps, and illustrated "webs of influence" to help students gain a more detailed understanding of an author's life and his or her place in literary history
- Gives students a chance to read additional literary works, as well as primary source documents, by featured authors

go.hrw.com

At **go.hrw.com** students put their reading, writing, listening, and speaking skills into action in real-world situations. The GO Site

- Reinforces the study of literature through additional biographical information about authors, a variety of cross-curricular projects connected to the literature in the student textbook, and literary elements activities
- Includes interactive reading workshops that guide students through informational texts
- Includes interactive writers' models that illustrate various types of writing
- Includes vocabulary-building activities, through which students explore synonyms, antonyms, etymologies, and multiple meanings

Holt Online Assessment

- Includes entry-level and summative assessments
- Provides tools to monitor student progress through tracking student mastery and recording and analyzing scores

Holt Online Essay Scoring

- Provides writing prompts for the types of writing most common in state assessments
- Instantly scores and gives holistic and analytic feedback on student essays
- Provides writing tips, activities, and model essays geared to students' results

Teaching Literacy to All Students, Grades 6–12

This online professional development program provides video demonstrations of best teaching practices combined with interactive exercises, graphic organizers, and lesson-planning templates; printable classroom handouts; and assessment instruments. The program contains 9 lesson-segments covering literacy topics such as

- Schoolwide literacy programs
- Assessment driving instruction
- English language learners and intensive learners
- Comprehension and fluency
- Strategies in language arts

Media

Visual Connections Videocassette Program

- Consists of author biographies, interviews, historical summaries, and cross-curricular connections that motivate students and enrich and extend learning

Fine Art Transparencies

- Features stunning examples of classic and contemporary art to complement the literature selections in *Elements of Literature*
- Helps students explore literary characters and ideas through visual representations
- Encourages students to make cross-curricular connections

One-Stop Planner CD-ROM with ExamView Test Generator

- Time-saving planning software that contains print-based teaching resources, clips from the video program, and valuable assessment tools

PowerNotes for Literature and Reading

- Fully editable instructional PowerPoint presentations that teach literary elements and reading skills and that introduce literary periods

Audio CD Library

- Includes dramatic readings by professional actors that bring to life nearly every reading selection in *Elements of Literature*

Audio CD Library, Selections and Summaries in Spanish

- Includes Spanish translations of key selections in *Elements of Literature*
- Includes recordings of summaries in Spanish of virtually every selection in *Elements of Literature*

Diagnosis and Prescription: Tracking Student Mastery

The Entry-Level and End-of-Year tests can be used to inform instructional planning, chart student progress, and provide individual and group snapshots of core language arts skills proficiency.

CORE SKILLS	Entry-Level Test	End-of-Year Test	Collection Diagnostic Test	Collection Summative Test	Reteaching	Remediation
Collection 1						
Plot and setting	Items 1, 2, 6, 9	Items 1, 2, 6–8	Items 1–6	Items 6–11, 14	• *The Holt Reader,* Collection 1	*Holt Reading Solutions:* • Lesson Plans (ELL) • Special Ed Lesson Plans • Adapted Readings *Holt Adapted Reader*
Informational reading	Items 11–19	Items 12, 13, 18–30	Items 6, 7, 8		• *The Holt Reader,* Collection 1	*Holt Reading Solutions:* • Lesson Plans (ELL) • Special Ed Lesson Plans • Adapted Readings *Holt Adapted Reader*
Vocabulary	Items 31–40	Items 4, 31–40	Items 9, 10	Items 1–5	• *The Holt Reader,* Collection 1	
Collection 2						
Character	Items 1, 6, 8, 9, 10, 24	Items 3, 9	Items 1–6	Items 6, 9, 10, 13, 14	• *The Holt Reader,* Collection 2 • *ATE,* Reteaching Lessons	*Holt Reading Solutions:* • Lesson Plans (ELL) • Special Ed Lesson Plans • Adapted Readings • MiniReads *Holt Adapted Reader*
Informational reading	Items 11–19	Items 12, 13, 18–30	Items 6, 7, 8		• *The Holt Reader,* Collection 2 • *ATE,* Reteaching Lessons	*Holt Reading Solutions:* • Lesson Plans (ELL) • Special Ed Lesson Plans • Adapted Readings *Holt Adapted Reader*
Vocabulary	Items 31–40	Items 4, 31–40	Items 9, 10	Items 1–5	• *The Holt Reader,* Collection 2	
Collection 3						
Narrator and voice	Items 1, 3, 4, 5, 6, 24, 29		Items 1, 2	Items 9–14	• *The Holt Reader,* Collection 3 • *ATE,* Reteaching Lessons	*Holt Reading Solutions:* • Lesson Plans (ELL) • Special Ed Lesson Plans • Adapted Readings *Holt Adapted Reader*
Informational reading	Items 11–19	Items 12, 13, 18–30	Items 6, 7, 8		• *The Holt Reader,* Collection 3	*Holt Reading Solutions:* • Lesson Plans (ELL) • Special Ed Lesson Plans • Adapted Readings *Holt Adapted Reader*
Vocabulary	Items 31–40	Items 4, 31–40	Items 9, 10	Items 1–5	• *The Holt Reader,* Collection 3	

CORE SKILLS	Entry-Level Test	End-of-Year Test	Collection Diagnostic Test	Collection Summative Test	Reteaching	Remediation
Collection 4						
Comparing themes	Items 10–30	Item 11	Items 1, 2	Items 12–14	• *The Holt Reader,* Collection 4 • *ATE*, Reteaching Lessons	*Holt Reading Solutions:* • Lesson Plans (ELL) • Special Ed Lesson Plans • MiniReads
Informational reading	Items 11–19	Items 12, 13, 18–30	Items 6, 7, 8		• *The Holt Reader,* Collection 4	*Holt Reading Solutions:* • Lesson Plans (ELL) • Special Ed Lesson Plans • Adapted Readings *Holt Adapted Reader*
Vocabulary	Items 31–40	Items 4, 31–40	Items 9, 10	Items 1–5		
Collection 5						
Irony and ambiguity	Items 25, 26, 28		Items 1–3	Item 13	• *The Holt Reader,* Collection 5	*Holt Reading Solutions:* • Lesson Plans (ELL) • Special Ed Lesson Plans • Adapted Readings *Holt Adapted Reader*
Informational reading	Items 11–19	Items 12, 13, 18–30	Items 6, 7, 8		• *The Holt Reader,* Collection 5 • *ATE*, Reteaching Lessons	*Holt Reading Solutions:* • Lesson Plans (ELL) • Special Ed Lesson Plans • Adapted Readings *Holt Adapted Reader*
Vocabulary	Items 31–40	Items 4, 31–40	Items 9, 10	Items 1–5	• *The Holt Reader,* Collection 5	
Collection 6						
Symbolism and allegory	Items 7, 22, 23	Item 10	Items 1, 2, 3	Items 11–13	• *The Holt Reader,* Collection 6	*Holt Reading Solutions:* • Lesson Plans (ELL) • Special Ed Lesson Plans
Informational reading	Items 11–19	Items 12, 13, 18–30	Items 6, 7, 8		• *The Holt Reader,* Collection 6	*Holt Reading Solutions:* • Lesson Plans (ELL) • Special Ed Lesson Plans • Adapted Readings *Holt Adapted Reader*
Vocabulary	Items 31–40	Items 4, 31–40	Items 9, 10	Items 1–5	• *The Holt Reader,* Collection 6	

CORE SKILLS	Entry-Level Test	End-of-Year Test	Collection Diagnostic Test	Collection Summative Test	Reteaching	Remediation
Collection 7						
Poetry: Imagery, figurative language, rhyme	Items 20–30		Items 1–10	Items 6–15	• *The Holt Reader,* Collection 7	*Holt Reading Solutions:* • Lesson Plans (ELL) • Special Ed Lesson Plans • Adapted Readings • MiniReads *Holt Adapted Reader*
Analyzing a poem	Items 20–30		Items 1–10	Items 6–15		
Collection 8						
Evaluating style	Items 5, 21, 27	Item 5	Items 1–3, 6	Items 12–15	• *The Holt Reader,* Collection 8	*Holt Reading Solutions:* • Lesson Plans (ELL) • Special Ed Lesson Plans
Informational reading	Items 11–19	Items 12, 13, 18–30	Items 6, 7, 8		• *The Holt Reader,* Collection 8	*Holt Reading Solutions:* • Lesson Plans (ELL) • Special Ed Lesson Plans • Adapted Readings *Holt Adapted Reader*
Vocabulary	Items 31–40	Items 4, 31–40	Items 9, 10		• *The Holt Reader,* Collection 8	
Collection 9						
Biographical and historical approach			Items 1–3	Items 12–14	• *The Holt Reader,* Collection 9	*Holt Reading Solutions:* • Lesson Plans (ELL) • Special Ed Lesson Plans • Adapted Readings *Holt Adapted Reader*
Informational reading	Items 11–19	Items 12, 13, 18–30	Items 6, 7, 8		• *The Holt Reader,* Collection 9	*Holt Reading Solutions:* • Lesson Plans (ELL) • Special Ed Lesson Plans
Vocabulary	Items 31–40	Items 4, 31–40	Items 9, 10		• *The Holt Reader,* Collection 9	

CORE SKILLS	Entry-Level Test	End-of-Year Test	Collection Diagnostic Test	Collection Summative Test	Reteaching	Remediation
Collection 10						
Epic and myth	Items 20–22	Items 1–11	Items 1, 2	Items 6–14	• *The Holt Reader*, Collection 10	*Holt Reading Solutions:* • Lesson Plans (ELL) • Special Ed Lesson Plans • Adapted Readings *Holt Adapted Reader*
Informational reading	Items 11–19	Items 12, 13, 18–30	Items 6, 7, 8		• *The Holt Reader*, Collection 10	*Holt Reading Solutions:* • Lesson Plans (ELL) • Special Ed Lesson Plans • Adapted Readings *Holt Adapted Reader*
Vocabulary	Items 31–40	Items 4, 31–40	Items 9, 10	Items 15–19		
Collection 11						
Drama			Items 1–4	Items 6–15	• *The Holt Reader*, Collection 11	*Holt Reading Solutions:* • Lesson Plans (ELL) • Special Ed Lesson Plans • Adapted Readings *Holt Adapted Reader*
Informational reading	Items 11–19	Items 12, 13, 18–30	Items 6, 7, 8		• *The Holt Reader*, Collection 11	*Holt Reading Solutions:* • Lesson Plans (ELL) • Special Ed Lesson Plans • Adapted Readings *Holt Adapted Reader*
Vocabulary	Items 31–40	Items 4, 31–40	Item 10	Items 1–5	• *The Holt Reader*, Collection 11	
Collection 12						
Consumer and workplace documents		Items 23–30	Items 1–10	Items 11–13	• *The Holt Reader*, Part 2	*Holt Reading Solutions:* • Lesson Plans (ELL) • Special Ed Lesson Plans

Best Practices in Writing

Harvey A. Daniels
Professor of Education
National-Louis University
Evanston, IL

RESEARCH

Atwell, N. 2002.
In the Middle: New Understandings About Writing, Reading, and Learning.
Portsmouth: Heinemann Educational Books.

Graves, D. 1983.
Writing: Teachers and Children at Work.
Portsmouth: Heinemann Educational Books.

Newman, F. 1996.
Authentic Achievement: Restructuring Schools for Intellectual Quality.
San Francisco: Jossey-Bass.

National Council of Teachers of English/ International Reading Association. 1999.
Standards for the English Language Arts.
Newark: NCTE/IRA.

Zemelman, S., H. Daniels, and A. Hyde. 1998.
Best Practice: New Standards for Teaching and Learning in America's Schools, 2nd ed.
Portsmouth: Heinemann Educational Books.

"There is a process to follow. There is a process to learn. That's the way it is with a craft, whether it be teaching or writing. There is a road, a journey to travel, and there is someone to travel with us, someone who has already made the trip." —**Donald Graves**

The Process of Writing

Over the past twenty-five years, the "process" model of writing has been strongly validated by educational research. A generation ago, many viewed writing as a somewhat magical act in which flawless texts flowed from the pens of a few muse-blessed artists. Today, we understand that writing is not so much a rare talent but a definable series of cognitive operations that can be learned by anyone who can read. For even the most skilled writer, composing is a sequential process of constructing meaning: gathering information, organizing material, trying out ideas in draft, revising and restructuring text, proofreading and editing, and sharing text with readers and using their feedback for further refinement. No, these stages aren't linear and lockstep; indeed, recursive and even idiosyncratic approaches are normal and useful. But the underlying cognitive reality remains: Just like reading, writing is a staged cognitive process of building up meaning.

New Teacher Roles

Once we understand that writing is more craft than magic, we can recast the teacher as a master craftsperson, helping apprentices to learn a trade. Process-writing teachers model, mentor, and coach; they create a classroom workshop where students build a repertoire of strategies for starting, developing, and polishing written products over a wide range of genres. The teacher's first job is to show how writing gets made, by serving as a live example of an adult writer at work. This doesn't mean teachers must be paragons or professionals, just journeyman composers eager to share their own writings and explain their own strategies. Then they can add rich literary models, bathing the workshop in fine literature, so students have great writers to learn from. That's why the *Elements of Literature* series includes collections of great and varied literature, followed by activities that help students draw directly upon these models to create their own original pieces.

Instructional Implications

Young writers need plenty of writing practice. In the workshop approach, students start many pieces, save all materials in a portfolio, and gradually develop selected drafts to a highly polished and public form. At the core of this work is deep revision: Students are constantly helped to re-see ideas and rethink organization, as well as to follow carefully the conventions of written language. Where possible, writing is not just graded, but shared with real audiences. This makes the work more rhetorically genuine and provides authentic feedback that can help writers grow. All these features of writing-process instruction remind us that—when the trade secrets are revealed, explained, and practiced—writing is not a mysterious practice reserved for the gifted, but a trade that's open to all.

Effective Vocabulary Instruction

Kylene Beers, Ph.D.
Senior Reading Researcher
Child Study Center
School Development Program
Yale University
New Haven, CT

RESEARCH

Beers, K. 2002.
When Kids Can't Read—What Teachers Can Do.
Portsmouth: Heinemann.

Blachowicz, C. L. Z., and Fisher, P. 2000.
"Vocabulary Instruction." *Handbook of Reading Research.* Eds. P. D. Pearson, R. Barr, M. Kamil, and P. Mosenthal.
White Plains: Longman. 503–524.

Tierney, R., and Cunningham, J. 1984.
"Research on Teaching Reading Comprehension." *Handbook of Reading Research.* Eds. P. D. Pearson, R. Barr, M. Kamil, and P. Mosenthal.
White Plains: Longman. 609–656.

"Preteaching vocabulary . . . requires that the words to be taught must be key words, . . . be taught in semantically and topically related sets, . . . and that only a few words be taught per lesson." **—Tierney and Cunningham**

Preteaching Vocabulary

When students don't know the meaning of words that are used in a text, their ability to understand that text is diminished. They can use the context as a clue to get the gist of the meaning, but sometimes the context doesn't provide enough information and other times the gist isn't helpful enough. In those cases, we must preteach the vocabulary. To do so effectively, focus on which words you teach, the number that you teach, and how you teach them.

The Right Words and the Right Number

Deciding which words to teach is linked to deciding how many to teach. Twenty new words per week are probably too many for struggling readers, especially when you consider that the list of twenty is just for English class. The more vocabulary words we give students to learn weekly, the less chance they have of learning a word to the level needed to move it from short term to long term memory. Keeping the number between five and ten means students have a better chance of retaining that word beyond the end of the week (Beers, 2002).

Consequently, choose wisely the words to be taught. Avid readers benefit by studying rare words—those highly unusual ones—because they already have a solid vocabulary of the more common ones. Struggling readers, however, benefit by focusing on high-utility words—those more common words that they are likely to see in other contexts. So, in this sentence, "The boys banked the canoe to the lee side of the rock," the inclination might be to teach the word *lee*, a rare word. However, if students don't know what *banked* means in this context or don't know the word *canoe*, it matters little what *lee* means. For struggling readers, a focus on high-utility words is more beneficial than a focus on rare words.

The Right Instructional Approach

Tierney and Cunningham (1984) explain that offering students a list of vocabulary words with their definitions is not as effective as placing each word within a semantic context. Students learn how to use words as they read or hear them used correctly. *Elements of Literature* provides a short list of words on the "Before You Read" page of each selection that are defined and then used in a sentence. It is this semantic placement that most helps students learn words. Choosing the right number of the right words and presenting words in a semantic context help students build their vocabulary and, as a consequence, improve their comprehension.

Teaching Comprehension

Kylene Beers, Ph.D.
Senior Reading Researcher
Child Study Center
School Development Program
Yale University
New Haven, CT

RESEARCH

Baumann, J. 1984.
"Effectiveness of a Direct Instruction Paradigm for Teaching Main Idea Comprehension." *Reading Research Quarterly*, 20: 93–108.

Beers, K. 2002.
When Kids Can't Read—What Teachers Can Do. Portsmouth: Heinemann.

Dole, J., Brown, K., and Trathen, W. 1996.
"The Effects of Strategy Instruction on the Comprehension Performance of At-risk Students." *Reading Research Quarterly*, 31: 62–89.

Duffy, G. 2002.
"The Case for Direct Explanation of Strategies." *Comprehension Instruction: Research-Based Best Practices.* Eds. C. Block and M. Pressley. New York: Guilford Press. 28–41.

Pearson, P. D. 1984.
"Direct Explicit Teaching of Reading Comprehension." *Comprehension Instruction: Perspectives and Suggestions.* Eds. G. Duffy, L. Roehler, and J. Mason. New York: Longman. 222–233.

"Comprehension is both a product and a process, something that requires purposeful, strategic effort on the reader's part as he or she predicts, visualizes, clarifies, questions, connects, summarizes, and infers."
—Kylene Beers

When the Text Is Tough

"Comprehension is only tough when you can't do it," explained the eleventh-grader. I almost dismissed his words until I realized what truth they offered. We aren't aware of all the thinking we do to comprehend a text until faced with a difficult text. Then, all too clearly, we're aware of what words we don't understand, what syntax seems convoluted, what ideas are beyond our immediate grasp. As skilled readers, we know what to do: We slow our pace, re-read, ask questions, connect whatever we do understand to what we don't understand, summarize what we've read thus far, make inferences about what the author is saying. In short, we make that invisible act of comprehension visible as we consciously push our way through the difficult text. At those times, we realize that, indeed, comprehension is tough.

Reading Strategies for Struggling Readers

It's even tougher if you lack strategies that would help you through the difficult text. Many struggling readers believe they aren't successful readers because that's just the way things are (Beers, 2002); they believe successful readers know some secret that they haven't been told (Duffy, 2002). While we don't mean to keep comprehension a secret, at times we do. For instance, though we tell students to "re-read," we haven't shown them how to alter their reading. We tell them to "make inferences" or "make predictions," but we haven't taught them how to do such things. In other words, we tell them what to do, but don't show them how to do it, in spite of several decades of research showing the benefit of direct instruction in reading strategies to struggling readers. (Baumann, 1984; Pearson, P. D., 1984; Dole, et al., 1996; Beers, 2002).

Direct Instruction

Direct instruction means telling students what you are going to teach them, modeling it for them, providing assistance as they practice it, then letting them practice it on their own. It's not saying, "Visualize while you read," but instead explaining, "Today, I'm going to read this part aloud to you. I'm going to focus on seeing some of the action in my mind as I read. I'm going to stop occasionally and tell you what I'm seeing and what in the text helped me see that." When we directly teach comprehension strategies to students via modeling and repeated practice, we show students that good readers don't *just* get it. They work hard to get it. *Elements of Literature* takes the secret out of comprehension as it provides teachers the support they need to reach struggling readers.

The Technology Connection

"Reading comprehension is a process that involves the orchestration of the reader's prior experience and knowledge about the world and about language." **—Bartoli and Botel**

Technology Promotes Thinking Skills

Without technology, there would be no reading. It takes technology to create text. Whether that technology has been the invention of the scroll, the moveable printing press, or e-books, each new innovation in text-creation technology brings new challenges for readers and writers. Computer technology is no exception, especially when it comes to helping readers access, and even create, the necessary prior knowledge needed for efficient reading.

Michael Joyce (1995) believes that Internet technology offers the possibility for students to use the same thinking skills "that experts routinely, subtly, and self-consciously apply in accomplishing intellectual tasks"—as it "promises to unlock these skills for novice learners and to empower and enfranchise their learning." The Internet offers this promise because it allows readers to act physically on the associations or mental connections they make when reading. Hyperlinks effectively placed in a piece of online text can help students make connections between what they are reading and what they already know. Hyperlinks support students' thinking by prompting them through the wording of the links, and when they activate a link, allowing them to immediately learn more information about a given topic.

Webbed Text and Thinking

Constance Weaver (1994) explains that prior knowledge develops through our experience with the world. Readers create some of those experiences through active participation with webbed texts. So, when the appropriate prior knowledge does not exist, students can gain knowledge via hyperlinks associated with a selection.

Jay Bolter (1991) believes that webbed texts bring the usually unconscious transaction between reader and writer to the forefront. The writer invites the reader to choose paths—or click on links. The reader considers the author's invitations and follows various paths through the links-as-invitation. Students experience the satisfaction of physically clicking on a link that addresses the same topic they may have been thinking about as they read. Those connections to more information increase their prior knowledge.

But webbed text can provide more than just information. We cannot ignore the importance of visual literacy in our culture today. In a world where images convey so much meaning, students must understand how images affect meaning. The more they are able to construct meaning with images, the better they will become at that mode of meaning construction (Henderson, 196). The effective combination of text and visually rich images on many Web pages, coupled with reflections on those elements, can help students build the literacies they need in this complex world.

Nancy Patterson, Ph.D.
Assistant Professor, School of Education
Grand Valley State University
Grand Rapids, MI

RESEARCH

Bolter, Jay David. 1991.
Writing Space: The Computer, Hypertext, and the History of Writing.
Mahwah: Lawrence Erlbaum Associates.

Henderson, Kathryn. 1995.
"The Visual Culture of Engineers."
The Cultures of Computing. Ed. Susan Leigh Star.
Cambridge: Blackwell Publishers. 196–218.

Joyce, Michael. 1995.
Of Two Minds: Hypertext Pedagogy and Poetics.
Ann Arbor: University of Michigan Press.

Snyder, Ilana. 1997.
Hypertext: The Electronic Labyrinth.
New York: New York University Press.

Weaver, Constance. 1994.
Reading Process and Practice: From Socio-Psycholinguistics to Whole Language, 2nd ed.
Portsmouth: Heinemann.

Multicultural Literacy

Dale Allender
Associate Executive Director
National Council of Teachers of English
Urbana, IL

RESEARCH

Allender, D.   2002
"The Myth Ritual Theory and the
Teaching of Multicultural Literature."
English Journal 5: 52–55.

Barthes, R.   1981
"Theory of the Text." *Untying the Text: A
Poststructuralist Reader.* Ed. R Young.
London: Routledge.

Bloome, D. and Egan-Robertson, A.   1993
"The Social Construction of Intertextuality in
Classroom Reading and Writing Lessons."
Reading Research Quarterly 28: 304–333.

Callahan, Meg   2002
"Intertextual Composition: The Power of the
Digital Pen." *English Education* 35: 46–64.

Spears-Bunton, L.   1999
"Calypso, Jazz, Reggae, and Salsa: Literature
Response and the African Diaspora." *Reader
Response in Secondary and College Classrooms.*
Ed. N. Karolides.
Mahway, New Jersey: Lawrence Erlbaum
Associates.

"Inherent in the theory of text is the notion of intertextuality."
—**Meg Callahan**

Finding a Way In

Multicultural literature affirms and celebrates the rich diversity of our classrooms. That very same literature, however, can be a source of confusion and frustration for some readers, as it often contains unfamiliar references and unfamiliar words or phrases. We can overcome these surface problems by using intertextual readings.

Intertextual Reading

At first glance, intertextual reading looks like paired reading via novel sets or themed reading. However, it is far more. It is an activity for before, during, and after reading; and it can be led by the teacher or students. When reading intertextually, teachers and students read widely within and across genres, canons and eras as a way of exploring one novel, short story or poem (Barthes 1981; Bloome and Egan-Robinson, 1993). This is a particularly helpful strategy when the core selection represents a nonwhite cultural group. Students begin to build an understanding of the core selection by reading various other selections. Some students will read primary-source documents from the era of the literary work; others will look at contemporary media with related content. Still others will look at student-produced research papers, Web sites, audio tapes, CDs, or poetry. Everything is fair game, as long as it has some relationship to the literature the whole class is reading. It is helpful if the additional material is short—a newspaper article, letter, poem, video clip, song, or excerpt from a reference book. Short pieces allow students to read and re-read quickly and not get bogged down in something intended to help with the primary reading task.

From Text to Talk

All of the additional reading can then be discussed in relation to the primary work as a way of illuminating, challenging, or affirming it through various reading, writing, and speaking activities. For example, students might use a Venn diagram to compare information in a newspaper account of a historic event to the representation of that event in the literature. Or they can interview each other about the literature in light of the related reading. They might ask a partner who read an article or studied a photograph how the literature shapes or expresses the event in a different way from the image or article. They might ask if the literature adds colorful language or if it changes facts and information. Such intertextual reading will help students understand multicultural literature. In fact, such reading extends the meaning of reading multiculturally so that now it includes reading multiple sources about a diversity of experiences and communities. *Elements of Literature,* with its thematic grouping of literature and its wide variety of genres, offers readers repeated opportunities for intertextual reading.

Literary Analysis: Beyond Response

Carol Jago
English Teacher
Santa Monica High School
Santa Monica, CA
and
Director
California Reading and Literature Project
University of California,
Los Angeles, CA

RESEARCH

Emig, J. 1990.
"Our Missing Theory." Conversations:
Contemporary Critical Theory and the Teaching
of Literature. Eds. C. Moran and E.F. Penfield.
Urbana: National Council of Teachers of English.
87–96.

Greene, M. 1988.
The Dialectic of Freedom.
New York: Teachers College Press.

Rosenblatt, L. 1968.
Literature as Exploration. 2nd ed.
New York: Noble & Noble.

Scholes, R. 1985.
Textual Power: Literary Theory and the Teaching
of English.
New Haven: Yale University Press.

"When there is active participation in literature—the reader living through, reflecting on, and criticizing his own responses to the text—there will be many kinds of benefits." —**Louise Rosenblatt**

Literary Analysis

Literary analysis is hard work that begins with readers' initial response to a literary work and deepens as readers measure that response against the richness of the text. That richness includes ideas presented in the text, symbols embedded in the text, and persuasive devices the author offers throughout the text. As readers do as Rosenblatt suggested and live through, reflect on, and criticize their own responses to the text, there are indeed many benefits. Those benefits become most evident when analysis follows response. As Robert Scholes explains in *Textual Power*, reading "requires both interpretation and criticism for completion."

Reading Stances

During the process of reading, readers take a series of stances toward the text. A reader's initial stance is a first impression including surface features of a text such as genre, content, and language. Moving through the text, the reader becomes caught up in the story or is carried along by a persuasive argument. Upon completion, readers step back and reflect on their own experience and prior knowledge. The text may cause them to rethink what they know. Finally, readers step back from their reading and reflect upon the context within which this piece of literature was created. Sometimes this stance includes thinking about the reading experience itself. These stances are not a hierarchy of skills, nor are they ever really independent of one another. Each adds a different dimension to the reader's understanding.

Critical Literary Stances

A stance can also refer to the point of view a reader adopts towards a text. Formal approaches to teaching literary analysis include psychological theories: psychoanalytic criticism drawing on the theories of Sigmund Freud, biographical approaches exploring the influence of the author's life upon the text, reader response approaches focusing upon what the reader brings to the text, and archetypal approaches examining universal responses to text. Other critical stances that readers may adopt include Marxist readings, new historicist readings, cultural readings, postcolonial readings, feminist readings, gender readings, and deconstructionist readings.

Maxine Greene argues that, "Learning to look through multiple perspectives, young people may be helped to build bridges among themselves; attending to a range of human stories, they may be provoked to heal and to transform." Throughout *Elements of Literature,* students are given the tools to build those bridges as they read texts and form initial responses and deepen them as they consider texts from multiple perspectives, examine literary techniques, and recognize the author's biases and purposes.

T87

Collection 1
Plot and Setting

**Informational Reading Focus:
Generating Research Questions**

About Collection 1

In Collection 1, students will master the following skills:

- **Literary Skills:** Analyze plot structure, flashback, and foreshadowing.
- **Reading Skills:** Generate research questions from informational texts.
- **Vocabulary Skills:** Use prefixes to understand word meanings; distinguish denotative and connotative meanings of words; and identify and use words from myths.
- **Writing Skills:** Develop, write, and revise an autobiographical narrative.
- **Listening and Speaking Skills:** Deliver an oral narrative.

Informational Text

Each collection of *Elements of Literature* provides a variety of informational texts related to the literature selections by theme or topic.

Minimum Course of Study

Most skills can be taught with a minimum number of selections and features. In the chart to the right, lessons highlighted in green constitute the minimum course of study that provides coverage of the skills taught in Collection 1.

Resource Manager (pp. 1C–1D)

Lesson and workshop resources are referenced in the Resource Manager on the pages that follow. These resources can be used to reinforce the skills taught in Collection 1, remediate students who are having difficulty, and provide supporting activities for English-language learners.

Scope and Sequence

Selection ▪ Feature	Literary Skills
Elements of Literature: Plot *by John Leggett*	• Understand plot structure and development of time and sequence
The Most Dangerous Game *by Richard Connell* ↔ *at grade level* **Informational Text: Can Animals Think?** *by Eugene Linden* ↔ *at grade level*	• Analyze plot structure and foreshadowing
Dog Star *by Arthur C. Clarke* ↔ *at grade level* **Informational Text: Far-out Housekeeping on the ISS** *by Ron Koczor* ↔ *at grade level*	• Analyze plot structure, flashback, and foreshadowing
Elements of Literature: Setting *by John Leggett*	• Understand setting and how it affects character, mood, and tone
A Christmas Memory *by Truman Capote* ↑ *above grade level*	• Analyze setting and how it affects mood
Writing Workshop: *Writing an Autobiographical Narrative*	
Listening and Speaking Workshop: *Presenting an Oral Narrative*	
Skills Review: *Informational Reading Skills* *Vocabulary Skills* *Writing Skills*	

Reading Skills	Vocabulary Skills	Writing ▪ Grammar and Language ▪ Listening and Speaking Skills
• Make predictions • Generate research questions	• Use prefixes to understand word meanings • Understand connotations of synonyms	• Write a story sequel
• Understand chronological order • Generate research questions, and research the answers	• Understand word derivations • Identify words from myths	• Write an autobiographical narrative
• Identify sensory details	• Use words in context	• Write a description of a place • Identify and use verb tenses
		• Write an autobiographical narrative
		• Present an oral narrative
• Generate research questions	• Understand multiple-meaning words	• Write an autobiographical narrative

Selection ▪ Feature	Planning	Differentiating Instruction ▪ Lesson Plans with ELL Strategies and Practice	Reading ▪ Vocabulary
Elements of Literature: Plot *by* John Leggett	• PowerNotes: Plot		
The Most Dangerous Game *by* Richard Connell **Informational Text:** Can Animals Think? *by* Eugene Linden	• One-Stop Planner with ExamView Test Generator	• The Holt Reader, pp. 6–37 • Holt Reading Solutions, pp. 29–36 • Supporting Instruction in Spanish, p. 3 • Audio CD Library, discs 1 and 2 • Audio CD Library, Selections and Summaries in Spanish	• The Holt Reader • Holt Reading Solutions • Vocabulary Development, pp. 1, 2 • PowerNotes: Making Predictions
Dog Star *by* Arthur C. Clarke **Informational Text:** Far-out Housekeeping on the ISS *by* Ron Koczor	• One-Stop Planner with ExamView Test Generator	• Holt Adapted Reader • Holt Reading Solutions, pp. 38–44 • Supporting Instruction in Spanish, p. 4 • Audio CD Library, discs 2 and 3 • Audio CD Library, Selections and Summaries in Spanish	• Holt Adapted Reader • Holt Reading Solutions • Vocabulary Development, p. 3
Elements of Literature: Setting *by* John Leggett	• PowerNotes: Setting		
A Christmas Memory *by* Truman Capote	• One-Stop Planner with ExamView Test Generator	• Holt Adapted Reader • Holt Reading Solutions, pp. 48–53 • Supporting Instruction in Spanish, p. 6 • Audio CD Library, discs 2 and 3 • Audio CD Library, Selections and Summaries in Spanish	• Holt Adapted Reader • Holt Reading Solutions • Vocabulary Development, p. 4
Writing Workshop: *Writing an Autobiographical Narrative*	• One-Stop Planner with ExamView Test Generator	• Workshop Resources: Writing, Listening, and Speaking, pp. 1–9 • Family Involvement Activities in English and Spanish • Supporting Instruction in Spanish, p. 69	
Listening and Speaking Workshop: *Presenting an Oral Narrative*	• One-Stop Planner with ExamView Test Generator	• Workshop Resources: Writing, Listening, and Speaking, pp. 10–15 • Supporting Instruction in Spanish	
Skills Review: *Informational Reading Skills Vocabulary Skills Writing Skills*			

The Holt Reader

The Holt Reader is a consumable paperback book which can be used alone or to accompany *Elements of Literature*. It offers guided support throughout the reading process and encourages students to become active readers by circling, underlining, questioning, and jotting down responses as they read. *The Holt Reader* works well for homework, students who have missed class, additional instructional time, reteaching, and remediation.

Holt Reading Solutions (HRS)

Holt Reading Solutions pulls together reading resources in the *Elements of Literature* program to create a powerful tool for intervention and whole-class instruction. *HRS* includes diagnostic assessment tools, lesson plans for English-language learners and special education students, adaptations of selected reading selections, vocabulary and comprehension worksheets, information on phonics and decoding, and additional instruction and practice in remedial reading skills.

Writing ▪ Grammar and Language ▪ Listening and Speaking	Assessment
• Daily Language Activities	• Holt Assessment: Literature, Reading, and Vocabulary • Holt Online Assessment • One-Stop Planner with ExamView Test Generator
• Daily Language Activities	• Holt Assessment: Literature, Reading, and Vocabulary • Holt Online Assessment • One-Stop Planner with ExamView Test Generator
• Daily Language Activities • Language Handbook Worksheets, pp. 34, 35	• Holt Assessment: Literature, Reading, and Vocabulary • Holt Online Assessment • One-Stop Planner with ExamView Test Generator
• Daily Language Activities • Workshop Resources: Writing, Listening, and Speaking, pp. 1–9	• Holt Assessment: Writing, Listening, and Speaking • Holt Online Assessment • One-Stop Planner with ExamView Test Generator
• Workshop Resources: Writing, Listening, and Speaking, pp. 10–15	• Holt Assessment: Writing, Listening, and Speaking • One-Stop Planner with ExamView Test Generator
	• Holt Assessment: Writing, Listening, and Speaking • One-Stop Planner with ExamView Test Generator

Technology

INTERNET

- go.hrw.com
- Holt Online Assessment
- Holt Online Essay Scoring
- Elements of Literature Online

MEDIA

 • One-Stop Planner with ExamView Test Generator

 • PowerNotes

 • Audio CD Library, discs 1, 2, and 3

 • Audio CD Library, Selections and Summaries in Spanish

 • Visual Connections Videocassette Program, Segment 1

 • Fine Art Transparencies, 1 and 2

 Transparency   Video

 CD-ROM   Audio CD

One–Stop Planner with ExamView Test Generator

The *One-Stop Planner* CD-ROM contains electronic versions of print-based teaching resources, clips from the video program, and valuable assessment tools. The *One-Stop Planner* resources are presented in easy-to-follow, point-and-click menu formats. To preview resources or print out worksheets and tests, you simply make a selection and click.

One–Stop Planner CD-ROM

Collection 1

SKILLS FOCUS

Grade-Level Skills

■ **Literary Skills**
Analyze plot structure and the development of time and sequence, including the use of foreshadowing and flashback.

■ **Literary Skills**
Analyze setting and how it affects character, mood, and tone.

■ **Reading Skills**
Generate relevant research questions after reading about an issue.

INTRODUCING THE COLLECTION

The first two stories in this collection are suspenseful tales that keep readers engaged. Aspects of time and sequence in the plot are examined in each story, with special attention to foreshadowing, flashbacks, and flashforwards. The informational piece that follows each of these first two stories shows students how to generate relevant questions for research. Setting is used in the last story to delineate character. The writing assignment at the end of the collection asks students to write their own biographical or autobiographical narratives or short stories, applying what they learned about sequencing events in a plot and using details of setting to reveal character. Students will also get a chance to present an oral narrative.

COLLECTION 1 RESOURCES: READING

Planning
■ *One-Stop Planner* CD-ROM with ExamView Test Generator

Differentiating Instruction
■ *Holt Reading Solutions*
■ *The Holt Reader*
■ *Holt Adapted Reader*

■ *Family Involvement Activities in English and Spanish*
■ *Supporting Instruction in Spanish*
■ *Audio CD Library, Selections and Summaries in Spanish*

Vocabulary
■ *Vocabulary Development*

Grammar and Language
■ *Language Handbook Worksheets*
■ *Daily Language Activities*

Assessment
■ *Holt Assessment: Literature, Reading, and Vocabulary*
■ *One-Stop Planner* CD-ROM with ExamView Test Generator
■ *Holt Online Assessment*

Collection 1

PLOT AND SETTING

INFORMATIONAL READING FOCUS

GENERATING RESEARCH QUESTIONS

A story to me means a plot
where there is some surprise. . . .
Because this is how life is—
full of surprises.

—Isaac Bashevis Singer

INTERNET
Collection
Resources
Keyword: LE5 9-1

Time Transfixed (1939) by René Magritte.
Oil on canvas (146.3 cm × 97.5 cm).
The Art Institute of Chicago.

1

What sort of surprises do you think Singer means? [Possible responses: a sudden disappointment; falling in love; escaping a dangerous situation.]

VIEWING THE ART

René Magritte (1898–1967) was a member of the surrealist movement and is considered the most important Belgian artist of the twentieth century. Magritte painted everyday objects realistically but often in paradoxical, impossible situations. His paintings challenge us to make meaningful connections between elements that are juxtaposed in unlikely ways. In *Time Transfixed,* an oddly small train careens through a fireplace into a seemingly empty room.

Activity. Invite students to imagine a scenario involving everyday objects in impossible situations. Then, have them write a story or create a piece of art based on that scenario.

Internet
- go.hrw.com (Keyword: LE5 9-1)
- *Elements of Literature Online*

Media
- *Audio CD Library*
- *Audio CD Library, Selections and Summaries in Spanish*

- *Fine Art Transparencies*
- *Visual Connections Videocassette Program*
- *PowerNotes*

Grade-Level Skills

■ Literary Skills

Analyze the development of time and sequence, including the use of foreshadowing and flashback.

Review Skills

■ Literary Skills

Evaluate the plot's structure and development, and the way in which conflicts are resolved.

Elements of Literature: Plot—Time and Sequence

Ask students when people might use the expression, "The plot thickens." [Possible response: They might use it to announce that a complication or mystery has arisen.] Then, review the definition of literary plot (a series of related events in a story). Point out that the plot of a story always thickens until a crisis or climax occurs. Writers don't always relate events in the order in which they happen, though. Sometimes they thicken the plot by rearranging the sequence of events. Ask students to recall movies or television shows that contain flashbacks or flash-forwards. How did they affect the development of the story?

Elements of Literature

Plot *by* John Leggett
TIME AND SEQUENCE

Hooking Your Curiosity

When we talk about stories, plot is the element to start with, for plot is story itself. **Plot** is a series of related events, like links in a chain. Each event hooks our curiosity and pulls us forward to the next event.

Conflict: The Fuel of Narrative

In most stories, we care about what happens next because we're hooked by a **conflict,** or struggle. In an **external conflict** the struggle takes place between two characters, between a character and a group, or between a character and something nonhuman—a typhoon or a computer virus, for example. An **internal conflict** takes place within a character's mind or heart: A desire to win someone's friendship might conflict with a fear of rejection.

Conflict is the fuel of narrative. The greater the conflict, the more we care about the outcome.

The Bare Bones of a Plot

Stories, like houses and human beings, need a structure, or framework, to hold them together. Plots are usually built on four major parts, which we might think of as their bare bones.

1 The first part of a plot is called the **basic situation,** or **exposition.** This is the opening of the story, when the characters and their conflict are introduced.

Young William didn't mind his hard work as the king's stableboy because he loved horses. The king, however, was miserable because his kingdom had been invaded by a large fire-breathing dragon who smelled to high heaven.

2 The second part of a plot is the **complication.** Now the main character takes some action to resolve the conflict but meets with more problems or complications: danger, hostility, fear, or even a new threatening situation.

William set out to kill the dragon in order to help the king. While he was riding into the woods, several robbers tried to hijack his horse. Poor William felt himself losing courage.

3 The third part of a story is the **climax.** This is the key scene in the story—that tense or exciting or terrifying moment when our emotional involvement is greatest. Now we learn what the outcome of the conflict is going to be.

When he had just about decided to give up the chase and return home, William found himself staring down the dragon's throat. Closing his eyes, he hurled his sword into the dragon's windpipe. The monster gagged and began to die.

4 The final part of the story is the **resolution.** Sometimes this is called the **denouement** (dā′nōō·män′). The resolution occurs at the end of the story. Now all the struggles are over, and we know what is going to happen to the characters.

INTERNET
More About Plot
Keyword: LE5 9-1

Literary Skills
Understand plot structure and development of time and sequence.

2 Collection 1 Plot and Setting • Generating Research Questions

---

DIFFERENTIATING INSTRUCTION

Learners Having Difficulty
Plot. Have students summarize the plot of a recent popular movie. Start by asking, "What is the basic situation?" Then, ask students, "What are the most important events that move the story forward?" As they recount the story, create a plot diagram, recording the key events and labeling the plot elements (basic situation, complications, climax, and resolution).

Advanced Learners
Acceleration. Discuss with students the reasons writers use flashbacks, flash-forwards, and foreshadowing. Why would a writer choose to tell a story out of straight chronological order?

When he returned to the palace with the dragon's head, William became a hero, although he had to spend the next two weeks soaking himself to get rid of the smell of a very dead dragon.

It's All in the Timing

Events in real life can go on and on, but stories cannot. That's why the plot of a story is framed by time. A story may cover fifty happy years in a marriage or five nerve-racking moments in a submarine, but every work of fiction is defined by a time span, a period of time that suits the writer's purpose.

Most stories are told in **chronological order,** the order in which events unfold in real time. The writer starts at the beginning and tells about each event in the order in which it happens. Yet writers frequently use other techniques to manipulate time and control our emotions, especially our feelings of suspense. For example, they might slow down time to emphasize a moment of danger, or they might speed up time to skip over events that don't move the story along.

Playing with Time

You have also read stories in which writers interrupt the flow of events to present an episode from the past. Such a scene is called a **flashback.** For example, a story might begin with a description of a woman hiding in an abandoned house. The writer might then use a flashback to show why the woman is hiding. A flashback could also be used to strengthen our understanding of the character by revealing a powerful memory.

Writers can play with time in another way as well. Instead of going back to the past, they can jump ahead days or years into the future by using a literary device called a **flash-forward.**

Finally, writers can bring the future into the present by using **foreshadowing,** hints or clues that suggest what is to come in the story. Foreshadowing can make a story more exciting by increasing suspense. For instance, a man is barely aware of wolves howling in the distance, but the reader wonders about them. Days later the man is pursued by those wolves. The reader realizes the howling foreshadowed the man's now-desperate situation.

So, whether writers make us look back or think ahead, they hook us into a story by playing with time.

Practice

Choose a children's story or a fairy tale that is familiar to you. First, draw a **plot diagram** like the one shown here, and add labels describing the key parts of the story's plot. Then, use your imagination to write a **flashback** that could occur in one part of the story.

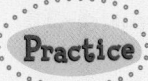

Possible response (based on "Cinderella"):

Basic Situation—Cinderella is mistreated by her stepmother and two stepsisters.

Event—They are all invited to a ball.

Event—The stepsisters keep Cinderella busy all day.

Complication—Cinderella has no proper clothes to wear to the ball and no time to get ready.

Event—Her fairy godmother magically creates a gown and carriage for her but warns her to be home by midnight.

Event—The prince and Cinderella dance all night until the stroke of midnight, when Cinderella runs away, leaving a glass slipper behind.

Event—The prince goes around the countryside asking every maiden to try on the slipper.

Climax—The slipper fits Cinderella.

Resolution—The prince and Cinderella marry and live happily ever after.

Possible flashback—After her stepsisters and stepmother leave for the ball, there is a flashback to Cinderella's childhood. In the flashback, Cinderella's mother tells her about a fairy godmother who will give her help when she needs it most.

Apply

Have students make a plot diagram of an episode from a television series that contains a flashback or flash-forward. Ask them to label the flashback or flash-forward and identify its purpose or effect.

Activity. Ask students to name a story or novel they have read in which flashbacks, flash-forwards, or foreshadowing is used. Have them summarize the plot and explain how and why the technique is used in the story.

Grade-Level Skills

■ Literary Skills

Analyze the development of time and sequence, including the use of foreshadowing and flashback.

■ Reading Skills

Make predictions.

Review Skills

■ Literary Skills

Identify events that advance the plot and determine how each event explains past or present actions, or foreshadows future actions.

Summary ⬌ *at grade level*

While traveling by yacht, Sanger Rainsford, an expert American hunter, accidentally falls overboard. He swims to a mysterious island, where he discovers the medieval-style château of a cultured but sinister Russian, General Zaroff, who is attended by Ivan, a fearsome manservant, and guarded by a pack of fierce hounds. Zaroff confides to Rainsford that his love of hunting has been thwarted by the lack of challenging prey. He boasts that he has stocked his island with the most dangerous and clever game of all—humans. When Rainsford refuses to join Zaroff in such a hunt, the Russian forces his "guest" to become the hunted. Zaroff stalks Rainsford, who must rely on his wits to escape capture and death. After a suspenseful chase, Rainsford outsmarts Zaroff, surprising the general in his bedchamber. The resolution is not depicted, but it is implied that Zaroff is fed to his hounds.

Before You Read

The Most Dangerous Game

Make the Connection

Quickwrite ✏️

Some of the most exciting narratives pit villain against hero in a life-or-death struggle. The tension in such stories often depends as much on the character of the bad guy or gal as on that of the hero. Write a few sentences describing a villain from a novel, story, or movie. Why does the character fascinate you?

Literary Focus

Foreshadowing: Hints About What's Ahead

People call them cliffhangers or nail-biters. They are stories of suspense that keep you glued to your chair. One way that writers create suspense is through **foreshadowing,** the use of clues that hint at later events in the story. Foreshadowing makes you curious, even anxious, to know what will happen next—it keeps you turning the pages. Once you've finished reading, you can piece together the clues and enjoy the story all the more. In this suspenseful tale the ominous foreshadowing will hook you early on.

Reading Skills

Making Predictions: Matching Wits with the Writer

When you read a suspense-filled story, you make predictions about what is going to happen, often without even realizing it. A **prediction** is a type of inference, a guess based on evidence. Some of the things readers base predictions on include

• clues the writer plants

- their own experience of life
- their understanding of how stories work

Before you start this famous adventure story, read its **title** again. What do you predict the title might mean? Be sure to compare your predictions with those of your classmates. (How many different interpretations did you have for the word *game*?) Then, as you read, stop at the open-book signs ( ) at the end of some paragraphs, and continue to make predictions.

Vocabulary Development

receding (ri·sēd′iŋ) *v.* used as *adj.*: becoming more distant.

disarming (dis·ärm′iŋ) *adj.*: removing or lessening suspicions or fears.

prolonged (prō·lôŋd′) *v.* used as *adj.*: extended.

imprudent (im·prood′'nt) *adj.*: unwise.

surmounted (sər·mount′id) *v.*: overcame.

unruffled (un·ruf′əld) *adj.*: calm; not disturbed.

invariably (in·ver′ē·ə·blē) *adv.*: always; without changing.

diverting (də·vurt′iŋ) *adj.*: entertaining.

impulse (im′puls′) *n.*: sudden desire to do something.

protruding (prō·trood′iŋ) *v.* used as *adj.*: sticking out.

go.hrw.com

INTERNET

Vocabulary Practice

Keyword: LE5 9-1

SKILLS FOCUS

Literary Skills Understand foreshadowing.

Reading Skills Make predictions.

RESOURCES: READING

Planning

■ *One-Stop Planner* CD-ROM with ExamView Test Generator

Differentiating Instruction

■ *Holt Reading Solutions*

■ *The Holt Reader*

■ *Supporting Instruction in Spanish*

■ *Audio CD Library, Selections and Summaries in Spanish*

Vocabulary

■ *Vocabulary Development*

Grammar and Language

■ *Daily Language Activities*

THE MOST DANGEROUS GAME

"Sailors have a curious dread of the place."

Richard Connell

"Off there to the right—somewhere—is a large island," said Whitney. "It's rather a mystery—"

"What island is it?" Rainsford asked.

"The old charts call it Ship-Trap Island," Whitney replied. "A suggestive name, isn't it? Sailors have a curious dread of the place. I don't know why. Some superstition—" Ⓐ

"Can't see it," remarked Rainsford, trying to peer through the dank tropical night that was palpable as it pressed its thick warm blackness in upon the yacht.

"You've good eyes," said Whitney, with a laugh, "and I've seen you pick off a moose moving in the brown fall bush at four hundred yards, but even you can't see four miles or so

Assessment

- *Holt Assessment: Literature, Reading, and Vocabulary*
- *One-Stop Planner* CD-ROM with ExamView Test Generator
- *Holt Online Assessment*

Internet

- *go.hrw.com* (Keyword: LE5 9-1)
- *Elements of Literature Online*

Media

- *Audio CD Library*
- *Audio CD Library, Selections and Summaries in Spanish*

PRETEACHING

Selection Starter

Motivate. At the outset of the story, one character says, "The world is made up of two classes—the hunters and the huntees." Have students discuss this idea. Do they agree?

Preview Vocabulary

Use these questions to reinforce students' mastery of the Vocabulary words listed on p. 4.

1. Does a man with a <u>receding</u> hairline have much hair? [no]
2. Would a <u>disarming</u> leader be able to calm an angry crowd? [yes]
3. Would you be displeased if a vacation was <u>prolonged</u>? [no]
4. Is it <u>imprudent</u> for bicyclists to wear helmets? [no]
5. Would you admire a person who <u>surmounted</u> a difficulty? [yes]
6. Is an easygoing person likely to remain <u>unruffled</u> during a crisis? [yes]
7. Would you be surprised if someone who was <u>invariably</u> late arrived halfway through a party? [no]
8. If a critic calls a play <u>diverting</u>, did she enjoy it? [yes]
9. Would a <u>timid</u> animal often have the <u>impulse</u> to run? [yes]
10. Would a careful construction worker leave a nail <u>protruding</u> from a floorboard? [no]

DIRECT TEACHING

Ⓐ **Literary Focus**

❷ **Foreshadowing.** Point out that the author immediately establishes a mood of fear here. What might the sailors' dread foreshadow? [Possible response: Awful things may happen on the island.]

A Reading Skills

? Expressing an opinion. Do you agree with Whitney or with Rainsford? Why? [Possible responses: I agree with Whitney because animals try to avoid pain and death. I agree with Rainsford because animals act on instinct, not feelings.]

B Reading Skills

Predicting. Suggest to students that in real life, people often have aimless conversations about topics that they never again discuss. In literature, however, conversations are seldom aimless. If the island is discussed, it will probably play a role in the story. Ask students to brainstorm all the roles the island could play. For example, the boat might be sunk by cannons fired from the island. [Possible response to question 1: The island will be the hostile setting for the rest of the story.]

through a moonless Caribbean night."

"Nor four yards," admitted Rainsford. "Ugh! It's like moist black velvet."

"It will be light in Rio," promised Whitney. "We should make it in a few days. I hope the jaguar guns have come from Purdey's.[1] We should have some good hunting up the Amazon. Great sport, hunting."

"The best sport in the world," agreed Rainsford.

"For the hunter," amended Whitney. "Not for the jaguar."

"Don't talk rot, Whitney," said Rainsford. "You're a big-game hunter, not a philosopher. Who cares how a jaguar feels?"

"Perhaps the jaguar does," observed Whitney.

Ⓐ "Bah! They've no understanding."

"Even so, I rather think they understand one thing—fear. The fear of pain and the fear of death."

"Nonsense," laughed Rainsford. "This hot weather is making you soft, Whitney. Be a realist. The world is made up of two classes—the hunters and the huntees. Luckily, you and I are the hunters. Do you think we've passed that island yet?"

"I can't tell in the dark. I hope so."

"Why?" asked Rainsford.

"The place has a reputation—a bad one."

"Cannibals?" suggested Rainsford.

"Hardly. Even cannibals wouldn't live in such a Godforsaken place. But it's gotten into sailor lore, somehow. Didn't you notice that the crew's nerves seemed a bit jumpy today?"

"They were a bit strange, now you mention it. Even Captain Nielsen—"

"Yes, even that tough-minded old Swede, who'd go up to the devil himself and ask him for a light. Those fishy blue eyes held a look I never saw there before. All I could get out of him was: 'This place has an evil name among seafaring men, sir.' Then he said to me, very gravely:

_____

1. **Purdey's** (pʉrʹdēz): British manufacturer of hunting equipment.

'Don't you feel anything?'—as if the air about us was actually poisonous. Now, you mustn't laugh when I tell you this—I did feel something like a sudden chill.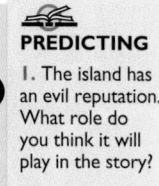

PREDICTING
1. The island has an evil reputation. What role do you think it will play in the story?

"There was no breeze. The sea was as flat as a plate-glass window. We were drawing near the island then. What I felt was a—a mental chill, a sort of sudden dread."

"Pure imagination," said Rainsford. "One superstitious sailor can taint the whole ship's company with his fear."

"Maybe. But sometimes I think sailors have an extra sense that tells them when they are in danger. Sometimes I think evil is a tangible thing—with wavelengths, just as sound and light have. An evil place can, so to speak, broadcast vibrations of evil. Anyhow, I'm glad we're getting out of this zone. Well, I think I'll turn in now, Rainsford."

"I'm not sleepy," said Rainsford. "I'm going to smoke another pipe on the afterdeck."

"Good night, then, Rainsford. See you at breakfast."

"Right. Good night, Whitney."

There was no sound in the night as Rainsford sat there but the muffled throb of the engine that drove the yacht swiftly through the darkness, and the swish and ripple of the wash of the propeller.

Rainsford, reclining in a steamer chair, indolently[2] puffed on his favorite brier.[3] The sensuous drowsiness of the night was on him. "It's so dark," he thought, "that I could sleep without closing my eyes; the night would be my eyelids—"

An abrupt sound startled him. Off to the

_____

2. **indolently** (inʹdə·lənt·lē) *adv.:* lazily.
3. **brier** (brīʹər) *n.:* tobacco pipe made from the root of a brier bush or tree.

Learners Having Difficulty
Invite learners having difficulty to read "The Most Dangerous Game" in interactive format in *The Holt Reader* and to use the sidenotes as aids to understanding the selection. The interactive version provides additional instruction, practice, and assessment of the literary skill taught in the Student Edition.

Monitor students' responses to the selection, and correct any misconceptions that arise.

English-Language Learners
Students may be unfamiliar with the terms relating to hunting, particularly multiple-meaning words such as *game, prey, report,* and *quarry*. Discuss the meanings of these

words and others, such as *huntees, twenty-two,* and *caliber*.

Special Education Students
For lessons designed for special education students, see *Holt Reading Solutions*.

right he heard it, and his ears, expert in such matters, could not be mistaken. Again he heard the sound, and again. Somewhere, off in the blackness, someone had fired a gun three times.

Rainsford sprang up and moved quickly to the rail, mystified. He strained his eyes in the direction from which the reports had come, but it was like trying to see through a blanket. He leapt upon the rail and balanced himself there, to get greater elevation; his pipe, striking a rope, was knocked from his mouth. He lunged for it; a short, hoarse cry came from his lips as he realized he had reached too far and had lost his balance. The cry was pinched off short as the blood-warm waters of the Caribbean Sea closed over his head.

He struggled up to the surface and tried to cry out, but the wash from the speeding yacht slapped him in the face and the salt water in his open mouth made him gag and strangle. Desperately he struck out with strong strokes after the receding lights of the yacht, but he stopped before he had swum fifty feet. A certain coolheadedness had come to him; it was not the first time he had been in a tight place. There was a chance that his cries could be heard by someone aboard the yacht, but that chance was slender and grew more slender as the yacht raced on. He wrestled himself out of his clothes and shouted with all his power. The lights of the yacht became faint and ever-vanishing fireflies; then they were blotted out entirely by the night.

Rainsford remembered the shots. They had come from the right, and doggedly he swam in that direction, swimming with slow, deliberate strokes, conserving his strength. For a seemingly endless time he fought the sea. He began to

count his strokes; he could do possibly a hundred more and then—

Rainsford heard a sound. It came out of the darkness, a high screaming sound, the sound of an animal in an extremity of anguish and terror.

He did not recognize the animal that made the sound; he did not try to; with fresh vitality he swam toward the sound. He heard it again; then it was cut short by another noise, crisp, staccato.

"Pistol shot," muttered Rainsford, swimming on.

Ten minutes of determined effort brought another sound to his ears—the most welcome he had ever heard—the muttering and growling of the sea breaking on a rocky shore. He was almost on the rocks before he saw them; on a night less calm he would have been shattered against them. With his remaining strength he dragged himself from the swirling waters. Jagged crags appeared to jut into the opaqueness.[4]

He forced himself upward, hand over hand. Gasping, his hands raw, he reached a flat place at the top. Dense jungle came down to the very edge of the cliffs. What perils that tangle of trees and underbrush might hold for him did not concern Rainsford just then. All he knew was that he was safe from his enemy, the sea, and that utter weariness was on him. He flung himself down at the jungle edge and tumbled headlong into the deepest sleep of his life.

---

4. **opaqueness** (ō·pāk′nis) *n.*: here, darkness. Something opaque does not let light pass through.

Vocabulary
receding (ri·sēd′iŋ) *v.* used as *adj.*: becoming more distant.

> For a seemingly endless time he fought the sea.

C Reading Skills
❷ **Evaluating.** What do you think of this fall as a plot device? [Possible responses: It seems unlikely that someone would stand on a rail to see better in the dark. People's curiosity sometimes leads them to do strange things.]

D Literary Focus
Foreshadowing. Point out this unusual diction. Referring to the sea as "blood-warm" is a way of foreshadowing violence. Have students look for other examples of description used to foreshadow events as they read.

E Literary Focus
❷ **Characters.** Remind students that they learn about characters both from what the narrator says about them and how the characters act. What do you learn about Rainsford in this passage? [Possible response: Both the narrator's words and Rainsford's actions reveal that he is coolheaded in an emergency.]

F Advanced Learners
❷ **Enrichment.** To what earlier part of the story does this passage allude? [Earlier Rainsford had insisted that animals have no feelings. Ironically, he now perceives the sound as that of "an animal in an extremity of anguish and terror."]

Advanced Learners
Acceleration. Have students compare what the characters say about themselves with their own assessments of the characters. They might use a chart like this one:

What Rainsford Says About Himself	What I Think About Rainsford
What Zaroff Says About Himself	What I Think About Zaroff

A Literary Focus

? Foreshadowing. The phrase "snarled and ragged jungle" suggests an area that has not been cultivated. What kind of men might Rainsford find in such a place? [Possible response: men who lead a simple, rough existence without the amenities of civilization.]

B Literary Focus

? Suspense. This passage generates suspense by leaving questions unanswered. What questions do you have? [Possible responses: What kind of animal was killed? Who was the hunter? What happened to the prey?]

C English-Language Learners

Building background knowledge. Tell students that gargoyles are waterspouts that are carved in the shapes of animals or monsters projecting from a building. They often appear on medieval Gothic cathedrals in Europe.

D Learners Having Difficulty

Questioning. Encourage students to interact with the text by asking questions raised by the appearance of a man carrying a revolver. [Possible questions: Is the man afraid of something? Is he protecting something? Did he fire the shots that Rainsford heard earlier?]

When he opened his eyes he knew from the position of the sun that it was late in the afternoon. Sleep had given him new vigor; a sharp hunger was picking at him. He looked about him, almost cheerfully.

"Where there are pistol shots, there are men. Where there are men, there is food," he thought. **A** But what kind of men, he wondered, in so forbidding a place? An unbroken front of snarled and ragged jungle fringed the shore.

He saw no sign of a trail through the closely knit web of weeds and trees; it was easier to go along the shore, and Rainsford floundered along by the water. Not far from where he had landed, he stopped.

B Some wounded thing, by the evidence a large animal, had thrashed about in the underbrush; the jungle weeds were crushed down and the moss was lacerated; one patch of weeds was stained crimson. A small, glittering object not far away caught Rainsford's eye and he picked it up. It was an empty cartridge.

"A twenty-two," he remarked. "That's odd. It must have been a fairly large animal too. The hunter had his nerve with him to tackle it with a light gun. It's clear that the brute put up a fight. I suppose the first three shots I heard was when the hunter flushed his quarry[5] and wounded it. The last shot was when he trailed it here and finished it."

He examined the ground closely and found what he had hoped to find—the print of hunting boots. They pointed along the cliff in the direction he had been going. Eagerly he hurried along, now slipping on a rotten log or a loose stone, but making headway; night was

---

5. **flushed his quarry:** drove the animal he was hunting out of its hiding place.

---

beginning to settle down on the island.

Bleak darkness was blacking out the sea and jungle when Rainsford sighted the lights. He came upon them as he turned a crook in the coastline, and his first thought was that he had come upon a village, for there were many lights. But as he forged along, he saw to his great astonishment that all the lights were in one enormous building—a lofty structure with pointed towers plunging upward into the gloom. His eyes made out the shadowy outlines of a palatial château;[6] it was set on a high bluff, and on three sides of it cliffs dived down to where the sea licked greedy lips in the shadows.

"Mirage," thought Rainsford. But it was no mirage, he found, when he opened the tall spiked iron gate. The stone steps were real enough; **C** the massive door with a leering gargoyle for a knocker was real enough; yet about it all hung an air of unreality.

He lifted the knocker, and it creaked up stiffly, as if it had never before been used. He let it fall, and it startled him with its booming loudness. He thought he heard steps within; the door remained closed. Again Rainsford lifted the heavy knocker and let it fall. The door opened then, opened as suddenly as if it were on a spring, and Rainsford stood blinking in the river of glaring gold light that poured out. The first thing Rainsford's eyes discerned was the largest man Rainsford had ever seen—a gigantic **D** creature, solidly made and black-bearded to the waist. In his hand the man held a long-barreled revolver, and he was pointing it straight at Rainsford's heart.

Out of the snarl of beard two small eyes regarded Rainsford.

---

6. **château** (sha·tō') *n.:* large country house.

"It's clear that the brute put up a fight."

READING MINI-LESSON

Developing Word-Attack Skills
Point out that long vowel sounds are often represented by a combination of two vowel letters. Use these words from the selection to illustrate this rule.

taint	*ai* stands for /ā/
steamer	*ea* stands for /ē/
believe	*ie* stands for /ē/
boast	*oa* stands for /ō/

Explain that a vowel pair, like *ai, ea, ie, oa,* or *oe,* sometimes represents two distinct vowel sounds. To illustrate this point, ask students to determine whether the underlined letters in the following words stand for one sound or two.

tailor [one]	naive [two]
series [one]	siesta [two]
anguished [one]	genuine [two]

"Don't be alarmed," said Rainsford, with a smile which he hoped was disarming. "I'm no robber. I fell off a yacht. My name is Sanger Rainsford of New York City."

The menacing look in the eyes did not change. The revolver pointed as rigidly as if the giant were a statue. He gave no sign that he understood Rainsford's words or that he had even heard them. He was dressed in uniform, a black uniform trimmed with gray astrakhan.[7]

"I'm Sanger Rainsford of New York," Rainsford began again. "I fell off a yacht. I am hungry."

The man's only answer was to raise with his thumb the hammer of his revolver. Then Rainsford saw the man's free hand go to his forehead in a military salute, and he saw him click his heels together and stand at attention. Another man was coming down the broad marble steps, an erect, slender man in evening clothes. He advanced to Rainsford and held out his hand.

In a cultivated voice marked by a slight accent that gave it added precision and deliberateness, he said: "It is a very great pleasure and honor to welcome Mr. Sanger Rainsford, the celebrated hunter, to my home."

Automatically Rainsford shook the man's hand.

"I've read your book about hunting snow leopards in Tibet, you see," explained the man. "I am General Zaroff."

Rainsford's first impression was that the man was singularly handsome; his second was that there was an original, almost bizarre quality about the general's face. He was a tall man past middle age, for his hair was a vivid white; but his thick eyebrows and pointed military moustache were as black as the night from which Rainsford had come. His eyes, too, were black and very bright. He had high cheekbones, a sharp-cut nose, a spare, dark face, the face of a man used to giving orders, the face of an aristocrat. Turning

---

7. **astrakhan** (as'trə·kən) *n.:* curly fur of very young lambs.

to the giant in uniform, the general made a sign. The giant put away his pistol, saluted, withdrew.

"Ivan is an incredibly strong fellow," remarked the general, "but he has the misfortune to be deaf and dumb. A simple fellow, but, I'm afraid, like all his race, a bit of a savage."

"Is he Russian?"

"He is a Cossack,"[8] said the general, and his smile showed red lips and pointed teeth. "So am I.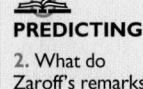

"Come," he said, "we shouldn't be chatting here. We can talk later. Now you want clothes, food, rest. You shall have them. This is a most restful spot."

Ivan had reappeared, and the general spoke to him with lips that moved but gave forth no sound.

"Follow Ivan, if you please, Mr. Rainsford," said the general. "I was about to have my dinner when you came. I'll wait for you. You'll find that my clothes will fit you, I think."

It was to a huge, beam-ceilinged bedroom with a canopied bed big enough for six men that Rainsford followed the silent giant. Ivan laid out an evening suit, and Rainsford, as he put it on, noticed that it came from a London tailor who ordinarily cut and sewed for none below the rank of duke.

The dining room to which Ivan conducted him was in many ways remarkable. There was a medieval magnificence about it; it suggested a baronial hall of feudal times, with its oaken panels, its high ceiling, its vast refectory table where two-score men could sit down to eat. About the hall were the mounted heads of many

---

8. **Cossack** (käs'ak'): member of a group from Ukraine, many of whom served as horsemen to the Russian czars and were famous for their fierceness in battle.

Vocabulary

disarming (dis·ärm'iŋ) *adj.:* removing or lessening suspicions or fears.

PREDICTING

2. What do Zaroff's remarks about Cossacks suggest about how he will behave later in the story?

E Literary Focus

? Conflict. How does this confrontation heighten the suspense? [Possible response: The giant menaces Rainsford with a gun. The fact that he does not seem to understand Rainsford makes him all the more mysterious and threatening.]

F Literary Focus

Characters. Have students draw conclusions about the character of General Zaroff from the narrator's description, the dialogue, and Zaroff's actions. [Possible responses: He is elegant, polite, handsome, educated, well-read, cultivated, and used to giving orders. There is a strange quality to his face.]

G Reading Skills

Predicting. Help students make this prediction by pointing out the strange detail about Zaroff's teeth. [Possible response to question 2: He might behave cruelly in an uncivilized way, without regard for society's rules.]

---

screaming [one]   idea [two]
mystified [one]   experiences [two]
throes [one]   poets [two]

Activity. Write these pairs of words on the chalkboard. Have students determine whether the underlined letters in each word stand for a single sound or for two distinct sounds.

1. Caribbean [two]   screaming [one]
2. bruised [one]   suicide [two]
3. society [two]   achieved [one]
4. weather [one]   Crimea [two]
5. Rainsford [one]   prosaic [two]
6. experiences [two]   retrieve [one]

DIRECT TEACHING

A **Vocabulary Development**

Word derivations: Prefixes.
Point out that the prefix *sur–* means "over" or "above." Something that *surpasses* the average passes over and above the average. Have students name the Vocabulary word with this prefix and use it in an original sentence. [Possible response: *Vocabulary word—*surmounted. *Sentence—*We *surmounted* the language barrier by communicating in sign language.]

B **Literary Focus**

? **Foreshadowing.** Rainsford is uncomfortable with the general's appraising, or judging, him. What does the general's inspection of Rainsford hint at? [Possible response: The general may be trying to decide how Rainsford will react to something.]

C **Reading Skills**

? **Predicting.** Help students predict what game Zaroff has brought to the island by having them rule out certain obvious possibilities. For example, when Zaroff says, "The biggest," he could be referring to elephants, but elephants are not normally dangerous. He has lions, tigers, moose, and bears mounted on the wall. When all the obvious possibilities have been eliminated, what remains? [Possible responses to question 3: a new breed of animal; an animal thought extinct; humans.]

---

animals—lions, tigers, elephants, moose, bears; larger or more perfect specimens Rainsford had never seen. At the great table the general was sitting, alone.

A "You'll have a cocktail, Mr. Rainsford," he suggested. The cocktail was surpassingly good; and, Rainsford noted, the table appointments were of the finest—the linen, the crystal, the silver, the china.

They were eating borscht, the rich red soup with sour cream so dear to Russian palates. Half apologetically General Zaroff said: "We do our best to preserve the amenities[9] of civilization here. Please forgive any lapses. We are well off the beaten track, you know. Do you think the champagne has suffered from its long ocean trip?"

"Not in the least," declared Rainsford. He was finding the general a most thoughtful and affable host, a true cosmopolite.[10] But there **B** was one small trait of the general's that made Rainsford uncomfortable. Whenever he looked up from his plate he found the general studying him, appraising him narrowly.

"Perhaps," said General Zaroff, "you were surprised that I recognized your name. You see, I read all books on hunting published in English, French, and Russian. I have but one passion in my life, Mr. Rainsford, and it is the hunt."

"You have some wonderful heads here," said Rainsford as he ate a particularly well-cooked filet mignon. "That Cape buffalo is the largest I ever saw."

"Oh, that fellow. Yes, he was a monster."

"Did he charge you?"

"Hurled me against a tree," said the general. "Fractured my skull. But I got the brute."

"I've always thought," said Rainsford, "that the Cape buffalo is the most dangerous of all big game."

For a moment the general did not reply; he

---

9. **amenities** (ə·men′ə·tēz) *n.:* comforts and conveniences.
10. **cosmopolite** (käz·mäp′ə·līt′) *n.:* knowledgeable citizen of the world.

---

was smiling his curious red-lipped smile. Then he said slowly: "No. You are wrong, sir. The Cape buffalo is not the most dangerous big game." He sipped his wine. "Here in my preserve on this island," he said in the same slow tone, "I hunt more dangerous game."

Rainsford expressed his surprise. "Is there big game on this island?"

The general nodded.
"The biggest."

"Really?"

"Oh, it isn't here naturally, of course. I have to stock the island."

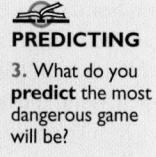

C **PREDICTING**
3. What do you **predict** the most dangerous game will be?

"What have you imported, general?" Rainsford asked. "Tigers?"

The general smiled. "No," he said. "Hunting tigers ceased to interest me some years ago. I exhausted their possibilities, you see. No thrill left in tigers, no real danger. I live for danger, Mr. Rainsford."

The general took from his pocket a gold cigarette case and offered his guest a long black cigarette with a silver tip; it was perfumed and gave off a smell like incense.

"We will have some capital hunting, you and I," said the general. "I shall be most glad to have your society."

"But what game—" began Rainsford.

"I'll tell you," said the general. "You will be amused, I know. I think I may say, in all modesty, that I have done a rare thing. I have invented a new sensation. May I pour you another glass of port, Mr. Rainsford?"

"Thank you, general."

The general filled both glasses and said: "God makes some men poets. Some He makes kings, some beggars. Me He made a hunter. My hand was made for the trigger, my father said. He was a very rich man, with a quarter of a million acres in the Crimea,[11] and he was an

---

11. **Crimea** (krī·mē′ə): peninsula in Ukraine jutting into the Black Sea.

CONTENT-AREA CONNECTIONS

Culture: The Essence of Civility
General Zaroff regards himself as a civilized man and refers to luxuries such as champagne and fine tableware as "amenities of civilization." Ask students to define and discuss the words *civilized* ("educated," "at an advanced stage of cultural development," "refined") and *civilization* ("an advanced stage of development in human society, with a high level of arts and sciences," "the culture of a

particular people or place"). Point out the differences between *civilization* and *civility,* which means "politeness" or "courtesy."
Whole-class activity. To spark a discussion of the true qualities of a civilized person, ask the following questions:

• In our culture, what material possessions, actions, or inner qualities suggest that someone is civilized?

• Which do you think are better indicators that someone is civilized: material possessions or inner qualities? Explain.

• Is Zaroff a civilized man? Explain.

Media: "The Most Dangerous Game" in the Movies
This short story has been the basis of many films. In a 1932 adaptation—the only one to keep Connell's title—Zaroff lures people to

---

Casanova (1997) by Julio Larraz. Oil on canvas (60″ × 69″).
Courtesy of the Nohra Haime Gallery, New York.

Cuban American artist **Julio Larraz** (1944–   ) has painted primarily in the United States, but his works often refer to his native land.

Activity. Tell students that the title of this painting, *Casanova*, refers to Giovanni Giacomo Casanova, an eighteenth-century Italian adventurer. Casanova gained a reputation as a man without scruples or moral sense who "hunted" women for his own pleasure. You might have students compare the man in the painting with the description of General Zaroff on pp. 9–10. Ask students to continue looking for similarities between the two men as they read.

ardent sportsman. When I was only five years old, he gave me a little gun, specially made in Moscow for me, to shoot sparrows with. When I shot some of his prize turkeys with it, he did not punish me; he complimented me on my marksmanship. I killed my first bear in the Caucasus[12] when I was ten. My whole life has been one <u>prolonged</u> hunt. I went into the army—it was expected of noblemen's sons—and for a time commanded a division of Cossack cavalry, but my real interest was always the hunt. I have hunted every kind of game in every land. It would be impossible for me to tell you how many animals I have killed."

---

12. **Caucasus** (kô′kə·səs): mountainous region between southeastern Europe and western Asia.

Vocabulary
prolonged (prō·lôŋd′) v. used as *adj.*: extended.

The Most Dangerous Game   **11**

---

his island, plies them with fine food and wine, and then hunts them with a rifle and bow and arrow. In *A Game of Death* (1945) a man shipwrecked on an island is stalked by its deranged inhabitant. In *Run for the Sun* (1956) a male writer and a female journalist who survive a plane crash in the jungles of Mexico are forced to run for their lives from a wounded Nazi and an English traitor.

Whole-class activity. Have the class list other movies that have elements in common with "The Most Dangerous Game." Ask them what elements the movie shares with the story. For example, *The Island of Dr. Moreau* (1977 and 1996) deals with a deranged man living on an island where cruelty and inhumanity prevail.

A Content-Area Connections

History: Russian Revolution
After the Russian Revolution of 1917, in which Communists overthrew the government of Czar Nicholas II, many Russian aristocrats—who traditionally had spoken French at the czar's court—fled to France or French-speaking areas of Europe, where they often had to work a variety of jobs in order to earn a living. Zaroff's obvious disdain for his fellow Russian émigrés reveals a startling arrogance on his part.

B Reading Skills

❓ Evaluating. Point out that Zaroff is making an assumption about what is a fair contest between an animal and a human. Do you agree with his assessment that jaguars are not cunning because they can't outwit a hunter with a high-powered rifle? [Possible responses: No, the only fair contest between a human and an animal is one in which the human does not use a weapon. Yes, since humans have the wit to invent weapons, it is fair to use them.]

C Reading Skills

❓ Making predictions. What do you think the general is leading up to? [Possible response: He is going to explain how he discovered prey that again made hunting exciting for him.]

D Literary Focus

❓ Suspense. How does the author create suspense, or anticipation, here? [Possible response: Both Rainsford and the readers are eager to find out what animal the general hunts. The general keeps putting off the moment of revelation.]

The general puffed at his cigarette.

"After the debacle[13] in Russia I left the country, for it was imprudent for an officer of the czar to stay there. Many noble Russians lost everything. I, luckily, had invested heavily in American securities, so I shall never have to open a tearoom in Monte Carlo[14] or drive a taxi in Paris. Naturally, I continued to hunt—grizzlies in your Rockies, crocodiles in the Ganges,[15] rhinoceroses in East Africa. It was in Africa that the Cape buffalo hit me and laid me up for six months. As soon as I recovered I started for the Amazon to hunt jaguars, for I had heard they were unusually cunning. They weren't." The Cossack sighed. "They were no match at all for a hunter with his wits about him and a high-powered rifle. I was bitterly disappointed. I was lying in my tent with a splitting headache one night when a terrible thought pushed its way into my mind. Hunting was beginning to bore me! And hunting, remember, had been my life. I have heard that in America businessmen often go to pieces when they give up the business that has been their life."

"Yes, that's so," said Rainsford.

The general smiled. "I had no wish to go to pieces," he said. "I must do something. Now, mine is an analytical mind, Mr. Rainsford. Doubtless that is why I enjoy the problems of the chase."

"No doubt, General Zaroff."

"So," continued the general, "I asked myself why the hunt no longer fascinated me. You are much younger than I am, Mr. Rainsford, and have not hunted as much, but you perhaps can guess the answer."

"What was it?"

---

13. **debacle** (di·bä′kəl) *n.:* overwhelming defeat. Zaroff is referring to the Russian Revolution of 1917, in which the czar and his government were overthrown.
14. **Monte Carlo** (mänt′ə kär′lō): gambling resort in Monaco, a country on the Mediterranean Sea.
15. **Ganges** (gan′jēz): river in northern India and Bangladesh.

"Simply this: Hunting had ceased to be what you call a sporting proposition. It had become too easy. I always got my quarry. Always. There is no greater bore than perfection."

The general lit a fresh cigarette.

"No animal had a chance with me anymore. That is no boast; it is a mathematical certainty. The animal had nothing but his legs and his instinct. Instinct is no match for reason. When I thought of this, it was a tragic moment for me, I can tell you."

Rainsford leaned across the table, absorbed in what his host was saying.

"It came to me as an inspiration what I must do," the general went on.

"And that was?"

The general smiled the quiet smile of one who has faced an obstacle and surmounted it with success. "I had to invent a new animal to hunt," he said.

"A new animal? You're joking."

"Not at all," said the general. "I never joke about hunting. I needed a new animal. I found one. So I bought this island, built this house, and here I do my hunting. The island is perfect for my purposes—there are jungles with a maze of trails in them, hills, swamps—"

"But the animal, General Zaroff?"

"Oh," said the general, "it supplies me with the most exciting hunting in the world. No other hunting compares with it for an instant. Every day I hunt, and I never grow bored now, for I have a quarry with which I can match my wits."

Rainsford's bewilderment showed in his face.

"I wanted the ideal animal to hunt," explained the general. "So I said: 'What are the attributes of an ideal quarry?' And the answer was, of course: 'It must have courage, cunning, and, above all, it must be able to reason.'"

Vocabulary
imprudent (im·prōōd′'nt) *adj.:* unwise.
surmounted (sər·mount′id) *v.:* overcame.

CONTENT-AREA CONNECTIONS

Science: Endangered Species
Some of the species of wildlife mentioned in the story are endangered. The rhinoceros population, for example, has shrunk from 65,000 in 1970 to less than 11,000 today because of hunting and the diminished size of its habitat.

Small-group activity. Encourage groups of students interested in big game animals, such as jaguars, lions, grizzly bears, or Cape buffalo, to choose one animal to research. Suggest that they investigate the animal's size, habits, and habitat and find out whether it is an endangered or threatened species. Groups can present their research in a visual format, such as a slide show, a series of digital images viewed on a computer, or Web page.

Tropical Storm with Tiger—Surprise by Henri Rousseau (Le Douanier) (1844–1910).
National Gallery, London/SuperStock.

"But no animal can reason," objected Rainsford.

"My dear fellow," said the general, "there is one that can."

"But you can't mean—" gasped Rainsford.

"And why not?"

"I can't believe you are serious, General Zaroff. This is a grisly joke."

"Why should I not be serious? I am speaking of hunting."

"Hunting? Good God, General Zaroff, what you speak of is murder."

The general laughed with entire good nature. He regarded Rainsford quizzically. "I refuse to believe that so modern and civilized a young man as you seem to be harbors romantic ideas about the value of human life. Surely your experiences in the war—"

"Did not make me condone[16] coldblooded murder," finished Rainsford stiffly.

Laughter shook the general. "How extraordinarily droll you are!" he said. "One does not

---

16. **condone** (kən·dōn′) *v.*: overlook an offense; excuse.

The Most Dangerous Game   13

VIEWING THE ART

French painter **Henri Rousseau** (1844–1910) is known as a primitive artist because he was self-taught. The childlike simplicity and imaginative power of his works have intrigued millions of viewers. (For more about Rousseau, see p. 15.)

Activity. After students read the story, ask them, "In what ways does Rousseau's *Tropical Storm with Tiger—Surprise* remind you of the contest between Rainsford and Zaroff?" [Possible response: The menacing atmosphere of the jungle resembles the mood of the story.]

E Literary Focus

? Foreshadowing. Remind students that part of a reader's enjoyment of foreshadowing comes from looking back and thinking, "I saw the clues pointing to this turn of events." What hints did the writer use to foreshadow this development? [Possible responses: the sailors' dread of the island; the shots and cries Rainsford heard; the evidence that a fairly large animal had been shot with a light gun; Zaroff's search for game that can reason.]

F Literary Focus

? Conflict. What is this conflict between Rainsford and Zaroff about? [Possible response: The two men disagree about the morality of hunting men for sport. Rainsford is outraged and appalled, but Zaroff laughs off his concerns as old-fashioned.]

A Advanced Learners

Enrichment. Invite students to analyze Zaroff's statements here. Suggest they keep the following questions in mind: In what way is Zaroff's interpretation of Darwin's theory of "survival of the fittest" flawed? (See Content-Area Connections below.) What would happen if everyone adhered to this philosophy? When has this or a similar philosophy been put into practice?

B Reading Skills

Predicting. Remind students to keep in mind what they learned about the island at the beginning of the story. [Possible response to question 4: The island is called Ship-Trap Island. General Zaroff may have found a way to trap and sink ships to force the sailors to come ashore. This would also explain the sailors' dread of the island.]

C Learners Having Difficulty

Using graphic aids. Work with the group to draw a picture showing how the general traps ships.

---

expect nowadays to find a young man of the educated class, even in America, with such a naive, and, if I may say so, mid-Victorian point of view. It's like finding a snuffbox in a limousine. Ah, well, doubtless you had Puritan ancestors. So many Americans appear to have had. I'll wager you'll forget your notions when you go hunting with me. You've a genuine new thrill in store for you, Mr. Rainsford."

"Thank you, I'm a hunter, not a murderer."

"Dear me," said the general, quite <u>unruffled</u>, "again that unpleasant word. But I think I can show you that your scruples[17] are quite ill-founded."

"Yes?"

"Life is for the strong, to be lived by the strong, and if need be, taken by the strong. The weak of the world were put here to give the strong pleasure. I am strong. Why should I not use my gift? If I wish to hunt, why should I not? I hunt the scum of the earth—sailors from tramp ships—lascars,[18] blacks, Chinese, whites, mongrels—a thoroughbred horse or hound is worth more than a score of them."

"But they are men," said Rainsford hotly.

"Precisely," said the general. "That is why I use them. It gives me pleasure. They can reason, after a fashion. So they are dangerous."

"But where do you get them?"

The general's left eyelid fluttered down in a wink. "This island is called Ship-Trap," he answered. "Sometimes an angry god of the high seas sends them to me. Sometimes, when Providence is not so kind, I help Providence a bit. Come to the window with me."

PREDICTING

4. Think about the information presented at the beginning of the story. How might Zaroff find men to hunt?

---

17. **scruples** (skrōō′pəlz) *n.:* feelings of doubt or guilt about a suggested action.
18. **lascars** (las′kərz) *n.:* East Indian sailors employed on European ships.

(Opposite) *The Snake Charmer* by Henri Rousseau (1844–1910).
Oil on canvas (160 cm × 189.5 cm).
Musée d'Orsay, Paris.

Rainsford went to the window and looked out toward the sea.

"Watch! Out there!" exclaimed the general, pointing into the night. Rainsford's eyes saw only blackness, and then, as the general pressed a button, far out to sea Rainsford saw the flash of lights.

The general chuckled. "They indicate a channel," he said, "where there's none; giant rocks with razor edges crouch like a sea monster with wide-open jaws. They can crush a ship as easily as I crush this nut." He dropped a walnut on the hardwood floor and brought his heel grinding down on it. "Oh, yes," he said, casually, as if in answer to a question, "I have electricity. We try to be civilized here."

"Civilized? And you shoot down men?"

A trace of anger was in the general's black eyes, but it was there for but a second, and he said, in his most pleasant manner: "Dear me, what a righteous young man you are! I assure you I do not do the thing you suggest. That would be barbarous. I treat these visitors with every consideration. They get plenty of good food and exercise. They get into splendid physical condition. You shall see for yourself tomorrow."

"What do you mean?"

"We'll visit my training school," smiled the general. "It's in the cellar. I have about a dozen pupils down there now. They're from the Spanish bark *San Lucar* that had the bad luck to go on the rocks out there. A very inferior lot, I regret to say. Poor specimens and more accustomed to the deck than to the jungle."

He raised his hand, and Ivan, who served as waiter, brought thick Turkish coffee. Rainsford,

Vocabulary
unruffled (un·ruf′əld) *adj.:* calm; not disturbed.

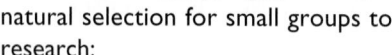

CONTENT-AREA CONNECTIONS

Science: Darwinian Theory
The English naturalist Charles Darwin (1809–1882) formulated the theory of evolution, an important part of which is the principle of natural selection. Many people, like General Zaroff in this story, have distorted this idea to suggest that only the strongest members of a species are worthwhile.
Small-group activity. Suggest the following questions about Darwin's theory of

natural selection for small groups to research:

• What is natural selection? What are some common examples?

• What kind of research did Darwin conduct before reaching his conclusions?

Have groups present their findings; then, challenge students to explain how Zaroff distorts Darwin's theory.

VIEWING THE ART

In his early forties, **Henri Rousseau** retired from his civil service job in order to devote himself to painting. Critics ridiculed his work, but Rousseau never lost faith in his ability. Avant-garde artists of his day, such as Pablo Picasso and Paul Gauguin, admired Rousseau's bold colors, flat designs, and fresh vision.

Activity. Rousseau's *The Snake Charmer* has a dreamlike quality that is also found in the artist's later, more sophisticated works. The colorful outsized plants and the sinuous form of the snake emerging from the shadows of the jungle create a sense of mystery. Suggest that students study the painting for a few minutes and then freewrite, expressing their responses to the painting's subject or to its color harmonies and use of shadow.

DEVELOPING FLUENCY

Whole-class activity. To show students how a writer builds suspense, have them re-read the passages in which Zaroff piques Rainsford's interest in the "new" animal. Have volunteers read aloud from p. 12, the twelfth paragraph ("It came to me as an inspiration"), through p. 16, the fifteenth paragraph ("I hope you have a good night's rest"). Establish the order in which students are to read; then, have each student read one paragraph (even if it is only a line of dialogue). Make sure students see how the author draws out the scene and then confirms the reader's suspicions at the very end.

A English-Language Learners

Interpreting multiple-meaning words. Discuss with students two of the meanings of *game* ("an activity done for amusement" and "wild animals hunted for sport"). Discuss with students how both meanings of the word apply to the title of this story.

B Reading Skills

❓ **Analyzing.** In what ways is this "game" an unequal contest? [Possible responses: The men Zaroff hunts do not have his experience in the jungle. They have only a knife, whereas he has a pistol and a pack of dogs.]

C Reading Skills

❓ **Making inferences.** What kind of heads do you suppose are in the general's new collection? [human heads]

A with an effort, held his tongue in check.

"It's a game, you see," pursued the general blandly. "I suggest to one of them that we go hunting. I give him a supply of food and an excellent hunting knife. I give him three hours' start. I am to follow, armed only with a pistol of the smallest caliber and range. If my quarry eludes me for three whole days, he wins the game. If I find him"—the general smiled—"he loses."

"Suppose he refuses to be hunted?"

"Oh," said the general, "I give him his option, of course. He need not play that game if he doesn't wish to. If he does not wish to hunt, I turn him over to Ivan. Ivan once had the honor of serving as official **B** knouter[19] to the Great White Czar, and he has his own ideas of sport. Invariably, Mr. Rainsford, invariably they choose the hunt."

"And if they win?"

The smile on the general's face widened. "To date I have not lost," he said.

Then he added, hastily: "I don't wish you to think me a braggart, Mr. Rainsford. Many of them afford only the most elementary sort of problem. Occasionally I strike a tartar.[20] One almost did win. I eventually had to use the dogs."

"The dogs?"

"This way, please. I'll show you."

The general steered Rainsford to a window. The lights from the windows sent a flickering illumination that made grotesque patterns on the courtyard below, and Rainsford could see moving about there a dozen or so huge black shapes; as they turned toward him, their eyes glittered greenly.

---

19. **knouter** (nout′ər) *n*.: person who beats criminals with a knout, a kind of leather whip.
20. **strike a tartar:** get more than one bargained for. A tartar is a violent, unmanageable person.

"A rather good lot, I think," observed the general. "They are let out at seven every night. If anyone should try to get into my house—or out of it—something extremely regrettable would occur to him." He hummed a snatch of song from the Folies-Bergère.[21]

C "And now," said the general, "I want to show you my new collection of heads. Will you come with me to the library?"

"I hope," said Rainsford, "that you will excuse me tonight, General Zaroff. I'm really not feeling at all well."

"Ah, indeed?" the general inquired solicitously.[22] "Well, I suppose that's only natural, after your long swim. You need a good, restful night's sleep. Tomorrow you'll feel like a new man, I'll wager. Then we'll hunt, eh? I've one rather promising prospect—"

Rainsford was hurrying from the room.

"Sorry you can't go with me tonight," called the general. "I expect rather fair sport—a big, strong black. He looks resourceful— Well, good night, Mr. Rainsford; I hope you have a good night's rest."

The bed was good and the pajamas of the softest silk, and he was tired in every fiber of his being, but nevertheless Rainsford could not quiet his brain with the opiate[23] of sleep. He lay, eyes wide open. Once he thought he heard

---

21. **Folies-Bergère** (fô′lē ber·zher′): famous nightclub in Paris.
22. **solicitously** (sə·lis′ə·təs·lē) *adv*.: in a concerned manner.
23. **opiate** (ō′pē·it) *n*.: anything that tends to soothe or calm someone. An opiate may also be a medicine containing opium or a related drug used to relieve pain.

Vocabulary
invariably (in·ver′ē·ə·blē) *adv*.: always; without changing.

> "If I find him" —the general smiled— "he loses."

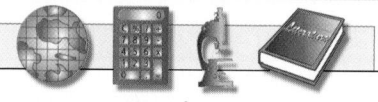

CONTENT-AREA CONNECTIONS

History: Czarist Russia
In czarist Russia, men convicted of crimes were subject to a two-part sentence. The first part, known as the punishment phase, was a beating, often a flogging, or knouting. The second phase—for those who survived the first—was a prison sentence. Members of the Russian aristocracy who were convicted of crimes were exempt from the punishment phase. Such inequities in the treatment of different social classes helped fuel the Russian Revolution.

Mixed-ability group activity. Put students in mixed-ability groups to research aspects of life in Russia before the revolution. Possible topics include the justice system, peasant life,

stealthy steps in the corridor outside his room. He sought to throw open the door; it would not open. He went to the window and looked out. His room was high up in one of the towers. The lights of the château were out now, and it was dark and silent, but there was a fragment of sallow moon, and by its wan light he could see, dimly, the courtyard; there, weaving in and out in the pattern of shadow, were black, noiseless forms; the hounds heard him at the window and looked up, expectantly, with their green eyes. Rainsford went back to the bed and lay down. By many methods he tried to put himself to sleep. He had achieved a doze when, just as morning began to come, he heard, far off in the jungle, the faint report of a pistol.

General Zaroff did not appear until luncheon. He was dressed faultlessly in the tweeds of a country squire. He was solicitous about the state of Rainsford's health.

"As for me," sighed the general, "I do not feel so well. I am worried, Mr. Rainsford. Last night I detected traces of my old complaint."

To Rainsford's questioning glance the general said: "Ennui. Boredom."

Then, taking a second helping of crêpes suzette,[24] the general explained: "The hunting was not good last night. The fellow lost his head. He made a straight trail that offered no problems at all. That's the trouble with these sailors; they have dull brains to begin with, and they do not know how to get about in the woods. They do excessively stupid and obvious things. It's most annoying. Will you have another glass of Chablis, Mr. Rainsford?"

"General," said Rainsford firmly, "I wish to leave this island at once."

The general raised his thickets of eyebrows; he seemed hurt. "But, my dear fellow," the general protested, "you've only just come. You've had no hunting—"

"I wish to go today," said Rainsford. He saw the dead black eyes of the general on him, studying him. General Zaroff's face suddenly brightened.

He filled Rainsford's glass with venerable Chablis from a dusty bottle.

"Tonight," said the general, "we will hunt—you and I."

Rainsford shook his head. "No, general," he said. "I will not hunt."

The general shrugged his shoulders and delicately ate a hothouse grape. "As you wish, my friend," he said. "The choice rests entirely with you. But may I not venture to suggest that you will find my idea of sport more diverting than Ivan's?"

He nodded toward the corner where the giant stood, scowling, his thick arms crossed on his hogshead of chest.

"You don't mean—" cried Rainsford.

"My dear fellow," said the general, "have I not told you I always mean what I say about hunting? This is really an inspiration. I drink to a foeman worthy of my steel—at last."

The general raised his glass, but Rainsford sat staring at him.

"You'll find this game worth playing," the general said enthusiastically. "Your brain against mine. Your woodcraft against mine. Your strength and stamina against mine. Outdoor chess! And the stake is not without value, eh?"

"And if I win—" began Rainsford huskily.

"I'll cheerfully acknowledge myself defeated if I do not find you by midnight of the third day," said General Zaroff. "My sloop will place you on the mainland near a town."

The general read what Rainsford was thinking.

"Oh, you can trust me," said the Cossack.

PREDICTING

5. Who will be the general's next victim?

Vocabulary
diverting (də·vʉrt′iŋ) *adj.:* entertaining.

---

24. **crêpes suzette** (krăp soo·zet′) *n.:* thin pancakes folded in a hot orange-flavored sauce and served in flaming brandy.

D Literary Focus

? Foreshadowing. Rainsford is locked in his room, high up in a tower. What future event do these circumstances hint at? [Possible responses: Since Rainsford is virtually a prisoner of the general, he may be forced to participate in one of the general's hunts or to battle Ivan.]

E Literary Focus

? Complications. Who do you think will prevail in this conflict? How might it be resolved? [Possible response: Since Zaroff is firmly in control, he will get his way. He will force Rainsford to hunt—or be hunted.]

F Reading Skills

Predicting. To help students answer question 5, ask them to recall what Ivan's idea of sport is. [Possible response to question 5: Rainsford will be the general's next victim.]

G Literary Focus

? Foreshadowing. What hints did the writer provide earlier that Zaroff would force Rainsford into a contest? [Possible responses: Rainsford was uneasy about the appraising look that Zaroff gave him during dinner. Zaroff showed himself to be indifferent to others' feelings in his reference to fellow Russian aristocrats reduced to poverty.]

the aristocracy, the rule of the czars, Alexander II's attempts at reform, the Eastern Orthodox religion, persecution of the Jews, and the arts. Have the groups present their findings to the class.

A **Literary Focus**

? Characters. What does Rainsford's response to Zaroff's demand for silence tell you about his character? [Possible response: Rainsford is a proud man of principle; he won't pretend to agree to something just to save himself.]

B **Literary Focus**

? Characters. What does this statement reveal about Zaroff's character? [Possible response: It shows how unbalanced he is. He grieves for his dog but feels nothing for the people he kills.]

C **Content-Area Connections**

Literature: Fables
Rainsford is alluding to one of Jean de La Fontaine's fables, in which a fox fleeing a pack of hounds tries a number of hiding places while a cat tries only one—a tree. Rainsford is comparing his efforts to escape to those of both the fox and the cat.

D **Reading Skills**

? Predicting. Remind students to base their predictions on their understanding of how stories work. From what they know of adventure and suspense stories, do they think Zaroff will spot Rainsford in the tree? [Possible responses to question 6: Zaroff will come close, but something will prevent him from spotting Rainsford. Zaroff will find Rainsford but will let him escape to continue the chase another day.]

"I will give you my word as a gentleman and a sportsman. Of course you, in turn, must agree to say nothing of your visit here."

A "I'll agree to nothing of the kind," said Rainsford.

"Oh," said the general, "in that case— But why discuss that now? Three days hence we can discuss it over a bottle of Veuve Clicquot,[25] unless—"

The general sipped his wine.

Then a businesslike air animated him. "Ivan," he said to Rainsford, "will supply you with hunting clothes, food, a knife. I suggest you wear moccasins; they leave a poorer trail. I suggest too that you avoid the big swamp in the southeast corner of the island. We call it Death Swamp. There's **B** quicksand there. One foolish fellow tried it. The deplorable[26] part of it was that Lazarus followed him. You can imagine my feelings, Mr. Rainsford. I loved Lazarus; he was the finest hound in my pack. Well, I must beg you to excuse me now. I always take a siesta after lunch. You'll hardly have time for a nap, I fear. You'll want to start, no doubt. I shall not follow till dusk. Hunting at night is so much more exciting than by day, don't you think? Au revoir,[27] Mr. Rainsford, au revoir."

General Zaroff, with a deep, courtly bow, strolled from the room.

From another door came Ivan. Under one arm he carried khaki hunting clothes, a haversack of food, a leather sheath containing a long-bladed hunting knife; his right hand rested on a cocked revolver thrust in the crimson sash about his waist. . . .

Rainsford had fought his way through the bush for two hours. "I must keep my nerve. I must keep my nerve," he said through tight teeth.

---

25. **Veuve Clicquot** (vöv klē·kô′): brand of fine champagne.
26. **deplorable** (dē·plôr′ə·bəl) *adj.:* regrettable; very bad.
27. **au revoir** (ō′rə·vwär′): French for "goodbye."

He had not been entirely clearheaded when the château gates snapped shut behind him. His whole idea at first was to put distance between himself and General Zaroff, and, to this end, he had plunged along, spurred on by the sharp rowels[28] of something very like panic. Now he had got a grip on himself, had stopped, and was taking stock of himself and the situation.

He saw that straight flight was futile; inevitably it would bring him face to face with the sea. He was in a picture with a frame of water, and his operations, clearly, must take place within that frame.

"I'll give him a trail to follow," muttered Rainsford, and he struck off from the rude paths he had been following into the trackless wilderness. He executed a series of intricate loops; he doubled on his trail again and again, recalling all the lore of the fox hunt and all the dodges of the fox. Night found him leg-weary, with hands and face lashed by the branches, on a thickly wooded ridge. He knew it would be insane to blunder on through the dark, even if he had the strength. His need for rest was imperative and he thought: "I have played the fox; now **C** I must play the cat of the fable." A big tree with a thick trunk and outspread branches was nearby, and taking care to leave not the slightest mark, he climbed up into the crotch and stretching out on one of the broad limbs, after a fashion, rested. Rest brought him new confidence and almost a feeling of security. Even so zealous a hunter as General Zaroff could not trace him there, he told himself; only the devil himself could follow that complicated trail through the jungle after dark. But, perhaps, the general was a devil—

PREDICTING

D 6. Will Zaroff spot Rainsford in the tree?

An apprehensive night crawled slowly by like a wounded snake, and sleep did not visit

---

28. **rowels** (rou′əlz) *n.:* small wheels with spurs that horseback riders wear on their heels.

Rainsford, although the silence of a dead world was on the jungle. Toward morning, when a dingy gray was varnishing the sky, the cry of some startled bird focused Rainsford's attention in that direction. Something was coming through the bush, coming slowly, carefully, coming by the same winding way Rainsford had come. He flattened himself down on the limb, and through a screen of leaves almost as thick as tapestry, he watched. The thing that was approaching was a man.

It was General Zaroff. He made his way along with his eyes fixed in utmost concentration on the ground before him. He paused, almost beneath the tree, dropped to his knees and studied the ground. Rainsford's impulse was to hurl himself down like a panther, but he saw the general's right hand held something metallic—a small automatic pistol.

The hunter shook his head several times, as if he were puzzled. Then he straightened up and took from his case one of his black cigarettes; its pungent incenselike smoke floated up to Rainsford's nostrils.

Rainsford held his breath. The general's eyes had left the ground and were traveling inch by inch up the tree. Rainsford froze there, every muscle tensed for a spring. But the sharp eyes of the hunter stopped before they reached the limb where Rainsford lay; a smile spread over his brown face. Very deliberately he blew a smoke ring into the air; then he turned his back on the tree and walked carelessly away, back along the trail he had come. The swish of the underbrush against his hunting boots grew fainter and fainter.

Then pent-up air burst hotly from Rainsford's lungs. His first thought made him feel sick and numb. The general could follow a trail through the woods at night; he could follow an extremely difficult trail; he must have uncanny powers; only by the merest chance had the Cossack failed to see his quarry.

Rainsford's second thought was even more terrible. It sent a shudder of cold horror through his whole being. Why had the general smiled? Why had he turned back?

Rainsford did not want to believe what his reason told him was true, but the truth was as evident as the sun that had by now pushed through the morning mists. The general was playing with him! The general was saving him for another day's sport! The Cossack was the cat; he was the mouse. Then it was that Rainsford knew the full meaning of terror.

"I will not lose my nerve. I will not."

He slid down from the tree and struck off again into the woods. His face was set and he forced the machinery of his mind to function. Three hundred yards from his hiding place he stopped where a huge dead tree leaned precariously[29] on a smaller living one. Throwing off his sack of food, Rainsford took his knife from its sheath and began to work with all his energy.

The job was finished at last, and he threw himself down behind a fallen log a hundred feet away. He did not have to wait long. The cat was coming again to play with the mouse.

---

29. **precariously** (pri·ker′ē·əs·lē) *adv.:* unsteadily; in an unstable manner.

Vocabulary
impulse (im′puls′) *n.:* sudden desire to do something.

A Vocabulary Development
Word derivations: Prefixes. Point out that the prefix *pro–* means "forward" or "forth." Where would a *protruding* bough be? [It would be sticking out from a tree.]

B Advanced Learners
Enrichment. Why is the narrator's comparison of Rainsford to a beaver appropriate here? [Possible response: European trappers decimated the population of beavers in North America by hunting them for their fur. This image confirms that Rainsford is the hunted rather than the hunter.]

C Content-Area Connections
History: World War I
The reference to Rainsford's digging himself in in France means that he is a veteran of the trench warfare of World War I. Soldiers dug trenches in which they lived and battled, sometimes for weeks or months at a time. Trench warfare was dirty and dangerous, so the reference to it as a "placid pastime" is meant to show the depth of Rainsford's present panic.

Following the trail with the sureness of a bloodhound came General Zaroff. Nothing escaped those searching black eyes, no crushed blade of grass, no bent twig, no mark, no matter how faint, in the moss. So intent was the Cossack on his stalking that he was upon the thing Rainsford had made before he saw it. His foot touched the protruding bough that was the trigger. Even as he touched it, the general sensed his danger and leapt back with the agility of an ape. But he was not quite quick enough; the dead tree, delicately adjusted to rest on the cut living one, crashed down and struck the general a glancing blow on the shoulder as it fell; but for his alertness, he must have been smashed beneath it. He staggered, but he did not fall; nor did he drop his revolver. He stood there, rubbing his injured shoulder, and Rainsford, with fear again gripping his heart, heard the general's mocking laugh ring through the jungle.

"Rainsford," called the general, "if you are within the sound of my voice, as I suppose you are, let me congratulate you. Not many men know how to make a Malay man-catcher. Luckily for me, I too have hunted in Malacca.[30] You are proving interesting, Mr. Rainsford. I am going now to have my wound dressed; it's only a slight one. But I shall be back. I shall be back."

When the general, nursing his bruised shoulder, had gone, Rainsford took up his flight again. It was flight now, a desperate, hopeless flight, that carried him on for some hours. Dusk came, then darkness, and still he pressed on. The ground grew softer under his moccasins; the vegetation grew ranker, denser; insects bit him savagely. Then, as he stepped forward, his foot sank into the ooze. He tried to wrench it back, but the muck sucked viciously at his foot as if it were a giant leech. With a violent effort, he tore loose. He knew where he was now. Death Swamp and its quicksand.

His hands were tight closed as if his nerve were something tangible that someone in the darkness was trying to tear from his grip. The softness of the earth had given him an idea. He stepped back from the quicksand a dozen feet or so, and, like some huge prehistoric beaver, he began to dig.

Rainsford had dug himself in in France,[31] when a second's delay meant death. That had been a placid pastime compared to his digging now. The pit grew deeper; when it was above his shoulders, he climbed out and from some hard saplings cut stakes and sharpened them to a fine point. These stakes he planted in the bottom of the pit with the points sticking up. With flying fingers he wove a rough carpet of weeds and branches and with it he covered the mouth of the pit. Then, wet with sweat and aching with tiredness, he crouched behind the stump of a lightning-charred tree.

He knew his pursuer was coming; he heard the padding sound of feet on the soft earth, and the night breeze brought him the perfume of the general's cigarette. It seemed to Rainsford that the general was coming with unusual swiftness; he was not feeling his way along, foot by foot. Rainsford, crouching there, could not see the general, nor could he see the pit. He lived a year in a minute. Then he felt an impulse to cry aloud with joy, for he heard the sharp crackle of the breaking branches as the cover of the pit gave way; he heard the sharp scream of pain as the pointed stakes found their mark. He leapt up from his place of concealment. Then he cowered back. Three feet from the pit a man was standing, with an electric torch in his hand.

"You've done well, Rainsford," the voice of the general called. "Your Burmese tiger pit has

---

30. **Malacca** (mə·lak′ə): state in what is now the nation of Malaysia in southeastern Asia.

31. **dug himself in in France:** dug a hole for shelter from gunfire during World War I (1914–1918).

Vocabulary
protruding (prō·trōōd′iŋ) *v.* used as *adj.*: sticking out.

CONTENT-AREA CONNECTIONS

History: Colonialism
Zaroff's and Rainsford's knowledge of both the Malay man-catcher and the Burmese tiger pit (p. 20) suggests that they have hunted for sport in parts of Asia colonized by the British. Colonialism had its roots in the European nations' demand for raw materials and pursuit of markets for their finished products. The colonial powers rationalized their plunder of colonized areas by citing a supposed obligation to "civilize" their inhabitants.

Whole-class activity. Have students discuss what they know about colonialism.

Then, discuss Zaroff's attitude as an extreme example of the colonial mind-set that values certain cultures over others.

Social Science: The Art of Tracking
Zaroff and Rainsford are both master trackers, able to read every bent twig and

D Reading Skills

❓ Drawing conclusions. Given what the general told Rainsford earlier about using the dogs, what do you conclude the general has decided? [Possible response: The general told Rainsford that he had to use the dogs when one man came close to winning the game. The general has apparently decided that Rainsford will win unless he uses his hounds.]

claimed one of my best dogs. Again you score. I think, Mr. Rainsford, I'll see what you can do against my whole pack. I'm going home for a rest now. Thank you for a most amusing evening."

At daybreak Rainsford, lying near the swamp, was awakened by the sound that made him know that he had new things to learn about fear. It was a distant sound, faint and wavering, but he knew it. It was the baying of a pack of hounds.

Rainsford knew he could do one of two things. He could stay where he was and wait. That was suicide. He could flee. That was postponing the inevitable. For a moment he stood there, thinking. An idea that held a wild chance came to him, and, tightening his belt, he headed away from the swamp.

The baying of the hounds drew nearer, then still nearer, nearer, ever nearer. On a ridge Rainsford climbed a tree. Down a watercourse, not a quarter of a mile away, he could see the bush moving. Straining his eyes, he saw the lean figure of General Zaroff; just ahead of him Rainsford made out another figure whose wide shoulders surged through the tall jungle weeds. It was the giant Ivan, and he seemed pulled forward by some unseen force. Rainsford knew that Ivan must be holding the pack in leash.

They would be on him any minute now. His mind worked frantically. He thought of a native

The Most Dangerous Game **21**

crushed blade of grass and follow their quarry wherever it flees. This skill was essential to hunting and gathering societies around the world. Native American hunters, for example, were expert at tracking buffalo, deer, wolverine, and other animals. Tracking game was so important that peoples who spoke different languages developed a sign language to communicate the whereabouts of game. In nineteenth-century Africa, Masai warriors tracked lions, and nonnative hunters stalked other big game, such as rhinos, Cape buffalo, and elephants.

Predicting. [Possible responses to question 7: The game is over, and Zaroff has won, except that he has lost Ivan and one of his best hounds. The game may not be over since Rainsford is a good swimmer.]

B Reading Skills

❓ Speculating. What effect does the "game" seem to have had on Rainsford? [Possible response: It has made him like a "beast at bay" and brought out a killer instinct.]

GUIDED PRACTICE

Monitoring students' progress. Guide students in answering these comprehension questions.

Short Answer

1. How does Rainsford happen to arrive on the island? [He falls overboard and swims to the island.]

2. What does Zaroff say he has become bored with? [hunting animals]

3. What species has Zaroff now chosen as his prey? [human beings]

4. What are the terms of the game? [The hunted man must elude Zaroff for three days.]

5. How does Rainsford finally escape from Zaroff? [He jumps into the sea.]

---

trick he had learned in Uganda. He slid down the tree. He caught hold of a springy young sapling and to it he fastened his hunting knife, with the blade pointing down the trail; with a bit of wild grapevine he tied back the sapling. Then he ran for his life. The hounds raised their voices as they hit the fresh scent. Rainsford knew now how an animal at bay feels.

He had to stop to get his breath. The baying of the hounds stopped abruptly, and Rainsford's heart stopped too. They must have reached the knife.

He shinnied excitedly up a tree and looked back. His pursuers had stopped. But the hope that was in Rainsford's brain when he climbed died, for he saw in the shallow valley that General Zaroff was still on his feet. But Ivan was not. The knife, driven by the recoil of the springing tree, had not wholly failed.

"Nerve, nerve, nerve!" he panted, as he dashed along. A blue gap showed between the trees dead ahead. Ever nearer drew the hounds. Rainsford forced himself on toward that gap. He reached it. It was the shore of the sea. Across a cove he could see the gloomy gray stone of the château. Twenty feet below him the sea rumbled and hissed. Rainsford hesitated. He heard the hounds. Then he leapt far out into the sea. . . .

PREDICTING
7. Trapped between his deadly pursuer and the sea, Rainsford jumps. Is the game over? Who has won?

When the general and his pack reached the place by the sea, the Cossack stopped. For some minutes he stood regarding the blue-green expanse of water. He shrugged his shoulders. Then he sat down, took a drink of brandy from a silver flask, lit a perfumed cigarette, and hummed a bit from *Madama Butterfly.*[32]

General Zaroff had an exceedingly good dinner in his great paneled dining hall that

---

32. ***Madama Butterfly:*** famous Italian opera by Giacomo Puccini (1858–1924).

---

evening. With it he had a bottle of Pol Roger and half a bottle of Chambertin. Two slight annoyances kept him from perfect enjoyment. One was the thought that it would be difficult to replace Ivan; the other was that his quarry had escaped him; of course the American hadn't played the game—so thought the general as he tasted his after-dinner liqueur. In his library he read, to soothe himself, from the works of Marcus Aurelius.[33] At ten he went up to his bedroom. He was deliciously tired, he said to himself as he locked himself in. There was a little moonlight, so before turning on his light, he went to the window and looked down at the courtyard. He could see the great hounds, and he called: "Better luck another time," to them. Then he switched on the light.

A man, who had been hiding in the curtains of the bed, was standing there.

"Rainsford!" screamed the general. "How in God's name did you get here?"

"Swam," said Rainsford. "I found it quicker than walking through the jungle."

The general sucked in his breath and smiled. "I congratulate you," he said. "You have won the game."

Rainsford did not smile. "I am still a beast at bay," he said, in a low, hoarse voice. "Get ready, General Zaroff."

The general made one of his deepest bows. "I see," he said. "Splendid! One of us is to furnish a repast[34] for the hounds. The other will sleep in this very excellent bed. On guard, Rainsford. . . ."

He had never slept in a better bed, Rainsford decided. ■

---

33. **Marcus Aurelius** (mär′kəs ô·rē′lē·əs): emperor of Rome from A.D. 161 to 180, who wrote about the philosophy of Stoicism, which held that people should make themselves indifferent to both pain and pleasure.

34. **repast** (ri·past′) *n.:* meal.

FAMILY/COMMUNITY ACTIVITY

Have students summarize the story for a family member up to the point where Rainsford is set loose by Zaroff. Have them ask the family member to predict the rest of the plot in as much detail as possible. Tell students to reveal the ending and discuss the meaning of the title afterward.

Meet the Writer

Richard Connell

Famous for One Story

By the time he dreamed up Rainsford's epic battle of wills with General Zaroff, Richard Connell (1893–1949) was already a seasoned writer, accustomed to seeing his work in print. He began writing early: As a ten-year-old cub reporter, he covered local baseball games for the newspaper his father edited in Poughkeepsie, New York. During his student days at Harvard, Connell wrote for both the college newspaper and *The Harvard Lampoon,* the school's famous humor magazine. He went on to write hundreds of short stories, as well as novels and screenplays. Despite Connell's tremendous output, only one story—"The Most Dangerous Game" (1924)—is still widely read. The story has not only fascinated readers for decades but has also intrigued filmmakers. This suspenseful tale has inspired four movies in the past seventy years.

What accounts for the story's enduring popularity? Nothing in it is especially believable—not the characters, not the plot, not even the violence. We are never really afraid that Rainsford will be chewed up by one of those hounds. Perhaps the answer is that "The Most Dangerous Game" is an adventure story, with all the appeal of a Hollywood scare-o-rama, complete with an elegant villain, his huge brute of a manservant, a castle, a dark jungle, bloodthirsty animals, and hideous mantraps. It is a fine example of a macho escape story. When we read it, we escape reality for a short time. We spend an hour or two away from real life and its problems.

Despite its literary flaws, people rarely forget this story.

What do you think of it?

The Most Dangerous Game **23**

Response and Analysis

Reading Check

1. *Characters*—Whitney; Sanger Rainsford; Ivan; General Zaroff.

   Conflict (What do the characters want, and what problems do they face?)—Rainsford wants to get off the island alive. Zaroff wants to hunt Rainsford down. Rainsford must find a way to elude the general, Ivan, and the general's hunting dogs for three days.

   Main events—1. Rainsford falls off a boat and swims to an island, where he discovers a medieval-style château. 2. General Zaroff tells Rainsford that hunting animals no longer challenges him and that he has found a new prey, humans. 3. When Rainsford refuses to hunt humans, Zaroff forces him to be the prey. 4. Using all the tricks he knows, Rainsford eludes the general for three days. 5. Trapped on the third day, Rainsford jumps into the sea.

   Climax—The general returns home disappointed. When he goes to his bedroom, he finds Rainsford there.

   Resolution—After winning the final battle, Rainsford spends the night in Zaroff's bed.

Thinking Critically

2. Possible answers: Humans are the most dangerous game (in the sense of "prey"). The most dangerous game is one that pits one human against another in a fight to the death.

3. Possible answers:
   - The name Ship-Trap Island, the island's bad reputation among sailors, the discussion of evil, the dread Whitney feels, and the three gunshots foreshadow danger.

Response and Analysis

Reading Check

1. Fill out a story map like the one below to review the **plot** of this famous chase story:

Characters:
Conflict: What do the characters want, and what problems do they face?
Main events: 1. 2. 3. [etc.]
Climax:
Resolution:

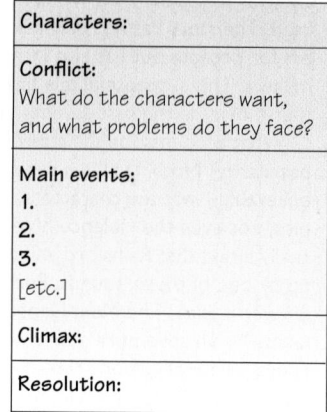

INTERNET
Projects and
Activities
Keyword: LE5 9-1

**SKILLS
FOCUS**

Literary Skills
Analyze plot
structure and
foreshadowing.

Reading Skills
Make
predictions.

Writing Skills
Write a story
sequel.

Thinking Critically

2. Did you **predict** the meaning of the story's **title**? What is the most dangerous game?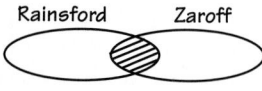

3. To hook our curiosity, writers drop clues that **foreshadow** what is going to happen later in a story.
   - What clues at the start of the story foreshadow danger for Rainsford?
   - How does Rainsford and Whitney's discussion about hunting at the start of the story foreshadow later developments?
   - What details in the physical description of Zaroff foreshadow the truth about his nature?

4. In your opinion, what happens to Zaroff? Do you think Rainsford changes his mind about hunting by the end of the story? Explain.

5. **Compare and contrast** the **characters** of Rainsford and Zaroff. Fill out a Venn diagram like the one below, listing the characteristics of each man in his circle. In the shaded area, list the characteristics the two men share.

   Rainsford   Zaroff

6. Think back to the villain you described in your Quickwrite. How does Zaroff compare with that evil character? ✎

Extending and Evaluating

7. Do the characters in this story make some comments that you have strong opinions about? Be sure to evaluate Zaroff's arguments for hunting men (pages 12–14).

8. Think about Zaroff's civilized tastes and his favorite game. Do Zaroffs— people whose refined manners mask their true nature—exist in real life? Explain.

WRITING

The Most Dangerous Game 2: The Sequel

In the morning, Rainsford awakes in Zaroff's comfortable bed. What happens next? Write a sequel to Rainsford's adventure. Does he stay on Ship-Trap Island and turn it into a theme park? Does he go home with a new taste for danger? Does General Zaroff manage to come up with yet another surprise? You might let Rainsford tell his own story, using "I."

- Rainsford says that the world is made up of two classes—hunters and "huntees," or prey—and that animals do not fear pain or death. Then Rainsford becomes the prey and feels fear.
- Zaroff's red lips and pointed teeth make him seem bloodthirsty, almost vampirelike.

4. Possible answers: Rainsford overpowers Zaroff and throws him to the dogs. Having

learned what it's like to be prey, Rainsford gives up hunting.

5. Possible answers:
   Rainsford—values human life; ethical; realistic.
   Zaroff—smug; cruel; manipulative; amoral.
   Both—hunters; risk takers; cunning; adventurous; indifferent to feelings of their prey.

6. Possible answers: Zaroff is similar to the villain I chose in that both lack a sense of

Vocabulary Development

Prefixes: Important Beginnings

What's the difference between *net* and *Internet*? Just a **prefix**—a few letters added to the beginning of a word that can greatly change a word's meaning. Knowing what a prefix means can help you define a new word. The chart below contains a number of common prefixes, some of which you'll find in the Word Bank words:

Prefix	Meaning	Example
bi–	two	bicycle
di–, dis–	no; not; away; apart	dishonest; dismiss
im–, in–	no; not; in	improper; include
inter–	between; among	international
mis–	badly; not; wrongly	misunder-standing
pre–	before	prearrange
pro–	forward; before	promote; proclaim
re–	back; again	return; redo
sur–	over; above	surface
un–	not; reverse of	untrue

Word Bank

receding
disarming
prolonged
imprudent
surmounted
unruffled
invariably
diverting
impulse
protruding

PRACTICE

Use the prefix chart at the left as you answer these questions:

1. What's the difference between *preceding* and *receding*? (Hint: The Latin word *cedere* originally meant "to go.")

2. How might a <u>disarming</u> smile affect you?

3. What's the difference between a long discussion and a <u>prolonged</u> discussion?

4. Give an example of an <u>imprudent</u> choice and a prudent one.

5. Use the meanings of the prefixes *sur–* and *dis–* to explain the difference between <u>surmounted</u> and *dismounted*.

6. What happens when a person remains <u>unruffled</u> in a tense situation? What happens if a person becomes ruffled?

7. If team A <u>invariably</u> loses to team B, what are team A's chances of remaining undefeated in a given season?

8. Ann, knowing that the Latin word *vertere* means "to turn," tells Joyce, "If you find that kids' movie <u>diverting</u>, you are reverting to childish behavior." Explain what Ann means.

9. Why might problems result from something you did on an <u>impulse</u>? If problems did result, would you want to redo or undo your actions?

10. Why would a <u>protruding</u> branch block the view from your window?

SKILLS FOCUS

Vocabulary Skills
Use prefixes to understand word meanings.

Vocabulary Development

Practice

1. *Preceding* means "going before"; *receding* means "going back."

2. Possible answer: A disarming smile might set me at ease.

3. A long discussion goes on for a long time; a prolonged discussion goes on longer than necessary.

4. Possible answer: It is imprudent to not wear a seat belt and prudent to wear one.

5. *Surmounted* means "triumphed over"; *dismounted* means "came down from."

6. An unruffled person remains calm. A ruffled person becomes upset.

7. There is no variation in team A's pattern of losing to team B.

8. If you like that movie, you are turning back to childish behavior.

9. Possible answer: Actions taken on impulse are hastily planned. You would want to undo your actions.

10. A protruding branch would stick out and cover the view.

ASSESSING

Assessment

■ *Holt Assessment: Literature, Reading, and Vocabulary*

---

right and wrong. Zaroff is different because the villain I described feels guilt for what he has done.

Extending and Evaluating

7. Possible answers: Students may have strong opinions about Zaroff's valuing some people's lives above others. Zaroff's argument for hunting humans is based on the false premise that life is only for the strong.

8. Possible answer: Real-life Zaroffs do exist; examples include dictators who display the trappings of culture but commit atrocities.

Grade-Level Skills

■ **Reading Skills**

Generate relevant research questions after reading about an issue.

Summary *at grade level*

In this magazine article, Eugene Linden presents four examples of intelligent behavior by animals. He also explores the idea that animals will apply their intelligence to serve their own purposes, not to please a scientist. Linden begins by describing an orangutan's repeated escapes from his enclosure in the Omaha Zoo. Next, he relates the story of Washoe, a chimp who learned more than 130 words in American Sign Language. Then, he describes an incident involving Orky, a killer whale that responded quickly to help rescue his baby. Finally, Linden tells about two orangutans that figured out how to get a double ration of oranges from their keepers.

PRETEACHING

Selection Starter

Motivate. Have students share stories about animals, wild or domesticated, that outsmarted humans or figured out ways to get what they wanted from them.

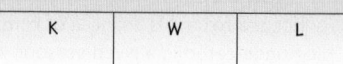

LINK TO "THE MOST DANGEROUS GAME"

Can Animals Think?

Generating Research Questions

Doing research is largely a question-and-answer process. You begin by looking at a subject and assessing what you already know about it. Then, you ask questions on topics you want to know more about and do research to answer those questions.

Asking good questions is the key to doing research that will lead to an interesting, informative report. When you generate research questions, your main goals should be to stay focused on a limited topic and to ask productive questions.

Helpful Hints

Here are some guidelines to help you develop research questions based on informational materials:

- Try using a **KWL** chart to begin your research. In the **K** column, list what you already know about the topic. In the **W** column, list the questions you have—what you want to learn. (When you've finished your research, complete the **L** column by telling what you've learned.)

K	W	L

- Stay focused on your subject matter. Don't wander into areas that are not related to the specific topic you're investigating.
- Focus on subsections of an informational article, which may be indicated by subheads. In this way you will narrow the scope of your subject so that you can explore it in more depth.
- Ask the **5W-How? questions** rather than yes-or-no questions: Who was in-

volved? What happened? When and where did it happen? Why and how did it happen? Such questions will help you get more information about your subject.

- Ask questions that can be answered within the scope of your research. Don't ask about issues so far-reaching that you cannot present a complete answer.

Remember: When you research, you aim to build your understanding of a subject from general, superficial knowledge to more specific, in-depth knowledge. Your research will be only as good as the questions you ask.

Vocabulary Development

balmy (bäm′ē) *adj.*: mild; pleasant.

intangible (in·tan′jə·bəl) *adj.*: cannot be touched or held.

awry (ə·rī′) *adv.*: in the wrong manner.

devious (dē′vē·əs) *adj.*: sneaky; deceptive.

beguile (bē·gīl′) *v.*: charm; deceive.

Connecting to the Literature

In "The Most Dangerous Game," General Zaroff has outwitted every animal he has hunted. So just how smart are animals? In the following article, Eugene Linden presents anecdotes—both amusing and heartwarming—that will make you think. Read on for glimpses into the often surprising thought processes of animals.

INTERNET
Interactive Reading Model
Keyword: LE5 9-1

SKILLS FOCUS

Reading Skills Generate research questions.

RESOURCES: READING

Planning
- *One-Stop Planner* CD-ROM with ExamView Test Generator

Differentiating Instruction
- *Holt Reading Solutions*
- *Supporting Instruction in Spanish*
- *Audio CD Library, Selections and Summaries in Spanish*

Vocabulary
- *Vocabulary Development*

Grammar and Language
- *Daily Language Activities*

Assessment
- *Holt Assessment: Literature, Reading, and Vocabulary*
- *Holt Online Assessment*

Internet
- go.hrw.com (Keyword: LE5 9-1)
- *Elements of Literature Online*

Media
- *Audio CD Library*
- *Audio CD Library, Selections and Summaries in Spanish*

Can Animals Think?

from *Time*, September 6, 1999

Eugene Linden

THE FIRST TIME Fu Manchu broke out, zookeepers chalked it up to human error. On a balmy day, the orangutans at the Omaha Zoo had been playing in their big outdoor enclosure. Not long thereafter, shocked keepers looked up and saw Fu and his family hanging out in some trees near the elephant barn. Later investigation revealed that the door that connects the furnace room to the orangutan enclosure was open. Head keeper Jerry Stones chewed out his staff, and the incident was forgotten. But the next time the weather was nice, Fu Manchu escaped again. Fuming, Stones recalls, "I was getting ready to fire someone."

Orangutans at a zoo in Tampa, Florida.

The next nice day, alerted by keepers desperate to keep their jobs, Stones finally managed to catch Fu Manchu in the act. First, the young ape climbed down some air-vent louvers into a dry moat. Then, taking hold of the bottom of the furnace door, he used brute force to pull it back just far enough to slide a wire into the gap, slip a latch, and pop the door open. The next day, Stones noticed something shiny sticking out of Fu's mouth. It was the wire lock pick, bent to fit between his lip and gum and stowed there between escapes.

Fu Manchu's jailbreaks made headlines in 1968, but his clever tricks didn't make a big impression on the scientists who specialize in looking for signs of higher mental processes in animals. At the time, much of the action in animal intelligence was focused on efforts to teach apes to use human languages. No researcher cared much about ape escape artists.

And neither did I. In 1970, I began following studies of animal intelligence, particularly the early reports of chimpanzees who learned how to use human words. The big breakthrough in these experiments came when two psychologists,[1] R. Allen and Beatrix Gardner, realized their chimps were

---

1. **psychologists** (sī·käl′ə·jists) *n.:* specialists who study the mind and emotions.

Vocabulary
balmy (bäm′ē) *adj.:* mild; pleasant.

Preview Vocabulary
Have students fill in the blanks in these sentences with words from the Vocabulary list on p. 26.
1. When their _____ plan for sneaking into the show went _____, they had to pay. [devious, awry]
2. To me, the first _____ day in April means it's the beginning of baseball season. [balmy]
3. The puppies tried to _____ her into giving them treats. [beguile]
4. The best gift Granddad gives us is _____: his complete attention. [intangible]

DIRECT TEACHING

A **Reading Informational Text**

❓ **Generating research questions.** Would this make a good research question? Why or why not? [No, the question "Can animals think?" is too broad to be answered effectively and in depth.]

B **Advanced Learners**
Generating research questions. Point out that between escapes, Fu Manchu hid the wire he used to pick the lock from his keepers. Ask students to generate a research question based on this piece of information. [Possible responses: What does this incident reveal about Fu Manchu's ability to plan ahead? What other incidents suggest that animals in captivity enjoy outwitting their keepers?]

DIFFERENTIATING INSTRUCTION

Learners Having Difficulty
Read the article aloud, stopping often to encourage students to ask questions. Work with students to edit their queries into focused research tools. Ask them:
• Does this question focus on the subject?
• Is this a **5W-How?** question?
• Could I answer this question in a report of a specific length?

English-Language Learners
For lessons designed for intermediate and advanced English-language learners, see *Holt Reading Solutions*.

Special Education Students
For lessons designed for special education students, see *Holt Reading Solutions*.

A Reading Informational Text

Generating research questions. This passage answers *who* and *what* questions. Ask students to formulate other *5W-How?* questions about the passage. [Possible responses: Where did the experiment take place? How did the scientists teach Washoe? Why were they conducting this experiment?]

B Reading Informational Text

❓ **Generating research questions.** Which of the following questions based on this passage would be more useful for research: (a) What did the other studies show? (b) What happened to Washoe? [(a)] Why? [Possible response: It would lead to more information about animal intelligence.]

C Reading Informational Text

Generating research questions. Point out that this passage contains a research question: In contrast to experiments that teach animals human activities, what other scientific investigations might help us better understand animals' minds?

D Reading Informational Text

❓ **Clarifying the main idea.** How does the story of Fu Manchu support this main idea? [Fu Manchu was acting in his own interest when he picked the lock.]

E Reading Skills

❓ **Analyzing.** What definition of intelligence does this statement imply? [Possible response: Intelligence involves assessing a situation and responding appropriately.]

A having trouble forming wordlike sounds and decided to teach a young female named Washoe sign language instead. Washoe eventually learned more than 130 words from the language of the deaf called American Sign Language.

B Washoe's success spurred more language studies and created such ape celebrities as Koko the gorilla and Chantek the orangutan. The work also set off a fierce debate in scientific circles about the nature of animal intelligence—one that continues to this day. Indeed, it has been easier to defeat communism than to get scientists to agree on what Washoe meant three decades ago when she saw a swan on a pond and made the signs for "water bird." Was she inventing a phrase to describe waterfowl, or merely generating signs vaguely associated with the scene in front of her?

C I began to wonder whether there might be better windows on animal minds than experiments designed to teach them human signs and symbols. When I heard about Fu Manchu, **D** I realized what to me now seems obvious: If animals can think, they will probably do their best thinking when it serves their purposes, not when some scientist asks them to.

Lending a Helping Tail

Why would an animal want to cooperate with a human? The behaviorist[2] would say that animals cooperate when, through reinforcement, they learn it is in their interest to cooperate. This is true as far as it goes, but I don't think it goes far enough. Certainly with humans, the <u>intangible</u> reinforcement that comes with respect, dignity, and accomplishment can be far more motivating than material rewards.

---

2. **behaviorist** (bē·hāv′yər·ist) *n.*: specialist who studies behavior.

Gail Laule, a consultant on animal behavior with Active Environments Inc., uses rewards to encourage an animal to do something, but also recognizes that animals are more than windup toys that blindly respond to tempting treats. "It's much easier to work with a dolphin if you assume that it is intelligent. . . . That was certainly the case with Orky," says Laule, referring to her work with one of the giant dolphins called orcas or **E** killer whales. "Of all the animals I've worked with, Orky was the most intelligent. . . . He would assess a situation and then do something based on the judgments he made."

Like the time he helped save a member of the family. Orky's mate Corky gave birth in the late 1970s, but the baby did not thrive at first, and the keepers took the little killer whale out of the tank by stretcher for emergency care and feeding. Things began to go <u>awry</u> when they returned the orca to the tank. The boom operator halted the stretcher when it was still a few feet above the water. Suddenly the baby began throwing up, through both its mouth and its blowhole. The keepers feared it would aspirate[3] some vomit, which could bring on a fatal case of pneumonia, but they could not reach the baby dangling above.

Orky had been watching the procedure, and, apparently sizing up the problem, he swam under the stretcher and allowed one of the men to stand on his head. This was remarkable since Orky had never been trained to carry people on his head like Sea World's Shamu. Then, using the amazing power of

---

3. **aspirate** (as′pə·rāt′) *v.*: breathe in.

Vocabulary

intangible (in·tan′jə·bəl) *adj.*: cannot be touched or held.

awry (ə·rī′) *adv.*: in the wrong manner.

CONTENT-AREA CONNECTIONS

Language: Sign Languages

An ape that learned American Sign Language (ASL) would not be able to communicate with someone using any other sign language. Approximately 103 sign languages are used by deaf people around the world today. They differ as widely from one another as do the spoken languages of the world. Each sign language has its own vocabulary and grammar. Each has rules for forming and sequencing signs. Even in cultures that use the same spoken language, sign languages may vary. For example, ASL and BSL (British Sign Language) are not mutually intelligible. Just like spoken languages, a sign language that is used by a far-flung population develops variations and dialects. **Small-group activity.** Have interested students work in small groups to generate research questions about sign languages.

Orky, a killer whale like the ones above, once helped save his baby.

his tail flukes to keep steady, Orky provided a platform that allowed the keeper to reach up and release the bridle so that the 420-pound baby could slide into the water within reach of help.

The Keeper Always Falls for That One

A sad fact of life is that it is easier to spot evidence of intelligence in <u>devious</u> behavior than in acts of cooperation or love.

While psychologists have studied various forms of animal deception, zookeepers are its targets every day. Helen Shewman, of the Woodland Park Zoo in Seattle, Washington, recalls that one day she dropped an orange through a feeding porthole for Meladi, one of the female orangutans. Instead of moving away, Meladi looked Helen in the eye and held out her hand. Thinking that the orange must have rolled off somewhere inaccessible, Helen gave her another one. When Meladi shuffled off, Helen noticed that she had hidden the original orange in her other hand.

Tawan, the colony's dominant male, watched this whole charade, and the next day he too looked Helen in the eye and pretended that he had not yet received an orange. "Are you sure you don't have one?" Helen asked. He continued to hold her gaze and held out his hand. Relenting, she gave him another, then noticed that he had been hiding his orange under his foot.

Countless creatures draw on their abilities not only to secure food and compete with their peers, but also to deal with, deceive, and <u>beguile</u> the humans they encounter. Every so often, they do something extraordinary, and we gain insight into our own abilities and what it's like to be an orangutan or an orca.

Vocabulary
devious (dē′vē·əs) *adj.:* sneaky; deceptive.
beguile (bē·gīl′) *v.:* charm; deceive.

F **Reading Informational Text**

? Generating research questions. Which of these questions would be a suitable topic for a research paper of three to four pages: What are the similarities and differences between dolphins and apes? How do dolphins behave in the wild? What kinds of studies have been done on dolphin intelligence? Did the baby orca survive? [What kinds of studies have been done on dolphin intelligence?]

G **Reading Informational Text**

Generating research questions. Ask students to generate some *5W-How?* questions from this statement. [Possible responses: What kinds of animals have gotten the better of zookeepers? Where could I find more accounts of this type of behavior? How have animals fooled zookeepers? Why do animals try to outsmart zookeepers?]

H **Reading Informational Text**

? Generating research questions. What research questions can you generate from this final summarizing statement? [Possible responses: How has research on animal intelligence given us insight into human abilities? What other animals have been the subjects of this research?]

Have students summarize this article for relatives or neighbors and then ask their listeners to tell any true stories they know showing that wild or domesticated animals have high intelligence.

Monitoring students' progress.
Have students write a one-sentence summary of each example of animal intelligence described by the writer. Then, have them circle the one that does not support the writer's main idea.

INDEPENDENT PRACTICE

Analyzing Informational Text

Reading Check

1. He climbed down some air-vent louvers into a dry moat, pulled back the bottom of a door connecting the enclosure to the furnace room, slid a wire into the gap, and slipped a latch on the door.

2. Orky figured out how to help his keepers save his baby. He let a keeper stand on his head; then he used his tail to hold himself steady so that the keeper could reach up and release the bridle holding the baby orca. The baby was then able to slide into the water.

3. After receiving an orange from the zookeeper, each hid the orange and acted as if it were lost, looking the zookeeper in the eye, and holding a hand out. The zookeeper then gave each another orange.

Answers and Model Rationales

1. **B** Students should realize that A and D are not stated in the article and that C is a detail.

2. **H** Students should realize that F, G, and J are general questions that broaden the topic.

3. **B** Questions with yes or no answers are not useful. A is wrong because broad questions are not desirable. C and D address irrelevant criteria.

Analyzing Informational Text

Reading Check

1. How did Fu Manchu get out of his enclosure?

2. What did Orky do that was so remarkable?

3. How did Meladi and Tawan deceive their zookeeper?

Test Practice

1. What is the **main idea** of "Can Animals Think"?
   A Studying animal behavior is interesting.
   B Animals are most likely to show intelligence not to please us but to serve their own needs.
   C Apes have had a difficult time mastering the sounds of human speech.
   D Human beings cannot or will not recognize animal intelligence.

2. If you wanted to do further research on the topic of animal intelligence, which question would help limit your investigation?
   F Do we value intelligence more than it deserves to be valued?
   G Will humans ever be able to communicate extensively with animals?
   H What are other instances in which orcas have made judgments?
   J What does *intelligence* mean?

3. Why is *How did the Gardners teach Washoe sign language?* a more useful first research question than *Did Washoe like learning sign language?*
   A It is a broad question about Washoe.
   B It will lead you to detailed information rather than a yes-or-no answer.
   C It covers a lengthy period of time.
   D It includes the psychologists who worked with Washoe.

4. Which research question would yield the *most* useful information about the intelligence of apes?
   F Who was smarter, Chantek or Koko?
   G What intelligent actions have observers seen orangutans perform in the wild?
   H How many times did Fu Manchu try to escape his enclosure?
   J What did Helen Shewman do the next time an orangutan tried to trick her into giving him an extra orange?

SKILLS FOCUS

Reading Skills
Generate research questions.

Constructed Response

Make a list of five questions that most intrigue you about animal intelligence. Once you have your list, share your questions with a few classmates. Which questions seem most likely to yield good research results?

4. **G** Students should realize that F and H are too specific to yield useful information. J asks about a human, not apes.

Constructed Response

Possible answers: What kinds of research on animal intelligence have been done? Which animals have shown the greatest intelligence? What definitions of intelligence have been used? Which domestic animals are the most intelligent? What do these experiments reveal about human intelligence?

Test-Taking Tips

For more information on how to answer multiple-choice questions, refer students to **Test Smarts.**

Vocabulary Development

Synonyms and Connotations

Is your town small, little, tiny, teeny, puny, or dinky? Do you live in a large, vast, gigantic, or sprawling city? How do you decide which is the best word to use when you are faced with what can seem like a dizzying number of choices?

The English language is filled with **synonyms**—words that mean the same thing or almost the same thing. When you choose a word or when you examine why a writer uses a particular word, you should think about its precise meaning as well as its context. You should also think about the word's **connotations,** or emotional overtones. *Dinky,* above, has negative connotations because it suggests something small, shabby, and insignificant. You would not like your beloved small town to be called dinky by a big-city visitor.

Look, for example, at what Gail Laule says about Orky in "Can Animals Think?":

> "He would assess a situation and then do something based on the judgments he made."

If you were using your own words to express that idea to a friend, you might have said that Orky would "think about" the situation. Why might *assess* be a better word to use to describe Orky's behavior? *Think* is a general word; it can be used in many different contexts. For example, *think* can mean "reflect." You might think about how a piece of advice applies to your life. *Assess,* however, is more precise. It implies the process of evaluation or calculation. *Assess* conveys the idea that Orky thinks logically. The word suits the scientific context of the sentence because the statement is an observation made by a specialist in animal behavior.

PRACTICE

Use a dictionary and a thesaurus to create a synonym chart, like the one below, for each word in the Word Bank. Write a sentence for each synonym. If there are slight (or not so slight) differences in meaning among the synonyms, or differences in connotation, try to make your sentences show that.

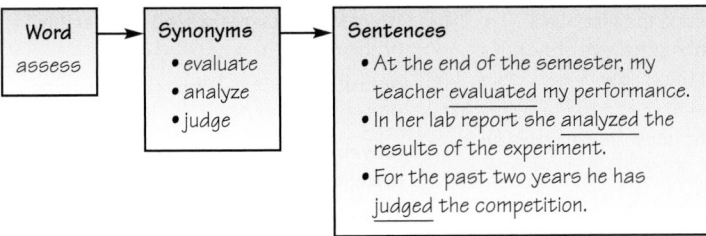

Word Bank

balmy
intangible
awry
devious
beguile

SKILLS FOCUS

Vocabulary Skills
Understand connotations of synonyms.

Can Animals Think?　**31**

Vocabulary Development

Practice

Possible Answers

- *Word*—balmy. *Synonyms*—mild; warm; tropical. *Sentences*—Because it was a <u>mild</u> day, everyone was in short sleeves. The day was unusually <u>warm</u> for November. The <u>tropical</u> weather put the vacationers in good spirits.
- *Word*—intangible. *Synonyms*—impalpable; abstract; vague. *Sentences*—An <u>impalpable</u> change of mood swept through the audience. The language was too <u>abstract</u> for the child. The man made <u>vague</u> promises about payment for the work.
- *Word*—awry. *Synonyms*—amiss; wrong; askew. *Sentences*—Her anxious expression revealed that something was <u>amiss</u>. We realized that something had gone <u>wrong</u> with the plan. Her hat was <u>askew</u>, and there were other signs that she had dressed hurriedly.
- *Word*—devious. *Synonyms*—sly; dishonest; insidious. *Sentences*—The <u>sly</u> fox tricked the crow into dropping its food. A <u>dishonest</u> merchant will soon have no customers. The <u>insidious</u> plot was hatched by the king's own son.
- *Word*—beguile. *Synonyms*—deceive; charm; trick. *Sentences*—The orangutan figured out how to <u>deceive</u> its keeper. The child could <u>charm</u> her grandmother into almost anything. The con artist <u>tricked</u> us into giving her money.

ASSESSING

Assessment

- *Holt Assessment: Literature, Reading, and Vocabulary*

RETEACHING

For another selection to teach generating research questions, see *The Holt Reader,* Part 2.

Grade-Level Skills

■ **Literary Skills**

Analyze the development of time and sequence, including the use of foreshadowing and flashback.

■ **Reading Skills**

Understand chronological order.

Review Skills

■ **Literary Skills**

Evaluate the plot's structure and development, and the way in which conflicts are resolved.

Summary ↔ *at grade level*

The narrator of this science fiction story dreams that he hears his dog, Laika, barking frantically. Awakening, he remembers that he is in his workplace on the far side of the moon and that he left Laika on Earth five years earlier. In a flashback, he recalls finding Laika as an abandoned puppy near California's Palomar Observatory and bonding with her, though he had never liked dogs. She accompanies him every day and once saves his life by barking to awaken him just before an earthquake strikes. When he leaves her to move to the moon station, they are both devastated; she dies shortly afterward. As the flashback ends and the narrator stirs from his reverie, he finds that he has awakened just in time to save himself from a deadly lunar quake. He escapes and saves all but two of his co-workers. He has rational explanations for his dream, but he still wishes he could have stayed in the dream with Laika for just a little longer.

Before You Read

Dog Star

Make the Connection

Quickwrite 🖉

Have you ever had a special relationship with an animal? Why do people love their pets so much? Jot down qualities that can make an animal a best friend.

Literary Focus

Flashback: Time Past, Time Present

It's impossible to turn back time. In your imagination, though, you can easily jump from the present to the past. When this jumping back happens in a story or movie, it's called a **flashback,** a scene that interrupts the present action of the plot to show what took place before.

One reason writers use flashbacks is to explain what led up to the present moment in a story. Flashbacks can also show the emotional impact of memories or past events. They can help writers create suspense, surprise, or mystery as well. As you read "Dog Star," think about Arthur C. Clarke's reasons for choosing to tell his story with a flashback.

go.hrw.com

INTERNET
More About
Arthur C. Clarke
Keyword: LE5 9-1

Reading Skills 📖

Chronological Order

Most stories follow **chronological order**—relating a series of events in time order, from start to finish. In "Dog Star," however, the writer interrupts the present time with a long flashback. To help you **organize the events** of this story, consider the following questions:

• The narrative begins in the present. At what moment does the narrative shift to the past?

SKILLS FOCUS

Literary Skills
Understand flashback.

Reading Skills
Understand chronological order.

• At what point does the narrator return to the present?

• How much time has passed between the final events in the flashback and the present moment in the story?

Background

Astronomers study space through powerful telescopes in observatories. The narrator of this story (published in 1962) is an astronomer. His dog, Laika, is named after the first animal sent into space—in 1957 aboard *Sputnik II,* a Russian satellite. The Dog Star, also known as Sirius, is the brightest star in the sky, located in the constellation Canis Major.

Vocabulary Development

desolating (des′ə·lāt′iŋ) *v.* used as *adj.:* producing a feeling of loneliness and sadness.

astronomers (ə·strän′ə·mərz) *n.:* scientists who study the stars and planets.

stellar (stel′ər) *adj.:* of or like a star.

luminous (lōō′mə·nəs) *adj.:* shining; glowing.

misanthropic (mis′ən·thräp′ik) *adj.:* disliking other human beings.

terrestrial (tə·res′trē·əl) *adj.:* earthly; of this world.

default (dē·fôlt′) *n.:* failure to do something.

labyrinthine (lab′ə·rin′thin) *adj.:* like a maze; complicated.

RESOURCES: READING

Planning
■ *One-Stop Planner* CD-ROM with ExamView Test Generator

Differentiating Instruction
■ *Holt Reading Solutions*
■ *Supporting Instruction in Spanish*
■ *Audio CD Library, Selections and Summaries in Spanish*

Vocabulary
■ *Vocabulary Development*

Grammar and Language
■ *Daily Language Activities*

Assessment
■ *Holt Assessment: Literature, Reading, and Vocabulary*

DOG STAR

ARTHUR C. CLARKE

Oddly enough, I was not frightened— at first.

When I heard Laika's frantic barking, my first reaction was one of annoyance. I turned over in my bunk and murmured sleepily, "Shut up." That dreamy interlude lasted only a fraction of a second; then consciousness[1] returned—and, with it, fear. Fear of loneliness, and fear of madness.

1. **consciousness** (kän′shəs·nis) *n.:* state of being awake or aware.

PRETEACHING

Selection Starter

Motivate. Bring in a newspaper or magazine article about an animal that assists humans, such as a guide dog or a CCI (Canine Companions for Independence) dog. Ask students for examples of other ways, tangible and intangible, in which animals help people. Then, assign the Quickwrite.

Preview Vocabulary

To help students master the Vocabulary words on p. 32, ask them to write responses to the following questions. (Possible responses are given.)

1. Describe an experience that might be <u>desolating</u> for a new student. [Being laughed at might make a newcomer sad and lonely.]

2. What <u>stellar</u> characteristics might <u>astronomers</u> study? [Those who study stars might note stars' brightness, size, and position.]

3. Why would a <u>luminous</u> face on a wristwatch be useful? [One could read it even in the dark.]

4. How might a <u>misanthropic</u> person respond when asked to donate to charity? [Disliking others, the person might refuse.]

5. List some basic requirements for supporting <u>terrestrial</u> life forms. [Earthly life forms need food, air, and water to survive.]

6. How might a wrestler lose a match by <u>default</u>? [by failing to appear or refusing to fight]

7. Name a game played by <u>labyrinthine</u> rules. [any game with complex rules]

- *One-Stop Planner* CD-ROM with ExamView Test Generator
- *Holt Online Assessment*

Internet
- go.hrw.com (Keyword: LE5 9-1)
- *Elements of Literature Online*

Media
- *Audio CD Library*
- *Audio CD Library, Selections and Summaries in Spanish*

Assign the Reading
Have the class read aloud the first four paragraphs, up to the flashback. Then, assign the rest of the story and the Reading Check questions (p. 41) as homework.

❓ **Time and sequence.** When the story opens, the narrator is dreaming. How long does his dream last? [a fraction of a second] For how long has he been separated from Laika? [five years]

B **Vocabulary Development**

❓ **Word derivations.** Which Vocabulary word could be used to describe the glowing wall paint that the narrator expects to see when he opens his eyes? [luminous] Think of other words derived from *lumen*, Latin for "light." [Possible responses: *illuminate, luminescence.*]

C **Reading Skills**

❓ **Recognizing chronological order.** Which phrases in this sentence suggest that a flashback is about to begin? ["back on Earth" and "from the past"]

D **Literary Focus**

❓ **Time and sequence.** Clarke wrote this story in the early 1960s but set it in the 1990s, in the future as he imagined it. In what year does the narrator find the abandoned puppy? [1992] How do you know? [He is driving a "new '92" car.]

E **Content-Area Connections**

Science: The Cage
Images from the Hale telescope at Mount Palomar Observatory appear on a mirror two hundred inches in diameter. When Clarke wrote this, astronomers rode an elevator to the "prime focus cage," a work area enclosed in metal mesh eighty feet above the mirror, where they could see the images clearly.

For a moment, I dared not open my eyes; I was afraid of what I might see. Reason told me that no dog had ever set foot upon this world, that Laika was separated from me by a quarter of a million miles of space—and, far more irrevocably, five years of time.

"You've been dreaming," I told myself angrily. "Stop being a fool—open your eyes! You won't see anything except the glow of the wall paint."

That was right, of course. The tiny cabin was empty, the door tightly closed. I was alone with my memories, overwhelmed by the transcendental[2] sadness that often comes when some bright dream fades into drab reality. The sense of loss was so desolating that I longed to return to sleep. It was well that I failed to do so, for at that moment, sleep would have been death. But I did not know this for another five seconds, and during that eternity I was back on Earth, seeking what comfort I could from the past.

No one ever discovered Laika's origin, though the Observatory staff made a few inquiries and I inserted several advertisements in the Pasadena newspapers. I found her a lost and lonely ball of fluff, huddled by the roadside one summer evening when I was driving up to Palomar. Though I have never liked dogs, or indeed any animals, it was impossible to leave this helpless little creature to the mercy of the passing cars. With some qualms, wishing that I had a pair of gloves, I picked her up and dumped her in the baggage compartment. I was not going to hazard

the upholstery of my new '92 Vik, and felt that she could do little damage there. In this, I was not altogether correct.

When I had parked the car at the Monastery —the astronomers' residential quarters, where I'd be living for the next week—I inspected my find without much enthusiasm. At that stage, I had intended to hand the puppy over to the janitor; but then it whimpered and opened its eyes. There was such an expression of helpless trust in them that—well, I changed my mind.

Sometimes I regretted that decision, though never for long. I had no idea how much trouble a growing dog could cause, deliberately and otherwise. My cleaning and repair bills soared; I could never be sure of finding an unravaged pair of socks or an unchewed copy of the *Astrophysical Journal*. But eventually Laika was both house-trained and Observatory-trained: She must have been the only dog ever to be allowed inside the two-hundred-inch dome. She would lie there quietly in the shadows for hours, while I was up in the cage making adjustments, quite content if she could hear my voice from time to time. The other astronomers became equally fond of her (it was old Dr. Anderson who suggested her name), but from the beginning she was my dog, and would obey no one else. Not that she would always obey me.

Vocabulary

desolating (des′ə·lāt′iŋ) *v.* used as *adj.*: producing a feeling of loneliness and sadness.

astronomers (ə·strän′ə·mərz) *n.*: scientists who study the stars and planets.

2. **transcendental** (tran′sen·dent′l) *adj.*: extraordinary; supreme.

DIFFERENTIATING INSTRUCTION

Learners Having Difficulty
Modeling. To help students read "Dog Star," model the reading skill of recognizing chronological order. Say, "Suppose you read that one character is separated from another 'by five years of time.' These words tell you that the characters last saw each other five years earlier." Encourage students as they read to ask themselves questions such as

"Which words tell me how these events are related in time?"

English-Language Learners
Be sure students know that this is a science fiction story. You might define science fiction as fiction in which a writer blends realistic elements with details of imaginary scientific or technological developments.

She was a beautiful animal, about ninety-five percent Alsatian.[3] It was that missing five percent, I imagine, that led to her being abandoned. (I still feel a surge of anger when I think of it, but since I shall never know the facts, I may be jumping to false conclusions.) Apart from two dark patches over the eyes, most of her body was a smoky gray, and her coat was soft as silk. When her ears were pricked up, she looked incredibly intelligent and alert; sometimes I would be discussing spectral types or stellar evolution with my colleagues, and it would be hard to believe that she was not following the conversation.

Even now, I cannot understand why she became so attached to me, for I have made very few friends among human beings. Yet when I returned to the Observatory after an absence, she would go almost frantic with delight, bouncing around on her hind legs and putting her paws on my shoulders—which she could reach quite easily—all the while uttering small squeaks of joy which seemed highly inappropriate from so large a dog. I hated to leave her for more than a few days at a time, and though I could not take her with me on overseas trips, she accompanied me on most of my shorter journeys. She was with me when I drove north to attend that ill-fated seminar at Berkeley.

We were staying with university acquaintances; they had been polite about it, but obviously did not look forward to having a monster in the house. However, I assured them that Laika never gave the slightest trouble, and rather reluctantly they let her sleep in the living room. "You needn't worry about burglars tonight," I said. "We don't have any in Berkeley," they answered, rather coldly.

In the middle of the night, it seemed that they were wrong. I was awakened by a hysterical, high-pitched barking from Laika which I had heard only once before—when she had first

seen a cow, and did not know what on earth to make of it. Cursing, I threw off the sheets and stumbled out into the darkness of the unfamiliar house. My main thought was to silence Laika before she roused my hosts—assuming that this was not already far too late. If there had been an intruder, he would certainly have taken flight by now. Indeed, I rather hoped that he had.

For a moment I stood beside the switch at the top of the stairs, wondering whether to throw it. Then I growled, "Shut up, Laika!" and flooded the place with light.

She was scratching frantically at the door, pausing from time to time to give that hysterical yelp. "If you want out," I said angrily, "there's no need for all that fuss." I went down, shot the bolt, and she took off into the night like a rocket.

It was very calm and still, with a waning Moon struggling to pierce the San Francisco fog. I stood in the luminous haze, looking out across the water to the lights of the city, waiting for Laika to come back so that I could chastise her suitably. I was still waiting when, for the second time in the twentieth century, the San Andreas fault woke from its sleep.[4]

Oddly enough, I was not frightened—at first. I can remember that two thoughts passed through my mind, in the moment before I realized the danger. Surely, I told myself, the geophysicists[5] could have given us *some* warning. And then I found myself thinking, with great surprise, "I'd no idea that earthquakes make so much noise!"

---

4. **second time . . . its sleep:** The San Andreas fault is a vast system of cracks running for about six hundred miles along California's coast. The fault's northern end was the center of a disastrous earthquake in San Francisco in 1906. The earthquake in "Dog Star" is fictional.
5. **geophysicists** (jē′ō·fiz′ə·sists) *n*.: scientists who study such aspects of the earth as the weather, earthquakes, and volcanoes.

Vocabulary
stellar (stel′ər) *adj*.: of or like a star.
luminous (lōō′mə·nəs) *adj*.: shining; glowing.

Dog Star   35

---

3. **Alsatian** (al·sā′shən): British name for German shepherd, a large dog resembling a wolf.

Dog Star   35

DIRECT TEACHING

F English-Language Learners
Understanding idioms. Point out the idiom *jumping to conclusions*; explain that it means "forming ideas on the basis of limited evidence."

G Literary Focus
? Characterization. How would you describe Laika's personality? [Possible responses: affectionate; intelligent; spirited.] How would you describe the narrator? [Possible responses: solitary; intelligent; logical.]

H Reading Skills
? Recognizing chronological order. Which words does the author use here to make the order of events clear? ["In the middle of the night," "by now," "for a moment," "then," "from time to time"]

I English-Language Learners
Understanding British English. Be sure students know that *to throw a switch* means "to turn a switch on or off," and to *shoot a bolt* means "to open or close a lock."

J Content-Area Connections
Science: Predicting Quakes
Clarke's speculation that the San Francisco area would experience a second major earthquake in the 1990s was not far off. The area's second cataclysmic quake of the twentieth century occurred in 1989.

Special Education Students
For lessons designed for special education students, see *Holt Reading Solutions*.

Advanced Learners
Acceleration. After discussing the term flashback, tell students that authors also use a device called flash-forward, shifting the

action of the plot briefly into the future. Charles Dickens uses both devices in *A Christmas Carol*: The Ghost of Christmas Past introduces a flashback, and the Ghost of Christmas Yet to Come introduces a flash-forward.

Activity. Ask students for other examples of flashbacks and flash-forwards from familiar books, films, or television shows.

A Advanced Learners

? **Foreshadowing.** Which words foreshadow a sad event to come? ["how soon it must end"] **What will end the narrator's happy times with Laika?** [He plans to leave Earth.]

B Literary Focus

? **Time and sequence.** How do thoughts of his future shape the narrator's decision? [He thinks that if he stays with Laika, she will die within a dozen years, and he will have lost his career as well.]

It was about then that I knew that this was no ordinary quake; what happened afterward, I would prefer to forget. The Red Cross[6] did not take me away until quite late the next morning, because I refused to leave Laika. As I looked at the shattered house containing the bodies of my friends, I knew that I owed my life to her; but the helicopter pilots could not be expected to understand that, and I cannot blame them for thinking that I was crazy, like so many of the others they had found wandering among the fires and the debris.

After that, I do not suppose we were ever apart for more than a few hours. I have been told—and I can well believe it—that I became less and less interested in human company, without being actively unsocial or <u>misanthropic</u>. Between them, the stars and Laika filled all my needs. We used to go for long walks together over the mountains; it was the happiest time I have ever known. There was only one flaw; I knew, though Laika could not, how soon it must end.

We had been planning the move for more than a decade. As far back as the nineteen-sixties it was realized that Earth was no place for an astronomical observatory. Even the small pilot instruments on the Moon had far outperformed all the telescopes peering through the murk and haze of the <u>terrestrial</u> atmosphere. The story of Mount Wilson, Palomar, Greenwich, and the other great names was coming to an end; they would still be used for training purposes, but the research frontier must move out into space.

I had to move with it; indeed, I had already been offered the post of Deputy Director, Far-side Observatory. In a few months, I could hope to solve problems I had been working on for years. Beyond the atmosphere, I would be like a blind man who had suddenly been given sight.

It was utterly impossible, of course, to take Laika with me. The only animals on the Moon

were those needed for experimental purposes; it might be another generation before pets were allowed, and even then it would cost a fortune to carry them there—and to keep them alive. Providing Laika with her usual two pounds of meat a day would, I calculated, take several times my quite comfortable salary.

The choice was simple and straightforward. I could stay on Earth and abandon my career. Or I could go to the Moon—and abandon Laika.

After all, she was only a dog. In a dozen years, she would be dead, while I should be reaching the peak of my profession. No sane man would have hesitated over the matter; yet I did hesitate, and if by now you do not understand why, no further words of mine can help.

In the end, I let matters go by <u>default</u>. Up to the very week I was due to leave, I had still made no plans for Laika. When Dr. Anderson volunteered to look after her, I accepted numbly, with scarcely a word of thanks. The old physicist[7] and his wife had always been fond of her, and I am afraid that they considered me indifferent and heartless—when the truth was just the opposite. We went for one more walk together over the hills; then I delivered her silently to the Andersons, and did not see her again.

Takeoff was delayed almost twenty-four hours, until a major flare storm had cleared the Earth's orbit; even so, the Van Allen belts were still so active that we had to make our exit through the North Polar Gap.[8] It was a

---

6. **Red Cross:** international society that aids people during wars or disasters.

7. **physicist** (fiz′ə·sist) *n.*: scientist who studies forms of matter and energy.
8. **Van Allen belts ... North Polar Gap:** The Van Allen belts, discovered by the American physicist James Van Allen, are two bands of radiation surrounding the earth. The North Polar Gap refers to an area above the North Pole where the radiation is weaker.

Vocabulary
misanthropic (mis′ən·thräp′ik) *adj.*: disliking other human beings.
terrestrial (tə·res′trē·əl) *adj.*: earthly; of this world.
default (dē·fôlt′) *n.*: failure to do something.

Cross-age group activity. You might arrange for a group of middle-school students to visit your class. Place the visitors and your students in small, mixed-ability groups, and have your students read "Dog Star" aloud to the visitors. Then, have each group work together on a large illustration for the story. Invite the groups to exhibit and discuss their illustrations.

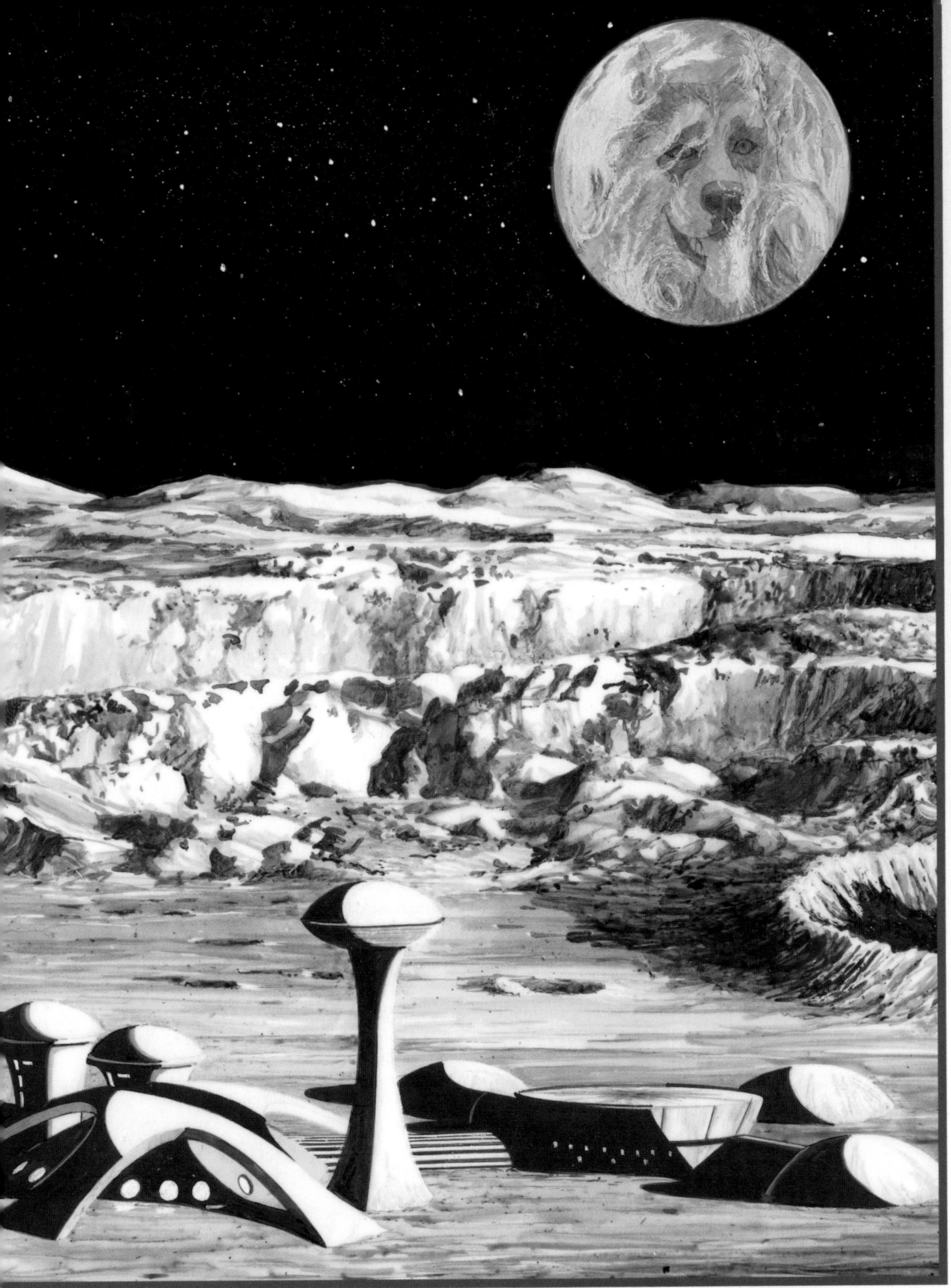

Astronomy: Sirius

A brilliant star that appears in the late fall and early winter sky just below the constellation Orion, Sirius sometimes seems to display a spectrum of colors as it sparkles. This brightest of stars has attracted attention since ancient times. The Egyptians, who called it Sothis, used it to predict Nile floods. The Greeks called it the Dog Star, noting that it followed Orion, a mythical hunter, across the sky. The Romans, who also knew Sirius as the Dog Star, associated it with the hottest time of year: the "dog days." In 1844, the German astronomer Friedrich Wilhelm Bessel discovered that Sirius is a binary, or double, star. The larger, brighter star of the pair is twenty-three times as bright as the Sun; the smaller one, a white dwarf, can be seen only with a telescope.

Individual activity. Encourage interested students to research stars and present brief oral reports. Possible topics to explore include binary stars, dwarf stars, and the ways astronomers classify stars.

A Learners Having Difficulty

❓ **Speculating.** Why do you think Laika dies? [She is heartbroken at being abandoned by the narrator.]

B Reading Skills

❓ **Recognizing chronological order.** With which words does the flashback end? ["in a little while the memory ceased to hurt."] Which words bring the story back to the present time and place? ["five years later, on the far side of the Moon"]

C Literary Focus

❓ **Time and sequence.** If the narrator's dream of Laika had lasted five seconds longer, what would have happened to him? [He would have died in the lunar quake.] What might his wish to have remained asleep longer suggest about his priorities now, as opposed to five years earlier? [Possible response: It suggests that he now values his bond with Laika more than his life.]

Monitoring students' progress. Guide students in responding to these true-false questions.

True-False

1. Laika saves the narrator from a deadly Berkeley earthquake. [T]

2. The narrator chooses his career over Laika. [T]

3. A dream of Laika saves the narrator's life on the moon. [T]

4. The narrator never regrets his decision to leave Laika. [F]

5. Laika dies in an earthquake. [F]

---

miserable flight; apart from the usual trouble with weightlessness, we were all groggy with antiradiation drugs. The ship was already over Farside before I took much interest in the proceedings, so I missed the sight of Earth dropping below the horizon. Nor was I really sorry; I wanted no reminders, and intended to think only of the future. Yet I could not shake off that feeling of guilt; I had deserted someone who loved and trusted me, and was no better than those who had abandoned Laika when she was a puppy, beside the dusty road to Palomar.

A The news that she was dead reached me a month later. There was no reason that anyone knew; the Andersons had done their best, and were very upset. She had just lost interest in living, it seemed. For a while, I think I did the same; but work is a wonderful anodyne,[9] and my program was just getting underway. Though I never forgot Laika, in a little while the memory ceased to hurt.

B Then why had it come back to haunt me, five years later, on the far side of the Moon? I was searching my mind for the reason when the metal building around me quivered as if under the impact of a heavy blow. I reacted without thinking, and was already closing the helmet of my emergency suit when the foundations slipped and the wall tore open with a short-lived scream of escaping air. Because I had automatically pressed the General Alarm button, we lost only two men, despite the fact that the tremor—the worst ever recorded on Farside—cracked all three of the Observatory's pressure domes.

9. **anodyne** (an'ō·dīn') *n.:* something that relieves pain.

> I had deserted someone who loved and trusted me . . .

It is hardly necessary for me to say I do not believe in the supernatural;[10] everything that happened has a perfectly rational explanation, obvious to any man with the slightest knowledge of psychology. In the second San Francisco earthquake, Laika was not the only dog to sense approaching disaster; many such cases were reported. And on Farside, my own memories must have given me that heightened awareness, when my never-sleeping subconscious[11] detected the first faint vibrations from within the Moon.

The human mind has strange and labyrinthine ways of going about its business; it knew the signal that would most swiftly rouse me to the knowledge of danger. There is nothing more to it than that; though in a sense one could say that Laika woke me on both occasions, there is no mystery about it, no miraculous warning across the gulf that neither man nor dog can ever bridge.

C Of that I am sure, if I am sure of anything. Yet sometimes I wake now, in the silence of the Moon, and wish that the dream could have lasted a few seconds longer—so that I could have looked just once more into those luminous brown eyes, brimming with an unselfish, undemanding love I have found nowhere else on this or on any other world. ■

---

10. **supernatural** (sōō'pər·nach'ər·əl) *n.:* forces or events that are not explained by the known laws of nature.

11. **subconscious** (sub·kän'shəs) *n.:* mental activity that occurs without our awareness.

Vocabulary
labyrinthine (lab'ə·rin'thin) *adj.:* like a maze; complicated.

Developing Word-Attack Skills
Show students that the accented syllable may differ in related words. Write the adjective *cosmopolitan* on the chalkboard, and read it aloud. Underline the syllable in *cosmopolitan* that is stressed the most heavily: *pol.* Then, write the related noun *cosmopolite,* meaning "a person who is cosmopolitan." Read the word *cosmopolite* aloud, and underline the syllable that is stressed the most heavily: *mop.*
Activity. Display these pairs of related words. Have students read the words aloud and identify the syllable that is the most heavily stressed in each one. Answers are underlined.

1. astronomy   astronomical
2. observatory   observation
3. transcend   transcendental

Meet the Writer

Arthur C. Clarke

The First Citizen of the Future

If the future is another country, Arthur C. Clarke (1917–   ) is its first citizen. Here are some of his credentials: He predicted many of the scientific developments of the second half of the twentieth century—such as satellites orbiting Earth and the moon landing—and he warned the world about the Y2K computer bug. Clarke has even predicted a few events that haven't happened yet. He expected humans to land on Mars in the 1990s; he has since revised the date to 2021. Soon after that, he says, dinosaurs will be re-created from computer-generated DNA, and mini-raptors will replace watchdogs.

Clarke was born in Minehead, England. At age thirteen, he built a telescope out of an old lens and a cardboard tube. Since his early start as an amateur astronomer, Clarke has written dozens of books of science fiction and science fact. In 1968, he was nominated for an Academy Award for writing the film version of his novel *2001: A Space Odyssey.*

Clarke says that he wants to be known not as a prophet but, rather, as an extrapolator—that is, someone who predicts the future based on what is happening in the present. In old age, when many others dwell nostalgically on the past, he continues to look hopefully into the future.

❝If an elderly but distinguished scientist says that something is possible, he is almost certainly right, but if he says that it is impossible, he is very probably wrong. **❞**

Arthur C. Clarke looks forward to celebrating his one hundredth birthday in December 2017 in a hotel orbiting the earth.

For Independent Reading

Arthur C. Clarke has written and edited more than ninety books, with about 100 million copies in print. In his exciting novel *Childhood's End,* the Overlords eliminate threats to humans—such as disease and poverty—but then they become a threat to humankind as well by controlling the minds of children. In Clarke's famous *2001: A Space Odyssey,* you'll take a journey with the crew of a spacecraft run by an all-too-human computer named HAL.

Meet the Writer

Background. Arthur C. Clarke continues to be an "extrapolator" of the future. He feels that the coming decade will be critical because of issues such as the population explosion, the energy crunch, and the environment.

For Independent Reading

Encourage students who have seen the movie *2001: A Space Odyssey* to read the book. You might also recommend the following titles:

- For science fiction fans, suggest *I, Robot* by Isaac Asimov, a classic set of interrelated stories by another master of the genre.
- Steer animal lovers toward *King Solomon's Ring* by Konrad Lorenz, a scientist's insightful and humorous memoir of unforgettable animals he has known.

---

4. impossible   impossibility
5. deliberate   deliberation
6. problems   problematic
7. calculate   calculation
8. atmosphere   atmospheric

DIFFERENTIATING INSTRUCTION

Advanced Learners
Enrichment. Tell students that the writer H. G. Wells greatly influenced Clarke.
Activity. Have students research the lives of Clarke and Wells and read Clarke's *Childhood's End* and Wells's *The War of the Worlds.* Ask students to report on similarities in the writers' works and lives.

Connection

Summary ⬇ *below grade level*

The speaker in this poem reflects on the importance of having "someone to hold and be held by." Using figurative language and images of a river, clouds, and an ocean, the poem shows the depth of the human need for connection.

DIRECT TEACHING

A Literary Focus

❓ **Theme.** According to the speaker in the poem, what can make the world an unpleasant place? [Possible responses: loneliness; isolation; having no one "to hold and be held by."]

B Literary Focus

❓ **Literary devices.** Personification is a form of figurative language in which something nonhuman is given human traits. In what ways are the ocean and clouds personified? [The ocean is referred to as female and is said to laugh and to weep; clouds are said to kiss the ocean's tears.]

C Literary Focus

❓ **Identifying themes across genres.** Why would the narrator of Arthur C. Clarke's short story "Dog Star" probably agree with the last stanza of this poem? [Possible responses: because he is lonely; because even after five years, he still mourns Laika; because he would give anything to be with Laika again.]

The World Is Not a Pleasant Place to Be
Nikki Giovanni

A the world is not a pleasant place
to be without
someone to hold and be held by

5 a river would stop
its flow if only
a stream were there
to receive it

B an ocean would never laugh
if clouds weren't there
10 to kiss her tears

C the world is not
a pleasant place to be without
someone

40 | Collection 1 | Plot and Setting • Generating Research Questions

Connecting and Comparing Texts

Nikki Giovanni's poem "The World Is Not a Pleasant Place to Be," like Arthur C. Clarke's short story "Dog Star," contrasts connection with isolation. The narrator of "Dog Star" would literally give his life for one more moment with his dog Laika, the only being with which he has ever bonded. His solitude is intensified by images of the vastness of space: He is an astronomer running a labora- tory on the far side of the moon. The speaker in "The World Is Not a Pleasant Place to Be" examines the bleakness of a life "without / someone to hold and be held by." This bleakness is intensified by images that suggest the vastness and impersonality of nature: a river, an ocean, a cloudy sky. Like the story, the poem suggests the joy of connection—the "kiss" of clouds that makes the ocean "laugh."

Response and Analysis

Reading Check

1. At what moment in the story does the **flashback** begin? (What present event triggers the flashback?) At what moment in the story are we back in present time?

2. Create a time line showing the events of the story in **chronological order.** Start with the earliest events in the story at the left end of your time line, and finish at the right end with the final event.

Thinking Critically

3. **Flashbacks** can serve several different purposes. For example, they can reveal a character's past or explain the cause of an event. What purposes does the flashback in this story serve?

4. Just before the flashback begins, there is a **foreshadowing** of what is about to happen in the present. Find the sentence in the fourth paragraph that foreshadows what is about to occur. Explain the clue.

5. List the details the **narrator** tells you about himself. Then, consider his actions. How would you **characterize** the narrator?

6. How would you describe Laika's **character**? Are there points in the story where she seems more like a person than a dog? Explain your response.

7. The narrator has a terrible **internal conflict** to resolve in choosing between Laika and his career. Does the author suggest that the narrator's decision was a mistake? Support your answer with details from the story.

8. At the end of the story, how does the narrator explain what happened in the lunar observatory? Do you think he really believes his own explanation? Why or why not?

9. What different meanings can you propose for the story's **title**?

10. Does this story have something to say about love's power to conquer even time? Explain what you think is the story's major revelation, or **theme**.

11. What do you think the narrator's response would be to the message of "The World Is Not a Pleasant Place to Be" (see the **Connection** on page 40)? Would you count a pet as "someone" who can make the world a pleasant place? Check your Quick-write notes.

Extending and Evaluating

12. In your opinion, would the story have been as effective if the writer had told it in strict chronological order instead of using a **flashback**? Explain your response.

WRITING

Blasts from the Past

Often something that we see, hear, or smell—a kite in the sky, a song on the radio, an apple pie baking in the oven—will trigger a memory, and suddenly we find ourselves flashing back to the past. Write a short **autobiographical narrative** about a past event in your own life. Has something in particular ever sparked your memory of the event?

▶ **Use "Writing an Autobiographical Narrative," pages 66–73, for help with this assignment.**

SKILLS FOCUS

Literary Skills
Analyze plot structure, flashback, and foreshadowing.

Reading Skills
Understand chronological order.

Writing Skills
Write an autobiographical narrative.

Dog Star 41

Response and Analysis

4. "It was well that I failed to do so, for at that moment, sleep would have been death." If he had gone back to sleep, he would have died.

5. He says he has few friends; he never liked animals, except Laika who gave him a love he has found nowhere else. Students might characterize him as intelligent, lonely, sad, introverted, and repressed.

6. Students might describe Laika as lively and intelligent. Some may cite as humanlike her "listening" to scientific discussions.

7. Possible answer: The author suggests that it was a mistake by having the narrator wish that his dream of Laika could have lasted longer, though it would have cost him his life.

8. He speculates that his subconscious picked up early signs of the quake and chose a dream of Laika's barking as the best way to wake him. Students may think that he "protests too much," suggesting that he doesn't entirely believe his own theory.

9. Possible answer: The memory of Laika shines like a star in the narrator's mind.

10. Possible answers: The special bond between a human and an animal can transcend time; loyalty to loved ones is more important than anything else.

11. Most students will say the narrator would concur with the poem.

Extending and Evaluating

12. Possible answers: Chronological order would make the narrative clearer; the flashback shows how strongly Laika's loss affects the narrator.

Reading Check

1. As the flashback begins, the narrator recalls his years with Laika. It is triggered by a dream of Laika, and it ends as a lunar quake jars the narrator into action.

2. The narrator adopts Laika; Laika's barking saves his life during the Berkeley quake; he leaves Laika to take a job on the moon; Laika dies; a dream of Laika awakens him; he senses a lunar tremor; he escapes unharmed and saves many others.

Thinking Critically

3. The flashback explains why the narrator hears Laika barking in his dream.

Vocabulary Development

Practice 1

(Lists of related words may vary.)

- *astronomers.* Origin—*astron* (Gr), "star" + *nomos* (Gr), "law"
- *stellar.* Origin—*stella* (L), "star"
- *luminous.* Origin—*lumen* (L), "light"
- *misanthropic.* Origin—*misanthrōpos* (Gr), "hating mankind"
- *terrestrial.* Origin—*terrestris* (L), "of the earth"
- *default.* Origin—*fallere* (L), "to fail"

Practice 2

Possible Answers
ant farms; genealogies of English kings and queens; Latin grammar; freeway system; human genome map; plate of spaghetti seen from a fly's viewpoint; computer game rules; mall; sewer system; microchip circuitry; IRS Form 1040 instructions

ASSESSING

Assessment

- *Holt Assessment: Literature, Reading, and Vocabulary*

RETEACHING

For another selection to teach plot and flashback, see *The Holt Reader,* Collection 1.

Vocabulary Development

Word Derivations: Back to the Source

The English language is made up of many words that originated in other languages, such as Latin, Greek, and French. You can use a **dictionary** to trace the **derivation,** or origin, of any word. (The derivation is also called the **etymology.**) The derivation usually appears in brackets after the entry word. The oldest form of the word appears last. (Be sure to check the meanings of the abbreviations used in your dictionary. *Gr* usually stands for "Greek," and *L* usually stands for "Latin.")

Look at the sample derivation below for *desolate.* (We are using *desolate* because most dictionaries do not have a separate listing for *desolating.*) The symbol "<" means "derived from or came from."

> **desolate** [ME *desolat* < L *desolare* < *de–*, intens. + *solare,* to make lonely < *solus,* alone]

You can read the above derivation as follows: *Desolate* comes from the Middle English *desolat,* which comes from the Latin *desolare,* which comes from a combination of the prefix *de–* (an intensive, or word part that emphasizes a meaning) and *solare,* which means "to make lonely." *Solare,* in turn, comes from the Latin *solus,* which means "alone."

PRACTICE 1

Use a dictionary to research the **derivation,** or origin, of each Word Bank word (except *desolating* and *labyrinthine*). Write the oldest form of the word and the language from which the word originally derives.

Word Bank
desolating
astronomers
stellar
luminous
misanthropic
terrestrial
default

Words and Myths: Telling Tales

When we talk about a herculean task, we're referring to the mythological muscleman Hercules. Many words in English have their origins in Greek, Roman, and Norse myths. We often associate other words, such as *labyrinth,* with these famous stories. A famous labyrinth (or maze) was built by Daedalus to house the Minotaur, a monster with the body of a man and the head of a bull. The Greek hero Theseus escaped from the labyrinth and killed the Minotaur. (For more about words from myths, see pages 716 and 732.)

Word Bank
labyrinthine

SKILLS FOCUS

Vocabulary Skills
Understand word derivations. Identify words from myths.

PRACTICE 2

Labyrinth and *labyrinthine,* an adjective meaning "like a maze" or "complicated," can be used both literally and figuratively (*the labyrinth of his mind,* for example). List as many things as you can that could be called labyrinthine—either literally or figuratively.

Informational Text

LINK TO "DOG STAR"

Far-out Housekeeping on the ISS

Researching Questions

Once you've generated research questions (see the guidelines on page 26), you're ready to look for the answers. Remember to consult as many reliable sources as possible.

Using Print Resources

Here are some useful resources you can find in a library or on the Internet:

- **Reference books**—such as encyclopedias, atlases, almanacs, and biographical references—contain specialized information. They are usually organized in a logical way, such as in alphabetical or chronological order. Examples include *American Men and Women of Science*, *National Geographic Atlas of the World*, *The World Almanac and Book of Facts*
- Other **nonfiction sources,** such as biographies, autobiographies, and history books, can help you get the full story. Use the library catalog to find these books.
- **Periodicals**—newspapers and magazines—can be excellent sources of information, especially for up-to-date facts. Libraries have either the *Readers' Guide to Periodical Literature,* a print index, or electronic indexes to help you locate articles on a particular subject.

Surfing the Web

The **Internet** provides up-to-the-minute information on a vast range of topics. Here are some useful research tips:

- Use a **search engine** to get a list of Web sites related to your topic. Often you can click on a site name on the

list and go directly to the site. If your search produces too many results, narrow it by choosing a more specific search term. You may need to try a different search engine to locate useful Web sites.
- Go directly to a **Web site** if you know the URL (uniform resource locator), the site's Internet address.

Checking Out a Web Site

On a Web page, look for **links** that lead directly to other sources on your topic. **Internal links** connect to other pages in the same site. **External links** lead to different Web sites. Usually you can reach a link by clicking on it. Look for these types of links:

- Some links are highlighted words or phrases within the text of an article. They may be underlined, in a color, or in italics.
- Other highlighted links may be listed in a side column or at the end of an article.
- **Audio** or **video links** connect to material you can listen to or watch.
- **Icons** are images, such as symbols or pictures, that function as links.

INTERNET

Interactive Reading Model

Keyword: LE5 9-1

> ### Connecting to the Literature
> When Arthur C. Clarke published "Dog Star" in 1962, he was imagining that people could live in space. Today people actually do live in space, on the International Space Station (ISS). This Internet article talks about real-life housekeeping in space.

SKILLS FOCUS

Reading Skills
Use research sources, including print resources and the Internet.

Far-out Housekeeping on the ISS   **43**

Grade-Level Skills

■ **Reading Skills**
Generate relevant research questions after reading about an issue.

Summary ⬌ *at grade level*

This NASA Web site, dated November 29, 2000, describes daily life aboard the International Space Station (ISS). ISS dwellers heat packaged meals or rehydrate pouches of dried food. Refrigerated food is not available, and water conservation is a priority. The space shuttle and unmanned supply vehicles deliver food to the ISS and remove trash; the unmanned vehicles later incinerate themselves along with the trash. ISS crewmembers e-mail home often, videophone home once a week, and bring everything from chess sets to DVDs for leisure time.

An audio link lets Web site viewers hear this article read aloud, and highlighted internal links open more articles about main topics. A list of titles and an icon serve as external links to related Web sites.

PRETEACHING

Selection Starter

Motivate. Invite students to imagine that they have won a week's stay on the International Space Station. They may bring only what will fit into a backpack. Ask them what they would take.

RESOURCES: READING

Planning
- ■ *One-Stop Planner* CD-ROM with ExamView Test Generator

Differentiating Instruction
- ■ *Holt Reading Solutions*
- ■ *Holt Adapted Reader*
- ■ *Supporting Instruction in Spanish*

Grammar and Language
- ■ *Daily Language Activities*

Assessment
- ■ *Holt Assessment: Literature, Reading, and Vocabulary*
- ■ *One-Stop Planner* CD-ROM with ExamView Test Generator
- ■ *Holt Online Assessment*

Internet
- ■ go.hrw.com (Keyword: LE5 9-1)
- ■ *Elements of Literature Online*

Media
- ■ *Audio CD Library*
- ■ *Audio CD Library, Selections and Summaries in Spanish*

A **Reading Informational Text**

? **Researching information.** What is the title of this Web site? ["Far-out Housekeeping on the ISS"] What does ISS stand for? [International Space Station]

B **Reading Informational Text**

? **Researching information.** Which print and online resources could offer you more information about the construction of Expedition 1? [Possible responses: Print resources include encyclopedias, 1990s periodical articles, and articles by or about Lu or Burbank. Online resources include other NASA Web sites, online encyclopedias, and online periodical archives.]

Back   Forward   Stop   Reload   Search

Location: http://science.nasa.gov/headlines/y2000/ast29nov_1.htm

Science @NASA
Inform Inspire Involve
science.nasa.gov

NASA Science News home

🔊 Listen to this story

A [Click on the audio link to listen to the article.]

Title of article

Far-out Housekeeping on the ISS

Life in space is a daring adventure, but somebody still has to cook dinner and take out the trash. Science@NASA interviews two astronauts about the thrill and routine of daily life in orbit.

November 29, 2000—It's open for business! And even though the construction crews aren't done yet, the International Space Station's first occupants have moved in and set up housekeeping. If all goes as planned, the arrival of Expedition 1 in orbit earlier this month signaled the beginning of a new era. From now on, there will always be humans in space.

B [Click on links within the article to learn more about a subject.]

Living in space is a daunting adventure with plenty of derring-do and glamour. Hollywood spacefarers rarely have to take out the trash or clean the kitchen. But, what about real-life astronauts? Are there chores to do on the ISS? In a recent interview with Science@NASA, Dr. Edward Lu and Coast Guard Lieutenant Commander Daniel Burbank—two astronauts who helped build the space station—discussed the excitement and the day-to-day routine of life in orbit.

"Space really is the most hostile environment humans have ever tried to live in," said Burbank. "You depend on the Station and the people on the ground for everything you need to survive. It is complicated and everything has to work!" It's a risky adventure with very little margin for error, but, said the astronauts, the thrill of being there is something that neither would give up.

HOT FOODS AND FRESH FRUIT

So what is it like being there for months or years at a time? For example, what does the ISS crew eat, and how is it cooked?

All food is delivered by the American space shuttle or Russian Progress vehicle. The crew helps select the foods they want from a wide-ranging menu.

(Right) The biggest challenge at mealtime for astronauts: catching your food! In this image Astronaut Loren Shriver (STS-46) demonstrates how objects act in free-fall while enjoying a snack of candy-coated peanuts. Residents of the ISS have more nutritious choices, too, including fresh fruits shuttled from Earth.

According to Vicki Kloeris, subsystem manager for shuttle and space station food at the Johnson Space Center, food aboard Space Station will come in several forms. "Most of the food will be processed and packaged in pouches or cans. Some will be dehydrated and the astronauts add hot water and eat. Some will be in pouches and cans and you simply heat and eat. A small amount will be fresh food delivered by the shuttle and Progress." The fresh food will include fruits and veggies, but nothing that requires

44 **Collection 1** Plot and Setting • Generating Research Questions

---

DIFFERENTIATING INSTRUCTION

Learners Having Difficulty
Using graphic aids. Remind students that graphics are also sources of information. Encourage students to see what they can learn from this site's photos and drawings.

English-Language Learners
You might point out this Web site's name: Science@NASA. Be sure students know that NASA is the acronym (a word made from the first letters of a series of words) for the National Aeronautics and Space Administration, the organization that develops and oversees U.S. space programs.

Special Education Students
For lessons designed for special education students, see *Holt Reading Solutions*.

Advanced Learners
Enrichment. Explain that allusions, or cultural and historical references, deepen the meaning of informational prose as well as fiction.
Activity. Show students this article's allusion to early Polynesian sailors charting the Pacific (under "R&R in Space," p. 45). Ask students

Location: http://science.nasa.gov/headlines/y2000/ast29nov_1.htm

refrigeration. ISS will contain more than one oven when it is fully operational. In the early stages, food is being cooked using either a small food warmer built by the Russians or a U.S.-built portable food warmer, about the size of a suitcase.

ISS, PHONE HOME

Information gained from the experiences of the Russian MIR space station crews indicates that isolation is one of the biggest problems a long-duration crew will face. To prevent this on ISS, the crew members will be encouraged to phone home. And while working on ISS will not exactly be like spending a couple of weeks away from home on business in the Big Apple or the Windy City, sailors traveling around the British Empire in the 17th and 18th centuries were more isolated than the ISS crew will be.

"Each crew member will have a video telephone call from home each week," said Burbank. "And the crew will be receiving and sending daily e-mail messages to and from family and friends. No one should feel isolated from home and family."

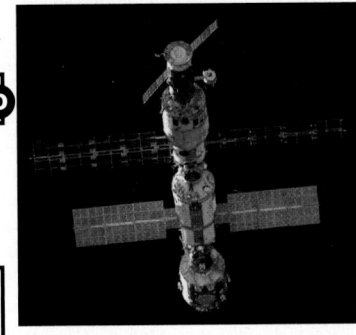

(Right) Members of the STS-106 crew, including Lu and Burbank, snapped this picture of the ISS from the space shuttle Atlantis in September 2000. [more information]

WHO TAKES OUT THE TRASH?

A recent Science@NASA story about water recycling on the ISS covered the great lengths that ISS designers are taking to minimize how much water and other consumables must be launched from Earth. Water-recycling efficiencies of greater than 95% are the goal.

But other wastes cannot be recycled so efficiently, particularly solid waste from food containers, experiments, empty fuel containers, and other ISS activities. So: Who takes out the trash?

Again, Progress and Shuttle come to the rescue. Every arrival of Shuttle brings fresh supplies. And when it leaves, it becomes the world's most expensive trash hauler! Bags and containers of sealed trash will be brought back to Earth.

More exciting, perhaps, is how the Russian Progress disposes of trash. Again, when it arrives, it brings fresh supplies (but no crews, since it is just a supply vehicle). And when the fresh supplies are unloaded, the trash bags are piled in and Progress is sealed. After it disconnects from ISS, it is placed into a lower orbit and makes a controlled reentry during which it and the trash are incinerated over the ocean.

R&R IN SPACE

Crews will be busy during their tours of duty on ISS. But all work and no play. . . . So what constitutes relaxation and recreation for the men and women living aboard ISS?

"Crew members will be allowed to take a certain amount of personal gear up with them," said Lu. "So things like checkers or chess sets, CDs and tape players, and the like are allowed. You can listen to your favorite music if you like. DVD movies will also be available for viewing."

So it's not exactly like home! And you can't take an evening walk outside to watch the sunset. But the

what questions the allusion suggests to them, and which resources might offer answers. Have students explore and assess these resources and briefly discuss their findings.

DIRECT TEACHING

C English-Language Learners

Slang. Tell students that the Big Apple is a nickname for New York City, and the Windy City is a nickname for Chicago.

D Advanced Learners

❷ **Enrichment.** What historical allusion appears in the last sentence of this paragraph? [an allusion to British seafarers of the seventeenth and eighteenth centuries] **What might be some of the most complete sources of information on these adventurers?** [Possible responses: Complete sources of information would include print sources such as encyclopedia articles, history books, and biographies.]

E Reading Informational Text

❷ **Researching information.** What does the underlining of these two phrases signify? [These are internal links.]

F Learners Having Difficulty

❷ **Identifying details.** What is the Russian Progress? [an unmanned space supply vehicle] **How are Progress vehicles used to dispose of trash from the ISS?** [The vehicles are loaded with trash and then allowed to burn up during reentry into Earth's atmosphere.]

A Reading Informational Text

? Researching information. Which external link would you expect to be most helpful if you wanted to know how ISS crews combat contamination of the space station by molds or bacteria? ["Microscopic Stowaways on the Space Station" would probably provide the most information. "Breathing Easy on the Space Station," "Water on the Space Station," and "Environmental Control and Life Support Systems" might briefly mention control of contaminants.]

GUIDED PRACTICE

Monitoring students' progress. Have students give an example of an internal link, an external link, an audio link, and an icon link provided by this Web site. For each link, have students identify a subject about which the link might provide more details. [Possible responses: internal—"All food" (menus); external—"Breathing easy on the Space Station" (air quality); audio—"Listen to this story" (entire article); icon—"More NASA news headlines" cartoon (other NASA projects).]

Location: http://science.nasa.gov/headlines/y2000/ast29nov_1.htm

"sailors" on ISS will have it better than those intrepid explorers that left Europe in the 15th century looking for new lands, or the Polynesian sailors that charted and settled the vast Pacific Ocean, or the Asian explorers and settlers who walked the land bridge from Siberia into Alaska and opened two new continents for their people.

They do, however, share two important traits. First, they are the vanguard of their respective civilizations, doing what they believe will improve the well-being of their people.

And second, they all had to forge ahead and ignore the shrill voices behind them warning that "beyond this point, there be dragons!"

Click on one of the underlined **links** in this box to go to a related Web page.

Web Links

Water on the Space Station—The first Science@NASA article in this series about the practical challenges of extended living in space. This article looks at how water will be conserved and recycled on the space station—including the crew's own urine!

Breathing Easy on the Space Station—The second Science@NASA article in this series about the practical challenges of extended living in space. The systems and methods used to ensure safe, breathable air for the crew are examined in this article.

Microscopic Stowaways on the Space Station—The third Science@NASA article in this series about the practical challenges of extended living in space.

International Space Station—NASA's Web page for the International Space Station.

Advanced Life Support Web Page—from the Johnson Space Flight Center.

Environmental Control and Life Support Systems—describes the life-support systems being developed at Marshall Space Flight Center.

A Join our growing list of subscribers—sign up for our express news delivery and you will receive a mail message every time we post a new story!!!

More NASA NEWS **Headlines**

Click on the **icon** to reach a related Web page.

For lesson plans and educational activities related to breaking science news, please visit Thursday's Classroom.	Author: Ron Koczor Production Editor: Dr. Tony Phillips Curator: Bryan Walls Media Relations: Steve Roy Responsible NASA official: Ron Koczor

---

Connecting and Comparing Texts

The nonfiction Web site "Far-out Housekeeping on the ISS" and Arthur C. Clarke's fictional story "Dog Star" both shed light on the challenges of living in space. The fictional narrator of Clarke's story works on the moon; the real people described on the Web site live aboard the International Space Station (ISS). Both texts address the human need for connection. The isolated narrator of "Dog Star" mourns deeply for the beloved pet he had to leave on Earth; the planners of the ISS confirm that isolation presents a major problem. How does the crew cope? [The occupants of the ISS maintain vital connections via e-mail and video telephone with families and friends on Earth.]

Analyzing Informational Text

Reading Check

1. Describe how food is brought to the International Space Station and how trash is removed.

2. According to the article, what traits do space travelers share with explorers who lived in earlier centuries?

Test Practice

1. If you wanted to learn more about living in space on a long-term basis, which search term would be the *most* useful?
   - **A** History of space exploration
   - **B** Space stations
   - **C** Astronauts
   - **D** Spacesuits

2. Which source would provide the *most* up-to-date information about extended living in space?
   - **F** An interview with astronauts who lived on the Mir space station
   - **G** A science textbook
   - **H** A history book about important space missions
   - **J** A Web page about new technology used on the ISS

3. If you wanted to find out more about how crews spend their free time in space, which source would be the *most* helpful?
   - **A** A newspaper article about plans for future space missions
   - **B** An autobiography describing an astronaut's experiences in space

   - **C** An encyclopedia entry about the history of the U.S. space program
   - **D** A Web page about the purpose of the U.S. space shuttle

4. If you wanted to learn about oxygen supplies for the ISS crew, which **link** on this Web page would be *least* likely to provide information?
   - **F** Breathing Easy on the Space Station
   - **G** Advanced Life Support Web Page
   - **H** Environmental Control and Life Support Systems
   - **J** Water on the Space Station

5. If you wanted to find out more about the handling of wastes on the ISS, which link would be the *most* useful?
   - **A** The Nasa News icon "More Headlines"
   - **B** The internal link "All food"
   - **C** The internal link "water recycling on the ISS"
   - **D** The audio link "Listen to this story"

Constructed Response

Generate a list of questions based on "Far-out Housekeeping on the ISS." (You might have questions about the experiences of the crews in the time since the article was written.) Then, choose one question, and research it in a library and on the **Internet**. Did you find information easily? What sources did you use? What additional resources could you have used to answer the question?

SKILLS FOCUS

Reading Skills
Generate research questions, and research the answers.

Far-out Housekeeping on the ISS **47**

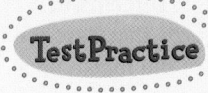
INDEPENDENT PRACTICE

Analyzing Informational Text

Reading Check

1. The U.S. space shuttle and the Russian Progress vehicle provide regular food deliveries and take away trash when they leave.

2. Both groups believe they are working to help their people and have forged ahead despite the misgivings of detractors.

Test Practice

Answers and Model Rationales

1. **B** A and C are too broad; D is off the topic. B would be most useful because space stations are places for living in space long-term.

2. **J** Students should quickly choose J because Web pages can be updated more often and easily than books (G and H) or any other source. An interview with Mir astronauts (F) would be less useful because Mir, an early space station, is now outdated.

3. **B** An autobiography would be likely to include detailed personal anecdotes about free time.

4. **J** Note the italicized word *least* in the question. F would be the link *most* likely to have information on oxygen. G and H, links involving life support, would probably also discuss oxygen. J, a link focusing on water, is *least* likely to mention oxygen.

5. **B** The All food link (B) may be *most* useful, since food generates trash and food delivery vehicles also remove wastes.

Test-Taking Tips

For more information on how to answer multiple-choice questions, refer students to **Test Smarts.**

Analyze the importance of the setting to the mood, tone, and meaning
of the text.

**Elements of Literature:
Setting**

Ask students to identify the basic
setting (time and place) of a popular
movie. Tell students that in addition
to establishing the time and place of
the action, setting helps create the
atmosphere (overall mood or feeling) of a work. Ask students to
come up with words that describe
the atmosphere of the movie under
discussion. Ask how the setting contributed to that atmosphere. Finally,
explain that setting often plays a
role in revealing characters and supporting the plot. For example, ask
students what types of characters
they might expect to see in the setting of a big-city hospital. [Possible
responses: dedicated and ambitious
doctors and nurses, cranky or seriously ill patients, excited or sorrowful
visitors.] What atmosphere might
the chaotic setting of the city hospital help create? [Possible responses:
tense, suspenseful, high pressure.]
Finally, ask students to discuss how
setting reveals a particular character
in the movie mentioned at the
beginning of the discussion.

Elements of Literature

Setting *by John Leggett*
PUTTING US THERE

A storyteller, like a travel agent, can help
gather us up from wherever we are and
put us down in another setting on earth
or, for that matter, on another planet or
on the moon (as Arthur C. Clarke does in
"Dog Star"). That other setting may be a
spot we've always wanted to visit, such as
a beach in Hawaii, or a place where we
don't want to be, such as the deck of a
sinking ship.

Setting tells us where and when a
story takes place. Setting can include the
locale of a story, the weather, the time of
day, and the time period (past, present, or
future). Setting can even include people's
customs—how they live, dress, eat, and
behave. One purpose of setting is to
provide background—a place where the
characters can live and act. Think, for
example, of Ship-Trap Island in "The Most
Dangerous Game," which provides a background filled with peril for Rainsford's
contest with Zaroff. A good setting helps
to make a story vivid and memorable.

Setting and Character

Places where people live can reveal a
great deal about their characters. In "The
Most Dangerous Game," for example,
Connell tells us that General Zaroff lives
in a "palatial château." The dining room
has "a medieval magnificence about it,"
with its "oaken panels," "high ceiling," and
table set with the "finest" silver and china.
The interior of Zaroff's castle gives the
impression that the general is a civilized
and cultured gentleman of refined taste.
Other details of the setting hint at

another, very different side of Zaroff,
however. The towers of the castle plunge
"upward into the gloom," and the cliffs
below the castle dive "down to where the
sea licked greedy lips in the shadows." A
"tall spiked iron gate" guards the entrance
to the castle. Although Zaroff is a man of
culture and elegance on the outside, these
eerie details hint at the evil lurking inside
him. The setting helps us understand
one of Connell's points in the story: Evil
is sometimes masked by polished manners, hidden from view by deceptive
appearances. As Connell does, writers
can use setting to help reveal meaning in
their stories.

Setting, Mood, and Tone

Setting can also provide **mood,** or
atmosphere—it can affect the way we
feel. Some settings make us fearful or
uneasy (midnight, a lonely house, the
scraping of a branch against the window).
Other settings make us feel happy (morning, a garden, the song of a bird). The
emotional effect created by a story's atmosphere draws us into the plot and
makes us care about the characters.

Writers can also use setting to help
express a **tone,** or attitude toward a subject or character. Imagine, for example,
that a writer places a character in a home
decorated with fake antiques and huge,
poorly painted portraits of family members. We can tell from the setting that the
writer is mocking the character's preten-
tious manners. By contributing to the
tone, setting helps shape our reactions to
a story.

INTERNET
**More About
Setting**
Keyword: LE5 9-1

**SKILLS
FOCUS**

Literary Skills
Understand
setting and
how it affects
character, mood,
and tone.

DIFFERENTIATING INSTRUCTION

Learners Having Difficulty
Setting. To help students identify setting,
you may wish to hand out photographs from
various magazines. Have students work in
small groups to identify the time and place of
the photograph (for example, a beach in
present-day Florida; a farmhouse kitchen in
the United States about fifty years ago; a
street in New York about one hundred

years ago). Tell students this is the basic
setting. Explain that the basic setting helps
create a particular atmosphere. Have each
group come up with words describing the
atmosphere of their photograph and explain
to the class how the setting helped create
that atmosphere. Tell students that writers
can use setting in even more ways than
photographers do. Writers can use setting to

help reveal characters, advance the plot, and
even contribute to the theme or overall
meaning of the story.

Advanced Learners
Acceleration. Help students analyze an
author's development of time and sequence.
Explain that a story's time frame, one of the
important elements of setting, may shift during the story.

How Is Setting Created?

One of the wonders of language is that it can summon up a place for us immediately. It can take us to Ship-Trap Island in "The Most Dangerous Game" and into Zaroff's château. Language can reach us through our five senses and put us right in the middle of the action, along with the characters themselves.

To create a believable setting or one that can make us feel pleasure, mystery, or fear, the writer must select the right details or images. **Images** are words or phrases that call forth a response from our senses—sight, smell, touch, hearing, and taste.

Suppose a writer wants us to imagine a setting as ordinary as the drugstore where Tamara is telling J. D. she never wants to see him again. We would get tired of reading a long list of all the objects on the drugstore shelves. Similarly, we would get tired of reading a list of all the trees, rocks, and puddles in the mountain pass where Casey is waiting to ambush the noon stagecoach. However, our own imagination will supply many details if the writer prompts us with the right images. In the drugstore scene the right image might be a row of bottles, each bearing the label "Poison." In the mountain pass the right image might be a circling vulture or the muddy water that seeps into the outlaw's cracked boots.

When a writer supplies a few right images, we will provide the rest of the scenery. We might draw from our own experience, or we might go beyond our memory into our imagination. There we will find all kinds of images—desert islands, palaces, and planets where we have never been.

This exercise of our imagination is what makes reading fiction a more personal and mind-enhancing experience than, for all its lazy pleasures, watching the ready-made images of movies and television.

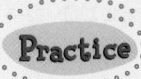

Think of a story that you've read in which the setting captured your imagination. Fill in a chart like the one here to describe the setting and show its role in the story:

SETTING
Title of story:
Where story takes place:
When story takes place:
Details of setting that reveal **character**:
Details of setting that reveal **mood** or **tone**:

HE DIDN'T KNOW HOW TO APPRECIATE NATURE.

Students' responses will vary.

Title of story—"The Most Dangerous Game"

Where story takes place—Ship-Trap Island

When story takes place—early in the twentieth century

Details of setting that reveal ***character***—gloomy gray stone of the château; tall spiked iron gate

Details of setting that reveal ***mood or tone***—"dingy gray was varnishing the sky," "cry of some startled bird," "vegetation grew ranker," and "muck sucked viciously at his foot as if it was a giant leech"

Apply

Encourage students to fill out another setting chart for a story or movie with a very different mood from the one they chose for the Practice activity.

Activity. Ask groups of students to identify examples of flashback and flash-forward in a recent story they have read. Have them analyze why the author chose to vary the time frame of the story. Students may present the results of their discussion to the class.

Grade-Level Skills

■ **Literary Skills**

Analyze the importance of the setting to the mood, tone, and meaning of the text.

■ **Reading Skills**

Identify sensory details.

Summary ⬆ *above grade level*

This semi-autobiographical story is set in the rural South during the Depression. The story focuses on Buddy's recollection of the final Christmas season he spent with his friend when he was seven and she was in her sixties. The story begins with the first chilly day of winter, which prompts Buddy's cousin's annual declaration, "it's fruitcake weather." Together they gather the ingredients they need to bake their thirty-one holiday fruitcakes. The day after they make the fruitcakes, Buddy and his cousin go into the woods to find a Christmas tree. Back home, they decorate the tree with handmade ornaments and then make gifts for family members. Although they would like to give each other extravagant gifts, they have no money and so build kites for each other. On Christmas Day, while flying their kites together, they both experience a transcendent moment of happiness. But this is to be their last Christmas together. Buddy is sent to military school and, a few years later, his cousin falls ill and dies. Buddy mourns her death and keeps searching the wintry sky, half-expecting to see a pair of kites sailing together toward heaven.

Before You Read

A Christmas Memory

Make the Connection

Quickwrite 🖉

"A Christmas Memory" is a story about two unlikely friends. The story reveals something about the nature of friendship and the enduring power of love—even when, to the rest of the world, the friendship seems odd, and the love is not noticed at all.

What do friends give each other? Think about your oldest friendship—why do some friendships last while others don't? Jot down your ideas on friendship, and save your notes.

Literary Focus

Setting Makes It Real

Setting can include the time when a story takes place, the weather, and the customs of the people—how they live, what they eat, how they dress, what they believe. Setting can help reveal character, affect the plot, contribute to a story's **mood** (or emotional effect), and enhance its meaning. In some stories the setting is so crucial that the story could not take place anywhere else.

Truman Capote opens "A Christmas Memory" by asking us to imagine a setting: "a morning in late November . . . more than twenty years ago" (he was referring to the early 1930s), a kitchen in a "spreading old house in a country town," and in the fireplace the season's first roaring fire. Capote's vivid description of the setting brings the characters to life and makes us feel as if we are there with them just as "fruitcake weather" begins.

go.hrw.com

INTERNET

Vocabulary Practice

•

More About Truman Capote

Keyword: LE5 9-1

SKILLS FOCUS

Literary Skills Understand setting and how it affects mood.

Reading Skills Identify sensory details.

Reading Skills 📖

Reading for Details

One of the first rules of good writing is "Show, don't tell." Through the use of **sensory details** (images that appeal to our senses of sight, taste, smell, hearing, and touch), writers reveal character and help their readers visualize actions and setting. As you read "A Christmas Memory," look for telling details in Capote's description of the setting—sensory details and comparisons that convey a feeling, or **mood,** and reveal a great deal about the characters. The questions at the open-book signs will help you.

Vocabulary Development

inaugurating (in·ô′gyə·rāt′iŋ) v.: formally beginning.

exhilarates (eg·zil′ə·rāts′) v.: gladdens; excites.

dilapidated (də·lap′ə·dāt′id) adj.: shabby; falling apart.

paraphernalia (par′ə·fər·nāl′yə) n.: equipment; gear.

sacrilegious (sak′rə·lij′əs) adj.: disrespectful toward religion.

carnage (kär′nij) n.: widespread killing; slaughter.

prosaic (prō·zā′ik) adj.: ordinary.

disposition (dis′pə·zish′ən) n.: usual frame of mind; temperament.

suffuse (sə·fyoōz′) v.: spread over or through.

noncommittal (nän′kə·mit′'l) adj.: not admitting or committing to any particular purpose or point of view.

RESOURCES: READING

Planning

■ *One-Stop Planner* CD-ROM with ExamView Test Generator

Differentiating Instruction

■ *Holt Reading Solutions*

■ *Holt Adapted Reader*

■ *Supporting Instruction in Spanish*

Vocabulary

■ *Vocabulary Development*

Grammar and Language

■ *Language Handbook Worksheets*

■ *Daily Language Activities*

Assessment

■ *Holt Assessment: Literature, Reading, and Vocabulary*

ᐧ CHRISTMAS MEMORY

We are each other's best friend.

TRUMAN CAPOTE

Christmas Morning (1930) by Charles E. Burchfield. Watercolor on paper (30″ × 22⅛″).

Private collection. Photo courtesy of the Charles E. Burchfield Foundation and Kennedy Galleries, New York.

■ *One-Stop Planner* CD-ROM with ExamView Test Generator
■ *Holt Online Assessment*

Internet
■ go.hrw.com (Keyword: LE5 9-1)
■ *Elements of Literature Online*

Media
■ *Audio CD Library*
■ *Fine Art Transparencies*
■ *Visual Connections Videocassette Program*
■ *Audio CD Library, Selections and Summaries in Spanish*

Selection Starter

Motivate. Use the *Visual Connections Videocassette Program* segment "Memories and Celebrations" to help students connect to the narrator's Christmas memory.

Preview Vocabulary

Have student use the Vocabulary words on p. 50 to complete these phrases.

1. a cheerful _____ [disposition]
2. bats, balls, and other sports _____ [paraphernalia]
3. rowdy behavior that seemed _____ in the temple [sacrilegious]
4. a neutral, _____ remark [noncommittal]
5. appalled at the _____ on the battlefield [carnage]
6. a company _____ its new hiring policy [inaugurating]
7. rundown and _____ [dilapidated]
8. a steep descent that _____ bikers [exhilarates]
9. a boring, _____ task [prosaic]
10. light that will _____ the room [suffuse]

VIEWING THE ART

Charles E. Burchfield
(1893–1967) often painted scenes from his childhood in Salem, Ohio.

Activity. Ask students to identify details in the painting that suggest the time and place of the story. [The Christmas tree and the clothes drying on a line show it's winter; the simple table and old-fashioned stove suggest the Depression era.]

A **Literary Focus**

? Setting and mood. What mood does Capote's opening description of the story's setting help to create? [Possible response: The mood is cozy, warm, and contented.]

B **Reading Skills**

? Interpreting. What do you think the narrator means when he says his elderly cousin is "still a child"? Is this a positive, negative, or neutral statement? Find details that support your opinion. [Possible responses: Her enthusiasm for making fruitcakes, her crying, and her closeness to a seven-year-old indicate that she is more like a child than an adult. This is a neutral statement of fact, but some students may interpret it as more positive (she is still alive and open to experience) or more negative (she never grew up).] As they read, suggest that students look for other ways in which Buddy's friend is "still a child" and other indications of whether the author considers this positive or negative.

C **Literary Focus**

? Setting and character. Remind students that setting not only tells the story's time and place but also can include details that reveal character. What do the details about the buggy tell you about the lives of those who push it? [Possible responses: The fact that the buggy is old and broken-down suggests that they are poor; the many things they do with it suggest that they are creative and enterprising.]

---

*I*magine a morning in late November. A coming of winter morning more than twenty years ago. Consider the kitchen of a spreading old house in a country town. A great black stove is its main feature; but there is also a big round table and a fireplace with two rocking chairs placed in front of it. Just today the fireplace commenced its seasonal roar.

A woman with shorn white hair is standing at the kitchen window. She is wearing tennis shoes and a shapeless gray sweater over a summery calico dress. She is small and sprightly, like a bantam hen; but, due to a long youthful illness, her shoulders are pitifully hunched. Her face is remarkable—not unlike Lincoln's, craggy like that, and tinted by sun and wind; but it is delicate too, finely boned, and her eyes are sherry-colored and timid. "Oh my," she exclaims, her breath smoking the windowpane, "it's fruit-cake weather!"

The person to whom she is speaking is myself. I am seven; she is sixty-something. We are cousins, very distant ones, and we have lived together—well, as long as I can remember. Other people inhabit the house, relatives; and though they have power over us, and frequently make us cry, we are not, on the whole, too much aware of them. We are each other's best friend. She calls me Buddy, in memory of a boy who was formerly her best friend. The other Buddy died in the 1880s, when she was still a child. She is still a child.

"I knew it before I got out of bed," she says, turning away from the window with a purposeful excitement in her eyes. "The courthouse bell sounded so cold and clear. And there were no birds singing; they've gone to warmer country, yes indeed. Oh, Buddy, stop stuffing biscuit and fetch our buggy. Help me find my hat. We've thirty cakes to bake."

It's always the same: A morning arrives in November, and my friend, as though officially inaugurating the Christmas time of year that exhilarates her imagination and fuels the blaze of her heart, announces: "It's fruitcake weather! Fetch our buggy. Help me find my hat."

The hat is found, a straw cartwheel corsaged with velvet roses out-of-doors has faded; it once belonged to a more fashionable relative. Together, we guide our buggy, a dilapidated baby carriage, out to the garden and into a grove of pecan trees. The buggy is mine; that is, it was bought for me when I was born. It is made of wicker, rather unraveled, and the wheels wobble like a drunkard's legs. But it is a faithful object; springtimes, we take it to the woods and fill it with flowers, herbs, wild fern for our porch pots; in the summer, we pile it with picnic paraphernalia and sugar-cane fishing poles and roll it down to the edge of the creek; it has its winter uses, too: as a truck for hauling firewood from the yard to the kitchen, as a warm bed for Queenie, our tough little orange and white rat terrier who has survived distemper and two rattlesnake bites. Queenie is trotting beside it now.

Three hours later we are back in the kitchen hulling a heaping buggyload of windfall pecans.[1] Our backs hurt from gathering them: How hard they were to find (the main crop having been shaken off the trees and sold by the orchard's owners, who are not us) among the concealing leaves, the frosted, deceiving grass. Caaarackle! A cheery crunch, scraps of miniature thunder sound as the shells collapse and the golden mound of sweet, oily, ivory meat mounts in the milk-glass bowl. Queenie begs to taste, and now

---

1. **windfall pecans:** pecans blown down from the trees by wind.

Vocabulary

inaugurating (in·ô′gyə·rāt′iŋ) v.: formally beginning.

exhilarates (eg·zil′ə·rāts′) v.: gladdens; excites.

dilapidated (də·lap′ə·dāt′id) adj.: shabby; falling apart.

paraphernalia (par′ə·fər·nāl′yə) n.: equipment; gear.

DIFFERENTIATING INSTRUCTION

Learners Having Difficulty
Modeling. To help students read "A Christmas Memory," model the reading skill of reading for details. Say, "The details Capote chose to include in the first paragraph—such as the big round table, fireplace, and rocking chairs—contribute to a warm and cozy atmosphere." Encourage students as they read to notice details of the setting and ask themselves, "How does this detail contribute to mood, character development, or plot?"

English-Language Learners
Students may need help with some of the expressions used in this story. Clarify the meaning of such idioms as "stuffing biscuit," "skinflint," "yonderways," "twobits cash," and "a dollar, my foot!" Encourage students to

and again my friend sneaks her a mite, though insisting we deprive ourselves. "We mustn't, Buddy. If we start, we won't stop. And there's scarcely enough as there is. For thirty cakes." The kitchen is growing dark. Dusk turns the window into a mirror: Our reflections mingle with the rising moon as we work by the fireside in the firelight. At last, when the moon is quite high, we toss the final hull into the fire and, with joined sighs, watch it catch flame. The buggy is empty; the bowl is brimful.

READING FOR DETAILS

1. Which **senses** does the author appeal to in the description of the kitchen in this paragraph? What **mood** is created?

We eat our supper (cold biscuits, bacon, blackberry jam) and discuss tomorrow. Tomorrow the kind of work I like best begins: buying. Cherries and citron, ginger and vanilla and canned Hawaiian pineapple, rinds and raisins and walnuts and whiskey and oh, so much flour, butter, so many eggs, spices, flavorings: Why, we'll need a pony to pull the buggy home.

But before these purchases can be made, there is the question of money. Neither of us has any. Except for skinflint sums persons in the house occasionally provide (a dime is considered very big money); or what we earn ourselves from various activities: holding rummage sales, selling buckets of handpicked blackberries, jars of homemade jam and apple jelly and peach preserves, rounding up flowers for funerals and weddings. Once we won seventy-ninth prize, five dollars, in a national football contest. Not that we know a fool thing about football. It's just that we enter any contest we hear about: At the moment our hopes are centered on the fifty-thousand-dollar Grand Prize being offered to name a new brand of coffee (we suggested "A.M."; and, after some hesitation, for my friend thought it perhaps sacrilegious, the slogan "A.M.! Amen!"). To tell the truth, our only *really* profitable enterprise was the Fun and Freak

Museum we conducted in a backyard woodshed two summers ago. The Fun was a stereopticon[2] with slide views of Washington and New York lent us by a relative who had been to those places (she was furious when she discovered why we'd borrowed it); the Freak was a three-legged biddy chicken[3] hatched by one of our own hens. Everybody hereabouts wanted to see that biddy: We charged grown-ups a nickel, kids two cents. And took in a good twenty dollars before the museum shut down due to the decease of the main attraction.

But one way and another we do each year accumulate Christmas savings, a Fruitcake Fund. These moneys we keep hidden in an ancient bead purse under a loose board under the floor under a chamber pot[4] under my friend's bed. The purse is seldom removed from this safe location except to make a deposit, or, as happens every Saturday, a withdrawal; for on Saturdays I am allowed ten cents to go to the picture show. My friend has never been to a picture show, nor does she intend to: "I'd rather hear you tell the story, Buddy. That way I can imagine it more. Besides, a person my age shouldn't squander their eyes. When the Lord comes, let me see Him clear." In addition to never having seen a movie, she has never: eaten in a restaurant, traveled more than five miles

---

2. **stereopticon** (ster′ē·äp′ti·kən) *n.:* old-fashioned kind of slide projector.
3. **biddy chicken:** hen; female chicken.
4. **chamber pot** *n.:* Before indoor plumbing and toilets, people used pots, usually kept in their bedrooms, or chambers.

Vocabulary
sacrilegious (sak′rə·lij′əs) *adj.:* disrespectful toward religion.

D Reading Skills

Reading for details. To help students name the senses appealed to, have them organize the images on a sense chart with a heading for each sense. [Possible responses to question 1: *Sight*—concealing leaves, frosted grass, golden mound, reflections. *Smell*—sweet, oily. *Sound*—Caarackle! cheery crunch, miniature thunder. *Taste*—sweet, oily. The mood is cozy and contented.]

E Literary Focus

? Setting. What do these details about the friends' activities tell you about the story's time and place? What does the setting suggest about the characters? [Possible responses: The story takes place in a poor rural area. The details suggest that the characters are imaginative, energetic, resourceful, and creative.]

F Content-Area Connections

Math: Admission Fees
Ask students to calculate how many people came to see the Fun and Freak Museum. You may first need to review the total that Buddy and his cousin made, as well as the charge for adults and for children. [Any combination of five cents (adults) and two cents (children) that adds up to twenty dollars is correct.]

---

check the footnotes for help with other idioms and to consult a dictionary of idioms or regionalisms if they can't figure out unfamiliar words and phrases from context.

Special Education Students
For lessons designed for special education students, see *Holt Reading Solutions*.

DIRECT TEACHING

A **Literary Focus**

? **Characterization.** What method of characterization does Capote use to reveal Buddy's cousin's character in this passage? [*Indirect*—Her character is revealed through her words, actions, and inactions.]

B **Reading Skills**

Reading for details. [Possible responses to question 2: The fact that they keep their money hidden in a bead purse beneath a loose board under a chamber pot reveals that they treasure the money and that they do not trust others in the house.]

C **Reading Skills**

Speculating. Point out to students that Buddy's cousin is very superstitious. Ask them if they think her ideas are a negative influence on Buddy. [Some students may feel that she is a bad influence on Buddy since she encourages him to be superstitious. Others may feel that her superstitions do little harm, while her kindness does a lot of good.]

D **Content-Area Connections**

History: Prohibition
In 1919, the Eighteenth Amendment to the U.S. Constitution prohibited the manufacture, sale, and transportation of intoxicating liquors. The amendment was repealed in 1933.

E **Literary Focus**

Setting and plot. Ask students to find three details about the setting of Haha's cafe that help build tension in the plot. [Possible response: "Garish-gay naked light bulbs," "gray mist," and "shabby and deserted" suggest that Buddy and his cousin might be in danger.]

A from home, received or sent a telegram, read anything except funny papers and the Bible, worn cosmetics, cursed, wished someone harm, told a lie on purpose, let a hungry dog go hungry. Here are a few things she has done, does do: killed with a hoe the biggest rattlesnake ever seen in this county (sixteen rattles), dip snuff[5] (secretly), tame hummingbirds (just try it) till they balance on her finger, tell ghost stories (we both believe in ghosts) so tingling they chill you in July, talk to herself, take walks in the rain, grow the prettiest japonicas[6] in town, know the recipe for every sort of old-time Indian cure, including a magical wart-remover.

READING FOR DETAILS
B **2.** What does the description of the hiding place for the Fruitcake Fund tell you about Buddy and his friend?

Now, with supper finished, we retire to the room in a faraway part of the house where my friend sleeps in a scrap-quilt-covered iron bed painted rose pink, her favorite color. Silently, wallowing in the pleasures of conspiracy, we take the bead purse from its secret place and spill its contents on the scrap quilt. Dollar bills, tightly rolled and green as May buds. Somber fifty-cent pieces, heavy enough to weight a dead man's eyes. Lovely dimes, the liveliest coin, the one that really jingles. Nickels and quarters, worn smooth as creek pebbles. But mostly a hateful heap of bitter-odored pennies. Last summer others in the house contracted to pay us a penny for every twenty-five flies we killed. Oh, the carnage of August: the flies that flew to heaven! Yet it was not work in which we took pride. And, as we sit counting pennies, it is as though we were back tabulating dead flies. Neither of us has a head for figures; we count slowly, lose track, start again. According to her calculations, we have $12.73. According to mine, exactly $13. "I do hope you're wrong, Buddy. We can't mess around with

5. **snuff** *n.*: powdered tobacco inhaled by sniffing.
6. **japonicas** (jə·pän′i·kəz) *n.*: flowering shrubs.

C thirteen. The cakes will fall. Or put somebody in the cemetery. Why, I wouldn't dream of getting out of bed on the thirteenth." This is true: She always spends thirteenths in bed. So, to be on the safe side, we subtract a penny and toss it out the window.

Of the ingredients that go into our fruitcakes, whiskey is the most expensive, as well as the hardest to obtain: State laws forbid its sale. But everybody knows you can buy a bottle from Mr. **D** Haha Jones. And the next day, having completed our more prosaic shopping, we set out for Mr. Haha's business address, a "sinful" (to quote public opinion) fish-fry and dancing cafe down by the river. We've been there before, and on the same errand; but in previous years our dealings have been with Haha's wife, an iodine-dark Indian woman with brassy peroxided hair and a dead-tired disposition. Actually, we've never laid eyes on her husband, though we've heard that he's an Indian too. A giant with razor scars across his cheeks. They call him Haha because he's so gloomy, a man who never laughs. As we approach his cafe (a large log cabin festooned[7] inside and out with chains of garish-gay naked light bulbs and standing by the river's muddy edge under the shade of river trees where moss drifts through the branches like gray mist) our **E** steps slow down. Even Queenie stops prancing and sticks close by. People have been murdered in Haha's cafe. Cut to pieces. Hit on the head. There's a case coming up in court next month. Naturally these goings-on happen at night when the colored lights cast crazy patterns and the Victrola[8] wails. In the daytime Haha's is shabby

7. **festooned** (fes·tōōnd′) *v.* used as *adj*: decorated.
8. **Victrola** (vik·trō′lə): old term for a record player.

Vocabulary
carnage (kär′nij) *n.*: widespread killing; slaughter.
prosaic (prō·zā′ik) *adj.*: ordinary.
disposition (dis′pə·zish′ən) *n.*: usual frame of mind; temperament.

DIFFERENTIATING INSTRUCTION

Advanced Learners
Acceleration. Use this activity to help advanced learners explain how the choice of a narrator affects the tone and credibility of a text.
Activity. Divide students into small groups. Have each group agree on one word that best captures the overall tone of this story such as *sad* or *nostalgic*. Then, have them

discuss how the author's choice of an older Buddy as the narrator contributes to that tone and to the story's credibility. After discussion, students may write a brief analysis of Capote's use of this narrator to create the tone of the story.

Bouquet and Stove (1929) by Yasuo Kuniyoshi.

and deserted. I knock at the door, Queenie barks, my friend calls: "Mrs. Haha, ma'am? Anyone to home?"

Footsteps. The door opens. Our hearts overturn. It's Mr. Haha Jones himself! And he *is* a giant; he *does* have scars; he *doesn't* smile. No, he glowers at us through Satan-tilted eyes and demands to know: "What you want with Haha?"

For a moment we are too paralyzed to tell. Presently my friend half finds her voice, a whispery voice at best: "If you please, Mr. Haha, we'd like a quart of your finest whiskey."

His eyes tilt more. Would you believe it? Haha is smiling! Laughing, too. "Which one of you is a drinkin' man?"

"It's for making fruitcakes, Mr. Haha. Cooking."

This sobers him. He frowns. "That's no way to waste good whiskey." Nevertheless, he retreats into the shadowed cafe and seconds later appears carrying a bottle of daisy-yellow unlabeled liquor. He demonstrates its sparkle in the sunlight and says: "Two dollars."

We pay him with nickels and dimes and pennies. Suddenly, jangling the coins in his hand like a fistful of dice, his face softens. "Tell you what," he proposes, pouring the money back into our bead purse, "just send me one of them fruitcakes instead."

"Well," my friend remarks on our way home, "there's a lovely man. We'll put an extra cup of raisins in *his* cake."

The black stove, stoked with coal and firewood, glows like a lighted pumpkin. Eggbeaters whirl, spoons spin round in bowls of butter and sugar, vanilla sweetens the air, ginger spices it; melting, nose-tingling odors saturate the kitchen, suffuse the house, drift out to the world on puffs of chimney smoke. In four days our work is done. Thirty-one cakes, dampened with whiskey, bask on window sills and shelves.

Who are they for?

Vocabulary
suffuse (sə·fyo͞oz′) *v.*: spread over or through.

[Side caption, vertical:] The Roland P. Murdock Collection, Wichita Art Museum, Wichita, Kansas. © Estate of Yasuo Kuniyoshi / Licensed by VAGA, New York, NY.

F Advanced Learners

? Acceleration. Tell students that irony occurs when there is a contrast between expectations and reality. Why is Haha Jones's name ironic? [He is the opposite of the laughing person his name suggests.] How does Haha's reputation contrast with his true character? [Possible response: Haha's dangerous reputation contrasts with his sense of humor and kindheartedness as he refuses to take money from Buddy's cousin.]

G Literary Focus

? Setting. What images does Capote use to place the reader in this kitchen setting? What mood do the sensory details of the images create? [Possible responses: The sensory details of light, warmth, and good aromas ("glows like a lighted pumpkin," "eggbeaters whirl," "vanilla sweetens the air,") help the reader to hear, smell, see, touch, and practically taste the fruitcakes. The sensory details create a homey, intimate mood.] You may ask students to write a similar paragraph full of sensory images about a pleasant childhood food memory.

VIEWING THE ART

The Japanese American modernist painter **Yasuo Kuniyoshi** (1893–1953) often combined Japanese motifs with American folk art and European modernist elements.

Activity. The contrast between the colorful, delicate lines of the flowers and the dark, solid mass of the stove emphasizes the qualities of each, enabling the viewer to perceive both stove and flowers more fully. Ask students to compare this visual effect to the literary effect Capote creates by pairing the seven-year-old Buddy with his aging cousin.

History: The Great Depression

On October 29, 1929 (a day later called Black Tuesday), the stock market crashed, after which the economy slid into a severe depression. The economic hard times lasted from 1929 to 1941. In 1933, when President Roosevelt took office promising "a new deal for the American people," thousands of "just plain folks" wrote to him about their trials and tribulations and their hopes for the future.

Mixed-ability group activity. Place students of differing abilities into groups of three or four and ask them to research some aspect of the Great Depression, such as its causes, its effects on American families, and its remedies—including the various programs of Roosevelt's New Deal. Have students present their findings in an oral report.

A Reading Skills

❓ Making inferences. What do the details about the recipients of the fruitcakes tell you about Buddy, his cousin, and their motivation for making the fruitcakes? [Possible response: They do not feel close to other members of the house or the town, but when they send out fruitcakes, they feel themselves linked to many interesting people all over the world.]

B Reading Skills

❓ Drawing conclusions. What conclusions can you draw about the family from this scattering of questions and exclamations? [Possible response: The other adults in the family are religious, self-righteous, and easily angered. The mention of certain relatives suggests a family history of alcoholism.]

C Vocabulary Development

❓ Literal and figurative meanings. Ask students for the literal meaning of *scald*. [to burn with hot liquid or steam] What is the figurative meaning of *scald* in "tongues that scald"? [Possible response: The relatives' angry, critical words burn with harshness and hurtfulness.]

D Reading Skills

Reading for details. [Possible response to question 3: His friend's feelings of humiliation and despair are conveyed through details such as the cowering dog, the fading fire, and the wet pillow.]

A Friends. Not necessarily neighbor friends: Indeed, the larger share are intended for persons we've met maybe once, perhaps not at all. People who've struck our fancy. Like President Roosevelt. Like the Reverend and Mrs. J. C. Lucey, Baptist missionaries to Borneo who lectured here last winter. Or the little knife grinder who comes through town twice a year. Or Abner Packer, the driver of the six o'clock bus from Mobile, who exchanges waves with us every day as he passes in a dust-cloud whoosh. Or the young Wistons, a California couple whose car one afternoon broke down outside the house and who spent a pleasant hour chatting with us on the porch (young Mr. Wiston snapped our picture, the only one we've ever had taken). Is it because my friend is shy with everyone *except* strangers that these strangers, and merest acquaintances, seem to us our truest friends? I think yes. Also, the scrapbooks we keep of thank-you's on White House stationery, time-to-time communications from California and Borneo, the knife grinder's penny postcards, make us feel connected to eventful worlds beyond the kitchen with its views of a sky that stops.

Now a nude December fig branch grates against the window. The kitchen is empty, the cakes are gone; yesterday we carted the last of them to the post office, where the cost of stamps turned our purse inside out. We're broke. That rather depresses me, but my friend insists on celebrating—with two inches of whiskey left in Haha's bottle. Queenie has a spoonful in a bowl of coffee (she likes her coffee chicory-flavored and strong). The rest we divide between a pair of jelly glasses. We're both quite awed at the prospect of drinking straight whiskey; the taste of it brings screwed-up expressions and sour shudders. But by and by we begin to sing, the two of us singing different songs simultaneously. I don't know the words to mine, just: *Come on along, come on along, to the dark-town strutters' ball*. But I can dance: That's what I mean to be, a tap-dancer in the movies. My dancing shadow

rollicks on the walls; our voices rock the chinaware; we giggle as if unseen hands were tickling us. Queenie rolls on her back, her paws plow the air, something like a grin stretches her black lips. Inside myself, I feel warm and sparky as those crumbling logs, carefree as the wind in the chimney. My friend waltzes round the stove, the hem of her poor calico skirt pinched between her fingers as though it were a party dress: *Show me the way to go home*, she sings, her tennis shoes squeaking on the floor. *Show me the way to go home*.

C **B** Enter: two relatives. Very angry. Potent with eyes that scold, tongues that scald. Listen to what they have to say, the words tumbling together into a wrathful tune: "A child of seven! whiskey on his breath! are you out of your mind? feeding a child of seven! must be loony! road to ruination! remember Cousin Kate? Uncle Charlie? Uncle Charlie's brother-in-law? shame! scandal! humiliation! kneel, pray, beg the Lord!"

Queenie sneaks under the stove. My friend gazes at her shoes, her chin quivers, she lifts her skirt and blows her nose and runs to her room. Long after the town has gone to sleep and the house is silent except for the chimings of clocks and the sputter of fading fires, she is weeping into a pillow already as wet as a widow's handkerchief.

READING FOR DETAILS

D **3.** What details in this paragraph help convey the feelings of Buddy's friend?

"Don't cry," I say, sitting at the bottom of her bed and shivering despite my flannel nightgown that smells of last winter's cough syrup, "don't cry," I beg, teasing her toes, tickling her feet, "you're too old for that."

"It's because," she hiccups, "I *am* too old. Old and funny."

"Not funny. Fun. More fun than anybody. Listen. If you don't stop crying you'll be so tired tomorrow we can't go cut a tree."

She straightens up. Queenie jumps on the bed (where Queenie is not allowed) to lick her cheeks.

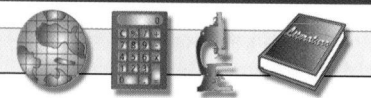
CONTENT-AREA CONNECTIONS

Culture: Music During the Depression
Buddy's cousin sings the song "Show Me the Way to Go Home," composed by Wendell Hall in 1926. During the Great Depression many people sought to forget their troubles through music. Although many of the popular songs of the era, such as "Brother, Can You Spare a Dime?" did reflect the agony of the times, upbeat musical pieces such as Irving Berlin's "Puttin' on the Ritz" (1929) helped

people persevere through poverty and despair.
Small-group activity. Provide students with copies of lyrics from songs of the Great Depression. You may also wish to play recordings of some of these songs for the class. Have small groups choose one song and explain how the lyrics reflect the times in which the song was written.

Christmas Trees by Theora Hamblett. Drawing.

Courtesy of the University Museums, University of Mississippi.

"I know where we'll find real pretty trees, Buddy. And holly, too. With berries big as your eyes. It's way off in the woods. Farther than we've ever been. Papa used to bring us Christmas trees from there: carry them on his shoulder. That's fifty years ago. Well, now: I can't wait for morning."

Morning. Frozen rime[9] lusters the grass; the sun, round as an orange and orange as hot-weather moons, balances on the horizon, burnishes[10] the silvered winter woods. A wild turkey calls. A renegade hog grunts in the undergrowth. Soon, by the edge of knee-deep, rapid-running water, we have to abandon the buggy. Queenie wades the stream first, paddles across, barking complaints at the swiftness of the current, the pneumonia-making coldness of it. We follow, holding our shoes and equipment (a hatchet, a burlap sack) above our heads. A mile more: of chastising thorns, burs and briers that catch at our clothes; of rusty pine needles brilliant with gaudy fungus and molted feathers. Here, there, a flash, a flutter, an ecstasy of

shrillings remind us that not all the birds have flown south. Always, the path unwinds through lemony sun pools and pitch vine tunnels. Another creek to cross: A disturbed armada[11] of speckled trout froths the water round us, and frogs the size of plates practice belly flops; beaver workmen are building a dam. On the farther shore, Queenie shakes herself and trembles. My friend shivers, too: not with cold but enthusiasm. One of her hat's ragged roses sheds a petal as she lifts her head and inhales the pine-heavy air. "We're almost there; can you smell it, Buddy?" she says, as though we were approaching an ocean.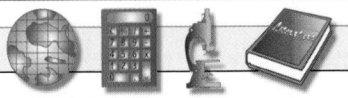

READING FOR DETAILS

4. Pick three **images** in this paragraph that appeal most forcefully to your senses. Explain why they help you imagine the setting.

And, indeed, it is a kind of ocean. Scented acres of holiday trees, prickly-leafed holly. Red berries shiny as Chinese bells: Black crows swoop upon them screaming. Having stuffed our burlap

---

9. **frozen rime:** frost.
10. **burnishes** (bʉr′nish·iz) *v.*: polishes.

---

11. **armada** (är·mä′də) *n.*: group, as of warships.

E **Learners Having Difficulty**

Re-reading. Have students re-read the last four paragraphs to identify how Buddy changes his cousin's mood from sad to happy. [He reminds her that the next day they will go cut a Christmas tree.]

F **Reading Skills**

Reading for details. [Possible responses to question 4: "pneumonia-making coldness" because it is simple and yet vivid; "rusty pine needles brilliant with gaudy fungus and molted feathers" because it is so detailed and colorful; "an ecstasy of shrillings" because it conveys intense excitement and appeals to the sense of hearing.]

VIEWING THE ART

Theora Hamblett (1895–1977) was born in the closing years of the nineteenth century, but did not begin to paint until the 1950s.

Activity. Encourage students to find a quotation from "A Christmas Memory" that they might use as a caption for this drawing.

Culture: The Christmas Tree

The tradition of the Christmas tree might have had its beginnings in the medieval German mystery plays, which used a tree to symbolize the Garden of Eden. Later, people cut down trees to set up in their homes. Over time, people began to decorate the tree with fruits, cookies, and candles. Some experts believe the Christmas tree is a survival of pagan tree worship and trace it to ancient Rome and Egypt.

Paired activity. Encourage students to work in pairs to research various midwinter celebrations around the world and their symbolic use of plants. After the research is finished, have the pairs share their findings with the class.

VIEWING THE ART

Leonard Ochtman (1854–1934) was an American artist who specialized in painting the Connecticut countryside. He was influenced by styles of painting that emphasized the effects of light on a landscape.

Activity. Ask students why they think this painting was titled *Morning Haze*. [Possible response: The title suggests the effects of weather on the wintry morning.]

Ⓐ Vocabulary Development

❓ Literal and figurative meanings. What is the literal meaning of *brute*? [a beast; relating to or characteristic of animals] How does Capote use *brute* figuratively here? [The tree is compared to a wild animal, and its cutting is compared to hunting and killing a wild animal.]

Ⓑ Literary Focus

❓ Characterization. What do you learn about the narrator's friend from her words and actions here? [Possible responses: She cares little for money and possessions; she can be strong and decisive; she has a spiritual respect for the uniqueness of living things.]

Ⓒ English-Language Learners

Idioms and colloquial expressions. Explain that because this story takes place in the rural South over seventy years ago, Capote uses expressions that were common in that time and place. Ask students to guess what "my foot," "blaze like a Baptist window," and "five-and-dime" mean. [Possible responses: "No way!" or another expression of disbelief; bright and colorful like a stained glass window; a store that once stood on most U.S. main streets, where you could buy items for five to ten cents during the Depression.]

Ⓐ sacks with enough greenery and crimson to garland a dozen windows, we set about choosing a tree. "It should be," muses my friend, "twice as tall as a boy. So a boy can't steal the star." The one we pick is twice as tall as me. A brave, handsome brute that survives thirty hatchet strokes before it keels with a creaking, rending cry. Lugging it like a kill, we commence the long trek out. Every few yards we abandon the struggle, sit down, and pant. But we have the strength of triumphant huntsmen; that and the tree's virile, icy perfume revive us, goad us on. Many compliments accompany our sunset return along the red clay road to town; but my friend is sly and Ⓑ noncommittal when passersby praise the treasure perched in our buggy: What a fine tree and where did it come from? "Yonderways," she murmurs vaguely. Once a car stops and the rich mill owner's lazy wife leans out and whines: "Giveya twobits cash for that ol tree." Ordinarily my friend is afraid of saying no; but on this occasion she promptly shakes her head: "We wouldn't take a dollar." The mill owner's wife persists. "A dollar, my foot! Fifty cents. That's my last offer. Goodness, woman, you can get another one." In answer, my friend gently reflects: "I doubt it. There's never two of anything."

Home: Queenie slumps by the fire and sleeps till tomorrow, snoring loud as a human.

A trunk in the attic contains: a shoe box of ermine tails[12] (off the opera cape of a curious lady who once rented a room in the house), coils

Morning Haze (1909) by Leonard Ochtman.

of frazzled tinsel gone gold with age, one silver star, a brief rope of dilapidated, undoubtedly dangerous candylike light bulbs. Excellent decorations, as far as they go, which isn't far enough: Ⓒ My friend wants our tree to blaze "like a Baptist window," droop with weighty snows of ornament. But we can't afford the made-in-Japan splendors at the five-and-dime. So we do what we've always done: sit for days at the kitchen table with scissors and crayons and stacks of colored paper. I make sketches and my friend cuts them out: lots of cats, fish too (because they're easy to draw), some apples, some watermelons, a few winged angels devised from saved-up sheets of Hershey-bar tinfoil. We use safety pins to attach these creations to the tree; as a final touch, we sprinkle the branches with shredded cotton (picked in August for this purpose). My friend, surveying the effect, clasps her hands together. "Now honest, Buddy. Doesn't it look good enough to eat?" Queenie tries to eat an angel.

Vocabulary
noncommittal (nän′kə·mit′l) *adj.*: not admitting or committing to any particular purpose or point of view.

---

12. **ermine** (ur′min) **tails:** black-tipped white tails of certain kinds of weasels, used to trim clothes.

DEVELOPING FLUENCY

Small-group activity. Ask students to work in groups of four or five to present a section of the story as a reader's theater project. Remind students that reader's theater involves a dramatic reenactment in which the actors may read from the book. Three students will take on the roles of the young Buddy, his cousin, and the grown-up Buddy, who serves as the narrator. The remaining student or students may direct the reading and make decisions regarding the use of props and gestures. Since there is no dialogue for Buddy in the story, students can write lines based on the boy's character. All students should work together to plan the reading and to assess how well it went. Encourage the groups to practice their performances and then present them to the class.

National Museum of American Art, Washington, D.C.

After weaving and ribboning holly wreaths for all the front windows, our next project is the fashioning of family gifts. Tie-dye scarves for the ladies, for the men a home-brewed lemon and licorice and aspirin syrup to be taken "at the first Symptoms of a Cold and after Hunting." But when it comes time for making each other's gift, my friend and I separate to work secretly. I would like to buy her a pearl-handled knife, a radio, a whole pound of chocolate-covered cherries (we tasted some once and she always swears: "I could live on them, Buddy, Lord yes I could—and that's not taking His name in vain"). Instead, I am building her a kite. She would like to give me a bicycle (she's said so on several million occasions: "If only I could, Buddy. It's bad enough in life to do without something *you* want; but confound it, what gets my goat is not being able to give somebody something you want *them* to have. Only one of these days, I will, Buddy. Locate you a bike. Don't ask how. Steal it, maybe"). Instead, I'm fairly certain that she is building me a kite—the same as last year, and the year before: The year before that we exchanged slingshots. All of which is fine by me. For we are champion kite-fliers who study the wind like sailors; my friend, more accomplished than I, can get a kite aloft when there isn't enough breeze to carry clouds.

Christmas Eve afternoon we scrape together a nickel and go to the butcher's to buy Queenie's traditional gift, a good gnawable beef bone. The bone, wrapped in funny paper, is placed high in the tree near the silver star. Queenie knows it's there. She squats at the foot of the tree, staring up in a trance of greed: When bedtime arrives she refuses to budge. Her excitement is equaled by my own. I kick the covers and turn my pillow as though it were a scorching summer's night. Somewhere a rooster crows: falsely, for the sun is still on the other side of the world.

"Buddy, are you awake?" It is my friend, calling from her room, which is next to mine;

and an instant later she is sitting on my bed holding a candle. "Well, I can't sleep a hoot," she declares. "My mind's jumping like a jack rabbit. Buddy, do you think Mrs. Roosevelt will serve our cake at dinner?" We huddle in the bed, and she squeezes my hand I-love-you. "Seems like your hand used to be so much smaller. I guess I hate to see you grow up. When you're grown up, will we still be friends?" I say always. "But I feel so bad, Buddy. I wanted so bad to give you a bike. I tried to sell my cameo Papa gave me. Buddy—" she hesitates, as though embarrassed. "I made you another kite." Then I confess that I made her one, too; and we laugh. The candle burns too short to hold. Out it goes, exposing the starlight, the stars spinning at the window like a visible caroling that slowly, slowly daybreak silences. Possibly we doze; but the beginnings of dawn splash us like cold water: We're up, wide-eyed and wandering while we wait for others to waken. Quite deliberately my friend drops a kettle on the kitchen floor. I tap-dance in front of closed doors. One by one the household emerges, looking as though they'd like to kill us both; but it's Christmas, so they can't. First, a gorgeous breakfast: just everything you can imagine—from flapjacks and fried squirrel to hominy grits and honey-in-the-comb. Which puts everyone in a good humor except my friend and me. Frankly, we're so impatient to get at the presents we can't eat a mouthful.

Well, I'm disappointed. Who wouldn't be? With socks, a Sunday school shirt, some handkerchiefs, a hand-me-down sweater, and a year's subscription to a religious magazine for children, *The Little Shepherd*. It makes me boil. It really does.

> **READING FOR DETAILS**
>
> 5. This paragraph includes interesting **figures of speech**, or comparisons, describing the stars and the dawn. What are the comparisons, and why are they effective?

D Literary Focus

❓ **Setting and character.** Buddy and his friend are in the kitchen again, this time making ornaments, wreaths, tie-dye scarves, cold medicine, and kites. Based on the descriptions of these homemade items, what can you conclude about the characters and their economic environment? [They are creative and resourceful, even though they are living in hard times.]

E Literary Focus

❓ **Characterization.** Remind students that writers often use what characters say to reveal more about them. What does Buddy's cousin say is worse than going without something you want? [not being able to give someone you care about what he or she wants] What does her statement reveal about her character? [She is selfless, loving, and giving.]

F Reading Skills

Reading for details. [Possible response to question 5: The comparisons are "the stars spinning at the window like a visible caroling that slowly, slowly daybreak silences" and "the beginnings of dawn splash us like cold water." They are effective because they strongly appeal to a number of senses in an unusual and memorable way.]

G Reading Skills

❓ **Making inferences.** Why do these presents make Buddy "boil"? [Possible responses: There is nothing personal about them; they are simply useful—not fun or imaginative.]

READING MINI-LESSON

Developing Word-Attack Skills
Remind students that a final e is often a signal that the preceding vowel has a long vowel sound. Use these word pairs to demonstrate the effect of a final e.

man	mane	pin	pine
met	mete	cod	code

Activity. Explain that a final e can also signal a long vowel in multisyllabic words, but that is not always the case. Write these words on

the chalkboard. Have students decide if the underlined syllable does or does not have a long vowel sound.

partic<u>i</u>pate [yes]   exhi<u>la</u>rate [yes]
sur<u>vive</u> [yes]   suf<u>fuse</u> [yes]
pro<u>pose</u> [yes]   car<u>nage</u> [no]
im<u>agine</u> [no]   hand<u>some</u> [no]

A **Literary Focus**

? Foreshadowing. Why do you think the author mentions Queenie's eventual death here? [Possible responses: It signals more sadness to come; it suggests that these happy times, of which Queenie is a part, will soon end—not only for Queenie, but for Buddy and his friend.]

B **Content-Area Connections**

Literature: Epiphany

? The Christian celebration of Epiphany, which occurs shortly after Christmas, commemorates the showing of the infant Jesus to the Magi, or Three Kings. The author James Joyce introduced the term *epiphany* in literature to mean a sudden, intuitive revelation. What is the revelation that Buddy's friend experiences this Christmas? [Possible response: She understands that the ordinary world of sky, kites, grass, dogs—"things as they are"—reveals God's presence.]

C **Reading Skills**

? Making inferences. What can you infer about Buddy's friend from the details in this passage? [Possible responses: Her mind and body are failing. We know she is very ill when she can't get out of bed even to make her holiday fruitcakes.]

D **Literary Focus**

? Setting and theme. The winter setting of the story has, so far, created a warm, nostalgic atmosphere. Now, what mood does the "fruitcake weather" create and how does the wintry setting add to the overall theme of the story? [Possible response: The mood is bleak and cheerless now that his friend is dead. The setting reinforces the theme of the preciousness of a true friend and the poignancy of loss.]

My friend has a better haul. A sack of satsumas,[13] that's her best present. She is proudest, however, of a white wool shawl knitted by her married sister. But she *says* her favorite gift is the kite I built her. And it *is* very beautiful; though not as beautiful as the one she made me, which is blue and scattered with gold and green Good Conduct stars; moreover, my name is painted on it, "Buddy."

"Buddy, the wind is blowing."

The wind is blowing, and nothing will do till we've run to a pasture below the house where Queenie has scooted to bury her bone (and where, a winter hence, Queenie will be buried, too). There, plunging through the healthy, waist-high grass, we unreel our kites, feel them twitching at the string like sky fish as they swim into the wind. Satisfied, sun-warmed, we sprawl in the grass and peel satsumas and watch our kites cavort. Soon I forget the socks and hand-me-down sweater. I'm as happy as if we'd already won the fifty-thousand-dollar Grand Prize in that coffee-naming contest.

"My, how foolish I am!" my friend cries, suddenly alert, like a woman remembering too late she has biscuits in the oven. "You know what I've always thought?" she asks in a tone of discovery, and smiling not at me but a point beyond. "I've always thought a body would have to be sick and dying before they saw the Lord. And I imagined that when He came it would be like looking at the Baptist window: pretty as colored glass with the sun pouring through, such a shine you don't know it's getting dark. And it's been a comfort: to think of that shine taking away all the spooky feeling. But I'll wager it never happens. I'll wager at the very end a body realizes the Lord has already shown Himself. That things as they are"—her hand circles in a gesture that gathers clouds and kites and grass and Queenie pawing earth over her bone—"just what they've always seen, was seeing Him. As for me, I could leave the world with today in my eyes."

This is our last Christmas together.

Life separates us. Those who Know Best decide that I belong in a military school. And so follows a miserable succession of bugle-blowing prisons, grim reveille-ridden[14] summer camps. I have a new home too. But it doesn't count. Home is where my friend is, and there I never go.

And there she remains, puttering around the kitchen. Alone with Queenie. Then alone. ("Buddy dear," she writes in her wild hard-to-read script, "yesterday Jim Macy's horse kicked Queenie bad. Be thankful she didn't feel much. I wrapped her in a Fine Linen sheet and rode her in the buggy down to Simpson's pasture where she can be with all her Bones. . . .") For a few Novembers she continues to bake her fruitcakes single-handed; not as many, but some: And, of course, she always sends me "the best of the batch." Also, in every letter she encloses a dime wadded in toilet paper: "See a picture show and write me the story." But gradually in her letters she tends to confuse me with her other friend, the Buddy who died in the 1880s; more and more, thirteenths are not the only days she stays in bed: A morning arrives in November, a leafless birdless coming of winter morning, when she cannot rouse herself to exclaim: "Oh my, it's fruitcake weather!"

And when that happens, I know it. A message saying so merely confirms a piece of news some secret vein had already received, severing from me an irreplaceable part of myself, letting it loose like a kite on a broken string. That is why, walking across a school campus on this particular December morning, I keep searching the sky. As if I expected to see, rather like hearts, a lost pair of kites hurrying toward heaven. ■

---

13. **satsumas** (sat′sə·mäz′) *n.:* oranges.

14. **reveille-ridden** (rev′ə·lē rid′'n): ruled by the drum or bugle signal used to rouse sleeping people in a military or summer camp. The writer uses this phrase to suggest a tightly disciplined camp.

FAMILY/COMMUNITY ACTIVITY

Encourage students and members of their family to explore connections between situations in "A Christmas Memory" and real-life situations using the think-aloud protocol. Each participant takes a turn reading aloud a favorite section of the story. As participants read their chosen passages, they freely express any connections they see to their own lives. For instance, some students may know what it feels like not to be able to buy the perfect gift for someone they love. You might send home a note to parents, explaining how the think-aloud protocol works and how the activity benefits students.

Meet the Writer

Truman Capote

"A Turtle on Its Back"

Truman Capote (1924–1984) said he was "sort of dragged up" by assorted elderly relatives who lived in "dirt-road Alabama." He was born in New Orleans, but his father deserted the family, and the boy was moved from place to place while his mother lived in New York. For several years, Capote attended military schools, which he hated. When he was seventeen, he abandoned formal schooling for good and moved to New York City to learn to write. He came to national prominence when he was just twenty-four years old, with the publication of his first novel, *Other Voices, Other Rooms* (1948).

Capote's most famous novel is probably *Breakfast at Tiffany's* (1958). It was made into a movie starring Audrey Hepburn as Holly Golightly, the story's unpredictable and "lost" heroine, who goes to New York from the South to make her fortune. His most talked-about book is not fiction at all, but an account of a mass murder that took place in Kansas. Called *In Cold Blood* (1965), the book took Capote six years to research and write and involved him in much controversy. Capote called the book a nonfiction novel—a narrative that reads like a novel but with events that are all true.

In an interview in *The New York Times Magazine*, Capote once said that his frustrations during his early years made him feel "like a turtle on its back."

66 I always felt that nobody was going to understand me, going to understand what I felt about things. I guess that's why I started writing. At least on paper I could put down what I thought. 99

61

Monitoring students' progress. Guide the class in answering these comprehension questions.

Short Answer

1. Who is Buddy's best friend? [his cousin, a woman in her sixties]
2. What do Buddy and his friend make as gifts for other people? [fruitcakes]
3. From whom do the two friends buy liquor? [Haha Jones]
4. What do the two friends give each other on their last Christmas together? [kites]
5. What finally happens to Buddy's friend? [She dies.]

Meet the Writer

Background. Capote agreed completely with the legions of writers who have said that writing does not come easily: "It's a very excruciating life facing that blank piece of paper every day and having to reach up somewhere into the clouds and bring something down out of them." Perhaps this is one reason Capote reached down to earth as often as he reached up into the clouds— writing nonfiction pieces of travel writing, crime writing, and autobiography. He also sometimes combined fiction and nonfiction, as in "A Christmas Memory," where he includes real details from his childhood such as growing up in the poor, rural, southern United States, living with elderly relatives, and being sent to military school.

Advanced Learners

Enrichment. Tell students that Capote sometimes took an active role in the adaptation of his stories and novels for screenplays.
Activity. Have students read excerpts of the television screenplay for "A Christmas Memory," which Capote himself wrote. Ask students to compare camera instructions with descriptive passages in the story to see what is the same and what is changed.

Connection

Summary ⬇ *below grade level*

In this free-verse tribute the speaker praises his father's simplicity, decency, and hard work. As the two walk through town, they discuss the price of pomegranates, the value of oranges, and death. The speaker realizes that he loves his father so much that he would give his life for him. He also realizes that his father's virtues—kindness, patience, and honesty—make him a great man.

DIRECT TEACHING

Ⓐ Reading Skills

❓ Reading for details. To what does the speaker's father compare people? [to orange trees.] **What does he mean by this?** [Possible response: The orange tree produces oranges, which have seeds that will produce more orange trees. Similarly, people have children who have more children, and so each person is "perpetual" too.]

Ⓑ Reading Skills

❓ Interpreting. How does the speaker seem to define greatness? [Possible response: Greatness is the simple wisdom that comes from living honestly, working hard, and providing for loved ones.]

VIEWING THE ART

William Low, an illustrator, is a first generation Chinese American. In this portrait, a man seems to be taking a break from playing music. **Activity.** Ask students how the man in the painting is like the father in Salinas's poem. [Possible response: An older man, he seems to possess a quiet dignity and to lack pretense.]

My Father Is a Simple Man

Luis Omar Salinas

The Jazz Musician by William Low.
Courtesy of the Artist.

I walk to town with my father
to buy a newspaper. He walks slower
than I do so I must slow up.
The street is filled with children.
5   We argue about the price
of pomegranates, I convince
him it is the fruit of scholars.
He has taken me on this journey
and it's been lifelong.
10   He's sure I'll be healthy
so long as I eat more oranges,
and tells me the orange
has seeds and so is perpetual;°
and we too will come back
15   like the orange trees.
I ask him what he thinks
about death and he says
he will gladly face it when
it comes but won't jump
20   out in front of a car.
I'd gladly give my life
for this man with a sixth
grade education, whose kindness
and patience are true . . .
25   The truth of it is, he's the scholar,
and when the bitter-hard reality
comes at me like a punishing
evil stranger, I can always
remember that here was a man
30   who was a worker and provider,
who learned the simple facts

in life and lived by them,
who held no pretense.°
And when he leaves without
35   benefit of fanfare° or applause
I shall have learned what little
there is about greatness.

---

13. perpetual (pər·pech′ōō·əl) *adj.*: continuing forever.
33. who held no pretense: who didn't show off.
35. fanfare (fan′fer′) *n.*: noisy display to draw attention (literally, a flourish of trumpets).

Connecting and Comparing Texts

In "My Father Is a Simple Man,", as in "A Christmas Memory," the first-person narrator pays tribute to an older person who has played an important role in his life. In both works, the younger person has more formal education than his elder but appreciates the wisdom of his older relative.

Activity. Have students write a poem or brief essay in tribute to an older, influential person. Encourage them to use quotations that illustrate the person's positive qualities.

Response and Analysis

Reading Check

1. What do you know about Buddy? What is his relationship to the old woman he calls "my friend"?

2. Why do Buddy and his friend make fruitcakes each year?

3. What obstacles must they overcome to make their gifts?

4. What does Buddy's friend discover after flying her kite on their last Christmas Day together?

Thinking Critically

5. How would you describe the **character** of Buddy's friend? Consider
   - what she says
   - the way her face is described
   - the things she does and has never done
   - Buddy's description of her as "still a child"

6. Look carefully at the sensory details in Capote's description of the kitchen at different points in the story. What **mood**—or feeling—do these details of **setting** convey in each scene?

7. Which details in the description of Mr. Haha Jones's cafe make it seem like a threatening place? Does the **setting** accurately reflect Haha Jones's character? Explain your answer.

8. As friends, what do Buddy and his cousin give to each other, and what do they get in return? In your opinion, why does this friendship have a lasting effect on Buddy? Support your answer with evidence from the story, and check your Quickwrite notes.

9. Explain the reference to kites in the last paragraph. What do kites represent for Buddy? What does this reference tell you about Buddy's feelings concerning the death of his friend?

10. In what ways is Buddy's friend similar to the speaker's father in "My Father Is a Simple Man" (see the **Connection** on page 62)? Do you think Buddy learns about "greatness" from his friend? Explain.

Extending and Evaluating

11. Do you think that Buddy's friend is a realistic character, or do you think that people like her don't exist in real life? Explain your response.

WRITING

There's No Place Like Home

People's homes reveal a great deal about their characters. We learn, for example, that Buddy's friend "sleeps in a scrap-quilt-covered iron bed painted rose pink," which may suggest her simplicity, her desire for beauty, or her own rosy, childlike personality. Write a **description** of the home of someone you know. Use **sensory details** to make the setting vivid and to create a mood. Be sure to convey the person's character through your description of his or her home. If you want to, you can create your own fictional character and setting.

▶ Use "Describing a Place," pages 384–391, for help with this assignment.

SKILLS FOCUS

Literary Skills
Analyze setting and how it affects mood.

Reading Skills
Identify sensory details.

Writing Skills
Write a description of a place.

Response and Analysis

Reading Check

1. Buddy is a man recalling a special childhood relationship with an older female cousin.

2. They make fruitcakes to send as gifts to people they admire.

3. They must save money for ingredients, gather windfall pecans, and get illegal whiskey.

4. God is revealed in everyday life.

Thinking Critically

5. She is wise and compassionate. She remains childlike in her vulnerability, her enthusiasms, and her appreciation of simple pleasures.

6. The cozy furniture, roaring fire, and dusk falling create a cheerful mood. The cooking activities and aromas convey an energetic mood. Singing and dancing in the kitchen create a celebratory mood.

7. Details include "garish-gay light bulbs," "lights cast crazy patterns," and "shabby and deserted." No, Jones is kind.

8. They give and receive unconditional love. The friendship is lasting because it is honest and without ulterior motives.

9. The kites represent the happy times Buddy shared with his friend. His friend gone, Buddy feels adrift like a kite on a broken string.

10. Both appreciate the simple things in life. From his cousin, Buddy learns the "greatness" of simply being himself.

Extending and Evaluating

11. Possible answers: Some may find aspects of Buddy's friend hard to believe, while others will find her good-natured simplicity and generosity believable.

Vocabulary Development

Practice

Possible Answers

- *exhilarates. Definition*—thoroughly happy. *Example*—Running always *exhilarates* me.
- *dilapidated. Definition*—in disrepair. *Example*—The family lived in a *dilapidated* old house.
- *paraphernalia. Definition*—related equipment. *Example*—All the art *paraphernalia* is in the closet.
- *sacrilegious. Definition*—against religious rules. *Example*—Is it *sacrilegious* to laugh in church?
- *carnage. Definition*—bloody slaughter. *Example*—The film portrays the *carnage* of war.
- *prosaic. Definition*—uninteresting. *Example*—Buddy's other relatives were *prosaic*.
- *disposition. Definition*—temperament. *Example*—She has a sunny *disposition*.
- *suffuse. Definition*—fill up with. *Example*—They watched the sky *suffuse* with color.
- *noncommittal. Definition*—indefinite. *Example*—"Maybe" is a *noncommittal* response.

Grammar Link

Practice

1. Answers will vary. The past tense makes the story less immediate, intimate, and nostalgic.

2. You might want to check students' underlining and labeling of verbs.

Vocabulary Development

Vocabulary Resource File

PRACTICE

Begin a vocabulary resource file you can refer to when you're writing and at a loss for words. Put each Word Bank word on a separate index card (or create a file on your computer). As in the example below, include the definition and sample sentences using the word. When you learn new words, add them to your file.

inaugurating *(verb)*
Definition: formally beginning
Examples
The principal will be <u>inaugurating</u> a new school policy tomorrow.
The theater will be <u>inaugurating</u> its first season with a performance of *Romeo and Juliet.*

Grammar Link

Verb Tenses: What Time Is It?

The tense of a verb indicates the time of the action or the state of being expressed by the verb. Different tenses serve different purposes. "A Christmas Memory" is told in the present tense, although Capote uses the past and future tenses at times.

SKILLS FOCUS

Vocabulary Skills
Use words in context.

Grammar Skills
Identify and use verb tenses.

Tense	Example	Purpose
Present	"On the farther shore, Queenie <u>shakes</u> herself and <u>trembles</u>."	• expresses an action that is occurring now • shows a customary action • expresses a general truth
Past	"'I <u>made</u> you another kite.'"	• expresses an action that occurred in the past but is not occurring now
Future	"'Buddy, do you think Mrs. Roosevelt <u>will serve</u> our cake at dinner?'"	• expresses an action that will occur

PRACTICE

1. Choose two paragraphs without dialogue in the story. Rewrite them in the past tense. How does the change in tense change the feeling of the story? Why do you think Capote chose to write in the present tense?

2. Take a sample of your writing, and underline the verbs. Label each verb tense. Are your tenses consistent?

▶ **For more help, see Tense, 3d and 3e, in the Language Handbook.**

ASSESSING

Assessment

- *Holt Assessment: Literature, Reading, and Vocabulary*

READ ON: FOR INDEPENDENT READING

FICTION

Just a Little Guy

In J.R.R. Tolkien's fantasy **The Hobbit,** Bilbo Baggins is just a little guy—a hobbit—who is minding his own business. Then one day the wizard Gandalf and a gang of thirteen dwarfs arrive at his door and carry him off. So begins Bilbo's great adventure, an adventure with some big challenges for a little guy: bee pastures, giant spiders, icy waterfalls, and the dreaded dragon Smaug.

NONFICTION

A Space Odyssey

It was a routine journey—the fifth time U.S. astronauts had set out for the moon. But on April 13, 1970, Jim Lovell, Fred Haise, and Jack Swigert felt a strange explosion in their spacecraft. The lights dimmed, and the air got thinner. The three astronauts abandoned ship—for a tiny lunar module with room and supplies for only two. *Apollo 13,* co-written by Jim Lovell and Jeffrey Kluger, tells the story of the epic journey.

FICTION

A Cheyenne Adventure

Has anyone ever had dreams for your future that you don't necessarily share? This is the situation that Young Elk, a Cheyenne youth, faces. His family wants him to become a warrior, but Young Elk wants to follow in the footsteps of Old Horsecatcher, a great man among the Cheyenne people, who tames wild horses with a gentle hand. In Mari Sandoz's **The Horsecatcher,** you'll meet a young man who will do anything—including tread on enemy territory, wrangle with untamed horses, and risk both life and honor—to stay true to his own spirit.

NONFICTION

Man's Best Friend

Can you imagine enduring a temperature of -50°F—or lower—on a dog-sled race that covers more than a thousand miles? Gary Paulsen brings an adventure like this to life in his book **Woodsong.** In this account of his experiences during the Iditarod, a dog-sled race through Alaska, Paulsen whisks us along on his long and lonely journey. His only companions are a team of dogs, and they turn out to be the best friends he has ever had.

Read On

For Independent Reading

If students enjoyed the themes and topics explored in this collection, you might recommend these titles for independent reading.

Assessment Options

The following projects can help you evaluate and assess your students' outside reading. Videotapes or audiotapes of completed projects may be included in students' portfolios.

- **Create picture postcards.** Have students make picture post-cards showing important places in the novels. On the back of each postcard, the student should write a brief message from the charac-ter for whom the location is most significant.

- **Plan a time capsule.** After students read one of the autobio-graphical accounts, have them list items that they think the narrator might include in a time capsule. Have students write an explana-tion for the inclusion of each item, geared toward someone who might open the time capsule.

- **Design a T-shirt.** Have students decide on a major theme from one work and create a design illustrating the theme. They can use fabric paint to transfer the design to a T-shirt. Have students explain how their designs exem-plify the themes.

- **Write companion copy.** Invite students to write a companion piece for one work—such as a short story that is a prequel or sequel to *The Horsecatcher* or a cycle of poems capturing thoughts or feelings of astronauts in *Apollo 13.*

DIFFERENTIATING INSTRUCTION

Estimated Word Counts and Reading Levels of Read On Books:

Fiction			Nonfiction		
The Hobbit	↔	112,400	Apollo 13	↔	158,700
The Horsecatcher	↑	70,400	Woodsong	↓	49,800

KEY: ↑ *above grade level*   ↔ *at grade level*   ↓ *below grade level*

Writing an Autobiographical Narrative

Writing Assignment
Write an autobiographical narrative that reveals an experience's significance for you.

It is human nature to want to share what happens in our lives. Many magazines and books—like this one—contain stories written by people who want to share their meaningful life experiences. You can share an experience that is important to you with others by writing an **autobiographical narrative.**

Prewriting

Search Your Memory for Experiences

Magic Moments Your autobiographical narrative will be based on a specific, meaningful experience from your life. To come up with some experiences that you might write about, jog your memory by visiting a specific place that was important to you when you were younger, thinking about the first time you did something—rode a bike, for example—or listing special occasions you remember well.

Choose an Experience

Do the Write Thing Ask yourself the following questions to evaluate each experience that you thought of.

• Is this experience important to me? Why?

• What specific details can I give about this experience?

• Is the experience too private or embarrassing to share?

When you finish, look over what you wrote about each experience. Choose the experience that brought out the most detailed and positive responses from you.

Define Your Purpose and Audience

Your Side of the Story In an autobiographical narrative your **purpose** is to relate the **sequence of events** that make up a personal experience and to express to your audience the **significance** of those events. Your **audience** consists of the people you think might read your autobiographical narrative. Ask yourself the questions below and on the next page to get a feel for your audience.

SKILLS FOCUS

Writing Skills
Write an autobiographical narrative.

1. **Who is my intended audience?** Your audience might include classmates, teachers, friends, parents, or even total strangers.

COLLECTION 1 RESOURCES: WRITING

Planning
■ *One-Stop Planner* CD-ROM with ExamView Test Generator

Differentiating Instruction
■ *Workshop Resources: Writing, Listening, and Speaking*
■ *Supporting Instruction in Spanish*

■ *Family Involvement Activities in English and Spanish*

Writing and Language
■ *Language Handbook Worksheets*
■ *Daily Language Activities*
■ *Workshop Resources: Writing, Listening, and Speaking*

2. **What will the audience need to know to understand the experience?**
   Plan to provide background information to help your readers understand your narrative, if necessary.

Gather Details

Let Your Memory Be Your Guide To search your memory for the details that will bring your narrative to life, answer the questions and use the tips in the chart below. List all of the vivid details you can recall about events, people, places, thoughts, and feelings. The second column contains details from one writer's answers to the questions.

ADDING DETAILS

Questions/Tips	Examples
Events	
What sequence of events make up the experience? Were there important events that led up to or followed the experience?	Sequence of events: walking in park, practicing building fires with Dad Later events: camp contest, camping in mountains
TIP: Match the **pace** of your narrative to the pace of the actual events—a quick pace for rapid events, a slow pace for more drawn-out events.	
Places	
Where did the events happen?	city park on cool summer morning; wilderness; thickly leaved trees; pines and aspens; smell of trees
TIP: Use **concrete sensory details** to create effective images of the sights, sounds, and smells of the places you are describing.	
People	
Who was involved in the events? What did those people look like? What did they do and say?	me—ages five, eleven, fourteen; Dad—young man dressed for work, wearing glasses; what Dad said as he taught me
TIP: Use sensory details to describe **actions** and **gestures**. Use **dialogue,** actual words people say, to show each person's personality.	
Thoughts and Feelings	
What did I think and feel as the events unfolded?	happiness during times with Dad; pleasure at collecting wood; luck for having such a dad; special bond
TIP: Use **interior monologue,** "thinking out loud," to share your thoughts with readers.	

Organize Details

Ducks in a Row Now, take a look at the events that you listed. When you write your narrative, discuss the events in **chronological order,** or time order. Events that came before your experience will appear first in your narrative because they will help your audience

Students can use a computer to create a list of evaluation questions similar to those in the chart. For each potential topic, students can make a copy of their chart and fill in the answer section. Students can then save each completed chart with a new file name and compare the charts side-by-side to help them choose an experience.

DIFFERENTIATING INSTRUCTION

Special Education Students
Students sometimes find it difficult to access their feelings. Allowing students to work through their writing assignments with an encouraging helper may help them recall events that they may use for their autobiographical narratives.

DIRECT TEACHING

Organize Details
As students organize the details for their autobiographical narratives, remind them that the details and dialogue they choose should be relevant to the main idea of the narrative. A detail is relevant if it provides important background information, helps give a clearer picture of the scene, or serves in a cause-and-effect chain to lead to the next event. If students are in doubt about the relevance of a detail, instruct them to include it in their drafts with an asterisk so they might take another look during revision.

Assessment
- *Holt Assessment: Writing, Listening, and Speaking*
- *One-Stop Planner* CD-ROM with ExamView Test Generator
- *Holt Online Assessment*
- *Holt Online Essay Scoring*

Internet
- go.hrw.com (Keyword LE5 9-1)
- *Elements of Literature Online*

CRITICAL THINKING

Point out to students that interesting details in a piece of writing often succeed through contrast. For example, a child's first trip to a big city might be marked by many contrasts between big and little things: the huge buildings towering over the awe-struck child. Or, a successful description may involve a contrast in emotion: a terrifying first day of school that turns out to be a very humorous experience. As students fill in their charts with details from their experiences, direct them to circle contrasting elements. Students can emphasize these contrasting elements in their writing.

DIRECT TEACHING

Consider the Significance of Your Experience

Explain and clarify for students the concepts of *explicit* and *implicit* in relation to the main idea of a piece of writing. Tell students that explicit main ideas are expressed in direct language to the reader, such as in the statement "This experience changed my life." Implicit main ideas, on the other hand, are suggested indirectly, most often through the accumulation of detail, and may emerge as a *controlling impression* in the writing. For example, descriptions of strong emotions in a scene will imply that the experience is a moving and meaningful one for those involved.

PRACTICE & APPLY 1

Guided and Independent Practice

Monitor students' understanding by asking students to write a brief sentence in which they relate the meaning of the experience about which they are writing. Check to make sure each student has a clear, concise sentence. Then, assign **Practice and Apply 1** as independent practice.

TIP You don't have to discuss events that came before your experience *and* events that came after your experience. Refer to your details list to see whether you will include earlier or later events.

DO THIS →

SKILLS FOCUS

Writing Skills
Establish a controlling impression.

---

understand what led up to your experience. You will discuss events that came after your experience later in your narrative to show how that experience related to other parts of your life.

Guide readers through the events by including in your narrative transitional words and phrases that suggest changes in time (*at first, to begin, then*) and place (*around, nearby, across from*). Also, keep in mind that the tone of your writing should be informal, as if you were talking to friends.

Consider the Significance of Your Experience

And So It Ends You chose a particular experience to write about because it was important to you in some way. You will want to share this significance with your readers, too. To consider the meaning of your autobiographical narrative, ask yourself these questions.

- Did the experience change me? If so, how?
- What did I learn from the experience?
- Has my **perspective,** my thoughts and feelings about the event, shifted over time? If so, how?

Thinking about your answers to the questions above, write a sentence telling what the experience meant to you. The writer narrating her experience with her father as he taught her to build a campfire developed the following statement about the meaning of her experience.

> A simple lesson in building campfires defined the relationship my dad and I have shared.

You don't have to include the sentence you wrote about the meaning of your experience in your final draft, but it will remind you of the controlling impression you want to create as you write. The **controlling impression** is the main idea or feeling you want to communicate about your experience. Every detail in the narrative should contribute to that impression. In the Writer's Model on the next page, the writer doesn't state her controlling impression directly. Instead, she expresses the controlling impression indirectly throughout the narrative through her choice of details.

PRACTICE & APPLY 1 Follow the guidelines in this section to choose an experience, analyze your audience, and gather and organize details for your autobiographical narrative.

Writing

Writing an Autobiographical Narrative

A Writer's Framework

Introduction	Body	Conclusion
• Begin with an engaging opening.	• Discuss the sequence of events that make up your experience.	• Look back at the experience from the present time.
• Supply background information so readers understand the context of the narrative.	• Discuss the important events that led up to or followed your experience.	• Reflect on what you learned or how you changed as a result of this experience.
• Hint at the significance of the experience.	• Include plenty of details about people, places, and events.	• Reveal the significance of the experience.

A Writer's Model

A Campfire Girl

Do people make campfires anymore? I suppose they do, but building campfires is prohibited in many places now. Even if rangers do not ban campfires, environmentally aware people agree that no one should be allowed to pick the ground bare of wood and scar the land with fire rings. Still, I am a campfire girl at heart. Even though I dutifully use camp stoves in the mountains and in the campgrounds, I still love a small blaze to warm my hands, to dry soggy socks, and to stare into when the night sky, far from the glow of city lights, is deep black.

My love for campfires all started because of a leisurely stroll in a park in New York City. When I was a tidy little skirt-wearing five-year-old, my family lived in New York for a summer. My father and I would go out early, when it was still cool, to walk the dog. Dad would be dressed for work, his shoes treading the asphalt path as I happily did a quickstep along beside him.

One morning as my father threw sticks for the dog, I started picking up sticks of my own. Always ready to play and teach, my dad crouched down and said, "Here, let me show you the right way to build a campfire. Once you learn how, you can build a fire in the middle of a tornado." He took my sticks and helped me gather others, graduated in size from tiny twigs to hefty branches. Gently propping the twigs

(continued)

INTRODUCTION
Engaging opening
Background information
Hint at meaning

BODY
First event of experience

People and place details
Feelings

Second event of experience

Dialogue

Specific action with sensory details

DIRECT TEACHING

A Writer's Model

Explain to students that using think sheets when reading models or drafts can help them organize their thoughts on the reading and remember ideas for their own writing and revision. A sample think sheet might look something like the following.

Text	Responses

PRACTICE & APPLY 2

Guided and Independent Practice

Monitor students' progress by asking the following questions.

1. How do you engage the reader in the introduction?

2. Which details are most effective in making the reader understand your feelings?

3. How do you convey what you learned from the experience?

Then, have students complete **Practice and Apply 2** for independent practice.

Specific movement
Dialogue

Thought

Later important event

Specific movement

Sensory details
Interior monologue

Later important event
Feelings

Sensory details

Sensory detail
CONCLUSION
A look back from the present

Significance of the experience

---

together, he started with a teepee shape. I watched his careful hands gently place slightly larger sticks on top of the others. "Don't pack the sticks too tightly together," he warned, "or the air can't flow and feed the fire." (This was the theory at least; we did not light our fires there in the middle of the city.) While I worked on the tepee and other structures—the log cabin, the **A**—the sounds of the city faded away.

Several years later at summer camp, we had a contest: Who could make a campfire the fastest using just one match? I have no doubt that my lessons in the park in New York City laid the foundation for my championship fire building at camp. I used the **A** structure. I blew gently on my kindling, giving the flame just enough air to turn the kindling into bright embers and make flames lick at the larger sticks. As other girls struggled to start a fire, I thought, "You're one lucky girl to have the dad you have. Some of my friends might have neat dads, but not like mine."

On later camping trips with my father, when I was no longer a tidy little girl, but a rugged teenager in jeans and work boots, I took special pleasure in collecting wood, placing each size in a separate pile. Then I would place the kindling and get it burning, making a small cook fire. Dad and I never built great, big bonfires in rings with three- to four-foot diameters. We made campfires just big enough for the heavy skillet we packed into the wilderness. (It cooked so much better than the aluminum pans that came in camp mess kits.) We ate many meals over our fires—usually potatoes and onions and just-caught trout. I can almost hear the sizzle of the fresh fish frying now.

That day in the city park, my dad could not have known of the backpacking trips he and I would share now—nine years later. Still, I see those little piles of sticks as my introduction to life outdoors. The thickly leaved trees of the park have given way to fragrant pines and aspen overhead, but the kinship I experienced with my dad remains the same. I was his campfire girl, sharing in his love of the outdoors and a well-built campfire. We were building something to warm us then and now.

INTERNET

More Writer's Models

Keyword: LE5 9-1

PRACTICE & APPLY 2

Write your autobiographical narrative, organizing details about people, places, and events chronologically. Refer to the framework on page 69 and the Writer's Model above as guides.

Revising

Evaluate and Revise Your Draft

Do Look Back To improve the draft of your autobiographical narrative, you must read it and read it again. Looking at your paper twice will help you strengthen the logic and coherence of its content and organization as well as its style. As you look over your draft, keep your **audience** and **purpose** in mind. Also, consider the **formality** of your words. Since you are telling your own true story, remember that the overall tone of your paper will be informal and personal.

> **First Reading: Content and Organization** On your first reading, concentrate on evaluating and revising your autobiographical narrative's content and organization. Use the guidelines in the chart below as a **think sheet**.

PEER REVIEW

Exchange your paper with a peer before you revise, and ask him or her to evaluate how effectively your narrative communicates the significance of your experience.

Rubric: Writing an Autobiographical Narrative

Evaluation Questions	▶ Tips	▶ Revision Techniques
❶ Does the introduction include an engaging opening, background information, and a hint at the significance of the experience?	▶ **Bracket** the engaging opening and background information. **Underline** the hint about the significance.	▶ **Add** an engaging opening and background information. **Add** a sentence or two that suggests the significance of the event.
❷ Does the narrative include details about events, people, and places?	▶ **Circle** details. If you have fewer than three circles in each paragraph, revise.	▶ **Add** details about events, people, and places to the paragraph. **Elaborate** on existing details with sensory language or dialogue.
❸ Does the narrative include details about the narrator's thoughts and feelings?	▶ **Highlight** sentences that contain the narrator's thoughts or feelings. If there isn't at least one such detail in the narrative, revise.	▶ **Elaborate** on details by answering the questions, "What did I think?" or "How did I feel?" Consider using interior monologue.
❹ Is the order of the events clear?	▶ **Number** the events in chronological order.	▶ **Rearrange** events in chronological order, if necessary, and **add** transitional words and phrases to show the order.
❺ Does the conclusion discuss the significance of the experience?	▶ **Underline** sentences in the conclusion that reveal the meaning of the experience.	▶ **Add** sentences that indirectly or directly explain the importance of the experience.

Evaluate and Revise Your Draft

Help students create interesting and informative titles for their autobiographical narratives. Point out to students that a good title captures the reader's attention and often may be read in more than one way, or may play off an existing title with which the reader might already be familiar: "The Crepes of Wrath," for example. Remind students to avoid generic titles such as "A Memory."

Elaboration

To help students elaborate in the body of their narratives, have them meet with partners. Students should describe the details and dialogue of their experience while their partner goes over a copy of their draft with a pencil. The partners should checkmark details and dialogue both mentioned out loud and included in the narrative. They should also make notes of details and dialogue not included. Partners can use each other's notes to help them fill out their accounts.

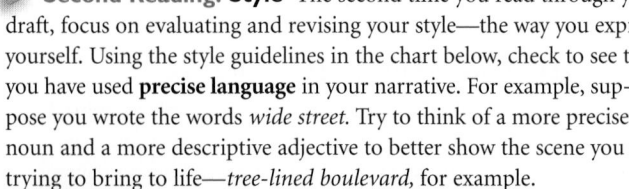

Second Reading: **Style** The second time you read through your draft, focus on evaluating and revising your style—the way you express yourself. Using the style guidelines in the chart below, check to see that you have used **precise language** in your narrative. For example, suppose you wrote the words *wide street.* Try to think of a more precise noun and a more descriptive adjective to better show the scene you are trying to bring to life—*tree-lined boulevard,* for example.

DIRECT TEACHING

Second Reading: Style

As students comb their narratives for imprecise nouns and adjectives, have them also list the verbs they use on a separate sheet of paper. Then, have students use a thesaurus to equate each listed verb with a more vivid or precise choice. This list should be useful in helping students make their verbs just as vivid and precise as their nouns and adjectives. Remind students, however, that words in a thesaurus do not always have exactly the same meaning, usage, or connotation as the word being replaced; students may wish to consult a dictionary if they are unsure of a word's usage.

GUIDED PRACTICE

Responding to the Revision Process

Answers

1. The phrase is more specific and vivid than the single word, and it also contributes to tone and setting.

2. The additions give the reader a better idea of how learning how to start a fire would be a new and unusual experience for the narrator. They also help to bring the scene to life for the reader.

PRACTICE & APPLY 3

Independent Practice

For peer assessment, have students work with a classmate to read each other's paper and answer the following questions.

1. What details helped you to imagine the writer's experience?

2. What details could the writer have included to make things more clear?

Style Guidelines

Evaluation Question	▶ Tip	▶ Revision Technique
● Does the narrative include precise language?	▶ Pick four sentences in each paragraph. In each, **circle** the nouns and adjectives. Are the nouns and adjectives vivid and precise?	▶ **Replace** at least two imprecise nouns and adjectives per paragraph with more precise language. (Use a dictionary or thesaurus if necessary.)

ANALYZING THE REVISION PROCESS

Study these revisions, and answer the questions that follow.

replace — My love for campfires all started because of a ~~walk~~ *leisurely stroll* in a park

add — in New York City. When I was ~~five~~ *a tidy little skirt-wearing five-year-old*, my family lived in New

York for a summer. My father and I would go out early, when

it was still cool, to walk the dog. Dad would be dressed for

elaborate — work, his shoes treading the asphalt path as I *happily* did a quickstep

along beside him.

Responding to the Revision Process

1. In the first sentence, why is "leisurely stroll" an improvement over "walk"?

2. How do the additions in the second and fourth sentences affect the reader's image of the narrator?

SKILLS FOCUS

Writing Skills
Use precise language.

PRACTICE & APPLY 3 Evaluate and revise the content, organization, and style of your essay, using the guidelines on these pages. Consider peer comments, too.

Publishing

Proofread and Publish Your Autobiographical Narrative

To Err Is Human Proofread your paper before you prepare a clean copy for publishing. Read your paper aloud slowly, focusing on each word you have written to make sure each sentence is complete. You might even ask for assistance in proofreading from a peer. Find and eliminate errors in grammar, mechanics, and usage. Such errors can prevent readers from enjoying or even understanding your ideas.

Get the Word Out You've just completed the story of a personal experience that is meaningful to you. Your work is something to be proud of and to share with other people. Try some of the following suggestions for reaching readers besides your teacher and classmates.

- Mail or e-mail your paper to interested relatives or friends. If your narrative is about an event in their lives or about someone your readers know, they might be especially interested in reading it. You might even consider giving your paper as a gift to someone else who was involved in the experience you describe.

- Look for magazines that publish this kind of personal essay. Well-written, authentic stories from students' lives are often welcomed in magazines for young people.

- If your narrative is about school life, consider submitting your narrative to your school's literary magazine or your school newspaper.

Reflect on Your Autobiographical Narrative

Count the Ways Use the following questions to look back at your autobiographical narrative and assess what you've learned in the process of writing it.

- How did writing this paper help you to understand this experience better or in a new way?

- Are you satisfied with how you expressed the meaning of your experience? Why or why not? What would you do differently if you wrote another autobiographical narrative?

PRACTICE & APPLY 4 Proofread your narrative to eliminate mistakes. Make a clean copy of your paper and publish it, using one of the suggestions above. Finally, answer the reflection questions.

TIP Proofreading will help ensure that your autobiographical narrative follows the **conventions** of standard American English. For example, look for and fix misplaced modifiers that describe people, places, and events in your narrative. For more on **misplaced modifiers,** see Placement of Modifiers, 5g, in the Language Handbook.

SKILLS FOCUS

Writing Skills
Proofread, especially for misplaced modifiers.

DIRECT TEACHING

Proofread and Publish Your Autobiographical Narrative

Give students a more structured, three-part approach to proofreading their papers. Students should re-read the entire text of their narrative three times: the first time for spelling errors, the second time for punctuation, and the third time for grammar, especially subject-verb agreement. By the third re-reading, students will have progressed from a surface analysis of their papers to a deeper evaluation and correction of the work's grammatical structure.

PRACTICE & APPLY 4

Guided and Independent Practice

To help you monitor students' reflection processes, you might have them create a sheet for their portfolio titled "I Have Learned These Grammar Concepts." On this sheet, students could list proofreading errors they found in their papers along with their corrections. Have students date their entries.

Then, have them complete **Practice and Apply 4** for independent practice.

DIFFERENTIATING INSTRUCTION

Advanced Learners
Enrichment. Students may want to research a number of magazines that publish work by teens, such as the *International Reading Association,* and submit their narratives. Direct students to first obtain a copy of the guidelines for contributors and make sure their narratives fit the descriptions.

Presenting an Oral Narrative

Speaking Assignment
Adapt an autobiographical narrative for an oral presentation, and present it to your class.

You have probably already told many true stories aloud, such as what happened when the family car broke down on vacation or how your team won the baseball championship. When you tell a story aloud, you are giving an **oral narrative.**

Adapt Your Autobiographical Narrative

Try a New Twist Because your audience will be listening to your narrative instead of reading it, you'll need to change it as you prepare for your presentation. Keep in mind the **occasion**—a speech for your class—and follow these suggestions to adapt your narrative.

- **Word Choice** Use **vocabulary** that sounds natural. Avoid words that might be unfamiliar to listeners, who won't be able to stop and look them up in a dictionary.

- **Setting** Locate events in **specific places.** For instance, say "in the cafeteria line" or "by my locker" rather than "at school."

- **Details** Readers have time to linger over language to form mental images of what a writer describes. Listeners don't. Look carefully at the **sensory details** you used in your written narrative to describe the sights, sounds, and smells of the events and people's actions. Read sensory passages aloud, and ask yourself whether your language is vivid enough to create images in listeners' minds.

  One writer decided that a more vivid description of starting a fire would interest her listeners. For her oral presentation, she changed "enough air to turn the kindling into bright embers and make flames lick at the larger sticks" to "enough air to turn the little pieces of wood into bright orange coals and make yellow and blue flames lick at the bigger sticks."

- **Organization** Use **chronological order** in your oral narrative, just as you did in your written one. You can even use the same transitional words and phrases you included in your paper to help listeners follow the events of your experience.

- **Conclusion** If you didn't directly state the **significance** of your experience in the conclusion of your written narrative, do so in the conclusion to your oral narrative. Strongly suggesting or indirectly stating the significance is acceptable in a written narrative that readers can re-read, but not in an oral narrative that they have to understand immediately.

SKILLS FOCUS

Listening and Speaking Skills
Present an oral narrative.

Deliver Your Narrative

Show and Tell When you wrote your autobiographical narrative, you expressed the significance of your experience through words alone. Since you'll deliver your narrative orally, you can also use **verbal and nonverbal techniques**—ways of using your voice as well as your face and body—to show how the experience made you feel and what it meant to you.

Use Verbal Techniques How you use your voice can give the audience as much information as what you say. The following chart explains some of the basic verbal techniques you can use.

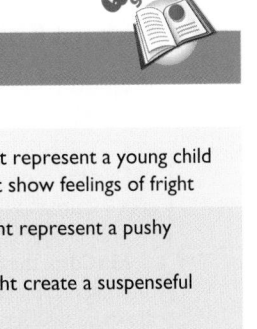

VERBAL TECHNIQUES		
Technique	**Uses**	**Examples**
Pitch	• change pitch for different characters • use pitch to show feelings	• a high pitch might represent a young child • a low pitch might show feelings of fright
Volume	• change volume for different characters • use volume to create mood	• a loud voice might represent a pushy character • a quiet voice might create a suspenseful mood
Rate, or Pace	• use rate to show emotions or create a mood • use a pace that reflects the speed at which various events occurred	• speaking slowly can create drama and suspense • speaking quickly (but distinctly) can communicate excitement or a quick series of events

Use Nonverbal Techniques You will also use facial expressions and gestures to add meaning to your oral narrative. A gesture such as forming an **A** with the hands can illustrate a method of placing sticks for a fire. Use your eyes to show emotion, and keep your listeners involved by making frequent eye contact with them.

Be sure to tailor your gestures and tone to your audience. For instance, exaggerated facial expressions and a "cutesy" voice might be appropriate for small children, but not for your classmates.

Take Note Sound natural and relaxed by delivering your narrative **extemporaneously,** using **concise notes**—notes that say a lot in a few words. Make note cards with short phrases or single words that remind you of details, and arrange the note cards in the order in which you will present them.

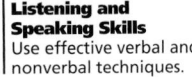

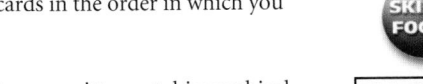 Adapt your written autobiographical narrative into an oral narrative. Practice your narrative, and then present it to your class.

SKILLS FOCUS

Listening and Speaking Skills
Use effective verbal and nonverbal techniques.

Deliver Your Narrative

Tell students to use their eyes to show emotion and to keep their audience engaged. Emphasize that maintaining eye contact helps the storyteller draw listeners into the narrative.

You may also want to allow students to hear a good storyteller in action. The library may have appropriate stories on audiotape, or you might find videotapes of stories told by professional actors. Discuss the performance and the performer's techniques with students.

RETEACHING

Take Note

To reteach the concept of making concise notes for an extemporaneous delivery, have students experiment with different ways of making brief notes for themselves that provide both mnemonic aid and performance directions. Students might draw sketches to help them deliver their oral narratives, or use symbols to stand for gestures or effects such as a rise in vocal volume, or they might only list short prompts, much like subheadings in a lengthy published article.

PRACTICE & APPLY

Guided and Independent Practice

Provide an opportunity for students to practice telling their stories aloud to one another in a small group. Have students prepare questions, based on the tips in this section, to rate the performances. Listeners should answer these questions and offer thoughtful, constructive comments. Finally, have a class discussion in which students share their views on what makes a successful oral narrative.

SKILLS FOCUS, pp. 76–79

Grade-Level Skills

■ **Reading Skills**
Generate relevant research questions after reading about an issue.

INTRODUCING THE SKILLS REVIEW

Use this review to assess students' grasp of ways to use informational text to generate research questions.

DIRECT TEACHING

A **Analyzing Informational Text**

❓ Generating research questions. What question is asked and answered in this section? [When will space tourism become a reality?] How might you change the question to provide a clearer focus for research? [Possible response: Define "space tourism".]

B **Analyzing Informational Text**

❓ Generating research questions. What research question might follow directly from this information? [Possible response: What is a G-suit?]

Pages 76–79 cover
Reading Skills
Generate research questions.

Test Practice

Generating Research Questions
DIRECTIONS: Read the following article. Then, read and respond to the questions that follow.

So You Want to Be an Astronaut?
Richard Knight

Richard Knight explains the problems that would-be space tourists will face.

A All but the most hardened skeptics[1] now admit that, sooner or later, space tourism will become a reality. But the question is: when exactly?
  The answer is: probably not for quite a while yet.
  MirCorp, the company which has leased the Mir space station, is offering one place on its mission to the station in September—it announced the spare seat earlier this year. But the return fare will cost up to £20 million[2]—and costs are not the only problems facing future space cadets.

The Body
According to Royal Air Force space expert Derek Clark, our bodies are not built for spaceflight and any would-be tourist will have to accept certain health risks and discomforts.

B Just getting to space is a physically demanding experience. Passengers will be pinned to the backs of their seats by a 3G force (increasing each tourist's apparent weight threefold) for 4 minutes 40 seconds from launch to orbit while being buffeted as they crash through the atmosphere.
  However, since extreme forces beyond 3G (which might be experienced in an emergency) can either starve the brain of oxygen or cause it to hemorrhage,[3] each tourist will probably have to be fitted with a tailor-made G-suit.
  In space, where there is almost no gravity, blood equalizes around the body, rather than being pulled into our legs. The effect is to give the brain more blood than usual. Our bodies cope with this by reducing blood mass through increased urination, reduced liquid intake, and nosebleeds. Passengers will take a day to get over this unpleasant process. Back on Earth, they will find their reduced blood mass is again drawn downwards, causing them to faint.

---

1. **skeptics** (skep′tiks) *n.*: people who doubt something.
2. **£20 million:** sum approximately equal to $30 million.
3. **hemorrhage** (hem′ər·ij′) *v.*: bleed heavily.

READING MINI-LESSON

Reviewing Word-Attack Skills

Activity. Display these pairs of words. Have students identify the word in which the underlined letters stand for two different sounds.

1. acqu<u>ai</u>ntances   pros<u>ai</u>c [prosaic]
2. r<u>ea</u>lism   r<u>ea</u>lity [reality]
3. n<u>eo</u>n   lunch<u>eo</u>n [neon]
4. fr<u>ui</u>tcake   gen<u>ui</u>ne [genuine]
5. canop<u>i</u>ed   exper<u>i</u>ence [experience]

Activity. Display these pairs of words. Have students identify the syllable said with the most stress in each word. Answers are underlined.

1. <u>in</u>spire   inspi<u>ra</u>tion
2. as<u>tron</u>omy   astro<u>nom</u>ical
3. obser<u>va</u>tion   ob<u>ser</u>vatory
4. ex<u>plore</u>   explo<u>ra</u>tion

Activity. Have students categorize these words into two groups: those that have a long vowel sound in the underlined syllable and those that do not.

vi<u>ri</u>le   <u>pur</u>chase   con<u>fide</u>
cor<u>sage</u>   i<u>ma</u>gine   <u>rel</u>ative
<u>ded</u>icate   <u>do</u>nate   <u>pur</u>pose

[*Long vowel sound*—confide, dedicate, donate.]

Before facing that challenge, however, 50 percent of space tourists will have spent most of their time feeling ill because of space sickness (an extreme form of travel sickness). This would contribute to weight loss: Each passenger will lose about 5 pounds on their first day in space and will continue to lose weight daily.

This is also because, with no gravity to fight against, muscles will deteriorate[4] fast, most seriously around the heart. In fact, tourists who stay in space long enough will find their hearts have become irreversibly weakened—which is the fate of some Mir astronauts. Each passenger would have to exercise for 6 hours a day to halt muscle deterioration.

Painful kidney stones are more likely to develop in space, and there is a need to protect would-be astronauts against infection. So tourists will either be isolated for a month prior to flight or given regular medicals during the lead-up. Having second thoughts, by any chance?

The Mind

Tourists will need to be quizzed by psychologists[5] in order to check whether they have the right mental stuff. This is because passengers may feel a profound sense of isolation as they look at Earth from space. Gazing out, they will be able to use the tips of their thumbs to blot the Earth from view, making everything they have ever known disappear.

As the sun rises and sets 16 times a day in space, sleep patterns will also be disrupted, possibly unhinging passengers. Some will suffer claustrophobia[6] from being confined to a narrow capsule in which one cannot walk, open a window or—of course—get out!

Another problem is that former astronauts are statistically more likely to suffer serious accidents when they return to Earth. This might be because, having flown to space and taken such a huge risk, they feel invincible[7] and take greater chances than normal. *Still* feel like going?

---

4. **deteriorate** (dē·tir′ē·ə·rāt′) *v.:* become weak or damaged.
5. **psychologists** (sī·käl′ə·jists) *n.:* specialists who study the mind and emotions.
6. **claustrophobia** (klôs′trə·fō′bē·ə) *n.:* abnormal fear of being in an enclosed place.
7. **invincible** (in·vin′sə·bəl) *adj.:* all-powerful; unbeatable.

Collection 1: Skills Review **77**

C Analyzing Informational Text

Generating research questions. Explain whether the following question, based on this passage, is useful for research: "In what ways did the profound sense of isolation affect the minds of Mir astronauts?" [Possible response: The question is useful because it is relevant to the passage, which mentions a sense of isolation as one challenge to space tourists, and because it focuses on the effects of one specific phenomenon on one group.]

D Analyzing Informational Text

? Generating research questions. What research questions might help you locate information to confirm or refute this statement? [Possible responses: What are the statistics on accident rates of former astronauts? To what other groups' accident rates have the accident rates of former astronauts been compared?]

Using Academic Language

Review of Literary Terms
Ask students to look back through the collection to find the meanings of the terms listed at right. Then, have students show their grasp of the terms by citing passages from the collection that illustrate the meanings of those terms.

Plot (p. 2); **Conflict** (p. 2); **Exposition** (p. 2); **Complication** (p. 2); **Climax** (p. 2); **Resolution** (p. 2); **Chronological Order** (pp. 3, 32); **Flashback** (pp. 3, 32); **Foreshadowing** (pp. 3, 4); **Setting** (p. 48); **Mood** (p. 48); **Tone** (p. 48); **Images** (p. 49).

Review of Informational Terms
Ask students to review the collection to find the meanings of the terms listed below.

Then, ask students to use those terms to explain how to generate research questions and how to identify resources.
KWL Chart (p. 26); *5W-How?* **Questions** (p. 26); **Reference Books** (p. 43); **Periodicals** (p. 43); **Search Engine** (p. 43); **Web Site** (p. 43); **Links** (p. 43).

Test-Taking Tips

Remind students that relevant research questions include specific terms, rather than abstractions, and are limited in scope. Encourage students to examine their own research questions again, checking for focus and relevance, before answering the Test Practice items.

For more information on answering multiple-choice items, refer students to **Test Smarts.**

Answers and Model Rationales

1. **A** Paragraph nine discusses heart muscle degeneration due to lack of gravity. The article does mention the incidence of kidney stones and depression, but not the causes of kidney stones (B) or the prevention of depression (C). It does not describe space planes (D).

2. **H** Students should see that F is both broad and off the topic; the topic is space tourism, not astronaut training. J is too broad, covering the whole space program, and includes the hard-to-define term *effective*. G is narrower but also includes vague terms such as "in the future" and "routine." Only H is focused enough to be researched easily.

Enough Demand?

Do sufficient numbers of people really want to travel to destination space? It is likely to be enormously expensive: Will enough people be able to find the money? Once the market is proved, the money required to fuel passenger space planes should be more forthcoming than it is at present. For now, however, we can only guess when the first scheduled flight beyond the atmosphere will take off . . . phew![8]

—from *The Times* (London), April 22, 2000

---

8. For now . . . phew! After the publication of this article, Dennis A. Tito, an American, became the first space tourist, blasting off into space on April 28, 2001. Paying $20 million for the trip, he joined a Russian crew on an eight-day journey to the International Space Station.

---

1. Which of the following questions is answered in the article?

   A What causes heart damage during prolonged space travel?

   B Why might space travelers develop kidney stones?

   C What can space travelers do to avoid becoming depressed?

   D What will the interior of a passenger space plane look like?

2. Which of the following research questions about space tourism is the *most* narrow and focused?

   F What kinds of people want to be astronauts?

   G In the future, will space tourism become as routine as international airplane flights are now?

   H How does a G-suit prevent a person from being injured during liftoff?

   J How effective are the U.S. government's current plans for the space program budget?

Collection 1: Skills Review

3. Assume your initial research question is *How do people feel once they return to earth after traveling in space?* Which follow-up question will *best* help you narrow your research?
   A Do people visit doctors frequently after space flights?
   B Are people satisfied with their lives once they are back on earth?
   C Do people ever regret traveling in space?
   D What specific physical effects do people experience after a space flight, and how long do the effects last?

4. If you wanted to do further research on the effects of space travel on the mind, which question would give you the *most* relevant information?
   F Will space tourists returning to earth be tested by psychologists?
   G Is there a cure for claustrophobia?
   H How do disrupted sleep patterns affect the human mind?
   J Which former astronauts have had serious accidents?

5. Which research question about the effects of space travel on the body follows *most* directly from the information in the article?
   A When will doctors and nurses be trained to work in space?
   B Does gravity have harmful effects on our bodies when we are on earth?
   C What are the symptoms of space sickness, and how long does it last?
   D What kinds of circulation problems do people face on earth?

6. If you wanted to use a search engine to learn how tourists will be transported to space, which would be the *most* helpful search term?
   F Mir space station
   G space planes
   H space missions
   J Royal Air Force

Constructed Response

7. Generate two original research questions from "So You Want to Be an Astronaut?" and explain why you believe one might be a more promising line of inquiry and further research than the other.

3. **D** Students should quickly eliminate A, B, and C—yes/no questions with vague terms such as *frequently* and *satisfied*. Only D is specific.

4. **H** F and G are yes/no questions. J is irrelevant because the names of the astronauts are less meaningful than statistical data such as number and type of accidents. H is most relevant: the article states that disrupted sleep patterns may "unhinge" passengers, but does not explain how or why.

5. **C** Students should note the italicized word *most* in the question. The article mentions space sickness but provides few specifics, so C follows most directly. Since the article deals primarily with people in space, B and D, about physical problems on earth, are irrelevant. A has relevance but does not follow directly from the article, which makes no mention of training medical professionals for space work.

6. **G** Students should see that J is only tangentially relevant; F and H are too broad.

Constructed Response

7. Possible response: How many people have paid to travel to outer space? What kinds of problems have space tourists encountered? The second question is better to research because it allows for in-depth study. The first question is too specific; it asks only for a number.

Assessment
- *Holt Assessment: Literature, Reading, and Vocabulary*

DIFFERENTIATING INSTRUCTION

Advanced Learners

Enrichment. Explain that one way to sharpen a research question is to focus on *specific characteristics* and *measurable data*. For example, an effective research question about space planes might explore their design and function (specific characteristics) and their size and capacities (measurable data).

Activity. Have each student choose a topic from the article and generate a narrow and focused research question about that topic. Then, have student pairs exchange questions and critique each other's work. Ask them to consider

- how the wording of the question might be clarified
- how the research focus might be sharpened

Have pairs work together to revise the research questions for your review.

Collection I: Skills Review

Vocabulary Skills

Multiple-Meaning Words
Modeling. Model the thought process of a good reader answering item I by saying, "In sentence I, *flushed* means 'forced (something) out of hiding.' In A and D, *flushed* means 'reddened.' In B, *flushed* means 'rinsed.' Only in C does *flushed* mean 'forced out of hiding,' so C is the best answer."

Answers and Model Rationales

I. **C** See the rationale above.

2. **J** Students should see that in sentence 2, *forged* means "advanced with speed." In F and H, *forged* means "created"; in G it means "counterfeited."

3. **A** In sentence 3, *preserve* is a noun meaning "sheltered area." Students should eliminate C and D because they use *preserve* as a verb. In B, *preserve* is a noun, but it refers to a kind of food.

4. **H** In sentence 4, *spring* is a noun meaning "a rebounding coil." G and J can be eliminated because they use *spring* as a verb. Of the two remaining choices, F is incorrect because people would not hike to a rebounding coil.

5. **B** In sentence 5, *tackle* is a verb meaning "to take on." Students can eliminate A, in which *tackle* is used as a noun, and C, in which *tackle* is used as an adjective and refers to fishing gear. In D, *tackle* is a verb, but its meaning is "to bring down an opposing player."

6. **J** In sentence 6, *sound* is a noun. Only in J is *sound* a noun.

Collection 1: Skills Review
Vocabulary Skills

Multiple-Meaning Words

Test Practice

DIRECTIONS: Choose the answer in which the underlined word is used in the same way it is used in the sentence from "The Most Dangerous Game."

1. "'I suppose the first three shots I heard was when the hunter flushed his quarry and wounded it.'"
   - **A** Shawna's face flushed with shame.
   - **B** We flushed the pipes with cleanser.
   - **C** The sudden noise flushed the sparrow out of his tree.
   - **D** Flushed and feverish, Dan cried.

2. "But as he forged along, he saw to his great astonishment that all the lights were in one enormous building. . . ."
   - **F** The horseshoes were forged in the blacksmith's shop.
   - **G** The detective said that the signature on the check had been forged.
   - **H** After lengthy negotiations the two companies forged a merger.
   - **J** The runner in last place suddenly forged ahead and grabbed the lead.

3. "'Here in my preserve on this island,' he said in the same slow tone, 'I hunt more dangerous game.'"
   - **A** The wild-animal preserve has become a popular tourist attraction.
   - **B** The ice cream was topped with a fruit preserve.
   - **C** Salt can preserve certain meats.
   - **D** The president swears to "preserve, protect, and defend the Constitution."

4. "The door opened then, opened as suddenly as if it were on a spring. . . ."
   - **F** We hiked to the spring and camped out in the woods.
   - **G** My dogs spring to the door when they hear my key in the lock.
   - **H** The child opened the box, and a clown on a spring popped up.
   - **J** New houses spring up each day as more people move to the town.

5. "'A twenty-two,' he remarked. 'That's odd. It must have been a fairly large animal too. The hunter had his nerve with him to tackle it with a light gun.'"
   - **A** Eli is a tackle on the football team.
   - **B** I tackled cleaning the garage, since someone had to do it.
   - **C** The fisherman packed up his tackle box as the boat docked.
   - **D** In the game, Claudia managed to tackle her opponent from behind.

6. "There was no sound in the night as Rainsford sat there but the muffled throb of the engine. . . ."
   - **F** Sometimes we sing so much that our voices sound hoarse.
   - **G** The child was so tired that he fell sound asleep in the car.
   - **H** Karen gave me sound advice.
   - **J** The silence was broken by the sound of shattering glass.

SKILLS FOCUS

Vocabulary Skills
Understand multiple-meaning words.

Vocabulary Review

Use this activity to assess whether students have retained the collection Vocabulary.
Activity. Have students select the correct word from the box to complete the following sentences.

awry	luminous	stellar
labyrinthine	prolonged	

I. The maze of trails on the island was mysterious and _____. [labyrinthine]

2. He fell, and his leg was twisted _____. [awry]

3. The _____ full moon lit up the night sky. [luminous]

4. If winds are too strong, the wait before liftoff may be _____. [prolonged]

5. Radio telescopes scan the stars for the sounds of _____ radio waves. [stellar]

Writing Skills

Test Practice

DIRECTIONS: The following paragraph is from a draft of a student's autobiographical narrative. Read the questions below it, and choose the best answer to each question.

(1) Of all the events of my childhood, the one I remember best is my first ride on the school bus. (2) It took our bus forty-five minutes to get from my house to the school. (3) As I stepped up the gritty black steps and looked for an empty seat, I saw countless strange faces glaring back at me. (4) I sat near the back of the bus next to a shy-looking kid with glasses that sat crookedly on his nose. (5) As the bus got rolling, I soon found myself in the midst of a raging paper war. (6) "When will this ever stop?" I wondered to myself as a thick, wet paper wad struck the back of my neck. (7) "Get under here!" the boy next to me shouted, signaling me to duck under the backpack he had put over his head for protection. (8) As we crouched, we laughed together at the chaos around us. (9) When we arrived, I promised to meet him after school so we could ride home together.

1. To improve the coherence of this paragraph, which sentence might the writer delete?
   A 2
   B 4
   C 7
   D 8

2. If the writer wanted to add sensory details to the paragraph, which of the following would be appropriate?
   F The bus had room for sixty-four.
   G I hated waiting for the bus even more than I hated riding in it.
   H I waded through crumpled litter and gray, chewed gum to get to my seat.
   J My friend's mom worked at the school, so she didn't ride the bus.

3. Why did the student put *"When will this ever stop?"* in quotation marks?
   A It sets the pace of the story.
   B It is the title of the story.
   C It is an important event.
   D It is interior monologue.

4. Which of the following sentences might the writer add to explain the significance of this experience?
   F I never met a single person I liked on that school bus.
   G In the midst of flying trash, I had somehow found a friend.
   H The bus system is in need of a strict disciplinary program.
   J The school bus is an efficient mode of transportation.

5. Imagine that you have been asked to present this experience as an oral narrative. Which of the following gestures would be appropriate to make when saying, "Get under here!"?
   A clapping your hands
   B giving the thumbs-up sign
   C waving your hands toward you
   D pointing at the audience

SKILLS FOCUS

Writing Skills
Write an autobiographical narrative.

Writing Skills

Answers

1. A
2. H
3. D
4. G
5. C

APPLICATION

Narrative Poem

Students can use what they have learned in this workshop to write a narrative poem about a personal experience. Suggest to students that they look up some examples of narrative poetry they can use for models. Encourage students to concentrate on precise, vivid descriptions and statements in their poems.

EXTENSION

Eyewitness Account

Point out to students that narratives, in the form of eyewitness accounts, are often used in reporting news or in supporting a persuasive argument. Used in these ways, the narratives have very different purposes than ones written to be read for entertainment. For homework, have students write their own eyewitness accounts of a newsworthy event or of a problem for which they would want to suggest a solution. Students can share their accounts with the class and tell how they differ in purpose, audience, and form from their autobiographical narratives.

Homework

RESOURCES: WRITING

Assessment
- *One-Stop Planner* CD-ROM with ExamView Test Generator
- *Holt Assessment: Writing, Listening, & Speaking*

Internet
- *Holt Online Assessment*
- *Holt Online Essay Scoring*

Collection 2
Character

**Informational Reading Focus:
Using Primary and Secondary
Sources**

About Collection 2

In Collection 2, students will master the
following skills:

- **Literary Skills:** Analyze how character
  traits are revealed through dialogue and
  what characters say about themselves;
  and analyze internal and external
  conflicts and motivation.
- **Reading Skills:** Make inferences about
  characters; and analyze the uses of
  primary and secondary sources.
- **Vocabulary Skills:** Understand shades
  of meanings of synonyms; use precise
  modifiers; create word maps; understand
  analogies; and use context clues.
- **Writing Skills:** Develop, write, and
  revise a short story.

Informational Text

Each collection of *Elements of Literature*
provides a variety of informational texts
related to the literature selections by
theme or topic.

Minimum Course of Study

Most skills can be taught with a minimum
number of selections and features. In the
chart to the right, lessons highlighted in
green constitute the minimum course of
study that provides coverage of the skills
taught in Collection 2.

Resource Manager
(pp. 82C–82D)

Lesson and workshop resources are
referenced in the Resource Manager on
the pages that follow. These resources can
be used to reinforce the skills taught in
Collection 2, remediate students who are
having difficulty, and provide supporting
activities for English-language learners.

Scope and Sequence

Selection ■ Feature	Literary Skills
Elements of Literature: Character *by* John Leggett	• Understand characterization
Thank You, M'am *by* Langston Hughes ↓ *below grade level* **Informational Text:** • Teaching Chess, and Life • Community Service & You • Feeding Frenzy *by* Carlos Capellan; T. J. Saftner; Peter Ames Carlin *and* Don Sider ↔ *at grade level*	• Analyze how character traits are revealed through dialogue
Helen on Eighty-sixth Street *by* Wendi Kaufman ↑ *above grade level*	• Analyze character traits from what characters say about themselves
Elements of Literature: Character Interactions *by* John Leggett	• Understand internal and external conflicts, motivation, flat and round characters, and dynamic and static characters
Marigolds *by* Eugenia W. Collier ↔ *at grade level*	• Analyze internal and external conflicts
Writing Workshop: *Writing a Short Story*	
Skills Review: *Literary Skills* *Vocabulary Skills* *Writing Skills*	• Analyze character traits, internal and external conflicts, and motivation

Reading Skills	Vocabulary Skills	Writing ▪ Grammar and Language ▪ Listening and Speaking Skills
• Make inferences • Understand the uses of primary and secondary sources	• Understand shades of meaning of synonyms • Use precise modifiers • Create word maps • Understand word origins	• Write a letter
• Understand allusions	• Understand word meanings	• Write a description • Write a short story • Understand and use coordinating conjunctions
• Make inferences about character motivation	• Understand word analogies • Understand figures of speech (simile and metaphor)	• Write an autobiographical narrative
		• Write a short story
	• Identify word meanings using context clues	• Write a short story

Resource Manager

Selection ▪ Feature	Planning	Differentiating Instruction ▪ Lesson Plans with ELL Strategies and Practice	Reading ▪ Vocabulary
Elements of Literature: Character *by* John Leggett	• PowerNotes: Character	• Family Involvement Activities in English and Spanish, p. 4	
Thank You, M'am *by* Langston Hughes **Informational Text:** • Teaching Chess, and Life • Community Service & You • Feeding Frenzy *by* Carlos Capellan; T. J. Saftner; Peter Ames Carlin *and* Don Sider	• One-Stop Planner with ExamView Test Generator	• The Holt Reader, pp. 54–62 • Holt Adapted Reader • Holt Reading Solutions, pp. 57–62 • Supporting Instruction in Spanish, p. 8 • Audio CD Library, disc 4 • Audio CD Library, Selections and Summaries in Spanish	• The Holt Reader • Holt Adapted Reader • Holt Reading Solutions • Vocabulary Development, p. 7
Helen on Eighty-sixth Street *by* Wendi Kaufman	• One-Stop Planner with ExamView Test Generator	• Holt Reading Solutions, pp. 69–74 • Supporting Instruction in Spanish, p. 9 • Audio CD Library, disc 5 • Audio CD Library, Selections and Summaries in Spanish	• Holt Reading Solutions • Vocabulary Development, p. 8
Elements of Literature: Character Interactions *by* John Leggett	• PowerNotes: Character		
Marigolds *by* Eugenia W. Collier	• One-Stop Planner with ExamView Test Generator	• Holt Adapted Reader • Holt Reading Solutions, pp. 77–82 • Supporting Instruction in Spanish, p. 10 • Audio CD Library, disc 5 • Audio CD Library, Selections and Summaries in Spanish	• Holt Adapted Reader • Holt Reading Solutions • Vocabulary Development, p. 9
Writing Workshop: *Writing a Short Story*	• One-Stop Planner with ExamView Test Generator	• Workshop Resources: Writing, Listening, and Speaking, pp. 16–23 • Supporting Instruction in Spanish, p. 69	
Skills Review: *Literary Skills* *Vocabulary Skills* *Writing Skills*			

The Holt Reader

The Holt Reader is a consumable paperback book which can be used alone or to accompany *Elements of Literature*. It offers guided support throughout the reading process and encourages students to become active readers by circling, underlining, questioning, and jotting down responses as they read. *The Holt Reader* works well for homework, students who have missed class, additional instructional time, reteaching, and remediation.

Holt Reading Solutions (HRS)

Holt Reading Solutions pulls together reading resources in the *Elements of Literature* program to create a powerful tool for intervention and whole-class instruction. *HRS* includes diagnostic assessment tools, lesson plans for English-language learners and special education students, adaptations of selected reading selections, vocabulary and comprehension worksheets, information on phonics and decoding, and additional instruction and practice in remedial reading skills.

Writing ▪ Grammar and Language ▪ Listening and Speaking	Assessment
• Daily Language Activities • Language Handbook Worksheets, pp. 3, 6	• Holt Assessment: Literature, Reading, and Vocabulary • Holt Online Assessment • One-Stop Planner with ExamView Test Generator
• Daily Language Activities • Language Handbook Worksheets, p. 106	• Holt Assessment: Literature, Reading, and Vocabulary • Holt Online Assessment • One-Stop Planner with ExamView Test Generator
• Daily Language Activities	• Holt Assessment: Literature, Reading, and Vocabulary • Holt Online Assessment • One-Stop Planner with ExamView Test Generator
• Daily Language Activities • Workshop Resources: Writing, Listening, and Speaking, pp. 16–23	• Holt Assessment: Writing, Listening, and Speaking • Holt Online Assessment • One-Stop Planner with ExamView Test Generator
	• Holt Assessment: Writing, Listening, and Speaking • One-Stop Planner with ExamView Test Generator

Technology

INTERNET

- go.hrw.com
- Holt Online Assessment
- Holt Online Essay Scoring
- Elements of Literature Online

MEDIA

 • One-Stop Planner with ExamView Test Generator

 • PowerNotes

 • Audio CD Library, discs 4 and 5

 • Audio CD Library, Selections and Summaries in Spanish

 • Visual Connections Videocassette Program, Segment 2

 • Fine Art Transparencies, 3 and 4

 Transparency   Video

 CD-ROM   Audio CD

One-Stop Planner with ExamView Test Generator

The *One-Stop Planner* CD-ROM contains electronic versions of print-based teaching resources, clips from the video program, and valuable assessment tools. The *One-Stop Planner* resources are presented in easy-to-follow, point-and-click menu formats. To preview resources or print out worksheets and tests, you simply make a selection and click.

One-Stop
Planner CD-ROM

Collection 2

SKILLS FOCUS

Grade-Level Skills

■ **Literary Skills**
Determine characters' traits by what the characters say about themselves.

■ **Literary Skills**
Analyze influences on characters (such as internal and external conflict and motivation) and how those influences affect the plot.

■ **Reading Skills**
Analyze and elaborate on ideas presented in primary or secondary sources.

INTRODUCING THE COLLECTION

The selections in this collection introduce students to a diverse array of fictional characters. These characters are struggling with a variety of conflicts, internal and external. In "Helen on Eighty-sixth Street," a preteen covets her rival's role in a play while dealing with the absence of her father. In "Marigolds," an impoverished rural teen confronts hard times and her own transition to adulthood. In "Thank You, M'am," a young boy tries to snatch a purse and finds himself the captive of his intended victim. As these characters struggle—experiencing victory and defeat, personal loss, and emotional growth—they reveal their inner traits, their capacity for change, and the vitality of the human spirit. Reading the selections, students will learn how to draw meaning from the characters' behavior, speech, and thoughts and how to examine their interactions. At the end of the collection, students are provided an opportunity to write their own short stories.

COLLECTION 2 RESOURCES: READING

Planning
■ *One-Stop Planner* CD-ROM with ExamView Test Generator

Differentiating Instruction
■ *Holt Reading Solutions*
■ *The Holt Reader*
■ *Holt Adapted Reader*

■ *Family Involvement Activities in English and Spanish*
■ *Supporting Instruction in Spanish*

Vocabulary
■ *Vocabulary Development*

Grammar and Language
■ *Language Handbook Worksheets*
■ *Daily Language Activities*

Collection 2

CHARACTER

INFORMATIONAL READING FOCUS

USING PRIMARY AND SECONDARY SOURCES

> Characters exist in their own right,
> apart from the page.... They will not
> be driven back between covers.
>
> —Irving Howe

INTERNET
Collection
Resources
Keyword: LE5 9-2

April (1990–1991) by Chuck Close.
Oil on canvas (100″ × 84″).

The Eli and Edythe L. Broad Collection. © Chuck Close.
Photograph © Bill Jacobson Studio.

83

THE QUOTATION
Ask students to name some characters they have encountered in fiction whose traits remind them of real people they know. Encourage discussion by providing examples of characters from this book, with lists of their traits.

VIEWING THE ART

This portrait by **Chuck Close** (1940–   ) is of his friend April Gornik. In the 1960s and 1970s, Close became famous for his large, highly realistic paintings based on photographs of faces. Propelled in part by an injury that restricted his movements, he adapted his painting style, exposing a grid structure and exploring the interactions of colors to create striking studies in character and technique.

Activity. Have students describe the painting when viewed from a few inches away, and then have them position the book from a distance of a few feet. Ask how the portrait changes with distance. Students should notice the interaction of colors and the way in which rough shapes resolve into a detailed image.

Assessment
- *Holt Assessment: Literature, Reading, and Vocabulary*
- *One-Stop Planner* CD-ROM with ExamView Test Generator
- *Holt Online Assessment*

Internet
- go.hrw.com (Keyword: LE5 9-2)
- *Elements of Literature Online*

Media
- *Audio CD Library*
- *Audio CD Library, Selections and Summaries in Spanish*
- *Fine Art Transparencies*
- *Visual Connections Videocassette Program*
- *PowerNotes*

Grade-Level Skills

■ **Literary Skills**
Determine characters' traits by
what the characters say about
themselves.

Review Skills

■ **Literary Skills**
Analyze the methods writers use to
reveal character.

**Elements of Literature:
Character**

Write the term *indirect characterization* on the chalkboard, and ask a
student to define it. Call on volunteers to name the five different
methods of indirect characterization. As they do, write each method
on the chalkboard: the character's
speech, actions, appearance, and
private thoughts and how other
characters in the story feel about
that character. Next, have students
define *direct characterization*. Discuss
the types of information likely to be
gained through each method of
characterization. Ask volunteers to
cite an example of each method from
a work the class has completed.

INTERNET
**More About
Character**
Keyword: LE5 9-2

**SKILLS
FOCUS**

Literary Skills
Understand
characterization.

Elements of Literature

Character *by* John Leggett
REVEALING HUMAN NATURE

Creating characters—telling what human
beings are like—is the whole point of
writing stories. A story is interesting to us
as readers largely because of what it tells
us about people and how we behave.

A magazine editor once told me that all
you need to tell a story is a character, an
adjective, and a series of choices that the
character must make. Of course, people
are much more complex than a single
adjective can suggest, and that is the joy,
and the difficulty, of storytelling. How
does a writer build a character out of
words—someone who will seem to
become flesh and blood and rise off
the page?

Interpreting Characters' Words

The most obvious method of characterization is the characters' **speech.** Think of
how you can recognize your friends from
what they say and how they say it. Think
of how Joe can be counted on to talk
about what things cost, whereas Sally
talks about their beauty. Think of how
Alice reveals her nature by using long,
fancy words and Sam reveals his by using
short, slangy ones. Here are four ways
writers use speech to reveal character:

1 When characters tell their own
stories through **first-person
narration,** they speak directly to the
reader. They present facts—describing
events in the story and perhaps even their
backgrounds—but they also tell us what
they think and feel. As they talk, they
reveal their personal traits.

2 Reading the characters' **dialogue**
in a story is like listening in on a
conversation. We can learn about the
characters not only by what they say
about themselves, but by how they
respond to each other.

3 In a **dramatic monologue,** a type
of poem, a speaker addresses one
or more silent listeners, often discussing a
specific problem or situation. As the words
come tumbling out, however, the speaker
tells us a great deal about his or her life
and values. We also learn about the
speaker's relationship with the listener(s).

4 In a play this kind of self-revealing
speech is a **soliloquy.** It is delivered
by a character alone onstage, addressing
himself or herself. Shakespeare's plays,
such as *Romeo and Juliet* (see page 787),
contain a number of soliloquies in which
characters reveal their deepest thoughts
to the audience in this way.

Other Clues to Character

1 Writers also use **appearance** to
create character. We can tell so
much about Scrooge, for example, from
the way Charles Dickens describes his
features:

The cold within him froze his old features,
nipped his pointed nose, shriveled his
cheek, stiffened his gait; made his eyes red,
his thin lips blue. . . .

Clearly Dickens wants us to think of
Scrooge as a character whose cold heart
is reflected in his whole appearance.

DIFFERENTIATING INSTRUCTION

**Learners Having Difficulty
Character.** Have students work in small
groups to examine each of the methods of
characterization described in the essay.
Students can skim through the stories the
class has already read to try to locate examples. For each story examined, students
should first choose and discuss a trait they
identify with a specific character. Students
should then look for specific ways in which
the author has revealed this trait. Ask groups
to create a chart listing each of the methods
and an example of its use from one of the
stories. Post the charts in the classroom.

The kinds of clothes a character wears can give us hints too. As readers we will respond one way to a character wearing a pinstriped suit and another way to a character wearing faded jeans.

2 In fiction a writer can even take us into the characters' minds to reveal their **private thoughts.** We might learn, for example, how one character secretly feels when he sees the bully picking on the smallest kid in the schoolyard or how another character feels as she watches her grandmother's coffin being lowered into the ground.

3 We can learn about characters by watching **how other characters in the story feel about them.** We might learn, for instance, that a salesman is a good guy in the eyes of his customers and a generous tipper in the eyes of the local waiter, but he is cranky and selfish in the eyes of his family.

4 One of the most important ways that we learn about characters is from their **actions,** from what we see them doing. For instance, when we first meet Scrooge on Christmas Eve, he is working on his accounts—an action that instantly reveals his obsession with money.

Direct and Indirect Characterization

Some writers also use **direct characterization** to tell us about the people who inhabit their fictional worlds. This means that a writer tells us directly what a character is like or what a person's motives are. In a famous listing of adjectives, Dickens tells us directly what kind of person Scrooge is:

Oh, but he was a tightfisted hand at the grindstone, Scrooge! a squeezing, wrenching, grasping, scraping, clutching, covetous old sinner!

Most modern writers do not rely on direct statements about their characters. They usually use the other methods listed here, which are called **indirect characterization.** This means that a writer *shows* us a character but allows us to interpret for ourselves the kind of person we are meeting. In fiction as in life itself, it is much more satisfying to discover for ourselves what people are truly like.

Practice

Who is the most unforgettable character you've ever met in a story? Write a few sentences about why you find the character so memorable. Before you begin writing, jot down your ideas on a chart like the one here:

Most memorable character	
Most outstanding character trait	
Character's appearance	
Important statements	
Important thoughts	
Important actions	
Reactions of other characters	

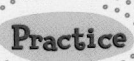

Practice

Students' responses will vary depending on the character chosen. Below are sample responses for Richard Connell's "The Most Dangerous Game."

Most memorable character—General Zaroff.

Most outstanding character trait—barbarity.

Character's appearance—"the face of a man used to giving orders," "red lips and pointed teeth."

Important statements—When speaking of a man and a dog who died in a swamp, Zaroff expresses sorrow only for the canine.

Important thoughts—Before he hunts men, Zaroff thinks it is "civilized" to provide them with good food and exercise.

Important actions—"Very deliberately . . . he turned his back on the tree and walked carelessly away."

Reactions of other characters—Rainsford, a hardened hunter, is sickened by Zaroff's game.

Apply

Encourage students to use the chart to examine other characters they encounter in this collection.

Advanced Learners

Acceleration. Use the following activity with advanced students to help them analyze the way in which authors have used archetypes from myth and tradition in literature.

Activity. Explain to students that an archetype is an original model. Archetypes are patterns that often spring from myth or traditional tales. Ask students how many stories they have encountered in which a main character defeats an evil counterpart. Whatever the story, both the hero and the villain have readily identifiable character traits. Have students discuss what these character traits are. Then, ask them to identify characters from myths, epics, or traditional tales, who serve as archetypes for fictional characters.

Grade-Level Skills

■ **Literary Skills**
Determine characters' traits by what the characters say about themselves.

■ **Reading Skills**
Make inferences.

Review Skills

■ **Literary Skills**
Analyze the methods a writer uses to reveal character.

Summary ⬇ *below grade level*

Late one night, Roger, who wants a pair of blue suede shoes, tries to snatch the purse of Mrs. Luella Bates Washington Jones as she walks home. The attempt fails, and Mrs. Jones collars the boy, who is no match for his captor. She drags him to her house, makes him wash his face, feeds him, and talks to him about his conduct—and her own. At the story's end she gives him money to buy the shoes and sends him on his way, closing her door on him before he can express his wonder and gratitude.

Before You Read

Thank You, M'am

Make the Connection
Quickwrite 🖉

There's a saying "When the going gets tough, the tough get going." In very difficult circumstances some people do indeed get going. They have a spirit that moves them ahead—pushing them to do heroic deeds. What makes these people so tough, so strong in spirit? Why do they turn out to be good? Why do others go so wrong? Jot down your thoughts about these hard questions.

Literary Focus
Dialogue: What Do They Say?

You get to know people best by talking with them and listening as they speak to others. In the same way, characters in a story reveal themselves to one another—and to the reader—through **dialogue,** or conversation. As a reader you eavesdrop on those conversations and form your own opinions about the characters.

In "Thank You, M'am" you eavesdrop on a brief encounter between two strangers. By the story's end they have learned some important things about each other. Notice what these two people say to each other—and what they don't say. Then, decide what you think of them.

INTERNET
More About
Langston Hughes
Keyword: LE5 9-2

SKILLS FOCUS

Literary Skills
Understand how character traits are revealed through dialogue.

Reading Skills
Make inferences.

Reading Skills 📖
Making Inferences: Educated Guesses

Most good writers don't tell you directly what their characters are like. Instead, authors often allow you to make your own inferences about characters from what they say and do. When you **make an inference,** you use your observations and prior experience to guess about something you don't know for sure. However, an inference isn't just a random guess. It's an educated guess—because it's based on evidence in the text. After you read this story, skim through it again, and jot down clues that you think reveal something important about the characters. Look at what they *say* (or what they don't say) and how they *act*.

> "Well, you didn't have to snatch *my* pocketbook to get some suede shoes."

86 **Collection 2** Character • Using Primary and Secondary Sources

RESOURCES: READING

Planning
■ *One-Stop Planner* CD-ROM with ExamView Test Generator

Differentiating Instruction
■ *Holt Reading Solutions*
■ *The Holt Reader*
■ *Holt Adapted Reader*
■ *Supporting Instruction in Spanish*

■ *Audio CD Library, Selections and Summaries in Spanish*

Grammar and Language
■ *Language Handbook Worksheets*
■ *Daily Language Activities*

Media
■ *Audio CD Library*

Thank You, M'am

Langston Hughes

Mom Alice (1944) by William Johnson. Oil on paperboard (25″ × 30¼″).

The Howard University Gallery of Art, Washington, D.C.

Thank You, M'am **87**

- *Visual Connections Videocassette Program*
- *Fine Art Transparencies*

Assessment

- *Holt Assessment: Literature, Reading, and Vocabulary*
- *One-Stop Planner CD-ROM with ExamView Test Generator*
- *Holt Online Assessment*

Internet

- *go.hrw.com (Keyword: LE5 9-2)*
- *Elements of Literature Online*

PRETEACHING

Selection Starter

Motivate. Discuss with students why people are tempted to steal. Why do some people give in to that temptation while others resist it? What influences a person's resistance to the desire to do something he or she knows is wrong? After this discussion, ask students to complete the Quickwrite activity.

Assign the Reading

Have students read this brief story in class. You may wish to work with small groups to help readers with dialect that appears in the story's dialogue. You may then wish to assign the dramatic monologue "Mother to Son" and the Response and Analysis questions as homework.

DIRECT TEACHING

A Literary Focus

❓ **Title.** Before you read a word of the story, what do the words of the title suggest? [Possible response: The words suggest a polite, young person speaking to an older woman.]

VIEWING THE ART

William Johnson (1901–1970) is best known for his works that portray the everyday lives of African Americans.

Activity. Ask students to brainstorm adjectives to describe Mom Alice in this painting. Suggest that as students read they keep these qualities in mind and compare them to the qualities that Mrs. Jones displays in "Thank You, M'am."

A Reading Skills

? Making inferences. What do the images presented in the first two sentences suggest about this woman? [Possible response: She is strong, practical, and self-reliant.]

B Reading Skills

? Making inferences. What can you infer about this boy's potential for violence, based on his first words? [Possible responses: The first word from the boy's mouth, "Yes'm," suggests that he is no hardened criminal and that he is childlike and respectful. He is sufficiently ashamed of his actions to offer the half apology "I didn't aim to," which makes him seem inexperienced and scarcely capable of the crime he attempted.]

C English-Language Learners

Understanding dialect. Point out the expression "I got a great mind to." Tell students that this expression is also commonly phrased as "I have a mind to." Ask them what they think it means. [Possible responses: "I'm thinking about"; "I plan to"; "I'm determined to."]

D Literary Focus

? Dialogue. What is it that Mrs. Jones is telling the boy in this key speech? [Possible responses: "You started this, and now you must take what comes"; "I'm going to teach you a lesson."]

A She was a large woman with a large purse that had everything in it but a hammer and nails. It had a long strap, and she carried it slung across her shoulder. It was about eleven o'clock at night, dark, and she was walking alone, when a boy ran up behind her and tried to snatch her purse. The strap broke with the sudden single tug the boy gave it from behind. But the boy's weight and the weight of the purse combined caused him to lose his balance. Instead of taking off full blast as he had hoped, the boy fell on his back on the sidewalk and his legs flew up. The large woman simply turned around and kicked him right square in his blue-jeaned sitter. Then she reached down, picked the boy up by his shirt front, and shook him until his teeth rattled.

After that the woman said, "Pick up my pocketbook, boy, and give it here." She still held him tightly. But she bent down enough to permit him to stoop and pick up her purse. Then she said, "Now ain't you ashamed of yourself?"

B Firmly gripped by his shirt front, the boy said, "Yes'm."

The woman said, "What did you want to do it for?"

The boy said, "I didn't aim to."

She said, "You a lie!"

By that time two or three people passed, stopped, turned to look, and some stood watching.

"If I turn you loose, will you run?" asked the woman.

"Yes'm," said the boy.

"Then I won't turn you loose," said the woman. She did not release him.

"Was I bothering *you* when I turned that corner?"

"Lady, I'm sorry," whispered the boy.

C "Um-hum! Your face is dirty. I got a great mind to wash your face for you. Ain't you got nobody home to tell you to wash your face?"

"No'm," said the boy.

"Then it will get washed this evening," said the large woman starting up the street, dragging the frightened boy behind her.

He looked as if he were fourteen or fifteen, frail and willow-wild, in tennis shoes and blue jeans.

The woman said, "You ought to be my son. I would teach you right from wrong. Least I can do right now is to wash your face. Are you hungry?"

"No'm," said the being-dragged boy. "I just want you to turn me loose."

"Was I bothering *you* when I turned that corner?" asked the woman.

"No'm."

D "But you put yourself in contact with *me*," said the woman. "If you think that that contact is not going to last awhile, you got another thought coming. When I get through with you, sir, you are going to remember Mrs. Luella Bates Washington Jones."

Sweat popped out on the boy's face and he began to struggle. Mrs. Jones stopped, jerked him around in front of her, put a half nelson about his neck, and continued to drag him up the street. When she got to her door, she dragged the boy inside, down a hall, and into a large kitchenette-furnished room at the rear of the house. She switched on the light and left the door open. The boy could hear other roomers laughing and talking in the large house. Some of their doors were open, too, so he knew he and the woman were not alone. The woman still had him by the neck in the middle of her room.

She said, "What is your name?"

DIFFERENTIATING INSTRUCTION

Learners Having Difficulty
Invite learners having difficulty to read "Thank You, M'am" in interactive format in *The Holt Reader* and to use the sidenotes as aids for understanding the selection. The interactive version provides additional instruction, practice, and assessment of the literature skill taught in the Student Edition. Monitor students' responses to the selection, and correct any misconceptions that arise.

English-Language Learners
Help students with the dialect in this story by listing on the chalkboard the standard English equivalents for the following colloquialisms: *Yes'm, didn't aim to, you a lie, gonna, late as it be, could've, I were young, set down.* You can also list any other words or phrases you think might be confusing to students. Ask students to suggest other colloquialisms from their own lives, and transcribe them to show how Hughes represents speech.

Digestive System (1989) by James Romberger. Pastel on paper (57″ × 60″).

"Roger," answered the boy.

"Then, Roger, you go to that sink and wash your face," said the woman, whereupon she turned him loose—at last. Roger looked at the door—looked at the woman—looked at the door—*and went to the sink.*

"Let the water run until it gets warm," she said. "Here's a clean towel."

"You gonna take me to jail?" asked the boy, bending over the sink.

"Not with that face, I would not take you nowhere," said the woman. "Here I am trying to get home to cook me a bite to eat, and you snatch my pocketbook! Maybe you ain't been to your supper either, late as it be. Have you?"

"There's nobody home at my house," said the boy.

"Then we'll eat," said the woman. "I believe you're hungry—or been hungry—to try to snatch my pocketbook."

Thank You, M'am **89**

DIRECT TEACHING

VIEWING THE ART

James Romberger (1958–   ) is a modern artist whose work includes not only paintings and drawings but also a series of comic book illustrations for a recent biography.

Activity. Have students speculate on certain aspects of the artwork, such as the point of view of the picture, the distortion of some vertical lines, the abundance of detail, the collision of lines, and the complements of light and dark colors. Invite students to discuss how the artist conveys a sense of both decay and renewal in a city neighborhood. Ask them what they think the painting's title means.

Special Education Students

For lessons designed for special education students, see *Holt Reading Solutions.*

Advanced Learners

Enrichment. According to biographer Arnold Rampersad, Langston Hughes lived "a lonely, passed-around childhood . . . [that] left him sensitive about his identity and self-worth." In this story is it possible that Roger also is sensitive, lonely, and unsure of his self-worth? Challenge students to prove or disprove this thesis by gathering evidence from the story to explain the inferences they make.

A Reading Skills

Making predictions. At this point, students know something about both Roger and Mrs. Jones, having made inferences about each. Several things could happen in the story from this scene on. Ask students to predict what they think the characters will do next and to explain how they arrived at these predictions. [Answers will vary.]

B Literary Focus

❓ Dialogue. What important idea is Mrs. Jones trying to convey to Roger in this speech? [Possible responses: She too has done things she shouldn't have; she understands what motivated him to snatch her purse.]

C Reading Skills

❓ Making inferences. Why does Roger offer to go to the store? [Possible responses: He wants to show that he can do something helpful; he wants to show that he is worthy of Mrs. Jones's trust.]

D Learners Having Difficulty

Paraphrasing. Ask students to express in their own words what Mrs. Jones means by "shoes got by devilish ways will burn your feet." [Possible response: Doing wrong to get things will eventually create trouble for you.]

"I want a pair of blue suede shoes," said the boy.

"Well, you didn't have to snatch *my* pocketbook to get some suede shoes," said Mrs. Luella Bates Washington Jones. "You could've asked me."

"M'am?"

A The water dripping from his face, the boy looked at her. There was a long pause. A very long pause. After he had dried his face and not knowing what else to do, dried it again, the boy turned around, wondering what next. The door was open. He could make a dash for it down the hall. He could run, run, run, *run!*

The woman was sitting on the daybed. After a while she said, "I were young once and I wanted things I could not get."

There was another long pause. The boy's mouth opened. Then he frowned, not knowing he frowned.

The woman said, "Um-hum! You thought I was going to say *but*, didn't you? You thought I was going to say, *but I didn't snatch people's pocketbooks.* Well, I wasn't going to **B** say that." Pause. Silence. "I have done things, too, which I would not tell you, son—neither tell God, if He didn't already know. Everybody's got something in common. So you set down while I fix us something to eat. You might run that comb through your hair so you will look presentable."

In another corner of the room behind a screen was a gas plate and an icebox. Mrs. Jones got up and went behind the screen. The woman did not watch the boy to see if he was going to run now, nor did she watch her purse, which she left behind her on the daybed. But the boy took care to sit on the far side of the room, away from the purse, where he thought she could easily see him out of the corner of her eye if she wanted to. He did not trust the woman *not* to trust him.

And he did not want to be mistrusted now.

"Do you need somebody to go the store," asked the boy, "maybe to get some milk or something?"

C "Don't believe I do," said the woman, "unless you just want sweet milk yourself. I was going to make cocoa out of this canned milk I got here."

"That will be fine," said the boy.

She heated some lima beans and ham she had in the icebox, made the cocoa, and set the table. The woman did not ask the boy anything about where he lived, or his folks, or anything else that would embarrass him. Instead, as they ate, she told him about her job in a hotel beauty shop that stayed open late, what the work was like, and how all kinds of women came in and out, blondes, redheads, and Spanish. Then she cut him a half of her ten-cent cake.

"Eat some more, son," she said.

When they were finished eating, she got up and said, "Now here, take this ten dollars and buy yourself some blue suede shoes. And next time, do not make the mistake of latching onto *my* pocketbook *nor* **D** *nobody else's*—because shoes got by devilish ways will burn your feet. I got to get my rest now. But from here on in, son, I hope you will behave yourself."

She led him down the hall to the front door and opened it. "Good night! Behave yourself, boy!" she said, looking out into the street as he went down the steps.

The boy wanted to say something other than "Thank you, m'am" to Mrs. Luella Bates Washington Jones, but although his lips moved, he couldn't even say that as he turned at the foot of the barren stoop and looked up at the large woman in the door. Then she shut the door. ∎

> He could make a dash for it down the hall. He could run, run, run, *run!*

DEVELOPING FLUENCY

Paired activity. As in a real conversation, there is plenty in this story's dialogue that is left unsaid. Point out that what the characters say only scratches the surface of what they are thinking, feeling, and communicating in other ways—the subtext. Invite students to work in pairs to create subtext for the dialogue in the story. Suggest that student pairs isolate the dialogue on one page of the story. Then, for everything said, ask them to record what could have been said but wasn't—any thoughts or feelings of the characters that are not directly revealed. Student pairs should then act out a single character—one reading the dialogue from the story and one reading the below-the-surface dialogue.

Meet the Writer

Langston Hughes

A Lonely Child

Langston Hughes (1902–1967) was a lonely child who moved often and felt distant from his parents, who eventually divorced. Hughes was born in Joplin, Missouri, and graduated from high school in Ohio. His father wanted to discourage his son's "impractical" dream of being a writer, so he sent him to Columbia University in New York City to study engineering.

The young writer was not happy, and he left college to join the crew of a ship that sailed to Europe and Africa. Eventually Hughes graduated from Lincoln University in Pennsylvania, but to support his writing, he worked at a variety of jobs: The man who was later known as one of the great original voices in American literature was also a cook, sailor, beachcomber, launderer, doorman, and busboy.

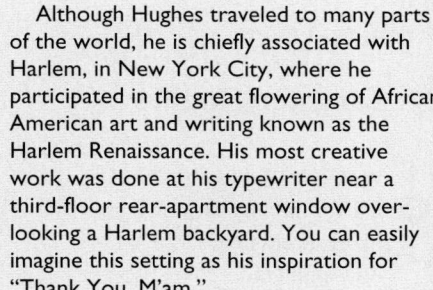

Although Hughes traveled to many parts of the world, he is chiefly associated with Harlem, in New York City, where he participated in the great flowering of African American art and writing known as the Harlem Renaissance. His most creative work was done at his typewriter near a third-floor rear-apartment window over-looking a Harlem backyard. You can easily imagine this setting as his inspiration for "Thank You, M'am."

Although he wrote stories, Hughes is probably best known as a poet. In an early collection of his poems, he wrote:

> ❝I have felt that much of our poetry has been aimed at the heads of the highbrows, rather than at the hearts of the people.❞

Hughes chose to let ordinary people speak for themselves. As in "Mother to Son" (see the **Connection** on page 92), his poems are often written in dialect, and many include slang—his speakers say what is on their minds, and they say it in the language they use every day.

For Independent Reading

If you would like to know more about Langston Hughes's interesting life, look for Arnold Rampersad's very readable biography, *The Life of Langston Hughes.*

Monitoring students' progress. Have students answer these true-false questions.

True-False

1. The boy tries to snatch a purse from a very frail woman. [F]
2. Mrs. Jones drags the boy home with her. [T]
3. Roger admits that he tried to steal Mrs. Jones's purse because he needed the money to buy food. [F]
4. After Mrs. Jones and Roger eat, she offers him the money he wants. [T]
5. Roger and Mrs. Jones become lifelong friends who visit each other often. [F]

Meet the Writer

Background. Although Hughes had written poetry and a novel, he did not start writing short stories until he was in his thirties. While he was on a tour of Russia, a friend lent him a collection of short stories by the English writer D. H. Lawrence. Those works affected Hughes so deeply that he wrote his first short stories soon afterward. In his stories, as in much of his poetry, Hughes re-created Harlem again and again. Critic Arthur P. Davis made this observation: "Called the poet laureate of Harlem, Hughes retained all his life a deep love for that colorful city within a city. . . . To Hughes, Harlem was place, symbol, and on occasion, protagonist."

For Independent Reading

- Students can learn more about Hughes's growing up in *The Big Sea,* which covers his life up to the age of twenty-eight.
- Advanced learners interested in the place Hughes loved so much might also enjoy Claude McKay's *Home to Harlem,* a novel about a returning soldier.

DIFFERENTIATING INSTRUCTION

Advanced Learners

Enrichment. Hughes claimed that the writing of others saved him and that this salvation occurred at a very young age. Beginning when he was about seven years old in Lawrence, Kansas, Hughes recalled, he "began to believe in nothing but books and the wonderful world in books—where if people suffered, they suffered in beautiful language, not in mono-syllables, as we did in Kansas."

Activity. Hughes is not the only writer to be saved by books. The writer Gary Paulsen said that a library card rescued him from an unhappy childhood and "handed him the world." Ask students to find quotations from other authors about the role that books played in their youth.

Connection

Summary ⬇ *below grade level*

In "Mother to Son," a mother tells her son about the difficulties of life and advises him on the attitude he should take toward it. Using the metaphor of a stair, she tells her son that although the way up has been rough and full of "tacks" and "splinters," she has never stopped striving. She advises her son not to turn back, not to rest, but to keep climbing, as she has done throughout her life.

Ⓐ Literary Focus

Dramatic monologue. Explain to students that this poetic form, a dramatic monologue, represents speech by a single person, rather than more than one, as in a dialogue. Point out that the speaker of the poem is speaking in dialect, as Mrs. Jones does in "Thank You, M'am."

Ⓑ English-Language Learners

Appreciating apostrophes. Show students that a key feature of written dialect is the use of apostrophes to indicate missing letters: Thus, *reachin'* (l.10) represents the word *reaching*. *I'se* (l.9) stands for *I has* or *I is* (*I have* or *I am* in standard English).

Ⓒ Literary Focus

❓ Metaphors. Hughes uses the metaphor of a stairway to describe the journey through life. What do you think this mother's life has been like? [Possible response: The mother probably has worked hard, both to earn a living and to raise her family.] What do the images she uses in the poem, such as splinters and bare floors, suggest? [Possible responses: She has lived in run-down apartments all of her life; her life has had many difficulties and setbacks.]

---

*In Hughes's poem "Mother to Son," a mother is talking to her son. The poem is an example of a **dramatic monologue**, a poem in which a speaker addresses one or more silent listeners. During the course of a dramatic monologue, the speaker reveals important thoughts and feelings.*

Mother to Son
Langston Hughes

Ⓐ
Well, son, I'll tell you:
Life for me ain't been no crystal stair.
It's had tacks in it,
And splinters,
5 And boards torn up,
And places with no carpet on the floor—
Bare.
But all the time
I'se been a-climbin' on,
10 And reachin' landin's,
Ⓑ And turnin' corners,
And sometimes goin' in the dark
Where there ain't been no light.
So boy, don't you turn back.
15 Don't you set down on the steps
'Cause you finds it's kinder hard.
Don't you fall now—
For I'se still goin', honey,
Ⓒ I'se still climbin',
20 And life for me ain't been no crystal stair.

Proletarian (1934) by Gordon Samstag.
Oil on canvas (48⅝" × 42").
The Toledo Museum of Art, Toledo, Ohio.
Museum Purchase Fund (1935.34).

Connecting and Comparing Texts

Help students recognize connections between "Thank You, M'am" and "Mother to Son." In addition to dialect, explore with students similarities in setting, in characters (including Roger and the son in the poem's title), and in theme. To help students recognize connections between the two pieces, have them make a chart of similarities between Mrs. Jones and the speaker in "Mother to Son." For each similarity shown on a chart, ask a student to cite evidence from the work that supports that idea. For example, both women appear not to be wealthy. Students might note Mrs. Jones's screened-off, gas-plate kitchenette and the lines from the poem that say "life for me ain't been no crystal stair."

VIEWING THE ART

Gordon Samstag (1906–1990), an American realist painter from New York, liked to paint people at work.

Activity. Ask students to compare the speaker in the poem with the woman in the painting. [Possible response: Both are hard-working, dignified African American women.]

Thank You, M'am   **93**

DIFFERENTIATING INSTRUCTION

Advanced Learners
Enrichment. Have students experiment by writing a dramatic monologue of their own. Suggest that they write either a stream-of-consciousness paragraph or a short poem, offering advice about life to a friend or younger sibling. Help students find a basic metaphor to extend through their works by having them complete the sentence "Life is a _____."

Response and Analysis

Reading Check

1. Possible answers: *What happened?*—A boy tried to steal a woman's purse. She stopped him, took him home, talked to him, fed him, gave him money, and sent him away. *Whom did it happen to?*—Roger and Mrs. Jones. *When and where did it happen?*—at night on a city street; in her apartment. *Why did it happen?*—He wanted money for shoes. Mrs. Jones wanted to teach him not to steal.

Thinking Critically

2. *Words. Mrs. Jones*—"Behave your-self, boy!" *Roger*—"I'm sorry," "There's nobody home at my house."
   Silences. Mrs. Jones—after Roger washes, as she begins to prepare food. *Roger*—Many, because he speaks little.
   Actions. Mrs. Jones—She forces Roger to her home; she doesn't restrain him; she gives him money. *Roger*—tries to steal her purse, does not try to escape.
   What they reveal. Mrs. Jones—She understands Roger, and wants to teach him right from wrong. *Roger*—He is a good person; he wants Mrs. Jones to trust him.

3. He might like to ask her why she acted as she did. He is surprised at her behavior. He has not been treated so well before.

4. The setting reveals a simple life of dignified poverty. Details might include water-stained walls and a worn carpet.

5. Both women are strong. Both have firm opinions about how people should behave. Mrs. Jones understands temptation; the mother sees how easy it is to give up. Mrs. Jones is trying to teach Roger right from wrong; the mother is urging her son to strive for a better life.

Response and Analysis

Reading Check

1. Write down the **main events** of this story as if you were reporting them for a newspaper. Answer these questions:
   - *What* happened?
   - *Whom* did it happen to?
   - *When* and *where* did it happen?
   - *Why* did it happen?

   Then, compare your list of events with your classmates' lists.

Thinking Critically

2. What does the **dialogue** between Roger and Mrs. Jones, as well as their actions, reveal about their **character traits**? Make a chart like the one here, showing what you **infer** from each character's words, silences, and actions.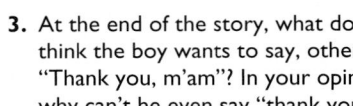

	Mrs. Jones	Roger
Words		
Silences		
Actions		
What they reveal		

3. At the end of the story, what do you think the boy wants to say, other than "Thank you, m'am"? In your opinion, why can't he even say "thank you"?

4. How does the **setting** of Mrs. Jones's home—her furnished room, the gas plate, the ten-cent cake, the noisy tenement—contribute to your sense of the kind of person she is? What details can your imagination add to her surroundings?

SKILLS FOCUS

Literary Skills
Analyze how character traits are revealed through dialogue.

Reading Skills
Make inferences.

Writing Skills
Write a letter.

5. Compare the character traits revealed by Mrs. Jones in the **dialogue** in the story with the traits revealed by the mother in "Mother to Son," Langston Hughes's **dramatic monologue** (see the **Connection** on page 92). Both women talk about difficulties in their own lives. What important message is each character trying to convey to her listener?

6. Look at your Quickwrite notes about what makes some people turn out to be good while others go wrong. What do you think made Mrs. Jones so good?

Extending and Evaluating

7. Based on your own experience, do you believe that these events could happen as Hughes describes them? Why or why not?

Literary Criticism

8. Review the biography of Langston Hughes on page 91. Do you think the way Mrs. Jones and the mother in "Mother to Son" approach life might reflect Hughes's own attitude toward life? Explain your answer.

WRITING

A Letter from Roger

What do you think Roger will be like ten years after his encounter with Mrs. Jones? What might he write in a letter to her? Compose a **letter** from Roger. Write as "I." Include Roger's present address in the letter. Be sure to state the purpose of his communication after all these years.

6. Possible answer: Perhaps she had loving parents who taught her right from wrong or perhaps she learned from experience.

Extending and Evaluating

7. Some students may find the story credible because Mrs. Jones seems so tough and down-to-earth; others may not believe that Roger wouldn't run off.

Literary Criticism

8. Answers may vary. Some students might say that Hughes showed perseverance pursuing his own dream of writing. Hughes also felt lonely as a child, which might explain why he often wrote about solitary characters, such as Mrs. Jones and Roger.

Vocabulary Development

Synonyms: Accept No Substitutes?

Although a **synonym** is a word that has the same or almost the same meaning as another word, synonyms are not always interchangeable. Often synonyms will have subtle but distinct shades of difference in meaning.

PRACTICE

Here are three words from the first paragraph of the story: *large*, *carried*, and *fell*. Find the sentences in which the words are used. Then, make a chart like the one below for each word. Could the synonyms work just as well in each sentence?

barren	
Definition	*empty; devoid of life*
Synonyms	*bare, sterile*
Substitutions	*He turned at the [bare/sterile] stoop.*
Response to substitutions	*Bare could work because it can refer to a lack of objects. Sterile doesn't work because it suggests cleanliness, not emptiness. Barren is best; it reminds me of something empty and lifeless.*

Grammar Link

Modifiers: Precise Meanings

Modifiers make your writing more specific. Notice how adjectives help you visualize those blue suede shoes that Roger wants. **Adjectives** (and adjective phrases) answer the question *what kind? which one? how many?* or *how much?* **Adverbs** (and adverb phrases) answer the question *where? when? how often? in what way?* or *to what extent?* The modifiers in these sentences from Hughes's story are single words, compound words, and phrases:

1. "The <u>large</u> woman <u>simply</u> turned <u>around</u> and kicked <u>him</u> <u>right square</u> in his <u>blue-jeaned</u> sitter."

2. "He looked as if he were <u>fourteen or fifteen, frail and willow-wild</u>, <u>in tennis shoes and blue jeans</u>."

PRACTICE

For each numbered sentence at the left, tell whether the underlined modifiers are acting as adjectives or adverbs. Then, rewrite each sentence three times, replacing the underlined modifiers with words and phrases of your own. Each time, give Mrs. Jones or the boy a totally different appearance. (For example, you might put Roger in hiking boots and a plaid shirt.)

When you write a description of a character, use precise adverbs and adjectives. Don't overdo it with modifiers, though. Sometimes a simple word is best.

▶ **For more help, see Using Modifiers, 5a–g, in the Language Handbook.**

SKILLS FOCUS

Vocabulary Skills
Understand shades of meaning of synonyms.

Grammar Skills
Use precise modifiers.

Vocabulary Development

Practice

- *large. Definition*—taking up a lot of space. *Synonyms*—big, enormous. *Substitutions*—"She was a [big, enormous] woman." *Response to substitutions*— Enormous is too forceful. *Big* seems to work, but *large* sounds more polite.

- *carried. Definition*—to hold or support while moving. *Synonyms*—transported, bore. *Substitutions*—"She [transported, bore] it slung across her shoulder." *Response to substitutions*— Bore is logical but suggests heavy labor. *Transported* seems too formal.

- *fell. Definition*—to come down suddenly. *Synonyms*—dropped, descended. *Substitutions*—"The boy [dropped, descended] on his back." *Response to substitutions*— Only *dropped* makes sense.

Grammar Link

Practice

Possible Answers

1. The <u>small</u> woman <u>quickly</u> turned <u>back</u> and kicked him <u>hard</u> in his <u>sweat-suited</u> sitter.

2. He looked as if he were <u>two or three, pale and limp, in diapers</u>.

ASSESSING

Assessment

- *Holt Assessment: Literature, Reading, and Vocabulary*

RETEACHING

For a lesson reteaching character traits, see **Reteaching,** p. 979A. For another selection to teach characterization, see *The Holt Reader,* Collection 2.

Grade-Level Skills

■ Reading Skills

Analyze and elaborate on ideas presented in primary and secondary sources.

Review Skills

■ Reading Skills

Determine whether a secondary source, such as a summary, is an accurate reflection of an original text.

Summary ⬌ *at grade level*

"Teaching Chess, and Life" is a firsthand account of how chess coach Jeremy Chiappetta helped a young man in a crime-infested neighborhood.

"Community Service & You" promotes volunteerism and describes the varied projects of Youth Service America.

"Feeding Frenzy" recounts the volunteer efforts of a Florida teenager, David Levitt, to begin a surplus food-sharing program in his own school district.

PRETEACHING

Selection Starter

Motivate. Ask students if they have ever performed volunteer work. Have them discuss the work they did, the results they achieved, and how their efforts made them feel.

Informational Text

LINK TO "THANK YOU, M'AM"

Teaching Chess, and Life ♦ Community Service & You ♦ Feeding Frenzy

Using Primary and Secondary Sources: Whose View?

Research sources generally fall into two basic categories: primary sources and secondary sources.

- A **primary source** is a firsthand account. In primary sources, writers present their experiences, opinions, and ideas. Primary sources include auto-biographies, letters, interviews, oral histories, eyewitness news reports, essays, editorials, and speeches.
- A **secondary source** is a secondhand account, often based on more than one viewpoint. In secondary sources, writers summarize, interpret, or analyze events in which they did not participate. Examples of secondary sources include encyclopedias and other reference works, textbooks, biographies, many magazine articles, and most newspaper articles.

Using the Sources

Follow these steps to get the most out of your sources:

- **Analyze.** First, decide whether the work is a primary or a secondary source. Then, look for the **main idea** of the work. Ask yourself, "How does the author support the main idea? Who is the author's audience? What is the author's purpose?"
- **Evaluate.** Look for clues indicating whether the author is presenting objective **facts** or subjective **opinions**. Is the factual information accurate? With primary sources especially, check the accuracy of the information by reading

INTERNET
Interactive
Reading Model
Keyword: LE5 9-2

SKILLS
FOCUS

Reading Skills
Understand the uses of primary and secondary sources.

other sources. Evaluate the author's opinions as well. Do you agree with the author's message?

- **Elaborate.** When you elaborate, you add information, usually in the form of details. You might present your own ideas on the topic, or you might do further research. Check to see if a secondary source has a **bibliography** or list of **works cited.** These contain other useful sources of information.

Vocabulary Development

mentorship (men′tər·ship) *n.:* advice or lessons from a mentor, or wise teacher.

intimidating (in·tim′ə·dāt′iŋ) *v.* used as *adj.:* frightening.

endeavors (en·dev′ərz) *n.:* serious attempts, efforts, or undertakings.

legislation (lej′is·lā′shən) *n.:* law or body of laws.

bureaucratic (byoor′ə·krat′ik) *adj.:* relating to rigid government routine.

undaunted (un·dôn′tid) *adj.:* not discouraged by a difficulty or setback.

Connecting to the Literature

Mrs. Jones in "Thank You, M'am" helps a boy who might otherwise end up on the wrong path. In the following primary and secondary sources, you'll meet people who also help others, and you'll learn about community service in the process.

RESOURCES: READING

Planning
- *One-Stop Planner* CD-ROM with ExamView Test Generator

Differentiating Instruction
- *Holt Reading Solutions*
- *Holt Adapted Reader*
- *Supporting Instruction in Spanish*

Vocabulary
- *Vocabulary Development*

Grammar and Language
- *Daily Language Activities*

Assessment
- *Holt Assessment: Literature, Reading, and Vocabulary*
- *One-Stop Planner* CD-ROM with ExamView Test Generator

- *Holt Online Assessment*

Internet
- go.hrw.com (Keyword: LE5 9-2)
- *Elements of Literature Online*

Media
- *Audio CD Library*
- *Audio CD Library, Selections and Summaries in Spanish*

PRIMARY SOURCE

PERSONAL ESSAY

TEACHING CHESS, AND LIFE

from an essay adapted by **The New York Times,** September 3, 2000

Carlos Capellan

Carlos Capellan, an assistant chess coach, shares a laugh with students during chess practice at Intermediate School 90.

If you were to walk down West 160th Street in Washington Heights, you would see drug dealers whistling to people in cars and handing off small packages to passersby. As you walk further down the block, you would see residents who are too scared to sit and talk to their neighbors on the front steps. These families stay inside most of the time. You would see parents pick up their children from P.S. 4 and hurry off the block before trouble can start. This is my block and this is my neighborhood.

Many kids my age in Washington Heights wind up in gangs, as drug dealers, in jail, or dead. I decided long ago that I would not end up in one of those situations because of the consequences I saw others suffer. I have stuck by this decision with help from several important people. One of the most influential people in my life is my former chess coach and current boss, Jeremy Chiappetta, who has taught me a lot about chess and more about life.

As an eighth-grader at a gang-infested junior high school, I joined the chess team as a way to stay out of trouble. I already knew the coach, Mr. Chiappetta, because he was my social studies teacher.

As a ninth- and tenth-grader, I volunteered to help Chia with his chess team at Intermediate School 90 on West 168th Street. During these years, I matured. I learned how to present myself in a positive way: taking off my hat inside buildings, judging when it was appropriate to make jokes (I had to learn this lesson a few times), and knowing how to speak in certain situations.

At one tournament I learned an important lesson from Chia. It was the last round of the U.S. Amateur Team East. I was playing for a top prize and was nervous. In the middle of the game I found a winning combination and I began to slam the pieces out of happiness. Then a big hand stopped the game clock and pulled me away. It was Chia. I could tell that he was angry, but I did not realize what I had done wrong. We talked

Teaching Chess, and Life **97**

Teaching Chess, and Life **97**

Ⓐ Reading Skills

Elaborate. [Possible response to question 1: Answers will vary. Many of your students may have done some mentoring, either formally in a school or community program or informally with a younger sibling or friend. Encourage students to elaborate on these experiences before they compare their feelings to those of Carlos.]

Ⓑ Reading Skills

Evaluate. [Possible response to question 2: Chia's mentorship had a beneficial effect on Carlos. Chia exposed Carlos to new ways of thinking, taught him sportsmanship and responsibility, and encouraged him to become a mentor himself. Without this support, Carlos might have become involved in gangs or crime.]

Ⓒ Reading Informational Text

❓ Extending ideas. Analyze the author's position on community service. Is it favorable or unfavorable? [The author clearly views community service favorably because he lists many positive outcomes of such work.]

Ⓓ Reading Informational Text

❓ Extending ideas. What will the author need to include to back up this assertion? [To be convincing, the author will have to provide examples and/or statistics.] **What do you think the author's purpose is for including this assertion?** [Possible response: The author is trying to persuade young people to believe that there must be something good about community service if so many others are doing it.]

---

about the meaning of sportsmanship. I apologized for my rudeness to my opponent and forfeited the game. I didn't win a prize.

With Chia's <u>mentorship</u>, I learned from my mistake. As a coach at I.S. 90, I've had to teach the same lesson to others. It makes me feel good about myself because I like helping the younger kids learn the game Chia taught me to love. ❶

Chia left I.S. 90 the year I became an eleventh-grader. He recommended me as an assistant chess coach, for which I am paid. This is my second year at I.S. 90 as an assistant coach. My responsibilities include teaching chess strategies and tactics three days a

> **❶ ELABORATE**
> Have you ever helped or taught a younger person? Were your feelings about the experience similar to Carlos's? Explain.

week. I also chaperone the team at tournaments almost every weekend.

All of this would not have been possible if not for Mr. Chiappetta. He turned me to chess and kept me involved. He gave me the opportunity to earn money doing something I love. Chess has kept me off the streets. It has challenged me and taught me to think in new ways. Because of chess, I was recently honored by the *Daily News* as one of the "21 New Yorkers to Watch in the 21st Century." Chess has made me a mentor to younger students, giving me the chance to become their Chia. ❷

> **❷ EVALUATE**
> How would you evaluate the impact Chia had on Carlos's life?

Vocabulary
mentorship (men'tər·ship) *n.:* advice or lessons from a mentor, or wise teacher.

SECONDARY SOURCE   MAGAZINE ARTICLE

Community Service & You

from *Career World,* September 1998

T. J. Saftner

Imagine you read the following help-wanted ad in your local newspaper:

Change the World Around You! Individual required to help out at nonprofit organization. No experience necessary. Interesting work with excellent benefit package. Short workweek and flexible hours.

Would you apply? What if the ad also said, "Must be willing to work without pay"? Before you say "No way!" consider this:

Last weekend, millions of Americans worked at soup kitchens, shelters, playgrounds, museums, prisons, and schools— and they didn't earn a cent. But they didn't go home empty-handed either. What these people received for their contribution wasn't money—according to a survey by Independent Sector—but a chance to learn new skills, prove their reliability, demonstrate their creativity, and build their self-esteem.

Record numbers of young people are getting involved in community service to gain a sense of belonging in their community, to foster personal development, and to help do all that needs to be done in today's world—

DIFFERENTIATING INSTRUCTION

Advanced Learners
Enrichment. After students have read the three selections, use the following questions to prompt a discussion on primary and secondary sources:

- Which article did you find most believable?
- Which article inspires you most to perform community service work?
- In general, do you find material presented in primary or secondary sources more compelling?

Pilots and volunteers unload food and supplies for the city of Watsonville, California, after the Loma Prieta earthquake.

from tutoring young readers, to building houses, to working at a blood drive.

Making a Difference

Volunteering can sound a little intimidating when you're a teenager. But look what's going on *already* in youth volunteerism:

Youth Service America is an alliance of organizations committed to community and national service whose goal is to "encourage the vitality, creativity, and goodwill of young people."

In 1995, Youth Service America joined basketball star Chris Webber and 1,000 young people in a massive river-cleanup project. In 1996, Youth Service America worked with four local nonprofit organizations to help construct playgrounds in Atlanta, Denver, Minneapolis, and Philadelphia.

Though these and many other events have attracted media attention, millions of young people volunteer without being recognized in the media for their efforts. Why do they do it?

Stephanie Star, a senior at Highland Park High School in the Chicago area, says, "It just feels good. You get a lot out of helping other people." Stephanie volunteers at a battered

women's shelter. She spends one evening a month at the shelter, serving dinner and talking to the women.

Not only can you make a contribution to your community and make a difference in someone's life, you can learn new skills, network° for future job contacts, and gain some valuable experience—all of which can help you in your future endeavors. Stephanie says her experience has helped to broaden her understanding of different kinds of people as well as social issues.

Making a Move

Volunteering can be a long-term commitment or an afternoon event. There are many areas available for community service: churches, soup kitchens, shelters, schools, the environment, politics, and lots more. You might be phoning, organizing, cooking, working with the young or the old. Whatever you do, it will most certainly affect someone's life. Who knows . . . it might even be your own. ●

> **● ANALYZE**
> Who is the author's **audience**? What is the author's **purpose** in writing this article?

° **network** *v.:* meet people or share information, often to advance a career.

Vocabulary
intimidating (in·tim′ə·dāt′iŋ) *v.* used as *adj.:* frightening.
endeavors (en·dev′ərz) *n.:* serious attempts, efforts, or undertakings.

Community Service & You **99**

A Reading Informational Text

? Primary and secondary sources. For this article to be a primary source, by whom would it have to be written? [David Levitt]

B English-Language Learners

Building background knowledge. Have students read the footnote for "liability lawsuits." Then, provide examples of liability lawsuits, such as those filed in the past against tobacco companies, to broaden student understanding. Ask students why school districts might be concerned about liability when donating cafeteria leftovers to shelters and food banks. [Possible response: If someone becomes sick from eating the leftover food, that person might sue the school district that donated it.]

C Reading Skills

Analyze. [Possible response to question: *Facts*—the surplus food program has sent more than a quarter-million pounds of leftovers; Levitt was singled out for praise by President Clinton; Kentucky Harvest funnels leftovers to charity. *Opinions*—Levitt's bill is a "no-brainer"; a nation shouldn't toss food into the garbage.]

SECONDARY SOURCE

MAGAZINE ARTICLE

Feeding Frenzy

from *People*, June 2, 1997

Peter Ames Carlin *and* Don Sider

A When 15-year-old David Levitt makes his weekly appearance at the Haven of Rest food bank in Pinellas Park, Florida, he is greeted as a good Samaritan.[1]

No one knows better than Levitt how to get food to the hungry. Since 1994 the surplus food-sharing program he designed as an 11-year-old for the Pinellas County public schools has sent more than a quarter-million pounds of cafeteria leftovers to the county's shelters and food banks. Singled out for praise last year by President Clinton, Levitt, a freshman at Seminole High, is currently backing state legislation to protect donors of **B** surplus food from liability lawsuits.[2] "It's a no-brainer," says State Representative Dennis Jones, who is shepherding Levitt's bill toward certain passage when the state legislature meets next spring. "You wonder why it's taken so long for someone to do it."

The same question crossed Levitt's mind in 1993, when he first read about Kentucky Harvest, a nonprofit organization that funnels leftover food from restaurants and other businesses to charities. He was only a sixth-grader, but Levitt understood that a nation that regularly sends 30 million people to bed hungry shouldn't toss nearly 20 percent of its edible food into the garbage.

Buttonholing[3] Osceola Middle School principal Fred Ulrich outside class one day, he asked if he could start a Harvest program using cafeteria leftovers. "I figured he didn't know me," says Levitt, "so he couldn't be mean." ●

● ANALYZE List three **facts** in the previous two paragraphs. Then, find two **opinions**.

Ulrich wasn't mean. He was merely realistic, pointing out that district health regulations prohibited using previously served food. ("Red tape,[4] red tape," Levitt sighs.) But, encouraged by his mother, Sandy, Levitt attended a Pinellas County school-board meeting and made his case for a local Harvest program. He not only won the board's approval but a spontaneous ovation to boot.

The board's approval, alas, merely gained him entrance to the bureaucratic maze. Next he had to contend with state health-department rules governing the handling of secondhand food. For a time it seemed that packaging requirements would doom the program—the state demanded specific containers, and the schools had no money to

---

1. **good Samaritan** *n.:* person who unselfishly helps others. The term comes from a Bible parable (Luke 10:30–37).
2. **liability lawsuits:** legal actions brought against a person or group to make up for loss or damage that has occurred.

3. **buttonholing** *v.* used as *adj.:* speaking intently with another person, often in an attempt to persuade him or her to do something.
4. **red tape** *n.:* complicated official forms and regulations.

Vocabulary
legislation (lej′is·lā′shən) *n.:* law or body of laws.
bureaucratic (byoor′ə·krat′ik) *adj.:* relating to rigid government routine.

pay for them. Undaunted, Levitt wrote to a major corporation, which promptly shipped eight cases of plastic bags to his doorstep, and on November 8, 1994, Levitt helped make the school's first delivery: cartons of milk and bags of salad for Haven of Rest. *"That,"* he says, "was satisfaction."

The younger child (sister Jamie is 18) of Sandy Levitt, a bookkeeper, and her husband, Rich, vice president of a medical-supply company, Levitt grew up in Seminole, a suburb of St. Petersburg, earning A's and B's in school and playing volleyball and a handful of musical instruments. "David's a typical teenager," notes his mother. Eventually he would like to attend the U.S. Air Force Academy and learn to fly. "That's today," he says. "Call me tomorrow—I might change."

What doesn't change is his ability to make things happen. And while he's fortunate to have a mother who helps push his projects along (Sandy is "the silent driving force," according to her husband), Levitt's energy has won him plenty of fans. "David has drawn attention to hunger and the availability of food in the community," says Mary Dowdell, director of Tampa Bay Harvest. Adds Stan

Curtis, the Kentucky stockbroker who started the first Harvest program: "Any parent in America would be glad to have him as a son."

Including the First Dad,[5] who invited Levitt to the White House last spring as part of a Points of Light ceremony.[6] Taking his medal from Hillary Rodham Clinton, Levitt wasn't shy about pushing his agenda. "What," he asked the First Lady, "do you do with the White House leftovers?"

D

---

5. **First Dad:** the president, if he has children; in this case, President Clinton.
6. **Points of Light ceremony:** awards ceremony sponsored by the Points of Light Foundation to honor people who have performed outstanding community service. The foundation, begun in 1990, took its name from a phrase used by former president George Herbert Walker Bush to describe private acts of goodwill: "a thousand points of light."

Vocabulary
undaunted (un·dôn′tid) *adj.:* not discouraged by a difficulty or setback.

David Levitt gathers bread for his Harvest program.

Analyzing Informational Text

Reading Check

1. Carlos learned to show good sportsmanship.

2. Possible answers: learning new skills, building self-esteem, gaining a sense of community belonging, or gaining valuable experience.

3. David Levitt was inspired to start his Harvest program by reading about a similar program called Kentucky Harvest, which donates food from restaurants to local charities.

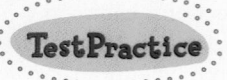

Answers and Model Rationales

1. **A** Students should realize that Carlos uses a mixture of opinions and facts. Students should realize that D is untrue and that C is self-contradictory, since by definition, facts are verifiable.

2. **F** Primary sources are firsthand accounts. Clearly F is the only choice that does not rely on the observations of a third party.

3. **C** D is a specific fact from the article, not the main idea. A may be true, but it is not the main idea. While regulations hinder Levitt, they are not presented as purposeless so B cannot be correct. Only C expresses the main idea.

4. **H** "Feeding Frenzy" describes numerous difficulties that Levitt faced so H is clearly correct. The ideas in F, G, and J do not concern obstacles to doing community service.

Test-Taking Tips

For more information on how to answer multiple-choice questions, refer students to **Test Smarts.**

Analyzing Informational Text

Reading Check

1. In "Teaching Chess, and Life," what lesson did Carlos Capellan learn after he slammed his chess pieces down during a tournament?

2. Give examples of how young people can benefit from doing volunteer work, according to "Community Service & You."

3. What motivated David Levitt to develop his food-sharing program, as described in "Feeding Frenzy"?

1. Which of the following statements is the *most* accurate **evaluation** of "Teaching Chess, and Life"?
   A The author uses both fact and opinion to make his point.
   B The author includes only opinions in his article.
   C The author includes facts that can't be checked for accuracy.
   D Because he does not support his point, the author fails to show why Chia has been so influential.

2. If the author of "Community Service & You" wrote a work that was a **primary source** instead of a **secondary source,** the writer would —
   F write only about his or her experience as a volunteer
   G write only about Stephanie Star's experience as a volunteer
   H interview volunteers who constructed playgrounds
   J provide a detailed report about the Independent Sector survey

3. Which sentence *best* expresses the **main idea** of "Feeding Frenzy"?
   A Good deeds should be given public recognition.
   B Many government regulations serve no purpose.
   C A good cause is worth pursuing, even in the face of difficulties.
   D Millions of people in America go to bed hungry.

4. Of the three articles, which gives the *best* picture of the difficulties faced by those who wish to do community service?
   F "Teaching Chess, and Life," because it tells about at-risk young people.
   G "Community Service & You," because it includes the statement "Volunteering can sound a little intimidating when you're a teenager."
   H "Feeding Frenzy," because it describes the obstacles to starting a food-sharing program.
   J "Teaching Chess, and Life," because the author needed Chia's help.

Constructed Response

SKILLS FOCUS

Reading Skills
Use primary and secondary sources.

Elaborate on the benefits of community service, as discussed in these articles, by doing your own original research. Interview someone, recommended by your teacher or a family member, who does volunteer work. Ask the volunteer to explain the benefits of his or her work. Then, use the primary-source information from the interview to extend the ideas presented in the articles. Write one or two paragraphs about the value of community service, and present a report to the class.

Constructed Response

If necessary, guide students in locating an appropriate interview subject. Suggest that students contact community groups that are already active in your school. Ensure that students prepare a list of questions ahead of time before conducting their interviews.

Remind students to practice good listening skills during their interviews. Allowing an interview subject to finish responses uninterrupted will often generate new questions for the interviewer.

Vocabulary Development

Mapping an Unfamiliar Word

PRACTICE 1

Making a word map like the one here, which organizes some ideas about *legislation,* will help you get to know a new word better. Fill out this map for *legislation,* and then make word maps of your own for the other words in the Word Bank. You will have to make up your own questions for each word.

Word Bank
intimidating
endeavors
legislation
bureaucratic
undaunted

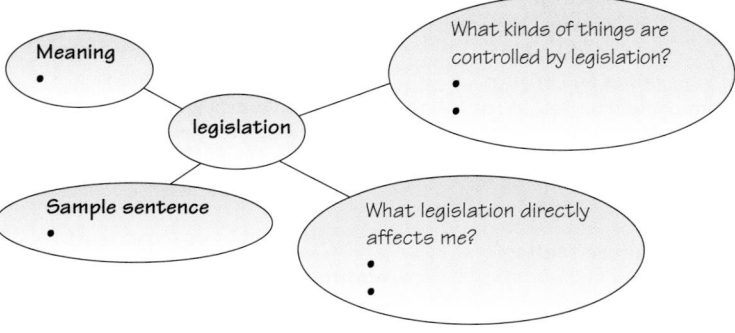

Word Origins: What's in a Word?

In "Teaching Chess, and Life," Carlos Capellan views Mr. Chiappetta as his mentor. The word *mentor,* which means "wise teacher," comes to us courtesy of Greek mythology. In Homer's great epic the *Odyssey* (see page 650), the goddess Athena assumes the form of Mentor and gives advice to Odysseus, Homer's hero, and to Odysseus's young son, Telemachus. Today a mentor is a teacher, a coach, or anyone else who acts as an advisor to other people.

Word Bank
mentorship

PRACTICE 2

Like *mentor,* the following words and phrases from the selections have interesting histories. Investigate the history of each one, and write a sentence or two about its origin and present meaning. To start, you may consult each selection's footnotes, but you will need to do your own research using a dictionary or other reference sources.

tournament	chaperone	good Samaritan
buttonholing	red tape	

Vocabulary Skills
Create word maps. Understand word origins.

Practice 1

Student word maps will vary.

Sample Answer

- *legislation. What kinds of things are controlled by legislation?*—the voting process, tax rates. *What legislation directly affects me?*—youth labor laws, helmet laws. *Sample sentence*—The governor hoped that his new legislation would be approved. *Meaning*—laws.

Practice 2

Possible Answers

- *Tournament,* which means "contest" today, finds its origins in the Middle Ages. Knights on horseback would participate in jousting contests, in which they would try to unseat their opponents.
- *Chaperone* comes from a French word for head covering. As a hat or hood accompanies or protects the head, a chaperone would serve to accompany and protect a younger person.
- *Good Samaritan* comes from the New Testament parable of a compassionate Samaritan (person from Samaria) who aids an injured man ignored by others.
- *Buttonholing* derives from the fact that garments of centuries past had buttons up the neck. To force someone to listen, one might grab another by the buttonholes.
- *Red tape* comes from the old bureaucratic practice of tying files together with red tape. To get to a needed file, a person would literally have to cut through the red tape.

ASSESSING

Assessment

- *Holt Assessment: Literature, Reading, and Vocabulary*

RETEACHING

For a lesson reteaching analyzing and elaborating on ideas, see **Reteaching,** p. 979A. For another selection to teach primary and secondary resources, see *The Holt Reader,* Part 2.

Grade-Level Skills

■ **Literary Skills**
Determine characters' traits by what the characters say about themselves.

■ **Reading Skills**
Understand allusions.

Review Skills

■ **Literary Skills**
Analyze the methods writers use to reveal character.

Summary ⬆ *above grade level*

Vita, the narrator, lives in an apartment with her mother. Vita deeply misses her father, who left them, and writes letters to him that she never sends. At school her class is staging a production of the story of Helen of Troy. Vita longs to play Helen, and envies Helen McGuire, who has the role. One day, remembering what her mother told her about ancient Greek sacrifices to the goddess Athena, Vita burns the letters to her father while chanting Greek words and asking Athena for the role of Helen, the return of her father, and the departure of her mother's boyfriend, Old Farfel. When Helen McGuire gets sick, Vita gets the role and believes that her ceremony caused the events to happen. When her mother stops seeing Farfel, Vita expects her father to appear the night of the play. When Vita delivers her climactic speech as Helen at the end of the play, she inserts a quiet, powerful goodbye that we know she means for her father. Vita discovers that sometimes you simply must accept a loss.

Before You Read

Helen on Eighty-sixth Street

Make the Connection

Quickwrite 🖉

We all have hopes and dreams. Some come true, some don't. What happens when our wishes don't come true, when we have to accept a loss or when we are disappointed in love or friendship? Jot down some of your hopes and dreams. Have any of them come true yet? What do these hopes and dreams tell you about yourself?

Literary Focus

Determining Character Traits: Got to Be Me

When characters tell their own stories, they also tell you a lot about their **character traits**—their personalities, values, likes, and dislikes. In "Helen on Eighty-sixth Street," the narrator, Vita, announces right off the bat, "I hate Helen. That's all I can say." While this statement reveals that Vita and Helen are not friends, Vita's forceful way of talking also tells you that she is outspoken and that she has strong feelings. As you read Vita's narration, determine more of her character traits, both from what she says and from the way she says it.

Reading Skills 📖

Understanding Allusions

Allusions are references to features of a culture—for example, to literature and history—that writers expect their readers to recognize. The writer of this story frequently alludes to Greek mythology.

INTERNET
Vocabulary Practice
Keyword: LE5 9-2

SKILLS FOCUS

Literary Skills
Determine character traits from what characters say about themselves.

Reading Skills
Understand allusions.

You may have already read some myths; in this textbook you'll find stories from the Greek epic the *Odyssey* (page 650). For more help with allusions, you can consult these resources in this text:

• A Closer Look, page 107
• the story's footnotes, pages 106–111

Don't get bogged down identifying allusions. Sometimes you can just guess what a name or event refers to by looking at the context clues.

Vocabulary Development

embodies (em·bäd′ēz) *v.*: conveys the impression of; represents.

odyssey (äd′i·sē) *n.*: extended journey marked by wandering, adventure, and changes of fortune.

litany (lit′′n·ē) *n.*: repetitive prayer or recitation.

incantation (in′kan·tā′shən) *n.*: chant of words or phrases that is meant to produce a magical result.

stifled (stī′fəld) *v.* used as *adj.*: smothered.

scourge (skʉrj) *n.*: cause of serious trouble or great suffering.

polytheism (päl′i·thē·iz′əm) *n.*: belief in more than one god.

ramparts (ram′pärts′) *n.*: broad embankments surrounding a castle, fort, or city for defense against attack.

supplication (sup′lə·kā′shən) *n.*: humble plea or request.

enunciate (ē·nun′sē·āt′) *v.*: pronounce; articulate.

104 Collection 2   Character • Using Primary and Secondary Sources

HELEN ON EIGHTY-SIXTH STREET

Wendi Kaufman

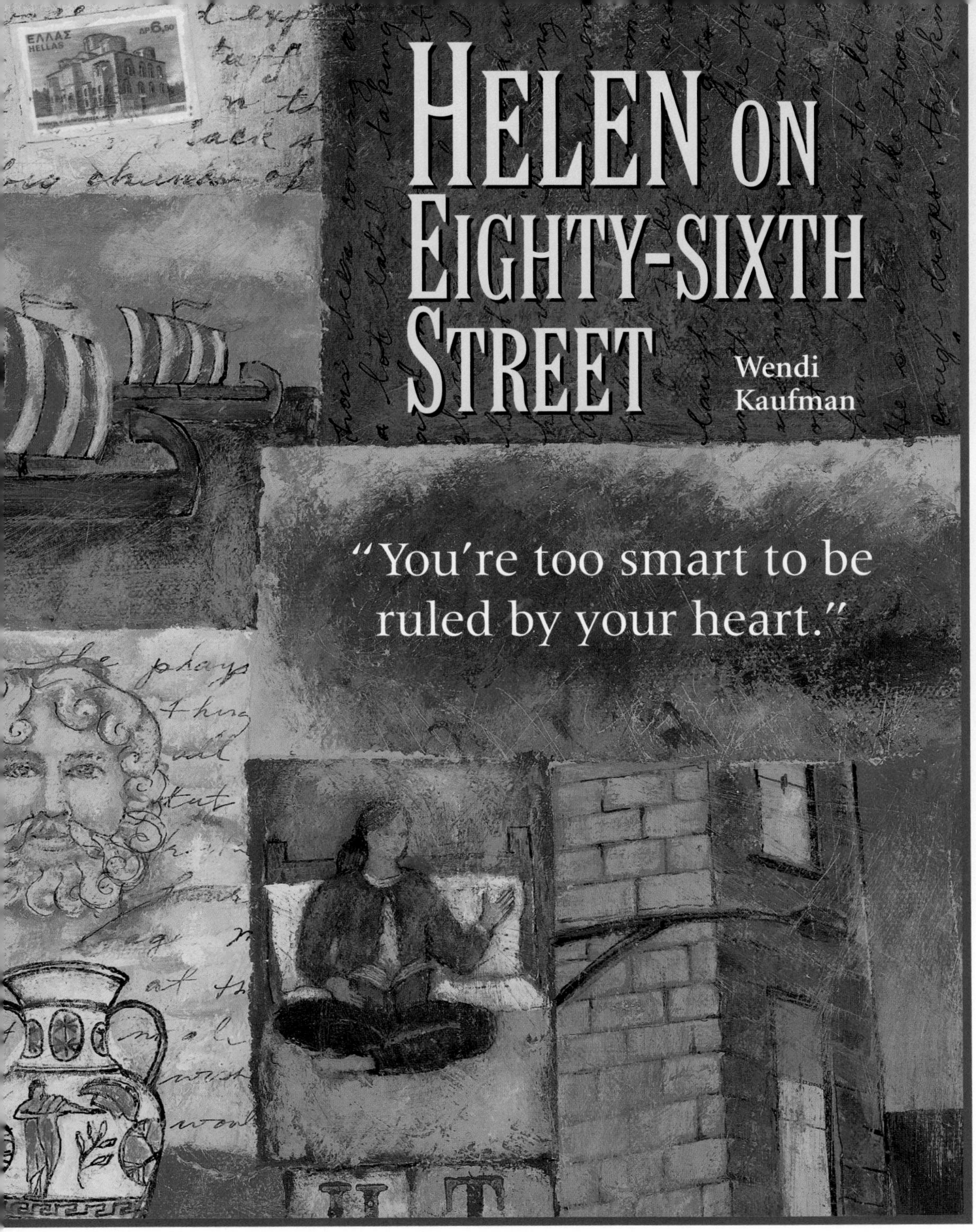

"You're too smart to be ruled by your heart."

- *One-Stop Planner* CD-ROM with ExamView Test Generator
- *Holt Online Assessment*

Internet
- go.hrw.com (Keyword: LE5 9-2)
- *Elements of Literature Online*

Media
- *Audio CD Library*
- *Audio CD Library, Selections and Summaries in Spanish*

Skills Starter

Motivate. Point out to students that as readers our first impression of a character is often an important one, just as is a first impression of a new acquaintance in real life. Ask students to focus on the kind of first impression that Vita makes upon them early in the story. Encourage them to examine the ways in which the author manages to produce this impression.

Preview Vocabulary

Use this activity to build understanding of the Vocabulary words on p. 104. Have students match each word in the lettered list with the correct set in the numbered list. Tell students that some sets offer synonyms for a Vocabulary word, while others use the same derivation as a Vocabulary word.

1. cantor, chant [c]
2. journey, quest [e]
3. theology [f]
4. bodily, bodiless [a]
5. announce [b]
6. psalm [d]
7. suppliant [j]
8. afflict, chastise [h]
9. fort, embankment [g]
10. muffled, suffocated [i]

a. embodies
b. enunciate
c. incantation
d. litany
e. odyssey
f. polytheism
g. ramparts
h. scourge
i. stifled
j. supplication

Assign the Reading

You may wish to assign the entire selection as homework to more advanced readers. Other students may benefit from reading and discussing A Closer Look, "The Beautiful Helen," in class, before moving on to the selection.

A Literary Focus

? Character traits. What method of characterization reveals the narrator's character traits? [Possible response: These traits are revealed through one form of indirect characterization—the first-person narrator reveals her feelings directly to the reader.]

B Reading Skills

Understanding allusions. Have students note this first example of allusion and the corresponding explanatory footnote. Demonstrate how students could use context clues to understand the allusion's significance: Vita's mother makes her remark in response to the news that Vita will not play Helen of Troy, so students could assume the quotation from Christopher Marlowe concerns Helen's beauty.

C Learners Having Difficulty

? Monitoring students' progress. How does reading the A Closer Look feature help you understand the content of this paragraph about Troy? [Possible response: The resource explains what the speaker means by being "in the horse." It also helps identify some of the Trojan characters she mentions.]

D Literary Focus

? Character. How can you tell that the narrator's mother is well acquainted with literature? [Earlier Helen of Troy triggered a literary allusion, and their cat is named for the English playwright who wrote the line that Vita's mother quotes. The *Odyssey* is a Greek epic by Homer. Their parakeets are named for the famous poet John Keats.]

A I hate Helen. That's all I can say. I hate her. Helen McGuire is playing Helen, so Mr. Dodd says, because, out of the entire sixth grade, she most embodies Helen of Troy. Great. Helen McGuire had no idea who Helen of Troy even was! When she found out, well, you should have seen her—flirting with all the boys, really acting the part. And me? Well, I know who Helen was. I am unhappy.

B My mother doesn't understand. Not that I expected she would. When I told her the news, all she said was "Ah, the face that launched a thousand ships." She didn't even look up from her book. Later, at dinner, she apologized for quoting Marlowe. Marlowe is our cat.[1]

At bedtime I told my mother, "You should have seen the way Helen acted at school. It was disgusting, flirting with the boys."

Mom tucked the sheets up close around my chin, so that only my head was showing, my body covered mummy style. "Vita," she said, "it sounds like she's perfect for the part."

C So, I can't play Helen. But, to make it worse, Mr. Dodd said I have to be in the horse. I can't believe it. The horse! I wanted to be one of the Trojan women—Andromache, Cassandra, or even Hecuba. I know all their names. I told Mr. Dodd this, and then I showed him I could act. I got really sad and cried out about the thought of the body of my husband, Hector, being dragged around the walls of my city. I wailed and beat my fist against my chest. "A regular Sarah Heartburn"[2] was all he said.

"Well, at least you get to be on the winning team," my mother said when I told her about the horse. This didn't make me feel any better.

---

1. **Marlowe:** The cat is named after Christopher Marlowe (1564–1593), an English dramatist. "The face that launched a thousand ships" is from one of Marlowe's plays and alludes to the Greek army's pursuit of Helen of Troy.
2. **Sarah Heartburn:** humorous reference to Sarah Bernhardt (1844–1923), a French actress known for her emotional style.

"It's better than being Helen. It's better than being blamed for the war," she told me.

Mom was helping me make a shield for my costume. She said every soldier had a shield that was big enough to carry his body off the field. I told her I wasn't going to be a body on the field, that I was going to survive, return home.

"Bring the shield, just in case," she said. "It never hurts to have a little help."

Mom and I live on West Eighty-sixth Street. We have lived in the same building, in the same apartment, my entire life. My father has been gone for almost three years. The truth is that he got struck with the wanderlust—emphasis on "lust," my mother says—and we haven't heard from him since.

D "Your father's on his own odyssey," my mother said. And now it's just me and Mom and Marlowe and the Keatses, John and John,[3] our parakeets, or "pair of Keats," as Mom says. When I was younger, when Dad first left and I still believed he was coming back, it made me happy that we still lived in the same building. I was happy because he would always know where to find us. Now that I am older, I know the city is not that big. It is easy to be found and easy to stay lost.

And I also know not to ask about him. Sometimes Mom hears things through old friends—that he has traveled across the ocean, that he is living on an island in a commune

---

3. **Keatses, John and John:** The parakeets are named after the English Romantic poet John Keats (1795–1821).

Vocabulary

embodies (em·bäd′ēz) *v.:* conveys the impression of; represents.

odyssey (äd′i·sē) *n.:* extended journey marked by wandering, adventure, and changes of fortune.

DIFFERENTIATING INSTRUCTION

Learners Having Difficulty
To help students read "Helen on Eighty-sixth Street," discuss the reading skill of understanding allusions. Note places where you would look for help in trying to understand an allusion, such as a dictionary, footnotes, or other explanatory material accompanying a text. Reassure students that it is not necessary to know everything about a particular allusion. Instead, students should just try to understand the central point of the reference. They should ask themselves, "Why did the author use this allusion here?"

with some people she called "the lotus-eaters,"[4] that he misses us.

Once I heard Mr. Farfel, the man who's hanging around Mom now, ask why she stayed in this apartment after my father left. "The rent's stabilized,"[5] she told him, "even if the relationship wasn't."

At school, Helen McGuire was acting weird because I'm going to be in the horse with Tommy Aldridge. She wanted to know what it's like: "Is it really cramped in there? Do you have to sit real close together?"

I told her it's dark, and we must hold each other around the waist and walk to make the horse move forward. Her eyes grew wide at this description. "Lucky you," she said.

Lucky me? She gets to stand in the center of the stage alone, her white sheet barely reaching the middle of her thighs, and say lines like "This destruction is all my fault" and "Paris, I do love you." She gets to cry. Why would she think I'm lucky? The other day at rehearsal, she was standing onstage waiting for her cue, and I heard Mrs. Reardon, the stage manager, whisper, "That Helen is as beautiful as a statue."

At home Old Farfel is visiting again. He has a chair in Mom's department.[6] The way she describes it, a chair is a very good thing. Mom translates old books written in Greek and Latin. She is working on the longest graduate degree in the history of Columbia University. "I'll be dead before I finish," she always says.

4. **lotus-eaters** *n.:* in the *Odyssey,* people who eat the fruit of the lotus tree, a sort of drug, which causes them to forget forever their homes and families. The Greek soldier Odysseus enters the land of the Lotus Eaters on his journey home from the Trojan War. (See page 658.)

5. **rent's stabilized:** In New York City, rent stabilization is a form of government-controlled rent regulation. Rent-stabilized apartments are less expensive than other types and are therefore much sought after.

6. **chair in Mom's department:** A chair is an important teaching position at a university.

A CLOSER LOOK

The Beautiful Helen

According to Greek mythology, the god Zeus fell in love with Leda, a mortal woman, and visited her in the form of a swan. Their daughter Helen grew up to be the most beautiful woman on earth. Helen married Menelaus, king of Sparta, but Paris, a handsome young prince, fell in love with her and ran away with her to Troy, his kingdom in Asia Minor. Helen's husband, Menelaus, banded together with other Greek kings and warriors under the leadership of his brother, Agamemnon. They sailed to Troy in a thousand ships to fetch Helen home.

For ten long years the Greeks camped outside the walls of Troy, but they were unable to break down the thick walls of the city. Finally the Greeks tricked the Trojans. They built a huge wooden horse with a hollow belly and hid some soldiers in it. They left the horse on the beach at Troy and pretended to sail away. The Trojans thought that the Greeks had at last retreated and had left the horse as a gift. They wheeled the huge horse into their city. That night the Greeks crept out of the horse, opened the city gate to their comrades, and slaughtered the Trojans. The old king, Priam, was killed. The Trojan women, including Queen Hecuba and her daughter Cassandra, were dragged into slavery. The queen of Troy had already seen her beloved son Hector killed by Achilles, his bleeding body dragged three times in the dust around the walls of the city.

In "Helen on Eighty-sixth Street," a class reenacts the tale of the beautiful Helen of Troy.

DIRECT TEACHING

E Reading Skills

Making inferences. Why does Helen McGuire say, "Lucky you"? [Helen is attracted to Tommy Aldridge.] **Vita doesn't understand Helen McGuire's behavior. Because of this, what can you infer about her?** [Possible responses: She is not yet interested in boys; she is young and naive.]

A CLOSER LOOK

The daughter of the Greek god Zeus and the mortal woman Leda, Helen of Troy was considered the most beautiful woman on earth. Swept away from her husband to Troy by the handsome prince Paris, Helen became the cause of one of the most legendary battles—and tales—in the history of Western civilization.

English-Language Learners

Help students understand the story's many allusive puns by pronouncing the words in question aloud. For instance, the phrase "pair of Keats" (p. 106) is used to suggest a second word, "parakeets" (p. 106), which sounds similar.

Special Education Students

For lessons designed for special education students and English-language learners, see *Holt Reading Solutions.*

Advanced Learners

Acceleration. Use the following activity with advanced students to help them understand archetypes. Ask students to discuss ways in which Helen of Troy serves as an archetype for an ideal woman of beauty and for the catalyst for war and great destruction. Encourage students to identify modern examples of this archetype from literature and film.

Literature: Shakespearean Allusions

Farfel combines two Shakespearean allusions: "The play's the thing" is from *Hamlet* (Act II, Scene 2), and "Life's but a walking shadow, a poor player / That struts and frets his hour upon the stage" is from *Macbeth* (Act V, Scene 5). Point out to students that the narrator is upset by the fact that her mother appreciates Farfel's literary allusions.

B **Learners Having Difficulty**

Breaking down difficult text. Help students work through this passage until they understand what Vita means by "spinning Argus": Her mother is twirling a vase that contains the ashes of the family dog.

Old Farfel has been coming around a lot lately, taking Mom and me to dinner at Italian places downtown. I don't like to be around when he's over.

"I'm going to Agamemnon's apartment to rehearse," I told Mom.

Old Farfel made a small laugh, one that gets caught in the back of the throat and never really makes it out whole. I want to tell him to relax, to let it out. He smells like those dark cough drops, the kind that make your eyes tear and your head feel like it's expanding. I don't know how she can stand him.

"Well, the play's the *thing*," Old Farfel said. "We're all just players strutting and fretting our hour on the stage."[7] Mom smiled at this, and it made me wish Old Farfel would strut his hours at his apartment and not at our place. I hate the way he's beginning to come around all the time.

When I get back from rehearsal, Mom is spinning Argus.[8] It's what she does when she gets into one of her moods. Argus, our dog, died last summer when I was away at camp. My mother can't stand to part with anything, so she keeps Argus, at least his ashes, in a blue-and-white vase that sits on our mantel.

Once I looked into the vase. I'd expected to see gray stuff, like the ash at the end of a cigarette. Instead, there was black sand and big chunks of pink like shells, just like at the beach.

My mother had the vase down from the mantel and was twirling it in her hands. I watched

---

7. **Well, the play's . . . on the stage:** references to lines in Shakespeare's plays *Hamlet* and *Macbeth*.

8. **Argus:** Odysseus's old dog. When Odysseus returns home after twenty years, Argus is the only one who recognizes him. (See page 694.)

DEVELOPING FLUENCY

Mixed-ability group activity. Students of different abilities can help each other understand this wryly humorous, richly allusive story. Divide the class into groups of four or five students for reciprocal teaching. One student reads aloud until any group member poses a comment or asks a question. The group stops to respond to the comment or answer the question. Another student in the group then reads aloud until a comment is offered or a question is raised, and so on.

Before assigning the entire class to reciprocal teaching groups, it's a good idea to model the technique with a selected group of students. Use the activity with the first three pages of the story or until readers become accustomed to the writer's style and to checking the footnotes to resolve some questions.

the white figures on it turn, following each other, running in a race that never ends.

"Life is a cycle," my mother said. The spinning made me dizzy. I didn't want to talk about life. I wanted to talk about Helen.

"Helen, again with Helen. Always Helen," my mother said. "You want to know about Helen?"

I nod my head.

"Well, her father was a swan and her mother was too young to have children. You don't want to be Helen. Be lucky you're a warrior. You're too smart to be ruled by your heart."

"And what about beauty? Wasn't she the most beautiful woman in the world?" I asked.

Mom looked at the Greek vase. "Beauty is truth, truth beauty—that is all ye need to know."[9]

She is not always helpful.

"Manhattan is a rocky island," Mom said at dinner. "There is no proper beach, no shore." My mother grew up in the South, near the ocean, and there are times when she still misses the beach. Jones, Brighton, or even Coney Island beaches don't come close for her. I know when she starts talking about the water that she's getting restless. I hope this means that Old Farfel won't be hanging around too long.

Every night I write a letter to my father. I don't send them—I don't know where to send them—but, still, I write them. I keep the letters at the back of my closet in old shoe boxes. I am on my third box. It's getting so full that I have to keep the lid tied down with rubber bands.

I want to write "Mom is talking about the water again. I think this means she is thinking of you. We are both thinking of you, though we don't mention your name. Are you thinking of us? Do you ever sit on the shore at night and wonder what we're doing, what we're thinking? Do you miss us as much as we miss you?"

9. **Beauty is truth . . . know:** The last two lines of Keats's poem "Ode on a Grecian Urn" are "'Beauty is truth, truth beauty'—that is all / Ye know on earth, and all ye need to know."

But instead I write, "I am in a play about the Trojan War. I get to wear a short white tunic, and I ambush people from inside a big fake horse. Even though we win the war, it will be many, many years before I return home. Until I see my family again. In this way, we are the same. I will have many adventures. I will meet giants and witches and see strange lands. Is that what you are doing? I wish you could come to the play."

Old Farfel is going to a convention in Atlanta. He wants Mom to go with him. From my bed, I can hear them talking about it in the living room. It would be good for her, he says. I know that Mom doesn't like to travel. She can't even go to school and back without worrying about the apartment—if she turned the gas off, if she fed the cat, if she left me enough money. She tells him that she'll think about it.

"You have to move on, Victoria," he tells her. "Let yourself go to new places."

"I'm still exploring the old places," she says.

He lets the conversation drop.

Mom said once that she traveled inside herself when Dad left. I didn't really understand, but it was one of the few times I saw her upset. She was sitting in her chair, at her desk, looking tired. "Mom, are you in there?" I waved my hand by her face.

"I'm not," she said. "I'm on new ground. It's a very different place."

"Are you thinking about Dad?"

"I was thinking how we all travel differently, Vita. Some of us don't even have to leave the house."

"Dad left the house."

"Sometimes it's easier to look outside than in," she said.

That night I dreamed about a swan. A swan that flies in circles over the ocean. This is not the dark water that snakes along the West Side Highway and slaps against the banks of New Jersey but the real ocean. Open water. Salty, like tears.

C Reading Skills

❓ Comparing and contrasting. Compare and contrast the kind of letter Vita *wants* to write to her father with the one she actually *does* write. How are they different? [The first focuses on her feelings; the second lists what's happening in school.] **How are they similar?** [In both, Vita tries to connect with her father by asking him questions that relate his experiences to hers and her mother's. In both she says she wishes to see him.]

D Literary Focus

❓ Character traits. What does this passage add to what you already know about Vita's mother? [Her name is Victoria; she doesn't like to travel, and she worries about things at home when she's away.]

E Advanced Learners

❓ Enrichment. How does Vita's mother, Victoria, convert the concept of traveling into a metaphor? [She speaks of traveling as a mental activity and uses it as a metaphor for the direction one takes in life.] **When Victoria says that sometimes it's easier to look outside than in, what could she mean?** [Possible response: She means that at times it is easier to look outside for the source of one's problems, rather than to examine one's own behavior. In other words, sometimes it is easier to run away from a problem than to look inward and try to solve it.]

F Reading Skills

❓ Understanding allusions. Who or what does the swan refer to? What resource would help you find out? [The swan refers to the father of Helen of Troy, the Greek god Zeus, who visited Helen's mother, Leda, in the form of a great swan. The resource A Closer Look on p. 107 explains this.]

A **Learners Having Difficulty**

Summarizing. To ensure students understand what is happening, be sure they read the tenth footnote and summarize these paragraphs. [Possible summary: While eating a takeout dinner, Vita looks at the paper cup holding her soup and remembers seeing a similar cup in a coffee shop at an earlier time. At the coffee shop her mother explained that the design on the cup was the Parthenon in Greece, where people once made sacrifices to the goddess Athena. Vita gets an idea looking at the cup, cuts out the little temple, and glues it on her notebook.]

B **Content-Area Connections**

Culture: Greek Cuisine
Explain that spanakopita is a traditional Greek pie made from thin sheets of dough, spinach, and feta cheese. Moussaka (the word comes to us through Greek from Turkish) is a Greek dish of ground meat and sliced eggplant. A gyro is a Greek sandwich of lamb or beef, tomato, and onion stuffed in pita bread.

At play practice, I watch the other girls dress up as goddesses and Trojan women. They wear gold scarves wound tight around their necks and **A** foreheads. They all wear flowers in their hair and flat pink ballet slippers. I wear a white sheet taken from my bed. It is tied around the middle with plain white rope. I also wear white sneakers. I don't get to wear a gold scarf or flowers. Mr. Dodd wrote this play himself and is very picky about details. Tommy Aldridge, my partner in the horse, was sent home because his sheet had Ninja Turtles on it. "They did not have Ninja Turtles in ancient Greece," Mr. Dodd said.

Mr. Dodd helps Helen McGuire with her role. "You must understand," he tells her, "Helen is the star of the show. Men have traveled great distances just to fight for her. At the end, when you come onstage and look at all the damage you've caused, we must believe you're really upset by the thought that this is all your fault."

Helen nods and looks at him blankly.

"Well, at least try to think of something really sad."

Old Farfel is taking Mom out to dinner again. It's the third time this week. Mom says it is a very important dinner, and I am not invited. Not that I would want to go, but I wasn't even asked. Mom brought in takeout, some soup and a cheese sandwich, from the coffee shop on the corner.

I eat my soup, alone in the kitchen, from a blue-and-white paper cup. I remember once at a coffee shop Mom held the same type of cup out in front of me.

"See this building, Vita?" she said. She pointed to some columns that were drawn on the front of her cup. It wasn't really a building—more like a cartoon drawing. "It's the Parthenon,"[10] she said. "It's where the Greeks made sacrifices to Athena."

"How did they make sacrifices?" I asked.

"They burned offerings on an altar. They believed this would bring them what they wanted. Good things. Luck."

I finish my soup and look at the tiny building on the cup. In between the columns are the words "Our Pleasure to Serve You." I run my fingers across the flat lines of the Parthenon and trace the roof. I can almost imagine a tiny altar and the ceremonies that were performed there.

It is then that I get an idea. I find a pair of scissors on Mom's desk and cut through the thick white lip of the cup toward the lines of the little temple. I cut around the words "Our Pleasure to Serve You." Then I take the temple and the words and glue them to the back of my notebook. The blue-and-white lines show clearly against the cardboard backing. I get Argus's big metal water bowl from the kitchen and find some matches from a restaurant Old Farfel took us to for dinner.

In my room I put on my white sheet costume and get all my letters to Dad out from the back of the closet. I know that I must say something, to make this more like a ceremony. I think of any **B** Greek words I know: *spanakopita, moussaka, gyro.* They're only food words, but it doesn't matter. I decide to say them anyway. I say them

---

10. **Parthenon:** temple of Athena, the Greek goddess of wisdom and warfare, who sided with the Greeks during the war. The Parthenon was built in the fifth century B.C.

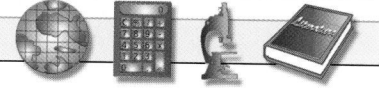

CONTENT-AREA CONNECTIONS

Geography: New York City
At the beginning of the story, Vita tells us that she lives on West Eighty-sixth Street (p. 106); on p. 109, she mentions several locations in the greater New York City metropolitan area.
Individual activity. Have interested students list all the place references in the story and locate a city map that shows these locations and tourist attractions, such as the Statue of Liberty. Have them draw and illustrate a simplified map to be posted in the classroom as a "tour guide" to the story.

Culture: Greek Religious Rituals
The ritual described in "Helen on Eighty-sixth Street" may interest students in learning more about ancient Greek religion.

over and over out loud until they blur into a litany, my own incantation: "Spanakopitamoussakaandgyro, Spanakopitamoussakaandgyro, Spanakopitamoussakaandgyro."

As I say this, I burn handfuls of letters in the bowl. I think about what I want: to be Helen, to have my father come back. Everything I have ever heard says that wishes are granted in threes, so I throw in the hope of Old Farfel's leaving.

I watch as the words burn. Three years of letters go up in smoke and flame. I see blue-lined paper turn to black ashes; I see pages and pages, months and years, burn, crumble, and then disappear. The front of my white sheet has turned black from soot, and my eyes water and burn.

When I am done, I take the full bowl of ashes and hide it in the vase on the mantel, joining it with Argus. My black hands smudge the white figures on the vase until their tunics become as sooty as my own. I change my clothes and open all the windows, but still Mom asks, when she comes home, about the burning smell. I told her I was cooking.

She looked surprised. Neither of us cooks much. "No more burnt offerings when I'm not home," she said. She looked upset and distracted, and Old Farfel didn't give that stifled laugh of his.

It's all my fault. Helen McGuire got chicken pox. Bad. She has been out of school for almost two weeks. I know my burning ceremony did this. "The show must go on," Mr. Dodd said when Achilles threw up the Tater Tots or when Priam's beard got caught in Athena's hair, but this is different. This is Helen. And it's my fault.

I know all her lines. Know them backward and forward. I have stood in our living room, towel tied around my body, and acted out the entire play, saying every line for my mother. When Mr. Dodd made the announcement about Helen at dress rehearsal, I stood up, white bedsheet slipping from my shoulders, and said in a loud, clear voice, "The gods must have envied me my beauty, for now my name is a curse. I have become hated Helen, the scourge of Troy."

Mr. Dodd shook his head and looked very sad. "We'll see, Vita. She might still get better," he said.

Helen McGuire recovered, but she didn't want to do the part because of all the pockmarks that were left. Besides, she wanted to be inside the horse with Tommy Aldridge. Mr. Dodd insisted that she still be Helen until her parents wrote that they didn't want her to be pressured, they didn't want to *do any further damage*, whatever that means. After that, the part was mine.

Tonight is the opening, and I am so excited. Mom is coming without Old Farfel. "He wasn't what I wanted," she said. I don't think she'll be seeing him anymore.

"What is beautiful?" I ask Mom before the play begins.

"Why are you so worried all the time about beauty? Don't you know how beautiful you are to me?"

"Would Daddy think I was beautiful?"

"Oh, Vita, he *always* thought you were beautiful."

"Would he think I was like Helen?"

She looked me up and down, from the gold lanyard[11] snaked through my thick hair to my too tight pink ballet slippers.

"He would think you're more beautiful than Helen. I'm almost sorry he won't be here to see it."

"*Almost* sorry?"

---

11. **lanyard** (lan′yərd) *n.:* here, a decorative cord.

Vocabulary

litany (lit′n·ē) *n.:* repetitive prayer or recitation.

incantation (in′kan·tā′shən) *n.:* chant of words or phrases that is meant to produce a magical result.

stifled (stī′fəld) *v.* used as *adj.:* smothered.

scourge (skʉrj) *n.:* cause of serious trouble or great suffering.

Helen on Eighty-sixth Street **111**

DIRECT TEACHING

C Learners Having Difficulty

? Finding details. What three wishes does Vita make as she burns her letters? [Vita wishes that she will get the part of Helen, that her father will return, and that Old Farfel will leave.]

D Reading Skills

? Understanding allusions. By "burnt offerings," Victoria is alluding to the ancient practice of burning meats and grains and offering them as gifts to the gods. Victoria uses the phrase humorously to refer to Vita's alleged cooking. What is ironically appropriate about her word choice? [She accidentally hits upon what Vita was doing when she sacrificed her letters written to her father for three wishes.]

E Literary Focus

? Character traits. What does this passage indicate about Vita? [Possible response: She feels guilty about Helen's illness, but not guilty enough to give up the possibility of replacing her in the play.]

Small-group activity. Have small groups of students use Internet or text resources to answer questions such as these:

- What were the names and attributes of the major Greek deities?
- What did ancient Greek worshipers ask for or expect?
- What kinds of offerings were considered appropriate?
- Where were ancient Greek rituals held—in fields, homes, or temples?
- Who conducted the ceremonies?

Groups can compile their answers into a fact sheet to be distributed to the class.

Helen on Eighty-sixth Street **111**

A Literary Focus

? Character. Re-read the exchange between Vita and her mother carefully. What discovery is Vita making here? [Vita has been convinced that the old gods still exist and that they can help her get her three wishes. Here with her mother's reminder, Vita is forced to consider that perhaps the gods can't help her, though she persists in hoping that Athena will come through. Vita reasons that since her first two wishes have come true, her third wish—her father's return—will be fulfilled as well.]

B English-Language Learners

Interpreting idioms. Explain to students that "break a leg" is a traditional good-luck wish exchanged by actors. Traditionally actors consider it dangerous to tempt fate by wishing for success, so they make the opposite wish.

C Reading Skills

? Making inferences. What are the hole, the empty pocket, and the absence? [Vita's father is not at the performance.]

D Literary Focus

? Character. Is Vita only saying goodbye to the audience? What change has occurred in Vita? [Possible response: She is saying goodbye to both the people attending the play and her absent father; the farewell marks Vita's acceptance of the loss of her father in her life.]

"Almost. At moments like this—you look so good those ancient gods are going to come alive again with envy."

"What do you mean, come alive again? What are you saying about the gods?"

"Vita, Greek polytheism is an extinct belief," she said, and laughed. And then she stopped and looked at me strangely. "When people stopped believing in the gods, they no longer had power. They don't exist anymore. You must have known that."

A Didn't I get the part of Helen? Didn't Old Farfel leave? I made all these things happen with my offering. I know I did. I don't believe these gods disappeared. At least not Athena.

"I don't believe you."

She looked at me, confused.

"You can't know for sure about the gods. And who knows? Maybe Daddy will even be here to see it."

"Sure," she said. "And maybe this time the Trojans will win the war."

I stand offstage with Mr. Dodd and wait for my final cue. The dry-ice machine has been turned on full blast and an incredible amount of fake smoke is making its way toward the painted backdrop of Troy. Hector's papier-mâché head has accidentally slipped from Achilles' hand and is now making a hollow sound as it rolls across the stage.

I peek around the thick red curtain, trying to see into the audience. The auditorium is packed, filled with parents and camcorders. I spot my mom sitting in the front row, alone. I try to scan the back wall, looking for a sign of him, a familiar shadow. Nothing.

Soon I will walk out on the ramparts, put my hand to my forehead, and give my last speech. "Are you sure you're ready?" Mr. Dodd asks. I think he's more nervous than I am. "Remember," he tells me, "this is Helen's big moment. Think loss." I nod, thinking nothing.

B "Break a leg," he says, giving me a little push toward the stage. "And try not to trip over the head."

The lights are much brighter than I had expected, making me squint. I walk through the smoky fog toward center stage.

"It is I, the hated Helen, scourge of Troy."

With the light on me, the audience is in shadow, like a big pit, dark and endless. I bow before the altar, feeling my tunic rise. "Hear my supplication," I say, pulling down a bit on the back of my tunic.

"Do not envy me such beauty—it has wrought only pain and despair."

I can hear Mr. Dodd, offstage, loudly whispering each line along with me.

"For this destruction, I know I will be blamed."

I begin to recite Helen's wrongs—beauty, pride, the abdication of Sparta—careful to enunciate clearly. "Troy, I have come to ask you to forgive me."

I'm supposed to hit my fist against my chest, draw a hand across my forehead, and cry loudly. Mr. Dodd has shown me this gesture, practiced it with me in rehearsal a dozen times—the last line, my big finish. The audience is very quiet.
C In the stillness there is a hole, an empty pocket, an absence. Instead of kneeling, I stand up, straighten my tunic, look toward the audience, and speak the line softly: "And to say goodbye."

D There is a prickly feeling up the back of my neck. And then applause. The noise surrounds me, filling me. I look into the darkened house and, for a second, I can hear the beating of a swan's wings, and, then, nothing at all. ■

Vocabulary

polytheism (päl′i·thē·iz′əm) *n.*: belief in more than one god.

ramparts (ram′pärts′) *n.*: broad embankments surrounding a castle, fort, or city for defense against attack.

supplication (sup′lə·kā′shən) *n.*: humble plea or request.

enunciate (ē·nun′sē·āt′) *v.*: pronounce; articulate.

FAMILY/COMMUNITY ACTIVITY

Ask students to share "Helen on Eighty-sixth Street" with their families. After family members have read the story, students can have them discuss moments in life when they made difficult discoveries, such as Helen's realization that dreams don't always come true. Encourage students to ask their family members how they reacted to these discoveries.

Meet the Writer

Wendi Kaufman

"Is Vita Based on Me?"

Wendi Kaufman (1964–) lives in Virginia, but her written "voice" was shaped by her childhood experiences—growing up in a small town in upstate New York. Kaufman is a graduate of George Mason University's master-of-fine-arts program. She is currently a correspondent for National Public Radio. Here is what she says about "Helen on Eighty-sixth Street":

❝I was reading the *Odyssey* and thought the stage production of a mythic tale would make a good backdrop for a short story. The *Odyssey* was originally an oral tale, an epic poem recited for hundreds of years before it was finally written down. I wanted to somehow incorporate that incantatory tone, to have my story sound like it was being spoken out loud—that's where the voice of Vita, the narrator, comes from.

Vita is twelve years old. I remember that as a hard age, a time on the cusp, when you're stuck in that middle ground between child and teen, and it's difficult to know where you belong, to find your own place. Vita wants to be Helen of Troy because she wants everything that Helen represents: beauty, popularity, adoration. I think these are things that many of us have desired at one time or another. The truth about Vita is that she *is* beautiful. She is warm, funny, knows her own mind, and is capable of great love—what could be more beautiful than that? She just doesn't know it yet.

I grew up in a sleepy town in the Hudson River Valley, about an hour from New York City, the kind of place Washington Irving wrote about. I always felt it was a boring town, a place where nothing ever happened. What I didn't realize was that the most important things were happening around me every day, the drama of daily life. As an adult, I have lived all over the country and have had many different experiences, but it is those childhood years, those early memories and discoveries, that I return to and write about most often.

Is Vita based on me? Not really. But as a young girl, I did love reading mythology. Myths are great stories for young writers. The plot twists, the drama—it's all there. Myths run the gamut of human emotion and experience. Love, loss, deceit, regret, betrayal, there's something in there for everybody. I would recommend them to any young writer—and to a few old ones.

For me, writing is an experience of the imagination, that chance to take a kernel of an idea or experience and explore it by becoming anyone or saying anything. That's what I love about writing. As for advice for young writers? Simple: Read, read, read. And, of course, keep writing. There are things that come out on the page, when pen hits paper, that you weren't expecting, that you didn't plan for. Those are the moments we all strive for.

Writing is about possibilities, about the freedom of the blank page. I can remember reading *Little Women* in the fourth grade and crying my eyes out. That was the first time I realized the power of literature. Never underestimate that power.❞

GUIDED PRACTICE

Monitoring students' progress.
Guide the class in answering these questions. Direct students to locate passages in the text that support their responses.

Short Answer

1. Vita lives with her _____ in Manhattan. [mother]
2. Vita wants to play the role of _____ in a class production, but is instead assigned to be a warrior inside the _____. [Helen of Troy, Trojan horse]
3. Every night she writes letters she cannot send to _____. [her father]
4. She sacrifices the letters to _____ in an attempt to make her wishes come true. [Athena]
5. The one wish that does not come true is _____. [the return of her father]

For Independent Reading

- For students interested in learning more about the mythology of ancient Greece, suggest John Pinsent's *Greek Mythology,* an illustrated introduction to the world of Greek gods and goddesses.
- Advanced readers will enjoy encountering the story of Helen of Troy in Homer's *Iliad;* this is the companion epic to Homer's *Odyssey,* which they will read in Collection 10 of this book.

DIFFERENTIATING INSTRUCTION

Advanced Learners

Enrichment. Have students read and discuss what Wendi Kaufman says in her reflection about writing "Helen on Eighty-sixth Street." What similarities do they find between the author and her character Vita? [Both Vita and Kaufman found twelve a difficult age; both appreciated mythology and the power of literature.]

Response and Analysis

Reading Check

1. Vita's father left her mother about three years earlier.

2. Vita wishes for the role of Helen, the departure of Old Farfel, and the return of her father.

3. The first two wishes come true. Her father does not return.

Thinking Critically

4. Answers will vary. For example, students may cite the episode in which Vita burns her letters as evidence of her emotional nature and determination to get what she wants. Others may use the same episode as evidence of her naiveté.

5. Possible answer: Vita still loves her father. Vita's early thoughts and statements reveal her inability to accept his abandonment. The strength of her belief in his return peaks after Vita's first two wishes come true and wavers after her conversation with her mother about the Greek gods. By the story's end, Vita accepts the fact that he will not return, showing that she's capable of learning hard truths.

6. Possible answer: Vita triumphs in her studies and in the role of Helen, but she loses her belief in the old myths and stops believing her father will return. The triumphs make her feel good, but the losses help her change and grow.

7. Possible answer: Vita's experience shows that one must accept some sadness in life and let go of trying to change things one cannot control.

8. Lists should include Helen of Troy, Marlowe, Trojan horse, Trojan women, Sarah Bernhardt, John Keats (p. 106); lotus-eaters, Paris (p. 107); Agamemnon, "the play's the *thing*,"

Response and Analysis

Reading Check

1. What is Vita's family situation?
2. What are her three wishes?
3. How does each wish turn out?

Thinking Critically

SKILLS FOCUS

Literary Skills
Analyze character traits from what characters say about themselves.

Reading Skills
Understand allusions.

Writing Skills
Write a description. Write a short story.

Vocabulary Skills
Understand word meanings.

Grammar Skills
Understand and use coordinating conjunctions.

4. As Vita tells us her story, we learn a great deal about her. We find out, for example, how she feels about herself and what she wants. Find passages in which Vita reveals what she is like. Based on those passages, what would you say are her three or four most important **character traits**?

5. How does Vita feel about her father? Does she really believe he will return? What do Vita's thoughts and statements about her father reveal about her own **character**?

6. Describe Vita's triumphs and losses. Which do you think are more important to her—the triumphs or the losses? Explain why.

7. Think about Vita and what she has learned by the story's end. How would you state the **theme** of this story—what truth does Vita's experience reveal to you?

8. Make a list of all the story's **allusions**—references to Greek mythology, to literature, even to New York City. With a partner, discuss how you figured out the meaning of each allusion. What resources in the text helped you? Are any of these allusions still puzzling you? (For example, what are those swan's wings at the story's end?)

Extending and Evaluating

9. Vita's mother tells her, "You don't want to be Helen. Be lucky you're a warrior. You're too smart to be ruled by your heart." What do you think of this advice?

10. This story can be boiled down to the following facts: A girl wants to star in the sixth-grade play. She misses her father, who has left the family, and she hopes that he will attend the play. Do you think the author's decision to add the myth of Helen of Troy to the story was a good idea? (Does the myth contribute to your understanding of Vita, or does it instead make the story too complicated?) Explain your answer.

WRITING

Impossible Dream?

Vita's dream of playing Helen in the school production comes true. Write about an ambition, hope, or dream of your own. Describe the dream, and explain how you tried to make it a reality. Did you succeed? Is it still too early to tell? Has your old dream been replaced by a more achievable one? (Be sure to check your Quickwrite notes.) 🖉

Trading Places

Write your own brief **story** about a character who wants to be like someone in a myth, novel, or movie you know. In your story, make it clear who your **character** wants to be and why. Create an interesting **conflict,** and end your story by having your character make an important discovery.

▶ **Use "Writing a Short Story," pages 132–139, for help with this assignment.**

Argus (p. 108); the quotation from Keats, Manhattan, New York beaches, West Side Highway (p. 109); and Ninja Turtles, Parthenon, Athena (p. 110). Most students will say that A Closer Look on p. 107 and the footnotes were helpful.

Extending and Evaluating

9. Students may feel that there are times when it is more important to follow one's heart than one's head.

10. Many students will feel that the use of the myth in the story rounds out Vita's character by revealing her dreams. Others may say that the allusions distract from the story's theme.

Vocabulary Development

Word Knowledge: Questions About Words

PRACTICE

How much do you know about the meanings of the Word Bank words? Make up two questions about each word, and organize your answers in a chart like the one below. After you have completed charts for all the words, invite a partner to answer your questions.

Word Bank
embodies
odyssey
litany
incantation
stifled
scourge
polytheism
ramparts
supplication
enunciate

stifled	
Questions	Answers
When is a cough sometimes stifled?	• during a play • during a speech
What other things are some-times stifled?	• sobs • screams • protests

Grammar Link

Coordinating Conjunctions: Getting It Together

Coordinating conjunctions join words, phrases, or clauses of equal importance. Suppose the following phrases are Kaufman's notes:

Told Helen McGuire it's dark. Hold each other around waist. Walk to make horse move forward.

Here is how she puts these notes together in one sentence using coordinating conjunctions:

"I told her it's dark, and we must hold each other around the waist and walk to make the horse move forward."

Here are two other sentences from the story that use coordinating conjunctions. Break these sentences into shorter ones to see how many details the writer combines:

1. "I will meet giants and witches and see strange lands."
2. "I change my clothes and open all the windows, but still Mom asks, when she gets home, about the burning smell."

PRACTICE

Using each coordinating conjunction listed below, summarize the main events in "Helen on Eighty-sixth Street." Be sure to compare your summaries with those of your classmates.

and	or	yet
so	for	
nor	but	

▶ **For more help, see The Compound Subject and The Compound Verb, 8e–f, and Run-on Sentences, 9b, in the Language Handbook.**

Vocabulary Development

Practice

Possible Answers
- *embodies. Question*—Who embodies the quality of beauty? *Answer*—Helen of Troy.
- *odyssey. Question*—What kind of journey is an odyssey? *Answer*—a long, adventure-filled trip.
- *litany. Question*—Who would deliver a litany of complaints? *Answer*—an angry customer.
- *incantation. Question*—Who in literature might chant incanta-tions? *Answer*—a witch.
- *scourge. Question*—What is a common childhood medical scourge? *Answer*—chicken pox.
- *polytheism. Question*—What culture practiced polytheism? *Answer*—ancient Greece.
- *ramparts. Question*—Where would you find ramparts? *Answer*—in a fort.
- *supplication. Question*—To whom do people bow in supplication? *Answer*—kings, queens, clergy.
- *enunciate. Question*—Why must actors enunciate well? *Answer*—so audiences can hear the lines.

Grammar Link

Practice

Possible answer: Vita wants to play Helen, *but* Helen McGuire gets the part. Helen envies Vita, *for* Vita gets to be in the horse with Tommy. Vita knows neither Greek *nor* the ritual, *yet* creates a ceremony. Her wishes for the role *and* for Old Farfel's departure come true, *so* she believes her third wish will also. Vita learns that some things you cannot change *or* cause to happen.

ASSESSING

Assessment
- *Holt Assessment: Literature, Reading, and Vocabulary*

RETEACHING

For a lesson reteaching character traits, see **Reteaching,** p. 979A. For another selection to teach characterization, see *The Holt Reader,* Collection 2.

■ **Literary Skills**

Analyze influences on characters (such as internal and external conflict and motivation) and how those influences affect the plot.

Review Skills

■ **Literary Skills**

Compare and contrast the motives of literary characters from different historical eras.

Elements of Literature: Character Interactions

On the chalkboard, list the following terms from the essay: *protagonist, antagonist, subordinate character, flat character, round character, dynamic character,* and *static character*. Point out that these terms apply to film and television as well as to literature. Ask volunteers to name favorite movies and television shows. Have students discuss the characters in the works they cite and try to reach a consensus on which of the terms apply to the characters. Note that each work won't provide a character for every term. An action thriller, for example, might not have round characters. A slapstick comedy might not have dynamic ones. Continue the discussion until several characters have been identified for each term.

Elements of Literature

Character Interactions *by* John Leggett
GIVE-AND-TAKE

A story with a suspenseful, fast-moving plot allows us to escape, at least briefly, from the tedium of our daily lives. For fiction to be more than just escape reading, though, it needs vivid, complex characters whose problems and triumphs draw forth our emotions and reveal some truth about humankind.

Characters in Conflict

Often a story revolves around one main character. Usually we care about this character, who may remind us of a person we know or even of ourselves.

What sets the main character's story in motion is **conflict.** The main character wants something, and the obstacles and choices he or she faces form the plot. We call the main character the **protagonist.** The character or force the protagonist struggles against and must overcome is the **antagonist.**

When the conflict is with an outside force—another person, society, a creature from the deep—it's an **external conflict.** When the protagonist faces a conflict within himself or herself—fear or self-doubt, for example—the character must overcome an **internal conflict.** Frequently an external conflict results in an internal struggle.

While the focus of our attention in a story is the conflict between the protagonist and the antagonist, writers often include **subordinate characters** who add depth and complication to the plot.

Imagine a situation in which Dorothy, our protagonist, is locked in a room by her antagonist, Uncle Godfrey. In an hour, Dorothy is due to sing in a contest to win a music scholarship. Her uncle is trying to prevent her from pursuing her music career because he wants her to work on the family's alligator farm. Dorothy's external conflict with her uncle creates an internal conflict for her as well. Her career goals conflict with her gratitude to her uncle for raising her and with her desire to obey him.

Enter a subordinate character: Dorothy's best friend, Madeleine, who pressures Dorothy to abandon her singing career and to become her partner in a get-rich-quick scheme. The way Dorothy resolves her conflicts with her uncle and with Madeleine will not only affect the plot but also reveal Dorothy's values and personality traits.

Motivation: The Driving Force

Motivation is what drives a character's actions. It explains behavior and reveals personality. What would motivate Dorothy to give up her singing career and become Madeleine's partner? Would it be loyalty to her best friend, or if she is ambitious, could it be greed?

Writers rarely make direct statements about a character's motivation. Instead, they plant clues and rely on readers to make inferences from those clues. If a writer doesn't provide motivation, a

go.hrw.com

INTERNET
More About Character Interactions
Keyword: LE5 9-2

SKILLS FOCUS

Literary Skills
Understand internal and external conflicts, motivation, flat and round characters, and dynamic and static characters.

DIFFERENTIATING INSTRUCTION

Learners Having Difficulty

Character interactions. To help students who have difficulty understanding character interactions, review with them the section of the essay on motivation. Then, distribute a short preselected story to student pairs. Work with them to identify what each character in the story wants. Once the student pairs understand each character's motivation,

ask them to identify each character's internal conflicts and conflicts with other characters. Finally, review the conversations between all the various characters, and discuss how these interactions affect the conflicts.

Advanced Learners

Acceleration. Use the following activity with advanced learners to help them evaluate

the philosophical, political, religious, ethical, and social influences that shaped the characters in American and world literature.

Activity. Suggest to students that the historical era in which a work is written cannot help but shape many aspects of that text. Challenge students to choose a work of literature from an earlier era that they have read and to relate the influences of the

character's actions may seem unbelievable or the story may seem boring.

Rounding Out Character

A **flat character** has only one or two character traits. If Uncle Godfrey's only motivation for locking up Dorothy is to get free labor on the farm, then we would view him as a flat character. Selfish and cruel, he is no more complicated than a character in a cartoon or fairy tale (think of the wicked stepmother in *Cinderella*).

Watch how our view of Uncle Godfrey changes if we learn that he is dying of a rare disease. Fearing that he won't be able to maintain the farm and that Dorothy's inheritance will become worthless, he wants her to look after the alligators. Proud and independent, however, he hides his diagnosis because he doesn't want Dorothy's pity. Suddenly we see him as a **round character,** a figure who has several sides to his personality. Uncle Godfrey has become complex, as have our reactions to him and to the story.

Characters and Change

In most stories, as the characters struggle to resolve their conflicts, they learn something about themselves or other people or even the world. As a result, they take action or change their behavior or their attitudes. Such characters are called **dynamic** because they grow or change.

Static characters don't progress or change. At the end of the story, they are the same as they were in the beginning. Subordinate characters are often static because a story doesn't revolve around them. Instead, their role is to further

the plot or to help us understand the main character.

A static character, Madeleine exits the story in pursuit of wealth, never changing her perspective or values. Dorothy, however, learns not to judge people too quickly. Discovering that Uncle Godfrey is ill, she realizes that sometimes people hide their emotions and fears. The changes that a dynamic character undergoes contribute to the **meaning** of the story.

The next time you read a story, think about the characters' choices—and those of the writer as well. If you had been in the shoes of either the protagonist or his or her creator, would you have made a different choice?

Practice

Think of a story you've read in which the protagonist faces powerful conflicts. Use a chart like the one here to map out the conflicts and their resolutions, as well as the protagonist's motivations:

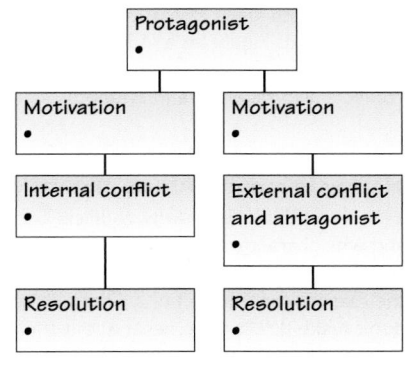

period (philosophical, political, religious, ethical, or social) to
- the types of conflicts in which characters are involved
- the emotional and intellectual motivations that propel the characters' actions
- the ways in which the characters interact with each other

Students' answers will vary depending on the story selected. Below are possible responses for Wendi Kaufman's "Helen on Eighty-sixth Street."

Protagonist—Vita.

Motivation—Vita wants to play Helen of Troy in a school production.

External conflict and antagonist—Helen McGuire has beaten her out of the role.

Resolution—Vita ends up with the role and delivers a successful performance.

Motivation—Vita's father left the family three years earlier.

Internal conflict—Vita can't get over her father's departure; she is torn by her desire for his return.

Resolution—By the story's end, Vita has finally accepted his absence.

Apply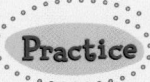

Encourage students to use a chart such as this to map out the character interactions in other stories that they read. You may want to have advanced students create a chart for "Marigolds" as homework. Students can fill in the boxes on the chart as they read, and turn in the completed graphic organizer when they have finished reading the story.

Grade-Level Skills

■ **Literary Skills**

Analyze influences on characters (such as internal and external conflict and motivation) and how those influences affect the plot.

■ **Reading Skills**

Make inferences about character motivation.

Review Skills

■ **Literary Skills**

Compare and contrast the motives of literary characters from different historical eras.

Summary ↔ *at grade level*

The narrator of the story is Lizabeth, a poor African American girl; the setting is rural Maryland during the Great Depression. One day Lizabeth, her brother, and their friends taunt Miss Lottie, an old woman who lives with her son John Burke, who is mentally disabled. Miss Lottie cultivates a spectacular plot of marigolds in her front yard, a bright contrast to her ramshackle house. The children throw stones at the marigolds and chant insults at Miss Lottie. Afterward, however, Lizabeth develops an internal conflict: She starts to feel ashamed of her behavior. That night she overhears her parents talking. For the first time she hears her father weep in despair about his inability to support his family. Her mother comforts her father, but Lizabeth cannot sleep. Finally she rouses her brother, and they return to Miss Lottie's house. Impelled by fear, need, bewilderment, anger, and hopelessness, Lizabeth destroys the remaining marigolds in a bitter, violent rage. When Miss Lottie comes outdoors, Lizabeth looks into the old lady's face and recognizes Miss Lottie's humanity for the first time. At that moment the young girl discovers compassion; she learns to sympathize with others, but she had to lose her innocence to do so.

Before You Read

Marigolds

Make the Connection

Quickwrite ✏

This story is about the passage from childhood to adulthood, a journey that is often marked by conflict. In fact, negotiating this passage can demand as much courage as a struggle with an outside enemy. Before you read this story, write down your response to the following question: What fears and conflicts do most young people deal with as they move into adult life? Keep your notes for use later on.

Literary Focus

Conflict: Battles Within and Without

Conflict, or struggle, is the heart of a story. When characters struggle against something outside themselves, their conflicts are **external.** Characters with **internal conflicts** struggle to resolve contradictory desires or to battle personal problems, such as fear or anger. The most intense conflicts occur when characters face both kinds of battles.

"Marigolds" includes a violent external confrontation, but important internal conflicts also take place in Lizabeth.

INTERNET
Vocabulary
Practice
Keyword: LE5 9-2

SKILLS FOCUS

Literary Skills
Understand external and internal conflicts.

Reading Skills
Make inferences about character motivation.

Reading Skills 📖

Making Inferences About Motivation

When you think about why conflicts occur and why characters behave as they do, you are trying to determine their **motivation,** the reasons for their actions. Often writers don't make direct statements about their characters. Instead, they expect you to make **inferences,** or educated guesses, based on clues in the text, such as a character's actions and words. As you

read "Marigolds," think about the characters' motivations. The questions at the open-book signs will help you.

Background

In the 1930s, a terrible economic depression swept the world. The booming stock market had collapsed in 1929, causing businesses to shut down all over America and factories to close their doors. Banks failed. People lost their life savings. Life was hard for almost every American during those years. As the narrator of this story says, however, the Great Depression was nothing new to her family: For the black families of rural Maryland, all times were hard times.

Vocabulary Development

arid (ar′id) *adj.:* lacking enough water for many types of plants to grow; dry.

futile (fyoot′l) *adj.:* useless; vain.

impoverished (im·päv′ər·ishd) *v.* used as *adj.:* poor; poverty-stricken.

poignantly (poin′yənt·lē) *adv.:* with a sharp sadness or pain; movingly.

clarity (klar′ə·tē) *n.:* clearness.

placidly (plas′id·lē) *adv.:* calmly; quietly.

inciting (in·sīt′iŋ) *v.* used as *n.:* stirring up.

malicious (mə·lish′əs) *adj.:* showing a desire to harm another; spiteful.

contrition (kən·trish′ən) *n.:* deep feelings of guilt and repentance.

RESOURCES: READING

Planning
■ *One-Stop Planner* CD-ROM with ExamView Test Generator

Differentiating Instruction
■ *Holt Reading Solutions*
■ *Holt Adapted Reader*
■ *Supporting Instruction in Spanish*

Vocabulary
■ *Vocabulary Development*

Grammar and Language
■ *Daily Language Activities*

Assessment
■ *Holt Assessment: Literature, Reading, and Vocabulary*

MARIGOLDS

Eugenia W. Collier

Miss Lottie didn't like intruders, especially children.

The Magic Garden (1978) by Romare Bearden. Watercolor and collage (10⅛″ × 7″).

Courtesy Linda Forrest Cummin and Pearson C. Cummin III. © Romare Bearden Foundation/Licensed by VAGA, New York, NY.

Marigolds **119**

- *One-Stop Planner* CD-ROM with ExamView Test Generator
- *Holt Online Assessment*

Internet
- go.hrw.com (Keyword: LE5 9-2)
- *Elements of Literature Online*

Media
- *Audio CD Library*
- *Audio CD Library, Selections and Summaries in Spanish*
- *Fine Art Transparencies*

Selection Starter

Motivate. Explain to students that the Great Depression was an economic tragedy that lasted the better part of a decade. To many who lived through the Depression, it seemed like a frustrating nightmare, one without hope of an end. Ask students how they would maintain hope in the midst of such hopelessness.

Preview Vocabulary

Have students read the Vocabulary words on p. 118 and study their pronunciations and meanings. Then, have them choose the word that best completes each of the following sentences.

1. During the Great Depression, looking for work seemed _____. [futile]
2. The _____ soil made it difficult to grow crops. [arid]
3. The contented old woman worked _____ in her garden. [placidly]
4. The girl's behavior had been _____; she had stirred up trouble by _____ the others. [malicious, inciting]
5. Afterward, the child felt _____ for her mean behavior. [contrition]
6. She saw her own actions with _____. [clarity]
7. The girl looked _____ at the _____ old woman, who never planted marigolds again. [poignantly, impoverished]

VIEWING THE ART

Romare Bearden (1914–1988) was an African American artist famous for his colorful collages depicting aspects of black life.
Activity. After students read "Marigolds," have them speculate why this work was chosen to illustrate the story.

A English-Language Learners

? Building background knowledge. Explain to students that an abstract painting is one that does not portray images realistically. It may emphasize a mix of color, line, shape, and form. By likening her memory to such a painting, the narrator is saying that her memory contains suggestions, emotions, and images rather than a precise picture. Ask students to reflect on their own memories of early childhood. Are they sharply drawn and specific or more like the abstract painting that the narrator describes?

B Vocabulary Development

? Figurative language. The narrator uses two metaphors in this sentence. To what does she compare poverty? [a cage] To what does she compare the hatred of poverty? [the natural instincts of a flamingo bred in captivity] What do the two images have in common? [the feeling of being trapped]

When I think of the hometown of my youth, all that I seem to remember is dust—the brown, crumbly dust of late summer—arid, sterile dust that gets into the eyes and makes them water, gets into the throat and between the toes of bare brown feet. I don't know why I should remember only the dust. Surely there must have been lush green lawns and paved streets under leafy shade trees somewhere in town; but memory is an abstract painting—it does not present things as they are, but rather as they *feel*. And so, when I think of that time and that place, I remember only the dry September of the dirt roads and grassless yards of the shantytown where I lived. And one other thing I remember, another incongruency[1] of memory—a brilliant splash of sunny yellow against the dust—Miss Lottie's marigolds.

Whenever the memory of those marigolds flashes across my mind, a strange nostalgia comes with it and remains long after the picture has faded. I feel again the chaotic emotions of adolescence, illusive as smoke, yet as real as the potted geranium before me now. Joy and rage and wild animal gladness and shame become tangled together in the multicolored skein[2] of fourteen-going-on-fifteen as I recall that devastating moment when I was suddenly more woman than child, years ago in Miss Lottie's yard. I think of those marigolds at the strangest times; I remember them vividly now as I desperately pass away the time. . . .

I suppose that futile waiting was the sorrowful background music of our impoverished little community when I was young. The Depression that gripped the nation was no new thing to us, for the black workers of rural Maryland had always been depressed. I don't know what it was that we were waiting for; certainly not for the prosperity that was "just around the corner," for those were white folks' words, which we never believed. Nor did we wait for hard work and thrift to pay off in shining success, as the American Dream promised, for we knew better than that, too. Perhaps we waited for a miracle, amorphous[3] in concept but necessary if one were to have the grit to rise before dawn each day and labor in the white man's vineyard until after dark, or to wander about in the September dust offering one's sweat in return for some meager share of bread. But God was chary[4] with miracles in those days, and so we waited—and waited.

We children, of course, were only vaguely aware of the extent of our poverty. Having no radios, few newspapers, and no magazines, we were somewhat unaware of the world outside our community. Nowadays we would be called culturally deprived and people would write books and hold conferences about us. In those days everybody we knew was just as hungry and ill clad as we were. Poverty was the cage in which we all were trapped, and our hatred of it was still the vague, undirected restlessness of the zoo-bred flamingo who knows that nature created him to fly free.

Perhaps we waited for a miracle . . .

---

1. **incongruency** (in'kän'grōo·ən·sē) *n.*: inconsistency; lack of agreement or harmony.
2. **multicolored skein** (skān): The writer is comparing her many feelings to a long, coiled piece (skein) of many- (multi) colored yarn.

---

3. **amorphous** (ə·môr'fəs) *adj.*: vague; shapeless.
4. **chary** (cher'ē) *adj.*: not generous.

Vocabulary

arid (ar'id) *adj.*: lacking enough water for many types of plants to grow; dry.

futile (fyōōt'l) *adj.*: useless; vain.

impoverished (im·päv'ər·ishd) *v.* used as *adj.*: poor; poverty-stricken.

DIFFERENTIATING INSTRUCTION

Learners Having Difficulty
Modeling. As they read "Marigolds," some students may have difficulty understanding the reasons behind the characters' actions. Help these students by modeling the reading skill of making inferences about motivation. After students have read to the end of p. 121, have them focus their attention on question 1. Tell students, "Lizabeth, her brother, and her friends have little to do but daydream. Knowing this and remembering what it was like to be fourteen with nothing to do, I understand why it might be a diversion to annoy a neighbor." Encourage students to draw upon their own experiences, as well as details in the text, for help in making further inferences about motivation.

English-Language Learners
Provide students who are unfamiliar with the history of the United States before World War II with additional background information about the 1930s. Distribute a simple time line of major events, beginning with the stock market crash of 1929 and ending with America's entry into the war.

As I think of those days I feel most poignantly the tag end of summer, the bright, dry times when we began to have a sense of shortening days and the imminence of the cold.

By the time I was fourteen, my brother Joey and I were the only children left at our house, the older ones having left home for early marriage or the lure of the city, and the two babies having been sent to relatives who might care for them better than we. Joey was three years younger than I, and a boy, and therefore vastly inferior. Each morning our mother and father trudged wearily down the dirt road and around the bend, she to her domestic job, he to his daily unsuccessful quest for work. After our few chores around the tumbledown shanty, Joey and I were free to run wild in the sun with other children similarly situated.

For the most part, those days are ill-defined in my memory, running together and combining like a fresh watercolor painting left out in the rain. I remember squatting in the road drawing a picture in the dust, a picture which Joey gleefully erased with one sweep of his dirty foot. I remember fishing for minnows in a muddy creek and watching sadly as they eluded my cupped hands, while Joey laughed uproariously. And I remember, that year, a strange restlessness of body and of spirit, a feeling that something old and familiar was ending, and something unknown and therefore terrifying was beginning.

One day returns to me with special clarity for some reason, perhaps because it was the beginning of the experience that in some inexplicable[5] way marked the end of innocence. I was loafing under the great oak tree in our yard, deep in some reverie which I have now forgotten, except that it involved some secret, secret thoughts of one of the Harris boys across the yard. Joey and a bunch of kids were bored now with the old tire suspended from an

oak limb, which had kept them entertained for a while.

"Hey, Lizabeth," Joey yelled. He never talked when he could yell. "Hey, Lizabeth, let's go somewhere."

I came reluctantly from my private world. "Where you want to go? What you want to do?"

The truth was that we were becoming tired of the formlessness of our summer days. The idleness whose prospect had seemed so beautiful during the busy days of spring now had degenerated to an almost desperate effort to fill up the empty midday hours.

"Let's go see can we find some locusts on the hill," someone suggested.

Joey was scornful. "Ain't no more locusts there. Y'all got 'em all while they was still green."

The argument that followed was brief and not really worth the effort. Hunting locust trees wasn't fun anymore by now.

"Tell you what," said Joey finally, his eyes sparkling. "Let's us go over to Miss Lottie's."

The idea caught on at once, for annoying Miss Lottie was always fun. I was still child enough to scamper along with the group over rickety fences and through bushes that tore our already raggedy clothes, back to where Miss Lottie lived. I think now that we must have made a tragicomic spectacle, five or six kids of different ages, each of us clad in only one garment—the girls in faded dresses that were too long or too short, the boys in patchy pants, their sweaty brown chests gleaming in the hot sun. A little cloud of dust followed our thin legs and bare feet as we tramped over the barren land.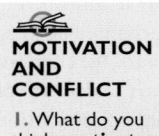

MOTIVATION AND CONFLICT

1. What do you think **motivates** the children to go to Miss Lottie's house to annoy her?

Vocabulary

poignantly (poin′yənt·lē) *adv.:* with a sharp sadness or pain; movingly.

clarity (klar′ə·tē) *n.:* clearness.

5. **inexplicable** (in·eks′pli·kə·bəl) *adj.:* not explainable or understandable.

DIRECT TEACHING

C Literary Focus

❓ **External conflict.** What external conflict does the narrator's father face? [He is struggling to find work.] Even though his unemployment is a result of the Depression, how might it cause an internal conflict? [The father feels torn because he cannot provide for his family.]

D Literary Focus

❓ **Internal conflict.** What internal conflict does the narrator of the story feel? [Possible response: She is becoming an adult, and she finds the thought of facing an unpredictable future terrifying.]

E Reading Skills

Motivation and conflict. [Possible response to question 1: Lizabeth, Joey, and the other children have little to do. They are poor with limited amusements and little parental supervision. The chance to annoy Miss Lottie is a welcome distraction from their day-to-day routine, considering that kids often look for trouble when they have little else to do. Also, Miss Lottie, with her conspicuous marigolds, stands out as an obvious target for mischief.]

Advanced Learners

Acceleration. Use the following activity with advanced learners to help them evaluate the philosophical, political, religious, ethical, and social influences that shaped the characters in American and world literature.

Activity. As students read "Marigolds," ask them to jot down any actions, statements, or thoughts of characters in the story that seem specifically related to the historical context in which it is set. Students should note how the setting in a poor rural community during the Great Depression influences the characters, as well as the specific hardships faced by African Americans at the time.

A Literary Focus

? Setting and mood. How do these details about Miss Lottie's house contribute to the story's mood? [They help to create a sad, despondent atmosphere.]

B Literary Focus

? Character traits. What do you learn in this passage about John Burke, Miss Lottie's son? [He is a mentally disabled man who lives in a dream world. He is easily angered, and when enraged, he speaks in his own language.]

C Reading Skills

? Making inferences about motivation. Why do you think the children make a game of disturbing John Burke? [Possible response: The children are bored and the game provides an amusing distraction; sadly, children are often insensitive—they don't realize how cruel it is to make fun of others. People like John Burke provide easy targets for their frustration.]

D Literary Focus

? Conflict. Point out the passage in which the narrator says that she and the other children reveled in their youth and mocked Miss Lottie's old age. Then, ask students how they would describe such a conflict in general terms. [youth versus old age] How would you characterize the other conflicts described in this passage? [Possible response: destruction versus creation, ugliness versus beauty, hope versus despair.]

When Miss Lottie's house came into view we stopped, ostensibly[6] to plan our strategy, but actually to reinforce our courage. Miss Lottie's house was the most ramshackle of all our ramshackle homes. The sun and rain had long since faded its rickety frame siding from white to a sullen gray. The boards themselves seemed to remain upright not from being nailed together but rather from leaning together, like a house that a child might have constructed from cards. A brisk wind might have blown it down, and the fact that it was still standing implied a kind of enchantment that was stronger than the elements. There it stood and as far as I know is standing yet—a gray, rotting thing with no porch, no shutters, no steps, set on a cramped lot with no grass, not even any weeds—a monument to decay.

In front of the house in a squeaky rocking chair sat Miss Lottie's son, John Burke, completing the impression of decay. John Burke was what was known as queer-headed. Black and ageless, he sat rocking day in and day out in a mindless stupor, lulled by the monotonous squeak-squawk of the chair. A battered hat atop his shaggy head shaded him from the sun. Usually John Burke was totally unaware of everything outside his quiet dream world. But if you disturbed him, if you intruded upon his fantasies, he would become enraged, strike out at you, and curse at you in some strange enchanted language which only he could understand. We children made a game of thinking of ways to disturb John Burke and then to elude his violent retribution.

But our real fun and our real fear lay in Miss Lottie herself. Miss Lottie seemed to be at least a hundred years old. Her big frame still held traces of the tall, powerful woman she must have been in youth, although it was now bent and drawn. Her smooth skin was a dark reddish brown, and her face had Indian-like features and the stern

stoicism[7] that one associates with Indian faces. Miss Lottie didn't like intruders either, especially children. She never left her yard, and nobody ever visited her. We never knew how she managed those necessities which depend on human interaction—how she ate, for example, or even whether she ate. When we were tiny children, we thought Miss Lottie was a witch and we made up tales that we half believed ourselves about her exploits. We were far too sophisticated now, of course, to believe the witch nonsense. But old fears have a way of clinging like cobwebs, and so when we sighted the tumbledown shack, we had to stop to reinforce our nerves.

"Look, there she is," I whispered, forgetting that Miss Lottie could not possibly have heard me from that distance. "She's fooling with them crazy flowers."

"Yeh, look at 'er."

Miss Lottie's marigolds were perhaps the strangest part of the picture. Certainly they did not fit in with the crumbling decay of the rest of her yard. Beyond the dusty brown yard, in front of the sorry gray house, rose suddenly and shockingly a dazzling strip of bright blossoms, clumped together in enormous mounds, warm and passionate and sun-golden. The old black witch-woman worked on them all summer, every summer, down on her creaky knees, weeding and cultivating and arranging, while the house crumbled and John Burke rocked. For some perverse reason, we children hated those marigolds. They interfered with the perfect ugliness of the place; they were too beautiful; they said too much that we could not understand; they did not make sense. There was something in the vigor with which the old woman destroyed the weeds that intimidated us. It should have been a comical sight—the old woman with the man's hat on her cropped white head, leaning over the bright mounds, her big

---

6. **ostensibly** (ä · sten′sə · blē) *adv.:* seemingly; apparently.

7. **stoicism** (stō′i · siz′əm) *n.:* calm indifference to pleasure or pain.

DEVELOPING FLUENCY

Paired activity. Students may have difficulties with some of Collier's vocabulary. You may wish to have students preview the story by skimming through the selection and listing unfamiliar words. Then, have students exchange lists with a partner. Partners can assist each other in pronouncing and defining the unknown words.

READING MINI-LESSON

Developing Word-Attack Skills
Use words from the selection to explore with students the sounds represented by the letter *i*, both alone and combined with other vowels.

- In *cultivate, i* by itself stands for the unaccented schwa sound.
- In *nostalgia, i* and *a* together stand for the unaccented schwa sound.

Southern Limited (1976) by Romare Bearden. Collage.

backside in the air—but it wasn't comical, it was something we could not name. We had to annoy her by whizzing a pebble into her flowers or by yelling a dirty word, then dancing away from her rage, reveling in our youth and mocking her age. Actually, I think it was the flowers we wanted to destroy, but nobody had the nerve to try it, not even Joey, who was usually fool enough to try anything.

> ### MOTIVATION
> **2.** What reasons can you give to explain why Miss Lottie works so hard in her garden?

E

"Y'all git some stones," commanded Joey now and was met with instant giggling obedience as everyone except me began to gather pebbles from the dusty ground. "Come on, Lizabeth."

I just stood there peering through the bushes, torn between wanting to join the fun and feeling that it was all a bit silly.

"You scared, Lizabeth?"

I cursed and spat on the ground—my favorite gesture of phony bravado. "Y'all children get the stones, I'll show you how to use 'em."

I said before that we children were not consciously aware of how thick were the bars of our cage. I wonder now, though, whether we were not more aware of it than I thought. Perhaps we had some dim notion of what we were, and how little chance we had of being anything else. Otherwise, why would we have been so preoccupied with destruction? Anyway, the pebbles were collected quickly, and everybody looked at me to begin the fun.

"Come on, y'all."

F

Marigolds 123

VIEWING THE ART

> **Romare Bearden** (1914–1988) studied art in New York City and Paris. He was influenced by artists like the German social commentator George Grosz and Georges Braque, the French proponent of *papier collé* (collage).
>
> **Activity.** Have students identify what is depicted in *Southern Limited.* [an African American couple, a train, a bird, a tree, a yard, a farmworker, and a ramshackle house or barn] Then, ask them to suggest possible interpretations of the title *Southern Limited.* [Possible responses: The title suggests the name of a railroad; the title recalls the limited existences that were once all that most African Americans could expect.]

E **Reading Skills**
Making inferences about motivation. [Possible response to question 2: Miss Lottie may be the poorest member of her community. She lives in a ramshackle house and must have struggled while raising a mentally disabled son. Given the hard times of the Depression, she would have little opportunity to improve her situation. Growing a garden may be Miss Lottie's one chance to introduce a little beauty into her difficult life. Her diligence may reflect a refusal to give up hope amid her desperate circumstances.]

F **Literary Focus**
❷ Internal conflict. Lizabeth struggles with the decision over whether or not to join the other children. What does Lizabeth's decision suggest about her at this point in the story? [Possible response: Lizabeth, caught between childhood and adulthood, struggles over whether or not to pester Miss Lottie. Her decision to participate indicates that at this stage of the story, Lizabeth is susceptible to peer pressure and not yet ready to be an adult.]

- In *passionate,* i and o together stand for the unaccented schwa sound.
- In *brilliant,* the second i stands for the consonant sound /y/.
- In *geranium,* i stands for long e.
- In *violent,* i stands for long i.

Activity. Display these sets of words. Have students identify the two words in which the letter i—alone or when combined with another vowel—stands for the same sound. Answers are underlined.

1. radio	accordion	emotion
2. trial	uproarious	violent
3. reliable	diet	exterior
4. insomnia	nostalgia	radius
5. rebellion	million	mission

A **Literary Focus**

? **Character's motivation.** Why do you think Lizabeth is acting like this? [Possible responses: She is taking out her negative feelings on Miss Lottie; she is caught up in the group excitement; it makes her feel important to show off in front of other children.]

B **Literary Focus**

? **Internal conflict.** What conflict is Lizabeth experiencing? [Possible responses: She is experiencing the conflict between childish ways and adult responses; she is feeling ashamed about her participation in the melee.]

C **Vocabulary Development**

Figurative language. Have students identify the type of figurative language used to describe the sound and effect of Lizabeth's mother's voice. [The author uses a simile comparing the voice to "a cool, dark room in summer."]

We crept to the edge of the bushes that bordered the narrow road in front of Miss Lottie's place. She was working placidly, kneeling over the flowers, her dark hand plunged into the golden mound. Suddenly *zing*—an expertly aimed stone cut the head off one of the blossoms.

"Who out there?" Miss Lottie's backside came down and her head came up as her sharp eyes searched the bushes. "You better git!"

We had crouched down out of sight in the bushes, where we stifled the giggles that insisted on coming. Miss Lottie gazed warily across the road for a moment, then cautiously returned to her weeding. *Zing*—Joey sent a pebble into the blooms, and another marigold was beheaded.

Miss Lottie was enraged now. She began struggling to her feet, leaning on a rickety cane and shouting. "Y'all git! Go on home!" Then the rest of the kids let loose with their pebbles, storming the flowers and laughing wildly and senselessly at Miss Lottie's impotent rage. She shook her stick at us and started shakily toward the road crying, "Git 'long! John Burke! John Burke, come help!"

A Then I lost my head entirely, mad with the power of inciting such rage, and ran out of the bushes in the storm of pebbles, straight toward Miss Lottie, chanting madly, "Old witch, fell in a ditch, picked up a penny and thought she was rich!" The children screamed with delight, dropped their pebbles, and joined the crazy dance, swarming around Miss Lottie like bees and chanting, "Old lady witch!" while she screamed curses at us. The madness lasted only a moment, for John Burke, startled at last, lurched out of his chair, and we dashed for the bushes just as Miss Lottie's cane went whizzing at my head.

I did not join the merriment when the kids gathered again under the oak in our bare yard.

B Suddenly I was ashamed, and I did not like being ashamed. The child in me sulked and said it was all in fun, but the woman in me flinched at the thought of the malicious attack that I had led. The mood lasted all afternoon. When we ate the beans and rice that was supper that night, I did not notice my father's silence, for he was always silent these days, nor did I notice my mother's absence, for she always worked until well into evening. Joey and I had a particularly bitter argument after supper; his exuberance got on my nerves. Finally I stretched out upon the pallet[8] in the room we shared and fell into a fitful doze.

When I awoke, somewhere in the middle of the night, my mother had returned, and I vaguely listened to the conversation that was audible through the thin walls that separated our rooms. At first I heard no words, only voices. My mother's voice was like a cool, dark room in summer— peaceful, soothing, quiet. I loved **C** to listen to it; it made things seem all right somehow. But my father's voice cut through hers, shattering the peace.

"Twenty-two years, Maybelle, twenty-two years," he was saying, "and I got nothing for you, nothing, nothing."

"It's all right, honey, you'll get something. Everybody out of work now, you know that."

"It ain't right. Ain't no man ought to eat his woman's food year in and year out, and see his children running wild. Ain't nothing right about that."

---

8. **pallet** (pal′it) *n.:* small bed or pad laid directly on the floor.

Vocabulary

placidly (plas′id·lē) *adv.:* calmly; quietly.

inciting (in·sīt′iŋ) *v.* used as *n.:* stirring up.

malicious (mə·lish′əs) *adj.:* showing a desire to harm another; spiteful.

CONTENT-AREA CONNECTIONS

History: The Great Depression
Explain to students that when the Great Depression began, people couldn't depend on a government-provided "safety net," which people can count on today. Programs like food stamps, unemployment compensation, and welfare had not been created. The unemployed were often reduced to eating weeds, such as dandelions, or standing in bread lines for a bowl of cabbage soup.

Small-group activity. Have students work in small groups to research the Great Depression and its consequences, including the development of safety net programs such as unemployment compensation. How did people who had been evicted from their homes manage to survive? If possible, students should interview older community members or relatives, in addition to doing research in libraries, in museums, and over the Internet.

You might suggest entering keywords such as *New Deal, President's Organization on Unemployment Relief,* or *Dust Bowl* into a search engine to aid students in their research. Have each group present a multimedia report that includes pictures, taped interviews, newspaper articles, and video clips.

"Honey, you took good care of us when you had it. Ain't nobody got nothing nowadays."

"I ain't talking about nobody else, I'm talking about *me*. God knows I try." My mother said something I could not hear, and my father cried out louder, "What must a man do, tell me that?"

"Look, we ain't starving. I git paid every week, and Mrs. Ellis is real nice about giving me things. She gonna let me have Mr. Ellis's old coat for you this winter—"

"Damn Mr. Ellis's coat! And damn his money! You think I want white folks' leavings? Damn, Maybelle"—and suddenly he sobbed, loudly and painfully, and cried helplessly and hopelessly in the dark night. I had never heard a man cry before. I did not know men ever cried. I covered my ears with my hands but could not cut off the sound of my father's harsh, painful, despairing sobs. My father was a strong man who could whisk a child upon his shoulders and go singing through the house. My father whittled toys for us, and laughed so loud that the great oak seemed to laugh with him, and taught us how to fish and hunt rabbits. How could it be that my father was crying? But the sobs went on, unstifled, finally quieting until I could hear my mother's voice, deep and rich, humming softly as she used to hum to a frightened child.

MOTIVATION

3. Why does Lizabeth's father break down and cry?

The world had lost its boundary lines. My mother, who was small and soft, was now the strength of the family; my father, who was the rock on which the family had been built, was sobbing like the tiniest child. Everything was suddenly out of tune, like a broken accordion. Where did I fit into this crazy picture? I do not now remember my thoughts, only a feeling of great bewilderment and fear.

Long after the sobbing and humming had stopped, I lay on the pallet, still as stone with my hands over my ears, wishing that I too could cry and be comforted. The night was silent now except for the sound of the crickets and of Joey's soft breathing. But the room was too crowded with fear to allow me to sleep, and finally, feeling the terrible aloneness of 4 A.M., I decided to awaken Joey.

"Ouch! What's the matter with you? What you want?" he demanded disagreeably when I had pinched and slapped him awake.

"Come on, wake up."

"What for? Go 'way."

I was lost for a reasonable reply. I could not say, "I'm scared and I don't want to be alone," so I merely said, "I'm going out. If you want to come, come on."

The promise of adventure awoke him. "Going out now? Where to, Lizabeth? What you going to do?"

I was pulling my dress over my head. Until now I had not thought of going out. "Just come on," I replied tersely.

I was out the window and halfway down the road before Joey caught up with me.

"Wait, Lizabeth, where you going?"

I was running as if the Furies[9] were after me, as perhaps they were—running silently and furiously until I came to where I had half known I was headed: to Miss Lottie's yard.

The half-dawn light was more eerie than complete darkness, and in it the old house was like the ruin that my world had become—foul and crumbling, a grotesque caricature. It looked haunted, but I was not afraid, because I was haunted too.

"Lizabeth, you lost your mind?" panted Joey.

I had indeed lost my mind, for all the smoldering emotions of that summer swelled in me and burst—the great need for my mother who was never there, the hopelessness of our poverty

---

9. **Furies** (fyŏŏr'ēz): in Greek and Roman mythology, spirits who pursue people who have committed crimes, sometimes driving them mad.

D Literary Focus

❓ **Conflict.** Describe the internal and external conflicts Lizabeth's father is facing. [Possible response: The external conflict he is facing is the challenge of providing for his family. The internal conflict is overcoming the torment and inadequacy he is feeling about his inability to do so.]

E Reading Skills

Making inferences about motivation. [Possible response to question 3: For many men, the ability to provide for their families is an important part of their sense of self-worth. Unable to provide for his family, Lizabeth's father feels like a failure. He cries because he is overcome by feelings of hopelessness and inadequacy.]

F Literary Focus

❓ **Internal conflict.** What do you think is haunting Lizabeth? [Possible responses: anger; fear of the future; frustration; despair at the realization that her father feels hopeless.] **What do you predict that she might do?** [Some students will predict her violence; others may think she means to make up with Miss Lottie in some way.]

A Reading Skills

Motivation and conflict.

[Possible response to question 4: Feelings of tension, fear, despondency, and frustration have built to a breaking point within Lizabeth; she explodes in a single violent act. She cries because of her feelings of remorse and the pain of her lost innocence.]

B Advanced Learners

? Enrichment. Miss Lottie has been fighting her entire life to preserve hope and beauty amid squalid poverty. Now she has finally lost her struggle because of Lizabeth. Why is this end to Miss Lottie's conflict both poignant and ironic? [Possible response: Miss Lottie's attempt to preserve hope was defeated by a young woman only fourteen years old. One might have expected Miss Lottie to have given up long ago and the younger woman to have held onto hope for longer.]

C Reading Skills

Motivation. [Possible responses to question 5: The episode marked the beginning of Lizabeth's journey into maturity and the process of developing empathy for others. Lizabeth may think about the marigolds because she still feels remorse for her actions and because only now in later years can she understand that Miss Lottie planted the flowers to endure the barren patch of her life.]

D Reading Skills

? Interpreting. What might Lizabeth mean by this last line? [Possible response: She has also tried to create beauty to overcome unhappiness.]

and degradation, the bewilderment of being neither child nor woman and yet both at once, the fear unleashed by my father's tears. And these feelings combined in one great impulse toward destruction.

"Lizabeth!"

I leaped furiously into the mounds of marigolds and pulled madly, trampling and pulling and destroying the perfect yellow blooms. The fresh smell of early morning and of dew-soaked marigolds spurred me on as I went tearing and mangling and sobbing while Joey tugged my dress or my waist crying, "Lizabeth, stop, please stop!"

And then I was sitting in the ruined little garden among the uprooted and ruined flowers, crying and crying, and it was too late to undo what I had done. Joey was sitting beside me, silent and frightened, not knowing what to say. Then, "Lizabeth, look."

I opened my swollen eyes and saw in front of me a pair of large, calloused feet; my gaze lifted to the swollen legs, the age-distorted body clad in a tight cotton nightdress, and then the shadowed Indian face surrounded by stubby white hair. And there was no rage in the face now, now that the garden was destroyed and there was nothing any longer to be protected.

"M-miss Lottie!" I scrambled to my feet and just stood there and stared at her, and that was the moment when childhood faded and womanhood began. That violent, crazy act was the last act of childhood. For as I gazed at the immobile face with the sad, weary eyes, I gazed upon a kind of reality which is hidden to childhood. The witch was no longer a witch but only a broken old woman who had dared to create beauty in the midst of ugliness and sterility. She had been born in squalor and

> 📖
> **MOTIVATION AND CONFLICT**
> **4.** Why does Lizabeth destroy the marigolds? Why do you think she cries as she does so?

lived in it all her life. Now at the end of that life she had nothing except a falling-down hut, a wrecked body, and John Burke, the mindless son of her passion. Whatever verve there was left in her, whatever was of love and beauty and joy that had not been squeezed out by life, had been there in the marigolds she had so tenderly cared for.

Of course I could not express the things that I knew about Miss Lottie as I stood there awkward and ashamed. The years have put words to the things I knew in that moment, and as I look back upon it, I know that that moment marked the end of innocence. Innocence involves an unseeing acceptance of things at face value, an ignorance of the area below the surface. In that humiliating moment I looked beyond myself and into the depths of another person. This was the beginning of compassion, and one cannot have both compassion and innocence.

The years have taken me worlds away from that time and that place, from the dust and squalor of our lives, and from the bright thing that I destroyed in a blind, childish striking out at God knows what. Miss Lottie died long ago and many years have passed since I last saw her hut, completely barren at last, for despite my wild contrition she never planted marigolds again. Yet, there are times when the image of those passionate yellow mounds returns with a painful poignancy. For one does not have to be ignorant and poor to find that his life is as barren as the dusty yards of our town. And I too have planted marigolds. ■

> 📖
> **MOTIVATION**
> **5.** What motivates Lizabeth to tell this story? Why does she still think of Miss Lottie's marigolds?

Vocabulary
contrition (kən·trish′ən) n.: deep feelings of guilt and repentance.

FAMILY/COMMUNITY ACTIVITY

"Marigolds" builds to the climactic event that marks the end of Lizabeth's childhood. Many cultures and religions around the world observe coming-of-age traditions that mark the transition from childhood to adulthood, such as a confirmation or a bar or bat mitzvah. Ask students to talk to community and family members about the coming-of-age traditions that they observe. Encourage students to ask

questions such as the following examples:

• When does the ceremony take place?
• How do you feel about the tradition?
• What should young people expect to gain from the experience?
• Is the coming-of-age tradition changing or evolving in any way? Has it changed in your lifetime?

Meet the Writer

Eugenia W. Collier

"I Must Have Done My Job Well"

"Marigolds" is a story that emerged from a difficult time in the life of its author, Eugenia W. Collier (1928–   ). Collier, who has taught English at Howard University, Baltimore Community College, and Morgan State University, tells how she came to write "Marigolds" and what the story means to her:

66 When I talk with people about 'Marigolds,' someone usually asks me whether the story is autobiographical. I am always pleased with the question, because it means that I must have done my job well—convinced the reader that the incidents in the story are actually happening. However, I always end up admitting that Lizabeth and I are two very different people. I was born and bred in the city of Baltimore, and my family never had the economic problems of Lizabeth's. In some ways we are different in temperament: I was never as daring as Lizabeth, never a leader among my peers. However, I hope that through her I have captured an experience which most young people have—the painful passage from childhood to adulthood, a passage which can be understood only in retrospect. Also, I was tapping into another deeply human experience: hoping desperately for something (planting marigolds) and then having that hope destroyed.

I wrote 'Marigolds' at a time of profound unhappiness. One night I had a tremendous urge to write. I wrote nonstop until the story was finished—about twenty-four hours. Later I sent 'Marigolds' (along with a fee I could hardly afford) to a well-advertised literary agency, which returned the story (not the fee) with a note saying that it had no plot, no conflict, and no hope of publication. Discouraged, I put 'Marigolds' away. Five years later, doing research for a project on black writing of the 1960s, I read stories in *Negro Digest* which were similar in subject matter to 'Marigolds.' I submitted my story, and *Negro Digest* published it. It won the Gwendolyn Brooks Prize for Fiction, it was selected for inclusion in an anthology of black fiction, and since then it has been included in a number of collections. Of all the fiction I have written, 'Marigolds' remains my favorite. 99

Connection

Summary ⬆ *above grade level*

The poem's speaker relates an event from his childhood that still troubles him today. He shot at and broke the wings of two birds. The birds, which could not fly, swam out to sea, and their cries could be heard for days.

Ⓐ Content-Area Connections

Literature: Literary Biography
Robert P. Tristram Coffin (1892–1955) was an American poet whose work focused on the farm and sea-faring life of New England. He saw poetry as a public service that should inspire people. In fact, he felt it was the poet's responsibility to say the best possible things about life. You might ask students how the poem could inspire readers. Coffin published more than fifty works and was awarded the Pulitzer Prize in poetry in 1936 for his collection *Strange Holiness* (1935).

Ⓑ Reading Skills

Summarizing. Play the poem from the *Audio CD Library,* or read it aloud in class. Then, have students work in pairs to summarize what happens in the poem and the effect it has on the speaker. [Possible response: As a boy the speaker shot two birds, badly injuring their wings instead of killing them. The guilt of this "sin" remains a part of his life; it still causes him to hear the cries of the injured birds above all other sounds of sorrow.]

Forgive My Guilt
Ⓐ Robert P. Tristram Coffin

Not always sure what things called sins may be,
I am sure of one sin I have done.
It was years ago, and I was a boy,
I lay in the frostflowers with a gun,
5   The air ran blue as the flowers, I held my breath,
Two birds on golden legs slim as dream things
Ran like quicksilver on the golden sand,
My gun went off, they ran with broken wings
Into the sea, I ran to fetch them in,
10   But they swam with their heads high out to sea,
They cried like two sorrowful high flutes,
With jagged ivory bones where wings should be.

Ⓑ For days I heard them when I walked that headland
Crying out to their kind in the blue,
15   The other plovers were going over south
On silver wings leaving these broken two.
The cries went out one day; but I still hear them
Over all the sounds of sorrow in war or peace
I ever have heard, time cannot drown them,
20   Those slender flutes of sorrow never cease.
Two airy things forever denied the air!
I never knew how their lives at last were spilt,
But I have hoped for years all that is wild,
Airy, and beautiful will forgive my guilt.

Connecting and Comparing Texts

Ask students to identify events, concepts, or themes of the poem that relate to those of "Marigolds." [Possible responses: The speaker in the poem and Lizabeth in "Marigolds" both commit an act of destruction; both feel guilty about what they did; both view the act as a loss of innocence; both events teach a lesson about being respectful and sympathizing with other living beings.]

Individual activity. Suggest that students create their own poems modeled after "Forgive My Guilt," using an experience that still haunts them. If you plan to ask students to read their poems in class, remind them to choose subject matter that they would be willing to share with their classmates.

Response and Analysis

Reading Check

1. What is the story's **setting**—that is, when and where does the story take place?

2. Who is Miss Lottie? Describe the children's daytime confrontation with her.

3. What does Lizabeth discover about her parents when she overhears their conversation?

4. What does Lizabeth do to Miss Lottie's flowers just before dawn?

Thinking Critically

5. What are Lizabeth's **internal conflicts**—what personal monsters are troubling her?

6. Lizabeth felt ashamed after she led the first attack against Miss Lottie. Why doesn't her sense of shame prevent her from destroying the garden at the end of the story? How is her **motivation** for this destructive act different from her motivation for taunting Miss Lottie earlier?

7. The narrator doesn't tell us much about the effect on Miss Lottie of the **external conflict** over the marigolds. Using the details the narrator *does* provide, explain how you think Miss Lottie was affected.

8. Lizabeth says that destroying the marigolds was her last act of childhood. Why does she think of herself as an adult from that moment on?

9. What does Lizabeth mean at the end of the story when she says that she too has planted marigolds? What do you think the marigolds have come to mean in the story? To answer, consider the feelings that the characters have had about the marigolds throughout the story:

   - Miss Lottie loves and cares for them.
   - The children do not understand why they are there.
   - Lizabeth wants to destroy them.

10. Lizabeth's parents are **subordinate characters** in the story, but their late-night conversation has a big impact on her. "The world had lost its boundary lines," she says in reaction to their conversation. What does she mean? What situations might make a child feel that boundaries have been lost?

Extending and Evaluating

11. Compare Lizabeth's feelings at the end of the story with those of the speaker of "Forgive My Guilt" (see the **Connection** on page 128). What did both children discover? In both cases, did you find it credible that a single act could cause a child to make such an important discovery? Explain your answer.

WRITING

Turning Points

Write an **autobiographical narrative** about a turning point in your life, an incident—whether minor or major, happy or sad—that made you grow up a little. What fears or conflicts did you face? What was the outcome of the incident? Include a reflection telling how the event brought you a little closer to being an adult. (Be sure to check your Quickwrite notes.) 🖉

▶ **Use "Writing an Autobiographical Narrative," pages 66–73, for help with this assignment.**

SKILLS FOCUS

Literary Skills
Analyze internal and external conflicts.

Reading Skills
Make inferences about character motivation.

Writing Skills
Write an autobiographical narrative.

Marigolds **129**

Response and Analysis

Thinking Critically

5. Possible answers: clinging to childhood; taking responsibility versus ignoring it; hope versus despair; the urge to create versus the desire to destroy.

6. Possible answer: Lizabeth's motivation for the first attack is boredom. Her motivation for the second attack is rage, fear, and helplessness at her family's situation. Her sense of shame is not strong enough to prevent this explosion.

7. Possible answer: The narrator tells us that Miss Lottie never plants marigolds again. While Miss Lottie may or may not have given up her spirit of hope, she seems to have decided not to express her feelings to others.

8. Possible answers: She has learned that actions have consequences; she is now aware of the hardships and frustrations that are part of adult life and can empathize with others.

9. Lizabeth means that she has taken a stand against despair by trying to create beauty. In the story, marigolds stand for beauty, hope, and strength.

10. Lizabeth's words might mean that she is confused by the role reversals and unexpected behavior of her parents. Other situations that might make a child feel this way are moving to a new town, the arrival of a new sibling, a divorce, or the loss of a family member.

Extending and Evaluating

11. Both children discovered that acts of physical destruction create lasting feelings of guilt. Many students may agree that single acts can bring about significant personal discoveries. They may use events from their own lives to justify their answers.

Reading Check

1. The story takes place in rural Maryland during the Great Depression of the 1930s.

2. Miss Lottie is an elderly neighbor who lives with her mentally disabled son. The children taunt Miss Lottie and call her a witch. They throw stones that damage her marigolds.

3. She discovers that her mother is currently the strong one of the family and that her father is overwhelmed with sadness at being unable to support his family.

4. In a violent fit of rage, Lizabeth destroys all of Miss Lottie's marigolds.

Vocabulary Development

Practice 1

2. contrition
3. clarity
4. impoverished
5. arid
6. malicious
7. futile
8. poignantly
9. inciting

Practice 2

Possible Answers

1. The marigolds were *as uncommon in this barren landscape as raindrops in the Sahara.*
2. The garden looked like *the sole color photograph in an album of black-and-white pictures.*
3. The days were as empty as *a deserted nest after the birds have flown south.*

ASSESSING

Assessment

■ *Holt Assessment: Literature, Reading, and Vocabulary*

RETEACHING

For another selection to teach character, see *The Holt Reader,* Collection 2.

Vocabulary Development

Analogies: Same or Different?

You can gain a better understanding of many words by completing an **analogy.** In an analogy the relationship between the words in the first pair is the same as the relationship in the second pair. In some common types of analogies, the words in the pairs are **synonyms** (words with the same meaning) or **antonyms** (words with opposite meanings). For more help with analogies, see pages 229 and 576.

PRACTICE 1

Use a word from the Word Bank to complete each analogy below. The first one has been done for you.

1. HARSHLY : ROUGHLY :: ___placidly___ : peacefully
2. BRAVERY : COURAGE :: _____ : regret
3. FLEXIBILITY : STIFFNESS :: _____ : vagueness
4. SOCIABLE : SHY :: _____ : wealthy
5. TARDY : PUNCTUAL :: _____ : wet
6. CHEERFUL : GLOOMY :: _____ : kind
7. FREQUENT : RARE :: _____ : useful
8. SWIFTLY : QUICKLY :: _____ : movingly
9. SINCERITY : FALSENESS :: _____ : suppressing

Word Bank

arid
futile
impoverished
poignantly
clarity
placidly
inciting
malicious
contrition

Figures of Speech: Making It Vivid

Collier's story is remarkable for its vivid figures of speech, which make the setting and the characters' feelings come alive. In a **figure of speech,** one thing is compared to another, very different thing. There are several kinds of figures of speech. A **simile** states the comparison using a word such as *like, as,* or *than:*

"But old fears have a way of <u>clinging like cobwebs</u>. . . ."

[Fears are compared to cobwebs.]

A **metaphor** compares two unlike things without using the word *like* or *as:*

"Memory is an abstract painting. . . ."

[Memory is directly compared to a painting.]

SKILLS FOCUS

Vocabulary Skills
Understand word analogies. Understand figures of speech (simile and metaphor).

PRACTICE 2

For each numbered item on the right, create at least one imaginative figure of speech. Remember that a figure of speech compares two *unlike* items.

1. The marigolds were _____.
2. The garden looked like _____.
3. The days were as empty as _____.

DIFFERENTIATING INSTRUCTION

Learners Having Difficulty

For extra practice, ask students to complete each sentence by creating a vivid simile or metaphor. Possible answers appear in brackets.

1. Children's games often resemble _____. [battles]
2. Conflict can simmer _____. [like a pot of soup on the stove]
3. Our usual supper of beans and rice tasted _____. [like dust from under the bed]
4. Innocence is _____. [a sleeping puppy]
5. Without the marigolds, Miss Lottie's yard looked _____. [like a face without eyes]

READ ON: FOR INDEPENDENT READING

FICTION
A Sapling Stands Tall

In Betty Smith's novel, a tree grows in Brooklyn—and so does young Francie Nolan. Living in a poor neighborhood with her parents and brother, Francie finds joys and an assortment of troubles as she comes of age. Her experiences are sometimes painful, but they become the building blocks of wisdom. *A Tree Grows in Brooklyn* takes place between 1902 and 1919, but don't be surprised if Francie and the Nolan family remind you of people you know.

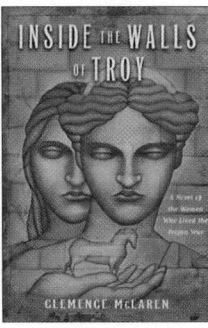

FICTION
A Beauty That Broke Hearts

Imagine having the kind of beauty that causes the death of fifty thousand men and the collapse of a great civilization. That is what happens to twelve-year-old Helen when she is kidnapped from her home and brought to the city of Troy. Clemence McLaren's novel *Inside the Walls of Troy* breathes new life into the ancient story of Helen, turning a mythical figure into a believable, flesh-and-blood young woman.

FICTION
Be Yourself

When you read the stories, poems, and plays in *American Dragons,* you'll hear the voices of twenty-five Asian American teenagers expressing their feelings. They are trying to figure out how to fit in and how to be themselves at the same time. In describing their struggles, they express a range of feelings—from rage to sorrow, from worry to wonder.

NONFICTION
The Boy Who Dreamed

Richard Wright's early years were plagued by hunger—for food, for knowledge, and for respect. He wrote stories filled with imagination and longing, and his intelligence left those around him feeling puzzled and threatened. After all, a black boy living in rural Mississippi in the 1920s couldn't go far in life—or could he? Wright's autobiography *Black Boy* is the stunning account of a young man who rose above oppression to live out his dreams.

Read On

For Independent Reading
If students enjoyed the themes and topics explored in the selections of this collection, you might recommend these titles for independent reading.

Assessment Options
The following projects can help you evaluate and assess your students' outside reading.

- **Make a map.** Have students create maps that depict the neighborhood described in *A Tree Grows in Brooklyn.* In addition to providing an overview of the geography of Brooklyn and its relationship to the greater New York area, maps should include legends that explain the function of lines and symbols. Students could also include in their maps illustrations of people, places, and scenes from the novel.

- **Create a reference guide.** Have students who read *Inside the Walls of Troy* work in groups to prepare a reference guide to Internet sources related to the Homeric myths. Students should divide their guide into different categories. For example, they could have one list of sites for exploring the historical background of the *Iliad* and *Odyssey,* another list of geographic resources, and a third for photos of artworks that depict Helen and other mythological figures.

DIFFERENTIATING INSTRUCTION

Estimated Word Counts and Reading Levels of Read On Books:

Fiction			Nonfiction		
A Tree Grows in Brooklyn	⬇	164,900	Black Boy	↔	87,000
American Dragons	↔	79,800			
Inside the Walls of Troy	↔	52,800			

KEY: ⬆ *above grade level*   ↔ *at grade level*   ⬇ *below grade level*

PRETEACHING

Skills Starter

Motivate. Have students brainstorm all the reasons that someone might tell a story. [Possible reasons: to teach a lesson, to scare someone, to pass the time] **List their suggestions on the chalkboard.** Allow a couple of students to relate a time when they told a story for a specific purpose and had good results.

DIRECT TEACHING

Integrating with Grammar, Usage, and Mechanics

As students start their short stories, they may have trouble using phrases and clauses skillfully. You may want to review Lessons 6 and 7 in the Language Handbook.

Writing a Short Story

Writing Assignment
Write a short story in which you use your imagination to express yourself and entertain others.

Have you ever been envious of a classmate, like Vita is of Helen in "Helen on Eighty-sixth Street"? You may have read many short stories and said to yourself, "That could be me." In fact, your life is probably filled with incidents that you could turn into stories. Now is your chance. In this workshop you'll write a **short story** of your own.

Prewriting

Find a Story Idea

On Fancy's Wings Short stories are works of **fiction.** The characters and events depicted in a short story might be based on real people and actual events, or they might be entirely the product of the writer's imagination. Brainstorm a list of ideas, and choose one as the starting point of your short story. You could write a story based on

- a great adventure you've always dreamed of having
- a historical event that fascinates or inspires you
- a personal experience from which you learned a lesson about life
- an incident from the life of a friend or relative

Plan Your Story

How to Begin There are five basic ingredients for any story: **plot, characters, point of view, setting,** and **theme.** You will need to use all of these ingredients, or elements, in your short story, but you can *start* by considering any one of them.

Plot What will happen in your story? The **plot** of a short story centers around a **conflict,** a struggle between opposing forces. Here are some of the different kinds of conflicts found in short stories.

TYPES OF CONFLICTS AND EXAMPLES	
External Conflict: character vs. character	Raul and Thomas compete for the final spot on the basketball team.
character vs. environment	Cassandra fights the storm as she tries to bring her small sailboat safely home.

(continued)

COLLECTION 2 RESOURCES: WRITING

Planning
- *One-Stop Planner* CD-ROM with ExamView Test Generator

Differentiating Instruction
- *Workshop Resources: Writing, Listening and Speaking*
- *Family Involvement Activities in English and Spanish*

- *Supporting Instruction in Spanish*

Writing and Language
- *Workshop Resources: Writing, Listening and Speaking*
- *Language Handbook Worksheets*
- *Daily Language Activities*

(continued)

character vs. situation	Shannon battles tradition to be allowed to play on a boys' baseball team.
Internal Conflict: **character vs. himself or herself (a struggle between conflicting ideas and feelings within a character)**	Jason is torn between his desire to help his friend pass an exam and his sense of right and wrong.

The conflict builds through a sequence of events, called the **rising action,** to a **climax,** the emotional high point of the story. After the climax, events unwind in the **resolution,** which shows the outcome of the conflict and brings the story to an end.

As you develop your plot, use the techniques listed below.

- Use plenty of **narrative details** about the actions, movements, gestures, and feelings of the characters to bring your story to life.
- Arrange your plot events in **chronological order,** the order in which the events actually occur.
- Use **flashbacks** to provide the background information necessary for readers to understand the story.
- **Pace** the action of your plot to reflect the mood you're trying to create. For example, a slow and leisurely pace might depict the events of a lazy summer afternoon. A fast and furious pace might depict the chaotic events of a chase scene.

Characters Who are the people in your story? Because short stories are just that—short—they usually concentrate on one **main character.** As you think of your main character, jot down answers to the following questions to bring that character to life.

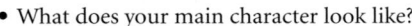 **DO THIS**

- What does your main character look like?
- What are his or her mannerisms?
- How does he or she act, think, feel, talk? (When characters in a story speak, they engage in **dialogue.** To be realistic, dialogue should sound the way real people talk.)

Supporting characters are developed in proportion to their importance in the story. In other words, if a supporting character appears briefly in your story, don't spend time developing that character. Give more detail about a supporting character who plays a key role in your story. To develop supporting characters, answer the same questions you answered to create your main character. You may not end up needing all the details, but you'll have them if you do.

Point of view Who will **narrate,** or tell, your story? Choose one of the following points of view, and use it consistently throughout your story.

 SKILLS FOCUS

Writing Skills
Write a short story. Develop plot, characters, point of view, setting, and theme.

Writing Workshop: Writing a Short Story **133**

MODELING AND DEMONSTRATION

Setting

Tell students that smells can bring back memories and elicit feelings. Encourage students to use words related to the sense of smell in their stories.

Write these two phrases on the chalkboard: *a restaurant kitchen, a deep forest.* Model making a list of sensory smell words that is relevant to each—perhaps *tangy, roasted,* and *cinnamon* for the kitchen and *musky, pine,* and *earthy* for the forest. Ask student volunteers to demonstrate understanding by sharing five to ten sensory words that fit the settings of their stories.

PRACTICE & APPLY 1

Guided and Independent Practice

Students might have difficulty coming up with story ideas. Provide these four possibilities for getting started, and monitor students' progress as they choose one and begin planning their stories.

- **Start with a plot.** Think of a conflict, or problem, that could be the center of the action. Have you heard, read, or seen anything lately that gives you ideas?

- **Start with a character.** Imagine what your main character would look like. Perhaps scan magazines looking for pictures of people who spark your imagination.

- **Start with a point of view.** Decide whether you are going to tell the story, either as yourself or as a character in the story, or whether you will have an omniscient narrator tell the story.

- **Start with a setting.** Where and when will your story take place? What time of the year is it? Is it set in the past, present, or future? Is the setting important to the story or not?

TIP Interior monologue is a technique writers use to reveal a character's thoughts. The character "thinks out loud" so the reader knows what the character is thinking. If you write from the first-person point of view, you must limit your use of interior monologue to the narrator. A third-person-omniscient narrator can use interior monologue for any character.

- A **first-person narrator** is either the main character, who tells his or her own story, or a supporting character, who tells the main character's story. The narrator uses the first-person pronoun *I* to tell the story. If you choose to use the first-person point of view, you limit yourself to telling only what the narrator could logically know and what he or she feels, thinks, or experiences.

- A **third-person-omniscient narrator** is not a character in the story, but an outside observer who sees and knows all. This narrator can tell the thoughts, feelings, and actions of any character in the story. He or she can narrate events occurring at the same time in different places. The omniscient narrator can also use **shifting perspectives,** revealing several characters' thoughts, feelings, and attitudes toward the same character or event. Use third-person pronouns—*he, she, they*—if you choose this point of view.

Read the examples below to see the difference your choice of point of view can make in your story.

> **First Person:** I walked to Mrs. Hawkins's house and knocked firmly on the door. When she opened it, I could tell she was surprised to see me. I quickly handed her the sandwich bag I had stored the card in.
>
> **Third Person Omniscient:** As Li walked to Mrs. Hawkins's house, she felt nervous. She knocked firmly on the door. Mrs. Hawkins was surprised to see Li standing on her doorstep. Quickly, Li handed her the sandwich bag that contained the card.

Setting Where and when does your story take place? **Setting** can play a major role in a short story, or it can be relatively unimportant. Use **sensory details**—words describing the sights, sounds, and smells of the setting—to help readers form specific mental pictures.

Setting often plays a role in establishing **mood**—the feeling or atmosphere of the story. For example, the setting of an isolated, old house surrounded by thick forests on a stormy night would contribute to a story's eerie, threatening mood.

Theme What is the **theme** of your story? What idea about life does it illustrate? Most often, stories suggest a theme through the details of characters, plot, setting, and point of view. The themes of most literature, including short stories, have to do with the emotions and experiences that make us human, such as fear, courage, loss, greed, love, and forgiveness.

SKILLS FOCUS

Writing Skills
Use sensory details.

PRACTICE & APPLY 1 Use the instructions in this section to develop the plot, characters, setting, and theme of a short story. Add sensory details to enhance your story.

DIFFERENTIATING INSTRUCTION

English-Language Learners

Have students tell a brief story from their native cultures in English. Discuss possible themes of the story. Then, explain that many themes are universal, and stories in various languages and from various cultures can share themes.

Writing

Writing a Short Story

A Writer's Framework

Beginning	Middle	End
• Begin with an intriguing event or an engaging introduction to the main character. • Establish the story's setting and the point of view. • Introduce the conflict that gives rise to the story's plot.	• Develop the events of the rising action. • Use narrative and sensory details to develop characters and describe the setting. • Bring the conflict to a head in an effective climax.	• Make the resolution of the conflict believable. • See that the resolution suggests the theme of the story.

A Writer's Model

The Long Lost Baseball Card

Li Hua, a thirteen-year-old baseball fanatic and rabid card collector, lay on her back in her bed. She was about to open the beat-up old book on baseball she'd paid a dollar for that morning at a garage sale. As she opened the dusty book, an object dropped out of it and hit her squarely on the end of her nose, making her sneeze and momentarily blinding her. She grabbed the object and held it away from her face. Her heart jumped in excitement when she saw that it was a Dizzy Dean baseball card. Dean was the great pitcher of the St. Louis Cardinals who won two games during the 1934 World Series. Fifteen minutes later, Li found the card on the Internet. It was worth well over a hundred dollars! What a find! Then she thought of Mrs. Hawkins, the kind woman who had sold her the book for a measly dollar, a book worth well over a hundred dollars, if you counted the card. Mrs. Hawkins's husband had died and she lived alone. She probably could use a hundred dollars.

Li remembered Mrs. Hawkins listening with a warm smile on her face while she rattled on about baseball and what a great find the book was. "I bought the book. The baseball card was in the book," Li said to herself. Mrs. Hawkins obviously doesn't know about the card. What harm would it do for me to keep it?"

Li picked up the phone to call Grandpa Lang and tell him about her discovery. Then, abruptly, she put it down. What would Grandpa Lang

(continued)

BEGINNING
Introduction to main character/Setting

Third-person point of view

Narrative and sensory details

Conflict suggested

MIDDLE

Interior monologue

Rising action

Learners Having Difficulty
Before beginning to draft their short stories, students may find it helpful to sketch storyboards of the events they plan to include in their stories. This can help students visually develop and organize the details for their stories.

DIFFERENTIATING INSTRUCTION

Advanced Learners

Enrichment. After students have read **A Writer's Model** on pp. 135–136, engage them in a class analysis of the model, using questions such as the ones below.

- How does the writer engage the reader in the introduction?
- Which narrative and sensory details are most effective in making the reader understand the significance of events in the story?
- Based on the resolution, what do you think the theme of the story is?

PRACTICE & APPLY 2

Guided and Independent Practice

Have students consult this checklist as they work on their story drafts.

- Characters: Add details to flesh out characters. Include physical descriptions and memories.
- Theme: Know where you are going as you write. The theme should develop naturally, not be added as an afterthought.
- Setting: Details of the setting should change as characters move from inside to outside, room to room, and so on.
- Point of View: Check frequently to make sure that you have not accidentally changed the point of view.

Monitor student progress by having mini-conferences to discuss student drafts in light of the four areas on the checklist.

Internal conflict

Flashback

Narrative and sensory details

Setting

Climax

Dialogue

END
Resolution

Sensory details
Theme

say? Would he be excited about the card, or would he be ashamed of her for keeping it? She couldn't stand for Grandpa Lang to be ashamed of her. The mere thought of disappointing him was terrible. At the same time, the card was like a strong magnet drawing her to it. That night she lay awake late into the night, wondering what to do.

As she tossed and turned, a scene from the past kept playing itself in her head. She and Grandpa Lang were standing in line to pay for the groceries they had bought. When it came time for Grandpa Lang to pay, he handed the cashier a ten-dollar bill. Grandpa didn't look at the change the cashier gave him. Instead, he stuffed it into his pocket, picked up the grocery bag, grabbed Li by the hand, and left the store. When they arrived at Grandpa Lang's house, Grandpa put the grocery bag on the table, emptied his pocket, and counted the change. "That young man gave me too much change," Grandpa Lang said. "He gave me change for a twenty instead of a ten. We must go back to the store, Li, and return the extra money."

Early the next morning, Li walked like a girl with a mission to Mrs. Hawkins's house and knocked firmly on the door. When the small woman answered the door, Li handed her the sandwich bag she'd stored the card in. "Here," she said, "is a card I found in the book you sold me yesterday. It's very valuable, so I knew you would want it back."

"That's so sweet of you, dear," Mrs. Hawkins said with a smile. "You know, my late husband was a great baseball fan. He even played on a minor-league team when we were young. He must have put that old card in that book to mark his place. I just know he would want someone who loves baseball as much as he did to have it. That card belongs to you, dear, but thank you for being such an honest young lady. I know your family must be very proud of you."

Li couldn't believe her ears. Her eyes welled up with tears as she poured out her thanks to Mrs. Hawkins and promised her that the card would become a prized part of her collection. Her heart felt so full she thought it might burst as she walked homeward, toward the waiting phone. Now she could call Grandpa Lang. She knew he would be as proud of her as she was of herself.

INTERNET

More Writer's Models

Keyword: LE5 9-2

PRACTICE & APPLY 2

Refer to the framework on page 135 and the Writer's Model above as you write the first draft of your short story. Return to the Prewriting section of this workshop as necessary to remind yourself of short story elements.

Revising

Revise Your Short Story

Author's Way Professional writers, authors who make their living by writing, are rarely satisfied with the first draft of anything they write. They spend hours rewriting, tweaking, and polishing their works, and even then they are not always satisfied. You should read and evaluate your story at least twice, once for content and organization and again for style. Use the charts below and on the next page as **think sheets** when you revise your story.

> **PEER REVIEW**
>
> Ask a classmate for feedback on your story's content, organization, and style. Have your classmate check for a consistent point of view.

▷ **First Reading: Content and Organization** The guidelines in the chart below can help you evaluate and revise the content and organization of your story.

Rubric: Writing a Short Story		
Evaluation Questions	▶ **Tips**	▶ **Revision Techniques**
❶ Does the introduction introduce the story's main character? Does it establish the setting and the narrator's point of view?	▶ **Underline** the words that introduce the main character. **Circle** the words that establish the setting. **Put a star** next to the pronoun that reveals the narrator's point of view.	▶ **Add** details to introduce the main character and to establish the setting. **Add** pronouns that clearly show the point of view of the story's narrator.
❷ Does the introduction clearly introduce the story's conflict?	▶ **Highlight** the sentence or sentences that introduce the conflict.	▶ **Add** sentences that make the conflict clear.
❸ Is the plot fully developed and organized in chronological order? Does the climax bring the conflict to a head?	▶ **Number** the events in the rising action. **Bracket** the climax.	▶ **Add** events to make the rising action clearer. **Rearrange** events that are out of order. **Add** details to make the climax more effective.
❹ Is the main character adequately developed?	▶ **Put a check mark** beside any dialogue and the narrative and sensory details that develop the main character.	▶ **Add** dialogue and narrative and sensory details where necessary to develop the main character.
❺ Is the resolution believable? Is the story's theme clear by the end of the story?	▶ **Highlight** the resolution. **Underline** the sentence or sentences that suggest the theme.	▶ **Replace** unrealistic events or details with more believable ones. **Add** a sentence or two to make the theme clearer.

DIRECT TEACHING

Elaboration

To further elaborate in their stories, students can add interior monologue. Have them read through their stories and mark any place where a character's thoughts could be revealed through an interior monologue. Caution students whose stories are in the first person that only the first person's thoughts can be presented; other characters' inner thoughts are unknown. Have them write interior monologue where appropriate.

RETEACHING

Evaluation Question #4

If students struggle with character development, you may have them answer this brief questionnaire about their main characters. If students cannot answer any of the questions, they should revise their stories by adding more details about their main characters.

- What are my physical characteristics? How old am I?
- What are my personality traits?
- What is the makeup of my family?
- What is my connection to other characters in the story?
- How am I affected by the main conflict in the story?

TECHNOLOGY TIP

Students may e-mail their short stories to parents, friends, or students in a colleague's class at another high school. Have students ask for feedback based on criteria that they develop and send with their narratives. When students receive feedback, have them review the comments for additional ways to improve their short stories.

GUIDED PRACTICE

Responding to the Revision Process

Answers

1. The revisions increase the emotional impact of the sentence. For example, the phrase "welled up with tears" is more descriptive than "watered."

2. The two additional sentences make it clear that Li is going to call her grandfather. The change is necessary because the reader might have forgotten about the grandfather and not made the connection that he was the reason Li wanted to make a phone call.

PRACTICE & APPLY 3

Independent Practice

You may ask students to use highlighters to mark the different structural parts of their short stories and to note in the margins the elements of the framework on p. 135 they have used. This will make it easy to recognize whether all necessary elements have been included.

Challenge students to change at least two verbs per paragraph. You may compare the new verb choices to the original verbs to see if students understand the concept of precise action verbs.

> **Second Reading: Style** Now, read and evaluate the style of your short story. Having good ideas for a plot, characters, and theme matters little if you don't engage the attention of your readers with a lively style. One way to ensure a lively, entertaining style is to use **vivid action verbs** that depict the action in your story with color and precision. Look at the examples below.

Dull Verbs	Vivid Verbs
walk	stroll
say	whisper
laugh	snicker

Style Guidelines

Evaluation Question	Tip	Revision Technique
Does the writer use vivid action verbs to depict action precisely?	**Put a star** by all of the verbs in a passage.	**Replace** dull verbs with precise action verbs.

ANALYZING THE REVISION PROCESS
Study these revisions, and answer the questions that follow.

replace

Her eyes *welled up with tears* watered as she *poured out her thanks to* thanked Mrs. Hawkins and promised her that the card would become a prized part of her collection.

Her heart felt so full she thought it might burst as she walked

add

homeward, toward the waiting phone. *Now she could call Grandpa Lang. She knew he would be as proud of her as she was of herself.*

Responding to the Revision Process

1. What did the writer accomplish by making the two revisions to the first sentence?

2. Why did the writer add two sentences at the end of the story? Do you think this revision was necessary? Why or why not?

Writing Skills
Revise for content and style.

PRACTICE & APPLY 3
Using the guidelines on these two pages, revise the content, organization, and style of your short story. Consider peer comments as you revise.

Publishing

Proofread and Publish Your Short Story

Tidy Tales After you've revised your short story, be sure to proofread it. Who will enjoy reading your short story if it is full of errors? You want your audience to focus on your story, not on mistakes you may have made. Check for and correct any errors in grammar, usage, and mechanics.

Welcome to the World of Publishing Your purpose for writing your short story was to express yourself and to entertain readers. Now that you've expressed your creative side to your classmates or teacher, it's time to publish your work so that others can read it. Here are some ways to present your story to a wider audience.

- Submit your story to a publication that accepts work from young writers. Your teacher or school librarian may have a list of such publications to get you started.

- Collect your class's short stories into a book. Arrange them in sections by theme: science fiction, adventure, drama, westerns, and mystery, for example. Then, put the book in the school library for others to read.

- Put your short story on the Internet by posting it to your own Web site, your school's Web site, or a site that accepts submissions from young writers.

- Rewrite your short story as a children's book. Simplify the plot and dialogue and add illustrations so that a younger audience will understand your story.

Reflect on Your Short Story

20/20 Hindsight Look back on what you've done, and reflect on what you've learned in the process of writing a short story. Use these questions to focus your thoughts.

- How did writing this short story help you understand the process that other authors go through when writing for publication?

- What short story elements do you think were the strongest in your story? Why?

PRACTICE & APPLY 4 First, proofread your story, paying particular attention to your punctuation of dialogue. Then, publish your story for a wider audience. Finally, reflect on your short story by answering the questions above.

TIP Proofreading will help ensure that your essay follows the **conventions** of standard American English. For example, check to see that you have correctly punctuated dialogue in your story. For more on **using quotation marks,** see Quotation Marks, 13c–j, in the Language Handbook.

COMPUTER TIP

If you have access to a computer and advanced publishing software, use those tools to design and format your class's short stories so that they look more professional. For more on **page design,** see *Designing Your Writing* in the Writer's Handbook.

SKILLS FOCUS

Writing Skills
Proofread, especially for the correct use of quotation marks with dialogue.

Writing Workshop: Writing a Short Story **139**

SKILLS FOCUS, pp. 140–143

Grade-Level Skills

■ **Literary Skills**
Analyze influences on characters (such as internal and external conflict and motivation) and how those influences affect the plot.

INTRODUCING THE SKILLS REVIEW

Use this review to assess students' understanding of the skills taught in this collection. You can use the annotations to guide students in their reading.

DIRECT TEACHING

A Reading Skills

❷ Making inferences about motivation. What can you infer about the people crossing the bridge? Why are they traveling? [Possible response: The clues "pontoon bridge" and "soldiers" suggest that the people are fleeing to escape a war. They probably are trying to get farther away from a front line or from an enemy advance.]

B Literary Focus

❷ Character traits. What does this passage reveal about the narrator? [Judging from the narration, he doesn't deviate from his orders. He carries out his duties in a matter-of-fact way.]

C Literary Focus

❷ Conflict. Compare the concerns that occupy each character. [The old man is concerned about his animals' welfare; the narrator is concerned about the approaching enemy, presumably the Fascists.] What outside force engages both characters in an external struggle? [The Spanish Civil War]

Test Practice

Character

DIRECTIONS: Read the following short story. Then, read and respond to the questions that follow.

During the Spanish Civil War (1936–1939), the Loyalists, who supported the government of Spain, fought against the Nationalists (Fascists), who were led by General Francisco Franco. "Old Man at the Bridge" is set during this conflict and shows the war's impact on the Spanish people.

Old Man at the Bridge
Ernest Hemingway

An old man with steel rimmed spectacles and very dusty clothes sat by the side of the road. There was a pontoon bridge across the river and carts, trucks, and men, women and children were crossing it. The mule-drawn carts staggered up the steep bank from the bridge with soldiers helping push against the spokes of the wheels. The trucks ground up and away heading out of it all and the peasants plodded along in the ankle deep dust. But the old man sat there without moving. He was too tired to go any farther.

It was my business to cross the bridge, explore the bridgehead beyond and find out to what point the enemy had advanced. I did this and returned over the bridge. There were not so many carts now and very few people on foot, but the old man was still there.

"Where do you come from?" I asked him.

"From San Carlos," he said, and smiled.

That was his native town and so it gave him pleasure to mention it and he smiled.

"I was taking care of animals," he explained.

"Oh," I said, not quite understanding.

"Yes," he said, "I stayed, you see, taking care of animals. I was the last one to leave the town of San Carlos."

He did not look like a shepherd nor a herdsman and I looked at his black dusty clothes and his gray dusty face and his steel rimmed spectacles and said, "What animals were they?"

"Various animals," he said, and shook his head. "I had to leave them."

I was watching the bridge and the African looking country of the Ebro Delta[1] and wondering how long now it would be before we would see the

SKILLS FOCUS

Pages 140–143 cover **Literary Skills** Analyze character traits, internal and external conflicts, and motivation.

---

1. **Ebro Delta:** the land at the mouth of the Ebro, the longest river entirely in Spain.

READING MINI-LESSON

Reviewing Word-Attack Skills Activity. Display these words. Have students group the words according to the sound represented by the letter *y*—the consonant sound /y/, the vowel sound /ī/, the vowel sound /i/, or the vowel sound /ē/. If a word has two *y*'s, students should identify the sound represented by each *y* and, if necessary, place the word in two groups, underlining the *y* that stands for that group's specific sound.

tyrant	hyphen	lawyer
uncertainty	identify	hypnotize
yearling	typical	rhyme
mystify	dignity	yodel
cylinder	lanyard	sympathy

Collection 2: Skills Review

enemy, and listening all the while for the first noises that would signal that ever mysterious event called contact, and the old man still sat there.

"What animals were they?" I asked.

"There were three animals altogether," he explained. "There were two goats and a cat and then there were four pairs of pigeons."

"And you had to leave them?" I asked.

"Yes. Because of the artillery.[2] The captain told me to go because of the artillery."

"And you have no family?" I asked, watching the far end of the bridge where a few last carts were hurrying down the slope of the bank.

"No," he said, "only the animals I stated. The cat, of course, will be all right. A cat can look out for itself, but I cannot think what will become of the others."

"What politics have you?" I asked.

"I am without politics," he said. "I am seventy-six years old. I have come twelve kilometers now and I think now I can go no further."

"This is not a good place to stop," I said. "If you can make it, there are trucks up the road where it forks for Tortosa."

"I will wait a while," he said, "and then I will go. Where do the trucks go?"

"Towards Barcelona," I told him.

"I know no one in that direction," he said, "but thank you very much. Thank you again very much."

He looked at me very blankly and tiredly, then said, having to share his worry with some one, "The cat will be all right, I am sure. There is no need to be unquiet about the cat. But the others. Now what do you think about the others?"

"Why they'll probably come through it all right."

"You think so?"

"Why not," I said, watching the far bank where now there were no carts.

"But what will they do under the artillery when I was told to leave because of the artillery?"

"Did you leave the dove cage unlocked?" I asked.

"Yes."

---

2. **artillery** (är·til'ər·ē) *n.*: mounted guns, such as cannons.

DIRECT TEACHING

D **Literary Focus**

? **Character interactions.** How would you characterize the narrator's attitude toward the old man, considering the questions he asks and the advice that he supplies? [Possible response: These exchanges indicate that the narrator is concerned about the old man's state of mind and his well-being. However, given the situation, the narrator cannot do much to help.]

[y for /y/—lawyer, yearling, yodel, lanyard. y for /ī/—tyrant, hyphen, identify, rhyme, mystify. y for /i/—hypnotize, typical, mystify, cylinder, sympathy. y for /ē/—uncertainty, dignity, sympathy.]

Activity. Explain that y can sometimes stand for different sounds in related words. Display these pairs of words. Have students tell if y stands for the same sound or different sounds in the two words.

1.	type	typical [different]
2.	myth	mythological [same]
3.	tyrant	tyrannize [different]
4.	cycle	cyclical [different]
5.	style	stylize [same]

Activity. Display these pairs of words. Have students tell if the underlined letters in the words stand for the same sound(s) or different sounds.

1.	maniac	enthusiasm [same]
2.	radio	patio [same]
3.	diet	relief [different]
4.	cranium	triumph [different]
5.	liar	familiar [different]

DIRECT TEACHING

A Literary Focus

❓ Character interactions.
What is the upshot of this final exchange between the two characters? [Possible response: The narrator feels powerless to help the old man, who will probably remain where he is. The narrator will have to move on to perform his duties.]

Test-Taking Tips

Remind students that the correct answers to inference questions *must* be supported by details in the text. In question 10, for example, H is clearly incorrect. At no point in the story does the narrator reveal dissatisfaction with his duties or any intention to desert the army.

For more instruction on how to answer multiple-choice items, refer students to **Test Smarts.**

Answers and Model Rationales

1. **B** The old man clearly states that artillery was the reason for his departure.

2. **G** Both characters are embroiled in the events of the war. There is no conflict between the characters mentioned in F, H, and J.

3. **C** The old man's remarks and questions to the narrator about the safety of the animals indicate that the necessity of leaving them behind concerns him greatly.

4. **G** From the narrator's description we learn that the old man is tired. His worries about the animals are revealed in his own statements.

A

"Then they'll fly."

"Yes, certainly they'll fly. But the others. It's better not to think about the others," he said.

"If you are rested I would go," I urged. "Get up and try to walk now."

"Thank you," he said and got to his feet, swayed from side to side and then sat down backwards in the dust.

"I was taking care of animals," he said dully, but no longer to me. "I was only taking care of animals."

There was nothing to do about him. It was Easter Sunday and the Fascists were advancing toward the Ebro. It was a gray overcast day with a low ceiling so their planes were not up. That and the fact that cats know how to look after themselves was all the good luck that old man would ever have.

---

1. Why did the old man at the bridge leave his home in San Carlos?
   A He was taken prisoner by the enemy.
   B He was fleeing an artillery attack.
   C He needed medical attention.
   D He wanted to get help for his animals.

2. The story's most serious **external conflict** is between —
   F the old man and the narrator
   G the two main characters and the war
   H the old man and the soldiers at the bridge
   J the narrator and the captain

3. The old man faces an **internal conflict** between —
   A rescuing the cat and saving the goats and pigeons
   B his loyalty to the government and his belief in the enemy's cause
   C his desire to take care of his animals and the need to leave his home
   D crossing the bridge to seek shelter and fleeing to Barcelona

4. The old man can *best* be **characterized** as —
   F angry and determined
   G tired and worried
   H hopeful and encouraging
   J unconcerned and unfriendly

Using Academic Language

Review of Literary Terms
Ask students to look back through the collection to find the meanings of the terms listed on the right. Then, have students show their grasp of the skills by citing passages from the collection that illustrate the meanings of those terms.

First-Person Narration (p. 84); **Dialogue** (pp. 84, 86); **Dramatic Monologue** (p. 84); **Characterization** (p. 85); **Character Traits** (p. 104); **External and Internal Conflict** (pp. 116, 118); **Subordinate Characters** (p. 116); **Motivation** (p. 116).

Collection 2: Skills Review

5. What is the narrator's **motivation** for urging the old man to move on?

   A   Concern for the old man's safety

   B   The need to carry out his orders

   C   Anger at the old man

   D   A desire to reunite the old man with his family in Barcelona

6. Several times the narrator says that he was "watching" the bridge or the far bank of the river. What **character trait** does the narrator reveal through this description?

   F   Curiosity

   G   Bravery

   H   Carelessness

   J   Alertness

7. What does the old man reveal about himself when he says in his **dialogue** with the narrator, "I am without politics"?

   A   He does not care about his native town.

   B   He has not taken sides during the war.

   C   He is rebelling against the leaders of his country.

   D   He is trying to hide his beliefs from the narrator.

8. Which of the following words *best* describes the behavior of the narrator toward the old man?

   F   Protective

   G   Hostile

   H   Indifferent

   J   Loving

9. From what the narrator says in the last paragraph about the old man's luck, we can infer that the **narrator** feels —

   A   sympathetic and optimistic

   B   relieved and carefree

   C   powerless and pessimistic

   D   superstitious and frightened

10. At the end of the story, we can infer that the **narrator** —

    F   leaves the old man to his fate

    G   stays to guard the old man

    H   deserts the army

    J   searches for someone to travel with the old man

Constructed Response

11. At different points in the story, both the old man and the narrator "give up." Identify details and words from the story that show each character's feeling of defeat.

5. **A**   D is contradicted by facts in the story. The narrator displays no anger so C is incorrect. It is possible that the narrator has instructions to move civilians along, but A is a better answer than B, since he encourages rather than orders the old man to depart.

6. **J**   Since the narrator is a soldier on duty, alertness rather than idle curiosity is the probable cause for his "watching." Doing so neither requires bravery nor indicates carelessness.

7. **B**   A and C are contradicted by facts in the story. B is a better choice than D, since the old man does not appear insincere and seems concerned only with his animals' welfare, not politics.

8. **F**   Since the narrator shows concern but not deep affection for the old man, F is a better choice than J.

9. **C**   The narrator's statement "There was nothing to do about him" indicates his feelings of powerlessness.

10. **F**   The last paragraphs support the inference that the narrator must continue to carry out his duties and that his interactions with the old man have ended.

Constructed Response

11. Details and words from the story that show the old man's feeling of defeat include his inability to move while other people are hastily crossing the bridge, his statement that "I think now I can go no further," his blank expression, and his falling down as the story concludes. The narrator reveals his feeling of defeat by saying, "There was nothing to do about him."

ASSESSING

Assessment

■ *Holt Assessment: Literature, Reading, and Vocabulary*

Review of Informational Terms

Ask students to review the collection to find the meanings of the terms listed on the right. Then, ask students to use those terms to explain how to extend ideas presented in primary and secondary sources.

Primary Source (p. 96); **Secondary Source** (p. 96); **Analyze** (p. 96); **Main Idea** (p. 96); **Evaluate** (p. 96); **Facts** (p. 96); **Opinions** (p. 96); **Elaborate** (p. 96).

Collection 2: Skills Review

Vocabulary Skills

Context Clues

Modeling. To model how to choose the correct answer for item 1, say, "There are many context clues for *incantation*. For example, it is performed in order to achieve a specific goal, and it contains magical words and is referred to as a prayer. Since the object of the incantation is not an enemy or a dead person, A and B can be eliminated. D is a better choice than C, since Vita wants to 'make something happen,' not give thanks."

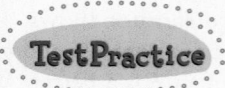

Answers and Model Rationales

1. **D** See rationale above.

2. **G** The context clue "the audience can understand Vita's lines" makes it clear that G is the correct choice.

3. **B** To capture the meaning of *odyssey*, the correct answer must be consistent with "a voyage of discovery." A and C do not fit this context. B is better than D, since it conveys a sense of motion.

4. **H** "Earn very little money" and "lost their jobs" are clues that *impoverished* refers to people in difficult financial straits. Only H conveys this meaning.

5. **A** The clause "he did not give up" is a context clue revealing that *undaunted* means "not discouraged."

6. **H** The context clue "such as" indicates that an example or examples follow. If "finishing school or pursuing a career" are examples of endeavors, then *endeavors* must mean "undertakings."

Collection 2: Skills Review

Vocabulary Skills

Context Clues

DIRECTIONS: Use the context clues in the following passages to identify the meaning of the underlined vocabulary words.

1. In "Helen on Eighty-sixth Street," Vita makes up an incantation in order to win the role of Helen and to bring her father back. Although the magical words she says are actually the names of Greek foods, Vita's prayer is heartfelt.
   In this passage, *incantation* means a —
   A curse against an enemy
   B speech praising a dead person
   C blessing giving thanks
   D chant to make something happen

2. In "Helen on Eighty-sixth Street," the audience can understand Vita's lines because she can speak precisely and clearly enunciate her words.
   In this passage, *enunciate* means —
   F shout
   G pronounce
   H quote accurately
   J mumble

3. In "Helen on Eighty-sixth Street," Vita sets forth on a kind of odyssey. However, instead of traveling throughout the world, she goes on a voyage of discovery into her own heart.
   In this passage, *odyssey* means —
   A ordeal
   B journey
   C change
   D education

4. In "Marigolds," Lizbeth tells about her impoverished hometown. People work hard but earn very little money, and many others have lost their jobs.
   In this passage, *impoverished* means —
   F terrified
   G guilty
   H poor
   J unlucky

5. "Feeding Frenzy" describes the obstacles David Levitt faced when he decided to start a food-sharing program. Undaunted, he did not give up and ultimately succeeded.
   In this passage, *undaunted* means —
   A not discouraged
   B proud
   C judgmental
   D furious

6. "Community Service & You" explains that you can learn new skills from volunteering that will help you in your future endeavors, such as finishing school or pursuing a career.
   In this passage, *endeavors* means —
   F years
   G obstacles
   H undertakings
   J knowledge

SKILLS FOCUS

Vocabulary Skills
Identify word meanings using context clues.

Vocabulary Review

Have students select the correct word from the box to complete the following sentences.

| mentorship | intimidating | ramparts |
| malicious | bureaucratic | undaunted |

1. The hill was [intimidating] to the bikers.

2. New rules made the process more [bureaucratic].

3. We stormed the castle's [ramparts].

4. Sunita cooks under the [mentorship] of a professional chef.

5. The turtle, [undaunted] by failure, repeatedly tried to flip itself over.

6. [Malicious] gossip is unkind.

Collection 2: Skills Review
Writing Skills

Test Practice

DIRECTIONS: The following paragraph is from a draft of a student's short story. Read the questions below it, and choose the best answer to each question.

(1) After riding twenty-two hours on a train, Amanda was glad to hear the conductor's booming voice call out "Union Station, Chicago." (2) "Spending a month in Canada was great, but I can't wait to see my family!" she thought. (3) She had just enough time on her phone card to call her dad at his office to let him know she was in and needed a ride. (4) She dragged the suitcase to a pay phone and made the call. (5) "Honey, I'm swamped with work, so take the commuter train and I'll pick you up at the depot," Dad said.

1. What words did the writer use to establish the setting?
   A "Amanda was glad to hear . . . 'Union Station, Chicago.'"
   B "had just enough time on her phone card"
   C "I can't wait to see my family!"
   D "a month in Canada was great"

2. Which of the following sentences would add sensory details?
   F Amanda's family lived about thirty miles outside of Chicago.
   G Amanda had brought a souvenir for her grandmother.
   H The steamy Chicago summer heat hit her like a slap in the face.
   J Her dad ran his own business.

3. Why did the writer put sentence 5 in quotation marks?
   A The sentence is dialogue.
   B It is the title of the story.
   C It is the conflict of the story.
   D The sentence creates suspense.

4. Which of the following sentences, if added, would tell the conflict of the story?
   F A child clutched his parent's hand as he exited the train.
   G When Amanda hung up, she realized that she had only Canadian money.
   H Amanda thought about the photos she would show her family.
   J Inside the station, it was noisy, crowded, and hot.

5. Which of the following sentences could be added to effectively describe the appearance of the main character?
   A The chubby conductor smiled broadly at the departing passengers.
   B Her dad was a small, wiry man who worked too hard.
   C Amanda said goodbye to the woman she had sat next to on the train.
   D The tall, brown-eyed girl getting off the train was tired and hungry.

SKILLS FOCUS

Writing Skills
Write a short story.

Writing Skills

Answers

1. A
2. H
3. A
4. G
5. D

APPLICATION

Once Upon a Time . . .

Have students create children's books based on experiences that are meaningful to them and suitable for youngsters. Tell students to keep their audience in suspense by saving any surprises for the conclusion. Remind them to include vivid details, limit the number of words on a page, and add colorful illustrations. You may have students bind their storybooks and give them to a younger class to read.

EXTENSION

Singing the Blues

Explain to students that blues and folk songs are a way for songwriters to share their stories with an audience. Have students choose favorite blues or folk songs and, for homework, write summaries of the songwriters' stories. Students may find examples of blues and folk songs in musical heritage dictionaries, biographical dictionaries of composers, encyclopedias, or documentaries on videotape. Students may form small groups and compare the stories from their songs.

Homework

RESOURCES: WRITING

Assessment
■ *One-Stop Planner* CD-ROM with ExamView Test Generator
■ *Holt Assessment: Writing, Listening, and Speaking*

Internet
■ *Holt Online Assessment*
■ *Holt Online Essay Scoring*

Collection 3
Narrator and Voice

Informational Reading Focus:
Synthesizing Sources

About Collection 3

In Collection 3, students will master the following skills:

- **Literary Skills:** Analyze the omniscient, third-person-limited, and first-person narrator (or point of view); understand surprise endings; and analyze voice.
- **Reading Skills:** Monitor your reading; summarize plot; draw conclusions; and synthesize information from several sources on a single topic.
- **Vocabulary Skills:** Use context clues; identify degrees of intensity among synonyms; create word maps; and understand Greek and Latin roots.
- **Writing Skills:** Develop, write, and revise an expository essay analyzing a biography.

Informational Text

Each collection of *Elements of Literature* provides a variety of informational texts related to the literature selections by theme or topic.

Minimum Course of Study

Most skills can be taught with a minimum number of selections and features. In the chart to the right, lessons highlighted in green constitute the minimum course of study that provides coverage of the skills taught in Collection 3.

Resource Manager
(pp. 146C–146D)

Lesson and workshop resources are referenced in the Resource Manager on the pages that follow. These resources can be used to reinforce the skills taught in Collection 3, remediate students who are having difficulty, and provide supporting activities for English-language learners.

Scope and Sequence

Selection ▪ Feature	Literary Skills
Elements of Literature: Narrator and Voice *by* John Leggett	• Understand narrators, or points of view (omniscient, first person, and third person limited), tone, and voice
The Interlopers *by* Saki ↑ *above grade level*	• Analyze the omniscient narrator (or point of view) • Understand the surprise ending
The Necklace *by* Guy de Maupassant ↔ *at grade level*	• Analyze the third-person-limited point of view
The Cask of Amontillado *by* Edgar Allan Poe ↑ *above grade level* **Informational Text:** • Poe's Final Days • Poe's Death Is Rewritten as Case of Rabies, Not Telltale Alcohol • If Only Poe Had Succeeded When He Said Nevermore to Drink • Rabies Death Theory *by* Kenneth Silverman; *The New York Times;* Burton R. Pollin *and* Robert E. Benedetto; R. Michael Benitez, M.D.	• Understand the first-person narrator • Analyze the unreliable narrator
Writing Workshop: *Analyzing Nonfiction*	
Skills Review: *Literary Skills* *Vocabulary Skills* *Writing Skills*	• Analyze narrator (or point of view) and voice

Reading Skills	Vocabulary Skills	Writing ▪ Grammar and Language ▪ Listening and Speaking Skills
• Monitor your reading	• Understand and use context clues	• Write a surprise ending
• Summarize plot	• Identify degrees of intensity among synonyms	• Write a position statement • Write a description • Use possessive pronouns and pronoun contractions correctly
• Draw conclusions • Synthesize information from several sources on a single topic	• Create word maps showing etymology, meaning, and context • Understand Greek and Latin word roots	• Write a new beginning for a short story • Write a speech • Punctuate dialogue correctly
		• Write an expository essay analyzing a biography
	• Understand synonyms	• Write an analysis of a biography

Selection ■ Feature	Planning	Differentiating Instruction ■ Lesson Plans with ELL Strategies and Practice	Reading ■ Vocabulary
Elements of Literature: Narrator and Voice *by* John Leggett	• PowerNotes: Point of View		
The Interlopers *by* Saki	• One-Stop Planner with ExamView Test Generator	• The Holt Reader, pp. 82–91 • Holt Adapted Reader • Holt Reading Solutions, pp. 85–90 • Supporting Instruction in Spanish, p. 11 • Audio CD Library, disc 6 • Audio CD Library, Selections and Summaries in Spanish	• The Holt Reader • Holt Adapted Reader • Holt Reading Solutions • Vocabulary Development, p. 12
The Necklace *by* Guy de Maupassant	• One-Stop Planner with ExamView Test Generator	• Holt Adapted Reader • Holt Reading Solutions, pp. 91–96 • Supporting Instruction in Spanish, p. 12 • Audio CD Library, disc 6 • Audio CD Library, Selections and Summaries in Spanish	• Holt Adapted Reader • Holt Reading Solutions • Vocabulary Development, p. 13 • PowerNotes: Summarizing a Story
The Cask of Amontillado *by* Edgar Allan Poe **Informational Text:** • Poe's Final Days • Poe's Death Is Rewritten as Case of Rabies, Not Telltale Alcohol • If Only Poe Had Succeeded When He Said Nevermore to Drink • Rabies Death Theory *by* Kenneth Silverman; *The New York Times;* Burton R. Pollin *and* Robert E. Benedetto; R. Michael Benitez, M.D.	• One-Stop Planner with ExamView Test Generator	• Holt Adapted Reader • Holt Reading Solutions, pp. 97–108 • Supporting Instruction in Spanish, pp. 12–13 • Audio CD Library, disc 7 • Audio CD Library, Selections and Summaries in Spanish • Family Involvement Activities in English and Spanish, p. 6	• Holt Adapted Reader • Holt Reading Solutions • Vocabulary Development, pp. 14, 15
Writing Workshop: *Analyzing Nonfiction*	• One-Stop Planner with ExamView Test Generator	• Workshop Resources: Writing, Listening, and Speaking, pp. 24–32 • Supporting Instruction in Spanish, p. 70	
Skills Review: *Literary Skills* *Vocabulary Skills* *Writing Skills*			

The Holt Reader

The Holt Reader is a consumable paperback book which can be used alone or to accompany *Elements of Literature*. It offers guided support throughout the reading process and encourages students to become active readers by circling, underlining, questioning, and jotting down responses as they read. *The Holt Reader* works well for homework, students who have missed class, additional instructional time, reteaching, and remediation.

Holt Reading Solutions (HRS)

Holt Reading Solutions pulls together reading resources in the *Elements of Literature* program to create a powerful tool for intervention and whole-class instruction. *HRS* includes diagnostic assessment tools, lesson plans for English-language learners and special education students, adaptations of selected reading selections, vocabulary and comprehension worksheets, information on phonics and decoding, and additional instruction and practice in remedial reading skills.

Writing ▪ Grammar and Language ▪ Listening and Speaking	Assessment
• Daily Language Activities	• Holt Assessment: Literature, Reading, and Vocabulary • Holt Online Assessment • One-Stop Planner with ExamView Test Generator
• Daily Language Activities • Language Handbook Worksheets, pp. 150, 151, 153	• Holt Assessment: Literature, Reading, and Vocabulary • Holt Online Assessment • One-Stop Planner with ExamView Test Generator
• Daily Language Activities • Language Handbook Worksheets, p. 146	• Holt Assessment: Literature, Reading, and Vocabulary • Holt Online Assessment • One-Stop Planner with ExamView Test Generator
• Daily Language Activities • Workshop Resources: Writing, Listening, and Speaking, pp. 24–32	• Holt Assessment: Writing, Listening, and Speaking • Holt Online Assessment • One-Stop Planner with ExamView Test Generator
	• Holt Assessment: Writing, Listening, and Speaking • One-Stop Planner with ExamView Test Generator

Technology

INTERNET

- go.hrw.com
- Holt Online Assessment
- Holt Online Essay Scoring
- Elements of Literature Online

MEDIA

 • One-Stop Planner with ExamView Test Generator

 • PowerNotes

 • Audio CD Library, discs 6 and 7

 • Audio CD Library, Selections and Summaries in Spanish

 • Visual Connections Videocassette Program, Segment 3

 • Fine Art Transparencies, 5

 Transparency   Video

 CD-ROM   Audio CD

One-Stop Planner with ExamView Test Generator

The *One-Stop Planner* CD-ROM contains electronic versions of print-based teaching resources, clips from the video program, and valuable assessment tools. The *One-Stop Planner* resources are presented in easy-to-follow, point-and-click menu formats. To preview resources or print out worksheets and tests, you simply make a selection and click.

One-Stop Planner CD-ROM

Collection 3

Grade-Level Skills

■ **Literary Skills**

Analyze the way tone, voice, persona, and choice of narrator affect characterization and plot.

■ **Reading Skills**

Synthesize the content from several sources or works by a single author on a single issue; paraphrase and connect the ideas with related topics in other sources.

INTRODUCING THE COLLECTION

The unsettling stories in this collection are by three masters of the unexpected: Saki (H. H. Munro), Guy de Maupassant, and Edgar Allan Poe. All three stories build to surprising conclusions while employing different points of view: omniscient, third-person limited, and first person. In the informational pieces that follow the Poe story, students synthesize information about the controversy surrounding his mysterious death. The collection culminates with an opportunity for students to write a biographical sketch in which they compare and contrast ideas presented in four sources and draw their own conclusions from those sources.

COLLECTION 3 RESOURCES: READING

Planning
■ *One-Stop Planner* CD-ROM with ExamView Test Generator

Differentiating Instruction
■ *Holt Reading Solutions*
■ *The Holt Reader*
■ *Holt Adapted Reader*
■ *Family Involvement Activities in English and Spanish*

■ *Supporting Instruction in Spanish*

Vocabulary
■ *Vocabulary Development*

Grammar and Language
■ *Language Handbook Worksheets*
■ *Daily Language Activities*

Assessment
■ *Holt Assessment: Literature, Reading, and Vocabulary*
■ *One-Stop Planner* CD-ROM with ExamView Test Generator
■ *Holt Online Assessment*

Collection 3

Narrator and Voice

INFORMATIONAL READING FOCUS

SYNTHESIZING SOURCES

> I want to feel I have my arm around a shoulder of this reader and I'm explaining, narrating, telling a wonderful story to this person. . . .
>
> —Russell Banks

INTERNET
Collection Resources
Keyword: LE5 9-3

Quilting Time (1986) by Romare Bearden.
Glass mosaic (c. 9′ 5″ × 13′ 11″).

Estate of Romare Bearden. © Romare Howard Bearden Foundation.
Licensed by VAGA, New York.

Internet
- go.hrw.com (Keyword: LE5 9-3)
- *Elements of Literature Online*

Media
- *Audio CD Library*
- *Audio CD Library, Selections and Summaries in Spanish*

- *Fine Art Transparencies*
- *Visual Connections Videocassette Program*
- *PowerNotes*

SKILLS FOCUS,
pp. 148–149

SKILLS FOCUS,
pp. 148–149

Grade-Level Skills

■ **Literary Skills**
Analyze the way tone, voice, persona, and choice of narrator affect characterization and plot.

Review Skills

■ **Literary Skills**
Contrast different points of view, and explain how they affect the overall theme of the work.

Elements of Literature:
Narrator and Voice

Call on a volunteer to describe waking up and getting ready for school in the morning. Then, ask the class to imagine the parents of the same student describing the same scene. How might the two accounts be different? Use this example to review the terms *first-person narrator* and *third-person narrator* and to point out that each person involved in an event views the event from a different perspective. Remind students that an author's choice of narrator affects how readers view the events in a story.

Narrator and Voice *by* John Leggett

WHO'S TALKING?

When you read a story, you hear someone—the narrator—telling the story. The narrator controls everything we know about the characters and events. There are three main types of narrators, or **points of view: omniscient** (äm·nish'ənt), **first person,** and **third person limited.**

Omniscient Point of View: The All-Knowing Storyteller

When the **omniscient point of view** is used, the narrator is not a character in the story and almost never refers to himself or herself directly. *Omniscient* means "all-knowing," and the omniscient narrator is able to tell us everything about every character (including how each one thinks and feels). Let's look at a story told from the omniscient point of view:

One day a young woman looked out her apartment window and saw a man playing a saxophone. "Cool," she thought as she swayed to his tune. A big brown dog joined the man and howled along with the music.
  Then a man in pajamas yelled from another window, complaining that the noise woke him up and he was going to call the police. This man, who worked the night shift and had to sleep all day, liked cats better than dogs anyway. The young saxophonist left.

The First-Person Point of View: "I" as the Storyteller

Unlike the all-knowing omniscient narrator, the **first-person narrator** is a character in the story who talks to us, using *I,*

the first-person pronoun. (Literary critics sometimes use the term **persona** to refer to a first-person narrator.)
  We get a very personal view of what is happening from a first-person narrator, but we know *only* what he or she thinks and experiences and is able—or chooses—to tell us. Always question whether a first-person narrator is **credible,** or can be trusted. An **unreliable narrator** is biased and does not (or cannot) tell the truth. Let's look at our story told by the man in pajamas, for example. Would you consider his opinion of the music reliable?

Oh, man! Just as I was finally dozing off, he starts playing that stupid saxophone. I've already been fired from one job because I fell asleep on the night shift. Now it's going to happen again. I don't know which sounds worse, that tone-deaf saxophonist or that yowling dog. I'm going to call the police.

Third Person Limited: Focus on One Character

In the **third-person-limited point of view,** the storyteller zooms in on just one character but talks about the character in the third person, using *he* or *she.* With this point of view, we share one character's reactions to everything that happens in the story, but what we know about the other characters is limited. Suppose we hear our story from this point of view, focusing on the saxophone player:

He found a good spot in front of Park View Apartments and started playing soulfully on his sax. He wanted an audi-

INTERNET
More About
Narrator and
Voice
Keyword: LE5 9-3

Literary Skills
Understand narrators, or points of view (omniscient, first person, and third person limited), tone, and voice.

148 Collection 3 Narrator and Voice • Synthesizing Sources

Learners Having Difficulty
Narrator and voice. Help students understand the concept of tone in literature by reminding them that their speaking tone sometimes reveals their attitude toward a person or an event. As an example, ask volunteers to say, "I need some help" in different tones of voice (for example, cheerful,

commanding, desperate, confident, nervous). Then, have them discuss what attitude each tone communicates. Remind students that since readers cannot "hear" the writer's tone of voice, they must pick it up from the words the narrator uses. Then, read a few paragraphs from several pieces of literature that the class has recently read, and help

students identify the tone of each work, pointing out places where the choice of words creates a certain tone.

Advanced Learners
Acceleration. This activity can help students analyze the ways tone is used to achieve specific rhetorical or aesthetic purposes.
Small-group activity. Have students form

ence and needed money. After one song, he spotted a cute girl at a window, applauding madly. A dog howled with the music, but the sax player let him stay, hoping the dog might attract some donations. Then he heard a man yelling about calling the police—clearly not a music lover.

Tone: Watch That Attitude!

A story's tone can be described in a single word: joyous, somber, humorous, serious, angry, tender, ironic. **Tone** is the attitude a speaker or writer takes toward a subject, character, or audience.

If you change a story's point of view, you may change the tone as well. For example, how might the tone of the saxophonist's story be different if the young woman were telling the story instead of the man in pajamas?

Voice: One-of-a-Kind Style

Tone is one aspect of the **voice** that characterizes a piece of writing. Voice refers to the writer's use of language and overall style, and it's created by the writer's tone and choice of words (**diction**). Often you can identify the author of a piece of writing from the voice. Sometimes writers purposely switch voices, or their voice may change over time, but usually a writer's voice remains the same from work to work.

In fiction, narrators can also be said to have a voice, which is created by their manner of speaking, word choice, and tone. The narrator's voice can affect our view of characters and plot events and

shape the tone of the story as a whole. Imagine, if you will, the big brown dog telling our story.

Practice

Write a paragraph telling the saxophone story from the point of view of the young woman or the big brown dog. Use either the first-person or the third-person-limited point of view, and try to create a distinct voice. Remember to show what the character is thinking and feeling.

I remember well my sensation as we first entered the house. I knew instantly that something was very wrong. I realized that my father's chair had been sat in, as well as my mother's and my own. The porridge we had left on the table to cool had been partially eaten. None of this, however, prepared me for what we were about to discover upstairs. . . .

Practice

Possible response: I'd been wandering the streets for hours, picking up one interesting scent after another, wondering when one of them might lead to a decent meal. Maintaining my freedom as a dog of the streets requires skill: avoiding the dog-catcher, satisfying the insistent call of the digestive juices, and finding a little human attention among the bustling crowds. Suddenly I heard a wail. A man was blowing a saxophone. The sound pierced my brain like a half-remembered primal cry from the distant past. Instinctively my vocal chords opened, my nose pointed skyward, and I was howling along with the sax. Images of moonlit nights, a furry pack of brothers, and the frozen Arctic tundra flooded over me. Then I noticed that people were throwing coins into the man's box. Maybe they'd throw some spare crumbs my way! I howled my most soulful wail. It was worth a try.

Apply

Encourage students to write a brief version of a well-known fairy tale from the first-person point of view of one of the characters.

small groups. Ask them first to define the meanings of the words *aesthetic* and *rhetorical* and to use these words as they discuss a piece of literature. Then, have students determine the tone of a story they have recently read. Encourage them to analyze the way that tone achieves a specific aesthetic or rhetorical purpose.

Grade-Level Skills

■ **Literary Skills**
Analyze the way tone, voice, persona, and choice of narrator affect characterization and plot.

■ **Reading Skills**
Monitor your reading.

Review Skills

■ **Literary Skills**
Contrast different points of view, and explain how they affect the overall theme of the work.

Summary ⬆ *above grade level*

Ulrich von Gradwitz and Georg Znaeym are engaged in a heated feud that dates back in their families for generations. The conflict involves a strip of forest that runs along the border between their properties. One night Ulrich is out patrolling his grounds, hunting for Georg, who he believes is poaching. Suddenly, in a dark, lonely spot in the forest, the two men come face to face, each intent on murdering the other. Before they can shoot, however, a tree falls, pinning both men to the ground. At first each claims his men will show up first and kill the other. As time passes, however, they begin to realize the folly of their feud. The men make peace and pledge eternal friendship. Together they call for help, and Ulrich rejoices when he sees figures approaching. In the surprise ending, Ulrich suddenly realizes that the figures are not rescuers— but wolves.

Before You Read

The Interlopers

Make the Connection
Quickwrite ✎

Most arguments can be settled when people agree to talk or compromise, but some disagreements become so bitter that they last for many years. Indeed, some regions of the world have been locked in conflict for generations. Write down a few examples of feuds that have torn families or even countries apart. What keeps such bitter hatred alive?

Literary Focus
Omniscient Narrator: Knowing It All

An **omniscient narrator** is someone who knows everything about everyone in the story. Since an omniscient narrator is not one of the characters, he or she can move easily from the mind of one character to the mind of the next. The narrator can also jump from place to place or zoom in and out. However, the fact that the narrator knows everything doesn't mean that you will learn all the information at once. Sometimes an omniscient narrator will save an important bit of information for the *very last moment* of the story.

Surprise Endings

A **surprise ending** resolves a story's conflict in a totally unexpected—yet logical—way. In Saki's story the surprise at the end may make you rethink the story.

Reading Skills 🕮
Monitoring Your Reading

Good readers use the following strategies to get through a difficult sentence or

INTERNET
Vocabulary
Practice
•
More About Saki
•
Keyword: LE5 9-3

SKILLS FOCUS

Literary Skills
Understand the omniscient narrator (or point of view) and the surprise ending.

Reading Skills
Monitor your reading.

passage. As you read Saki's story, have a notebook or some self-sticking notes handy so that you can follow these guidelines:

• When you don't understand a word, look for **context clues.**
• Break down long sentences into simpler ones.
• Look for the subject and verb in complicated sentences.
• Stop at the end of a passage you think is important, and **summarize** it.
• **Re-read** difficult passages.

Vocabulary Development

precipitous (prē·sip′ə·təs) *adj.:* very steep.

acquiesced (ak′wē·est′) *v.* (used with *in*): accepted; complied with.

marauders (mə·rôd′ərz) *n.:* people who roam in search of loot, or goods to steal.

exasperation (eg·zas′pər·ā′shən) *n.:* great annoyance.

pious (pī′əs) *adj.:* showing religious devotion.

retorted (ri·tôr′tid) *v.:* replied sharply.

condolences (kən·dō′ləns·iz) *n.:* expressions of sympathy.

languor (laŋ′gər) *n.:* weakness; weariness.

reconciliation (rek′ən·sil′ē·ā′shən) *n.:* friendly end to a quarrel.

succor (suk′ər) *n.:* help given to someone in distress; relief.

RESOURCES: READING

Planning
■ *One-Stop Planner* CD-ROM with ExamView Test Generator

Differentiating Instruction
■ *Holt Reading Solutions*
■ *The Holt Reader*
■ *Holt Adapted Reader*
■ *Supporting Instruction in Spanish*

■ *Audio CD Library, Selections and Summaries in Spanish*

Vocabulary
■ *Vocabulary Development*

Grammar and Language
■ *Daily Language Activities*

Moon Shadows (1992) by Lois Dodd. Oil on canvas (36" × 50").

Courtesy Fischbach Gallery, New York.
© Lois Dodd/Licensed by VAGA, New York, NY.

THE INTERLOPERS

Saki

Ulrich von Gradwitz patrolled the dark forest in quest of a human enemy.

In a forest of mixed growth somewhere on the eastern spurs of the Carpathians,[1] a man stood one winter night watching and listening, as though he waited for some beast of the woods to come within the range of his vision and, later, of his rifle. But the game for whose presence he kept so keen an outlook was none that figured in the sportsman's calendar as lawful and proper for the chase; Ulrich von Gradwitz patrolled the dark forest in quest of a human enemy.

The forest lands of Gradwitz were of wide extent and well stocked with game; the narrow strip of precipitous woodland that lay on its outskirt was not remarkable for the game it

---

1. **Carpathians** (kär·pā′thē·ənz): mountain range that starts in Slovakia and extends through Poland, Ukraine, and Romania.

Vocabulary
precipitous (prē·sip′ə·təs) adj.: very steep.

The Interlopers   **151**

A Literary Focus

? Omniscient narrator. What perspective do you get from the omniscient narrator that you would probably not get if one of the two men were telling the story? [Possible response: The omniscient narrator can present both sides of the story. If only one man told the story, the other man's perspective would be neglected.]

B Reading Skills

? Monitoring your reading. Point out that this long passage describes an event and its results, which take place within an instant. Ask students to summarize the passage by answering these questions: What major event happens? What is the result of this event? [Possible response: A tree falls on Ulrich and Georg. Both are pinned beneath the tree.]

---

harbored or the shooting it afforded, but it was the most jealously guarded of all its owner's territorial possessions. A famous lawsuit, in the days of his grandfather, had wrested it from the illegal possession of a neighboring family of petty landowners; the dispossessed party had never acquiesced in the judgment of the courts, and a long series of poaching affrays[2] and similar scandals had embittered the relationships between the families for three generations. The neighbor feud had grown into a personal one since Ulrich had come to be head of his family; if there was a man in the world whom he detested and wished ill to, it was Georg Znaeym, the inheritor of the quarrel and the tireless game snatcher and raider of the disputed border forest. The feud might, perhaps, have died down or been compromised if the personal ill will of the two men had not stood in the way; as boys they had thirsted for one another's blood, as men each prayed that misfortune might fall on the other, and this wind-scourged winter night Ulrich had banded together his foresters to watch the dark forest, not in quest of four-footed quarry, but to keep a lookout for the prowling thieves whom he suspected of being afoot from across the land boundary. The roebuck,[3] which usually kept in the sheltered hollows during a storm wind, were running like driven things tonight, and there was movement and unrest among the creatures that were wont to sleep through the dark hours. Assuredly there was a disturbing element in the forest, and Ulrich could guess the quarter from whence it came.

He strayed away by himself from the watchers whom he had placed in ambush on the crest of the hill and wandered far down the steep slopes amid the wild tangle of undergrowth, peering through the tree trunks and listening through the

---

whistling and skirling[4] of the wind and the restless beating of the branches for sight or sound of the marauders. If only on this wild night, in this dark, lone spot, he might come across Georg Znaeym, man to man, with none to witness—that was the wish that was uppermost in his thoughts. And as he stepped round the trunk of a huge beech he came face to face with the man he sought.

The two enemies stood glaring at one another for a long silent moment. Each had a rifle in his hand, each had hate in his heart and murder uppermost in his mind. The chance had come to give full play to the passions of a lifetime. But a man who has been brought up under the code of a restraining civilization cannot easily nerve himself to shoot down his neighbor in cold blood and without a word spoken, except for an offense against his hearth and honor. And before the moment of hesitation had given way to action, a deed of Nature's own violence overwhelmed them both. A fierce shriek of the storm had been answered by a splitting crash over their heads, and ere they could leap aside, a mass of falling beech tree had thundered down on them. Ulrich von Gradwitz found himself stretched on the ground, one arm numb beneath him and the other held almost as helplessly in a tight tangle of forked branches, while both legs were pinned beneath the fallen mass. His heavy shooting boots had saved his feet from being crushed to pieces, but if his fractures were not as serious as they might have been, at least it was evident that he could not move from his present position till someone came to release him. The descending twigs had slashed the skin of his face, and he had to wink away some drops of blood from his eyelashes before he could take in a general view of

---

4. **skirling** (skurl'iŋ) v. used as n.: shrill, piercing sound.

Vocabulary
acquiesced (ak'wē·est') v. (used with in): accepted; complied with.
marauders (mə·rôd'ərz) n.: people who roam in search of loot, or goods to steal.

---

2. **poaching affrays** (ə·frāz'): noisy quarrels or brawls about poaching, which means "fishing or hunting illegally on private property."
3. **roebuck** (rō'buk') n.: male (or males) of the roe deer, small deer that live in Europe and Asia.

DIFFERENTIATING INSTRUCTION

Learners Having Difficulty
Invite learners having difficulty to read "The Interlopers" in interactive format in *The Holt Reader* and to use the sidenotes as aids to understanding the selection. The interactive version provides additional instruction, practice, and assessment of the literary skill taught in the Student Edition.

Monitor students' responses to the selection, and correct any misconceptions that arise.

English-Language Learners
Help set the scene for students' reading by discussing the concept of a feud. Define and use phrases such as *feuding over, long-standing feud, family feud,* and *blood feud.* Ask volun-

teers to provide examples of each term from history, literature, and film.

Special Education Students
For lessons designed for special education students, see *Holt Reading Solutions.*

the disaster. At his side, so near that under ordinary circumstances he could almost have touched him, lay Georg Znaeym, alive and struggling, but obviously as helplessly pinioned[5] down as himself. All round them lay a thick-strewn wreckage of splintered branches and broken twigs.

Relief at being alive and exasperation at his captive plight brought a strange medley of pious thank offerings and sharp curses to Ulrich's lips. Georg, who was nearly blinded with the blood which trickled across his eyes, stopped his struggling for a moment to listen, and then gave a short, snarling laugh.

"So you're not killed, as you ought to be, but you're caught, anyway," he cried, "caught fast. Ho, what a jest, Ulrich von Gradwitz snared in his stolen forest. There's real justice for you!"

And he laughed again, mockingly and savagely.

"I'm caught in my own forest land," retorted Ulrich. "When my men come to release us, you will wish, perhaps, that you were in a better plight than caught poaching on a neighbor's land, shame on you."

Georg was silent for a moment; then he answered quietly:

"Are you sure that your men will find much to release? I have men, too, in the forest tonight, close behind me, and *they* will be here first and do the releasing. When they drag me out from under these branches, it won't need much clumsiness on their part to roll this mass of trunk right over on the top of you. Your men will find you dead under a fallen beech tree. For form's sake I shall send my condolences to your family."

"It is a useful hint," said Ulrich fiercely. "My men had orders to follow in ten minutes' time, seven of which must have gone by already, and when they get me out—I will remember the hint. Only as you will have met your death poaching on my lands, I don't think I can decently send any message of condolence to your family."

---

5. **pinioned** (pin′yənd) *v.* used as *adj.*: pinned, as if chained or tied up.

"Good," snarled Georg, "good. We fight this quarrel out to the death, you and I and our foresters, with no cursed interlopers to come between us. Death and damnation to you, Ulrich von Gradwitz."

"The same to you, Georg Znaeym, forest thief, game snatcher."

Both men spoke with the bitterness of possible defeat before them, for each knew that it might be long before his men would seek him out or find him; it was a bare matter of chance which party would arrive first on the scene.

Both had now given up the useless struggle to free themselves from the mass of wood that held them down; Ulrich limited his endeavors to an effort to bring his one partially free arm near enough to his outer coat pocket to draw out his wine flask. Even when he had accomplished that operation, it was long before he could manage the unscrewing of the stopper or get any of the liquid down his throat. But what a heaven-sent draft[6] it seemed! It was an open winter,[7] and little snow had fallen as yet, hence the captives suffered less from the cold than might have been the case at that season of the year; nevertheless, the wine was warming and reviving to the wounded man, and he looked across with something like a throb of pity to where his enemy lay, just keeping the groans of pain and weariness from crossing his lips.

"Could you reach this flask if I threw it over to you?" asked Ulrich suddenly. "There is good wine in it, and one may as well be as comfortable as one can. Let us drink, even if tonight one of us dies."

---

6. **draft** *n.*: drink.
7. **open winter**: mild winter.

Vocabulary

exasperation (eg·zas′pər·ā′shən) *n.*: great annoyance.

pious (pī′əs) *adj.*: showing religious devotion.

retorted (ri·tôr′tid) *v.*: replied sharply.

condolences (kən·dō′ləns·iz) *n.*: expressions of sympathy.

C Advanced Learners

? **Acceleration.** What is ironic about Georg's statement? Why is it the opposite of what you might expect? [Possible response: He rejoices at Ulrich's being trapped, even though he is also trapped.] **What does the statement reveal about Georg?** [Possible responses: He is so thoroughly blinded by hatred that he cannot recognize his own peril; the defeat of his enemy is more important to him than his own survival.] **What view of human nature does this passage suggest?** [Possible response: It suggests a bleak, pessimistic view of people, as more interested in revenge than in their own well-being.]

D Literary Focus

? **Surprise ending.** The Before You Read page indicates that the story has a surprise ending. Given what you know about surprise endings, do you think the situation will be resolved the way either man predicts? Give a reason for your opinion. [Possible response: It probably won't be, because there would be no surprise if the situation were resolved the way they describe.]

E Reading Skills

Monitoring your reading. This sentence, like many lengthy sentences in the story, may be difficult for some readers to follow. Suggest that readers try to summarize the sentence. If they cannot, suggest that they re-read it. [Possible summary: Because the winter has been mild, the men are not suffering from the cold. Even so, as the wine warms Ulrich, he pities his injured enemy and admires him for not complaining.]

Advanced Learners

Acceleration. Use the following activity with advanced learners to help them analyze how a theme represents a view on life.
Activity. After students read the story, ask them to articulate the theme. Encourage them to discuss what the story and its theme suggest about the author's view of life.

A Literary Focus

❷ Omniscient narrator. How does the author's use of an omniscient narrator affect your understanding of Ulrich's character? [Possible response: Knowing what Ulrich is thinking prepares the reader for his change in attitude.]

B Reading Skills

❷ Speculating. Who might the interlopers Georg mentions be? [Possible responses: He might mean poachers who want to hunt on the disputed land; perhaps he's referring to people like the lawyers who handled the original case but could not bring peace.]

C Reading Skills

❷ Monitoring your reading. How might you break this sentence into shorter, simpler sentences? [Possible response: The wind tore through the branches of the cold, gloomy forest. It whistled round the tree trunks. The two men waited for others to rescue them.]

"No, I can scarcely see anything; there is so much blood caked round my eyes," said Georg; "and in any case I don't drink wine with an enemy."

(A) Ulrich was silent for a few minutes and lay listening to the weary screeching of the wind. An idea was slowly forming and growing in his brain, an idea that gained strength every time that he looked across at the man who was fighting so grimly against pain and exhaustion. In the pain and languor that Ulrich himself was feeling, the old fierce hatred seemed to be dying down.

"Neighbor," he said presently, "do as you please if your men come first. It was a fair compact. But as for me, I've changed my mind. If my men are the first to come, you shall be the first to be helped, as though you were my guest. We have quarreled like devils all our lives over this stupid strip of forest, where the trees can't even stand upright in a breath of wind. Lying here tonight, thinking, I've come to think we've been rather fools; there are better things in life than getting the better of a boundary dispute. Neighbor, if you will help me to bury the old quarrel, I—I will ask you to be my friend."

Georg Znaeym was silent for so long that Ulrich thought perhaps he had fainted with the pain of his injuries. Then he spoke slowly and in jerks.

"How the whole region would stare and gabble if we rode into the market square together. No one living can remember seeing a Znaeym and a von Gradwitz talking to one another in friendship. And what peace there would be among the forester folk if we ended our feud tonight. And if we choose to make peace among **(B)** our people, there is none other to interfere, no interlopers from outside. . . . You would come and keep the Sylvester night[8] beneath my roof,

---

8. **Sylvester night:** feast day honoring Saint Sylvester (Pope Sylvester I, d. 335), observed on December 31.

and I would come and feast on some high day at your castle. . . . I would never fire a shot on your land, save when you invited me as a guest; and you should come and shoot with me down in the marshes where the wildfowl are. In all the countryside there are none that could hinder if we willed to make peace. I never thought to have wanted to do other than hate you all my life, but I think I have changed my mind about things too, this last half-hour. And you offered me your wine flask. . . . Ulrich von Gradwitz, I will be your friend."

For a space both men were silent, turning over in their minds the wonderful changes that this dramatic reconciliation would bring about. In the cold, gloomy forest, with the wind tearing in fitful gusts through the naked branches and whistling **(C)** round the tree trunks, they lay and waited for the help that would now bring release and succor to both parties. And each prayed a private prayer that his men might be the first to arrive, so that he might be the first to show honorable attention to the enemy that had become a friend.

Presently, as the wind dropped for a moment, Ulrich broke the silence.

"Let's shout for help," he said; "in this lull our voices may carry a little way."

"They won't carry far through the trees and undergrowth," said Georg, "but we can try. Together, then."

The two raised their voices in a prolonged hunting call.

"Together again," said Ulrich a few minutes later, after listening in vain for an answering halloo.

"I heard something that time, I think," said Ulrich.

Vocabulary

languor (laŋ′gər) *n.:* weakness; weariness.

reconciliation (rek′ən·sil′ē·ā′shən) *n.:* friendly end to a quarrel.

succor (suk′ər) *n.:* help given to someone in distress; relief.

READING MINI-LESSON

Developing Word-Attack Skills
Write the selection word *compromised* on the chalkboard. Point out that *compromised* looks like a combination of the prefix *com–* and the word *promised,* and in fact, it is. The prefix *com–* adds the meaning "together" to *promise,* forming a word that means "to make a mutual promise; to decide something together." Explain that *compromised* is not pronounced like a combination of *com–*

and *promised.* Compare the pronunciations of *promised* (präm′ist) and *compromised* (käm′prə·mīzd′), and help students identify the changes in stress and letter sounds.

Explain that the addition of prefixes and suffixes may change the way a word is pronounced. Write these pairs of words on the chalkboard, and compare their pronunciations.

    human   inhumanity

fatigue   indefatigable

sign   insignificant

Activity. Display these pairs of related words. Have students decide how the pronunciation of the two words differ.

1. habit   habituate   4. serve preservation
2. oblige obligation   5. recite recitation
3. solution resolution   6. mania maniacal

Chish Yah XV (1992) by Rick Bartow. Pastel and graphite on paper (20″ × 40″).

D Literary Focus

? Surprise ending. Explain why the ending is surprising. [Possible responses: Readers are expecting rescuers, but instead the wolves seal the men's doom; readers have been led to expect an ending in which one man would triumph over the other in some way.]

VIEWING THE ART

Rick Bartow (1946–   ) is a Native American artist and teacher who lives in the state of Oregon.

Activity. What qualities of the wolf does this artwork stress? [Possible responses: It stresses that the wolf is a carnivorous predator; it stresses the wolf's sharp teeth and the wolf's ability to stalk and focus on its prey.]

GUIDED PRACTICE

Monitoring students' progress. Guide the class in answering these comprehension questions. Have students support their responses with passages from the text.

True-False

1. The von Gradwitz and Znaeym families have a long history of friendship. [F]
2. Ulrich hopes to come across Georg alone in the forest. [T]
3. Ulrich makes a peace offering of some bread. [F]
4. Georg's and Ulrich's attitudes toward each other change dramatically while they are together in the forest. [T]
5. At the end the men are rescued. [F]

"I heard nothing but the pestilential[9] wind," said Georg hoarsely.

There was silence again for some minutes, and then Ulrich gave a joyful cry.

"I can see figures coming through the wood. They are following in the way I came down the hillside."

Both men raised their voices in as loud a shout as they could muster.

"They hear us! They've stopped. Now they see us. They're running down the hill toward us," cried Ulrich.

---

9. **pestilential** (pes′tə·len′shəl) *adj.*: Strictly speaking, *pestilential* means "deadly; causing disease; harmful." Here, Georg uses the word to mean "cursed."

"How many of them are there?" asked Georg.

"I can't see distinctly," said Ulrich; "nine or ten."

"Then they are yours," said Georg; "I had only seven out with me."

"They are making all the speed they can, brave lads," said Ulrich gladly.

"Are they your men?" asked Georg. "Are they your men?" he repeated impatiently, as Ulrich did not answer.

"No," said Ulrich with a laugh, the idiotic chattering laugh of a man unstrung with hideous fear.

"Who are they?" asked Georg quickly, straining his eyes to see what the other would gladly not have seen.

"*Wolves.*" ∎

D

The Interlopers   **155**

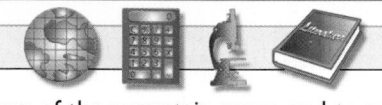

CONTENT-AREA CONNECTIONS

Social Science: The Carpathians
The Carpathians carve a nine-hundred-mile path through eastern Europe. Though this mountain range is the eastern continuation of the Alps, it is not nearly as high. The tallest peak, Mount Gerlach, is 8,711 feet.
Mixed-ability group activity. Invite a group of students of mixed abilities to research the region. Encourage them to find images of the mountain range and to research the countries through which it passes. You may wish to have them interview a member of the community or a history teacher in the school who is knowledgeable about the area. Invite the group to present an oral report or to display their findings as a photo essay or bulletin board feature.

Background. The aunts who raised young Munro later served as models for some of his characters. His aunt Augusta, for example, inspired a character in his famous short story "Sredni Vashtar."

For Independent Reading

If students choose to read "The Open Window," you might suggest that they notice what kind of narrator tells the story and think about the effect of the narrator on their perceptions of the characters and the events.

Connection

Summary ⬄ *at grade level*

> In this traditional African fable, Goat and Fox are quarreling. Goat, hoping to get revenge, plans a trick. However, he is the one who is ultimately the victim. The tale concludes with a moral warning.

DIRECT TEACHING

A **Reading Skills**

❓ **Comparing and contrasting.**
How is the relationship of Goat and Fox like that of Ulrich and Georg?
[Possible responses: Both pairs are feuding; both relationships are competitive.]

B **Reading Skills**

❓ **Expressing an opinion.**
Would this be a good moral, or theme, for "The Interlopers"?
[Possible responses: Yes, because Ulrich and Georg presumably die as a result of their feud. No, because they had resolved their quarrel.]

Meet the Writer

Saki

An Exotic Imagination

Hector Hugh Munro (1870–1916) wrote stories with snappy endings that were either wickedly funny or terrifying. Munro was born in Burma, where his father was an officer in the military police. When his mother died suddenly, he went to live with his grandmother and two stern aunts in a house in England whose windows were never opened. The aunts considered Hector sickly; he played with few children and was not sent to school until he was ten.

When he began writing stories, Munro took a foreign pen name, Saki, after the character who served wine to the gods in the then-popular poem the *Rubáiyát of Omar Khayyám*. (Omar Khayyám was a Persian poet.)

For Independent Reading

If you enjoyed "The Interlopers," try Saki's story "The Open Window," about a young girl with an unusual imagination.

CONNECTION / FABLE

The Trapper Trapped

**Vai (African) traditional,
retold by Roger D. Abrahams**

A Goat and Fox were quarreling, and Goat told Fox that he intended to get him into trouble so bad he would never be able to get out. Fox said, "All right; you do that, and I will return the favor to you."

Goat went for a walk and saw Leopard. Being frightened, Goat asked, "Auntie, what are you doing here?" "My little one is sick," said Leopard. Then Goat, thinking quickly, said, "Fox has medicine that will make your little one well." Leopard said to call Fox, so Goat went to Fox and said, "They are calling you."

"Who is calling me?" replied Fox. "I don't know," said Goat; "I think it is your friend. Go this way and you will run into him." Fox went down the path and at length came upon Leopard. Fox was frightened, and inquired: "Did you call me?" "Yes, my son. Goat came just a while ago and told me you had medicine that would make my little one well." "Yes," said Fox, "I have medicine that will cure your little one, but I must have a little goat horn to put it in. If you get me a goat horn, I will let you have the medicine." "Which way did Goat go?" asked Leopard. "I left him up there," replied Fox. "You wait here with my little one, and I will bring you the horn," said Leopard, and away she ran. Soon after, Leopard killed Goat and returned with his horns to Fox.

B *Beware, lest you fall into the trap you set for someone else.*

Connecting and Comparing Texts

Help students make connections between Saki's story and the fable by asking them the following questions:

- **What are the consequences of hatred for the characters in both "The Interlopers" and "The Trapper Trapped"?** [Death is the explicit consequence in the fable and the implicit outcome in "The Interlopers."]
- **How does the ending of "The Interlopers" differ from the way one would expect a fable to end?** [Possible responses: "The Interlopers" has a surprise ending, but endings of fables are usually predictable and moralistic. In a fable, two enemies who resolve their differences might be expected to survive; in "The Interlopers," however, cooperation between the characters only helps to draw the attention of the wolves.]

Response and Analysis

Reading Check

1. Make a story map for "The Interlopers" by filling in a chart like the one here:

Title: "The Interlopers"
Characters:
Setting:
Conflicts:
Main events:
Climax and resolution:

2. Review the notes you made while you read the story. Did you find Saki's writing style difficult to understand? What reading strategies did you use to resolve your difficulties?

Thinking Critically

3. **Irony** is what we feel when something turns out to be different from what we expect or think appropriate. What is surprising and ironic about the ending of the story—what did you expect to happen, and what happens instead?

4. Find places in the text where the word *interlopers* is used. What is an interloper? Who are the interlopers in the story? (Are there several kinds of interlopers in the story?)

5. Find instances when the **omniscient narrator** tells what Georg and Ulrich are thinking. What similarities between the **characters** are revealed by the narrator? How would your reaction to events in the **plot** be different if you didn't know what both characters were thinking?

6. **Tone**—the writer's attitude toward a subject or character—is affected by the choice of narrator. What tone does Saki create through the use of an **omniscient narrator**? How do you think the tone would be different if the story were told from the point of view of Ulrich or Georg?

7. Most fables have a **moral,** a message about how we should live our lives. What is the moral of "The Trapper Trapped" (see the **Connection** on page 156)? How does that moral compare with the message of "The Interlopers"?

Extending and Evaluating

8. Refer to your Quickwrite notes. Do you think Saki's story has a serious message about the kinds of feuds you described in your notes, or do you think the story is told just for entertainment? Give reasons for your answer.

WRITING

One More Twist

Saki's story has several surprising twists, the most stunning one being the **surprise ending.** Choose a point in the last two pages of the story, and create your own plot twist by changing the action and writing a **new ending.** You might decide not to have Ulrich and Georg reconcile; you might come up with a new twist beyond the final one. In your version, imitate Saki's omniscient narrator by showing what each character is thinking.

INTERNET
Projects and Activities
Keyword: LE5 9-3

SKILLS FOCUS

Literary Skills
Analyze the omniscient narrator (or point of view).

Reading Skills
Monitor your reading.

Writing Skills
Write a surprise ending.

The Interlopers **157**

Response and Analysis

Thinking Critically

3. Possible answer: Readers expect the men to be rescued, but they will likely be killed.

4. The word *interlopers,* which appears on pp. 153 and 154, means "intruders" or "meddlers." Possible *interlopers:* The men see each other as interlopers; the wolves.

5. Possible answers: The narrator says that neither man is certain he will be rescued (p. 153). When the narrator shows that Ulrich pities Georg, we understand why he offers him wine (p. 153). The men hate each other; neither likes to kill; both fear defeat. After reconciliation, each prays that he might be the first to honor his new friend. Their reconciliation makes the ending more tragic because the two families may continue to feud.

6. Possible answer: Saki creates respect for the men and contempt toward the feud. Readers might sympathize with one point of view and believe that one was right and the other was wrong.

7. The moral is "Beware, lest you fall into the trap you set for someone else." It is similar to the message of "The Interlopers," since the men are the victims of their wishes to best each other.

Extending and Evaluating

8. Possible answer: The story presents a serious message: Feuds can cost lives. However, the story's coincidences—the men meeting, the tree falling—suggest that it is meant to entertain.

Reading Check

1. Possible answers: *Characters*—Ulrich von Gradwitz, Georg Znaeym. *Setting*—a forest in the Carpathian Mountains. *Conflicts*—between Ulrich and Georg; between the two men and nature. *Main events*—Ulrich and Georg meet; they are trapped under a tree; Ulrich offers Georg wine; they become friends; they call for help; wolves attack. *Climax and resolution*—The conflict between the men climaxes when Ulrich offers Georg wine, and the conflict is resolved when they end their feud; the conflict between the men and nature climaxes when Ulrich sees the wolves, and the conflict is left unresolved.

2. Students might use context clues, break down long sentences, summarize passages, and re-read difficult sections.

Vocabulary Development

Practice

Possible Answers

1. Instead of sloping gently, the mountain road was <u>precipitous</u>. [contrast]

2. Joe's friends were surprised that he <u>acquiesced</u>; they didn't expect him to agree. [restatement]

3. Like ancient barbarians, the <u>marauders</u> roamed the countryside in search of loot. [comparison]

4. A look of <u>exasperation</u>, or great annoyance, crossed her face. [restatement]

5. All praised his <u>pious</u> behavior—his praying morning and evening, his unfailing presence at church on Sunday, his frequent reading of the Bible. [example]

6. Asked if he had <u>retorted</u>, the witness claimed that he had not replied sharply. [definition]

7. <u>Condolences</u> for her loss arrived in the mail in the form of cards, notes, and long letters. [example]

8. The mother's <u>languor</u> contrasted sharply with her son's robust health. [contrast]

9. Their friends hoped that the <u>reconciliation</u> would provide a friendly end to the quarrel. [definition]

10. Like rain falling on parched earth, the <u>succor</u> provided by emergency workers began the healing process. [comparison]

Vocabulary Development

Context Clues: Solving Word Mysteries

When you come across an unfamiliar word, **context clues**—the words and phrases around the word—can give you a good sense of that word's meaning. Here are a few ways in which context clues can point toward the meaning of an unfamiliar word—in this case, *interlopers*:

- Context clues may **define** the word.

  The people who interfered in the family's private concerns were accused of being <u>interlopers</u>.

- Context clues may **restate** the word.

  The <u>interlopers</u>, *intruders on horseback*, waved their swords as they rode into town.

- Context clues may provide **examples** of the word.

  Protecting the privacy of the millionaire, the guards viewed all strangers who approached the mansion as <u>interlopers</u>, including *curious tourists, journalists, and photographers.*

- Context clues may **compare** the word to something similar.

  Like mice, the <u>interlopers</u> slipped into the building unnoticed.

- Context clues may **contrast** a word with something dissimilar.

  Far from being welcome guests, the men at the party were seen as <u>interlopers</u>.

Look at the following passage from "The Interlopers," and note how the italicized context clues point toward the meaning of the Word Bank word *languor*:

> "An idea was slowly forming and growing in his brain, an idea that gained strength every time that he looked across at the man who was fighting so grimly against pain and *exhaustion*. In the pain and <u>languor</u> that Ulrich himself was feeling, the old fierce hatred seemed to be dying down."

Ulrich's "languor" is compared to Georg's "exhaustion," hinting that *languor* and *exhaustion* have similar meanings.

Word Bank

precipitous
acquiesced
marauders
exasperation
pious
retorted
condolences
languor
reconciliation
succor

SKILLS FOCUS

Vocabulary Skills
Understand and use context clues.

PRACTICE

Review the definition of each Word Bank word. Then, write an original sentence that provides **context clues** to the word's meaning. Use each of the following types of context clues at least once: definition, restatement, example, comparison, and contrast. You might want to exchange papers with a partner to evaluate each other's context clues.

ASSESSING

Assessment

- *Holt Assessment: Literature, Reading, and Vocabulary*

RETEACHING

For a lesson reteaching narrator and tone, see **Reteaching,** p. 979A. For another selection to teach narrator, see *The Holt Reader,* Collection 3.

Before You Read

The Necklace

Make the Connection

Quickwrite

All of us, at one time or another, have felt that the grass is greener on the other side of the fence—in other words, that someone else's life is better than our own. We believe that having what someone else has will make us happy—until we experience the unexpected negative results of envy. In a few lines, jot down your feelings about envy. Have you ever seen or felt its negative effects?

Literary Focus

Third-Person-Limited Point of View: Zooming In on One Character

Guy de Maupassant specialized in showing what makes human beings tick. It's not surprising, then, that he tells this famous story from the **third-person-limited point of view,** zooming in on the thoughts of a single character, Mathilde Loisel. We learn in the first seven paragraphs about Mathilde's past, her dreams, what makes her unhappy, what she envies in other people, and what she thinks will make her happy. We follow Mathilde so closely through a crisis in her life that the story's ending hits us almost as powerfully as it strikes the unsuspecting Mathilde.

Reading Skills

Summarizing: A Plot Formula

Many short stories and movies have a plot that can be summed up with this formula: *Somebody wants . . . , but . . . , so . . .* The plot begins with *somebody* (the main character) who *wants* something desperately, *but* something or someone stands in the way (the conflict), *so* the character takes steps to overcome the obstacles. Remember that this formula may repeat itself several times in a story until the resolution of the plot. After you finish "The Necklace," decide how the story fits this pattern.

Background

"The Necklace" takes place in Paris in the late 1880s. At that time and in that place, social classes were all-important; people were born into a certain class, and that was usually where they remained for the rest of their lives.

Vocabulary Development

incessantly (in·ses′ənt·lē) *adv.:* constantly; continually.

disconsolate (dis·kän′sə·lit) *adj.:* causing sadness or depression; also, very unhappy.

vexation (vek·sā′shən) *n.:* disturbance; distress.

pauper (pô′pər) *n.:* very poor person.

adulation (a′jōō·lā′shən) *n.:* intense or excessive admiration or praise.

aghast (ə·gast′) *adj.:* terrified; horrified.

privations (prī·vā′shənz) *n.:* hardships; lack of the things needed for a happy, healthy life.

exorbitant (eg·zôr′bi·tənt) *adj.:* much too high in price or amount.

go.hrw.com

INTERNET

Vocabulary Practice
•
More About Guy de Maupassant
•

Keyword: LE5 9-3

SKILLS FOCUS

Literary Skills Understand the third-person-limited point of view.

Reading Skills Summarize plot.

Grade-Level Skills

■ **Literary Skills**
Analyze the way tone, voice, persona, and choice of narrator affect characterization and plot.

■ **Reading Skills**
Summarize plot.

Review Skills

■ **Literary Skills**
Contrast different points of view, and explain how they affect the overall theme of the work.

Summary *at grade level*

This story, told from the third-person-limited point of view, opens with the inner conflict of Mathilde Loisel, a beautiful woman married to a minor bureaucrat. She despises her life, and dreams of wealth and social status. Invited to an elegant reception, she borrows a diamond necklace from a wealthy friend. Mathilde is a sensation at the party but loses the necklace. The Loisels borrow an enormous sum of money to replace it and toil in extreme poverty for ten years to repay the debt. At the end a haggard and coarsened Mathilde meets the owner of the necklace by chance and tells her the whole story. In an ultimate irony, the friend reveals that the original necklace was a fake.

Planning
■ *One-Stop Planner* CD-ROM with ExamView Test Generator

Differentiating Instruction
■ *Holt Reading Solutions*
■ *Holt Adapted Reader*
■ *Supporting Instruction in Spanish*

Vocabulary
■ *Vocabulary Development*

Grammar and Language
■ *Language Handbook Worksheets*
■ *Daily Language Activities*

Assessment
■ *Holt Assessment: Literature, Reading, and Vocabulary*

■ *Holt Online Assessment*

Internet
■ go.hrw.com (Keyword: LE5 9-3)
■ *Elements of Literature Online*

Media
■ *Audio CD Library*
■ *Audio CD Library, Selections and Summaries in Spanish*

Mr. and Mrs. Potter Palmer Collection (Bequest of Berthe Honoré Palmer) (1922, 410). Photograph © 1994, The Art Institute of Chicago. All Rights Reserved.

Selection Starter

Motivate. To help students understand the main character, have them brainstorm what people envy in others. Students may name possessions, such as clothing and expensive cars, or attributes, such as personality and special talents. After the discussion, have students complete the Quickwrite.

Preview Vocabulary

To help familiarize students with the words listed on p. 159, have them choose a vocabulary word that is similar in meaning to each underlined word or phrase in the sentences below.

1. A poor person could not treat friends to a meal that was excessive in price. [pauper, exorbitant]

2. Lack of food and shelter caused trouble for the first American colonists. [privations, vexation]

3. Dejected when her dog died, a pet owner talked endlessly about her grief. [disconsolate, incessantly]

4. Mrs. Jones was shocked at her son's idolization of someone she held in contempt. [aghast, adulation]

VIEWING THE ART

The French artist **Jean-Baptiste-Camille Corot** (1796–1875) established his reputation as a neoclassical landscape painter, but he later developed a style that anticipated Impressionism. Corot was particularly interested in capturing the effects of light and in rendering subtle tonal gradations.

Activity. Ask students to describe the mood of *Interrupted Reading*. Suggest that they consider the use of light and shadow and speculate about what the young woman might be thinking. [Students might say that the tone is serious and a little sad. Perhaps, like Mme. Loisel, the woman is unhappy, and tries to escape through reading.]

THE NECKLACE

GUY DE MAUPASSANT

Interrupted Reading (c. 1870) by Jean-Baptiste-Camille Corot. Oil on canvas mounted on board (92.2 cm × 65.1 cm).

She so much longed to please, be envied, be fascinating . . .

160

Learners Having Difficulty
Modeling. To help students read "The Necklace," model the reading skill of summarizing by saying, "Suppose you read that a young woman in 'The Necklace' dreams of a fancy home but has little money. You can use the *Somebody wants . . . , but . . .* formula to summarize her inner conflict: 'She *wants* luxury, *but* she is poor.'" Encourage students as they read to ask themselves, "Who wants what at this point in the story?" and "What stands in the way?"

English-Language Learners
Maupassant's formal diction and complex style may challenge students. You might put students in mixed-ability pairs, encouraging them to pause and re-read as needed.

She was one of those pretty and charming girls, born, as if by an accident of fate, into a family of clerks. With no dowry,[1] no prospects, no way of any kind of being met, understood, loved, and married by a man both prosperous and famous, she was finally married to a minor clerk in the Ministry of Education.

She dressed plainly because she could not afford fine clothes, but she was as unhappy as a woman who has come down in the world; for women have no family rank or social class. With them, beauty, grace, and charm take the place of birth and breeding. Their natural poise, their instinctive good taste, and their mental cleverness are the sole guiding principles which make daughters of the common people the equals of ladies in high society.

She grieved incessantly, feeling that she had been born for all the little niceties and luxuries of living. She grieved over the shabbiness of her apartment, the dinginess of the walls, the worn-out appearance of the chairs, the ugliness of the draperies. All these things, which another woman of her class would not even have noticed, gnawed at her and made her furious. The sight of the little Breton girl[2] who did her humble housework roused in her disconsolate regrets and wild daydreams. She would dream of silent chambers, draped with Oriental tapestries[3] and lighted by tall bronze floor lamps, and of two handsome butlers in knee breeches, who, drowsy from the heavy warmth cast by the central stove, dozed in large overstuffed armchairs.

She would dream of great reception halls hung with old silks, of fine furniture filled with priceless curios,[4] and of small, stylish, scented sitting rooms just right for the four o'clock chat with intimate friends, with distinguished and sought-after men whose attention every woman envies and longs to attract.

When dining at the round table, covered for the third day with the same cloth, opposite her husband, who would raise the cover of the soup tureen, declaring delightedly, "Ah! a good stew! There's nothing I like better . . . ," she would dream of fashionable dinner parties, of gleaming silverware, of tapestries making the walls alive with characters out of history and strange birds in a fairyland forest; she would dream of delicious dishes served on wonderful china, of gallant compliments whispered and listened to with a sphinxlike[5] smile as one eats the rosy flesh of a trout or nibbles at the wings of a grouse.

She had no evening clothes, no jewels, nothing. But those were the things she wanted; she felt that was the kind of life for her. She so much longed to please, be envied, be fascinating and sought after.

She had a well-to-do friend, a classmate of convent-school days whom she would no longer go to see, simply because she would feel so

She had no evening clothes, no jewels, nothing.

---

1. **dowry** (dou'rē) *n.:* property that a woman brings to her husband at marriage.
2. **Breton** (bret''n) **girl:** girl from Brittany, a region in northwestern France.
3. **tapestries** (tap'əs·trēz) *n.:* heavy woven cloths with decorative designs and pictures, used as wall hangings or furniture coverings.

4. **curios** (kyoor'ē·ōz') *n.:* unusual items.
5. **sphinxlike** *adj.:* mysterious. The sphinx was a creature in Greek mythology who asked riddles.

Vocabulary

incessantly (in·ses'ənt·lē) *adv.:* constantly; continually.

disconsolate (dis·kän'sə·lit) *adj.:* causing sadness or depression; also, very unhappy.

A Literary Focus

❷ Third-person-limited point of view. To introduce Mathilde Loisel, the narrator uses the passive voice: "of being met, understood, loved, and married" and "was finally married." What does the passive voice help readers to understand about Mathilde's life? [Possible response: It helps to emphasize her lack of control over her life.]

B Reading Skills

❷ Summarizing. If Mathilde is the "somebody" in the *Somebody wants . . . , but . . . , so . . .* plot formula, how might you summarize what she wants? [Possible response: She wants luxury, wealth, and status.]

C Literary Focus

❷ Third-person-limited point of view. What does the narrator reveal about Mathilde by reporting that the visit to her friend distresses her? [Possible responses: Mathilde envies her friend; she covets her friend's more luxurious life; she feels entitled to such a life.]

Special Education Students
For lessons designed for special education students and English-language learners, see *Holt Reading Solutions.*

Advanced Learners
Acceleration. Use the following activity to help advanced learners analyze the use of irony to achieve rhetorical or aesthetic purposes. Remind students that authors sometimes use irony to highlight themes. **Activity.** Ask students to write sentences about the effects of class restrictions. Then, have students explain how ironies in the story call attention to the themes.

A Literary Focus

? Third-person-limited point of view. The narrator reports Mathilde's thoughts and feelings as she talks with M. Loisel. What does this information reveal about her character and her regard for her husband? [Possible responses: She is self-centered and vain; she seems not to appreciate how hard her husband tries to please her.]

B Literary Focus

? Third-person-limited point of view. The narrator briefly departs from Mathilde's limited point of view for a glimpse into M. Loisel's feelings and thoughts. What purpose might this departure serve? [Possible response: By showing the lengths to which Mathilde's husband will go to make her happy, while she gives little thought to pleasing him, the narrator emphasizes her spoiled, self-centered nature.]

C English-Language Learners

Idioms. Point out the idiom *all out of sorts.* Explain that it means "in a bad mood."

D Literary Focus

? Third-person-limited point of view. By reporting this conversation, the narrator indirectly reveals the character of M. Loisel. How would you compare his character with Mathilde's? [Possible response: Mathilde is so vain that she would rather miss a good time than create the wrong impression; in contrast, M. Loisel is unpretentious and practical and appreciates simpler pleasures.]

distressed on returning home. And she would weep for days on end from vexation, regret, despair, and anguish.

Then one evening, her husband came home proudly holding out a large envelope.

"Look," he said, "I've got something for you."

She excitedly tore open the envelope and pulled out a printed card bearing these words:

"The Minister of Education and Mme. Georges Ramponneau[6] beg M. and Mme. Loisel[6] to do them the honor of attending an evening reception at the Ministerial Mansion on Friday, January 18."

Instead of being delighted, as her husband had hoped, she scornfully tossed the invitation on the table, murmuring, "What good is that to me?"

"But, my dear, I thought you'd be thrilled to death. You never get a chance to go out, and this is a real affair, a wonderful one! I had an awful time getting a card. Everybody wants one; it's much sought after, and not many clerks have a chance at one. You'll see all the most important people there."

She gave him an irritated glance and burst out impatiently, "What do you think I have to go in?"

He hadn't given that a thought. He stammered, "Why, the dress you wear when we go to the theater. That looks quite nice, I think."

He stopped talking, dazed and distracted to see his wife burst out weeping. Two large tears slowly rolled from the corners of her eyes to the corners of her mouth; he gasped, "Why, what's the matter? What's the trouble?"

By sheer willpower she overcame her outburst and answered in a calm voice while wiping the tears from her wet cheeks, "Oh, nothing. Only I don't have an evening dress and therefore I can't go to that affair. Give the card to some friend at the office whose wife can dress better than I can."

6. **Mme. Georges Ramponneau** (mà·dàm' zhôrzh ràm'pə·nô) . . . **M.** (mə·syʉr') . . . **Mme. Loisel** (mà·dàm' lwä·zel'): *M.* and *Mme.* are abbreviations for "Monsieur" and "Madame" and are the French equivalents of *Mr.* and *Mrs.*

He was stunned. He resumed, "Let's see, Mathilde. How much would a suitable outfit cost—one you could wear for other affairs too—something very simple?"

She thought it over for several seconds, going over her allowance and thinking also of the amount she could ask for without bringing an immediate refusal and an exclamation of dismay from the thrifty clerk.

Finally, she answered hesitatingly, "I'm not sure exactly, but I think with four hundred francs I could manage it."

He turned a bit pale, for he had set aside just that amount to buy a rifle so that the following summer, he could join some friends who were getting up a group to shoot larks on the plain near Nanterre.[7]

However, he said, "All right. I'll give you four hundred francs. But try to get a nice dress."

As the day of the party approached, Mme. Loisel seemed sad, moody, ill at ease. Her outfit was ready, however. Her husband said to her one evening, "What's the matter? You've been all out of sorts for three days."

And she answered, "It's embarrassing not to have a jewel or a gem—nothing to wear on my dress. I'll look like a pauper. I'd almost rather not go to the party."

He answered, "Why not wear some flowers? They're very fashionable this season. For ten francs you can get two or three gorgeous roses."

She wasn't at all convinced. "No. . . . There's nothing more humiliating than to look poor among a lot of rich women."

But her husband exclaimed, "My, but you're silly! Go see your friend Mme. Forestier,[8] and ask her to lend you some jewelry. You and she know each other well enough for you to do that."

7. **Nanterre** (nän·ter'): town near Paris.
8. **Forestier** (fô·rəs·tyā').

Vocabulary
vexation (vek·sā'shən) *n.:* disturbance; distress.
pauper (pô'pər) *n.:* very poor person.

Museum of Fine Arts, Boston: Zoe Oliver Sherman Collection.

The New Necklace (1910) by William McGregor Paxton. Oil on canvas (91.76 cm × 73.02 cm).

VIEWING THE ART

The American artist **William McGregor Paxton** (1869–1941) was a member of the Boston School, a group of painters who continued the tradition of French academic painting in the United States. Paxton moved to France in 1887 to study painting, returning to Boston in 1893 and establishing himself as an important portrait painter. It is evident in *The New Necklace* that Paxton was interested in Asian culture and the decorative use of color and pattern. The scene is full of luxurious decorative objects, suggesting the women's elegance and reflecting a Western taste for Asian art and antiquities at the time.

Activity. Ask students what the surroundings and dress in the painting suggest about the two women. [Possible response: They are wealthy and have an interest in other cultures.]

The Necklace   **163**

A Literary Focus

❓ Third-person-limited point of view. How would the effect of this passage differ if it were told from the first-person point of view by Mme. Loisel? [Possible response: Mme. Loisel would seem to be bragging if she delivered this information herself. Coming from a third-person narrator, it seems like an objective observation.]

A CLOSER LOOK

After students have read the story, discuss the roles of women in late-nineteenth-century France. Ask students to create a chart to compare and contrast those roles with the roles of women in modern United States society. You may want to have students use the information on their charts to write a comparison-and-contrast essay.

B Reading Informational Text

❓ Generating research questions. Ask students what research questions they can generate from the essay's last four sentences. [Possible response: Were there women in nineteenth-century France who tried to improve work conditions for women? If so, who were they, and what did they do?]

She gave a cry of joy. "Why, that's so! I hadn't thought of it."

The next day she paid her friend a visit and told her of her predicament.

Mme. Forestier went toward a large closet with mirrored doors, took out a large jewel box, brought it over, opened it, and said to Mme. Loisel, "Pick something out, my dear."

At first her eyes noted some bracelets, then a pearl necklace, then a Venetian cross, gold and gems, of marvelous workmanship. She tried on these adornments in front of the mirror, but hesitated, unable to decide which to part with and put back. She kept on asking, "Haven't you something else?"

"Oh, yes, keep on looking. I don't know just what you'd like."

All at once she found, in a black satin box, a superb diamond necklace; and her pulse beat faster with longing. Her hands trembled as she took it up. Clasping it around her throat, outside her high-necked dress, she stood in ecstasy looking at her reflection.

Then she asked, hesitatingly, pleading, "Could I borrow that, just that and nothing else?"

"Why, of course."

She threw her arms around her friend, kissed her warmly, and fled with her treasure.

The day of the party arrived. Mme. Loisel was a sensation. She was the prettiest one there, fashionable, gracious, smiling, and wild with joy. All the men turned to look at her, asked who she was, begged to be introduced. All the Cabinet officials wanted to waltz with her. The minister took notice of her.

She danced madly, wildly, drunk with pleasure, giving no thought to anything in the triumph of her beauty, the pride of her success, in a kind of happy cloud composed of all the adulation, of all the admiring glances, of all the

Vocabulary
adulation (aʹjoo·lāʹshən) *n.*: intense or excessive admiration or praise.

A CLOSER LOOK
Separate Spheres

During the late nineteenth century the doctrine of "separate spheres" shaped French society. According to this idea, men were aggressive and intellectual, qualified to work in the public sphere of universities, business, and politics. Women were seen as weak and emotional, suited for the private sphere. They raised children and made sure that their homes were clean and beautiful. The law reinforced these boundaries: Husbands controlled their wives' property, and women could not vote or enter professions like the law or civil service. For middle- and upper-class women, supported by their husbands or fathers and aided by servants, this lifestyle was restrictive but not impossible. For poor women the situation was different. Millions of them became factory workers, laundresses, cooks, bread carriers, or seamstresses. These women led extremely difficult lives. At work, conditions could be hazardous, even fatal. Seamstresses endured daily shifts of thirteen hours or more; weavers were exposed to toxic substances; silk workers were surrounded by clouds of steam and frequently caught pneumonia. In the end, women received little in return for working strenuously and endangering their health. Many earned only about four hundred francs in an entire year, the cost of Mathilde Loisel's party dress.

Hush! (The Concert) (c.1875) by James Tissot. Oil on canvas (73.6 cm × 112.2 cm).
Manchester City Art Galleries, Manchester, England.

The French painter **James Tissot** (1836–1902) is best known for his paintings of fashionable gatherings of the upper classes. Having established himself as a painter of historical scenes, he shifted his focus in the mid-1860s to painting scenes of contemporary life. He fled to England after 1871 because of his involvement in the Paris Commune, an attempted revolution that was suppressed. Living in London until 1882, he worked as a caricaturist and a successful portrait painter. In *Hush! (The Concert),* it is evident that Tissot paid close attention to contemporary fashions and manners.

Activity. Ask students to pick a character or group of characters in the painting and write a brief description of their reactions to the concert and to other partygoers.

C Learners Having Difficulty
? Paraphrasing. These two sentences are complicated, but the ideas they express are not. How would you state them in your own words? [Possible response: He put her wraps on her, and they were much shabbier than her dress. She knew she looked poor, and she wanted to get away before the wealthy women noticed.]

---

awakened longings, of a sense of complete victory that is so sweet to a woman's heart.

She left around four o'clock in the morning. Her husband, since midnight, had been dozing in a small, empty sitting room with three other gentlemen whose wives were having too good a time.

He threw over her shoulders the wraps he had brought for going home, modest garments of everyday life whose shabbiness clashed with the stylishness of her evening clothes. She felt this and longed to escape unseen by the other women, who were draped in expensive furs.

Loisel held her back.

"Hold on! You'll catch cold outside. I'll call a cab."

But she wouldn't listen to him and went rapidly down the stairs. When they were on the street, they didn't find a carriage; and they set out to hunt for one, hailing drivers whom they saw going by at a distance.

They walked toward the Seine,[9] disconsolate and shivering. Finally, on the docks, they found one of those carriages that one sees in Paris only after nightfall, as if they were ashamed to show their drabness during daylight hours.

It dropped them at their door in the Rue des Martyrs,[10] and they climbed wearily up to their apartment. For her, it was all over. For him,

---

9. **Seine** (sen): river that runs through Paris.
10. **Rue des Martyrs** (rü′ dā mär·tēr′): street in Paris. The name means "Street of the Martyrs." People who suffer for their beliefs or people who suffer for a long time are called martyrs.

The Necklace   **165**

Developing Word-Attack Skills
Point out that the letter *x* is unusual in English because it doesn't stand for its own unique sound. Explain that the letter *x* rarely occurs at the beginning of words, but when it does, it usually stands for the sound /z/. Illustrate this point with the words *xylophone* and *xenon.* The letter *x* occurs more often at the end of words and syllables. In this position it usually stands for the sound /ks/. Use

the selection word *sphinxlike* (p. 161) as an example of a word in which *x* stands for /ks/.

Write the selection word *anxiety* and the related word *anxious* on the chalkboard, and have students compare the sounds of *x* in the two words. Help them recognize that in *anxiety,* *x* stands for /z/, but in *anxious,* *x* stands for /ksh/.

Activity. Have students read each word aloud and decide if *x* sounds as it does in *sphinxlike* (/ks/), *anxiety* (/z/), or *anxious* (/ksh/). They may consult a dictionary.

1. oxymoron [/ks/]
2. obnoxious [/ksh/]
3. xenophobia [/z/]
4. taxidermy [/ks/]
5. juxtapose [/ks/]
6. hexagon [/ks/]
7. lynx [/ks/]
8. toxin [/ks/]
9. vexation [/ks/]
10. axiom [/ks/]

The Necklace   **165**

A Reading Skills

Summarizing. A plot complication arises here. Encourage students to use the *Somebody wants . . . , but . . .* part of the plot formula to summarize this complication. [Possible summary: *Mathilde wants* to return the borrowed necklace, *but* she has lost it.]

VIEWING THE ART

Sometimes called the father of Impressionism, **Camille Pissarro** (1830–1903) was born in St. Thomas in the Virgin Islands and moved to France in 1855. Like other Impressionists, Pissarro was especially interested in the effects created by natural light. In the late 1880s, Pissarro began experimenting with pointillism, in which paint is applied in small, carefully separated dots, but he later returned to a more impressionistic approach.

Activity. Explain that Montmartre has long been an artists' district in Paris. Ask students to describe the mood, or emotional atmosphere, of this work. [Students might note the suggestions of light, liveliness, crowds, and gaiety.]

The Boulevard Montmartre at Night (1897) by Camille Pissarro. Oil on canvas (53.3 cm × 64.8 cm).
© The National Gallery, London.

there was the thought that he would have to be at the Ministry at ten o'clock.

Before the mirror, she let the wraps fall from her shoulders to see herself once again in all her glory. Suddenly she gave a cry. The necklace was gone.

Her husband, already half undressed, said, "What's the trouble?"

She turned toward him despairingly, "I . . . I . . . I don't have Mme. Forestier's necklace."

"What! You can't mean it! It's impossible!"

They hunted everywhere, through the folds of the dress, through the folds of the coat, in the pockets. They found nothing.

He asked, "Are you sure you had it when leaving the dance?"

"Yes, I felt it when I was in the hall of the Ministry."

"But if you had lost it on the street, we'd have heard it drop. It must be in the cab."

"Yes, quite likely. Did you get its number?"

"No. Didn't you notice it either?"

"No."

They looked at each other aghast. Finally Loisel got dressed again.

"I'll retrace our steps on foot," he said, "to see if I can find it."

And he went out. She remained in her evening clothes, without the strength to go to bed, slumped in a chair in the unheated room, her mind a blank.

Her husband came in around seven o'clock. He had had no luck.

He went to the police station, to the newspapers to post a reward, to the cab companies, everywhere the slightest hope drove him.

That evening Loisel returned, pale, his face lined; still he had learned nothing.

"We'll have to write your friend," he said, "to tell her you have broken the catch and are having it repaired. That will give us a little time to turn around."

She wrote to his dictation.

At the end of a week, they had given up all hope.

And Loisel, looking five years older, declared, "We must take steps to replace that piece of jewelry."

The next day they took the case to the jeweler whose name they found inside. He consulted his records. "I didn't sell that necklace, madame," he said. "I only supplied the case."

Then they went from one jeweler to another hunting for a similar necklace, going over their recollections, both sick with despair and anxiety.

They found, in a shop in Palais Royal,[11] a string of diamonds which seemed exactly like the one they were seeking. It was priced at forty thousand francs. They could get it for thirty-six.

They asked the jeweler to hold it for them for

---

11. **Palais Royal** (pả·lā′ rwä·yål′): fashionable shopping district in Paris.

three days. And they reached an agreement that he would take it back for thirty-four thousand if the lost one was found before the end of February.

Loisel had eighteen thousand francs he had inherited from his father. He would borrow the rest.

He went about raising the money, asking a thousand francs from one, four hundred from another, a hundred here, sixty there. He signed notes, made ruinous deals, did business with loan sharks, ran the whole gamut of money-lenders. He compromised the rest of his life, risked his signature without knowing if he'd be able to honor it, and then, terrified by the outlook of the future, by the blackness of despair about to close around him, by the prospect of all the privations of the body and tortures of the spirit, he went to claim the new necklace with the thirty-six thousand francs, which he placed on the counter of the shopkeeper.

When Mme. Loisel took the necklace back, Mme. Forestier said to her frostily, "You should have brought it back sooner; I might have needed it."

She didn't open the case, an action her friend was afraid of. If she had noticed the substitution, what would she have thought? What would she have said? Would she have thought her a thief?

Mme. Loisel experienced the horrible life the needy live. She played her part, however, with sudden heroism. That frightful debt had to be paid. She would pay it. She dismissed her maid; they rented a garret under the eaves.[12]

She learned to do the heavy housework, to perform the hateful duties of cooking. She washed dishes, wearing down her shell-pink nails scouring the grease from pots and pans; she

---

12. **garret under the eaves:** attic under the overhanging lower edges of a roof.

Vocabulary

aghast (ə·gast′) *adj.*: terrified; horrified.

privations (prī·vā′shənz) *n.*: hardships; lack of the things needed for a happy, healthy life.

B Literary Focus

❓ Third-person-limited point of view. The narrator, focusing on Mathilde's point of view, sketches the risks Loisel is taking but doesn't report his feelings. What feelings for Mathilde do Loisel's actions reveal? [Possible response: He has given up his inheritance for her and has assumed responsibility for her misfortune, so he must be deeply devoted to her.]

C Vocabulary Development

❓ Literal meanings of words. Point out that *blackness* and *despair* are synonyms. What other words have a similar meaning? [Possible responses: *hopelessness; discouragement; despondency.*] Ask students to rank the words named from highest to lowest intensity. [Possible response: *blackness; hopelessness; despair; despondency; discouragement.*]

D Advanced Learners

❓ Acceleration. Why is it ironic that Mathilde is in this position? [Possible response: Ironically, her love of finery and of the easy life has led to a hard life in which she must deprive herself of everything fine.] What point about the role of wealth in this society might this irony underscore? [Possible responses: Those who lose wealth lose respect; this society measures human worth in terms of wealth.]

DEVELOPING FLUENCY

Individual activity. Review the different ways a reader can convey the meaning of a text through oral interpretation: vocal pitch and tone, facial expression, body language and posture, and gestures. Then, assign each student two to three sentences of the story for dramatic reading. (You may want to assign a section to more than one student.) Allow students time to read their sections silently and to examine the text for ways to interpret it effectively. Finally, have students take turns delivering their sections.

A Reading Skills

❓ Summarizing. What have the past ten years been like for the Loisels? Use the *Somebody wanted . . . , but . . . , so . . .* formula. [Possible response: *The Loisels wanted* to replace the lost necklace, *but* they couldn't afford to, *so* they borrowed huge sums at high interest and sank into a life of poverty struggling to pay the debts.]

B Literary Focus

❓ Third-person-limited point of view. How might this description of Mme. Loisel be different if she were narrating it in the first person? [Possible responses: She might downplay the loss of her looks; she might be full of self-pity.]

C Reading Skills

Speculating. Explain what you think Mathilde's life might have been like if she had not lost the necklace and why you think as you do. [Possible responses: She might have attained higher status, since her beauty and charm could have helped her husband advance; or she might have remained middle-class and unhappy, thwarted by French class and gender restrictions and by her own shallow and self-centered outlook.]

D Literary Focus

Irony. Point out the layers of irony in the ending. One is the realization that the necklace the Loisels suffered to replace was a fake. Another is that Mathilde, who yearned for wealth and refinement, was reduced to poverty and coarseness by her yearnings. A third is the ironic parallel between the fake diamonds and Mathilde, a social fake.

---

scrubbed dirty linen, shirts, and cleaning rags, which she hung on a line to dry; she took the garbage down to the street each morning and brought up water, stopping on each landing to get her breath. And, clad like a peasant woman, basket on arm, guarding sou[13] by sou her scanty allowance, she bargained with the fruit dealers, the grocer, the butcher, and was insulted by them.

Each month notes had to be paid, and others renewed to give more time.

Her husband labored evenings to balance a tradesman's accounts, and at night, often, he copied documents at five sous a page.

A And this went on for ten years.

Finally, all was paid back, everything including the <u>exorbitant</u> rates of the loan sharks and accumulated compound interest.

B Mme. Loisel appeared an old woman now. She became heavy, rough, harsh, like one of the poor. Her hair untended, her skirts askew, her hands red, her voice shrill, she even slopped water on her floors and scrubbed them herself. But, sometimes, while her husband was at work, she would sit near the window and think of that long-ago evening when, at the dance, she had been so beautiful and admired.

C What would have happened if she had not lost that necklace? Who knows? Who can say? How strange and unpredictable life is! How little there is between happiness and misery!

Then, one Sunday, when she had gone for a walk on the Champs Élysées[14] to relax a bit from the week's labors, she suddenly noticed a woman strolling with a child. It was Mme. Forestier, still young looking, still beautiful, still charming.

Mme. Loisel felt a rush of emotion. Should she speak to her? Of course. And now that everything was paid off, she would tell her the whole story. Why not?

She went toward her. "Hello, Jeanne."

The other, not recognizing her, showed astonishment at being spoken to so familiarly by this common person. She stammered, "But . . . madame . . . I don't recognize . . . You must be mistaken."

"No, I'm Mathilde Loisel."

Her friend gave a cry, "Oh, my poor Mathilde, how you've changed!"

"Yes, I've had a hard time since last seeing you. And plenty of misfortunes—and all on account of you!"

"Of me . . . How do you mean?"

"Do you remember that diamond necklace you loaned me to wear to the dance at the Ministry?"

"Yes, but what about it?"

"Well, I lost it."

"You lost it! But you returned it."

"I brought you another just like it. And we've been paying for it for ten years now. You can imagine that wasn't easy for us who had nothing. Well, it's over now, and I am glad of it."

Mme. Forestier stopped short. "You mean to say you bought a diamond necklace to replace mine?"

"Yes. You never noticed, then? They were quite alike."

And she smiled with proud and simple joy.

D Mme. Forestier, quite overcome, clasped her by the hands. "Oh, my poor Mathilde. But mine was fake. Why, at most it was worth only five hundred francs!" ∎

> **"Oh, my poor Mathilde, how you've changed!"**

---

13. **sou** (soō) *n.:* old French coin of little value.
14. **Champs Élysées** (shän zā·lē·zā′): famous avenue in Paris.

Vocabulary
exorbitant (eg·zôr′bi·tənt) *adj.:* much too high in price or amount.

FAMILY/COMMUNITY ACTIVITY

If possible, invite a community financial expert or a loan officer from a community lending institution to speak to the class about lending practices and interest rates in your area. Ask the speaker to discuss mainstream lending as well as other options. Afterward, encourage students to compare today's lending practices with those that the Loisels encountered in "The Necklace."

Meet the Writer

Guy de Maupassant

Seeing Things Anew

Guy de Maupassant (gē də mō·pä·sän′) (1850–1893), one of the world's greatest short story writers, was born in Normandy, the French province that is the setting for much of his fiction. After his parents separated, Maupassant was raised by his mother, who was a close friend of the great novelist Gustave Flaubert.

Flaubert set out to instruct the young Maupassant in the art of fiction. He explained that good writing depends upon seeing things anew, rather than recording what people before us have thought. Flaubert also gave his student this advice:

> 66 Whatever you want to say, there is only one word to express it, only one verb to give it movement, only one adjective to qualify it. 99

For years, Maupassant sent Flaubert his writing exercises every week, and then they met to discuss his work over lunch. With the success of his story "Ball of Fat," Maupassant, now age thirty, quit his job as a clerk with the naval ministry and began to put great energy into writing. He quickly achieved enormous popularity. For eleven years he wrote at a hectic pace and produced nearly three hundred stories and six novels. Advising writers, Maupassant said, "Get black on white."

His story "The Horla" has been called one of the most terrifying stories of madness ever written. It foretold Maupassant's own tragic fate of illness, insanity, and early death. He died in a Paris asylum when he was only forty-two years old.

For Independent Reading

Among Maupassant's many stories you might want to read "The Piece of String," in which a simple piece of string helps seal a man's fate. In "Two Friends" a carefree fishing trip proves fateful.

DIFFERENTIATING INSTRUCTION

Advanced Learners

Enrichment. Tell students that Maupassant's terse writing style is due in part to the fact that many of his stories were first published in newspapers, which severely restricted the length of his material.

Activity. Encourage students to learn more about Maupassant's earlier years (1850–1879) and to present their findings as a jacket blurb for a volume of his stories.

Monitoring students' progress. Guide students in responding to these questions. Have them find support in the text for their answers.

True-False

1. Mathilde marries into a wealthy family. [F]
2. Until she is invited to the ball, Mathilde is content with her life. [F]
3. Mathilde borrows a necklace from her friend Mme. Forestier. [T]
4. The Loisels scrimp for ten years to pay the debts created by the loss of the necklace. [T]
5. Mme. Forestier says the necklace Mathilde borrowed years ago was an inexpensive fake. [T]

Meet the Writer

Background. As Maupassant labored to "get black on white," he developed the habit of writing to fill the page, regardless of whether he felt he was doing quality work. He came to believe that no matter how hurriedly he composed, his literary voice would somehow ring true and be understood by the reader. Judging by the tremendous popularity of his works during his lifetime, and by their enduring appeal, he was right.

For Independent Reading

Students reading other stories by Maupassant will notice that most end with a sharp twist, a technique that he developed and that for decades was the hallmark of the short story genre.

- For an American Gothic approach to literary irony, suggest Nathaniel Hawthorne's classic short story "The Birth-mark."
- Fans of nineteenth-century French literature may enjoy the novella *A Simple Heart,* by Maupassant's mentor, Gustave Flaubert.

Response and Analysis

Reading Check

1. Possible answer: *Mme. Loisel wants* an upper-class lifestyle, *but* she lacks wealth. *So* when she is invited to a reception, she borrows a necklace from a friend to seem wealthier. She loses the necklace. *Mme. Loisel* doesn't *want* her friend to know, *but* she can't afford a replacement. *So* she and her husband borrow the money and work ten years to pay off the loans. Years later Mme. Loisel sees her friend again and learns that the necklace was a fake.

Thinking Critically

2. The Loisels struggled to replace a fake necklace with a real one.

3. Possible answers: The narrator paints a mostly unsympathetic picture of Mathilde, emphasizing her vanity and shallowness; due to misfortune, Mathilde matures into a proud woman, becoming a mostly sympathetic character.

4. Possible answer: If the story were told from the point of view of Mathilde's husband, readers might learn more about him and find a more sentimental portrait of Mathilde. Told by Mathilde, the story might be more melodramatic and sympathetic toward her.

5. Students may describe the tone as detached. Some students may say the story criticizes Mathilde only, since vanity causes her problems; others may say the story criticizes a society that measures worth in terms of wealth.

6. Possible answer: In the story he is "thrifty." He seems practical, hard-working, and devoted to Mathilde.

Extending and Evaluating

7. Possible answers: Yes, because envy has caused much misery; no, because Maupassant over-dramatized his characters.

Response and Analysis

Reading Check

1. **Summarize** the plot using the *Somebody wants . . . , but . . . , so . . .* formula. Compare your summaries in class.

Thinking Critically

2. When Mme. Forestier reveals that the necklace was a fake, the reader feels the force of **irony**—the sense that something has turned out to be the opposite of what we expected. Explain what makes the story's closing sentences ironic.

3. The **third-person-limited narrator** lets us see the world through the eyes of Mathilde Loisel. Does the narrator paint a mostly sympathetic or a mostly unsympathetic picture of Mathilde? Explain.

4. Think about this story's **point of view** as if you were Maupassant trying to decide how to tell your story. Explain how the story and our understanding of Mathilde would change if the story were told by her husband or by Mathilde herself.

5. The choice of narrator affects a story's **tone**—the writer's attitude toward a subject or character. What tone is created through Maupassant's use of a **third-person-limited narrator**? For help deciding, consider whether the story is critical of Mathilde only or whether the writer is criticizing the values of a whole society.

6. How would you **characterize** Mathilde's husband? Consider what you know about him:
   - his loyalty to Mathilde
   - the way he indulges her
   - his years of sacrifice and hard work
   - his plans to buy something for himself

Extending and Evaluating

7. Look back at your Quickwrite notes about envy. Do you think Maupassant has painted a believable picture of the effects of envy? (Is the plot believable? Are the characters' motives convincing?) Why or why not?

WRITING

What's the Difference?

Do you think Mme. Forestier should return the difference in value between the original necklace and the one she received as a replacement? Take one side of this question, and write a statement for or against a payment to the Loisels. Be ready to defend your position in class.

Then and Now

Plan a twenty-first-century version of "The Necklace." The plot should focus on someone who borrows what he or she thinks is a valuable item and then briefly enters a different social world. Decide which point of view you will use to tell the story. Then, write a brief description of the major characters, the setting, and the plot. Try to come up with your own ironic ending.

INTERNET
Projects and Activities
Keyword: LE5 9-3

SKILLS FOCUS

Literary Skills Analyze the third-person-limited point of view.

Reading Skills Summarize plot.

Writing Skills Write a position statement. Write a description.

DIFFERENTIATING INSTRUCTION

Learners Having Difficulty
In each sentence, have students choose the correct possessive pronoun or contraction.

1. Can you ask (your/you're) friend to lend you some jewelry? [your]
2. (Whose/Who's) been invited? [Who's]
3. The ladies look stunning in (their/they're) evening gowns. [their]
4. I can't return the necklace yet because (its/it's) clasp is broken. [its]

Advanced Learners
Acceleration. Use the following activity to help advanced learners evaluate historical and social influences that shape characters, plots, and settings.

Vocabulary Development

Ranking Synonyms

PRACTICE

You can reinforce your ownership of a word by comparing the word with other words that have similar meanings. One way to compare words is to rank them from high to low intensity. For an example, see the chart below.

Work with a partner to make an "intensity scale" for each Word Bank word. We've done the first word for you. Add at least two words that are synonyms but show an increase or decrease in intensity. Be sure to compare and defend your intensity scales in class.

Word Bank

incessantly
disconsolate
vexation
pauper
adulation
aghast
privations
exorbitant

High Intensity	Medium Intensity	Low Intensity
incessantly	constantly	always

Grammar Link

Pronoun Problems

Some pronouns in English sound exactly like other words: *its* and *it's*; *their* and *they're*; *whose* and *who's*; *your* and *you're*. Words that sound alike are not a problem when you are speaking, but they can be troublesome when you are writing. To avoid making mistakes, you must be aware of the difference between a possessive pronoun and a pronoun contraction:

• A **possessive pronoun** (such as *its, their, whose, your*) shows ownership or relationship.

• A **pronoun contraction** (such as *it's, they're, who's,* and *you're*) is a shortened form of a pronoun and a verb (*it is, they are, who is,* and *you are*). A pronoun contraction *always* contains an **apostrophe.**

PRACTICE

Choose the correct pronoun from each underlined pair in parentheses.

1. "But her husband exclaimed, 'My, but (your/you're) silly!'"

2. "'(Its/It's) embarrassing not to have a jewel or a gem—nothing to wear on my dress.'"

3. "'Why not wear some flowers? (Their/They're) very fashionable this season.'"

4. "The next day they took the case to the jeweler (whose/who's) name they found inside."

Check the pronouns in your writing. Have you used a possessive where a contraction should have been used? Have you spelled a possessive pronoun with an apostrophe?

➤ **For more help, see Contractions, 14g, in the Language Handbook.**

SKILLS FOCUS

Vocabulary Skills
Identify degrees of intensity among synonyms.

Grammar Skills
Use possessive pronouns and pronoun contractions correctly.

Vocabulary Development

Practice

Possible Answers

■ *disconsolate. High*—disconsolate. *Medium*—saddened. *Low*—unhappy.

■ *vexation. High*—vexation. *Medium*—annoyance. *Low*—discomfort.

■ *pauper. High*—pauper. *Medium*—needy person. *Low*—underprivileged person.

■ *adulation. High*—adulation. *Medium*—admiration. *Low*—respect.

■ *aghast. High*—aghast. *Medium*—alarmed. *Low*—upset.

■ *privations. High*—privations. *Medium*—hardships. *Low*—shortages.

■ *exorbitant. High*—exorbitant. *Medium*—excessive. *Low*—costly.

Grammar Link

Practice

1. you're   3. They're
2. It's   4. whose

ASSESSING

Assessment

■ *Holt Assessment: Literature, Reading, and Vocabulary*

RETEACHING

For a lesson reteaching narrator and tone, see **Reteaching,** p. 979A. For another selection to teach narrator, see *The Holt Reader,* Collection 3.

Activity. Ask students to apply their understanding of late-nineteenth-century French social conditions to help Mathilde solve her problems. Invite students to brainstorm alternative solutions to her conflicts: how she might have come to terms with her economic status, how she might have handled her desire to impress people at the ball, and what she might have done when the necklace was lost. Stipulate that the solutions must take into account French class and gender restrictions of the late 1800s. Have students use these considerations to develop a series of advice-column letters and responses.

Grade-Level Skills

■ **Literary Skills**

Analyze the way tone, voice, persona, and choice of narrator affect characterization and plot.

■ **Reading Skills**

Draw conclusions.

Review Skills

■ **Literary Skills**

Contrast different points of view, and explain how they affect the overall theme of the work.

Summary ⬆ *above grade level*

Montresor, the Italian nobleman narrating this classic tale of horror, claims that Fortunato has injured and insulted him and vows revenge. Meeting Fortunato during the winter carnival, Montresor feigns friendship and lures him home to taste some amontillado, a rare wine that is kept in a cask in an underground vault. Once they are underground, Montresor chains Fortunato to a wall and bricks him in, burying him alive. Fifty years later, the crime remains undiscovered. Is Montresor to be believed, or is he an unreliable narrator? Is he lying—or simply mad?

Before You Read

The Cask of Amontillado

Make the Connection

Quickwrite 🖉

Poe was a master at writing stories of revenge. What experiences could lead someone to seek revenge? How could an obsession with vengeance lead to tragedy? Jot down your responses, and include examples from stories or movies.

Literary Focus

Unreliable Narrator

Writers sometimes assume a **persona,** which is a mask or a voice for a first-person narrator. When you read a story told by a **first-person narrator,** you need to ask yourself if you can trust the narrator. Sometimes a writer will purposely use an unreliable narrator to tell a story.

An **unreliable narrator** may not always know the whole truth or may purposely choose to deceive us. A narrator's actions, statements, and **voice**—his or her style of speaking, **diction** (word choice), and **tone** (attitude)—will provide you with clues about his or her reliability.

INTERNET

Vocabulary Practice

•

More About Edgar Allan Poe

•

Keyword: LE5 9-3

Reading Skills 📖

Drawing Conclusions

When you read, you act like a detective. You gather evidence and draw **conclusions,** or make judgments, based on that evidence. To decide if the narrator of Poe's story is unreliable, look closely at all the narrator *says* and *does*. Then, examine what his enemy, Fortunato, *says*. What details could support a charge of unreliability—even insanity? The questions at the open-book signs will help you.

SKILLS FOCUS

Literary Skills
Understand the first-person narrator and the unreliable narrator.

Reading Skills
Draw conclusions.

Background

Centuries ago Christians in Italy buried their dead in catacombs—long, winding underground tunnels. Later wealthy families built private catacombs beneath their homes. Dark and cool, these chambers were suitable not only for burial but also for the storage of fine wines, such as amontillado (ə·män′tə·lä′dō). Poe's story is set during carnival, which is celebrated before the start of Lent, the season during which Christians give up various pleasures. During carnival, many people wear costumes and dance in the streets.

Vocabulary Development

precluded (prē·klo͞od′id) v.: made impossible in advance; prevented.

impunity (im·pyo͞o′ni·tē) n.: freedom from punishment or harm.

retribution (re′trə·byo͞o′shən) n.: punishment.

immolation (im′ə·lā′shən) n.: destruction.

connoisseurship (kän′ə·sʉr′ship) n.: expert knowledge.

impose (im·pōz′) v. (used with *upon*): take advantage of.

recoiling (ri·koil′iŋ) v. used as *adj.*: moving backward, as in fear.

endeavored (en·dev′ərd) v.: tried.

obstinate (äb′stə·nət) adj.: stubborn.

succession (sək·sesh′ən) n.: series.

RESOURCES: READING

Planning
■ *One-Stop Planner* CD-ROM with ExamView Test Generator

Differentiating Instruction
■ *Holt Reading Solutions*
■ *Holt Adapted Reader*
■ *Supporting Instruction in Spanish*

Vocabulary
■ *Vocabulary Development*

Grammar and Language
■ *Language Handbook Worksheets*
■ *Daily Language Activities*

Assessment
■ *Holt Assessment: Literature, Reading, and Vocabulary*

■ *One-Stop Planner* CD-ROM with ExamView Test Generator
■ *Holt Online Assessment*

Internet
■ go.hrw.com (Keyword: LE5 9-3)
■ *Elements of Literature Online*

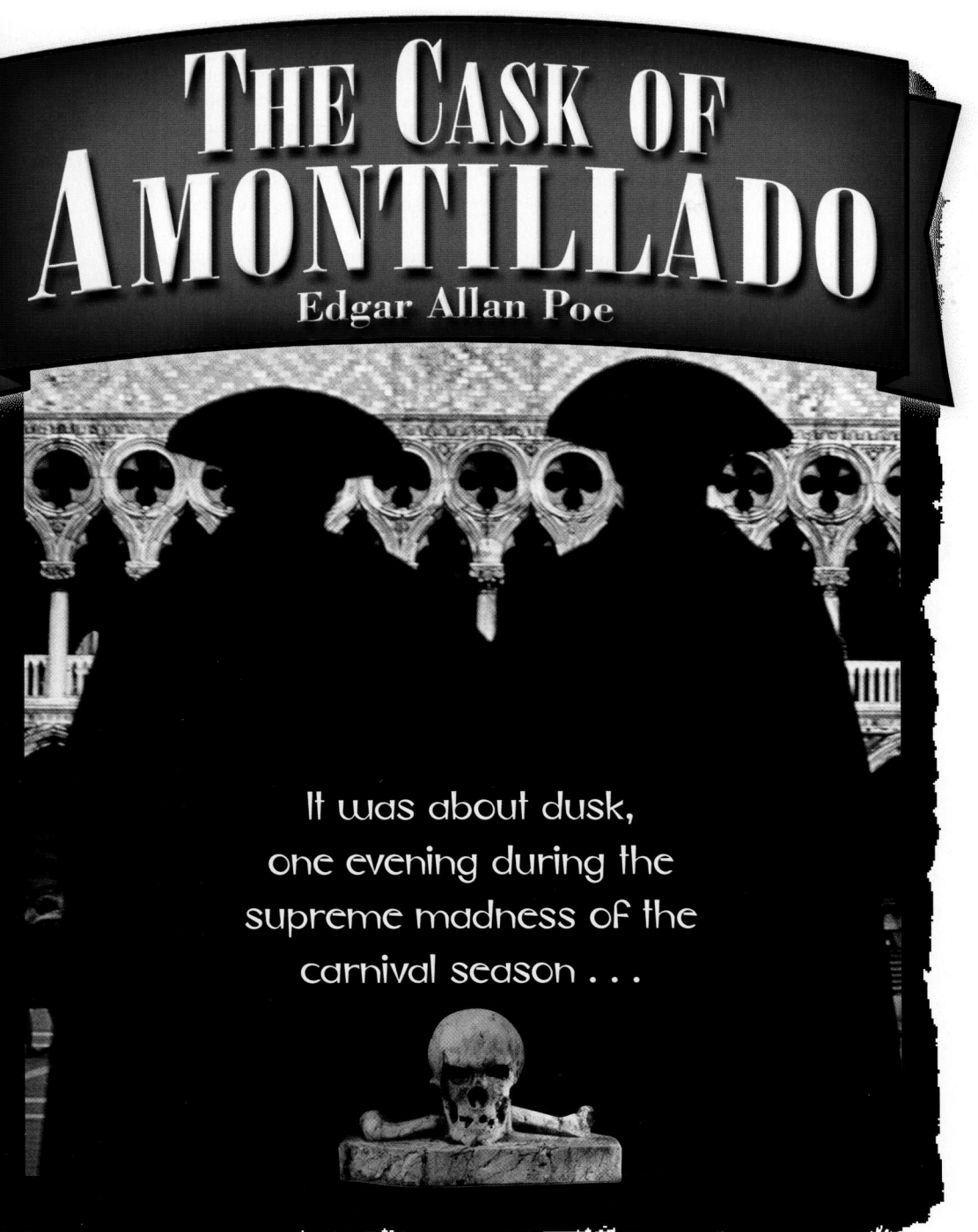

THE CASK OF AMONTILLADO

Edgar Allan Poe

It was about dusk,
one evening during the
supreme madness of the
carnival season . . .

Media
- *Audio CD Library*
- *Audio CD Library, Selections and Summaries in Spanish*
- *Fine Art Transparencies*
- *Visual Connections Videocassette Program*

PRETEACHING

Selection Starter

Motivate. Use the *Visual Connections* Videocassette, Segment 3, "Irony in Italy" to pique students' interest in Poe's story and its setting.

Preview Vocabulary

Ask students to choose the best Vocabulary word from the list on p. 172 to replace each underlined word or phrase.

1. The criminals knew that they could operate with no fear of punishment. [impunity]

2. A whole series of lawyers had struggled in vain to prove that he was an accessory to the crime. [succession; endeavored]

3. The defense lawyer felt that the public's desire for revenge ruled out the possibility of acquittal. [retribution; precluded]

4. Although the state argued that the man's expert knowledge of art proved his guilt, the jury was unyielding in rejecting the argument. [connoisseurship; obstinate]

5. Shrinking away from the crime scene photos, the witness testified that the destruction of the museum was the act of a lone criminal. [recoiling; immolation]

6. If I can do a task myself, I'd rather not presume upon the kindness of others to do it for me. [impose]

A Literary Focus

❓ Unreliable narrator. Poe hints that the narrator may be unreliable. How do the narrator's opening statements suggest that he is over-reacting? [Possible response: "The thousand injuries" is a classic exaggeration; his fixation on "retribution" and desire to be an "avenger" seem extreme.]

B Literary Focus

❓ Unreliable narrator. Notice how the narrator secretively schemes for revenge. Is this how most people would respond to an insult? [Possible response: No, most people would openly confront the insulter and demand an apology.]

C Reading Skills

Drawing conclusions. [Possible responses to question 1: The narrator is intensely vindictive; he is filled with hatred for Fortunato.]

D Reading Skills

❓ Drawing conclusions. Why is the narrator glad to see Fortunato? [Possible response: The meeting provides him with an opportunity to exact his revenge.] Most people do not act friendly toward those they hate. What conclusion might the narrator's behavior lead you to draw about his mental state? [Possible responses: It shows that the narrator may be mentally unbalanced; it shows that the narrator is calculating and has a secret motive for being friendly.]

A The thousand injuries of Fortunato I had borne as best I could; but when he ventured upon insult, I vowed revenge. You, who so well know the nature of my soul, will not suppose, however, that I gave utterance to a threat. At length I would be avenged; this was a point definitively settled—but the very definitiveness with which it was resolved precluded the idea of risk. I must not only punish, but punish with impunity. A wrong is unredressed[1] when retribution overtakes its redresser. It is equally unredressed when the avenger fails to make himself felt as such to him who has done the wrong.

B It must be understood that neither by word nor deed had I given Fortunato cause to doubt my goodwill. I continued, as was my wont, to smile in his face, and he did not perceive that my smile *now* was at the thought of his immolation.

C

DRAWING CONCLUSIONS

1. What does the narrator's smiling at the thought of Fortunato's death tell you about his character?

He had a weak point—this Fortunato—although in other regards he was a man to be respected and even feared. He prided himself on his connoisseurship in wine. Few Italians have the true virtuoso spirit. For the most part their enthusiasm is adopted to suit the time and opportunity—to practice imposture upon the British and Austrian millionaires. In painting and gemmary, Fortunato, like his countrymen, was a quack—but in the matter of old wines he was sincere. In this respect I did not differ from him materially: I was skillful in the Italian vintages myself and bought largely whenever I could.

It was about dusk, one evening during the supreme madness of the carnival season, that I encountered my friend. He accosted me with excessive warmth, for he had been drinking

much. The man wore motley.[2] He had on a tight-fitting parti-striped dress, and his head was surmounted by the conical cap and bells. I was so pleased to see him that I thought I should never have done wringing his hand.

D I said to him, "My dear Fortunato, you are luckily met. How remarkably well you are looking today! But I have received a pipe[3] of what passes for amontillado, and I have my doubts."

"How?" said he. "Amontillado? A pipe? Impossible! And in the middle of the carnival!"

"I have doubts," I replied; "and I was silly enough to pay the full amontillado price without consulting you in the matter. You were not to be found, and I was fearful of losing a bargain."

"Amontillado!"

"I have my doubts."

"Amontillado!"

"And I must satisfy them."

"Amontillado!"

"As you are engaged, I am on my way to Luchesi. If anyone has a critical turn, it is he. He will tell me—"

"Luchesi cannot tell amontillado from sherry."

---

2. **motley** (mät′lē) *n.*: multicolored costume worn by a clown or jester.
3. **pipe** *n.*: barrel.

Vocabulary

precluded (prē·klōōd′id) *v.*: made impossible in advance; prevented.

impunity (im·pyōō′ni·tē) *n.*: freedom from punishment or harm.

retribution (re′trə·byōō′shən) *n.*: punishment.

immolation (im′ə·lā′shən) *n.*: destruction.

connoisseurship (kän′ə·sur′ship) *n.*: expert knowledge.

---

1. **unredressed** (un′ri·drest′) *v.* used as *adj.*: not set right or not made up for.

DIFFERENTIATING INSTRUCTION

Learners Having Difficulty
Modeling. To help students read "The Cask of Amontillado," model the reading skill of drawing conclusions. Say, "Suppose you read that the narrator in this story holds a grudge for years. Knowing that few people hold grudges for so long, you can draw the conclusion that he is unusually vengeful." Encourage students as they read to ask

themselves, "What do the narrator's actions lead me to conclude about his mental state?"

English-Language Learners
You might use echo reading to ease these students into Poe's complex writing style. Pair students with different reading proficiency levels. Have the more proficient reader read aloud and the other student echo what the first reader says.

Special Education Students
For lessons designed for special education students, see *Holt Reading Solutions*.

Advanced Learners
Acceleration. Use the following activity to help advanced students analyze the ways authors have used archetypes drawn from myth and tradition.

E Content-Area Connections

Culture: Wine
Amontillado is a type of sherry. (Sherry is a fortified wine originally made in the Andalusia region of Spain.) Amontillado is classed as a medium sherry, which means that it has been aged.

F Reading Skills

Drawing conclusions. [Possible responses to question 2: The narrator plays on Fortunato's competitive nature and on his vanity about his wine expertise. This strategy shows that the narrator has pinpointed Fortunato's weaknesses and is a shrewd manipulator.]

"And yet some fools will have it that his taste is a match for your own."

"Come, let us go."

"Whither?"

"To your vaults."[4]

"My friend, no; I will not impose upon your good nature. I perceive you have an engagement. Luchesi—"

"I have no engagement; come."

"My friend, no. It is not the engagement, but the severe cold with which I perceive you are afflicted. The vaults are insufferably damp. They are encrusted with niter."[5]

"Let us go, nevertheless. The cold is merely nothing. Amontillado! You have been imposed upon. And as for Luchesi, he cannot distinguish sherry from amontillado."

Thus speaking, Fortunato possessed himself of my arm. Putting on a mask of black silk and drawing a roquelaure[6] closely about my person, I suffered him to hurry me to my *palazzo.*[7]

DRAWING CONCLUSIONS

2. How does the narrator lure Fortunato to his palace? What does the narrator's strategy tell you about him?

---

6. **roquelaure** (räk'ə·lôr') *n.*: heavy knee-length cloak.
7. *palazzo* (pä·lät'sð): Italian for "palace."

Vocabulary

impose (im·pōz') *v.* (used with *upon*): take advantage of.

---

4. **vaults** (vôlts) *n.*: storage cellars.
5. **niter** (nīt'ər) *n.*: salt deposits.

Activity. Elicit examples of horror stories and novels students have read (such as the works of Stephen King or H. P. Lovecraft) and of horror films they have seen. Invite students to discuss these works and to list recurring archetypal patterns and motifs of horror, such as thirst for revenge, burial places, and the wearing of masks or costumes. As students read Poe's story, have them use their lists to identify its archetypal elements.

A Literary Focus

❓ Unreliable narrator. What does the narrator's attitude toward his servants reveal about his view of humanity? [Possible responses: He expects people to be untrustworthy; he is cynical.]

B Literary Focus

❓ Unreliable narrator. What is bizarre about the narrator's reference to Fortunato as his "poor friend"? [Possible response: Since Montresor has vowed revenge on Fortunato, the man is no friend. Also, "poor" indicates sympathy, an unlikely feeling toward an enemy.]

C Reading Skills

❓ Predicting. Do you predict that Fortunato will have a long life? What do you predict will happen to Fortunato? [Possible responses: No, because he will get pneumonia and die; no, because Montresor will kill him in the catacombs.]

D Advanced Learners

❓ Acceleration. What archetypal images appear on the Montresor coat of arms? [Possible response: A striking snake is an archetypal image, as is a foot crushing a snake.] What is suggested by the images and motto? [Possible response: The Montresors (the foot) always punish those (the snake) who try to harm them.]

A There were no attendants at home; they had absconded to make merry in honor of the time. I had told them that I should not return until the morning and had given them explicit orders not to stir from the house. These orders were sufficient, I well knew, to ensure their immediate disappearance, one and all, as soon as my back was turned.

I took from their sconces two flambeaux[8] and, giving one to Fortunato, bowed him through several suites of rooms to the archway that led into the vaults. I passed down a long and winding staircase, requesting him to be cautious as he followed. We came at length to the foot of the descent and stood together on the damp ground of the catacombs of the Montresors.

The gait of my friend was unsteady, and the bells upon his cap jingled as he strode.

"The pipe," said he.

"It is farther on," said I; "but observe the white web-work which gleams from these cavern walls."

He turned toward me, and looked into my eyes with two filmy orbs that distilled the rheum[9] of intoxication.

"Niter?" he asked, at length.

"Niter," I replied. "How long have you had that cough?"

"Ugh! ugh! ugh!—ugh! ugh! ugh!—ugh! ugh! ugh!—ugh! ugh! ugh!—ugh! ugh! ugh!"

B My poor friend found it impossible to reply for many minutes.

"It is nothing," he said, at last.

"Come," I said, with decision, "we will go back; your health is precious. You are rich, respected, admired, beloved; you are happy, as once I was. You are a man to be missed. For me it is no matter. We will go back; you will be ill, and I cannot be responsible. Besides, there is Luchesi—"

"Enough," he said; "the cough is a mere nothing; it will not kill me. I shall not die of a cough."

"True—true," I replied; "and, indeed, I had no intention of alarming you unnecessarily—but you should use all proper caution. A draft of this Médoc[10] will defend us from the damps."

Here I knocked off the neck of a bottle which I drew from a long row of its fellows that lay upon the mold.

"Drink," I said, presenting him the wine.

He raised it to his lips with a leer. He paused and nodded to me familiarly, while his bells jingled.

"I drink," he said, "to the buried that repose around us."

C "And I to your long life."

He again took my arm, and we proceeded.

"These vaults," he said, "are extensive."

"The Montresors," I replied, "were a great and numerous family."

"I forget your arms."[11]

D "A huge human foot d'or, in a field azure; the foot crushes a serpent rampant whose fangs are embedded in the heel."[12]

"And the motto?"

"The drops of moisture trickle among the bones."

---

8. **sconces** (skän′siz) *n.:* wall fixtures that hold **flambeaux** (flam′bōz′) *n.,* candlesticks or flaming pieces of wood.
9. **rheum** (rōōm) *n.:* watery discharge.
10. **Médoc** (mā·dôk′): type of red wine.
11. **arms** *n.:* coat of arms, a group of symbols used to represent a family.
12. **foot d'or . . . heel:** The Montresor coat of arms shows a huge golden foot against a blue background, with the foot crushing a snake that is rearing up and biting the heel.

CONTENT-AREA CONNECTIONS

Culture: Carnival

Carnival is a time of merrymaking in late winter, just before the Christian season of austerity called Lent. Carnival is a celebration of indulgence—people eat, drink, dance, and wear colorful costumes. In the United States the most famous carnival celebration is Mardi Gras in New Orleans. (The phrase *mardi gras* is French for "fat Tuesday.")

There the holiday is celebrated with parades, Dixieland jazz, and dancing along the city streets. In Brazil, Rio de Janeiro's world-famous Carnaval features thousands of samba dancers, organized in groups or schools, competing for the Carnaval championship. In the West Indies, Trinidad's celebrations include steel band and calypso music competitions.

Activity. Have students research and report on carnival celebrations or on the history of periods of austerity, atonement, or fasting, such as Lent, Yom Kippur, or Ramadan.

"*Nemo me impune lacessit.*"[13]

"Good!" he said.

The wine sparkled in his eyes and the bells jingled. My own fancy grew warm with the Médoc. We had passed through walls of piled bones, with casks and puncheons[14] intermingling, into the inmost recesses of the catacombs. I paused again, and this time I made bold to seize Fortunato by an arm above the elbow.

"The niter!" I said. "See, it increases. It hangs like moss upon the vaults. We are below the river's bed. The drops of moisture trickle among the bones. Come, we will go back ere it is too late. Your cough—"

"It is nothing," he said; "let us go on. But first, another draft of the Médoc."

I broke and reached him a flagon of de Grave.[15] He emptied it at a breath. His eyes flashed with a fierce light. He laughed and threw the bottle upward with a gesticulation I did not understand.

I looked at him in surprise. He repeated the movement—a grotesque one.

"You do not comprehend?" he said.

"Not I," I replied.

"Then you are not of the brotherhood."

"How?"

"You are not of the Masons."[16]

"Yes, yes," I said, "yes, yes."

"You? Impossible! A Mason?"

"A Mason," I replied.

"A sign," he said.

"It is this," I answered, producing a trowel[17] from beneath the folds of my roquelaure.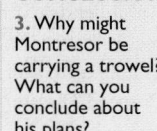

"You jest," he exclaimed, recoiling a few paces. "But let us proceed to the amontillado."

"Be it so," I said, replacing the tool beneath the cloak and again offering him my arm. He leaned upon it heavily. We continued our route in search of the amontillado. We passed through a range of low arches, descended, passed on, and, descending again, arrived at a deep crypt in which the foulness of the air caused our flambeaux rather to glow than flame.

At the most remote end of the crypt there appeared another less spacious. Its walls had been lined with human remains, piled to the vault overhead, in the fashion of the great catacombs of Paris. Three sides of this interior crypt were still ornamented in this manner. From the fourth the bones had been thrown down and lay promiscuously[18] upon the earth, forming at one point a mound of some size. Within the wall thus exposed by the displacing of the bones, we perceived a still interior recess, in depth about four feet, in width three, in height six or seven. It seemed to have been constructed for no especial use within itself, but formed merely the interval between two of the colossal supports of the roof of the catacombs and was backed by one of their

---

DRAWING CONCLUSIONS

3. Why might Montresor be carrying a trowel? What can you conclude about his plans?

---

13. *Nemo me impune lacessit* (nā**′**mō mā im·pōō**′**nā lä·ke**′**sit): Latin for "Nobody attacks me without punishment."
14. **puncheons** (pun**′**chənz) *n.:* large wine casks.
15. **flagon of de Grave:** narrow-necked bottle with a handle and sometimes a lid, containing a wine from the Graves region of France.
16. **Masons:** Freemasons, a secret society of people who believe in brotherhood, giving to the poor, and helping one another. Members use secret signs and gestures to recognize one another.

17. **trowel** (trou**′**əl) *n.:* flat tool with a pointed blade, especially used by a mason, a person who builds with stone or concrete. The Freemasons probably began as associations of stoneworkers.
18. **promiscuously** (prō·mis**′**kyōō·əs·lē) *adv.:* randomly; in a disorganized way.

Vocabulary
recoiling (ri·koil**′**iŋ) *v.* used as a*dj.:* moving backward, as in fear.

The Cask of Amontillado **177**

E Literary Focus

❷ **Unreliable narrator.** Why does Montresor profess concern for Fortunato's health? [Possible response: He is trying to disarm Fortunato by appearing concerned, so that Fortunato will not suspect him.] **How does this passage suggest that Montresor is an unreliable narrator?** [Possible response: He will deceive people if it suits his purposes.]

F English-Language Learners

Build background knowledge. Explain that Fortunato uses the word *Mason* to mean a member of an exclusive, secret society called the Freemasons. Montresor, in an ominous pun, uses it in its more common meaning of "bricklayer; stone worker."

G Reading Skills

Drawing conclusions. [Possible responses to question 3: Montresor may be planning to kill Fortunato and to bury the body in concrete; Montresor has carefully planned and prepared for the day he would lure Fortunato into the catacombs.]

CONTENT-AREA CONNECTIONS

Art: Heraldry
Coats of arms are symbolic designs originally used to decorate shields. Heraldry, the system of symbolic emblems used in coats of arms, was developed in medieval times to help combatants distinguish friend from foe.
Activity. Have students research heraldry and create a display of various coats of arms with captions explaining the symbols.

History: Freemasons
The Freemasons, the subject of Montresor's pun, are a secret fraternal society that grew out of medieval craft guilds. Founded in 1717, the Freemasons are the largest secret society in the world.
Activity. Have students research and report on the Freemasons' activities and influence during the time in which the story is set (the eighteenth or nineteenth century).

A **Reading Skills**

? **Drawing conclusions.** What kind of person has Fortunato shown himself to be? [Possible responses: He is arrogant—he claims to be a wine expert; he is mean—he calls Luchesi an ignoramus.]

B **Vocabulary Development**

? **Word derivations.** The word *depended* has an unusually literal meaning here. The word *depend* comes from Latin *pendere,* "to hang." The prefix *de–* means "down." What might the narrator mean when he says that the chain depended from the staple? [It hung down.] What other words in English derive from *pendere?* [Possible responses: pendulum, pendant, pending, appendix.]

A CLOSER LOOK

This information came from Joseph S. Schick's "The Origin of 'The Cask of Amontillado.'"

The letter was written by Rev. Joel Tyler Headley (1814–1897), a popular writer in his day. It was one of several contained in his book, *Letters from Italy* (1845). The letter, called "A Sketch, a Man Built in a Wall," was published in *The Columbian Magazine* and *The New York Evening Mirror,* two publications Poe knew well.

Activity. Many well-known works of literature are based upon real-life events. With the class, make a list of such stories, books, movies, and plays, and discuss how closely the literary work follows the true story. (Examples might include the play *The Miracle Worker,* the movie *Titanic,* and the novel *To Kill a Mockingbird.*)

---

circumscribing walls of solid granite.

It was in vain that Fortunato, uplifting his dull torch, endeavored to pry into the depth of the recess. Its termination the feeble light did not enable us to see.

"Proceed," I said; "herein is the amontillado. As for Luchesi—"

A "He is an ignoramus," interrupted my friend, as he stepped unsteadily forward, while I followed immediately at his heels. In an instant he had reached the extremity of the niche, and finding his progress arrested by the rock, stood stupidly bewildered. A moment more and I had fettered[19] him to the granite. In its surface were two iron staples, distant from each other about **B** two feet horizontally. From one of these depended a short chain, from the other a padlock. Throwing the links about his waist, it was but the work of a few seconds to secure it. He was too much astounded to resist. Withdrawing the

---

19. **fettered** (fet'ərd) *v.:* chained.

---

key, I stepped back from the recess.

"Pass your hand," I said, "over the wall; you cannot help feeling the niter. Indeed it is *very* damp. Once more let me *implore* you to return. No? Then I must positively leave you. But I must first render you all the little attentions in my power."

"The amontillado!" ejaculated my friend, not yet recovered from his astonishment.

"True," I replied; "the amontillado."

As I said these words, I busied myself among the pile of bones of which I have before spoken. Throwing them aside, I soon uncovered a quantity of building stone and mortar. With these materials and with the aid of my trowel, I began vigorously to wall up the entrance of the niche.

I had scarcely laid the first tier of the masonry when I discovered that the intoxication

---

Vocabulary
endeavored (en·dev'ərd) *v.:* tried.

A CLOSER LOOK
The Other Man in the Wall

On July 12, 1845, a letter appeared in a New York newspaper. The letter writer was describing his recent travels in Italy. He said that he had an amazing experience in the little town of San Giovanni when he visited the church of San Lorenzo. He was shown a niche covered with a sort of trap-door in the wall of the church. Inside the niche was an upright human skeleton. The writer examined the skeleton and concluded that the victim had been walled in alive and suffocated. The writer supposed that the motive had been revenge. He guessed that the man had been tied securely and then walled in, brick by brick. The writer also guessed that the men involved were nobles (like Fortunato and Montresor)—no one else, he figured, could have gotten control of a church to perform the gruesome deed.

The year after this letter was published, Poe wrote his famous revenge story "The Cask of Amontillado."

Crypt of the popes, Catacomb of S. Callisto, Rome, Italy.

READING MINI-LESSON

Developing Word-Attack Skills
Write these selection words on the chalkboard: *roquelaure, flambeaux, Médoc.* Point out that they are of French origin. Pronounce the words for students, and help them use the words to make the following generalizations about letter-sound correspondences in words with French origins.

• The letters *qu* stand for /k/.
• The letters *eau* stand for /ō/.
• The letter *x,* forming the plural, stands for /z/.
• The letter *é* stands for /ā/.

Activity. Write these sentences on the chalkboard. Have students underline each word from French and read it aloud.

of Fortunato had in a great measure worn off. The earliest indication I had of this was a low moaning cry from the depth of the recess. It was *not* the cry of a drunken man. There was then a long and obstinate silence. I laid the second tier, and the third, and the fourth; and then I heard the furious vibrations of the chain. The noise lasted for several minutes, during which, that I might hearken to it with the more satisfaction, I ceased my labors and sat down upon the bones. When at last the clanking subsided, I resumed the trowel and finished without interruption the fifth, the sixth, and the seventh tier. The wall was now nearly upon a level with my breast. I again paused and, holding the flambeaux over the masonwork, threw a few feeble rays upon the figure within.

> **DRAWING CONCLUSIONS**
> 4. What can you conclude about Montresor's state of mind when he stops his work to enjoy Fortunato's cries?

A succession of loud and shrill screams, bursting suddenly from the throat of the chained form, seemed to thrust me violently back. For a brief moment I hesitated—I trembled. Unsheathing my rapier,[20] I began to grope with it about the recess; but the thought of an instant reassured me. I placed my hand upon the solid fabric of the catacombs and felt satisfied. I reapproached the wall; I replied to the yells of him who clamored. I reechoed—I aided—I surpassed them in volume and in strength. I did this, and the clamorer grew still.

It was now midnight, and my task was drawing to a close. I had completed the eighth, the ninth, and the tenth tier. I had finished a portion of the last and the eleventh; there remained but a single stone to be fitted and plastered in. I struggled with its weight; I placed it partially in its destined position. But now there came from out the niche a low laugh

---

20. **rapier** (rā′pē·ər) *n.*: slender two-edged sword.

---

that erected the hairs upon my head. It was succeeded by a sad voice, which I had difficulty in recognizing as that of the noble Fortunato. The voice said—

"Ha! ha! ha!—he! he! he!—a very good joke indeed—an excellent jest. We will have many a rich laugh about it at the *palazzo*—he! he! he!—over our wine—he! he! he!"

"The amontillado!" I said.

"He! he! he!—he! he! he!—yes, the amontillado. But is it not getting late? Will not they be awaiting us at the *palazzo*—the Lady Fortunato and the rest? Let us be gone."

"Yes," I said, "let us be gone."

"*For the love of God, Montresor!*"

"Yes," I said, "for the love of God!"

But to these words I hearkened in vain for a reply. I grew impatient. I called aloud—

"Fortunato!"

No answer. I called again—

"Fortunato!"

No answer still. I thrust a torch through the remaining aperture and let it fall within. There came forth in return only a jingling of the bells. My heart grew sick—on account of the dampness of the catacombs. I hastened to make an end of my labor. I forced the last stone into its position; I plastered it up. Against the new masonry I reerected the old rampart[21] of bones. For the half of a century no mortal has disturbed them. *In pace requiescat.*[22] ∎

> **DRAWING CONCLUSIONS**
> 5. Do you think Montresor's "heart grew sick" because of the dampness or for some other reason? Support your conclusion.

---

21. **rampart** (ram′pärt′) *n.*: wall resembling one built for protection or defense.
22. ***In pace requiescat*** (in pä′chā rā′kwē·es′kät): Latin for "May he rest in peace."

Vocabulary
obstinate (äb′stə·nət) *adj.*: stubborn.
succession (sək·sesh′ən) *n.*: series.

The Cask of Amontillado **179**

FAMILY/COMMUNITY ACTIVITY

1. The star was traveling with her protégé.
2. A porter carried their portmanteau.
3. They saw a boutique in the station.
4. Its windows featured clever tableaux.
5. The actress spied a red chapeau.
6. With élan she placed it on her head.
7. The star approved of nothing risqué.

You might suggest that groups of students prepare dramatic readings of "The Cask of Amontillado." If you wish, you might arrange for one or more groups to read the story to another class or to visitors from the community. If the story is read well, the horror and suspense can keep listeners spellbound. Have students in the groups take different roles— one student can serve as director; two students can read the dialogue of Montresor and Fortunato; some students can take turns reading the narration; and other students can choose and play suitable music as introduction and background to the story.

Monitoring students' progress.
Guide students in responding to these comprehension questions. Have them locate passages in the story that support their responses.

Short Answer

1. Who is the narrator of this story? [Montresor, an Italian noble]

2. How does the narrator describe Fortunato? [Fortunato inspires respect but has weaknesses, including excessive pride in his knowledge of wines.]

3. What is amontillado? [wine]

4. What is the Montresor coat of arms? [a human foot crushing a snake that is biting it, with a motto about revenge]

5. How does Montresor get revenge? [He buries Fortunato alive behind a wall in a catacomb.]

Meet the Writer

Background. Poe's explorations of horror have inspired generations of writers. Lois Duncan, author of *I Know What You Did Last Summer,* describes her first encounter with "The Cask of Amontillado" as her "most terrifying reading experience": "I find the story resurfacing in fever dreams in hideous detail, affecting all of my senses—the sight of that last square of light, so quickly obliterated; the sound of a trowel slathering plaster across a brick; then, the dark closing in as the final stone is slowly and deliberately inserted into place. . . . And finally, the chilling realization that, no matter how loudly [Fortunato and I] scream, there will be no escape."

For Independent Reading

Tell students that a prize given annually by the Mystery Writers of America is called the Edgar Award, in honor of Poe.

Students who like horror will enjoy Daphne du Maurier's classic short story "The Birds."

Meet the Writer

Edgar Allan Poe

A Haunted Life

Edgar Allan Poe (1809–1849) was the son of traveling actors. His father deserted the family, and his beautiful young mother died in a theatrical rooming house in Richmond, Virginia, before Edgar was three years old. The little boy was taken in as a foster child by the wealthy and childless Allan family of Richmond.

At first, Edgar's foster parents were pleased with his brilliant scholarship and athletic ability. But later they became angry at his moodiness and irresponsibility with money. Poe went to the University of Virginia but dropped out with heavy gambling debts. (John Allan apparently refused to

support him any longer.) Eventually Poe and his foster father split up completely, and Poe was left penniless. After several failed courtships, Poe married a thirteen-year-old cousin, Virginia Clemm, and moved to New York City. There, in 1837, they set up house, together with Virginia's mother, whom Poe fondly called Muddy.

Poe drank excessively at times, and he was always in need of money. He wrote regularly, however, and had increasing success, although his unusual poems and stories were mocked by conservative critics. "The Cask of Amontillado" was published in 1846, during a time when Poe was enduring vicious insults from critics. The story might have been Poe's way of getting even not only with hostile critics but also with his foster father. The Montresor motto is the motto of Scotland; John Allan was Scottish and, like the hated Fortunato, a businessman and a Mason.

Poe's one refuge in life was threatened when Virginia became ill with tuberculosis. (Almost 25 percent of Americans in the nineteenth century died from tuberculosis.) When she died, Poe broke down completely. Two years later he was found delirious in a tavern in Baltimore on a rainy election day. The great master of horror died a few days later.

For Independent Reading

For more tales of terror by Poe, read "The Pit and the Pendulum," in which the narrator faces heart-stopping threats to his life, and "The Tell-Tale Heart," in which a haunted man tries to convince us he's not mad. Mystery lovers will enjoy "The Gold Bug," one of Poe's tales that set the stage for the modern detective story.

180 Collection 3 Narrator and Voice • Synthesizing Sources

DIFFERENTIATING INSTRUCTION

Advanced Learners

Enrichment. Tell students that before Poe's wife died, he tried to support her and himself by editing various magazines.

Activity. Encourage students to learn more about Poe's career as a magazine editor. Suggest that they enter *Edgar Allan Poe* and *editor* as keywords in a search engine to

research the magazines with which Poe was involved. Tell students to make a list of these magazines and to include a brief annotation with each listing. The annotations should state the type of magazine it was, the role Poe had, the years Poe edited, and any other information that seems relevant.

Response and Analysis

Reading Check

1. What does Montresor admit is his **motive** for this crime?

2. According to Montresor, what makes a perfect crime?

3. According to Montresor, what kind of person is Fortunato?

4. How does Montresor lure Fortunato farther and farther into the catacombs?

5. What evidence suggests that Montresor has committed the perfect crime?

Thinking Critically

6. How would you describe the **persona** that Poe has created for Montresor? Why might Poe have chosen someone like Montresor to tell his story?

7. What **character traits** in Fortunato make him fall prey to Montresor?

8. In your opinion, what is Montresor thinking when he says, "*In pace requiescat*"? Explain your interpretation.

9. To whom could Montresor be talking, fifty years after the murder, and for what reasons?

10. Montresor's **voice**—the way he speaks and his **tone**—is frequently **ironic**. Which of Montresor's comments to the unsuspecting Fortunato mean something different from what they seem to mean?

11. Think about whether or not Montresor is an **unreliable narrator.** Do any details suggest that he might have imagined "the thousand injuries" and the insult—or even the whole story? Can you find evidence in the story to support Montresor's claim that Fortunato *did* in fact injure and insult him? To support your answers, con-

sider Montresor's actions, statements, and **voice.**

12. Think about Poe's decision to set his story during carnival. What is **ironic** about the **setting**? In what ways does the setting suit the plot of the story?

Extending and Evaluating

13. Is this just a gripping horror story told only for entertainment, or do you think it reveals some truth about people who are consumed by a desire for revenge? Give reasons for your opinions. (Be sure to check your Quickwrite notes.) ✏

WRITING

Fortunato's Version

Suppose this story were told from Fortunato's **first-person point of view.** Write a **new beginning.** Start at the point where the two men meet at dusk, and end when they begin their journey underground. Let the reader know what Fortunato thinks of Montresor. Is he guilty of the thousand injuries and the insult that Montresor refers to? Create an individual **voice** for Fortunato (one that is different from Montresor's) by giving him a distinct tone and style of speaking. For example, is he frank, confused, or overconfident?

Crime and Punishment

Suppose the person to whom Montresor is telling his story has turned him over to the police. Montresor's lawyer will argue that he is insane. The prosecution will argue that Montresor knew exactly what he was doing and that he even planned the murder in advance. Write a **speech** for either lawyer, and argue your case before your classmates.

go.hrw.com

INTERNET
Projects and Activities
Keyword: LE5 9-3

SKILLS FOCUS

Literary Skills
Analyze the first-person narrator and the unreliable narrator.

Reading Skills
Draw conclusions.

Writing Skills
Write a new beginning for a short story. Write a speech.

The Cask of Amontillado **181**

Response and Analysis

Thinking Critically

6. Montresor is secretive, intense, obsessive, vengeful and possibly insane. Possible answer: Poe might have chosen Montresor to narrate because he wanted to depict a vengeful mind.

7. Fortunato is open, easygoing, self-assured, and vain. Montresor takes advantage of the last two traits.

8. Possible answers: Montresor is gloating about his success; he hopes the crime will remain undiscovered.

9. Possible answers: He could be confessing to a priest, perhaps on his deathbed; he could be unburdening himself—or boasting—to a friend or a relative.

10. Possible answers: "My dear Fortunato . . . " (p. 174); "[Y]our health is precious." (p. 176); "You are a man to be missed." (p. 176); "I [drink] to your long life." (p. 176); "Once more let me *implore* you to return." (p. 178)

11. Possible answer: There is scant evidence of Fortunato's "thousand injuries," which casts doubt on Montresor's motives. Montresor shows that he is willing to deceive others, maybe even the readers, to suit his purposes.

12. The "supreme madness" of carnival suits the madness of the tale. The festivities contrast ironically with the horror and suffering, and it is grimly ironic that the victim wears a clown costume.

Extending and Evaluating

13. Possible answer: Beyond mere entertainment, the story shows how vengefulness can erode humane impulses and drive people to commit unspeakable crimes.

Reading Check

1. He says he has vowed revenge for Fortunato's insults.

2. It is a crime in which the perpetrator is not caught and the victim realizes that the motive is revenge.

3. Montresor portrays Fortunato as arrogant, insulting, and vain.

4. Montresor appeals to Fortunato's vanity, saying that he will ask Luchesi to taste the amontillado if Fortunato cannot.

5. Fortunato's bones are still undisturbed fifty years after the crime.

Vocabulary Development

Practice

Student word maps will vary.

- *retribution. Etymology*—L *re–*, "back" + *tribuere*, "to pay." *Meaning*—punishment. *Sample sentence*—If you cheat, you will face <u>retribution</u>.
- *immolation. Etymology*—L *immolatus*, from *immolare*, "to sprinkle a victim with sacrificial meal." *Meaning*—destruction. *Sample sentence*—An earthquake caused the city's <u>immolation</u>.
- *impose (upon). Etymology*—L *in–*, "on" + *ponere*, "to put." *Meaning*—take advantage of. *Sample sentence*—If guests <u>impose</u> upon him, he doesn't invite them back.
- *obstinate. Etymology*—L *ob–*, "against" + *stare*, "to stand." *Meaning*—stubborn. *Sample sentence*—That <u>obstinate</u> mule won't budge.
- *succession. Etymology*—L *succedere*, "to follow after." *Meaning*—series. *Sample sentence*—After a <u>succession</u> of errors, the coach called a timeout.

Grammar Link

Practice

Possible Answers

2. Dialogue 1:

   "Amontillado!" breathed Fortunato.

   "I have my doubts," I sighed.

   "Amontillado!" panted Fortunato.

   Dialogue 2:

   "You do not comprehend?" smirked Fortunato.

   "Not I," I admitted.

   "Then you are not of the brotherhood," Fortunato declared.

3. Students' answers will vary.

Vocabulary Development

Word Maps

PRACTICE

A word map can supply several different kinds of information. It can give the word's **etymology,** or origin, by listing **root words** and **prefixes.** It can also give a definition and a sample sentence. Use a dictionary to make a word map for each word in the Word Bank. (A map of *precluded* appears below.)

Word Bank

precluded
impunity
retribution
immolation
connoisseurship
impose
recoiling
endeavored
obstinate
succession

```
                    precluded
        ┌───────────────┼───────────────┐
   Etymology         Meaning         Sample sentence
< Latin prae–,    made impossible   Cara's injury precluded
  "before"        in advance;       her entering the
< Latin claudere, prevented         gymnastics meet.
  "to close"
```

Grammar Link

Dialogue—Who's Talking?

Dialogue in a story can advance the plot, reveal the thoughts of a character, or present important information to a reader. In American usage, **dialogue** is enclosed in double quotation marks (" "). Usually a new paragraph lets us know when a different person begins to speak, as in this example from "The Cask of Amontillado":

> "You do not comprehend?" he said.
> "Not I," I replied.
> "Then you are not of the brotherhood."

Most writers use **tag lines** (such as *he said* and *I replied*) to identify the speakers in a dialogue. Some writers do not always use tag lines, however. Poe, for example, has written long passages of conversation between Montresor and Fortunato in which neither speaker is directly identified. Remember that tag lines should not be enclosed in quotation marks.

SKILLS FOCUS

Vocabulary Skills
Create word maps showing etymology, meaning, and context.

Grammar Skills
Punctuate dialogue correctly.

PRACTICE

Look back at the dialogue beginning "Amontillado!" on page 174 and at the dialogue beginning "You do not comprehend?" on page 177.

1. Get together with a partner, and read the dialogues aloud. Use your voices to distinguish one speaker from another.

2. Now, add tag lines to Poe's dialogue. (Be sure to punctuate them correctly.) Compare your edited versions of Poe's dialogue in class.

3. Finally, look at what Poe's dialogue accomplished. What did you learn about the characters or plot from this exchange?

▶ **For more help, see Quotation Marks, 13c–j, in the Language Handbook.**

ASSESSING

Assessment

- *Holt Assessment: Literature, Reading, and Vocabulary*

RETEACHING

For a lesson reteaching narrator and tone, see **Reteaching,** p. 979A. For another selection to teach narrator, see *The Holt Reader,* Collection 3.

Informational Text

LINK TO "THE CASK OF AMONTILLADO"

Four Readings About Poe's Death

Synthesizing Sources: Seeing the Big Picture

When you research a subject, you read many different sources carefully. Then you need to **synthesize** the information, putting all the pieces together to see the big picture. Follow these steps:

- **Find the main idea.** Look for each writer's main idea, and take notes about it. To work your way through a difficult passage, **paraphrase** it—restate the passage in your own words.
- **Look for supporting evidence.** Ask yourself, "Does the writer support his or her ideas with facts, statistics, examples, anecdotes (brief real-life stories), or quotations? Does the writer use logic and reasoning to prove a point?" For help identifying the writer's main ideas and support, try making a chart.

Main Idea 1	Main Idea 2
Support 1	Support 1
Support 2	Support 2

- **Compare and contrast.** Look for similarities and differences between your sources. In particular, compare and contrast the main ideas and the types of support the authors use.
- **Make connections.** Does the information in your sources remind you of ideas that you've read about in the past—perhaps in other articles or books or even in a story or poem?
- **Put it all together.** Once you've completed these steps, you're ready to put all the pieces together. To **synthesize** what you've learned, you may want to write a research report, an editorial, a speech, or a letter.

Vocabulary Development

insensible (in·sen′sə·bəl) *adj.*: not fully conscious or aware.

imposing (im·pō′ziŋ) *adj.*: large and impressive looking.

stupor (stoo′pər) *n.*: dull, half-conscious state.

spectral (spek′trəl) *adj.*: ghostly; unreal.

expired (ek·spīrd′) *v.*: died.

maligned (mə·līnd′) *v.* used as *adj.*: falsely accused of bad conduct; slandered.

belligerent (bə·lij′ər·ənt) *adj.*: angry and aggressive or ready to start a fight.

conspicuous (kən·spik′yoo·əs) *adj.*: obvious; noticeable; notable.

ascribe (ə·skrīb′) *v.*: assign or attribute something to a cause.

chronic (krän′ik) *adj.*: frequently occurring.

transmitted (trans·mit′id) *v.*: passed on.

Connecting to the Literature

The life of Edgar Allan Poe, author of "The Cask of Amontillado," is shrouded in mystery. Most scholars believe that Poe died as a result of drinking too much alcohol. According to another theory, Poe died of rabies, a disease people can get when they are bitten or scratched by an animal infected with the rabies virus. The following four selections present a debate about what killed this tragic genius.

SKILLS FOCUS

Reading Skills
Synthesize information from several sources on a single topic.

Four Readings About Poe's Death **183**

SKILLS FOCUS, pp. 183–192

Grade-Level Skills

- **Reading Skills**
Synthesize the content from several sources or works by a single author on a single issue.

Summary ⬆ *above grade level*

These four pieces discuss theories about the death of Edgar Allan Poe.

The first piece is an excerpt from a biography by Kenneth Silverman. Silverman draws on reports from Poe's contemporaries to chronicle Poe's last days—a fever left untreated, a week's disappearance, confusion, delirium, and sudden death. Most people blamed alcoholism, though at least one of Poe's doctors diagnosed Poe's condition as encephalitis due to exposure.

The second piece, a news article, discloses the theory of a modern physician, Dr. R. Michael Benitez. He states that Poe showed symptoms of rabies, not alcohol abuse. Support for his theory comes from a rabies expert and from the curator of the Poe museum, who states that Poe rarely drank in his later years.

The third is a letter to the editor in which two professors counter Dr. Benitez's theory, arguing that Poe's letters reveal he binged on alcohol, that Poe had no bite marks, and that doctors of Poe's day were not likely to ignore rabies symptoms in making a diagnosis.

The final piece is Dr. Benitez's response to the letter, giving more support for his theory.

Skills Starter

Motivate. You might bring in an article about a current event, such as an investigation or a trial. Ask students what they think about the issue. As they discuss their ideas, encourage them to connect and synthesize information from the article and from other sources familiar to them.

Preview Vocabulary

To reinforce students' understanding of the Vocabulary words on p. 183, have them write responses to the following questions.

1. In what kind of movie might an imposing spectral form appear? [An impressive ghostly form might appear in a horror movie.]

2. Why might someone grow belligerent if you maligned him? [Many people get angry when they are insulted.]

3. Why might chronic colds make you insensible of smells? [A perpetually stuffy nose would make it difficult to smell.]

4. What are some conspicuous ways for a silent message to be transmitted? [Light signals are one obvious way to send a message.]

5. A character in a story says, "Alas, the queen has fallen into a stupor and expired! To what do you ascribe it?" Restate the dialogue in your own words. ["The queen has fainted and died! What do you think caused it?"]

A **Reading Informational Text**

❓ **Synthesizing sources.** What is the first evidence Silverman cites to support the idea that Poe seemed drunk? [He cites the report of Joseph Walker, who saw and spoke with Poe.]

BIOGRAPHY

This biography traces the last few days of Poe's life, in 1849. He had just parted from Elmira Shelton, to whom he was recently engaged. Shelton lived in Richmond, Virginia, and Poe set out from there for Baltimore, Maryland, eventually planning to go to New York City. He never reached it.

Poe's Final Days

from *Edgar A. Poe: Mournful and Never-Ending Remembrance*

Kenneth Silverman

In the early morning of September 27, a Thursday, Poe began the first leg of his return to the North, setting out from Richmond for Baltimore on the 4 A.M. steamer,[1] with a trunk containing some clothing, books, and manuscripts.

No reliable evidence exists about what happened to or within Poe between that time and October 3, a week later, when a printer named Joseph Walker saw him at Gunner's Hall, a Baltimore tavern, strangely dressed and semiconscious.

It was Election Day for members of Congress, and like other local watering holes[2] the tavern served as a polling place. Poe seemed to Walker "rather the worse for wear" and "in great distress." Apparently flooded with drink, he may also have been ill from exposure. Winds and soaking rains the day before had sent Baltimoreans prematurely hunting up overcoats and seeking charcoal fires for warmth. . . . Poe managed to tell Walker that he knew Joseph Evans

Snodgrass, the Baltimore editor and physician with whom he had often corresponded while living in Philadelphia. As it happened, Walker had worked as a typesetter for Snodgrass's *Saturday Visitor.* He sent Snodgrass a dire note, warning that Poe needed "immediate assistance."

When Snodgrass arrived at Gunner's Hall, he found Poe sitting in an armchair, surrounded by onlookers. Poe had a look of "vacant stupidity." He wore neither vest nor tie, his dingy trousers fit badly, his shirt was crumpled, his cheap hat soiled. Snodgrass thought he must be wearing castoff clothing, having been robbed or cheated of his own. He ordered a room for Poe at the tavern, where he might stay comfortably until his relatives in Baltimore could be notified. Just then, however, one of them arrived—Henry Herring, Poe's uncle by marriage, who somehow had also learned of his condition. A lumber dealer now nearly sixty years old, he had wed Muddy's[3] sister, and spent time with Poe

---

1. **steamer** (stēm′ər) *n.*: steamship, or ship driven by steam power.
2. **watering holes:** informal for "bars, taverns."

3. **Muddy's:** Muddy was Poe's nickname for Maria Clemm, his aunt and mother-in-law. Poe had married his cousin, Virginia Clemm.

DIFFERENTIATING INSTRUCTION

Learners Having Difficulty

Students may be challenged by dealing with four informational pieces in one lesson. Point out that all four pieces respond to the question, "What killed Edgar Allan Poe?" Suggest that students divide a sheet of paper into four columns labeled *Biography, Article, Letter 1,* and *Letter 2.* Have them jot notes in the columns as they read.

English-Language Learners

Point out that in American culture, alcoholism carries a social stigma, which underlies some of the controversy surrounding Poe's death. Explain that public sentiment against alcohol grew so strong that from 1920 to 1933, the U.S. government upheld a constitutional amendment prohibiting the sale and use of alcoholic beverages.

during his early days in Baltimore and later when both families lived in Philadelphia. But he refused now to take over his care, saying that on former occasions, when drunk, Poe had been abusive and ungrateful. Instead, he suggested sending Poe to a hospital. A carriage was called for. Poe had to be carried into it, Snodgrass said—insensible, muttering.

Through the chilly wet streets Poe was driven to the hospital of Washington Medical College, set on the highest ground of Baltimore. An imposing five-story building with vaulted gothic windows, it afforded both public wards and private rooms, advertised as being spacious, well ventilated, and directed by an experienced medical staff. Admitted at five in the afternoon, Poe was given a private room, reportedly in a section reserved for cases involving drunkenness. He was attended by the resident physician, Dr. John J. Moran, who apparently had living quarters in the hospital together with his wife. Moran had received his medical degree from the University of Maryland four years earlier and was now only about twenty-six years old. But he knew the identity of his patient—a "*great* man," he wrote of Poe, to whose "rarely gifted mind are we indebted for many of the brightest thoughts that adorn our literature." He as well as the medical students, nurses, and other physicians—all considered Poe, he said, "an object of unusual regard."

According to Moran and his wife, Poe reached the hospital in a stupor, unaware of who or what had brought him there. He remained thus "unconscious" until three o'clock the next morning, when he developed

> ### His face was pale and he was drenched in sweat.

a tremor[4] of the limbs and what Moran called "a busy, but not violent or active delirium."[5] His face was pale and he was drenched in sweat. He talked constantly, Moran said, addressing "spectral and imaginary objects on the walls." Apparently during Poe's delirium, his cousin Neilson Poe came to the hospital, having been contacted by Dr. Moran. A lawyer and journalist involved in Whig politics,[6] Neilson was just Poe's age. In happier circumstances Poe would not have welcomed the visit. Not only had Neilson offered Virginia[7] and Muddy a home apart from him; his cousin also, he believed, envied his literary reputation. Years before he had remarked that he considered "the little dog," as he called Neilson, the "bitterest enemy I have in the world." The physicians anyway thought it inadvisable for Neilson to see Poe at the moment, when "very excitable." Neilson sent some changes of linen and called again the next day, to find Poe's condition improved.

---

4. **tremor** (trem′ər) *n.*: involuntary trembling, especially from a physical illness.
5. **delirium** (di·lir′ē·əm) *n.*: irrational, raving behavior, often caused by high fever.
6. **Whig politics:** The Whigs were one of the two major American political parties at the time, the other being the Democrats.
7. **Virginia:** Poe's wife, Virginia Clemm. She died of tuberculosis in 1847.

Vocabulary
insensible (in·sen′sə·bəl) *adj.*: not fully conscious or aware.

imposing (im·pō′ziŋ) *adj.*: large and impressive looking.

stupor (stoō′pər) *n.*: dull, half-conscious state.

spectral (spek′trəl) *adj.*: ghostly; unreal.

B Reading Informational Text

? Synthesizing sources. How does Henry Herring's refusal support the assertion that Poe had a history of alcohol abuse? [Herring refused to care for Poe because of earlier episodes when Poe was drunk and caused trouble.]

C Reading Informational Text

? Synthesizing sources. According to Dr. Moran, what symptoms did Poe show during his first night in the hospital? [At first, Poe was comatose; he then began trembling, turned pale, sweated profusely, and grew delirious.]

D English-Language Learners

Archaic language. Students may know that in today's English, *changes of linen* refers to fresh bedsheets and towels. Explain that Silverman has used the phrase's antiquated meaning—in the past, the phrase referred to clean shirts and underwear.

Special Education Students
For lessons designed for special education students and English-language learners, see *Holt Reading Solutions*.

Advanced Learners
Acceleration. Use this activity to help students verify facts and make reasonable assertions about an author's arguments by using elements of the text to defend and clarify interpretations.

Activity. Suggest that students consult various reference works to learn more about the transmission and symptoms of rabies in humans. Have students use this information to assess the arguments of Silverman, Dr. Benitez, and Pollin and Benedetto. Have each student explain his or her assessment in a paragraph in which the topic sentence makes an assertion about the validity of one author's theory about the cause of Poe's death. Tell students to use details from the selections to defend their assertions.

A **Reading Informational Text**

? **Synthesizing sources.** What were the final changes in Poe's condition, according to Dr. Moran? [On Saturday, Poe went from a quiet state to wild delirium, which lasted until early Sunday. He then grew quiet again and suddenly died.]

B **Reading Informational Text**

? **Synthesizing sources.** Which evidence supports the idea that Poe died of alcoholism, and which supports the idea that he died of encephalitis? [The alcoholism theory is supported by the opinion of Dr. Snodgrass and Poe's symptoms of delirium tremens. The encephalitis theory is supported by the opinions of Dr. Moran and a senior doctor, details of the weather, and a report that Poe left home with a fever.]

C **Reading Informational Materials**

? **Synthesizing sources.** How would you paraphrase Silverman's main idea about the cause of Poe's death? [Possible responses: The cause of death is not clear; alcoholism, exposure, and encephalitis may all have played a part; drinking may have led Poe to neglect his health and contract encephalitis.]

Poe being quieted, Moran began questioning him about his family and about where he lived, but found his answers mostly incoherent. Poe did not know what had become of his trunk or when he had left Richmond, but said he had a wife there, as Moran soon learned was untrue. He said that his "degradation," as Moran characterized it, made him feel like sinking into the ground. Trying to rouse Poe's spirits, Moran told him he wished to contribute in every way to his comfort, and hoped Poe would soon be enjoying the company of his friends. . . .

Then Poe seemed to doze, and Moran left him briefly. On returning he found Poe violently delirious, resisting the efforts of two nurses to keep him in bed. From Moran's description, Poe seems to have raved a full day or more, through Saturday evening, October 6, when he began repeatedly calling out someone's name. It may have been that of a Baltimore family named Reynolds or, more likely, the name of his uncle-in-law Henry Herring. Moran later said that he sent for the Herring family, but that only one of Herring's two daughters came to the hospital. Poe continued deliriously calling the name until three o'clock on Sunday morning. Then his condition changed. Feeble from his exertions he seemed to rest a short time and then, Moran reported, "quietly moving his head he said '*Lord help my poor Soul*' and expired!"

The cause of Poe's death remains in doubt. Moran's account of his profuse perspiration, trembling, and hallucinations indicates

> **On returning he found Poe violently delirious . . .**

delirium tremens, *mania à potu*.[8] Many others who had known Poe, including the professionally trained Dr. Snodgrass, also attributed his death to a lethal amount of alcohol. Moran later vigorously disputed this explanation, however, and some Baltimore newspapers gave the cause of death as "congestion of the brain" or "cerebral inflammation."[9] Although the terms were sometimes used euphemistically[10] in public announcements of deaths from disgraceful causes, such as alcoholism, they may in this case have come from the hospital staff itself. According to Moran, one of its senior physicians diagnosed Poe's condition as encephalitis, a brain inflammation, brought on by "exposure." This explanation is consistent with the prematurely wintry weather at the time, with Snodgrass's account of Poe's partly clad[11] condition, and with Elmira Shelton's recollection that on leaving Richmond Poe already had a fever. Both explanations may have been correct: Poe may have become too drunk to care about protecting himself against the wind and rain.

8. **delirium tremens,** *mania à potu:* Delirium *tremens* refers to an alcoholic state in which the victim behaves irrationally and sometimes violently, hallucinates (sees imaginary things), and trembles. *Mania à potu* is a Latin phrase meaning "madness from drinking."

9. **"congestion of the brain" or "cerebral inflammation":** These are terms for conditions of the brain caused by injury or infection.

10. **euphemistically** (yōō′fə·mis′tə·klē) *adv.:* in a manner meant to mask or substitute for something unpleasant or offensive.

11. **clad** (klad) *adj.:* dressed.

Vocabulary
expired (ek·spīrd′) *v.:* died.

The following newspaper article announced a new theory about Poe's death, developed by Dr. R. Michael Benitez. In response to this article, Burton R. Pollin and Robert E. Benedetto wrote a letter disputing Dr. Benitez's theory. Dr. Benitez replied by writing a letter defending his ideas. Both letters follow this article.

NEWSPAPER ARTICLE

Poe's Death Is Rewritten as Case of Rabies, Not Telltale Alcohol

from *The New York Times*, September 15, 1996

Edgar Allan Poe did not die drunk in a gutter in Baltimore but rather had rabies, a new study suggests.

The researcher, Dr. R. Michael Benitez, a cardiologist[1] who practices a block from Poe's grave, says it is true that the writer was seen in a bar on Lombard Street in October 1849, delirious and possibly wearing somebody else's soiled clothes.

But Poe was not drunk, said Dr. Benitez, an assistant professor of medicine at the University of Maryland Medical Center. "I think Poe is much maligned in that respect," he added.

The writer entered Washington College Hospital comatose,[2] Dr. Benitez said, but by the next day was perspiring heavily, hallucinating, and shouting at imaginary companions. The next day, he seemed better but could not remember falling ill.

On his fourth day at the hospital, Poe again grew confused and belligerent, then quieted down and died.

That is a classic case of rabies, the doctor said. His study is in the September issue of *The Maryland Medical Journal*.

In the brief period when he was calm and awake, Poe refused alcohol and could drink water only with great difficulty. Rabies victims frequently exhibit hydrophobia, or fear of water, because it is painful to swallow.

There is no evidence that a rabid animal had bitten Poe. About one fourth of rabies victims reportedly cannot remember being bitten. After an infection, the symptoms can take up to a year to appear. But when the symptoms do appear, the disease is a swift and brutal killer. Most patients die in a few days.

Poe "had all the features of encephalitic[3] rabies," said Dr. Henry Wilde, who frequently treats rabies at Chulalongkorn University Hospital in Bangkok, Thailand.

Although it has been well established that Poe died in the hospital, legend has it that he

---

3. **encephalitic** (en·sef'ə·lit'ik) *adj.*: related to encephalitis, an inflammation, or swelling, of the brain.

Vocabulary

maligned (mə·līnd') *v.* used as *adj.*: falsely accused of bad conduct; slandered.

belligerent (bə·lij'ər·ənt) *adj.*: angry and aggressive or ready to start a fight.

---

1. **cardiologist** (kär'dē·äl'ə·jist) *n.*: doctor who specializes in diseases of the heart.
2. **comatose** (kō'mə·tōs') *adj.*: deeply unconscious and unable to be wakened.

D Reading Informational Text

❓ Synthesizing sources. Which of these details about Poe's symptoms do not appear in the excerpt from Silverman's biography? [the fact that Poe refused alcohol and could barely drink water]

E Advanced Learners

❓ Acceleration. The article does not directly cite the source of this information. How might you confirm it? [Possible response: One might examine Dr. Benitez's article in *The Maryland Medical Journal*, read more of Silverman's biography, or read Dr. Moran's report.]

F Reading Informational Text

❓ Synthesizing sources. How does Dr. Benitez's theory account for the lack of evidence that Poe was bitten by a rabid animal? (To answer, you might connect the information in this paragraph with what you know about the way small wounds heal.) [Possible response: Since the first symptoms of rabies may appear up to a year after a bite, and since small wounds heal in a few weeks (often with no scar), Poe might have been lightly nipped or scratched months earlier.]

G Reading Informational Text

❓ Synthesizing sources. Which other source names encephalitis as a possible cause of Poe's death? [It was diagnosed by one of Poe's attending doctors, as reported in the excerpt from Silverman's biography.]

DEVELOPING FLUENCY

Small-group activity. Place students in teams to debate Dr. Benitez's theory (Poe died of rabies) versus the contention of Pollin and Benedetto (Poe died of alcoholism). Have teams prepare by first developing position statements with supporting evidence. Remind students that they should anticipate possible arguments from the opposition, and ask them to prepare counterarguments. Students should re-read the four selections carefully, noting evidence that supports their position and counterarguments. Finally, stage the debate. Have both teams read aloud the passages that support their points.

A Reading Informational Text

❷ Synthesizing sources. For which of Dr. Benitez's ideas do Jeff Jerome's statements function as supporting evidence? [Possible response: They support the idea that Poe's symptoms were not caused by alcohol abuse.]

The Edgar Allan Poe House and Museum in Baltimore as it appears today.

succumbed in the gutter, a victim of his debauched[4] ways.

The legend may have been fostered by his doctor, who in later years became a temperance advocate[5] and changed the details to make an object lesson of Poe's death.

The curator of the Edgar Allan Poe House and Museum in Baltimore, Jeff Jerome, said that he had heard dozens of tales but that

---

4. **debauched** (dē·bôchd′) *adj.:* characterized by extreme indulgence in pleasures.
5. **temperance advocate:** someone who believes that people should not drink alcohol.

"almost everyone who has come forth with a theory has offered no proof."

Some versions have Poe unconscious under the steps of the Baltimore Museum before being taken to the hospital. Other accounts place him on planks between two barrels outside a tavern on Lombard Street. In most versions, Poe is wearing someone else's clothes, having been robbed of his suit.

Poe almost surely did not die of alcohol poisoning or withdrawal, Mr. Jerome said. The writer was so sensitive to alcohol that a glass of wine would make him violently ill for days. Poe may have had problems with alcohol as a younger man, Mr. Jerome said, but by the time he died at forty he almost always avoided it.

Dr. Benitez worked on Poe's case as part of a clinical pathologic conference. Doctors are presented with a hypothetical[6] patient and a description of the symptoms and are asked to render a diagnosis.

Dr. Benitez said that at first he did not know that he had been assigned Poe, because his patient was described only as "E. P., a writer from Richmond." But by the time he was scheduled to present his findings a few weeks later, he had figured out the mystery.

"There was a conspicuous lack in this report of things like CT scans and MRI's,"[7] the doctor said. "I started to say to myself, 'This doesn't look like it's from the 1990s.' Then it dawned on me that E. P. was Edgar Poe."

---

6. **hypothetical** (hī′pə·thet′i·kəl) *adj.:* in theory; not actual.
7. **CT scans and MRI's:** medical tests that use modern technology. Both tests produce an image of a cross-section of soft tissue such as the brain.

Vocabulary
conspicuous (kən·spik′yōō·əs) *adj.:* obvious; noticeable; notable.

LETTER TO THE EDITOR

If Only Poe Had Succeeded When He Said Nevermore to Drink

from *The New York Times,* September 23, 1996

To the Editor:

Dr. R. Michael Benitez, an assistant professor of medicine at Maryland University Medical Center, is wrong to ascribe the death of Edgar Allan Poe to rabies through animal infection rather than to the traditionally maintained cause of alcoholism (news article, September 15).

Poe was found outside a Baltimore saloon in an alcoholic stupor on October 3, 1849, and died four days later. Dr. John J. Moran's account of his final days is given in a letter to Poe's aunt and mother-in-law, Maria Clemm, a *New York Herald* article in 1875, and a book by Moran in 1885. Supplementary accounts of Poe's alcoholic condition came from Joseph Walker, a Baltimore printer who first found him; Dr. Joseph Snodgrass, an editor well known to Poe; and two of Poe's relatives. None of these confirm Dr. Benitez's statement that "Poe was not drunk." Evidence of Poe's chronic binges is strewn through his letters, in periodic admissions of "recoveries" and promises to his wife, Virginia, and her mother to "reform." **B**

Dr. Benitez admits the primary weakness of his theory—lack of evidence of a bite or scratch. In those days, rabies was well known as to causes and symptoms, including itching and other sensations that could affect an entire limb or side of the body. How could Moran and his staff ignore such symptoms in a patient? **C**

And what of Poe's cat, dearly loved but left behind in the Bronx over three months earlier? Guiltless was the pet Caterina, who, uninfected and showing no sign of rabies, died of starvation when deserted by Clemm after Poe's death. **D**

In short, there is no need to whitewash° the self-destructive behavior of this literary genius and major American poet, critic, and teller of tales.

Burton R. Pollin
Robert E. Benedetto
Bronxville, New York
September 20, 1996

The writers are, respectively, professor emeritus of English, City University of New York, and an associate film professor at the University of South Carolina.

°**whitewash** (hwīt′wôsh′) *v.:* cover up the faults or defects of something; give a favorable appearance to something.

Vocabulary

ascribe (ə·skrīb′) *v.:* assign or attribute something to a cause.

chronic (krän′ik) *adj.:* frequently occurring.

DIRECT TEACHING

B Reading Informational Text

Synthesizing sources. What information do Pollin and Benedetto provide that appears in neither the biography excerpt nor the news article? [They provide the year of Poe's death; a list, with dates, of Dr. Moran's writings on Poe's death; and details from Poe's personal letters to his wife and her mother.]

C Reading Informational Text

Synthesizing sources. In this paragraph, how do Pollin and Benedetto undermine the theory that Poe died of rabies? [Possible response: They describe rabies symptoms that neither Silverman nor Dr. Benitez report in Poe; they state that Poe's doctors knew rabies symptoms and would have noticed them in Poe.]

D Learners Having Difficulty

Reading inverted sentences. Students can clarify the ideas in this inverted sentence by breaking it into three shorter sentences with standard subject-verb order. Have students use the following starters:

- The pet Caterina was . . . [guiltless].
- She was uninfected and . . . [showing no signs of rabies].
- She died of starvation when . . . [she was deserted by Clemm after Poe's death].

Ⓐ Reading Informational Text

❷ Synthesizing sources. Which of Dr. Benitez's assertions do the data in this paragraph explain and support? [They support the assertion that the lack of a visible bite or scratch mark does not weaken the rabies death theory.]

Ⓑ Reading Informational Text

❷ Synthesizing sources. How does the information in this paragraph rebut Pollin's and Benedetto's contention that Poe's doctors would have recognized rabies symptoms? [Possible response: Dr. Benitez shows that rabies is often hard to recognize and that doctors of Poe's time knew much less about rabies than today's doctors do.]

GUIDED PRACTICE

Monitoring students' progress. Guide students in answering these comprehension questions. Direct students to locate passages in the text that support their responses.

Short Answer

1. What does Silverman conclude is the cause of Poe's death? [encephalitis due to exposure, a result of alcohol abuse]

2. What does Dr. Benitez believe caused Poe's death? [rabies or rabies encephalitis]

3. What do Pollin and Benedetto think Poe died of? [alcoholism]

4. According to Dr. Benitez, what diagnosis is not disproved by the lack of evidence of a bite? [rabies]

LETTER TO THE EDITOR

Rabies Death Theory

from *The New York Times*, September 30, 1996

To the Editor:

Contrary to a September 23 letter, I do not "admit" that the lack of bite or scratch is a weakness in my theory that Edgar Allan Poe may have died of rabies encephalitis.

Data published by the Centers for Disease Control and Prevention indicate that over the past 20 years in the United States there have been 33 reported cases of human rabies, yet only 24 percent of these victims could recall an appropriate history of animal exposure. Bat-related subtypes of rabies have been identified in 15 cases of human rabies since 1980, although patient contact of any sort with bats could be documented in only 7 of these patients.

A diagnosis is not always easy or straightforward. The incubation period[1] in humans may be as long as a year, if the inoculation[2] is small and occurs on the hand or foot. Thus the lack of evidence of a bite or scratch is not inconsistent with the diagnosis. Finally, although physicians knew how rabies was transmitted at the time of Poe's death, even at the time of Louis Pasteur's first use of a rabies "vaccine" in 1885 the causative agent, a rhabdovirus, was unknown.[3]

I was saddened to hear of the fate of Caterina, Poe's cat, yet nowhere have I suggested that Poe contracted rabies from her, although it is worth noting that there was no available vaccine for pets at that time.

R. Michael Benitez, M.D.
Baltimore, Maryland
September 26, 1996

The writer is an assistant professor of medicine at the University of Maryland Medical Center.

3. **even at the time of Louis Pasteur's ... was unknown:** Louis Pasteur (1822–1895) was a French chemist who helped develop the important medical theory linking germs and disease. Pasteur developed a rabies vaccine using tissue from infected animals. Benitez is pointing out, however, that at the time of Poe's death, scientists had not isolated and identified the virus that causes rabies.

Vocabulary
transmitted (trans·mit′id) *v.*: passed on.

1. **incubation period:** amount of time between a person's exposure to a disease and the appearance of symptoms.
2. **inoculation** (i·näk′yə·lā′shən) *n.:* here, skin puncture from an animal bite or scratch through which a disease is passed on.

CONTENT-AREA CONNECTIONS

Science: Louis Pasteur
Known as the father of microbiology, Pasteur (1822–1895) pioneered the study of bacteria as agents of disease. Pasteur also developed pasteurization, a technique for preserving foods that involves heating them to specific temperatures to kill microorganisms. He proved that many diseases are caused by bacteria that infect the body, and also developed the first vaccines for anthrax and rabies. In 1888, a center for the study of bacteria, viruses, immunity, and allergies, called the Pasteur Institute, was founded in France in his honor. **Individual activity.** Encourage interested students to research and report on Pasteur's life and his many accomplishments.

Analyzing Informational Text

Reading Check

1. Make a time line of Poe's last days, based on the information in the biography "Poe's Final Days."

2. Summarize the **evidence** cited to support Dr. Benitez's theory in the article ("Poe's Death Is Rewritten as Case of Rabies, Not Telltale Alcohol").

3. According to Burton R. Pollin and Robert E. Benedetto, what is the major weakness of Dr. Benitez's theory?

SKILLS FOCUS

Reading Skills
Synthesize information from several sources on a single topic.

Test Practice

1. What is the **main idea** of the letter by Pollin and Benedetto?

   A   Poe has been unjustly accused of being an alcoholic.

   B   There is a great deal of evidence that Poe's death was due to alcoholism.

   C   Poe's cat could not have bitten him and given him rabies.

   D   Poe was a great writer, but he had human faults.

2. What is the *strongest* **evidence** Dr. Benitez presents in his letter to defend his theory?

   F   Rabies has a long incubation period, and many victims do not remember being attacked by an animal.

   G   There was no available vaccine for pets at the time of Poe's death.

   H   During Poe's lifetime, doctors knew how rabies was passed on.

   J   Louis Pasteur first used a rabies vaccine in 1885.

3. What information in the biography could support Dr. Benitez's theory that rabies caused Poe's death?

   A   It had been raining, and Poe may have suffered from exposure.

   B   Dr. Moran stated that Poe sweated and addressed "imaginary objects on the walls."

   C   Poe was so ill that he was taken to the hospital.

   D   No one knows where Poe was the week before he appeared at the tavern.

4. Which of the following statements that **contrast** the biography with Pollin and Benedetto's letter is *not* true?

   F   The biography states that Dr. Moran eventually claimed Poe didn't die from drinking too much, but the letter states that Dr. Moran provided evidence for this theory.

   G   Pollin and Benedetto refer to Poe's letters as evidence, but the biography does not.

   H   The biography does not discuss the rabies death theory, but the letter does.

   J   The letter does not refer to Joseph Walker's description of Poe, but the biography does.

   (continued)

Reading Check

1. Possible answer: Sept. 27—Poe boards steamer from Richmond to Baltimore. Sept. 28 through Oct. 2—lost days. Oct. 3—Poe found, seemingly drunk, outside a Baltimore tavern; taken to hospital semi-conscious. Oct. 4—Poe develops tremors, sweating, and delirium. Oct. 5—Poe grows calmer but recalls little of past week, then becomes delirious again. Oct. 6—Delirium continues. Oct. 7—At 3:00 A.M., Poe grows quiet and suddenly dies.

2. Possible answer: Poe had all the symptoms of encephalitic rabies—heavy sweating, wild hallucinations with quiet interludes, trouble drinking liquids, and sudden death. Poe had no bite mark, but one-fourth of rabies victims do not, since

Analyzing Informational Text

symptoms may be delayed for a year after a bite. Dr. Henry Wilde, a rabies expert, agrees. Jeff Jerome, curator of the Poe Museum, concurs that Poe was "almost surely" not drunk, since he avoided alcohol as an older man.

3. Pollin and Benedetto say that the major weakness of Dr. Benitez's theory is that Poe had no bite mark.

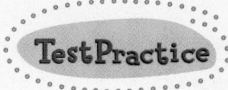

Test Practice

Answers and Model Rationales

1. **B**   The letter focuses on support for the alcoholism theory (B). A contradicts the main idea. C is a supporting detail. D paraphrases the final sentence but not the main idea.

2. **F**   Dr. Benitez provides copious data to support this statement (F). G and J support his idea that Poe might have encountered a rabid animal, but the evidence for them is weaker than that for F. H is untrue.

3. **B**   B directly supports Dr. Benitez's theory, since he lists heavy sweating and delirium as classic rabies symptoms. A supports the encephalitis theory. C could support any of the theories. D is too vague to support any theory directly.

4. **J**   This item requires comparison and identification of supporting evidence. F, G, and H are all true. J is untrue, since both the letter and the biography refer to Joseph Walker's description of Poe.

   (continued)

5. C This item requires comparison. A, B, and C are all similarities, but C is the most important, since it concerns one of Dr. Benitez's main points. D is implied in both pieces but is stated in neither.

6. G The best synthesis will focus on the issue at hand and take into account the main ideas of all sources. F fails to focus on the issue of Poe's death. H excludes the main ideas of two sources—the article and Dr. Benitez's letter. J is speculation, not synthesis.

Test-Taking Tips

For more information on how to answer multiple-choice questions, refer students to **Test Smarts**.

Vocabulary Development

Practice

Possible Answers

- *–spec–: conspicuous,* "obvious; noticeable"; *despicable; spectral,* "ghostly"; *spectator*
- *–spir–: expired,* "died"; *inspire*
- *–pon–: imposing,* "large and impressive-looking"; *deposit*
- *–mit–: transmitted,* "passed on"; *submit*
- *–mal–: maligned,* "falsely accused of bad conduct"; *malpractice*
- *–chron–: chronic,* "frequently occurring"; *chronological*
- *–stup–: stupor,* "dull, half-conscious state"; *stupid*
- *–bel–: belligerent,* "angry and aggressive"; *antebellum*
- *–sent–: insensible,* "not fully conscious or aware"; *sensitive*
- *–scrib–: ascribe,* "assign or attribute as a cause"; *describe*

---

5. Which statement is the *most* important **similarity** between the article and Dr. Benitez's letter?

A Both inform the reader that Dr. Benitez is an assistant professor of medicine.

B Both use statistics as support.

C Both point out that the lack of a bite or scratch does not weaken the rabies death theory.

D Both state that only highly skilled doctors can diagnose rabies.

6. Which of the following statements is the *best* **synthesis** of the information in these four sources?

F Poe was a tortured genius.

G Poe's symptoms could point to several different causes of death.

H All theories should take into account that Poe died drunk.

J Poe's illness would have been correctly diagnosed by modern doctors.

Constructed Response

Imagine that you are writing a biography of Poe. Write the last few paragraphs of your book, in which you tell about Poe's death. In your discussion, **synthesize** the information from the four sources by **paraphrasing** the ideas and **comparing and contrasting** the points. End your account by drawing your own **conclusions** from the information.

▶ **Use "Analyzing Nonfiction," pages 194–201, for help with this assignment.**

Vocabulary Development

Understanding Word Derivations: Useful Roots

PRACTICE

A **root** is the part of a word that establishes its core meaning. Knowing what some common roots mean will help you figure out the definitions of new words. Match each root in the chart below with a word from the Word Bank. (Note that two words share a root.) Then, define the word, and write another word with the same root.

SKILLS FOCUS

Vocabulary Skills
Understand Greek and Latin word roots.

Word Roots	
Latin Roots	**–spec–,** "look"
–bel–, "war"	**–spir–,** "breathe"
–mal–, "ill"	**–stup–,** "be stunned or amazed"
–mit–, "send"	
–pon–, "place"	
–scrib–, "write"	**Greek Root**
–sent–, "feel"	**–chron–,** "time"

Word Bank

insensible
imposing
stupor
spectral
expired
maligned
belligerent
conspicuous
ascribe
chronic
transmitted

ASSESSING

Assessment

- *Holt Assessment: Literature, Reading, and Vocabulary*

RETEACHING

For another selection to teach synthesizing sources, see *The Holt Reader,* Part 2.

READ ON: FOR INDEPENDENT READING

FICTION
Crisis in a Small Town

Harper Lee's *To Kill a Mockingbird* is a riveting story of race relations as viewed by a wise, plucky child. Eight-year-old Scout and her brother, Jem, learn an unforgettable lesson about courage, justice, and compassion when their father takes part in a shocking trial that will change their hometown forever. You're not likely to forget this Pulitzer Prize–winning novel.

FICTION
California Dreams

When Panchito lived in Mexico, the most excitement he ever had was hunting for chicken eggs and going to church on Sundays. Then Panchito's father moves the family to California, where jobs for migrant workers abound and the promise of an American education awaits. In Francisco Jiménez's *The Circuit,* Panchito describes his family's odyssey from one labor camp to another as they pursue the American dream.

FICTION
The Monster's Revenge

Mary Shelley's classic novel, *Frankenstein,* has two narrators: Dr. Frankenstein, an obsessed scientist who creates a monster in the image of a man (and later comes to fear his creation); and the monster himself, a huge, misshapen creature who fights the men who have hurt him. Who is the real monster in this story? The answer just might surprise you.

This title is available in the HRW Library.

NONFICTION
On the Outside Looking In

Adeline Yen Mah, a young girl living in Shanghai, was a family outcast. Her father had trouble remembering her name, and her stepmother treated her no better than a servant. However, her memoir, *Chinese Cinderella,* is not about hardship alone: It also describes her friends, her aunt and grandfather, and the teachers who encouraged her talent as a writer that would one day lead Adeline into a whole new world.

Read On

For Independent Reading

If students enjoyed the themes and topics explored in this collection, you might recommend these titles for independent reading.

Assessment Options

The following projects can help you evaluate and assess your students' outside reading. Videotapes, disks, or audiotapes of completed projects may be included in students' portfolios.

- **Create an electronic slide presentation.** If computers and software are available, encourage students to design presentations combining images, text, and sound effects related to one of the novels. A presentation should include an overview of the novel's literary elements. Students might add music, animation, buttons, and hyperlinks.

- **Design a lantern.** Students might make Chinese paper lanterns in the shape of hexagonal cylinders, decorated with meaningful quotes and images related to the memoir *Chinese Cinderella.* Have students hang their lanterns in the classroom.

- **Where in the world?** Invite students to create a triptych—an artwork made up of three panels—illustrating the background and setting of any of the Read On selections. One panel might focus on geographic area, one on historical era, and one on social milieu. Each panel should include a brief explanatory caption.

DIFFERENTIATING INSTRUCTION

Estimated Word Counts and Reading Levels of Read On Books:

Fiction			Nonfiction		
To Kill a Mockingbird	↔	122,800	*Chinese Cinderella*	↓	67,600
The Circuit	↔	23,400			
Frankenstein	↑	87,000			

KEY: ↑ *above grade level*   ↔ *at grade level*   ↓ *below grade level*

Skills Starter

Motivate. Bring to class a cartoon that features a recognizable politician or celebrity. Show the cartoon to the students, and then ask the following questions: 1) Who is the person featured in the cartoon? 2) What characteristics of the person has the cartoonist chosen to emphasize? 3) What is the cartoonist's message? 4) What is the cartoonist's attitude toward the person characterized in the cartoon?

Explain to students that when they analyze a biography, they must remember to analyze *the work of the biographer* and not *the subject of the biography*. Remembering their analysis of the cartoonist's presentation of the subject may keep them on task.

DIRECT TEACHING

Integrating with Grammar, Usage, and Mechanics

As students start their biography analyses, they may have trouble with subject-verb agreement and pronoun-antecedent agreement. You may want to review the Agreement section in the Language Handbook.

Choose a Biography

Please be aware that Internet resources are sometimes public forums, and their content can be unpredictable.

Analyzing Nonfiction

Writing Assignment
Write an analytical essay in which you examine how the parts of a biography fit together to support the writer's thesis.

Earlier in this collection, you read a newspaper article, an excerpt from a book, and several letters, all about the writer Edgar Allan Poe. As you can see in these nonfiction resources, few things interest people more than other peoples' lives. We listen to friends' life stories, scan magazine articles about the lives of celebrities, and read **biographies**—nonfiction narratives that tell the life stories of famous and not-so-famous people. In this workshop you will **analyze a biography** about a person whose life you find interesting.

Prewriting

Choose a Biography

Get a Life Whose life journey would you like to follow? Think about the variety of history makers, past and present, that you could learn more about—a queen or a conquistador, a political activist or an artist. If you're interested in a particular historical period, scan a book about that period for colorful personalities. You might also explore magazines, newspapers, and the Internet to find people who are currently noteworthy or have made an impact in recent decades. Then, check to see whether there are biographies in print about them.

Analyze Character, Events, and Setting

A Closer Look Biographers combine details about character, events, and setting—the **elements of biography**—to give readers a greater understanding of their subjects. When you analyze a biography, you look at how the writer uses these elements to express his or her unique perspective, or point of view, about the person. Create a two-column **analysis log,** like the one on page 195, in which you record the details you find as you read the biography. In your log, you may **quote** the writer's *exact* words (record the page number of the quotation). You may also **paraphrase** *all* of the writer's ideas in your own words, or **summarize** only the writer's *most important* ideas in your own words.

The details you find about the character of the biography's subject, the events in his or her life, and the setting in which that person lived will point you to what the writer is saying about him or her.

SKILLS FOCUS

Writing Skills
Write an expository essay analyzing a biography.

● **Character** A biographer should give you a clear idea of the person's **character**—what he or she is or was like as a person. In your log,

COLLECTION 3 RESOURCES: WRITING

Planning
- *One-Stop Planner* CD-ROM with ExamView Test Generator

Differentiating Instruction
- *Workshop Resources: Writing, Listening, and Speaking*
- *Family Involvement Activities in English and Spanish*

- *Supporting Instruction in Spanish*

Writing and Language
- *Workshop Resources: Writing, Listening, and Speaking*
- *Daily Language Activities*
- *Language Handbook Worksheets*

take notes about what the person did, thought, felt, and said and about what others said about him or her.

● **Events** The **events** in a biography are the real-life incidents that affected the person. In your analysis log, list four to six of the most important events in the person's life. For example, look for births and deaths of people important to him or her, marriages and divorces, and successes or failures.

● **Setting** The events in the person's life take place in the context of a specific time and place—the **setting** of the biography. Write down in your log any details that relate to the living conditions of the average person of that time and place, the conditions in which the subject of the biography lived, and the historical events of the time.

TIP You may find it difficult to analyze the entire biography in great detail. Instead, you may wish to focus your analysis on one stage of the person's life: early, middle, or end.

Tying It Together After recording notes on the elements of biography—character, events, and setting—look for places in the biography where the writer **draws conclusions** about the elements' importance to the person's life. Write these conclusions in the right-hand column of your log, next to the details you've gathered. Sometimes a writer doesn't state conclusions directly. In those cases you must **infer,** or make an educated guess about, the significance of the elements. The following is part of an analysis log a student created while analyzing a biography about Edgar Allan Poe.

 DO THIS

Elements of Biography	Biographer's Conclusions
Character	
• Although Poe's foster father (John Allan) used his influence to get Poe into West Point, Poe was court-martialed because of his bad behavior.	• Poe wanted "to use his own harm to punish John Allan" (page 65).
Events	
• His mother died while he was very young.	• Poe never recovered from the early death of his mother; then, the deaths of Stanard and Allan reopened these wounds.
• He became attached to Jane Stanard, a friend's mother, who soon died.	
• His chronically ill foster mother, Fanny Allan, died.	
Setting	
• The economy of the times forced John Allan to relocate his business and family several times.	• Poe didn't have a stable home life.
• Poe lived in the early 1800s, a time when the profession of writer was relatively new in the U.S.	• Poe had to take unimaginative jobs that didn't pay well.

DIFFERENTIATING INSTRUCTION

Special Education Students
You may wish to allow students to work in self-selected pairs on their prewriting activities. If two students select the same biography, they can discuss the biography and any analyses of it they may find. Although each student will analyze a different aspect of the biography, discussing its meaning can lead to a deeper understanding of the biography.

Assessment
■ *Holt Assessment: Writing, Listening, and Speaking*
■ *One-Stop Planner* CD-ROM with ExamView Test Generator
■ *Holt Online Assessment*
■ *Holt Online Essay Scoring*

Internet
■ *go.hrw.com* (Keyword: LE5 9-3)
■ *Elements of Literature Online*

DIRECT TEACHING

The Big Idea
You may suggest that students specifically indicate that the opinion presented in their thesis is the biographer's. Additionally, advise students that they may want to include the title and author of their biography in their thesis statements, as shown in the student example. If they choose not to, they should make sure this information appears elsewhere in their introductions.

RETEACHING

Get It Together
To help students who may have trouble preparing to write, hold individual conferences with them after they have answered the following questions.

• What is your thesis statement?

• What main points support the thesis?

• What evidence supports each main point?

• How will you organize your paper?

PRACTICE & APPLY 1

Guided and Independent Practice
Suggest these preparatory steps as students begin their prewriting.

1. Read the foreword to find insight into the biographer's relation to the subject.

2. While reading, jot down on an index card any details or topics (and page number) from the biography that might later support a thesis.

3. When you finish reading, review and organize your notes. See if any topics suggest themselves as a thesis.

Write and Support a Thesis Statement

The Big Idea Once you've analyzed the biography, try to determine how the conclusions fit together to form a main idea about the person. Ask yourself, "What is the biographer's point of view on this person?" Then, write a **thesis statement,** one or two sentences in which you identify the biographer's main idea about the subject of the biography. Here's the thesis statement from the analysis of the Poe biography.

> In <u>Edgar A. Poe: Mournful and Never-ending Remembrance</u>, biographer Kenneth Silverman portrays Poe as a victim of circumstances.

Backing It Up Support for your thesis statement will come in the form of **evidence** and **elaboration.**

● **Evidence:** Gather evidence to back up your thesis by looking over your analysis log. For each of the elements of biography, select the details—the quotations, summaries, and paraphrases—that best support your thesis. Make sure the information you choose relates directly to the thesis. For each quotation, provide **parenthetical citations**—the page number (within parentheses) to indicate where you found that detail.

● **Elaboration:** Make the connections for your readers. Help them understand your analysis by explaining how the evidence supports your thesis statement. You can elaborate on individual pieces of evidence or on groups of evidence.

Organize Your Analysis

Get It Together Next, organize your analysis in a logical order. One good logical order is **order of importance,** in which you present your ideas from most important to least important, or vice versa. Decide which element includes the strongest evidence for supporting your thesis statement, and plan to discuss that element either first or last in your analysis. Discuss the strongest element first if you think it's something that will really grab your audience's attention and create a strong first impression. Discuss this element last if it's something that you'd most like your audience to remember and think about after reading your essay.

Reference Note
For more on using **parenthetical citations,** see page 619.

SKILLS FOCUS

Writing Skills
Write and support a thesis statement.

PRACTICE & APPLY 1

Using the information on pages 194–196, choose and analyze a biography. Gather details for each of the elements of biography; then, write a thesis statement. Support your thesis statement with evidence and elaboration. Finally, organize your analysis.

196 Collection 3 Narrator and Voice • Synthesizing Sources

Writing

Analyzing Nonfiction

A Writer's Framework

Introduction	Body	Conclusion
• Provide background information about the biography's subject. • Introduce the biography's title and author. • State your thesis.	• Support your thesis statement with information about the elements of biography—character, events, and setting. • Support your discussion of each element with relevant evidence. • Elaborate on the evidence.	• Summarize your ideas about the elements of biography. • Restate your thesis in different words.

A Writer's Model

The Tragic Life of Edgar Allan Poe

Edgar Allan Poe, the author of such grim and frightful tales as "The Cask of Amontillado," was a great American writer and a desperately unhappy man. In <u>Edgar A. Poe: Mournful and Never-ending Remembrance</u>, biographer Kenneth Silverman portrays Poe as a victim of circumstances. This sympathetic biography shows a man struggling unsuccessfully for love and acceptance.

Silverman suggests that Poe was a victim of the tragic events of his early life. Illness, death, abandonment, and separation seemed to plague him. Poe was not quite three years old when his mother, Eliza, died after being ill for several months, "perhaps with some infectious fever" (8). Being abandoned earlier by his father and now orphaned and separated from his brother and sister deprived Poe of a family and an inheritance. Poe was taken in, though never adopted, by John Allan, a harsh, self-made man. Allan's wife, Fanny, was "often ill and sometime absent" (20). Poe's new family was not an ideal family for emotional support. As a teenager, Poe became attached to Jane Stanard, the mother of a school friend. She soon died at the age of thirty-one. Approximately five years later, Fanny Allan passed away. According to Silverman, Poe never accepted or recovered from his mother's death; then, the deaths of Stanard and Allan reopened these old wounds. These deaths left Poe emotionally scarred.

INTRODUCTION
Background information

Thesis statement

BODY
Element 1: Events
Evidence
Parenthetical citation
Elaboration
Evidence

Elaboration
Evidence

Biographer's conclusion
Elaboration

(continued)

Writing Workshop: Analyzing Nonfiction   197

A Writer's Model

The following is biographical information for the book analyzed in **A Writer's Model:**

Silverman, Kenneth. *Edgar A. Poe: Mournful and Never-ending Remembrance.* New York: Harper Collins, 1991.

MODELING AND DEMONSTRATION

A Writer's Model

Model for students the correct punctuation for parenthetical documentation by reviewing **A Writer's Model** with them and pointing out the placement of the end quotation marks, the parentheses, and the end punctuation. Then, write these two examples on the chalkboard and have students copy them down and punctuate them correctly.

1. Gerald insisted that his involvement "had nothing to do with politics."—found on source page 341

2. After several years of dedicated drifting, she "made her meandering way home."—found on source page 16

Have volunteers demonstrate understanding by marking the correct punctuation on the chalkboard.

DIRECT TEACHING

A Writer's Model

Point out to students that after every cycle of presenting key points and evidence, the writer provides the *biographer's* conclusion. The writer's conclusion is not drawn until the end of the essay, and it is a conclusion about the biography—not about the biography's subject.

DIFFERENTIATING INSTRUCTION

Learners Having Difficulty

Students might benefit from talk-writing their drafts. Pair each student with a partner who will ask questions and record responses, either in writing or on audiotape. Have students question each other about major supporting points and about evidence and elaboration.

PRACTICE & APPLY 2

Guided and Independent Practice

Before students complete **Practice and Apply 2** for independent practice, guide them through **A Writer's Framework,** using a sample topic. After students have completed their first drafts, have them compare their work to the framework. Suggest that they notate their drafts in the margins to show how each paragraph of their draft corresponds to a step of the framework. You can use students' marginal notations to help you monitor their progress.

Element 2: Character

Evidence

Biographer's conclusion

Elaboration

Biographer's conclusion

Element 3: Setting

Evidence

Elaboration
Evidence

Elaboration

CONCLUSION
Summary of elements of biography

Restatement of thesis

Poe's self-destructive character was a reaction to the events of his early years. For example, Poe asked for and received John Allan's help in gaining admission to the U.S. Military Academy. At first he did well at West Point, but after about a year, Poe stopped going to classes and was court-martialed. Silverman believes that Poe's decline began when he received the "dramatic and upsetting" news that John Allan had remarried. Silverman explains that "John Allan's marriage meant that others would now receive the attention and comforts he had looked to have himself" (63). Instead of being happy for John Allan when he remarried, Poe felt that the affection that he wanted and the inheritance that he needed from Allan would instead go to Allan's new wife and possible heirs. Silverman believes that Poe decided to quit West Point in order "to use his own harm to punish John Allan" (65).

In addition, the setting in which Poe lived also tended to make his circumstances miserable. The economy of the times forced John Allan to relocate his business and family several times. When Edgar was six and a half, the family relocated to England for five years. Much of this time Edgar spent in various boarding schools, which left him "away from his caretakers, under new and unfamiliar custodians, in a strange country, angered and frightened"(18). In early 1819, Allan's business began to fail, so the family returned to the United States, where "unsettled and financially troubled, the Allans made several moves in Richmond as Edgar grew into his teens" (23). The upheavals only worsened the stress in Poe's life. Later, as Poe began his literary career, he found it hard to make a living. In the early 1800s, the profession of writer was new. Poe had to take jobs writing unimaginative features for magazines—a task he truly hated.

Silverman shows that Poe's selfish and self-destructive behaviors are understandable. Born in a time when he could not earn a decent living by writing, shuttled around from place to place, scarred by the loss of his mother, and unloved by his foster father, Poe lived a tragic life. Edgar A. Poe: Mournful and Never-ending Remembrance makes Poe the hero—and victim—of a life as full of misery as one of the writer's own tales.

INTERNET
More Writer's Models
Keyword: LE5 9-3

PRACTICE & APPLY 2

Refer to the framework and the Writer's Model on pages 197–198 as you write your analysis. Be sure to elaborate on all the evidence you present.

Revising

Evaluate and Revise Content, Organization, and Style

Read It Again To make sure your writing is the best it can be, read through your paper at least twice. The first time, use the guidelines below to evaluate the content and organization of your analysis. Then, in your second reading, use the guidelines on the next page to evaluate the style of your analysis.

First Reading: Content and Organization To make sure your analysis is clear and easy to follow, use the content and organization guidelines below. Begin by asking the questions in the left-hand column. To help you answer those questions, follow the tips in the middle column. If your essay needs revision, use the revision techniques detailed in the right-hand column.

> **PEER REVIEW**
>
> Exchange your essay with a peer before you revise. A peer might be able to find places where you need additional evidence and elaboration to support your thesis.

Rubric: Analyzing Nonfiction

Evaluation Questions	▶ Tips	▶ Revision Techniques
❶ Does the introduction contain the title and author of the biography and a clear thesis statement?	**Underline** the title and author of the biography. **Double underline** the thesis statement.	If needed, **add** a thesis statement or **add** the biography's author and title to the introduction.
❷ Does the essay include information about all the elements of biography—character, events, and setting? Does the evidence support the discussion of each element?	**Bracket** each element. **Put a check mark** by each piece of evidence—quotation, paraphrase, and summary.	**Add** information about each element. **Replace** or **delete** any evidence that does not support the discussion of the element.
❸ Is evidence clearly explained through elaboration?	**Draw an arrow** from each piece of evidence—quote, paraphrase, and summary—to its elaboration.	**Elaborate** by explaining what the evidence means or why it is important.
❹ Is the organizational pattern of the analysis easy to follow?	**Look back** at the elements, which you have already bracketed. If they are not organized in a logical order, revise.	**Rearrange** body paragraphs into a logical order, such as order of importance.
❺ Does the conclusion summarize the elements of biography and restate the thesis?	**Underline** the summary of the elements of biography. **Double underline** the restatement of the thesis.	If needed, **add** sentences that summarize the elements and that restate the thesis of the analysis.

Rubric: Analyzing Nonfiction

Advise students to use **Rubric: Analyzing Nonfiction** on this page as a think sheet by having students answer the questions in their notebooks. Explain to students that using think sheets to summarize their notes allows students to place their thoughts, observations, and questions on paper—which in turn helps improve the content and organization of their essays.

DIFFERENTIATING INSTRUCTION

Learners Having Difficulty

Students may have difficulty recognizing when they should modify their thesis statement instead of replacing or omitting evidence. Have them complete the following steps to see if it is their thesis or their key points that need revision.

1. On an index card, write the thesis.
2. On additional index cards, write each key point.
3. Place all the cards on a desk with the thesis card at the top and the key points under it.
4. If any of the key points seem not to fit under the thesis, check to see if the thesis can be reasonably revised to cover the key point.

DIRECT TEACHING

Elaboration

To elaborate further in their essays, students might use analogies to make their essays more interesting to readers. They might draw comparisons between specific events in the life of the subject and similar yet commonly experienced events to which readers can relate.

English-Language Learners

Draw two parallel lines on the chalkboard. Ask students why the two sides of a railroad track must run parallel to each other. They will say that the rails run parallel to keep the train on track. Explain that writers should use parallel structure to keep their readers on track. Have the students practice achieving simple parallel structure by revising these lists to make the elements within each list parallel.

List 1
invent
believe
arrangement [arrange]

List 2
the round, orange basketball
the cold, sweet lemonade
the big diamond [, bright]

GUIDED PRACTICE

Responding to the Revision Process

Answers

1. makes all words nouns, thus parallel

2. to provide a quotation to elaborate on a key point

3. the page number of the quotation; it is important to include so that the reader can check the source for accuracy

PRACTICE & APPLY 3

Independent Practice

Use the rubric on pp. 199 and 200 to assess students' revisions. You may want to create a simple checklist based on this rubric to save time during assessment.

▷ **Second Reading: Style** In your second reading, pay attention to your style and its impact on your message. One way to improve your style is to write balanced, parallel sentences. **Parallel sentences** use the same grammatical forms or parts of speech to express related ideas. Create parallelism by balancing a noun with a noun, a phrase with a phrase, a clause with a clause, and so on. Use the following guidelines to revise unbalanced sentences.

Style Guidelines

Evaluation Question	▷ Tip	▷ Revision Technique
● Are the ideas in the analysis expressed in balanced, parallel sentences?	▷ **Circle** the words *or* and *and* in all the sentences. Check to see that all items in the series joined by these words have the same grammatical form or part of speech.	▷ **Reword** sentences for parallelism. Pair nouns with nouns, phrases with phrases, clauses with clauses, and so on.

ANALYZING THE REVISION PROCESS

Study these revisions, and answer the questions that follow.

replace
Silverman suggests that Poe was a victim of the tragic events
abandonment,
of his early life. Illness, death, ~~abandoning,~~ and separation

seemed to plague him. Poe was not quite three years old when

add
his mother, Eliza, died *after being ill for several months,*
"perhaps with some infectious fever" (8).

Responding to the Revision Process

1. How did replacing *abandoning* with *abandonment* improve the second sentence?

2. Why did the writer add information to sentence three?

3. What does the information in parentheses tell the reader? Why is that information important?

SKILLS FOCUS

Writing Skills
Revise for content and style.

PRACTICE & APPLY 3 Using the rubric on page 199, revise the content and organization of your analysis. Then, use the guidelines above to revise your style. Use the example paragraph above as a model for your own revisions.

Publishing

Proofread and Publish Your Analysis

Get It Right If you want readers to take your analysis seriously, you must make sure it is free of mistakes in grammar, spelling, and punctuation. If you have time, set your analysis aside for a day or two. Having time to refresh your mind and eyes often will allow you to catch more errors. Then, carefully proofread your analysis.

Get the Word Out You've worked hard to make your analysis the best that it can be. Why be satisfied having it read by only your teacher, a couple of peer editors, or your parents? Look for a larger audience that may have an interest in reading about the person of the biography you analyzed. Try one of these ideas to share your analysis.

- Ask permission to post your analysis on a Web site dedicated to the person studied in your analysis. You may even wish to create your own site about him or her.

- Offer your analysis to local book clubs. Often an employee or a bulletin board at your local library or bookstore can direct you to a book club that would be interested in your analysis.

- Along with your classmates, gather analyses of people who have something in common, such as a group of authors or a group of current history makers. Then, create a classroom collection or display featuring information from these analyses.

Reflect on Your Analysis

Think Twice Write answers to the following questions to reflect on what you have learned in this workshop.

- What was the most interesting element of the biography you analyzed—the character of the person, the events in his or her life, or the setting? How was this element significant?

- How might you apply the analysis skills you learned in this workshop the next time you read other nonfiction works or even a novel or short story?

- Has analyzing this biography allowed you to look at the person in a different way? If so, what have you learned from his or her life story?

PRACTICE & APPLY 4 Proofread your analysis to ensure that it follows English-language conventions. Publish your analysis by using one of the ideas suggested above. Lastly, reflect on your analysis and what you have learned.

> **TIP** Proofreading will help ensure that your analysis follows the **conventions** of standard American English. For example, your analysis might be confusing if your sentences include verbs that do not agree in number with their subjects. For more on **subject-verb agreement,** see Agreement of Subject and Verb, 2a–m, in the Language Handbook.

SKILLS FOCUS

Writing Skills
Proofread, especially for correct subject-verb agreement.

Suggest that students use the grammar-checking capabilities of their word-processing program to check subject-verb agreement as well as pronoun-antecedent agreement. Caution that the grammar check will not locate every error all the time, but it is still a useful tool.

DIRECT TEACHING

Get the Word Out

Please be aware that Internet resources are sometimes public forums, and their content can be unpredictable.

PRACTICE & APPLY 4

Guided and Independent Practice

- Monitor students' understanding by asking students to write a short list of grammar, usage, and mechanics errors they commonly find when proofreading their papers. Have them list strategies for correcting these errors. Briefly check students' lists.

- Take a quick poll to make sure each student has an idea for publishing his or her analysis.

- Have students complete **Practice and Apply 4** for independent practice.

Literary Skills

SKILLS FOCUS, pp. 202–203

Grade-Level Skills

■ **Literary Skills**
Analyze the way tone, voice, persona, and choice of narrator affect characterization and plot.

INTRODUCING THE SKILLS REVIEW

Use this review to assess students' grasp of the way voice and the choice of narrator affect a story. If necessary, use the annotations to guide students in their reading before they answer the questions.

DIRECT TEACHING

Ⓐ Literary Focus

❓ Point of view. In this paragraph, what details does the first-person narrator share about herself? [Her name is Yolanda; she is an immigrant to New York; she goes to a Catholic school and is in fourth grade at the time of the story.]

Ⓑ Literary Focus

❓ Point of view. We see the Cuban missile crisis through Yolanda's eyes. How would you describe her tone—her attitude toward the events she describes? [Possible response: She is serious, sincere, and naive.]

Ⓒ Literary Focus

❓ Point of view. Which of Yolanda's observations reveal why she likes Sister Zoe? [Possible responses: Sister Zoe reassures her and does not scold her for making a scene; the remark about snowflakes shows that Sister Zoe values diversity and individuality.]

Collection 3: Skills Review
Literary Skills

Narrator and Voice

Test Practice

DIRECTIONS: Read the following selection. Then, read and respond to the questions that follow.

Snow

Julia Alvarez

Ⓐ Our first year in New York we rented a small apartment with a Catholic school nearby, taught by the Sisters of Charity, hefty women in long black gowns and bonnets that made them look peculiar, like dolls in mourning. I liked them a lot, especially my grandmotherly fourth-grade teacher, Sister Zoe. I had a lovely name, she said, and she had me teach the whole class how to pronounce it. *Yo-lan-da.* As the only immigrant in my class, I was put in a special seat in the first row by the window, apart from the other children, so that Sister Zoe could tutor me without disturbing them. Slowly, she enunciated the new words I was to repeat: *laundro-mat, cornflakes, subway, snow.*

Ⓑ Soon I picked up enough English to understand holocaust[1] was in the air. Sister Zoe explained to a wide-eyed classroom what was happening in Cuba. Russian missiles were being assembled, trained supposedly on New York City. President Kennedy, looking worried too, was on the television at home, explaining we might have to go to war against the Communists. At school, we had air-raid drills: An ominous bell would go off and we'd file into the hall, fall to the floor, cover our heads with our coats, and imagine our hair falling out, the bones in our

arms going soft. At home, Mami and my sisters and I said a rosary[2] for world peace. I heard new vocabulary: *nuclear bomb, radioactive fallout, bomb shelter.* Sister Zoe explained how it would happen. She drew a picture of a mushroom on the blackboard and dotted a flurry of chalk marks for the dusty fallout that would kill us all.

The months grew cold, November, December. It was dark when I got up in the morning, frosty when I followed my breath to school. One morning, as I sat at my desk daydreaming out the window, I saw dots in the air like the ones Sister Zoe had drawn—random at first, then lots and lots. I shrieked, "Bomb! Bomb!" Sister Zoe jerked around, her full black skirt ballooning as she hurried to my side. A few girls began to cry.

Ⓒ But then Sister Zoe's shocked look faded. "Why, Yolanda dear, that's snow!" She laughed. "Snow."

"Snow," I repeated. I looked out the window warily. All my life I had heard about the white crystals that fell out of American skies in the winter. From my desk I watched the fine powder dust the sidewalk and parked cars below. Each flake was different, Sister Zoe had said, like a person, irreplaceable and beautiful.

Pages 202–203 cover
Literary Skills
Analyze narrator (or point of view) and voice.

---

1. **holocaust** (hä′lə·käst′) *n.:* great or total destruction of life.

2. **rosary** (rō′zər·ē) *n.:* in the Roman Catholic religion, series of prayers counted off on a special set of beads.

READING MINI-LESSON

Reviewing Word-Attack Skills
Activity. Display these pairs of related words. Have students tell if the underlined parts of the words are pronounced in the same way [S] or differently [D].

1. line	delineate	[D]
2. punish	impunity	[D]
3. minus	minuscule	[D]
4. suffer	insufferable	[S]
5. number	numerous	[D]
6. fable	fabulous	[D]
7. perfect	imperfections	[D]
8. extra	extraordinary	[D]

Activity. Display these sound symbols and words. Have students identify the word in which the given sound is heard.

1. /ō/ beautiful beau [√]

Collection 3: Skills Review

Test-Taking Tips

For more information on answering multiple-choice items, refer students to **Test Smarts**.

1. Why does Yolanda yell, "Bomb! Bomb!" when she sees snow?
   A The winter landscape is bare, as if a bomb had destroyed everything.
   B The snowflakes look like her teacher's pictures of the fallout from a bomb.
   C New in school, she wants to gain her classmates' attention.
   D She wants to show that she has understood her teacher's lessons.

2. How does the use of a **first-person narrator** affect the telling of the story?
   F The reader sees events through the eyes of several characters.
   G The description of events is unbiased.
   H The reader is presented with Yolanda's personal view of events.
   J Yolanda lies in the story.

3. Why is it important that the story is told from the **point of view** of a recent immigrant to the United States?
   A Yolanda is unfamiliar with some aspects of life in the United States.
   B Living in the United States makes Yolanda frightened and insecure.
   C Yolanda's classmates don't explain things to her.
   D Yolanda's teacher treats her unfairly.

4. What is the *best* description of the narrator's **voice** in this passage: "I saw dots in the air like the ones Sister Zoe had drawn—random at first, then lots and lots"?
   F Sophisticated
   G Childlike
   H Hopeful
   J Playful

5. What is the **tone** of the story?
   A Sarcastic and superior
   B Angry and suspicious
   C Homesick and sad
   D Innocent and sincere

6. What impression does the narrator create of Sister Zoe?
   F Sister Zoe has knowingly exaggerated the danger in order to scare the children.
   G Sister Zoe is a nervous, easily frightened person.
   H Sister Zoe mocks Yolanda and doesn't think she's intelligent.
   J A caring teacher, Sister Zoe helps her students learn.

Constructed Response

7. Suppose that Sister Zoe were the narrator of the story instead of Yolanda. What would she be able to tell you that Yolanda couldn't? How would the story be different? Support your opinions using specific examples from the story.

Answers and Model Rationales

1. **B** She is alarmed, not seeking attention (C) or approval (D). She is gazing not at the landscape (A) but into the air, where snowflakes resemble what her teacher drew (B).

2. **H** F would be the effect of a third-person-omniscient narrator; G is one possible effect of a third-person narrator. J is untrue. H is the effect of a first-person narrator's perspective.

3. **A** Yolanda's unfamiliarity with snow (A) is key to the plot. D is inaccurate. B and C are not necessarily suggested by the story.

4. **G** "[D]ots in the air" and "lots and lots" sound childlike (G), not sophisticated (F). She sees the dots as fallout—not a hopeful (H) or playful (J) reaction.

5. **D** The narrator's tone includes no sarcasm (A), anger (B), or homesickness (C). She views events with innocence and sincerity (D).

6. **J** Sister Zoe seems direct, not deceitful (F); kind, not mocking (H); and confident, not nervous (G). Her treatment of Yolanda reveals a love of children (J).

Constructed Response

7. If Sister Zoe were the narrator of the story, readers would learn more about her feelings toward Yolanda and her other students. Perhaps she would convey her own fears about nuclear war. The story might suffer if Sister Zoe were the narrator because the climax would not be as dramatic. Whereas Yolanda is scared by what she thinks is nuclear fallout, Sister Zoe quickly realizes that the powder in the air is merely snow.

2.	/ā/	école [√]	echo
3.	/k/	plague	plaque [√]
4.	/z/	flambeaux [√]	flummox
5.	/ō/	cockatoo	portmanteau [√]
6.	/ā/	fiancé [√]	finance
7.	/k/	baguette	bouquet [√]
8.	/ā/	résumé [√]	resume

ASSESSING

Assessment

- *Holt Assessment: Literature, Reading, and Vocabulary*

Synonyms

Modeling. Model the thought process of a good reader getting the answer to item 1 by saying, "The word *retorted* means 'replied sharply.' I can eliminate A and C because *bragged* and *pretended* are very different in meaning from *retorted*. I can also eliminate D, because *retorted* does not imply loudness."

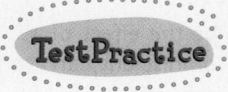
TestPractice

Answers and Model Rationales

1. **B** See rationale above.

2. **F** *Succor* means the same as "help" (A). *Food* (G), *advice* (H), and *sympathy* (J) are more specific kinds of help.

3. **B** *Disconsolate* means "very sad," which is different from the meanings of A, C, and D but is similar to the meaning of B.

4. **J** *Incessantly* means "without stopping." It does not imply nastiness (F), injustice (G), or volume (H).

5. **B** *Recoiling* means "moving backward as if in fear," not necessarily staring (A) or pausing (D). *Laughing* (C) is unrelated.

6. **J** *Retribution* means "punishment." *Forgiveness* (H) is an antonym. *Imprisonment* (F) is too specific. *Payment* (G) could mean punishment or reward.

7. **D** *Endeavored* means "tried." *Began* (B) and *hoped* (C) do not mean "tried," and *failed* (A) is its antonym.

8. **G** Poe wrote, traveled, and drank, but *expired* means "died." A clue is that the theories concern Poe's death.

9. **D** If students recall that Dr. Benitez noticed clues to Poe's identity, it may help them recall that *conspicuous* means "obvious."

Synonyms

Test Practice

DIRECTIONS: Choose the *best* synonym for the underlined word in each sentence.

1. When Ulrich threatened him, Georg retorted that his men would kill Ulrich first.
   A bragged
   B replied
   C pretended
   D shouted

2. Ulrich says that his men will offer succor to Georg first.
   F help
   G food
   H advice
   J sympathy

3. Mathilde is disconsolate when she loses her friend's necklace.
   A ashamed
   B unhappy
   C angry
   D frightened

4. Mathilde talks incessantly about her desire for wealth.
   F nastily
   G unjustly
   H loudly
   J constantly

5. Recoiling at first upon seeing the trowel, Fortunato then follows Montresor into the catacombs.
   A staring
   B retreating

   C laughing
   D pausing

6. Montresor believes that Fortunato deserves retribution for insulting him.
   F imprisonment
   G payment
   H forgiveness
   J punishment

7. Struggling to break the chains, Fortunato endeavored to free himself.
   A failed
   B began
   C hoped
   D tried

8. There are several different theories that explain why Poe expired.
   F wrote
   G died
   H traveled
   J drank

9. The medical report on an unnamed patient contained conspicuous clues identifying the patient as Poe.
   A many
   B few
   C minor
   D obvious

SKILLS FOCUS

Vocabulary Skills
Understand synonyms.

Vocabulary Review

Use the following activity to assess students' retention of the collection Vocabulary. Have students select the correct word to complete the following sentences.

precluded	privations	chronic
precipitous	maligned	

1. Mathilde constantly bemoaned her fate; she was a _____ complainer. [chronic]

2. Her husband's lack of wealth _____ an expensive lifestyle. [precluded]

3. He always spoke kindly of Mathilde, although she often _____ him. [maligned]

4. The couple's descent into poverty was _____. [precipitous]

5. Their harsh new life included hunger and other _____. [privations]

Collection 3: Skills Review
Writing Skills

Collection 3: Skills Review
Writing Skills

Test Practice

DIRECTIONS: The following paragraph is from a draft of a student's analysis of a biography. Read the questions below it, and choose the best answer to each question.

(1) Harold C. Livesay wrote the biography *Andrew Carnegie and the Rise of Big Business.* (2) Even though Carnegie came to the United States as a poor Scottish immigrant, he did not let his circumstances keep him down. (3) While working as a bobbin boy at the age of fourteen, "Andrew decided to learn double-entry bookkeeping and enrolled in a night school course across the river in Pittsburgh" (16). (4) He lived with his mother, father, and younger brother, Tom. (5) Carnegie never settled into a position when he thought he could climb higher. (6) His will, determining, and strength led him to become one of the most successful people in the United States.

1. Which of the following could follow sentence 1 to convey the biographer's distinctive perspective?
   - **A** Livesay is a biographer who writes primarily about the U.S. economy.
   - **B** This biography shows Carnegie's determined character.
   - **C** Livesay believes that Carnegie was a ruthless businessperson.
   - **D** Carnegie was the greatest entrepreneur of his time.

2. Which sentence, if added, would explain the details in sentence 3?
   - **F** Carnegie's father couldn't adapt to the market changes.
   - **G** Carnegie wasn't very sociable because he spent all his time working.
   - **H** The Carnegie family survived due to the support of friends.
   - **J** Young Carnegie became a model of self-improvement and determination.

3. To support the idea that Carnegie was strongly driven, the writer could
   - **A** quote Carnegie stating that he had "determined to make a fortune"
   - **B** describe the working conditions in the U.S. in the 1850s and 1860s
   - **C** relate details about the ten richest people in American history
   - **D** summarize an article that criticizes Carnegie's business ethics

4. Which sentence might the writer delete to improve the passage's organization?
   - **F** 2
   - **G** 3
   - **H** 4
   - **J** 6

5. To create parallelism in sentence 6, the writer should replace "will, determining, and strength" with
   - **A** will, determine, and strength
   - **B** will, determination, and strength
   - **C** will, determining, and being strong
   - **D** willingness, determine, and being strong

SKILLS FOCUS

Writing Skills
Write an analysis of a biography.

RESOURCES: WRITING

Assessment
- *One-Stop Planner* CD-ROM with ExamView Test Generator
- *Holt Assessment: Writing, Listening, & Speaking*

Internet
- *Holt Online Assessment*
- *Holt Online Essay Scoring*

Writing Skills
Answers
1. B
2. J
3. A
4. H
5. B

DIRECT TEACHING

Test Practice

Explain that Andrew Carnegie (1835–1919) was a successful industrialist and philanthropist who gave generously to public institutions across the U.S. and the U.K.

APPLICATION

Speech

For homework, have students watch a documentary about a famous person. Have students prepare to deliver a short speech discussing the documentary maker's point of view. Did the documentary maker seem to admire the subject? dislike the subject? sympathize with the subject? What specific details suggest this attitude?

For students who may not have access to a television at home, suggest that they report on a biography from a magazine.

 Homework

EXTENSION

Scrapbook

Students can complete this activity for homework. Have them select six to eight cartoons that depict famous people. They should glue the cartoons on sheets of construction paper and fasten the sheets into a book. Under each, they should identify the subject and briefly describe the cartoonist's attitude toward the subject.

Collection 4
Comparing Themes

**Informational Reading Focus:
Synthesizing Sources**

About Collection 4
In Collection 4, students will master the following skills:

- **Literary Skills:** Understand, analyze, and compare universal themes; and compare themes across genres.
- **Reading Skills:** Make predictions; make inferences about character motivation; synthesize ideas from different sources; connect literature and the news; and distinguish fact and opinion.
- **Vocabulary Skills:** Understand word origins; understand word analogies; create semantic charts; and understand multiple-meaning words.
- **Writing Skills:** Develop, write, and revise a comparison-contrast essay.

Informational Text
Each collection of *Elements of Literature* provides a variety of informational texts related to the literature selections by theme or topic.

Minimum Course of Study
Most skills can be taught with a minimum number of selections and features. In the chart to the right, lessons highlighted in green constitute the minimum course of study that provides coverage of the skills taught in Collection 4.

Resource Manager
(pp. 206C–206D)
Lesson and workshop resources are referenced in the Resource Manager on the pages that follow. These resources can be used to reinforce the skills taught in Collection 4, remediate students who are having difficulty, and provide supporting activities for English-language learners.

206A

Scope and Sequence

Selection ▪ Feature	Literary Skills
Elements of Literature: Theme *by* John Leggett	• Understand theme and universal themes • Compare a theme across genres
Elements of Literature: Comparing Universal Themes	• Understand and compare universal themes
The Sniper *by* Liam O'Flaherty ↔ *at grade level*	• Analyze theme and conflict • Compare universal themes
Cranes *by* Hwang Sunwŏn ↔ *at grade level*	• Analyze theme and character • Compare universal themes
Informational Text: • A Country Divided • Lives in the Crossfire • Internment • Peace Isn't Impossible *by* Patricia McMahon; Laurel Holliday; Margaret McCrory; George J. Mitchell ↔ *at grade level*	
Elements of Literature: Comparing a Theme Across Genres	• Understand how genre relates to theme • Compare and contrast a theme across genres
Liberty *by* Julia Alvarez ↔ *at grade level*	• Analyze how a story's title relates to its theme
Exile *by* Julia Alvarez ↔ *at grade level*	• Analyze the characteristics of narrative poetry, including theme • Analyze metaphors and similes
An American Story *by* Anthony Lewis ↔ *at grade level*	• Analyze characteristics of news features, including the main idea
Writing Workshop: *Comparing Media Coverage*	
Skills Review: *Literary Skills* *Vocabulary Skills* *Writing Skills*	• Compare the presentation of a theme across genres • Compare universal themes

Reading Skills	Vocabulary Skills	Writing ▪ Grammar and Language ▪ Listening and Speaking Skills
• Compare and contrast themes		• Write a comparison-contrast essay
• Make predictions • Make inferences about character motivation • Synthesize ideas from different sources dealing with a single topic	• Demonstrate word knowledge • Understand word origins • Understand word analogies • Create semantic charts	• Write a summary • Write a descriptive paragraph • Identify participles and participial phrases • Write a speech • Write about a character's motivations
• Compare and contrast a theme across genres		• Write a comparison-contrast essay
• Connect literature and the news • Distinguish between fact and opinion	• Use a thesaurus to find synonyms • Identify denotations and connotations • Identify word origins of English words from foreign languages	• Write a reflective essay • Compare reports from different news media • Use a thesaurus to find synonyms • Use clear pronoun references • Write a poem, letter, or journal entry from a character's point of view • Retell a news feature in another genre • Support an opinion • Use commas correctly in a series; in dates; and with cities, states, and countries
		• Write an essay comparing and contrasting the ways in which different news media cover the same event
	• Understand multiple-meaning words	• Write a comparison-contrast essay

Resource Manager

Selection ▪ Feature	Planning	Differentiating Instruction ▪ Lesson Plans with ELL Strategies and Practice	Reading ▪ Vocabulary
Elements of Literature: Theme *by* John Leggett	• PowerNotes: Theme		
Elements of Literature: Comparing Universal Themes **The Sniper** *by* Liam O'Flaherty **Cranes** *by* Hwang Sunwŏn **Informational Text:** • A Country Divided • Lives in the Crossfire • Internment • Peace Isn't Impossible *by* Patricia McMahon; Laurel Holliday; Margaret McCrory; George J. Mitchell	• One-Stop Planner with ExamView Test Generator	• The Holt Reader, pp. 110–114 • Holt Adapted Reader • Holt Reading Solutions, pp. 111–128 • Supporting Instruction in Spanish, pp. 14–16 • Audio CD Library, disc 8 • Audio CD Library, Selections and Summaries in Spanish • Family Involvement Activities in English and Spanish, p. 6	• The Holt Reader • Holt Adapted Reader • Holt Reading Solutions • Vocabulary Development, pp. 18, 19, 20
Elements of Literature: Comparing a Theme Across Genres **Liberty** *by* Julia Alvarez **Exile** *by* Julia Alvarez **An American Story** *by* Anthony Lewis	• One-Stop Planner with ExamView Test Generator	• Holt Reading Solutions, pp. 129–143 • Supporting Instruction in Spanish, pp. 17–18 • Audio CD Library, disc 9 • Audio CD Library, Selections and Summaries in Spanish	• Holt Reading Solutions • Vocabulary Development, p. 21 • PowerNotes: Summarizing a Story
Writing Workshop: *Comparing Media Coverage*	• One-Stop Planner with ExamView Test Generator	• Workshop Resources: Writing, Listening, and Speaking, pp. 33–40 • Family Involvement Activities in English and Spanish, pp. 17–18 • Supporting Instruction in Spanish, p. 70	
Skills Review: *Literary Skills* *Vocabulary Skills* *Writing Skills*			

The Holt Reader

The Holt Reader is a consumable paperback book which can be used alone or to accompany *Elements of Literature*. It offers guided support throughout the reading process and encourages students to become active readers by circling, underlining, questioning, and jotting down responses as they read. *The Holt Reader* works well for homework, students who have missed class, additional instructional time, reteaching, and remediation.

Holt Reading Solutions (HRS)

Holt Reading Solutions pulls together reading resources in the *Elements of Literature* program to create a powerful tool for intervention and whole-class instruction. *HRS* includes diagnostic assessment tools, lesson plans for English-language learners and special education students, adaptations of selected reading selections, vocabulary and comprehension worksheets, information on phonics and decoding, and additional instruction and practice in remedial reading skills.

206C

Writing ▪ Grammar and Language ▪ Listening and Speaking	Assessment
• Daily Language Activities • Language Handbook Worksheets, pp. 57, 68	• Holt Assessment: Literature, Reading, and Vocabulary • Holt Online Assessment • One-Stop Planner with ExamView Test Generator
• Daily Language Activities • Language Handbook Worksheets, pp. 48, 132, 133, 134, 136, 137, 139	• Holt Assessment: Literature, Reading, and Vocabulary • Holt Online Assessment • One-Stop Planner with ExamView Test Generator
• Daily Language Activities • Workshop Resources: Writing, Listening, and Speaking, pp. 33–40	• Holt Assessment: Writing, Listening, and Speaking • Holt Online Assessment • One-Stop Planner with ExamView Test Generator
	• Holt Assessment: Writing, Listening, and Speaking • One-Stop Planner with ExamView Test Generator

One-Stop Planner with ExamView Test Generator

The *One-Stop Planner* CD-ROM contains electronic versions of print-based teaching resources, clips from the video program, and valuable assessment tools. The *One-Stop Planner* resources are presented in easy-to-follow, point-and-click menu formats. To preview resources or print out worksheets and tests, you simply make a selection and click.

One-Stop Planner CD-ROM

Collection 4

Grade-Level Skills

■ **Literary Skills**
Compare and contrast similar themes across genres.

■ **Literary Skills**
Compare works that express a universal theme, and provide evidence to support that theme.

■ **Reading Skills**
Synthesize the content from several sources or works by a single author on a single issue.

INTRODUCING THE COLLECTION

Selections in this collection are grouped in three sections to help students master the skills of comparing universal themes, synthesizing information from several sources, and comparing the development of a theme in works of different genres. The first two stories encourage students to reflect on a universal theme in world literature—the tragic conflicts and personal costs people face during a time of war, especially civil war.

In the four informational selections that follow the stories, students are asked to synthesize information about the causes and effects of the ongoing conflict in Northern Ireland.

In the third section of the collection, students read a short story, a poem, and a news feature, which all focus on the effects of being exiled from one's home country and beginning a new life in a new land. Students are asked to compare how a similar theme is developed in these three different genres.

Finally, the collection closes with opportunities for students to write a comparison-contrast essay about how two different news media cover a single news event.

COLLECTION 4 RESOURCES: READING

Planning
■ *One-Stop Planner* CD-ROM with ExamView Test Generator

Differentiating Instruction
■ *Holt Reading Solutions*
■ *The Holt Reader*
■ *Holt Adapted Reader*

■ *Family Involvement Activities in English and Spanish*
■ *Supporting Instruction in Spanish*

Vocabulary
■ *Vocabulary Development*

Grammar and Language
■ *Language Handbook Worksheets*
■ *Daily Language Activities*

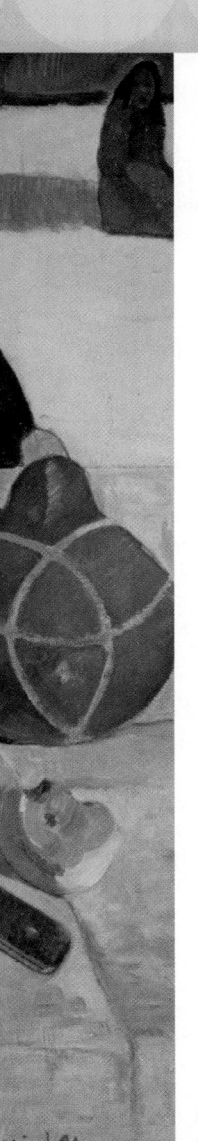

Collection 4

COMPARING THEMES

INFORMATIONAL READING FOCUS

SYNTHESIZING SOURCES

Human life is fiction's only theme.

—Eudora Welty

INTERNET
Collection
Resources
Keyword: LE5 9-4

The Meal or *The Bananas* (1891) by Paul Gauguin.
Oil on canvas.

Musée d'Orsay, Paris.
© Erich Lessing/Art Resource, New York.

THE QUOTATION

Ask students whether they agree with Eudora Welty's statement. [Possible responses: No, because themes are also found in nonhuman life such as animals. Yes, because within human life are found all the themes that matter.]

VIEWING THE ART

Paul Gauguin (1848–1903) was born in Paris but grew up in Lima, Peru, before moving back to France. After working on a ship from 1865 to 1871, Gauguin settled down; he became a stockbroker and started painting. Adopting an impressionist style, he later developed an innovative painting style characterized by nonnaturalistic form, heightened color, and symbolic subject matter. In 1891, Gauguin traveled to Tahiti to escape a society in France that he felt was too conventional and restrictive. Gauguin's best-known paintings were inspired by his time in the South Pacific.

Activity. Ask students to identify symbols of human life in Gauguin's painting. [Possible response: The people are young and sitting before food that will sustain life.]

Assessment
■ *Holt Assessment: Literature, Reading, and Vocabulary*
■ *One-Stop Planner* CD-ROM with ExamView Test Generator
■ *Holt Online Assessment*

Internet
■ go.hrw.com (Keyword: LE5 9-4)

■ *Elements of Literature Online*

Media
■ *Audio CD Library*
■ *Audio CD Library, Selections and Summaries in Spanish*
■ *Fine Art Transparencies*
■ *PowerNotes*

- **Literary Skills**
Compare and contrast works that express a universal theme, and provide evidence to support that theme.

Review Skills

- **Literary Skills**
Analyze recurring themes across traditional and contemporary works.

Elements of Literature: Theme

Write the following sentence on the chalkboard: *True love will conquer all obstacles and triumph in the end.* Ask students to name some popular songs that convey this message or central idea about life. List the titles under the sentence. Then, ask students to name movies they have seen or books they have read that also convey this idea about life. Explain that the message, or central idea about life, that a work of art conveys is called its **theme.**

Add that many kinds of art from many different times and places express ideas about love because love is an important experience that is common to all people everywhere. Then, ask students to suggest songs or movies that convey other ideas about love and to express each idea, or theme, in a sentence. [Possible responses: The course of true love is never easy. Love always involves sacrifice. Losing someone you love is extremely difficult.]

Elements of Literature

Theme *by* John Leggett
AN IDEA ABOUT LIFE

A story can excel in any number of ways—in the strength of its plot, in the reality of its characters, in the gracefulness of its language. But what often makes us remember a story long after we've read it is the idea on which it's built—its theme.

Revealing a Truth About Human Behavior

The **theme** of a story is the central idea, or insight, about life that it reveals. This insight is a truth about human behavior that the writer has usually discovered from experience—for example, that sometimes it is a mistake to marry for love alone or that as one grows old, death becomes less terrifying. To communicate this idea, the writer tells a story.

The theme is usually not stated directly in a story. Instead, the characters act out the theme for us. If the story works, we feel the characters' experiences so strongly that the truth revealed to them is revealed to us as well.

When the theme of a story seems fresh and true, we say, "Yes, I see what the writer means, but I hadn't quite thought of it that way before." Then we have penetrated the surface of human behavior and have seen what the writer wants us to recognize about our lives.

Although a theme is usually invisible and unstated, it can be the story's most forceful element. Themes are also important to other forms of literature, and a similar theme can be found across **genres**—in stories, novels, plays, poems, even in nonfiction. A powerful theme can

be the reason that a work of literature gets to our hearts and lingers in our minds.

Universal Themes

Because a theme is a **generalization** about life or human nature and because certain experiences are common to all people everywhere, authors often express similar themes. These **universal themes** deal with such basic human concerns as good and evil, life and death, love and loss. These great themes, the ones that recur in every culture and in every period of history, shine a light on our common experiences and can help guide us through our lives.

How to Find a Story's Theme

It's not always easy to step back from a literary work and express its central idea in a sentence. Figuring out the theme, however, will help you understand a work more fully. Here are some guidelines to help you search for and state the theme of a work:

1 The theme of a work is not the same as its subject. The **subject** is simply the topic, which can be stated in a single word, such as *love*. The theme makes some revelation about the subject—for example: "Love may be more likely to bloom when we least expect it." Remember that a theme must always be an idea that can be expressed in at least one sentence.

INTERNET
More About
Theme
Keyword: LE5 9-4

SKILLS FOCUS

Pages 208–230 and 244–268 cover
Literary Skills Understand theme and universal themes. Compare a theme across genres.

208 Collection 4 Comparing Themes • Synthesizing Sources

Learners Having Difficulty

Theme. To help students understand that the resolution of a conflict can be a clue to a story's theme, have them meet in small groups to discuss classic cartoons in which a strong, aggressive character tries to catch a smaller, weaker opponent. Ask how this type of conflict is usually resolved in the cartoons. Then, have students identify the universal

theme about the strong and the weak that such cartoons convey. [Possible response: A small, physically weak character can often triumph over a strong, aggressive character by using cleverness and ingenuity.]

English-Language Learners

For more instruction on theme for English-language learners and special education students, see *Holt Reading Solutions*.

Advanced Learners

Acceleration. Help students analyze the way in which the theme of a selection reflects a view or comment on life. Explain that some universal themes in literature comment on the relative importance of values that are often in conflict in life. For example, a character may face a conflict that forces him or her to answer the question

2 Think about whether the main **character** changes in the course of a work or realizes something he or she hadn't known before. Often a writer expresses the theme through what a character learns.

3 Think about how the **conflict** is resolved. Conflict is central to literature, and how the conflict is resolved often provides a clue to the theme.

4 When you have finished reading a work, think about the **title.** Does it have a special meaning? Does it point to the theme? (Not all titles do.)

5 Test your statement of the theme—does it apply to the whole work, not just to parts of it?

6 Keep in mind that there is no single way to state the theme of a work. You and your classmates may express the same theme in different words, or you may even have different opinions about what the main theme is. The literary works that are richest in meaning often have more than one theme.

Thinking Critically About Theme

The wise reader makes a judgment about a writer's view of the world and doesn't accept a story's theme as valid just because it's in print. The wise reader asks, "Is this story's view of life too romantic? Is it too cynical? Is it too simple? Is it narrow-minded? Is this writer an overenthusiastic salesperson who is trying to get me to buy an idea that is false or shoddy?"

Much of popular fiction is "formula fiction," fiction written to a plan that satisfies the general preference for happy or upbeat stories over true-to-life ones. As wise readers we must learn to make our own critical judgments about the fiction we read—just as we do about the television shows we watch and the movies we see.

Practice

Think of a story you've read that had an impact on you. Then, use a map like the one here to help you figure out the story's **theme.** Compare your map with the ones your classmates made. Did you and any of your classmates map stories with similar themes?

Title:

Topic:

How the main character changes:

How the conflict is resolved:

What the title suggests:

Theme:

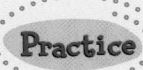

Practice

If students have difficulty choosing a story to analyze, suggest that they use a story or novel that they remember from their childhood. Fairy tales with strong, memorable themes include "Beauty and the Beast," "The Emperor's New Clothes," and "The Ugly Duckling." Contemporary children's classics with important themes include *Charlotte's Web, Where the Wild Things Are,* and *The Little Engine That Could.*

Possible answers for "Beauty and the Beast":

Title—"Beauty and the Beast"

Topics—love versus fear, appearance versus reality

How the main character changes—At first Beauty is afraid of the Beast and repelled by his appearance; but as she comes to know him, she is able to see the gentleness that lies beneath his ugly exterior and falls in love with him.

How the conflict is resolved—When Beauty expresses her love for the Beast, he turns into a handsome prince, and the two live happily ever after.

What the title suggests—It suggests the central questions and conflicts that are resolved in the story, such as "What is true beauty?" "How much can you tell about a person from his or her outward appearance?" and "What happens when two seemingly opposite qualities are brought together?"

Themes—Love enables people to see what lies beneath the surface of another person to see the person's true self. You can't always judge a person's character by his or her outward appearance. Love can transform people and bring out their inner beauty.

"What is more important in life, my individual freedom or my responsibility to my family?"
Activity. Have students meet in small groups to identify and discuss books or movies in which characters have to weigh the relative importance of conflicting values—such as freedom versus responsibility, revenge versus reconciliation, or friendship versus competition. Ask students to identify which value each character chooses and what view of life each choice represents.

Grade-Level Skills

■ **Literary Skills**
Compare and contrast works that express a universal theme, and provide evidence to support that theme.

Review Skills

■ **Literary Skills**
Analyze recurring themes across traditional and contemporary works.

Comparing Universal Themes

Overview

The next two selections that students will read are linked by both their subject matter and their themes. Although set in different time periods and places, both "The Sniper" and "Cranes" explore the terrible personal conflicts experienced by individuals caught up in tragic civil wars.

"The Sniper" is a gripping, suspenseful story set in Ireland during the civil war of the 1920s. It describes in vivid detail the thoughts, feelings, and actions of a sniper who is struggling to survive a showdown with an enemy counterpart on a nearby rooftop—an enemy with whom he shares more than he can imagine.

"Cranes" is a quieter, more reflective story set in Korea during the civil war of the 1950s. In this story a South Korean soldier must decide the fate of a North Korean prisoner who happens to be a close friend from childhood.

The chart on this page will help students, as they read the two selections, to compare and contrast the conflicts and motivations of the stories' main characters and to derive a statement of each story's theme.

Elements of Literature

Comparing Universal Themes

"The Sniper" . . . *by* Liam O'Flaherty . . . short story . . . page 212
"Cranes" . . . . *by* Hwang Sunwŏn . . . . short story . . . page 222

Universal Ties, Universal Themes

No matter what we look like or where we come from, we are all made of the same stuff—we all have hearts and minds, feelings and thoughts. We all have hopes and fears, worries and dreams. We all experience both sorrows and joys. These universal concerns and experiences are the ties that bind us.

Writers translate these shared experiences into works of art that express **universal themes.** These themes are not restricted to literature from a particular time or place but appear over and over again. Writers, however, make these themes their own by adding their unique insights and perspectives and conveying the themes in an original way.

Divided Loyalties

We are all individuals, but we also live in communities. Sometimes our ties and needs as individuals conflict with our social responsibilities. This is particularly true during civil wars, when serving one's country can conflict with loyalty to family and friends. The next two stories concern men caught up in civil war. Read on to discover the theme each author wants to express about that experience.

Remember that the **theme** of a particular literary work is too complicated to be summed up in a single word and should be stated in a sentence. A story about war, for example, might express the following theme: "In wartime it can sometimes be difficult to distinguish the innocent from the guilty."

Reading Skills

Comparing and Contrasting Themes

After you have read and discussed each story, use a chart like the one below to help you compare and contrast the themes in the two works. Fill in comments about the characters' conflicts, motives, and decisions. The guidelines on pages 208–209 will help you state the theme of each work. Then, turn to page 230.

	"The Sniper"	"Cranes"
Main character		
Character's conflict(s)		
Character's motives		
What character learns		
How conflict(s) is resolved		
Statement of theme		

SKILLS FOCUS

Pages 210–230 cover
Literary Skills
Understand and compare universal themes.

Reading Skills
Compare and contrast themes.

Before You Read

The Sniper

Make the Connection

Quickwrite 🖉

What qualities enable people to perform well when facing heart-pounding fear or stress? Think about your own experiences or those of someone you know, as well as news stories or fiction you've read. Then, jot down your thoughts about people taking action when the stakes are high.

Literary Focus

Theme and Conflict: What's at Stake?

In many stories, particularly those involving high-stakes struggles, the **theme**, or central idea, is often revealed by the way the **conflict** in the story is resolved. "The Sniper" is such a story. It focuses for a brief but heart-stopping time on a soldier fighting in Ireland's civil war. The stakes of his conflict could not be higher: He either lives or dies. As you read, decide what idea about war the writer communicates through the sniper's experiences.

Reading Skills 🏊

Making Predictions

When you read a suspenseful story like "The Sniper," you make **predictions,** or guesses, about what is going to happen: Will the main character escape the enemy? Will each new action help the main character or create new problems? How will it all end? As you read this story, keep these questions in mind. Does the writer give you any hints about the outcome?

Background

This story is set in Dublin, Ireland, in the 1920s, during a time of bitter civil war. On one side were the Republicans; they wanted all of Ireland to become a republic, totally free from British rule. On the other side were the Free Staters; they had compromised with Britain and had agreed to allow the English to continue to rule six counties in the northern province of Ulster. (For reference, see the map on page 234.)

Like all civil wars, this one tore families apart. It pitted children against parents, sister against sister, brother against brother. As the story opens, the writer immediately puts you into the war—high on a Dublin rooftop.

INTERNET

Vocabulary Practice

Keyword: LE5 9-4

Vocabulary Development

beleaguered (bē·lē′gərd) v. used as adj.: surrounded and under attack.

ascetic (ə·set′ik) adj.: severe; also, self-disciplined.

fanatic (fə·nat′ik) n.: person whose extreme devotion to a cause is excessive or unreasonable.

ruse (ro͞oz) n.: trick.

silhouetted (sil′ə·wet′id) v. used as adj.: outlined.

remorse (ri·môrs′) n.: deep guilt.

SKILLS FOCUS

Literary Skills
Understand theme and conflict.

Pages 210–230 cover Compare universal themes.

Reading Skills
Make predictions.

The Sniper   **211**

SKILLS FOCUS, pp. 211–219

Grade-Level Skills

■ **Literary Skills**
Compare and contrast works that express a universal theme, and provide evidence to support that theme.

■ **Reading Skills**
Make predictions.

Review Skills

■ **Literary Skills**
Analyze recurring themes across traditional and contemporary works.

Summary ⬌ *at grade level*

This brief, suspenseful story is set in Dublin, Ireland, during the civil war of the 1920s. In realistic detail, it portrays the horrors of war through the actions of a Republican sniper, who is caught in a life-or-death conflict. Positioned on a Dublin rooftop, the sniper engages an unseen enemy on a rooftop across the street. They exchange gunfire, and the sniper is wounded. He recovers enough strength to kill his enemy, only to discover at the end of the story that he has killed his own brother. The story's ironic surprise ending brings home its theme: The inhumanity of war can even pit brother against brother, with tragic consequences.

Selection Starter

Build background. Have students read the Background information about the Irish civil war on p. 211 and study the map on p. 234. Then, ask students to explain why the conflicts in civil wars can be especially tragic.

Preview Vocabulary

Have students complete each sentence with the correct Vocabulary word from p. 211.

1. David is self-indulgent, but his brother is quite _____. [ascetic]

2. Her face was _____ on the window shade. [silhouetted]

3. Don't try to discuss an issue with a _____ because that kind of person will not listen. [fanatic]

4. Kate felt _____ for hurting her friend's feelings. [remorse]

5. The _____ army was forced to surrender. [beleaguered]

6. Tom used a clever _____ to get his friends to do his chores. [ruse]

DIRECT TEACHING

Ⓐ Vocabulary Development

Word derivations. The noun *snipe* refers to a marsh bird that is hunted as game. Because snipe hunters would hide to keep from scaring away the birds, the verb *snipe* came to mean "to shoot from a hidden place." In 1824, the suffix *–er* was added to form the noun *sniper,* meaning "a person who shoots from a hidden place at an enemy."

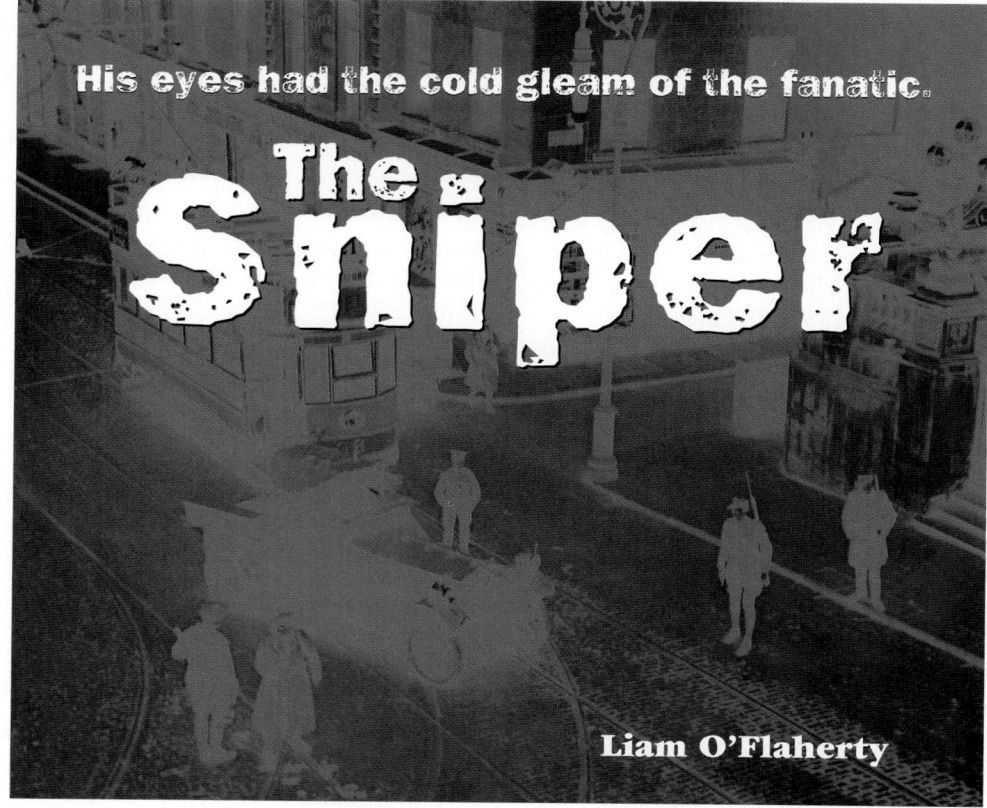

His eyes had the cold gleam of the fanatic.
The Sniper

Liam O'Flaherty

The Black and Tan—members of a British auxiliary police force—occupy a major Dublin street (November 1920).

The long June twilight faded into night. Dublin lay enveloped in darkness but for the dim light of the moon that shone through fleecy clouds, casting a pale light as of approaching dawn over the streets and the dark waters of the Liffey.[1] Around the beleaguered Four Courts[2] the heavy guns roared. Here and there through the city, machine guns and rifles broke the silence of the night, spasmodically, like dogs barking on lone farms. Republicans and Free Staters were waging civil war.

_____

1. **Liffey:** river that runs through Dublin.
2. **Four Courts:** government buildings in Dublin.

Ⓐ On a rooftop near O'Connell Bridge, a Republican sniper lay watching. Beside him lay his rifle and over his shoulders was slung a pair of field glasses. His face was the face of a student, thin and ascetic, but his eyes had the cold gleam of the fanatic. They were deep and thoughtful, the eyes of a man who is used to looking at death.

_____

Vocabulary

beleaguered (bē·lē'gərd) *v.* used as *adj.:* surrounded and under attack.

ascetic (ə·set'ik) *adj.:* severe; also, self-disciplined.

fanatic (fə·nat'ik) *n.:* person whose extreme devotion to a cause is excessive or unreasonable.

DIFFERENTIATING INSTRUCTION

Learners Having Difficulty

Invite learners having difficulty to read "The Sniper" in interactive format in *The Holt Reader* and to use the sidenotes as aids to understanding the selection. The interactive version provides additional instruction, practice, and assessment of the literature skill taught in the Student Edition. Monitor students' responses to the selection and correct any misconceptions that arise.

English-Language Learners

To help students visualize the action in this fast-moving story, you may wish to set the scene for them and introduce important terminology before they begin reading. Tell students that the sniper is hiding on a rooftop that includes a *parapet* with *breastwork,* behind which he can hide. (Refer students to the footnotes on p. 213 for definitions of these terms.) An unseen enemy is firing at him from

He was eating a sandwich hungrily. He had eaten nothing since morning. He had been too excited to eat. He finished the sandwich, and, taking a flask of whiskey from his pocket, he took a short draft. Then he returned the flask to his pocket. He paused for a moment, considering whether he should risk a smoke. It was dangerous. The flash might be seen in the darkness, and there were enemies watching. He decided to take the risk.

Placing a cigarette between his lips, he struck a match, inhaled the smoke hurriedly, and put out the light. Almost immediately, a bullet flattened itself against the parapet[3] of the roof. The sniper took another whiff and put out the cigarette. Then he swore softly and crawled away to the left.

Cautiously he raised himself and peered over the parapet. There was a flash and a bullet whizzed over his head. He dropped immediately. He had seen the flash. It came from the opposite side of the street.

He rolled over the roof to a chimney stack in the rear and slowly drew himself up behind it, until his eyes were level with the top of the parapet. There was nothing to be seen—just the dim outline of the opposite housetop against the blue sky. His enemy was under cover.

Just then an armored car came across the bridge and advanced slowly up the street. It stopped on the opposite side of the street, fifty yards ahead. The sniper could hear the dull panting of the motor. His heart beat faster. It was an enemy car. He wanted to fire, but he knew it was useless. His bullets would never pierce the steel that covered the gray monster.

Then round the corner of a side street came an old woman, her head covered by a tattered shawl. She began to talk to the man in the turret[4] of the car. She was pointing to the roof where the sniper lay. An informer.

The turret opened. A man's head and shoulders appeared, looking toward the sniper. The sniper raised his rifle and fired. The head fell heavily on the turret wall. The woman darted toward the side street. The sniper fired again. The woman whirled round and fell with a shriek into the gutter.

Suddenly from the opposite roof a shot rang out and the sniper dropped his rifle with a curse. The rifle clattered to the roof. The sniper thought the noise would wake the dead. He stooped to pick the rifle up. He couldn't lift it. His forearm was dead. "I'm hit," he muttered.

Dropping flat onto the roof, he crawled back to the parapet. With his left hand he felt the injured right forearm. The blood was oozing through the sleeve of his coat. There was no pain—just a deadened sensation, as if the arm had been cut off.

Quickly he drew his knife from his pocket, opened it on the breastwork[5] of the parapet, and ripped open the sleeve. There was a small hole where the bullet had entered. On the other side there was no hole. The bullet had lodged in the bone. It must have fractured it. He bent the arm below the wound. The arm bent back easily. He ground his teeth to overcome the pain.

Then taking out his field dressing, he ripped open the packet with his knife. He broke the neck of the iodine bottle and let the bitter fluid

There was a flash and a bullet whizzed over his head.

---

3. **parapet** (par′ə·pet′) *n.:* low wall or railing.

4. **turret** (tur′it) *n.:* low, usually revolving structure for guns on a tank or warship.

5. **breastwork** *n.:* low wall put up as a military defense.

The Sniper 213

❓ Making inferences. Why must the sniper leave by morning? [Possible response: When the bodies on the street are discovered in the morning, enemy troops will come looking for him.] **Why can't he use his rifle?** [He was shot in the right arm, and his arm is broken. He does not have the strength to hold and fire the heavy rifle.]

Ⓑ Reading Skills

❓ Making predictions. What do you think the sniper will do next to avoid being trapped on the rooftop? [Answers will vary. Some students may suspect that he will either try to sneak off the rooftop or try to trick his enemy in some way.]

Ⓒ Learners Having Difficulty

Monitoring students' progress. Ask students to explain the purpose of the sniper's actions in this paragraph. [He is trying to make his enemy think that he has been killed.]

Ⓓ Reading Skills

❓ Making predictions. What do you think the sniper will do now that his trick has succeeded? [Many students will predict that the sniper will take a shot at the enemy.]

Ⓔ Literary Focus

❓ Conflict and theme. How does the sniper's reaction to the death of his enemy change your view of him and his situation? [Possible response: At first the sniper is overjoyed to see his enemy fall, but moments later he feels remorse and revulsion for what he has done. His internal conflict makes him seem more human and shows that war has transformed him into a person that he despises.]

drip into the wound. A paroxysm[6] of pain swept through him. He placed the cotton wadding over the wound and wrapped the dressing over it. He tied the ends with his teeth.

Then he lay still against the parapet, and, closing his eyes, he made an effort of will to overcome the pain.

In the street beneath all was still. The armored car had retired speedily over the bridge, with the machine gunner's head hanging lifeless over the turret. The woman's corpse lay still in the gutter.

Ⓐ The sniper lay still for a long time nursing his wounded arm and planning escape. Morning must not find him wounded on the roof. The enemy on the opposite roof covered his escape. He must kill that enemy and he could not use his rifle. He had only a revolver to do it. Then he Ⓑ thought of a plan.

Taking off his cap, he placed it over the muzzle of his rifle. Then he pushed the rifle slowly upward over the parapet, until the cap was visible from the opposite side of the Ⓒ street. Almost immediately there was a report,[7] and a bullet pierced the center of the cap. The sniper slanted the rifle forward. The cap slipped down into the street. Then, catching the rifle in the middle, the sniper dropped his left hand over the roof and let it hang, lifelessly. After a few moments he let the rifle drop to the street. Then he sank to the roof, dragging his hand with him.

Crawling quickly to the left, he peered up at the corner of the roof. His ruse had succeeded. Ⓓ The other sniper, seeing the cap and rifle fall, thought that he had killed his man. He was now standing before a row of chimney pots, looking

---

6. **paroxysm** (par′ək·siz′əm) n.: sudden attack; fit.
7. **report** (ri·pôrt′) n.: loud noise; in this case, from a gunshot.

across, with his head clearly silhouetted against the western sky.

The Republican sniper smiled and lifted his revolver above the edge of the parapet. The distance was about fifty yards—a hard shot in the dim light, and his right arm was paining him like a thousand devils. He took a steady aim. His hand trembled with eagerness. Pressing his lips together, he took a deep breath through his nostrils and fired. He was almost deafened with the report and his arm shook with the recoil.

Then when the smoke cleared he peered across and uttered a cry of joy. His enemy had been hit. He was reeling over the parapet in his death agony. He struggled to keep his feet, but he was slowly falling forward, as if in a dream. The rifle fell from his grasp, hit the parapet, fell over, bounded off the pole of a barber's shop beneath, and then clattered on the pavement.

Then the dying man on the roof crumpled up and fell forward. The body turned over and over in space and hit the ground with a dull thud. Then it lay still.

The sniper looked at his enemy falling and he shuddered. The lust of battle died in him. He became bitten by remorse. The sweat Ⓔ stood out in beads on his forehead. Weakened by his wound and the long summer day of fasting and watching on the roof, he revolted from the sight of the shattered mass of his dead enemy. His teeth chattered, he began to gibber to himself, cursing the war, cursing himself, cursing everybody.

He looked at the smoking revolver in his hand, and with an oath he hurled it to the roof

> Morning must not find him wounded on the roof.

Vocabulary
ruse (rooz) n.: trick.
silhouetted (sil′ə·wet′id) v. used as adj.: outlined.
remorse (ri·môrs′) n.: deep guilt.

READING MINI-LESSON

Developing Word-Attack Skills
Write the Vocabulary word *ruse* on the chalkboard, and ask a volunteer to read it aloud. Point out that *ruse* ends with the letters *se* and the sound /z/. Explain that a final *se* can stand for the /z/ or the /s/ sound. Have students compare the sound of *se* in these words:

choose	noose	tease
porpoise	peruse	curse

In some words, *se* is pronounced as /z/ or /s/, depending on whether the word is a noun or a verb. The noun ends with /s/; the verb ends with /z/. Share these examples:

1. They had no <u>use</u> for the contraption. They didn't know how to <u>use</u> it.

Irish Free State soldier keeping guard over a post office (September 1922).

at his feet. The revolver went off with the concussion and the bullet whizzed past the sniper's head. He was frightened back to his senses by the shock. His nerves steadied. The cloud of fear scattered from his mind and he laughed.

Taking the whiskey flask from his pocket, he emptied it at a draft. He felt reckless under the influence of the spirit. He decided to leave the roof now and look for his company commander, to report. Everywhere around was quiet. There was not much danger in going through the streets. He picked up his revolver and put it in his pocket. Then he crawled down through the skylight to the house underneath.

When the sniper reached the laneway on the street level, he felt a sudden curiosity as to the identity of the enemy sniper whom he had killed. He decided that he was a good shot, whoever he was. He wondered did he know him. Perhaps he had been in his own company before the split in the army. He decided to risk going over to have a look at him. He peered around the corner into O'Connell Street. In the upper part of the street there was heavy firing, but around here all was quiet.

The sniper darted across the street. A machine gun tore up the ground around him with a hail of bullets, but he escaped. He threw himself face downward beside the corpse. The machine gun stopped.

Then the sniper turned over the dead body and looked into his brother's face. ∎

The Sniper   215

DIRECT TEACHING

F English-Language Learners
Interpreting words with multiple meanings. This passage includes three words with multiple meanings that may confuse students: *draft* (amount drunk in one swallow), *spirit* (type of alcoholic beverage), and *company* (a group of soldiers who fight together).

G Reading Skills
❷ Making predictions. Do you think the sniper may have killed someone he knows? Why or why not? [Possible response: It is very likely, since many of the soldiers fought together in the same army before the civil war. The passage seems to foreshadow a terrible surprise for the sniper.]

H Literary Focus
❷ Conflict and theme. How does this final revelation contribute to the message or theme that the author wants to convey about war? [Possible response: It dramatically conveys the horror and inhumanity of war, especially civil war; because of his fanatical devotion to a cause, the sniper has unknowingly killed someone he loves—his brother.]

---

2. The gym teacher would not <u>excuse</u> him.
   The student had no <u>excuse</u> for missing gym.
Activity. Write these sentences on the chalkboard. Have students read the sentences and tell if the final *se* in the underlined word is pronounced /s/ or /z/.
1. As a puppy, the dog had suffered <u>abuse</u>. [/s/]
2. Its owner used any <u>excuse</u> to beat it. [/s/]

3. The owner <u>chose</u> to call it discipline. [/z/]
4. In truth, he liked to <u>abuse</u> the dog. [/z/]
5. Soon the owner had no <u>use</u> for the dog. [/s/]
6. He turned the dog <u>loose</u> to fend for itself. [/s/]
7. No one can <u>excuse</u> such behavior. [/z/]
8. Dogs respond to <u>praise</u>, not cruelty. [/z/]

Monitoring students' progress. Guide the class in answering these comprehension questions. Direct students to locate passages in the text that support their responses.

Short Answer

1. **Where does the action take place?** [It takes place on the rooftops of houses in a street in Dublin, Ireland.]

2. **What happens to the old woman who informs on the sniper?** [The sniper kills her.]

3. **How is the sniper injured?** [The enemy across the street shoots him in the arm.]

4. **How does the sniper manage to kill the enemy?** [He plays a trick to make the enemy believe he is dead.]

Meet the Writer

Background. Trained for the priesthood, Liam O'Flaherty rejected this vocation for a succession of different trades and professions. After being wounded in the Irish civil war, he gave up the soldier's life and sailed to Brazil. Over the next few years, he worked in places such as Gibraltar, New York, and Smyrna (now Izmir) as a deckhand, porter, lumberjack, dishwasher, and bank clerk. His writing illustrates the struggle to keep alive one's spiritual values in the real world, a struggle he knew well.

Meet the Writer

Liam O'Flaherty

Soldier and Writer

Liam O'Flaherty (1896–1984) was born into a large, impoverished family on one of Ireland's rocky Aran Islands. The family faced great hardships—several of O'Flaherty's siblings died when they were quite young, and money and food were scarce. The O'Flaherty home was rich, instead, with stories. The Aran Islands have a long tradition of oral storytelling, and neighbors regularly gathered at his family's home to share tales and songs. In praise of his mother, O'Flaherty wrote:

“Even when there was no food in the house, she would gather us about her at the empty hearth and weave fantastic stories. . . .”

As a storyteller in his own right, O'Flaherty turned to the Aran Islands for inspiration, writing frequently about Irish peasant life. In his fiction he also captured the struggles of the Irish Civil War. *The Informer* (1925), his best-known novel, is a tale of betrayal set during the Irish "Troubles."

O'Flaherty himself lived during the war, and like the title character of "The Sniper," he fought on the Republican side. He participated in the Four Courts Rebellion, in which Republicans occupied Dublin's central courts of justice. The rebellion ended in failure: The courts were blown up, and the Republicans were forced to surrender. The writer responsible for the gripping, realistic detail in "The Sniper" had experienced the roar of gunfire firsthand.

DIFFERENTIATING INSTRUCTION

Advanced Learners
Acceleration. Use this activity to help students relate literary works and authors to the major themes and issues of their eras.

Activity. Have students read W. B. Yeats's poem "Easter, 1916." Then, ask them to compare the two authors' ideas about the violence of the Irish civil war as depicted in the poem and the story.

Response and Analysis

Reading Check

1. Why does the sniper kill the old woman? What happens to him after he fires his weapon?

2. What does the sniper do to trick his enemy?

3. What discovery does the sniper make at the end of the story? Did you **predict** this outcome?

Thinking Critically

4. Explain the **irony** in the story's last sentence.

5. What facts are we told directly about the sniper? What can you infer about his **character**? Think, in particular, about his ability to perform in the face of fear and stress. (Refer to your Quickwrite notes for help answering.) ✏

6. How do you think O'Flaherty wants the reader to view the sniper—is he a coldblooded killer, a soldier doing his duty, or a man caught in a tragic situation? How do the sniper's actions change your opinion of him at various moments in the story?

7. This story revolves around an **external conflict,** the sniper's life-or-death struggle. Explain the **internal conflict** the sniper also faces. How is his internal conflict resolved?

8. How would you state the **theme** of this story—that is, the point the writer is making about war, especially civil war, and what it can do to human beings? How do the resolutions of the story's conflicts help reveal the theme?

Extending and Evaluating

9. Do you think the story is improved by the **surprise ending,** or does the ending seem an unfair trick to make you pay attention to the story's message? Explain your answer.

WRITING

Before and After

Two important parts of this story are missing. One is the "before" narrative, telling why the two brothers ended up on opposite sides in the war. The other is the "after" narrative, describing what happens to the sniper after he discovers he has killed his brother. Write a paragraph **summarizing** what you imagine would be told in the "before" or "after" narrative.

Views from the Battlefield

Gunshots break the nighttime silence. Barbershops become battlefields. What might it be like to live in a neighborhood like the sniper's? Write a paragraph **describing** such an experience from the point of view of a teenager. For a true account of such an experience, read "Internment" on pages 238–240.

SKILLS FOCUS

Literary Skills
Analyze theme and conflict.

Reading Skills
Make predictions.

Writing Skills
Write a summary. Write a descriptive paragraph.

Response and Analysis

Thinking Critically

4. The sniper thought he killed an enemy; in fact he killed his brother.

5. We are told that he is thin and ascetic, has the cold eyes of a fanatic, and is used to looking at death. One can infer that he is experienced in battle, quick-thinking, and resourceful.

6. At first the sniper is described as a coldhearted fanatic, and his killing of the old woman supports this. After he kills the enemy, he does feel remorse and seems to hate what he has become.

7. The sniper's internal conflict is revealed in the remorse and self-hatred he feels after killing the enemy. He believes in his cause, but he hates the cruelty to which war has driven him. At first this conflict seems to be resolved when he nearly shoots himself by accident, shocking him out of self-doubt. But after seeing that he has killed his brother, the internal conflict will likely reemerge.

8. Possible answers: Fighting a war causes people to sacrifice their humanity to advance their cause. War forces people to make tragic choices between survival and compassion. That the sniper survives only by killing an old woman and an enemy who turns out to be his brother starkly reveals this theme.

Extending and Evaluating

9. Some students may find the ending poignant; others may feel manipulated by the unlikely coincidence of this plot twist. Have them tell why the story would or would not have been more effective with a different ending.

Reading Check

1. The old woman is an informer who points out the sniper's location to an enemy in an armored car. After he fires his weapon, he is wounded by a gunshot from an enemy sniper across the street.

2. He makes the enemy think that he is dead by placing his cap over his rifle, drawing gunfire, and then letting the cap and rifle drop to the street.

3. He discovers that the enemy he has killed is his own brother. Near the end of the story, students are likely to have predicted that the enemy was someone the sniper knew.

Vocabulary Development

Practice 1

Possible answers are listed below. Questions will vary.

1. Living conditions in a beleaguered town would be difficult. Because the town would be surrounded by enemy forces, the people would be unable to receive supplies, travel, or escape.

2. Students might list eating at restaurants, buying stylish clothes, or playing video games.

3. A fanatic is more unreasonable in his or her devotion to a person or a cause than a fan is.

4. Students may describe the schemes of tricksters in myths or con artists in fiction. They may also describe daring escapes based on tricking the enemy, a common feature of thrillers.

5. Students might suggest that the friend apologize and perform a kind act for the person.

Practice 2

Possible word stories:

- *Silhouette* derives from the name of Étienne de Silhouette (1709–1767), a French finance minister whose hobby was cutting out paper shadow portraits. *Current meaning*—an outline of a person or object filled in with the same color.

- *Sandwich* derives from the title of English nobleman John Montagu (1718–1792), the fourth Earl of Sandwich. The earl loved to gamble, and he asked for slices of bread and meat to be brought to him so that he could play while he ate. *Current meaning*—two slices of bread with a filling.

- *Maverick* derives from the name of Samuel A. Maverick (1803–1870), a Texas rancher who refused to brand his cattle. *Current meaning*—a staunchly independent person.

- *Chauvinism* derives from the name of Nicolas Chauvin, an excessively patriotic nineteenth-century

---

Vocabulary Development

Word Knowledge: Can You Explain It?

PRACTICE 1

One way to get to know a word is to ask and answer questions about it. Write detailed answers to the following five questions. Then, write your own questions about the Word Bank words, and ask a partner to answer them.

1. What would living conditions be like in a beleaguered town?

2. What would be the first two luxuries you would give up if you decided to lead a more ascetic lifestyle?

3. What is the difference between a fanatic and a fan?

4. Think about a ruse in a story you've read or a movie you've seen. What made it particularly clever?

5. What advice would you give a friend who felt remorse for teasing a classmate?

> **Word Bank**
> beleaguered
> ascetic
> fanatic
> ruse
> remorse

Word Stories

Many words in English have interesting stories to tell. Most words come down to us from other languages with their spellings, pronunciations, and meanings altered. Some words, however, are ripped right out of the headlines, turning people's last names into new words. One such word is *boycott*, which means "refuse to deal with someone; refuse to buy, sell, or use something in order to punish a person or a group." The word comes from the name of Captain C. C. Boycott, who managed the estate of an Irish nobleman. In 1880, when the captain refused to lower the rent for tenants living on the nobleman's land, shopkeepers wouldn't sell him supplies, and people destroyed his property. The *boycott* of Captain Boycott hit the news, and a new word was born.

PRACTICE 2

In a notebook or computer file, start keeping a collection of interesting word stories. Look up *silhouette*, from the Word Bank, and write a few sentences telling the story of its origin and explaining its current meaning. As you learn about other words, add their word stories to your notebook or file. You can start now by researching *sandwich, maverick,* and *chauvinism.*

> **Word Bank**
> silhouetted

SKILLS FOCUS

Vocabulary Skills
Demonstrate word knowledge. Understand word origins.

French soldier. *Current meaning*—excessive partiality to a group to which one belongs; a superior attitude toward the opposite sex.

Grammar Link

Participial Phrases: Yes! Dangling Participles: No!

A **participle** is a verb form that can be used as an adjective. Participles come in two varieties: **present participles** (*darkening* sky) and **past participles** (*shattered* glass). A **participial phrase** is made up of a participle and all of its modifiers and objects—for example, "*taking* off his cap" or "*weakened* by his wound."

Participles and participial phrases are economical, vivid ways of including more ideas and images in a sentence, and writers use them to avoid strings of short, choppy sentences. They are particularly good to use in action-driven writing, like that in "The Sniper." Read the following sentences aloud, and notice how much more fluid O'Flaherty's version is:

> The sniper lay still for a long time. He nursed his wounded arm. He planned his escape.

> O'FLAHERTY
> "The sniper lay still for a long time nursing his wounded arm and planning escape."

Remember that participles and participial phrases act as adjectives and must always modify a noun or pronoun. They should be placed close to the noun or pronoun they modify. A **dangling participle** or a **dangling participial phrase** is a grammatical error that occurs when there is no word in the sentence for a participle to modify. To correct the sentence, you have to add or replace words, as in the following example:

DANGLING
Then, catching the rifle in the middle, his left hand dropped over the roof. . . .
[Who is catching the rifle?]

O'FLAHERTY (CORRECT)
"Then, catching the rifle in the middle, the *sniper* dropped his left hand over the roof. . . ."

PRACTICE 1

Identify the participial phrases in the following sentences, along with the word each one modifies. If the sentence contains a dangling participle, rewrite the sentence by adding a word or words that the participle can modify.

1. Hearing an armored car approach, his heart beat faster.
2. Wounded by the bullet, the pain was intense.
3. Hiding on a rooftop, the sniper killed three people.
4. The sniper, losing his taste for battle, threw down his gun.
5. Acting as an informer, the sniper's location was revealed.

PRACTICE 2

Take a sample of your own writing, and underline any short, choppy sentences. Then, see if you can use participles to combine some sentences. Check to see that your revised sentences don't contain any dangling participles.

▶ **For more help, see Placement of Modifiers, 5f, in the Language Handbook.**

Grammar Skills
Identify participles and participial phrases.

The Sniper   219

Grammar Link

Practice 1

1. *Participial phrase*—"Hearing an armored car approach." *Logically modifies*—the sniper. *Possible rewrite*—Hearing an armored car approach, the sniper felt his heart beat faster.
2. *Participial phrase*—"Wounded by the bullet." *Logically modifies*—the sniper. *Possible rewrite*—Wounded by the bullet, the sniper felt intense pain.
3. *Participial phrase*—"Hiding on a rooftop." *Word modified*—sniper.
4. *Participial phrase*—"losing his taste for battle." *Word modified*—sniper.
5. *Participial phrase*—"Acting as an informer." *Logically modifies*—the old woman. *Possible rewrite*—Acting as an informer, the old woman revealed the sniper's location.

Practice 2
Sentences will vary.

Assessment
■ *Holt Assessment: Literature, Reading, and Vocabulary*

For a lesson reteaching universal themes, see **Reteaching,** p. 979A. For another selection to teach comparing themes, see *The Holt Reader,* Collection 4.

Grade-Level Skills

■ **Literary Skills**
Compare and contrast works that express a universal theme, and provide evidence to support that theme.

■ **Reading Skills**
Make inferences about character motivation.

Review Skills

■ **Literary Skills**
Compare and contrast the motives of literary characters, from different historical eras, confronting similar conflicts.

Summary ⟷ *at grade level*

This poignant story is set in a village on the border of North and South Korea during the Korean civil war of the 1950s. Toward the end of the war, Sŏngsam, a South Korean soldier, returns to his hometown. He discovers that his boyhood friend, Tŏkchae, has been taken prisoner for being a Communist leader for the North. Sŏngsam agrees to escort the prisoner to the authorities in a nearby town.

As the former friends walk, Tŏkchae refuses to look at his captor, but Sŏngsam is flooded with memories of experiences the two shared as boys. When he finally gets Tŏkchae to speak, he learns that Tŏkchae chose not to escape when the Communists invaded because his bedridden father depended on him. Sŏngsam also learns that Tŏkchae has married a girl they both knew and is about to become a father.

When they reach a field of cranes, a memory from the past finally inspires Sŏngsam to release his prisoner. Through the progression of Sŏngsam's memories and conversation, the reader infers that he has decided that loyalty to a friend victimized by the war is more important than strict adherence to a cause.

Before You Read

Cranes

Make the Connection

Quickwrite ✏️

Which is worse: betraying one's duty or betraying one's friend? Imagine a situation in which you were forced to make such a choice. What issues would you weigh as you tried to make a decision? Freewrite for a few minutes about this dilemma.

Literary Focus

Theme and Character: Life Lessons

Reading a story is often like following characters on a journey. Sometimes the characters travel to a new place; other times they stay where they are. Either way, they take a journey of the heart or mind.

In the course of their journey, characters may face overwhelming obstacles or heart-rending decisions, and they learn something in the process—about themselves or others or life in general. Through what their **characters** learn, writers communicate their **theme,** or central idea.

In "Cranes," the main character travels only a short distance on foot, but the journey he takes in his heart and mind is much greater. As you read the story, think about what the main character learns and remembers during his walk. What theme does the writer convey?

Reading Skills 📖

Making Inferences About Motivation

To understand characters fully, you need to determine their **motivation,** or the reasons for their behavior. Usually

INTERNET
Vocabulary Practice
Keyword: LE5 9-4

SKILLS FOCUS

Literary Skills
Understand theme and character.

Pages 210–230 cover Compare universal themes.

Reading Skills
Make inferences about character motivation.

writers don't make direct statements about motivation. Instead, you need to make **inferences,** or educated guesses, based on clues in the story. As you read "Cranes," think about why the main character makes certain decisions and why he behaves as he does. The questions at the open-book signs will help you make inferences.

Vocabulary Development

averted (ə·vʉrt′id) *v.* used as *adj.*: turned away.

obstruction (əb·struk′shən) *n.*: obstacle; barrier.

constitutes (kän′stə·to͞ots′) *v.*: makes up; forms.

mainstay (mān′stā′) *n.*: principal support.

refuge (ref′yo͞oj) *n.*: shelter; protection from danger or difficulty.

220 (Collection 4) Comparing Themes • Synthesizing Sources

Background

The conflict in this story is shaped by the civil war that took place in the early 1950s in Korea, a nation west of Japan bordering on China and Russia.

At the end of World War II, the country was divided in half, at the thirty-eighth parallel of latitude, with Soviet troops occupying the north and U.S. troops occupying the south. There had been plans to reunite the country eventually, but instead, in 1948, a Communist government was established in the north and a pro-Western government was established in the south.

In 1950, Communist troops from North Korea invaded the south. They were opposed by soldiers from South Korea, supported by United Nations (mostly U.S.) forces. Ultimately the conflict centered around the thirty-eighth parallel. During the war many villages along the thirty-eighth parallel changed hands several times between North and South Korea. "Cranes" is set in one such village.

A large number of Korean civilians and military personnel died during the war, and both North and South Korea suffered great devastation. A truce agreement was signed in 1953, the year "Cranes" was published, and the final military front line of battle became the boundary between North and South Korea. The two countries have still not achieved reunification.

NORTH AND SOUTH KOREA

Cranes **221**

Selection Starter

Build background. Have students read the Background information about the Korean civil war and study the map on p. 221. Then, have them compare and contrast the political situation in Korea in the 1950s with the situation in Ireland in the 1920s. Ask how the conflicts and choices experienced by the characters in "Cranes" might be similar to those experienced by the main character of "The Sniper."

Preview Vocabulary

To reinforce students' understanding of the Vocabulary words listed on p. 220, have them write their responses to the following questions.

1. Why might a young boy keep his face <u>averted</u> when meeting someone new? [Possible response: because he is shy.]

2. What would a train engineer do if there was an <u>obstruction</u> on the tracks? [Possible response: stop the train until the tracks were cleared.]

3. In your opinion, what <u>constitutes</u> a good story? [Possible response: an exciting plot, appealing characters, good dialogue.]

4. Who or what is a <u>mainstay</u> in your life? [Possible responses: family, friends, religion, music, membership in a club or team.]

5. Where might you seek <u>refuge</u> during a tornado? [Possible response: in a basement.]

Assign the Reading

You might want to assign the Quickwrite on p. 220 as homework before having students read the story. Encourage students to pause at the open-book signs as they read the story independently. Have them consider why the main character behaves as he does at each point in the story and what they might have done if they were in his situation.

■ *One-Stop Planner* CD-ROM with ExamView Test Generator
■ *Holt Online Assessment*

Internet
■ go.hrw.com (Keyword: LE5 9-4)
■ *Elements of Literature Online*

Media
■ *Audio CD Library*
■ *Audio CD Library, Selections and Summaries in Spanish*
■ *Fine Art Transparencies*

Make sure students understand that the words of the old man are a mini-flashback. As Sŏngsam returns to the town where he grew up and passes by a chestnut tree, he remembers how the owner of the tree used to chastise him for climbing it.

B English-Language
Learners

Interpreting idioms. Make sure students understand that the phrase *passed away* is a euphemistic idiom meaning "died."

C Literary Focus

❓ **Theme and character.** How does Sŏngsam's discovery about the prisoner force him into a situation in which he may have to make some difficult decisions? [The fact that the prisoner Tŏkchae is an old friend means that Sŏngsam will have to decide whether to acknowledge the friendship and how to treat the prisoner—for example, whether to speak to him, ignore him, or try to help him.]

D Reading Skills

❓ **Making inferences about motivation.** Why do you think Sŏngsam offers to accompany the prisoner? [Possible response: He wants to talk to his old friend or to protect him.] Why doesn't he tell the other soldiers about his relationship to the prisoner? [Possible response: If he did, the other soldiers might not trust him with the prisoner.]

Cranes

Hwang Sunwŏn
translated by Peter H. Lee

A young man stood, tied up.

The northern village at the border of the thirty-eighth parallel[1] was snugly settled under the high, bright autumn sky.

One white gourd lay against another on the dirt floor of an empty farmhouse. The occasional village elders first put out their bamboo pipes before passing by, and the children too turned aside some distance off. Their faces were ridden with fear.

The village as a whole showed few traces of destruction from the war, but it did not seem like the same village Sŏngsam[2] had known as a boy.

At the foot of a chestnut grove on the hill behind the village he stopped and climbed a chestnut tree. Somewhere far back in his mind he heard the old man with a wen[3] shout, "You bad boy, you're climbing up my chestnut tree again!"

The old man must have passed away, for among the few village elders Sŏngsam had met, the old man was not to be found. Holding the trunk of the tree, Sŏngsam gazed at the blue sky for a while. Some chestnuts fell to the ground as the dry clusters opened of their own accord.

In front of the farmhouse that had been turned into a public peace-police office, a young man stood, tied up. He seemed to be a stranger, so Sŏngsam approached him to have a close look. He was taken aback; it was none other than his boyhood playmate, Tŏkchae.[4]

Sŏngsam asked the police officer who had come with him from Ch'ŏnt'ae[5] what it was all about. The prisoner was vice-chairman of the Farmers Communist League and had just been flushed out[6] of his hideout in his own house, Sŏngsam learned.

Sŏngsam sat down on the dirt floor and lit a cigarette.

Tŏkchae was to be escorted to Ch'ŏngdan[7] by one of the peace policemen.

After a time, Sŏngsam lit a new cigarette from the first and stood up.

"I'll take the fellow with me."

Tŏkchae, his face averted, refused to look at Sŏngsam. They left the village.

---

1. **northern village ... thirty-eighth parallel:** village close to the northern border of South Korea.
2. **Sŏngsam** (sən'säm').
3. **wen** *n.:* harmless skin tumor.
4. **Tŏkchae** (tək'chə').
5. **Ch'ŏnt'ae** (chən'tə').
6. **flushed out:** forced from a hiding place.
7. **Ch'ŏngdan** (chən'dän').

Vocabulary
averted (ə·vurt'id) *v.* used as *adj.:* turned away.

DIFFERENTIATING INSTRUCTION

Learners Having Difficulty
Modeling. To help students read "Cranes," model the reading skill of making inferences about motivation. Say, "Suppose that a character in a war story sneaked up behind an enemy and then paused in shock as he saw the enemy's face. You could infer that the reason for the character's change in behavior was that the enemy turned out to be someone he knew." Encourage students as they read to ask themselves, "Why is Sŏngsam saying this now?" and "Why is Sŏngsam suddenly changing his behavior toward the prisoner?"

English-Language Learners
Be sure students understand that much of the story's action occurs in flashbacks; as Sŏngsam walks through the landscape of his old hometown, he recalls incidents from his childhood. Use photographs, if necessary, to introduce

Scenes of Daily Life by Lee Dong-Shick (1941–   ).

VIEWING THE ART

This image by **Lee Dong-Shick** (1941–   ) shows a rural scene of daily life in a style indebted to the traditions of Korean art. Korean art was influenced by Chinese artistic traditions, but diverged from them. By the eighteenth century, Korean artists began to focus on depicting the natural world and the daily life of ordinary people more than their contemporaries in China. Artists such as Dong-Shick have continued to develop this tendency.

Activity. What are some of the activities of daily life depicted here? [People are working, tending to cattle and children, and conversing.]

© Christie's Images.

Cranes 223

story words that name plants and animals in the rural Korean setting, such as *gourd, bamboo, chestnut, fodder,* and *cranes.*

Special Education Students
For lessons designed for special education students, see *Holt Reading Solutions.*

A Literary Focus

❓ **Flashback.** What event from childhood does Sŏngsam recall in this passage, and what role did Tŏkchae play in the event? [Sŏngsam recalls getting caught in the chestnut tree by its owner, falling to the ground, and getting chestnut needles in his bottom. Tŏkchae pulled the needles out and then offered his friend the chestnuts he had collected.]

B Reading Skills

Character motivation. [Possible response to question 1: He decides not to smoke because he cannot offer Tŏkchae a cigarette, and he feels it is unfair to enjoy something that his prisoner and former friend cannot enjoy. This act of kindness is motivated by his memory of the kindness and loyalty Tŏkchae showed to him when they got caught raiding the chestnut tree.]

C Reading Skills

Character motivation. [Possible response to question 2: Seeing the hill where he used to cut fodder for the cows reminds Sŏngsam of when he was forced to leave his home because of the Communist invasion. This reminds him that Tŏkchae is a Communist now and therefore his enemy.]

D Literary Focus

❓ **Theme and character.** What does Sŏngsam learn about the recent developments in Tŏkchae's life once his friend begins speaking to him? [He learns that Tŏkchae did not volunteer to be vice-chairman of the Communist League but was drafted into the position. His father is old, bedridden, and lives only for his son.] How is this information likely to complicate Sŏngsam's feelings about his prisoner? [The information is likely to arouse Sŏngsam's sympathy and make it more difficult to regard Tŏkchae as an enemy.]

Sŏngsam kept on smoking, but the tobacco had no taste. He just kept drawing in the smoke and blowing it out. Then suddenly he thought that Tŏkchae too must want a puff. He thought of the days when they used to share dried gourd leaves behind walls, hidden from the adults. But today, how could he offer a cigarette to a fellow like this?

Once, when they were small, he went with Tŏkchae to steal some chestnuts from the grandpa with the wen. It was Sŏngsam's turn to go up the tree. Suddenly there came shouts from the old man. He slipped and fell to the ground. Sŏngsam got chestnut needles all over his bottom, but he kept on running. It was only when they reached a safe place where the old man could not overtake them that he turned his bottom to Tŏkchae. Plucking out those needles hurt so much that he could not keep tears from welling up in his eyes. Tŏkchae produced a fistful of chestnuts from his pocket and thrust them into Sŏngsam's... Sŏngsam threw away the cigarette he had just lit. Then he made up his mind not to light another while he was escorting Tŏkchae.

📖 **CHARACTER MOTIVATION**

1. How is Sŏngsam's decision related to his memory of the time Tŏkchae gave him chestnuts?

They reached the hill pass, the hill where he and Tŏkchae used to cut fodder for the cows until Sŏngsam had had to move near Ch'ŏnt'ae, south of the thirty-eighth parallel, two years before the liberation.

Sŏngsam felt a sudden surge of anger in spite of himself and shouted, "So how many have you killed?" 📖

📖 **CHARACTER MOTIVATION**

2. What do you think motivates Sŏngsam to ask this question?

For the first time, Tŏkchae cast a quick glance at him and then turned away.

"How many did you kill, you?" he asked again.

Tŏkchae turned toward him once again and glared. The glare grew intense and his mouth twitched.

"So you managed to kill many, eh?" Sŏngsam felt his heart becoming clear from within, as if an obstruction had been removed. "If you were vice-chairman of the Communist League, why didn't you run? You must have been lying low with a secret mission."

Tŏkchae did not answer.

"Speak up, what was your mission?"

Tŏkchae kept walking. Tŏkchae is hiding something, Sŏngsam thought. He wanted to take a good look at him, but Tŏkchae would not turn his averted face.

Fingering the revolver at his side, Sŏngsam went on: "No excuse is necessary. You are sure to be shot anyway. Why don't you tell the truth, here and now?"

"I'm not going to make any excuses. They made me vice-chairman of the league because I was one of the poorest and I was a hardworking farmer. If that constitutes a crime worthy of death, so be it. I am still what I used to be—the only thing I'm good at is digging in the soil." After a short pause, he added, "My old man is bedridden at home. He's been ill almost half a year." Tŏkchae's father was a widower, a hardworking, poor farmer who lived only for his son. Seven years ago his back had given out and his skin had become diseased.

"You married?"

"Yes," replied Tŏkchae after a while.

"To whom?"

"Shorty."

"To Shorty?" How interesting! A woman so small and plump that she knew the earth's vastness but not the sky's altitude. Such a cold fish! He and Tŏkchae used to tease her and make her cry. And Tŏkchae had married that girl.

"How many kids?"

Vocabulary

obstruction (əb·strŭk′shən) n.: obstacle; barrier.
constitutes (kän′stə·tōōts′) v.: makes up; forms.

DIFFERENTIATING INSTRUCTION

Advanced Learners

Acceleration. Use this activity to help students analyze how the theme of a selection represents a view or comment on life, using textual evidence to support the claim.

Activity. Have students copy the following quotation from British writer E. M. Forster: "If I had to choose between betraying my country and betraying my friend, I hope I should have the guts to betray my country." Ask students to explain whether Sŏngsam, the main character of this story, would agree with this fully, agree with reservations, or disagree with the quotation. Have them cite details from the story that support their conclusion.

Spring Landscape by Yi Sang-Bom (1897–1972). Ink and watercolor on paper.

"The first is arriving this fall, she says."

Sŏngsam had difficulty swallowing a laugh about to explode in spite of himself. Although he had asked how many kids Tŏkchae had, he could not help wanting to burst into laughter at the image of her sitting down, with a large stomach, one span around. But he realized this was no time to laugh or joke over such matters.

"Anyway, it's strange you did not run away."

"I tried to escape. They said that once the South invaded, no man would be spared. So men between seventeen and forty were forcibly taken to the North. I thought of evacuating, even if I had to carry my father on my back. But father said no. How could the farmers leave the land behind when the crops were ready for harvest? He grew old on that farm depending on me as the prop and <u>mainstay</u> of the family. I wanted to be with him in his last moments so that I could close his eyes with my own hand. Besides, where can farmers like us go, who know only living on the land?"

Last June Sŏngsam had had to take <u>refuge</u>. At night he had broken the news privately to his father. But his father had said the same thing! Where can a farmer go, leaving all the chores behind? So Sŏngsam left alone. Roaming about the strange streets and villages in the South, Sŏngsam had been haunted by thoughts of his old parents and the young children, left with all the chores. Fortunately, his family was safe then, as now.

They crossed the ridge of a hill. This time Sŏngsam walked with his face averted. The autumn sun was hot on his forehead. This was an ideal day for the harvest, he thought.

>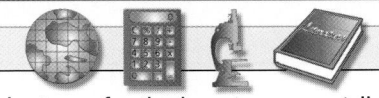
> **CHARACTER MOTIVATION**
> 3. Why do you think Sŏngsam turns his face away from Tŏkchae?

When they reached the foot of the hill, Sŏngsam hesitatingly stopped. In the middle of a field he spied a group of cranes that looked like men in white clothes bending over.

Vocabulary
mainstay (mān′stā′) *n.*: principal support.
refuge (ref′yo͞oj) *n.*: shelter; protection from danger or difficulty.

Cranes   225

DIRECT TEACHING

E **Literary Focus**
❷ **Theme and character.** How is this information about Tŏkchae and his father likely to influence Sŏngsam? [Possible response: It is likely to inspire Sŏngsam's sympathy and admiration for Tŏkchae and to make it even more difficult for Sŏngsam to regard his old friend as an enemy who must be turned over to the authorities and put to death.]

F **Reading Skills**
Character motivation. [Possible response to question 3: Sŏngsam is ashamed to look at his friend because Tŏkchae has actually behaved more honorably toward his father and his family than Sŏngsam did in a similar situation.]

VIEWING THE ART

A leader of modern Korean landscape painters, **Yi Sang-Bom** (1897–1972) reconciled the influx of Western artistic styles with the traditions of Korean art. In 1923, he founded a group of artists who studied both modern and older art. He and his followers developed a style of painting that depicted realistic views of nature within a framework of traditional Korean landscape painting.

Activity. How do you know that this scene is set in the spring? [The predominance of plants suggests a springtime setting.]

CONTENT-AREA CONNECTIONS

Culture: Confucian Ideals
When Sŏngsam learns that Tŏkchae has remained in the village to take care of his old bedridden father, he is filled with admiration and sympathy for his friend, even though Tŏkchae has now become his political enemy. Sŏngsam also feels shame for abandoning his own family for political reasons. That is because Korean culture is dominated by an emphasis on family devotion, especially toward one's parents and other elders. This principle, known as filial piety, or *hsiao*, is a Confucian ideal, a product of the long influence of Chinese culture in Korea.
Individual activity. Ask students to research filial piety in Korean culture and to report their findings to the class.

VIEWING THE ART

Chang Woo-Soung (1912–   ) combines the traditions of Korean painting with modern techniques and subjects, making him one of the most revered Korean artists. *Two Cranes* depicts two striding birds in a spare setting. An emphasis on negative space—the blank area around the objects—is characteristic of paintings from Korea, China, and Japan.

Activity. To explain the concept of negative space, have students trace the outline of the birds onto a sheet of paper, then color in the area outside the birds. Point out how negative space creates a dynamic composition.

Ⓐ Learners Having Difficulty

Finding sequence of events. Point out that this passage is a flashback to an incident that happened when Sŏngsam and Tŏkchae were twelve years old. Have students summarize the sequence of events that occurred after the boys secretly captured the crane. [They tied it up and visited it every day. Then they found out that government officials would soon be hunting cranes. They ran to set their crane free. At first the crane couldn't fly, even when the boys helped it. They heard a shot and feared the crane was dead. Finally, though, it flew away.]

Two Cranes by Chang Woo-Soung (1912–   ). Ink and watercolor on paper.

This used to be the neutralized zone along the thirty-eighth parallel. The cranes were still living here, as before, while the people were all gone.

Ⓐ Once, when Sŏngsam and Tŏkchae were about twelve, they had set a trap here, without the knowledge of the adults, and had caught a crane, a Tanjŏng crane. They had roped the crane, even its wings, and had paid daily visits, patting its neck and riding on its back. Then one day they overheard the neighbors whispering. Someone had come from Seoul[8] with a permit from the

---

8. **Seoul** (sōl): capital of South Korea.

governor-general's office to catch cranes as specimens or something. Then and there the two boys dashed off to the field. That they would be found out and punished was no longer a weighty concern; all they worried about was the fate of their crane. Without a moment's delay, still out of breath from running, they untied the crane's feet and wings. But the bird could hardly walk. It must have been worn out from being bound.

The two held it up in the air. Then, all of a sudden, a shot was fired. The crane fluttered its wings a couple of times and came down again.

It was shot, they thought. But the next

READING MINI-LESSON

Developing Word-Attack Skills
Write these homophone pairs on the chalkboard, and have volunteers read them aloud.

border   boarder
gourd   gored
yore   your

Activity. Point out that all the words on the chalkboard have something in common. They all contain the /ôr/ sound. Have students identify and underline the letters that represent the sound /ôr/.
[border, boarder; gourd, gored; yore, your]

Activity. Display these word pairs. Except for the first letter, the words in each pair are spelled alike. Have volunteers tell if the words in each pair rhyme.

worth   forth [no rhyme]
door   poor [rhyme]
word   cord [no rhyme]
pour   hour [no rhyme]

Activity. Display these sets of words. Have students identify the two words in each set that have the sound /ôr/. Answers are underlined.

1. court	courteous	escort
2. mourn	adjourn	shore
3. soured	poured	horde
4. boredom	border	borrow
5. worse	remorse	hoarse

moment, as another crane from a nearby bush fluttered its wings, the boys' crane stretched its long neck with a whoop and disappeared into the sky. For a long time the two boys could not take their eyes away from the blue sky into which their crane had soared.

"Hey, why don't we stop here for a crane hunt?" Sŏngsam spoke up suddenly.

Tŏkchae was puzzled, struck dumb.

"I'll make a trap with this rope; you flush a crane over here."

Having untied Tŏkchae's hands, Sŏngsam had already started crawling among the weeds.

> ### CHARACTER MOTIVATION
>
> **4.** Why did the boys set the bird free? Why might Sŏngsam be remembering this incident?

B

Tŏkchae's face turned white. "You are sure to be shot anyway"—these words flashed through his mind. Pretty soon a bullet would fly from where Sŏngsam has gone, he thought.

Some paces away, Sŏngsam quickly turned toward him. "Hey, how come you're standing there like you're dumb? Go flush the crane!"

Only then did Tŏkchae catch on. He started crawling among the weeds.

A couple of Tanjŏng cranes soared high into the clear blue autumn sky, fluttering their huge wings. ■

> ### CHARACTER MOTIVATION
>
> **5.** What is Sŏngsam's real motivation for urging Tŏkchae to flush the crane?

D

C

Meet the Writer

Hwang Sunwŏn

The Voice of His Divided Nation

Throughout his lifetime, Hwang Sunwŏn (1915–2000) saw his beloved homeland, Korea, torn by political turmoil. That turmoil touched him deeply and greatly affected his writing.

As a small boy, Hwang saw his father imprisoned for political activities. Korea was struggling against its powerful neighbor, Japan, which had made Korea part of its empire in 1910. By the early 1940s, the Japanese had banned all writing in the Korean language, and Hwang was forced to work in secret. After World War II, when Korea was no longer under Japan's control, communism spread through the northern part of the country. Hwang and his family fled to the south, but they became refugees again when North Korea invaded South Korea at the beginning of the Korean War.

A poet in his youth, Hwang later turned his attention to writing prose, producing seven novels and gaining a reputation as a master writer of the modern Korean short story. His country's complex history is the frequent subject of his fiction, which (like "Cranes") is set in modern times as well as in the distant past. Although his work is rooted in the history and culture of his country, Hwang also explores universal themes, such as the loneliness of the individual. He is highly regarded for his insight into the hearts and minds of his characters.

Cranes **227**

Response and Analysis

Reading Check

1. The events take place in a village at the border of North and South Korea near the end of the Korean civil war, in the 1950s.

2. They were friends.

3. Sŏngsam is fighting for South Korea.

4. Tŏkchae is vice-chairman of the Farmers Communist League. He didn't leave home because his old and bedridden father refuses to leave his farm at harvest time. Tŏkchae says that farming is the only life he and his father know.

Thinking Critically

5. Both are kind, compassionate men who love their families and were forced to make difficult choices because of the war.

6. Sŏngsam is torn between his duty to deliver an enemy prisoner and his love for a childhood friend. He allows Tŏkchae to escape.

7. First, Sŏngsam recalls how Tŏkchae pulled the chestnut needles out of his bottom and shared his chestnuts after the boys escaped from the chestnut tree's owner. Then Sŏngsam recalls how the boys set free a crane they had caught, saving its life. Both memories motivate him to have compassion for his friend and to allow him to escape.

8. He learns that Tŏkchae was made vice-chairman of the Farmers Communist League simply because he was poor and hardworking. He also learns that Tŏkchae has married and is about to become a father. When Sŏngsam hears this news, he cannot bear to look at his friend because he feels ashamed.

9. Possible answer: People's love and loyalty to their friends and

Response and Analysis

Reading Check

1. What is the **setting** of the story—when and where do the events take place?

2. What was Sŏngsam's relationship with Tŏkchae when they were children?

3. For which side in the war is Sŏngsam fighting?

4. Why is Tŏkchae a prisoner? What reasons does he give for not leaving his home with his father?

Thinking Critically

5. Although Sŏngsam and Tŏkchae represent opposite sides of the war, they share similarities. Compare their **characters** and their situations.

6. What is Sŏngsam's **internal conflict** regarding Tŏkchae? How is the conflict resolved at the end of the story?

7. What does Sŏngsam recall in the two **flashbacks** to his childhood? Explain how these memories **motivate** Sŏngsam's actions in the present.

8. What does Sŏngsam learn about Tŏkchae during their walk? How does this information affect Sŏngsam's actions?

9. What is the story's **theme**—that is, what is it saying about civil war and friendships?

10. In many Asian cultures the crane **symbolizes,** or represents, long life. Birds in flight often symbolize freedom. Re-read the last sentence of the story, and explain how the cranes might symbolize both characters.

SKILLS FOCUS

Literary Skills
Analyze theme and character.

Reading Skills
Make inferences about character motivation.

Writing Skills
Write a speech. Write about a character's motivations.

Extending and Evaluating

11. Do you think the ending of the story is effective? Would it be more effective if the writer directly stated what was happening or if Sŏngsam and Tŏkchae shared their thoughts with each other? Give reasons for your answer.

WRITING

The Right Choice?

Sŏngsam wrestles with divided loyalties in this story. Do you think he makes the right decision in the end? Imagine that he is on trial for letting Tŏkchae escape. Write a **speech** in which Sŏngsam defends his actions. Alternatively, compose a speech in which a prosecutor condemns Sŏngsam for his decision. Refer to your Quickwrite notes as you plan your speech. 🖉

Decisive Moments

Think up your own fictional character who faces an important decision, perhaps one that involves a moral choice, as Sŏngsam's does. Write one page in which you present the character's thoughts at the moment the decision is made. What motivates the character to make this decision?

> **Comparing Themes**
> For a writing assignment comparing the themes in "The Sniper" and "Cranes," see page 230.

families are much more real and important than the shifting political loyalties that lead to civil war.

10. Possible answers: Both Sŏngsam and Tŏkchae have been set free by Sŏngsam's decision to allow his friend to escape. Tŏkchae gains his physical freedom, while Sŏngsam asserts his freedom to place personal love and loyalty above political loyalty.

Extending and Evaluating

11. Students' responses will vary, depending on how neatly they like plots to be resolved and on their preference for either overtly emotional or more subtle endings. Some students will find the final image of the two soaring cranes effective; others may wish for an overt reconciliation between the two friends.

Vocabulary Development

Analogies: Pairs of Related Words

Analogy questions ask you to analyze the relationship between one pair of words and then complete a second pair of words. The same relationship must be expressed in the two pairs. Follow the steps below to complete a word analogy. (For more about analogies, see page 576.)

> **Word Bank**
> averted
> obstruction
> constitutes
> mainstay
> refuge

MOUTH : FACE :: _____ : television

   a. entertainment   **c.** telephone

   b. living room   **d.** screen

1. Identify the relationship between the words in the first pair. In the example, the relationship is that of a part (*mouth*) to a whole (*face*).

2. Use a sentence to see the relationship in the analogy more clearly: A *mouth* is a part of a *face*, just as a _____ is a part of a *television*.

3. Select the word that completes the second pair so that it expresses the same relationship as that in the first pair. Choice d, *screen*, is correct because it refers to a part of a television.

The chart below shows some of the relationships used in analogies:

Type of Relationship	Example
Synonyms	TIRED : SLEEPY :: happy : joyous
Antonyms	RIGHT : WRONG :: few : many
Part to whole	LEAF : TREE :: kitchen : house
Member to category	EARTH : PLANET :: truck : vehicle
Object (or thing) to a characteristic of it	SUN : HOT :: desert : dry

PRACTICE 1

Complete each analogy below with the Word Bank word that fits best:

1. ANNOUNCES : DECLARES :: _____ : forms
2. SUCCEEDED : FAILED :: _____ : faced
3. SKYSCRAPER : TALL :: _____ : safe
4. CONTEST : COMPETITION :: _____ : obstacle
5. PAIL : BUCKET :: _____ : support

PRACTICE 2

Using the chart above as a reference, identify the type of relationship in each word pair:

1. crane : bird   **3.** scream : loud   **5.** wheel : bus
2. glass : fragile   **4.** soccer : sport

SKILLS FOCUS

Vocabulary Skills
Understand word analogies.

Vocabulary Development

Practice 1

1. constitutes
2. averted
3. refuge
4. obstruction
5. mainstay

Practice 2

1. member to category
2. object to a characteristic of it
3. thing to a characteristic of it
4. member to category
5. part to whole

ASSESSING

Assessment

■ *Holt Assessment: Literature, Reading, and Vocabulary*

RETEACHING

For a lesson reteaching universal themes, see **Reteaching,** p. 979A. For another selection to teach comparing themes, see *The Holt Reader,* Collection 4.

Comparing Universal Themes

Writing Tips

This page helps students prepare to write an essay comparing and contrasting the themes of "The Sniper" and "Cranes." Focusing on the block method of organizing a comparison-contrast essay and on the three-part essay structure of introduction, body, and conclusion, this page gives step-by-step guidance in writing the essay.

Students may need additional help in writing the thesis statement for their essay's introductory paragraph. Point out the importance of this statement. Explain that the thesis statement announces what the rest of the essay will prove or demonstrate and that all of the details in the essay should support this statement.

To help students write a thesis statement about how the themes of the two stories are similar and different, ask them to consider the following questions:

- How are the situations of the two main characters similar? Is the situation of one character more tragic than that of the other? What evidence in the story makes you think so?

- Is the resolution of one story more hopeful than the resolution of the other? What evidence in the story makes you think so?

- Do both main characters learn similar lessons? Have their feelings about war changed by the end of the story? What evidence in the story makes you think so?

Writing a Comparison-Contrast Essay

Comparing Universal Themes

Now that you have read "The Sniper" and "Cranes," you can compare and contrast their themes in an essay. When you write a **comparison-contrast essay,** you look for similarities (**comparisons**) and differences (**contrasts**) between the works.

Gather and Organize Your Information

To write your essay, use the chart on page 210 that you created to compare elements of the two stories. It will contain the basic information you need to compose your essay.

Comparison-contrast essays can be organized in two ways. One way is called the **block method,** which you will use to write this essay. The other way is the **point-by-point method,** which you will learn about on page 268.

The Block Method

When you use the block method, you discuss the *stories,* one at a time. First you write about the relevant elements of one story in the order you think most effective. Then you discuss the same elements in the other story, following the same order. The chart at the right gives an example.

Use Three-Part Structure

Most essays have three basic parts. Use this structure when you write your comparison-contrast essay:

1. In your **introduction,** tell the reader what works you will be comparing,

giving titles, authors, and any necessary background information. The introduction, usually a single paragraph, should end with a **thesis statement,** in which you state how the stories' themes are similar or different.

2. The **body** of your essay consists of paragraphs supporting your thesis statement with evidence from the stories—the information you listed in your chart.

3. In your **conclusion,** sum up your major points, and end with a new (but related) thought.

Develop Your Ideas

You should develop and **elaborate** on every general statement in your essay. Provide examples, details, or quotations to prove your thesis.

▶ **For more help writing a comparison-contrast essay, see pages 270–277.**

Block Method
Story 1: "The Sniper"
Element 1: Main character and his situation
Element 2: Character's motives and conflict(s)
Element 3: What character learns
Element 4: Resolution of conflict(s)
Element 5: Theme
Story 2: "Cranes"
Element 1: Main character and his situation
Element 2: Character's motives and conflict(s)
Element 3: What character learns
Element 4: Resolution of conflict(s)
Element 5: Theme

SKILLS FOCUS

Literary Skills
Compare universal themes.

Writing Skills
Write a comparison-contrast essay.

DIFFERENTIATING INSTRUCTION

Advanced Learners
Enrichment. As students discuss the meaning of the story's crane symbolism in question 10 on p. 228, explain that since 1955, cranes have also come to symbolize peace and the hope of reconciliation for war-torn countries. An international peace movement was inspired by the experiences of Sadako Sasaki, a Japanese girl suffering from aftereffects of the atomic bomb that was dropped on Hiroshima.

She attempted to fold one thousand origami cranes to find healing. (Origami is the Japanese art of folding paper figures.)
Activity. Have students read the book *Children of the Paper Crane* or research Sadako's story on the Internet. Then, have them report to the class on how the experiences of one girl inspired a worldwide peace movement.

Informational Text

LINK TO "THE SNIPER"

A Country Divided ◆ Lives in the Crossfire ◆ Internment ◆ Peace Isn't Impossible

Synthesizing Sources

When you research a subject, get a balanced view by using several types of sources and examining different points of view. Here are some guidelines:

- **Categorize your sources.** Is a work a **primary source**—a firsthand, or eyewitness, account? Is it a **secondary source** providing interpretation or analysis of events in which the writer did not participate? (For more on primary and secondary sources, see pages 96 and 578–579.)
- **Determine the author's purpose and audience.** Was the piece written, for example, to tell a personal story, to change an unsympathetic reader's mind, or to provide background information?
- **Compare and contrast.** Write a **paraphrase** of the sources' main ideas. If your subject is controversial, do your sources agree or disagree? Compare the information in your sources, and think about what you can learn from each one. Does a source provide only objective facts or the author's feelings and thoughts? Are **facts** and **opinions** combined?
- **Connect to other sources or related topics.** Connect your resources to other works of nonfiction or fiction that you've read, perhaps ones about another time or place.
- **Synthesize.** Consider your sources as a group. How does each source contribute to your understanding of the subject? Do your sources present different opinions to give you a balanced view of the issues?

Draw **conclusions** from your sources and from connections to other sources you've read. What do you now understand about your subject? What do you still need to find out?

Vocabulary Development

intolerance (in·täl′ər·əns) n.: prejudice; hostility to other groups.

negotiations (ni·gō′shē·ā′shənz) n.: discussions aimed at reaching an agreement.

designate (dez′ig·nāt′) v.: point out; indicate.

absorb (ab·sôrb′) v.: take in.

reunification (rē·yōō′nə·fi′kā′shən) n.: joining together of things that had been divided.

divergent (dī·vʉr′jənt) adj.: separate; going in different directions.

coerced (kō·ʉrsd′) v.: forced.

abhor (ab·hôr′) v.: hate.

optimist (äp′tə·mist) n.: person who is always hopeful.

condone (kən·dōn′) v.: overlook or excuse an offense.

INTERNET
Interactive Reading Model
Keyword: LE5 9-4

Connecting to the Literature

The long-standing conflicts between Catholics and Protestants in Ireland, the setting of "The Sniper" (page 212), are called the Troubles. The following selections discuss the conflict and tell what it's like to live in a place where your home is a battleground.

SKILLS FOCUS

Reading Skills
Synthesize ideas from different sources dealing with a single topic.

Grade-Level Skills

- **Reading Skills**
Synthesize the content from several sources or works by a single author on a single issue.

Summary *at grade level*

> "A Country Divided" chronicles the causes of conflict in Northern Ireland.
>
> "Lives in the Crossfire" describes the effects of violence in Northern Ireland.
>
> "Internment" is a memoir by a woman who was in Belfast when the British suspended protections for suspected Irish criminals.
>
> "Peace Isn't Impossible" is a 1997 essay urging that the violent minority on both sides of the conflict not be allowed to thwart peace.

PRETEACHING

Preview Vocabulary

Discuss the following questions:

1. Could useful <u>negotiations</u> occur between groups if a spirit of <u>intolerance</u> exists between them?
2. Would you <u>abhor</u> or <u>condone</u> a government that <u>coerced</u> elders?
3. How might leaders promote the <u>reunification</u> of groups that had developed <u>divergent</u> interests?
4. What qualities can be used to <u>designate</u> an <u>optimist</u>?
5. What attitudes can children <u>absorb</u> from their parents?

RESOURCES: READING

Planning
- *One-Stop Planner* CD-ROM with ExamView Test Generator

Differentiating Instruction
- *Holt Reading Solutions*
- *Holt Adapted Reader*
- *Supporting Instruction in Spanish*

Vocabulary
- *Vocabulary Development*

Grammar and Language
- *Daily Language Activities*

Assessment
- *Holt Assessment: Literature, Reading, and Vocabulary*
- *One-Stop Planner* CD-ROM with ExamView Test Generator

- *Holt Online Assessment*

Internet
- go.hrw.com (Keyword: LE5 9-4)
- *Elements of Literature Online*

Media
- *Audio CD Library*
- *Audio CD Library, Selections and Summaries in Spanish*

DIRECT TEACHING

A Reading Informational Text

❷ Synthesizing sources. Is this text a primary source or a secondary source? [secondary source] How can you tell? [It provides analysis of events in which the writer did not participate.]

B Vocabulary Development

❷ Recognizing word families. Tell students that the word *Protestant* can be used as either a noun or an adjective and that it is derived from the verb *protest*. Ask students to name other words derived from this verb. [Possible responses: *protester, protesting, protestation.*]

C Reading Informational Text

❷ Synthesizing sources. What purpose do you think the author has for providing these facts? [Possible responses: The facts about how the Irish Catholics were treated by their English Protestant rulers help explain why the conflict between the English and the Irish, and between Catholics and Protestants in Ireland, became so intense. It provides background about the causes of the continuing conflict.]

D Vocabulary Development

❷ Recognizing word families. What other words do you know that are related to the word *rebellions?* [Possible responses: *rebel, rebellious.*]

A Country Divided

from *One Belfast Boy*
Patricia McMahon

The flag of Ireland. The green is for Catholics, the orange is for Protestants, and the white symbolizes peace between them.

A Around the year 1170 the king of England, Henry II, declared himself king of Ireland as well. Gradually, with great bloodshed, Ireland was brought under the control of England, or Great Britain, as England came to be known. Through the centuries, Ireland was held as a colony of the British Empire—held against the wishes of the Irish people.

There were also other people living in Ireland, however. English settlers had been going to Ireland for centuries, and beginning in 1609, James I, then king of England, offered land to Scottish settlers if they would move to Ireland and farm the land—land that was being taken from the native Irish.

To the Irish, these new arrivals came to be known as the strangers: people with a different language, a different way of life, and, most important, a different religion. **B** For the people of Ireland were Catholic and the strangers taking over their land were Protestant. At that time in England and in much of Europe, a terrible intolerance existed between different religions.

The English gradually put laws into place that said Catholics could not own land, could not vote, could not be elected to public office or work for the government. Catholics were not allowed to be lawyers. They were not allowed to speak the Irish language or study Irish history or literature. They were **C** forbidden to hold Mass. Bishops, priests, and monks[1] were forced to leave the country. By 1780 the Irish people owned only 5 percent of their own land, and in 1800 the British government passed the Act of Union, declaring Ireland part of the United Kingdom of Great Britain and Ireland.

Through the long years of British rule, the Irish fought for their freedom. They fought with what weapons they had, in rebellions **D** great and small—rebellions that the vast British army always put down. The Irish fought with words as well as weapons. They organized and signed petitions, held massive nonviolent protests, and after Catholics

---

1. **hold Mass . . . monks:** Mass is the Catholic Church's ritual service. Bishops and priests are Catholic clergy. Monks live in religious communities governed by a set of strict rules.

Vocabulary
intolerance (in·täl′ər·əns) *n.:* prejudice; hostility to other groups.

DIFFERENTIATING INSTRUCTION

Learners Having Difficulty
Some students may have difficulty following the long sequence of causes and effects that have contributed to the many centuries of conflict between the English and the Irish and between Protestants and Catholics in Ireland and Northern Ireland. As students read the brief history, help them construct a time line of important events, from 1170 to 1998, in this centuries-old struggle.

English-Language Learners
Students unfamiliar with Christianity may not understand the intolerance described between the two denominations of Christians—Catholics and Protestants. Explain that until the 1500s, most Christians accepted the leadership and authority of the Catholic pope, seated in Rome. In 1517, a German pastor named Martin Luther rebelled against the pope's authority and eventually established

---

View of damage in Dublin, Ireland, after the uprising in 1916.

regained the vote in 1829, they lobbied[2] in the English Parliament[3] for their freedom.

In 1916, during World War I, a small rebellion broke out in Dublin[4] on Easter Monday. The Irish rebels were quickly defeated. Sixteen of the leaders were shot, and many men and women were jailed, including some who had not been involved. Anger grew in Ireland. People began to join Sinn Fein, a political group working for Irish freedom. In the Irish language, Sinn Fein means "ourselves alone." Those who felt it

---

2. **lobbied** (läb′ēd) *v.*: attempted to influence public officials to do something.
3. **English Parliament:** branch of the English government with the power to make laws for the country.
4. **Dublin:** Ireland's capital.

was necessary to fight with weapons joined the IRA—the Irish Republican Army—and fought the British army where and when they could. The outnumbered IRA, led by a man named Michael Collins, managed to inflict losses on the superior British forces. The Irish people began to believe that this time would be different, this time freedom would finally come.

But the Protestants of Ireland did not approve of the rebellion. They had lived in Ireland for generations. They owned land and businesses. And they knew who they were: They were British subjects, and they believed Ireland should remain part of the United Kingdom. They were willing to fight to keep it so. "No surrender" became

E **Learners Having Difficulty**

Monitoring students' progress. You may want to have students pause here in their reading to check their understanding of the importance of the Easter Monday rebellion. The rebellion itself was small and the Irish were defeated, but Britain's harsh reaction to it radicalized many Irish citizens, who until then had not been involved in the conflict.

F **Advanced Learners**

❓ Enrichment. Why do you think this organization continues to call itself Sinn Fein today, even though very few Irish people speak the old Irish language? [Possible responses: The Irish name reminds people of their heritage and what they are fighting for. It reminds people of how the struggle began.]

G **Reading Informational Text**

❓ Synthesizing sources. Does this author present a range of opinions on the issue of Irish independence? Explain. [Yes. This paragraph explains the point of view of Protestants with English ancestry, who wished to remain British subjects. Earlier paragraphs presented the point of view of Sinn Fein members and the IRA.]

---

the Lutheran Church. This new branch of Christianity was called Protestantism because Luther protested against the Catholic Church. In 1534, King Henry VIII of England broke away from the Roman Catholic Church, when the pope refused to grant him a divorce. He founded the Anglican Church, another branch of Protestantism, with himself as head. As a result, for the English, Protestantism was both a religious and a political loyalty.

Advanced Learners

Enrichment. Invite groups of students to create a set of researchable questions about the conflict in Northern Ireland, generated from information in the four selections here. Each group can collaborate on a research paper based on one of these questions or prepare a presentation for the class.

A Reading Skills

❓ Identifying cause and effect.
Why did the British government agree to hold peace talks with the rebels in 1920? [The Irish rebels were inflicting serious damages on property and killing British soldiers. The English wanted to put a stop to the violence, so they were willing to negotiate a settlement.]

B Learners Having Difficulty

❓ Finding details. Why did the British want Ulster, the northern part of Ireland, to remain part of the United Kingdom? [Many British Protestants lived there.] Why was a new border drawn, not including the counties of Donegal, Cavan, and Monaghan in Northern Ireland? [The British wanted Northern Ireland to be a place where there were more Protestants than Catholics, and there were too many Catholics in those counties.]

C Reading Informational Text

❓ Synthesizing sources.
Connect the information in this paragraph to the situation in the story "The Sniper." Which side of the argument described here did the main character of the story support? [He believed that Ireland should not be divided and should have rejected the British deal.] Which side of the argument did the sniper's brother support? [He believed that the creation of Northern Ireland was a temporary measure and that the British proposal should be accepted.]

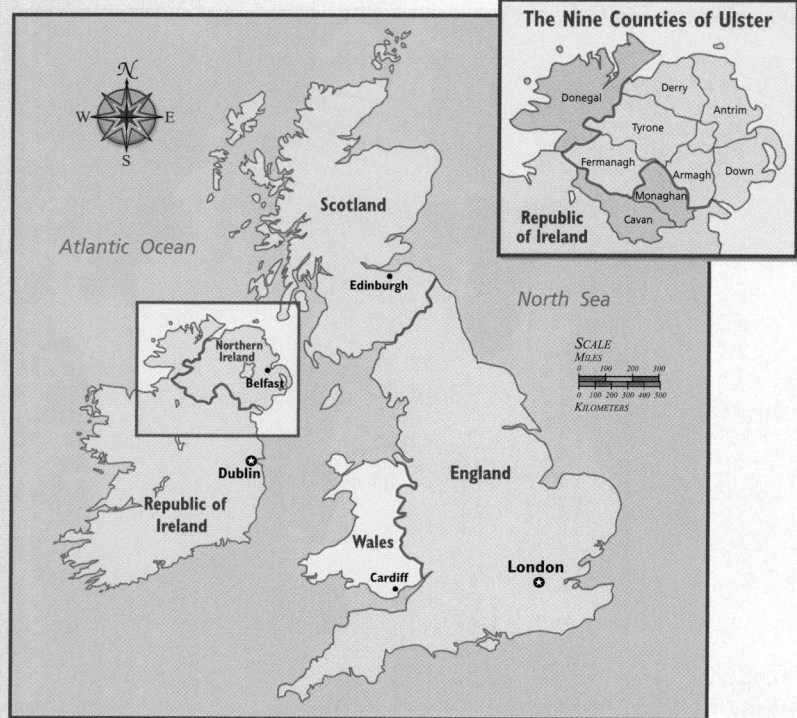

their motto. Great numbers of Protestants were living in the North; their cry was "Ulster[5] will fight, and Ulster will be right."

The damages inflicted by the Irish rebels grew, and the British government agreed in 1920 to meet with the Irish for peace talks. After difficult <u>negotiations</u>, the British agreed to the Irish demands for self-government and freedom. But they did not agree to freedom for all of Ireland. Ulster, where so many British Protestants lived, would become Northern Ireland and would become part of the United Kingdom of Great Britain and Northern Ireland. But not *all* of Ulster would become Northern

Ireland. A new border would be drawn to create a place where there would be more Protestants than Catholics. Three counties—Donegal, Cavan, and Monaghan—of the original nine making up Ulster were not included in Northern Ireland. This was the deal the British offered. If it was not accepted, the talks would be ended, and the fighting would begin again.

In Ireland, the arguments over the proposal were fierce. Some believed there should be no division of the country—no deal. Others thought it was the best deal possible at that time. They believed that

5. **Ulster:** name often given to the northern, predominantly Protestant, portion of Ireland.

Vocabulary
negotiations (ni·gō'shē·ā'shənz) *n.*: discussions aimed at reaching an agreement.

CONTENT-AREA CONNECTIONS

Social Science: Primary Sources About the Troubles
Among the primary sources existing about the conflict in Northern Ireland are many interviews, memoirs, and oral histories available in print or on the Internet.
Paired activity. Have pairs of students research primary sources about one historical event described in the four selections. One student should research eyewitness accounts written by Catholic residents of Northern Ireland, and the other should research sources by Protestant residents. Then, have each pair discuss what they have learned about the views of the people on each side of the conflict.

creating Northern Ireland was a temporary measure and Ireland would soon be reunited. In the end, Ireland took the offer. But anger over the division of the country was so strong that civil war broke out. Friends who had fought together against the British now turned on one another.

And so in 1921, while most of the Irish gained their freedom, the Catholics of Northern Ireland remained under British rule. In the new Ulster, Catholics could not vote unless they owned land, and few did. Businesses, government, public housing, and jobs were all controlled by Protestants.

In 1968, Catholics began to form civil rights organizations, inspired by the work of people like Dr. Martin Luther King, Jr., in the United States. Catholics wanted to have the same rights as Protestants. They began a series of protest marches across Northern Ireland. The government forbade the marches. Catholic demonstrators were attacked and gassed.[6] Catholic homes, neighborhoods, and churches were attacked by mobs who believed that the Catholics were not entitled to equal rights.

The Catholics began to fight back, arming themselves. The Irish Republican Army, whose numbers had dwindled since the country was divided, gained new recruits and became active again. The British army moved in to try to stop the fighting, but the battles grew worse. After fourteen unarmed protesters were killed by a British army regiment in 1972, on a day that became known as Bloody Sunday, the IRA's membership swelled. Soon the cities and towns of Northern Ireland were battlegrounds.

---

6. **gassed** v.: exposed to tear gas or some other airborne substance released in order to cause great discomfort.

Both the Protestants and the Catholics made bombs, blew up buildings, and created armies. The IRA began to argue within its ranks about tactics, splitting into different groups. One group, called the Provisional IRA, or the Provos, became the present-day IRA. Both Catholics and Protestants were guilty of murder and mayhem. At one point there were as many as seven armed groups on the streets of Belfast.[7] Even the question of civil rights seemed to have been lost amidst the violence and the constant calls for revenge.

More than 3,200 people have died in the Troubles[8]—men, women, and children—Protestant and Catholic alike. They died over the question "Are we British or are we Irish?" And after all this time, there are still two very different answers to that question. The deaths have not changed this.

The habit of hating is a hard one to break. But many people believe it is worth a try. People on both sides of the walls[9] who want peace keep working to stop the fighting. In 1997, a new cease-fire went into effect. Peace talks began, which led to the signing of a peace accord in 1998. A new government for Northern Ireland was formed, intending to guarantee the rights of Catholics. Some say there will be no peace until the entire island of Ireland is united. Some say there will be no peace if that ever happens.

Although a peace accord was signed in 1998, as of 2001, peace has not been established in Northern Ireland. Both sides continue to work on resolving the conflict.

---

7. **Belfast:** capital of Northern Ireland.
8. **More than . . . Troubles:** This figure refers to the number of deaths at the time of the book's publication, in 1999.
9. **both sides of the walls:** walls in some parts of Belfast that separate Catholics and Protestants.

D Reading Skills

? Identifying cause and effect. What happened on Bloody Sunday, and how did this incident affect the situation in Northern Ireland? [A British army regiment killed fourteen unarmed Irish protesters. As a result, membership in the IRA swelled, and the violence increased dramatically.]

E Reading Informational Text

? Synthesizing sources. How can you tell that the author of this paragraph is an objective outsider to the conflict in Northern Ireland? [She describes violent acts committed by both sides in the conflict. She says, "Both Catholics and Protestants were guilty of murder and mayhem."]

F Reading Informational Text

? Synthesizing sources. How does the author's purpose change at the end of the selection? [At the beginning her purpose is to provide background information. Now her purpose is to persuade people to work for peace.]

G Reading Informational Text

? Synthesizing sources. What range of opinion about the conflict in Northern Ireland does the author explain at the end of the selection? [She says that some people believe that there will always be fighting unless Ireland is unified, while others believe that there will always be fighting if reunification should happen.] How hopeful does she seem that the conflict will be resolved soon? [By explaining that people are still polarized in positions for which there is no compromise, she seems to hold little hope that the conflict will be resolved soon.]

A Reading Informational Text

? Synthesizing sources. Is this passage a primary source or a secondary source? [primary source] How can you tell? [A resident of Northern Ireland uses the pronoun *I* to give an eyewitness account of what it is like to live amid the violence of Northern Ireland.]

B Reading Informational Text

? Synthesizing sources. Compare and contrast the content of this diary entry with that of the earlier one. [In both entries a girl expresses her fear of the violence in her neighborhood. The first girl is afraid of the IRA's bombs; the second is afraid of being shot by Protestants.] Why do you think this author included primary sources in her book about Northern Ireland? [The primary sources provide direct evidence of the fear, insecurity, and lack of understanding felt by young people on both sides of the conflict.]

C Reading Informational Text

? Synthesizing sources. Is the remainder of this selection a primary source or a secondary source? [secondary source] Why does the author emphasize the physical separation of Catholics and Protestants in Northern Ireland? [Possible response: She wants readers to understand that there is little opportunity for those on opposing sides of the conflict to interact and communicate with one another. From childhood on, people on each side learn only the point of view of their own side in the conflict.]

NONFICTION

Lives in the Crossfire

from *Children of "the Troubles"*
Laurel Holliday

A **December 20, 1976**

I would love to risk sleeping some Christmas night with curtains flung back from the windows, nothing but shiny black glass between me and the stars and sky, the drizzle and the horses, but [IRA] bombs ruthlessly silence my wishes, for a while at least.

—*from the diary of Sharon Ingram, eighteen years old, Ballygawley*

B **28th April, 1994**

I am frightened living on this street across from the Protestants. I am frightened they will come and kill us because this is the eleventh time they have shot people in our street. I don't know why they want to kill us.

—*from the diary of Bridie Murphy, eleven years old, Belfast*

C From the moment children are born in Northern Ireland, they begin to live in a majority Protestant or a majority Catholic neighborhood. They go to either a Catholic or a Protestant school, and their friends are likely to be exclusively one or the other. They are taught to shop only in their "own" shops in some towns and, eventually, to socialize only in their "own" pubs. And, of course, when they die they will go to a segregated graveyard.

Amazingly, I think, to those who haven't been raised there, in Belfast even the taxis divide along religious lines, with one fleet heading to Catholic and another to Protestant neighborhoods. In some parts of the country even the sidewalks are painted to designate political/religious loyalties.

In addition to these very obvious distinctions that children need to learn in order to survive in Northern Ireland, they also absorb differences in language and perspective[1] that set them apart from one another for the rest of their lives. If you are Catholic, for example, you call Northern Ireland's second largest city Derry; if you are Protestant, it is Londonderry to you. If you are Catholic, you call the nearly three decades of the Troubles a war; if you are Protestant, you are careful to point out that there has been a terrorist uprising, not a war, in Northern Ireland.

1. **perspective** (pər·spek′tiv) *n.:* point of view.

Vocabulary
designate (dez′ig·nāt′) *v.:* point out; indicate.
absorb (ab·sôrb′) *v.:* take in.

DEVELOPING FLUENCY

Paired activity. Invite pairs of students to take turns reading aloud Laurel Holliday's selection, which contrasts the Catholic point of view with the Protestant point of view. Provide photocopies of the selection for students to mark up.

First, have them read the selection aloud one sentence at a time, deciding together where they need to pause within each sentence to convey its meaning. Also, have students decide which words they should emphasize in each sentence. Have students indicate pauses by drawing vertical lines between words and emphases by underlining words that are especially important or that indicate points of contrast. Finally, have each student read the entire selection aloud without stopping.

In fact, even the name you call your country will be in question. If you are raised in a Catholic family wanting the reunification of Ireland, you will refer to the North of Ireland as your homeland or call it the Six Counties, rather than making it sound as if it were a separate country called Northern Ireland. And if you were raised in a Protestant environment, you will be more likely to call your country Northern Ireland or Ulster.

Not only are most children in Northern Ireland set on divergent sectarian[2] courses from birth, but from the age of seven some Protestant and Catholic children are coerced into running secret errands for terrorists and assembling and hiding their weapons.

---

2. **sectarian** (sek·ter′ē·ən) *adj.:* pertaining to a particular religious group.

Although the majority of people in Northern Ireland abhor the violence and take no part in it themselves, virtually every family in Northern Ireland has had members beaten, tortured, or murdered, and the country's children have been witness to it all. For this is not a private war, conducted behind closed doors, nor a war where the men go away to fight the enemy. This is an everyday, in-your-face war, where the enemy lives on the next block and speaks (almost) the same language.

Vocabulary

reunification (rē·yōō′nə·fi′kā′shən) *n.:* joining together of things that had been divided.

divergent (dī·vur′jənt) *adj.:* separate; going in different directions.

coerced (kō·urst′) *v.:* forced.

abhor (ab·hôr′) *v.:* hate.

D Reading Informational Text

? Synthesizing sources. What facts does the author include at the end of the selection to summarize the effects of the war in Northern Ireland? [Most people hate the violence and do not take part in it; but almost every family includes victims of the violence, and the children witness it every day.]

E Reading Skills

? Comparing and contrasting. How does the focus of this selection differ from that of "A Country Divided"? [This selection focuses on how the conflict affects the day-to-day life of people in Northern Ireland today; "A Country Divided" focuses on the historical development of the conflict over hundreds of years.]

Lives in the Crossfire   **237**

DIRECT TEACHING

Ⓐ Reading Informational Text

❓ Synthesizing sources. Is this selection a primary source or a secondary source? [primary source] How long ago did the events that the writer witnessed occur? [They occurred in 1971, more than thirty years ago.]

Ⓑ Reading Informational Text

❓ Synthesizing sources. Does this selection focus on objective facts or on personal feelings? [personal feelings] How were the members of the writer's family feeling the day of the Internment? [Possible responses: tense, afraid, nervous, worried.]

Ⓒ English-Language Learners

Interpreting colloquial language. Make sure students understand that *mum* is an affectionate, colloquial term for "mother," commonly used in Ireland. The word *zombie* refers literally to a corpse brought back to life. Here it is used colloquially to refer to someone who appears to be in a trance. The idiomatic expression *took it in turns* means "alternated doing something—first one person, then the other."

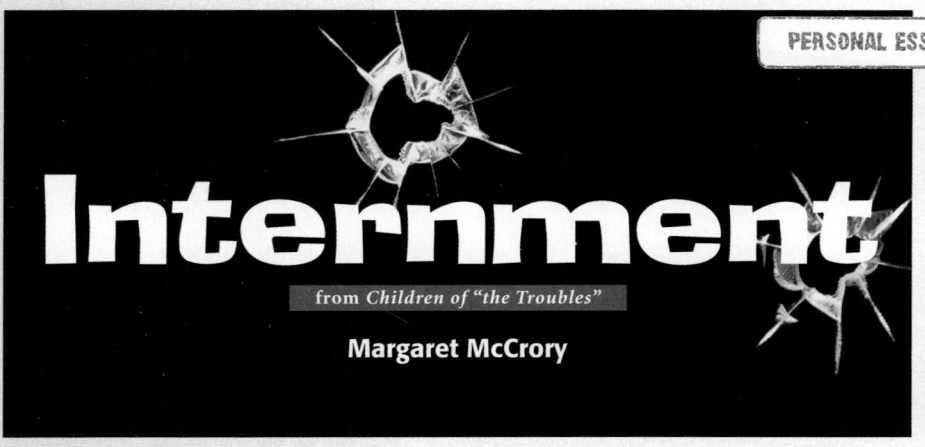

PERSONAL ESSAY

Internment

from *Children of "the Troubles"*

Margaret McCrory

Internment was a policy authorized by the British government in reaction to the violence in Northern Ireland. The policy allowed the police to jail suspected criminals without charging them with a crime or producing evidence against them. Margaret McCrory was a teenager in Belfast, and she witnessed the violent reaction to this policy.

Ⓐ August 9, 1971, is a day I will remember as long as I live. We were emigrating[1] to America the next day but that's not why I'll remember that date. That was the night of Internment. I was only thirteen at the time, but just thinking about that day still brings back the knotted feelings in my stomach.

I was supposed to feel excited about leaving and also sad to be saying goodbye to our friends and neighbors. But we woke up that morning to a strange silence outside. We found ourselves whispering to each other and sneaking looks out the windows. There was nothing out there at all—no people, no cars, not even the dogs were barking. It was eerie.

We felt something big was about to happen, but when? The waiting was the worst feeling I've ever felt. I don't know if we would have sensed so much tension if my mum hadn't kept repeating over and over again, "Please, Lord, get us out of here." She **Ⓑ** looked and acted like she was scared to death and I suppose some of that rubbed off on us. We were very subdued[2] all day. The funny thing was there wasn't a bite in the house, yet no one complained they were hungry.

Late afternoon, and there was still no activity outside. By this time we were all nervous wrecks. We had nothing in the house to occupy us—just a couple of mattresses and our suitcases. Hugh, who was nine, was so nervous that he made himself sick. Mum made him lie down on the mattress in the boys' room on the second floor. Eileen, eleven, was walking around like a zombie, **Ⓒ** staring straight ahead with huge eyes. She was scary. David, eight, and Maria, seven, were playing quietly on the bare floor, which was really unusual for them. Mum and I took it in turns to peek out of the windows.

1. **emigrating** (em′i·grāt′iŋ) *v.:* leaving a country to live in another place.

2. **subdued** (səb·dood′) *adj.:* quiet; reserved or restrained.

238　Collection 4　Comparing Themes • Synthesizing Sources

DIFFERENTIATING INSTRUCTION

Advanced Learners
Enrichment. When the British began their Internment policy in Northern Ireland, they suspended habeas corpus, one of the oldest and most cherished elements of English common law, which is also included in the U.S. Constitution. The principle of habeas corpus, which dates back to the reign of Henry VII (1485–1509), holds that a person cannot be

deprived of his or her personal liberty unless charged before a judge with a specific crime.
Activity. Have students research the history and applications of habeas corpus in the United Kingdom and the United States, as well as circumstances in which this basic protection may be suspended. Have them present their findings in an oral report.

Mum had gone into the kitchen to brush[3] the floor when the shooting began. We could hear the bullets whizzing over the house and ricocheting[4] off the corrugated iron on the factory wall behind our house. The bullets smashed through the kitchen window. Mum dropped the brush and ran. To this very day she still complains about leaving a pile of dirt on the floor.

Hugh was crying upstairs and Eileen was screaming her head off. Between the deafening noise inside and the explosive noises from outside, we felt like we were in the middle of World War III. All the shooting seemed to be at the back of the house where the boys' room was so we dragged Hugh and the mattress up to the third floor where our room overlooked the front of the house. We all huddled together on the mattresses.

It was very hot but when Mum opened the window a little bit we could feel our throats begin to burn. Which meant that there was tear gas out there, and from past experience we knew what that could do to you. Your throat would begin to burn and your eyes would sting like mad. Then you would feel violently sick. It was a horrible feeling so we quickly shut the window.

The Uzis[5] were going mad out there—the noise was incredible!—and Eileen couldn't stop screaming. I was scared but I also felt excited and very curious. I really wanted to know what was going on out there so every chance I got I would sneak a look outside. I could see men with guns running up our street. They saw me and shooed me in by gesturing with their hands to get down. Mum made me sit with them on the mattresses, but Eileen's screaming was driving me mad so I finally told her that they weren't going to kill her because I was going to do it first. She quieted down to loud whimpering instead.

We could see the orange glow of petrol bombs exploding and hear the bang of plastic bullets being fired. The boys were good at recognizing the sounds because they used to collect spent cartridges after nights of violence. But this was the worst we had ever seen.

Finally Maria, David, and Hugh went to sleep. Mum had to comfort Eileen, who was scared out of her mind. There was too much going on to even think of sleep. Every so often there would be a slight lull and I would run to the window. The sky was really bright now. The barricades were burning so as to keep the soldiers out. I could see men outside shooting their guns up the avenue. They were hiding behind walls, bins, poles—anything at all. It was like watching television. When several bullets hit the wall outside our window Mum made me lie down again.

We heard people shouting for Father Murphy, our parish priest, to come and give someone the Last Rites.[6] Ten minutes later we heard shouts of "They killed Father Murphy!" "They shot him!" "Three bodies on top of each other!" Mum and I could only look at each other in shock. Father Murphy was our friend. He taught Hugh and David how to box. He had been

---

3. **brush** *v.:* sweep.
4. **ricocheting** (rik'ə·shā'iŋ) *v.* used as *adj.:* bouncing from one surface to another.
5. **Uzis** (o͞o'zēz): trademark name for submachine guns.

6. **parish priest ... the Last Rites:** The parish is the area served by one particular church and priest. In the Catholic Church the Last Rites are the final religious rituals and prayers for a person near death.

Internment   239

D Reading Informational Text

? Synthesizing sources. What does this first-person account of the violence in Northern Ireland add to your understanding that the previous selections could not? [It dramatically conveys the feelings of terror and uncertainty experienced by those who are caught up in the middle of the violence.]

E English-Language Learners

Building background knowledge. Explain that tear gas is a nonlethal gas used by police officers to subdue people engaged in violent or illegal activities. It irritates the eyes and temporarily blinds people with tears.

F Learners Having Difficulty

? Finding details. How can you tell that this is not the first time the family has experienced violence in their neighborhood? [The writer says that the family knew about the effects of tear gas from "past experience" and then describes its effects.]

G English-Language Learners

Interpreting colloquial language. Explain that the idiom *going mad,* in this context, means "being used furiously, fast, and hard." The word *shooed* means "scared or drove away," based on the interjection *Shoo.* The colloquial expression *driving me mad* means "affecting me unbearably, to the point of insanity."

? **Identifying cause and effect.**
How and why does the death of
Father Murphy change the mood of
the family? [Until then, the narrator
had felt fear but also a sense of
excitement, because the violence had
felt unreal, as if she were watching a
TV program. When Father Murphy is
killed, the shocking reality of what is
happening sinks in.]

B **Learners Having
Difficulty**

? **Monitoring students'
progress.** Why was the violence in
the streets especially threatening to
the writer's family? [The barricades
and devastation in the streets made it
almost impossible for the family to
escape.]

C **Reading Informational
Text**

? **Synthesizing sources.** What
conclusion can you draw from the
perspective that this primary source
adds to your understanding of the
situation in Northern Ireland?
[Possible response: The violence in
some areas of Northern Ireland was
so bad that residents were desperate
to escape their own country.]

---

at our house only yesterday—they must
be wrong.

They weren't. Ten men died that night, all
from our street. Father Murphy had been
shot dead while giving a man the Last Rites.
And when another man went to help Father
Murphy, he had been killed as well.

It was very hard lying there listening to
the *rat-a-tat* of the gunfire and not think
that someone else might be dead. The excitement was gone and fear and deep sadness
were left. We lay there until morning when,
finally, all noises stopped and we could hear
our neighbors outside.

They were clustered together exchanging
war stories and talking about Father Murphy.
We were next on their agenda. We were never
going to get out, they said, and no one was
going to risk his life to get us out. I think
they were a bit jealous.

Mum didn't give up. She asked everybody

until one man with an old post office van
said yes.

We had an awful time getting through
burnt-out barricades and around overturned
lorries[7]—sometimes even human barricades.
After many detours we finally reached the
airport to find no planes were flying that day.
We were bundled into a minibus and driven
to Dublin.

We were still in shock from the night
before. Even after twenty-four hours with
no food none of us complained that we
were hungry. Every time we heard Father
Murphy's name mentioned on the radio we
cried our eyes out but Mum just kept repeating "Thank God we're out!" That's all
she would say.

She was dead right though. Thank God
we did get out.

_____
7. **lorries** (lôr′ēz) *n.:* British for "trucks."

OPINION ESSAY

Peace Isn't Impossible

from *Newsweek*, June 30, 1997

George J. Mitchell

*In 1997, when he wrote the essay excerpted
here, George J. Mitchell was serving as chair-
man of the peace negotiations in Northern
Ireland. He was nominated for a Nobel Peace
Prize for his work. Since then he has worked
to prevent international crises, including the
violence in the Middle East.*

Is the peace process dead? The question
hangs over Northern Ireland like a heavy
fog, blanketing the land with fear and anxiety.

I may be an incurable optimist, but I believe a historic opportunity to end centuries
of conflict in Northern Ireland still exists. If
it's not seized now, though, it may be years
before we have another chance, and the
failure could cost many lives on both sides.

It's worth pursuing a political settlement

Vocabulary
optimist (äp′tə·mist) *n.:* person who is always
hopeful.

History: The Nobel Peace Prize
The Nobel prizes are awarded annually from
a fund established in 1895 by Swedish industrialist and inventor Alfred Nobel. Originally
awarded in five categories—physics, chemistry, medicine, literature, and promoting
peace—a sixth category, economics, was
added in 1969. In 1998, the Nobel Peace
Prize was awarded to John Hume and David

Trimble, the Catholic and Protestant leaders
who helped bring about a peace agreement
in Northern Ireland. Among other recent
winners of the prize have been the organizations Doctors Without Borders (1999)
and the International Campaign to Ban
Landmines (1997), as well as individuals such
as Mother Teresa and Elie Wiesel.

Small-group activity. Have groups of
students research the achievements of individuals and organizations that have been
awarded the Nobel Peace Prize from 1980
to the present. Have them create a classroom museum exhibit titled "Pioneers for
Peace," with photographs and brief reports
about each winner of the prize.

for one overriding reason: The overwhelming majority of people in Northern Ireland want political stability and reconciliation.[1] To give up now, to succumb[2] to despair and sectarian[3] war, would be to declare that a handful of men of violence are winners and the rest of the people are losers. That's a result I'm not prepared to accept.

During the past two years I've come to know and admire the people of Northern Ireland. They're energetic and productive. They deserve a better life than they've had. Of course, there are those who don't want anything to change, ever. They want to re-create a past that is gone forever. But their way will only guarantee never-ending conflict. It will ensure that the next half century is as full of death and fear as was the past half century. If, on the other hand, we can end the violence and people can live free of fear, then gradually the walls of division will finally come down.

I'm constantly asked by Americans concerned about Northern Ireland, "What can I do?" Here's my answer: The American people, and especially the leaders of the Irish American community, must say clearly and repeatedly that they condemn violence, that they demand its end, that they will not support those who engage in or condone violence. They must say it publicly, loudly, and forcefully. Political violence, from whatever source, is morally

> **It's not too late to negotiate an end to centuries of bloodshed and despair in Northern Ireland.**

wrong. It's counterproductive.[4] It deepens divisions. It increases hatred. It hurts innocent people. It makes peace and reconciliation more difficult to attain. It must end.

After his election, to emphasize its importance, Prime Minister Blair[5] chose Northern Ireland for his first trip outside London. In a speech there he said: "I am ready to make one further effort to proceed with this inclusive talks process.[6] My message to Sinn Fein is clear. The settlement train is leaving. I want you on that train. But it is leaving anyway, and I will not allow it to wait for you. You cannot hold the process to ransom[7] any longer. So end the violence. Now."

So the process must and will move on. Only the outcome is in doubt. Some have said that the political talks are all that's preventing widespread war. But as the participants in those talks know better than anyone, they cannot go on indefinitely. They must either move forward or end in failure. For the people of Northern Ireland, the time for decision is now.

---

4. **counterproductive** (kount′ər · prə · duk′tiv) *adj.*: producing results that are the opposite of what was intended.
5. **Prime Minister Blair:** Tony Blair became Britain's prime minister, or head of the government, when his Labor Party won the British national elections in 1997.
6. **inclusive talks process:** series of discussions that included representatives from all the major groups involved in the conflict.
7. **ransom** (ran′səm) *n.*: money (or another demand) paid to free someone being held prisoner. Here, Blair is saying that the peace process will not be halted by Sinn Fein's threat of violence.

Vocabulary
condone (kən · dōn′) *v.*: overlook or excuse an offense.

---

1. **reconciliation** (rek′ən · sil′ē · ā′shən) *n.*: bringing together to settle a conflict.
2. **succumb** (sə · kum′) *v.*: give in to.
3. **sectarian** (sek · ter′ē · ən) *adj.*: pertaining to a particular religious group.

D Reading Informational Text

? Synthesizing sources. What is the author's purpose for writing this selection? [He wants to persuade the American public that it is possible to negotiate a political settlement that will bring peace to Northern Ireland and to urge those involved to seize the opportunity now before it fades away.]

E Reading Skills

? Identifying cause and effect. According to Senator Mitchell, will ending the violence in Northern Ireland be the cause or the effect of ending the political divisions there? [He says that ending the violence must come first, since only then will people's sense of fear diminish and political divisions fade.]

F Learners Having Difficulty

Reading aloud. Have a volunteer read this passage aloud. Then, ask why Senator Mitchell is opposed to political violence. [He says it is both morally wrong and counterproductive. Instead of helping to solve the problem, political violence makes peace more difficult to attain.]

G Reading Informational Text

? Synthesizing sources. Explain the metaphor used by Prime Minister Tony Blair to express England's viewpoint about the peace process in Northern Ireland. [He says the opportunity to negotiate a peace settlement is like a train getting ready to leave the station: It will be available only for a short time. Sinn Fein must get "on that train" and join the peace process by ending the violence now, or it will be too late.] **Does Senator Mitchell agree or disagree with Prime Minister Blair?** [He agrees with the prime minister.]

Tell students that the process of negotiating a peace settlement often depends on mediation, a process in which two opposing sides in a conflict agree to present their cases to a neutral third party, who then helps the two sides reach a compromise agreement. Tell students that this process is also used to resolve disputes in smaller, more personal cases.

Invite a lawyer or other professional involved in mediating disputes to speak to the class about the principles involved in bringing two opposing sides to an agreement. (In many urban areas, you can find organizations involved in mediation listed under the category "Mediation Services" in the Yellow Pages.)

Analyzing Informational Text

Reading Check

1. In 1920, the British agreed to grant independence to most of Ireland, except for six northern counties, which would remain part of the United Kingdom. Civil war broke out because some Irish citizens wanted to accept the offer, but others were violently opposed to it.

2. Possible answers: Catholics and Protestants go to different schools, and they shop and socialize only in their "own" places of business. Some taxis go only to Catholic or Protestant neighborhoods. Sidewalks are painted different colors to reflect people's loyalties. The names each side uses to refer to parts of Ireland differ according to their loyalties.

3. During a gun battle, Father Murphy was shot and killed in the street while giving last rites to a dying Catholic rebel.

4. He admires them for being energetic and productive, and he believes that most of them want peace.

Answers and Model Rationales

1. **B**   Most of the details in the selection focus on the effects the conflict has on the daily lives of children and adults.

2. **H**   This purpose is stated in the editorial's first paragraph. Although Mitchell quotes Prime Minister Blair, praising him is not his main point, so F is incorrect. Mitchell does not criticize Americans, so G is incorrect. Although Mitchell believes that the time for making peace is short, the pace of the negotiations is not his main point, so J is incorrect.

Analyzing Informational Text

Reading Check

SKILLS FOCUS

Reading Skills
Synthesize ideas from different sources dealing with a single topic.

1. What caused civil war to break out in Ireland in the 1920s, according to "A Country Divided"?

2. Give two examples of how the division between Catholics and Protestants affects daily life, according to "Lives in the Crossfire."

3. Explain what happened to Father Murphy, as Margaret McCrory describes in "Internment."

4. What is George Mitchell's view of the people of Northern Ireland?

Test Practice

1. What is the **main idea** of "Lives in the Crossfire"?
   - **A** Violence is not productive.
   - **B** The Troubles affect the daily life of children, as well as that of adults, in Northern Ireland.
   - **C** Most people in Northern Ireland oppose violence.
   - **D** It is impossible to judge which side is right in the conflict.

2. What is the **purpose** of Mitchell's editorial?
   - **F** To praise Prime Minister Blair's role in the peace talks
   - **G** To criticize Americans for not helping to restore peace in Northern Ireland
   - **H** To urge an end to the violence and the establishment of peace
   - **J** To argue that the peace process is taking too long

3. Which of the following statements comparing "A Country Divided" to "Lives in the Crossfire" is *not* true?
   - **A** Neither author expresses a bias in the selection.
   - **B** Both include facts.
   - **C** Both are secondary sources.
   - **D** Both explain the causes of the conflict.

4. Reading "A Country Divided" helps you understand and evaluate Mitchell's argument in "Peace Isn't Impossible" because it —
   - **F** presents an opposing argument that shows the weaknesses of Mitchell's points
   - **G** provides historical background for Mitchell's argument
   - **H** explains why Tony Blair became Britain's prime minister
   - **J** places blame for the conflict on one side

5. What do you learn from "Internment" that you *don't* learn from any of the other selections?
   - **A** The ways Protestants and Catholics are separated in daily life
   - **B** The feelings and thoughts of a family caught in the conflict
   - **C** How many people have been killed during the conflict
   - **D** The history of the conflict

3. **D**   A, B, and C are all true. But only "A Country Divided" explains the causes of the conflict. The other selection focuses on its effects. Therefore, D is the untrue statement.

4. **G**   The essay is too evenhanded to be F. H is false because Tony Blair isn't mentioned. J is incorrect because blame is placed on both sides of the conflict. The background that the essay provides is useful, so G is correct.

5. **B**   "Internment" is the only primary source among the selections that focuses on the feelings of a family caught in the conflict.

6. Whose viewpoint is *not* represented in the four sources?

   F A member of the Irish Republican Army's

   G A peace negotiator's

   H Prime Minister Tony Blair's

   J A teenager's

7. Which topic is *not* related to the issues raised in these four sources?

   A Growing up in countries torn by war

   B The use of nonviolent protest to create change

   C Irish emigration to other countries in the past forty years

   D Recent changes in the daily life of the average American teenager

8. What **conclusion** can you draw from **synthesizing** the content of the selections?

   F Peace has not been established because no one is trying to achieve it.

   G The long-standing conflict has been deadly, and it has divided the Irish people.

   H The conflict is between political leaders, and it does not affect the lives of citizens.

   J If the conflict doesn't end soon, many Irish will leave the country.

Constructed Response

In a brief essay, **summarize** or **paraphrase** the main ideas in these sources about the conflict in Northern Ireland. Then, **connect** this information about the Troubles to what you may already know about civil wars in other places or times. Finally, draw a **conclusion** by giving your opinion of what future leaders can learn from these struggles.

Vocabulary Development

Word Families: Meet the Relatives

PRACTICE

Most words are members of **word families,** groups of related words that have slightly different forms and that function as different parts of speech.

For each Word Bank word, make a word-family chart like the one here, for *optimist.* Define the Word Bank word, and give its part of speech. Then, use a dictionary for help listing related words, their definitions, and their parts of speech. Write a sentence for each word in the family.

Word Bank

intolerance
negotiations
designate
absorb
reunification
divergent
coerced
abhor
optimist
condone

Word Bank Word	Sentence
optimist *n.:* person who is always hopeful	Senator Mitchell, an <u>optimist</u>, believes that peace is possible.

Related Words	Sentences
optimism *n.:* hopeful or cheerful viewpoint	The captain's <u>optimism</u> lifted my spirits.
optimistic *adj.:* expecting the best outcome	<u>Optimistic</u>, Amy was not discouraged.

SKILLS FOCUS

Vocabulary Skills
Create semantic charts.

---

6. F Students can discover this answer through the process of elimination: "Peace Isn't Impossible" gives the viewpoints of both a peace negotiator and Prime Minister Blair, so G and H are incorrect. "Internment" gives a teenager's point of view, so J is incorrect. Only the viewpoint of the IRA is not represented in the selections.

7. D None of the selections have anything to do with American life, so this topic is clearly not related. A is related to issues raised in "Lives in the Crossfire." B is a topic mentioned in "A Country Divided," and C is related to the plight of the family whose story is told in "Internment."

8. G The death and division caused by the conflict are described in all four selections.

Constructed Response

Students' essays should include main ideas about the conflict and its history. Possible connections include the American Civil War and civil wars in the Balkans and Africa. Conclusions should suggest the futility of war.

Vocabulary Development

Practice

Sample word-family chart:
Word Bank Word—intolerance *n.:* prejudice; hostility to other groups. *Sentence*—<u>Intolerance</u> led to war in Northern Ireland. *Related Words*—tolerant *adj.:* showing respect for other people's ideas and beliefs; tolerate *v.:* allow; bear; endure. *Sentences*—Her parents were <u>tolerant</u>. How long can people <u>tolerate</u> the violence in Northern Ireland?

ASSESSING

Assessment

■ *Holt Assessment: Literature, Reading, and Vocabulary*

RETEACHING

For another selection to teach synthesizing sources, see *The Holt Reader,* Part 2.

Grade-Level Skills

■ **Literary Skills**
Compare and contrast similar themes across genres.

Comparing a Theme Across Genres

Overview

In this feature, students read selections from three different genres that deal with the same subject: the experience of immigrants leaving their countries to make a new home in the United States. The first two selections, "Liberty" and "Exile," are Julia Alvarez's explorations, in fiction and in poetry, of a young girl's experience of leaving her home and coming to the United States. The final selection is a newspaper feature by the columnist Anthony Lewis. Following his story about how a family of Vietnamese immigrants struggled to get to the United States is a Connection feature, a newspaper article about the same family eight years later.

This page introduces the ways in which genre shapes readers' reactions to each selection, how the choice of genre relates to the author's purpose for writing, how genre relates to the theme or main idea, and how the writer uses the characteristics of the particular genre to develop the theme or main idea.

Elements of Literature

Comparing a Theme Across Genres

Giving Form to Theme

Genre—the kind, or type, of literature—shapes our reactions to a work. To understand the role of genre, consider the following questions:

- **How does the choice of genre relate to the author's purpose for writing?** Nonfiction writers want their readers to *think* about issues. Fiction writers usually want readers to *experience* events with certain characters and make some discovery. Poets often want readers to *see* and *feel* something and to gain insight in the process.

- **What is the theme or the main idea, and is it stated or implied?** Authors of nonfiction generally state their main ideas. In fiction and poetry, however, themes are usually implied—you need to examine the works carefully to figure out the themes.

- **How does the writer use the characteristics of the genre to develop the theme or the main idea?** Nonfiction authors usually support their ideas with facts and examples. Fiction writers use literary elements, such as characters and conflict, to develop their themes. Poets use imagery, figurative language, and sound devices.

Examining Theme and Genre

You are about to read a short story, a poem, and a news feature about the experience of immigrants coming to the United States. As you read, ask yourself, "What insight about the immigrant experience does each work convey? How does the choice of genre affect my response to each work?"

Reading Skills

Comparing and Contrasting a Theme Across Genres

After you have read and discussed each work, fill in a chart like the one below to compare how the genre affects the work's theme or main idea. For help stating the theme, re-read the guidelines on pages 208–209. Then, turn to page 268.

SKILLS FOCUS

Pages 244–268 cover
Literary Skills
Understand how genre relates to theme.

Reading Skills
Compare and contrast a theme across genres.

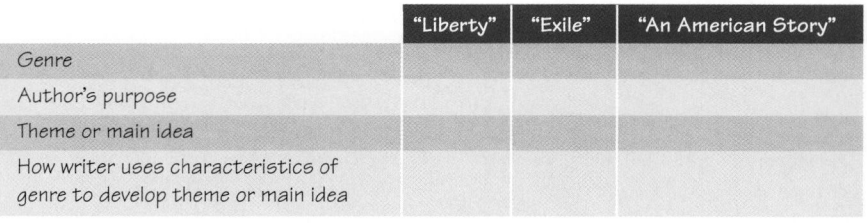

	"Liberty"	"Exile"	"An American Story"
Genre			
Author's purpose			
Theme or main idea			
How writer uses characteristics of genre to develop theme or main idea			

Before You Read

Liberty

Make the Connection

Quickwrite ✏️

Imagine that your family is leaving home because you're all in great danger. You must leave now, and there's no chance of returning. You can take only one special belonging with you. What will it be? List your top three choices. Then, quickwrite about what you'll miss most about your home.

Literary Focus

Theme and Title: Did You Catch My Meaning?

The **title** often gives a clue to a story's **theme,** or central idea. Sometimes the title's meaning may not be clear to you until after you've read the story. Other times, as with "Liberty," the title is a familiar word or expression that brings to mind certain images or associations. By the end of the story, though, the title may take on deeper levels of meaning that help you understand the story's theme.

Reading Skills 📖

Connecting Literature and the News

In recent decades many people have emigrated from the Dominican Republic (Julia Alvarez's birthplace) and other Caribbean and Latin American countries. They've left their homelands because of political oppression, war, or harsh living conditions.

Journalists aren't the only writers who have dealt with this topic. Many fiction writers have based their stories on the actual experiences of emigrants. In

"Liberty," Julia Alvarez tells about one young girl's experience of leaving her home, a story that could appear in today's newspaper. As you read, think about how Alvarez, through the fiction writer's craft, is able to pull us into these events in an intensely personal way. What techniques does she use?

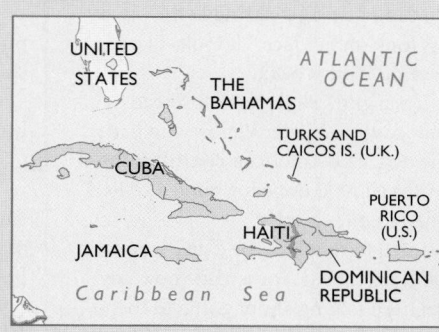

UNITED STATES
ATLANTIC OCEAN
THE BAHAMAS
TURKS AND CAICOS IS. (U.K.)
CUBA
PUERTO RICO (U.S.)
JAMAICA
HAITI
DOMINICAN REPUBLIC
Caribbean Sea

INTERNET

Vocabulary Practice
•
More About Julia Alvarez
•
Keyword: LE5 9-4

Vocabulary Development

elect (ē·lekt′) v.: choose.

hyperactive (hī′pər·ak′tiv) adj.: abnormally active; very lively.

distracted (di·strakt′id) adj.: unable to concentrate on something.

putrid (pyōō′trid) adj.: offensive to the senses; disgusting.

admonitions (ad′mə·nish′ənz) n.: scoldings; warnings.

clenched (klencht) v. used as adj.: tightly closed.

inconsolable (in′kən·sōl′ə·bəl) adj.: unable to be comforted; brokenhearted.

SKILLS FOCUS

Literary Skills
Understand how a story's title relates to its theme.

Reading Skills
Connect literature and the news.

Liberty **245**

Grade-Level Skills

■ **Literary Skills**
Understand how a story's title relates to its theme.

■ **Literary Skills**
Compare and contrast similar themes across genres.

■ **Reading Skills**
Connect literature and the news.

PRETEACHING

Preview Vocabulary

Use these sentences to reinforce students' grasp of the Vocabulary words listed on p. 245.

1. The small child was so _____ that even her sister could not keep up with her. [hyperactive]

2. No _____ to take proper care of the puppy were needed; she fed it every day. [admonitions]

3. When the child's puppy ran away, she was _____, crying incessantly. [inconsolable]

4. When we told her the puppy might not return, she threatened us with a _____ fist. [clenched]

5. Without the puppy she seemed _____ and unable to concentrate on anything. [distracted]

6. She wrinkled her face, as if she had just smelled something _____. [putrid]

7. She did not _____ to get another puppy for a long time. [elect]

Summary ⟷ *at grade level*

Although the story's setting is not named, it is clear that the narrator's family is living in a repressive country and that the father is trying to get visas so the family can immigrate to the United States. The narrator spends much of her time playing with her beloved puppy Liberty. One morning Mami announces that the family will leave for the United States that evening and that each child may pack one toy. The narrator says she wants to bring Liberty, but her mother refuses. Her aunt consoles her by saying that she will find liberty in the United States. In the middle of the night, as the family is waiting to go to the airport, the narrator opens the door to Liberty's pen and tells him to go away. He does not want to leave, and she kicks him until he runs away. She slowly begins to realize what sort of liberty will be waiting for her in the United States.

DIRECT TEACHING

Ⓐ Reading Skills

❓ Connecting literature and the news. How does the family's need for visas connect to real-world events you've read about? [Students should be familiar with news stories about refugees fleeing nations that are experiencing political upheaval. These people often seek visas in order to leave their countries and start a better life elsewhere.]

Ⓑ Literary Focus

Genre and theme. Ask students to summarize the basic situation of the story so far and to think about the theme Alvarez is developing. [Possible response: The main characters are the narrator, Mami, Papi, and the dog; the conflict seems to be between Mami and the others, but there are hints of a larger conflict between the family and the repressive government.]

LIBERTY

Julia Alvarez

Papi came home with a dog whose kind we had never seen before. A black-and-white-speckled electric current of energy. It was a special breed with papers, like a person with a birth certificate. Mami just kept staring at the puppy with a cross look on her face. "It looks like a mess!" she said. "Take it back."

"Mami, it is a gift!" Papi shook his head. It would be an insult to Mister Victor, who had given us the dog. The American consul[1] wanted to thank us for all we'd done for him since he'd been assigned to our country.

Ⓐ "If he wanted to thank us, he'd give us our visas,"[2] Mami grumbled. For a while now, my parents had been talking about going to the United States so Papi could return to school. I couldn't understand why a grown-up who could do whatever he wanted would <u>elect</u> to go back to a place I so much wanted to get out of.

On their faces when they talked of leaving there was a scared look I also couldn't understand.

Ⓑ "Those visas will come soon," Papi promised. But Mami just kept shaking her head about the dog. She had enough with four girls to take on puppies, too. Papi explained that the dog would stay at the end of the yard in a pen. He would not be allowed in the house. He would not be pooping in Mami's orchid garden. He would not be barking until late at night. "A well-behaved

---

1. **American consul:** person appointed by the United States government to represent American interests and provide assistance to Americans living in a foreign country.
2. **visas** (vē′zəz) *n.:* certificates granting official approval to enter a country.

dog," Papi concluded. "An American dog."

The little black-and-white puppy yanked at Papi's trouser cuff with his mouth. "What shall we call you?" Papi asked him.

"Trouble," Mami suggested, kicking the puppy away. He had left Papi's trousers to come slobber on her leg.

"We will call him Liberty. Life, liberty, and the pursuit of happiness." Papi quoted the U.S.A. Constitution. "Eh, Liberty, you are a lucky sign!"

Liberty barked his little toy barks and all us kids laughed. "Trouble." Mami kept shaking her head as she walked away. Liberty trotted behind her as if he agreed that that was the better name for him.

Mami was right, too—Liberty turned out to be trouble. He ate all of Mami's orchids, and that little <u>hyperactive</u> baton of a tail knocked things off the low coffee table whenever Liberty climbed on the couch to leave his footprints in among the flower prints. He tore up Mami's garden looking for buried treasure. Mami screamed at Liberty and stamped her foot. "Perro sin vergüenza!"[3] But Liberty just barked back at her.

"He doesn't understand Spanish," Papi said lamely. "Maybe if you correct him in English, he'll behave better!"

---

3. **"Perro sin vergüenza!"** (per′rô sēn ver·hwen′sä): Spanish for "shameless dog."

Vocabulary
elect (ē·lekt′) *v.:* choose.
hyperactive (hī′pər·ak′tiv) *adj.:* abnormally active; very lively.

DIFFERENTIATING INSTRUCTION

Learners Having Difficulty
Modeling. To help students read "Liberty," model the reading skill of connecting literature and the news. Say to students, "In writing this story, Alvarez drew upon her family's experience of leaving the Dominican Republic because it was run by an oppressive government that limited people's freedom." Encourage students as they read to make connections between the circumstances that cause the narrator's family to leave their country and news reports about circumstances that have led other people to flee their home countries.

English-Language Learners
In order for students to fully understand this story, they must understand the various meanings of the word *liberty*. Tell students

"We will call him Liberty. Life, liberty, and the pursuit of happiness."

that *freedom* is a common synonym for *liberty* and that liberty involves both the freedom to do certain things and the freedom from certain other things. Place students in small groups, and have them brainstorm a list of words and phrases that illustrate and explain what *liberty* means. Students may include specific examples from their own lives. Students should end up with a list including ideas such

as "freedom to act, speak, or think as you please"; "freedom from restriction or control"; "freedom to choose a livelihood"; "freedom to enjoy social, political, and economic rights"; and "freedom from unjust governmental control."

Special Education Students
For lessons designed for special education students and English-language learners, see *Holt Reading Solutions.*

A Literary Focus

❓ Theme and title. So far the story has been about the dog, Liberty, but now Papi is speaking seriously about the concept of liberty. Ask students to paraphrase his statement. [Possible response: To gain freedom, you must be willing to give up something.] **What is Papi sacrificing for liberty?** [Possible responses: the family's ability to continue living in their country; his family's security.] **What theme does Papi's statement suggest?** [Possible response: Liberty is so important that great sacrifices are made willingly.]

B English-Language Learners

Slang and idioms. Invite students to use context clues to guess the meanings of the terms *tomboy* [a girl who acts like a boy], *live wire* [an energetic person], *troublemaker* [someone who continually causes trouble], and *drive Mami to drink* [upset Mami]. You may ask students for similar terms in their first languages.

C Literary Focus

❓ Theme. **What does this passage reveal about Liberty?** [Possible response: He does not like to go into his pen.] **What theme about liberty might the author be developing?** [Possible response: One cannot experience liberty when restricted or confined.]

Mami turned on him, her slipper still in midair. Her face looked as if she'd light into him after she was done with Liberty. "Let him go be a pet in his own country if he wants instructions in English!" In recent weeks, Mami had changed her tune about going to the United States. She wanted to stay in her own country. She didn't want Mister Victor coming around our house and going off into the study with Papi to talk over important things in low, worried voices.

"All liberty involves sacrifice," Papi said in a careful voice. Liberty gave a few perky barks as if he agreed with that.

Mami glared at Papi. "I told you I don't want trouble—" She was going to say more, but her eye fell on me and she stopped herself. "Why aren't you with the others?" she scolded. It was as if I had been the one who had dug up her lily bulbs.

The truth was that after Liberty arrived, I never played with the others. It was as if I had found my double in another species. I had always been the tomboy, the live wire, the troublemaker, the one who was going to drive Mami to drink, the one she was going to give away to the Haitians. While the sisters dressed pretty and stayed clean in the playroom, I was out roaming the world looking for trouble. And now I had found someone to share my adventures.

"I'll take Liberty back to his pen," I offered. There was something I had figured out that Liberty had yet to learn: when to get out of Mami's way.

She didn't say yes and she didn't say no. She seemed distracted, as if something else was on her mind. As I led Liberty away by his collar, I could see her talking to Papi. Suddenly she started to cry, and Papi held her.

"It's okay," I consoled Liberty. "Mami doesn't mean it. She really does love you. She's just nervous." It was what my father always said when Mami scolded me harshly.

At the back of the property stood Liberty's pen—a chain-link fence around a dirt square at the center of which stood a doghouse. Papi had built it when Liberty first came, a cute little house, but then he painted it a putrid green that reminded me of all the vegetables I didn't like. It was always a job to get Liberty to go into that pen.

Sure enough, as soon as he saw where we were headed, he took off, barking, toward the house,

---

Vocabulary

distracted (di·strakt′id) *adj.:* unable to concentrate on something.

putrid (pyoo′trid) *adj.:* offensive to the senses; disgusting.

DEVELOPING FLUENCY

Small-group activity. The sections of the story that include dialogue are excellent portions for students to read aloud. Divide students into three or four groups, and have each group choose a passage of the story that includes dialogue. Have students take parts and practice reading through the passage a number of times, experimenting with different volumes and tones of voice. Have students perform their excerpts for the class.

then swerved to the front yard to our favorite spot. It was a grassy knoll[4] surrounded by a tall hibiscus hedge. At the center stood a tall, shady samán tree. From there, no one could see you up at the house. Whenever I did something wrong, this was where I hid out until the punishment winds blew over. That was where Liberty headed, and I was fast behind on his trail.

Inside the clearing I stopped short. Two strange men in dark glasses were crouched behind the hedge. The fat one had seized Liberty by the collar and was pulling so hard on it that poor Liberty was almost standing on his hind legs. When he saw me, Liberty began to bark, and the man holding him gave him a yank on the collar that made me sick to my stomach. I began to back away, but the other man grabbed my arm. "Not so fast," he said. Two little scared faces—my own—looked down at me from his glasses.

"I came for my dog," I said, on the verge of tears.

"Good thing you found him," the man said. "Give the young lady her dog," he ordered his friend, and then he turned to me. "You haven't seen us, you understand?"

I didn't understand. It was usually I who was the one lying and grown-ups telling me to tell the truth. But I nodded, relieved when the man released my arm and Liberty was back in my hands.

"It's okay, Liberty." I embraced him when I put him back in his pen. He was as sad as I was. We had both had a hard time with Mami, but this was the first time we'd come across mean and scary people. The fat man had almost broken Liberty's neck, and the other one had left his fingerprints on my arm. After I locked up the pen, I watched Liberty wander back slowly to his house and actually go inside, turn around, and stick his little head out the door. He'd always avoided that ugly doghouse before. I walked back to my own house, head down, to find my parents and tell them what I had seen.

---
4. **knoll** (nōl) *n.:* small hill.

Overnight, it seemed, Mister Victor moved in. He ate all his meals with us, stayed 'til late, and when he had to leave, someone from the embassy was left behind "to keep an eye on things." Now, when Papi and Mister Victor talked or when the *tíos*[5] came over, they all went down to the back of the property near Liberty's pen to talk. Mami had found some wires in the study, behind the portrait of Papi's great-grandmother fanning herself with a painted fan. The wires ran behind a screen and then out a window, where there was a little box with lots of other wires coming from different parts of the house.[6]

Mami explained that it was no longer safe to talk in the house about certain things. But the only way you knew what things those were was when Mami leveled her eyes on you as if she were pressing the off button on your mouth. She did this every time I asked her what was going on.

"Nothing," she said stiffly, and then she urged me to go outside and play. Forgotten were the admonitions to go study or I would flunk out of fifth grade. To go take a bath or the *microbios*[7] might kill me. To drink my milk or I would grow up stunted and with no teeth. Mami seemed absent and tense and always in tears. Papi was right—she was too nervous, poor thing.

I myself was enjoying a heyday of liberty. Several times I even got away with having one of Mister Victor's Coca-Colas for breakfast instead of my boiled milk with a beaten egg, which Liberty was able to enjoy instead.

"You love that dog, don't you?" Mister Victor asked me one day. He was standing by the pen with Papi waiting for the uncles. He had a funny

---
5. *tíos* (tē'ôs): Spanish for "uncles."
6. **little box . . . house:** probably a reference to a device used to listen in secretly on conversations in the house.
7. *microbios* (mē·krô'bē·ôs): Spanish for "germs."

Vocabulary
admonitions (ad'mə·nish'ənz) *n.:* scoldings; warnings.

Liberty 249

DIRECT TEACHING

D Vocabulary Development
❓ **Literal and figurative meanings.** Bring students' attention to the word *winds*. Ask for its literal meaning. [moving air] How is Alvarez using the word figuratively? [Possible response: She is characterizing the parents' anger as a figurative wind that blows strongly at first but diminishes over time. The narrator hides until the "punishment winds" blow over and fade away.]

E Reading Skills
❓ **Making inferences.** Based on their appearance and actions, what can you infer about who these men are and what they are doing? [Possible response: They are bodyguards, spies, thieves, or government agents keeping the family under surveillance.]

F Reading Skills
❓ **Identifying cause and effect.** What is the cause of the narrator's "heyday of liberty"? [Her mother is preoccupied and so is not keeping close watch over her daughter's activities.] What are the effects of her liberty? [She gets to go outside and play instead of study. She even sneaks a soda for breakfast and gives Liberty her usual breakfast of boiled milk with an egg.] How do you think the narrator would define *liberty* at this point in the story? [Possible responses: the freedom to do whatever she wants; freedom from parental control.]

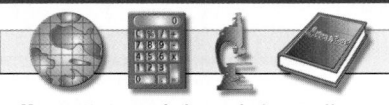

CONTENT-AREA CONNECTIONS

Geography/History: The Dominican Republic
Have a student identify the Dominican Republic on a map or a globe. If any of your students are from the Dominican Republic, invite them to tell the class something about the geography or history of their country.

Small-group activity. Ask small groups of students to choose one aspect of the Dominican Republic's history or geography to research. Have them report their findings to the class.

A Learners Having Difficulty

❓ Questioning. What is happening in this conversation? [Possible response: The men are speaking in code to cover up the real meaning of their conversation, which probably has to do with plans for their escape to the United States.]

B Literary Focus

❓ Genre and theme. What is the major conflict in the story at this point? [an external conflict between the narrator and her mother over what to do with Liberty] How do you think the conflict will be resolved? Explain how the resolution will affect the story's theme. [Possible responses: The narrator will sneak Liberty on the plane, leading to a theme about the importance of acting according to one's own wishes; the narrator will have to leave Liberty behind, contributing to the theme that attaining liberty involves making sacrifices.]

C Reading Skills

❓ Connecting literature and the news. On the basis of your knowledge of current world events, is Mami's "or else" statement realistic? Give examples to explain. [Possible response: Yes, it is realistic; people have been punished in their own countries for political actions and beliefs.]

---

accent that sounded like someone making fun of Spanish when he spoke it.

I ran Liberty through some of the little tricks I had taught him, and Mister Victor laughed. His face was full of freckles—so that it looked as if he and Liberty were kin. I had the impression that God had spilled a lot of his colors when he was making American things.

Soon the uncles arrived and the men set to talking. I wandered into the pen and sat beside Liberty with my back to the house and listened. The men were speaking in English, and I had picked up enough of it at school and in my parents' conversations to make out most of what was being said. They were planning some hunting expedition for a goat with guns to be delivered by Mister Charlie. Papi was going to have to leave the goat to the others because his tennis shoes were missing. Though I understood the words—or thought I did—none of it made sense. I knew my father did not own a pair of tennis shoes, we didn't know a Mister Charlie, and who ever heard of hunting a goat?

As Liberty and I sat there with the sun baking the tops of our heads, I had this sense that the world as I knew it was about to end. The image of the two men in mirror glasses flashed through my head. So as not to think about them, I put my arm around Liberty and buried my face in his neck.

Late one morning Mami gave my sisters and me the news. Our visa had come. Mister Victor had arranged everything, and that very night we were going to the United States of America! Wasn't that wonderful! She flashed us a bright smile, as if someone were taking her picture.

We stood together watching her, alarmed at this performance of happiness when really she looked like she wanted to cry. All morning aunts had been stopping by and planting big kisses on our foreheads and holding our faces in their hands and asking us to promise we would be very good. Until now, we hadn't a clue why they were so worked up.

Mami kept smiling her company smile. She had a little job for each of us to do. There would not be room in our bags for everything. We were to pick the one toy we wanted to take with us to the United States.

I didn't even have to think twice about my choice. It had suddenly dawned on me we were leaving, and that meant leaving *everything* behind. "I want to take Liberty."

Mami started shaking her head no. We could not take a dog into the United States of America. That was not allowed.

"Please," I begged with all my might. "Please, please, Mami, please." Repetition sometimes worked—each time you said the word, it was like giving a little push to the yes that was having a hard time rolling out of her mouth.

"I said no!" The bright smile on Mami's face had grown dimmer and dimmer. "*N–O*." She spelled it out for me in case I was confusing no with another word like yes. "I said a toy, and I mean a toy."

I burst into tears. I was not going to the United States unless I could take Liberty! Mami shook me by the shoulders and asked me between clenched teeth if I didn't understand we had to go to the United States or else. But all I could understand was that a world without Liberty would break my heart. I was inconsolable. Mami began to cry.

Tía[8] Mimi took me aside. She had gone to school in the States and always had her nose in a book. In spite of her poor taste in how to spend her free time, I still loved her because she had smart things to say. Like telling Mami that punishment was not the way to make kids behave. "I'm going to tell you a little secret," she offered

---

8. **tía** (tē′ä): Spanish for "aunt."

Vocabulary

clenched (klencht) *v.* used as *adj.*: tightly closed.

inconsolable (in′kən·sōl′ə·bəl) *adj.*: unable to be comforted; brokenhearted.

Alvarez's own experience of leaving her home prompted her to write this story. Have students seek out and interview members of their family or community who came to the United States from another country. Have students tell the class about one of their interviewees' experiences of immigration. Make sure that students have gotten permission to share the stories of their interviewees.

Developing Word-Attack Skills
Write the words *count* and *country* on the chalkboard. Have students read the words and tell what is alike and different about them. Help them recognize that the letters that spell *count* also appear in the word *country*, but the vowel sound in *count* is not heard in *country*. Point out that *count* and *country* illustrate two

common sounds for the *ou* spelling: the sound /ou/ as in *count* and /u/ as in *country*. Then, write the words *should* and *shoulder* on the chalkboard, and have students compare the spellings and pronunciations. Help them recognize that *should* rhymes with *good* and *wood*. The vowel sound is /oo/ and the *l* is silent. In *shoulder*, *ou* stands for /ō/ and the *l* is pronounced.

now. "You're going to find liberty when you get to the United States."

"Really?" I asked.

She hesitated a minute, and then she gave me a quick nod. "You'll see what I mean," she said. And then, giving me a pat on the butt, she added, "Come on, let's go pack. How about taking that wonderful book I got you on the Arabian Nights?"

Late in the night someone comes in and shakes us awake. "It's time!"

Half asleep, we put on our clothes, hands helping our arms to go into the right sleeves, buttoning us up, running a comb through our hair.

We were put to sleep hours earlier because the plane had not come in.

But now it's time.

"Go sit by the door," we are ordered, as the hands, the many hands that now seem to be in control, finish with us. We file out of the bedroom, one by one, and go sit on the bench where packages are set down when Mami comes in from shopping. There is much rushing around. Mister Victor comes by and pats us on the head like dogs. "We'll have to wait a few more minutes," he says.

In that wait, one sister has to go to the bathroom. Another wants a drink of water. I am left sitting with my baby sister, who is dozing with her head on my shoulder. I lay her head down on the bench and slip out.

Through the dark patio down the path to the back of the yard I go. Every now and then a strange figure flashes by. I have said good-bye to Liberty a dozen times already, but there is something else I have left to do.

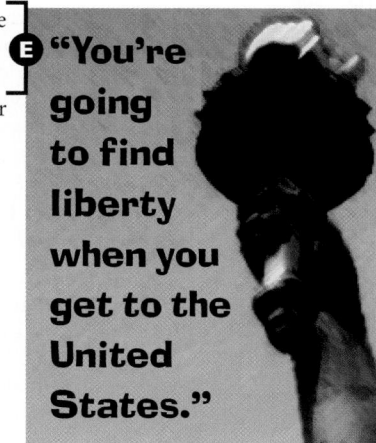

"You're going to find liberty when you get to the United States."

Sitting on the bench, I had an image again of those two men in mirror glasses. After we are gone, they come onto the property. They smash the picture of Papi's great-grandmother fanning herself. They knock over the things on the coffee table as if they don't know any better. They throw the flowered cushions on the floor. They smash the windows. And then they come to the back of the property and they find Liberty.

Quickly, because I hear calling from the big house, I slip open the door of the pen. Liberty is all over me, wagging his tail so it beats against my legs, jumping up and licking my face.

"Get away!" I order sharply, in a voice he is not used to hearing from me. I begin walking back to the house, not looking around so as not to encourage him. I want him to run away before the gangsters come.

He doesn't understand and keeps following me. Finally I have to resort to Mami's techniques. I kick him, softly at first, but then, when he keeps tagging behind me, I kick him hard. He whimpers and dashes away toward the front yard, disappearing in areas of darkness, then reappearing when he passes through lighted areas. At the front of the house, instead of turning toward our secret place, he keeps on going straight down the drive, through the big gates, to the world out there.

He will beat me to the United States is what I am thinking as I head back to the house. I will find Liberty there, like Tía Mimi says. But I already sense it is a different kind of liberty my aunt means. All I can do is hope that when we come back—as Mami has promised we will— my Liberty will be waiting for me here. ∎

Liberty 251

Write the word *coupon* on the chalkboard, and read it aloud. Explain that *coupon* was originally a French word, and in words of French origin, the letters *ou* stand for /o͞o/, as in *cool*.
Activity. Display these pairs of words. Have students read the words and tell if *ou* stands for the same sound [s] or different sounds [d] in the words.

1. found
   foundation [s]
2. double
   doubt [d]
3. coupe
   couple [d]
4. boulder
   boudoir [d]
5. crouch
   crouton [d]
6. bounty
   county [s]
7. poultry
   pouch [d]
8. trouble
   enough [s]

Monitoring students' progress.
Guide the class in answering these comprehension questions. Direct students to locate passages in the text that support their responses.

True-False

1. The story is about a young girl and a dog named Trouble. [F]
2. The narrator's mother doesn't want to leave her home. [T]
3. Government agents wearing sunglasses are watching the narrator's family. [T]
4. Government agents arrest the family and force them to go into exile in the United States. [F]
5. Before she leaves, the narrator frees the dog from his pen and drives him away. [T]

Meet the Writer

Background. Although the setting of "Liberty" is not named, it probably takes place in the Dominican Republic. Julia Alvarez lived there until her family was forced into exile because of her father's opposition to the dictator Rafael Trujillo. During Trujillo's reign (1930–1961), people had few civil liberties, and the secret police suppressed all opposition.

Julia Alvarez says, "I am a Dominican, hyphen, American. As a fiction writer, I find that the most exciting things happen in the realm of that hyphen, the place where two worlds collide or blend together." Have students discuss what they think Alvarez means by this statement. Then, have students research the life story of a famous Asian-American, Hispanic-American, Irish-American, or any other "hyphenated American" and present a biographical sketch to the class, focusing on, as Alvarez puts it, "the realm of the hyphen"—the influence the person's ethnicity had on his or her life.

Meet the Writer

Julia Alvarez

"Magic Happened in My Life"

When Julia Alvarez (1950–   ) says, "I write stories for different reasons," she means it. Like the girl in "Liberty," she knows political terror and exile firsthand, for her family fled from the Dominican Republic when she was ten. Alvarez says she "can't shut up" about important human events. One of her novels, *In the Time of the Butterflies* (1994), is based on the true story of the 1960 murders of the three Mirabal sisters, wives of political prisoners in her homeland.

Some of her fiction, she says, is "like cupping my hands around a moth" to save it, and some stories she writes to keep her heart from breaking.

❝I think of myself at ten years old, newly arrived in this country, feeling out of place, feeling that I would never belong in this

world. . . . And then, magic happened in my life. . . . An English teacher asked us to write little stories about ourselves. I began to put into words some of what my life had been like in the Dominican Republic. Stories about my gang of cousins and the smell of mangoes and the iridescent, vibrating green of hummingbirds. Since it was my own little world I was making with words, I could put what I wanted in it. . . . I could save what I didn't want to lose—memories and smells and sounds, things too precious to put anywhere else. ❞

Julia Alvarez teaches English at Middlebury College in Vermont, yet having two cultures and two languages is central to her world and writing. Two novels—*How the García Girls Lost Their Accents* (1991) and *¡Yo!* (1997)—follow four sisters who grow up in America speaking Spanglish, a mixture of Spanish and English.

❝No matter what my motive is when I begin, I end up understanding myself and the world around me much better. I think that's why I like being a writer: With each revision, the world gets clearer and, ironically, though writing is so solitary, people get closer, more real. ❞

For Independent Reading

What was it really like for Julia Alvarez to find herself suddenly living in a new country—and in a new culture? To find out, read her essays in *Something to Declare*.

For additional information about Julia Alvarez, see Meet the Writer, page 258.

Response and Analysis

Reading Check

1. Sketch a map that shows the story's **setting.** Include the following elements: (a) the house, (b) the dog pen, (c) the grassy knoll and hedge, and (d) the drive and big gates. Then, make a map legend, identifying the important **events** that occur at each location.

Thinking Critically

2. What is really happening in this story? Read between the lines (the hidden wires, the American consul's visits, and so on), and explain the family's situation.

3. The narrator says about Liberty, "It was as if I had found my double in another species." Describe the narrator's **character.** What traits does she share with Liberty? Why does she identify with her dog?

4. The word *liberty* is central to this story. You first encounter *liberty* in the **title,** but it is also the dog's name and a central concept throughout the story. Explain how the story's **theme,** or insight about life, relates to liberty.

5. Which elements of "Liberty" are characteristic of a short story as opposed to a news report? How would the account of the narrator's experiences be different if it appeared in a newspaper?

Extending and Evaluating

6. What is your opinion of the writer's decision to tell this story from a child's point of view? Would the story be less effective or more effective if it were told from the point of view of the mother or the father? Explain.

WRITING

Leaving It All Behind

Whether you love where you live or long to be somewhere different, moving is a jolt. As you load the last box, see the rooms suddenly bare, and take one last look at your neighborhood, memories flood in. If you've ever moved, you know how it feels to ache for the familiar. If you haven't, look around. What would break your heart to leave behind? Expand your Quickwrite notes, and in a few paragraphs, describe your thoughts about leaving it all behind.

Newcomers to America

The United States was built—and continues to be built—by immigrants. How do the media cover stories about people immigrating to this country today? Write a few paragraphs **comparing** and **contrasting** reports from two different news media—a newspaper, the Internet, TV, or the radio, for example. Consider the focus and purpose of each report as well as the way in which information is presented.

▶ **Use "Comparing Media Coverage," pages 270–277, for help with this assignment.**

SKILLS FOCUS

Literary Skills
Analyze how a story's title relates to its theme.

Reading Skills
Connect literature and the news.

Writing Skills
Write a reflective essay. Compare reports from different news media.

Group being sworn in as citizens of the United States.

Liberty   253

Response and Analysis

Thinking Critically

2. Possible answers: The family is in trouble with the government; they are being spied upon and may be in danger.

3. Possible answers: Like Liberty, the narrator is lively, curious, strong-willed, and playful. She identifies with her dog because they are so similar and perhaps also because they both raise Mami's ire.

4. Possible answer: The story's theme relates to the preciousness of liberty and the sacrifices people make to gain it. The family makes the sacrifice of leaving their home, and the narrator makes the sacrifice of leaving her dog behind so that he too can have liberty.

5. Possible answers: The story's first-person point of view, emotional tone, characters and their motivations, plot and its conflicts, and overall theme are characteristic of a short story. If the narrator's experiences appeared as a news report, the point of view would be third person, the tone would be matter-of-fact, and the content would be drier and factual.

Extending and Evaluating

6. Possible answer: Telling the story from a child's point of view makes it more effective because it creates dramatic irony in which the reader knows more than the narrator, thus creating tension and making the story more compelling and poignant.

Reading Check
Legend

1. Possible map:

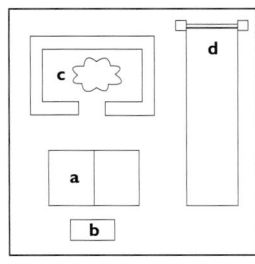

a) *house*—surveillance wires discovered; narrator learns she can't take Liberty to the United States.

b) *dog pen*—narrator overhears plans of Papi, Mister Victor, and uncles; narrator frees Liberty and kicks him.

c) *grassy knoll and hedge*—Two strangers grab Liberty and the narrator.

d) *the drive and big gates*—Liberty leaves through gates; family drives out to leave for the United States.

Vocabulary Development

Possible Answers

- *elect.* See *choose. Synonyms*—select; pick.
- *hyperactive.* See *overactive. Synonyms*—hyper; frenetic; hyperkinetic.
- *distracted.* See *inattentive. Synonyms*—unmindful; indifferent.
- *putrid.* See *terrible. Synonyms*—atrocious; disgusting; repulsive.
- *clenched.* See *hold. Synonyms*—grasp; grip; cling.
- *inconsolable.* See *disconsolate. Synonyms*—heartsick; comfortless. See *sorrowful. Synonyms*—anguished; grievous.

Grammar Link

Practice

Possible Answers

1. Papi brought home a puppy, and the dog caused a lot of trouble.

2. When I spotted Liberty and the strange man with sunglasses, Liberty looked frightened.

3. Because the sisters were leaving for America, all morning their aunts stopped by to kiss them.

4. Tía Mimi, who said she had a secret, also told me that Mami was upset.

Vocabulary Development

Using a Thesaurus to Find Synonyms

A **synonym** is a word that has the same, or nearly the same, meaning as another word. To find synonyms, writers use a **thesaurus.** Most thesauri list synonyms based on a word's different shades of meaning. Follow the cross-references given until you find the exact meaning you want to convey.

This chart shows how one student used a thesaurus to find synonyms for *admonitions.* Make a thesaurus chart for the other words in the Word Bank.

> **Word Bank**
>
> elect
> hyperactive
> distracted
> putrid
> admonitions
> clenched
> inconsolable

Grammar Link

Making Pronouns Clear

Inexact pronoun reference, a common mistake, causes misunderstandings. *You* always know whom you're referring to when you use *he, she,* or *they,* but your readers may have someone else in mind.

A **pronoun** should refer clearly to its **antecedent** (the noun or pronoun to which a pronoun refers). Avoid unclear, or **ambiguous,** pronoun references. These occur when a pronoun can refer to either of two antecedents. Usually you can pin down your meaning by replacing the pronoun with the noun to which it refers.

UNCLEAR
Papi and Mister Victor are fluent in two languages, but <u>he</u> speaks Spanish with an accent.

CLEAR
Papi and Mister Victor are fluent in two languages, but <u>Mister Victor</u> speaks Spanish with an accent.

CLEAR
Papi and Mister Victor, <u>who speaks</u> Spanish with an accent, are fluent in two languages.

PRACTICE

Reword the following sentences to correct the inexact pronoun references:

1. Papi brought home a puppy, and he caused a lot of trouble.

2. When I spotted Liberty and the strange man with the sunglasses, he looked frightened.

3. All morning, aunts stopped by to kiss the sisters because they were leaving for America.

4. Tía Mimi said that Mami was upset, and she had a secret.

▶ **For more help, see Clear Pronoun Reference, 4i, in the Language Handbook.**

SKILLS FOCUS

Vocabulary Skills
Use a thesaurus to find synonyms.

Grammar Skills
Use clear pronoun references.

ASSESSING

Assessment

- *Holt Assessment: Literature, Reading, and Vocabulary*

RETEACHING

For another selection to teach comparing themes, see *The Holt Reader,* Collection 4.

Before You Read

Exile

Make the Connection

Quickwrite ✏️

Think about the word *exile,* and brainstorm for a few minutes about the images it calls to mind. Imagine that you have been exiled from something precious to you: a beloved place or a particular group of people. Write a few sentences about what that experience would be like.

Literary Focus

Narrative Poetry: Telling a Story Poetically

A **narrative poem** tells a story in poetic form. It has the elements of a story—a narrator, characters, a plot, and usually a setting—but it also has the characteristics of poetry. It relies heavily on imagery and figures of speech to touch your emotions and capture your imagination.

As you read the narrative poem "Exile," notice the various story elements as well as the parallels to Alvarez's short story "Liberty" (page 246). Then, think about how the poem differs from the story—or from any short story.

Theme: Comparisons Say It All

Poems, like short stories, have **themes,** or central ideas. Since poets have much less space to develop their themes than short story writers do, poets often use **metaphors** and **similes,** comparisons that connect two unlike things in an imaginative way, to help express their ideas. As you read "Exile," think about the larger meaning that swimming and a trip to the beach have. How do these comparisons help Alvarez convey the meaning of her poem?

Background

Julia Alvarez's family left their home in the Dominican Republic in 1960 because her father had become involved in a plot to overthrow Rafael Trujillo, the Dominican dictator. After Trujillo seized power in his country in 1930, the Dominican people lost many of their rights, and his opponents were frequently murdered. "Exile" begins with the speaker's family fleeing the capital city, Ciudad Trujillo (syōō′däd′ trōō·hē′yô), or Trujillo City, named in honor of the dictator in 1936. The city's original name, Santo Domingo, was restored after Trujillo was assassinated, in 1961.

The Tower of Homage, a fort that is several centuries old, stands in Santo Domingo, Dominican Republic.

INTERNET
More About Julia Alvarez
Keyword: LE5 9-4

SKILLS FOCUS

Literary Skills
Understand the characteristics of narrative poetry, including theme. Identify metaphors and similes.

Grade-Level Skills
■ **Literary Skills**
Understand how genre and theme relate in a narrative poem.

Review Skills
■ **Literary Skills**
Identify the literary devices (such as metaphor and simile) that define a writer's style.

Summary 🔁 *at grade level*

In this narrative poem the speaker is a young girl who tells the story of the night her family fled their country. She then narrates some of their experiences and feelings in the first weeks of their new life in the United States. On the evening they fled, the speaker remembers her father explaining that they were going to the beach. She knows this is not true but goes along with it and finds herself floating away—to the airport. She knows there is danger but "swims" on anyway. A few weeks after the family arrives in the United States, the speaker and her father stop at a department store window to admire a display of mannequins outfitted for the beach. The speaker imagines their own reflected faces in the window as the faces of swimmers just before plunging in—"eager, afraid, not yet sure of the outcome."

Exile **255**

Skills Starter

Build prerequisite skills. Remind students that a narrative poem tells a story in a poetic way, using imagery and figures of speech. You might mention "Paul Revere's Ride" or "Casey at the Bat" as examples of narrative poems that students may have read.

DIRECT TEACHING

A Literary Focus

Narrative poetry. Remind students that narrative poetry uses many of the same literary elements as fiction, including setting, character, and plot. Ask students what they know so far about the setting, the two main characters, and the plot. [*Setting*—Ciudad Trujillo and New York City in 1960; *Characters*—the speaker and Papi (her father); *Plot*—The speaker and her father have to leave their home country.]

B Literary Focus

❓ Simile and theme. What two things is the speaker comparing in this simile? [Her arms and Jesus' arms on the cross.] **How does the comparison contribute to the poem's theme?** [Possible response: One must learn to accept one's fate, as the speaker accepts her exile and as Jesus accepted his crucifixion.]

Exile

Julia Alvarez

Ciudad Trujillo, New York City, 1960

A The night we fled the country, Papi,
you told me we were going to the beach,
hurried me to get dressed along with the others,
while posted at a window, you looked out

5 at a curfew-darkened Ciudad Trujillo,
speaking in worried whispers to your brothers,
which car to take, who'd be willing to drive it,
what explanation to give should we be discovered . . .

On the way to the beach, you added, eyeing me.
10 The uncles fell in, chuckling phony chuckles,
What a good time she'll have learning to swim!
Back in my sisters' room Mami was packing

a hurried bag, allowing one toy apiece,
her red eyes belying° her explanation:
15 *a week at the beach so Papi can get some rest.*
She dressed us in our best dresses, party shoes.

Something was off, I knew, but I was young
and didn't think adult things could go wrong.
So as we quietly filed out of the house
20 we wouldn't see again for another decade,

B I let myself lie back in the deep waters,
my arms out like Jesus' on His cross,
and instead of sinking down as I'd always done,
magically, that night, I could stay up,

---
14. **belying** (bē·lī′iŋ) *v.* used as *adj.*: showing to be untrue.

DIFFERENTIATING INSTRUCTION

Learners Having Difficulty
Some students may need help identifying and understanding the basic situation of the poem. Point out that the main characters, setting, and plot are very similar to those of "Liberty." Explain that this poem's time frame is larger than that of "Liberty," as part of it takes place later in New York City.

English-Language Learners
Make sure students understand that all the references to swimming are metaphoric— they refer to something else. You may explain that in the speaker's home country, everything came to her naturally. In her new country, she will have to "learn to swim"— that is, learn new ways of living, speaking, and getting along.

Special Education Students
For lessons designed for special education students, see *Holt Reading Solutions.*

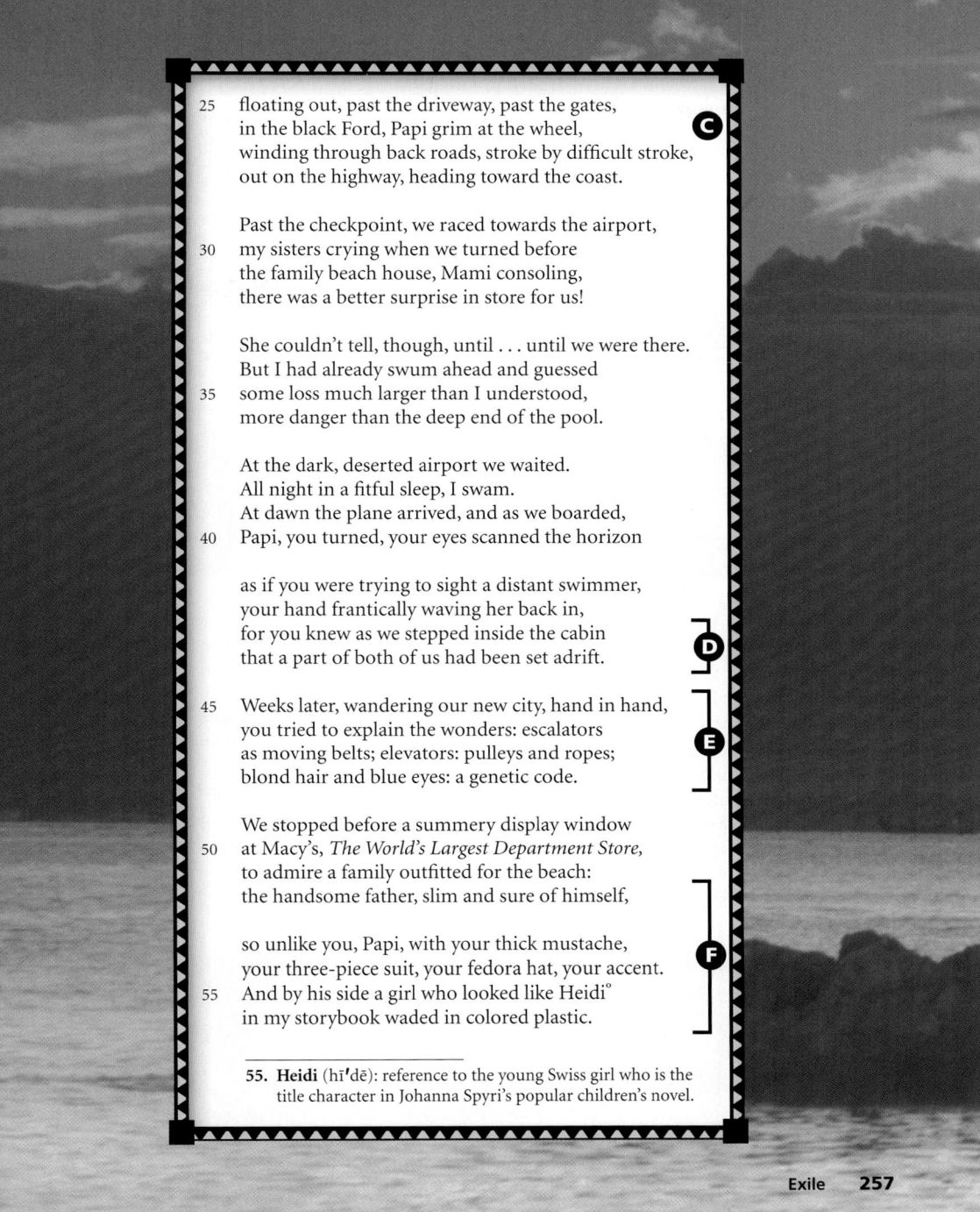

25 floating out, past the driveway, past the gates,
in the black Ford, Papi grim at the wheel,
winding through back roads, stroke by difficult stroke,
out on the highway, heading toward the coast.

Past the checkpoint, we raced towards the airport,
30 my sisters crying when we turned before
the family beach house, Mami consoling,
there was a better surprise in store for us!

She couldn't tell, though, until . . . until we were there.
But I had already swum ahead and guessed
35 some loss much larger than I understood,
more danger than the deep end of the pool.

At the dark, deserted airport we waited.
All night in a fitful sleep, I swam.
At dawn the plane arrived, and as we boarded,
40 Papi, you turned, your eyes scanned the horizon

as if you were trying to sight a distant swimmer,
your hand frantically waving her back in,
for you knew as we stepped inside the cabin
that a part of both of us had been set adrift.

45 Weeks later, wandering our new city, hand in hand,
you tried to explain the wonders: escalators
as moving belts; elevators: pulleys and ropes;
blond hair and blue eyes: a genetic code.

We stopped before a summery display window
50 at Macy's, *The World's Largest Department Store*,
to admire a family outfitted for the beach:
the handsome father, slim and sure of himself,

so unlike you, Papi, with your thick mustache,
your three-piece suit, your fedora hat, your accent.
55 And by his side a girl who looked like Heidi°
in my storybook waded in colored plastic.

55. **Heidi** (hī′dē): reference to the young Swiss girl who is the
title character in Johanna Spyri's popular children's novel.

Exile   257

C Vocabulary Development

? Connotative meanings.
How might the connotation of this description have changed if the author had used the synonym *somber* for *grim*? [Possible response: Both words imply seriousness, but *somber* has a sad connotation; *grim* implies seriousness of purpose, not sadness or dejection.]

D Literary Focus

? Narrative poetry. Remind students that a narrative poem narrates something—that is, it tells a story. Summarize the story so far. [Possible response: A young girl and her family have just escaped from a repressive government and are about to fly to another country.]

E Learners Having Difficulty

? Finding details. Make sure students understand the shift in setting. Where is the family now? [New York City] What are some of the new things they see? [escalators, elevators, and blond hair and blue eyes]

F Reading Skills

? Comparing and contrasting. How is the mannequin family in the window different from the speaker's family? [The mannequin father is slim, confident, and dressed for the beach, while the narrator's father is formally dressed and has a thick mustache. The mannequin girl is blond while the narrator probably has dark hair.]

Advanced Learners
Enrichment. Point out Alvarez's water imagery. You may assign students to research the symbolism of water in ancient civilizations, religious traditions, Freudian and Jungian thought, and the visual arts and poetry. [Students may discover that water is symbolic of dissolution, or death, and, at the same time, of renovation, regeneration, and rebirth. It also represents the unconscious.]
Activity. Have students write an analysis of the water imagery and its symbolism in this poem. The essay should conclude with ways in which Alvarez's use of water contributes to the poem's theme.

A Literary Focus

Comparing a theme across genres. Ask students to compare Alvarez's main theme here with her theme in "Liberty." [Possible responses: In "Liberty," Alvarez examines the sacrifices that must be made to attain freedom; in "Exile," she conveys the risks and uncertainties of choosing to live in exile.]

GUIDED PRACTICE

Monitoring students' progress. Divide students into small groups. Have each group work on a chart showing similarities and differences in the settings, characters, and plots of "Liberty" and "Exile." As the groups work, monitor their progress. Finished charts can be presented to the class.

For Independent Reading
Books of poetry by Alvarez include *Homecoming: New and Collected Poems* and *The Other Side / El Otro Lado*.

We stood awhile, marveling at America,
both of us trying hard to feel luckier
than we felt, both of us pointing out
60   the beach pails, the shovels, the sandcastles

no wave would ever topple, the red and blue boats.
And when we backed away, we saw our reflections
superimposed,° big-eyed, dressed too formally
with all due respect as visitors to this country.

65   Or like, Papi, two swimmers looking down
at the quiet surface of our island waters,
seeing their faces right before plunging in,
eager, afraid, not yet sure of the outcome.

---

63. superimposed (sōō′per·im·pōzd′) *v.* used as *adj.*: put on top of something else.

Meet the Writer

Julia Alvarez

At Home with Words

Julia Alvarez (1950–   ) explains that she began writing as a way of acquiring a new "homeland" after her family fled from the Dominican Republic when she was ten to settle in the United States. She comments, "English, not the United States, was where I landed and sunk deep roots." As a college student she began writing seriously—and began winning awards for her poetry too. Nurturing a love of poetry in others, she has conducted poetry workshops for schoolchildren, prisoners, and senior citizens, in addition to teaching creative writing to college students.

Alvarez says of her younger self:

" I realized that I had lost the island we had come from, but . . . I had discovered an even better world: the one words can create in a story or poem. **"**

Response and Analysis

Reading Check

1. **Summarize** the story told in this poem by filling out a **story map** like the one here:

"Exile"
Narrator:
Main characters:
Settings:
Narrator's problem:
Main events:

2. Is the speaker telling about recent events or ones that happened many years ago? Support your answer with details from the poem.

Thinking Critically

3. How would you describe the relationship between the speaker and Papi?

4. The idea of a trip to the beach grows in meaning throughout the poem. As the family flees, what is associated with the idea of going to the beach?

5. Using a **metaphor**, the speaker compares the beach scene displayed in the store window to America (line 57). Why does the scene represent America for her?

6. Once in the United States, the speaker refers to herself and her father as "visitors to this country" (line 64). What details in the poem help convey the sense that they don't fit in?

7. In the last four lines of the poem, the speaker says that she and Papi are like "two swimmers . . . / eager, afraid, not yet sure of the outcome." What is she really saying through the use of this **simile**? What feelings is she expressing?

8. How would you state the **theme** of this poem—that is, what point is the speaker making about her experience of immigrating to the United States?

9. In what ways are the story "Liberty" and the poem "Exile" different? Consider
   - events covered
   - **setting(s)**
   - what narrator/speaker knows
   - **tone** or **mood**

Extending and Evaluating

10. Why might Alvarez have chosen to write about fleeing her home in two genres—a story and a poem? Do the story and the poem affect you differently? Explain.

WRITING

Papi's Version

Write a **poem, letter,** or **journal entry** from the point of view of Papi, the speaker's father. Have him set down his thoughts and feelings about his family's move to the United States. You may want to focus on Papi's thoughts about the speaker. Is he concerned about her safety as well as her reactions to being exiled? How does he feel when he looks in the department-store window? Check your Quickwrite notes for help capturing Papi's experience of being exiled.

SKILLS FOCUS

Literary Skills
Analyze the characteristics of narrative poetry, including theme. Analyze metaphors and similes.

Writing Skills
Write a poem, letter, or journal entry from a character's point of view.

Exile   **259**

Reading Check

1. Possible story map:
   Narrator—a young girl. *Main characters*—Narrator and her father. *Setting*—Ciudad Trujillo and New York City in 1960. *Narrator's problem*—coping with leaving her home and learning to live in a new place. *Main events*—family packs at night for a "trip to the beach"; family drives through back roads to the airport and leaves their homeland; in the United States, they explore their new city and gaze at mannequins dressed for the beach behind a store window, feeling out of place and uncertain.

2. The events happened years ago. *Support*— "I was young and didn't think adult things could go wrong"; "we quietly filed out of the house we wouldn't see again for another decade."

Response and Analysis

Thinking Critically

3. Possible answer: They have a close and loving relationship.

4. At first, a trip to the beach seems like an ordinary, fun activity. It then becomes a metaphor for the uncertainty of going into exile.

5. Possible answer: The scene represents an American ideal.

6. Possible answers: They do not have blond hair and blue eyes; they dress formally and have foreign accents.

7. Possible answer: So much about their new life is unknown. The speaker is expressing the mixed feelings they have about their adopted home.

8. Possible answer: The condition of exile is complex, with feelings of fear and loss competing with eagerness for a better life.

9. Possible answers: "Liberty" covers the weeks before the family flees; its setting is the family home; the narrator knows only as much as a ten-year-old can know; the tone is light until the very end. "Exile" covers the evening of the family's flight and their first experiences of life in the United States; its setting is Ciudad Trujillo and New York City; the speaker is an adult who knows all the nuances of the exile; the tone is sober.

Extending and Evaluating

10. Possible answers: The two genres allow Alvarez to express two aspects of the immigrant experience. Poetry allows her to focus on the emotional aspect, and fiction allows her to convey her belief in liberty. Some students will identify more with the swimming imagery of the poem while others will identify with the losses in the story.

Vocabulary Development

Practice

Possible Answers

2. *Eyeing* indicates that Papi was looking at her with special intent.

3. *Phony* conveys that the speaker is aware that the uncles are putting on a show to protect the children from knowing the danger of the situation.

4. *Filed* brings to mind an orderly exit one by one. Filing out of a building carries a connotation of responding to an emergency drill.

5. *Wandering* suggests aimlessness. People who wander are not sure of where they are or where they want to go.

6. Unlike *diving*, *plunging* includes the idea that one enters something suddenly or forcibly. There is also the sense that once entered, there is no going back; one has "taken the plunge."

ASSESSING

Assessment

■ *Holt Assessment: Literature, Reading, and Vocabulary*

RETEACHING

For another selection to teach comparing themes, see *The Holt Reader*, Collection 4.

Denotation and Connotation: Word Pictures

A word's **denotation** is its strict dictionary definition. A word's **connotations** are the feelings and associations that the word suggests. Take, for example, the word *fled* at the beginning of Alvarez's poem "Exile": "The night we fled the country . . ." The denotation of *fled*—its literal meaning—is "ran away; escaped from danger."

Why is *fled* a better word to use in this line than the synonym *ran away*? The phrase *running away* can be used in many different contexts, and it calls to mind a wide range of images or associations. For example, an untamed horse might run away from a ranch, or a person might run away from responsibility. *Fled*, on the other hand, has much more emotional power. Its connotations are more specific and include fear, panic, and confusion—associations that deepen our response to the speaker's experience.

Denotations are **objective.** They are not based on someone's individual opinions and experiences. In contrast, connotations are **subjective**—they are based on personal thoughts and feelings—and may vary from individual to individual. Over time your own associations with a word may change. For instance, the word *fled* may have new connotations for you now that you have read "Exile."

PRACTICE

Vocabulary Skills
Identify denotations and connotations.

For help thinking about why Alvarez used each of the underlined words rather than a synonym in the lines from "Exile" in the right column, answer the following questions about connotations. The first item is completed for you as an example.

1. "while <u>posted</u> at a window, you looked <u>out</u>" (line 4)

    What images do you associate with *posted* that you would not associate with *standing* if it were used in this line instead?

    Answer: *Posted makes me think of a guard or soldier who is responsible for protecting others from danger.*

2. "*On the way to the beach,* you added, <u>eyeing</u> me." (line 9)

    In this line, what does *eyeing* tell you about Papi that the phrase *looking at* would not?

3. "The uncles fell in, chuckling <u>phony</u> chuckles," (line 10)

    What connotations does *phony* have that *false* does not?

4. "So as we quietly <u>filed</u> out of the house" (line 19)

    What connotations does *filed* have that *walked* does not? What do you associate with the action of filing out of a building?

5. "Weeks later, <u>wandering</u> our new city, hand in hand," (line 45)

    What connotations does *wandering* have that *exploring* does not? When you think of people wandering, what images come to mind?

6. "seeing their faces right before <u>plunging</u> in," (line 67)

    What connotations does *plunging* have that *diving* would not have in this line?

Before You Read

An American Story

Make the Connection

Quickwrite

Countries, like people, have complex identities based on many factors, such as culture, traditions, values, and history. Think about the title "An American Story." How would you describe America's identity? What do you think of when you hear something described as American? Jot down your thoughts about these questions.

Literary Focus

The News Feature: Read All About It

In **news reports,** journalists present information—facts, statistics, statements by other people—in a straightforward style. In **news features,** journalists also present information, but they give their reports a personal slant by including their own views and by writing in an individual style. A news feature provides a unique perspective on a current or past event. The writer's choice of subject says, in effect, "I could write about anything in the world, but I chose to write about this particular subject. Find out why."

As you read the following news feature, think about why Anthony Lewis chose to write about Viet Dinh and his family, refugees from Vietnam. What is Lewis's personal perspective in the article? What is his **main idea?**

Reading Skills

Distinguishing Between Fact and Opinion

A **fact** is something that can be proved true. An **opinion** is a personal belief or judgment that can be supported but not proved. Facts are definite, but opinions can differ greatly.

Newspapers include both fact-based and opinion-based writing. News reports are strictly factual, telling the *who, what, when, where, why,* and *how* of a particular event. Most other writing that appears in newspapers, such as editorials and movie reviews, mixes fact and opinion. As you read this news feature, fill out a two-column chart. In one column, list the main facts, and in the other, list opinions.

Facts	Opinions

Background

During the Vietnam War, which began in the 1950s and ended in 1975, South Vietnam and the United States tried unsuccessfully to prevent the Communists of North Vietnam from taking over South Vietnam.

After the war, hundreds of thousands of South Vietnamese sought escape from Vietnam—from communism and from "reeducation" camps in which political opponents were imprisoned and at times tortured or executed. Fleeing the country in small boats, many of the "boat people" perished at sea. Survivors reaching new lands were often turned away by foreign governments or confined to refugee camps that were little better than prisons. "An American Story" tells about the plight of one family of boat people.

SKILLS FOCUS

Literary Skills Understand characteristics of news features, including the main idea.

Reading Skills Distinguish between fact and opinion.

SKILLS FOCUS, pp. 261–268

Grade-Level Skills

■ **Literary Skills**
Understand characteristics of news features, including the main idea.

■ **Literary Skills**
Compare and contrast similar themes across genres.

■ **Reading Skills**
Distinguish between fact and opinion.

Summary *at grade level*

Journalist Anthony Lewis writes about the Dinh family's escape from Communist Vietnam, the hardships they endured, and the struggle to reunite the family. Lewis says that he received an essay from Viet Dinh in 1991, describing his sister and nephew's plight in a refugee camp in Hong Kong. Viet Dinh's essay was published in the op-ed section of *The New York Times,* and soon after, his sister and her son joined the family in Portland. Lewis then describes the careers of the family members. To this point, Lewis's article is factual, telling the *who, what, when, where, why,* and *how* of the story. In the two paragraphs before the final one, Lewis reveals why he chose to write about the Dinh family. Using the Dinhs as a model, Lewis argues that America is enriched by immigrants and urges Americans to continue accepting them. He supports his opinion with one last factual paragraph, revealing that Viet Dinh has graduated from Harvard Law School and will soon clerk for the U.S. Supreme Court.

RESOURCES: READING

Planning
■ *One-Stop Planner* CD-ROM with ExamView Test Generator

Differentiating Instruction
■ *Holt Reading Solutions*
■ *Supporting Instruction in Spanish*
■ *Audio CD Library, Selections and Summaries in Spanish*

Assessment
■ *Holt Assessment: Literature, Reading, and Vocabulary*
■ *One-Stop Planner* CD-ROM with ExamView Test Generator
■ *Holt Online Assessment*

Internet
■ go.hrw.com (Keyword: LE5 9-4)
■ *Elements of Literature Online*

Media
■ *Audio CD Library*
■ *Audio CD Library, Selections and Summaries in Spanish*

Build prerequisite skills. Remind students that genre influences how an author conveys his or her theme or main idea. Review how Alvarez uses literary elements such as plot, character, setting, and figurative language to convey her themes about immigration in fiction and poetry. Point out that this nonfiction selection instead uses facts and examples to convey its main idea, which is also about immigration.

DIRECT TEACHING

A Literary Focus

The news feature. Point out that this selection begins as a typical news report—with a lead paragraph laying out the *5W-How?* questions of good news reporting. Ask students to identify the *who, what, when, where,* and *why* of this news feature. [*Who* is Viet Dinh and his family; *what* is their immigration; *when* is Thanksgiving of 1978; *where* is the United States; *why* is because the family were refugees from Vietnam; *how* is with little money. The paragraph doesn't say exactly how they arrived, but it does state that they came with few resources (for example, they had to spend their few dollars on clothing for a colder climate), which suggests that they came under duress.]

B Learners Having Difficulty

Using graphic aids. Have students sketch the Dinh family and label each person with their name and relationship to Viet Dinh. As they continue reading, students may add professions to the labels. You may also suggest that students trace or copy the map on p. 263 onto a separate piece of paper and use it as a graphic aid to trace the family's journey from Vietnam to Malaysia and the sister's journey from Vietnam to Hong Kong.

AN AMERICAN STORY

The family was reunited after fifteen years.

Anthony Lewis

Vietnamese boat people rescued by the cargo ship *Medicins du Monde.*

Patrick Barviel/Gamma Liaison.

Fifteen years ago this Thanksgiving weekend,[1] a ten-year-old Vietnamese boy named Viet Dinh arrived in this country as a refugee. He was with his mother, four sisters, and a brother. They had two hundred dollars, which they spent on used winter coats.

They were boat people. They had left Vietnam on a small fishing boat, which lost its engine in a storm. They drifted for days until they made it to Malaysia—swimming in at night to avoid patrol boats that had fired at them. After months in a refugee camp, they were cleared for admission to the United States and flown to Portland, Oregon.

Two members of the family were left behind in Vietnam: Viet Dinh's father, Phong Dinh, and his older sister Van Dinh, who was twenty then. She stayed behind to help their father.

Phong Dinh had been a city councilman in Vung Tau during the Saigon regime.[2] When the Communists took over in 1975, he was sent to a reeducation camp. He escaped from the camp on June 12, 1978, and was on the run when his wife and six children left.

Over the next five years, Phong Dinh tried unsuccessfully twenty-five times to get out of Vietnam by boat. He paid boatmen who never turned up or who were arrested. Finally, in 1983, he made it to the Philippines, and then to the United States.

That left the oldest child, Van Dinh. She had helped her father pay the boatmen. But it was six years before she managed to leave herself: on a boat that reached Hong Kong in August 1989.

---

1. **Fifteen years . . . weekend:** November 1978.

2. **Saigon regime:** period of time when the anti-Communist government of South Vietnam, based in the capital city of Saigon, was in power.

DIFFERENTIATING INSTRUCTION

Learners Having Difficulty
Modeling. To help students read "An American Story," model the reading skill of distinguishing between fact and opinion. Say, "Often people think that everything they read in a newspaper is factual. But in news features, the author presents both facts and opinions.

To distinguish between the two, ask yourself, 'Can this point be proven true, or is it just a feeling or thought?'" Encourage students as they read to be on the lookout for the writer's opinions and to decide for themselves if the writer's examples and facts support his or her opinions.

The family here knew that she had left Vietnam because they got a message to that effect. But for a year they did not know she was in a Hong Kong refugee camp; indeed, they did not know whether she had landed anywhere or had gone down at sea, as many boat people had.

Van Dinh was kept in the locked Hong Kong camp for three years, waiting for clearance[3] as a refugee. With her was her five-year-old son, Quan, who had a congenital heart condition.[4] That made her desperate to reach the United States, but for years she could not even get an interview with those in charge of the refugee process in Hong Kong.

At the end of 1991, Viet Dinh, then twenty-three years old, sent me an essay he had written about his sister Van's plight in Hong Kong. I forwarded it to *The New York Times* op-ed[5] page, and the editors published it in January 1992.

Last month I had another letter from Viet Dinh. It had good news about his sister. After his op-ed piece was published, other papers picked up the story. The Hong Kong authorities, feeling the pressure, finally interviewed Van Dinh—and found that she was entitled to refugee status. In September 1992, she made it to Portland. The family was reunited after fifteen years.

There is more to tell about the Dinh family, as I learned when I interviewed Viet. His parents are running a small grocery in Salem, Oregon.

---

3. **clearance** (klir′əns) *n.:* official, especially governmental, approval; in this case, permission to be released from the refugee camp.
4. **congenital heart condition:** serious heart problem that a person is born with.

5. **op-ed:** opposite the editorial (page). In a newspaper a page featuring columns and articles expressing opinions and observations.

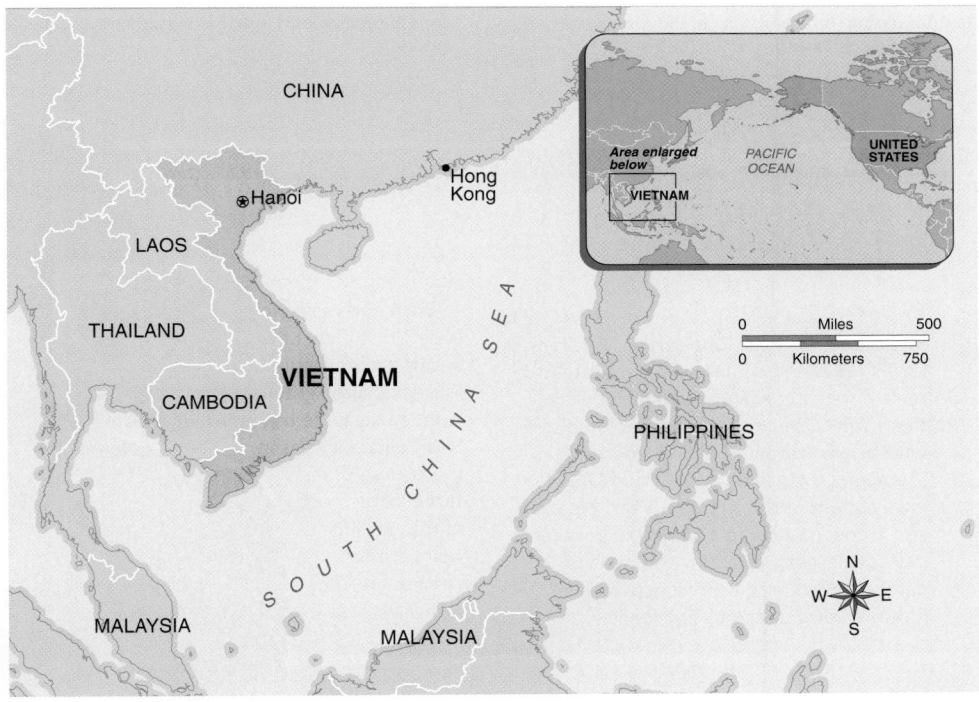

C **Reading Skills**

❓ **Identifying cause and effect.** Why did Viet Dinh write to Anthony Lewis at *The New York Times*? [Possible response: He was concerned about his sister and her child and wanted to publicize the fact that they were stuck in a Hong Kong refugee camp.] **What effect did this letter have?** [The publicity worked, and Hong Kong authorities gave Van Dinh refugee status, allowing her to join her family in Portland.]

English-Language Learners
For lessons designed for intermediate and advanced English-language learners, see *Holt Reading Solutions*.

Special Education Students
For lessons designed for special education students, see *Holt Reading Solutions*.

A Reading Skills

? Distinguishing between fact and opinion. Elicit from students that, so far, this news feature has been factual. Now, however, Lewis offers some opinions. What opinions does Lewis put forward in this passage? [Possible responses: This is an American story; the Dinh family is doing exactly what immigrants on the Lower East Side did; there is no other country that has taken so many people from so many places as the United States has; there is no other country that has gained so much from immigrants; to turn away immigrants would damage the United States.]

B Literary Focus

? Genre and main idea. What is Lewis's main idea? [Possible response: Immigrants enrich this country, and the nation should welcome them.] What example and facts does Lewis offer in his final paragraph to support his opinions in the preceding paragraphs? [To support his opinion that the United States has much to gain from immigrants, Lewis gives the example of Viet Dinh and the fact that he has graduated from Harvard Law School and will soon be clerking for a U.S. Supreme Court justice.]

C Literary Focus

? Comparing a theme across genres. Why do you think Alvarez and Lewis chose to convey their themes in a particular genre? [Possible responses: Alvarez chose fiction to convey an insight into life—the sacrifices that must be made to attain liberty; she chose poetry to convey the intense feelings of going into and living in exile; Lewis chose nonfiction to examine the issue of immigration and to make the point that the great majority of immigrants are strong, determined, and hardworking people who should be welcomed into the United States.]

A sister, Anh, helps them. Another sister, Thu, is an accountant. Kathleen and Leanne are computer programmers. Viet's one brother, Bao, is an architect.

The child with the heart condition, Van's son Quan, has been treated in Portland. He is doing fine.

Van herself, after fourteen months in the United States, is studying at a community college in Salem and working as an assembler in an electronics plant. "After she gets her English and cultural skills together," Viet said, "I think she'd like to open a business."

It is an American story, and one that I wish members of Congress and their constituents[6] who are fulminating[7] these days about "the immigrant threat" would think about. The Dinh family is doing exactly what immigrants on the Lower East Side[8] and so many other places did in past years: struggling for themselves and making this country better.

There is no other country that has taken in so many people from so many places and cultures, and gained so much in the process. To turn away from that tradition now would do the United States great damage.

One more thing about Viet Dinh. His recent letter ended: "I graduated from the Harvard Law School in June and am now a law clerk[9] for Judge Laurence H. Silberman of the U.S. Court of Appeals in Washington. Next year I clerk for Justice Sandra Day O'Connor at the Supreme Court." ■

—from *The New York Times*,
November 26, 1993

---

6. **constituents** (kən·stich′o͞o·ənts) *n.:* people represented by a particular elected official.
7. **fulminating** (ful′mə·nāt′iŋ) *v.:* shouting or expressing criticisms.
8. **Lower East Side:** area in New York City that was home to European immigrants, especially Germans and eastern Europeans, in the late nineteenth and early twentieth centuries.
9. **law clerk:** assistant to a judge or attorney. Clerking for a Supreme Court justice is a greatly respected position.

Meet the Writer

Anthony Lewis

A Strong Voice

In the course of his long career, Anthony Lewis (1927–   ) has never hesitated to raise his strong voice and express views that might anger others. As a columnist who briefly reported from Hanoi, in Vietnam, Lewis sharply criticized U.S. involvement in the Vietnam War. He has also frequently taken a stance to protect individual rights, including the right of defendants to legal representation even if they cannot afford to pay for it.

Born and raised in New York City, Lewis became a professional journalist after graduating from college. He has won two Pulitzer Prizes in the course of his career. For most of the last fifty years, he has written for *The New York Times*.

264 Collection 4 Comparing Themes • Synthesizing Sources

Ex-Refugee Is Nominated for Justice Post

Dena Bunis *and* Anh Do

WASHINGTON— Viet Dinh wiped tears from his eyes as a United States senator chronicled his remarkable journey from a 10-year-old fleeing Vietnam in a boat to a law professor facing a congressional panel Wednesday as a nominee for assistant attorney general.

For a young Dinh and his family it was the point of no return. They had fled Vietnam by boat in 1978. After 12 days with no food or water, they landed in a port in Malaysia, where they were met by gunfire and cast back into the South China Sea.

That night they swam ashore, sure their boat could not withstand another sea voyage. Dinh's mother, Nguyen, stayed aboard and, "wielding an ax that was almost as tall as she was," put a hole in the side of the boat to sink it so they would not be forced back to sea, Dinh said.

"That image of my mother destroying our last link to Vietnam really stands in my mind to this day as to the courage she possesses, but also the incredible lengths which my parents, like so many other people, have gone to in order to find that promise of freedom and opportunity."

D "This is a spectacular American story," Senator Pete Domenici said Wednesday as he introduced Dinh. "You've got a Vietnamese scholar who just 23 years ago was a young man out on a boat at sea who could just as well have drowned, and we never would have heard from him. But because of a loving

family around him, they eventually ended up American citizens."

As Domenici talked, Dinh's parents—who split their time between Garden Grove and Salem, Oregon—sat proudly next to their son. Dinh's lower lip quivered as he fought the emotion of the moment.

His journey and the patriotism for his new country came flooding back, he said, as he heard Domenici's words.

For many in the Vietnamese legal community in Orange County, Dinh is viewed as a trailblazer and risk taker.

"With his achievements, he puts the idea that a Vietnamese-American can be successful in law and on a national level," said Hao-Nhien Vu, a Garden Grove lawyer. If confirmed, Dinh will be the highest-ranking Vietnamese-American legal official in the nation. "A lot of people will be watching what he does and learning from his example."

Dinh says he's not looking beyond his new job.

E "It will be in the public service," Dinh said. "I am really enamored by the institutions of government. They protect the most precious aspect of America, the promise of opportunity and freedom.

"Even when I was in the refugee camp, I knew the value of this promise."

—from *The Orange County Register,* May 10, 2001

Viet Dinh's nomination as assistant attorney general was overwhelmingly confirmed by the Senate in May 2001.

Summary ⬌ *at grade level*

Eight years after Anthony Lewis wrote the preceding news feature, this newspaper article appeared, reporting on Viet Dinh's nomination for assistant attorney general of the United States. The article begins by describing Viet Dinh's emotional response to hearing U.S. Senator Pete Domenici tell the Dinh family's harrowing story. That story includes some new details, such as the twelve days the family went without food and water and the mother destroying their little boat with an ax. Dinh says he wants to be in public service because the institutions of government protect America's promise of freedom and opportunity.

DIRECT TEACHING

D Reading Skills

❓ **Identifying the main idea.** Senator Domenici uses the same words that Lewis used in his article to describe the Dinh family's story. What do you think Senator Domenici meant by an "American story"? [Possible response: the rags to riches story in which a poor, frightened boy comes to the United States and through hard work and perseverance ends up as a role model for others.] **Is this the same American story that Lewis had in mind?** [Possible response: Yes, in part, Lewis's American story is about immigrants struggling for themselves and in doing so making this country better.]

E Reading Skills

Distinguishing between fact and opinion. Have students identify the opinions in this newspaper article and state who holds these opinions and whether they agree or disagree with them. [Opinions include Domenici saying, "This is a spectacular American story," and Dinh saying that "the institutions of government . . . protect . . . the promise of opportunity and freedom."]

Connecting and Comparing Texts

Ask students to identify the *5W-How?* questions of this newspaper article. [*Who* is Viet Dinh; *what* is his nomination for assistant attorney general of the United States; *where* is Washington, D.C.; *when* is May 10, 2001; *why* is because Dinh is about to become the highest-ranking Vietnamese American legal official in the nation; *how* is with great emotion and dignity.] **Then, ask students what the main idea of this report is and how it is similar to or different**

from the main idea in Lewis's article. [Possible response: The main idea is that Viet Dinh, a once-penniless refugee, is about to become a high-ranking government official, proving that Dinh's adopted country is a land of freedom and opportunity. In other words, immigration to the United States is a good thing for immigrants— which is slightly different in emphasis from the main idea in Lewis's story, which is that immigration is a good thing for the United States.]

Response and Analysis

Reading Check

1. Viet Dinh is ten years old when his family leaves Vietnam in a small boat. The boat loses its engine, patrol boats fire at the boat, the family reaches a refugee camp in Malaysia and finally makes it to Portland, Oregon.

2. The Communists had sent Phong Dinh to a reeducation camp.

3. The publicity surrounding Viet Dinh's essay in *The New York Times* led to Hong Kong officials granting Van Dinh refugee status.

Thinking Critically

4. The Dinh family is selfless, loving, tightly knit, hardworking, and persevering.

5. Possible answer: Their history is the story of so many immigrants who overcame difficulties, worked hard, and made their lives and the United States better.

6. Opinions include the Dinh family's story is "an American story"; the family did exactly what immigrants on the Lower East Side did; no other country takes so many people in; to not accept immigrants would damage the United States. The facts of the Dinh family's struggle provide support for the first two opinions.

7. Possible answer: Immigrants are hardworking, caring people who make the United States stronger.

8. America represents freedom and opportunity to Viet Dinh and his family. America is associated with different things for Alvarez's narrators. For the narrator in "Liberty," America represents a place where liberty is waiting

---

Response and Analysis

Reading Check

1. Briefly summarize the key events in Viet Dinh's struggle to reach America. How old was he when he arrived in this country?

2. Why didn't Phong Dinh leave Vietnam when Viet and other members of the family fled the country?

3. Why was Van Dinh finally allowed to come to the United States?

Thinking Critically

4. How would you **characterize** the Dinh family? Think in particular about Viet Dinh, Phong Dinh, and Van Dinh. What qualities are revealed by their actions and goals?

5. Lewis states that the history of the Dinh family is "an American story." What makes the story typically American? (Be sure to check your Quickwrite notes.)

6. What **opinions** does the article express? Which **facts** provide the strongest support for these opinions?

7. In your own words, state the **theme**, or **main idea**, about immigrants that Lewis expresses in this news feature.

8. What does America represent for Viet Dinh and his family? Is America associated with similar or different things in "Liberty" and "Exile"? Explain.

9. In "Ex-Refugee Is Nominated for Justice Post" (see the *Connection* on page 265), Viet Dinh is presented as a role model. Based on your reading of the article and "An American Story," what do you think makes Viet Dinh a good example for other people?

SKILLS FOCUS

Literary Skills
Analyze characteristics of news features, including the main idea.

Reading Skills
Distinguish between fact and opinion.

Writing Skills
Retell a news feature in another genre. Support an opinion.

Extending and Evaluating

10. Do you find Lewis's article effective and his opinions convincing? Explain why or why not.

11. Lewis's news feature is filled with **details** that leave vivid impressions in the mind of the reader. Which details had the greatest impact on you? Why?

WRITING

From Fact to Fiction

Retell part of Viet Dinh's family experience in **another genre**—a poem, song, journal entry, or short story, for example. For help getting started, think about the characteristics of the new genre. Then, decide what you need to add—or what you need to leave out—in order to tell about the experience in a new form.

In My Opinion

The United States is made up of people from many different countries and cultures, as Anthony Lewis points out. Look around your school and community, or think about our country as a whole. How have we benefited from the influence of people from many parts of the world? Write one or two paragraphs in which you explain the benefits you've observed. Remember to include details.

> **Comparing Themes**
> For a writing assignment comparing the themes in "Liberty," "Exile," and "An American Story," see page 268.

---

for her. In "Exile," the speaker views the United States with a mixture of eagerness and apprehension.

9. Possible answers: He is hardworking and persevering; he cares deeply for people; he is devoted to protecting freedom in his adopted country.

Extending and Evaluating

10. Most students will find the article effective because Lewis supports his opinions with the compelling facts of the Dinh family's struggle and success.

11. Answers may include the many repeated attempts of the father to escape, the fact that Viet Dinh wrote to *The New York Times* to help his sister, and that it took fifteen years for the family to be reunited.

Vocabulary Development

Word Origins: Borrowed Words

PRACTICE

Just as the United States is made up of people from all over the world, the English language contains many words that have come from foreign lands. For example, the words *refugee* and *regime* (in "An American Story") come from the French words *réfugié* and *régime*.

> **Word:** *parachute*
> **Language of origin:** *French*
> **Definition:** *device made out of cloth, used to slow the fall of an object from a great height*
> **What you associate with the word:** *safety; excitement; danger*

The words in the following list also come to English from other languages. For each word in the list, use a dictionary for help making a chart like the one for parachute.

- kindergarten
- pajamas
- patio
- plaza
- rodeo
- souvenir
- tea
- umbrella
- yacht

Grammar Link

Commas: Keeping Things Tidy

Commas keep words from running into one another like bumper cars. Here are some comma rules used in "An American Story":

1. Use commas to separate three or more items in a series.

   "He was with his mother, four sisters, and a brother."

2. When writing a date, separate the day of the month from the year with a comma. Use another comma to separate the year from the rest of the sentence.

   "He escaped from the camp on June 12, 1978, and was on the run when his wife and six children left."

   If only the month and year are given, don't separate them with a comma.

   "But it was six years before she managed to leave herself: on a boat that reached Hong Kong in August 1989."

3. Use a comma to separate the name of a city and a state or country. If the sentence continues, separate the name of the state or country from the rest of the sentence with a comma.

   "His parents are running a small grocery in Salem, Oregon."

PRACTICE

Rewrite each sentence, adding commas where necessary.

1. This article was originally published on November 26 1993.

2. Viet Dinh's father his mother and Anh all work in Salem Oregon.

3. Immigrants have made new homes in Oregon New York and other states.

4. Van Dinh arrived in Portland Oregon in September 1992.

> **For more help, see Commas, 12f–l, in the Language Handbook.**

SKILLS FOCUS

Vocabulary Skills
Identify word origins of English words from foreign languages.

Grammar Skills
Use commas correctly in a series; in dates; and with cities, states, and countries.

Vocabulary Development

Practice
Possible Answers

- *Word*—kindergarten. *Origin*—German. *Definition*—a school for young children.
- *Word*—pajamas. *Origin*—Hindi. *Definition*—clothing worn for sleeping.
- *Word*—patio. *Origin*—Spanish. *Definition*—an outdoor area near a house.
- *Word*—plaza. *Origin*—Spanish. *Definition*—a public square.
- *Word*—rodeo. *Origin*—Spanish. *Definition*—an exhibition of the skills of cowhands.
- *Word*—souvenir. *Origin*—French. *Definition*—a token of remembrance or memento.
- *Word*—tea. *Origin*—Chinese. *Definition*—dried leaves from which a beverage is made.
- *Word*—umbrella. *Origin*—Italian. *Definition*—something that protects one from the rain.
- *Word*—yacht. *Origin*—Dutch. *Definition*—a private boat for recreation.

Grammar Link

Practice

1. This article was originally published on November 26, 1993.

2. Viet Dinh's father, his mother, and Anh all work in Salem, Oregon.

3. Immigrants have made new homes in Oregon, New York, and other states.

4. Van Dinh arrived in Portland, Oregon, in September 1992.

ASSESSING

Assessment
- *Holt Assessment: Literature, Reading, and Vocabulary*

RETEACHING

For another selection to teach comparing themes, see *The Holt Reader,* Collection 4.

Comparing a Theme Across Genres

Writing Tips

Before students begin to write their essays, encourage them to freewrite about the ways in which genre shaped their reactions to each selection. Then, have them take their ideas and arrange them using the point-by-point structure. As students write their essays, remind them to elaborate on every general statement they make, supporting it with examples, details, facts, or quotations from the selections. Finally, encourage students to work on their thesis statement after they have completed their first draft of the essay.

Writing a Comparison–Contrast Essay

Comparing a Theme Across Genres

Now that you have read "Liberty," "Exile," and "An American Story," you are ready to write a comparison-contrast essay discussing how a similar topic is treated in three genres. When you write a **comparison-contrast essay,** you look for similarities (comparisons) and differences (contrasts) between the works.

Gather and Organize Your Information

The chart on page 244 that you created to show how genre shapes the theme or the main idea in each of the three selections will give you the basic information you need for your essay.

Your points in a comparison-contrast essay can be organized in two ways. For this essay, you will use the **point-by-point method.** (The **block method** was covered on page 230.)

The Point-by-Point Method

When you use the point-by-point method, you organize your essay by *ideas,* not by works (as you do in the block method). You discuss each idea, or element, in turn. The chart at the right gives an example.

Use Three-Part Structure

Use a three-part structure for your comparison-contrast essay:

- **introduction**—including background and a **thesis statement** briefly explaining how genre shapes content in the works

- **body**—including separate paragraphs for each element

- **conclusion**—summing up and adding a new thought or personal insight

Revise Your Essay

The following questions will help you revise your essay:

- Does the thesis statement clearly state the point of the essay?

- Is a point about an element in Work 1 followed by points about that element in Work 2 and Work 3?

- Have you developed and elaborated on each point?

- Is the conclusion clear and effective?

▶ **For more help writing a comparison-contrast essay, see pages 270–277.**

SKILLS FOCUS

Literary Skills
Compare and contrast a theme across genres.

Writing Skills
Write a comparison-contrast essay.

Point-by-Point Method
Element 1: How Genre Relates to Author's Purpose
Work 1: "Liberty" Work 2: "Exile" Work 3: "An American Story"
Element 2: Theme / Main Idea and Whether Stated or Implied
Work 1: "Liberty" Work 2: "Exile" Work 3: "An American Story"
Element 3: Genre Characteristics Used to Develop Theme / Main Idea
Work 1: "Liberty" Work 2: "Exile" Work 3: "An American Story"

DIFFERENTIATING INSTRUCTION

Advanced Learners
Enrichment. For a fuller discussion of question 10 on p. 266, you may wish to have students debate the issue of immigration.
Activity. Divide advanced learners into two groups. One team will support Lewis's main idea that immigration is good for the United States. The other team will support the idea that immigration weakens America. Each side should gather facts and examples to support their stance, and then teams should debate the issue.

READ ON: FOR INDEPENDENT READING

FICTION

A Family Divided

To live in North Korea in 1945 is to live in a world seemingly without springtime, where each day is as grim and forbidding as winter. It is the year that the Japanese military occupies Pyongyang and begins to tear families apart, including ten-year-old Sookan's. *Year of Impossible Goodbyes* by Sook Nyul Choi is the story of one fiercely determined family that does everything in its power to be reunited, even in the face of great danger.

NONFICTION

Difficult Days

All of the Uchida family's dreams about life in California have come true: Their two daughters, Yoshiko and Keiko, enjoy all the riches of America. Their lives are happy in every respect—until that day in 1941 when Yoshiko comes home from the library and finds an eerie silence in her house. Her father is gone—sent away to an army internment camp—and the rest of her family, along with hundreds of other innocent Japanese Americans, soon joins him. Yoshiko Uchida's *Desert Exile: The Uprooting of a Japanese-American Family* is a powerful true account of a shameful chapter in our nation's history.

FICTION

Head of His Tribe

Okonkwo seems to have it all—wealth, privilege, and status within his Nigerian village. Then, in the blink of an eye, everything changes, and Okonkwo is separated from his family and sent into exile for seven years. Will his village and its tribal customs be the same when he returns? Will his family accept him? You'll find surprising answers to these questions in Chinua Achebe's classic novel *Things Fall Apart.*

This title is available in the HRW Library.

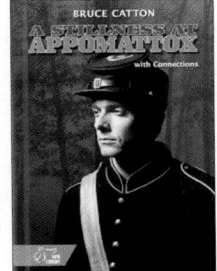

NONFICTION

The Last Great Battle

The author Bruce Catton, known for his true tales of the Civil War, considered himself more of a storyteller than a historian. You'll see why when you read his book *A Stillness at Appomattox.* Written with freshness and dramatic flair, this is a history that takes you into the hearts and minds of those who fought in the last and most devastating year of the Civil War. You'll hear the stories of hard-bitten generals and brave young soldiers, many of whom meet at the final, fateful battle at Appomattox.

This title is available in the HRW Library.

Read On

For Independent Reading

If students enjoyed the themes and topics explored in this collection, you might recommend these titles for independent reading.

Assessment Options

The following projects can help you evaluate and assess your students' outside reading. Videotapes or audiotapes of completed projects may be included in student portfolios.

- **Compare themes.** Have students write an essay comparing the theme of *The Year of Impossible Goodbyes* or *Things Fall Apart* to the theme of one of the short stories in Collection 4. Encourage them to explain how the development of a theme in the genre of the novel differs from the development of a theme in a short story.

- **Adapt to a different genre.** Have students write a short story, poem, or news feature based on the events or the theme of the book they read. Students who write a poem may use the poem "Exile" by Julia Alvarez as a model.

- **Make a time line.** Have students make a time line showing the most important events described in *A Stillness at Appomattox* or *Desert Exile: The Uprooting of a Japanese-American Family.*

DIFFERENTIATING INSTRUCTION

Estimated Word Counts and Reading Levels of Read On Books:

Fiction			Nonfiction		
Year of Impossible Goodbyes	⬇	55,900	*Desert Exile: The Uprooting of a Japanese-American Family*	⬌	55,200
Things Fall Apart	⬆	70,900	*A Stillness at Appomattox*	⬌	158,800

KEY: ⬆ *above grade level*   ⬌ *at grade level*   ⬇ *below grade level*

270 Collection 4 Comparing Themes • Synthesizing Sources

PRETEACHING

Skills Starter

Motivate. Have students write down three details from a news story that they have read or heard that stirred their emotions. Then, discuss with students the following: Should a news story be presented in a way designed to stir the emotions? Why or why not? [Some students may respond that viewers pay more attention to the news when a story pulls them in emotionally. Other students may say that journalists should remain as objective as possible and not rely on emotional appeal.]

CORRECTING MISCONCEPTIONS

Remind students that the purpose of a comparison-contrast essay is to inform, not to persuade. Explain that comparisons and contrasts should be supported with facts, examples, and other details rather than with opinions. To fulfill this informative purpose, students should maintain objectivity throughout their essays.

DIRECT TEACHING

Compare and Contrast Coverage

If students express a desire to locate Internet news sites on their own, keep in mind that Internet resources are sometimes public forums, and their content can be unpredictable.

Comparing Media Coverage

Writing Assignment Write an essay in which you compare and contrast the coverage of a single news event by two different news media.

Suppose that the event depicted in Liam O'Flaherty's "The Sniper" actually happened last week, and you saw media coverage of it—twice. The first report was on the nightly news of a major television network, and the second report you read on the Internet. The two stories were not the same, though. One was short and dramatic. The other contained more information and interviews from several people. Why, you wonder, are two reports on the same event so different?

Prewriting

Select a News Event

Topping the News Tonight As you search for a news story for your essay, look for major national and international events—it's likely you'll find more coverage about them. Watch a national news program or read a national newspaper first to select an event. Then, survey other media, such as magazines, radio programs, and Internet sites, to find additional coverage of the event. Pick an event that's interesting to you; you'll be spending a lot of time thinking about it.

Compare and Contrast Coverage

Two Horses, Different Colors The basic purpose of all responsible news organizations is to communicate information about current events, yet no two media report a news event the same way. Every news story is shaped and limited by the technology and traditions of the medium itself, as well as by the writers, editors, directors, and producers involved in creating the story.

For example, while a network news story might use dramatic video and audio to involve the viewer emotionally, the story will probably last less than a minute. Internet news, on the other hand, is usually more complex. An Internet news site can engage a viewer for a longer amount of time by allowing the viewer to move back and forth through text, audio clips, and images and to link to additional information related to the news story. By comparing how different media present the same story, you can see how different kinds of editorial decisions come across to readers, listeners, or viewers.

Answer the questions in the chart on the next page to compare the coverage of one event by two news media. Each of the boldface terms can be a specific **point of comparison** for your essay.

SKILLS FOCUS

Writing Skills
Write an essay comparing and contrasting the ways in which different news media cover the same event.

COLLECTION 4 RESOURCES: WRITING

Planning
- *One-Stop Planner* CD-ROM with ExamView Test Generator

Differentiating Instruction
- *Workshop Resources: Writing, Listening, and Speaking*
- *Family Involvement Activities in English and Spanish*

- *Supporting Instruction in Spanish*

Writing and Language
- *Workshop Resources: Writing, Listening, and Speaking*
- *Daily Language Activities*
- *Language Handbook Worksheets*

QUESTIONS TO ASK WHEN COMPARING MEDIA

Quick guide!

Attention-getting techniques	• How are images, words, and sounds arranged to get the audience's attention?
Objectivity	• Is the main subject portrayed objectively, or is there a positive or negative slant?
	• If two people or groups are involved, does the story give the impression that one side is more honorable or honest than the other?
Complexity	• Does the story provide background information?
	• Does it help you see how this event fits into a bigger picture?
	• Does the story present multiple points of view?
	• What types of sources are interviewed?
Sequence of information	• How does the story begin and end?
	• What kinds of details make up the bulk of the story—interviews, facts, dramatic images, others?
Emotional impact	• Does the story seem to be designed to arouse a certain feeling or impression in its audience?
	• What techniques does it use to do this?

The example below shows what one student discovered when he compared the coverage of an avalanche in the French Alps by a network news program and an Internet news site. Notice that the student listed specific details and examples as he analyzed the two news stories using the points of comparison in the chart above.

TV Network News versus Internet News

Similarities

1. set up as humans vs. nature stories
2. focus on the devastation to the town and the effort to rescue skiers
3. feature interviews with local citizens and victims' families
4. inform the audience that this area of the Alps is prone to avalanches
5. show the site of the avalanche on a map of Europe

Differences

TV News	**Internet News**
1. Begins with views of Alps, then cuts to footage of the avalanche and shots of the devastation and rescue workers. Ends with shot of heavy snowfall and warning that time is running out.	1. Begins with a description of the avalanche and then focuses on the rescue effort. Links connect to photos of rescue workers and survivors.

(continued)

Integrating with Grammar, Usage, and Mechanics

As students start their comparison-contrast essays, they may have difficulty using verbs and pronouns correctly. You may want to review lessons 3 and 4 in the Language Handbook.

CRITICAL THINKING

Remind students that journalists and media professionals aren't the only people who have to make editorial decisions as part of their jobs. For example, historians have to make decisions about what to include and what to leave out of history books. Ask students to name other professions in which people make editorial decisions. [Possible answers include fiction writing, filmmaking, advertising, publishing, and marketing.]

Assessment

■ *Holt Assessment: Writing, Listening, and Speaking*
■ *One-Stop Planner* CD-ROM with ExamView Test Generator
■ *Holt Online Assessment*
■ *Holt Online Essay Scoring*

Internet

■ go.hrw.com (Keyword: LE5 9-4)
■ *Elements of Literature Online*

2. Includes an interview with a rescued American couple.

3. Does not give additional sources of information.

2. Includes interviews with rescued American couple, the head of the rescue operation, and local merchants.

3. Gives links to informational sites and related stories.

Form a Thesis

Remind students that their theses will not merely state that two news stories about the same event differed, but will also tell *how* the two reports differed. In the body of their essays, students can give support for their general description of how the reports varied. Then, in the conclusion of their essays, students should strive to suggest reasons *why* the two stories differed in the ways they found.

Form a Thesis

What's the Point? Now that you have compared and contrasted your two media, what basic conclusion or judgment can you arrive at? Was one medium more objective, complex, or dramatic than the other? The conclusion or judgment you make based on your analysis is your **thesis.** You communicate your thesis in a **thesis statement,** a sentence or two that states the point you intend to prove to your readers. Write a thesis statement that is **clear** and **coherent.** The student comparing the stories about an avalanche wrote the following thesis statement.

| DO THIS →

The online story was more complex than the network news story and depended less on emotional impact.

Organize Your Essay

Medium by Medium or Point by Point? In order for readers to understand the similarities and differences between the two reports, you will need to organize your ideas clearly. There are two basic plans you can use to organize your comparison-contrast essay.

- **Block method:** Discuss the similarities between the two stories first and then move on to the differences, or tell everything about one medium first and then move on to the second medium. The block method works best for shorter pieces with fewer comparisons.

- **Point-by-point method:** Explain how the subjects are alike and different for one point of comparison, then the next point of comparison, and so on. For example, your essay might deal first with how the stories begin, move on to discuss the sequence of information in each story, then cover each story's complexity. The point-by-point method works best for longer essays with more comparisons.

PRACTICE & APPLY 1

Guided and Independent Practice

Monitor students' understanding by writing the following question on the chalkboard for discussion: *If you had seen only one of these stories, how would your impression of the event be different?* Then, assign **Practice and Apply 1** as independent practice.

SKILLS FOCUS

Writing Skills
Establish a thesis. Organize the essay by the block method or the point-by-point method.

PRACTICE & APPLY 1

Use the instructions on the previous pages to select a news event, and analyze its coverage by two different news media. Then, write a thesis statement that communicates your conclusion about the coverage. Finally, organize the information you've gathered.

Writing

Comparing Media Coverage

A Writer's Framework

Introduction	Body	Conclusion
• Create an opening that engages readers' attention.	• Make your method of organization clear: block or point-by-point.	• Remind readers of your thesis.
• Introduce the news event and the subjects you will compare and contrast.	• Discuss the similarities and differences between the two news stories.	• Mention factors that might account for the differences you found.
• State your thesis clearly.	• Provide support for each point of comparison.	• Make a final point, or leave readers with an idea to think about.

A Writer's Model

The highlighted words and phrases below help the reader understand the essay's organization.

More News Is Good News

Have you ever watched a news story on network news that left you wondering, "What's the rest of the story?" I have. Just the other night I watched a story about a terrible avalanche in the French Alps. When it was over I wanted to know more, so I went to the Internet. The coverage I found on a major online news site was both similar to and different from the network news. Overall, the online story was more complex than the network news story and depended less on emotional impact.

The similarities in the two stories were obvious. Both reported the story as a human beings-versus-nature story, focusing on the awesome power of the avalanche and on the heroic efforts of rescue workers. Both featured interviews of people on the scene and informed their audiences that this area of the French Alps is prone to avalanches. Finally, both stories showed the site of the avalanche on a map of Europe.

The differences in the coverage of the avalanche by the two media were more striking. The network news story began with peaceful Alpine views, then cut to dramatic footage of the avalanche and the devastation and rescue efforts afterwards. It ended with a shot of

(continued)

INTRODUCTION
Engaging opening
News event

Subjects
Thesis statement

BODY
Similarities

Differences:
1. sequence
2. attention-getting techniques

Writing Workshop: Comparing Media Coverage   **273**

DIFFERENTIATING INSTRUCTION

Advanced Learners
Enrichment. Encourage students to look for professional comparison-contrast models in newspapers, magazines, or published reports. Have them note whether the examples they find use the block or the point-by-point method. Then, have volunteers briefly present their examples to the class, and lead a discussion about what makes the professional models so effective. *Note: If students search the Internet for a model, remember that the content in this public forum can be unpredictable.*

MODELING AND DEMONSTRATION

A Writer's Framework
Demonstrate how to organize the body of an essay by writing the following sample outline on the chalkboard.

Ice-Skating versus Roller-Skating

Block Method
A. Ice-skating
　1. Ice rink
　2. Skates with blades
B. Roller-skating
　1. Wooden rink
　2. Skates with wheels

Point-by-Point Method
A. Ice-skating
　1. Ice rink
B. Roller-skating
　1. Wooden rink
A. Ice-skating
　2. Skates with blades
B. Roller-skating
　2. Skates with wheels

Have a student volunteer demonstrate understanding of the two organizational patterns by writing similar outlines on the chalkboard comparing and contrasting a topic of your choice.

RETEACHING

Body
If students need help focusing their comparison-contrast essays, ask them to read **A Writer's Model** on pp. 273–274 and determine how the writer focuses on differences between the two types of media being discussed. Students may point out the following:

* The thesis statement focuses on differences.
* The essay emphasizes differences much more strongly than similarities.
* The writer uses contrast clue words.

Students may find it helpful to keep these examples in mind as they develop their own essays.

Learners Having Difficulty

To help students decide which organizational pattern to use, explain that although both organizational methods are good ways to structure comparison-contrast essays, each method seems to suit slightly different situations. The block method may work better when the audience is more familiar with one of the two subjects under discussion. In this case, the more familiar subject can be addressed first, and the relevant points of comparison or contrast can be presented without a great deal of explanation. When both subjects are relatively unfamiliar to the audience, the point-by-point method, which does not require readers to remember new information for as long as the block method does, may be easier for readers to follow.

Guided and Independent Practice

Monitor students' progress by having them write down their thesis statements. Also, discuss with students the different personal and social categories from which media professionals choose examples or anecdotes in order to make an emotional impact on the audience. Tell students to take note of the following emotional-appeal categories in their analyses:

• love and relationships
• death
• children
• animals
• the unknown

Then, assign **Practice and Apply 2** as independent practice.

(continued)

3. emotional impact

Differences in complexity

CONCLUSION
Restatement of thesis

Factors that account for differences

Idea for readers to think about

INTERNET
More Writer's Models
Keyword: LE5 9-4

heavy afternoon snowfall and a warning that time was running out for victims still buried. The online news story, on the other hand, began with a brief description of the avalanche before moving on to focus on rescue efforts. The site provided links to photographs of rescue workers and survivors. The television story was much more dramatic, obviously appealing to the emotions of the viewers. The online story, by comparison, was calm and reasoned, focusing on the business at hand—the rescue.

The online story provided more background information and a wider variety of points of view than the television story. For example, the television story aired clips from an interview with a rescued American couple. The online story provided the same interview and others as well—with the head of the rescue effort and with local merchants worried about their businesses. Moreover, the online story provided links to articles on related topics such as previous avalanches in the area, their effects on the local economy, and steps taken to prevent and prepare for avalanches. The television story did not refer viewers to any other sources of information.

The online story was less dramatic and more complex than the television story. It provided more context and a wider variety of points of view. The television news coverage was no doubt influenced by the time limitations of a thirty-minute program and by a greater need to use drama and emotional impact to attract an audience. The Internet news site obviously also wants to attract an audience, but is free from the space and time limitations that restrict the television news coverage. Watching television news coverage is a good way to find out what important events have taken place on a given day, but an interested viewer may want to consider going to a reliable online news source for more complete information.

PRACTICE & APPLY 2 Using the framework on page 273 and the Writer's Model above as guides, write the first draft of your essay comparing media coverage.

Revising

Revise Your Comparison-Contrast Essay

The Professional Touch For professional writers, the revision process is as important as any other phase of the writing process. Follow their example by first evaluating and revising the content and organization of your essay using the guidelines below. Then, evaluate and revise your essay's style using the guidelines in the chart on page 276.

▶ **First Reading: Content and Organization** Use the chart below to look for ways to improve the content and the **logic** and **coherence** of the organization of your comparison-contrast essay. As you consider the evaluation questions, take into account your essay's intended **audience,** your **purpose** for writing the essay, and the degree of **formality** required of an analytical essay such as this one. Use the tips in the middle column to help you answer the evaluation questions and the revision techniques in the last column to help you make necessary revisions.

> **PEER REVIEW**
>
> Exchange your essay with a peer before you revise. He or she may have ideas on how you can improve the block or point-by-point organization of your paper.

Rubric: Comparing Media Coverage

Evaluation Questions	▶ Tips	▶ Revision Techniques
❶ Is the opening engaging? Does the introduction present the two news media and the news event?	**Underline** the engaging opening. **Bracket** the introduction of the media and the news event.	**Add** a startling fact, interesting quotation, or intriguing question. **Add** a sentence introducing the media and news event.
❷ Does the thesis include a conclusion about the media coverage?	**Highlight** the thesis statement.	If needed, **add** a thesis statement that provides a conclusion about the media coverage.
❸ Is there an obvious, easy-to-follow organizational pattern?	**Label** the points of comparison. If there is no consistent pattern, revise.	**Rearrange** events into point-by-point organization or block organization.
❹ Is each point of comparison adequately supported?	**Put a check mark** by each detail or reference to a news story.	**Add** a detail or reference, or **elaborate** to explain existing support.
❺ Does the conclusion mention factors that might account for similarities and differences? Does it remind readers of the thesis and leave them with an idea to consider?	**Circle** factors that might account for similarities or differences. **Draw a line through** the sentence restating the thesis. **Double underline** the sentence with the idea for readers to consider.	**Add** factors accounting for similarities or differences. **Add** a sentence restating the thesis or an idea for readers to ponder, as necessary. **Delete** material that does none of the above.

Audience and Purpose

You may want to remind students that there is more than one way to present a comparison-contrast essay. Certain methods may be more preferable depending on students' purpose and audience. For example, a multimedia presentation might be an appropriate form to present information to co-workers or classmates. If the audience is a teacher, a formal comparison-contrast essay is probably the most appropriate form for presenting information.

Rubric: Comparing Media Coverage

Advise students to use the **Rubric: Comparing Media Coverage** chart on this page as a think sheet by answering the questions in their notebooks. Explain to students that using think sheets to summarize their notes allows them to place their thoughts, observations, and questions on paper, which, in turn, helps improve the content and organization of their essays.

Elaboration

Students can use a question-asking strategy to help them include sufficient detail in their essays. Have them look for places in their drafts that lead them to ask the questions *How? Why? For example? When?* When a question arises, students should check whether the rest of the sentence or a following sentence answers it. If not, students should add a sentence or sentences to answer the question.

Many word-processing programs have functions that show overprint markings and revisions in a color different from that of the original text. If students have access to these programs, they can make suggested revisions without deleting their original text. This will allow them to see clearly how the evaluation questions, tips, and revision techniques affected their papers.

GUIDED PRACTICE

Responding to the Revision Process

Answers

1. The phrase provides an example of how the online story provides a wider variety of points of view and more background information than the television story.

2. The addition gives more details that elaborate on the support.

PRACTICE & APPLY 3

Independent Practice

Brainstorm with students a list of transitional words and phrases and write them on the chalkboard for students to use during revision. To assess whether students have followed the content, organization, and style guidelines, ask students to mark revisions on their papers in a different color of ink. Students can use the margins of their papers for additional comments or revisions.

> **Second Reading: Style** Once you have revised the content and organization of your essay, you can concentrate on its style. One way to improve the style is to use transitional words and phrases, such as *next, finally,* and *most important.* **Transitional words and phrases** connect one idea to another, making your ideas easy to read and understand. Transitional words and phrases are particularly important in comparison-contrast essays, where you constantly move back and forth between the subjects or points of your essay. To help you add transitional words and phrases to your essay, use the guidelines in the chart below.

Style Guidelines

Evaluation Question	Tip	Revision Technique
Does the writer use transitional words and phrases to guide the reader?	**Draw a box** around transitional words and phrases such as *on the other hand, by contrast, however,* and so on.	**Add** transitional words and phrases to make the points of comparison clearer to readers.

ANALYZING THE REVISION PROCESS
Study these revisions, and answer the questions that follow.

The online story provided more background information and a wider variety of points of view than the television story.

add — *For example,* The television story aired clips from an interview with a rescued American couple. The online story provided the same

elaborate — interview and others as well, *—with the head of the rescue effort and with local merchants worried about their businesses.*

Responding to the Revision Process

1. How did adding a transitional phrase connect the ideas in the first two sentences?
2. Why do you think the writer added to the last sentence?

SKILLS FOCUS

Writing Skills
Revise for content and style.

PRACTICE & APPLY 3

Revise the content, organization, and style of your essay, using the guidelines in this section. Be sure to read through your paper twice.

DIFFERENTIATING INSTRUCTION

English-Language Learners
To help students improve the sentence fluency of their essays, suggest that they read their essays aloud to a partner. Both students should take turns reading their essays aloud to each other and listening for places where the points of comparison would be made clearer by adding transitional words or phrases.

Publishing

Proofread and Publish Your Essay

The Final Touch Informative and thought-provoking content that is well organized and communicated with an engaging style is the most impressive element of any essay. However, the best content can be seriously spoiled by careless errors in grammar, usage, and mechanics. Make your essay as free of such errors as you can by proofreading it carefully and correcting errors as you discover them. You might even ask a peer to help you find and correct mistakes. Once you have completed this process, make a final copy.

An Essay in Search of an Audience You've worked hard to write and polish your essay. Now, you can reap the rewards of your hard work by sharing your analysis with others. How do you find an audience? Consider the following suggestions for publication.

- Post your essay to an online site that specializes in media analysis, and ask for reader feedback.

- Form a group of three to four classmates to read and comment on each other's essays.

- E-mail your essay to the news organizations whose coverage you analyzed, and ask for their feedback.

- Adapt your essay into an oral presentation. Think about incorporating technology into your presentation so your audience can view video clips or Web pages.

Reflect on Your Essay

Food for Thought Look back and reflect on what you have learned in the process of analyzing media coverage and writing a comparison-contrast essay. Use these questions to focus your thoughts.

- How did writing this essay help you understand the editorial decisions that media professionals are required to make?

- Which of your points of comparison do you think was the strongest argument for looking to more than one source for the news of any event? Why?

- Considering your experience comparing and contrasting news media, which medium would you choose as your news source if you were forced to choose only one? Why?

PRACTICE & APPLY 4 Use the suggestions and questions on this page to proofread, publish, and reflect on your essay comparing media coverage of a news event.

TIP Careful proofreading will help ensure that you have used English-language **conventions** properly. For example, check to see that you have correctly capitalized and punctuated the names of news programs or Internet news sites in your essay. For more on **capitalizing and punctuating titles,** see Capitalization, 11f, in the Language Handbook.

SKILLS FOCUS

Writing Skills
Proofread to correct grammar, usage, and mechanics errors. Publish and reflect on the essay.

SKILLS FOCUS, pp. 278–279

Grade-Level Skills

- **Literary Skills**
Compare and contrast works that express a universal theme, and provide evidence to support that theme.

- **Literary Skills**
Compare and contrast similar themes across genres.

INTRODUCING THE SKILLS REVIEW

Use this review to assess students' grasp of the skills taught in this collection.

Ⓐ Literary Focus

❷ Comparing points of view. From what point of view is the story told? [first-person point of view] Who is the narrator? [the eldest child of the family]

Ⓑ Literary Focus

❷ Universal themes. How does the narrator feel about her father? [She loves him deeply.] How can you tell? [The thought of losing him makes her hold him tightly.]

Ⓒ Literary Focus

❷ Comparing points of view. From what point of view is the poem written? [first-person point of view] Who is the speaker? [He is an adult looking back on his childhood.]

Ⓓ Literary Focus

❷ Universal themes. How did the speaker feel about his father when he was younger? [He took his father for granted and never thanked him.] How does the speaker feel now? [He finally appreciates his father's love and regrets his lack of appreciation as a boy.]

Collection 4: Skills Review
Literary Skills

Comparing Themes

Test Practice

DIRECTIONS: Read the following short story and poem. Then, read and respond to the questions that follow.

Papa Who Wakes Up Tired in the Dark
Sandra Cisneros

Your *abuelito*[1] is dead, Papa says early one morning in my room. *Está muerto,*[2] and then as if he just heard the news himself, crumples like a coat and cries, my brave Papa cries. I have never seen my Papa cry and don't know what to do.

I know he will have to go away, that he will take a plane to Mexico, all the uncles and aunts will be there, and they will have a black-and-white photo taken in front of the tomb with flowers shaped like spears in a white vase because this is how they send the dead away in that country.

Because I am the oldest, my father has told me first, and now it is my turn to tell the others. I will have to explain why we can't play. I will have to tell them to be quiet today.

My Papa, his thick hands and thick shoes, who wakes up tired in the dark, who combs his hair with water, drinks his coffee, and is gone before we wake, today is sitting on my bed.

And I think if my own Papa died what would I do. I hold my Papa in my arms. I hold and hold and hold him.

1. **abuelito** (ä·bwel·ē′tō): Spanish for "grandpa."
2. **Está muerto** (es·tä′ mwer′tō): Spanish for "He is dead."

Those Winter Sundays
Robert Hayden

Sundays too my father got up early
and put his clothes on in the
    blueblack cold,
then with cracked hands that ached
from labor in the weekday weather
    made
5 banked fires blaze. No one ever
    thanked him.

I'd wake and hear the cold splintering,
    breaking.
When the rooms were warm, he'd call,
and slowly I would rise and dress,
fearing the chronic° angers of
    that house,

10 Speaking indifferently to him,
who had driven out the cold
and polished my good shoes as well.
What did I know, what did I know
of love's austere° and lonely offices?°

9. **chronic** (krän′ik) *adj.:* constant.
14. **austere** (ô·stir′) *adj.:* self-sacrificing.
    offices *n.:* services; duties.

SKILLS FOCUS

Pages 278–279 cover
Literary Skills
Compare the presentation of a theme across genres. Compare universal themes.

READING MINI-LESSON

Reviewing Word-Attack Skills
Activity. Write these sentences on the chalkboard. Have students read the sentences and tell if the last *se* letters in the two underlined words have the same sound [s] or different sounds [d].

1. That <u>excuse</u> is <u>nonsense</u>. [s]
2. Anyone can <u>lose</u> some <u>course</u> notes. [d]
3. But to <u>accuse</u> your pet is <u>perverse</u>. [d]
4. She claimed her cat <u>chose</u> to <u>use</u> her notes for a litter box. [s]
5. But the teacher <u>refused</u> to <u>excuse</u> her from taking the test. [s]

Activity. Display these pairs of words. Each pair shares some of the same letters. Have students underline the letters in each word that are the same and tell if these letters stand for the same sound [s] or different sounds [d].

Collection 4: Skills Review

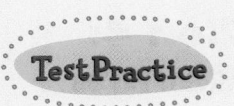

1. In "Papa Who Wakes Up Tired in the Dark," how does the narrator feel when she sees her father cry?
   A Guilty
   B Confused
   C Angry
   D Suspicious

2. When he was young, the speaker in "Those Winter Sundays" —
   F did not appreciate his father
   G felt grateful to his father
   H did not obey his father
   J gave orders to his father

3. Both works describe a father who wakes up early in the dark. What do these two fathers have in common?
   A Both are ambitious.
   B Both are restless and aimless.
   C Neither father wants to spend time with his family.
   D Both work hard and love their families.

4. What feeling is expressed at the end of both selections?
   F Fear or nervousness
   G Pity
   H Embarrassment
   J Love or appreciation

5. Which of the following statements about the two selections is *false*?
   A Unlike the story's narrator, the poem's speaker is an adult looking back on the past.
   B Unlike the relationship described in the poem, the parent-child relationship in the story is warm.
   C The tone of the poem, unlike the tone of the story, is regretful.
   D The poem's speaker, unlike the story's narrator, has seen his father cry.

6. Although these works are different **genres** (a story and a poem), they share each of the following elements *except* —
   F a first-person narrator or speaker
   G a repeated phrase
   H dialogue
   J an image of the father's hands

7. If Robert Hayden wanted to turn "Those Winter Sundays" into a story, he might add all of the following elements *except* —
   A a scene showing a conflict between the father and son
   B end rhyme
   C a climax to the plot
   D more characters

Constructed Response

8. In your opinion, what is the common **theme** of both selections? Provide specific examples to support your response.

Answers and Model Rationales

1. **B** When the narrator sees her father cry, she says, "I have never seen my Papa cry and don't know what to do," so B is correct.

2. **F** The speaker's lack of appreciation in childhood for his father is expressed in ll. 5, 10, and 13–14. He feels grateful only now as an adult, so G is not correct.

3. **D** D is the only possible answer. Both speakers have hardworking fathers who love their families.

4. **J** Both selections end with an expression of love: The story describes the narrator holding her father tightly, and the poem ends with the speaker's statement that as a child he did not appreciate his father's love, but now he does.

5. **D** The false statement is D because the poem's speaker does not mention seeing his father cry. A, B, and C are all true.

6. **H** H is the only possible answer because the poem has no dialogue.

7. **B** B is the only possible answer because end rhyme is an element of poetry, whereas the other choices are short story elements.

Constructed Response

8. A common theme in the two selections is that relationships between parents and children are filled with unspoken but powerful emotions. The narrator of the poem notices his father's good deeds but doesn't take the time to thank him. The narrator of the story clearly has strong feelings for her father, because she cannot imagine living without him.

 **ASSESSING**

Assessment
■ *Holt Assessment: Literature, Reading, and Vocabulary*

---

1. journey ad<u>jou</u>rn [s]
2. fl<u>ou</u>r flourish [d]
3. c<u>ou</u>rt c<u>ou</u>rtesy [d]
4. b<u>o</u>re b<u>o</u>redom [s]
5. bor<u>ou</u>gh b<u>o</u>rrow [d]

6. s<u>ou</u>r s<u>ou</u>rce [d]
7. g<u>o</u>rgeous g<u>o</u>ry [s]
8. c<u>ou</u>rse c<u>ou</u>rage [d]
9. torment tort<u>oi</u>se [s]
10. w<u>o</u>rn w<u>o</u>rm [d]

Activity. Display these sets of words. Have students identify the two words in which the letters *ou* stand for the same sound. Answers are underlined.

1. <u>county</u>   country   <u>couch</u>
2. <u>trouble</u>   trout   <u>trousers</u>
3. <u>boulder</u>   soul   soufflé
4. <u>soup</u>   souse   <u>souvenir</u>
5. <u>grout</u>   group   <u>grouch</u>

Collection 4: Skills Review

Vocabulary Skills

Multiple-Meaning Words

Modeling. Model the thought process of a good reader answering item I by saying, "In the excerpt, *light* is a noun meaning the opposite of *darkness*. In A, *light* is used as a verb, not a noun. In B, *light* refers to a way of looking at someone. In C, *light* is an adjective, meaning the opposite of *dark*. Only D uses the word as the excerpt does."

Answers and Model Rationales

1. **D** See rationale above.
2. **G** In F, *dull* means "boring." In H, it means "not sharp." In J, *dull* means "unable to feel."
3. **A** In B, *fired* means "deprived of a job." In C, it means "spoke rapidly." In D, it means "aroused."
4. **J** In F, *drew* means "sketched." In G, it means "inferred from evidence." In H, it means "attracted."
5. **D** In A, *flash* refers to a brief amount of time. In B, it refers to a verbal outburst. In C, it is a verb meaning "briefly display."
6. **J** In F, *broke* means "lacking money." In G, *broke* means "to suddenly move away." In H, *broke* means "to give way to one's feelings."

Collection 4: Skills Review
Vocabulary Skills

Multiple-Meaning Words

DIRECTIONS: Choose the answer in which the underlined word is used in the same way it is used in the sentence from "The Sniper."

1. "Dublin lay enveloped in darkness but for the dim light of the moon that shone through fleecy clouds. . . ."
   - **A** Please light the candles on the birthday cake.
   - **B** The biography presented the author in a favorable light.
   - **C** She always dressed in light colors.
   - **D** When we go camping, we read by the light of the fire.

2. "The sniper could hear the dull panting of the motor."
   - **F** We left the party early because it was dull.
   - **G** We heard the dull roar of crowds in the distance.
   - **H** I couldn't cut the fruit with the dull knife.
   - **J** In shock after the accident, he felt dull to pain and grief.

3. "The sniper raised his rifle and fired."
   - **A** Each person fired two shots at the target.
   - **B** The supervisor fired the employee last week.
   - **C** Journalists fired questions at the mayor during the press conference.
   - **D** The speaker fired up the crowd, inspiring the audience to take action.

4. "Quickly he drew his knife from his pocket. . . ."
   - **F** The engineer drew a diagram to show how the machine worked.
   - **G** The students drew several conclusions from their survey.
   - **H** The movie star always drew large crowds wherever he went.
   - **J** I waited in suspense as my mother slowly drew a surprise from the bag.

5. "There was a flash and a bullet whizzed over his head."
   - **A** If I hurry, I can be there in a flash.
   - **B** Usually serious, my friend suddenly displayed a flash of wit.
   - **C** To enter the building, just flash your badge.
   - **D** A flash of lightning lit up the sky.

6. "Here and there through the city, machine guns and rifles broke the silence of the night. . . ."
   - **F** Her company went bankrupt, and she is broke.
   - **G** We broke away from the crowds and wandered off by ourselves.
   - **H** Chris was so upset that he broke down in tears.
   - **J** The sound of lighthearted laughter broke the tension in the room.

SKILLS FOCUS

Vocabulary Skills
Understand multiple-meaning words.

Using Academic Language

Review of Literary Terms
Ask students to review the collection to find the meanings of the terms listed below. Then, have students show their grasp of these terms by citing passages from the collection that illustrate their meanings.
Theme (p. 208); **Universal Themes** (pp. 208, 210); **Comparison** (pp. 230, 268); **Contrast** (pp. 230, 268); **Genre** (p. 244).

Review of Informational Terms
Ask students to use the terms below to explain how to synthesize the content from several sources.
Primary Source (p. 231); **Secondary Source** (p. 231); **Synthesize** (p. 231); **Paraphrase** (p. 231); **Compare** (p. 231); **Contrast** (p. 231); **Connect** (p. 231).

Vocabulary Review

Ask students to choose Vocabulary words from the box that are synonyms for the items below.

| averted | coerced | beleaguered |
| obstruction | abhor | |

1. surrounded [beleaguered]
2. blockage [obstruction]
3. hate [abhor]
4. turned away [averted]
5. forced [coerced]

Collection 4: Skills Review
Writing Skills

Test Practice

DIRECTIONS: The following paragraph is from a draft of a student's comparison-contrast essay. Read the questions below it, and choose the best answer to each question.

(1) Recently, an online article and a newspaper article discussed wildfires in the West. (2) If you have access to the Web, you can read the online article. (3) The online article, "Western Wildfires Continue," presents a variety of information that provides an objective picture of the wildfire. (4) The newspaper article, "Local Firefighters Battle Bravely," presents a very personal look at the dangerous task of fighting wildfires. (5) Stirring photos and emotional language in the article create a strong emotional impact.

1. To present a clear, coherent thesis, which of these could the student add after sentence 1?
   A While both stories discuss wildfires in the West, the newspaper story has greater emotional impact.
   B The Web site is viewed by people worldwide, but the newspaper is read mostly locally.
   C A firefighter from my hometown has volunteered to battle the wildfires.
   D I enjoyed reading the two articles and finding out their differences.

2. Which of the following sentences would add to the ideas in sentence 3?
   F Both writers gathered some of their material from the Associated Press.
   G Too many paid advertisements surround the online story and distract the reader.
   H The newspaper article has pictures of the local firefighters hugging their families goodbye.
   J It offers links to other reports, satellite photos, and interviews with sources.

3. Which of these transitional words or phrases should the writer add to the beginning of sentence 4?
   A Meanwhile,
   B In addition,
   C On the other hand,
   D For example,

4. Which sentence should be deleted to improve the passage's organization?
   F 2
   G 3
   H 4
   J 5

5. To discuss similarities between the media, which of the following could the writer add?
   A an explanation that the newspaper article is distributed only locally
   B a statement that both articles discuss the need for more help
   C a description of the online story's graphics
   D a defense of the credibility of each source quoted in the articles

Writing Skills
Write a comparison-contrast essay.

RESOURCES: WRITING

Assessment
- *One-Stop Planner* CD-ROM with ExamView Test Generator
- *Holt Assessment: Writing, Listening, & Speaking*

Internet
- *Holt Online Assessment*
- *Holt Online Essay Scoring*

Writing Skills
Answers
1. A
2. J
3. C
4. F
5. B

APPLICATION

Oral Comparison and Contrast
Homework

For homework, have students apply what they have learned in this workshop in an oral comparison of a book and the movie made from it. Suggest that interested students present their comparisons as if they were television or radio journalists reporting their findings to the public. They may even want to "interview" other students as part of their support for their analyses.

EXTENSION

Historical Figures and the Media

Allow students to work with a partner to compare two historical figures' use of the media. To help students get started, offer the example of Franklin D. Roosevelt's use of fireside chats. To find another president who also used mass media to communicate with the public, students might search encyclopedias for biographies of John F. Kennedy, who participated in the first televised debates with Richard Nixon, and of Jimmy Carter, who often spoke with people on telephone call-in programs. Have pairs of students prepare a report that compares the two historical figures.

Collection 5

Irony and Ambiguity

Informational Reading Focus: Evaluating an Argument

About Collection 5

In Collection 5, students will master the following skills:

- **Literary Skills:** Analyze irony and ambiguity; analyze surprise endings; and interpret contradictions.
- **Reading Skills:** Make predictions; make inferences about character motivation; and evaluate an author's argument and evidence.
- **Vocabulary Skills:** Understand diction; use context clues to understand the meanings of words; and identify synonyms.
- **Writing Skills:** Develop, write, and revise a persuasive essay.
- **Listening and Speaking Skills:** Debate an issue.

Informational Text

Each collection of *Elements of Literature* provides a variety of informational texts related to the literature selections by theme or topic.

Minimum Course of Study

Most skills can be taught with a minimum number of selections and features. In the chart to the right, lessons highlighted in green constitute the minimum course of study that provides coverage of the skills taught in Collection 5.

Resource Manager

(pp. 282C–282D)

Lesson and workshop resources are referenced in the Resource Manager on the pages that follow. These resources can be used to reinforce the skills taught in Collection 5, remediate students who are having difficulty, and provide supporting activities for English-language learners.

Scope and Sequence

Selection ▪ Feature	Literary Skills
Elements of Literature: Irony and Ambiguity *by* John Leggett	• Understand irony (verbal irony, situational irony, and dramatic irony) and ambiguity
The Gift of the Magi *by* O. Henry ↑ *above grade level*	• Analyze situational irony and the surprise ending
The Lady, or the Tiger? *by* Frank R. Stockton ↑ *above grade level*	• Analyze ambiguity
Informational Text: A Defense of the Jury System *by* Thomas M. Ross, Esq. ↔ *at grade level*	
The Road Not Taken *by* Robert Frost ↔ *at grade level*	• Interpret contradictions
Writing Workshop: *Writing a Persuasive Essay*	
Listening and Speaking Workshop: *Debating an Issue*	
Skills Review: *Literary Skills* *Vocabulary Skills* *Writing Skills*	• Analyze irony and ambiguity

Reading Skills	Vocabulary Skills	Writing ▪ Grammar and Language ▪ Listening and Speaking Skills
• Make predictions	• Demonstrate word knowledge • Understand diction	• Write a character description • Write a letter
• Make inferences about character motivation • Evaluate an author's argument and evidence	• Use context clues to understand the meaning of words • Use context clues to understand the meanings of words	• Write a persuasive essay • Write a sequel • Use correct subject-verb agreement with an interrupting prepositional phrase
		• Write a letter • Write a poem
		• Write a persuasive essay
		• Debate an issue
	• Identify synonyms	• Write a persuasive essay

Resource Manager

Selection ▪ Feature	Planning	Differentiating Instruction ▪ Lesson Plans with ELL Strategies and Practice	Reading ▪ Vocabulary
Elements of Literature: Irony and Ambiguity *by John Leggett*	• PowerNotes: Irony	• Family Involvement Activities in English and Spanish, p. 7	
The Gift of the Magi *by O. Henry*	• One-Stop Planner with ExamView Test Generator	• The Holt Reader, pp. 142–151 • Holt Adapted Reader • Holt Reading Solutions, pp. 147–152 • Supporting Instruction in Spanish, p. 20 • Audio CD Library, disc 10 • Audio CD Library, Selections and Summaries in Spanish	• The Holt Reader • Holt Adapted Reader • Holt Reading Solutions • Vocabulary Development, p. 24 • PowerNotes: Making Predictions
The Lady, or the Tiger? *by Frank R. Stockton* **Informational Text:** A Defense of the Jury System *by Thomas M. Ross, Esq.*	• One-Stop Planner with ExamView Test Generator	• Holt Adapted Reader • Holt Reading Solutions, pp. 153–163 • Supporting Instruction in Spanish, pp. 20–21 • Audio CD Library, disc 10 • Audio CD Library, Selections and Summaries in Spanish	• Holt Adapted Reader • Holt Reading Solutions • Vocabulary Development, pp. 25, 26
The Road Not Taken *by Robert Frost*	• One-Stop Planner with ExamView Test Generator	• Holt Reading Solutions, pp. 164–166 • Supporting Instruction in Spanish, p. 21 • Audio CD Library, disc 10 • Audio CD Library, Selections and Summaries in Spanish	• Holt Reading Solutions
Writing Workshop: *Writing a Persuasive Essay*	• One-Stop Planner with ExamView Test Generator	• Workshop Resources: Writing, Listening, and Speaking, pp. 41–48 • Family Involvement Activities in English and Spanish, pp. 19–20 • Supporting Instruction in Spanish, p. 71	
Listening and Speaking Workshop: *Debating an Issue*	• One-Stop Planner with ExamView Test Generator	• Workshop Resources: Writing, Listening, and Speaking, pp. 49–55 • Supporting Instruction in Spanish	
Skills Review: *Literary Skills Vocabulary Skills Writing Skills*			

The Holt Reader

The Holt Reader is a consumable paperback book which can be used alone or to accompany *Elements of Literature*. It offers guided support throughout the reading process and encourages students to become active readers by circling, underlining, questioning, and jotting down responses as they read. *The Holt Reader* works well for homework, students who have missed class, additional instructional time, reteaching, and remediation.

Holt Reading Solutions (HRS)

Holt Reading Solutions pulls together reading resources in the *Elements of Literature* program to create a powerful tool for intervention and whole-class instruction. *HRS* includes diagnostic assessment tools, lesson plans for English-language learners and special education students, adaptations of selected reading selections, vocabulary and comprehension worksheets, information on phonics and decoding, and additional instruction and practice in remedial reading skills.

Writing ▪ Grammar and Language ▪ Listening and Speaking	Assessment
• Daily Language Activities	• Holt Assessment: Literature, Reading, and Vocabulary • Holt Online Assessment • One-Stop Planner with ExamView Test Generator
• Daily Language Activities • Language Handbook Worksheets, pp. 15, 16, 17, 18	• Holt Assessment: Literature, Reading, and Vocabulary • Holt Online Assessment • One-Stop Planner with ExamView Test Generator
• Daily Language Activities	• Holt Assessment: Literature, Reading, and Vocabulary • Holt Online Assessment • One-Stop Planner with ExamView Test Generator
• Daily Language Activities • Workshop Resources: Writing, Listening, and Speaking, pp. 41–48	• Holt Assessment: Writing, Listening, and Speaking • Holt Online Assessment • One-Stop Planner with ExamView Test Generator
• Workshop Resources: Writing, Listening, and Speaking, pp. 49–55	• Holt Assessment: Writing, Listening, and Speaking • One-Stop Planner with ExamView Test Generator
	• Holt Assessment: Writing, Listening, and Speaking • One-Stop Planner with ExamView Test Generator

Technology

INTERNET

- go.hrw.com
- Holt Online Assessment
- Holt Online Essay Scoring
- Elements of Literature Online

MEDIA

- • One-Stop Planner with ExamView Test Generator
- • PowerNotes
- • Audio CD Library, disc 10
- • Audio CD Library, Selections and Summaries in Spanish
- • Visual Connections Videocassette Program, Segment 4
- • Fine Art Transparencies, 7 and 8

Transparency	Video
CD-ROM	Audio CD

One-Stop Planner with ExamView Test Generator

The *One-Stop Planner* CD-ROM contains electronic versions of print-based teaching resources, clips from the video program, and valuable assessment tools. The *One-Stop Planner* resources are presented in easy-to-follow, point-and-click menu formats. To preview resources or print out worksheets and tests, you simply make a selection and click.

One-Stop Planner CD-ROM

282D

Collection 5

SKILLS FOCUS

Grade-Level Skills

■ **Literary Skills**
Identify ambiguities, contradictions, and ironies in the text.

■ **Reading Skills**
Evaluate the credibility of an author's argument by examining generalizations, the scope of the evidence, and the intentions of the author.

INTRODUCING THE COLLECTION

In this collection, students read classic works of fiction and poetry that are famous for their surprise twists. The masterful use of irony and ambiguity in these works creates a lasting emotional impression that has haunted generations of readers.

The surprise ending of O. Henry's memorable love story "The Gift of the Magi" allows students to evaluate the emotional impact of situational irony. In the modern fable "The Lady, or the Tiger?" students debate the lingering question that the tale's ambiguous ending forces them to consider. In the famous Robert Frost poem "The Road Not Taken," students ponder the ambiguities created by Frost's subtle use of verbal irony.

Students are also guided through the steps of evaluating an argument. As they read a persuasive essay, they analyze the reasons and evidence presented to support the author's defense of the jury system.

Finally, the collection closes with opportunities for students to write persuasive essays and to debate issues.

COLLECTION 5 RESOURCES: READING

Planning
■ *One-Stop Planner* CD-ROM with ExamView Test Generator

Differentiating Instruction
■ *Holt Reading Solutions*
■ *The Holt Reader*
■ *Holt Adapted Reader*

■ *Family Involvement Activities in English and Spanish*
■ *Supporting Instruction in Spanish*

Vocabulary
■ *Vocabulary Development*

Grammar and Language
■ *Language Handbook Worksheets*
■ *Daily Language Activities*

Collection 5

IRONY and AMBIGUITY

INFORMATIONAL READING FOCUS

EVALUATING AN ARGUMENT

How shall a man live if he can no longer rely upon things turning out differently from what he thought?

—Thomas Mann

INTERNET
Collection
Resources
Keyword: LE5 9-5

New Shoes for H (1973–1974) by Don Eddy (American, 1944–). Acrylic on canvas (111.7 cm × 121.9 cm).
© The Cleveland Museum of Art, 2002, Purchase with a grant from the National Endowment for the Arts and matched by gifts from members of The Cleveland Society for Contemporary Art (1974.53).

283

Grade-Level Skills

■ **Literary Skills**
Identify ambiguities, contradictions, and ironies in the text.

Review Skills

■ **Literary Skills**
Identify the literary devices (such as metaphor, dialect, and irony) that define a writer's style.

Elements of Literature: Irony and Ambiguity

Ask students if they have ever seen a movie with a surprise ending. The movie *The Sixth Sense,* for instance, is a perfect example of the dramatic impact of an ironic surprise ending. Students may also mention mysteries or thrillers in which viewers are led to identify one character as the villain until almost the very end, when a previously unsuspected villain is suddenly revealed.

Ask students to discuss why they do or do not like surprise endings. Help students conclude that a well-executed surprise ending can remind us that in life, as well as in art, things are not always what they seem and events don't always turn out the way we expect them to.

Elements of Literature

INTERNET
More About Irony and Ambiguity
Keyword: LE5 9-5

SKILLS FOCUS

Literary Skills
Understand irony (verbal irony, situational irony, and dramatic irony) and ambiguity.

Irony and Ambiguity *by* John Leggett
SURPRISES, TWISTS, AND MYSTERIES

Fiction, really good fiction, reflects the human experience. Good fiction is a great mirror in which we see—in ways that entertain and inform us—how the lives of others have unfolded, and so it suggests how life may unfold for ourselves.

The fiction writer who wants to bring about such a wonder must first convince the reader that the story being told is a truth. That means that we must believe in the story as a reflection of human experience. The sound of truth in a story—often described in the writing business today as "telling it like it is"—means giving the characters and events all the peculiarities of real life. These include the surprise and contrariness and uncertainty that confound us in our daily rounds—and that keep us guessing about our own futures.

Irony: Not What We Expect

Irony is the word that describes the difference between what we expect or what seems suitable and what actually happens. Imagine, for example, that the fellow we elected mayor because he ran on a platform of honesty is caught with the missing pension fund. Sometimes irony so surprises us that it is comic. The floored prizefighter lifts his head from the canvas to say, "I think I've got him worried."

Our pleasure in irony comes from our recognition that it is *true*—that life rarely fulfills our expectations and often astounds us.

We find three kinds of irony in stories. **Verbal irony**—the simplest kind—is used when someone *says* one thing but *means* the opposite. The prizefighter's comment is an example of verbal irony.

Situational irony describes an event that is not just surprising but actually contrary to what we expected. When the mayor is caught with his hand in the pension fund, we have situational irony.

A third kind of irony is **dramatic irony.** This type of irony often occurs in plays, a fact that explains how it gets its name. When *we* know what is in store for a character, but the character does *not* know, we are experiencing dramatic irony. When Joan plans a huge surprise birthday party for Fred, and Fred returns to a darkened home and wearily says, "All I want is a quiet evening," we recognize dramatic irony at work. We also feel the tug of suspense: We want to know what will happen when thirty people leap out to surprise Fred.

Ambiguity: Conflicting Interpretations

In a story, just as in actual experience, the outcome of our expectations can also be ambiguous. Irony is the reverse of what we expected; **ambiguity** offers us several conflicting consequences or meanings—and leaves us to sort them out.

In actual life we tend to have ambiguous feelings about many of our experiences. "I'm a reasonably honest person, but I never did return Rudy's watch." "Megan's a lovely girl, but she's so irresponsible." Both of these are examples of ambiguous feelings.

284 Collection 5   Irony and Ambiguity • Evaluating an Argument

DIFFERENTIATING INSTRUCTION

Learners Having Difficulty
Irony. Help students understand that although the term *irony* may be new to them, verbal and situational irony are common in everyday life. To demonstrate verbal irony, write the following expressions on the chalkboard: *Thanks a lot* and *I'm so thrilled to be here.*

Ask students to describe a situation in which they might say one of these sentences when, in fact, they meant the exact opposite. Then, have them read the sentences aloud using an ironic tone of voice.

Advanced Learners
Acceleration. Help move students toward analyzing the ways in which irony, tone, mood,

the author's style, and the "sound" of language achieve specific rhetorical or aesthetic purposes or both.

Activity. Point out that many of today's comedy writers and stand-up comedians use an ironic tone and style of language in their work. Have students analyze a contemporary comedy performance or piece of comic

Irony and ambiguity can apply to every aspect of storytelling. Suppose a story tells about a shy girl, Emily. Emily has bright expectations for the school dance, based upon the dress her mother is making for her and on Donald, the neighbor who will take her to the dance. If once within the gym, Donald abandons Emily and leaves her to languish alone by the water fountain, the story's ending is ironic. It is the opposite of what we would hope for and expect.

An ambiguous ending offers us a choice of outcomes. In Emily's case the storyteller might suggest that Donald's neglect actually toughened Emily for a rewarding life of research on spiders and beetles. Perhaps instead the story hints that Emily didn't really like Donald anyway and was using him to feel socially accepted. Both of these are ambiguous endings.

It's possible that the whole story—its very theme—is ironic or ambiguous, so that when you've finished and put the story aside, the *why* of the story is puzzling. Does the writer mean that Emily is happier with spiders and beetles? Is Emily really manipulative, or is she just protective of herself?

Some readers think those stories with ironic or ambiguous endings or themes are the ones we remember —because we can never be quite sure what they mean. It seems that the best stories are not the easiest ones to understand. The best stories are the ones that present life and people the way they are: complicated, unpredictable, mysterious.

Practice

Review the definition of **verbal irony**. Then, write a paragraph describing a scene between two characters. Include an ironic statement made by one character. You might take inspiration from one of the characters or situations described above.

Complete Peace

Practice

Emily fidgets nervously as her mother fits her daughter into the shiny red party dress.

Possible Answer

"I can't believe I'm really going to the dance!" Emily said.

"What do you mean?" her mother answered. "You're a bright, pretty girl. Why wouldn't any boy be proud to take you to a dance?"

"Yeah, right, Mom. I'm the most popular girl in school. That's why so many boys are breaking down our door, begging to take me out."

Apply

Groups of students might enjoy expanding one of their scenes into a skit and performing it for the class. After each performance, have the class identify when verbal irony was used in the skit.

writing. Have them identify elements of verbal, situational, or dramatic irony in the piece. Then, ask them to speculate about what purposes— besides making people laugh—the comic writers might have for using an ironic tone and style.

Grade-Level Skills

■ **Literary Skills**
Identify ambiguities, contradictions, and ironies in the text.

■ **Reading Skills**
Make predictions.

Review Skills

■ **Literary Skills**
Identify the literary devices (such as metaphor, dialect, and irony) that define a writer's style.

Summary ⬆ *above grade level*

This O. Henry classic, famous for its characteristic surprise ending, is a tale of selfless love between a husband and a wife. At Christmas, Della sells her long, beautiful hair to buy her husband Jim a platinum fob chain for his prized watch. Ironically, Jim has sold his watch to buy an expensive set of combs for his wife's hair. Their love for each other has made the two sacrifice their most precious possessions.

Before You Read

The Gift of the Magi

Make the Connection
Quickwrite ✏️

If you could save just one item from a disaster—a fire, a flood, an earthquake— what would it be? In a few sentences, describe your most cherished possession, and tell why you treasure it. Was it a gift? If so, how does that make it especially important to you?

Literary Focus
Situational Irony: Not What We Expect

Often when we read a story, we think one thing will happen only to be surprised when something entirely different takes place. This is an example of **situational irony,** which reminds us that chance, or the unexpected, often has the last word.

O. Henry, who wrote "The Gift of the Magi," specialized in a particular type of ironic situation: the **surprise ending.** Whether O. Henry's endings are happy or sad, they are always emotionally satisfying.

Reading Skills 📖
Making Predictions: What Will Happen Next?

Why do we read? One reason is that we are curious. At the start of a story, a writer sets up a situation that raises a lot of questions. We read on because we want to know what happens.

Read the first paragraph of this story, and then write down a **prediction.** What do you think will happen next? Stop at least twice more, and write down your predictions. As you do this, ask yourself

these questions: "Is the writer keeping me in suspense? Is he succeeding in surprising me?" Keep your notes.

Background

The Magi referred to in the title of this story are the three "wise men" who, according to the Bible (Matthew 2:1–13), brought gifts of frankincense and myrrh (substances prized for their fragrance) as well as gold to the infant Jesus. Traditionally the Magi's gifts are regarded as the first Christmas presents.

Vocabulary Development

instigates (in′stə·gāts′) *v.:* urges on to some action, usually negative, or sets something in motion; here, gives rise to.

agile (aj′əl) *adj.:* moving with ease.

depreciate (dē·prē′shē·āt′) *v.:* make something seem less important; lower the value of.

cascade (kas·kād′) *n.:* waterfall.

ransacking (ran′sak′iŋ) *v.:* searching thoroughly.

discreet (di·skrēt′) *adj.:* showing good judgment in what one says or does; especially being silent or careful.

scrutiny (skroot′′n·ē) *n.:* close inspection.

nimble (nim′bəl) *adj.:* quickly moving.

coveted (kuv′it·id) *v.* used as *adj.:* longed-for.

singed (sinjd) *v.* used as *adj.:* slightly burned.

INTERNET
Vocabulary
Practice
•
More About
O. Henry
•
Keyword: LE5 9-5

SKILLS FOCUS

Literary Skills
Understand situational irony and the surprise ending.

Reading Skills
Make predictions.

RESOURCES: READING

Planning
■ *One-Stop Planner* CD-ROM with ExamView Test Generator

Differentiating Instruction
■ *Holt Reading Solutions*
■ *The Holt Reader*
■ *Holt Adapted Reader*
■ *Supporting Instruction in Spanish*

■ *Audio CD Library, Selections and Summaries in Spanish*

Vocabulary
■ *Vocabulary Development*

Grammar and Language
■ *Daily Language Activities*

The Gift of the Magi

O. Henry

The Magi, as you know, were wise men . . .

Hairdresser's Window (1907) by John Sloan. Oil on canvas.

The Ella Gump Sumner and Mary Catlin Sumner Collection Fund.
© Wadsworth Atheneum, Hartford, Connecticut.

Assessment

- *Holt Assessment: Literature, Reading, and Vocabulary*
- *One-Stop Planner* CD-ROM with ExamView Test Generator
- *Holt Online Assessment*

Internet

- go.hrw.com (Keyword: LE5 9-5)
- *Elements of Literature Online*

Media

- *Audio CD Library*
- *Audio CD Library, Selections and Summaries in Spanish*

Selection Starter

Motivate. Ask students if they find selecting gifts for family and friends difficult or rewarding. Ask volunteers to share memorable gift-giving moments.

Preview Vocabulary

Have students complete each of the following sentences with the correct Vocabulary word from p. 286.

1. One very upset shopper _____ a storewide search for her missing diamond earring. [instigates]
2. The girl dreamed that the many birthday gifts she _____ would shower over her like a _____ of riches. [coveted, cascade]
3. The _____ shopper used _____ steps to maneuver through the crowded aisles. [agile, nimble]
4. The thieves left after _____ the jewelry display. [ransacking]
5. The shoplifter tried to be _____ but did not escape the _____ of the security guards. [discreet, scrutiny]
6. Will a _____ frame _____ the value of a painting? [singed, depreciate]

VIEWING THE ART

The artist **John Sloan** (1871–1951) was a member of The Eight, a group of American realist painters who broke away from the art establishment in 1908. Sloan and the other artists in his group who painted the gritty nature of life were derisively called the Ashcan School by art critics. Sloan lived most of his life in New York City.

Activity. There are three figures in the painting: the hairdresser, her assistant, and a customer. Working in small groups, students should write two pages of dialogue between the three women. Ask volunteers to read their "scene" aloud to the class.

A Reading Skills

? Making inferences. Why do you think Della flops down on the couch and howls? [Possible responses: Christmas is coming, and Della is frustrated by her impoverished situation. Perhaps she is depressed because she cannot afford to buy someone a gift.]

B Literary Focus

? Situational irony. Why is it ironic that the card on the letter box bears the name "Mr. James Dillingham Young"? [Possible response: The use of the middle name "Dillingham" attempts to impart a sense of stability, prominent lineage, and affluence, yet the occupants of this apartment are desperately poor.]

C Correcting Misconceptions

Some students may be confused by the narrator's use of "you." Explain that this is a purely stylistic device favored by the author to draw in the reader. At several points in the story, the narrator directly addresses the reader, sometimes offering comments, other times asking the reader to consider a particular observation.

One dollar and eighty-seven cents. That was all. And sixty cents of it was in pennies. Pennies saved one and two at a time by bulldozing the grocer and the vegetable man and the butcher until one's cheeks burned with the silent imputation of parsimony[1] that such close dealing implied. Three times Della counted it. One dollar and eighty-seven cents. And the next day would be Christmas.

A There was clearly nothing to do but flop down on the shabby little couch and howl. So Della did it. Which instigates the moral reflection that life is made up of sobs, sniffles, and smiles, with sniffles predominating.

While the mistress of the home is gradually subsiding from the first stage to the second, take a look at the home. A furnished flat[2] at $8 per week. It did not exactly beggar description, but it certainly had that word on the lookout for the mendicancy squad.[3]

B In the vestibule[4] below was a letter box into which no letter would go, and an electric button from which no mortal finger could coax a ring. Also appertaining[5] thereunto was a card bearing the name "Mr. James Dillingham Young."

The "Dillingham" had been flung to the breeze during a former period of prosperity when its possessor was being paid $30 per week. Now, when the income was shrunk to $20, the letters of "Dillingham" looked blurred, as though they were thinking seriously of contracting to a modest and unassuming *D.* But whenever Mr. James Dillingham Young came home and reached his flat above, he was called Jim and greatly hugged by Mrs. James **C** Dillingham Young, already introduced to you as Della. Which is all very good.

1. **imputation** (im′pyo͞o·tā′shən) **of parsimony** (pär′sə·mō′nē): suggestion of stinginess.
2. **flat** *n.*: apartment.
3. **mendicancy** (men′di·kən·sē) **squad:** police who arrested beggars and homeless people.
4. **vestibule** (ves′tə·byo͞ol′) *n.*: small entrance hall.
5. **appertaining** (ap′ər·tān′iŋ) *v.* used as *adj.*: belonging.

Della finished her cry and attended to her cheeks with the powder rag. She stood by the window and looked out dully at a gray cat walking a gray fence in a gray back yard. Tomorrow would be Christmas Day and she had only $1.87 with which to buy Jim a present. She had been saving every penny she could for months, with this result. Twenty dollars a week doesn't go far. Expenses had been greater than she had calculated. They always are. Only $1.87 to buy a present for Jim. Her Jim. Many a happy hour she had spent planning for something nice for him. Something fine and rare and sterling—something just a little bit near to being worthy of the honor of being owned by Jim.

There was a pier glass[6] between the windows of the room. Perhaps you have seen a pier glass in an $8 flat. A very thin and very agile person may, by observing his reflection in a rapid sequence of longitudinal strips, obtain a fairly accurate conception of his looks. Della, being slender, had mastered the art.

Suddenly she whirled from the window and stood before the glass. Her eyes were shining brilliantly, but her face had lost its color within twenty seconds. Rapidly she pulled down her hair and let it fall to its full length.

Now, there were two possessions of the James Dillingham Youngs in which they both took a mighty pride. One was Jim's gold watch that had been his father's and his grandfather's. The other was Della's hair. Had the Queen of Sheba lived in the flat across the air shaft,[7] Della would have let her hair hang out the window some day to dry just to

6. **pier glass** *n.*: tall mirror hung between two windows.
7. **air shaft** *n.*: narrow gap between two buildings.

Vocabulary

instigates (in′stə·gāts′) *v.:* urges on to some action, usually negative, or sets something in motion; here, gives rise to.

agile (aj′əl) *adj.:* moving with ease.

Learners Having Difficulty
Invite learners having difficulty to read "The Gift of the Magi" in interactive format in *The Holt Reader* and to use the sidenotes as aids to understanding the selection. The interactive version provides additional instruction, practice, and assessment of the literature skill taught in the Student Edition.

Monitor students' responses to the selection, and correct any misconceptions that arise.

English-Language Learners
Encourage students to use context clues to decipher unfamiliar words in the story. Model the process using this sentence (p. 288): "In the vestibule below was a letter box into which no letter would go." Ask students,

"Where would you find a letter box, or mailbox?" [A mailbox would be in an entrance hall or near the front door of an apartment.]

Special Education Students
For lessons designed for special education students, see *Holt Reading Solutions.*

Horse-Drawn Cabs, New York (1891) by Frederick Childe Hassam. Oil pastel on canvas.

depreciate Her Majesty's jewels and gifts. Had King Solomon been the janitor, with all his treasures piled up in the basement, Jim would **D** have pulled out his watch every time he passed, just to see him pluck at his beard from envy.

So now Della's beautiful hair fell about her rippling and shining like a cascade of brown waters. It reached below her knee and made itself almost a garment for her. And then she did it up again nervously and quickly. Once she faltered for a minute and stood still while a tear or two splashed on the worn red carpet.

On went her old brown jacket; on went her old brown hat. With a whirl of skirts and with **E** the brilliant sparkle still in her eyes, she fluttered out the door and down the stairs to the street.

Where she stopped, the sign read: "Mme. Sofronie. Hair Goods of All Kinds." One flight up Della ran, and collected herself, panting. Madame, large, too white, chilly, hardly looked the "Sofronie."

"Will you buy my hair?" asked Della.

"I buy hair," said Madame. "Take yer hat off and let's have a sight at the looks of it."

Down rippled the brown cascade.

"Twenty dollars," said Madame, lifting the mass with a practiced hand.

"Give it to me quick," said Della.

Vocabulary

depreciate (dē·prē'shē·āt') v.: make something seem less important; lower the value of.

cascade (kas·kād') n.: waterfall.

The Gift of the Magi   **289**

A Vocabulary Development

Diction. Point out the highly ornate diction, or choice of words, used by O. Henry in this paragraph. Ask students to paraphrase it in simpler terms. [Possible response: When Della got home, her happiness lessened, and her mind turned to practical matters. To fix the damage that love and generosity had caused, she tried to curl the hair she had left, but it wasn't easy.]

B Literary Focus

❓ Situational irony. How might Della's sacrifice create an ironic situation? [Possible response: Jim may react differently than Della expects: He may be angry with her, or he might even prefer her hair short.]

C Reading Skills

❓ Making predictions. What do you think will happen when Jim sees Della? [Possible responses: He won't care about her hair; he will be angry that she sold her most prized possession just to buy him a present.]

Oh, and the next two hours tripped by on rosy wings. Forget the hashed metaphor. She was ransacking the stores for Jim's present.

She found it at last. It surely had been made for Jim and no one else. There was no other like it in any of the stores, and she had turned all of them inside out. It was a platinum fob chain,[8] simple and chaste in design, properly proclaiming its value by substance alone and not by meretricious[9] ornamentation—as all good things should do. It was even worthy of The Watch. As soon as she saw it she knew that it must be Jim's. It was like him. Quietness and value—the description applied to both. Twenty-one dollars they took from her for it, and she hurried home with the 87 cents. With that chain on his watch, Jim might be properly anxious about the time in any company. Grand as the watch was, he sometimes looked at it on the sly on account of the old leather strap that he used in place of a chain.

When Della reached home, her intoxication gave way a little to prudence and reason. She got out her curling irons and lighted the gas and went to work repairing the ravages[10] made by generosity added to love. Which is always a tremendous task, dear friends—a mammoth task.

Within forty minutes her head was covered with tiny, close-lying curls that made her look wonderfully like a truant schoolboy. She looked at her reflection in the mirror long, carefully, and critically.

"If Jim doesn't kill me," she said to herself, "before he takes a second look at me, he'll say I look like a Coney Island chorus girl. But what could I do—oh! what could I do with a dollar and eighty-seven cents?"

At 7 o'clock the coffee was made and the frying pan was on the back of the stove hot and ready to cook the chops.

8. **fob chain:** short chain meant to be attached to a pocket watch.
9. **meretricious** (mer′ə·trish′əs) *adj.:* attractive in a cheap, flashy way.
10. **ravages** (rav′ij·iz) *n.:* terrible damage.

Jim was never late. Della doubled the fob chain in her hand and sat on the corner of the table near the door that he always entered. Then she heard his step on the stair away down on the first flight, and she turned white for just a moment. She had a habit of saying little silent prayers about the simplest everyday things, and now she whispered: "Please God, make him think I am still pretty."

The door opened and Jim stepped in and closed it. He looked thin and very serious. Poor fellow, he was only twenty-two—and to be burdened with a family! He needed a new overcoat and he was without gloves.

Jim stepped inside the door, as immovable as a setter at the scent of quail. His eyes were fixed upon Della, and there was an expression in them that she could not read, and it terrified her. It was not anger, nor surprise, nor disapproval, nor horror, nor any of the sentiments that she had been prepared for. He simply stared at her fixedly with that peculiar expression on his face.

Della wriggled off the table and went for him.

"Jim, darling," she cried, "don't look at me that way. I had my hair cut off and sold it because I couldn't have lived through Christmas without giving you a present. It'll grow out again—you won't mind, will you? I just had to do it. My hair grows awfully fast. Say 'Merry Christmas!' Jim, and let's be happy. You don't know what a nice—what a beautiful, nice gift I've got for you."

"You've cut off your hair?" asked Jim, laboriously, as if he had not arrived at that patent[11] fact yet even after the hardest mental labor.

"Cut it off and sold it," said Della. "Don't you like me just as well, anyhow? I'm me without my hair, ain't I?"

Jim looked about the room curiously.

11. **patent** (pat′′nt) *adj.:* obvious.

Vocabulary
ransacking (ran′sak′iŋ) *v.:* searching thoroughly.

READING MINI-LESSON

Developing Word-Attack Skills
Remind students that the letter *c* stands for two different sounds, depending on the vowel letter that follows it: *c* before *a, o,* or *u* stands for /k/, and *c* before *e, i,* or *y* stands for /s/. **Activity.** Write these words from the selection on the chalkboard. Each word contains two *c*'s. Have students read the words and tell which sound each *c* stands for.

mendicancy [/k/, /s/]   calculated [/k/, /k/]
conception [/k/, /s/]   cascade [/k/, /k/]
practiced [/k/, /s/]   ecstatic [/k/, /k/]
sacrificed [/k/, /s/]   critically [/k/, /k/]

Point out that in some situations, the letter *c* before *i* stands not for the sound /s/ but the sound /sh/. Illustrate this using these words from the selection: *depreciate,* in which *ci* stands

The Closed Shutters by Elizabeth Nourse (c. 1860–1938). Oil on canvas.
Musée d'Orsay/Art Resource, New York.

VIEWING THE ART

The painter **Elizabeth Nourse** (1859–1938) was born in a suburb of Cincinnati, Ohio. At the age of fifteen, Elizabeth began to study art at what was later to become the Art Academy of the Cincinnati Art Museum. In 1887, Elizabeth traveled to Paris, where she continued her studies at the Académie Julian. She painted in a bold and confident style that was welcomed by the Paris Salon, and they accepted her work for exhibition.

In *The Closed Shutters,* the subject of the painting is illuminated by light that enters through the slats in the shutters.

Activity. Use this painting as a springboard for oral storytelling. Ask students, "Who is the woman in the painting?" "What does the setting suggest about her circumstances?" and "What is she thinking as she gazes into the mirror?"

---

for /shē/; *meretricious* and *mathematician,* in which the letters *ci* together stand for /sh/.
Activity. Display these words. Have students group them into the following three categories: *c* stands for /k/; *c* stands for /s/; *c* or *ci* stands for /sh/.

peculiar [/k/] appreciate [/sh/] facetious [/s/]

curiously [/k/] deprecate [/k/] rapacious [/sh/]

delicious [/sh/] cinema [/s/] glacier [/sh/]

facial [/sh/] spacious [/sh/] recipe [/s/]

cylinder [/s/] incinerate [/s/] secretary [/k/]

ducal [/k/] intoxicate [/k/] nucleus [/k/]

adjacent [/s/] logical [/k/] special [/sh/]

A Advanced Learners

? Acceleration. How would you characterize the narrator's tone here? [Possible responses: condescending; superior; amused; distant.]

B Literary Focus

? Situational irony. Why is this an ironic situation? [Possible responses: With short hair, Della has no use for the combs; Della sold her hair to buy Jim a gift.]

C Literary Focus

? Situational irony. How does this surprise twist make the situation even more ironic? [Both Della and Jim sacrificed their most cherished possession to buy something for use with the other's most cherished possession.]

D Literary Focus

? Theme. How does O. Henry explain his earlier reference to the Magi here? [Possible response: He suggests that the love that inspires sacrifice and generosity is the real gift of the wise.]

"You say your hair is gone?" he said, with an air almost of idiocy.

"You needn't look for it," said Della. "It's sold, I tell you—sold and gone, too. It's Christmas Eve, boy. Be good to me, for it went for you. Maybe the hairs on my head were numbered," she went on with a sudden serious sweetness, "but nobody could ever count my love for you. Shall I put the chops on, Jim?"

Out of his trance Jim seemed quickly to wake. He enfolded his Della. For ten seconds let us regard with <u>discreet</u> <u>scrutiny</u> some inconsequential object in the other direction. Eight dollars a week or a million a year—what is the difference? A mathematician or a wit would give you the wrong answer. The Magi brought valuable gifts, but that was not among them. This dark assertion will be illuminated later on.

Jim drew a package from his overcoat pocket and threw it upon the table.

"Don't make any mistake, Dell," he said, "about me. I don't think there's anything in the way of a haircut or a shave or a shampoo that could make me like my girl any less. But if you'll unwrap that package, you may see why you had me going awhile at first."

White fingers and <u>nimble</u> tore at the string and paper. And then an ecstatic scream of joy; and then, alas! a quick feminine change to hysterical tears and wails, necessitating the immediate employment of all the comforting powers of the lord of the flat.

For there lay The Combs—the set of combs, side and back, that Della had worshiped for long in a Broadway window. Beautiful combs, pure tortoise shell, with jeweled rims—just the shade to wear in the beautiful vanished hair. They were expensive combs, she knew, and her heart had simply craved and yearned over them without the least hope of possession. And now, they were hers, but the tresses that should have adorned the coveted adornments were gone.

But she hugged them to her bosom, and at length she was able to look up with dim eyes and a smile and say: "My hair grows so fast, Jim!"

And then Della leaped up like a little <u>singed</u> cat and cried, "Oh, oh!"

Jim had not yet seen his beautiful present. She held it out to him eagerly upon her open palm. The dull precious metal seemed to flash with a reflection of her bright and ardent spirit.

"Isn't it a dandy, Jim? I hunted all over town to find it. You'll have to look at the time a hundred times a day now. Give me your watch. I want to see how it looks on it."

Instead of obeying, Jim tumbled down on the couch and put his hands under the back of his head and smiled.

"Dell," said he, "let's put our Christmas presents away and keep 'em a while. They're too nice to use just at present. I sold the watch to get the money to buy your combs. And now suppose you put the chops on."

The Magi, as you know, were wise men—wonderfully wise men—who brought gifts to the Babe in the manger. They invented the art of giving Christmas presents. Being wise, their gifts were no doubt wise ones, possibly bearing the privilege of exchange in case of duplication. And here I have lamely related to you the uneventful chronicle of two foolish children in a flat who most unwisely sacrificed for each other the greatest treasures of their house. But in a last word to the wise of these days, let it be said that of all who give gifts, these two were the wisest. Of all who give and receive gifts, such as they are wisest. Everywhere they are wisest. They are the Magi. ■

Vocabulary

discreet (di·skrēt′) *adj.*: showing good judgment in what one says or does; especially being silent or careful.

scrutiny (skrōōt′'n·ē) *n.*: close inspection.

nimble (nim′bəl) *adj.*: quickly moving.

coveted (kuv′it·id) *v.* used as *adj.*: longed-for.

singed (sinjd) *v.* used as *adj.*: slightly burned.

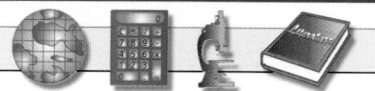

CONTENT-AREA CONNECTIONS

Culture: Giving of Gifts
Ask students to share what they know about the gift-giving traditions of various cultures. Examples include the gift exchanges and donations to the poor associated with the Jewish celebration of Hanukkah; the potlatch ceremony among some Native American peoples, in which an individual gives away every possession; or the *kula* tradition among Pacific Islanders in Melanesia, in which symbolic exchanges solidify mutual, lifelong obligations.
Paired activity. Interested students can work in pairs to research and explore another culture's gift-giving traditions. You might have students create a bulletin board display to illustrate their findings.

Meet the Writer

O. Henry

He ♥ New York

O. Henry (1862–1910), whose real name was William Sydney Porter, grew up in Greensboro, North Carolina. At the age of twenty, he went to Texas, where he became a rancher, worked as a bank teller, and founded a humorous weekly called *The Rolling Stone.*

When he was accused of stealing a thousand dollars from the First National Bank of Austin, where he was a teller, Porter panicked and fled to Central America. In Honduras he traveled with the outlawed Jennings brothers and helped them spend the loot from a recent robbery. When news of his wife's illness brought him back to Austin, he was arrested, tried, and sentenced to five years in prison. Ironically, if he had not run away, Porter might have been acquitted. The bank was poorly run, and the loss of money might have been a case of mismanagement, not a crime.

Porter served only three years of his sentence. In prison he wrote more than a dozen stories and absorbed the underworld lore that he would use in stories such as "A Retrieved Reformation." He also may have found his pen name there: One of the prison guards was named Orrin Henry.

Porter left prison in 1901 and went to New York. He loved the city at once, and he wrote about it and its inhabitants for the few years remaining in his life. He once remarked:

> ❝ There are stories in everything. I've got some of my best yarns from park benches, lampposts, and newspaper stands. ❞

O. Henry wrote more than six hundred stories altogether—sixty-five in 1904 alone. A heavy drinker, he died of tuberculosis when he was only forty-seven. His last words were "Pull up the shades so I can see New York. I don't want to go home in the dark."

For Independent Reading

Want to read more O. Henry stories with surprising twists? Try "The Ransom of Red Chief," in which O. Henry paints a comical picture of two kidnappers who get much more than they bargain for. In "A Retrieved Reformation" an expert burglar has an unexpected change of heart.

The Gift of the Magi **293**

Monitoring students' progress. Guide the class in answering these comprehension questions.

True-False

1. The story is set on Christmas Eve. [T]
2. Della sells her hair to buy Jim a gift. [T]
3. Jim's watch is a family heirloom. [T]
4. Jim sells his watch to buy Della a locket. [F]

Meet the Writer

Background. Like his characters, O. Henry knew what it is like to need money. Although he made money from his writing, his costly lifestyle left him perpetually broke. When he was admitted to the hospital at the end of his life, he had only twenty-three cents in his pockets.

O. Henry's biographer David Stuart says that the author "wrote the best stories about New York City that have ever been written, and . . . his stories give a very good picture of life in the city in the period from 1900 to 1910, a picture that cannot be secured elsewhere."

DIFFERENTIATING INSTRUCTION

Advanced Learners
Enrichment. O. Henry's many tales set in New York City can provide excellent points of departure for further inquiry into the famous city's history and culture.
Activity. Have students read an O. Henry selection that has New York City as its setting. Then, encourage students to research the economic, political, and cultural influences evident in the city at that time. Finally, have students write an essay explaining how those influences might have helped shape the story O. Henry wrote.

Connection

Summary ⬌ *at grade level*

Pat Mora's poem describes an elderly couple as they navigate a plaza crowded with tourists. The speaker contrasts the pair with the tourists to emphasize the aged couple's enduring love.

DIRECT TEACHING

A **Reading Skills**

? **Drawing conclusions.** What do you think the speaker means by "bodies returning to the land"? [Possible response: The couple is elderly, and in both a physical and chronological sense, they are headed toward the ground in which they will be buried.]

B **Reading Skills**

Comparing and contrasting. Ask students to compare the dress of the tourists with that of the elderly couple. [Possible responses: The tourists are wearing minimal clothing; the elderly couple is fully clothed, perhaps to protect against the effects of the sun, or because they are of a generation that tends to favor a more modest, conservative mode of dress.]

CONNECTION / POEM

This poem is about the love of an elderly couple—los ancianos in Spanish. As you read, consider why the poet chose these Spanish words for her title rather than their English equivalent.

Los Ancianos

Pat Mora

They hold hands
as they walk with slow steps.
Careful together they cross the plaza
both slightly stooped, bodies returning to the land,
5   he in faded khaki° and straw hat,
she wrapped in soft clothes, black
rebozo° round her head and shoulders.

Tourists in halter tops and shorts
pose by flame trees and fountains,
10   but the old couple walks step by step
on the edge.
Even in the heat, only their wrinkled
hands and faces show. They know
of moving through a crowd at their own pace.

15   I watch him help her
off the curb and I smell love
like dried flowers, old love
of holding hands with one man for fifty years.

---
5. khaki (kak′ē) *n.:* tan-colored clothing.
7. *rebozo* (re·bô′thô): Spanish for "shawl."

Connecting and Comparing Texts

The questions that follow can help prompt students to make connections between "The Gift of the Magi" and "Los Ancianos":

• **What message does each work express about the importance of appearance and the importance of love?** [Possible response: In "The Gift of the Magi," both Della and Jim make sacrifices to improve the appearance of their partner. Della sacrifices her hair so Jim will have a proper chain to show off his treasured watch. Jim sacrifices his watch so that Della will have ornaments for her beautiful hair. In the end, however, neither partner has anything to show to the world. Still, each has the love of the other. In "Los Ancianos," the elderly couple, unlike the skimpily clad tourists, displays little to the world except wrinkled skin and faded clothing. Still, to the poem's speaker, their decades-old love is clearly evident.]

• **How are these messages similar?** [Possible response: Both the story and the poem make the point that love is more valuable than appearances and that in comparison to love, good looks and signs of affluence are trivial.]

Response and Analysis

Reading Check

1. Suppose you are telling the story of Della and Jim to a group of your friends. Identify the two **characters,** tell what each one **wants** to do, and summarize the **main events** and the **outcome** of their story.

2. What **predictions** did you make as you read the story? Did your predictions come close to what actually happens? Check your reading notes.

Thinking Critically

3. An **ironic situation** is one that turns out to be just the opposite of what we—or the characters in the story—expect. Describe the **situational irony** in this story. What lesson about life and love do you think it teaches Della and Jim?

4. What is the real "gift" referred to in the **title**? (Notice that O. Henry uses the word *gift,* not *gifts.*)

5. A **contradiction** occurs when two statements or situations have opposite meanings. In the last paragraph of the story, the narrator first describes Della and Jim as "foolish children" who "unwisely sacrificed" their treasures for each other. The narrator then says they are "the wisest" of all who give and receive gifts. How can you explain the contradiction in the narrator's description of the characters?

6. What do you think this story, written a century ago, has to say about our consumer society today? Do you think some people equate love with money? Consider advertising, the amount of money we spend on gifts, and the value placed on having many possessions.

7. In the poem "Los Ancianos" (see the **Connection** on page 294), the elderly Hispanic couple, dressed in old clothing and walking slowly, seems to represent traditional values. In contrast, the tourists in halter tops posing for cameras seem to represent a more modern, materialistic world. What point might the poet be making by this **contrast**? Do you see any similarity between the poet's point and Della and Jim's situation? Explain.

Extending and Evaluating

8. What is your reaction to O. Henry's **surprise ending**? Do you enjoy this kind of **irony** in stories or movies, or does it seem contrived—a trick played on the reader? Explain your response.

WRITING

Life Goes On

The glimpse O. Henry gives us of Della and Jim is of just one brief time in their lives, early in their marriage. As life goes on, people change and grow—sometimes in opposite directions. Provide readers with a glimpse of Della and Jim ten years later. In what ways has each character changed or stayed the same? What is each one doing? Where do they live? Write a paragraph about Della and Jim called "Life Goes On." When they are old, will they be like the couple in "Los Ancianos" (see the **Connection** on page 294)?

What It Means to Me

Imagine that you are writing a **letter** to your grandchild, telling him or her the story of a cherished possession. Explain how you got it and why it's so important to you. (Be sure to check your Quickwrite notes.)

INTERNET
Projects and Activities
Keyword: LE5 9-5

SKILLS FOCUS

Literary Skills
Analyze situational irony and the surprise ending.

Reading Skills
Make predictions.

Writing Skills
Write a character description.
Write a letter.

The Gift of the Magi **295**

Response and Analysis

Thinking Critically

3. The situational irony occurs because both Della and Jim expect to delight the other with a gift. Instead, their sacrifices render both gifts useless. Della and Jim may have learned that their love does not rely on material gifts or that love can lead to unexpected results.

4. Possible answer: The real gift is the gift of love, as displayed by generosity, unselfishness, and sacrifice.

5. Jim and Della have made foolish choices and are now stuck with two expensive and useless items. However, they are truly wise since their selfless acts have demonstrated the strength of their love.

6. Possible answer: The story is very relevant in modern society. Love and money are often equated together, and during the holidays, people often feel compelled to buy things they can't afford in order to demonstrate their love.

7. Possible answer: The speaker in "Los Ancianos" contrasts the tourists with the elderly couple to emphasize the value of enduring love, more important than any material item. This point is echoed by the situation of Della and Jim who have selflessly shown their love, despite having exchanged worthless gifts.

Extending and Evaluating

8. Possible answers: The ending is enjoyable because it casts the story in a new light; a surprise ending is unsatisfying because it makes you feel as if you have been tricked.

Reading Check

1. Possible answer: Della wants to buy her husband Jim a Christmas present but has no money. She sells her hair and uses the money to buy Jim a chain for his watch. When he comes home, Jim is stunned to see Della without long hair. He has bought her the fancy hair combs she wanted and has sold his watch to do so. Neither one can use their gifts, but together the couple has a love more precious than any gift.

2. Answers will vary. Some students will have correctly predicted the outcome of the story. Others may have predicted that Jim would become angry when he found out about Della's hair.

Vocabulary Development

Practice 1

Possible Answers

1. He sets his plan in motion.
2. An agile person might swing easily from rung to rung.
3. a bad accident
4. The boat would likely sink.
5. I might ransack my memory to remember someone's name.
6. A discreet person would keep the secret to herself.
7. A scrutiny of my room would reveal my habits.
8. A nimble person could easily learn a new dance.
9. On a hot summer day, I coveted a visit to a public lake.
10. I would throw the shirt out.

Practice 2

Possible Answers

1. "And now, they were hers, but the tresses that should have adorned the coveted adornments were gone."

   Now she had them, but she had no hair to wear them in.

2. "In the vestibule below was a letter box into which no letter would go, and an electric button from which no mortal finger could coax a ring."

   The doorbell and mailbox were both broken.

3. "It was a platinum fob chain, simple and chaste in design, properly proclaiming its value by substance alone."

   It was a simple and elegant platinum chain—clearly valuable.

Vocabulary Development

In Your Own Words

PRACTICE 1

How well do you understand the meaning of the Word Bank words? Try answering the following questions:

1. If a criminal instigates a plan to rob a bank, what does he do?
2. What might an agile person do on monkey bars?
3. What would depreciate the value of a car?
4. What would happen to a small boat that sailed into a cascade?
5. When might you find yourself ransacking your memory?
6. What does a discreet person do when told a secret?
7. What would a scrutiny of your room reveal about you?
8. When might it be particularly helpful to be nimble?
9. Describe something you once coveted.
10. If you singed your shirt when ironing it, what would you do with it?

Word Bank

instigates
agile
depreciate
cascade
ransacking
discreet
scrutiny
nimble
coveted
singed

Diction—Ornate or Plain?

Diction, or word choice, can make a great difference in a piece of writing. A realistic writer might use slang. A science reporter might use precise, technical language. A romantic person might want to be poetic.

O. Henry loved flowery and ornate diction. In the first paragraph he writes:

"One's cheeks burned with the silent imputation of parsimony that such close dealing implied."

A writer who preferred a plain style might have said:

You'd blush to think that bargaining suggested you were stingy.

SKILLS FOCUS

Vocabulary Skills
Demonstrate word knowledge. Understand diction.

PRACTICE 2

Find three ornate sentences in the story, and rewrite each of them using plain, straightforward diction, as if you were modernizing the story for today's readers. Compare your rewritten versions in class.

Writers' Tip: William Strunk, Jr., and E. B. White, the authors of a famous writing handbook called *The Elements of Style,* tell writers never to use a twenty-dollar word when a ten-cent word will do just as well. As you work on your writing, think about your **diction.** Consider the diction that is most appropriate for your characters, your setting, and your tone. Can a strong, simple word work as well as a fancy one?

PEANUTS® reprinted by permission of UFS, Inc.

ASSESSING

Assessment

- *Holt Assessment: Literature, Reading, and Vocabulary*

RETEACHING

For another selection to teach irony, see *The Holt Reader,* Collection 5.

Before You Read

The Lady, or the Tiger?

Make the Connection

Quickwrite ✏️

Did you ever have to make a choice between something that was good for you and something that was good for someone you cared about? Are you glad that you chose as you did? Jot down your thoughts about making this choice.

Literary Focus

Ambiguity: Mixed Signals

Ambiguity is a quality that allows something to be interpreted in several different—sometimes even conflicting—ways. Ambiguity adds complexity to a story. It can make fiction seem more like real life, where we often encounter people and events that are puzzling or mysterious.

An ambiguous story can linger in your mind for days or years. You might return to the story again and again, answering its questions differently each time. Ambiguity made "The Lady, or the Tiger?" an instant hit, and it has kept people trying to answer one simple—or not so simple—question for more than a century.

Reading Skills

Making Inferences About Motivation: The *Whys* and *Wherefores*

When you make an **inference** about a character's **motivation,** you make an educated guess about the character's reasons for behaving in a certain way. You base this guess on what the narrator tells you as well as on clues (such as what a character says or does) that the writer has planted in the text.

As you read "The Lady, or the Tiger?" think about the motivation of the characters—in particular, that of the king's daughter. The questions at the open-book signs will help you make inferences.

Background

During the Middle Ages an accused person's guilt or innocence was often determined by a trial by ordeal. If the person was not hurt during a physical test, it was believed the accused was saved from harm by God and was therefore innocent. Those who were injured or killed were viewed as guilty. In this story, justice is determined in a similar way.

Vocabulary Development

exuberant (eg·zoo'bər·ənt) *adj.:* elaborate; extreme; also, high-spirited.

genial (jēn'yəl) *adj.:* cheerful and friendly.

impartial (im·pär'shəl) *adj.:* fair; unbiased.

allegiance (ə·lē'jəns) *n.:* loyalty.

procured (prō·kyoord') *v.:* gotten; obtained.

dire (dīr) *adj.:* terrible.

retribution (re'trə·byoo'shən) *n.:* punishment.

fervent (fur'vənt) *adj.:* passionate.

aspiring (ə·spīr'iŋ) *v.* used as *n.:* seeking to gain; desiring.

deliberation (di·lib'ər·ā'shən) *n.:* careful thought, especially in making a decision.

go.hrw.com

INTERNET

Vocabulary Practice

Keyword: LE5 9-5

SKILLS FOCUS

Literary Skills
Understand ambiguity.

Reading Skills
Make inferences about character motivation.

The Lady, or the Tiger? **297**

Grade-Level Skills

■ **Literary Skills**
Identify ambiguities, contradictions, and ironies in the text.

■ **Reading Skills**
Make inferences about character motivation.

Review Skills

■ **Literary Skills**
Identify the literary devices (such as metaphor, dialect, and irony) that define a writer's style.

Summary ⬆️ *above grade level*

In this fairy tale a king edifies his subjects through public trials with verdicts that are determined by chance. The accused subject must choose to open one of two identical doors. Behind one door is the reward—a beautiful maiden to marry. Behind the other door lies the punishment—a ferocious tiger. When the princess's lover is discovered and jailed, the trial takes on personal significance for the king. The young man's hopes for survival rest with the princess. The author adds a layer of ambiguity to her action by revealing that the maiden behind the "door of innocence" is the princess's rival.

RESOURCES: READING

Planning
■ *One-Stop Planner* CD-ROM with ExamView Test Generator

Differentiating Instruction
■ *Holt Reading Solutions*
■ *Holt Adapted Reader*
■ *Supporting Instruction in Spanish*

Vocabulary
■ *Vocabulary Development*

Grammar and Language
■ *Daily Language Activities*
■ *Language Handbook Worksheets*

Assessment
■ *Holt Assessment: Literature, Reading, and Vocabulary*
■ *One-Stop Planner* CD-ROM with ExamView Test Generator
■ *Holt Online Assessment*

Internet
■ go.hrw.com (Keyword: LE5 9-5)
■ *Elements of Literature Online*

Media
■ *Audio CD Library*
■ *Audio CD Library, Selections and Summaries in Spanish*
■ *Fine Art Transparencies*

THE LADY, OR THE TIGER?

Frank R. Stockton

Proserpine (1874) by Dante Gabriel Rossetti. Oil on canvas (125.1 cm × 61 cm).

In the very olden time, there lived a semibarbaric[1] king, whose ideas, though somewhat polished and sharpened by the progressiveness of distant Latin neighbors, were still large, florid, and untrammeled,[2] as became the half of him which was barbaric. He was a man of exuberant fancy, and, withal,[3] of an authority so irresistible that, at his will, he turned his varied fancies into facts. He was greatly given to self-communing; and, when he and himself agreed upon any thing, the thing was done. When every member of his domestic and political systems moved smoothly in its appointed course, his nature was bland and genial; but whenever there was a little hitch, and some of his orbs got out of their orbits, he was blander and more genial still, for nothing pleased him so much as to make the crooked straight, and crush down uneven places.

Among the borrowed notions by which his barbarism had become semified[4] was that of the public arena, in which, by exhibitions of manly and beastly valor, the minds of his subjects were refined and cultured.

1. **semibarbaric** (sem′ĭ·bär·ber′ik) *adj.*: partly uncivilized.
2. **untrammeled** (un·tram′əld) *adj.*: not restrained or kept under control.
3. **withal** (with·ôl′) *adv.*: in addition.
4. **semified**: probably an invented word suggesting "reduced in half."

Vocabulary

exuberant (eg·zoo′bər·ənt) *adj.*: elaborate; extreme; also, high-spirited.
genial (jēn′yəl) *adj.*: cheerful and friendly.

Stalking Tiger by Rosa Bonheur (1822–1899). Oil on wood.

But even here the exuberant and barbaric fancy asserted itself. The arena of the king was built, not to give the people an opportunity of hearing the rhapsodies of dying gladiators, nor to enable them to view the inevitable conclusion of a conflict between religious opinions and hungry jaws, but for purposes far better adapted to widen and develop the mental energies of the people. This vast amphitheater,[5] with its encircling galleries, its mysterious vaults, and its unseen passages, was an agent of poetic justice, in which crime was punished, or virtue rewarded, by the decrees of an impartial and incorruptible chance.

When a subject was accused of a crime of sufficient importance to interest the king, public notice was given that on an appointed day the fate of the accused person would be decided in the king's arena—a structure which well deserved its name; for, although its form and plan were borrowed from afar, its purpose emanated solely from the brain of this man, who, every barleycorn a king,[6] knew no tradition to which he owed more allegiance than pleased his fancy, and who ingrafted on every adopted form of human thought and action the rich growth of his barbaric idealism.

When all the people had assembled in the galleries, and the king, surrounded by his court, sat high up on his throne of royal state on one side of the arena, he gave a signal, a door beneath him opened, and the accused subject stepped out into the amphitheater. Directly opposite him, on the other side of the enclosed space, were two doors, exactly alike and side by side. It was the duty and the privilege of the person on trial to walk directly to these doors and open one of them. He could open either door he pleased: He was subject to no guidance or influence but that of the aforementioned impartial and incorruptible chance. If he opened the one, there came out of it a hungry tiger, the fiercest and most cruel that could be procured, which immediately sprang upon him, and tore him to pieces, as a punishment for his guilt. The

---

5. **amphitheater** (am′fə·thē′ə·tər) *n.:* round building with an open space surrounded by rows of seats.
6. **every barleycorn a king:** every bit of him a king; a barleycorn is a small unit of measure used in earlier times.

Vocabulary
impartial (im·pär′shəl) *adj.:* fair; unbiased.
allegiance (ə·lē′jəns) *n.:* loyalty.
procured (prō·kyoord′) *v.:* gotten; obtained.

The Lady, or the Tiger?   **299**

DIRECT TEACHING

A Vocabulary Development

Context clues. Point out that an antonym can help to determine the meaning of an unfamiliar word. Here, "retribution" and "reward" are presented as the two outcomes of the king's system. Since the two outcomes are opposites, a reader could assume that *punishment,* the antonym of *reward,* is the same as *retribution.*

B Reading Skills

Inferring character motivation.

[Possible responses to question 1: The king is described as being semibarbaric and despotic, yet prone to extravagant ideas about culture and society. He probably created this system to satisfy both aspects of his character. The public executions feed his barbarism; the fact that the outcome is determined by the accused satisfies his notions of justice and impartiality.]

C Advanced Learners

? Acceleration. Ask students to consider how the narrator's comments on the public's enjoyment of the trials might connect to and satirize contemporary cultural appetites. What entertainment mediums in our society provide cliffhanger endings, involve real-life participants, reward success, and punish failure? [Possible responses: "reality" television programs, game shows that involve weeding out participants, live coverage of criminal trials.]

moment that the case of the criminal was thus decided, doleful iron bells were clanged, great wails went up from the hired mourners posted on the outer rim of the arena, and the vast audience, with bowed heads and downcast hearts, wended slowly their homeward way, mourning greatly that one so young and fair, or so old and respected, should have merited so dire a fate.

But, if the accused person opened the other door, there came forth from it a lady, the most suitable to his years and station that his majesty could select among his fair subjects; and to this lady he was immediately married, as a reward of his innocence. It mattered not that he might already possess a wife and family, or that his affections might be engaged upon an object of his own selection: The king allowed no such subordinate arrangements to interfere with his great scheme of retribution and reward. The exercises, as in the other instance, took place immediately, and in the arena. Another door opened beneath the king, and a priest, followed by a band of choristers, and dancing maidens blowing joyous airs on golden horns and treading an epithalamic measure,[7] advanced to where the pair stood, side by side; and the wedding was promptly and cheerily solemnized. Then the gay brass bells rang forth their merry peals, the people shouted glad hurrahs, and the innocent man, preceded by children strewing flowers on his path, led his bride to his home.

This was the king's semibarbaric method of administering justice. Its perfect fairness is obvious. The criminal could not know out of which

---

7. **treading an epithalamic measure:** performing a wedding dance.

THERE WAS NO ESCAPE FROM THE JUDGMENTS OF THE KING'S ARENA.

door would come the lady: He opened either he pleased, without having the slightest idea whether, in the next instant, he was to be devoured or married. On some occasions the tiger came out of one door, and on some out of the other. The decisions of this tribunal[8] were not only fair, they were positively determinate:[9] The accused person was instantly punished if he found himself guilty; and, if innocent, he was rewarded on the spot, whether he liked it or not. There was no escape from the judgments of the king's arena.

The institution was a very popular one. When the people gathered together on one of the great trial days, they never knew whether they were to witness a bloody slaughter or a hilarious wedding. This element of uncertainty lent an interest to the occasion which it could not otherwise have attained. Thus, the masses were entertained and pleased, and the thinking part of the community could bring no charge of unfairness against this plan; for did not the accused person have the whole matter in his own hands?

This semibarbaric king had a daughter as blooming as his most florid fancies, and with a soul as fervent and imperious[10] as his own. As is

---

8. **tribunal** (trī·byōō′nəl) *n.:* court of justice.
9. **determinate** (dē·tur′mi·nit) *adj.:* final; definite.
10. **imperious** (im·pir′ē·əs) *adj.:* arrogant; self-important.

Vocabulary

dire (dīr) *adj.:* terrible.

retribution (re′trə·byōō′shən) *n.:* punishment.

fervent (fur′vənt) *adj.:* passionate.

INFERRING CHARACTER MOTIVATION

1. Based on what you know about the king, tell why you think he created this system of justice.

---

usual in such cases, she was the apple of his eye, and was loved by him above all humanity. Among his courtiers was a young man of that fineness of blood and lowness of station common to the conventional heroes of romance who love royal maidens. This royal maiden was well satisfied with her lover, for he was handsome and brave to a degree unsurpassed in all this kingdom; and she loved him with an ardor that had enough of barbarism in it to make it exceedingly warm and strong. This love affair moved on happily for many months, until one day the king happened to discover its existence. He did not hesitate nor waver in regard to his duty in the premises. The youth was immediately cast into prison, and a day was appointed for his trial in the king's arena. This, of course, was an especially important occasion; and his majesty, as well as all the people, was greatly interested in the workings and development of this trial.

Never before had such a case occurred; never before had a subject dared to love the daughter of a king. In after-years such things became commonplace enough; but then they were, in no slight degree, novel and startling.

INFERRING CHARACTER MOTIVATION

2. Why doesn't the king approve of the youth's love for his daughter?

The tiger cages of the kingdom were searched for the most savage and relentless beasts, from which the fiercest monster might be selected for the arena; and the ranks of maiden youth and beauty throughout the land were carefully surveyed by competent judges, in order that the young man might have a fitting bride in case fate did not determine for him a different destiny. Of course, everybody knew that the deed with which the accused was charged had been done. He had loved the princess, and neither he, she, nor anyone else thought of denying the fact; but the king would not think of allowing any fact of this kind to interfere with the workings of the

tribunal, in which he took such great delight and satisfaction. No matter how the affair turned out, the youth would be disposed of; and the king would take an aesthetic[11] pleasure in watching the course of events, which would determine whether or not the young man had done wrong in allowing himself to love the princess.

The appointed day arrived. From far and near the people gathered, and thronged the great galleries of the arena; and crowds, unable to gain admittance, massed themselves against its outside walls. The king and his court were in their places, opposite the twin doors—those fateful portals, so terrible in their similarity.

All was ready. The signal was given. A door beneath the royal party opened, and the lover of the princess walked into the arena. Tall, beautiful, fair, his appearance was greeted with a low hum of admiration and anxiety. Half the audience had not known so grand a youth had lived among them. No wonder the princess loved him! What a terrible thing for him to be there!

As the youth advanced into the arena, he turned, as the custom was, to bow to the king: But he did not think at all of that royal personage; his eyes were fixed upon the princess, who sat to the right of her father. Had it not been for the moiety[12] of barbarism in her nature, it is probable that lady would not have been there; but her intense and fervid soul would not allow her to be absent on an occasion in which she was so terribly interested. From the moment that the decree had gone forth, that her lover should decide his fate in the king's arena, she had thought of nothing, night or day, but this great event and the various subjects connected with it. Possessed of more power, influence, and force of character than anyone who had ever before been interested in such a case, she had done what no other person had done—she had

---

11. **aesthetic** (es·thet'ik) *adj.:* relating to an appreciation for beauty.
12. **moiety** (moi'ə·tē) *n.:* half part.

D Literary Focus

❓ **Recurring theme.** How would you describe the "conventional heroes of romance who love royal maidens" who tend to reappear in fairy tales? [Possible response: They tend to be brave and handsome, but they possess humble backgrounds.]

E Reading Skills

Inferring character motivation. [Possible responses to question 2: As is typical in fairy tales, the king doesn't want his daughter to be involved with someone from a lower social class; he wants to have a say in whom his daughter is involved with.]

F Reading Skills

❓ **Evaluating.** Does the king's refusal to interfere in the case involving his daughter demonstrate the fairness of his system? [Possible response: No; it shows that he is not personally corrupt, but it does not change the fact that his system of justice is completely arbitrary.]

DEVELOPING FLUENCY

Cross-age activity. While the subject matter of the story is suitable for readers of all ages, the vocabulary level and sentence construction would make it inaccessible to younger students. Have students work in small groups to create concise retellings of the story that would be enjoyable to students at lower grade levels. Before writing the simpler

versions, students should re-read the story and reach a consensus on which events and details are essential to the retelling. If possible, allow groups to share their versions with students from lower grades.

A Reading Skills
Inferring character motivation.

[Possible responses to question 3: The princess shares her father's barbaric side, which includes a morbid curiosity for and enjoyment of brutal entertainment. She is also deeply in love with the accused, and this side of her character motivates her to learn the secret in order to influence her lover's decision.]

B Literary Focus
? Ambiguity. How does this paragraph make the possible future actions of the princess ambiguous? [Possible response: Since she knows the secret of the doors, one would expect the princess to save her lover's life. This description of the princess's jealousy over the maiden reveals her internal conflict and makes the reader wonder if the princess would allow her lover to end up marrying her hated rival.]

C Reading Skills
Inferring character motivation.

[Possible responses to question 4: The accused trusts the princess because he knows the depth of her love for him. Furthermore, since he doesn't know the identity of the woman behind the door, he has no reason to imagine that the princess is torn by jealousy. The princess probably realizes this and is confident of the young man's trust.]

possessed herself of the secret of the doors. She knew in which of the two rooms, that lay behind those doors, stood the cage of the tiger, with its open front, and in which waited the lady. Through these thick doors, heavily curtained with skins on the inside, it was impossible that any noise or suggestion should come from within to the person who should approach to raise the latch of one of them; but gold, and the power of a woman's will, had brought the secret to the princess.

> **INFERRING CHARACTER MOTIVATION**
>
> **A 3.** Why would the princess's barbaric half draw her to the arena, where her lover might be killed? Why would she be **motivated** to learn the secret of the doors?

And not only did she know in which room stood the lady ready to emerge, all blushing and radiant, should her door be opened, but she knew who the lady was. It was one of the fairest and loveliest of the damsels of the court who had been selected as the reward of the accused youth, should he be proved innocent of the crime of aspiring to one so far above him; and the princess hated her. Often had she seen, or imagined that she had seen, this fair creature throwing glances of admiration upon the **B** person of her lover, and sometimes she thought these glances were perceived and even returned. Now and then she had seen them talking together; it was but for a moment or two, but much can be said in a brief space; it may have been on most unimportant topics, but how could she know that? The girl was lovely, but she had dared to raise her eyes to the loved one of the princess; and, with all the intensity of the savage blood transmitted to her through long lines of wholly barbaric ancestors, she hated the woman who blushed and trembled behind that silent door.

When her lover turned and looked at her, and his eye met hers as she sat there paler and whiter than anyone in the vast ocean of anxious faces about her, he saw, by that power of quick perception which is given to those whose souls are one, that she knew behind which door crouched the tiger, and behind which stood the lady. He had expected her to know it. He understood her nature, and his soul was assured that she would never rest until she had made plain to herself this thing, hidden to all other lookers-on, even to the king. The only hope for the youth in which there was any element of certainty was based upon the success of the princess in discovering this mystery; and the moment he looked upon her, he saw she had succeeded, as in his soul he knew she would succeed.

Then it was that his quick and anxious glance asked the question: "Which?" It was as plain to her as if he shouted it from where he stood. There was not an instant to be lost. The question was asked in a flash; it must be answered in another.

Her right arm lay on the cushioned parapet before her. She raised her hand, and made a slight, quick movement toward the right. No one but her lover saw her. Every eye but his was fixed on the man in the arena.

He turned, and with a firm and rapid step he walked across the empty space. Every heart stopped beating, every breath was held, every eye was fixed immovably upon that man. Without the slightest hesitation, he went to the door on the right, and opened it.

> **INFERRING CHARACTER MOTIVATION**
>
> **C 4.** Why do you think the young man trusts the princess to save his life? Do you think the princess is sure he will trust her?

Now, the point of the story is this: Did the tiger come out of that door, or did the lady?

Vocabulary
aspiring (ə·spīr′iŋ) v. used as n.: seeking to gain; desiring.

READING MINI-LESSON

Developing Word-Attack Skills
Write the words *cordial, genial,* and *jovial* on the chalkboard, and have students read the words aloud. Point out that all three words have the suffix *–ial,* but that it is pronounced differently in each word. In *cordial,* the suffix *–ial* is pronounced /əl/; in *genial,* it is pronounced /yəl/; in *jovial,* it is pronounced /ē·əl/.

Explain that the vowel combination *ia* has different pronunciations in other endings as well. Write the words *defiance, variance,* and *allegiance* on the chalkboard, and help students compare the sounds of the letters *–iance* in the three words. In *defiance, –iance* is pronounced /ī·əns/; in *variance,* the letters are pronounced /ē·əns/; in *allegiance,* they are pronounced /əns/. Help students recognize

Caracalla and Geta (1907) by Sir Lawrence Alma-Tadema.

Private Collection / © Bridgeman Art Gallery.

The more we reflect upon this question, the harder it is to answer. It involves a study of the human heart which leads us through devious mazes of passion, out of which it is difficult to find our way. Think of it, fair reader, not as if the decision of the question depended upon yourself, but upon that hot-blooded, semibarbaric princess, her soul at a white heat beneath the combined fires of despair and jealousy. She had lost him, but who should have him?

How often, in her waking hours and in her dreams, had she started in wild horror, and covered her face with her hands as she thought of her lover opening the door on the other side of which waited the cruel fangs of the tiger!

But how much oftener had she seen him at the other door! How in her grievous reveries[13] had she gnashed her teeth, and torn her hair, when she saw his start of rapturous delight as he opened the door of the lady! How her soul had burned in agony when she had seen him rush to meet that woman, with her flushing cheek and sparkling eye of triumph; when she had seen him lead her forth, his whole frame kindled with the joy of recovered life; when she had heard the glad shouts from the multitudes, and the wild ringing of the happy bells; when she had seen the priest, with his joyous follow-

D

---

13. **reveries** (rev′ə·rēz) *n.:* daydreams.

The Lady, or the Tiger? **303**

DIRECT TEACHING

VIEWING THE ART

Born in Holland, **Sir Lawrence Alma-Tadema** (1836–1912) lived most of his working life in England. In 1863, he visited Italy, and he was deeply influenced by the archaeological history of that country. He painted many paintings that feature scenes set in the classical past. This painting shows the brothers Caracalla (on the right) and Geta (on the left) at a stadium. Caracalla, the older brother, arranged to have Geta murdered to settle the power struggle that occurred after the death of their father, the emperor Septimus Severus.

Activity. Have students study the painting. How does the artist hint at the struggle that is to occur between the two brothers? [Possible response: Caracalla is shown at the right of the painting leaning against a pillar, in shadows and partly hidden from the crowds. Geta is depicted in the foreground showing himself to the spectators.]

D Literary Focus

❓ **Ambiguity.** Does this statement make it seem likely that the princess has sent the young man to the tiger? Explain your opinion. [Possible responses: Yes, she is more disturbed by the idea of him ending up with the young woman than by the idea of seeing him dead; no, she probably has this vision more often because she is inclined to save him.]

that in *defiance* and *variance,* the base word determines how the *i* is pronounced. The word *defiance* is derived from *defy,* which ends with the sound /ī/, and *variance* is derived from *vary,* which ends with the sound /ē/.
Activity. Display these sets of words. Have students read the words and identify the two in which the vowel combination *ia* has the same sound or sounds. Answers are underlined.

1.	initial	initiate	gladiator
2.	genial	menial	denial
3.	partial	trial	martial
4.	radiant	median	reliant
5.	arterial	memorial	artificial
6.	spatial	social	associate
7.	abbreviate	judicial	mediate

A **Reading Skills**

Inferring character motivation.

[Possible responses to question 5: A desire to spare her lover from death would motivate the princess to send the youth to the lady; an inability to overcome her savage jealousy toward her rival would motivate the princess to send him to the tiger.]

GUIDED PRACTICE

Monitoring students' progress. Guide the class in answering these comprehension questions. Direct students to locate passages in the story that support their responses.

True-False

1. The king uses a panel of judges to determine the guilt of accused criminals. [F]

2. A young man is accused of having an affair with the princess. [T]

3. The young man is put on trial in the arena. [T]

4. The princess is unable to learn what lies behind each of the two doors. [F]

5. The princess refuses to speak with her father. [F]

Meet the Writer

Background. Stockton's famous tale, as well as his other works, earned him a lasting audience that admire him for his uniqueness, if not necessarily for the substance of his writing. *The Cambridge History of English and American Literature* describes his short stories as "like nothing else in American literature" and as "amusing, delightful, ephemeral."

Stockton was also one of the earliest writers of science fiction, and in many of his works, he imagined the fantastic and unexpected. For example, in his novel *The Great War Syndicate,* he described machines that were invented not to fight war but to prohibit it.

ers, advance to the couple, and make them man and wife before her very eyes; and when she had seen them walk away together upon their path of flowers, followed by the tremendous shouts of the hilarious multitude, in which her one despairing shriek was lost and drowned!

Would it not be better for him to die at once, and go to wait for her in the blessed regions of semibarbaric futurity?

And yet, that awful tiger, those shrieks, that blood!

Her decision had been indicated in an instant, but it had been made after days and nights of anguished <u>deliberation</u>. She had known she would be asked, she had decided what she would answer, and, without the slightest hesitation, she had moved her hand to the right.

The question of her decision is one not to be lightly considered, and it is not for me to presume to set myself up as the one person able to answer it. And so I leave it with all of you: Which came out of the opened door—the lady, or the tiger? ■

INFERRING CHARACTER MOTIVATION
5. What would **motivate** the princess to direct the youth to the lady? Why would she send him to the tiger?

Vocabulary

deliberation (di·lib′ər·ā′shən) *n.:* careful thought, especially in making a decision.

Meet the Writer

Frank R. Stockton

Famous Overnight

When Frank R. Stockton (1834–1902) wrote "The Lady, or the Tiger?" he never imagined that his inspired idea for a story would bring him lasting fame.

Born in Philadelphia, Stockton started out as a sickly, imaginative boy who amused himself by inventing stories. He eventually became a successful writer of works for adults and children.

In 1882, Stockton concocted a lively story, which he called "In the King's Arena," to entertain some friends at a party. *Century Magazine* published it as "The Lady, or the Tiger?" and Stockton became famous overnight. Hundreds of readers pestered him, demanding that he decide the story's outcome once and for all. Stockton did finally respond to his readers, but his answer was not the one they had hoped for.

❝If you decide which it was—the lady, or the tiger—you find out what kind of a person you are yourself.❞

Stockton was admired by his contemporaries. Near the end of his life, one critic praised him for his "inventiveness," a quality that the modern reader of "The Lady, or the Tiger?" can certainly appreciate.

FAMILY/COMMUNITY ACTIVITY

Readers of all ages will enjoy Frank R. Stockton's fairy tale and will come up with their own ideas about the story's mysterious ending—ideas that are influenced by readers' personal interpretations and experiences. Ask students to share the story with their family members and to discuss the ambiguous ending after they have read it. Encourage students to share any interesting rationales regarding the choice of ending that their family members express.

Response and Analysis

Reading Check

1. How are people punished or rewarded under the king's system of justice?

2. Why is the young man put on trial in the king's arena?

3. What does the princess learn?

4. Why does the young man decide to open the door on the right?

Thinking Critically

5. How would you describe the **character** of the king and the way he rules his people? Do you think the narrator believes he is a good leader? Explain your answer.

6. **Characterize** the princess. In what ways is she similar to her father? What kind of love does she feel for the young man?

7. When the narrator says of the king's system of justice, "Its perfect fairness is obvious," he is using **verbal irony**—saying one thing but meaning something completely different. Explain what the narrator is implying in this line. Then, find another example of verbal irony in the story.

8. What do you think is behind the door the young man opens: the lady or the tiger? Consider these factors, and support your answer with evidence:

   - the **character** of the princess
   - the princess's **motivation** for directing the young man to the lady or the tiger
   - clues in the narrator's description of the princess's thoughts and behavior

   Watch for **subtleties,** or fine distinctions, which can tell you a lot about a character, even though the meaning is often implied rather than stated directly.

9. What is the **tone** of the story— the attitude expressed toward the characters and events? List one or two adjectives to describe the tone, and explain your choice of adjectives.

Extending and Evaluating

10. Why might Stockton have left the ending of his story **ambiguous**—was he trying to make a particular point or create a particular effect? Explain whether you think the ambiguous ending makes the story memorable.

WRITING

Your Verdict

Do you think most people, faced with the princess's dilemma, would save their loved one or send him or her to death? In other words, are people motivated mostly by their own desires or by concern for others? Write one or two **persuasive** paragraphs in which you defend your point of view. (Be sure to check your Quickwrite notes.)

▶ **Use "Writing a Persuasive Essay," pages 320–327, for help with this assignment.**

The End

Write a **sequel** to this story. You might decide once and for all whether the lady or the tiger is behind the door, or you might decide to make your sequel **ambiguous** in its own way. You could even invent an entirely new way of ending the story. Tell about the final events from the point of view of one of the following characters: the young man, the princess, the king, a member of the audience in the arena—or even the tiger.

SKILLS FOCUS

Literary Skills
Analyze ambiguity.

Reading Skills
Make inferences about character motivation.

Writing Skills
Write a persuasive essay. Write a sequel.

The Lady, or the Tiger? **305**

Response and Analysis

6. Like her father, the princess tries to be rational, but she is driven by powerful emotions and "savage blood." While she loves her suitor, this love may not be strong enough to overcome her jealousy.

7. The narrator is implying that the king's system is ludicrously unjust. An additional example of verbal irony is the statement "The thinking part of the community could bring no charge of unfairness against this plan."

8. Some students may say the tiger is behind the door, citing the narrator's emphasis on the princess's savage side and the strength of her jealousy. Others may argue that the maiden is behind the door, noting that the princess's last thoughts before making her decision are about the "awful tiger, those shrieks, that blood!"

9. Students may identify the narrator's tone as humorous, ironic, tongue-in-cheek, or satirical. They may cite words and phrases such as "semibarbaric king," "orbs got out of their orbits," and "florid fancies."

Extending and Evaluating

10. Most students will say that Stockton chooses an ambiguous ending in order to create a unique effect on the reader. With the ending unclear, Stockton creates a talking point for his readers. Others may argue that Stockton chooses the ambiguous ending to emphasize a question about human nature: Is it possible to act selflessly if it means we have to give up what we desire?

Reading Check

1. The guilt or innocence of the accused man is determined by chance in a public arena.

2. He is accused of having a love affair with the king's daughter.

3. She learns which door hides the tiger and which door hides the maiden.

4. He follows the signal of the princess.

Thinking Critically

5. Possible answers: The king is an arbitrary, capricious tyrant. The narrator seems to approve of the king's leadership; the narrator's approval is ironic, adding to the story's satirical effect.

Vocabulary Development

Practice

1. *retribution. Context clue*—"good, innocent character was rewarded."

2. *impartial. Context clues*—"never favored any team"; "making just decisions."

3. *dire. Context clue*—"families lost their homes, roads were flooded, and the town lost electricity."

4. *deliberation. Context clue*—"thought about the issue for days."

5. *exuberant. Context clues*—"Enthusiastic and energetic"; "the liveliest person in the room."

6. *procured. Context clue*—"lost . . . but."

7. *aspiring. Context clues*—"Practicing the violin every day"; "become a professional musician."

8. *genial. Context clues*—"made friends easily"; "good-natured and outgoing."

9. *allegiance. Context clue*—"patriotic."

10. *fervent. Context clues*—"opposites"; "rarely showed emotion."

Vocabulary Development

Context Clues: Looking for Signs

Context clues are like signs that can help explain the meaning of a new word. **Context clues** can be **synonyms,** which **restate** the meaning of a word, or **antonyms,** which **contrast** with the word. They can also be **examples** or descriptive words and phrases that help **define** the word. Note how the context clues (underlined) in this sentence from "The Lady, or the Tiger?" help you understand the meaning of *dire:*

> "The moment that the case of the criminal was thus decided, . . . great wails went up from the hired mourners posted on the outer rim of the arena, and the vast audience, with bowed heads and downcast hearts, wended slowly their homeward way, mourning greatly that one . . . should have merited so **dire** a fate."

The context clues—the descriptive phrases that emphasize people's sadness—help you understand that *dire* means "terrible."

PRACTICE

For each sentence below, choose the Word Bank word that best completes the sentence. Then, identify the **context clues** in each sentence that helped you determine the answer.

1. The ending of the movie was predictable: The good, innocent character was rewarded whereas the evil criminal received _____.

2. The _____ referee never favored any team and was respected for making just decisions.

3. The hurricane created a _____ situation: Many families lost their homes, roads were flooded, and the town lost electricity.

4. After making a list of pros and cons, I thought about the issue for days, and finally, after much _____, I decided to move.

5. Enthusiastic and energetic, Lynette was so _____ that she always turned out to be the liveliest person in the room.

6. Eric lost his father's favorite scarf, but he _____ a similar one at a neighborhood store.

7. Practicing the violin every day, Anna hoped to play in an orchestra, and I admired her for _____ to become a professional musician.

8. The _____ student made friends easily because he was so good-natured and outgoing.

9. The soldier was suspected of being a spy even though he had shown _____ to his captain and had appeared to be patriotic.

10. Although Jamie and Jesse were twins, they were opposites in that Jamie rarely showed emotion but Jesse was always _____.

Word Bank

exuberant
genial
impartial
allegiance
procured
dire
retribution
fervent
aspiring
deliberation

SKILLS FOCUS

Vocabulary Skills
Use context clues to understand the meaning of words.

Grammar Link

Subject-Verb Agreement:
Interrupting Prepositional Phrases

In standard American English, verbs **agree** with their subjects in number. That is, if the subject is singular, the verb is singular; if the subject is plural, the verb is plural. Making sure that subjects and verbs agree can be tricky when **prepositional phrases** come between the subject and the verb in a sentence. Usually such phrases do not determine the number of the subject. Look at these examples from "The Lady, or the Tiger?":

"The tiger cages of the kingdom were searched for the most savage and relentless beasts. . . ." [plural subject, plural verb]

"This vast amphitheater, with its encircling galleries, its mysterious vaults, and its unseen passages, was an agent of poetic justice. . . ." [singular subject, singular verb]

When a prepositional phrase separates a subject and a verb, imagine there is a box around the interrupting words, as in the examples above. That way you'll be able to see the subject and verb as a pair, and it will be easier to decide whether the verb should be singular or plural. Remember, too, that the object of a prepositional phrase is never the subject of a sentence.

PRACTICE

In the following sentences, decide whether the verb should be singular or plural, and choose the correct form of the verb:

1. The young man, like other prisoners, (was/were) put on trial in the arena.

2. One of the most beautiful maidens (was/were) chosen to stand behind the door.

3. The princess's visions of her lover's fate (was/were) tormenting her.

4. The princess, in addition to crowds of people, (was/were) present at the trial.

5. The story, with its alternative endings, (has/have) intrigued readers for more than a century.

6. My friend, among other readers, (thinks/think) the lady was behind the door.

7. My view, unlike my classmates' opinions, (is/are) that the tiger was behind the door.

8. Our questions about the story (remains/remain) unresolved.

▶ **For more help, see Agreement of Subject and Verb, 2a–m, in the Language Handbook.**

SKILLS FOCUS

Grammar Skills
Use correct subject-verb agreement with an interrupting prepositional phrase.

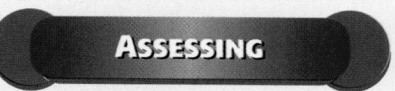

Grammar Link

Practice

1. was   5. has
2. was   6. thinks
3. were   7. is
4. was   8. remain

Assessment

■ *Holt Assessment: Literature, Reading, and Vocabulary*

RETEACHING

For another selection to teach ambiguity, see *The Holt Reader,* Collection 5.

DIFFERENTIATING INSTRUCTION

Learners Having Difficulty
If students need additional practice in deciding whether a verb should be singular or plural, have them choose the correct verb form in each of the following sentences.

1. The princess's ideas on the subject of love and passion (was/were) primitive. [were]

2. Nearly every one of the king's many subjects (was/were) loyal to him. [was]

3. The maiden, along with many others in the king's court, (has/have) prayed that the young man would choose her door. [has]

4. The heavy doors with a thick layer of padding (was/were) made soundproof. [were]

5. Do you agree that the king, despite what he says about his notions of justice, (has/have) been unfair to the young man? [has]

Grade-Level Skills

■ **Reading Skills**

Evaluate the credibility of an author's argument by examining generalizations, the scope of the evidence, and the intentions of the author.

Review Skills

■ **Reading Skills**

Assess the quality of the author's evidence to support claims, noting instances of bias and stereotyping.

Summary ✎ *at grade level*

As the title indicates, this persuasive essay defends the jury system. The author, an assistant district attorney, first addresses some typical criticisms that jurors base their decisions on emotion rather than reason and that jurors cannot be trusted to understand complex issues. He then compares people who criticize jurors to people who criticize voters for making irrational or ill-informed choices, recognizing that these systems have obvious imperfections, but stating that he wouldn't advocate abolishing either one of them. Having acknowledged that the jury system is fallible, the author states that most criticism of juries is unjustified. As evidence, he cites surveys of jurors and judges, showing that most of them would prefer to be tried by a jury panel rather than by a judge. The author also points out that relying on the verdict of a judge does not guarantee fairness because judges are subject to human error. A jury, however, reflects the makeup of a community and helps ensure that a verdict will not be based on one person's biases or lack of understanding. The author concludes that though the jury system has problems, it is the best system of justice for a democracy because it guarantees that the perspectives of all citizens will be respected.

Informational Text

LINK TO "THE LADY, OR THE TIGER?"

A Defense of the Jury System

Evaluating an Argument: And the Verdict Is . . .

An **argument** is a series of statements designed to convince you of something. When you evaluate an author's argument, you act somewhat like a juror serving on a trial. Like a juror you need to analyze the evidence presented to you and decide whether the argument is sound. The following tips and the chart on the next page will help you determine whether an author's argument is **credible,** or believable:

1. **Understand the claim, or opinion.** First, read through the argument to make sure that you understand the matter being discussed. Identify what the author is trying to prove, which is called the **claim,** or **opinion.** Often the author's opinion is stated in the form of a **generalization,** or a broad statement that covers many situations. For example, the following statement is a generalization that expresses an opinion: *All jurors should be allowed to take notes during a trial.* Try to restate the author's opinion in your own words.

2. **Identify the support.** An author must provide support for a claim in order to create a persuasive argument. Here are some common types of support that authors use:

   Logical appeals. To show that their opinions are valid, authors present **reasons,** statements that explain *why* the author holds an opinion. For example, the following statement provides a reason for the author's opinion: *All jurors should be allowed to take notes during a trial because notes can help them remember important information for reaching a verdict.*

Evidence is the information that authors use to support their reasons. Every generalization, to be believable, should be backed up by evidence. There are several types of evidence:

- facts
- statistics (number facts)
- examples
- quotations from or opinions of experts

Sometimes writers use analogies, another type of logical appeal, to help them explain a point. An **analogy** is a type of comparison in which writers usually explain something complex or unfamiliar in terms of something familiar.

Emotional appeals. To win readers over to their opinions, authors sometimes appeal to readers' emotions rather than their reason. Writers, for instance, might want their readers to feel outrage over an injustice or to feel sympathy for a victim. Emotional appeals can be effective tools, but watch out for arguments that rely heavily on emotion at the expense of logic. It's usually a sign that an argument is weak. Emotional appeals include

- **loaded words** (words with strong emotional connotations)
- **anecdotes** (brief stories)

3. **Evaluate the evidence.** An argument is only as strong as its evidence. Ask yourself: "Does the evidence directly support the author's reasons? Does the author present sufficient evidence to back up generalizations and to prove the claim? Has the author loaded the argument with emotional appeals instead of providing valid evidence?"

INTERNET
Interactive
Reading Model
Keyword: LE5 9-5

SKILLS FOCUS

Reading Skills
Evaluate an author's argument and evidence.

RESOURCES: READING

Planning

■ *One-Stop Planner* CD-ROM with ExamView Test Generator

Differentiating Instruction

■ *Holt Reading Solutions*

■ *Holt Adapted Reader*

■ *Supporting Instruction in Spanish*

Vocabulary

■ *Vocabulary Development*

Grammar and Language

■ *Daily Language Activities*

Assessment

■ *Holt Assessment: Literature, Reading, and Vocabulary*

4. Identify the author's intent. Finally, think about why the author is making this argument. As far as you can tell, has the author carefully weighed all the evidence before arriving at an opinion? Does the author, instead, seem to be biased or prejudiced? Note how the author's **intent,** or purpose, influences the **tone** of the argument. For example, if the author wants to urge readers to take action, the tone might be strongly emotional.

5. Create a chart. To help you evaluate an argument, make a chart like the one shown here. Such a chart will help you see the strengths and weaknesses of an argument.

Evaluating an Author's Argument
Claim, or opinion:
Logical appeals
Reason 1:
Evidence:
Reason 2:
Evidence:
Emotional appeals
Loaded words:
Anecdotes:
Tone:

➤ **For more about persuasive writing, see "Writing a Persuasive Essay," pages 320–327, at the end of this collection.**

Vocabulary Development

irrational (i·rash′ə·nəl) *adj.:* not based on reason or logic.

superficial (sōō′pər·fish′əl) *adj.:* not deep or thorough; shallow.

obscure (əb·skyoor′) *v.:* conceal; cover up.

advocates (ad′və·kāts′) *v.:* supports; argues in favor of.

conscientiously (kän′shē·en′shəs·lē) *adv.:* carefully and thoughtfully.

affluent (af′lōō·ənt) *adj.:* wealthy.

Connecting to the Literature

"The Lady, or the Tiger?" describes a system of justice in which the fate of the accused is decided entirely by chance. How fair is our own system, trial by jury? Read the following persuasive essay to find out what one expert thinks.

A Defense of the Jury System   **309**

- *One-Stop Planner* CD-ROM with ExamView Test Generator
- *Holt Online Assessment*

Internet
- go.hrw.com (Keyword: LE5 9-5)
- *Elements of Literature Online*

Media
- *Audio CD Library*
- *Audio CD Library, Selections and Summaries in Spanish*

Selection Starter

Motivate. Discuss the pros and cons of the jury system. Point out to students that most important tasks in our society are done by specialists—pilots fly airplanes, carpenters build homes. Yet when it comes to deciding if a person is guilty or not guilty in a court of law, we rely on a jury of average citizens. Ask for a show of hands of those students who feel that a jury is a good way to decide cases and of those who feel that there might be a better way. Before students read the selection, have advocates for each side offer reasons and examples to support their positions.

Preview Vocabulary

Have pairs of students take turns reading aloud the definitions of the Vocabulary words on p. 309. Then, have students work together on the following exercise.

1. Tell about a time when you made an irrational decision.
2. How would you know if someone had only superficial knowledge of baseball?
3. Should the tobacco industry be allowed to obscure the dangers of cigarette smoking? Explain.
4. Suppose a group in your school advocates a uniform dress code. How would you respond?
5. Tell about a time when you acted conscientiously.
6. Who do you think is the most affluent person in the United States?

Assign the Reading

Point out the title of the selection to students before they begin reading. Ask them to write a statement of what they predict will be the author's main opinion or claim. Encourage students to take notes on the author's claim and to cite his supporting evidence for it.

A Reading Informational Text

? **Evaluating an argument.** Point out that the author begins his essay by noting criticism of the jury system. Why do you think he does this? [Possible response: to acknowledge that the jury system is not perfect and therefore disarm critics who would use the same example to call for abolishing the jury system.]

B Reading Informational Text

Evaluating an argument. If necessary, remind students that a generalization is a broad statement that covers many situations. [Possible response to question 1: Juries are criticized for being overly emotional and irrational. Juries are criticized for not understanding complex issues.]

C Reading Informational Text

? **Evaluating an argument.** What analogy does the author make in this paragraph? [Critics of the jury system are like critics of the democratic process of voting.] How does the author use this analogy to state his opinion or claim? [He refers to the common statement that "democracy is the worst form of government—except for all the others" and says the same is true of the jury system.]

PERSUASIVE ESSAY

A DEFENSE OF THE JURY SYSTEM

Thomas M. Ross, Esq.

A The jury system is often attacked for delivering seemingly irrational verdicts in both criminal and civil cases.[1] Much of this criticism stems from some well-publicized verdicts that the public has felt were unjustified and unreasonable. For example, when a fast-food company was forced to pay $2.7 million in damages in a case brought by a woman who had spilled a cup of coffee on her lap, the verdict was widely ridiculed. One congressman remarked, "Most people say this doesn't make a lot of sense."

Juries are criticized for deciding cases based upon their prejudices or emotions, rather than rationally applying the law to the evidence presented in a case. They are also criticized for being incapable of understanding the complex financial and scientific issues that sometimes arise in today's court cases. For example, a jury in one case awarded a small company $35 million in damages from a communications conglomerate[2] for a patent infringement.[3] A lawyer involved in the case remarked that the jury of "unemployed laborers and housewives didn't understand that stuff."**B**

B **EVALUATING ARGUMENTS**

In your own words, explain the author's two main **generalizations** in this paragraph.

1. **civil cases:** court cases relating to the rights and duties of individuals.
2. **conglomerate** (kən·gläm′ər·it) *n.:* large business made up of several smaller companies.
3. **patent infringement:** Patents are legal documents granting inventors exclusive rights to make and profit from their inventions. Making or using an invention without the permission of the patent owner is called patent infringement.

C People who make these criticisms, however, are very much like people who criticize voters for being irrational or ill-informed. Critics claim that many voters have only a superficial grasp of the issues and, accordingly, are easily swayed by simplistic slogans and "thirty-second sound bites"[4] that obscure the complexity of the issues. Despite these criticisms of voters, hardly anyone advocates abolishing the vote. After all, it has been said that "democracy is the worst form of government—except for all the others." The same can be said of the jury system: It's the worst system of justice—except for all the others.

Much of the criticism of the jury system is unjustified and stems from unfamiliarity with the system. When people actually serve on a jury, they usually find that the cases receiving widespread negative publicity are atypical[5]—most of their peers perform their duties conscientiously, honestly, and fairly. For example, a survey of eight hundred

4. **sound bites** *n.:* brief, attention-getting statements, often made by politicians, that are broadcast on television and radio.
5. **atypical** (ā·tip′i·kəl) *adj.:* not typical; unusual.

Vocabulary
irrational (i·rash′ə·nəl) *adj.:* not based on reason or logic.
superficial (sōō′pər·fish′əl) *adj.:* not deep or thorough; shallow.
obscure (əb·skyoor′) *v.:* conceal; cover up.
advocates (ad′və·kāts′) *v.:* supports; argues in favor of.
conscientiously (kän′shē·en′shəs·lē) *adv.:* carefully and thoughtfully.

Learners Having Difficulty
Modeling. To help students understand how to evaluate the credibility of an author's argument, you may wish to review the ways in which logical arguments are supported—with facts, examples, statistics, and expert testimony. Say, "Pets help people live longer, healthier lives. How can I support this argument?" Encourage students to brainstorm for examples of support, such as statistics that show pet owners living longer, testimony from pet owners and mental-health professionals, and studies showing the benefits of pet ownership.

jurors by the *National Law Journal* in 1993 revealed that 75 percent of them would prefer to be tried by a panel of their peers rather than by a panel of judges. Even judges themselves, who observe juries daily, have confidence in most jurors. A survey of state judges in Texas found that 98 percent believed that juries do at least "moderately well" in reaching a "just and fair" verdict. Furthermore, if those judges were a party in a civil lawsuit or were accused of a crime, 60 percent said that they would rather have their civil case decided by a jury than by a judge, and 80 percent said they would rather have their criminal case decided by a jury. ❷

> **❷ EVALUATING EVIDENCE**
> What type of **evidence** is presented in this paragraph?

D

Some people believe that having cases decided exclusively by judges would improve our justice system. However, like jurors, judges are human beings, capable of making misjudgments. Relying on judges, instead of juries, to decide cases does not guarantee that every verdict will be considered fair by all. Furthermore, judges are not representative of society as a whole. Although more women and minority members are being appointed as judges—as more women and minority members

enter the legal profession itself—judges are still mostly Caucasian and male. Moreover, most judges, like most lawyers, generally come from middle-class and affluent backgrounds. Thus, the experiences and perspectives of women, minorities, and poor and working-class people would be underrepresented in a system in which all cases were decided by judges.

E

On the other hand, jurors are drawn from both sexes, all ethnic groups, all economic backgrounds, all adult ages, all religions, and all neighborhoods within a jurisdiction.[6] (Indeed, the only qualification a person needs to be a juror is the ability to be fair and impartial.) Consequently, a jury will reflect diverse viewpoints and experiences, rather than just the viewpoint and experiences of a single judge. The jury system thus helps ensure that a verdict will not be based on an individual's biases or lack of understanding of particular people's experiences.

Human beings are not perfect—we make mistakes, and sometimes we are swayed by our emotions—and that means that the jury system is also not perfect. Despite its flaws, the jury system is the best means we have for maintaining justice in a democracy. No other system guarantees that the perspectives of all citizens will be represented. ❸

> **❸ EVALUATING ARGUMENTS**
> In your own words, state the author's main **claim,** or **opinion,** in this essay.

F

The author is an assistant district attorney in Kings County (Brooklyn), New York.

G

6. **jurisdiction** (joor′is·dik′shən) *n.:* here, geographic area under the authority of a particular court system.

Vocabulary
affluent (af′loo·ənt) *adj.:* wealthy.

D **Reading Informational Text**
Evaluating an argument.
[Response to question 2: statistical evidence based on surveys of jurors and judges.]

E **Reading Informational Text**
❷ **Evaluating an argument.**
What reasons does the author give to support his opinion that judges would be no better than juries?
[Judges are capable of making the same misjudgments as jurors. Judges are generally white, affluent males, who often cannot relate to the diverse experiences of defendants.]

F **Reading Informational Text**
Evaluating an argument. [Possible response to question 3: While the jury system is not perfect, it is the best system we have to administer justice.]

G **Advanced Learners**
❷ **Enrichment.** How might the author's position in the legal system influence his purpose in arguing for the jury system? [Possible response: As a lawyer and assistant district attorney, he may be biased toward the existing system and have a vested interest in keeping it as it is.]

GUIDED PRACTICE

Monitoring students' progress. Have students form small groups to fill out charts like the one on p. 309. Groups can then compare their charts.

English-Language Learners
To understand this essay, students may need some background information on the U.S. jury system. Explain that the fate of a person accused of a crime is decided by "a jury of his peers"—that is, a group of twelve people of equal standing with the defendant. Those twelve men and women, drawn from the community at large, are instructed to listen to the evidence and decide the case.

Analyzing Informational Text

Reading Check

1. Juries are criticized for delivering irrational verdicts and for not understanding complex issues.

2. Juries are representative of society as a whole. Juries ensure that a verdict is not based on one person's biases or lack of understanding.

3. The jury system guarantees "that the perspectives of all citizens will be represented."

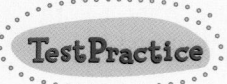

Answers and Model Rationales

1. **D** A expresses an opinion that the author disagrees with; B is evidence supporting the author's overall opinion; and although the author does not think it should be replaced, he admits that there are things wrong with the jury system (C).

2. **J** J is clearly the right answer, because the comparison does not use facts (F), anecdotes (G), or loaded words (H).

3. **A** The author does not use loaded words (D), anecdotes (C), or experts' quotations (B), so A is the correct answer.

4. **F** The statistics the author presents all measure the trust jurors and judges have for juries.

5. **A** Only A contains words with strong emotional connotations. All the other phrases are neutral.

6. **H** The tone of the essay is not sarcastic (F) or resentful (J). While some readers may find the message comforting (G), the overall tone of the essay is reasonable (H).

Analyzing Informational Text

Reading Check

1. According to the first two paragraphs, why are juries frequently criticized?

2. List the advantages of having cases decided by juries instead of by judges, as described in the essay.

3. According to the author, what does the jury system guarantee that no other judicial system can guarantee?

Test Practice

1. Which statement *best* expresses the author's **claim,** or **opinion**?
   A A few highly publicized cases prove that the jury system is not fair.
   B Many judges believe that the jury system is fair.
   C There is nothing wrong with the jury system, and it should not be replaced.
   D Despite its problems, trial by jury is the fairest system of justice.

2. The author's comparison of the jury system to the popular vote is an example of —
   F a fact
   G an anecdote
   H loaded words
   J an analogy

3. To support his **claim,** the author relies most heavily on —
   A reasons and facts
   B experts' quotations
   C anecdotes
   D loaded words

4. What conclusion does the author want you to draw from the **statistics** he presents in the essay?
   F Jurors and judges trust juries.
   G More criminal cases than civil cases are decided by judges.
   H After serving as jurors, most people feel that the jury system is not effective.
   J Surveys are a good way to learn about the jury system.

5. Which of the following phrases from the essay is an example of **loaded language**?
   A "simplistic slogans"
   B "unfamiliarity with the system"
   C "like most lawyers"
   D "an individual's biases"

6. Which word *best* describes the **tone** of the essay?
   F sarcastic
   G comforting
   H reasonable
   J resentful

SKILLS FOCUS

Reading Skills
Evaluate an author's argument and evidence.

Constructed Response

Imagine that Ross's essay was published in your local newspaper. Write a letter to the editor in which you tell whether you think Ross's argument is **credible.** Explain your point of view by **evaluating** the **claim** and supporting **evidence** in his essay. How strong or weak do you find his argument?

312 Collection 5 Irony and Ambiguity • Evaluating an Argument

Test-Taking Tips

Tell students to read each possible answer completely. They should be aware that test writers sometimes create an answer that is partially correct. If part of the answer is correct and part is incorrect (as in C for question 1), then the entire answer is incorrect.

For more information on how to answer multiple-choice items, refer students to **Test Smarts.**

Vocabulary Development

Using Contexts

PRACTICE

Each practice item below includes one of the Word Bank words used in three different **contexts**. (The first example is a quotation from the essay.) For each item, review the three examples. Then, choose the best meaning of the Word Bank word to complete the sentence in the third example.

1. "The jury system is often attacked for delivering seemingly <u>irrational</u> verdicts. . . . "

   Confused and panicked, he made <u>irrational</u> comments.

   An <u>irrational</u> argument is
   a. illogical
   b. predictable
   c. convincing
   d. simplistic

2. "Critics claim that many voters have only a <u>superficial</u> grasp of the issues. . . ."

   As she had only a <u>superficial</u> knowledge of the law, she consulted a legal expert.

   Someone with a <u>superficial</u> view of life might be called
   a. biased
   b. shallow
   c. false
   d. thorough

3. "Critics claim that many voters . . . are easily swayed by simplistic slogans and 'thirty-second sound bites' that <u>obscure</u> the complexity of the issues."

   On rainy days, clouds <u>obscure</u> the mountaintop from view.

To <u>obscure</u> something is to
a. highlight it
b. change it
c. exaggerate it
d. conceal it

Word Bank
irrational
superficial
obscure
advocates
conscientiously
affluent

4. "Hardly anyone <u>advocates</u> abolishing the vote."

   Only one candidate <u>advocates</u> using the plot of land for a shopping mall instead of a park.

   A politician who <u>advocates</u> something
   a. disagrees with it
   b. understands it
   c. prevents it
   d. supports it

5. "Most of their peers perform their duties <u>conscientiously</u>, honestly, and fairly."

   Sensitive and attentive, the nurse cared for her patients <u>conscientiously</u>.

   To do your job <u>conscientiously</u> means to do it
   a. independently
   b. carefully and thoughtfully
   c. with authority
   d. modestly

6. "Moreover, most judges, like most lawyers, generally come from middle-class and <u>affluent</u> backgrounds."

   Only <u>affluent</u> people shop at the elegant, expensive store.

   An <u>affluent</u> family is
   a. wealthy
   b. close-knit
   c. proud
   d. happy

SKILLS FOCUS

Vocabulary Skills
Use context clues to understand the meaning of words.

A Defense of the Jury System   313

Vocabulary Development

Practice

1. a
2. b
3. d
4. d
5. b
6. a

ASSESSING

Assessment

■ *Holt Assessment: Literature, Reading, and Vocabulary*

RETEACHING

For a lesson to reteach evaluating an argument, see **Reteaching,** p. 979A. For another selection to teach argument, see *The Holt Reader,* Part 2.

Grade-Level Skills

■ **Literary Skills**
Identify ambiguities, contradictions, and ironies in the text.

Summary ↔ *at grade level*

> When the speaker encounters a forked path in the woods, he is undecided about which road to take, because one seems just as good as the other. After long consideration, the speaker chooses the road less traveled. Reflecting on his decision, the speaker realizes that someday this choice will have made a tremendous difference in his life.

PRETEACHING

Selection Starter

Motivate. Point out to students that people often compare life to a road or a pathway. Cite phrases such as "taking a new turn or direction," "coming to a fork in the road," and "life at a crossroads." Have students think about moments when their own lives reached a "turning point." Encourage them to complete the Quickwrite.

Before You Read

The Road Not Taken

Make the Connection

Quickwrite ✏
Think of a choice you made that marked a turning point in your life—trying out for a sports team, signing up as a volunteer in your community, standing up for a friend. Go back to the moment when you made the choice, and imagine that you made a different one instead. Jot down notes about how you envision your life would be different if that turning point had never happened.

Literary Focus

Contradictions: Yes = No
Life is full of contradictions. A particular choice you once made might have improved your life in some ways but made it worse in others. Was it a good choice or a bad one? It was both—and it was neither. Such **contradictions**—two feelings, events, or statements that are opposites—are often captured in literature.

When you come across contradictory statements in a literary work, you might first assume that one statement is true and the other is not, or you might try to figure out which statement the writer *really* meant. However, sometimes both statements are true in some way, and the writer meant both of them.

The poet Robert Frost called "The Road Not Taken" a tricky poem. Read it several times, and try to figure out exactly what Frost's attitude is about life and the choices we make.

INTERNET
More About
Robert Frost
Keyword: LE5 9-5

Literary Skills
Understand
contradictions.

314　Collection 5　Irony and Ambiguity • Evaluating an Argument

---

RESOURCES: READING

Planning
■ *One-Stop Planner* CD-ROM with ExamView Test Generator

Differentiating Instruction
■ *Holt Reading Solutions*
■ *Supporting Instruction in Spanish*
■ *Audio CD Library, Selections and Summaries in Spanish*

Grammar and Language
■ *Daily Language Activities*

Assessment
■ *Holt Assessment: Literature, Reading, and Vocabulary*
■ *One-Stop Planner* CD-ROM with ExamView Test Generator
■ *Holt Online Assessment*

Internet
■ go.hrw.com (Keyword: LE5 9-5)
■ *Elements of Literature Online*

Media
■ *Audio CD Library*
■ *Audio CD Library, Selections and Summaries in Spanish*

The Road Not Taken

Robert Frost

Two roads diverged° in a yellow wood,
And sorry I could not travel both
And be one traveler, long I stood
And looked down one as far as I could
5   To where it bent in the undergrowth;

Then took the other, as just as fair,
And having perhaps the better claim,
Because it was grassy and wanted wear;
Though as for that the passing there
10 Had worn them really about the same,

And both that morning equally lay
In leaves no step had trodden black.
Oh, I kept the first for another day!
Yet knowing how way leads on to way,
15 I doubted if I should ever come back.

I shall be telling this with a sigh
Somewhere ages and ages hence:
Two roads diverged in a wood, and I—
I took the one less traveled by,
20 And that has made all the difference.

1. **diverged** (dī·vʉrjd′) *v.:* branched off in different directions.

A Learners Having Difficulty

Reading inverted sentences. Words in poetry often appear in a different order than in everyday speech. "Long I stood" is an example of this unexpected word order. Ask students if they can explain why the poet may have placed the word *stood* at the end of the line. [Possible responses: The poet wanted to rhyme *stood* with *wood* (l. 1) and *could* (l. 4); the rhythm of the poem called for a strong beat at the end of the line.]

B Literary Focus

❷ Verbal irony. What does the speaker really mean in this exclamatory statement? Does he believe that he will ever come back? [Possible responses: The speaker means the opposite of what he says and is being ironic; the speaker ironically contrasts youthful expectations with mature knowledge.]

C Reading Skills

❷ Making inferences. Why do you think Frost titled this poem "The Road Not Taken," rather than "The Road Taken"? [Possible responses: Perhaps the speaker remains curious about how things would have turned out if he had made a different choice; perhaps he regrets his choice.]

DIFFERENTIATING INSTRUCTION

Learners Having Difficulty
Tell students that sarcasm is a form of verbal irony. Say, "Suppose I say there will be a test tomorrow. How might you reply that would be the opposite of what you really mean?" [Possible responses: "Great!" "I can't wait."] Point out that tone of voice makes it easy to recognize verbal irony. Explain that writers may use written devices, such as punctuation, to help readers recognize verbal irony.

Advanced Learners
Enrichment. After students have read the poem and the letter, point out that both pieces present the reader with dual images of a single person.

Activity. Ask students to imagine meeting a much older version of themselves. How might they describe their future appearance, interests, regrets, and accomplishments? Ask students to write a dialogue between themselves and their older counterpart.

Monitoring students' progress.
Guide the class in answering these comprehension questions.

Short Answer

1. Where is the "road not taken"? [in the woods]

2. Why does the speaker choose the path he took? [because it appears less frequently traveled]

3. Does the speaker think he will get a chance to travel the other road? [No, he seems to realize that once he has made a choice there is no going back.]

4. What is the result of the speaker's choice? [It has made a great difference in his life by influencing later choices.]

Meet the Writer

Background. Robert Frost felt strongly about the process of writing poetry. He emphasized both intuition and emotion. "A poem is never a put-up job so to speak. It begins as a lump in the throat, a sense of wrong, a homesickness, a lovesickness. It is never a thought to begin with. It is at its best when it is a tantalizing vagueness. It finds its thought and succeeds, or doesn't find it and comes to nothing."

Meet the Writer

Robert Frost

First Poet

Robert Frost (1874–1963), who became so strongly identified with New England, was actually born in San Francisco, California, far from the craggy northeastern countryside he celebrated. After the death of his father when Frost was a child, he and his mother moved to Lawrence, Massachusetts. Known in high school as the class poet, Frost attended college on and off, never earning a degree. To make a living, he worked as a teacher, editor, and shoemaker, and he also ran a farm, struggling all the while to get his poems published.

Frost's literary fortunes changed dramatically in 1912, when he sold his farm and moved his family to England. Several volumes of his poetry were soon published overseas, and Frost began to be recognized critically in America as well. In 1915, he came home to New England to stay, and his career in America took off. Hugely popular, he accumulated numerous awards, including four Pulitzer Prizes.

As he aged, the craggy-faced poet turned into a beloved American icon. Two years before his death he received the great honor of reciting his poem "The Gift Outright" at the inauguration of President John F. Kennedy in 1961. He was the first poet ever to read a poem at a presidential inauguration.

Frost's poetry is deeply rooted in the New England landscape. In his poems he conveys the harsh beauty of rural New England and creates vivid New England characters, often by capturing natural spoken language in his writing. However, his direct, economical style can be misleading, as in "The Road Not Taken." Frost's poems are often ironic and ambiguous, lending complexity to his work. In Frost's view,

❝ Poetry provides the one permissible way of saying one thing and meaning another. . . . ❞

You'll find other poems by Frost on pages 423 and 441.

316

Advanced Learners

Enrichment. Frost wrote, "Poetry begins in trivial metaphors, pretty metaphors, 'grace metaphors,' and goes on to the profoundest thinking that we have."

Activity. Ask a small group of students to explore additional poems of Robert Frost in which he uses metaphor, irony, simple language, and images of nature to convey his profoundest themes. Suggest that students enter *Robert Frost* as a keyword in a search engine. After students have read several of Frost's poems and some criticism of his work, have each student choose one poem on which to become an expert. Have students share their interpretations of their selected Frost poems with the group.

Robert Frost wrote this letter to the literary editor Susan Hayes Ward.

Crossing Paths

Robert Frost

Plymouth, New Hampshire
10 February 1912

Dear Miss Ward:

Two lonely crossroads that themselves cross each other I have walked several times this winter without meeting or overtaking so much as a single person on foot or on runners. The practically unbroken condition of both for several days after a snow or a blow proves that neither is much traveled. Judge then how surprised I was the other evening as I came down one to see a man, who to my own unfamiliar eyes and in the dusk looked for all the world like myself, coming down the other, his approach to the point where our paths must intersect[1] being so timed that unless one of us pulled up we must inevitably collide. I felt as if I was going to meet my own image in a slanting mirror. Or say I felt as we slowly converged[2] on the same point with the same noiseless yet laborious strides as if we were two images about to float together with the uncrossing of someone's eyes. I verily expected to take up or absorb this other self and feel the stronger by the addition for the three-mile journey home. But I didn't go forward to the touch. I stood still in wonderment and let him pass by; and that, too, with the fatal omission of not trying to find out by a comparison of lives and immediate and remote interests what could have brought us by crossing paths to the same point in the wilderness at the same moment of nightfall. Some purpose I doubt not, if we could but have made it out. I like a coincidence almost as well as an incongruity. . . .[3]

A

B

Nonsensically yours, **C**

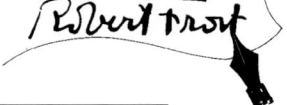

---

1. **intersect** (in′tər•sekt′) *v.*: cross each other.
2. **converged** (kən•vurjd′) *v.*: moved toward each other.
3. **incongruity** (in′kän•grōō′i•tē) *n.*: something not in agreement with what is expected.

The Road Not Taken **317**

Connection

Summary ⬆ *above grade level*

> In this letter, Frost relates an incident that occurred during an evening walk. Having passed by a stranger on a lonely rural crossroads, the poet imagines that he saw his own image or double.

DIRECT TEACHING

A **English-Language Learners**
Archaic language. Tell students that the word *verily* and the expression *feel the stronger* suggest an archaic prose style. Explain that the word *verily* means "honestly" or "truly" and that *feel the stronger* means the same as "feel stronger." Point out that *verily*—as well as *veracity, verify,* and *very*—originates from the Latin *verus,* meaning "true."

B **Reading Skills**
❓ **Comparing and contrasting.** What are some similarities between "The Road Not Taken" and "Crossing Paths"? [Possible responses: Both involve walks taken on roads that are little traveled; both involve paths that come together; both involve choices.]

C **Reading Skills**
❓ **Expressing an opinion.** Do you think Frost's musings are fanciful or serious? Explain your opinion. [Possible response: Fanciful, because he closes the letter with "Nonsensically yours."]

Connecting and Comparing Texts

Use these questions to help students discuss and connect Frost's two works:

• How are the situations in the poem and the letter similar and different? [Possible response: Both present the reader with a man who must make a decision, walking on a lonely road. In the poem the roads diverge and the speaker has to choose which road to take. In the letter, Frost's path crosses that of a stranger, and he must choose how to react.]

• In both the poem and the letter, what does the speaker reflect is the effect of his decision? [In both works, the speaker reflects that his decision has prevented him from exploring another possible choice and has made a "fatal" or lasting impact on his life.]

• Frost states in the letter, "I verily expected to take up or absorb this other self." How is Frost's use of the archaic term *verily* similar to his use of an exclamation point in l.13 of the poem? [The term *verily*, like the exclamation point in the poem, calls attention to Frost's use of verbal irony. Frost means the opposite of *verily*—he does not truly expect to "absorb this other self."]

Response and Analysis

Thinking Critically

1. The word *woods* suggests a place with lots of trees that keep one from seeing ahead. They symbolize dark, dangerous places where people may get lost. Similarly, decision making is not always clear; people cannot always envision the consequences.

2. The speaker is telling himself that he can return to the same place and take the other route the next time. But he later realizes (ll. 14–15) that one choice leads to others, so each choice is final.

3. In ll. 6–8, the speaker says the second road is better because it "wanted wear." But in ll. 9–10, he contradicts himself by saying that both roads have the same wear.

4. Possible answer: The line appears to be sincere, based on l. 16, "telling this with a sigh"—since the traveler will presumably understand the gravity of his choice in the future.

5. Possible answers: Lines 6–8 have a hopeful tone; ll. 9–10 and l. 13 have an ironic tone; ll. 16–17 have a regretful tone.

6. Possible answers: Both the poem and the letter have lonely roads in them; both have a tone of regret about decisions not made. Students might ask Frost whether this experience gave him the idea for the poem "The Road Not Taken."

Extending and Evaluating

7. Possible answers: People are sometimes given a second chance in life. Some may alter a decision later on, but the circumstances will not be exactly the same as they were the first time around, so the effects of the choice may be different from what they would have been.

Response and Analysis

Thinking Critically

1. Why might Frost have chosen to write about roads that go through woods rather than roads that go through a garden or a wide-open plain? (Consider what woods might **symbolize,** or stand for. Think also of the expression *We're not out of the woods yet.*)

2. What do you think the speaker means when he says that he "kept" the first road for another day (line 13)? How do we know that he realizes his choice of paths is utterly final?

3. From what the speaker says in lines 6–10, is one road really "less traveled" than the other? Explain the **contradiction** in these lines.

4. Do you think the poem's final line is meant as **verbal irony,** or is it a sincere statement? Give reasons to support your response.

5. How would you describe the **tone** of the poem—the speaker's attitude toward the subject? (Keep in mind that according to Frost, the most insightful question one could ask about the poem concerns line 16: Why the sigh?) Which words, phrases, or lines in the poem convey this tone to you?

6. Talk over your responses to Frost's letter "Crossing Paths" (see the **Connection** on page 317). What connections do you see between the poem and the incident Frost describes in the letter? What questions would you like to ask Frost? Why?

INTERNET
Projects and Activities
Keyword: LE5 9-5

SKILLS FOCUS

Literary Skills
Interpret contradictions.

Writing Skills
Write a letter.
Write a poem.

Extending and Evaluating

7. What is your opinion of the speaker's **contradiction** in lines 13–15 about having a chance to take the other road? Do you think people can ever go back and try another road? Explain your response.

WRITING

Turning Points

Write a **letter** to a friend telling about a choice you made that resulted in a turning point in your life. Explain how this choice affected your life. Are you glad that you made the choice? Do you have any regrets? Be sure to check your Quickwrite notes.

On the Road

Think of another setting and another traveler. Write a road **poem** of your own (maybe about a road taken). You can base your poem on your own experiences, or you can write about an imaginary traveler. Use vivid **images** to set the scene for your reader.

DIFFERENTIATING INSTRUCTION

Learners Having Difficulty

Before students answer the questions, review metaphor, contradiction, and irony in class. *Monitoring tip:* If students have trouble answering question 6, have them work in pairs to re-read the selections and then create a list of similarities between the two writings.

Advanced Learners

Enrichment. To explore question 7 further, have students determine factors that make some decisions impossible to reverse.
Activity. Have students interview a parent, grandparent, or older friend about turning points in their lives. What irreversible decisions have they made? At what points did they have a chance to go back and try another "road"? Invite students to share their findings.

FICTION

The Secrets of Camp Green Lake

The trouble begins when Stanley is falsely accused of stealing sneakers that belong to the basketball legend Clyde Livingston, otherwise known as Sweet Feet. As punishment, Stanley is sent to Camp Green Lake, a remote juvenile detention center. There he is expected to dig enormous holes. "If you find anything interesting," says his camp counselor, "hand it over to the warden." What could possibly be interesting in a dried-up lake bed? Read Louis Sachar's suspenseful, Newbery Medal–winning novel, **Holes,** to unearth the answer.

This title is available in the HRW Library.

FICTION / NONFICTION

Wit and Wisdom

James Thurber's *My World and Welcome to It* is a collection of essays, sketches, and stories from one of America's great comic writers. Whether recording his funny observations about life abroad or complaining about the phone company, Thurber chooses his targets with gentle good humor. His combination of ironic wit and plain-spoken charm will make you feel as if you're spending the day with a favorite uncle.

FICTION

Fair Enough

What is justice? Is there more than one kind? Sharon Creeden, a storyteller and a trial attorney, takes a close look at what justice means to the world. The result is her book *Fair Is Fair: World Folktales of Justice,* an entertaining collection of myths, fables, and folklore from many lands. Creeden shows us that what's fair and just is a little more ambiguous than we might think—differing from nation to nation as well as from case to case.

NONFICTION

Out of the Fields

Elva was a small child when her family packed up and moved from Mexico to Minnesota, hoping to earn their living as migrant laborers. Along with her brothers and sisters, Elva endures filthy living conditions and tiring work—only occasionally stealing moments to run and play barefoot in the broad, grassy fields. Then school begins, and Elva discovers that she has a special talent. What she does with this talent and the difficult decisions she has to make are beautifully outlined in Elva Treviño Hart's memoir *Barefoot Heart: Stories of a Migrant Child.*

Read On

For Independent Reading

If students enjoyed the themes and topics explored in this collection, you might recommend these titles for independent reading.

Assessment Options

The following projects can help you evaluate and assess your students' outside reading. Videotapes or audiotapes of completed projects may be included in student portfolios.

- **Write a new ending.** The plot of Louis Sachar's *Holes* includes many ironic twists and a surprise ending in which injustices are corrected. The stories in *Fair Is Fair: World Folktales of Justice* also resolve injustices in surprising ways. Encourage students to write a new ending to the novel or one of the stories. Their endings should also be ironic, surprising, and reflective of students' own sense of justice.

- **Role-play an interview.** Have pairs of students who have read *My World and Welcome to It* or *Barefoot Heart: Stories of a Migrant Child* role-play an interview with the book's author. The interview with James Thurber should focus on the author's humorous and ironic view on life. The interview with Elva Treviño Hart should focus on the choices she made to acquire an education and escape the poverty of her childhood and how she later came to embrace her past by writing about it.

DIFFERENTIATING INSTRUCTION

Estimated Word Counts and Reading Levels of Read On Books:

Fiction			Fiction/Nonfiction			Nonfiction		
Holes	⬇	66,900	My World and Welcome to It	⬆	82,900	Barefoot Heart: Stories of a Migrant Child	↔	106,200
Fair Is Fair: World Folktales of Justice	↔	46,400						

KEY: ⬆ *above grade level*   ↔ *at grade level*   ⬇ *below grade level*

Skills Starter

Motivate. Ask students to recall times in which they have been persuaded to take action. For example, students might have decided to try a new food based on a friend's suggestion or an advertisement they saw on TV. Call on volunteers to share their experiences and to answer these questions:

- What specific elements in the piece of persuasion convinced them?
- Where do students see the same persuasive elements at work in the world around them?

DIFFERENTIATING INSTRUCTION

Learners Having Difficulty

Students may have trouble choosing issues on which to write persuasive essays. Have each student compile a list of possible issues and then use this checklist to evaluate his or her issues:

- Eliminate issues from the list that are vague, general, or that do not spark a significant amount of differing opinion.
- Rate each remaining issue from 1 to 5, with 5 being of the highest interest and importance.
- Circle the issue rated 5, or choose the most interesting of those rated 5.
- Check to make sure the issue is one about which you do not mind sharing your thoughts and feelings.

Writing a Persuasive Essay

Writing Assignment
Write a persuasive essay on a topic about which you have a strong opinion.

As you read in his essay "A Defense of the Jury System," Thomas M. Ross has strong feelings about the jury system. What issue do you care about, and how can you get others to care about the issue, too? One way to share your views and convince others to accept them is to write persuasively. In a **persuasive essay** your goal will be to state your opinion clearly and support it with reasons and evidence.

Prewriting

Choose an Issue

A Powerful Issue For your persuasive essay, consider **issues** that stir up strong feelings in you and in others. What situations make you and other people angry, sad, or enthusiastic? List a few issues that you really care about. Then, pick the one you have the strongest views about and the one about which you can gather enough evidence to defend your position. Keep in mind that your essay should be at least 1,500 words, so choose an issue that is interesting enough to hold readers' interest in a paper of that length.

Write an Opinion Statement

Get on Your Soapbox You probably already know where you stand on your issue. Share your clear and well-defined **perspective** with readers by drafting an opinion statement (also known as a thesis statement). Your **opinion statement** should clearly state both the issue and your position on it. One student brainstormed the following issues and positions as he developed an opinion statement.

Issue	Position
Recycling	helps to protect our natural resources.
People who ride motorcycles	should be required to wear helmets.
Banning bicycles on sidewalks	would force riders onto unsafe streets.

Writing Skills
Write a persuasive essay.

Keep your own opinion statement in mind to help you focus your ideas as you plan and draft your essay.

COLLECTION 5 RESOURCES: WRITING

Planning
- *One-Stop Planner* CD-ROM with ExamView Test Generator

Differentiating Instruction
- *Family Involvement Activities in English and Spanish*
- *Workshop Resources: Writing, Listening, and Speaking*

Writing and Language
- *Workshop Resources: Writing, Listening, and Speaking*
- *Daily Language Activities*
- *Language Handbook Worksheets*

Assessment
- *Holt Assessment: Writing, Listening, and Speaking*

Consider Your Purpose and Audience

Your Readers Await You In a persuasive essay your **purpose** is to convince readers to share your opinion or to take the action you suggest. In order to persuade your readers effectively, you must understand them. Think about your **audience** by jotting down answers to the following questions.

◉ **What will make my audience care about this issue?** Identify specific ways in which the topic affects your readers' lives.

◉ **What concerns might my audience have?** Consider how your issue looks from their point of view, or **bias.** For example, some readers may think that recycling is too expensive. Take this objection, or **counterclaim,** into account as you support your position.

◉ **What will my audience expect from my essay?** Consider aspects of the issue about which readers might want more information. They will expect your essay to provide solid information to help them make a decision.

◀ ─── DO THIS

TIP Readers' counterclaims can also be called **counterarguments.**

Gather Support for Your Position

Back It Up To be convincing, give at least three strong **reasons** to support your opinion statement. Your reasons will tell why you believe your position is correct and may include **rhetorical devices** that appeal to your readers' logic, emotions, or ethical beliefs.

• A **logical appeal** speaks to readers' common sense and logic. Logical appeals make sense.

• An **emotional appeal** is aimed at readers' hearts. Emotional appeals speak to emotions such as fear, love, sympathy, and pride.

• An **ethical appeal** addresses readers' sense of right and wrong. Ethical appeals also rely on a reader's belief that the writer is ethical.

Here are the reasons the student writer developed.

> **Opinion Statement:** Recycling is the best way to preserve natural resources and to reduce the costs of processing garbage.
>
> **Reasons:**
> 1. It saves precious resources. (logical appeal)
> 2. It keeps us from being buried in trash. (emotional appeal)
> 3. It reduces the garbage we produce. (ethical appeal)

Create a chart like the one above in which you write your opinion statement and list at least three reasons to support it. As you create your chart, keep in mind that your teacher may want you to have more logical appeals than emotional or ethical appeals.

SKILLS FOCUS

Writing Skills
Identify purpose and audience. Use logical, emotional, and ethical appeals.

Writing Workshop: Writing a Persuasive Essay **321**

■ *One-Stop Planner* CD-ROM with ExamView Test Generator
■ *Holt Online Assessment*
■ *Holt Online Essay Scoring*
Internet
■ go.hrw.com (Keyword LE5 9-5)
■ *Elements of Literature Online*

TECHNOLOGY TIP

In addition to visiting the library or using local resources such as government agencies or local experts, students are likely to search the Internet for support. Explain that students must use caution when they use information from the Internet because it is largely unregulated. Suggest that students use a reliable Web site created exclusively for research by a reliable institution.

You need to be aware that Internet resources sometimes function as public forums, and their content can be unpredictable.

DIRECT TEACHING

Plan Your Draft

As students organize their support, have them use a visual organizer such as the following to help them shape their body paragraphs.

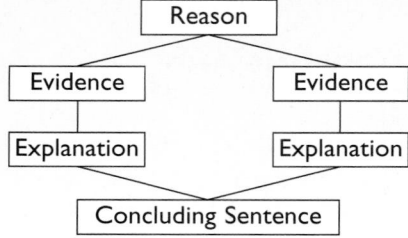

PRACTICE & APPLY 1

Guided and Independent Practice

Lead students through these steps to help them generate reasons that support their opinion statements:

1. Add two or three *because* clauses to your opinion statement.

2. Delete the *because* from each clause, and rewrite it as a sentence.

3. Add introductory or transitional words, such as *one important reason, first, second,* and *the most important reason,* to each topic sentence, indicating its order.

 **TIP** Make sure to identify any source you quote. For more on **citing sources,** see page 619.

The Evidence Suggests . . . Provide at least two pieces of **evidence** to support each of your reasons. The following chart shows examples of the kinds of evidence you can provide to present a tightly reasoned argument. No matter which types of evidence you include, make sure your evidence is **relevant,** or clearly related to your issue. Precise, specific evidence will help readers better understand your position and will be more convincing than vague evidence.

EVIDENCE FOR PERSUASIVE APPEALS

Types of Evidence	Examples
Analogies Comparisons that show similarities between otherwise unrelated facts or ideas	We should be as concerned about the garbage problem today as they once were about finding a vaccine for polio.
Anecdotes Personal examples or stories that illustrate a point	My grandfather says the forests that once surrounded my hometown have nearly vanished.
Case studies Examples from scientific research	Government studies show that collecting and using recycled materials saves energy.
Commonly accepted beliefs Ideas that most people share	Most people think that garbage is useless and has no value.
Examples Specific instances or illustrations of a general idea	For example, recycling could help save some of the fifty thousand trees that are sacrificed every week to produce Sunday newspapers in the U.S.
Expert opinions Statements made by a recognized authority on the subject	Brenda Platt of the Institute for Local Self-Reliance says, "Studies have concluded that recycling costs less than traditional trash collection and disposal. . . ."
Facts Statements that can be proven true; some facts are in the form of statistics, or numerical information	Garbage usually goes into landfills. Of the garbage produced each year in the U.S., 42% is paper.

Plan Your Draft

Get Your Information in Order To be its most persuasive, your essay should move **smoothly and logically** from one idea to the next. Decide now how to organize the reasons that support your opinion statement. Readers will best remember ideas presented at the end of the essay and at the beginning. Therefore, you might want to put your second strongest reason in the first body paragraph and your strongest reason in the final body paragraph. Place remaining reasons in between.

 **SKILLS FOCUS**

Writing Skills
Provide relevant evidence.
Organize the evidence.

PRACTICE & APPLY 1

Choose an issue for your persuasive essay, write an opinion statement, and gather and organize reasons and evidence to support your opinion.

322 **Collection 5** Irony and Ambiguity • Evaluating an Argument

Writing

Writing a Persuasive Essay

A Writer's Framework

Introduction	Body	Conclusion
• Grab your readers' interest with an attention getter. • Give background information so readers understand the issue. • Present an opinion statement that identifies the issue and states your opinion on it.	• Provide at least three reasons that support your opinion statement. • Give at least two pieces of evidence to support each reason. • Organize the reasons and evidence logically.	• Restate your opinion. • Summarize your reasons, or include a call to action—a sentence that tells readers what you want them to do.

A Writer's Model

Do Something Good for the Earth

INTRODUCTION
Attention getter
Background information

Garbage! It smells bad and looks disgusting. Most people think about trash only when they take it out. People in the United States should be thinking about garbage more, however, because they throw away 40 percent of all the garbage in the world. The solution to this problem is recycling. Recycling is the best way to preserve natural resources and to reduce the costs of processing garbage.

Opinion statement

BODY/ Reason 1: Emotional appeal
Evidence: Statistics

By recycling, we can prevent our country from being buried in trash. Much of the garbage that is now tossed out could be recycled. Of the 200 million tons of garbage that U.S. citizens produce yearly, about 42 percent is paper (from trees), 8 percent is glass, 9 percent is metal (from ore, a natural resource), 7 percent is plastic (from petroleum, a natural resource), 8 percent is food waste, and 18 percent is yard waste. Government officials estimate that 60 percent of all this trash could be recycled. Environmentalists suggest a much higher figure—as much as 70 to 90 percent.

Reason 2: Logical appeal
Evidence: Anecdote
Evidence: Example

Recycling more of our garbage can also save precious resources. My grandfather says the thick forests that once surrounded my hometown have nearly vanished. By recycling newspapers, we can rescue trees from destruction. For example, recycling could help save some of the fifty thousand trees that are sacrificed every week to produce Sunday newspapers in the United States. We can also save water and energy by

(continued)

DIFFERENTIATING INSTRUCTION

Advanced Learners

Enrichment. To help students understand the development of an opinion statement, or thesis, have them analyze the Declaration of Independence, which is an example of a persuasive essay. Distribute copies of the document to groups of four or five students. Using **A Writer's Framework** on this page, have students identify the different parts of a persuasive essay. Students may present their analyses as graphic organizers.

RETEACHING

A Writer's Model

If students have difficulty understanding the framework for a persuasive essay, have students use **A Writer's Framework** to evaluate **A Writer's Model,** noting the parts of the framework as they appear alongside the model. Discuss with students their assessments of the essay's success and thoroughness, and ask them to brainstorm ways in which the essay may be improved. Write students' suggestions on the chalkboard, and encourage them to keep such concerns in mind as they write their own essays.

DIFFERENTIATING INSTRUCTION

Special Education Students

For students who need help in understanding the concept of adequate and logical support for an opinion, have a helper guide them in drawing a pyramid graphic and recording their opinion statements at the top. The helper can then ask each student to verbalize several reasons for an opinion and list these below the statement to support it. Finally, for each reason, students can be helped to locate at least two supporting facts or examples.

(continued)

Evidence: Facts and statistics

recycling. Recycling paper instead of making it from trees reduces the amount of water used to make the paper by 60 percent and the amount of energy by 70 percent. Aluminum cans show the biggest savings from recycling. To produce a can from recycled aluminum takes 95 percent less energy than from ore.

Reason 3: Ethical appeal

Evidence: Facts
Counterclaim addressed
Evidence: Expert opinion

Recycling more can reduce the mountains of garbage we produce—and reduce the costs associated with all the landfills where the garbage is dumped. Garbage does not just disappear after it is hauled away. It usually goes into landfills—many of which have created toxic pollution problems and enormous cleanup costs. People often object to recycling by saying that it costs too much. Brenda Platt of the Institute for Local Self-Reliance says, "Studies have concluded that recycling costs less than traditional trash collection and disposal when communities achieve high levels of recycling." Therefore, people should understand that recycling actually saves money by reducing waste and by eliminating the costs that go along with solid-waste disposal and landfill cleanup.

CONCLUSION
Restated opinion
Summary of reasons

Call to action

Much of what is thrown away now can be recycled. Anyone who loves the earth can help make it a better place by recycling. Garbage makes our shared home, this planet, less livable for the people of today and for the children of tomorrow. People have caused this garbage crisis, and only people can solve it. Do you care enough to do your part by recycling?

As you write the first draft of your persuasive essay, refer to the framework on page 323 and the Writer's Model above. They will help you expand and organize your ideas.

Guided and Independent Practice

To verify that students follow the framework on p. 323, have students label their essays in the margins as **A Writer's Model** has been labeled on pp. 323–324. If students have trouble getting started, suggest that they begin their writing with their opinion statements and wait until after they have completed the rest of their papers to compose attention-getting openers.

Revising

Evaluate and Revise Your Draft

Checking It Twice When you invest your strong feelings and your time in writing a persuasive essay, you want to make sure that the final product is as clear and well written as possible in order to convince your audience. Read your essay at least twice. During the first reading, consider your essay's content and organization. On your second reading, focus on style, using the guidelines on page 326.

PEER REVIEW

Trade papers with a classmate. Check to see whether the opinion statement is supported by at least three reasons and evidence.

▶ **First Reading: Content and Organization** Use the following guidelines to evaluate and revise the content and organization of your persuasive essay. Ask yourself the evaluation questions in the left-hand column, and use the tips in the middle column to help you with your answers. Then, use the revision techniques in the right-hand column to make any improvements.

Rubric: Writing a Persuasive Essay

Evaluation Questions	▶ Tips	▶ Revision Techniques
❶ Does the introduction express a clear opinion statement?	▶ **Bracket** the opinion statement.	▶ **Add** an opinion statement that identifies the issue and states an opinion on it.
❷ Do at least three reasons support the opinion statement? Do the reasons include logical, emotional, or ethical appeals?	▶ **Underline** each reason. **Label** logical appeals with an *L*, emotional appeals with an *E*, and ethical appeals with an *H*.	▶ **Add** reasons. **Elaborate** on existing reasons so that they appeal to readers' logic, emotions, or ethics. Make sure the appeals are balanced.
❸ Do at least two pieces of evidence support each reason?	▶ **Circle** each piece of evidence, and **draw an arrow** to the reason it supports.	▶ **Add** evidence for each reason. **Rearrange** evidence so that it is in the paragraph with the reason it supports.
❹ Is the organization logical and effective?	▶ **Number** each reason with a rank (1 for strongest, and so on).	▶ **Rearrange** paragraphs to put the strongest reason first or last.
❺ Are possible reader counterclaims addressed?	▶ **Put a plus sign** by any sentence that addresses a reader counterclaim.	▶ **Add** sentences that identify and respond to reader counterclaims.
❻ Does the conclusion restate the writer's opinion? Does it include a summary of reasons or a call to action?	▶ **Put a box** around the restatement of the writer's opinion. **Highlight** the summary of reasons or the call to action.	▶ **Add** a sentence that restates the position. **Add** a summary of reasons or a call to action.

English-Language Learners

When helping students revise their first drafts, avoid correcting every grammatical error. Instead, pay strict attention to content and organization to help students focus on what they are saying. You might state the main idea of each paragraph to help each student notice how the essay as a whole is organized. Once the content and organization of students' essays are clear, they can work on grammar.

DIRECT TEACHING

Elaboration

Help students elaborate on their supporting evidence by using this activity. Lead the class through a practice of adding evidence by choosing a paragraph from **A Writer's Model** and challenging volunteers to add an example of each of the types of evidence from the **Evidence for Persuasive Appeals** chart on p. 322. Write students' examples on the chalkboard so that those having difficulty adding evidence to their own papers have a ready model for doing so.

Rubric: Writing a Persuasive Essay

Advise students to use the **rubric** chart on this page as a think sheet by having them answer the questions in their notebooks. Explain that using think sheets to summarize their notes allows students to place their thoughts, observations, and questions on paper, which in turn helps improve the content and organization of their essays.

Second Reading: Style The style of your persuasive essay should be formal. To maintain a serious tone, use the guidelines in the following chart to eliminate clichés in your essay. **Clichés** are overused expressions that have lost meaning and impact. "Last but not least," "once in a blue moon," and "tough as nails" are examples of clichés. Replace clichés with original words or phrases as in the following example.

> **Cliché:** Manuel was *as busy as a bee* while he worked on his project.
> **Original words:** Manuel *worked diligently* on his project.

Style Guidelines

Evaluation Question	▶ Tip	▶ Revision Technique
● Does the essay include any worn-out, overused expressions?	▶ **Draw a line through** clichés.	▶ **Replace** each cliché with a fresh, original expression.

GUIDED PRACTICE

Responding to the Revision Process

Answers

1. The phrase "vanish into thin air" is a cliché; replacing the phrase with more original wording maintains a serious tone and helps keep the writing fresh and interesting.

2. The addition of the sentence addresses a possible reader counterclaim.

ANALYZING THE REVISION PROCESS
Look at these revisions, and answer the questions that follow.

replace   Garbage does not just ~~vanish into thin air~~. It usually goes into
disappear after it is hauled away.

landfills—many of which have created toxic pollution
People often object to recycling by saying that it costs too much.
add   problems and enormous cleanup costs. Brenda Platt of the

Institute for Local Self-Reliance says, "Studies have concluded

that recycling costs less than traditional trash collection and

disposal when communities achieve high levels of recycling."

Responding to the Revision Process

1. Why did the writer replace the words *vanish into thin air* in the first sentence?

2. Why did the writer add a sentence to the paragraph?

SKILLS FOCUS

Writing Skills
Revise for content and style.

PRACTICE & APPLY 3

Independent Practice

As students revise their papers, direct them to pay special attention to those places in their essays at which they are tempted to read more quickly or skip over details. Point out that a section that is easily skipped over by the writer might also prompt the same reaction in the intended audience. Students should be on the lookout for weak reasoning, uninspired writing, and clichés at such points.

PRACTICE & APPLY 3 Read your essay once to revise its content and organization, using the guidelines on page 325. Then, revise its style, using the guidelines above.

Publishing

Proofread and Publish Your Persuasive Essay

Last Look Now that you have polished the content, organization, and style of your essay, proofread it to be sure that it is free of grammar, spelling, and punctuation errors. (For information on **proofreading,** see *The Writing Process* in the Writer's Handbook.)

Have your Say Persuasive writing is meant to be shared. Here are some ways you might share your persuasive essay with an audience.

- Send your essay to an organization with an interest in your issue or with the power to make the change you want.

- Publish your essay on a school or community Web site or on a Web site devoted to the issue you addressed. Use a graphics program to include photographs or illustrations on your Web page.

- Use a publishing program to format your essay into columns so that it looks like an article. Then, submit your article to your school newspaper or to a newspaper or magazine that publishes articles on issues such as yours.

Reflect on Your Persuasive Essay

Taking a Deeper Look To reflect on what you have learned about persuasion and how your writing skills have developed through completing this workshop, answer these questions.

- What difficulties did you have finding reasons to support your opinion or evidence to support your reasons? How did you solve these problems?

- How did addressing your readers' counterclaims or concerns help you to strengthen your persuasive argument? What did you learn about your audience and the other side of the issue from this part of the writing process?

- What revisions do you think strengthened your essay the most? Why?

   If you include your persuasive essay in a writing portfolio, attach your responses to it.

PRACTICE & APPLY 4 Proofread your essay, checking for grammar, usage, and mechanics mistakes. Then, publish your essay, using one of the suggestions above. Finally, reflect on the skills you have used to create your persuasive essay.

 TIP Proofreading your essay will help ensure that you have used the **conventions** of standard American English correctly. For example, to avoid delivering a reason that is the opposite of what you mean, check to make sure that you haven't used two negative words *(no, none, nothing, not)* in a sentence. For more on **double negatives,** see double negative, Glossary of Usage, in the Language Handbook.

 COMPUTER TIP

If you have access to a computer and advanced publishing software, you can format your essay so that it looks professional. For more on **page design,** see *Designing Your Writing* in the Writer's Handbook.

SKILLS FOCUS

Writing Skills
Proofread, design, and publish the essay.

Writing Workshop: Writing a Persuasive Essay **327**

PRETEACHING

Motivate. Ask students if they have ever had a friendly disagreement with someone, only to think of the perfect argument *after* the conversation. Point out to students that in a formal debate, ample opportunity for rebuttal ensures that participants always get to speak their minds.

DIRECT TEACHING

Define the Proposition

You may need to point out that the given example, "*Resolved:* That Northside High School should turn an existing classroom into a computer lab," is meant to provide a starting point for learning about debate procedures, not to be used as the focus of an actual formal debate.

RETEACHING

Take Sides

If students have difficulty preparing for the debate, you may wish to create a debate proposition, and write it on the chalkboard. Then, group students and assign each group the position of either affirmative or negative. Let the groups brainstorm how they would defend their sides, what type of evidence would best suit their reasons, and where they could find such evidence. Each group can share their information on the chalkboard. Allow time for discussion.

Debating an Issue

Speaking Assignment

With other students, stage a debate in which two teams present opposite sides of an issue.

Conversations about controversial topics break down for a variety of reasons: perhaps someone is long-winded, or someone else gets angry and logic flies out the window. In a debate, however, there are rules that keep the discussion from breaking down. A **debate** is a balanced argument covering opposite sides of an issue. In a debate two teams compete to win the support of the audience.

Prepare for the Debate

Define the Proposition A debate focuses on a single, narrow issue, **the proposition.** The proposition is worded as a **resolution,** a positive statement calling for a change in the way things are. Most often, the proposition will be chosen for you and will involve a topic with equally strong arguments on both sides. Here is an example resolution one group of students used for a debate.

> *Resolved:* That Northside High School should turn an existing classroom into a computer lab.

Take Sides A traditional debate requires two teams of two people each and a chairperson.

- The **affirmative team,** which speaks first in the debate, argues for the proposition. Because this team is arguing for a change in the current state of things, it has the **burden of proof.** It is the team's task to prove why the change must be made.

- The **negative team** argues that the proposal of the affirmative side should be rejected—that things are fine the way they are.

- The **chairperson** directs the debate and ensures that all rules and time limits are followed. If a debater believes an opponent has broken the rules, he or she may appeal to the chairperson.

Participants in a debate are generally assigned to a team, without regard to how each member personally feels about the issue. You might think it would be better to argue the side of the issue you support. However, sometimes it is easier to argue for something you don't really support because you know all of the weaknesses in the case and how your opponents might approach them. Whichever side of the case you are assigned, your task is to present rational arguments that are easy to follow and understand.

SKILLS FOCUS

Listening and Speaking Skills
Debate an issue.

COLLECTION 5 RESOURCES: LISTENING & SPEAKING

Planning
- *One-Stop Planner* CD-ROM with ExamView Test Generator

Differentiating Instruction
- *Workshop Resources: Writing, Listening, and Speaking*
- *Family Involvement Activities in English and Spanish*

- *Supporting Instruction in Spanish*

Listening and Speaking
- *Workshop Resources: Writing, Listening, and Speaking*
- *Daily Language Activities*

Assessment
- *Holt Assessment: Writing, Listening, and Speaking*

Research the Proposition To prepare effectively for a debate, you must research the proposition fully. Identify the **key issues**—the main differences between your position and the position of the opposing team. Key issues often involve the following questions.

- Does a problem exist?
- What is causing the problem?
- Will this proposition solve the problem?
- What will this proposition cost?

Your research should provide answers to these questions. Use the answers to develop specific **reasons** that support your side of the proposition. Reasons, even those that include **rhetorical devices,** can't stand alone. They must be supported by evidence, or **proof.** Refer to the following chart to see the four most common types of proof.

Reference Note

For more on **rhetorical devices** and **types of evidence,** see pages 321 and 322.

PROOF USED IN DEBATES

Type of Proof	Example
Specific instances—examples that illustrate a point	Many students currently attending Northside High School have so little computer experience that they can't even perform basic research tasks using the Internet.
Testimony—comments from someone who has already studied or experienced the problem	According to Sarah Jones, a former student of Northside High School, "I felt very ill prepared when I entered college because my computer skills were so far behind those of my classmates."
Facts—statements that can be proven true	The school board voted not to buy computers to be placed in the classrooms.
Statistics—facts presented as numerical information	976 students are enrolled at Northside, yet the current computer lab has space for only 30 students per class period.

To meet the standard **tests for evidence** and be appropriate for the debate, your proof must be credible, valid, and relevant to the topic you are discussing.

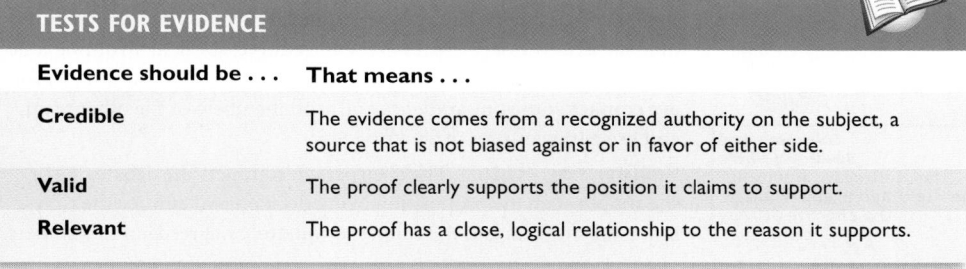

TESTS FOR EVIDENCE

Evidence should be . . .	That means . . .
Credible	The evidence comes from a recognized authority on the subject, a source that is not biased against or in favor of either side.
Valid	The proof clearly supports the position it claims to support.
Relevant	The proof has a close, logical relationship to the reason it supports.

Listening and Speaking Workshop: Debating an Issue **329**

- *One-Stop Planner* CD-ROM with ExamView Test Generator

Internet
- go.hrw.com (Keyword: LE5 9-5)
- *Elements of Literature Online*

Prepare Debate Speeches

Model for students the three different types of speeches that use the classical speech form on this page. Then, call on student volunteers to demonstrate understanding in front of the class by outlining further examples of each of the three types of speeches.

DIRECT TEACHING

Prepare Debate Speeches

Point out to students that there are three ways to prepare their remarks:

- A **manuscript speech** is read word-for-word; it allows for few mistakes but may seem dull to the audience.

- A **memorized speech** gives one the freedom to make eye contact with the audience but may sound stiff and rehearsed.

- The **extemporaneous speech** is carefully outlined and rehearsed but not memorized.

Encourage students to use the extemporaneous method. You may want to model for students examples of each method.

Conduct the Debate

Emphasize these points for students:

- **Eye contact** communicates honesty and sincerity. Make eye contact with as many members of the audience as possible.

- **Facial expressions** are so important they can even take the place of the verbal message. Make sure your expressions are appropriate and under control.

- **Simple gestures** such as nodding for "yes," shaking one's head for "no," and pointing one's finger can be very effective.

- **Posture**—standing up straight and looking alert communicates confidence to the audience.

Be sure to make notes on the evidence that might be used against your position as well as evidence that supports your position. If you know what proof the other team might present, you'll be better prepared to respond to their arguments. Once you've fully researched your topic, organize your evidence into these three categories:

- **Constructive arguments,** which support your side

- **Refutations,** which attack the other side

- **Rebuttals,** which reply to challenges to your side

Prepare Debate Speeches An effective structure for persuasive speeches is the **classical speech form,** in which the argument has a brief but engaging introduction, smooth transitions, a concise body, and a strong conclusion. There are two types of speeches in a debate that you'll need to organize in this manner: **constructive speeches,** delivered during the first part of the debate, and **rebuttal speeches,** delivered in response to the constructive speeches.

- **Affirmative constructive speeches** build the argument in favor of the proposition. A constructive speech for the affirmative side should present two to four reasons in support of the position. Each reason should be supported by strong evidence.

- **Negative constructive speeches** defend the way things are. They deny the existence of a problem or make the case that existing solutions are all that's needed to correct a problem. Reasons that support the argument for the negative side also need to be backed up by strong evidence.

- **Rebuttal speeches** respond to the constructive speeches. They have two objectives: refutation and rebuttal. **Refutation** means to attack the other side's argument by questioning the quantity and quality of their evidence and the logic of their reasoning. **Rebuttal** means to rebuild your argument after the other team has attacked it.

Conduct the Debate

Present Yourself When it's time for you to present your constructive and rebuttal speeches, focus on your task and speak clearly and naturally. Use your **voice, facial expressions,** and **gestures** to make your message expressive. For example, speak at a **volume** loud enough to be heard and at a **rate** that is not too fast or too slow. Make **eye contact** with your audience and with members of the other team, and use hand gestures in a natural way.

Follow the Rules The chairperson conducts the debate. He or she should state the proposition being debated and enforce the time limits for speakers and the rules of **etiquette,** or agreed-upon manners.

TIP Plan your rebuttal speeches in advance, before you hear what the other side says about your argument. The time allowed for rebuttal speeches is short, so you must focus only on the opposing team's most important points. Don't try to address every point they make.

SKILLS FOCUS

Listening and Speaking Skills
Use constructive arguments, refutations, and rebuttals. Use effective delivery techniques.

CORRECTING MISCONCEPTIONS

Students may have a combative conception of argumentation and may take too lightly or even ignore a discussion of debate etiquette. Remind students that ridicule, sarcasm, and personal attacks are never appropriate in a formal debate. If possible, show students a videotape of part of a government debate (for example, the prime minister's answering of questions in the English House of Commons) to demonstrate that no matter how heated a debate may be, the participants still observe rules of civility and politeness.

To follow debate etiquette, you should be respectful and polite and use gestures, a tone of voice, and vocabulary that are appropriate for your audience. It is traditional in debates to refer to a speaker on the other team as "my worthy opponent."

Speaking in Turn A traditional debate follows this schedule. Each team member delivers one constructive and one rebuttal speech.

TRADITIONAL DEBATE SCHEDULE

First Part: Constructive Speeches		Second Part: Rebuttal Speeches
(10 minutes each)	I n t e r m i s s i o n	(5 minutes each)
1st Affirmative Team Speaker		1st Negative Team Speaker
1st Negative Team Speaker		1st Affirmative Team Speaker
2nd Affirmative Team Speaker		2nd Negative Team Speaker
2nd Negative Team Speaker		2nd Affirmative Team Speaker

Judge a Debate

Win or Lose Unlike a football game, a debate does not always have a clear winner. Normally, in order to determine a winner, three appointed judges listen to the debate and evaluate how well each speaker met certain standards. To judge for yourself which team won a debate, answer the questions in the following chart.

QUESTIONS FOR JUDGING A DEBATE

Content	Delivery
1. Did the team prove that a significant problem does/does not exist? How thorough was the team's analysis of the problem?	1. Did the speakers seem confident and well prepared? Explain.
2. How did the team convince you that the proposition is/is not the best solution to solving the problem?	2. Did the speakers maintain eye contact and speak at an appropriate rate and volume? Explain.
3. How effectively did the team present reasons and evidence supporting the case? Was evidence credible, valid, and relevant?	3. Did the speakers observe proper debate etiquette? Explain.
4. How effectively did the team refute and rebut arguments made by the opposing team?	

PRACTICE & APPLY 5 Participate in a debate on a controversial proposition. First, research the proposition and prepare speeches. Then, present your speeches, following the rules of etiquette for a debate.

Advanced Learners

Enrichment. Encourage students to incorporate graphics or audiovisual devices in their speeches. Suitable graphics include photographs or drawings, charts of statistics, and maps or diagrams. Appropriate audiovisual devices might include slides, computer images, or audiotaped recordings. Caution students that their audiovisuals should not distract the audience from their main points but should instead emphasize their main points.

PRACTICE & APPLY 5

Guided and Independent Practice

Students may find it easier to begin preparing for a debate if they first identify and analyze the type of proposition. Tell students there are three types of formal debate propositions:

- A **proposition of fact** makes a statement about what is happening, what has happened, or what will happen, and debaters should attempt to prove it true or false. Example: "David Cruz is guilty of damaging Ellie Kung's bicycle."

- A **proposition of value** expresses a judgment about a person, place, or thing, and though it cannot be found as a matter of fact, debaters should strive to use precise evaluative language. Example: "*Resolved:* That Central High School has the best math department in the state."

- A **proposition of policy** focuses on a specific plan of action and is marked by the word *should;* debaters should investigate the pros and cons of the plan of action in question. Example: "*Resolved:* That Central High School should implement a new recycling policy."

SKILLS FOCUS, pp. 332–335

Grade-Level Skills

■ **Literary Skills**
Identify ambiguities, contradictions, and ironies in the text.

INTRODUCING THE SKILLS REVIEW

Use this review to assess students' grasp of the skills taught in this collection. If necessary, you can use the annotations to guide students in their reading before they answer the questions.

DIRECT TEACHING

Ⓐ Literary Focus

❓ Irony and tone. What details in this paragraph would you not expect to find in a traditional folk tale? [The sentence "Her nursery looked like Cartier's window" and the colloquial word *cheap* are intrusions of a contemporary outlook in a seemingly traditional story.] **What tone, or attitude, do these details convey?** [They convey a humorous, ironic tone because they are both unexpected and funny.]

Ⓑ Learners Having Difficulty

❓ Summarizing. What kinds of possessions did the princess have up until her eighteenth birthday? [She had been showered with expensive presents and surrounded by luxurious possessions made of precious materials.]

Irony and Ambiguity

Test Practice

DIRECTIONS: Read the following fable. Then, read and respond to the questions that follow.

The Princess and the Tin Box

James Thurber

Once upon a time, in a far country, there lived a King whose daughter was the prettiest princess in the world. Her eyes were like the corn-flower, her hair was sweeter than the hyacinth, and her throat made the swan look dusty.

Ⓐ From the time she was a year old, the Princess had been showered with presents. Her nursery looked like Cartier's[1] window. Her toys were all made of gold or platinum or diamonds or emeralds. She was not permitted to have wooden blocks or china dolls or rubber dogs or linen books, because such materials were considered cheap for the daughter of a king.

When she was seven, she was allowed to attend the wedding of her brother and throw real pearls at the bride instead of rice. Only the nightingale, with his lyre[2] of gold, was permitted to sing for the Princess. The common blackbird, with his boxwood flute, was kept out of the palace grounds. She walked in silver-and-samite[3] slippers to a sapphire-and-topaz bathroom and slept in an ivory bed inlaid with rubies.

Ⓑ On the day the Princess was eighteen, the King sent a royal ambassador to the courts of five neighboring kingdoms to announce that he would give his daughter's hand in marriage to the prince who brought her the gift she liked the most.

The first prince to arrive at the palace rode a swift white stallion and laid at the feet of the Princess an enormous apple made of solid gold which he had taken from a dragon who had guarded it for a thousand years. It was placed on a long ebony table set up to hold the gifts of the Princess' suitors. The second prince, who came on a gray charger, brought her a nightingale made of a thousand diamonds, and it was placed beside the golden apple. The third prince, riding on a black horse, carried a great jewel box made of platinum and sapphires, and it was placed next to the diamond nightingale. The fourth prince, astride a fiery yellow horse, gave the Princess a gigantic heart made of rubies

Pages 332–335 cover
Literary Skills
Analyze irony and ambiguity.

---

1. **Cartier's** (kär′tē·āz): store selling expensive jewelry in New York City.
2. **lyre** (līr) *n.:* small stringed instrument.
3. **samite** (sam′īt) *n.* used as *adj.:* heavy silk fabric.

READING MINI-LESSON

Reviewing Word-Attack Skills
Activity. Display these pairs of related words. Have students tell if the underlined letter *c* stands for the same sound or different sounds in each pair.

1. critical   criticism   [different]
2. politics   politician   [different]
3. toxic   intoxicate   [same]
4. logic   logician   [different]
5. circle   circuit   [same]
6. sincere   sincerity   [same]
7. tropics   tropical   [same]
8. physical   physician   [different]
9. particle   participle   [different]
10. ethics   ethical   [same]

and pierced by an emerald arrow. It was placed next to the platinum-and-sapphire jewel box.

Now the fifth prince was the strongest and handsomest of all the five suitors, but he was the son of a poor king whose realm had been overrun by mice and locusts and wizards and mining engineers so that there was nothing much of value left in it. He came plodding up to the palace of the Princess on a plow horse, and he brought her a small tin box filled with mica and feldspar and hornblende[4] which he had picked up on the way.

The other princes roared with disdainful laughter when they saw the tawdry gift the fifth prince had brought to the Princess. But she examined it with great interest and squealed with delight, for all her life she had been glutted with precious stones and priceless metals, but she had never seen tin before or mica or feldspar or hornblende. The tin box was placed next to the ruby heart pierced with an emerald arrow.

"Now," the King said to his daughter, "you must select the gift you like best and marry the prince that brought it."

---

4. **mica . . . hornblende:** types of ordinary rocks.

Drawing for "The Princess and the Tin Box" (1948) by James Thurber.

From *The Beast in Me and Other Animals.* Copyright © 1948 James Thurber. Copyright © renewed 1976 by Rosemary A. Thurber.
Reprinted by arrangement with Rosemary A. Thurber and the Barbara Hogenson Agency.

C Reading Skills

? Comparing and contrasting. How is the fifth prince different from the other four? [He is the strongest and the most handsome prince, but he's also the only poor one.] **How is his gift different from the others?** [Instead of bringing an expensive gift made from precious materials, he brings ordinary rocks in a tin box.]

D Literary Focus

? Irony. How does the princess react to the fifth prince's gift? [She is delighted with it because she has never seen such ordinary things.] **Which gift do you expect her to select as the best?** [Responses may vary. Many students will expect her to choose the fifth prince's gift.]

Activity. Display these words. Have students read the words and count the number of syllables in each word.

1. appreciate [4]
2. partial [2]
3. partiality [5]
4. initial [3]
5. initiate [4]
6. diagonal [4]
7. substantial [3]
8. pliant [2]
9. material [4]
10. giant [2]
11. abbreviate [4]
12. diamond [2]

Activity. Display these sound symbols and words. Have students identify the word in which the letter *i* stands for the sound given. Answers are underlined.

1. /ē/ <u>gladiator</u> dialogue
2. /ī/ <u>denial</u> genial
3. /ē/ patrician <u>patriarch</u>
4. /ī/ <u>diagram</u> media
5. /ē/ <u>menial</u> viable

Skills Review

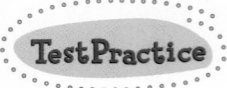

DIRECT TEACHING

Test-Taking Tips

Remind students to look for italicized words such as *best* and *most* in the questions. When two or more choices are reasonable answers to a question, students should choose the one for which the passage provides the most evidence.

For more instruction on how to answer multiple-choice items, refer students to **Test Smarts**.

Ⓐ Literary Focus

❓ **Irony.** How is the ending of the story surprising? [Based on the princess's initial delight with the ordinary gift and on the plot patterns of most folk tales, readers might expect the princess to choose the gift of the poor prince, but she does not.]

TestPractice

Answers and Model Rationales

1. **A** The second and third paragraphs of the story describe how the princess was constantly showered with expensive presents. The points raised in B, C, and D are not suggested in the story.
2. **F** The princess's choice of the expensive box shows that materialism is her defining characteristic.

Ⓐ

The Princess smiled and walked up to the table and picked up the present she liked the most. It was the platinum-and-sapphire jewel box, the gift of the third prince.

"The way I figure it," she said, "is this. It is a very large and expensive box, and when I am married, I will meet many admirers who will give me precious gems with which to fill it to the top. Therefore, it is the most valuable of all the gifts my suitors have brought me, and I like it the best."

The Princess married the third prince that very day in the midst of great merriment and high revelry. More than a hundred thousand pearls were thrown at her and she loved it.

Moral: All those who thought that the Princess was going to select the tin box filled with worthless stones instead of one of the other gifts will kindly stay after class and write one hundred times on the blackboard, "I would rather have a hunk of aluminum silicate than a diamond necklace."

---

1. The details of the princess's life before her eighteenth birthday imply that she was —
   - **A** raised to value only material goods
   - **B** indifferent to the feelings of others
   - **C** easily bored
   - **D** not interested in getting married

2. Which adjective *best* describes the princess's **character**?
   - **F** materialistic
   - **G** curious
   - **H** indecisive
   - **J** modest

3. How are the gifts of the first four princes similar?
   - **A** They are made from precious materials.
   - **B** They are more valuable than anything the princess has ever been given.
   - **C** They are useful objects.
   - **D** They please the king more than the princess.

334 Collection 5 Irony and Ambiguity • Evaluating an Argument

---

Using Academic Language

Review of Literary Terms
Ask students to look back through the collection to find the meanings of the terms listed at right. Then, have students show their grasp of the terms by citing passages from the collection that illustrate the meanings of those terms.

Irony (p. 284); **Verbal Irony** (p. 284); **Situational Irony** (pp. 284, 286); **Dramatic Irony** (p. 284); **Ambiguity** (pp. 284, 297); **Contradictions** (p. 314).

Review of Informational Terms
Ask students to look back through the collection to find the meanings of the terms listed at right. Then, ask students to use

those terms to explain how to evaluate the credibility of an author's argument.

Credibility (p. 308); **Claim** (p. 308); **Generalization** (p. 308); **Logical Appeals** (p. 308); **Reasons** (p. 308); **Evidence** (p. 308); **Emotional Appeals** (p. 308); **Intent** (p. 309).

Collection 5: Skills Review

4. Which is the *most* important reason for expecting the princess to choose the fifth prince's gift?

   F The fifth prince is the strongest and the most handsome of the suitors.

   G His gift is not valuable.

   H She seems most impressed by his gift.

   J She feels sorry for the fifth prince because he is poor.

5. The princess's choice of the third prince's gift is an example of —

   A verbal irony

   B ambiguity

   C dramatic irony

   D situational irony

6. What **theme,** or insight about life, does the fable (and especially the moral) suggest?

   F It's impossible to understand others.

   G Some people rush to judge others.

   H Everyone really values material goods, and it is foolish to pretend otherwise.

   J People value love more than wealth.

7. Why is the moral **ironic**?

   A The reader expects the author to criticize the fifth prince for giving the princess a tin box.

   B The reader expects the author to find fault with the princess's values.

   C The reader expects the author to praise the king for thinking of his daughter's happiness.

   D The reader expects the author to express admiration for the third prince's clever gift.

8. What is the **tone** of the fable?

   F Ironic and grim

   G Ironic and sorrowful

   H Ironic and joyful

   J Ironic and humorous

Constructed Response

9. **Ambiguity** occurs in a story when there are several possible meanings or outcomes. Explain how the author's intentions could be considered ambiguous.

ASSESSING

Assessment

■ *Holt Assessment: Literature, Reading, and Vocabulary*

3. **A** The story describes the four gifts as made from precious metals and gems. B is incorrect because the princess has always had precious things; C is incorrect because the gifts are chosen for their flashy materials, not for their use; and D is incorrect because the story does not mention the king's reaction.

4. **H** The princess "examined it [the tin box] with great interest and squealed with delight" because she had never seen such a common thing. She had not reacted at all to the other gifts. F is true, but the princess does not respond to the fifth prince's appearance, only to his gift. G is true, but it is not a reason for expecting the princess to choose the fifth prince's gift. J is incorrect because the story does not describe how the princess feels about the prince's poverty.

5. **D** Situational irony occurs when something happens that is contrary to what we expect to happen. We expect the princess to choose the fifth prince's gift, but she does not, so D is correct.

6. **H** The moral forces the reader to acknowledge that while some people may claim not to be materialistic, almost everyone would rather have a diamond necklace than tin. J is incorrect because love plays no role in the story, and F is incorrect because the princess's materialistic motives are easy to understand. Although the author may imply that we shouldn't be too quick to judge the princess (G), that is not the main theme.

7. **B** In traditional folk tales, we expect greedy people to be judged harshly, not rewarded, so B is the best choice.

8. **J** The exaggerations, colloquialisms, and contemporary references such as "Cartier's window" give the story a humorous tone. Because the selection is lighthearted, F and G are incorrect. The story presents the princess's materialism as realistic rather than joyful, so H is not correct.

9. Possible response: The meaning of the author's message is ambiguous. Because the reader's expectations of the princess's choice differ from her actual choice, the reader questions the author's intentions. Does the author think it is best to take the most expensive gift, or does he think that greediness is universal?

Collection 5: Skills Review

Vocabulary Skills

Synonyms

Modeling. Model the thought process of a good reader answering item 1. Say, "All of the words could describe the combs, but only one is similar in meaning to the word *coveted*. A clue in the sentence is that Della 'greatly admired' the combs. A coveted item is one that a person strongly wishes for, so B, longed-for, is correct."

Answers and Model Rationales

1. **B** See rationale above.
2. **H** Only *waterfall* means the same as *cascade*. The clue "wavy" helps to eliminate the other options.
3. **D** The word *intense* is a clue to the answer, *passionate*.
4. **F** A system based on chance could not be described as predictable (G), merciful (H), or reasonable (J).
5. **D** Only the word *terrible* is powerful enough to describe the threat of "being torn to pieces by a tiger."
6. **H** A person who believes the jury system is "the fairest" would not oppose or criticize it, so F and G are wrong. J is too neutral a word to fit the context.
7. **C** The word *only* in the sentence helps to eliminate A and B. The word *complex* is a clue that *superficial* means the opposite of "deep and complicated." *Superficial* and *shallow* are similar in meaning.
8. **F** The fact that most juries deliver fair verdicts is positive. Negative publicity would not reveal, exaggerate, or suggest a positive aspect, so G, H, and J are incorrect.

Collection 5: Skills Review
Vocabulary Skills

Test Practice

Synonyms

DIRECTIONS: Choose the *best* synonym for the underlined word in each sentence.

1. In "The Gift of the Magi," Jim buys Della the coveted combs that she had greatly admired.
   A beautiful
   B longed-for
   C expensive
   D unusual

2. Before Della cuts off her long, shining, wavy hair in "The Gift of the Magi," it is compared to a cascade.
   F crown
   G silk
   H waterfall
   J ribbons

3. In "The Lady, or the Tiger?" the princess's fervent nature causes her to have intense feelings of love and jealousy.
   A sensitive
   B unforgiving
   C stubborn
   D passionate

4. The king in "The Lady, or the Tiger?" believes that his system of justice is impartial because each prisoner's fate is decided entirely by chance.
   F unbiased
   G predictable
   H merciful
   J reasonable

5. In "The Lady, or the Tiger?" prisoners face the dire threat of being torn to pieces by a tiger.
   A suspenseful
   B unjust
   C unexpected
   D terrible

6. In "A Defense of the Jury System," the author advocates preserving the jury system because he feels that it's the fairest system of justice.
   F opposes
   G criticizes
   H supports
   J describes

7. In "A Defense of the Jury System," the author states that juries are criticized for having only a superficial understanding of complex issues.
   A wrong
   B forgetful
   C shallow
   D prejudiced

8. The author of "A Defense of the Jury System" says that negative publicity should not obscure the fact that most juries deliver fair verdicts.
   F conceal
   G reveal
   H exaggerate
   J suggest

SKILLS FOCUS

Vocabulary Skills
Identify synonyms.

336 Collection 5 Irony and Ambiguity • Evaluating an Argument

---

Vocabulary Review

Use this activity to assess whether students have retained the collection Vocabulary. Ask students to choose a Vocabulary word from the box that is an antonym for the word that is underlined in each of the sentences below.

irrational	discreet	impartial
conscientiously	fervent	

1. In making his rulings, the judge had to be biased. [impartial]

2. That lawyer was unemotional in his prosecution of the case. [fervent]

3. A defense lawyer must be outspoken about a client's confidences. [discreet]

4. The judge carelessly instructed the jury. [conscientiously]

5. The jury must reach a decision that is reasonable. [irrational]

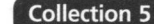

Test Practice

DIRECTIONS: Read the following paragraph from a student's persuasive essay. Then, answer the questions below it.

(1) More people should ride bicycles. (2) Using a bicycle as a means of transportation helps you to exercise each day. (3) If you ride as quick as a flash, you can burn 240 calories an hour. (4) Another reason why people should use bicycles is that riding a bicycle does not cause pollution. (5) Exhaust from cars, on the other hand, contributes to air, ground, and water pollution. (6) So get a move on for your health and the environment—dust off that old three-speed, pump up the tires, and ride to school tomorrow.

1. To help convey an opinion, the writer could revise sentence 1 to say
   A Bicycling can be good for both you and the environment.
   B I have two bicycles—a mountain bike and a road bike.
   C Repairing a flat bicycle tire is easy when you know how.
   D Many families enjoy bicycling as a hobby they can do together.

2. How might the writer of this paragraph address the concern of some readers that riding a bicycle is dangerous?
   F by citing statistics of people who ride bicycles twice a week
   G by comparing bicycles to cars
   H by explaining how helmets and bike lanes have made bicycling safer
   J by telling readers about two friends who bike to school every day

3. Which of the following sentences could be added to support the logical appeal that bicycling is a good form of exercise?
   A Ride slowly when you begin.

   B I prefer riding a bike to jogging.
   C Three-mile trips are quicker by bike.
   D Riding a bicycle tones the leg muscles.

4. How could the writer revise sentence 3 so that it conveys a serious tone?
   F If you ride as quick as a flash, you can burn some major calories.
   G If you ride lickety-split, you can burn 240 calories an hour.
   H If you ride at 6 miles per hour, you can burn 240 calories in an hour.
   J If you ride at 6 miles per hour, you can burn a whole lot of calories.

5. In a debate, which of the following sentences would the above paragraph support?
   A *Resolved:* That bicycling is a safe form of exercise.
   B *Resolved:* That cars cause air, ground, and water pollution.
   C *Resolved:* That people should use bicycles as transportation.
   D *Resolved:* That people should wear helmets while bicycling.

SKILLS FOCUS

Writing Skills
Write a persuasive essay.

Answers
1. A
2. H
3. D
4. H
5. C

APPLICATION

Advertisement

Have students apply what they have learned in this workshop by designing, for homework, a written or spoken advertisement, either for a product or service of their own invention or an existing product or service. Remind students that their advertisements should be concise, attention grabbing, and error free. Ask volunteers to present their advertisements to the class.

EXTENSION

Take a Public Stand

Students can use their persuasive skills to express their positions on any number of local and community issues. They can write a persuasive appeal on an issue in the form of a letter to the editor and send the letter to the school or local newspaper, or they might prepare remarks for a student council or city council meeting. Direct students to investigate beforehand the form they choose; they might study sample letters to the editor to get an idea of the appropriate length and tone, or they might attend a council meeting to determine how much time a speaker has to give his or her opinion. Ask volunteers to share their plans and results with the class.

RESOURCES: WRITING

Assessment
■ *One-Stop Planner* CD-ROM with ExamView Test Generator
■ *Holt Assessment: Writing, Listening, and Speaking*

Internet
■ *Holt Online Assessment*
■ *Holt Online Essay Scoring*

Collection 6
Symbolism and Allegory

**Informational Reading Focus:
Synthesizing Sources**

About Collection 6

In Collection 6, students will master the
following skills:

- **Literary Skills:** Analyze symbols
  and allegories.
- **Reading Skills:** Make inferences from
  details; identify main idea; identify cause
  and effect; and synthesize information
  from several sources.
- **Vocabulary Skills:** Identify and
  interpret similes; identify word
  denotations and connotations; understand
  word origins; and use context clues.
- **Writing Skills:** Develop, write, and
  revise a descriptive essay.
- **Listening and Speaking Skills:**
  Present a description.

Informational Text

Each collection of *Elements of Literature*
provides a variety of informational texts
related to the literature selections by
theme or topic.

Minimum Course of Study

Most skills can be taught with a minimum
number of selections and features. In the
chart to the right, lessons highlighted in
green constitute the minimum course of
study that provides coverage of the skills
taught in Collection 6.

Resource Manager
(pp. 338C–338D)

Lesson and workshop resources are
referenced in the Resource Manager on
the pages that follow. These resources can
be used to reinforce the skills taught in
Collection 6, remediate students who are
having difficulty, and provide supporting
activities for English-language learners.

Scope and Sequence

Selection ▪ Feature	Literary Skills
Elements of Literature: Symbolism and Allegory *by* John Malcolm Brinnin	• Understand symbolism and allegory
The Scarlet Ibis *by* James Hurst ↔ *at grade level*	• Analyze symbolism
The Grandfather *by* Gary Soto ↔ *at grade level*	• Analyze symbols with multiple meanings
The Golden Kite, the Silver Wind *by* Ray Bradbury ↔ *at grade level*	• Analyze allegory
Informational Text: • Weapons of the Spirit • Letter to President Roosevelt • On the Abolition of the Threat of War • The Arms Race *by* Albert Einstein ↑ *above grade level*	
Writing Workshop: *Describing a Place*	
Listening and Speaking Workshop: *Presenting a Description*	
Skills Review: *Literary Skills* *Vocabulary Skills* *Writing Skills*	• Analyze symbolism and allegory

Reading Skills	Vocabulary Skills	Writing ■ Grammar and Language ■ Listening and Speaking Skills
• Make inferences from details	• Use words in context • Identify and interpret similes	• Describe a setting • Retell the story from a different point of view
• Identify main idea	• Identify word denotations and connotations	• Write an explanation • Write about a symbol • Use parallel structure
• Identify cause and effect	• Understand word origins • Demonstrate word knowledge	• Write a summary
• Synthesize information from several sources (by one author) on a single topic	• Create semantic maps	
		• Write a descriptive essay
		• Present a description
	• Use context clues to understand word meanings	• Write a descriptive essay

Selection ■ Feature	Planning	Differentiating Instruction Lesson Plans with ELL Strategies and Practice	Reading ■ Vocabulary
Elements of Literature: Symbolism and Allegory *by John Malcolm Brinnin*			
The Scarlet Ibis *by James Hurst*	• One-Stop Planner with ExamView Test Generator	• The Holt Reader, pp. 168–186 • Holt Reading Solutions, pp. 171–176 • Supporting Instruction in Spanish, p. 23 • Audio CD Library, disc 11 • Audio CD Library, Selections and Summaries in Spanish	• The Holt Reader • Holt Reading Solutions • Vocabulary Development, p. 29
The Grandfather *by Gary Soto*	• One-Stop Planner with ExamView Test Generator	• Holt Reading Solutions, pp. 177–182 • Supporting Instruction in Spanish, p. 24 • Audio CD Library, disc 11 • Audio CD Library, Selections and Summaries in Spanish	• Holt Reading Solutions • PowerNotes: Identifying the Main Idea
The Golden Kite, the Silver Wind *by Ray Bradbury* **Informational Text:** • Weapons of the Spirit • Letter to President Roosevelt • On the Abolition of the Threat of War • The Arms Race *by Albert Einstein*	• One-Stop Planner with ExamView Test Generator	• Holt Adapted Reader • Holt Reading Solutions, pp. 183–188 • Supporting Instruction in Spanish, pp. 25–26 • Audio CD Library, disc 11 • Audio CD Library, Selections and Summaries in Spanish	• Holt Adapted Reader • Holt Reading Solutions • Vocabulary Development, pp. 31, 32
Writing Workshop: *Describing a Place*	• One-Stop Planner with ExamView Test Generator	• Workshop Resources: Writing, Listening, and Speaking, pp. 56–62 • Family Involvement Activities in English and Spanish • Supporting Instruction in Spanish, p. 71	
Listening and Speaking Workshop: *Presenting a Description*	• One-Stop Planner with ExamView Test Generator	• Workshop Resources: Writing, Listening, and Speaking, pp. 63–68 • Supporting Instruction in Spanish	
Skills Review: *Literary Skills Vocabulary Skills Writing Skills*			

The Holt Reader

The Holt Reader is a consumable paperback book which can be used alone or to accompany *Elements of Literature*. It offers guided support throughout the reading process and encourages students to become active readers by circling, underlining, questioning, and jotting down responses as they read. *The Holt Reader* works well for homework, students who have missed class, additional instructional time, reteaching, and remediation.

Holt Reading Solutions (HRS)

Holt Reading Solutions pulls together reading resources in the *Elements of Literature* program to create a powerful tool for intervention and whole-class instruction. *HRS* includes diagnostic assessment tools, lesson plans for English-language learners and special education students, adaptations of selected reading selections, vocabulary and comprehension worksheets, information on phonics and decoding, and additional instruction and practice in remedial reading skills.

Writing ▪ Grammar and Language ▪ Listening and Speaking	Assessment
• Daily Language Activities	• Holt Assessment: Literature, Reading, and Vocabulary • Holt Online Assessment • One-Stop Planner with ExamView Test Generator
• Daily Language Activities • Language Handbook Worksheets, p. 108	• Holt Assessment: Literature, Reading, and Vocabulary • Holt Online Assessment • One-Stop Planner with ExamView Test Generator
• Daily Language Activities	• Holt Assessment: Literature, Reading, and Vocabulary • Holt Online Assessment • One-Stop Planner with ExamView Test Generator
• Daily Language Activities • Workshop Resources: Writing, Listening, and Speaking, pp. 56–62	• Holt Assessment: Writing, Listening, and Speaking • Holt Online Assessment • One-Stop Planner with ExamView Test Generator
• Workshop Resources: Writing, Listening, and Speaking, pp. 63–68	• Holt Assessment: Writing, Listening, and Speaking • One-Stop Planner with ExamView Test Generator
	• Holt Assessment: Writing, Listening, and Speaking • One-Stop Planner with ExamView Test Generator

Technology

INTERNET

- go.hrw.com
- Holt Online Assessment
- Holt Online Essay Scoring
- Elements of Literature Online

MEDIA

- One-Stop Planner with ExamView Test Generator
- PowerNotes
- Audio CD Library, disc 11
- Audio CD Library, Selections and Summaries in Spanish
- Visual Connections Videocassette Program, Segment 5
- Fine Art Transparencies, 9

 Transparency   Video

 CD-ROM   Audio CD

One–Stop Planner with ExamView Test Generator

The *One-Stop Planner* CD-ROM contains electronic versions of print-based teaching resources, clips from the video program, and valuable assessment tools. The *One-Stop Planner* resources are presented in easy-to-follow, point-and-click menu formats. To preview resources or print out worksheets and tests, you simply make a selection and click.

One–Stop Planner CD-ROM

Collection 6

■ **Literary Skills**
Analyze various literary devices, including allegory and symbolism.

■ **Reading Skills**
Synthesize the content from several sources or works by a single author on a single issue.

INTRODUCING THE COLLECTION

Students will find that the selections in this collection contain many layers of meaning. In "The Scarlet Ibis," a fragile, struggling bird is a symbol for the narrator's physically disabled brother. In Gary Soto's essay "The Grandfather," a growing avocado tree in the family yard acquires a multitude of meanings. In "The Golden Kite, the Silver Wind," Ray Bradbury transforms a simple story about rival Chinese rulers into an allegory about the nuclear arms race. By reading these selections and discussing their ideas, students will learn to appreciate how symbols speak to the reader's imagination and take on different shades of meaning.

The last selection of the collection is comprised of four related informational pieces by the great scientist Albert Einstein. Students are asked to synthesize the views that he expresses about peace, war, and weaponry.

The collection concludes with an opportunity for students to write descriptive essays and to give descriptive presentations.

COLLECTION 6 RESOURCES: READING

Planning
■ *One-Stop Planner* CD-ROM with ExamView Test Generator

Differentiating Instruction
■ *Holt Reading Solutions*
■ *The Holt Reader*
■ *Holt Adapted Reader*

■ *Family Involvement Activities in English and Spanish*
■ *Supporting Instruction in Spanish*

Vocabulary
■ *Vocabulary Development*

Grammar and Language
■ *Language Handbook Worksheets*
■ *Daily Language Activities*

Collection 6

Symbolism and Allegory

INFORMATIONAL READING FOCUS

SYNTHESIZING SOURCES

What we have not named as a symbol escapes our notice.

—W. H. Auden

INTERNET
Collection Resources
Keyword: LE5 9-6

Paris Through the Window (1913) by Marc Chagall. Oil on canvas (53½″ × 55¾″).

The Solomon R. Guggenheim Museum, New York. Gift, Solomon R. Guggenheim, 1937 (37.438).

339

Grade-Level Skills

■ **Literary Skills**
Analyze various literary devices, including allegory and symbolism.

Review Skills

■ **Literary Skills**
Identify the literary devices that define a writer's style.

**Elements of Literature:
Symbolism and Allegory**

Review the definition of the term *symbol* with students. Then, write the names of several popular symbols on the chalkboard, such as a heart for love, an owl for wisdom, the color green for envy and money, or the American flag for America and patriotism. Ask students to share some associations they make with these symbols, and write their ideas on the chalkboard. Point out that one symbol can call to mind several associations. Explain that in everyday life as well as in literature, symbols can mean different things to different individuals.

Elements of Literature

Symbolism and Allegory *by* John Malcolm Brinnin
LAYERS OF MEANING

What Symbols Stand For

A **symbol** is often an ordinary object, event, person, or animal to which we have attached extraordinary meaning and significance. We use a rectangle of dyed cloth to symbolize a country. We use a picture of a skull and crossbones to stand for poison or danger. We send red roses as a symbol of love.

Where Do Symbols Come From?

Symbols can be inherited or invented. The most familiar symbols have been inherited—that is, they have been handed down over time. For example, no one knows exactly who first thought of using the lion to symbolize power, courage, and domination. Once these qualities were associated with the animal, images of lions appeared on flags, banners, coats of arms, and castle walls, and the lion became a **public symbol,** one that shows up in art and literature even today.

People throughout history have endowed ordinary objects with meanings far beyond their simple functions: A crown symbolizes royalty; an olive branch symbolizes peace; five linked rings symbolize the Olympics.

Symbols can also be invented. You probably have a symbol for your school. Writers often take a new object, character, or event and make it the embodiment of some human concern. Some invented symbols in literature have become so widely known that they have gained the status of public

symbols. Peter Pan as the symbol of eternal childhood is an example.

Why Create Symbols?

You may ask why writers don't just come right out and say what they mean. Symbols allow writers to suggest layers and layers of meaning—possibilities that a simple, literal statement could never convey. A symbol is like a pebble cast into a pond: It sends out ever-widening ripples of meaning.

In the short story "Marigolds" (page 119), a poor woman has no beauty in her world except the dazzling marigolds that she plants around her ramshackle house. The children in the story, who are as poor as the old woman, hate the flowers and all that they stand for. In a moment of thoughtless hatred and violence, one girl destroys all the bright flowers.

Those flowers are real flowers in the story, but we also get a sense that they symbolize something else, something larger than the flowers themselves. Some readers might feel that they symbolize hope and beauty and that the children are so angry about their poverty that they want to destroy anything that expresses the beauty of another world. Other readers will have different ideas about what the marigolds stand for, but most will agree that the marigolds work on more than just a literal level in the story.

You may not be able to articulate fully what a certain symbol means, but you will find that the symbol, if it is powerful and well chosen, will speak forcefully to your

INTERNET
More About
Symbolism and
Allegory
Keyword: LE5 9-6

SKILLS FOCUS

Literary Skills
Understand
symbolism and
allegory.

DIFFERENTIATING INSTRUCTION

Learners Having Difficulty
Symbolism and allegory. Choose a familiar story, such as "Cinderella," that has examples of symbols. Have students work in small groups to discuss what might be the symbolic meanings of the characters and objects. For example, Cinderella might be viewed as a symbol of an abused person, her fairy godmother as a symbol of maternal

love, her stepmother as a symbol of evil, and her glass slipper as a symbol of individuality. Next, present allegory as an extension of symbolism, in which the story as a whole takes on a second level of meaning. To help clarify the concept for students, use the example of fables, in which the animal characters often represent moral qualities such as good, evil, laziness, and greed.

English-Language Learners
For more instruction on symbolism and allegory for English-language learners and special education students, see *Holt Reading Solutions.*

Advanced Learners
Acceleration. Use the following activity to help advanced learners analyze characteristics of subgenres such as allegory.

emotions and to your imagination. You may also find that you will remember and think about the symbol long after you have forgotten other parts of the story's plot.

Allegory: Split-level Stories

An **allegory** is a story in which characters, settings, and actions stand for something beyond themselves. In some types of allegories, the characters and setting represent abstract ideas or moral qualities. In other types, characters and situations stand for historical figures and events.

An allegory can be read on one level for its literal, or straightforward, meaning and on a second level for its symbolic, or allegorical, meaning. Allegories are often intended to teach a moral lesson or to make a comment about goodness and vice.

Some of the most famous allegories feature characters and places whose names describe what they symbolize. In an old English play called *Everyman,* the main character is named Everyman (he stands for exactly what his name indicates). One day, Everyman is summoned by Death to give an accounting of his life. Everyman asks his friends Fellowship, Beauty, Strength, and Good Deeds to go with him to tell Death that he has led a good life. Only Good Deeds stays with him to the end. The allegory in *Everyman* doesn't get in the way of a very good story! In fact, *Everyman,* written in the 1400s, is still revived in theaters today, and it still gets good reviews.

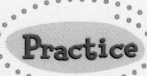
Practice

A. Think about the great number of symbols we're surrounded by in everyday life. For starters, identify what the items below stand for. Then, see if you can explain the basis for the symbol—why is this symbol appropriate for what it stands for?
1. A snake
2. An eagle
3. Spring
4. An owl
5. A white flag

B. Here is a brief poem that works on two levels: a literal level and a symbolic level. A *fen* is a swampy place. What does the fen symbolize in this poem?

> **I May, I Might, I Must**
>
> If you will tell me why the fen
> appears impassable, I then
> will tell you why I think that I
> can get across it if I try.
> —Marianne Moore

Practice

A. Possible responses are listed below:
1. Snakes have many negative connotations including evil, sneakiness, and untrustworthiness. One reason we make these associations may be because many snakes move silently and are often camouflaged in the wild. Another reason may be because of the snake's role in the biblical story about the fall of Adam and Eve.
2. An eagle symbolizes strength and boldness, two characteristics that the bird seems to possess in the wild.
3. Spring symbolizes hope and new beginnings. This symbolism is appropriate because spring is the season in which plants create new life after disappearing in winter.
4. The owl symbolizes wisdom. This association is due solely to this bird's solemn, dignified appearance as it gazes upon the nocturnal world.
5. The white flag symbolizes surrender or truce. It was first used as a signal for a cease-fire in order to talk with the enemy.

B. Possible response: In Marianne Moore's poem, a fen symbolizes the challenges and obstacles people face in life.

Apply

Encourage students to think of another piece of literature, a movie, or a song that includes a distinct symbol. Have students explain the ideas they associate with that symbol.

Activity. Discuss the definition of the term *allegory* as described in the essay. Emphasize that on the surface the characters in an allegory, like those in *Everyman,* show little in the way of individual personality. Instead, they embody values or moral qualities. Ask students to cite examples of works from literature or cinema that they believe contain allegorical characters. Have students describe the moral lesson the work intends to teach. Challenge students to try to reach a consensus on the characteristics of allegorical works, based on the examples that they have named.

Grade-Level Skills

■ **Literary Skills**
Analyze various literary devices, including allegory and symbolism.

■ **Reading Skills**
Make inferences from details.

Review Skills

■ **Literary Skills**
Identify the literary devices that define a writer's style.

Summary *at grade level*

The story's first-person narrator relates this story from the past. His little brother, Doodle, is born physically disabled. Doodle is expected to die, yet he lives. The narrator must care for his brother, taking him everywhere in a go-cart. He is often frustrated by this burden, but after much effort, he succeeds in teaching Doodle how to walk. Proud of this success, the narrator works to teach him how to run, swim, climb trees, and fight. In a symbolic episode that foreshadows the story's tragic resolution, Doodle buries a fallen bird—the brilliant scarlet ibis of the title. Later that day, the strain of trying to learn physical skills leaves Doodle gravely weakened. In the climactic final scene, Doodle collapses and dies while running to catch up with his brother, who has abandoned him in the midst of a thunderstorm. The narrator feels guilt for his brother's death, and he discovers too late the depth of his feelings for his brother.

Before You Read

The Scarlet Ibis

Make the Connection

Quickwrite ✏️
Make a list of situations that might make someone feel proud. Is pride positive or negative—can it be both? Jot down your thoughts about what it means to be proud.

Literary Focus

Symbols: Deeper Meanings
A **symbol** is an object, person, animal, or event that stands for something more than itself. We're surrounded by symbols in our everyday lives. The dove, often pictured on greeting cards, is a universal symbol of peace.

In literature, symbols add deeper levels of meaning to a work. Sometimes a symbol will be associated with a particular character. In "The Scarlet Ibis" you'll notice similarities and links between one character and a bird. These are hints that the author is making a symbolic connection between the two that can deepen your understanding of the character.

In the hands of a skillful writer, symbols have the power to move us deeply. If you're like most readers, this story about two young brothers will move you as well.

Reading Skills

Making Inferences from Details
When you notice details in a story, you're aware of the little things. Such details may seem insignificant at first, but they can develop more meaning as you read further. It's up to you to make **inferences,** or educated guesses, about what the writer wants to convey through the details.

INTERNET
Vocabulary
Practice
Keyword: LE5 9-6

SKILLS FOCUS

Literary Skills
Understand symbolism.

Reading Skills
Make inferences from details.

As you read "The Scarlet Ibis," keep track of the little things—color, gesture, weather—and see what larger meanings they might point to. The questions at the open-book signs will help you.

Background

This story is set in the American South. Its climax takes place in 1918, the year World War I ended. You'll find references in the story to battles being fought far from its peaceful southern setting. As you read, think about why the author chose this setting. (See Meet the Writer on page 354.)

Vocabulary Development

sullenly (sul′ən·lē) *adv.*: resentfully; gloomily.

imminent (im′ə·nənt) *adj.*: near; about to happen.

iridescent (ir′i·des′ənt) *adj.*: rainbow-like; displaying a shifting range of colors.

serene (sə·rēn′) *adj.*: peaceful; calm.

infallibility (in·fal′ə·bil′i·tē) *n.*: inability to make a mistake.

blighted (blīt′id) *v.* used as *adj.*: suffering from conditions that destroy or prevent growth.

doggedness (dôg′id·nis) *n.*: stubbornness; persistence.

reiterated (rē·it′ə·rāt′id) *v.*: repeated.

precariously (pri·ker′ē·əs·lē) *adv.*: unsteadily; insecurely.

mar (mär) *v.*: damage; spoil.

RESOURCES: READING

Planning
■ *One-Stop Planner* CD-ROM with ExamView Test Generator

Differentiating Instruction
■ *Holt Reading Solutions*
■ *The Holt Reader*
■ *Supporting Instruction in Spanish*

■ *Audio CD Library, Selections and Summaries in Spanish*

Vocabulary
■ *Vocabulary Development*

Grammar and Language
■ *Daily Language Activities*

The Scarlet Ibis

James Hurst

Doodle was just about the craziest brother a boy ever had.

343

Ⓐ Learners Having Difficulty

Paraphrasing. Explain that *clove* is the past tense of *cleave*, which means "to split," and that *bleeding* suggests a vivid red. Ask students to paraphrase this sentence. [Possible response: The ibis settled in the red tree between summer and fall.]

Ⓑ Literary Focus

❓ Symbols. The adult narrator repeats the word *bleeding* to mean "red." What associations are triggered by the color red? Think of red objects, expressions like "seeing red," and titles of books or movies. [Possible responses: stop signs, exit signs, "code red," *The Hunt for Red October, The Scarlet Letter.*] What qualities does red seem to symbolize? [Possible responses: danger, love, courage, and death.] Watch to see what meaning red takes on in this story.

Ⓒ Literary Focus

❓ Voice and tone. Notice the shift in voice and tone from that of an adult looking back in time to that of the child who was actually there during that long-ago summer. What differences do you notice between this paragraph and the first two paragraphs of the story? [The sentences become shorter, the vocabulary easier, and the language more conversational.]

Ⓓ English-Language Learners

Idioms. Explain that to be "all there" is a colloquial expression that means to be "mentally healthy."

Ⓐ It was in the clove of seasons, summer was dead but autumn had not yet been born, that the ibis lit in the bleeding tree. The flower garden was stained with rotting brown magnolia petals, and ironweeds grew rank[1] amid the purple phlox. The five o'clocks by the chimney still marked time, but the oriole nest in the elm was untenanted and rocked back and forth like an empty cradle. The last graveyard flowers were blooming, and their smell drifted across the cotton field and through every room of our house, speaking softly the names of our dead.

It's strange that all this is still so clear to me, now that that summer has long since fled and time has had its way. A grindstone stands where **Ⓑ** the bleeding tree stood, just outside the kitchen door, and now if an oriole sings in the elm, its song seems to die up in the leaves, a silvery dust. The flower garden is prim, the house a gleaming white, and the pale fence across the yard stands straight and spruce. But sometimes (like right now), as I sit in the cool, green-draped parlor, the grindstone begins to turn, and time with all its changes is ground away—and I remember Doodle.

Doodle was just about the craziest brother a boy ever had. Of course, he wasn't a crazy crazy like old Miss Leedie, who was in love with President Wilson and wrote him a letter every day, but was a nice crazy, like someone you meet in your dreams. He was born when I was six and **Ⓒ** was, from the outset, a disappointment. He seemed all head, with a tiny body which was red and shriveled like an old man's. Everybody thought he was going to die—everybody except Aunt Nicey, who had delivered him. She said he would live because he was born in a caul[2] and cauls were made from Jesus' nightgown. Daddy had Mr. Heath, the carpenter, build a little

mahogany coffin for him. But he didn't die, and when he was three months old, Mama and Daddy decided they might as well name him. They named him William Armstrong, which was like tying a big tail on a small kite. Such a name sounds good only on a tombstone.

I thought myself pretty smart at many things, like holding my breath, running, jumping, or climbing the vines in Old Woman Swamp, and I wanted more than anything else someone to race to Horsehead Landing, someone to box with, and someone to perch with in the top fork of the great pine behind the barn, where across the fields and swamps you could see the sea. I wanted a brother. But Mama, crying, told me that even if William Armstrong lived, he would never do these things with me. He might not, **Ⓓ** she sobbed, even be "all there." He might, as long as he lived, lie on the rubber sheet in the center of the bed in the front bedroom where the white

---

1. **rank** (raŋk) *adj.:* thick and wild. *Rank* also means "smelly."
2. **caul** (kôl) *n.:* membrane (thin, skinlike material) that sometimes covers a baby's head at birth.

DIFFERENTIATING INSTRUCTION

Learners Having Difficulty
Invite learners having difficulty to read "The Scarlet Ibis" in interactive format in *The Holt Reader* and to use the sidenotes as aids to understanding the selection. The interactive version provides additional instruction, practice, and assessment of the literary skill taught in the Student Edition. Monitor students'

responses to the selection, and correct any misconceptions that arise.

English-Language Learners
Students may have difficulty understanding the meanings of multiple-meaning words such as *clove, spruce, ground, invalid, stroke, weave, stream, film,* and *rustling.* To help these students, pair them with fluent English readers,

marquisette[3] curtains billowed out in the afternoon sea breeze, rustling like palmetto fronds.[4]

It was bad enough having an invalid brother, but having one who possibly was not all there was unbearable, so I began to make plans to kill him by smothering him with a pillow. However, one afternoon as I watched him, my head poked between the iron posts of the foot of the bed, he looked straight at me and grinned. I skipped through the rooms, down the echoing halls, shouting, "Mama, he smiled. He's all there! He's all there!" and he was.

When he was two, if you laid him on his stomach, he began to try to move himself, straining terribly. The doctor said that with his weak heart this strain would probably kill him, but it didn't. Trembling, he'd push himself up, turning first red, then a soft purple, and finally collapse back onto the bed like an old worn-out doll. I can still see Mama watching him, her hand pressed tight across her mouth, her eyes wide and unblinking. But he learned to crawl (it was his third winter), and we brought him out of the front bedroom, putting him on the rug before the fireplace. For the first time he became one of us.

MAKING INFERENCES

1. What can you **infer** about the little boy from the **details** in this paragraph?

As long as he lay all the time in bed, we called him William Armstrong, even though it was formal and sounded as if we were referring to one of our ancestors, but with his creeping around on the deerskin rug and beginning to talk, something had to be done about his name. It was I who renamed him. When he crawled, he crawled backward, as if he were in reverse and couldn't change gears. If you called him, he'd turn around as if he were going in the other direction, then he'd back right up to you to be picked up. Crawling backward made him look like a doodlebug[5] so I began to call him Doodle, and in time even Mama and Daddy thought it was a better name than William Armstrong. Only Aunt Nicey disagreed. She said caul babies should be treated with special respect since they might turn out to be saints. Renaming my brother was perhaps the kindest thing I ever did for him, because nobody expects much from someone called Doodle.

Although Doodle learned to crawl, he showed no signs of walking, but he wasn't idle. He talked so much that we all quit listening to what he said. It was about this time that Daddy built him a go-cart, and I had to pull him around. At first I just paraded him up and down the piazza,[6] but then he started crying to be taken out into the yard and it ended up by my having to lug him wherever I went. If I so much as picked up my cap, he'd start crying to go with me, and Mama would call from wherever she was, "Take Doodle with you."

He was a burden in many ways. The doctor had said that he mustn't get too excited, too hot, too cold, or too tired and that he must always be treated gently. A long list of don'ts went with him, all of which I ignored once we got out of the house. To discourage his coming with me, I'd run with him across the ends of the cotton rows and career him around corners on two wheels. Sometimes I accidentally turned him over, but he never told Mama. His skin was very sensitive, and he had to wear a big straw hat whenever he went out. When the going got rough and he had to cling to the sides of the go-cart, the hat slipped all the way down over his ears. He was a sight. Finally, I could see I was licked. Doodle was my brother, and he was going to cling to me forever, no matter what I did, so I dragged him across the burning cotton field to share with him

3. **marquisette** (mär′ki·zet′) *adj.*: thin, netlike fabric.
4. **palmetto fronds:** fanlike leaves of a palm tree.

5. **doodlebug** (dood′′l·bug′) *n.*: larva of a type of insect that moves backward.
6. **piazza** (pē·az′ə) *n.*: large covered porch.

The Scarlet Ibis   **345**

A **Reading Skills**

❓ Making inferences. What can you infer about Doodle based on his reaction to the swamp? [Possible response: He is bright, emotional, and sensitive to beauty.]

B **Literary Focus**

❓ Narrator. How would this passage, and the story in general, differ if it were told by an omniscient narrator? [Possible responses: There would be less information about the character's feelings and motivations; the story would be told from a more objective viewpoint.]

C **Reading Skills**

❓ Making predictions. In this episode, the narrator is cruel to his brother, and Doodle responds with fear. Why is Doodle so afraid of being left? [Possible responses: He is unable to move from the barn loft on his own. He cannot walk and is totally dependent on his older brother.]
What do you think might happen in the future based on what happens in this episode? [Possible responses: The narrator may treat Doodle cruelly again. The narrator may leave Doodle.]

---

the only beauty I knew, Old Woman Swamp. I pulled the go-cart through the sawtooth fern, down into the green dimness where the palmetto fronds whispered by the stream. I lifted him out and set him down in the soft rubber grass beside a tall pine. His eyes were round with wonder as he gazed about him, and his little hands began to stroke the rubber grass. Then he **A** began to cry.

"For heaven's sake, what's the matter?" I asked, annoyed.

"It's so pretty," he said. "So pretty, pretty, pretty."

After that day Doodle and I often went down into Old Woman Swamp. I would gather wildflowers, wild violets, honeysuckle, yellow jasmine, snakeflowers, and waterlilies, and with wire grass we'd weave them into necklaces and crowns. We'd bedeck ourselves with our handiwork and loll about thus beautified, beyond the touch of the everyday world. Then when the slanted rays of the sun burned orange in the tops of the pines, we'd drop our jewels into the stream and watch them float away toward the sea.

B There is within me (and with sadness I have watched it in others) a knot of cruelty borne by the stream of love, much as our blood sometimes bears the seed of our destruction, and at times I was mean to Doodle. One day I took him up to the barn loft and showed him his casket, telling him how we all had believed he would die. It was covered with a film of Paris green[7] sprinkled to kill the rats, and screech owls had built a nest inside it.

Doodle studied the mahogany box for a long time, then said, "It's not mine."

---

7. **Paris green:** poisonous green powder used to kill insects.

"It is," I said. "And before I'll help you down from the loft, you're going to have to touch it."

"I won't touch it," he said <u>sullenly</u>.

C "Then I'll leave you here by yourself," I threatened, and made as if I were going down.

Doodle was frightened of being left. "Don't go leave me, Brother," he cried, and he leaned toward the coffin. His hand, trembling, reached out, and when he touched the casket, he screamed. A screech owl flapped out of the box into our faces, scaring us and covering us with Paris green. Doodle was paralyzed, so I put him on my shoulder and carried him down the ladder, and even when we were outside in the bright sunshine, he clung to me, crying, "Don't leave me. Don't leave me."

When Doodle was five years old, I was embarrassed at having a brother of that age who couldn't walk, so I set out to teach him. We were down in Old Woman Swamp and it was spring and the sick-sweet smell of bay flowers hung everywhere like a mournful song. "I'm going to teach you to walk, Doodle," I said.

He was sitting comfortably on the soft grass, leaning back against the pine. "Why?" he asked.

I hadn't expected such an answer. "So I won't have to haul you around all the time."

"I can't walk, Brother," he said.

"Who says so?" I demanded.

"Mama, the doctor—everybody."

"Oh, you can walk," I said, and I took him by the arms and stood him up. He collapsed onto the grass like a half-empty flour sack. It was as if he had no bones in his little legs.

"Don't hurt me, Brother," he warned.

Vocabulary
sullenly (sul′ən·lē) *adv.:* resentfully; gloomily.

DIFFERENTIATING INSTRUCTION

Advanced Learners
Acceleration. Use the following activity to help advanced learners analyze how imagery and figures of speech evoke readers' emotions.
Activity. Ask students to jot down several examples of figurative language and imagery that they encounter as they read. For each example, have students state the comparison and describe the image and emotional impression it creates. Then, ask students to rework each example in order to change the image or the evoked emotion.

"Shut up. I'm not going to hurt you. I'm going to teach you to walk." I heaved him up again, and again he collapsed.

This time he did not lift his face up out of the rubber grass. "I just can't do it. Let's make honeysuckle wreaths."

"Oh yes you can, Doodle," I said. "All you got to do is try. Now come on," and I hauled him up once more.

It seemed so hopeless from the beginning that it's a miracle I didn't give up. But all of us must have something or someone to be proud of, and Doodle had become mine. I did not know then that pride is a wonderful, terrible thing, a seed that bears two vines, life and death. Every day that summer we went to the pine beside the stream of Old Woman Swamp, and I put him on his feet at least a hundred times each afternoon. Occasionally I too became discouraged because it didn't seem as if he was trying, and I would say, "Doodle, don't you *want* to learn to walk?"

He'd nod his head, and I'd say, "Well, if you don't keep trying, you'll never learn." Then I'd paint for him a picture of us as old men, white-haired, him with a long white beard and me still pulling him around in the go-cart. This never failed to make him try again.

Finally, one day, after many weeks of practicing, he stood alone for a few seconds. When he fell, I grabbed him in my arms and hugged him, our laughter pealing through the swamp like a ringing bell. Now we knew it could be done. Hope no longer hid in the dark palmetto thicket but perched like a cardinal in the lacy toothbrush tree, brilliantly visible. "Yes, yes," I cried, and he cried it too, and the grass beneath us was soft and the smell of the swamp was sweet.

With success so imminent, we decided not to tell anyone until he could actually walk. Each

MAKING INFERENCES

2. What can you **infer** about the narrator from his comments about his pride and from his behavior toward Doodle?

day, barring rain, we sneaked into Old Woman Swamp, and by cotton-picking time Doodle was ready to show what he could do. He still wasn't able to walk far, but we could wait no longer. Keeping a nice secret is very hard to do, like holding your breath. We chose to reveal all on October eighth, Doodle's sixth birthday, and for weeks ahead we mooned around the house, promising everybody a most spectacular surprise. Aunt Nicey said that, after so much talk, if we produced anything less tremendous than the Resurrection,[8] she was going to be disappointed.

At breakfast on our chosen day, when Mama, Daddy, and Aunt Nicey were in the dining room, I brought Doodle to the door in the go-cart just as usual and had them turn their backs, making them cross their hearts and hope to die if they peeked. I helped Doodle up, and when he was standing alone I let them look. There wasn't a sound as Doodle walked slowly across the room and sat down at his place at the table. Then Mama began to cry and ran over to him, hugging him and kissing him. Daddy hugged him too, so I went to Aunt Nicey, who was thanks-praying in the doorway, and began to waltz her around. We danced together quite well until she came down on my big toe with her brogans,[9] hurting me so badly I thought I was crippled for life.

Doodle told them it was I who had taught him to walk, so everyone wanted to hug me, and I began to cry.

"What are you crying for?" asked Daddy, but I couldn't answer. They did not know that I did it for myself; that pride, whose slave I was, spoke to me louder than all their voices; and that Doodle walked only because I was ashamed of having a crippled brother.

---

8. Resurrection: reference to the Christian belief in the rising of Jesus from the dead after his burial.
9. brogans (brō′gənz) *n.:* heavy ankle-high shoes.

Vocabulary
imminent (im′ə·nənt) *adj.:* near; about to happen.

D Reading Skills

? **Interpreting.** What do you think the narrator means by this statement? [Possible response: Pride can be healthy because it leads you to accomplish things, but it can also lead to something negative.]

E Reading Skills

Making inferences. [Possible response to question 2: The narrator is working with Doodle more for his own sense of accomplishment than for the hope of helping Doodle learn to walk. He loves Doodle but feels that because of his inability to walk, Doodle is a burden to him.]

F Literary Focus

? **Symbols.** Ask students to identify and explain the symbol for hope. [Hope is symbolized by the cardinal, a bird whose brilliant red plumage suggests a vibrant life force.]

G English-Language Learners

Cultural concepts. Explain that in some cultures, children draw an imaginary X in the air and say "Cross my heart and hope to die" when they want to seal a promise.

H Reading Skills

? **Making judgments.** Do you think the narrator judges himself too harshly? Explain. [Possible response: Yes, his motives are not entirely selfish. The scenes he describes show that he truly likes being with Doodle and that he is willing to work hard to help Doodle accomplish things.]

DEVELOPING FLUENCY

Mixed-ability group activity. Arrange students in mixed-ability groups that include advanced learners, learners having difficulty, and English-language learners. Invite a fluent reader to choose a passage from the selection and to read it aloud to the group while the others follow along in their texts. Then, have the group members discuss the meaning of the passage and resolve questions they may have about difficult words, figurative language, or sentence structure. Finally, have the group members take turns reading parts of the passage aloud.

348 `Collection 6` **Symbolism and Allegory • Synthesizing Sources**

Developing Word-Attack Skills

Review the sounds of *–ed* using words from the selection.

- *–ed* stands for /d/ in *stained* and *shriveled*
- *–ed* stands for /t/ in *looked* and *skipped*
- *–ed* stands for /id/ in *decided* and *wanted*

Write the selection word *ashamedly* on the chalkboard, and read it aloud. Explain that *ashamed* is pronounced /ə•shāmd′/, and *–ed* stands for /d/. When *–ly* is added, the sound of *–ed* changes to /id/: /ə•shām′id•lē/.

Activity. Write these sentences on the chalkboard. Have volunteers tell if the suffix *–ed* in the underlined word is pronounced as one syllable or two.

1. He <u>learned</u> a great deal from reading. [1]
   He became a very <u>learned</u> man. [2]

2. A wizened man gave a <u>crooked</u> smile. [2]
   Then he <u>crooked</u> a finger to beckon us. [1]

3. Grandma had <u>aged</u> much in the past year. [1]
   Now she looked like an <u>aged</u> person. [2]

4. The girl wore a pale green <u>peaked</u> hat. [1]
   The color made her look a bit <u>peaked</u>. [2]

Within a few months Doodle had learned to walk well and his go-cart was put up in the barn loft (it's still there) beside his little mahogany coffin. Now, when we roamed off together, resting often, we never turned back until our destination had been reached, and to help pass the time, we took up lying. From the beginning Doodle was a terrible liar, and he got me in the habit. Had anyone stopped to listen to us, we would have been sent off to Dix Hill.

My lies were scary, involved, and usually pointless, but Doodle's were twice as crazy. People in his stories all had wings and flew wherever they wanted to go. His favorite lie was about a boy named Peter who had a pet peacock with a ten-foot tail. Peter wore a golden robe that glittered so brightly that when he walked through the sunflowers they turned away from the sun to face him. When Peter was ready to go to sleep, the peacock spread his magnificent tail, enfolding the boy gently like a closing go-to-sleep flower, burying him in the gloriously iridescent, rustling vortex.[10] Yes, I must admit it. Doodle could beat me lying.

Doodle and I spent lots of time thinking about our future. We decided that when we were grown, we'd live in Old Woman Swamp and pick dog's-tongue[11] for a living. Beside the stream, he planned, we'd build us a house of whispering leaves and the swamp birds would be our chickens. All day long (when we weren't gathering dog's-tongue) we'd swing through the cypresses on the rope vines, and if it rained we'd huddle beneath an umbrella tree and play stickfrog. Mama and Daddy could come and live with us if they wanted to. He even came up with the idea that he could marry Mama and I could marry Daddy. Of course, I was old enough to know this wouldn't work out, but

10. **vortex** (vôr′teks′) n.: something resembling a whirlpool.
11. **dog's-tongue** n.: wild vanilla.

the picture he painted was so beautiful and serene that all I could do was whisper yes, yes.

Once I had succeeded in teaching Doodle to walk, I began to believe in my own infallibility and I prepared a terrific development program for him, unknown to Mama and Daddy, of course. I would teach him to run, to swim, to climb trees, and to fight. He, too, now believed in my infallibility, so we set the deadline for these accomplishments less than a year away, when, it had been decided, Doodle could start to school.

That winter we didn't make much progress, for I was in school and Doodle suffered from one bad cold after another. But when spring came, rich and warm, we raised our sights again. Success lay at the end of summer like a pot of gold, and our campaign got off to a good start. On hot days, Doodle and I went down to Horsehead Landing, and I gave him swimming lessons or showed him how to row a boat. Sometimes we descended into the cool greenness of Old Woman Swamp and climbed the rope vines or boxed scientifically beneath the pine where he had learned to walk. Promise hung about us like leaves, and wherever we looked, ferns unfurled and birds broke into song.

That summer, the summer of 1918, was blighted. In May and June there was no rain and the crops withered, curled up, then died under the thirsty sun. One morning in July a hurricane came out of the east, tipping over the oaks in the yard and splitting the limbs of the elm trees. That afternoon it roared back out of the west,

Vocabulary

iridescent (ir′i·des′ənt) adj.: rainbowlike; displaying a shifting range of colors.

serene (sə·rēn′) adj.: peaceful; calm.

infallibility (in·fal′ə·bil′i·tē) n.: inability to make a mistake.

blighted (blīt′id) v. used as adj.: suffering from conditions that destroy or prevent growth.

The Scarlet Ibis **349**

DIRECT TEACHING

A **Reading Skills**

? **Making inferences.** Why might Doodle lie? [Possible response: Perhaps he tells stories about people flying because he is physically limited.]

B **Reading Skills**

? **Making predictions.** Do you think the narrator's goals for Doodle will be realized? Why or why not? [Possible response: In time Doodle may learn these things, but probably not in a year.]

C **Vocabulary Development**

Figurative language. Point out the simile "Promise hung about us like leaves." Ask volunteers to define promise and leaves. Discuss how these two words have little in common. Explain that by comparing dissimilar things, the writer expands the meaning of the words beyond the literal. The leaves are associated with life and growth and, therefore, hope.

D **Literary Focus**

? **Symbols.** If the summer is taken as a symbol of what is to come, what do you think may lie in Doodle's future? [He may suffer bad times and may even die, as did the crops that summer.]

CONTENT-AREA CONNECTIONS

History: Political Parties
Explain to students that at the time the events in this story take place, most southern farmers belonged to the Democratic Party, and the Republicans were the party of Abraham Lincoln and the North—the people who had defeated the South during the Civil War. For the rest of the nineteenth century and into the twentieth, the United States was politically divided along regional lines.

The North voted primarily Republican, while the South was solidly Democratic. In the later decades of the twentieth century, political lines shifted: The Democratic Party made significant inroads in the North, and the Republicans gained support in the South.

History: World War I
The French names that the narrator refers to were well-known to Americans in the

summer of 1918, because U.S. soldiers were engaged in battles at these sites. At Château-Thierry, American soldiers displayed great courage and skill in combat, halting the German advance and inspiring the war-weary British and French armies. The Allies suffered many casualties, but by August the Germans were in full retreat. The armistice was signed on November 11, 1918.

The Scarlet Ibis **349**

A **Reading Skills**

Making inferences. [Possible response to question 3: First there was no rain; then a storm destroyed the crops. The local blight brought destruction to the crops; the war in Europe destroyed lives and property.]

B **Reading Skills**

❓ Analyzing. In the opening paragraph of the story, the narrator refers to "the clove of seasons." Why might the phrase be repeated here? [Possible responses: to emphasize the time frame established earlier; to suggest that the narrator is now leading up to the climax of the story.]

C **Learners Having Difficulty**

Breaking down difficult text. To help students having difficulty, model the process of breaking down the text. Draw a net or a web on the chalkboard, and discuss how easy it might be to become entangled or caught in such a pattern. Then, discuss the allusion to crumbs—trail markers used by Hansel and Gretel in the fairy tale. Finally, have students paraphrase the sentence. [Possible response: We had gone too deeply into our plan to turn back, and we had left ourselves no way out.]

---

blew the fallen oaks around, snapping their roots and tearing them out of the earth like a hawk at the entrails[12] of a chicken. Cotton bolls were wrenched from the stalks and lay like green walnuts in the valleys between the rows, while the cornfield leaned over uniformly so that the tassels touched the ground. Doodle and I followed Daddy out into the cotton field, where he stood, shoulders sagging, surveying the ruin. When his chin sank down onto his chest, we were frightened, and Doodle slipped his hand into mine. Suddenly Daddy straightened his shoulders, raised a giant knuckly fist, and with a voice that seemed to rumble out of the earth itself began cursing heaven, hell, the weather, and the Republican party.[13] Doodle and I, prodding each other and giggling, went back to the house, knowing that everything would be all right.

And during that summer, strange names were heard through the house: Château-Thierry, Amiens, Soissons, and in her blessing at the supper table, Mama once said, "And bless the Pearsons, whose boy Joe was lost in Belleau Wood."[14]

MAKING INFERENCES

3. Which **details** in the last two paragraphs show that the summer of 1918 "was blighted"? What connection can you make between the local blight and events in France?

B So we came to that clove of seasons. School was only a few weeks away, and Doodle was far behind schedule. He could barely clear the ground when climbing up the rope vines, and his swimming was certainly not passable. We decided to double our efforts, to make that last drive and reach our pot of gold. I made him swim until he turned blue and row until he couldn't lift an oar. Wherever we went, I

purposely walked fast, and although he kept up, his face turned red and his eyes became glazed. Once, he could go no further, so he collapsed on the ground and began to cry.

"Aw, come on, Doodle," I urged. "You can do it. Do you want to be different from everybody else when you start school?"

"Does it make any difference?"

"It certainly does," I said. "Now, come on," and I helped him up.

As we slipped through the dog days,[15] Doodle began to look feverish, and Mama felt his forehead, asking him if he felt ill. At night he didn't sleep well, and sometimes he had nightmares, crying out until I touched him and said, "Wake up, Doodle. Wake up."

It was Saturday noon, just a few days before school was to start. I should have already admitted defeat, but my pride wouldn't let me. The excitement of our program had now been gone for weeks, but still we kept on with a tired doggedness. It was too late to turn back, for we had both wandered too far into a net of expectations and had left no crumbs behind.

Daddy, Mama, Doodle, and I were seated at the dining-room table having lunch. It was a hot day, with all the windows and doors open in case a breeze should come. In the kitchen Aunt Nicey was humming softly. After a long silence, Daddy spoke. "It's so calm, I wouldn't be surprised if we had a storm this afternoon."

"I haven't heard a rain frog," said Mama, who believed in signs, as she served the bread around the table.

"I did," declared Doodle. "Down in the swamp."

"He didn't," I said contrarily.

---

12. **entrails** (en′trālz) *n.:* inner organs; guts.
13. **Republican party**: At this time most southern farmers were loyal Democrats.
14. **Château-Thierry** (sha′tō′ tē·er′ē), **Amiens** (à·myan′), **Soissons** (swä·sôn′), . . . **Belleau** (be·lô′) **Wood**: World War I battle sites in France.

15. **dog days** *n.:* hot days in July and August, named after the Dog Star (Sirius), which rises and sets with the sun during this period.

Vocabulary
doggedness (dôg′id·nis) *n.:* stubbornness; persistence.

CONTENT-AREA CONNECTIONS

Culture: Weather and Folklore
Discuss the fact that the rain frog Mama mentions in the story serves as an indicator of rain. Point out that many cultures have signals that people have depended on throughout history to help them forecast the weather. Provide such examples as the sayings "A ring around the moon means that it is going to rain" or "Red sky at morning, sailors take warning; red sky at night, sailors delight."

Paired activity. Have pairs of students research weather folklore for examples of sayings or signals like the one in the story. Have them note several examples and write an explanation of what each means. Invite volunteers to share their findings with the class.

"You did, eh?" said Daddy, ignoring my denial.

"I certainly did," Doodle reiterated, scowling at me over the top of his iced-tea glass, and we were quiet again.

Suddenly, from out in the yard came a strange croaking noise. Doodle stopped eating, with a piece of bread poised ready for his mouth, his eyes popped round like two blue buttons. "What's that?" he whispered.

I jumped up, knocking over my chair, and had reached the door when Mama called, "Pick up the chair, sit down again, and say excuse me."

By the time I had done this, Doodle had excused himself and had slipped out into the yard. He was looking up into the bleeding tree. "It's a great big red bird!" he called.

The bird croaked loudly again, and Mama and Daddy came out into the yard. We shaded our eyes with our hands against the hazy glare of the sun and peered up through the still leaves. On the topmost branch a bird the size of a chicken, with scarlet feathers and long legs, was perched precariously. Its wings hung down

loosely, and as we watched, a feather dropped away and floated slowly down through the green leaves.

"It's not even frightened of us," Mama said.

"It looks tired," Daddy added. "Or maybe sick."

Doodle's hands were clasped at his throat, and I had never seen him stand still so long. "What is it?" he asked.

Daddy shook his head. "I don't know, maybe it's—"

At that moment the bird began to flutter, but the wings were uncoordinated, and amid much flapping and a spray of flying feathers, it tumbled down, bumping through the limbs of the bleeding tree and landing at our feet with a thud. Its long, graceful neck jerked twice into an S, then straightened out, and the bird was still. A white veil came over the eyes, and the long white

D

Vocabulary

reiterated (rē·it′ə·rāt′id) v.: repeated.

precariously (pri·ker′ē·əs·lē) adv.: unsteadily; insecurely.

CONTENT-AREA CONNECTIONS

Science: Botany

Individual activity. Have students skim the text, jotting down the names of the various plants mentioned in the story. Then, have them research these plants in library reference sources or on the Internet. Ask students to write an essay describing the environment in which this group of plants thrives. Have students include a paragraph that tells how researching the plants helped them better understand the story's setting. Some students may enjoy illustrating their essays with drawings of some of the plants.

D **Reading Skills**

❷ Making inferences. The physical details of Doodle's response to the bird's presence seem to unsettle the narrator. What does the description hint at? [Possible responses: The fate of the scarlet ibis foreshadows the fate of Doodle; there is a powerful tie between Doodle and the scarlet ibis; only Doodle is able to empathize with the sick and exhausted bird.]

DIRECT TEACHING

A Vocabulary Development

❓ Figurative language. What two things are compared in this simile? [the scarlet ibis and a broken vase of red flowers] How does the comparison help you understand something about the scarlet ibis? [Possible response: It creates for the reader an image of how the scarlet ibis must have looked as it lay on the ground, and it conveys the idea that the bird cannot be mended or healed.]

B Reading Skills

Making inferences. [Possible responses to question 4: The bird's struggle to fly is similar to Doodle's struggle to walk and run. The bird's sudden entrance into the story, the link between the bird's name and the title of the story, and the detailed description of the bird's death are all clues that the bird might stand for something beyond itself—for Doodle, perhaps.]

C Reading Skills

Making inferences. [Possible responses to question 5: Doodle is fascinated by the scarlet ibis because it is strange and beautiful and it is not a bird that Doodle or anyone in his family has seen before. He takes pains to bury it because he feels a kinship with the bird. Both seem displaced, tired, sick, and fragile.]

D Advanced Learners

❓ Acceleration. Call students' attention to the narrator's descriptions of the setting in these two paragraphs. What contrasting mental pictures does this imagery create? [Possible responses: The calm, comforting images of the autumn light, the still waters, and the sounds of birds and insects are contrasted to the ominous and violent images of the approaching and then breaking storm.]

---

beak unhinged. Its legs were crossed and its claw-like feet were delicately curved at rest. Even death did not <u>mar</u> its grace, for it lay on the earth like a broken vase of red flowers, and we stood around it, awed by its exotic beauty.

"It's dead," Mama said.

"What is it?" Doodle repeated.

"Go bring me the bird book," said Daddy.

I ran into the house and brought back the bird book. As we watched, Daddy thumbed through its pages. "It's a scarlet ibis," he said, pointing to a picture. "It lives in the tropics— South America to Florida. A storm must have brought it here."

Sadly, we all looked back at the bird. A scarlet ibis! How many miles it had traveled to die like this, in *our* yard, beneath the bleeding tree.

"Let's finish lunch," Mama said, nudging us back toward the dining room.

"I'm not hungry," said Doodle, and he knelt down beside the ibis.

"We've got peach cobbler for dessert," Mama tempted from the doorway.

Doodle remained kneeling. "I'm going to bury him."

"Don't you dare touch him," Mama warned. "There's no telling what disease he might have had."

"All right," said Doodle. "I won't."

Daddy, Mama, and I went back to the dining-room table, but we watched Doodle through the open door. He took out a piece of string from his pocket and, without touching the ibis, looped one end around its neck. Slowly, while singing softly "Shall We Gather at the River," he carried the bird around to the front yard and dug a hole in the flower garden, next to the

MAKING INFERENCES

4. The sensory **details** in the description of the bird seem to give it extra meaning. Does the bird's struggle to fly remind you of a character in the story? What special significance might the bird have?

petunia bed. Now we were watching him through the front window, but he didn't know it. His awkwardness at digging the hole with a shovel whose handle was twice as long as he was made us laugh, and we covered our mouths with our hands so he wouldn't hear.

When Doodle came into the dining room, he found us seriously eating our cobbler. He was pale and lingered just inside the screen door. "Did you get the scarlet ibis buried?" asked Daddy.

Doodle didn't speak but nodded his head.

"Go wash your hands, and then you can have some peach cobbler," said Mama.

"I'm not hungry," he said.

"Dead birds is bad luck," said Aunt Nicey, poking her head from the kitchen door. "Specially *red* dead birds!"

As soon as I had finished eating, Doodle and I hurried off to Horsehead Landing. Time was short, and Doodle still had a long way to go if he was going to keep up with the other boys when he started school. The sun, gilded with the yellow cast of autumn, still burned fiercely, but the dark green woods through which we passed were shady and cool. When we reached the landing, Doodle said he was too tired to swim, so we got into a skiff and floated down the creek with the tide. Far off in the marsh a rail was scolding, and over on the beach locusts were singing in the myrtle trees. Doodle did not speak and kept his head turned away, letting one hand trail limply in the water.

After we had drifted a long way, I put the oars in place and made Doodle row back against the tide. Black clouds began to gather in the southwest, and he kept watching them,

MAKING INFERENCES

5. Why is Doodle so fascinated by the scarlet ibis? Why does he take such pains to bury it?

Vocabulary
mar (mär) *v.*: damage; spoil.

352 Collection 6 Symbolism and Allegory • Synthesizing Sources

---

CONTENT-AREA CONNECTIONS

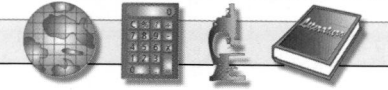

Science: Ornithology

The central symbol of this selection is the ibis, an exotic bird that is unfamiliar to most Americans. The story also mentions the egret, the oriole, the screech owl, the rail, the marsh crow, and other birds.

Small-group activity. Ask interested students to learn more about one type of bird mentioned in the selection. Students can work in small groups to compile a fact sheet on the

bird of their choice, including such information as size, distinguishing features, habitat or range, population estimate, feeding habits, and vocal calls. Have students present their findings to the class. They might enhance their presentations with multimedia elements, such as sound or video clips or photographs of the bird.

352 Collection 6 Symbolism and Allegory • Synthesizing Sources

trying to pull the oars a little faster. When we reached Horsehead Landing, lightning was playing across half the sky and thunder roared out, hiding even the sound of the sea. The sun disappeared and darkness descended, almost like night. Flocks of marsh crows flew by, heading inland to their roosting trees, and two egrets, squawking, arose from the oyster-rock shallows and careened away.

Doodle was both tired and frightened, and when he stepped from the skiff he collapsed onto the mud, sending an armada[16] of fiddler crabs rustling off into the marsh grass. I helped him up, and as he wiped the mud off his trousers, he smiled at me ashamedly. He had failed and we both knew it, so we started back home, racing the storm. We never spoke (what are the words that can solder[17] cracked pride?), but I knew he was watching me, watching for a sign of mercy. The lightning was near now, and

from fear he walked so close behind me he kept stepping on my heels. The faster I walked, the faster he walked, so I began to run. The rain was coming, roaring through the pines, and then, like a bursting Roman candle, a gum tree ahead of us was shattered by a bolt of lightning. When the deafening peal of thunder had died, and in the moment before the rain arrived, I heard Doodle, who had fallen behind, cry out, "Brother, Brother, don't leave me! Don't leave me!"

The knowledge that Doodle's and my plans had come to naught was bitter, and that streak of cruelty within me awakened. I ran as fast as I could, leaving him far behind with a wall of rain dividing us. The drops stung my face like nettles, and the wind flared the wet, glistening leaves of the bordering trees. Soon I could hear his voice no more.

I hadn't run too far before I became tired, and the flood of childish spite evanesced[18] as well. I stopped and waited for Doodle. The sound of

---

16. **armada** (är · mä′də) *n.:* group. *Armada* is generally used to mean "fleet, or group, of warships."
17. **solder** (säd′ər) *v.:* patch or repair. *Solder* is a mixture of metals melted and used to repair metal parts.

18. **evanesced** (ev′ə·nest′) *v.:* faded away; disappeared.

The Scarlet Ibis **353**

E **Learners Having Difficulty**

Breaking down difficult text. Point out the phrase "the words that can solder cracked pride." Direct students' attention to the footnote, pronounce the word *solder,* and call on volunteers to tell about the actual use of solder, such as to mend a dripping pipe. Point out that solder is used here in a figurative sense, and ask a volunteer to paraphrase the phrase in which the word appears. [Possible response: What could the boys say to each other that would restore their wounded pride?] **Invite students to suggest what the narrator might have said to Doodle as "a sign of mercy."** [Possible responses: "You did your best;" "I expected too much of you;" "I pushed you too hard—it's my fault that you failed."]

Understanding the effects of similes. Review with students that a simile uses words such as *like, resemble,* and *as* to compare two things that are unlike in most ways, yet similar in one way. For example, "That child has as many toys as a flower has bees." However, if a simile is used too often, it loses its sparkle. For example, most people are tired of hearing "I'll stick to you like glue." Encourage students to watch for fresh, creative similes as they read.

Activity. Have students complete each simile below with a word or phrase that creates a fresh, interesting comparison. Possible responses are given.

1. Mona is always as fresh as _____. [new bread]

2. Jake is as thin as _____. [a strand of linguine]

3. The buckles on his jacket clattered like _____. [lobsters' claws]

4. He walks like _____. [a sick caterpillar]

5. Pete is as jumpy as _____. [a lovesick giraffe]

The Scarlet Ibis **353**

A **Reading Skills**

Making inferences. [Possible response to question 6: The details in the description of Doodle resemble the details in the description of the fallen scarlet ibis. The writer makes this connection to show that both Doodle and the scarlet ibis are rare and beautiful creatures that are too frail to survive in their environment.]

GUIDED PRACTICE

Monitoring students' progress. Guide the class in answering these comprehension questions. Direct students to locate passages in the text that support their responses.

True-False

1. The narrator's mother wonders whether the sickly child is mentally disabled. [T]

2. The narrator nicknames his brother "Doodle" because Doodle likes the song "Yankee Doodle Dandy." [F]

3. The narrator teaches Doodle to walk because Aunt Nicey insists on it. [F]

4. Doodle buries the dead scarlet ibis by himself. [T]

5. The narrator leaves Doodle behind in a rainstorm and returns to find him dead. [T]

rain was everywhere, but the wind had died and it fell straight down in parallel paths like ropes hanging from the sky. As I waited, I peered through the downpour, but no one came. Finally I went back and found him huddled beneath a red nightshade bush beside the road. He was sitting on the ground, his face buried in his arms, which were resting on his drawn-up knees. "Let's go, Doodle," I said.

He didn't answer, so I placed my hand on his forehead and lifted his head. Limply, he fell backward onto the earth. He had been bleeding from the mouth, and his neck and the front of his shirt were stained a brilliant red.

"Doodle! Doodle!" I cried, shaking him, but there was no answer but the ropy rain. He lay very awkwardly, with his head thrown far back, making his vermilion[19] neck appear unusually

---

19. **vermilion** (vər·mil′yən) *adj.*: bright red.

long and slim. His little legs, bent sharply at the knees, had never before seemed so fragile, so thin. 📖

I began to weep, and the tear-blurred vision in red before me looked very familiar. "Doodle!" I screamed above the pounding storm, and threw my body to the earth above his. For a long, long time, it seemed forever, I lay there crying, sheltering my fallen scarlet ibis from the heresy[20] of rain. ∎

---

20. **heresy** (her′ə·sē) *n.*: here, mockery. *Heresy* generally means "denial of what is commonly believed to be true" or "rejection of a church's teaching."

MAKING INFERENCES

A 6. What do the **details** in the description of Doodle in the last two paragraphs remind you of? Explain why you think the writer makes this association.

Meet the Writer

James Hurst

Brothers at War

James Hurst (1922–   ) was born on a farm by the sea in North Carolina. Although he studied singing both in New York at the famous Juilliard School of Music and in Rome, Italy, he eventually became a banker. For thirty-four years he worked in the international department of a large bank in New York. During this time, Hurst also published some short stories, including "The Scarlet Ibis." He wants readers of "The Scarlet Ibis" to think of how the war raging among "brothers" in Europe is related to the conflict between Doodle and *his* brother. Perhaps, he reflects, people always suffer when others try to make them over in their own image.

Hurst finally retired from banking and returned to North Carolina—to New Bern, a town near his birthplace.

FAMILY/COMMUNITY ACTIVITY

Encourage students to investigate the resources that exist in your community for assisting people with physical limitations or disabilities. Write a letter to students' parents or guardians explaining the activity. Provide a starting point for students by suggesting some community-based agencies that may offer assistance or provide information. Suggest that students work in pairs or with family members to obtain information by interviewing (in person or by phone) local rehabilitation clinic administrators, physical therapists, and other health professionals. Afterward, have pairs of students prepare a report to share with the class. Remind students to get permission from their interviewees before sharing their findings.

If There Be Sorrow

Mari Evans

If there be sorrow
let it be
for things undone . . .
undreamed
  unrealized
    unattained
to these add one;
Love withheld . . .
. . . restrained

C **B**

The Kiss (1908)
by Constantin Brancusi.
Musée National d'Art Moderne, Paris.
© 2003 Artists Rights Society (ARS),
New York/ADAGP, Paris.

Connecting and Comparing Texts

Discuss with students what the speaker of "If There Be Sorrow" and the narrator of "The Scarlet Ibis" have in common. [Both realize that deep sadness should be reserved for restrained love or love held back. The narrator of the story realizes at the end of the story that instead of being cruel to Doodle, he should have protected his brother from harm.]

Connection

Summary ⬌ *at grade level*

This short and bittersweet poem reminds the reader that it is important to show one's love.

DIRECT TEACHING

VIEWING THE ART

Constantin Brancusi (1876–1957), born in Romania, became one of the most influential figures in modern art. Brancusi's interest in the carvings of preliterate peoples led him to develop an abstract style that reduces the subject to its essential form and reveals the full beauty of the material. *The Kiss* is a good example; it simplifies the human form of two bodies to closely linked faces, arms, and torsos.

Activity. Point out that Brancusi's technique of reducing figures to essential shapes is an example of visual symbolism—he portrays the universal rather than the personal. His work provides a powerful counterpoint to Mari Evans's poem. Ask students to suggest examples of images that would symbolize love "withheld . . . restrained." [Possible response: two figures facing away from each other, arms folded.]

B Learners Having Difficulty

Paraphrasing. To find the essential meaning of the poem, have students read through it at least twice and paraphrase it in their own words. [Possible response: If you grieve, be sorry about things you didn't do or dream or attain, and especially for love you withheld.]

C Reading Skills

? Analyzing. What is the effect of the repetition and the visual pattern of these three words? [They lend emphasis to the last lines of the poem, which state the importance of love.]

Response and Analysis

Reading Check

1. Doodle's older brother

2. The story takes place near the end of World War I, in 1918.

3. Embarrassed by his brother's physical limits, the narrator teaches Doodle to walk out of shame. He cries out of guilt.

4. He tries to teach Doodle to run, swim, climb trees, and fight.

5. Doodle responds with love, compassion, and respect; he gives the bird a proper burial.

Thinking Critically

6. Students may find the narrator responsible for Doodle's death. His emotions are probably grief and guilt.

7. Students may pity the narrator because of the guilt and sorrow he has felt since Doodle's death. Doodle's life was better than anyone expected.

8. The narrator realizes Doodle was a precious being who should have been cherished.

9. Both Doodle and the scarlet ibis are thin and fragile. Doodle seems to identify with the bird when he buries it. The bird could not survive in the wrong climate, and Doodle is unable to survive his disabilities. Doodle's "brilliant red" blood reminds the narrator of the scarlet ibis.

10. Possible themes: No human emotion is entirely pure; our lives are shaped by conflicting emotions. Two passages containing the themes are "There is within me . . . a knot of cruelty borne by the stream of love" (p. 346) and "pride is a wonderful, terrible thing, a seed that bears two vines, life and death" (p. 347).

11. Possible answer: Pride can lead to sorrow because it can prevent us from taking action out of fear of failure. Fears can

Response and Analysis

Reading Check

1. Who is narrating the story?

2. When does the story about Doodle take place?

3. Why does the narrator teach Doodle to walk, and why does he cry when his family congratulates him for his effort?

4. After Doodle has learned to walk, what does his brother try to teach him to prepare him for school?

5. How does Doodle respond to the scarlet ibis and to its death?

Thinking Critically

6. Explain your opinion of the narrator's behavior at the end of the story. Is he in some way responsible for Doodle's death? Is his emotion at the very end sorrow, guilt, or something else?

7. By the end, whom do you pity more—the narrator or Doodle? Why?

8. Do you think the narrator makes any kind of discovery at the story's end, as he cradles his brother's little body?

9. In the last sentence the narrator calls his brother his "fallen scarlet ibis." In what ways could the ibis be a **symbol** for Doodle? Consider **details** about the following factors:

   • the resemblance between Doodle and the ibis

   • Doodle's identification with the bird

   • Doodle's and the ibis's struggles to survive in their worlds

   • the similarity between Doodle's and the ibis's deaths

10. In Meet the Writer (page 354), there is an indication of what Hurst thinks his famous story means. How would you state the **theme** of his story? What

---

go.
hrw
.com

INTERNET
Projects and Activities
Keyword: LE5 9-6

SKILLS FOCUS

Literary Skills
Analyze symbolism.

Reading Skills
Make inferences from details.

Writing Skills
Describe a setting. Retell the story from a different point of view.

---

truth about life do the story's events reveal to you? Find passages from the story to support your response.

11. Re-read what the narrator says on page 347 about pride. Then, explain whether you think pride can lead to the kinds of sorrow that Mari Evans writes about in her poem "If There Be Sorrow" (see the **Connection** on page 355). Be sure to check your Quickwrite notes before answering.

Extending and Evaluating

12. Some people say that they will never forget "The Scarlet Ibis." Why might people find this story so memorable? Does the story and its **symbolism** appeal to your emotions? Explain.

WRITING

You Are Here

The writer creates a vivid, lush setting in "The Scarlet Ibis" by using sensory details. Choose a place, either real or imaginary, urban or rural, and **describe** it in one or two paragraphs. Use a variety of **sensory details** to help make your setting seem real.

▶ **Use "Describing a Place," pages 384–391, for help with this assignment.**

Doodle's Point of View

"The Scarlet Ibis" would be a very different story if it were told from Doodle's point of view. Pick a key **scene** in the story, and tell it through Doodle's eyes. You may choose to write in the first person, using Doodle's voice, or you may use a third-person-limited point of view, in which you have a narrator describe Doodle's thoughts and feelings.

---

make one timid (to share love or to reach for goals, for example) and later regret missed opportunities.

Extending and Evaluating

12. Possible answers: Readers can identify with the narrator. Many will recall frustrations and joys between themselves and

their siblings. Some students may not like the story because of the narrator's cruelty toward his brother. Others may like the story because the wish to be considered normal is powerful in our culture. Doodle's death is a warning to not ignore those who are different. The story's symbolism heightens that message.

Vocabulary Development

Word Knowledge: Own These Words

PRACTICE 1

Follow the directions in each item for using the Word Bank words.

1. Describe a moment from your childhood, using the word *sullenly*.
2. Write a headline for a newspaper article, using the word *imminent*.
3. Use the word *iridescent* in a sentence in an ad for jewelry.
4. Use the word *serene* in a sentence about the aftermath of a storm.
5. Use the word *infallibility* in a description of a person.
6. Write a sentence about a landscape, and include the word *blighted*.
7. Use the word *doggedness* in an ad for a political candidate.
8. Write an instruction from a teacher, using the word *reiterated*.
9. Write a sentence about Doodle, using the word *precariously*.
10. Write an apology, using the word *mar*.

Word Bank

sullenly
imminent
iridescent
serene
infallibility
blighted
doggedness
reiterated
precariously
mar

Figurative Language—Picture This

"They named him William Armstrong, which was like tying a big tail on a small kite." How is the name William Armstrong like a big tail? This question is not a riddle. James Hurst is using a simile—the simplest form of **figurative language**—to help us understand that an impressive name is being given to frail, vulnerable Doodle. A **simile** is a comparison between two dissimilar things, using a word such as *like, as,* or *resembles.*

Here are three more sentences with similes from "The Scarlet Ibis":

1. "[The ibis] lay on the earth like a broken vase of red flowers. . . ."
2. "The sick-sweet smell of bay flowers hung everywhere like a mournful song."
3. "Success lay at the end of summer like a pot of gold. . . ."

PRACTICE 2

1. In each sentence above, locate the simile, and tell what is being compared. What exactly do the two things have in common?
2. Reword each passage using a new simile. Can you change the emotional tone of the passage by using a different comparison?
3. Highlight places in a sample of your own descriptive writing that you could make more vivid by using a simile. Rewrite each passage by adding a fresh comparison. Avoid trite, or overused, comparisons.

SKILLS FOCUS

Vocabulary Skills
Use words in context. Identify and interpret similes.

The Scarlet Ibis   **357**

Vocabulary Development

Practice 1
Possible Answers

1. I <u>sullenly</u> went to my room after being scolded.
2. Economists Warn Stock Market Crash <u>Imminent</u>
3. Choose from our selection of <u>iridescent</u> stones.
4. After the downpour, the neighborhood was <u>serene</u>.
5. I believed in my father's <u>infallibility</u> until he admitted he caused the car accident.
6. Our lawn, <u>blighted</u> by the drought, was yellow and brittle.
7. Judge Brown pursues criminals with great <u>doggedness</u>.
8. Mr. Martin <u>reiterated</u>, "It is important to read the poem several times in order to understand it."
9. Doodle stood up and took his first step <u>precariously</u>.
10. I am sorry if my actions <u>mar</u> your opinion of me.

Practice 2
1. The ibis is compared to a broken vase of red flowers; both are red and fractured, and both retain their beauty. The smell is compared to a mournful song; both fill the air and evoke feelings of sadness and nostalgia. Success is being compared to a pot of gold; both are things that people would like to achieve or own.
2. Possible answers: The ibis lay on the earth like an exotic tropical plant; the sick-sweet smell of bay flowers hung everywhere like smog; success lay at the end of summer like an ever-distant star.

ASSESSING

Assessment

- *Holt Assessment: Literature, Reading, and Vocabulary*

RETEACHING

For a lesson reteaching literary devices, see **Reteaching,** p. 979A.

Grade-Level Skills

■ **Literary Skills**

Analyze various literary devices, including allegory and symbolism.

■ **Reading Skills**

Identify the main idea.

Review Skills

■ **Literary Skills**

Identify the literary devices that define a writer's style.

Summary ⬌ *at grade level*

Soto reminisces about growing up with his grandfather, an immigrant from Mexico who settles in Fresno, California, and works for thirty years at a raisin-packing plant. His grandfather has a passion for growing fruit trees: lemon, orange, and avocado. Each day after work, he sits in the yard and looks after them. To Soto's grandfather, the trees symbolize money. As he gathers the fruit, he relishes the dollars he is saving on store-bought fruit. Ironically, his favorite tree is the only one that does not save him money. The avocado, whose slow, steady growth parallels Soto's own, bears its first edible specimen after fifteen years, a fruit that Soto shares with his grandfather. The tree finally begins yielding after twenty years. By the time of his grandfather's death, the tree is tall and strong, symbolizing the growth of the family. Its branches might blow in the wind, but its thick trunk, like the grandfather himself, is rooted solidly in the ground.

Before You Read

The Grandfather

Make the Connection

Quickwrite

Think about someone who means a great deal to you. What is this person like? Why is he or she so important to you? Write down a few sentences explaining what this person means to you.

Literary Focus

Symbols with Multiple Meanings: One Trunk, Many Branches

A wedding ring, we all know, symbolizes marriage, but what does the ocean represent? Some people might say that it symbolizes freedom and possibility; others might think it represents the frightening power of nature. Sometimes a **symbol**—an object, person, animal, or event that stands for something more than itself—has one clear-cut association (like a wedding ring). Other symbols (like the ocean) are more open-ended and may have **multiple meanings.**

Symbols in literature allow writers to suggest layers of meaning. Sometimes a symbol's meaning changes as a work unfolds. Other times a symbol represents one thing for one character and something else for another character. Symbols are also open to the reader's interpretation. In fact, they may have different shades of meaning for each of us. All of these meanings are valid as long as they are based on clues the writer plants in the text. While it may be difficult to figure out all the meanings of a symbol that operates on many levels, such a symbol can have an especially powerful appeal to our emotions and imaginations.

go.
hrw
.com

INTERNET

Vocabulary
Practice
•
More About
Gary Soto
•
Keyword: LE5 9-6

SKILLS
FOCUS

Literary Skills
Understand symbols with multiple meanings.

Reading Skills
Identify main idea.

As you read "The Grandfather," pay special attention to what the author, Gary Soto, says about the avocado tree planted by his grandfather. Notice how the tree's meaning seems to expand as the tree itself grows over time.

Reading Skills

Main Idea: The Heart of the Matter

Many works of nonfiction are focused on a **main idea,** a central message that the writer wants to communicate to the reader. When a main idea is stated directly, you almost can't miss it. Look for it near the beginning or at the end of an essay or speech, for example. When the main idea is **implied,** or suggested, you can discover it on your own by making **inferences,** or educated guesses. You'll find clues that point to the main idea in the details included in the piece and in the type of language the writer uses. As you read "The Grandfather," try to determine what single idea lies at the heart of Soto's essay.

Vocabulary Development

gurgle (gur′gəl) *v.:* make a bubbling sound while flowing.

hovered (huv′ərd) *v.:* stayed suspended over something.

sulked (sulkt) *v.:* showed resentment and ill-humor.

meager (mē′gər) *adj.:* thin; small; inadequate.

358 Collection 6 Symbolism and Allegory • Synthesizing Sources

---

RESOURCES: READING

Planning

■ *One-Stop Planner* CD-ROM with ExamView Test Generator

Differentiating Instruction

■ *Holt Reading Solutions*

■ *Supporting Instruction in Spanish*

■ *Audio CD Library, Selections and Summaries in Spanish*

Vocabulary

■ *Vocabulary Development*

Grammar and Language

■ *Daily Language Activities*

■ *Language Handbook Worksheets*

Assessment

■ *Holt Assessment: Literature, Reading, and Vocabulary*

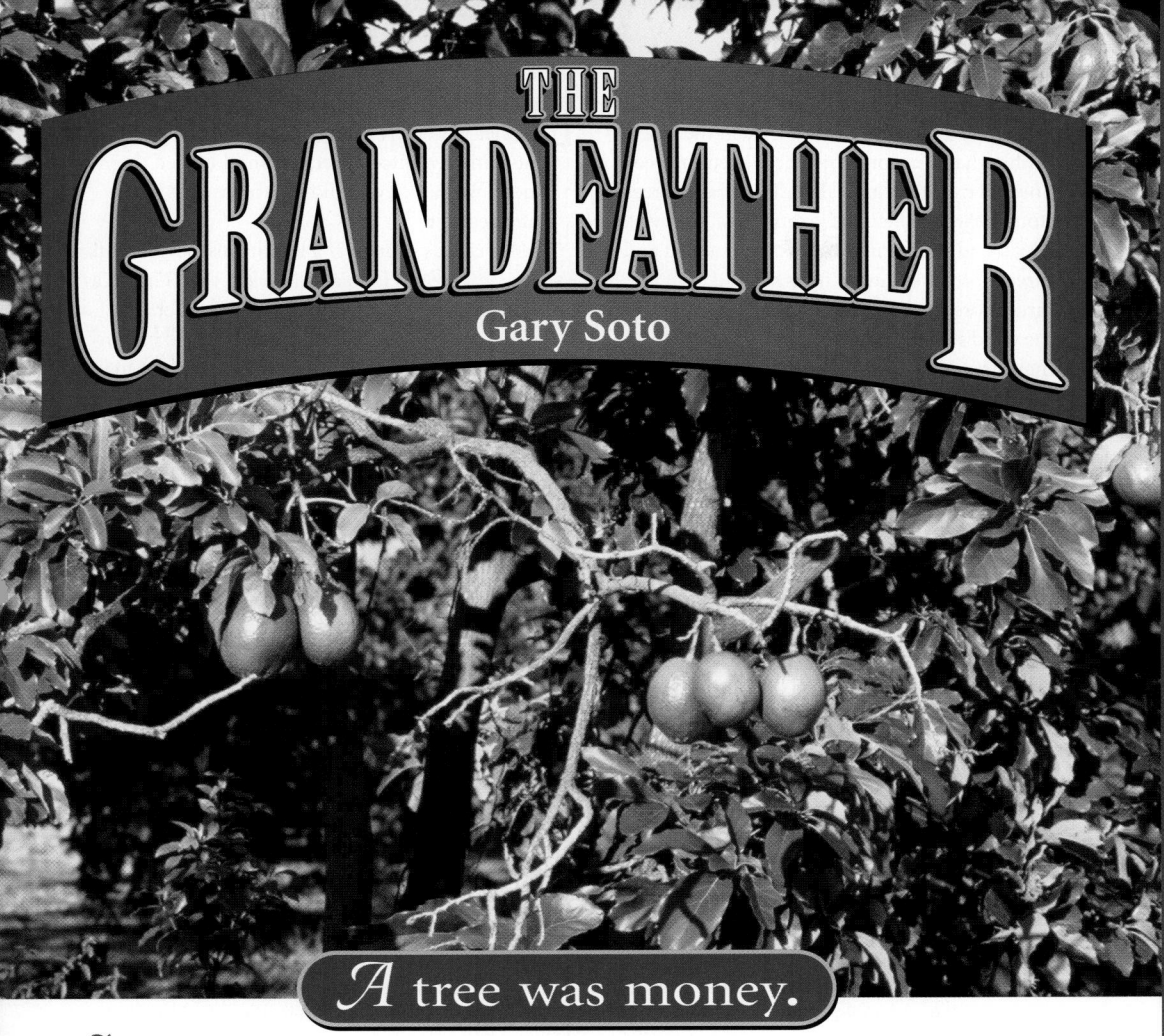

THE GRANDFATHER

Gary Soto

A tree was money.

Grandfather believed a well-rooted tree was the color of money. His money he kept hidden behind portraits of sons and daughters or taped behind the calendar of an Aztec[1] warrior. He tucked it into the sofa, his shoes and slippers, and into the tight-lipped pockets of his suits. He kept it in his soft brown wallet

that was machine tooled with "MEXICO" and a campesino[2] and donkey climbing a hill. He had climbed, too, out of Mexico, settled in Fresno[3] and worked thirty years at Sun Maid Raisin, first as a packer and later, when he was old, as a watchman with a large clock on his belt.

---

1. **Aztec** (az'tek'): of the Aztecs, a culture existing in Mexico before the Spanish conquest of the early 1500s.

---

2. **campesino** (käm'pe·sē'nð) *n.:* Spanish for "peasant" or "farmworker."
3. **Fresno** (frez'nō): city in central California.

The Grandfather   359

- *One-Stop Planner* CD-ROM with ExamView Test Generator
- *Holt Online Assessment*

Internet
- go.hrw.com (Keyword: LE5 9-6)
- *Elements of Literature Online*

Media
- *Audio CD Library*
- *Audio CD Library, Selections and Summaries in Spanish*
- *Visual Connections Videocassette Program*

PRETEACHING

Skills Starter
Build prerequisite skills. Ask volunteers to list examples of symbolic objects from everyday life (for example, the sun, a star, a flag, a sports mascot, an anchor, the color white). Ask the class to brainstorm ideas and associations related to each word. Point out that a symbol often inspires a variety of associations.

Preview Vocabulary
Have students study the Vocabulary words on p. 358. Then, ask them to answer the questions below. Possible responses are given.

1. If you hear water <u>gurgle</u> in the bathtub, what is it doing? [going down the drain]
2. How would you feel if someone <u>hovered</u> over you as you were <u>reading</u>? [bothered, annoyed]
3. When was the last time you <u>sulked</u>? [when I got grounded]
4. Describe a <u>meager</u> breakfast. [a piece of dry toast and a cup of tea]

DIRECT TEACHING

A Literary Focus
❓ Symbolism. What does the grandfather associate with money? [a well-rooted tree]

B Literary Focus
❓ Symbolism. In what way might the grandfather's rise to packer then to watchman resemble a donkey's labored climb? [Possible response: Like a donkey climbing a hill, the grandfather made a slow ascent out of poverty.]

A Literary Focus

? **Symbolism.** What details suggest that the author intends the avocado tree to have symbolic meaning? [Possible responses: Unlike the orange and lemon trees, the avocado is described in detail. It is the grandfather's favorite tree, and he sulks because the city prevents it from bearing fruit, suggesting that the tree is very important to him.]

B Literary Focus

? **Symbolism.** What do the tree and Soto have in common? [Both have grown larger and older, as shown by the tree's branches now casting a shadow and by Soto's having learned to write.]

C Learners Having Difficulty

? **Questioning.** Why is it odd that the avocado tree is the grandfather's favorite? [Money is important to the grandfather, and his other trees save him money by bearing fruit. The avocado tree only provides one edible fruit in fifteen years and does not save the grandfather much money.]

After work, he sat in the backyard under the arbor,[4] watching the water gurgle in the rosebushes that ran along the fence. A lemon tree hovered over the clothesline. Two orange trees stood near the alley. His favorite tree, the avocado, which had started in a jam jar from a seed and three toothpicks lanced in its sides, rarely bore fruit. He said it was the wind's fault, and the mayor's, who allowed office buildings so high that the haze of pollen[5] from the countryside could never find its way into the city. He sulked about this. He said that in Mexico buildings only grew so tall. You could see the moon at night, and the stars were clear points all the way to the horizon. And wind reached all the way from the sea, which was blue and clean, unlike the oily water sloshing against a San Francisco pier.

During its early years, I could leap over that tree, kick my bicycling legs over the top branch and scream my fool head off because I thought for sure I was flying. I ate fruit to keep my strength up, fuzzy peaches and branch-scuffed plums cooled in the refrigerator. From the kitchen chair he brought out in the evening, Grandpa would scold, "Hijo,[6] what's the matta with you? You gonna break it."

By the third year, the tree was as tall as I, its branches casting a meager shadow on the ground. I sat beneath the shade, scratching words in the hard dirt with a stick. I had learned "Nile"[7]

4. **arbor** (är′bər) *n.:* shelter made of branches or covered with vines.
5. **pollen** (päl′ən) *n.:* powdery grains from a seed plant. The fruit-bearing parts of plants must be dusted with pollen in order to produce fruit.
6. **Hijo** (ē′hô): Spanish for "child" or "son."
7. **Nile** (nīl): very long river in Africa, flowing through Egypt into the Mediterranean Sea.

in summer school and a dirty word from my brother who wore granny sunglasses. The red ants tumbled into my letters, and I buried them, knowing that they would dig themselves back into fresh air.

A tree was money. If a lemon cost seven cents at Hanoian's Market, then Grandfather saved fistfuls of change and more because in winter the branches of his lemon tree hung heavy yellow fruit. And winter brought oranges, juicy and large as softballs. Apricots he got by the bagfuls from a son, who himself was wise for planting young. Peaches he got from a neighbor, who worked the night shift at Sun Maid Raisin. The chile plants, which also saved him from giving up his hot, sweaty quarters, were propped up with sticks to support an abundance of red fruit.

But his favorite tree was the avocado because it offered hope and the promise of more years. After work, Grandpa sat in the backyard, shirtless, tired of flagging trucks loaded with crates of raisins, and sipped glasses of ice water. His yard was neat: five trees, seven rosebushes, whose fruit were the red and white flowers he floated in bowls, and a statue of St. Francis[8] that stood in a circle of crushed rocks, arms spread out to welcome hungry sparrows.

8. **St. Francis:** Saint Francis of Assisi (1181?–1226), a lover of nature who was said to have preached to sparrows.

Vocabulary

gurgle (gʉr′gəl) *v.:* make a bubbling sound while flowing.

hovered (huv′ərd) *v.:* stayed suspended over something.

sulked (sulkt) *v.:* showed resentment and ill-humor.

meager (mē′gər) *adj.:* thin; small; inadequate.

DIFFERENTIATING INSTRUCTION

Learners Having Difficulty
Modeling. To help students read "The Grandfather," model the reading skill of finding the main idea. Say, "When I look for a work's main idea, I use important details as clues to help me make inferences. Because the essay is named for the grandfather and because he is described in its first paragraph, the essay's central message is probably

related to him." Encourage students as they read to ask themselves, "What is the most important thing Soto wants me to know about his grandfather?"

English-Language Learners
Pair these students with more fluent speakers for help in clarifying language that is unusual or unfamiliar. The pairs may discuss

colloquial expressions ("scream my fool head off"); inverted sentences ("Apricots he got by the bagfuls . . ."); and Soto's image-laced prose ("ate the smile from an ice cold watermelon").

Special Education Students
For lessons designed for special education students, see *Holt Reading Solutions.*

After ten years, the first avocado hung on a branch, but the meat was flecked with black, an omen, Grandfather thought, a warning to keep an eye on the living. Five years later, another avocado hung on a branch, larger than the first and edible when crushed with a fork into a heated tortilla. Grandfather sprinkled it with salt and laced it with a river of chile.

"It's good," he said, and let me taste.

I took a big bite, waved a hand over my tongue, and ran for the garden hose gurgling in the rosebushes. I drank long and deep, and later ate the smile from an ice cold watermelon.

Birds nested in the tree, quarreling jays with liquid eyes and cool, pulsating throats. Wasps wove a horn-shaped hive one year, but we smoked them away with swords of rolled up newspapers lit with matches. By then, the tree was tall enough for me to climb to look into the neighbor's yard. But by then I was too old for that kind of thing and went about with my brother, hair slicked back and our shades dark as oil.

After twenty years, the tree began to bear. Although Grandfather complained about how much he lost because pollen never reached the poor part of town, because at the market he had to haggle over the price of avocados, he loved that tree. It grew, as did his family, and when he died, all his sons standing on each other's shoulders, oldest to youngest, could not reach the highest branches. The wind could move the branches, but the trunk, thicker than any waist, hugged the ground. ■

Meet the Writer

Gary Soto

A California Boy

Gary Soto (1952–   ) grew up in a Mexican American family in Fresno, a city in California's San Joaquin Valley. He went to college, planning to major in geography. Then a poem—"Unwanted" by Edward Field—changed his life. The poem helped him discover the power of language. He began to see how he could reach other people by writing about his own experiences, and that's exactly what he did—and is still doing. Soto even named his first book, *The Elements of San Joaquin* (1977), after his birthplace. Much of his award-winning fiction and poetry draws on childhood memories, the everyday details of Mexican American life. As Soto puts it:

“ I tried to remain faithful to the common things of my childhood—dogs, alleys, my baseball mitt, curbs, and the fruit of the valley. . . . I wanted to give these things life. ”

For Independent Reading

If you enjoyed "The Grandfather," take a look at the book it came from: *A Summer Life*. You might also enjoy reading Soto's *Baseball in April and Other Stories* and *A Fire in My Hands*, one of his collections of poems for young adults.

The Grandfather **361**

Response and Analysis

Reading Check

1. Ten years passed before the avocado tree produced its first fruit.

2. Soto's grandfather saved money by harvesting his trees' fruit.

3. The grandfather believed the tree offered hope and promise.

Thinking Critically

4. Possible answers: The grandfather is a hardworking man who values self-sufficiency. He is not afraid to take risks, as evidenced by his move to California.

5. In contrast to rural Mexico, California is sullied by urban development and pollution that block views of the sky and spoil the water. For example, the grandfather said that the sea in Mexico "was blue and clean, unlike the oily water sloshing against a San Francisco pier."

6. Possible answer: Soto believes that his grandfather is the foundation of his family who was responsible for its growth and for setting down its roots in the United States.

7. Possible answers: *The grandfather*—Like the tree that begins in a jar and roots itself in the yard, Soto's grandfather begins in one place (Mexico) and then builds roots in another (Fresno). His bounty, the family, takes time to develop just like the tree's fruit. *Soto*—The tree grows slowly, a developmental path that mirrors Soto's own journey from childhood to maturity. *The grandfather's family*—Like the tree, the family grows large over the years, and though its members might go in different directions (like the tree's branches), it has a strong foundation (like the tree's trunk).

Response and Analysis

Reading Check

1. How many years passed before the avocado tree produced its first fruit?

2. Why did Soto's grandfather believe that "a tree was money"?

3. Why was the avocado tree the grandfather's favorite?

Thinking Critically

4. How would you **characterize** Soto's grandfather? To answer, consider his move to California and his attitude toward his backyard and the avocado tree.

5. What differences did Soto's grandfather see between Mexico and California? How did he feel about these differences? Support your answers with evidence from the essay.

6. What do you think is the **main idea** of the essay? In other words, what point is Soto making about his grandfather?

7. The avocado tree is a **symbol** that has **multiple meanings** in the essay. Soto develops these meanings throughout the work, and he brings some of them together in the last paragraph. Use evidence from the essay to explain how the tree might symbolize the following people:
   - the grandfather
   - Soto
   - the grandfather's family

8. How would you describe the writer's **tone,** or attitude toward his subject? List two or three adjectives.

SKILLS FOCUS

Literary Skills
Analyze symbols with multiple meanings.

Reading Skills
Identify main idea.

Writing Skills
Write an explanation.
Write about a symbol.

9. Soto's essay is filled with **imagery**—language that appeals to our senses of sight, sound, touch, taste, and smell. Choose the two or three images that most appeal to you, and explain why you think they are effective.

Extending and Evaluating

10. The essay is titled "The Grandfather," but a great deal of it focuses on the avocado tree. Do you think the essay would have been more effective if Soto had included more direct description of his grandfather and less description of the tree? Why or why not?

WRITING

VIP (Very Important Person)
Soto associates his grandfather with his backyard and, more specifically, with his avocado tree. Write a few paragraphs explaining why a particular person is important to you. Look back at your Quickwrite notes for help. Then, consider whether you associate that person with a particular place or object. If so, make that **symbolic** connection clear to your reader.

A Symbol of Your Own
Think about a natural place (such as a park or a beach) or an element of nature (such as a flower or a bird) that has symbolic meaning for you. What do you associate with this place or element? Does this **symbol** have **multiple meanings** for you? Write a paragraph or a poem in which you reveal the symbol's meaning or meanings and its appeal for you. Remember that symbols are appealing because they often carry powerful associations and affect our emotions. Try to use specific images to make your symbol vivid to your reader.

---

8. Possible answers: nostalgic, admiring, sympathetic, loving

9. Possible images: *Touch*—"hot, sweaty quarters." *Sight*—"red ants tumbled into my letters"; "fuzzy peaches and branch-scuffed plums." *Sound*—"garden hose gurgling in the rosebushes"; "quarrelling jays." *Taste/sight/touch*—"ate the smile from an ice cold watermelon." Explanations will vary.

Extending and Evaluating

10. Possible answers: No, because the avocado tree has powerful symbolic value. Yes, because direct description would leave the reader with no doubt about Soto's feelings and meanings.

Vocabulary Development

Connotations and Denotations: Ripples of Meaning

PRACTICE

The power of a word begins with its dictionary definition, its **denotation.** In addition, each word sets off ripples of feelings and associations—its **connotations.** For each Word Bank word, look back at the sentence in which the word is used, and check the word's denotation. Then, write down the connotations the word has for you. Finally, rewrite the sentence, substituting a word with different connotations, and describe how the meaning of the sentence has changed. Follow this example, for *sloshing:*

SOTO'S SENTENCE
"And wind reached all the way from the sea, which was blue and clean, unlike the oily water sloshing against a San Francisco pier."

DENOTATION: splashing about

CONNOTATIONS: splashing gently, irregularly, lazily

NEW SENTENCE
And wind reached all the way from the sea, which was blue and clean, unlike the oily water slapping against a San Francisco pier.

NEW MEANING
Now the water seems to hit the pier in a louder and more forceful, regular manner. The water seems almost angry.

> **Word Bank**
> gurgle
> hovered
> sulked
> meager

Grammar Link

Parallel Structure: Keeping Things Balanced

"I took a big bite, waved a hand over my tongue, and ran for the garden hose gurgling in the rosebushes."

The sentence above uses a series of verbs to re-create Soto's actions when he bites into an avocado. This is an example of **parallel structure,** in which related ideas are expressed in a similar way. To create balanced sentences, a noun should be matched with a noun, an adjective with an adjective, a phrase with a phrase, a clause with a clause, and so on.

FAULTY
My favorite activities are playing baseball and to read.
PARALLEL
My favorite activities are playing baseball and reading.

PRACTICE

Complete the following sentences. Make sure that you use parallel structure.

1. The grandfather's backyard was neat, colorful, and _____.

2. The grandfather's daily routine was divided between working at Sun Maid Raisin and _____.

3. The grandfather grew heavy lemons, juicy oranges, and _____.

4. The grandfather planted the avocado tree, took care of it for many years, and _____.

5. At first, Soto could leap over the avocado tree, then he could sit in its shade, and finally _____.

➤ **For more help, see Improving Sentence Style, 10f, in the Language Handbook.**

SKILLS FOCUS

Vocabulary Skills
Identify word denotations and connotations.

Grammar Skills
Use parallel structure.

The Grandfather   **363**

Vocabulary Development

Practice
Possible Answers

- *gurgle. Soto's sentence*—"After work, he sat in the backyard under the arbor, watching the water gurgle in the rosebushes that ran along the fence." *Denotation*—making a bubbling sound. *Connotation*—pleasant flow. *Replacement*—gush. *New meaning*—The water seems more forceful.

- *hovered. Soto's sentence*—"A lemon tree hovered over the clothesline." *Denotation*—suspended over. *Connotation*—was very near. *Replacement*—towered. *New meaning*—The tree seems intimidating.

- *sulked. Soto's sentence*—"He sulked about this." *Denotation*—showed resentment. *Connotation*—acted like an unhappy child. *Replacement*—despaired. *New meaning*—Now the grandfather's unhappiness is both more profound and more adult.

- *meager. Soto's sentence*—"By the third year, the tree was as tall as I, its branches casting a meager shadow on the ground." *Denotation*—small, inadequate. *Connotation*—feeble. *Replacement*—slender. *New meaning*—The shadow is still small, but the image is more flattering to the tree.

Grammar Link

Practice
Possible Answers

1. festive
2. caring for his fruit trees
3. buttery avocados
4. watched it bear fruit
5. he could climb it

ASSESSING

Assessment

- *Holt Assessment: Literature, Reading, and Vocabulary*

RETEACHING

For a lesson reteaching literary devices, see **Reteaching,** p. 979A.

Grade-Level Skills

■ **Literary Skills**
Analyze various literary devices, including allegory and symbolism.

■ **Reading Skills**
Identify cause and effect.

Review Skills

■ **Literary Skills**
Identify the literary devices that define a writer's style.

Summary ⬌ *at grade level*

In Bradbury's cold war allegory, an ancient Chinese ruler, or Mandarin, grows distraught after learning about events in a nearby town. A rival ruler has changed the shape of his city walls to resemble the outline of a pig. The Mandarin is upset because his own town walls resemble an orange. Because a pig can eat an orange, this change is an evil omen. On his daughter's advice, the Mandarin orders his own town walls to be rebuilt in the shape of a club, which can beat a pig. Instead of solving the problem, it launches a type of "walls race" as each town tries to outdo the other. The cycle continues until both towns grow desperately weak because the inhabitants have no time for productive activity—they are too busy building walls. Finally, the daughter tells the now-ailing Mandarin to summon his rival to try to end the vicious cycle. She takes the two rulers out into a field where children are flying kites and points out that kites and wind cooperate and complement each other's beauty. The Mandarin rebuilds his walls a final time, in the shape of a kite. His rival rebuilds his walls in the shape of the wind. Peace reigns at last, and prosperity returns to both towns.

Before You Read

The Golden Kite, the Silver Wind

Make the Connection

Quickwrite

We compete in many aspects of our lives. Are there benefits to competition? Are there disadvantages? What happens when competition turns into hostile rivalry? Jot down your thoughts.

Literary Focus

Allegory: A Symbolic Story

An **allegory** is often written to teach a lesson. The events in an allegory can be read on two levels. They have a straightforward, surface meaning, but they also stand for something larger than themselves.

Writers of allegories tend to use simple situations, which they may exaggerate to make a point. Allegorical characters often have just one or two distinct traits that clearly show the characters' natures.

Ray Bradbury wrote "The Golden Kite, the Silver Wind" during the cold war (see Background on this page). As you read this allegory, try to figure out the lesson Bradbury wants to teach.

Reading Skills 📖

Cause and Effect: Why and What

A **cause** explains *why* something happens, and an **effect** is the *result* of something that has happened. Use these guidelines to identify cause-and-effect relationships:

- Watch for words that signal cause-and-effect relationships, such as *because, for, since, so, as a result, therefore.*
- Notice how characters or situations change. *Why* do they change? *What* event causes the change?
- Try to predict the effects of events.

go.
hrw
.com

INTERNET
Vocabulary
Practice
•
More About
Ray Bradbury
•
Keyword: LE5 9-6

SKILLS
FOCUS

Literary Skills
Understand allegory.

Reading Skills
Identify cause and effect.

Background

This story was published during the height of the cold war between the United States and the former Soviet Union. After World War II, the two nations began competing with each other for power. They never met in direct military combat, but each nation built up its nuclear arsenal, creating a dangerous situation.

In ancient China, this story's setting, sons were much more highly prized than daughters, and most women were prevented from having any public role.

Vocabulary Development

omens (ō′mənz) *n.*: things or events believed to be signs of future occurrences.

lurked (lʉrkt) *v.*: lay in wait, ready to attack.

portents (pôr′tents) *n.*: things that warn of events about to occur.

acclaimed (ə·klāmd′) *v.*: received strong approval; applauded.

pandemonium (pan′də·mō′nē·əm) *n.*: great confusion; chaos.

spurn (spʉrn) *v.*: reject someone or something for being unworthy; scorn.

eclipse (i·klips′) *v.*: conceal from view; overshadow.

sustain (sə·stān′) *v.*: support; nourish.

monotony (mə·nät′'n·ē) *n.*: lack of variety.

enduring (en·door′iŋ) *adj.*: strong and lasting.

364 Collection 6 Symbolism and Allegory • Synthesizing Sources

RESOURCES: READING

Planning
■ *One-Stop Planner* CD-ROM with ExamView Test Generator

Differentiating Instruction
■ *Holt Reading Solutions*
■ *Supporting Instruction in Spanish*
■ *Audio CD Library, Selections and Summaries in Spanish*

Vocabulary
■ *Vocabulary Development*

Grammar and Language
■ *Daily Language Activities*

Assessment
■ *Holt Assessment: Literature, Reading, and Vocabulary*

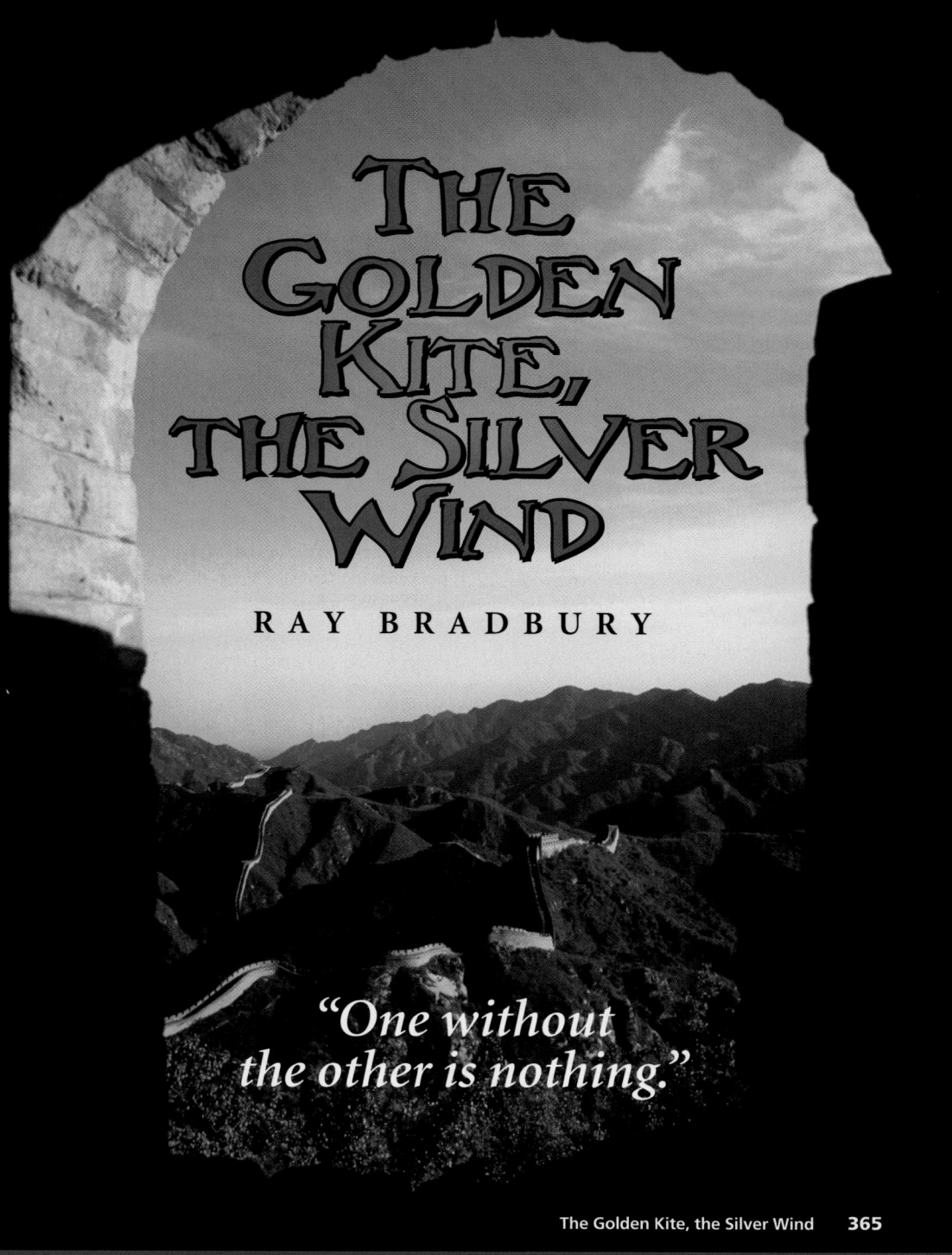

THE GOLDEN KITE, THE SILVER WIND

RAY BRADBURY

"One without
the other is nothing."

- *One-Stop Planner* CD-ROM with ExamView Test Generator
- *Holt Online Assessment*

Internet
- go.hrw.com (Keyword: LE5 9-6)
- *Elements of Literature Online*

Media
- *Audio CD Library*
- *Audio CD Library, Selections and Summaries in Spanish*

Selection Starter

Build background. Further background on the cold war may help students appreciate the allegorical aspects of the fable. In 1949, the Soviet Union broke the U.S. nuclear monopoly by building an atomic bomb. The United States responded by testing the first hydrogen bomb in 1952. The Soviet Union followed suit one year later. Both countries continued developing more lethal and more expensive weapon systems. Some credit the arms race for bringing about the fall of the Soviet Union's communist system—by bankrupting it.

Preview Vocabulary

To familiarize students with the Vocabulary words on p. 364, have them answer these questions. Answers will vary.

1. What are some omens of bad luck?
2. What was the last gift you received that had enduring value?
3. What are some portents that bad weather is on the way?
4. Name a movie that critics acclaimed.
5. What might create pandemonium in a crowded theater?
6. What might eclipse your view of a fish in a fish tank?
7. What animal lurked by the mouse hole?
8. How do you sustain your body?
9. How might you break the monotony of cleaning your room?
10. Describe a reason why you might spurn an opportunity.

A **Reading Skills**

❓ Making inferences. The Mandarin is the ruler of a city. Why might the growth of a neighboring city bother him? [Possible response: He may see it as a rival.]

B **Reading Skills**

❓ Identifying cause and effect. What causes the Mandarin to be so upset over the new wall's shape? [Possible response: In his society, people are highly attuned to symbolic meaning. In this case the wall's symbolism could have negative effects on the Mandarin's town.]

A "In the shape of a *pig*?" cried the Mandarin.[1]

"In the shape of a pig," said the messenger, and departed.

"Oh, what an evil day in an evil year," cried the Mandarin. "The town of Kwan-Si, beyond the hill, was very small in my childhood. Now it has grown so large that at last they are building a wall."

"But why should a wall two miles away make my good father sad and angry all within the hour?" asked his daughter quietly.

"They build their wall," said the Mandarin, "in the shape of a pig! Do you see? Our own city wall is built in the shape of an orange. That pig will devour us, greedily!"

---
1. **Mandarin** (man′də·rin): high-ranking government official in the Chinese Empire.

"Ah."

They both sat thinking.

B Life was full of symbols and omens. Demons lurked everywhere, Death swam in the wetness of an eye, the turn of a gull's wing meant rain, a fan held *so*, the tilt of a roof, and, yes, even a city wall was of immense importance. Travelers and tourists, caravans, musicians, artists, coming upon these two towns, equally judging the portents, would say, "The city shaped like an orange? No! I will enter the city shaped like a pig and prosper, eating all, growing fat with good luck and prosperity!"

The Mandarin wept. "All is lost! These symbols and signs terrify. Our city will come on evil days."

Vocabulary

omens (ō′mənz) *n.*: things or events believed to be signs of future occurrences.

lurked (lʉrkt) *v.*: laid in wait, ready to attack.

portents (pôr′tents) *n.*: things that warn of events about to occur.

366

Learners Having Difficulty
Modeling. To help students read "The Golden Kite, the Silver Wind," model the reading skill of identifying cause and effect. Say, "The Mandarin is very upset at the opening of the story, and I want to know why. It is clear from his statements that the nearby town's actions are the cause of his unhappiness." Encourage students as they read to ask themselves, "What caused the character to act this way?" and "What was the effect of the town's actions?"

English-Language Learners
Bradbury's evocative imagery and figurative language may be misunderstood by students who are learning English because they might take his words literally. Discuss with students some examples of figurative language from the selection, such as "Death rattled his cane" and "Poverty made a sound like a wet cough." Explain that authors use figurative language to create visual images that bring ideas and details to life in readers' minds.

"Then," said the daughter, "call in your stonemasons[2] and temple builders. I will whisper from behind the silken screen and you will know the words."

The old man clapped his hands despairingly. "Ho, stonemasons! Ho, builders of towns and palaces!"

The men who knew marble and granite and onyx and quartz[3] came quickly. The Mandarin faced them most uneasily, himself waiting for a whisper from the silken screen behind his throne. At last the whisper came.

"I have called you here," said the whisper.

"I have called you here," said the Mandarin aloud, "because our city is shaped like an orange, and the vile city of Kwan-Si has this day shaped theirs like a ravenous pig—"

---

2. **stonemasons** *n.*: people who build with stone.
3. **marble and granite and onyx** (än′iks) **and quartz** *n.*: high-quality stones.

Here the stonemasons groaned and wept. Death rattled his cane in the outer courtyard. Poverty made a sound like a wet cough in the shadows of the room.

"And so," said the whisper, said the Mandarin, "you raisers of walls must go bearing trowels[4] and rocks and change the shape of *our* city!"

The architects and masons gasped. The Mandarin himself gasped at what he had said. The whisper whispered. The Mandarin went on: "And you will change our walls into a club which may beat the pig and drive it off!"

The stonemasons rose up, shouting. Even the Mandarin, delighted at the words from his mouth, applauded, stood down from his throne. "Quick!" he cried. "To work!"

---

4. **trowels** (trou′əlz) *n.*: tools for laying plaster or mortar.

The Golden Kite, the Silver Wind **367**

A Learners Having Difficulty

Summarizing. Ask students to summarize the major events in the story so far. [Possible response: A ruler is upset because a neighboring town has built a wall in the shape of a pig, which can symbolically eat his own orange-shaped wall. The Mandarin's daughter advises him to build a club-shaped wall, which can beat the pig.]

B Reading Skills

❓ Identifying cause and effect. Does the construction of the club-shaped wall have the effect desired by the Mandarin? [No; instead of eliminating the threat posed by Kwan-Si, it creates a new one.]

C Literary Focus

❓ Figurative language. Have students identify the simile in this paragraph. What do they associate with the images of the "autumn fruit" and the "ancient tree"? [Possible response: decay, aging, and death.]

D Reading Skills

❓ Making predictions. How might Kwan-Si respond to this new wall? [Possible response: They might create a wall in the shape of an object that could destroy a lake.]

E Reading Skills

Identifying cause and effect. This series of exchanges between the messenger and the Mandarin contains a string of cause-and-effect relationships. A cause creates an effect that, in turn, becomes a cause that leads to a new effect. For example, the Mandarin's lake-shaped wall causes Kwan-Si to build a mouth-shaped wall, which causes the Mandarin to build a needle-shaped wall. Encourage students to create a diagram that shows the cause-and-effect chain.

When his men had gone, smiling and bustling, the Mandarin turned with great love to the silken screen. "Daughter," he whispered, "I will embrace you." There was no reply. He stepped around the screen, and she was gone.

Such modesty, he thought. She has slipped away and left me with a triumph, as if it were mine.

The news spread through the city; the Mandarin was acclaimed. Everyone carried stone to the walls. Fireworks were set off and the demons of death and poverty did not linger, as all worked together. At the end of the month the wall had been changed. It was now a mighty bludgeon[5] with which to drive pigs, boars, even lions, far away. The Mandarin slept like a happy fox every night.

"I would like to see the Mandarin of Kwan-Si when the news is learned. Such pandemonium and hysteria; he will likely throw himself from a mountain! A little more of that wine, oh Daughter-who-thinks-like-a-son."

But the pleasure was like a winter flower; it died swiftly. That very afternoon the messenger rushed into the courtroom. "Oh Mandarin, disease, early sorrow, avalanches, grasshopper plagues, and poisoned well water!"

The Mandarin trembled.

"The town of Kwan-Si," said the messenger, "which was built like a pig and which animal we drove away by changing our walls to a mighty stick, has now turned triumph to winter ashes. They have built their city's walls like a great bonfire to burn our stick!"

The Mandarin's heart sickened within him, like an autumn fruit upon the ancient tree. "Oh, gods! Travelers will spurn us. Tradesmen, reading the symbols, will turn from the stick, so easily destroyed, to the fire, which conquers all!"

"No," said a whisper like a snowflake from behind the silken screen.

"No," said the startled Mandarin.

---

5. **bludgeon** (bluj′ən) *n.:* short club.

"Tell my stonemasons," said the whisper that was a falling drop of rain, "to build our walls in the shape of a shining lake."

The Mandarin said this aloud, his heart warmed.

"And with this lake of water," said the whisper and the old man, "we will quench the fire and put it out forever!"

The city turned out in joy to learn that once again they had been saved by the magnificent Emperor of ideas. They ran to the walls and built them nearer to this new vision, singing, not as loudly as before, of course, for they were tired, and not as quickly, for since it had taken a month to rebuild the wall the first time, they had had to neglect business and crops and therefore were somewhat weaker and poorer.

There then followed a succession of horrible and wonderful days, one in another like a nest of frightening boxes.

"Oh, Emperor," cried the messenger, "Kwan-Si has rebuilt their walls to resemble a mouth with which to drink all our lake!"

"Then," said the Emperor, standing very close to his silken screen, "build our walls like a needle to sew up that mouth!"

"Emperor!" screamed the messenger. "They make their walls like a sword to break your needle!"

The Emperor held, trembling, to the silken screen. "Then shift the stones to form a scabbard to sheathe that sword!"[6]

"Mercy," wept the messenger the following morn, "they have worked all night and shaped

---

6. **scabbard ... sword:** A scabbard is a case for a sword's blade. *To sheathe a sword* means "to put it in a case."

Vocabulary

acclaimed (ə·klāmd′) *v.:* received strong approval; applauded.

pandemonium (pan′də·mō′nē·əm) *n.:* great confusion; chaos.

spurn (spʉrn) *v.:* reject someone or something for being unworthy; scorn.

---

368 Collection 6 Symbolism and Allegory • Synthesizing Sources

---

CONTENT-AREA CONNECTIONS

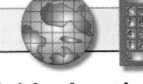

History: Building the Great Wall
Because this selection is set in China and deals with building walls, students might be reminded of the Great Wall of China. The Great Wall was built around two thousand years ago with the intent of protecting China's border from invasion.

Individual activity. Encourage interested students to learn more about China's Great Wall, including who built the wall and from whom China wanted to protect itself. Invite volunteers to share their findings with the class.

their walls like lightning which will explode and destroy that sheath!"

Sickness spread in the city like a pack of evil dogs. Shops closed. The population, working now steadily for endless months upon the changing of the walls, resembled Death himself, clattering his white bones like musical instruments in the wind. Funerals began to appear in the streets, though it was the middle of summer, a time when all should be tending and harvesting. The Mandarin fell so ill that he had his bed drawn up by the silken screen and there he lay, miserably giving his architectural orders. The voice behind the screen was weak now, too, and faint, like the wind in the eaves.

"Kwan-Si is an eagle. Then our walls must be a net for that eagle. They are a sun to burn our net. Then we build a moon to eclipse their sun!"

Like a rusted machine, the city ground to a halt.

At last the whisper behind the screen cried out:

"In the name of the gods, send for Kwan-Si!"

Upon the last day of summer the Mandarin Kwan-Si, very ill and withered away, was carried into our Mandarin's courtroom by four starving footmen. The two mandarins were propped up, facing each other. Their breaths fluttered like winter winds in their mouths. A voice said:

"Let us put an end to this."

The old men nodded.

"This cannot go on," said the faint voice. "Our people do nothing but rebuild our cities to a different shape every day, every hour. They have no time to hunt, to fish, to love, to be good to their ancestors and their ancestors' children."

"This I admit," said the mandarins of the towns of the Cage, the Moon, the Spear, the Fire, the Sword, and this, that, and other things.

"Carry us into the sunlight," said the voice.

The old men were borne out under the sun and up a little hill. In the late summer breeze a

Vocabulary
eclipse (i·klips′) v.: conceal from view; overshadow.

369

F Literary Focus

❓ **Allegory.** Remind students that allegories tend to exaggerate simple situations in order to make a point. What point might Bradbury be trying to make about the inevitable result of an arms race? [A nation that engages in an arms race will weaken and impoverish itself.]

G English-Language Learners

Interpreting figurative language. Point out to students that this paragraph is filled with examples of figurative language—language that should not be taken literally. Remind them that Kwan-Si is the neighboring town and the statements mean that the rivals' walls resemble an eagle, a net, a sun, and a moon.

H Reading Skills

❓ **Identifying cause and effect.** Why are the two leaders ready to try to put an end to their conflict? [The "walls race" has placed both towns on the brink of ruin.]

I Reading Skills

❓ **Making inferences.** Whose voice directs the party to be carried into the sunlight? [The voice is that of the Mandarin's daughter, who has been directing the Mandarin throughout the course of events.]

READING MINI-LESSON

Developing Word-Attack Skills
Write the Vocabulary word *pandemonium* on the chalkboard, and ask students to find two smaller words within the larger word. [*pan* and *demon*] Explain that the prefix *pan–*, meaning "all," and the word *demon* hint at the original meaning of *pandemonium*, which was "abode of all the demons." However, *pan–* and *demon* do not help in pronouncing the word. In *demon*, the first syllable is

stressed: /dē′mən/. In *pandemonium,* the syllable *de* in *demon* is an unaccented syllable: /pan′də•mō′nē•əm/.
Activity. Display these pairs of words written in syllables. Have students underline the syllable that is said with greatest stress. Answers are underlined.

1. pol-y-<u>phon</u>-ic   po-<u>lyph</u>-o-ny
2. tel-e-<u>path</u>-ic   te-<u>lep</u>-a-thy
3. <u>dem</u>-on-strate   de-<u>mon</u>-stra-tive
4. <u>syl</u>-la-ble   syl-<u>lab</u>-ic
5. <u>con</u>-science   con-sci-<u>en</u>-tious
6. <u>hyp</u>-o-crite   hy-<u>poc</u>-ri-sy

A Literary Focus

❓ Allegory. What might this idea represent in the world outside the story? [Possible responses: Rival nations should end the arms race; cooperation between nations is better than competition.]

B Vocabulary Development

Word origins. Point out the word *nourishment,* and explain that it comes from the Latin word *nutrire,* meaning "to feed." Ask students to define the word *nourishment.* [food that is needed for growth and life] What other words may come from the Latin *nutrire?* [nourish, nutrient, nutrition, nutritious, nurture]

C Literary Focus

❓ Figurative language. How does this simile help a reader to visualize the effect of peace on the town? [The comparison of disease to a "frightened jackal" shows that health has returned with a vengeance; disease is too scared to hang around.]

few very thin children were flying dragon kites in all the colors of the sun, and frogs and grass, the color of the sea, and the color of coins and wheat.

The first Mandarin's daughter stood by his bed.

"See," she said.

"Those are nothing but kites," said the two old men.

"But what is a kite on the ground?" she said. "It is nothing. What does it need to <u>sustain</u> it and make it beautiful and truly spiritual?"

"The wind, of course!" said the others.

"And what do the sky and the wind need to make *them* beautiful?"

"A kite, of course—many kites, to break the <u>monotony</u>, the sameness of the sky. Colored kites, flying!"

"So," said the Mandarin's daughter. "You, Kwan-Si, will make a last rebuilding of your town to resemble nothing more nor less than the wind. And we shall build like a golden kite. The wind will beautify the kite and carry it to wondrous heights. And the kite will break the sameness of the wind's existence and give it purpose and meaning. One without the other is nothing. Together, all will be beauty and cooperation and a long and <u>enduring</u> life."

Whereupon the two mandarins were so overjoyed that they took their first nourishment in days, momentarily were given strength, embraced, and lavished praise upon each other, called the Mandarin's daughter a boy, a man, a stone pillar, a warrior, and a true and unforgettable son. Almost immediately they parted and hurried to their towns, calling out and singing, weakly but happily.

And so, in time, the towns became the Town of the Golden Kite and the Town of the Silver Wind. And harvestings were harvested and business tended again, and the flesh returned, and disease ran off like a frightened jackal. And on every night of the year the inhabitants in the Town of the Kite could hear the good clear wind sustaining them. And those in the Town of the Wind could hear the kite singing, whispering, rising, and beautifying them.

"So be it," said the Mandarin in front of his silken screen. ■

Vocabulary

sustain (sə·stān′) *v.:* support; nourish.
monotony (mə·nät′n·ē) *n.:* lack of variety.
enduring (en·door′iŋ) *adj.:* strong and lasting.

FAMILY/COMMUNITY ACTIVITY

Encourage students to talk with their parents, grandparents, or other adults about the cold war between the United States and the former Soviet Union. Together with chosen adults, students can re-read "The Golden Kite, the Silver Wind" and identify more of its cold war allegorical elements. Encourage volunteers to share any new or interesting insights with the class.

Meet the Writer

Ray Bradbury

Preventing the Future

When Ray Bradbury (1920–   ) was asked about predicting future events and future technological inventions in his writing, he responded, "That's not my business. My business is to prevent the future." In other words, throughout his career, Bradbury has tried to guide his readers toward a future that is more humane. Whether he is writing about the self-destructive effects of our behavior, as in "The Golden Kite, the Silver Wind," or the potentially devastating effects of our reliance on science and technology, his stories "are intended as much to instruct how to prevent dooms, as to predict them."

At age twelve, Bradbury began writing stories "long after midnight" on a toy typewriter. In his early days as a writer, he wrote about ghosts and dinosaurs, growing up in the Midwest, and going to Mars. Some of these stories ended up as highly respected "accidental novels": The Green Town, Illinois, stories became *Dandelion Wine,* and those about the Red Planet ended up as *The Martian Chronicles.*

A prolific author, Bradbury has worked in a variety of genres, writing short stories, novels, plays, film scripts, nonfiction—and poetry. Readers of "The Golden Kite, the Silver Wind"—a story filled with poetic, figurative language—will not be surprised by Bradbury's explanation of the central role that poetry has played for him:

66 I've found inspiration for many of my short stories in other people's poetry . . . Poetry is an old love of mine, one which is central to my life. 99

For another story by Bradbury, see page 499.

For Independent Reading

In addition to *Dandelion Wine* and *The Martian Chronicles,* you'll enjoy reading Bradbury's *Fahrenheit 451,* a novel set in a future in which books are banned and burned (at a temperature of 451 degrees Fahrenheit).

Advanced Learners

Enrichment. In his imaginative works about the future, Ray Bradbury often warns about such dangers in the modern world as nuclear weapons, unrestrained technology, racism, and censorship.

Activity. Encourage students to learn more about how Bradbury creates worlds of fantasy and societies of the future in order to explore his perceptions about today's world. Suggest that they enter the keywords *Ray Bradbury* in an Internet search engine. Working in small groups, students may create an annotated bibliography of Bradbury's major works, noting the important themes in them. Suggest that each student read one of these works, evaluate it for the group, and add information about it to the bibliography.

Meet the Writer

Background. Bradbury writes voraciously, often getting an idea for a story in the morning and finishing it before noon. Says Bradbury of the characters he dreams up, "I jump out of bed and I run and trap them before they are gone."

The distrust of technology found in Bradbury's work is evident in his life. He scorns computers, choosing to write on a typewriter, and has referred to the Internet as a "big scam." Several Bradbury novels have been made into films, including *Fahrenheit 451.*

For Independent Reading

Encourage students who read *Fahrenheit 451* to consider the degree to which the technological future described in the novel has actually come to pass.

- Advanced learners who wish to explore allegory further will enjoy *Animal Farm,* George Orwell's fable about totalitarian society.
- For students interested in Chinese folk tales, suggest *Chinese Fairy Tales and Fantasies,* translated and edited by Moss Roberts.

GUIDED PRACTICE

Monitoring students' progress. Guide the class in answering these comprehension questions. Have students locate passages in the text that support their responses.

True-False

1. At the story's beginning, the Mandarin is very upset. [T]
2. The Mandarin orders his workers to build city walls in the shape of a club. [T]
3. The daughter urges the Mandarin to attack the neighboring town. [F]
4. The Mandarin's own town is set on fire. [F]
5. At the story's end, the two towns achieve peace. [T]

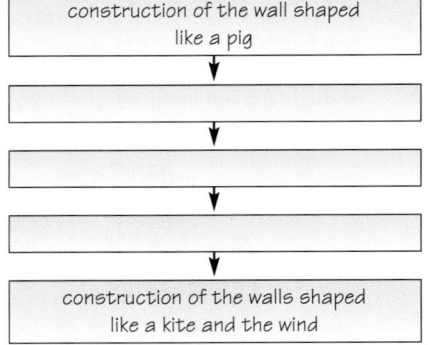

INDEPENDENT PRACTICE

Response and Analysis

Reading Check

1. Possible chart items: construction of club wall; construction of bonfire wall; construction of lake wall; construction of many more walls; people lose time for harvesting and other productive activities; sickness and death spread through the towns; the mandarins meet to try to end the vicious cycle.

Thinking Critically

2. Possible answer: Each town is motivated by fear of falling behind the other. Negative effects are that people have no time to work their trades, thus shops close; they grow tired and ill; and some even die.

3. Without the wind, the kite cannot fly. Without the kite, the wind has no purpose. By having the two towns rebuild their walls in these shapes, she is indicating that they should stop trying to compete with one another. If they try to complement each other instead, both can prosper.

4. Possible answer: When her father is despairing, the daughter is a natural leader, remaining calm and confident. She is clever, as demonstrated by her ability to come up with solutions for the town's problems. She is also open to change, as she shows when her strategy of counter-building proves hopeless.

5. In an allegorical reading the two mandarins can be seen as the leaders of the United States and the former Soviet Union. The town leaders' race to build walls represents the race to build nuclear arms, which the two countries engaged in for nearly four decades.

Response and Analysis

Reading Check

1. Fill in the story's events in the proper order on a **cause-and-effect** chart like the one below. The first and last events have been filled in for you. (Use as many boxes as you need.) Then, write a sentence explaining each cause-and-effect relationship on the chart.

> construction of the wall shaped like a pig
>
> ↓
>
> ↓
>
> ↓
>
> construction of the walls shaped like a kite and the wind

Thinking Critically

2. What do you think **motivates** the two towns to engage in the wall-building competition? What are the negative effects of the competition on the townspeople? (Compare your answers with your Quickwrite notes.)

3. Referring to the kite and the wind, the Mandarin's daughter says, "One without the other is nothing." Explain her statement and her solution to the **conflict** between the two towns.

4. Describe the **character** of the Mandarin's daughter. For help answering, consider
   - why she offers her father advice
   - the type of advice she gives

SKILLS FOCUS

Literary Skills
Analyze allegory.

Reading Skills
Identify cause and effect.

Writing Skills
Write a summary.

5. How can this story be seen as an **allegory** about the cold war (see Background on page 364)? In other words, what connections do you see between events in the story and the conflict between the United States and the former Soviet Union?

6. What do you think is the **theme** of this **allegory**? That is, what lesson do you think Bradbury wanted to teach the people of his day?

7. Bradbury's story is filled with figures of speech. Find at least one place in the story where he uses **personification** —a kind of metaphor in which a non-human thing is given human characteristics—to describe poverty and death. What effect does he create by using personification in his description?

Extending and Evaluating

8. Now that the cold war is over, do you think Bradbury's allegory still has something to teach us today? Explain your response.

WRITING

Your Version

In writing an allegory about the cold war, Bradbury chose to tell about two rival towns in ancient China. If you were writing the allegory, what situation would you describe? Pick a time, a place, and a type of conflict. Feel free to use your imagination—after all, Bradbury's townspeople build walls resembling the wind and a kite. Then, write a few paragraphs summarizing events in your **allegory.** How will you resolve the conflict so that your allegory teaches a lesson?

6. Possible answer: The lesson is that an arms race can only lead to self-destruction and that both the United States and the Soviet Union would be well served by cooperating rather than competing.

7. Death is said to clatter "his white bones like musical instruments" and to swim "in the wetness of an eye." Poverty is said to make "a sound like a wet cough." Students may say that these figures of speech make phenomena like death and poverty more vivid and frightening.

Extending and Evaluating

8. Answers will vary. Many students will say that despite the end of the cold war, international cooperation is more necessary than ever and that it is important not to let perceived dangers lead to self-destructive national choices.

Vocabulary Development

Word Ancestors

PRACTICE 1

Like people, words have ancestors. In the English language many words are derived from Latin and Greek words (**root words**) that existed long before the English words we now use every day. Use a dictionary to research the **derivation,** or **origin,** of the Word Bank words. (Note that the derivation of some words may include a prefix and a root word.) Then, think of other English words that derive from the same root words. Put your information in a word map like the sample one for *ancestor* below. (For more help researching word derivations, see page 42.)

Word Bank

portents
acclaimed
sustain
monotony
enduring

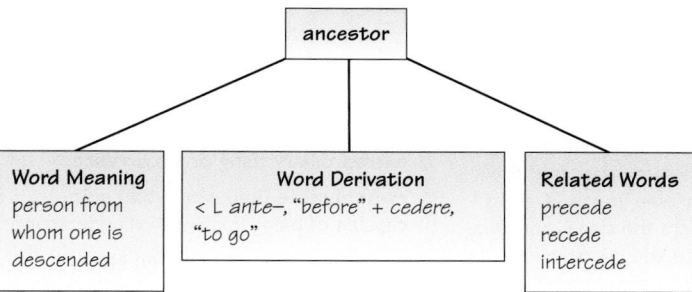

ancestor

Word Meaning	Word Derivation	Related Words
person from whom one is descended	< L *ante–*, "before" + *cedere,* "to go"	precede recede intercede

Word Knowledge: What Would Happen?

PRACTICE 2

Write one or two sentences answering the following questions. Be sure to justify your responses.

1. Would a superstitious person disregard or pay attention to <u>omens</u>?

2. If someone <u>lurked</u> near a store, was the person more likely to rob it or purchase something?

3. If <u>pandemonium</u> broke out during a rally, would the crowds of people be calm?

4. Would you be friendly toward people who <u>spurn</u> you?

5. If the moon were to <u>eclipse</u> the sun, would it be dark or bright outside?

Word Bank

omens
lurked
pandemonium
spurn
eclipse

SKILLS FOCUS

Vocabulary Skills
Understand word origins. Demonstrate word knowledge.

Practice 1

- *portents.* Word Meaning—omens. Derivation—L *por–,* "through" + *tendere,* "to stretch." *Related Words*—portend, portentous.

- *acclaimed.* Word Meaning—received strong approval. Derivation—L *ad–,* "to" + *clamare,* "to cry out." *Related Words*—claim, exclaim, acclamation.

- *sustain.* Word Meaning—support; nourish. Derivation—L *sus–,* "under" + *tenere,* "to hold." *Related Words*—maintain, sustenance.

- *monotony.* Word Meaning—lack of variety. Derivation—Gr *mono–,* "single" + *tonos,* "tone." *Related Words*—monotonous, monograph, monotone.

- *enduring.* Word Meaning—lasting. Derivation—L *in–,* "in" + *durare,* "to hold out, last." *Related Words*—endurance, durable.

Practice 2

Possible Answers

1. A superstitious person would pay attention to omens because he or she would believe that such signs revealed the future.

2. Thieves, who prefer to remain unnoticed, are more likely to lurk than a paying customer.

3. During pandemonium, people might scream or riot.

4. No; I would not be friendly toward people who reject me.

5. During such an eclipse, it would be dark because the sun's rays would be blocked.

ASSESSING

Assessment

- *Holt Assessment: Literature, Reading, and Vocabulary*

RETEACHING

For a lesson reteaching literary devices, see **Reteaching,** p. 979A. For another selection to teach allegory, see *The Holt Reader,* Collection 6.

Grade-Level Skills

■ **Reading Skills**
Synthesize the content from several sources or works by a single author on a single issue.

Review Skills

■ **Reading Skills**
Clarify main ideas by identifying their relationships to other topics.

Summary ⬆ *above grade level*

This lesson consists of four short works by Albert Einstein. In the first piece, an interview, he urges people to channel their energy toward peace rather than war. In the second piece, a letter dated 1939, he warns President Franklin D. Roosevelt that Nazi Germany is trying to develop atomic bombs and asks that the U.S. government help scientists create similar weapons. In the third piece, an essay written in 1952, Einstein explains why he wrote the letter to Roosevelt and states his belief that preparing for war makes war inevitable. In the fourth piece, Einstein urges governments to renounce policies of violence.

PRETEACHING

Preview Vocabulary

Have students match the Vocabulary words with their synonyms below.

1. possible [conceivable]
2. discontinue [abolish]
3. destroy [eradicate]
4. marvel [phenomenon]
5. drastic [radical]
6. certainty [conviction]
7. conquered [vanquished]
8. rejection [renunciation]
9. undefeatable [invincible]
10. expected [inevitable]

Informational Text

LINK TO "THE GOLDEN KITE, THE SILVER WIND"

Weapons of the Spirit ◆ Letter to President Roosevelt ◆ On the Abolition of the Threat of War ◆ The Arms Race

Synthesizing Works by One Author

Sometimes authors address an important issue several times in the course of their careers. Follow these guidelines to synthesize the content of several works that express one person's ideas:

- **Paraphrase.** To understand complex ideas, **paraphrase**—restate in your own words—the points presented in your sources. A paraphrase is not a quotation, which is the author's own wording and must appear within quotation marks. Instead, a paraphrase is entirely made up of your own words. A good paraphrase covers the significant material in the source and restates ideas in the order in which they appear.
- **Compare and contrast.** Relate your sources to one another. Does the author express different opinions about the issue in your sources? If so, why have the author's views changed? If the author expresses similar views in all the sources, what is the author's **purpose** in writing about the issue each time? Is the **audience** different? Is the author covering different aspects of the issue in each source?
- **Connect.** Relate the ideas in your sources to your prior knowledge about the author or the issue. Connect your sources to other works by the author or to works about the author that you may have read.
- **Synthesize.** Finally, look at the sources as a group, and consider what they tell you about the author's views

on the issue. Keep in mind that if you look at a source in isolation or out of context, you may misinterpret the author's views or see only half the picture. By synthesizing the content of several works, you will gain a fuller understanding of the author's ideas.

go.hrw.com

INTERNET
Interactive
Reading Model
Keyword: LE5 9-6

SKILLS FOCUS

Reading Skills
Synthesize information from several sources (by one author) on a single topic.

Vocabulary Development

eradicate (ē·rad′i·kāt′) v.: eliminate completely; get rid of.

phenomenon (fə·näm′ə·nən) n.: extraordinary thing or occurrence.

conceivable (kən·sēv′ə·bəl) adj.: capable of being imagined or understood.

abolish (ə·bäl′ish) v.: put an end to. *Abolition* is the noun form of this word.

radical (rad′i·kəl) adj.: extreme; thorough.

conviction (kən·vik′shən) n.: strong belief.

invincible (in·vin′sə·bəl) adj.: unconquerable.

inevitable (in·ev′i·tə·bəl) adj.: unavoidable; certain to happen.

vanquished (vaŋ′kwisht) v.: defeated.

renunciation (ri·nun′sē·ā′shən) n.: formal act of giving up something.

Connecting to the Literature

"The Golden Kite, the Silver Wind" is an allegory about the nuclear arms race. The following selections present Albert Einstein's views on nuclear weapons and explain his belief that nations must cooperate and work for peace.

374 Collection 6 Symbolism and Allegory • Synthesizing Sources

---

RESOURCES: READING

Planning
■ *One-Stop Planner* CD-ROM with ExamView Test Generator

Differentiating Instruction
■ *Holt Reading Solutions*
■ *Holt Adapted Reader*
■ *Supporting Instruction in Spanish*

Vocabulary
■ *Vocabulary Development*

Grammar and Language
■ *Daily Language Activities*

Assessment
■ *Holt Assessment: Literature, Reading, and Vocabulary*

Albert Einstein (1879–1955) is widely regarded as one of the greatest scientists of all time. Born and raised in Germany, Einstein studied physics, the science of matter and energy. Einstein, who was Jewish, escaped from Nazi Germany in 1933. He settled in the United States, where he spent the remainder of his life. Einstein was a pacifist, a person strongly opposed to war.

Weapons of the Spirit

from an interview with George Sylvester Viereck
from *Einstein on Peace*

Albert Einstein

It may not be possible in one generation to eradicate the combative instinct.[1] It is not **(A)** even desirable to eradicate it entirely. Men should continue to fight, but they should fight for things worthwhile, not for imaginary geographical lines, racial prejudices, and private greed draped in the colors of patriotism. Their arms should be weapons of the spirit, not shrapnel[2] and tanks. ●

> ● **PARAPHRASING**
> According to Einstein, what are the wrong types of battles? **Paraphrase** this paragraph.

Think of what a world we could build if the power unleashed in war were applied to **(C)** constructive tasks! One tenth of the energy that the various belligerents[3] spent in the

World War, a fraction of the money they **(A)** exploded in hand grenades and poison gas, would suffice to raise the standard of living in every country and avert the economic catastrophe of worldwide unemployment.

We must be prepared to make the same heroic sacrifices for the cause of peace that we make ungrudgingly for the cause of war. **(B)** There is no task that is more important or closer to my heart.

Nothing that I can do or say will change the structure of the universe. But maybe, by raising my voice, I can help the greatest of all causes—goodwill among men and peace on earth.

—1931

(D)

---

1. **combative instinct:** Einstein views the tendency of human beings to fight with one another as an inborn trait.
2. **shrapnel** (shrap′nəl) *n.:* shells that explode, releasing many small metal balls.
3. **belligerents** (bə·lij′ər·ənts) *n.:* persons engaged in fighting one another.

Vocabulary
eradicate (ē·rad′i·kāt′) *v.:* eliminate completely; get rid of.

■ *One-Stop Planner* CD-ROM with ExamView Test Generator
■ *Holt Online Assessment*

Internet
■ go.hrw.com (Keyword: LE5 9-6)
■ *Elements of Literature Online*

Media
■ *Audio CD Library*
■ *Audio CD Library, Selections and Summaries in Spanish*

A **Reading Skills**
❷ Determining author's purpose. Einstein is arguing against war. Why then does he begin by acknowledging that fighting is a human instinct? [Possible responses: This opening allows him both to disarm critics who would argue that fighting is part of human nature and to discuss ways that the combative instinct can be channeled into constructive work.]

B **Reading Skills**
Paraphrasing. [Possible response to question: Wrong types of battles include those fought because of territory, racial prejudice, and greed. Possible paraphrase: Fighting is a human instinct that cannot be erased, but it can be redirected toward worthwhile goals.]

C **Reading Informational Text**
❷ Synthesizing content: Connect. How is Einstein's point here similar to the lesson of "The Golden Kite, the Silver Wind"? [Possible response: Einstein suggests that if a fraction of the money and effort spent on war went instead toward peace, we would live in a better world. In "The Golden Kite, the Silver Wind," Ray Bradbury illustrates a similar idea. In two rival cities, people are on the verge of starvation and ruin because their resources have gone into competing with each other. Only when they cooperate is prosperity restored.]

D **Reading Informational Text**
❷ Synthesizing content: Paraphrase. How would you paraphrase the last two paragraphs? [Possible response: We must fight for peace with as much energy as we spend fighting war, because peace and goodwill are the most important things in the world.]

A Reading Informational Text

Synthesizing content: Paraphrase.
Have students paraphrase the first two paragraphs of Einstein's letter. [Possible response: The recent work of various scientists has led to the possible use of uranium as a way to generate large amounts of energy. I feel that it's my responsibility to alert you to this situation so that the government can take appropriate action.]

Einstein Warns President Roosevelt

During the 1930s, the Nazis built up German military power with the aim of dominating Europe. Despite Einstein's belief in pacifism, the political situation in Germany convinced him of the importance of researching the possibility of developing nuclear weapons.

At that time, scientists in the United States and Europe, like Leo Szilard, Enrico Fermi, and Frédéric Joliot-Curie, were making great strides in investigating how to create a nuclear chain reaction, which would release a tremendous amount of energy that could be used to create powerful bombs. Scientists suspected that the government of Nazi Germany was sponsoring similar experiments.

Shortly before World War II broke out, scientists persuaded Einstein to sign a letter addressed to President Franklin D. Roosevelt warning of the Nazis' research in nuclear weapons. This famous letter ultimately led to the establishment of the Manhattan Project, which developed the atomic bombs dropped on Japan in August 1945, ushering in the nuclear age.

LETTER

Letter to President Roosevelt
Albert Einstein

```
                              Albert Einstein
                              Old Grove Rd.
                              Nassau Point
                      Peconic, Long Island

                      August 2nd, 1939

F. D. Roosevelt,
President of the United States,
White House
Washington, D.C.

Sir:
  Some recent work by E. Fermi and L. Szilard, which has been
communicated to me in manuscript, leads me to expect that the element
uranium may be turned into a new and important source of energy in
the immediate future. Certain aspects of the situation which has
arisen seem to call for watchfulness and, if necessary, quick action
on the part of the Administration. I believe therefore that it is
my duty to bring to your attention the following facts and
recommendations:
  In the course of the last four months it has been made probable--
through the work of Joliot in France as well as Fermi and Szilard in
```

DIFFERENTIATING INSTRUCTION

Learners Having Difficulty
Some students may have difficulty with the rather formal structure of Einstein's language. Encourage these students to pair up with more fluent readers and work together to create paraphrases paragraph by paragraph of each piece. In this way, students can also practice their paraphrasing skills with the support of more fluent readers.

English-Language Learners
In order for students to understand these selections, they must understand a number of words and phrases related to war. You may wish to define and give examples of words such as *arms, armament, hand grenades, uranium,* and *nuclear chain reaction* before students begin reading.

America--that it may become possible to set up a nuclear chain reaction in a large mass of uranium, by which vast amounts of power and large quantities of new radium-like elements would be generated. Now it appears almost certain that this could be achieved in the immediate future.

This new phenomenon would also lead to the construction of bombs, and it is conceivable--though much less certain--that extremely powerful bombs of a new type may thus be constructed. A single bomb of this type, carried by boat and exploded in a port, might very well destroy the whole port together with some of the surrounding territory. However, such bombs might very well prove to be too heavy for transportation by air.

The United States has only very poor ores of uranium in moderate quantities. There is some good ore in Canada and the former Czechoslovakia while the most important source of uranium is Belgian Congo.

In view of this situation you may think it desirable to have some permanent contact maintained between the Administration and the group of physicists working on chain reactions in America. One possible way of achieving this might be for you to entrust with this task a person who has your confidence and who could perhaps serve in an inofficial capacity. His task might comprise the following:

a) to approach Government Departments, keep them informed of the further development, and put forward recommendations for Government action giving particular attention to the problem of securing a supply of uranium ore for the United States;

b) to speed up the experimental work, which is at present being carried on within the limits of the budgets of University laboratories, by providing funds, if such funds be required, through his contacts with private persons who are willing to make contributions for this cause, and perhaps also by obtaining the co-operation of industrial laboratories which have the necessary equipment.

I understand that Germany has actually stopped the sale of uranium from the Czechoslovakian mines which she has taken over. That she should have taken such early action might perhaps be understood on the ground that the son of the German Under-Secretary of State, von Weizsäcker, is attached to the Kaiser-Wilhelm-Institut in Berlin where some of the American work on uranium is now being repeated. ●

●ANALYZING

What is Einstein's **purpose** in writing to President Roosevelt?

Yours very truly,

A. Einstein

(Albert Einstein)

Vocabulary

phenomenon (fə·näm′ə·nən) *n.*: extraordinary thing or occurrence.
conceivable (kən·sēv′ə·bəl) *adj.*: capable of being imagined or understood.

B **Reading Informational Text**

Synthesizing content: Compare and contrast. Point out to students that in "Weapons of the Spirit," Einstein makes clear his distaste for war and his love of peace. In contrast, in writing this letter he appears to be encouraging President Roosevelt to take an active part in the development of massive weapons of destruction.

C **Reading Skills**

❓ Distinguishing between fact and opinion. Early in the letter, Einstein says he would present facts and recommendations on how the president should proceed. What are the facts, and for each fact, what does Einstein recommend? [Possible response: *Fact 1*—Scientists are working on uranium chain reactions. *Recommendation 1*—The Administration should contact these scientists. *Fact 2*—The United States has poor uranium supplies. *Recommendation 2*—The United States should secure a supply of good uranium ore. *Fact 3*—Uranium research is being done on university budgets. *Recommendation 3*—Additional funding should be provided.]

D **Reading Skills**

Analyzing. [Possible response to question: Einstein wants to inform the president of current work with uranium and its potential use in creating very destructive bombs; Einstein specifically wants to warn him of the danger that Germany might develop such bombs and to urge the president to devote more resources to such experiments in the United States.]

Special Education Students
For lessons designed for special education students, see *Holt Reading Solutions*.

A Reading Informational Text

? Synthesizing content: Connect. What public perception do you think Einstein is addressing in the opening quotation? [Possible response: He is addressing the perception that he was an advocate of the atomic bomb or that he was partly responsible for the bomb's development by encouraging the president to support the research.]

B Reading Informational Text

? Synthesizing content: Connect. How does the opening paragraph connect to the previous letter? [Possible response: Einstein refers to the letter and states that by signing it, he did play a role in producing the atomic bomb.] **In the next paragraph, how does Einstein justify writing that letter?** [He says that he feared the Germans might develop the bomb.]

C Reading Informational Text

Synthesizing content: Paraphrase. Paraphrase the main ideas in the third and fourth paragraphs. [Possible response: As long as nations prepare for war, war will continue. The only way to stop war is to abolish the entire concept of war.]

On the Abolition of the Threat of War

from Ideas and Opinions

Albert Einstein

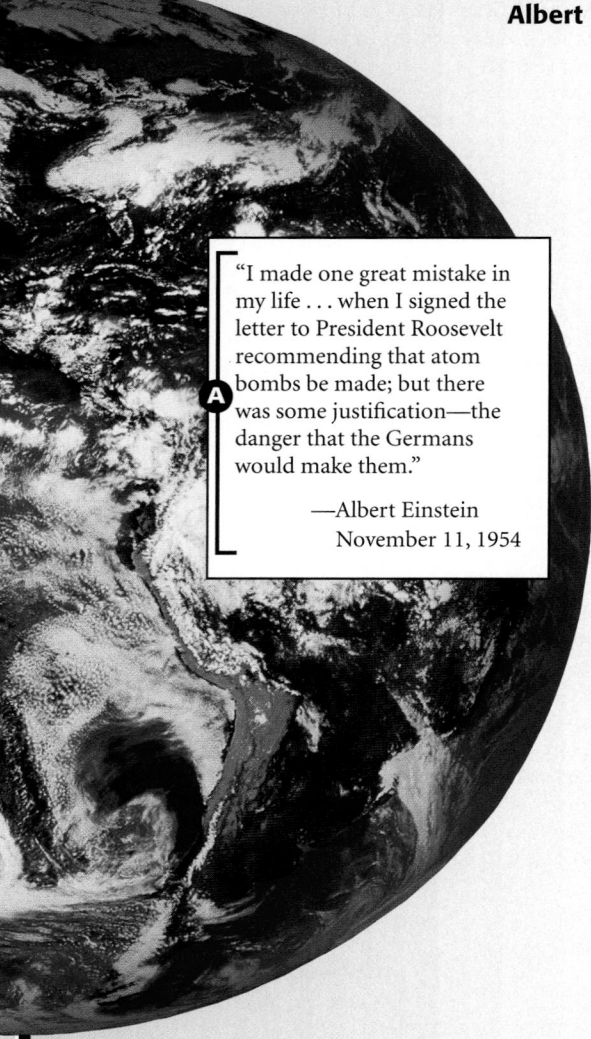

> "I made one great mistake in my life . . . when I signed the letter to President Roosevelt recommending that atom bombs be made; but there was some justification—the danger that the Germans would make them."
>
> —Albert Einstein
> November 11, 1954

My part in producing the atomic bomb consisted in a single act: I signed a letter to President Roosevelt, pressing the need for experiments on a large scale in order to explore the possibilities for the production of an atomic bomb.

I was fully aware of the terrible danger to mankind in case this attempt succeeded. But the likelihood that the Germans were working on the same problem with a chance of succeeding forced me to this step. I could do nothing else although I have always been a convinced pacifist. To my mind, to kill in war is not a whit better than to commit ordinary murder.

As long, however, as the nations are not resolved to <u>abolish</u> war through common actions and to solve their conflicts and protect their interests by peaceful decisions on a legal basis, they feel compelled to prepare for war. They feel obliged to prepare all possible means, even the most detestable ones, so as not to be left behind in the general armament race.[1] This road necessarily leads to war, a war which under the present conditions means universal destruction.

Under these circumstances the fight against *means* has no chance of success. Only the <u>radical</u> abolition of wars and of the

---

1. **armament race:** rivalry between hostile nations to build up larger and larger stores of weapons.

Vocabulary
abolish (ə·bäl′ish) *v.:* put an end to. *Abolition* is the noun form of this word.
radical (rad′i·kəl) *adj.:* extreme; thorough.

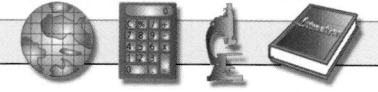

CONTENT-AREA CONNECTIONS

History: Hot and Cold Wars

Hot wars are fought with guns and bombs. Cold wars are fought with warnings and threats. In 1947, Walter Lippmann introduced the term *cold war* as the title of a pamphlet he wrote, and the term soon came into common use.
Individual activity. Interested students may research aspects of the cold war, including former British Prime Minister Winston Churchill's "iron curtain" speech, the signing of the NATO treaty, Fidel Castro's victory in Cuba, and the Cuban missile crisis. Encourage students to report their findings to the class.

Science: Einstein and the Fourth Dimension

Until the early 1900s, physicists thought about the world and its properties in three dimensions. Sir Isaac Newton determined the basic

threat of war can help. This is what one has to work for. One has to be resolved not to let himself be forced to actions that run counter to this goal. This is a severe demand on an individual who is conscious[2] of his dependence on society. But it is not an impossible demand.

Gandhi,[3] the greatest political genius of our time, has pointed the way. He has shown of what sacrifices people are capable once they have found the right way. His work for the liberation of India is a living testimony[4] to the fact that a will governed by firm conviction is stronger than a seemingly invincible material power.[5] ●

—1952

---

2. **conscious** (kän′shəs) *adj.*: aware.
3. **Gandhi** (gän′dē): Mohandas Gandhi (1869–1948) led the struggle for India's independence from Britain. He practiced the use of nonviolent protest to achieve political goals.
4. **testimony** (tes′tə·mō′nē) *n.*: evidence; proof.
5. **material power:** here, a nation; also, physical power.

Vocabulary
conviction (kən·vik′shən) *n.*: strong belief.
invincible (in·vin′sə·bəl) *adj.*: unconquerable.

TELEVISION INTERVIEW

Although the United States and the former Soviet Union were allies during World War II, they later became involved in a power struggle known as the cold war. The two superpowers engaged in an arms race to develop more and more powerful nuclear weapons. In 1952, the United States successfully tested the first hydrogen bomb, a weapon much more powerful than the atomic bomb. In 1953, the Soviet Union exploded its own hydrogen bomb.

The Arms Race

from *Einstein on Peace*
Albert Einstein

The arms race between the United States and the Soviet Union, initiated originally as a preventive measure, assumes hysterical proportions. On both sides, means of mass destruction are being perfected with feverish haste and behind walls of secrecy. And now the public has been advised that the production of the hydrogen bomb is the new goal which will probably be accomplished. An accelerated development toward this end has been solemnly proclaimed by the President. If these efforts should prove successful, radioactive poisoning of the atmosphere and, hence, annihilation[1] of all life on earth will have been

---

1. **annihilation** (ə·nī′ə·lā′shən) *n.*: absolute destruction.

---

laws of three-dimensional physics in the late 1600s. Then, in 1905, Einstein changed everything. While still in his twenties and studying in Switzerland, Einstein published his theory of general relativity, the work for which he is most famous. The theory introduced the fourth dimension of time into various equations, the most famous being $E = mc^2$. (In this equation, *E* is energy, *m* is mass, and *c* is the speed of light.)

Individual activity. Invite interested students to learn more about Newton's laws of three-dimensional physics and Einstein's work with the fourth dimension. Have volunteers share their findings with the class.

Ⓐ Reading Skills

Paraphrasing. [Possible response to question: Each step of the arms race causes another step that escalates the race, which causes another step, and so on, until the end result is the destruction of life on earth.]

Ⓑ Reading Informational Text

Synthesizing content. Ask students to consider the main points of the preceding selections and synthesize the information to make a summative statement about Einstein's opinions on war and peace. [Possible response: Einstein believes that war should be abolished, but he knows that this cannot happen as long as people mistrust each other and develop weapons to defend themselves. Therefore, he believes that people must find ways to trust each other and work out their differences by peaceful means.]

GUIDED PRACTICE

Monitoring students' progress. Guide the class in answering these comprehension questions. Direct students to locate passages in the text that support their responses.

True-False

1. Upon reflection, Einstein believes he made a mistake in writing his letter to President Roosevelt. [T]

2. Einstein respects nonviolent political methods based on mutual trust. [T]

3. Einstein believes that world peace can be achieved only by stopping the development of weapons. [F]

4. Einstein explains that he promoted atomic bomb development only because he believed that Nazi Germany was researching the technology. [T]

---

brought within the range of what is technically possible. The weird aspect of this development lies in its apparently in-exorable[2] character. Each step appears as the inevitable consequence of the one that went before. And at the end, looming ever clearer, lies general annihilation. ●

Is there any way out of this impasse[3] created by man himself? All of us, and particularly those who are responsible for the policies of the United States and the Soviet Union, must realize that, although we have vanquished an external enemy,[4] we have proved unable to free ourselves from the war mentality. We shall never achieve real peace as long as every step is taken with a possible future conflict in view, especially since it becomes ever clearer that such a war would spell universal annihilation. The

> **● PARAPHRASING**
>
> Einstein is describing a cause-and-effect relationship in the last three sentences of this paragraph. **Paraphrase** these sentences to explain his point.

2. **inexorable** (in·eks′ə·rə·bəl) *adj.:* unable to be stopped.
3. **impasse** (im′pas′) *n.:* difficult situation or problem with no obvious solution.
4. **external enemy:** hostile nations. Einstein is referring to Germany, Japan, and their allies in World War II, which were defeated by the United States, Great Britain, France, the former Soviet Union, and their allies.

guiding thought in all political action should therefore be: What can we do in the prevailing situation to bring about peaceful coexistence among all nations? The first goal must be to do away with mutual fear and distrust. Solemn renunciation of the policy of violence, not only with respect to weapons of mass destruction, is without doubt necessary.

In the last analysis the peaceful coexistence of peoples is primarily dependent upon mutual trust and, only secondarily, upon institutions such as courts of justice and the police. This holds true for nations as well as for individuals. And the basis of trust is a loyal relationship of give-and-take.

—1950

Vocabulary

inevitable (in·ev′i·tə·bəl) *adj.:* unavoidable; certain to happen.

vanquished (van′kwisht) *v.:* defeated.

renunciation (ri·nun′sē·ā′shən) *n.:* formal act of giving up something.

DIFFERENTIATING INSTRUCTION

Advanced Learners

Enrichment. Tell students that most people—even great thinkers such as Einstein—expand, refine, and sometimes redefine their positions on various topics.

Activity. Have students first discuss, in small groups, opinions or beliefs of their own that have changed over time. Then, ask students to analyze the ways in which reading more than

one work by an author can help the reader understand the evolution of a person's opinions and beliefs. Encourage students to consider how personal experiences, world events, and scientific advances could change a person's opinions on a particular topic.

Analyzing Informational Text

Reading Check

1. In "Weapons of the Spirit," what does Einstein say nations should devote their resources to, instead of preparing for war?

2. List two recommendations that Einstein makes in "Letter to President Roosevelt."

3. In "On the Abolition of the Threat of War," what reason does Einstein give for signing the letter to President Roosevelt?

4. According to Einstein in "The Arms Race," what is the first goal that must be achieved to bring about peace?

Reading Skills
Synthesize information from several sources (by one author) on a single topic.

Test Practice

1. Which statement represents the *best* **paraphrase** of the first sentence of "Letter to President Roosevelt"?

   A Some recent work by E. Fermi and L. Szilard leads me to expect that the element uranium may be turned into a new and important source of energy.

   B There have been important scientific developments lately.

   C The United States should investigate the possible military uses of scientific discoveries.

   D Research by E. Fermi and L. Szilard suggests that it may soon be possible to convert uranium into a powerful new energy source.

2. Which statement *best* expresses the **main idea** of "The Arms Race"?

   F We can't control the arms race between the United States and the Soviet Union.

   G To prevent universal destruction, the United States and the Soviet Union must trust each other and reject violence.

   H Individuals and the police must work to establish peace.

   J The United States and the Soviet Union entered the arms race to protect themselves.

3. Which idea is included in *both* "On the Abolition of the Threat of War" and "The Arms Race"?

   A Gandhi is a role model.

   B The only part Einstein played in the creation of the atom bomb was signing a letter to President Roosevelt.

   C The United States is working on producing a hydrogen bomb.

   D The arms race will result in universal destruction.

4. Which selections contain ideas about war and peace that differ the *most*?

   F "Weapons of the Spirit" and "On the Abolition of the Threat of War"

   G "Weapons of the Spirit" and "Letter to President Roosevelt"

   H "The Arms Race" and "On the Abolition of the Threat of War"

   J "Weapons of the Spirit" and "The Arms Race"

Analyzing Informational Text

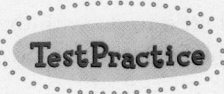

TestPractice

Answers and Model Rationales

1. **D** A duplicates Einstein's wording. B is too general, while the idea in C is not found in the sentence. D accurately conveys the content without plagiarizing.

2. **G** H and J are secondary points. F is incorrect because Einstein suggests a way to end the arms race. The main idea, from the second paragraph, is G.

3. **D** A and B are mentioned only in "On the Abolition of the Threat of War"; C is only mentioned in "The Arms Race." Only D occurs in both selections.

4. **G** The letter to the president is the only document which advocates anything to do with war. Since only G mentions the letter, that is clearly the best choice.

Reading Check

1. He says that resources should go to positive, constructive tasks such as raising people's standard of living.

2. Recommendations include contacting nuclear physicists, obtaining a supply of uranium, and speeding up research in atomic chain reactions.

3. Einstein explains that he was compelled to sign the letter to President Roosevelt because, at that time, he believed that German scientists were working on developing an atomic bomb and were likely to succeed.

4. The first goal to bring lasting peace is to work toward mutual trust among people and nations.

5. D A, B, and C are correct conclusions. Only D would be an incorrect conclusion, as the other selections show that Einstein was a pacifist.

6. H The selections have nothing to do with the training of physicists (G) and little to do with the breakup of the Soviet Union or the economic policies of the Roosevelt administration (F and J).

Test-Taking Tips

For more instruction on how to answer multiple-choice items, refer students to **Test Smarts**.

Vocabulary Development

Practice

Possible Answers. Sentences and questions will vary.

■ *phenomenon. Definition*—a rare thing or occurrence. *Synonyms*—incident, happening.

■ *conceivable. Definition*—capable of being imagined or understood. *Synonyms*—likely, probable.

■ *abolish. Definition*—put an end to. *Synonyms*—cancel, dissolve.

■ *radical. Definition*—extreme. *Synonyms*—revolutionary, immoderate.

■ *conviction. Definition*—strong belief. *Synonyms*—certitude, assurance.

■ *invincible. Definition*—unconquerable. *Synonyms*—indomitable, invulnerable.

■ *inevitable. Definition*—unavoidable. *Synonyms*—definite, inescapable.

■ *vanquished. Definition*—defeated. *Synonyms*—overthrew, beat.

■ *renunciation. Definition*—the act of giving up something. *Synonyms*—repudiation, surrender.

---

5. If you read *only* "Letter to President Roosevelt," you might draw the *incorrect* conclusion that Einstein —

A felt the United States needed to protect itself

B thought the government should be aware of scientific research

C believed nuclear weapons could be dangerous

D was a firm believer in war

6. If you wanted to **connect** the content of these selections to another topic, which topic would be the *most* closely related?

F The breakup of the Soviet Union in the 1990s

G The training of physicists

H The development of nuclear arms today

J The economic policies of President Roosevelt's administration

Constructed Response

Synthesize the content of these selections by writing a paragraph summarizing Einstein's views on war. End your paragraph by **connecting** Einstein's views to the state of our world today. Does he make any statements that you think are relevant to current relationships between nations?

Vocabulary Development

Semantic Map: Charting Words

PRACTICE

Semantic mapping is a simple strategy that can help you master new words. A semantic map might include (1) a word's definition, (2) its synonyms, (3) its use in a sentence, (4) a question about the word. A sample is shown here. Make a semantic map for the other words in the Word Bank. Use a thesaurus or a dictionary to help you identify synonyms.

Word Bank
eradicate
phenomenon
conceivable
abolish
radical
conviction
invincible
inevitable
vanquished
renunciation

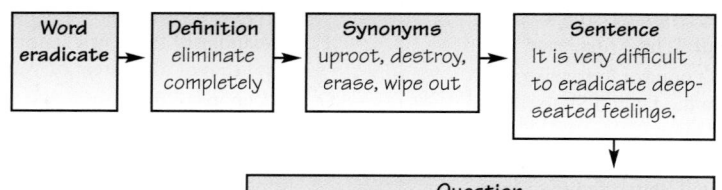

SKILLS FOCUS

Vocabulary Skills
Create semantic maps.

382 Collection 6 Symbolism and Allegory • Synthesizing Sources

---

ASSESSING

Assessment

■ *Holt Assessment: Literature, Reading, and Vocabulary*

RETEACHING

For another selection to teach synthesizing sources, see *The Holt Reader,* Part 2.

READ ON: FOR INDEPENDENT READING

FICTION

The Prince and the Pilot

A pilot whose plane has crashed in the African desert is awakened from sleep by a strange, small voice: "Please," a boy says, "draw me a sheep!" So begins Antoine de Saint-Exupéry's timeless book, ***The Little Prince.*** This story of a lonely, stranded pilot and a gentle prince who has traveled to different planets—meeting a businessman, a king, a lamplighter, and a geographer—can be read as an imaginative allegory about growing up.

NONFICTION

A Study in Courage

Johnny Gunther was a tall, thin teenager with bright blue eyes and hair the color of wheat. Johnny was also kind, funny, and gifted—so gifted, in fact, that his admission to Harvard seemed guaranteed. Then tragedy struck. At age sixteen, Johnny was diagnosed with malignant brain cancer. ***Death Be Not Proud,*** written by his father, John Gunther, is an inspiring account of a boy who chose to live the last year of his life with dignity, hope, and humor. Once you've met Johnny Gunther, you will never forget him.

FICTION

Leap of Faith

A baseball game goes afoul for Reuven Malter when a wildly thrown ball hits him square in the eye. The pitcher is Danny Saunders—an opponent who unexpectedly becomes a friend. Reuven and Danny have much in common—their Brooklyn upbringing and their interest in their studies—but they are divided by their faiths. Danny is part of a Hasidic sect of Judaism, while Reuven belongs to a more liberal Orthodox sect. Chaim Potok's ***The Chosen*** is a compassionate story about tradition, tolerance, and understanding.

This title is available in the HRW Library.

NONFICTION

Stories That Hit Home

You can count on Gary Soto to offer up lively, realistic coming-of-age tales. ***Living up the Street*** is no exception. These stories, drawn from Soto's own experiences growing up, cover everything from joys (tomato fights, first love, and Little League games) to hardship (the sudden death of his hardworking father). Soto depicts barrio life in Fresno, California, with warmth and sympathy, sharing tales not only about himself but also about his whole community.

Read On 383

Read On

For Independent Reading

If students enjoyed the themes and topics explored in this collection, you might recommend these titles for independent reading.

Assessment Options

The following projects can help you assess your students' outside reading. Videotapes or audiotapes of completed projects may be included in student portfolios.

- **Analyze an allegory.** Readers have attributed a variety of allegorical meanings to *The Little Prince.* Many have seen it as a story about growing up and accepting responsibility. Others have read religious significance into the story. Recently environmental lessons have been attributed to the tale. Invite students to discuss this book's meaning.

- **Write a plot sequel.** Have students create a basic plot structure for a sequel to *The Chosen.* Remind students to identify the setting, the conflict, and any important details. Have students write their plot structures on the chalkboard and explain them to the class.

- **Write a letter.** Invite interested students to write a letter to the author of *Death Be Not Proud.* Encourage students to share with Mr. Gunther what they learned about life from reading the story of his son's life. Ask students to consider these questions before they begin their letters: "What surprised you about Johnny's choices?" and "What life lessons have you learned from Johnny?"

- **Translate a story for the stage.** Have students who read *Living up the Street* choose one short story or scene to rewrite for the stage. Students can work in pairs or small groups and perform their adaptations for the class.

PRETEACHING

Skills Starter

Motivate. To help students realize the importance and the many possibilities of descriptive writing, write on the chalkboard a sentence that lacks descriptive details, such as "The hot air balloon landed." Then, divide the class into four or five groups and challenge each group to rewrite the sentence to provide more sensory information. Each group can choose a spokesperson to share a few of its results with the class. Point out to students that descriptive detail not only provides the reader with more information but makes writing more vivid and fun to read.

MODELING AND DEMONSTRATION

Choose a Place

Use the bulleted list below to model for students the process of assembling a list of places to describe in an essay. Write your example ideas on the chalkboard for students to discuss. Then, have a volunteer use the steps to demonstrate choosing his or her own place to describe.

- **Look close to home.** Stick to a place you know well.
- **See the place with your own eyes.** Concentrate on what makes your viewpoint of the place unique.
- **Start small.** You should be able to describe the subject in a few pages.

Describing a Place

Writing Assignment
Write an essay in which you describe a place that is both familiar and meaningful to you.

Our thoughts and feelings about a place determine our impression of it. For example, in James Hurst's short story "The Scarlet Ibis," the narrator's feelings of sadness and loss are conveyed through the descriptions of his childhood home. In this workshop you will share your personal picture of a place by writing a **descriptive essay.** This type of description, in which you express your attitude toward your subject, is called **subjective description.**

Prewriting

Choose a Place

Stake Your Claim As you search for a subject to describe, think of places that are meaningful to you in some way and that you know well. Also, think of places you can describe within a few pages. For example, you couldn't describe the entire city of San Francisco within a few pages, but you could describe the Golden Gate Bridge. Make a list of a few places that you could describe well. Choose the one place from the list that seems to stand out from the rest—the one you feel will be the most interesting for you to write about and for others to read.

Consider Purpose, Audience, and Tone

Facts or Feelings? Since you are writing a subjective description, your **purpose** is not only to describe a place, but also to share your thoughts and feelings about it. Subjective descriptions are usually written from a first-person point of view, using such pronouns as *I, me, we,* and *us.* Plan to write a description of 1,500 words.

Think about who is likely to read your essay. The **audience** you select should drive your choice of descriptive details. For example, if your intended audience is already familiar with the place you're describing, you won't include the same kinds of details that you would for an audience unfamiliar with the place.

Your purpose helps determine your **tone**—the attitude toward your subject that comes through in your writing. In a subjective description, your tone should generally be informal and conversational. Your feelings about the place you're describing will also determine your tone. For example, you might feel nostalgic, amused, or respectful about the place. Whatever tone you choose, make sure you maintain it consistently throughout your description.

SKILLS FOCUS

Writing Skills
Write a descriptive essay.

COLLECTION 6 RESOURCES: WRITING

Planning
- *One-Stop Planner* CD-ROM with ExamView Test Generator

Differentiating Instruction
- *Workshop Resources: Writing, Listening, and Speaking*
- *Family Involvement Activities in English and Spanish*

Writing and Language
- *Workshop Resources: Writing, Listening, and Speaking*
- *Daily Language Activities*
- *Language Handbook Worksheets*

Assessment
- *Holt Assessment: Writing, Listening, and Speaking*

Gather Details

Do You See What I See?   You will use three kinds of details to create your description: sensory, factual, and figurative details.

- **Sensory details** are words and phrases that appeal to the five senses—sight, hearing, touch, smell, and taste. In your writing, you should try to include details from all the senses—not just sight details.

- **Factual details** include names, dates, numbers, and quotations, as well as true statements. For example, in a description of a public park, a writer might say: "About a dozen seniors meet every morning to exercise near the fountain." That statement combines a number and a fact the writer has learned.

- **Figurative details** include similes, metaphors, and examples of personification. Figurative details lose their effectiveness if they are overused, so think of them as spice to be sprinkled lightly on your description.

Be on the Lookout   To find the details you need for your essay, you can either observe directly the place you are describing or recall details from your memory. To collect secondhand details, consider doing research by reading about the place you've chosen or by interviewing other people who have been there.

Organize your sensory, factual, and figurative details in the first three rows of a chart like the one below. In the fourth row, add your thoughts and feelings about the place you're describing.

Reference Note

For more on **similes, metaphors,** and **personification,** see pages 428–429.

 DO THIS

Details for a description of our kitchen

Sensory details	• pine cabinets • stepfather sings as he cooks • tangy smell of hot sauce
Factual details	• have lived in the house for 10 years • have dinner together once a week
Figurative details	The kitchen warms me like a big blanket on a winter morning.
Thoughts and feelings	• A visitor might not think our kitchen is special. • It holds special sounds, smells, and memories. • The kitchen is the place our family comes together.

Consider **shifting vantage points** as you list your details. Your vantage point is the position from which you view a place. When you look at a place from different vantage points—whether high, low, near, or far—you almost always find a different set of details.

SKILLS FOCUS

Writing Skills
Use sensory, factual, and figurative details.

Gather Details

To help students gather details for their writing, suggest that they think of a favorite place and brainstorm reasons why it is so special. This will help them to think of descriptive details as well as to describe the place fully. You might prompt students by encouraging them to think of a place rich with sensory impressions, such as a flower garden, forest, basketball court, or city street. Have students spend time observing the places they choose, making notes of sensory impressions and factual details.

Integrating with Grammar, Usage, and Mechanics

As students start their descriptive essays, they may have trouble with capitalization. You may want to review 11a–f in the Language Handbook.

DIFFERENTIATING INSTRUCTION

Learners Having Difficulty

Students who are having trouble gathering sensory details should work in groups to develop word banks containing sensory details. Each member of the group should give at least three details for each sense—for example, *taste: tangy, sharp, bitter.* For variety, students should not duplicate words within a group.

Students may not understand that the description they are writing is to be a subjective one and may assume that the essay needs to be more formal. Point out to students that the central purpose of the essay is to describe what the place means to them. This significance will not be treated as a fact—that is, no one can argue whether or not the place really is important to them. Students should feel free to write exactly what they think and how they feel about the place.

TECHNOLOGY TIP

Suggest to students that they input their details on a computer or word processor before they state their controlling impression. Most word-processing software has a cut-and-paste procedure. Show students how to move phrases and fragments, using the cut-and-paste method, from place to place within a document, or from one document to another. By inputting their details before writing their controlling impression, students might find that the impression "writes itself."

PRACTICE & APPLY 1

Guided and Independent Practice

Monitor students' understanding by asking them to list the controlling impression and descriptive details for their essays and the organization they plan to use. Students having trouble deciding on a controlling impression should follow these steps:

- Determine how the details you have listed relate to one another.
- Use your answer to identify at least one descriptive thread.
- Write a sentence that states a controlling impression in terms of the thread you have identified.

State Your Controlling Impression

Make a Statement In descriptive writing, the details you choose point to a **controlling impression,** the main idea or feeling you want to communicate about your subject. As with a thesis statement, keeping the controlling impression in mind keeps the writer focused and on track. The following diagram shows the relationship between the details in a description and the controlling impression.

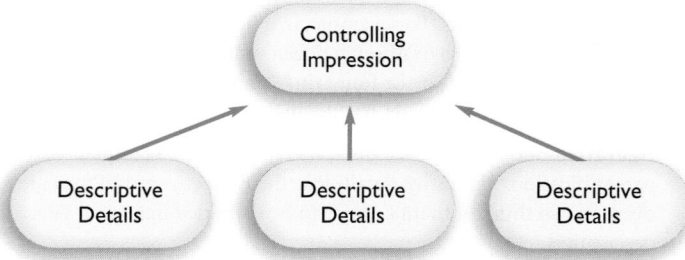

State your controlling impression for your readers. The student writing about her family's kitchen wrote the following statement of her controlling impression. Notice how it clearly conveys her **perspective,** or point of view, about the place.

> Our kitchen is a warm, welcoming place. It is the heart of our home—our place to come together.

Organize Your Details

Make Arrangements Arrange your details in an order that will make sense to your audience. For a description of a place, there are two common ways to arrange details.

- **Spatial order** organizes details according to their location. You can describe a place from top to bottom, from left to right, or from far away to close up.

- **Order of importance** arranges details from least important to most important or from most important to least important.

As you write, include words and phrases that help your readers follow your essay's organization. Spatial order signal words and phrases include *on the top, under,* and *next to.* Words and phrases that signal order of importance include *finally, most important,* and *then.*

SKILLS FOCUS

Writing Skills
Organize details around a controlling impression.

PRACTICE & APPLY 1

Using the information on these pages, choose a place to describe. Then, gather details and organize them in a logical way.

Writing

Describing a Place

A Writer's Framework

Introduction

- Start with a statement or question that will grab readers' attention.
- Make the subject and your point of view on it clear immediately.
- Include a statement of your controlling impression.

Body

- Use a variety of details (sensory, factual, and figurative).
- Include your thoughts and feelings about your subject.
- Organize your details in either spatial order or order of importance.

Conclusion

- Sum up your thoughts about the place you are describing.
- Restate your controlling impression.

A Writer's Model

The Kitchen

Great food, fellowship, and laughter are three things that come to mind right away when I think of my family's kitchen. It may seem strange to think of the kitchen as a special place, but for my family it is. We say goodbye there before school, and we say hello there when we get home. It's a place for food, of course, but it's also a place for sharing and for laughing. Our kitchen is a warm, welcoming place. It is the heart of our home—our place to come together.

A visitor seeing our kitchen for the first time might wonder why I choose to describe our kitchen as warm. The kitchen looks quite ordinary, with the usual assortment of fixtures and appliances. It has pine cabinets, a two-sided stainless-steel sink, a refrigerator/family bulletin board, and an old but sturdy stove. At the center of the room sits a butcher-block table, scuffed from years of use. That's where our family eats most meals. In short, almost any visitor would probably say it seems like a plain, ordinary kitchen.

However, the five of us in my family see that room in a different way. We've lived in the house for ten years, and for us, the kitchen is a place that holds ten years of special sounds, smells, and memories. We enjoy the sound of my stepfather singing songs from his childhood as he cooks, and the tangy smell of his special hot sauce, which never seems to leave the room entirely. We often talk in the kitchen while we

(continued)

INTRODUCTION
Attention grabber
Subject

Controlling impression

BODY
Thoughts and feelings
Sensory details

Factual details
Thoughts and feelings
Sensory details

Factual details

RETEACHING

A Writer's Model

Because the difference between "showing" and "telling" is often difficult for students to understand, you might use the statement "Have a nice day" to show that "nice day" means different things to different people. Have students freewrite a brief description of a "nice day"; then, ask volunteers to share their results. Some students may describe weather and some may describe events, but their specific examples of what is "nice" will certainly differ. The word *nice* is thus a "telling" word, vague and abstract, and students should avoid such words in their own descriptive writing.

As students read **A Writer's Model,** have them place self-adhesive notes next to places in which the writer has done a good job of using specific, concrete details, "showing" instead of "telling."

prepare our mandatory once-weekly family dinner—the only time it seems we're all together at one time anymore. If it's cold outside, we might pull up our chairs around the stove, basking in its friendly heat as we talk.

Phrase signaling order of importance

Figurative detail

Most important, though, our kitchen is the heart of our home. It may not seem like a special place to someone else, but when I'm lonely or tired, it warms me—like a big blanket on a winter morning. It's just as important to everyone else in my family. We can't imagine a home without such a central meeting spot. Our kitchen is our place to come together and share our lives, to celebrate holidays and triumphs, to console one another over defeats and sorrows.

Thoughts and feelings

CONCLUSION
Summary

Many people probably would not think of a kitchen as an extraordinary place. For some, it might be just a place for a sleepy kid to have a quick breakfast, for a hungry and tired parent to heat up a plate of leftovers, or for a teenager who wants a snack to make popcorn on a Friday night. However, for me and my family, our kitchen will always be a warm, wonderful place—not merely a functional place, or a place to pass through quickly on the way to somewhere else.

Restatement of controlling impression

INTERNET
More Writer's Models
Keyword: LE5 9-6

PRACTICE & APPLY 2

Guided and Independent Practice

Monitor students' progress by discussing with them what they think are the strengths and weaknesses of **A Writer's Model.** What will they try to do that is similar to the model in their own writing? You may want to review the framework as six quick steps:

* Grab the reader's attention.
* Present the controlling impression.
* Use sensory details to "show."
* Share thoughts and feelings.
* Move readers toward understanding the controlling impression.
* End with a bang.

Then, assign **Practice and Apply 2** as independent practice.

PRACTICE & APPLY 2 Refer to the framework and Writer's Model as you write your descriptive essay. Make sure you support your controlling impression with a variety of sensory, factual, and figurative details.

PEANUTS reprinted by permission of United Feature Syndicate, Inc.

Revising

Evaluate and Revise Your Draft

Double-Check It When you revise your writing, always read through your writing twice. Read your descriptive essay once for content and organization and once for style. Sometimes reading an essay aloud—to yourself, to a member of your family, or to a friend—helps you find places that need further attention. You may also get feedback on how effectively you used sensory, factual, and figurative details.

First Reading: Content and Organization Use the chart below as a **think sheet** to look for ways to improve the content and organization of your descriptive essay. Respond to questions in the left-hand column. If you need help answering the questions, use the tips in the middle column. If necessary, make the changes suggested in the right-hand column.

Rubric: Describing a Place

Evaluation Questions	▶ Tips	▶ Revision Techniques
❶ Does the introduction include a statement of the controlling impression?	▶ **Underline** the statement of the writer's perspective on the subject.	▶ **Add** a sentence that states your perspective on the subject.
❷ Does the description include a variety of details (sensory, factual, and figurative)?	▶ **Put an S** above sensory details, an **F** above details that show facts, and an **I** above details that make imaginative comparisons.	▶ **Add** details that appeal to several senses. **Elaborate** with facts, such as specific dates, names, or numbers. **Add** similes, metaphors, or examples of personification.
❸ Does the description include details about the writer's thoughts and feelings?	▶ **Put an asterisk** next to sentences that contain details about the writer's thoughts and feelings.	▶ **Elaborate** by including your thoughts or feelings about the subject of the essay.
❹ Is the paper clearly organized using either spatial order or order of importance?	▶ **Number** the details. Then, draw a simple map of the place described and place the numbers on it.	▶ If you cannot see a clear pattern to the numbers, **rearrange** details so that they fall into either a clear spatial order or a clear order of importance.
❺ Does the conclusion include a summary of thoughts about the subject? Does it include a restatement of the controlling impression?	▶ **Highlight** the sentence that summarizes the writer's thoughts about the place he or she is describing. **Bracket** the sentence that restates the controlling impression.	▶ **Add** a sentence that summarizes your thoughts about the place you're describing. **Add** a sentence that restates the controlling impression, if necessary.

Elaboration

Students can use an analogy strategy to add details to their essays. Have them look for appropriate places in their papers to draw a comparison that helps illustrate what they are describing. For example, if their essay describes a favorite hiking trail, they might include a passage such as: "When I hike along the trail behind my house, I feel like an eagle soaring above the treetops. I become carefree, and my problems seem to shrink and drift away."

Responding to the Revision Process

Answers

1. The word *heart* creates a metaphor within the sentence. The revised sentence makes an imaginative comparison.

2. The writer adds a subjective and figurative detail in the form of a simile that provides a tactile and emotional description of her home.

3. The word *significant* is redundant. Omitting it trims deadwood and makes the sentence stronger.

DIFFERENTIATING INSTRUCTION

Advanced Learners

Enrichment. After students have analyzed the sentences in **Analyzing the Revision Process,** pair students and have them revise the sentences in a different way. This activity will reinforce that there are many ways to revise and improve writing. The following is a possible revision:

"Most importantly, our kitchen comforts me like a heartfelt hug. It may not seem like a special place to someone else, but to me it is like a dependable oasis on a long desert trek."

PRACTICE & APPLY 3

Independent Practice

After students use the steps in the evaluation chart to revise their papers, direct students to pay special attention to the parts of their papers that are *not* marked in any way—that are *not* part of the controlling impression, the thoughts or feelings, or the supporting details. Students should consider whether their papers might be stronger without the unmarked sentences.

Second Reading: Style On your second reading of your paper, your goal is to improve your essay's style. You've probably used a number of good descriptive adjectives—but have you also used unnecessarily repetitive adjectives? Using two or more adjectives that pointlessly repeat the same meaning—such as "an *old, ancient* stove," or "a *scraped* and *scuffed* cabinet"—just adds useless deadwood to your writing. Like dead limbs on a tree, these words weigh your writing down and sap it of its strength. Use the following guidelines to cut out **deadwood adjectives** so that your writing stays strong.

Style Guidelines

Evaluation Question	▶ Tip	▶ Revision Technique
● Do some sentences contain unnecessarily repetitive adjectives?	▶ **Circle** all pairs of adjectives (adjectives joined by a comma or by *and* or *but*). Revise any circled pair having almost the same meaning.	▶ **Cut** one of the adjectives from a pair, or **replace** one with an adjective that has a different meaning.

ANALYZING THE REVISION PROCESS

Study these revisions, and answer the questions that follow.

> *heart*
> replace   Most important, though, our kitchen is the ~~center~~ of our
>
> home. It may not seem like a special place to someone else, but
>   *—like a big blanket on a winter morning.*
> add   when I'm lonely or tired, it warms me‸ It's just as important
>
> delete   ~~and significant~~ to everyone else in my family.

Responding to the Revision Process

1. Why do you think the writer changed the word *center* to *heart* in the first sentence? What is the effect of the change?

2. What type of detail did the writer add to the second sentence? Why do you think she added it?

3. How did the writer's omission of the word *significant* improve the sentence?

SKILLS FOCUS

Writing Skills
Revise for content and style.

PRACTICE & APPLY 3 Revise the content, organization, and style of your paper, using the guidelines on these two pages. Be sure to check for a variety of details.

Publishing

Proofread and Publish Your Essay

Get It Right Your paper should be as error-free as you can make it before you prepare a final copy. Check it thoroughly for grammar, usage, and mechanics errors, and correct them as you find them.

Spread the Word You've worked hard to write and polish your descriptive essay. Now you can reap the rewards of your hard work by sharing your description with readers. Try one or more of these publishing ideas.

- If your description is of a place in your community, send a copy of the description to your local newspaper.

- Publish your description as a Web page. Scan photographs of the place you described, and include them on the page. If your paper includes descriptions of sounds, record some of the sounds and create hyperlinks to sound files of the recordings.

- If any of your classmates have written descriptions that are related to your description, bind all of your descriptions together as a booklet. Give the booklet a title that summarizes the connection between the descriptions, and distribute copies of the booklet to your class.

- Videotape the place you've described in your essay. Show the videotape to an audience of your classmates as you provide a soundtrack by reading the description aloud.

Reflect on Your Essay

Decisions, Decisions Look back at the decisions you made while writing your essay. You will see that in this workshop you have practiced skills you can carry over into other writing assignments. To reflect on some of your decisions, write responses to the following questions.

- What was the best descriptive detail in your essay? Why do you think it was so effective?

- How would you use descriptive details to describe an object? to describe a person?

- If you were to describe another place, would you choose the same method of organizing your details as you used for this descriptive essay? Why or why not?

PRACTICE & APPLY 4 Proofread, publish, and reflect on your essay, using the guidelines on this page. Remember to follow the conventions of standard American English as you seek a wider distribution of your essay.

TIP Proofreading will help ensure that your essay follows the **conventions** of standard American English. For example, because first-person pronouns are common in a subjective description, check that you have used correct pronoun cases in your essay. For more on **case forms,** see Case, 4a–e, in the Language Handbook.

SKILLS FOCUS

Writing Skills
Proofread, especially for correct pronoun case.

Proofread and Publish Your Essay

If students choose to publish their essays as Web pages, provide them with these hints for design:

- Avoid using too many graphics, as this will increase loading time.

- Avoid cluttered pages, and use short blocks of text whenever possible.

- Design Web pages from side to side instead of from top to bottom, since Web pages are wider than they are tall.

- Create a standard footer for the bottom of each page with such information as the date of the last update, an e-mail address for feedback, and links to other pages.

You need to be aware that Internet resources are sometimes public forums, and their content can be unpredictable.

PRACTICE & APPLY 4

Guided and Independent Practice

Remind students checking the case of the pronouns in their papers of these rules:

- The subject of a verb should be in the nominative case. *(I, he, she, we, they)*

- The direct object of a verb should be in the objective case. *(me, him, her, us, them)*

- Compound subjects and direct objects have the same case. *(him and me,* for example, not *him and I)*

DIFFERENTIATING INSTRUCTION

English-Language Learners

In Spanish most personal pronouns have the same form for both the nominative and objective cases, as in "She spoke to she." Most Spanish-speakers are unaccustomed to making a distinction between personal pronoun cases when they speak their native language. Have students practice saying aloud the corrected versions of the sentences they have written with personal pronouns. Oral repetition will help English-language learners establish a correct nominative-objective distinction for personal pronouns.

PRETEACHING

Motivate. Direct students to close their eyes and concentrate on their visual memories of the classroom. Call on volunteers to share details as they keep their eyes closed. Point out that giving an oral description of a place is their chance to shape an audience's understanding of that place and to get an audience to see the place in a new way.

DIRECT TEACHING

Adapt Your Essay
To help students choose the points they want to cover, suggest that students record themselves reading their essays and then listen with pen and paper in hand to select ideas to present. This will also help students decide what details to replace or delete.

RETEACHING

Adapt Your Essay
To reteach the concept of tailoring a presentation to an audience, have students write what their audience is likely to have experienced at the place they will describe (or at a place like it). Point out that what they have on their papers is the audience's expectation of their presentation. Students should aim both to connect their experiences to those of their audience and to surprise their audience with a new perspective.

Presenting a Description

Speaking Assignment
Adapt your descriptive essay for a descriptive presentation, and deliver it to an audience.

Your listeners hear the rumble in your stomach and the buzz of conversation around you. They feel the weight of your tray as you push it toward the basket of glistening, red apples twenty feet ahead. A good **descriptive presentation**—even one that describes the cafeteria lunch line—must make your listeners see, feel, and hear what you describe. In this workshop you will have an opportunity to do just that.

Adapt Your Essay

I Spy Something In order to help your listeners see, hear, and feel the place you're describing, your presentation should include plenty of **concrete imagery**—specific details that help listeners create mental pictures of the place you are describing.

If you have limited time to speak, choose the **sensory, factual,** and **figurative details** from your written description that will be most effective in helping your audience visualize the place you are describing. If you need more details to fill the amount of time you are given, consider adding details that you might find by shifting vantage points or perspectives. By **shifting vantage points and perspectives,** you help the audience "see" the place from more than one position or from another person's viewpoint.

Get Involved Make your **point of view** and **relationship** with the place you're describing clear. Since you will be presenting a subjective description, you must show your **personal involvement** with the subject. To do that, include all of the thoughts and feelings about the place that you included in your essay. Then, consider whether you should add more information to make your thoughts and feelings about the place clear for a listening audience.

The Point Is Once you have reconsidered your details, locate the statement of your **controlling impression** in your essay's introduction. You may want to begin your presentation with this statement so that your audience is clear about your feelings early on.

SKILLS FOCUS

Listening and Speaking Skills
Present a description.

Plan Your Presentation

Come to Order An **extemporaneous** presentation is one in which the speaker has practiced, but not memorized, the speech. The speaker may also use **concise note cards.** To prepare your extemporaneous presentation, write your controlling impression on

392 Collection 6 Symbolism and Allegory • Synthesizing Sources

---

COLLECTION 6 RESOURCES: LISTENING & SPEAKING

Planning
- *One-Stop Planner* CD-ROM with ExamView Test Generator

Differentiating Instruction
- *Workshop Resources: Writing, Listening, and Speaking*
- *Family Involvement Activities in English and Spanish*

- *Supporting Instruction in Spanish*

Listening and Speaking
- *Workshop Resources: Writing, Listening, and Speaking*
- *Daily Language Activities*

Assessment
- *Holt Assessment: Writing, Listening, and Speaking*

one note card and the details that support it on separate note cards. These cards should include **summaries** that contain key words and phrases taken from your written description.

Should you order your details the same way as in your written description or use a different order? To answer this question you must once again consider what would be most effective for people listening to your description rather than reading it. If you use **spatial order** your audience may find it easier to create an accurate mental picture of the place. If you use **order of importance** you will emphasize to your listeners the details about the place that are most significant to you. Once you've chosen an order, number each of your note cards in the order in which you will present them.

More Than Words As you arrange your cards, watch for opportunities to incorporate **visuals,** such as props, graphs, or electronic media, into your presentation. In a presentation about a circus, for example, you might use the **occasion** to wear a red coat and carry a cane just as the ringmaster might do. In a presentation about a cave, you might want to create a slide show of the stalagmites and stalactites you describe. For best results, use the visuals that appeal to the **interests of your audience.**

Practice Your Presentation

Say It Like This Before you deliver your speech in public, try practicing in private. Keep in mind the following techniques to help you plan your delivery.

- **Verbal techniques** emphasize important details and add interest to your presentation. For example, you can change the pitch of your voice from high to low to add suspense or change the tone of your voice from serious to humorous.

- **Nonverbal techniques,** such as changing facial expressions and gestures, communicate different moods or feelings. For example, you can raise your eyebrows to show surprise or shrug your shoulders to show uncertainty.

Practice your presentation several times so that you know how to elaborate on the details from your note cards and smoothly connect those details to your visuals. Practice speaking loudly and clearly, making eye contact with audience members, and using your voice, gestures, and facial expressions to communicate your feelings.

 PRACTICE & APPLY Follow the instructions on these two pages to adapt the descriptive essay you wrote in the Writing Workshop for a descriptive presentation. Practice your presentation, and then deliver it to an audience.

Reference Note
For more on **summarizing,** see page 615.

DIFFERENTIATING INSTRUCTION

Learners Having Difficulty
If students decide to use visuals, caution them that their visuals should not overwhelm their presentations or substitute for it but should supplement it. In their delivery notes on their cards, students can mark appropriate places in which to draw attention to a prop, graph, drawing, or other form of visual. Also, point out to students that appropriate additions to a presentation might include media appealing to other senses: recorded music, for example, if their description is of a symphony hall, or samples of a special dish, if their description is of a kitchen.

SKILLS FOCUS

Listening and Speaking Skills
Prepare your presentation. Use appropriate verbal and nonverbal techniques.

 **PRACTICE & APPLY**

Guided and Independent Practice
Allow students to practice giving their descriptions to one another in small groups. They might ask each other these questions:

- What can I do to better capture and hold my audience's interest?

- What areas of my presentation can be omitted or expanded?

Students can use the answers to these questions to fine-tune their presentations.

Listening and Speaking Workshop: Presenting a Description 393

- *One-Stop Planner* CD-ROM with ExamView Test Generator

Internet
- go.hrw.com (Keyword LE5 9-6)
- *Elements of Literature Online*

Collection 6: Skills Review
Literary Skills

SKILLS FOCUS,
pp. 394–397

Grade-Level Skills

■ **Literary Skills**
Analyze various literary devices, including allegory and symbolism.

INTRODUCING THE SKILLS REVIEW

Use this review to assess students' understanding of the literary skills taught in this collection. If necessary, you can use the annotations to guide students in their reading before they answer the questions.

DIRECT TEACHING

A Literary Focus
Symbolism and allegory.
Remind students that folk tales and fables are often allegorical—the characters stand for moral qualities or abstract ideas, and the story is intended to teach or provide a moral lesson. As students read this folk tale, encourage them to consider what qualities or ideas the characters might represent.

B Literary Focus
❷ Symbolism and allegory. Is the king a truly individual character with a distinct personality, or is he the typical fairy tale king? [He is a characterless king, typical of such stories, exercising his position to get what he wants.] If he represents a quality, what quality might that be? [Possible responses: arrogance, authority.]

Test Practice

Symbolism and Allegory
DIRECTIONS: Read the following folk tale. Then, read and respond to the questions that follow.

A The Happy Man's Shirt

retold by Italo Calvino

translated by George Martin

A king had an only son that he thought the world of. But this prince was always unhappy. He would spend days on end at his window staring into space.

"What on earth do you lack?" asked the king. "What's wrong with you?"

"I don't even know myself, Father."

"Are you in love? If there's a particular girl you fancy, tell me, and I'll arrange for you to marry her, no matter whether she's the daughter of the most powerful king on earth or the poorest peasant girl alive!"

"No, Father, I'm not in love."

The king tried in every way imaginable to cheer him up, but theaters, balls, concerts, and singing were all useless, and day by day the rosy hue drained from the prince's face.

The king issued a decree,[1] and from every corner of the earth came the most learned philosophers, doctors, and professors. The king showed them the prince and asked for their advice. The wise men withdrew to think, then returned to the king. "Majesty, we have given the matter close thought and we have studied the stars. Here's what you must do. Look for a happy man, a man who's happy through and through, and exchange your son's shirt for his."

That same day the king sent ambassadors to all parts of the world in search of the happy man.

A priest was taken to the king. "Are you happy?" asked the king.

"Yes, indeed, Majesty."

"Fine. How would you like to be my bishop?"[2]

"Oh, Majesty, if only it were so!"

"Away with you! Get out of my sight! I'm seeking a man who's happy just as he is, not one who's trying to better his lot."

SKILLS FOCUS

Pages 394–397 cover **Literary Skills** Analyze symbolism and allegory.

---

1. **decree** (dē·krē′) *n.:* official order.
2. **bishop** (bish′əp) *n.:* high-ranking Christian clergyman.

READING MINI-LESSON

Reviewing Word-Attack Skills
Activity. Display these sentences. Have students underline the word in which the suffix *–ed* adds the syllable /id/. Answers are underlined.

1. The school flag <u>needed</u> to be replaced.
2. The flag was <u>ragged</u> and tattered.
3. The student council convened and <u>appointed</u> a committee to buy a new flag.
4. They asked for contributions and <u>collected</u> almost two hundred dollars.
5. The whole school <u>waited</u> impatiently until the flag finally arrived.
6. With all the students gathered around, the committee <u>presented</u> the flag to the principal.

C Literary Focus

? Symbolism and allegory.
Have students note that the young man is nameless. What quality does he probably represent? [Possible responses: happiness, contentment.]

Thus the search resumed, and before long the king was told about a neighboring king, who everybody said was a truly happy man. He had a wife as good as she was beautiful and a whole slew of children. He had conquered all his enemies, and his country was at peace. Again hopeful, the king immediately sent ambassadors to him to ask for his shirt.

The neighboring king received the ambassadors and said, "Yes, indeed, I have everything anybody could possibly want. But at the same time I worry because I'll have to die one day and leave it all. I can't sleep at night for worrying about that!" The ambassadors thought it wiser to go home without this man's shirt.

At his wit's end, the king went hunting. He fired at a hare but only wounded it, and the hare scampered away on three legs. The king pursued it, leaving the hunting party far behind him. Out in the open field he heard a man singing a refrain. The king stopped in his tracks. "Whoever sings like that is bound to be happy!" The song led him into a vineyard, where he found a young man singing and pruning the vines.

"Good day, Majesty," said the youth. "So early and already out in the country?"

"Bless you! Would you like me to take you to the capital? You will be my friend."

"Much obliged, Majesty, but I wouldn't even consider it. I wouldn't even change places with the Pope." **C**

"Why not? Such a fine young man like you . . ."

"No, no, I tell you. I'm content with just what I have and want nothing more."

"A happy man at last!" thought the king. "Listen, young man. Do me a favor."

"With all my heart, Majesty, if I can."

"Wait just a minute," said the king, who, unable to contain his joy any

7. The principal passed it to an honor guard, who <u>hoisted</u> it up the flagpole.

8. Then everyone cheered and <u>applauded</u>.

Activity. Display these pairs of related words. The syllable said with the greatest stress appears in boldface in the first word. Have students tell if the stressed syllable is the same [s] or different [d] in the second word.

1. **en**ergize	energetic	[d]
2. **ma**niac	maniacal	[d]
3. **sym**bol	symbolic	[d]
4. hys**ter**ia	hysterics	[s]
5. **rep**tile	reptilian	[d]
6. no**tor**ious	notoriety	[d]
7. **man**nerly	mannerism	[s]
8. **gal**axy	galactic	[d]

TestPractice

Answers and Model Rationales

1. **D** The king shows his love for his son through his exhaustive attempts to solve the son's problems. B would be correct if the question asked about the son's feelings. Although the king may feel affection for his son or frustration over his own inability to help, he does not express anger or irritation toward his son, so A and C are incorrect.

2. **H** Since royalty usually has wealth and the happy man is so poor that he doesn't even have a shirt, H is the best choice. Issues of romance, pride, and respect are not present in the story, so F, G, and J are improbable symbolic meanings.

3. **B** Being royalty, the prince is likely to be richer, more powerful, and better clothed than most people. It is unlikely that his unhappiness is related to appearance or feelings of superiority, so A and D can be eliminated. Since putting oneself in someone else's clothing (shoes or shirt, for example) means "to see what it's like to be that person," B is a better choice than C.

4. **H** The description of the priest does not indicate that he is a modest person or a flatterer, so F and G are incorrect. Although it's possible to describe the priest as hopeful (J), his eagerness to become a bishop and the king's response to him clearly indicate that he symbolizes ambition.

5. **A** B and C are wrong as the prince is neither in love nor worried about dying. A is better than D because the neighboring king knows why he is sad.

---

longer, ran to get his retinue.[3] "Come with me! My son is saved! My son is saved!" And he took them to the young man. "My dear lad," he began, "I'll give you whatever you want! But give me . . . give me . . ."

"What, Majesty?"

"My son is dying! Only you can save him. Come here!"

The king grabbed him and started unbuttoning the youth's jacket. All of a sudden he stopped, and his arms fell to his sides.

The happy man wore no shirt.

---

3. **retinue** (ret″n·ōō′) *n.:* assistants attending an important person.

---

1. Which pair of words *best* describes the king's feelings for his son?
   - **A** Anger and frustration
   - **B** Confusion and depression
   - **C** Affection and irritation
   - **D** Love and concern

2. The unhappy man is a prince. What might his position in life **symbolize** in the folk tale?
   - **F** Respect
   - **G** Pride
   - **H** Material wealth
   - **J** Romance

3. The wise men tell the king that his son should wear a happy man's shirt. What does wearing someone else's shirt **symbolize**?
   - **A** Looking like someone else
   - **B** Being like someone else
   - **C** Complimenting someone
   - **D** Feeling superior to someone

4. What might the character of the priest **symbolize**?
   - **F** Flattery
   - **G** Modesty
   - **H** Ambition
   - **J** Hopefulness

396 Collection 6 Symbolism and Allegory • Synthesizing Sources

Using Academic Language

Review of Literary Terms
Ask students to look back through the collection to find the meanings of the terms listed to the right. Then, have students cite passages from the collection that illustrate the meanings of those terms.

Symbol (pp. 340, 342, 358); **Public Symbol** (p. 340); **Allegory** (pp. 341, 364); **Multiple Meanings** (p. 358).

Review of Informational Terms
Ask students to review the collection to find the meanings of the terms listed to the right.

5. What is similar about these two **characters:** the prince and the neighboring king?
   - **A** Both seem to have everything they could want, but neither is content.
   - **B** Both are in love, but they are still not happy.
   - **C** Both worry about dying, which makes them unhappy.
   - **D** Both are sad, and neither knows why.

6. Why does the king think that the young man who sings as he works is happy?
   - **F** He is polite.
   - **G** He is satisfied with his life.
   - **H** He is healthy and young.
   - **J** He enjoys working outdoors in the country.

7. What does the happy man's lack of a shirt **symbolize?**
   - **A** External things cannot create happiness.
   - **B** True happiness does not exist in the real world.
   - **C** The man will soon experience unhappiness.
   - **D** The man does not understand what happiness is.

8. Which statement *best* expresses the **theme,** or **moral,** of the folk tale?
   - **F** People should not rely on others to help them solve their problems.
   - **G** It is difficult to know what other people are truly feeling.
   - **H** True happiness must come from within you.
   - **J** Although you may fail to attain your goals at first, you should not give up.

9. The **symbols** in this folk tale might **appeal** to us in part because they —
   - **A** make the setting of the story vivid
   - **B** give the narrator a distinct personality
   - **C** contribute to the meaning and emotional impact of the story
   - **D** provide information about the author's life

10. Which word *best* describes the **tone** of the folk tale?
    - **F** optimistic
    - **G** pessimistic
    - **H** sympathetic
    - **J** ironic

Constructed Response

11. In what way can this tale be seen as an **allegory?** Support your response using examples from the text.

6. **G** Though the points made in F, H, and J are true, the young man turns down the king's offer because he is happy where he is.

7. **A** B can be eliminated because the young man is obviously happy. Since no hint of coming discontent or confusion is evident in the text, C and D can also be eliminated.

8. **H** G is contradicted by the text; many people know that the prince is unhappy. Nothing in the story points to the idea that persistence leads to success. While no one is able to help the prince, H is a better choice than F because it is a stronger statement of what the shirtless young man represents.

9. **C** The symbols in this tale do not relate to the setting (A). The narrator does not have a particular personality, and we learn nothing about the author's life from the tale, so B and D are incorrect. The symbols do help the author convey the tale's theme, or moral, so C is correct.

10. **J** The tale is not optimistic (F) because the king doesn't find a way to help his son. Because the young man proves that true happiness is possible, the tale cannot be described as pessimistic (G). Because the ending is unexpected, J is a better choice than H.

Constructed Response

11. "The Happy Man's Shirt" can be seen as an allegory because the characters are representations of abstract ideas and the story tells a lesson. The prince represents material wealth; the young man represents happiness. The story uses these characters to teach the lesson that happiness depends on a person, not on material possessions.

Then, ask students to use those terms to explain how to synthesize the content from several sources by a single author. **Paraphrase** (p. 374); **Compare and Contrast** (p. 374); **Connect** (p. 374); **Synthesize** (p. 374).

Test-Taking Tips

Point out that students should never skim a test question. Hasty readers, for example, might see the words *feelings* and *son* in question 1 and assume that the question is about the son's feelings. They might then incorrectly choose B.

For more instruction on how to answer multiple-choice items, refer students to **Test Smarts.**

Vocabulary Skills

Context Clues

Modeling. Model the answer to question 1 by saying, "*Blighted* is an adjective describing a summer featuring no rain, dead crops, and a hurricane. D describes the kind of summer in which such events occur."

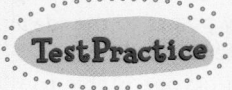

Answers and Model Rationales

1. See rationale above.

2. **F** G is incorrect because the narrator is helping his brother. There is no information related to the narrator's thought process, so J is incorrect. H is plausible, but the context clues "Determined" and "refuses to give up" support F as the best choice.

3. **C** The context clue "praise" makes it clear that *acclaimed* has positive connotations.

4. **G** The context clues "view the town as weak and unlucky" and "won't want to visit it" indicate that travelers will look down upon the town and reject it.

5. **B** The context clue "principle" indicates that Einstein's views were deeply held beliefs, not guilt (A), doubts (C), or worries (D).

6. **G** The clue that *inevitable* is a synonym for *unavoidable* is "certain." No context clues support F and J, and *unlikely* (H) is the opposite of *certain*.

ASSESSING

Assessment

■ *Holt Assessment: Literature, Reading, and Vocabulary*

Test Practice

Context Clues

DIRECTIONS: Use the context clues in the following passages to help you identify the meaning of the underlined vocabulary words.

1. In "The Scarlet Ibis" the summer of 1918 is blighted. Crops die because there is no rain. Then a hurricane uproots trees.
   In this passage, *blighted* means —
   A causing confusion
   B difficult to understand
   C filled with anger and resentment
   D suffering from conditions that prevent growth

2. In "The Scarlet Ibis" the narrator reveals his doggedness in his attitude toward his brother. Determined, he refuses to give up his efforts to teach his brother how to walk and swim.
   In this passage, *doggedness* means —
   F persistence
   G cruelty
   H sensitivity
   J logic

3. In "The Golden Kite, the Silver Wind" the Mandarin's plans to save his town are acclaimed at first. When he orders the wall to be redesigned, the townspeople praise him for his efforts.
   In this passage, *acclaimed* means —
   A rejected
   B criticized
   C applauded
   D mocked

4. In "The Golden Kite, the Silver Wind" the Mandarin fears that travelers will spurn the town. They won't want to visit it because they'll view the town as weak and unlucky.
   In this passage, *spurn* means —
   F attack
   G scorn
   H praise
   J discourage

5. In "On the Abolition of the Threat of War," Einstein expresses his conviction that we must end the arms race. Achieving peace was an important principle for him throughout his life.
   In this passage, *conviction* means —
   A deep guilt
   B strong belief
   C lasting doubt
   D constant worry

6. In "The Arms Race," Einstein states that a nuclear war seems inevitable. As each side continues to build up a supply of nuclear weapons, it seems certain that war will break out.
   In this passage, *inevitable* means —
   F destructive
   G unavoidable
   H unlikely
   J frightening

SKILLS FOCUS

Vocabulary Skills
Use context clues to understand word meanings.

Vocabulary Review

Have students select from the box an antonym for each numbered word.

meager	imminent	invincible
pandemonium	eradicate	

1. ample [meager]
2. create [eradicate]
3. vulnerable [invincible]
4. tranquility [pandemonium]
5. remote [imminent]

Test Practice

DIRECTIONS: Read the following paragraph from a draft of a student's descriptive essay. Then, answer the questions below it.

(1) Some people enjoy extravagant theme parks; others like quiet city parks, but my favorite is the ballpark. (2) From the parking lot, I see the huge stadium looming against the sky, its brilliant flags beckoning me toward the metal entrance gates. (3) As you move into the concession area, the smell of popcorn fills your nostrils, and you can hear the muffled cheers of fans. (4) In the stands, I feel an excited tension swirl inside me as I join in the wave and hold up posters in support of my favorite player. (5) The ballpark may not have trees or roller coasters, but it thrills me every time I go.

1. If the writer wanted to add sensory details to the passage, which sentence below would be most appropriate?
   A The field is watered every night by the stadium's head groundskeeper.
   B The fans cheer when they hear the piercing *crack!* of the bat.
   C There are nine players per team.
   D As the stadium fills, I feel more and more anxious for the game to begin.

2. Which of the following sentences could be added after sentence 1 to form a stronger controlling impression?
   F At the ballpark the surroundings are just as exciting as the game itself.
   G A baseball game is no fun unless you are playing in it.
   H A baseball stadium is a very popular attraction for people of all ages.
   J Attending sporting events is a favorite pastime of many Americans.

3. Which of the sentences should be changed to first-person point of view?
   A 1   C 4
   B 3   D 5

4. Which sentence would best fit between sentences 4 and 5 to match the spatial organization of the details in the passage?
   F From my seat, I see the ballplayers spread out onto the field and run to their respective positions.
   G Most of all, I dream about being a pro baseball player.
   H You glance through the program and figure out the rankings of each player you are about to see.
   J I hope to catch a stray ball that might be knocked into the stands.

5. In an oral presentation of this description, the writer could incorporate visuals with
   A a chart of baseball statistics
   B a slide show of famous players
   C the flags and posters described
   D a graph of the concession sales

SKILLS FOCUS

Writing Skills
Write a descriptive essay.

RESOURCES: WRITING

Assessment
- *One-Stop Planner* CD-ROM with ExamView Test Generator
- *Holt Assessment: Writing, Listening, and Speaking*

Internet
- *Holt Online Assessment*
- *Holt Online Essay Scoring*

Writing Skills
Answers
1. B
2. F
3. B
4. F
5. C

APPLICATION

Detailed Maps
You may want to suggest that, for homework, students draw a detailed map of a room in their home. After they have finished, ask them to write paragraphs containing the same information as the maps. Remind students that the more detailed the descriptions, the more accurately audiences will envision the rooms.

EXTENSION

Field Notes
Students can use their powers of subjective descriptive writing to take objective field notes on a certain place. Point out to students that archaeologists, geologists, and naturalists all use field notes in order to record their precise firsthand observations made in the field. Students can choose any subject, from a quiet wood to a busy street corner, on which to take notes. Direct students to use a compact notebook, write in pencil, mark the date and location of their observations, and jot down their impressions quickly.

Collection 7
Poetry

About Collection 7

In Collection 7, students will master the following skills:

- **Literary Skills:** Analyze imagery; analyze characteristics of catalog poems, haiku, sonnets, lyric poems, ballads, and free verse; compare two poems; analyze figures of speech; analyze tone and diction; analyze rhyme and meter; and analyze a speaker's persona, tone, and voice.
- **Reading Skills:** Use strategies for reading poems.
- **Vocabulary Skills:** Create a word bank for word study; and understand multiple meanings of words.
- **Writing Skills:** Develop, write, and revise an analysis of a poem.
- **Listening and Speaking Skills:** Present an oral response to a poem.

Minimum Course of Study

Most skills can be taught with a minimum number of selections and features. In the chart to the right, lessons highlighted in green constitute the minimum course of study that provides coverage of the skills taught in Collection 7.

Resource Manager
(pp. 400E–400H)

Lesson and workshop resources are referenced in the Resource Manager on the pages that follow. These resources can be used to reinforce the skills taught in Collection 7, remediate students who are having difficulty, and provide supporting activities for English-language learners.

Selection ▪ Feature	Literary Skills
Elements of Literature: Imagery *by* John Malcolm Brinnin	• Understand imagery
A Blessing *by* James Wright ↔ *at grade level*	• Analyze sensory imagery
Woman Work *by* Maya Angelou ↓ *below grade level* **Daily** *by* Naomi Shihab Nye ↔ *at grade level*	• Analyze the characteristics of catalog poems
in Just- *by* E. E. Cummings ↑ *above grade level*	• Analyze imagery, especially unusual and fresh imagery
Haiku *by* Miura Chora, Chiyo, Matsuo Bashō, Kobayashi Issa	• Analyze the characteristics of haiku
Once by the Pacific *by* Robert Frost ↑ *above grade level*	• Analyze the characteristics of sonnets
Country Scene *by* Hồ Xuân Hu'o'ng ↑ *above grade level*	• Analyze the characteristics of lyric poems • Compare two poems
Elements of Literature: Figures of Speech *by* John Malcolm Brinnin	• Understand figures of speech, including similes, metaphors, and personification
Tiburón *by* Martin Espada ↔ *at grade level*	• Analyze similes
Folding Won Tons In *by* Abraham Chang ↔ *at grade level*	• Analyze figures of speech, including similes and metaphors
"Hope" is the thing with feathers *by* Emily Dickinson ↔ *at grade level*	• Analyze extended metaphor
Internment *by* Juliet S. Kono ↔ *at grade level*	• Analyze diction • Analyze denotations and connotations • Compare poems
Fog *by* Carl Sandburg ↓ *below grade level*	• Analyze implied metaphors • Compare poems
Fire and Ice *by* Robert Frost ↓ *below grade level*	

Reading Skills	Vocabulary Skills	Writing ▪ Grammar and Language ▪ Listening and Speaking Skills
		• Write a description containing sensory imagery
		• Write a catalog poem
	• Create a word bank for word study	• Write an analysis of a poem • Write a poem containing fresh images • Present an oral interpretation of a poem
		• Write a haiku
		• Write a poem containing similes and images
• Use strategies for reading a poem		• Write a poem with figures of speech and images
		• Write a poem using an extended metaphor • Reformulate a poem
		• Write a poem containing a metaphor • Write a paragraph supporting an opinion

(continued)

Selection ▪ Feature	Literary Skills	Reading Skills
The Seven Ages of Man *by* William Shakespeare ↑ *above grade level*	• Analyze extended metaphors	
Women *by* Alice Walker ↔ *at grade level*	• Analyze tone and diction	
Boy at the Window *by* Richard Wilbur ↔ *at grade level*	• Analyze personification	
Elements of Literature: The Sounds of Poetry *by* John Malcolm Brinnin	• Understand rhyme, rhythm, meter, free verse, onomatopoeia, and alliteration	
I Wandered Lonely as a Cloud *by* William Wordsworth ↑ *above grade level*	• Analyze rhythm and meter	
The Courage That My Mother Had *by* Edna St. Vincent Millay ↓ *below grade level*	• Analyze rhyme	
Ballad of Birmingham *by* Dudley Randall ↓ *below grade level*	• Analyze the characteristics of ballads	
The Gift *by* Li-Young Lee ↑ *above grade level*	• Analyze the characteristics of free verse	
Legal Alien / Extranjera legal *by* Pat Mora ↔ *at grade level*	• Analyze a speaker's persona, tone, and voice	
The Base Stealer by Robert Francis ↔ *at grade level* **American Hero** *by* Essex Hemphill ↔ *at grade level*	• Analyze alliteration, onomatopoeia, and sentence structure	
Writing Workshop: *Analyzing a Poem*		
Listening and Speaking Workshop: *Presenting a Poem*		
Skills Review: *Literary Skills* *Writing Skills*	• Understand characteristics of poetry, including imagery, figurative language, and sound effects	

Vocabulary Skills	Writing ■ Grammar and Language ■ Listening and Speaking
• Understand multiple meanings of words	• Write a poem containing an extended metaphor • Paraphrase a poem
	• Write a descriptive paragraph
	• Write an analysis of a poem • Prepare a poem for oral presentation
	• Write a description • Write a comparison
	• Write a descriptive paragraph
	• Write a ballad • Write a comparison-contrast essay
	• Write a free-verse poem • Write an analysis of a free-verse poem
	• Write a poem
	• Write a free-verse poem
	• Write an analysis of a poem
	• Present an oral response to a poem
	• Write an analysis of a poem

Selection ▪ Feature	Planning	Differentiating Instruction ▪ Lesson Plans with ELL Strategies and Practice	Reading ▪ Vocabulary
Elements of Literature: Imagery *by* John Malcolm Brinnin	• PowerNotes: Imagery		
A Blessing *by* James Wright	• One-Stop Planner with ExamView Test Generator	• The Holt Reader, pp. 201–204 • Holt Reading Solutions, pp. 197–198 • Supporting Instruction in Spanish, p. 27 NOTE: All poetry selections appear on • Audio CD Library, disc 12 • Audio CD Library, Selections and Summaries in Spanish	• The Holt Reader • Holt Reading Solutions
Woman Work *by* Maya Angelou **Daily** *by* Naomi Shihab Nye	• One-Stop Planner with ExamView Test Generator	• Holt Reading Solutions, pp. 199–202 • Supporting Instruction in Spanish, p. 27	• Holt Reading Solutions
in Just- *by* E. E. Cummings	• One-Stop Planner with ExamView Test Generator	• Holt Reading Solutions, pp. 203–206 • Supporting Instruction in Spanish, p. 28	• Holt Reading Solutions
Haiku *by* Miura Chora; Matsuo Bashō; Chiyo; Kobayashi Issa	• One-Stop Planner with ExamView Test Generator	• Holt Reading Solutions, pp. 207–208 • Supporting Instruction in Spanish, p. 28	• Holt Reading Solutions
Once by the Pacific *by* Robert Frost **Country Scene** *by* Hồ Xuân Hu'o'ng	• One-Stop Planner with ExamView Test Generator	• Holt Reading Solutions, pp. 209–212 • Supporting Instruction in Spanish, p. 29	• Holt Reading Solutions
Elements of Literature: Figures of Speech *by* John Malcolm Brinnin	• PowerNotes: Figures of Speech	• Family Involvement Activities in English and Spanish, p. 9	
Tiburón *by* Martín Espada	• One-Stop Planner with ExamView Test Generator	• Holt Reading Solutions, pp. 215–216 • Supporting Instruction in Spanish, p. 29	• Holt Reading Solutions
Folding Won Tons In *by* Abraham Chang	• One-Stop Planner with ExamView Test Generator	• Holt Reading Solutions, pp. 217–218 • Supporting Instruction in Spanish, pp. 29–30	• Holt Reading Solutions • PowerNotes: How to Read a Poem
"Hope" is the thing with feathers *by* Emily Dickinson **Internment** *by* Juliet S. Kono	• One-Stop Planner with ExamView Test Generator	• Holt Reading Solutions, pp. 219–222 • Supporting Instruction in Spanish, p. 30	• Holt Reading Solutions
Fog *by* Carl Sandburg **Fire and Ice** *by* Robert Frost	• One-Stop Planner with ExamView Test Generator	• Holt Reading Solutions, pp. 223–225 • Supporting Instruction in Spanish, p. 31	• Holt Reading Solutions
The Seven Ages of Man *by* William Shakespeare	• One-Stop Planner with ExamView Test Generator	• Holt Adapted Reader • Holt Reading Solutions, pp. 226–229 • Supporting Instruction in Spanish, p. 31	• Holt Adapted Reader • Holt Reading Solutions

Writing ▪ Grammar and Language ▪ Listening and Speaking	Assessment
	• Holt Assessment: Literature, Reading, and Vocabulary • Holt Online Assessment • One-Stop Planner with ExamView Test Generator
	• See "A Blessing" above
	• See "A Blessing" above
	• See "A Blessing" above
	• See "A Blessing" above
	• See "A Blessing" above
	• See "A Blessing" above
	• See "A Blessing" above
	• See "A Blessing" above
	• See "A Blessing" above

Technology

INTERNET

- go.hrw.com
- Holt Online Assessment
- Holt Online Essay Scoring
- Elements of Literature Online

MEDIA

 • One-Stop Planner with ExamView Test Generator

 • PowerNotes

 • Audio CD Library, disc 12

 • Audio CD Library, Selections and Summaries in Spanish

 • Visual Connections Videocassette Program, Segments 6, 7, and 8

• Fine Art Transparencies, 10 and 11

 Transparency   Video

 CD-ROM   Audio CD

(continued)

Selection Feature	Planning	Differentiating Instruction Lesson Plans with ELL Strategies and Practice	Reading Vocabulary
Women *by Alice Walker*	• One-Stop Planner with ExamView Test Generator	• Holt Reading Solutions, pp. 230–231 • Supporting Instruction in Spanish, p. 31	• Holt Reading Solutions
Boy at the Window *by Richard Wilbur*	• One-Stop Planner with ExamView Test Generator	• Holt Reading Solutions, pp. 232–234 • Supporting Instruction in Spanish, p. 32	• Holt Reading Solutions
Elements of Literature: **The Sounds of Poetry** *by John Malcolm Brinnin*	• PowerNotes: Sound Effects in Poetry		
I Wandered Lonely as a Cloud *by William Wordsworth*	• One-Stop Planner with ExamView Test Generator	• Holt Adapted Reader • Holt Reading Solutions, pp. 237–239 • Supporting Instruction in Spanish, p. 32	• Holt Adapted Reader • Holt Reading Solutions
The Courage That My Mother Had *by Edna St. Vincent Millay*	• One-Stop Planner with ExamView Test Generator	• Holt Reading Solutions, pp. 240–242 • Supporting Instruction in Spanish, p. 33	• Holt Reading Solutions
Ballad of Birmingham *by Dudley Randall*	• One-Stop Planner with ExamView Test Generator	• Holt Reading Solutions, pp. 243–246 • Supporting Instruction in Spanish, p. 33	• Holt Reading Solutions
The Gift *by Li-Young Lee*	• One-Stop Planner with ExamView Test Generator	• Holt Reading Solutions, pp. 247–248 • Supporting Instruction in Spanish, p. 34	• Holt Reading Solutions
Legal Alien / Extranjera legal *by Pat Mora*	• One-Stop Planner with ExamView Test Generator	• Holt Reading Solutions, pp. 249–250 • Supporting Instruction in Spanish, p. 34	• Holt Reading Solutions
The Base Stealer *by Robert Francis* **American Hero** *by Essex Hemphill*	• One-Stop Planner with ExamView Test Generator	• Holt Reading Solutions, pp. 251–254 • Supporting Instruction in Spanish, pp. 34-35	• Holt Reading Solutions
Writing Workshop: *Analyzing a Poem*	• One-Stop Planner with ExamView Test Generator	• Workshop Resources: Writing, Listening, and Speaking, pp. 69–76 • Supporting Instruction in Spanish, p. 72	
Listening and Speaking Workshop: *Presenting a Literary Response*	• One-Stop Planner with ExamView Test Generator	• Workshop Resources: Writing, Listening, and Speaking, pp. 77–82 • Supporting Instruction in Spanish	
Skills Review: *Literary Skills* *Writing Skills*			

The Holt Reader

The Holt Reader is a consumable paperback book which can be used alone or to accompany *Elements of Literature*. It offers guided support throughout the reading process and encourages students to become active readers by circling, underlining, questioning, and jotting down responses as they read. *The Holt Reader* works well for homework, students who have missed class, additional instructional time, reteaching, and remediation.

Holt Reading Solutions (HRS)

Holt Reading Solutions pulls together reading resources in the *Elements of Literature* program to create a powerful tool for intervention and whole-class instruction. *HRS* includes diagnostic assessment tools, lesson plans for English-language learners and special education students, adaptations of selected reading selections, vocabulary and comprehension worksheets, information on phonics and decoding, and additional instruction and practice in remedial reading skills.

Writing ▪ Grammar and Language ▪ Listening and Speaking	Assessment
	• Holt Assessment: Literature, Reading, and Vocabulary • Holt Online Assessment • One-Stop Planner with ExamView Test Generator
	• See "Women" above
	• See "Women" above
	• See "Women" above
	• See "Women" above
	• See "Women" above
	• See "Women" above
	• See "Women" above
• Daily Language Activities • Workshop Resources: Writing, Listening, and Speaking, pp. 69–76	• Holt Assessment: Writing, Listening, and Speaking • Holt Online Assessment • One-Stop Planner with ExamView Test Generator
• Workshop Resources: Writing, Listening, and Speaking, pp. 77–82	• Holt Assessment: Writing, Listening, and Speaking • One-Stop Planner with ExamView Test Generator
	• See Listening and Speaking Workshop above

One-Stop Planner with ExamView Test Generator

The *One-Stop Planner* CD-ROM contains electronic versions of print-based teaching resources, clips from the video program, and valuable assessment tools. The *One-Stop Planner* resources are presented in easy-to-follow, point-and-click menu formats. To preview resources or print out worksheets and tests, you simply make a selection and click.

One-Stop
Planner CD-ROM

SKILLS FOCUS

Grade-Level Skills

■ **Literary Skills**
Analyze various literary devices, including figurative language and imagery.

INTRODUCING THE COLLECTION

In this collection, students will explore the characteristics of a wide range of poetic forms, from the fleeting whisper of the haiku to the steady rhythm of the iambic line. Along the way, students will examine the unique visions of a diverse group of poets, including Maya Angelou, Li-Young Lee, and Robert Frost. They will discover that poets draw from a reservoir of rhythms and sounds to create images and associations that linger in readers' and listeners' minds. Each lesson focuses on different aspects of the poetic palette—from the simple, yet striking, metaphors of Emily Dickinson to the inventive constructions of E. E. Cummings. The collection culminates with an opportunity for students to give an oral presentation of a poem.

COLLECTION 7 RESOURCES: READING

Planning
■ *One-Stop Planner* CD-ROM with ExamView Test Generator

Differentiating Instruction
■ *Holt Reading Solutions*
■ *The Holt Reader*
■ *Holt Adapted Reader*

■ *Family Involvement Activities in English and Spanish*
■ *Supporting Instruction in Spanish*

Assessment
■ *Holt Assessment: Literature, Reading, and Vocabulary*
■ *One-Stop Planner* CD-ROM with ExamView Test Generator

■ *Holt Online Assessment*

Internet
■ go.hrw.com (Keyword: LE5 9-7)
■ *Elements of Literature Online*

Media
■ *Audio CD Library*
■ *Audio CD Library, Selections and Summaries in Spanish*

Collection 7

Poetry

A word is dead
When it is said,
Some say.
I say it just
Begins to live
That day.

—Emily Dickinson

INTERNET
Collection
Resources

Keyword: LE5 9-7

Dialogue of Two Poets Disguised as Birds (1988) by Alfredo Castañeda. Oil on canvas (15¾″ × 19¾″).

Mary Ann Martin/Fine Art, New York.

401

SKILLS FOCUS,
pp. 402–403

Grade-Level Skills

■ **Literary Skills**
Analyze various literary devices, including imagery.

Review Skills

■ **Literary Skills**
Analyze common literary devices (such as symbolism, imagery, and metaphor) in a variety of texts.

Elements of Literature: Imagery

Choose a popular song with lyrics appropriate for classroom discussion, and write the lyrics on the chalkboard. If possible, play a recording of the song for students. Ask students what the words make them see, smell, or hear. Ask students how they feel about these images and what words in particular produce images and emotions. Then, have students describe the images and discuss the moods they help to evoke.

You might relate the discussion to the examples provided in the text, pointing out the images that contribute to the feeling of loneliness in the lines from "The House on the Hill." For example, the "broken walls" suggest that no one tends to the house; the color gray indicates there is little light; and "all gone away" emphasizes the sense of desolation.

VIEWING THE ART

American artist **Edward Hopper** (1882–1967) did not receive critical and popular attention until the early 1920s. Today, he is considered one of the twentieth century's foremost realists, known especially for his bleak scenes of urban life.

Activity. Ask students what aspects of the house Hopper emphasizes and what feelings the painting evokes. [Possible response: Hopper emphasizes its size and its remote location. The painting evokes feelings of loneliness and abandonment.]

Imagery *by* John Malcolm Brinnin
SEEING THINGS FRESHLY

Imagery is one of the elements that give poetry its forcefulness. Images are basically copies of things you can see. But images in poetry can do even more than help us see things. An **image** is a single word or a phrase that appeals to one of our senses. An image can help us see color or motion. Sometimes it can also help us hear a sound, smell an odor, feel texture or temperature, or even taste a sweet, sour, or salty flavor.

Suppose you were an artist and wanted to paint a picture of a house. You would emphasize certain aspects of the house. You might emphasize the age of the house by making its shingles look as worn and wrinkled and cracked as an old shoe. You might emphasize the emptiness of the house by painting curtainless windows that reflect the clouds and doors opening onto empty hallways. In each case, as an artist you would give the actual image (the house) a certain twist, a particular shading.

Poets do the same thing. Edwin Arlington Robinson in "The House on the Hill" saw an empty house and emphasized its loneliness:

Through broken walls and gray
The winds blow bleak and shrill;
They are all gone away.

Robert Frost in "The Black Cottage" saw an empty house and emphasized the new life that had moved in:

"There are bees in this wall." He struck the
    clapboards,
Fierce heads looked out; small bodies
    pivoted.
We rose to go. Sunset blazed on the
    windows.

INTERNET
More About Imagery
Keyword: LE5 9-7

SKILLS FOCUS

Literary Skills
Understand imagery.

House by the Railroad (1925) by Edward Hopper. Oil on canvas (24″ x 29″).

The Museum of Modern Art, New York. Given anonymously. Photograph © 2000 The Museum of Modern Art, New York.

DIFFERENTIATING INSTRUCTION

Learners Having Difficulty
Imagery. Have students make charts that list the five senses to which imagery appeals [sight, hearing, taste, smell, touch]. Then, write the images listed below on the chalkboard, and guide students in matching each image with the sense to which it appeals:

• The phantom fog hid the tops of the buildings. [sight]

• The autumn leaves crackled underfoot. [hearing]

• The aroma of fresh-baked cookies greeted me at the door. [smell]

• With each sip the lemonade reminded me of that sour summer long ago. [taste]

• The soft, cool grass welcomed my bare feet. [touch]

Imagery is part of a poet's style. It is the product of the poet's own way of seeing the world. Just as we learn to recognize certain painters at once by noticing the colors and shapes that mark their works, so we learn to identify poets by paying attention to their imagery. Of course, the time and place in which poets live influence the kind of imagery they use. Poets who live in cities will usually draw upon the street scenes and industrial landscapes they know so well. Poets who live far from cities will usually draw their images from what they see of country life.

Imagery and Feelings

An image can be so fresh, so powerful, that it can speak to our deepest feelings. An image can be so phrased that it makes us feel joy or grief, wonder or horror, love or disgust.

Here is a poem that uses images to help us see a scene on the Great Lakes and hear the sounds made by a boat lost in the mist. Yet what readers remember most about this little poem is the way the images make them feel:

Lost
Desolate and lone
All night long on the lake
Where fog trails and mist creeps,
The whistle of a boat
Calls and cries unendingly,
Like some lost child
In tears and trouble
Hunting the harbor's breast
And the harbor's eyes.
—Carl Sandburg

The poet . . . should stop and examine what others have missed, whether it be veins on a leaf or the surge of a mob; he should hear what others miss—not just skylarks but the breath of an old man or sleet against the window; he should respond to the feel of a rusted iron railing, a cut, or a gull's feather; he should identify the variety of city smells and country odors and consider what it is that makes an unoccupied house different from one lived in; and he should taste not only food but pine gum and smog.

—Stephen Minot

Practice

To see how **images** can be drawn from all sorts of things we observe in life, create two images for each of the following categories. Have one image suggest something pleasant and the other suggest something unpleasant. Try to include images that show how a thing **looks, smells, tastes, sounds,** or **feels** to the touch.

Images	Pleasant	Unpleasant
Animal images		
Flower images		
Water images		
Sky images		
Earth images		
City images		
Country images		

Practice
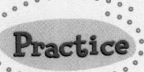

Possible responses:

Animal images. Pleasant—a fuzzy kitten curled up in sleep. *Unpleasant*—a foul-smelling cage of hissing rats.

Flower images. Pleasant—the perfume of a spring bouquet. *Unpleasant*—the stench of rotting petals.

Water images. Pleasant—the gentle splash of spring rain. *Unpleasant*—murky canal.

Sky images. Pleasant—the bright orange rays of the morning sun. *Unpleasant*—the empty dirty gray horizon.

Earth images. Pleasant—the soft, springy feel of a lush green lawn. *Unpleasant*—stinging sand blown into my eyes.

City images. Pleasant—the majesty of the skyscraper-filled skyline. *Unpleasant*—the piles of rank-smelling uncollected garbage.

Country images. Pleasant—the cheerful chatter of baby ducks. *Unpleasant*—the droning hum of swarming flies.

Have students continue to use these charts to record striking images from the poems in the chapter.

Advanced Learners
Acceleration. Use the following activity to help advanced learners analyze the use of imagery, personification, figures of speech, and sounds to evoke the reader's emotions.

Activity. Have students work in small groups to review poems with which they are familiar. Ask students to discuss the predominant feelings or emotions they associate with these poems. Then, have students return to each poem to identify examples of imagery that contribute to these feelings.

Grade-Level Skills

■ **Literary Skills**
Analyze various literary devices, including imagery.

Review Skills

■ **Literary Skills**
Analyze common literary devices in a variety of texts.

Summary *at grade level*

The speaker and a companion pull off a Minnesota highway at dusk and watch two ponies as they graze contentedly in a pasture. The speaker, overwhelmed by the animals' grace, happiness, and love for one another, experiences a transformative moment when one of the ponies affectionately approaches him.

PRETEACHING

Skills Starter

Build background. Explain to students that although many forms of writing make use of imagery, poetry often relies heavily on this literary device. The brevity of many poems forces each word to contribute to the poet's intended effect. Words that appeal to the senses—because they can trigger strong emotions and associations in the minds of readers—are therefore valuable tools for the poet.

Before You Read

A Blessing

Make the Connection
Quickwrite
Close your eyes, and try to visualize something in nature. Describe what you are seeing. You could be describing something as big as the sky or as small as an ant, as soft as a rabbit or as squishy as a swamp, as . . . Well, you've got the idea. Explain how what you are describing makes you feel.

Literary Focus
Imagery
Poetry is often said to be magical. When a poem helps us see something in a new way, we sometimes feel a shiver of awe, and we say, "How did the poet do that?"

Poets create their magic by using words to excite our emotions and our imaginations. One of the ways they do that is through **imagery**—language that appeals to our senses.

Sight is the sense many people rely on most, so not surprisingly it is the most common source of imagery in poetry. Images can also appeal to our senses of **hearing, touch, smell,** and **taste.** Sometimes an image appeals to two or more senses at the same time.

All these images re-create an experience the poet wants to share with us. They give us the feeling that we're right there, a part of it all.

Literary Skills
Understand
sensory imagery.

RESOURCES: READING

Planning
■ *One-Stop Planner* CD-ROM with ExamView Test Generator

Differentiating Instruction
■ *Holt Reading Solutions*
■ *The Holt Reader*
■ *Supporting Instruction in Spanish*

■ *Audio CD Library, Selections and Summaries in Spanish*

Assessment
■ *Holt Assessment: Literature, Reading, and Vocabulary*
■ *One-Stop Planner* CD-ROM with ExamView Test Generator
■ *Holt Online Assessment*

Internet
■ go.hrw.com (Keyword: LE5 9-7)
■ *Elements of Literature Online*

Media
■ *Audio CD Library*
■ *Audio CD Library, Selections and Summaries in Spanish*

A Blessing

James Wright

Just off the highway to Rochester, Minnesota,
Twilight bounds softly forth on the grass,
And the eyes of those two Indian ponies
Darken with kindness.
5   They have come gladly out of the willows
To welcome my friend and me.
We step over the barbed wire into the pasture
Where they have been grazing all day, alone.
They ripple tensely, they can hardly contain their happiness
10   That we have come.
They bow shyly as wet swans. They love each other.
There is no loneliness like theirs.
At home once more,
They begin munching the young tufts of spring in the darkness.
15   I would like to hold the slenderer one in my arms,
For she has walked over to me
And nuzzled my left hand.
She is black and white,
Her mane falls wild on her forehead,
20   And the light breeze moves me to caress her long ear
That is delicate as the skin over a girl's wrist.
Suddenly I realize
That if I stepped out of my body I would break
Into blossom.

A Blessing   405

Monitoring students' progress.
To assess students' understanding of
the selection, ask them to write two
or three sentences summarizing the
events described in the poem and
the effects these events have on
the speaker.

Meet the Writer

Background. The darkness found
in many of Wright's other poems
may find their source in the poet's
difficult childhood. Neither of
Wright's parents received a high
school education, and Wright himself missed a year of high school
after suffering a nervous breakdown.
Wright was skeptical of the attention he received after winning the
Pulitzer Prize in 1972. "It'll fade," he
said, "and I'll be a footnote in some
high-school anthology."

For Independent Reading

Wright was profoundly influenced
by the poetry of Robert Frost.
Suggest that students read several
of Frost's poems and then compare
and contrast the two poets.

Meet the Writer

James Wright

"We Know What He's Talking About"

Travelers who pull off I-90 at the High
Forest Rest Area in Stewartville, Minnesota,
may not find two ponies in a pasture.
Thanks to the radio host Garrison Keillor,
however, they will find a plaque engraved
with the poem "A Blessing."

Keillor dedicated the plaque in 1998. A
pair of horses was on hand, as were more
than two hundred local high school students. One sophomore said he liked
Wright's poem because it spoke "about the
beauty of Minnesota. And it's so close to
us; we know what he's talking about."

The Pulitzer Prize–winner James
Wright (1927–1980) often wrote
about the places in his life—Minnesota, where he taught college for
eight years (Keillor was his student
there); New York City, his home in
later life; but especially Martin's Ferry,
the mill town in Ohio where he grew
up in a poor family during the Great
Depression.

Much of Wright's poetry is dark,
and it explores themes of loneliness
and alienation. "A Blessing" escapes
this darkness—perhaps that is the
reason for its popularity. Keillor has
said of the poem:

❝I've seen it done in needlework, and in
rye seeds glued to particle board and entered in the crop show at the state fair. I've
heard it read at weddings in meadows, weddings attended by horses. . . . It is a love
poem.❞

Response and Analysis

Reading Check

1. What is the **setting** of the poem—*where* and *when* does it take place?

2. What were the ponies doing all day?

3. How do the ponies feel about the visit? How do they feel about each other?

4. Why does the speaker feel especially fond of one of the ponies?

Thinking Critically

5. Most of the **images** in this poem appeal to the senses of sight and touch. Make a two-column chart like the one here, with the headings "Sight" and "Touch." Then, list images from the poem in the appropriate columns. Some images might be listed in both columns.

Sight	Touch

6. You may have read myths in which a character is fantastically changed from one form to another. This change is called **metamorphosis.** What metamorphosis do you *see* in the last three lines of the poem? What emotion do you think the speaker is expressing there?

7. What human qualities and feelings does the speaker give to the ponies?

8. The **tone** of this poem is joyful. It expresses the pleasure that comes from springtime and love. What **images** in the poem help to create its tone?

Extending and Evaluating

9. What do you think of the **title** "A Blessing"? What does it have to do with the experience described in the poem? What other titles can you suggest for the poem?

WRITING

Capturing a Feeling

Write a **poem** or a **paragraph** that describes something in nature that you feel strongly about. You can start with an image you found for the Quickwrite on page 404, or you can come up with a new subject. Be sure to tell *where* you are as you observe your scene. Use images that appeal to the **senses** and that reveal how you feel about your subject. How does your subject **look, sound, smell, feel,** or **taste**?

SKILLS FOCUS

Literary Skills
Analyze sensory imagery.

Writing Skills
Write a description containing sensory imagery.

A Blessing **407**

A Blessing **407**

Grade-Level Skills

■ **Literary Skills**
Understand and explain the characteristics of different forms of poetry, including a catalog poem.

Summary ⬇ *below grade level*

In "Woman Work," the speaker lists her many onerous tasks. Her days are so dominated by ceaseless labor that she cannot call her life her own. For solace she looks to nature, calling on sun, rain, and other elements to ease her pain.

Summary ⬌ *at grade level*

In "Daily," the speaker catalogs her daily domestic chores. Repetition is a key element of the poem's structure and content, but it is ultimately transcendent rather than tedious. The theme—that hands-on tasks connect a person to the world—is contained in a final metaphor.

PRETEACHING

Selection Starter

Motivate. Ask students to review the items on their Quickwrite lists. Would they classify these activities as enjoyable, drudgery, necessities of life, or something else?

Before You Read

Woman Work
Daily

Make the Connection

Quickwrite ✏️

Make a list of the things that you do during an ordinary day. What is the first thing you do in the morning? What is the last thing you do before bed? What is your favorite part of the day? The following two poems tell about the things that people do every day. As you read, think about your list. How does it compare with the poems?

Literary Focus

Catalog Poem

You've probably seen the kind of catalogs that come from stores, filled with pictures of almost anything in the world you'd want to buy. Like those catalogs, a **catalog poem** brings together many different images and presents them for your attention. Unlike a retail catalog, though, a poem does not want you to part with your money; it wants you only to enter the poem and, with your imagination, share an experience with the speaker.

The repetition of images in a catalog poem creates a rolling rhythm when the poem is read aloud. Try reading the two poems that follow aloud, and see how the piling up of images creates the poems' rhythmic beat.

Literary Skills
Understand the characteristics of catalog poems.

Woman Work Ⓐ

Maya Angelou

I've got the children to tend
The clothes to mend
The floor to mop
The food to shop Ⓑ
5 Then the chicken to fry
The baby to dry
I got company to feed
The garden to weed
I've got the shirts to press
10 The tots to dress
The cane to be cut
I gotta clean up this hut
Then see about the sick
And the cotton to pick

15 Shine on me, sunshine
Rain on me, rain
Fall softly, dewdrops
And cool my brow again.

Storm, blow me from here
20 With your fiercest wind
Let me float across the sky
'Til I can rest again.

Fall gently, snowflakes
Cover me with white
25 Cold icy kisses and
Let me rest tonight.

Sun, rain, curving sky
Mountain, oceans, leaf and stone
Star shine, moon glow
30 You're all that I can call my own.

Woman Work   409

A Literary Focus

? Simile. What comparison does the speaker use to describe how she addresses her envelope? What does it indicate about her feelings toward her work? [Possible response: She uses a simile, likening the job to balancing a cloud in the center of the sky. It shows that she takes pleasure in her work and tries to do it well, seeing beauty even in mundane tasks.]

B Literary Focus

? Metaphor. What might the metaphor in l. 21 mean? [Possible responses: A day can be defined by naming the tasks performed during the course of it; daily tasks are essential to life, just as nouns are essential to sentences.] What might the metaphor in l. 22 mean? [Possible response: Working hands connect people to the material world, just as churches connect people to the spiritual world.]

VIEWING THE ART

Mexican artist **Diego Rivera** (1886–1957) is best known for his historical murals. This painting shows a woman grinding *masa harina* (corn meal) for tortillas.

Activity. Ask students how the focus of this painting is similar to that of "Daily." [Possible responses: Both focus on the hands as being central to the routines of daily life; both convey a sense of respect for work done by hand.]

Daily

Naomi Shihab Nye

These shriveled seeds we plant,
corn kernel, dried bean,
poke into loosened soil,
cover over with measured fingertips
5   These T-shirts we fold
into perfect white
squares
These tortillas we slice and fry to crisp strips
This rich egg scrambled in a gray clay bowl
10 This bed whose covers I straighten
smoothing edges till blue quilt fits brown blanket
and nothing hangs out
A This envelope I address
so the name balances like a cloud
15 in the center of the sky
This page I type and retype
This table I dust till the scarred wood shines
This bundle of clothes I wash and hang and wash again
like flags we share, a country so close
20 no one needs to name it
B The days are nouns: touch them
The hands are churches that worship the world

The Grinder (1924) by Diego Rivera. Encaustic on canvas (90 cm × 117 cm).

Courtesy Museo de Arte Moderno (INBA), Mexico City.
©1995 The Detroit Institute of Arts. Photograph by Dirk Bakker.

DIFFERENTIATING INSTRUCTION

Learners Having Difficulty
Students often lose confidence in their reading ability when they cannot recall what they have just read. Have them write the heads "First Reading" and "Second Reading" on a piece of paper. Ask them to read one of the poems, concentrating on three images. After reading, students should close their books and list the images in their own words.

Advanced Learners
Acceleration. This activity can help students analyze the characteristics of subgenres.
Activity. Have students read some of Walt Whitman's catalog poems (many are archived online). Students can choose one poem to compare with the two presented here, listing similarities in the elements of catalog poems.

Meet the Writers

Maya Angelou
Naomi Shihab Nye

Born Winner

Maya Angelou.

"One would say of my life, 'born loser, had to be'—but it's not the truth. In the black community, however bad it looks, there's a lot of love and so much humor."

Maya Angelou (1928–) is anything but a loser. After she left Stamps, Arkansas, she won a scholarship to the California Labor School, where she took evening classes in dance and drama. In 1954 and 1955, she toured Europe and Africa in a State Department–sponsored production of the opera *Porgy and Bess*. She later wrote and produced a ten-part television series on Africanisms in American life; wrote songs that were recorded by B. B. King; and published short stories, magazine articles, and poems. In 1992, she was asked to write a poem for the inauguration of President Bill Clinton. On Inauguration Day in 1993, Maya Angelou presented her eloquent poem "On the Pulse of Morning." Here are the final lines:

"Here on the pulse of this new day
You may have the grace to look up and out
And into your sister's eyes,
And into your brother's face,
Your country,
And say simply
Very simply
With hope—
Good morning."

Angelou is an imposing woman—six feet tall—with a gracious, formal manner. She speaks six languages fluently. Although she declares a continuing interest in exploring the character of the black woman, Angelou's focus is not narrow:

"I speak to the black experience, but I am always talking about the human condition—about what we can endure, dream, fail at, and still survive."

Noticing the World

Naomi Shihab Nye (1952–), born and raised in St. Louis, Missouri, has written several collections of poems, including *Red Suitcase* (1994) and *Words Under the Words: Selected Poems* (1995). Nye is also a songwriter with two albums to her credit—*Rutabaga-Roo* and *Lullaby Raft*. Many of Nye's poems are inspired by her childhood memories and by her travels, including visits to her Palestinian grandmother in Jerusalem. Nye lives in San Antonio, Texas, with her husband and her son. She regularly reads her poetry in schools, where she also runs workshops to help students find the poetry hiding in their own imaginations. She says:

"Being alive is a common road. It's what we notice [that] makes us different."

Naomi Shihab Nye.

GUIDED PRACTICE

Monitoring students' progress. To assess students' understanding of the selections, ask them to create a Venn diagram to compare and contrast the two poems. In the interior section of the diagram, students can include elements of structure or content common to both poems, such as repetition and the performance of certain tasks. In the exterior section of the diagram, students can indicate aspects that are unique to each poem.

Meet the Writers

Background. Maya Angelou's life has been filled with hardships, successes, and unique experiences. She grew up in rural Arkansas during the era of segregation, left school at the age of fifteen, and headed for California. There she worked as a streetcar conductor before continuing her education. Today Angelou lives and teaches in North Carolina.

Naomi Shihab Nye's work reflects her Palestinian-American background and the people of her ethnically diverse neighborhood in Texas. Nye's fascination with multiculturalism led her to edit *This Same Sky: A Collection of Poems from Around the World,* an anthology that includes the work of poets from sixty nations (Four Winds Press, 1992).

For Independent Reading

- Students may enjoy reading *What Have You Lost,* a poetry collection compiled by Naomi Shihab Nye. The poems in the compilation revolve around the theme of losses, some big, some small. Many of the poems are suitable for lower-level readers and are accompanied by photographs.
- Students who like "Woman Work" may enjoy a further exploration of Maya Angelou's writing. Suggest the *Complete Collected Poems of Maya Angelou.*

DIFFERENTIATING INSTRUCTION

Advanced Learners

Enrichment. Although she addresses the human condition in her work, Angelou writes highly personal works that stem from her own unique experience.

Activity. Encourage students to find out more about Angelou's life. They may wish to read excerpts from her autobiographical account *I Know Why the Caged Bird Sings* (you may wish to preview any sections you assign to students). Alternatively, they can use one of the many Internet resources devoted to Angelou. Invite students to work in groups to create a bulletin board on the writer, her life, and her work.

Response and Analysis

Reading Check

1. Possible answers: child care, sewing, shopping, cooking, gardening, ironing, cutting cane, housecleaning, tending the sick, picking cotton.

2. Possible answers: planting seeds, folding shirts, cooking, making beds, addressing envelopes, typing, dusting, doing laundry.

Thinking Critically

3. Possible answers: The images of child care and housework in "Woman Work" suggest that the speaker does domestic work. Images of cutting cane and picking cotton show that she works on a farm. In "Daily," images of frying tortillas suggest that she lives in the Southwest. Images of housework suggest that she cares for a family; images of typing suggest that she writes.

4. Students may describe the tone of "Woman Work" as desperate or despondent, citing the repetitive "I've got . . . to [do]" structure and the pleas for relief. The tone of "Daily" may be described as content, citing details such as making "perfect white squares" as evidence that the work brings the speaker pleasure.

5. She asks the elements for relief from her daily struggles.

6. Possible answers: Each day of work is of substantive, meaningful value; daily chores give the speaker a strong connection with the world.

7. Students may say that men's poems would focus on things men do in the workplace, rather than on child care or household chores.

Response and Analysis

Woman Work
Daily

Reading Check

1. Name five activities listed by the speaker of "Woman Work."

2. Name five activities listed by the speaker of "Daily."

Thinking Critically

3. What does the **catalog** of **images** in "Woman Work" tell you about the life of the speaker? Where do you think she lives? What do you learn from the images in "Daily" about the life of its speaker?

4. Both **catalog poems** list daily activities in a woman's life, but the tone of each poem is different—the speakers express different attitudes toward their lives. How would you describe the **tone** of each poem? Is it complaining? bitter? angry? resigned? accepting? loving? joyful? Is it something else? Cite details from each poem to explain the tone you hear in it.

5. The second through fifth stanzas of "Woman Work" use **apostrophe** (ə·päs′trə·fē)—they address, or speak directly to, someone or something. What things does this speaker address? What does she ask for?

6. The last two lines of "Daily" are not part of the poem's catalog; rather, they sum up the speaker's message. What do you think the poet is saying about daily work in these lines?

7. Both of these poems were written by women about their daily work. If the poems had been written by men and were called "Man Work," how might they be different?

Literary Skills
Analyze the characteristics of catalog poems.

Writing Skills
Write a catalog poem.

WRITING

My Day

Expand your notes for the Quickwrite on page 408 into a **catalog poem** that lists the things you do every day. Choose images that make your day come alive for the reader. You might want to imitate the structure of one of the poems in the following ways:

- If you imitate "Woman Work," begin with *I've got . . .* Then, list the things— such as "a bus to catch"—that you have to do.

- If you imitate "Daily," begin each line with *These/This . . .* Write, for example, "This heavy backpack I carry . . ."

How do you feel about your daily work? Try to express that feeling.

Woman with Basket (Mujer con Canasta) (1921) by Diego Rivera. Watercolor.

©Christie's Images/SuperStock.

ASSESSING

Assessment

■ *Holt Assessment: Literature, Reading, and Vocabulary*

Before You Read

in Just-

Make the Connection

Quickwrite ✏️

Jot down some of the things you associate with your favorite season of the year. Think of activities, sights, smells, tastes, sounds—even special people you see during that time of year.

Literary Focus

Fresh Images

An important part of a poet's job is to find **fresh images** that help us see the world in an unusual or original way. Notice how E. E. Cummings combines *mud* with *luscious* and *puddle* with *wonderful* to make brand-new images. These images remind us how much fun it was to play in the mud and splash in puddles when we were little kids.

SKILLS FOCUS

Literary Skills
Understand imagery, especially unusual and fresh imagery.

Meet the Writer

E. E. Cummings

Nobody-but-Himself

E. E. Cummings (1894–1962) began writing a poem a day when he was eight years old—and he kept at it until he was twenty-two. Multiply 365 poems a year by fourteen, and see what you get! Many of these poems were very short, and a lot of them weren't very good. However, if practice makes perfect, then Cummings must have been perfect—on some days anyhow.

Cummings once got a letter from a high school editor asking him what advice he had for young people who wanted to become poets. Cummings's reply tells us something about what poetry meant to him:

❝A poet is somebody who feels, and who expresses his feeling through words. This may sound easy. It isn't . . . [because] the moment you feel, you're nobody-but-yourself. To be nobody-but-yourself—in a world which is doing its best, night and day, to make you everybody else—means to fight the hardest battle which any human being can fight; and never stop fighting. . . . If, at the end of your first ten or fifteen years of fighting and working and feeling, you find you've written one line of one poem, you'll be very lucky indeed. . . . Does this sound dismal? It isn't. It's the most wonderful life on earth.❞

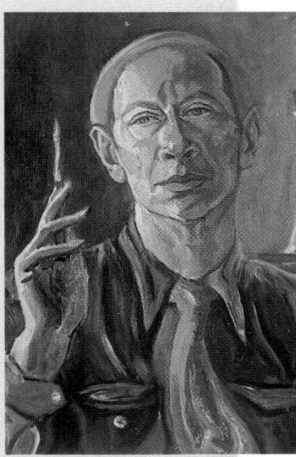

Self-Portrait by E. E. Cummings.
© Bettmann/CORBIS.

SKILLS FOCUS,
pp. 413–417

Grade-Level Skills

■ **Literary Skills**
Analyze various literary devices, including imagery.

Summary ⬆ *above grade level*

Spring has arrived, and children come rushing outside to enjoy nature. Cummings captures their enthusiasm and energy in the rhythm of his poem, alternately running words together and spacing them unusually far apart. In the playful spirit of childhood, he coins compound words that create fresh images for familiar scenes. The flood of youthful emotions, thawed by the warm weather, is a true miracle of spring. But perhaps a somewhat melancholy tone is introduced by the sound of the whistling balloonman, whose cry is repeated at the beginning, middle, and end of the poem.

GUIDED PRACTICE

Monitoring students' progress. Have students create a word web with "in Just-/spring" in the center circle. In the outer circles of the web, students should write, in their own words, some of the associations that the poet makes with this season.

in Just- **413**

RESOURCES: READING

Planning
■ *One-Stop Planner* CD-ROM with ExamView Test Generator

Differentiating Instruction
■ *Holt Reading Solutions*
■ *Supporting Instruction in Spanish*
■ *Audio CD Library, Selections and Summaries in Spanish*

Assessment
■ *Holt Assessment: Literature, Reading, and Vocabulary*
■ *One-Stop Planner* CD-ROM with ExamView Test Generator
■ *Holt Online Assessment*

Internet
■ go.hrw.com (Keyword: LE5 9-7)

■ *Elements of Literature Online*

Media
■ *Audio CD Library*
■ *Audio CD Library, Selections and Summaries in Spanish*
■ *Fine Art Transparencies*

in Just-

E. E. Cummings

A in Just-
    spring   when the world is mud-
luscious the little
lame balloonman

5 whistles   far   and wee
B
and eddieandbill come
running from marbles and
piracies and it's
spring

10 when the world is puddle-wonderful

the queer
old balloonman whistles
far   and   wee
and bettyandisbel come dancing

15 from hop-scotch and jump-rope and

it's
spring
and
    the

20   goat-footed
C
balloonMan   whistles
far
and
wee

414

A **Literary Focus**

❷ **Diction.** The poet chooses his words with great care. What two meanings does the word *Just* have? [Possible responses: *Just* means "barely" since the poem takes place in the very first moments of spring. *Just* means "only" in the sense that it is only at this time of the year, after being cooped up all winter long, that children are so happy and excited to be outside.]

B **Literary Focus**

❷ **Fresh images.** What do the images "mud-luscious" and "puddle-wonderful" make you think of? [Possible response: They conjure up early spring when it rains a lot and the ground is moist and full of new life.] **Why are these images fresh?** [Possible response: The images bestow a playfulness, even magical aura on mud and puddles, which often have negative associations.]

C **Content-Area Connections**

Literature: Allusions
By calling the balloonman "goat-footed," Cummings is alluding to Pan, a Greek deity, who was part animal, with goat's horns and hoofs. The words *panic* and *pandemonium* stem from his name, because he was considered a source of scary noises. Though ugly, Pan chased after nymphs and was a wonderful musician.

DIFFERENTIATING INSTRUCTION

English-Language Learners
The invented words and unusual word spacing of the poem may be visually intimidating. Have students listen to the recording from the *Audio CD Library* before they read the poem.

Advanced Learners
Enrichment. An artist as well as a poet, Cummings used the typography of his poems to enhance their meaning. The look of the poems may suggest to readers that the poems are difficult and abstract, but in fact their subject matter is often simple human feelings and basic human relationships.
Activity. Have students read other works by E. E. Cummings and select a single poem to read aloud to the class. Students may want to find an example that highlights Cummings's use of unusual typographical layouts and distribute photocopies of the poem before their reading.

Eyeglasses for the Mind

Stephen King

I did the Mike Wallace radio show in New York at the CBS building. We went in and the electric eye had a case of the hiccups. The door was one of these doors where you'd step on the pad and the door would slide open. And this door was almost pitching a fit. It was jerking back and forth, not closing or opening all the way.

And my feeling about that is that somebody else would look at that and say: "Oh, that door has the hiccups." Whereas a little kid would walk up to that door and might very well shrink away from even going near it. And say: "It wants to eat me, it's alive!" Children see things from a different perspective.

And in that sense I'm childlike. I looked at the door and I thought: "Gee, that would make a good story if that thing came alive and somebody walked up to it and CHUNG!" Which is a very childish sort of fantasy.

People respond to this perspective. It doesn't really die. It atrophies[1] and lies dormant.[2] And I get paid to show people that different perspective. It's like exercising a muscle, rather than letting it go slack. But I'll tell you a funny thing. There are writers who look like children. They've used this facility so much for so long that they literally look like children.

Ray Bradbury is sixty years old and he has the face of a child. You see it in the eyes a lot of the time. Isaac Singer has the eyes of a child in that old face. They look out of that old face and they're very young.

That's why people pay writers and artists. That's the only reason we're around. We're excess baggage. I can't even fix a pipe in my house when it freezes. I am a dickey bird on the back of civilization.

I have no skill that improves the quality of life in a physical sense at all. The only thing I can do is say: "Look here, this is the way you didn't look at it before. It's just a cloud to you, but look at it, doesn't it look like an elephant?" Somebody says: "Boy! it does look like an elephant!" And for that, people pay because they've lost all of it themselves.

You know, I'm like a person who makes eyeglasses for the mind.

—1979 interview from *Feast of Fear: Conversations with Stephen King*

---

1. **atrophies** (a′trə·fēz) *v.:* wastes away.
2. **dormant** (dôr′mənt) *adj.:* inactive.

in Just-   **415**

Connecting and Comparing Texts

Ask students to explain how this interview with Stephen King relates to the poem "in Just-" by E. E. Cummings. [Possible response: King's description of a writer as someone who retains the imaginative perspective of a child and helps readers to see things from this perspective readily applies to "in Just-." In that poem, Cummings helps readers reawaken to the enthusiasm and energy children feel with the onset of spring. He does this using creative word spacing and the coining of fresh new words.] Then, invite students to discuss King's characterization of the writer's role. Ask them to cite other examples, in addition to Cummings's poem, of how writers provide "eyeglasses for the mind" to reawaken the child's perspective in readers.

Response and Analysis

Reading Check

1. The season is spring. The weather is often rainy, and it is just turning warm.

2. Possible answers: running, playing marbles, playing pirates, hopscotch, and jumping rope.

3. The central figure is the balloonman.

4. He whistles. Children are attracted to the sound.

Thinking Critically

Possible Answers

5. "Mud-luscious" appeals to multiple senses. *Mud* invokes the senses of sight and touch; *luscious* invokes the sense of taste. "Whistles far and wee" appeals to the sense of hearing. "Puddle-wonderful" appeals to both sight and touch since readers are apt to imagine both the look and feel of splashing water. Together these images create a playful mood that inspires memories of childhood joy.

6. The unusual word spacing mimics the leaps and hops that children make while dancing and playing. The compounding of the children's names conveys the children's joy and emphasizes how they play together.

7. Like Pan, the balloonman makes music and provokes people to dance. Although the balloonman is a participant in the children's enjoyment of spring, if the children stop listening to the music and notice his strange appearance, they might be afraid of him.

8. Writers present a fantastic perspective of the world; with this goal in mind, writers provide "eyeglasses" for readers to see their perspective. With use of playful language, Cummings draws the reader into the world of his poem.

Response and Analysis

Reading Check

1. What season of the year is the **setting** for this poem? What's the weather like at that time of year?

2. List three activities that are mentioned in the poem.

3. Who is the central figure in this poem—the person who is mentioned three times?

4. What sound does this person make? Who is attracted to this sound?

Thinking Critically

5. What senses do the **images** "mud-luscious," "whistles far and wee," and "puddle-wonderful" appeal to? What impact do these images have on the poem's **mood,** or atmosphere?

6. Cummings is known for his unusual punctuation and arrangement of words. What are the children doing in the poem that matches the leaps and jumps of the words? Why might Cummings have made single words out of the names Eddie and Bill, Betty and Isbel?

7. Where does Pan, a famous goat-footed character from Greek mythology, enter this poem? Pan, who has the cloven hooves and shaggy legs of a goat, is a god of the woodlands and of merrymaking. He is usually shown playing a flute and leading shepherds in a dance. How is the balloon man like Pan?

8. According to Stephen King (see the **Connection** on page 415), what do writers do that is important? How do you interpret the title of his piece, "Eyeglasses for the Mind"? Do you think Cummings provides readers of "in Just-" with "eyeglasses for the mind"?

INTERNET

Projects and Activities

Keyword: LE5 9-7

Literary Skills
Analyze imagery, especially unusual and fresh imagery.

Writing Skills
Write an analysis of a poem. Write a poem containing fresh images.

Listening and Speaking Skills
Present an oral interpretation of a poem.

416 Collection 7 Poetry

WRITING

What Makes It Work?

Cummings is famous for his unusual style as well as for his fresh imagery. In a few paragraphs, analyze "in Just-," paying particular attention to its **imagery, word choice, mood,** and **style** (use of punctuation and word arrangement). Explain what you think makes Cummings so popular and unique.

▶ **Use "Analyzing a Poem," pages 480–487, for help with this assignment.**

A Seasonal Salute

Stephen King recognizes the importance of seeing things with imaginative eyes (see the **Connection** on page 415). Take your turn doing that. Write a **poem** that presents **fresh images** to describe your favorite season. Your notes for the Quickwrite on page 413 should give you a start. Be sure to avoid **clichés**—overused, burned-out expressions.

You might open your poem the way Cummings does: "in Just- [your season] when the world is . . ." Play with words, punctuation, and spacing to help readers share your pleasure in this season.

LISTENING AND SPEAKING

Say It Aloud

Prepare to read "in Just-" aloud. Decide where you will pause (watch those big spaces), when you will speed up, and when you might even draw the words out, as if you were singing. Then, read the poem to a partner.

DIFFERENTIATING INSTRUCTION

Learners Having Difficulty

Have students work in small groups to answer the Interpretation questions. If students have difficulty with question 7, give students more information about Pan. You may wish to draw a two-column chart on the chalkboard and list details about Pan on one side. Have students suggest details about the balloonman for the other side.

Advanced Learners

Enrichment. Extend question 7 by having students comment further on the balloonman's role in the poem. To stimulate discussion, ask the following questions:

• Which words used to describe the balloonman have unflattering connotations? How do these words affect the tone?

• What is the effect of capitalizing the letter *M* in the final "balloonMan"?

Vocabulary Development

Word Knowledge: Hunting Interesting Words

PRACTICE

Poets are always searching for words. Start your own **word bank** in which you enter unusual and interesting words. You can set your word bank up in a computer file or on index cards. To get started, leaf through an old magazine or newspaper, and choose just one page. Then, define and enter in your word bank any unusual or interesting words from the page. Map each word as shown in the chart below. Give its **meaning,** a **synonym,** and two sample sentences using the word. Use a **dictionary** and a **thesaurus** if you like.

Word: implacable
Meaning: relentless; can't be satisfied or stopped
Synonyms: inflexible, rigid
Sample sentences: • Robert is an implacable force on the student council. • We could not defeat the implacable enemy.

SKILLS FOCUS

Vocabulary Skills
Create a word bank for word study.

Vocabulary Development

Practice

Students' answers will vary. Check students' comprehension of the words in their individual word banks by examining how the student uses the word in a sample sentence. Sample word chart:

Word—pandemonium. *Meaning*—incredible disorder; extreme turmoil. *Synonyms*—tumult, chaos. *Uses*—Pandemonium broke out in the crowded restaurant when customers noticed smoke and flames escaping from the kitchen.

ASSESSING

Assessment
■ *Holt Assessment: Literature, Reading, and Vocabulary*

RETEACHING

For a lesson reteaching literary devices, see **Reteaching,** p. 979A.

Review Skills

■ Literary Skills

Understand and explain the characteristics of different forms of poetry, including haiku.

Summary  *at grade level*

These four haiku present images of nature and ambiguous messages that are typical of the genre. Chora's poem expresses the speaker's reaction to the toad that interrupts his work. Chiyo uses the image of a twining flower to suggest the bonds that can grow between neighbors. In Bashō's poem, a frog jumping into a pond transforms silence into sound. Issa sees the larger world reflected in the miniature eyes of a dragonfly.

PRETEACHING

Skills Starter

Motivate. Use *Visual Connections* to introduce students to the traditions of haiku. Show the videocassette segment "Images in Haiku" (Segment 7).

Before You Read

Haiku

Make the Connection

Quickwrite 🖉

Pick a special day of the year. Write down what you might **hear, see, taste, smell,** or **touch** on that day. Try to find images that reveal the way you might feel at a particular moment on that special day.

Literary Focus

Haiku

Haiku, the most famous form of Japanese poetry, can capture moments of life with the speed and precision of a snapshot. While snapshots usually record only the *outside* appearance of the moments, haiku can take you *inside* to reveal an insight or truth.

To unlock the meaning of a haiku, read each word or phrase carefully. Let yourself see, hear, smell, taste, or touch each single element of the original moment. Let these **images** serve as a starting point for your own thoughts and associations. In the end you will find yourself standing inside a special moment in someone else's life—whether the experience was captured three minutes ago or three hundred years ago.

In the Japanese language a **haiku**
- has seventeen syllables—five in lines 1 and 3; seven in line 2
- presents **images** from nature and from everyday life—usually two contrasting images
- often contains a seasonal word or symbol (*kigo*)
- presents a moment of discovery or enlightenment (*satori*)

The Original Language

Here, in the original Japanese with the English translation, is Bashō's haiku from the next page. (*Ya* is a word frequently used in haiku to mean something like *Lo!* in English, which means "Look!" or "See!" Some translators indicate it with a colon, since it suggests a kind of equation.)

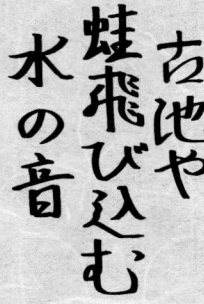

Furu	ike	ya
old	pond	:
Kawazu	tobikomu	
frog	jump in	
Mizu	no	oto
water	of	sound

SKILLS FOCUS

Literary Skills
Understand the characteristics of haiku.

Morning Glories (detail) (19th century) by Suzuki Kiitsu. Japanese painted screen.
Color and gold leaf on paper (6′ high × 13′ wide).
The Metropolitan Museum of Art, New York, Seymour Fund, 1954 (54.69.1).

Haiku

Get out of my road
and allow me to plant these
bamboos, Mr. Toad.
　　　　　　—Miura Chora

The old pond;
A frog jumps in:
Sound of water.
—Matsuo Bashō

A morning glory
Twined round the bucket:
I will ask my neighbor for water.
　　　　　　—Chiyo

A dragonfly!
The distant hills
Reflected in his eyes.
　　　　—Kobayashi Issa

Haiku　**419**

VIEWING THE ART

Suzuki Kiitsu (1796–1858) captures the fleeting moment in which the blossoms of morning glories open.

Activity. Invite students to draw connections between the artwork and the haiku. [Possible responses: Both freeze a moment in nature; both highlight simple natural images.]

DIRECT TEACHING

A Literary Focus

❓ **Haiku.** In haiku, comparisons are not stated directly. What comparison is suggested here? [The relationship between neighbors is likened to the morning glory's wrapping itself around the bucket.]

B Literary Focus

Haiku. Traditional haiku contain *kigo,* or words associated with a particular season. A Japanese reader, for example, would know that *snow* indicates winter and that evening *showers* mean that it is summer. Here, the word *frog* suggests spring.

C Literary Focus

Haiku. Punctuation in a haiku—colons, dashes, and exclamation marks—indicates a shift in subject or mood. Ask students to practice reading the haiku aloud, capturing the change in the speaker's mood after the surprise of seeing the dragonfly.

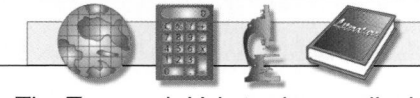

CONTENT-AREA CONNECTIONS

Literature: Haiku

Haiku remains extremely popular in Japan. Newspapers that publish haiku columns receive hundreds of new submissions. Magazines and even television shows focus on the haiku form.

Bashō's haiku of the "old pond" has probably received more critical comment than any other Japanese language poem. Discuss these observations with your students:

- The Zen monk Hakuin always talked about the sound of one hand clapping. The sound of water in this haiku is also like that: It is there, and it is not there.
- There is a sudden shift from stillness (no sound) to movement (sound), and then there's a return from movement (sound) to anticipated stillness (no sound).
- The poem is like a flash of lightning illuminating a quiet corner.

Asian Prints. The Metropolitan Museum of Art, New York, Rogers Fund, 1931 (JIB 81.10).

GUIDED PRACTICE

Monitoring students' progress. Guide the class in answering these comprehension questions.

Short Answer

1. What animal is on the road? [a toad]

2. What does the dragonfly reflect? [the hills]

3. What does the morning glory twine around? [a bucket]

4. What sound is heard? [a splash of water]

Meet the Writer

Background. Matsuo Bashō traveled extensively and wrote accounts of his journeys, which are as remarkable as his poetry. He viewed the short syllable count of haiku as an advantage, not a restriction, saying, "Is there any good in saying everything?"

For Independent Reading

- Students who enjoyed the haiku selections might read *The Essential Haiku: Versions of Bashō, Buson, and Issa,* edited and translated by Robert Haas.

- Haiku fans will appreciate seeing how haiku has evolved. *Haiku World: An International Poetry Almanac,* edited by William J. Higginson, presents over a thousand haiku by poets from fifty countries.

VIEWING THE ART

Katsushika Hokusai (1760–1849) presents his own twist on the Japanese art of paper folding, origami. Ask students, "What is the artist imagining here?" [Possible response: The sheets of paper become living birds.]

Meet the Writers

> Miura Chora
> Chiyo
> Matsuo Bashō
> Kobayashi Issa

Captured Moments

Miura Chora (1729–1780), like most writers of haiku, drew his images from the ordinary objects and activities of daily life—in this case, planting bamboo shoots. In Japanese every haiku has exactly seventeen syllables, but English translators can't always achieve that. Count the number of syllables on page 419, and see if this translator has performed a miracle of translation.

Chiyo (1703–1775) is the most celebrated of the women writers of haiku. Some critics say her poems are too explicit and lack the mystery of true haiku. They want their haiku to be more subtle, indirect, and suggestive—like the classical Bashō poem on page 419. Yet Chiyo's admirers think that some people mistake haziness in haiku for profound thought.

Matsuo Bashō (1644–1694) is considered the developer of the haiku form as well as its greatest master. Bashō was a deeply spiritual man who became a Zen monk in his later years. His haiku show a zest for every speck of life—a sense that nothing in this world is unimportant.

Kobayashi Issa (1763–1827) had a very sad life. Despite his poverty and the fact that he saw all his beloved children die, Issa's extraordinarily simple poems are full of human tenderness and wry humor.

A Magician Turning Paper into Cranes (detail) (1819) from the *Manga* (a book of humorous sketches) by Katsushika Hokusai.

DIFFERENTIATING INSTRUCTION

Advanced Learners
Enrichment. After reading the four poems, students may be interested in learning more about the history of haiku. Explain to students that haiku evolved in seventeenth-century Japan from long multiverse poems called *renga.* Poets detached the first three lines from these longer poems, transforming them into independent structures.

Activity. Have students work in small groups to research haiku, its relation to other forms of Japanese poetry, and its most noted composers. Students can share the information they find by posting it on a classroom bulletin board, including information about individual poets, a sample of their poetry, and examples of other related poetry forms.

Response and Analysis

Reading Check

1. These haiku are, of course, translated. Which of the four **haiku** follow the rule of five syllables in lines 1 and 3, seven syllables in line 2?

2. Describe two **images** you see in each haiku.

3. Which haiku relies most on the sense of hearing?

Thinking Critically

4. What season of the year do you think each haiku describes? Which word or words give you a clue?

5. Haiku often balance two **contrasting images.** In Chora's haiku, for example, the toad in the road, probably resting, contrasts with the human, busy planting his bamboo. What contrasting images can you find in the other three haiku?

6. Think about the person who is speaking in each haiku. Put yourself in each person's shoes, one by one. Consider:

- In Chora's haiku, do you wait for the toad to move, or do you poke it?

- In Chiyo's haiku, do you ever use that bucket for water again?

- In Bashō's haiku, what might you be doing before the frog jumps in?

- In Issa's haiku, for how long are you able to see the hills?

WRITING

A Special-Day Haiku

Write a **haiku** celebrating the special day you made notes about for the Quickwrite on page 418. You should limit your haiku to three lines, but it is not necessary to use just seventeen syllables—unless you want a challenge! Keep in mind that a haiku usually does the following things:

- It brings two images together, usually for contrast.

- It contains a word describing the season or weather.

- It presents a moment of discovery.

Detail of frogs and a hare from the *Choju Giga* scrolls (late 12th to mid-13th century).

Burstein Collection / CORBIS.

SKILLS FOCUS

Literary Skills
Analyze the characteristics of haiku.

Writing Skills
Write a haiku.

Haiku   421

Response and Analysis

Thinking Critically

4. Possible answers: *Chora's haiku*—spring, as this is the season when people plant things. *Bashō's haiku*—spring, as this is the season when a frog is most active. *Chiyo's haiku*—summer, as this is the season when the morning glory is fully grown. *Issa's haiku*—spring or summer, as these are the seasons when one would most likely see a dragonfly.

5. Possible answers: *Bashō's haiku*—the lively motion of a jumping frog with the stillness of a pond. *Chiyo's haiku*—an immobile plant with an active human. *Issa's haiku*—a tiny dragonfly with immense landscape features (hills).

6. Possible answers:
   - wait and appreciate the moment
   - not until the flower dies
   - taking a nap
   - a moment before the dragonfly flies away

Assessment

■ *Holt Assessment: Literature, Reading, and Vocabulary*

Reading Check

1. Chora's haiku follows the rule of five syllables in lines 1 and 3, seven syllables in line 2.

2. Possible answers: *Chora's haiku*—a road, bamboo trees, a toad. *Bashō's haiku*—a pond, a frog, a splashing sound. *Chiyo's haiku*—a morning glory, a bucket. *Issa's haiku*—a dragonfly, the reflection of hills in the dragonfly's eyes.

3. Bashō's haiku relies most on the sense of hearing.

Grade-Level Skills

■ **Literary Skills**
Understand and explain the characteristics of different forms of poetry, including sonnets.

Summary  *above grade level*

In Robert Frost's English sonnet "Once by the Pacific," the speaker describes the awesome power of the ocean as waves crash against the shore. The force of the waves and the implication of a coming storm make the speaker think of the end of the world. In a biblical allusion to God's words of "Let there be light" at creation, the speaker warns that the world may end at God's command to "Put out the Light."

Before You Read

Once by the Pacific

Make the Connection
"Let There Be Light"
In the Bible, when God creates the universe, God says, "Let there be light" (Genesis 1:3). After each stage of creation, the Bible says, "And God saw that it was good." Keep these words in mind as you read Robert Frost's vision of an event that is the opposite of creation.

Literary Focus
Sonnet
Robert Frost loved writing sonnets because he enjoyed the challenge of fitting his thoughts into a very strict form. Here are the rules for the sonnet:

- It has fourteen lines.
- It follows a regular rhyme pattern.
- It is usually written in **iambic pentameter.**

An **iamb** is an unstressed syllable followed by a stressed one (da DAH), as in the word *before*. Writing an iambic line isn't as hard as you might think because the iamb is common in ordinary English speech:

Amanda wore her favorite pair of jeans.

Pentameter means there are five stressed syllables, or beats, in each line— *penta* is Greek for "five," and *meter* is Greek for "measure." (Occasional variations help keep the rhythm from becoming monotonous.) Here are lines from two sonnets written in iambic pentameter. Read the lines aloud to hear their beat.

Shall I compare thee to a summer's day?
—William Shakespeare

The shattered water made a misty din.
—Robert Frost

There are two traditional types of sonnet. In the **Italian,** or **Petrarchan, sonnet** the first eight lines (the **octave**) pose a problem, which is responded to in the last six lines (the **sestet**). In the **English,** or **Shakespearean, sonnet,** three four-line units are followed by a **couplet,** or two-line unit. Some modern poets, like Frost, create their own types of sonnet.

For biographies of Robert Frost, see pages 316 and 442.

INTERNET
More About Robert Frost
Keyword: LE5 9-7

SKILLS FOCUS

Literary Skills
Understand the characteristics of different types of sonnets.

Once by the Pacific

Robert Frost

The shattered water made a misty din.
Great waves looked over others coming in,
And thought of doing something to the shore
That water never did to land before.
5 The clouds were low and hairy in the skies,
Like locks blown forward in the gleam of eyes.
You could not tell, and yet it looked as if
The shore was lucky in being backed by cliff,
The cliff in being backed by continent;
10 It looked as if a night of dark intent
Was coming, and not only a night, an age.
Someone had better be prepared for rage.
There would be more than ocean-water broken
Before God's last *Put out the Light* was spoken.

A Literary Focus

❓ Sonnet. How can you tell that this poem is a sonnet? [It has four-teen lines; it rhymes; it is written in iambic pentameter.]

B Literary Focus

❓ Personification. In these lines, what forces of nature seem to be human and alive? [Possible responses: The waves seem human as the larger waves look over the others and think about taking violent action. The "hairy" clouds seem alive as "the gleam" of their "eyes" seems to foretell the evil that the waves contemplate.]

C Reading Skills

❓ Making inferences. What backing do the shore and cliff have? [Possible responses: They are backed by the entire continent; they have strong, secure backing.] **What does the need for this backing imply?** [It implies that the waves are very powerful and threatening.]

D Literary Focus

❓ Mood. What is the mood of this poem? [Possible responses: somber; pessimistic; awed and fearful; apocalyptic.] **What words and images help reveal the poem's mood?** [Possible responses: "The clouds were low and hairy"; "a night of dark intent"; "better be prepared for rage"; "more than ocean-water broken"; and "God's last *Put out the Light.*"]

DIFFERENTIATING INSTRUCTION

Learners Having Difficulty
Pair these learners with more fluent readers to read the sonnet and review the images and actions described in this sophisticated poem. Encourage pairs to break down the images one by one and describe or rephrase them in their own words. For instance, "shattered water" could be rephrased as "crashing waves." Have student pairs also review the characteristics that make this poem an English sonnet. You may wish to make sure that all students understand iambic pentameter. Give each pair a photocopy of the poem, and monitor students as they scan several of the lines. As you play the audio CD recording of the poem, you might have students gently tap out the beat with their index fingers.

SKILLS FOCUS, pp. 424–427

Review Skills

■ **Literary Skills**
Understand and explain the characteristics of different forms of poetry, including lyric poems.

Summary ⇧ *above grade level*

In the lyric poem "Country Scene," Vietnamese poet Hồ Xuân Hương describes a river in the rural countryside. The fading sound of a tolling bell reminds the speaker of the impermanence of love, and she laments that "only poetry lasts."

PRETEACHING

Selection Starter

Build background. Invite students to share what they already know about Vietnam. If necessary, tell students that Vietnam is a country in Southeast Asia, and point it out on a map. Explain that historically Vietnam has been an agricultural country. Farmers grow rice in its river deltas. Fishing is also an important part of rural Vietnamese life.

Before You Read

Country Scene

Make the Connection

Lasting Impressions

In "Country Scene" the poet, like many other poets throughout the centuries, expresses her views about what lasts—and what doesn't last. Think about nature, your own life, and the world around you. Which things are permanent? Which things are fleeting?

Literary Focus

Lyric Poem

Robert Frost's "Once by the Pacific" (page 423) is a sonnet, which is a type of lyric poem. There are many kinds of lyric poem. In general, a **lyric poem** is a short poem that expresses a speaker's thoughts or feelings. In ancient Greece, lyric poems were sung to the music of a stringed instrument called a *lyre*. Today we call the words to all types of songs *lyrics*.

In its original Vietnamese, "Country Scene," the lyric poem that follows, is called a *lu-shih*. The English translation cannot begin to show how challenging *lu-shih* is to write. Vietnamese is a tonal language, and the tones in a poem must fall at certain places in each seven-syllable line. Every *lu-shih* poem has eight lines, with rhymes usually at the end of the first, second, fourth, sixth, and eighth lines.

While we may not be able to appreciate the complexity of this *lu-shih* poem in its English translation, we can certainly think about its message and share the beauty of its imagery.

SKILLS FOCUS

Literary Skills Understand the characteristics of lyric poems.

The Original Language

Below, at the left, is "Country Scene" in its original language, Nom, which is written in an ancient Vietnamese script. Below, at the right, is a translation in modern Vietnamese. For more information about these texts, see Meet the Writer on page 426.

即 景

濕 洸 頭 崇 頓 噴 湄
妬 埃 [illegible] 特 景 蕭 踈
撑 菩 古 樹 嶟 [illegible] 傘
[illegible] 撮 長 江 滂 朗 詞
[illegible] 牧 呦 [illegible] 沔 曠 野
[illegible] 漁 扛 [illegible] [illegible] 平 沙
鐘 埃 組 緌 邊 箕 佐
殃 [illegible] 鍾 情 沒 襊 詩

Tức cảnh

Thấp thoáng đầu ghềnh lún phún mưa
Đố ai vẽ được cảnh tiêu sơ
Xanh om cổ thụ chon von tán
Trắng toát tràng giang phẳng lặng tờ
Còi mục thét lừng miền khoáng dã
Lưới ngư giang gió bãi bình sa
Chuông ai đất nối bên kia tá
Ương lở chung tình một túi thơ.

DIFFERENTIATING INSTRUCTION

English-Language Learners
Some students may have trouble with some of the vocabulary in this poem. If necessary, pair students with fluent English speakers to define such words as *desolate, canopy, shepherd,* and *tolling.*

Special Education Students
For lessons designed for special education students, see *Holt Reading Solutions.*

Country Scene

Hồ Xuân Hu'o'ng

translated by John Balaban

The waterfall plunges in mist.
Who can describe this desolate scene:

the long white river sliding through
the emerald shadows of the ancient canopy  **A**

. . . a shepherd's horn echoing in the valley,
fishnets stretched to dry on sandy flats. **B**

A bell is tolling, fading, fading
just like love. Only poetry lasts. **C**

Monitoring students' progress. Guide the class in answering these comprehension questions. Direct students to locate words and passages in the poems that support their responses.

True-False

Once by the Pacific

1. The stormy ocean becomes calm and serene by the end of the poem. [F]
2. The speaker is awed by the ocean's power. [T]

Country Scene

3. People fish on the river described in this poem. [T]
4. The speaker believes that poetry fades but love endures. [F]

Meet the Writer

Hồ Xuân Hu'o'ng

The Mysterious Spring Essence

The Vietnamese poet Hồ Xuân Hu'o'ng (c. 1770s–1820s) lived in a time of political turmoil and social collapse. South Vietnam, aided by foreign powers, was at war with the north. Rulers battled for power while ordinary people struggled to stay alive through decades of chaos and destruction.

Sound familiar? It did to John Balaban, an American conscientious objector who, during another war in Vietnam two centuries later, brought medical care to wounded Vietnamese children. Along with supplies he brought a tape recorder to capture the classic poems he heard the villagers recite. Many of their favorites, they told him, had been written by the great poet Hồ Xuân Hu'o'ng, whose name means "spring essence."

Little is known about Hồ. She is thought to have been born in north central Vietnam, to the "second wife," or concubine, of a scholar. She became a concubine as well, to an official she ridiculed in a poem as Mr. Toad. At that time, Vietnamese women had little status. Yet Hồ, who often attacked male authority in her writing, earned fame and admiration instead of punishment—a mark of how deeply the people of her country loved poetry.

Today only a few dozen people know how to read Nom, the traditional Vietnamese writing system Hồ used. Balaban hopes to turn that situation around. His collection of Hồ's poetry, *Spring Essence*, includes her poems in both the modern Vietnamese and the Nom scripts next to his English translations. It is the first time the ancient script, which was originally reproduced by woodblock, has ever come off a printing press. (The Nom and modern Vietnamese texts of "Country Scene" on page 424 are reproduced from *Spring Essence*.)

Vietnamese clay plate (16th century).
Musée des Arts Asiatiques-Guimet, Paris. © Erich Lessing/Art Resource, New York.

DEVELOPING FLUENCY

Paired activity. Have students work in pairs to practice reading aloud either of these poems. If they choose "Once by the Pacific," remind them to moderate their reading so that the poem's rhyme and iambic pentameter do not create a sing-song effect. If they choose "Country Scene," suggest that they think of ways to communicate the speaker's mood. Ask students if the speaker in the poem is happy or sad. Once pairs have had practice time, invite interested students to perform for the class.

Response and Analysis

Once by the Pacific

Reading Check

1. Where is the speaker in "Once by the Pacific" standing as he observes the ocean? What are the waves doing?

2. According to lines 10–11, what do the wild waves make the speaker think of?

3. Look at the last two lines of the **sonnet,** the concluding **couplet.** What dreadful thoughts is the speaker sharing with us there?

Thinking Critically

4. What **images** in lines 1–4 help you picture the waves—and even hear them?

5. What **images** in lines 5–6 help you picture the clouds?

6. Whose "rage" is described in line 12? What could cause that rage?

7. Look back at Make the Connection on page 422. How does the last line of the sonnet differ from God's words of creation in the Bible?

8. What do you think the **theme,** or message, of this sonnet is?

9. Look at how this poem is structured. What characteristics of a **sonnet** does it have? Is it an **Italian sonnet** or an **English sonnet,** or is it a modern variation on the sonnet form? Explain your answer.

Country Scene

Reading Check

1. What is this speaker looking at? What does she hear?

2. What does the speaker think of when she hears the bell?

Thinking Critically

3. According to this speaker, what outlasts both nature and love? In your opinion, which is more lasting—love or poetry?

4. How would you describe the **tone** of this **lyric**? Is it a pessimistic poem or a positive poem? Cite details from the poem to support your answer.

Comparing Poems

Fill out a chart like the one below to help you compare these two **lyrics:**

	Frost	Hồ
What is the speaker observing?		
What **images** create the scene?		
How does the speaker feel?		
What lesson does the speaker draw from the experience?		
What is the **tone** of the poem?		

SKILLS FOCUS

Literary Skills
Analyze the characteristics of sonnets and lyric poems. Compare two poems.

Once by the Pacific

Reading Check

1. on a cliff; crashing against the shore
2. a night with angry or evil intentions
3. thoughts of the world's end

Thinking Critically

4. Possible answers: "shattered water"; "misty din"; "great waves looked over others."

5. Possible answers: "low and hairy"; "like locks blown forward."

6. Possible answers: The speaker describes God's or nature's rage, caused by human acts.

7. God's words of creation are "Let there be light," while the last line of the sonnet are words of destruction, "Put out the Light."

8. Possible answers: All life on earth could someday end. God and nature are more powerful than human beings.

Response and Analysis

9. The poem is a sonnet: it has fourteen lines in iambic pentameter and a regular rhyme pattern. It is an English sonnet because it has three four-line units followed by a couplet.

Country Scene

Reading Check

1. She sees a river and waterfall in the woods. She hears a shepherd's horn and a tolling bell.

2. She thinks of love and then poetry.

Thinking Critically

3. The speaker thinks poetry outlasts both nature and love. Possible answers: Poetry lasts longest; love can last a lifetime, but a poem can last for centuries. Love lasts longest; poetry is ephemeral but love is eternal.

4. Possible answers: The poem is pessimistic; the speaker feels that love is always "fading, fading." The poem is positive; the speaker feels that beautiful scenes and emotions can be captured forever because "poetry lasts."

Comparing Poems

Possible chart:

Frost. Speaker observes—waves crashing on shore. *Images*—waves, mist, cliff, clouds, night. *Speaker's feelings*—threatened, awed. *Speaker's lesson*—The world is powerless against God's rage. *Poem's tone*—somber.

Hồ. Speaker observes—waterfall, river scenes. *Images*—waterfall, mist, river, forest, nets. *Speaker's feelings*—sad but empowered. *Speaker's lesson*—Love fades; poetry endures. *Poem's tone*—sad but hopeful.

Assessment

■ *Holt Assessment: Literature, Reading, and Vocabulary*

Grade-Level Skills

■ **Literary Skills**

Analyze various literary devices, including figures of speech, such as similes, metaphors, and personification.

Review Skills

■ **Literary Skills**

Identify the literary devices that define a writer's style.

**Elements of Literature:
Figures of Speech**

On the chalkboard, write the names of the types of figurative language discussed in the essay: simile, direct metaphor, implied metaphor, and personification. Point out that students probably encounter each of these figures of speech every time they watch the news. When a sportscaster says that an athlete's "ability is beginning to blossom," this is an implied metaphor, likening the athlete to a flower. When the sportscaster calls the athlete a "warrior," that is a direct metaphor. A weatherperson uses personification when describing the sun as "smiling down on us" and simile when describing March as "in like a lion, out like a lamb."

Ask volunteers to come up with their own examples for each of the terms. Have other students explain the connection that is being made in each example.

Elements of Literature

Figures of Speech *by* John Malcolm Brinnin

SEEING CONNECTIONS

One of the ways that poets play with words is by using figurative language—expressions that put aside literal meanings in favor of imaginative connections. A **figure of speech** is always based on a comparison, and it is not literally true. If your older brother says to you, "Listen, I'm going to give you a piece of my mind," you don't say, "OK, I'll bring a plate to put it on." You understand that he is using a figure of speech, that he's going to tell you what he's *really* thinking and that it's not going to be nice.

Figurative language can be a kind of shorthand. While it can take a lot of words to express an idea in literal terms, the same idea can be communicated instantly by a figure of speech. Think of all the words you'd have to use to explain literally what these common expressions mean: "My heart is broken." "The check bounced." "Chill out."

Figures of Speech in Everyday Language

Many figures of speech that were once fresh and original have been completely absorbed into our everyday language. We use them without realizing that they aren't literally true. When we think about our language, in fact, we realize that figures of speech are the foundation of thousands of expressions.

When we refer to the "roof of the mouth" or the "arm of the chair" or the "foot of the bed," we are using figurative language. In each case we are imaginatively relating a part of the body to something that has nothing to do with the body.

Even the languages of science and business are based on figures of speech. Stockbrokers talk about "the market crash." Our newest technological field, computer science, has its own figures of speech in terms such as *virus, window,* and *mouse.*

Similes: "X Is Like Y"

A simile is the simplest form of figurative language. In a **simile** two dissimilar things are compared using a word such as *like, as, than,* or *resembles.* "The moon shines *like* a fifty-cent piece." "Eva's eyes are *as* glassy *as* marbles." "Lucy feels lighter *than* a grasshopper."

Here is a poet who looked at an ordinary fork and thought of a simile:

Fork

This strange thing must have crept
Right out of hell.
It resembles a bird's foot
Worn around the cannibal's neck.
As you hold it in your hand,
As you stab with it into a piece of meat,
It is possible to imagine the rest
    of the bird:
Its head which like your fist
Is large, bald, beakless, and blind.
                              —Charles Simic

Metaphors: "X Is Y"

Similes are easily recognized because of their connectives (*like, as, than, resembles*): "You eat like a pig!" When the connective is omitted, we have a metaphor: "You're a pig!" A **metaphor,** then, is a comparison between two unlike things in which one

INTERNET
More About
Figures of
Speech
Keyword: LE5 9-7

**SKILLS
FOCUS**

Literary Skills
Understand
figures of
speech,
including similes,
metaphors, and
personification.

DIFFERENTIATING INSTRUCTION

**Learners Having Difficulty
Figurative language.** Guide students in constructing their own examples of similes, metaphors, and personification. On the chalkboard, write several fill-in-the-blank sentences like those shown below.

• Love is a _____.

• She has a mind like a _____.

• The wind _____ (suggest a human quality or action).

Have students suggest possible words and phrases to complete each sentence. Discuss the type of figurative language that is created through each of the students' responses.

thing becomes another thing without the use of a word such as *like* or *as*. The difference between a metaphor and a simile is a matter of emphasis. In a simile the two things remain separate, but in a metaphor they are united.

A metaphor can be direct or implied. A **direct metaphor** directly compares the two things using a verb such as *is*. An **implied metaphor** implies or suggests the comparison between the two things without stating it directly. If we say, "The city is a sleeping woman," we are using a direct metaphor. If we say, "The city sleeps peacefully," we use an implied metaphor. Both metaphors identify a city that has its lights out with a person who has fallen into the darkness of sleep.

Metaphor is the most flexible type of figurative language. It is a means by which all experience can be imaginatively connected.

Personification: Making the World Human

Personification is a special kind of metaphor in which human qualities are given to something that is not human—an animal, an object, or even an idea. Explain the personification you find in each of these headlines:

- Every Computer "Whispers" Its Secrets
- China Now a Struggling Giant
- White House Digs In Its Heels on Budget Issue

When we say that a cough is stubborn or a computer is user-friendly or love is blind, we are using a kind of personification. Personification is yet another example of how we use our imaginations to give meaning to the whole nonhuman world.

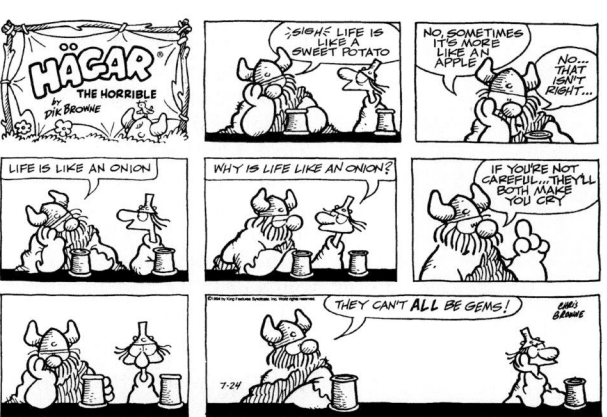

Reprinted with special permission of King Features Syndicate.

 **Practice**

Figures of speech are widely used. Look through a newspaper or magazine, including the advertisements, and gather at least six figures of speech. Look for examples of **similes, metaphors,** and **personification.**

Practice

Possible responses:

Similes—The storm is charging the coast like a bull; for lawmakers the issue stank like a festering wound.

Metaphors—The quarterback was a real general on the field; the tennis player ruled the court; the president is the lead actor on the world stage.

Personification—The ball limped into the goal; luck smiled on the defending champion; bad weather will rear its ugly head.

Apply

Ask students to look at the cartoon on p. 429 and examine each of the comparisons the main character makes. Then, have them suggest other possibilities for the simile "Life is like _____." The simile can be of their own creation or one that they are familiar with from another source. Encourage students to discuss the possible meanings of each simile they create.

Advanced Learners

Acceleration. Use the following activity with advanced learners to help them analyze ways poets use personification and figures of speech to evoke readers' emotions.

Activity. Present students with a list of emotions, such as fear, surprise, sadness, contentment, and envy. Then, ask students to find a poem that evokes one of these emotions in the reader. Have them identify examples of figurative language from the poem that help create this emotional response. As an extension, challenge students to write their own short poems, using simile, metaphor, or personification to evoke a specific emotional response.

SKILLS FOCUS, pp. 430–431

Grade-Level Skills

■ **Literary Skills**

Analyze figurative language, including similes.

Summary ⬌ *at grade level*

> A long, red car lies stalled in the street with its hood up and its radio blaring. The speaker compares the car to a shark and its current driver to a fisherman.

DIRECT TEACHING

Ⓐ Literary Focus

❓ **Simile.** Point out that the car is compared not simply to a shark but to a prize shark. What might this mean? [Possible response: A prize shark is one that has been sought after by fishermen; the car has been "won" or "captured" and is highly valued.] Then, write the following sentence on the chalkboard, and invite volunteers to complete the comparison: "A car is like a ———." Help students determine whether each response is a simple, literal comparison or a simile.

Meet the Writer

Background. Martín Espada writes primarily in English, but he often laces his poetry with a few Spanish words. He says: "I do that a lot so you will find Spanish words and phrases sprinkled throughout my poems. . . . It happens because there's a good reason for it to happen aesthetically."

Tiburón

Make the Connection

Quickwrite 🖉

Think of something manufactured. It can be something large, like a snowmobile or a jet plane, or something small, like a pencil sharpener or a cell phone. Jot down some notes about how this item **looks, sounds,** and **smells** (if it has a smell) and what it **feels** like. Does it remind you of anything?

Literary Focus

SKILLS FOCUS

Literary Skills
Understand similes.

Similes

When you compare two *unlike* things using a specific word of comparison such as *like, as,* or *resembles,* you are using a **simile.** A simile is much more imaginative than a simple, literal comparison. If you say, "That car is as red as an apple," you are expressing a simple comparison. It is a literal truth that the color of the apple and the color of the car are similar. If, however, you say, "That car is as sweet and delicious as an apple," you are using a simile. The car cannot be bitten into as an apple can, and it certainly would not taste delicious if you could eat it. What the simile does is communicate to us how much you love that red car.

The following poem is based on one simile. The simile is first suggested in the title, which means "shark" in Spanish.

Tiburón

Martín Espada

East 116th
and a long red car
stalled with the hood up
roaring salsa
Ⓐ 5   like a prize shark
mouth yanked open
and down in the stomach
the radio
of the last fisherman
10   still tuned
to his lucky station

RESOURCES: READING

Planning
■ *One-Stop Planner* CD-ROM with ExamView Test Generator

Differentiating Instruction
■ *Holt Reading Solutions*
■ *Supporting Instruction in Spanish*
■ *Audio CD Library, Selections and Summaries in Spanish*

Assessment
■ *Holt Assessment: Literature, Reading, and Vocabulary*
■ *One-Stop Planner* CD-ROM with ExamView Test Generator
■ *Holt Online Assessment*

Internet
■ go.hrw.com (Keyword: LE5 9-7)

■ *Elements of Literature Online*

Media
■ *Audio CD Library*
■ *Audio CD Library, Selections and Summaries in Spanish*

Meet the Writer

Martín Espada

"You Can't Tell a Poet to Shut Up"

Lots of poets earn their living by teaching English at a college, as Martín Espada (1957–   ) does. Not many others have also worked as a gas-station attendant, nightclub bouncer, monkey caretaker in a laboratory, radio journalist in Nicaragua, encyclopedia salesperson, and lawyer.

Martín Espada was born and raised in Brooklyn, New York, the son of Puerto Rican parents. He dropped out of college, discouraged by literature classes that taught only works by white male authors. Then a friend introduced him to Latin American revolutionary poetry, and he realized that his kind of writing—politically charged as well as deeply personal—did have its own tradition. He completed college, and he went on to law school. As both a lawyer and a poet he tries to speak for those who cannot speak for themselves.

Espada's poems often cause controversy, but he always speaks his mind. He says,

The worst thing you can say to a poet is 'Don't say that.' You can't tell a poet to shut up. That just makes us want to say it all the more. 🙴

Response and Analysis

Reading Check

1. Describe the scene in the poem.
2. Where does the salsa music come from?

Thinking Critically

3. Think about the **images** in this poem. What can you see? hear?
4. This poem is based on a **simile** comparing a car to a shark. In what ways is this car like a shark?
5. What do you think has happened to the "last fisherman"? Why is his station "lucky"?

WRITING

It Looks Like . . .

Write a **poem** about the manufactured item you described in your Quickwrite notes. Use at least one **simile** that compares your subject to something that is alive. Include **images** that appeal to at least two senses. Will you title your poem after the subject of your poem ("A Long Red Car") or after the living thing you compare it to ("Shark")? ✏️

Literary Skills
Analyze similes.

Writing Skills
Write a poem containing similes and images.

Tiburón   **431**

INDEPENDENT PRACTICE

Response and Analysis

Reading Check

1. A red car is stalled on the street with its hood open and radio playing.
2. from the car's radio

Thinking Critically

3. Possible answers: *Sight*—the long red car; the open hood; a shark with a gaping mouth; the dial of a car radio. *Sound*—salsa music blasting from the radio.
4. The car is long, sleek, and threatening as is a shark; the car's open hood is like a shark's mouth; with the driver beneath its hood, the car resembles a shark that is being examined by a fisherman.
5. The driver may be working on the car; the driver may have left to get assistance; the driver may be lucky to have "hooked" such a fine vehicle.

ASSESSING

Assessment
■ *Holt Assessment: Literature, Reading, and Vocabulary*

RETEACHING

For a lesson reteaching literary devices, see **Reteaching,** p. 979A. For another selection to teach figures of speech, see *The Holt Reader,* Collection 7.

DIFFERENTIATING INSTRUCTION

English-Language Learners
The Spanish words in the poem may be especially confusing to non-Spanish-speaking students who are learning English. Make sure all students know that *tiburón* (the word that is the title of the poem) means "shark" in English and that *salsa* can mean a particular style of music, as it does here, or a type of spicy sauce.

Grade-Level Skills

■ **Literary Skills**
Analyze figurative language, including similes and metaphors.

■ **Reading Skills**
Use strategies for reading a poem.

Summary *at grade level*

Drawing on the memory of his mother's technique for making won tons, the speaker makes his own for the first time. A variety of images and figurative language is used to describe each step in the process. The spoonfuls of filling are "the color of the fat sun in October," and the won tons themselves are twice likened metaphorically to flowers. While the speaker admits his own won tons are not perfect, he takes pride in his accomplishment. At the poem's end, he has to decide how many he wants to save for later consumption.

PRETEACHING

Selection Starter

Motivate. Ask students if they've ever tried to perform a new task solely from memory—relying on mental images of how someone else did the thing they wanted to do. Was doing so difficult? Were they successful? Have students share examples with their classmates.

Before You Read

Folding Won Tons In

Make the Connection

Quickwrite ✏️
Think of something that another person taught you to do, such as dance, mow the lawn, rock climb, play a game, surf the Internet, build a campfire, or cook a special food. Then, list all the words and phrases you can think of that are associated with that activity. If you choose cooking a special food, for instance, you might start with *winter night, Dad, radio playing, sausage, sizzling onions, pasta.*

Literary Focus

Figurative Language
Images can be created by using both literal language (such as "mud-luscious" from "in Just-" on page 414) and figurative language. **Figurative language** is language that is based on imaginative comparisons and is not literally true. Two kinds of figurative language are **similes,** comparisons using a word such as *like* or *as,* and **metaphors,** comparisons that do not use *like* or *as.* "The road was a ribbon of moonlight" is a famous metaphor from a poem called "The Highwayman." If that poem's author had written, "The road was *like* a ribbon of moonlight," he would have written a simile. Both of those figures of speech help put pictures in readers' minds.

SKILLS FOCUS

Literary Skills
Identify figurative language, including similes and metaphors.

Reading Skills
Use strategies for reading a poem.

Reading Skills 📖

Reading a Poem
When you're reading poetry, keep the following strategies in mind:

• Look for punctuation telling you where sentences begin and end. Most poems are written in full sentences.

• If lines of a poem are difficult to understand, look for the subject, verb, and object (if there is one) of each sentence. Try to decide what words the clauses and phrases modify.

• Do not make a full stop at the end of a line if there is no period, question mark, exclamation point, comma, colon, semicolon, or dash there. If a line has no punctuation at its end, read on to the next line to complete the sense of the sentence. A line of poetry without punctuation at its end is called a **run-on line.** A line of poetry that has punctuation at its end is called an **end-stopped line.**

• Read the poem aloud. The sound of a poem is very important to its meaning. Then, read the poem a second or a third time. Each time you read a poem, you'll get more meaning—and probably more pleasure—from it.

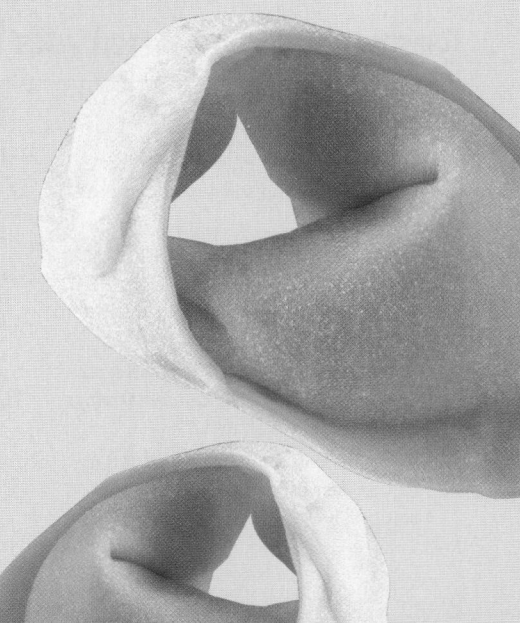

RESOURCES: READING

Planning
■ *One-Stop Planner* CD-ROM with ExamView Test Generator

Differentiating Instruction
■ *Holt Reading Solutions*
■ *Supporting Instruction in Spanish*
■ *Audio CD Library, Selections and Summaries in Spanish*

Assessment
■ *Holt Assessment: Literature, Reading, and Vocabulary*
■ *One-Stop Planner* CD-ROM with ExamView Test Generator
■ *Holt Online Assessment*

Internet
■ go.hrw.com (Keyword: LE5 9-7)

■ *Elements of Literature Online*

Media
■ *Audio CD Library*
■ *Audio CD Library, Selections and Summaries in Spanish*

Folding Won Tons In

Abraham Chang

I've seasoned the pork as I imagine my mother
      would—
sesame oil, ginger, pepper,
scallions chopped imperfectly.
Sheets of doughy skin,
5   I only have the skill
to buy.

Thumb and forefinger peel
each tender, white scrap of noodle
from the clinging stack.
10   I pat their centers pink
with fragrant spoonfuls
the color of the fat sun in October.

Mimicking from memory:
A twist, a tuck, a folding over—
15   a finger lick of water to seal
my misshapen flowers.

My hands powderdusted;
acquainted with each new blossom.
I line them up
20   like newborns huddled
together, waiting to be fed
to their distant fathers.

The soup bubbles to overflowing,
I slide the dumplings in
25   and stir them in their dizzy descent.

Drowned, swollen,
and glistening; steam hidden
for an instant—

I set them on the table
30   and decide how many
I will save
for one more day.

A

B

C

Meet the Writer

Abraham Chang

Filled with Memories

Abraham Chang (1976–   ) is a "replanted" New Yorker. This young poet was born and raised in New York City, but he spent his college years in Boston and abroad. In 1998, after receiving an Academy of American Poets Prize, Chang returned to New York to attend a master's program in creative writing at New York University. There he worked with several award-winning poets, including Galway Kinnell, Sharon Olds, Donald Hall, and his mentor, Philip Levine.

For Chang's reflection on his poem, see the **Connection** *on page 434.*

Folding Won Tons In   **433**

DIRECT TEACHING

A **Reading Skills**

? **Reading a poem.** What is the subject and the verb of the sentence in ll. 10–12? [*Subject*—I; *Verb*—pat] What word does the phrase "Mimicking from memory" modify? [I] How does the punctuation in l. 13 help you understand what follows in ll. 14–16? [The colon clarifies that what follows is a list of the actions that the speaker is mimicking.]

B **Literary Focus**

? **Metaphor.** What does the speaker compare the won tons to? [misshapen flowers] What does this comparison suggest? [Possible response: The speaker's skills at making won tons are not as good as his mother's. The won tons are imperfect, hence misshapen.]

C **Literary Focus**

? **Figurative language.** How have the hands become "acquainted with each new blossom"? To what senses does this image appeal? [The hands have become acquainted with the blossoms (won tons) while folding them, the fingers touching each skin. The image appeals to sight and touch.]

GUIDED PRACTICE

Monitoring students' progress. To assess students' understanding of "Folding Won Tons In," have them identify the speaker's actions in each stanza of the poem.

DIFFERENTIATING INSTRUCTION

Learners Having Difficulty
Modeling. To help students read "Folding Won Tons In," model each of the reading strategies that comprise the skill of reading a poem. Read the first stanza aloud, demonstrating how to pause at punctuation marks and how to read through lines with no punctuation. Say, "The last three lines are more difficult than the first three lines. I'll re-read them to see if I can find the subject, verb, and object of the sentence. Doing so, I can see that the subject is 'I' and that 'Sheets of doughy skin' is the object of 'to buy.' I may paraphrase the sentence two ways to make sure I understand it: 'I only have the skill to buy the skin; I don't have the skill to make the skin.'" Encourage students to use these strategies as they read the rest of the poem.

Connection

Summary  *at grade level*

> Chang reflects on the period in which he wrote "Folding Won Tons In." One day he makes won tons, relying on the memory of how his mother made them. The results are imperfect, yet satisfying. They represent an attempt to incorporate the past into his newly independent life.

INDEPENDENT PRACTICE

Response and Analysis

Reading Check

1. Season the pork, chop the scallions, peel the noodles from the stack, fill the centers, fold the won tons, line them up, slide them in the soup, and stir.

2. He puts them on the table and decides how many to save for the next day.

Thinking Critically

3. Possible answers: "A twist, a tuck, a folding over—a finger lick of water" (ll. 14–15), because it conveys the rapid and complex movements required to create each dumpling; "each new blossom" (l. 18), because it presents an image of the dumplings as delicate, flowerlike creations.

4. The metaphors "misshapen flowers" (l. 16) and "each new blossom" (l. 18) and the simile "like newborns huddled together" (ll. 20–21) describe the won tons. The center of each won ton is compared to "the fat sun in October" (l. 12). These figures of speech suggest that the speaker views his won tons with an almost paternal pride.

5. The subject is "I."

CONNECTION / REFLECTION

On "Folding Won Tons In"

Abraham Chang

The poem was based on my attempt at making won-ton soup while I was living by myself for the first time. I felt powerful but also a bit anxious at the prospect of being alone in the "real world." I had just returned to New York for graduate school, and I was living in my grandparents' former apartment. I was left to care for this place that had been in our family for over two decades. The apartment felt different, mainly because I was different. The place was "my own" now, but it was filled with the memories of growing up there. The crayon drawings that I had scribbled inside closet doors as a kid still remained, but here I was—in my early twenties, feeling like a new creation and figuring out what it meant to be independent.

I tried my best to remember how my mother used to make dumplings; the recipe and technique were much more difficult than I thought they would be. I couldn't get it exactly right—I couldn't make the skins; I couldn't get the spices or ingredients in the right proportions. But I was determined to do this by myself, so I chopped and mixed and shaped those won tons with my own hands. I "folded" the memories of my family's customs and culture, my anxiety, and my new independence into those won tons, and I nourished myself in more ways than one. They were nowhere near perfect, but they expressed what I was going through at the time: how I cherished my past, kept my focus on the present, and stirred hope for my future by creating something for myself—even if it was only dinner.

434 Collection 7 Poetry

SKILLS FOCUS

Literary Skills
Analyze figures of speech, including similes and metaphors.

Reading Skills
Use strategies for reading a poem.

Writing Skills
Write a poem with figures of speech and images.

Response and Analysis

Reading Check

1. List all the steps the speaker follows as he makes the won tons.

2. What does the speaker do with the won tons after they're made?

Thinking Critically

3. Imagine that you are the poet. Which **image**—a word or phrase that appeals to your senses—in this poem would you feel most pleased with? Why does it especially please you?

4. This poem is full of **figures of speech** that create vivid images. List all the figures of speech you find in this poem—all the things that the won tons are compared to. How does the speaker feel about his won-ton soup?

5. Read the first stanza aloud, paying attention to the **end-stopped lines** and the **run-on line.** What is the subject of the sentence that begins on line 4?

WRITING

Remembering the Lesson

Starting with the notes you jotted down for your Quickwrite on page 432, write a **poem** in which you describe the "lesson" you learned. Does your lesson have a special meaning, like that described by Chang (see the **Connection** at the left)?

Remember that a poem, unlike a how-to manual, does not just give information. Take your readers *inside* the experience. Choose **figures of speech** and **images** that help them feel that they are experiencing the lesson with you. Be sure to read your lines aloud so that you can hear the way they sound.

ASSESSING

Assessment
- *Holt Assessment: Literature, Reading, and Vocabulary*

RETEACHING

For another selection to teach figures of speech, see *The Holt Reader,* Collection 7.

Before You Read

"Hope" is the thing with feathers

Make the Connection

Quickwrite 🖉

Think of an emotion or a state of mind. You might choose feelings like grief, joy, anger, dreaminess, selfishness, or ambition. Then, jot down three metaphors in which you identify your subject with something else. Open like this: "Joy is . . ."

Literary Focus

Extended Metaphor

This famous poem is built around a **metaphor** that is carried throughout the entire work. Emily Dickinson states her metaphor in the first line: "Hope," she says, is the "thing with feathers." Notice all the ways she imagines how the gift of hope is like a bird ("the thing with feathers"). When a metaphor is developed over several lines or even through an entire poem like this, it is called an **extended metaphor**.

Bird Singing in the Moonlight (1938–1939) by Morris Graves. Tempera and watercolor on mulberry paper (26 ³/₄″ × 30 ¹/₈″).
The Museum of Modern Art, New York. Purchase. Photograph © 1997 The Museum of Modern Art, New York.

"Hope" is the thing with feathers

Emily Dickinson

"Hope" is the thing with feathers—
That perches in the soul—
And sings the tune without the words—
And never stops—at all—

5   And sweetest—in the Gale—is heard—
And sore must be the storm—
That could abash the little Bird
That kept so many warm—

I've heard it in the chillest land—
10 And on the strangest Sea—
Yet, never, in Extremity,
It asked a crumb—of Me.

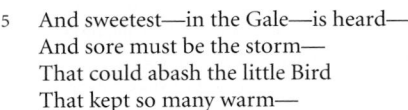

INTERNET
More About
Emily Dickinson
Keyword: LE5 9-7

SKILLS FOCUS

Literary Skills
Understand extended metaphors.

"Hope" is the thing with feathers   435

**SKILLS FOCUS,
pp. 435–439**

Grade-Level Skills

■ **Literary Skills**
Analyze figurative language, including extended metaphors.

Summary ⬆ *above grade level*

In the metaphor that extends through all three stanzas of the poem, Dickinson likens hope to a bird whose song never stops. Both are fragile yet able to endure the harshest conditions and warm those who hear their music.

DIRECT TEACHING

A Literary Focus

❓ **Extended metaphor.** What is the speaker saying about where hope resides? [Hope resides deeply within each of us.]

B Learners Having Difficulty

❓ **Paraphrasing.** What does the speaker mean by suggesting that the song is sweetest "in the Gale" [Possible response: Hope is most important when things are at their worst.]

C Literary Focus

❓ **Extended metaphor.** How does the metaphor of a bird give life to the abstract idea of hope? [Possible responses: The metaphor makes the reader envision hope as something that can perch, sing, and soar into the air.]

RESOURCES: READING

Planning
■ *One-Stop Planner* CD-ROM with ExamView Test Generator

Differentiating Instruction
■ *Holt Reading Solutions*
■ *Supporting Instruction in Spanish*
■ *Audio CD Library, Selections and Summaries in Spanish*

Assessment
■ *Holt Assessment: Literature, Reading, and Vocabulary*
■ *One-Stop Planner* CD-ROM with ExamView Test Generator
■ *Holt Online Assessment*

Internet
■ go.hrw.com (Keyword: LE5 9-7)

■ *Elements of Literature Online*

Media
■ *Audio CD Library*
■ *Audio CD Library, Selections and Summaries in Spanish*
■ *Visual Connections Videocassette Program*

Grade-Level Skills

■ **Literary Skills**
Evaluate the aesthetic qualities of style, including the effect of diction and figurative language.

■ **Literary Skills** Understand denotations and connotations.

Summary *at grade level*

The poem centers around the relocation of Japanese Americans to internment camps during World War II, focusing on a woman brought from California to one camp in Crystal City, Texas. Word choices such as "branding" and "herded" associate her dehumanizing experience with the treatment of cattle. Despite her indignation and sadness, the woman cannot keep from noticing the stark beauty of the Texas landscape.

PRETEACHING

Skills Starter

Build background. To introduce diction, denotation, and connotation, write these sentences on the chalkboard:

• She made a <u>brave</u> choice.

• She made a <u>rash</u> choice.

• She made a <u>foolhardy</u> choice.

Have students note differences in the meanings of the three words. *Brave* has strong positive connotations. *Foolhardy* has strong negative ones. *Rash* is also viewed negatively but the context implies a decision made on the spur of the moment.

Before You Read

Internment

Make the Connection
Branded

Imagine a situation in which you feel "disrespected," treated as less than the person that you know you are. How might you feel in that situation?

Literary Focus
Diction

Diction is a writer's choice of words. In all writing, but especially in poetry, every word counts, so poets choose their words very carefully. Poems rarely appear fully formed and perfect in a poet's head. Instead, they are developed painstakingly, through many revisions. Poets work hard to find words that have the exact meanings and connotations (or associations) that they want to convey.

Denotation and Connotation

Words are not as simple as they look sitting on a page. Words often have many meanings and represent complicated ideas. First there are the literal meanings of words—the definitions found in a dictionary. These are called **denotations.** Then there are the **connotations**—all the associations and emotions that have come to be attached to a word.

For example, in the poem that follows, the poet uses the word *barracks.* Dictionaries say that this word means "large, simple buildings providing temporary housing for people, often soldiers." That's the denotation of the word. What associations and emotions come to mind when you hear the word *barracks,* though? The connotations of the word might include *cold, bare, ugly, lonely, homesick.* In order to

appreciate the full meaning of a poem, pay attention to the writer's **diction,** or word choice. Did the poet choose some words with very specific connotations? How can you explain the choice?

SKILLS FOCUS

Literary Skills
Understand diction.
Understand denotations and connotations.

Background

On December 8, 1941, the day after Japan attacked Pearl Harbor, the United States entered World War II. Early in 1942, the U.S. government sent notices to thousands of Japanese Americans living on the West Coast, requiring them to report to relocation centers, where they were assigned to internment camps in inland areas. The Japanese Americans had committed no crime, and most of them were American citizens, but an executive order signed by the president made it legal for the government to imprison them in these camps. While many Nisei (second-generation Japanese Americans) served heroically in the United States armed forces, more than 110,000 of their family members were confined behind barbed wire until 1946, after World War II had already ended. When these people returned to their homes, many of them found that their property had been stolen. After forty years the U.S. government formally apologized, and it paid a small compensation to the Americans who had been interned in the camps.

436 Collection 7 Poetry

Planning
■ *One-Stop Planner* CD-ROM with ExamView Test Generator

Differentiating Instruction
■ *Supporting Instruction in Spanish*
■ *Audio CD Library, Selections and Summaries in Spanish*

Assessment
■ *Holt Assessment: Literature, Reading, and Vocabulary*
■ *One-Stop Planner* CD-ROM with ExamView Test Generator
■ *Holt Online Assessment*

Media
■ *Audio CD Library*

DIFFERENTIATING INSTRUCTION

Learners Having Difficulty
Broaden students' understanding of the World War II internment of Japanese Americans with one of the many available resources that are suitable for below-level readers. Here are two suggestions:

• *The Children of Topaz: The Story of the Japanese-American Internment Camp,* by Michael O. Tunnell and George W.

Internment

Juliet S. Kono

Corralled, they are herded inland  **A**
from Santa Rosa.
After the long train ride
on the Santa Fe,
5 the physical exam,
the delousing with DDT, **B**
the branding of her indignation, **C**
she falls asleep.

Days later, she awakens
10 in an unfamiliar barracks—
Crystal City, Texas—
on land once a pasture.
Not wanting to,
not meaning to see beauty
15 in this stark landscape,
she sees, nonetheless,
through her tears—
on the double row
of barbed wire fencing **D**
20 which holds them in
like stolid cattle—
dewdrops, impaled
and golden.

A Japanese American mother carries her sleeping daughter during the relocation from Bainbridge Island, Washington, to internment camps in 1942.
© Seattle Post-Intelligencer Collection; Museum of History and Industry/CORBIS.

DIRECT TEACHING

A Vocabulary Development

❓ Denotation and connotation.
What is a corral? What images does the word *corralled* bring to mind? [Possible responses: A corral is an enclosure for holding horses or cattle; the word evokes images of animals rounded up, penned in, and grouped tightly together.]

B Content-Area Connections

Science: Agricultural Pesticides
Explain to students that DDT is an abbreviation for a highly effective pesticide introduced in the 1940s. Its use was banned in the United States in 1972.

C Literary Focus

❓ Diction. What does branding mean here? What are the word's associations? [Possible response: stamping permanently; the word is associated with burning marks into the hides of cattle for identification purposes.]

D Reading Skills

Reading a poem. To help students see that the word *dewdrops* is the object of the verb *sees,* have them read these lines with the words between the dashes (ll. 18–21) omitted.

Chilcoat, contains diary entries kept by students interned at the camps.

- *Invisible Thread: A Memoir,* by Yoshiko Uchida, describes the author's experiences growing up in California and her family's stay in a Nevada internment camp.

You might also have students explore Internet resources that focus on the internment. Suggest that students use keywords such as *Japanese American internment, War Relocation Authority,* and *Executive Order 9066* in Internet search engines.

English-Language Learners
You may want to show students a collection of images that will help them to grasp the associations that English-speakers make with the cattle-related vocabulary in the poem. These images, which are easily available from Internet photo galleries, might include photographs of southwestern ranches and pastureland, cows with branding marks, cattle being herded, and corrals filled with animals.

Monitoring students' progress. Guide the class in answering these comprehension questions. Direct students to locate passages in the poems that support their responses.

True-False

"Hope" is the thing with feathers

1. The poet compares hope to a song. [F]
2. The speaker has lost hope. [F]
3. A bird asks the speaker for something. [F]

Internment

4. The woman travels by train. [T]
5. The woman is free to come and go as she likes. [F]
6. The barracks are surrounded by barbed wire. [T]

Meet the Writers

Background. The biographer Richard Sewall says that Emily Dickinson "does not tell us how to live . . . so much as what it feels like to be alive." She defines emotions, including both joy and longing, with metaphors that startle the reader with their clarity. For example, "Exultation is the going of an inland soul to sea" or "Longing is like the Seed/That wrestles in the Ground."

Juliet Kono's poetry captures two generations of her Japanese American family's life on a sugar plantation in Hawaii. In 1991, Kono paired with fellow Hawaiian poet Cathy Song to edit the multicultural anthology *Sister Stew: Poetry and Fiction by Women* (Bamboo Ridge Press, 1991). Much of this book highlights the common bonds of women of Hawaiian heritage.

For Independent Reading

Students who appreciate poetry may enjoy browsing through *Americans' Favorite Poems,* edited by Robert Pinsky and Maggie Dietz.

Meet the Writers

Emily Dickinson
Juliet S. Kono

She Knows Poetry

Unlike most people today, **Emily Dickinson** (1830–1886) was born, lived most of her life, and died in the same house. From the time she was twenty-six, she rarely went out of that house in Amherst, Massachusetts. Yet for the next thirty years she traveled to the ends of the earth and the universe—in her imagination. She jotted down poems in the margins of newspapers, on brown paper bags, and even on the insides of envelopes.

Dickinson also wrote many letters. In one of them, she defined poetry:

66 If I read a book and it makes my whole body so cold no fire can ever warm me, I know it is poetry. If I feel physically as if the top of my head were taken off, I know that it is poetry. These are the only ways I know it. 99

A famous editor, T. W. Higginson, once asked Emily Dickinson for a photograph of herself. In her reply the poet created a photograph in words.

66 Could you believe me—without? I had no portrait, now, but am small, like the Wren, and my Hair is bold, like the Chestnut Bur—and my eyes like the Sherry in the Glass, that the Guest leaves. 99

While she was alive, only seven of her poems were published—all anonymously. Dickinson died not knowing that she would be recognized as one of the greatest poets who ever wrote in English.

Emily Dickinson.

Amherst College Archives and Special Collections.

"They Just Love It When I Misspell Something"

The poet and college teacher **Juliet Kono** (1943–   ) writes when her students write. She says,

66 They like to listen and see these first drafts because they can see how raw and 'chicken scratch' even my work can be. They just love it when I misspell something or if the ideas do not flow. They like it even better when they suggest something and my piece gets better. 99

Kono was born and raised in Hilo, on the Big Island of Hawaii. As a young girl she and her Japanese American family survived a thirty-foot-high tsunami, a tidal wave that swept away their house and car and killed 159 people. "My mother carried my sister on her back," she says, "and my Aunt Dot held me, as she says, under her arm like a suckling pig." This extraordinary experience turns up in many of her poems, collected in the books *Hilo Rains* and *Tsunami Years.*

Advanced Learners
Enrichment. Share the information about Emily Dickinson in the Meet the Writer feature of the Teacher's Edition, and ask students to discuss the metaphors on exultation and longing.
Activity. Engage students in a further exploration of Dickinson's poetry (see the source at the left in For Independent Reading). As

they explore her poetry, have them gather examples of the kinds of metaphors that define emotions and "startle the reader with their clarity." Have students choose their favorites and post them, along with the poems from which they come, on a bulletin board. You may wish to have students choose photographs or art reproductions to accompany the poems they select.

Response and Analysis

"Hope" is the thing . . .

Reading Check

1. Dickinson uses a **metaphor** that compares hope to a bird. Where does the bird perch? Under what conditions has the speaker heard it sing?

2. What does hope (or the bird) ask for in return for its song?

Thinking Critically

3. A gale is a strong wind. What do you think the "gale" **symbolizes,** or stands for, in this poem?

4. Think of all the ways Dickinson **extends** the **metaphor.** How is hope's song endless? How does it keep you warm?

5. How do you interpret what the speaker says about hope in the last stanza?

Internment

Reading Check

1. In the first stanza, what events happen to the girl before she falls asleep?

2. Describe the place where she finds herself upon waking.

Thinking Critically

3. What words in the first stanza have **connotations** that suggest that Kono is comparing the imprisoned travelers to cattle? Find the **simile** in the second stanza that restates this comparison. How do these words help you to understand the girl's feelings?

4. In Kono's poem, what does the girl see that she considers beautiful? Why is she reluctant to find beauty in her situation?

5. Look at the poet's **diction,** or word choice, in line 22. What **connotations,** or associations, do you have with the verb *impaled*? What other words could the poet have used to describe how the dewdrop is fixed on the barbed wire?

6. What could the dewdrops in Kono's poem **symbolize,** or stand for? (Consider the significance of the fact that the fragile dewdrops are "impaled" on the barbed wire but are still "golden.")

Comparing Poems

After reading Dickinson's poem, a sixteen-year-old student in California wrote:

> It reminds me that although bad things happen and I feel lonely and alone, hope is there protecting me.

Do you think the speaker in Kono's poem has a similar feeling? In what ways might Dickinson's and Kono's poems address the same thoughts and feelings?

WRITING

With Metaphors

Like Dickinson, write a **poem** in which you compare an emotion to something else, perhaps something in the world of nature. You might find ideas in your Quickwrite on page 435. Begin your first line with a **metaphor,** and extend it in the poem as far as you can.

Text Reformulation

When you **reformulate** a text, you rewrite it using a different format. For example, you could reformulate the poem "Internment" as a news article or an interview. Try it. You will find that when you reformulate a poem, you come to understand it very well.

SKILLS FOCUS

Literary Skills
Analyze extended metaphor. Analyze diction and connotations. Compare poems.

Writing Skills
Write a poem using an extended metaphor. Reformulate a poem.

Response and Analysis

"Hope" is the thing with feathers

Reading Check

1. The bird perches in the soul. It is heard during a gale, in the chillest land, and on the strangest sea.

2. Hope asks for nothing.

Thinking Critically

3. Possible answers: hard times, moments of despair or hopelessness.

4. Hope continues to sing in the most dire situations. The bird warms people with a cheering song amid cold despair.

5. Possible answer: Even in the most dire times, hope asks for nothing in return.

Internment

Reading Check

1. She travels by train, receives a physical exam, and is deloused.

2. She is in the barracks of an internment camp in Texas, surrounded by barbed wire fencing.

Thinking Critically

3. *First stanza*—"corralled," "herded," "branding." *Second stanza*—"like stolid cattle." The words clarify that the speaker feels she and others are being treated like animals.

4. The speaker sees beauty in the dewdrops on the barbed wire fence. She does not want to recognize beauty because she has been treated in an ugly way.

5. Possible answer: "Impaled" evokes violent images of being speared. Other possible words: "fixed," "stuck," or "caught."

6. Possible answers: The dewdrops represent the internees; they represent beauty.

Comparing Poems

Both poems speak of natural beauty and offer symbols of hope in times of darkness and despair.

ASSESSING

Assessment

- *Holt Assessment: Literature, Reading, and Vocabulary*

RETEACHING

For lessons reteaching literary devices, see **Reteaching,** p. 979A.

Grade-Level Skills

■ **Literary Skills**
Analyze figurative language, including implied metaphors.

Summary *below grade level*

Carl Sandburg's free-verse poem re-creates the movement of fog over a harbor and city. In an extended metaphor the poet implicitly compares the fog to a cat. Like fog that muffles sound, the poem's mood is tranquil.

In "Fire and Ice," Robert Frost uses an implied metaphor. He equates desire with fire and hate with ice. He declares that he has experienced both of these destructive emotions and that they can bring an end to the world.

DIRECT TEACHING

A Literary Focus

? Implied metaphor. Do you think the comparison of fog to a cat makes sense? Explain. [Possible responses: Yes, both fog and cats move silently and seem mysterious and elusive; no, fog is more dangerous than a cat.]

Before You Read

Fog
Fire and Ice

Make the Connection
Quickwrite ✏
The titles of these two poems cite three natural conditions: fog, fire, and ice. What thoughts and pictures come into your mind when you hear those words? What do you associate with each word? Jot down your ideas.

Literary Focus
Implied Metaphor
By now you know that **figures of speech** compare one thing to another, very different thing.

A **simile** expresses the comparison by using a word such as *like, as, than,* or *resembles:*

> *The moon looks like a balloon.*

A **direct metaphor** tells us directly that one thing *is* something else:

> *The moon is a balloon.*

An **implied metaphor,** however, does not tell us directly that one thing is something else. Instead, it *suggests* the comparison:

> *Without a string, the moon drifts across the sky.*

The following poems are two of the shortest that Carl Sandburg and Robert Frost ever wrote. As you read the poems, use your powers of inference to figure out the implied metaphor in each one.

go.hrw.com

INTERNET
More About
Robert Frost
Keyword: LE5 9-7

SKILLS FOCUS

Literary Skills
Understand implied metaphors.

Fog
Carl Sandburg

> The fog comes
> on little cat feet.
>
> **A** It sits looking
> over harbor and city
> on silent haunches
> and then moves on.

RESOURCES: READING

Planning
■ *One-Stop Planner* CD-ROM with ExamView Test Generator

Differentiating Instruction
■ *Holt Reading Solutions*
■ *Supporting Instruction in Spanish*
■ *Audio CD Library, Selections and Summaries in Spanish*

Assessment
■ *Holt Assessment: Literature, Reading, and Vocabulary*
■ *One-Stop Planner* CD-ROM with ExamView Test Generator
■ *Holt Online Assessment*

Internet
■ go.hrw.com (Keyword: LE5 9-7)

■ *Elements of Literature Online*
Media
■ *Audio CD Library*
■ *Audio CD Library, Selections and Summaries in Spanish*

Fire and Ice

Robert Frost

Some say the world will end in fire,
Some say in ice.
From what I've tasted of desire
I hold with those who favor fire. **A**
But if it had to perish twice,
I think I know enough of hate **B**
To say that for destruction ice
Is also great
And would suffice. **C**

The Polar Sea (1824) by Caspar David Friedrich.
Hamburg Kunsthalle, Hamburg, Germany.

A Literary Focus

❓ Implied metaphor. With what emotion does the speaker indirectly compare fire? [desire] ice? [hatred] What does the speaker suggest by saying the world may end in either fire or ice? [Possible response: Fire and ice are implied metaphors for destructive emotions and represent ways humans may destroy the earth.]

B Reading Skills

❓ Making inferences. What can you infer from the speaker's statement, "I think I know enough of hate"? [Possible response: The speaker appreciates how powerful the emotion of hatred can be, perhaps suggesting that he himself has felt it or that he has experienced it directed at himself.]

C Vocabulary Development

❓ Word associations. How does the word *suffice* reinforce the meaning of the last four lines? [Possible responses: In its sound and appearance, *suffice* suggests the word *suffer*, reinforcing the terrible power of hate.]

VIEWING THE ART

Caspar David Friedrich (1774–1840) was a German painter whose work often shows man being overwhelmed by the forces of nature.

Activity. Ask students what story they can read into this painting. [Possible response: A ship has been trapped and destroyed by the movement of powerful ice sheets.]

DIFFERENTIATING INSTRUCTION

Learners Having Difficulty
The short lengths of both poems make them perfect for developing student fluency in oral reading. Have pairs of students take turns reading each poem aloud. Then, have them listen to the recording of each poem on the *Audio CD Library*. Have students discuss how reading and listening to the two poems increases their understanding and appreciation of them.

English-Language Learners
Frost uses colloquial speech to give his poem a conversational voice. However, the idioms in ll. 3–4 might confuse students learning English. Before reading "Fire and Ice," explain that *tasted* can mean "to experience" and *hold with* means "agree with." Also, preteach the word *suffice*, meaning "to be adequate."

Monitoring students' progress.
Guide the class in answering these comprehension questions. Direct students to locate words in the poems that support their responses.

Short Answer

Fog

1. To what does Sandburg compare fog? [a cat]

2. What does the fog do at the end of Sandburg's poem? [It moves on.]

Fire and Ice

3. In Frost's poem, which emotion is linked with ice? [hatred]

4. According to the poem, what does ice have the power to do? [destroy]

Meet the Writers

Background. Besides being a poet, Sandburg worked as a newspaper reporter. This experience influenced Sandburg's poetry. On the day Sandburg wrote "Fog," he had an appointment to interview a juvenile court judge. As he walked to his appointment, Sandburg watched the fog settle over the Chicago harbor. While he was waiting to talk to the judge, Sandburg took out a pencil and wrote "Fog" on a piece of newsprint. He always kept his pockets stuffed with various clippings and poems, and on that day he pulled out some Japanese haiku. Sandburg decided to write, as he puts it, his own "free-going, independent American Hoku" (an alternate spelling of *haiku*) as he waited for the judge.

In Robert Frost's poem simple things take on deep significance. Describing the trajectory of his writing, the poet remarked, "Poetry begins in trivial metaphors and goes on to the profoundest thinking we have."

Meet the Writers

Carl Sandburg
Robert Frost

Sandburg on Poetry

Carl Sandburg (1878–1967) wrote a poem called "Ten Definitions of Poetry." Here are three of the definitions:

❝ Poetry is a search for syllables to shoot at the barriers of the unknown and the unknowable. . . .

Poetry is the synthesis of hyacinths and biscuits. . . .

Poetry is the opening and closing of a door, leaving those who look through to guess about what is seen during a moment. ❞

Sandburg, the son of Swedish immigrants, was born in Galesburg, Illinois. Between the ages of thirteen and nineteen, he worked on a milk wagon, in a barbershop, at a theater, in a brickyard, and as a hotel dishwasher and a harvest hand.

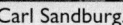
Carl Sandburg.

He became known as the poet of Chicago in the days when that city was the expanding center of steel mills, stockyards, and railroads. Though he was unknown to the poetry world until he was thirty-six, Sandburg's name was a household word by the time he died. His sometimes tough, often tender poems about nature and the American people—especially working-class people—were loved by millions.

Frost on Poetry

New England, where **Robert Frost** (1874–1963) lived most of his life, still bears the scars of the Ice Age glacier that stripped the land bare and buried everything in its path. Enormous boulders litter the landscape where the glacier dropped them many thousands of years ago. Indeed, Frost had only to look out his farmhouse window to see the destructive effects of ice—and he had only to take a short walk to find the charred

Robert Frost.

clearings left by lightning fires. Then, like all human beings, he had only to look inside himself to discover the destructive forces of desire and hate.

In his essay "The Figure a Poem Makes," Frost talks about poetry:

❝ [A poem] . . . begins in delight and ends in wisdom . . . a clarification of life—not necessarily a great clarification, such as sects and cults are founded on, but in a momentary stay against confusion. ❞

Late in his life, Robert Frost played an important role on the national stage when he recited one of his poems at John F. Kennedy's inauguration as president in 1961.

For another biography of Frost, see page 316.

Advanced Learners

Enrichment. Frost and Sandburg are two of the true giants of twentieth-century American literature. Before his death, Frost was considered America's favorite poet by many. Certainly he was the last American poet to achieve the status of a national celebrity. Sandburg, also a popular and beloved poet, collected examples of American folklore in *The American Songbag* and wrote a six-volume Pulitzer Prize–winning biography of Abraham Lincoln.

Activity. Have students choose one of the two poets and research one or more aspects of his life or work. Students can use such keywords as *biography* and *Frost* or *Sandburg* in an Internet search engine. Invite students to report to the class on their subject's importance to American literature in a panel discussion format.

Response and Analysis

Fog

Reading Check

1. What animal does Sandburg compare the fog to, and how do you know?

2. What parts of the animal's body does he mention?

3. What does this animal do?

Thinking Critically

4. What qualities does fog share with the animal in Sandburg's poem? Could fog also be compared to an elephant? a snake? a dog?

Fire and Ice

Reading Check

1. According to the speaker in "Fire and Ice," what disagreement do some people have about how the world will end?

2. Which side of the argument does the speaker agree with?

Thinking Critically

3. How could the world end in fire?

4. How could the world end in ice?

5. How would you define *desire* as Frost uses the word in his poem? How is desire like fire? How could desire bring on the end of the world?

6. Why would the speaker feel that hate and ice have something in common? How could hate cause the destruction of the world?

Comparing Poems

Now that you have read these two poems, go back to your Quickwrite notes for page 440. How have your ideas about fog, fire, and ice changed? How has the poets' use of **metaphor** changed the thoughts, images, and emotions you associate with those words? (You can gather your ideas in a chart like the one below.) Which poem do you find more powerful? Which do you think you will remember longer? Why?

	Fog	Fire	Ice
Old associations			
Poet's metaphors			
New associations			

WRITING

The Heat Wave Comes In . . .

Write a **poem** in the style of Sandburg's in which you compare a force of nature to an animal. Extend your metaphor as far as it will go, without forcing it. You can use a **direct metaphor:** " . . . is . . . ," or you can use an **implied metaphor,** as Sandburg does.

Your Opinion

Fire and ice are two extremes of nature. Either force could put an end to all living things. Desire and hate are two human emotions; we can be consumed by desire and hardened by hate. Which emotion—desire or hate—do you feel is more destructive? (Think in terms of an individual's life as well as the life of the world.) Write a paragraph explaining your opinion.

go.hrw.com

INTERNET

Projects and Activities

Keyword: LE5 9-7

SKILLS FOCUS

Literary Skills
Analyze implied metaphors. Compare poems.

Writing Skills
Write a poem containing a metaphor. Write a paragraph supporting an opinion.

Fog / Fire and Ice   **443**

Grade-Level Skills

■ **Literary Skills**
Analyze figurative language, including extended metaphors.

Summary ⬆ *above grade level*

In this blank-verse poem, Shakespeare compares the world to a stage, people to actors, and their lives to roles in a play. He divides a man's life into seven acts or ages: infant, schoolboy, lover, soldier, judge, pantaloon (a foolish old man), and second childhood. The extended metaphor embodies the poem's theme: Life follows a fixed pattern.

DIRECT TEACHING

Ⓐ Literary Focus

❓ Extended metaphor. How does the poet extend the "world as a stage" metaphor? [The world is compared to a stage, and people are compared to actors. He develops his metaphor by dividing a man's life into seven ages or acts.]

Before You Read

The Seven Ages of Man

INTERNET

More About William Shakespeare

Keyword: LE5 9-7

SKILLS FOCUS

Literary Skills
Understand extended metaphors.

Make the Connection
Quickwrite 🖊

Seven acts—that's how long this poet imagines the play of your life is going to be. According to Jaques (pronounced jā′kwēz), a character in Shakespeare's comedy *As You Like It,* you're now in the middle of the second act of your life. Before you read what he predicts about the rest of your life, try to second-guess him. Write down what you think are the seven stages of a person's life.

Literary Focus
Extended Metaphor

In *As You Like It,* Jaques makes a speech that is considered one of the finest examples of extended metaphor ever written.

An **extended metaphor** is a comparison developed over several lines of writing. (In the play, Jaques's speech is a **monologue**—a long speech delivered by a single character. Here it is presented as a separate poem.)

Jaques opens with the famous metaphor: "All the world's a stage." As he goes on, Jaques extends that metaphor to compare the stages of our lives to seven acts, with seven different roles all played by the same actor. In the play, Jaques is a moody character. See if you think this speech reflects his gloomy outlook on life.

For a biography of William Shakespeare, see page 776.

The Seven Ages of Man
William Shakespeare

Ⓐ
All the world's a stage,
And all the men and women merely players;
They have their exits and their entrances,
And one man in his time plays many parts,
5 His acts being seven ages. At first the infant,
Mewling and puking in the nurse's arms;
And then the whining schoolboy, with his satchel
And shining morning face, creeping like snail
Unwillingly to school. And then the lover,
10 Sighing like furnace, with a woeful ballad
Made to his mistress' eyebrow. Then a soldier,
Full of strange oaths, and bearded like the pard,°
Jealous in honor, sudden and quick in quarrel,
Seeking the bubble reputation

12. **pard** (pärd) *n.:* leopard.

First Steps by Vincent van Gogh (1853–1890), after Millet. Oil on canvas (28½″ × 35⅞″).

15 Even in the cannon's mouth. And then the justice,°
    In fair round belly with good capon° lined,
    With eyes severe and beard of formal cut,
    Full of wise saws° and modern instances;
    And so he plays his part. The sixth age shifts
20 Into the lean and slippered pantaloon,°
    With spectacles on nose and pouch on side;
    His youthful hose,° well saved, a world too wide
    For his shrunk shank; and his big manly voice,
    Turning again toward childish treble, pipes
25 And whistles in his sound. Last scene of all,
    That ends this strange eventful history,
    Is second childishness and mere oblivion,
    Sans° teeth, sans eyes, sans taste, sans everything.

15. justice *n.:* judge.
16. capon (kā′pän′) *n.:* fat chicken.

18. saws (sôz) *n.:* old sayings.

20. pantaloon (pan′tə·lōōn′) *n.:* silly old man.

22. hose (hōz) *n.:* stockings.

28. sans (sanz) *prep.:* without.

Response and Analysis

Reading Check

1. players (actors)
2. infant, schoolboy, lover, soldier, judge, pantaloon, and second childhood

Thinking Critically

3. The infant "mewls" and "pukes," and the schoolboy "whines." He is shown "creeping like [a] snail" to school. Jaques seems to dislike both infants and schoolboys.

4. We know that the justice eats well. He appears intellectual, but his judgments are just old sayings illustrated by modern examples.

5. The changes include weight loss; poor sight; ill-fitting clothes; weak voice; raspy breathing; senility; loss of teeth, sight, and taste. Students may say that Shakespeare ridicules the aged as sickly and infantile whereas today's seniors are regarded more respectfully.

6. Some students may feel that the infant, schoolboy, and soldier remain true today. Some students may feel that the portrayal of old age is untrue in the modern era.

Vocabulary Development

Practice

- *strange.* Other meanings—peculiar; foreign. *Jaques's meaning l. 12*—foreign; alien.

- *fair.* Other meanings—attractive; clear; just; moderately large; average. *Jaques's meaning l. 16*—moderately large.

- *saws.* Other meanings—cutting tools; maxims. *Jaques's meaning l. 18*—maxims; sayings.

- *hose.* Other meanings—stockings; flexible tube. *Jaques's meaning l. 22*—stockings.

Response and Analysis

Reading Check

1. In Shakespeare's famous **metaphor** that compares the world to a stage, what does he compare men and women to?

2. Shakespeare uses an **extended metaphor** when he has Jaques describe a person's life as though it were a play made up of seven acts. Name those seven acts.

Thinking Critically

3. In this **monologue,** what **images** help you picture childhood (the first two acts) as Jaques sees it? What **simile** describes the schoolboy's attitude toward school? How do you think Jaques feels about infants and schoolboys?

4. If the justice's belly is lined "with good capon," what do we know about him? What details make the judge seem like a ridiculous character?

5. According to Jaques, what physical and mental changes take place when a man reaches the sixth and seventh ages? Does he make old age seem dignified or silly? What do you think of Jaques's view of old age?

6. Shakespeare's famous lines were written more than four hundred years ago. Of the seven ages of man that he characterizes, which do you think remain true to life today? Have any changed? (Be sure to check your Quickwrite notes.) 🖉

WRITING

The Seven Ages of Woman

Shakespeare wrote about the seven ages of man. Write your own **poem**—or a paragraph—focusing on the seven ages of woman. Begin with the **metaphor** of life as a stage, and extend it as far as you can. Start with the infant, and describe seven ages. What attitude will you take toward the stages of a woman's life?

This Is What It Says

When you **paraphrase** a text, you restate it in your own words. Write a paraphrase of Jaques's speech. Explain his comparisons in your own words. Here is a possible paraphrase of lines 1–2: "The whole world can be compared to a stage, and all the people in the world can be compared to actors on that stage."

Vocabulary Development

Multiple Meanings

PRACTICE

The common words in boldface below have multiple meanings. Each word is used at least once by Jaques. Find where he uses each word, examine its **context,** and then create a word map for each word like the one here. The footnotes will help you.

strange   fair   saws   hose

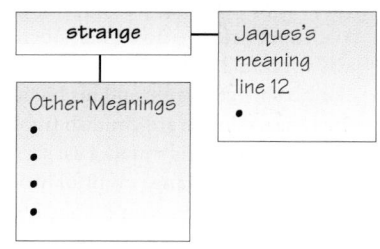

---

go.hrw.com

INTERNET
Projects and Activities
Keyword: LE5 9-7

SKILLS FOCUS

Literary Skills
Analyze extended metaphors.

Writing Skills
Write a poem containing an extended metaphor. Paraphrase a poem.

Vocabulary Skills
Understand multiple meanings of words.

ASSESSING

Assessment

- *Holt Assessment: Literature, Reading, and Vocabulary*

RETEACHING

For a lesson reteaching literary devices, see **Reteaching,** p. 979A. For another selection to teach figures of speech, see *The Holt Reader*, Collection 7.

Before You Read

Women

Make the Connection

Quickwrite ✏️

Make notes about people whom you consider heroes because they helped you become the person you are today. You'll probably think of relatives, friends, or teachers, but you might also include people you've never met—people in the news or people from the past, for instance. What makes these people heroes to you?

Literary Focus

Tone

Tone is a writer's or speaker's attitude toward a subject or toward an audience. You know from your own life how impor-

tant it is to be sensitive to tone. If you're talking to a friend, for example, and you misread a tone of sarcasm for a tone of sincerity, you've made a big mistake. In speech, voice and body language help to convey tone. In writing, however, tone can be revealed only by an author's choice of words, or **diction.**

You've read poems in this book that reveal many tones, from cynical to sincere to playful. In the following poem, what tone does the poet take toward her subject?

go.hrw.com

INTERNET

More About Alice Walker

Keyword: LE5 9-7

SKILLS FOCUS

Literary Skills
Understand tone and diction.

Rosa Parks's refusal to give up her seat to a white man prompted the Montgomery bus boycott in 1955.

John H. Glenn, Jr., became the first American to orbit the earth in 1962.

Blind, deaf, and mute by the age of two, Helen Keller eventually became a world-famous author and activist.

Women **447**

SKILLS FOCUS, pp. 447–449

Grade-Level Skills
■ **Literary Skills**
Evaluate the aesthetic qualities of style, including the effect of diction and tone.

Summary ⬌ *at grade level*

In an admiring tone the poet celebrates the courageous love of mothers who struggle to gain a better life for their children. The poem's imagery indirectly compares the mothers' struggle for their children's education with a military operation.

PRETEACHING

Skills Starter

Build background. Explain that a writer's diction, or word choice, is often the best clue to tone. Words are chosen for their literal meanings and for their negative or positive connotations and associations.

RESOURCES: READING

Planning
■ *One-Stop Planner* CD-ROM with ExamView Test Generator

Differentiating Instruction
■ *Holt Reading Solutions*
■ *Supporting Instruction in Spanish*
■ *Audio CD Library, Selections and Summaries in Spanish*

Assessment
■ *Holt Assessment: Literature, Reading, and Vocabulary*
■ *One-Stop Planner* CD-ROM with ExamView Test Generator
■ *Holt Online Assessment*

Internet
■ go.hrw.com (Keyword: LE5 9-7)

■ *Elements of Literature Online*

Media
■ *Audio CD Library*
■ *Audio CD Library, Selections and Summaries in Spanish*

A Literary Focus

❓ **Tone.** Consider the adjectives and nouns used to describe this generation. Is this a positive or negative portrayal? [Possible response: It is a positive portrayal since it emphasizes the strength of women.]

B Literary Focus

❓ **Tone.** What does the use of a military metaphor imply about the women's struggle and its importance? [Possible response: The use of a military metaphor emphasizes how hard the women worked to achieve their goals and how important their efforts are.]

C Reading Skills

❓ **Interpreting.** Who are the people referred to as "we" in l. 22? [Possible responses: the women's children; future generations.]

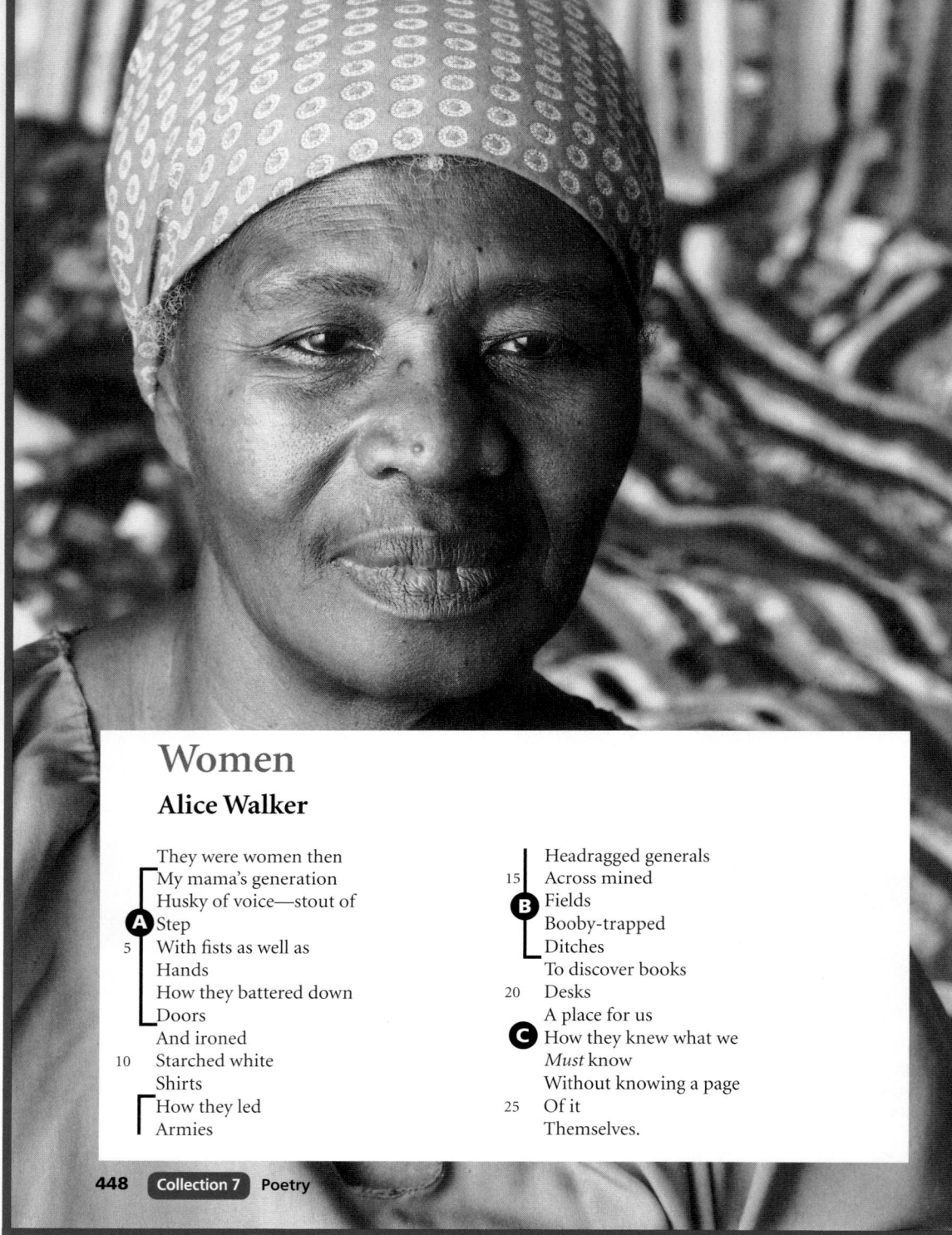

Women

Alice Walker

They were women then
My mama's generation
Husky of voice—stout of
A Step
5   With fists as well as
Hands
How they battered down
Doors
And ironed
10 Starched white
Shirts
How they led
Armies

Headragged generals
15 Across mined
B Fields
Booby-trapped
Ditches
To discover books
20 Desks
A place for us
C How they knew what we
Must know
Without knowing a page
25 Of it
Themselves.

448   Collection 7   Poetry

DIFFERENTIATING INSTRUCTION

Learners Having Difficulty
Some students may have difficulty reading "Women" because it lacks punctuation until the final line. Identifying logical breaks in the poem will help increase students' fluency, as well as their understanding of the poem.
Activity. Pair learners having difficulty with more fluent readers, and have them work together to prepare the poem for an oral

reading. Students should analyze the poem and choose logical breaks or stopping places. They should consider various factors when deciding where to pause, such as the poem's imagery, its rhythm, and ideas and words that they think are important. Students can read the poem aloud and explain their choices to the class.

Meet the Writer

Alice Walker

"I Had Terrific Teachers"

Alice Walker (1944–   ) is a poet, novelist, short story writer, and essayist. She is best known for her novel *The Color Purple,* which won a Pulitzer Prize in 1983. Walker was born in Eatonville, a small town in Georgia. She was the youngest of eight children. Her father was a sharecropper, and her mother was a maid.

Walker says that "Women" is for her mother, one of several important people in her life:

❝I also had terrific teachers. When I was four and my mother had to go work in the fields, my first-grade teacher let me start in her class. Right on through grammar school and high school and college, there was one—sometimes even two—teachers who saved me from feeling alone, from worrying that the world I was stretching to find might not even exist . . .

My teachers lent me books: *Jane Eyre* was my friend for a long time. Books became my world, because the world I was in was very hard. My mother was working as a maid, so she was away from six-thirty in the morning until after dark. . . . I was supposed to take care of the house and do the cooking. I was twelve, coming home to an empty house and cleaning and fixing dinner—for people who didn't really appreciate the struggle it was to fix it. I missed my mother very much. ❞

Response and Analysis

Reading Check

1. What generation of women does the speaker describe?

2. List three things that these women tried to obtain for their children.

3. How did they go about obtaining what they knew their children needed?

Thinking Critically

4. In lines 12–18, Walker uses an **implied metaphor,** suggesting rather than stating a comparison. What does she compare the women to?

5. Think about the **historical context** of this poem. What "doors" did these women have to batter down? What do you think the "mined fields" and "booby-trapped ditches" stand for?

6. What do you think these women *knew* their children had to know?

7. What is the speaker's **tone,** her attitude toward these women? What words or phrases in the poem help you identify the speaker's tone?

WRITING

Celebrate Heroes

How would you describe the heroic women and men of today? What do they struggle for? What obstacles do they face? Write a paragraph describing these people. (Check your Quickwrite notes.) ✏

SKILLS FOCUS

Literary Skills
Analyze tone and diction.

Writing Skills
Write a descriptive paragraph.

Women   449

INDEPENDENT PRACTICE

Response and Analysis

Reading Check

1. The speaker is describing her mother's generation.

2. They tried to obtain books, desks, and "a place for us" (educational opportunity).

3. They removed barriers to opportunity and led their children along dangerous paths.

Thinking Critically

4. She compares the women fighting for their children's education to generals leading soldiers on a battlefield.

5. Possible answers: The doors represent barriers to educational opportunity, such as school segregation, racism, and poverty. The "mined fields" and "booby-trapped ditches" may stand for the hostile actions of politicians and segregationists who opposed equal educational opportunity and for the poor quality of schools in black neighborhoods.

6. Possible answer: The women knew that education was the key to their children's success in American society.

7. Possible answer: With words and phrases like "husky of voice," "stout of step," and "battered-down doors," the poet emphasizes the strength of the women she describes and reveals her admiration for their actions.

ASSESSING

Assessment

■ *Holt Assessment: Literature, Reading, and Vocabulary*

Grade-Level Skills

■ **Literary Skills**

Analyze figurative language, including personification.

Summary  *at grade level*

At twilight a young boy is weeping for the lone snowman outside his window. A storm is approaching, and the boy fears for the snowman's safety amid the wind and cold. The poem alludes to the fall of Adam, likening the snowman, in the boy's despairing eyes, to an outcast from the paradise of the warm house.

The snowman is imbued with human qualities. He is comfortable in the cold and knows that indoors he would die. But moved by the boy's fear, he sheds a single tear for the suffering of the child.

PRETEACHING

Selection Starter

Motivate. Ask students to recall themselves as young children. Did they ever think that inanimate objects, such as dolls, teddy bears, and snowmen, had human thoughts or emotions? Have volunteers share some details about their childhood memories.

Before You Read

Boy at the Window

Make the Connection

A Cold Winter Night

What do you think children fear? What makes children feel safe? When a child looks out the window on a cold winter night, what might he or she be thinking?

Literary Focus

Personification

Personification is a type of figurative language in which the writer speaks of something nonhuman as if it had human qualities. If you say, "The sun smiled down on us," you are personifying the sun, which can't really smile at all. If you say, "Time is a thief," you are personifying time, which isn't able to rob us of our valuables at all. In "Once by the Pacific" (see page 423), Robert Frost personifies waves when he writes:

> Great waves looked over others
>   coming in,
> And thought of doing something to
>   the shore
> That water never did to land before.

Waves don't have eyes; they can't "look." Nor do waves have brains; they can't "think." By personifying the great waves, Frost helps us see the stormy ocean as a kind of dangerous monster.

SKILLS FOCUS

Literary Skills
Understand personification.

RESOURCES: READING

Planning

■ *One-Stop Planner* CD-ROM with ExamView Test Generator

Differentiating Instruction

■ *Holt Reading Solutions*
■ *Supporting Instruction in Spanish*
■ *Audio CD Library, Selections and Summaries in Spanish*

Assessment

■ *Holt Assessment: Literature, Reading, and Vocabulary*
■ *One-Stop Planner* CD-ROM with ExamView Test Generator
■ *Holt Online Assessment*

Internet

■ go.hrw.com (Keyword: LE5 9-7)

■ *Elements of Literature Online*

Media

■ *Audio CD Library*
■ *Audio CD Library, Selections and Summaries in Spanish*

Boy at the Window

Richard Wilbur

Seeing the snowman standing all alone
In dusk and cold is more than he can bear.
The small boy weeps to hear the wind prepare
A night of gnashings° and enormous moan.
His tearful sight can hardly reach to where
The pale-faced figure with bitumen° eyes
Returns him such a god-forsaken stare
As outcast Adam gave to Paradise.°

The man of snow is, nonetheless, content,
Having no wish to go inside and die.
Still, he is moved to see the youngster cry.
Though frozen water is his element,
He melts enough to drop from one soft eye
A trickle of the purest rain, a tear
For the child at the bright pane surrounded by
Such warmth, such light, such love, and so much fear.

---

4. gnashings (nash′iŋz) *n.*: grinding of teeth, as in anger.
6. bitumen (bi·tōō′mən) *n.*: coal.
8. outcast . . . Paradise: reference to the biblical account of Adam and Eve's expulsion from Paradise.

A Literary Focus

❷ Personification. What human qualities is the boy attributing to the snowman in this stanza? [Possible response: The boy imagines that the snowman is capable of feeling cold, lonely, and sad.]

B English-Language Learners

❷ Multiple-meaning words. What two meanings of the word *melt* are suggested here? [to turn from ice to water; to be touched or emotionally affected]

C Literary Focus

❷ Repetition. Ask students to identify the repetition in l. 16. What is the effect of this repetition? [Possible responses: The speaker uses the word *such* three times. This repetition emphasizes the depth of love, light, and warmth that exists inside the house, thereby heightening the contrast with fear; it creates rhythm that heightens the meaning in the line.]

DIFFERENTIATING INSTRUCTION

Learners Having Difficulty
To help students understand the poem, have them apply the strategy of reformulating text. Have student pairs reformulate the poem into a story, explaining what the boy and snowman think, feel, and do in narrative form.

Advanced Learners
Acceleration. To help students analyze ways that poets use sound to evoke readers'
emotions, have students examine sound effects in the poem.

Activity. Ask students the following questions:
• Which lines rhyme in the first stanza? [ll. 1 and 4; ll. 2, 3, 5, and 7; ll. 6 and 8] What is the poem's rhyme scheme? [abbabcbc]
• What rhyming sounds in the first stanza are repeated in the second? [*Die, cry, eye,*
and *by* in the second stanza are slant rhymes for *eyes* and *Paradise* in the first stanza, and *tea,* and *fear* for *where* and *stare.*]
• Which line contains both alliteration and onomatopoeia? [l. 4] What is the effect of these sounds? [Possible responses: They help readers experience the sounds of the wind and understand the boy's feelings.]

Monitoring students' progress.
To assess students' understanding of "Boy at the Window," ask them to create a four-column chart with the column heads "What the boy sees," "What the boy feels," "What the snowman sees," and "What the snowman feels." Have students use their knowledge of the poem to complete their charts.

Meet the Writer

Background. Richard Wilbur might have embarked on any number of careers, but he viewed poetry as the one thing he *had* to do. "I was a competent teacher, and might have been competent in journalism, and a few other professions. But in poetry I had a gift, and if you have a gift (as opposed to a competence), there's an obligation to exercise it."

Millions of readers have certainly benefited from Wilbur's decision to follow his muse. His best known poem may be "A Stable Lamp Is Lighted," a Christmas poem that is a staple in hymnals across North America.

Meet the Writer

Richard Wilbur

A Model Poet

When the two-time Pulitzer Prize–winner and national poet laureate Richard Wilbur (1921–   ) first appeared before the American public, he was standing on a can of beans. Wilbur's father worked as a commercial artist in New York City, and he used his son as a model for the advertisements he drew. "Often I posed as a child flushed with health because he was taking the right vitamins," Wilbur says, or as "a child running excitedly home from the grocery with the right cereal."

Young Richard wasn't just another handsome face. When he was only eight, he sold his first poem (about owls and nightingales) to a children's magazine for one dollar. He went on to college and other adventures—one Depression summer he lived as a teenage hobo, jumping freight trains and traveling through nearly every state in the country. He returned to writing poetry at an unlikely moment: in a World War II foxhole, with enemy artillery falling all around him.

Back home from the war, he stuffed his writing in a desk drawer and started graduate school. Then one day an editor friend came to visit, and Wilbur's wife mentioned the poems

in his desk. "He took them home to his apartment," Wilbur says, "reappeared an hour later, kissed me on both cheeks"—the friend was European—"and declared me a poet. And then he sent the things off to New York."

Wilbur's work was an immediate success. Readers enjoyed his wit, his skill with words, and the way he focused on the details of the world around him. "I was always averse to high-minded abstract talk," he says; he prefers "poetry of close observation . . . poetry that acknowledges the importance of things however small." As small as a drop of water trickling down a snowman's cheek?

DIFFERENTIATING INSTRUCTION

Advanced Learners
Enrichment. Richard Wilbur admired poets such as William Carlos Williams, Elizabeth Bishop, Marianne Moore, and Francis Ponge, poets who shared his affinity for the "poetry of close observation . . . poetry that acknowledges the importance of things however small."
Activity. Have students explore the work of the poets listed above by finding examples in their poems that like "Boy at the Window"

embody this quality of close observation. (Students might research in collections of modern poetry or on the Internet by using the poets' names as keywords in a search engine.) Suggest that students choose a single example to read for their classmates. After the readings, students can discuss how each of the poems exemplify Wilbur's criteria.

Response and Analysis

Reading Check

1. The first stanza focuses on the boy. Where is he?

2. Why does the boy feel so sad that he weeps?

3. The second stanza focuses on the snowman. Why is the "man of snow" content?

4. What word in the last line reveals why the snowman feels so sad for the boy that *he* weeps?

Thinking Critically

5. Which words in line 4 **personify** the weather conditions as a threatening person or animal? What words might a television weather reporter use to describe the same conditions?

6. What details in the poem **personify,** or give human qualities to, the snowman?

7. In line 8, the poet **alludes,** or refers, to the biblical account of Adam and Eve's expulsion from Paradise. Why does the poet compare the snowman to Adam? What does the expression "god-forsaken" mean?

8. The boy and the snowman cry for each other. In the poem, who actually has more reason to feel sorry for the other? In what ways is this **ironic**— just the opposite of what we might expect the situation to be?

9. What do you think this poem is saying about fear, pity, and sympathy?

WRITING

Analyzing a Poem

Many readers are moved by "Boy at the Window." In a brief **essay,** analyze what makes the poem effective. Consider elements like **figurative language, imagery, tone,** and **theme.** Pay particular attention to the poem's use of **personification.**

▶ Use "Analyzing a Poem," pages 480–487, for help with this assignment.

LISTENING AND SPEAKING

Oral Presentation

Prepare this poem for **oral presentation.** You might have two speakers: one for the first verse (the boy's point of view) and one for the second (the snowman's point of view). Before you present the poem, note when you will pause at the end of a line because a mark of punctuation (a period or a comma) tells you to and when you will read on to the next line to complete the meaning of the phrase or sentence. This poem was written with great care for the way it sounds. Where do you find the poem's rhyming words?

Literary Skills
Analyze personification.

Writing Skills
Write an analysis of a poem.

Listening and Speaking Skills
Prepare a poem for oral presentation.

Boy at the Window   453

Response and Analysis

Reading Check

1. The boy is inside his house looking through the window.

2. He is sad that the snowman has to stay outside during a storm.

3. Cold is the snowman's natural element. He would melt if he went inside.

4. fear

Thinking Critically

5. Possible answer: "gnashings," "enormous moan." A reporter might describe "howling" or "gale-force" winds.

6. "Returns him such a god-forsaken stare"; "The man of snow is . . . content"; "Having no wish to . . . die"; "he is moved"; "to drop . . . a tear/For the child."

7. Possible answers: The boy feels that the warm house is paradise and sees the snowman as exiled or cast out like Adam. "God-forsaken" refers to Adam's feelings on being expelled from paradise; the boy imagines that the snowman must similarly feel similarly forsaken and alone, outside in the cold.

8. Possible answer: The boy's fear for the snowman is ironic because the snowman is happy and can survive only in the cold. The snowman has greater reason to feel sorry for the boy, whose fear is causing him genuine suffering.

9. Possible answers: Often our pity for others is misplaced, and our perceptions of their state are incorrect; fear can cause unhappiness, even among those surrounded by warmth, light, and love.

Assessment

■ *Holt Assessment: Literature, Reading, and Vocabulary*

For another selection to teach figures of speech, see *The Holt Reader,* Collection 7.

Grade-Level Skills

■ **Literary Skills**
Analyze various literary devices, including rhyme, rhythm, meter, onomatopoeia, and alliteration.

■ **Literary Skills**
Analyze free verse.

Elements of Literature: The Sounds of Poetry

Music can be a useful tool for introducing the sounds of poetry since the two share many of the same elements. Begin by playing a familiar popular song, and ask students to listen for and jot down rhyming words. If the song contains examples of the terms *approximate rhyme, onomatopoeia,* or *alliteration,* you may also wish to point them out.

Then, introduce rhythm through the beat of music. Have volunteers drum on a desk to demonstrate examples of three-four time, four-four time, stressed and unstressed beats, and syncopation. Ask students to demonstrate the rhythmic patterns of one or two popular songs.

Finally, tell students that poetry is a form of music that is created with words rather than musical notes. Explain that poets, like musicians, use rhyme and rhythm to create sounds and evoke feelings in their listeners.

Elements of Literature

The Sounds of Poetry *by* John Malcolm Brinnin
RHYME, RHYTHM, AND MORE

Make It Rhyme

Everyone loves rhyme—even babies respond to rhyme, so the first books read to you were probably written in rhyme. **Rhyme** is the repetition of the sound of the stressed vowel and any sounds that follow it in words that are close together in a poem: *nails* and *whales; material* and *cereal; icicle* and *bicycle*.

Until very recently rhyme was considered essential to poetry, but for poets today its use is a matter of choice. Modern poets who use rhyme feel that it helps make a poem sing. It enhances the music of a poem by adding chiming sounds. A regular pattern of end rhyme, or **rhyme scheme,** defines the shape of a poem and holds it together.

Many poets feel that just about all the words in the English language that can be rhymed were used long ago. The contemporary poet who writes in rhyme may have to repeat rhymes that have echoed down the centuries.

Approximate Rhyme: Not Quite Exact

Some poets solve the problem of creating new rhymes by using **approximate rhyme**—that is, words that repeat some sounds but are not exact echoes. Approximate rhymes are also called *half rhymes, off rhymes, slant rhymes,* or—by readers who dislike them—*imperfect rhymes.* In any case, they are substitutes for **exact rhymes** like *moon* and *June* or *hollow* and *follow.* Instead of being an exact echo, approximate rhyme is a partial echo: *moon* and *morn; hollow* and *mellow.*

INTERNET
More About the
Sounds of Poetry
Keyword: LE5 9-7

Literary Skills
Understand
rhyme, rhythm,
meter, free verse,
onomatopoeia,
and alliteration.

Internal Rhyme Versus End Rhyme: Chimes Inside and Out

Rhymes usually occur at the ends of lines. This type of rhyme is called **end rhyme.** The rhyming words are seldom spaced more than four lines apart—if the interval is longer than that, the chiming sound cannot be clearly heard. Rhyme can also occur inside the lines. This is called **internal rhyme.** Here are some lines from "The Raven" by Edgar Allan Poe in which two internal rhymes (*remember* and *ember*) chime with *December:*

Ah, distinctly I remember it was in the
   bleak December;
And each separate dying ember wrought
   its ghost upon the floor.

You've Got Rhythm

As long as your heart is beating, you've got rhythm. Musicians and poets, perhaps in imitation of that heartbeat, create rhythm in their compositions. **Rhythm** is a musical quality based on repetition.

Meter: A Pattern of Stressed Syllables

A common form of rhythm is **meter,** a regular pattern of stressed and unstressed syllables in each line. The poem on the next page by Robert Frost is written in meter. The stressed syllables are marked ′; the unstressed syllables are marked ˘. Read the poem aloud to feel its steady beat.

454 **Collection 7** Poetry

DIFFERENTIATING INSTRUCTION

Learners Having Difficulty
The sounds of poetry. Some students may have particular difficulty with the section on meter. Before you introduce the concept, be sure that students understand the basics of syllabication. Have students use a dictionary to find the stressed syllables in several common words, such as *classroom, occupation,* and *discuss.* Allow pairs of students to take turns sounding out the syllabication of multisyllable words. Then, read aloud some of the accented poetry lines in the essay, showing students how to lightly emphasize the rhythm as they read. Call on volunteers to read other lines, emphasizing the stressed syllables as they read.

Advanced Learners
Acceleration. Use the following activity with advanced learners to help them analyze

Dust of Snow

The way a crow
Shook down on me
The dust of snow
From a hemlock tree

Has given my heart
A change of mood
And saved some part
Of a day I had rued.
            —Robert Frost

Frost wrote his poem mostly in iambs. An **iamb** (ī′amb′) is an unstressed syllable followed by a stressed syllable (da DAH). An iamb is one kind of poetic foot. A **foot** usually consists of one stressed syllable and one or more unstressed syllables.

English poetry has other kinds of feet. A **trochee** (trō′kē) is a stressed syllable followed by an unstressed syllable (DAH da); it is the opposite of an iamb. This line from Poe's "The Raven" uses trochees:

Once upon a midnight dreary

An **anapest** (an′ə·pest′) is two unstressed syllables followed by a stressed syllable (da da DAH). Here is a line from Byron's poem "The Destruction of Sennacherib" that uses anapests:

The Assyrian came down like
       the wolf on the fold

A **dactyl** (dak′təl) is one stressed syllable followed by two unstressed syllables (DAH da da). Here is the beginning of a nursery rhyme that uses dactyls:

Hickory, dickory, dock

A **spondee** (spän′dē) is two stressed syllables (DAH DAH). Here are some lines from "We Real Cool" by Gwendolyn Brooks that use spondees:

We real cool. We

Left school. We

Lurk late. . . .

When you analyze a poem to show its meter, you are **scanning** the poem. Scanning is a way of taking a poem apart to see how the poet has created its music.

Free Verse Isn't Free

Until the nineteenth century almost all poetry in English used a strict rhyme scheme and meter pattern. Eventually, however, poets began to abandon the old poetic rules to write **free verse,** which does not follow a regular pattern of rhyme and meter. This kind of poetry sometimes sounds similar to prose or to everyday spoken language.

Free verse is free only in the sense that it is liberated from formal rules. Poets writing free verse still pay close attention to the sound and rhythm of their lines—to the rhythmic rise and fall of the voice, to pauses, and to the balance between long and short phrases. Rhythm is also created in free verse by the repetition of words or even lines.

The poem on the next page by David Ignatow is written in free verse. You'll notice how close to ordinary spoken language it sounds at first. But then you'll notice how the rhythm of the poem imitates the rhythm of a bagel rolling—the words come faster and faster—and at the end the reader feels as "strangely happy" as the speaker of the poem.

(continued)

ways in which poets use sound to evoke readers' emotions.
Activity. Ask students to work in groups to create a bulletin board that features their favorite poets along with examples of their poetry. Students should classify the poems by their use of readily identifiable rhythmic patterns, rhyme types, or other poetic sound effects. Each student should choose one poem and read it to the group, demonstrating the particular effect they wish to highlight. Groups can follow each reading with a discussion of how the sound effects contribute to the emotional tone of the poem.

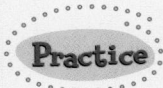

Possible Answers

1. Michélle—iamb; Trácy, Míchael, Lászĺo, Márvĭn, Shéilă—trochees; Aňtŏinétte—anapest; Gwéndŏlўn, Ďorŏthў, Timŏthў—dactyls; Jojo—spondee.

2. Rhyme—No taxation without representation; Alliteration—Save Saratoga schools.

3. *ocean. Exact rhymes*—motion, lotion. *Approximate rhymes*—caution, sheen.

   wash. Exact rhymes—posh, josh. *Approximate rhymes*—splash, moss.

   warm. Exact rhymes—storm, swarm. *Approximate rhymes*—farm, arm.

   beard. Exact rhyme—weird. *Approximate rhyme*—sear.

   power. Exact rhymes—tower, sour. *Approximate rhymes*—shore, poorer.

4. *rainy, windy night*—The splash and howl of the storm woke me from my sleep. *Cat munching dry cat food*—The calico snapped at the dry chunks.

Apply 🔖 Homework

Point out that poetic effects such as exact rhyme, approximate rhyme, internal rhyme, onomatopoeia, and alliteration are staples of the advertising world. Share some examples of print ads containing these effects from your local newspaper, or show videotaped examples from television commercials. Then, distribute old newspaper sections to student pairs. Have partners work together to find several examples of each term.

POETRY IN MOTION

The Bagel

David Ignatow

I stopped to pick up the bagel
rolling away in the wind,
annoyed with myself
for having dropped it
as it were a portent.
Faster and faster it rolled,
with me running after it

bent low, gritting my teeth,
and I found myself doubled over
and rolling down the street
head over heels, one complete somersault
after another like a bagel
and strangely happy with myself.

New York City Transit   Incorporated with the Poetry Society of America

This poem, along with many others, has appeared in New York City subway cars and on buses as part of a program called Poetry in Motion.

Other Sounds Singing

Rhyme and rhythm are not the only ways to create the sounds of poetry. Two other important techniques are **onomatopoeia** (än'ō·mat'ō·pē'ə) and **alliteration** (ə·lit'ər·ā'shən). The names may be difficult to say, but the techniques are easy to learn and use.

Onomatopoeia: Imitating Sounds

Onomatopoeia is the use of words that sound like what they mean. We use onomatopoeia when we say a cannon "booms" or bacon "sizzles." The words can echo a natural sound (*hiss, slap, rumble, snarl, moan*) or a mechanical sound (*whack, clickety-clack, putt-putt, toot*).

Alliteration: Repeating Sounds

Alliteration is the repetition of the same consonant sound in several words, usually at the beginnings of the words: *fragrant flowers, hot and heavy, dog days.* Alliteration can also be the repetition of similar but not identical sounds: a series of *p*'s and *b*'s or *s*'s and *z*'s. The repetition of vowel sounds is called **assonance.**

Alliteration and onomatopoeia can sometimes be used together to echo sounds. Here is another example from "The Raven":

The silken sad uncertain rustling of each
    purple curtain

The alliteration of "silken sad uncertain" and the onomatopoeia of "rustling" combine to imitate the sound that wind makes blowing past heavy silk draperies.

Practice

Find elements of poetry in the world around you:

1. List ten names. Which syllables are stressed? Which are not stressed? What "tunes" do the names make?

2. Collect some political slogans with **rhyme** and **alliteration** in them.

3. Think of two **exact rhymes** and two **approximate rhymes** to go with these words: *ocean, wash, warm, beard, power.*

4. Describe the following scenes, using **onomatopoeia:**
   • a rainy, windy night
   • a cat munching on dry cat food

Before You Read

I Wandered Lonely as a Cloud

Make the Connection

Quickwrite ✏️

Recall a scene you once saw that made a strong impression on you. Perhaps it was the earth seen from a plane window, the ocean just before a storm, the desert at night, or a sky filled with migrating birds. Close your eyes, and be there again. Make notes about what you see.

Literary Focus

Rhythm and Meter

Rhythm, or the repetition of sound patterns, is what gives poems their musical quality. William Wordsworth, like most poets of his time, created rhythm by arranging his words so that the lines repeat a regular pattern of stressed and unstressed syllables. This regular pattern is called **meter.** You can hear meter just as you can hear the steady beat of a heart.

When you **scan** a poem to describe its meter, you mark the stressed syllables with the symbol ′ and the unstressed syllables with the symbol ˘.

Scanning a poem requires you to read the poem aloud. As you read Wordsworth's famous poem, listen for its beat. What syllables do you stress?

Background

This poem captures with enormous precision a special moment that occurred two hundred years ago—on April 15, 1802, to be precise. We *can* be precise because there was another witness to that miracle—the poet's sister, Dorothy, also a wonderful writer—who captured the very same scene in her journal.

SKILLS FOCUS

Literary Skills
Understand rhythm and meter.

SKILLS FOCUS, pp. 457–460

Grade-Level Skills
- **Literary Skills**
Analyze rhythm and meter.

Summary ⬆ *above grade level*

The poem opens with a simile comparing the speaker's solitude to a drifting cloud. The solitude is broken when the speaker comes upon "a crowd" of daffodils. Personification gives the flowers a life force, and they become "jocund company" for the speaker. In the final stanza, the speaker tells how he later reexperiences the glory of the daffodils in his imagination.

I Wandered Lonely as a Cloud

William Wordsworth

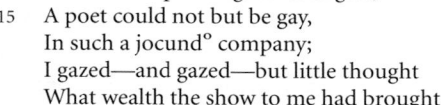

I wandered lonely as a cloud
That floats on high o'er vales and hills,
When all at once I saw a crowd,
A host, of golden daffodils,
5 Beside the lake, beneath the trees,
Fluttering and dancing in the breeze.

Continuous as the stars that shine
And twinkle on the Milky Way,
They stretched in never-ending line
10 Along the margin of a bay;
Ten thousand saw I at a glance,
Tossing their heads in sprightly dance.

The waves beside them danced, but they
Outdid the sparkling waves in glee; **A**
15 A poet could not but be gay,
In such a jocund° company;
I gazed—and gazed—but little thought
What wealth the show to me had brought:

For oft, when on my couch I lie
20 In vacant or in pensive mood,
They flash upon that inward eye
Which is the bliss of solitude;
And then my heart with pleasure fills, **B**
And dances with the daffodils.

---

16. jocund (jäk′ənd) *adj.:* merry.

I Wandered Lonely as a Cloud   **457**

DIRECT TEACHING

Ⓐ Literary Focus

❓ **Personification.** What things are personified in these lines, and what human qualities are they given? [The daffodils and the waves on the lake are portrayed as dancing. The daffodils are also given the human quality of glee.]

Ⓑ Literary Focus

❓ **Rhyme.** Point out that poets often use inverted word order to create rhyme and to emphasize an idea. What idea is emphasized by the inverted word order in l. 23? [By putting "fills" at the end of the line, the poet stresses the speaker's happiness.]

RESOURCES: READING

Planning
- *One-Stop Planner* CD-ROM with ExamView Test Generator

Differentiating Instruction
- *Holt Reading Solutions*
- *Holt Adapted Reader*
- *Supporting Instruction in Spanish*

Assessment
- *Holt Assessment: Literature, Reading, and Vocabulary*
- *One-Stop Planner* CD-ROM with ExamView Test Generator
- *Holt Online Assessment*

Internet
- go.hrw.com (Keyword: LE5 9-7)

- *Elements of Literature Online*

Media
- *Audio CD Library*
- *Audio CD Library, Selections and Summaries in Spanish*

Monitoring students' progress.
Guide the class in answering these comprehension questions.

Short Answer

1. In the opening line, what is the speaker doing? [wandering]

2. Who or what is dancing in the poem? [daffodils]

3. How does the speaker feel when near the daffodils? [cheerful]

4. In the last stanza, what does the speaker recall? [the daffodils]

Meet the Writer

Background. William Wordsworth, his wife Mary, and his sister Dorothy lived together for many years in England's scenic Lake District. The walk described in the poem and in the journal entry on p. 459 took place there. Dorothy was a prolific journal writer, and in his poems, Wordsworth frequently reflected upon and referred to the entries she made about experiences they had shared. Writing about Wordsworth, Matthew Arnold wrote that his "poetry is great because of the extraordinary power with which Wordsworth feels the joy offered us in Nature . . . and because of the extraordinary power with which he shows us this joy."

Meet the Writer

William Wordsworth

Nature: The Best Teacher

The English Romantic poet William Wordsworth (1770–1850) believed that nature is the best teacher. He also believed that uneducated people who live close to nature have at least as much to teach us as sages, or wise people.

> "One impulse from a vernal wood
> May teach you more of man,
> Of moral evil and of good,
> Than all the sages can. "

Wordsworth's mother died when he was seven. Six years later his father was also dead. Wordsworth had started writing poems by the age of fifteen. When he was twenty-eight, he and his close friend Samuel Taylor Coleridge published a collection of poems called *Lyrical Ballads*. This slim book contained only twenty-four poems, all very different from the fancy, aristocratic poetry that most poets then wrote. Wordsworth and Coleridge used simple people and ordinary experiences as their subjects. They used common speech. They said that the human mind is intimately related to the workings of the natural world. They said that God is revealed in the laws and forces of nature.

According to Wordsworth, poetry begins when we get in touch with a memory and relive the experience:

William Wordsworth (1842) by B. R. Haydon.
By Courtesy of the National Portrait Gallery, London.

> "Poetry is the spontaneous overflow of powerful feelings: It takes its origin from emotion recollected in tranquillity. "

By "tranquillity," Wordsworth means that it's better to write about an experience later than when you're right in the middle of it. Of course, you can still take notes, as Wordsworth and his sister, Dorothy, regularly did. Then you can take your time to relive what you experienced and put it down on paper just the way you want to.

Learners Having Difficulty

Distribute a sheet that has the first line of the poem broken down into syllables and scanned with markings showing stressed and unstressed syllables. Have students follow along as they listen to the audio CD recording of the line. Then, have students follow in their books as they listen to the complete poem. Encourage students to notice how the stress pattern creates the rolling rhythm.

Advanced Learners

Enrichment. Explain to students that Wordsworth was a frequent collaborator with British poet Samuel Taylor Coleridge. Together, they wrote *Lyrical Ballads*, a work that helped spark the Romantic movement in England.

Activity. Ask students to further explore the poetry of Wordsworth and Coleridge and research their importance to the

Romantic movement. Students may choose a pair of poems, one by each poet, to share with the class. Have them explain how these poems reflect the ideas and characteristics of the Romantic period.

I Never Saw Daffodils So Beautiful

Dorothy Wordsworth

April 15, 1802: . . . The wind seized our breath. The lake was rough. There was a boat by itself floating in the middle of the bay below Water Millock. We rested again in the Water Millock Lane. The hawthorns are black and green, the birches here and there greenish, but there is yet more of purple to be seen on the twigs. We got over into a field to avoid some cows—people working. A few primroses by the roadside—wood sorrel flower, the anemone, scentless violets, strawberries, and that starry, yellow flower which Mrs. C. calls pile wort. When we were in the woods beyond Gowbarrow Park, we saw a few daffodils close to the waterside. We fancied that the lake had floated the seeds ashore, and that the little colony had so sprung up. But as we went along there were more and yet more; and at last, under the boughs of the trees, we saw that there was a long belt of them along the shore, about the breadth of a country turnpike road. I never saw daffodils so beautiful. They grew along the mossy stones about and about them; some rested their heads upon these stones as on a pillow for weariness; and the rest tossed and reeled and danced, and seemed as if they verily laughed with the wind that blew upon them over the lake, they looked so gay, ever glancing, ever changing. This wind blew directly over the lake to them. There was here and there a little knot, and a few stragglers a few yards higher up; but they were so few as not to disturb the simplicity, unity, and life of that one busy highway. We rested again and again. The bays were stormy, and we heard the waves at different distances, and in the middle of the water. Rain came on—we were wet when we reached Luff's. . . .

I Wandered Lonely as a Cloud   **459**

Connecting and Comparing Texts

Despite shared content and the journal entry's possible role in aiding William Wordsworth in composing his poem, the two works have many dissimilarities. Have students comment on the following points:

• The poem describes a solitary experience. How is the journal entry different? [In the journal entry, "we" is used rather than "I," indicating that the writer is accompanied by other people.]

• What reasons may there be for the differences between these two descriptions of the same event? [Possible responses: Dorothy wrote right after the experience happened, while William had time to consider its lasting impact; the two writers had different purposes—the journal writer wished to record an actual event, and the poet wanted to evoke a feeling or mood.]

Connection

Summary ⬅ *at grade level*

Dorothy Wordsworth's journal entry is dated two years before her brother William Wordsworth wrote his poem about the same experience. She describes in detail a springtime walk in the Lake District. The poet might have used her journal to jog his memory when he wrote "I Wandered Lonely as a Cloud."

DIRECT TEACHING

A Reading Informational Text

❓ Find differences between texts. How does the journal entry's introduction of the daffodils differ from the poem's introduction? [Possible responses: The journal entry gives a lot of details about the surroundings, while the poem focuses on the daffodils; the journal entry describes the walkers' route, while the poem describes the speaker's mood and emotions.]

B Literary Focus

❓ Simile. What two things are being compared here? [Daffodils laying upon stones are compared to weary people resting their heads on pillows.]

C Reading Informational Text

❓ Finding differences between texts. What is the difference between the way the poem ends and the way the journal ends? [Possible responses: The poem ends in a mood of blissful tranquility, while the journal entry ends with a description of a storm; the poem ends with a recollection some time after the walk, while the journal entry ends when the walk is over.]

Response and Analysis

Reading Check

1. The speaker's mood is a feeling of loneliness.

2. He sees "a crowd" or a large group of daffodils.

3. He becomes cheerful in the "company" of the daffodils.

4. Later, he reexperiences the blissful emotions of pleasure and joy that he felt at the time.

Thinking Critically

5. "lonely as a cloud/That floats on high o'er vales and hills"

6. Possible answers: *Poem*—"a crowd"; "A host"; "dancing in the breeze"; "Tossing their heads in sprightly dance"; "Outdid the sparkling waves in glee"; "a jocund company"; "dances with the daffodils." *Journal entry*—"rested their heads"; "as on a pillow for weariness"; "tossed and reeled and danced"; "verily laughed"; "gay, ever glancing"; "stragglers."

7. Possible answers: The speaker is referring to the riches of the mind or to treasured memories. People get this wealth by experiencing the wonders of nature.

8. Students may describe the "inward eye" as imagination, memory, or the ability to visualize.

9. Ĭ wándĕred lónelў ás ă clóud Thăt flóats ŏn high ŏ'er váles ănd hĭlls, Whĕn áll ăt ońce Ĭ sáw ă crŏẃd, Ă hóst, ŏf góldĕn dáffŏdĭls,

---

Response and Analysis

Reading Check

1. What is the **speaker's** mood at the beginning of the poem?

2. As the speaker wanders, what does he see "all at once"?

3. How does the speaker's mood change that day because of what he sees?

4. How does the memory of what he saw affect him later?

Thinking Critically

5. What **simile** does the speaker use to describe his loneliness?

6. Which words in the poem **personify** the daffodils, or make them seem like people—even friends and companions —to the lonely speaker? Which words in Dorothy Wordsworth's journal entry (see the **Connection** on page 459) also personify the daffodils?

7. The word *wealth* can mean many different things. What kind of wealth is the speaker referring to in line 18? Name other ways people can get that kind of wealth.

8. How would you explain the "inward eye" in line 21 of the poem?

9. **Scan** the first four lines of "I Wandered Lonely as a Cloud" to show the poem's **meter.** Mark each stressed syllable ' and each unstressed syllable ˘. How does the meter affect the sound of the poem?

SKILLS FOCUS

Literary Skills
Analyze rhythm and meter.

Writing Skills
Write a description.
Write a comparison.

WRITING

Be There Again

Write a **description**—in prose or poetry —of the scene you visualized for your Quickwrite notes. Ask yourself, "What time of year is it? What time of day is it? Is anybody with me? What do I see? What does the scene remind me of? How has the scene affected me?"

Journal and Poem

Write at least one paragraph **comparing** Dorothy Wordsworth's journal entry (see the **Connection** on page 459) with her brother's poem. Before you write, make a chart like the one here to identify how the journal compares with the poem:

	Journal Entry
Details not in poem	
Details that contradict poem	
Figurative language similar to that in poem	
Figurative language different from that in poem	
Lesson drawn from experience (if any)	

ASSESSING

Assessment

■ *Holt Assessment: Literature, Reading, and Vocabulary*

RETEACHING

For a lesson reteaching literary devices, see **Reteaching**, p. 979A. For another selection to teach the sounds of poetry, see *The Holt Reader,* Collection 7.

Before You Read

The Courage That My Mother Had

Make the Connection

Quickwrite 🖉

Is there something in your family that you would like to inherit? It could be something material, like a picture. (In this poem the speaker has inherited a brooch, or large decorative pin, from her mother.) It could also be a wonderful quality or talent—like the ability to play the piano. Jot down your thoughts.

Literary Focus

Rhyme

Rhyme is often the first thing we notice about a poem. We all know rhyme when we hear it; **rhyme** is the repetition of accented vowel sounds, and all sounds following them, in words that are close together: *raid/evade; funny/money*.

Rhymes usually come at the end of a line of poetry. When these **end rhymes** fall in a pattern, it is called a **rhyme scheme**. A rhyme scheme is indicated using different letters of the alphabet, beginning with *a*, for each new rhyme at the end of a line. Here is how the rhyme scheme of this old children's rhyme is indicated:

Little Miss Muffet	*a*
Sat on a tuffet	*a*
Eating her curds and whey.	*b*
Along came a spider	*c*
Who sat down beside her	*c*
And frightened Miss Muffet away.	*b*

The rhyme scheme of Miss Muffet's poem is *aabccb*.

Listen for the rhymes in Millay's poem. What pattern do they make?

Literary Skills
Understand rhyme.

The Courage That My Mother Had

Edna St. Vincent Millay

The courage that my mother had
Went with her, and is with her still:
Rock from New England quarried;
Now granite in a granite hill.

5   The golden brooch my mother wore
She left behind for me to wear;
I have no thing I treasure more:
Yet, it is something I could spare.

Oh, if instead she'd left to me
10 The thing she took into the grave!—
That courage like a rock, which she
Has no more need of, and I have.

The Courage That My Mother Had   **461**

SKILLS FOCUS,
pp. 461–462

Grade-Level Skills
■ **Literary Skills**
Analyze rhyme.

Summary ⬇ *below grade level*

The speaker mourns the loss of her mother and her mother's courage, which is buried with her. She says that her mother left her a brooch, which she treasures, but that she would gladly exchange the jewelry for the courage—which her mother no longer needs and she does.

DIRECT TEACHING

A **Literary Focus**

❷ Rhyme. Where do rhymes occur in this stanza? Are they near rhymes, exact rhymes, end rhymes, or internal rhymes? [The stanza features two sets of end rhymes. *Still* and *hill* are an exact rhyme; *had* and *quarried* are a near rhyme.]

B **English-Language Learners**

Rhyming words. Make sure students realize that *wear* (l. 5) and *spare* (l. 8) rhyme. Also, point out that *grave* (l. 10) and *have* (l. 12) are near rhymes.

RESOURCES: READING

Planning
■ *One-Stop Planner* CD-ROM with ExamView Test Generator

Differentiating Instruction
■ *Holt Reading Solutions*
■ *Supporting Instruction in Spanish*
■ *Audio CD Library, Selections and Summaries in Spanish*

Assessment
■ *Holt Assessment: Literature, Reading, and Vocabulary*
■ *One-Stop Planner* CD-ROM with ExamView Test Generator
■ *Holt Online Assessment*

Internet
■ go.hrw.com (Keyword: LE5 9-7)

■ *Elements of Literature Online*

Media
■ *Audio CD Library*
■ *Audio CD Library, Selections and Summaries in Spanish*

Monitoring students' progress. Ask students to write a note from the speaker to her mother, in which the speaker conveys the feelings she has expressed in the poem.

INDEPENDENT PRACTICE

Response and Analysis

Reading Check

1. She left a golden brooch.
2. She has died and is buried.
3. She wishes for her mother's courage.

Thinking Critically

4. Her mother's courage is twice compared to rock. This comparison suggests that the courage is strong and long lasting.
5. Possible answers: The feeling is a deep, heartfelt yearning; the feeling is mourning for the loss of a quality the speaker does not possess.
6. The poem has an *abab* rhyme scheme. There are four words without exact rhyming partners: They are *had* and *quarried* in the first stanza, and *grave* and *have* in the third stanza.
7. Some students may suggest that relatives can hand down such traits as courage. Other students may say that this is not a genetic trait but a behavioral one that is learned. Through the actions and words of family members modeling the quality of courage, it sets an example for children and grandchildren.

Meet the Writer

Edna St. Vincent Millay

Family Ties
Edna St. Vincent Millay (1892–1950) was born and grew up in Rockland, Maine. She started writing poetry as a child. Millay wrote "Renascence" (ri·nas′əns), one of her most famous poems, when she was only nineteen, and she published her first book of poetry the year she graduated from Vassar College.

As you might have guessed from "The Courage That My Mother Had," the strength of women is an important theme in Millay's writing. Millay worshiped her mother, a strong New Englander who worked as a nurse to support her three daughters after their father deserted the family.

Response and Analysis

Reading Check

1. What has the mother left her daughter?
2. Where is the mother now?
3. What does the daughter wish her mother had left her?

Thinking Critically

4. What **metaphor** in line 3, later expressed as a **simile** in line 11, does Millay use to describe her mother's courage? What does her comparison suggest to you about Millay's view of courage?
5. Like all **lyric poems** this one expresses a strong emotion. How would you describe this feeling?
6. Describe the **rhyme scheme** in this poem by using letters from the alphabet to indicate each end rhyme. Which pairs of words are **approximate rhymes**?
7. Where do you think the quality of courage comes from? Is courage something that can be passed on from one person to another? Can it be learned? Give reasons for your answer.

WRITING

Passing It On
Expand your Quickwrite notes by writing a paragraph describing the material possession, personal quality, or talent that you'd most like to inherit from your family. Try to find a **metaphor** for the possession, quality, or talent that shows how you feel about it. ✏

SKILLS FOCUS

Literary Skills
Analyze rhyme.

Writing Skills
Write a descriptive paragraph.

ASSESSING

Assessment
■ *Holt Assessment: Literature, Reading, and Vocabulary*

RETEACHING

For another selection to teach the sounds of poetry, see *The Holt Reader,* Collection 7.

Before You Read

Ballad of Birmingham

Make the Connection

Quickwrite 🖊

Think of an event that has taken place in your lifetime that tells a story. Jot down your ideas. Now imagine your story as a song. What type of song would it be?

Literary Focus

Ballad

A **ballad** is a song that tells a story, often a story about love, death, or betrayal. Ballads can be sad or humorous. They tell their stories using a steady **rhythm** and a simple pattern of **rhymes,** which make them easy to memorize. A typical ballad uses **repetition,** often in the form of a **refrain**—a phrase or a stanza that is repeated throughout the work, usually at the end of each verse.

Ballads have been popular since the Middle Ages, and in the twenty-first

century the form is still alive and well. Old **folk ballads,** which were composed by unknown singers and passed along orally for many years before being written down, are still sung today. Singers writing new ballads today have a rich tradition to draw on. **Literary ballads,** like the one that follows, are written in imitation of the old ballads.

Every ballad, old or new, tells a tale that can be as gripping as a front-page newspaper story. Dudley Randall wrote his ballad in response to the tragic events that made headlines on September 15, 1963. In the midst of the struggle for civil rights for African Americans, a bomb exploded in a church in Birmingham, Alabama. Four teenage girls were killed.

Like many of the traditional ballads, this one uses dialogue to tell a story.

The Sixteenth Street Baptist Church in 1964, after damaged parts were rebuilt with gifts from around the world.

SKILLS FOCUS

Literary Skills
Understand the characteristics of ballads.

Ballad of Birmingham   463

SKILLS FOCUS,
pp. 463–467

Grade-Level Skills

■ **Literary Skills**
Understand and explain the characteristics of different forms of poetry, including ballads.

Summary ⬇ *below grade level*

Dudley Randall's literary ballad describes the horrifying 1963 bombing of the Sixteenth Street Baptist Church in Birmingham, Alabama, which caused the deaths of four children. Using a simple *abcb* rhyme pattern, the ballad creates a mood of despair. It begins with an ironic conversation between a mother and her daughter. The mother urges her child to go to church, thinking this is a safer place to be than the protest-filled "streets of Birmingham"—a repeated phrase. The final two stanzas relate the mother's frantic efforts to find her child in the wreckage of the church.

PRETEACHING

Skills Starter

Build background. Ask students to share examples of ballads with which they are familiar, for example, "Casey Jones" or "The Wreck of the Hesperus." Have students discuss what characteristics these works share. Provide additional examples of narrative folk songs that take the ballad form. You may wish to play one or more recordings for the class.

RESOURCES: READING

Planning
■ *One-Stop Planner* CD-ROM with ExamView Test Generator

Differentiating Instruction
■ *Holt Reading Solutions*
■ *Supporting Instruction in Spanish*
■ *Audio CD Library, Selections and Summaries in Spanish*

Assessment
■ *Holt Assessment: Literature, Reading, and Vocabulary*
■ *One-Stop Planner* CD-ROM with ExamView Test Generator
■ *Holt Online Assessment*

Internet
■ go.hrw.com (Keyword: LE5 9-7)

■ *Elements of Literature Online*

Media
■ *Audio CD Library*
■ *Audio CD Library, Selections and Summaries in Spanish*

A **Literary Focus**

❓ **Ballad.** What's the rhyme scheme of this stanza? [*abcb*] What quality do the rhymes, along with the rhythm, give the poem? [Possible responses: a musical quality; the sense of a song; a steady drumbeat.]

B **Content-Area Connections**

History: March for Freedom
A freedom march was an organized protest against racial segregation and for civil rights. Often, marchers faced intense hostility. They were blasted with high-pressure water from fire hoses, attacked by police dogs, and beaten with nightsticks.

C **Learners Having Difficulty**

❓ **Questioning.** Why might the speaker describe the dressing process in such detail? [Possible response: The speaker wants to emphasize how much the daughter is valued and treasured, which adds greater poignancy to the mother's loss.]

D **Literary Focus**

❓ **Ballad.** Which words from earlier lines of the poem are repeated in l. 27? ["the streets of Birmingham"] What is the effect of this repetition? [Possible responses: The repetition suggests the refrain of a song; the repetition emphasizes the place where the horrendous act occurred, connecting the name with the act in perpetuity.]

Ballad of Birmingham
(On the bombing of a church in Birmingham, Alabama, 1963)

Dudley Randall

"Mother dear, may I go downtown
Instead of out to play,
And march the streets of Birmingham
In a Freedom March today?"

5 "No, baby, no, you may not go,
For the dogs are fierce and wild,
And clubs and hoses, guns and jails
Aren't good for a little child."

"But, mother, I won't be alone.
10 Other children will go with me,
And march the streets of Birmingham
To make our country free."

"No, baby, no, you may not go,
For I fear those guns will fire.
15 But you may go to church instead
And sing in the children's choir."

She has combed and brushed her
    night-dark hair,
And bathed rose-petal sweet,
And drawn white gloves on her small
    brown hands,
20 And white shoes on her feet.

The mother smiled to know her child
Was in the sacred place,
But that smile was the last smile
To come upon her face.

25 For when she heard the explosion,
Her eyes grew wet and wild.
She raced through the streets of Birmingham
Calling for her child.

She clawed through bits of glass and brick,
30 Then lifted out a shoe.
"O, here's the shoe my baby wore,
But, baby, where are you?"

The Migration Series (1940–1941), Panel 54, by Jacob Lawrence. Tempera on gesso on composition board (12″ × 18″). "For the migrants the church was the center of life." (Text and title revised by the artist 1993.)
The Museum of Modern Art, New York. Gift of Mrs. David M. Levy.

Learners Having Difficulty
Engage students in the narrative by having them create an oral presentation of the poem. Have students work in groups of three to read the parts of mother, daughter, and narrator. Allow the groups time to practice their parts, encouraging them to interpret the words expressively. Then, have the groups present their interpretations to the class, thus allowing listeners to hear different interpretations.

English-Language Learners
These students may not be familiar with the events of the civil rights movement that provide the ballad's historical context. You may wish to display photos or show video footage of such events as freedom marches.

Advanced Learners
Enrichment. Spike Lee's documentary *4 Little Girls* also recounts the story of the

Meet the Writer

Dudley Randall

"I Liked the Feel of Those Books"

The newsboys hawking the *Detroit Free Press* always sold as many copies as they could. One morning, though, one of the boys, Dudley Randall (1914–2000), had a special reason to persuade folks to buy a paper: He'd published his first poem in it.

No one who knew the Randalls would have been surprised to see thirteen-year-old Dudley's name in print. His father, a minister, loved to recite poems and often used them in his sermons. "There were a

lot of books around the house," Randall recalled, including beautifully bound volumes of poetry by Alfred, Lord Tennyson and Robert Browning. "I liked the feel of those books."

After serving in the army during World War II, Randall devoted himself to the books he loved. He worked his way through college and graduate school, and he became a university librarian as well as a poet. Then, in 1965, he started his own publishing company, Broadside Press, "so black people could speak to and for their people."

"Ballad of Birmingham" was the first poem Broadside Press published. (It was an actual broadside—a large poster with the poem printed on it.) Randall poured his time, energy, and money into the publishing venture. At first he ran the press from his home; later he moved to a small building next door. A friend recalled, "I would often walk in and see him doing everything from writing invoices and packing boxes to sweeping the floor."

Many outstanding poets of the time sent their work to Broadside: Alice Walker, Gwendolyn Brooks, Robert Hayden, Nikki Giovanni, Amiri Baraka (Leroi Jones), Audre Lorde, Etheridge Knight, and dozens more. Randall encouraged and supported African American writers, and they in turn saw Broadside Press as their own.

Monitoring students' progress. To assess students' understanding of the ballad, ask them to create a sequence-of-events chain that outlines the events of the poem in the order in which they occur.

Meet the Writer

Background. Dudley Randall was said to have started the Broadside Press with only twelve dollars. Eventually the publisher had ninety poetry titles and had printed half a million books. In 1981, the mayor of Detroit pronounced Randall poet laureate of the city.

For Independent Reading

■ You may wish to recommend to students a Newbery Honor Book, *The Watsons Go to Birmingham*, by Christopher Paul Curtis. Set in Birmingham, Alabama, in 1963, this young adult novel uses fictional characters to tell the historical events of that year, including the bombing of the Sixteenth Street Baptist Church.

September 15, 1963, bombing. You might wish to preview and recommend the film. **Activity.** Students who have seen the film may compare that experience to reading about the events. Ask students to discuss which version of the events they find most effective—the film, the ballad, or the factual account.

Connection

Summary ⟷ *at grade level*

"The History Behind the Ballad" provides a factual account of the September 15, 1963, bombing that inspired Dudley Randall's poem. The author describes the activities of the four girls attending Youth Day at the Sixteenth Street Baptist Church before the bombing, the terrible moment when the bombing occurred, and the grim aftermath as Maxine McNair searches for her child.

DIRECT TEACHING

Ⓐ Reading Informational Text

❷ Analyzing author's intent. Why does the author provide details about the girls' activities when readers already know of their tragic fate? [Possible response: To prolong the readers' feeling of dread and heighten their feelings of being helpless to stop the tragedy.]

Ⓑ Literary Focus

❷ Irony. Why is it ironic that the bombing took place in a church? [Possible response: The people in the church are striving for goodness and do not deserve to be the objects of hatred.]

Ⓒ Reading Informational Text

❷ Find differences between texts. What perspective does this historical account give you that you do not receive in Dudley Randall's ballad about the same events? [Possible response: The account gives readers the perspective of the adults who were attending church when the bombing occurred.]

The History Behind the Ballad

Taylor Branch

The following account is from Parting the Waters, *a book that won the Pulitzer Prize in history in 1989.*

Ⓐ That Sunday was the annual Youth Day at the Sixteenth Street Baptist Church. Mamie H. Grier, superintendent of the Sunday school, stopped in at the basement ladies' room to find four young girls who had left Bible classes early and were talking excitedly about the beginning of the school year. All four were dressed in white from head to toe, as this was their day to run the main service for the adults at eleven o'clock. Grier urged them to hurry along and then went upstairs to sit in on her own women's Sunday-school class. They were engaged in a lively debate Ⓑ on the lesson topic, "The Love That Forgives," when a loud earthquake shook the entire church and showered the classroom with plaster and debris. Grier's first thought was that it was like a ticker-tape parade. Maxine McNair, a schoolteacher sitting next to her, reflexively went stiff and was the only Ⓒ one to speak. "Oh, my goodness!" she said. She escaped with Grier, but the stairs down to the basement were blocked and the large stone staircase on the outside literally had vanished. They stumbled through the church to the front door and then made their way around outside through the gathering noise of moans and sirens. A hysterical church member shouted to Grier that her husband had already gone to the hospital in the first ambulance. McNair searched desperately for her only child until finally she came upon a sobbing old man and screamed, "Daddy, I can't find Denise!" The man helplessly replied, "She's dead, baby. I've got one of her shoes." He held a girl's white dress shoe, and the look on his daughter's face made him scream out, "I'd like to blow the whole town up!"

The windows of the Sixteenth Street Baptist Church, where four young girls were killed.

Connecting and Comparing Texts

Encourage students to discuss their responses to each of the two selections. Ask, "Did Dudley Randall and Taylor Branch have different purposes for writing?" [Possible response: Randall composed his ballad to trigger a strong emotional response in the reader. While Branch's account may also trigger such feelings as anger or sadness, the article was written to provide an accurate, detail-filled account of the events that occurred.]

Response and Analysis

Reading Check

1. Who are the two people who speak in this ballad?

2. What does the younger person ask permission to do? Why does the older person say no?

3. What happens that day in the church?

4. What does the older person find after clawing through glass and brick?

Thinking Critically

5. This ballad's emotional effect is based in part on **dramatic irony,** which occurs when the reader knows something that a character does not know. What does the reader know that the mother in the ballad doesn't know? Explain why the mother's refusing to let her child join a demonstration and sending her to church instead is a powerful example of dramatic irony.

6. Find and explain an example of **irony** (the contrast between what is expected or considered appropriate and what actually happens) in "The History Behind the Ballad," Taylor Branch's historical account of the church bombing (see the *Connection* on page 466).

7. This ballad does not have a refrain, but it does contain **repetition.** Which two lines are repeated? What does the repetition of the words *baby, child,* and *children* add to the emotional effect of the poem?

8. Like many folk ballads this **literary ballad** is written in four-line stanzas with **end rhymes.** Which lines rhyme in every stanza of this ballad?

9. Read the ballad aloud, paying special attention to its **rhythm** and **end rhyme.** How would you describe the sound of the ballad?

WRITING

Recasting the News

Go back to your Quickwrite notes. Turn one of the subjects on your list into a **ballad.** If you want a challenge, try to find rhyming words to end either lines 1 and 3 or lines 2 and 4. You might want to imitate the style of Randall's ballad and use **dialogue** to tell your story.

Poetry and History

In a short essay, **compare** and **contrast** Randall's ballad with Branch's historical account (see the *Connection* on page 466). Although the authors use very different forms to tell the same story, what similarities do you see between the two works? Consider, for example, the use of **descriptive details, dialogue,** and **irony.** What are the key differences between the two works? Conclude by explaining whether the ballad or the historical account seems most powerful to you.

▶ For help writing a comparison-contrast essay, see pages 230 and 268.

	Ballad	Historical Account
Descriptive details		
Dialogue		
Irony		
Impact on me		

SKILLS FOCUS

Literary Skills
Analyze the characteristics of ballads.

Writing Skills
Write a ballad. Write a comparison-contrast essay.

Response and Analysis

Reading Check

1. The speakers are a child and her mother.

2. The child asks for permission to participate in a freedom march. Her mother, fearing for her safety, denies permission and tells her to go to church.

3. An explosion rocks the church.

4. The mother finds her daughter's shoe.

Thinking Critically

5. The mother's sending her daughter to church is dramatic irony because the reader knows that church is the *least* safe place. The reader realizes that the church will be bombed and the child will die there. Sadly, the mother's concern results in her daughter's death.

6. Possible answers: On a day when the women's Sunday school topic is love and forgiveness, an almost unforgivably heinous act of racial hatred occurs; the girls are excited about a school year that they will not be alive to finish.

7. "And march the streets of Birmingham" occurs twice, in ll. 3 and 11 (the closely matching "through the streets of Birmingham" occurs in l. 27). "No, baby, no, you may not go" occurs twice, in ll. 5 and 13. The repetition of the words *baby, child,* and *children* emphasizes that the victims were the most innocent and helpless members of society.

8. The second and fourth lines of each stanza rhyme.

9. Possible answer: The rhythm and end rhyme create a sound pattern that makes the reader anticipate the poem's conclusion.

Assessment

■ *Holt Assessment: Literature, Reading, and Vocabulary*

Grade-Level Skills

■ **Literary Skills**
Understand and explain the characteristics of free verse.

Summary  *above grade level*

As the speaker removes a splinter from his wife's thumb, he remembers a similar incident from his childhood, when his father pulled a splinter from his palm. The speaker remembers his father's tenderness rather than the pain. Love transforms the operation— the metal splinter is imagined as a gift planted in the boy's hand by his father. This recollection might explain the speaker's own tenderness as he delicately performs a similar operation for his wife.

PRETEACHING

Selection Starter

Motivate. Ask students to recall some occasions that were especially frightening to them when they were young children, such as getting a vaccination, visiting the dentist, or being treated after they had fallen and skinned their knees. What did a parent, friend, or healthcare worker do to try to keep them calm on these occasions?

Before You Read

The Gift

Make the Connection
Quickwrite 🖉
Try to recall a time when a parent, a teacher, or a friend did something special for you that you would like to be able to do for others someday. (Maybe you have already done it.) Write down what you remember about that person's actions and your feelings about them.

Literary Focus
Free Verse

Free verse is poetry that does not adhere to strict patterns of rhyme and meter. No rhyme scheme. No regular meter. No rules about line length and stanzas to worry about. What could be easier to write than free verse?

You have probably learned by now that writing anything well is not easy— especially poetry. A free-verse poem may not have rhyme and meter, but it does have clearly focused images, original figures of speech, and words chosen carefully for both what they mean and what they suggest.

Free verse also has rhythm. The **rhythm** in free verse comes from the natural rise and fall of the voice, from pauses, and from the balance between long and short lines. Rhythm also comes from the repetition of sounds, words, phrases, and even entire lines.

Read "The Gift" aloud, watching for punctuation marks. Pause briefly at commas. Make full stops at periods. Let your voice rise and fall in a natural way, like the voice of an oral storyteller. Do you feel the poem's rhythm?

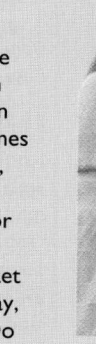

SKILLS FOCUS

Literary Skills
Understand the characteristics of free verse.

RESOURCES: READING

Planning
■ *One-Stop Planner* CD-ROM with ExamView Test Generator

Differentiating Instruction
■ *Holt Reading Solutions*
■ *Supporting Instruction in Spanish*
■ *Audio CD Library, Selections and Summaries in Spanish*

Assessment
■ *Holt Assessment: Literature, Reading, and Vocabulary*
■ *One-Stop Planner* CD-ROM with ExamView Test Generator
■ *Holt Online Assessment*

Internet
■ go.hrw.com (Keyword: LE5 9-7)

■ *Elements of Literature Online*
Media
■ *Audio CD Library*
■ *Audio CD Library, Selections and Summaries in Spanish*

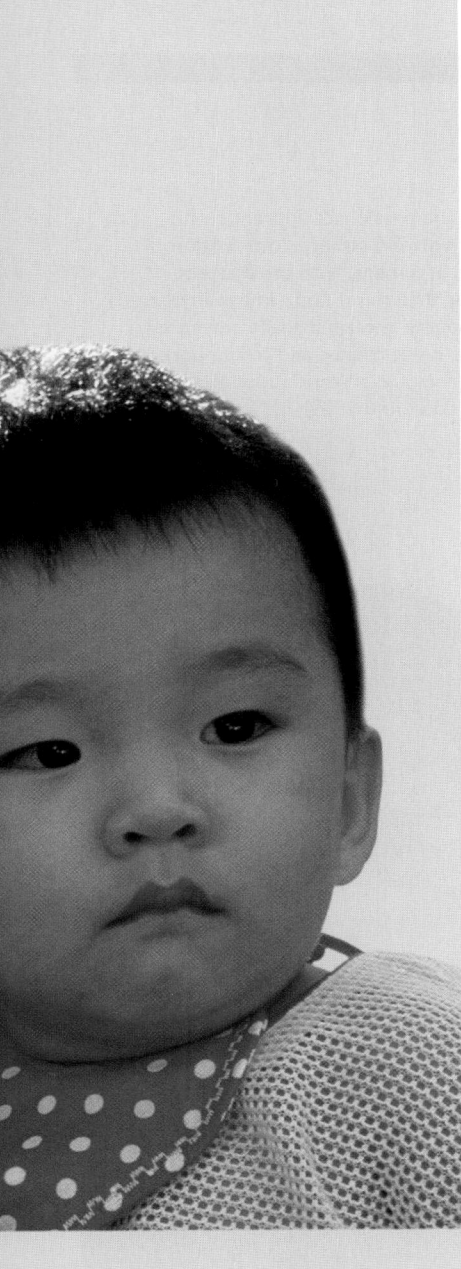

The Gift

Li-Young Lee

To pull the metal splinter from my palm
my father recited a story in a low voice.
I watched his lovely face and not the blade.
Before the story ended he'd removed
5 the iron sliver I thought I'd die from.

I can't remember the tale
but hear his voice still, a well
of dark water, a prayer.
And I recall his hands,
10 two measures of tenderness
he laid against my face,
the flames of discipline
he raised above my head.

Had you entered that afternoon
15 you would have thought you saw a man
planting something in a boy's palm,
a silver tear, a tiny flame.
Had you followed that boy
you would have arrived here,
20 where I bend over my wife's right hand.

Look how I shave her thumbnail down
so carefully she feels no pain.
Watch as I lift the splinter out.
I was seven when my father
25 took my hand like this,
and I did not hold that shard
between my fingers and think,
Metal that will bury me,
christen it Little Assassin,
30 Ore Going Deep for My Heart.
And I did not lift up my wound and cry,
Death visited here!
I did what a child does
when he's given something to keep.
35 I kissed my father.

DIRECT TEACHING

A Literary Focus

❓ Free verse. Notice how the poem appears on the page. Do the lines of this stanza have the same number of syllables as the lines in the previous stanza? [The lines in this stanza have fewer syllables.] Does every stanza have the same number of lines? [no] How can you tell that this is a poem and not prose? [Possible responses: It has rhythm, as shown by the lines and pauses, and it is filled with original figures of speech. The ideas are suggested in compressed images rather than spelled out.]

B Reading Skills

❓ Interpreting. Call students' attention to the words "Look" and "Watch" that begin ll. 21 and 23. What does the speaker want the reader to notice? [Possible responses: He wants to show how carefully he removes the splinter from his wife's hand. He is demonstrating that he has learned tenderness from his father.]

C Literary Focus

❓ Free verse. Call attention to the four punctuation marks in the last five lines. Read the stanza aloud for the class, letting your voice rise for the line that ends in an exclamation mark and pause significantly before the last line. What effect is produced by this punctuation? [Possible response: It imparts a sense of urgency, which culminates at the exclamation mark and is followed by a renewed sense of tenderness and calm.]

DIFFERENTIATING INSTRUCTION

Learners Having Difficulty
The poem's shifts in time may confuse some students. Help them recognize that only ll. 18–23 pertain to the present, while the lines preceding and following that section pertain to the past. You may wish to give students a photocopy of the poem and have students use a highlighter to differentiate these lines from the rest.

English-Language Learners
Students learning English may have a more difficult time appreciating the rhythmic and musical qualities of free-verse poetry when reading it themselves. After their initial reading of the poem, suggest that students listen to the recording of the poem in the *Audio CD Library*.

Monitoring students' progress.
Guide the class in answering these comprehension questions.

True-False

1. The speaker tells of an injury to his knee. [F]

2. The son clearly remembers the tale his father tells him. [F]

3. Both father and son remove a splinter from someone's hand. [T]

4. The boy kisses his father. [T]

Meet the Writer

Li-Young Lee

"The Winged Seed"

The great-grandfather of Li-Young Lee (1957–   ) was the first president of the Republic of China. His father, on whom the character in "The Gift" is based, was the personal physician to the revolutionary leader Mao Tse-tung. In the 1950s, the family fled the political turmoil in China when the Communist People's Republic was established. They went first to Indonesia, and Li-Young Lee was born in Jakarta. There his father was thrown into jail by the corrupt dictator Sukarno. His father spent nineteen months in prison, seventeen of them in a leper colony. When the family fled again, they went to Hong Kong. When Lee was six, they arrived in the United States, where his father became a Presbyterian minister.

Lee has recorded his family's history in *The Winged Seed: A Remembrance* (1995). His first book of poems, *Rose,* won the 1986 Delmore Schwartz Memorial Poetry Award, and a second book, *The City in Which I Love You,* was the 1990 Lamont Poetry Selection of the Academy of American Poets.

Lee, who now lives in Chicago with his family, has said about his writing:

❝I know I am not a poet. How do I know this? Because I know a poet when I read one. There are living poets in the world today. I am not one of them. But I want to be one, and I know only of one path: serious and passionate apprenticeship, which involves a strange combination of awe and argument, with the Masters.

Other than this, I don't know anything about poetry, though if space permitted, I could go on earnestly, and to the boredom and horror of everyone, about all those things I don't know.❞

Advanced Learners
Enrichment. The speaker in "The Gift" shifts between the past and the present. Ask students to chart the time shifts and the linking elements of the poem. They could use a time line or create their own original graphic organizer. To help them get started, ask the following questions:

• How many time periods are represented in "The Gift"? [two] What is the action that links the different time periods? [removing a splinter from a hand]

• In what direction does the poem move in time? ["The Gift" moves from the past to the present and then back to the past.]

• What purpose does this time shifting serve? [Possible responses: It shows how the present can trigger memories of the past; it reveals a major influence on the speaker in his growth from boy to man.]

Response and Analysis

Reading Check

1. What does the **speaker** of the poem remember about his father when he removed a splinter from the speaker's hand?

2. Later in the poem, whose splinter does the speaker remove?

3. What was the speaker given to keep? What did the speaker give his father in return?

Thinking Critically

4. In the first stanza, why do you think the father recited a story to his son?

5. Throughout the poem, Lee uses precise **images.** List at least four images that appeal to your senses of sight, hearing, and touch and therefore help you imagine what happened to the little boy and to the speaker's wife.

6. In the second stanza, what **metaphors** does the speaker use to describe his father's voice? What metaphor describes his father's hands? What do these figures of speech reveal about the speaker's feelings toward his father?

7. In the third stanza, whom do you think the speaker is talking to when he says "you"? What scene is taking place in the present?

8. What does the speaker say he *didn't* do with the shard, or piece of metal, in his hand? Why, instead, did he kiss his father?

9. How is the speaker's behavior in the present, described in the third and fourth stanzas, similar to his father's behavior in the first two stanzas?

10. Read the poem aloud, and listen to the sounds it creates. The poet is so skillful that we hardly notice his

technique—but it is there. In line 1, what sounds are **alliterated**? What **sentence pattern** is repeated in the third stanza? What pattern is repeated in the fourth stanza? What initial sound is **alliterated** in line 17?

Extending and Evaluating

11. In lines 26–32, the poem has a brief but intense change in tone. What is the **tone,** or the speaker's attitude, in these lines, and how does it differ from the tone in the rest of the poem? List words that help create the tone in this section. Then, explain whether you find these lines distracting. Why might the poet have included them?

WRITING

A Gift to You

Write a **free-verse poem** about a gift you received. The gift could have come in the form of advice or in the form of an experience in which you learned something valuable, such as the one you described in your Quickwrite notes. Use **images** and **figures of speech** to show how you feel about the person who gave you the gift. Try to repeat sentence patterns to create **rhythm.** Read the lines of your poem over, revising them until you're pleased with the way they sound. Can you feel the rhythm?

Analyzing Free Verse

Write a few paragraphs analyzing the strategies Li-Young Lee uses in "The Gift" to create verbal music. Look specifically for the **repetition** of words and **alliteration.** Discuss the ways he creates a natural rhythm in his poem.

▶ Use "Analyzing a Poem," pages 480–487, for help with this assignment.

SKILLS FOCUS

Literary Skills
Analyze the characteristics of free verse.

Writing Skills
Write a free-verse poem. Write an analysis of a free-verse poem.

Assessment

■ *Holt Assessment: Literature, Reading, and Vocabulary*

Response and Analysis

Reading Check

1. The speaker remembers his father's hands and voice.

2. The speaker removes his wife's splinter.

3. The speaker was given his father's tender care. He gave his father a kiss in return.

Thinking Critically

4. The father is distracting his son while he removes a splinter.

5. Possible answers: "a silver tear, a tiny flame"; "hear his voice still, a well/of dark water, a prayer"; "his hands,/two measures of tenderness/he laid against my face."

6. *Voice*—"a well of dark water"; "a prayer." *Hands*—"two measures of tenderness." These figures of speech depict the speaker's father as a kindly figure.

7. The speaker is talking to the reader. As an adult, he is removing a splinter from his wife's hand.

8. He did *not* hold the shard up and acknowledge the pain it caused him. He kissed his father instead to thank him.

9. The speaker soothes and distracts his wife as he removes the splinter from her hand.

10. The *p* sound is repeated in l. 1 (*pull, splinter, palm*). In the third stanza, "Had you" and "you would have" are each used twice to begin lines. In the fourth stanza, "And I did not" is used twice to begin sentences.

Extending and Evaluating

11. Possible answer: In ll. 26–32, the calm tone becomes more dramatic with the use of words such as *assassin* and *death*. These lines may indicate the childish panic the speaker might have felt had his father been a less-reassuring presence.

Grade-Level Skills

■ **Literary Skills**
Analyze tone, voice, persona, and choice of narrator.

Summary  *at grade level*

The speaker's tone conveys the anxiety and discomfort felt by people who are bilingual and bicultural living in the United States. Although the speaker can function effectively in either an Anglo or a Mexican context, she does not feel fully at home in either of them. She straddles two worlds that are separate and suspicious of each other, and both worlds view her, at least to some extent, with prejudice. The two versions of the poem, one in English and one in Spanish, reinforce the speaker's bilingual background.

PRETEACHING

Selection Starter

Motivate. Before students begin reading, ask them to consider the title of the poem. Ask, "What might the poet be referring to? What is the difference between a legal and illegal alien?" [Students may suggest that unlike illegal aliens, or people who have entered the country unlawfully, a "legal alien" is someone who has every right to be here but who may be treated or may feel like an outsider.]

Before You Read

Legal Alien/Extranjera legal

Make the Connection

Quickwrite ✏️

Think of all the worlds you belong to: the worlds of home, family, school, sports, and friends, for example. Make a chart like the one here, in which you list at least three ways you feel or behave in *two* of your worlds:

INTERNET
More About
Pat Mora
Keyword: LE5 9-7

My Worlds	
School	Sports
average student	great pitcher
good in math	OK fielder
quiet, shy	confident

Literary Focus

SKILLS FOCUS

Literary Skills
Understand a speaker's persona, tone, and voice.

Speaker

Poets can imagine anyone or anything as their **speaker,** the voice talking to us in a poem. The speaker is often the poet—but not always. The poet may assume a **persona,** or mask, and speak as someone much younger or older than himself or herself. Sometimes the speaker is an animal or even an object that doesn't have the power of speech in real life.

The choice of a speaker affects a poem's **tone,** the attitude expressed toward its subject or audience. The speaker's tone and his or her style of speaking create the speaker's **voice.**

As you read a poem, listen carefully to the voice. Do you hear the formal, somber voice of an older man reflecting on his life? Do you hear the excited chatter of a young child? Often the speaker's identity and voice are keys to the meaning of a poem.

As you start to read Pat Mora's poem, ask yourself, "Who's talking to me?" Keep in mind that a legal alien is a person from another country who enters the United States through legal channels.

RESOURCES: READING

Planning
■ *One-Stop Planner* CD-ROM with ExamView Test Generator

Differentiating Instruction
■ *Holt Reading Solutions*
■ *Supporting Instruction in Spanish*
■ *Audio CD Library, Selections and Summaries in Spanish*

Assessment
■ *Holt Assessment: Literature, Reading, and Vocabulary*
■ *One-Stop Planner* CD-ROM with ExamView Test Generator
■ *Holt Online Assessment*

Internet
■ go.hrw.com (Keyword: LE5 9-7)

■ *Elements of Literature Online*

Media
■ *Audio CD Library*
■ *Audio CD Library, Selections and Summaries in Spanish*

Legal Alien

Pat Mora

Bi-lingual, Bi-cultural,
able to slip from "How's life?"
to *"Me'stan volviendo loca,"*°
able to sit in a paneled office
5   drafting memos in smooth English,
able to order in fluent Spanish
at a Mexican restaurant,
American but hyphenated,
viewed by Anglos as perhaps exotic,
10 perhaps inferior, definitely different,
viewed by Mexicans as alien
(their eyes say, "You may speak
Spanish but you're not like me"),
an American to Mexicans
15 a Mexican to Americans
a handy token
sliding back and forth
between the fringes of both worlds
by smiling
20 by masking the discomfort
of being pre-judged
Bi-laterally.°

3. *Me'stan ... loca* (me·stän′ vōl·vē·en′ dō lō′cä):
   Spanish for "They're driving me crazy."
22. **Bi-laterally** (bī·lat′ər·əl·ē) *adv.:* by both sides.
    (Mora has added a hyphen to this word.)

Extranjera legal

Pat Mora

Bi-lingüe, bi-cultural,
capaz de deslizarse de *"How's life?"*
a "Me'stan volviendo loca,"
capaz de ocupar un despacho bien apuntado,
5   redactando memorandums en inglés liso,
capaz de ordenar la cena en español fluido
en restaurante mexicano,
americana pero con guión,
vista por los anglos como exótica,
10 quizás inferior, obviamente distinta,
vista por mexicanos como extranjera
(sus ojos dicen "Hablas español
pero no eres como yo"),
americana para mexicanos
15 mexicana para americanos
una ficha servible
pasando de un lado al otro
de los márgenes de dos mundos
sonriéndome
20 disfrazando la incomodidad
del pre-juicio
bi-lateralmente.

United States BILINGUAL Spanish

Legal Alien / Extranjera legal   **473**

Legal Alien / Extranjera legal   **473**

Response and Analysis

Reading Check

1. They view her as exotic, inferior, and different.

2. The speaker believes that they are suspicious of the ease with which she fits into Anglo society.

3. The speaker's smile masks the discomfort of a bicultural life.

Thinking Critically

4. Possible answers: The speaker is a person of Mexican American heritage who speaks both Spanish and English and functions well in both Anglo and Mexican society. Details such as "Bi-lingual, Bi-cultural," "drafting memos in smooth English," and "able to order in fluent Spanish / at a Mexican restaurant" reveal the speaker's identity.

5. The speaker means that she has a dual cultural background, suggesting the two-word terms we often use to describe people's ethnic heritages. Some students may say that, with the exception of Native Americans, everyone is "hyphenated." Most will say that Americans should be proud of a bicultural identity.

6. In the sense of "symbol," *token* suggests that the speaker has no individual identity or value; in the sense of "something used in place of money," *token* suggests that the speaker is a medium of exchange between cultures.

7. Possible answers: The voice of the persona is sarcastic and slightly angry. The words "exotic," "inferior," and "alien" (ll. 9–11) suggest a slightly sarcastic tone; "token," "fringes," "discomfort," and "pre-judged" (ll. 16–21) suggest an angry tone.

Meet the Writer

Pat Mora

Beyond Borders

Pat Mora (1942–   ) maintains that people's identities grow out of all the worlds they inhabit—the ones they inherit from the past as well as the ones they encounter as they go through life. Born and raised in the border town of El Paso, Texas, Mora has spent her life observing the interactions between Mexican and Anglo cultures. While never denying the painful side of bicultural existence, Mora stresses the harmonies between the cultures—harmonies that are the result of centuries of shared living. She finds the differences among people less important than the things all cultures share—marrying, raising children, working, growing old, and dying.

The poem "Legal Alien" is from *Chants* (1984), Mora's first book of poems. Her other books include *Communion* (1991), a book of poems, and *House of Houses* (1997), a memoir of her family.

Response and Analysis

Reading Check

1. According to the speaker, how do Americans view her?

2. Why does the speaker believe that Mexicans view her as "alien"?

3. What does her smile "mask," or hide?

Thinking Critically

SKILLS FOCUS

Literary Skills
Analyze a speaker's persona, tone, and voice.

Writing Skills
Write a poem.

4. Who do you think the **speaker** of "Legal Alien" is? How do you know?

5. What does the speaker mean when she says, "American but hyphenated"? Who could say they are unhyphenated Americans? In the great "melting pot" of cultures that is America, why might "hyphenated Americans" feel proud of their two heritages?

6. In line 16, the speaker uses a **metaphor** in which she compares herself to a token. However, *token* is a word with multiple meanings. What different meanings of *token* is the poet suggesting?

7. Read the poem aloud, and listen carefully to how the speaker expresses her thoughts. How would you describe the **voice** of the **persona**? To answer, consider her **tone** and her style of speaking.

WRITING

Your Worlds

Use the notes you made for the Quickwrite on page 472 as the basis for a **poem** about the worlds you live in. You might want to use this framework:

In the world of . . . ,
I am . . .

In the world of . . . ,
I am . . .

Some people think I'm . . . ,
But I am really . . .

ASSESSING

Assessment

- *Holt Assessment: Literature, Reading, and Vocabulary*

RETEACHING

For a lesson reteaching narrator and tone, see **Reteaching,** p. 979A.

Before You Read

The Base Stealer
American Hero

Make the Connection

Quickwrite

Take a few minutes to imagine that you're a sports hero. You pick the sport—one that you've played or one that you've watched a lot. Imagine that you're at the critical point in an important game. The pressure's on. You go into action. Jot down what happens and what you are feeling.

Literary Focus

Sound and Sense

Baseball games, basketball games, football games, hockey games—all are exciting because they are like stories: They have a beginning, a middle, and an end, and they contain action and tension. When poets tackle sports, they use elements of poetry

to try to re-create the excitement—and even the beauty—of the game.

One of the poems that follows is about a base stealer. The base stealer is modeled on Jackie Robinson, who played mostly second base for the Brooklyn Dodgers from 1947 to 1956. (For an essay about Robinson, see page 744.) The other poem is about an unnamed basketball player whose slam-dunk wins the game. The poets use sentence structure, alliteration, and onomatopoeia to help us see and hear what happens on the court and on the field.

Poets sometimes use **sentence structure** to reflect the meaning of a line of poetry. To describe a short, quick action, a poet might place just one short sentence in a line of a poem. To describe a long, continuous action, a poet might continue the description for several lines. As you read "The Base Stealer," listen to how the poet uses sentence structure to reflect the actions described in the poem.

Alliteration is the repetition of consonant sounds in several words, usually at the beginnings of the words. The sentence *Harry hurried home for a hamburger* uses alliteration. Advertisers make use of alliteration all the time because they know it is pleasing to our ears.

Onomatopoeia is the use of a word whose sound imitates or suggests its meaning (*clang, honk, meow*). One television sportscaster became famous for his use of onomatopoeia when he said "swish" every time a player made a basket. You'll find more examples of onomatopoeia in "American Hero."

Literary Skills
Understand alliteration, onomatopoeia, and sentence structure.

The Base Stealer / American Hero **475**

SKILLS FOCUS,
pp. 475–478

Grade-Level Skills

■ **Literary Skills**
Analyze various literary devices, including alliteration and onomatopoeia.

■ **Literary Skills**
Analyze sentence structure in a poem.

Summary ↔ *at grade level*

In "The Base Stealer," a baseball player readies himself to try and steal a base. The tension is evident as the player navigates the moment between the two bases. He is balanced in two directions. His movements are compared to those of a tightrope-walker: "Both ways taut." The poet uses alliteration to heighten the sense of the moment. The tense anticipation of the crowd is conveyed through the repetition of their unspoken thoughts as they await the moment of theft.

"American Hero" opens with an exhilarating description of a basketball player's star performance. The game's fast pace and immediacy are conveyed through metaphor, alliteration, an accumulation of sensory details, and onomatopoeia. The player is pumped up by the wildly cheering audience but is quickly deflated when he thinks of less friendly crowds. He realizes that his presence is unwelcome in some neighborhoods, where he is judged on the basis of race rather than talent.

Jackie Robinson slides into home plate.

The Base Stealer

Robert Francis

Poised between going on and back, pulled
Both ways taut like a tightrope-walker,
Fingertips pointing the opposites,
Now bouncing tiptoe like a dropped ball
5   Or a kid skipping rope, come on, come on,
Running a scattering of steps sidewise,
How he teeters, skitters, tingles, teases,
Taunts them, hovers like an ecstatic bird,
He's only flirting, crowd him, crowd him,
10 Delicate, delicate, delicate, delicate—now!

American Hero

Essex Hemphill

I have nothing to lose tonight.
All my men surround me, panting,
as I spin the ball above our heads
on my middle finger.
5   It's a shimmering club light
and I'm dancing, slick in my sweat.
Squinting, I aim at the hole
fifty feet away. I let the tension go.
Shoot for the net. Choke it.
10 I never hear the ball
slap the backboard. I slam it
through the net. The crowd goes wild
for our win. I scored
thirty-two points this game
15 and they love me for it.
Everyone hollering
is a friend tonight.
But there are towns,
certain neighborhoods
20 where I'd be hard pressed
to hear them cheer
if I move on the block.

Meet the Writers

Robert Francis
Essex Hemphill

A One-man Show

Robert Francis (1901–1987) liked to do things for himself. He lived alone in a cottage on the outskirts of Amherst, Massachusetts, baking his own bread, growing his own vegetables, and walking seven miles round-trip to town for groceries and library books because he didn't earn enough money from his writing to buy a car.

When publishers rejected his fourth collection of poems, Francis paid a printer to run copies labeled "Published by the Author." When the volume failed to draw attention, he went one step further: He wrote a negative review of his own book ("The subjects, for the most part, are most unpoetic . . . Strange as anything else are, if

you please, two baseball poems."), and he sent it to the local newspaper under an assumed name, hoping someone would write in to defend him. No one did. So Francis wrote another letter criticizing the first. Unfortunately, the paper did not print the second letter. Eventually Francis found many publishers for his writings.

Francis once said,

❝Poetry is at its best when it provides enjoyable excitement and when that excitement comes as much from what the poet makes of words as from what he says in words. Poetry at its best is a highly skilled game a poet plays with life and language, a game that the reader can follow play by play. . . . ❞

"Take Care of Your Blessings"

When **Essex Hemphill** (1957–1995) said goodbye to friends, he used to add, "Take care of your blessings." He believed that everyone has special gifts that need to be nurtured and used to the fullest. "Our blessings," he said, "are only as good to us as we are to them."

Hemphill found one of his blessings when he was fourteen. Feeling out of place in his working-class neighborhood in Washington, D.C., he turned to writing as a way to explore who he really was. "Tablets, journals, those became my confidants," he said.

As a student at the University of Maryland, he made friends with a group of local

African American poets (one recalls him as "a young brother with a big heart"), and he discovered another blessing—a talent for performance. Hemphill loved to read his poems aloud. He said that "poetry doesn't solely live on the page. Poetry is meant to be heard."

Before his tragic death at thirty-eight, Hemphill had become widely known as a writer, editor, and activist. He said,

❝I'm part of a generation that is making it possible for the young to feel empowered earlier . . . I know long after I'm gone, the space I'm carving out will help other voices come through. ❞

Monitoring students' progress. Guide the class in answering these comprehension questions. Direct students to locate words and passages in the poems that support their responses.

True-False

The Base Stealer

1. The speaker is a tightrope-walker. [F]
2. A base runner is caught stealing. [F]

American Hero

3. The hero has disappointed his fans tonight. [F]
4. A basket is made from fifty feet away. [T]
5. The speaker realizes that he would not be considered a hero in some neighborhoods. [T]

For Independent Reading

Students who appreciated the two sports-related selections will enjoy reading Mel Glenn's *Jump Ball: A Basketball Season in Poems*. Glenn uses poetry to follow the championship season of a fictional high school basketball team. Along the way, he explores a variety of serious themes relevant to teenage readers.

SKILLS REVIEW

Technical vocabulary. Explain to students that most sports, fields of study, and occupations have their own technical or specialized vocabulary—a set of words and phrases that are used to describe things specific to that field. Tell students that context can help them understand unfamiliar technical vocabulary. For example, a person unfamiliar with basketball might not know that *hole* (l. 7 in

"American Hero") means "basketball hoop." Using the surrounding words and sentences, however, a reader can easily determine that the speaker is aiming the ball at the basket.
Activity. The following three steps can help students review their understanding of using word meanings in context: (1) Ask experts in the class to list technical basketball terms, such as *pick-and-roll, screen, key,* and *post up.*

(2) Have the experts write sentences that contain the terms and context clues, such as examples and restatements, to their meanings. (3) Have students unfamiliar with the game try to define the terms using only the context of the sentences.

Response and Analysis

Reading Check

1. The runner is taking a lead from first base, poised to steal second.

2. Possible answers: spin, dancing, squinting, aim, shoot, choke, slam.

Thinking Critically

3. In l. 1 of "The Base Stealer," the *p* sound repeats in *poised* and *pulled*; in l. 2, the *t* sound repeats in *taut* and *tightrope*; in l. 4, the *b* sound repeats in *bouncing* and *ball* and the *t* sound in *tiptoe*. In l. 2 of "American Hero," the *m* sound repeats in *my*, *men*, and *me*; in ll. 6–7, the *s* sound repeats in *slick*, *sweat*, and *squinting*; in ll. 10–11, the *b* sound repeats in *ball* and *backboard*.

4. Possible answer: *slap, slam,* and *hollering* are onomatopoeic. They help re-create the aural excitement of a basketball game, immersing the reader in the sounds of the event.

5. The phrases suggest the runner's indecisive motion, emphasized by the repeated *p* sound in *poised* and *pulled*. Two commands are "come on" and "crowd him."

6. The base stealer's movements are compared to the movements of a tightrope-walker (l. 2), a dropped ball (l. 4), a kid skipping rope (l. 5), and a bird (l. 8).

7. Students' readings will vary.

8. Possible answers: "American Hero" implies that some people will applaud talented athletes but judge them by their race outside the arena. The title is ironic, because to these people, the athletes are no longer heroes once they become neighbors.

Response and Analysis

The Base Stealer
American Hero

Reading Check

1. In the first four lines of "The Base Stealer," what is the character's situation? What is he doing?

2. List at least three verbs that describe what the player in "American Hero" is doing before the crowd goes wild in line 12.

go.hrw.com

INTERNET
Projects and Activities
Keyword: LE5 9-7

SKILLS FOCUS

Literary Skills
Analyze alliteration, onomatopoeia, and sentence structure.

Writing Skills
Write a free-verse poem.

Thinking Critically

3. Find three lines in "The Base Stealer" that use **alliteration** to describe the base stealer's actions. Where is alliteration used in "American Hero" to describe the basketball player and his game? Read the lines in both poems aloud, and explain the effects created by the repeated sounds.

4. Find at least three examples of **onomatopoeia** in "American Hero." How do those words contribute to the poem's appeal?

5. Notice how the **sentence structure** in "The Base Stealer" suggests motion and helps to convey the actions being described. How does the sentence structure in lines 1–2 reflect the meaning of those lines? Why do you think Francis lists four verbs in line 7? Find two different commands that Francis repeats to make us feel part of the crowd cheering the player on.

6. Find three **similes** in "The Base Stealer" that compare the movements of the base stealer to other movements.

7. Read "American Hero" aloud to hear how the short sentences re-create the tension of a basketball game. Which part of speech—noun, verb, adjective, or adverb—is emphasized the most in these sentences? Why?

8. Both of these poems are about sports. Which poem also has a serious message, and what is it? How does that poem's title create a sense of **irony**—a sense that the title does not mean exactly what it says?

WRITING

Poetry in Sports

Review your Quickwrite notes. Then, write a **free-verse poem** about the turning point of a game that you've played or watched or imagined. Make yourself the hero. Use short sentences and alliteration to help re-create fast-paced action.

Jackie Robinson steals home plate during the 1955 World Series.

478

ASSESSING

Assessment

■ *Holt Assessment: Literature, Reading, and Vocabulary*

RETEACHING

For a lesson reteaching literary devices, see **Reteaching,** p. 979A. For another selection to teach the sounds of poetry, see *The Holt Reader,* Collection 7.

READ ON: FOR INDEPENDENT READING

POETRY

Distant Times and Remote Places

Ever read any African chants, European lullabies, or Native American myths set to verse? If you'd like to, *Talking to the Sun* is the place to start. Poems covering almost all aspects of life and nature—including the sky, sand, flowers, animals, forests, and love—are arranged by topic. Works by such poets as Langston Hughes, Edna St. Vincent Millay, and William Shakespeare are represented alongside tribal hymns and American folk songs. This beautiful collection is enhanced by artwork from New York's Metropolitan Museum of Art.

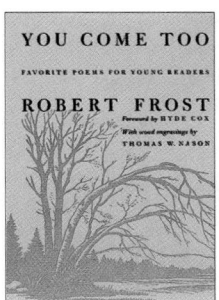

POETRY

Almost There

Discover some of the best of Robert Frost's poetry in *You Come Too.* In this collection for readers of all ages, you'll encounter poems like "Christmas Tree," "Hyla Brook," and his famous, inviting title poem. Frost brings to life the trees, mountains, cliffs, dirt roads, old fences, grassy fields, and abandoned houses of his beloved New England. Reading his work, you'll have the sense that you are there—deep in the woods or at the edge of a babbling brook.

POETRY

From the Morning Papers

"Poet's Choice" was a weekly newspaper column designed to add poetry to your morning cereal. The poet Robert Hass chose one poem each week to appear in twenty-five major American newspapers. Each poem addressed a different subject, from the changing of the seasons to the celebration of a holiday to the death of a great writer. Hass has collected these poems in one volume, *Poet's Choice: Poems for Everyday Life.*

POETRY

Man of the People

Carl Sandburg, a poet known for his direct, conversational style, wanted to celebrate the simple things in life. He also wanted to pay tribute to the unsung heroes of our country. Reading his collection *Harvest Poems: 1910–1960* is like sifting through snapshots of the everyday people—waitresses, farmers, mothers, and children—who represent the heart of America. This collection includes all of his most popular poems, including "Chicago" and selections from his book *The People, Yes.*

Read On   479

DIFFERENTIATING INSTRUCTION

Estimated Word Counts and Reading Levels of Read On Books:

Poetry					
Talking to the Sun	⬌	25,900	*You Come Too*	⬇	11,700
Poet's Choice: Poems for Everyday Life	⬌	36,300	*Harvest Poems: 1910–1960*	⬌	38,900

KEY: ⬆ *above grade level*   ⬌ *at grade level*   ⬇ *below grade level*

Read On

For Independent Reading

If students enjoyed the poems presented in this collection, you might recommend these titles for independent reading.

Assessment Options

The following projects can help you evaluate and assess your students' outside reading. Videotapes or audiotapes of completed projects may be included in student portfolios.

- **Find figurative language.** Ask students who read *Talking to the Sun* to keep a notebook of the most striking similes, metaphors, and other examples of figurative speech that they encounter in their reading. Students should classify the examples by type and explain how the comparisons appeal to the reader's imagination and emotions.

- **Pair poems and images.** Ask students who read *Poet's Choice: Poems for Everyday Life* to find photographs or illustrations from magazines, books, or Internet sources to accompany their favorite poems from the collection. Students can photocopy the poems and images and post them on a bulletin board.

- **Respond to poetry through poetry.** Invite students who read *You Come Too* to choose one poem to respond to by writing an original poem on the same topic. Encourage students to use Robert Frost's poem as a model but to draw from their own experiences. Challenge students to bring their world to life for readers as Frost did with his native New England.

- **Present a poetry reading.** Invite students who read *Harvest Poems: 1910–1960* to write their own poems inspired by "everyday people" in their community. Encourage students to sponsor a poetry reading of their poems, or of their favorite poems by Sandburg.

PRETEACHING

PRETEACHING

Skills Starter

Motivate. Read aloud a short poem to the class. Ask students to complete the following sentences: Listening to this poem made me feel _____ because _____. I think a point the poet was trying to make is _____ because _____.

Permit volunteers to share their responses. Point out that students have informally analyzed the poem, and explain that in this workshop they will learn a more formal approach to analysis.

DIRECT TEACHING

So Many Options

You need to be aware that Internet resources are sometimes public forums, and their content can be unpredictable.

DIFFERENTIATING INSTRUCTION

Special Education Students

Since analysis is a challenging task, some students may need assistance in selecting poetry that is at an appropriate level. Ask a helper to work with these students as they search for poems. When a student has found a piece that he or she is considering for analysis, the helper should ask the student to read the poem and retell its main idea and some supporting details to ensure that the student understands the piece well enough to analyze it.

Analyzing a Poem

Writing Assignment
Write a response to literature in which you analyze the literary elements of a poem.

In this collection, you've focused on two important elements of literature—imagery and figurative language. In this Writing Workshop you'll write an **analysis of a poem** in which you examine the poem's elements to discover how those elements combine to convey the poem's theme and overall effect.

Prewriting

Choose and Analyze a Poem

So Many Options The poem you select for analysis should be just right: not so short that it contains too little to examine, nor so long that you can't cover it in detail in an essay of 1,500 words. Poems of ten to twenty lines that are rich in meaning are often suited to analyses of that length. To find a poem to analyze, re-read poems you have enjoyed before; ask for recommendations from your teacher, a librarian, family members, and friends; or look for collections of poems in your school or community library or on the Internet.

The Poet's Tools To analyze the poem you've selected, you'll need to re-read it several times. As you re-read, pay close attention to the poem's **literary elements.** Careful analysis of the elements used in a particular work will make you aware of how the poet uses those elements to shape meaning and create certain effects. The following chart lists some common literary elements found in poetry and gives questions to help you analyze them.

LITERARY ELEMENTS

Element	Analysis Questions
Speaker: the voice talking in the poem; the narrator of the poem (not necessarily the poet)	Who is speaking in the poem? Is the speaker the poet or a character created by the poet?
Theme: the meaning, or main idea, of the poem, usually involving some insight into human existence	Does the poem examine some common life experience or problem? Does it suggest solutions or answers?
Tone: the poet's attitude toward the subject, the audience, or a character	What is the poet's attitude toward the subject (sarcastic, respectful)? the audience (friendly, hostile)? the characters (sympathetic, cruel)?

(continued)

COLLECTION 7 RESOURCES: WRITING

Planning
- *One-Stop Planner* CD-ROM with ExamView Test Generator

Differentiating Instruction
- *Workshop Resources: Writing, Listening, and Speaking*
- *Family Involvement Activities in English and Spanish*

- *Supporting Instruction in Spanish*

Assessment
- *Holt Assessment: Writing, Listening, and Speaking*
- *One-Stop Planner* CD-ROM with ExamView Test Generator
- *Holt Online Assessment*
- *Holt Online Essay Scoring*

(continued)

Stylistic devices: the techniques the poet uses to control language to create certain effects	How does **diction**, the poet's choice of key words, influence the poem's meaning? Does the poet use **figurative language**, such as **metaphors** and **similes**, to make imaginative comparisons? What **sound devices**, such as **rhythm**, **rhyme**, and **repetition**, does the poet use? What effects do they have on the poem?

Identify one or more **key literary elements** that are essential to understanding the poem's theme. Below you will find an analysis log one student created while analyzing the poem "A Dream Deferred" by Langston Hughes. It shows the poem and some of the student's notes on the poem's stylistic devices—what he determined to be the key literary element.

 **DO THIS**

ANALYSIS LOG

1	What happens to a dream deferred?	**Line 1**	DICTION: "dream" = hope, aspiration for the future. "defer" = to delay temporarily, to give in to someone else.
2	Does it dry up	**Lines 2–3**	SIMILE: Deferred dream shrivels.
3	like a raisin in the sun?	**Lines 4–5**	SIMILE: Deferred dream becomes diseased, infected.
4	Or fester like a sore—		
5	And then run?	**Line 6**	SIMILE: Deferred dream stinks of decay.
6	Does it stink like rotten meat?	**Lines 7–8**	SIMILE: Deferred dream is sickeningly sweet.
7	Or crust and sugar over—	**Lines 9–10**	SIMILE: Deferred dream is a burden; it weighs the dreamer down.
8	like a syrupy sweet?		
9	Maybe it just sags	**Line 11**	METAPHOR: Deferred dream is a bomb that explodes and destroys.
10	like a heavy load.		Possible THEME: A dream deferred causes destruction. This is the answer to the poem's question.
11	Or does it explode?		

Write Your Thesis

The Key Point Now, summarize your main idea about the poem in a coherent **thesis statement**—one or two sentences that make the focus of your analysis clear to your audience. The student analyzing "A Dream Deferred" wrote the following thesis statement while prewriting. He later fine-tuned it to better fit the introduction to his analysis.

> In "A Dream Deferred," Langston Hughes uses the stylistic devices of diction, figurative language, and sound to show that keeping people from achieving their dreams can have destructive consequences.

 SKILLS FOCUS

Writing Skills
Write an analysis of a poem. Establish a thesis statement.

Internet
- go.hrw.com (Keyword: LE5 9-7)
- *Elements of Literature Online*

English-Language Learners
Students who are learning English may find it challenging to analyze poetic language. To facilitate the task, you may want to have these students work with a poem that has been published in both English and their native language. Many books print the original poem and the English translation side by side. Encourage students to focus on the poem's overall meaning and how the poet uses the speaker, imagery, theme, and tone to convey that meaning.

Advanced Learners
Enrichment. Students should understand the stylistic devices *connotation* and *denotation*. Have pairs of students look up both words in a thesaurus. Then, ask them to discuss how a poet might use connotation and denotation to influence a poem's meaning.

DIRECT TEACHING

Integrating with Grammar, Usage, and Mechanics
As students start their poetry analyses, they may have trouble punctuating phrases and clauses. You may want to review 12h–i and 12m–o in the Language Handbook.

Write Your Thesis
If students need help coming up with a thesis statement, suggest that they use the following fill-in-the-blank model as a guide:
In (title of poem), (name of author) uses (key literary elements) to show/illustrate/communicate (the poem's theme).

Gather Supporting Evidence

To help students evaluate their evidence, suggest that they use index cards to keep track of details or quotations, writing only one detail per card. Then, to decide which literary element is most important, students could look at the amount of elaboration they have provided for each. The element with the most elaboration will usually be the most important one.

Guided and Independent Practice

Students can follow these steps as they begin to analyze their poems:

• Read the poem accurately by following the punctuation marks.

• Copy down the entire poem in order to underline, circle, and annotate (make notes about) parts of it.

• Break the poem into sections—sentences, stanzas, or others—that express complete thoughts.

• Seek a second opinion and share interpretations.

As students work, move about the room and monitor progress by assessing their annotated poems and checking their thesis statements.

Then, have students finish their analyses as they complete **Practice and Apply I** independently.

Gather Supporting Evidence

The Poem as Witness An analysis of a poem should contain accurate **references** to the poem. These references—quotations from the poem and details restated in your own words—will support the thesis. Each reference should be followed by **elaboration:** an explanation of how the quotation or detail supports your thesis. Elaboration shows you have a good grasp of the poem's **significant ideas** and enables you to address the poem's **ambiguities, nuances, and complexities.**

● **Ambiguities** are lines or words that lend themselves to more than one interpretation.

● **Nuances** are changes in tone or meaning. For example, a poem might start with a light tone and then turn more serious.

● **Complexities** result when a poem is rich in meaning but difficult to interpret. For example, a poem may discuss problems that don't have simple solutions, or ask questions that don't have easy answers.

Below is the beginning of a chart one student created to show the references and the elaboration he will include in his analysis.

Literary Element	Detail or Quotation	Elaboration
Stylistic device: Diction	"What happens to a dream deferred?"(1)	A dream can be a hope or an aspiration for the future. <u>Defer</u> is an ambiguous word. It can mean "to delay" or "to give in to what someone else wants."
Stylistic device: Simile	"Does it dry up /like a raisin in the sun?"(2–3)	This is a complex image. The reader is meant to think of the dried and wrinkled raisin in contrast to the fat, juicy grape that the dream once was, before it dried up.

Organize Your Analysis

Putting Things in Order Before beginning your first draft, put your ideas in order. You might arrange your analysis by **order of importance,** beginning or ending with the key literary element most important to the poem's theme and effect. You might also arrange your analysis by discussing the key literary elements in the order in which they appear in the poem.

SKILLS FOCUS

Writing Skills
Support ideas with references to the poem. Arrange ideas in their order of importance.

PRACTICE & APPLY 1 Using the instructions on pages 480–481, choose and analyze a poem. Then, decide on the poem's key literary elements, write a thesis statement, and gather evidence to support the thesis. Organize your analysis.

Writing

Analyzing a Poem

A Writer's Framework

Introduction
- Grab readers' attention by relating the poem's meaning to experiences people have in common.
- Introduce the poem's title and author.
- State your thesis, including the key elements and theme you will discuss.

Body
- Organize the key literary elements by order of importance or in the order in which they appear in the poem.
- Discuss each key literary element.
- Provide references for each key element, and elaborate on each key element.

Conclusion
- Remind readers of your thesis by restating it.
- Summarize your main points.
- Show how the poem relates to broader themes in life.

A Writer's Model

Stylistic Devices in "A Dream Deferred"

What is life worth without dreams and the hope that those dreams can come true someday? What happens when the achievement of a dream is postponed—again and again? In "A Dream Deferred," Langston Hughes answers these questions by using the stylistic devices of diction, figurative language, and sound to show that keeping people from achieving their dreams can have destructive consequences.

Hughes starts with a question to get his readers thinking about his message: "What happens to a dream deferred?" (line 1). His diction here is important. He uses the word "dream" to mean a hope for or vision of a better future. He chooses the word defer for its two meanings. It can mean both "to put something off until sometime in the future" and "to give in to what someone else wants." Hughes uses the word in both ways: Someone else postpones the dream, but the dreamer gives in to the delay. The question then is, "How long will the dreamer accept the postponement of his or her dream?"

In the next part of the poem, Hughes answers this basic question about deferred dreams with a series of similes written as questions. The first simile asks if a deferred dream dries up "like a raisin in the sun" (3). The image of the dried and wrinkled raisin contrasts with the fat, juicy grape the dream once was. The images created by the following three similes are worse. Does the deferred dream "fester like

(continued)

INTRODUCTION
Attention-getting opener

Thesis (with title and author)

BODY
First stylistic device: diction

Ambiguity explained

Second stylistic device: figurative language

Complexities explained

Writing Workshop: Analyzing a Poem **483**

CRITICAL THINKING

Tell students that the questions posed by the writer in this introduction are technically *rhetorical questions*, questions that are generally not intended to be answered. However, in a literary analysis of this type, the purpose of the essay is to answer the rhetorical questions posed by the essay's author.

CORRECTING MISCONCEPTIONS

Explain to students that metaphors are not always exact comparisons that result from calling one thing another, as in "Her smile is the morning sun." A metaphor can also be the result of assigning recognizable characteristics. For example, in line 11 of his poem, Hughes asks whether something explodes. He does not directly call a dream deferred an exploding bomb, but the metaphor is clear because of the assigned characteristic.

(continued)

Similes

a sore— / And then run?" (4–5) or "stink like rotten meat?" (6) or "crust and sugar over— / like a syrupy sweet?" (7–8)? The images in these similes seem to say that if a dream is postponed, it rots or spoils or infects the dreamer. The last simile is not a question but a guess. "Maybe" a deferred dream "just sags / like a heavy load." (9–10). This simile makes the deferred dream seem like a heavy burden carried on the dreamer's back, making him or her bow under its weight. All of these similes suggest that a deferred dream becomes something terrible.

Metaphor

Ambiguity explained

In the poem's last line, Hughes uses another piece of figurative language, a metaphor—"Or does it explode?" (11)—to address his message. He emphasizes the metaphor even more by using different print from the rest of the poem. He seems to be saying that this is exactly what happens: a deferred dream is a bomb that finally explodes. He might also mean that it is not the dream but the dreamer that explodes—in anger.

Third stylistic device: sound

Rhyme
Nuance explained

Rhythm

The sound of the poem intensifies its meaning even more. Like a piece of jazz music, the poem uses rhyme and short bursts of rhythm. The rhymes—"sun/run," "meat/sweet," and "load/explode"—pull the ideas behind the similes and the metaphor together, repeating and building up the importance of the ideas like a series of notes repeated in music. Similarly, just as pauses in music provide dynamic rhythms, the lines in the poem have pauses between them, shown by the use of dashes and the skipped lines that set off the central section. The last important question of the poem, asked after a skipped-line pause, is like a final drumbeat that ends a piece of jazz music.

Nuance explained

CONCLUSION
Restatement of thesis

Summary of main points

Just what does happen when the achievement of a dream is postponed again and again? Hughes uses the stylistic devices of diction, figurative language, and sound to tell his readers what might happen to a deferred dream. The word "deferred" hints that the dreamer might not always accept the postponement of his or her dream. The five similes seem to say that only the dreamer is hurt. In the final metaphor, however, the deferred dream is a bomb that will eventually explode and hurt many people. Hughes ties the poem together with jazzy rhyme and rhythm. "A Dream Deferred" carries an idea we should all consider—not to let our own dreams become deferred, and not to block others in their quests to follow their own dreams.

Relation to broader themes in life

INTERNET
More Writer's Models
Keyword: LE5 9-7

PRACTICE & APPLY 2

Guided and Independent Practice

1. Have students write down for your approval the title and main idea of the poem they will analyze.

2. Have students work with a partner to evaluate their plans and drafts. Partners can take turns asking questions about the writer's intentions, using **A Writer's Framework** as a guide.

3. Encourage students to make revisions to their prewriting plans based on the feedback they receive.

PRACTICE & APPLY 2 Now it is your turn to write an analysis. Use the framework on page 483 and the Writer's Model as guidelines while you write the first draft of your analysis of a poem.

Revising

Evaluate and Revise Your Draft

Rework and Refine Poets write and rewrite their poems, changing words and phrases until they find exactly the right meaning that rests in exactly the right words. As a writer, you may find that your first draft also may need a rewrite or two. To make your analysis of a poem as clear, precise, and effective as it can be, review your paper. Evaluate and revise the content and organization of your analysis first. Then, evaluate and revise its style.

> **PEER REVIEW**
>
> Before you revise, ask a classmate to read your analysis and the poem you analyzed. He or she may offer you more ideas about how the key literary elements you identified influence the poem.

➤ First Reading: **Content and Organization** The following chart will help you evaluate and revise your analysis. Answer the questions in the first column, check the tips in the second column, and look at the third column for suggestions.

Rubric: Analyzing a Poem

Evaluation Questions	▶ Tips	▶ Revision Techniques
❶ Does the introduction mention the poem's title and author? Does it include a clear thesis statement that names the key elements and the poem's theme?	▶ **Circle** the poet, title, and thesis statement. **Put a check mark** next to the key elements and theme in the thesis statement.	▶ **Add** a sentence that names the poem's title and author. **Add** a clear thesis statement that names the key elements and the theme.
❷ Does each body paragraph discuss a key literary element that supports the thesis?	▶ **Bracket** the key literary element in each body paragraph.	▶ **Replace** body paragraphs that don't address key elements.
❸ Is each key literary element supported with references to the poem? Does the writer explain each reference?	▶ **Highlight** quotations or restated details from the poem, and **draw an arrow** to their explanations.	▶ **Add** quotations or restated details. **Elaborate** by explaining how the quotations and details support the thesis.
❹ Is the analysis organized by order of importance or in the order that the key elements appear in the poem?	▶ **Number** the body paragraphs. If the numbers do not reflect an appropriate sequence, revise.	▶ **Rearrange** the body paragraphs in the order of importance or in the order the key elements appear in the poem.
❺ Does the conclusion effectively remind readers of the thesis and summarize the main points? Does it show how the poem relates to broader themes in life?	▶ **Underline** the sentence in the conclusion that restates the thesis. **Put a star** beside the sentences that summarize the main points. **Put two stars** by the sentences that relate the poem to broader themes.	▶ If necessary, **add** a sentence restating the thesis. **Add** sentences that summarize the main points and that relate the poem to broader themes.

Writing Workshop: Analyzing a Poem **485**

MODELING AND DEMONSTRATION

Second Reading: Style

To make sure students understand how to eliminate unnecessary clauses, write these two sentences on the chalkboard:

I bought the suit that is blue.

All of us who are on the committee voted for the proposition.

Model revising the first sentence by identifying the unnecessary clause *that is blue* and then eliminating the pronoun *that* and the *be* verb *is*. Then, rearrange the remaining words to read *I bought the blue suit*. Have a volunteer demonstrate understanding by revising the second sentence. [Possible revision: *All of us on the committee voted for the proposition*.]

GUIDED PRACTICE

Responding to the Revision Process

Answers

1. The revisions make the statement more specific and, therefore, clearer.

2. The sentence was reworded to remove the unnecessary clause.

PRACTICE & APPLY 3

Independent Practice

- Suggest that students include all the revision marks and highlights suggested by both the rubric and the style guidelines charts on their revised drafts. These marks will allow you to skim students' revisions quickly to see that they followed the rubric and the style guidelines.

- Students should check for wordy sentences and correct as needed to make the revisions read smoothly.

▷ **Second Reading: Style** In your second reading, pay attention to your writing style and its impact on your tone. Sentences with wordy, unnecessary clauses can create a **tone** that intimidates readers. For example, note how clumsy the following sentence is: "What transpires when the achievement of what a person creates in the mind's eye, what the person desires in reality, is postponed, and that postponement happens repeatedly?" Now, compare the stiff formality of that sentence to its rewrite: "What happens when the achievement of a dream is postponed—again and again?" Eliminating the unnecessary clauses improved the tone. Your analysis's tone should be knowledgeable yet friendly, not intimidating. Use the following guidelines to help you cut down on wordiness.

Style Guidelines

Evaluation Question	▶ Tip	▶ Revision Technique
● Does the analysis contain wordy sentences with unnecessary clauses?	▶ **Double underline** clauses beginning with *which is, which are, that is, that are, who is,* and *who are.*	▶ **Reduce** half of these clauses to participles or participial phrases by **deleting** the pronouns *who, which,* or *that* and the *be* verb. If necessary, **rearrange** the remaining words.

ANALYZING THE REVISION PROCESS

Study these revisions, and answer the questions that follow.

> In "A Dream Deferred," Langston Hughes answers these ques-
> **replace**   *the stylistic devices of diction, figurative language, and sound*
> tions by using ~~different elements~~ to show that keeping people
>   *destructive*
> **rearrange/delete**   from achieving their dreams can have consequences ~~that are~~
> **delete**   ~~destructive.~~

Responding to the Revision Process

1. How do the writer's revisions improve the thesis statement?

2. Why do you think the writer reworded the end of the sentence?

SKILLS FOCUS

Writing Skills
Revise for content and style.

PRACTICE & APPLY 3

Revise the content, organization, and style of your analysis by using the preceding guidelines and those on page 485. Look at the Writer's Model on page 483 and the revisions shown in the example above as models for your own revisions.

Publishing

Proofread and Publish Your Analysis

The Finishing Touches Avoid letting minor mistakes in your final draft distract readers or discredit your ideas. **Proofread** your paper carefully to eliminate any errors in grammar, usage, and mechanics. Even a few errors in your analysis can damage its effectiveness.

Sharing Your Work After you've done all the hard work of analyzing a poem and putting your insights onto paper, it would be a shame to have only your teacher and a small number of classmates read your analysis. Here are some suggestions on how you might share your analysis of a poem with a larger audience.

- Ask an older sibling or relative who has taken high school or college literature classes to read and critique your analysis.

- Submit your analysis to your school's literary magazine.

- Post your analysis to a teen literary magazine on the Internet, or find a Web site devoted to the writer of the poem you analyzed and inquire as to whether you could post your analysis to the site.

- Organize a poetry night at your school. Read aloud the poems you and your classmates have analyzed. Select several analyses of the poetry to read, also.

Reflect on Your Analysis

Relive the Experience Write brief responses to the following questions to reflect on what you have learned in this workshop. Recognizing your strengths and weaknesses can help you improve future writing.

- How did writing this paper change your feelings about the poem you selected? How did your understanding of the poem change after you performed an in-depth analysis of it?

- Was the tone of your analysis knowledgeable yet friendly? How might you adjust your tone if you were writing this analysis for a different audience, for example, a class of sixth-graders?

- What new techniques or ideas about analyzing poetry did you learn in this workshop? How could you apply them to analyzing other forms of literature?

PRACTICE & APPLY 4 Proofread your analysis carefully, and eliminate any errors you find. Select one or two publishing options to get your analysis out to a larger audience. Finally, answer the preceding reflection questions.

TIP Proofreading will help ensure that your essay follows the **conventions** of standard American English. For example, you should make sure that you have correctly punctuated the quotations in your analysis. For more on **punctuating quotations,** see Quotation Marks, 13f, in the Language Handbook.

SKILLS FOCUS

Writing Skills
Proofread, especially for correct punctuation of quotations. Publish and reflect on the essay.

Writing Workshop: Analyzing a Poem   **487**

DIRECT TEACHING

Sharing Your Work
You need to be aware that Internet resources are sometimes public forums, and their content can be unpredictable.

PRACTICE & APPLY 4

Guided and Independent Practice
Monitor students' progress by checking the publishing options that they choose. Sample answers to the reflective questions follow:

- Some students may observe that writing an analysis of a poem reveals layers of meaning that were not apparent upon first reading.

- Students might suggest that an analysis written for a younger audience should focus on simpler literary elements and offer definitions or explanations of literary elements.

- Students may say that they learned writing techniques such as reducing wordiness and using quotations.

488 Collection 7 Poetry

<table>
</table>

PRETEACHING

Motivate. Ask students to think of sporting event broadcasts that they have listened to on the radio or TV. Ask them to discuss the different roles of the announcer and the sports analyst. They should say that the announcer simply describes the plays while the analyst comments on specific players and their motivations, the effectiveness of certain plays, and so on. In presenting their poetry analyses, the students will be like sports analysts, commenting on specific techniques and the effectiveness of literary elements.

DIRECT TEACHING

REVIEW SKILL

One way for students to develop their introductions and find supporting ideas and viewpoints is to consult existing literary criticism. Suggest that students use the school librarian as a resource for finding relevant works of literary criticism.

Presenting a Poem

Speaking Assignment
Deliver an oral interpretation of a poem to an audience.

Long before paper was invented, there was a tradition of poems being spoken aloud in order to pass on the important cultural events of a people. Many of us would agree that poetry—with its distinctive rhymes, rhythms, and imagery—lends itself to being heard, not just being read silently. Presenting a poem orally is another way to help others fully appreciate a poem's message and effects. It can also deepen your own understanding as you bring the poem dramatically to life.

Preparing to Read Aloud

Think It Over Your first step in preparing to read a poem aloud to an audience is to build your private, personal understanding of the poem.

- **Make a Choice** As you worked through the collection, you may have already found a poem that you feel strongly about. If you still haven't found a poem that's right for you, read aloud several from this collection again to see which one you'd most enjoy reading in public.

- **Shape Your Interpretations** Make a copy of the poem, and use it as a working script. Underline the parts you find most dramatic—**words, images, sounds, rhythms,** and **figures of speech.** Note places where you want to go slowly, speed up, or pause. Be sure to note which lines do not end with a punctuation mark. This means that you don't come to a full pause: You read on to the next line to complete the thought.

SKILLS FOCUS

Listening and Speaking Skills
Present an oral interpretation of a poem.

- **Get to Know the Speaker** Make notes describing the speaker of the poem. Is the speaker a particular age? How does the speaker feel in the poem? Do his or her feelings change as the poem goes on?

- **Get an Attitude!** What will your own tone, or attitude, be? Thoughtful? Serious? Sarcastic? How will you use your voice to convey your tone? Your tone should convey that of the poem.

COLLECTION 7 RESOURCES: LISTENING & SPEAKING

Planning
- *One-Stop Planner* CD-ROM with ExamView Test Generator

Differentiating Instruction
- *Workshop Resources: Writing, Listening, and Speaking*
- *Family Involvement Activities in English and Spanish*

- *Supporting Instruction in Spanish*

Listening and Speaking
- *Workshop Resources: Writing, Listening, and Speaking*

Assessment
- *Holt Assessment: Writing, Listening, and Speaking*

Rehearse Your Presentation

Memorizing (or Not) You may or may not decide to memorize your poem. Even if you plan to hold and look at a copy of the poem throughout your reading, you should be extremely familiar with it. Should you choose to memorize your poem, this secret will help you: Thoroughly understanding a text makes it much easier to memorize.

Practice, Practice, Practice You'll give a more effective presentation if you've rehearsed it several times. To increase the effectiveness of your delivery, practice using the following **verbal** and **nonverbal techniques** as you rehearse.

GUIDELINES TO IMPROVE DELIVERY

Verbal Techniques	Nonverbal Techniques
Diction: In speaking, diction refers to the clarity of your pronunciation. Always speak clearly and carefully so that your listeners can understand you.	**Eye contact:** Look directly into the eyes of as many audience members as you can. Eye contact communicates confidence and sincerity.
Emphasis: Stress key words or phrases in your presentation by saying them with a different volume or tone than you have been using.	**Facial expressions:** Be relaxed and natural, using a smile, a grimace, or a raised eyebrow to convey the meaning of the poem.
Pauses: Use pauses—small silences in your presentation—to help listeners understand the meaning of the poem.	**Gestures:** Don't be stiff or fidget; make relaxed and natural gestures with your head, hands, and arms as you speak. Move around a bit, rather than being rooted in one place.

Present Your Poem

A Lasting Impression Make a clean copy of the poem. Across the top, write your finished version of the following sentence that begins "If the audience gets just one single impression. . . ." Add any final important interpretive and performance notes. This is your script.

 **PRACTICE & APPLY 5** Try reading your poem aloud to friends. Prepare notes for your presentation based on their feedback. Practice verbal and nonverbal techniques. Then, deliver your poem.

SKILLS FOCUS

Listening and Speaking Skills
Use appropriate verbal and nonverbal techniques.

- *One-Stop Planner* CD-ROM with ExamView Test Generator

Internet
- go.hrw.com (Keyword: LE5 9-7)
- *Elements of Literature Online*

English-Language Learners
Students from some cultures may have been taught that making direct eye contact, especially with adults, is insolent or rude. Assure them that when they make eye contact during an oral presentation they will be perceived as confident and sincere, not disrespectful. You might let them practice with you as their audience.

RETEACHING

Guidelines to Improve Delivery
You might reteach the concept of using gestures and facial expressions effectively by taping an appropriate feature story from the television news. Play the tape for students and lead a discussion on the speaker's use of gestures and facial expressions.

PRACTICE & APPLY 5

Guided and Independent Practice
You may find it useful to guide students in the following ways:

1. Have students tape a dress rehearsal of their presentations on audio or video. They can trade tapes with a partner and evaluate each other's delivery.

2. Monitor students' progress by sitting in on some of the partner conferences.

3. For independent practice, have students present their final oral presentations to the class.

Collection 7: Skills Review

Literary Skills

SKILLS FOCUS, pp. 490–492

Grade-Level Skills

■ **Literary Skills**
Analyze various literary devices, including sound effects, figures of speech, and imagery.

INTRODUCING THE SKILLS REVIEW

Use this review to assess students' understanding of the skills taught in this collection. If necessary, you can use the annotations to guide students in their reading before they answer the questions.

DIRECT TEACHING

A Literary Focus

❓ Imagery. What details does Endrezze use to create an image of a second-grade classroom? [Possible responses: the smell of glue; the sight and feel of wooden desks; the litter of eraser rubbings, rulers, pencils, and chalk; walls covered with pictures and charts with stickers.]

B Literary Focus

❓ Tone. What words and phrases does the poet use in these lines to create a melancholy, or somber, tone? [Possible responses: "cold metal," "rained," "bruised petals," "formless sky," "cool," "umbrellas," "sky falling," "smelled the sourness."]

Test-Taking Tips

Remind students to exercise time-management skills when taking multiple-choice tests. Rather than spending too much time on a single question, students can return to the item after answering easier ones.

For more instruction on how to answer multiple-choice items, refer students to **Test Smarts.**

Test Practice

Poetry

DIRECTIONS: Read the following poem. Then, read and respond to the questions that follow.

The Girl Who Loved the Sky

Anita Endrezze

Outside the second-grade room,
the jacaranda tree blossomed
into purple lanterns, the papery petals
drifted, darkening the windows.
5 Inside, the room smelled like glue.
The desks were made of yellowed wood,
the tops littered with eraser rubbings,
rulers, and big fat pencils.
Colored chalk meant special days.
10 The walls were covered with precise
bright tulips and charts with shiny stars
by certain names. There, I learned
how to make butter by shaking a jar
until the pale cream clotted
15 into one sweet mass. There, I learned
that numbers were fractious° beasts
with dens like dim zeros. And there,
I met a blind girl who thought the sky
tasted like cold metal when it rained
20 and whose eyes were always covered
with the bruised petals of her lids.
She loved the formless sky, defined
only by sounds, or the cool umbrellas
of clouds. On hot, still days
25 we listened to the sky falling
like chalk dust. We heard the noon
whistle of the pig-mash factory,
smelled the sourness of homebound men.
I had no father; she had no eyes;
30 we were best friends. The other girls
drew shaky hopscotch squares
on the dusty asphalt, talked about

---

16. **fractious** (frak′shəs) *adj.*: hard to manage; rebellious.

Pages 490–492 cover **Literary Skills** Understand characteristics of poetry, including imagery, figurative language, and sound effects.

Using Academic Language

Review of Literary Terms
Ask students to review the collection to find the meanings of the terms listed below. Then, have students cite passages from the collection that illustrate the meanings.

Imagery (pp. 402, 404); **Catalog Poem** (p. 408); **Fresh Images** (p. 413); **Haiku** (p. 418); **Sonnet** (p. 422); **Iambic**

Pentameter (p. 422); **Petrarchan Sonnet** (p. 422); **Shakespearean Sonnet** (p. 422); **Lyric Poem** (p. 424); **Figures of Speech** (pp. 428, 440); **Simile** (pp. 428, 430, 432, 440,); **Metaphor** (pp. 429, 432, 440); **Personification** (pp. 429, 450); **Figurative Language** (p. 432); **Extended Metaphor** (pp. 435, 444); **Diction** (p. 436); **Implied**

pajama parties, weekend cookouts,
and parents who bought sleek-finned cars.
35   Alone, we sat in the canvas swings,
our shoes digging into the sand, then pushing,
until we flew high over their heads,
our hands streaked with red rust
from the chains that kept us safe.
40   I was born blind, she said, an act of nature.
Sure, I thought, like birds born
without wings, trees without roots.
I didn't understand. The day she moved
I saw the world clearly; the sky
45   backed away from me like a departing father.
I sat under the jacaranda, catching
the petals in my palm, enclosing them
until my fist was another lantern
hiding a small and bitter flame.

Answers and Model Rationales

1. **C** "Other girls" (l. 30) is a clue that the speaker is a girl herself, so B can be eliminated. A is incorrect because the speaker describes the blind girl as her friend. D can be eliminated, as the speaker associates many of her memories with the natural world.

2. **G** Only G is supported by evidence in the poem. F and H are incorrect because only the speaker, not her friend (F), lost a parent; and the teacher (H) is not mentioned. Ll. 38–39 suggest that the children are not self-confident (J).

3. **C** Only lightweight (C), not stiff (B) or heavy (D), petals would drift from a tree. The petals are purple, not white (A).

1. The **speaker** in this poem is —
  A a blind woman looking back at her lonely childhood
  B a popular girl in second grade
  C a girl who felt like an outsider
  D a child who grew up feeling uneasy in the natural world

2. In line 35, "Alone, we sat in the canvas swings," the poet uses the word *alone* to convey that the speaker and the blind girl —
  F have lost their parents
  G are separated from their classmates
  H are not supervised by their teacher
  J are independent, self-confident children

3. The poet uses the word *papery* in the **image** "the papery petals/drifted" (lines 3–4) to show that the petals are —
  A white
  B stiff
  C lightweight
  D heavy

(continued)

Metaphor (p. 440); **Ballad** (p. 463); **Speaker** (p. 472); **Persona** (p. 472); **Tone** (pp. 447, 472); **Voice** (p. 472).

Answers and Model Rationales

4. J   Only J makes a comparison between two unlike things.

5. B   In B, eyelids are implicitly compared to flower petals. None of the other answer choices makes comparisons.

6. H   Alliteration is the repetition of consonant sounds, and all examples contain alliteration except for "whistle of the pig-mash factory (H)".

7. D   The example contains no rhyme or onomatopoeia, thus eliminating A and C. The example's comparison uses *like,* so it is not a metaphor (B). Since the sky, a nonhuman object, is associated with human behavior—backing away—personification (D) is the best choice.

8. J   F and G can be eliminated because of the length and structure of the poem. It doesn't really tell a story or have a rhythm (H), so J is clearly the best choice.

9. B   Only B shows how the speaker equates the departure of her friend, who loves the sky, with the departure of her father.

Constructed Response

10. The tone of the speaker in the poem is sad. Images such as "the sky / tasted like cold metal" and "the sourness of homebound men" create a feeling of melancholy. The speaker also evokes a sense of loneliness and isolation when she describes the other students playing hopscotch while she and her friend sit on swings by themselves. The speaker's loneliness increases after her friend leaves: She feels that the sky has itself "backed away" from her.

---

4. An example of **metaphor** in this poem is —
   F "the pale cream clotted" (line 14)
   G "The walls were covered with precise/bright tulips" (lines 10–11)
   H "I saw the world clearly" (line 4)
   J "my fist was another lantern" (line 48)

5. An example of **implied metaphor** is —
   A "The desks were made of yellowed wood,/the tops littered with eraser rubbings" (lines 6–7)
   B "and whose eyes were always covered/with the bruised petals of her lids" (lines 20–21)
   C "dens like dim zeros" (line 17)
   D "the jacaranda tree blossomed" (line 2)

6. Which phrase does *not* include **alliteration**?
   F "our hands streaked with red rust" (line 38)
   G "the cool umbrellas/of clouds" (lines 23–24)
   H "whistle of the pig-mash factory" (line 27)
   J "birds born/without wings" (lines 41–42)

7. "The sky/backed away from me like a departing father" (lines 44–45) is an example of **simile** and —
   A rhyme
   B metaphor
   C onomatopoeia
   D personification

8. This poem is a —
   F sonnet
   G haiku
   H ballad
   J free-verse poem

9. Why does the speaker say, "the sky/backed away from me like a departing father" (lines 44–45)?
   A She is describing an approaching storm.
   B The blind girl loves the sky, and the speaker feels that the girl's leaving is like the loss of her father.
   C She is swinging and feeling sad as she thinks about her father.
   D She thinks her friend's blindness is unnatural, like a sky that moves away from you.

Constructed Response

10. Describe the speaker's **tone** in this poem. Cite specific lines or words to support your opinion.

ASSESSING

Assessment

■ *Holt Assessment: Literature, Reading, and Vocabulary*

Collection 7: Skills Review
Writing Skills

Test Practice

DIRECTIONS: Read the following paragraph from a draft of a student's analysis of a poem. Then, answer the questions below it.

(1) In "The Seven Ages of Man," a poem that was written by William Shakespeare, Shakespeare uses figurative language to talk about human nature in a satire. (2) The poem is actually from a speech by Jaques in Shakespeare's comedy *As You Like It*. (3) The metaphor "All the world's a stage / And all the men and women merely players" in the first two lines compares life to a play. (4) Shakespeare also uses similes to make human life seem simple.

1. How could the tone and wordiness of sentence 1 be corrected?

   A "The Seven Ages of Man" is a poem by Shakespeare that uses language that is figurative.

   B Shakespeare wrote "The Seven Ages of Man" and uses figurative language to poke fun at human nature.

   C Shakespeare, with figurative language, ridicules human nature in "The Seven Ages of Man."

   D Shakespeare's "The Seven Ages of Man" uses figurative language to satirize human nature.

2. To support the statement that Shakespeare uses similes, the student could

   F refer to several specific similes within the poem

   G quote similes from another of Shakespeare's works

   H show examples of Shakespeare's metaphors in the poem

   J rewrite Shakespeare's similes to be more familiar to modern audiences

3. Which sentence could be added to develop the reference in sentence 3?

   A The words "merely players" suggest that people simply perform the roles they are given.

   B This is a good metaphor because Shakespeare knew about stages.

   C Later, Shakespeare compares humans to leopards to show that both are simple beasts.

   D Although this line refers to women, the "seven ages" apply only to men.

4. To improve the passage's organization, which sentence should be moved?

   F 1   H 3
   G 2   J 4

5. To present this passage as part of an oral literary presentation, the student could

   A avoid distractions by not looking at the audience

   B use verbal techniques to stress key ideas or points

   C tell a series of jokes to entertain the audience

   D pause after each sentence to ensure the information sinks in

SKILLS FOCUS

Writing Skills
Write an analysis of a poem.

Answers

1. D
2. F
3. A
4. G
5. B

APPLICATION

Analysts at Work

For homework, have students do research to find out about professionals whose jobs require them to perform analyses on a regular basis. Have students create a list of such jobs on a chart. Students might also interview these professionals so they can include on the chart a brief description of how the professional uses analysis in his or her job.

Homework

EXTENSION

A Picture's Worth a Thousand Words

Have students select another poem and express their reactions to the poem through art. This approach may help them express emotions they might not be able to articulate in words. Students might create drawings that summarize their overall impressions of their poems or that illustrate key lines or images from the works. They may also use colors, shapes, and lines to express their impressions. Have students use the visual representations with the text to explain what the poem they selected means to them.

RESOURCES: WRITING, LISTENING & SPEAKING

Assessment
- *One-Stop Planner* CD-ROM with ExamView Test Generator
- *Holt Assessment: Writing, Listening, and Speaking*

Internet
- *Holt Online Assessment*
- *Holt Online Essay Scoring*

Collection 8

Literary Criticism
Evaluating Style

**Informational Reading Focus:
Evaluating Arguments:
Pro and Con**

About Collection 8

In Collection 8, students will master the following skills:

- **Literary Skills:** Analyze elements of style, including diction, figurative language, sentence structure, figures of speech, imagery, tone, and mood.
- **Reading Skills:** Understand cause-and-effect relationships; evaluate the credibility of opposing arguments; and visualize the story.
- **Vocabulary Skills:** Understand Greek and Latin prefixes and root words; understand word denotations and connotations; and use context clues.
- **Writing Skills:** Develop, write, and revise an analysis of a short story.

Informational Text

Each collection of *Elements of Literature* provides a variety of informational texts related to the literature selections by theme or topic.

Minimum Course of Study

Most skills can be taught with a minimum number of selections and features. In the chart to the right, lessons highlighted in green constitute the minimum course of study that provides coverage of the skills taught in Collection 8.

Resource Manager
(pp. 494C–494D)

Lesson and workshop resources are referenced in the Resource Manager on the pages that follow. These resources can be used to reinforce the skills taught in Collection 8, remediate students who are having difficulty, and provide supporting activities for English-language learners.

494A

Scope and Sequence

Selection ▪ Feature	Literary Skills
Elements of Literature: Evaluating Style *by* Kylene Beers	• Understand elements of style, including diction, figurative language, tone, and mood
A Sound of Thunder *by* Ray Bradbury ↔ *at grade level* **Informational Text:** • Rising Tides • An Arctic Floe of Climate Questions *by* Bob Herbert; Robert Cooke ↔ *at grade level*	• Analyze elements of style, including figurative language and mood
To Da-duh, in Memoriam *by* Paule Marshall ↑ *above grade level*	• Analyze elements of style, including diction, sentence structure, and figures of speech
How to Eat a Guava *by* Esmeralda Santiago ↔ *at grade level*	• Analyze elements of style, including diction, imagery, and tone
Writing Workshop: *Analyzing a Short Story*	
Skills Review: *Literary Skills* *Vocabulary Skills* *Writing Skills*	• Evaluate elements of style, including diction, figurative language, tone, and mood

Reading Skills	Vocabulary Skills	Writing ▪ Grammar and Language ▪ Listening and Speaking Skills
• Understand cause-and-effect relationships • Evaluate the credibility of opposing arguments	• Understand Greek and Latin prefixes and root words • Demonstrate word knowledge	• Write a descriptive essay • Use verbs in the active and passive voices
• Visualize the story	• Create semantic maps • Understand word denotations and connotations	• Analyze a story's style
		• Write a descriptive paragraph • Compare and contrast a memoir with a poem
		• Write an analysis of a short story
	• Use context clues to understand the meanings of words	• Write an analysis of a short story

Resource Manager

Selection ■ Feature	Planning	Differentiating Instruction ■ Lesson Plans with ELL Strategies and Practice	Reading ■ Vocabulary
Elements of Literature: Evaluating Style *by* Kylene Beers		• Family Involvement Activities in English and Spanish, p. 10	
A Sound of Thunder *by* Ray Bradbury **Informational Text:** • Rising Tides • An Arctic Floe of Climate Questions *by* Bob Herbert; Robert Cooke	• One-Stop Planner with ExamView Test Generator	• The Holt Reader, pp. 222–239 • Holt Adapted Reader • Holt Reading Solutions, pp. 257–268 • Supporting Instruction in Spanish, pp. 36–37 • Audio CD Library, disc 13 • Audio CD Library, Selections and Summaries in Spanish	• The Holt Reader • Holt Adapted Reader • Holt Reading Solutions • Vocabulary Development, pp. 35, 36
To Da-duh, in Memoriam *by* Paule Marshall	• One-Stop Planner with ExamView Test Generator	• Holt Reading Solutions, pp. 269–274 • Supporting Instruction in Spanish, p. 38 • Audio CD Library, disc 14 • Audio CD Library, Selections and Summaries in Spanish	• Holt Reading Solutions • Vocabulary Development, p. 37
How to Eat a Guava *by* Esmeralda Santiago	• One-Stop Planner with ExamView Test Generator	• Holt Reading Solutions, pp. 275–280 • Supporting Instruction in Spanish, p. 38 • Audio CD Library, disc 14 • Audio CD Library, Selections and Summaries in Spanish	• Holt Reading Solutions
Writing Workshop: *Analyzing a Short Story*	• One-Stop Planner with ExamView Test Generator	• Workshop Resources: Writing, Listening, and Speaking, pp. 83–91 • Supporting Instruction in Spanish, p. 72	
Skills Review: *Literary Skills Vocabulary Skills Writing Skills*			

The Holt Reader

The Holt Reader is a consumable paperback book which can be used alone or to accompany *Elements of Literature*. It offers guided support throughout the reading process and encourages students to become active readers by circling, underlining, questioning, and jotting down responses as they read. *The Holt Reader* works well for homework, students who have missed class, additional instructional time, reteaching, and remediation.

Holt Reading Solutions (HRS)

Holt Reading Solutions pulls together reading resources in the *Elements of Literature* program to create a powerful tool for intervention and whole-class instruction. *HRS* includes diagnostic assessment tools, lesson plans for English-language learners and special education students, adaptations of selected reading selections, vocabulary and comprehension worksheets, information on phonics and decoding, and additional instruction and practice in remedial reading skills.

494C

Writing ▪ Grammar and Language ▪ Listening and Speaking	Assessment
• Daily Language Activities • Language Handbook Worksheets, p. 36	• Holt Assessment: Literature, Reading, and Vocabulary • Holt Online Assessment • One-Stop Planner with ExamView Test Generator
• Daily Language Activities	• Holt Assessment: Literature, Reading, and Vocabulary • Holt Online Assessment • One-Stop Planner with ExamView Test Generator
• Daily Language Activities	• Holt Assessment: Literature, Reading, and Vocabulary • Holt Online Assessment • One-Stop Planner with ExamView Test Generator
• Daily Language Activities • Workshop Resources: Writing, Listening, and Speaking, pp. 83–91	• Holt Assessment: Writing, Listening, and Speaking • Holt Online Assessment • One-Stop Planner with ExamView Test Generator
	• Holt Assessment: Writing, Listening, and Speaking • One-Stop Planner with ExamView Test Generator

Technology

INTERNET

- go.hrw.com
- Holt Online Assessment
- Holt Online Essay Scoring
- Elements of Literature Online

MEDIA

 • One-Stop Planner with ExamView Test Generator

• PowerNotes

• Audio CD Library, discs 13 and 14

• Audio CD Library, Selections and Summaries in Spanish

• Visual Connections Videocassette Program, Segment 9

• Fine Art Transparencies, 12 and 13

 Transparency   Video

 CD-ROM   Audio CD

One-Stop Planner with ExamView Test Generator

The *One-Stop Planner* CD-ROM contains electronic versions of print-based teaching resources, clips from the video program, and valuable assessment tools. The *One-Stop Planner* resources are presented in easy-to-follow, point-and-click menu formats. To preview resources or print out worksheets and tests, you simply make a selection and click.

 One-Stop Planner CD-ROM

Collection 8

SKILLS FOCUS

Grade-Level Skills

■ **Literary Skills**
Evaluate the aesthetic qualities of style, including the effect of diction, figurative language, tone, and mood.

■ **Reading Skills**
Evaluate the credibility of opposing arguments by examining the logic of the arguments, the scope of the evidence, and the intentions of the authors.

INTRODUCING THE COLLECTION

Many students know *style* as a word to describe fashions in clothing and hair. As they read the stories in this collection, however, they will come to understand what is meant by a *writing* or *literary* style. Students will identify the elements that make up a writer's style and analyze how that style contributes to a work's mood, tone, and theme. In Ray Bradbury's time-travel story "A Sound of Thunder," they will see that sensory images and figurative language evoke the story's exotic settings and mood. In Paule Marshall's story "To Da-duh, in Memoriam," students will learn how dialect and sentence structure can help to achieve very special effects. In Esmeralda Santiago's essay "How to Eat a Guava," they will explore how the author uses sensory imagery to express her feelings about her dual cultural identity.

The collection also includes two persuasive articles that present opposing viewpoints on the issue of global warming. Students will be asked to analyze and evaluate the evidence for each side. The collection concludes with an opportunity for students to write an analysis of a short story.

COLLECTION 8 RESOURCES: READING

Planning
■ *One-Stop Planner* CD-ROM with ExamView Test Generator

Differentiating Instruction
■ *Holt Reading Solutions*
■ *The Holt Reader*
■ *Holt Adapted Reader*

■ *Family Involvement Activities in English and Spanish*
■ *Supporting Instruction in Spanish*

Vocabulary
■ *Vocabulary Development*

Grammar and Language
■ *Language Handbook Worksheets*
■ *Daily Language Activities*

Collection 8

LITERARY CRITICISM

Evaluating Style

INFORMATIONAL READING FOCUS

EVALUATING ARGUMENTS: PRO AND CON

I don't wish to sign my name,
though I am afraid everybody
will know who the writer is:
One's style is one's signature always.

—Oscar Wilde

INTERNET

Collection Resources

Keyword: LE5 9-8

The Starry Night (1889) by Vincent van Gogh.
Oil on canvas (2′5″ × 3′¼″).

The Museum of Modern Art, New York.
Acquired through the Lillie P. Bliss Bequest.

495

THE QUOTATION

Have students sign their names, then, exchange papers and try to copy each other's signatures. Point out that, just as each person's handwriting is unique and hard to copy, so is each person's writing style. Each writer uses words to tell a story or express an idea in a distinct way.

VIEWING THE ART

Vincent van Gogh (1853–1890) struggled to remain true to his artistic vision, despite poverty and ill health. Using bold brushwork, intense colors, and coarse expressive shapes, van Gogh created his most stunning works of art in the last two years of his life. His vivid letters to his brother Theo chronicle the extreme joy and pain of an artist's life.

Activity. Bring a sample of van Gogh's letters to class and read them aloud. Ask students to discuss how his writing style compares to his painting style in *Starry Night.* [Some students may compare the heightened emotion in both the painting and the letters. Others may contrast the sensitivity in his language to the visual boldness in the artwork.]

Assessment

■ *Holt Assessment: Literature, Reading, and Vocabulary*

■ *One-Stop Planner* CD-ROM with ExamView Test Generator

■ *Holt Online Assessment*

Internet

■ go.hrw.com (Keyword: LE5 9-8)

■ *Elements of Literature Online*

Media

■ *Audio CD Library*

■ *Audio CD Library, Selections and Summaries in Spanish*

■ *Fine Art Transparencies*

■ *Visual Connections Videocassette Program*

■ *PowerNotes*

■ **Literary Skills**
Evaluate the aesthetic qualities of style, including the effect of diction, figurative language, tone, and mood.

Review Skills

■ **Literary Skills**
Identify the literary devices that define a writer's style.

Elements of Literature: Evaluating Style

Videotape and play for students a sampling of hosts on television, ranging from a serious news anchor to a host on a late-night comedy show, and from a fast-paced sports commentator to a celebrity spokesperson. Ask students to listen carefully for the kinds of word choices that the different "talking heads" choose. On the chalkboard, note and discuss some of these differences. Then, point out that just as different speakers use different word choices, so do different writers. Explain that each person's way of expression is called style.

INTERNET
More About Evaluating Style
Keyword: LE5 9-8

SKILLS FOCUS

Literary Skills
Understand elements of style, including diction, figurative language, tone, and mood.

Elements of Literature

Evaluating Style *by* Kylene Beers
THE WRITER'S PERSONAL STAMP

Here are two questions you might be asked about style:

1. What kind of music do you like?

a. I'm a boot-stomping, line-dancing, country-and-western fan.

b. I live for the beat of a rock-and-roll band.

c. I never listen to any music composed after 1890.

2. How does the inside of your locker look?

a. Neat. Inside of door is decorated. Books are all lined up.

b. Might have been neat once, but I really can't remember.

c. I have a locker?

The way you answered each question reveals a little about who you are and what your personal style is. Just as your style emerges through what you say and do, a writer's **style** emerges through the way he or she uses words to recreate an experience.

Diction: It's the Way You Say It

Style in writing is revealed chiefly through word choice, or **diction,** and through **sentence patterns.** Some authors write in informal English or even in slang. Others use formal English. While some writers might say, "He could never have done that of which he is accused," others might prefer the less formal "He couldn't have done it."

Some writers use elegant, multisyllabic words; others prefer short, everyday words—*home* instead of *abode*; *sleepy* instead of *somnolent*.

Some writers like to use **figures of speech:** "The eerie sound pulled me down the hall as if I were a dog on a leash." Others prefer to stick with the literal: "I walked down the hall, trying to trace the eerie sound."

Some writers use short, punchy sentences; others use long, complex ones. The choice depends on the topic and the effects writers want to create.

Here are two paragraphs by two writers. Read each passage, and note their different styles. Which style is more formal? Which is more modern? What details are you basing your answers on?

Restless, shifting, fugacious as time itself is a certain vast bulk of the population of the red brick district of the lower West Side. Homeless, they have a hundred homes. They flit from furnished room to furnished room, transients forever—transients in abode, transients in heart and mind.

—from "The Furnished Room" by O. Henry

But Easter's early morning sun had shown the dress to be a plain ugly cut-down from a white woman's once-was-purple throw-away. It was old-lady-long too, but it didn't hide my skinny legs, which had been greased with Blue Seal Vaseline and powdered with the Arkansas red clay.

—from *I Know Why the Caged Bird Sings* by Maya Angelou

DIFFERENTIATING INSTRUCTION

Learners Having Difficulty
To help students differentiate between mood and tone, tell them that tone is how the *author* feels about a subject. Mood is the feeling that the author wants to evoke in *readers*. For example, one writer might use a sarcastic tone about a subject in order to make readers laugh. This writer would create a humorous mood. Another writer might use a sarcastic tone in order to inform readers about a serious problem in the world. This writer might create a solemn mood.

Advanced Learners
Acceleration. Use the following activity to help students analyze the ways in which the author's tone, mood, and style achieve specific rhetorical purposes. Tell students that in a nonfiction work, the author's tone often reflects his or her purpose for writing. For

Tone: It's an Attitude

Another element of style is **tone,** a writer's attitude toward a subject, a character, or the audience. Tone isn't only what you say but also *how* you say it. A writer creates tone through word choice.

Read the following sentence from Charles Dickens's description of Uriah Heep, a character in *David Copperfield.* What details reveal how Dickens feels about Uriah? What is Dickens's tone?

I observed that he had not such a thing as a smile about him, and that he could only widen his mouth and make two hard creases down his cheeks, one on each side, to stand for one.

Tone can also be revealed in the way a writer handles plot and **theme.** If a writer provides a happy ending to a conflict, the story might convey a romantic, positive, or hopeful theme. There is a possibility, this writer seems to say, that life will reward us with great joys. But what if all a writer's characters come to tragic or disappointing ends? Then you might determine that the writer is pessimistic, that he or she feels that life, in the long run, is unfulfilling.

Mood: An Emotional Atmosphere

Mood is the feeling a story evokes. Mood is also created by diction and figures of speech. Many writers are famous for their ability to evoke particular moods. Read this description from Edgar Allan Poe's "The Fall of the House of Usher." What is the mood in this passage? Which words create that mood?

During the whole of a dull, dark, and soundless day in the autumn of the year, when the clouds hung oppressively low in the heavens, I had been passing alone, on horseback, through a singularly dreary tract of country; and at length found myself, as the shades of evening drew on, within view of the melancholy House of Usher.

How to Talk About Style: The Vocabulary of Criticism

Literary critics often focus on style. They evaluate how well a writer uses language, sets a mood, and establishes tone. As you take on the role of a literary critic, you might find the following words helpful in describing **tone** and **mood:**

Words for Tone		
admiring	comic	sarcastic
affectionate	forgiving	serious
bitter	mocking	vengeful

Words for Mood		
eerie	joyful	peaceful
gloomy	mysterious	sad

Practice

Choose one of these topics: tests, friends, school lunches. Then, write about it twice. Write one paragraph in the **formal** style you would use in a research paper. Write the other in the **informal** style you would use when talking with friends.

Practice

Sample paragraphs about friends:

Formal Style

Friends are among the greatest sources of joy and satisfaction that life has to offer. With a true friend, one feels completely at home, totally at ease. Friends support one another during times of difficulty, celebrate their achievements together, console one another during times of sorrow, and share secrets that they would not disclose to anyone else.

Informal Style

Nothing can beat the fun of just hanging with your friends. No matter what happens, they're always there for you. They cheer you on when you're up and cheer you up when you're down. Friends are the greatest because you can tell them anything and they're always on your side.

Apply

Ask students to look back at stories and poems they have read in recent months. Have them choose words from the lists on this page to describe the mood and tone of each work.

example, an author whose purpose is to inform will probably use an objective tone. A writer whose purpose is to entertain might take a lighthearted tone about a subject. A writer whose purpose is to persuade might use an angry or a somber tone.

Activity. Have students write three different paragraphs about contemporary music. Have them write each paragraph with a different purpose in mind: to inform, to entertain, or to persuade. Then, have partners exchange paragraphs and analyze the writer's purpose and tone in each paragraph.

Grade-Level Skills

■ **Literary Skills**
Evaluate the aesthetic qualities of style, including the effect of figurative language and mood.

■ **Reading Skills**
Understand cause-and-effect relationships.

Review Skills

■ **Literary Skills**
Identify significant literary devices that define a writer's style.

Summary *at grade level*

This science fiction story begins in the year 2055, the day after an election in which Keith, a democrat, wins out over Deutscher, a fascist. Time travel is possible and Eckels, a wealthy hunter, goes on a prehistoric safari to shoot a dinosaur. As Eckels's party travels back in time, Travis, the leader, warns the hunters not to stray from a prelaid anti-gravity Path, theorizing that the minutest damage to the environment could have serious reverberations for the future. Even the tyrannosaur they are going to shoot is chosen because it would have died minutes later anyway. When the time comes to make the kill, Eckels panics and runs away, stumbling off the Path. Travis is furious. After the party returns to 2055, Eckels senses that things are subtly different. He then discovers a dead butterfly on the sole of his shoe. After finding out that now Deutscher has triumphed over Keith, Eckels realizes the magnitude of his actions—he has changed the course of his country's history. The story's climax comes when Travis shoots Eckels.

Before You Read

A Sound of Thunder

Make the Connection

Quickwrite ✏️

"A Sound of Thunder" is a story about time travel. Jot down some thoughts about where you'd go if you could travel through time. Would you choose the past or the future as your destination? Would you stay in the region where you live, or would you go someplace else? How would traveling through time affect your life?

Literary Focus

Style: Figurative Language and Mood

Ray Bradbury tells this science fiction story in a lush style. In a literary work, **style** refers to the particular way a writer uses language. Style is largely created through **diction,** or word choice, and sentence patterns.

Bradbury's style owes much to vivid **images** and imaginative **figurative language.** (For more about figurative language—similes, metaphors, and personification—see pages 428–429.) These elements help him create one of the most exotic **settings** you will ever enter—a setting with a prehistoric creature whose "armored flesh glittered like a thousand green coins"—and a minor setting placed far into the future.

Setting and figurative language help to shape a story's **mood,** the feeling or the atmosphere it evokes. For example, the night sky might be a soft blanket or an icy lake—each metaphor suggests a different mood. Notice how Bradbury's language propels you into a frightening, exotic world—where anything can happen.

go.hrw.com

INTERNET

Vocabulary Practice
•
More About Ray Bradbury
•
Keyword: LE5 9-8

SKILLS FOCUS

Literary Skills
Understand elements of style, including figurative language and mood.

Reading Skills
Understand cause-and-effect relationships.

Reading Skills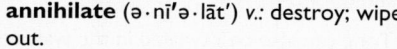

Cause and Effect: Chain Reaction

The events in a plot are interconnected, like links in a chain: One event causes another event, which causes another event, and so on. When you read, ask, "Why do these events happen? How do they affect the plot or the characters?" This story is very much *about* causes and effects. The questions at the open-book signs will help you examine them.

Vocabulary Development

annihilate (ə·nī′ə·lāt′) *v.*: destroy; wipe out.

expendable (ek·spen′də·bəl) *adj.*: worth sacrificing to gain an objective.

depression (dē·presh′ən) *n.*: major economic downturn. (*Depression* also means "sadness.")

paradox (par′ə·däks′) *n.*: something that has or seems to have contradictory qualities.

delirium (di·lir′ē·əm) *n.*: extreme mental disturbance, often accompanied by hallucinations (seeing things that are not there).

resilient (ri·zil′yənt) *adj.*: able to return to its original shape quickly after being stretched or compressed; elastic.

remit (ri·mit′) *v.*: return payment.

revoke (ri·vōk′) *v.*: cancel; withdraw.

primeval (prī·mē′vəl) *adj.*: primitive; of the earliest times.

subliminal (sub·lim′ə·nəl) *adj.*: below the level of awareness.

498 **Collection 8** Evaluating Style • Evaluating Arguments: Pro and Con

---

RESOURCES: READING

Planning
■ *One-Stop Planner* CD-ROM with ExamView Test Generator

Differentiating Instruction
■ *Holt Reading Solutions*
■ *The Holt Reader*
■ *Supporting Instruction in Spanish*

■ *Audio CD Library, Selections and Summaries in Spanish*

Vocabulary
■ *Vocabulary Development*

Grammar and Language
■ *Daily Language Activities*
■ *Language Handbook Worksheets*

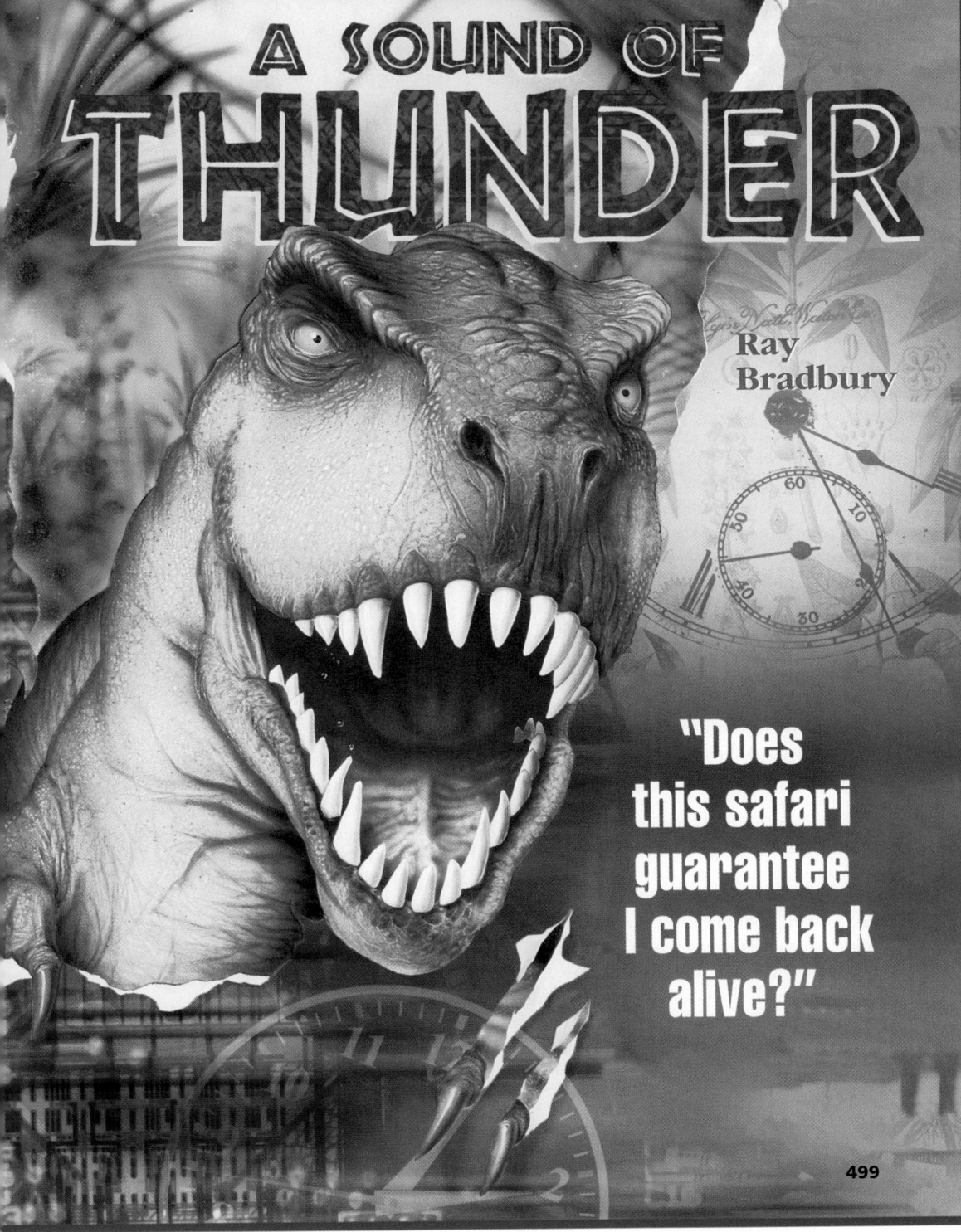

A SOUND OF THUNDER

Ray Bradbury

"Does this safari guarantee I come back alive?"

499

A Reading Skills

? Analyzing. What do Eckels's actions here reveal about him? [Possible responses: He is scared; he is rich and accustomed to getting guarantees of safety.]

B Literary Focus

Style. Bradbury is considered by many to be a master of fiction because he indulges in an almost stream-of-consciousness style, which is evident in this passage about the time machine. Help students see that this passage contains a series of images and impressions about the machine, rather than a literal description of it. Discuss whether a description such as this conveys the awesome qualities of the machine better than a conventional description would.

C Literary Focus

Style. [Possible responses to question 1: *Similes*— "a sound like a gigantic bonfire burning all of Time"; "like golden salamanders, the old years, the green years, might leap." *Metaphors*— "an aura that flickered"; "everything fly back to seed." *Personification*— "a snaking and humming of wires"; "moons eat."]

D Content-Area Connections

History: Deutscher
Point out that in the German language, the name *Deutscher* means "German." In post–World War II United States, when this story was published, Hitler's Germany was considered the quintessential example of the evils of dictatorship.

The sign on the wall seemed to quaver under a film of sliding warm water. Eckels felt his eyelids blink over his stare, and the sign burned in this momentary darkness:

> **TIME SAFARI, INC.**
> Safaris to any
> year in the past.
> You name the animal.
> We take you there.
> You shoot it.

A A warm phlegm gathered in Eckels's throat; he swallowed and pushed it down. The muscles around his mouth formed a smile as he put his hand slowly out upon the air, and in that hand waved a check for ten thousand dollars to the man behind the desk.

"Does this safari guarantee I come back alive?"

"We guarantee nothing," said the official, "except the dinosaurs." He turned. "This is Mr. Travis, your Safari Guide in the Past. He'll tell you what and where to shoot. If he says no shooting, no shooting. If you disobey instructions, there's a stiff penalty of another ten thousand dollars, plus possible government action, on your return."

B Eckels glanced across the vast office at a mass and tangle, a snaking and humming of wires and steel boxes, at an aura[1] that flickered now orange, now silver, now blue. There was a sound like a gigantic bonfire burning all of Time, all the years and all the parchment calendars, all the hours piled high and set aflame.

A touch of the hand and this burning would, on the instant, beautifully reverse itself. Eckels

---

1. **aurora** (ô·rôr′ə) *n.*: Bradbury is comparing the glow coming from the time machine to an aurora, a colorful display of light that appears at night in the skies near the North and South Poles.

remembered the wording in the advertisements to the letter. Out of chars and ashes, out of dust and coals, like golden salamanders, the old years, the green years, might leap; roses sweeten the air, white hair turn Irish-black, wrinkles vanish; all, everything fly back to seed, flee death, rush down to their beginnings, suns rise in western skies and set in glorious easts, moons eat themselves opposite to the custom, all and everything cupping one in another like Chinese boxes,[2] rabbits into hats, all and everything returning to the fresh death, the seed death, the green death, to the time before the beginning. A touch of a hand might do it, the merest touch of a hand.

STYLE

C 1. Find at least three examples of **figurative language** (similes, metaphors, and personification) in the previous two paragraphs.

"Unbelievable." Eckels breathed, the light of the Machine on his thin face. "A real Time Machine." He shook his head. "Makes you think. If the election had gone badly yesterday, I might be here now running away from the results. Thank God Keith won. He'll make a fine President of the United States."

D "Yes," said the man behind the desk. "We're lucky. If Deutscher had gotten in, we'd have the worst kind of dictatorship. There's an anti-everything man for you, a militarist, anti-Christ, anti-human, anti-intellectual. People called us up, you know, joking but not joking. Said if Deutscher became President they wanted to go live in 1492. Of course it's not our business to conduct Escapes, but to form Safaris. Anyway, Keith's President now. All you got to worry about is—"

"Shooting my dinosaur," Eckels finished it for him.

"A *Tyrannosaurus rex.* The Tyrant Lizard, the most incredible monster in history. Sign

---

2. **Chinese boxes:** set of boxes, each of which fits into the next-largest one.

DIFFERENTIATING INSTRUCTION

Learners Having Difficulty
Invite learners having difficulty to read "A Sound of Thunder" in interactive format in *The Holt Reader* and to use the sidenotes as aids to understanding the selection. The interactive version provides additional instruction, practice, and assessment of the literary skill taught in the Student Edition. Monitor students' responses to the selection, and correct any misconceptions that arise.

English-Language Learners
Bradbury's figurative language may confuse students. To help them understand it, you might monitor their reading in small groups.

Special Education Students
For lessons designed for special education students, see *Holt Reading Solutions.*

E **Learners Having Difficulty**

❓ **Finding details.** What details in this paragraph tell you that Eckels is very scared? [Possible responses: a pale face, stiff jaw, trembling arms, hands tightly grasping the rifle.] **What is he scared of?** [Possible responses: time travel, encountering the dinosaur.]

this release. Anything happens to you, we're not responsible. Those dinosaurs are hungry."

Eckels flushed angrily. "Trying to scare me!"

"Frankly, yes. We don't want anyone going who'll panic at the first shot. Six Safari leaders were killed last year, and a dozen hunters. We're here to give you the severest thrill a *real* hunter ever asked for. Traveling you back sixty million years to bag the biggest game in all of Time. Your personal check's still there. Tear it up."

Mr. Eckels looked at the check. His fingers twitched.

"Good luck," said the man behind the desk. "Mr. Travis, he's all yours."

They moved silently across the room, taking their guns with them, toward the Machine, toward the silver metal and the roaring light.

First a day and then a night and then a day and then a night, then it was day-night-day-night-day. A week, a month, a year, a decade! A.D. 2055. A.D. 2019. 1999! 1957! Gone! The Machine roared.

They put on their oxygen helmets and tested the intercoms.

Eckels swayed on the padded seat, his face pale, his jaw stiff. He felt the trembling in his arms, and he looked down and found his hands tight on the new rifle. There were four other

A Sound of Thunder   **501**

A Literary Focus

❓ Figurative language and mood. Ask students to identify examples of personification and metaphor in these two paragraphs. What effect does this use of figurative language have on the mood of the story? [Examples include "The Machine howled."; "Time was a film run backward."; "Suns fled and ten million moons fled after them."; "its scream fell to a murmur." The comparisons help to create a mood of fear and anxiety—a feeling that things are not as they should be.]

B Reading Skills

❓ Cause and effect. According to Travis, what might be a result of going off the Path or of unintentionally killing an animal or plant? [It could destroy an important link in a species and maybe affect the future.]

C Reading Skills

Cause and effect. Travis's explanation is an excellent example of a cause-and-effect chain of events. To help students better understand the concept of a cause-and-effect sequence of events, you may wish to map out this chain on the chalkboard. Begin with the events below, and have students add to the chain.

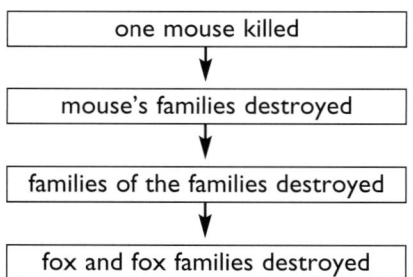

one mouse killed
↓
mouse's families destroyed
↓
families of the families destroyed
↓
fox and fox families destroyed
↓

men in the Machine. Travis, the Safari Leader; his assistant, Lesperance; and two other hunters, Billings and Kramer. They sat looking at each other, and the years blazed around them.

"Can these guns get a dinosaur cold?" Eckels felt his mouth saying.

"If you hit them right," said Travis on the helmet radio. "Some dinosaurs have two brains, one in the head, another far down the spinal column. We stay away from those. That's stretching luck. Put your first two shots into the eyes, if you can, blind them, and go back into the brain."

A The Machine howled. Time was a film run backward. Suns fled and ten million moons fled after them. "Think," said Eckels. "Every hunter that ever lived would envy us today. This makes Africa seem like Illinois."

The Machine slowed; its scream fell to a murmur. The Machine stopped.

The sun stopped in the sky.

The fog that had enveloped the Machine blew away and they were in an old time, a very old time indeed, three hunters and two Safari Heads with their blue metal guns across their knees.

"Christ isn't born yet," said Travis. "Moses has not gone to the mountain to talk with God. The Pyramids are still in the earth, waiting to be cut out and put up. *Remember* that. Alexander, Caesar, Napoleon, Hitler—none of them exists."

The men nodded.

"That"—Mr. Travis pointed—"is the jungle of sixty million two thousand and fifty-five years before President Keith."

He indicated a metal path that struck off into green wilderness, over streaming swamp, among giant ferns and palms.

"And that," he said, "is the Path, laid by Time Safari for your use. It floats six inches above the earth. Doesn't touch so much as one grass blade, flower, or tree. It's an anti-gravity metal. Its purpose is to keep you from touching this world of the Past in any way. Stay on the Path. Don't go off it. I repeat. *Don't go off.* For *any* reason! If you fall off, there's a penalty. And don't shoot any animal we don't okay."

"Why?" asked Eckels.

They sat in the ancient wilderness. Far birds' cries blew on a wind, and the smell of tar and an old salt sea, moist grasses, and flowers the color of blood.

"We don't want to change the Future. We don't belong here in the Past. The government doesn't *like* us here. We **B** have to pay big graft[3] to keep our franchise. A Time Machine is finicky business. Not knowing it, we might kill an important animal, a small bird, a roach, a flower even, thus destroying an important link in a growing species."

"That's not clear," said Eckels.

"All right," Travis continued, "say we accidentally kill one mouse here. That means all the future families of this one particular mouse are **C** destroyed, right?"

"Right."

"And all the families of the families of the families of that one mouse! With a stamp of your foot, you <u>annihilate</u> first one, then a dozen,

---

3. graft *n.:* bribes.

Vocabulary
annihilate (ə·nī′ə·lāt′) *v.:* destroy; wipe out.

CONTENT-AREA CONNECTIONS

History: Identifying Domino Effects
After students have finished reading the story, ask them to think of examples in history of the domino effect described in the story—situations in which a seemingly small incident proves to have tremendous implications through a chain of linked events.

Small-group activity. Have small groups of students create posters with illustrations showing how these linked events lead step by step to a final result.

then a thousand, a million, a *billion* possible mice!"

"So they're dead," said Eckels. "So what?"

"So what?" Travis snorted quietly. "Well, what about the foxes that'll need those mice to survive? For want of ten mice, a fox dies. For want of ten foxes, a lion starves. For want of a lion, all manner of insects, vultures, infinite billions of life forms are thrown into chaos and destruction. Eventually it all boils down to this: Fifty-nine million years later, a cave man, one of a dozen in the *entire world,* goes hunting wild boar or saber-toothed tiger for food. But you, friend, have *stepped* on all the tigers in that region. By stepping on *one* single mouse. So the cave man starves. And the cave man, please note, is not just *any* expendable man, no! He is an *entire future nation.* From his loins would have sprung ten sons. From *their* loins one hundred sons, and thus onward to a civilization. Destroy this one man, and you destroy a race, a people, an entire history of life. It is comparable to slaying some of Adam's grandchildren. The stomp of your foot, on one mouse, could start an earthquake, the effects of which could shake our earth and destinies down through Time, to their very foundations. With the death of that one cave man, a billion others yet unborn are throttled in the womb. Perhaps Rome never rises on its seven hills. Perhaps Europe is forever a dark forest, and only Asia waxes healthy and teeming.[4] Step on a mouse and you crush the Pyramids. Step on a mouse and you leave your print, like a Grand Canyon, across Eternity. Queen Elizabeth might never be born, Washington might not cross the Delaware, there might never be a United States at all. So be careful. Stay on the Path. *Never* step off!"

> ### CAUSE AND EFFECT
>
> **2.** In this cause-and-effect chain, what small **cause** leads to what enormous **effect**?

4. **teeming** (tēm′iŋ) *adj.:* swarming; overflowing.

"I see," said Eckels. "Then it wouldn't pay for us even to touch the *grass*?"

"Correct. Crushing certain plants could add up infinitesimally.[5] A little error here would multiply in sixty million years, all out of proportion. Of course maybe our theory is wrong. Maybe Time *can't* be changed by us. Or maybe it can be changed only in little subtle ways. A dead mouse here makes an insect imbalance there, a population disproportion later, a bad harvest further on, a depression, mass starvation, and, finally, a change in *social* temperament in far-flung countries. Something much more subtle, like that. Perhaps only a soft breath, a whisper, a hair, pollen on the air, such a slight, slight change that unless you looked close you wouldn't see it. Who knows? Who really can say he knows? We don't know. We're guessing. But until we do know for certain whether our messing around in Time *can* make a big roar or a little rustle in history, we're being careful. This Machine, this Path, your clothing and bodies, were sterilized, as you know, before the journey. We wear these oxygen helmets so we can't introduce our bacteria into an ancient atmosphere."

"How do we know which animals to shoot?"

"They're marked with red paint," said Travis. "Today, before our journey, we sent Lesperance here back with the Machine. He came to this particular era and followed certain animals."

"Studying them?"

"Right," said Lesperance. "I track them through their entire existence, noting which of them lives longest. Very few. How many times they mate. Not often. Life's short. When I find one that's going to die when a tree falls on him,

5. **infinitesimally** (in′fin·i·tes′i·məl·ē) *adv.:* in amounts too small to be measured.

Vocabulary

expendable (ek·spen′də·bəl) *adj.:* worth sacrificing to gain an objective.

depression (dē·presh′ən) *n.:* major economic downturn. (*Depression* also means "sadness.")

DIRECT TEACHING

D **Reading Skills**
Cause and effect. [Possible response to question 2: Accidentally killing one mouse might prevent the most momentous historical events from happening, such as the formation of civilization in Europe and the founding of the United States.]

E **Literary Focus**
❷ **Foreshadowing.** What purpose do you think Bradbury had in including such detailed discussions of these scientific theories? [Possible response: Bradbury's emphasis on the theory of a small change affecting the future might foreshadow later events in the plot.]

DEVELOPING FLUENCY

Mixed-ability group activity. Arrange students in mixed-ability groups of four, and ask them to prepare a reader's theater performance. Assign the best reader the role of narrator, and have two others read the dialogue of Eckels and Travis. The remaining student in each group can read the dialogue of every other character. If possible, provide students with photocopies of the story so they can highlight their parts. Encourage students to rehearse the presentation, offering one another direction and advice as necessary. Have students either record their presentation or perform it live for the class.

A **Advanced Learners**

❓ Acceleration. What idea discussed in this paragraph could be considered a characteristic of science fiction? [the time-travel paradox] Is there scientific merit in the idea that people cannot meet themselves during time travel? [Possible response: Yes; the same matter cannot be in the same place twice.]

B **Vocabulary Development**

Prefixes and root words. Point out the word *bisect.* Explain that the prefix *bi–* means "two" and the root word *sect* means "cut." Ask students to define *bisect* based on this etymology. ["to cut into two pieces"] Then, have students suggest what *bisect* means in the sentence. [Possible response: "cut into."]

or one that drowns in a tar pit, I note the exact hour, minute, and second. I shoot a paint bomb. It leaves a red patch on his side. We can't miss it. Then I correlate our arrival in the Past so that we meet the Monster not more than two minutes before he would have died anyway. This way, we kill only animals with no future, that are never going to mate again. You see how *careful* we are?"

"But if you came back this morning in Time," said Eckels eagerly, "you must've bumped into *us,* our Safari! How did it turn out? Was it successful? Did all of us get through —alive?"

Travis and Lesperance gave each other a look.

A "That'd be a paradox," said the latter. "Time doesn't permit that sort of mess—a man meeting himself. When such occasions threaten, Time steps aside. Like an airplane hitting an air pocket. You felt the Machine jump just before we stopped? That was us passing ourselves on the way back to the Future. We saw nothing. There's no way of telling *if* this expedition was a success, *if we* got our monster, or whether all of us— meaning *you,* Mr. Eckels—got out alive."

Eckels smiled palely.

"Cut that," said Travis sharply. "Everyone on his feet!"

They were ready to leave the Machine.

The jungle was high and the jungle was broad and the jungle was the entire world forever and forever. Sounds like music and sounds like flying tents filled the sky, and those were pterodactyls soaring with cavernous gray wings, gigantic bats of delirium and night fever. Eckels, balanced on the narrow Path, aimed his rifle playfully.

"Stop that!" said Travis. "Don't even aim for fun, blast you! If your guns should go off—"

Eckels flushed.

"Where's our *Tyrannosaurus?*"

Lesperance checked his wristwatch. "Up ahead. **B** We'll bisect his trail in sixty seconds. Look for the red paint! Don't shoot till we give the word. Stay on the Path. *Stay on the Path!*"

They moved forward in the wind of morning.

"Strange," murmured Eckels. "Up ahead, sixty million years, Election Day over. Keith made President. Everyone celebrating. And here we are, a million years lost, and they don't exist. The things we worried about for months, a lifetime, not even born or thought of yet."

"Safety catches off, everyone!" ordered Travis. "You, first shot, Eckels. Second, Billings. Third, Kramer."

"I've hunted tiger, wild boar, buffalo, elephant, but now, this is *it,*" said Eckels. "I'm shaking like a kid."

Vocabulary

paradox (par′ə·däks′) *n.:* something that has or seems to have contradictory qualities.

delirium (di·lir′ē·əm) *n.:* extreme mental disturbance, often accompanied by hallucinations (seeing things that are not there).

504 **Collection 8** Evaluating Style • Evaluating Arguments: Pro and Con

CONTENT-AREA CONNECTIONS

Literature: The Time Machine
The first time machine in science fiction is described in H. G. Wells's 1895 novel *The Time Machine.* That machine facilitated travel only to the future. An exciting adventure story, *The Time Machine* also reflected the fears held by many in the late nineteenth century about the possibilities of science and technology.

Activity. Have students who have read *The Time Machine* compare and contrast the ways in which Wells and Bradbury use time travel to develop their stories. Encourage them to discuss whether it might be easier to write about traveling into the future or into the past and to give reasons for their opinions.

"Ah," said Travis.

Everyone stopped.

Travis raised his hand. "Ahead," he whispered. "In the mist. There he is. There's His Royal Majesty now."

The jungle was wide and full of twitterings, rustlings, murmurs, and sighs.

Suddenly it all ceased, as if someone had shut a door.

Silence.

A sound of thunder.

Out of the mist, one hundred yards away, came *Tyrannosaurus rex*.

"It," whispered Eckels. "It . . ."

"Sh!"

It came on great oiled, <u>resilient</u>, striding legs. It towered thirty feet above half of the trees, a great evil god, folding its delicate watchmaker's claws close to its oily reptilian chest. Each lower leg was a piston, a thousand pounds of white bone, sunk in thick ropes of muscle, sheathed over in a gleam of pebbled skin like the mail[6] of a terrible warrior. Each thigh was a ton of meat, ivory, and steel mesh. And from the great breathing cage of the upper body those two delicate arms dangled out front, arms with hands which might pick up and examine men like toys, while the snake neck coiled. And the head itself, a ton of sculptured stone, lifted easily upon the sky. Its mouth gaped, exposing a fence of teeth like daggers. Its eyes rolled, ostrich eggs, empty of all expression save hunger. It closed its mouth in a death grin. It ran, its pelvic bones crushing aside trees and bushes, its taloned feet clawing damp earth, leaving prints six inches deep wherever it settled its weight. It ran with a gliding ballet step, far too poised and balanced for its ten tons. It moved into a sunlit arena warily, its beautifully reptilian hands feeling the air.

📖 **STYLE**

3. What **descriptive details** and **figures of speech** make the dinosaur seem terrifying?

---

6. mail *n.:* here, flexible metal armor.

"Why, why," Eckels twitched his mouth. "It could reach up and grab the moon."

"Sh!" Travis jerked angrily. "He hasn't seen us yet."

"It can't be killed." Eckels pronounced this verdict quietly, as if there could be no argument. He had weighed the evidence and this was his considered opinion. The rifle in his hands seemed a cap gun. "We were fools to come. This is impossible."

"Shut up!" hissed Travis.

"Nightmare."

"Turn around," commanded Travis. "Walk quietly to the Machine. We'll <u>remit</u> one half your fee."

"I didn't realize it would be this *big*," said Eckels. "I miscalculated, that's all. And now I want out."

"It *sees* us!"

"There's the red paint on its chest!"

The Tyrant Lizard raised itself. Its armored flesh glittered like a thousand green coins. The coins, crusted with slime, steamed. In the slime, tiny insects wriggled, so that the entire body seemed to twitch and undulate,[7] even while the monster itself did not move. It exhaled. The stink of raw flesh blew down the wilderness.

"Get me out of here," said Eckels. "It was never like this before. I was always sure I'd come through alive. I had good guides, good safaris, and safety. This time, I figured wrong. I've met my match and admit it. This is too much for me to get hold of."

"Don't run," said Lesperance. "Turn around. Hide in the Machine."

"Yes." Eckels seemed to be numb. He looked

---

7. undulate (un'jə·lāt') *v.:* move in waves.

Vocabulary

resilient (ri·zil'yənt) *adj.:* able to return to its original shape quickly after being stretched or compressed; elastic.

remit (ri·mit') *v.:* return payment.

C Literary Focus

❓ **Figurative language and mood.** Ask students to point out the simile and metaphor in this passage. ["as if someone had shut a door"; "A sound of thunder."] **What mood do these comparisons create?** [Possible responses: The abrupt change from a noisy jungle to a silent one creates a mood of tension and apprehension.]

D Content-Area Connections

Literature: Bradbury on Bradbury

Here is what Bradbury had to say about his description of the tyrannosaur: "So Shakespeare has given me the courage—and Melville—to do the aside. . . . I say to the audience 'I'm going to stop the plot here, okay? . . . and you know what I'm going to do? I'm going to describe a dinosaur as it's never been described. Now watch this.' And then I sit down and write a prose poem about this wonderful creature that comes gliding out of the jungle."

E Literary Focus

Style. [Possible responses to question 3: "a great evil god"; "delicate watchmaker's claws"; "Each lower leg was a piston, a thousand pounds of white bone"; "pebbled skin like the mail of a terrible warrior"; "Each thigh was a ton of meat, ivory, and steel mesh"; "hands which might pick up and examine men like toys"; "the head . . . a ton of sculptured stone"; "a fence of teeth like daggers"; "death grin."]

F Literary Focus

❓ **Conflict.** Who are in conflict here? [Eckels and Travis] What is the conflict? [Possible responses: Eckels is overwhelmed by the dinosaur, and Travis thinks Eckels is speaking and acting foolishly; Eckels wants to give up, and Travis fears that Eckels is endangering the expedition.]

CONTENT-AREA CONNECTIONS

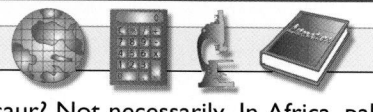

Science: Mega-monsters

Tyrannosaurus rex might not have been the "most incredible monster in history." In 1994–1995, paleontologists discovered in Argentina's Patagonia region the skeleton of *Giganotosaurus*. They estimate that this prehistoric predator weighed about 8 tons—perhaps a ton or so more than the heaviest *T. rex*—and measured about 47 feet in length. So was *Giganotosaurus* the largest meat-eating dinosaur? Not necessarily. In Africa, paleontologists have found the skull of yet another carnivorous dinosaur—*Carcharodontosaurus*. The skull alone is over 60 inches in length, almost the same size as that of *Giganotosaurus*. Without a complete skeleton, scientists can only speculate about this dinosaur's size, but they believe it to be similar in size to the other two mega-monsters.

This article focuses on one explanation for the extinction of the dinosaurs. From the discovery of deposits of iridium—a mineral that is rare on earth but common in outer space—scientists have theorized that dinosaurs disappeared because an asteroid or comet hit earth. The impact would have caused a massive dust cloud that would have blocked sunlight, thus killing plants, the source of food. After the dust settled, there would have been a greenhouse effect, with temperatures soaring too high to support most life.

DIRECT TEACHING

A Reading Skills

? Cause and effect. What causes Eckels to step off the Path? [Possible response: He is overwhelmed by his fear of the tyrannosaur.] What might be an effect of his stepping off the Path? [Possible responses: He might crush something and alter the future; the dinosaur might kill him.]

B Reading Informational Text

Paraphrasing ideas. Ask students to paraphrase this paragraph. [In layers of rock, geologists find evidence of the earth's past. Scientists from the University of California at Berkeley have found evidence in rock that dinosaurs became extinct after an asteroid or comet hit earth.]

---

at his feet as if trying to make them move. He gave a grunt of helplessness.

"Eckels!"

He took a few steps, blinking, shuffling.

"Not *that* way!"

The Monster, at the first motion, lunged forward with a terrible scream. It covered one hundred yards in six seconds. The rifles jerked up and blazed fire. A windstorm from the beast's mouth engulfed them in the stench of slime and old blood. The Monster roared, teeth glittering with sun.

Eckels, not looking back, walked blindly to the edge of the Path, his gun limp in his arms, stepped off the Path, and walked, not knowing it, in the jungle. His feet sank into green moss. His legs moved him, and he felt alone and remote from the events behind.

The rifles cracked again. Their sound was lost in shriek and lizard thunder. The great level of the reptile's tail swung up, lashed sideways. Trees exploded in clouds of leaf and

branch. The Monster twitched its jeweler's hands down to fondle at the men, to twist them in half, to crush them like berries, to cram them into its teeth and its screaming throat. Its boulder-stone eyes leveled with the men. They saw themselves mirrored. They fired at the metallic eyelids and the blazing black iris.

Like a stone idol, like a mountain avalanche, *Tyrannosaurus* fell. Thundering, it clutched trees, pulled them with it. It wrenched and tore the metal Path. The men flung themselves back and away. The body hit, ten tons of cold flesh and stone. The guns fired. The Monster lashed its armored tail, twitched its snake jaws, and lay still. A fount of blood spurted from its throat. Somewhere inside, a sac of fluids burst. Sickening gushes drenched the hunters. They stood, red and glistening.

The thunder faded.

The jungle was silent. After the avalanche, a green peace. After the nightmare, morning.

A CLOSER LOOK

How Did They Disappear?

What caused the extinction of the dinosaurs? How could such a dominant, thriving population disappear? Scientists have wondered whether their extinction was the result of a gradual decline or a sudden catastrophe. Now some geologists think they've found the answer—in rocks.

Geologists know the secret of time travel: They know that layers—or sediments—of rock can reveal the history of the earth. It is in these layers that a team of scientists from the University of California at Berkeley found evidence indicating that the dinosaurs were wiped out after an asteroid or a comet—nobody knows which it was—slammed into the earth 65

million years ago. It's a theory that combines some of science fiction's favorite subjects: time travel, asteroids, and dinosaurs.

The rocks tell the story. All over the world the sediment that forms the boundary between the age of the dinosaurs and the age following their extinction contains deposits of iridium, a mineral that is extremely rare on earth but common in outer space. Some scientists believe that the iridium was deposited when a huge asteroid or a comet—about six miles across—struck the earth.

Scientists even believe that they have discovered the site where the comet or asteroid hit, in Chicxulub (chek′shoo·loob′), on the coast of the Yucatán Peninsula in Mexico. The proof is in the rocks, which contain not just deposits of iridium but also all the other right minerals and chemicals to prove the theory.

READING MINI-LESSON

Developing Word-Attack Skills
Write the selection words *subtle* and *phlegm* on the chalkboard. Read them aloud and ask students which letters are not heard when the word is pronounced. Help them recognize that *b* in *subtle* and *g* in *phlegm* are silent letters.

Write the following sentences on the chalkboard. Have volunteers read them aloud and identify the word in each sentence that has a silent letter.

We owe a great *debt* to the explorers. They *climbed* mountains and forded rivers. In the uncharted terrain, terror *reigned*. Fear did not *gnaw* at their resolve.

Use the examples in the sentences to generalize that the letter *b* is silent in final *bt* and *mb* and the letter *g* is silent in initial or final *gn*.

Activity. Display these sets of words. Have students identify which underlined letter is silent. (Answers are italicized.)

1. ignorant	*gnome*	ignominious
2. *dumbstruck*	grumble	humbug
3. *malign*	malignant	malinger
4. *plumber*	lumber	slumber
5. double	dubitable	*doubtful*
6. subterfuge	*subtlety*	subterranean
7. *campaign*	pagination	pigmentation
8. dignity	indignation	*deign*

Billings and Kramer sat on the pathway and threw up. Travis and Lesperance stood with smoking rifles, cursing steadily.

In the Time Machine, on his face, Eckels lay shivering. He had found his way back to the Path, climbed into the Machine.

Travis came walking, glanced at Eckels, took cotton gauze from a metal box, and returned to the others, who were sitting on the Path.

"Clean up."

They wiped the blood from their helmets. They began to curse too. The Monster lay, a hill of solid flesh. Within, you could hear the sighs and murmurs as the furthest chambers of it died, the organs malfunctioning, liquids **F** running a final instant from pocket to sac to spleen, everything shutting off, closing up forever. It was like standing by a wrecked locomotive or a steam shovel at quitting time, all valves being released or levered tight. Bones cracked; the tonnage of its own flesh, off balance, dead weight, snapped the delicate

forearms, caught underneath. The meat settled, quivering.

Another cracking sound. Overhead, a gigantic tree branch broke from its heavy mooring, fell. It crashed upon the dead beast with finality.

"There." Lesperance checked his watch. "Right on time. That's the giant tree that was scheduled to fall and kill this animal originally." He glanced at the two hunters. "You want the trophy picture?"

"What?"

CAUSE AND EFFECT

4. Why doesn't the hunters' killing the dinosaur affect the future?

G

"We can't take a trophy back to the Future. The body has to stay right here where it would **E** have died originally, so the insects, birds, and bacteria can get at it, as they were intended to. Everything in balance. The body stays. But we *can* take a picture of you standing near it."

The two men tried to think, but gave up, shaking their heads.

The impact would have caused massive fires, tidal waves, and floods, but the dust created by the impact—composed of iridium and other minerals—caused even bigger problems. The dust blocked the sunlight; the earth became cool and dark, plants died, and the food chain was devastated. Eventually the dust settled, but then a greenhouse effect set in, creating temperatures too high to support most life forms. Almost all life on earth vanished. The 150-million-year reign of the dinosaurs had reached its catastrophic end.

A Sound of Thunder   507

CONTENT-AREA CONNECTIONS

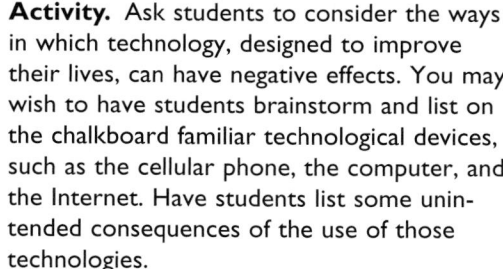

Science: Technology
Like much of Bradbury's fiction, "A Sound of Thunder" warns of the unintended consequences that may arise from technology. Bradbury's feelings about technology are evident in his well-known antipathy toward the automobile, an instrument he feels is often misused, with tragic results.

Activity. Ask students to consider the ways in which technology, designed to improve their lives, can have negative effects. You may wish to have students brainstorm and list on the chalkboard familiar technological devices, such as the cellular phone, the computer, and the Internet. Have students list some unintended consequences of the use of those technologies.

DIRECT TEACHING

C Literary Focus
Figurative language and mood. Ask students to identify the two similes that help readers picture the falling dinosaur. ["Like a stone idol," "like a mountain avalanche"] What mood does this passage create? [Possible responses: terror, suspense, excitement, tension.]

D Reading Informational Text
Examining the sequence of information. Ask students to place the events cited in this paragraph in the order in which they actually happened. [Few, if any, iridium deposits existed on earth. A large asteroid or comet containing iridium landed on earth. Dinosaurs became extinct. Iridium now exists in the layer of rock that coincides with the last of the dinosaurs but does not exist in layers that come after it.]

E English-Language Learners
Breaking down difficult text. Students may have trouble with the imagery and vocabulary in this passage. Suggest that they read aloud and discuss the passage with partners. Students should also look up such difficult words as *sac, spleen, locomotive,* and *tonnage.*

F Vocabulary Development
Prefixes and root words. Ask students to use their knowledge of prefixes and root words to determine the meaning of *malfunctioning.* [Possible response: The prefix *mal*— means "bad," and the root *func* means "to perform," so *malfunctioning* means "performing badly."]

G Reading Skills
Cause and effect. [Possible response to question 4: The dinosaur was identified as one that will die soon anyway, so there is little chance that the future will be affected.]

A Literary Focus

? Conflict. Why is Travis angry at Eckels? [Eckels has stepped off the Path and perhaps jeopardized not only the business but also the future of the world.]

B Reading Skills

? Making judgments. What does Eckels's offer of payment reveal about him? [He thinks money can fix everything.] **Do you think money can fix something like this? Explain.** [Possible responses: Money cannot fix the future; money cannot change what Eckels has done.]

C Content-Area Connections

History: Dates
Have students identify the historical importance of each date listed here. [1492—Columbus sailed to the Americas; 1776—the Declaration of Independence was written; 1812— the War of 1812 took place.]

D Reading Skills

? Cause and effect. What does Travis fear might be the effects of Eckels having stepped off the path? [He fears that Eckels might have greatly altered the future.]

They let themselves be led along the metal Path. They sank wearily into the Machine cushions. They gazed back at the ruined Monster, the stagnating mound, where already strange reptilian birds and golden insects were busy at the steaming armor.

A sound on the floor of the Time Machine stiffened them. Eckels sat there, shivering.

"I'm sorry," he said at last.

"Get up!" cried Travis.

Eckels got up.

"Go out on that Path alone," said Travis. He had his rifle pointed. "You're not coming back in the Machine. We're leaving you here!"

Lesperance seized Travis's arm. "Wait—"

"Stay out of this!" Travis shook his hand away. "This fool nearly killed us. But it isn't *that* so much, no. It's his *shoes*! Look at them! He ran off the Path. That *ruins* us! We'll forfeit! Thousands of dollars of insurance! We guarantee no one leaves the Path. He left it. Oh, the fool! I'll have to report to the government. They might revoke our license to travel. Who knows *what* he's done to Time, to History!"

"Take it easy, all he did was kick up some dirt."

"How do we *know*?" cried Travis. "We don't know anything! It's all a mystery! Get out of here, Eckels!"

Eckels fumbled his shirt. "I'll pay anything. A hundred thousand dollars!"

Travis glared at Eckels's checkbook and spat. "Go out there. The Monster's next to the Path. Stick your arms up to your elbows in his mouth. Then you can come back with us."

"That's unreasonable!"

"The Monster's dead, you idiot. The bullets! The bullets can't be left behind. They don't belong in the Past; they might change anything. Here's my knife. Dig them out!"

The jungle was alive again, full of the old tremorings and bird cries. Eckels turned slowly to regard the primeval garbage dump, that

hill of nightmares and terror. After a long time, like a sleepwalker he shuffled out along the Path.

He returned, shuddering, five minutes later, his arms soaked and red to the elbows. He held out his hands. Each held a number of steel bullets. Then he fell. He lay where he fell, not moving.

"You didn't have to make him do that," said Lesperance.

"Didn't I? It's too early to tell." Travis nudged the still body. "He'll live. Next time he won't go hunting game like this. Okay." He jerked his thumb wearily at Lesperance. "Switch on. Let's go home."

1492. 1776. 1812.

They cleaned their hands and faces. They changed their caking shirts and pants. Eckels was up and around again, not speaking. Travis glared at him for a full ten minutes.

"Don't look at me," cried Eckels. "I haven't done anything."

"Who can tell?"

"Just ran off the Path, that's all, a little mud on my shoes—what do you want me to do—get down and pray?"

"We might need it. I'm warning you, Eckels, I might kill you yet. I've got my gun ready."

"I'm innocent. I've done nothing!"

1999. 2000. 2055.

The Machine stopped.

"Get out," said Travis.

The room was there as they had left it. But not the same as they had left it. The same man sat behind the same desk. But the same man did not quite sit behind the same desk.

Travis looked around swiftly. "Everything okay here?" he snapped.

Vocabulary

revoke (ri·vōk′) v.: cancel; withdraw.

primeval (prī·mē′vəl) adj.: primitive; of the earliest times.

"Fine. Welcome home!"

Travis did not relax. He seemed to be looking at the very atoms of the air itself, at the way the sun poured through the one high window.

"Okay, Eckels, get out. Don't ever come back."

Eckels could not move.

"You heard me," said Travis. "What're you *staring* at?"

Eckels stood smelling of the air, and there was a thing to the air, a chemical taint so subtle, so slight, that only a faint cry of his <u>subliminal</u> senses warned him it was there. The colors, white, gray, blue, orange, in the wall, in the furniture, in the sky beyond the window, were . . . were . . . And there was a *feel.* His flesh twitched. His hands twitched. He stood drinking the oddness with the pores of his body. Somewhere, someone must have been screaming one of those whistles that only a dog can hear. His body screamed silence in return. Beyond this room, beyond this wall, beyond this man who was not quite the same man seated at this desk that was not quite the same desk . . . lay an entire world of streets and people. What sort of world it was now, there was no telling. He could feel them moving there, beyond the walls, almost, like so many chess pieces blown in a dry wind. . . .

But the immediate thing was the sign painted on the office wall, the same sign he had read earlier today on first entering.

Somehow, the sign had changed:

> # TYME SEFARI INC.
> ### Sefaris tu any yeer en the past.
> #### Yu naim the animall.
> #### Wee taekyuthair.
> #### Yu shoot itt.

Eckels felt himself fall into a chair. He fumbled crazily at the thick slime on his boots. He held up a clod of dirt, trembling, "No, it *can't* be. Not a *little* thing like that. No!"

Embedded in the mud, glistening green and gold and black, was a butterfly, very beautiful and very dead.

"Not a little thing like *that*! Not a butterfly!" cried Eckels.

It fell to the floor, an exquisite thing, a small thing that could upset balances and knock down a line of small dominoes and then big dominoes and then gigantic dominoes, all down the years across Time. Eckels's mind whirled. It *couldn't* change things. Killing one butterfly couldn't be *that* important! Could it?

His face was cold. His mouth trembled, asking: "Who—who won the presidential election yesterday?"

The man behind the desk laughed. "You joking? You know very well. Deutscher, of course! Who else? Not that fool weakling Keith. We got an iron man now, a man with guts!" The official stopped. "What's wrong?"

Eckels moaned. He dropped to his knees. He scrabbled at the golden butterfly with shaking fingers. "Can't we," he pleaded to the world, to himself, to the officials, to the Machine, "can't we take it *back*, can't we *make* it alive again? Can't we start over? Can't we—"

He did not move. Eyes shut, he waited, shivering. He heard Travis breathe loud in the room; he heard Travis shift his rifle, click the safety catch, and raise the weapon.

There was a sound of thunder. ∎

Vocabulary

subliminal (sub·lim′ə·nəl) *adj.:* below the level of awareness.

A Sound of Thunder   **509**

E **Literary Focus**

? **Figurative language and mood.** Have students identify the figurative language in this section. ["His body screamed silence in return." "He could feel them moving . . . like so many chess pieces blown in a dry wind."] **What mood do these comparisons create?** [Possible response: They create a mood of desolation and hopelessness.]

F **Reading Skills**

? **Cause and effect.** What chain of events do the dominoes refer to? [They refer to the way that killing a small creature can set off a chain of events that profoundly affects the future.]

Monitoring students' progress. Guide the class in answering these comprehension questions. Direct students to locate passages in the text that support their responses.

True-False

1. Time Safari, Inc. offers hunting trips into the distant past. [T]
2. Keith, a candidate for president, has dictatorial tendencies. [F]
3. Eckels shows little fear of the giant dinosaur. [F]
4. The hunters are unable to kill their prey. [F]
5. By stepping on a butterfly, Eckels changes the course of history. [T]

Meet the Writer

Background. If the time machine from this story were real, Bradbury would probably never take a trip on it. In his long lifetime, this author has never driven a car or ridden in an airplane. Indeed, he shows a healthy suspicion, if not an outright distaste, for most modern technology.

The critic Sam Lundwall claims that "All of Bradbury's works [are] utterly naive and from a scientist's point of view, crazy." How might this criticism pertain to "A Sound of Thunder"?

Meet the Writer

Ray Bradbury

Teller of Tales

Ray Bradbury (1920–   ) calls himself a teller of tales and a magic realist. He also claims to remember everything—every book he's read, every movie he's seen, all the events of his life back to and including his birth, in Waukegan, Illinois, on August 22, 1920. All those memories and a big imagination are the materials for the fiction and poetry he's been publishing for more than fifty years. Bradbury gives credit for his writing to his boyhood self:

> 66 I don't know if I believe in previous lives; I'm not sure I can live forever. But that young boy believed in both, and I have let him have his head. He has written my stories and books for me. 99

Bradbury's work is full of childhood imaginings, fantasies, and nightmares—portraits of Venus and Mars, time travel, ageless children, never-ending rains—but Bradbury the grown-up is a concerned citizen. His fantasy stories are often warnings against blind faith in science, but they're optimistic. By giving strange twists to everyday objects and events, Bradbury

challenges his readers to look at them as if for the first time. As a writer he lets readers see science through the excited eyes of children, but he also informs, suggesting ways we might use technology more responsibly.

For another Bradbury story, see page 365.

DIFFERENTIATING INSTRUCTION

Advanced Learners

Enrichment. Write the following words of Ray Bradbury on the chalkboard, and have students copy the quotation: "Without libraries what have we? We have no past and no future."

Activity. Have students write a short essay discussing what Bradbury means, especially in light of the story they have just read. Students may first want to research and learn more about Bradbury's purposes in writing. Suggest that they enter *Ray Bradbury* and *science fiction* as keywords in a search engine on the Internet. Students may also want to re-read the story, taking notes on what Bradbury is conveying to readers about history and politics and about the relationships among the past, the present, and the future. Students may also look for clues to the meaning of the quotation in Ray Bradbury's other stories.

from Jurassic Park
Michael Crichton

In Michael Crichton's novel Jurassic Park *(1990), John Hammond, a rich corporate executive, hires a team of scientists to clone dinosaurs from DNA, and he succeeds in bringing the giant reptiles back from extinction. Hammond populates an island reserve, Jurassic Park, with his clones, letting them roam on lands surrounded by electric fences. He plans to have visitors pay to view the monstrous creatures, using Land Cruisers that run on electric tracks throughout the reserve. Just before the park's scheduled opening, something goes seriously wrong: A park employee's attempt to enter an off-limits laboratory automatically shuts down portions of the park's electricity. As a result, the power feeding the fences and the tracks fails. The dinosaurs are loose.*

As this excerpt opens, the Land Cruisers stop. Inside one are two visiting scientists, Dr. Malcolm and Dr. Grant; in the other are Hammond's grandchildren, Tim and his sister, Lex. A tyrannosaur approaches.

The huge head raised back up, jaws open, and then stopped by the side windows. In the glare of lightning, they saw the beady, expressionless reptile eye moving in the socket.

It was looking in the car.

His sister's breath came in ragged, frightened gasps. He reached out and squeezed her arm, hoping she would stay quiet. The dinosaur continued to stare for a long time through the side window. Perhaps the dinosaur couldn't really see them, he thought. Finally the head lifted up, out of view again.

"Timmy . . . ," Lex whispered.

"It's okay," Tim whispered. "I don't think it saw us."

He was looking back toward Dr. Grant when a jolting impact rocked the Land Cruiser and shattered the windshield in a spider web as the tyrannosaur's head crashed against the hood of the Land Cruiser. Tim was knocked flat on the seat. The night-vision goggles slid off his forehead.

He got back up quickly, blinking in the darkness, his mouth warm with blood.

"Lex?"

He couldn't see his sister anywhere.

The tyrannosaur stood near the front of the Land Cruiser, its chest

A Sound of Thunder   511

Connection

Summary ⟷ *at grade level*

The idea of contemporary people confronting the prehistoric past has served as an imaginative springboard for many writers. In this excerpt from *Jurassic Park*, Michael Crichton shows how frightening this confrontation might be.

DIRECT TEACHING

A **Reading Skills**

❓ **Making connections.** Which scene in "A Sound of Thunder" does this remind you of? [Possible response: The scene in which the hunters first meet the tyrannosaur and Travis tries to quiet Eckels.]

B **Reading Skills**

❓ **Cause and effect.** What causes Tim's mouth to bleed? [The tyrannosaur rocks the Land Cruiser, which shatters the windshield and knocks Tim flat, cutting his mouth.]

CONTENT-AREA CONNECTIONS

Science: Dinosaur Descendants

Improbable as it may seem, chickens, pigeons, and parakeets may be cousins to the mighty *Tyrannosaurus rex*. Scientists in China have discovered evidence of feathers on the remains of two 120-million-year-old dinosaurs. These and other findings—such as the presence of a wishbone in a velociraptor skeleton—support the theory that modern birds are direct dinosaur descendants, their family tree branching off during the Jurassic Period.

Individual activity. Have interested students investigate this subject more thoroughly. Ask them to report their findings to the class, using visual aids that compare the structures of the two species and listing the evidence that has led scientific researchers to propose this theory.

A **Reading Skills**

❓ Drawing conclusions. What is the tyrannosaur trying to do? [Possible response: It is trying to get at the children inside the car.]

B **Reading Skills**

Making connections. Point out that Crichton and Bradbury use similar images. For example, both writers describe the dinosaur's breath as stinking. Have students discuss whether Crichton may have read "A Sound of Thunder" before writing *Jurassic Park* or whether these images are so obvious that different people could come up with them independently.

moving as it breathed, the forelimbs making clawing movements in the air.

"Lex!" Tim whispered. Then he heard her groan. She was lying somewhere on the floor under the front seat.

A Then the huge head came down, entirely blocking the shattered windshield. The tyrannosaur banged again on the front hood of the Land Cruiser. Tim grabbed the seat as the car rocked on its wheels. The tyrannosaur banged down twice more, denting the metal.

Then it moved around the side of the car. The big raised tail blocked his view out of all the side windows. At the back, the animal snorted, a deep rumbling growl that blended with the thunder. It sank its jaws into the spare tire mounted on the back of the Land Cruiser and, in a single headshake, tore it away. The rear of the car lifted into the air for a moment; then it thumped down with a muddy splash.

"Tim!" Dr. Grant said. "Tim, are you there?"

Tim grabbed the radio. "We're okay," he said. There was a shrill metallic scrape as claws raked the roof of the car. Tim's heart was pounding in his chest. He couldn't see anything out of the windows on the right side except pebbled leathery flesh. The tyrannosaur was leaning against the car, which rocked back and forth with each breath, the springs and metal creaking loudly.

Lex groaned again. Tim put down the radio and started to crawl over into the front seat. The tyrannosaur roared and the metal roof dented downward. Tim felt a sharp pain in his head and tumbled to the floor, onto the transmission hump. He found himself lying alongside Lex, and he was shocked to see that the whole side of her head was covered in blood. She looked unconscious.

There was another jolting impact, and pieces of glass fell all around him. Tim felt rain. He looked up and saw that the front windshield had broken out. There was just a jagged rim of glass and, beyond, the big head of the dinosaur.

Looking down at him.

B Tim felt a sudden chill and then the head rushed forward toward him, the jaws open. There was the squeal of metal against teeth, and he felt the hot stinking breath of the animal, and a thick tongue stuck into the car through the windshield opening. The tongue slapped wetly around inside the car—he felt the hot lather of dinosaur saliva—and the tyrannosaur roared—a deafening sound inside the car—

The head pulled away abruptly.

Tim scrambled up, avoiding the dent in the roof. There was still room to sit on the front seat by the passenger door. The tyrannosaur stood in the rain near the front fender. It seemed confused by what had happened to it. Blood dripped freely from its jaws.

The tyrannosaur looked at Tim, cocking its head to stare with one big eye. The head moved close to the car, sideways, and peered in. Blood splattered on the dented hood of the Land Cruiser, mixing with the rain.

It can't get to me, Tim thought. It's too big.

Then the head pulled away, and in the flare of lightning he saw the hind leg lift up. And the world tilted crazily as the Land Cruiser slammed over on its side, the windows splatting in the mud. He saw Lex fall helplessly against the side window, and he fell down beside her, banging his head. Tim felt dizzy. Then the tyrannosaur's jaws clamped onto the window frame, and the whole Land Cruiser was lifted up into the air and shaken.

"Timmy!" Lex shrieked so near to his ear that it hurt. She was suddenly awake, and he grabbed her as the tyrannosaur crashed the car down again. Tim felt a stabbing pain in his side, and his sister fell on top of him. The car went up again, tilting crazily. Lex shouted *"Timmy!"* and he saw the door give way beneath her, and she fell out of the car into the mud, but Tim couldn't answer because in the next instant everything swung crazily—he saw the trunks of the palm trees sliding downward past him—moving sideways through the air—he glimpsed the ground very far below—the hot roar of the tyrannosaur—the blazing eye—the tops of the palm trees—

And then, with a metallic scraping shriek, the car fell from the tyrannosaur's jaws, a sickening fall, and Tim's stomach heaved in the moment before the world became totally black, and silent.

C

A Sound of Thunder   **513**

DIRECT TEACHING

C Reading Skills

❓ Cause and effect. What might have caused the dinosaur to drop the Land Cruiser from its jaws? [Possible responses: It was feeling pain from the glass cuts; it was distracted by something else going on around it.]

Connecting and Comparing Texts

Ask students to compare the portrayal of the tyrannosaur in the *Jurassic Park* excerpt with the description of the dinosaur in Bradbury's story. Which depiction do you find more frightening? Why? [Possible responses: Descriptive phrases such as "great evil god" and "stink of raw flesh" make Bradbury's depiction more vivid, and therefore more frightening. It is easier to visualize and imagine the fear of the passengers trapped in the Land Cruiser.] Many students will be familiar with the film version of *Jurassic Park*. Invite them to discuss whether "A Sound of Thunder" would translate onto the screen as effectively as Michael Crichton's novel did.

A Sound of Thunder   513

Response and Analysis

Reading Check

1. Possible Answers
- The hunting party travels to the past and encounters a dinosaur.
- Eckels panics upon seeing the dinosaur and steps off the Path.
- Back in their present time, things are different, and Eckels discovers he has killed a butterfly.
- Travis aims his gun at Eckels.

Thinking Critically

2. If the mouse is killed, its descendants won't exist. Then a fox will not have mice to eat, a lion will not have foxes to eat, and so on until a cave man dies for lack of game to hunt. Therefore, an entire human race and civilization may die out.

3. The setting has changed in subtle ways: faint smells, colors slightly wrong, words spelled strangely.

4. Travis shoots Eckels because he broke the rules, leading to a chain of events that caused the dictator Deutscher to be elected.

5. Possible meanings: the blast of Travis's rifle as he kills Eckels; a figurative reference to a momentous historical event; a warning about the dangers of technology.

6. Possible answer: Both stories warn of the potential dangers of technology and the impact of individual action.

Extending and Evaluating

7. Possible answers: If changing one thing in the past can have vast repercussions, why don't little changes in the present cause great ripples? Also, according to Travis, the butterfly's death should have caused changes that would make their world unrecognizable. Most students will say that the story's flaws did not lessen their enjoyment.

Response and Analysis

Reading Check

1. Fill in a **cause-and-effect** chart like the one here to show the sequence of events in the story. The first and the last event are already filled in. Add other boxes as you need them to include all the main events.

| Eckels signs up for a safari to the past. |
| ↓ |
| |
| ↓ |
| |
| ↓ |
| We hear "a sound of thunder." |

go.hrw.com

INTERNET
Projects and Activities
Keyword: LE5 9-8

SKILLS FOCUS

Literary Skills Analyze elements of style, including figurative language and mood.

Reading Skills Understand cause-and-effect relationships.

Writing Skills Write a descriptive essay.

Thinking Critically

2. Identify the steps in the chain of **causes and effects** that Travis says would occur if a time traveler accidentally killed even one mouse (see pages 502–503). Do you think his theory might really be accurate? Explain.

3. When the time travelers return to the world of 2055, how has that **setting** changed? What details reveal the changes?

4. What happens to Eckels at the end of the story? What is the **cause** of the final event?

5. What different meanings can you give for the story's **title**?

6. Do you think Bradbury's **purpose** is simply to entertain, or does his story have a serious **theme**, or message? Explain your answer. Consider the same question for the *Jurassic Park* excerpt (see the **Connection** on page 511).

Extending and Evaluating

7. There's no doubt that Bradbury has written what critics would call a blockbuster story. Now, take it apart. Do you find flaws in its logic? Work in teams, and share your findings. Be sure to consider this question: Do flaws in the story (if any) lessen your enjoyment of it?

Literary Criticism

8. Bradbury's writing **style** is full of vivid descriptions and **images**. What descriptive details help you see, hear, and smell Bradbury's prehistoric swamp?

9. How would you describe the **mood** of Bradbury's story? How do elements of his **style** such as **figurative language** help to create that mood?

10. Bradbury's story has an exciting adventure plot, which could have been related in simple concrete language without **figures of speech**. What might the story have gained if it had been written in such a **style**? What might it have lost?

WRITING

Excursions in Time

Imagine that you're entering an essay contest in which the grand prize is a time-travel journey. Write a brief **essay** telling exactly where you'd go, to what point in time (select a year in the future or the past), and why. Describe what you imagine you will see when you arrive. What do you want to accomplish when you reach your destination? (Check your Quickwrite notes for ideas.)

Literary Criticism

8. Possible details: "pterodactyls soaring with cavernous gray wings," "sounds like music and sounds like flying tents," "the stink of raw flesh."

9. Possible answer: The mood of the story is tense and anxious. Comparisons such as "great evil god," and "terrible warrior," and descriptive phrases such as "stench of slime and old blood" help to create this mood.

10. Possible answers: The story might have gained simplicity, making it easier to read. It would have lost the powerful sense of place and events created by the descriptive figures of speech.

Vocabulary Development

Prefixes and Root Words: Keys to Meaning

PRACTICE

Knowing the meanings of some Greek and Latin **prefixes** and **root words** can help you decipher the meanings of many English words. Use a dictionary to look up the **etymology** (word origin) of each Word Bank word. Then, make a chart like the one here for each word (skip *expendable*). (Most, but not all, of the words begin with a prefix.)

expendable
Meaning: worth sacrificing to gain an objective
Prefix: Latin *ex–*, "out"
Root word: Latin *pendere*, "to weigh"
Words with same root word or prefix: expenditure, expense, exclude
Sentence: No member of the crew was expendable.

Word Bank

annihilate
expendable
depression
paradox
delirium
resilient
remit
revoke
primeval
subliminal

Grammar Link

Verbs Play Active and Passive Roles

Like people, **action verbs** have voices. A verb in the **active voice** expresses an action performed *by* its subject.

> Ray Bradbury <u>wrote</u> "A Sound of Thunder."
> "Mr. Eckels <u>looked</u> at the check."

A verb in the **passive voice** expresses an action done *to* its subject. (Hint: A passive-voice verb always includes a form of *be* and the past participle of the verb.)

> "A Sound of Thunder" <u>was written</u> by Ray Bradbury.
> "'Six safari leaders <u>were killed</u> last year. . . .'"

The active voice is strong and direct. A verb in the passive voice sounds weak partly because it needs a helping verb.

The passive voice is useful when a writer doesn't know who or what performed an action (*My bicycle was stolen*) or when a writer doesn't want readers to know who performed an action (*The TV was left on*).

PRACTICE

Rewrite each sentence, changing the verb from the passive voice to the active voice. Notice how the active voice results in shorter, more vigorous sentences.

1. The idea of hunting the dinosaur was abandoned by Eckels.
2. The dinosaur's footsteps could be heard and felt by the hunters.
3. The silence was shattered by the dinosaur's scream.
4. This story has been reviewed favorably by most students.

▶ **For more help, see Active and Passive Voice, 3f–g, in the Language Handbook.**

SKILLS FOCUS

Vocabulary Skills
Understand Greek and Latin prefixes and root words.

Grammar Skills
Use verbs in the active and passive voices.

A Sound of Thunder 515

Grammar Link

Practice

1. Eckels abandoned the idea of hunting dinosaurs.
2. The hunters heard and felt the dinosaur's footsteps.
3. The dinosaur's scream shattered the silence.
4. Most students have reviewed this story favorably.

ASSESSING

Assessment

■ *Holt Assessment: Literature, Reading, and Vocabulary*

RETEACHING

For lessons reteaching author's style, see p. 979A and *The Holt Reader*, Collection 8.

Vocabulary Development

Practice

- *annihilate. Meaning*—destroy, wipe out; *Prefix*—L. *ad–*, "to, toward"; *Root word*—L. *nihil*, "nothing." *Related words*—annex, annul; nihilism.

- *depression. Meaning*—major economic downturn; *Prefix*—L. *de–*, "from, down, away"; *Root word*—L. *premere*, "to press." *Related words*—departed, pressure.

- *paradox. Meaning*—something that has or seems to have contradictory qualities; *Prefix*—Gr. *para–*, "beside, beyond"; *Root word*—Gr. *dokein*, "to seem." *Related words*—paragraph, parallel.

- *delirium. Meaning*—extreme mental excitement, often accompanied by hallucinations; *Prefix*—L. *de–*, "from, down, away"; *Root word*—L. *lira–*, "furrow." *Related words*—deflate, delirious.

- *resilient. Meaning*—elastic; *Prefix*—L. *re–*, "back, again"; *Root word*—L. *salire*, "to leap." *Related words*—salient, repeat.

- *remit. Meaning*—send back; *Prefix*—L. *re–*, "back, again"; *Root word*—L. *mittere*, "to send." *Related words*—relieve, submit.

- *revoke. Meaning*—cancel, withdraw; *Prefix*—L. *re–*, "back, again"; *Root word*—L. *vocare*, "to call." *Related words*—remove, vocal.

- *primeval. Meaning*—primitive; *Prefix*—L. *primus*, "first"; *Root word*—L. *aevum*, "age." *Related words*—primary, medieval.

- *subliminal. Meaning*—below the level of consciousness; *Prefix*—L. *sub–*, "under, below, secretly"; *Root word*—L. *limin*, "threshold." *Related words*—submarine, preliminary.

Grade-Level Skills

■ **Reading Skills**

Evaluate the credibility of opposing arguments by examining the logic of the arguments, the scope of the evidence, and the intentions of the author.

Summary ◁▷ *at grade level*

Two articles address the scope of the threat posed by global warming. In "Rising Tides," Bob Herbert makes an emotional call for readers to appreciate that global warming is a present-day reality, not some future possibility. Supporting his argument with reasons and evidence, Herbert describes the manifestations of recent climactic phenomena, such as the melting of Antarctic ice and the snow atop Mount Kilimanjaro. He also includes opinions from an international panel to support his chief contention—that the effects of global warming will be most catastrophic for developing nations, not the industrial countries that have caused the phenomena. As a result, Herbert argues, Americans have a special responsibility to address the issue.

Robert Cooke's article, "An Arctic Floe of Climate Questions," takes a less alarmist stance, suggesting that it is far too early to sound the warning. Cooke addresses the issue of melting polar ice, and while conceding the existence of a near-term warming trend, he argues that weather processes are incredibly complex. A short-term fluctuation does not equal a long-term trend, Cooke maintains, and he uses quotations from experts to point out that there may be numerous forces at work that are changing polar conditions.

Informational Text

LINK TO "A SOUND OF THUNDER"

Rising Tides ◆ An Arctic Floe of Climate Questions

Evaluating Arguments: Pro and Con

When you read or listen to opposing views on an important issue, how can you decide which side to believe?

1. **Understand the arguments.** Begin by making sure that you understand the issue and the **opinion,** or **claim,** presented in each argument. It helps to **paraphrase** the arguments, using your own words.

2. **Identify the support.** Start by identifying the **logical appeals**—the **reasons** why the writer holds that opinion—and the **evidence** given to back up each reason. The evidence may consist of the following items:
   • **facts** (statements that can be verified objectively)
   • **statistics** (numerical facts)
   • **examples**
   • **comments from experts**
   To what extent has the author also used **emotional appeals,** such as **loaded words** and **anecdotes** (colorful or emotional stories)?

Who Is More Persuasive?

You can create a chart like the one on the next page to help you evaluate the **credibility** of each argument. To decide which argument is stronger and why, consider these questions:

1. **Is the argument logical?** Do the **reasons** make sense, and are they relevant to the issue? Learn to recognize these common **fallacies,** or errors in logical thinking:
   • **Circular reasoning.** Watch out for statements that look like

reasons or conclusions but simply restate an author's opinion.

> "After-school sports are essential because they're a necessary part of school activities."

• **False cause and effect.** Just because one event happens *after* another event, the first event did not necessarily *cause* the second event. The two events may be (and often are) totally unrelated.

> "When after-school sports were dropped at Adams High School, the dropout rate increased."

• **Hasty generalization.** A **generalization** is a broad statement. An author can't generalize about everyone or everything based on one or two cases. An author must examine many cases before he or she can make a **valid** (true) generalization.

> "Everyone agrees that dropping after-school sports is a bad idea. I know because I asked my friend Chad, and he agrees with me."

• **Attacking the person.** A good argument stays focused on an issue and on an opponent's argument—not on an opponent's character or judgment.

> "Mr. McAloo, who proposed cutting after-school sports, is a mean, stingy person."

2. **How comprehensive is the support?** Does the writer provide reasons and sufficient **evidence** to support every generalization? An

INTERNET
Interactive
Reading Model
Keyword: LE5 9-8

SKILLS FOCUS

Reading Skills
Evaluate the credibility of opposing arguments.

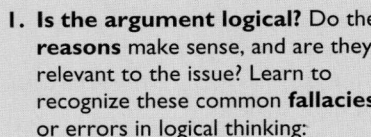

RESOURCES: READING

Planning
■ *One-Stop Planner* CD-ROM with ExamView Test Generator

Differentiating Instruction
■ *Holt Reading Solutions*
■ *Holt Adapted Reader*
■ *Audio CD Library, Selections and Summaries in Spanish*

■ *Supporting Instruction in Spanish*

Vocabulary
■ *Vocabulary Development*

Grammar and Language
■ *Daily Language Activities*

Assessment
■ *Holt Assessment: Literature, Reading, and Vocabulary*

unsupported generalization seriously weakens an argument.

3. **Does the writer deal with opposing evidence?** To strengthen his or her argument, does the writer discuss opposing evidence to anticipate objections? Dealing with the opponent's viewpoint is important when an issue is a controversial one about which many people have clear **pro** (for) or **con** (against) views.

4. **Is the structure effective?** A good writer carefully structures an argument to be most persuasive. Readers generally remember the beginning and the end of a piece most clearly, so an effective technique is to put the strongest reasons in those positions. (Writers also commonly structure arguments using **comparison and contrast** and **cause and effect**.)

5. **What is the author's intent?** Is the writer's purpose clear throughout? Often the writer's goal is just to change your thinking, but sometimes it is a **call to action**, asking you to go out and *do* something. Are you being asked to change your behavior in any way? to write a letter? to offer your help? Do there seem to be hidden agendas in the writer's argument?

6. **What is the tone?** An author's intent directly affects a work's **tone**, a writer's attitude toward his or her subject or audience. If the intent is to persuade, look for a tone that is serious, calm, and reasonable. You should question the credibility of the argument if the author uses a humorous, angry, or highly emotional tone or if the author exaggerates or tries to make light of various issues.

Answering all of these questions will help you evaluate the strengths and weaknesses of opposing arguments.

Evaluating Arguments	Piece 1 Pro	Piece 2 Con
Claim		
Logical appeals		
Emotional appeals		
Tone		
Author's intent		
Credibility		

Vocabulary Development

receding (ri·sēd′iŋ) *v.*: moving back; becoming less.

catastrophic (kat′ə·sträf′ik) *adj.*: disastrous.

implications (im′pli·kā′shənz) *n.*: possible connections or consequences.

indiscriminate (in′di·skrim′i·nit) *adj.*: careless.

deficient (dē·fish′ənt) *adj.*: lacking.

equitable (ek′wit·ə·bəl) *adj.*: fair; just.

demise (dē·mīz′) *n.*: death; end.

ominous (äm′ə·nəs) *adj.*: threatening.

impending (im·pend′iŋ) *v.* used as *adj.*: about to happen.

ignorance (ig′nə·rəns) *n.*: lack of knowledge.

Connecting to the Literature

"A Sound of Thunder" and the *Jurassic Park* excerpt depict a future in which humans tamper with their environment—with disastrous results. The following articles take different positions on the impact humans have on the environment today.

Selection Starter

Motivate. Encourage students to share what they know about global warming, including the causes that scientists believe are responsible for the phenomenon. Ask the class whether they think it is a serious threat to the environment.

Preview Vocabulary

Have students read the definitions of the Vocabulary words on p. 517. Then, ask partners to work together to use these words to complete the following sentences.

1. The destruction and _____ of plant life makes dunes vulnerable to erosion. [demise]

2. _____ can be cured with education. [Ignorance]

3. Weather satellites gather advance information about the _____ storm. [impending]

4. Powerful winds and crashing waves are _____ signs of a hurricane approaching. [ominous]

5. An _____ balance between conserving and using resources can be achieved. [equitable]

6. _____ walking or running on the dunes makes them subject to erosion. [Indiscriminate]

7. After the storm, a shipwreck became visible beneath the _____ waters. [receding]

8. Small boats are _____ in the equipment needed to weather a storm. [deficient]

9. Damage along the shore will have negative _____ for summer employment. [implications]

10. A breach of the breakwater can cause _____ destruction on land. [catastrophic]

Assign the Reading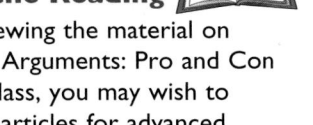

After reviewing the material on Evaluating Arguments: Pro and Con with the class, you may wish to assign the articles for advanced readers to read on their own. Other students may read the articles in small groups.

- *One-Stop Planner* CD-ROM with ExamView Test Generator
- *Holt Online Assessment*

Internet
- go.hrw.com (Keyword: LE5 9-8)
- *Elements of Literature Online*

Media
- *Audio CD Library*
- *Audio CD Library, Selections and Summaries in Spanish*

A **Learners Having Difficulty**

? **Breaking down difficult text.**
What does Herbert say is hard to acknowledge? [that Mount Kilimanjaro's ice cap, which seemed a permanent feature of the planet, will vanish]

B **Reading Skills**
Emotional appeals. [Possible response to question 1: Loaded words include "at a scary rate," scientists were "astonished," a "mammoth fragment," and "collapsed like a window shattered by a rock."]

C **Reading Skills**
Evaluating an argument.
[Possible response to question 2: Herbert claims that global warming is already occurring. As evidence, he cites environmental changes, such as changes in the seasons, intense rainstorms, rising sea levels, receding glaciers, thawing permafrost, and earlier appearances of flowering trees and emerging insects.]

OP-ED ARTICLE

The following two opinion articles, "Rising Tides" by Bob Herbert and "An Arctic Floe of Climate Questions" by Robert Cooke, present opposing views on global warming. Most scientists believe that we have altered the earth's atmosphere by releasing huge amounts of carbon dioxide and other greenhouse gases from our factories and cars. These gases trap heat in the earth's lower atmosphere and increase the earth's average temperatures, causing global warming. Some people, however, question whether our current global warming reflects a permanent change in our climate.

Rising Tides

from *The New York Times*, **February 22, 2001**

Bob Herbert

A The easiest approach for the time being is to pretend it's not happening. It's better for the nerves in the short run . . . than to acknowledge that the majestic ice cap atop Mount Kilimanjaro,[1] which seemed for so long to be an almost permanent feature of the planet, will vanish in less than 15 years.

It's February and it's cold in New York, which can help us maintain the fiction that the planet is not warming at a scary rate. But the snows are disappearing from Kilimanjaro, and a few years ago scientists were astonished when a mammoth[2] fragment of the Larsen Ice Shelf at the edge of the Antarctic Peninsula[3] collapsed like a window shattered by a rock. The fragment had measured 48

miles by 22 miles and was hundreds of feet thick. It eventually disappeared. **1**

Many strange things are happening. The seasons are changing, rainstorms are becoming more intense, sea levels are rising, mighty glaciers are receding, the permafrost (by definition, the *permanently* frozen subsoil in the polar regions) is thawing, trees are flowering earlier, insects are emerging sooner, and so on.

Global warming is not coming, it's here. **2**

There are likely to be some beneficial results in some areas from the warming, such as longer growing seasons and increased crop yields in certain

1 **EMOTIONAL APPEALS**

B What **loaded words** can you find in this paragraph?

2 **EVALUATING AN ARGUMENT**

C What is the author's main **claim** so far? What **evidence** supports that claim?

1. **Mount Kilimanjaro** (kil′ə·män·jär′ō): highest mountain in Africa (19,340 feet), located in Tanzania.
2. **mammoth** (mam′əth) *adj.:* enormous.
3. **Antarctic Peninsula** (ant·ärk′tik pə·nin′sə·lə): narrow body of land (about eight hundred miles long) extending from Antarctica toward South America. The icy continent of Antarctica is a landmass surrounding the South Pole.

Vocabulary
receding (ri·sēd′iŋ) *v.:* moving back; becoming less.

DIFFERENTIATING INSTRUCTION

Learners Having Difficulty
Discuss Evaluating Arguments: Pro and Con (p. 516) with students. Work through the lists point by point, providing (or asking volunteers to provide) additional examples of logical appeals (evidence), emotional appeals, circular reasoning, false cause and effect, and hasty generalization. You may wish to preselect a

short opinion piece from a newspaper and analyze it with students.

English-Language Learners
To help students with the content-related vocabulary, focus their attention on a globe or a world map. Point out the two polar regions, the Arctic Ocean and the North Pole, and Antarctica. Use latitudinal lines to demonstrate

An African elephant roams in a meadow by Mount Kilimanjaro.

mid-latitude regions,[4] and a decline in deaths related to extreme cold. But over all, the effects of this sharp and accelerating and largely artificial warming of the planet—including the consequences of such extreme events as droughts, floods, heat waves, avalanches, and tropical storms—are potentially catastrophic.

The Intergovernmental Panel on Climate Change, in a report released Tuesday in Geneva,[5] said, "More people are projected to be harmed than benefited by climate change, even for global mean temperature increases[6] of less than a few degrees centigrade."

The report also discussed an issue that has profound policy and ethical[7] implications.

___

4. **mid-latitude regions:** areas of the world with moderate temperatures.
5. **Geneva** (jə·nēʹvə): city in southwest Switzerland.
6. **global mean temperature increases:** increases in average temperatures all over the world.
7. **ethical** (ethʹi·kəl) *adj.:* moral; relating to principles of what's right and just.

The worst effects of global warming will probably not be felt by those most responsible for the pollution of the atmosphere by heat-trapping greenhouse gases. The great industrial societies, which have benefited so long from the rapacious devouring of resources[8] and the indiscriminate release of pollutants, are also the societies best positioned to cope with the treacherous forces of global warming.

As the panel noted in its report, "The ability of human systems to adapt to and cope with climate change depends on such factors as wealth, technology, education,

___

8. **rapacious devouring of resources:** greedy using up of natural resources.

Vocabulary
catastrophic (kat'ə·sträf'ik) *adj.:* disastrous.
implications (im'pli·kā'shənz) *n.:* possible connections or consequences.
indiscriminate (in'di·skrim'i·nit) *adj.:* careless.

A **Reading Skills**

Evaluating an argument.
[Possible response to question 3: The negative effects of global warming will be felt most in developing countries.]

B **Reading Informational Text**

? **Evaluating an argument.**
What evidence does Herbert provide for this generalization? [none]

C **Reading Skills**

Author's intent. [Possible responses to question 4: The author wants Americans to take responsibility for their contribution to global warming. He wants Americans to make sacrifices that will help preserve the global environment.]

---

information, skills, infrastructure,[9] access to resources, and management capabilities."

Developing countries, deficient in those areas, are doomed to suffer disproportionately[10] from the warming of the planet. "The effects of climate change," the panel said, "are expected to be greatest in developing countries in terms of loss of life and relative effects on investment and the economy." **❸**

> **❸ EVALUATING AN ARGUMENT**
>
> **A** **Paraphrase** the **generalization** that the author makes in this paragraph.

Despite the powerful and increasing evidence of the role of carbon dioxide and other greenhouse gases in the warming of the earth, the concentrations of those gases in the atmosphere are expected to increase, not decrease, over the next several decades. Government leaders are not responding to **B** the problem with the sense of urgency that is called for.

Carbon dioxide doesn't just float away in a day or two. It remains in the atmosphere for more than 100 years. The consequences of our failure to act will last for centuries.

Americans have a special responsibility here. The United States is the mightiest nation on the planet and the greatest contributor to the industrial component of global warming.[11] The nation is wealthy and

---

9. **infrastructure** (in′frə·struk′chər) *n.:* basic installations such as roads, schools, power plants, and transportation and communication systems needed to support a modern, developed society.
10. **disproportionately** (dis′prə·pôr′shə·nət·lē) *adv.:* not in fair balance; here, to an excessive degree.
11. **industrial component of global warming:** the release of pollutants during the manufacturing process, which increases the overall warming of the earth.

---

at peace. A mature approach would require certain sacrifices designed to provide a better environment for future generations of Americans and a more equitable relationship with neighbors around the world. **❹**

> **❹ AUTHOR'S INTENT**
>
> **C** What is the **call to action** here? What does the author want Americans to do?

But that's only one approach. Another is to just ignore the problem and continue to feast like gluttons[12] at the table of the world's resources. That will work for a while. Why not? All you have to do is convince yourself that damaging the planet is somebody else's problem.

---

12. **gluttons** (glut′′nz) *n.:* persons who greedily eat too much.

Vocabulary
deficient (dē·fish′ənt) *adj.:* lacking.
equitable (ek′wit·ə·bəl) *adj.:* fair; just.

This aerial view shows the Brunt Ice Shelf in Antarctica.

OP-ED ARTICLE

An Arctic Floe of Climate Questions

from *Newsday*, April 18, 2001

Robert Cooke

Recent reports of the North Pole's demise are, to borrow from Mark Twain, "exaggerated."[1] ❶

Although the blanket of floating ice that usually covers the North Pole was found last summer to be gone—there was just open water—climate specialists say that's not such a big deal. As the ice shifts, leads, or channels of water, open up, and ice-free areas called polynyas form.

Eventually, the ice moves and such gaps close.

But some alarm bells did ring, because there is growing concern that we humans are fouling things up through our burning of gas, oil, and coal, which releases so-called greenhouse gases such as carbon dioxide into the air. These gases, which trap heat, may be causing the whole world's temperature to steadily creep higher and higher. And an absence of ice at the North Pole seemed like one more ominous sign of impending trouble. ❷

> **❶ EVALUATING AN ARGUMENT**
> From this first sentence, what can we anticipate the author's **opinion**, or **claim**, will be?

> **❷ EVALUATING AN ARGUMENT**
> Explain how the author addresses **opposing arguments** here.

Temperature records also show, clearly, that globally temperatures have gone up by about 3 degrees Fahrenheit in the past 150 years, or since temperatures have been recorded. And, perhaps coincidentally, the last few years have been the warmest on record, accentuating[2] concerns. One scenario[3] suggests that the greatest impact from warming will be apparent at high latitudes near the poles.[4]

A recent University of Wisconsin study has shown that in the Northern Hemisphere[5] many of the rivers and lakes that freeze are doing so later—by 8.7 days—than they did more than a century ago. Also, "ice-out," or breakup, is occurring about 9.8 days sooner. This suggests that winters are now a bit shorter.

What people need to know, however, is that the global weather equation is enormously complex, and no one knows exactly how to work it out. A few years with extra-hot

---

1. **Recent reports ... "exaggerated":** reference to an 1897 cable sent by the American humorist Mark Twain (1835–1910) to a journalist in response to rumors of Twain's death, often quoted as "The reports of my death are greatly exaggerated."

2. **accentuating** (ak·sen'chŏŏ·āt'iŋ) *v.* used as *adj.*: heightening; emphasizing.
3. **scenario** (sə·ner'ē·ō') *n.*: outline of events, real or imagined.
4. **poles** *n.*: regions around the North and South Poles.
5. **Northern Hemisphere:** the half of the earth north of the equator.

Vocabulary

demise (dē·mīz') *n.*: death; end.

ominous (äm'ə·nəs) *adj.*: threatening.

impending (im·pend'iŋ) *v.* used as *adj.*: about to happen.

An Arctic Floe of Climate Questions   521

CONTENT-AREA CONNECTIONS

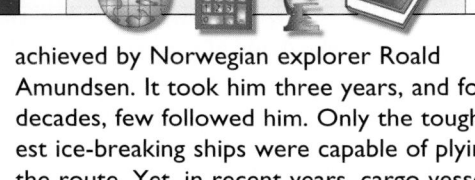

Science: The Northwest Passage
For centuries, explorers wanted to find a way to navigate the ice-filled waters north of the Canadian mainland from east to west. This Northwest Passage would cut thousands of miles off a westbound ocean journey. Time after time, however, sailors were defeated by the hazardous sections of solid Arctic ice. In 1906, the voyage was first achieved by Norwegian explorer Roald Amundsen. It took him three years, and for decades, few followed him. Only the toughest ice-breaking ships were capable of plying the route. Yet, in recent years, cargo vessels and even cruise ships have been making the trip. The recent warming trend has resulted in the dwindling volume and the thinning of polar ice. By the summer of 1998, the once-fearsome Northwest Passage was a nearly ice-free open water journey.

A **Reading Skills**

Evaluating an argument.

[Possible response to question 3: Global weather is very complex and subject to short-term fluctuation. One cannot infer trends on the basis of just a few years of data.]

B **Reading Skills**

Evaluating an argument.

[Possible response to question 4: A quote from an expert, a University of Colorado climatologist, is used to support Cooke's claim that the disappearance of polar ice is a complex issue.]

C **Reading Skills**

Evaluating an argument.

[Possible response to question 5: Greater decreases in polar ice have occurred in the past. Cooke may have chosen to end the article with an expert's quote to lend greater weight to his own opinion.]

---

summers or an episode of ice shrinking at the poles does not make a disaster. Such things could be normal fluctuations[6] in a very changeable system. ❸

A ❸ **EVALUATING AN ARGUMENT**
What is the author's main **claim**?

The reason it's so hard to find answers is, in part, a matter of <u>ignorance</u>. Only in the past half-century have instruments begun to be set out at sea and on land to monitor[7] what's actually happening. And only since about 1972 have orbiting satellites[8] been able to even roughly track what's happening to ice at the poles. Because there is no reliable, long-term history of climate variability,[9] we can't know whether what seems unusual now is actually unusual in global climate. Tests in sediments[10] and ice cores show that the world's temperature has been higher in the past and, of course, sometimes lower during ice ages.

What recent data have suggested is that ice in the Arctic has been thinning, and the extent or area of sea ice has shrunk by a measurable degree. On the other hand, there's substantial disagreement among scientists there too. Measurements taken by submarines under the ice are being debated; some experts think the ice has thinned, others think it hasn't. In any case, the submarines have been cruising beneath the ice cap for less than 50 years.

Still, "if you look at the records, it seems that since 1972, when satellite observations began, there has definitely been a significant

decrease in sea ice. It's a statistically significant decrease and that is pretty well accepted," said climatologist[11] Mark Serreze, at the University of Colorado.

But, he added, "the problem is that when you look at what the sea ice is doing, it's not just temperature that governs what the ice is doing. The winds are involved in blowing it around." So a large storm is capable of moving the ice, breaking it up and opening a polynya, an open sea area, at the North Pole. ❹

B ❹ **EVALUATING EVIDENCE**
What type of **evidence** does the author present in the last two paragraphs?

"These are known to exist, even at the pole," said George Kukla, a paleoclimatologist[12] at Columbia University's Lamont Doherty Earth Observatory.

"From what I understand, in the past 20 years we've been observing a trend in the thinning of the ice and a decrease in the area covered by ice," Kukla said.

"But according to comparisons, it doesn't seem to be reaching the situation [seen] in the 1940s and 1950s, when there was relatively little ice in that area," Kukla said. "So we can't say it is something that was unprecedented."[13] ❺

C ❺ **EVALUATING EVIDENCE**
Paraphrase the quotations in the last two paragraphs. Why might the author have chosen to end his article with this **expert's opinion**?

---

6. **fluctuations** (fluk′chōō·ā′·shənz) *n.*: temporary increases and decreases.
7. **monitor** (män′i·tər) *v.*: check on; observe.
8. **orbiting satellites**: artificial, unmanned spacecraft that circle the earth, transmitting images and data from space.
9. **variability** (ver′ē·ə·bil′ə·tē) *n.*: changeability.
10. **sediments** (sed′ə·mənts) *n.*: soil, rock, and other solids deposited by water or wind.

11. **climatologist** (klī′mə·täl′ə·jist) *n.*: scientist who studies climate and its effects.
12. **paleoclimatologist** (pā′lē·ō·klī′mə·täl′ə·jist) *n.*: scientist who studies earth's ancient, prehistoric climates.
13. **unprecedented** (un·pres′ə·den′tid) *adj.*: never happening before.

Vocabulary
ignorance (ig′nə·rəns) *n.*: lack of knowledge.

DIFFERENTIATING INSTRUCTION

Advanced Learners

Enrichment. Students may benefit from evaluating the structure of Cooke's essay.

Activity. Have students answer questions like these:

• What concerns do the initial paragraphs address? [They focus on recent data that the earth is, in fact, heating up.]

• Where does the focus of the essay change? How? [In the seventh paragraph, Cooke begins supporting his contention that recent temperature fluctuations do not necessarily signal long-term disaster.]

• What kind of information is presented in the last five paragraphs? Why might it appear last? [Quotations from experts support the thesis that long-term weather

trends are complex. Readers tend to recall what they have just read, so the evidence that best supports Cooke's thesis is saved for last.]

Analyzing Informational Text

Reading Check

1. Name six effects of global warming mentioned in "Rising Tides."
2. What two opposing approaches to global warming does Herbert say Americans can take?
3. According to Cooke's article, what do temperature records show for the "last few years"?
4. According to Cooke, what do people need to know about the "global weather equation"?

SKILLS FOCUS

Reading Skills
Evaluate the credibility of opposing arguments.

Test Practice

1. The two writers have opposing views about —
   - A the causes of global warming
   - B whether we are now experiencing serious global warming
   - C the ability of people to adapt to climate changes
   - D the impact of global warming on developing nations

2. In "Rising Tides," to support his **claim** that global warming is already here, Herbert cites many —
   - F facts about weather-related changes
   - G facts about the world's population
   - H anecdotes about weather
   - J quotations from experts

3. Herbert supports his statement that the effects of global warming will be more disastrous for developing nations by using —
   - A his personal observations
   - B quotations from a panel of experts
   - C a number of emotional appeals
   - D an anecdote

4. In the last paragraph of "Rising Tides," Herbert's **tone** is —
   - F sympathetic
   - G serious
   - H humorous
   - J ironic

5. What is Cooke's **intent** in writing his article "An Arctic Floe of Climate Questions"?
   - A To prove that global warming has really begun
   - B To reassure his audience that global warming, even if it occurs, poses no threat to life as we know it
   - C To present what he feels is a balanced view of the likelihood of global warming
   - D To warn his audience about the possibility of global warming and its terrible consequences

6. In the second half of his article, Cooke uses the **example** of shrinking Arctic ice to show that —
   - F data collected by submarines is unreliable
   - G global warming is a highly emotional issue
   - H scientists have been measuring the ice for hundreds of years
   - J scientists disagree about the meaning of the data

Rising Tides / An Arctic Floe of Climate Questions   523

Reading Check

1. Possible answers: melting snow on Mount Kilimanjaro, crumbling Antarctic ice, changing seasons, more intense rainstorms, rising sea levels, receding glaciers, thawing permafrost, earlier flowering trees, earlier emerging insects.

2. Americans can make sacrifices that will help the environment, or they can ignore the problem.

3. The last few years have been the warmest on record.

4. People need to know that it is enormously complex.

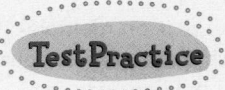

INDEPENDENT PRACTICE

Analyzing Informational Text

Test Practice

Answers and Model Rationales

1. **B** Cooke does not address points in C and D. Both writers agree that the burning of fuels that release gases is a possible or probable cause for global warming so A is incorrect. They disagree, however, on whether current manifestations of global warming are part of a threatening, long-term trend, so B is the best answer.

2. **F** Facts include information about Mount Kilimanjaro and the collapsing Antarctic ice shelf. Although the article does quote expert opinion, the quotations discuss the effects of global warming, not its existence, so J is incorrect.

3. **B** Students should see that Herbert uses quotations from the Intergovernmental Panel on Climate Change's report to support his statement.

4. **G** Phrases such as "feast like gluttons" and "damaging the planet" should help students see that Herbert takes a serious tone in the final paragraph.

5. **C** A, B, and D are incorrect since Cooke does not attempt to prove, reassure, or warn. Students should see that C is the best choice, since Cooke tries to present a balanced, non-alarmist look at the phenomenon.

6. **J** F is incorrect since Cooke says that the data is being debated. G is false since none of the information presented is emotional in nature. H is directly contradicted by information in the passage. J is clearly the best choice.

7. B A, C, and D are statements of fact. Only B, with the loaded language "mightiest nation on the planet," is an appeal to the emotions of the reader.

Test-Taking Tips

Remind students that on multiple-choice tests, each question is of equal value, so they should answer the easy questions first. Then, they can return to finish the harder questions. For more instruction on how to answer multiple-choice items, refer students to **Test Smarts.**

Vocabulary Development

Practice

Possible Answers

1. I might use an anti–hair loss ointment or wear a hat.

2. I might try to find a place to take shelter. I might close all my windows.

3. I might explain that getting As in English and Cs in Science suggests where my strengths lie. One implication might be that I have to study harder.

4. I might want to repaint it. Next time, I might get some help.

5. I would begin a strenuous weightlifting program. I might spend more time exercising.

6. I would have to do more chores than I do now. I would receive more help from my brother who does very little.

7. I would be sad. I would have to find new entertainment.

8. I might be frightened. I might turn and run away.

9. I would pack my bags. I would say goodbye to friends.

10. I would pay more attention in class. I would study harder.

---

7. Which of the following items contains an **emotional appeal**?

   A Herbert's statement: "Carbon dioxide . . . remains in the atmosphere for more than 100 years."

   B Herbert's statement: "The United States is the mightiest nation on the planet. . . ."

   C Cooke's statement: "As the ice shifts, leads, or channels of water, open up. . . ."

   D Cooke's statement: "Eventually, the ice moves and such gaps close."

Constructed Response

Write a brief essay in which you **evaluate** the **credibility** of the two arguments. What is the author's **intent** in each case? What is each writer's **opinion,** or **claim**? Is each argument logical and convincing? How strong and comprehensive is the **evidence** and other support each writer presents in his argument? Whose view—Herbert's or Cooke's—do you find more credible and persuasive? (A chart like the one below will help you organize your ideas.)

	Herbert	Cooke
Writer's intent		
Writer's opinion, or claim		
Evidence and other support		
Credibility of argument		

Vocabulary Development

Word Knowledge: What If?

PRACTICE

Demonstrate your understanding of the Word Bank words by listing at least two possible outcomes for each of the following situations:

1. What if you noticed that your hairline was <u>receding</u>?

2. What if you heard that a <u>catastrophic</u> storm was approaching?

3. What if you had to explain the <u>implications</u> of your report card?

4. What if you painted your room in an <u>indiscriminate</u> way?

5. What if you decided your physical strength was <u>deficient</u>?

6. What if the distribution of household chores in your family became more <u>equitable</u>?

7. What if you heard a rumor about the <u>demise</u> of your favorite television program?

8. What if you noticed someone approaching you with an <u>ominous</u> look?

9. What if you faced an <u>impending</u> move to another state?

10. What if your <u>ignorance</u> prevented you from doing well on your history test?

SKILLS FOCUS

Vocabulary Skills
Demonstrate word knowledge.

Word Bank

receding
catastrophic
implications
indiscriminate
deficient
equitable
demise
ominous
impending
ignorance

ASSESSING

Assessment

■ *Holt Assessment: Literature, Reading, and Vocabulary*

RETEACHING

For a lesson to reteach evaluating an argument, see **Reteaching,** p. 979A. For another selection to teach evaluating an argument, see *The Holt Reader,* Part 2.

Before You Read

To Da-duh, in Memoriam

Make the Connection

Quickwrite 🖉

Do you consider yourself a city slicker or a country bumpkin? Make a list of things you associate with life in the country. Then, make a list of things you associate with city life. Save your lists.

Literary Focus

Diction and Sentence Patterns: A Matter of Style

Style refers to the way a writer uses language. **Diction,** a writer's choice of words, is an important element of style. Writers must decide whether to use a plain word (*upset*) or a complex one (*distraught*). They must choose between words with different **connotations,** the emotions and associations suggested by words (*crawl* or *creep*).

Sometimes a writer's diction is distinguished by his or her use of **dialect,** the way of speaking characteristic of a particular region or group of people. Paule Marshall brings her grandmother to life by reproducing her rhythmic Barbados dialect.

Another element of style is **sentence structure.** Some writers use short, punchy sentences. Others use long, rhythmic sentences. Finally, **figures of speech,** or unusual comparisons, make a writer's style more descriptive.

As you read this story, think about how you would describe Marshall's style.

Reading Skills 📖

Visualizing the Story

This story presents a series of striking images that help you imagine an unfamiliar setting and an unusual character. The story will be easier to read if you try **visualizing** it—seeing the story happen in your mind as if it were a movie. The questions at the open-book signs will help you.

Background

This story is set in Barbados, a tropical island in the Caribbean that was a British colony for almost 340 years before gaining its independence in 1966. The rich culture of Barbados is the product of English, African, and Caribbean influences. Most of today's Barbadians are descendants of Africans who were slaves on British-owned sugar plantations.

INTERNET
Vocabulary Practice
Keyword: LE5 9-8

Vocabulary Development

unrelenting (un·ri·len′tiŋ) *adj.*: not letting up or weakening.

formidable (fôr′mə·də·bəl) *adj.*: impressive; causing fear or dread.

reproved (ri·proovd′) *v.*: disapproved of.

truculent (truk′yoo·lənt) *adj.*: fierce.

decrepit (dē·krep′it) *adj.*: falling apart.

admonished (ad·män′isht) *v.*: scolded mildly.

perennial (pə·ren′ē·əl) *adj.*: year-round; continual.

austere (ô·stir′) *adj.*: very plain; severe.

protracted (prō·trakt′id) *adj.*: extended.

menacing (men′əs·iŋ) *v.* used as *adj.*: threatening.

SKILLS FOCUS

Literary Skills
Understand elements of style, including diction and sentence structure.

Reading Skills
Visualize the story.

SKILLS FOCUS, pp. 525–540

Grade-Level Skills

■ **Literary Skills**
Evaluate the aesthetic qualities of style, including the effect of diction, sentence structure, and figurative language.

■ **Reading Skills**
Visualize the story.

Summary ⬆ *above grade level*

In this short story, Paule Marshall uses a lyrical style and the diction of her ancestral Barbados to examine thematic conflicts between youth and old age, between city and country, and between colonizer and colonized. The story's nine-year-old narrator journeys from New York City to Barbados with her mother and older sister to visit Da-duh, her grandmother. During the visit, the narrator and Da-duh develop a ritual of taking walks around Da-duh's land. Da-duh proudly points out fruit trees and sugar canes and demands that her granddaughter admit that these things don't exist in New York. In return, the narrator both captivates and scares Da-duh with her descriptions of life in a big city. One day, the narrator describes the Empire State Building, a building taller than the surrounding hills. This knowledge seems to defeat Da-duh, and she takes to languishing in a lounge chair. The walks become listless and empty. Soon after the narrator returns to New York, Da-duh dies during an uprising of Barbadian workers against the British.

RESOURCES: READING

Planning
■ *One-Stop Planner* CD-ROM with ExamView Test Generator

Differentiating Instruction
■ *Holt Reading Solutions*
■ *Supporting Instruction in Spanish*

Vocabulary
■ *Vocabulary Development*

Grammar and Language
■ *Daily Language Activities*

Assessment
■ *Holt Assessment: Literature, Reading, and Vocabulary*
■ *One-Stop Planner* CD-ROM with ExamView Test Generator
■ *Holt Online Assessment*

Internet
■ go.hrw.com (Keyword: LE5 9-8)
■ *Elements of Literature Online*

Media
■ *Audio CD Library*
■ *Audio CD Library, Selections and Summaries in Spanish*
■ *Fine Art Transparencies*

Selection Starter

Build background. Tell students that this story is set in the 1930s, three decades before Barbados gained independence. Suggest that students consider, as they read, how this time period might influence Da-duh's attitudes and experiences.

Preview Vocabulary

To familiarize students with the Vocabulary words on p. 525, have them work in pairs to answer these questions:

1. In what situation is it good to be <u>unrelenting</u>?

2. What person, place, or thing do you find <u>formidable</u>?

3. Name an action that might be <u>reproved</u> by your teacher.

4. Describe a situation that would leave you <u>truculent</u>.

5. If a building is <u>decrepit</u>, what does it look like?

6. Describe a time when someone <u>admonished</u> you.

7. Describe something in your life that is <u>perennial</u>.

8. If a person's clothing were <u>austere</u>, what would it look like?

9. What does it mean if two people have a <u>protracted</u> argument?

10. Describe something or someone that you find <u>menacing</u>.

VIEWING THE ART

Charles Alston (1907–1977) was an African-American artist who served as an educator and advocate for the arts. Trained during the Harlem Renaissance, Alston participated in the Fine Arts Project, part of the federally sponsored Works Progress Administration during the Great Depression. Alston's use of abstract geometric forms derives from his interest in Cubism, while the frontal monumentality of the figures reveals Alston's interest in Egyptian art and his desire to portray an African-American family as a strong, supportive unit.

Collection of the Whitney Museum of American Art. Purchased with funds from the Artists and Students Assistance Fund (55.47). © 1995 Whitney Museum of American Art, New York.

Family (1955) by Charles H. Alston. Oil on canvas (48¼″ × 35¾″).

526 Collection 8 Evaluating Style • Evaluating Arguments: Pro and Con

To Da-duh,

in Memoriam

Paule Marshall

Da-duh stared at me as if I were a creature from Mars . . .

"... Oh Nana! all of you is not involved in this evil business Death,
Nor all of us in life."

—from "At My Grandmother's Grave"
by Lebert Bethune

I did not see her at first I remember. For not only was it dark inside the crowded disembarkation shed[1] in spite of the daylight flooding in from outside, but standing there waiting for her with my mother and sister I was still somewhat blinded from the sheen of tropical sunlight on the water of the bay which we had just crossed in the landing boat, leaving behind us the ship that had brought us from New York lying in the offing.[2] Besides, being only nine years of age at the time and knowing nothing of islands I was busy attending to the alien sights and sounds of Barbados, the unfamiliar smells.

---

1. **disembarkation shed:** place where passengers wait or assemble after leaving a ship or plane.
2. **in the offing:** at some distance but in sight.

A Literary Focus

? Setting. How do you know from the first sentence that the story takes place in the past? [The phrase "I remember" indicates that the narrator is speaking of the past.]

B Literary Focus

? Setting. What do other details tell about the story's setting? [Such words as "tropical sunlight," "bay," "islands," and "Barbados" indicate that the story is set in Barbados, a tropical island.]

Ⓐ Literary Focus

❓ Diction. What does Marshall's use of the word "purposeful" suggest about the old woman? [Possible response: It suggests that she is a proud, determined person.]

Ⓑ Literary Focus

❓ Sentence structure. What are the sentences in this section like? [They are long and rhythmic, almost breathless.] How does this sentence structure reflect the emotional state of the narrator? [Possible response: The narrator is both nervous and excited at meeting her grandmother. The breathless, rambling sentences reflect these emotions and her impressions.]

Ⓒ Literary Focus

❓ Diction. Consider the simile "fleshless as a death mask" and the connotations of such words as "maggots," "ruined skin," and "deep wells." What images and associations do these word choices evoke? [Possible response: They conjure up the image of a skull and associations of death. They suggest that the woman appears extremely old, as if she should already be dead.]

Sharecropper (1970) by Elizabeth Catlett. Woodcut.

Evans-Tibbs Collection, Washington, D.C. © Elizabeth Catlett/Licensed by VAGA, New York, NY.

Ⓐ I did not see her, but I was alerted to her approach by my mother's hand which suddenly tightened around mine, and looking up I traced her gaze through the gloom in the shed until I finally made out the small, purposeful, painfully erect figure of the old woman headed our way.

Her face was drowned in the shadow of an ugly rolled-brim brown felt hat, but the details of her slight body and of the struggle taking place within it were clear enough—an intense, Ⓑ unrelenting struggle between her back which was beginning to bend ever so slightly under the weight of her eighty-odd years and the rest of her which sought to deny those years and hold that back straight, keep it in line. Moving swiftly toward us (so swiftly it seemed she did not intend stopping when she reached us but would sweep past us out the doorway which opened onto the sea and like Christ walk upon the water!), she was caught between the sunlight at her end of the building and the darkness inside— and for a moment she appeared to contain them both: the light in the long severe old-fashioned white dress she wore which brought the sense of a past that was still alive into our bustling present and in the snatch of white at her eye; the darkness in her black high-top shoes and in her face which was visible now that she was closer.

Ⓒ It was as stark and fleshless as a death mask, that face. The maggots might have already done their work, leaving only the framework of bone beneath the ruined skin and deep wells at the temple and jaw. But her eyes were alive, unnervingly so for one so old, with a sharp light that flicked out of the dim clouded depths like a lizard's tongue to snap up all in her view. Those eyes betrayed a child's curiosity about the world, and I wondered vaguely seeing them, and seeing the way the bodice of her ancient dress had collapsed in on her flat chest (what had happened to her breasts?), whether she might not be some kind of child at the same time that she was a woman, with

Vocabulary
unrelenting (un·ri·len′tin) *adj.*: not letting up or weakening.

DIFFERENTIATING INSTRUCTION

Learners Having Difficulty
Modeling. To help students read "To Da-duh, in Memoriam," model the reading skill of visualizing. After students have read the first paragraph, say, "I focus on details like the dark disembarkation shed, the narrator being blinded by the tropical sunlight, the bay, and the ship, and try to imagine each. Together, these details form a picture and help me to imagine the dark interior of a building, beyond which is a bright, sun-dappled bay with a big ship off in the distance." Ask students to pause and visualize other scenes as they read.

English-Language Learners
Students may have trouble with the diction of this story, especially Da-duh's Barbadian dialect. Suggest that students work in pairs to read the story, using context and story clues to make sense of unfamiliar words and phrases.

Special Education Students
For lessons designed for special education students, see *Holt Reading Solutions*.

Advanced Students
Acceleration. Use the following activity to help advanced students describe how works

fourteen children, my mother included, to prove it. Perhaps she was both, both child and woman, darkness and light, past and present, life and death—all the opposites contained and reconciled in her.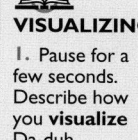

"My Da-duh," my mother said formally and stepped forward. The name sounded like thunder fading softly in the distance.

"Child," Da-duh said, and her tone, her quick scrutiny of my mother, the brief embrace in which they appeared to shy from each other rather than touch, wiped out the fifteen years my mother had been away and restored the old relationship. My mother, who was such a <u>formidable</u> figure in my eyes, had suddenly with a word been reduced to my status.

"Yes, God is good," Da-duh said with a nod that was like a tic. "He has spared me to see my child again."

We were led forward then, apologetically because not only did Da-duh prefer boys but she also liked her grandchildren to be "white," that is, fair-skinned; and we had, I was to discover, a number of cousins, the outside children of white estate managers and the like, who qualified. We, though, were as black as she.

My sister being the oldest was presented first. "This one takes after the father," my mother said and waited to be <u>reproved</u>.

Frowning, Da-duh tilted my sister's face toward the light. But her frown soon gave way to a grudging smile, for my sister with her large mild eyes and little broad winged nose, with our father's high-cheeked Barbadian cast to her face, was pretty.

"She's goin' be lucky," Da-duh said and patted her once on the cheek. "Any girl child that takes after the father does be lucky."

She turned then to me. But oddly enough she did not touch me. Instead leaning close, she

VISUALIZING
1. Pause for a few seconds. Describe how you **visualize** Da-duh.

peered hard at me, and then quickly drew back. I thought I saw her hand start up as though to shield her eyes. It was almost as if she saw not only me, a thin <u>truculent</u> child who it was said took after no one but myself, but something in me which for some reason she found disturbing, even threatening. We looked silently at each other for a long time there in the noisy shed, our gaze locked. She was the first to look away.

"But Adry," she said to my mother and her laugh was cracked, thin, apprehensive. "Where did you get this one here with this fierce look?"

"We don't know where she came out of, my Da-duh," my mother said, laughing also. Even I smiled to myself. After all I had won the encounter. Da-duh had recognized my small strength—and this was all I ever asked of the adults in my life then.

"Come, soul," Da-duh said and took my hand. "You must be one of those New York terrors you hear so much about."

She led us, me at her side and my sister and mother behind, out of the shed into the sunlight that was like a bright driving summer rain and over to a group of people clustered beside a <u>decrepit</u> lorry.[3] They were our relatives, most of them from St. Andrews although Da-duh herself lived in St. Thomas, the women wearing bright print dresses, the colors vivid against their darkness, the men rusty black suits that encased

---

3. **lorry** (lôr′ē) n.: British for "truck."

Vocabulary

formidable (fôr′mə·də·bəl) adj.: impressive; causing fear or dread.

reproved (ri·proōvd′) v.: disapproved of.

truculent (truk′yoō·lənt) adj.: fierce.

decrepit (dē·krep′it) adj.: falling apart.

VISUALIZING
2. Pause and think about what you see happening here. What do the details suggest about the way Da-duh regards her granddaughter?

DIRECT TEACHING

D **Reading Skills**

Visualizing. [Possible response to question 1: as a very skinny, frail, child-like old woman with alert, shrewd, observant eyes.]

E **Learners Having Difficulty**

Retelling. Marshall's sophisticated sentence structure and diction may cause problems for some students. Suggest that they work in pairs to retell what has happened in the story so far in their own words.

F **Literary Focus**

? **Character.** What does the information contained in this paragraph reveal about Da-duh? [She is sexist and very color-conscious.] How might this affect the narrator's relationship with her grandmother? [Possible response: The narrator, being dark-skinned and a girl, may not get treated well by Da-duh; Da-duh's prejudices may harm the narrator's self-image.]

G **Literary Focus**

Dialect. Point out that Da-duh's dialect helps to characterize her as a native of Barbados. Ask students to rephrase her speech in standard English. ["She's going to be lucky. Any young girl who takes after her father is lucky."]

H **Reading Skills**

Visualizing. [Possible response to question 2: The details conjure up a staring match between two combatants, each trying to figure out the other; it suggests that Da-duh is unsure about her granddaughter and is trying to test her or figure her out.]

---

by members of different cultures relate to one another.

Activity. After students finish the selection, have them read or re-read "Women" by Alice Walker on p. 448 as well as the Meet the Writer material accompanying the poem. Point out that both Walker and Marshall share a similar desire to celebrate, remember, and reclaim their female ancestors. Have students

compare and contrast the women celebrated in each work. Ask, "How are they alike and different? What battles are they fighting? In what way are they culturally similar? In what ways are they culturally different?"

A **Reading Skills**

❷ **Interpreting.** What do the words and behavior of the relatives suggest about the way they view people from outside the island? [Possible responses: Outsiders are the objects of awe and scrutiny; the relatives feel both shy and curious in the presence of these visitors from a place that is both culturally and geographically distant.]

B **Vocabulary Development**

❷ **Denotation and connotation.** Point out that the author could have chosen to use the word *curiosity* rather than *wonder* since their denotations are very similar. What connotations does *wonder* have that *curiosity* lacks? Why might the author have chosen it? [Possible answer: *Wonder* carries suggestions of awe, disbelief, and the witnessing of miracles. The author might have chosen it to emphasize the cultural gap that exists between these relatives and the New York visitors.]

C **Literary Focus**

❷ **Figurative language.** Have students identify the two metaphors in this paragraph. How do they illustrate two very different sides of Da-duh's character? [Da-duh is compared to a ruling monarch and the narrator is compared to Da-duh's anchor. The first comparison indicates strength—she is a powerful matriarch, the "ruler" of the Barbados clan; the second, which shows her relying on a small child for security, illustrates her weakness, her fear of modernity and machines.]

A them like straitjackets. Da-duh, holding fast to my hand, became my anchor as they circled round us like a nervous sea, exclaiming, touching us with their calloused hands, embracing us shyly. They laughed in awed bursts: "But look Adry got big-big children!" / "And see the nice things they wearing, wristwatch and all!" / "I tell you, Adry has done all right for herself in New York. . . ."

B Da-duh, ashamed at their wonder, embarrassed for them, <u>admonished</u> them the while. . . . She said, "Why you all got to get on like you never saw people from 'Away' before? You would think New York is the only place in the world to hear wunna. That's why I don't like to go anyplace with you St. Andrews people, you know. You all ain't been colonized."

We were in the back of the lorry finally, packed in among the barrels of ham, flour, cornmeal, and rice and the trunks of clothes that my mother had brought as gifts. We made our way slowly through Bridgetown's clogged streets, part of a funereal procession of cars and open-sided buses, bicycles and donkey carts. The dim little limestone shops and offices along the way marched with us, at the same mournful pace, toward the same grave ceremony—as did the people, the women balancing huge baskets on top their heads as if they were no more than hats they wore to shade them from the sun. Looking over the edge of the lorry I watched as their feet slurred the dust. I listened, and their voices, raw and loud and dissonant[4] in the heat, seemed to be grappling with each other high overhead.

C Da-duh sat on a trunk in our midst, a monarch amid her court. She still held my hand, but it was different now. I had suddenly become her anchor, for I felt her fear of the lorry with its

---

4. **dissonant** (dis′ə·nənt) *adj.:* lacking harmony; clashing.

Vocabulary
admonished (ad·män′isht) *v.:* scolded mildly.

Landscape with Royal Palms (1977) by Roosevelt. Oil on wood panel (21.1″ × 14″).

Private Collection / Edmond Van Hoorick / SuperStock.

VIEWING THE ART

Roosevelt Sanon (1952–   ), who is known by his first name, is from Jacmel, a city in southern Haiti. A leader of Haitian folk art, Roosevelt paints the landscape of his country in bright colors and playful, harmonious compositions. He depicts Haiti as a tropical paradise free of troubles and strife. In this painting, the palm trees form a rhythmic pattern that structures the details of the scene.

Activity. Ask students for some adjectives that might describe this scene. [Suggested answers: colorful, peaceful, idyllic, tropical]

A Reading Skills
Comparing and contrasting. Contrast the narrator's feelings on leaving the city with those of her grandmother. [Da-duh finds the rural environment comforting, but the narrator sees the countryside as an alien and frightening place.]

B Literary Focus
Dialect. Ask students what Da-duh means by "They's canes father, bo"? [Possible response: She means that the canes on St. Thomas are so large that they are big enough to be the father of the canes now in view.]

C Content-Area Connections
History: Panama Canal
The Panama Canal is a 51-mile-long man-made waterway that provides passage for ships between the Pacific and Atlantic oceans (through the Caribbean Sea). The canal was a complicated and expensive engineering feat, built by the United States between 1904 and 1914. The job attracted tens of thousands of laborers from Europe, the Americas, and the Caribbean. Their work was difficult and dangerous. Thousands died during the project, many to disease. In 2000, the United States turned control of the canal over to Panama under an agreement negotiated in 1977.

D Literary Focus
? Conflict. How are the narrator's views about the countryside changing? What does this suggest about the competition between the narrator and Da-duh? [Possible response: The narrator, prompted by her grandmother, is beginning to appreciate the beauty of the fertile Barbadian countryside. It no longer appears frightening or poor in comparison with New York. This change suggests that so far, Da-duh is winning the battle of wills.]

asthmatic motor (a fear and distrust, I later learned, she held of all machines) beating like a pulse in her rough palm.

As soon as we left Bridgetown behind though, she relaxed, and while the others around us talked she gazed at the canes[5] standing tall on either side of the winding marl road. "C'dear," she said softly to herself after a time. "The canes this side are pretty enough."

A They were too much for me. I thought of them as giant weeds that had overrun the island, leaving scarcely any room for the small tottering houses of sun-bleached pine we passed or the people, dark streaks as our lorry hurtled by. I suddenly feared that we were journeying, unaware that we were, toward some dangerous place where the canes, grown as high and thick as a forest, would close in on us and run us through with their stiletto blades. I longed then for the familiar: for the street in Brooklyn where I lived, for my father who had refused to accompany us ("Blowing out good money on foolishness," he had said of the trip), for a game of tag with my friends under the chestnut tree outside our aging brownstone house.

B "Yes, but wait till you see St. Thomas canes," Da-duh was saying to me. "They's canes father, bo," she gave a proud arrogant nod. "Tomorrow, God willing, I goin' take you out in the ground and show them to you."

True to her word Da-duh took me with her the following day out into the ground. It was a fairly large plot adjoining her weathered board-and-shingle house and consisting of a small orchard, a good-sized cane piece, and behind the canes, **C** where the land sloped abruptly down, a gully. She had purchased it with Panama money sent by her eldest son, my uncle Joseph, who had died work-

---
5. **canes** *n.:* tall stems of sugar-cane plants.

ing on the canal. We entered the ground along a trail no wider than her body and as devious and complex as her reasons for showing me her land. Da-duh strode briskly ahead, her slight form filled out this morning by the layers of sacking petticoats she wore under her working dress to protect her against the damp. A fresh white cloth, elaborately arranged around her head, added to her height, and lent her a vain, almost roguish[6] air.

Her pace slowed once we reached the orchard, and glancing back at me occasionally over her shoulder, she pointed out the various trees.

"This here is a breadfruit," she said. "That one yonder is a papaw. Here's a guava. This is a mango. I know you don't have anything like these in New York. Here's a sugar apple." (The fruit looked more like artichokes than apples to me.) "This one bears limes. . . ." She went on for some time, intoning the names of the trees as though they were those of her gods. Finally, turning to me, she said, "I know you don't have anything this nice where you come from." Then, as I hesitated: "I said I know you don't have anything this nice where you come from. . . ."

"No," I said and my world did seem suddenly lacking.

Da-duh nodded and passed on. The orchard ended and we were on the narrow cart road that led through the cane piece, the canes clashing like swords above my cowering head. Again she turned and her thin muscular arms spread wide, her dim gaze embracing the small field of canes, she said—and her voice almost broke under the weight of her pride, "Tell me, have you got anything like these in that place where you were born?"

"No."

---
6. **roguish** (rō'gish) *adj.:* mischievous.

> "I know you don't have anything like these in New York."

DEVELOPING FLUENCY

Small-group activity. Have students form small groups and choose one of the long descriptive passages from the story to read aloud, such as the episode in which the narrator first walks into the woods or the scene in which she dances for her grandmother. Group members should review the passage together, familiarizing themselves with the sentence structures, the pronunciation of unfamiliar words and dialect, and the rhythm of Marshall's prose. Students should then individually rehearse reading the passage. When they are ready, they can present their readings to other group members.

"I din' think so. I bet you don't even know that these canes here and the sugar you eat is one and the same thing. That they does throw the canes into some machine at the factory and squeeze out all the little life in them to make sugar for you all so in New York to eat. I bet you don't know that."

"I've got two cavities and I'm not allowed to eat a lot of sugar."

But Da-duh didn't hear me. She had turned with an inexplicably angry motion and was making her way rapidly out of the canes and down the slope at the edge of the field which led to the gully below. Following her apprehensively down the incline amid a stand of banana plants whose leaves flapped like elephants' ears in the wind, I found myself in the middle of a small tropical wood—a place dense and damp and gloomy and tremulous with the fitful play of light and shadow as the leaves high above moved against the sun that was almost hidden from view. It was a violent place, the tangled foliage fighting each other for a chance at the sunlight, the branches of the trees locked in what seemed an immemorial struggle, one both necessary and inevitable. But despite the violence, it was pleasant, almost peaceful in the gully, and beneath the thick undergrowth the earth smelled like spring.

VISUALIZING

3. Describe two pictures that this description of the wood puts in your mind.

This time Da-duh didn't even bother to ask her usual question, but simply turned and waited for me to speak.

"No," I said, my head bowed. "We don't have anything like this in New York."

"Ah," she cried, her triumph complete. "I din' think so. Why, I've heard that's a place where you can walk till you near drop and never see a tree."

"We've got a chestnut tree in front of our house," I said.

"Does it bear?" She waited. "I ask you, does it bear?"

"Not anymore," I muttered. "It used to, but not anymore."

She gave the nod that was like a nervous twitch. "You see," she said. "Nothing can bear there." Then, secure behind her scorn, she added, "But tell me, what's this snow like that you hear so much about?"

Looking up, I studied her closely, sensing my chance, and then I told her, describing at length and with as much drama as I could summon not only what snow in the city was like, but what it would be like here, in her perennial summer kingdom.

". . . And you see all these trees you got here," I said. "Well, they'd be bare. No leaves, no fruit, nothing. They'd be covered in snow. You see your canes. They'd be buried under tons of snow. The snow would be higher than your head, higher than your house, and you wouldn't be able to come down into this here gully because it would be snowed under. . . ."

She searched my face for the lie, still scornful but intrigued. "What a thing, huh?" she said finally, whispering it softly to herself.

"And when it snows you couldn't dress like you are now," I said. "Oh no, you'd freeze to death. You'd have to wear a hat and gloves and galoshes and earmuffs so your ears wouldn't freeze and drop off, and a heavy coat. I've got a Shirley Temple[7] coat with fur on the collar. I can dance. You wanna see?"

Before she could answer I began, with a dance called the Truck which was popular back then in the 1930s. My right forefinger waving, I trucked around the nearby trees and around Da-duh's awed and rigid form. After the Truck I did the Suzy-Q, my lean hips swishing, my sneakers sidling zigzag over the ground. "I can sing," I

---

7. **Shirley Temple:** child movie star popular during the 1930s.

Vocabulary
perennial (pə·ren′ē·əl) *adj.*: year-round; continual.

E Literary Focus
Sentence structure. Ask students to comment on the construction of this sentence. [Possible responses: The sentence is long and meandering, containing a simile and numerous descriptive adjectives. It mirrors the narrator's journey as she slowly follows her grandmother deeper into the woods, pausing in places to describe the sensory experience she is having.]

F Reading Skills
Visualizing. [Possible responses to question 3: the huge, flapping leaves of the banana plants, the tangled limbs of the trees, the speckled mix of light and shadow.]

G Learners Having Difficulty
Re-reading. Ask students to recall Da-duh's question. ["Have you got anything like these in that place where you were born?"] If students have difficulty remembering, have them return to the previous page and re-read the section where she asks it.

H Literary Focus
❼ Conflict. What "chance" does the narrator sense? Why does she incorporate as much detail and drama as possible into her explanation? [The narrator senses a weakness in her grandmother in her curiosity about snow, something New York has but Barbados lacks. It is an opportunity to regain the advantage in the "city versus country" battle her grandmother is currently winning, and for that reason, the narrator plays up the drama and detail as much as possible.]

? **Figurative language.** What comparison does the narrator use to convey the depth and intensity of the grandmother's curiosity? [The grandmother's gaze is likened to a surgeon's knife cutting into the narrator's skull.]

B **Reading Skills**

? **Interpreting.** What do you think the grandmother fears? [Possible responses: modernity, technology, the world outside her familiar cane fields.] If the narrator's stories frighten Da-duh, why does she continue to walk and talk with her? [Possible response: Her fear is outweighed by her desire to know more about the world in which the narrator lives.]

C **Advanced Learners**

? **Enrichment.** Ask students to draw on their prior knowledge of the colonial experience in the Caribbean to make inferences about the social conditions that Da-duh must have lived through. Why is she so shocked at the narrator's revelation that she "beat up a white girl"? [Possible response: Da-duh grew up in a society in which white European colonists and their descendants occupied the upper-most rung of the hierarchy. For her, a black person beating up a white person would be unthinkable; it would overturn this hierarchy.]

said and did so, starting with "I'm Gonna Sit Right Down and Write Myself a Letter," then without pausing, "Tea for Two," and ending with "I Found a Million Dollar Baby in a Five and Ten Cent Store."

For long moments afterwards Da-duh stared at me as if I were a creature from Mars, an emissary from some world she did not know but which intrigued her and whose power she both felt and feared. Yet something about my performance must have pleased her, because bending down she slowly lifted her long skirt and then, one by one, the layers of petticoats until she came to a drawstring purse dangling at the end of a long strip of cloth tied round her waist. Opening the purse she handed me a penny. "Here," she said half-smiling against her will. "Take this to buy yourself a sweet at the shop up the road. There's nothing to be done with you, soul."

From then on, whenever I wasn't taken to visit relatives, I accompanied Da-duh out into the ground, and alone with her amid the canes or down in the gully I told her about New York. It always began with some slighting remark on her part: "I know they don't have anything this nice where you come from," or "Tell me, I hear those foolish people in New York does do such and such. . . ." But as I answered, recreating my towering world of steel and concrete and machines for her, building the city out of words, I would feel her give way. I came to know the signs of her surrender: the total stillness that would come over her little hard dry form, the probing gaze that **A** like a surgeon's knife sought to cut through my skull to get at the images there, to see if I were lying; above all, her fear, a fear nameless and profound, the same one I had felt beating in the **B** palm of her hand that day in the lorry.

Over the weeks I told her about refrigerators, radios, gas stoves, elevators, trolley cars, wringer washing machines, movies, airplanes, the cyclone at Coney Island,[8] subways, toasters, electric lights: "At night, see, all you have to do is flip this little switch on the wall and all the lights in the house go on. Just like that. Like magic. It's like turning on the sun at night."

"But tell me," she said to me once with a faint mocking smile, "do the white people have all these things too or it's only the people looking like us?"

I laughed. "What d'ya mean," I said. "The white people have even better." Then: "I beat up a white girl in my class last term."

"Beating up white people!" Her tone was incredulous.[9]

"How you mean!" I said, using an expression of hers. "She called me a name."

For some reason Da-duh could not quite get **C** over this and repeated in the same hushed, shocked voice, "Beating up white people now! Oh, the lord, the world's changing up so I can scarce recognize it anymore."

One morning toward the end of our stay, Da-duh led me into a part of the gully that we had never visited before, an area darker and more thickly overgrown than the rest, almost impenetrable. There in a small clearing amid the dense bush, she stopped before an incredibly tall royal palm which rose cleanly out of the ground, and drawing the eye up with it, soared high above the trees around it into the sky. It appeared to be touching the blue dome of sky, to **D**

> "We've got buildings hundreds of times this tall in New York."

---

8. **cyclone at Coney Island:** roller-coaster ride in an amusement park in Brooklyn, New York.
9. **incredulous** (in·krej′oo·ləs) *adj.:* unbelieving; doubting.

Developing Word-Attack Skills
Write the selection word *disembarkation* on the chalkboard. Tell students that it is built by adding prefixes and suffixes to one simple word—*bark,* which means "a sailing ship." Work through these steps with students:

• The prefix *em–* is added to *bark* to create a word that means "to go on board a ship."

• The prefix *dis–* is added to *embark* to create a word that means the opposite, "to get off a ship and go ashore."

• The suffix *–ation* is added to *disembark* to change it from a verb to a noun that means "the act of going ashore."

Explain that breaking a word like *disembarkation* into its parts helps readers figure out a word's meaning. It also helps them understand how to read the word.

Activity. Have students read these words by breaking them into their components.

1. disentanglement
2. nonthreatening
3. unrestrainedness
4. underachievement
5. unguardedly
6. inalienable
7. multiculturalism
8. unremarkable
9. unreasonable
10. reoccurrence
11. unenlightened
12. misrecollection
13. disdainfulness
14. reinforcement

A Garden in Nassau (1885) by Winslow Homer. Watercolor, gouache, and pencil on paper.

© Christie's Images, Inc.

be flaunting[10] its dark crown of fronds right in the blinding white face of the late morning sun.

Da-duh watched me a long time before she spoke, and then she said very quietly, "All right, now, tell me if you've got anything this tall in that place you're from."

I almost wished, seeing her face, that I could have said no. "Yes," I said. "We've got buildings hundreds of times this tall in New York. There's one called the Empire State Building that's the tallest in the world. My class visited it last year and I went all the way to the top. It's got over a hundred floors. I can't describe how tall it is. Wait a minute. What's the name of that hill I went to visit the other day, where they have the police station?"

"You mean Bissex?"

---

10. **flaunting** (flônt′iŋ) *v.*: showing off proudly or disrespectfully.

"Yes, Bissex. Well, the Empire State Building is way taller than that."

"You're lying now!" she shouted, trembling with rage. Her hand lifted to strike me.

"No, I'm not," I said. "It really is, if you don't believe me I'll send you a picture postcard of it soon as I get back home so you can see for yourself. But it's way taller than Bissex."

All the fight went out of her at that. The hand poised to strike me fell limp to her side, and as she stared at me, seeing not me but the building that was taller than the highest hill she knew, the small stubborn light in her eyes (it was the same amber as the flame in the kerosene lamp she lit at dusk) began to fail. Finally, with a vague gesture that even in the midst of her defeat still tried to dismiss me and my world, she turned and started back through the gully, walking slowly, her steps groping and uncertain, as if she were suddenly

E

D Literary Focus

❓ Figurative language. What type of figurative language does the writer use in the description of the royal palm? [The author personifies the tree by describing it as "flaunting its dark crown of fronds right in the blinding white face of the late morning sun."]

E Literary Focus

❓ Conflict. Why is Da-duh so enraged? [After Da-duh proudly flaunts the jewel of her forest, an incredibly tall royal palm, the narrator "one-ups" her by talking about the Empire State Building. It must be clear to her now that even her landscape's finest specimens cannot compete with the wonders that exist in the narrator's world.]

VIEWING THE ART

The work of **Winslow Homer** (1836–1910) has made him one of the most acclaimed American artists of the nineteenth century. A realist painter, Homer began his career with engravings of the Civil War and established his reputation with his oil paintings of American life.

Activity. Ask students to compare Homer's visual description of the palm tree with the description of a tree in the story. [Both emphasize the size and stateliness of the palm.]

CONTENT-AREA CONNECTIONS

Geography: Barbados

At the time of the British arrival in 1627, Barbados was completely uninhabited. Its early occupants, probably Arawaks and Caribs, had long since abandoned the island. They may have fled after contact with Spanish explorers who tried to enslave them. The British quickly developed the island as a cane-producing colony. For three centuries,

sugar plantation owners and people of British origin were the most powerful segments of the population. Only in the 1930s, the period in which Marshall's story is set, did the African-descended majority begin making progress toward achieving political representation and access to the ownership of land.

Today, the sugar industry is still a major part of Barbados's economy. Gradually, how-

ever, as in other Caribbean islands, sugar's leading role is being supplanted by tourism. **Small-group activity.** Ask students to work in groups to create a Barbados bulletin board. Students can include a map showing the island's location; facts about the island, its history, population, and culture; and images that illustrate the natural landscape described in the story.

A **Learners Having Difficulty**

Breaking down difficult text. Guide students in understanding this long, complex sentence that represents a crucial turning point in the story. Help them divide it into parts and to paraphrase each part in their own words. [Possible responses: She was defeated. She turned and walked away. Her steps seemed uncertain. I followed, happy at my victory but also feeling sad.]

B **Reading Skills**

Visualizing. [Possible responses to question 4: Her hand falls limp, the light in her eyes begins to fail, and she walks slowly with groping and uncertain steps.]

C **Literary Focus**

❓ Diction. Ask students to discuss the connotations of the word *abstract*. What does it indicate about Da-duh's sorrow? [Possible responses: *Abstract* may suggest something that is mysterious, difficult to understand, and hard to define. The exact cause or nature of Da-duh's unhappiness is difficult to describe.]

VIEWING THE ART

This view of an autumn field was painted by **Vincent van Gogh** (1853–1890) when he lived in Arles, France. Van Gogh preferred to base paintings on his observations of the natural world, and this work demonstrates his attentiveness to the colors and atmosphere of late autumn.

Activity. Van Gogh painted the sun's light as visible rays. How do these rays interact with the rest of the painting? [They are broken by the lines of the tree branches and echoed by the brushstrokes indicating the straw in the painting's lower half.]

© Francis G. Mayer/CORBIS

Enclosed Field with Rising Sun (1889) by Vincent van Gogh. Oil on canvas. (71 cm × 90.5 cm)

A no longer sure of the way, while I followed triumphant yet strangely saddened behind.

The next morning I found her dressed for our morning walk but stretched out on the Berbice chair in the tiny drawing room where she sometimes napped during the afternoon heat, her face turned to the window beside her. She appeared thinner and suddenly indescribably old.

"My Da-duh," I said.

"Yes, nuh," she said. Her voice was listless and the face she slowly turned my way was, now that I think back on it, like a Benin mask,[11] the features drawn and almost distorted by an

VISUALIZING

B **4.** What details in the paragraph help you **visualize** that "all the fight went out of" Da-duh?

C ancient abstract sorrow.

"Don't you feel well?" I asked.

"Girl, I don't know."

"My Da-duh, I goin' boil you some bush tea," my aunt, Da-duh's youngest child, who lived with her, called from the shed-roof kitchen.

"Who tell you I need bush tea?" she cried, her voice assuming for a moment its old authority. "You can't even rest nowadays without some malicious person looking for you to be dead. Come girl," she motioned me to a place beside her on the old-fashioned lounge chair, "give us a tune."

I sang for her until breakfast at eleven, all my brash irreverent Tin Pan Alley songs,[12] and then just before noon we went out into the ground. But it was a short, dispirited walk. Da-duh didn't

---

11. **Benin mask:** reference to the beautiful ivory-and-wood masks carved in the West African kingdom of Benin, which flourished from the fourteenth to the seventeenth centuries.

12. **Tin Pan Alley songs:** Tin Pan Alley is a district in New York City, associated since the late nineteenth century with popular songwriters. Tin Pan Alley songs were "brash" (bold) and "irreverent" (mocking; disrespectful).

even notice that the mangoes were beginning to ripen and would have to be picked before the village boys got to them. And when she paused occasionally and looked out across the canes or up at her trees, it wasn't as if she were seeing them but something else. Some huge, monolithic[13] shape had imposed itself, it seemed, between her and the land, obstructing her vision. Returning to the house she slept the entire afternoon on the Berbice chair.

She remained like this until we left, languishing[14] away the mornings on the chair at the window gazing out at the land as if it were already doomed; then, at noon, taking the brief stroll with me through the ground during which she seldom spoke, and afterwards returning home to sleep till almost dusk sometimes.

On the day of our departure she put on the austere, ankle-length white dress, the black shoes and brown felt hat (her town clothes she called them), but she did not go with us to town. She saw us off on the road outside her house and in the midst of my mother's tearful protracted farewell, she leaned down and whispered in my ear, "Girl, you're not to forget now to send me the picture of that building, you hear."

By the time I mailed her the large colored picture postcard of the Empire State Building, she was dead. She died during the famous '37 strike,[15] which began shortly after we left. On the day of her death England sent planes flying low over the island in a show of force—so low, according to my aunt's letter, that the downdraft from them shook the ripened mangoes from the trees in Da-duh's orchard. Frightened, everyone in the village fled into the canes.

---

13. **monolithic** (män′ə·lith′ik) *adj.:* like a single large block of stone.
14. **languishing** (laŋ′gwish·iŋ) *adj.:* losing strength and energy; here, lying stretched out, without much energy.
15. **famous '37 strike:** Political factors and economic hardships led Barbadian workers to riot against the British in 1937.

Except Da-duh. She remained in the house at the window so my aunt said, watching as the planes came swooping and screaming like monstrous birds down over the village, over her house, rattling her trees and flattening the young canes in her field. It must have seemed to her lying there that they did not intend pulling out of their dive, but like the hardback beetles which hurled themselves with suicidal force against the walls of the house at night, those menacing silver shapes would hurl themselves in an ecstasy of self-immolation[16] onto the land, destroying it utterly.

VISUALIZING

5. What do you see happening in this passage? Which details create the most vivid pictures?

When the planes finally left and the villagers returned, they found her dead on the Berbice chair at the window.

She died and I lived, but always, to this day even, within the shadow of her death. For a brief period after I was grown I went to live alone, like one doing penance,[17] in a loft above a noisy factory in downtown New York and there painted seas of sugar cane and huge, swirling van Gogh[18] suns and palm trees striding like brightly-plumed Tutsi[19] warriors across a tropical landscape, while the thunderous tread of the machines downstairs jarred the floor beneath my easel, mocking my efforts. ∎

---

16. **self-immolation** (self·im′ə·lā′shən) *n.:* violent self-destruction, usually by fire.
17. **penance** (pen′əns) *n.:* action done to make up for wrong behavior.
18. **van Gogh:** Dutch artist Vincent van Gogh (1853–1890) painted suns that seemed to roll through skies filled with swirling colors.
19. **Tutsi** (tōōt′sē): Watusi (or Watutsi), a people of Burundi and Rwanda, in central Africa.

Vocabulary

austere (ô·stir′) *adj.:* very plain; severe.
protracted (prō·trakt′id) *adj.:* extended.
menacing (men′əs·iŋ) *v.* used as *adj.:* threatening.

D Reading Skills

❷ Making inferences. What is the "huge, monolithic shape"? How has it come between Da-duh and the land? [The shape is the Empire State Building. Knowledge of its existence now prevents Da-duh from enjoying the beauty of the rural landscape she so loved.]

E Literary Focus

❷ Character. What action indicates how important seeing the Empire State Building is to Da-duh? [She interrupts her daughter's emotional farewell to remind her granddaughter to send a picture of it.]

F Reading Skills

❷ Speculating. How do you think Da-duh would have reacted had she lived to receive the postcard? [Possible response: It would have left her awestruck; it would have confirmed her worst fears about the relation of her world to the modernity and grandeur of New York.]

G Reading Skills

Visualizing. [Possible responses to question 5: A squadron of fighter planes roaring overhead, almost grazing the house, trees, and canes. The most vivid details are "swooping and screaming," "rattling her trees," "flattening the young canes," and "hurled themselves with suicidal force against the walls of the house."]

H Literary Focus

❷ Sentence structure. Focus students' attention on the two phrases that break up the middle of the sentence. What is the author choosing to emphasize by including them? [Possible response: The two phrases—"but always, to this day even"—are redundant, but they emphasize the profound and lasting effect the experience of her grandmother's death has had on the narrator.]

Encourage students to share "To Da-duh, in Memoriam" with their parents or other older family members. After they have read the story, students can ask their relatives to discuss their memories of their own parents or grandparents. You might have students ask these relatives to try to remember any difficulties people from those generations had

adjusting to or dealing with aspects of a changing modern world. Students can encourage their parents to share any particular anecdotes they remember.

Meet the Writer

Background. The core idea for "To Da-duh, in Memoriam" came from Paule Marshall's sense of rivalry between her and her grandmother. "Years later, when I got around to writing the story, I tried giving the contest I had sensed between us a wider meaning. I wanted the basic theme of youth and old age to suggest rivalries, dichotomies of a cultural and political nature, having to do with the relationship of western civilization and the Third World."

GUIDED PRACTICE

Monitoring students' progress. Guide the class in answering these comprehension questions. Direct students to locate passages in the story that support their responses.

Short Answer

1. Where is the narrator from? [New York City]

2. Why has she come to Barbados? [She has come with her mother and sister to visit her grandmother.]

3. Where do Da-duh and the narrator walk every day? [through the cane fields and forest near Da-duh's home]

4. What does Da-duh ask the narrator to send her? [a postcard of the Empire State Building]

5. Who sends planes flying low over the island? [the British]

Meet the Writer

Paule Marshall

"I Am . . . an Unabashed Ancestor Worshipper"

Paule Marshall (1929–   ) calls this story the "most autobiographical" of her works. The Latin words *in memoriam* in the title mean "in memory of." The story is written in memory of Marshall's grandmother, who was called Da-duh by her family. Marshall based her story on a yearlong visit she made when she was nine to see her grandmother in Barbados. While she was there, she sensed "a subtle kind of power struggle" between her and her grandmother.

❝It was as if we both knew, at a level beyond words, that I had come into the world not only to love her and to continue her line but to take her very life in order that I might live.❞

Marshall adds that she has based other characters on her grandmother:

❝She's an ancestor figure, symbolic for me of the long line of black women and men—African and New World—who made my being possible, and whose spirit I believe continues to animate my life and work. I wish to acknowledge and celebrate them. I am . . . an unabashed ancestor worshipper.❞

Marshall was born in Brooklyn, New York, and she grew up among people who had emigrated from Caribbean islands like Barbados to the United States. Her writings have always reflected her background, which combines African American and Caribbean influences.

After graduating from college, Marshall found work as a journalist, and she began writing her first novel, *Brown Girl, Brownstones.* Her fiction focuses on the links among all the different African cultures in the Western Hemisphere.

Response and Analysis

Reading Check

1. When Da-duh takes the narrator "out into the ground," what question does the old woman repeatedly ask?

2. What causes "all the fight" to go out of Da-duh?

3. What happens to Da-duh on the day that British planes fly over her house?

Thinking Critically

4. Explain the **conflict** between the narrator and her grandmother. How is their competition finally resolved?

5. Why is Da-duh so frightened by the narrator's stories about New York?

6. Why, once her grandmother is defeated, does the narrator feel "triumphant yet strangely saddened"?

7. Why does the narrator live "within the shadow" of Da-duh's death? Why is it significant that the factory machines mock her efforts to paint sugar cane, suns, and palm trees?

8. Consider what the story says about the following conflicts. Then, state what you think is the story's **theme**. (Check your Quickwrite notes.)
   - youth versus old age
   - colonial rule versus independence
   - urban life versus rural life

9. Which scene in the story creates the most vivid pictures in your mind? How does the writer's **style** help you **visualize** the scene?

Literary Criticism

10. Marshall describes her own relationship with her grandmother as "close, affectionate yet rivalrous." Using evidence from the story, show how the relationship between the **narrator** and Da-duh reflects the author's relationship with her grandmother. (For more about the relationship between the author's life and work, see Meet the Writer on page 538.)

11. Look back at your statement of the story's theme (question 8). Find examples of specific words (**diction**) or **figures of speech** that help convey that **theme**. (For example, what might the author's comparison of the British planes to "monstrous birds" at the end of the story tell you about the conflict between colonies and the nations that rule them?)

12. How would you describe the story's **mood**—the feeling evoked by the setting? Give examples to show how the author's **diction** and **figures of speech** help create that mood.

WRITING

Analyzing a Story: It's Got Style

How would you describe Paule Marshall's **style**? Is it poetic, suspenseful, realistic, or fanciful, for example? Consider her **diction**, especially her use of **dialect**, her **figures of speech**, and her sentence structure. Then, write a few paragraphs analyzing Marshall's style. Before you write, gather examples from the story to support your points. Place your examples in a chart like the one below:

Elements of Style	Examples from Story
Descriptive words	
Dialect	
Figures of speech	
Sentence structure	

▶ Use "Analyzing a Short Story," pages 548–555, for help with this assignment.

SKILLS FOCUS

Literary Skills
Analyze elements of style, including diction and figures of speech.

Reading Skills
Visualize the story.

Writing Skills
Analyze a story's style.

To Da-duh, in Memoriam **539**

Response and Analysis

6. The narrator is triumphant to have won but saddened that losing has taken a toll on Da-duh.

7. Possible answer: She feels guilty, believing she hastened Da-duh's death. The machines mocking her is an ironic twist; now she is in her grandmother's position, having modern technology encroach on a tropical world.

8. Possible answers: Colonization is wrong; progress has its price; change is inevitable.

9. Possible answer: Da-duh at the window while the British planes are flying low is vividly depicted by similes and action verbs.

Literary Criticism

10. Possible answer: The narrator's walks with Da-duh and Da-duh's treatment of the narrator reveal their bond; their competition about the merits of New York and Barbados mirrors the real life "power struggle" between Marshall and her grandmother.

11. Possible answers: Descriptions of Da-duh reinforce the idea that youth and age are in conflict, especially the phrase that "all the fight went out of" Da-duh after she learns of the Empire State Building. The reference to machines as "mocking" suggests that technological progress is frightening, has a high social price, and is used by colonizers to subjugate.

12. Possible answer: Despite the story's lush setting, the mood is tense and ominous. The descriptions of Da-duh's face as "like a Benin mask" and of her behavior as "languishing" create this mood, as do the similes describing the planes as "monstrous birds" and "hardback beetles," and words such as *dangerous* and *violent* used to describe the landscape.

Reading Check

1. Do you have anything this nice where you come from?

2. Learning about the existence of the Empire State Building.

3. She dies sitting in her chair at the window watching the planes.

Thinking Critically

4. They compete about which is better, Barbados or New York. The narrator wins when she tells Da-duh about the Empire State Building.

5. Possible answer: The things her granddaughter describes seem so alien that they turn her ideas about the world—and her place in it—upside down.

Vocabulary Development

Practice 1

Possible Word Maps

- *formidable. Meaning*—causing fear or dread. *Related word*—formidably. *Example*—A rival can be <u>formidable</u>.

- *reproved. Meaning*—disapproved of. *Related words*—reprovingly, reprove. *Example*—A child can be <u>reproved</u>.

- *truculent. Meaning*—fierce, ready to fight. *Related word*—truculence. *Example*—A warrior can be <u>truculent</u>.

- *decrepit. Meaning*—falling apart. *Related word*—decrepitude. *Example*—Old buildings can be <u>decrepit</u>.

- *admonished. Meaning*—scolded mildly. *Related word*—admonish. *Example*—You could be <u>admonished</u> for being late.

- *perennial. Meaning*—continual. *Related word*—perennially. *Example*—I am a <u>perennial</u> host.

- *austere. Meaning*—very plain, severe. *Related words*—austerely, austerity. *Example*—A sparsely furnished home can be <u>austere</u>.

- *protracted. Meaning*—extended. *Related words*—protract, protractor. *Example*—Delays can be <u>protracted</u>.

- *menacing. Meaning*—threatening. *Related words*—menace, menacingly. *Example*—Storms can seem <u>menacing</u>.

Practice 2

Possible Answers

1. *Alien* has connotations of the foreign, while *strange* can just mean weird or nonsensical.

2. *Fierce* is not necessarily *cruel*. Brave people can look *fierce*. *Cruel* suggests meanness.

3. *Overrun* suggests a taking over or out-of-control aspect.

4. *Solemn* can simply mean serious, while *funereal* hints at death, sadness and mourning.

5. *Monstrous* denotes size but calls to mind something terrifying.

Vocabulary Development

Word Mapping

PRACTICE 1

The following word map for *unrelenting* shows its meaning, related words, and examples of things or situations that can be unrelenting. Make a similar map for each of the remaining Word Bank words. Be sure to compare your word maps with those of a partner.

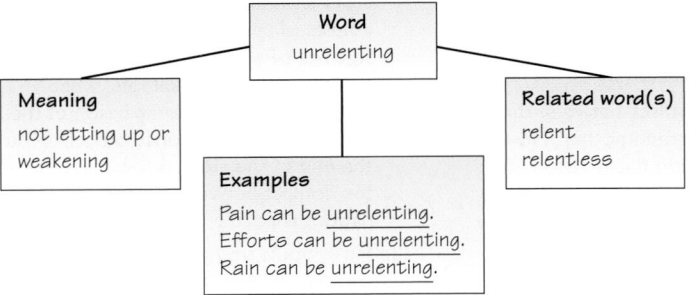

Word Bank

unrelenting
formidable
reproved
truculent
decrepit
admonished
perennial
austere
protracted
menacing

Denotation and Connotation: Fine-tuning

PRACTICE 2

All words have **denotations**—literal meanings. Some words also have **connotations**—emotions and associations that have come to be attached to them. The words *cheap, inexpensive*, and *reasonable*, for example, all mean "not costly." However, *cheap* has negative connotations, whereas *inexpensive* and *reasonable* do not. *Cheap* suggests that something is not worth very much. The phrase "cheap sweater" suggests that a sweater is not well made or that it's of poor quality.

Paule Marshall's **diction** is characterized by her use of words with rich connotations, which add emotional depth to her writing. When you write, think carefully about the connotations of the words you use—doing so can make your writing more vivid and complex.

For help thinking about the connotations of the words that Marshall uses, answer the following questions:

1. The narrator describes the sights of Barbados as "alien." What do you associate with *alien* that you don't associate with *strange*?

2. Da-duh notices the narrator's "fierce" look. How is a <u>fierce</u> look different from a cruel look?

3. Marshall says that sugar-cane plants "overrun" the island. What does *overrun* suggest that *cover* doesn't?

4. The procession of cars, buses, bicycles, and donkey carts leaving Bridgetown is called "funereal." What does *funereal* suggest that *solemn* doesn't?

5. Marshall describes the British planes as looking like "monstrous birds." What images does *monstrous* call to mind that aren't suggested by *large* or *huge*?

SKILLS FOCUS

Vocabulary Skills
Create semantic maps. Understand word denotations and connotations.

ASSESSING

Assessment

- *Holt Assessment: Literature, Reading, and Vocabulary*

RETEACHING

For a lesson reteaching author's style, see p. 979A and *The Holt Reader*, Collection 8.

Before You Read

How to Eat a Guava

Make the Connection

Quickwrite ✏️

What is your absolutely favorite food? Think about eating that food, and write down all the sensations you experience while eating it. Do you associate that food with a certain time or place in your life or with certain experiences? Make a list of all the memories and feelings you connect with your favorite food.

Literary Focus

Style: Diction and Imagery

An important element of an author's style is **diction,** or word choice, and an important element of diction is imagery. **Imagery** is language that appeals to one or more of our senses—sight, sound, taste, touch, and smell. An image can help to re-create a place, a thing, or a person. Images give printed words on a page the glow and hum of real life.

In "How to Eat a Guava," Esmeralda Santiago takes a relatively simple subject —the eating of a tropical fruit—and turns it into a feast for all the senses. If you have eaten a guava, see how well her imagery re-creates the experience for you. If, on the other hand, this is your introduction to the guava—enjoy!

Tone: An Attitude

Diction and imagery have a powerful effect on creating tone in a piece of writing. **Tone** is a writer's attitude toward a subject. Since tone can be difficult to identify, it's helpful to think of a tone as "an attitude," which might be positive or negative, joyful or sorrowful, serious or humorous. A writer's tone can usually be expressed in a single word. As you read this excerpt from Santiago's memoir, you'll notice that her vivid imagery conveys an attitude about the guavas of her youth in Puerto Rico. What tone does Santiago create?

Background

The author of "How to Eat a Guava" comes from Puerto Rico, a Caribbean island where guavas and other tropical fruits grow in abundance. Located about one thousand miles southeast of Florida, Puerto Rico is a commonwealth of the United States, and its inhabitants are U.S. citizens. Spanish is the chief language of Puerto Rico, reflecting its long history as a Spanish colony; English is its other official language.

INTERNET
More About Esmeralda Santiago
Keyword: LE5 9-8

Literary Skills
Understand elements of style, including diction, imagery, and tone.

SKILLS FOCUS, pp. 541–546

Grade-Level Skills

■ **Literary Skills**
Evaluate the aesthetic qualities of style, including the effect of diction, imagery, and tone.

Review Skills

■ **Literary Skills**
Identify the literary devices that define a writer's style.

Summary *at grade level*

The author moved to the United States mainland from Puerto Rico at the age of thirteen. Here she describes her emotional response as an adult when she encounters a display of guavas in a supermarket. Using vivid imagery, she recaptures the sights, smells, tastes, and touches she associates with these fruits that grew in her childhood home of Puerto Rico. In the end, however, she decides not to buy a guava, choosing instead the "predictable and bittersweet" tastes of apples and pears, the American fruits of her adulthood. The essay is a bittersweet evocation of the divided identity of someone who has lived in two very different worlds.

RESOURCES: READING

Planning
■ *One-Stop Planner* CD-ROM with ExamView Test Generator

Differentiating Instruction
■ *Holt Reading Solutions*
■ *Supporting Instruction in Spanish*
■ *Audio CD Library, Selections and Summaries in Spanish*

Vocabulary
■ *Vocabulary Development*

Grammar and Language
■ *Daily Language Activities*

Assessment
■ *Holt Assessment: Literature, Reading, and Vocabulary*

■ *One-Stop Planner* CD-ROM with ExamView Test Generator
■ *Holt Online Assessment*

Internet
■ go.hrw.com (Keyword: LE5 9-8)
■ *Elements of Literature Online*

Media
■ *Audio CD Library*

Selection Starter

Motivate. Bring in an apple, an orange, a pear, and a bunch of grapes. Divide the class into four groups, and give each group one of the four fruits. Ask each group to list vivid sensory details to describe how their fruit looks, sounds, smells, feels, and tastes. Then, have them discuss any childhood memories and feelings they associate with the fruit. After the discussion, encourage students to complete the Quickwrite individually.

542

HOW TO EAT A GUAVA

from When I Was Puerto Rican
Esmeralda Santiago

"You grimace, your eyes water, and your cheeks disappear as your lips purse into a tight ○."

Barco que no anda, no llega a puerto.
A ship that doesn't sail, never reaches port.

There are guavas at the Shop & Save. I pick one the size of a tennis ball and finger the prickly stem end. It feels familiarly bumpy and firm. The guava is not quite ripe; the skin is still a dark green. I smell it and imagine a pale pink center, the seeds tightly embedded in the flesh.

A ripe guava is yellow, although some varieties have a pink tinge. The skin is thick, firm, and sweet. Its heart is bright pink and almost solid with seeds. The most delicious part of the guava surrounds the tiny seeds. If you don't know how to eat a guava, the seeds end up in the crevices between your teeth.

When you bite into a ripe guava, your teeth must grip the bumpy surface and sink into the thick edible skin without hitting the center. It takes experience to do this, as it's quite tricky to determine how far beyond the skin the seeds begin.

Some years, when the rains have been plentiful and the nights cool, you can bite into a guava and not find many seeds. The guava bushes grow close to the ground, their branches laden with green then yellow fruit that seem to ripen overnight. These guavas are large and juicy, almost seedless, their roundness enticing you to have one more, just one more, because next year the rains may not come.

As children, we didn't always wait for the fruit to ripen. We raided the bushes as soon as the guavas were large enough to bend the branch.

A green guava is sour and hard. You bite into it at its widest point, because it's easier to grasp with your teeth. You hear the skin, meat, and seeds crunching inside your head, while the inside of your mouth explodes in little spurts of sour.

You grimace, your eyes water, and your cheeks disappear as your lips purse into a tight O. But you have another and then another,

How to Eat a Guava   **543**

A **Literary Focus**

? **Style and imagery.** Which details show how a guava looks, feels, and tastes? [*looks*—"the size of a tennis ball," "dark green," "pale pink center," "seeds tightly embedded in the flesh," "yellow," "pink tinge," "skin is thick," "heart is bright pink," "almost solid with seeds," "tiny seeds"; *feels*—"prickly stem end," "bumpy and firm," "grip the bumpy surface," "sink into the thick edible skin"; *tastes*—"sweet"]

B **Literary Focus**

? **Tone.** What attitude does the author seem to have toward the guavas she ate in her childhood? [Possible responses: She remembers them fondly because their taste was so enticing and irresistible. She expresses an affectionate, homesick attitude toward these vivid reminders of her homeland.]

C **Literary Focus**

? **Style and imagery.** To which senses does the imagery in these paragraphs appeal? [taste, touch, sound]

English-Language Learners
Invite students whose families have immigrated from a tropical area such as Puerto Rico to describe for the class the appearance and taste of tropical fruits such as guavas, papayas, and mangoes. Encourage them to use both Spanish and English adjectives in their descriptions. Also, have students describe any vivid memories they have of eating such fruits.

Special Education Students
For lessons designed for special education students, see *Holt Reading Solutions*.

? Drawing conclusions. Why does the author describe the taste of ripe apples and pears as "bittersweet"? [Possible response: The actual taste of these fruits is sweet, but the contrast between them and the intense, unpredictable experience of eating a guava gives the author a feeling of great loss.]

GUIDED PRACTICE

Monitoring students' progress. Activity. To monitor students' comprehension of the text, have them first summarize the events that occur in the present adult life of the author. [The author sees a display of guavas in a grocery store. She picks one up and remembers eating guavas in Puerto Rico. She puts the guava back and steers her cart to the apples and pears.] **Then, ask students to summarize the author's memories of her past.** [She recalls eating ripe and green guavas as a child in Puerto Rico, as well as the last guava she ate on the day she left her homeland.]

Meet the Writer

Background. Esmeralda Santiago says that she writes about her childhood "for other kids, for the next generation." Why? "I really want young people to see that these feelings you have right now, other people have felt them—maybe the person sitting next to you. But also that you can get over them, write about them and not be embarrassed by them."

enjoying the crunchy sounds, the acid taste, the gritty texture of the unripe center. At night, your mother makes you drink castor oil,° which she says tastes better than a green guava. That's when you know for sure that you're a child and she has stopped being one.

I had my last guava the day we left Puerto Rico. It was large and juicy, almost red in the center, and so fragrant that I didn't want to eat it because I would lose the smell. All the way to the airport I scratched at it with my teeth, making

___
° **castor oil** *n.:* yellow or colorless oil made from castor beans, used as a home remedy for digestive problems.

little dents in the skin, chewing small pieces with my front teeth, so that I could feel the texture against my tongue, the tiny pink pellets of sweet.

Today, I stand before a stack of dark green guavas, each perfectly round and hard, each $1.59. The one in my hand is tempting. It smells faintly of late summer afternoons and hopscotch under the mango tree. But this is autumn in New York, and I'm no longer a child.

The guava joins its sisters under the harsh fluorescent lights of the exotic fruit display. I push my cart away, toward the apples and pears of my adulthood, their nearly seedless ripeness predictable and bittersweet. ■

Meet the Writer

Esmeralda Santiago

Between Two Worlds

Esmeralda Santiago (1948–   ) grew up in Puerto Rico, the eldest of eleven children. At the age of thirteen, she moved to New York City with her mother, her brothers, and her sisters. Living in Puerto Rico and in New York, she says, has to some extent made her feel that she doesn't quite fit into either culture—a feeling she highlights in the title of her memoir, *When I Was Puerto Rican.* In a note to readers of the book she writes:

❝ When I returned to Puerto Rico after living in New York for seven years, I was told I was no longer Puerto Rican because my Spanish was rusty, my gaze too direct, my personality too assertive. . . . Yet, in the United States, my darkness, my accented speech, my frequent lapses into confused silence between English and Spanish identified me as foreign, non-American. In writing the book I wanted to get back to that feeling of Puertoricanness I had before I came here. Its title reflects who I was then, and asks, who am I today? ❞

After graduating from Harvard University, Santiago earned a master's degree from Sarah Lawrence College. She currently lives in Westchester County, New York. Now, after years of struggling with not being entirely at home in her two cultures, Santiago says she defines *home* "as the place where I am."

DIFFERENTIATING INSTRUCTION

Advanced Learners

Acceleration. This activity can help students analyze the way the author's tone and style achieves specific rhetorical or aesthetic purposes.

Activity. Point out that Santiago is writing for an audience of Americans who "don't know how to eat a guava" and that she is contrasting the fruit with the "nearly seedless" and "predictable" apples and pears

that many Americans eat. Ask students to analyze the style and tone of the essay in order to determine what underlying message the author might be trying to convey to readers who do not share her ethnic background. [Possible response: The cultures that immigrants leave behind feature a richness and complexity that many Americans lack the experience to understand.]

The Tropics in New York

Claude McKay

Bananas ripe and green, and ginger-root,
   Cocoa in pods and alligator pears,°
And tangerines and mangoes and grape fruit,
   Fit for the highest prize at parish° fairs,

5 Set in the window, bringing memories
   Of fruit-trees laden by low-singing rills,°
And dewy dawns, and mystical blue skies
   In benediction° over nun-like hills.

My eyes grew dim, and I could no more gaze;
10   A wave of longing through my body swept,
And, hungry for the old, familiar ways,
   I turned aside and bowed my head and wept.

B

C

2. **alligator pears:** avocados.
4. **parish** (par'ish) *n.:* church district; here, county.
6. **rills** *n.:* small streams.
8. **benediction** (ben'ə · dik'shən) *n.:* blessing.

How to Eat a Guava **545**

Connection

Summary ➡ *at grade level*

Like Santiago's essay, this poem describes the reaction of an immigrant from the tropics, after he sees a display of tropical fruits. In the first stanza, the speaker lists the fruits he sees. In the second stanza, he describes the landscape of his homeland, which the fruits call to mind. In the third stanza, he describes the feelings of longing and homesickness that these memories cause and the fact that he turns away from the display and weeps.

DIRECT TEACHING

B Literary Focus

❓ Style, imagery, and tone. What sensory details and simile does the speaker use to describe his homeland? [Sensory details: "fruit-trees laden by low-singing rills," "dewy dawns," "mystical blue skies." Simile: "nun-like hills."] What tone, or attitude toward his homeland, does the imagery create? [Possible responses: loving, longing, reverential, worshipful, awed.]

C Reading Skills

❓ Identifying cause and effect. Why does the speaker turn away from the store window and weep? [He cannot bear the feelings of longing and homesickness that the sight of the tropical fruits arouses in him. He misses his homeland.]

Connecting and Comparing Texts

Have students point out similarities between the experiences described in Esmeralda Santiago's essay and in Claude McKay's poem. [In both works, an immigrant from a tropical homeland sees a display of tropical fruit, which reminds him or her of the homeland left behind. Both the essayist and the speaker of the poem have vivid sensory memories of their homeland. In the end, both turn away from the fruit display because they cannot bear the sadness that their memories evoke.]

Then, ask which work provides more vivid sensory images of the author's homeland. [Possible response: Santiago's essay provides imagery that appeals to all of the five senses, while McKay provides only a few images that appeal mainly to the senses of sight and sound.]

Response and Analysis

Reading Check

1. If you bite too far, tiny seeds will get stuck between your teeth.

2. She is living in New York City.

3. She puts it back.

Thinking Critically

4. She remembers rain, cool nights, and bushes of fruit. She recalls children eating the hard, sour, unripened fruits. She has fond memories of her childhood, and she misses her homeland.

5. Possible answers: Apples and pears are "American" fruits that suit her adult identity; guavas suit her Puerto Rican identity and past that she feels she cannot recapture.

Literary Criticism

6. *Ripe. Sight*—yellow with pink tinge, bright pink inside. *Taste*—sweet, juicy. *Smell*—fragrant. *Touch*—firm, bumpy. *Green. Sight*—dark green, pale pink center. *Taste*—"explodes in little spurts of sour." *Smell*—"It smells faintly of late summer afternoons . . . under the mango tree." *Touch*—hard, prickly, bumpy, gritty. *Sound*—crunching. Emphasis is on sight, taste, and touch.

7. The tone is nostalgic and affectionate: "familiarly bumpy and firm," "enticing you to have one more, just one more," and "Some years when the rains have been plentiful and the nights cool."

8. Possible answers: bittersweet, conflicted. The tone changes with the shift from past to present. Sentences that begin with "But this is autumn in New York . . ." and "I push my cart away . . ." signal this change.

9. Possible answers: It is impossible to recapture childhood. A person's sense of home is connected to vivid memories.

Response and Analysis

Reading Check

1. Why do you have to be careful when you bite into a ripe guava?

2. Where is Santiago living at the time of the incident at the Shop & Save?

3. At the end, what does the author do with the guava in her hand?

Thinking Critically

4. What memories does Santiago associate with the guavas she ate in her youth in Puerto Rico? What do her recollections reveal about her feelings about her youth and her homeland?

5. At the end of the piece, what can you **infer** from the fact that Santiago heads toward the apples and pears? Why do you think she doesn't eat guavas anymore?

Literary Criticism

6. **Compare and contrast** Santiago's **images** of a ripe guava and a green one. List words and phrases that she uses to describe each one. Which senses does she emphasize? Make a chart like the one here to organize your thoughts:

	Ripe	Green
Sight		
Taste		
Smell		
Touch		
Sound		

7. How would you identify the **tone** of the essay until the point when Santiago describes having her last guava? Look carefully at the **diction**, especially the **imagery**. Find words and phrases that help to create the tone.

SKILLS FOCUS

Literary Skills Analyze elements of style, including diction, imagery, and tone.

Writing Skills Write a descriptive paragraph. Compare and contrast a memoir with a poem.

8. How would you describe the **tone** at the end of the piece? Has it changed? What words help create the tone at the end?

9. On the surface, Santiago's description of eating a guava is pure sensation. However, her description is also a way of communicating some serious ideas about time, growing up, and home. What **theme** do you think Santiago expresses through the **imagery** in "How to Eat a Guava"?

WRITING

Tasty Time Remembered

Choose a particular food memory—eating pumpkin pie at Thanksgiving or ripe watermelon at a July Fourth picnic—and write a paragraph in which you share the experience with your readers. Pay special attention to **sensory details.** (Check your Quickwrite notes.) ✏

Comparing Literature

In a paragraph or two, **compare and contrast** Santiago's memoir "How to Eat a Guava" with McKay's poem "The Tropics in New York" (see the **Connection** on page 545), two pieces about tropical fruit. Consider the following factors: the **imagery** used; the situation described; the writer's or speaker's memories; the **tone,** or the attitude, of the piece. Be sure to consider ways in which the memoir and poem may differ. Use a chart like the one here to organize your ideas:

	"How to Eat a Guava"	"The Tropics in New York"
Imagery		
Situation		
Memories		
Tone		

ASSESSING

Assessment

■ *Holt Assessment: Literature, Reading, and Vocabulary*

RETEACHING

For a lesson reteaching author's style, see **Reteaching,** p. 979A. For another selection to teach author's style, see *The Holt Reader,* Collection 8.

FICTION

Belonging

Twelve-year-old Frankie Addams is filled with contradictions. She wants to be accepted for who she is—and she wants to change into somebody different. She wants to be treated as a grown-up—and she wants to remain a child forever. Most of all, she wants a sense of belonging. When Frankie's older brother announces his engagement, a wave of excitement passes through her sleepy Georgian town. No one is more excited than Frankie, who sees the wedding as her chance to become a "we." You can find out what happens to Frankie by reading **The Member of the Wedding** by Carson McCullers.

FICTION

A Part of the Family

In Seoul, Korea, there is a season known as *changma*, the rainy season. For eleven-year-old Junehee and her family, the season of *changma* brings more than the usual rainfall—it brings Pyungsoo, a young boy orphaned by a mudslide. When the strange, quiet boy joins her household, Junehee does not welcome him at first. Then, as her parents' marriage begins to disintegrate—in part because of Pyungsoo's arrival—Junehee turns to the friendless boy for comfort. **The Long Season of Rain** by Helen Kim is the story of two "siblings" brought together at first by fate and then by love.

FICTION

Other Worlds

One of H. G. Wells's most inspired creations is a character known as the Time Traveler, the inventor of the Time Machine. This machine propels him from Victorian England thousands of years into the future, where he lands at the heart of a conflict between good and evil. Another of Wells's stories—one about a nightmarish invasion from Mars—is so convincing that it created a panic in America when the actor Orson Welles read it aloud in a radio broadcast in 1938. Take your own journey into worlds beyond with Wells's **The Time Machine** and **The War of the Worlds**.

These titles are available in the HRW Library.

NONFICTION

Writer at Work

In Alice Walker's **In Search of Our Mothers' Gardens** you'll meet the writer—up close and personal. This collection of essays, articles, reviews, and speeches covers a wide range of topics. You'll read moving tributes to famous African American writers such as Langston Hughes and Zora Neale Hurston, and you'll learn about Walker's own writing process as well. The collection also includes an autobiographical piece about the author's childhood injury and one about her experiences as a civil rights activist during the 1960s.

Read On   547

If students enjoyed the themes and topics explored in this collection, you might recommend these titles for independent reading.

Assessment Options

The following projects can help you evaluate and assess your students' outside reading. Videotapes and audiotapes of completed projects may be included in student portfolios.

- **Perform a monologue.** Invite students to write a first-person monologue that might be spoken by one of the characters in the novel they read. The character should introduce himself or herself, describe the conflict he or she faces in the novel, and explain his or her hopes and dreams for the future. Have students perform their monologues, live or on videotape, for the class.

- **Critique the writer's style.** Suggest that students analyze the style of the writer whose book they read. Have them consider sentence types and lengths, whether the writer's diction is formal or informal, and the prevalence of imagery and figurative language in the writer's work. Finally, have students evaluate why they did or did not enjoy the writer's style.

- **Write a response.** Encourage students who read Alice Walker's book to write a response to one of the essays, articles, reviews, or speeches in the collection. First, have students explain the main ideas the author expresses in the work. Then, have them explain why they do or do not agree with the author's opinions.

DIFFERENTIATING INSTRUCTION

Estimated Word Counts and Reading Levels of Read On Books:

Fiction			Non-Fiction		
The Member of the Wedding	↔	70,000	*In Search of Our Mothers' Gardens*	↑	87,800
The Time Machine and					
The War of the Worlds	↔	117,200			
The Long Season of Rain	↓	90,900			

KEY: ↑ *above grade level*   ↔ *at grade level*   ↓ *below grade level*

Analyzing a Short Story

Skills Starter

Motivate. Ask students to think of books they have read that they would recommend to others. Then, ask volunteers to give reasons why they would recommend the book. Point out to students that they have just engaged in a form of literary analysis.

Integrating with Grammar, Usage, and Mechanics

As students start their short story analyses, they may have trouble with capitalization and punctuation. You may want to review Lessons 11–14 in the Language Handbook.

Analyze Literary Elements

To help students analyze the tone—the attitude toward the subject, characters, or readers—of a story, ask these questions:

- What word best describes the author's attitude: sympathy? contempt? friendliness? arrogance? something else?
- What words, phrases, and sentences can you find that clue you in to the author's tone?

Point out that the author's tone can influence mood and theme, and it affects how the reader will respond to the story.

Writing Assignment
Write a response to literature in which you analyze the literary elements in a short story.

Did the short stories you read earlier in this collection—"A Sound of Thunder" and "To Da-Duh, in Memoriam"—make a deep impression on you? Some stories can create a variety of emotions in their readers: tingling excitement, gut-wrenching fear, profound sadness, or exceptional delight. How do authors create such intense feelings in their readers? You can better understand the effects a story causes if you write an **analysis** of it.

Prewriting

Choose a Story

It's Up To You Since you'll be putting a lot of time and thought into your short story analysis, be sure to find a short story that interests you. To find a good short story:

- look for stories by an author whose work you have enjoyed in the past
- ask your friends, parents, or teachers to recommend a short story
- scan short story collections at your school or community library

Analyze Literary Elements

Take Two Begin by reading the story to get an overall impression of it. Then, go back and take a closer look at the literary elements to **grasp the significant ideas** in the story. You are probably familiar with the basic literary elements of character, plot, and setting. To analyze these elements, ask yourself these questions.

- **Character**—What are the major characters like? What motivates them? Do any of them change? If so, how?
- **Plot**—What conflict or problem do the characters face? How is the conflict resolved? Does the resolution make sense?
- **Setting**—Where and when does the story take place? Does the setting affect the story's plot or characters? If so, how?

The story may include additional literary elements such as those listed in the chart on the next page. Read the description of each element, and jot down answers to the questions in the right-hand column as you begin to look deeper into the short story.

SKILLS FOCUS

Writing Skills
Write an analysis of a short story.

COLLECTION 8 RESOURCES: WRITING

Planning
- *One-Stop Planner* CD-ROM with ExamView Test Generator

Differentiating Instruction
- *Workshop Resources: Writing, Listening, and Speaking*
- *Family Involvement Activities in English and Spanish*

- *Supporting Instruction in Spanish*

Writing and Language
- *Workshop Resources: Writing, Listening, and Speaking*
- *Daily Language Activities*
- *Language Handbook Worksheets*

LITERARY ELEMENTS

Description	Analysis Questions
Mood is the dominant feeling created in the story.	• Is the mood tense? hectic? happy and fun? frightening? quiet and calm? • What helps to create the story's mood?
Point of view is the vantage point or angle from which the narrator tells the story.	• Is the narrator of the story a character in the story (first-person point of view), or is he or she outside of the story (third-person point of view)? • How does the point of view affect your understanding of the story?
Stylistic devices are the language techniques the author uses to create certain effects.	• How does the author's word choice, or **diction,** influence the story's meaning? • What **metaphors, similes,** or examples of **personification** does the author use to prompt you to look at things differently?
Symbolism is the use of an object, person, or event to represent something beyond itself.	• Is a specific object closely related to a character or event? • Does one character or one event represent an abstract idea, such as bravery, greed, or education?
Theme is the main idea the story reveals or suggests about life or human nature.	• What common life experience or problem does the story examine? • How do the other elements in the story work together to reveal the theme?

Write a Thesis Statement

Focus In Select the element you think has the most influence on the story. This will be the **focus element** of your analysis. To do this, ask yourself, "Why do I like this story?" and "What makes this story successful?" For example, a student analyzing "The Scarlet Ibis" (page 343) decided that mood is the element that gives that story its impact.

Next, think about what the author does to create the focus element or make it effective. You may notice that other elements work together to develop the focus element. The student writing about "The Scarlet Ibis" decided that diction, point of view, and symbolism all contribute to the mood of the story. He will develop a **key point,** or main idea, about each of these elements to support his discussion of mood.

Finally, write a **thesis statement** that identifies both the focus element and the key points about it. The student wrote the following draft of a thesis statement for his analysis of "The Scarlet Ibis."

> In "The Scarlet Ibis," James Hurst uses diction, point of view, and symbolism to create a mood of tragedy, sadness, and loss.

TIP You may find that two or more elements contribute equally to the story's impact. If so, try to focus your essay equally on each element. Be sure you have enough time and space to create an in-depth analysis of each element.

SKILLS FOCUS

Writing Skills
Establish a thesis statement.

MODELING AND DEMONSTRATION

Literary Elements

Model for students the process of analyzing literary elements with these steps:

1. Pick a story familiar to students.
2. Complete on the chalkboard a chart based on the elements in the **Literary Elements** chart.
3. Answer the questions for each element as it relates to the story you have selected.

Then, ask for a volunteer to demonstrate understanding by answering one or two questions about his or her story.

RETEACHING

Write a Thesis Statement

Provide these steps to help students having difficulty compose thesis statements for their analyses:

1. Compare your first impression of the story with your chart of its literary elements. Your most interesting answers to the analysis questions will likely support your overall reaction to the story.
2. Decide what you want to say about the element or elements you find most important. Your thoughts about these elements will be your main idea, or thesis.
3. Form your thesis statement by joining the literary element or elements with your main idea about them.

Point out to students that a literary analysis has many possible thesis statements. Here is a possible alternative to the one given for "The Scarlet Ibis": "Through vivid imagery and enduring symbolism James Hurst's 'The Scarlet Ibis' presents the reader with an unforgettable human portrait of innocence lost."

Assessment

- *Holt Assessment: Writing, Listening, and Speaking*
- *One-Stop Planner* CD-ROM with ExamView Test Generator
- *Holt Online Assessment*
- *Holt Online Essay Scoring*

Internet

- go.hrw.com (Keyword: LE5 9-8)
- *Elements of Literature Online*

DIFFERENTIATING INSTRUCTION

Learners Having Difficulty

If students are having trouble finding support, point out that the key points they make should relate directly to their theses. To determine their key points, students can use these tips:

- To discover the most effective key points, ask questions such as these about the thesis: How should the analysis show that the thesis is correct? Where in the story can such support be found?

- Consider how the literary elements relate to the thesis. For example, a story usually shows a change in a character or situation. How does the change relate to the thesis?

CRITICAL THINKING

To ensure that students have used evidence that is both relevant and sound, suggest that they consider these questions:

- Is each statement supported with at least two pieces of evidence?

- Does the evidence include facts, examples, or direct quotations?

- Does each piece of evidence effectively support the thesis statement?

PRACTICE & APPLY 1

Guided and Independent Practice

Monitor students' progress by quickly checking that each student has chosen a short story, chosen useful focus elements, and developed effective key points. Then, have students complete **Practice and Apply 1** as independent practice.

DO THIS ➡

Support Your Thesis Statement

What's the Point? To support your key points, gather **evidence** by taking notes on details from the short story. Evidence comes in three forms:

- **Direct quotation:** Exact words from the short story, set within quotation marks.

- **Paraphrase:** A restatement of all the author's ideas in your own words.

- **Summary:** A condensed restatement of the author's most important ideas.

It's not enough just to present evidence. **Elaborate** on the evidence you've included by explaining what it means and how it supports your key points. You can use elaboration to clarify and explain any ambiguities, nuances, and complexities you find in the story. **Ambiguities** are words, sentences, or passages that lend themselves to more than one interpretation. **Nuances** are changes in tone or meaning. **Complexities** result when a story is rich in meaning but difficult to interpret. (The Writer's Model on page 551 contains examples of a nuance and a complexity.)

Here is how one student supported a key point with evidence from the story and with elaboration.

Key point	Supporting evidence	Elaboration
The author uses the stylistic device of diction to help create the mood.	The narrator describes the flowers around his childhood home as "rotting brown magnolia petals" and "graveyard flowers."	This description refers to the aspects of nature with words that remind the reader of death. Hurst is creating an atmosphere of approaching tragedy.

Organize Your Analysis

Line It Up Next, you must organize your analysis. One way to organize the information is **chronologically,** in the order that the key points appear in the story. Another way is to arrange the information by **order of importance**—presenting the analysis of the most important point either first, to create a strong first impression, or last, to end your analysis on a strong note. Use order of importance if one key point is clearly more important than the others.

SKILLS FOCUS

Writing Skills
Support the thesis statement. Arrange ideas logically and effectively.

PRACTICE & APPLY 1 Choose a short story and analyze the literary elements in it. Choose a focus element and develop key points about it. Write a thesis, select strong supporting evidence, and organize the ideas for your analysis.

Writing

Analyzing a Short Story

A Writer's Framework

Introduction

- Grab readers' attention by relating an anecdote or by asking a question.
- Identify the story's author and title.
- State your thesis, presenting the focus element and key points.

Body

- Discuss one key point in each paragraph.
- Support each key point with evidence from the text.
- Elaborate by explaining how evidence supports each key point.

Conclusion

- Restate your thesis in a fresh way.
- Summarize your key points.
- End with a thoughtful comment that connects your analysis to real life.

A Writer's Model

Birds of a Feather Fall Together

When you pass an abandoned mansion, do you see a creepy haunted house or an intriguing historical home? Your view of the mansion depends on its atmosphere—the mood surrounding it. The same can be said of a short story—a story's mood influences the reader's feelings about the story itself. In "The Scarlet Ibis," James Hurst uses diction, point of view, and symbolism to create a mood of tragedy, sadness, and loss.

Throughout the story, the author creates the mood through diction, a stylistic device. In the first paragraph, the narrator describes the flowers around his childhood home as "rotting brown magnolia petals" and "graveyard flowers." He describes an abandoned bird's nest as "an empty cradle." Even the scent of the flowers that surround him is described as "speaking softly the names of our dead." This complex description refers to the aspects of nature with words that remind the reader of death. Hurst is creating an atmosphere of approaching tragedy. Because the story revolves around the relationship between the narrator and his frail brother, Doodle, the mood makes the reader worry about Doodle's future.

The point of view from which the story is told also influences its mood. Everything the reader knows about the relationship between the brothers comes directly from the first-person point of view of the

(continued)

INTRODUCTION

Title and author
Thesis statement

BODY
Key point: diction
Direct quotation

Elaboration

Key point: point of view

CORRECTING MISCONCEPTIONS

When striving for an appropriate tone in their papers, students may misuse the formal language of literary analysis. You can use any paragraph of **A Writer's Model** to point out that writing a complex analysis with a formal tone does not require needlessly elevated diction or repetition. Encourage students to incorporate such language into their writing while striving for a similar level of precision and lack of redundancy.

DIFFERENTIATING INSTRUCTION

English-Language Learners

Remind students that they should avoid the words *I, me, my,* and *mine* when writing a literary analysis. They can avoid these words by rewording statements or by using the pronoun *one.* Provide students with these examples and corrections:

- I don't understand the motives of Dr. Frankenstein. [Dr. Frankenstein's motives are unclear.]

- I expected the ending to be happier. [One expects a happier ending.]

PRACTICE & APPLY 2

Guided and Independent Practice

Monitor students' progress by making sure that each student has an outline or set of notes from which to work and has kept organized note cards of direct quotations.

Then, have students complete **Practice and Apply 2** as independent practice.

(continued)

Complexity	
Direct quotation	
Elaboration	
Key point: symbolism	
Nuance	
Paraphrase	
Direct quotation	
Elaboration	
Direct quotation	
CONCLUSION	
Restatement of thesis	
Summary of points	
Final comment	

narrator. The narrator is an older person looking back to his past to tell the story of his brother, for whose death he feels responsible. The narrator confesses both his positive and negative feelings for his brother. In his first description of Doodle, he refers to his brother as "nice crazy, like someone you meet in your dreams" and yet also as "a disappointment." The narrator loves his brother, but is disappointed in him because of his physical disabilities. This mixture of disappointment and love had fueled the narrator's actions towards his brother, and now he feels grief and guilt over the results.

The most direct way readers understand the story's mood is through the symbol of the scarlet ibis. With its arrival the mood in the short story becomes gloomier. A storm has blown the bird out of its natural place into the bleeding tree in the narrator's front yard. His family is fascinated by it until the dying bird falls to the ground, its "long, graceful neck" straightening and its feet curling underneath its body. When Doodle dies a short time later, probably from exhaustion and heart failure after his brother abandons him, his limp neck looks "unusually long and slim," and his legs are "bent sharply at the knees." The blood from Doodle's mouth colors his neck and shirt red like the bird's feathers. The connection between the ibis and Doodle becomes even clearer as the narrator cries over his brother, referring to him as "my fallen scarlet ibis." Doodle, like the bird, is a rare and fragile creature who could not survive the harshness of life. The symbolic relationship between the ibis and Doodle creates sympathy and compassion for the frail boy and helps the reader understand why the narrator suffers grief and guilt over Doodle's death.

In "The Scarlet Ibis," the author uses diction, point of view, and symbolism to create a gloomy, somber mood. Through diction, Hurst gives us an overwhelming sense that something sad is going to happen. Through point of view, we come to understand how the narrator's conflicted feelings about his deceased brother have brought him grief and guilt. Finally, through symbolism, we see the tragic fate of fragile creatures in our harsh world. By presenting this complex relationship, James Hurst helps all readers better explore their own feelings about love and cruelty and about loyalty and loss.

INTERNET
More Writer's Models
Keyword: LE5 9-8

PRACTICE & APPLY 2 Write the first draft of your analysis of the short story you have examined. Use the framework on page 551 and the Writer's Model above as guides.

Revising

Evaluate and Revise Your Draft

Once Is Not Enough Reading over your draft just once is not enough. Carefully read your analysis at least twice. First, evaluate and revise the content and organization of your essay by using the guidelines in the chart below. Then, on your second reading, use the guidelines in the chart on the next page to improve the style of the writing in your analysis.

> **PEER REVIEW**
>
> Exchange your analysis with a peer before you revise. He or she can help you make sure that your key points are adequately supported by direct quotations, paraphrases, and summaries.

▶ **First Reading: Content and Organization** Use the chart below to help you evaluate and revise the content and organization of your short story analysis. Ask yourself the questions in the column to the left. If you need help answering the questions, use the tips in the middle column. If you need to revise, use the techniques in the column to the right.

Rubric: Analyzing a Short Story

Evaluation Questions	▶ Tips	▶ Revision Techniques
❶ Does the introduction grab the reader's attention and name the author and title of the story?	▶ **Put a check mark** by the sentences that capture the reader's interest. **Highlight** the title and the author in the introduction.	▶ **Add** sentences that will capture the reader's interest. **Add** the story's title or the author's name to the introduction.
❷ Does the thesis list the focus element and key points the analysis will discuss?	▶ **Draw a wavy line** under the focus element. **Put a star** beside the key points.	▶ **Add** specific information about the focus element and key points the analysis will cover.
❸ Does each body paragraph discuss one key point?	▶ **Number** each key point. Be sure that each paragraph covers only one key point.	▶ **Rearrange** key points so that only one is discussed in each body paragraph.
❹ Are the key points supported with evidence from the text and with elaboration?	▶ **Underline** the supporting evidence for each key point, and **double underline** the elaboration that explains the evidence.	▶ **Add** evidence to support each key point. **Elaborate** by explaining how evidence supports each key point.
❺ Does the conclusion restate the thesis and summarize the key points? Does it end with a final comment that relates the analysis to real life?	▶ **Highlight** the restated thesis. **Bracket** the summary of the key points, and **double bracket** the final comment.	▶ **Add** a restatement of the thesis and a summary of key points. **Add** a thoughtful final comment that connects the analysis to real life.

Writing Workshop: Analyzing a Short Story   **553**

Second Reading: Style Imagine that "The Scarlet Ibis" had been called "The Pink Ibis." Although both pink and scarlet are shades of red, pink doesn't capture the color of the bird. "Scarlet" better describes the ibis's blood-red color—a color that brings symbolic meaning to the story. As you re-read your analysis and examine your style, check that you have used **appropriate modifiers**—precise adjectives and adverbs that accurately describe what they modify.

Style Guidelines

Evaluation Question	▶ Tip	▶ Revision Technique
● Do all adjectives and adverbs precisely describe the words or word groups they are supposed to modify?	▶ **Circle** all adjectives and adverbs in your analysis.	▶ **Replace** adjectives and adverbs that are inaccurate or weak with precise and accurate ones.

ANALYZING THE REVISION PROCESS
Study these revisions, and answer the questions that follow.

> The connection between the ibis and Doodle becomes even
>
> clearer as the narrator cries over his brother, referring to
>
> him as "my fallen scarlet ibis." Doodle, like the bird, is a rare
>
> *fragile*   *who could not survive the harshness of life.*
> and ~~weak~~ creature‚ The symbolic relationship between the ibis
>
> *frail*
> and Doodle creates sympathy and compassion for the ‚~~weak~~
>
> *and helps the reader understand why the narrator suffers*
> boy‚ *grief and guilt over Doodle's death.*

replace/elaborate

replace

elaborate

Responding to the Revision Process
1. How does replacing *weak* with *fragile* and *frail* change the meaning of this passage?
2. How does the elaboration in this section add to the reader's understanding of the story?

SKILLS FOCUS

Writing Skills
Revise for content and style.

> **PRACTICE & APPLY 3** Use the guidelines on page 553 to help you evaluate and revise the content and organization of the first draft of your analysis. Then, use the style guidelines above for further revisions. Finally, examine the revisions in the paragraph above as a model for your own revisions.

GUIDED PRACTICE

Responding to the Revision Process

Answers
1. The replacement words emphasize the bird's and the boy's uniqueness and beauty, instead of merely underlining the helplessness of both.
2. The elaboration makes a specific point that relates the details directly to the thesis of the essay.

PRACTICE & APPLY 3

Independent Practice
Remind students that when engaging in peer review, they should strive to make their comments constructive. Any criticism should come with a suggestion for change, worded such as, "I wonder if there is a better way to say this," "You might want to…," or "How about changing this to…?" Point out to students that while their peers' suggestions may not always be the perfect solution to a problem, their comments may help determine the nature of a problem the writer did not notice.

Publishing

Proofread and Publish Your Analysis

Look Carefully Before you publish your short story analysis, make sure it is error-free. If you have too many errors in your analysis, your readers may not take your ideas seriously. Read over it several times, looking for mistakes in grammar, usage, and mechanics. To make sure you catch every error, have a classmate proofread your analysis, too.

Show It Off Once you know your analysis is error-free, it's time to share it with its intended audience. Here are a few ways to get your work before the public.

- Form a literary club with your friends. Take turns sharing your literary analyses at your meetings.

- Submit your short story analysis to a Web site dedicated to student publishing. Also, look for online book stores that encourage readers to submit analyses and reviews.

- Compile your class's short story analyses into a booklet. Ask your school librarian to add it to your school library. Also, ask your librarian to index your compilation on the library database as a reference tool for other students.

- Deliver your short story analysis as an oral response to literature. For more on **presenting a literary response,** see page 488.

Reflect on Your Analysis

Thinking Back Take time to think about writing your short story analysis. The questions below can help you think about what you learned as you wrote your literary analysis.

- How did you choose the story you analyzed? Would this process help you choose other stories to read informally? Why or why not?

- What did you find easy or difficult about writing an analysis? Why?

- Did you enjoy the story more or less after you analyzed it in depth? Explain your answer.

PRACTICE & APPLY 4 First, proofread your analysis. Then, consider your publishing options, and follow through on the one you think is most appropriate. Finally, reflect upon what you have learned in this workshop by answering the questions above.

TIP Proofreading will help ensure that your essay follows the **conventions** of standard American English. For example, you most likely used pronouns at times to stand in for characters' names. Your reader may get confused if your pronouns' antecedents are not clear. Correct all inexact pronoun references in your analysis. For more on **clear pronoun reference,** see Clear Pronoun Reference, 4i, in the Language Handbook.

SKILLS FOCUS

Writing Skills
Proofread, especially for clear pronoun reference.

SKILLS FOCUS, pp. 556–557

Grade-Level Skills

■ **Literary Skills**
Evaluate the aesthetic qualities of style, including the effect of diction, figurative language, tone, and mood.

INTRODUCING THE SKILLS REVIEW

Use this review to assess students' grasp of the skills taught in this collection.

DIRECT TEACHING

A Literary Focus

? Diction. What verbs does the author use to describe what Salvador does each morning? [*shakes, ties, combs, feeds*] What do these verbs tell you about Salvador? [He is responsible for getting his brothers ready for school each morning. He is constantly busy helping his family.]

B Literary Focus

? Style. How many sentences does the author use in this paragraph? [one complete sentence, two that are incomplete] What figurative language does she use to describe Salvador's feelings? ["inside that body too small to contain the hundred balloons of happiness, the single guitar of grief"] What imagery does she use to help you visualize Salvador and his brothers running across the schoolyard? ["scuttles off," "dodging," "elbows and wrists crisscrossing," "the several shoes running," "Grows small and smaller," "dissolves," "flutters."]

Test-Taking Tips

For more instruction on how to answer multiple-choice items, refer students to **Test Smarts**.

Test Practice

Literary Criticism: Evaluating Style

DIRECTIONS: Read the following story. Then, read and respond to the questions that follow.

Salvador Late or Early

Sandra Cisneros

A Salvador with eyes the color of caterpillar, Salvador of the crooked hair and crooked teeth, Salvador whose name the teacher cannot remember, is a boy who is no one's friend, runs along somewhere in that vague direction where homes are the color of bad weather, lives behind a raw wood doorway, shakes the sleepy brothers awake, ties their shoes, combs their hair with water, feeds them milk and cornflakes from a tin cup in the dim dark of the morning.

Salvador, late or early, sooner or later arrives with the string of younger brothers ready. Helps his mama, who is busy with the business of the baby. Tugs the arms of Cecilio, Arturito, makes them hurry, because today, like yesterday, Arturito has dropped the cigar box of crayons, has let go the hundred little fingers of red, green, yellow, blue, and nub of black sticks that tumble and spill over and beyond the asphalt puddles until the crossing-guard lady holds back the blur of traffic for Salvador to collect them again.

B Salvador inside that wrinkled shirt, inside the throat that must clear itself and apologize each time it speaks, inside that forty-pound body of boy with its geography of scars, its history of hurt, limbs stuffed with feathers and rags, in what part of the eyes, in what part of the heart, in that cage of the chest where something throbs with both fists and knows only what Salvador knows, inside that body too small to contain the hundred balloons of happiness, the single guitar of grief, is a boy like any other disappearing out the door, beside the schoolyard gate, where he has told his brothers they must wait. Collects the hands of Cecilio and Arturito, scuttles off dodging the many schoolyard colors, the elbows and wrists crisscrossing, the several shoes running. Grows small and smaller to the eye, dissolves into the bright horizon, flutters in the air before disappearing like a memory of kites.

SKILLS FOCUS

Pages 556–557 cover
Literary Skills
Evaluate elements of style, including diction, figurative language, tone, and mood.

READING MINI-LESSON

Reviewing Word-Attack Skills
Display these sets of words. Have students identify the word in which the underlined letter is silent.

1. de<u>b</u>it   de<u>b</u>tor   [debtor]
2. be<u>n</u>ign   be<u>g</u>uile   [benign]
3. num<u>b</u>ness   num<u>b</u>erless   [numbness]
4. cam<u>p</u>aign   pra<u>g</u>matic   [campaign]
5. thum<u>b</u>   tum<u>b</u>ler   [thumb]
6. so<u>v</u>ereign   in<u>d</u>ignant   [sovereign]

Display these words and have volunteers divide each one into its component parts.

7. unconditionally
8. preexistence
9. disengagement
10. cosponsorship
11. misinformation
12. disenchantment

[un/condition/al/ly; pre/exist/ence; dis/engage/ment; co/sponsor/ship/; mis/in/form/ation; dis/en/chant/ment]

Answers and Model Rationales

1. **C** Only C fits Salvador's character; he is too busy taking care of his brothers to care about his appearance.

2. **G** Verbs such as *shakes, ties, combs,* and *feeds* describe a boy busy helping his family. He knows what to do and does everything promptly, so F is wrong. His throat must "apologize each time it speaks," so H is wrong. He doesn't seem to have opportunities, so J is wrong.

3. **C** Words and phrases such as "Grows small and smaller to the eye," reinforce earlier suggestions that Salvador is easily forgotten.

4. **F** The phrases "where homes are the color of bad weather" and "the dim dark of the morning" create a gloomy mood.

5. **B** Most important to the story is the idea that no one notices Salvador or his actions.

6. **F** The author clearly feels sympathy for Salvador's hard life.

7. **D** As an example, the first paragraph of the story is one long sentence that is full of visual imagery. The author's ideas are clearly expressed and consistent throughout, so A is incorrect. There is no dialogue, so B is incorrect. The author uses repetition, but not irony, so C is incorrect.

Constructed Response

8. The author describes Salvador as "a boy who is no one's friend," "with the string of younger brothers," "inside that wrinkled shirt," "a boy like any other disappearing out the door," and "small and smaller to the eye." I would describe Salvador as a boy who is burdened with the responsibilities of an adult.

---

1. Cisneros's **diction** in the phrase "Salvador inside that wrinkled shirt" helps you understand that Salvador is —
   A wearing someone else's clothes
   B too big for his shirt
   C too busy to care about his appearance
   D irresponsible and undependable

2. One characteristic of Cisneros's **diction** in this piece is her use of verbs to describe Salvador. What do these verbs tell you about his **character**?
   F He is indecisive.
   G He is seldom at rest.
   H He is confident.
   J He takes advantage of opportunities.

3. Cisneros uses a **simile** comparing Salvador to "a memory of kites" to show that he —
   A is not forgotten
   B is lively and cheerful
   C leaves a fleeting impression
   D moves swiftly

4. Which word *best* describes the **mood** Cisneros creates through her description of the homes and the morning in the first paragraph?
   F gloomy
   G suspenseful
   H hopeful
   J terrifying

5. Which of the following is the *best* expression of the selection's **theme**?
   A Children like Salvador will eventually triumph over the many obstacles in their lives and find happiness.
   B There are children like Salvador whose difficult life and small acts of courage go almost unnoticed.
   C In many families the oldest child often takes responsibility for younger siblings.
   D Although children may seem different on the outside, they are actually similar.

6. Which word *best* describes the **tone** the author creates through her description of Salvador?
   F sympathetic
   G mocking
   H bitter
   J objective

7. Cisneros's **style** in this selection is characterized by her use of —
   A ambiguity and contradiction
   B dialogue and symbolism
   C repetition and irony
   D imagery and long sentences

Constructed Response

8. List five ways that the author describes Salvador. Then, write down one way that you would describe him.

Using Academic Language

Review of Literary Terms
Have students show their grasp of style by citing passages from the collection that illustrate the meanings of the following terms. **Style** (pp. 496, 525); **Diction** (pp. 496, 525, 541); **Sentence structure** (p. 525); **Figures of speech** (pp. 496, 525); **Tone** (pp. 497, 541); **Mood** (p. 497); **Connotations** (p. 525); **Imagery** (p. 541).

Review of Informational Terms
Ask students to use these terms to explain how to evaluate the credibility of an author's argument.
Claim (p. 516); **Logical appeals** (p. 516); **Evidence** (p. 516); **Facts** (p. 516); **Credibility** (p. 516); **Emotional appeals** (p. 516); **Intent** (p. 516).

Collection 8: Skills Review

Vocabulary Skills

Context Clues

Modeling. Model the thoughts of a good reader answering item 1. Say, "Travis warns Eckels that he might *annihilate* a 'whole race of people.' Then he explains the consequences of *killing* a mouse: a billion people might not exist. These clues suggest that *annihilate* means *destroy*, option B. Travis is unlikely to 'meet,' 'frighten,' or 'discourage' an entire race."

Answers and Model Rationales

1. **B** See rationale above.
2. **F** Since there are dinosaurs and no people, a *primeval* world must be ancient and *primitive*. A world without people would not be *familiar* or necessarily *better* (options G and H), and the dinosaur has not been *forgotten* (J).
3. **B** The "widespread destruction and loss of life" are strong clues that *catastrophic* means *disastrous*. The effects are explained, so *mysterious* (A) is wrong. The effects are obviously not *immediate* (C), and there is no mention of *preventing* global warming (D).
4. **J** "We do not know" is a strong clue that *ignorance* means "lack of knowledge." None of the other choices fits with the statement.
5. **C** The statement that "Da-duh commands respect" implies that she is *impressive*. A person is not necessarily respected for being *frail, motherly,* or *sensitive*, so A, B, and D are incorrect.
6. **J** The words *plain* and *simple* hint that *austere* means *severe*. Plain, simple clothes are not *elegant* (F) and need not be *ugly* (H), and *shabby* clothes (G) do not suit a proud personality.

Collection 8: Skills Review

Vocabulary Skills

 **Test Practice**

Context Clues

DIRECTIONS: Use the context clues in the following passages for help identifying the meaning of the underlined Vocabulary words.

1. In "A Sound of Thunder," Travis warns Eckels to stay on the path so that he doesn't accidentally annihilate a whole race of people. By killing just one mouse, Eckels could prevent the birth of a billion people.

   In this passage, *annihilate* means —

   A meet
   B destroy
   C frighten
   D discourage

2. In "A Sound of Thunder," Eckels travels to the past and enters a primeval world. Dinosaurs rule the earth, and there is no evidence of human civilization.

   In this passage, *primeval* means —

   F primitive
   G better
   H familiar
   J forgotten

3. In "Rising Tides," Bob Herbert argues that the effects of global warming could be catastrophic. As the world grows warmer and the oceans rise, there could be widespread destruction and loss of life.

   In this passage, *catastrophic* means —

   A mysterious
   B disastrous
   C immediate
   D prevented

4. In "An Arctic Floe of Climate Questions," Robert Cooke discusses our ignorance about climate changes. We do not know if warmer temperatures, which seem unusual to us now, are actually typical of long-term weather patterns.

   In this passage, *ignorance* means —

   F warnings
   G neglect
   H desire to prevent
   J lack of knowledge

5. In "To Da-duh, in Memoriam," Da-duh is a formidable woman. Her adult daughter greets her like an obedient child, for Da-duh commands respect from everyone.

   In this passage, *formidable* means —

   A frail
   B motherly
   C impressive
   D sensitive

6. In "To Da-duh, in Memoriam," Da-duh dresses in an austere manner. Her plain, simple clothes suit her strong, proud personality and her old-fashioned way of life.

   In this passage, *austere* means —

   F elegant
   G shabby
   H ugly
   J severe

SKILLS FOCUS

Vocabulary Skills
Use context clues to understand the meanings of words.

Vocabulary Review

Use this activity to assess whether students have retained the collection Vocabulary. Ask students to choose the word from the box that fits the context of each sentence.

| protracted | resilient | truculent |
| ominous | deficient | |

1. Fiercely competitive, the boxers faced each other in _____ poses. [truculent]

2. Though old, the ball was _____, quickly bouncing back. [resilient]

3. They lost to the other team, because their passing skills were _____. [deficient]

4. Dark and _____, the clouds threatened to halt our softball game. [ominous]

5. The battle for first place was _____ as the game went into extra innings. [protracted]

Test Practice

DIRECTIONS: Read the following paragraph from a draft of a student's analysis of a short story. Then, answer the questions below it.

(1) In "A Sound of Thunder," Ray Bradbury uses similes to create a frightening tone that alerts readers to the dangers of toying with nature. (2) After traveling back in time for a prehistoric safari, a group of silly men shoots a Tyrannosaurus rex. (3) The dinosaur falls "[l]ike a stone idol," and the men stare in awe "like [they were] standing by a wrecked locomotive." (4) Bradbury also uses diction in his short story. (5) When Travis describes the consequences of killing animals before their time, he says, "Step on a mouse, and you leave your print, like a Grand Canyon, across Eternity."

1. To support the idea that Bradbury's use of similes creates a frightening tone, the student could also
   A explain the definition of tone
   B provide a paraphrase of another passage that includes a simile
   C give examples of various stylistic devices that appear in the story
   D tell another one of Bradbury's stories

2. Which sentence could be added to elaborate on the direct quotations in sentence 3?
   F The men are uncaring when they kill the dinosaur, and hunting only makes them want to kill even bigger animals.
   G The similes show that nature is more powerful than humans.
   H These similes give the impression that the death of the dinosaur has a greater impact than expected.
   J The men have to be careful to stay on the anti-gravity path so that they do not disturb anything from the past.

3. Which of the following words would be the best replacement for the weak modifier *silly* in sentence 2?
   A foolish   C angry
   B stupid   D adventuresome

4. To demonstrate an understanding of the short story, the writer could add which of the following sentences as a conclusion?
   F If the humans in this story hadn't been so careless, everything would have worked out fine.
   G The similes demonstrate humans' dangerous potential to alter the past, and worse, the future.
   H Greed ultimately costs one safari hunter his life.
   J The stylistic devices create a suspenseful mood throughout the story.

5. Which sentence should be moved to another paragraph in order to improve the passage's organization?
   A 1   C 4
   B 3   D 5

SKILLS FOCUS

Writing Skills
Write an analysis of a short story.

1. B
2. H
3. A
4. G
5. C

APPLICATION

Web Writing

Have interested students start their own literary magazine on the World Wide Web. Students can write, edit, and publish literary analyses, poetry, short stories, and essays. Submissions could be solicited from high school students from around the country for future issues. (Optionally, students may send out issues to "subscribers" in e-mail form.) *Please be aware that Internet resources are sometimes public forums, and their content can be unpredictable.*

EXTENSION

Comparison Charts

The German "Aschenputtel," the Chinese "Yeh-Shen," and the English "Cinderella" are different versions of the same story. Have students read these stories or several versions of another story. Then, for homework have students create charts comparing the stories' characters, settings, plots, mood, points of view, use of stylistic devices and symbolism, themes, and tone.

Homework

RESOURCES: WRITING

Assessment
■ *One-Stop Planner* CD-ROM with ExamView Test Generator
■ *Holt Assessment: Writing, Listening, and Speaking*

Internet
■ *Holt Online Assessment*
■ *Holt Online Essay Scoring*

Collection 9

Literary Criticism

Biographical and Historical Approach

Informational Reading Focus: Using Primary and Secondary Sources

About Collection 9

In Collection 9, students will master the following skills:

- **Literary Skills:** Analyze a literary work, using biographical and historical approaches.
- **Reading Skills:** Summarize a story; analyze primary and secondary sources; and make inferences.
- **Vocabulary Skills:** Complete word analogies; create semantic maps; understand jargon, or technical vocabulary; and identify synonyms.
- **Writing Skills:** Develop, write, and revise a research paper.
- **Listening and Speaking Skills:** Present a research report.

Informational Text

Each collection of *Elements of Literature* provides a variety of informational texts related to the literature selections by theme or topic.

Minimum Course of Study

Most skills can be taught with a minimum number of selections and features. In the chart to the right, lessons highlighted in green constitute the minimum course of study that provides coverage of the skills taught in Collection 9.

Selection ▪ Feature	Literary Skills
Elements of Literature: Literary Roots *by* Kylene Beers	• Understand biographical and historical approaches to literary works
American History *by* Judith Ortiz Cofer ↔ *at grade level*	• Analyze a literary work, using biographical and historical approaches
Informational Text: • A Warm, Clear Day in Dallas • Address to Congress, November 27, 1963 • Students React to President Kennedy's Death *by* Marta Randall; Lyndon B. Johnson ↔ *at grade level*	
Beware of the Dog *by* Roald Dahl ↔ *at grade level*	• Analyze historical setting
Writing Workshop: *Writing a Research Paper*	
Listening and Speaking Workshop: *Presenting Research*	
Skills Review: *Informational Reading Skills* *Vocabulary Skills* *Writing Skills*	

Resource Manager
(pp. 560C–560D)

Lesson and workshop resources are referenced in the Resource Manager on the pages that follow. These resources can be used to reinforce the skills taught in Collection 9, remediate students who are having difficulty, and provide supporting activities for English-language learners.

Reading Skills	Vocabulary Skills	Writing ▪ Grammar and Language ▪ Listening and Speaking Skills
• Summarize a story	• Complete word analogies	• Write an explanatory paragraph • Understand and use adverb clauses
• Analyze primary and secondary sources	• Clarify word meanings	
• Make inferences	• Create semantic maps • Understand jargon, or technical vocabulary	• Write a research paper
		• Write a research paper
		• Present a research report
• Analyze primary and secondary sources	• Identify synonyms	• Write a research paper

Resource Manager

Selection ■ Feature	Planning	Differentiating Instruction Lesson Plans with ELL Strategies and Practice	Reading ■ Vocabulary
Elements of Literature: Literary Roots *by* Kylene Beers		• Family Involvement Activities in English and Spanish, p. 11	
American History *by* Judith Ortiz Cofer **Informational Text:** • A Warm, Clear Day in Dallas • Address to Congress, November 27, 1963 • Students React to President Kennedy's Death *by* Marta Randall; Lyndon B. Johnson	• One-Stop Planner with ExamView Test Generator	• The Holt Reader, pp. 252–265 • Holt Adapted Reader • Holt Reading Solutions, pp. 283–294 • Supporting Instruction in Spanish, pp. 40–41 • Audio CD Library, disc 15 • Audio CD Library, Selections and Summaries in Spanish	• The Holt Reader • Holt Adapted Reader • Holt Reading Solutions • Vocabulary Development, pp. 40, 42 • PowerNotes: Summarizing a Story
Beware of the Dog *by* Roald Dahl	• One-Stop Planner with ExamView Test Generator	• Holt Reading Solutions, pp. 295–300 • Supporting Instruction in Spanish, p. 42 • Audio CD Library, disc 16 • Audio CD Library, Selections and Summaries in Spanish	• Holt Reading Solutions • Vocabulary Development, p. 43
Writing Workshop: *Writing a Research Paper*	• One-Stop Planner with ExamView Test Generator	• Workshop Resources: Writing, Listening, and Speaking, pp. 92–101 • Family Involvement Activities in English and Spanish, pp. 23–24 • Supporting Instruction in Spanish, p. 73	
Listening and Speaking Workshop: *Presenting Research*	• One-Stop Planner with ExamView Test Generator	• Workshop Resources: Writing, Listening, and Speaking, pp. 102–107 • Supporting Instruction in Spanish	
Skills Review: *Informational Reading Skills Vocabulary Skills Writing Skills*			

The Holt Reader

The Holt Reader is a consumable paperback book which can be used alone or to accompany *Elements of Literature*. It offers guided support throughout the reading process and encourages students to become active readers by circling, underlining, questioning, and jotting down responses as they read. *The Holt Reader* works well for homework, students who have missed class, additional instructional time, reteaching, and remediation.

Holt Reading Solutions (HRS)

Holt Reading Solutions pulls together reading resources in the *Elements of Literature* program to create a powerful tool for intervention and whole-class instruction. *HRS* includes diagnostic assessment tools, lesson plans for English-language learners and special education students, adaptations of selected reading selections, vocabulary and comprehension worksheets, information on phonics and decoding, and additional instruction and practice in remedial reading skills.

Writing ▪ Grammar and Language ▪ Listening and Speaking	Assessment
• Daily Language Activities • Language Handbook Worksheets, p. 77	• Holt Assessment: Literature, Reading, and Vocabulary • Holt Online Assessment • One-Stop Planner with ExamView Test Generator
• Daily Language Activities	• Holt Assessment: Literature, Reading, and Vocabulary • Holt Online Assessment • One-Stop Planner with ExamView Test Generator
• Daily Language Activities • Workshop Resources: Writing, Listening, and Speaking, pp. 92–101	• Holt Assessment: Writing, Listening, and Speaking • Holt Online Assessment • One-Stop Planner with ExamView Test Generator
• Workshop Resources: Writing, Listening, and Speaking, pp. 102–107	• Holt Assessment: Writing, Listening, and Speaking • One-Stop Planner with ExamView Test Generator
	• Holt Assessment: Writing, Listening, and Speaking • One-Stop Planner with ExamView Test Generator

Technology

INTERNET

- go.hrw.com
- Holt Online Assessment
- Holt Online Essay Scoring
- Elements of Literature Online

MEDIA

- One-Stop Planner with ExamView Test Generator
- PowerNotes
- Audio CD Library, discs 15 and 16
- Audio CD Library, Selections and Summaries in Spanish
- Visual Connections Videocassette Program, Segment 10
- Fine Art Transparencies, 14 and 15

 Transparency   Video

 CD-ROM   Audio CD

One-Stop Planner with ExamView Test Generator

The *One-Stop Planner* CD-ROM contains electronic versions of print-based teaching resources, clips from the video program, and valuable assessment tools. The *One-Stop Planner* resources are presented in easy-to-follow, point-and-click menu formats. To preview resources or print out worksheets and tests, you simply make a selection and click.

 One-Stop Planner CD-ROM

Collection 9

Grade-Level Skills

■ **Literary Skills**

Analyze the way a work of literature relates to the themes and issues of its historical period. (Historical approach)

■ **Reading Skills**

Analyze and elaborate on ideas presented in primary or secondary sources.

INTRODUCING THE COLLECTION

The selections in this collection all serve to remind readers of the importance of a work's historical setting—that is, its time and place.

Several of the works pivot around a single historical moment in American history, the death of President John F. Kennedy. This event seemed to mark the end of one era, the post–World War II boom, and usher in the turbulence of the 1960s. Students will experience this period in fiction, in Judith Ortiz Cofer's "American History," and in a variety of informational materials that include primary- and secondary-source documents.

Students will also explore two works that center on British fighter pilots in World War II. In the suspenseful short story "Beware of the Dog," Roald Dahl draws on his wartime experience as a fighter pilot. The other work is a "you are there" report by the legendary war correspondent Ernie Pyle.

The collection culminates with an opportunity for students to write a research paper in which they present documented evidence that supports a thesis and adapt their report to deliver in an oral presentation.

COLLECTION 9 RESOURCES: READING

Planning

■ *One-Stop Planner* CD-ROM with ExamView Test Generator

Differentiating Instruction

■ *Holt Reading Solutions*

■ *The Holt Reader*

■ *Holt Adapted Reader*

■ *Family Involvement Activities in English and Spanish*

■ *Supporting Instruction in Spanish*

Vocabulary

■ *Vocabulary Development*

Grammar and Language

■ *Language Handbook Worksheets*

■ *Daily Language Activities*

Collection 9

LITERARY CRITICISM

BIOGRAPHICAL AND HISTORICAL APPROACH

INFORMATIONAL READING FOCUS

USING PRIMARY AND SECONDARY SOURCES

There is no book
which is not of its own time....

—Jorge Luis Borges

The Bitter Nest, Part II: The Harlem Renaissance Party (1988) by Faith Ringgold.
Acrylic on canvas with printed, dyed, and pieced fabric (94″ × 83″).
Smithsonian American Art Museum, Washington, D.C.

INTERNET
Collection Resources
Keyword: LE5 9-9

561

THE QUOTATION

Argentine poet and author Jorge Luis Borges (1899–1986) was known for his short stories, which often resembled imaginative metaphysical puzzles transforming time and space. Ask students to comment on the meaning of Borges's statement. [Possible response: We cannot separate literature from its historical and social contexts.]

VIEWING THE ART

As an African American woman, **Faith Ringgold** (1930–   ) adopted quilts as her medium because her ancestors had created quilts that she feels have largely been ignored as a type of art. This quilt is part of a five-part series. The story in these quilts traces the life of a fictitious mother. Set in the 1920s, the scene depicted shows the mother entertaining W.E.B. DuBois, Langston Hughes, Aaron Douglass, Zora Neale Hurston, Florence Mills and other important writers and artists of the Harlem Renaissance.

Activity. Which character stands out most in Ringgold's quilt? Why? [The woman in the lower right stands out from the rest, as she is dancing and wears a colorful dress. She is the central character of the series.]

Assessment
- Holt Assessment: Literature, Reading, and Vocabulary
- One-Stop Planner CD-ROM with ExamView Test Generator
- Holt Online Assessment

Internet
- go.hrw.com (Keyword: LE5 9-9)

- Elements of Literature Online

Media
- Audio CD Library
- Audio CD Library, Selections and Summaries in Spanish
- Fine Art Transparencies
- Visual Connections Videocassette Program
- PowerNotes

Grade-Level Skills

■ **Literary Skills**

Analyze the way a work of literature relates to the themes and issues of its historical period. (Historical approach)

Review Skills

■ **Literary Skills**

Analyze how a literary work reflects the attitudes and beliefs of its author. (Biographical approach)

Elements of Literature: Literary Roots

To help students focus on the idea of historical setting, ask them to think about how a movie is influenced by the time and place in which it is set. Invite students to choose a movie with a historical setting that most of them have seen, and have them discuss questions like these:

• What historical events of the period are reflected in the movie?

• What topics or issues of the times influence the plot or the characters?

• How would the movie be different if it were set at a different time or place?

Tell students that as they read this essay, they will explore similar kinds of questions in regard to literature.

Literary Roots *by* Kylene Beers
THE WRITER'S LIFE AND TIMES

Once upon a time not too long ago, a hard drive meant a long trip in a car with too many children and not enough air conditioning. A mouse scared you, and a desktop was the top of your desk. You needed waves to surf, a speedy car to be an instant messenger, and a pencil to draw. As times change, our world and the language we use to describe it change too.

When and Where Are Important

Without doubt, our **historical setting**—the time and the place—affects our language and our vision of the world. Historical setting also has an impact on the way people write and what they write about. Read the following few lines:

> That man over there say
>   a woman needs to be helped into carriages
> and lifted over ditches
>   and to have the best place everywhere.
> Nobody ever helped me into carriages
>   or over mud puddles
>   or gives me a best place....
>   —from "Ain't I a Woman?"
>   Sojourner Truth

Pause now, and ask yourself, "Who are the people in this text? What's the situation? Is the speaker male or female? angry or happy? frustrated or content? Why is the speaker saying this?"

Now here's a little historical background: This is the first part of a speech given at a women's rights convention in Akron, Ohio, in 1851. Unfortunately, there is no exact copy of the speech in existence today. It has been adapted here in the form

of a poem. The speaker is a woman. She is responding to other speakers—all men—who are explaining why women shouldn't have the same rights as men.

Read the lines again, and ask yourself more questions: "What do the details about how a woman should be treated ('helped into carriages and lifted over ditches') tell me? What might a man say today about how to treat a woman?" Understanding the historical setting of this speech helps us grasp the issues that were important at the time it was given.

The Writer's Life Experience Is Important

Now let's add another dimension—a **biographical** one—to our discussion by focusing on the author, Sojourner Truth. Not only was Sojourner Truth a woman, but she was also an African American woman. Think about the time—1851. At that time in America, most African Americans were held as slaves. Sojourner Truth, however, had gained her freedom and changed her name. The word *sojourner* means "traveler; person on a journey." Suddenly the speaker's name, meaning "traveler on a journey toward truth," adds to what we know about her.

Read the text one more time, and answer those original questions again:

1. Who are the people in this text?
2. What's the situation?
3. Is the speaker male or female? angry or happy? frustrated or content?
4. Why is the speaker saying this?

SKILLS FOCUS

Literary Skills Understand biographical and historical approaches to literary works.

562　Collection 9　Biographical and Historical Approach • Using Primary and Secondary Sources

---

DIFFERENTIATING INSTRUCTION

Learners Having Difficulty

Have students read the essay in small groups. After they have read through the section titled "The Writer's Life Experience Is Important," ask them to pause and go back through the essay to identify the passages containing the answers to the four questions.

Remind students that this kind of information helps readers to place a text in its proper context. Help them recognize that understanding the historical setting and something about the writer's life can make the text easier to understand.

Advanced Learners

Acceleration. Use the following activity to help advanced students evaluate the philosophical, political, religious, ethical, and social influences of a historical period.

Activity. Have students work in small groups to discuss the big political and social

You'll probably find that your answers, now that you know the historical setting and some biographical information about the author, have a fuller meaning.

Put It All Together

Read more of what Sojourner Truth said:

Look at me
Look at my arm!
I have plowed and planted
and gathered into barns
and no man could head me. . . .
And ain't I a woman? . . .
that little man in black there say
a woman can't have as much rights as
a man
cause Christ wasn't a woman
Where did your Christ come from?
From God and a woman!
Man had nothing to do with him!
If the first woman God ever made
was strong enough to turn the world
upside down, all alone
together women ought to be able to
turn it
rightside up again.

We can see the issue of women's rights emerging in this part of the speech as well. Look carefully at the phrase "that little man in black there," above. Who is this man? Look at his argument against women having the same rights as men. He's offering a religious justification for his views. Is the "man in black" a clergyman? Again, understanding the historical context helps us see an issue of the time—the conflict between men and women and the use of religious justifications for some laws that gave men more rights than women. Sojourner Truth also discusses her own experience in this

speech. Understanding a writer's life, including his or her attitudes, heritage, and traditions, adds meaning to what we are reading.

Don't Jump to Conclusions

Remember, however, that an author's life is not always mirrored in a text. Ray Bradbury, for example, has written some famous stories about Mars, but Bradbury is from Waukegan, Illinois, and he is certainly not a Martian. However, a close look at Bradbury's work shows concern for some issues specific to our time, such as the conflict between personal freedom and technology.

Practice

Working with a partner or in a small group, make a list of some short stories or novels you've read that have a **historical setting.** Then, jot down notes about each work, using a chart like the one below. Be sure to compare your findings with those of your classmates.

Title of story or novel:
When was the work written?
What is the writer's background?
What issues of the writer's time are reflected in the work?

Practice

Charts will vary. Here is a possible chart for the story "The Necklace" by Guy de Maupassant:

- *Title of story or novel*—"The Necklace"
- *When was the work written?*—in the late nineteenth century
- *What is the writer's background?*—Maupassant was a young upper-class Frenchman who was mentored by the famous French novelist Gustave Flaubert. Maupassant achieved great success with his writing, especially his short stories.
- *What issues of the writer's time are reflected in the work?*—"The Necklace" reflects the great division between social classes and the limited employment opportunities for women. For example, the main character, Mme. Loisel, is smart and ambitious, but society keeps people like her from advancing to a higher place in life and does not allow such a woman to have a successful career.

Apply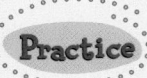

Suggest that as students study this collection, they think about its ideas in relation to media that they explore outside class. Students should consider the historical setting of each work they read, watch, and listen to. Have them keep a running log of how the historical setting affects both the media they are exposed to and their reactions to it. Invite students to share the information in their logs as they complete their work for the collection.

ideas present in the novels or stories that they identify in the Practice activity. For instance, if the main character is a woman, have students summarize a woman's position in society at the time. Could she vote? Did women hold important jobs? Also, have them discuss the big political issues, such as slavery or war, that were important during the time.

Grade-Level Skills

■ **Literary Skills**
Analyze the way a work of literature relates to the themes and issues of its historical period. (Historical approach)

■ **Reading Skills**
Summarize a story.

Summary ⟷ *at grade level*

The story's first-person narrator, Elena, is a Puerto Rican girl in the ninth grade who lives with her family in an apartment building in Paterson, New Jersey. She develops a crush on a blond-haired boy named Eugene, who lives in a house next door. On the day President John F. Kennedy is assassinated, her mother is grieving, but Elena insists on leaving their apartment in order to go to Eugene's house to study for an American history test. Elena is turned away by Eugene's mother, who says she does not want her son to become close to anyone in the neighborhood. Later that evening, Elena tries to summon up grief for the dead president, but her tears are for herself and the loss of her friend. The story ends without resolving the conflict between Elena's personal feelings and what she thinks she should feel about the assassination. Elena discovers that prejudice and personal loss are not put "on hold" even when the country seems united in a great public loss.

PRETEACHING

Skills Starter

Build background. The *Visual Connections* segment "A Shared Memory" provides historical background for the story, as it reviews the events surrounding the assassination of President John F. Kennedy. Play this segment for students before they read the story.

Before You Read

American History

Make the Connection

Quickwrite ✏️
List moments in your life that you'll always remember. Your list might include events that have historical significance as well as personal importance. Jot down notes explaining why each event is memorable.

Literary Focus

Biographical and Historical Approach: The Roots of Literature
Where do writers get ideas for their works? Sometimes they turn to their own lives because they want to share an insight they've gained. Although names and details may be changed, these works reveal something about their authors, such as their childhoods, heritages, or beliefs.

Other times the **themes** and issues of a literary work are related to the **historical period** in which its writer is living. These issues may be central to the work, or they may provide background for the characters' lives.

The title "American History" hints that the personal experiences of Elena, the main character, are related in some way to life in this country. Meet the Writer (page 572) and the personal essay "Volar" (see the **Connection** on page 573) show that Elena's experiences also reflect those of the author. As you read, consider how the life and times of the author shape her story.

Reading Skills 📖

Summarizing: The Big Picture
When you finish a story, you should pause to summarize what happens. For

help focusing on a story's most important elements, review who the main characters are and what happens to them.

Background
President John F. Kennedy was assassinated on November 22, 1963, while riding in a motorcade in Dallas, Texas. That unforgettable day has become an important part of the way we view ourselves as a nation. Even today people from all walks of life share stories about where they were and what they were doing when Kennedy was killed. (For more about Kennedy, see pages 580–587.)

Vocabulary Development

literally (lit′ər·əl·ē) *adv.*: actually; in fact.

discreet (di·skrēt′) *adj.*: careful; showing good judgment.

linger (liŋ′gər) *v.*: continue to stay; be reluctant to leave.

infatuated (in·fach′o͞o·āt′id) *adj.*: carried away by shallow or foolish love.

vigilant (vij′ə·lənt) *adj.*: watchful.

enthralled (en·thrôld′) *v.*: fascinated.

elation (ē·lā′shən) *n.*: great joy.

distraught (di·strôt′) *adj.*: deeply troubled, as with worry or grief.

dilapidated (də·lap′ə·dāt′id) *adj.*: in poor condition; shabby and neglected.

solace (säl′is) *n.*: comfort; easing of grief.

go.hrw.com

INTERNET
Vocabulary Practice
•
More About Judith Ortiz Cofer
•
Keyword: LE5 9-9

SKILLS FOCUS

Literary Skills
Understand biographical and historical approaches to literary works.

Reading Skills
Summarize a story.

RESOURCES: READING

Planning
■ *One-Stop Planner* CD-ROM with ExamView Test Generator

Differentiating Instruction
■ *Holt Reading Solutions*
■ *The Holt Reader*
■ *Holt Adapted Reader*
■ *Supporting Instruction in Spanish*

■ *Audio CD Library, Selections and Summaries in Spanish*

Vocabulary
■ *Vocabulary Development*

Grammar and Language
■ *Daily Language Activities*
■ *Language Handbook Worksheets*

AMERICAN HISTORY

Judith Ortiz Cofer

"Listen," he repeated, "something awful has happened."

Teach Our Children (1990) by Juan Sanchez. Oil and mixed media on canvas.

Collection of the Museum of Tourism, San Juan, Puerto Rico.

once read in a "Ripley's Believe It or Not" column that Paterson, New Jersey, is the place where the Straight and Narrow (streets) intersect. The Puerto Rican tenement known as El Building was one block up on Straight. It was, in fact, the corner of Straight and Market; not "at" the corner, but *the* corner. At almost any hour of the day, El Building was like a monstrous jukebox, blasting out salsas[1] from open windows as the residents, mostly new immigrants just up from the island, tried to drown out whatever they were currently

enduring with loud music. But the day President Kennedy was shot, there was a profound silence in El Building; even the abusive tongues of viragoes,[2] the cursing of the unemployed, and the screeching of small children had been somehow muted. President Kennedy was a saint to these people. In fact, soon his photograph would be hung alongside the Sacred Heart and over the spiritist altars[3] that many women kept in their apartments. He would become part of

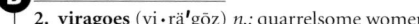

1. **salsas** (säl′səz) *n:* lively dance music from Latin America.

2. **viragoes** (vi·rä′gōz) *n.:* quarrelsome women.
3. **the Sacred Heart . . . altars:** The Sacred Heart is an image depicting the wounded heart of Jesus, often encircled by a crown of thorns. "Spiritist altars" most likely refers to memorials for dead relatives.

American History **565**

Assessment
- *Holt Assessment: Literature, Reading, and Vocabulary*
- *One-Stop Planner* CD-ROM with ExamView Test Generator
- *Holt Online Assessment*

Internet
- go.hrw.com (Keyword LE5 9-9)

- *Elements of Literature Online*

Media
- *Audio CD Library*
- *Audio CD Library, Selections and Summaries in Spanish*
- *Fine Art Transparencies*
- *Visual Connections Videocassette Program*

A Literary Focus

Historical approach. The author reminds us that the events of the story are related to the events of history that are also taking place.

B Literary Focus

Biographical approach. Cofer's description of the school routine, the weather, and the way the girls play and interact is so true to life that readers may feel she is drawing from her own experience. She realistically conveys the humiliation endured by young people in an unfamiliar and unfriendly culture. When the girls chant about pork chops, they are making fun of Elena's heritage; beans, rice, and pork chops are a popular Puerto Rican meal.

the hierarchy of martyrs[4] they prayed to for favors that only one who had died for a cause would understand.

A On the day that President Kennedy was shot, my ninth-grade class had been out in the fenced playground of Public School Number 13. We had been given "free" exercise time and had been ordered by our PE teacher, Mr. DePalma, to "keep moving." That meant that the girls should jump rope and the boys toss basketballs through a hoop at the far end of the yard. He in the meantime would "keep an eye" on us from just inside the building.

It was a cold gray day in Paterson. The kind that warns of early snow. I was miserable, since I had forgotten my gloves and my knuckles were turn-**B** ing red and raw from the jump rope. I was also taking a lot of abuse from the black girls for not turning the rope hard and fast enough for them.

"Hey, Skinny Bones, pump it, girl. Ain't you got no energy today?" Gail, the biggest of the black girls who had the other end of the rope yelled, "Didn't you eat your rice and beans and pork chops for breakfast today?"

The other girls picked up the "pork chop" and made it into a refrain: "Pork chop, pork chop, did you eat your pork chop?" They entered the double ropes in pairs and exited without tripping or missing a beat. I felt a burning on my cheeks and then my glasses fogged up so that I could not manage to coordinate the jump rope with Gail. The chill was doing to me what it always did: entering my bones, making me cry, humiliating me. I hated the city, especially in winter. I hated Public School Number 13. I hated my skinny, flat-chested body, and I envied the black girls, who could jump rope so fast that their legs became a blur. They always seemed to be warm, while I froze.

---

4. **hierarchy** (hī′ər·är′kē) **of martyrs** (märt′ərz): *Hierarchy* means "ranking in order of importance." Martyrs are people who have suffered or died rather than give up their faith or principles.

There was only one source of beauty and light for me that school year—the only thing I had anticipated at the start of the semester. That was seeing Eugene. In August, Eugene and his family had moved into the only house on the block that had a yard and trees. I could see his place from my window in El Building. In fact, if I sat on the fire escape I was literally suspended above Eugene's backyard. It was my favorite spot to read my library books in the summer. Until that August the house had been occupied by an old Jewish couple. Over the years I had become part of their family, without their knowing it, of course. I had a view of their kitchen and their backyard, and though I could not hear what they said, I knew when they were arguing, when one of them was sick, and many other things. I knew all this by watching them at mealtimes. I could see their kitchen table, the sink, and the stove. During good times, he sat at the table and read his newspapers while she fixed the meals. If they argued, he would leave and the old woman would sit and stare at nothing for a long time. When one of them was sick, the other would come and get things from the kitchen and carry them out on a tray. The old man had died in June. The last week of school I had not seen him at the table at all. Then one day I saw that there was a crowd in the kitchen. The old woman had finally emerged from the house on the arm of a stocky middle-aged woman, whom I had seen there a few times before, maybe her daughter. Then a man had carried out suitcases. The house had stood empty for weeks. I had had to resist the temptation to climb down into the yard and water the flowers the old lady had taken such good care of.

By the time Eugene's family moved in, the yard was a tangled mass of weeds. The father had spent several days mowing, and when he finished, from where I sat I didn't see the red,

Vocabulary
literally (lit′ər·əl·ē) *adv.*: actually; in fact.

DIFFERENTIATING INSTRUCTION

Learners Having Difficulty
Invite learners having difficulty to read "American History" in interactive format in *The Holt Reader* and to use the sidenotes as aids to understanding the story. The interactive version provides additional instruction, practice, and assessment of the literary skill taught in the Student Edition. Monitor

students' responses to the story, and correct any misconceptions that arise.

English-Language Learners
To help students get into the story, read the first paragraph aloud and discuss any unfamiliar words. You might show a picture of a jukebox from the 1960s to help students

understand the simile that compares the building to a "monstrous jukebox."

Special Education Students
For lessons designed for special education students, see *Holt Reading Solutions*.

yellow, and purple clusters that meant flowers to me. I didn't see this family sit down at the kitchen table together. It was just the mother, a redheaded, tall woman who wore a white uniform—a nurse's, I guessed it was; the father was gone before I got up in the morning and was never there at dinner time. I only saw him on weekends, when they sometimes sat on lawn chairs under the oak tree, each hidden behind a section of the newspaper; and there was Eugene. He was tall and blond, and he wore glasses. I liked him right away because he sat at the kitchen table and read books for hours. That summer, before we had even spoken one word to each other, I kept him company on my fire escape.

Once school started, I looked for him in all my classes, but PS 13 was a huge, overpopulated place and it took me days and many discreet questions to discover that Eugene was in honors classes for all his subjects, classes that were not open to me because English was not my first language, though I was a straight-A student. After much maneuvering I managed to "run into him" in the hallway where his locker was—on the other side of the building from mine—and in study hall at the library, where he first seemed to notice me but did not speak, and finally, on the way home after school one day when I decided to approach him directly, though my stomach was doing somersaults.

I was ready for rejection, snobbery, the worst. But when I came up to him, practically panting in my nervousness, and blurted out: "You're Eugene. Right?" he smiled, pushed his glasses up on his nose, and nodded. I saw then that he was blushing deeply. Eugene liked me, but he was shy. I did most of the talking that day. He nodded and smiled a lot. In the weeks that followed, we walked home together. He would linger at the corner of El Building for a few minutes, then walk down to his two-story house. It was not until Eugene moved into that house that I noticed that El Building blocked most of the

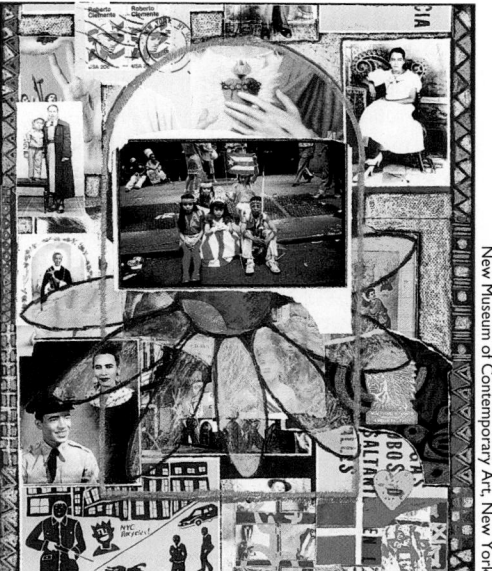

Untitled (1992) by Juan Sanchez.
Mixed media on paper.

Originally commissioned for the Testimonio Exhibit, New Museum of Contemporary Art, New York.

sun and that the only spot that got a little sunlight during the day was the tiny square of earth the old woman had planted with flowers.

I did not tell Eugene that I could see inside his kitchen from my bedroom. I felt dishonest, but I liked my secret sharing of his evenings, especially now that I knew what he was reading since we chose our books together at the school library.

One day my mother came into my room as I was sitting on the windowsill staring out. In her abrupt way she said: "Elena, you are acting 'moony.'" "Enamorada" was what she really said, that is—like a girl stupidly infatuated. Since I had turned fourteen . . . , my mother had been

---

Vocabulary

discreet (di·skrēt′) *adj.:* careful; showing good judgment.

linger (liŋ′gər) *v.:* continue to stay; be reluctant to leave.

infatuated (in·fach′o͞o·āt′id) *adj.:* carried away by shallow or foolish love.

American History **567**

VIEWING THE ART

Juan Sanchez combines patriotic and spiritual images in this collage. The arch contains a detail from an image of the Sacred Heart. The photographs suggest spiritist altars and martyrs.

Activity. Have students identify images in the collage. [Possible responses: a flower, a group of children with Puerto Rican flags, a soldier.]

C **Reading Skills**

❓ **Comparing and contrasting.** What are some ways Elena and Eugene are alike? [Possible response: Both wear glasses and like to read.] In what important way do they differ? [They come from different cultural and ethnic backgrounds.]

D **Reading Skills**

❓ **Summarizing.** How would you summarize the story thus far? [Summaries should include the following items: a description of the building Elena lives in; the effect of President Kennedy's assassination on the building and its residents; Elena's personal struggles with her classmates; the cold weather; the city; her school; her habit of watching the elderly couple; her interest in Eugene.]

E **Literary Focus**

❓ **Biographical approach.** How does this passage reveal the author's attitude toward discrimination? [Possible response: The writer is probably revealing her beliefs and attitudes through Elena. Cofer is saying that it is unfair for capable students to be held back because of their race or native language.]

A Literary Focus

❓ Biographical approach.

How does this passage reflect the heritage, traditions, and attitudes of the writer? [Possible response: Cofer describes the way a Puerto Rican family unites in mourning the loss of a loved one. In the story the elder Puerto Ricans have remained closely connected with their heritage while Elena, representing a younger generation, feels disconnected from it and is ready to cut ties to the past.]

B Vocabulary Development

Synonyms and antonyms. Point out the word *hysterical*. Then, ask students to identify synonyms and antonyms for *hysterical* from the words *apathetic, crazed, emotional, excitable, frenzied, frantic, impassive, imperturbable, indifferent, nonchalant, stoic, uncontrolled, unruffled,* and *wild*.

C English-Language Learners

Colloquialisms. Be sure that students understand the meaning of *hick,* an insulting term for an unsophisticated person, usually from a rural area.

D Literary Focus

Historical approach. The first sentence of this paragraph reorients the reader. After supplying background information, Elena returns us to the time of the story's opening paragraph—a particular day in America's history.

---

more vigilant than ever. She acted as if I was going to go crazy or explode or something if she didn't watch me and nag me all the time about being a señorita[5] now. She kept talking about virtue, morality, and other subjects that did not interest me in the least. My mother was unhappy in Paterson, but my father had a good job at the bluejeans factory in Passaic and soon, he kept assuring us, we would be moving to our own house there. Every Sunday we drove out to the suburbs of Paterson, Clifton, and Passaic, out to where people mowed grass on Sundays in the summer and where children made snowmen in the winter from pure white snow, not like the gray slush of Paterson, which seemed to fall from the sky in that hue. I had learned to listen to my parents' dreams, which were spoken in Spanish, as fairy tales, like the stories about life in the island paradise of Puerto Rico before I was born. I had been to the island once as a little girl, to Grandmother's funeral, and all I remembered was wailing women in black, my mother becoming hysterical and being given a pill that made her sleep two days, and me feeling lost in a crowd of strangers all claiming to be my aunts, uncles, and cousins. I had actually been glad to return to the city. We had not been back there since then, though my parents talked constantly about buying a house on the beach someday, retiring on the island—that was a common topic among the residents of El Building. As for me, I was going to go to college and become a teacher.

But after meeting Eugene I began to think of the present more than of the future. What I wanted now was to enter that house I had watched for so many years. I wanted to see the other rooms where the old people had lived and where the boy spent his time. Most of all I wanted to sit at the kitchen table with Eugene like two adults, like the old man and his wife had done, maybe drink some coffee and talk about

books. I had started reading *Gone with the Wind*. I was enthralled by it, with the daring and the passion of the beautiful girl living in a mansion, and with her devoted parents and the slaves who did everything for them. I didn't believe such a world had ever really existed, and I wanted to ask Eugene some questions since he and his parents, he had told me, had come up from Georgia, the same place where the novel was set. His father worked for a company that had transferred him to Paterson. His mother was very unhappy, Eugene said, in his beautiful voice that rose and fell over words in a strange, lilting way. The kids at school called him "the Hick" and made fun of the way he talked. I knew I was his only friend so far, and I liked that, though I felt sad for him sometimes. "Skinny Bones and the Hick" was what they called us at school when we were seen together.

The day Mr. DePalma came out into the cold and asked us to line up in front of him was the day that President Kennedy was shot. Mr. DePalma, a short, muscular man with slicked-down black hair, was the science teacher, PE coach, and disciplinarian at PS 13. He was the teacher to whose homeroom you got assigned if you were a troublemaker, and the man called out to break up playground fights and to escort violently angry teenagers to the office. And Mr. DePalma was the man who called your parents in for "a conference."

That day, he stood in front of two rows of mostly black and Puerto Rican kids, brittle from their efforts to "keep moving" on a November day that was turning bitter cold. Mr. DePalma, to our complete shock, was crying. Not just silent adult tears, but really sobbing. There were a few titters from the back of the line where I stood shivering.

---

5. **señorita** (se´nyô·rē´tä) *n.:* Spanish for "unmarried woman."

Vocabulary
vigilant (vij´ə·lənt) *adj.:* watchful.
enthralled (en·thrôld´) *v.:* fascinated.

CONTENT-AREA CONNECTIONS

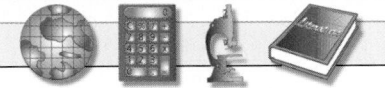

History: President John F. Kennedy

Small-group activity. To help students understand the importance of President Kennedy to the American public, have them research his role in developing the space program or the controversy surrounding his assassination. Have them report to the class in a panel discussion, speaking and using such visual aids as maps, diagrams, and magazine and newspaper articles from the 1960s.

Social Science: Puerto Rico

Puerto Rico, an island in the Caribbean Sea, is a self-governing commonwealth in union with the United States. Its people are born citizens of the United States. Since World War II, Puerto Rican immigration has had a significant impact on the economy and culture of the New York metropolitan area and other urban areas. In the 1950s and 1960s, thousands immigrated in hope of economic opportunities.

"Listen," Mr. DePalma raised his arms over his head as if he were about to conduct an orchestra. His voice broke, and he covered his face with his hands. His barrel chest was heaving. Someone giggled behind me.

"Listen," he repeated, "something awful has happened." A strange gurgling came from his throat, and he turned around and spat on the cement behind him.

"Gross," someone said, and there was a lot of laughter.

"The president is dead, you idiots. I should have known that wouldn't mean anything to a bunch of losers like you kids. Go home." He was shrieking now. No one moved for a minute or two, but then a big girl let out a "Yeah!" and ran to get her books piled up with the others against the brick wall of the school building. The others followed in a mad scramble to get to their things before somebody caught on. It was still an hour to the dismissal bell.

A little scared, I headed for El Building. There was an eerie feeling on the streets. I looked into Mario's drugstore, a favorite hangout for the high school crowd, but there were only a couple of old Jewish men at the soda bar talking with the short-order cook in tones that sounded almost angry, but they were keeping their voices low. Even the traffic on one of the busiest intersections in Paterson—Straight Street and Park Avenue—seemed to be moving slower. There were no horns blasting that day. At El Building, the usual little group of unemployed men was not hanging out on the front stoop making it difficult for women to enter the front door. No music spilled out from open doors in the hallway. When I walked into our apartment, I found my mother sitting in front of the grainy picture of the television set.

Retroactive I (1964) by Robert Rauschenberg. Oil on canvas (84″ × 60″).

Wadsworth Atheneum, Hartford. Gift of Susan Morse Hilles.
© Robert Rauschenberg/Licensed by VAGA, New York.

She looked up at me with a tear-streaked face and just said: "Dios mío,"[6] turning back to the set as if it were pulling at her eyes. I went into my room.

Though I wanted to feel the right thing about President Kennedy's death, I could not fight the feeling of elation that stirred in my chest. Today was the day I was to visit Eugene in his house. He had asked me to come over

---

6. **dios mío** (dē′ōs mē′ō): Spanish for "Oh, my God."

Vocabulary
elation (ē·lā′shən) *n.:* great joy.

VIEWING THE ART

Robert Rauschenberg (1925–   ) was born in Port Arthur, Texas. One of the twentieth century's most influential artists, he is best known for his "combines"—collages that juxtapose familiar images and objects in new and surprising ways. He has said of his work, "Painting relates to both art and life. . . . I try to act in that gap between the two."

Activity. Images of John F. Kennedy and of an astronaut appear as icons of modern life in several of Rauschenberg's works. Here, the images were transferred to the canvas from print reproductions, and their faintness suggests the passage of time. You might point out that Rauschenberg produced this work the year after President Kennedy was assassinated. If students were to create a collage suggesting what we think of ourselves as a nation today, what images would they use, and why?

Ⓔ Reading Skills

❷ Interpreting. Elena characterizes Mr. DePalma as a stern disciplinarian. What is significant about his behavior here? [Possible response: He is so distraught over the death of President Kennedy that he loses his composure before the students.]

Ⓕ Literary Focus

Biographical approach. The writer goes into great detail describing people's reaction to the shocking news that President Kennedy had been shot. Such intimate knowledge suggests that the writer may be recalling what she herself observed that day.

DEVELOPING FLUENCY

Small-group activity. Although most of this story is presented in the form of direct narration, there are several passages of dialogue. Divide the class into small groups, with two or three students assigned to read the Elena passages and the others to read the dialogue of the other characters. Encourage students to read with expression, and have them practice their readings until they can present a polished performance. Allow interested groups to present their reading to the rest of the class.

❓ Irony. Why is it ironic that Elena and Eugene have chosen the subject of American history to study together? [Possible response: They are living through what would turn out to be one of the most significant days in American history.]

B Literary Focus

❓ Theme. Point out to students that this is a key passage in the story; it is one of several passages that reveal the essence of the theme. What does Elena's mother understand that Elena, as yet, does not? [Possible response: Elena's mother knows that Eugene's parents may not want him to associate with a Puerto Rican immigrant.]

C Learners Having Difficulty

❓ Questioning. What is most likely the reason for the mother's face being red and swollen? [Possible response: She is mourning the death of President Kennedy.] Why does the writer make a point of including this detail? [Possible response: To draw a parallel with the scene Elena has just left—her own mother had been crying.]

A after school to study for an American history test with him. We had also planned to walk to the public library together. I looked down into his yard. The oak tree was bare of leaves and the ground looked gray with ice. The light through the large kitchen window of his house told me that El Building blocked the sun to such an extent that they had to turn lights on in the middle of the day. I felt ashamed about it. But the white kitchen table with the lamp hanging just above it looked cozy and inviting. I would soon sit there, across from Eugene, and I would tell him about my perch just above his house. Maybe I should.

In the next thirty minutes I changed clothes, put on a little pink lipstick, and got my books together. Then I went in to tell my mother that I was going to a friend's house to study. I did not expect her reaction.

"You are going out *today?*" The way she said "today" sounded as if a storm warning had been issued. It was said in utter disbelief. Before I could answer, she came toward me and held my elbows as I clutched my books.

"Hija,[7] the president has been killed. We must show respect. He was a great man. Come to church with me tonight."

She tried to embrace me, but my books were in the way. My first impulse was to comfort her, she seemed so distraught, but I had to meet Eugene in fifteen minutes.

"I have a test to study for, Mama. I will be home by eight."

B "You are forgetting who you are, Niña.[8] I have seen you staring down at that boy's house. You are heading for humiliation and pain." My mother said this in Spanish and in a resigned tone that surprised me, as if she had no intention of stopping me from "heading for humiliation and pain." I started for the door. She sat in front of the TV holding a white handkerchief to her face.

---

7. **hija** (ē′hä) *n.:* Spanish for "daughter."
8. **niña** (nē′nyä) *n.:* Spanish for "girl."

I walked out to the street and around the chain-link fence that separated El Building from Eugene's house. The yard was neatly edged around the little walk that led to the door. It always amazed me how Paterson, the inner core of the city, had no apparent logic to its architecture. Small, neat single residences like this one could be found right next to huge, dilapidated apartment buildings like El Building. My guess was that the little houses had been there first, then the immigrants had come in droves, and the monstrosities had been raised for them—the Italians, the Irish, the Jews, and now us, the Puerto Ricans and the blacks. The door was painted a deep green: verde, the color of hope. I had heard my mother say it: verde-esperanza.

C I knocked softly. A few suspenseful moments later the door opened just a crack. The red, swollen face of a woman appeared. She had a halo of red hair floating over a delicate ivory face—the face of a doll—with freckles on the nose. Her smudged eye makeup made her look unreal to me, like a mannequin[9] seen through a warped store window.

"What do you want?" Her voice was tiny and sweet sounding, like a little girl's, but her tone was not friendly.

"I'm Eugene's friend. He asked me over. To study." I thrust out my books, a silly gesture that embarrassed me almost immediately.

"You live there?" She pointed up to El Building, which looked particularly ugly, like a gray prison, with its many dirty windows and rusty fire escapes. The woman had stepped halfway out and I could see that she wore a white nurse's uniform with "St. Joseph's Hospital" on the name tag.

---

9. **mannequin** (man′ə·kin) *n.:* life-size model of a person.

Vocabulary

distraught (di·strôt′) *adj.:* deeply troubled, as with worry or grief.

dilapidated (də·lap′ə·dāt′id) *adj.:* in poor condition; shabby and neglected.

READING MINI-LESSON

Developing Word-Attack Skills
Review the sounds represented by the letters *ch* and *qu*. Point out that although the digraph *ch* often stands for the sound /ch/, there are a large number of words that have Greek roots in which *ch* stands for /k/, and there are some words derived from French in which *ch* stands for /sh/.

Also, point out that *qu* stands for the sound /kw/ in most English words, but in words that derive from French, *qu* stands simply for the sound /k/.
Activity. Display these sets of words. In each set, have students identify the two words in which *ch* or *qu* stand for the same sound. Answers are underlined.

1. archives	orchid	chives
2. bouquet	bequest	brusque
3. chicanery	charade	charisma
4. orchestra	orchard	archaic
5. parquet	perquisite	plaque
6. sequins	harlequin	mannequin
7. parchment	architect	archetype
8. mechanical	technical	treachery

Untitled (1993) by Juan Sanchez.
Mixed media on paper.

"Yes. I do."

She looked intently at me for a couple of heartbeats, then said as if to herself, "I don't know how you people do it." Then directly to me: "Listen. Honey. Eugene doesn't want to study with you. He is a smart boy. Doesn't need help. You understand me. I am truly sorry if he

told you you could come over. He cannot study with you. It's nothing personal. You understand? We won't be in this place much longer, no need for him to get close to people—it'll just make it harder for him later. Run back home now."

I couldn't move. I just stood there in shock at hearing these things said to me in such a honey-drenched voice. I had never heard an accent like hers, except for Eugene's softer version. It was as if she were singing me a little song.

"What's wrong? Didn't you hear what I said?" She seemed very angry, and I finally snapped out of my trance. I turned away from the green door and heard her close it gently.

Our apartment was empty when I got home. My mother was in someone else's kitchen, seeking the solace she needed. Father would come in from his late shift at midnight. I would hear them talking softly in the kitchen for hours that night. They would not discuss their dreams for the future, or life in Puerto Rico, as they often did; that night they would talk sadly about the young widow and her two children, as if they were family. For the next few days, we would observe luto in our apartment; that is, we would practice restraint and silence—no loud music or laughter. Some of the women of El Building would wear black for weeks. **D**

That night, I lay in my bed trying to feel the right thing for our dead president. But the tears that came up from a deep source inside me were strictly for me. When my mother came to the door, I pretended to be sleeping. Sometime during the night, I saw from my bed the streetlight come on. It had a pink halo around it. I went to my window and pressed my face to the cool glass. Looking up at the light, I could see the white snow falling like a lace veil over its face. I did not look down to see it turning gray as it touched the ground below. ■ **E**

Vocabulary
solace (säl′is) *n.*: comfort; easing of grief.

D **Content-Area Connections**
History: The Kennedys
The widow and her children are Jacqueline, Caroline, and John Kennedy, Jr.

E **Literary Focus**
? **Biographical approach.** What is revealed here about the writer's attitude toward discrimination and prejudice? [Possible response: Cofer is saying that the pain of a personal heartbreak can be harder to cope with than the grief of a public tragedy.]

GUIDED PRACTICE

Monitoring students' progress. Guide the class in answering these comprehension questions. Direct students to locate passages in the text that support their responses.

True-False

1. The story is set in an apartment building in Puerto Rico. [F]
2. Eugene's family lives in the only house on the block that has a yard and trees. [T]
3. Elena manages to meet Eugene in one of her honors classes. [F]
4. Elena finally tells Eugene that she can see into his family's kitchen window. [F]
5. Eugene's mother refuses to let Elena enter the house. [T]

VIEWING THE ART

Born in Brooklyn, **Juan Sanchez** creates artistically innovative prints and collages to explore issues of Puerto Rican identity and politics. His art mixes autobiographical and cultural artifacts, such as photographs, with an overlay of symbolic imagery.

Activity. Ask students to discuss the meaning they attribute to the overpainted symbols. [Possible response: love, happiness]

DIFFERENTIATING INSTRUCTION

Learners Having Difficulty
Use this activity to review the historical and biographical approach to a work of literature. Tell students that in writing "American History," Judith Ortiz Cofer drew on her own beliefs and cultural heritage as a source of inspiration for her plot and characters. In addition, she relates the characters and events of her story to the issues of a time in history.

Small-group activity. At the time Cofer was growing up and when her story takes place, the problem of racial prejudice was an important issue in American society. Ask students to write down three historical facts they have learned from this story and to find those facts reported in another source, such as an encyclopedia, a history book, or a reliable Internet site. Have students share what they have learned in small groups.

Meet the Writer

Background. Judith Ortiz Cofer claims to have learned about the power of words from her grandmother, who "could silence an entire room when she said 'Tengo un cuento'" ("I have a story to tell"). Cofer has said that her first poem published in a national journal "came straight from Mama's technique of telling a story, claiming it was the absolute truth, the *la verdad,* but changing it every time to suit the occasion and the audience. She was teaching us that reality is relative, that we change it through our own interpretation. She couldn't have said it that way because she's no literary critic, but I absorbed her technique. And I learned that was art. Art is taking the ordinary and trying to give it enough levels so that it becomes universal. I make people laugh when I say that my unschooled grandmother and Virginia Woolf were two of my literary ancestors. As different as they were they shared one thing: They knew that the word was empowering in a way that nothing else was."

For Independent Reading

Encourage students who read *Silent Dancing: A Partial Remembrance of a Puerto Rican Childhood* to choose one essay or poem with which they felt a personal connection and write a brief response to the piece.

Meet the Writer

Judith Ortiz Cofer

"The Human Experience"

Judith Ortiz Cofer (1952–   ) was born in Puerto Rico, but her family moved to the mainland United States when she was a toddler. In her autobiography, *Silent Dancing: A Partial Remembrance of a Puerto Rican Childhood,* Cofer explains that her family moved to Paterson, New Jersey—to a large apartment building that was known as El Building (like Elena's home in "American History"). Cofer says that her "memories of life in Paterson during those first few years are in shades of gray." Her father had encountered prejudice while looking for an apartment, but in El Building the family joined a community of fellow Puerto Rican immigrants. Cofer says of her early home:

> ❝The walls were thin, and voices speaking and arguing in Spanish could be heard all day. Salsas blasted out of radios turned on early in the morning and left on for company. Women seemed to cook rice and beans perpetually—the strong aroma of red kidney beans boiling permeated the hallways. ❞

It was a challenge for Cofer to master English in her new home, but she achieved her goal. She earned a master's degree, and she attended Oxford University in England, where she received recognition as a Scholar of the English-Speaking Union. She has taught English at colleges in Florida and Georgia, and she has published several books of poetry, as well as fiction and nonfiction.

Cofer's stories often reflect the issues of her time. However, she explains that this does not make her a "political writer":

> ❝I am not a political writer in that I never take an issue and write a story about it. The people in my stories deal with political issues but only in accordance with the needs of their personal lives. My politics are imbedded in my work as part of the human experience. A story like 'American History' . . . takes place on the day Kennedy was shot. The girl in the story wants to feel the right way about the president's death, but she's in love and she can't help thinking about this boy. Yet she is faced at the end of the story with a political situation. The mother of the boy she loves rejects her because she's Puerto Rican. The story doesn't end with a speech on prejudice but with the heartbreak of a girl still unable to comprehend that it all comes together and affects her life: the death of a president, life in America, prejudice, the plight of the immigrant. ❞

For Independent Reading

If you want to read more by and about Cofer, try *Silent Dancing: A Partial Remembrance of a Puerto Rican Childhood,* her award-winning collection of autobiographical essays and poems.

DIFFERENTIATING INSTRUCTION

Advanced Learners

Enrichment. Judith Ortiz Cofer says that she was a Navy brat and that when her father became involved in the Cuban missile crisis, the family lost contact with him for six months. She has said, "The truth is what I felt about my father disappearing, not that he was actually on a ship in Cuba at that time. . . . If I'm going to talk about the Cuban missile crisis, I talk about it as a historical event that took place in particular years. The thoughts and the feelings of the people involved are mine to make up. The only license that the poet has is to make truth what she wants it to be, as long as you can convince someone else that it's important."

Activity. Have students investigate the Cuban missile crisis, paying attention both to the historical facts and to the effect the crisis had on the American people. Suggest that students enter *Cuban missile crisis* and *American History* as keywords in an Internet search engine.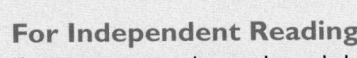

Volar

Judith Ortiz Cofer

At twelve I was an avid consumer of comic books—*Supergirl* being my favorite. I spent my allowance of a quarter a day on two twelve-cent comic books or a double issue for twenty-five. I had a stack of *Legion of Super Heroes* and *Supergirl* comic books in my bedroom closet that was as tall as I. I had a recurring dream in those days: that I had long blond hair and could fly. In my dream I climbed the stairs to the top of our apartment building as myself, but as I went up each flight, changes would be taking place. Step by step I would fill out: my legs would grow long, my arms harden into steel, and my hair would magically go straight and turn a golden color. . . . Supergirl had to be aerodynamic.[1] Sleek and hard as a supersonic missile. Once on the roof, my parents safely asleep in their beds, I would get on tip-toe, arms outstretched in the position for flight and jump out my fifty-story-high window into the black lake of the sky. From up there, over the rooftops, I could see everything, even beyond the few blocks of our barrio;[2] with my

X-ray vision I could look inside the homes of people who interested me. Once I saw our landlord, whom I knew my parents feared, sitting in a treasure-room dressed in an ermine coat and a large gold crown. He sat on the floor counting his dollar bills. I played a trick on him. Going up to his building's chimney, I blew a little puff of my super-breath into his fireplace, scattering his stacks of money so that he had to start counting all over again. I could more or less program my Supergirl dreams in those days by focusing on the object of my current obsession. This way I "saw" into the private lives of my neighbors, my teachers, and in the last days of my childish fantasy and the beginning of adolescence, into the secret room of the boys I liked. In the mornings I'd wake up in my tiny bedroom with the incongruous[3]— at least in our tiny apartment —white "princess" furniture my mother had chosen for me, and find myself back in my body: my tight curls still clinging to my head, skinny arms and legs and flat chest unchanged.

(continued)

1. **aerodynamic** (er'ō·dī·nam'ik) *adj.:* having characteristics that easily enable flight.
2. **barrio** (bär'ē·ō) *n.:* area of a city inhabited by people who speak Spanish.
3. **incongruous** (in·käŋ'grōō·əs) *adj.:* lacking harmony; not fitting in.

Connection

Summary ⬌ *at grade level*

In this personal essay, Judith Ortiz Cofer speaks of herself at age twelve, when her avid reading of comic books gave rise to a recurrent dream in which she herself became Supergirl.

DIRECT TEACHING

A **Literary Focus**

❓ Figurative language. What types of figurative language does Cofer use in describing her dream? [*Simile*—when she compares Supergirl to a supersonic missile. *Metaphor*—when she describes jumping into the "black lake of the sky."]

B **Reading Skills**

❓ Speculating. Most superheroes use their powers to fight crime, avenge evil, and perform daring, breathtaking deeds. Cofer's activity in her Supergirl dreams is far less dramatic. Why do you suppose she uses her power in the way that she does? [Possible response: Because having knowledge of other people's lives is a form of "power." Apparently, this type of power was important to Cofer as a girl. Also, Cofer did avenge evil in her dream about scattering the landlord's money.]

Connecting and Comparing Texts

Invite students to hold a discussion comparing "American History" and "Volar." You may wish to use the following prompts to stimulate discussion:

• **What do the people (characters) in these two selections have in common?** [Both selections are about people with dreams of a better life.]

• **What do Elena and Cofer have in common?** [Both enjoy observing the lives of others. Elena likes to sit on the fire escape and watch the families in the house next door. As a girl, Cofer had dreams of flying out of her building and peering into the private lives of neighbors and teachers.]

• **How are the endings of both selections similar?** [Both selections end with striking images of reflection and longing. Elena looks out her bedroom window at the falling snow rather than at the snow turning gray as it touches the ground. In the essay, Cofer's mother looks out the kitchen window over the "dismal alley. . . littered with refuse" and says, "Oh, if only I could fly."]

Ⓐ Reading Skills

Comparing and contrasting. Point out to students the way in which Cofer compares herself and her mother. In her dreams, Cofer leaps through an open window and flies. In real life, Cofer's mother looks out of a window and wishes she could fly. Both mother and daughter have dreams they cling to.

Ⓑ Literary Focus

❓ Symbolism. What might windows and the ability to fly symbolize for Cofer and her mother? [Possible responses: The window might represent their view into the world outside; flying might symbolize the power to escape from their lives and fulfill their dreams.]

In the kitchen my mother and father would be talking softly over a *café con leche*.[4] She would come "wake me" exactly forty-five minutes after they had gotten up. It was their time together at the beginning of each day and even at an early age I could feel their disappointment if I interrupted them by getting up too early. So I would stay in my bed recalling my dreams of flight, perhaps planning my next flight. In the kitchen they would be discussing events in the barrio. Actually, he would be carrying that part of the conversation; when it was her turn to speak she would, more often than not, try shifting the topic toward her desire to see her *familia*[5] on the Island: *How about a vacation in Puerto Rico together this year, Querido?*[6] *We could rent a car, go to the beach. We could . . .* And he would answer patiently, gently, *Mi amor,*[7] *do*

you know how much it would cost for all of us to fly there? It is not possible for me to take the time off . . . Mi vida,[8] *please understand. . . .* And I knew that soon she would rise from the table. Not abruptly. She would light a cigarette and look out the kitchen window. The view was of a dismal alley that was littered with refuse thrown from windows. The space was too narrow for anyone larger than a skinny child to enter safely, so it was never cleaned. My mother would check the time on the clock over her sink, the one with a prayer for patience and grace written in Spanish. A birthday gift. She would see that it was time to wake me. She'd sigh deeply and say the same thing the view from her kitchen window always inspired her to say: *Ay, si yo pudiera volar.*[9]

---

4. *café con leche* (kä·fä′ kän·lä′chä): Spanish for "coffee with hot milk."
5. *familia* (fä·mē′ lyä) *n.:* Spanish for "family.
6. *querido* (ke·rē′ dō) *n.:* Spanish for "dear."
7. *mi amor* (mē ä·mor′): Spanish for "my love."

8. *mi vida* (mē vē′dä): Spanish for "my life"; used as an affectionate term for a loved one.
9. *Ay, si yo pudiera volar* (ī sē yō pōōd·yē′rä vō·lär′): Spanish for "Oh, if only I could fly."

Response and Analysis

Reading Check

1. **Summarize** the story by identifying the main **characters** and describing the **setting** and main **events**. In your summary, answer the following questions:
   - How do Elena and Eugene know each other?
   - What is El Building, and where is it?
   - What happened in the United States on November 22, 1963?
   - What happens to Elena on November 22, 1963?

Thinking Critically

2. Eugene, nicknamed "the Hick," and Elena, nicknamed "Skinny Bones," come from very different cultures, yet they have some things in common. What are they?

3. Why is Elena turned away from Eugene's house?

4. Re-read the last sentence in the story. Why doesn't Elena want to see the snow turning gray? What does this statement reveal about Elena's character—about how she faces a loss in her life?

Literary Criticism

5. The story takes place on a day of great **historical** importance. How do Elena's family and community react to the death of President Kennedy? What **conflict** does Elena experience concerning her own reaction to the president's death?

6. Answer the questions in each of the following bulleted items. Doing so will help you figure out the story's **theme.**

- President Kennedy was committed to eliminating prejudice and establishing equal rights for all Americans. How does Elena encounter prejudice in the story?
- President Kennedy's assassination is often described as marking a loss of innocence in this country—that is, the discovery that dreams can be destroyed in one horrible moment. In what way does Elena make such a discovery?
- Review Cofer's discussion of the story in Meet the Writer on page 572. How do Elena's personal situation and the political issues of the time come together at the end of the story?
- Now, considering your answers to the previous questions, state the **theme** of the story. How does the **title** relate to the theme?

7. How are Cofer's feelings and attitudes when she was young, as described in "Volar" (see the **Connection** on page 573), reflected in the character of Elena in "American History"? What similarities do you see between Cofer's parents in the essay and Elena's parents in the story?

WRITING

"I Will Never Forget"

Review your Quickwrite notes, and choose one memorable moment on your list. Write one or two paragraphs explaining why the event had such a significant impact on you. Did you gain a particular insight from the event? Did it affect you emotionally? Did it change your life in some way? Use specific details to make the meaning of the event clear to your reader.

go.
hrw
.com

INTERNET
Projects and Activities
Keyword: LE5 9-9

SKILLS FOCUS

Literary Skills
Analyze a literary work using biographical and historical approaches.

Reading Skills
Summarize a story.

Writing Skills
Write an explanatory paragraph.

Response and Analysis

Thinking Critically

2. They are both outsiders, love reading, and excel academically.

3. Possible answer: Eugene's mother does not want him to associate with immigrants.

4. Possible answer: Elena does not want to see what is beautiful become defiled.

Literary Criticism

5. The family and community are grief-stricken. Elena feels guilt because her sorrow is for her personal loss, not her country's.

6. Possible answers:
   - Elena encounters prejudice on the playground and from Eugene's mother.
   - Elena's dream to enter Eugene's house is destroyed in one horrible moment when she is turned away because of her ethnic background.
   - Elena tries to feel sorrow over the loss of the president but realizes that she is more affected by her own loss.
   - Possible theme: People will continue to experience private pains and joys despite the events of history unfolding around them. The story's title refers to two kinds of American history made that day: the shocking event that was public and political and the shameful event that was personal and private.

7. As a young girl, Cofer dreamed of a bigger, sleeker, more powerful body. Likewise, Elena is unhappy with her skinny body. Both sets of parents are dissatisfied with their lives and long to return to their native land.

Reading Check

1. Possible answers:
   - Elena first knows Eugene from watching him while sitting on her fire escape. She then meets up with him on the way home from school one day.
   - El Building is a tenement located at the intersection of Straight and Narrow streets in Paterson, New Jersey.

   - On November 22, 1963, President John F. Kennedy was assassinated.
   - On November 22, 1963, Elena is turned away from a friend's house because of racial discrimination.

Vocabulary Development

Practice 1

1. elation
2. distraught
3. dilapidated
4. literally
5. infatuated
6. vigilant
7. enthralled
8. discreet
9. solace
10. linger

Practice 2

1. Worker to tool
2. Object to function
3. Performer to action
4. Performer to action
5. Worker to tool

Vocabulary Development

Analogies: Word Pairs

In an **analogy** the same relationship must be expressed in two pairs of words. Follow this example for completing analogies:

TERRIFIED : AFRAID :: hot : _____

a. cold   b. warm   c. dry   d. thirsty

1. The relationship between the first pair of words is one of degree. *Terrified* describes a more intense, overwhelming type of fear than the word *afraid* implies.

2. In the second pair, *hot* refers to having a high temperature. The one word choice that indicates less intense heat is *warm*.

The following chart shows some relationships used in analogies. (For more information about analogies, see page 229.)

(For more information about analogies, see page 229.)

Word Bank

literally
discreet
linger
infatuated
vigilant
enthralled
elation
distraught
dilapidated
solace

Type of Relationship	Example
Synonyms	HELP : AID :: speak : talk
Degree	DISAPPOINTED : HEARTBROKEN :: pretty : beautiful
Object (or thing) to a characteristic of it	APPLE : CRISP :: lemon : sour
Cause and effect	COLD : SHIVER :: happiness : smile
Object to function	SCALE : WEIGH :: knife : cut
Worker to tool	CARPENTER : SAW :: firefighter : hose
Performer to action	CLOWN : JUGGLE :: pitcher : throw

PRACTICE 1

Complete each analogy below with the Word Bank word that fits best:

1. LABOR : FATIGUE :: victory : _____
2. DAMP : WET :: worried : _____
3. PIN : SHARP :: shack : _____
4. HONESTLY : TRUTHFULLY :: actually : _____
5. CHILLY : FREEZING :: attracted : _____
6. LOYAL : FAITHFUL :: careful : _____
7. AMUSING : HILARIOUS :: interested : _____
8. ARTIST : CREATIVE :: guard : _____
9. WRITER : AUTHOR :: comfort : _____
10. ADMIT : CONFESS :: stay : _____

PRACTICE 2

Using the chart above as a reference, identify the type of relationship in each word pair below:

1. photographer : camera
2. fan : cool
3. mayor : govern
4. ballerina : dance
5. farmer : plow

SKILLS FOCUS

Vocabulary Skills
Complete word analogies.

Grammar Link

Adverb Clauses

To avoid writing a series of short, choppy sentences and to show relationships between ideas, writers use adverb clauses.

An **adverb clause** is a subordinate clause that tells *where, when, how, why, to what extent,* or *under what conditions* an action occurs. Throughout her story, Cofer uses adverb clauses (underlined below) and a variety of subordinating conjunctions (boldface below) to make the relationships between her ideas clear. The first item in each pair shows how a passage from Cofer's story would have looked if she had not put one of her ideas in a subordinate clause.

1. I sat on the fire escape. In fact, I was literally suspended above Eugene's backyard.
    COFER: "In fact, **if** I sat on the fire escape I was literally suspended above Eugene's backyard." [Subordinate clause tells *under what conditions.*]

2. He sat at the kitchen table and read books for hours. I liked him right away.
    COFER: "I liked him right away **because** he sat at the kitchen table and read books for hours." [Subordinate clause tells *why.*]

3. I got home. Our apartment was empty.
    COFER: "Our apartment was empty **when** I got home." [Subordinate clause tells *when.*]

Remember to use **commas,** where appropriate, when you combine two sentences using an adverb clause. Place a comma after an introductory adverb clause. An adverb clause in the middle or at the end of a sentence is generally not set off by a comma. The box in the next column lists some of the most widely used subordinating conjunctions:

Subordinating Conjunctions

after	before	until
although	once	when
as	since	where
because	though	while

PRACTICE

Combine each pair of sentences by turning one of them into an adverb clause. Refer to the list of subordinating conjunctions above to help you rewrite the sentences. Use commas where appropriate.

1. President Kennedy was killed on November 22, 1963. The whole world mourned.
2. The students were in the yard. The girls jumped rope and the boys played basketball.
3. The gym teacher was a tough man. He cried openly about President Kennedy's death.
4. Elena's old neighbor died. His wife moved away.
5. The other girls made fun of Elena. She was different from them.
6. Elena felt alone and unhappy. Eugene moved into her neighborhood.
7. Elena watched Eugene from her fire escape. He sat in his kitchen reading library books.
8. Elena went to Eugene's house. Her mother tried to persuade her to stay home.
9. Elena felt sad at the end of the story. Her friendship with Eugene was over.
10. Elena looked out her window. Snow fell softly to the ground.

▶ **For more help, see Kinds of Clauses, 7e, in the Language Handbook.**

SKILLS FOCUS

Grammar Skills
Understand and use adverb clauses.

American History   **577**

Grammar Link

Practice

Possible Answers

1. When President Kennedy was killed on November 22, 1963, the whole world mourned.
2. The students were in the yard, where the girls jumped rope and the boys played basketball.
3. Although the gym teacher was a tough man, he cried openly about President Kennedy's death.
4. After Elena's old neighbor died, his wife moved away.
5. The other girls made fun of Elena because she was different from them.
6. Elena felt alone and unhappy until Eugene moved into her neighborhood.
7. Elena watched Eugene from her fire escape as he sat in his kitchen reading library books.
8. Elena went to Eugene's house, although her mother tried to persuade her to stay home.
9. Elena felt sad at the end of the story because her friendship with Eugene was over.
10. Elena looked out her window as snow fell softly to the ground.

ASSESSING

Assessment

■ *Holt Assessment: Literature, Reading, and Vocabulary*

RETEACHING

For a lesson reteaching biographical approach, see **Reteaching,** p. 979A. For another selection to teach historical approach, see *The Holt Reader,* Collection 9.

Grade-Level Skills

■ **Reading Skills**

Analyze and elaborate on ideas presented in primary and secondary sources.

Summary ⬍ *at grade level*

Three selections address the death of President John F. Kennedy in November 1963. Marta Randall's "A Warm, Clear Day in Dallas" is a history book account (secondary source) that chronicles the events that occurred on the day of the assassination. It also provides an overview of Kennedy's abbreviated term as president and uses quotations from politicians and academics to build an understanding of the tragic event's significance.

"Address to Congress" is a primary-source document, an excerpt from the speech made by President Lyndon B. Johnson five days after Kennedy's death. In the speech, President Johnson urges Congress to move forward with Kennedy's civil rights bill as a memorial to the slain president. Johnson expresses his resolve to work for Kennedy's goals and calls on Americans to respond to tragedy by putting hatred and violence aside.

Summary ⬇ *below grade level*

"Students React to President Kennedy's Death" consists of essays written by students two months after the assassination. Two students express the thoughts, sorrows, and fears they experienced in the wake of the national tragedy.

Informational Text

LINK TO "AMERICAN HISTORY"

A Warm, Clear Day in Dallas ◆ Address to Congress, November 27, 1963 ◆ Students React to President Kennedy's Death

Primary and Secondary Sources: Through Whose Eyes?

When you do research, you use sources that fall into two main categories: primary sources and secondary sources.

- A **primary source** is a firsthand account, such as a speech, an autobiography, or a letter. A primary source is useful because it directly expresses the thoughts and feelings of a writer, and it may include details that only an eyewitness can provide. Remember, though, that a primary source expresses the viewpoint of only one person, who may be biased or whose knowledge may be limited.

- A **secondary source** is a second-hand account. Authors of secondary sources, such as history books, biographies, and textbooks, summarize or analyze events in which they did not participate. Most magazine and newspaper articles are secondary sources, unless they are eyewitness reports, editorials, or opinion pieces. (Note that a historian would consider any newspaper or magazine article from the past to be a primary-source document from a particular historical period.)

Some types of secondary sources, such as encyclopedias, are more objective than primary sources because they are based on several different viewpoints. Secondary sources can also give you a broader view of a subject than primary sources might provide.

INTERNET
Interactive
Reading Model
Keyword: LE5 9-9

SKILLS FOCUS

Reading Skills
Understand and use primary and secondary sources.

The following chart lists some types of primary and secondary sources:

Primary Sources	Secondary Sources
Diaries	Encyclopedia articles
Autobiographies	Biographies
Letters	Reference books
Personal essays	History books
Speeches	Textbooks
Interviews	Most newspaper articles
Oral histories	Most magazine articles
Editorials	Literary criticism
Eyewitness news reports	
Literary works	
Public documents	

Using the Sources

To get the most out of using primary and secondary sources, follow these steps:

1. **Analyze.** First, determine whether your resources are primary or secondary sources. Examine what the authors say, why they say it, and how they express themselves.

   - Ask yourself, "Who is the author?" (For example, is the author a historian or a participant in an event?)

   - Also ask, "What is the **main idea** of the work? How does the author support the main idea?"

   - Determine the author's **purpose** and **audience**. For example, is the author writing to inform the general public, to describe an experience to a friend, or to persuade a group of senators to take action?

578 [Collection 9] Biographical and Historical Approach • Using Primary and Secondary Sources

---

RESOURCES: READING

Planning
■ *One-Stop Planner* CD-ROM with ExamView Test Generator

Differentiating Instruction
■ *Holt Reading Solutions*
■ *Supporting Instruction in Spanish*
■ *Audio CD Library, Selections and Summaries in Spanish*

Vocabulary
■ *Vocabulary Development*

Grammar and Language
■ *Daily Language Activities*

Assessment
■ *Holt Assessment: Literature, Reading, and Vocabulary*

- Describe the author's **tone** (attitude toward the subject) and writing **style**. In a speech, for example, an author might use a formal style and express opinions in a confident, uplifting tone. However, when writing about the same subject in a diary entry, an author might use an informal style and express doubts or worries in a cautious, concerned tone. Keep in mind that the tone and style of a work are affected by an author's audience and purpose.

2. **Evaluate.** First, determine whether points in your sources are objective **facts** (which can be proved) or subjective **opinions** (which cannot be proved). Both primary and secondary sources usually include a mixture of facts and opinions. Then, evaluate whether the facts and opinions are **credible,** or reliable. Follow these guidelines:
   - Verify that **facts** are **accurate** by checking other sources. Remember to note when each source was written. Do your sources present the latest findings?
   - Decide whether you think **opinions** are **valid** by considering whether you trust the authors and the experts or eyewitnesses who are quoted in your sources. Ask yourself, "Do these people know the subject well? Are they **biased,** or prejudiced, in some way?"
   - Consider how an author's **purpose** and **audience** affect the way that he or she presents facts and opinions. Watch out for sources that present opinions as if they were objective facts.

3. **Elaborate.** Draw connections between what you've learned from your sources and your prior knowledge of the subject. Do further research, or discuss your own opinions about the subject.

Vocabulary Development

denouncing (dē·nouns′iŋ) v. used as adj.: accusing publicly; condemning.

virtuous (vʉr′chōō·əs) adj.: good and moral; honorable.

controversial (kän′trə·vʉr′shəl) adj.: stirring up disagreement between groups holding opposing views.

conspiracy (kən·spir′ə·sē) n.: secret, often unlawful plan carried out by a group.

immortal (i·môrt′'l) adj.: lasting or living forever.

vitalized (vīt′'l·īzd′) v.: given life to; energized.

resolve (ri·zälv′) n.: strength of purpose; determination.

tolerance (täl′ər·əns) n.: respect for others who differ from you; freedom from prejudice.

bigotry (big′ə·trē) n.: strong prejudice against a particular group of people.

defiant (dē·fī′ənt) adj.: openly and boldly resisting or opposing.

Connecting to the Literature

In "American History," Elena's family and community are devastated by the assassination of President John F. Kennedy. The following selections tell what President Kennedy meant to our nation and to individual Americans as well.

Skills Starter

Build background. Before students read the Before You Read section, ask volunteers to share the resources they used to complete recent research. Then, list them on the chalkboard. After the class has read Before You Read, ask students to identify the listed sources as primary or secondary.

Preview Vocabulary

To familiarize students with the Vocabulary words on p. 579, have them use the words to complete the following sentences.

1. Racism and other forms of _____ should have no place in public or private life. [bigotry]
2. It's diplomatic to show _____ in the face of differing opinions. [tolerance]
3. The _____ two-year-old refused to listen to her mother. [defiant]
4. "Be good," said Mom. "Only _____ children get presents." [virtuous]
5. President Kennedy's youth and energy _____ the country. [vitalized]
6. The president refused to change his mind; nothing could shake his _____. [resolve]
7. Many dream of being _____, but no one can live forever. [immortal]
8. The new highway proposal was _____; some argued for it, others against it. [controversial]
9. The pacifist made speeches _____ war. [denouncing]
10. It seemed like a _____; everyone had turned against him. [conspiracy]

Assign the Reading

You may wish to assign the three selections as independent reading for advanced readers. Have other students read the selections in class.

- *One-Stop Planner* CD-ROM with ExamView Test Generator
- *Holt Online Assessment*

Internet
- go.hrw.com (Keyword LE5 9-9)
- *Elements of Literature Online*

Media
- *Audio CD Library*
- *Audio CD Library, Selections and Summaries in Spanish*
- *Fine Art Transparencies*

A **Reading Skills**
Evaluating. [Possible response to question 1: The sentence provides facts—the exact time and place—of events that occurred in the past. The sentence creates questions in readers' minds and establishes a mood of suspense.]

B **Reading Informational Text**
? Primary and secondary sources. Remind students that a history book is a secondary source. Ask, "Since the author wasn't an eyewitness to the event, where might she have acquired the information for this description?" [Possible responses: from newspaper accounts on the day of the assassination; from video footage of the motorcade; from interviews with eyewitnesses; from other books on the assassination.]

C **Reading Informational Text**
? Evaluate. What facts does the author use to illustrate that there was some hostility toward President Kennedy in Dallas? [Possible response: She cites the existence of "hate posters and leaflets denouncing the president" and the fact that there was a full-page anti-Kennedy newspaper advertisement published the day of the assassination.]

BIOGRAPHY

SECONDARY SOURCE

A Warm, Clear Day in Dallas

from John F. Kennedy

Marta Randall

The Texas School Book Depository Building.

On November 22, 1963, at 12:30 in the afternoon, a man with a rifle crouched behind a window in the Texas School Book Depository above Dealey Plaza in Dallas, Texas. **❶**

❶ EVALUATE
A Why is this an effective first sentence for a historical account?

It was a clear, brilliant autumn day, and the crowds in the street below cheered and waved as President John F. Kennedy's limousine passed by. The president and his wife, Jacqueline, smiled and waved back; earlier the president had stopped the motorcade[1] twice, once to shake hands with a little girl, and a second time to greet a Catholic nun and her group of

schoolchildren. During both of these stops, the Secret Service worked frantically to keep the crowd at a distance. Dallas, with a murder rate twice the national average and a vocal and hostile anti-Kennedy element, was not a safe city. Just a day earlier the city had been covered with hate posters and leaflets[2] denouncing the president. That morning's *Dallas News* had carried a full-page advertisement criticizing Kennedy for his abandonment of the Constitution and softness toward Moscow and communism.[3] But this afternoon the crowd seemed friendly, and the president wanted to be close to the people, to touch their hands and talk with them.

The motorcade entered Main Street and approached Dealey Plaza. Texas Governor

1. **motorcade** (mōt'ər·kād') *n.:* procession of cars or other vehicles, usually to escort an important person.

2. **leaflets** (lēf'lits) *n.:* printed material distributed to the public, often used to spread the views of a particular group.

3. **Moscow and communism:** Moscow is the capital of Russia, formerly the Soviet Union. Kennedy was president during a tense stage in the cold war, the bitter rivalry between the United States and its allies (supporters of democracy and capitalism) and the Soviet Union and its allies (supporters of communism).

Vocabulary
denouncing (dē·nouns'in) *v.* used as *adj.:* accusing publicly; condemning.

Learners Having Difficulty
Students will benefit from a discussion of the primary and secondary sources listed in the chart on p. 578. Discuss the use of each of these types of sources. For each one, ask students to suggest the kinds of research for which it would be useful. Then, present students with several different research questions. Have students suggest which materials

might be most useful for researching each topic or question.

English-Language Learners
Students who have not lived in the United States their entire lives may be less familiar with the historical era described. You may wish to preview this period for students. Draw a time line of the second half of the

twentieth century on the chalkboard. Ask a volunteer to indicate where events mentioned in the selections fall on the time line. Events might include the cold war, the building of the Berlin Wall, the Cuban missile crisis, Kennedy's inauguration, the Kennedy assassination, and the passage of the Civil Rights Act. Ask students to share what they know about each of these events.

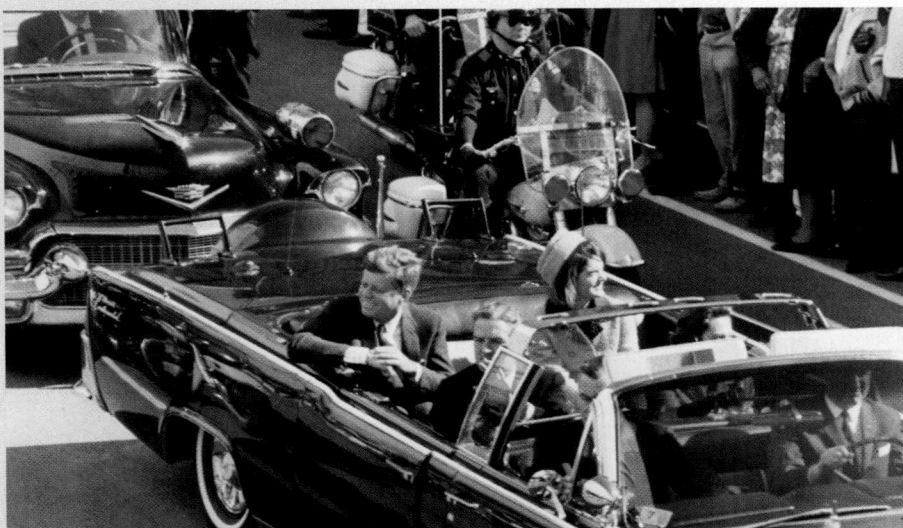

President Kennedy and Mrs. Kennedy smile at the crowds lining their motorcade route in Dallas, Texas, on November 22, 1963.

John Connally and his wife, Nellie, were riding in the limousine with the president, and Mrs. Connally said, "Mr. President, you can't say Dallas doesn't love you." The president waved at the crowd and said, "That's obvious." It seemed to be true.

John F. Kennedy had been president for a little more than a thousand days, and in that time he had brought the country through crises that shook the world. From the early humiliation of a badly planned and disastrous invasion of Cuba, he had gone on to challenge the nuclear might of the Soviet Union over missile bases in Cuba, confronted the Soviet Union over the explosive issue of the Berlin Wall,[4] founded

an Alliance for Progress that knit together the United States and Latin America, committed the United States to outer space exploration, and signed a nuclear test ban treaty with the Soviet Union and other countries. Perhaps the most important of his achievements was his support for civil rights and his effort to move the United States away from racial segregation and toward freedom and equal rights for all Americans. Kennedy called his program "the New Frontier"; he emphasized fresh solutions to the new, increasingly complex problems faced by the United States. Though he demanded hard work from himself, his staff, and all Americans, his youth, intellectual vigor,[5] and spirit of practical optimism imbued[6] many Americans with

4. **Berlin Wall:** In 1961, the Communist government in East Germany constructed a wall dividing East and West Berlin to prevent people living in East Germany from fleeing to West Germany (a Western-style democracy). The Berlin Wall was opened in 1989.

5. **intellectual vigor:** strong mental ability; high intelligence.
6. **imbued** (im·byood′) v.: inspired; filled with.

A Warm, Clear Day in Dallas **581**

A Reading Skills

Evaluating. [Possible response to question 2: *Facts*—Kennedy was president for a little more than a thousand days; Kennedy founded an Alliance for Progress; Kennedy signed a nuclear test ban treaty; Kennedy called his program "the New Frontier." *Opinion*—The most important of his achievements was his support for civil rights.]

B Reading Informational Text

? Analyzing: Sources. What sources does the author use to help readers visualize the scene of the shooting? [The author includes quotations from two eyewitnesses, the wives of the two victims.]

C Reading Informational Text

? Analyzing: Author's purpose. Ask students to pause to consider the author's purpose thus far. Is the author trying to simply inform the reader or trying to persuade the reader of something? [Possible response: The author is trying to inform a general audience about the events of the assassination.]

D Reading Informational Text

? Evaluating. What position does the author take on the question of whether Oswald was working alone? [Possible response: The author does not take a concrete stand.]

E Reading Skills

Evaluating. [Possible response to question 3: The author expresses the opinion that there will never be an explanation for the Kennedy assassination that will satisfy everyone.]

---

the belief that real progress could be made toward creating a better, more just society. Some people compared the Kennedy White House with Camelot, the idyllic court of King Arthur, the legendary Celtic king,[7] where for "one brief, shining moment" the strongest and most virtuous knights had gathered. ❷

❷ EVALUATE
List four **facts** contained in this paragraph. Then, find one **opinion.**

Not everyone was pleased with Kennedy and his administration, and segregation and U.S.-Soviet relations were both controversial subjects in Texas. But as the motorcade rolled on, the president was not worried. As he passed out of sight of the people in Dealey Plaza, the man in the sixth-floor window of the Texas School Book Depository aimed his rifle and fired.

Kennedy was hit first in the throat; the second bullet shattered his skull. Governor Connally was shot through the back. Jacqueline Kennedy cried, "Oh no, no . . . Oh, my God, they have shot my husband," and held the president tightly. As the two women cradled their husbands, the limousine pulled out of the motorcade and rushed to Parkland Hospital. Mrs. Connally later recalled, ". . . we must have been a horrible sight flying down the freeway with those dying men in our arms. There was no screaming in that horrible car. It was just a silent, terrible drive."

At one o'clock, the president was pronounced dead; an hour and a half later,

---

7. **Camelot . . . Celtic king:** According to legend, Arthur was a noble, brave king of Britain and the leader of the knights of the Round Table in the sixth century. Camelot has come to symbolize the glories of his rule.

---

aboard Air Force One,[8] Vice President Lyndon Johnson was sworn in as the 36th president of the United States. Jacqueline Kennedy stood beside him, still wearing her blood-soaked suit.

At 2:15 that afternoon, a young man named Lee Harvey Oswald was arrested for the murder of John Kennedy; two days later, on national television, Oswald was shot to death by a Dallas nightclub owner named Jack Ruby. One of President Johnson's first acts in office was to create a commission[9] headed by Earl Warren, chief justice of the Supreme Court, to investigate Kennedy's assassination. Despite the commission's finding that Oswald worked alone in killing the president, many people still believe that the assassination was the result of a conspiracy. It is likely that there will never be an explanation that satisfies everyone. ❸

❸ EVALUATE
What **opinion** does the author express in this paragraph?

John Kennedy was buried in Arlington National Cemetery on November 25, 1963. Leaders from 92 countries attended the funeral and millions of people lined the route. Jacqueline lit an eternal flame over his grave while his two young children looked on.

---

8. **Air Force One:** airplane on which the president of the United States travels.
9. **commission** (kə·mish′ən) *n.:* group of people officially appointed to perform a duty.

Vocabulary
virtuous (vʉr′chōō·əs) *adj.:* good and moral; honorable.
controversial (kän′trə·vʉr′shəl) *adj.:* stirring up disagreement between groups holding opposing views.
conspiracy (kən·spir′ə·sē) *n.:* secret, often unlawful plan carried out by a group.

CONTENT-AREA CONNECTIONS

 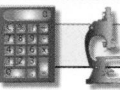 

History: Decade of Assassinations
The death of President John F. Kennedy was the first of four assassinations that shook the country and helped to brand the 1960s as a violent decade. In 1965, African American leader Malcolm X was shot and killed in New York City. In April 1968, civil rights leader Martin Luther King, Jr., was assassinated in Memphis. Later that year, Robert F. Kennedy (John F. Kennedy's younger brother and a

candidate for the Democratic presidential nomination) was shot and killed in California. **Small-group activity.** Have students work in small groups to collect primary-source documents related to the assassination of each of the leaders mentioned. These documents might include speeches, interviews, eyewitness accounts, or government documents. You may wish to create a classroom file of this student research.

Historian Herbert S. Parmet has written: "Few deaths have ever shocked so much of the world." People everywhere reacted with disbelief, shock, and grief. Jimmy Carter, a Georgia farmer who later became president of the United States, said, "I wept openly for the first time in ten years, for the first time since my own father died." Businesses and schools closed as American daily life virtually came to a halt. For four days, until the president was buried, people huddled around television sets and radios in grief and disbelief. In Copenhagen, Denmark, thousands of people brought flowers to the U.S. Embassy, so many that by the next morning the building was surrounded by flowers six feet deep. In West Berlin, people placed lit candles in darkened windows. Almost any American born before 1957 can remember where she or he was the day John Kennedy died. ❹

> ❹ **ANALYZE**
> How would you describe the author's **purpose** in this **secondary source**? Is the **tone** of the piece generally objective or subjective?

Jacqueline Kennedy and her children, Caroline and John, along with other members of the Kennedy family, at the funeral of President John F. Kennedy.

A Warm, Clear Day in Dallas **583**

A Reading Informational Text

? Analyzing: Audience. To whom is Johnson's speech directed? [Possible response: Johnson's primary audience is Congress. However, many ordinary citizens will also read the speech or hear broadcasts of it.]

B Learners Having Difficulty

Breaking down difficult text. Direct students' attention to the first line of the speech. Explain that Johnson is telling his audience that he would gladly give up his position as president if only John F. Kennedy were still alive. In other words, Johnson wishes that the event that placed him in this high position—Kennedy's assassination—had never happened.

C Reading Skills

Analyzing. [Possible response to question 1: Johnson's tone is somber, yet reassuring. The repetition of the phrase "lives on" emphasizes that all is not lost with the president's death; His influence will continue to be felt.]

D Reading Informational Text

? Evaluating. Ask students how repetition and parallel structure are used in this paragraph. [Possible response: The structure "the dream of . . ." is used seven times to emphasize Kennedy's goals.] **Why do you think Johnson calls these goals "American dreams"?** [Possible response: By calling them "American dreams," Johnson makes it more difficult for critics to oppose them.]

SPEECH

PRIMARY SOURCE

Immediately after President Kennedy's death, Vice President Lyndon B. Johnson was sworn in as the new president. Five days later Johnson made the following speech to a joint session of the House of Representatives and the Senate.

Address to Congress
November 27, 1963

from "Address Before a Joint Session of the Congress"
Lyndon B. Johnson

Mr. Speaker, Mr. President, Members of the House, Members of the Senate, my fellow Americans:

All I have I would have given gladly not to be standing here today.

The greatest leader of our time has been struck down by the foulest deed of our time. Today John Fitzgerald Kennedy lives on in the immortal words and works that he left behind. He lives on in the mind and memories of mankind. He lives on in the hearts of his countrymen. ❶

No words are sad enough to express our sense of loss. No words are strong enough to express our determination to continue the forward thrust of America that he began.

The dream of conquering the vastness of space—the dream of partnership across the Atlantic—and across the Pacific as well—the dream of a Peace Corps[1] in less developed nations—the dream of education for all of our children—the dream of jobs for all who seek them and need them—the dream of care for our elderly—the dream of an all-out attack on mental illness—and above all, the dream of equal rights for all Americans, whatever their race or color—these and other American dreams have been vitalized by his drive and by his dedication.

And now the ideas and the ideals which he so nobly represented must and will be translated into effective action.

On the 20th day of January, in 1961, John F. Kennedy told his countrymen that our national work would not be finished "in the first thousand days, nor in the life of this administration, nor even perhaps in our lifetime on this planet. But," he said, "let us begin."

Today, in this moment of new resolve, I would say to all my fellow Americans, let us continue.

❶ ANALYZE
What is the **tone** of this paragraph? How does Johnson's repetition of the phrase "lives on" contribute to the tone?

Vocabulary
immortal (i·môrt′l) *adj.*: lasting or living forever.
vitalized (vīt′l·īzd′) *v.*: given life to; energized.
resolve (ri·zälv′) *n.*: strength of purpose; determination.

---

1. **Peace Corps:** U.S. agency, established in 1961, that sends volunteers abroad to assist people in underdeveloped areas.

DEVELOPING FLUENCY

Small-group activity. Have students work in small groups to practice reading Johnson's address to Congress aloud. Encourage students to copy the speech on a separate sheet of paper. Have them work together to mark on the manuscript pauses, pronunciations of difficult words, and other cues. Then, have each student take a turn reading the speech aloud to their group members.

President Johnson addressing Congress on November 27, 1963.

We meet in grief, but let us also meet in renewed dedication and renewed vigor. Let us meet in action, in tolerance, and in mutual understanding. John Kennedy's death commands what his life conveyed—that America must move forward. The time has come for Americans of all races and creeds[4] and political beliefs to understand and to respect one another. So let us put an end to the teaching and the preaching of hate and evil and violence. Let us turn away from the fanatics[5] of the far left and the far right, from the apostles[6] of bitterness and bigotry, from those defiant of law, and those who pour venom[7] into our nation's bloodstream. **❷**

> **❷ ANALYZE**
> In this paragraph, what is Johnson urging his audience to do? What is his **tone** here?

This is our challenge—not to hesitate, not to pause, not to turn about and linger over this evil moment, but to continue on our course so that we may fulfill the destiny that history has set for us. Our most immediate tasks are here on this Hill.[2]

First, no memorial oration or eulogy[3] could more eloquently honor President Kennedy's memory than the earliest possible passage of the civil rights bill for which he fought so long. We have talked long enough in this country about equal rights. We have talked for one hundred years or more. It is time now to write the next collection, and to write it in the books of law.

I profoundly hope that the tragedy and the torment of these terrible days will bind us together in new fellowship, making us one people in our hour of sorrow. So let us here highly resolve that John Fitzgerald Kennedy did not live—or die—in vain.

---

4. **creeds** (krēdz) *n.:* religious beliefs.
5. **fanatics** (fə·nat'iks) *n.:* people whose extreme devotion to a cause is excessive or unreasonable.
6. **apostles** (ə·päs'əls) *n.:* people sent forth to spread a view or belief.
7. **venom** (ven'əm) *n.:* poison.

Vocabulary

tolerance (täl'ər·əns) *n.:* respect for others who differ from you; freedom from prejudice.

bigotry (big'ə·trē) *n.:* strong prejudice against a particular group of people.

defiant (dē·fī'ənt) *adj.:* openly and boldly resisting or opposing.

---

2. **Hill:** Capitol Hill in Washington, D.C., where Congress meets and where Johnson was giving the speech.
3. **oration** (ō·rā'shən) **or eulogy** (yōō'lə·jē): *oration* means "formal speech"; *eulogy* means "speech praising someone who has died."

❸ Learners Having Difficulty
❓ Questioning. What does Johnson mean when he says, "Our most immediate tasks are here on this Hill"? [Possible response: He is urging Congress to act immediately to move forward with the slain president's legislative agenda.]

❺ Vocabulary Development
Jargon. Point out the phrase "the far left and the far right." Explain that in politics, those who hold liberal views on issues are described as "leftist" or "left wing"; those with conservative views are "right wing." "Far left" and "far right" identify those with *extreme* liberal or conservative views.

❻ Reading Skills
Analyzing. [Possible response to question 2: Johnson is urging his audience to renounce hatred, racism, inflammatory speech, and violence. His tone is urgent, forceful, and demanding.]

❼ Reading Informational Text
❓ Evaluating. How do these closing lines make it difficult for people to oppose Johnson's requests? [Possible response: By framing his program in terms of not allowing President Kennedy to die in vain, Johnson makes criticism of his requests seem to be an insult to the memory of the president.]

CONTENT-AREA CONNECTIONS

Social Science: Congress
President Johnson's "Address to Congress" provides students with a good opportunity to review or extend their knowledge of how the United States Congress works.
Paired activity. Assign pairs of students one particular Congress-related topic to research. Possible topics include parts of Congress, duties of members, term lengths, responsibilities of Congress as a whole, and roles of the Senate and House of Representatives in lawmaking and enforcement. Students should present their findings to the class during a whole-class discussion.

A **Reading Informational Text**

? **Primary and secondary sources.** What makes this essay a primary-source document? [Possible response: The essay is a firsthand account that expresses the experiences and emotions of a person who lived through a historical event.]

B **Learners Having Difficulty**

? **Summarizing.** What emotions did the girl feel when she heard about the assassination? [Possible response: She felt anger and sorrow.]

C **Reading Informational Text**

? **Evaluating.** Consider this girl's account of what she experienced, along with the statements made in "A Warm, Clear Day in Dallas" about the emotional impact of the assassination on people around the world. Are the two accounts consistent? [Possible response: Yes; the girl's description of her profound sorrow echoes Randall's statements.]

D **Reading Skills**

? **Making inferences.** As does the title and first line of "A Warm, Clear Day in Dallas," this essay emphasizes the beauty of the fall day on which the assassination occurs. Why might both writers choose to emphasize the weather? [Possible response: The writers want to point out how the favorable weather of November 22, 1963 stood in stark contrast to the events that were about to occur, making them seem even more ugly and shocking.]

PRIMARY SOURCES

PERSONAL ESSAYS

The following personal essays were written by students two months after President Kennedy was assassinated. The essays appear here exactly as the students wrote them and include some spelling and grammatical errors.

Students React to President Kennedy's Death

from *Children and the Death of a President*

Girl Age Twelve, Grade Seven
How I felt about President Kennedy's Assassination.

A When I found out about President Kennedy's assassination I was full of sorrow and I was very worried.

When this drastic event took place I was sorry because I did not think anybody could stoop to such a low thing to do as **B** murder. When I heard that our President was dead, I just could not believe it. I felt just like crying. To think that our President was dead, struck down by an assassin's bullet, made me burn up inside.

I was worried about our country. Maybe it was just for a little while but I was worried because for a while we did not have a President. Some question kept flashing through my mind. What was to become of our country? Why should anybody do such a thing? Would Lindin Baynes Johnson be as good a president as the late President Kennedy? These are questions to be answered in the future. Maybe not even then.

I wish President Kennedy was not taken **C** away from the world, his family and his country.

Girl Age Fourteen, Grade Eight
What I Remmember About the Weekend President Kennedy Was Assassinated.

D It was a sunny and beautiful day, November 22, 1963. The air was chilled with a slight breeze, but there wasn't a cloud in the sky. For almost everyone on the earth there was no anxiety or fear of and unexpected tradgedy. It was a normal Friday and everyone went about their business as usual, but, the day was brought to an abrupt standstill.

Our class was in math our sixth period class. We were in the middle of the test when a neighboring teacher came in and handed our math teacher a note. A sudden expression of horror filled her face. She followed the other teacher into the hall, leaving us unattended. I began to feel uneasy and quite nervous when the teacher returned. She had a look of utter disbelief and shock on her face. At once the thought of another World War came into my head. I got very fidgety and was distracted from my work on the test.

CONTENT-AREA CONNECTIONS

History: Civil Rights Act of 1964
Explain to students that President Johnson signed into law the Civil Rights Act, the most far-reaching civil rights legislation in the nation's history, on July 2, 1964, after both houses of Congress voted in favor of it. The law prohibits segregation in public places and bans discrimination on the basis of color, race, religion, or national origin in education and employment. Support for the bill was far from unanimous. In fact, much of the strongest opposition came from members of the president's own party, Democratic senators and congressmen from the South. Criticism also came from many African Americans who felt the legislation didn't go far enough.

The eternal flame at the John F. Kennedy Memorial in Arlington, Virginia.

For the next five minutes or so she just sat staring into space. Then she stood up and kind of moped around the classroom watching us. Almost immediately after she stood up the test was discontinued. There was a piercing silence in the room as we passed forward our papers. I think we all knew something was wrong. Then she told us the horrible and tradgedy filled event. "The President had been killed." I was standing almost frozen stiff with shock and disbelief. Presently I began to move again and I found my seat. The school was dismissed very shortly. We all moved in silence back to our homeroom where we gathered our books and coats. The halls in school were never so quiet. We went home and tried to console ourselves but it was too much. Most of us cried. I shed one tear I couldn't allow myself to cry although I certainly felt like it. ●

● **ANALYZE**
Review the title and the first two paragraphs of this essay. What are the first two clues that this is a **primary source?**

That whole weekend you were glued to the television. It showed from the tragic moment until his casket was lowered into the ground. I never felt so empty in all my life. I felt as if he was one of the family. Never could such a thing happen I said to myself. It's just impossible.

I'm Catholic so Monday night our church had a Mass said for him. When I walked into church and saw the imposter casket° sitting in the middle of the isle I almost died. My sunk to my knees.

From that Black day to this day I still can't bring myself to really believe deeply inside my heart what had happened that day President Kennedy was assassinated.

° **Mass ... imposter casket:** Mass is the traditional church service of worship for Roman Catholics. In most funeral masses the casket holding the body of the dead person remains in front of the congregation during the service. Here an empty casket symbolized Kennedy's death.

DIRECT TEACHING

E Reading Informational Text

Elaborating. Have students consider this description of the scene at school when news of the assassination was announced. Ask them to think how it must have felt to hear this news. You may wish to encourage students to compare this account to their own experiences on September 11, 2001, the day of the World Trade Center and Pentagon terrorist attacks.

F Reading Skills

Analyzing. [Possible response to question: The title "What I Remember About the Weekend President Kennedy Was Assassinated" indicates that the essay will contain the personal feelings of the writer; the first two paragraphs provide a firsthand description of what she herself experienced.]

G Reading Informational Text

❷ Evaluating. What details from the other student essay and "A Warm, Clear Day in Dallas" are echoed in this paragraph? [Possible responses: People found Kennedy's death impossible to believe; people spent days glued to the television; people felt a profound sense of loss.]

DIFFERENTIATING INSTRUCTION

Learners Having Difficulty
Work with students to make connections between the details and ideas presented in these selections. You might begin by reviewing "A Warm, Clear Day in Dallas" and identifying the important details and key points included in that piece. Then, you can help students find details and ideas in Johnson's address and in the students' letters that support or extend the information in Randall's selection.

DEVELOPING FLUENCY

Paired activity. After students have read the selections, ask them to imagine that they have been asked to describe the events surrounding the Kennedy assassination to someone who knows little about them. Then, have students take turns describing the events to their partners.

Analyzing Informational Text

Reading Check

1. Lee Harvey Oswald shot President Kennedy as he rode in a motorcade through Dallas. Lyndon B. Johnson was sworn in as president and Oswald was arrested for the murder.

2. Johnson called for early passage of the civil rights bill.

3. The girl worries for the country that is without a president and wonders whether President Johnson would perform as well as President Kennedy.

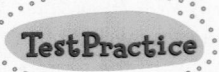

Answers and Model Rationales

1. **C** Randall includes opinions but provides more facts, so A is incorrect. B is wrong because details about Kennedy's funeral support her statement. Quotations by a historian, the presidential widow, and a former president are included, so D is incorrect.

2. **J** Only J expresses the major thrusts of Johnson's speech.

3. **A** A speech focused on the passage of a political agenda is appropriate for an audience of lawmakers. B is wrong, since many could keep Kennedy's memory alive. C is wrong, because many do not agree with Johnson's views; and D is wrong, because he does not discuss this topic.

4. **H** School closings, mass television watching, and clear fall weather are all detailed in Randall's text. H is the only possible answer.

Analyzing Informational Text

Reading Check

Reading Skills
Analyze primary and secondary sources.

1. Explain how President Kennedy died, as recounted in "A Warm, Clear Day in Dallas." Then, list two important events that occurred in the first hours after his death.

2. According to his speech, what does President Johnson think would be the best way to honor President Kennedy's memory?

3. What concerns does the twelve-year-old girl express in her personal essay?

Test Practice

1. Which statement represents the *most* accurate **evaluation** of "A Warm, Clear Day in Dallas"?

   A The author includes many more opinions than facts in the selection.

   B The author does not support her statement "People everywhere reacted with disbelief, shock, and grief" to the news of President Kennedy's death.

   C The author presents both facts and opinions in her account of Kennedy's assassination.

   D The author includes quotations from people who seem unreliable.

2. The **purpose** of President Johnson's speech was to —

   F tell how much he mourned the loss of Kennedy

   G convey that he would be a better president than Kennedy was

   H describe his outrage over violent, evil acts

   J express his commitment to pursuing Kennedy's goals for the country

3. Why is Johnson's speech appropriate for his **audience,** members of Congress?

   A He discusses the need to turn ideas into actions, and his audience makes laws for the country.

   B Only his audience, the country's political leaders, could help Americans keep Kennedy's memory alive.

   C His audience, who worked closely with Kennedy, was especially affected by his death and would agree with Johnson's views.

   D Using Kennedy as a model, he wants to tell his audience how to become better leaders.

4. Which statement in the fourteen-year-old's personal essay *cannot* be **verified** with information from "A Warm, Clear Day in Dallas"?

   F "That whole weekend you were glued to the television."

   G "It was a sunny and beautiful day, November 22, 1963."

   H "It was a normal Friday and everyone went about their business as usual. . . ."

   J "The school was dismissed very shortly."

ASSESSING

Assessment

■ *Holt Assessment: Literature, Reading, and Vocabulary*

RETEACHING

For a lesson reteaching analyzing and elaborating on ideas, see **Reteaching,** p. 979A. For another selection to teach analyzing and elaborating on ideas, see *The Holt Reader,* Part 2.

5. Which of the following statements describing a **difference** between "A Warm, Clear Day in Dallas" and Johnson's speech is *true*?

A One can learn about the views of an individual person only from Johnson's speech.

B "A Warm, Clear Day in Dallas" is more objective than Johnson's speech.

C Only Johnson's speech describes Kennedy's commitment to civil rights.

D Only "A Warm, Clear Day in Dallas" discusses Kennedy's dedication to improving society.

6. Which statement can be supported by **facts** or **opinions** in *all* of the selections?

F President Kennedy's untimely death was a tragedy from which the United States has never recovered.

G Millions of people, adults as well as children, were deeply saddened by President Kennedy's death.

H There will always be some people who believe that President Kennedy was not killed by a lone gunman.

J President Kennedy has come to be admired more in death than he was in life.

Constructed Response

Extend the information in these selections by doing your own original research. Ask two adults whom you know well to describe what they remember about the day President Kennedy was shot. Then, write one or two paragraphs in which you **elaborate** on the ideas in the selections, using your new **primary-source** information. Does your research support the information and the ideas in the selections, or does it offer a different perspective?

Vocabulary Development

Word Knowledge: What's the Difference?

PRACTICE

Answer each of the following questions by explaining the differences in meaning between the two words. The two words may be **antonyms** (opposites) or **synonyms** with different **connotations** (associations), or they may be different in other ways.

1. What's the difference between *denouncing* and *criticizing*?
2. What's the difference between *virtuous* and *immoral*?
3. What's the difference between *controversial* and *contradictory*?
4. What's the difference between *conspiracy* and *plan*?
5. What's the difference between *immortal* and *mortal*?
6. What's the difference between *vitalized* and *weakened*?
7. What's the difference between *resolve* and *desire*?
8. What's the difference between *tolerance* and *bigotry*?
9. What's the difference between *defiant* and *uncooperative*?

Word Bank

denouncing
virtuous
controversial
conspiracy
immortal
vitalized
resolve
tolerance
bigotry
defiant

SKILLS FOCUS

Vocabulary Skills
Clarify word meanings.

8. *Bigotry* and *tolerance* are antonyms. The former means "hatred for others;" the latter means "acceptance and respect."

9. *Defiant* and *uncooperative* are synonyms. *Defiant* connotes an outright refusal to cooperate.

5. B A balanced, historical account is likely to be more objective than a presidential speech with a political agenda. Because individual views and detailed information about Kennedy's programs are contained in both Randall's text and Johnson's speech, A, C, and D are incorrect.

6. G America has recovered from the tragedy, eliminating F. The detail in H is discussed only in "A Warm, Clear Day in Dallas." None of the selections agree with the statement in J.

Test-Taking Tips

For more instruction on how to answer multiple-choice items, refer students to **Test Smarts**.

Vocabulary Development

Practice

Possible Answers

1. *Denouncing* is a far stronger form of condemnation than is *criticizing*.

2. *Virtuous,* meaning "good and moral," is an antonym for *immoral,* which means "corrupt or unjust."

3. The two words share the same Latin root—*contra*–, meaning "against." *Controversial* means "sparking disagreement." *Contradictory* means "opposing."

4. A *conspiracy* is a *plan* hatched by individuals working in concert. Unlike *plan, conspiracy* connotes secrecy and deceit.

5. *Immortal* and *mortal* are antonyms. The former lives forever; the latter does not.

6. *Vitalized* and *weakened* are antonyms. The former means "having gained energy," while the latter means "having lost energy or strength."

7. *Resolve* is stronger than *desire.* It involves an unwavering determination, not just a longing.

■ **Literary Skills**

Analyze the way a work of literature relates to the themes and issues of its historical period. (Historical approach)

■ **Reading Skills**

Make inferences.

Summary  *at grade level*

The historical setting of this gripping story is very important. It takes place during World War II, at the time when Germany occupied most of Europe, including France. The plot revolves around the experiences of a British fighter pilot who has been hit by enemy fire while on a bombing raid somewhere over Germany. The story opens as he is trying to fly back to his home base in England while bleeding severely from a badly injured leg. When he realizes that he will soon lose consciousness, he bails out of the plane with no idea as to where he is or where he will land. He returns to consciousness in a hospital. The nurse tells him he is in Brighton, a seaside town in England. But certain details make him suspicious about his true location. The next morning, he crawls to the window. There, he glimpses a sign: "Garde au chien." He realizes then that he is in occupied France and that the hospital staff are likely to be intelligence officers. In the last line of the story, he gives only his name, rank, and number so as not to betray his country by giving information to the enemy.

Before You Read

Beware of the Dog

Make the Connection

Quickwrite 🖋

There's an old saying, "Appearances can be deceiving." Have you ever been misled by the appearance of someone or something? List some situations in which people might be deceived. Why might they be misled? How might they discover that their initial impressions were wrong? Jot down your responses.

Literary Focus

Understanding Historical Setting

Usually when a writer sets a story in a distinct **historical period,** the story's **conflicts** reflect the conflicts faced by the people living in that particular time and place.

Many works of fiction are driven by the high-stakes struggles of actual wars. Roald Dahl's "Beware of the Dog" tells the story of a British fighter pilot during World War II. As you read this story, remember its historical setting. Keep in mind that every breath the pilot takes, every thought he has, is influenced by the fact that his country is at war, and he is fighting for his life.

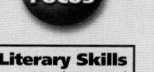

INTERNET

Vocabulary Practice
•
More About Roald Dahl
•
Keyword: LE5 9-9

SKILLS FOCUS

Literary Skills
Understand historical setting.

Reading Skills
Make inferences.

Reading Skills 📖

Making Inferences: Telltale Signs

When you make an **inference,** you make an educated guess about something. Some stories contain telltale signs or hints that something may be going on that the writer is not spelling out for you. In such cases, as in "Beware of the Dog," it's your job to infer what those hints might mean, using your experience and imagination. As you read this story, the questions at the open-book signs will help you make inferences.

Background

World War II began when Germany invaded Poland, in 1939, prompting Great Britain and France to declare war on Germany. France surrendered to Germany in 1940, and it was occupied by the German army until it was liberated by Allied forces, in 1944. The war finally ended on September 2, 1945.

This story is told from the vantage point of a British fighter pilot, probably after the Battle of Britain (1940). As the story opens, the pilot is trying to get back home after a bombing mission against German targets somewhere in Europe.

Vocabulary Development

undulating (un′jə·lāt′iŋ) *v.* used as *adj.*: moving in waves.

giddy (gid′ē) *adj.*: dizzy.

unconscious (un·kän′shəs) *adj.*: not awake and alert.

idly (īd′′lē) *adv.*: without aim or purpose.

delirious (di·lir′ē·əs) *adj.*: temporarily confused and seeing imaginary things, often because of injury or fever.

obsession (əb·sesh′ən) *n.*: persistent idea or desire that consumes a person's attention.

hoisted (hoist′id) *v.*: lifted or pulled up.

beckoned (bek′ənd) *v.*: gestured or signaled to request someone to approach or follow.

RESOURCES: READING

Planning
■ *One-Stop Planner* CD-ROM with ExamView Test Generator

Differentiating Instruction
■ *Holt Reading Solutions*
■ *Supporting Instruction in Spanish*
■ *Audio CD Library, Selections and Summaries in Spanish*

Vocabulary
■ *Vocabulary Development*

Grammar and Language
■ *Daily Language Activities*

Assessment
■ *Holt Assessment: Literature, Reading, and Vocabulary*

BEWARE OF THE DOG

Roald Dahl

Something had occurred to him; something so fantastic and absurd...

591

■ *One-Stop Planner* CD-ROM with ExamView Test Generator
■ *Holt Online Assessment*

Internet
■ go.hrw.com (Keyword LE5 9-9)
■ *Elements of Literature Online*

Media
■ *Audio CD Library*

A **Reading Skills**

❓ **Making inferences.** Remind students that when they make a logical guess based on clues plus use their own experiences, they are making an inference. Based on the first paragraph, where do you think the character in the story is? [He is in the air, probably in an airplane.] What clues led you to this inference? [Clouds are below him and the sun is white.]

B **Reading Skills**

❓ **Making inferences.** One way a writer develops a character is to show the character's thoughts and actions. What inferences can you make about the pilot's character from what he is imagining about his actions after landing? [Possible response: He is, or wants to be, lighthearted, brave, imperturbable, and in control.]

C **Literary Focus**

❓ **Figurative language.** To what does the pilot compare his severe injury? [to "finding a dead cat on the sofa"] What does this simile reveal about the pilot's state of mind and why is this state of mind advantageous? [Possible response: He is looking at his injury as though it were something apart from himself. This helps him to remain rational and unafraid.]

D **Reading Skills**

Making inferences. [Possible response to question 1: His condition is worsening and his thoughts are becoming irrational and disconnected, perhaps due to the trauma and loss of blood.]

E **Reading Skills**

❓ **Drawing conclusions.** What will happen if the pilot passes out? [The plane will crash and he will die.] How does the repetition of "I'm going to pass out" heighten the suspense of the story? [Possible response: It emphasizes the extreme danger the pilot is in.]

A Down below there was only a vast white undulating sea of cloud. Above there was the sun, and the sun was white like the clouds, because it is never yellow when one looks at it from high in the air.

He was flying the Spitfire.[1] His right hand was on the stick and he was working the rudder bar[2] with his left leg alone. It was quite easy. The machine was flying well. He knew what he was doing.

B Everything is fine, he thought. I'm doing all right. I'm doing nicely. I know my way home. I'll be there in half an hour. When I land, I shall taxi in and switch off my engine and I shall say, help me to get out, will you. I shall make my voice sound ordinary and natural and none of them will take any notice. Then I shall say, someone help me to get out. I can't do it alone because I've lost one of my legs. They'll all laugh and think that I'm joking and I shall say, all right, come and have a look. . . . Then Yorky will climb up on to the wing and look inside. He'll probably be sick because of all the blood and the mess. I shall laugh and say, for God's sake, help me get out.

C He glanced down again at his right leg. There was not much of it left. The cannon shell had taken him on the thigh, just above the knee, and now there was nothing but a great mess and a lot of blood. But there was no pain. When he looked down, he felt as though he were seeing something that did not belong to him. It had nothing to do with him. It was just a mess which happened to be there in the cockpit; something strange and unusual and rather interesting. It was like finding a dead cat on the sofa.

He really felt fine, and because he still felt fine, he felt excited and unafraid.

I won't even bother to call up on the radio for the bloodwagon, he thought. It isn't necessary. And when I land, I'll sit there quite normally

1. **Spitfire:** British fighter plane used in World War II.
2. **stick . . . rudder bar:** "Stick" refers to the plane's joystick, which controls its movement up or down. The rudder bar helps control movement to the right or the left.

and say, some of you fellows come and help me out, will you, because I've lost one of my legs. That will be funny. I'll laugh a little while I'm saying it; I'll say it calmly and slowly, and they'll think I'm joking. When Yorky comes up on to the wing and gets sick, I'll say, Yorky . . . have you fixed my car yet. Then when I get out, I'll make my report. Later I'll go up to London and see Bluey. I'll say, Bluey I've got a surprise for you. I lost a leg today. But I don't mind so long as you don't. It doesn't even hurt. We'll go everywhere in cars. I always hated walking except when I walked down the street of the coppersmiths in Baghdad,[3] but I could go in a rickshaw.[4] I could go home and chop wood, but the head always flies off the ax. Hot water, that's what it needs; put it in the bath and make the handle swell. I chopped lots of wood last time I went home and I put the ax in the bath . . .

D

MAKING INFERENCES

1. What can you **infer** about the pilot's condition from the way his thoughts are wandering?

Then he saw the sun shining on the engine cowling[5] of his machine. He saw the sun shining on the rivets in the metal, and he remembered the airplane and he remembered where he was. He realized that he was no longer feeling good; that he was sick and giddy. His head kept falling forward on to his chest because his neck seemed no longer to have any strength. But he knew that he was flying the Spitfire. He could feel the handle of the stick between the fingers of his right hand.

E I'm going to pass out, he thought. Any moment now I'm going to pass out.

3. **Baghdad** (bag'dad'): capital of Iraq.
4. **rickshaw** *n.*: small, two-wheeled carriage, pulled by a person.
5. **cowling** *n.*: metal covering of an airplane engine.

Vocabulary

undulating (un'jə·lāt'iŋ) *v.* used as *adj.*: moving in waves.

giddy (gid'ē) *adj.*: dizzy.

DIFFERENTIATING INSTRUCTION

Learners Having Difficulty

Modeling. To help students read "Beware of the Dog," model the reading skill of making inferences. Say, "The pilot keeps telling himself that everything is fine. When people are in trouble, they often say things that they wish were true in order to reassure themselves and keep themselves going. Readers may infer that the pilot is not fine, but is in great danger." Encourage students as they read to ask themselves questions such as "What can I infer about the characters and setting based on clues in the story plus my own knowledge?"

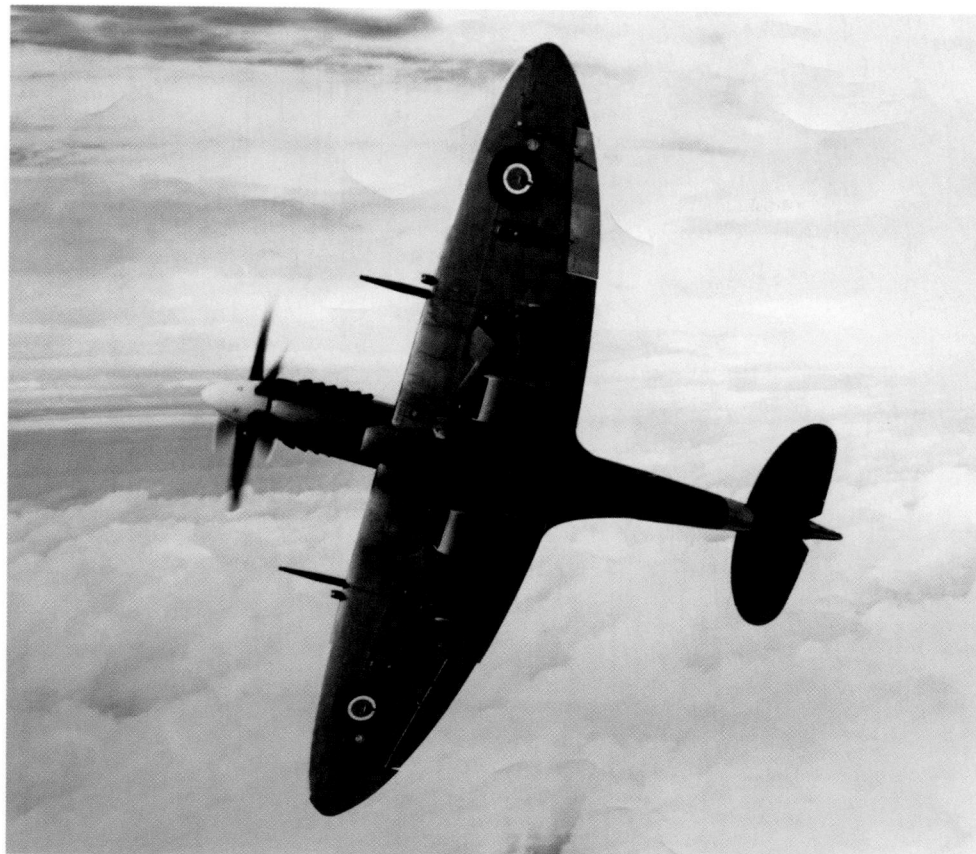

British Spitfire, the famous fighter plane used in the Battle of Britain. (A Spitfire is also shown in the photograph on page 591.)

He looked at his altimeter.[6] Twenty-one thousand. To test himself he tried to read the hundreds as well as the thousands. Twenty-one thousand and what? As he looked, the dial became blurred and he could not even see the needle. He knew then that he must bail out;[7] that there was not a second to lose, otherwise he would become unconscious. Quickly, frantically, he tried to slide back the hood with his left

hand, but he had not the strength. For a second he took his right hand off the stick and with both hands he managed to push the hood back. The rush of cold air on his face seemed to help. He had a moment of great clearness. His actions became orderly and precise. That is what happens with a good pilot. He took some quick deep breaths from his oxygen mask, and as he did so, he looked out over the side of the

---

6. **altimeter** (al·tim′ət·ər) *n.*: instrument that measures altitude, or height.
7. **bail out** *v.*: parachute out of an airplane in an emergency.

Vocabulary
unconscious (un·kän′shəs) *adj.*: not awake and alert.

DIFFERENTIATING INSTRUCTION

Advanced Learners

Acceleration. Use the following activity to help advanced learners relate literary works and authors to the major themes and issues of their eras.

Activity. Invite students to work in small groups to go through the story and list any incident or aspect of setting that may relate to issues that the British faced in World War II. Then, have students research such topics as the role of British fighter pilots during that war, the downing of planes, the capture of pilots, how military intelligence was obtained, and Roald Dahl's experience as a fighter pilot. Invite the group to hold a panel discussion for the class, in which researchers discuss the relationship of the story to major issues of its time period.

cockpit. Down below there was only a vast white sea of cloud and he realized that he did not know where he was.

It'll be the Channel,[8] he thought. I'm sure to fall in the drink.[9]

He throttled back,[10] pulled off his helmet, undid his straps, and pushed the stick hard over to the left. The Spitfire dipped its port[11] wing and turned smoothly over on to its back. The pilot fell out.

As he fell, he opened his eyes, because he knew that he must not pass out before he had pulled the cord. On one side he saw the sun; on the other he saw the whiteness of the clouds, and as he fell, as he somersaulted in the air, the white clouds chased the sun and the sun chased the clouds. They chased each other in a small circle; they ran faster and faster and there was the sun and the clouds and the clouds and the sun, and the clouds came nearer until suddenly there was no longer any sun but only a great whiteness. The whole world was white and there was nothing in it. It was so white that sometimes it looked black, and after a time it was either white or black, but mostly it was white. He watched it as it turned from white to black, then back to white again, and the white stayed for a long time, but the black lasted only for a few seconds. He got into the habit of going to sleep during the white periods, of waking up just in time to see the world when it was black. The black was very quick. Sometimes it was only a flash, a flash of black lightning. The white was slow and in the slowness of it, he always dozed off.

One day, when it was white, he put out a hand and he touched something. He took it between his fingers and crumpled it. For a time he lay there, idly letting the tips of his fingers play with

---

8. **Channel:** English Channel, the narrow body of water separating England and France.
9. **fall in the drink:** British expression meaning "fall into the water."
10. **throttled back:** reduced the speed of an airplane.
11. **port** *adj.:* left, on a ship or an airplane.

the thing which they had touched. Then slowly he opened his eyes, looked down at his hand, and saw that he was holding something which was white. It was the edge of a sheet. He knew it was a sheet because he could see the texture of the material and the stitchings on the hem. He screwed up his eyes and opened them again quickly. This time he saw the room. He saw the bed in which he was lying: He saw the gray walls and the door and the green curtains over the window. There were some roses on the table by his bed.

Then he saw the basin on the table near the roses. It was a white enamel basin and beside it there was a small medicine glass.

This is a hospital, he thought. I am in a hospital. But he could remember nothing. He lay back on his pillow, looking at the ceiling and wondering what had happened. He was gazing at the smooth grayness of the ceiling which was so clean and gray, and then suddenly he saw a fly walking upon it. The sight of this fly, the suddenness of seeing this small black speck on a sea of gray, brushed the surface of his brain, and quickly, in that second, he remembered everything. He remembered the Spitfire and he remembered the altimeter showing twenty-one thousand feet. He remembered the pushing back of the hood with both hands and he remembered the bailing out. He remembered his leg.

It seemed all right now. He looked down at the end of the bed, but he could not tell. He put one hand underneath the bedclothes and felt for his knees. He found one of them, but when he felt for the other, his hand touched something which was soft and covered in bandages.

Just then the door opened and a nurse came in. "Hello," she said. "So you've waked up at last."

MAKING INFERENCES

2. Look carefully at the description in the last two paragraphs. Where do you think the pilot is?

Vocabulary
idly (īd'lē) *adv.:* without aim or purpose.

A **Literary Focus**

❷ **Historical setting.** What do you know about the historical context of this story—that is, the time and place in which it is set—that would explain why the pilot is afraid he'll land in the water? [Possible response: He fears that instead of landing safely in England, he may come down in the Channel or on the French side of the Channel. There, he risks capture or death at the hands of enemy soldiers.]

B **Learners Having Difficulty**

Determining sequence of events. Many things happen quickly in this paragraph. Ask students to make a numbered list showing each thing that happened in the order it occurred.

C **Reading Skills**

❷ **Interpreting.** What is the pilot describing as the sun and clouds chase each other? [His perceptions as he is in free fall.] What do you think might have happened after the clouds and the sun became whiteness and blackness? [The pilot may have lost consciousness after he went through the clouds or after he landed. He may be only dimly aware of day and night.]

D **Reading Skills**

Making inferences. [Possible response to question 2: He is in a bed in a hospital room.] Ask students to point out the details that led them to their inference. [Possible responses: The white and gray shades of the room; the sheets; the spare furnishings; the medicine glass.]

A **Literary Focus**

? **Historical setting.** The pilot has been unconscious for days. Why does it make sense that this would be his first question upon regaining consciousness? [Possible responses: He needs to orient himself. He needs to know if he is in enemy territory or not.]

B **Vocabulary Development**

? **Literal meanings.** Remind students that the word *last* has a number of meanings in English. What does *last* mean in this passage? [Possible response: Here it means "the one before" and refers to the previous war, or World War I.]

C **Reading Skills**

? **Making inferences.** How would the ribbons and the doctor's appearance in general be likely to strike the British pilot? [The pilot would probably feel reassured and impressed by the doctor's appearance.]

D **Literary Focus**

? **Historical setting.** Tell students that Roald Dahl was himself a fighter pilot for the British RAF (Royal Air Force) during World War II. How do details in this passage help reveal the author's time period and background? [Possible response: The description of the German Junkers 88 is so detailed and precise that it could only have been written by someone who had lived during World War II and had developed a keen awareness of the sounds of different aircraft. The passage clearly reflects Dahl's years as a fighter pilot for the RAF.]

She was not good-looking, but she was large and clean. She was between thirty and forty and she had fair hair. More than that he did not notice.

A "Where am I?"

"You're a lucky fellow. You landed in a wood near the beach. You're in Brighton.[12] They brought you in two days ago, and now you're all fixed up. You look fine."

"I've lost a leg," he said.

"That's nothing. We'll get you another one. Now you must go to sleep. The doctor will be coming to see you in about an hour." She picked up the basin and the medicine glass and went out.

But he did not sleep. He wanted to keep his eyes open because he was frightened that if he shut them again everything would go away. He lay looking at the ceiling. The fly was still there. It was very energetic. It would run forward very fast for a few inches, then it would stop. Then it would run forward again, stop, run forward, and every now and then it would take off and buzz around viciously in small circles. It always landed back in the same place on the ceiling and started running and stopping all over again. He watched it for so long that after a while it was no longer a fly, but only a black speck upon a sea of gray, and he was still watching it when the nurse opened the door, and stood aside while the doctor came in. He was an **B** army doctor, a major, and he had some last war ribbons on his chest. He was bald and small, but he had a cheerful face and kind eyes.

C

"Well, well," he said. "So you've decided to wake up at last. How are you feeling?"

"I feel all right."

"That's the stuff. You'll be up and about in no time."

The doctor took his wrist to feel his pulse. "By the way," he said, "some of the lads from

---

12. **Brighton** (brīt′n): English city on the English Channel.

---

your squadron[13] were ringing up[14] and asking about you. They wanted to come along and see you, but I said that they'd better wait a day or two. Told them you were all right and that they could come and see you a little later on. Just lie quiet and take it easy for a bit. Got something to read?" He glanced at the table with the roses. "No. Well, nurse will look after you. She'll get you anything you want." With that he waved his hands and went out, followed by the large clean nurse.

When they had gone, he lay back and looked at the ceiling again. The fly was still there and as he lay watching it he heard the noise of an airplane in the distance. He lay listening to the sound of its engines. It was a long way away. I wonder what it is, he thought. Let me see if I can place it. Suddenly he jerked his head sharply to one side. Anyone who has been bombed can tell the noise of a Junkers 88. They can tell most other German bombers for that matter, but especially a Junkers 88. The engines seem to sing a duet. There is a **D** deep vibrating bass voice and with it there is a high-pitched tenor. It is the singing of the tenor which makes the sound of a Ju-88 something which one cannot mistake.

He lay listening to the noise and felt quite certain about what it was. But where were the sirens and where the guns? That German pilot certainly had a nerve coming near Brighton alone in daylight.

The aircraft was always far away and soon the noise faded away into the distance. Later on there was another. This one, too, was far away, but there was the same deep undulating bass and the high swinging tenor and there was no mistaking it. He had heard that noise every day during the Battle.[15]

---

13. **squadron** (skwäd′rən) *n.*: military unit.
14. **ringing up:** British expression meaning "telephoning."
15. **Battle:** Battle of Britain (1940), in which Germany tried to conquer Great Britain. The Germans launched heavy air attacks, but they could not defeat Britain's Royal Air Force.

CONTENT-AREA CONNECTIONS

Geography: The English Channel
In the story, the pilot bailed out of his plane over the English Channel. Historically, during World War II, this narrow strip of water was the major obstacle that prevented the German land army from rolling into Britain as they had rolled into France.
Small-group activity. Have groups draw a scale map showing a close-up of the Channel and the coastline and cities on both sides of it.

If they wish, students may illustrate the border of the map with scenes from the story.

Science: Trauma
Tell students that the pilot in this story is under a great deal of stress, both physical and mental. Simply flying a bomber over enemy territory is stressful enough, but getting hit and sustaining a massive injury is severely traumatic.

Individual activity. Invite interested students to research an aspect of the physiological or psychological effects of trauma. They may focus on adrenaline, endorphins, blood loss, or other matters of special interest.

History/Technology: Aircraft
World War II was the first war in which air power played a decisive role. The editor of the book *Fighters of World War II* referred to the Spitfire as "this magnificent thoroughbred fighting machine . . . perhaps the best-known British aircraft of all time."

Mixed-ability group activity. Have students of varying abilities work on researching details about the Spitfire or other fighters used in World War II. They should focus both on the plane itself and on its role in the war. Groups may then report their findings to the class.

Making inferences. [Possible responses to question 3: If the planes are German, either Britain was defeated while the pilot was unconscious or the pilot is not in Brighton but in enemy territory. From the nurse's responses, you can infer that she is trying to avoid the pilot's questions.]

An area in London hit by German bombs during an air raid in 1940.

He was puzzled. There was a bell on the table by the bed. He reached out his hand and rang it. He heard the noise of footsteps down the corridor. The nurse came in.

"Nurse, what were those airplanes?"

"I'm sure I don't know. I didn't hear them. Probably fighters or bombers. I expect they were returning from France. Why, what's the matter?"

"They were Ju-88s. I'm sure they were Ju-88s. I know the sound of the engines. There were two of them. What were they doing over here?"

The nurse came up to the side of his bed and began to straighten out the sheets and tuck them in under the mattress.

"Gracious me, what things you imagine. You mustn't worry about a thing like that. Would you like me to get you something to read?"

"No, thank you."

She patted his pillow and brushed back the hair from his forehead with her hand.

"They never come over in daylight any longer. You know that. They were probably Lancasters or Flying Fortresses."[16]

"Nurse."

"Yes."

"Could I have a cigarette?"

"Why certainly you can."

She went out and came back almost at once with a packet of Players and some matches. She handed one to him and when he had put it in his mouth, she struck a match and lit it.

"If you want me again," she said, "just ring the bell," and she went out.

---

16. **Lancasters or Flying Fortresses:** Lancasters are British heavy bombers; Flying Fortresses are American heavy bombers.

> **MAKING INFERENCES**
>
> **3.** If the planes are German bombers, what might that signify? What can you **infer** about the nurse from her responses to the pilot's questions about the planes?

598 Collection 9 Biographical and Historical Approach • Using Primary and Secondary Sources

CONTENT-AREA CONNECTIONS

History: The German Problem
When the pilot is trying to prove his sanity to himself, he says he will make a speech about something "complicated and intellectual" and chooses the topic of "what to do with Germany after the war." This question was discussed by many people during and after the war. Even the best and the brightest of the intellectuals were at a loss to explain how Germany, one of the most progressive countries in Europe, had fallen prey to such aggression and barbarism. People wanted to do something that would change Germany so that such crimes could never happen again. **Individual activity.** Have students use the Internet and history books to discover what *did* happen to Germany after the war. Encourage students to report their findings to the class.

Once toward evening he heard the noise of another aircraft. It was far away, but even so he knew that it was a single-engined machine. It was going fast; he could tell that. He could not place it. It wasn't a Spit, and it wasn't a Hurricane.[17] It did not sound like an American engine either. They make more noise. He did not know what it was, and it worried him greatly. Perhaps I am very ill, he thought. Perhaps I am imagining things. Perhaps I am a little delirious. I simply do not know what to think.

That evening the nurse came in with a basin of hot water and began to wash him.

"Well," she said, "I hope you don't think that we're being bombed."

She had taken off his pajama top and was soaping his right arm with a flannel.[18] He did not answer.

She rinsed the flannel in the water, rubbed more soap on it, and began to wash his chest.

"You're looking fine this evening," she said. "They operated on you as soon as you came in. They did a marvelous job. You'll be all right. I've got a brother in the RAF,"[19] she added. "Flying bombers."

He said, "I went to school in Brighton."

She looked up quickly. "Well, that's fine," she said. "I expect you'll know some people in the town."

"Yes," he said, "I know quite a few."

She had finished washing his chest and arms. Now she turned back the bedclothes so that his left leg was uncovered. She did it in such a way that his bandaged stump remained under the sheets. She undid the cord of his pajama trousers and took them off. There was no trouble because they had cut off the right trouser leg so that it could not interfere with the bandages. She began to wash his left leg and the

17. **Hurricane:** type of British fighter plane.
18. **flannel** *n.:* piece of soft woolen fabric; here, used as a washcloth.
19. **RAF:** abbreviation for Royal Air Force, Great Britain's air force.

rest of his body. This was the first time he had had a bed bath and he was embarrassed. She laid a towel under his leg and began washing his foot with the flannel. She said, "This wretched soap won't lather at all. It's the water. It's as hard as nails."

He said, "None of the soap is very good now and, of course, with hard water[20] it's hopeless." As he said it, he remembered something. He remembered the baths which he used to take at school in Brighton, in the long stone-floored bathroom which had four baths in a row. He remembered how the water was so soft that you had to take a shower afterward to get all the soap off your body, and he remembered how the foam used to float on the surface of the water, so that you could not see your legs underneath. He remembered that sometimes they were given calcium tablets because the school doctor used to say that soft water was bad for the teeth.

"In Brighton," he said, "the water isn't . . ."

He did not finish the sentence. Something had occurred to him; something so fantastic and absurd that for a moment he felt like telling the nurse about it and having a good laugh.

She looked up. "The water isn't what?" she said.

"Nothing," he answered. "I was dreaming."

She rinsed the flannel in the basin, wiped the soap off his leg, and dried him with a towel.

"It's nice to be washed," he said. "I feel better." He was feeling his face with his hand. "I need a shave."

20. **hard water:** water that contains minerals that prevent soap from making a good lather.

Vocabulary
delirious (di·lir′ē·əs) *adj.:* temporarily confused and seeing imaginary things, often because of injury or fever.

MAKING INFERENCES

4. What do you think the pilot was about to say? What "fantastic" thought has occurred to him, and why doesn't he share it with the nurse?

Beware of the Dog **599**

B **Reading Skills**

? **Making inferences.** Why is the pilot so worried by the sound of a plane he cannot identify? [Possible response: The pilot is an experienced flyer who can identify distant planes by their engine sounds. It worries him that he cannot identify a plane because it means he may not be in England or he may be losing his mind.]

C **Reading Skills**

? **Speculating.** Why do you think the nurse looks up quickly when the pilot says he went to school in Brighton? [Possible responses: She did not expect him to be from Brighton; she is surprised or upset.]

D **Vocabulary Development**

Literal meanings. Discuss the fact that in American English, *fantastic* is often used informally to mean "great" or "wonderful," and it may also mean "bizarre or strange." But the root of the word is *fantasy*, "an illusion or a flight of fancy," and that is the sense in which *fantastic* is used here. Name a synonym for *fantasy*. [Possible response: *illusion*.]

E **Reading Skills**

Making inferences. [Possible responses to question 4: He may have been about to say that the water in Brighton isn't hard. The "fantastic" thought may be that he is not in Brighton, not even in England but quite possibly on the other side of the English Channel in occupied France. He doesn't share his thoughts with the nurse because he has begun to realize that she might be the enemy.]

DEVELOPING FLUENCY

Small-group activity. There are many passages in this story that give great insight into the workings of the pilot's mind. Have each group choose a passage of the story that lets them enter into the pilot's mind. Have students practice reading the passage. They may experiment with different speeds and intonations to find the ones that best match their concept of the pilot's character. When students are ready, have them perform their reading for the class.

Beware of the Dog **599**

A Literary Focus

? Conflict. What internal and external conflicts are keeping the pilot awake? [Possible response: The external conflict is the war and the possibility that he is in danger; the internal conflict is over whether he can trust his senses.]

B Literary Focus

Historical setting. When the pilot says he will make a speech about something "complicated and intellectual," he chooses the subject of what to do with Germany after the war. Tell students that this was an important topic for people of this time period. Because Germany was an aggressor in both World War I and World War II, many Europeans wondered what could be done with the country in order to prevent a third world war.

C Reading Skills

? Analyzing. The pilot himself is making inferences about where he is and what is going on around him. To make these inferences, he is drawing upon his own observations and experiences. What experiences has he drawn upon? [He has recalled that when he was boy in Brighton the water was very soft, and he has used his experience as a fighter pilot, from which he has learned how to distinguish aircraft by their sounds.] What inference do you think the pilot may make based on these clues? [Possible responses: He may think he is going crazy; he may think he is not in England.]

D Literary Focus

? Character. What do the pilot's actions reveal about his character? [He is determined, strong-willed, self-disciplined, and brave.]

"We'll do that tomorrow," she said. "Perhaps you can do it yourself then."

That night he could not sleep. He lay awake thinking of the Junkers 88s and of the hardness of the water. He could think of nothing else. They were Ju-88s, he said to himself. I know they were. And yet it is not possible, because they would not be flying around so low over here in broad daylight. I know that it is true and yet I know that it is impossible. Perhaps I am ill. Perhaps I am behaving like a fool and do not know what I am doing or saying. Perhaps I am delirious. For a long time he lay awake thinking these things, and once he sat up in bed and said aloud, "I will prove that I am not crazy. I will make a little speech about something complicated and intellectual. I will talk about what to do with Germany after the war." But before he had time to begin, he was asleep.

He woke just as the first light of day was showing through the slit in the curtains over the window. The room was still dark, but he could tell that it was already beginning to get light outside. He lay looking at the gray light which was showing through the slit in the curtain and as he lay there he remembered the day before. He remembered the Junkers 88s and the hardness of the water; he remembered the large pleasant nurse and the kind doctor, and now a small grain of doubt took root in his mind and it began to grow.

He looked around the room. The nurse had taken the roses out the night before. There was nothing except the table with a packet of cigarettes, a box of matches, and an ashtray. The room was bare. It was no longer warm or friendly. It was not even comfortable. It was cold and empty and very quiet.

Slowly the grain of doubt grew, and with it came fear, a light, dancing fear that warned but did not frighten; the kind of fear that one gets not because one is afraid, but because one feels that there is something wrong. Quickly the

doubt and the fear grew so that he became restless and angry, and when he touched his forehead with his hand, he found that it was damp with sweat. He knew then that he must do something; that he must find some way of proving to himself that he was either right or wrong, and he looked up and saw again the window and the green curtains. From where he lay, that window was right in front of him, but it was fully ten yards away. Somehow he must reach it and look out. The idea became an obsession with him and soon he could think of nothing except the window. But what about his leg? He put his hand underneath the bedclothes and felt the thick bandaged stump which was all that was left on the right-hand side. It seemed all right. It didn't hurt. But it would not be easy.

He sat up. Then he pushed the bedclothes aside and put his left leg on the floor. Slowly, carefully, he swung his body over until he had both hands on the floor as well; then he was out of bed, kneeling on the carpet. He looked at the stump. It was very short and thick, covered with bandages. It was beginning to hurt and he could feel it throbbing. He wanted to collapse, lie down on the carpet, and do nothing, but he knew that he must go on.

With two arms and one leg, he crawled over toward the window. He would reach forward as far as he could with his arms, then he would give a little jump and slide his left leg along after them. Each time he did it, it jarred his wound so that he gave a soft grunt of pain, but he continued to crawl across the floor on two hands and one knee. When he got to the window, he reached up, and one at a time he placed both hands on the sill. Slowly he raised himself up until he was standing on his left leg. Then quickly he pushed aside the curtains and looked out.

Vocabulary
obsession (əb·sesh'ən) n.: persistent idea or desire that consumes a person's attention.

READING MINI-LESSON

Developing Word-Attack Skills
Use the selection words *undulating* and *natural* to explore the effect of *u* on the consonants *d* and *t*. Write *undulating, under,* and *unduly* on the chalkboard and compare the sound of *d* in *undulating* with the sound of *d* in the other words. In *under,* the letter *d* has its usual sound /d/. It also has the sound /d/ in *unduly,* where *un-* is a prefix added to the word *duly.*

In the word *undulating,* however, the letter *d* has the sound /j/, as it does in words like *graduate* and *educate,* where *d* is followed by *u.*

In a similar way, explore the effect of *u* on the consonant *t.* Write *nature, natal,* and *native* on the chalkboard, and compare the sounds of *t* in the words. Point out that in *natal* and *native,* the letter *t* has its usual sound /t/, but in *nature, t* has the sound /ch/, as it does in

He saw a small house with a gray tiled roof standing alone beside a narrow lane, and immediately behind it there was a plowed field. In front of the house there was an untidy garden, and there was a green hedge separating the garden from the lane. He was looking at the hedge when he saw the sign. It was just a piece of board nailed to the top of a short pole, and because the hedge had not been trimmed for a long time, the branches had grown out around the sign so that it seemed almost as though it had been placed in the middle of the hedge. There was something written on the board with white paint. He pressed his head against the glass of the window, trying to read what it said. The first letter was a *G,* he could see that. The second was an *A,* and the third was an *R.* One after another he managed to see what the letters were. There were three words, and slowly he spelled the letters out aloud to himself as he managed to read them.

G-A-R-D-E A-U C-H-I-E-N, *Garde au chien.*[21] That is what it said.

He stood there balancing on one leg and holding tightly to the edges of the windowsill with his hands, staring at the sign and at the whitewashed lettering of the words. For a moment he could think of nothing at all. He stood there looking at the sign, repeating the words over and over to himself. Slowly he began to realize the full meaning of the thing. He looked up at the cottage and at the plowed field. He looked at the small orchard on the left of the cottage and he looked at the green countryside beyond. "So this is France," he said. "I am in France."

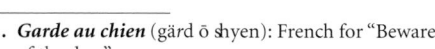

MAKING INFERENCES

5. Why does the pilot conclude that he is in France?

---

21. *Garde au chien* (gärd ō shyen): French for "Beware of the dog."

Beware of the Dog   601

DIRECT TEACHING

E Learners Having Difficulty

❓ **Finding details.** What does the pilot see outside his window? [a small house, narrow lane, plowed field, garden, hedge] **Based on these details, where might the pilot be?** [almost anywhere in Europe]

F Literary Focus

Historical setting. Ask students to think about why Dahl chose to have the sign read "Beware of the Dog," rather than, say, "Don't Walk on the Grass." Have them use the historical approach to explain Dahl's choice. [Possible response: Dahl had fought against Germany and was writing mainly for English-speaking readers unsympathetic toward Germany who would find it fitting that the sign the pilot reads is warning him about "dogs."] **Explain to non-native speakers of English that "dog" is sometimes used derogatorily to mean someone who is contemptible and vile.**

G Reading Skills

Making inferences. [Possible response to question 5: The sign is written in French.]

---

such words as *posture* and *punctual,* where *t* is followed by *u.*

Activity. Write these sets of words on the chalkboard. Have volunteers identify the words in which *d* stands for /j/ or *t* stands for /ch/. Answers are underlined.

1. <u>perpetual</u>	<u>petulance</u>	pestilence
2. <u>picture</u>	pictorial	<u>picturesque</u>
3. <u>contextual</u>	<u>conjecture</u>	contestant
4. <u>gradual</u>	gradient	<u>graduation</u>
5. <u>posture</u>	<u>postulate</u>	impostor
6. <u>gesticulate</u>	<u>gesture</u>	digestive
7. <u>modular</u>	modernism	<u>modulate</u>
8. <u>educable</u>	reducible	<u>reeducate</u>

A Literary Focus

❓ Climax. Remind students that the climax occurs when the conflict is resolved. **What conflict has been resolved now that the pilot has read the sign?** [The internal conflict over whether he can trust his senses.] **How has the conflict been resolved?** [Because the sign is in French, it means the pilot landed in occupied France and is in enemy territory, not in Brighton.]

B Vocabulary Development

❓ Jargon. Explain that the word *intelligence* has a different meaning in the military. Elicit from students that it means gathered information, generally about the enemy. **What do you think the job of an "intelligence officer" probably is.** [To find out as much as possible about the enemy and to block the enemy from gathering accurate information about one's own side.]

C Reading Skills

Making inferences. [Possible responses to question 6: He might recall Johnny's words because he is now in a situation in which those words apply.]

D Literary Focus

❓ Historical setting. Remember that the setting is occupied France in wartime. **What might be the significance of the nurse offering the pilot another egg?** [Possible response: In wartime, there may be shortages of many food items. Eggs were probably a rare treat; by offering the pilot not one, but two, she is trying to ingratiate herself with him.]

Now the throbbing in his right thigh was very great. It felt as though someone was pounding the end of his stump with a hammer and suddenly the pain became so intense that it affected his head. For a moment he thought he was going to fall. Quickly he knelt down again, crawled back to the bed, and **hoisted** himself in.

A He pulled the bedclothes over himself and lay back on the pillow, exhausted. He could still think of nothing at all except the small sign by the hedge and the plowed field and the orchard. It was the words on the sign that he could not forget.

It was some time before the nurse came in. She came carrying a basin of hot water and she said, "Good morning, how are you today?"

He said, "Good morning, nurse."

The pain was still great under the bandages, but he did not wish to tell this woman anything. He looked at her as she busied herself with getting the washing things ready. He looked at her more carefully now. Her hair was very fair. She was tall and big-boned and her face seemed pleasant. But there was something a little uneasy about her eyes. They were never still. They never looked at anything for more than a moment and they moved too quickly from one place to another in the room. There was something about her movements also. They were too sharp and nervous to go well with the casual manner in which she spoke.

She set down the basin, took off his pajama top, and began to wash him.

"Did you sleep well?"

"Yes."

"Good," she said. She was washing his arms and his chest.

"I believe there's someone coming down to see you from the Air Ministry after breakfast," she went on. "They want a report or something.

I expect you know all about it. How you got shot down and all that. I won't let him stay long, so don't worry."

He did not answer. She finished washing him and gave him a toothbrush and some tooth powder. He brushed his teeth, rinsed his mouth, and spat the water out into the basin.

Later she brought him his breakfast on a tray, but he did not want to eat. He was still feeling weak and sick and he wished only to lie still and think about what had happened. And there was a sentence running through his head. It was a sentence which **B** Johnny, the intelligence officer of his squadron, always repeated to the pilots every day before they went out. He could see Johnny now, leaning against the wall of the dispersal hut with his pipe in his hand, saying, "And if they get you, don't forget, just your name, rank, and number. Nothing else. For God's sake, say nothing else." **C**

"There you are," she said as she put the tray on his lap. "I've got you an egg. Can you manage all right?"

"Yes."

She stood beside the bed. "Are you feeling all right?"

"Yes."

D "Good. If you want another egg, I might be able to get you one."

"This is all right."

"Well, just ring the bell if you want any more." And she went out.

> **There was something a little uneasy about her eyes.**

MAKING INFERENCES

6. Why might the pilot now recall the sentence Johnny used to repeat to the pilots every day?

Vocabulary
hoisted (hoist′id) *v.:* lifted or pulled up.

FAMILY/COMMUNITY ACTIVITY

Roald Dahl drew upon his experiences as a Royal Air Force (RAF) pilot in World War II to write this story. Have students seek out and interview members of their family or community who have had war experiences. Students should first ask interviewees if they are comfortable talking about their experiences. If so, students may ask them to talk about some of their memories. Then, have students tell the class about one of their interviewees' experiences.

He had just finished eating, when the nurse came in again.

She said, "Wing Commander Roberts is here. I've told him that he can only stay for a few minutes."

She beckoned with her hand and the wing commander came in.

"Sorry to bother you like this," he said.

He was an ordinary RAF officer, dressed in a uniform which was a little shabby. He wore wings and a DFC.[22] He was fairly tall and thin with plenty of black hair. His teeth, which were irregular and widely spaced, stuck out a little even when he closed his mouth. As he spoke, he took a printed form and a pencil from his pocket and he pulled up a chair and sat down.

"How are you feeling?"

There was no answer.

---

22. **wings and a DFC:** Wings are an emblem worn by the pilot and the crew of an aircraft. DFC stands for Distinguished Flying Cross, a medal awarded to officers of the Royal Air Force for distinguished conduct in combat.

"Tough luck about your leg. I know how you feel. I hear you put up a fine show before they got you."

The man in the bed was lying quite still, watching the man in the chair.

The man in the chair said, "Well, let's get this stuff over. I'm afraid you'll have to answer a few questions so that I can fill in this combat report. Let me see now, first of all, what was your squadron?"

The man in the bed did not move. He looked straight at the wing commander and he said, "My name is Peter Williamson. My rank is squadron leader and my number is nine seven two four five seven." ■

MAKING INFERENCES

7. What can you **infer** from the pilot's answer to the wing commander's question at the end of the story? What has the pilot realized?

Vocabulary

beckoned (bek′ənd) v.: gestured or signaled to request someone to approach or follow.

Meet the Writer

Roald Dahl

A Dragon to Be Slain

"Beware of the Dog" appeared in *Over to You: Ten Stories of Flyers and Flying*, the first collection of stories published by Roald (rōō′ôl) Dahl (1916–1990). Reviewing the collection, one critic commented, "This, one never doubts, is the way British pilots talked, felt, acted."

In his fiction, Dahl was able to capture the life of flying because he himself had been a flier. Dahl was born in Wales of Norwegian parents. When World War II began, he joined Great Britain's Royal Air Force and became a fighter pilot. Dahl suffered grave injuries when his plane crashed in 1940. Although a widely circulated story states that Dahl's plane was shot down by enemy fire, his crash actually occurred because he was given the wrong information about the location of an airfield. In his autobiography, *Going Solo*, Dahl explains what happened when he was forced to make an emergency landing in the desert once his fuel supply ran low:

Beware of the Dog **603**

Meet the Writer

Background. Before he became a writer, Roald Dahl had a varied career, including a job in east Africa. But it was his life as a fighter pilot that defined him. In the introduction to his autobiography *Going Solo* he writes that every moment of the time he spent flying with the Royal Air Force (RAF) in World War II was "totally enthralling."

For Independent Reading

Encourage students who read Dahl's autobiography or other stories in *Over to You: Ten Stories of Flyers and Flying* to pay close attention to how the war influenced Dahl's writing and his life.

"My undercarriage hit a boulder and collapsed completely and the Gladiator buried its nose in the sand at what must have been about seventy-five miles an hour.

My injuries in that bust-up came from my head being thrown forward violently against the reflector-sight when the plane hit the ground (in spite of the fact that I was strapped tightly, as always, into the cockpit), and apart from the skull fracture, the blow pushed my nose in and knocked out a few teeth and blinded me completely for days to come.

It is odd that I can remember very clearly quite a few of the things that followed seconds after the crash. Obviously I was unconscious for some moments, but I must have recovered my senses very quickly because I can remember hearing a mighty *whoosh* as the petrol tank in the port wing exploded, followed almost at once by another mighty *whoosh* as the starboard tank went up in flames. I could see nothing at all, and I felt no pain. All I wanted was to go gently off to sleep and to hell with the flames. But soon a tremendous heat around my legs galvanized my soggy brain into action. With great difficulty I managed to undo first my seat-straps and then the straps of my parachute, and I can even remember the desperate effort it took to push myself upright in the cockpit and roll out headfirst on to the sand below. "

Dahl dragged himself away from the burning plane—and then he collapsed. He was later told that the flames from his plane lit up the desert for miles. When British soldiers set out to investigate the crash site, they were astonished to find Dahl's "still-breathing body."

Dahl lived to fly—and be injured—again. He was eventually encouraged to write about his military adventures. The story of his military experiences marked the beginning of Dahl's career as a writer.

At first, Dahl mostly wrote fiction for adults, specializing in stories with a surprising twist. After his own children were born, he began to write children's stories and novels, and these works—such as *Charlie and the Chocolate Factory*—made him famous.

As a child and an adult, Dahl experienced many personal tragedies. His life was not easy, but as one person put it, "He fought misfortune as if it was a dragon to be slain."

For Independent Reading

For more gripping adventures about the lives of pilots, read Dahl's autobiography, *Going Solo*, and his short story collection *Over to You: Ten Stories of Flyers and Flying*.

DIFFERENTIATING INSTRUCTION

Advanced Learners

Enrichment. Most students probably know Roald Dahl only as the author of children's books such as *Charlie and the Chocolate Factory.* Dahl, however, also wrote two autobiographies plus stories that incorporated his experiences in the Royal Air Force as well as stories that blended the macabre with mystery and suspense.

Individual activity. Suggest that students enter *RAF, Roald Dahl,* and *Hurricane* as keywords in a search engine. Have students share information they discover about Dahl's experiences in the RAF.

Ernie Pyle (1900–1945) was an award-winning American journalist and war correspondent who covered World War II. In the following report he describes the courage of a British pilot whose plane was shot down.

Wounded and Trapped
Ernie Pyle

A World War II RAF pilot.

ON THE WESTERN FRONT—(by wireless)— **A** We ran to the wrecked British plane, lying there upside down, and dropped on our hands and knees and peeked through a tiny hole in the side.

A man lay on his back in the small space of the upside-down cockpit. His feet disappeared somewhere in the jumble of dials and rubber pedals above him. His shirt was open and his chest was bare to the waist. He was smoking a cigarette.

He turned his eyes toward me when I peeked in, and he said in a typical British manner of offhand friendliness, "Oh, hello."

"Are you all right," I asked, stupidly.

He answered, "Yes, quite. Now that you chaps are here."

I asked him how long he had been trapped in the wrecked plane. He said he didn't know for sure as he had got mixed up about the passage of time. But he did know the date of the month he was shot down. He told me the date. And I said out loud, "Good God!"

For, wounded and trapped, he had been lying there for eight days!

His left leg was broken and punctured by an ack-ack burst. His back was terribly burned by raw gasoline that had spilled. The foot of his injured leg was pinned rigidly under the rudder bar. **B**

His space was so small he couldn't squirm around to relieve his own weight from his paining back. He couldn't straighten out his legs, which were bent above him. He couldn't see out of his little prison. He had not had a bite to eat or a drop of water. All this for eight days and nights. **C**

Yet when we found him, his physical condition was strong, and his mind was as calm and rational as though he were sitting in a London club. He was in agony, yet in his correct Oxford accent he even apologized for taking up our time to get him out.

The American soldiers of our rescue party cussed as they worked, cussed with open admiration for this British flier's greatness of heart which had kept him alive and sane

Beware of the Dog 605

Summary ⬌ *at grade level*

The article begins as Ernie Pyle and others run up to a crashed British plane and find a pilot who has been trapped in the cockpit for eight days, with his back burned and his broken leg pinned under the rudder. Despite his harrowing ordeal, the man is rational and in good spirits. While the rescuers work to extract him from the wreckage, they gradually hear the story of how he was shot down and trapped in no-man's land while the war raged around him.

DIRECT TEACHING

A **Reading Skills**
❓ **Determining the author's purpose.** This is an unusual way to begin a news story. Why do you think Pyle chose to begin it this way? [Possible response: to grab readers' attention and involve them, as if they were participating in the story.]

B **Literary Focus**
❓ **Objective and subjective reporting.** Is this reporting purely factual and objective or is it subjective, revealing the writer's feelings? [Possible responses: Objective, because it gives facts and details; subjective, because the author reveals his feelings, saying "Good God!" and using exclamation points as punctuation.]

C **Literary Focus**
❓ **Comparing and contrasting.** What similarities do you see between this man and the main character in Dahl's story? [Possible responses: Both are fighter pilots; both were shot and wounded in the leg; both lost control of their aircraft; both are very courageous and mentally tough.]

Connecting and Comparing Texts

Invite students to compare and contrast this nonfiction news story with "Beware of the Dog." You might stimulate discussion by asking students to consider similarities and differences between

• the real and the fictional pilot
• the historical setting (time and place)

• the author's purpose
• the moods and themes of the two selections

A Learners Having Difficulty

? Summarizing. To help students follow the events, ask, "How would you summarize these three paragraphs in words the pilot may have used to relate his story?" [Possible response: "I was flying at night and the Germans began firing from the ground. They hit my engine, but I was too low to parachute out, so I went down for a crash-landing. I put my lights on to see where I would land, and then the Germans really let me have it. They got my leg and my hand. Then, my plane skidded across the ground and flipped upside down and here I am."]

B Reading Skills

? Drawing conclusions. What was happening in the field around the pilot while he was trapped? [The field was a battleground between the Americans and the Germans.] Who finally won the field and what did this mean for the pilot? [The Americans won and so the pilot had a good chance of being rescued by the Allied forces.]

C Reading Skills

? Determining the author's purpose. Why do you think the writer included this section about the pilot's delirium at the end of the article? [Possible responses: to show that the pilot had suffered terribly during his ordeal, even though he was now perfectly calm; to increase the believability of the account.]

---

through his lonely and gradually hope-dimming ordeal.

One of them said, "These Limies[1] have got guts!"

It took us almost an hour to get him out. We don't know whether he will live or not, but he has a chance. During the hour we were ripping the plane open to make a hole, he talked to us. And here, in the best nutshell I can devise from the conversation of a brave man whom you didn't want to badger with trivial questions, is what happened—

He was an RAF flight lieutenant, piloting a night fighter. Over a certain area the Germans began letting him have it from the ground with machine-gun fire.

The first hit knocked out his motor. He was too low to jump, so—foolishly, he said—he turned on his lights to try a crash landing. Then they really poured it on him. The second hit got him in the leg. And a third bullet cut right across the balls of his right-hand forefingers, clipping every one of them to the bone.

He left his wheels up, and the plane's belly hit the ground going uphill on a slight slope. We could see the groove it had dug for about 50 yards. Then it flopped, tail over nose, onto its back. The pilot was absolutely sealed into the upside-down cockpit.

"That's all I remember for a while," he told us. "When I came to, they were shelling all around me."

Thus began the eight days. He had crashed right between the Germans and Americans in a sort of pastoral[2] no man's land.[3]

---

1. **Limies** (līm′ēz): slang for "English sailors" or, sometimes, "English soldiers."
2. **pastoral** (pas′tər·əl) *adj.*: rural.
3. **no man's land:** unoccupied area separating opposing armies.

For days afterwards the field in which he lay surged back and forth between German hands and ours.

His pasture was pocked with hundreds of shell craters. Many of them were only yards away. One was right at the end of his wing. The metal sides of the plane were speckled with hundreds of shrapnel holes.

He lay there, trapped in the midst of this inferno of explosions. The fields around him gradually became littered with dead. At last American strength pushed the Germans back, and silence came. But no help. Because, you see, it was in that vacuum behind the battle, and only a few people were left.

The days passed. He thirsted terribly. He slept some; part of the time he was unconscious; part of the time he undoubtedly was delirious. But he never gave up hope.

After we had finally got him out, he said as he lay on the stretcher under a wing, "Is it possible that I've been out of this plane since I crashed?"

Everybody chuckled. The doctor who had arrived said, "Not the remotest possibility. You were sealed in there and it took men with tools half an hour to make an opening. And your leg was broken and your foot was pinned there. No, you haven't been out."

"I didn't think it was possible," the pilot said, "and yet it seems in my mind that I was out once and back in again."

That little memory of delirium was the only word said by that remarkable man in the whole hour of his rescue that wasn't as dispassionate and matter-of-fact as though he had been sitting comfortably at the end of the day in front of his own fireplace.

—Scripps-Howard wire copy, August 22, 1944

Response and Analysis

Reading Check

1. Describe the situation as the story opens. Who is the **main character**, what is he doing, and what has just happened to him?

2. Where does the nurse tell the pilot he is?

3. What does the wing commander ask the pilot at the end of the story? What is the pilot's response?

Thinking Critically

4. Summarize the clues in the story and the **inferences** you made that helped you understand the pilot's situation.

5. What do the people working in the hospital do and say to create the appearance that the pilot is in England? How does the pilot figure out that he has been deceived? (Be sure to check your Quickwrite notes.)

6. Describe the **character** of the pilot. Consider
   - his reactions to his situation at the beginning of the story
   - his attempt to get to the window
   - his responses to the nurse and the wing commander at the end of the story

7. For the **title** of his story, Dahl chose the wording of a common sign. What other meanings, in addition to its literal one, might this title have? (Hint: Figuratively speaking, who is the dog? Who must beware, and why?)

8. This story grips the reader from the start. How does Dahl create **suspense** in the story? Give examples from the text.

Literary Criticism

9. Describe the **conflicts** the pilot faces in the course of the story. How does each conflict reflect the issues or themes of the story's **historical period**?

10. "Wounded and Trapped" (see the **Connection** on page 605) is about a real World War II fighter pilot. What similarities can you find between the situation of Dahl's fictional pilot and the real pilot's situation during this **historical period**?

11. How might Dahl have drawn on his own experiences as a fighter pilot when writing this story? Review the biographical information in Meet the Writer (see pages 603–604) to help you answer, and point to specific places in the story as examples.

WRITING

Research Paper

Select a topic related to World War II that you would like to know more about. Keep your topic limited so that you can explore it in a short **research paper** ("the Battle of Britain," for example, instead of "World War II aviation battles"). Make a list of questions that you want to answer, and identify sources that you could use to research your topic. Take notes as you read your sources, and then organize your information into a short report. Be sure to credit your sources.

▶ **Use "Writing a Research Paper," pages 610–629, for help with this assignment.**

SKILLS FOCUS

Literary Skills
Analyze historical setting.

Reading Skills
Make inferences.

Writing Skills
Write a research paper.

Response and Analysis

5. They say he is in Brighton, squadron members have called, the nurse's brother is RAF. They dress in English uniforms. The pilot gets suspicious when he hears Ju-88s, and when he is told Brighton water is hard, but he knows it is soft. The French sign lets him know that he is in occupied France.

6. The pilot is smart, brave, self-disciplined, and loyal.

7. Possible answers: Be aware that your enemy may try to fool you; watch out for low-down people and their dirty tricks.

8. Dahl creates suspense by telling events from the pilot's point of view, letting the reader experience only his observations and feelings.

Literary Criticism

9. The pilot faces the external conflicts of war, of being shot down and wounded by enemy fire, of being a prisoner of war: All are issues of the historical period. He faces an internal conflict regarding his sanity, which reflects the uncertainty of wartime when people may have a hard time telling friend from foe.

10. Both are British fighter pilots who are injured on missions; both go down with their planes; both are at one time trapped behind enemy lines; both use inner resources to survive.

11. Dahl draws on his experience to describe flying the Spitfire while wounded; to tell about feeling no pain after injury, about going in and out of consciousness, about identifying enemy planes by sound.

Reading Check

1. The main character is a British pilot. He is flying his plane, and he has just been hit by enemy fire and is injured.

2. In Brighton, an English city.

3. He asks for the pilot's squadron and the pilot answers with his name, rank, and number.

Thinking Critically

4. The sound of German bombers and the water's hardness are clues that the pilot is not in Brighton. The sign in French helps readers infer that the place is occupied France.

Vocabulary Development

Semantic Map

Practice 1

Sample Answers

- *giddy—dizzy. When might a person feel giddy? While dancing.*
- *What could you do to stop feeling giddy? Sit down.*

Jargon

Practice 2

- *stick. Sentence—*"His right hand was on the stick. . . ." *Meaning—lever to guide the plane. Other meaning—a piece of wood. Sample sentence—Rex fetched the stick.*
- *bail out. Sentence—*"He knew then that he must bail out. . . ." *Meaning—parachute out of a plane. Other meaning—remove water from something that is flooded. Sample sentence—To stay afloat, we had to bail out the boat.*
- *throttled. Sentence—*"He throttled back. . . ." *Meaning—to reduce the fuel to the plane's engine. Other meaning—to strangle. Sample sentence—The film's villain throttled the hero.*
- *port. Sentence—*"The Spitfire dipped its port wing. . . ." *Meaning—left-hand side. Other meaning—where ships dock. Sample sentence—We sailed into port.*
- *wings. Sentence—*"He wore wings and a DFC. . . ." *Meaning—an emblem worn by an aircraft's pilot and crew. Other meaning—bird's appendages. Sample sentence—The hawk soared on its outstretched wings.*

Vocabulary Development

Semantic Map

PRACTICE 1

For each Word Bank word, make a **semantic map** like the one below for *undulating*. First, define the word. Then, write at least two questions about the word, and answer them. You'll have to make up different questions for each word. Compare your maps with those of your classmates.

> **undulating:** moving in waves

What can be described as undulating?
- a flag in a breeze
- long, wavy hair
- a wheat field on a windy day

What would you *not* describe as undulating?
- a falling rock
- a bouncing ball
- a high-speed train

Word Bank
undulating
giddy
unconscious
idly
delirious
obsession
hoisted
beckoned

Jargon: Working Words

When is a *nose* not as plain as the thing in the middle of your face? When it's actually the front of an airplane. This use of the word *nose* is an example of **jargon,** the specialized words, or **technical vocabulary,** used by people who hold particular jobs or who have particular interests. Newspaper reporters, chefs, and basketball players, for example, all have their own specialized vocabulary. In "Beware of the Dog," Dahl uses the jargon of pilots to make his story as specific and realistic as possible.

PRACTICE 2

Many jargon words have no meaning outside their specialized field. Often, however, words can take on a specialized meaning in a particular field while still maintaining other, more common meanings. For each example of jargon listed in the box below, fill out a chart like the one for *taxi* at the right. Use a dictionary and the footnotes in the story to help you complete your charts.

SKILLS FOCUS

Vocabulary Skills
Create semantic maps. Understand jargon, or technical vocabulary.

stick	throttled	wings
bail out	port	

taxi
Sentence in story: "When I land, I shall <u>taxi</u> in and switch off my engine. . . ."
Meaning in story: move slowly along the ground after landing
Other meaning: travel in a taxicab
Sample sentence for other meaning: We <u>taxied</u> from the train station to our hotel.

ASSESSING

Assessment

- *Holt Assessment: Literature, Reading, and Vocabulary*

RETEACHING

For another selection to teach historical approach, see *The Holt Reader,* Collection 9.

FICTION
America Has Many Streets

Reading the stories in *America Street* is like taking a walk through fourteen American neighborhoods—each with its own distinct character. On one street, Toni Cade Bambara will introduce you to Squeaky, who's absolutely determined to win the neighborhood race. On another street you'll meet Grace Paley's Shirley, who's memorizing lines for her first school play. Duane Big Eagle will take you to Raoul's neighborhood, where Raoul is boarding a train in search of his mysterious medicine-woman aunt. Why not go for a walk and meet your neighbors?

FICTION
Fateful Storm

War, romance, typhoons, and an edge-of-your-seat courtroom drama are interwoven in the novel *The Caine Mutiny.* When the behavior of the captain aboard the USS *Caine* threatens the ship and its crew, a mutiny takes place. Although the lieutenant responsible for the mutiny is court-martialed (taken to court for breaking military law), the character of the captain is really on trial. Herman Wouk won a Pulitzer Prize for this novel, which was partly inspired by his own U.S. Navy experiences during World War II.

NONFICTION
A Survivor's Story

The Endless Steppe by Esther Hautzig is a true account of a family taken captive during World War II. Ten-year-old Esther and her family—like many other innocent Polish Jews—are arrested in their home, crowded onto a train car usually used to transport cattle, and sent to a Russian-owned labor camp in frigid Siberia. Whether describing harsh winds and hunger or her family's love for one another, Esther Hautzig shows spirit, courage, and faith—she'll remind you of Anne Frank.

NONFICTION
Taking Her Place

Charlayne Hunter-Gault was the first African American woman to attend the University of Georgia. As you'll see in her autobiography, *In My Place,* being the first wasn't easy. After the triumph of being admitted to the university came the pain of prejudice. Some of her classmates and professors didn't want her at the school, and she had to fight for her civil rights. Hunter-Gault explains why her struggle was worth it.

Read On   609

DIFFERENTIATING INSTRUCTION

Estimated Word Counts and Reading Levels of Read On Books:

Fiction			Nonfiction		
America Street	⬇	45,300	The Endless Steppe	⬌	75,300
The Caine Mutiny	⬌	249,200	In My Place	⬆	113,200

KEY: ⬆ *above grade level*   ⬌ *at grade level*   ⬇ *below grade level*

Read On

For Independent Reading

If students enjoyed the themes and topics explored in this collection, you might recommend these titles for independent reading.

Assessment Options

The following projects can help you evaluate and assess your students' outside reading. Videotapes or audiotapes of completed projects may be included in students' portfolios.

- **Create character monologues.** Students who read *America Street* can create a character monologue for one of the main characters from the stories. The monologue should deal with the plot of the story and be true to the character as she or he is portrayed in the story. Students can perform their character monologues for the class.

- **Hold a mock trial.** Students who read *The Caine Mutiny* may form a group to hold their own mock court-martial of Captain Queeg. The group should assign each member a character and then create a script based on events in the novel. After preparation, the group can hold the court-martial for the class.

- **Write a book review.** Students can write a review of the book they have read. Remind them that a good book review gives both a brief synopsis of the story and the reviewer's opinion of both the content and the style. Students might first consult professional book reviews to see how they are written.

- **Make a display.** Several students might collaborate to produce a bulletin-board display highlighting books, such as *In My Place* and *The Endless Steppe,* about individuals who are forced to confront the prejudices of others and who manage to overcome the ordeal. Students may wish to illustrate scenes from the books or include copies of photographs that show the settings and authors.

PRETEACHING

Skills Starter

Motivate. Ask students to think of at least three famous discoveries. Then, have students try to imagine (or remember from a class) what the discoverers were trying to find. You can use the example of Columbus, who might have put his goal in the form of the question, "Is it possible to find a trade route to the East by sailing westward?" Point out to students that trying to answer a question they themselves pose requires research to discover the answers. Discuss with students the kinds of questions they have on various topics and how they might propose going about looking for the answers.

Writing a Research Paper

Writing Assignment Write a research paper in which you present documented evidence that supports a thesis.

Suppose that after reading "American History" earlier in this collection, you found yourself wanting to know more about Puerto Rico or the assassination of President John F. Kennedy. It's not unusual for new subjects to grab your interest and make you want to learn more. Whether it's learning the history that leads to current events, discovering the truth behind the latest urban legend, or exploring the background of a story you've just read, asking questions and finding the answers help feed your interest. Writing a research paper about a topic that interests you works much the same way. You begin by asking questions and tracking down the answers; then, you tell others about your new knowledge by writing a paper.

Prewriting

DIRECT TEACHING

Select a Topic

Spend a few moments talking with students about topics that are appropriate for school. Acknowledge that all of their questions are valid and worth investigating, but help students to understand what is acceptable within the context of a school research project. Caution students also to choose a topic that lends itself to research. That is, students should be able to find adequate information on the topic from a variety of sources. Students should not choose a topic about which they already feel themselves well informed.

If students choose or research their topics using the Internet, you need to be aware that the World Wide Web sometimes functions as a public forum and that its content may be unpredictable.

Select a Topic

A Need to Know With so many topics you can research, where will you start? First, consider the task you will be undertaking—researching and writing a paper of at least 1,500 words. Because you'll be spending a lot of time and energy on this task, the topic of your research paper should be something that interests you and will also interest others. Here are ways to generate ideas for a topic if you don't already have one in mind.

- **Follow current events.** Consider any topic on the news that catches your attention, such as legislation affecting teenagers or a new scientific breakthrough.

- **Dream up a vacation.** Look over maps or visit Web sites for a location you'd like to visit. Learn all you can about the people, geography, and attractions in the area.

- **Make a list of your personal interests.** Consider hobbies, sports, music, or other interests you already have. Use your research paper as a way to learn more about one of your pastimes or to get involved in a new area of interest.

SKILLS FOCUS

Writing Skills
Write a research paper.

- **Think about historical or literary figures.** You've learned about many interesting people in this class and in others. Which historical or literary figure interests you?

610 Collection 9 Biographical and Historical Approach • Using Primary and Secondary Sources

---

COLLECTION 9 RESOURCES: WRITING

Planning
- *One-Stop Planner* CD-ROM with ExamView Test Generator

Differentiating Instruction
- *Workshop Resources: Writing, Listening, and Speaking*
- *Family Involvement Activities in English and Spanish*

- *Supporting Instruction in Spanish*

Writing and Language
- *Workshop Resources: Writing, Listening, and Speaking*
- *Daily Language Activities*
- *Language Handbook Worksheets*

Form a Research Question

In a Nutshell Once you've thought of a topic, consider what you want and need to know about it. Develop one question that will focus your project and keep you on track as you gather information. This **research question** should ask exactly what you want to find out from your research. To get started, ask yourself the questions shown in the left column of the chart below. One writer's responses are shown to the right as an example. Notice that the writer's research question cannot be answered with a single word.

DEVELOPING A RESEARCH TOPIC

Questions	Answers
What is my topic?	the poet Robert Frost
+ What do I hope to learn from my research?	I want to know how he got ideas for poems.
= What is my research question?	Where did Robert Frost get ideas for his poems?

From One Come Many Next, let your research question lead you to form several related, more-detailed questions. These detailed questions, in turn, will help you find the specific evidence you need for your paper. The student writer broke up his research question into the following three detailed questions.

—Did Frost base any poems on actual events from his life?
—Did Frost write about the places where he lived?
—Did Frost ever explain where he got the ideas for his poems?

Identify Purpose and Audience

Why Write? Before you head to the library or hit the Internet, think about why you are researching this topic and who will be reading about your findings. The **purpose** of your research paper is to uncover information from various sources. You'll **synthesize,** or combine, the information you gather from multiple sources, draw conclusions based on your research, and inform others about your findings.

Who Will Read It? The others that you'll inform are your **audience**—consisting of your classmates, your teacher, and anyone else with whom you wish to share your research. For your audience to understand you, you must first understand them. Ask yourself the following questions about your audience so you can tailor your research to anticipate and address their wants and needs.

SKILLS FOCUS

Writing Skills
Develop a research question. Consider your purpose and audience.

Assessment

- *Holt Assessment: Writing, Listening, and Speaking*
- *One-Stop Planner* CD-ROM with ExamView Test Generator
- *Holt Online Assessment*
- *Holt Online Essay Scoring*

Internet

- *go.hrw.com* (Keyword LE5 9-9)
- *Elements of Literature Online*

CRITICAL THINKING

Allow students to discover for themselves how secondary sources can vary in their interpretations of an event. Select an event currently in the news, and ask specific students to each find one of these: news stories from different television channels, articles from different newspapers, and Internet pieces on the event. Have students present their findings to the class, and have the class analyze both similarities and differences in main points, details, and the tone of the secondary sources.

You need to be aware that Internet resources sometimes act as public forums and that their content may be unpredictable.

DIRECT TEACHING

Find Sources

Provide students with this checklist so that they may better divide the project of writing a research paper into a series of manageable tasks. The checklist will also allow you to easily check their progress.

Steps	Date Completed
Select topic and research question.	
Find and evaluate sources.	
Make source cards.	
Finish taking research notes.	
Write thesis statement.	
Make outline.	
Prepare *Works Cited* list.	
Write first draft.	
Revise draft.	
Prepare final draft, and publish.	

- What information will my readers already have about my topic?
- What questions will they expect me to answer about it?
- How can I clear up potential misunderstandings or biases they might have?
- What unfamiliar terms or technical notations will I need to define for my readers?

TIP Add the questions you think your audience will expect you to answer to the list of detailed questions you created on page 611.

Find Sources

A Wealth of Information Where will you find the answers to your research questions? You'll need to gather information from both primary and secondary sources. **Primary sources** contain original, firsthand information that is unfiltered and unedited. Primary sources include legal documents, letters, diaries, eyewitness accounts, and surveys. **Secondary sources** provide indirect or secondhand information. They are other people's interpretations of primary material—for example, encyclopedia entries, newspaper articles, documentaries, and biographies.

Let's Get Started Begin your search at your school library, but also plan on visiting your community library and any college or university libraries in your area. Although your search might start at a library, it certainly should not end there. Check out community resources that might be valuable sources, such as various local, state, and national government agencies, as well as electronic media. The charts below and on the next page list resources that might be available in your area libraries and in your community, along with the sources or types of information they provide.

LIBRARY RESOURCES	
Resource	**Source or Type of Information**
Card catalog or online catalog	books listed by title, author, and subject; in some libraries this catalog also lists audiovisual materials—videotapes, records, CDs, audiotapes, filmstrips, and films
Readers' Guide to Periodical Literature	articles in magazines and journals
Microfilm, microfiche, or online databases	encyclopedias (electronic or print), biographical references, atlases, almanacs
General and specialized reference books or CD-ROMs	indexes to major newspapers such as *The New York Times,* back issues of newspapers
World Wide Web and online services	articles, interviews, bibliographies, pictures, videos, sound recordings; access to the Library of Congress and other libraries

DIFFERENTIATING INSTRUCTION

Special Education Students
Ask helpers to act as research assistants for students who need extra support on this assignment. The "research assistant" might do some tasks such as writing requests to get materials or searching for and bookmarking Internet sites to keep the project from getting bogged down in clerical details.

COMMUNITY RESOURCES

Resource	Source or Type of Information
Local, state, and national government agencies	voting records, recent or pending legislation, experts on state and federal government
Local newspaper offices	accounts of events of local interest, historical information on city or area
Museums, historical societies, service groups	historical events, scientific achievements, art and artists, special exhibits, and experts
Video stores, audiotape rental stores	documentary and instructional videotapes and audiotapes

TIP Consider **interviewing experts** in the subject areas you are researching. Experts can be valuable primary sources, and often they can direct you to other useful sources. Be sure to arrive at the interview on time with relevant questions prepared in advance. Take careful notes of the responses to your questions. Conduct yourself in a mature and respectful way, speaking courteously and sensitively to the person you are interviewing—this person is providing you with priceless help. Finally, compile the most useful responses while they're fresh in your mind so you can accurately report them.

Evaluate Sources

A Source to Trust? Just as members of a jury have to decide which witnesses are **credible,** or believable, and which are not, you have to determine the extent to which you can trust your sources of information. Here are some questions you can use to put them to the test.

1. **Is the source up-to-date?** Information is generated so quickly now that it is easy to find current material. If information on your topic is constantly changing, be sure that your sources are up-to-date.

2. **Does the source seem factual?** Check its information against your own knowledge and against other sources. If you find a **discrepancy,** or difference, between sources, check additional sources to determine which information is most accurate or most useful. For example, one writer might state that Robert Frost quit college and never graduated. However, another writer might give an explanation: Frost left college to help his wife, who was having difficulties with her pregnancy.

3. **Does the source provide explanations?** Look for explanations that might help you and your readers understand the **complexities** of the topic. For example, even though many of Frost's poems deal with nature, they may have several interpretations. By explaining the interpretations, you may help your audience gain insight into Frost's poems.

SKILLS FOCUS

Writing Skills
Interview experts. Evaluate sources.

Integrating with Grammar, Usage, and Mechanics
As students begin their research papers, they might have trouble with punctuation. You may want to review lessons 12–14 in the Language Handbook.

TECHNOLOGY TIP

Point out to students that if they research their topic on the World Wide Web, they can make their searches more efficient by using combinations of keywords. For example, if a computer search using the keyword *asthma* yields too much irrelevant information, they might narrow the search by using *asthma + athletics.* Direct students to look for information on advanced-searching strategies on the first screen of their search engines.

Learners Having Difficulty

Students may not know where to find the information necessary for source cards. To provide students with practice looking up material, you might want to allocate class time to a guided research exercise. Gather a small collection of books, magazines, newspapers, encyclopedia volumes, CD-ROMs, videotapes, and Web site printouts. Assist students in locating the information they would need to record source information from these materials for their research projects. Remind the class that the placement of source information can vary among different kinds of print and nonprint resources.

DIRECT TEACHING

Guidelines for Recording Source Information

If you prefer that students use a different style for documenting sources, such as footnotes, you may want to give students an example of the style to use as a model. The following is an example of a footnote for a book with one author. The number 1 at the beginning of the footnote refers to a number in the report where there is information to document. The footnote gives the author's first and last names, the book's title, publication information, and a page reference.

1. Jay Parini. *Robert Frost: A Life*. New York: Henry Holt and Company, 1999: 258.

Whatever style students use, if there is source information that is not relevant or available, such as an author or date of publication for an online source, remind students that it is acceptable to leave out that information from their documentation.

4. **Do the sources cover different perspectives?** Some sources may be biased, or slanted, toward one point of view. Therefore, you may find that different sources present varying **perspectives** on the same subject. For example, a short biography included in a book of Robert Frost's poetry might be entirely positive about the poet and mention only his awards. However, a newspaper critic who is reviewing the book might mention negative aspects of Frost's writing. It is important to include in your research all relevant perspectives concerning any controversial or strongly slanted information.

Prepare Source Cards

Keeping Track of Everything Since your paper will include a *Works Cited* list, a list of all the sources you use in your paper, you need a way to keep track of all your information. One way is to write information about each source on a 3- x 5-inch index card and number each card. If you keep track of your sources on a computer, create a separate file or record for each source. Keeping your source files or records separate will ensure that you don't get confused about where a piece of information came from.

The following chart tells you the information you need to record for each type of source. Pay close attention to the punctuation used in each type of record. The listings follow the **Modern Language Association (MLA)** format. Your teacher may ask you to use a different format, such as that of *The Chicago Manual of Style*. Be sure you know which format your teacher requires. Noting source information in the correct format now will make it easier for you to create your *Works Cited* list later.

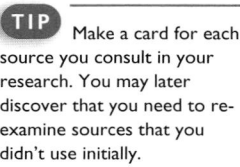

TIP Make a card for each source you consult in your research. You may later discover that you need to re-examine sources that you didn't use initially.

Reference Note

For more on *Works Cited* lists, see page 626.

GUIDELINES FOR RECORDING SOURCE INFORMATION

1. **Book with One Author.** Write author's name, last name first; book title; place of publication; name of publishing company; and year of publication.

   Parini, Jay. <u>Robert Frost: A Life</u>. New York: Henry Holt and Company, 1999.

2. **Book with More Than One Author.** Write first author's name, last name first; then list other authors, first name first. Record other information as for a book with one author.

   Thompson, Lawrance, and R. H. Winnick. <u>Robert Frost: The Later Years, 1938–1963</u>. New York: Holt, Rinehart and Winston, 1976.

3. **Magazine or Newspaper Article.** Write author's name, last name first; article title; magazine or newspaper name; day, month, and year of publication; edition; and beginning page number. For magazine articles, also list the end page number. For newspaper articles, indicate the section as part of the page number. If no author is listed, start with the article title.

   "A Lover's Quarrel With the World." <u>Time</u> 8 Feb. 1963: 84.

(continued)

English-Language Learners

The punctuation of source titles varies from country to country. Students who have recently come to the United States might punctuate titles as they have done in their native countries. For example, some students might use quotation marks to punctuate book titles. Also, while italics are used for book titles in English, languages such as Chinese and Arabic do not have italics. So that students can punctuate titles correctly in their documentation, use the punctuation shown in the guidelines to review the rules for punctuating each type of title. You may find that a display listing titles that require underlining (italics) on one side and those that require quotation marks on the other is helpful.

(continued)

4. **Encyclopedia Article.** Write author's name, last name first; article title; encyclopedia name; edition number, followed by the abbreviation *ed.;* and year of publication. If no author is listed, start with article title.

Costello, Bonnie. "Frost, Robert Lee." <u>The World Book Encyclopedia</u>. 2000 ed. 2000.

5. **Radio or Television Program.** Write episode or segment title; program name; series title (if any); network name; local station call letters and city (if any); and day, month, and year of broadcast.

"Poet Laureate Reads an Ode to Spring." <u>All Things Considered</u>. National Public Radio. 21 Apr. 1996.

6. **Film, Audio, or Video.** Write title; director (first name first); distributor; and year of release. When citing an audio or video recording, include the original release date (if relevant) and the medium (for example, audiocassette, videocassette, DVD) before the distributor.

<u>Understanding Literature and Life: Drama, Poetry, and Narrative: Part IIb: Poetry</u>. Arnold Weinstein. Audiocassette. The Teaching Company, 1997.

7. **Personal or Telephone Interview.** Write interviewee's last name, then first name; interview type (personal or telephone); and day, month, and year of interview.

Thompson, Carole. Telephone and e-mail interviews. 12 May 2002.

8. **Portable database.** Write author's name, last name first; title of document, article, or part of work; database title; publication medium (for example, CD-ROM, diskette, or magnetic tape); edition, release, or version; place of publication (if known), name of publisher, and date of publication.

Greiner, Donald J. "Robert (Lee) Frost." <u>Dictionary of Literary Biography, Volume 54: American Poets, 1880–1945, Third Series</u>. CD-ROM. 1987 ed. Gale Group, 2001.

9. **Online sources.** Write author's name, last name first (if listed); title of document; title of database or site; date of electronic publication (if available); name of sponsoring institution; date information was accessed; <URL> [or] name of online service.

"Ripton, Vermont." <u>The Friends of Robert Frost</u>. The Friends of Robert Frost. 23 May 2002 <http://www.frostfriends.org/ripton.html>.

Take Notes

The Researcher's Best Friend Take **accurate and coherent notes** of information and ideas you find in your sources. You'll use these facts and details as evidence to support your thesis. Note specific data, facts, and ideas that seem significant and will provide valuable support to answer your questions. Take notes on each piece of information by using one of the following methods.

- **Quote** the information directly, writing the author's exact words.

- **Paraphrase** the information by restating all of the author's ideas in your own words.

- **Summarize** the information by briefly restating only the author's main idea and most important details.

Writing Skills
Use appropriate documentation for sources.

Take Notes

Give students these additional steps to follow in taking their notes and keeping them organized:

- Record your notes on something easy to retrieve. You may use 3x5 note cards or computer files in a database.

- Use a separate note card, computer file, or database record for each item of information and for each source.

- Keep computer printouts in a folder. Highlight key words and make notes in the margin.

CORRECTING MISCONCEPTIONS

Students may be confused on the subject of what exactly constitutes plagiarism. To extend students' understanding of the concept and to clear up any misunderstanding, assign pairs of students to create for a given quotation an example of plagiarism and an example of giving proper credit. Use the quotation below as a model.

Sample quotation: "Writing nonfiction is like being a detective. You have to sleuth out the information and then put all the pieces together to form a book that makes sense." —Lee Martin, Ph.D.

Plagiarism: After completing many research projects, one might come to the conclusion that writing nonfiction is very similar to detective work because both activities involve investigation.

Proper credit: An experienced researcher might come to the conclusion reached by Lee Martin, Ph.D., when she stated that "writing nonfiction is like being a detective." Martin believes that the two activities are similar because they both involve investigation.

TIP If you choose to make notes on your computer, record the information from each source in a separate file.

Write your direct quotations, paraphrases, and summaries on **note cards.** In the upper left-hand corner of each card, write a key word or phrase as the heading for the card so that you can tell at a glance what the note is about. In the upper right-hand corner, write the number (from your source cards) of the source where you found the information. Then, write the text of the note. Finally, in the bottom right-hand corner, record the page number when appropriate. Here are sample note cards that show a direct quotation, a paraphrase, and a summary of information a student found in the book *Robert Frost: The Later Years 1938–1963.*

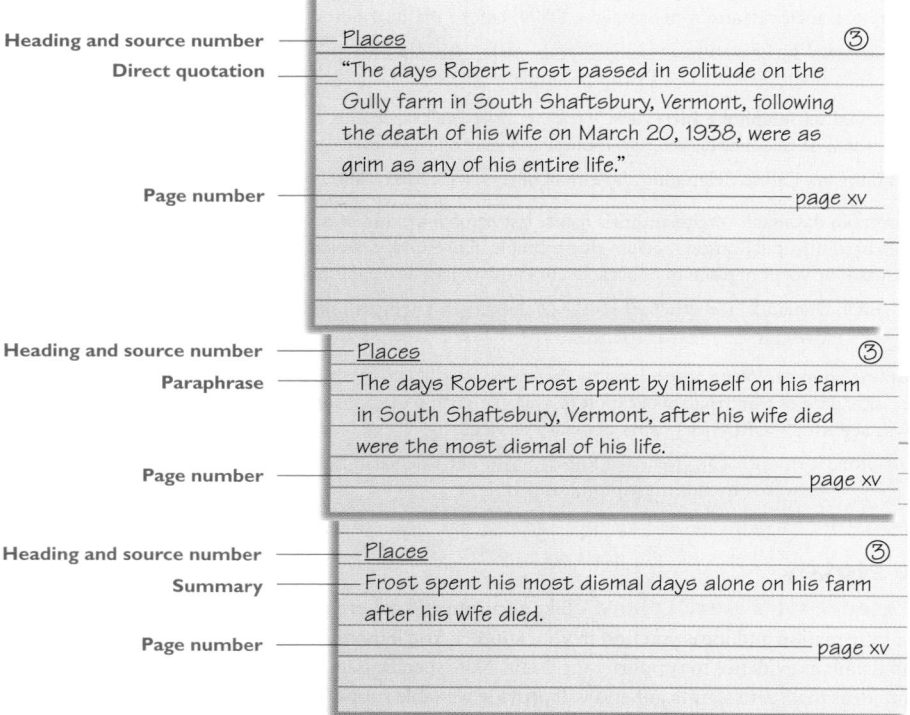

Heading and source number — Places ③
Direct quotation — "The days Robert Frost passed in solitude on the Gully farm in South Shaftsbury, Vermont, following the death of his wife on March 20, 1938, were as grim as any of his entire life."
Page number — page xv

Heading and source number — Places ③
Paraphrase — The days Robert Frost spent by himself on his farm in South Shaftsbury, Vermont, after his wife died were the most dismal of his life.
Page number — page xv

Heading and source number — Places ③
Summary — Frost spent his most dismal days alone on his farm after his wife died.
Page number — page xv

SKILLS FOCUS

Writing Skills
Take notes. Develop main ideas.

TIP A variety of types of evidence will hold your readers' interest while developing the main points in your paper. In addition to facts and details, note these types of evidence, if they're relevant to your research questions.

- **scenarios:** general descriptions of potential events or common situations
- **commonly held beliefs:** broad ideas that most people accept
- **hypotheses:** educated guesses about causes or outcomes
- **definitions:** objective explanations of unfamiliar terms

616 Collection 9 **Biographical and Historical Approach • Using Primary and Secondary Sources**

Write a Thesis Statement

The Bottom Line Your **thesis** is the main idea of your report and the answer to your original research question. Through research, the writer who began with the research question *Where did Robert Frost get ideas for his poems?* found that Frost was inspired by the places where he lived and the natural areas nearby. To state his thesis, he turned his research question into a statement and added information that answered the question. Below is his preliminary thesis statement. As you will see in the Writer's Model on page 622, the writer later fine-tuned his thesis statement to fit the focus of his final draft.

> Robert Frost got many of the ideas for his poems from the places where he lived and the natural areas nearby.

What Tone of Voice? Since you want your readers to take your ideas seriously, be sure that your thesis statement has a formal tone that reflects confidence in what you say. Use this **formal tone** throughout your paper. That means you should avoid slang words, contractions, and first-person pronouns, such as *I* or *we,* and you should use correct grammar. Use technical terms where appropriate, defining or thoroughly explaining them for readers.

Organize Information and Develop an Outline

Get It Together Next you'll need to organize the information you've gathered. Begin by reviewing your note cards and sorting them into groups with similar headings. If a group doesn't have enough note cards to provide adequate support for its heading, you may decide to omit that group or to do additional research for more support.

Organize the groups of cards in the order in which you will present them in the paper. Choose the organizational method below that best fits your topic.

- **Chronological order** presents events in the order that they happened.

- **Logical order** groups related ideas together—explaining the parts of a whole or comparing two subjects, for example.

- **Order of importance** places the most important ideas first and moves to the least important (or vice versa).

You can combine orders in your report if doing so will make your information clearer. For example, you could arrange your main points in logical order but organize the support for those points chronologically.

DO THIS

SKILLS FOCUS

Writing Skills
Establish a coherent thesis statement.

Write a Thesis Statement

Point out to students that there are many possible thesis statements for the same topic and that their statements may change as their research progresses. For example, an alternative to the given example is, "Although Robert Frost got ideas for his poetry from the many different places where he lived, most important by far were nearby natural areas."

Remind students that not all of the questions they subdivided from their original research question need to be addressed in their thesis statements. The answers to most of these questions will appear as supporting details throughout the research paper.

Organize Information and Develop an Outline

Advise students unsure of which method of organization to use to create informal outlines using each of the three types in order to decide which best fits their purpose and audience, and which best fits their thesis. Students will probably find one method easier or more appropriate than the others. Remind students that an informal outline does not need to have a set form. Ideas or facts should be sorted into groups and then the groups arranged in order.

Get It Together

As students plan their reports, have them use a visual organizer such as the following to help them shape their body paragraphs.

Subtopic:
#1 Support:
Conclusion:
Conclusion:
#2 Support:
Conclusion:
Conclusion:
Concluding Sentence:

Learners Having Difficulty

Remind students that *voice* is the sound and rhythm of a writer's language. Though they are writing with a formal tone, students should not make their language so stiff and abstract that their own voice does not show through. One way students can maintain their own voice is by not using any words they are not absolutely sure they know how to use. If students wish to expand their vocabulary, they should find a number of uses of the word in varied contexts before adding it to their own lexicon.

Pick a Card After sorting your note cards, it's time to create an outline of your ideas. An outline for a writing project is like a traveler's map. Good outlines and good maps give guidance and keep people going in the right direction but also leave them free to change their plans. Your outline will include the answers to your detailed questions and the important facts and details that support those answers.

Begin outlining by creating an early plan based on your sorted note cards. This early plan, or **informal outline,** should include the major headings and broad categories of support from your notes. Here is a student's early plan for his report on Robert Frost:

> Thesis: Frost's poetry inspired by places where he lived, nature
>   Early life (San Francisco, aunt's farm)
>   Places he lived as an adult (Derry and other farms, England)
>   Natural areas (poems inspired by nature walks)
> Conclusion: Frost's importance

You will use your informal outline as a guide to create a more detailed **formal outline.** In a formal outline, you plan the arrangement of more specific information from your notes and show the hierarchy of ideas using a formal structure. As you create your formal outline, use numerals and letters to identify main points (headings), supporting ideas (subheadings), and details (facts and examples). This format is shown in the following student outline:

TIP Watch for opportunities to include graphs, charts, maps, or time lines in your paper, and note on your outline where to place them. Visuals such as these can help your readers understand important ideas. Word-processing programs often include features that make it simple for you to include visuals in your paper.

SKILLS FOCUS

Writing Skills
Create an outline.

> I. Introduction
>   A. Thesis statement: Robert Frost got many of the ideas for his poems from the places where he lived and natural areas nearby.
>   B. Background information
> II. Body
>   A. Early life
>   1. San Francisco
>   a. "Once by the Pacific"
>   b. "At Woodward's Gardens"
>   2. Aunt's farm
>   B. Adulthood—Places he lived
>   1. Background information
>   2. Farm in Derry
>   a. Description
>   b. "Mending Wall"

        3. England
            a. Reasons for move
            b. Accomplishments
        4. Return to U.S.
            a. Newfound fame
            b. "Directive"
            c. Reputation
    C. Adulthood—Nature
        1. Nature walks
        2. "Stopping by Woods on a Snowy Evening"
        3. Robert Frost Trail
III. Conclusion
    A. Restatement of thesis
    B. Obituary quote
    C. Frost's impact

Document Sources

Where Credit Is Due In a research paper, you use information and ideas that you obtained from outside sources. Give credit to these sources by citing them in the body of your paper and by listing them at the end of your finished paper—by doing so, you'll avoid the serious academic offense of plagiarism, or claiming someone else's words or ideas as your own.

Citing Sources in the Body When you are writing the body of your report, you must decide what to give credit for and how to give it.

● **What to credit:** If the same information can be found in several easy-to-find sources, it is considered common knowledge. You do not have to document it. For example, it is common knowledge that Robert Frost was an American poet. However, any information that you obtain from outside sources that is not common knowledge must be documented.

● **How to credit:** There are several ways to give credit. One of the most widely used methods is **parenthetical citation.** In this workshop you'll see examples of the parenthetical citation format recommended by the Modern Language Association (MLA). When using parenthetical citations, you should place each citation as close as possible to the information it documents. In most cases you will insert the citation in parentheses before the end punctuation of the sentence in which you have used someone else's words or ideas. Parenthetical citations should be brief so as not to interrupt the flow of the sentences. The chart on the next page tells the information you will need to cite for different sources.

Writing Skills
Use appropriate
documentation for sources.

GUIDELINES FOR GIVING CREDIT WITHIN A PAPER

1. Source with One Author. Last name of the author, followed by the page number (if any) of the work being cited: (Parini 258)

2. Source with No Author Given. Title, or shortened form of it, followed by the page number (if any): ("Lover's Quarrel" 84)

3. Source with Two or More Authors. All authors' last names, followed by the page number (if any): (Thompson and Winnick 14)

4. An Indirect Source. Abbreviation *qtd. in* [quoted in] before the source, followed by the page number: (qtd. in Parini 73)

5. Author's Name Given in Sentence. Page number only: (14)

6. An Interview. Interviewee's full name: (Carole Thompson)

Include a *Works Cited* List At the end of your research paper, you'll include a *Works Cited* list that identifies all the print and nonprint sources used in your paper. If you use only print sources in your paper, you can title your list of sources "Bibliography." You provide this list to help readers learn more about your topic. Be sure your citations are accurate; imagine the trouble your readers would have looking for your sources if one or more elements were missing from a citation.

PREPARING THE WORKS CITED LIST

1. Put your *Works Cited* list on a separate page at the end of your final draft. Center the words *Works Cited* at the top of the page.

2. Follow the correct format for each source. (See pages 620–621.)

3. List your sources in alphabetical order by the authors' last names (or by the title for a work with no author listed). Ignore *A, An,* and *The,* and use the first letter of the next word.

4. Begin each listing on a separate line, aligned with the left margin. If the listing is longer than one line, indent the remaining lines five spaces, or one half inch if you are using a computer. Double-space all entries.

SKILLS FOCUS

Writing Skills
Use appropriate
documentation for sources.

TIP  Before drafting, find out your teacher's formatting requirements. For example, you may need to number every page except the first one in the top right-hand corner or include a footer with your name. You'll also need to prepare a separate title page that includes your name, the date, the title of your report, and the teacher's name. If you take care of details such as these now, you won't have to worry about them when you're preparing your final draft.

Integrate Quotations

Straight from the Horse's Mouth Look back at the direct quotations you have in your notes. While quotations make your paper more credible, too many can make your paper choppy and difficult to read. Directly quote a source only when you can't more effectively summarize or paraphrase an idea. Synthesize the ideas in each quotation you use by connecting the quoted words with your own thoughts or by providing your own interpretation of the quotation.

Be careful when inserting quotations that you don't interrupt the paper's flow of ideas. The chart below shows examples of ways to integrate quotations into your paper once you begin writing. The examples are from a newspaper article you can find in the *Works Cited* list on page 626.

INTEGRATING QUOTATIONS

Type of Quotation	Directions	Example
phrase or clause	Place the quotation within your own sentence, and enclose it in quotation marks.	Frost's images of New England were considered part of "a great American tradition" ("Robert Frost Dies" 5).
short quotation (four lines or less)	Introduce the quotation with your own words, then place it within quotation marks.	One newspaper account of Robert Frost's death says, "he exemplified a great American tradition with his superb, almost angular verses written out of the New England scene" ("Robert Frost Dies" 5).
long quotation (more than four lines)	Introduce the quotation in your own words, followed by a colon. Indent each line ten spaces from the left margin, or one inch if you are using a computer. Do not use quotation marks. Place the parenthetical citation *after* the end punctuation.	In the account of Robert Frost's death in *The New York Times,* the writer chose Frost's images of New England farms and nature to leave a final impression of the poet on his readers:　To countless persons who had never seen New Hampshire birches in the snow or caressed a perfect ax he exemplified a great American tradition with his superb, almost angular verses written out of the New England scene. ("Robert Frost Dies" 5)

PRACTICE & APPLY 1 Use the preceding prewriting information to plan your research paper. First, choose a topic and develop research questions. As you research, create source cards and note cards. Then, develop a thesis and form an outline.

Writing a Research Paper

A Writer's Framework

As students study the framework, you may want to help them gather and organize the materials they will need to write their papers, including their search journals, source cards and notes, and final outlines. Have students mark on their outlines the parts that match the items in the framework. Suggest that students organize their note cards in the same order as they will in their outlines. You may also want to direct some students to write their papers section by section, checking with you after each part, rather than trying to write their papers all at once.

A Writer's Framework

Introduction	Body	Conclusion
• Capture your readers' attention with a question, anecdote, or interesting fact.	• Develop each main point from your outline in a separate body paragraph.	• Remind readers of your thesis by restating it in different words.
• Supply readers with background information on your topic.	• Support each main point with evidence—facts and details in the form of smoothly integrated direct quotations, paraphrases, and summaries.	• Leave your readers with a closing thought—an idea or point to ponder.
• Include a clear thesis statement that gives the answer to your original research question.	• Arrange your main points and evidence in a logical order.	

A Writer's Model

A Walk with Frost

INTRODUCTION

As a high school boy walked home from school in Lawrence, Massachusetts, in 1890, a few lines of poetry about the conquest of Mexico unexpectedly popped into his head. He wrote them down and submitted them to his school paper, where the finished poem was published (Parini 25). No one who read the poem could have possibly known that this boy, Robert Frost, would eventually become "the most popular American poet of his time" (Costello 543).

Source with one author

Background information

Source with no author listed

Frost's popularity and widespread fame did not come early or easily. He spent almost forty years soaking up the sights and sounds of life around him before publishing his first book of poetry ("Lover's Quarrel" 84). Those forty years, however, created memories and experiences that would shape his writing for the remaining forty-five years of his life. Looking back on the sum of his work, readers should see that Robert Frost found much of the inspiration for his poetry from the places where he lived and the natural areas nearby.

Thesis statement

BODY
First main point

This inspiration began where Frost's life began—in San Francisco. The Frost family took many trips to local parks and beaches, including the Cliff House beach, where Frost walked with his father near the pounding surf. This sparked a poem called "Once by

(continued)

the Pacific" (Parini 14). As a boy, with his sister, Jeanie, and his parents, Will and Isabelle, he often visited a zoo in a Victorian park called Woodward's Gardens. This park became the setting for his poem "At Woodward's Gardens," in which a boy teases two monkeys with a magnifying glass and the monkeys snatch it from him (Untermeyer 35).

When Frost was only eleven, his father died, leaving the family penniless. His mother returned with her children to her home state of Massachusetts, where her family could take them in (Parini 19). Frost spent many happy days at his aunt's farm, where he learned to love farming and formed the basis for many of the images found in his poetry (Parini 22). He finished high school as co-valedictorian of his class.

As an adult, Frost continued finding inspiration in farming and nature. After briefly attending Dartmouth College, he taught school to help his mother and rented his first farm in 1893. He later tried his hand at journalism, married his high school sweetheart, and briefly attended Harvard University, leaving Harvard to help his wife during a difficult pregnancy.

Life changed for Frost when he was able to buy a larger, more beautiful farm in Derry, New Hampshire. The farm in Derry was a lovely place with an apple orchard and a brook running along the property. This farm and this time of Frost's life eventually provided experiences and images for much of his poetry. Frost himself once commented, "There was something about the experience at Derry which stayed in my mind, and was tapped for poetry in the years that came after" (qtd. in Parini 73).

The Derry farm was the inspiration of several of Frost's most well-known poems, including "Mending Wall," in which two neighbors repair the wall between their properties:

> Something there is that doesn't love a wall,
> That sends the frozen-ground-swell under it,
> And spills the upper boulders in the sun;
> And makes gaps even two can pass abreast. (lines 1–4)

The actual wall that needed mending is still located at the Derry farm, which is open to the public as a museum filled with Frost memorabilia ("Derry").

The Frosts spent eleven simple and pleasant years on the Derry farm. In 1912, however, Frost made the risky decision to sell the farm and move to England. He wanted a new adventure that would

(continued)

Second main point
Summary

Short quotation

Indirect source

Long quotation

Online source

DIFFERENTIATING INSTRUCTION

Advanced Learners

Enrichment. Ask students to identify the organizational order used in **A Writer's Model** and to suggest reasons why the writer may have used that particular organization. [The model is in chronological order, which allows the writer to follow the events in Robert Frost's life in the order that they happened and to make connections between those events and the poet's work.] **Discuss with students how the model may have been written using another order.** [A logical order may have arranged the locales of Frost's life into categories; order of importance may have prioritized the place in which Frost lived as he produced his most important poems.] **Make sure students have good reasons to support their choice of the best order for the model.**

You may also want to point out to students that the writer of the model uses an anecdote to grab the reader's attention at the beginning of the paper. Suggest that students also consider quotations, surprising statements, and interesting facts as hooks for readers' attention.

DIRECT TEACHING

A Writer's Model

Remind students of the proper format for a research paper. **A Writer's Model** has not been double-spaced due to space constraints. Most writing guides, however, recommend double-spacing for both the body and the list of sources in a research paper.

CRITICAL THINKING

Tell students that writers of lengthy papers often use subheadings to guide their reader through their essays. Ask students to study the model and determine where three or four subheadings might be added to help the reader [possibilities include "Early Life," "Derry," and "The Farmer-Poet"]. Invite students to consider whether subheadings would be useful as they draft their own writing.

DIFFERENTIATING INSTRUCTION

Learners Having Difficulty

Students may benefit from studying how many quotations the author of **A Writer's Model** incorporates into an average paragraph. Point out to students as well the nice balance of critical commentary and quotations from poems. Students can use the model to guide them in deciding how many quotations to include in each paragraph and also to help them decide on a balanced proportion of primary and secondary sources. Remind students that any quoted information should be guided and controlled by their own original ideas and that their papers should not merely contain the ideas of others.

Phrase/quotation	give him "peace to write, the excitement of change" (Parini 113).
Source with two authors	While he had managed to publish a few poems, he felt he had the ability to write great poetry and to "realize his childhood dream of achieving honor and glory as a poet" (Thompson and Winnick xvi). England turned out to provide the inspiration Frost needed. Within a few months of his family's move, Frost had published his first book, *A Boy's Will,* and was working on a second. During his two years in England, he made many important literary friends and began to believe he would actually be able to make his way as a poet. World War II was brewing, however, and the Frosts quickly made their escape back to America ("England").
Summary	Frost returned home to unexpected fame. The two books he completed while in England were widely available and well-reviewed. Suddenly Frost was considered at the forefront of "the new era in American poetry" (qtd. in Untermeyer xxii). Despite this success, he settled back into his familiar way of life, buying a farm in New Hampshire. As before, he supported his family through the combination of farming and teaching. At last, though, his talents were being recognized by editors and reviewers (Parini 160).
Paraphrase	Frost's love of farms remained, even though he could not make a living at it (Parini 173). He continued writing poems with imagery and settings he knew well, including many poems with what was becoming Frost's trademark—the voice of the New England farmer. Among these was "Directive," which describes with great sadness an abandoned farmhouse: "There is a house that is no more a house/Upon a farm that is no more a farm" (qtd. in Parini 361). According to biographer Jay Parini, the landscape Frost describes serves as "a map of his inner landscape," whose sorrow he then can leave behind (361).
Short quotation	As his reputation grew, Frost began lecturing at many colleges and universities, cementing his reputation as a farmer-poet (Thompson and Winnick xvii). This carefully crafted image lasted right up to one of his last poems, still about a farm, called "A Cabin in the Clearing" ("Ripton").
Third main point	Along with his love of farms, Frost was fond of nature. One of his favorite pastimes throughout his life was walking in woods or along nature trails, which he called "botanizing" walks ("Ripton"). Two of his most quoted poems are about traveling alone in a natural setting—"Stopping by Woods on a Snowy Evening" and "The Road Not Taken." Both poems sparked lively debates about whether Frost's

(continued)

(continued)

message was simple or complex. In "Stopping by Woods on a Snowy Evening," for example, there are many interpretations to these lines:

> The woods are lovely, dark and deep,
> But I have promises to keep,
> And miles to go before I sleep,
> And miles to go before I sleep. (lines 13–16)

Some people argue that the last lines simply mean the traveler has a long way to go before getting home. Others take a more complex view that "travelers in life" often do not know where they are going. During public readings of the poem, Frost would not say what he really meant, but that he wanted to leave the interpretation open to the listener (Parini 213).

Frost's love of nature is so tied to his poetry that many of the places dedicated to his memory follow the themes of his poems and continue to inspire other nature lovers. According to the president of The Friends of Robert Frost, the Green Mountain National Forest has a Robert Frost Trail along scenic paths where visitors can stop and read plaques inscribed with poems. One such plaque displays the poem "A Winter Eden" and stands near a swamp much like the one described in the poem. At one spot, walkers arrive at a fork in a path where they can consider the words of "The Road Not Taken" (Carole Thompson).

The boy who was first inspired to write poetry by an account of the conquest of Mexico had earned a reputation as the poetic voice of the common farmer through imagery inspired by his surroundings. The young man who had subsisted on farming and teaching came to be considered "America's best-known and best-loved poet" (Thompson and Winnick xvi). In the account of Robert Frost's death in *The New York Times,* the writer chose Frost's images of New England farms and nature to leave his readers with a final impression:

> To countless persons who had never seen New Hampshire birches in the snow or caressed a perfect ax he exemplified a great American tradition with his superb, almost angular verses written out of the New England scene. ("Robert Frost Dies" 5)

Frost certainly succeeded in his aim to "lodge a few poems where they can't be gotten rid of easily" (Parini xi). With four Pulitzer prizes, countless honorary degrees, and poetry that has been read all over the world, Robert Frost found his honor and glory in writing poetry, just as he always knew he would.

Complexity explained

Interview

CONCLUSION
Restatement of thesis

Concluding thought

(continued)

DIRECT TEACHING

Works Cited

Ask students to study each piece listed on the **Works Cited** list and to evaluate each entry based on the type of source, date, and type of material. For instance, students may respond that the Web site listings are very recent and should provide up-to-date material but that the title of the Web site indicates that the articles might be one-sided in their uncritical praise for the poet. Some listings that are more than twenty-five years old might be dated, but the titles indicate they are relevant to the essay. The inclusion of personal interviews indicates a reliable breadth and depth of research.

RETEACHING

Practice & Apply 2

Students may have trouble transferring their notes into original paragraphs. Suggest that students sit down with a blank sheet of paper and a stack of their notes. Then, have them read the notes in order and turn them face down. Have students write one to three sentences that describe or explain what the notes say. These sentences should capture the essential information in the notes.

PRACTICE & APPLY 2

Guided and Independent Practice

Make sure each student has an outline for his or her first draft along with organized note cards. Emphasize to students the importance of a thorough and accurate method of citation. Ask students: "Would you trust the account of Robert Frost's life and work in **A Writer's Model** if you found errors in its citations?" Point out that their readers will similarly lose trust in them if they are not careful and thorough.

TIP Generally, research papers and their *Works Cited* lists are double-spaced. They are shown here single-spaced because of limited room. See *go.hrw.com* for a double-spaced model of a research paper.

(continued)

Works Cited

Costello, Bonnie. "Frost, Robert Lee." The World Book Encyclopedia. 2000 ed. 2000.

"Derry, New Hampshire." The Friends of Robert Frost. The Friends of Robert Frost. 23 May 2002 <http://www. frostfriends.org/ derry.html>.

"England." The Friends of Robert Frost. The Friends of Robert Frost. 23 May 2002 <http://www.frostfriends.org/ england.html>.

"A Lover's Quarrel With the World." Time 8 Feb. 1963: 84.

Parini, Jay. Robert Frost: A Life. New York: Henry Holt and Company, 1999.

"Robert Frost Dies at 88; Kennedy Leads in Tribute." New York Times 30 Jan. 1963. Western ed.: 1+.

"Ripton, Vermont." The Friends of Robert Frost. The Friends of Robert Frost. 23 May 2002 <http://www.frostfriends.org/ ripton.html>.

Thompson, Carole. Telephone and e-mail interviews. 12 May 2002.

Thompson, Lawrance, and R. H. Winnick. Robert Frost: The Later Years, 1938–1963. New York: Holt, Rinehart and Winston, 1976.

Untermeyer, Louis, ed. The Road Not Taken. New York: Holt, Rinehart and Winston, 1962.

INTERNET
More Writer's Models
Keyword: LE5 9-9

PRACTICE & APPLY 2 Write the first draft of your research paper and *Works Cited* list. Look back at the framework on page 622 to make sure you include all the essential elements of a research paper. Also, use the Writer's Model and its annotations as guides for writing your own paper. Be sure to smoothly integrate any direct quotations, and use a variety of quotations, paraphrases, and summaries from your sources. Include parenthetical citations to document your sources for all of these types of information.

Revising

Evaluate and Revise Your Draft

Touch-up or Major Overhaul? Many famous writers revise their works several times. Sometimes they even revise works that have already been published. Very few writers get it just right the first time. To refine your own writing, you should read through your paper at least twice. First, evaluate the content and organization using the following guidelines. Then, use the guidelines on the next page to revise your essay for style.

> **PEER REVIEW**
>
> Ask a peer to read your paper before you begin revising. He or she may be able to point out places where you need more evidence to support a main point.

▶ **First Reading: Content and Organization** The following chart should help you evaluate and revise the content and organization of your draft. Ask yourself the questions in the left-hand column. If you need help answering them, use the tips in the middle column. Then, make the changes suggested in the right-hand column.

Rubric: Writing a Research Paper

Evaluation Questions	▶ Tips	▶ Revision Techniques
❶ Is the thesis clearly stated? Does it seem to answer a specific research question?	▶ **Underline** the thesis statement. **Draw a box** around the part that answers a specific research question.	▶ **Add** a thesis statement or **replace** an existing statement with one that clearly answers the research question.
❷ Is each main point well supported with evidence—facts and details in the form of direct quotations, summaries, and paraphrases?	▶ **Highlight** each main point with a different colored marker. Then, **highlight** evidence with the color of its corresponding main point.	▶ **Add** additional evidence for any main points that have too little support.
❸ Are direct quotations smoothly integrated into the paper?	▶ **Draw an arrow** from each direct quotation to the words that introduce the quotation.	▶ **Reword** the text around quotations so that the flow of ideas is not disrupted.
❹ Are all sources given proper credit?	▶ **Look back** at all highlighted direct quotations, paraphrases, and summaries. **Place check marks** by their parenthetical citations.	▶ **Add** parenthetical citations for direct quotations, paraphrases, or summaries from sources.
❺ Does the conclusion restate the thesis and give the readers a closing thought?	▶ **Underline** the restatement of the thesis. **Put a wavy line** under the closing thought.	▶ **Add** a restatement of the thesis. **Elaborate** on the ideas in the essay by leaving readers with an idea or point to ponder.

Writing Workshop: Writing a Research Paper **627**

GUIDED PRACTICE

Responding to the Revision Process

Answers

1. The writer revised the beginning of the second sentence to avoid the monotonous, passive phrase "There were."

2. The writer included the citation to show the source of the information in the sentence; the citation tells the reader the source of the information so the reader can verify it for him- or herself.

Second Reading: Style In your second reading, look at your sentence style. Since your research paper is so full of information, you don't want to risk losing your readers' attention. Starting many sentences with phrases like *there is* and *there was* can make your research paper monotonous to readers and cause their attention to fade. Instead of overusing these tired sentence structures, add variety to your sentence beginnings by starting with your subject and following it with a lively verb. The following style guidelines will help.

Style Guidelines

Evaluation Question	▶ Tip	▶ Revision Technique
● Do many sentences begin with the words *there is, there was, there are,* or *there were?*	▶ **Double underline** each sentence that begins this way. If you have more than two or three in your entire paper, revise.	▶ **Rearrange** the sentence so that the subject comes first. Then, **replace** *is, are, was,* or *were* with a more lively verb.

ANALYZING THE REVISION PROCESS

Study these revisions, and answer the questions that follow.

> This inspiration began where Frost's life began—in San
>
> *replace* — *The Frost family took*
>
> Francisco, ~~There were~~ many trips to local parks and beaches,
>
> including the Cliff House beach, where Frost walked with his
>
> father near the pounding surf. This sparked a poem called
>
> *add* — "Once by the Pacific." *(Parini 14).*

Responding to the Revision Process

1. Why did the writer revise the beginning of the second sentence?

2. Why did the writer add the parenthetical citation to the last sentence? What does the citation tell the reader about the information in that sentence?

SKILLS FOCUS

Writing Skills
Revise for content and style.

PRACTICE & APPLY ③ Revise the content, organization, and style of your research paper by using the charts on the last two pages to guide you. Look at the revisions in the paragraph above as a model for your own revisions.

PRACTICE & APPLY ③

Independent Practice

As students revise their papers, encourage them to study each sentence's basic subject-verb-object structure. Point out to students that when including many facts and details, it is sometimes easy to forget basic things such as writing in complete, clear sentences. Students should make sure the structures of their sentences are as well organized and as easy to follow as the structures of their papers.

Publishing

Proofread and Publish Your Essay

A Fine-toothed Comb   Before you prepare the final copy of your research paper, make sure it's free of grammar, spelling, and punctuation errors. Particularly, watch for errors in documenting your sources. Compare the format of your entries in the *Works Cited* list against the MLA format guidelines shown on pages 614–615. Double check that the information in your parenthetical citations matches the information you give in your *Works Cited* list.

Share the Wealth   Once you've corrected any errors, make sure your final draft meets your teacher's manuscript requirements. Include a correctly formatted title page, and use pagination, spacing, and margins appropriate to a research report. Now that you've spent so much time and energy researching and writing your paper, consider how you can share what you've learned with a larger audience. Here are some suggestions:

- Locate a group or organization that would have a special interest in your research. For example, organizations of Frost fans might be interested in publishing all or parts of the the Writer's Model on page 622.

- Collect other research papers from your class for a special display at your school or in your classroom. Using advanced publishing software and graphics software, polish the design of your papers to heighten their appeal.

- Send a copy of your paper to any professional you may have interviewed. For example, the writer of the Frost paper might mail a copy to the Frost organization president whom he interviewed.

Reflect on Your Essay

Give It Some Thought   Writing short responses to the following questions will help you build on what you've learned in this workshop.

- What difficulties did you encounter while writing this paper? How might you avoid these problems when writing future research reports?

- How might you use the research skills you've acquired in this workshop in your other classes?

- What discoveries did you make about the topic and about yourself as a writer while completing this workshop?

PRACTICE & APPLY 4   Proofread your research paper, and consider all your publishing options. Plan and carry out the publishing option or options that most appeal to you. Then, answer the reflection questions above.

TIP   Proofreading helps ensure that your essay follows the **conventions** of standard American English. For example, because you are presenting so much information on your topic, you may have a tendency to merge two complete sentences into one run-on sentence. Proofread your paper to make sure that it's free of run-on sentences. For more on **run-on sentences,** see Run-on Sentences, 9b, in the Language Handbook.

COMPUTER TIP

For information on creating an appealing document design using computer software, see Designing Your Writing in the Writer's Handbook.

SKILLS FOCUS

Writing Skills
Proofread, especially to correct run-on sentences.

Motivate. Direct students to remember times they have watched news broadcasts on TV. Ask students: "Do the news anchors speak just like any person would in any situation?" Lead students to discuss the various strategies, both verbal (for example, pace and voice modulation) and nonverbal (such as eye contact and gestures), that news reporters use to get their messages across. Have students evaluate the need for and the usefulness of such strategies and share when they have used such strategies themselves.

DIRECT TEACHING

Adapt Your Research Paper

Tell students that their two main concerns when delivering information orally will be to deliver that information clearly and to maintain their audience's interest. As students go about adapting their papers for their oral presentations, direct them to keep these two main concerns at the forefront of their minds. Any time they have a question about what to do, students should ask themselves: "What would make the information more clear to my audience? What would make my delivery more interesting?"

Speaking Assignment
Adapt the information from a written research report to effectively deliver it in an oral presentation.

Presenting Research

All day long you listen—to teachers, to other students, to your parents. Everybody has information that you need to hear. What do you do when it's your turn to speak? How do you share information—like the contents of a research paper—effectively? This workshop explains how to share your research in an **oral presentation.**

Adapt Your Research Paper

Similar but Different The information in your oral presentation will likely be the same as the information in your paper. You will, though, need to adapt your written ideas so you can deliver them effectively orally. To start, consider the following suggestions.

Shorten and Simplify Make your points directly, keeping your words and sentences simple to make sure that listeners don't get lost. Plan to use standard American English and avoid slang. If you must use certain unfamiliar words, technical terms, or notations, be sure you define and explain them carefully and clearly.

Give Previews and Repeat Yourself Break the information in your presentation into small units; then, prepare a one- or two-sentence preview of each section to let listeners know what to expect. At the end of each section sum up the ideas you have given. Obvious previews and repetition help listeners absorb and remember information.

Drop Clues Listeners need to know where you are leading them. Help them by presenting your ideas in a logical, easy-to-follow order. Do not stray too far from the simplest, most straightforward uses of chronological order or order of importance. Insert transitional words and phrases, such as *first, second, next, most important,* and *finally,* to help make the organization of your ideas crystal clear.

Anticipate Your Listeners' Reactions Be prepared to deal with listeners who may misunderstand you or have a bias against your ideas. You should be able to restate or paraphrase information if your listeners look confused. Handle doubters by referring to your facts. Remember to respect their ideas, but also express confidence and defend the research you have gathered.

Mapping Your Course As you review your material for adaptation, make sure that you maintain a strong basic presentation structure of introduction, body, and conclusion. Use the chart on the next page to plan the content of each section.

SKILLS FOCUS

Listening and Speaking Skills
Present a research report.

Planning
■ *One-Stop Planner* CD-ROM with ExamView Test Generator

Differentiating Instruction
■ *Workshop Resources: Writing, Listening, and Speaking*
■ *Family Involvement Activities in English and Spanish*

■ *Supporting Instruction in Spanish*

Listening and Speaking
■ *Workshop Resources: Writing, Listening, and Speaking*
■ *Daily Language Activities*

Assessment
■ *Holt Assessment: Writing, Listening, and Speaking*

ORGANIZING SPEECH CONTENT

Introduction	• Plan to grab your listeners' attention with a startling statement, an interesting and relevant anecdote, or a connection to the interests of the listeners. • Consider incorporating your original research question into your introduction.
Body	• Support your thesis with only the most relevant and significant evidence from your paper. • Use ideas from both primary and secondary sources to show listeners that you've considered all important ideas and perspectives. • Keep your ideas logically organized in either chronological order or order of importance. • Add to your credibility by telling where your information came from. Smoothly introduce source information by saying something like "Biologist Kim Griffith suggests that . . ."
Conclusion	• Summarize your main points. • Pose an interesting thought or question to keep your listeners thinking about the ideas you've presented after you're finished.

Prepare for Delivery

In the Spotlight In an oral presentation, preparing your content is only half the battle. Now, you must prepare to stand before an audience and say your ideas aloud. Practice communicating your ideas effectively, using verbal and nonverbal techniques.

Show 'Em! Consider using the technology available at your school to include **visuals**—such as charts, maps, or graphs—to enhance the appeal and clarity of your presentation. Short video clips and graphics shown on a television or an overhead projector can help you express ideas more effectively. For example, rather than simply reporting responses from an interview you've conducted, why not videotape the interview and show the most relevant segments of it to your audience? Also, consider using **props** in your presentation. For example, a speaker could enhance a presentation about Japanese culture by wearing a kimono. Whatever audiovisual support you use, be sure that it is relevant and easy to understand.

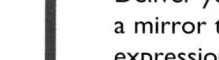 Adapt the information from your research paper for an oral presentation. Practice your verbal and nonverbal techniques; then, deliver your presentation to an audience.

Reference Note

For information on **verbal and nonverbal delivery techniques,** see page 75.

SKILLS FOCUS

Listening and Speaking Skills
Organize the speech. Use visual aids.

■ *One-Stop Planner* CD-ROM with ExamView Test Generator

Internet
■ go.hrw.com (Keyword LE5 9-9)
■ *Elements of Literature Online*

Prepare for Delivery

One method of helping students understand the best ways in which to give an oral report is to provide them with a concrete example of some of the *worst* ways. Read aloud for students a short article from a newspaper or magazine. Make sure you do not make any eye contact or pause at any point but instead rush through the reading, occasionally mumbling a word or two. Then, ask students what improvements they think could have been made in the presentation, and write students' suggestions on the chalkboard. Have students then compare their comments to the tips given in this workshop.

DIFFERENTIATING INSTRUCTION

Learners Having Difficulty

The best help for many students will be practice. Students uncomfortable with or unskilled at public speaking may benefit from using these rehearsal techniques:

• Record yourself as you deliver the speech. Then, play the tape back and make notes about what you might want to change.

• Deliver your speech to friends or family, and ask for feedback.

• Deliver your speech in front of a mirror to judge your facial expressions and body language.

PRACTICE & APPLY

Guided and Independent Practice

Have each student freewrite for five minutes about the changes they intend to make in their written reports in order to present the research orally. Discuss with students the various strategies they can use.

Informational Reading Skills

SKILLS FOCUS, pp. 632–635

Grade-Level Skills

■ Reading Skills
Analyze and elaborate on ideas presented in primary and secondary sources.

INTRODUCING THE SKILLS REVIEW

Use this review to assess students' understanding of the skill taught in this collection. If necessary, you can use the annotations to guide students in their reading before they answer the questions.

DIRECT TEACHING

Ⓐ Analyzing Informational Text

❷ Analyzing. Based on the opening sentence, how would you characterize the author's tone? [Possible response: The tone is dry, objective, and direct.]

Ⓑ Analyzing Informational Text

❷ Analyzing. Does this paragraph contain just facts, just opinions, or a mix of both? [just facts]

Ⓒ Analyzing Informational Text

❷ Evaluating. Who does the author's intended audience seem to be? [The article is intended for a general audience—readers who want to learn the basic facts about the assassination.]

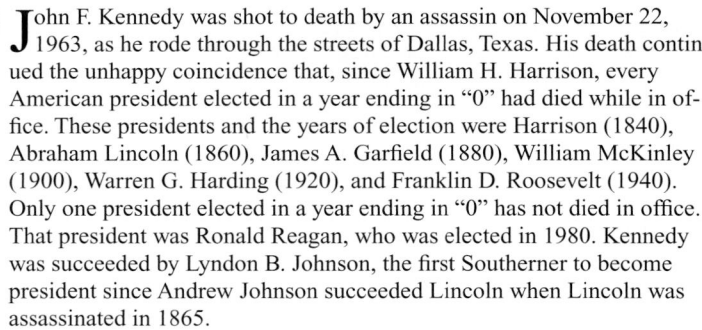

Using Primary and Secondary Sources

Test Practice   DIRECTIONS: Read the following encyclopedia article and personal recollection. Then, read and respond to the questions that follow.

Kennedy's Assassination

Eric Sevareid

Ⓐ John F. Kennedy was shot to death by an assassin on November 22, 1963, as he rode through the streets of Dallas, Texas. His death continued the unhappy coincidence that, since William H. Harrison, every American president elected in a year ending in "0" had died while in office. These presidents and the years of election were Harrison (1840), Ⓑ Abraham Lincoln (1860), James A. Garfield (1880), William McKinley (1900), Warren G. Harding (1920), and Franklin D. Roosevelt (1940). Only one president elected in a year ending in "0" has not died in office. That president was Ronald Reagan, who was elected in 1980. Kennedy was succeeded by Lyndon B. Johnson, the first Southerner to become president since Andrew Johnson succeeded Lincoln when Lincoln was assassinated in 1865.

The new president. Television and radio flashed the news of the shooting to a shocked world. Vice President Johnson raced to the hospital and remained until Kennedy died. Then, he went to the airport where the presidential plane waited. Mrs. Kennedy and the coffin holding her husband's body arrived later. At 2:39 P.M., U.S. District Judge Sarah T. Ⓒ Hughes administered the oath of office to Johnson, who became the 36th president of the United States. As Johnson took the oath in the airplane, he was flanked by his wife and by Mrs. Kennedy.

Then the plane carrying the new chief executive and his wife, the body of the dead president, and the late president's widow returned to Washington. When the plane arrived, Johnson told the nation: "This is a sad time for all people. We have suffered a loss that cannot be weighed. . . ."

The world mourns. The sudden death of the young and vigorous American president shocked the world. Kennedy's body was brought back to the White House and placed in the East Room for 24 hours. On the Sunday after the assassination, the president's flag-draped coffin was carried to the Capitol Rotunda to lie in state.° Throughout the day and night, hundreds

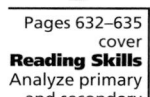

Pages 632–635 cover
Reading Skills
Analyze primary and secondary sources.

°**Capitol Rotunda to lie in state:** The Capitol Rotunda is the round room beneath the dome of the Capitol, the building in which the U.S. Congress meets in Washington, D.C. *Lie in state* means "be displayed to the public before burial."

632 Collection 9 Biographical and Historical Approach • Using Primary and Secondary Sources

---

READING MINI-LESSON

Reviewing Word-Attack Skills
Activity. Display these pairs of words. Have students tell if the underlined letters in the words stand for the same sound or different sounds. Encourage students to check pronunciations in a dictionary.

  I. intelle<u>ct</u>ual   intelligen<u>t</u>sia
  [Different: /ch/ and /t/]

2. <u>ch</u>orus   <u>ch</u>ores
  [Different: /k/ and /ch/]

3. <u>qu</u>atrain   manne<u>qu</u>in
  [Different: /kw/ and /k/]

4. mo<u>d</u>ulation   mo<u>d</u>ernistic
  [Different: /j/ and /d/]

5. se<u>qu</u>ester   se<u>qu</u>oia   [Same: /kw/]

6. pa<u>ch</u>yderm   la<u>ch</u>rymose   [Same: /k/]

---

of thousands of people filed past the guarded casket. Representatives from over 90 countries attended the funeral on November 25.

Kennedy was buried with full military honors at Arlington National Cemetery across the Potomac River from Washington, D.C. At the close of the funeral service, Mrs. Kennedy lighted an "eternal flame" to burn over the president's grave. In one of his first acts, President Johnson named the National Aeronautics and Space Administration installation in Florida the John F. Kennedy Space Center.

Other public buildings and geographical sites throughout the world were named for President Kennedy. Congress voted funds for the John F. Kennedy Center for the Performing Arts in Washington, D.C. Great Britain made one acre of ground permanent United States territory as part of a Kennedy memorial at Runnymede. In 1979, the John F. Kennedy Library opened in Boston.

—from "John Fitzgerald Kennedy,"
The World Book Encyclopedia (2001)

For Me, It Was a Dramatic Day
Pierre Salinger

Pierre Salinger, President Kennedy's press secretary, remembers where he was and how he felt when he heard the news of Kennedy's assassination.

For me, it was a dramatic day. I had left the White House on November 19 to accompany six members of JFK's cabinet[1] to an economic conference in Tokyo. President Kennedy had asked me to join the trip to organize his visit to Tokyo, planned for February 1964. This would have been the first visit by an American president to Japan since the end of World War II.

We stopped in Honolulu[2] for three days for an important meeting on the Vietnam crisis. Early in the morning of November 22, the White

---

1. **cabinet** *n.:* The president's cabinet includes the heads of the various departments of the executive branch, such as the departments of State, Treasury, and Defense.
2. **Honolulu** (hän′ə·lōō′lōō): capital of Hawaii.

DIRECT TEACHING

D **Analyzing Informational Text**

❷ **Elaborating.** Consider the facts presented about the foreign response to Kennedy's assassination. What can you conclude about the event's global impact? [Possible responses: People in other countries were sorrowful over Kennedy's death; Kennedy must have been greatly admired the world over.]

E **Analyzing Informational Text**

❷ **Primary and secondary sources.** You know that this selection is an entry from an encyclopedia. So would the article be an example of a primary or secondary source? [Encyclopedias are secondary sources. They contain information that is synthesized from other sources.]

F **Analyzing Informational Text**

❷ **Analyzing.** From the title, what kind of information do you expect this recollection to contain? [Possible response: The "For Me" suggests that it will contain the author's personal thoughts, feelings, and experiences.] **Consider the author's position. Is his selection a primary or secondary source?** [The author was on the president's staff. His account is a primary source.]

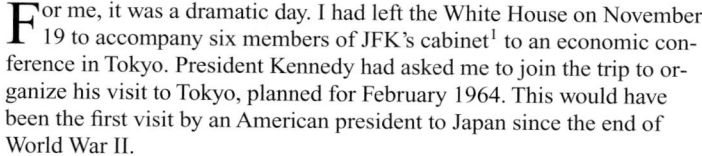

7. impetuous   imperturbable
[Different: /ch/ and /t/]

8. verdurous   endurance
[Different: /j/ and /d/]

9. eventually   eventuality   [Same: /ch/]
10. brochure   crochet   [Same: /sh/]
11. factual   perpetually   [Same: /ch/]
12. bisque   risqué   [Same: /k/]

Activity. Display these sound symbols and words. Have students identify the word in which the given sound is heard. Answers are underlined.

1. /sh/   cartouche   touchstone   toucan
2. /ch/   recherché   ricochet   ritual
3. /kw/   mystique   antique   antiquarian
4. /t/   portrayal   natural   cultural

5. /d/	undulate	unduly	undulant
6. /k/	achieve	archival	chivalrous
7. /j/	pendulum	pendant	pugnacious
8. /k/	acquaint	sequential	piquant
9. /ch/	anchor	anachronism	anchovy
10. /k/	chasm	chasuble	chastise
11. /ch/	chartreuse	century	chauffeur
12. /j/	pendant	pendulous	impending

DIRECT TEACHING

A Analyzing Informational Text

? Evaluating. What information does the author provide that would be hard to obtain from other sources? [Possible response: He provides an insider's view of what happened in the period immediately after the shooting—confusion and disarray within the administration.]

B Analyzing Informational Text

? Evaluating. How does the account shift at this point? [Up to this point, the author has provided a chronological, factual account of his experience. Now, he reveals his feelings, the devastating emotions triggered in him by the events.]

C Analyzing Informational Text

? Evaluating. Both pieces refer to Jackie Kennedy. What does this description of her behavior reveal that the encyclopedia entry does not? [Possible response: It reveals the first lady's compassion. It is she who has suffered the greatest loss, yet she tries to help the author deal with the tragedy.]

D Learners Having Difficulty

? Questioning. Why is the author shocked to hear that the president wants to speak with him? [He is thinking of Kennedy as the president, even though Kennedy is dead. At last, he realizes that it is the new president, Lyndon Johnson, calling.]

House plane headed for Tokyo. I was in the back of the plane reading the economic papers when suddenly somebody came and told me the six cabinet secretaries had to see me. They were in the office in the front of the plane. When I walked in, it was grim. They handed me a wire bulletin[3] saying Kennedy had been shot.

A The plane turned around and headed back to Honolulu, and I was instructed to take over the communications system to the White House and find out what had happened. When I connected with the White House, there was total confusion. For many minutes nothing was coming through clearly. About a half hour after the plane had turned around, I heard in my ear: "Wayside. Standby." Wayside was my code name. About every thirty seconds for the next five minutes, I heard the same thing. Then suddenly came a new message. "Wayside. Lancer is dead." Lancer was the code name for President Kennedy.

B I was destroyed. I so admired and liked JFK. I had a feeling that not only was he lost, but that my life was lost.

C When we reached Washington, a car took me to the White House. JFK's body had just arrived in the East Room and there was a short prayer service. Jackie Kennedy came up to me after the prayer and said I had had a terrible day and should sleep in the White House.

I went upstairs where I talked with colleagues like Ken O'Donnell and Larry O'Brien until five in the morning. Finally, I went to sleep.

D At 7 A.M. the phone rang. I heard the operator say: "Mr. Salinger, the president wants to talk to you." For an instant, I thought I'd had a nightmare. Then, on the phone I heard: "Pierre, this is Lyndon."[4] It was over. It was now clear to me that Kennedy was dead.

—from *Where Were You When President Kennedy Was Shot?*

---

3. **wire bulletin:** news bulletin from a wire service, an organization that transmits news stories to newspapers and radio and television stations by telegraph or electronic means.
4. **Lyndon:** Lyndon B. Johnson, Kennedy's vice president, who became president after Kennedy was killed.

Using Academic Language

Review of Literary Terms
Ask students to look back through the collection to find the meanings of the terms listed below. Then, have students show their grasp of the terms by citing passages from the collection that illustrate the meanings of the terms. **Historical Setting or Period** (pp. 562, 590); **Biographical Approach** (pp. 562, 564); **Theme** (p. 564); **Conflict** (p. 590).

Review of Informational Terms
Ask students to review the collection to find the meanings of the terms listed at right. Then, ask students to use the terms to explain how to extend ideas presented in primary and secondary sources.

Collection 9: Skills Review

1. Why is "Kennedy's Assassination" a valuable source for research?

   A It is written for an audience made up of experts.

   B Its purpose is to show why Kennedy was a great president.

   C It reveals Lyndon B. Johnson's opinion of the assassination.

   D It presents a factual, historical perspective on the assassination and its aftermath.

2. What is the **tone** of "Kennedy's Assassination"?

   F dramatic

   G objective

   H sorrowful

   J enraged

3. Which statement is the *most* accurate **evaluation** of "For Me, It Was a Dramatic Day"?

   A It is a primary source because it is a firsthand account of one person's experiences.

   B It is a secondary source because the author did not actually witness the assassination.

   C It is a secondary source because it is a strictly factual description of an event.

   D It is a primary source because it includes only opinions and no facts.

4. The **purpose** of "For Me, It Was a Dramatic Day" is to —

   F reveal the author's sense of shock and loss at the news of Kennedy's death

   G show that Lyndon B. Johnson effectively took control of the country

   H warn that the government could easily be thrown into confusion

   J emphasize the author's personal relationship with Kennedy and his family

5. Which point in "For Me, It Was a Dramatic Day" can be **verified** by reading "Kennedy's Assassination"?

   A Kennedy's code name was Lancer.

   B Kennedy had planned to visit Japan.

   C Kennedy's body was placed in the East Room in the White House.

   D Pierre Salinger communicated with the White House about Kennedy's death.

Constructed Response

6. Examine the two sources, "Kennedy's Assassination" and "For Me, It Was a Dramatic Day," and explain how they differ. How might each source be used in a research paper about John F. Kennedy's assassination?

Primary Source (p. 578); **Secondary Source** (p. 578); **Analyze** (p. 578); **Author's Purpose** (p. 578); **Audience** (p. 578); **Evaluate** (p. 579); **Facts** (p. 579); **Opinions** (p. 579); **Elaborate** (p. 579).

Test-Taking Tips

Advise students that if they have difficulty with a question, they should cross out any answers they know to be incorrect. This will help them focus on the remaining choices. For more instruction on how to answer multiple-choice items, refer students to **Test Smarts**.

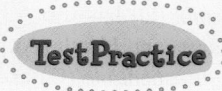

Answers and Model Rationales

1. **D** Its value lies in its being objective and fact based. A is incorrect because encyclopedia entries are written for a general audience; B and C are incorrect, because the article does not focus on Kennedy's greatness nor is Johnson's opinion revealed.

2. **G** Like most encyclopedia entries, "Kennedy's Assassination" maintains a neutral, or objective, tone. It expresses neither rage nor sorrow and does not try to enhance the inherent drama of the event it describes.

3. **A** B and C can be eliminated since a firsthand account is by definition a primary source. D is incorrect since the relative balance of fact and opinion has no bearing on whether it is a primary source.

4. **F** Because the article focuses on Salinger's shock and grief, F is the best choice.

5. **C** Both selections state that Kennedy's body was placed in the East Room of the White House. The points in A, B, and D are not in "Kennedy's Assassination."

Constructed Response

6. "Kennedy's Assassination" is a factual account of Kennedy's death, while "For Me, It Was a Dramatic Day" is a personal account. The encyclopedia article could provide objective facts for a report; the firsthand account could provide details about how people close to the president reacted to his death.

Collection 9: Skills Review

Vocabulary Skills

Synonyms

Modeling. Model the thoughts of a good test taker answering item 1. Say, "*Vigilant* means to watch over something. *Watchful* (D) has the same meaning as *vigilant*. *Harsh* (A), *forgiving* (B), and *irresponsible* (C) are not similar in meaning, so they are wrong."

Answers and Model Rationales

1. **D**   See rationale above.

2. **G**   To be *enthralled* is "to be fascinated," so G is the answer. H is an antonym of *enthralled* and F and J are unrelated words.

3. **C**   *Solace* means "comfort," so C is the correct answer. The words in options A and B are not related to *solace*. *Pity* (D), while sometimes related to *solace*, is not a synonym of it.

4. **F**   *Condemning* is a synonym for *denouncing*, so F is correct. G is an antonym and H and J are unrelated words.

5. **D**   Since *resolve* means "determination," D is correct. A is an unrelated word, while B and C imply the opposite of *resolve*.

6. **G**   *Giddy* means "dizzy," so G is correct. F is an unrelated word, and while the pilot might feel numb or distressed (H and J), these words are not synonyms of *giddy*.

7. **B**   To *hoist* is to *lift*, so B is correct. A, C, and D are related terms but not synonyms.

8. **F**   To *beckon* means "to signal without words." Therefore, option F is correct. Options G, H, and J are incorrect because they involve words.

Collection 9: Skills Review
Vocabulary Skills

Synonyms

Test Practice

DIRECTIONS: Choose the *best* synonym for the underlined word in each sentence.

1. In "American History," Elena's mother is vigilant in making sure that Elena's behavior is appropriate for a young lady.
   - A   harsh
   - B   forgiving
   - C   irresponsible
   - D   watchful

2. Elena loves to read, and she is enthralled by one novel in particular.
   - F   enraged
   - G   fascinated
   - H   bored
   - J   educated

3. Elena's mother visits a neighbor, seeking solace after the assassination of President Kennedy.
   - A   entertainment
   - B   knowledge
   - C   comfort
   - D   pity

4. In "A Warm, Clear Day in Dallas" the author states that some people were denouncing the president before his assassination.
   - F   condemning
   - G   praising
   - H   warning
   - J   mocking

5. In his speech, President Johnson explains his resolve to continue the work begun by President Kennedy.
   - A   dream
   - B   doubts
   - C   refusal
   - D   determination

6. In "Beware of the Dog" the pilot, feeling giddy from his injury, fears that he will pass out.
   - F   threatened
   - G   dizzy
   - H   numb
   - J   distressed

7. After he looked out the window, the pilot hoisted himself back onto his bed.
   - A   rolled
   - B   lifted
   - C   slid
   - D   threw

8. The nurse beckoned to the wing commander to indicate that he could enter the pilot's hospital room.
   - F   gestured
   - G   wrote
   - H   shouted
   - J   whispered

SKILLS FOCUS

Vocabulary Skills
Identify synonyms.

Vocabulary Review

Use this activity to assess whether students have retained the collection Vocabulary. Have students fill in the blank in each sentence with the word from the box that best completes the meaning.

discreet	distraught	defiant
controversial	delirious	

1. The injured pilot became _____, imagining things that weren't there. [delirious]

2. The woman became grief-stricken and _____ after the president's death. [distraught]

3. If you are _____, you will be careful in choosing someone to confide in. [discreet]

4. Was President Kennedy _____ in going to Dallas despite the warnings? [defiant]

5. The subject of who killed Kennedy is _____, stirring up great debate. [controversial]

Test Practice

DIRECTIONS: Read the following paragraph from a draft of a student's research paper. Then, answer the questions below it.

(1) The introduction of the first commercially produced radios, in 1920, altered the way people learned about world events. (2) For the first time in history, everyone could receive the same information simultaneously. (3) In the 1920s, sociologists Robert and Helen Lynd said, "With but little equipment one can call the life of the rest of the world from the air. . . ." (4) Live coverage gave news events an immediacy far greater than the newspapers could provide. (5) My great-grandfather told me that each night his family listened to radio news programs. (6) In fact, according to the researcher Phyllis Stark, most people first learned of historic events from the radio.

1. To improve the coherence of this paragraph, which sentence could be deleted?
   A   2   C   5
   B   3   D   6

2. If the student wanted to add a quotation from a primary source, which of these sources would be appropriate?
   F   the autobiography of an early radio pioneer
   G   an analysis of statistics on early radio audiences
   H   a Web site dedicated to a famous radio star
   J   a documentary on popular music in the 1920s

3. To show a different perspective on this topic, the next paragraph could discuss
   A   a short history of the rise of television
   B   an excerpt from a radio transcript of the attack on Pearl Harbor

   C   a discussion of the negative impact radio had on newspapers
   D   a list of other inventions from the 1920s that changed the world

4. To credit the source of the quotation in sentence 3, the student could
   F   insert the title of the source name in the margin
   G   include a parenthetical citation at the end of the quotation
   H   take credit for the information as an original thought
   J   include a parenthetical citation at the end of the paragraph

5. If the student were presenting the report orally, how could she help the audience understand the topic?
   A   play relaxing music in the background to soothe her audience
   B   bring a map of Pearl Harbor, Hawaii
   C   bring an example of a radio recording from the 1920s
   D   read directly from the paper to avoid forgetting important ideas

SKILLS FOCUS

Writing Skills
Write a research paper.

RESOURCES: WRITING

Assessment
- *One-Stop Planner* CD-ROM with ExamView Test Generator
- *Holt Assessment: Writing, Listening, and Speaking*

Internet
- *Holt Online Assessment*
- *Holt Online Essay Scoring*

Answers
1. C
2. F
3. C
4. G
5. C

APPLICATION

Research for Fiction Writing

Point out to students that to make fictional works seem real, writers must do the research necessary to lend a feeling of reality to their characters and details of place, time, and action. Ask students to work with two classmates to conduct research for fiction writing. Have them imagine that they are collaborating on a story about three fifteen-year-olds growing up in a poor neighborhood in a city in the northeastern United States in 1900. Have groups brainstorm, then list, at least five questions they would need to answer to give the story an air of reality. Then, students should identify three or more sources they might consult to answer each question.

EXTENSION

Playing the Ad Game

Have students suppose that a documentary producer decides to make their research papers into television documentaries. As a homework assignment, have students create print ads, which will appear as full pages in several national magazines, for a campaign to advertise their documentaries. Students should select images and words to make the topics of their research papers as appealing as possible to a general audience.

Homework

Collection 10

Epic and Myth

**Informational Reading Focus:
Evaluating an Argument**

About Collection 10

In Collection 10, students will master the
following skills:

- **Literary Skills:** Understand the way
  a work of literature is related to its
  historical period; and analyze
  characteristics of epic poetry and myths.
- **Reading Skills:** Monitor reading
  comprehension; evaluate an author's
  argument; and identify cause and effect.
- **Vocabulary Skills:** Analyze Homeric
  (epic) similes; understand synonyms and
  epithets; understand words from myths;
  and understand idioms.
- **Writing Skills:** Develop, write, and
  revise a cause-and-effect essay.
- **Listening and Speaking Skills:**
  Deliver a persuasive speech.

Informational Text

Each collection of *Elements of Literature*
provides a variety of informational texts
related to the literature selections by
theme or topic.

Minimum Course of Study

Most skills can be taught with a minimum
number of selections and features. In the
chart to the right, lessons highlighted in
green constitute the minimum course of
study that provides coverage of the skills
taught in Collection 10.

Scope and Sequence

Selection ▪ Feature	Literary Skills
An Introduction to the Odyssey *by* David Adams Leeming	• Understand characteristics of epic poetry • Understand the way a work of literature is related to the themes and issues of its historical period
from the **Odyssey, Part One** *by* Homer ↔ *at grade level*	• Analyze characteristics of epic poetry, including heroes and their external conflicts
from the **Odyssey, Part Two** *by* Homer ↔ *at grade level*	• Analyze characteristics of epic poetry, including character traits
Informational Text: • Where I Find My Heroes • Heroes with Solid Feet *by* Oliver Stone; Kirk Douglas ↔ *at grade level*	
The Fenris Wolf Norse myth *retold by* Olivia Coolidge ↔ *at grade level*	• Analyze characteristics of myths, including archetypes • Analyze how a work of literature is related to its historical period
Writing Workshop: *Persuading with Cause and Effect*	
Listening and Speaking Workshop: *Giving a Persuasive Speech*	
Skills Review: *Informational Reading Skills* *Vocabulary Skills* *Writing Skills*	

Resource Manager

(pp. 638C–638D)
Lesson and workshop resources are
referenced in the Resource Manager on
the pages that follow. These resources
can be used to reinforce the skills taught
in Collection 10, remediate students
who are having difficulty, and provide
supporting activities for English-language
learners.

Reading Skills	Vocabulary Skills	Writing ▪ Grammar and Language ▪ Listening and Speaking Skills
• Monitor your comprehension	• Create semantic maps • Analyze Homeric (epic) similes	• Write a paragraph with personification • Analyze a persuasive argument
• Evaluate an author's argument, including intent and tone	• Understand synonyms • Understand epithets • Understand words from Greek and Roman myths • Use words in context • Understand idioms	• Discuss the hero's character traits in a brief essay • Write a continuation of the story • Write a story plan • Write a movie proposal • Discuss how the epic relates to life today in a brief essay
• Identify cause and effect	• Understand words from Norse myths	• Write an explanatory essay • Compare and contrast epics
		• Write a persuasive cause-and-effect essay
		• Deliver a persuasive speech
• Evaluate an author's argument, including intent and tone	• Identify synonyms	• Write a cause-and-effect essay

Resource Manager

Selection ▪ Feature	Planning	Differentiating Instruction ▪ Lesson Plans with ELL Strategies and Practice	Reading ▪ Vocabulary
An Introduction to the Odyssey *by* David Adams Leeming	• PowerNotes: The Epic		
from the **Odyssey, Part One** *by* Homer	• One-Stop Planner with ExamView Test Generator	• The Holt Reader, pp. 284–301 • Holt Adapted Reader • Holt Reading Solutions, pp. 303–308 • Supporting Instruction in Spanish, pp. 43–47 • Audio CD Library, disc 17 • Audio CD Library, Selections and Summaries in Spanish	• The Holt Reader • Holt Adapted Reader • Holt Reading Solutions • Vocabulary Development, p. 46
from the **Odyssey, Part Two** *by* Homer **Informational Text:** • Where I Find My Heroes • Heroes with Solid Feet *by* Oliver Stone; Kirk Douglas	• One-Stop Planner with ExamView Test Generator	• Holt Adapted Reader • Holt Reading Solutions, pp. 309–320 • Supporting Instruction in Spanish, pp. 47–49 • Audio CD Library, disc 17 • Audio CD Library, Selections and Summaries in Spanish	• Holt Adapted Reader • Holt Reading Solutions • Vocabulary Development, pp. 47, 48
The Fenris Wolf *retold by* Olivia Coolidge	• One-Stop Planner with ExamView Test Generator	• Holt Reading Solutions, pp. 321–326 • Supporting Instruction in Spanish, p. 50 • Audio CD Library, disc 17 • Audio CD Library, Selections and Summaries in Spanish	• Holt Reading Solutions
Writing Workshop: *Persuading with Cause and Effect*	• One-Stop Planner with ExamView Test Generator	• Workshop Resources: Writing, Listening, and Speaking, pp. 108–114 • Supporting Instruction in Spanish, p. 73	
Listening and Speaking Workshop: *Giving a Persuasive Speech*	• One-Stop Planner with ExamView Test Generator	• Workshop Resources: Writing, Listening, and Speaking, pp. 115–120 • Supporting Instruction in Spanish	
Skills Review: *Informational Reading Skills* *Vocabulary Skills* *Writing Skills*			

The Holt Reader

The Holt Reader is a consumable paperback book which can be used alone or to accompany *Elements of Literature*. It offers guided support throughout the reading process and encourages students to become active readers by circling, underlining, questioning, and jotting down responses as they read. *The Holt Reader* works well for homework, students who have missed class, additional instructional time, reteaching, and remediation.

Holt Reading Solutions (HRS)

Holt Reading Solutions pulls together reading resources in the *Elements of Literature* program to create a powerful tool for intervention and whole-class instruction. *HRS* includes diagnostic assessment tools, lesson plans for English-language learners and special education students, adaptations of selected reading selections, vocabulary and comprehension worksheets, information on phonics and decoding, and additional instruction and practice in remedial reading skills.

Writing ▪ Grammar and Language ▪ Listening and Speaking	Assessment
• Daily Language Activities	• Holt Assessment: Literature, Reading, and Vocabulary • Holt Online Assessment • One-Stop Planner with ExamView Test Generator
• Daily Language Activities	• Holt Assessment: Literature, Reading, and Vocabulary • Holt Online Assessment • One-Stop Planner with ExamView Test Generator
• Daily Language Activities	• Holt Assessment: Literature, Reading, and Vocabulary • Holt Online Assessment • One-Stop Planner with ExamView Test Generator
• Daily Language Activities • Workshop Resources: Writing, Listening, and Speaking, pp. 108–114	• Holt Assessment: Writing, Listening, and Speaking • Holt Online Assessment • One-Stop Planner with ExamView Test Generator
• Workshop Resources: Writing, Listening, and Speaking, pp. 115–120	• Holt Assessment: Writing, Listening, and Speaking • One-Stop Planner with ExamView Test Generator
	• Holt Assessment: Writing, Listening, and Speaking • One-Stop Planner with ExamView Test Generator

Technology

INTERNET

- go.hrw.com
- Holt Online Assessment
- Holt Online Essay Scoring
- Elements of Literature Online

MEDIA

 • One-Stop Planner with ExamView Test Generator

 • PowerNotes

• Audio CD Library, disc 17

• Audio CD Library, Selections and Summaries in Spanish

 • Visual Connections Videocassette Program, Segment 11

 • Fine Art Transparencies, 16

Transparency   Video

CD-ROM   Audio CD

One–Stop Planner with ExamView Test Generator

The *One-Stop Planner* CD-ROM contains electronic versions of print-based teaching resources, clips from the video program, and valuable assessment tools. The *One-Stop Planner* resources are presented in easy-to-follow, point-and-click menu formats. To preview resources or print out worksheets and tests, you simply make a selection and click.

 One–Stop Planner CD-ROM

Collection 10

SKILLS FOCUS

Grade-Level Skills

■ **Literary Skills**
Analyze interactions between characters (such as internal and external conflict and motivation) and the way those interactions affect the plot.

■ **Literary Skills**
Understand and explain characteristics of epic poetry.

■ **Reading Skills**
Evaluate the credibility of an author's argument by examining generalizations, the scope of the evidence, and the intentions of the author.

INTRODUCING THE COLLECTION

The selections in this collection take students on an epic journey—Odysseus's long and perilous journey from Troy back to his home and family in Ithaca after the Trojan War. David Adams Leeming's richly detailed introductory essay sets the stage, and several twentieth-century poems offer imaginative interpretations of and insights into themes and characters in Homer's classic. The informational selections focus on heroism in today's world and give students an opportunity to evaluate persuasive arguments. At the end of the collection, students will have the opportunity to write a persuasive essay and to give a persuasive speech.

COLLECTION 10 RESOURCES: READING

Planning
■ *One-Stop Planner* CD-ROM with ExamView Test Generator

Differentiating Instruction
■ *Holt Reading Solutions*
■ *The Holt Reader*
■ *Holt Adapted Reader*

■ *Family Involvement Activities in English and Spanish*
■ *Supporting Instruction in Spanish*

Vocabulary
■ *Vocabulary Development*

Grammar and Language
■ *Language Handbook Worksheets*
■ *Daily Language Activities*

Collection 10

Epic and Myth

INFORMATIONAL READING FOCUS

EVALUATING AN ARGUMENT

If we are fortunate, if the gods and muses are smiling, about every generation someone comes along to inspire the imagination for the journey each of us takes.

—Bill Moyers

INTERNET

Collection Resources

Keyword: LE5 9-10

Ulysses and the Sirens. Detail from a mosaic (4th century A.D.).

639

Grade-Level Skills

■ **Literary Skills**
Understand and explain characteristics of epic poetry.

■ **Literary Skills**
Analyze the way a work of literature relates to the themes and issues of its historical period. (Historical approach)

An Introduction to the Odyssey

This introductory essay provides students with background for their reading of the *Odyssey*. It includes information on the epic and its place in Greek culture, on the Trojan War, and on the role of the storyteller and the audience in the ancient world.

DIRECT TEACHING

A **Content-Area Connections**
History: The Discovery of Troy
Only in the last hundred years have archaeologists established that Troy was an actual city that was destroyed about 1200 B.C.—a date very close to 1184 B.C., the traditional date for the climax of the Trojan War. A map of the area is shown on p. 650.

B **Content-Area Connections**
Literature: Epic
Characteristics of an epic usually include

• a physically impressive hero of national or historical importance

• a vast setting encompassing much of the known physical world and sometimes the Land of the Dead

• a quest or journey undertaken in search of something of value

• the involvement of supernatural forces

• glorification of the hero at the end

• a basis in a specific culture or society

An Introduction to the
ODYSSEY

by David Adams Leeming

These battles might have taken place as early as 1200 B.C.—a time that was at least as long ago for Homer's audience as the Pilgrims' landing at Plymouth Rock is for us.

SKILLS FOCUS

Pages 640–646 cover
Literary Skills
Understand characteristics of epic poetry. Understand the way a work of literature is related to the themes and issues of its historical period.

Almost three thousand years ago, people who lived in the starkly beautiful part of the world we now call Greece were telling stories about a great war. The person credited with later gathering all these stories together and telling them as one unified epic is a man named Homer (*Homēros,* in Greek). Homer's great war stories are called, in English, the *Iliad* and the *Odyssey*. (In Greek, the *Iliad* is *Ilias* and the *Odyssey* is *Odysseia*.)

A Homer's stories probably can be traced to historical struggles for control of the waterway leading from the Aegean Sea to the Sea of Marmara and the Black Sea. These battles might have taken place as early as 1200 B.C.—a time that was at least as long ago for Homer's audience as the Pilgrims' landing at Plymouth Rock is for us.

Homer's first epic was the *Iliad,* which tells of a ten-year war fought on the plains outside the walls of a great city called Troy (also known as Ilion). The ruins of Troy can still be seen in western Turkey. In Homer's story the Trojan War was fought between the people of Troy and an alliance of Greek kings (at that time each island and area of the Greek mainland had its own king). The *Iliad* tells us that the cause of the war was sexual jealousy: The world's most beautiful woman, Helen, abandoned her husband, Menelaus, a Greek king, and ran off with Paris, a prince of Troy. (See "The Beautiful Helen," page 107.)

The *Odyssey,* Homer's second epic, is the story of the attempt of one Greek soldier, Odysseus, to get home after the Trojan War. All epic poems in the Western world owe something to the basic patterns established by these two stories.

EPICS AND VALUES

B **Epics** are long narrative poems that tell of the adventures of heroes who in some way embody the values of their civilizations. The Greeks for centuries used the *Iliad* and the *Odyssey* in schools to teach Greek virtues. So it is not surprising that later cultures that admired the Homeric epics created their own epics, imitating Homer's style but conveying their own value systems.

DIFFERENTIATING INSTRUCTION

Learners Having Difficulty
Have students read the introduction to the *Odyssey*. Then, divide the students into pairs, and ask them to come up with at least five questions for their partners. Tell them to write each question on a separate note card and then exchange cards before reading the introduction a second time. Suggest that students use the questions and answers for review. Encourage students to consider the

art as well as the text as they write their questions.

English-Language Learners
Help build students' confidence by modeling the correct pronunciation of names and having students repeat the pronunciations several times.

Advanced Learners
Ask each student to become an expert on one of the characters or places mentioned in

Still, for all the epics written since Homer's time and for all the ones composed before it, when people in the Western world think of the word *epic*, they think primarily of the *Iliad* and the *Odyssey*. Rome's *Aeneid*, France's *Song of Roland*, Italy's *The Divine Comedy*, the ancient Mesopotamian tale of Gilgamesh, India's *Mahabharata* and *Ramayana*, Mali's *Sundiata*—all are great stories in the epic tradition. But Homer's epics are at the heart of the epic tradition.

The *Iliad* is the primary model for the epic of war. The *Odyssey* is the model for the epic of the long journey. The theme of the journey has been basic in Western literature—it is found in fairy tales, in such novels as *The Incredible Journey, Moby-Dick,* and *The Hobbit,* and in such movies as *The Wizard of Oz* and *Star Wars.* Thus, the *Odyssey* has been the more widely read of Homer's two great stories.

THE WAR-STORY BACKGROUND: VIOLENCE AND BRUTALITY

The background for Odysseus's story is found in the *Iliad,* which is set in the tenth and final year of the Trojan War. According to the *Iliad,* the Greeks attacked Troy to avenge the insult suffered by Menelaus, king of Sparta, when his wife, Helen, ran off with Paris, a young prince of Troy. The Greek kings banded together under the leadership of Agamemnon,

C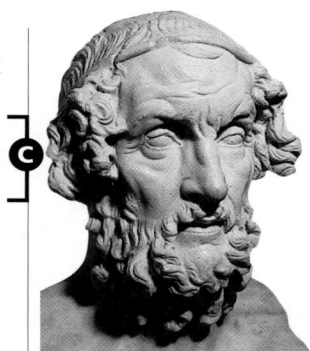

The blind poet Homer. Detail from statue found near Naples (probably 2nd century A.D.).
British Museum, London.

Home to Ithaca (1977) from the *Odysseus Collages* by Romare Bearden. Collage on board (14″ × 22³⁄₄″).
Estate of Romare Bearden. © Romare Howard Bearden Foundation. Licensed by VAGA, New York.

An Introduction to the Odyssey **641**

DIRECT TEACHING

C Content-Area Connections

Literature: Gilgamesh
The tale of Gilgamesh, which dates back as far as the third millennium B.C., is the earliest extant example of epic poetry. The epic describes the journeys of a Mesopotamian king in search of the secret of immortality.

VIEWING THE ART

Romare Bearden (1914–1988) was born in North Carolina and educated at New York University and the Sorbonne, in Paris. He became the premier collagist in the United States in the 1960s. In his collages, which he made from pieces of photographs and painted paper, Bearden often depicted aspects of American life and culture. In this collage, part of a series he did on the Trojan War, Bearden sets the Homeric epic in an African context. Other works by Bearden appear on pp. 119, 123, and 147.

Activity. Ask students what events in the Trojan War they can identify in the picture. [Note the wooden horse, the burning towers of Ilium, the ruined city, and the boats setting off.] Point out that Bearden has depicted the soldiers as African warriors.

CONTENT-AREA CONNECTIONS

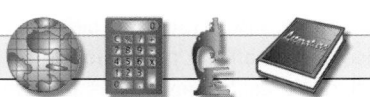

the introduction. Have students research the character or place they choose in encyclopedias and other reference books, such as Edith Hamilton's *Mythology.* Also tell them to take notes on their subject as they read the epic. Students who want to know more about a particular place or character can then ask the expert for information.

Language: Homeric Terms
Individual activity. Have students make a two-column chart to record names and terms in Homer's epic (such as *odyssey* and *Trojan horse*) that they come across in everyday life. Instruct them to list these expressions in the left column and to write down where they found each term (a

novel, a news article or report, an advertisement, and so forth), along with a definition of the term in the right column.

Ⓐ Content-Area Connections

Greek Mythology: Achilles

Achilles, the hero of the *Iliad,* is the source of the term *Achilles' heel,* which means "vulnerable or weak spot." (The worst pitcher in a baseball team's starting rotation might be called the team's Achilles' heel.) When Achilles was a baby, his mother, Thetis, dipped him in the river Styx to make him invulnerable, but neglected the spot on the baby's heel where she was holding him. Paris killed Achilles by shooting a divinely directed poisoned arrow into his heel.

Ⓑ Content-Area Connections

Literature: Agamemnon

In Homer's tale it is actually Aegisthus, the wife's lover, who kills Agamemnon. Another Greek writer, Aeschylus, wrote a play in which Agamemnon's unfaithful wife, Clytemnestra, is the murderer. The play, called *Agamemnon,* opens the *Oresteia* trilogy.

Ⓒ Content-Area Connections

Literature: Authorship

Earlier, the English writer Samuel Butler presented a similar theory in *The Authoress of the Odyssey* (1897). Although the question of female authorship can never be resolved, even today experts disagree on whether the same poet wrote the *Iliad* and the *Odyssey.* The arguments on either side are based primarily on stylistic similarities and differences between the two epics. In ancient times, however, the authorship of both epics was universally credited to a single poet named Homer.

---

the brother of Menelaus. In a thousand ships, they sailed across the Aegean Sea and laid siege to the walled city of Troy.

The audience of the *Odyssey* would have known this war story. Listeners would have known that the Greeks were eventually victorious—that they gained entrance to Troy, reduced the city to smoldering ruins, and butchered all the inhabitants, except for those they took as slaves back to Greece. They would have known all about the greatest of the Greek warriors, Achilles, who died young in the final year of the war. The audience would probably have heard other epic poems (now lost) that told of the homecomings of the various Greek heroes who survived the war. They would especially have known about the homecoming of Agamemnon, the leader of the Greek forces, who was murdered by his unfaithful wife when he returned from Troy.

Finally, Homer's listeners might well have been particularly fascinated by another homecoming story—this one about a somewhat unusual hero, known as much for his brain as for his brawn. In fact, many legends had already grown up around this hero, whose name was Odysseus. He was the subject of Homer's new epic, the *Odyssey.*

ODYSSEUS: A HERO IN TROUBLE

In Homer's day, heroes were thought of as a special class of aristocrats. They were placed somewhere between the gods and ordinary human beings. Heroes experienced pain and death, but they were always sure of themselves, always "on top of the world."

Odysseus is different. He is a hero in trouble. We can relate to Odysseus because like him we also face a world of difficult choices. Like Odysseus we have to cope with unfair authority figures. Like him we have to work very hard to get what we want.

The *Odyssey* is a story marked by melancholy and a feeling of postwar disillusionment. Odysseus was a great soldier in the war, but his war record is not of interest to the monsters that populate the world of his wanderings. Even the people of his home island, Ithaca, seem to lack respect for him. It is as if society were saying to the returning hero, "You were a great soldier once—or so they say—but times have changed. This is a difficult world, and we have more important things to think about than your record."

In the years before the great war, Odysseus had married the beautiful and ever-faithful Penelope, one of several very strong women in the man's world of the Greek epic. (One critic, Robert Graves, was so impressed by the unusual importance of women and home and hearth in the *Odyssey* that he believed Homer must have been a woman.)

Penelope and Odysseus had one son, Telemachus (tə·lem′ə·kəs). He was still a toddler when Odysseus was called by Agamemnon and

The *Odyssey* is a story marked by melancholy and a feeling of postwar disillusionment.

One critic, Robert Graves, was so impressed by the unusual importance of women and home and hearth in the *Odyssey* that he believed Homer must have been a woman.

DIFFERENTIATING INSTRUCTION

Learners Having Difficulty

Have students work in small groups listing words in the introduction that give them trouble. Have groups share their lists with the class. Then, divide the problem words into categories, such as names, literary terms, or social-studies terms. Have each student group create an illustrated dictionary page for the words from one of these categories and make copies of the page to share with classmates.

Menelaus to join them in the war against Troy. But Odysseus was a homebody. He preferred not to go to war, especially a war fought for an unfaithful woman. Even though he was obligated under a treaty to go, Odysseus tried draft-dodging. It is said that when Agamemnon and Menelaus came to fetch him, he pretended to be insane and acted as if he did not recognize his visitors. Instead of entertaining them, he dressed as a peasant and began plowing a field and sowing it with salt. But the "draft board" was smarter than Odysseus. They threw his baby, Telemachus, in front of his oncoming plow. Odysseus revealed his sanity by quickly turning the plow aside to avoid running over his son.

THE WOODEN-HORSE TRICK

Once in Troy, Odysseus performed extremely well as a soldier and commander. It was he, for example, who thought of the famous wooden-horse trick that would lead to the downfall of Troy. For ten years the Greeks had been fighting the Trojans, but they were fighting outside Troy's massive walls. They had been unable to break through the walls and enter the city. Odysseus's plan was to build an enormous wooden horse and hide a few Greek soldiers inside its hollow belly. After the horse was built, the Greeks pushed it up to the gates of Troy and withdrew their armies, so that their camp appeared to be abandoned. Thinking that the Greeks had given up the fight and that the horse was a peace offering, the Trojans brought the horse into their city. That night the Greeks hidden inside the hollow belly came out, opened the gates of Troy to the whole Greek army, and began the battle that was to win the war.

THE ANCIENT WORLD AND OURS

The world of Odysseus was harsh, a world familiar with violence. In a certain sense, Odysseus and his men act like pirates on their journey home. They think nothing of entering a town and carrying off all its worldly goods. The "worldly goods" in an ancient city might have been only pots and pans and cattle and sheep. The "palaces" the Greeks raided might have been little more than elaborate mud and stone farmhouses. Yet, in the struggles of Odysseus, Penelope, and Telemachus in their "primitive" society that had little in common

Trojan Horse (16th century) by Niccolò dell' Abbate. Tempera on panel.
Galleria Estense, Modena, Italy.

D

DIRECT TEACHING

D Content-Area Connections

Literature: Views of Odysseus Although Homer intended his audience to admire Odysseus, the hero was later attacked for his craftiness and guile by several important ancient writers. In his play *Ajax*, Sophocles (496–406 B.C.) portrays Odysseus as deceitful, and in the *Aeneid*, Virgil portrays Odysseus as the embodiment of Greek treachery.

VIEWING THE ART

The Italian painter **Niccolò dell' Abbate** (c. 1512–1571) is best known for his large-scale decorative projects, many of which are lively depictions of scenes from mythology and history.

Activity. Ask students what details in the painting identify it as a scene from the Trojan War. [Note the horse, the strongly built city, and the soldiers, some of whom are grilling the Greek spy Sinon, while others are dragging the horse into the city.] Be sure to compare the style of this painting with that of Bearden's collage on p. 641.

CONTENT-AREA CONNECTIONS

History: Greek Ages
The events of the *Iliad* and the *Odyssey* are said to have taken place around 1200 B.C., near the end of the Greek Bronze Age (called *the age of heroes* by the Greeks). Ancient Greek culture is considered to have reached its peak in the two centuries between 500 and about 300 B.C., a period known as the classical age.

Small-group activity. Have one group of students create a time line of the stages in the development of ancient Greece, marking major historical, cultural, and literary events. Other groups can research topics such as these:

• **Warfare.** How was war conducted in the twelfth century B.C.? What kinds of armor did soldiers wear? What sorts of

weapons did they have? What strategies and tactics did they use?

• **Diet.** What did soldiers eat during the Trojan War? What did Odysseus and his men eat on their journey? What foods were available in the area of the Aegean Sea at this time? In what ways was food prepared?

Ⓐ Content-Area Connections

Literature: Gods and Mortals
The phrase *double determination* refers to the joint action of a god and a mortal to produce a certain result. In Homer, events are often caused by the actions of a mortal abetted by the intervention of a god. Thus, Athena may help a hero strike a target with an arrow, but the hero had to be an excellent archer in the first place.

Ⓑ Content-Area Connections

History: Homer's Origins
In Homer's time, Chios was part of a region called Ionia. One reason people believe Homer came from Chios is that many of the grammatical structures and vocabulary words in the epics are Ionian in origin. Another is that a society of storytellers calling themselves the "sons of Homer" sprang up in Chios in the sixth century B.C.

Odysseus and his family are people searching for the right relationships with one another and with the people around them.

Odysseus is in search of a way out of what we might today call his midlife crisis.

Some scholars think Homer was just a legend. But scholars have also argued about whether a man called Shakespeare ever existed. It is almost as if they were saying that Homer and Shakespeare are too good to be true.

with the high Athenian culture that would develop several centuries later, there is something that has a great deal to do with us.

A SEARCH FOR THEIR PLACES IN LIFE

Odysseus and his family are people searching for the right relationships with one another and with the people around them. They want to find their proper places in life. It is this **theme** that sets the tone for the *Odyssey* and determines the unusual way in which the poem is structured.

Instead of beginning at the beginning with Odysseus's departure from Troy, the story begins with his son, Telemachus. Telemachus is now twenty years old. He is threatened by rude, powerful men swarming about his own home, pressuring his mother to marry one of them. These men are bent on robbing Telemachus of his inheritance. Telemachus is a young man who needs his father, the one person who can put things right at home.

Meanwhile, we hear that his father is stranded on an island, longing to find a way to get back to his wife, child, and home. It is ten years since Odysseus sailed from Troy, twenty years since he left Ithaca to fight in Troy. While Telemachus is in search of his father, Odysseus is in search of a way out of what we might today call his midlife crisis. He is searching for inner peace, for a way to reestablish a natural balance in his life. The quests of father and son provide a framework for the poem and bring us into it as well—because we all are in search of our real identities, our true selves.

RELATIONSHIPS WITH THE GODS

This brings us to mythic and religious questions in the *Odyssey*. **Myths** are traditional stories, rooted in a particular culture, that usually explain a belief, a ritual, or a mysterious natural phenomenon. Myths are essentially religious because they are concerned with the relationship between human beings and the unknown or spiritual realm.

Ⓐ As you will see, Homer is always concerned with the relationship between humans and gods. Homer is religious: For him, the gods control all things. Athena, the goddess of wisdom, is always at the side of Odysseus. This is appropriate, because Odysseus is known for his mental abilities. Thus, in Homer's stories a god can be an **alter ego,** a reflection of a hero's best or worst qualities. The god who works against Odysseus is Poseidon, the god of the sea, who is known for arrogance and a certain brutishness. Odysseus himself can be violent and cruel, just as Poseidon is.

WHO WAS HOMER?

Ⓑ No one knows for sure who Homer was. The later Greeks believed he was a blind minstrel, or singer, who came from the island of Chios.

CONTENT-AREA CONNECTIONS

Culture: Storytelling
The wandering storyteller who keeps history and legend alive through oral recitation is a tradition in many cultures. The *jali*, or griot, of West Africa is a combination poet, professional musician, cultural historian, and keeper of genealogical information. A griot's repertoire might include records of family lineages, to be sung at weddings and other occasions, as well as legends and myths. The griot's singing is often accompanied by the *balafon,* a type of xylophone, or the *kora,* a stringed instrument with similarities to a banjo or a harp. Traditionally griots formed a hereditary professional caste, and an apprentice griot might receive his musical education from another family member. The *Sundiata* epic, which tells the story of the thirteenth-century Malian king Sundiata Keita, has been told for centuries by griots.

Small-group activity. Encourage students to learn more about the *Sundiata* epic or to find recordings of griot music and griot-influenced music from West Africa to share with the class.

Some scholars feel there must have been two Homers; some think he was just a legend. But scholars have also argued about whether a man called Shakespeare ever existed. It is almost as if they were saying that Homer and Shakespeare are too good to be true. On the whole, it seems sensible to take the word of the Greeks themselves. We can at least accept the existence of Homer as a model for a class of wandering bards or minstrels later called rhapsodes (rap′sōdz′).

These **rhapsodes,** or "singers of tales," were the historians and entertainers as well as the mythmakers of their time. There was probably no written history in Homer's day. There were certainly no movies and no television, and the Greeks had nothing like a Bible or a book of religious stories. So it was that the minstrels traveled about from community to community singing of recent events or of the doings of heroes, gods, and goddesses. It is as if the author of the Book of Kings in the Bible, the writer of a history of World War II, and a famous pop singer were combined in one person. The people in Homer's day saw no conflict among religion, history, and good fun.

HOW WERE THE EPICS TOLD?

Scholars have found that oral epic poets are still composing today in Eastern Europe and other parts of the world. These scholars suggest that stories like the *Iliad* and the *Odyssey* were originally told aloud by people who could not read and write. The stories followed a basic story line, but most of the actual words were improvised—made up on the spot—in a way that fit a particular rhythm or meter. The singers of these stories had to be very talented, and they had to work very hard. They also needed an audience that could listen closely.

We can see from this why there is so much repetition in the Homeric epics. The oral storyteller, in fact, had a store of formulas ready in his memory. He knew formulas for describing the arrival and greeting of guests, the eating of meals, and the taking of baths. He knew formulas for describing the sea (it is "wine-dark") and for describing Athena (she is "gray-eyed Athena").

Formulas such as these had another advantage: they gave the singer and his audience some breathing time. The audience could relax for a moment and enjoy a familiar and memorable passage, while the singer could think ahead to the next part of his story.

When we think about the audience that listened to these stories, we can also understand the value of the extended comparisons that we today call **Homeric** or **epic similes.** These similes compare heroic or epic events to simple and easily understandable everyday events—

Singer with lyre. Bronze statue from the Minoan period.
Archaeological Museum, Heraklion, Crete.

The oral storyteller, in fact, had a store of formulas ready in his memory. He knew formulas for describing the arrival and greeting of guests, the eating of meals, and the taking of baths.

An Introduction to the Odyssey   645

C Content-Area Connections
Culture: Rhapsodes
Although written versions of the epics became available in the sixth century B.C., rhapsodes were active for many centuries after Homer. Contests between reciters of epic poetry became common at Greek festivals, and the philosopher Plato (c. 428–c. 348 B.C.) describes a rhapsode named Ion who made his living by reciting long passages of epics to music.

D Content-Area Connections
Literature: Verse Meter
Both the *Odyssey* and the *Iliad* are written in dactylic hexameter, a type of verse in which each line consists of six metrical feet. The first four feet may be either dactyls (made up of one stressed syllable and two unstressed syllables) or spondees, (made up of two stressed syllables). The fifth foot is usually a dactyl, and the sixth is a spondee.

E Content-Area Connections
Language: Formulaic Repetition
One formula used for Odysseus, when his name appears in the nominative case (as the subject of a sentence), is *polymetis Odysseus* ("many-counseled Odysseus"). If the poet has a longer stretch of verse to fill, he might use the formula *polytlas dios Odysseus* ("much-enduring, god-like Odysseus"). Formulas may run as long as an entire passage.

VIEWING THE ART

The Minoan culture flourished in Greece from 2000 B.C. to 1500 B.C. This culture was named for the legendary King Minos, who was said to keep a beast, half man, half bull, in a labyrinth. This sculpture shows a singer playing a lyre, a small stringed instrument similar to a harp.

A Content-Area Connections

Literature: Homeric Similes

Homeric similes are often based on images from nature (lions, storms, deer, rivers) and everyday activities (fishing, herding). Another notable feature of Homeric similes is their length. Some, such as the comparison of the blinding of Polyphemus to the actions of a blacksmith (ll. 368–408), continue for many lines.

B Content-Area Connections

Humanities: Audiences

❓ What contemporary situations does the scene described here make you think of? [Possible response: the expectant audience at a Broadway show, an important concert, or the opening night of an eagerly awaited film.]

---

events the audience would recognize instantly. For example, at one point in the *Iliad,* Athena prevents an arrow from striking Menelaus. The singer compares the goddess's actions to an action that would have been familiar to every listener:

A

> She brushed it away from his skin as lightly as when a mother
> Brushes a fly away from her child who is lying in sweet sleep.

Epic poets such as Homer would come to a city and would go through a part of their repertory while there. A story as long as the *Odyssey* (11,300 lines) could not be told at one sitting. We have to assume that if the singer had only a few days in a town, he would summarize some of his story and sing the rest in detail, in as many sittings as he had time for.

This is exactly what will happen in the selections from the *Odyssey* that are presented here. We'll assume that Homer wants to get his story told to us, but that his time is limited. We'll also assume that the audience, before retiring at the end of each performance, wants to talk about the stories they've just heard. You are now part of that audience.

A LIVE PERFORMANCE

What was it like to hear a live performance of the *Odyssey*? We can guess what it was like because there are many instances in the epic itself in which traveling singers appear and sing their tales. In the court of the Phaeacian king, Alcinous (al·sin'ō·əs), in Book 8, for instance, there is a particularly wonderful singer who must make us wonder if the blind Homer is talking about himself. Let's picture the setting of a performance before we start the story.

Imagine a large hall full of people who are freshly bathed, rubbed with fine oils, and draped in clean tunics. Imagine the smell of meat being cooked over charcoal, the sound of voices. Imagine wine being freely poured, the flickering reflections of the great cooking fires, and the torches that light the room. A certain anticipation hangs in the air. It is said that the blind minstrel Homer is in the city and that he has new stories about that long war in Troy. Will he appear and entertain tonight?

B

I̶magine a large hall full of people who are freshly bathed, rubbed with fine oils, and draped in clean tunics. Imagine the smell of meat being cooked over charcoal, the sound of voices. Imagine wine being freely poured, the flickering reflections of the great cooking fires, and the torches that light the room.

Ruins of an amphitheater at the temple of Hephaestus in Athens.

Check Test: Short Answer

Guide the class in answering these comprehension questions. Have students support their responses with passages from the text.

1. **Who is traditionally accepted as the author of the *Odyssey*?** [Homer]

2. **How is the *Odyssey* related to the *Iliad*?** [The *Odyssey* tells the story of a hero returning from the war described in the *Iliad*.]

3. **When and where does the *Iliad* take place?** [approximately 1200 B.C. in Troy]

4. **Where is Odysseus's home?** [in Ithaca]

5. **What is a Homeric simile?** [an extended comparison between heroic or epic events and images from nature or everyday occurrences]

PEOPLE AND PLACES IN THE ODYSSEY

The following cast of characters lists some of those who take part in the sections of the *Odyssey* included in this book. Note that the Greeks in the *Odyssey* are often referred to as **Achaeans** (ə·kē′ənz) or **Argives** (är′gīvz′). *Achaeans* is the most general term, which also includes the people of Ithaca, the island off the west coast of Greece where Odysseus ruled. The word *Achaeans* is taken from the name of an ancient part of northeastern Greece called Achaea. The name *Argives* usually refers to the Greeks who went to fight at Troy.

Penelope by John Roddam Spencer Stanhope.

THE WANDERINGS: CHARACTERS AND PLACES

Aeaea (ē·ē′ə): home of Circe, the enchantress and goddess.

Alcinous (al·sin′ō·əs): king of Phaeacia. Odysseus tells the story of his adventures to Alcinous's court.

Calypso (kə·lip′sō): beautiful nymph goddess who keeps Odysseus on her island for seven years.

Circe hands the magic potion to Odysseus. Detail from a lecythus, a vase used for oils and ointments (5th century B.C.).

Charybdis (kə·rib′dis): female monster who sucks in water three times a day to form a deadly whirlpool. (Scholars believe the character is based on a real whirlpool in the Strait of Messina.)

Cicones (si·kō′nēz′): people living on the southwestern coast of Thrace who battled Odysseus and his men on their journey.

Circe (sʉr′sē): enchantress and goddess who turns Odysseus's men into swine.

Cyclops: See **Polyphemus,** below.

Erebus (er′ə·bəs): dark area of the underworld where the dead reside.

Eurylochus (yōō·ril′ə·kəs): a member of Odysseus's loyal crew.

Lotus Eaters: people who feed Odysseus's men lotus plants to make them forget Ithaca.

Phaeacia (fē·ā′shə): island kingdom ruled by King Alcinous. The Phaeacians are shipbuilders and traders.

Polyphemus (päl′i·fē′məs): son of the sea god Poseidon and blinded by Odysseus. Polyphemus is a **Cyclops** (sī′kläps′), one of a race of brutish one-eyed giants, the **Cyclopes** (sī·klō′pēz′), who live solitary lives as shepherds, supposedly on the island now known as Sicily.

VIEWING THE ART

Activity. Ask students to compare Penelope's attitude in this nineteenth-century Pre-Raphaelite painting with the attitude of the female figure (who may be Penelope) in the terra-cotta relief from the fifth century B.C. on p. 692. [In both works, the figure holds her head in her hand.] Students can also discuss the changing conventions of art by contrasting the depiction of Circe on the vase from the fifth century B.C. with this realistic depiction of Penelope. [Spencer Stanhope's Penelope resembles a real female human being, whereas the fifth-century image is highly stylized and not immediately recognizable as that of a female.]

DIFFERENTIATING INSTRUCTION

Learners Having Difficulty
Using graphic aids. Suggest that students photocopy the list of characters on these two pages and refer to it as they read the epic. Encourage students to jot down notes on the characters as they read.

English-Language Learners
Tape-record a native English-speaker (perhaps an advanced student) pronouncing the names on the list to help students become familiar with the names. Ask the person making the tape to pause for a few seconds after pronouncing each name to allow listeners to repeat it.

Advanced Learners
Activity. Have students prepare a guide to the pronunciation of the listed names. The guide should include rules for pronouncing certain letter combinations (for example, *ch* at the beginning of a word is pronounced /k/; *eu* is pronounced /yoo/) and additional examples. The guide might also explain how to identify the accented syllable in a name. Ask students to share their guides with English-language learners.

DIRECT TEACHING

A Content-Area Connections
Mythology: Athena
As goddess of war and wisdom, Athena allies herself with the brave and intelligent Odysseus and frequently comes to his aid.

B Content-Area Connections
Language: Greek Root Words
The name Cronus has been connected with the Greek word *chronos,* meaning "time," from which the English words *chronic, crony,* and *chronicle* derive. A number of English words derive from *hēlios,* the Greek word for "sun"; for example, plants whose flowers turn toward the sun are called *heliotropes.* Ask students to find other words that derive from *hēlios.* [Possible responses: *helium, heliocentric, perihelion.*]

C Content-Area Connections
Mythology: Poseidon
At first Poseidon supported the Greeks against the Trojans, who had cheated him of his pay for building their city walls. But Poseidon turned against the Greeks when they defiled Athena's temple; he turned against Odysseus after Odysseus incurred the curse of the Cyclops Polyphemus, Poseidon's son.

VIEWING THE ART

Athena assists warriors defending civilized values. She is said to have emerged from Zeus's head, fully grown and dressed for battle.

Activity. What details in this beautiful sculpture reveal that Athena is associated with warriors? [the helmet and the spear] Note that the goddess is mourning one of the great warriors in ancient Greek literature, Achilles.

Poseidon. Detail from a bronze statue. (5th century B.C.)

Scylla (sil'ə): female monster with six serpent heads, each head having a triple row of fangs. (Scholars believe this character is based on a dangerous rock in the Strait of Messina.)

Sirens: sea nymphs whose beautiful and mysterious music lures sailors to steer their ships toward dangerous rocks.

Teiresias (tī·rē'sē·əs): famous blind prophet from the city of Thebes. Odysseus meets him in the Land of the Dead.

Thrinakia (thri·nā'kē·ə): island where the sun god Helios keeps his cattle.

ITHACA: THE PEOPLE AT HOME
Antinous (an·tin'ō·əs): one of Penelope's main suitors; an arrogant and mean young noble from Ithaca.

Eumaeus (yōō·mē'əs): swineherd, one of Odysseus's loyal servants.

Eurycleia (yōō'ri·klē'yə): Odysseus's old nurse.

Eurymachus (yōō·rim'ə·kəs): suitor of Penelope.

Eurynome (yōō·rin'ə·mē): Penelope's housekeeper.

Penelope (pə·nel'ə·pē): Odysseus's faithful wife.

Philoeteus (fi·lē'shē·əs): cowherd, one of Odysseus's loyal servants.

Telemachus (tə·lem'ə·kəs): Odysseus's son.

THE GODS
Apollo (ə·päl'ō): god of poetry, music, prophecy, medicine, and archery.

Athena (ə·thē'nə): favorite daughter of Zeus; the great goddess of wisdom as well as war and peace. She favored the Greeks during the Trojan War. She is often called Pallas Athena.

Cronus (krō'nəs): Titan (giant god) who ruled the universe until his son Zeus overthrew him.

Helios (hē'lē·äs'): sun god.

Hephaestus (hē·fes'təs): god of metalworking.

Hermes (hʉr'mēz'): messenger god.

Poseidon (pō·sī'dən): god of the sea; brother of Zeus. Poseidon is called Earth Shaker because he is believed to cause earthquakes. He is an enemy of Odysseus.

Zeus (zōōs): the most powerful god. His home is on Olympus.

Athena mourning the death of Achilles at Troy. Detail from a marble stele, or pillar.

648 Collection 10 Epic and Myth • Evaluating an Argument

RESOURCES: READING

Planning
- *One-Stop Planner* CD-ROM with ExamView Test Generator

Differentiating Instruction
- *Holt Reading Solutions*
- *The Holt Reader*
- *Holt Adapted Reader*
- *Supporting Instruction in Spanish*

- *Audio CD Library, Selections and Summaries in Spanish*

Vocabulary
- *Vocabulary Development*

Grammar and Language
- *Daily Language Activities*

Before You Read

from the Odyssey, Part One

Make the Connection

Quickwrite ✏️

What makes a hero? Write down the names of people, real or fictional, whom you consider heroic. Then, list character traits that you think a hero should have. Are these traits universal, or do they reflect only our own culture? Add to your notes as you read the *Odyssey*.

Literary Focus

Heroes at Large

We admire them in books and movies, on TV shows, and in the news, and if we look closely, even in our own lives. They're our heroes—real or fictional.

In fiction, as in real life, heroes often set off on a journey that we're all on: the quest to discover who we are and what we can do. Encountering challenges and dangers, heroic characters face **external conflicts** —struggles with other characters (these are often **subordinate characters** who play a secondary role in the story) or with the forces of nature.

Whether heroes fail or succeed on their journeys, they do it on a grand scale, giving us new perspectives on our own lives. As you read these tales of Odysseus's wanderings, think about how he overcomes his conflicts. What makes him heroic?

Reading Skills

Monitor Your Comprehension

As you read this epic, stop now and then to ask yourself questions and to sum up what you've read. Ask:

- What has happened so far?

- Why did it happen?
- What are the important events in this episode?
- When do the events take place?
- What might happen next?
- Can I visualize what is being described?
- What is my evaluation of the characters' decisions and actions?
- What connections can I make between what I've read and my own life?

The questions at the open-book signs will help you monitor your comprehension. If you can't answer the questions, go back through the text to find the answers.

INTERNET
Vocabulary Practice
•
More About Homer
•
Keyword: LE5 9-10

Vocabulary Development

adversity (ad·vʉr′sə·tē) *n.*: hardship; great misfortune.

formidable (fôr′mə·də·bəl) *adj.*: awe-inspiring by reason of excellence; strikingly impressive.

ravage (rav′ij) *v.*: destroy violently; ruin.

profusion (prō·fyōō′zhən) *n.*: large supply; abundance.

adversary (ad′vər·ser′ē) *n.*: enemy; opponent.

rancor (raŋ′kər) *n.*: bitter hatred; ill will.

abominably (ə·bäm′ə·nə·blē) *adv.*: in an extremely unpleasant or disgusting manner.

ardor (är′dər) *n.*: passion; enthusiasm.

tumult (tōō′mult) *n.*: commotion; uproar; confusion.

restitution (res′tə·tōō′shən) *n.*: compensation; repayment.

Literary Skills
Understand characteristics of epic poetry, including heroes and their external conflicts.

Reading Skills
Monitor your comprehension.

Odyssey, Part One   **649**

SKILLS FOCUS, pp. 649–688

Grade-Level Skills

■ **Literary Skills**

Analyze interactions between characters (such as internal and external conflict and motivation) and the way those interactions affect the plot.

■ **Literary Skills**

Understand and explain characteristics of epic poetry.

■ **Reading Skills**

Monitor your comprehension.

Summary 🔁 *at grade level*

> The *Odyssey* can be divided into four major sections: Books 1–4 (Telemachus's journey in search of his father); Books 5–8 (Odysseus's departure from Calypso's island and arrival in Phaeacia); Books 9–12 (a flashback in which Odysseus tells the Phaeacians of his adventures); and Books 13–24 (Odysseus's return to Ithaca, his battle with the suitors, and his reunion with Penelope, Telemachus, and his father, Laertes).

PRETEACHING

Preview Vocabulary

The Vocabulary words have been divided into two batches: the first ten words (*adversity* through *restitution*) for Part One and the remainder (*candor* through *tremulous*) for Part Two. Have volunteers write the Vocabulary words on the chalkboard. Then, tell students to write each of the Vocabulary words on a separate index card and to draw a picture illustrating the word's meaning on the back of the card (for example, a dog ripping apart sofa cushions might represent *ravage*). Afterward, divide students into pairs and instruct them to take turns showing the picture side of each card to their partners and having them guess which Vocabulary word is depicted.

Assessment

- *Holt Assessment: Literature, Reading, and Vocabulary*
- *One-Stop Planner* CD-ROM with ExamView Test Generator
- *Holt Online Assessment*

Internet

- go.hrw.com (Keyword: LE5 9-10)
- *Elements of Literature Online*

Media

- *Audio CD Library*
- *Fine Art Transparencies*
- *Visual Connections Videocassette Program*

Motivate. Ask students to describe a fantastic voyage they'd like to take. Where would they go? What adventures would they have? What changes would they expect to see upon their return? Show the *Visual Connections* segment "Where in the World Did Odysseus Go?" to help students learn more about Odysseus's journey.

from the

ODYSSEY

Homer

translated by Robert Fitzgerald

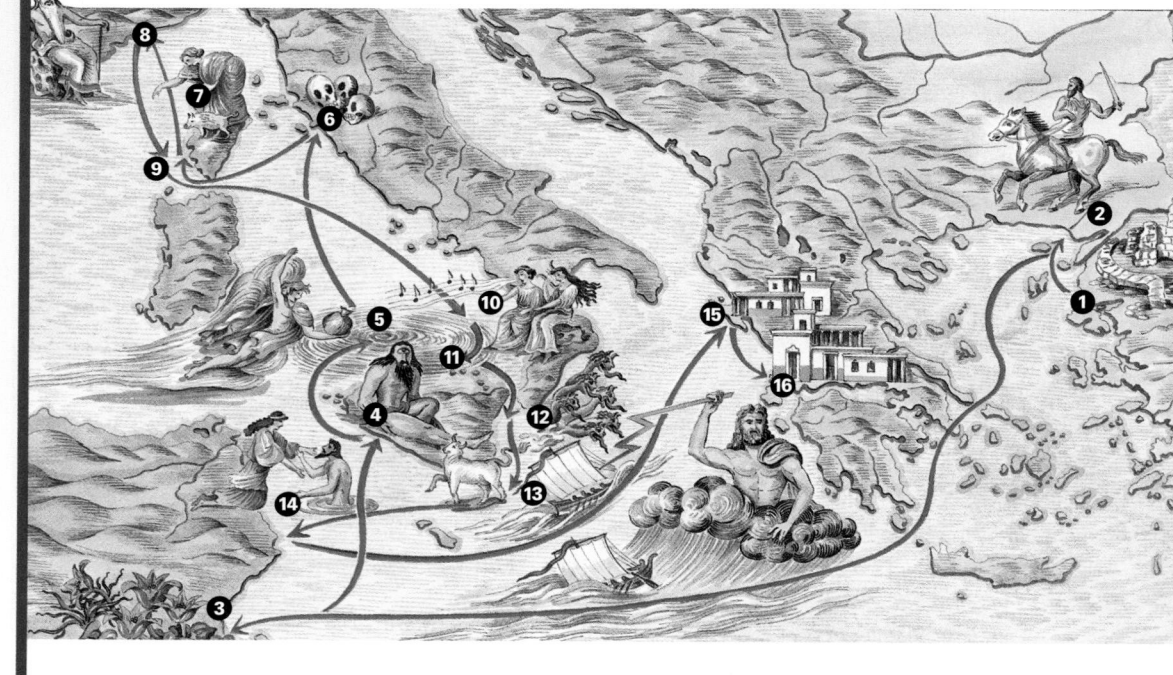

❶ *Troy*	❺ *Island of Aeolia*	❾ *Circe*	⓭ *Thrinakia*
❷ *Cicones*	❻ *Laestrygonians*	❿ *Sirens*	⓮ *Calypso*
❸ *Lotus Eaters*	❼ *Circe*	⓫ *Charybdis*	⓯ *Phaeacia*
❹ *Cyclops*	❽ *Teiresias and the Land of the Dead*	⓬ *Scylla*	⓰ *Ithaca*

650   Collection 10   Epic and Myth • Evaluating an Argument

DIFFERENTIATING INSTRUCTION

Learners Having Difficulty
Invite learners having difficulty to read the excerpt from the *Odyssey* in *The Holt Reader* and to use the sidenotes as aids to understanding the selection. The interactive version provides additional instruction, practice, and assessment of the literary skill taught in the Student Edition. Monitor students' responses to the selection, and correct any misconceptions that arise.

English-Language Learners
Build students' confidence by modeling the pronunciation of names such as Odysseus, Telemachus, and Polyphemus.

Special Education Students
For lessons designed for special education students, see *Holt Reading Solutions*.

Advanced Learners
Activity. Have students keep a list of motifs, or repeated patterns, in the epic that also appear in modern stories and films. Suggest that they look for similarities in terms of story lines, characters, and themes. Ask students to share their lists with the class.

TELL THE STORY

Homer opens with an invocation, or prayer, asking the Muse° to help him sing his tale. Notice how the singer gives his listeners hints about how his story is to end.

Sing in me, Muse, and through me tell the story
of that man skilled in all ways of contending,°
the wanderer, harried for years on end,
after he plundered the stronghold
on the proud height of Troy.

5   He saw the townlands
and learned the minds of many distant men,
and weathered many bitter nights and days
in his deep heart at sea, while he fought only
to save his life, to bring his shipmates home.

10   But not by will nor valor could he save them,
for their own recklessness destroyed them all—
children and fools, they killed and feasted on
the cattle of Lord Helios, the Sun,
and he who moves all day through heaven

15   took from their eyes the dawn of their return.

Of these adventures, Muse, daughter of Zeus,
tell us in our time, lift the great song again.
Begin when all the rest who left behind them
headlong death in battle or at sea

20   had long ago returned, while he alone still hungered
for home and wife. Her ladyship Calypso
clung to him in her sea-hollowed caves—
a nymph, immortal and most beautiful,
who craved him for her own.

                                          And when long years and seasons

25   wheeling brought around that point of time
ordained for him to make his passage homeward,
trials and dangers, even so, attended him
even in Ithaca, near those he loved.
Yet all the gods had pitied Lord Odysseus,

30   all but Poseidon, raging cold and rough
against the brave king till he came ashore
at last on his own land. . . .

                                          (*from* Book 1)

°The Greeks believed that there were nine Muses, daughters of Zeus, the chief god. The Muses inspired people to produce music, poetry, dance, and all the other arts.

2. contending (kən·tend′iŋ) *v.* used as *n.:* fighting; dealing with difficulties.

Oral presentation.
1–32. *Read this prayer to the Muse aloud. (You and a partner could read it as a chorus, or you could alternate with single voices.) What does Homer tell you about the hero and about what is going to happen to him?*

Ⓐ

Homer invokes the Muse, asking her to help him tell the story of Odysseus's adventures. Homer mentions Odysseus's hardships, his valor, and his struggle to return home safely with his shipmates. He reminds us that the shipmates died because of their own recklessness. He asks the Muse to begin the story at the point where the other Greek warriors have returned from battle but Odysseus is still longing to get back to his home and wife. Odysseus is being held captive by Calypso, who wants him to stay with her. Homer foreshadows the trials and dangers that lie ahead for Odysseus despite the sympathy he receives from all the gods except Poseidon.

DIRECT TEACHING

Ⓐ Literary Focus

❓ Epic. The *Odyssey* opens with a convention of epic poetry—the poet's prayer to the Muse. **What does the poet ask of the Muse?** [He asks her to sing through him and tell the story of Odysseus.]

Response to Margin Question

Lines 1–32. Possible response: The hero is a soldier whose men have all died on the long, terrible voyage from Troy. He longs to return home after all his battles, but he is held captive by the nymph Calypso, who wants him for her own. The gods all take pity on the soldier—except for Poseidon. Now the time is decreed for him to make his way home.

Trapped on Calypso's island, Odysseus yearns to escape and make his way home. Our first glimpse of the hero finds him weeping, scanning the horizon of the sea (ll. 71–74). At Athena's behest, Zeus sends Hermes to order the goddess to release Odysseus. Calypso reluctantly agrees to let him go. Odysseus builds a raft and sets sail, but Poseidon raises a storm and wrecks the raft. Odysseus lands on the island of Scheria and falls asleep in a pile of leaves. (Explain to students that in this book the *Odyssey* has been divided into two parts, which do not correspond to the books, or sections, that make up the epic.)

DIRECT TEACHING

A **Reading Skills**

Speculating. Point out that Book 5 contains many images that appeal to the senses. Ask students why there might be an emphasis on sensory images in this section of the epic. Have them re-read the notes on "Calypso, the Sweet Nymph" above. [The abundance of sensory images helps explain why Odysseus was willing at first to remain on the island as Calypso's captive.]

B **Literary Focus**

❓ Homeric simile. What is Hermes' flight compared to here? [the flight of a gull skimming just above white-capped waves, dipping into the water from time to time to catch a fish]

C **Literary Focus**

❓ Sensory images. What do you see, hear, feel, and smell in this famous description of Calypso's home? [a blazing fire; cedar and thyme smoke; singing; a golden shuttle]

PART ONE: THE WANDERINGS

CALYPSO, THE SWEET NYMPH

Books 1–4 of the epic tell about Odysseus's son, Telemachus. Telemachus has been searching the Mediterranean world for his father, who has never returned from the ten-year Trojan War. (Today, Odysseus would be listed as missing in action.)

When we first meet Odysseus, in Book 5 of the epic, he is a prisoner of the beautiful goddess Calypso. The old soldier is in despair: He has spent ten years (seven of them as Calypso's not entirely unwilling captive) trying to get home.

The goddess Athena has supported and helped Odysseus on his long journey. Now she begs her father, Zeus, to help her favorite, and Zeus agrees. He sends the messenger god Hermes to Calypso's island to order Odysseus released. Although Calypso is not described as evil, her seductive charms—even her promises of immortality for Odysseus—threaten to keep the hero away from his wife, Penelope.

No words were lost on Hermes the Wayfinder
who bent to tie his beautiful sandals on,
35 ambrosial,° golden, that carry him over water
or over endless land in a swish of the wind,
and took the wand with which he charms asleep—
or when he wills, awake—the eyes of men.
So wand in hand he paced into the air,
40 shot from Pieria° down, down to sea level,
and veered to skim the swell. A gull patrolling
between the wave crests of the desolate sea
will dip to catch a fish, and douse his wings;
no higher above the whitecaps Hermes flew
45 until the distant island lay ahead,
then rising shoreward from the violet ocean
he stepped up to the cave. Divine Calypso,
the mistress of the isle, was now at home.
Upon her hearthstone a great fire blazing
50 scented the farthest shores with cedar smoke
and smoke of thyme, and singing high and low
in her sweet voice, before her loom aweaving,
she passed her golden shuttle to and fro.
A deep wood grew outside, with summer leaves
55 of alder and black poplar, pungent cypress.
Ornate birds here rested their stretched wings—
horned owls, falcons, cormorants—long-tongued
beachcombing birds, and followers of the sea.
Around the smooth-walled cave a crooking vine
60 held purple clusters under ply° of green;

35. ambrosial (am·brō′zhəl) *adj.*: fit for the gods; divine. Nectar and ambrosia are the drink and food that kept the gods immortal.

40. Pieria (pī·ir′ē·ə): place in central Greece not far from Olympus; a favorite spot of Hermes'.

Man with a headband. Detail from a bronze statue (c. 460–450 B.C.).

Museo Archeologico Nazionale, Reggio Calabria, Italy.

60. ply (plī) *n.*: twisted strands.

652 Collection 10 Epic and Myth • Evaluating an Argument

and four springs, bubbling up near one another
shallow and clear, took channels here and there
through beds of violets and tender parsley.
Even a god who found this place
65   would gaze, and feel his heart beat with delight:
so Hermes did; but when he had gazed his fill
he entered the wide cave. Now face-to-face
the magical Calypso recognized him,
as all immortal gods know one another
70   on sight—though seeming strangers, far from home.
But he saw nothing of the great Odysseus,
who sat apart, as a thousand times before,
and racked his own heart groaning, with eyes wet
scanning the bare horizon of the sea. . . .

Hermes tells Calypso that she must give up Odysseus forever.
Now we are directly introduced to Odysseus. Notice what this
great warrior is doing when we first meet him.

75   The strong god glittering left her as he spoke,
and now her ladyship, having given heed
to Zeus's mandate, went to find Odysseus
in his stone seat to seaward—tear on tear
brimming his eyes. The sweet days of his lifetime
80   were running out in anguish over his exile,
for long ago the nymph had ceased to please.
Though he fought shy of her and her desire,
he lay with her each night, for she compelled him.
But when day came he sat on the rocky shore
85   and broke his own heart groaning, with eyes wet
scanning the bare horizon of the sea.
Now she stood near him in her beauty, saying:

  "O forlorn man, be still.
Here you need grieve no more; you need not feel
90   your life consumed here; I have pondered it,
and I shall help you go. . . ."

Calypso promises Odysseus a raft and provisions to help him
homeward without harm—provided the gods wish it. Now
Odysseus and Calypso say goodbye.

  Swiftly she turned and led him to her cave,
and they went in, the mortal and immortal.
He took the chair left empty now by Hermes,

33–66. *There is a great*
deal of nature **imagery** *in this*
episode. Jot down some of the im-
ages that help you see Hermes'
flight. What images describing
Calypso's island appeal to your
senses of sight, hearing, and smell?
How does the natural beauty of
Calypso's island compare with the
reality of Odysseus's situation?

Hermes. Bronze statue
(5th century B.C.).

National Archaeological Museum, Athens.

88–91. *Zeus ordered*
Calypso to free Odysseus, but the
nymph claims that the idea is her
own. Why do you think she does
this? What is your opinion of her
deception?

Odyssey, Part One   **653**

CONTENT-AREA CONNECTIONS

Mythology: Greek Gods
The pantheon of Greek gods, goddesses, nymphs, and demigods can be likened to a great family. Athena, the goddess of war and wisdom, for example, is the daughter of Zeus; the messenger god, Hermes, is Zeus's son. The sea god, Poseidon, the father of the Cyclops Polyphemus, is also the brother of Zeus and Hades.
Small-group activity. Have groups of students create family trees that show the tangled ties connecting these figures. Ask them to annotate the trees with specific information on the deities, their characteristics and histories, the location in ancient Greece with which they're associated, and the role, if any, they play in the *Iliad* and the *Odyssey*. Students in each group can be assigned the roles of researcher, graphic artist, editor, and presenter.

D **Reading Skills**
Monitoring your comprehension. At this point, you might have students check their understanding. Suggest that they ask themselves questions—for example, "Why has Hermes traveled to Calypso's island?" [At Athena's urging, Zeus has sent Hermes to tell Calypso that she must free Odysseus.]

E **Content-Area Connections**
Mythology: Greek Gods
Have students note the goddess Calypso's love for Odysseus and her very humanlike desire to take credit for the decision to release him. Unlike deities in many other religions, Greek gods and goddesses often behave as capriciously as humans. They even display such unsavory qualities as possessiveness, jealousy, pride, anger, and vindictiveness. Such behavior plays an important part in the *Odyssey*, since it is the actions of the gods that keep Odysseus from returning home to Ithaca.

Responses to Margin Questions

Lines 33–66. The god's flight is described in ll. 39–45. For details appealing to the senses in the description of Calypso's home, see note C on p. 652. Images describing Calypso's island that appear in ll. 55–63 include "pungent cypress," "Ornate birds," "a crooking vine," "purple clusters," "springs bubbling up," "beds of violets," and "tender parsley."

Lines 88–91. Possible response: Maybe Calypso is too proud to tell Odysseus that she was ordered to free him, or perhaps she wants him to think she is kind and generous. Some students will feel that her deceit is understandable; others will feel that it underscores her selfishness.

A Reading Skills

? Speculating. Considering their similarity in appearance and emotions, what do you think distinguishes humans from gods? [Possible responses: Gods are immortal; gods have exceptional powers that humans lack.]

B Literary Focus

? Homeric simile. What is being compared in these lines? [The way Odysseus hides himself in the leaves to sleep is being compared to the way a piece of burning wood is buried in embers to preserve a spark for the next day.]

VIEWING THE ART

Explain to students that there were two main styles of pottery painting in ancient Greece: the black-figured style and the red-figured style. In the red-figured style the pottery was partially covered with a black glaze and the figures were painted on the remaining red clay.

Activity. Ask students to think about the ancient Greeks' use of images from mythology to decorative everyday objects: vases, urns, water jugs, mirrors. How are these objects different from the mass-produced everyday objects of our own time? [Objects made today are usually decorated with images from the natural world or with abstract designs.]

Response to Margin Question

Lines 101–118. Possible response: Calypso offers Odysseus immortality if he will stay with her. His reply tells us that he is devoted to Penelope, yet he manages to avoid offending Calypso by implying that it is a defect in him that makes him prefer his wife to the eternally youthful and beautiful goddess.

---

95 where the divine Calypso placed before him
victuals and drink of men; then she sat down
facing Odysseus, while her serving maids
brought nectar and ambrosia to her side.
Then each one's hands went out on each one's feast
100 until they had had their pleasure; and she said:

"Son of Laertes,° versatile Odysseus,
after these years with me, you still desire
your old home? Even so, I wish you well.
If you could see it all, before you go—
105 all the adversity you face at sea—
you would stay here, and guard this house, and be
immortal—though you wanted her forever,
that bride for whom you pine each day.
Can I be less desirable than she is?
110 **A** Less interesting? Less beautiful? Can mortals
compare with goddesses in grace and form?"

To this the strategist Odysseus answered:

"My lady goddess, there is no cause for anger.
My quiet Penelope—how well I know—
115 would seem a shade before your majesty,
death and old age being unknown to you,
while she must die. Yet, it is true, each day
I long for home, long for the sight of home. . . ."

So Odysseus builds the raft and sets sail. But the sea god Poseidon is by no means ready to allow an easy passage over his watery domain. He raises a storm and destroys the raft. It is only with the help of Athena and a sea nymph that Odysseus arrives, broken and battered, on the island of Scheria (skē'rē•ə). There he hides himself in a pile of leaves and falls into a deep sleep.

120 **B** A man in a distant field, no hearth fires near,
will hide a fresh brand° in his bed of embers
to keep a spark alive for the next day;
so in the leaves Odysseus hid himself,
while over him Athena showered sleep
that his distress should end, and soon, soon.
125 In quiet sleep she sealed his cherished eyes.

(*from* Book 5)

Vocabulary
adversity (ad·vʉr'sə·tē) *n.:* hardship; great misfortune.

---

101. Laertes (lā·ʉr'tēz').

Calypso and Odysseus. Detail from a red-figured vase (5th century B.C.).

101–118. *According to Calypso, what would Odysseus gain by staying with her? What does Odysseus's response tell you about his feelings for his wife? How has Odysseus managed to say no to Calypso and still not offend her?*

120. fresh brand: burning stick.

Check Test: True-False

Guide the class in answering these comprehension questions. Have students support their responses with passages from the text.

1. Odysseus is trying to return to his home in Ithaca after fighting in Troy. [T]

2. Zeus sends Hermes to deliver a message to Calypso. [T]

3. Odysseus, content in Calypso's care, has no desire to return home. [F]

4. Calypso promises Odysseus that he will become immortal if he remains with her. [T]

5. With the aid of the sea god, Poseidon, Odysseus is able to escape from Calypso. [F]

Calypso

Suzanne Vega

My name is Calypso
And I have lived alone
I live on an island
And I waken to the dawn
5 A long time ago
I watched him struggle with the sea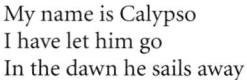
I knew that he was drowning
And I brought him into me
Now today
10 Come morning light
He sails away
After one last night
I let him go.

My name is Calypso
15 My garden overflows
Thick and wild and hidden
Is the sweetness there that grows
My hair it blows long
As I sing into the wind
20 I tell of nights
Where I could taste the salt on his skin

Salt of the waves
And of tears
And though he pulled away
25 I kept him here for years
I let him go.

My name is Calypso
I have let him go
In the dawn he sails away
30 To be gone forever more
And the waves will take him in again
But he'll know their ways now
I will stand upon the shore
With a clean heart
35 And my song in the wind
The sand will sting my feet
And the sky will burn
It's a lonely time ahead
I do not ask him to return
40 I let him go
I let him go.

The Departure of Ulysses from the Isle of Calypso (1848–1849) by Samuel Palmer.

The Whitworth Art Gallery, the University of Manchester.

Odyssey, Part One   **655**

Connecting and Comparing Texts

Although the *Odyssey* was written centuries ago, readers can still easily understand the feelings and conflicts experienced by the characters. Have students compare the emotions and conflicts described in the song "Calypso" with those described in the Calypso episode of the *Odyssey*. Why would a songwriter of today choose to write about Calypso? [Losing someone you love is a timeless theme.] What is the song about? [letting go of a loved one for unselfish reasons] **Does the song help you understand the *Odyssey*? If so, how?** [Possible response: It makes Calypso and her loss vivid and very sad.]

At King Alcinous's feast, Odysseus replies to the king, who has asked him to identify himself. Odysseus begins by stating where he is from. He then describes being detained by Calypso and Circe and speaks of the many years he has spent on his journey home from Troy. He tells of the Cicones and of a storm raised by Zeus that caused Odysseus's ships to drift for nine days.

DIRECT TEACHING

A Reading Skills

❓ Analyzing character. What impression of Odysseus do you get from his description of himself? [Students may notice the word *guile* and suggest that Odysseus considers himself cunning. They may consider him a braggart. Explain that the ancient Greeks would not have thought this self-identification by an epic hero boastful.]

B Literary Focus

❓ Theme. What central idea of the poem does Odysseus express in this passage? [He expresses the desire for home that motivates his actions throughout the entire poem. Note that he excuses himself by claiming that although the goddesses loved him, he "never gave consent" in his heart.]

"I AM LAERTES' SON. . . ."

Odysseus is found by the daughter of Alcinous, king of the Phaeacians. That evening he is a guest at court (Books 6–8).

To the ancient people of Greece and Asia Minor, all guests were godsent. They had to be treated with great courtesy before they could be asked to identify themselves and state their business. That night, at the banquet, the stranger who was washed up on the beach is seated in the guest's place of honor. A minstrel, or singer, is called, and the mystery guest gives him a gift of pork, crisp with fat, and requests a song about Troy. In effect, Odysseus is asking for a song about himself.

Odysseus weeps as the minstrel's song reminds him of all his companions, who will never see their homes again. Now Odysseus is asked by the king to identify himself. It is here that he begins the story of his journey.

Now this was the reply Odysseus made: . . .

"I am Laertes' son, Odysseus.

                      Men hold me

A formidable for guile in peace and war:
this fame has gone abroad to the sky's rim.
130 My home is on the peaked seamark of Ithaca
under Mount Neion's windblown robe of leaves,
in sight of other islands—Doulikhion,
Same, wooded Zakynthos—Ithaca
being most lofty in that coastal sea,
135 and northwest, while the rest lie east and south.
A rocky isle, but good for a boy's training;
I shall not see on earth a place more dear,
though I have been detained long by Calypso,
loveliest among goddesses, who held me
140 in her smooth caves, to be her heart's delight,
as Circe of Aeaea, the enchantress,
desired me, and detained me in her hall.

B But in my heart I never gave consent.
Where shall a man find sweetness to surpass
145 his own home and his parents? In far lands
he shall not, though he find a house of gold.

What of my sailing, then, from Troy?

                    What of those years
of rough adventure, weathered under Zeus?

Vocabulary
formidable (fôr′mə·də·bəl) *adj.*: awe-inspiring by reason of excellence; strikingly impressive.

εἴμ᾽ Ὀδυσεὺς Λαερτιάδης,
ὃς πᾶσι δόλοισιν
ἀνθρώποισι μέλω, καί
μευ κλέος οὐρανὸν
ἵκει. ναιετάω δ᾽
Ἰθάκην εὐδείελον·
ἐν δ᾽ ὄρος αὐτῇ,
Νήριτον εἰνοσίφυλλον
ἀριπρεπές· ἀμφὶ δὲ
νῆσοι πολλαὶ
ναιετάουσι μάλα
σχεδὸν ἀλλήλῃσι,
Δουλίχιόν τε· Σάμη
τε καὶ ὑλήεσσα
Ζάκυνθος.

The passage beginning "I am Laertes' son" in Greek.

CONTENT-AREA CONNECTIONS

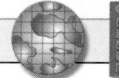  

Geography: Ionian Islands
Paired activity. Have students locate the Ionian islands of Ithaca (also spelled Itháki) and Zákynthos (also spelled Zákinthos) on a map. Then, have them locate the area, in western Turkey near the Dardanelles, thought to be the site of Troy. Have students use the compass rose and map scale to trace Odysseus's journey from Ithaca to Troy: the direction he might have taken and the distance he covered. Some students may wish to work with a partner to make an enlarged map of the area. Suggest that one partner draw the map and the other label the places.

The wind that carried west from Ilion°
150 brought me to Ismaros, on the far shore,
a strongpoint on the coast of the Cicones.
I stormed that place and killed the men who fought.
Plunder we took, and we enslaved the women,
to make division, equal shares to all—
155 but on the spot I told them: 'Back, and quickly!
Out to sea again!' My men were mutinous,
fools, on stores of wine. Sheep after sheep
they butchered by the surf, and shambling cattle,
feasting—while fugitives went inland, running
160 to call to arms the main force of Cicones.
This was an army, trained to fight on horseback
or, where the ground required, on foot. They came
with dawn over that terrain like the leaves
and blades of spring. So doom appeared to us,
165 dark word of Zeus for us, our evil days.
My men stood up and made a fight of it—
backed on the ships, with lances kept in play,
from bright morning through the blaze of noon
holding our beach, although so far outnumbered;
170 but when the sun passed toward unyoking time,
then the Achaeans, one by one, gave way.
Six benches were left empty in every ship
that evening when we pulled away from death.
And this new grief we bore with us to sea:
175 our precious lives we had, but not our friends.
No ship made sail next day until some shipmate
had raised a cry, three times, for each poor ghost
unfleshed by the Cicones on that field.
Now Zeus the lord of cloud roused in the north
180 a storm against the ships, and driving veils
of squall moved down like night on land and sea.
The bows went plunging at the gust; sails
cracked and lashed out strips in the big wind.
We saw death in that fury, dropped the yards,°
185 unshipped the oars, and pulled for the nearest lee:°
then two long days and nights we lay offshore
worn out and sick at heart, tasting our grief,
until a third Dawn came with ringlets shining.
Then we put up our masts, hauled sail, and rested,
190 letting the steersmen and the breeze take over.

149. Ilion (il′ē·än′): another name for Troy.

152–160. What do you think of the way Odysseus and his men behave toward the Cicones? Do armies behave like this in modern times?

184. yards (yärdz) *n.:* rods supporting the sails.
185. lee (lē) *n.:* place of shelter from the wind.

Odyssey, Part One   657

C Content-Area Connections
Geography: Ismaros
The town of Ismaros was near Troy, and the Greeks may have considered the inhabitants no different from the Trojans. Help students follow the events by referring to the map on p. 650.

D Reading Skills
? Expressing an opinion. Here Odysseus, who considers himself a great leader, blames his unruly crew for the Cicones' attack. Does their insubordination reflect unfavorably on Odysseus? [Possible responses: Odysseus may have expected too much of his men in the way of self-control; Odysseus's loss of control over his men points to his shortcomings as a leader.]

E Literary Focus
Foreshadowing. The tragic episode with the Cicones foreshadows an even greater tragedy on Thrinakia, where Odysseus's men, once again disobeying him, slaughter the sun god's cattle and bring about their own destruction.

Responses to Margin Question
Lines 152–160. Possible responses: Because they regard the Cicones as enemies, Odysseus and his men treat them cruelly, in accordance with the custom of the day. Seizing the enemy's riches and enslaving their women (l. 153) were routine actions. Armies today may sometimes behave similarly, but such behavior violates international law.

DIFFERENTIATING INSTRUCTION

Learners Having Difficulty
Activity. Encourage students having trouble by pointing out that Odysseus could be considered a superhero or action hero, much like Superman, Batman, James Bond, or Indiana Jones. Suggest to students that they make a comic book depicting Odysseus's adventures as they read the epic. Students will probably enjoy this activity and may produce some surprising work.

Summary ⬌ *at grade level*

After losing many men in the battle with the Cicones on Ismaros and being driven off course by a fierce storm, Odysseus and his crew arrive at the land of the Lotus Eaters. A few sailors partake of the lotus, which causes them to forget their homeland. Odysseus has to drag them to the ships and tie them to the rowing benches.

DIRECT TEACHING

Responses to Margin Question

Lines 204–215. Possible responses: Odysseus ties down the three men to keep them from returning to the Lotus Eaters; he's afraid they'll lead more crewmen to the Lotus. This tells us that Odysseus cares about the welfare of his men; he knows he'll need all his men in order for him to return home.

I might have made it safely home, that time,
but as I came round Malea the current
took me out to sea, and from the north
a fresh gale drove me on, past Cythera.°
195   Nine days I drifted on the teeming sea
before dangerous high winds."

(from Book 9)

194. Cythera (si·thir′ə).

THE LOTUS EATERS

"Upon the tenth
we came to the coastline of the Lotus Eaters,
who live upon that flower. We landed there
200   to take on water. All ships' companies
mustered° alongside for the midday meal.
Then I sent out two picked men and a runner
to learn what race of men that land sustained.
They fell in, soon enough, with Lotus Eaters,
205   who showed no will to do us harm, only
offering the sweet Lotus to our friends—
but those who ate this honeyed plant, the Lotus,
never cared to report, nor to return:
they longed to stay forever, browsing on
210   that native bloom, forgetful of their homeland.
I drove them, all three wailing, to the ships,
tied them down under their rowing benches,
and called the rest: 'All hands aboard;
come, clear the beach and no one taste
215   the Lotus, or you lose your hope of home.'
Filing in to their places by the rowlocks
my oarsmen dipped their long oars in the surf,
and we moved out again on our seafaring. . . ."

(from Book 9)

201. mustered (mus′tərd) *v.*: gathered; assembled.

204–215. *Why does Odysseus tie down the three men? What does this action tell you about him?*

CONTENT-AREA CONNECTIONS

Word Origins: Greek Names
Many modern English terms derive from Greek names found in the *Odyssey*. For example, the Greek word for a place where people could study the arts inspired by the Muses has survived as the word *museum.* The word *music* comes from a Greek word meaning "belonging to or coming from the Muses." The Muses are the daughters of Zeus and Mnemosyne, the goddess of memory, a figure of special importance to an oral poet who depended on his memory. The silent *M* that appears at the beginning of Mnemosyne's name also appears in a modern word that comes from her name: *mnemonic,* meaning "device that aids the memory." Adding the Greek prefix *a–,* meaning "without," to the stem of the name Mnemosyne produces words having to do with forgetting. Examples include *amnesia* (referring to loss of memory) and *amnesty* (referring to the excusing, or "forgetting," of offenses).
Mixed-ability group activity. Pair advanced students with learners having difficulty. Have advanced learners identify words related to names in the selection, and ask learners having difficulty to look up the words. Then, have the students discuss the connection between the names in the epic and the words derived from them.

A CLOSER LOOK

Troy: It Casts a Spell

The ancient Greeks and Romans had no doubt that the Trojan War really happened. They believed it took place around 1200 B.C. The Greek historian Thucydides (c. 460–c. 400 B.C.) believed that the real causes of the war were economic and political—he rejected Homer's story of Helen's abduction and the vengeance taken on Troy by the Greeks. By the middle of the nineteenth century, however, most historians had dismissed the Trojan War as a legend.

Enter Heinrich Schliemann (1822–1890). Schliemann was a wealthy German merchant who turned archaeologist when he was middle-aged and archaeology was in its infancy. Armed with a well-thumbed copy of Homer's *Iliad,* Schliemann arrived in northwestern Turkey in 1871. A few miles from the Dardanelles, the narrow and windy sea lane that divides Europe from Asia, Schliemann began excavations at a small hill called Hissarlik, perched about a hundred feet above a wide plain.

After five long years, Schliemann made an electrifying discovery. He unearthed gold cups, bracelets, and a spectacular gold headdress. Homer had called Troy "rich in gold," and Schliemann now told the world he had found the treasure of Priam, the last king of Troy. (The gold's eventful history was not over. Schliemann took the treasure to Berlin, where it disappeared at the end of World War II. "Priam's gold" surfaced again in 1993 in Moscow's Pushkin Museum.)

Schliemann went on to excavate Mycenae, the home of King Agamemnon in Greece. There he also found treasure.

Despite his successes, he was plagued by doubts about whether he had really found Troy. The level, or stratum, where the gold was discovered seemed too ancient to date from the traditional time of the Trojan War.

We now know that Schliemann's treasure came from a stratum (called Troy II) that dated back to a thousand years before the Trojan War. Another level (Troy VIIA) showed violent destruction by fire around 1200 B.C. Could this have been Homer's Troy? During the 1930s, another team of archaeologists (this time from the United States) thought so. Despite the inconsistencies that remain, the hill of Hissarlik is now widely accepted as the most likely location of the Trojan War.

In the 1990s, a fifteen-year archaeological project began in Turkey, directed by Professor Manfred Korfmann from the University of Tübingen in Germany. Whatever Korfmann and his international team of seventy scientists and ninety local workers discover, their presence at Troy in the third millennium is powerful proof that this ancient war still casts a spell.

Odyssey, Part One   659

A CLOSER LOOK

The etching in the background of this feature shows the ruins of Troy: the man at the left is Schliemann. This feature may give students ideas for research projects on Troy, Agamemnon (what happened to him when he returned home?), and King Priam and his children Cassandra and Hector. Students may also be interested in researching current excavations in Troy. What discoveries have been made, and what light do they shed on this ancient epic? Ask students what other historical mysteries might be solved one day by archaeologists. They might mention Stonehenge, Easter Island, and the serpentine mounds found in Ohio and Illinois. Another area students may want to investigate is urban archaeology, a relatively new field. You might recommend C. W. Ceram's *Gods, Graves, and Scholars,* a highly readable book on archaeology.

Ⓐ Reading Informational Text

❓ Extending ideas. How does this detail support the author's point that by the nineteenth century, few historians believed in the existence of the ancient city of Troy? [Possible response: Schliemann's "electrifying discovery" was the first tangible evidence that Troy may have existed.]

Ⓑ Reading Informational Text

❓ Extending ideas. How does the detail in the closing paragraph support the author's argument? [Possible response: The description of an ambitious international archaeological project in Turkey is striking evidence that Troy continues to "cast a spell" in the twenty-first century.]

DIFFERENTIATING INSTRUCTION

Learners Having Difficulty
Have students pause after each section to review the material with a partner. Instruct students to work with their partners to write a brief summary of the section. You may want to collect and review these summaries to make sure students comprehend the material.

Advanced Learners
Comparing and contrasting texts.
Suggest that students read Tennyson's poem "The Lotus Eaters" and look for details that relate to the *Odyssey.* Have them compare and contrast the themes of the two poems. Encourage students to present their ideas to the class in the form of a panel discussion.

The Cyclops Polyphemus imprisons Odysseus and his followers in his cave. The men watch, horror-struck and helpless, as the monster consumes two of their number each morning and night. Odysseus conceives of a plan of escape. With his companions, he fashions a sharp wooden stake, which he heats in the fire and thrusts into the Cyclops's eye while the monster is sleeping, blinding him. Odysseus and his men make their escape from the cave by clinging to the underbellies of the Cyclops's rams. As they sail away, Odysseus cannot resist taunting the monster, who curses his former captive and implores his father, Poseidon, the sea god, to keep the hero wandering on the seas for many years.

DIRECT TEACHING

A Reading Skills

❷ Drawing conclusions. Why do you think Odysseus and his men make an offering to the gods? [Possible responses: to thank the gods for allowing them to survive the voyage; to appease the gods so that they will be allowed to return home.]

VIEWING THE ART

Odilon Redon (1840–1916), a French painter and graphic artist, wrote that his originality consisted of "bringing to life, in a human way, improbable beings and making them live according to the laws of probability." Redon painted ethereal, dreamlike scenes inspired by mythology, the Bible, and his own imagination.

Activity. Ask students what elements in the painting suggest that Redon's Cyclops is very different from the ferocious creature described in the *Odyssey*. [Possible responses: the pastel colors and blurred outlines; the peaceful landscape; Cyclops's mild expression.]

THE CYCLOPS

In his next adventure, Odysseus describes his encounter with the Cyclops named Polyphemus, Poseidon's one-eyed monster son. Polyphemus may represent the brute forces that any hero must overcome before he can reach home. Now Odysseus must rely on the special intelligence associated with his name. Odysseus is the cleverest of the Greek heroes because he is guided by the goddess of wisdom, Athena.

It is Odysseus's famed curiosity that leads him to the Cyclops's cave and that makes him insist on waiting for the barbaric giant.

Odysseus is still speaking to the court of King Alcinous.

A "We lit a fire, burnt an offering,
220   and took some cheese to eat; then sat in silence
around the embers, waiting. When he came
he had a load of dry boughs on his shoulder
to stoke his fire at suppertime. He dumped it
with a great crash into that hollow cave,
225   and we all scattered fast to the far wall.
Then over the broad cavern floor he ushered
the ewes he meant to milk. He left his rams

The Cyclops (detail) (late 19th or early 20th century) by Odilon Redon.

Rijksmuseum Kröller-Müller, Otterlo, the Netherlands.

660 [Collection 10] Epic and Myth • Evaluating an Argument

DIFFERENTIATING INSTRUCTION

English-Language Learners
Students who are learning English will find the *Odyssey's* structure and vocabulary challenging. You may want to pair these students with native English speakers to read aloud a section of the epic. Have students take turns reading aloud with the more confident reader coaching the English-language learner.

and he-goats in the yard outside, and swung
high overhead a slab of solid rock
230   to close the cave. Two dozen four-wheeled wagons,
with heaving wagon teams, could not have stirred
the tonnage of that rock from where he wedged it
over the doorsill. Next he took his seat
and milked his bleating ewes. A practiced job
235   he made of it, giving each ewe her suckling;
thickened his milk, then, into curds and whey,
sieved out the curds to drip in withy baskets,°
and poured the whey to stand in bowls
cooling until he drank it for his supper.
240   When all these chores were done, he poked the fire,
heaping on brushwood. In the glare he saw us.

'Strangers,' he said, 'who are you? And where from?
What brings you here by seaways—a fair traffic?
Or are you wandering rogues, who cast your lives
245   like dice, and ravage other folk by sea?'

We felt a pressure on our hearts, in dread
of that deep rumble and that mighty man.
But all the same I spoke up in reply:

'We are from Troy, Achaeans, blown off course
250   by shifting gales on the Great South Sea;
homeward bound, but taking routes and ways
uncommon; so the will of Zeus would have it.
We served under Agamemnon,° son of Atreus°—
the whole world knows what city
255   he laid waste, what armies he destroyed.
It was our luck to come here; here we stand,
beholden for your help, or any gifts
you give—as custom is to honor strangers.
We would entreat you, great Sir, have a care
260   for the gods' courtesy; Zeus will avenge
the unoffending guest.'

He answered this

from his brute chest, unmoved:

'You are a ninny,
or else you come from the other end of nowhere,
telling me, mind the gods! We Cyclopes

---

237. **withy baskets:** baskets made from willow twigs.

253. **Agamemnon** (ag′ə·mem′nän′). **Atreus** (ā′trē·əs).

Vocabulary
ravage (rav′ij) v.: destroy violently; ruin.

B Reading Skills

❓ **Analyzing.** How does Homer make it clear that Odysseus faces a formidable opponent in the Cyclops? [Possible responses: The poet shows the brute strength of the Cyclops by having him lift a huge, extremely heavy slab of rock; the poet describes the Cyclops's strength as greater than that of twenty-four wagons pulled by teams of horses.]

C Reading Skills

❓ **Interpreting.** What does the phrase "fair traffic" mean? What does the Cyclops mean by these questions? ["Fair traffic" means legitimate business, such as that of traders or sailors. The Cyclops wants to know if the strangers' business in his cave is legitimate or if they have come to harm him in some way.]

D Reading Skills

Monitoring your comprehension. Suggest that students stop at this point to ask themselves questions. They might ask, for example, "What did I learn in an earlier episode that explains why Odysseus gives the Cyclops this warning?" [Odysseus is treated as an honored guest by King Alcinous and the Phaeacians, in line with the ancient Greek belief that guests were protected by the gods and had to be treated with great courtesy.]

READING SKILLS REVIEW

Predicting. Tell students that, when they read they are acting as detectives. They follow the trail of clues in a text and combine this evidence with their own knowledge to predict what will happen. For example, when reading "The Lotus Eaters," they may have predicted that Odysseus would escape from the Lotus Eaters' land, using evidence of Odysseus's character and their own knowledge of how people behave.

Activity. Ask students to make four-column charts with the headings "Clues in the Text," "Own Knowledge," "Prediction," and "Actual Outcome" and to fill in the charts as they read. Help students get started by having them read ll. 311–322 and predict the reason Odysseus is making the pointed stake. Then, read ll. 357–361 and predict the reason Odysseus names himself Nohbdy. Tell students to list the clues in the text and facts they know that helped them make their predictions and to read on to learn the outcome.

VIEWING THE ART

Pellegrino Tibaldi (1527–1596) was an Italian painter who was greatly influenced by Michelangelo. Starting in approximately 1550, he painted frescoes of the stories of Odysseus in the style of Michelangelo's paintings on the Sistine Chapel ceiling. He later served as architect for the Milan Cathedral and court painter for Philip II of Spain.

Activity. How does Tibaldi's depiction of the Cyclops differ from that by Redon on p. 660? [Possible responses: Tibaldi depicts the Cyclops as angry, monstrous, and ferocious, whereas Redon depicts him as gentle and shy; Tibaldi uses dark colors to highlight the Cyclops's massive muscles and brute strength, whereas Redon emphasizes the creature's fantastical nature; Tibaldi's Cyclops has one eye and two eye sockets, whereas Redon's has just an eye.]

Palazzo Poggi, Bologna, Italy.

Ulysses and His Companions on the Island of the Cyclops (16th century) by Pellegrino Tibaldi.

662 Collection 10 Epic and Myth • Evaluating an Argument

CONTENT-AREA CONNECTIONS

Architecture: The Parthenon
The Parthenon was built in Athens during the fifth century B.C. as a tribute to Athena, the city's chief deity. The art historian Thomas Craven said of the temple, "Behold the Parthenon, the only perfect building erected by man."

Individual activity. Ask students to find photographs of the Parthenon and to do research on its style of architecture and the way it has been used during its long history. Suggest that students consider researching one of the following questions:

• What did the original Parthenon look like?
• What happened to the building in the sixth century A.D.?
• What happened to the building in the seventeenth century?
• What are the Elgin marbles? Where are they today?

265 care not a whistle for your thundering Zeus
     or all the gods in bliss; we have more force by far.
     I would not let you go for fear of Zeus—
     you or your friends—unless I had a whim to.
     Tell me, where was it, now, you left your ship—
270 around the point, or down the shore, I wonder?'

     He thought he'd find out, but I saw through this,
     and answered with a ready lie:

                                        'My ship?

     Poseidon Lord, who sets the earth atremble,
     broke it up on the rocks at your land's end.
275 A wind from seaward served him, drove us there.
     We are survivors, these good men and I.'

     Neither reply nor pity came from him,
     but in one stride he clutched at my companions
     and caught two in his hands like squirming puppies
280 to beat their brains out, spattering the floor.
     Then he dismembered them and made his meal,
     gaping and crunching like a mountain lion—
     everything: innards, flesh, and marrow bones.
     We cried aloud, lifting our hands to Zeus,
285 powerless, looking on at this, appalled;
     but Cyclops went on filling up his belly
     with manflesh and great gulps of whey,
     then lay down like a mast among his sheep.
     My heart beat high now at the chance of action,
290 and drawing the sharp sword from my hip I went
     along his flank to stab him where the midriff
     holds the liver. I had touched the spot
     when sudden fear stayed me: if I killed him
     we perished there as well, for we could never
295 move his ponderous doorway slab aside.
     So we were left to groan and wait for morning.

     When the young Dawn with fingertips of rose
     lit up the world, the Cyclops built a fire
     and milked his handsome ewes, all in due order,
300 putting the sucklings to the mothers. Then,
     his chores being all dispatched, he caught
     another brace° of men to make his breakfast,
     and whisked away his great door slab
     to let his sheep go through—but he, behind,
305 reset the stone as one would cap a quiver.°

The Cyclops Polyphemus. Detail from a marble statue (2nd century B.C.).

Museum of Fine Arts, Boston.

A

B

289–295. *Why doesn't Odysseus kill the Cyclops at this moment? What factors must Odysseus consider in devising a successful plan of escape?*

302. **brace** (brās) *n.:* pair.

305. **quiver** (kwiv′ər) *n.:* case for arrows.

Odyssey, Part One   663

DIRECT TEACHING

A **Literary Focus**
❓ **Character.** What is happening at this point? [Odysseus knows the Cyclops is asking where the ship is because he wants to destroy it, so he prepares to reply with a lie.] **What does Odysseus's remark suggest about his character?** [Possible responses: The fact that Odysseus is not deceived by the Cyclops's casual manner shows that he is quick-witted and perceptive; Odysseus is a practical man and will lie when necessary in order to save his men.]

B **Reading Skills**
Monitoring your comprehension. Ask students which details help them visualize this gruesome scene. [Possible responses: "squirming puppies"; "spattering the floor"; "gaping and crunching like a mountain lion."] Suggest that students pause here to ask themselves questions about this horrifying picture. For example, they might ask, "Why does Homer include such gruesome details?" [Possible response: He includes these details to enable the reader to fully grasp the horror of what is happening.]

Response to Margin Question

Lines 289–295. Although Polyphemus is asleep and vulnerable, Odysseus cannot kill him because the escape route is blocked. Odysseus must devise a way to defeat Polyphemus while the escape route is open and before the Cyclops eats all of his men.

CONTENT-AREA CONNECTIONS

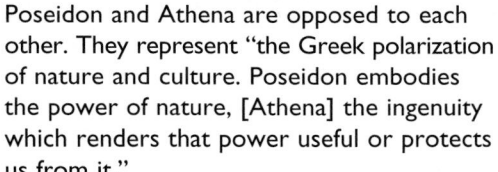

Literature: Character Analysis
According to the critic Erwin F. Cook, the *Odyssey* portrays a series of contrasts between *metis*, "cunning intelligence," and *bie* (or *bia*), "violent might." Odysseus demonstrates *metis* throughout his adventures, as does his patron, Athena. Poseidon and other figures who oppose Odysseus represent *bie*. Cook argues that in the *Odyssey* and other works,

Poseidon and Athena are opposed to each other. They represent "the Greek polarization of nature and culture. Poseidon embodies the power of nature, [Athena] the ingenuity which renders that power useful or protects us from it."
Whole-class activity. Invite students to discuss Cook's ideas and to decide whether they agree with them. Have students cite

examples from the episodes they've read so far to support their opinions. Then, ask students to keep Cook's ideas in mind as they read the remaining episodes and to look for details that confirm or refute his contentions.

A **Reading Skills**

❓ **Predicting.** What do you think Odysseus plans to do with the pointed staff? [Possible responses: He plans to stab the Cyclops with it; he plans to poke out his eye.]

B **Reading Skills**

❓ **Evaluating.** As the captain, Odysseus could have simply chosen the men he wanted for the job rather than drawing lots. Is it wise of him to let the men "toss" for this job, or is he foolishly risking the future of the whole group by not appointing the men best suited to help him? [Possible responses: Letting the men toss for the job is wise, because it ensures that the men will not feel resentful about the outcome; no, it is foolish to risk undertaking something so dangerous without selecting the men best suited for the job.]

C **Literary Focus**

❓ **Foreshadowing.** Odysseus says that the rams may have entered the cave at "a god's bidding." What does this mean, and what does it suggest about the role the rams will play? [Possible response: It means that the gods may be directing the rams' actions. The rams may play a part in helping Odysseus and his men escape.]

There was a din of whistling as the Cyclops
rounded his flock to higher ground, then stillness.
And now I pondered how to hurt him worst,
if but Athena granted what I prayed for.
310   Here are the means I thought would serve my turn:

      a club, or staff, lay there along the fold—
      an olive tree, felled green and left to season
      for Cyclops' hand. And it was like a mast
      a lugger° of twenty oars, broad in the beam—
315   a deep-seagoing craft—might carry:
      so long, so big around, it seemed. Now I
      chopped out a six-foot section of this pole
      and set it down before my men, who scraped it;
      and when they had it smooth, I hewed again
320   to make a stake with pointed end. I held this
      in the fire's heart and turned it, toughening it,
      then hid it, well back in the cavern, under
      one of the dung piles in profusion there.
      Now came the time to toss for it: who ventured
325   along with me? Whose hand could bear to thrust
      and grind that spike in Cyclops' eye, when mild
      sleep had mastered him? As luck would have it,
      the men I would have chosen won the toss—
      four strong men, and I made five as captain.

330   At evening came the shepherd with his flock,
      his woolly flock. The rams as well, this time,
      entered the cave: by some sheepherding whim—
      or a god's bidding—none were left outside.
      He hefted his great boulder into place
335   and sat him down to milk the bleating ewes
      in proper order, put the lambs to suck,
      and swiftly ran through all his evening chores.
      Then he caught two more men and feasted on them.
      My moment was at hand, and I went forward
340   holding an ivy bowl of my dark drink,
      looking up, saying:

                                    'Cyclops, try some wine.
      Here's liquor to wash down your scraps of men.
      Taste it, and see the kind of drink we carried

314. lugger (lug′ər) *n.:* type of sailboat.

Odysseus handing the drink to Polyphemus. Relief on a Grecian marble sarcophagus (1st century A.D.).
Museo Archeologico Nazionale, Naples, Italy.

Vocabulary
profusion (prō·fyōō′zhən) *n.:* large supply; abundance.

Making generalizations. Remind students that making a generalization is similar to drawing a conclusion. The reader uses details in the text and prior knowledge to make a judgment. What is different about making generalizations is that the reader analyzes different facts, events, or situations. Analyzing a range of information enables the reader to make a broad statement that applies to a number of situations. For example, examining the way Odysseus reacts to the Cicones, Polyphemus, and the Sirens may help the reader make a generalization about how Odysseus responds to dangerous situations. **Activity.** Ask students to think about the behavior of Athena, Zeus, and Poseidon; recall what they have read about the gods in other Greek myths; and make a generalization about the character traits of the Greek gods. As students continue reading the *Odyssey,* ask them to make other generalizations from what they have read and their prior knowledge. Then, have students discuss the process they used to make their generalizations.

under our planks. I meant it for an offering
345 if you would help us home. But you are mad,
unbearable, a bloody monster! After this,
will any other traveler come to see you?'

He seized and drained the bowl, and it went down
so fiery and smooth he called for more:

350 'Give me another, thank you kindly. Tell me,
how are you called? I'll make a gift will please you.
Even Cyclopes know the wine grapes grow
out of grassland and loam in heaven's rain,
but here's a bit of nectar and ambrosia!'

355 Three bowls I brought him, and he poured them down.
I saw the fuddle and flush come over him,
then I sang out in cordial tones:

                                        'Cyclops,
you ask my honorable name? Remember
the gift you promised me, and I shall tell you.
360 My name is Nohbdy: mother, father, and friends,
everyone calls me Nohbdy.'

                              And he said:

'Nohbdy's my meat, then, after I eat his friends.
Others come first. There's a noble gift, now.'

Even as he spoke, he reeled and tumbled backward,
365 his great head lolling to one side; and sleep
took him like any creature. Drunk, hiccuping,
he dribbled streams of liquor and bits of men.

Now, by the gods, I drove my big hand spike
deep in the embers, charring it again,
370 and cheered my men along with battle talk
to keep their courage up: no quitting now.
The pike of olive, green though it had been,
reddened and glowed as if about to catch.
I drew it from the coals and my four fellows
375 gave me a hand, lugging it near the Cyclops
as more than natural force nerved them; straight
forward they sprinted, lifted it, and rammed it
deep in his crater eye, and I leaned on it
turning it as a shipwright turns a drill
380 in planking, having men below to swing
the two-handled strap that spins it in the groove.
So with our brand we bored that great eye socket

Odysseus and three companions
blinding Polyphemus. Detail from a
Cyrenean cup (6th century B.C.).
Bibliothèque Nationale, Paris.

A **Literary Focus**

❓ Homeric simile. What is the blinding of the Cyclops compared to? [the act of plunging a white-hot ax head into a cold tub of water]

B **Literary Focus**

Irony. Ask students to explain the irony of these lines. [When Polyphemus tells the other Cyclopes that Nohbdy has ruined him, they think he is saying that no one has ruined him.]

C **Reading Skills**

❓ Expressing an opinion. Do you think it is wise for Odysseus to laugh, considering that he and his men are obviously not yet out of danger? [Possible responses: No, his laughter is premature, since he and his men are still trapped; no, his laughter may anger Polyphemus even more; yes, such a clever trick deserves celebration, and the Cyclops, who is now blind, cannot easily find Odysseus.]

D **Literary Focus**

❓ Character. How would you characterize Odysseus here? [Possible responses: a strategist; a trickster; a planner.]

---

while blood ran out around the red-hot bar.
Eyelid and lash were seared; the pierced ball
hissed broiling, and the roots popped.

385   In a smithy°
one sees a white-hot axhead or an adze°
plunged and wrung in a cold tub, screeching steam—
the way they make soft iron hale and hard—
just so that eyeball hissed around the spike.

390 The Cyclops bellowed and the rock roared round him,
and we fell back in fear. Clawing his face
he tugged the bloody spike out of his eye,
threw it away, and his wild hands went groping;
then he set up a howl for Cyclopes

395 who lived in caves on windy peaks nearby.
Some heard him; and they came by divers° ways
to clump around outside and call:

                      'What ails you,
Polyphemus? Why do you cry so sore
in the starry night? You will not let us sleep.

400 Sure no man's driving off your flock? No man
has tricked you, ruined you?'

                    Out of the cave
the mammoth Polyphemus roared in answer:
'Nohbdy, Nohbdy's tricked me. Nohbdy's ruined me!'

To this rough shout they made a sage° reply:

405 'Ah well, if nobody has played you foul
there in your lonely bed, we are no use in pain
given by great Zeus. Let it be your father,
Poseidon Lord, to whom you pray.'

                   So saying
they trailed away. And I was filled with laughter

410 to see how like a charm the name deceived them.
Now Cyclops, wheezing as the pain came on him,
fumbled to wrench away the great doorstone
and squatted in the breach with arms thrown wide
for any silly beast or man who bolted—

415 hoping somehow I might be such a fool.
But I kept thinking how to win the game:
death sat there huge; how could we slip away?
I drew on all my wits, and ran through tactics,
reasoning as a man will for dear life,

385. smithy (smith′ē) *n.:* black-smith's shop, where iron tools are made.
386. adze (adz) *n.:* axlike tool with a long, curved blade.

396. divers (dī′vərz) *adj.:* diverse; various.

404. sage (sāj) *adj.:* wise.

Odysseus and his men blinding the Cyclops. Hydria, or water jar (530–510 B.C.).
Collection Villa Guilia, Rome.

SKILLS REVIEW

Analyzing similes. Remind students that a simile is a figure of speech comparing two very different things, with a comparison word, such as *like* or *as.* You might write a couple of common examples on the chalkboard: *skin as smooth as silk, a smile like sunshine.*

Activity. Ask students to complete the following sentences by creating similes.
1. The monstrous creature was _____.
2. Odysseus's days away from home seemed _____.
3. Calypso was _____.

Activity. Have pairs of students evaluate each other's similes. Tell students to ask themselves, "In what way are these two unlike things alike? Does the simile work to make the idea come alive? Is the simile fresh and original?"

Odysseus escaping the cave of Polyphemus under the belly of the ram. Detail from a krater, a vessel for holding wine (c. 510 B.C.).
Badisches Landesmuseum, Karlsruhe, Germany.

420   until a trick came—and it pleased me well.
   The Cyclops' rams were handsome, fat, with heavy
   fleeces, a dark violet.

   Three abreast

   I tied them silently together, twining
   cords of willow from the ogre's bed;
425   then slung a man under each middle one
   to ride there safely, shielded left and right.
   So three sheep could convey each man. I took
   the woolliest ram, the choicest of the flock,
   and hung myself under his kinky belly,
430   pulled up tight, with fingers twisted deep
   in sheepskin ringlets for an iron grip.
   So, breathing hard, we waited until morning.

   When Dawn spread out her fingertips of rose
   the rams began to stir, moving for pasture,
435   and peals of bleating echoed round the pens
   where dams with udders full called for a milking.
   Blinded, and sick with pain from his head wound,
   the master stroked each ram, then let it pass,
   but my men riding on the pectoral fleece°
440   the giant's blind hands blundering never found.
   Last of them all my ram, the leader, came,

439. pectoral fleece: wool on an animal's chest.

Odyssey, Part One   **667**

DIRECT TEACHING

E **Learners Having Difficulty**
? **Sequence.** What steps does Odysseus take to prepare for their escape? [He lashes sets of three rams together, ties a man under the belly of each middle sheep, and then takes the choicest ram and hangs on tightly to its belly.]

F **Literary Focus**
Figures of speech. Ask students what figure of speech this is and to explain how they know. [It is an example of personification; the comparison bestows a human attribute, fingertips, on a nonhuman thing, dawn.] Ask students to tell how the personification helps them visualize the scene. [The image of rosy fingertips spread out against the sky calls up a picture of the red streaks that appear in the sky at dawn.]

SKILLS REVIEW

Chronological order. Remind students that chronological order is the order in which events occur. Point out that the *Odyssey* is not structured in strict chronological order. Book 5, for example, tells of Odysseus's interactions with Calypso, events that occur later than the adventures that Odysseus relates to King Alcinous's court in Books 9–12.

These adventures are themselves told as part of a flashback. Clues in the narrative make it clear that Odysseus is talking about events that have occurred in the distant past. The rhetorical question that Odysseus uses to preface his story is one such clue: "What of those years / of rough adventure, weathered under Zeus?"

Activity. Have students work in groups to create a chronology of the main events in Part One. Tell them to present their chronology in paragraph form or on a time line.

A Literary Focus

? Irony. What is ironic about this statement? [By using a double negative, the Cyclops unintentionally predicts what is about to happen: Everybody will get out alive.]

B Reading Skills

Monitoring your comprehension. This is a good point at which to stop students and make sure they understand what is going on. Have them ask themselves questions, such as these: "Why are the 'fellows' faces' full of joy and then grief? Why does Odysseus hush his men?" [The "fellows" are the shipmates, who rejoice when they see that Odysseus and his party are safe but become mournful when they realize that some men are missing. Odysseus hushes them because he does not want the Cyclops to hear them and figure out where they are and what they are doing.]

VIEWING THE ART

In the "black-figured" style of pottery painting, black silhouettes were painted directly onto the red clay. A *lecythus* is a small cylindrical bottle used for storing oils and perfumes.

Activity. Ask students to write down what Odysseus is thinking as he clings to the ram's wool.

Response to Margin Question

Lines 421–442. After blinding the Cyclops, Odysseus and his men cling to the bellies of Polyphemus's rams who, on their way out to pasture, carry the men safely from the cave. Possible response: The men look very frightened, especially when the Cyclops strokes each ram. Some of the men bite large mouthfuls of wool to keep silent and not scream or moan with terror.

---

weighted by wool and me with my meditations.
The Cyclops patted him, and then he said:

'Sweet cousin ram, why lag behind the rest
445 in the night cave? You never linger so,
but graze before them all, and go afar
to crop sweet grass, and take your stately way
leading along the streams, until at evening
you run to be the first one in the fold.
450 Why, now, so far behind? Can you be grieving
over your Master's eye? That carrion rogue°
and his accurst companions burnt it out
when he had conquered all my wits with wine.
A Nohbdy will not get out alive, I swear.
455 Oh, had you brain and voice to tell
where he may be now, dodging all my fury!
Bashed by this hand and bashed on this rock wall
his brains would strew the floor, and I should have
rest from the outrage Nohbdy worked upon me.'

460 He sent us into the open, then. Close by,
I dropped and rolled clear of the ram's belly,
going this way and that to untie the men.
With many glances back, we rounded up
his fat, stiff-legged sheep to take aboard,
465 and drove them down to where the good ship lay.
B We saw, as we came near, our fellows' faces
shining; then we saw them turn to grief
tallying those who had not fled from death.
I hushed them, jerking head and eyebrows up,
470 and in a low voice told them: 'Load this herd;
move fast, and put the ship's head toward the breakers.'
They all pitched in at loading, then embarked
and struck their oars into the sea. Far out,
as far offshore as shouted words would carry,
475 I sent a few back to the adversary:

'O Cyclops! Would you feast on my companions?
Puny, am I, in a Caveman's hands?
How do you like the beating that we gave you,
you damned cannibal? Eater of guests
480 under your roof! Zeus and the gods have paid you!'

Vocabulary
adversary (ad'vər·ser'ē) *n.*: enemy; opponent.

421–442. *Explain Odysseus's trick. What do you* **visualize** *happening in this scene?*

451. **carrion rogue:** rotten scoundrel. *Carrion* is decaying flesh.

Odysseus escaping under the ram. Detail from a black-figured convex lecythus (c. 590 B.C.), by the Ambush Vase Painter.
Staatliche Antikensammlung, Munich, Germany.

The blind thing in his doubled fury broke
a hilltop in his hands and heaved it after us.
Ahead of our black prow it struck and sank
whelmed in a spuming geyser, a giant wave
485 that washed the ship stern foremost back to shore.
I got the longest boathook out and stood
fending us off, with furious nods to all
to put their backs into a racing stroke—
row, row or perish. So the long oars bent
490 kicking the foam sternward, making head
until we drew away, and twice as far.
Now when I cupped my hands I heard the crew
in low voices protesting:

                                    'Godsake, Captain!
Why bait the beast again? Let him alone!'

495 'That tidal wave he made on the first throw
all but beached us.'

                                    'All but stove us in!'

'Give him our bearing with your trumpeting,
he'll get the range and lob° a boulder.'

                                                    'Aye
He'll smash our timbers and our heads together!'

500 I would not heed them in my glorying spirit,
but let my anger flare and yelled:

                                    'Cyclops,
if ever mortal man inquire
how you were put to shame and blinded, tell him
Odysseus, raider of cities, took your eye:
505 Laertes' son, whose home's on Ithaca!'

At this he gave a mighty sob and rumbled:

'Now comes the weird° upon me, spoken of old.
A wizard, grand and wondrous, lived here—Telemus,°
a son of Eurymus;° great length of days
510 he had in wizardry among the Cyclopes,
and these things he foretold for time to come:
my great eye lost, and at Odysseus' hands.
Always I had in mind some giant, armed
in giant force, would come against me here.
515 But this, but you—small, pitiful, and twiggy—

498. lob (läb) *v.:* toss.

507. weird (wird) *n.:* fate.
508. Telemus (tel′ə·məs).
509. Eurymus (yoo′rē·məs).

Odyssey, Part One   669

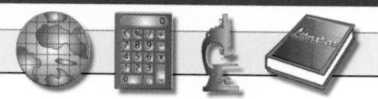

C Literary Focus

❓ Irony. What is ironic about the order that Odysseus gives? [Possible response: It is because of his boasting that the men must "row or perish."]

D Reading Skills

❓ Predicting. How might Odysseus's revelation of his name create problems for him and his men? [Now that he knows who blinded him, Polyphemus can seek revenge through his father, Poseidon.]

E Literary Focus

Character. Point out to students that Polyphemus's underestimation of his adversary, which is a character flaw, has led to his downfall. He was so sure of his own strength that when his blinding was foretold, he believed that only another giant would be able to do it. As a result, he was not as cautious as he should have been with Odysseus and his men.

CONTENT-AREA CONNECTIONS

Culture: Conceptions of the World
To a modern reader the universe as conceived by the ancient Greeks might appear mysterious but rather small. The Greeks imagined the earth as a disk only a third larger in area than the United States. Delphi was regarded as the center of the world. A turbulent river bounded Homer's earth; beyond was the dark region known as Erebus, through which the dead passed on their way to Hades, or the underworld.

Small-group activity. Suggest that students research various cultures' conceptions of the world throughout history. Students may want to draw maps illustrating the conceptions of the world.

A Reading Skills

? **Evaluating.** Do you believe Polyphemus's promise? Is he trustworthy? Explain. [No, he has offered false promises before, so there is no reason to believe him now.]

B Reading Skills

? **Making connections.** Go back and re-read the invocation that Homer uses to open the *Odyssey*. What parts of Polyphemus's curse come true? [Although Odysseus does see his home again, he must wait ten years, and his companions have all perished.]

Responses to Margin Questions

Line 538. Answers will vary. Most students will probably choose Odysseus's escape from Polyphemus as the highlight for several reasons: The episode, vividly told, is full of suspense, violence, and terror; the escape is daring, dangerous, and brilliantly executed. Students may wish to get together in pairs or small groups to discuss both their own customs and their observations about hospitality in the *Odyssey*.

you put me down with wine, you blinded me.
Come back, Odysseus, and I'll treat you well,
praying the god of earthquake to befriend you—
his son I am, for he by his avowal
520   fathered me, and, if he will, he may
heal me of this black wound—he and no other
of all the happy gods or mortal men.'

Few words I shouted in reply to him:

'If I could take your life I would and take
525   your time away, and hurl you down to hell!
The god of earthquake could not heal you there!'

At this he stretched his hands out in his darkness
toward the sky of stars, and prayed Poseidon:

'O hear me, lord, blue girdler of the islands,
530   if I am thine indeed, and thou art father:
grant that Odysseus, raider of cities, never
see his home: Laertes' son, I mean,
who kept his hall on Ithaca. Should destiny
intend that he shall see his roof again
535   among his family in his fatherland,
far be that day, and dark the years between.
Let him lose all companions, and return
under strange sail to bitter days at home.' . . ."

(from Book 9)

Here we will imagine that Homer stops reciting for the night. The blind poet might take a glass of wine before turning in. The listeners would go off to various corners of the local nobleman's house. They might discuss highlights of the poet's tale among themselves and look forward to the next evening's installment.

Polyphemus. Terra-cotta head (4th century B.C.).

Louvre, Paris, France.

538. *Take a few minutes to list what you think are the highlights of Odysseus's journey so far. What questions do you have? What do you think will happen next?*

Read **"Welcome: A Religious Duty"** *on page 671. Then, as you continue reading the story, trace the ways Homer repeatedly dramatizes the importance of mutual respect among people. Think about your own ideas of hospitality today—what are the customs in your family and neighborhood? What are the customs in American society as a whole?*

A CLOSER LOOK

Welcome: A Religious Duty

Today's visitors to Greece are often struck by the generous hospitality of its people. An ancient tradition lies behind the traveler's welcome in Greece—and it is a tradition that was fundamentally religious before it became a part of social custom.

Zeus, the king of the gods, demanded that strangers be treated graciously. Hosts had a religious duty to welcome strangers, and guests had a responsibility to respect hosts. The close interconnections and mutual respect in this host-guest relationship are reflected in the fact that the word *xenos* (zen′ōs) in ancient Greek can mean both "host" and "guest." The relationship is often symbolized in the *Odyssey* by the presentation of gifts. Alcinous, the king of the Phaeacians, for example, gives Odysseus a magically swift ship in which to sail home.

What happens when the host-guest relationship is abused or otherwise breaks down? In Homer's epic songs about the Trojan War, the *Iliad* and the *Odyssey*, the customs of hospitality are violated at least three times. The first occasion caused the war itself: Paris, prince of Troy, ran off with the beautiful Helen from Sparta while he was the guest of Helen's husband, Menelaus. For the Greeks this insult to *xenia* (hospitality) was at least as serious as Helen's unfaithfulness, and it meant that Zeus would, in the end, allow the Greeks to triumph in the long war.

The second example of violated hospitality has its humorous and ironic side.

In the *Odyssey* the Cyclops is monstrous not only because of his huge size and brutish appearance. He is set apart from civilized beings precisely because of his barbaric outlook on *xenia*. When Odysseus begs the Cyclops for hospitality and warns that Zeus will avenge an injured guest, the Cyclops replies that he and his kind "care not a whistle for . . . Zeus" (line 265). With dark humor the Cyclops uses the word *xeineion* (Greek for "guest-gift" or "noble gift") when he tells Odysseus that he will have the privilege of being eaten last (lines 362–363). The poetic justice of the Cyclops's blinding would not be lost on Homer's Greek audience.

The final example of a breach in the law of hospitality underlies the entire plot structure of the *Odyssey:* Back in Ithaca, year after year the suitors abuse the hospitality of Odysseus—an absent "host"—and threaten to take away his wife. The bloody vengeance that Odysseus wreaks on these suitors should be understood in the context of their outrageous violation of religious law. The suitors have turned hospitality into a crude mockery. Perhaps it is not accidental that Odysseus invokes the host-guest relationship just before the battle, when he quietly gives his son, Telemachus, the signal to fight (lines 1208–1209):

> "Telemachus, the stranger [*xeinos*] you welcomed in your hall has not disgraced you."

A CLOSER LOOK

Ask students to think of ways people from various cultures greet strangers and treat guests. What do these customs show about the cultures' beliefs? Discuss with students how these beliefs are manifested in everyday life, even in actions as simple as a friendly handshake, which demonstrates a certain democratic feeling by signaling that both participants are at the same level. You might tell students that the handshake was originally intended to show that neither person was carrying a weapon. Have students share their ideas in a class discussion, making sure they display an open-minded, tolerant attitude toward various cultures' beliefs and customs. Write students' ideas on the chalkboard, and have students compare their customs with those of the ancient Greeks.

C **Reading Informational Text**
? **Clarifying the main idea.** How do the details in this passage support the main idea? [Possible responses: The meaning of the Greek word *xenos* reflects the deep importance of the host-guest relationship; Alcinous's gift in the *Odyssey* illustrates the ancient tradition of welcoming strangers.]

D **Reading Informational Text**
? **Generating research questions.** What research questions can you generate from this closing section? [Possible responses: How has the violation of hospitality led to battles between different peoples in history? What laws of hospitality have deep importance in other cultures?]

Connection

Summary ⬌ *at grade level*

In this poem, Nikki Giovanni compares a violent tropical storm to the Cyclops.

DIRECT TEACHING

A Literary Focus

❓ **Figures of speech.** What does the comparison of a tropical storm to the Cyclops suggest? [Possible responses: that the storm is powerful and destructive; that the storm will randomly kill people.]

B Reading Skills

❓ **Speculating.** Ulysses is the Roman name of Odysseus. What might have happened if the Cyclops in the *Odyssey* had not met Odysseus (Ulysses)? [Possible response: The Cyclops might have gone on attacking everyone around him indefinitely.] **What does the allusion to the *Odyssey* imply about the tropical storm?** [Possible responses: By saying that the storm "meets no Ulysses," the poet suggests that it, too, will go on destroying as long as it can; the allusion suggests that no human force is capable of stopping the storm.]

C Reading Skills

❓ **Evaluating.** Why is the metaphor of the Cyclops appropriate for describing a tropical storm? [Possible responses: Like the Cyclops, a hurricane has an eye; both the storm and the Cyclops are strong, wantonly destructive forces that can be dealt with only through intelligence and resourcefulness.]

A # The Cyclops in the Ocean
Nikki Giovanni

B Moving slowly . . . against time . . . patiently majestic . . .
the cyclops . . . in the ocean . . . meets no Ulysses . . .

Through the night . . . he sighs . . . throbbing against the
shore . . . declaring . . . for the adventure . . .

5 A wall of gray . . . gathered by a slow touch . . . slash and
slither . . . through the waiting screens . . . separating into
nodules . . . making my panes . . . accept the touch . . .

Not content . . . to watch my frightened gaze . . . he clamors
beneath the sash . . . dancing on my sill . . .

C 10 Certain to die . . . when the sun . . . returns . . .

Tropical Storm Dennis
August 15–18, 1981, Florida

Connecting and Comparing Texts

"The Cyclops in the Ocean" personifies Tropical Storm Dennis by comparing it to the Cyclops. With the class, identify the traits of the Cyclops that resemble those of a storm. Make a list of similar characteristics or qualities on the chalkboard or on an overhead transparency. Write down any other qualities of the Cyclops that students can think of. Then, ask students to make lists of other creatures or natural phenomena that exhibit qualities like those of the Cyclops. After students have shared their ideas, ask the class to select one creature or phenomenon and to create a class poem comparing it to the Cyclops.

THE ENCHANTRESS CIRCE

*After sailing from the Cyclops's island, Odysseus and his men land on the island of
Aeolia. There the wind king, Aeolus (ē'ɔ·ləs), does Odysseus a favor. He puts all
the stormy winds in a bag so that they will not harm the Ithacans. The bull's-hide
bag containing the winds is wedged under Odysseus's afterdeck. During the voyage, when the curious and suspicious sailors open the bag, thinking it contains
treasure, the evil winds roar up into hurricanes that blow the ships back to Aeolia.
Aeolus drives them away again.*

D

*On the island of the Laestrygonians (les·trig·ō'nē·ənz), gigantic cannibals, all
the ships but one are destroyed and their crews devoured. Odysseus's ship escapes
and lands on Aeaea, the home of the enchantress and goddess Circe. Here a party
of twenty-three men, led by Eurylochus, goes off to explore the island. Odysseus is
still telling his story to Alcinous and his court.*

"In the wild wood they found an open glade,
540 around a smooth stone house—the hall of Circe—
and wolves and mountain lions lay there, mild
in her soft spell, fed on her drug of evil.
None would attack—oh, it was strange, I tell you—
but switching their long tails they faced our men
545 like hounds, who look up when their master comes
with tidbits for them—as he will—from table.
Humbly those wolves and lions with mighty paws
fawned on our men—who met their yellow eyes
and feared them.
                    In the entranceway they stayed
550 to listen there: inside her quiet house
they heard the goddess Circe.
                              Low she sang

in her beguiling voice, while on her loom
she wove ambrosial fabric sheer and bright,
by that craft known to the goddesses of heaven.
555 No one would speak, until Polites°—most
faithful and likable of my officers—said:

'Dear friends, no need for stealth:° here's a young weaver
singing a pretty song to set the air
atingle on these lawns and paven courts.
560 Goddess she is, or lady. Shall we greet her?'

So reassured, they all cried out together,
and she came swiftly to the shining doors
to call them in. All but Eurylochus—
who feared a snare—the innocents went after her.

E

F

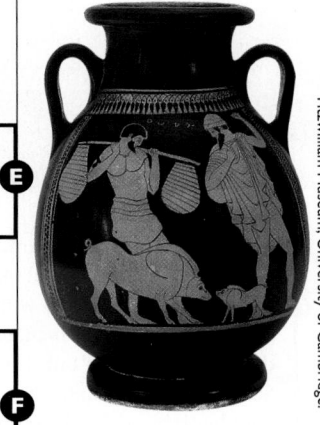

Fitzwilliam Museum, University of Cambridge.

Pigs, swineherd, and Odysseus by
the Pig Painter. Pelike, or jar
(470–460 B.C.).

555. Polites (pō·lī'tēz').

557. stealth (stelth) *n.*: sneaky
behavior.

Odyssey, Part One   **673**

Odysseus and his men reach the
island of the witch Circe. The
sailors are beguiled by the sorcer-
ess, who turns them into swine
and shuts them in a pigsty.

DIRECT TEACHING

D **Reading Skills**

❷ **Interpreting.** What does the
sailors' opening of the bull's-hide
bag suggest about their relationship
with Odysseus? [Possible responses:
The sailors don't trust Odysseus to
share treasures with them; Odysseus
does not always share information
with his sailors.]

E **Literary Focus**

❷ **Simile.** What comparison does
Odysseus make to emphasize the
strange gentleness of the wild
beasts' behavior? [He compares
them to domesticated dogs who
depend on a master for sustenance.]

F **Reading Skills**

❷ **Making inferences.** Circe, like
Calypso, is first seen at her loom,
singing and weaving. What inference
could you make about women in
ancient Greece from this fact?
[Possible response: Weaving was an
important part of women's work in
ancient Greece.]

Check Test: True-False

Guide the class in answering these comprehension questions. Have students support
their responses with passages from the text.

1. Odysseus refuses King Alcinous's request
to identify himself. [F]

2. Odysseus and his sailors are welcomed by
the Cicones. [F]

3. Odysseus is forced to leave three men
behind with the Lotus Eaters. [F]

4. The Cyclops Polyphemus is the son of the
god Poseidon. [T]

5. Fellow Cyclopes come to Polyphemus's aid
after he is wounded. [F]

DIRECT TEACHING

Ⓐ Reading Skills

❓ Making connections. At what other point in the epic have some of Odysseus's men eaten something that made them lose their desire for home? [During the episode with the Lotus Eaters in Book 9, some of Odysseus's men sampled the lotus and lost their desire to return home.]

Ⓑ Reading Skills

Monitoring your comprehension. Suggest that students stop to check their understanding of events and to ask themselves questions at this point—for example: "What has happened to the men?" [The men have been turned into pigs.] "Will Eurylochus somehow rescue them?" [Possible response: It seems likely that he will, since he was clever enough to avoid Circe's trap.]

Responses to Margin Question

Lines 549–583. Students may suggest that the men violated the code of hospitality by sneaking around Circe's home rather than showing her the proper respect; others may say that the men did nothing to justify such horrible treatment. Circe violated the laws of hospitality by drugging the men's drink, turning them into pigs, and locking them up.

Circe offers the magic potion to Odysseus. Detail from Greek vase from Thebes.
British Museum, London.

565 ┌ On thrones she seated them, and lounging chairs,
  │ while she prepared a meal of cheese and barley
Ⓐ │ and amber honey mixed with Pramnian wine,°
  │ adding her own vile pinch, to make them lose
  └ desire or thought of our dear fatherland.
570 ┌ Scarce had they drunk when she flew after them
  │ with her long stick and shut them in a pigsty—
Ⓑ │ bodies, voices, heads, and bristles, all
  │ swinish now, though minds were still unchanged.
  │ So, squealing, in they went. And Circe tossed them
575 │ acorns, mast,° and cornel berries—fodder
  └ for hogs who rut and slumber on the earth.

   Down to the ship Eurylochus came running
   to cry alarm, foul magic doomed his men!
   But working with dry lips to speak a word
580 he could not, being so shaken; blinding tears
   welled in his eyes; foreboding filled his heart.
   When we were frantic questioning him, at last
   we heard the tale: our friends were gone. . . ."

(from Book 10)

567. Pramnian wine: strong wine from Mount Pramnos in ancient Greece.

575. mast *n.:* various kinds of nuts used as food for hogs.

549–583. *Note your responses to this horrible experience. What have the men done to deserve being turned into pigs? How does Circe violate the laws of hospitality?*

READING SKILLS REVIEW

Homonyms. Remind students that homonyms are words that sound alike but have different meanings and spellings. To assess their ability to distinguish between some common homonyms, have students complete the following activity.

Activity. Correct each of the following items by replacing the incorrect homonym with the correct word.

1. ". . . You need grieve no more; you need not feel / your life consumed <u>hear</u>. . . ." (ll. 89–90) [here]

2. "And this new grief we <u>boar</u> with us to sea. . . ." (l.174) [bore]

3. ". . . He had a load of dry <u>bows</u> on his shoulder / to stoke his fire. . . ." (ll. 222–223) [boughs]

4. "'We are from Troy, Achaeans, blown off <u>coarse</u> / by shifting gales. . . .'" (ll. 249–250) [course]

5. ". . . Eurylochus came running / to cry alarm, <u>fowl</u> magic doomed his men!" (ll. 577–578) [foul]

Odysseus leaves the ship and rushes to Circe's hall. The god Hermes stops him to give him a plant that will weaken Circe's power. (Homer calls it a moly; it might have been a kind of garlic.) Protected by the plant's magic, Odysseus resists Circe's sorcery. The goddess, realizing she has met her match, frees Odysseus's men. Now Circe, "loveliest of all immortals," persuades Odysseus to stay with her. Odysseus shares her meat and wine, and she restores his heart. After many seasons of feasting and other pleasures, Odysseus and his men beg Circe to help them return home.

C

She responds to their pleas with the command that Odysseus alone descend to the Land of the Dead, "the cold homes of Death and pale Persephone," queen of the underworld. There Odysseus must seek the wisdom of the blind prophet Teiresias.

D

Odysseus pursuing Circe.
Greek vase.
Louvre, Paris, France.

THE LAND OF THE DEAD

In the Land of the Dead, Odysseus seeks to learn his destiny. The source of his information is Teiresias, the famous blind prophet from the city of Thebes. The prophet's lack of external sight suggests the presence of true insight. Circe has told Odysseus exactly what rites he must perform to bring Teiresias up from the dead. Odysseus continues telling his story to Alcinous's court.

"Then I addressed the blurred and breathless dead,
585   vowing to slaughter my best heifer for them
before she calved, at home in Ithaca,
and burn the choice bits on the altar fire;
as for Teiresias, I swore to sacrifice
a black lamb, handsomest of all our flock.
590   Thus to assuage the nations of the dead
I pledged these rites, then slashed the lamb and ewe,
letting their black blood stream into the well pit.
Now the souls gathered, stirring out of Erebus,
brides and young men, and men grown old in pain,
595   and tender girls whose hearts were new to grief;
many were there, too, torn by brazen lanceheads,
battle-slain, bearing still their bloody gear.

Odyssey, Part One   675

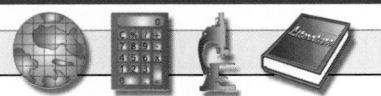

CONTENT-AREA CONNECTIONS

Art: *Odyssey*-Inspired Works
Small-group activity. Have student groups research some of the artworks inspired by the *Odyssey* and use copies of them to create a display called The *Odyssey* Art Gallery. Suggest that they can look at illustrated editions of the epic and library art resources (including books and CD-ROMs) and make drawings or photocopies of what they find.

History: Sailing Vessels
Odysseus's ship was a galley—a long, low, usually single-decked ship, probably made of pine or oak, propelled by oars and sails. Lacking a fully enclosed cabin, it was uncomfortable for overnight stays. Tell students that the scene in which Odysseus builds a raft to leave Calypso's island may be the earliest literary depiction of boat making.

Summary ⬆ *above grade level*

In the underworld, Odysseus is addressed by the seer Teiresias, who warns him to stay away from the cattle of Helios, the sun god. Teiresias tells Odysseus that when he finally arrives home, he will find his household in disarray. Teiresias also tells Odysseus that after slaying his wife's suitors, he must make sacrifices to Poseidon.

VIEWING THE ART

The Greeks often drank a mixture of wine and water, served in a pitcher. This type of jug was known as an oinochoe (ē·nä′ə·wē′).

Activity. Ask students to identify the style of pottery painting here. [red-figured style]

DIRECT TEACHING

C Learners Having Difficulty
❓ **Finding details.** What other role has Hermes played in the *Odyssey*? [He was sent by Zeus to tell Calypso to free Odysseus.]

D Content-Area Connections
Greek Mythology: Persephone
Persephone, the queen of the underworld, is the daughter of Demeter, the goddess of crops and fertility. In a well-known myth, Persephone is abducted by Hades, the god of the underworld (and the brother of Zeus and Poseidon), who has fallen in love with her. The grief-stricken Demeter neglects her duties and allows a blight to descend on the earth. Finally Zeus intervenes and a compromise is reached: Persephone will remain in the underworld for only part of each year. During the time she is there, Demeter goes into mourning and nothing grows. The myth helps explain the changing seasons.

? **Making inferences.** Whom is Odysseus referring to when he uses the term *sovereign Death?* [Hades, king of the underworld]

B **Content-Area Connections**

Literature: Odysseus's Mother
One of the phantoms Odysseus must keep away from the lamb's blood is his own mother, Anticlea. Having been away for so long, Odysseus does not know that she has died and is surprised and saddened to see her here.

From every side they came and sought the pit
with rustling cries; and I grew sick with fear.
600 But presently I gave command to my officers
to flay° those sheep the bronze cut down, and make
burnt offerings of flesh to the gods below—
A to sovereign Death, to pale Persephone.°
Meanwhile I crouched with my drawn sword to keep
605 **B** the surging phantoms from the bloody pit
till I should know the presence of Teiresias. . . .

Soon from the dark that prince of Thebes came forward
bearing a golden staff; and he addressed me:

'Son of Laertes and the gods of old,
610 Odysseus, master of landways and seaways,
why leave the blazing sun, O man of woe,
to see the cold dead and the joyless region?
Stand clear, put up your sword;
let me but taste of blood, I shall speak true.'

615 At this I stepped aside, and in the scabbard
let my long sword ring home to the pommel silver,
as he bent down to the somber blood. Then spoke
the prince of those with gift of speech:

                                    'Great captain,
a fair wind and the honey lights of home
620 are all you seek. But anguish lies ahead;

601. **flay** (flā) *v.:* strip the skin from.

603. **Persephone** (pər·sef′ə·nē).

Persephone, queen of the underworld, with her husband, Hades (4th century B.C.). British Museum, London.

DEVELOPING FLUENCY

Mixed-ability group activity. Assign students to small mixed-ability groups—each including advanced learners, learners having difficulty, and English-language learners—to read aloud several of Aesop's fables and discuss the moral and social lessons they convey. Have advanced students model reading aloud sentences and paragraphs. Then, have other students re-read the passages aloud as fluently as possible. Ask students to compare and contrast Aesop's lessons with those in the *Odyssey.*

the god who thunders on the land prepares it,
not to be shaken from your track, implacable,°
in rancor for the son whose eye you blinded.
One narrow strait may take you through his blows:
625 denial of yourself, restraint of shipmates.
When you make landfall on Thrinakia first
and quit the violet sea, dark on the land
you'll find the grazing herds of Helios
by whom all things are seen, all speech is known.

630 Avoid those kine,° hold fast to your intent,
and hard seafaring brings you all to Ithaca.
But if you raid the beeves,° I see destruction
for ship and crew. Though you survive alone,
bereft of all companions, lost for years,

635 under strange sail shall you come home, to find
your own house filled with trouble: insolent men
eating your livestock as they court your lady.
Aye, you shall make those men atone in blood!
But after you have dealt out death—in open

640 combat or by stealth—to all the suitors,
go overland on foot, and take an oar,
until one day you come where men have lived
with meat unsalted, never known the sea,
nor seen seagoing ships, with crimson bows

645 and oars that fledge light hulls for dipping flight.
The spot will soon be plain to you, and I
can tell you how: some passerby will say,
"What winnowing fan° is that upon your shoulder?"
Halt, and implant your smooth oar in the turf

650 and make fair sacrifice to Lord Poseidon:
a ram, a bull, a great buck boar; turn back,
and carry out pure hecatombs° at home
to all wide heaven's lords, the undying gods,
to each in order. Then a seaborne death

655 soft as this hand of mist will come upon you
when you are wearied out with rich old age,
your countryfolk in blessed peace around you.
And all this shall be just as I foretell.' . . ."

(*from* Book 11)

Vocabulary
rancor (raŋ′kər) *n.*: bitter hatred; ill will.

622. **implacable** (im · plak′ə · bəl) *adj.*: unyielding; merciless.

630. **kine** (kīn) *n.*: old term for "cattle."

632. **beeves** *n.*: another old term for "cattle."

648. **winnowing fan:** device used to remove the useless dry outer covering from grain. (These people would never have seen an oar.)

652. **hecatombs** (hek′ə·tōmz′) *n.*: sacrifices of one hundred cattle at a time to the gods. In Greek, *hekaton* means "one hundred."

 **618–658.** *What prophecy does Odysseus receive? Take notes on how you might film this important scene in the underworld. How many actors would you need? What props would you use? You might sketch the scene as you* **visualize** *it.*

Odyssey, Part One **677**

C Reading Skills

Monitoring your comprehension. Ask students if they have any questions about the meaning of ll. 621–623. They might ask themselves, "Which god is Teiresias referring to?" [Poseidon, the god of the sea and of earthquakes and father of the Cyclops Polyphemus, whom Odysseus blinded]

D Reading Skills

❓ Making connections. Remind students of Homer's words at the beginning of the epic, in Book 1 (p. 651), where the poet reveals how the story ends. According to this excerpt from Book 1, do Odysseus's men heed Teiresias's warning, or does the seer's prophecy come true? [The men ignore the warning and slaughter Helios's cattle. The prophecy comes true: Odysseus alone survives, and it takes him many more years to get home.]

E Reading Skills

❓ Expressing an opinion. So far, everything Teiresias says has already been recounted by the poet in Book 1. Does knowing in advance what happens lessen your enjoyment of the epic? [Possible responses: No; although readers know what will happen, they don't know how it will happen. Yes; knowing in advance that the prophecy comes true takes away much of the suspense.]

Responses to Margin Question

Lines 618–658. Possible responses: Teiresias tells Odysseus that he and his men will return home only if they leave the cattle of the sun god, Helios, unharmed. Teiresias prophesies that the men will perish and that Odysseus will be long delayed in reaching home.

Suggest that students consider scenery, lighting, costumes, and props as they make notes on dramatizing this scene.

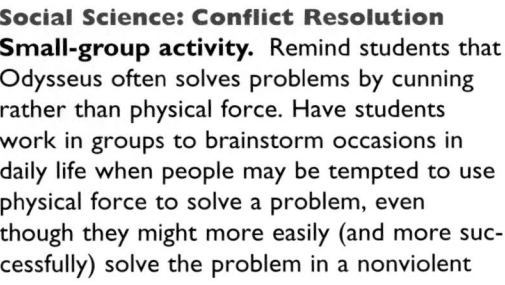

CONTENT-AREA CONNECTIONS

Social Science: Conflict Resolution
Small-group activity. Remind students that Odysseus often solves problems by cunning rather than physical force. Have students work in groups to brainstorm occasions in daily life when people may be tempted to use physical force to solve a problem, even though they might more easily (and more successfully) solve the problem in a nonviolent way. Make a two-column table on the chalkboard, labeling one column "Problems" and the other "Solutions." Have groups submit ideas to be listed in the "Problems" column. Then, have the class suggest ways to solve each of the problems nonviolently. List these ideas in the "Solutions" column.

Summary ⬅➡ at grade level

Odysseus returns to Circe's island. The witch tells him how to avoid the dangers of the Sirens and Scylla and Charybdis. He has himself tied to the mast so that he can hear the Sirens' singing without succumbing to it. Odysseus plugs his men's ears with beeswax to keep them from hearing the Sirens' bewitching voices. Odysseus and his crew escape this danger, but they lose six men to Scylla when they pass through the straits of Scylla and Charybdis.

DIRECT TEACHING

Ⓐ Reading Skills

❓ Context clues. What is the meaning of the word *innocent* in l. 663? [any unsuspecting person; someone who is unaware that listening to the Sirens' singing is dangerous] What context clues helped you figure out the meaning of the word? [Possible responses: bewitch; woe.]

Ⓑ Reading Skills

❓ Predicting. From what you know of Odysseus, do you think he will take the risk of listening to the Sirens' song? [Possible responses: Yes, Odysseus will listen because he is adventurous and will not want to miss the experience; no, Odysseus wants to get home too badly and is too clever to be tempted.]

THE SIRENS; SCYLLA AND CHARYBDIS

Odysseus and his men return to Circe's island, where Circe warns Odysseus of the perils that await him. In the following passage, Odysseus, quoting Circe, is still speaking at Alcinous's court.

            "'Listen with care

660   to this, now, and a god will arm your mind.
      Square in your ship's path are Sirens, crying
      beauty to bewitch men coasting by;
   Ⓐ woe to the innocent who hears that sound!
      He will not see his lady nor his children
665   in joy, crowding about him, home from sea;
      the Sirens will sing his mind away
      on their sweet meadow lolling. There are bones
      of dead men rotting in a pile beside them
      and flayed skins shrivel around the spot.

                        Steer wide;
670   keep well to seaward; plug your oarsmen's ears
      with beeswax kneaded soft; none of the rest
      should hear that song.

                        But if you wish to listen,
      let the men tie you in the lugger, hand
      and foot, back to the mast, lashed to the mast,
675 Ⓑ so you may hear those Harpies'° thrilling voices;
      shout as you will, begging to be untied,
      your crew must only twist more line around you
      and keep their stroke up, till the singers fade. . . .'"

The next peril lies between two headlands. Circe continues her warning.

         "'. . . That is the den of Scylla, where she yaps
680   abominably, a newborn whelp's° cry,
      though she is huge and monstrous. God or man,
      no one could look on her in joy. Her legs—
      and there are twelve—are like great tentacles,
      unjointed, and upon her serpent necks
685   are borne six heads like nightmares of ferocity,
      with triple serried° rows of fangs and deep
      gullets of black death. Half her length, she sways
      her heads in air, outside her horrid cleft,

675. Harpies (här′pēz): monsters, half bird and half woman, who are greedy for victims.

680. whelp's (hwelps) *n.:* puppy's.

686. serried (ser′ēd) *adj.:* crowded together; densely packed.

Vocabulary
abominably (ə·bäm′ə·nə·blē) *adv.:* in an extremely unpleasant or disgusting manner.

678 Collection 10 Epic and Myth • Evaluating an Argument

CONTENT-AREA CONNECTIONS

Geography: Odysseus's Sea
Many efforts have been made, with varying success, to identify the actual sites of Odysseus's adventures in the Mediterranean. Experts generally agree that the tale of Scylla and Charybdis is a folk legend inspired by the narrow Strait of Messina between mainland Italy and Sicily.

Mixed-ability group activity. Help students locate the Strait of Messina on a map of the Mediterranean Sea. Have them discuss why this strait might pose danger to galleys, like the ones in which Odysseus and his men are sailing.

hunting the sea around that promontory°
690   for dolphins, dogfish, or what bigger game
thundering Amphitrite° feeds in thousands.
And no ship's company can claim
to have passed her without loss and grief; she takes,
from every ship, one man for every gullet.

695   The opposite point seems more a tongue of land
you'd touch with a good bowshot, at the narrows.
A great wild fig, a shaggy mass of leaves,
grows on it, and Charybdis lurks below
to swallow down the dark sea tide. Three times
700   from dawn to dusk she spews it up
and sucks it down again three times, a whirling
maelstrom;° if you come upon her then
the god who makes earth tremble could not save you.
No, hug the cliff of Scylla, take your ship
705   through on a racing stroke. Better to mourn
six men than lose them all, and the ship, too. . . .

C

D

689. promontory (präm′ən·tôr′ē)
n.: high area of land that juts out
into a body of water.

691. Amphitrite (am′fi·trīt′ē):
goddess of the sea and wife of
Poseidon.

702. maelstrom (māl′strəm) *n.:*
large, violent whirlpool.

The Sirens (c. 1875) by Sir Edward Burne-Jones.

National Gallery of South Africa, Cape Town.

C Reading Skills

❓ **Idioms.** People sometimes use
the expression *caught between Scylla
and Charybdis.* What does it mean?
[It means "between two dangers or
undesirable alternatives." A similar
expression is *between a rock and a
hard place.*]

D Reading Skills

❓ **Expressing an opinion.** Do
you agree with Circe that it is better to sacrifice six men than to risk
losing them all? Explain. [Students
may say that her advice is harsh but
logical or that Odysseus ought to try
to find a third, better solution.]

VIEWING THE ART

Sir Edward Burne-Jones
(1833–1898) was a member of the
Pre-Raphaelites, a group of English
artists who sought to reform art.
The Pre-Raphaelites were inspired
in particular by the art of the early
Italian Renaissance, before the
time of Raphael, and strove for a
simple, direct style. Like other
Pre-Raphaelites, Burne-Jones often
painted medieval themes in a
romantic style.

Activity. How does the romantic
imagery in this painting contrast
with Circe's depiction of the
Sirens? [The Sirens are pictured as
beautiful and gentle, whereas Circe
compares them to Harpies.]

Odyssey, Part One   **679**

A **Learners Having Difficulty**

❓ Who else has warned Odysseus to leave Helios's cattle alone? [Teiresias, the prophet of Thebes, whom Odysseus visited in the underworld]

B **Reading Skills**

❓ **Expressing an opinion.** Do you agree that it's best to know about dangers you may face? **Explain.** [Possible responses: It is good to know about dangers if you can do something to avoid them or protect yourself from them—but otherwise, knowing doesn't help and may make you feel worse; I think most people would want to know about dangers they face, whether they can do anything about them or not, because knowing what to expect is better than fearing the unknown.]

Responses to Margin Question

Lines 659–716. The dangers facing Odysseus and his crew, in order from least to most severe, are the Sirens followed by Scylla and Charybdis. Although the Sirens can sing men's minds away and lead them to certain death, they are easily avoided by either plugging the men's ears or immobilizing the men so they cannot heed the Sirens' call. However, the passage between Scylla and Charybdis presents the choice between total destruction of the ship and crew or the unavoidable death of six sailors.

Then you will coast Thrinakia, the island
where Helios's cattle graze, fine herds, and flocks
of goodly sheep. The herds and flocks are seven,
with fifty beasts in each.

710 No lambs are dropped,
or calves, and these fat cattle never die. . . .

A Now give those kine a wide berth, keep your thoughts
intent upon your course for home,
and hard seafaring brings you all to Ithaca.
715 But if you raid the beeves, I see destruction
for ship and crew. . . .'"

The Ithacans set off. Odysseus does not tell his men of Circe's last prophecy—that he will be the only survivor of their long journey. Still speaking to Alcinous's court, Odysseus continues his tale.

"The crew being now silent before me, I
addressed them, sore at heart:

'Dear friends,
B more than one man, or two, should know those things
720 Circe foresaw for us and shared with me,
so let me tell her forecast: then we die
with our eyes open, if we are going to die,
or know what death we baffle if we can. Sirens
weaving a haunting song over the sea
725 we are to shun, she said, and their green shore
all sweet with clover; yet she urged that I
alone should listen to their song. Therefore
you are to tie me up, tight as a splint,
erect along the mast, lashed to the mast,
730 and if I shout and beg to be untied,
take more turns of the rope to muffle me.'

I rather dwelt on this part of the forecast,
while our good ship made time, bound outward down
the wind for the strange island of Sirens.
735 Then all at once the wind fell, and a calm
came over all the sea, as though some power
lulled the swell.

The crew were on their feet
briskly, to furl the sail, and stow it; then,
each in place, they poised the smooth oar blades
740 and sent the white foam scudding by. I carved
a massive cake of beeswax into bits

680 Collection 10 Epic and Myth • Evaluating an Argument

📖 **659–716.** *According to Circe, what dangers lie ahead for Odysseus and his crew? List the dangers in order from least severe to most severe, and give your reasons for placing the threats in this order.*

Circe Pouring Poison into a Vase and Awaiting the Arrival of Ulysses (19th century) by Sir Edward Burne-Jones.

The Bridgeman Art Library.

SKILLS REVIEW

Character's traits. Odysseus, the hero of the *Odyssey*, deals ably with beings of all kinds and with various cultures. Have students discuss the qualities that enable Odysseus to deal successfully with the gods, people, and other creatures that he meets on his journey. **Activity.** Ask each student to choose a quality—such as open-mindedness, intelligence, courage, self-confidence, or determination— and to find two examples in the text that show Odysseus using that characteristic to deal with a dangerous situation. Have students share their examples with the class and discuss how these qualities would help people resolve problems and crises in today's world.

and rolled them in my hands until they softened—
no long task, for a burning heat came down
from Helios, lord of high noon. Going forward
745   I carried wax along the line, and laid it
thick on their ears. They tied me up, then, plumb°
amidships, back to the mast, lashed to the mast,
and took themselves again to rowing. Soon,
as we came smartly within hailing distance,
750   the two Sirens, noting our fast ship
off their point, made ready, and they sang. . . .

The lovely voices in ardor appealing over the water
made me crave to listen, and I tried to say
'Untie me!' to the crew, jerking my brows;
755   but they bent steady to the oars. Then Perimedes°
got to his feet, he and Eurylochus,
and passed more line about, to hold me still.
So all rowed on, until the Sirens
dropped under the sea rim, and their singing
dwindled away.
760   My faithful company
rested on their oars now, peeling off
the wax that I had laid thick on their ears;
then set me free.
                            But scarcely had that island
faded in blue air when I saw smoke
765   and white water, with sound of waves in tumult—
a sound the men heard, and it terrified them.
Oars flew from their hands; the blades went knocking
wild alongside till the ship lost way,
with no oar blades to drive her through the water.

746. plumb (plum) *adv.:* vertically.

755. Perimedes (per·i·mē′dēz′).

Odysseus and the Sirens, Athenian red-figure stamnos vase by the Siren Painter, late Archaic, c. 490 B.C. (earthenware).
British Museum, London, UK.

Vocabulary
ardor (är′dər) *n.:* passion; enthusiasm.
tumult (tōō′mult) *n.:* commotion; uproar; confusion.

Odyssey, Part One   681

C Reading Skills
❓ **Drawing conclusions.** Why does Odysseus put wax in his men's ears? [to keep them from hearing the Sirens' singing]

D Reading Skills
Monitoring your comprehension. Remind students to pause periodically to make sure they understand what is happening and to visualize the action. Here they might try to imagine the haunting music of the Sirens and to picture Odysseus tied to the mast. Or they might ask themselves, "Why does Odysseus try to gesture with his brows for the crew to untie him?" [The crew cannot hear anything he says because they have wax plugs in their ears.]

E Reading Skills
❓ **Interpreting.** What does "the Sirens dropped under the sea rim" mean? [Possible responses: It means that they have dropped below the horizon; it means that Odysseus and his men can no longer see them.]

VIEWING THE ART

This red-figure stamnas vase shows Odysseus tied to the mast as the oarsmen frantically row away.

Activity. Have students compare this ancient Greek depiction of the Sirens with that of Sir Edward Burne-Jones on p. 679. [Possible responses: The Greeks depict the Sirens as part woman, part bird. Burne-Jones shows them as beautiful young women dressed in gauzy drapery; the ships are different.]

CONTENT-AREA CONNECTIONS

Music: "Sirènes"
After students read the section about the Sirens in the *Odyssey*, have them listen to a recording of "Sirènes" ("Sirens"), the third nocturne from Claude Debussy's three *Nocturnes for Orchestra*. In his dreamy, poetic music, the French composer Claude Debussy (1862–1918) focused on conveying mood and atmosphere. Debussy described "Sirènes" as music about "the sea and its innumerable rhythms," in the midst of which the wordless "mysterious song of the Sirens is heard," after which "they laugh, and the song passes on."
Individual activity. Ask students to jot down words and phrases describing the impressions or feelings evoked by the music as they listen. Then, encourage students to state whether they think Debussy effectively captures the Sirens' song and to explain why or why not.

A **Reading Skills**

? Extending the text. Is it necessary for great leaders like Odysseus to inspire their followers? **Explain.** [Possible response: Yes, being able to inspire people is one of the qualities that makes a leader great. Here Odysseus calms and inspires his men by reminding them of how they escaped the Cyclops.]

B **English-Language Learners**

Idioms. Explain that *by hook or crook* means "in any way possible."

C **Literary Focus**

? Character. What does Odysseus's failure to remember Circe's warning against using weapons reveal about his self-image? [Possible responses: It suggests that he continues to think of himself as the clever warrior who solves problems unaided; it suggests that he is not used to situations in which he has no control and must stand by helplessly.]

Response to Margin Question

Lines 770–793. Odysseus reassures his men by reminding them that they've faced and survived danger before. Then he prays aloud to Zeus for help. He does not tell them that six of them will be eaten by Scylla, as he doesn't want them to stop rowing.

---

770 Well, I walked up and down from bow to stern,
    trying to put heart into them, standing over
    every oarsman, saying gently,

                                        'Friends,

A have we never been in danger before this?
    More fearsome, is it now, than when the Cyclops
775 penned us in his cave? What power he had!
    Did I not keep my nerve, and use my wits
    to find a way out for us?

                                    Now I say

B by hook or crook this peril too shall be
    something that we remember.

                                Heads up, lads!

780 We must obey the orders as I give them.
    Get the oar shafts in your hands, and lie back
    hard on your benches; hit these breaking seas.
    Zeus help us pull away before we founder.°

    You at the tiller, listen, and take in
785 all that I say—the rudders are your duty;
    keep her out of the combers° and the smoke;
    steer for that headland; watch the drift, or we
    fetch up in the smother,° and you drown us.'

    That was all, and it brought them round to action.
790 But as I sent them on toward Scylla, I
    told them nothing, as they could do nothing.
    They would have dropped their oars again, in panic,
    to roll for cover under the decking. Circe's
    bidding against arms had slipped my mind,
795 **C** so I tied on my cuirass° and took up
    two heavy spears, then made my way along
    to the foredeck—thinking to see her first from there,
    the monster of the gray rock, harboring
    torment for my friends. I strained my eyes
800 upon that cliffside veiled in cloud, but nowhere
    could I catch sight of her.

                                And all this time,
    in travail,° sobbing, gaining on the current,
    we rowed into the strait—Scylla to port
    and on our starboard beam Charybdis, dire
805 gorge° of the salt sea tide. By heaven! when she
    vomited, all the sea was like a caldron
    seething over intense fire, when the mixture
    suddenly heaves and rises.

Scylla. Greek bronze.
National Archaeological Museum, Athens.

783. founder (foun′dər) *v.:* sink.

786. combers (kōm′ərz) *n.:* large waves.

788. smother (smu*th*′ər) *n.:* commotion; violent action or disorder.

770–793. *Think about what kind of leader Odysseus is. What does he tell his men, to reassure them? What does he decide not to tell them? Why?*

795. cuirass (kwi·ras′) *n.:* armor for the breast and back.

802. travail (trə·vāl′) *n.:* hard, exhausting work or effort; tiring labor.

805. gorge (gôrj) *n.:* throat and jaws of a greedy, all-devouring being.

CONTENT-AREA CONNECTIONS

History: Nautical Terminology
The ancient Greeks were skilled sailors, and Homer demonstrates his knowledge of seafaring through his use of nautical terminology in Odysseus's exhortation to his men.
Paired activity. Write the following terms and definitions on the chalkboard. Have pairs of students match the numbered terms and

the lettered definitions. Suggest that students use a dictionary if they need to.

1. aft [g]
2. bow [b]
3. deck [d]

a. part of a ship that supports the sail
b. front part of a ship
c. front part of a ship's main deck

                                        The shot spume
soared to the landside heights, and fell like rain.

810   But when she swallowed the sea water down   **D**
      we saw the funnel of the maelstrom, heard
      the rock bellowing all around, and dark
      sand raged on the bottom far below.
      My men all blanched° against the gloom, our eyes   **814. blanched** (blancht) *v.:* grew
815   were fixed upon that yawning mouth in fear   pale.
      of being devoured.
                                    Then Scylla made her strike,
      whisking six of my best men from the ship.

      I happened to glance aft at ship and oarsmen
      and caught sight of their arms and legs, dangling
820   high overhead. Voices came down to me
      in anguish, calling my name for the last time.

      A man surf-casting on a point of rock
      for bass or mackerel, whipping his long rod
      to drop the sinker and the bait far out,   **E**
825   will hook a fish and rip it from the surface
      to dangle wriggling through the air;
                                        so these
      were borne aloft in spasms toward the cliff.

      She ate them as they shrieked there, in her den,
      in the dire grapple,° reaching still for me—   **829. dire grapple:** terrible struggle.
830   and deathly pity ran me through
      at that sight—far the worst I ever suffered   **F**
      questing the passes of the strange sea.
                                    We rowed on.
      The Rocks were now behind; Charybdis, too,
      and Scylla dropped astern.
                                    Then we were coasting
835   the noble island of the god, where grazed
      those cattle with wide brows, and bounteous flocks
      of Helios, lord of noon, who rides high heaven.
      From the black ship, far still at sea, I heard   843. *Suppose you wanted
      the lowing of the cattle winding home   to write a* **screenplay** *dramatizing
840   and sheep bleating; and heard, too, in my heart   this famous part of the* Odyssey—
      the words of blind Teiresias of Thebes   *the crew's struggle against the
      and Circe of Aeaea: both forbade me   Sirens and against Scylla and
      the island of the world's delight, the Sun. . . ."   Charybdis. Who would be your
                                                                 main characters? How would you
                                    (*from* Book 12)   use music and visuals—especially
                                                                 in the Sirens scene? Write down
                                                                 your ideas about filming the epic.*

---

4. foredeck [c]   **d.** floor of a ship that   **8. starboard** [i]   **h.** rear end of a ship
                            covers a lower portion   **9. stern** [h]   **i.** right-hand side of a ship
5. mast [a]   **e.** a bar or handle for   **10. tiller** [e]   **j.** left-hand side of a ship
                            turning a boat's rudder
6. port [j]   **f.** flat piece of wood or
                            metal used for steering
7. rudder [f]   **g.** at, near, or toward the
                            stern of a ship

D Reading Skills
Monitoring your comprehension.
Suggest that students stop to check their understanding of events and to visualize the action. They might identify details that help them picture the whirlpool Charybdis. [Details include "when she / vomited," "like a caldron / seething over intense fire," "heaves and rises," "spume / soared," "fell like rain," "funnel of the maelstrom," "rock bellowing," and "dark / sand raged."]

E Literary Focus
❷ **Homeric simile.** What things are being compared in this passage? [The action of Scylla grabbing the men is compared to a fisherman surf-casting.] **What is the effect of this comparison?** [Possible responses: It emphasizes the quick and unexpected nature of what has happened; it highlights the helplessness of the men and the fact that they are food for Scylla.]

F Reading Skills
❷ **Expressing an opinion.** Do you agree that this scene seems like the worst described in the *Odyssey* so far? Why or why not? [Possible responses: For Odysseus it is the worst, because he knew that it would happen, and he probably feels guilty that he could do nothing to stop it; some of the scenes with the Cyclops seemed worse, especially the one in which Odysseus describes Polyphemus dribbling bits of men.]

Response to Margin Question
Line 843. Main characters might include Odysseus, his men, Circe, the Sirens, Scylla, and Charybdis. Students may suggest the use of music to represent the singing of the Sirens and the sounds of Scylla and Charybdis and a creative visual or costume for Scylla.

Odysseus warns his men not to touch the sun god's cattle. Storms rage for a month, and their food supply is exhausted. One sailor, Eurylochus, convinces the others that eating the cattle is preferable to starvation. Odysseus wakes up to discover that his men have feasted on the cattle. He curses the gods for letting him sleep during the feast so that he could not restrain his men.

DIRECT TEACHING

A **Reading Skills**

❓ Challenging the text. Since Odysseus is the captain, shouldn't he have just ordered his men to bypass Thrinakia? Explain your response. [Possible responses: Odysseus probably feared that the men would not obey such an order, because they had just been through a terrible ordeal and were emotionally and physically exhausted; no matter how his men felt, Odysseus had heard the warnings of both Teiresias and Circe and should have insisted on bypassing the island.]

B **Reading Skills**

❓ Interpreting. What does Odysseus mean when he says that no man can avoid the eye of Helios? [Since Helios is the sun god, he can see everything; no one can escape observation by the sun god.]

VIEWING THE ART

For information on the artist, see p. 662.

Activity. Ask students to describe the look in the eyes of the animal in the foreground. [Possible responses: fearful; alarmed.] What does the soldier in the foreground seem to be signaling? [Possible response: Perhaps he is cautioning the viewer not to tell Odysseus what the men are doing.]

THE CATTLE OF THE SUN GOD

A *Odysseus urges his exhausted crew to bypass Thrinakia, the island of the sun god, Helios. When the men insist on landing, Odysseus makes them swear not to touch the god's cattle. Odysseus is still speaking to Alcinous's court.*

"In the small hours of the third watch, when stars
845   that shone out in the first dusk of evening
had gone down to their setting, a giant wind
blew from heaven, and clouds driven by Zeus
shrouded land and sea in a night of storm;
so, just as Dawn with fingertips of rose
850   touched the windy world, we dragged our ship
to cover in a grotto, a sea cave
where nymphs had chairs of rock and sanded floors.
I mustered all the crew and said:

                         'Old shipmates,
our stores are in the ship's hold, food and drink;
855   the cattle here are not for our provision,
or we pay dearly for it.

                        Fierce the god is
who cherishes these heifers and these sheep:

B Helios; and no man avoids his eye.'

To this my fighters nodded. Yes. But now
860   we had a month of onshore gales, blowing
day in, day out—south winds, or south by east.
As long as bread and good red wine remained
to keep the men up, and appease their craving,
they would not touch the cattle. But in the end,
865   when all the barley in the ship was gone,
hunger drove them to scour the wild shore
with angling hooks, for fishes and sea fowl,

The Companions of Ulysses Slaying the Cattle of the Sun God Helios (16th century) by Pellegrino Tibaldi.
Palazzo Poggi, Bologna, Italy.

whatever fell into their hands; and lean days
wore their bellies thin.

870 So one day I withdrew to the interior
to pray the gods in solitude, for hope
that one might show me some way of salvation.
Slipping away, I struck across the island
to a sheltered spot, out of the driving gale.

875 I washed my hands there, and made supplication°
to the gods who own Olympus, all the gods—
but they, for answer, only closed my eyes
under slow drops of sleep.

Now on the shore Eurylochus
made his insidious° plea:

'Comrades,' he said,
880 'You've gone through everything; listen to what I say.
All deaths are hateful to us, mortal wretches,
but famine is the most pitiful, the worst
end that a man can come to.

Will you fight it?
Come, we'll cut out the noblest of these cattle
885 for sacrifice to the gods who own the sky;
and once at home, in the old country of Ithaca,
if ever that day comes—
we'll build a costly temple and adorn it
with every beauty for the Lord of Noon.

890 But if he flares up over his heifers lost,
wishing our ship destroyed, and if the gods
make cause with him, why, then I say: Better
open your lungs to a big sea once for all
than waste to skin and bones on a lonely island!'

895 Thus Eurylochus; and they murmured 'Aye!'
trooping away at once to round up heifers.
Now, that day tranquil cattle with broad brows
were grazing near, and soon the men drew up
around their chosen beasts in ceremony.

900 They plucked the leaves that shone on a tall oak—
having no barley meal—to strew° the victims,
performed the prayers and ritual, knifed the kine
and flayed each carcass, cutting thighbones free
to wrap in double folds of fat. These offerings,
905 with strips of meat, were laid upon the fire.
Then, as they had no wine, they made libation°

875. supplication (sup′lə·kā′shən)
n.: humble requests; prayers.

879. insidious (in·sid′ē·əs) *adj.*:
treacherous; more dangerous than
is apparent.

C

D

878–894. *What is Eurylochus's "insidious plea"? If you
were a member of the crew, would
you be swayed by this argument, or
would you heed Odysseus's warning?
Do you think murdering the cattle is
justified, or is it an offense against
the god Helios?*

901. strew (stro͞o) *v.*: scatter about.

906. libation (lī·bā′shən) *n.*:
offering of wine or oil to the gods.

**C Learners Having
Difficulty**

? Questioning. Who is the
"Lord of Noon"? [Helios, the sun
god]

D Reading Skills

? Interpreting. What does
Eurylochus mean by this comment?
[He is talking about drowning.]

**Response to
Margin Question**

Lines 878–894. Eurylochus argues
that it is better to live and risk
Helios's anger by slaughtering his
cattle than to die of starvation.
Some students might agree. Since
the men are facing certain death,
why not kill the cattle and try to
appease Helios later? At least they
would have a chance of surviving.
Others will feel that the men should
explore other alternatives, such as
waiting a little longer or appealing
to Helios before they kill his cattle.

Check Test: Short Answer

Guide the class in answering these comprehension questions. Have students support
their responses with passages from the text.
Answers may vary slightly.

1. **Why is Odysseus able to withstand
   Circe's magical powers?** [Odysseus is pro-
   tected by a magic herb given him by
   Hermes.]

2. **Whom does Odysseus visit in the Land of
   the Dead?** [Odysseus consults the blind
   prophet Teiresias.]

3. **What prediction does Circe make to
   Odysseus about his journey home?** [Circe
   prophesies that only Odysseus will survive
   the trip.]

4. **Which two monsters does Odysseus pass
   between after facing the Sirens?** [Odysseus
   and his crew navigate between Scylla and
   Charybdis.]

5. **What does Odysseus order his men not
   to do on Thrinakia?** [He orders them not
   to kill the cattle of Helios.]

A Literary Focus

? Character. In the *Odyssey*, Odysseus constantly takes credit when things go well. Now, when a tragedy occurs, he blames the gods for making him fall asleep. What does this reveal about his character? [Possible responses: Odysseus has a big ego and takes responsibility only for successes; Odysseus cannot accept failure and must find someone or something else to blame.]

Response to Margin Question

Lines 921–930. Helios is angry because Odysseus's men have slaughtered his cattle.

Assessment

■ *Holt Assessment: Literature, Reading, and Vocabulary*

---

with clear spring water, broiling the entrails° first;
and when the bones were burnt and tripes° shared,
they spitted the carved meat.

                              Just then my slumber
910   left me in a rush, my eyes opened,
and I went down the seaward path. No sooner
had I caught sight of our black hull, than savory
odors of burnt fat eddied around me;
grief took hold of me, and I cried aloud:

915   'O Father Zeus and gods in bliss forever,
you made me sleep away this day of mischief!
O cruel drowsing, in the evil hour!
Here they sat, and a great work they contrived.'

Lampetia° in her long gown meanwhile
920   had borne swift word to the Overlord of Noon:

'They have killed your kine.'

                        And the Lord Helios
burst into angry speech amid the immortals:

'O Father Zeus and gods in bliss forever,
punish Odysseus' men! So overweening,°
925   now they have killed my peaceful kine, my joy
at morning when I climbed the sky of stars,
and evening, when I bore westward from heaven.
Restitution or penalty they shall pay—
and pay in full—or I go down forever
930   to light the dead men in the underworld.' . . ."

                             (*from* Book 12)

When Odysseus and his men set sail again, they are punished with death—a thunderbolt from Zeus destroys their boat, and all the men drown. Only Odysseus survives. Exhausted and nearly drowned, he makes his way to Calypso's island, where we met him originally, in Book 5.

   Odysseus has brought us up to date. He can now rest and enjoy the comforts of Alcinous's court—but not for long. Ahead lies his most difficult task—reclaiming his own kingdom.

   At this moment of suspense, Homer might have put aside his harp until the next night.

Vocabulary
restitution (res′tə·too′shən) *n.*: compensation; repayment.

907. **entrails** (en′trālz) *n.*: intestines; guts.
908. **tripes** (trīps) *n.*: stomach parts.

919. **Lampetia** (lam·pē′shē·ə): daughter of Helios. Lampetia guarded her father's herds of cattle.

924. **overweening** (o′vər·wēn′iŋ) *adj.*: excessively proud.

921–930. *What exactly has happened to cause the god's fury?*

Zeus seated on his throne, holding thunderbolts. Bronze statuette found on Mount Lyceum (6th century B.C.).

National Archaeological Museum, Athens.

Response and Analysis

from the Odyssey, Part One

Reading Check

1. In a chart like the one below, **summarize** the **external conflict** and its **resolution** in each episode. 🏛️

Adventure	Summary
Calypso	
Lotus Eaters	
Cyclops	
Circe	
Sirens; Scylla and Charybdis	
Cattle of the Sun God	

2. What does Odysseus learn about his future from blind Teiresias in the Land of the Dead?

Thinking Critically

3. "Nobody" in Greek is *outis,* which sounds like *Odysseus.* In his **conflict** with the Cyclops, how does Odysseus overcome the monster through a clever use of language? What curse at the end of this adventure **foreshadows** trouble?

4. What conclusions about the deceptive nature of beauty can you draw from the Circe episode?

5. Book 5 of the *Odyssey* focuses on Odysseus's captivity on Calypso's island. Suzanne Vega (see the **Connection** on page 655) expresses Calypso's view of the affair. How does her song compare with Homer's story? Whom do you sympathize with—Odysseus or Calypso?

6. From what you've observed of Odysseus, how would you describe what the Greeks valued in a hero? Do we value these same traits today? Check your Quickwrite notes for page 649. ✏️

Extending and Evaluating

7. How many of the monsters or threats to Odysseus in this part of the epic are female? What do you think of the way women are portrayed so far?

WRITING

It's Alive!

In "The Cyclops in the Ocean" (see the **Connection** on page 672), the modern poet Nikki Giovanni **personifies** a tropical storm—that is, she describes the storm as if it were a living creature. Write a paragraph personifying some other violent force of nature. Describe how it looks and sounds and what it does with its victims.

Cause and Effect

Characters in the *Odyssey* often use cause-and-effect arguments when they try to **persuade.** For example, when Odysseus asks the Cyclops for help, he warns the Cyclops of the effects of offending the gods by harming a guest. Calypso tries to persuade Odysseus to remain with her by mentioning the effects he will suffer if he leaves her. Choose one argument from the epic, and describe why it is persuasive or how you think it could be strengthened.

▶ Use "Persuading with Cause and Effect," pages 734–741, for help with this assignment.

INTERNET
Projects and Activities
Keyword: LE5 9-10

Odyssey, Part One **687**

Response and Analysis

2. Odysseus learns that Poseidon will cause him rough seas; that his men will be killed; that he will be lost for years but eventually return home to chaos; that he will appease Poseidon; and that he will die at sea when he is old.

Thinking Critically

3. Odysseus calls himself "Nohbdy," thus preventing the other Cyclopes from helping Polyphemus. The Cyclops's curse foreshadows the difficulties Odysseus will face before reaching home.

4. Possible answers: Physical beauty does not signify inner virtue; it is unwise to be seduced by physical beauty.

5. In the song, Calypso is motivated by love to let Odysseus go; in the epic she is ordered to do so. The song tells the tale from her point of view; the epic, from his. Students' sympathies will likely be divided.

6. Possible answers: discipline, loyalty, wit, intelligence, bravery, love of home, and obedience to divine powers. Many students will say that these qualities are still valued today.

Extending and Evaluating

7. Except for the Cicones and Polyphemus, all are female. Some students may say that females are portrayed as monsters; others may point to the positive portrayal of Athena.

Reading Check

1. Possible Answers

Calypso. Calypso releases Odysseus. Odysseus leaves on a raft. Poseidon raises a storm, and the hero is shipwrecked on Scheria.

Lotus Eaters. Three of Odysseus's men eat the lotus and lose their desire to leave. Odysseus forces them onto the ships.

Cyclops. Trapped in Polyphemus's cave, Odysseus and his men blind the monster and escape. Odysseus taunts the Cyclops, who curses him.

Circe. Circe turns Odysseus's crew into swine. Odysseus compels her to restore them to human form.

Sirens; Scylla and Charybdis. Odysseus plugs the crew's ears and has himself tied to the mast so that he may hear the Sirens' song. Between Scylla and Charybdis he loses six men.

Cattle of the Sun God. Odysseus's men kill Helios's cattle. Zeus sinks their ship; only Odysseus survives.

Vocabulary Development

Practice I

Word maps will vary. Here is a sample for *rancor*.

Who displays rancor in the *Odyssey*? • Polyphemus • Poseidon	What might make me feel rancor? • being treated unfairly

rancor

Whom would I expect to show rancor? • people who believe they've been wronged • nations at war • bigots	Who is unlikely to show rancor? • a puppy • an easygoing person

Practice 2

1. Scylla is compared to a fisherman and the men to fish on a line. None of us has ever seen Scylla snatch men from a ship, but most of us can picture a fisherman hauling his wriggling catches out of the sea.

2. Possible answers: With a burst of flame and smoke, the rocket rose like a powerful bird trailing a tail of fire. The craters sprinkled across the surface of the moon look like the round depressions made by raindrops falling onto a sandy beach. The one-celled creatures moved about under the lens of the microscope like insects scurrying and jostling one another.

Vocabulary Development

Semantic Mapping

PRACTICE 1

With a partner, create a semantic map for each Word Bank word. Make up questions about each word, and provide your own answers. A sample map is done for *formidable*. Compare your maps in class.

Who is formidable in the *Odyssey*? • Odysseus • the gods	Do I want to be called formidable? • Yes, I'd like to be formidable as a center forward.

formidable

What have I seen that is formidable? • Josh on football field • Emma in math class • volcano	What is not formidable? • ant • baby • peaceful pond

Figures of Speech—Homeric Similes

In a **figure of speech,** a writer compares one thing to something else, something quite different from it in all but a few important ways. For example, Homer compares the army of the Cicones to "the leaves and blades of spring" (lines 163–164). He is saying that enemy soldiers suddenly appeared everywhere, as green grass and leaves do in spring. The comparison is surprising because a fierce army seems very different from the tender leaves and grass of spring.

The **Homeric simile** (also called **epic simile**) is an extended comparison between something that the audience cannot have seen (such as Odysseus boring out the Cyclops's eye) and something ordinary that they would know (such as a shipbuilder drilling a plank; see lines 379–381 on page 665).

SKILLS FOCUS

Vocabulary Skills
Create semantic maps. Analyze Homeric (epic) similes.

PRACTICE 2

1. Re-read lines 822–827 on page 683. Explain how this Homeric simile brings the audience into the story by comparing a strange, unfamiliar occurrence to something familiar.

2. Make up three Homeric similes of your own, in which you compare something strange or unfamiliar to something ordinary and familiar. (Remember that a simile makes a comparison using a word such as *like, as,* or *resembles*.) You might consider describing one of the following things:

   • a space launch

   • the surface of the moon

   • something you see through a microscope

DIFFERENTIATING INSTRUCTION

Learners Having Difficulty
Read these similes from the *Odyssey*, and explain how each compares an unfamiliar occurrence to something familiar.

1. "A man in a distant field, no hearth fires near, / will hide a fresh brand in his bed of embers / to keep a spark alive for the next day; / so in the leaves Odysseus hid himself. . . ." [Odysseus is compared to a burning stick buried in embers to preserve a spark of fire.]

2. "Athena . . . made [Odysseus] seem taller, and massive too, with crisping hair / in curls like petals of wild hyacinth / but all red-golden. Think of gold infused / on silver by a craftsman. . . ." [The images of flower petals and finely wrought precious metals help us visualize the radiance of the hero.]

Before You Read

from the Odyssey, Part Two

Make the Connection

Quickwrite 🖊

Imagine that someone has been absent from home for many years. What might that person think or feel upon returning home? Make a list of possible reactions, and save your notes.

Literary Focus

Living Characters

Odysseus is brave and clever. Penelope is faithful—and clever, too. Circe is lovely and bewitching. Homer has depicted his characters—mortals, gods, goddesses, and monsters alike—with bold, vivid strokes.

Storytellers reveal **character traits** in many ways. As you read, look carefully at what characters *say* and *do* and *think*. Note how they *interact* and how they are *described*. Then, think about what all this information tells you. Is a character noble or evil? wise or foolish? arrogant or humble? Does the character possess a combination of both positive and negative traits?

Part Two of the *Odyssey* contains the climax of the epic. Suspenseful and exciting, it is also deeply moving, as Odysseus returns home to Ithaca and is reunited with his wife, Penelope. As you read, think about what these characters are like and why they have lived in the imagination of readers for centuries.

Vocabulary Development

candor (kan′dər) *n.:* honesty; frankness.

disdainful (dis·dān′fəl) *adj.:* scornful; regarding someone as beneath you.

adorn (ə·dôrn′) *v.:* add beauty to; decorate.

revelry (rev′əl·rē) *n.:* merrymaking; festivity.

glowered (glou′ərd) *v.:* glared; stared angrily.

avails (ə·vālz′) *v.:* is of use; helps.

lavished (lav′isht) *v.:* gave generously.

aloof (ə·lōōf′) *adj.:* at a distance; unfriendly.

pliant (plī′ənt) *adj.:* flexible.

tremulous (trem′yōō·ləs) *adj.:* trembling; shaking.

INTERNET

Vocabulary Practice
•
More About Homer
•
Keyword: LE5 9-10

SKILLS FOCUS

Literary Skills
Understand characteristics of epic poetry, including character traits.

SKILLS FOCUS,
pp. 689–717

Grade-Level Skills

■ **Literary Skills**
Analyze interactions between characters (such as internal and external conflict and motivation) and the way those interactions affect the plot.

■ **Literary Skills**
Understand and explain characteristics of epic poetry.

■ **Reading Skills**
Monitor your comprehension.

Summary *at grade level*

After trying to find out whether his father is still alive, Telemachus returns to Ithaca. He visits Eumaeus, the swineherd, who explains that Penelope is besieged by suitors. Still grieving for her lost husband, she refuses to remarry. Odysseus, disguised in beggar's rags, is also in the swineherd's hut, but Telemachus does not recognize his father. The three men share a meal, and then the swineherd is sent to tell Penelope about her son's return. Athena appears and transforms Odysseus into his youthful self. Telemachus is incredulous and suspects a trick, but Odysseus reassures him. Father and son tearfully rejoice.

RESOURCES: READING

Planning
■ *One-Stop Planner* CD-ROM with ExamView Test Generator

Differentiating Instruction
■ *Holt Reading Solutions*
■ *Holt Adapted Reader*
■ *Supporting Instruction in Spanish*

■ *Audio CD Library, Selections and Summaries in Spanish*

Vocabulary
■ *Vocabulary Development*

Assessment
■ *Holt Assessment: Literature, Reading, and Vocabulary*

■ *One-Stop Planner* CD-ROM with ExamView Test Generator
■ *Holt Online Assessment*

Internet
■ go.hrw.com (Keyword: LE5 9-10)
■ *Elements of Literature Online*

Media
■ *Audio CD Library*

Selection Starter

Motivate. Remind students that in "The Land of the Dead," in Part One, Teiresias, warns Odysseus that he will find his "house filled with trouble: insolent men / eating your livestock as they court your lady." Ask students to speculate about what Odysseus will do, judging from the hero's character traits and his dealings with adversaries in previous episodes. Ask students what they themselves would do if they were faced with a similar situation.

Preview Vocabulary

Have students work in pairs on the following exercises to reinforce their understanding of the Vocabulary words for Part Two (p. 689).

1. Describe the way an <u>aloof</u> person acts.
2. Name a <u>pliant</u> material.
3. What might make you <u>tremulous</u>?
4. Describe a time when you engaged in <u>revelry</u>.
5. Show how someone <u>glowered</u> at another person.
6. Tell how a sharp beak <u>avails</u> a bird of prey.
7. Describe the way you would feel if someone <u>lavished</u> praise on you.
8. Describe a situation in which <u>candor</u> would be important.
9. Show how a <u>disdainful</u> person acts.
10. Describe the way you might <u>adorn</u> a window for a holiday.

PART TWO: COMING HOME

In Book 13, Odysseus, laden with gifts, is returned in secret to Ithaca in one of the magically swift Phaeacian ships. In Ithaca, Athena appears to the hero. Because his home is full of enemies, she advises him to proceed disguised as a beggar. Now Odysseus must succeed not only by physical power but also by intelligence.

In Book 14, Odysseus, in his beggar's disguise, finds his way to the hut of Eumaeus, his old and trusty swineherd. Eumaeus is the very image of faithfulness in a servant—a quality much admired by Homer's society. The introduction of members of the so-called servant class as important actors is unusual in epic poetry, and it indicates Homer's originality. Odysseus is politely entertained by Eumaeus, but the king remains disguised from his old servant.

In Book 15, Athena appears to Odysseus's son, Telemachus. The young man has gone to Pylos and Sparta to talk to old comrades of his father's to try to discover if Odysseus is alive or dead. Athena advises him to return to Ithaca. His home—the palace of Odysseus—has been overrun by his mother's suitors. These arrogant men are spending money from Telemachus's inheritance on feasting and drinking, and they are demanding that his mother, Penelope, take one of them as a husband. Athena warns Telemachus that the suitors plan to ambush him. Telemachus boards a ship for home, lands secretly on Ithaca, and heads toward the hut of the swineherd.

As father and son move closer and closer together, the suspense becomes great. Now Homer is ready to recount what could be the most dramatic moment in the epic. Remember that Odysseus has not seen his son for twenty years. Telemachus has been away from Ithaca for a year.

Penelope at Her Loom (detail), from *The Story of Virtuous Women* series (c. 1480–1483). Wool tapestry.

Marie Antoinette Evans Fund. Courtesy, Museum of Fine Arts, Boston.

SKILLS REVIEW

Using prior knowledge. Before students begin reading Part Two of the *Odyssey*, suggest that reviewing what they have read so far can help them set the stage for the events to come and enhance their understanding of what they read. Remind them that like audiences in Homer's time, they already know a great deal about what lies ahead in the epic. You might suggest that they re-read Homer's invocation on p. 651.

Activity. Write a few phrases or sentences describing what you already know about

• the situation in Odysseus's home
• Penelope
• Telemachus
• the suitors

But there were two men in the mountain hut—
Odysseus and the swineherd. At first light
blowing their fire up, they cooked their breakfast
and sent their lads out, driving herds to root
in the tall timber.

935   When Telemachus came,
the wolfish troop of watchdogs only fawned on him
as he advanced. Odysseus heard them go
and heard the light crunch of a man's footfall—
at which he turned quickly to say:

                              "Eumaeus,

940 here is one of your crew come back, or maybe
another friend: the dogs are out there snuffling
belly down; not one has even growled.
I can hear footsteps—"

                 But before he finished
his tall son stood at the door.

                      The swineherd

945 rose in surprise, letting a bowl and jug
tumble from his fingers. Going forward,
he kissed the young man's head, his shining eyes
and both hands, while his own tears brimmed and fell.
Think of a man whose dear and only son,

950 born to him in exile, reared with labor,
has lived ten years abroad and now returns:
how would that man embrace his son! Just so
the herdsman clapped his arms around Telemachus
and covered him with kisses—for he knew

955 the lad had got away from death. He said:

"Light of my days, Telemachus,
you made it back! When you took ship for Pylos°
I never thought to see you here again.
Come in, dear child, and let me feast my eyes;

960 here you are, home from the distant places!
How rarely, anyway, you visit us,
your own men, and your own woods and pastures!
Always in the town, a man would think
you loved the suitors' company, those dogs!"

Odysseus and Telemachus.
Mosaic (1st century A.D.)
(31.5 cm wide).
Kunsthistorisches Museum,
Vienna, Austria.

957. Pylos (pī′lōs): home of Nestor, one of Odysseus's fellow soldiers in the Trojan War. Telemachus had gone to see if Nestor knew anything about Odysseus's whereabouts.

A Reading Skills

? Finding details. What details in this passage indicate Telemachus's and Eumaeus's hospitality? [When Telemachus enters the room, he asks the beggar, Odysseus, to remain seated; Eumaeus builds a couch for Telemachus; Eumaeus feeds Telemachus and Odysseus and gives them wine.]

Response to Margin Question

Lines 974–990. Students should note that Odysseus is still in disguise during the scene. Telemachus and Eumaeus treat him courteously. Odysseus might be thinking of how best to reveal his identity to his son and wife and how to oust the suitors. Telemachus and Eumaeus might also be thinking about how to get rid of the suitors.

---

965   Telemachus with his clear <u>candor</u> said:

"I am with you, Uncle.° See now, I have come
because I wanted to see you first, to hear from you
if Mother stayed at home—or is she married
off to someone, and Odysseus' bed

970   left empty for some gloomy spider's weaving?"
Gently the forester replied to this:

"At home indeed your mother is, poor lady
still in the women's hall. Her nights and days
are wearied out with grieving."

                                        Stepping back

975   he took the bronze-shod lance, and the young prince
entered the cabin over the worn door stone.
Odysseus moved aside, yielding his couch,
but from across the room Telemachus checked him:

980   "Friend, sit down; we'll find another chair
in our own hut. Here is the man to make one!"

The swineherd, when the quiet man sank down,
built a new pile of evergreens and fleeces—
a couch for the dear son of great Odysseus—
A   then gave them trenchers° of good meat, left over

985   from the roast pork of yesterday, and heaped up
willow baskets full of bread, and mixed
an ivy bowl of honey-hearted wine.
Then he in turn sat down, facing Odysseus,
their hands went out upon the meat and drink

990   as they fell to, ridding themselves of hunger. . . .

Not realizing that the stranger is his father, Telemachus tries to protect him as best he can. He says that the beggar cannot stay in the palace hall because he will be abused by the drunken suitors.

  The swineherd is sent to Penelope with news of her son's return. Now even Athena cannot stand the suspense any longer. She turns to Odysseus, who is still in beggar's rags:

. . . She tipped her golden wand upon the man,
making his cloak pure white, and the knit tunic
fresh around him. Lithe° and young she made him,

966. Uncle: here, a term of affection.

The return of Odysseus. Terracotta relief believed to be from the island of Melos (first half of the 5th century B.C.).

The Metropolitan Museum of Art, New York. Fletcher Fund, 1930 (30.11.9). Photograph ©1982 The Metropolitan Museum of Art.

984. trenchers (tren′chərz) *n.:* wooden platters.

974–990. *Who is still in disguise in this scene? How does the ancient Greeks' regard for hospitality affect the way the other characters treat him? What do you think each character is feeling and thinking as he eats?*

993. lithe (līth) *adj.:* limber.

Vocabulary
candor (kan′dər) *n.:* honesty; frankness.

DIFFERENTIATING INSTRUCTION

Learners Having Difficulty
Pair students with more proficient readers, and have the pairs take turns reading aloud ten lines at a time. Have the listening partner summarize what takes place in the passage before the roles are switched. Tell students to discuss sections that were unclear in the first reading.

English-Language Learners
Have students work in pairs to identify key scenes in the epic, such as Telemachus's arrival at the swineherd's hut or the blinding of the Cyclops. Then, have students draw or paint the scene and write a caption describing the action. Afterward, encourage students to use their illustration as part of an oral summary of a section of the epic.

ruddy with sun, his jawline clean, the beard
995 no longer gray upon his chin. And she
withdrew when she had done.

                 Then Lord Odysseus
reappeared—and his son was thunderstruck.
Fear in his eyes, he looked down and away
as though it were a god, and whispered:

                               "Stranger,
1000 you are no longer what you were just now!
Your cloak is new; even your skin! You are
one of the gods who rule the sweep of heaven!
Be kind to us, we'll make you fair oblation°
and gifts of hammered gold. Have mercy on us!"

1003. oblation (äb·lā′shən) *n.:* offering of a sacrifice. Telemachus thinks the stranger is a god.

1005 The noble and enduring man replied:

"No god. Why take me for a god? No, no.
I am that father whom your boyhood lacked
and suffered pain for lack of. I am he."

Held back too long, the tears ran down his cheeks
as he embraced his son.

1010   Only Telemachus,
uncomprehending, wild
with incredulity,° cried out:

1012. incredulity (in′krə·dōō′lə·tē) *n.:* disbelief.

                         "You cannot
be my father Odysseus! Meddling spirits
conceived this trick to twist the knife in me!
1015 No man of woman born could work these wonders
by his own craft, unless a god came into it
with ease to turn him young or old at will.
I swear you were in rags and old,
and here you stand like one of the immortals!"

1020 Odysseus brought his ranging mind to bear
and said:
                  "This is not princely, to be swept
away by wonder at your father's presence.
No other Odysseus will ever come,
for he and I are one, the same; his bitter
1025 fortune and his wanderings are mine.
Twenty years gone, and I am back again
on my own island. . . ."

                Then, throwing
his arms around this marvel of a father,
Telemachus began to weep. Salt tears

Telemachus Sees His Father (1875). Lithograph by Friedrich Preller the Elder.
Archiv f.Kunst and Geschichte, Berlin.

Odyssey, Part Two 693

B Reading Skills

? Making inferences. What does Telemachus's response to Odysseus's transformation suggest about the relationship between the ancient Greeks and their gods? [Possible responses: The gods did not normally appear to mortals, and when they did, it was often to punish them; the ancient Greeks feared their gods and felt that they had to be appeased and showered with gifts even if humans were not aware of having done anything wrong.]

C Literary Focus

? Epithets. What epithets are used to characterize Odysseus here? ["noble and enduring"]

D Reading Skills

Monitoring your comprehension. Suggest that students stop at this point to check their understanding of events and to ask questions—for example, "Why has Athena changed Odysseus's appearance?" [Possible response: Perhaps she wants to move events along more quickly.]

Special Education Students

For lessons designed for special education students, see *Holt Reading Solutions*.

Advanced Learners

Most of the excerpts in Part One are told from the first-person point of view, as Odysseus recounts his adventures to the court of King Alcinous. Those in Part Two are told from the third-person point of view. Have students compare and contrast the experience of reading each part. How does the change in point of view affect their responses to the characters and events?

Odysseus disguises himself as a beggar once again and heads toward home. Odysseus's old hound, Argos, who lies abandoned outside the gates, recognizes his master's voice. Wagging his tail, the faithful dog greets his master and then dies.

DIRECT TEACHING

Ⓐ Literary Focus

❓ Homeric simile. To what are Odysseus's and Telemachus's cries compared? [the cries of a hawk whose young have been stolen from the nest]

Ⓑ Literary Focus

❓ Determining author's purpose. Why would a great epic concern itself with an old dog? [Possible responses: Perhaps the dog will play a role in the coming events; the dog may be a symbol of loyalty; the way a society treats animals can reveal its values.]

Ⓒ Reading Skills

❓ Responding to the text. How does this description of Argos make you feel? [Possible responses: sad about the dog's condition; angry with the people who have neglected him.]

Ⓓ Literary Focus

❓ Character. What does this scene reveal about Odysseus's character? [Possible response: Odysseus is sensitive, but he is able to hide his feelings; he has self-control.]

Responses to Margin Question

Lines 1005–1035. Possible response: Students should explain their choice. The problems that now face Odysseus and Telemachus are ousting the suitors and restoring order to the kingdom. Odysseus must also renew his relationship with Penelope.

1030   rose from the wells of longing in both men,
Ⓐ   and cries burst from both as keen and fluttering
        as those of the great taloned hawk,
        whose nestlings° farmers take before they fly.
        So helplessly they cried, pouring out tears,
1035   and might have gone on weeping so till sundown. . . .

                                        (*from* Book 16)

1033. nestlings (nestʹliŋz) *n.:* young birds that are not ready to leave the nest.

1005–1035. *Which part of this recognition scene between father and son do you find most moving or most dramatic? Sum up the problems that now face father and son in the palace at Ithaca.*

THE BEGGAR AND THE FAITHFUL DOG

Telemachus returns to the family compound and is greeted tearfully by his mother, Penelope, and his old nurse, Eurycleia. A soothsayer has told his mother that Odysseus is alive and in Ithaca. However, Telemachus does not report that he has seen his father. The suspense builds as Odysseus, once again disguised as a beggar, returns to his home, accompanied only by the swineherd. He has been away for twenty years. Only one creature recognizes him.

                                        While he spoke
        an old hound, lying near, pricked up his ears
        and lifted up his muzzle. This was Argos,
Ⓑ   trained as a puppy by Odysseus,
1040   but never taken on a hunt before
        his master sailed for Troy. The young men, afterward,
        hunted wild goats with him, and hare, and deer,
        but he had grown old in his master's absence.
        Treated as rubbish now, he lay at last
1045   upon a mass of dung before the gates—
Ⓒ   manure of mules and cows, piled there until
        field hands could spread it on the king's estate.
        Abandoned there, and half destroyed with flies,
        old Argos lay.
                                But when he knew he heard
1050   Odysseus' voice nearby, he did his best
        to wag his tail, nose down, with flattened ears,
        having no strength to move nearer his master.
        And the man looked away,
Ⓓ   wiping a salt tear from his cheek; but he
1055   hid this from Eumaeus. Then he said:

        "I marvel that they leave this hound to lie
        here on the dung pile;
        he would have been a fine dog, from the look of him,

Laconian hound scratching his head. Detail from an Attic red-figured ceramic scyphus, or drinking cup, by the Euergides Painter (c. 500 B.C.).
Ashmolean Museum, Oxford, England.

Odysseus is recognized by
Eurycleia when she washes his feet.
Roman relief.

Museo Nazionale Romano, Rome, Italy.

1060 though I can't say as to his power and speed
when he was young. You find the same good build
in house dogs, table dogs landowners keep
all for style."

And you replied, Eumaeus:

"A hunter owned him—but the man is dead
1065 in some far place. If this old hound could show
the form he had when Lord Odysseus left him,
going to Troy, you'd see him swift and strong.
He never shrank from any savage thing
he'd brought to bay in the deep woods; on the scent
1070 no other dog kept up with him. Now misery
has him in leash. His owner died abroad,
and here the women slaves will take no care of him.
You know how servants are: without a master
they have no will to labor, or excel.
1075 For Zeus who views the wide world takes away
half the manhood of a man, that day
he goes into captivity and slavery."

Eumaeus crossed the court and went straight forward
into the megaron° among the suitors;
1080 but death and darkness in that instant closed
the eyes of Argos, who had seen his master,
Odysseus, after twenty years. . . .

(*from* Book 17)

 **1044–1071.** *Here again we*
hear about people who mock the
sacred laws of respect and hospital-
ity. In showing us how the old dog
is treated, what is Homer telling us
about conditions in Ithaca?

1078. megaron (meg′ə·rän) *n.:* great
hall or central room.

E

F

Odyssey, Part Two   **695**

DIRECT TEACHING

E **Literary Focus**

? **Irony.** Why is this scene ironic?
[Eumaeus does not realize, although
the reader does, that he is speaking
to Odysseus about Odysseus.]

F **Reading Skills**

? **Expressing an opinion.** What
do you think of Eumaeus's statement about servants? [Possible
responses: It's unjust to assume that
all servants are lazy and unable to
think for themselves; being a servant
is hard enough, so it's no wonder
most servants do only what's
required of them; slavery by its very
nature keeps human beings from
realizing their full potential.]

Response to
Margin Question

Lines 1044–1071. Possible
response: The overall condition of
Ithaca, like that of Argos, suggests
neglect and abandonment.

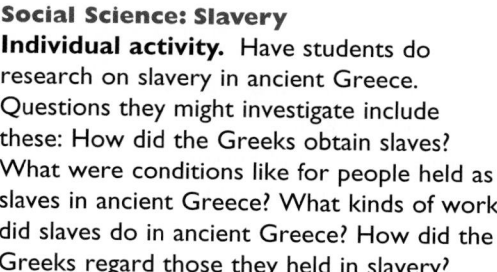

CONTENT-AREA CONNECTIONS

Social Science: Slavery
Individual activity. Have students do
research on slavery in ancient Greece.
Questions they might investigate include
these: How did the Greeks obtain slaves?
What were conditions like for people held as
slaves in ancient Greece? What kinds of work
did slaves do in ancient Greece? How did the
Greeks regard those they held in slavery?

Encourage students to prepare reports
from their research and to share them with
the class in oral, print, or multimedia
presentations.

A Literary Focus

? Character. What qualities does Penelope reveal through her actions? [Possible responses: generosity; hospitality; discretion; kindness; loyalty to her husband.]

B Reading Skills

? Making predictions. Judging from what you know about Odysseus, how do you predict he will deal with the suitors? [Possible responses: He will rally the people of Ithaca to drive out the suitors; he will take on the suitors single-handedly; he will use stealth and cunning to get them to leave.]

C Reading Skills

? Speculating. Why do you think Odysseus continues to conceal his identity from Penelope? [Possible responses: He is afraid that she will not believe him; he is worried that she might accidentally spoil the plans he has made for vanquishing the suitors.]

The Epic Continues

In the hall the "beggar" is taunted by the evil suitors, but Penelope supports him. She has learned that the ragged stranger claims to have news of her husband. Unaware of who the beggar is, she invites him to visit her later in the night to talk about Odysseus.

In Book 18, Penelope appears among the suitors and reproaches Telemachus for allowing the stranger to be abused. She certainly must have warmed her husband's heart by doing this and by singing the praises of her lost Odysseus.

In Book 19, the suitors depart for the night, and Odysseus and Telemachus discuss their strategy. The clever hero goes as appointed to Penelope with the idea of testing her and her maids. (Some of the maids have not been loyal to the household and have been involved with the suitors.) The faithful wife receives her disguised husband. We can imagine the tension Homer's audience must have felt. Would Odysseus be recognized?

The "beggar" spins a yarn about his origins, pretending that he has met Odysseus on his travels. He cannot resist praising the lost hero, and he does so successfully enough to bring tears to Penelope's eyes. We can be sure that this does not displease her husband.

The storytelling beggar reveals that he has heard that Odysseus is alive and is even now sailing for home. Penelope calls for the old nurse and asks her to wash the guest's feet—a sign of respect and honor. As Eurycleia does so, she recognizes Odysseus from a scar on his leg.

Quickly Odysseus swears the old nurse to secrecy. Meanwhile, Athena has cast a spell on Penelope so that she has taken no notice of this recognition scene. Penelope adds to the suspense by deciding on a test for the suitors on the next day. Without realizing it, she has now given Odysseus a way to defeat the men who threaten his wife and kingdom.

In Book 20, Odysseus, brooding over the shameless behavior of the maidservants and the suitors, longs to destroy his enemies but fears the revenge of their friends. Athena reassures him. Odysseus is told that the suitors will die.

Odysseus is recognized by Eurycleia. Detail from a scyphus, a drinking cup.
Museo Archeologico, Chiusi, Italy.

READING SKILLS REVIEW

Appositive phrases. In the *Odyssey*, Homer frequently uses epithets to characterize people. These epithets often consist of adjectives, appositives, or appositive phrases. An appositive is a noun or pronoun placed beside another noun or pronoun to explain or identify it: "Father Zeus, grant our old wish!"

An appositive phrase consists of an appositive and its modifiers: " '. . . Grant that Odysseus, <u>raider of cities</u>, never / see his home. . . .' "

Appositives and appositive phrases can precede or follow the noun they modify.
Activity. In the following items, double underline epithets consisting of adjectives and add a single underline to epithets consisting of appositives or appositive phrases.

1. crooked-minded Cronus
2. light of my days, Telemachus
3. Agamemnon, son of Atreus
4. thundering Zeus
5. Telemus, a son of Eurymus
6. great-hearted Odysseus

Penelope to Ulysses

Penelope, distressed by the suitors' demands that she marry one of them, plays a trick on them. She has told them that she is weaving a shroud (a cloth used to wrap a body for burial) for Laertes, her father-in-law. She promises that she will choose a husband when she has completed the work. "So every day I wove on the great loom, but every night by torchlight I unwove it. . . ." With this simple trick she has deceived her suitors for three years. What do this trick and this poem reveal about Penelope? As you read the Odyssey, look for places where she displays these same traits.

Like a spider committing suicide
each night I unweave the web of my day.
I have no peace.
About me the insistent buzz of flies
5 drones louder every day.
I am starving.
I watch them, always, unblinking stare.
All my dwindling will
I use in not moving, not trying, unweaving.
10 I pull in my empty nets
eating myself, waiting.

—Meredith Schwartz
Highland Park High School
Highland Park, New Jersey

An Ancient Gesture
Edna St. Vincent Millay

I thought, as I wiped my eyes on the corner of my apron:
Penelope did this too.
And more than once: you can't keep weaving all day
And undoing it all through the night;
5 Your arms get tired, and the back of your neck gets tight;
And along towards morning, when you think it will never be light,
And your husband has been gone, and you don't know where, for years,
Suddenly you burst into tears;
There is simply nothing else to do.

10 And I thought, as I wiped my eyes on the corner of my apron:
This is an ancient gesture, authentic, antique,
In the very best tradition, classic, Greek;
Ulysses did this too.
But only as a gesture,—a gesture which implied
15 To the assembled throng that he was much too moved to speak.
He learned it from Penelope . . .
Penelope, who really cried.

Odyssey, Part Two 697

Connection

Summary ⬌ *at grade level*

> This poem is written from the perspective of Penelope and describes her long, lonely wait for Odysseus.

DIRECT TEACHING

D Literary Focus

? Simile. How are Penelope's actions like those of a spider committing suicide? [A spider that destroys its own web cannot catch food and will starve; by unraveling her weaving, Penelope is precluding the possibility of a new marriage, choosing instead to cling to a past that may offer no promise.]

Connection

Summary ⬌ *at grade level*

> The speaker, like Penelope a woman who has been waiting years for her husband to return, reflects on the bond linking all women in this situation.

E Literary Focus

? Tone. How does this litany of words and phrases with positive connotations alter the tone of the poem? [Possible responses: The tone changes from one of weary resignation to one of self-affirmation; the speaker seems to be reciting the positive terms as a way of pulling herself together.]

Connecting and Comparing Texts

Ask students to discuss how this student poem connects with Homer's epic. What dimension does the student poem add to the portrayal of Penelope in the excerpts from the *Odyssey* in the text? [Possible response: It reveals the depth of her suffering and the toll Odysseus's absence and the handling of the suitors have taken on her.]

Next discuss how Millay's poem connects with the *Odyssey*. How does the speaker's situation compare with Penelope's? Point out that the speaker of the poem thinks of her experience as timeless and universal. Have students think of other gestures, emotions, and situations described in the *Odyssey* that are similarly timeless and universal—for

example, tears and hugs upon being reunited with a long-lost relative or friend (Odysseus and Telemachus); facing a bully (Odysseus and Polyphemus); wanting something that is dangerous (Odysseus and the Sirens).

Write students' ideas on the chalkboard, and ask for examples from modern life that parallel those in the epic.

Penelope has set a seemingly impossible test for her suitors— to string her husband's old bow and shoot an arrow through the sockets of twelve iron ax handles. A number of suitors try and fail; then Odysseus, still in his beggar's disguise, asks to try. Penelope agrees and then retires inside. Ignoring the taunts of the suitors, Odysseus performs the feat.

DIRECT TEACHING

VIEWING THE ART

The Italian painter **Bernadino Pínturicchio** (1454–1513) is best known for his works depicting historical themes rendered in the classical style.

Activity. Ask students to note the domestic details in this busy scene. What might the suitors be saying to Penelope? Has anyone yet noticed the ship outside the window?

Penelope with the Suitors (c. 1509) by Pínturicchio.

THE TEST OF THE GREAT BOW

In Book 21, Penelope, like many unwilling princesses of myth and fairy tale, proposes an impossible task for those who wish to marry her. By so doing, she causes the bloody events that lead to the restoration of her husband. The test involves stringing Odysseus's huge bow, an impossible feat for anyone except Odysseus himself. Odysseus had left his bow home in Ithaca twenty years earlier.

> Now the queen reached the storeroom door and halted.
> Here was an oaken sill, cut long ago
> and sanded clean and bedded true. Foursquare
> 1085 the doorjambs and the shining doors were set
> by the careful builder. Penelope untied the strap
> around the curving handle, pushed her hook
> into the slit, aimed at the bolts inside,
> and shot them back. Then came a rasping sound
> 1090 as those bright doors the key had sprung gave way—
> a bellow like a bull's vaunt° in a meadow—

1091. vaunt (vônt) *n.*: boast.

followed by her light footfall entering
over the plank floor. Herb-scented robes
lay there in chests, but the lady's milk-white arms

1095   went up to lift the bow down from a peg
in its own polished bow case.

                                    Now Penelope

sank down, holding the weapon on her knees,
and drew her husband's great bow out, and sobbed
and bit her lip and let the salt tears flow.

1100   Then back she went to face the crowded hall
tremendous bow in hand, and on her shoulder hung
the quiver spiked with coughing death. Behind, her
maids bore a basket full of ax heads, bronze
and iron implements for the master's game.

1105   Thus in her beauty she approached the suitors,
and near a pillar of the solid roof
she paused, her shining veil across her cheeks,
her maids on either hand and still,
then spoke to the banqueters:

                          "My lords, hear me:

1110   suitors indeed, you recommended this house
to feast and drink in, day and night, my husband
being long gone, long out of mind. You found
no justification for yourselves—none
except your lust to marry me. Stand up, then:

1115   we now declare a contest for that prize.
Here is my lord Odysseus' hunting bow.
Bend and string it if you can. Who sends an arrow
through iron ax-helve sockets,° twelve in line?
I join my life with his, and leave this place, my home,

1120   my rich and beautiful bridal house, forever
to be remembered, though I dream it only." . . .

*Many of the suitors boldly try the bow, but not one man can even
bend it enough to string it.*

Two men had meanwhile left the hall:
swineherd and cowherd, in companionship,
one downcast as the other. But Odysseus

1125   followed them outdoors, outside the court,
and coming up said gently:

                     "You, herdsman,
and you, too, swineherd, I could say a thing to you,
or should I keep it dark?

Odysseus slaying the suitors. Detail
from an Attic red-figured scyphus,
or drinking cup, by the Penelope
Painter, from Tarquinii, an ancient
city in central Italy (c. 440 B.C.).
Antikensammlung Staatliche Museen
zu Berlin Preussischer Kulturbesitz.

1118. ax-helve sockets: An ax helve
is an ax handle; a socket is a hollow
piece lined with iron at the end of the
handle. Shooting an arrow through a
line of ax-helve sockets would be a
task possible only for a superhero like
Odysseus.

A **Literary Focus**

❓ **What images does Homer use to
help his audience imagine even
something as ordinary as this scene
at the storeroom?** [*Sight*—"oaken
sill," "Foursquare," "shining doors,"
"curving handle," "bright doors,"
"plank floor," "milk-white arms," "polished bow case." *Sound*—"rasping," "a
bellow like a bull's vaunt," "light footfall." *Touch*—"sanded clean." *Smell*—
"herb-scented robes."]

B **Reading Skills**

❓ **Making inferences. Why is
Penelope crying?** [Possible responses:
Seeing Odysseus's bow again after so
many years makes her miss him even
more; letting others handle his bow
seems like a sign that she has given
up waiting for him; perhaps she is
worried that one of the suitors might
actually pass her test.]

C **Literary Focus**

❓ **Conflict. What internal conflict
is Odysseus experiencing here?** [He
doesn't know whether to reveal himself, because he is not sure that he
can trust the men and that they will
support him.]

Odyssey, Part Two   **699**

Learners Having Difficulty
Have students participate in a story-round to
review what they have read each day. Begin
by asking, "What happened first?" Call on a
student to answer the question; then, have
him or her call on another student, asking,
"And then what happened?" Have students
continue until each important point has been
covered. Remind students to summarize, not
recount, listing only the most important
events.

A Reading Skills

? Identifying cause and effect.
Why does Odysseus decide to reveal
his identity to the two men now?
[Possible responses: Their prayers to
the gods convince him that they are
sincere; he needs their help to carry
out his plan for the suitors.]

B Reading Skills

? Interpreting. What does
Odysseus mean here? [He means
that he will need Zeus's guidance to
get rid of the suitors.]

**Response to
Margin Question**

Lines 1122–1140. Odysseus asks
the swineherd and the cowherd
whether or not they would support
Odysseus if he returned. The men
respond, and pass the test, by asking
Zeus for the opportunity to join
forces with Odysseus.

No, no; speak,
my heart tells me. Would you be men enough
1130   to stand by Odysseus if he came back?
Suppose he dropped out of a clear sky, as I did?
Suppose some god should bring him?
Would you bear arms for him, or for the suitors?"

The cowherd said:

"Ah, let the master come!
1135   Father Zeus, grant our old wish! Some courier°
guide him back! Then judge what stuff is in me
and how I manage arms!"

Likewise Eumaeus
fell to praying all heaven for his return,
so that Odysseus, sure at least of these,
told them:

1140   "I am at home, for I am he.
I bore adversities, but in the twentieth year
I am ashore in my own land. I find
the two of you, alone among my people,
longed for my coming. Prayers I never heard
1145   except your own that I might come again.
So now what is in store for you I'll tell you:
If Zeus brings down the suitors by my hand
I promise marriages to both, and cattle,
and houses built near mine. And you shall be
1150   brothers-in-arms of my Telemachus.
Here, let me show you something else, a sign
that I am he, that you can trust me, look:
this old scar from the tusk wound that I got
boar hunting on Parnassus°— . . ."

Shifting his rags
1155   he bared the long gash. Both men looked, and knew
and threw their arms around the old soldier, weeping,
kissing his head and shoulders. He as well
took each man's head and hands to kiss, then said—
to cut it short, else they might weep till dark—

1160   "Break off, no more of this.
Anyone at the door could see and tell them.
Drift back in, but separately at intervals
after me.

Now listen to your orders:

1135. courier (kŏŏr'ē·ər) *n.:* guide
or messenger.

1122–1140. *How does
Odysseus test the loyalty of the
swineherd and the cowherd? How
do they prove that they can be
trusted?*

1154. Parnassus (pär·nas'əs): As a
young man, Odysseus had gone
hunting on Parnassus, his mother's
home, and was gored above the knee
by a boar.

1165　when the time comes, those gentlemen, to a man,
　　　will be dead against giving me bow or quiver.
　　　Defy them. Eumaeus, bring the bow
　　　and put it in my hands there at the door.
　　　Tell the women to lock their own door tight.
　　　Tell them if someone hears the shock of arms
1170　or groans of men, in hall or court, not one
　　　must show her face, but keep still at her weaving.
　　　Philoeteus, run to the outer gate and lock it.
　　　Throw the crossbar and lash it." . . .

C

Now Odysseus, still in his beggar's clothes, asks to try the bow. The suitors refuse to allow a mere beggar to try where they have failed, but Penelope insists that the stranger be given his chance. The suspense is very great—by this act, Penelope has accepted her husband as a suitor.

D

　　　Eumaeus, the swineherd, hands Odysseus the bow and tells the nurse to retire with Penelope and the maids to the family chambers (the harem) and to bolt the doors. Odysseus had earlier told Telemachus to remove the suitors' weapons from the great hall. Now he takes the bow.

　　　　　　　　　　　　　And Odysseus took his time,
1175　turning the bow, tapping it, every inch,
　　　for borings that termites might have made
　　　while the master of the weapon was abroad.
　　　The suitors were now watching him, and some
　　　jested among themselves:

　　　　　　　　　　　　　　　　"A bow lover!"

　　　"Dealer in old bows!"

1180　　　　　　　　　　　　　　　"Maybe he has one like it
　　　at home!"

　　　　　　　　　　　"Or has an itch to make one for himself."

　　　"See how he handles it, the sly old buzzard!"

　　　And one <u>disdainful</u> suitor added this:

　　　"May his fortune grow an inch for every inch he bends it!"

1185　But the man skilled in all ways of contending,
　　　satisfied by the great bow's look and heft,

E

Vocabulary
disdainful (dis·dān′fəl) *adj.*: scornful; regarding someone as
　beneath you.

1174–1220. *As you read this scene, make notes about how you* **visualize** *it. Where are various characters placed? How are they reacting? It might help to draw a picture of the great hall and indicate where various actions take place.*

C Reading Skills
Monitor your comprehension. Suggest that students pause here to check their understanding of events and to ask themselves questions— for example, "How does Odysseus plan to vanquish the suitors?" [Possible response: He plans to have Philoeteus lock the suitors in and to use his bow to attack the suitors.]

D Literary Focus
❓ Irony. Why is Penelope's acceptance of the beggar as a suitor ironic? [The suitor, Odysseus, is actually her husband.]

E Literary Focus
❓ Epithet. What epithet is used for Odysseus here? ["the man skilled in all ways of contending"] **Where else has Homer used this epithet for Odysseus?** [In the invocation at the beginning of the epic, Homer asks the Muse to help him "tell the story of that man skilled in all ways of contending."]

Response to Margin Question
Lines 1174–1220. This scene might be staged as follows: Odysseus, at center stage, examines the bow, strings it, and shoots the arrow. The suitors, standing on the side, jeer at Odysseus as he studies the bow but are stunned into silence when he succeeds in stringing it. After shooting the bow, Odysseus summons Telemachus and whispers to him.

DIFFERENTIATING INSTRUCTION

Advanced Learners
Enrichment. Have pairs or small groups of students hold a panel discussion on the use of disguises by characters in literature. Instruct students to begin with a discussion of Odysseus's decision to disguise himself upon his return to Ithaca. Students should address the following question: "Why doesn't Odysseus reveal his identity at once

to his family members?" [Students may say that he doesn't want to alert the suitors to his presence or that he is simply following Athena's advice.] **Next, ask students to cite examples of other works that use the device of a character in disguise.** [Students may mention *Robin Hood;* the biblical story in which Jacob disguises himself as Esau; Shakespeare's *As You Like It,* in which Rosalind disguises herself as Ganymede,

a young man; or the Chinese legend and poem of Mu Lan, in which a girl disguises herself as a man to go to war.] **Have students identify the purpose of the disguises in the stories they mention and discuss the themes the disguises serve.**

A Literary Focus

? Imagery. How many auditory images can you find in this passage? [Auditory images include "hummed and sang / a swallow's note," "hushed hall," "Zeus thundered / overhead, one loud crack," "twanging bow," and "to thud with heavy brazen head beyond."]

Response to Margin Question

Line 1220. Possible response: Odysseus will try to kill the suitors. Clues include the bolting of the doors, the removal of the suitors' weapons, the remaining arrows in Odysseus's quiver, and Odysseus's statement that "the hour has come to cook their lordships' mutton."

---

like a musician, like a harper, when
with quiet hand upon his instrument
he draws between his thumb and forefinger
1190   a sweet new string upon a peg: so effortlessly
Odysseus in one motion strung the bow.
Then slid his right hand down the cord and plucked it,
so the taut gut vibrating hummed and sang
a swallow's note.
                    In the hushed hall it smote the suitors
1195   and all their faces changed. Then Zeus thundered
overhead, one loud crack for a sign.
And Odysseus laughed within him that the son
of crooked-minded Cronus° had flung that omen down.
He picked one ready arrow from his table
1200   where it lay bare: the rest were waiting still
in the quiver for the young men's turn to come.
He nocked° it, let it rest across the handgrip,
and drew the string and grooved butt of the arrow,
aiming from where he sat upon the stool.
                                        Now flashed
1205   arrow from twanging bow clean as a whistle
through every socket ring, and grazed not one,
to thud with heavy brazen head beyond.
                                        Then quietly
Odysseus said:
                    "Telemachus, the stranger
you welcomed in your hall has not disgraced you.
1210   I did not miss, neither did I take all day
stringing the bow. My hand and eye are sound,
not so contemptible as the young men say.
The hour has come to cook their lordships' mutton—
supper by daylight. Other amusements later,
1215   with song and harping that adorn a feast."

He dropped his eyes and nodded, and the prince
Telemachus, true son of King Odysseus,
belted his sword on, clapped hand to his spear,
and with a clink and glitter of keen bronze
1220   stood by his chair, in the forefront near his father.

                                        (*from* Book 21)

1198. Cronus (krō′nəs): father of Zeus, called crooked-minded because of his schemes to destroy his children.

1202. nocked (näkt) *v.*: fitted to the bowstring.

1220. *What do you predict will happen next? Review the episode, looking for clues in what Odysseus says and does.*

Vocabulary
adorn (ə·dôrn′) *v.*: add beauty to; decorate.

702 Collection 10 Epic and Myth • Evaluating an Argument

CONTENT-AREA CONNECTIONS

Science/History: Archery

Archery was a popular sport in many ancient cultures. Although Odysseus's skill as an archer provides a dramatic moment in the *Odyssey*, the bow and arrow did not play a major role in warfare during Homer's time. Early bows were made of wood and animal sinew; the arrows, also wooden, were tipped with heads of stone or flint. It is possible that the bow described by Homer was Scythian. Scythian bows were curved in one direction when strung and in the opposite direction when unstrung. Restringing a Scythian bow required a great deal of strength; both arms and legs were needed to bend it back in the right direction.

Individual activity. Suggest that interested students research and explain the physics behind this early hand-powered weapon. Students should describe how energy is accumulated through the pulling of the bowstring and how the stored energy is released with the flight of the arrow. Students may want to investigate improvements made in the bow and arrow through the use of modern materials and advanced designs.

DEATH AT THE PALACE

The climax of the story is here, in Book 22. Although Odysseus is ready to reclaim his rightful kingdom, he must first confront more than a hundred hostile suitors. The first one he turns to is Antinous. All through the story, Antinous has been the meanest of the suitors and their ringleader. He hit Odysseus with a stool when the hero appeared in the hall as a beggar, and he ridiculed the disguised king by calling him a bleary vagabond, a pest, and a tramp.

B

Now shrugging off his rags the wiliest fighter of the islands
leapt and stood on the broad doorsill, his own bow in his
   hand.
He poured out at his feet a rain of arrows from the quiver
and spoke to the crowd:

      "So much for that. Your clean-cut game is over.
1225 Now watch me hit a target that no man has hit before,
if I can make this shot. Help me, Apollo."°

He drew to his fist the cruel head of an arrow for Antinous
just as the young man leaned to lift his beautiful drinking
     cup,
embossed, two-handled, golden: the cup was in his fingers,
1230 the wine was even at his lips, and did he dream of death?
How could he? In that revelry amid his throng of friends
who would imagine a single foe—though a strong foe
     indeed—
could dare to bring death's pain on him and darkness on
     his eyes?
Odysseus' arrow hit him under the chin
1235 and punched up to the feathers through his throat.

Backward and down he went, letting the wine cup fall
from his shocked hand. Like pipes his nostrils jetted
crimson runnels,° a river of mortal red,
and one last kick upset his table
1240 knocking the bread and meat to soak in dusty blood.
Now as they craned to see their champion where he lay
the suitors jostled in uproar down the hall,
everyone on his feet. Wildly they turned and scanned
the walls in the long room for arms; but not a shield,

Vocabulary
revelry (rev′əl·rē) *n.*: merrymaking; festivity.

C

1221–1303. As you read this action scene, imagine it as a film. After you finish reading, choose one part of the scene, and sketch it in your notebook. Make a list of the props you would need if you were filming the battle.

1226. Help me, Apollo: Odysseus prays to Apollo because this particular day is one of the god's feast days. Apollo is also the god of archery.

1238. runnels (run′əlz) *n.*: streams.

Odyssey, Part Two   **703**

Summary ⬌ *at grade level*

To reclaim his kingdom, Odysseus must fend off Penelope's angry suitors, who have united against the hero, with Antinous as their ringleader. Telemachus and his father, joined by the swineherd and the cowherd, trap the suitors in the hall and kill them.

DIRECT TEACHING

B **Literary Focus**

? **Plot.** What is the main question you expect the climax to answer? [Possible response: Will Odysseus defeat the suitors?]

C **Reading Skills**

? **Analyzing.** What makes this description of Antinous's death especially powerful? [Possible response: The power comes from the juxtaposition of the elaborate description of Antinous drinking his wine, oblivious to his peril, and the stark description of the arrow's impact.]

Response to Margin Question

Lines 1221–1303. The main props would probably be plates of food and wine goblets on the long table. Other props might include the bow, quiver, and arrows. Ask students to support their positioning of the characters with details from the text.

DEVELOPING FLUENCY

Paired activity. Pair advanced students with learners having difficulty. Have student pairs collaborate on preparing a script for a television news report of the death of Antinous. Have the advanced student serve as prompter and scribe as the other student describes the scene in contemporary prose. After the script is written, the advanced learner can act as the anchorperson, introducing his or her partner as the on-site reporter who reads the script.

A Reading Skills

? Interpreting. What does Homer mean when he says the suitors "imagined as they wished"? [Possible responses: He means that their initial response to Antinous's death is denial; he means that they refuse to believe that Odysseus killed Antinous purposely, because if they did, they would realize that their own lives are in danger.]

B Literary Focus

? Character. What does Eurymachus's speech reveal about his character? [Possible response: His attempt to save his own life by assigning all the blame to Antinous shows that he is quick-thinking, duplicitous, and wily.]

not a good ashen spear was there for a man to take and

1245   throw.
All they could do was yell in outrage at Odysseus:

"Foul! to shoot at a man! That was your last shot!"

"Your own throat will be slit for this!"

        "Our finest lad is down!
You killed the best on Ithaca."

        "Buzzards will tear your eyes out!"

1250 For they imagined as they wished—that it was a wild shot,
an unintended killing—fools, not to comprehend
they were already in the grip of death.
But glaring under his brows Odysseus answered:

"You yellow dogs, you thought I'd never make it
1255 home from the land of Troy. You took my house to plunder,
twisted my maids to serve your beds. You dared
bid for my wife while I was still alive.
Contempt was all you had for the gods who rule wide
        heaven,
contempt for what men say of you hereafter.
1260 Your last hour has come. You die in blood."

As they all took this in, sickly green fear
pulled at their entrails, and their eyes flickered
looking for some hatch or hideaway from death.
Eurymachus alone could speak. He said:

1265 "If you are Odysseus of Ithaca come back,
all that you say these men have done is true.
Rash actions, many here, more in the countryside.
But here he lies, the man who caused them all.
Antinous was the ringleader, he whipped us on
1270 to do these things. He cared less for a marriage
than for the power Cronion° has denied him
as king of Ithaca. For that
he tried to trap your son and would have killed him.
He is dead now and has his portion. Spare
1275 your own people. As for ourselves, we'll make
restitution of wine and meat consumed,
and add, each one, a tithe of twenty oxen
with gifts of bronze and gold to warm your heart.
Meanwhile we cannot blame you for your anger."

Suitor hiding behind a table: The return of Odysseus. Limestone relief from Turkey (380 B.C.).
Kunsthistorisches Museum, Vienna, Austria.

1271. Cronion (krō′nē·ən): another name for Zeus, meaning "son of Cronus."

SKILLS REVIEW

Generate relevant questions. Ask students what questions about ancient Greek culture, mythology, or history have occurred to them as they read the *Odyssey*. Write students' responses on the chalkboard, or have a volunteer do so. Review with students the kinds of questions that can be researched and the kinds that cannot. For example, as interesting as it would be to know what Homer would think of modern adventure stories, this question cannot be answered.
Activity. Have students work in groups to determine which of their listed questions can be researched and to rewrite the other questions to make them researchable. Then, have students think of specific reference works they could use to find the answers.

Once students have finished their research, have them record their questions and answers on separate index cards. Suggest that they note on the cards the section of the *Odyssey* that inspired their curiosity. Have students record on the flip side of each card the sources they used to find the answers. Post the cards on an *Odyssey* Q-and-A bulletin board.

1280 Odysseus glowered under his black brows
and said:

"Not for the whole treasure of your fathers,
all you enjoy, lands, flocks, or any gold
put up by others, would I hold my hand.
There will be killing till the score is paid.
1285 You forced yourselves upon this house. Fight your way out,
or run for it, if you think you'll escape death.
I doubt one man of you skins by." . . .

*Telemachus joins his father in the fight. They are helped by the
swineherd and cowherd. Now the suitors, trapped in the hall without weapons, are struck right and left by arrows, and many of them
lie dying on the floor.*

At this moment that unmanning thundercloud,
the aegis, Athena's shield,
took form aloft in the great hall.
1290   And the suitors mad with fear
at her great sign stampeded like stung cattle by a river
when the dread shimmering gadfly strikes in summer,
in the flowering season, in the long-drawn days.
After them the attackers wheeled, as terrible as falcons
from eyries° in the mountains veering over and diving
1295   down
with talons wide unsheathed on flights of birds,
who cower down the sky in chutes and bursts along the
            valley—
but the pouncing falcons grip their prey, no frantic wing
            avails,
and farmers love to watch those beakèd hunters.
1300 So these now fell upon the suitors in that hall,
turning, turning to strike and strike again,
while torn men moaned at death, and blood ran smoking
over the whole floor. . . .

(*from* Book 22)

Ulysses Slaying the Suitors (detail)
(1802) by Henry Fuseli.
© 2003 Kunsthaus Zurich.

1295. eyries (er'ēz) *n.:* nests built in
high places.

1221–1303. How does this
bloody episode relate to the epic's
theme about the value of hospitality and about what happens to
people who mock divine laws?

Vocabulary
glowered (glou'ərd) *v.:* glared; stared angrily.
avails (ə·vālz') *v.:* is of use; helps.

C Reading Skills
Monitor your comprehension.
Have students ask themselves
questions to check their understanding—for example, "What two
things has Odysseus done to make
it impossible for the suitors to 'fight
[their] way out or run for it'?" [He
has had their weapons removed and
the gate locked.]

D Literary Focus
❷ **Homeric simile.** To what are
Odysseus and his men compared?
[to falcons sweeping down from their
high nests to attack prey]

VIEWING THE ART

The Anglo-Swiss artist **Henry
Fuseli** (1741–1825) was one of
the most popular painters of his
time. Among his pupils was John
Constable.

Activity. Ask students to select
a quotation from the text to use
as a subtitle for the painting—for
example, "There will be killing till
the score is paid."

**Response to Margin
Question**
Lines 1221–1303. Possible
response: The horrific scene makes
it clear that those who abuse hospitality and mock divine laws will be
punished mercilessly.

At first Penelope is so shocked by the appearance of her long-lost husband that she is unable to speak or move. Telemachus reproaches her for being stand-offish, but she wants proof that he is truly her husband. Odysseus bathes and dresses in fresh clothing, yet Penelope is still resistant. Finally Odysseus proves his identity by revealing the secret of their marriage bed, which is built around the base of a tree. Upon hearing this, Penelope embraces Odysseus, shedding tears of joy.

DIRECT TEACHING

A **Reading Skills**

❷ **Making predictions.** How do you think Odysseus will react to Penelope's testing? [Possible responses: He will be stunned; he will be impatient; he will be angry; he will be hurt.]

B **Reading Skills**

❷ **Drawing conclusions.** Why does Penelope have so much trouble recognizing Odysseus? [Possible responses: It's been twenty years since she last saw him, and people can change a great deal in that time; she may fear that the man is an impostor or a test sent by the gods; perhaps she imagined that Odysseus would look different when he returned; doubt and hope are warring within her, clouding her senses and affecting her judgment.]

Response to Margin Question

Line 1304. Possible response: Penelope may be thinking that the gods are playing a cruel trick on her; she may believe that the stranger really is her husband but fears being disappointed.

ODYSSEUS AND PENELOPE

Odysseus now calls forth the maids who have betrayed his household by associating with the suitors. He orders them to clean up the house and dispose of the dead. Telemachus then "pays" them by hanging them in the courtyard.

A *Eurycleia tells Penelope about the return of Odysseus and the defeat of the suitors. The faithful wife—the perfect mate for the wily Odysseus—suspects a trick from the gods. She decides to test the stranger who claims to be her husband.*

1305 Crossing the doorsill she sat down at once
in firelight, against the nearest wall,
across the room from the lord Odysseus.

                        There
leaning against a pillar, sat the man
and never lifted up his eyes, but only waited
for what his wife would say when she had seen him.

B 1310 And she, for a long time, sat deathly still
in wonderment—for sometimes as she gazed
she found him—yes, clearly—like her husband,
but sometimes blood and rags were all she saw.
Telemachus's voice came to her ears:

                             "Mother,

1315 cruel mother, do you feel nothing,
drawing yourself apart this way from Father?
Will you not sit with him and talk and question him?
What other woman could remain so cold?
Who shuns her lord, and he come back to her
1320 from wars and wandering, after twenty years?
Your heart is hard as flint and never changes!"

Penelope answered:

                            "I am stunned, child.
I cannot speak to him. I cannot question him.
I cannot keep my eyes upon his face.
1325 If really he is Odysseus, truly home,
beyond all doubt we two shall know each other
better than you or anyone. There are
secret signs we know, we two."

                             A smile
came now to the lips of the patient hero, Odysseus,
1330 who turned to Telemachus and said:

"Peace: let your mother test me at her leisure.
Before long she will see and know me best.

📖 **1304.** *Make notes about Penelope as you read this episode. What might she be thinking?*

Penelope (1878) by Anthony Frederick Augustus Sandys. Colored chalk on paper.
Cecil Higgins Art Gallery, Bedford, Bedfordshire, England.

READING MINI-LESSON

Developing Word-Attack Skills
Copy this line from the selection on the chalkboard: "So wand in hand, he paced into the air. . . ." Read the line aloud, and have students identify the two words that look as though they should rhyme but don't. [*wand* and *hand*] Explain that the presence of the letter *w* often affects the pronunciation of a vowel following it.

Activity. Show students the following sets of words to demonstrate that *a* and *o* are often pronounced differently after *w* from the way they are pronounced after other consonant letters.

bad	glad	had	mad	wad
chant	grant	pant	rant	want
bar	car	far	jar	war
carp	harp	sharp	tarp	warp
chord	ford	lord	sword	word

These tatters, dirt—all that I'm caked with now—
make her look hard at me and doubt me still. . . ."

*Odysseus orders Telemachus, the swineherd, and the cowherd to
bathe and put on fresh clothing.*

1335   Greathearted Odysseus, home at last,
        was being bathed now by Eurynome
        and rubbed with golden oil, and clothed again
        in a fresh tunic and a cloak. Athena
        lent him beauty, head to foot. She made him
1340   taller, and massive, too, with crisping hair
        in curls like petals of wild hyacinth
        but all red-golden. Think of gold infused
        on silver by a craftsman, whose fine art
        Hephaestus taught him, or Athena: one
1345   whose work moves to delight: just so she lavished
        beauty over Odysseus' head and shoulders.
        He sat then in the same chair by the pillar,
        facing his silent wife, and said:

                                        "Strange woman,
        the immortals of Olympus made you hard,
1350   harder than any. Who else in the world
        would keep aloof as you do from her husband
        if he returned to her from years of trouble,
        cast on his own land in the twentieth year?

        Nurse, make up a bed for me to sleep on.
        Her heart is iron in her breast."

1355
        spoke to Odysseus now. She said:

                                        Penelope

                                        "Strange man,
        if man you are . . . This is no pride on my part
        nor scorn for you—not even wonder, merely.
        I know so well how you—how he—appeared
1360   boarding the ship for Troy. But all the same . . .

        Make up his bed for him, Eurycleia.
        Place it outside the bedchamber my lord
        built with his own hands. Pile the big bed
        with fleeces, rugs, and sheets of purest linen."

Vocabulary
lavished (lav′isht) *v.*: gave generously.
aloof (ə·lōof′) *adj.*: at a distance; unfriendly.

Penelope by John Roddam Spencer
Stanhope.
The De Morgan Foundation, London, UK.

DIRECT TEACHING

C Literary Focus

❓ Homeric simile. To what does
this simile compare Odysseus? [a
beautiful gold-plated work of art]

**D Vocabulary
Development**

Connotation. In Greek the word
for "strange woman" is *daimonie*.
By using this word, Odysseus is suggesting that Penelope's wits have
been taken away by a *daimon*, a
supernatural force. Penelope echoes
the expression back to Odysseus in
l. 1356.

E Reading Skills

❓ Making inferences. What is
Penelope implying in these lines?
[She is implying that the stranger is
not a man but a god disguised as a
man.]

VIEWING THE ART

John Roddam Spencer
Stanhope (1829–1908) specialized in mythological and allegorical
subjects. A Pre-Raphaelite painter,
he was influenced by Sir Edward
Burne-Jones (see p. 679) but
developed his own style.

Activity. Have students compare
and contrast this depiction of
Penelope with the one by
Pinturicchio on p. 698. [Possible
response: In the Pinturicchio, she is
weaving; in this painting, she sits
next to her loom looking forlorn.]

Point out that the words in each set are
spelled the same except for the beginning
letters. Have volunteers read the words in
each set. Help students recognize that all the
words in the set have the same vowel sound
except the word beginning with *w*.
Activity. Write the following word pairs on
the chalkboard. Ask volunteers to read each

pair aloud and state whether the vowel is
pronounced the same way in both words.

1. paddle   waddle [different]
2. gallop   wallop [different]
3. paste   waste [same]
4. battle   wattle [different]
5. hobble   wobble [same]

6. callow   wallow [different]
7. garden   warden [different]
8. pander   wander [different]
9. catch   watch [different]
10. ponder   wonder [different]
11. horse   worse [different]
12. safer   wafer [same]

A Literary Focus

? Imagery. How does the use of imagery in this passage emphasize Odysseus's feelings for Penelope? [Possible response: The detail and care with which Odysseus describes how he built the bedroom and bed demonstrates his dedication to Penelope.]

B Reading Skills

? Drawing conclusions. What do Penelope's physical sensations suggest she is feeling? [Possible response: Finally convinced that the man before her is Odysseus, she is flooded with relief and joy that her husband has returned and her twenty-year wait is over.]

C Literary Focus

? Irony. What is ironic about Penelope's statement? [Possible response: It is ironic because Penelope has been every bit as cautious as Odysseus.]

Response to Margin Question

Lines 1374–1384. Possible response: He carved one bedpost from the stump of an olive tree, fastened the other posts to it with oxhide, and decorated the wood with inlays. Characteristics that suggest strength and endurance are the pillarlike olive trunk and the inlay of silver, gold, and ivory.

1365   With this she tried him to the breaking point,
       and he turned on her in a flash, raging:

       "Woman, by heaven you've stung me now!
       Who dared to move my bed?
       No builder had the skill for that—unless
1370   a god came down to turn the trick. No mortal
       in his best days could budge it with a crowbar.
       There is our pact and pledge, our secret sign,
       built into that bed—my handiwork
       and no one else's!
                                    An old trunk of olive
1375   grew like a pillar on the building plot,
       and I laid out our bedroom round that tree,
       lined up the stone walls, built the walls and roof,
       gave it a doorway and smooth-fitting doors.
       Then I lopped off the silvery leaves and branches,
1380   hewed and shaped the stump from the roots up
       into a bedpost, drilled it, let it serve
       as model for the rest, I planed them all,
       inlaid them all with silver, gold, and ivory,
       and stretched a bed between—a <u>pliant</u> web
       of oxhide thongs dyed crimson.
1385   There's our sign!
       I know no more. Could someone else's hand
       have sawn that trunk and dragged the frame away?"

       Their secret! as she heard it told, her knees
       grew <u>tremulous</u> and weak, her heart failed her.
1390   With eyes brimming tears she ran to him,
       throwing her arms around his neck, and kissed him,
       murmuring:
                     "Do not rage at me, Odysseus!
       No one ever matched your caution! Think
       what difficulty the gods gave: they denied us
1395   life together in our prime and flowering years,
       kept us from crossing into age together.
       Forgive me, don't be angry. I could not
       welcome you with love on sight! I armed myself
       long ago against the frauds of men,
1400   impostors who might come—and all those many

1374–1384. *This description of Odysseus and Penelope's bed is famous—and complex.* **Paraphrase** *Odysseus's description of the bed. What characteristics of the bed suggest the strength and endurance of their love?*

Vocabulary
pliant (plī′ənt) *adj.:* flexible.
tremulous (trem′yōō·ləs) *adj.:* trembling; shaking.

Check Test: Short Answer

Guide the class in answering these comprehension questions. Have students support their responses with passages from the text. Answers may vary slightly.

1. Why doesn't Telemachus recognize his father right away? [Odysseus is disguised as a beggar; Telemachus was just a baby when Odysseus went off to war.]

2. Who is Antinous? [the leader of the suitors assembled in Odysseus's home]

3. What is Odysseus able to do that the suitors cannot do? [He can string the bow.]

4. What signs of approval do the gods give Odysseus? [Zeus thunders; Athena's aegis, or shield, appears.]

5. Who aids Odysseus in his battle with the suitors? [Telemachus, the swineherd, and the cowherd]

6. What is the secret of the marriage bed of Odysseus and Penelope? [One bedpost is carved from the rooted stump of an olive tree.]

whose underhanded ways bring evil on! . . .
But here and now, what sign could be so clear
as this of our own bed?
No other man has ever laid eyes on it—

1405 only my own slave, Actoris, that my father
sent with me as a gift—she kept our door.
You make my stiff heart know that I am yours."

Now from his breast into his eyes the ache
of longing mounted, and he wept at last,

1410 his dear wife, clear and faithful, in his arms,
longed for
        as the sun-warmed earth is longed for by a swimmer
spent in rough water where his ship went down
under Poseidon's blows, gale winds and tons of sea.
Few men can keep alive through a big surf

1415 to crawl, clotted with brine, on kindly beaches
in joy, in joy, knowing the abyss behind:
and so she too rejoiced, her gaze upon her husband,
her white arms round him pressed, as though forever. . . .

(*from* Book 23)

1408–1418. *The journey
ends with an embrace. What
simile helps you understand the
joy Odysseus feels in the arms of
his wife?*

Penelope and Her Suitors (1912) by J. W. Waterhouse.

City of Aberdeen Art Gallery and Museums Collection, Scotland.

D Reading Skills

? Interpreting. What does
Penelope mean when she refers to
her "stiff heart"? [Possible responses:
She means her heart is stiff from
disuse because she has had no husband to love for so long; she means
she has had to harden her heart to
protect herself from the anguish of
accepting that Odysseus might never
return.]

VIEWING THE ART

The English painter **J. W.
Waterhouse** (1849–1917) is best
known for his atmospheric paintings of scenes from classical
mythology.

Activity. Ask students to imagine
what Penelope is thinking as she
concentrates on her weaving,
her back turned to the imploring
suitors. [Possible response: She
may be thinking of her husband or
wishing the suitors would leave her
alone.]

**Response to Margin
Question**

Lines 1408–1418. The simile in
ll. 1411–1416 compares Odysseus's
feelings to the joy a half-drowned
sailor feels on reaching land at last.
The simile is especially fitting
because Odysseus has had to contend repeatedly with trials brought
on by Poseidon, god of the sea.

In the *Odyssey,* Homer lists many kinds of
plants and animals found in the Greek isles.
They include horned owls, falcons, cormorants,
thyme, olive trees, cedar, and clover. Encourage
students to work with a family member or
friend to identify plants and animals that live in
their area, city, or state. Suggest that students
and family members or friends contact the
local or state nature conservancy and visit
community parks to gather information. The
results of their survey can be presented as a
brochure or poster for tourists.

VIEWING THE ART

J. M. W. Turner (1775–1851) painted landscapes and seascapes with a sense of theatrical grandeur and an understanding of nature as a sublime, overwhelming force. In his later paintings, in particular, he increasingly abandoned descriptive details to suggest extreme atmospheric conditions and stunning light effects. Note how Polyphemus is merged into the landscape, as if the giant were a natural force himself.

Activity. What attitude toward nature does this painting express? [awe, admiration] Where do humans seem to fit into Turner's vision of nature? [subordinate to natural forces] See if students can find Polyphemus, the Cyclops. [He is in the upper right, on the crag, hurling a rock at the Greeks.]

CONNECTION / POEM

Ulysses Deriding Polyphem (detail) (19th century) by J.M.W. Turner. Oil on canvas.
Tate Gallery, London.

Ithaca

C. P. Cavafy

translated by Edmund Keeley
and Philip Sherrard

When you set out for Ithaca,
pray that your road's a long one,
full of adventure, full of discovery.
Laistrygonians, Cyclops,
5 angry Poseidon—don't be scared of them:
you won't find things like that on your way
as long as your thoughts are exalted,
as long as a rare excitement
stirs your spirit and your body.
10 Laistrygonians, Cyclops,
wild Poseidon—you won't encounter them
unless you bring them along inside you,
unless your soul raises them up in front of you.

Pray that your road's a long one.
15 May there be many a summer morning when—
full of gratitude, full of joy—
you come into harbors seen for the first time;
may you stop at Phoenician trading centers
and buy fine things,
20 mother-of-pearl and coral, amber and ebony,
sensual perfumes of every kind,
as many sensual perfumes as you can;
may you visit numerous Egyptian cities
to fill yourself with learning from the wise.

25 Keep Ithaca always in mind.
Arriving there is what you're destined for.
But don't hurry the journey at all.
Better if it goes on for years
so you're old by the time you reach the island,
30 wealthy with all you've gained on the way,
not expecting Ithaca to make you rich.
Ithaca gave you the marvelous journey.
Without her you wouldn't have set out.
She hasn't anything else to give.

35 And if you find her poor, Ithaca won't have
      fooled you.
Wise as you'll have become, and so
      experienced,
you'll have understood by then what an
      Ithaca means.

Connection

Summary ⬆ *above grade level*

Using an extended metaphor, the speaker counsels the reader to savor the "marvelous journey" of life.

DIRECT TEACHING

Ⓐ Reading Skills

❓ Making inferences. What do you think Cavafy is suggesting in the line "pray that your road's a long one"? [Possible responses: He means that you should hope that your life is long and varied; he means that you should not dread getting older but consider each added year a gift.]

Ⓑ Reading Skills

❓ Interpreting. What does Cavafy mean by these lines? [Possible responses: He means that life is what you make of it; he means that many of our troubles are self-inflicted.]

Ⓒ Literary Focus

❓ Symbol. What do you think Ithaca symbolizes in this poem? [Possible responses: heaven; death; one's goal in life; one's ideal place in the world; old age.]

Connecting and Contrasting Texts

Discuss with students how the journey to Ithaca in Cavafy's poem can be interpreted as the journey that everyone takes in life. This journey may include experiences like those Odysseus had during his journey home: visiting new places, learning about people different from oneself, and facing and overcoming obstacles. Encourage students to analyze Cavafy's poem and to list in their journals the many types of life experiences the poet mentions.

Have them think of similar experiences in their own lives so far or in the lives they imagine leading in the future. Remind students to include only experiences they do not mind sharing.

Experiences in Cavafy's Poem	Experiences in My Own Life

Connection

Summary ⬆ *above grade level*

In this excerpt from *The Odyssey: A Modern Sequel,* a Greek poet extends the story to show the hero, home at last, unexpectedly feeling trapped.

DIRECT TEACHING

A Literary Focus

❓ Imagery. What details does the poet use to help readers visualize the fire? ["glowering fire fade," "withering flames," "the ash that spread like powder on the dying coals"]

B Literary Focus

❓ Alliteration. Where is alliteration used in these lines? [in l. 19, "dwindled" and "died"; in l. 20, "son's smooth-skinned" and "softness"]

C Reading Skills

❓ Making connections. Where in the *Odyssey* does Odysseus sit weeping by the water? [In Book 5, when he is being held captive by Calypso, Odysseus sits by the water each day "with eyes wet," longing for home (ll. 72–74).] **What might Odysseus be longing for here?** [Possible responses: for escape from Teiresias's prophecy; for adventure and far-off lands; for the exciting life he led in his younger days; for relief from the conflict between his duty to stay home and his desire to go to sea.]

The Sea Call

Nikos Kazantzakis
translated by Kimon Friar

When Odysseus meets Teiresias in the underworld, the **A** *prophet tells him that he will reach home but will then take yet another journey to a land where people live who know nothing of the sea. (See pages 676–677.) In this excerpt from a modern sequel to the Odyssey by the twentieth-century Greek poet Nikos Kazantzakis, Odysseus has returned to Ithaca.* **B** *Sitting by the hearth with his family, his eyes alight with excitement, he relates his adventures. But then . . .*

Odysseus sealed his bitter lips and spoke no more,
but watched the glowering fire fade, the withering flames,
the ash that spread like powder on the dying coals,
then turned, glanced at his wife, gazed on his son and father,
5   and suddenly shook with fear and sighed, for now he knew
that even his native land was a sweet mask of Death.
Like a wild beast snared in a net, his eyes rolled round
and tumbled down his deep eye-sockets, green and bloodshot.
His tribal palace seemed a narrow shepherd's pen,
10   his wife a small and wrinkled old housekeeping crone,
his son an eighty-year-old drudge who, trembling, weighed
with care to find what's just, unjust, dishonest, honest,
as though all life were prudence, as though fire were just,
and logic the highest good of eagle-mounting man!
15   The heart-embattled athlete laughed, dashed to his feet,
and his home's sweetness, suddenly, his longed-for land,
the twelve gods, ancient virtue by his honored hearth,
his son—all seemed opposed now to his high descent.
The fire dwindled and died away, and the four heads
20   and his son's smooth-skinned calves with tender softness glowed
till in the trembling hush Penelope's wan cries
broke in despair like water flowing down a wall.
Her son dashed and stood upright by his mother's throne,
touched gently with a mute compassion her white arm,
25   then gazed upon his father in the dim light, and shuddered,
for in the last resplendence of the falling fire
he could discern the unmoving eyes flash yellow, blue,
and crimson, though the dark had swallowed the wild body.
With silent strides Odysseus then shot back the bolt,
30   passed lightly through the courtyard and sped down the street.
Some saw him take the graveyard's zigzag mountain path,
some saw him leap on rocks that edged the savage shore,
some visionaries saw him in the dead of night
swimming and talking secretly with the sea-demons,
C 35   but only a small boy saw him in a lonely dream
sit crouched and weeping by the dark sea's foaming edge.

Connecting and Comparing Texts

Guide students in comparing and contrasting the mood of the last episode from the *Odyssey* in the text with the mood of Kazantzakis's poem. You might ask, "Why does Odysseus weep when Penelope finally recognizes him as her husband? Why does he weep in this poem?" [Possible response: In the epic, Odysseus weeps with joy and relief that he is safe in the warmth and security of his home, surrounded by his family. In the poem, Odysseus crouches by the edge of the ocean, weeping because he realizes that he was happier with his adventurous, seafaring life or that he will never again feel truly at home in either world.]

Response and Analysis

from the Odyssey, Part Two

Reading Check

1. Describe Argos's condition when Odysseus sees him.

2. What is the contest of the bow, and how will Penelope reward the winner?

3. Just before trying the bow, Odysseus reveals himself to two people. Who are they? Why does he confide in them?

4. List at least five images or events from Odysseus's battle with the suitors.

5. How does Penelope test Odysseus after the battle?

Thinking Critically

6. What **Homeric simile** in lines 1031–1033 describes the feelings of Odysseus and his son as they embrace after twenty years? How would you describe exactly what the father and his son are feeling here?

7. **Situational irony** occurs when what happens is different from what we expect. Why is it ironic that Odysseus returns to his kingdom dressed as a beggar?

8. **Dramatic irony** refers to a situation in which readers know more than the characters know. Where in the scene in the swineherd's hut is there dramatic irony?

9. In epics it is rare for heroes to have relationships with ordinary people, but in the *Odyssey,* servants play important roles. How does Odysseus treat Eumaeus and the cowherd? What values might Homer be trying to teach through that treatment?

10. What **character traits** does Penelope reveal in her interactions with Odysseus disguised as a beggar?

11. What does the interaction between Odysseus and Penelope in lines 1348–1418 tell you about their relationship? Calypso wondered what it was about Penelope that drew Odysseus homeward (see page 654). Now that you've met Penelope, how would you answer Calypso?

12. The *Odyssey* is many centuries old. Do you think the feelings and needs shown by the people in the *Odyssey* are shared by people today? Which feelings does the speaker in "An Ancient Gesture" identify with (see the **Connection** on page 697)? Which experiences or people in this story did you identify with most? Why?

13. Suppose a modern general, like Odysseus, had fought a war for ten years and was missing for another ten years. What emotions might he (or she) have experienced upon returning home? What changes might he (or she) have found at home after twenty years? (Check your Quickwrite notes for page 689.) ✏

14. In "Ithaca" (see the **Connection** on page 711), a modern Greek poet uses Ithaca as a **symbol,** a place that functions as itself in the poem but also stands for something beyond itself. Explain what you think "arriving in Ithaca" could mean for all of us.

Extending and Evaluating

15. Do you think Odysseus's revenge on the suitors and maids is excessive or too brutal? Explore this question from Odysseus's viewpoint (remember that he is the rightful king) and from your own modern viewpoint.

SKILLS FOCUS

Literary Skills
Analyze characteristics of epic poetry, including character traits.

Writing Skills
Discuss the hero's character traits in a brief essay. Write a continuation of the story. Write a story plan. Write a movie proposal. Discuss how the epic relates to life today in a brief essay.

Odyssey, Part Two   **713**

Response and Analysis

Thinking Critically

6. The two men's feelings are compared to those of a hawk whose young have been stolen. Odysseus and Telemachus are probably feeling a mixture of joy at their reunion and grief at their years of separation.

7. Odysseus is a king.

8. The swineherd greets Telemachus as a father would greet his son after a long absence, while Odysseus, disguised as a beggar, looks on.

9. They are treated with respect. Everyone should be treated with respect.

10. Penelope shows graciousness, kindness, fairness, and caution.

11. They are equally matched in intelligence, tenacity, and devotion to each other.

12. Possible answer: People today still feel love for home and family. Students may identify with Penelope's loyalty and with Odysseus's longing for home.

13. Possible answer: The general might suffer from depression or post-traumatic stress disorder. His or her spouse might not have waited.

14. Possible answers: Achieving a state of mind in which one appreciates all that life has to offer; reaching a state of grace or spiritual enlightenment.

Extending and Evaluating

15. Possible answers: Yes, because neither Penelope nor Telemachus was physically harmed by the suitors; no, because the suitors abused one of the Greeks' highest values, hospitality, and the maids were disloyal. Today Odysseus's retribution seems excessive because the maids committed no crime, and imprisonment would be a more appropriate punishment for the suitors.

Odyssey, Part Two   **713**

Reading Check

1. The dog lies fly-bitten and neglected.

2. The test is to string Odysseus's bow and shoot an arrow through twelve ax-handle sockets. She will marry the winner.

3. Needing their help, Odysseus reveals himself to the swineherd and the cowherd.

4. Odysseus casting off his rags, Antinous's "one last kick," Odysseus's rebuke of the suitors, the suitors stampeding like cattle, and blood running over the floor.

5. She tells her servant to move their bed, provoking him into telling how he built it.

Writing

1. Noble or Not?

Have students work in pairs on finding the epithets and the actions illustrating each character trait.

2. Prophetic Puzzler

Before students start to write their extensions, have them work in pairs on a detailed interpretation of the prophecy. They may want to use a chart like the following one to record their ideas. An example is given.

Teiresias's Advice	Interpretation
Go overland on foot and take an oar . . . ." (l. 641)	This may mean that Odysseus must humble himself.

3. Her Odyssey

Encourage students to begin by writing responses to the bulleted list on p. 714. Emphasize to students that they are writing a story plan, not a complete story.

4. And Now—The Movie

Have students describe the highlights of their film to a partner and evaluate their ideas with him or her.

5. Timeless Messages

Ask students to cite specific lines to support their ideas. You may want to suggest that students use a chart like the following one to organize their ideas:

Value	Example	Lesson

WRITING

Choose from among the following assignments to respond to the *Odyssey*:

1. Noble or Not?

In a brief **essay,** discuss at least four of Odysseus's **character traits.** Find situations in the epic that reveal each trait. In your final paragraph, sum up your opinion of Odysseus's character. Do you think he is totally admirable? To what extent would he be considered a hero today?

2. Prophetic Puzzler

In Part One, lines 639–658 (page 677), Teiresias makes a famous prophecy: Odysseus will take off on yet another journey after he returns home. (For part of one writer's extension of the *Odyssey,* see "The Sea Call," the **Connection** on page 712.) What do you think happens to Odysseus after he takes back his kingdom? Write your own continuation of Odysseus's story based on Teiresias's prophecy.

3. Her Odyssey

Write a **story plan** showing how an odyssey could have a woman as its voyaging hero. You may set your story in any time and place, from Odysseus's Greece to your hometown today to a distant galaxy in the future. Consider these points in your plan:

- occupation of the hero; her reason for being away from home; her situation at home
- trials of her journey; how she deals with the "monsters" she meets
- what happens when she returns home

4. And Now—The Movie

Write a **proposal** in which you suggest ways that the *Odyssey* could be made into a movie—set in contemporary times. In your proposal, written for the people who will produce the movie, you will have to explain how you would modernize the *Odyssey*.

Write two or three paragraphs. Use a chart like the one below to organize your ideas:

1200 B.C.	Today
a. Trojan War as a background	a.
b. Hero is soldier who fought in war	b.
c. Hero journeys home around Mediterranean and down to the underworld	c.
d. Hero uses ships with oars and sails	d.
e. Hero meets Lotus Eaters, Sirens, Scylla, and Charybdis	e.
f. Hero is tempted by Circe and Calypso	f.
g. Fortune hunters at home hound hero's wife	g.
h. Hero's son is insulted	h.
i. Gods dominate the action	i.

5. Timeless Messages

A work of literature becomes important to us when we feel that it relates to our lives. In a brief **essay,** discuss at least three ways in which the *Odyssey* relates to life today. You might consider what it says about these values:

- courtesy and respect for all groups of people
- courage, trust, and discipline
- loyalty to family and community
- obedience to law—human or divine

DIFFERENTIATING INSTRUCTION

Learners Having Difficulty
Have students interested in the Prophetic Puzzler activity work in pairs or small groups paraphrasing Teiresias's prophecy before they begin interpreting the prophecy.

Advanced Learners
Enrichment. Have students look in a library or on the Internet for information on writing movie proposals and scripts. Suggest that students write a script for a scene in their proposed movie.

Vocabulary Development

Synonyms

PRACTICE 1

Synonyms are words with similar meanings, such as *beast* and *monster*. You have to use synonyms with care since they do not always mean exactly the same thing. Create a chart like the one here, listing synonyms for each Word Bank word. Can you substitute the synonyms in the original sentence?

candor
Original Sentence: "Telemachus with his clear candor said . . ."
Synonyms: honesty, frankness, fairness, impartiality
Response to Substitutions: Here, *candor* describes a way of expressing oneself. *Frankness* works best. *Honesty* could also apply. Judgment is not involved, so *fairness* and *impartiality* don't work.

Word Bank

candor
disdainful
adorn
revelry
glowered
avails
lavished
aloof
pliant
tremulous

Epithets

An **epithet** (ep′ə·thet′) is an adjective or phrase used to characterize someone. *Catherine the Great* and *baby boomers* are epithets used to characterize an empress and a generation. Homer uses epithets as formulas to characterize places and people. The epithet "faithful Penelope" instantly reminds us of Penelope's outstanding character trait.

A Famous Epithet Mystery

One of Homer's famous epithets is "the wine-dark sea." Since wine is red or white or yellowish, and the sea is none of these hues, the description is puzzling. Some say that the ancient Greeks diluted their wine with water and that the alkali in the water changed the color of the wine from red to blue. Others think the sea was covered with red algae. Robert Fitzgerald, the great translator of the *Odyssey*, thought about the question when he was sailing on the Aegean Sea:

> "The contrast of the bare arid baked land against the sea gave the sea such a richness of hue that I felt as though we were sailing through a bowl of dye. The depth of hue of the water was like the depth of hue of a good red wine."

PRACTICE 2

1. Odysseus is called "versatile Odysseus," "wily Odysseus," "the strategist," and "the noble and enduring man." What does each underlined word mean?

2. Telemachus is called "clearheaded Telemachus." How would you define *clearheaded*? What is its opposite?

3. Dawn is described as "rosy-fingered." What does this epithet help you see?

4. Make up your own epithets for these characters: the Cyclops, Circe, Argos, Penelope, and the suitors.

SKILLS FOCUS

Vocabulary Skills
Understand synonyms. Understand epithets.

Vocabulary Development

Practice 1

Possible Answers
Students' responses to substitutions will vary. Students should try to find at least two synonyms for each word in the Word Bank.

Word	Synonyms
disdainful	haughty; scornful
adorn	bedeck; decorate
revelry	festivity; merrymaking
glowered	glared; scowled
avails	aids; helps
lavished	bestowed; wasted
aloof	detached; remote
pliant	flexible; docile
tremulous	trembling; fearful

Practice 2

1. versatile: "skilled in many areas"; wily: "crafty; sly"; strategist: "person skilled in preparing plans for action"; enduring: "standing fast; persistent"

2. clearheaded: "rational; not easily confused"; its opposite: "confused; irrational"

3. Possible answer: The epithet creates an image of pink rays of light streaming up from the horizon.

4. Students' epithets will vary. Remind students that their epithet should name or describe each character's outstanding character traits.

DIFFERENTIATING INSTRUCTION

Learners Having Difficulty
Epithets. Write the following quotations on the chalkboard. Have students identify the epithets in these quotations, taken from Homer's other epic, the *Iliad*.

1. "At last his own generous wife came running to meet him, / Andromache, the daughter of high-hearted Eëtion. . . ." [daughter of high-hearted Eëtion]

2. "Then tall Hector of the shining helm answered her. . . ." [Hector of the shining helm]

3. ". . . where all the other / lovely-haired women of Troy propitiate the grim goddess . . ." [lovely-haired women; the grim goddess]

4. "Quick-footed Achilles spoke sternly. . . ." [quick-footed Achilles]

5. "Thus they buried Hector, tamer of horses." [Hector, tamer of horses]

Vocabulary Development

Practice 1

1. The word *museum* is derived from the Greek *mouseion*, meaning "place for the Muses."

2. Sirens were dangerous. They lured sailors to their death. A siren is a warning of danger.

3. It means that we live under the protection of the Constitution.

Vocabulary Development

Words from Greek and Roman Myths

Myths are stories associated with a particular society that are essentially religious. Myths often explain the mysteries of nature, the origins of rituals, and the relationships between gods and humans. Myths taught Homer's audiences important lessons about religion and conduct.

The Greek and Roman myths live on in the English language, as the charts below show. As we read the *Iliad* and the *Odyssey,* we come across names of gods, goddesses, mythical heroes, human heroes—and monsters and villains. Many English words have their origins in these names. For example, a long, difficult journey in search of something of value is called an *odyssey,* whether it be Alex Haley's odyssey in search of his African roots or a scientist's odyssey in search of the secrets of DNA.

Names from Greek and Roman Myths (and English Words That Derive from Them)			
Name	*English Word*	*Name*	*English Word*
aegis	aegis	Muses	museum; music
Ceres	cereal	Narcissus	narcissistic
Hector	hector	Olympia	Olympics
Jove	jovial	Siren	siren
Mars	martial	Tantalus	tantalize
Mentor	mentor	Titans	titanic
Mercury	mercury	Vulcan	volcano; vulcanize

Planets Named for Gods from Greek and Roman Myths	
Mercury	Saturn
Venus	Uranus
Mars	Neptune
Jupiter	Pluto

NASA Expeditions Named for Gods from Greek and Roman Myths	
Apollo	Mercury

PRACTICE 1

Read the following information, and answer the questions about words derived from the Greek myths and epics. To help you answer, look up the underlined words in a good dictionary.

1. Homer opens his epic poems with a prayer to the **Muse.** In mythology the nine Muses were goddesses who inspired people working in the arts and sciences. One word derived from the name Muse is *music.*

   How is the meaning of our word museum *related to the Muses?*

2. The **Sirens** were island creatures with enchanting female voices who lured sailors to steer their ships toward dangerous rocks.

   Why do you think the horn of an ambulance is called a siren?

3. The **aegis** (ē′jis) was the great shield of Zeus, king of the gods. Anyone who acted "under the aegis" had Zeus's power and support. Athena later carried the aegis (see the *Odyssey,* line 1289).

   What do we mean today when we say we live under the aegis *of the Constitution?*

SKILLS FOCUS

Vocabulary Skills
Understand words from Greek and Roman myths.

DIFFERENTIATING INSTRUCTION

Learners Having Difficulty
Write the following sentences on the chalkboard, and have students choose the correct word.

1. The word *cereal* comes from the name Ceres/Sirens. [Ceres]

2. The word *martial* comes from the name Muses/Mars. [Mars]

3. Something large and powerful could be described using a word that comes from the name Tantalus/Titan. [Titan]

4. A person who has a very changeable personality might be described as mercurial/martial. [mercurial]

5. If a pet reminded you of the sun, you might name it Helios/Hector. [Helios]

4. **Hector,** the oldest of Priam's sons in the *Iliad,* was the bravest Trojan hero, a great leader who loved his family. Hector didn't deserve the meaning that his name took on during the seventeenth century. The word *hector* came to be associated with the unpleasant act of bullying.

What do children do when they hector *others to get what they want?*

5. **Tantalus,** a mortal son of Zeus, was punished in Hades for having revealed his father's secrets. There he is forced to stand in water, with luscious fruit dangling over his head. Whenever he tries to drink the water or eat the fruit, he cannot reach them.

How is the word tantalize *related to Tantalus?*

6. **Narcissus,** son of a river god, was a handsome youth who was cold to all who loved him. To punish him, the gods doomed him to fall in love with his own reflection in the water. When Narcissus tried to embrace his beloved, the reflection in the water disappeared. After Narcissus died from grief, he was changed into a flower, which we call narcissus.

What kind of teenager might be called narcissistic?

PRACTICE 2

The ancient Romans adopted many Greek myths, but they changed Greek names to Latin ones. Read the following information about words derived from Roman myths, and answer the questions. Check your answers by looking up each underlined word in a good dictionary.

1. **Jove** was another name for the Roman god Jupiter (the Greek god Zeus). According to those who believe the stars and planets influence our lives, people who are born under the sign of the planet Jupiter are jovial.

Why is it fun to have a jovial *guest at your party?*

2. **Mars** was the Roman god of war (the Greek god Ares). To the Romans he was second in importance to Jove. The third month of the year is named in his honor, as is the fourth planet from the sun.

What happens when a peace-loving nation becomes martial?

3. **Vulcan** was the Roman god of fire and metalworking. A blacksmith, he created beautiful things and instruments of war. He lived under various mountains. When he worked, smoke and fire came out of the mountain.

How is our word volcano *related to Vulcan?*

4. **Ceres** was the Roman goddess of corn and grain, who also controlled fertility and the harvest. After Pluto (his Greek name was Hades) kidnapped her daughter, Proserpina (the Greek Persephone), Ceres was so stricken with grief that she caused crops to stop growing and let the earth become barren. When Proserpina, goddess of springtime, returns to Ceres for six months each year, the earth bears fruit again.

Why might people have given the name cereal *to a breakfast food?*

PRACTICE 3

Why are these names, based on the names of Greek and Roman gods and goddesses, appropriate?

1. Vulcan's Forge—a blacksmith shop
2. Mercury's Messengers—a delivery service
3. Ceres' Place—a vegetarian cafe

4. When children hector someone, they bully or browbeat the person.
5. The word *tantalize* is derived from the name Tantalus; it means "tease or disappoint by seeming to offer something and then withholding it."
6. A teenager who is self-involved and egotistical might be called narcissistic.

Practice 2

1. A jovial person is cheerful and high-spirited.
2. As the Roman god of war, Mars is associated with bloodshed. When a nation becomes martial, it becomes warlike.
3. The word *volcano* derives from the name Vulcan; it refers to an opening in the earth's surface through which molten rock and gases are ejected.
4. *Cereal* refers to any grain that is used for food. People probably associated the growing and harvesting periods of grains with Ceres' periods of barrenness and fertility.

Practice 3

1. Vulcan is the Roman god of fire and metalworking (identified with the Greek god Hephaestus).
2. Mercury is the Roman messenger of the gods (identified with the Greek god Hermes).
3. Ceres is the Roman goddess of agriculture (identified with the Greek goddess Demeter).

ASSESSING

RETEACHING

Assessment

■ *Holt Assessment: Literature, Reading, and Vocabulary*

For another selection to teach epic and myth, see *The Holt Reader,* Collection 10.

Grade-Level Skills

■ **Reading Skills**

Evaluate the credibility of an author's argument by examining the author's intent and tone.

Review Skills

■ **Reading Skills**

Analyze an author's argument, point of view, or perspective.

Summary 🔄 *at grade level*

> These two essays describe the personal meaning of heroism for two prominent figures in the entertainment industry. Director Oliver Stone has altered his view of heroism to include not just the great heroes of the past, like George Washington and Harriet Tubman, but ordinary people who show "simple acts of heroism." Actor Kirk Douglas recalls being told by a Holocaust survivor about the Berlin residents—"little heroes" she calls them—who saved her life.

PRETEACHING

Preview Vocabulary

Have students choose the Vocabulary word from p. 718 that best completes each of the sentences below.

1. The backpackers looked _____ after being lost in the woods for two weeks without food. [emaciated]

2. The tornado threatened to _____ all the buildings in its path. [annihilate]

3. A smart athlete _____ strenuous exercise until after stretching his or her muscles. [defers]

4. Our environmental group is our town's strongest _____ of the recycling program. [advocate]

5. Most children want to _____ their role models. [emulate]

Informational Text

LINK TO "FROM THE ODYSSEY"

Where I Find My Heroes ◆ Heroes with Solid Feet

Evaluating an Author's Argument: Intent and Tone

Arguments can appeal to both our hearts and our minds—to both emotion and reason. Writers make **appeals to reason,** or **logic,** by supporting their opinions with objective evidence (such as facts and statistics). In contrast, **emotional appeals** (such as anecdotes and loaded words) can win readers' hearts, even though they do not offer objective evidence.

1. **What's the intent?** The author's **intent,** or **purpose,** determines which mix of logical and emotional appeals is appropriate. For example, a writer trying to convince us of the dangers of drunk driving would use an argument based mostly on **logical appeals.** A reliance on emotional appeals would suggest that the writer was unable to back up his or her ideas with hard evidence.

   However, a writer who wants us to see a personal, subjective issue—such as honor or love—in a new light would probably not use facts and statistics, which could seem cold and unfeeling. Instead, he or she would probably appeal more to our hearts than our minds, using the following **emotional appeals:**

   Anecdotes. Brief, often colorful stories that personalize an issue, anecdotes put a human face on cold facts. For example, a story about one firefighter's heroic rescue of a child is more powerful than statistics showing the number of lives saved by firefighters.

   Loaded words. Words like *hero, evil, victim,* and *freedom* have strong positive or negative **connotations,** or emotional associations. Loaded words work on our feelings. Writers must

avoid overusing them because readers sense when their feelings are being manipulated.

2. **What's the tone?** The author's intent has a direct impact on **tone.** A serious subject demands a sober, objective tone. An attempt to inspire requires an uplifting, encouraging tone. A desire to entertain requires a humorous tone.

   Tone is created primarily through the author's choice of words. In addition to **loaded language, sensory images** and **figurative language** also contribute to tone by painting vivid pictures in readers' minds.

   As you read the following arguments, note each author's tone and the way he supports his argument.

INTERNET
Interactive
Reading Model
Keyword: LE5 9-10

SKILLS FOCUS

Reading Skills
Evaluate an author's argument, including intent and tone.

Vocabulary Development

advocate (ad′və·kit) *n.:* supporter.

defers (dē·fʉrz′) *v.:* delays; puts off.

emaciated (ē·mā′shē·āt′id) *adj.:* extremely thin; wasted away.

annihilate (ə·nī′ə·lāt′) *v.:* destroy completely.

emulate (em′yo͞o·lāt′) *v.:* follow the example of; imitate.

Connecting to the Literature

In Homer's *Odyssey,* Odysseus is a larger-than-life hero who does larger-than-life deeds. In the following nonfiction pieces, two highly successful film artists discuss the "little heroes" in our lives.

RESOURCES: READING

Differentiating Instruction

■ *Holt Reading Solutions*

■ *Holt Adapted Reader*

■ *Supporting Instruction in Spanish*

■ *Audio CD Library, Selections and Summaries in Spanish*

Vocabulary

■ *Vocabulary Development*

Grammar and Language

■ *Daily Language Activities*

Assessment

■ *Holt Online Assessment*

■ *Holt Assessment: Literature, Reading, and Vocabulary*

■ *One-Stop Planner* CD-ROM with ExamView Test Generator

Where I Find My Heroes

from *McCall's Magazine*, November 1992

Oliver Stone

Oliver Stone became a movie director after serving in the Vietnam War. His films have explored historical subjects, such as the Vietnam War and President Kennedy's assassination.

It's not true that there are no heroes anymore—but it is true that my own concept of heroism has changed radically over time. When I was young and I read the Random House biographies, my heroes were always people like George Washington and General Custer[1] and Abraham Lincoln and Teddy Roosevelt. Men, generally, and doers. Women—with the exception of Clara Barton, Florence Nightingale, and Joan of Arc[2]—got short shrift.[3] Most history was oriented toward male heroes.

But as I've gotten older, and since I've been to war, I've been forced to reexamine the nature of life and of heroism. What is true? Where are the myths?

The simple acts of heroism are often overlooked—that's very clear to me not only in war but in peace. I'm not debunking[4] all of history: Crossing the Delaware[5] *was* a magnificent action. But I am saying that I think the meaning of heroism has a lot to do with evolving into a higher human being. I came into contact with it when I worked with Ron Kovic, the paraplegic[6] Vietnam vet, on *Born on the Fourth of July*. I was impressed by his life change, from a patriotic and strong-willed athlete to someone who had to deal with the total surrender of his body, who grew into a nonviolent and peaceful advocate of change in the Martin Luther King, Jr., and Gandhi[7]

---

1. **General Custer:** General George Armstrong Custer (1839–1876) was killed in a fierce battle against the Sioux and Cheyenne.
2. **Clara Barton** (1821–1912), **Florence Nightingale** (1820–1910), **and Joan of Arc** (1412–1431): Barton, a Civil War nurse, founded the Red Cross. Nightingale, an English nurse, is regarded as the founder of modern nursing. Joan of Arc led French troops to victory against the English during the Hundred Years' War.
3. **short shrift** *n.*: colloquial expression meaning "little time or attention."

4. **debunking** (dē·buŋk′iŋ) *v.*: discrediting something by exposing it as false or exaggerated.
5. **Crossing the Delaware:** On Christmas night in 1776, George Washington led soldiers from Valley Forge, Pennsylvania, across the Delaware River, surprising and defeating Hessian troops.
6. **paraplegic** (par′ə·plē′jik) *adj.*: having paraplegia, a condition in which a person loses sensation and movement in the lower half of the body.
7. **Gandhi:** Mohandas Gandhi (1869–1948) led India to independence from British rule using nonviolent resistance.

Vocabulary
advocate (ad′və·kit) *n.*: supporter.

DIRECT TEACHING

A Reading Informational Text

? Evaluating the credibility of an author's argument. What is Stone's argument, as he states it in the first paragraph? [His ideas of heroism have changed over time.] What do you think his intention will be in the remainder of the essay? [Possible responses: to convince readers that his concept of heroism has changed; to persuade readers to have a broader view of heroism.]

B Reading Informational Text

? Evaluating the credibility of an author's argument. Do you think the experiences that Stone cites give his argument credibility? Explain. [Possible responses: No, because many people grow older and have been in a war, and their views have not necessarily changed. Yes, getting older and being in a war are major life experiences that can add credibility to what a person says.]

C Reading Informational Text

? Evaluating the credibility of an author's argument. Which words in Stone's description of Ron Kovic have emotional associations? [Possible responses: *paraplegic, Vietnam vet, patriotic, athlete, nonviolent, peaceful*.] Do you think Stone's word choices help his argument? Explain. [Possible responses: Yes, because the words make Kovic come alive as a hero. No, because Stone doesn't provide additional details or examples.]

DIFFERENTIATING INSTRUCTION

Learners Having Difficulty
Some students may have difficulty with the pronoun *it* in the fourth sentence of the third paragraph. Point out that the pronoun refers to the idea "the meaning of heroism has a lot to do with evolving into a higher human being." Ask students what the last word in the essay refers to. [virtue] You may also need to point out that the clauses in the next-to-last paragraph are not complete sentences. They

are answers to the question that begins the paragraph. Have students turn each clause into a sentence by adding "is a hero" or "are heroes."

Advanced Learners
Enrichment. Have students discuss Stone's statement that heroism is "not to be recognized." Students should state their reasons for agreeing or disagreeing with the statement.

Internet
- go.hrw.com (Keyword: LE5 9-10)
- *Elements of Literature Online*

Media
- *Audio CD Library*

? Evaluating the credibility
of an author's argument. How
does Stone's argument appeal to
both heart and mind? [Possible
response: Facts that Stone uses to
appeal to the mind as well as to the
heart include being a war veteran
and being a father.]

tradition. So heroism *is* tied to an evolution
of consciousness. . . .[8]

A Since the war, I've had children, and I'm
wrestling now with the everyday problems of
trying to share my knowledge with them
without overwhelming them. It's difficult to
be a father, to be a mother, and I think that
to be a kind and loving parent is an act of
heroism. So there you go—heroes are everyday, common people. Most of what they do
goes unheralded, unappreciated. And that,
ironically, *is* heroism: not to be recognized.

Who is heroic? Scientists who spend years
of their lives trying to find cures for diseases.
The teenager who says no to crack. The
inner-city kid who works at McDonald's
instead of selling drugs. The kid who stands

alone instead of joining a gang, which would
give him an instant identity. The celebrity
who remains modest and treats others with
respect, or who uses his position to help
society. The student who defers the immediate
pleasure of making money and finishes college or high school. People who take risks
despite fears. People in wheelchairs who
don't give up. . . .

We have a lot of corruption in our society.
But we mustn't assume that everything is always basely motivated. We should allow for
the heroic impulse—which is to be greater
than oneself, to try to find another version of
oneself, to grow. That's where virtue comes
from. And we must allow our young generation to strive for virtue, instead of ridiculing it.

8. **evolution of consciousness:** growth in awareness
of one's self and one's role.

Vocabulary
defers (dē·fʉrz′) v.: delays; puts off.

Saul Mendoza of the United States and Francesca Porcellato of Italy talk after the
presentation of awards for winning competitions in the men's and women's Wheelchair
Division of the New York City Marathon, November 4, 2001.

Berlin served as Germany's capital for most of the twentieth century. In 1933, the National Socialist German Workers Party, known as the Nazis, came to power, and Adolf Hitler became head of Germany. The Nazis began a series of discriminatory measures against Jews, which denied them rights given to other Germans. The Nazis eventually implemented what they called their Final Solution—confining Jews and other people considered undesirable in concentration camps, in which they were killed by gassing and other means or worked to death. By the end of World War II, over six million European Jews had perished in the Holocaust.

Kirk Douglas (1916–) is a Hollywood star known for his fiery performances in such roles as the artist Vincent van Gogh and Spartacus, a slave who led a rebellion against the Roman Empire. Like his father, Michael Douglas is an award-winning actor.

Heroes with Solid Feet

from *The New York Times*, April 23, 2001

Kirk Douglas

Beverly Hills, California

Recently, I journeyed to Berlin to accept the Golden Bear, a lifetime achievement award, from the Berlin Film Festival. Those awards make me smile—lifetime achievement? Is this the end? Not long ago my son Michael received a lifetime achievement award. If you last long enough, you may get dozens.

I accepted the Golden Bear because I was curious to see Berlin again. During my earlier visits there, the city had been divided by a wall.[1]

In a press conference at the film festival, one journalist asked loudly, "As a Jew, how does it affect you to be in Berlin?" A montage of pictures we have all seen raced through my mind. Shattering glass windows, Hitler salutes, Jews being herded into freight cars, piles of emaciated Jews, ovens, dark smoke coming out of chimneys.

"The last century has been a disaster," I said. "My generation did not do a good job—so many wars, so much killing and of course, here in Germany, the Holocaust, perhaps the worst crime of all, the attempt to annihilate a people as a final solution."

---

1. **divided by a wall:** reference to the wall built by the Communists in 1961 that separated Communist East Berlin and democratic West Berlin. The Berlin Wall was opened in 1989, when Germany was reunited under a democratic government.

Vocabulary

emaciated (ē·mā′shē·āt′id) *adj.*: extremely thin; wasted away.

annihilate (ə·nī′ə·lāt′) *v.*: destroy completely.

A **Reading Informational Text**

? **Evaluating the credibility of an author's argument.** This is an anecdote within an anecdote. What idea or argument does the anecdote support? [Possible response: Inge Borck's anecdote supports the idea that ordinary people can do heroic things.] **How does the anecdote make you feel about Inge Borck's credibility?** [Possible response: She is credible because she lived through these experiences.]

They were all listening.

"But I don't think children should be punished for the sins of their fathers. We should do all we can to give our children that chance."

The questioner persisted. "So why did you come back to Berlin?" I ignored him. But the question bothered me. I didn't know a proper reason for a Jew to be in Berlin.

The audience at the awards ceremony gave me a standing ovation when I gave my speech in German, a language I learned when I made two movies in Germany. The papers were filled with my smiling face. The television reports were very complimentary. That night my wife and I had a wonderful Wiener schnitzel[2]

---

2. **Wiener schnitzel** (vē'nər shnit'səl): German dish consisting of breaded veal cutlet.

with some friends and a Jewish friend of theirs, Inge Borck, who lived in Berlin throughout the war. She was such a happy person, smiling and laughing. But when I was told that her parents and grandparents had all been killed in the concentration camps, I blurted out, "So why do you stay in Berlin?"

Smiling, she gave me this answer: "I owe that to the little heroes."

"I don't understand," I said. With a sigh, she came over and sat closer.

A "When the Gestapo[3] came to get them, my parents sent me to a small hotel to save my life. The owner was the first little hero. She kept me safe for a couple of nights.

---

3. **Gestapo** (gə·stä'pō): Nazi secret police.

The plaques in the Garden of the Righteous, in Israel, honor non-Jews who risked their lives to help Jews during the Holocaust.

During World War II, the Danish people helped more than seven thousand Jews escape the Nazis by smuggling them to Sweden. This boat was used in the rescue operation.

When it became dangerous, I met my second little hero. Or should I say heroine? She was our former housekeeper. She hid me for a while and endangered her own life. Then I lived in a cloister.[4] My little heroes were the nuns who took care of me when I was very sick. They never asked questions. When the situation became dangerous, my next little hero was a policeman who didn't agree with the Nazis. All through the war, I was lucky to find little heroes who helped me till the Russians came in."[5]

"So, why do you stay here?" I asked again. She looked at my perplexed face and said, "I thought about it, but I feel I owe it to the little heroes who helped me. Not everyone here was wicked."

Her story had a great impact on me. Of course, we are always looking for a big hero to emulate, and very often we see them topple from clay feet.[6] How much better to reach for the little heroes in life—and to try to be one. It's not always as hard as it was for the people in wartime Berlin. You aren't obligated to save a life—you only need to try to help other people.

And if everyone tried—well, just think of the lifetime achievements.

---

4. **cloister** (kloisʹtər) n.: place where a religious group, such as a group of nuns or monks, lives apart from the rest of society.
5. **Russians came in:** In the spring of 1945, Germany was defeated by British, United States, and Russian troops, ending World War II.

6. **topple from clay feet:** *Clay feet* is a figurative expression that refers to heroes who are discredited when their weaknesses are revealed. A statue in which the feet are made of clay, which can crumble easily, will not stand for long.

Vocabulary
emulate (emʹyoo·lāt′) v.: follow the example of; imitate.

DIRECT TEACHING

B Reading Informational Text

❓ Evaluating the credibility of an author's argument. Douglas states his argument at the end of his essay. Do you think it is more effective here than it would have been at the beginning? Why? [Possible responses: Placing the argument at the end is more effective, because he builds up to it gradually, and when he finally states his argument, it leaves readers with a strong impression. Placing the argument at the end is less effective because the first part of the essay doesn't contribute much to it.]

CONTENT-AREA CONNECTIONS

History: Berlin, Germany
The city of Berlin was very heavily damaged during World War II. Within months after Germany surrendered to the Russian Army in May of 1945, the city was divided among the Allied powers. The United States, Great Britain, France, and the Soviet Union each took one section of the city. Conflict over how to govern Berlin quickly arose between the Western Allies and Russia, resulting in a city that became divided into West and East Berlin. The division also separated Germany into two parts, West and East Germany. West Germany moved its capital to Bonn, but East Germany retained East Berlin as its capital. Suffering from a poor economy, anti-Communist riots, and the escape of hundreds of thousands of people to West Germany, Communist-controlled East Germany erected a wall through Berlin in 1961. Twenty-six and one-half miles long, the wall became known among Berliners—East and West—as the "Wall of Shame." Twenty-eight years later, as the Communist regime began to crumble, East Germany allowed its citizens to pass freely into West Germany. West Germany and East Germany were reunited in October of 1990, and by the end of that year, the Wall of Shame had been completely dismantled.

Analyzing Informational Text

Reading Check

1. Stone's heroes were mostly male historical figures, such as George Washington, General Custer, and Abraham Lincoln.

2. Heroes are everyday, common people.

3. He ignored the question.

4. Inge Borck is a resident of Berlin and a Holocaust survivor. The "little heroes" are the people of Berlin who protected her from the Nazis.

TestPractice

Answers and Model Rationales

1. **C** Stone's stated argument is that his own idea of heroism has changed. He does not attempt to show his own heroism (A) and does not mention any of his movies (D). Kovic (B) is only one of several examples Stone cites.

2. **F** The essay shows no evidence of anger (J) or humor (H). Stone does seem concerned (G) that heroes are unheralded and that there is corruption in American society, but his overall tone is uplifting.

3. **A** B and C are details within his anecdote. D is part of his conclusion.

4. **G** The words *herded* and *emaciated* (G) are loaded words. None of the words in the other choices are loaded. In H, *proper* simply means "logical" or "acceptable."

5. **C** The anecdote about Inge Borck serves to demonstrate a small act of heroism (C). There are insufficient facts and anecdotes to support A, B, and D.

Analyzing Informational Text

Reading Check

1. What kinds of heroes does Oliver Stone say he had when he was young?

2. What is the **main idea** of "Where I Find My Heroes"?

3. What was Kirk Douglas's response when asked why he returned to Berlin?

4. Who is Inge Borck, and who were the "little heroes" she told Douglas about?

Test Practice

1. Oliver Stone's **intent,** or **purpose,** in writing "Where I Find My Heroes" is to —
   A show how heroic he is
   B praise Ron Kovic's heroism
   C convince us of his vision of heroism
   D publicize his movies

2. Which word *best* describes the **tone** of Oliver Stone's essay?
   F uplifting
   G concerned
   H humorous
   J angry

3. Kirk Douglas uses an **anecdote** when he —
   A describes what happened at the Berlin Film Festival
   B tells why he accepted the Golden Bear award
   C explains that he learned German while making movies in Germany
   D says everyone should try to be a "little hero"

4. Kirk Douglas uses **loaded words** in which of the following items?
   F "If you last long enough, you may get dozens."
   G "Jews being herded into freight cars, piles of emaciated Jews, ovens, dark smoke coming out of chimneys."
   H "I didn't know a proper reason for a Jew to be in Berlin."
   J " 'So, why do you stay here?' I asked again."

5. Douglas's **purpose,** or **intent,** in writing his op-ed article is to —
   A persuade people never to forget the Holocaust
   B prove that he was right to go to Berlin
   C point out the importance of small acts of heroism
   D explain how traditional heroes have clay feet

Constructed Response

SKILLS FOCUS

Reading Skills
Evaluate an author's argument, including intent and tone.

Select either Oliver Stone's essay or Kirk Douglas's op-ed article, and write an **evaluation** of the author's argument. First, explain the writer's **purpose,** or **intent,** and the main **opinion,** or **claim,** the writer is defending. Then, describe the means of support the author uses (facts, examples, loaded words, anecdotes, and so forth). Next, describe the **tone** of the piece. Finally, comment on how successful the author was in convincing you with his argument. Was your heart touched? Your mind? Both?

Constructed Response

Students' evaluations should show evidence of understanding the author's main argument. Both authors support their arguments with a mixture of facts and anecdotes, occasionally using words with positive and negative connotations. Both authors use an uplifting tone which appeals more to the heart than to the mind.

Test-Taking Tips

For more instruction on how to answer multiple-choice items, refer students to **Test Smarts.**

Vocabulary Development

Word Knowledge: Using Context

PRACTICE 1

Use context clues in each sentence to help you fill in each blank with the appropriate word from the Word Bank.

1. Years of poor nutrition made the refugees weak and _____.

2. I always try to _____ people whom I admire, but I don't always succeed.

3. Sandra always _____ having fun after school until she has finished her homework.

4. There are laws to protect endangered species so that humans do not _____ certain animals.

5. Malcolm became an enthusiastic _____ of exercise after he started running and going to the gym regularly.

> **Word Bank**
> advocate
> defers
> emaciated
> annihilate
> emulate

Understanding Idioms

An **idiom** is an expression peculiar to a particular language that means something different from the literal meaning of its words. Kirk Douglas uses the idiom *clay feet,* which refers to a hero who is found to have hidden faults. The expression comes from the idea that a statue with clay feet will topple, since clay can easily crack and crumble.

Other common idioms include *a fish out of water* ("out of one's element"), *cry wolf* ("give a false alarm," based on a fable by Aesop), and *long in the tooth* ("somewhat old," based on judging a horse's age by the length of its teeth).

PRACTICE 2

Explain the meaning of each underlined idiom in the following sentences. Then, explain where you think each expression may have come from.

1. "Hold your horses," the teacher said. "The class hasn't been dismissed yet."

2. Sally is a couch potato who does nothing but watch television.

3. "Step on it!" called her mother. "You're going to be late for school!"

4. Natasha sent her letter to the editor by both e-mail and snail mail.

5. Pavel was star-struck after meeting the best surfer on the beach.

SKILLS FOCUS

Vocabulary Skills
Use words in context. Understand idioms.

Where I Find My Heroes / Heroes with Solid Feet **725**

Vocabulary Development

Practice 1

1. emaciated
2. emulate
3. defers
4. annihilate
5. advocate

Practice 2

1. *Meanings*—"wait" or "go slowly." *Possible origin*—from the days of horse-drawn wagons and stage-coaches.

2. *Meanings*—"someone who is inactive, passive, or disengaged," "someone who spends a lot of time watching television." *Possible origin*—derived from *vegetable,* meaning "lifeless person," and the habit of watching television passively from a sofa.

3. *Meanings*—"Do it quickly!" "Get going!" *Possible origin*—Derived from the use of the gas pedal in automobiles.

4. *Meaning*—"ordinary stamped mail sent through the post office." *Possible origin*—*snail,* connoting slowness, rhymes with *mail;* the slowness of regular mail is contrasted with the speed of e-mail.

5. *Meaning*—"awed." *Possible origin*—from the awe of observing stars in the sky; from the allure of Hollywood stars; from hypothetical impact of being hit by a star.

ASSESSING

Assessment

- *Holt Assessment: Literature, Reading, and Vocabulary*

RETEACHING

For a lesson reteaching evaluating an argument, see **Reteaching,** p. 979A. For another selection to teach evaluating an argument, see *The Holt Reader,* Part 2.

DIFFERENTIATING INSTRUCTION

Advanced Learners

Activity. Challenge advanced students to identify more idioms and to create illustrations or verbal descriptions of the meanings and possible origins of these idioms. Students can share their work with English-language learners.

Grade-Level Skills

■ **Literary Skills**
Understand characteristics of myths, including archetypes.

■ **Literary Skills**
Analyze the way a work of literature relates to the themes and issues of its historical period. (Historical approach)

■ **Reading Skills**
Identify cause and effect.

Summary *at grade level*

> The Fenris Wolf is an enormous, ferocious monster, fathered by Loki, an evil but indispensable god. After two failed attempts to restrain the wolf, the gods obtain a thin, soft rope created by the dwarf people. Fenris scoffs at the rope and correctly suspects it might be enchanted, so he demands a hostage as he agrees to test the rope's strength. The god Tyr volunteers to be the hostage, placing his bare hand in the wolf's menacing jaws. As the wolf strains to release himself from the rope, he bites off Tyr's hand but is unable to free himself. The wolf remains bound throughout Odin's rule, but eventually frees himself when, as the fates decree, the gods are destroyed.

Before You Read

The Fenris Wolf

Make the Connection

Quickwrite 🖉

How do you feel when you hear someone talk about wolves or serpents? Note whether you associate each creature with good or with evil. Then, write down why you think you have formed these associations.

Literary Focus

Myths

Every society has its **myths,** stories that are connected to the traditions and religion of the culture that produced them. Myths tell people where they came from, where they are going, and how they should live. Myths predate science: They often provide imaginative explanations for the origins of things. They answer questions like *Why is there evil in the world?* or *Why do we die?* or *Why do the seasons change?*

Many archetypes (är′kə·tīps′) come from myths. **Archetypes** are very old patterns or images that recur over and over again in literature. Archetypes can be characters (such as the sacrificial hero), plots (such as the heroic quest), animals (such as lambs, wolves, and serpents), or settings (such as the place of perfect happiness).

In this myth you will find the archetype of the "big bad wolf." You will also find the archetype of the sacrificial hero—a hero who sacrifices himself or herself for the greater good.

SKILLS FOCUS

Literary Skills
Understand characteristics of myths, including archetypes. Understand how a work of literature is related to its historical period.

Reading Skills
Identify cause and effect.

Reading Skills

Identifying Cause and Effect

Myths are narratives, which are built on a series of causes and effects. One event happens in a narrative, which causes another event to happen, which causes another event to happen, and so on. To keep track of causes and their effects, make a chart like the one below:

| Event 1 | → | Causes event 2 | → | Causes event 3 |

Background

Norse Mythology

"The Fenris Wolf" is a story from Norse mythology, the system of myths that developed thousands of years ago among the peoples of Scandinavia and Germany. The oldest surviving written versions of these tales came from Iceland in the thirteenth century. One collection, *The Elder Edda,* consists of poems compiled by an unknown person. The other collection, *The Younger Edda,* was written down by Snorri Sturluson, a wealthy and cultured man who was politically active in both Iceland and Norway. The tale of Fenris, or Fenrir as he is sometimes called, is found in Snorri Sturluson's collection.

There are variations in the Norse myths, as there are in the myths of most cultures. According to one version of the Norse creation story, life began in the boundary between fire and ice. Eventually, the first gods were born from a family of giants. These gods include those listed on the opposite page. Odin, Ve, and Vili created the earth and the first

---

Planning
■ *One-Stop Planner* CD-ROM with ExamView Test Generator

Differentiating Instruction
■ *Holt Reading Solutions*
■ *Supporting Instruction in Spanish*
■ *Audio CD Library, Selections and Summaries in Spanish*

Vocabulary
■ *Vocabulary Development*

Grammar and Language
■ *Daily Language Activities*

Assessment
■ *Holt Assessment: Literature, Reading, and Vocabulary*

■ *One-Stop Planner* CD-ROM with ExamView Test Generator
■ *Holt Online Assessment*

Internet
■ go.hrw.com (Keyword: LE5 9-10)
■ *Elements of Literature* Online

Media
■ *Audio CD Library*

man and woman. They also created **Asgard** (äs′gärd′), where the gods live, and **Midgard** (mid′gärd′), where humans live.

One of the most remarkable and tragic aspects of Norse mythology is its bleak prophecy about how the world will end. In this prophecy, giants and monsters led by the evil god Loki will do battle with the other gods and goddesses. All the gods and goddesses, giants, and monsters will slay each other, and the entire earth will be consumed by fire. This final struggle is called **Ragnarok** (rag′nə·räk′).

However, Norse mythology does contain a faint glimmer of hope. The myths contain a prophecy that a new world will be created, free of misery and evil, following the destruction.

Norse Gods

Odin (ō′din): also known as **Woden** (wōd′'n), god of wisdom and victory; leader of the family of gods.

Ve (vā) and **Vili** (vil′ē): Odin's brothers.

Frigga (frig′ə) or **Frigg** (frig): Odin's wife, goddess of marriage and motherhood.

Thor (thôr): Odin's oldest son, god of thunder and lightning.

Balder (bôl′dər): Odin and Frigga's son, god of goodness and harmony; the most beautiful of the gods.

Tyr (tir) or **Tiu** (tē′ōō): god of war; the bravest of the gods.

Loki (lō′kē): god of fire, mischief, and evil.

Frey (frā), or **Freyr** (frār): god of sun, rain, and harvests.

Freya (frā′ə): Frey's sister, goddess of love and fertility.

Bragi (brä′gē): god of poetry, eloquence, and music.

A CLOSER LOOK

Norse Mythology

The world of Norse mythology is a strange world. Asgard, the home of the gods, is unlike any other heaven men have dreamed of. No radiancy of joy is in it, no assurance of bliss. It is a grave and solemn place, over which hangs the threat of an inevitable doom. The gods know that a day will come when they will be destroyed . . . Asgard will fall in ruins. The cause the forces of good are fighting to defend against the forces of evil is hopeless. Nevertheless, the gods will fight for it to the end.

Necessarily the same is true of humanity. If the gods are finally helpless before evil, men and women must be more so. The heroes and heroines of the early stories face disaster. They know that they cannot save themselves, not by any courage or endurance or great deed. Even so, they do not yield. They die resisting. A brave death entitles them—at least the heroes—to a seat in Valhalla, one of the halls in Asgard, but there too they must look forward to final defeat and destruction. In the last battle between good and evil they will fight on the side of the gods and die with them.

This is the conception of life which underlies the Norse religion, as somber a conception as the mind of man has ever given birth to. The only sustaining support possible for the human spirit, the one pure unsullied good men can hope to attain, is heroism; and heroism depends on lost causes. The hero can prove what he is only by dying. The power of good is shown, not by triumphantly conquering evil, but by continuing to resist evil while facing certain defeat.

—Edith Hamilton, from *Mythology*

The Fenris Wolf **727**

Skills Starter

Build background. Iceland, an island characterized by numerous volcanoes, glaciers, thermal springs, lakes and rivers, was first colonized by Norwegian and other Scandanavian Vikings around A.D. 870. In A.D. 930, the diverse political units of the island unified under one commonwealth government, the Althing, which was the first parliament in the world. The island prospered despite the absence of a head of state. In 1262, Iceland surrendered to Norwegian authority, which also brought about the decline of the golden age of Icelandic literature.

The Elder Edda, also called the prose Edda, written around 1222 by Snorri Sturluson (1179 to 1241) was actually intended as a textbook for Icelandic poets. The word *edda* may be related to the Icelandic word meaning "song" or "poems," or it may refer to *Oddi*, a cultured town in southern Iceland where Snorri Sturluson was raised. The tale of Fenris comes from the third section of the Edda, which is in the form of a dialogue between a Swedish king, Gylfi, and the gods of Asgard.

Assign the Reading

You might wish to have advanced learners read the selection independently and complete the Response and Analysis as homework. You may wish to have other students read the selection aloud in small groups, each student reading aloud a paragraph in turn.

CONTENT-AREA CONNECTIONS

The Functions of Myth

"Myth basically serves four functions," says mythologist Joseph Campbell. "The first is the mystical function—that is the one I've been speaking about, realizing what a wonder the universe is, and what a wonder you are, and experiencing awe before this mystery. . . . The second is a cosmological dimension, the dimension with which science is concerned— showing you what the shape of the universe is, but showing it in such a way that the mystery again comes through. . . . The third function is the sociological one—supporting and validating a certain social order. And here's where the myths vary enormously from place to place. . . . But there is a fourth function of myth, and this is the one that I think everyone must try today to relate to— and that is the pedagogical function, of how to live a human lifetime under any circumstances. Myths can teach you that."

Activity. Ask students to analyze the *Odyssey,* the Fenris Wolf myth, or another myth in terms of how it fulfills each of these functions, especially the fourth.

A **Literary Focus**

? **Myth.** Loki is clever but trouble-some. His character is an archetype of the trickster, which is found in myths and folk tales of many cultures. Other examples are the coyote in Zuni myths, Brer Rabbit in African American folk tales, and the spider Anansi in African folk tales. What can you infer about the other gods from their dependence on Loki? [Possible response: They are not perfect; they're prone to getting in trouble and needing help.]

THE FENRIS WOLF

A NORSE MYTH

RETOLD BY OLIVIA COOLIDGE

The Norse god Tyr and the Fenris Wolf. Manuscript.

A Though Loki, the fire god, was handsome and ready-witted, his nature was really evil. He was, indeed, the cause of most of the misfortunes which befell the gods. He was constantly in trouble, yet often forgiven because the gods valued his cleverness. It was he who found ways out of difficulty for them, so that for a long time they felt that they could not do without him.

Learners Having Difficulty
Modeling. Some students may have difficulty identifying causes and effects in a series of events. Draw students' attention to key words and phrases such as *because, so that, therefore,* and *since.* Point out that sometimes a cause-and-effect relationship is implied and there is no key word or phrase. Model the

process of recognizing an implied cause-and-effect relationship by saying, "When I read that 'The howls of the beast were so dreadful . . . that the gods . . . dared not go near him, lest he devour them,' I know that the wolf's howls are the cause and the gods' fear is the effect."

In the early days Loki, though a god, had wedded a monstrous giantess, and the union of these two evil beings produced a fearful brood. The first was the great world serpent, whom Odin cast into the sea, and who became so large that he completely encircled the earth, his tail touching his mouth. The second was Hel, the grisly goddess of the underworld, who reigned in the horrible land of the dead. The third was the most dreadful of all, a huge monster called the Fenris Wolf.

When the gods first saw the Fenris Wolf, he was so young that they thought they could tame him. They took him to Asgard, therefore, and brave Tyr undertook to feed and train him. Presently, however, the black monster grew so enormous that his open jaws would stretch from heaven to earth, showing teeth as large as the trunks of oak trees and as sharply pointed as knives. The howls of the beast were so dreadful as he tore his vast meals of raw meat that the gods, save for Tyr, dared not go near him, lest he devour them.

At last all were agreed that the Fenris Wolf must be fettered[1] if they were to save their very lives, for the monster grew more ferocious towards them every day. They forged a huge chain, but since none was strong enough to bind him, they challenged him to a trial of strength. "Let us tie you with this to see if you can snap the links," said they.

The Fenris Wolf took a look at the chain and showed all his huge white teeth in a dreadful grin. "Bind me if you wish," he growled, and he actually shut his eyes as he lay down at ease to let them put it on.

---

1. **fettered** (fet′ərd) *v.*: chained.

> The wolf howled in triumph until the sun and moon in heaven trembled at the noise.

The gods stepped back, and the wolf gave a little shake. There was a loud cracking sound, and the heavy links lay scattered around him in pieces. The wolf howled in triumph until the sun and moon in heaven trembled at the noise.

Thor, the smith,[2] called other gods to his aid, and they labored day and night at the second chain. This was half as strong again as the first, and so heavy that no one of the gods could drag it across the ground. "This is by far the largest chain that was ever made," said they. "Even the Fenris Wolf will not be able to snap fetters such as these."

Once more they brought the chain to the wolf, and he let them put it on, though this time it was clear that he somewhat doubted his strength. When they had chained him, he shook himself violently, but the fetters held. His great, red eyes burned with fury, the black hair bristled on his back, and he gnashed his teeth until the foam flew. He strained heavily against the iron until the vast links flattened and lengthened, but did not break. Finally with a great bound and a howl he dashed himself against the ground, and suddenly the chain sprang apart so violently that broken pieces were hurled about the heads of the watching gods.

Now the gods realized in despair that all their strength and skill would not avail to bind the wolf. Therefore Odin sent a messenger to the dwarf people under the earth, bidding them forge him a chain. The messenger returned with

---

2. **smith** *n.*: blacksmith, someone who works at a forge, making and repairing metal objects, such as horseshoes.

A **Reading Skills**

? **Irony.** What is ironic about the materials from which the dwarfs' chain is made? [Possible response: The materials cannot be seen or heard and therefore do not imply great strength for a chain, as would a material such as steel.]

B **Literary Focus**

? **Dramatic and situational irony.** What do the gods know that they think the wolf doesn't know? [The chain is enchanted and the wolf will not be able to break free.] What is ironic about Tyr's action at this point? [He knows that he will lose his hand.]

C **Literary Focus**

? **Myth.** How is Tyr's action heroic? [Because Tyr knowingly sacrifices his hand, the Fenris Wolf is fettered and the gods are safe for a while.]

GUIDED PRACTICE

Monitoring students' progress. Guide the class in answering these comprehension questions.

True-False

1. Loki was handsome and well-behaved. [F]

2. The Fenris Wolf was the most horrible of all Loki's children. [T]

3. The wolf was unable to free himself from Thor's chains. [F]

4. Tyr lost his leg when the Fenris Wolf bit it off. [F]

5. The dwarfs had more power than the gods. [T]

A a little rope, smooth and soft as a silken string, which was hammered on dwarfish anvils[3] out of strange materials which have never been seen or heard. The sound of a cat's footfall, the breath of a fish, the flowing beard of a woman, and the roots of a mountain made the metal from which it was forged.

The gods took the tiny rope to the Fenris Wolf. "See what an easy task we have for you this time," they said.

"Why should I bother myself with a silken string?" asked the wolf sullenly. "I have broken your mightiest chain. What use is this foolish thing?"

"The rope is stronger than it looks," answered they. "We are not able to break it, but it will be a small matter to you."

"If this rope is strong by enchantment," said the wolf in slow suspicion, "how can I tell that you will loosen me if I cannot snap it after all? On one condition you may bind me: You must give me a hostage from among yourselves."

"How can we do this?" they asked.

---

3. **anvils** (an'vəlz) *n.*: iron or steel blocks on which hot metal objects are hammered into shape.

The Fenris Wolf stretched himself and yawned until the sun hid behind clouds at the sight of his great, red throat. "I will let you bind me with this rope," he said, "if one of you gods will hold his hand between my teeth while I do it."

B The gods looked at one another in silence. The wolf grinned from ear to ear. Without a word Tyr walked forward and laid his bare hand inside the open mouth.

C The gods bound the great wolf, and he stretched himself and heaved as before. This time, however, he did not break his bonds. He gnashed his jaws together, and Tyr cried out in pain as he lost his hand. Nevertheless, the great black wolf lay howling and writhing and helplessly biting the ground. There he lay in the bonds of the silken rope as long as the reign of Odin endured. The Fates declared, however, that in the last days, when the demons of ice and fire should come marching against the gods to the battlefield, the great sea would give up the serpent, and the Fenris Wolf would break his bonds. The wolf would swallow Odin, and the gods would go down in defeat. Sun and moon would be devoured, and the whole earth would perish utterly. ■

Meet the Writer

Olivia Coolidge

A Reteller of Tales
Olivia Coolidge (1908–   ) is best known for her retellings of the myths from ancient Greece, specifically aimed at young adults. Her interest in ancient legends has been evident from the beginning of her career. One of her earliest works, *Legends of the North,* is a collection of the Norse myths that contains "The Fenris Wolf" and other strange tales of the Northern gods, including the Norse creation myth and stories of the great Norse heroes. Coolidge has written about people from the distant past—ancient Egypt and Rome, for example—and from more recent historical periods as well. Her biographies of such figures as Abraham Lincoln, Tom Paine, and Gandhi, written for young adults, have been highly praised.

READING MINI-LESSON

Developing Word-Attack Skills
Write the selection word *gnashed* on the chalkboard. Point out that when the letters *gn* appear together at the beginning, as they do in *gnashed,* or at the end of a word, the *g* is silent. Then, explain that the *g* is usually not silent when *gn* occurs in the middle of a word—for example, *magnet, ignore, recognize.*

Activity. Write the following pairs of words on the chalkboard. Have students read them and tell which word in each pair has a silent *g.* Answers are underlined.

1. agnostic   benign
2. ignoble   gnome
3. deign   dignity
4. maligned   malignant
5. arraigned   interregnum

Response and Analysis

Reading Check

1. In a chart like the one below, outline the story as a series of **causes** and their **effects**. The first event and the final event are listed for you. Use as many boxes as you need to chart the causes and effects that lead from the first event to the final one.

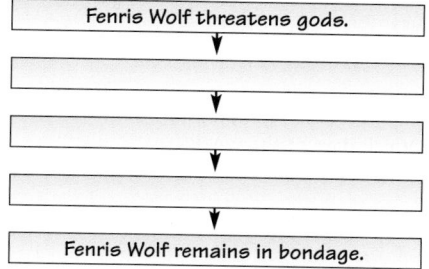

Thinking Critically

2. Traditional folk and mythic literature often includes events that happen in threes. What event takes place three times in this myth? What is the result of the third event?

3. **Compare** and **contrast** the Fenris Wolf and his father, Loki. Remember to consider their relationship with the gods.

4. In Norse mythology, heroes face terrible enemies with great courage—even though they know they will be defeated in the end. What action in this myth shows that kind of heroic behavior?

5. In Norse mythology the dwarfs who live under Midgard have great cunning and skill. What is their rope made of? What do all these ingredients have in common? Why can't the Fenris Wolf break their rope?

6. This story is dramatically visual. What **similes** does the storyteller use to help you imagine the wolf's teeth?

What vivid **images** help you picture the Fenris Wolf?

7. The third binding of the Fenris Wolf is successful, yet the myth ends tragically. How does the story's ending reflect the bleak outlook of Norse mythology?

WRITING

Evildoers

In literature, wolves and serpents are often demonized—that is, they are associated with sneaky behavior, evil, and destruction. In a brief **essay,** explain why you think wolves and snakes are presented in a negative way. In your first paragraph, describe how wolves and serpents are usually presented, and give examples from stories you know. In your second paragraph, discuss why wolves and serpents might have gotten such bad reputations. You can **research** the wolf and the serpent on the Internet or in an encyclopedia. (Check your Quickwrite notes.)

Monsters and Endings

The Norse myth "The Fenris Wolf" and the Greek epic the *Odyssey* come from different traditions and different parts of the world. They have many similarities—for example, monsters with amazing powers are important in both works. The two works also have many differences. The Greek epic ends happily, while the Norse myth, true to Norse tradition, ends tragically, with a reference to the destruction of the earth. In a few paragraphs, **compare** and **contrast** both the role of monsters in the two works and the stories' endings. Be sure to include details to support your points.

SKILLS FOCUS

Literary Skills
Analyze characteristics of myths, including archetypes. Analyze how a work of literature is related to its historical period.

Reading Skills
Identify cause and effect.

Writing Skills
Write an explanatory essay. Compare and contrast epics.

Response and Analysis

Thinking Critically

2. The Fenris Wolf is fettered three times. After the third time, he remains fettered.

3. Both are evil. Loki is clever and well-liked; the Fenris Wolf is ferocious and terrifying.

4. Tyr volunteers to put his hand in the wolf's mouth even though he knows the wolf will bite it off.

5. The dwarfs' rope is made of the sound of a cat's footfall, the breath of a fish, the flowing beard of a woman, and the roots of a mountain. None of these materials have ever been seen or heard. The dwarfs' rope is magical.

6. *Similes*—"teeth as large as the trunks of oak trees and as sharply pointed as knives." *Images*—the wolf's jaws stretching from heaven to earth; the sun and the moon trembling at the wolf's laughter; the wolf gnashing his teeth "till foam flew"; the sun hiding behind a cloud at the sight of the wolf's great, red throat; Tyr crying out as the wolf bites off his hand; the wolf swallowing Odin; the sun and moon being devoured.

7. In the end the gods are destroyed and the world perishes.

Reading Check

1. Sample Answers

   Cause 1—Fenris Wolf threatens gods. *Effect 1*—Gods try to fetter the wolf.

   Cause 2—Fenris Wolf breaks two sets of fetters. *Effect 2*—Gods ask the dwarfs for help.

   Cause 3—Fenris Wolf suspects a trick and demands a hostage. *Effect 3*—Tyr volunteers.

   Cause 4—Fenris Wolf struggles to free himself. *Effect 4*—Tyr loses his hand when Fenris Wolf bites it off as he is struggling to free himself.

   Cause 5—Fenris Wolf remains in bondage. *Effect 5*—The gods are safe for a while.

Vocabulary Development

Practice 1

1. **a.** *Odin,* or *Woden*—Wednesday. **b.** *Frigg*—Friday. **c.** *Tyr,* or *Tiu*—Tuesday. **d.** *Thor*—Thursday.

2. *Monday* is a rough translation of the late Latin *Lunae dies,* which means "moon day." *Sunday* is a rough translation of the late Latin *dies solis,* which means "day of the sun." *Saturday* is a half-translated adoption of the Latin *Saturni dies,* which means "day of (the planet) Saturn."

Practice 2

1. Hel, the underworld goddess

2. Thor, the god of thunder, war, and strength

ASSESSING

Assessment

■ *Holt Assessment: Literature, Reading, and Vocabulary*

Vocabulary Development

Words from Norse Myths

The English language that we speak today has been enriched over the years by contributions from many languages, among them German, Latin, Greek, French, and Spanish. Old English, the ancestor of our modern English, was the language spoken by Anglo-Saxon tribes who migrated to England from areas in what are now Germany, Denmark, and other northern European countries. Because they originated in northern Europe, the Anglo-Saxon people shared much of the culture from which Norse mythology sprang. In modern English we still use many terms that derive from that ancient culture.

PRACTICE 1

1. Four of our weekdays are named for gods from Norse mythology. Look at the following list of Norse gods. Which days of the week are named for these gods? Use a dictionary to check your answers.

   a. Odin, or Woden   **c.** Tyr, or Tiu
   b. Frigga (or Frigg)   **d.** Thor

2. What is the origin of the names of the other days of the week? Look up *Monday, Saturday,* and *Sunday* in a dictionary. Then, write one or two sentences explaining the **origin,** or **derivation,** of each name. (For help researching word origins, see page 42.)

PRACTICE 2

Refer to the story and to a dictionary for help answering the following questions:

1. What Norse name is our word *hell* related to?

2. What Norse god gave us our word *thunder*?

SKILLS FOCUS

Vocabulary Skills
Understand words from Norse myths.

Thor with his magic hammer.

DIFFERENTIATING INSTRUCTION

Advanced Learners
Enrichment. Have students discuss the similarities and differences between the gods portrayed in the *Odyssey* and those in "The Fenris Wolf." You may want to have students prepare a graphic aid such as a two-column chart, with one column labeled "Greek Gods" and the other "Norse Gods."

READ ON: FOR INDEPENDENT READING

FICTION

Wealth at a Price

In the tiny village of La Plata, a fisherman, Kino, is doing his best to support his wife, Juana, and their baby son, Coyotito—but times are tough, and money is scarce. Kino's discovery of a valuable pearl seems to be the answer to all his prayers. The only trouble is that everyone else in his village thinks so too, and Kino must make a perilous escape from would-be thieves in order to protect his family and his fortune. John Steinbeck's novella *The Pearl* is a heart-rending moral tale of greed and its consequences.

FICTION

Tales from Greece and Rome

The author Edith Hamilton was one of our leading experts on classical myths, and her love of the subject can be found on every page of her collection *Mythology.* Most of the best-known Roman, Greek, and Norse myths are here—from the labors of Hercules to Jason's quest to the triumph of Perseus. Odysseus's long travels are also included, as are tales of Odin, Thor, and Loki. Hamilton's brisk retellings make each story an adventure with glorious heroes and monstrous villains.

NONFICTION

A True-Life Epic

Long Walk to Freedom by Nelson Mandela is an inspiring chronicle of a man who fought to put an end to apartheid, the official policy of racial segregation and discrimination against blacks in South Africa. Mandela, whose humanitarian activism resulted in a twenty-seven-year imprisonment, wrote much of this autobiography while behind bars. His story is an epic journey that begins with Mandela's country childhood and ends with his winning the presidency in South Africa's first multiracial election.

This title is available in the HRW Library.

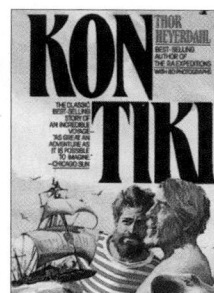

NONFICTION

Another Odyssey at Sea

Kon-Tiki is a real-life adventure story with a suspenseful plot that rivals anything in fiction or in film. Thor Heyerdahl journeyed 4,300 nautical miles across the Pacific Ocean—supported by nothing more than a handmade balsa-wood raft. Read this now-classic tale of Heyerdahl's voyage, and relive the dangers that threatened the Kon-Tiki crew: encounters with strange "monsters," leaks in the raft, and life-or-death struggles with a treacherous sea.

Read On   733

DIFFERENTIATING INSTRUCTION

Estimated Word Counts and Reading Levels of Read On Books:

Fiction			Nonfiction		
The Pearl	⬇	25,900	*Long Walk to Freedom*	⬆	176,800
Mythology	↔	148,800	*Kon-Tiki*	↔	112,600

KEY: ⬆ *above grade level*   ↔ *at grade level*   ⬇ *below grade level*

Persuading with Cause and Effect

Skills Starter

Motivate. Point out to students that they have been asking cause-and-effect questions since they first started exploring the world as small children: Why does it get dark? Why can't I do this or that? What if I become a lawyer? Point out that at the root of these answers is a simple cause-and-effect relationship. Tell students that in this workshop they will learn to use cause-and-effect relationships to bring about desired changes.

Consider Purpose, Audience, and Tone

You may want to remind students that there is more than one form in which to persuade with cause and effect. Some forms may be more appropriate than others, depending on students' purpose and audience. For example, a multimedia presentation might be an appropriate form in which to present information to a large group. If the audience is a school administrator, a formal essay is probably the most appropriate form for presenting information.

Writing Assignment
Write an essay in which you examine the causes and effects of a situation and persuade the reader to take action to change it.

In the *Odyssey*, when Calypso tries to persuade Odysseus to remain with her, she explains the effects Odysseus will suffer if he leaves her island. If you were to use the same persuasive technique, you probably would want to be more successful than Calypso was with Odysseus. However, what *can* you do if you find yourself in a situation that you think needs to be changed? You might first want to ask yourself: "What caused this situation to happen? What effects will this situation have?" Then, ask: "What actions would fix this situation?"

Prewriting

Choose a Situation

Wanted: Change Agents Change agents are people who make things happen, often by persuading others to take action to change situations. By writing a **persuasive cause-and-effect essay,** you can become a change agent. To find a possible topic, create an *If-Then* log by looking at the world around you and asking yourself, *"If* 'X' occurred, *then* what would happen?" Next, consider the effects of the situation and the actions that might result in change. You might also brainstorm with other students about local situations or problems.

Make a list of promising topics for your persuasive paper. Then, review your list and choose the topic that you find most interesting and that might inspire the strongest response in your readers.

Consider Purpose, Audience, and Tone

Part of the Solution The **purpose** of your essay is both expository and persuasive; that is, you will *explain* the cause and effects of a situation to readers in order to *convince* them to take action. However, simply explaining the cause and effects of a situation may not motivate your readers. They also need to know a specific action they can take to correct or change the situation, and be persuaded to take that action.

In order to write persuasively about the action, you need to understand what your **audience**—your readers—will need and want to know. Ask yourself: "How much do my readers already know about the situation?" and "What are my readers' concerns or biases about the

SKILLS FOCUS

Writing Skills
Write a persuasive cause-and-effect essay. Consider purpose, audience, and tone.

COLLECTION 10 RESOURCES: WRITING

Planning
- *One-Stop Planner* CD-ROM with ExamView Test Generator

Differentiating Instruction
- *Workshop Resources: Writing, Listening, and Speaking*
- *Family Involvement Activities in English and Spanish*

- *Supporting Instruction in Spanish*

Writing and Language
- *Workshop Resources: Writing, Listening, and Speaking*
- *Daily Language Activities*
- *Language Handbook Worksheets*

situation?" Knowing generally who your readers are and what reactions to expect from them can help you address any objections—or **counterclaims**—they may make. Addressing those objections in your essay will make your arguments more persuasive.

Your choice of words, details, and sentence structure express the **tone** of your writing—your attitude toward your subject and your audience. For most audiences, use a slightly formal tone so they will take your ideas seriously.

Analyze the Cause and Effects

What Happened and So What? The situation you've chosen is most likely part of a larger cause-effect relationship; that is, the situation has been caused by some previous action or decision. Ask yourself: "What is the initial *cause* of the situation I've chosen?" Analyze that cause so that you can explain to your readers why the situation or problem exists in the first place.

Next, turn your attention to the *effects* of the situation. When you write persuasively using cause and effect, you want your readers to agree that the situation you're describing needs to be changed. Therefore, think about the two or three most significant effects resulting from your situation. Those effects are probably negative ones; that's why there is a need for change.

Gather and Evaluate Evidence

Here's Why To be persuasive, provide precise and relevant **evidence** that supports your explanation of the cause and effects, and structure that evidence in a logical fashion. Evidence provides the proof your reader needs to accept your opinion. The following guide shows the kinds of supporting evidence you can use in your essay.

Quick guide

KINDS OF SUPPORTING EVIDENCE

Expert opinions are statements made by an authority on a subject.

Quotations present a person's word-for-word statement on a topic.

Facts are statements that can be proven true; **statistics** are facts in number form.

Anecdotes are brief stories that illustrate general ideas.

Commonly held beliefs are ideas that most people share.

A **case study** is an individual example used as the basis for generalizations.

An **analogy** is an explanation of something that readers do not know in terms of something familiar to them.

SKILLS FOCUS

Writing Skills
Structure ideas and arguments in a logical fashion. Use supporting evidence.

Writing Workshop: Persuading with Cause and Effect **735**

DIFFERENTIATING INSTRUCTION

Learners Having Difficulty
Use the following analogies to help students understand how anticipating and recognizing counterclaims can strengthen a position.

- Athletic coaches spend time and energy scouting the plays and personnel of other teams. This enables them to prepare their own teams to take advantage of opponents' weaknesses or neutralize their strengths.

- Lawyers must prepare to respond to claims made by opposing counsel. They must anticipate the arguments their opponents will make so that the arguments can be refuted.

DIRECT TEACHING

Integrating with Grammar, Usage, and Mechanics
As students begin their persuasive essays, they may have trouble with punctuation and correct spelling. You may want to review lessons 12–15 in the Language Handbook.

Assessment
- *Holt Assessment: Writing, Listening, and Speaking*
- *One-Stop Planner* CD-ROM with ExamView Test Generator
- *Holt Online Assessment*
- *Holt Online Essay Scoring*

Internet
- *go.hrw.com* (Keyword: LE5 9-10)
- *Elements of Literature Online*

CRITICAL THINKING

Tell students that their choice of logical, emotional, or ethical persuasive appeals should be based on a consideration of both the subject matter and the audience. For example, if students were trying to persuade an audience that a hospital needed a new multi-million-dollar pediatric unit, an emotional appeal to individual donors might work best, whereas a logical appeal to a city council might be most effective. Have students think of other subjects and audiences that require different types of appeals.

DIRECT TEACHING

Write Your Opinion Statement

Point out to students that their opinion statements should clearly present a cause-and-effect relationship. For example, they might write "Extending the passing periods from five to six minutes will lead to fewer students arriving tardy to classes and fewer disruptions for teachers." Another possibility is "The new ordinance requiring pet owners to keep their dogs on a leash will result in healthier, happier people and pets."

PRACTICE & APPLY 1

Guided and Independent Practice

Monitor students' progress by asking each student to list the topic of his or her essay, its audience, and its tone, and to outline briefly the causes and effects of the situation. Meet individually with students to check for appropriateness of topics and solid cause-and-effect relationships. Then, have students complete **Practice and Apply 1** for independent practice.

TIP Whenever you use evidence, keep in mind that one of your goals is to use **logical reasoning** to build a persuasive case.

| DO THIS |

SKILLS FOCUS

Writing Skills
Establish your opinion statement.

Look at the following notes one student made. Notice how the evidence supports the effect the student lists.

> **Effect:** Heavy backpacks will cause health problems in students.
> **Evidence:** A local chiropractor reports an increase in the number of students complaining of back and shoulder pain due to backpacks. (expert opinion)

A Matter of Appeal When you propose changes that you want your readers to adopt, you'll write persuasively, shaping your explanations and evidence with **rhetorical devices,** such as logical, emotional, or ethical appeals. To be convincing, use one or a combination of all three kinds of appeals within your essay. For example, look at the way one student experimented with the three different appeals to shape an explanation of a negative effect.

Effect: Health problems for students

Logical Appeal	Statistic showing the weight of a student's backpack and the resulting muscle strain
Emotional Appeal	Description of a student's chronic back pain from a heavy backpack
Ethical Appeal	Statement about the school's responsibility to maintain the physical well-being of the student in areas besides sports

Write Your Opinion Statement

Sound Off To voice your opinion, write an **opinion statement** to share your perspective on the changes needed for a situation. An opinion statement lets your readers know how you feel about the situation, and hints at the effects you will discuss.

Decide on a Call to Action

Do What I Say! After explaining the cause and effects of your situation, urge your readers to take action to improve the situation. To be convincing, address your readers' counterclaims, and clearly state the actions you think are necessary for changing the situation. You may want to give the readers a choice between two courses of action. For example, the student writing about heavy backpacks proposed that the school administration either reinstall school lockers or issue an extra set of textbooks for each classroom.

PRACTICE & APPLY 1
Use the information on these pages to plan a persuasive cause-and-effect essay.

Writing

Persuading with Cause and Effect

A Writer's Framework

Introduction

- Begin with a bold statement or anecdote.

- Provide background information for the situation if necessary.

- Include a clear opinion statement. Indicate how you feel about the situation and hint at the effects you will discuss.

Body

- Explain the cause and the effects of the situation.

- Use persuasive appeals—logical, emotional, and ethical.

- Use evidence as support—facts, statistics, anecdotes, expert opinions, logical reasoning, or commonly accepted beliefs.

Conclusion

- Propose a specific call to action.

- Address any counterclaims a reader may have to your call to action.

- Restate your essay's opinion statement.

- End with a strong statement.

A Writer's Model

The highlighted words below indicate cause and effect.

A Weighty Case

Crowds of students once streamed toward Smith High School just before the first bell, headed for their lockers to deposit their bulging backpacks. However, now they are out of luck. Now there is no rest for the weary and heavy-laden at Smith High School, where lockers have been removed by school administrators because of their concerns about crowded hallways and tardiness. As a result, Smith High School students carry their heavy backpacks all day—an unfortunate situation that will cause other serious problems for students and should be changed.

According to a school announcement, the decision to remove the lockers was prompted by congested hallways. During every passing period between classes, clumps of students filled the halls so that other students could not get to class on time. Tardiness had become a real issue for the administration and teachers. The school administration's answer was to remove the lockers from the high school.

Without lockers, students have been forced to carry heavy backpacks all day. This situation creates not only an inconvenience, but also a health risk. A recent study shows that carrying an overloaded backpack can result in serious muscle strain in a student's

INTRODUCTION
Anecdote

Background information

Opinion statement

BODY
Description of cause

Effect 1: Logical appeal

Evidence: Case study

(continued)

Introduction

Hearing their drafts read aloud by another person can help students evaluate the tone of their writing. You may want to pair students so that they can read aloud each other's writing to check for a serious and consistent tone.

DIFFERENTIATING INSTRUCTION

Advanced Learners

Enrichment. Challenge students to draft outlines for persuasive essays arguing the point of view opposite to that of **A Writer's Model.** Have students include statistics, examples, and stories they would use to support the argument. After students have completed this task, ask them what they learned that would help them revise **A Writer's Model.** For example, they may have discovered another opposing point, or counterclaim, that could be addressed.

CORRECTING MISCONCEPTIONS

Students may be tempted to include phrases such as "In my opinion," "It is the opinion of this writer," and so on. Explain that these phrases actually weaken essays and direct attention to the author rather than to the opinion. Readers will generally not care too much about who the author of a persuasive essay is unless the author is a celebrity.

DIRECT TEACHING

A Writer's Model

To reinforce the skill of providing supportive evidence, turn students' attention back to **A Writer's Model.** Point out the different types of evidence the writer uses in the third paragraph (case study, expert opinion, quotation, statistics). Ask students how each piece of evidence works to strengthen the essay.

PRACTICE & APPLY 2

Guided and Independent Practice

- As students draft their essays, hold brief, individual conferences with them. Prior to the conference, ask them to draw a box around the separate causes and effects they are presenting in the essay.

- Students may find it easier to draft the bodies of their essays first, describing causes and effects and providing details. Then, students can see whether there is sufficient support for their opinion statements. If not, students should revise their opinion statements or find additional supporting evidence before drafting their introductions and conclusions.

Evidence: Expert opinion

Evidence: Quotation

Evidence: Statistics

Ethical appeal

Effect 2: Emotional appeal

Evidence: Example

Emotional appeal
CONCLUSION
Call to action

Counterclaim addressed

Another call to action

Commonly held belief

Restatement of opinion
Final statement

INTERNET
More Writer's Models
Keyword: LE5 9-10

---

back and shoulders. Alexa Nuñez, a local chiropractor, reports an increase in the number of high school students who suffer from back and neck pain caused by carrying heavy backpacks. She says, "Students are carrying heavy backpacks slung over one shoulder and increasing their risk of injury." Nuñez also says that the American Chiropractic Association recommends that a backpack should weigh no more than 10 percent of the student's body weight, or no more than 15 pounds. A backpack full of textbooks and supplies, however, weighs 25 or 30 pounds. Asking students to carry this weight all day means ignoring basic health guidelines.

Besides the harm caused by carrying these backpacks, there is an additional danger once students get to class. Because a stuffed backpack cannot fit under a desk, it ends up jamming the aisle. As a result, students and teachers cannot move freely around the classroom, and they may trip and fall. In case of a fire or even a fire drill, what if a student stumbles on a backpack, falls, and smashes her head? In the rush to escape, what if no one notices her? Is this a risk that Smith High administrators are willing to take?

Because of the hardships imposed on students by the school administration's decision, I ask for one of the following actions. First, I urge the school administration to reconsider its decision and restore the lockers for student use at least before school, during lunch, and after school. If students used their lockers at these times, they would not fill the halls during the passing periods, risk being tardy, or jam the aisles. The students would have to carry only half of their day's required books and perhaps cut the weight of their backpacks in half. Second, if the school cannot reinstall the lockers for some reason, I request that the school remedy the situation with a widely discussed and widely used method: Issue two sets of textbooks—one for the classroom and one for home. Everyone is concerned about student health, but the school should not expose students to real health risks in order to prevent possible, but highly unlikely, risks. Removing the lockers was a mistake because of the problems it has created for the students. To correct its mistake, Smith High School should reinstall the lockers or issue another set of textbooks for each student.

PRACTICE & APPLY 2

Write the first draft of your essay, using the framework and Writer's Model as guides. Remember to explain the cause and effects of the situation you have chosen and to use persuasive appeals.

Revising

Evaluate and Revise Your Draft

Checking It Twice If you are urging an audience to accept both your evaluation of a situation and your call to action, you'll want to present your explanation and persuasion in the best manner possible. Since errors detract from your presentation, try to read through your paper at least twice. If you have time, set your paper aside so that you can look at it with fresh eyes. Then, use the guidelines below to evaluate and revise your draft for content and organization. Use the guidelines on page 740 to revise for style, making sure you have used plenty of **cause-effect clue words.**

> **First Reading: Content and Organization** Use the chart below to evaluate the content and organization of your essay. Answer the evaluation questions. Then, use the tips to pinpoint the revisions you need to make. As you revise, keep in mind your audience and your purpose for writing.

PEER REVIEW

Ask a classmate to read your essay and check to see if you have clearly explained the situation's cause and effects, used supporting evidence, and persuaded the reader to take action.

Rubric: Persuading with Cause and Effect

Evaluation Questions	▶ Tips	▶ Revision Techniques
❶ Does the essay include an opinion about the situation and hint at its effects?	▶ **Highlight** the opinion statement. **Underline** the opinion. **Double underline** the hint at the effects of the situation.	▶ **Add** an opinion statement that clearly states an opinion about the situation and hints at the effects.
❷ Does the essay explain the cause and effects of the situation?	▶ **Circle** the situation. **Bracket** the cause. **Double bracket** the effects.	▶ **Add** an explanation of the situation's cause. **Elaborate** by explaining the situation's effects.
❸ Does the essay include a variety of supporting evidence?	▶ **Put a check** by each piece of evidence. **Label** each kind of evidence.	▶ **Add** evidence—facts, statistics, anecdotes, expert opinions, and so on.
❹ Does the essay use logical, emotional, or ethical appeals?	▶ **Put a box around** and **label** the sentences that show logical, emotional, or ethical appeals.	▶ **Add** sentences that use one or a combination of logical, emotional, or ethical appeals.
❺ Does the conclusion address the reader's counterclaims and include a specific call to action and a last strong statement?	▶ **Put a star by** the counterclaims. **Draw parentheses around** the call to action. In the margin, **draw an arrow** pointing to the final strong statement.	▶ **Add** sentences that address counterclaims. **Reword** sentences to include a specific call to action and a final, strong statement.

DIRECT TEACHING

Rubric: Persuading with Cause and Effect

Advise students to use the **Rubric** chart on this page as a think sheet by answering the questions in their notebooks. Explain to students that using think sheets to summarize their notes allows them to place their thoughts, observations, and questions on paper, which in turn helps improve the content and organization of their essay.

Elaboration

Students should understand that elaboration is a key element of sustaining their arguments in a logical fashion. Point out that students can bolster their cause-and-effect explanations with evidence—facts, statistics, expert opinions, and anecdotes. This approach might be particularly effective as causal chains become longer and readers are led further away from the initial cause.

TECHNOLOGY TIP

Encourage students to use the borders, shading, and style formatting options in their word-processing programs to mark their essays as suggested in the **Rubric** chart on this page. Suggest that they evaluate only one area at a time; otherwise, the markings may become too confusing.

Second Reading: Style To keep your readers interested and really drive home the ideas in your essay, work on revising and improving your **style**—the way you express your thoughts. Use cause-effect clue words to link your ideas for the reader and to connect your sentences more clearly. Follow the guidelines below to revise for style.

Style Guidelines

Evaluation Question	▶ Tip	▶ Revision Technique
● Does the essay use cause-effect clue words to help explain the situation and its negative effects?	▶ **Highlight** any words that show either cause or effect.	▶ **Reword** sentences so that you use words that show cause and effects.

ANALYZING THE REVISION PROCESS
Study these revisions, and answer the questions that follow.

> Now there is no rest for the weary and heavy-laden at Smith
>
> High School, where lockers have been removed by school ad-
>
> reword ministrators. *because of their concerns* ~~The school administrators are concerned~~ about
>
> reword crowded hallways and tardiness. *As a result,* Smith High School students
>
> add carry their heavy backpacks all day. *—an unfortunate situation that will cause other serious problems for students and should be changed.*

Responding to the Revision Process
1. What is the effect of adding the words "because of their concerns" in the passage above?
2. How do the words "As a result," added to the last sentence, relate to the previous sentence?
3. How did the addition to the end of the last sentence clarify the opinion statement?

SKILLS FOCUS

Writing Skills
Revise for content and style.

PRACTICE & APPLY 3 Use the guidelines on pages 739 and 740 to revise the content, organization, and style of your essay. Make sure that you have clearly explained your situation's cause and effects, and have used cause-effect clue words.

GUIDED PRACTICE

Responding to the Revision Process

Answers

1. The addition sets up a cause-and-effect relationship and shows that the author is not argumentative.
2. "As a result" makes the cause-and-effect relationship clear.
3. It made clear the negative effect of carrying a backpack and appealed to readers' emotions.

PRACTICE & APPLY 3

Independent Practice
Check to see whether students have marked their essays according to the tips in the **Rubric** chart on p. 739. To make sure that students do not simply recopy the draft as a final copy, ask that they submit lists of their revisions with their essays.

Publishing

Proofread and Publish Your Essay

Getting It Right Remember that you never get a second chance to make a first impression. Make sure, therefore, that your essay is as error-free as possible so that you will create the right first impression on your readers and accomplish your goals. Before you make a final copy, check your essay thoroughly for grammar, usage, and mechanical errors. Correct any errors that you find.

Change Your World Try one of the following suggestions to share the ideas you presented in your essay.

- Submit your essay to people who can make the changes you propose. For instance, an essay about a school-related topic might be submitted to your school newspaper or to your school administration, while an essay about a neighborhood issue could be submitted to the neighborhood newsletter.

- Adapt your essay into an oral presentation that can be delivered to people who might be affected by the situation you are discussing, such as the school environment club or the city council.

- Videotape a reading of your presentation and show it to a public-speaking class for their review. Use their suggestions to make adjustments in your next presentation. For information on **adapting your essay for a persuasive speech,** see page 742.

- Exchange your paper with a pen pal from another country. Correspond with each other about the similarities and differences in persuading with cause and effect in the two cultures.

Reflect on Your Essay

A Job Well Done To reflect upon the decisions you made and the skills you gained while writing your essay, answer the following questions.

- Did you have trouble finding a situation with negative effects to discuss? Explain your answer.

- What was your best supporting piece of evidence? Why do you think that this was the case?

- Did writing this essay help you see how you could really take action and change a situation that has negative effects? Explain your reasoning.

PRACTICE & APPLY 4 Proofread, publish, and reflect on your essay, using the instructions on this page. Remember to have one of your peers review your essay and provide feedback so that you may have a final check on your work.

> **TIP** A dangling modifier—a modifying word, phrase, or clause that does not clearly and sensibly modify—can muddle your explanation and confuse your readers. Carefully proofread your essay to correct dangling modifiers and to ensure that you follow the **conventions** of standard American English. For more on **dangling modifiers,** see Placement of Modifiers, 5f, in the Language Handbook.

SKILLS FOCUS

Writing Skills
Proofread, especially to correct dangling modifiers.

Tip
To make sure students understand how to eliminate dangling modifiers, write these two sentences on the chalkboard:

> After waiting in line for five hours, the ticket seller announced that the concert was sold out.

> Though she studied a long time for the test, the teacher said that her grade was disappointing.

Model finding the dangling modifier in the first sentence by circling the phrase "After waiting in line for five hours" and then asking whom the phrase describes. Students should realize that the phrase does not describe the ticket seller though it appears to at first. Rewrite the sentence like this: "After waiting in line for five hours, my sister cried when the ticket seller announced that the concert was sold out."

Ask a volunteer to demonstrate understanding for the class by identifying the dangling modifier in the second sentence and then rewriting it to eliminate the confusion.

PRACTICE & APPLY 4

Guided and Independent Practice

As students read their peers' essays, ask them to focus on how effective they think the evidence offered will be on the intended audience. You may circulate among students to monitor progress. Ask students to write their thoughts on an index card and return it along with the essay. Check with individual students to elicit their response to their partner's comments.

English-Language Learners
Some students may lack confidence in their English skills and choose not to publish their essays even if their ideas are persuasive. Pair these students with English-proficient students who will review their essays to make sure correct, standard English is used. The English-proficient partners can identify nonstandard usage and work with the English-language learners to correct it. Have the students select a venue for sharing the essay together.

PRETEACHING

PRETEACHING

Motivate. Ask students what television commercials have persuaded them to do something new or different, or persuaded them to try a new food or product. Select one that most of the students are familiar with, and discuss its approach to persuading viewers. Ask students how they were convinced by the commercial. Urge students to remember the effective aspects of the commercial as they plan to deliver persuasive speeches.

RETEACHING

Tailor-Made

Reteach the concept of appropriate tone by pointing out to students that the tone of their speeches will affect the way their audience responds. It is important to have sound, clear reasoning so that the audience will take the speaker's words into consideration. To review the difference between a well-supported opinion and an argumentative attack, have students add examples to the table below.

Persuasive	Argumentative
The widespread fear of wolves is based on misinformation and the influence of fairy tales.	People who fear wolves are silly and misinformed.

DIFFERENTIATING INSTRUCTION

Advanced Learners

Enrichment. Have students reflect on the process of preparing and delivering a persuasive speech by answering the following question: Suppose you were asked to deliver your speech again to a different audience. How might you improve your preparation and delivery?

Giving a Persuasive Speech

Speaking Assignment
Adapt your persuasive cause-and-effect essay for a persuasive speech, and deliver it to your class.

A persuasive speech, like an essay that uses cause and effect to persuade, may change the audience members' beliefs, unite them behind a common cause, or inspire them to take action to solve a problem. A speech and an essay share the basic techniques of persuasion. In this workshop you will learn how to take advantage of those techniques and some additional strategies.

Adapt Your Essay

Tailor-Made To adapt your cause-effect essay for a speech, first think about your **audience.** Because a listening audience can't rehear a word, phrase, or sentence, be sure that your vocabulary is simple and easily understood. For a formal speech, however, maintain the same formal **tone** as you used in your essay.

Beginnings The art of verbal persuasion begins with the first words that you speak to your audience. Adapt the **introduction** of your essay so that you can make a dramatic impact from the very beginning. For example, use an intriguing literary quotation, an interesting anecdote, or a reference to an authority on the subject of your speech. Sometimes repeating your opinion statement to your audience reinforces the importance of your ideas.

Endings Conclude your speech by summarizing the effects of your situation. Restate your opinion in a memorable fashion. Then, make a lasting impression by saying your final sentence slowly enough that the audience can feel its impact. A great last line usually is rewarded by the audience's applause.

In the Middle, Make Your Case You will spend the majority of your time explaining why your audience should agree with your opinion statement. How will you formulate your arguments for your listeners? Keep the following suggestions in mind as you review the body paragraphs of your essay.

- Remember that you have a limited amount of time to present your material. You may need to evaluate your description of the situation's cause, the explanation of its effects, and the supporting evidence you have used. Present only the information that will be most compelling to your audience, but make sure your evidence is both valid and credible. Each piece of evidence, as well as the **logical reasoning** that you use, should be relevant to your explanations of your situation and its effects.

INTERNET
Speeches
Keyword: LE5 9-10

SKILLS FOCUS

Listening and Speaking Skills
Deliver a persuasive speech.

COLLECTION 10 RESOURCES: LISTENING & SPEAKING

Planning
- *One-Stop Planner* CD-ROM with ExamView Test Generator

Differentiating Instruction
- *Workshop Resources: Writing, Listening, and Speaking*
- *Family Involvement Activities in English and Spanish*

- *Supporting Instruction in Spanish*

Listening and Speaking
- *Workshop Resources: Writing, Listening, and Speaking*

Assessment
- *Holt Assessment: Writing, Listening, and Speaking*

- Choose the most effective **rhetorical devices**—emotional, logical, and ethical appeals—from your essay. Your appeals should suit your listening audience. For example, an audience of your classmates may respond to an effective emotional appeal. However, if you are addressing a school board, logical and ethical appeals would be more effective rhetorical devices for your persuasive speech.

One Jump Ahead Public speakers—from presidents to principals—know that one of the most effective strategies for convincing others is to anticipate and address the **concerns** and **counterclaims** of audience members who might disagree with them. If the audience for your speech is different from the audience for your essay, consider what different concerns or counterclaims the different audience might have and make adjustments in your speech.

Additional Evidence If you find that you need additional evidence to be convincing, consider interviewing an authority on your subject. Before the interview, arrange a time and prepare a set of logical, appropriate questions. During the interview, record the responses, either by taking careful notes, or by asking permission to audiotape or videotape your interviewee. Listen carefully and politely; conduct the interview in a mature, respectful, and responsible manner. Answer any questions that may be asked of you by showing you have knowledge of the subject. After the interview, express your appreciation. Review your notes, and evaluate the effectiveness of the interview process. What, if anything, would you change and why?

Appealing Order To organize your speech, stick to the same basic organizational structure that you used for your essay. Use cause-effect clue words to help show the order of ideas and to make clear the relationship between the situation and its cause and effects.

Present Your Speech

Special Delivery To present a **formal speech**—a memorized speech—make a careful outline. You will memorize and practice the speech before you deliver it. To help you with your formal speech, create concise notes on the content of your speech and on the verbal and nonverbal techniques you intend to use at particular points. **Verbal techniques** include the tone, pitch, and volume of your voice. **Nonverbal techniques** include gestures, pauses, and eye contact. Use your notes to rehearse your speech before a mirror, an audience, a video camera, or an audio recorder. (For more on **verbal and nonverbal techniques,** see page 75.)

PRACTICE & APPLY 5 Use the instruction in this workshop to adapt your persuasive cause-and-effect essay for a persuasive speech. Then, rehearse and deliver your speech.

TIP Counterclaims are also called **counterarguments.**

SKILLS FOCUS

Listening and Speaking Skills
Practice your presentation.

Listening and Speaking Workshop: Giving a Persuasive Speech **743**

- *One-Stop Planner* CD-ROM with ExamView Test Generator

Internet
- go.hrw.com (Keyword: LE5 9-10)
- *Elements of Literature Online*

Appealing Order
Share the following outline with students to show them how they may organize their speeches in a cause-and-effect pattern. Tell students that having an organizational plan can help them avoid any audience confusion and will help the audience focus on the topic of persuasion.

Analyzing Causes and Effects
I. Introduction: Give the opinion statement.
II. Body
   A. Examine the causes or effects.
   B. Address counterarguments.
III. Conclusion
   A. Reinforce the belief or idea.
   B. Give a call to action.

PRACTICE & APPLY 5

Guided and Independent Practice
Share these practice and preparation tips with students before they begin preparing their speeches.

- Speak at a reasonable rate and volume.
- Enunciate.
- Be enthusiastic.
- Use an effective pitch and tone of voice.
- Maintain eye contact with your audience.
- Use appropriate gestures and facial expressions.
- Use good posture.
- Breathe deeply to reduce nervousness.

Then, have students complete **Practice and Apply 5** independently.

Collection 10: Skills Review

Informational Reading Skills

Informational Reading Skills

SKILLS FOCUS, pp. 744–747

Grade-Level Skills

■ **Reading Skills**
Evaluate the credibility of an author's argument by examining the author's intent and tone.

INTRODUCING THE SKILLS REVIEW

Use this review to assess students' grasp of the skills taught in this collection. If necessary, you can use the annotations to guide students in their reading before they answer the questions.

DIRECT TEACHING

Ⓐ Reading Skills

❷ Evaluating the author's argument. Aaron states his intent or purpose in the second paragraph. What does he want to do? [He wants to persuade the reader that Jackie Robinson was a hero who was "bigger than life."] What important fact does he present that appeals to the reader's mind? [Possible response: In 1947, U.S. society was racially segregated.]

Ⓑ Reading Skills

❷ Evaluating the author's argument. Aaron's repetition of the word *bigger* sets a serious tone that has an emotional appeal, yet this paragraph is also filled with facts. What are these facts? [Robinson's teammates tried to kick him off the club; pitchers tried to hit him; base runners tried to spike him; people wrote him death threats.]

Test Practice

Evaluating an Argument

DIRECTIONS: Read the following article. Then, read and respond to the questions that follow.

Jackie Robinson

Henry Aaron

I was fourteen years old when I first saw Jackie Robinson. It was the spring of 1948, the year after Jackie changed my life by breaking baseball's color line. His team, the Brooklyn Dodgers, made a stop in my hometown of Mobile, Alabama, while barnstorming its way north to start the season, and while he was there, Jackie spoke to a big crowd of black folks over on Davis Avenue. I think he talked about segregation, but I didn't hear a word that came out of his mouth. Jackie Robinson was such a hero to me that I couldn't do anything but gawk at him.

Ⓐ They say certain people are bigger than life, but Jackie Robinson is the only man I've known who truly was. In 1947 life in America—at least my America, and Jackie's—was segregation. It was two worlds that were afraid of each other. There were separate schools for blacks and whites, separate restaurants, separate hotels, separate drinking fountains, and separate baseball leagues. Life was unkind to black people who tried to bring those worlds together. It could be hateful. But Jackie Robinson, God bless him, was bigger than all of that.

Ⓑ Jackie Robinson had to be bigger than life. He had to be bigger than the Brooklyn teammates who got up a petition to keep him off the ball club, bigger than the pitchers who threw at him or the base runners who dug their spikes into his shin, bigger than the bench jockeys who hollered for him to carry their bags and shine their shoes, bigger than the so-called fans who wrote him death threats.

When Branch Rickey first met with Jackie about joining the Dodgers, he told him that for three years he would have to turn the other cheek and silently suffer all the vile things that would come his way. Believe me, it wasn't Jackie's nature to do that. He was a fighter, the proudest and most competitive person I've ever seen. This was a man who, as a lieutenant in the army, risked a court-martial[1] by refusing to sit in the back of a military bus. But when Rickey read to him from *The Life of Christ,* Jackie understood the wisdom and the necessity of forbearance.[2]

SKILLS FOCUS

Pages 744–747 cover **Reading Skills** Evaluate an author's argument, including intent and tone.

---

1. **court-martial** (kôrt′mär′shəl) *n.:* military trial.
2. **forbearance** (fôr · ber′əns) *n.:* patience and self-control.

744 Collection 10 Epic and Myth • Evaluating an Argument

READING MINI-LESSON

Reviewing Word-Attack Skills
Activity. Write the following sets of words on the chalkboard. The first word in each set begins with *w.* Have students read the words and identify the word that rhymes with the *w* word. Encourage them to use a dictionary to check pronunciations whenever necessary. Answers are underlined.

1.	wattle	battle	<u>bottle</u>
2.	wombat	<u>combat</u>	comet
3.	wallop	gallop	<u>dollop</u>
4.	worse	horse	<u>curse</u>
5.	wallow	mallow	<u>hollow</u>
6.	wattage	adage	<u>cottage</u>
7.	wizard	<u>lizard</u>	buzzard
8.	warden	garden	<u>cordon</u>
9.	wander	pander	<u>ponder</u>
10.	warren	barren	<u>foreign</u>

To this day, I don't know how he withstood the things he did without lashing back. I've been through a lot in my time, and I consider myself to be a patient man, but I know I couldn't have done what Jackie did. I don't think anybody else could have done it. Somehow, though, Jackie had the strength to suppress his instincts, to sacrifice his pride for his people's. It was an incredible act of selflessness that brought the races closer together than ever before and shaped the dreams of an entire generation.

Before Jackie Robinson broke the color line, I wasn't permitted even to think about being a professional baseball player. I once mentioned something to my father about it, and he said, "Ain't no colored ball-players." There were the Negro Leagues, of course, where the Dodgers discovered Jackie, but my mother, like most, would rather her son be a schoolteacher than a Negro Leaguer. All that changed when Jackie started stealing bases in a Brooklyn uniform.

Jackie's character was much more important than his batting average, but it certainly helped that he was a great ballplayer, a .311 career hitter whose trademark was rattling pitchers and fielders with his daring base running. He wasn't the best Negro League talent at the time he was chosen, and baseball wasn't really his best sport—he had been a football and track star at UCLA—but he played the game with a ferocious creativity that gave the country a good idea of what it had been missing all those years. With Jackie in the infield, the Dodgers won six National League pennants.

I believe every black person in America had a piece of those pennants. There's never been another ballplayer who touched people as Jackie did. The only comparable athlete, in my experience, was Joe Louis.[3] The difference was that Louis competed against white men; Jackie competed with them as well. He was taking us over segregation's threshold[4] into a new land whose scenery made every black person stop and stare in reverence.[5] We were all with Jackie. We slid into every base that he swiped, ducked at every fastball that hurtled toward his head. The circulation of the Pittsburgh *Courier,* the leading black newspaper,

---

3. **Joe Louis:** Nicknamed "the Brown Bomber," Joe Louis (1914–1981) was world heavyweight champion from 1937 to 1949.
4. **threshold** (thresh'ōld') *n.*: doorsill; here, a boundary marking the end of one thing and the start of something new.
5. **reverence** (rev'ə · rəns) *n.*: tremendous respect.

C Reading Skills

? Evaluating the author's argument. In this paragraph, which words or groups of words appeal to your emotions? [Possible responses: "lashing"; "I know I couldn't have done what Jackie did"; "strength"; "suppress"; "sacrifice"; "incredible act of selflessness"; "brought the races together"; "dreams."]

11. wobble   hobble   trouble
12. wonder   fonder   thunder

Activity. Write the following pairs of words on the chalkboard. Have students choose the word with the silent letter. Invite students to use a dictionary to check pronunciations. Answers are underlined

1. agnostic   gnostic
2. wistful   whistle

3. wrestle   kestrel
4. gnomonic   ignominious
5. pestilent   pestle
6. gneissic   ignescent
7. ogre   gnome
8. hastening   easterly
9. hustler   hosteler
10. malignant   alignment

A Reading Skills

? Evaluating the author's argument. How did Robinson affect other black players? [He inspired them to play for the betterment of their people, not just for themselves as baseball players.]

Do you agree with Aaron that this helped make Robinson a hero? Explain. [Most students will agree that one of the qualities of a hero is that he or she inspires others.]

B Reading Skills

? Evaluating the author's argument. Like most of the paragraphs in this essay, this one has an appeal to the reader's mind and heart. What are some of the facts Aaron describes? [Older black players attended Robinson's funeral, but few younger ones did; Aaron was close to matching Ruth's record for home runs; Aaron dedicated his home run record to a great cause.]

Which words and phrases have emotional appeal? [Possible responses: "funeral," "appalled," "tribute," "dream," "inspired," "dedicate," "great cause."]

---

increased by 100,000 when it began reporting on him regularly. All over the country, black preachers would call together their congregations just to pray for Jackie and urge them to demonstrate the same forbearance that he did.

Later in his career, when the "Great Experiment"[6] had proved to be successful, Jackie allowed his instincts to take over in issues of race. He began striking back and speaking out. And when Jackie Robinson spoke, every black player got the message. He made it clear to us that we weren't playing just for ourselves or for our teams; we were playing for our people. I don't think it's a coincidence that the black players of the late '50s and '60s—me, Roy Campanella, Monte Irvin, Willie Mays, Ernie Banks, Frank Robinson, Bob Gibson, and others—dominated the National League. If we played as if we were on a mission, it was because Jackie Robinson had sent us out on one.

Even after he retired in 1956 and was inducted into the Hall of Fame in 1962, Jackie continued to chop along the path that was still a long way from being cleared. He campaigned for baseball to hire a black third-base coach, then a black manager. In 1969 he refused an invitation to play in an old-timers' game at Yankee Stadium to protest the lack of progress along those lines.

A great star from my generation, Frank Robinson (who was related to Jackie only in spirit), finally became the first black manager, in 1975. Jackie was gone by then. His last public appearance was at the 1972 World Series; he showed up with white hair, carrying a cane and going blind from diabetes. He died nine days later.

Most of the black players from Jackie's day were at the funeral, but I was appalled by how few of the younger players showed up to pay him tribute. At the time, I was 41 home runs short of Babe Ruth's[7] career record, and I felt that it was up to me to keep Jackie's dream alive. I was inspired to dedicate my home-run record to the same great cause to which he dedicated his life. I'm still inspired by Jackie Robinson. Hardly a day goes by that I don't think of him.

—from *American Legends: From the Time 100*

---

6. **"Great Experiment":** term used to describe the breaking of the color barrier in major-league baseball.
7. **Babe Ruth's:** George Herman Ruth (1895–1948), nicknamed "the Babe," was one of the most successful and popular baseball players in history. In 1974, Ruth's home-run record was finally beaten by Henry ("Hank") Aaron.

Review of Literary Terms

Ask students to review the collection to find the meanings of the terms listed at the right. Then, have students show their grasp of the skills by citing passages from the collection that illustrate the meanings of those terms.

Epics (p. 640); **Myths** (pp. 644, 726), **Alter Ego** (p. 644); **Rhapsodes** (p. 645); **Homeric Similes** (p. 645); **External Conflicts** (p. 649); **Subordinate Characters** (p. 649).

Review of Informational Terms

Ask students to use these terms to explain how to evaluate the credibility of an author's argument.

Logical Appeals (p. 718); **Emotional Appeals** (p. 718); **Anecdotes** (p. 718); **Loaded Words** (p. 718); **Connotations** (p. 718); **Tone** (p. 718).

Collection 10: Skills Review

1. Henry Aaron's **intent,** or **purpose,** in writing this article is to —
   A praise Jackie Robinson
   B describe segregation in baseball
   C explain the importance of being patient
   D explain why he became a ballplayer

2. Which of the following words *best* describes the **tone** of this article?
   F critical
   G mournful
   H admiring
   J regretful

3. Which of the following statements uses **loaded words**?
   A "I was fourteen years old when I first saw Jackie Robinson."
   B "I didn't hear a word that came out of his mouth."
   C "For three years he would have to turn the other cheek and silently suffer all the vile things that would come his way."
   D "Jackie's character was much more important than his batting average. . . ."

4. All of the following statements are **facts** *except* —
   F "He campaigned for baseball to hire a black third-base coach. . . ."
   G "With Jackie in the infield, the Dodgers won six National League pennants."
   H "I believe every black person in America had a piece of those pennants."
   J "He retired in 1956 and was inducted into the Hall of Fame in 1962. . . ."

5. Aaron uses the **anecdote** about Robinson risking a court-martial to show that Robinson —
   A did not respect laws
   B was a proud person who fought for respect
   C could not control his temper
   D did not like being a soldier

6. Which of the following statements is the *most* accurate **evaluation** of Aaron's argument?
   F It relies almost entirely on emotional appeals.
   G Facts, statistics, and other objective evidence make up the argument's main support.
   H It uses a mix of facts and emotional appeals to convince the reader.
   J Aaron includes little support in his argument.

Constructed Response

7. According to Aaron, why did Jackie Robinson have to be "bigger than life"? Explain your answer using details from the text.

Answers and Model Rationales

1. **A** The entire article is not about segregation in baseball (B), nor it is about the importance of being patient (C) or why Aaron himself became a baseball player (D). The entire article praises Robinson (A).

2. **H** Aaron's overall tone is one that expresses wonder to delight at knowing Robinson the ballplayer and man. Aaron mourns Robinson's death (G), but it does not dominate the entire article. He expresses neither regret (J) nor criticism (F).

3. **C** The words *suffer* and *vile* (C) are loaded with connotations. The words in the other choices are all neutral.

4. **H** Both F and G express an opinion but support it with a fact; J states two facts. H is an opinion, indicated by "I believe."

5. **B** The entire point of the anecdote is to illustrate Robinson's fierce pride, so B is correct.

6. **H** F is inaccurate because the article does use many facts that have logical appeal; G is inaccurate because the article does more than just state facts; J is inaccurate because the article uses factual support effectively.

Constructed Response

7. Jackie Robinson had to endure numerous threats to his life and his livelihood without fighting back in order to keep playing baseball. He was the target of ridicule and violence from fans, opposing players, and even his own teammates. Robinson put aside his fierce pride so that other African Americans would be allowed to play. That decision is what makes him "bigger than life."

Test-Taking Tips

For more instruction on how to answer multiple-choice items, refer students to **Test Smarts.**

ASSESSING

Assessment

■ *Holt Assessment: Literature, Reading, and Vocabulary*

RETEACHING

For a lesson reteaching evaluating an argument, see **Reteaching,** p. 979A. For another selection to teach evaluating an argument, see *The Holt Reader,* Part 2.

Collection 10: Skills Review

Vocabulary Skills

Synonyms

Modeling. Model the thought process of a good reader answering item 1. Say, "Doubt (A), fear (C), and disappointment (D) are internal obstacles, but Odysseus faced external difficulties as well. *Adversity,* an external difficulty, means 'hardship'; therefore, B is a synonym."

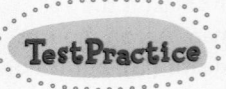

Answers and Model Rationales

1. **B** See rationale above.

2. **F** The song conveyed great passion (F). Promise (G), sorrow (H), and terror (J) are not characteristic of something beautiful.

3. **D** *Disdainful* denotes contempt, and *scornful* is the only word that shares this meaning.

4. **H** *Frightening* is the key word in the sentence. Only *disgustingly* (H) could describe a frightening act, not *cheerfully* (F), *loudly* (G), or *constantly* (J).

5. **B** Something formidable causes awe or dread; only *impressive* (B) is close in meaning.

6. **H** An adversary is an enemy or opponent. G and J do not denote opposition.

7. **A** Odysseus was not prone to screaming (D); a glance (B) or laugh (C) would be too casual; therefore, stared (A) is the best answer.

8. **H** Most likely, Penelope would act distant (H) toward a stranger rather than threaten (G) or show affection (F). Penelope was not disloyal (J) to Odysseus.

9. **B** *Restitution* means "compensation" or "repayment" (B), not aid (A), sympathy (C), or forgiveness (D).

Synonyms

DIRECTIONS: Choose the *best* synonym for the underlined word in each sentence.

1. Odysseus overcame great <u>adversity</u> on his long, hard journey homeward.
   - A doubt
   - B hardship
   - C fear
   - D disappointment

2. The beautiful song of the sirens was haunting and filled with <u>ardor</u>.
   - F passion
   - G promise
   - H sorrow
   - J terror

3. Because Odysseus appeared as a poor old man, the suitors were <u>disdainful</u> of him.
   - A suspicious
   - B respectful
   - C ignorant
   - D scornful

4. The monster Scylla yapped <u>abominably</u>, frightening Odysseus's crew.
   - F cheerfully
   - G loudly
   - H disgustingly
   - J constantly

5. A brilliant general and a clever statesman, Odysseus was <u>formidable</u> in war and peace.
   - A helpful
   - B impressive
   - C untrustworthy
   - D beloved

6. The Cyclops was a fearsome <u>adversary</u>, but Odysseus tricked the one-eyed monster and escaped from his cave.
   - F burden
   - G giant
   - H opponent
   - J fighter

7. Odysseus only <u>glowered</u> at the suitors when they pleaded for their lives.
   - A stared
   - C laughed
   - B glanced
   - D screamed

8. Penelope was <u>aloof</u> to Odysseus until he proved his <u>true</u> identity by telling the secret of their bed.
   - F affectionate
   - G threatening
   - H distant
   - J disloyal

9. When Odysseus's men killed Helios's cattle, the god insisted that he should receive <u>restitution</u>.
   - A aid
   - B repayment
   - C sympathy
   - D forgiveness

SKILLS FOCUS

Vocabulary Skills
Identify synonyms.

Vocabulary Review

Use this activity to assess whether students have retained the collection Vocabulary. Ask students to complete each of the analogies at right with a Vocabulary word from the box.

| profusion | defers | annihilate |
| emaciated | emulate | |

1. sew : pattern :: _____ : model [emulate]

2. stature : position :: abundance : _____ [profusion]

3. gorged : bloated :: starved : _____ [emaciated]

4. reveals : discloses :: _____ : delays [defers]

5. praise : rebuke :: create : _____ [annihilate]

Test Practice

DIRECTIONS: Read the following paragraph from a draft of a student's cause-and-effect essay. Then, answer the questions below it.

(1) School administrators changed the dress code policy for students at Wabash High School in order to focus students' attention on academics instead of appearance. (2) The policy has proved most ineffective in reducing students' attention to appearance. (3) The students show how fashion-conscious they still are by buying a special kind of expensive blue shirt to add to the basic uniform. (4) Many students report in fact that wearing the school uniforms increases student body unity. (5) Some students also still discriminate against others who cannot create the elaborate hairstyles of the "in-crowd."

1. Which of the following sentences shows a cause-effect clue word or phrase?
   A   1   C   3
   B   2   D   4

2. Which sentence could be added to support the argument that students are still fashion-conscious despite wearing school uniforms?
   F   Parents love uniforms because their teens spend less on clothing.
   G   Students comb area stores for "cool" accessories—watches, earrings, and blazer lapel pins.
   H   The school uniform is a smart combination of school colors for the required blazer, skirt or trousers, and shoes.
   J   School uniforms have no effect on the fashion industry.

3. Which sentence could the writer add to address a reader's counterclaim that wearing school uniforms *has* refocused students' attention on academics?

   A   Grade point averages have not changed since students began wearing school uniforms.
   B   Administrators have lowered the academic standards since requiring school uniforms.
   C   Students care more about their social lives than their academics.
   D   Parents care more about student athletics than academics.

4. Which sentence should be deleted to improve the organization of the passage?
   F   2   H   4
   G   3   J   5

5. To present this passage formally as a speech, the writer could
   A   read from note cards for the presentation
   B   enliven the presentation with props or visuals
   C   make sudden loud noises to gain the audience's attention
   D   sustain a low and flat speaking voice to soothe the audience

SKILLS FOCUS

Writing Skills
Write a cause-and-effect essay.

Collection 10: Skills Review   **749**

RESOURCES: WRITING

Assessment
- *One-Stop Planner* CD-ROM with ExamView Test Generator
- *Holt Assessment: Writing, Listening, and Speaking*

Internet
- *Holt Online Assessment*
- *Holt Online Essay Scoring*

Answers
1. A
2. G
3. A
4. H
5. B

APPLICATION

Media Blitz

Have students develop ideas for public service announcements, such as the ones designed to discourage underage smoking or to encourage people to obey the speed limit. Students should then prepare media presentations that introduce a message and persuade an audience of its importance and benefits. Remind students to create visuals to help convince their audience. If students have access to a computer, they might use software designed to help produce media presentations. Then, have students deliver their presentations to the class.

EXTENSION

Motivations and Consequences

For homework, have students choose a character from a work of fiction and write a short analysis of the causes, or motives, of the character's behavior. Students should answer the following question: What effects do his or her actions have on fellow characters or the plot? Instruct students to focus on just a few causes and effects of the character's behavior. Remind them that limiting their focus will force them to evaluate more critically the causes and effects they choose to discuss. Suggest that students present their analyses in the form of a book review that others in the class may read.

Homework

Collection 11

Drama

Informational Reading Focus: Synthesizing Sources

About Collection 11

In Collection 11, students will master the following skills:

- **Literary Skills:** Analyze elements of drama, including dramatic structure, tragedy, comedy, scene design, dialogue, and stage directions.
- **Reading Skills:** Paraphrase speeches; synthesize information from several sources on a single topic.
- **Vocabulary Skills:** Understand word origins and archaic language; understand the history of the English language; understand word denotations and connotations; and understand multiple-meaning words.
- **Writing Skills:** Develop, write, and revise an essay comparing a scene from a play with its film adaptation.
- **Listening and Speaking Skills:** Analyze a historically significant speech.

Informational Text

Each collection of *Elements of Literature* provides a variety of informational texts related to the literature selections by theme or topic.

Minimum Course of Study

Most skills can be taught with a minimum number of selections and features. In the chart to the right, lessons highlighted in green constitute the minimum course of study that provides coverage of the skills taught in Collection 11.

Resource Manager
(pp. 750C–750D)

Lesson and workshop resources are referenced in the Resource Manager on the pages that follow. These resources can be used to reinforce the skills taught in Collection 11, remediate students who are having difficulty, and provide supporting activities for English-language learners.

Scope and Sequence

Selection ▪ Feature	Literary Skills
Elements of Literature: Drama *by* Diane Tasca	• Understand elements of drama, including dramatic structure, tragedy, comedy, scene design, dialogue, and stage directions
Visitor from Forest Hills *by* Neil Simon ↔ *at grade level*	• Analyze characteristics of comedy and farce
William Shakespeare's Life: • **A Genius from Stratford** • **Shakespeare and His Theater: A Perfect Match** • **How to Read Shakespeare** *by* Robert Anderson	• Understand the function of scene design in drama
The Tragedy of Romeo and Juliet **The Prologue** **Act I** *by* William Shakespeare ↔ *at grade level*	• Analyze characteristics of tragedy, including complication • Understand how a work of literature is related to its historical period
The Tragedy of Romeo and Juliet, Act II *by* William Shakespeare ↔ *at grade level*	• Analyze characteristics of tragedy, including dramatic irony • Describe scene design
The Tragedy of Romeo and Juliet, Act III *by* William Shakespeare ↔ *at grade level*	• Analyze characteristics of tragedy, including complication, turning point, and suspense
The Tragedy of Romeo and Juliet, Act IV *by* William Shakespeare ↔ *at grade level*	• Analyze characteristics of tragedy, including complication, dramatic irony, and suspense
The Tragedy of Romeo and Juliet, Act V *by* William Shakespeare ↔ *at grade level* **Informational Text:** • Dear Juliet • Romeo and Juliet in Bosnia *by* Lisa Bannon; Bob Herbert ↔ *at grade level*	• Analyze characteristics of tragedy, dramatic irony, and climax • Analyze soliloquy, monologue, and dialogue
Writing Workshop: *Comparing a Play and a Film*	
Listening and Speaking Workshop: *Analyzing and Evaluating Speeches*	
Skills Review: *Literary Skills* *Vocabulary Skills* *Writing Skills*	• Understand elements of drama

Reading Skills	Vocabulary Skills	Writing ▪ Grammar and Language ▪ Listening and Speaking Skills
	• Create semantic maps	• Write a farcical scene
	• Understand word origins	• Present a speech from the play
	• Understand archaic language	
	• Understand word origins	• Write a prologue • Present scenes from the play
• Paraphrase speeches		• Write the thoughts of a character
• Synthesize information from several sources on a single topic	• Understand figures of speech • Understand the history of the English language • Understand word denotations and connotations	• Compare a play with a film • Prepare a plan for a modern version of a play • Write an essay analyzing the structure of the play • Write a character analysis • Prepare an oral report about character types
		• Write an essay comparing a scene from a play with its film adaptation
		• Analyze a historically significant speech
	• Understand multiple-meaning words	• Write an essay comparing a scene from a play with its film adaptation

Selection ▪ Feature	Planning	Differentiating Instruction ▪ Lesson Plans with ELL Strategies and Practice	Reading ▪ Vocabulary
Elements of Literature: Drama *by* Diane Tasca	• PowerNotes: Drama		
Visitor from Forest Hills *by* Neil Simon	• One-Stop Planner with ExamView Test Generator	• The Holt Reader, pp. 314–326 • Holt Reading Solutions, pp. 329–334 • Supporting Instruction in Spanish, p. 51 • Audio CD Library, disc 18 • Audio CD Library, Selections and Summaries in Spanish	• The Holt Reader • Holt Reading Solutions • Vocabulary Development, p. 51
William Shakespeare's Life: • **A Genius from Stratford** • **Shakespeare and His Theater: A Perfect Match** • **How to Read Shakespeare** *by* Robert Anderson	• PowerNotes: The Language of William Shakespeare		
The Tragedy of Romeo and Juliet *by* William Shakespeare **Informational Text:** • Dear Juliet • Romeo and Juliet in Bosnia *by* Lisa Bannon; Bob Herbert	• One-Stop Planner with ExamView Test Generator	• Holt Adapted Reader • Holt Reading Solutions, pp. 337–366 • Supporting Instruction in Spanish, pp. 52–63 • Audio CD Library, disc 19 • Audio CD Library, Selections and Summaries in Spanish	• Holt Adapted Reader • Holt Reading Solutions • Vocabulary Development, p. 52
Writing Workshop: *Comparing a Play and a Film*	• One-Stop Planner with ExamView Test Generator	• Workshop Resources: Writing, Listening, and Speaking, pp. 121–128 • Supporting Instruction in Spanish, p. 74	
Listening and Speaking Workshop: *Analyzing and Evaluating Speeches*	• One-Stop Planner with ExamView Test Generator	• Workshop Resources: Writing, Listening, and Speaking, pp. 129–134 • Supporting Instruction in Spanish	
Skills Review: *Literary Skills* *Vocabulary Skills* *Writing Skills*			

The Holt Reader

The Holt Reader is a consumable paperback book which can be used alone or to accompany *Elements of Literature*. It offers guided support throughout the reading process and encourages students to become active readers by circling, underlining, questioning, and jotting down responses as they read. *The Holt Reader* works well for homework, students who have missed class, additional instructional time, reteaching, and remediation.

Holt Reading Solutions (HRS)

Holt Reading Solutions pulls together reading resources in the *Elements of Literature* program to create a powerful tool for intervention and whole-class instruction. *HRS* includes diagnostic assessment tools, lesson plans for English-language learners and special education students, adaptations of selected reading selections, vocabulary and comprehension worksheets, information on phonics and decoding, and additional instruction and practice in remedial reading skills.

Writing ▪ Grammar and Language ▪ Listening and Speaking	Assessment
• Daily Language Activities	• Holt Assessment: Literature, Reading, and Vocabulary • Holt Online Assessment • One-Stop Planner with ExamView Test Generator
• Daily Language Activities	• Holt Assessment: Literature, Reading, and Vocabulary • Holt Online Assessment • One-Stop Planner with ExamView Test Generator
• Daily Language Activities • Workshop Resources: Writing, Listening, and Speaking, pp. 121–128	• Holt Assessment: Writing, Listening, and Speaking • Holt Online Assessment • One-Stop Planner with ExamView Test Generator
• Workshop Resources: Writing, Listening, and Speaking, pp. 129–134	• Holt Assessment: Writing, Listening, and Speaking • One-Stop Planner with ExamView Test Generator
	• Holt Assessment: Writing, Listening, and Speaking • One-Stop Planner with ExamView Test Generator

Technology

INTERNET

- go.hrw.com
- Holt Online Assessment
- Holt Online Essay Scoring
- Elements of Literature Online

MEDIA

 • One-Stop Planner with ExamView Test Generator

 • PowerNotes

 • Audio CD Library, discs 18 and 19

• Audio CD Library, Selections and Summaries in Spanish

• Visual Connections Videocassette Program, Segment 12

• Fine Art Transparencies, 17 and 18

 Transparency   Video

 CD-ROM   Audio CD

One–Stop Planner with ExamView Test Generator

The *One-Stop Planner* CD-ROM contains electronic versions of print-based teaching resources, clips from the video program, and valuable assessment tools. The *One-Stop Planner* resources are presented in easy-to-follow, point-and-click menu formats. To preview resources or print out worksheets and tests, you simply make a selection and click.

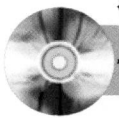 One–Stop Planner CD-ROM

Collection 11

Grade-Level Skills

■ **Literary Skills**

Analyze the characteristics of dramatic literature, such as dramatic structure, tragedy, comedy, scene design, dialogue, and stage directions.

■ **Reading Skills**

Synthesize the content from several sources or works by a single author on a single topic; paraphrase and connect the ideas with related topics in other sources.

INTRODUCING THE COLLECTION

The two plays in this collection present one of drama's most emotionally charged themes: how love between two young people is affected by conflicts between the parents of one or both lovers. Neil Simon's comedy, *Visitor from Forest Hills,* set in the Plaza Hotel in New York City, explores the theme with contemporary humor. Shakespeare's *The Tragedy of Romeo and Juliet,* on the other hand, set in sixteenth-century Italy, is the classic exposition on the death of innocent young lovers. The collection's informational selections echo the theme in two more contemporary settings. Finally, the collection ends by providing students with the opportunity to write an essay comparing a play and a film and to analyze and evaluate a speech.

COLLECTION 11 RESOURCES: READING

Planning
■ *One-Stop Planner* CD-ROM with ExamView Test Generator

Differentiating Instruction
■ *Holt Reading Solutions*
■ *The Holt Reader*
■ *Holt Adapted Reader*

■ *Family Involvement Activities in English and Spanish*
■ *Supporting Instruction in Spanish*

Vocabulary
■ *Vocabulary Development*

Grammar and Language
■ *Language Handbook Worksheets*
■ *Daily Language Activities*

Assessment
■ *Holt Assessment: Literature, Reading, and Vocabulary*
■ *One-Stop Planner* CD-ROM with ExamView Test Generator
■ *Holt Online Assessment*

Internet
■ go.hrw.com (Keyword: LE5 9-11)

Collection 11

DRAMA

INFORMATIONAL READING FOCUS
SYNTHESIZING SOURCES

What does theater give us that nothing
else can—not so intensely anyway, or so
pleasurably? It gives us human beings in
three dimensions: bodies that live in
front of us, that move, speak, change
shape, create tension, or bestow peace.

—Margo Jefferson

INTERNET
Collection
Resources
Keyword: LE5 9-11

Russian Ballet I (1912) by August Macke.
Oil on paper (103 cm × 81 cm).
Kunsthalle, Bremen, Germany.

751

THE QUOTATION
Why do you think theater might
provide a more intense or pleasur-
able experience than reading a
book or watching a movie? [Possible
responses: Unlike a book, theater provides visual stimulation or spectacle;
the actors in a play are performing
right in front of you, making the
experience more immediate and intimate than watching a movie.]

VIEWING THE ART
German painter **August Macke**
(1887–1914) was a member of a
group of artists from Munich who
called themselves *Blaue Reiter*
("Blue Rider"). Macke painted
with bright, undiluted colors and
an ambiguous sense of space. This
painting depicts a performance by
the Ballet Russes, an innovative
dance company.

- *Elements of Literature Online*

Media
- *Audio CD Library*
- *Audio CD Library, Selections and Summaries
  in Spanish*
- *Fine Art Transparencies*
- *Visual Connections Videocassette Program*
- *PowerNotes*

Grade-Level Skills

■ **Literary Skills**

Analyze the characteristics of dramatic literature, such as dramatic structure, tragedy, comedy, scene design, dialogue, and stage directions.

Review Skills

■ **Literary Skills**

Evaluate the plot's structure and development, and the way in which conflicts are resolved.

Elements of Literature: Drama

Before students read this essay, have them meet in small groups to discuss plays they have seen or performed in. Ask them to consider the following questions as they discuss each play:

- Who are the main characters?
- What problem or conflict does the main character have?
- How is the conflict resolved?
- Does the play have a happy ending or a sad ending?
- How is watching a play different from watching a movie?

Explain that drama denotes performances that take place on a stage in a theater. On the chalkboard, list the plays that students discussed, and indicate whether each had a happy ending or a sad ending. Tell students that plays with happy endings are called comedies and that plays with sad endings are called tragedies.

Elements of Literature

Drama *by* Diane Tasca
FORMS AND STAGECRAFT

Plays: Stories Acted Out

A **play** is a story acted out, live and onstage. It presents characters performed by flesh-and-blood people in a physical setting, interacting before our eyes.

Like stories, plays consist of characters carrying out a series of actions, driven by a conflict of some kind. However, stories and plays differ markedly in their format. A play, as you know, is a prose narrative. A narrator in a short story describes the characters, action, and settings; the characters' words are usually marked by quotation marks.

In contrast, a play consists entirely of the characters' words and actions. The playwright may describe the setting and the characters' actions, but the audience never hears these stage directions. The audience sees and hears only the actors' interpretations of them.

go.hrw.com

INTERNET

More About Drama

Keyword: LE5 9-11

SKILLS FOCUS

Literary Skills
Understand elements of drama, including dramatic structure, tragedy, comedy, scene design, dialogue, and stage directions.

> A play is
> a story acted out,
> live and onstage.

Dramatic Structure

You can expect the plot of a play to follow a rising-and-falling structure, much like that of a story. The plot is based on a **conflict,** whether a battle fought for a crown, as in Shakespeare's *Macbeth,* or one fought for a family heirloom, as in August Wilson's *The Piano Lesson.* Various conflicts—both internal and external—create tension for the characters. As the conflicts grow more complicated, the tension increases. Finally the tension reaches a **climax,** such as an argument, a chase, or a passionate love scene. Then the conflict is resolved, the action winds down, and the play ends.

The March Toward Tragedy

The oldest plays we know of were performed in ancient Greece as part of religious festivals. They included tragedies and comedies. The tragedies dealt with heroic characters and subjects that could not have been larger: fate, life, and death.

A **tragedy** is the presentation of serious and important actions that end unhappily. Some tragedies, like *Romeo and Juliet,* portray the suffering of innocent characters, but in most tragedies the central character is a noble figure, known as the **tragic hero,** who has a personal failing that leads to his or her downfall. This **tragic flaw** might be excessive pride, ambition, rebelliousness, or passion—imperfections that lead the otherwise noble hero to make choices that doom him or her to a tragic end.

The Dance of Comedy

A **comedy** is simply a play that ends happily. Many people would define a comedy as a funny play, and in fact most comedies are meant to make us laugh. However, comedies can have other, more important purposes as well, including making us think about issues and question things we take for granted.

DIFFERENTIATING INSTRUCTION

Learners Having Difficulty

Drama. Some students may need more background information and examples of dramatic scenes before they are ready to break down the dramatic elements of a movie or play in the Practice. As an example, discuss a popular movie. Ask students familiar with the movie to describe the costumes and the sets. Prompt students to recall memorable lines of dialogue, then have the entire class discuss why the lines are memorable.

English-Language Learners

To help students understand the terms associated with drama, have them write each boldface term and its definition on the front of a three-by-five-inch note card. Students may refer to these cards as they read *Visitor*

Whereas the principal characters in classical tragedies were noble, the central characters in a comedy could be from any class—they could be princes, ordinary townspeople, servants. Like tragic heroes, characters in comedies almost always have flaws. Instead of marching to their doom, however, these flawed characters usually discover the error of their ways, and order is restored.

Like tragedy, comedy is rooted in **conflict,** but the conflict in comedies is usually romantic: Someone wants to marry someone else but faces an obstacle—for example, an opposing parent or a rival suitor. In comedy the obstacle is always overcome, but not before **complications** —often ridiculous but sometimes serious —heighten the suspense. The complications can involve misunderstandings, mistaken identities, disguises, and other transformations.

Modern Drama

Many of today's dramas do not have clear-cut distinctions between comedy and tragedy. Some plays have relatively happy endings, and others have relatively sad endings, but many plays mix the serious with the humorous. Unlike most of the classic tragedies of ancient Greece or Shakespeare's England, serious modern plays are not concerned with kings and queens. Instead, they tend to focus on the personal and domestic conflicts of ordinary people. The characters in contemporary plays, both serious and comedic, are usually ones their audiences will identify with rather than look up to. Thus a modern play like *The Diary of Anne Frank* exposes us to the horror of the Holocaust by showing its effect on the daily lives of a small group of characters who are much like the viewers watching the play.

From the Page to the Stage

Dramas are meant to be performed. While we can enjoy reading the written text of a play and can learn a great deal from it, we need to remember that it was written to be performed. It is the job of the people bringing the play to the stage—the actors, directors, and designers—to translate the playwright's intentions.

A **stage** can be grand or intimate in size. It can be positioned at one end of the theater in front of the audience, or it can be placed in the middle of the theater, surrounded by the audience. A stage is like a small world unto itself, with its own coordinates: not north, south, east, and west, but *upstage* (away from the audience), *downstage* (toward the audience), *stage right* and *stage left* (the actors' right and left when facing the audience).

Scene Design: Dressing the Stage

Every play takes place somewhere and at some time, and a **set** transforms a bare stage into that place and time. A set might be realistic and detailed, looking just like a handsome living room, a bustling office, or an autumn forest. It might be abstract or minimal, meeting the needs of the action with just a few movable boxes and screens. A set can change from scene to scene; sometimes the change is accomplished with elaborate motorized lifts and turntables, sometimes with just a change in the lighting.

Until the last few centuries most plays (including those of Shakespeare) were performed outdoors in natural light. Today most plays are performed indoors and so require artificial **lighting.** Lights can wash the entire stage with golden

A Literary Focus

? Forms of drama. Articulate the relationship between purposes and characteristics of different forms of drama. Why do you think playwrights traditionally choose larger-than-life characters—for example, gods, kings, and heroes—as the protagonists for tragedy, but choose common people as the protagonists for comedy? [Possible responses: Larger-than-life people are rare and so is tragedy, whereas comedy is a more everyday experience; tragedy's lessons are more serious and profound, while comedy's are lighter and more ephemeral.]

B Vocabulary Development

Word origins. Have students note the definition and spelling of *playwright.* Explain that a wright (from the Old English *wyrhta,* a worker or maker) is a person who constructs something. The word is used mainly in compounds. Thus a shipwright constructs ships; a playwright constructs plays. Also point out that the word *upstage* has acquired a second meaning. Used as a verb, it describes an actor's drawing attention to himself or herself and away from another actor by moving toward the back of the stage, causing the other actor to turn his or her back to the audience. Generally, it means to draw attention to oneself and away from another person.

from Forest Hills and write examples of each term on the backs of the cards. Also, the cards may be combined into a class reference file.

Advanced Learners

Enrichment. After students have read the essay "Drama: Forms and Stagecraft," ask them to consider ways in which drama and fiction are similar and different. Have students hypothesize about the varying challenges of writing for the stage and writing for the printed page.

A Vocabulary Development

Word origins. Explain that the word *dialogue* derives from *dia,* a Greek word, meaning "through" or "across," which in turn derives from an Indo-European base *dwo,* meaning "two," and the Greek word *legein,* meaning "to choose" or "to talk." The prefix *mono–* is from the Greek word *monos,* meaning "single" or "alone."

B Literary Focus

Forms of drama. Articulate the relationship between purposes and characteristics of different forms of drama. After students have read the material on pp. 752–754, ask them to make a checklist like the one below. Students can complete the checklist as they read *Visitor from Forest Hills.* Encourage them to revise their responses as they read—changing their first guess of the protagonist, for example, or identifying a second antagonist.

Elements of Drama Checklist

• Identify the **protagonist:** _____
_____

• List **antagonists:** _____
_____

• Summarize the information presented in the **exposition:** _____
_____

• Describe a **conflict:** _____
_____

• Describe a **complication:** _____
_____

• Identify the **climax:** _____
_____

• Briefly describe the **resolution:** _
_____

Practice

Answers will vary. Encourage students to be as specific as possible, using examples to illustrate their points.

---

sunlight or cast blue twilight shadows, depending on their brightness, placement, and filter colors. They can create a warm, relaxed mood or a chilling, ominous tone.

Actors dress in **costumes** appropriate for their characters as well as for the time and place of the play. Costumes also suggest the social positions and professions of the characters. Like sets, costumes can be elaborate or minimal. In one production of a play, for example, a king might wear embroidered, fur-trimmed robes and a jeweled crown, but in another production the same king might wear black pants, a T-shirt, and a yellow cardboard crown.

When an actor waves a sword or talks on a cell phone, he or she is using a prop. **Props** (short for *properties*) are the portable items that actors carry or handle onstage (for example, books, letters, goblets, scepters, purses, umbrellas, suitcases).

All the elements of the scene design—sets, lights, costumes, and props—work together to support the action and create the appropriate mood. Above all, they help sustain the audience's belief in the reality of a play.

Characters Onstage

A The conversation between characters in a play is called **dialogue.** A long speech by one character to one or more other characters onstage is a **monologue.** A speech by a character who is alone onstage, speaking to himself or herself or to the audience, is a **soliloquy.** Playwrights often use monologues and soliloquies to develop ideas or express complex emotions.

Sometimes a character speaks to the audience or to another character in an **aside,** dialogue that is not supposed to be heard by the other characters onstage.

Texts of plays include **stage directions,** which describe how the characters move around the stage and how they speak their lines. (When a play is published, stage directions usually appear in italics.) Actors, directors, and designers usually regard stage directions as suggestions rather than rigid specifications. Since every actor on-stage is always doing something, even if he or she is not speaking, a playwright cannot specify every action every character performs. It is up to the actors to figure out how to fill out their characters' lives physically and emotionally onstage.

The actor decides (with the director's help) how to interpret the lines of a play—what the words mean, why the character says them, how the character feels while saying them. If you were to see two productions of the same play, the words would be the same, but the actors' actions and interpretations would certainly differ.

B Drama is one of the oldest forms of literature, but it continues to speak to people today. Plays explore the human heart and psyche in a direct way. Following the memorable description Shakespeare's *Hamlet* gave four centuries ago, plays "hold, as 'twere, the mirror up to nature."

Practice

Choose a play or movie you remember seeing, and discuss its dramatic elements. Start by describing the **set** (or sets). Then, describe the actors' **costumes.** Next, evaluate the characters' **dialogue**—was it convincing? clever? silly? Finally, write a few **stage directions,** based on what you imagine them to have been.

SKILLS REVIEW

Outlining. Remind students that creating an outline is a useful strategy for recognizing main ideas and supporting details while reading a nonfiction text. Explain that outlining involves organizing the logical connections between ideas. On the chalkboard, draw a skeleton outline (see p. 755) for the first two paragraphs of the essay "Drama: Forms and Stagecraft" (p. 752), and review the use of

Roman numerals for main topics and of capital letters and Arabic numerals for subtopics. Call on volunteers to complete the outline for this section on the essay.

Activity. Ask students to outline the information presented in the rest of the essay. Have students compare their outlines.

Before You Read

Visitor from Forest Hills

Make the Connection
Quickwrite 🖉

Imagine an elegant album filled with typical wedding photographs: the bride and groom gazing at each other lovingly, the happy couple slicing the wedding cake, the dressed-up parents beaming proudly. Now, imagine the photos of a wedding at which everything has gone comically wrong: The bride's dog has eaten the wedding cake; sprinklers have gone off, soaking all the guests; the groom's father recognizes the bride's uncle as the third-grade bully. List a few of your own ideas for photos of the world's worst wedding.

Literary Focus

Comedy: Happy Endings

A **comedy** is a play that ends happily—with some laughter along the way. However, the best comedies are not aimed solely at the audience's funny bone. Like any good work of literature, a good comedy shows us something true about life—something that may not be funny at all. For example, in George Bernard Shaw's great comedy *Pygmalion* (the basis for the musical *My Fair Lady*), a highly educated professor successfully teaches a poor flower seller how to speak and behave like a lady. The play has many funny moments, but ultimately the professor discovers something serious: the human cost and responsibility of turning someone's life upside down.

Farce.
Comedies can take various forms. One popular and very old type of comedy is **farce,** in which a playwright concentrates largely on ridiculous situations, comical physical actions (pies thrown in faces, wild chase scenes), and screwball dialogue. The characters in a farce are usually broad, one-dimensional **types,** who are representative of a group of people. In a way, type characters make literature possible—we recognize ourselves and others in stories. Stereotypes, however, are another matter. A **stereotype** represents a fixed, usually prejudicial idea about a group of people that is offensive and hurtful.

Both farce and comedy thrive on the contrast between characters with opposite natures. Opposites, of course, usually promise **conflict,** and conflict is the basis of drama. You are familiar with the humor that comes from a conflict of opposites in movies and television shows. In *The Odd Couple,* for example, two men share an apartment: One is a compulsively neat housekeeper; the other is very sloppy. This teaming of opposites is good for endless laughs. Other examples are the cowboy and the lady, the taxi driver and the princess, and the tough guy and the soft-hearted woman.

The battle of the sexes. Neil Simon's comedy *Visitor from Forest Hills* uses one set of opposites that has served comedy for many years: a man and a woman—usually husband and wife—who wage the so-called battle of the sexes. In such comedies the man is usually portrayed as a quick-tempered (though loving) husband and father, the domineering head of the household, and the woman is usually portrayed as a slightly muddled, or confused, wife and mother. Of course, it usually

(*continued*)

INTERNET

Vocabulary Practice

Keyword: LE5 9-11

SKILLS FOCUS

Literary Skills
Understand characteristics of comedy and farce.

SKILLS FOCUS
pp. 755–775

Grade-Level Skills
■ **Literary Skills**
Analyze the characteristics of dramatic literature, such as comedy and farce.

Summary *at grade level*

> Minutes before their daughter Mimsey is to be wed, Norma and Roy Hubley find that she has locked herself in the bathroom of their hotel suite. Mimsey refuses to communicate with her parents as they take turns trying to coax her to come out and get on with the wedding. Norma's and Roy's efforts to get Mimsey out of the bathroom reveal each parent's motives, and the conflict between those motives creates much of the comedy in the play. Roy's concern is largely with the money the delay is costing him. Norma's attitude is more complex. Mimsey finally agrees to have a talk with her dad—in the bathroom. After the talk, Mimsey remains in the bathroom but Roy goes to the phone and calls the groom to come up to the suite. In the meantime, Roy explains to Norma that Mimsey is afraid that after getting married, she and her husband will become like the bickering Roy and Norma. The groom arrives, utters just two words, returns to the reception room, and Mimsey comes out of the bathroom.

I. Plays: Stories in Motion
   A. Story acted out
   B. Characters impelled by conflict
      1. In a story, narrator describes the action
      2. In a play, characters speak

II. Dramatic Structure
   A. Plot based on conflict
      1. Internal conflict
      2. External conflict
   B. Climax
   C. Resolution

Assign the Reading

You might wish to extend the Quickwrite as a homework assignment before having students read the selection. Have student pairs use their imaginary photos to write a scenario for a short play. Encourage students to share their scenarios with the class and to vote for the one that seems the most disastrous.

Skills Starter

Build prerequisite skills. Remind students that a comedy, like other forms of drama, has a *plot*—a series of related events. Review the basic elements of plot structure: *exposition* or basic situation; *conflict* or problem, *complications* or new obstacles; *climax*; and *resolution*.

Preview Vocabulary

Have pairs of students take turns reading aloud the definitions of the Vocabulary words on p. 756. Then, have the partners work together on the following exercises to reinforce understanding of the words.

1. Describe how someone's volatile behavior might look.
2. Describe a time when you looked at something incredulously.
3. In what situation might you see a torrent of leaves?
4. Explain why someone might show vehemence during an argument.
5. Explain how you felt when you did something despondently.
6. Describe an event or situation that seemed interminable.

develops in these plays that although the wife *seems* flighty and disorganized, she is really more sensible than the husband.

When you read *Romeo and Juliet* (page 787), you will recognize the sixteenth-century squabbling of Lord and Lady Capulet, Juliet's parents, as not much different from the squabbling of Roy and Norma in *Visitor from Forest Hills.* It is all part of the battle of the sexes—and that battle, serious or hilarious, will probably go on forever.

Neil Simon, one of the most successful writers of comedy today, has said that he writes about potentially sad situations from a comic point of view. Think about his comment as you read *Visitor from Forest Hills.* What not-so-funny truth does it lead us to, laughing along the way?

Vocabulary Development

volatile (väl'ə·təl) *adj.:* explosive; likely to change rapidly.

incredulously (in·krej'oo·ləs·lē) *adv.:* unbelievingly; skeptically.

torrent (tôr'ənt) *n.:* flood; downpour.

vehemence (vē'ə·məns) *n.:* strong feeling or passion.

despondently (di·spän'dənt·lē) *adv.:* hopelessly.

interminable (in·tur'mi·nə·bəl) *adj.:* with no end in sight.

Background

The Plaza Hotel is one of New York City's most elegant landmarks. Located near Central Park, the Plaza has been the setting of many movies, plays, and works of fiction. *Visitor from Forest Hills* is one of three short plays, all set in the Plaza Hotel, that make up Neil Simon's *Plaza Suite.* (A *suite* is a series of related things —in this case, connecting bedrooms and a sitting room in a hotel.)

The photographs throughout the play are from the 1968 national tour of *Plaza Suite,* starring Betty Garrett as Norma Hubley and Forrest Tucker as Roy Hubley, with Dana Ivey as Mimsey Hubley.

RESOURCES: READING

Planning
■ *One-Stop Planner* CD-ROM with ExamView Test Generator

Differentiating Instruction
■ *Holt Reading Solutions*
■ *Supporting Instruction in Spanish*
■ *Audio CD Library, Selections and Summaries in Spanish*

Vocabulary
■ *Vocabulary Development*

Grammar and Language
■ *Daily Language Activities*

Assessment
■ *Holt Assessment: Literature, Reading, and Vocabulary*

Visitor from Forest Hills

from Plaza Suite

Neil Simon

" *Mimsey! Are you coming out or do we have the wedding in the bathroom?* "

CAST OF CHARACTERS

Roy Hubley

Mimsey Hubley

and **Borden Eisler**

Norma Hubley

Suite 719 at the Plaza. It is three o'clock on a warm Saturday afternoon in spring.

The living room is bedecked with vases and baskets of flowers. In the bedroom one opened valise containing a young woman's street clothes rests on the floor. A very large box, which had held a wedding dress, rests on the luggage rack, and a man's suit lies on the bed. A fur wrap and gloves are thrown over the back of the sofa. Telegrams of congratulations and newspapers are strewn about.

The suite today is being used more or less as a dressing room, since a wedding is about to occur downstairs in one of the reception rooms.

As the lights come up, NORMA HUBLEY is at the phone in the bedroom, impatiently tapping the receiver. She is dressed in a formal cocktail dress and a large hat, looking her very best, as any woman would want to on her daughter's wedding day. But she is extremely nervous and harassed, and with good cause—as we'll soon find out.

- *One-Stop Planner* CD-ROM with ExamView Test Generator
- *Holt Online Assessment*

Internet
- go.hrw.com (Keyword: LE5 9-11)
- *Elements of Literature Online*

Media
- *Audio CD Library*
- *Audio CD Library, Selections and Summaries in Spanish*

DIRECT TEACHING

A Literary Focus

? Scene design. After reading the cast of characters and the description of the set, what do you think the characters will be like? [Possible response: The characters will probably be middle-class or upper-class people who can afford to stay at the Plaza.] **What kinds of costumes will they wear?** [Possible response: They will be elegantly dressed for a formal wedding.]

A Literary Focus

❓ Characteristics of comedy: Conflict. What conflict arises between Norma's mood and Mr. Eisler's comments to her? [Norma is very nervous about something, but Mr. Eisler doesn't know this and is trying to engage her in a friendly conversation.] **How do you know Mr. Eisler is *not* the person she wants to speak to?** [She tells him everything is fine.]

Norma (*on the phone*). Hello? . . . Hello, operator? . . . Can I have the Blue Room, please . . . The Blue Room . . . Is there a Pink Room? I want the Hubley-Eisler wedding . . . The Green Room, that's it. Thank you . . . Could you please hurry, operator, it's an emergency . . . (*She looks over at the bathroom nervously. She paces back and forth.*) Hello? . . . Who's this? . . . Mr. Eisler . . . It's Norma Hubley . . . No, everything's fine . . . Yes,

we're coming right down . . . (*She is smiling and trying to act as pleasant and as calm as possible.*) Yes, you're right, it certainly *is* the big day . . . Mr. Eisler, is my husband there? . . . Would you please? . . . Oh! Well, I'd like to wish you the very best of luck too . . . Borden's wonderful boy . . . Well, they're *both* wonderful kids . . . No, no. She's as calm as a cucumber . . . That's the younger generation, I guess . . . Yes, everything seems to be going along beautifully . . . Absolutely beautifully . . . Oh, thank you. (*Her husband has obviously just come on the other end because the expression on her face changes violently and she screams a rasping whisper filled with doom. Sitting on the bed*) Roy? You'd better get up here right away, we're in big trouble . . . Don't ask questions, just get up here . . . I hope you're not drunk because I can't handle this alone . . . Don't say anything. Just smile

758

> ❝ If there's gonna be a wedding, let's have a wedding. Come on! ❞

Learners Having Difficulty
Help students recognize exaggeration as an element in comedy. Say, "Suppose you read that a character complains that he'd rather face a swarm of killer bees than attend a party." The exaggerated comparison is not only funny, it also tells us something about the character. Encourage students as they read to

find when exaggeration is being used to create humor and to develop characters.

English-Language Learners
For lessons designed for intermediate and advanced English-language learners, see *Holt Reading Solutions*.

and walk leisurely out the door . . . and then get the hell up here as fast as you can. (*She hangs up, putting the phone back on the night table. She crosses to the bathroom and then puts her head up against the door. Aloud through the bathroom door*) All right, Mimsey, your father's on his way up. Now, I want you to come out of that bathroom and get married. (*There is no answer.*) Do you hear me? . . . I've had enough of this nonsense . . . Unlock that door! (*That's about the end of her authority. She wilts and almost pleads.*) Mimsey, darling, please come downstairs and get married, you know your father's temper . . . I know what you're going through now, sweetheart, you're just nervous . . . Everyone goes through that on their wedding day . . . It's going to be all right, darling. You love Borden and he loves you. You're both going to have a wonderful future. So please come out of the bathroom! (*She listens; there is no answer.*) Mimsey, if you don't care about your life, think about mine. Your father'll kill me. (*The front doorbell rings.* NORMA *looks off nervously and moves to the other side of the bed.*) Oh, God, he's here! . . . Mimsey! Mimsey, please, spare me this . . . If you want, I'll have it annulled[1] next week, but please come out and get married! (*There is no answer from the bathroom but the front doorbell rings impatiently.*) All right, I'm letting your father in. And heaven help the three of us!

[*She crosses through the bedroom into the living room. She crosses to the door and opens it as* ROY HUBLEY *bursts into the room.* ROY *is dressed in striped trousers, black tailcoat, the works. He looks elegant but he's not too happy in this attire. He is a* volatile, *explosive man equipped to handle the rigors of the competitive business world, but a nervous, frightened man when it comes to the business of marrying off his only daughter.*]

Roy. Why are you standing here? There are sixty-eight people down there drinking my liquor. If

---

1. **annulled** (ə·nuld′) *v.:* ended legally.

---

there's gonna be a wedding, let's have a wedding. Come on! (*He starts back out the door but sees that* NORMA *is not going anywhere. She sits on the sofa. He comes back in.*) . . . Didn't you hear what I said? There's another couple waiting to use the Green Room. Come on, let's go! (*He makes a start out again.*)

Norma (*very calm*). Roy, could you sit down a minute? I want to talk to you about something.

Roy (*she must be mad*). You want to talk *now*? You had twenty-one years to talk while she was growing up. I'll talk to you when they're in Bermuda. Can we please have a wedding?

Norma. We can't have a wedding until you and I have a talk.

Roy. Are you crazy? While you and I are talking here, there are four musicians playing downstairs for seventy dollars an hour. I'll talk to you later when we're dancing. Come on, get Mimsey and let's go. (*He starts out again.*)

Norma. That's what I want to talk to you about.

Roy (*comes back*). Mimsey?

Norma. Sit down. You're not going to like this.

Roy. Is she sick?

Norma. She's not sick . . . exactly.

Roy. What do you mean, she's not sick exactly? Either she's sick or she's not sick. Is she sick?

Norma. She's not sick.

Roy. Then let's have a wedding! (*He crosses into the bedroom.*) Mimsey, there's two hundred dollars worth of cocktail frankfurters getting cold downstairs . . . (*He looks around the empty room.*) Mimsey? (*He crosses back to the living room to the side of the sofa. He looks at* NORMA.) . . . Where's Mimsey?

Norma. Promise you're not going to blame me.

Roy. Blame you for what? What did you do?

Norma. I didn't do anything. But I don't want to get blamed for it.

Vocabulary
volatile (väl′ə·təl) *adj.:* explosive; likely to change rapidly.

A **Literary Focus**

❓ Structural elements: Aside. Here Norma is thinking out loud, and her speech is directed toward the audience, not to Roy. What is this kind of speech called? [aside] How do Norma's thoughts add to the humor of the situation? [Possible responses: Her imagination is running wild; she is exaggerating.]

B **Literary Focus**

❓ Plot structure: Complication. How is Roy complicating the situation? [By accusing Norma of causing Mimsey to lock herself in the bathroom, Roy increases the conflict between his wife and himself.]

C **Literary Focus**

❓ Plot structure: Exposition. Roy's description provides insight into Mimsey's character and increases the audience's curiosity. What do you think the audience wants to know? [Possible response: Why is such a conventional young woman acting this way?]

D **Literary Focus**

❓ Character traits. What can you infer about Roy's social background from his diction, or his choice of words? [Possible response: He's probably from a working-class background.] Do you think his diction adds to the humor of the situation? Explain. [Possible responses: Yes; he's like a bull in a china shop. Roy's behavior clashes humorously with the politeness and sophistication that the set and the occasion suggest.]

Roy. What's going on here? Are you going to tell me where Mimsey is?

Norma. Are you going to take an oath you're not going to blame me?

Roy. *I take it! I take it!* NOW WHERE THE HELL IS SHE?

Norma. . . . She's locked herself in the bathroom. She's not coming out and she's not getting married.

[ROY *looks at* NORMA *incredulously. Then, because it must be an insane joke, he smiles at her. There is even the faint glint of a chuckle.*]

Roy (*softly*). . . . No kidding, where is she?

A **Norma** (*turns away*). He doesn't believe me. I'll kill myself.

[ROY *turns and storms into the bedroom. He crosses to the bathroom and knocks on the door. Then he tries it. It's locked. He tries again. He bangs on the door with his fist.*]

Roy. Mimsey? . . . Mimsey? . . . *MIMSEY?* (*There is no reply. Girding himself, he crosses back through the bedroom into the living room to the* **B** *sofa. He glares at* NORMA.) . . . All right, what did you say to her?

Norma (*jumping up and moving away*). I knew it! I knew you'd blame me. You took an oath. God'll punish you.

Roy. I'm not blaming you. I just want to know what *stupid* thing you said to her that made her do this.

Norma. I didn't say a word. I was putting on my lipstick, she was in the bathroom, I heard the door go click, it was locked, my whole life was over, what do you want from me?

Roy. And you didn't say a word?

Norma. Nothing.

C **Roy** (*ominously moving toward her as* NORMA *backs away*). I see. In other words, you're trying to tell me that a normal, healthy, intelligent twenty-one-year-old college graduate, who has driven me crazy the last eighteen months with wedding lists, floral arrangements, and choices of assorted hors d'oeuvres,[2] has suddenly decided to spend this, the most important day of her life, locked in the Plaza Hotel john?

Norma (*making her stand at the mantel*). Yes! Yes! Yes! Yes! Yes!

D **Roy** (*vicious*). YOU MUSTA SAID SOMETHING!

[*He storms into the bedroom.* NORMA *goes after him.*]

Norma. Roy . . . Roy . . . What are you going to do?

Roy (*stopping below the bed*). First I'm getting the college graduate out of the bathroom! Then we're gonna have a wedding and then you and I are gonna have a big talk! (*He crosses to the bathroom door and pounds on it.*) Mimsey! This is your father. I want you and your four-hundred-dollar wedding dress out of there in five seconds!

Norma (*standing at the side of the bed*). Don't threaten her. She'll never come out if you threaten her.

Roy (*to* NORMA). I got sixty-eight guests, nine waiters, four musicians, and a boy with a wedding license waiting downstairs. This is no time

---

2. **hors d'oeuvres** (ôr′dɜrvz′) *n.:* appetizers.

Vocabulary
incredulously (in·krej′oo·ləs·lē) *adv.:* unbelievingly; skeptically.

> **"You go downstairs and marry the short, skinny kid."**

DEVELOPING FLUENCY

Small-group activity. The dialogue in this play provides a good opportunity for students to practice reading fluently. Allow students to choose a character and practice in small groups, reading aloud that character's lines. Students should practice using appropriate intonation and enunciation.

to be diplomatic. (*Bangs on the door*) Mimsey!
. . . Are you coming out or do we have the wedding in the bathroom?

Norma. Will you lower your voice! Everyone will hear us.

Roy (*to* NORMA). How long you think we can keep this a secret? As soon as that boy says "I do" and there's no one standing next to him, they're going to suspect something. (*He bangs on the door.*) You can't stay in there forever, Mimsey. We only have the room until six o'clock . . . *You hear me?*

[*There is still no reply from the bathroom.*]

Norma. Roy, will you please try to control yourself.

Roy (*with great display of patience, moves to the foot of the bed and sits*). All right, I'll stay here and control myself. You go downstairs and marry the short, skinny kid. (*Exploding*) *What's the matter with you?* Don't you realize what's happening?

Norma (*moving to him*). Yes. I realize what's happening. Our daughter is nervous, frightened, and scared to death.

Roy. Of what? OF WHAT? She's been screaming for two years if he doesn't ask her to marry him, she'll throw herself off the Guggenheim Museum . . . What is she scared of?

Norma. I don't know. Maybe she's had second thoughts about the whole thing.

Roy (*getting up and moving to the bathroom door*). Second thoughts? This is no time to be having *second thoughts*. It's costing me eight thousand dollars for the *first thoughts*. (*He bangs on the door.*) Mimsey, open this door.

Norma. Is that all you care about? What it's costing you? Aren't you concerned about your daughter's happiness?

Roy (*moving back to her below the bed*). Yes! Yes, I'm concerned about my daughter's happiness. I'm also concerned about that boy waiting downstairs. A decent, respectable, intelligent

young man . . . who I hope one day is going to teach that daughter of mine to grow up.

Norma. You haven't the faintest idea of what's going through her mind right now.

Roy. Do you?

Norma. It could be anything. I don't know, maybe she thinks she's not good enough for him.

Roy (*looks at her incredulously*). . . . Why? What is he? Some kind of Greek god? He's a plain kid, nothing . . . That's ridiculous. (*Moves back to the door and bangs on it*) Mimsey! Mimsey, open this door. (*He turns to* NORMA.) Maybe she's not in there.

Norma. She's in there. (*Clutches her chest and sits on the side of the bed*) Oh, God, I think I'm having a heart attack.

Roy (*listening at the door*). I don't hear a peep out of her. Is there a window in there? Maybe she tried something crazy.

Norma (*turning to him*). That's right. Tell a woman who's having a heart attack that her daughter jumped out the window.

Roy. Take a look through the keyhole. I want to make sure she's in there.

Norma. She's in there, I tell you. Look at this, my hand keeps bouncing off my chest. (*It does.*)

Roy. Are you gonna look in there and see if she's all right or am I gonna call the house detective?

Norma (*getting up and moving below the bed*). Why don't *you* look?

Roy. Maybe she's taking a bath.

Norma. Two minutes before her own wedding?

Roy (*crossing to her*). What wedding? She just called it off.

Norma. Wouldn't I have heard the water running?

Roy (*making a swipe at her hat*). With that hat you couldn't hear Niagara Falls! . . . Are you going to look to see what your daughter's doing in the bathroom or do I ask a stranger?

Norma (*crossing to the door*). I'll look! I'll look! I'll look! (*Reluctantly she gets down on one knee and*

E Literary Focus

❓ Characteristics of comedy: Wit. Roy's wit adds to the play's humor. What makes this speech funny? [Possible response: The image of the groom saying "I do" without the bride present is absurd. The phrase "they're going to suspect something" is also humorously sarcastic.]

F Literary Focus

❓ Character traits. These words show a side of Roy that you haven't seen yet. What is it? [Possible response: He shows tenderness, compassion, care.] How are his comments here different from those he made earlier about Borden? [Earlier, he was intemperate and sarcastic, calling Borden a "short, skinny kid" and "a plain kid."]

G Literary Focus

❓ Characteristics of comedy. In a comedy the playwright has characters react in unexpected ways in order to keep the seriousness of the conflict in check. Why doesn't Roy take Norma seriously when she says she's having a heart attack? [Possible responses: He knows she's exaggerating; he's heard it all before.]

CONTENT-AREA CONNECTIONS

Math: Budgeting

Mixed-ability group activity. Weddings are expensive—especially when held at a posh hotel. Roy says Mimsey's wedding cost eight thousand dollars—and this was in 1968. Suggest that students use information from the selection and from their own research to plan a wedding and prepare a budget for the costs. Students should decide on the number of guests and the total amount they are willing to spend on the wedding. Then, students can research costs by phoning vendors and using the Internet. The budget should be as detailed as possible, with costs specified for items such as hotel suite rental, flowers, catered food, and rented clothing.

A Literary Focus

? Characteristics of comedy.
What unexpected reaction does
Norma have here? [She reacts to
her torn stocking and to the threatened wedding as if they are matters
of equal seriousness.]

B Literary Focus

**? Characteristics of comedy:
Physical humor.** In a realistic or
serious play, Roy's attempt to break
down the door would be consistent
with the tone of the play. Why is it
humorous in this play? [Possible
responses: Roy is so determined, and
his character is so exaggerated, that
his failure to open the door—and his
injury—are slapstick.]

C Literary Focus

**? Plot development:
Complication.** The conflict has
intensified. How is Roy both sarcastic and ridiculous? [He's sarcastic in
accusing Mimsey of causing all the
trouble; he's ridiculous in exaggerating
what has happened—Norma's torn
stocking and his "broken" arm.]

---

looks through the keyhole with one eye.) Oh,
my God!

A **Roy.** What's the matter?
Norma (*to him*). I ripped my stockings. (*Getting
up and examining her stocking*)
Roy. Is she in there?
Norma. She's in there! She's in there! (*Hobbling
to the far side of the bed and sitting down on the
edge*) Where am I going to get another pair of
stockings now? How am I going to go to the
wedding with torn stockings?
Roy (*crossing to the bathroom*). If *she* doesn't
show up, who's going to look at *you?* (*He kneels
at the door and looks through the keyhole.*) There
she is. Sitting there and crying.
Norma. I *told* you she was in there . . . The only
one in my family to have a daughter married in
the Plaza and I have torn stockings.
Roy (*he is on his knees, his eye to the keyhole*).
Mimsey, I can see you . . . Do you hear me? . . .
Don't turn away from me when I'm talking to you.
Norma. Maybe I could run across to Bergdorf's.[3]
They have nice stockings. (*Crosses to her purse on
the bureau in the bedroom and looks through it*)
Roy (*still through the keyhole*). Do you want me
to break down the door, Mimsey, is that what
you want? Because that's what I'm doing if
you're not out of there in five seconds . . . Stop
crying on your dress. Use the towel!
Norma (*crossing to* ROY *at the door*). I don't have
any money. Give me four dollars, I'll be back in
ten minutes.
Roy (*gets up and moves below the bed*). In ten
minutes she'll be a married woman, because I've
had enough of this nonsense. (*Yells in*) All right,
Mimsey, stand in the shower because I'm breaking down the door.
Norma (*getting in front of the door*). Roy, don't
get crazy.
Roy (*preparing himself for a run at the door*). Get
out of my way.

---
3. **Bergdorf's:** Bergdorf Goodman, an expensive store
near the Plaza Hotel.

Norma. Roy, she'll come out. Just talk nicely to
her.
Roy (*waving her away*). We already had nice
talking. Now we're gonna have door breaking.
(*Through the door*) All right, Mimsey, I'm coming in!
Norma. No, Roy, don't! Don't!

B [*She gets out of the way as* ROY *hurls his body, led
by his shoulder, with full force against the door. It
doesn't budge. He stays against the door silently a
second; he doesn't react. Then he says, calmly and
softly:*]

Roy. Get a doctor.
Norma (*standing below the door*). I knew it. I
knew it.
Roy (*drawing back from the door*). Don't tell me I
knew it, just get a doctor. (*Through the door*) I'm
not coming in, Mimsey, because my arm is
broken.
Norma. Let me see it. Can you move your
fingers? (*Moves to him and examines his fingers*)
C **Roy** (*through the door*). Are you happy now?
Your mother has torn stockings and your father
has a broken arm. How much longer is this
gonna go on?
Norma (*moving* ROY's *fingers*). It's not broken,
you can move your fingers. Give me four dollars
with your other hand, I have to get stockings.

[*She starts to go into his pockets. He slaps her
hands away.*]

Roy. Are you crazy moving a broken arm?
Norma. Two dollars, I'll get a cheap pair.
Roy (*as though she were a lunatic*). I'm not carrying any cash today. Rented, everything is rented.
Norma. I can't rent stockings. Don't you even
have a charge plate? (*Starts to go through his
pockets again*)
Roy (*slaps her hands away. Then pointing dramatically*). Wait in the Green Room! You're no
use to me here, go wait in the Green Room!
Norma. With torn stockings?

762 Collection 11 Drama • Synthesizing Sources

SKILLS REVIEW

Cause-and-effect relationships. Review
cause-and-effect relationships with the class.
Ask volunteers to describe the difference
between a cause and an effect and to give
examples. Then, have them provide examples
of causes with multiple effects and effects with
multiple causes.
Activity. Have students create a cause-and-
effect chain for events in the play by copying

the graphic organizer shown below. As students continue reading, they can add more
boxes and fill them in with causes and effects.

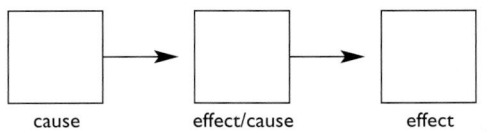

cause   effect/cause   effect

Roy. Stand behind the rented potted plant. (*Takes her by the arm and leads her below the bed. Confidentially*) They're going to call from downstairs any second asking where the bride is. And *I'm* the one who's going to have to speak to them. *Me! Me! Me!* (*The phone rings. Pushing her toward the phone*) That's them. *You* speak to them!

Norma. What happened to *me me me*?

[*The phone rings again.*]

Roy (*moving to the bathroom door*). Answer it. Answer it.

[*The phone rings again.*]

Norma (*moving to the phone*). What am I going to say to them?

Roy. I don't know. Maybe something'll come to you as you're talking.

Norma (*picks the phone up*). Hello? . . . Oh, Mr. Eisler . . . Yes, it certainly is the big moment. (*She forces a merry laugh.*)

Roy. Stall 'em. Stall 'em. Just keep stalling him. Whatever you do, stall 'em! (*Turns to the door*)

Norma (*on the phone*). Yes, we'll be down in two minutes. (*Hangs up*)

> **"No, Roy, don't! Don't!"**

Visitor from Forest Hills   **763**

D Literary Focus

❓ **Sound effects.** What effect does the ringing phone have on the characters? on the audience? [It increases the tension for the characters; it makes the audience laugh.]

E Literary Focus

❓ **Character foil.** A foil is a character who is used as a contrast to another character. For which character is Mr. Eisler a foil? [Roy] From the two conversations he has with Norma, what do you learn about him that makes him a foil? [He is polite and prone to clichés.]

READING SKILLS REVIEW

Making inferences about character. Remind students that when they make an inference while reading, they combine their own knowledge with evidence in the text. To make an inference about a character, they need to pay close attention to the character's speech, appearance, thoughts, and actions, as well as to what other characters say and think about that character. Then they combine this evidence with their knowledge of people to make some decision about the character. Ask volunteers to give examples of the process of making an inference.

Activity. As students read *Visitor from Forest Hills,* ask them to make inferences about Roy, Norma, Mimsey, and other characters. Have students make charts like the one shown here to explain how they arrived at their inferences.

Details about the character from the text	
My knowledge of people	
Inference	

A **Literary Focus**

❓ **Elements of drama: Protagonist and antagonist.** In drama, the protagonist is the character who sets the plot in motion. Usually the protagonist is a well-rounded, dynamic main character who is onstage most of the time. How is the protagonist in this play different? [Mimsey is the protagonist, but so far she has not appeared on stage and has not said a word.] Who are the antagonists—the characters who block the protagonist? [Roy and Norma] How is the situation between protagonist and antagonists turned on its head in this comedy? [The protagonist is actually blocking the antagonists.]

B **Literary Focus**

❓ **Dialogue.** What is the dialogue showing about the characters? [Possible response: They're still in conflict. Even though Roy is using "we" to imply a bond between his wife and himself, it's a false—or ambiguous—bond because he still wants to blame Norma for Mimsey's behavior.]

C **Literary Focus**

❓ **Character traits.** From the way the Hubleys discuss their problems, how would you describe their relationship? [Possible response: They have been arguing with each other for years; their relationship is full of conflict even though each cares about the other.]

Roy (*turns back to her*). Are you crazy? What did you say that for? I told you to stall him.

Norma. I stalled him. You got two minutes. What do you want from me?

Roy (*shakes his arm at her*). You always panic. The minute there's a little crisis, you always go to pieces and panic.

Norma (*shaking her arm back at him*). Don't wave your broken arm at me. Why don't you use it to get your daughter out of the bathroom?

Roy (*very angry, kneeling to her on the bed*). I could say something to you now.

Norma (*confronting him, kneels in turn on the bed*). Then why don't you say it?

Roy. Because it would lead to a fight. And I don't want to spoil this day for you. (*He gets up and crosses back to the bathroom door.*) Mimsey, this **A** is your father speaking . . . I think you know I'm not a violent man. I can be stern and strict, but I have never once been violent. Except when I'm angry. And I am really angry now, Mimsey. You can ask your mother.

[*Moves away so* NORMA *can get to the door.*]

Norma (*crossing to the bathroom door*). Mimsey, this is your mother speaking. It's true, darling, your father is very angry.

Roy (*moving back to the door*). This is your father again, Mimsey. If you have a problem you want to discuss, unlock the door and we'll discuss it. I'm not going to ask you this again, Mimsey. I've reached the end of my patience. I'm gonna count to three . . . and by God, I'm warning you, young lady, by the time I've reached three. . . *this door better be open!* (*Moving away to below the bed*) All right—One! . . . Two! . . . THREE! (*There is no reply or movement from behind the door.* ROY *helplessly sinks down* **B** *on the foot of the bed.*) . . . Where did we fail her?

Norma (*crosses to the far side of the bed, consoling him as she goes, and sits on the edge*). We didn't fail her.

Roy. They're playing "Here Comes the Bride"

downstairs and she's barricaded in a toilet—we must have failed her.

Norma (*sighs*). All right, if it makes you any happier, we failed her.

Roy. You work and you dream and you hope and you save your whole life for this day, and in one click of a door, suddenly everything crumbles. Why? What's the answer?

Norma. It's not your fault, Roy. Stop blaming yourself.

C **Roy.** I'm not blaming myself. I know *I've* done my best.

Norma (*turns and looks at him*). What does that mean?

Roy. It means we're not perfect. We make mistakes, we're only human. I've done my best and we failed her.

Norma. Meaning *I* didn't do my best?

Roy (*turning to her*). I didn't say that. I don't know what your best is. Only *you* know what your best is. Did you do your best?

Norma. Yes, I did my best.

Roy. And I did my best.

Norma. Then we *both* did our best.

Roy. So it's not our fault.

Norma. That's what I said before.

[*They turn away from each other. Then:*]

Roy (*softly*). Unless one of us didn't do our best.

Norma (*jumping up and moving away*). I don't want to discuss it any more.

Roy. All right, then what are we going to do?

Norma. I'm having a heart attack, *you* come up with something.

Roy. How? All right, I'll go down and tell them. (*Gets up and moves to the bedroom door*)

Norma (*moving to the door in front of him*). Tell them? Tell them what?

[*As they move into the living room, she stops him above the sofa.*]

Roy. I don't know. Those people down there deserve some kind of an explanation. They got all

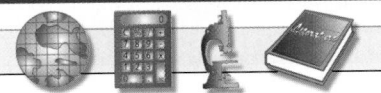

CONTENT-AREA CONNECTIONS

Health: Heart Attack
Remind students that a heart attack is a very serious occurrence. It can cause permanent disability or death, yet people jokingly refer to a heart attack when using hyperbole, as Norma does in *Visitor from Forest Hills*.
Small-group activity. Have students work in small groups to look at the serious side of heart attacks by preparing a public letter or

public service announcement entitled "Now, if you were *really* having a heart attack." Students may assign among themselves the roles of researcher, recorder, designer or editor, and speaker (if they prepare an announcement). Their product should describe some of the main causes of, and steps to prevent, a heart attack.

dressed up, didn't they?

Norma. What are you going to say? You're going to tell them that my daughter is not going to marry their son and that she's locked herself in the bathroom?

Roy. What do you want me to do, start off with two good jokes? They're going to find out *some* time, aren't they?

Norma (*with great determination*). I'll tell you what you're going to do. If she's not out of there in five minutes, we're going to go out the back door and move to Seattle, Washington! . . . You don't think I'll be able to show my face in this city again, do you? (ROY *ponders this for a moment, then reassures her with a pat on the arm. Slowly he turns and moves into the bedroom. Suddenly, he loses control and lets his anger get the best of him. He grabs up the chair from*

"ROY!"

765

D Literary Focus

? Characteristics of comedy: Farce. What elements of farce do you see in this scene? [Norma's plan to move to Seattle is absurd; Roy engages in comic physical action; both characters are types who do not undergo any change.]

A Literary Focus

❓ Characterization. How does this speech first break and then reinforce Roy's stereotype? [At first he is uncharacteristically tender. Then he resorts to a typically angry threat.]

B Literary Focus

❓ Characteristics of comedy: Physical comedy. If your clothes ripped just before an important event, you wouldn't laugh. Why can you laugh here? [Possible response: Simon has set the play's comic tone by making Roy's and Norma's characters absurd. He has given the audience permission to see Roy's misfortune as a joke.]

the dresser, and brandishing it above his head, he dashes for the bedroom door, not even detouring around the bed but rather crossing right over it. NORMA *screams and chases after him.)* ROY!

[*At the bathroom door,* ROY *manages to stop himself in time from smashing the chair against the door, trembling with frustration and anger. Finally, exhausted, he puts the chair down below the door and straddles it, sitting leaning on the back.* NORMA *sinks into the bedroom armchair.*]

Roy. . . . Would you believe it, last night I cried. Oh yes. I turned my head into the pillow and lay there in the dark, crying, because today I was losing my little girl. Some stranger was coming and taking my little Mimsey away from me . . . so I turned my back to you—and cried . . . Wait'll you hear what goes on *tonight!*

Norma (*lost in her own misery*). I should have invited your cousin Lillie. (*Gestures to the heavens*) She wished this on me, I know it. (*Suddenly* ROY *begins to chuckle.* NORMA *looks at him. He chuckles louder, although there is clearly no joy in his laughter.*) Do you find something funny about this?

Roy. Yes, I find something funny about this. I find it funny that I hired a photographer for three hundred dollars. I find it hysterical that the wedding pictures are going to be you and me in front of a locked bathroom! (*Gets up and puts the chair aside*) All right, I'm through sitting around waiting for that door to open. (*He crosses to the bedroom window and tries to open it.*)

Norma (*following after him*). What are you doing?

Roy. What do you think I'm doing?

> ❝You can pass out after the wedding. . .❞

[*Finding it impossible to open it, he crosses to the living room and opens a window there. The curtains begin to blow in the breeze.*]

Norma (*crosses after him*). If you're jumping, I'm going with you. You're not leaving *me* here alone.

Roy (*looking out the window*). I'm gonna crawl out along that ledge and get in through the bathroom window. (*He starts to climb out the window.*)

Norma. Are you crazy? It's seven stories up. You'll kill yourself. (*She grabs hold of him.*)

Roy. It's four steps, that's all. It's no problem, I'm telling you. Now will you let go of me.

Norma (*struggling to keep him from getting out the window*). Roy, no! Don't do this. We'll leave her in the bathroom. Let the hotel worry about her. Don't go out on the ledge. (*In desperation, she grabs hold of one of the tails of his coat.*)

Roy (*half out the window, trying to get out as she holds on to his coat*). You're gonna rip my coat. Let go or you're gonna rip my coat. (*As he tries to pull away from her, his coat rips completely up the back, right up to the collar. He stops and slowly comes back into the room.* NORMA *has frozen in misery by the bedroom door after letting go of the coat.* ROY *draws himself up with great dignity and control. He slowly turns and moves into the bedroom, stopping by the bed. With great patience, he calls toward the bathroom.*) Hey, you in there . . . Are you happy now? Your mother's got torn stockings and your father's got a rented ripped coat. Some wedding it's gonna be. (*Exploding, he crosses back to the open window in the living room.*) Get out of my way!

Norma (*puts hand to her head*). I'm getting dizzy. I think I'm going to pass out.

READING MINI-LESSON

Developing Word-Attack Skills
Explain that most two-syllable words in English are said with greater stress on the first syllable. Write these selection words on the chalkboard, and read them aloud. Draw a vertical line between the syllables in each word, and have volunteers underline the syllable that is said with greatest stress.

scandal [scan|dal] solemn [sol|emn]
occur [oc|cur] control [con|trol]

With some words the stress pattern differs depending on what part of speech the word is. For example, the first syllable is stressed in the adjective *perfect* (pur′fikt). The second syllable is stressed in the verb *perfect* (pər•fekt′).

Roy (*getting her out of the way*). . . . You can pass out *after* the wedding . . . (*He goes out the window and onto the ledge.*) Call room service. I want a double Scotch the minute I get back.

[*And he disappears from view as he moves across the ledge.* NORMA *runs into the bedroom and catches a glimpse of him as he passes the bedroom window, but then he disappears once more.*]

Norma (*bemoaning her fate*). . . . He'll kill himself. He'll fall and kill himself, that's the way my luck's been going all day. (*She staggers away from the window and leans on the bureau.*) I'm not going to look. I'll just wait until I hear a scream. (*The telephone rings and* NORMA *screams in fright.*) Aggghhh! . . . I thought it was him . . . (*She crosses to the phone by the bed. The telephone rings again.*) Oh, God, what am I going to say? (*She picks it up.*) Hello? . . . Oh, Mr. Eisler. Yes, we're coming . . . My husband's getting Mimsey now . . . We'll be right down. Have some more hors d'oeuvres . . . Oh, thank you. It certainly *is* the happiest day of my life. (*She hangs up.*) No, I'm going to tell him I've got a husband dangling over Fifty-ninth Street. (*As she crosses back to the opened window, a sudden torrent of rain begins to fall. As she gets to the window and sees it*) I knew it! I knew it! It had to happen . . . (*She gets closer to the window and tries to look out.*) Are you all right, Roy? . . . Roy? (*There's no answer.*) He's not all right, he fell. (*She staggers into the bedroom.*) He fell, he fell, he fell, he fell . . . He's dead, I know it. (*She collapses onto the armchair.*) He's laying there in a puddle in front of Trader Vic's[4] . . . I'm passing out. This time I'm really passing out. (*And she passes out on the chair, legs and arms spread-eagled. The doorbell rings; she jumps right up.*) I'm coming! I'm coming! Help me, whoever you are, help me! (*She rushes through the bedroom into the living room and to the front door.*) Oh, please, somebody, help me, please!

———————————————
4. **Trader Vic's:** restaurant formerly in the Plaza Hotel.

[*She opens the front door and* ROY *stands there dripping wet, fuming, exhausted, and with clothes disheveled[5] and his hair mussed.*]

Roy (*staggering into the room and weakly leaning on the mantelpiece. It takes a moment for him to catch his breath.* NORMA, *concerned, follows him.*). She locked the window too. I had to climb in through a strange bedroom. There may be a lawsuit.

[*He weakly charges back into the bedroom, followed by* NORMA, *who grabs his coattails in an effort to stop him. The rain outside stops.*]

Norma (*stopping him below the bed*). Don't yell at her. Don't get her more upset.
Roy (*turning back to her*). Don't get her *upset*? I'm hanging seven stories from a gargoyle in a pouring rain and you want me to worry about *her*? . . . You know what she's doing in there? She's playing with her false eyelashes. (*Moves to the bathroom door*) I'm out there fighting for my life with pigeons and she's playing with eyelashes . . . (*Crossing back to* NORMA) . . . I already made up my mind. The minute I get my hands on her, I'm gonna kill her. (*Moves back to the door*) Once I show them the wedding bills, no jury on earth would convict me . . . And if by some miracle she survives, let there be no talk of weddings . . . She can go into a convent. (*Slowly moving back to* NORMA *below the bed*) . . . Let her become a librarian with thick glasses and a pencil in her hair, I'm not paying for any more canceled weddings . . . (*Working himself up into a frenzy, he rushes to the table by the armchair and grabs up some newspapers.*) Now get her out of there or I start to burn these newspapers and smoke her out.

[NORMA *stops him, soothes him, and manages to*

———————————————
5. **disheveled** (di·shev′əld) *adj.:* disordered; messy.

Vocabulary
torrent (tôr′ənt) *n.:* flood; downpour.

C Literary Focus

❓ Soliloquy. Who is Norma talking to? [herself] What does her soliloquy reveal about her character? [Possible responses: She is out of control. She is ridiculously anxious and self-centered.]

D Literary Focus

❓ Dialogue. Even if the audience had an inclination to be sympathetic with Roy's ordeal, what in his own description would deter them? [Possible response: the hyperbole of "I'm out there fighting for my life with pigeons and she's playing with eyelashes."]

E Literary Focus

❓ Character traits. How would you characterize Roy based on this comment? [He thinks in stereotypes.]

Activity. Write these sentences on the chalkboard. Have volunteers tell which syllable is stressed in the underlined word.

1. A rare antique <u>console</u> table was ruined. [first]
   No one could <u>console</u> the owner. [second]

2. Their presence should <u>allay</u> all fear. [second]
   Two guards are watching the <u>alley</u>. [first]

3. The track team needs a <u>discus</u> thrower. [first]
   The team met to <u>discuss</u> the problem. [second]

4. The team was very <u>upset</u> about losing. [second]
   The game was a terrible <u>upset</u>. [first]

A Literary Focus

Plot development. After another parallel episode in which he yells through the bathroom door a list of the effects of Mimsey's behavior, Roy appears to be giving up. The rapid variations in his behavior—from open physical rage to controlled rage to vocalized rage—signals the approach of the climax.

B Reading Skills

? Responding to the text. What did you feel when you read this passage? [Possible responses: sadness; compassion.] **Why do you think the passage made you feel that way?** [Norma, for once, is talking like a concerned, loving parent, not like a self-centered lunatic. The change is abrupt, unexpected.]

C Literary Focus

? Plot structure: Climax. What makes this a climax of the play—a moment of great emotional intensity or suspense? [Possible response: The climax is established through the abrupt change in tone of Norma's and Roy's speech to each other and to Mimsey, and Mimsey's two knocks on the door—her first communication with her parents.]

---

get him calmed down. She gently seats him on the foot of the bed.]

Norma (*really frightened*). I'll get her out! I'll get her out! (*She crosses to the door and knocks.*) Mimsey! Mimsey, please! (*She knocks harder and harder.*) Mimsey, you want to destroy a family? You want a scandal? You want a story in the *Daily News*? . . . Is that what you want? Is it? . . . Open this door! *Open it!* (*She bangs very hard, then stops and turns to* ROY.) . . . Promise you won't get hysterical.

Roy. What did you do? (*Turns wearily to her*)

Norma. I broke my diamond ring.

Roy (*letting the papers fall from his hand*). Your good diamond ring?

Norma. How many do I have?

Roy (*yells through the door*). Hey, you with the false eyelashes! (*Getting up and moving to the door*) . . . You want to see a broken diamond ring? You want to see eighteen hundred dollars' worth of crushed baguettes?[6] . . . (*He grabs* NORMA's *hand and holds it to the keyhole.*) Here! Here! *This* is a worthless family heirloom (*Kicks the door*)—and *this* is a diamond bathroom door! (*Controlling himself. To* NORMA) Do you know what I'm going to do now? Do you have any idea? (NORMA *puts her hand to her mouth, afraid to hear.* ROY *moves away from the door to the far side of the bed.*) I'm going to wash my hands of the entire Eisler-Hubley wedding. You can take all the Eislers and all the hors d'oeuvres and go to Central Park and have an eight-thousand-dollar picnic . . . (*Stops and turns back to* NORMA) I'm going down to the Oak Room with my broken arm, with my drenched rented ripped suit—and I'm gonna get blind! . . . I don't mean drunk, I mean totally blind . . . (*Erupting with great vehemence*) because I don't want to see you or your crazy daughter again, if I live to be a thousand.

---

6. **baguettes** (ba·gets′) *n.*: here, diamonds in the shape of long, narrow rectangles.

[*He turns and rushes from the bedroom, through the living room to the front door. As he tries to open it,* NORMA *catches up to him, grabs his tailcoat, and pulls him back into the room.*]

Norma. That's right. Run out on me. Run out on your daughter. Run out on everybody just when they need you.

Roy. You don't need me. You need a rhinoceros with a blowtorch—because no one else can get into that bathroom.

Norma (*with rising emotion*). I'll tell you who can get into that bathroom. Someone with love and understanding. Someone who cares about that poor kid who's going through some terrible decision now and needs help. Help that only *you* can give her and that *I* can give her. *That's* who can get into that bathroom now.

[ROY *looks at her solemnly . . . Then he crosses past her, hesitates and looks back at her, and then goes into the bedroom and to the bathroom door.* NORMA *follows him back in. He turns and looks at* NORMA *again. Then he knocks gently on the door and speaks softly and with some tenderness.*]

Roy. Mimsey! . . . This is Daddy . . . Is something wrong, dear? . . . (*He looks back at* NORMA, *who nods encouragement, happy about his new turn in character. Then he turns back to the door.*) . . . I want to help you, darling. Mother and I both do. But how can we help you if you won't talk to us? Mimsey, can you hear me? (*There is no answer. He looks back at* NORMA.)

Norma (*at the far side of the bed*). Maybe she's too choked up to talk.

Roy (*through the door*). Mimsey, if you can hear me, knock twice for yes, once for no.(*There are two knocks on the door. They look at each other encouragingly.*) Good. Good . . . Now, Mimsey, we

---

Vocabulary
vehemence (vē′ə·məns) *n.*: strong feeling or passion.

DEVELOPING FLUENCY

Whole-class activity. Explain that one key to interpreting dialogue is paying careful attention to the stage directions. Stage directions may give precise instructions for how a character should speak certain lines. Have students note speaking cues such as "yells through the door," "controlling himself," "erupting with great vehemence," and "with rising emotion" in the stage directions for the dialogue on p. 768. You might have pairs of students take turns reading lines of dialogue aloud using the speaking cues given in the stage directions, or ask each student to choose two lines of dialogue to interpret orally for the class.

---

want to ask you a very, very important question. Do you want to marry Borden or don't you?

[*They wait anxiously for the answer. We hear one knock, a pause, then another knock.*]

Norma (*happily*). She said yes.
Roy (*despondently*). She said no. (*Moves away from the door to the foot of the bed*)
Norma. It was two knocks. Two knocks is yes. She wants to marry him.
Roy. It wasn't a double knock "yes." It was two single "no" knocks. She doesn't want to marry him.

Norma. Don't tell me she doesn't want to marry him. I heard her distinctly knock "yes." She went (*Knocks twice on the foot of the bed*) "Yes, I want to marry him."
Roy. It wasn't (*Knocks twice on the foot of the bed*) . . . It was (*Knocks once on the foot of the bed*) . . . and then another (*Knocks once more on the foot of the bed*) . . . That's "no," twice, she's not marrying him. (*Sinks down on the side of the bed*)

Vocabulary
despondently (di·spän′dənt·lē) *adv.:* hopelessly.

"Don't tell me she doesn't want to marry him."

A Literary Focus

? Plot structure: Resolution. The plot now moves toward the resolution of the conflict, but not without surprises. What do you think of Mimsey's decision? [Possible response: It is surprising because the audience was lead to expect that she would decide to talk to Norma—as did Norma.]

B Reading Skills

? Interpreting. Has Norma really changed? [Possible responses: Yes; she has been hurt by Mimsey's decision, and she is regretful. No; she is still self-centered—her tears are for herself.]

C Reading Skills

? Making predictions. What do you predict that Mr. Hubley will say to Borden? [Possible response: He will tell Borden that the wedding is delayed or postponed indefinitely.]

Norma (*crossing to the door*) Ask her again. (*Into the door*) Mimsey, what did you say? Yes or no? (*They listen. We hear two distinct loud knocks.* NORMA *turns to* ROY.) . . . All right? There it is in plain English . . . You never *could* talk to your own daughter. (*Moves away from the door*)

Roy (*getting up wearily and moving to the door*). Mimsey, this is not a good way to have a conversation. You're gonna hurt your knuckles . . . Won't you come out and talk to us? . . . Mimsey?

Norma (*leads* ROY *gently to the foot of the bed*). Don't you understand, it's probably something she can't discuss with her father. There are times a daughter wants to be alone with her mother. (*Sits* ROY *down on the foot of the bed and crosses back to the door*) Mimsey, do you want me to come in there and talk to you, just the two of us, sweetheart? Tell me, darling, is that what you want? (*There is no reply. A strip of toilet paper appears from under the bathroom door.* ROY *notices it, pushes* NORMA *aside, bends down, picks it up, and reads it.*) What? What does it say? (ROY *solemnly hands it to her.* NORMA *reads it aloud.*) "I would rather talk to Daddy."

[NORMA *is crushed. He looks at her sympathetically. We hear the bathroom door unlock.* ROY *doesn't quite know what to say to* NORMA. *He gives her a quick hug.*]

Roy. I—I'll try not to be too long.

[*He opens the door and goes in, closing it behind him quietly.* NORMA, *still with the strip of paper in her hand, walks slowly and sadly to the foot of the bed and sits. She looks glumly down at the paper.*]

Norma (*aloud*). . . . "I would rather talk to

Daddy". . . Did she have to write it on this kind of paper? (*She wads up the paper.*) . . . Well—maybe I didn't do my best . . . I thought we had such a good relationship . . . Friends. Everyone thought we were friends, not mother and daughter . . . I tried to do everything right . . . I tried to teach her that there could be more than just love between a mother and a daughter . . . There can be trust and respect and friendship and understanding . . . (*Getting angry, she turns and yells toward the closed door.*) Just because *I* don't speak to my mother doesn't mean *we* can't be different!

> **"It's so bad you can't even tell me . . ."**

[*She wipes her eyes with the paper. The bathroom door opens. A solemn* ROY *steps out, and the door closes and locks behind him. He deliberately buttons his coat and crosses to the bedroom phone wordlessly.* NORMA *has not taken her eyes off him. The pause seems* interminable.]

Roy (*into the phone*). The Green Room, please . . . Mr. Borden Eisler. Thank you. (*He waits.*)

Norma (*getting up from the bed*). . . . I'm gonna have to guess, is that it? . . . It's so bad you can't even tell me . . . Words can't form in your mouth, it's so horrible, right? . . . Come on, I'm a strong person, Roy. Tell me quickly, I'll get over it . . .

Roy (*into the phone*) Borden? Mr. Hubley . . . Can you come up to 719? . . . Yes, now . . . (*He hangs up and gestures for* NORMA *to follow him. He crosses into the living room and down to the ottoman,[7] where he sits.* NORMA *follows and stands*

---

7. **ottoman** (ät'ə·mən) *n.:* cushioned footstool.

Vocabulary
interminable (in·tʉr'mi·nə·bəl) *adj.:* with no end in sight.

FAMILY/COMMUNITY ACTIVITY

Encourage students to take a poll among family or community members of their favorite slapstick comedies in two categories: characters played by humans and cartoons. Almost everyone has a favorite slapstick team, such as Laurel and Hardy, and a favorite scene. Encourage students to share their own favorites with family members and to bring in the results of their poll for the rest of the class.

SKILLS REVIEW

Inferring relationships among characters. To show the relationships among characters at this point in the play (pp. 770–771), have students work in groups of three to generate a character sociogram like the one shown here. All members of the group should work together to brainstorm a few words that describe the

waiting behind him. Finally) She wanted to talk to me because she couldn't bear to say it to both of us at the same time . . . The reason she's locked herself in the bathroom . . . is she's afraid.

Norma. Afraid? What is she afraid of? That Borden doesn't love her?

Roy. Not that Borden doesn't love her.

Norma. That she doesn't love Borden?

Roy. Not that she doesn't love Borden.

Norma. Then what is she afraid of?

Roy. . . . She's afraid of what they're going to become.

Norma. I don't understand.

Roy. Think about it.

Norma (*crossing above the sofa*). What's there to think about? What are they going to become? They love each other, they'll get married, they'll have children, they'll grow older, they'll become like us. (*Comes the dawn. Stops by the side of the sofa and turns back to* ROY)—I never thought about that.

Roy. Makes you stop and think, doesn't it?

Norma. I don't think we're so bad, do you? . . . All right, so we yell and scream a little. So we fight and curse and aggravate each other. So you blame me for being a lousy mother and I accuse you of being a rotten husband. It doesn't mean we're not happy . . . does it? . . . (*Her voice rising*) Well? . . . Does it? . . .

Roy (*looks at her*). . . . She wants something better. (*The doorbell rings. He crosses to open the door.* NORMA *follows.*) Hello, Borden.

Borden (*stepping into the room*). Hi.

Norma. Hello, darling.

Roy (*gravely*). Borden, you're an intelligent young man. I'm not going to beat around the bush. We have a serious problem on our hands.

Borden. How so?

Roy. Mimsey—is worried. Worried about your future together. About the whole institution of marriage. We've tried to allay her fears, but obviously we haven't been a very good example. It

seems you're the only one who can communicate with her. She's locked herself in the bathroom and is not coming out . . . It's up to you now.

[*Without a word,* BORDEN *crosses below the sofa and up to the bedroom, through the bedroom below the bed and right up to the bathroom door. He knocks.*]

Borden. Mimsey? . . . This is Borden . . . Cool it! 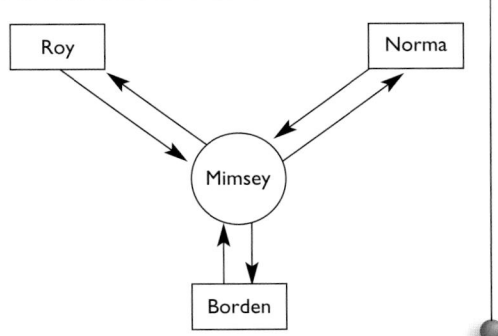 (*Then he turns and crosses back to the living room. Crossing above the sofa, he passes the Hubleys, and without looking at them, says*) See you downstairs!

[*He exits without showing any more emotion. The Hubleys stare after him as he closes the door. But then the bathroom door opens and* NORMA *and* ROY *slowly turn to it as* MIMSEY, *a beautiful bride, in a formal wedding gown, with veil, comes out.*]

Mimsey. I'm ready now!

[NORMA *turns and moves into the bedroom toward her.* ROY *follows slowly, shaking his head in amazement.*]

Roy. *Now* you're ready? *Now* you come out?

Norma (*admiring* MIMSEY). Roy, please . . .

Roy (*getting angry, leans toward her over the bed*). I break every bone in my body and you come out for "Cool it"?

Norma (*pushing* MIMSEY *toward* ROY). You're beautiful, darling. Walk with your father, I want to look at both of you.

Roy (*fuming. As she takes his arm, to* NORMA) That's how he communicates? That's the brilliant understanding between two people? "Cool it"?

Norma (*gathering up* MIMSEY'*s train as they move toward the living room*). Roy, don't start in.

Roy. What kind of a person is that to let your daughter marry?

DIRECT TEACHING

D **Literary Focus**

❓ Theme. Exactly what is the "that" which Norma never considered? [that Mimsey and Borden would become like Norma and Roy] Did this line change your perception of the play? Explain. [Possible response: Yes; the play has suddenly become serious after so much humor, and the shift is stunning.]

E **Literary Focus**

❓ Character traits. How would you answer Norma? Are the Hubleys so bad? [Possible responses: At this point in the play, they are very sympathetic characters because they've been forced to look at themselves, and it has given them pause. This is just a brief moment in the play; up to this point they have shown that they are not very likable people.]

F **Literary Focus**

❓ Plot structure: Resolution. How has the conflict been resolved? [Borden, with just two words—"cool it!"—has persuaded Mimsey to come out of the bathroom and proceed with the wedding.]

---

relationships or feelings among Mimsey (as the main character), Roy, Norma, and Borden. Point out that a sociogram has arrows pointing from the main character to the subordinate characters and from the subordinate characters to the main character, so students should, for example, identify Norma's relationship to or feelings toward Mimsey, as well as Mimsey's relationship to or feelings toward

Norma. Advise students, if necessary, that some of these characters seem to have two conflicting feelings toward each other. (Students should list both feelings.) Ask each group to make a poster of their character sociogram to be used when they present their ideas to the class.

```
  Roy                Norma
     ↘            ↗
        Mimsey
          ↑↓
        Borden
```

Ⓐ Reading Skills

❓ Responding to the text.
What do you think of Roy's statement? [Possible responses: His comment is ironic because Mimsey locked herself in the bathroom because of deep concern about her future. Roy doesn't get the message when it's right in front of him.]

GUIDED PRACTICE

Monitoring students' progress.
Guide the class in answering these comprehension questions. Direct students to locate passages in the text that support their responses.

True-False

1. Roy is downstairs when Mimsey locks herself in the bathroom. [T]

2. Roy states that he doesn't care about the money, only about Mimsey's happiness. [F]

3. Norma forces Roy to try to break down the bathroom door. [F]

4. Mimsey answers some of her parents' questions by knocking on the bathroom door. [T]

5. At the end of the play, Norma and Roy swear never to argue again. [F]

[*They stop above the sofa.* MIMSEY *takes her bridal bouquet from the table behind the sofa while* NORMA *puts on her wrap and takes her gloves from the back of the sofa.*]

Norma. Roy, don't aggravate me. I'm warning you, don't spoil this day for me.
Ⓐ Roy. Kids today don't care. Not like they did in my day.
Norma. Walk. Will you walk? In five minutes he'll marry one of the flower girls. Will you walk—

[MIMSEY *takes* ROY *by the arm and they move to the door as* NORMA *follows.*]

Roy [*turning back to* NORMA] Crazy. I must be out of my mind, a boy like that. (*Opens the door*) She was better off in the bathroom. You hear me? Better off in the bathroom . . . (*They are out the door . . .*)■

CURTAIN

"She was better off in the bathroom."

772

Meet the Writer

Neil Simon

Laughing on the Outside

Over the years, Neil Simon (1927–   ) has had a string of successful plays running on Broadway. His plays are also performed in community and university theaters, on film, and on television. Simon has been making people laugh for more than fifty years.

Born and raised in New York City, Simon began writing comedy for television in the early 1950s. He moved on to the theater with his first play, *Come Blow Your Horn,* in 1961. Since then he has written hits for Broadway and the movies, such as *The Odd Couple, Chapter Two,* and *The Goodbye Girl.* Two of his comedies, *Barefoot in the Park* and *Plaza Suite,* had record-breaking runs on Broadway. Some of his more recent plays, *Brighton Beach Memoirs, Biloxi Blues,* and *Broadway Bound,* are based on his own boyhood and on his stint in the army.

Simon says that he is always looking at life as a play—he is always on the alert for new characters and new stories. In his half century as a professional writer, he has discovered almost everything there is to know about why people laugh. He says that audiences often laugh as a relief from the tension in a play. Simon tells about the time when *Plaza Suite* was about to open on Broadway:

66 The first act was too long—it wasn't that it was too long, we were getting too many laughs in a scene that we thought was basically serious. So Mike [Nichols, the director] and I started to cut out all of the laugh lines, and they started to laugh at other lines that they had never laughed at. They just wanted to laugh! 99

For Independent Reading

For more laughs, read *Barefoot in the Park,* a comic play about the difficult first weeks of a new marriage (for a short excerpt, see page 938). You'll also enjoy *The Odd Couple,* a hilarious comedy about two men who are separated from their wives and are sharing an apartment, and *Broadway Bound,* Simon's humorous portrait of himself as a young writer dealing with his difficult family.

DIFFERENTIATING INSTRUCTION

Advanced Learners
Enrichment. Neil Simon has said that whenever he goes to schools to speak at drama classes, there is little interest in the theater. "There'll be about four kids in the group who are interested in plays, but most of them want to know about films."

Activity. Have students discuss how they would interest other students in the theater—in seeing plays, writing plays, acting in plays, and in producing plays. Suggest that students present their ideas in an essay, as a poster, or as a short dramatic piece.

Response and Analysis

Reading Check

1. Norma tells Mr. Eisler that Mimsey is "calm as a cucumber," but in fact Mimsey has locked herself in the bathroom, refusing to get married.

2. Norma uses the strict-parent approach by telling Mimsey her father is on his way up and she must come out of the bathroom; then Norma softens her tone and tells Mimsey how she understands that brides can be nervous; then she begs Mimsey to spare her from Roy's wrath.

3. Roy is concerned about money. Examples: "Mimsey, there's two hundred dollars worth of cocktail frankfurters getting cold downstairs"; "I find it funny that I hired a photographer for three hundred dollars"; "I want you and your four-hundred-dollar wedding dress out of there."

4. They realize that she is afraid that her marriage will turn out like theirs.

5. He tells Mimsey to "cool it."

Thinking Critically

6. Norma and Roy engage in slapstick antics such as trying to break down the door, peeking through the keyhole, and going out on a ledge outside the hotel. At the end of the play, they are disheveled and exhausted: Roy has a torn, wet tuxedo, and Norma has a ripped stocking and broken diamond ring.

7. Possible answers: Mimsey is in love with Borden; he has a relationship with her that she doesn't have with her parents.

8. Time is crucial because the wedding has been scheduled to begin within minutes, and the groom, his father, and the guests are waiting for the bride and her parents.

Response and Analysis

Reading Check

1. The **exposition** of a play presents the characters and their basic situation and **conflicts.** In *Visitor from Forest Hills,* the exposition is given in Norma's opening speech. How does Norma describe the way Mimsey feels? What is the *real* problem?

2. What different approaches does Norma first use to try to coax Mimsey out of the bathroom?

3. Many **farces,** or comedies, have a jack-in-the-box character, a character who establishes one attitude and then repeats it each time he or she "pops up" in the play. We laugh at the character because he or she is so predictable. Roy Hubley is the jack-in-the-box in this play. What is he always concerned about? Find at least three lines that repeat Roy's chief concern.

4. What do the Hubleys finally realize that Mimsey is afraid of?

5. Borden's appearance onstage signals the **climax** of the play. How does he resolve the Hubleys' problem?

Thinking Critically

SKILLS FOCUS

Literary Skills
Analyze characteristics of comedy and farce.

Writing Skills
Write a farcical scene.

6. What **farcical** (farcelike) actions do Norma and Roy Hubley engage in to get Mimsey to come out of the bathroom? **Contrast** how they look when the play begins with how they look when the play is over and they start downstairs.

7. Why do you think Borden's simple "Cool it!" works, whereas Norma and Roy's hysterics do not?

8. **Tension** is often created when a play's action runs against the clock. Why is time a crucial element in this play?

9. On the surface this play is about a frightened bride and her parents' comic efforts to get her to her wedding ceremony. Who, though, receives most of the playwright's attention? Who or what would you say is the *real* subject of *Visitor from Forest Hills?*

10. Neil Simon's plays are usually **satiric**—that is, they make us laugh because they expose the foolishness of certain characters. What flaws in Roy and Norma is Simon making us laugh at?

Extending and Evaluating

11. Do you think most parents would behave like Roy and Norma if their daughter locked herself in a bathroom on her wedding day? Describe how some other parents might respond to the Hubleys' unusual problem.

WRITING

Extending the Play

Write a **farcical scene** showing Mimsey, Borden, Roy, and Norma twenty-five years after *Visitor from Forest Hills.* Begin the action at the wedding of Mimsey and Borden's daughter or son. Choose any part of the wedding ceremony or reception to dramatize, including the hour just before the wedding. (You might develop one of the photo ideas that you listed in your Quickwrite.) Invent a **conflict** so that your scene will have movement (a beginning, a middle, and an end), and express the conflict through the characters' **dialogue.** Be sure to include **stage directions** and **scene designs.**

---

9. Possible answer: Roy and Norma receive most of Neil Simon's attention because he wrote most of the dialogue (and monologues and asides) for them. The real subject of the play is the relationship between married people.

10. Roy's flaws are that he does not know how to control his anger, and he thinks only about money. Norma's flaws are that she is self-centered and given to hyperbole.

Extending and Evaluating

11. Possible answers: No, most parents would be more compassionate and reasonable toward their daughter, perhaps asking her about her fears. Yes, most parents would react more or less as Roy and Norma did.

Vocabulary Development

Semantic Map

Making a semantic map is a good strategy for learning and using new words. A **semantic map** is a chart that can include a word's definition, questions and answers about when to use the word, the word's synonyms and antonyms (if there are any), and a sentence using the word. A sample map for the word *volatile* is shown here:

Word Bank
volatile
incredulously
torrent
vehemence
despondently
interminable

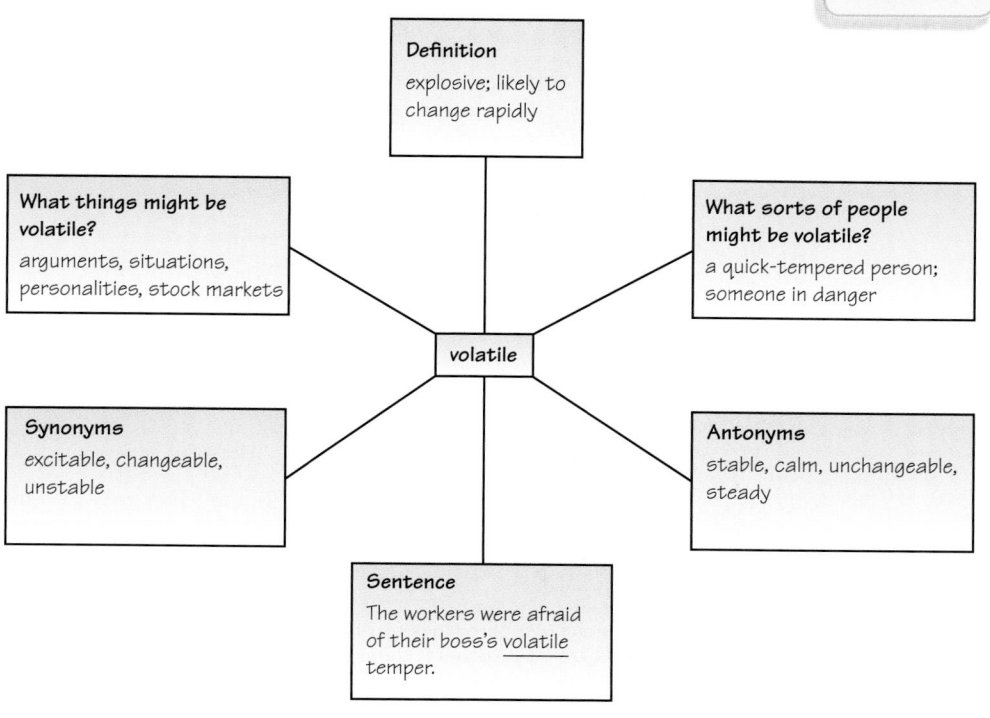

Definition
explosive; likely to change rapidly

What things might be volatile?
arguments, situations, personalities, stock markets

What sorts of people might be volatile?
a quick-tempered person; someone in danger

volatile

Synonyms
excitable, changeable, unstable

Antonyms
stable, calm, unchangeable, steady

Sentence
The workers were afraid of their boss's volatile temper.

PRACTICE

Work with a small group to make a **semantic map** for each of the other Word Bank words. Use a thesaurus or a dictionary for help identifying **synonyms** and **antonyms.**

SKILLS FOCUS

Vocabulary Skills
Create semantic maps.

Practice
Possible Answers

- *incredulously. Definition*—unbelievingly. *Things*—none. *People*—someone who receives either very good or very bad news; someone with a skeptical nature. *Synonyms*—dubiously; doubtfully. *Antonyms*—credulously; certainly; positively; trustingly. *Sentence*—My mother reacted incredulously when she was told she had won the lottery.

- *torrent. Definition*—flood; downpour. *Things*—rivers; rainstorms. *People*—someone who is very upset; someone who is talkative. *Synonyms*—deluge; downpour. *Antonyms*—trickle; spurt. *Sentence*—The man whose car had been vandalized let loose a torrent of angry words.

Vocabulary Development

- *vehemence. Definition*—strong feeling or passion. *Things*—none. *People*—someone who is very emotional. *Synonyms*—fervor; zeal; violence. *Antonyms*—passivity; blandness; neutrality. *Sentence*—Maria spoke with great vehemence at the political rally for her candidate.

- *despondently. Definition*—very sadly. *Things*—none. *People*—someone who has suffered a great loss. *Synonyms*—sorrowfully; gloomily; dolefully; *Antonyms*—happily; cheerfully; joyfully. *Sentence*—Ethan spoke despondently about his team's loss.

- *interminable. Definition*—with no end in sight. *Things*—a long car trip; a boring speech or performance; a list of chores. *People*—someone who seems to talk nonstop; someone who is always complaining. *Synonyms*—endless; long; prolonged; unceasing; continuous. *Antonyms*—short; brief; concise; abrupt. *Sentence*—After two hours the city council meeting began to seem interminable.

ASSESSING

Assessment
- *Holt Assessment: Literature, Reading, and Vocabulary*

RETEACHING

For a lesson reteaching analyzing dramatic literature, see **Reteaching,** p. 979A. For another selection to teach analyzing dramatic literature, see *The Holt Reader,* Collection 11.

Grade-Level Skills

■ **Literary Skills**
Analyze the function of dialogue in dramatic literature.

Overview

The first of the two introductory essays summarizes what is known of Shakespeare's life, stressing his consummate professionalism and placing the writing of *Romeo and Juliet* in context. The second essay describes the Globe Theatre, which was built by Shakespeare's company, and compares and contrasts it with modern theaters. The essay also discusses the differences between the media of theater and film. Have students look through the essays and notice the illustrations, headings, and captions. Suggest students make a list of questions that they hope to find answers to as they read.

DIRECT TEACHING

A **Content-Area Connections**

History: Biographical Records
During Shakespeare's time, people saw little need to keep biographical records unless the person was a member of the aristocracy or had a strong connection to either the church or the state. The occupation of playwright was not held in high regard.

B **Content-Area Connections**

Literature: Shakespeare's Critics
Critics did write about Shakespeare during his lifetime. In 1598, a critic named Francis Meres compared Shakespeare favorably to the poets of classical antiquity. Shakespeare's colleague Ben Jonson called Shakespeare "the soul of the age," equal in importance to the ancient Greek playwrights Aeschylus, Euripides, and Sophocles.

WILLIAM SHAKESPEARE'S LIFE: A GENIUS FROM STRATFORD

by Robert Anderson

William Shakespeare (1783). Sketch by Ozias Humphrey.
By permission of the Folger Shakespeare Library, Washington, D.C.

A He is the most famous writer in the world, but he left us no journals or letters—he left us only his poems and his plays. What we know about William Shakespeare's personal life comes mostly from church and legal documents—a **B** baptismal registration, a marriage license, and records of real estate transactions. We also have a few remarks that others wrote about him during his lifetime.

We know that William was born the third of eight children around April 23, 1564, in Stratford, a market town about one hundred miles northwest of London. His father, John, was a shopkeeper and a man of some importance in Stratford, serving at various times as justice of the peace and high bailiff (mayor).

William attended grammar school, where he studied Latin grammar, Latin

776 Collection 11 Drama • Synthesizing Sources

DIFFERENTIATING INSTRUCTION

Learners Having Difficulty
Activity. To help students improve their understanding of the main ideas, suggest that they make a time line using the dates and information provided in the two essays, "Shakespeare's Life" and "Shakespeare and His Theater." Caution students to leave space between dates because the chronology of information in the two essays overlaps.

Activity. Pair students of different abilities and have them read through the introductory pages on Shakespeare and the theater of his time. One student should read a section aloud while the other makes brief notes on interesting new facts in a chart like the following. Partners should take turns reading aloud and taking notes and then complete their individual charts, adding comments about their original observations.

literature, and rhetoric (the uses of language). As far as we know, he had no further formal education.

At the age of eighteen, he married Anne Hathaway, who was eight years older than he was. Sometime after the birth of their second and third children (twins), Shakespeare moved to London, apparently leaving his family in Stratford.

We know that several years later, by 1592, Shakespeare had already become an actor and a playwright. By 1594, he was a charter member of the theatrical company called the Lord Chamberlain's Men, which was later to become the King's Men. (As the names of these acting companies indicate, theatrical groups depended on the support of a wealthy patron—the King's Men were supported by King James himself.) Shakespeare worked with this company for the rest of his writing life. Year after year he provided it with plays, almost on demand. Shakespeare was the ultimate professional writer. He had a theater that needed plays, actors who needed parts, and a family that needed to be fed.

Romeo and Juliet was probably among the early plays that Shakespeare wrote, between 1594 and 1596. By 1612, when he returned to Stratford to live the life of a prosperous retired gentleman, Shakespeare had written thirty-seven plays, including such masterpieces as *Julius Caesar, Hamlet, Othello, King Lear,* and *Macbeth.*

Shakespeare's plays are still produced all over the world. During a Broadway season in the 1980s, one critic estimated that if Shakespeare were alive, he would be receiving $25,000 a week in royalties for a production of *Othello* alone. The play was attracting larger audiences than any other nonmusical production in town.

Shakespeare died on April 23, 1616, at the age of fifty-two. He is buried under the old stone floor in the chancel of Holy Trinity Church in Stratford. Carved over his grave is the following verse (the spelling has been modernized):

> Good friend, for Jesus' sake forbear
> To dig the dust enclosèd here!
> Blessed be the man that spares these
>   stones
> And cursed be he that moves my bones.

These are hardly the best of Shakespeare's lines (if indeed they are his at all), but like his other lines, they seem to have worked. His bones have lain undisturbed to this day.

C Content-Area Connections

Culture: Education
Like other young boys of his social class, Shakespeare probably began grammar school at about age seven. Classes were held for about nine hours each day, year-round. Corporal punishment was used to enforce the strict discipline. Students studied Latin because it was needed for careers in medicine, law, or the church and because an educated person was expected to be well versed in Latin.

D Content-Area Connections

Social Studies: Plague
From 1592 to 1594, London authorities repeatedly closed the theaters because of outbreaks of the plague. Since there was little demand for plays, Shakespeare turned his attention to poetry. Two of his long poems, *Venus and Adonis* and *The Rape of Lucrece,* were written during this time.

E Content-Area Connections

Literature: Shakespeare's Plays
While many critics consider Shakespeare's tragedies to be his greatest plays, students should also know that Shakespeare wrote comedies—plays that are funny and end happily—and histories—plays about the lives of kings. Shakespeare was both a prolific and wide-ranging playwright.

F Content-Area Connections

Customs: Burial
Today, burial sites are generally left undisturbed. In Shakespeare's day, however, a body would eventually have been removed from under the church floor and the remains moved into a charnel house (a place where corpses or bones are deposited) to allow room for the burial of another body.

CONTENT-AREA CONNECTIONS

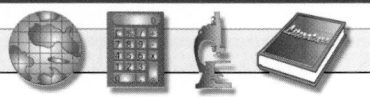

Theater: Theater in Shakespeare's Time
In Shakespeare's time the theater was popular but often condemned by government and religious officials who feared the spread of diseases and immorality.
Paired activity. Have students research the causes and effects of attempts to control the theater made by London officials in the years between 1570 and 1640.

Theater: Publishing Shakespeare's Plays
As producer and director Joseph Papp explained, none of Shakespeare's plays were published until seven years after his death: "In an age where there were no copyright laws, publishing a popular play meant that rival acting companies could get hold of it and perform it without the fear of legal consequences."

A Content-Area Connections

Theater: Early English Theaters

By 1574, playgoers at the inns had become so unruly that the London authorities began to charge innkeepers licensing fees for performances, a fact that probably contributed to Burbage's decision to build a theater. Since public plays were frowned upon by London officials, Burbage's theater was built outside the city limits, south of London Bridge. In 1608, Shakespeare and his colleagues opened an indoor private playhouse at Blackfriars. Shakespeare's company continued to play for part of the year, however, at the "wooden O," the Globe Theatre.

B Content-Area Connections

Theater: The End of Burbage's Theater

Before he began his theater career, James Burbage was trained as a carpenter. His original theater, called simply The Theater, was built on leased land. Soon after Burbage's death, the lease expired, and the landlord was not eager to renew it. Legally, he could take possession of the building if it was not removed after expiration of the lease. That is why Burbage's sons decided to tear down The Theater while the landlord was away in the country. To help finance the building of the Globe from the old planks of The Theater, the Burbage sons formed a financial partnership with the members of Shakespeare's acting company, the Lord Chamberlain's Men.

SHAKESPEARE AND HIS THEATER: A PERFECT MATCH

by Robert Anderson

The Globe Theatre (18th century), based on C. J. Visscher's engraved panoramic view of London (published 1616).
British Museum, London. The Granger Collection, New York.

Sometimes playwrights influence the shape and form of a theater, but more often existing theaters seem to influence the shape and form of plays. It is important that we understand Shakespeare's theater because it influenced how he wrote his plays. Shakespeare took the theater of his time, and he used it brilliantly.

"The Wooden O"

In 1576, outside the city walls of London, an actor-manager named James Burbage built the first permanent theater in England. He called it the Theatre. Up to that time, touring acting companies had played wherever they could rent space. Usually this would be in the courtyards of inns. There the actors would erect a temporary platform stage at one end of the yard and play to an audience that stood around the stage or sat in the tiers of balconies that surrounded the courtyard. (Normally these balconies were used as passageways to the various rooms of the inn.) It was natural, then, that the first theater built by Burbage should derive its shape and form from the inns.

In 1599, Burbage's theater was torn down and its timbers were used by Shakespeare and his company to build the Globe Theatre. This was the theater for which Shakespeare wrote most of his plays.

In his play *Henry V*, Shakespeare called his theater a "wooden O." It was a large, round (or polygonal) building, three stories high, with a large platform stage that projected from one end into a yard open to the sky. In the back wall of this stage was a curtained-off inner stage. Flanking the inner stage were two doors for entrances and exits. Above this inner stage was a small balcony or upper stage, which

SKILLS FOCUS

Pages 778–780
cover
Literary Skills
Understand the function of scene design in drama.

778 Collection 11 Drama • Synthesizing Sources

CONTENT-AREA CONNECTIONS

History: Events

Small-group activity. After students have read the introductory essays on Shakespeare and the theater during his lifetime, provide the class with a list of related topics that they may research in the library or on the Internet. Possible topics include Elizabeth I, Stratford-on-Avon, the Globe Theatre, and the bubonic plague. Divide students into small groups. Have each group choose a topic and compile a list of facts relating to it during a specific historical period.

When students return to the classroom, ask a presenter from each group to read the list of facts. Remind students to jot down notes as they listen and to save their notes for the Writer's Workshop. These notes may later help students decide on topics for their research reports, to be completed after reading *Romeo and Juliet*.

could be used to suggest Juliet's balcony or the high walls of a castle or the bridge of a ship. Trapdoors were placed in the floor of the main stage for the entrances and exits of ghosts and for descents into hell.

The plays were performed in the afternoon. Since the stage was open to the sky, there was no need for stage lighting. There were very few sets (scenery, furniture, and so on). The stage was "set" by the language. A whole forest scene was created in one play when a character announced, "Well, this is the Forest of Arden." But costumes were often elaborate, and the stage might have been hung with colorful banners and trappings. (The groundlings, those eight hundred or more people who stood shoulder to shoulder around the stage for the price of a penny, loved a good show. Most people still do.)

We can see that this stage, with its few sets and many acting areas—forestage, inner stage, and upper stage—made for a theater of great fluidity. That is, scene could follow scene with almost cinematic ease.

In one interesting aspect the theater in Shakespeare's day was very different from the theater we know today. Plays were originally performed by the all-male medieval trade guilds, so all women's parts were played by boys. It would be many years before women appeared onstage in the professional English theater. In Shakespeare's day, Juliet would have been played by a trained boy actor.

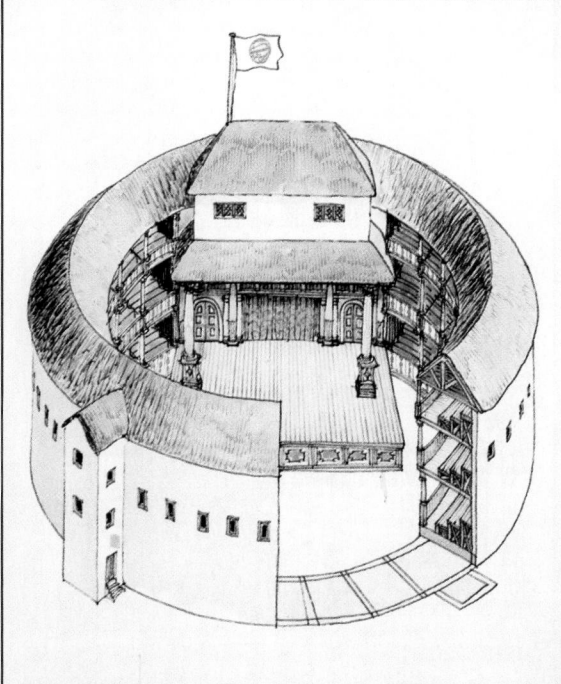

C "The Wooden O," the Globe Theatre. Drawing by David Gentleman.

The Modern Stage:
Back to Shakespeare's Theater

It has been said that all you need for a theater is "two planks and a passion." Since Shakespeare's time "the planks" (the stage) have undergone various changes. First, the part of the stage that projected into the yard grew narrower, and the small curtained inner stage grew larger, until there developed what is called the **proscenium**
D **stage.** Here there is no outer stage; there is only the inner stage, and a large curtain separates it from the audience. The effect is like looking inside a window or inside a picture frame. This is the stage most of us know today. It has been standard for well over a hundred years.

Shakespeare and His Theater   **779**

C **Content-Area Connections**

Theater: Reviews

During Shakespeare's time, visitors from abroad wrote in praise of London's theaters. Thomas Platter wrote: "The playhouses are so constructed that they play on a raised platform so that everyone can see the whole spectacle. The actors are most expensively and beautifully dressed. . . ." The German tourist Paul Hentzner wrote: "Without the city are some theaters where English actors almost every day represent tragedies and comedies to very numerous audiences; these are concluded with excellent music, variety of dances, and the great applause of the audience."

D **Reading Skills**

❷ Analyzing cause and effect.
Some critics contend that since Shakespeare knew that boys would play the women's roles, it affected how he delineated his female characters. For example, a large number of the heroines in Shakespeare's comedies are often disguised as boys and therefore dressed in masculine garb. Do you agree with the cause-and-effect relationship these critics see, or can you think of some other reason for having women disguise themselves as men? [Students may agree with the critics, or they may suggest that Shakespeare simply enjoyed creating plot complications by having characters go about in disguise.]

English-Language Learners
For lessons designed for English-language learners and special education students, see *Holt Reading Solutions.*

A Reading Skills

Expressing an opinion. Ask students who have acting experience (or a professional actor invited to the class) to respond to the following questions: How does the type of theater affect your acting style and your relationship with the audience? What do you like and dislike about a large auditorium? a small, intimate theater? an outdoor performance? [Responses will vary.]

B Content-Area Connections

Film: Shakespeare on Film
For more information on film adaptations of Shakespeare's plays, including *Romeo and Juliet,* see the A Closer Look feature "Shakespeare in the Video Store" on p. 892.

GUIDED PRACTICE

Guide the class in answering these comprehension questions.

True-False

1. Shakespeare was the son of a nobleman. [F]
2. Shakespeare's wife and children apparently remained in Stratford when he moved to London. [T]
3. Plays were performed at night, after the end of the workday. [F]
4. There were no actresses on the London stage during Shakespeare's time. [T]
5. The main stage in the Shakespearean theater projected into the audience. [T]

A cutaway of the Globe, showing the three stage levels and the dressing and prop rooms. Drawing by David Gentleman.

A But recently we have seen a reversal of this design. Now more and more theaters (especially university and regional theaters) are building "thrust" stages, or arena stages. In this kind of theater, the audience once again sits on three or even four sides of the stage.

The Movies and the Theater: Words Versus Action

Like Shakespeare's stage, this kind of thrust stage, with its minimal scenery, allows playwrights (if they want) to move their stories rapidly from place to place. They can establish each new scene with a line like "Well, this is the Forest of Arden." As a result, playwrights have been tempted to write plays that imitate the style of movies. But this imitation rarely works. Theater and movies are different media. A theater audience does not necessarily want to be whisked from place to place. People who go to plays often prefer to spend a long, long time watching the subtle development of conflicts among a small group of people, all in one setting. For example, all of the action in Lorraine Hansberry's play *A Raisin in the Sun* takes place inside one small apartment on Chicago's South Side.

B Movies are basically a *visual* medium and so must chiefly engage and delight the eye rather than the ear. (One movie director once referred to a dialogue in a movie as "foreground *noise*"!) The theater is much more a medium of *words*. When we go to see a play, it is the movement of the words rather than the movement of the scenery that delights us.

This difference between the appeal of a movie and the appeal of a play may account for the failure of some successful plays when they are translated to the screen. The movie producer will say, "Open up the story." In "opening up the story," the producer sometimes loses the concentration, the intensity, that was the prime virtue of the play.

DIFFERENTIATING INSTRUCTION

Learners Having Difficulty
Students who have had limited exposure to plays might have difficulty understanding why a play and a movie of the same story are performed differently. If possible, encourage students to attend a theater performance of *Romeo and Juliet,* or show a taped stage performance in class. Then, show a videotape of a film adaptation. As the class reads the play, work with students to make a chart, like the one on the right, that lists some of the major differences between a play and a movie. Some categories to consider include setting, facial expressions, dialogue, and volume of voices.

Play	Movie
Setting must fit on stage.	Setting(s) can be anywhere; camera can pan or zoom.
Facial expressions have to be seen from a distance.	Camera can shoot close-ups.

How to Read Shakespeare

The Poetry

Whatever Shakespeare learned of rhetoric, or language, in grammar school, he parades with relish in *Romeo and Juliet*. He is obviously having a fine time here with puns and wordplay and all the other variations he can ring on the English language.

Romeo and Juliet is written in both prose and poetry. Prose is for the most part spoken by the common people and, occasionally, by Mercutio when he is joking. Most of the other characters speak in poetry.

Blank verse. The poetry is largely written in unrhymed iambic pentameter. In **iambic meter** each unstressed syllable is followed by a stressed syllable, as in the word *prefér*. In **iambic pentameter** there are five of these iambic units in each line. Unrhymed iambic pentameter is called **blank verse.** The word *blank* just means that there is no rhyme at the ends of lines.

Read aloud this perfect example of iambic pentameter, spoken by Romeo. The syllables marked with a stress (**'**) should be stressed.

But soft! What light through yonder window breaks?

Couplets. When Shakespeare uses rhymes, he generally uses **couplets,** two consecutive lines of poetry that rhyme. The couplets often punctuate a character's exit or signal the end of a scene. Read aloud Juliet's exit line from the balcony:

Good night, good night! Parting is such sweet sorrow
That I shall say good night till it be morrow.

Reading the lines. We have all heard people ruin a good poem by mechanically pausing at the end of each line, whether or not the meaning of the line called for a pause. (Maxwell Anderson, who wrote verse plays, had his plays typed as though they were prose, so that actors would not be tempted to pause at the end of each line. Consider using this technique when you stage a scene.)

How to Read Shakespeare **781**

History of the English language.
Although all of these words are archaic, the phrase "give short shrift" is still occasionally used orally or seen in contemporary prose, and means "to give very little attention to," as if to ignore or deem insignificant.

Lines of poetry are either end-stopped or run-on. An **end-stopped line** has some punctuation at its end. A **run-on line** has no punctuation at its end. In a run-on line the meaning is always completed in the line or lines that follow.

Try reading aloud this passage from Act II, Scene 2, where Juliet speaks in end-stopped lines—lines ending with punctuation that requires her to pause:

O, Romeo, Romeo! Wherefore art thou Romeo?
Deny thy father and refuse thy name;
Or, if thou wilt not, be but sworn my love,
And I'll no longer be a Capulet.

Romeo's speech in the same scene has many run-on lines. Read these lines aloud; where does Romeo pause?

The brightness of her cheek would shame those stars
As daylight doth a lamp; her eyes in heaven
Would through the airy region stream so bright
That birds would sing and think it were not night.

The glory of *Romeo and Juliet* is its poetry and its theatricality. The play is fast moving, and the poetry suits the story of young people dealing with a matter very important to them—passionate, once-in-a-lifetime love.

The Words

Shakespeare wrote this play about four hundred years ago. It's not surprising, then, that many words are by now **archaic,** which means that they (or their particular meanings) have disappeared from common use. The sidenotes in the play will help you with these archaic words and with other words and expressions that might be unfamiliar to you. Here are some of the archaic words that are repeatedly used in the play:

'a: he.
a': on.
an' or **and:** if.
anon: soon; right away; coming.
but: if; except; only.
Good-den or **go-den** or **God-den:** Good evening (said in the late afternoon).
hap or **happy:** luck; lucky.
humor: mood; moisture.
Jack: common fellow; ordinary guy.
maid: unmarried girl.
mark: listen to.

Marry: mild oath, shortened from "by the Virgin Mary."
nice: trivial; foolish.
owes: owns.
shrift: confession or forgiveness for sins that have been confessed to a priest. After confession a person was said to be **shriven.**
soft: quiet; hush; slow up.
stay: wait.
still: always.
withal: with that; with.
wot: know.

Before You Read

The Tragedy of Romeo and Juliet

Make the Connection

Quickwrite ✏️

"Kids these days! They think that love conquers all, that nothing matters except how they feel about each other. They have no sense of responsibility to their families, no respect for tradition, no regard for those who are older and wiser. They don't know the problems they're going to have that all the love in the world won't solve for them."

What do you think of this complaint? Have you heard older people say these things about kids today? How would one of the kids respond to this speaker? Write a quick response from a kid's point of view.

Literary Focus

Tragedy

A **tragedy** is a narrative about serious and important actions that end unhappily. Usually a tragedy ends with the deaths of the **main characters.** In some tragedies the disaster hits totally innocent characters; in others the main characters are in some ways responsible for their downfall. Shakespeare's tragic plays usually follow this five-part pattern:

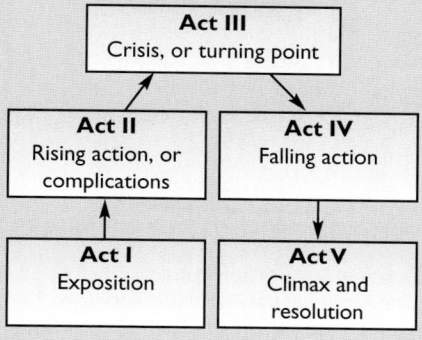

```
                    ┌─────────────────────────┐
                    │        Act III          │
                    │  Crisis, or turning point│
                    └─────────────────────────┘
          ┌──────────────────┐   ┌──────────────────┐
          │     Act II        │   │     Act IV        │
          │ Rising action, or │   │  Falling action   │
          │   complications   │   │                   │
          └──────────────────┘   └──────────────────┘
          ┌──────────────────┐   ┌──────────────────┐
          │     Act I         │   │     Act V         │
          │   Exposition      │   │   Climax and      │
          │                   │   │   resolution      │
          └──────────────────┘   └──────────────────┘
```

1. The **exposition** establishes the setting, introduces some of the main characters, explains background, and introduces the characters' main conflict.

2. The **rising action** consists of a series of complications. These occur as the main characters take action to resolve their problems.

3. The **crisis,** or **turning point,** is the moment when a choice made by the main characters determines the direction of the action: upward to a happy ending, which would be a **comedy,** or downward to **tragedy.** This turning point is the dramatic and tense moment when the forces of conflict come together. Look for the turning point in Act III.

4. The **falling action** presents events that result from the action taken at the turning point. These events usually lock the characters deeper and deeper into disaster; with each event we see the characters falling straight into tragedy.

5. The final and greatest **climax** occurs at the end of the play—usually, in tragedy, with the deaths of the main characters. In the **resolution** (or **denouement**) all the loose parts of the plot are tied up. The play is over.

The **Staging the Play** sidenotes throughout the play will help you visualize the play being performed—including the way the stage would be set, the way the actors would move and interact onstage, and the way they would say their lines.

(continued)

INTERNET

More About William Shakespeare

Keyword: LE5 9-11

SKILLS FOCUS

Literary Skills
Understand characteristics of tragedy. Understand how a work of literature is related to its historical period.

Many sidenotes throughout the play cover **Literary Skills** Understand characteristics of tragedy.

SKILLS FOCUS, pp. 783–917

Grade-Level Skills
■ **Literary Skills**
Analyze the characteristics of dramatic literature, including tragedy.

■ **Literary Skills**
Analyze the function of dialogue, scene design, soliloquies, asides, and character foils in dramatic literature.

■ **Literary Skills**
Analyze the way a work of literature relates to the themes and issues of its historical period.

Review Skills

■ **Literary Skills**
Evaluate the plot's structure and development, and the way in which conflicts are resolved.

■ **Literary Skills**
Analyze how a literary work reflects the attitudes and beliefs of its author.

The Tragedy of Romeo and Juliet **783**

RESOURCES: READING

Planning
■ *One-Stop Planner* CD-ROM with ExamView Test Generator

Differentiating Instruction
■ *Holt Reading Solutions*
■ *Supporting Instruction in Spanish*
■ *Audio CD Library, Selections and Summaries in Spanish*

Vocabulary
■ *Vocabulary Development*

Grammar and Language
■ *Daily Language Activities*

Assessment
■ *Holt Assessment: Literature, Reading, and Vocabulary*
■ *One-Stop Planner* CD-ROM with ExamView Test Generator

■ *Holt Online Assessment*

Internet
■ go.hrw.com (Keyword: LE5 9-11)
■ *Elements of Literature Online*

Media
■ *Audio CD Library*
■ *Visual Connections Videocassette Program*
■ *Fine Art Transparencies*

Selection Starter

Motivate. Engage students in a discussion of how love is portrayed in poems, novels, plays, movies, and television. How might circumstances in the lives of two people—each person's family, community, or nation—have a negative impact on their relationship? Might some obstacles be good for the young lovers? On the chalkboard, list students' ideas in a chart such as the following.

What the Lovers Want	Obstacles	
	Good?	Bad?

You may also wish to have students watch "The Bard: William Shakespeare" (Videocassette, Segment 12), which provides an introduction to the life and works of Shakespeare. Dramatic excerpts from Acts I and II of *Romeo and Juliet* are available in the *Audio CD Library* (disc 19).

Build background. Although students do not need to know the history of Italy in the sixteenth century to understand the play, you can enhance their understanding by telling them that the feud that dominates the play has struck a familiar chord with audiences in various times and places, and also accurately reflects specific historical conditions in Italy in the thirteenth and fourteenth centuries when control of cities was divided among rival noble families.

Assign the Reading

You may wish to have advanced learners read aloud as other students listen. Have readers pause after the prologue and after each scene in order to discuss the sidenotes. Encourage students to re-read (silently or aloud) after they have discussed the sidenotes.

Background

Most of Shakespeare's plays are based on stories that were already well-known to his audiences. (Shakespeare usually wrote about historical subjects.) *Romeo and Juliet* is based on a long narrative poem by Arthur Brooke, which was published in 1562 as *The Tragicall Historye of Romeus and Juliet*. Brooke's popular poem itself was based on older Italian stories.

Romeo and Juliet, a very young man and a nearly fourteen-year-old girl, fall in love at first sight. They are caught up in an idealized, almost unreal, passionate love. They are in love with love. In his prologue, Brooke preaches a moral, which people of his time expected. He says that Romeo and Juliet had to die because they broke the laws and married unwisely, against their parents' wishes. Shakespeare does away with this moralizing. He presents the couple as "star-crossed lovers," doomed to disaster by fate.

To understand what *star-crossed* means, you have to realize that most people of Shakespeare's time believed in astrology. They believed that the course of their lives was partly determined by the hour, day, month, and year of their birth—hence "the stars" under which they were born. Shakespeare himself may not have shared this belief. In a later play, *Julius Caesar*, he has a character question this age-old idea about astrology and the influence of the stars:

> The fault, dear Brutus, is not in our
> stars,
> But in ourselves that we are underlings.

Although Shakespeare says in his prologue that Romeo and Juliet are star-crossed, he does not make them mere victims of fate. Romeo and Juliet make decisions that lead to their disaster. More important, other characters have a hand in the play's tragic ending. How important do *you* think fate is in affecting what happens to us? To what degree do you think we control our own destinies?

Romeo and Juliet (1977) by Milton Hebald, at the Delacorte Theater in Central Park, New York City.

✲ CHARACTERS ✲

THE MONTAGUES

Lord Montague
Lady Montague
Romeo, son of Montague
Benvolio, nephew of Montague and friend of Romeo
Balthasar, servant of Romeo
Abram, servant of Montague

THE CAPULETS

Lord Capulet
Lady Capulet
Juliet, daughter of Capulet
Tybalt, nephew of Lady Capulet
Nurse to Juliet
Peter, servant to the Nurse
Sampson, **Gregory** } servants of Capulet
An Old Man of the Capulet family

THE OTHERS

Prince Escalus, ruler of Verona
Mercutio, a relative of the Prince and friend of Romeo
Friar Laurence, a Franciscan priest
Friar John, another Franciscan priest
Count Paris, a young nobleman, a relative of the Prince
An Apothecary (a druggist)
Page to Paris
Chief Watchman
Three Musicians
An Officer
Citizens of Verona, Relatives of both families, **Maskers, Guards, Watchmen,** and **Attendants**

Scene: Verona and Mantua, cities in northern Italy

The Tragedy of Romeo and Juliet 785

Summary ⟷ *at grade level*

The Prologue

The Chorus, played by a single actor, briefly summarizes the plot of the play. The story is set in Verona, Italy. The recent fighting that has broken out between two feuding noble families dooms a pair of young lovers, each the off-spring of one of the families. The unfolding of "their death-marked love" is the play's subject; its tragic climax is their untimely deaths, which cause their respective families to resolve the feud.

Act I, Scene I

On a street in Verona, Sampson and Gregory, servants of Lord Capulet, provoke a fight with two of Lord Montague's servants, Balthasar and Abram. Benvolio, a relative of the Montagues and a friend of Romeo's, enters and stops the fight; but when Tybalt, a relative of the Capulets, enters and insults Benvolio, a general free-for-all ensues. It is stopped by an officer and several citizens. Lord and Lady Capulet and Lord and Lady Montague enter, and the two men exchange angry words. Prince Escalus enters, warns the lords that any further fighting will be punished by death, and dismisses the crowd.

Left alone on stage, the Montagues and Benvolio discuss Romeo's recent strange and lovelorn behavior. After the Montagues exit, Romeo enters and confesses to Benvolio that he is in despair because he loves a young woman, Rosaline, who has sworn herself to a life of chastity. Benvolio advises his friend to forget her and find someone else, but Romeo says that other women only remind him of his beloved.

> "A pair of star-crossed lovers"
> ✵

786

Learners Having Difficulty
As students read the play, have them write down their questions about the content and form of the text. Then, ask students to form small groups (with the addition of an advanced learner) to try to answer their questions.

English-Language Learners
Have these students watch one of the film versions of the play before reading it to help them visualize the setting and action and understand the main conflicts. Also, read the summary of each scene aloud before assigning it.

THE TRAGEDY OF ROMEO AND JULIET

William Shakespeare

THE PROLOGUE

Enter CHORUS.

Chorus.

Two households, both alike in dignity,°
   In fair Verona, where we lay our scene,
From ancient grudge break to new mutiny,
   Where civil blood makes civil hands unclean.°
5 From forth the fatal loins of these two foes
   A pair of star-crossed lovers take their life;
Whose misadventured piteous overthrows
   Do with their death bury their parents' strife.
The fearful passage of their death-marked love,
10   And the continuance of their parents' rage,
Which, but° their children's end, naught could remove,
   Is now the two hours' traffic° of our stage;
The which if you with patient ears attend,
What here shall miss, our toil shall strive to mend.

[*Exit.*]

A   **1. dignity:** status.

4. Where...unclean: That is, where civilians' passions ("civil blood") make their hands unclean (because they have been used for killing).

B   **11. but:** except for.

12. traffic: business.

C   **Staging the Play**
14. *This prologue is spoken by a single actor called the Chorus. The Chorus welcomes the audience and gives them a taste of the story. What will the "two hours' traffic" of this stage be about? What will happen to the two lovers?*

The photographs throughout the play are from the New York Shakespeare Festival's 1988 production of *Romeo and Juliet,* starring Cynthia Nixon as Juliet, Peter MacNicol as Romeo, and Anne Meara as the Nurse. All photographs taken by Martha Swope / TimePix.

The Tragedy of Romeo and Juliet, The Prologue   **787**

A Literary Focus

Puns. Elizabethans greatly enjoyed puns, especially the rapid-fire exchange of wordplay typical of Shakespeare's comic characters. Have students look for more examples of punning exchanges between characters as they continue to read Act I.

B Literary Focus

? Dialogue. The servants of the house of Capulet are already using insulting language to generalize about members of the Montague family. What does their dialogue show about attitudes in the two households? [Even the servants of the two families are ready for a fight.]

Responses to Margin Questions

Stage direction. The servants are probably pretending to fight with imaginary foes, gesturing with their swords and shields.

Stage direction. Instead of attacking, Sampson and Gregory start quarreling with each other; each doubts the other's bravery. Sampson is probably backing away or hiding behind Gregory and pushing him forward.

✴ ACT I ✴

Scene 1. *Verona. A public place.*

Enter SAMPSON *and* GREGORY, *of the house of Capulet, with swords and bucklers (shields).*

Sampson. Gregory, on my word, we'll not carry coals.°
Gregory. No, for then we should be colliers.°
Sampson. I mean, and° we be in choler,° we'll draw.°
Gregory. Ay, while you live, draw your neck out of collar.°
5 **Sampson.** I strike quickly, being moved.
Gregory. But thou art not quickly moved to strike.
Sampson. A dog of the house of Montague moves me.
Gregory. To move is to stir, and to be valiant is to stand. Therefore, if thou art moved, thou run'st away.
10 **Sampson.** A dog of that house shall move me to stand. I will take the wall° of any man or maid of Montague's.
Gregory. That shows thee a weak slave; for the weakest goes to the wall.°
Sampson. 'Tis true; and therefore women, being the
15 weaker vessels, are ever thrust to the wall. Therefore I will push Montague's men from the wall and thrust his maids to the wall.
Gregory. The quarrel is between our masters and us their men.
20 **Sampson.** 'Tis all one. I will show myself a tyrant. When I have fought with the men, I will be civil with the maids—I will cut off their heads.
Gregory. The heads of the maids?
Sampson. Ay, the heads of the maids or their maidenheads.
25 Take it in what sense thou wilt.
Gregory. They must take it in sense that feel it.
Sampson. Me they shall feel while I am able to stand; and 'tis known I am a pretty piece of flesh.
Gregory. 'Tis well thou art not fish; if thou hadst, thou
30 hadst been Poor John.° Draw thy tool!° Here comes two of the house of Montagues.

[Enter two other servingmen, ABRAM *and* BALTHASAR.]

Sampson. My naked weapon is out. Quarrel! I will back thee.

Stage direction: Two servants enter, bragging and teasing each other. What actions do you imagine they are engaged in as they cross the city square?

1. **carry coals:** do dirty work (put up with insults). People often made jokes about men who carted coal.
2. **colliers:** coal dealers (men with dirty jobs). Notice how the servants start making jokes based on words that sound similar (*colliers, choler,* and *collar*).
3. **and:** if. **choler:** anger. **draw:** pull out swords.
4. **collar:** hangman's noose.
11. **take the wall:** take the best place on the path (which is closest to the wall).
13. **goes to the wall:** is defeated.

30. **Poor John:** kind of salted fish, a poor person's food. **tool:** sword.

? Staging the Play
Stage direction: Sampson's and Gregory's swaggering stops when they spy their enemies. How do their next speeches show that they are really cowards? What's Sampson doing when he says, "Quarrel! I will back thee"?

CONTENT-AREA CONNECTIONS

Literature: Structure of the Play
The critic Northrop Frye analyzed this scene in his essay "Romeo and Juliet": "The stage direction tells us that servants are on the street armed with swords and bucklers (small shields). Even if you came in late and missed the prologue, you'd know from seeing those servants that all was not well in Verona. Because that means there's going to

be a fight. If you let servants swank around like that, fully armed, they're bound to get into fights. So in view of Tudor policy and Queen Elizabeth's personal dislike of duels and brawling, this play would have no trouble with the censor, because it shows the tragic results of the kind of thing that the authorities thoroughly disapproved of anyway.

The first scene shows Shakespeare in his usual easy command of the situation starting off with a gabble of dialogue that doesn't contribute much to the plot, but gets over the latecomer problem and quiets the audience very quickly because the jokes are bawdy jokes, the kind the audience most wants to hear."

Gregory. How? Turn thy back and run?

Sampson. Fear me not.°

35 **Gregory.** No, marry. I fear thee!

Sampson. Let us take the law of our sides;° let them begin.

Gregory. I will frown as I pass by, and let them take it as they list.

Sampson. Nay, as they dare. I will bite my thumb° at them,
40   which is disgrace to them if they bear it.

Abram. Do you bite your thumb at us, sir?

Sampson. I do bite my thumb, sir.

Abram. Do you bite your thumb at us, sir?

Sampson (*aside to* GREGORY). Is the law of our side if I say
45   ay?

Gregory (*aside to* SAMPSON). No.

Sampson. No, sir, I do not bite my thumb at you, sir; but I
   bite my thumb, sir.

Gregory. Do you quarrel, sir?

50 **Abram.** Quarrel, sir? No, sir.

Sampson. But if you do, sir, I am for you. I serve as good a
   man as you.

Abram. No better.

Sampson. Well, sir.

[*Enter* BENVOLIO.]

55 **Gregory.** Say "better." Here comes one of my master's
   kinsmen.

Sampson. Yes, better, sir.

Abram. You lie.

Sampson. Draw, if you be men. Gregory, remember thy
60   swashing° blow.

[*They fight.*]

Benvolio.
   Part, fools!
   Put up your swords. You know not what you do.

[*Enter* TYBALT.]

Tybalt.
   What, art thou drawn among these heartless hinds?°
   Turn thee, Benvolio; look upon thy death.

Benvolio.
65   I do but keep the peace. Put up thy sword,
   Or manage it to part these men with me.

---

34. Fear me not: Do not distrust me.

36. Let . . . sides: Let us stay on the right side of the law.

39. bite my thumb: insulting gesture.

❓ **Staging the Play**
41. *It takes the Montague servants some time to speak. How might their actions show that these four servants are very wary of one another?*

❓ **Staging the Play**
44. *An* **aside** *is dialogue spoken by a character to the audience or to another character that others onstage are not supposed to hear. Sampson and Gregory speak to each other in asides. Who is not supposed to overhear them?*

❓ **55.** *How does Gregory's behavior change when he spots Tybalt in the distance?*

60. swashing: slashing with great force.

❓ **Staging the Play**
62. *What action is Benvolio involved in here?*

63. heartless hinds: cowardly hicks.

❓ **Staging the Play**
64. *In some productions, Tybalt's second line is spoken after a dramatic silence. Why should this line demand our attention?*

The Tragedy of Romeo and Juliet, Act I, Scene I   **789**

C **Reading Skills**

❓ **Making inferences.** What are the attitudes of these characters toward the law? [Possible response: In spite of their bragging, they do not want to get into trouble with the law.]

D **Learners Having Difficulty**

Reading aloud. To help students follow the escalating tensions in this section, read the passage aloud. Emphasize the whispered asides and the fine distinction made by Sampson between "I do bite my thumb, sir" and "I do not bite my thumb at you, sir."

E **Reading Skills**

Reading Shakespeare's poetry. Point out that Shakespeare begins to use blank verse (unrhymed iambic pentameter) when the aristocratic characters begin to speak. Help students count the iambs in each line of Tybalt's and Benvolio's lines. For example, "Pŭt úp / yoŭr swórds. / Yŏu knów / nŏt whát / yŏu dó."

Responses to Margin Questions

Line 41. The Montague servants respond to the weak insults with questions, not with immediate action. The Capulet servants continue to show their insecurity in their wary asides and evasive answers.

Line 44. Abram is not supposed to hear the brief dialogue between Sampson and Gregory.

Line 55. Tybalt is one of the "master's kinsmen" referred to here. Assuming Tybalt will protect them, Gregory now tells Sampson to issue a real insult to Abram—that Lord Capulet is a "better" man than Lord Montague.

Line 62. Benvolio is separating Sampson and Abram, who have started to fight.

Line 64. Tybalt has drawn his sword and threatens to kill Benvolio.

The Tragedy of Romeo and Juliet, Act I, Scene I   **789**

A Literary Focus

❓ Dialogue. What differences in character between Lady Capulet and Lady Montague are revealed in the dialogue each has with her husband? [Possible response: Lady Capulet is sharply critical of her husband's ability, while Lady Montague discourages her husband because she believes he is wrong to go looking for a fight.]

B Reading Skills

Reading Shakespeare's poetry. Have students analyze the Prince's monologue to find end-stopped lines and run-on lines. Then, have a student read the speech aloud, pausing only at the end of end-stopped lines.

Responses to Margin Questions

Line 67. Tybalt is full of hate and eager to fight. Benvolio is a peacemaker.

Line 73. Lady Capulet is pointing out to her husband that he is too old and out of shape to fight.

Line 76. Lady Montague is restraining her husband; she does not want him involved in a brawl.

Stage direction. The prince should enter with ceremony and appear to be in control. You can tell he is ignored at first because he asks, "Will they not hear?"

Line 85. The brawlers have thrown down their weapons and are listening to the prince.

Tybalt.
What, drawn, and talk of peace? I hate the word
As I hate hell, all Montagues, and thee.
Have at thee, coward!

[*They fight.*]

[*Enter an* OFFICER, *and three or four* CITIZENS *with clubs, bills, and partisans, or spears.*]

70 **Officer.** Clubs, bills, and partisans! Strike! Beat them down!
Down with the Capulets! Down with the Montagues!

[*Enter old* CAPULET, *in his gown, and his wife,* LADY CAPULET.]

Capulet.
What noise is this? Give me my long sword, ho!
Lady Capulet.
A crutch, a crutch! Why call you for a sword?
Capulet.
My sword, I say! Old Montague is come
75 And flourishes his blade in spite of° me.

[*Enter old* MONTAGUE *and his wife,* LADY MONTAGUE.]

Montague.
Thou villain Capulet!—Hold me not; let me go.
Lady Montague.
Thou shalt not stir one foot to seek a foe.

[*Enter* PRINCE ESCALUS, *with his* TRAIN.]

Prince.
Rebellious subjects, enemies to peace,
Profaners of this neighbor-stainèd steel—
80 Will they not hear? What, ho! You men, you beasts,
That quench the fire of your pernicious rage
With purple fountains issuing from your veins!
On pain of torture, from those bloody hands
Throw your mistempered° weapons to the ground
85 And hear the sentence of your movèd prince.
Three civil brawls, bred of an airy° word
By thee, old Capulet, and Montague,
Have thrice disturbed the quiet of our streets
And made Verona's ancient citizens
90 Cast by their grave beseeming° ornaments
To wield old partisans, in hands as old,

❓ 67. *This is a key speech. What is Tybalt's mood? How is he shown to be opposite in nature to Benvolio?*

❓ 73. *In the midst of the tension over Tybalt, we have a comic touch. Why is Lady Capulet talking about a crutch?*
75. in spite of: in defiance of.

❓ 76. *Who is holding Montague back?*

❗ Staging the Play
Stage direction: If you were directing this play, how would you stage the entrance of the prince? His dignified procession must contrast with the bloody rioting. How do you know from his speech that the prince is at first ignored by the brawlers?

84. mistempered: used with bad temper.

❗ Staging the Play
85. *There is a dramatic pause before the next line is spoken. What are the brawlers doing now?*
86. airy: light or harmless.
90. grave beseeming: dignified, as they should be.

DIFFERENTIATING INSTRUCTION

Learners Having Difficulty
Divide students into small groups. Ask each group to design and write a formal decree that could have been written by Prince Escalus, warning quarreling factions that those who do not follow his orders will "pay the forfeit of the peace." Each group member can contribute a few lines to the decree. Students may need help imitating Shakespeare's language and style. They can decorate their decrees with

official seals and perhaps write them in a decorative script, such as calligraphy.

Advanced Learners
Enrichment. Suggest that students organize a Shakespeare festival, involving all ninth-grade English classes. Students should plan events and organize supporting tasks, including scenes from Shakespeare's plays to be performed; appropriate music to be performed

"Throw your mistempered weapons to the ground . . ."
✧

Cankered° with peace, to part your cankered° hate.
If ever you disturb our streets again,
Your lives shall pay the forfeit of the peace.
95   For this time all the rest depart away.
You, Capulet, shall go along with me;
And, Montague, come you this afternoon,
To know our farther pleasure in this case,
To old Freetown, our common judgment place.
100 Once more, on pain of death, all men depart.

[*Exeunt all but* MONTAGUE, LADY MONTAGUE, *and* BENVOLIO.]

Montague.
Who set this ancient quarrel new abroach?°
Speak, nephew, were you by when it began?
Benvolio.
Here were the servants of your adversary
And yours, close fighting ere I did approach.
105 I drew to part them. In the instant came
The fiery Tybalt, with his sword prepared,
Which, as he breathed defiance to my ears,
He swung about his head and cut the winds,
Who, nothing hurt withal, hissed him in scorn.
110 While we were interchanging thrusts and blows,
Came more and more, and fought on part and part,°
Till the prince came, who parted either part.
Lady Montague.
O, where is Romeo? Saw you him today?
Right glad I am he was not at this fray.

92. cankered: The first *cankered* means "rusted" (from lack of use in peaceful times); the second means "diseased," like a canker, a running sore.

❓ 100. *What has been happening in Verona? What is the prince's warning?*

C **101. new abroach:** newly opened.

D **111. on part and part:** some on one side, some on the other.

❓ Staging the Play
114. *For the first time, Romeo is mentioned—by his mother, whose parental concern is accented by a rhyme. Lady Montague does not say anything else in this scene. What do you imagine she is doing while her husband and Benvolio discuss her son?*

E

---

or recordings to be played; costumes to be worn; Elizabethan greetings to be exchanged; Elizabethan food to be prepared. Additional tasks include decorating the classroom, writing invitations and press releases, designing and building sets, and videotaping festival events. Planners should attempt to involve students of all ability levels.

C **Content-Area Connections**
History: Society
Remind students that society was made up of royalty, clergy, soldiers, and servants; it was not a democracy, and fights between noble families were frequent. Because England at the time was a monarchy, Elizabethans would have recognized the social order in the play as similar to the one under which they lived.

D **Reading Skills**
❓ Making judgments. Does Benvolio seem to be telling the truth about what happened? [Possible responses: Yes, he has given an accurate summary of the street brawl; yes, but he is leaving out details that would show how willing most of the Montague people were to fight.]

E **Reading Skills**
❓ Drawing conclusions. How might you describe Lady Montague's personality at this point? [Possible responses: She seems anxious and worried about her son; she is a concerned mother.]

Responses to Margin Questions
Line 100. Three civil disturbances have resulted from the conflict between the Capulets and the Montagues. The prince decrees that the punishment for any future fighting will be death.

Line 114. Lady Montague might be listening carefully to her husband and Benvolio discuss Romeo, or she might pace behind the two men, looking for Romeo.

Ⓐ Literary Focus

❓ Characterization. What main character is talked about here for the first time? [Romeo] What do we learn about him? [He is acting strangely; he wants to be alone and is evading his friend.]

Ⓑ Literary Focus

Imagery. Point out that images of darkness and light play an important part in this love story. At this point, Romeo's yearning for darkness and solitude recalls the Elizabethan stereotype of the courtly lover, whose affection is typically unrequited.

Ⓒ Literary Focus

❓ Character traits. What do these lines reveal about Lord Montague's character? [Possible responses: He wonders what is on his son's mind because he wants to help him; he is an attentive, concerned, and nonjudgmental parent.]

Response to Margin Question

Line 139. Romeo rises early to walk by himself and then shuts himself in his room at daybreak. He is moody and tearful, and he will not talk to anyone about his sorrow.

Benvolio.

115   Madam, an hour before the worshiped sun
      Peered forth the golden window of the East,
      A troubled mind drave me to walk abroad;
      Where, underneath the grove of sycamore
      That westward rooteth from this city side,
120   So early walking did I see your son.
      Towards him I made, but he was ware° of me
      And stole into the covert of the wood.
      I, measuring his affections by my own,
      Which then most sought where most might not be found,°
125   Being one too many by my weary self,
      Pursued my humor° not pursuing his,
      And gladly shunned who gladly fled from me.

Montague.
      Many a morning hath he there been seen,
      With tears augmenting the fresh morning's dew,
130   Adding to clouds more clouds with his deep sighs;
      But all so soon as the all-cheering sun
      Should in the farthest East begin to draw
      The shady curtains from Aurora's° bed,
      Away from light steals home my heavy° son
135   And private in his chamber pens himself,
      Shuts up his windows, locks fair daylight out,
      And makes himself an artificial night.
      Black and portentous must this humor prove
      Unless good counsel may the cause remove.

Benvolio.
140   My noble uncle, do you know the cause?

Montague.
      I neither know it nor can learn of him.

Benvolio.
      Have you importuned° him by any means?

Montague.
      Both by myself and many other friends;
      But he, his own affections' counselor,
145   Is to himself—I will not say how true—
      But to himself so secret and so close,
      So far from sounding° and discovery,
      As is the bud bit with an envious° worm
      Ere he can spread his sweet leaves to the air
150   Or dedicate his beauty to the sun.
      Could we but learn from whence his sorrows grow,
      We would as willingly give cure as know.

121. ware: aware.

124. He sought a place where no one could be found. (He wanted to be alone.)
126. humor: mood.

133. In Roman mythology, Aurora (ô·rôr′ə) is goddess of the dawn.
134. heavy: heavy-hearted.

❓ 139. *Romeo has been described by his father and his friend. What do we know of him so far?*

142. importuned: questioned.

147. So far from sounding: so far from being sounded out for his mood (as a river is sounded for its depth).
148. envious: evil.

Music: Renaissance Music
Point out that as Renaissance-era English was different from today's English, the music of the Renaissance was quite different from contemporary music.
Whole-class activity. Play recordings of music composed by William Byrd, Renaissance folk songs, or liturgical music of the time. You can play the music as students enter or leave the classroom or as they engage in creative activities related to the collection.

Architecture: Elizabethan Theaters
Small-group activity. Some students may be interested in how Elizabethan theaters looked. Have them work in small groups to research additional information about the Globe Theatre. Topics might include outside appearance; seating arrangements; mechanical devices, such as trapdoors; or how sound effects were made. Students should create a visual aid to accompany a report to the class.

[*Enter* ROMEO.]

Benvolio.
    See, where he comes. So please you step aside;
    I'll know his grievance, or be much denied.
Montague.
155   I would thou wert so happy° by the stay
    To hear true shrift.° Come, madam, let's away.

               [*Exeunt* MONTAGUE *and* LADY MONTAGUE.]

Benvolio.
    Good morrow, cousin.
Romeo.   Is the day so young?
Benvolio.
    But new struck nine.
Romeo.   Ay me! Sad hours seem long.
    Was that my father that went hence so fast?
Benvolio.
160   It was. What sadness lengthens Romeo's hours?
Romeo.
    Not having that which having makes them short.
Benvolio. In love?
Romeo. Out—
Benvolio. Of love?
Romeo.
165   Out of her favor where I am in love.
Benvolio.
    Alas that love, so gentle in his view,°
    Should be so tyrannous and rough in proof!°

> "Here's much to do with hate,
> but more with love."

Romeo.
    Alas that love, whose view is muffled still,°
    Should without eyes see pathways to his will!
170   Where shall we dine? O me! What fray was here?
    Yet tell me not, for I have heard it all.
    Here's much to do with hate, but more with love.°
    Why then, O brawling love, O loving hate,
    O anything, of nothing first created!

Staging the Play
Stage direction: *Romeo at first doesn't see his parents or Benvolio. How do you think he would be acting as he enters?*

155. **happy:** lucky.
156. **shrift:** confession.

Staging the Play
157. *Benvolio is trying to be casual. What attitude should Romeo convey in his answer to Benvolio's cheery greeting?*

165. *Romeo blurts out the truth. What is the cause of his strange behavior?*

166. **view:** appearance.
167. **in proof:** in reality.

168. **muffled still:** always blindfolded. Romeo is talking about Cupid (the god of love in Roman mythology), who was often depicted as blindfolded.

170. *Romeo wants to change the subject. Then he notices the signs of the street fighting. What does he say about the rivalry between the two families?*

172. **more with love:** They enjoyed fighting.

DIRECT TEACHING

D Reading Skills
❷ Reading Shakespeare's poetry. What purpose do these two sets of couplets serve? [They signal the exit of Romeo's parents and the beginning of a new part of the scene, featuring Romeo and Benvolio.]

Responses to Margin Questions
Stage direction. Romeo should be introverted and distracted, concentrating on his feelings for Rosaline.

Line 157. Romeo should be uninterested in Benvolio's conversation.

Line 165. The young woman Romeo loves does not love him.

Line 170. Romeo distances himself from the feuding, attributing the street conflict to hatred between the families and to the brawlers' love of fighting.

DIFFERENTIATING INSTRUCTION

English-Language Learners
You may need to pause for frequent, informal check tests to ensure that English-language learners are comprehending the text. Especially after long monologues or dialogues, have them stop to answer these questions:

• Who is speaking?

• What is the character speaking about?

• To whom is the character speaking?

• What does the monologue or dialogue tell me about the character(s)?

Advanced Learners
Enrichment. These students may wish to explore the problems that scholars encounter when trying to determine the authorship of plays written during this time period. Have them research how the lack of copyright laws in Elizabethan England makes it difficult to determine the original writer of some Elizabethan plays. Have them offer their own suggestions for ways that Shakespeare and other playwrights might have ensured that their work was not plagiarized.

A **Literary Focus**

Figures of speech. Tell students that a figure of speech that combines two contradictory elements is called an oxymoron. An example is "deafening silence." Have them list the oxymorons in this passage. [*brawling love, loving hate, heavy lightness, serious vanity, feather of lead, bright smoke, cold fire, sick health, still-waking sleep*]

B **Reading Skills**

❓ Connecting with the text. When might a friend's sympathy add to a person's feelings of depression? [Possible responses: when the depressed person worries that he or she is now making others feel bad; when the reason for depression is very personal, and it is frustrating not to be able to explain it.]

C **Reading Skills**

❓ Reading Shakespeare's poetry. Have a student read aloud Romeo's comments about love. Are the lines written in blank verse or in couplets? [couplets] Are the lines end-stopped or run-on? [end-stopped] Remind students that the reader should pause at the end of end-stopped lines. Ask another volunteer to read the lines aloud so that students can appreciate the poetic elements.

Responses to Margin Questions

Lines 175–178. Romeo presents these oxymorons, or contradictions, to show that love, which should cause joy, often produces its opposite.

Line 191. Romeo uses figurative language to compare love to smoke, fire, the sea, madness, gall (meaning "bile" or "bitterness"), and a sweet.

175

A
O heavy lightness, serious vanity,
Misshapen chaos of well-seeming forms,
Feather of lead, bright smoke, cold fire, sick health,
Still-waking sleep, that is not what it is!
This love feel I, that feel no love in this.
Dost thou not laugh?

180 **Benvolio.**   No, coz,° I rather weep.

Romeo.
Good heart, at what?

Benvolio.   At thy good heart's oppression.

Romeo.

B
Why, such is love's transgression.
Griefs of mine own lie heavy in my breast,
Which thou wilt propagate,° to have it prest°
185 With more of thine. This love that thou hast shown
Doth add more grief to too much of mine own.

C
Love is a smoke made with the fume of sighs;
Being purged, a fire sparkling in lovers' eyes;
Being vexed, a sea nourished with loving tears.
190 What is it else? A madness most discreet,°
A choking gall, and a preserving sweet.
Farewell, my coz.

Benvolio.   Soft!° I will go along.
And if you leave me so, you do me wrong.

Romeo.
Tut! I have lost myself; I am not here;
195 This is not Romeo, he's some other where.

Benvolio.
Tell me in sadness,° who is that you love?

Romeo.
What, shall I groan and tell thee?

Benvolio.   Groan? Why, no;
But sadly tell me who.

Romeo.
Bid a sick man in sadness make his will.
200 Ah, word ill urged to one that is so ill!
In sadness, cousin, I do love a woman.

Benvolio.
I aimed so near when I supposed you loved.

Romeo.
A right good markman. And she's fair I love.

Benvolio.
A right fair mark, fair coz, is soonest hit.

❓ 175–178. *All of these are* **contradictions,** *things that are really the opposite of the way they are described. How does Romeo bitterly relate these to the love he feels?*

180. coz: cousin (or other relative).

184. propagate: increase. **prest:** pressed; burdened.

190. discreet: discriminating.

❓ 191. *Romeo refuses to reveal more about his troubles and suggests to Benvolio that he is driven mad by love. What things does he compare love to, before he tries to get away from Benvolio?* **192. Soft:** Wait.

196. sadness: seriousness.

DEVELOPING FLUENCY

Peer-tutoring activity. To help students develop facility with Elizabethan blank verse, pair strong readers with those who find the reading more difficult. Have the partners read through short segments of the play, stopping to discuss the meaning and significance of each segment before moving on to the next.

Have struggling readers take notes on passages that provide significant background information or that move the plot forward.

Romeo.

205   Well, in that hit you miss. She'll not be hit
With Cupid's arrow. She hath Dian's wit,°
And, in strong proof° of chastity well armed,
From Love's weak childish bow she lives uncharmed.
She will not stay° the siege of loving terms,
210   Nor bide th' encounter of assailing eyes,
Nor ope her lap to saint-seducing gold.°
O, she is rich in beauty; only poor
That, when she dies, with beauty dies her store.°

Benvolio.

Then she hath sworn that she will still° live chaste?

Romeo.

215   She hath, and in that sparing makes huge waste;
For beauty, starved with her severity,
Cuts beauty off from all posterity.
She is too fair, too wise, wisely too fair,
To merit bliss° by making me despair.
220   She hath forsworn to love, and in that vow
Do I live dead that live to tell it now.

Benvolio.

Be ruled by me; forget to think of her.

Romeo.

O, teach me how I should forget to think!

Benvolio.

By giving liberty unto thine eyes.
Examine other beauties.

225   **Romeo.**   'Tis the way
To call hers, exquisite, in question° more.
These happy masks° that kiss fair ladies' brows,
Being black, put us in mind they hide the fair.
He that is strucken blind cannot forget
230   The precious treasure of his eyesight lost.
Show me a mistress that is passing fair:
What doth her beauty serve but as a note
Where I may read who passed that passing fair?
Farewell. Thou canst not teach me to forget.

Benvolio.

235   I'll pay that doctrine, or else die in debt.°

[*Exeunt.*]

---

206. Dian's wit: the cunning of Diana, the Roman goddess of chastity, the moon, and hunting, who was not interested in men.

207. proof: armor.

209. stay: submit to.

211. Nor ope . . . gold: In Greek mythology, the god Zeus visited Danae in the form of a shower of gold, and Danae bore Zeus a son.

213. when she dies . . . her store: Her store of beauty dies with her, since she'll have no children.

214. still: always.

219. bliss: heaven.

? **221.** *What vow has the young woman made?*

226. call . . . in question: bring her beauty to mind.

227. masks: Women often wore masks to protect their faces from the sun.

? **233.** *Why won't looking at other women help Romeo?*

235. or else die in debt: or die trying.

? **Staging the Play**
235. *Benvolio can exit here as if running after Romeo. The pair will reenter later, Romeo still being pursued. How would the audience feel about Benvolio?*

The Tragedy of Romeo and Juliet, Act I, Scene I   **795**

DIRECT TEACHING

D **Literary Focus**

? **Exposition.** According to Romeo, why does the young woman he is in love with refuse him? [She has vowed to remain chaste, that is, to refuse all lovers and never marry.]

E **Reading Skills**

? **Drawing conclusions.** Based on his response, how much time does Romeo spend thinking about the young woman he loves? [He thinks about her all of the time.]

Responses to Margin Questions

Line 221. The young woman, Rosaline, has made a vow of chastity.

Line 233. Romeo says that looking at other women will only remind him of Rosaline's superior beauty.

Line 235. Students might say the audience would feel that Benvolio is a sympathetic, devoted, levelheaded friend who wants to help Romeo forget his unfulfilled love for Rosaline.

CONTENT-AREA CONNECTIONS

Psychology: Love

Point out to students that the play contains three different forms of love: (1) Romeo's unrequited love for Rosaline, which follows the convention of courtly love, in which the lover's mistress is proud and cruel and repels all advances; (2) the real love between Romeo and Juliet, the kind of love that culminates in marriage; and (3) a coarse and earthy kind of love, as epitomized by Mercutio and by the nurse.

Individual activity. Have students compare Romeo's comments about adult love in this scene with the image of the lover in Shakespeare's "The Seven Ages of Man," on p. 444.

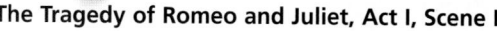

Summary ⬅ at grade level

Act I, Scene 2

Paris asks Lord Capulet for permission to marry Juliet. Capulet hesitates because he feels that Juliet is too young for marriage. He relents, however, advising Paris that he must win Juliet's heart. Capulet invites Paris to a feast. He hands his servant a list of the people to be invited and exits with Paris. The illiterate servant asks Romeo and Benvolio for help. Romeo discovers that Rosaline, Capulet's niece, has been invited. Benvolio, hoping his friend will fall in love with someone else, persuades Romeo to "crash" the party.

DIRECT TEACHING

A Content-Area Connections

Culture: Marriage
At what age does Capulet consider it proper for Juliet to marry? [sixteen] Discuss how attitudes regarding the proper age for marrying vary across cultures and throughout history. During Elizabethan times, life spans were shorter than they are today, so people married earlier.

B Reading Skills

? Reading Shakespeare's poetry. Have a volunteer read Capulet's monologue aloud. When does the speech switch from blank verse to couplets? [at l. 16] Have volunteers practice reading the run-on lines 26–30 (up to the period).

Responses to Margin Questions

Line 12. Paris wants to marry Capulet's daughter, Juliet.

Line 15. Capulet believes that Juliet, not yet fourteen, is too young to marry; she is his only living child, and he fears losing her to Paris.

Capulet is reasonable, no longer quick-tempered. He is a loving father and desirous of peace.

Scene 2. *A street.*

Enter CAPULET, COUNT PARIS, *and the clown, his* SERVANT.

Capulet.
But Montague is bound° as well as I,
In penalty alike; and 'tis not hard, I think,
For men so old as we to keep the peace.

Paris.
Of honorable reckoning° are you both,
5 And pity 'tis you lived at odds so long.
But now, my lord, what say you to my suit?

Capulet.
But saying o'er what I have said before:
My child is yet a stranger in the world,
She hath not seen the change of fourteen years;
10 Let two more summers wither in their pride
Ere we may think her ripe to be a bride.

Paris.
Younger than she are happy mothers made.

> **"Earth hath swallowed all my hopes but she;
> She is the hopeful lady of my earth."**

Capulet.
And too soon marred are those so early made.
Earth hath swallowed all my hopes but she;
15 She is the hopeful lady of my earth.
But woo her, gentle Paris, get her heart;
My will to her consent is but a part.
And she agreed, within her scope of choice°
Lies my consent and fair according° voice.
20 This night I hold an old accustomed° feast,
Whereto I have invited many a guest,
Such as I love; and you among the store,
One more, most welcome, makes my number more.
At my poor house look to behold this night
25 Earth-treading stars° that make dark heaven light.
Such comfort as do lusty young men feel

796 Collection 11 Drama • Synthesizing Sources

1. **is bound:** is pledged to keep the peace.

4. **reckoning:** reputation.

A

? 12. *Paris is very much at ease with old Capulet and more composed than the lovesick Romeo we just saw. What does Paris want?*

? 15. *Why doesn't Capulet want his daughter to marry right away? How is Capulet now different from the man who drew his sword in Scene 1?*

18. **within her scope of choice:** among all she can choose from.
19. **according:** agreeing.
20. **accustomed:** traditional.

25. **Earth-treading stars:** that is, young girls.

CONTENT-AREA CONNECTIONS

History: Notable Historical Events
To help students put the writings of William Shakespeare in historical context, ask them to create a time line of notable historical events. Students can use a history textbook or an encyclopedia to locate the dates and descriptions of the following events and place them on a time line in chronological order:

Battle of Hastings [1066]
Marco Polo travels in Asia [1271–1295]
Birth of English poet Geoffrey Chaucer [1340?]
Birth of Joan of Arc [1412]
Birth of Ferdinand Magellan [1480]
Christopher Columbus first sails the Atlantic [1492]
Birth of Galileo Galilei [1564]
Birth of Sir Isaac Newton [1642]

796 Collection 11 Drama • Synthesizing Sources

When well-appareled April on the heel
Of limping winter treads, even such delight
Among fresh fennel° buds shall you this night
30 Inherit° at my house. Hear all, all see,
And like her most whose merit most shall be;
Which, on more view of many, mine, being one,
May stand in number,° though in reck'ning none.°
Come, go with me.

[*To* SERVANT, *giving him a paper.*]

Go, sirrah, trudge about
35 Through fair Verona; find those persons out
Whose names are written there, and to them say
My house and welcome on their pleasure stay.°

[*Exit with* PARIS.]

Servant. Find them out whose names are written here? It is
written that the shoemaker should meddle with his yard
40 and the tailor with his last, the fisher with his pencil and
the painter with his nets;° but I am sent to find those
persons whose names are here writ, and can never find°
what names the writing person hath here writ. I must to
the learned. In good time!°

[*Enter* BENVOLIO *and* ROMEO.]

Benvolio.
45 Tut, man, one fire burns out another's burning;
   One pain is less'ned by another's anguish;
Turn giddy, and be holp by backward turning;°
   One desperate grief cures with another's languish.
Take thou some new infection to thy eye,
50 And the rank poison of the old will die.
Romeo.
Your plantain leaf is excellent for that.
Benvolio.
For what, I pray thee?
Romeo.   For your broken° shin.
Benvolio.
Why, Romeo, art thou mad?
Romeo.
Not mad, but bound more than a madman is;
55 Shut up in prison, kept without my food,

---

29. **fennel:** an herb. Capulet compares the young girls to fennel flowers.
30. **Inherit:** have.

33. **stand in number:** be one of the crowd (of girls). **though in reck'ning none:** though none will be worth more than Juliet is.

? Staging the Play
34. *Capulet can be played many ways by actors. Some play him here as a loving, considerate father. Other actors interpret him as a man who chiefly wants a socially advantageous marriage for his daughter. How would you play this scene?*

37. **stay:** wait.

? Staging the Play
38. *Like the other servants this one plays for comedy. He can't read or write. How should he show his bewilderment?*

39–41. **shoemaker . . . nets:** The servant is quoting mixed-up proverbs. He's trying to say that people should attend to what they do best.
42. **find:** understand.
44. **In good time:** Just in time.

? Staging the Play
44. *The servant looks up from the note to see the young gentlemen enter. He now tries to get them to read the note, while Benvolio chases Romeo across the stage. How do Romeo's comments in the following conversation show that he is trying to change the subject?*

47. **be holp by backward turning:** be helped by turning in the opposite direction.
52. **broken:** scratched.

DIRECT TEACHING

C Reading Skills

? Interpreting. What advice is Benvolio trying to give Romeo here? [Possible responses: If you let yourself fall in love with someone else, you won't feel the pain of your first love; stay lovesick if you want, but pick someone else to concentrate on.]

Responses to Margin Questions

Line 34. Responses may vary. Some students may observe that Capulet could have conflicting motives.

Line 38. The servant could use exaggerated gestures, such as shrugging, wringing his hands, scratching his head, and waving his arms.

Line 44. Romeo speaks sarcastically about medicines used for physical injuries and makes the point that no medicine can assuage his suffering.

DIFFERENTIATING INSTRUCTION

Advanced Learners
Enrichment. Explain to students that Act I sets up an opposition between youth and age. Have students write a short essay contrasting Lord Capulet, who embodies the characteristics of older people, and Romeo, who epitomizes the attitudes of youth. Ask students to give examples showing how the actions and statements of each character represent either youth or age. Invite students to read their essays to the class.

A Literary Focus

Rising action. Point out that this scene brings a new complication to the plot. Through sheer coincidence, the illiterate Capulet servant has come upon two Montagues and asked them to read the list of guests. As a result, Romeo finds out that his beloved, Rosaline, is to be at the Capulet party that evening.

B Literary Focus

Dramatic irony. The servant has no idea he is speaking to the only son of Lord Montague. But Romeo, Benvolio, and the audience are aware of the irony of the servant's revelation.

Responses to Margin Questions

Line 56. Romeo mocks the servant, but gently, and offers to help him. Benvolio is no doubt amused, appreciating the wit that the servant cannot.

Line 70. Romeo might read the list of names with mockery or with lack of interest until he gets to Rosaline's name. Then his voice could betray his excitement. Whether he asks the question casually or sharply, Romeo should convey his ulterior motive: He wants to know where Rosaline will be.

Line 89. Benvolio claims that other beautiful young women at the party will make Rosaline look like a crow in comparison.

Whipped and tormented and—God-den,° good fellow.

Servant. God gi' go-den. I pray, sir, can you read?

Romeo.
Ay, mine own fortune in my misery.

60 **Servant.** Perhaps you have learned it without book. But, I pray, can you read anything you see?

Romeo.
Ay, if I know the letters and the language.

Servant. Ye say honestly. Rest you merry.

Romeo. Stay, fellow; I can read. **A**

[*He reads the letter.*]

"Signior Martino and his wife and daughters;
65 County Anselm and his beauteous sisters;
The lady widow of Vitruvio;
Signior Placentio and his lovely nieces;
Mercutio and his brother Valentine;
Mine uncle Capulet, his wife and daughters;
70 My fair niece Rosaline; Livia;
Signior Valentio and his cousin Tybalt;
Lucio and the lively Helena."
A fair assembly. Whither should they come?

Servant. Up.

75 **Romeo.** Whither? To supper?

Servant. To our house.

Romeo. Whose house?

Servant. My master's.

Romeo.
Indeed I should have asked you that before.

80 **Servant.** Now I'll tell you without asking. My master is the great rich Capulet; and if you be not of the house of Montagues, I pray come and crush a cup of wine. Rest you merry. **B**

[*Exit.*]

Benvolio.
At this same ancient° feast of Capulet's
85 Sups the fair Rosaline whom thou so loves;
With all the admirèd beauties of Verona.
Go thither, and with unattainted° eye
Compare her face with some that I shall show,
And I will make thee think thy swan a crow.

Romeo.
90 When the devout religion of mine eye

56. God-den: good evening.

? **Staging the Play**
56. *Romeo turns to get away and runs into the servant, who has been listening to them in stupefied silence. How should the two gentlemen treat the servant in this little encounter?*

? **Staging the Play**
70. *Rosaline, Capulet's niece, is the young woman Romeo is in love with. Some actors read this line to betray to the audience Romeo's secret. How would you have Romeo read this line? How would he ask his question in line 73?*

84. ancient: old; established by an old custom.

87. unattainted: untainted; unspoiled (by prejudice).

? **89.** *What does Benvolio say to lure Romeo to the party?*

CONTENT-AREA CONNECTIONS

History: Education
Individual activity. Have students research education during the Renaissance, particularly in Elizabethan England. How widespread was the ability to read and write? What differences in education prevailed between the upper and lower classes of society?

Theater: Costumes
Individual activity. Students particularly interested in the staging of Elizabethan plays may wish to explore how social class and status were revealed by costuming. In this brief scene, for example, how would the clothing of the illiterate servant contrast with that of the two young noblemen, Benvolio and Romeo? At the evening party, how would the dress of female servants contrast with that of female guests?

Maintains such falsehood, then turn tears to fires;
And these, who, often drowned, could never die,
    Transparent heretics,° be burnt for liars!
One fairer than my love? The all-seeing sun
95   Ne'er saw her match since first the world begun.

Benvolio.
Tut! you saw her fair, none else being by,
Herself poised° with herself in either eye;
But in that crystal scales° let there be weighed
Your lady's love against some other maid
100 That I will show you shining at this feast,
And she shall scant° show well that now seems best.

Romeo.
I'll go along, no such sight to be shown,
But to rejoice in splendor of mine own.

                                    [*Exeunt.*]

93. Transparent heretics: His eyes would be easily "seen through"—they would betray the truth.

C 97. poised: balanced (for comparison).
98. crystal scales: Romeo's eyes.

101. scant: scarcely.

? Staging the Play
103. *If we know from the letter that Rosaline is to be at the party and that she is the one Romeo loves, we know why Romeo decides to go to Capulet's. Actors usually say these lines to indicate that the decision to go is crucial and fateful. What mood is Romeo in?*

"One fairer
than my love?
The all-seeing sun
Ne'er saw her
match since first
the world begun."
✡

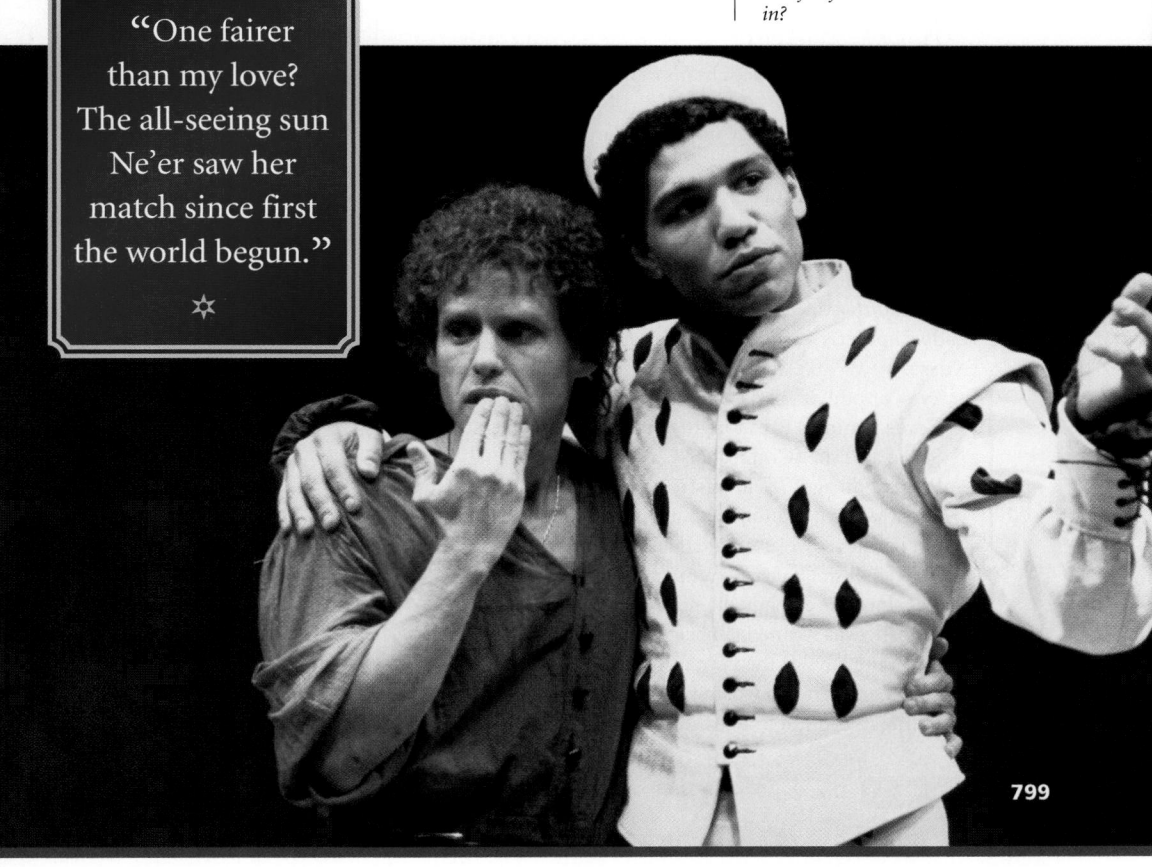

C Reading Skills

? Reading Shakespeare's poetry. Have a pair of students read aloud the dialogue between Benvolio and Romeo. Point out that Benvolio's first speech begins in blank verse and ends in a couplet. Romeo's speech has the rhyme scheme *ababcc*. Benvolio's next speech is in couplets, as are Romeo's parting lines. What is significant about the change from blank to rhymed verse? [Rhyme usually signals the end of a scene or a character's exit. It serves both purposes here.]

Response to Margin Question
Line 103. Romeo is hopeful, excited, and optimistic.

799

Summary ⇔ *at grade level*

Act I, Scene 3

Lady Capulet asks Juliet's nurse to summon Juliet, who subsequently enters. Her initial address to her mother shows that she is submissive and obedient. The nurse rambles on, telling a story about Juliet as a child. Lady Capulet tells the nurse to be quiet and then tells Juliet of Paris's marriage offer, asking her daughter to consider his proposal. Both the mother and the nurse praise Paris's appearance, and Juliet dutifully agrees to her mother's request.

Ⓐ Literary Focus

❓ Exposition. The nurse's long monologue provides background information about Juliet's family and upbringing and about the nurse's position in the family. Why might the nurse feel especially strong affection for Juliet? [Her own daughter, who would have been the same age as Juliet, died, probably making the nurse feel much closer to Juliet.]

Response to Margin Question

Line 10. The nurse exhibits complete ease with the issue of sexuality. In her earthiness, her bawdiness, and her frankness, she provides a significant contrast to Lady Capulet and reveals her place in the household.

Scene 3. A room in Capulet's house.

Enter Capulet's wife, LADY CAPULET, *and* NURSE.

Lady Capulet.
 Nurse, where's my daughter? Call her forth to me.

Nurse.
 Now, by my maidenhead at twelve year old,
 I bade her come. What,° lamb! What, ladybird!
 God forbid, where's this girl? What, Juliet!

[*Enter* JULIET.]

Juliet.
 How now? Who calls?

Nurse.   Your mother.

5 **Juliet.**   Madam, I am here.
 What is your will?

Lady Capulet.
 This is the matter.—Nurse, give leave awhile;
 We must talk in secret. Nurse, come back again.
 I have rememb'red me; thou's° hear our counsel.
10   Thou knowest my daughter's of a pretty age.

Nurse.
 Faith, I can tell her age unto an hour.

Lady Capulet.
 She's not fourteen.

Nurse.   I'll lay fourteen of my teeth—
 And yet, to my teen° be it spoken, I have but four—
 She's not fourteen. How long is it now
 To Lammastide?°

15 **Lady Capulet.**   A fortnight and odd days.

Nurse.
 Even or odd, of all days in the year,
 Come Lammas Eve at night shall she be fourteen.
 Susan and she (God rest all Christian souls!)
 Were of an age.° Well, Susan is with God;
20   She was too good for me. But, as I said,
 On Lammas Eve at night shall she be fourteen;
 That shall she, marry; I remember it well.
 'Tis since the earthquake now eleven years;
 And she was weaned (I never shall forget it),
25   Of all the days of the year, upon that day;
 For I had then laid wormwood to my dug,°
 Sitting in the sun under the dovehouse wall.

3. What: impatient call, like "Hey!" or "Where are you?"

9. thou's: thou shalt.

❓ Staging the Play
10. *The nurse and Lady Capulet are opposites in nature. Lady Capulet sends the nurse off and then calls her back. Some actresses use this impulsive move to indicate Lady Capulet's reluctance to speak to her daughter about marriage. In contrast, how does the nurse react in this scene?*

13. teen: sorrow.
15. Lammastide: Christian church feast, held in England on August 1.

19. Were of an age: were the same age.

26. laid wormwood to my dug: applied a bitter substance (wormwood) to her breast to wean the baby.

DIFFERENTIATING INSTRUCTION

Learners Having Difficulty
To help them keep track of the characters, ask students to convert the list of characters on p. 785 into a chart or graphic organizer. Like the list, the chart should distinguish between Capulets and Montagues. As students continue reading the play, they should add graphic elements to the chart—such as straight or broken lines, arrows, stars, swords, or lightning bolts—to show how specific characters connect or come into conflict as the plot develops.

Advanced Learners
As Act I closes with both Romeo and Juliet realizing their love and its dangers, have students think about the thoughts and feelings of either character. Then, as that character, they should write a diary entry or a letter that reveals the character's inner hopes, dreams, and plans for the future.

My lord and you were then at Mantua.
Nay, I do bear a brain. But, as I said,
30   When it° did taste the wormwood on the nipple
Of my dug and felt it bitter, pretty fool,
To see it tetchy° and fall out with the dug!
Shake, quoth the dovehouse!° 'Twas no need, I trow,
To bid me trudge.
35   And since that time it is eleven years,
For then she could stand high-lone;° nay, by th' rood,°
She could have run and waddled all about;
For even the day before, she broke her brow;
And then my husband (God be with his soul!

40   'A was a merry man) took up the child.
"Yea," quoth he, "dost thou fall upon thy face?
Thou wilt fall backward when thou hast more wit;°
Wilt thou not, Jule?" and, by my holidam,°
The pretty wretch left° crying and said, "Ay."
45   To see now how a jest shall come about!
I warrant, and I should live a thousand years,
I never should forget it. "Wilt thou not, Jule?" quoth he,
And, pretty fool, it stinted° and said, "Ay."

Lady Capulet.
Enough of this. I pray thee hold thy peace.

Nurse.
50   Yes, madam. Yet I cannot choose but laugh
To think it should leave crying and say, "Ay."
And yet, I warrant, it had upon its brow
A bump as big as a young cock'rel's stone;
A perilous knock; and it cried bitterly.
55   "Yea," quoth my husband, "fall'st upon thy face?
Thou wilt fall backward when thou comest to age,
Wilt thou not, Jule?" It stinted and said, "Ay."

Juliet.
And stint thou too, I pray thee, nurse, say I.

Nurse.
Peace, I have done. God mark thee to his grace!
60   Thou wast the prettiest babe that e'er I nursed.

> ## "Thou wast the prettiest babe that e'er I nursed."
> ✧

---

30. it: she, the young Juliet.

32. tetchy: angry.

33. Shake, quoth the dovehouse: The dovehouse shook (from the earthquake).

36. high-lone: alone. **by th' rood:** by the cross (a mild oath).

B

42. wit: understanding.

43. by my holidam: by my holy relic (object associated with a saint).

44. left: stopped.

48. stinted: stopped.

? Staging the Play
48. *Shakespeare often includes **comic scenes** and speeches in his tragedies. The nurse laughs heartily at her husband's joke. How would Lady Capulet react?*

C

? Staging the Play
58. *How would Juliet react to her nurse's chatter? Do you think she finds the story funny?*

DIRECT TEACHING

B Reading Skills

? Drawing conclusions. Based on this allusion to her husband, what might the Capulet family have become to the nurse over the years? [Since she has lost both her husband and her child, she probably thinks of the members of the Capulet household as her family.]

C Literary Focus

? Monologue. The nurse's monologue establishes her character. What are your first impressions of her? [Some students may find her funny and lovable; others may find her tedious, vulgar, and long-winded.]

Responses to Margin Questions

Line 48. Lady Capulet is reserved and, at this point, impatient with the nurse's ramblings, as her next line (49) indicates.

Line 58. Based on her comment in this line, she finds the nurse's comments annoying or embarrassing. She might find the story funny if her mother were not there, since she and the nurse have a relationship that is probably less restrained than the one she has with her mother.

A **Literary Focus**

❓ **Word play.** What double meanings of the word *marry* does Lady Capulet use here? Check the list on p. 782 if you are not sure. [She uses the word as a mild oath, meaning "by the Virgin Mary," as well as the standard meaning "to be wed."]

B **Reading Skills**

Reading Shakespeare's poetry. Have a student read Lady Capulet's speech aloud, and then have the class analyze its poetic structure. [The speech is written in iambic pentameter. The first four lines are in blank verse; the rest are in rhyming couplets. Most of the lines are end-stopped, except for run-on lines 85 and 89.]

Responses to Margin Questions

Line 62. Juliet should be serious, reserved, and respectful; perhaps she should be a little frightened, too.

Line 79. Juliet is probably experiencing a mixture of emotions: excitement, happiness, fear, and hope.

Line 94. The images are "fair volume," "margent of his eyes," "book of love," "unbound lover," "cover," "gold clasps," and "golden story."

And I might live to see thee married once,
I have my wish.

Lady Capulet.
    Marry, that "marry" is the very theme
    I came to talk of. Tell me, daughter Juliet,
65   How stands your disposition to be married?

Juliet.
    It is an honor that I dream not of.

Nurse.
    An honor? Were not I thine only nurse,
    I would say thou hadst sucked wisdom from thy teat.

Lady Capulet.
    Well, think of marriage now. Younger than you,
70   Here in Verona, ladies of esteem,
    Are made already mothers. By my count,
    I was your mother much upon these years
    That you are now a maid. Thus then in brief:
    The valiant Paris seeks you for his love.

Nurse.
75   A man, young lady! Lady, such a man
    As all the world.—Why, he's a man of wax.°

Lady Capulet.
    Verona's summer hath not such a flower.

Nurse.
    Nay, he's a flower, in faith—a very flower.

Lady Capulet.
    What say you? Can you love the gentleman?
80   This night you shall behold him at our feast.
    Read o'er the volume of young Paris' face,
    And find delight writ there with beauty's pen;
    Examine every married lineament,°
    And see how one another lends content;°
85   And what obscured in this fair volume lies
    Find written in the margent of his eyes.
    This precious book of love, this unbound lover,
    To beautify him only lacks a cover.
    The fish lives in the sea, and 'tis much pride
90   For fair without the fair within to hide.°
    That book in many's eyes doth share the glory,
    That in gold clasps locks in the golden story;
    So shall you share all that he doth possess,
    By having him, making yourself no less.

❓ **Staging the Play**
62. *Line 62 suggests another dramatic pause. Often a director will have Juliet rush to the nurse and kiss her. Her fondness for and gaiety with the nurse must contrast with her reserve toward her mother. How should Juliet react when she speaks in line 66?*

76. man of wax: man like a wax statue, with a perfect figure.

❓ **Staging the Play**
79. *Notice that Juliet isn't answering. How do you suppose she is feeling during the conversation between the nurse and her mother about this man they want her to marry?*

83. married lineament: harmonious feature.
84. how one another lends content: how one feature makes another look good.
90. For fair without the fair within to hide: for those who are handsome outwardly also to be handsome inwardly.

❓ **94.** *Lady Capulet has made an elegant appeal to Juliet, to persuade her to consider marrying Paris. Which* **images** *in this speech compare Paris to a fine book?*

READING SKILLS REVIEW

Drawing conclusions. Remind students that drawing conclusions is the process of combining their prior knowledge with evidence from the text in order to decide what is really going on or what characters are really like. Tell them that readers have been drawing their own conclusions about Shakespeare's characters for hundreds of years. Because Shakespeare's characters are dynamic individuals capable of growth and change, readers must often adjust their conclusions about them as the play continues.

Activity. Ask students to jot down their first impressions of the major characters introduced so far. Their lists should include Lord and Lady Montague, Romeo, Benvolio, Lord and Lady Capulet, Juliet, the nurse, Tybalt, and Prince Escalus. Have them save their lists and add to or change them as the plot unfolds in the next four acts.

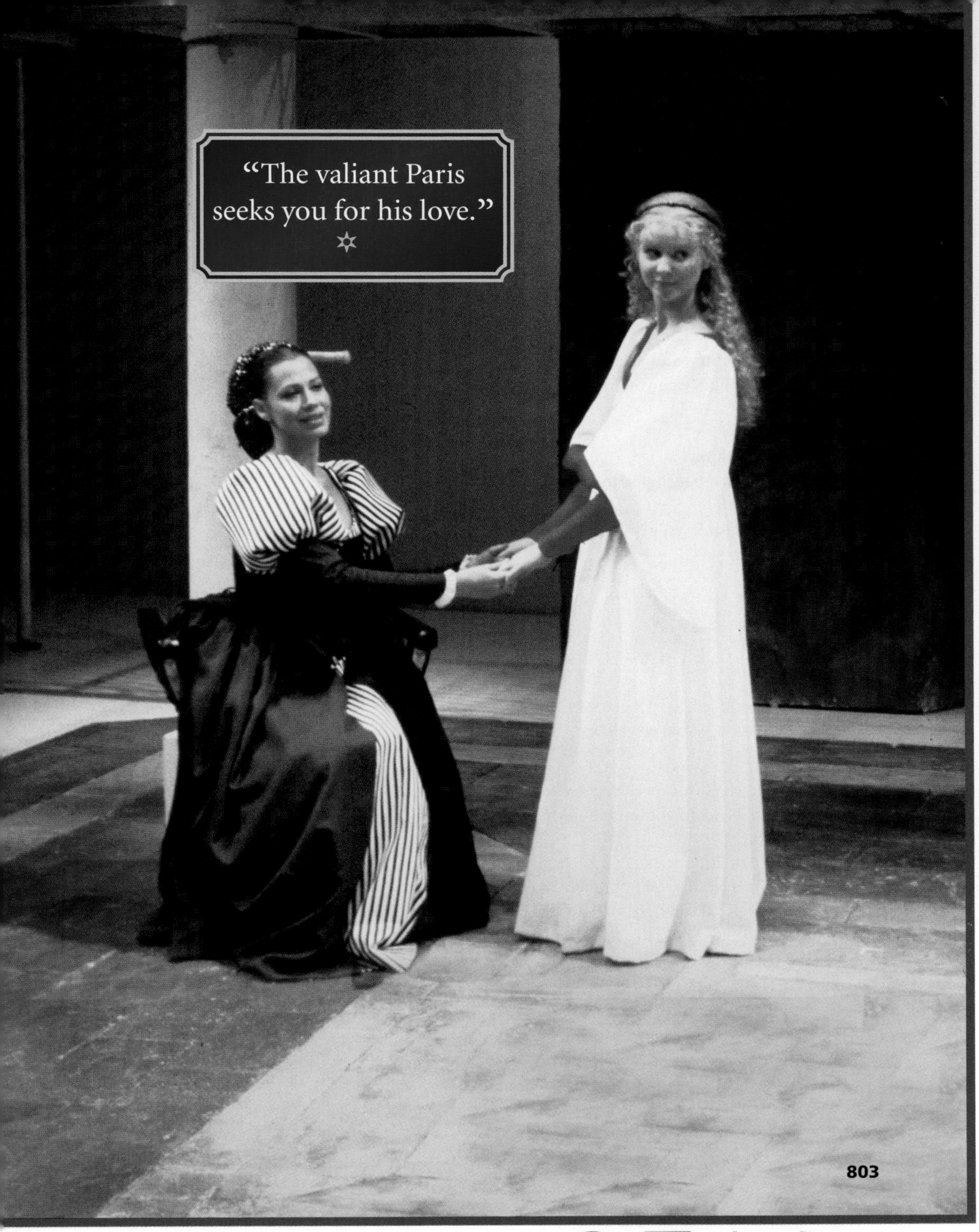

> "The valiant Paris
> seeks you for his love."
> ☆

803

Social Studies/Health: Life Expectancy
Small-group activity. Have students research changes in life expectancy for Europeans since the 1400s. Which centuries showed the most dramatic changes in life expectancy? What social and scientific developments caused these changes? Students might also research family life and child-rearing customs in Elizabethan England. How close were parents and children? How did class affect this relationship? When did children begin to assume adult responsibilities and privileges?

A Literary Focus

Rising action. A new complication is being added to the plot. While Romeo will be searching for Rosaline at the party, Juliet will be deciding whether Paris will make a suitable husband. (Ironically, Romeo and Juliet will find each other instead of the ones they are looking for.)

Responses to Margin Questions

Line 96. The nurse is frank, assertive, and down-to-earth. Lady Capulet is indirect and refined.

Line 99. Juliet says she will not, in looking, go beyond what her mother would approve of.

Line 100. Juliet seems obedient yet speaks clearly for herself. She seems loving, both from her actions and from the reactions of others.

Line 105. Some students may like and admire Juliet's gentle disposition, while others may find her politeness and obedience boring.

Summary ↔ *at grade level*

Act I, Scene 4

Romeo, Benvolio, and their friend Mercutio don masks in preparation for attending the Capulets' party. Romeo is still lovesick and tells his friends that a dream has filled him with forebodings about the party. Mercutio, trying to get Romeo to forget his troubles, describes Queen Mab, who is the fairy in control of the dream world. Mercutio insists that dreams have no bearing on reality. Romeo, who foresees his own "untimely death" (l. 111), disagrees but decides to confront whatever fate awaits him and sets off for the party with his friends.

Response to Margin Question

Stage direction. Romeo says he is "heavy" (l. 12), has "a soul of lead" (l. 15), and is so "enpiercèd" with Cupid's arrow that he cannot rise above his woe (ll. 19–22).

Nurse.

95   No less? Nay, bigger! Women grow by men.

Lady Capulet.

Speak briefly, can you like of Paris' love?

Juliet.

 I'll look to like, if looking liking move;
But no more deep will I endart mine eye
Than your consent gives strength to make it fly.

[*Enter* SERVINGMAN.]

100   **Servingman.** Madam, the guests are come, supper served up, you called, my young lady asked for, the nurse cursed in the pantry, and everything in extremity. I must hence to wait. I beseech you follow straight.

[*Exit.*]

Lady Capulet.

We follow thee. Juliet, the county stays.°

Nurse.

105   Go, girl, seek happy nights to happy days.

[*Exeunt.*]

Scene 4. *A street.*

Enter ROMEO, MERCUTIO, BENVOLIO, *with five or six other* MASKERS; TORCHBEARERS.

Romeo.

What, shall this speech be spoke for our excuse?°
Or shall we on without apology?

Benvolio.

The date is out of such prolixity.°
We'll have no Cupid hoodwinked° with a scarf,

5   Bearing a Tartar's painted bow of lath,
Scaring the ladies like a crowkeeper;°
Nor no without-book prologue,° faintly spoke
After the prompter, for our entrance;
But, let them measure° us by what they will,

10   We'll measure them a measure° and be gone.

Romeo.

Give me a torch. I am not for this ambling.
Being but heavy, I will bear the light.

804 Collection 11 Drama • Synthesizing Sources

---

96. *A* **character foil** *is a character who sets off another character by contrast so that each will stand out vividly. How does the nurse serve as a foil to Lady Capulet?*

99. *Juliet says she'll look at Paris to see if she likes him (if liking is brought about by looking). How does she show that she is a dutiful daughter?*

Staging the Play
100. *Another comical servant enters, speaking breathlessly, but our attention still must be on Juliet. In some productions we now hear the sounds of music coming from offstage, and Juliet exits excitedly, with little dancing motions. Do we really know much about Juliet yet?*

104. the county stays: the count waits.

105. *We meet Juliet for the first time in this scene. What is your first impression of her?*

Staging the Play
Stage direction: It's night. The stage is lit with torches and filled with masked young men. The mood is one of excitement—but we are watching Romeo. What does he say in the next speeches to indicate that he is still heavy-hearted?

1. shall . . . excuse?: Shall we introduce ourselves with the usual speeches? (Uninvited maskers were usually announced by a messenger.)
3. The date . . . prolixity: Such long-winded speeches are out of fashion now.
4. hoodwinked: blindfolded.
6. crowkeeper: scarecrow.
7. without-book prologue: memorized speech.
9. measure: examine; appraise.
10. measure them a measure: dance a dance.

READING SKILLS REVIEW

Comparing and contrasting. Remind students that when they compare, they show how two or more items are alike. When they contrast, they show how the items are different. Shakespeare's plays are full of contrasting pairs of characters, called foils, whose differences strengthen our impression of each character. Differences between characters can be determined by what they say and do, by their outward appearance, and by what others say about them.

Activity. Assign different students to compare and contrast different pairs of characters, such as the following examples:

• Romeo and Mercutio
• the nurse and Lady Capulet
• Benvolio and Tybalt
• the nurse and Mercutio
• Lord Capulet and Tybalt

Mercutio.
  Nay, gentle Romeo, we must have you dance.
Romeo.
  Not I, believe me. You have dancing shoes
15 With nimble soles; I have a soul of lead
  So stakes me to the ground I cannot move.
Mercutio.
  You are a lover. Borrow Cupid's wings
  And soar with them above a common bound.
Romeo.
  I am too sore enpiercèd with his shaft
20 To soar with his light feathers; and so bound
  I cannot bound a pitch° above dull woe.
  Under love's heavy burden do I sink.
Mercutio.
  And, to sink in it, should you burden love—
  Too great oppression for a tender thing.
Romeo.
25 Is love a tender thing? It is too rough,
  Too rude, too boist'rous, and it pricks like thorn.
Mercutio.
  If love be rough with you, be rough with love;
  Prick love for pricking, and you beat love down.
  Give me a case to put my visage in.
30 A visor° for a visor! What care I
  What curious eye doth quote deformities?°
  Here are the beetle brows shall blush° for me.
Benvolio.
  Come, knock and enter; and no sooner in
  But every man betake him to his legs.°
Romeo.
35 A torch for me! Let wantons light of heart
  Tickle the senseless rushes° with their heels;
  For I am proverbed with a grandsire phrase,°
  I'll be a candleholder and look on;
  The game was ne'er so fair, and I am done.°
Mercutio.
40 Tut! Dun's the mouse, the constable's own word!

The Tragedy of Romeo and Juliet, Act I, Scene 4   **805**

❓ Staging the Play
13. *Mercutio is a key character. Here he comes out of the crowd and speaks to Romeo. They engage in a verbal duel about love. In the following dialogue, how do Mercutio and Romeo differ in their attitudes toward love?*

Ⓑ
21. bound a pitch: fly as high as a falcon.

❓ 23. *In what ways does Mercutio show that he is a good friend to Romeo? Would you want to be Mercutio's friend?*

❓ Staging the Play
29. *Mercutio pauses and asks for a mask. What activity would he be engaged in here?*

30. visor: mask.
31. quote deformities: see imperfections (in the way he looks).
32. Here . . . blush: The mask's heavy eyebrows will blush for him.
34. betake . . . legs: begin dancing.
Ⓒ
36. rushes: The dance floor is covered with rushes, plants with small, green flowers.
37. grandsire phrase: old man's saying.
39. The game . . . I am done: The game (dancing) was never very good, and I'm exhausted.

❓ 39. *Despite Mercutio's teasing and Benvolio's urging, what is Romeo determined to do at the dance?*

DIRECT TEACHING

Ⓑ Reading Skills
❓ Making judgments. Do you think someone truly depressed, as Romeo claims to be, would be so quick with a witty comeback? [Possible responses: Yes, because sometimes people who are upset make jokes to cover their feelings; no, because if he had really lost someone he loved, he would not have the energy to think of quick jokes.]

Ⓒ Learners Having Difficulty
Paraphrasing. Struggling readers may find this combination of archaic vocabulary and figurative language difficult to decipher. Read the passage aloud, and then use the margin notes to help students paraphrase Romeo's words. [Possible paraphrase: Bring me a torch. Let my lighthearted friends dance. As the old men say, I'll be the candlestick and just watch you; the dancing was never that great anyway, and I'm exhausted.]

Responses to Margin Questions
Line 13. Romeo feels oppressed by unrequited love and powerless to combat his feelings. Mercutio believes in taking action and being realistic about love: "If love be rough with you, be rough with love" (l. 27).

Line 23. Mercutio enjoys Romeo's intelligence and wit; he shows his friendship by trying to tease Romeo out of his depression. Some students may say that they would want Mercutio for a friend because of his sense of humor and his loyalty; others may say that they would prefer a less teasing friend.

Line 29. Mercutio is selecting and putting on a mask.

Line 39. Romeo will watch, not dance.

> "O, then
> I see
> Queen Mab
> hath been
> with you."
> ✦

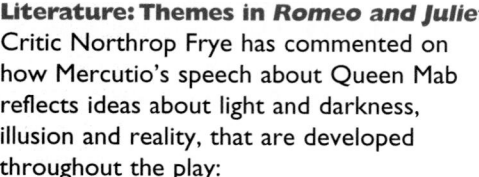

CONTENT-AREA CONNECTIONS

Literature: Themes in *Romeo and Juliet*

Critic Northrop Frye has commented on how Mercutio's speech about Queen Mab reflects ideas about light and darkness, illusion and reality, that are developed throughout the play:

"The light and dark imagery comes into powerful focus with Mercutio's speech on Queen Mab. Queen Mab, Mercutio tells us, is the instigator of dreams, and Mercutio takes what we would call a very Freudian approach to dreams.

"They are primarily wish fulfillment fantasies. . . . But such dreams are an inseparable mixture of the illusion and a reality profounder than the ordinary realities of the day. When we wake we carry into the daylight world, without realizing it, the feelings engendered by the dream, the irrational and absurd conviction that the world as we want it to be has its own reality, and perhaps is what could be there instead. Both the lovers carry on an inner debate in which one voice tells them that they are embarking on a dangerous illusion, and another says that they must embark on it anyway whatever the dangers, because by doing so they are martyrs, or witnesses, to an order of things that matters more than the sunlit reality."

If thou art Dun,° we'll draw thee from the mire
Of this sir-reverence love,° wherein thou stickest
Upon to the ears. Come, we burn daylight, ho!

Romeo.
Nay, that's not so.

Mercutio.   I mean, sir, in delay

45   We waste our lights° in vain, like lights by day.
Take our good meaning, for our judgment sits
Five times in that° ere once in our five wits.

Romeo.
And we mean well in going to this masque,
But 'tis no wit° to go.

Mercutio.   Why, may one ask?

Romeo.
I dreamt a dream tonight.

50 **Mercutio.**   And so did I.

Romeo.
Well, what was yours?

Mercutio.   That dreamers often lie.

Romeo.
In bed asleep, while they do dream things true.

Mercutio.
O, then I see Queen Mab hath been with you.
She is the fairies' midwife, and she comes

55   In shape no bigger than an agate stone
On the forefinger of an alderman,
Drawn with a team of little atomies°
Over men's noses as they lie asleep;
Her wagon spokes made of long spinners'° legs,

60   The cover, of the wings of grasshoppers;
Her traces,° of the smallest spider web;
Her collars, of the moonshine's wat'ry beams;
Her whip, of cricket's bone; the lash, of film;°
Her wagoner, a small gray-coated gnat,

65   Not half so big as a round little worm
Pricked from the lazy finger of a maid;°
Her chariot is an empty hazelnut,
Made by the joiner squirrel or old grub,
Time out o' mind the fairies' coachmakers.

70   And in this state she gallops night by night
Through lovers' brains, and then they dream of love;
On courtiers' knees, that dream on curtsies straight;
O'er lawyers' fingers, who straight dream on fees;
O'er ladies' lips, who straight on kisses dream,

---

41. Dun: pun on Romeo's "done"; Dun was the common name used for a horse in an old game called "Dun is in the mire."

42. sir-reverence love: "Save your reverence" is an apologetic expression. Mercutio means "We'll save you from—pardon me for saying so—love."

45. lights: torches.

47. in that: in our good meaning.

A

49. no wit: not a good idea.

? **Staging the Play**
50. *Romeo's mood seems to have changed abruptly, and he has a sense of approaching doom. How would he speak this line about a dream? Would Mercutio's reply be kind or sharp?*

? **53.** *Mercutio, as a ringleader and a born entertainer, serves as a **character foil** for the more serious and emotional Romeo. Mercutio grabs everyone's attention with this famous **monologue**—a long speech directed at other characters onstage. What point is Mercutio making about dreams and their significance? What does he claim Queen Mab has to do with Romeo? (Try reading this speech aloud. You might also want to draw a picture of Queen Mab.)*

B

57. atomies: tiny creatures.
59. spinners': spiders'.
61. traces: reins and harnesses for a wagon.
63. film: filament, or thread.
66. lazy finger of a maid: Lazy maids were said to have worms breeding in their fingers.

A **Literary Focus**
Rising action. Romeo says that he has decided to attend the party despite a warning dream. His fateful decision to attend sets in motion the rest of the plot and seals his fate.

B **Reading Skills**
Reading Shakespeare's poetry. Point out to students that the beginning of Mercutio's monologue contains three run-on lines. Have volunteers take turns reading ll. 53–58 aloud to make them sound conversational. Remind students not to pause at the end of the run-on lines (ll. 54, 55, 57).

Responses to Margin Questions
Line 50. Romeo is serious, but Mercutio is still joking. Mercutio's wit is always sharp but not necessarily unkind.

Line 53. Through fanciful description, humorous puns, and mockery, Mercutio is making the point that dreams are not at all significant.
   Mercutio says that Queen Mab has brought Romeo's dream and that it is not to be taken seriously.

The Tragedy of Romeo and Juliet, Act I, Scene 4   **807**

Ⓐ Reading Skills

❓ Making connections. What connection is there between the different visits that Queen Mab makes? [All of the people visited by Queen Mab end up dreaming about what they secretly desire.]

Ⓑ Reading Skills

Reading Shakespeare's poetry. Reading this passage aloud will give students more practice in handling the run-on lines of blank verse. It is especially challenging because it contains four consecutive run-on lines.

Responses to Margin Questions

Line 94. While Mercutio's earlier examples make fun of people's own follies, his example of the "hag" suggests a genuinely evil presence that can harm innocent people.

Line 103. Mercutio warns Romeo that he could lose his friends if he continues to rebuff them. Mercutio uses words that evoke a sense of alienation—*inconstant, frozen, angered.*

Line 106. Romeo expresses his fear as an intuition, a misgiving without logical explanation; however, his phrase "a despiséd life, closed in my breast" (l. 110) suggests that he has always expected tragedy in his life.

His fatalism is evident in his references to "the stars" and to "he that hath the steerage of my course."

75   Which oft the angry Mab with blisters plagues,
Because their breaths with sweetmeats tainted are.
Sometime she gallops o'er a courtier's nose,
And then dreams he of smelling out a suit;°
And sometime comes she with a tithe pig's° tail
80   Tickling a parson's nose as 'a lies asleep,
Ⓐ Then dreams he of another benefice.°
Sometime she driveth o'er a soldier's neck,
And then dreams he of cutting foreign throats,
Of breaches, ambuscadoes, Spanish blades,
85   Of healths° five fathom deep; and then anon
Drums in his ear, at which he starts and wakes,
And being thus frighted, swears a prayer or two
And sleeps again. This is that very Mab
That plaits the manes of horses in the night
90   And bakes the elflocks° in foul sluttish hairs,
Which once untangled much misfortune bodes.
This is the hag,° when maids lie on their backs,
That presses them and learns them first to bear,
Making them women of good carriage.°
This is she—
95   **Romeo.**   Peace, peace, Mercutio, peace!
Thou talk'st of nothing.
Mercutio.   True, I talk of dreams;
Which are the children of an idle brain,
Begot of nothing but vain fantasy;
Which is as thin of substance as the air,
100   And more inconstant than the wind, who woos
Even now the frozen bosom of the North
And, being angered, puffs away from thence,
Turning his side to the dewdropping South.
Benvolio.
This wind you talk of blows us from ourselves.
105   Supper is done, and we shall come too late.
Romeo.
Ⓑ   I fear, too early; for my mind misgives
Some consequence yet hanging in the stars
Shall bitterly begin his fearful date
With this night's revels and expire the term
110   Of a despiséd life, closed in my breast,
By some vile forfeit of untimely death.

78. suit: person who might want to buy his influence at court.
79. tithe pig's: A tithe is a tenth of one's income, given to the church. Farmers often gave the parson one pig as a tithe.
81. benefice: church office that enabled a minister to make a living.
85. healths: toasts to his health.

90. elflocks: locks of hair that were tangled by mischievous elves.

92. hag: nightmare. Nightmares were thought to be spirits who molested women at night.
94. women of good carriage: women who can bear children well.

❓ 94. *Mercutio's tone changes here. How are these last details getting into subjects that are more shocking and cynical? Romeo doesn't like this turn of events and cuts Mercutio off.*

❓ 103. *Mercutio could be comparing Romeo to the frozen north. If he is, what warning does he give his friend about remaining cold too long?*

❓ 106. *Romeo here expresses his feeling that something terrible will happen. Does he give any reasons for his fear? Which words in this speech suggest that he is going to the party because he is in the hands of fate?*

But he that hath the steerage of my course
Direct my sail! On, lusty gentlemen!
Benvolio. Strike, drum.

[*They march about the stage and retire to one side.*]

Scene 5. *A hall in Capulet's house.*

SERVINGMEN *come forth with napkins.*

First Servingman. Where's Potpan, that he helps not to
take away? He shift a trencher!° He scrape a trencher!

Second Servingman. When good manners shall lie all in
one or two men's hands, and they unwashed too, 'tis a
5 foul thing.

First Servingman. Away with the join-stools,° remove the
court cupboard, look to the plate. Good thou, save me a
piece of marchpane,° and as thou loves me, let the porter
let in Susan Grindstone and Nell, Anthony, and Potpan!

10 **Second Servingman.** Ay, boy, ready.

First Servingman. You are looked for and called for, asked
for and sought for, in the great chamber.

Third Servingman. We cannot be here and there too.
Cheerly, boys! Be brisk awhile, and the longer liver
15 take all.

[*Exeunt.*]

[*Enter* CAPULET, LADY CAPULET, JULIET, TYBALT, NURSE, *and
all the* GUESTS *and* GENTLEWOMEN, *meeting the* MASKERS.]

Capulet.
  Welcome, gentlemen! Ladies that have their toes
  Unplagued with corns will walk a bout° with you.
  Ah, my mistresses, which of you all
  Will now deny to dance? She that makes dainty,°
20 She I'll swear hath corns. Am I come near ye now?
  Welcome, gentlemen! I have seen the day
  That I have worn a visor and could tell
  A whispering tale in a fair lady's ear,
  Such as would please. 'Tis gone, 'tis gone, 'tis gone.
25 You are welcome, gentlemen! Come, musicians, play.

? Staging the Play
  Stage direction: As you
read these servants' speeches, note
that one speaks in short emphatic
phrases and bosses everyone else
around. Which one is this? What
mood do you think is suggested in
this short scene?

  2. trencher: wooden plate.

  6. join-stools: wooden stools
made by a carpenter (a joiner).

  8. marchpane: marzipan.

  17. bout: dance.

  19. makes dainty: pretends to
be shy.

C

The Tragedy of Romeo and Juliet, Act I, Scene 5 **809**

Summary 🔄 *at grade level*

Act I, Scene 5

Three servants enter, bantering
with one another as they set up
for the Capulets' party. Lord
Capulet cheerfully greets his
guests, welcomes the maskers, and
reminisces about his youth. Romeo
sees Juliet and falls in love with her
at first sight. Although he inquires
about her, he does not learn her
identity. Tybalt, recognizing his
enemy's voice, prepares for a fight.
He is restrained by Capulet, however, who compliments Romeo's
manners. Tybalt obeys his uncle's
command but swears he will have
revenge. Romeo confesses his love
to Juliet; their exchange forms a
sonnet, which uses religious imagery
to describe the passionate devotion of lovers. They kiss but are
separated by the nurse, who summons Juliet to her mother. Romeo
finds out from the nurse that Juliet
is Lord Capulet's daughter, laments
his bad fortune, and departs with
his friends. Juliet questions her
nurse as to Romeo's identity; discovering that he is a Montague,
she, too, mourns her bad luck
in love.

DIRECT TEACHING

C Reading Skills
? Connecting with the text.
How would you feel about being
welcomed to a party in this way?
[Some students may say that they
would feel as if the host were really
glad to see them and that all the
young people could just relax and
enjoy themselves. Other students
may say that they would expect the
host to be a teaser and the party to
be a lot of fun.]

**Response to
Margin Question**
Stage direction. The first servant
speaks in short commands. The
mood is excited, hectic, and frantic.

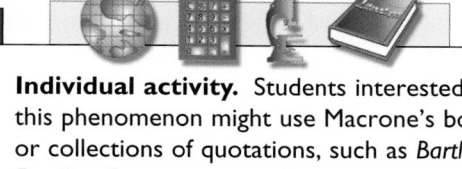

CONTENT-AREA CONNECTIONS

Language: Shakespeare's Phrases
So many of Shakespeare's phrases have
entered the English language as common
expressions that entire books have been written on the topic, including Michael Macrone's
Brush Up Your Shakespeare! "Cold comfort,"
"crack of doom," and "milk of human kindness" are but a few of the Shakespearean
expressions Macrone presents.

Individual activity. Students interested in
this phenomenon might use Macrone's book
or collections of quotations, such as *Bartlett's
Familiar Quotations,* in order to make a list
of well-known expressions that come from
Romeo and Juliet and other Shakespeare plays.
Encourage students to compare Shakespeare's
use of each phrase with the way it is currently
used in ordinary speech.

A Literary Focus

Imagery. Point out to students Shakespeare's use of images of light and darkness, particularly in relationship to Romeo and Juliet. You might ask students to record such images in their notebooks from this point on.

B Reading Skills

? Responding to the text.
What is your response to Romeo's declaration about Juliet's beauty? [Possible responses: It seems as if he falls in love very easily; since he was so attracted to Rosaline before, Juliet must have a truly stunning appearance; this time Romeo may have truly fallen in love.]

Responses to Margin Questions

Stage direction. Capulet remembers flirting at masked balls but now can do nothing but sit because he is long past his "dancing days." His comments emphasize Romeo and Juliet's youth.

Line 41. Juliet is dancing and must be downstage from the other couples, or somehow separated from them, so that the audience sees her clearly as Romeo is smitten.

Line 53. Romeo has fallen instantly in love with Juliet, claiming that he knows true love and beauty for the first time.

Line 54. The audience knows Tybalt's hatred of the Montagues and his rash temper. He could kill Romeo or, because of the prince's order, sentence Romeo to death simply by provoking a fight.

[*Music plays, and they dance.*]

A hall,° a hall! Give room! And foot it, girls.
More light, you knaves, and turn the tables up,
And quench the fire; the room is grown too hot.
Ah, sirrah, this unlooked-for sport° comes well.

30 Nay, sit; nay, sit, good cousin Capulet;
For you and I are past our dancing days.
How long is't now since last yourself and I
Were in a mask?

Second Capulet. By'r Lady, thirty years.

Capulet.

What, man? 'Tis not so much, 'tis not so much;
35 'Tis since the nuptial of Lucentio,
Come Pentecost as quickly as it will,
Some five-and-twenty years, and then we masked.

Second Capulet.

'Tis more, 'tis more. His son is elder, sir;
His son is thirty.

Capulet. Will you tell me that?
40 His son was but a ward° two years ago.

Romeo (*to a* SERVINGMAN).

What lady's that which doth enrich the hand
Of yonder knight?

Servingman. I know not, sir.

Romeo.

A 45 O, she doth teach the torches to burn bright!
It seems she hangs upon the cheek of night
As a rich jewel in an Ethiop's ear—
Beauty too rich for use, for earth too dear!
So shows a snowy dove trooping with crows
As yonder lady o'er her fellows shows.
50 The measure° done, I'll watch her place of stand
And, touching hers, make blessèd my rude° hand.
B Did my heart love till now? Forswear it, sight!
For I ne'er saw true beauty till this night.

Tybalt.

This, by his voice, should be a Montague.
55 Fetch me my rapier, boy. What! Dares the slave
Come hither, covered with an antic face,°
To fleer° and scorn at our solemnity?
Now, by the stock and honor of my kin,
To strike him dead I hold it not a sin.

Capulet.

60 Why, how now, kinsman? Wherefore storm you so?

Staging the Play
Stage direction: The dance, slow and stately, takes place at center stage. Old Capulet and his relative reminisce at one side, but our attention is focused on Romeo (in a mask) and Juliet, who is dancing with someone else. How does the following conversation contrast the two old men with Romeo and Juliet?

26. A hall: clear the floor (for dancing).
29. unlooked-for sport: He hadn't expected to find some of the dancers masked.

40. ward: minor.

Staging the Play
41. In some productions, Romeo puts his torch down here, to draw our attention to his urgent question. Where would Juliet be onstage at this point?

50. measure: dance.
51. rude: rough or simple.

? 53. What has happened to Romeo?

? 54. Why would we feel a sense of fear when we see Tybalt stepping onto center stage again?
56. antic face: hideous mask.
57. fleer: jeer.

"What lady's that which doth enrich the hand Of yonder knight?" ☆

Tybalt.
     Uncle, this is a Montague, our foe,
     A villain, that is hither come in spite
     To scorn at our solemnity this night.
Capulet.
     Young Romeo is it?
Tybalt.   'Tis he, that villain Romeo.
Capulet.
65   Content thee, gentle coz, let him alone.
     'A bears him like a portly° gentleman,
     And, to say truth, Verona brags of him
     To be a virtuous and well-governed youth.
     I would not for the wealth of all this town
70   Here in my house do him disparagement.
     Therefore be patient; take no note of him.
     It is my will, the which if thou respect,
     Show a fair presence and put off these frowns,

C 66. **portly:** well-mannered.

The Tragedy of Romeo and Juliet, Act 1, Scene 5   **811**

CONTENT-AREA CONNECTIONS

Literature: Poetry in *Romeo and Juliet*
The literary critic Phyllis Rackin noted the importance of poetry in *Romeo and Juliet*: "Of all Shakespeare's tragedies, *Romeo and Juliet* depends most upon its poetry. . . . In no other tragedy does Shakespeare use the imagery and the elaborate rhymed verse of lyric poetry to the extent he does in *Romeo* *and Juliet*. One useful approach to this play is, in fact, to regard it as a poem—a great lyrical, metaphorical definition of romantic love. Imagery of darkness and light, of night and day, pervades the language, and it serves more than anything else to define the nature of the lovers' passion."

A Literary Focus

? Rising action. How do Tybalt's actions and thoughts increase the tension in the play? [Possible response: He is forced to back away from a confrontation with Romeo, but his hatred of Montagues remains intense. He promises to renew the confrontation at another time. His threat establishes him as Romeo's hot-headed enemy and poises readers for greater trouble ahead.]

Responses to Margin Questions

Line 74. Capulet says that Romeo is behaving like a gentleman and should be left alone. Capulet is trying to be reasonable and fair, but his pride and temper are also evident in his speeches to Tybalt.

In Scene 1, Capulet automatically assumed that Montague was affronting him, but when Tybalt reacts in a similar way, Capulet is angry and chides him for his posturing, childish behavior.

Line 92. Students may wish to work in pairs or in small groups. Advise them to make general sense of each line and then think of how an angry teenager and an angry adult might express the same ideas today.

An ill-beseeming semblance for a feast.

Tybalt.

75   It fits when such a villain is a guest.
         I'll not endure him.

Capulet.   He shall be endured.
         What, goodman boy!° I say he shall. Go to!°
         Am I the master here, or you? Go to!
         You'll not endure him, God shall mend my soul!

80   You'll make a mutiny among my guests!
         You will set cock-a-hoop.° You'll be the man!

Tybalt.
         Why, uncle, 'tis a shame.

Capulet.   Go to, go to!
         You are a saucy boy. Is't so, indeed?
         This trick may chance to scathe° you. I know what.

85   You must contrary me! Marry, 'tis time—
         Well said, my hearts!—You are a princox°—go!
         Be quiet, or—More light, more light!—For shame!
         I'll make you quiet. What!—Cheerly, my hearts!

Tybalt.
         Patience perforce° with willful choler° meeting
90 Ⓐ   Makes my flesh tremble in their different greeting.
         I will withdraw; but this intrusion shall,
         Now seeming sweet, convert to bitt'rest gall.

                                                      [*Exit.*]

? 74. *What is Capulet's sensible reply to Tybalt's hostility? What feelings is Capulet revealing in his next speeches? Have Capulet's feelings about the Montagues changed since Scene 1?*

77. goodman boy: a scornful phrase. *Goodman* is below the rank of gentleman; *boy* is insulting. **Go to:** similar to "Go on" or "Cut it out."

81. set cock-a-hoop: start trouble.

84. scathe: hurt.

86. princox: rude youngster.

89. patience perforce: enforced patience. **choler:** anger.

? 92. *Paraphrase lines 54–92, putting the exchange between Capulet and Tybalt in modern-day language.*

> "For saints have hands that pilgrims' hands do touch, And palm to palm is holy palmers' kiss."
> ✦

812

Theme. *Romeo and Juliet* deals with several issues beyond that of two young people involved in a passionate, once-in-a-lifetime love. You might discuss these additional related themes:

• Love can confer integrity upon two very young people.

• Tragedy can occur when older people's rage is carried over to the next generation.

• Humans are often powerless to make the kind of world they would like to live in.

• Innocence, virtue, and beauty can be quickly and thoughtlessly destroyed.

• A disordered and chaotic world can bring disaster down on those who live in it.

Romeo.
　　If I profane with my unworthiest hand
　　　　This holy shrine, the gentle sin is this:°
95　My lips, two blushing pilgrims, ready stand
　　　　To smooth that rough touch with a tender kiss.
Juliet.
　　Good pilgrim, you do wrong your hand too much,
　　　　Which mannerly devotion shows in this;
　　For saints have hands that pilgrims' hands do touch,
100　　　And palm to palm is holy palmers'° kiss.
Romeo.
　　Have not saints lips, and holy palmers too?
Juliet.
　　Ay, pilgrim, lips that they must use in prayer.
Romeo.
　　O, then, dear saint, let lips do what hands do!
　　They pray; grant thou, lest faith turn to despair.
Juliet.
105　Saints do not move,° though grant for prayers' sake.
Romeo.
　　Then move not while my prayer's effect I take.
　　Thus from my lips, by thine my sin is purged.

　　[*Kisses her.*]

Juliet.
　　Then have my lips the sin that they have took.
Romeo.
　　Sin from my lips? O trespass sweetly urged!
　　Give me my sin again. [*Kisses her.*]
110　**Juliet.**　　　　　　You kiss by th' book.°
Nurse.
　　Madam, your mother craves a word with you.
Romeo.
　　What is her mother?
Nurse.　　　　　　Marry, bachelor,
　　Her mother is the lady of the house,
　　And a good lady, and a wise and virtuous.
115　I nursed her daughter that you talked withal.°
　　I tell you, he that can lay hold of her
　　Shall have the chinks.°
Romeo.　　　　　　Is she a Capulet?
　　O dear account! My life is my foe's debt.°
Benvolio.
　　Away, be gone; the sport is at the best.

? Staging the Play
93. *In contrast to the raging Tybalt, Romeo is now at center stage with Juliet. Romeo takes Juliet's hand, and in their next fourteen lines (lines 93–106), the two young speakers' words form a **sonnet**. Romeo pretends to be a pilgrim going to a saint's shrine. What religious images do the two young lovers use to talk of their feelings for each other?*

94. the gentle sin is this: this is the sin of a gentleman.

100. palmers': pilgrims going to a holy place. They often carried palm leaves to show they had been to the Holy Land.

? 100. *Romeo and Juliet bring the palms of their hands together here. What in their words suggests that this is what they are doing?*

105. do not move: do not make the first move.

? Staging the Play
107. *In the midst of the swirling dancers, Romeo and Juliet kiss. All of the audience's attention must be on this kiss. What do you fear as you watch, remembering that Tybalt is nearby?*

110. You kiss by th' book: You take my words literally (to get more kisses).

? Staging the Play
111. *As the nurse interrupts, the dance ends. Juliet runs off, and Romeo is left alone with the nurse. What do we know about the Capulets' plans for Juliet that Romeo does not know?*

115. withal: with.

117. chinks: money.

118. My life is my foe's debt: My foe now owns my life.

DIRECT TEACHING

B Reading Skills
Reading Shakespeare's poetry. Point out that this dialogue is actually a sonnet. It consists of fourteen lines of iambic pentameter and has the rhyme scheme *abab cbcb dede ff*. Ask a pair of volunteers to read it aloud.

C Reading Skills
? Responding to the text. How do you feel about the nurse's comment to Romeo about the wealth of the Capulet family? [Possible responses: She is showing a sense of humor about the reasons people marry; she should be a little more cautious about making this comment to a stranger.]

Responses to Margin Questions
Line 93. Students should note the following words and phrases: *profane, holy shrine, sin, pilgrims, devotion, saints, palm, holy palmers', prayer, pray, grant, faith.*

Line 100. Juliet says that Romeo has made a "mannerly devotion" and likens their "palm to palm" contact to a kiss.

Line 107. The audience fears that Tybalt will see the kiss and be unable to restrain his anger.

Line 111. The Capulets want Juliet to marry Paris.

FAMILY/COMMUNITY ACTIVITY

Suggest that students organize a visit to a community theater for a behind-the-scenes look at what goes into a theatrical production. Students can contact the director of the theater to arrange for an interview and tour. In some cases the school auditorium might also be the community theater. Students should prepare questions in advance, make observations, take notes, and make comparisons between the way modern staging is done and the way plays were staged in Shakespeare's time.

A Literary Focus

? **Tragedy.** What is the serious, important action that the play is addressing? [Possible response: love between two young people.] What fate has been foreshadowed for the main characters? [They will die.]

B Literary Focus

Rising action. Have students summarize the plot complications that have occurred by the end of Act I. [Romeo has gone to the Capulet party to see his love, Rosaline, but instead has fallen in love with Juliet, Lord Capulet's daughter, at first sight. Tybalt recognizes Romeo and wants to attack him but is restrained by Lord Capulet. Juliet was supposed to look over Paris at the party but instead has fallen in love with Romeo at first sight. Both Romeo and Juliet learn each other's identity after it is too late.]

Responses to Margin Questions

Line 120. Romeo's friends are preparing to leave, and the other guests are going into the banquet hall.

Line 128. While pretending to be idly curious, Juliet must also communicate intense interest and excitement.

Line 132. Dramatically it increases the tension of the moment; her politeness and reserve cause her to be indirect in her questioning; love has dulled her reason; she is afraid of being disappointed.

Line 143. Juliet could be thoughtful, secretive, and sorrowful. She has just realized that Romeo is a Montague and that therefore her "only love" is a "loathèd enemy."

Romeo.

120   Ay, so I fear; the more is my unrest.

Capulet.

         Nay, gentlemen, prepare not to be gone;
         We have a trifling foolish banquet towards.°
         Is it e'en so? Why then, I thank you all.
         I thank you, honest gentlemen. Good night.

125   More torches here! Come on then; let's to bed.
         Ah, sirrah, by my fay,° it waxes late;
         I'll to my rest.

                    [*Exeunt all but* JULIET *and* NURSE.]

Juliet.

         Come hither, nurse. What is yond gentleman?

Nurse.

         The son and heir of old Tiberio.

Juliet.

130   What's he that now is going out of door?

Nurse.

         Marry, that, I think, be young Petruchio.

Juliet.

         What's he that follows there, that would not dance?

Nurse.

         I know not.

Juliet.

         Go ask his name.—If he be married,

135   My grave is like to be my wedding bed.

Nurse.

         His name is Romeo, and a Montague,
         The only son of your great enemy.

Juliet.

         My only love, sprung from my only hate!
         Too early seen unknown, and known too late!

140   Prodigious° birth of love it is to me
         That I must love a loathèd enemy.

Nurse.

         What's this? What's this?

Juliet.   A rhyme I learnt even now
         Of one I danced withal.

[*One calls within,* "Juliet."]

Nurse.   Anon, anon!°
         Come, let's away; the strangers all are gone.

                                        [*Exeunt.*]

? **120.** *Romeo stands alone here, horrified. What activity goes on around him?*

122. towards: in preparation.

126. fay: faith.

? **Staging the Play**
128. *Juliet has moved to the side of the stage. What feelings must she convey in this question? (She is not pointing to Romeo.)*

? **132.** *Juliet has asked her nurse the names of several men at the dance. Why do you think she asks about Romeo last?*

140. Prodigious (prō·dij′əs): huge and monstrous.

? **Staging the Play**
143. *What tone of voice would Juliet use here? What has she just realized?*

143. anon: at once.

READING MINI-LESSON

Developing Word-Attack Skills
In the beginning of the play, the characters Sampson and Gregory play with words that have similar sounds. Two of the words, *choler* and *collar,* are homophones—that is, they are words that sound alike but are spelled differently and have different meanings. Explain that the English language is rich with homophones because it freely adopted words from other languages. *Choler,* for example, was originally a Greek word. It uses the letters *ch* for /k/, which is a typical letter-sound correspondence in Greek words. *Choler* and *collar* have different spellings for the unaccented syllable /ər/.

Explore another homophone pair from the play: *masque* and *mask. Masque* was originally a French word, with the letters *que* standing for the final /k/. The spelling was Anglicized to

"Thus from my lips, by thine my sin is purged."
✫

815

Monitoring students' progress. Guide the class in answering these comprehension questions. Direct students to find passages in the text that support their responses.

Short Answer

1. **Why do the servants argue in the opening scene of Act I?** [They are carrying on the feud between their masters, Lord Capulet and Lord Montague.]

2. **What warning does Prince Escalus give the feuding families?** [He warns the families that the punishment for future fighting will be death.]

3. **Why is Romeo acting strangely at the beginning of Act I?** [He is distracted and moody because of his unreturned love for Rosaline.]

4. **Why does Lady Capulet want Juliet to attend the evening celebration?** [She wants Juliet to see Paris, who has asked to marry Juliet.]

5. **What realization does Juliet have at the end of Act I?** [She realizes that Romeo, the boy she has fallen in love with at first sight, is a Montague and a bitter enemy of the Capulet family.]

mask, but the French spelling is still used for the word that means a masquerade or a form of dramatic entertainment that was popular in Shakespeare's time.

Activity. Write these words on the chalkboard. For each word, have a volunteer write a homophone.

1. counsel [council]
2. suite [sweet]
3. discreet [discrete]
4. sword [soared]
5. pride [pried]
6. morning [mourning]
7. liars [lyres]
8. plaits [plates]
9. heir [air]
10. medlars [meddlers]
11. presence [presents]
12. chaste [chased]
13. meddle [medal]
14. groan [grown]

The Tragedy of Romeo and Juliet, Act I, Scene 5   815

Response and Analysis

Reading Check

1. The prologue says that the lovers' death ends the family feud.

2. Tybalt is the nephew of Lady Capulet. He hates the Montagues and starts a fight with Benvolio.

3. The Prince warns the fighters that they will be killed if they disturb the peace again.

4. Mercutio encourages Romeo to dance, to treat love roughly, and to pay no attention to dreams.

5. Romeo and Juliet meet at the Capulet's masked ball.

Thinking Critically

6. Possible Answer

Characters	Lines of Dialogue	What We Learn
Gregory and Sampson	11. 5–13	Capulet's servants hate the Montagues.
Benvolio and Tybalt	11. 63–69	Tybalt views Benvolio as a bitter enemy.
Benvolio and Montague	11. 120–156	Romeo is acting strangely, and no one knows why.

7. In Scene 2, Lord Capulet approves of Paris as a suitor for Juliet, and while he says he will not force her to marry Paris, he makes it clear that he determines her choices (ll. 18–19). In Scene 3, the complication deepens because Juliet desires to be obedient and she pledges not to let her emotions rule her.

8. Possible answers: Whereas Romeo focuses on his inner life and emotions, Mercutio focuses on his appearance and his "performances" for others; Romeo expects to be a bystander at the party, while Mercutio has a reputation for being the life of the party; Romeo is moody and admits to feeling hopeless, while Mercutio displays confidence.

Response and Analysis

Act I

Reading Check

1. What does the prologue say ends the rage between two families of Verona?

2. Who is Tybalt? What does he do that is dangerous?

3. What warning does Prince Escalus give the street brawlers in Scene 1?

4. In Scene 4, how does Mercutio try to snap Romeo out of his depression?

5. Where do Romeo and Juliet first meet?

Thinking Critically

6. Scene 1 shows how information can be conveyed through **dialogue**, or conversation between characters. Look at these three interactions: Gregory and Sampson; Benvolio and Tybalt; Benvolio and Montague. In a chart like the following one, list each pair of characters on the left. In the next column, write the line numbers of some of their dialogue. In the third column, explain what we learn from the dialogue.

go.
hrw
.com

INTERNET
Projects and
Activities
Keyword: LE5 9-11

Characters	Lines of Dialogue	What We Learn
Gregory and Sampson		
Benvolio and Tybalt		
Benvolio and Montague		

**SKILLS
FOCUS**

Literary Skills
Analyze
characteristics
of tragedy,
including
complication.

**Listening and
Speaking Skills**
Present a speech
from the play.

7. Before Romeo and Juliet meet in Scene 4, Shakespeare must set up obstacles to their love so that when they do meet, we will groan at the problems they are going to face. What problem, or **complication**, is presented in Scenes 2 and 3?

8. Mercutio is used as a character foil to Romeo. In drama a **character foil** is a character who sets off another character by strong contrast. In what way is Mercutio a foil to Romeo?

9. The title of this play tells us that it is a **tragedy**—a play in which the main characters come to an unhappy end. How do Romeo's and Juliet's reactions in Scene 5, when they learn each other's identity, **foreshadow,** or give clues to, their tragic end?

10. Shakespeare usually inserts **comic elements** into his tragedies. His servants and workers, for example, often tell funny stories, make puns, and kid around. List three examples of scenes from Act I that show comic elements.

Extending and Evaluating

11. Although the action of this play takes place in Italy in the fourteenth century, we can recognize similarities between the culture of that time and that of our own. Which **conflicts** in Act I could you imagine taking place today? What details would have to change, if any?

LISTENING AND SPEAKING
Speak the Speech

Choose a speech from this act, and prepare it for performance. Your first step is to write out or type the speech. Then, read it aloud several times so that you feel the rhythm created by the **blank verse.** However, watch for **end-stopped lines** and **run-on lines,** and don't let your reading become sing-song. If you have a partner you'd like to perform with, pick a **dialogue**—perhaps the love "duet" by Romeo and Juliet in Scene 5, lines 93–110.

9. Romeo says, "My life is my foe's debt," and Juliet says, "Too early seen unknown, and known too late!" Both characters recognize their doom.

10. Possible answers: Gregory and Sampson in their skittish encounter with Abram (Scene 1); the nurse's recollection of an event in Juliet's youth (Scene 3); Lord Capulet's greeting of the guests (Scene 5).

Extending and Evaluating

11. Conflicts that might take place today include the street fighting, Mercutio's sharp teasing with Romeo, and the hot exchange between Lord Capulet and Tybalt. However, many details—language, dress, and marriage customs—would be different.

Vocabulary Development

Shakespeare's Words—Then and Now

As you saw in the list on page 782, many words in Shakespeare's plays have different meanings today. *Humor,* for example, comes from a Latin word for "moisture; fluid." In Shakespeare's time, people believed there were four fluids, or humors, in the body, which regulated a person's temperament, or disposition. *Humorous* eventually came to refer to a person who can see comedy in situations.

PRACTICE

Choose five words from the list on page 782, and use a good dictionary to research their **derivations,** or origins. (Which words are very old English words, rooted in Anglo-Saxon, or Old English?) Make a diagram like the one below, showing their origins, what each word meant in Shakespeare's day, and what it means today.

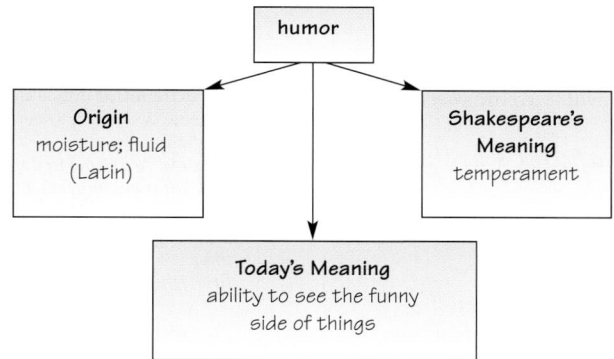

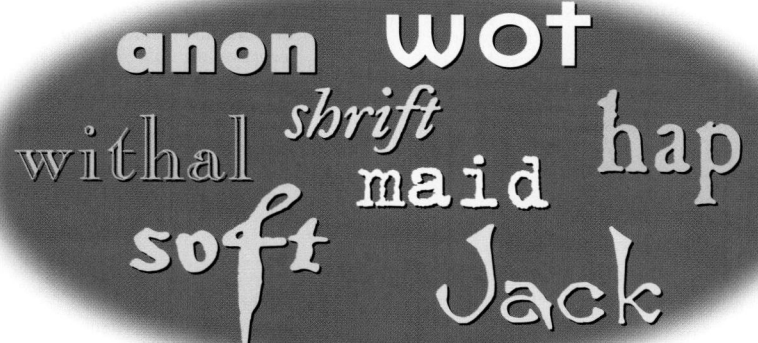

SKILLS FOCUS

Vocabulary Skills
Understand word origins.

The Tragedy of Romeo and Juliet, Act I   **817**

Vocabulary Development

Practice

Possible Answers

- *but. Shakespeare's meaning*—if, only. *Today's meaning*—except, yet. *Origin*—without, outside (Old English).

- *maid. Shakespeare's meaning*—unmarried girl. *Today's meaning*—a person whose job is cleaning. *Origin*—maiden (Middle English).

- *mark. Shakespeare's meaning*—listen to. *Today's meaning*—a visible impression on a surface; to set off as distinctive. *Origin*—borderland (Latin).

- *nice. Shakespeare's meaning*—trivial, foolish. *Today's meaning*—agreeable, good. *Origin*—ignorant, not knowing (Latin).

- *owes. Shakespeare's meaning*—owns. *Today's meaning*—is indebted to. *Origin*—to own, possess (Old English).

ASSESSING

Assessment
- *Holt Assessment: Literature, Reading, and Vocabulary*

RETEACHING

For a lesson reteaching analyzing dramatic literature, see **Reteaching,** p. 979A. For another selection to teach analyzing dramatic literature, see *The Holt Reader,* Collection 11.

DIFFERENTIATING INSTRUCTION

Learners Having Difficulty
You may wish to simplify this assignment by focusing only on the Reading Check questions on p. 816. You may also wish to use the questions and answers under the Guided Practice on p. 815. *Monitoring tip:* If students have trouble identifying characters, refer them to the list of characters on p. 785.

Advanced Learners
When discussing question 7 on p. 816, encourage students to speculate on why Paris is absent from the scene in which Romeo meets Juliet. Mention that critics have sometimes identified flaws in Shakespeare's works. Is this one of them? Ask students how Paris's presence might add further complications to the scene.

Selection Starter

Motivate. Act I was concerned mainly with the exposition of the play. Act II will present rising action, or complications, some of which have been introduced in Act I. Ask students to describe further complications they think might occur in Act II.

Summary ⟷ *at grade level*

Act II, Chorus

Romeo, cured of his longing for Rosaline, is now in love with someone who seems likewise unattainable. Yet the young couple's love ensures that they will find a way to meet.

Act II, Scene I

Romeo enters the Capulets' orchard. Mercutio calls after him. When Romeo does not respond, Mercutio and Benvolio depart, believing that Romeo is depressed over Rosaline.

DIRECT TEACHING

Reading Skills

Reading Shakespeare's poetry. Have a volunteer read the Chorus aloud. Ask the class to analyze its rhyme scheme and compare it with that of the Prologue for Act I. [Both are sonnets with the rhyme scheme *abab cdcd efef gg.*]

Responses to Margin Questions

Line 14. Romeo's love for Rosaline has died. He loves Juliet, the daughter of his father's enemy. He will have difficulty seeing Juliet and gaining permission to marry her. The Chorus says that the lovers are "Alike bewitchèd by the charm of looks."

Stage direction. The wall could be angled so that Romeo would be visible on one side and Mercutio and Benvolio on the other.

✦ ACT II ✦

Enter CHORUS.

Chorus.
　　Now old desire doth in his deathbed lie,
　　　　And young affection gapes to be his heir;
　　That fair° for which love groaned for and would die,
　　　　With tender Juliet matched, is now not fair.
5　　Now Romeo is beloved and loves again,
　　　　Alike° bewitchèd by the charm of looks;
　　But to his foe supposed he must complain,°
　　　　And she steal love's sweet bait from fearful hooks.
　　Being held a foe, he may not have access
10　　　To breathe such vows as lovers use to swear,°
　　And she as much in love, her means much less
　　　　To meet her new belovèd anywhere;
　　But passion lends them power, time means, to meet,
　　Temp'ring extremities° with extreme sweet.° [*Exit.*]

Scene 1. *Near Capulet's orchard.*

Enter ROMEO *alone.*

Romeo.
　　Can I go forward when my heart is here?
　　Turn back, dull earth, and find thy center° out.

[*Enter* BENVOLIO *with* MERCUTIO. ROMEO *retires.*]

Benvolio.
　　Romeo! My cousin Romeo! Romeo!
Mercutio.　　　　　　　　　　　He is wise
　　And, on my life, hath stol'n him home to bed.
Benvolio.
5　　He ran this way and leapt this orchard wall.
　　Call, good Mercutio.
Mercutio.　　　　　Nay, I'll conjure too.
　　　　Romeo! Humors! Madman! Passion! Lover!
　　Appear thou in the likeness of a sigh;
　　Speak but one rhyme, and I am satisfied!
10　　Cry but "Ay me!" pronounce but "love" and "dove";
　　Speak to my gossip° Venus one fair word,

3. That fair: Rosaline.

6. Alike: both (both Romeo and Juliet).
7. complain: ask Juliet's father, his foe, for her hand in marriage.

10. use to swear: are used to promising.

14. extremities: difficulties. **extreme sweet:** very sweet delights.
? 14. *According to the Chorus, what has happened to Romeo's old love? What is his new problem? What line suggests that these young people fell in love at first sight?*

2. center: Juliet. The "dull earth" is Romeo, and Juliet is his soul.

? Staging the Play
Stage direction: Although the stage direction says that Romeo "retires," a few lines later Benvolio says that Romeo ran and leapt over the wall. Since leaping a wall is difficult, most actors simply move behind it. How might the stage be designed so that we see Romeo hiding in Capulet's orchard and Benvolio and Mercutio on the other side of the wall?

11. gossip: good friend. In Roman mythology, Venus is the goddess of love.

RESOURCES: READING

Planning
- *One-Stop Planner* CD-ROM with ExamView Test Generator

Differentiating Instruction
- *Holt Reading Solutions*
- *The Holt Reader*
- *Holt Adapted Reader*
- *Supporting Instruction in Spanish*

- *Audio CD Library, Selections and Summaries in Spanish*

Assessment
- *Holt Assessment: Literature, Reading, and Vocabulary*
- *One-Stop Planner* CD-ROM with ExamView Test Generator
- *Holt Online Assessment*

One nickname for her purblind° son and heir,
Young Abraham Cupid,° he that shot so true
When King Cophetua loved the beggar maid!°

15   He heareth not, he stirreth not, he moveth not;
The ape is dead,° and I must conjure him.
I conjure thee by Rosaline's bright eyes,
By her high forehead and her scarlet lip,
By her fine foot, straight leg, and quivering thigh,

20   And the demesnes° that there adjacent lie,
That in thy likeness thou appear to us!

Benvolio.
    And if he hear thee, thou wilt anger him.

Mercutio.
    This cannot anger him. 'Twould anger him
To raise a spirit in his mistress' circle°

25   Of some strange nature, letting it there stand
Till she had laid it and conjured it down.
That were some spite;° my invocation
Is fair and honest: in his mistress' name,
I conjure only but to raise up him.

Benvolio.
30   Come, he hath hid himself among these trees
To be consorted° with the humorous° night.
Blind is his love and best befits the dark.

> "If love be blind, love cannot hit the mark."

Mercutio.
    If love be blind, love cannot hit the mark.
And wish his mistress were that kind of fruit

35   As maids call medlars when they laugh alone.
O, Romeo, that she were, O that she were
An open et cetera, thou a pop'rin pear!
Romeo, good night. I'll to my truckle bed;
This field bed is too cold for me to sleep.
Come, shall we go?

40 **Benvolio.**   Go then, for 'tis in vain
To seek him here that means not to be found.

[*Exit with others.*]

---

12. **purblind** (pur′blīnd′): blind.
13. **Young Abraham Cupid:** To Mercutio, Romeo seems the very figure of love—old like Abraham in the Bible and young like Cupid, the god of love in Roman mythology.
14. **When . . . maid:** from a popular ballad.
16. **The ape is dead:** Romeo is "playing" dead.
20. **demesnes** (di·mānz′): domains; regions.

? Staging the Play
22. *What is Benvolio's tone here? Why would Romeo be angry at Mercutio's remarks?*

24. **circle:** magical place.

27. **spite:** cause to be angry.

31. **consorted:** familiar. **humorous:** damp.

DIRECT TEACHING

B Learners Having Difficulty
Reading aloud. Read this passage aloud to help students appreciate Mercutio's humorous, mocking tone. He is parodying Romeo's earlier flowery speeches about love.

C Literary Focus
? Irony. What is ironic about this particular taunt by Mercutio? [Mercutio does not realize that Romeo has completely forgotten about Rosaline and is now in love with Juliet.]

D Reading Skills
? Interpreting. What is meant by the popular saying referred to here, "Love is blind"? [Possible response: When people fall in love, they cannot see any imperfections in the person they love.]

Response to Margin Question
Line 22. Benvolio is trying to both subdue and to warn Mercutio. Romeo would be angry because Mercutio is mocking Romeo's passion and making a bawdy joke at Rosaline's expense.

The Tragedy of Romeo and Juliet, Act II, Scene 1   **819**

Internet
- go.hrw.com (Keyword: LE5 9-11)
- *Elements of Literature Online*

Media
- *Audio CD Library*
- *Visual Connections Videocassette Program*
- *Fine Art Transparencies*

DIFFERENTIATING INSTRUCTION

English-Language Learners
Continue to use videos, audiotaped performances, and reading aloud to help these students follow the play.

Advanced Learners
Have students write a love sonnet either from Romeo to Juliet or from Juliet to Romeo. They may use Elizabethan language or contemporary English.

Act II, Scene 2

Romeo glimpses Juliet at her window. Enraptured, he delivers a monologue praising her beauty. Unaware of Romeo's presence, Juliet begins speaking of her love for him. Romeo emerges from the shadows, and Juliet recognizes his voice. Aware of the dangerous position Romeo is in, she asks why he is there at all. Romeo begins to swear his love, but Juliet stops his rash declarations, fearful of their intensity. Hearing her nurse call, she withdraws. When she reappears at the window, she declares that if Romeo really loves her, he will marry her. The nurse calls again, and Juliet withdraws but appears at the window one last time. The lovers are reluctant to part, but they must.

DIRECT TEACHING

Ⓐ Advanced Learners

Imagery. Students tracing the play's images of light and darkness will find Romeo's monologue of special interest, since he compares Juliet to both the sun and the stars. He also mocks the moon, traditionally a symbol of chastity.

Ⓑ Reading Skills

Reading Shakespeare's poetry. Point out how Shakespeare uses a few tricks to make his lines fit the rhythmic pattern of iambic pentameter. Accent marks (`) indicate that a syllable or letter should be pronounced, even though it is usually silent. Apostrophes (') indicate that a syllable or letter has been dropped and should not be pronounced.

Responses to Margin Questions

Line 1. Romeo refers to Mercutio. He is talking of the "wound" of love.

Line 2. Juliet is standing outside her window on her balcony.

Line 25. Romeo says that Juliet is a "bright angel" and "a wingèd messenger of heaven."

Scene 2. *Capulet's orchard.*

Romeo (*coming forward*).
  He jests at scars that never felt a wound.

[*Enter* JULIET *at a window.*]

Ⓐ
  But soft! What light through yonder window breaks?
  It is the East, and Juliet is the sun!
  Arise, fair sun, and kill the envious moon,
5 Who is already sick and pale with grief
  That thou her maid° art far more fair than she.
  Be not her maid, since she is envious.
  Her vestal livery° is but sick and green,°
  And none but fools do wear it. Cast it off.
10 It is my lady! O, it is my love!
  O, that she knew she were!
  She speaks, yet she says nothing. What of that?
  Her eye discourses;° I will answer it.
  I am too bold; 'tis not to me she speaks.
15 Two of the fairest stars in all the heaven,
  Having some business, do entreat her eyes
  To twinkle in their spheres till they return.
  What if her eyes were there, they in her head?
  The brightness of her cheek would shame those stars
20 As daylight doth a lamp; her eyes in heaven
  Would through the airy region stream so bright
  That birds would sing and think it were not night.
  See how she leans her cheek upon her hand!
  O, that I were a glove upon that hand,
  That I might touch that cheek!
Juliet.   Ay me!
25 **Romeo.**   She speaks.
Ⓑ
  O, speak again, bright angel, for thou art
  As glorious to this night, being o'er my head,
  As is a wingèd messenger of heaven
  Unto the white-upturnèd wond'ring eyes
30 Of mortals that fall back to gaze on him
  When he bestrides the lazy puffing clouds
  And sails upon the bosom of the air.
Juliet.
  O Romeo, Romeo! Wherefore° art thou Romeo?
  Deny thy father and refuse thy name;
35 Or, if thou wilt not, be but sworn my love,
  And I'll no longer be a Capulet.

❓ 1. *Romeo has heard all the joking. Whom is he referring to here, and what kind of "wound" is he talking about?*

❓ Staging the Play
2. *Romeo's **soliloquy** begins the balcony scene—one of the most famous and most beautiful in all dramatic literature—in which the two lovers woo and win each other. (In the Elizabethan theater [see page 778], a balcony was already built into the stage, so the **scene design** was not a problem. In modern theaters, however, it is often difficult to have a balcony high enough and yet still visible to people sitting in the back of the theater.) What is Juliet doing while Romeo is speaking aloud to himself?*

6. thou her maid: Juliet, whom Romeo sees as the servant of the virgin goddess of the moon, Diana in Roman mythology.
8. vestal livery: maidenly clothing. **sick and green:** Unmarried girls supposedly had "greensickness," or anemia.
13. discourses: speaks.

❓ 25. *Romeo and Juliet rarely talk of each other in straightforward prose. What are some of the **figures of speech** and **images** that Romeo uses to express his love here?*

33. Wherefore: why. In other words, "Why is your name Romeo?" (It is the name of her enemy.)

DIFFERENTIATING INSTRUCTION

Learners Having Difficulty
Following the changes in location in Act II can be difficult. Ask these students to make columns on a sheet of paper with the following headings and then to list events that occur in each location as they read: "Near Capulet's Orchard," "Friar Laurence's Cell," "Street."

Invite learners having difficulty to read *The Tragedy of Romeo and Juliet,* Act II, Scene 2, in interactive format in *The Holt Reader* and to use the sidenotes as aids to understanding the selection.

"But soft! What light through yonder window breaks? It is the East, and Juliet is the sun!"

✧

821

Advanced Learners

Ask pairs of students to perform the balcony scene, either in Shakespeare's language, in a modern translation, or in pantomime. Videotape their performances to share with other classes. Make tapes available for students to share with their families.

A Content-Area Connections

Language: Archaic Language
Have students translate this famous passage into contemporary English. [Possible response: Does it really matter what name we call something? A rose would still smell as sweet, even if it had a different name. And Romeo would be just as perfect if he had a different name. Give up your name, Romeo, and in exchange, take me.]

B Reading Skills

? Responding to the text. Are you surprised by Romeo's immediate willingness to give up being a Montague? [Possible responses: No, because he seems to keep his distance from his family; yes, because he has barely met Juliet.]

Responses to Margin Questions

Line 37. Juliet loves Romeo so much that she is willing to renounce her family for his love.

Line 42. Juliet says that things exist independently from their names: A different name would not change Romeo's appearance or character.

Line 49. Lines 54–57 indicate that Romeo is speaking directly to Juliet.

"O Romeo, Romeo! Wherefore art thou Romeo?" ☆

Romeo (*aside*).
　Shall I hear more, or shall I speak at this?
Juliet.
　'Tis but thy name that is my enemy.
　Thou art thyself, though not° a Montague.
40　What's Montague? It is nor hand, nor foot,
　Nor arm, nor face. O, be some other name
　Belonging to a man.
　What's in a name? That which we call a rose
　By any other word would smell as sweet.
45　So Romeo would, were he not Romeo called,
Ⓐ　Retain that dear perfection which he owes°
　Without that title. Romeo, doff thy name;
　And for thy name, which is no part of thee,
　Take all myself.
Romeo.　　　　I take thee at thy word.
50　Call me but love, and I'll be new baptized;
Ⓑ　Henceforth I never will be Romeo.

? Staging the Play
Stage direction. *Here Romeo is speaking an **aside**—a remark made to the audience or to another character that others onstage are not meant to hear.*
? 37. *Juliet does not know that Romeo is standing beneath her balcony. What has Romeo now learned about her feelings for him?*

39. though not: even if you were not.

? Staging the Play
42. *Short lines like this one usually indicate an interruption or pause. Here Juliet pauses to think about a question. What does she say in answer to this question about the true significance of a name?*

46. owes: owns.

? Staging the Play
49. *All of Romeo's and Juliet's speeches in this scene so far have been soliloquies. A **soliloquy** is a speech in which a character, who is usually alone onstage, expresses private thoughts or feelings that the audience hears. (A soliloquy is different from a **monologue**, which is directed to other characters onstage.) Here the lovers speak their thoughts out loud, but not to each other. Which of the lines that follow tell us that Romeo is now speaking to Juliet?*

CONTENT-AREA CONNECTIONS

Drama: Staging
Individual activity. Students interested in theater arts may enjoy researching the different ways that the balcony scene has been staged throughout the play's history. If photographs or illustrations are not available, students can sketch or paint the scene as they imagine it might have looked in performance.

Geography: Italy
Paired activity. Students can enhance their understanding of the relationship between geography and culture by exploring a map of Italy, where the action in the play takes place. Ask students to locate Italy on a world map and to note its relationship to the rest of southern Europe and its extension into the Mediterranean Sea. Have pairs of

students do research to answer this question: How did Italy's location influence the development of trade and the emergence of a merchant class? Encourage students to use maps and other graphic aids to present their findings to the class.

Juliet.
What man art thou, that, thus bescreened in night,
So stumblest on my counsel?°

Romeo.   By a name
I know not how to tell thee who I am.
55   My name, dear saint, is hateful to myself
Because it is an enemy to thee.
Had I it written, I would tear the word.

Juliet.
My ears have yet not drunk a hundred words
Of thy tongue's uttering, yet I know the sound.
60   Art thou not Romeo, and a Montague?

Romeo.
Neither, fair maid, if either thee dislike.

Juliet.
How camest thou hither, tell me, and wherefore?
The orchard walls are high and hard to climb,
And the place death, considering who thou art,
65   If any of my kinsmen find thee here.

Romeo.
With love's light wings did I o'erperch° these walls;
For stony limits cannot hold love out,
And what love can do, that dares love attempt.
Therefore thy kinsmen are no stop to me.

Juliet.
70   If they do see thee, they will murder thee.

Romeo.
Alack, there lies more peril in thine eye
Than twenty of their swords! Look thou but sweet,
And I am proof° against their enmity.

Juliet.
I would not for the world they saw thee here.

Romeo.
75   I have night's cloak to hide me from their eyes;
And but° thou love me, let them find me here.
My life were better ended by their hate
Than death proroguèd,° wanting of thy love.

Juliet.
By whose direction found'st thou out this place?

Romeo.
80   By Love, that first did prompt me to inquire.
He lent me counsel, and I lent him eyes.
I am no pilot; yet, wert thou as far

53. counsel: private thoughts.

C

66. o'erperch: fly over.

D

73. proof: armored.

? **Staging the Play**
74. *Juliet is practical. She fears Romeo will be murdered. What is Romeo's tone—is he also fearful and cautious, or is he reckless and elated?*

E
76. but: if only.
78. proroguèd: postponed.

? **78.** *The two lovers will repeatedly remind us that they prefer death to separation. What does this speech tell us of Romeo's intentions? Do you think he is seriously thinking of death here, or is he being impulsive and exaggerating—behaving as many people do when they've fallen head over heels in love?*

The Tragedy of Romeo and Juliet, Act II, Scene 2   **823**

DIRECT TEACHING

C **Reading Skills**
Making connections. Point out that by calling Juliet "dear saint," Romeo is continuing the religious wordplay they started at the party.

D **Literary Focus**
? **Rising action.** What complication threatens the lovers' happiness? [Their families are enemies, and Romeo could be killed if he were caught under Juliet's window.] **Which one of them seems to take this threat more seriously? Explain.** [Juliet seems more concerned; she warns Romeo about it twice, but he is so carried away by love that he feels no fear.]

E **Content-Area Connections**
Language: Archaic Language
Have students translate this difficult passage into contemporary English. [Possible response: As long as I know you love me, I don't care if I'm caught here. I'd rather die knowing you love me than go on living without your love.]

Responses to Margin Questions
Line 74. Romeo is reckless and elated, as though love makes him invulnerable.

Line 78. Romeo intends to risk everything for Juliet's love. The play will eventually prove the truth of Romeo's assertions, but at this point, expect students to debate his seriousness.

CONTENT-AREA CONNECTIONS

Music: Settings of the Balcony Scene from *Romeo and Juliet*
Whole-class activity. After students have read Act II, Scene 2, play for them the two following song adaptations of that scene, and have them compare how the two composers captured the lovers' emotions. The selections are "Ah! léve-toi, soleil" ("Ah, rise, sun!") from *Roméo et Juliette* by Charles

Gounod and "Tonight" from *West Side Story* by Leonard Bernstein. French composer Charles Gounod (shärl gōō • nō′) (1818–1893) won fame with operas inspired by literature, like *Faust* and *Roméo et Juliette*. In the balcony scene of the latter, Romeo sings the aria "Ah! léve-toi, soleil." *West Side Story* is a musical by the American conductor and composer Leonard Bernstein (1918–1990),

with lyrics by Stephen Sondheim. It is based on the story of Romeo and Juliet, but set in 1950s New York, where the lovers, Tony and Maria, are from rival gangs, one white, one Hispanic. The balcony scene is set on a fire escape, where the couple sings "Tonight."

The Tragedy of Romeo and Juliet, Act II, Scene 2   823

A Literary Focus

Rising action. Have students notice Juliet's interruptions here. Rather than rudeness, the interruptions convey the lovers' excitement, as well as the growing recklessness and urgency they feel about their love. It is this speed and urgency that quickly pushes the plot forward to its tragic conclusion.

Responses to Margin Questions

Line 85. She shifts from embarrassment to frankness at l. 89, "but farewell compliment"; to pleading at l. 90, "Dost thou love me?"; to anxiety at ll. 91–92, "Yet, if thou swear'st, / Thou mayst prove false"; to doubt at l. 94. Juliet is worried because she has not been coy but has inadvertently revealed her true feelings.

Line 109. Juliet wants Romeo's vow to be unchangeable, which the moon is not. Most students will not imagine a comic delivery because Juliet has so far been fervent and serious.

As that vast shore washed with the farthest sea,
I should adventure for such merchandise.

Juliet.

85 Thou knowest the mask of night is on my face;
Else would a maiden blush bepaint my cheek
For that which thou hast heard me speak tonight.
Fain would I dwell on form—fain, fain deny
What I have spoke; but farewell compliment.°
90 Dost thou love me? I know thou wilt say "Ay";
And I will take thy word. Yet, if thou swear'st,
Thou mayst prove false. At lovers' perjuries,
They say Jove laughs. O gentle Romeo,
If thou dost love, pronounce it faithfully.
95 Or if thou think'st I am too quickly won,
I'll frown and be perverse and say thee nay,
So thou wilt woo; but else, not for the world.
In truth, fair Montague, I am too fond,°
And therefore thou mayst think my havior° light;
100 But trust me, gentleman, I'll prove more true
Than those that have more cunning to be strange.°
I should have been more strange, I must confess,
But that thou overheard'st, ere I was ware,
My truelove passion. Therefore pardon me,
105 And not impute this yielding to light love,
Which the dark night hath so discoverèd.°

> "O gentle Romeo,
> If thou dost love, pronounce
> it faithfully."

Romeo.
Lady, by yonder blessèd moon I vow,
That tips with silver all these fruit-tree tops—

Juliet.
Ⓐ O, swear not by the moon, the inconstant moon,
110 That monthly changes in her circle orb,
Lest that thy love prove likewise variable.

Romeo.
What shall I swear by?

Juliet.   Do not swear at all;
Or if thou wilt, swear by thy gracious self,

Staging the Play
85. *Juliet's thoughts race now, and she probably speaks rapidly here. Read this* **monologue** *aloud. Where does Juliet shift from embarrassment to frankness, to pleading, to anxiety, to doubt? Why is she worried that Romeo will think poorly of her?*

89. compliment: good manners.

98. fond: affectionate, tender.
99. havior: behavior.

101. strange: aloof or cold.

106. discoverèd: revealed.

Staging the Play
109. *Why is Juliet afraid of having Romeo swear by the moon? If you were speaking these lines, would you make them comic, or would you make Juliet sound genuinely frightened?*

DEVELOPING FLUENCY

Mixed-ability group activity. As students read Act II, ask them to note lines they find difficult to comprehend. After students have finished reading each scene, have group members share their notes with one another. Group members can work together to analyze these lines for meaning. Then, have students re-read aloud dialogue containing the lines they previously found difficult.

Which is the god of my idolatry,
And I'll believe thee.

Romeo. If my heart's dear love—

Juliet.
Well, do not swear. Although I joy in thee,
I have no joy of this contract tonight.
It is too rash, too unadvised, too sudden;
Too like the lightning, which doth cease to be
Ere one can say it lightens. Sweet, good night!
This bud of love, by summer's ripening breath,
May prove a beauteous flower when next we meet.
Good night, good night! As sweet repose and rest
Come to thy heart as that within my breast!

Romeo.
O, wilt thou leave me so unsatisfied?

Juliet.
What satisfaction canst thou have tonight?

Romeo.
The exchange of thy love's faithful vow for mine.

Juliet.
I gave thee mine before thou didst request it;
And yet I would it were to give again.

Romeo.
Wouldst thou withdraw it? For what purpose, love?

Juliet.
But to be frank° and give it thee again.
And yet I wish but for the thing I have.
My bounty° is as boundless as the sea,
My love as deep; the more I give to thee,
The more I have, for both are infinite.
I hear some noise within. Dear love, adieu!

[NURSE *calls within.*]

Anon, good nurse! Sweet Montague, be true.
Stay but a little, I will come again. [*Exit.*]

Romeo.
O blessèd, blessèd night! I am afeard,
Being in night, all this is but a dream,
Too flattering-sweet to be substantial.

[*Enter* JULIET *again.*]

Juliet.
Three words, dear Romeo, and good night indeed.

? **120.** *Romeo is quick with vows and promises. Why has Juliet become fearful and cautious?*

131. frank: generous.

133. bounty: capacity for giving.

DIRECT TEACHING

B Literary Focus

Foreshadowing. **How does Shakespeare use images of light and darkness here to hint at dangers to come?** [Juliet expresses her fear at the rashness of their love by comparing it to lightning, which flashes briefly and then "doth cease to be." Her description foreshadows the coming deaths of the lovers.]

C Literary Focus

Character traits. **What does Juliet's response to Romeo reveal about her character?** [Possible responses: It shows that she is deeply romantic and loving; it shows that she is intelligent and articulate—indeed, poetic—in expressing her feelings.]

D Reading Skills

Making connections. **How do Romeo's words here echo those of Mercutio in his Queen Mab speech in Act I, Scene 4?** [Possible response: Although Romeo and Juliet love the night because it allows them to be together, Romeo also fears that what is happening may be as unreal as a dream. Mercutio described dreams as coming from "vain fantasy" and having no bearing on reality.]

Response to Margin Question

Line 120. She fears they are "too sudden" in their vows and believes that time should test their love.

CONTENT-AREA CONNECTIONS

Literature: Comparing Two Plays
Advanced learners may wish to compare and contrast *Romeo and Juliet* with *Antony and Cleopatra.* Philip Edwards, writing in the *Oxford Illustrated History of English Literature,* suggests an initial comparison:

"*Romeo and Juliet* is Shakespeare's love tragedy of youth as *Antony and Cleopatra* is his love tragedy of middle age. To Juliet, a girl of fourteen, hedged around by nurse and parents and a family feud, comes the liberation of first love—which Shakespeare enshrines in a sonnet shared between Romeo and Juliet when they kiss. The plot moves forward by a simple mechanism of ironic reversals which mark the stages of a clear path of 'responsibility' for the tragic outcome. . . . If there is less than full tragedy at the end, it is . . . because, for all their impetuousness, the young lovers in their desperately sad conclusion are simply victims—not of fate, but of their elders and betters. There is nothing of that fatal collaboration in one's own destruction which is so marked in the great later tragedies. Intense pity, little terror . . ."

The Tragedy of Romeo and Juliet, Act II, Scene 2 825

A **Reading Skills**

❓ **Speculating.** What might have prompted Juliet to talk about marriage upon her return to the balcony? [Possible responses: Seeing her nurse inside reminds Juliet of the talk with her mother about marriage earlier that day; she remembers that plans to engage her to Paris are in the works.]

B **Content-Area Connections**

Literature: Greek Mythology
In Greek myth, Echo was a nymph who was deprived of the power of speech as a punishment from the goddess Hera. Afterward, Echo fell in love with Narcissus, but she was unable to declare her love. She went to live in solitary caves, where she died of a broken heart.

C **Reading Skills**

❓ **Interpreting.** Although Romeo and Juliet have to wait only a few hours to see each other again, Juliet says that it will feel like twenty years. How has Juliet's perception of time changed since she met Romeo? [Possible response: Time is distorted for Juliet; any time away from Romeo seems much longer than it actually is.]

Responses to Margin Questions

Line 148. Juliet says that she will give herself to Romeo only through marriage. She shows her fears in ll. 143–144 and 150–151.

Line 154. The similes in ll. 157–158 indicate this movement. Romeo says he is as reluctant to go away from Juliet as a schoolboy is to go toward school.

If that thy bent° of love be honorable,
Thy purpose marriage, send me word tomorrow,
145 By one that I'll procure to come to thee,
Where and what time thou wilt perform the rite;
And all my fortunes at thy foot I'll lay
And follow thee my lord throughout the world.

Nurse (*within*). Madam!

Juliet.
150 I come anon.—But if thou meanest not well,
I do beseech thee—

Nurse (*within*). Madam!

Juliet. By and by I come.—
To cease thy strife° and leave me to my grief.
Tomorrow will I send.

Romeo. So thrive my soul—

Juliet.
155 A thousand times good night! [*Exit.*]

Romeo.
A thousand times the worse, to want thy light!
Love goes toward love as schoolboys from their books;
But love from love, toward school with heavy looks.

[*Enter* JULIET *again.*]

Juliet.
Hist! Romeo, hist! O for a falc'ner's voice
160 To lure this tassel gentle° back again!
Bondage is hoarse° and may not speak aloud,
Else would I tear the cave where Echo° lies
And make her airy tongue more hoarse than mine
With repetition of "My Romeo!"

Romeo.
165 It is my soul that calls upon my name.
How silver-sweet sound lovers' tongues by night,
Like softest music to attending ears!

Juliet.
Romeo!

Romeo. My sweet?

Juliet. What o'clock tomorrow
Shall I send to thee?

Romeo. By the hour of nine.

Juliet.
170 I will not fail. 'Tis twenty years till then.

143. bent: intention.

❓ **148.** *What is Juliet making clear to Romeo here? Where does she show that she still fears he may be false with her?*

153. strife: efforts to win her.

❓ **Staging the Play**
154. *With this fervent vow, Romeo swears by his immortal soul. What lines that follow indicate that Romeo turns around and heads away from Juliet's balcony?*

160. tassel gentle: male falcon.
161. Bondage is hoarse: Juliet is in "bondage" to her parents and must whisper.
162. Echo: In Greek mythology, a girl who could only repeat others' final words.

826 Collection 11 Drama • Synthesizing Sources

READING SKILLS REVIEW

Understanding inverted sentences.
Tell students that even when we recognize Shakespeare's vocabulary, we often stumble over his sentences because he inverts the standard syntax, or word order, that we are used to in English sentences. The patterns we know best are the following ones:

subject	verb	
The night	fades away.	

subject	verb	object
I	kiss	your hand.

But Shakespeare often favors inverted patterns:

verb	subject	
Quickly fades	the night.	

object	subject	verb
Your hand	I	do kiss.

I have forgot why I did call thee back.

Romeo.

Let me stand here till thou remember it.

Juliet.

I shall forget, to have thee still stand there,
Rememb'ring how I love thy company.

Romeo.

175 And I'll still stay, to have thee still forget,
Forgetting any other home but this.

Juliet.

'Tis almost morning. I would have thee gone—
And yet no farther than a wanton's° bird,
That lets it hop a little from his hand,
180 Like a poor prisoner in his twisted gyves,°
And with a silken thread plucks it back again,
So loving-jealous of his liberty.

Romeo.

I would I were thy bird.

Juliet.   Sweet, so would I.
Yet I should kill thee with much cherishing.
185 Good night, good night! Parting is such sweet sorrow
That I shall say good night till it be morrow.   [*Exit.*]

Romeo.

Sleep dwell upon thine eyes, peace in thy breast!
Would I were sleep and peace, so sweet to rest!
Hence will I to my ghostly friar's° close cell,
190 His help to crave and my dear hap° to tell.   [*Exit.*]

Scene 3. *Friar Laurence's cell.*

Enter FRIAR LAURENCE *alone, with a basket.*

Friar.

The gray-eyed morn smiles on the frowning night,
Check'ring the eastern clouds with streaks of light;
And fleckèd darkness like a drunkard reels
From forth day's path and Titan's burning wheels.°
5 Now, ere the sun advance his burning eye
The day to cheer and night's dank dew to dry,
I must upfill this osier cage° of ours
With baleful° weeds and precious-juicèd flowers.
The earth that's Nature's mother is her tomb.

---

174. *When Juliet first discovers that Romeo is in the garden, she urges him to leave for his own safety. Why does she now want him to stay?*

178. wanton's: careless child's.

180. gyves (jīvz): chains, like the threads that hold the bird captive.

184. *What terrible event does this line foreshadow?*
185. *Why is parting "sweet" to Juliet? (Is she enjoying this prolonged farewell?)*

189. ghostly friar's: spiritual father's.
190. hap: luck.

Staging the Play
1. *In the absence of lighting, Shakespeare had his characters "set the stage" in their speeches. What "scene" does the friar set in this* **soliloquy**? *How are his* **images** *of night different from Romeo's images in his "O blessèd, blessèd night" speech in the last scene?*

4. Titan's burning wheels: wheels of the sun god's chariot.
7. osier (ō′zhər) **cage:** cage woven of willow branches.
8. baleful: evil or poisonous.

The Tragedy of Romeo and Juliet, Act II, Scene 3   **827**

Activity. Have students write the following sentences from the play in standard syntax:

1. "And all my fortunes at thy foot I'll lay." [And I'll lay all my fortunes at thy foot.]

2. "Else would I tear the cave where Echo lies." [Else I would tear the cave where Echo lies.]

3. "How silver-sweet sound lovers' tongues by night." [How silver-sweet lovers' tongues sound by night.]

D Reading Skills
Reading Shakespeare's poetry.
Ask two students to read these famous farewell speeches aloud. Have students discuss any other lines in the play they have especially enjoyed so far. Encourage them to look for others as they read on and to jot them down in their notebooks.

Summary ⬌ *at grade level*

Act II, Scene 3
Early the next morning, Romeo goes to the cell of Friar Laurence, his spiritual adviser. The friar is in his garden, contemplating nature. He soliloquizes that all of nature's creations are beneficial if put to their proper use; if misused, however, the result can be deadly. Men, like nature, are also capable of both good and evil. Romeo greets him, and the friar perceives that there is something amiss, or the young man would not be out so early. Romeo tells of his love for Juliet and asks the friar to marry them. The friar chides Romeo for his change of heart, but agrees, for he thinks their union will unite their families and end the feud.

Responses to Margin Questions

Line 174. In the brief time that they have spoken in this scene, Juliet has come to love having Romeo near.

Line 184. Juliet's image foreshadows that her love will be the cause of Romeo's death.

Line 185. Juliet's oxymoron expresses her pleasure in extending her good-byes, for they allow her to stay with Romeo as long as possible.

Line 1. The friar describes dawn. Romeo said the night was so wonderful he feared it was a dream. Friar Laurence, however, presents night as "frowning" and "dank," a "drunkard" who reels off the path set by the cheering sun.

The Tragedy of Romeo and Juliet, Act II, Scene 3   **827**

A **Literary Focus**

Foreshadowing. The references to death and the dangers of herbs that are misused foreshadow some of the tragedy to come. Friar Laurence's knowledge of herbs will turn out to be crucial to the plot.

"Within the infant rind of this weak flower
Poison hath residence and medicine power . . ."
☆

10	What is her burying grave, that is her womb;	
	And from her womb children of divers kind	
	We sucking on her natural bosom find,	
	Many for many virtues excellent,	
	None but for some, and yet all different.	
15 **A**	O, mickle° is the powerful grace that lies	**15. mickle:** great.
	In plants, herbs, stones, and their true qualities;	
	For naught so vile that on the earth doth live	
	But to the earth some special good doth give;	
	Nor aught so good but, strained° from that fair use,	**19. strained:** turned aside.
20	Revolts from true birth,° stumbling on abuse.	**20. true birth:** true purpose.
	Virtue itself turns vice, being misapplied,	

828 Collection 11 Drama • Synthesizing Sources

CONTENT-AREA CONNECTIONS

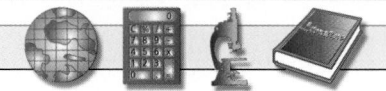

Science: Medicinal Powers of Plants
Individual activity. Have interested students research the medicinal uses of specific plants or modern medicines derived from plants. They might explore, for example, the development of digitalis, a heart stimulant, from foxglove and a kind of antiseptic from camphor.

And vice sometime by action dignified.

[*Enter* ROMEO.]

Within the infant rind° of this weak flower
Poison hath residence and medicine° power;
25 For this, being smelt, with that part cheers each part;°
Being tasted, stays all senses with the heart.
Two such opposèd kings encamp them still°
In man as well as herbs—grace and rude will;
And where the worser is predominant,
30 Full soon the canker° death eats up that plant.

Romeo.
Good morrow, father.

Friar.   Benedicite!°
What early tongue so sweet saluteth me?
Young son, it argues a distemperèd head°
So soon to bid good morrow to thy bed.
35 Care keeps his watch in every old man's eye,
And where care lodges, sleep will never lie;
But where unbruisèd° youth with unstuffed° brain
Doth couch his limbs, there golden sleep doth reign.
Therefore thy earliness doth me assure
40 Thou art uproused with some distemp'rature;
Or if not so, then here I hit it right—
Our Romeo hath not been in bed tonight.

Romeo.
That last is true. The sweeter rest was mine.

Friar.
God pardon sin! Wast thou with Rosaline?

Romeo.
45 With Rosaline, my ghostly father? No.
I have forgot that name and that name's woe.

Friar.
That's my good son! But where hast thou been then?

Romeo.
I'll tell thee ere thou ask it me again.
I have been feasting with mine enemy,
50 Where on a sudden one hath wounded me
That's by me wounded. Both our remedies
Within thy help and holy physic° lies.
I bear no hatred, blessèd man, for, lo,
My intercession° likewise steads° my foe.

Friar.
55 Be plain, good son, and homely° in thy drift.

? 22. *How, according to the friar, can good turn to evil and evil turn to good?*

? Staging the Play
23. *Romeo enters quietly, unseen by the friar. As the friar explains that his flower contains the power to heal as well as kill, why might the audience fear for Romeo and Juliet?*

23. rind: outer covering.
24. medicine: medicinal.
25. For . . . part: When the flower is smelled, each part of the body is stimulated.
27. still: always.
30. canker: cankerworm, a larva that feeds on leaves.
31. Benedicite (be·ne·dis'i·tā): Latin for "bless you."
33. distemperèd head: troubled mind.

37. unbruisèd: innocent.
unstuffed: untroubled.

B ? Staging the Play
44. *Does the friar approve? If you were playing the friar, how would you speak to Romeo?*

52. holy physic: the friar's healing power (physic) to make Romeo and Juliet husband and wife.
54. intercession: request.
steads: helps.
55. homely: simple and straightforward.

B Reading Skills

? Making inferences. How close a friendship do Romeo and Friar Laurence seem to have? How can you tell? [Possible response: Romeo feels close enough to have confided in the friar about Rosaline when he would not tell his parents and was reluctant to tell his friend Benvolio.]

Responses to Margin Questions

Line 22. The friar says that when virtue, or good, is misapplied it turns to vice, or evil; evil can be transformed into good by dignified action.

Line 23. Friar Laurence says that like plants, people contain within themselves both creative and destructive powers. The audience is reminded that Romeo and Juliet must handle their passion carefully so that it is enriching, not consuming.

Line 44. Friar Laurence cannot approve, and he speaks sharply to Romeo.

SKILLS REVIEW

Chronological order. Remind students that the chronology of a story refers to the sequence of events in the plot and how much time passes from one event to the next. Tell them that the entire plot of *Romeo and Juliet* takes place in just four days. Encourage students to keep track of the passage of time in the play, using clues in the text and their own logic and reasoning.

Activity. The following questions will help start this time-tracking process.
1. How much time passes in Act I? [It all takes place during the same day and night.]
2. How much time passes in Scenes 1 and 2 of Act II? [It is still the same night as the party in Act I.]

3. How much time has passed between the closing of Act II, Scene 2, and the opening of Scene 3? [It is the next morning. Only one day has passed since the play began.]

As students continue reading, have them note the passage of time and keep track of the events that happen on each of the four days the plot covers.

A **Literary Focus**

Rising action. Friar Laurence's startled reaction to Romeo's request for an immediate marriage to Juliet emphasizes the speed at which complications are developing in the plot.

B **Reading Skills**

? **Making inferences.** What does Friar Laurence's statement suggest about his view of men and women? [Possible response: He believes that men should set an example of strong character for women.]

C **Learners Having Difficulty**

Paraphrasing. Have students paraphrase Romeo's reply in language a teenager might use today. [Possible response: Come on, please don't criticize me. The girl I love now loves me as much as I love her. Rosaline didn't.]

Responses to Margin Questions

Line 56. The dialogue is written in rhymed couplets.

Line 65. Friar Laurence is making fun of Romeo's extravagant behavior when he pined for Rosaline, pretending he can still see Romeo's tears and hear his groans. Different interpretations are possible. Romeo could take the teasing with goodwill, or he could react impatiently, knowing, as the friar cannot, the seriousness of his feelings for Juliet.

Riddling confession finds but riddling shrift.°

Romeo.
　Then plainly know my heart's dear love is set
　On the fair daughter of rich Capulet;
　As mine on hers, so hers is set on mine,
60　And all combined,° save what thou must combine
　By holy marriage. When and where and how
　We met, we wooed, and made exchange of vow,
　I'll tell thee as we pass; but this I pray,
　That thou consent to marry us today.

Friar.
65　Holy Saint Francis! What a change is here!
　Is Rosaline, that thou didst love so dear,
　So soon forsaken? Young men's love then lies
　Not truly in their hearts, but in their eyes.
　Jesu Maria! What a deal of brine
70　Hath washed thy sallow cheeks for Rosaline!
　How much salt water thrown away in waste
　To season° love, that of it doth not taste!
　The sun not yet thy sighs from heaven clears,
　Thy old groans ring yet in mine ancient ears.
75　Lo, here upon thy cheek the stain doth sit
　Of an old tear that is not washed off yet.
　If e'er thou wast thyself, and these woes thine,
　Thou and these woes were all for Rosaline.
　And art thou changed? Pronounce this sentence then:
80　Women may fall when there's no strength in men.

Romeo.
　Thou chid'st me oft for loving Rosaline.

Friar.
　For doting, not for loving, pupil mine.

Romeo.
　And bad'st me bury love.

Friar.　　　　　　　　　　Not in a grave
　To lay one in, another out to have.

Romeo.
85　I pray thee chide me not. Her I love now
　Doth grace° for grace and love for love allow.
　The other did not so.

Friar.　　　　　　　　　O she knew well
　Thy love did read by rote, that could not spell.°
　But come, young waverer, come go with me.
90　In one respect I'll thy assistant be;
　For this alliance may so happy prove

---

56. shrift: forgiveness (in the religious rite of confession).

? **56.** *As we have seen, the play is mostly written in* **blank verse,** *but Shakespeare varies his verse forms from time to time. The prologues are written in* **sonnet form.** *The endings of scenes are marked by* **rhymed couplets.** *What is the* **rhyme scheme** *of this dialogue?*

60. combined: agreed.

? **Staging the Play**
65. *In the early part of the play, Shakespeare keeps Romeo's intense love in perspective by letting us see how others regard him. We have heard Mercutio's sarcastic "The ape is dead." How does Friar Laurence continue with this scolding and ridicule? What actions do you imagine Romeo is engaged in as he listens to the priest?*

72. season: preserve; keep fresh. (In Shakespeare's day, food was seasoned with salt to keep it from spoiling.)

86. grace: favor.

88. Romeo recited words of love without understanding them.

To turn your households' rancor to pure love.

Romeo.

O, let us hence! I stand on° sudden haste.

Friar.

Wisely and slow. They stumble that run fast. [*Exeunt.*]

Scene 4. A street.

Enter BENVOLIO *and* MERCUTIO.

Mercutio.

Where the devil should this Romeo be?
Came he not home tonight?

Benvolio.

Not to his father's. I spoke with his man.

Mercutio.

Why, that same pale hardhearted wench, that Rosaline,
5   Torments him so that he will sure run mad.

Benvolio.

Tybalt, the kinsman to old Capulet,
Hath sent a letter to his father's house.

Mercutio. A challenge, on my life.

Benvolio. Romeo will answer it.

10 **Mercutio.** Any man that can write may answer a letter.

Benvolio. Nay, he will answer the letter's master, how he dares, being dared.

Mercutio. Alas, poor Romeo, he is already dead: stabbed with a white wench's black eye; run through the ear with
15 a love song; the very pin° of his heart cleft with the blind bow-boy's butt-shaft; and is he a man to encounter Tybalt?

> "Alas, poor Romeo, he is already dead . . . run through the ear with a love song . . ."

Benvolio. Why, what is Tybalt?

Mercutio. More than Prince of Cats.° O, he's the coura-
20 geous captain of compliments. He fights as you sing pricksong°—keeps time, distance, and proportion; he

The Tragedy of Romeo and Juliet, Act II, Scene 4   **831**

---

92. *In Shakespeare's time it was not at all unusual to form alliances and settle disputes by arranging marriages. How does this explain Friar Laurence's decision to help the young couple?*

93. I stand on: I am firm about.

Staging the Play
94. *Romeo has gotten what he wants, and he dashes offstage. Nonetheless, why do the friar's last words leave us with a sense that danger lies ahead?*

D **7.** *Now that the play's love story seems to be heading toward a marriage, Shakespeare turns again to the feuding families. Why is Tybalt looking for Romeo?*

15. pin: center (of a target).

19. Prince of Cats: Tybalt is the name of a cat in a fable who is known for his slyness.
21. sing pricksong: sing with attention to every note on a printed sheet of music.

Summary ⬌ *at grade level*

> **Act II, Scene 4**
> Mercutio and Benvolio, looking for Romeo, reveal that Tybalt will challenge Romeo to a duel. They fear that their lovesick friend is in no state for a fight with Tybalt, who is a talented swordsman. Romeo enters, and Mercutio teases him about his behavior the previous night. Next, the nurse enters. Mercutio, still unaware of the relationship between Romeo and Juliet, insults the nurse, suggesting that she is a bawd for her mistress. Mercutio and Benvolio exit, and the nurse asks Romeo if his love is true. He assures her it is and tells her to have Juliet come to Friar Laurence's cell that afternoon to be married.

DIRECT TEACHING

D **Literary Focus**

Rising action. For the past two scenes, we have been swept along with Romeo and Juliet's love story. Now we are reminded of another plot complication—Juliet's cousin Tybalt has an angry grudge against Romeo that could doom the couple's love.

Responses to Margin Questions

Line 92. The friar hopes that Romeo and Juliet's marriage will end the feud between the Montagues and the Capulets.

Line 94. Friar Laurence's aphorism suggests that Romeo may be moving too fast for his own good. (This is exactly what Juliet feared in the last scene.)

Line 7. Tybalt wants to challenge Romeo to a duel; he has harbored a grudge about Romeo's uninvited appearance at the Capulet party.

CONTENT-AREA CONNECTIONS

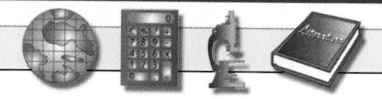

Sociology: Conflict Resolution
Small-group activity. Have students discuss how conflicts can be resolved nonviolently. You may wish to have students research or recall conflicts in their community that were resolved peacefully such as labor disputes, educational reform, and allocation of city or state funds. Students should identify roles played by spokespersons for both sides, negotiators, or intermediaries, such as clergy or elected officials.

A **Learners Having Difficulty**

Changing your reading strategy. Read this passage aloud so students can hear Mercutio's humorous, mocking tone. Tell them that when Mercutio speaks, it's usually more important to catch the tone, tempo, and rhythm of his speeches rather than worry about the meaning of every word.

B **Content-Area Connections**

Customs: Courtly Love
Note that in this speech, Mercutio mocks the conventions of courtly love. A lover in the Renaissance was expected to proclaim his lady superior to women in classical literature who were famous for their beauty, such as Petrarch's Laura, Dido, Cleopatra, Helen of Troy, and Hero. Refer students to the sidenote for l. 41 to identify these women.

C **Advanced Learners**

Rewriting. Challenge these students to write a modern equivalent of this fast-paced, witty dialogue, in which two good friends tease each other and exchange puns at each other's expense.

Responses to Margin Questions

Line 26. Tybalt is an accomplished, if affected, duelist: "one, two and the third in your bosom!" (ll. 22–23). Since Mercutio takes Tybalt's abilities seriously, he probably is fearful for Romeo, even as he acts out Tybalt's showy fencing style. When Mercutio moves on to mock the dandies, he becomes even livelier; even though he's still having fun, he seems truly disgusted with their pretentiousness.

Line 52. Romeo immediately deflects Mercutio's ridicule of his bowing "in the hams" by defining the bow as a curtsy (l. 56) and then continues with a pun, "courteous exposition" (l. 58).

A rests his minim rests,° one, two and the third in your bosom! The very butcher of a silk button, a duelist, a duelist! A gentleman of the very first house,° of the first
25 and second cause.° Ah, the immortal passado!° The punto reverso!° The hay!°

Benvolio. The what?

Mercutio. The pox of° such antic, lisping, affecting fantasticoes°—these new tuners of accent! "By Jesu, a
30 very good blade! A very tall° man! A very good whore!" Why, is not this a lamentable thing, grand sir, that we should be thus afflicted with these strange flies, these fashionmongers, these pardon-me's, who stand so much on the new form° that they cannot sit at ease on the old
35 bench? O, their bones,° their bones!

[*Enter* ROMEO.]

Benvolio. Here comes Romeo! Here comes Romeo!

Mercutio. Without his roe,° like a dried herring. O flesh,
B flesh, how art thou fishified! Now is he for the numbers°
that Petrarch flowed in. Laura, to his lady, was a kitchen
40 wench (marry, she had a better love to berhyme her),
Dido° a dowdy, Cleopatra a gypsy, Helen and Hero
hildings° and harlots, Thisbe a gray eye° or so, but not to
the purpose. Signior Romeo, bonjour! There's a French
salutation to your French slop.° You gave us the
45 counterfeit° fairly last night.

Romeo. Good morrow to you both. What counterfeit did I give you?

Mercutio. The slip, sir, the slip. Can you not conceive?°

Romeo. Pardon, good Mercutio. My business was great, and
50 in such a case as mine a man may strain courtesy.

Mercutio. That's as much as to say, such a case° as yours constrains a man to bow in the hams.

C **Romeo.** Meaning, to curtsy.

Mercutio. Thou hast most kindly hit it.
55 **Romeo.** A most courteous exposition.

Mercutio. Nay, I am the very pink of courtesy.

Romeo. Pink for flower.

Mercutio. Right.

---

22. minim rests: shortest pauses in a bar of music.
24. first house: first rank.
25. first and second cause: dueling terms ("first," offense is taken; "second," a challenge is given). **passado:** lunge.
26. punto reverso: backhand stroke. **hay:** home thrust.

? **Staging the Play**
26. *Mercutio mocks Tybalt's dueling style. What do you picture Mercutio doing as he talks of duels? Is he also concerned for Romeo? How do his actions change in the next speech as he mocks people who want to wear the latest fashions?*

28. pox of: plague on (curse on).
29. fantasticoes: dandies; men who copy French fashions.
30. tall: brave.
34. new form: new fashions.
35. bones: pun on their use of the French *bon* ("good").
37. roe: pun on *roe,* female deer. *Roe* also means "fish eggs," so Mercutio is also suggesting that love has made Romeo gutless.
38. numbers: verses. Petrarch was an Italian poet who wrote verses to a woman named Laura.
41. Dido: queen of Carthage in the *Aeneid,* who loved Aeneas. (The women who follow also were famous lovers in history, legend, and literature: Cleopatra was the queen of Egypt, loved by Antony; Helen of Troy was loved by Paris; Hero was loved by Leander; Thisbe was loved by Pyramus.)
42. hildings: good-for-nothings. **gray eye:** gleam in the eye.
44. slop: loose trousers then popular in France.
45. counterfeit: slip.
48. conceive: understand.
51. case: set of clothes.

? **52.** *Romeo is being lured by Mercutio to match wits. How can you tell that Romeo soon gets into the spirit of the game and for the moment forgets his romantic problems? In the following verbal duel the two friends use puns.*

DIFFERENTIATING INSTRUCTION

Learners Having Difficulty
Have students work in small groups to develop a summary of Act II, Scene 4. Help students see where stage directions mark shifts in the scene—episodes or segments created by the entrances and exits of the characters. Students should then take these episodes one at a time, using the margin notes as they discuss what happens, until they can summarize its action in a sentence or two.

English-Language Learners
Show students a single scene from a videotaped film version of the play, such as Act II, Scene 4. Have students focus on the general meaning and action of the scene, rather than individual speeches. Help them draw inferences about the action and the mood. Then, guide them in finding textual support for their conclusions.

Romeo. Why, then is my pump° well-flowered.°

60 **Mercutio.** Sure wit, follow me this jest now till thou hast worn out thy pump, that, when the single sole of it is worn, the jest may remain, after the wearing, solely singular.

Romeo. O single-soled jest, solely singular for the singleness!°

65 **Mercutio.** Come between us, good Benvolio! My wits faint.

Romeo. Swits° and spurs, swits and spurs; or I'll cry a match.

Mercutio. Nay, if our wits run the wild-goose chase, I am done; for thou hast more of the wild goose in one of thy 70 wits than, I am sure, I have in my whole five. Was I with you there for the goose?°

Romeo. Thou wast never with me for anything when thou wast not there for the goose.°

Mercutio. I will bite thee by the ear for that jest.

75 **Romeo.** Nay, good goose, bite not!

Mercutio. Thy wit is a very bitter sweeting;° it is a most sharp sauce.

Romeo. And is it not, then, well served in to a sweet goose?°

Mercutio. O, here's a wit of cheveril,° that stretches from an 80 inch narrow to an ell broad!°

Romeo. I stretch it out for that word "broad," which, added to the goose, proves thee far and wide a broad° goose.

Mercutio. Why, is not this better now than groaning for love? Now art thou sociable, now art thou Romeo; now 85 art thou what thou art, by art as well as by nature. For this driveling love is like a great natural° that runs lolling up and down to hide his bauble° in a hole.

Benvolio. Stop there, stop there!

Mercutio. Thou desirest me to stop in my tale against the 90 hair.°

Benvolio. Thou wouldst else have made thy tale large.°

Mercutio. O, thou art deceived! I would have made it short; for I was come to the whole depth of my tale, and meant indeed to occupy the argument no longer.

95 **Romeo.** Here's goodly gear!°

[*Enter* NURSE *and her man* PETER.]

A sail, a sail!

---

59. pump: shoe. **well-flowered:** pun on *well floored*. Men's shoes were "pinked," or cut with decorations.

64. singleness: pun on "silliness."
? Staging the Play
65. *What exaggerated action might Mercutio perform here?*
66. Swits: switches (a pun on wits).

71. Was . . . goose?: Was I right in calling you a goose?

73. goose: here, woman.

76. bitter sweeting: kind of apple.
78. sweet goose: sour sauce was considered best for sweet meat.
79. cheveril: kid leather (another reference to fashion).
80. ell broad: forty-five inches across.
82. broad: indecent.
86. natural: idiot.
87. bauble: cheap jewel.
? 87. *What does the loyal Mercutio think he has accomplished for Romeo by this game of wits?*

90. against the hair: against my inclination.
91. large: indecent.
95. gear: matter for teasing.
? 96. *After establishing the bad news that Tybalt is looking for Romeo, this scene turns into a playful duel of wits between Romeo and Mercutio. Wordplay of this sort was very popular with Elizabethan audiences but can be difficult for modern audiences to follow due to the many changes in word usage in four hundred years. The scene moves into a third phase as the nurse and her servant "sail" onstage. What does Romeo's comment suggest about the nurse's size?*

The Tragedy of Romeo and Juliet, Act II, Scene 4   833

D Literary Focus

? Irony. Mercutio still thinks that Romeo's absence the previous night had to do with Rosaline, and now he thinks Romeo has given up on the idea of love. What does the audience know that explains Romeo's better humor? [The audience knows that Romeo and Juliet have exchanged promises of love and that Friar Laurence is ready to conduct a wedding ceremony.]

Responses to Margin Questions

Line 65. Mercutio could be pretending to faint.

Line 87. Mercutio thinks he has gotten Romeo's mind off his foolish love for Rosaline and restored him to his usual sociable, clever self.

Line 96. Romeo suggests that the nurse is quite large.

Special Education Students
For lessons designed for special education students, see *Holt Reading Solutions*.

Advanced Learners
Enrichment. Challenge advanced learners to begin the ongoing project of developing a study guide that contains one page for each scene of the play. Each page should include the following items: two significant questions the scene poses and answers (with answers included); two quotations that are significant for revealing motivation or for advancing the plot; and two symbols or pictures that suggest the essence of the scene (such as a balcony and a rose for Act II, Scene 2).

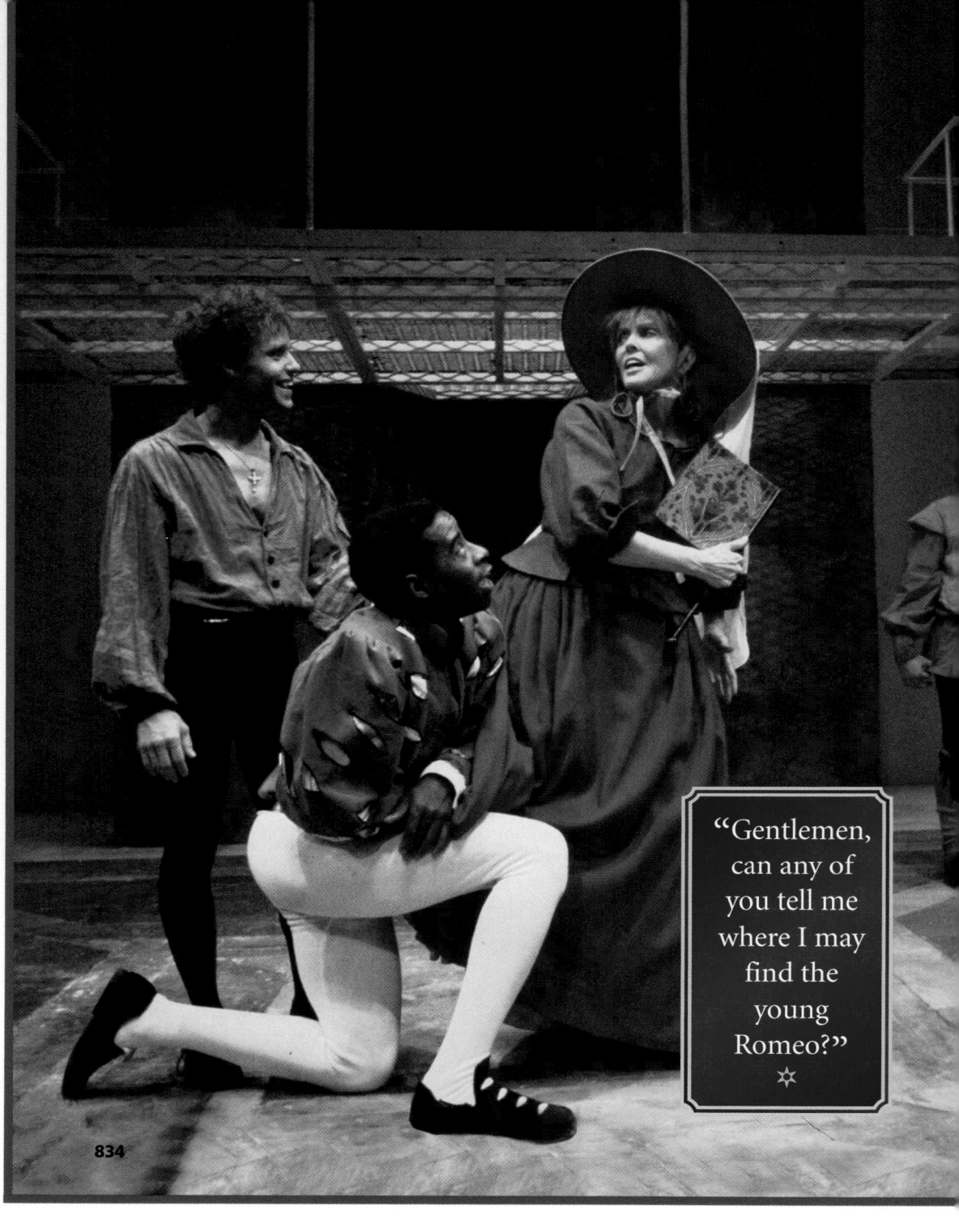

"Gentlemen, can any of you tell me where I may find the young Romeo?"
✧

834

Mercutio. Two, two! A shirt and a smock.°

Nurse. Peter!

Peter. Anon.

100   **Nurse.** My fan, Peter.

Mercutio. Good Peter, to hide her face; for her fan's the
    fairer face.

Nurse. God ye good morrow, gentlemen.

Mercutio. God ye good-den,° fair gentlewoman.

105   **Nurse.** Is it good-den?

Mercutio. 'Tis no less, I tell ye; for the bawdy hand of the
    dial is now upon the prick of noon.

Nurse. Out upon you! What a man are you!

Romeo. One, gentlewoman, that God hath made, himself
110   to mar.

Nurse. By my troth, it is well said. "For himself to mar,"
    quoth 'a? Gentlemen, can any of you tell me where I may
    find the young Romeo?

Romeo. I can tell you; but young Romeo will be older when
115   you have found him than he was when you sought him. I
    am the youngest of that name, for fault of a worse.°

Nurse. You say well.

Mercutio. Yea, is the worst well? Very well took, i' faith!
    Wisely, wisely.

120   **Nurse.** If you be he, sir, I desire some confidence with you.

Benvolio. She will endite° him to some supper.

Mercutio. A bawd, a bawd, a bawd! So ho!

Romeo. What hast thou found?

Mercutio. No hare,° sir; unless a hare, sir, in a Lenten pie,°
125   that is something stale and hoar° ere it be spent.

[*He walks by them and sings.*]

          An old hare hoar,
          And an old hare hoar,
          Is very good meat in Lent;
          But a hare that is hoar
130   Is too much for a score
          When it hoars ere it be spent.

    Romeo, will you come to your father's? We'll to dinner
    thither.

Romeo. I will follow you.

135   **Mercutio.** Farewell, ancient lady. Farewell (*singing*) "Lady,
    lady, lady."   [*Exeunt* MERCUTIO, BENVOLIO.]

Nurse. I pray you, sir, what saucy merchant was this that

---

97. A shirt and a smock: a man (shirt) and a woman (smock).

104. God ye good-den: God grant you a good evening.

116. for fault of a worse: for want of a better.

121. endite (en·dīt′): invite. Benvolio mocks the nurse, for she said "confidence" but meant "conference."

? Staging the Play
122. *Mercutio, who knows nothing of Romeo's plan to marry Juliet, thinks the nurse has come to arrange a secret date between Romeo and her mistress. He mocks and insults the nurse by suggesting that she is a bawd, or "procurer," for Juliet. Mercutio dominates the stage when he's on it. What do you imagine he's doing here?*

124. hare: slang for "morally loose woman." **Lenten pie:** rabbit pie, eaten sparingly during Lent, so that it is around for a long time and gets stale.

125. hoar (hôr): gray with mold (the old nurse has gray hair).

? Staging the Play
131. *Mercutio teases the nurse about being a flirt by singing the chorus of an old song about a "chaste" lady. The nurse is outraged and struggles to keep her fine airs. How does Romeo try to calm her?*

A **Reading Skills**

? **Interpreting.** The nurse is trying to act dignified and put on airs in front of the young gentlemen by calling for her fan, but the young men mock her pretensions. Why do you think Romeo joins in the teasing (beginning with l. 114 on this page) when he knows the nurse has come on a very serious mission? [Possible responses: He has gotten carried away in his lighthearted teasing with Mercutio and finds it hard to stop; he has to keep up the behavior his friends expect from him so that they don't suspect what is really going on.]

Responses to Margin Questions

Line 122. Mercutio makes his saucy comment to Benvolio and then may walk around the nurse as he sings, clowning behind her back.

Line 131. Romeo assures her that Mercutio is not to be taken seriously.

The Tragedy of Romeo and Juliet, Act II, Scene 4   **835**

CONTENT-AREA CONNECTIONS

Music: Madrigals

Small-group activity. Have students research recordings of humorous madrigals and other Renaissance songs that Mercutio might have enjoyed. Such recordings are often available through the community library. Have a group of students learn the parts for one of the madrigals and perform it for the class.

❓ **Paraphrasing.** How would you paraphrase Romeo's description of Mercutio? [Possible responses: Mercutio is just full of talk; Mercutio says a lot of things he doesn't really mean.]

B **English-Language Learners**

Idioms. Tell students that forms of the expressions *a fool's paradise* and *deal double* are still used in English today. A person living in *a fool's paradise* thinks everything is perfect but has been sadly misled. The expression *double dealing* refers to an intentional act of deception—pretending to feel or promise something when, in fact, you have no intention of following through on your promise.

C **Reading Skills**

❓ **Making inferences.** What will Romeo use the rope ladder for? [for climbing up the balcony wall to Juliet's room on the night of their wedding]

Responses to Margin Questions

Line 147. The nurse is talking to Peter.

Line 152. The nurse shouts "Scurvy knave!" after Mercutio and turns to Romeo with "Pray you, sir." When she addresses Romeo, she could become respectful, secretive, and even a bit puffed up with her own importance.

Line 160. The nurse warns Romeo not to trifle with Juliet's feelings, not to say he loves her unless he means it. The nurse's motives may be her genuine love for Juliet, her sense that Juliet is too young and inexperienced to take betrayal easily, and her awareness that Juliet indeed loves Romeo.

---

was so full of his ropery?°

A **Romeo.** A gentleman, nurse, that loves to hear himself talk
140 and will speak more in a minute than he will stand to in
a month.

Nurse. And 'a speak anything against me, I'll take him
down, and 'a were lustier than he is, and twenty such
Jacks; and if I cannot, I'll find those that shall. Scurvy
145 knave! I am none of his flirt-gills;° I am none of his
skainsmates.° And thou must stand by too, and suffer
every knave to use me at his pleasure!

Peter. I saw no man use you at his pleasure. If I had, my
weapon should quickly have been out, I warrant you. I
150 dare draw as soon as another man, if I see occasion in a
good quarrel, and the law on my side.

Nurse. Now, afore God, I am so vexed that every part about
me quivers. Scurvy knave! Pray you, sir, a word; and, as I
told you, my young lady bid me inquire you out. What
155 she bid me say, I will keep to myself; but first let me tell
B ye, if ye should lead her in a fool's paradise, as they say, it
were a very gross kind of behavior, as they say; for the
gentlewoman is young; and therefore, if you should deal
double with her, truly it were an ill thing to be offered to
160 any gentlewoman, and very weak dealing.

Romeo. Nurse, commend me to thy lady and mistress. I
protest unto thee—

Nurse. Good heart, and i' faith I will tell her as much. Lord,
Lord, she will be a joyful woman.

165 **Romeo.** What wilt thou tell her, nurse? Thou dost not
mark° me.

Nurse. I will tell her, sir, that you do protest, which, as I take
it, is a gentlemanlike offer.

Romeo.
Bid her devise
170 Some means to come to shrift this afternoon;
And there she shall at Friar Laurence' cell
Be shrived° and married. Here is for thy pains.

Nurse. No, truly, sir; not a penny.

Romeo. Go to! I say you shall.

175 **Nurse.** This afternoon, sir? Well, she shall be there.

Romeo.
C And stay, good nurse, behind the abbey wall.
Within this hour my man shall be with thee
And bring thee cords made like a tackled stair,°
Which to the high topgallant° of my joy

---

138. **ropery:** roguery; vulgar ways.

145. **flirt-gills:** flirty girls.
146. **skainsmates:** loose women.
❓ 147. *Whom is the nurse talking to here?*

❓ **Staging the Play**
152. *In which part of this speech does the nurse refer to Mercutio? When does the nurse turn to Romeo? How might her manner change?*

❓ 160. *What warning does the nurse give Romeo, and why do you think she does this?*

166. **mark:** listen to.

172. **shrived** (shrīvd): forgiven of her sins.

178. **tackled stair:** rope ladder.
179. **topgallant:** highest platform on a sailing ship's mast.

180　Must be my convoy° in the secret night.
　　　Farewell. Be trusty, and I'll quit° thy pains.
　　　Farewell. Commend me to thy mistress.
　　Nurse.
　　　Now God in heaven bless thee! Hark you, sir.
　　Romeo.
　　　What say'st thou, my dear nurse?
　　Nurse.
185　Is your man secret? Did you ne'er hear say,
　　　Two may keep counsel, putting one away?
　　Romeo.
　　　Warrant thee my man's as true as steel.
　　Nurse. Well, sir, my mistress is the sweetest lady. Lord,
　　　Lord! When 'twas a little prating thing—O, there is a
190　nobleman in town, one Paris, that would fain lay knife
　　　aboard;° but she, good soul, had as lieve see a toad, a very
　　　toad, as see him. I anger her sometimes, and tell her that
　　　Paris is the properer man; but I'll warrant you, when I
　　　say so, she looks as pale as any clout° in the versal° world.
195　Doth not rosemary and Romeo begin both with a letter?
　　Romeo. Aye, nurse; what of that? Both with an R.
　　Nurse. Ah, mocker! That's the dog's name.° R is for the—
　　　no; I know it begins with some other letter; and she hath
　　　the prettiest sententious° of it, of you and rosemary, that
200　it would do you good to hear it.
　　Romeo. Commend me to thy lady.
　　Nurse. Ay, a thousand times. [*Exit* ROMEO.] Peter!
　　Peter. Anon.
　　Nurse. Before, and apace.　　　　　　　[*Exit after* PETER.]

Scene 5. *Capulet's orchard.*

Enter JULIET.

Juliet.
　　　The clock struck nine when I did send the nurse;
　　　In half an hour she promised to return.
　　　Perchance she cannot meet him. That's not so.
　　　O, she is lame! Love's heralds should be thoughts,
5　　Which ten times faster glide than the sun's beams
　　　Driving back shadows over low'ring hills.
　　　Therefore do nimble-pinioned doves° draw Love,
　　　And therefore hath the wind-swift Cupid wings.
　　　Now is the sun upon the highmost hill

The Tragedy of Romeo and Juliet, Act II, Scene 5　**837**

---

180. convoy: means of conveyance.
181. quit: repay.

191. lay knife aboard: take a slice (lay claim to Juliet).

194. clout: rag cloth. **versal:** universal.

? **194.** *The nurse becomes confiding as she rattles on and on. What trouble for Romeo and Juliet does she talk about? What is Juliet's feeling for Paris now?*
197. In other words, a dog's growl has an *r* sound (*r-r-r-r*).
199. sententious: The nurse means "sentence."

? **Staging the Play**
204. *Romeo abruptly rushes offstage, leaving the nurse with Peter. She bossily pushes Peter ahead of her as she exits, to show that she still has authority over someone. How has this scene advanced the love story? What action has been set in motion?*

7. nimble-pinioned doves: Nimble-winged doves were said to pull the chariot of Venus, the Roman goddess of love.

DIRECT TEACHING

D Content-Area Connections
Culture: Herbs
In British folklore the herb rosemary symbolizes remembrance. Ironically, it is associated both with weddings and with funerals, so linking rosemary with Romeo foreshadows both great happiness and great tragedy.

Responses to Margin Questions
Line 194. The nurse reminds the audience that Paris wants to marry Juliet. While Juliet promised her mother to consider Paris, she now has no inclination to like him because she loves Romeo.

Line 204. Romeo's serious intentions are confirmed, the friar and the nurse have become the lovers' accomplices, and the marriage has been arranged.

Summary　↔ *at grade level*

Act II, Scene 5
Juliet waits impatiently for her nurse to return. When the nurse enters, she further frustrates Juliet with her digressive questions and comments. After chiding Juliet for being ungrateful, the nurse tells her Romeo's plans. Having been given leave to go to church that afternoon, Juliet will instead go to Friar Laurence's cell.

E Literary Focus

? **Theme.** How does Juliet's speech here extend the theme of youth versus age? [Possible response: The youthful Juliet is desperately impatient for news of Romeo and comments on the swiftness of youth and love, contrasting them with the slowness of the old nurse, who cannot feel the youthful passion Juliet does.]

CONTENT-AREA CONNECTIONS

Inventions: Mechanical Clocks
Time plays an important role in *Romeo and Juliet*. At the beginning of Scene 5, for example, Juliet makes reference to the clock's striking nine.
Paired activity. Students may be interested in finding out what kind of clock Juliet might have had. Water-powered mechanical clocks were invented in China around the eleventh century, but the development of the all-mechanical escapement clock got underway in Italy during the Renaissance. Have students research information about the state of mechanical clocks in the fifteenth and sixteenth centuries. Students may present their findings in the form of a multimedia report, including text, diagrams, scale models, and photography.

The Tragedy of Romeo and Juliet, Act II, Scene 5　837

A **Reading Skills**

? **Connecting with the text.**
Do you think this is how most teenagers view older generations? **Explain.** [Possible responses: Yes, especially when they are made to wait for something important; no, because sometimes the older people are the ones in a rush.]

B **Literary Focus**

? **Character traits.** What does this line of reasoning show about Juliet? [Possible responses: She is logical and practical; in the throes of love, she has become impatient and inconsiderate with her elders.]

C **English-Language Learners**

Interpreting. These students may be confused by the nurse's seemingly nonsensical remarks. Point out that she is being facetious and teasing Juliet, first saying that Juliet has made a bad choice and then listing all of Romeo's good points. She uses words such as *yet, though,* and *but,* as if she is going to offer opposing information, but everything she says about Romeo is positive.

Responses to Margin Questions

Line 17. Juliet is impatient.

Line 30. Ask students to support their answers by referring to the nurse's characterization in earlier scenes.

Line 38. The nurse digresses and rattles on; she is also frequently bawdy.

---

10 Of this day's journey, and from nine till twelve
Is three long hours; yet she is not come.
Had she affections and warm youthful blood,
She would be as swift in motion as a ball;
My words would bandy her° to my sweet love,
15 And his to me.
But old folks, many feign as they were dead—
Unwieldy, slow, heavy, and pale as lead.

[*Enter* NURSE *and* PETER.]

O God, she comes! O honey nurse, what news?
Hast thou met with him? Send thy man away.
Nurse.
20 Peter, stay at the gate.   [*Exit* PETER.]
Juliet.
Now, good sweet nurse—O Lord, why look'st thou sad?
Though news be sad, yet tell them merrily;
If good, thou sham'st the music of sweet news
By playing it to me with so sour a face.
Nurse.
25 I am aweary, give me leave awhile.
Fie, how my bones ache! What a jaunce° have I!
Juliet.
I would thou hadst my bones, and I thy news.
Nay, come, I pray thee speak. Good, good nurse, speak.
Nurse.
Jesu, what haste! Can you not stay° awhile?
30 Do you not see that I am out of breath?
Juliet.
How art thou out of breath when thou hast breath
To say to me that thou art out of breath?
The excuse that thou dost make in this delay
Is longer than the tale thou dost excuse.
35 Is thy news good or bad? Answer to that.
Say either, and I'll stay the circumstance.°
Let me be satisfied, is't good or bad?
Nurse. Well, you have made a simple° choice; you know not
how to choose a man. Romeo? No, not he. Though his
40 face be better than any man's, yet his leg excels all men's;
and for a hand and a foot, and a body, though they be
not to be talked on, yet they are past compare. He is not
the flower of courtesy, but, I'll warrant him, as gentle as a
lamb. Go thy ways, wench; serve God. What, have you
45 dined at home?

14. bandy her: send her back and forth, like a tennis ball.

? **Staging the Play**
17. *Juliet either has run onstage or is standing on the balcony. What is her mood in this* **soliloquy** *as she waits for the nurse to return?*

26. jaunce: tiring journey.

29. stay: wait.
? **Staging the Play**
30. *The actor playing the nurse can interpret her actions here in several ways. She could be genuinely weary; she could be teasing Juliet; or she could be fearful about the part she has agreed to play in the elopement. How do you think the nurse should play this scene?*

36. stay the circumstance: wait for the details.
38. simple: foolish.

? **38.** *In* **comedy** *a character sometimes has one peculiarity that can always be counted on for a laugh. You push a button, and you get the same response. Such a character is sometimes called a jack-in-the-box. What is the nurse's almost inevitable way of responding when she is asked for information?*

Juliet.

No, no. But all this did I know before.
What says he of our marriage? What of that?

Nurse.

Lord, how my head aches! What a head have I!
It beats as it would fall in twenty pieces.
50 My back a'° t' other side—ah, my back, my back!
Beshrew° your heart for sending me about
To catch my death with jauncing up and down!

Juliet.

I' faith, I am sorry that thou art not well.
Sweet, sweet, sweet nurse, tell me, what says my love?

55 **Nurse.** Your love says, like an honest gentleman, and a
courteous, and a kind, and a handsome, and, I warrant, a
virtuous—where is your mother?

Juliet.

Where is my mother? Why, she is within.
Where should she be? How oddly thou repliest!
60 "Your love says, like an honest gentleman,
'Where is your mother?'"

Nurse.   O God's Lady dear!
Are you so hot?° Marry come up, I trow.°
Is this the poultice for my aching bones?
Henceforward do your messages yourself.

Juliet.

65 Here's such a coil!° Come, what says Romeo?

Nurse.

Have you got leave to go to shrift today?

50. **a':** on.

51. **Beshrew:** shame on.

❓ 52. *What line in this speech indicates that Juliet has tried to humor the nurse by rubbing her back?*

❓ **Staging the Play**
61. *Juliet can play this scene in several ways. Do you imagine she is angry here? Is she bewildered? impatient? Is she mocking the old nurse?*

62. **hot:** angry. **Marry come up, I trow:** something like "By the Virgin Mary, come off it, I swear."
65. **coil:** fuss.

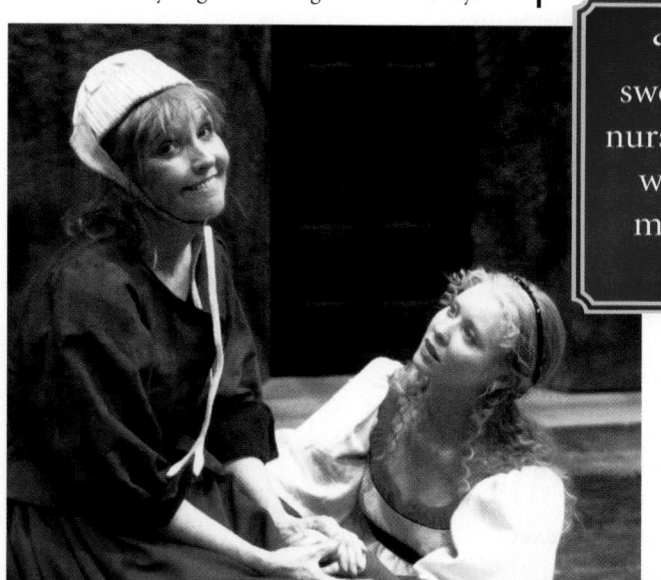

"Sweet, sweet, sweet nurse, tell me, what says my love?" ✪

Responses to Margin Questions

Line 52. "My back a' t' other side—ah, my back, my back!" (l. 50).

Line 61. Responses will vary. Most likely, Juliet is both confused and impatient, wanting to keep the conversation wholly on the subject of Romeo.

839

A Literary Focus

Rising action. The plot continues to develop at a breakneck pace as Romeo and Juliet's wedding plans are completed. List some possible complications that could interfere with their happiness. [Possible responses: Paris has asked to marry Juliet; Tybalt is challenging Romeo to a duel; the nurse or the friar could accidentally reveal the secret plans and tip off the warring families.]

Summary ◆→ *at grade level*

Act II, Scene 6

Romeo is at Friar Laurence's cell. The friar cautions the young man that the intensity of his love will lead to no good. When Juliet enters, Romeo urges her to describe the extent of their love. Juliet replies that fancy words are unable to do justice to the substance of her love. The friar quickly leads them off to be married.

B Literary Focus

Foreshadowing. Romeo and Juliet's love is now compared to gunpowder, and a violent, consuming end is predicted for it.

Responses to Margin Questions

Line 69. The nurse says Juliet is blushing, and students might suppose that she hugs the nurse.

Line 78. Elated, Juliet puns on the words *hie* (hasten) and *high* (excellent).

Line 8. Romeo says that marrying Juliet will be full happiness for him, even if "love-devouring death" then claims his life.

Line 15. Friar Laurence warns that passionate love is so intense that it may wear itself out quickly. He fears that love without moderation is all-consuming and volatile.

Juliet.
　　I have.

A Nurse.
　　Then hie° you hence to Friar Laurence' cell;
　　There stays a husband to make you a wife.
70　　Now comes the wanton blood up in your cheeks.
　　They'll be in scarlet straight at any news.
　　Hie you to church; I must another way,
　　To fetch a ladder, by the which your love
　　Must climb a bird's nest soon when it is dark.
75　　I am the drudge, and toil in your delight;
　　But you shall bear the burden soon at night.
　　Go; I'll to dinner; hie you to the cell.

Juliet.
　　Hie to high fortune! Honest nurse, farewell.　　[*Exeunt.*]

Scene 6. *Friar Laurence's cell.*

Enter FRIAR LAURENCE *and* ROMEO.

Friar.
　　So smile the heavens upon this holy act
　　That afterhours with sorrow chide us not!

Romeo.
　　Amen, amen! But come what sorrow can,
　　It cannot countervail° the exchange of joy
5　　That one short minute gives me in her sight.
　　Do thou but close our hands with holy words,
　　Then love-devouring death do what he dare—
　　It is enough I may but call her mine.

Friar.
B　　These violent delights have violent ends
10　　And in their triumph die, like fire and powder,°
　　Which, as they kiss, consume. The sweetest honey
　　Is loathsome in his own deliciousness
　　And in the taste confounds° the appetite.
　　Therefore love moderately: long love doth so;
15　　Too swift arrives as tardy as too slow.

[*Enter* JULIET.]

　　Here comes the lady. O, so light a foot
　　Will ne'er wear out the everlasting flint.°
　　A lover may bestride the gossamers°
　　That idle in the wanton summer air,

840 Collection 11 **Drama • Synthesizing Sources**

---

68. hie (hī): hurry.

? Staging the Play
69. *At last the nurse tells Juliet what she has been waiting to hear. What do you see Juliet doing as she hears the news?*

? Staging the Play
78. *Even Juliet puns. What pun does she exit on? What is her mood?*

4. countervail: match or equal.

? 8. *We are continually prepared for the steps Romeo and Juliet might take if they are separated. What does Romeo say here to remind us again of how desperate their love is?*

10. powder: gunpowder.

13. confounds: destroys.

? 15. *What warning does the friar give about passionate love? What fear does he express for the future?*

17. flint: stone.

18. gossamers: finest spider threads.

CONTENT-AREA CONNECTIONS

Literature: Love in *Romeo and Juliet*
Echoing Friar Laurence's warning, critic Derick Marsh sums up the love of Romeo and Juliet in the following way: "I think that the play concerns itself with the nature of a particular kind of love, first love, that intense sexual attraction that by its very nature cannot long remain as it is. In the ordinary course of life, this change is accepted because it is inevitable; either the love withers away, or changes into some other kind of love, of equal or perhaps even greater value, but different in kind. In this play, it is protected from change, heightened and intensified by the sense of doom that pervades the play, but for that very reason, immune to time's decay, because neither we nor the lovers are ever allowed to believe that their love can last long

---

20   And yet not fall; so light is vanity.°
Juliet.
      Good even to my ghostly confessor.
Friar.
      Romeo shall thank thee, daughter, for us both.
Juliet.
      As much to him,° else is his thanks too much.
Romeo.
      Ah, Juliet, if the measure of thy joy
25   Be heaped like mine, and that thy skill be more
      To blazon° it, then sweeten with thy breath
      This neighbor air, and let rich music's tongue
      Unfold the imagined happiness that both
      Receive in either by this dear encounter.
Juliet.
30   Conceit,° more rich in matter than in words,
      Brags of his substance, not of ornament.°
      They are but beggars that can count their worth;
      But my true love is grown to such excess
      I cannot sum up sum of half my wealth.
Friar.
35   Come, come with me, and we will make short work;
      For, by your leaves, you shall not stay alone
      Till holy church incorporate two in one.   [*Exeunt.*]

20. **vanity:** fleeting human love.

23. **As much to him:** the same to him.

26. **blazon:** describe.

? 29. *What is Romeo asking Juliet to do?*

30. **Conceit:** genuine understanding.
31. **ornament:** fancy language.

C

? 34. *What is Juliet's response to Romeo's request?*

? **Staging the Play**
37. *What do you think the friar's tone is in this last speech? Is there a slightly humorous or teasing note here?*

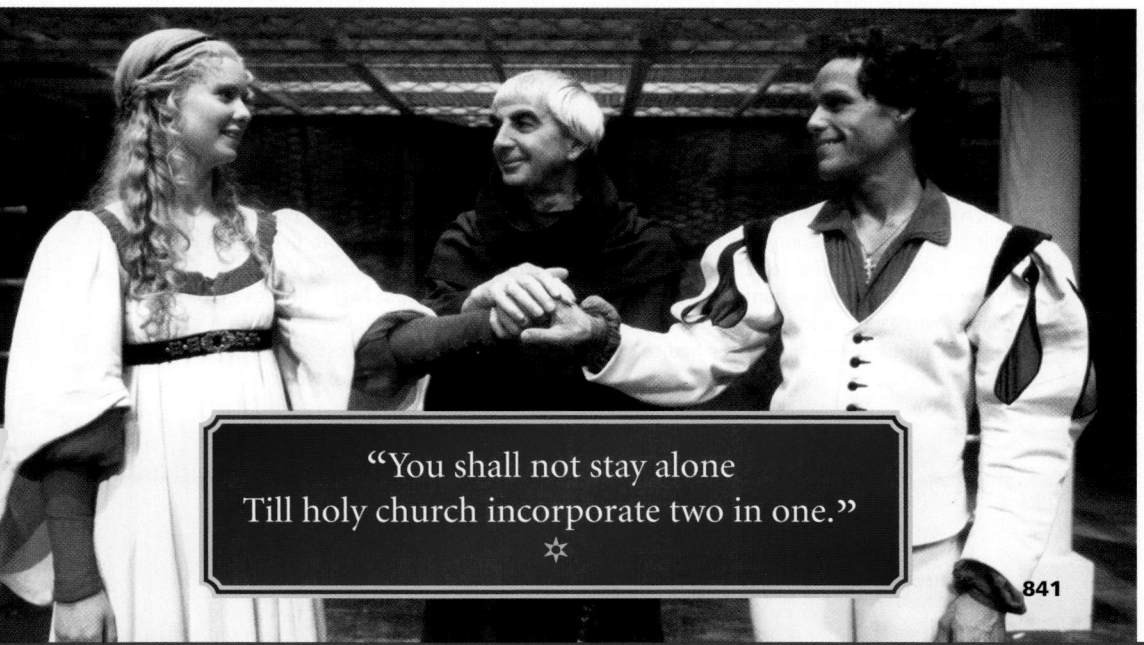

"You shall not stay alone
Till holy church incorporate two in one."
✦

841

enough to exhaust its first intensity. In that sense their love wins a victory over time, but since such a victory can only be won out of time, the love must end in death; in this sense it is self-defeating."

A CLOSER LOOK

Male actors stopped playing women's roles in the 1660s, when actresses began to appear regularly in the English theater. Shakespeare's acting company was small, with about fifteen full members. These actors shared in the profits of performances, and Shakespeare often wrote parts tailored to fit the talents and skills of particular company members. *Shakespeare in Love,* a 1998 movie starring Gwyneth Paltrow and Joseph Fiennes, provides an enjoyable look at the acting life in Elizabethan London, especially the custom of using boys to act the parts of women. The story is based on the genesis of *Romeo and Juliet*— a totally unhistorical view but a pleasure to watch all the same. The movie has an R rating.

Ⓐ Reading Informational Text

❓ Primary and secondary sources. In this secondary source essay, what primary-source citation is introduced in the first paragraph? [The primary source is Thomas Coryate, an English traveler in 1608.] What point does the quote support? [Until 1660, boys played female roles on the London stage.]

Ⓑ Reading Informational Text

❓ Primary sources. What primary sources might the essay have cited to illustrate the popularity of boy actors? [Possible responses: a passage from the records of the legal case of the Thomas Clifton kidnapping; a quotation from a contemporary theatergoer noting the excellent acting of a boy actor.]

A CLOSER LOOK
No Female Actors and No R-Rated Love Scenes

Ⓐ On a visit to Venice in 1608, the English traveler Thomas Coryate recorded his astonishment: "For I saw women act, a thing I never saw before, though I have heard that it hath been sometimes used in London." Coryate was surprised because at the time in London, boy actors between the ages of about ten and eighteen regularly took the parts of women onstage.

The roots of this custom were bound up with the origins of medieval drama. Centuries earlier in English cathedrals, stories from the Bible were acted in brief plays. The performers—all male—came from the clergy, and they were assisted by choirboys. It wasn't until 1660 that women were permitted on the English stage—by the express order of King Charles II, whose fondness for the theater (and female actors) was to become a mark of his reign.

Ⓑ Boy actors were divided into two categories. There were members of all-boy companies, like the Children of St. Paul's Cathedral and the Children of the Chapel Royal. These young players enjoyed such popularity (and made so much money for their business managers) that star actors were in great demand. From the records of a 1602 legal case, we know that a schoolboy named Thomas Clifton was kidnapped and forced to join the Chapel Children. His father had to sue to get him back.

Other boy actors were apprentices to individual actors in the adult companies. These boys were preparing for a professional career. They took women's parts onstage for several years before and during adolescence. (It was one of these boy actors who took the part of Juliet.) When they were in their late teens, they switched to men's roles.

Some evidence suggests that Elizabethan actors trained their voices to be higher pitched, for both speaking and singing—so the difference between boys' voices and those of adults might have been less noticeable in Shakespeare's time. In any case, for a part such as Juliet—who is not yet fourteen when she makes her first appearance—the costume and makeup of a boy actor could have easily sustained the illusion. Unlike male and female actors in movies today, the young lovers in Shakespeare's play would have avoided physical contact. The words suggested the intensity of their feelings.

Casting boys as women on the Shakespearean stage had another unexpected twist. Plays with women in male disguise were highly popular at the time. Shakespeare wrote five such dramas, including *The Merchant of Venice, As You Like It,* and *Twelfth Night.* In these cases, boys played women who disguised themselves as young men. The mind boggles at the layers of illusion.

Response and Analysis

Act II

Reading Check

1. What plans do Romeo and Juliet make in Scene 2?

2. What fault does Friar Laurence find in Romeo in Scene 3?

3. We hear in Scene 4 that Tybalt is looking for Romeo. Why does he want Romeo?

4. How does Mercutio feel about Tybalt?

5. What part does the nurse play in Romeo and Juliet's schemes?

Thinking Critically

6. An **aside** is a short speech, usually delivered to the audience but sometimes to another character, that others onstage are not supposed to hear. Whom is Romeo talking to in his aside in Scene 2, line 37? Why is the aside effective?

7. This play in general and the balcony scene in particular are greatly admired for the beauty of the poetry. Pick one passage in Act II that especially appeals to you, and explain the poetic and literary devices involved. Is there **rhyme, rhythm,** or **alliteration**? What do the **figures of speech** mean? What senses do the **images** appeal to?

8. The nurse is one of Shakespeare's great **comic** characters. Do you think the nurse is a principled character, a person with a strong sense of right and wrong? Or does she seem to be easily corrupted, someone who will do whatever people want her to do? Find passages to support your answer.

9. Though Act II is a happy act, Shakespeare at times reminds us that this is

a **tragedy** (a play that ends unhappily). Point out lines that **foreshadow,** or give clues to, possible trouble ahead.

10. The friar agrees to marry Romeo and Juliet because he wants them to be happy, but he also has another **motive.** What is that motive? What does it reveal about his **character**?

11. **Dramatic irony** occurs when the audience knows something that a character does not know. Since the prologue told us how the play will end, we sense this irony when we hear the friar's motive. What other moments of dramatic irony occur in this act?

Extending and Evaluating

12. Romeo's and Juliet's families hate each other, for reasons that we aren't told about. (The families themselves may even have forgotten.) Do you find the young lovers' situation believable? Can you think of any parallels today, and can you think of any real-life Romeos and Juliets?

Scene Design

Paint the Picture

Elizabethan playwrights created their **scene designs** mostly from words rather than the scenery, props, and lighting that might be used today. Pick a scene from Act II, and decide how you would design and stage it. If there is a wall or balcony in your scene, where would you place it? Where would the characters stand? Would you add furniture, trees, or other props? Would you include a backdrop showing a city street, a garden, a forest, or a castle? How would you light your scene? Make a drawing of your design, and add any description necessary to make your ideas clear to the viewer.

INTERNET
Projects and Activities
Keyword: LE5 9-11

SKILLS FOCUS

Literary Skills
Analyze characteristics of tragedy, including dramatic irony. Describe scene design.

The Tragedy of Romeo and Juliet, Act II   843

Response and Analysis

7. Sample answer for Scene 2, ll. 38–49: Line 39 has alliteration (thou . . . thyself . . . though); Juliet compares Romeo to a rose that "would smell as sweet" were it called by another name, an appeal to the senses of sight and smell.

8. Possible answer: The nurse is principled in her loyalty to Juliet. She tries to protect Juliet (Scene 4, ll. 155–160).

9. Possible answers: Scene 2, ll. 77–78; Scene 6, ll. 9–15.

10. He wants to help end the feud between the families. This motive shows that the friar truly cares about the well-being of the two families.

11. Possible answers: Mercutio and Benvolio believe that Romeo is still in love with Rosaline when he is actually in love with Juliet; in many of their speeches, Romeo and Juliet look forward to their happiness and profess a readiness to die for love.

Extending and Evaluating

12. Most students will find the lovers' situation believable. Real-life Romeos and Juliets may include young people from different religious, ethnic, or socioeconomic backgrounds.

Reading Check

1. Juliet will send a messenger to Romeo to find out the time and place for their wedding.

2. He finds Romeo too quick to fall in and out of love.

3. Tybalt wants to challenge him to a duel.

4. Mercutio dislikes Tybalt and, although he ridicules his fencing style, considers him dangerous.

5. She is a messenger for them.

Thinking Critically

6. Romeo is speaking either to himself or to the audience. The aside is effective because he hears Juliet, but she does not know that he is listening.

Vocabulary Development

Practice

Possible Answers

1. Tell me, who was that rude merchant?

2. Are you sure your assistant can keep a secret? Haven't you heard of the saying "Two can keep a secret if one of them is dead"?

3. She's smart, and would rather see a toad than look at him.

4. I'm tired; leave me alone for a while. Whew! My bones are aching! I've had a rough trip.

5. Then, go quickly to Friar Laurence's place where someone waits to be your husband.

ASSESSING

Assessment

■ *Holt Assessment: Literature, Reading, and Vocabulary*

RETEACHING

For a lesson reteaching analyzing dramatic literature, see **Reteaching,** p. 979A. For another selection to teach analyzing dramatic literature, see *The Holt Reader,* Collection 11.

Vocabulary Development

Shakespeare's Language

Shakespeare's language is different from the English we use today. For one thing, many of Shakespeare's words and expressions are now **archaic.** They are out of use, or their meaning has changed. For another thing, Shakespeare often omits words. For example, in the Prologue the speaker says:

> "If you with patient ears attend,
> What here shall miss, our toil shall strive to mend."

Shakespeare depends on your instinct and your ear to provide the missing words. He has also used the word *attend* in a way not commonly used today. Here's how we might say the same thing:

> If you listen patiently,
> Whatever you've missed from my speech, we'll try to make clear by our work onstage.

PRACTICE

The passages below are spoken by Juliet's nurse. Rewrite each one in the kind of English that you would use. Check the context, the side-notes, and a good dictionary for help.

1. "I pray you, sir, what saucy merchant was this that was so full of his ropery?" (pages 835–836, lines 137–138)

2. "Is your man secret? Did you ne'er hear say,
   Two may keep counsel, putting one away?" (page 837, lines 185–186)

3. "But she, good soul, had as lieve see a toad, a very toad, as see him." (page 837, lines 191–192)

4. "I am aweary, give me leave awhile.
   Fie, how my bones ache! What a jaunce have I!" (page 838, lines 25–26)

5. "Then hie you hence to Friar Laurence' cell;
   There stays a husband to make you a wife." (page 840, lines 68–69)

SKILLS FOCUS

Vocabulary Skills
Understand archaic language.

DIFFERENTIATING INSTRUCTION

Learners Having Difficulty

Have students rewrite these passages from Act II in contemporary English. They should use the scene and line references to place the words in context. Possible answers are given in brackets.

1. "Go then, for 'tis in vain / To seek him here that means not to be found." (Scene 1, ll. 40–41) [Let's go. It's pointless to look for him here. He's hiding, and he doesn't want us to find him.]

2. "I take thee at thy word." (Scene 2, l. 49) [I believe what you're saying.]

3. "What o'clock tomorrow / Shall I send to thee?" (Scene 2, ll. 168–169) [What time tomorrow should I send my messenger to meet you?]

4. "I have forgot that name and that name's woe." (Scene 3, l. 46) [I've forgotten about her and all the troubles she caused me.]

5. "Warrant thee my man's as true as steel." (Scene 4, l. 187) [I swear that my friend is trustworthy.]

✴ ACT III ✴

Scene 1. *A public place.*

Enter MERCUTIO, BENVOLIO, *and* MEN.

Benvolio.
 I pray thee, good Mercutio, let's retire.
 The day is hot, the Capels° are abroad,
 And, if we meet, we shall not 'scape a brawl,
 For now, these hot days, is the mad blood stirring.

5 **Mercutio.** Thou art like one of these fellows that, when he
 enters the confines of a tavern, claps me his sword upon
 the table and says, "God send me no need of thee!" and
 by the operation of the second cup draws him on the
 drawer,° when indeed there is no need.

10 **Benvolio.** Am I like such a fellow?

 Mercutio. Come, come, thou art as hot a Jack in thy mood
 as any in Italy; and as soon moved to be moody, and as
 soon moody to be moved.

 Benvolio. And what to?

15 **Mercutio.** Nay, and there were two such, we should have
 none shortly, for one would kill the other. Thou! Why,
 thou wilt quarrel with a man that hath a hair more or a
 hair less in his beard than thou hast. Thou wilt quarrel
 with a man for cracking nuts, having no other reason but
20 because thou hast hazel eyes. What eye but such an eye
 would spy out such a quarrel? Thy head is as full of
 quarrels as an egg is full of meat; and yet thy head hath
 been beaten as addle° as an egg for quarreling. Thou hast
 quarreled with a man for coughing in the street, because
25 he hath wakened thy dog that hath lain asleep in the sun.
 Didst thou not fall out with a tailor for wearing his new
 doublet° before Easter? With another for tying his new
 shoes with old riband? And yet thou wilt tutor me from
 quarreling!

30 **Benvolio.** And I were so apt to quarrel as thou art, any man
 should buy the fee simple of° my life for an hour and a
 quarter.

 Mercutio. The fee simple? O simple!°

[*Enter* TYBALT *and others.*]

---

2. Capels: Capulets.

? **4.** *Romeo's friends enter the stage. Again Shakespeare "sets the stage" by having the characters tell us what the weather is like. Why does this weather seem to breed trouble?*

 9. draws him on the drawer: draws his sword on the waiter (who "draws" the drink).

? **Staging the Play**
 16. *Mercutio mocks Benvolio, who is anything but a troublemaker. (Mercutio is the one who can't seem to resist a quarrel.) If you were playing Benvolio, what would you be doing as Mercutio goes on and on? If you were playing Mercutio, how would you behave as your comments became more and more exaggerated?*

 23. addle: rotten.
 27. doublet: jacket.

 31. buy the fee simple of: buy insurance on.

 33. O simple: O stupid.

Summary ⬅➡ *at grade level*

Act III, Scene 1

Benvolio warns Mercutio that if they encounter any of the Capulets, there will be a fight. When Tybalt enters, Mercutio aggressively confronts him. When Romeo enters, Tybalt insults him and challenges him to a duel, but Romeo refuses to fight. Mercutio fights Tybalt in Romeo's stead. When Romeo intervenes to stop the fight, Tybalt wounds Mercutio and flees. Mercutio dies, and Romeo laments that his response was the cause of his friend's death. When Tybalt returns, Romeo and Tybalt fight; Romeo kills him and flees. As the Montagues arrive, Benvolio explains what has happened. The prince decrees that Romeo is banished from Verona and will be killed if found.

DIRECT TEACHING

Responses to Margin Questions

Line 4. The hot weather is making people irritable and testy.

Line 16. Benvolio could be laughing at Mercutio's foolishness or pretending to ignore it. Mercutio is surely embellishing his description of Benvolio with exaggerated gestures.

RESOURCES: READING

Planning
■ *One-Stop Planner CD-ROM with ExamView Test Generator*

Differentiating Instruction
■ *Holt Reading Solutions*
■ *Holt Adapted Reader*
■ *Supporting Instruction in Spanish*

■ *Audio CD Library, Selections and Summaries in Spanish*

Assessment
■ *Holt Assessment: Literature, Reading, and Vocabulary*
■ *One-Stop Planner CD-ROM with ExamView Test Generator*
■ *Holt Online Assessment*

Media
■ *Audio CD Library*
■ *Visual Connections Videocassette Program*
■ *Fine Art Transparencies*

A **Reading Skills**

? **Drawing conclusions.** What clues tell you that Mercutio really does want to fight? [Possible responses: He dares Tybalt to throw a punch; he engages in a battle of wits to rile Tybalt.]

B **Learners Having Difficulty**

Finding details. Help students use the sidenotes to analyze Mercutio's intentional misinterpretation of the word *man,* as used by Tybalt. This misunderstanding helps fuel the violence to come.

C **Literary Focus**

? **Dramatic irony.** Dramatic irony occurs when the audience or the reader knows something important that a character in a play does not know. What effect does your knowledge of Romeo and Juliet's wedding have on you during this scene? [Possible responses: Some students may say it increases their feelings of dread about what is about to happen; others may say it increases their sense of involvement in the scene.]

Responses to Margin Questions

Stage direction. Romeo, who is buoyant and happy, probably has a bounce in his step and a smile on his face. Because he does not know of Tybalt's intent and is feeling benevolent in general, he may feel removed from the tense situation and be unable to perceive Tybalt's fury.

Lines 58–65. Tybalt first calls Romeo a "villain."

Benvolio. By my head, here come the Capulets.

35 **Mercutio.** By my heel, I care not.

Tybalt.
Follow me close, for I will speak to them.
Gentlemen, good-den. A word with one of you.

Mercutio.
And but one word with one of us?
Couple it with something; make it a word and a blow.

40 **Tybalt.** You shall find me apt enough to that, sir, and you
will give me occasion.

A **Mercutio.** Could you not take some occasion without giving?

Tybalt. Mercutio, thou consortest with Romeo.

Mercutio. Consort?° What, dost thou make us minstrels?
45 And thou make minstrels of us, look to hear nothing but
discords. Here's my fiddlestick;° here's that shall make
you dance. Zounds,° consort!

Benvolio.
We talk here in the public haunt of men.
Either withdraw unto some private place,
50 Or reason coldly of your grievances,
Or else depart. Here all eyes gaze on us.

Mercutio.
Men's eyes were made to look, and let them gaze.
I will not budge for no man's pleasure, I.

[*Enter* ROMEO.]

Tybalt.
Well, peace be with you, sir. Here comes my man.

B **Mercutio.**
55 But I'll be hanged, sir, if he wear your livery.°
Marry, go before to field,° he'll be your follower!
Your worship in that sense may call him man.

Tybalt.
Romeo, the love I bear thee can afford
No better term than this: thou art a villain.°

Romeo.
60 Tybalt, the reason that I have to love thee
Doth much excuse the appertaining° rage
To such a greeting. Villain am I none.
Therefore farewell. I see thou knowest me not.

Tybalt.
Boy, this shall not excuse the injuries
C 65 That thou hast done me; therefore turn and draw.

846 Collection 11 Drama • Synthesizing Sources

---

44. **Consort:** Mercutio pretends to think that Tybalt means a *consort,* or group of musicians.
46. **fiddlestick:** bow for playing violinlike instruments (referring to his sword).
47. **Zounds:** slang for "by God's wounds."

? **Staging the Play**
Stage direction: Romeo is returning from his secret marriage—he has no thought about hatred and killing. What would he be doing as he enters? How would he react to the tense situation?

55. **livery:** servant's uniform. By *man,* Tybalt meant "target," but Mercutio uses the word to mean "servant."
56. **field:** dueling field.

59. **villain:** boor; clumsy, stupid fellow.

61. **appertaining:** appropriate.

? **58–65.** *What insult does Tybalt use to try to make Romeo draw his sword?*

DIFFERENTIATING INSTRUCTION

English-Language Learners
Continue to use videos, audiotaped performances, and reading aloud to help these students follow the play.

Special Education Students
For lessons designed for English-language learners and special education students, see *Holt Reading Solutions.*

Advanced Learners
Enrichment. Act III brings the death of Mercutio, who critic Clifford Leech has claimed is the true tragic hero of *Romeo and Juliet.* Leech says that Mercutio's isolation and anger link him to later Shakespeare heroes, such as Hamlet, Othello, Lear, and Macbeth. Ask advanced students to discuss and write about Mercutio's significance in the play.

Romeo.
I do protest I never injured thee,
But love thee better than thou canst devise°
Till thou shalt know the reason of my love;
And so, good Capulet, which name I tender°
70 As dearly as mine own, be satisfied.

Mercutio.
O calm, dishonorable, vile submission!
Alla stoccata° carries it away.

[*Draws.*]

Tybalt, you ratcatcher, will you walk?°

Tybalt.
What wouldst thou have with me?

75 **Mercutio.** Good King of Cats, nothing but one of your nine lives. That I mean to make bold withal,° and, as you shall use me hereafter, dry-beat° the rest of the eight. Will you pluck your sword out of his pilcher° by the ears? Make haste, lest mine be about your ears ere it be out.

80 **Tybalt.** I am for you.

[*Draws.*]

Romeo.
Gentle Mercutio, put thy rapier up.

Mercutio. Come, sir, your passado!

[*They fight.*]

Romeo.
Draw, Benvolio; beat down their weapons.
Gentlemen, for shame! Forbear this outrage!
85 Tybalt, Mercutio, the prince expressly hath
Forbid this bandying° in Verona streets.
Hold, Tybalt! Good Mercutio!

[TYBALT *under Romeo's arm thrusts* MERCUTIO *in, and flies.*]

Mercutio.   I am hurt.
A plague a' both houses! I am sped.°
Is he gone and hath nothing?

Benvolio.   What, art thou hurt?

Mercutio.
90 Ay, ay, a scratch, a scratch. Marry, 'tis enough.
Where is my page? Go, villain, fetch a surgeon.

[*Exit* PAGE.]

67. **devise:** imagine.

69. **tender:** value.

❓ 70. *Why does Romeo refuse to duel with Tybalt?*

❓ Staging the Play
71. *Mercutio doesn't know about Romeo's marriage to Juliet (a Capulet). Why is Mercutio so outraged? What feeling should Tybalt express (fear? annoyance?) as he asks Mercutio what he wants?*

72. **Alla stoccata** (ä′lä stə·kä′tä): Italian for "at the thrust"; a fencing term.

73. **walk:** make a move.

76. **make bold withal:** make free with (take away).

77. **dry-beat:** thrash.

78. **pilcher:** scabbard (sword holder).

❓ Staging the Play
Stage direction: *The stage direction simply says "They fight," but how would you—as director—choreograph the action? The sword fight can range all over the stage, but where must the three characters be placed when Tybalt stabs Mercutio?*

86. **bandying:** brawling.

88. **sped:** wounded.

The Tragedy of Romeo and Juliet, Act III, Scene 1   847

Ⓓ English-Language Learners
Cultural allusions. Remind students that Tybalt is named for a character in a fable who was called the "King of Cats." Tell them that some Western cultures share a folk belief that cats have nine lives. Ask if there are any similar beliefs in their cultures.

Ⓔ Literary Focus
Character traits. Point out to students that Mercutio says he has a scratch but is really mortally wounded. Mercutio's ironic banter in spite of dire circumstances is typical of his character.

Responses to Margin Questions
Line 70. Romeo says he has not injured Tybalt. Also, because he and Juliet are married, he now considers himself part of Tybalt's family, but he can only hint at this reason.

Line 71. Mercutio thinks Romeo is cowardly not to meet Tybalt's challenge. Fiery Tybalt is not likely to be afraid, but he could be annoyed or angered.

Stage direction. The director would have Mercutio first draw Tybalt away from Romeo so that Romeo can then come between the two swordsmen, attempting to stop the fight. If you show a film of the play, students could enjoy seeing how the director blocks this scene.

CONTENT-AREA CONNECTIONS

History: Duels
Paired activity. In Act II, Mercutio and Benvolio discuss the fact that Tybalt has challenged Romeo to a duel. Have student pairs research information on the history of dueling. Challenge students to find out when dueling formally came into existence and why a duel between Romeo and Tybalt would have been illegal—and not just because Prince Escalus forbade fighting between the two families.

The Tragedy of Romeo and Juliet, Act III, Scene 1   **847**

A Reading Skills

? Interpreting. What does Romeo mean here by saying that Juliet's beauty has made him "effeminate"? [Possible responses: He is pre-occupied with thoughts of his new bride; love has made him conciliatory, a virtue associated with women; love has drained him of the aggressiveness the other young men exhibit.]

Responses to Margin Questions

Line 101. Romeo is shocked, sad, remorseful, and perhaps ashamed. He might speak softly and ruefully, almost as if he were speaking to himself.

Line 105. Mercutio repeatedly curses the houses of Montague and Capulet, specifically their destructive feud. He uses variations of the curse "A plague a' [on] both your houses!" in ll. 88, 96–97, 103, and 105.

Responses about Mercutio's tone will vary. You may want to point out, however, that Mercutio has been a loyal friend to Romeo and seldom expresses his feelings directly. Even if Mercutio does not actually feel bitter, it is in character for him to go out with a roar, not with a whimper.

Stage direction. Tybalt's return is unlikely in some ways but certainly not impossible. Mercutio dies offstage; Tybalt could have seen his death and returned to challenge Romeo again. Students may also mention that impetuous Tybalt might behave erratically or return to prove that he is not a coward.

Accept all staging ideas, but remind students of Benvolio's description of "the furious Tybalt" (l. 118).

Romeo.
    Courage, man. The hurt cannot be much.

Mercutio. No, 'tis not so deep as a well, nor so wide as a
    church door; but 'tis enough, 'twill serve. Ask for me
95   tomorrow, and you shall find me a grave man. I am
    peppered,° I warrant, for this world. A plague a' both
    your houses! Zounds, a dog, a rat, a mouse, a cat, to
    scratch a man to death! A braggart, a rogue, a villain, that
    fights by the book of arithmetic!° Why the devil came
100   you between us? I was hurt under your arm.

Romeo.
    I thought all for the best.

Mercutio.
    Help me into some house, Benvolio,
    Or I shall faint. A plague a' both your houses!
    They have made worms' meat of me. I have it,
105   And soundly too. Your houses!
                    [*Exeunt* MERCUTIO *and* BENVOLIO.]

Romeo.
    This gentleman, the prince's near ally,°
    My very friend, hath got this mortal hurt
    In my behalf—my reputation stained
    With Tybalt's slander—Tybalt, that an hour
110   Hath been my cousin. O sweet Juliet,
    Thy beauty hath made me effeminate
    And in my temper soft'ned valor's steel!

    [*Enter* BENVOLIO.]

Benvolio.
    O Romeo, Romeo, brave Mercutio is dead!
    That gallant spirit hath aspired° the clouds,
115   Which too untimely here did scorn the earth.

Romeo.
    This day's black fate on more days doth depend;°
    This but begins the woe others must end.

    [*Enter* TYBALT.]

Benvolio.
    Here comes the furious Tybalt back again.

Romeo.
    Alive in triumph, and Mercutio slain?
120   Away to heaven respective lenity,
    And fire-eyed fury be my conduct now!

96. peppered: given a deadly wound (peppered food is ready to eat; Mercutio is "ready" to die).

99. fights by the book of arithmetic: fights according to formal rules of fencing.

? Staging the Play
101. *How would Romeo say this pathetic line?*

? Staging the Play
105. *What curse has Mercutio pronounced four times? Some actors playing Mercutio make him seem bitter about his approaching death and hostile to Romeo. Other Mercutios are gallant to the end and extend a hand to Romeo in friendship. How would you play this death speech?*

106. ally: relative. Mercutio is related to Verona's Prince Escalus.

114. aspired: climbed to.

116. depend: hang over.

? Staging the Play
Stage direction: Does it seem unlikely that Tybalt would return so soon? He must return, of course, so that Romeo can avenge Mercutio. An alternative would have been to have Romeo attack Tybalt as soon as he stabbed Mercutio, but then Shakespeare would have lost Mercutio's great dying speech. How would you stage Tybalt's return so that it seems believable?

READING MINI-LESSON

Developing Word-Attack Skills

Write the letters *ile* on the chalkboard. Remind students that in one-syllable words, *–ile* always stands for /īl/—for example, *file, mile, pile, tile,* and *while.* In words of more than one syllable, the final *–ile* may or may not stand for /īl/. Demonstrate this using the words *exile* and *agile* from Act III. Write the words on the chalkboard, and have a volunteer read them aloud. Help students recognize that in *exile,* *–ile* stands for /īl/, but in *agile,* the letters spell the unaccented syllable /əl/. Invite students to suggest other examples of words in which *–ile* stands for /īl/ or /əl/. [/īl/—*reptile, infantile, projectile.* /əl/—*fragile, facile, mobile.*]

Activity. Display these words. Have students group them according to the sound of *–ile:* /īl/, as in *exile,* or /əl/, as in *agile.* Encourage them to check a dictionary for the pronunciation of unfamiliar words.

"O, I am fortune's fool!"
✧

849

beguile   servile   sterile
reconcile domicile   immobile
puerile   docile   turnstile
crocodile imbecile   juvenile
fertile   missile   gracile

[/īl/—beguile, reconcile, domicile, turnstile, crocodile.
/əl/—sterile, immobile, docile, imbecile, fertile, missile, gracile. /īl/ or /əl/—servile, puerile, juvenile.]

Ⓐ Literary Focus

Turning point. Romeo's words leave little doubt that he will duel with Tybalt, which will set in motion a whole chain of events, turning the play toward its tragic ending.

Ⓑ Literary Focus

❓ Turning point. What questions might be in the audience's mind at this turning point in the play? [Possible responses: Will Romeo be caught and put to death, or will the prince spare his life? Will Romeo ever see Juliet again? Will Romeo tell everyone about his marriage to Juliet?]

Responses to Margin Questions

Line 132. Romeo is standing in amazement (l. 131), apparently immobilized by the shock of having killed Tybalt.

Line 133. He means he is unlucky; by chance, he has been provoked to an action that will further inflame the Capulet-Montague feud and endanger his marriage to Juliet.

Stage direction. The stage would be filled with confusion, with people milling about as they see and react to Tybalt's corpse.

Ⓐ
        Now, Tybalt, take the "villain" back again
        That late thou gavest me; for Mercutio's soul
        Is but a little way above our heads,
125   Staying for thine to keep him company.
        Either thou or I, or both, must go with him.

Tybalt.
        Thou, wretched boy, that didst consort him here,
        Shalt with him hence.

Romeo.   This shall determine that.

[They fight. TYBALT *falls.]*

Ⓑ
Benvolio.
        Romeo, away, be gone!
130   The citizens are up, and Tybalt slain.
        Stand not amazed. The prince will doom thee death
        If thou art taken. Hence, be gone, away!

Romeo.
        O, I am fortune's fool!

Benvolio.   Why dost thou stay?

                              [Exit ROMEO.*]*

[Enter CITIZENS.*]*

Citizen.
        Which way ran he that killed Mercutio?
135   Tybalt, that murderer, which way ran he?

Benvolio.
        There lies that Tybalt.

Citizen.   Up, sir, go with me.
        I charge thee in the prince's name obey.

[Enter PRINCE, *old* MONTAGUE, CAPULET, *their* WIVES, *and all.]*

Prince.
        Where are the vile beginners of this fray?

Benvolio.
        O noble prince, I can discover° all
140   The unlucky manage° of this fatal brawl.
        There lies the man, slain by young Romeo,
        That slew thy kinsman, brave Mercutio.

Lady Capulet.
        Tybalt, my cousin! O my brother's child!
        O prince! O cousin! Husband! O, the blood is spilled
145   Of my dear kinsman! Prince, as thou art true,

132. *What details in Benvolio's speech tell us what Romeo is doing and how he is feeling after this second death?*

133. *What do you think Romeo means by calling himself "fortune's fool"? What does he realize will now happen to him and Juliet?*

Staging the Play
Stage direction: What do you imagine the stage looks like as the prince and the two families enter?

139. discover: reveal.
140. manage: course.

CONTENT-AREA CONNECTIONS

Social Studies: Family Feuds
The basis for the main conflict of the play lies in the feud between the Capulets and the Montagues. Explain to students that a feud is a bitter, long-standing, often deadly quarrel that is frequently passed on from one generation to the next.

Individual activity. Ask students to use library resources to find information about a more recent feud—that of the Hatfields and the McCoys in the Appalachian Mountains during the nineteenth century. Ask students to find reasons for the conflict and to discover how the conflict was resolved at last.

Sports: Fencing
Small-group activity. Have students work in small groups to research the sport of fencing, the history of which owes much to sixteenth-century Italian fencing schools. Ask them to report on the kinds of implements used, the basic strategies and terminology, and the sport's popularity in modern times.

For blood of ours shed blood of Montague.
O cousin, cousin!

Prince.

Benvolio, who began this bloody fray?

Benvolio.

Tybalt, here slain, whom Romeo's hand did slay.
150   Romeo, that spoke him fair, bid him bethink
How nice° the quarrel was, and urged° withal
Your high displeasure. All this—utterèd
With gentle breath, calm look, knees humbly bowed—
Could not take truce with the unruly spleen°
155   Of Tybalt deaf to peace, but that he tilts°
With piercing steel at bold Mercutio's breast;
Who, all as hot, turns deadly point to point,
And, with a martial scorn, with one hand beats
Cold death aside and with the other sends
160   It back to Tybalt, whose dexterity
Retorts it. Romeo he cries aloud,
"Hold, friends! Friends, part!" and swifter than his
    tongue,
His agile arm beats down their fatal points,
And 'twixt them rushes; underneath whose arm
165   An envious° thrust from Tybalt hit the life
Of stout Mercutio, and then Tybalt fled;

C

151. **nice:** trivial. **urged:** mentioned.

154. **spleen:** anger.
155. **tilts:** thrusts.

165. **envious:** full of enmity or hatred.

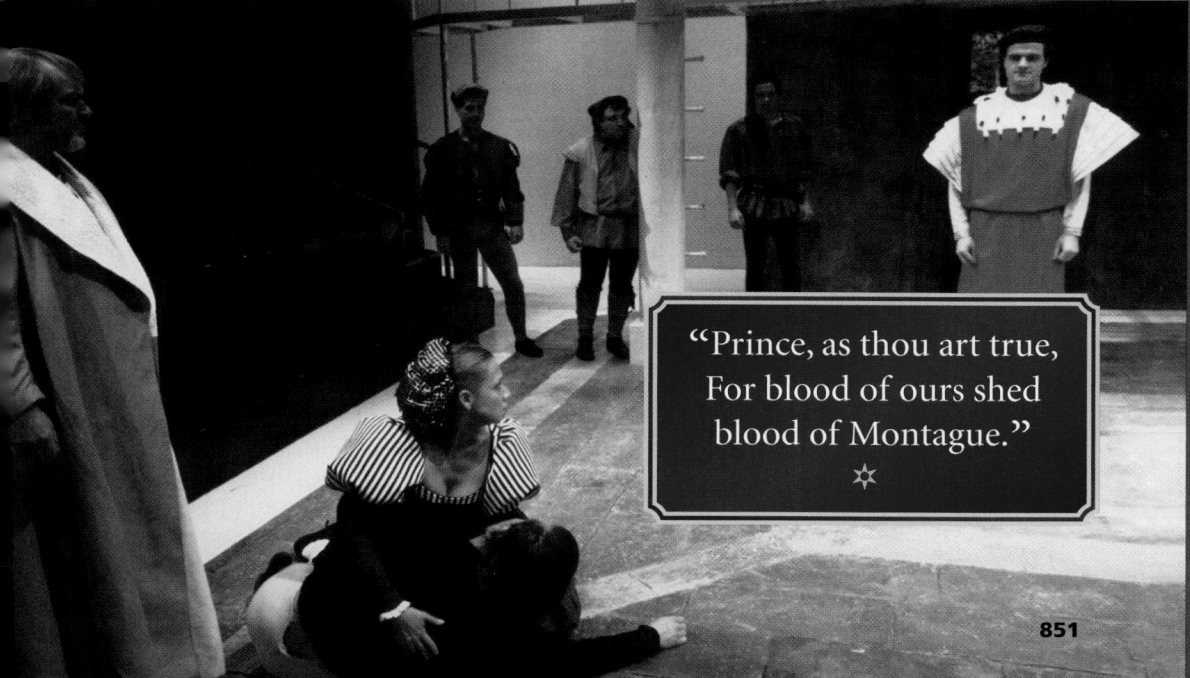

"Prince, as thou art true, For blood of ours shed blood of Montague."
✧

851

A Reading Skills

? Making judgments. Do you feel this punishment is fair or unfair? Why? [Possible responses: It is unfair, because the prince originally said that anyone starting another fight would die, so Tybalt would have died anyway; it is fair, because the prince reduced the punishment for fighting (from death to exile) in Romeo's special case.]

B Reading Skills

Reading Shakespeare's poetry. Have a volunteer read the prince's monologue aloud. Then, ask students to describe the meter and poetic style Shakespeare uses in the speech. [It is written in iambic pentameter and contains rhymed couplets, or pairs of rhyming lines.]

Responses to Margin Questions

Line 172. In most details it is accurate, but Benvolio does not explain that it was Mercutio who first baited Tybalt and that Romeo fled only at Benvolio's urging.

Line 176. Lady Capulet believes Tybalt was overcome by twenty young men and that Romeo killed him, in effect, in a cowardly way. She distrusts Benvolio because he is a Montague and Romeo's good friend.

Line 194. Romeo is exiled; if he does not leave Verona, he will be killed. The prince refuses mercy because the feud has now resulted in the death of one of his own kinsmen, Mercutio.

Stage direction. In the fighting scene the youths are spurred to action by their emotions; here the adults use logic to plead their cases.

But by and by comes back to Romeo,
Who had but newly entertained° revenge,
And to 't they go like lightning; for, ere I
170   Could draw to part them, was stout Tybalt slain;
And, as he fell, did Romeo turn and fly.
This is the truth, or let Benvolio die.

Lady Capulet.
He is a kinsman to the Montague;
Affection makes him false, he speaks not true.
175   Some twenty of them fought in this black strife,
And all those twenty could but kill one life.
I beg for justice, which thou, prince, must give.
Romeo slew Tybalt; Romeo must not live.

Prince.
Romeo slew him; he slew Mercutio.
180   Who now the price of his dear blood doth owe?

Montague.
Not Romeo, prince; he was Mercutio's friend;
His fault concludes but what the law should end,
The life of Tybalt.

A Prince.   And for that offense
Immediately we do exile him hence.
185   I have an interest in your hate's proceeding,
My blood° for your rude brawls doth lie a-bleeding;
But I'll amerce° you with so strong a fine
That you shall all repent the loss of mine.
B I will be deaf to pleading and excuses;
190   Nor tears nor prayers shall purchase out abuses.
Therefore use none. Let Romeo hence in haste,
Else, when he is found, that hour is his last.
Bear hence this body and attend our will.
Mercy but murders, pardoning those that kill.
                                [*Exit with others.*]

---

168. entertained: thought of.

? 172. *Is Benvolio's testimony about events fully accurate?*

? 176. *How does Lady Capulet think Tybalt was killed? Why does she think Benvolio is lying?*

186. My blood: that is, Mercutio, his blood relative.
187. amerce: punish.

? 194. *The prince has heard arguments from both families and has given judgment in the case. What is Romeo's punishment? Why won't the prince show Romeo greater mercy?*

? Staging the Play
Stage direction: *The families exit in separate processions, carrying their dead. How does this scene contrast with the fighting that has just taken place?*

DIFFERENTIATING INSTRUCTION

Advanced Learners
Enrichment. Students working in groups of three can role-play a news interview that covers the events in Act III. They can use the dialogue as a guide for their interviews. Each group member should take a turn playing the news reporter. Other group members can play the roles of the witnesses, such as Benvolio or innocent bystanders. Invite volunteer groups to reconstruct their interviews for the class. These interviews will help students review and comprehend the events surrounding the deaths.

Scene 2. *Capulet's orchard.*

Enter JULIET *alone.*

Juliet.

    Gallop apace, you fiery-footed steeds,°
    Towards Phoebus' lodging! Such a wagoner
    As Phaethon° would whip you to the west
    And bring in cloudy night immediately.
5   Spread thy close curtain, love-performing night,
    That runaways' eyes may wink,° and Romeo
    Leap to these arms untalked of and unseen.
    Lovers can see to do their amorous rites,
    And by their own beauties; or, if love be blind,
10   It best agrees with night. Come, civil° night,
    Thou sober-suited matron all in black,
    And learn me how to lose a winning match,
    Played for a pair of stainless maidenhoods.
    Hood° my unmanned° blood, bating° in my cheeks,
15   With thy black mantle till strange° love grow bold,
    Think true love acted simple modesty.
    Come, night; come, Romeo; come, thou day in night;
    For thou wilt lie upon the wings of night
    Whiter than new snow upon a raven's back.
20   Come, gentle night; come, loving, black-browed night;
    Give me my Romeo; and, when he shall die,
    Take him and cut him out in little stars,
    And he will make the face of heaven so fine
    That all the world will be in love with night

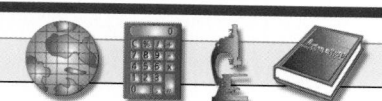

> "O, I have bought
> the mansion of a love,
> But not possessed it . . . "

25   And pay no worship to the garish sun.
    O, I have bought the mansion of a love,
    But not possessed it; and though I am sold,
    Not yet enjoyed. So tedious is this day
    As is the night before some festival
30   To an impatient child that hath new robes
    And may not wear them. O, here comes my nurse,

C

? **1.** *In this famous* **soliloquy,** *Juliet yearns for the night, when she and Romeo will be together. What do we in the audience know that Juliet does not yet know?*

  1. steeds: horses. (In Greek mythology, horses pull the sun god Phoebus's chariot across the sky each day.)
  3. Phaethon (fā′ə·thän′): Phoebus's reckless son, who couldn't hold the horses' reins.
  6. That runaways' eyes may wink: so that the eyes of the sun god's horses may shut.
  10. civil: well-behaved.
  14. Hood: cover. **unmanned:** unmated. **bating:** fluttering.
  15. strange: unfamiliar.

? **24.** *Work with a small group to make a word map for the word* night. *Include all the associations, images, and synonyms that you can come up with. How do they compare with Juliet's view of night?*

? **Staging the Play**
26. *What is the "mansion of a love" that Juliet has bought?*

? **31.** *Where does Juliet, in lines of unconscious* **foreshadowing,** *make us think of Romeo's death?*

CONTENT-AREA CONNECTIONS

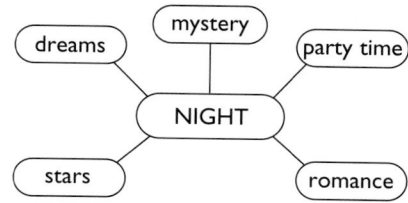

Music: *West Side Story*
Whole-class activity. Play an audio or video recording of the song "Tonight" from the Broadway musical or movie *West Side Story.* Have students compare the imagery and emotions in the song with those expressed in Juliet's soliloquy in Scene 2. How successfully have the composer and

lyricist matched the mood Shakespeare intended for this scene?

> **Act III, Scene 2**
> Juliet, anxious to consummate her marriage, delivers a soliloquy in which she urges night to hasten its approach. The nurse enters, saying that someone is dead. For some time Juliet believes Romeo is dead. The nurse finally explains that it is Tybalt who is dead and that Romeo, who killed him, is banished. Juliet threatens to kill herself, but the nurse comforts her by saying that she will go to the friar's cell and tell Romeo to come to Juliet's chamber that evening, as planned.

DIRECT TEACHING

C Reading Skills
Reading Shakespeare's poetry. Although Juliet's soliloquy is not in strict iambic pentameter, it is a beautiful love poem that offers a moment of respite from the growing sense of doom. Divide the soliloquy (ll. 1–31) into several parts, and ask students to read it aloud, paying attention to the run-on lines and end-stopped lines. Then, have the class analyze the soliloquy's imagery.

Responses to Margin Questions
Line 1. Romeo has killed Tybalt and has been banished from Verona.
Line 24. Possible cluster diagram:

```
        mystery
dreams           party time
       NIGHT
stars            romance
```

Contemporary associations with night are likely to resemble Juliet's view.
Line 26. Romeo is the mansion. (The image suggests his body.)
Line 31. In ll. 21–25, Juliet mentions Romeo's death as she describes how he brings light to her life.

A **Literary Focus**

❷ **Interactions between characters.** Why does Juliet's joy suddenly turn to despair? [Juliet sees the nurse approaching, wringing her hands, and the nurse announces, "He's dead."]

B **Literary Focus**

Characteristics of drama. Point out that in the dialogue between Juliet and the nurse, Shakespeare heightens the dramatic tension by making the nurse so distracted that she is unable to tell Juliet simply that Romeo has killed Tybalt and has been banished. The tension resonates in the audience because they know what has happened.

C **Vocabulary Development**

Homonyms. Tell students that the word *bier* is pronounced the same way as its homonym *beer*. A *bier* is a coffin; the word can also refer to the supporting platform on which a coffin is placed.

Responses to Margin Questions

Line 35. The nurse speaks distractedly because of her grief.
Line 39. The nurse says only "He's dead," and Juliet assumes she means Romeo.
Line 60. Believing Romeo is dead, Juliet says that she wants to share his "heavy bier," meaning his coffin.

[*Enter* NURSE, *with a ladder of cords.*]

And she brings news; and every tongue that speaks
But Romeo's name speaks heavenly eloquence.
Now, nurse, what news? What hast thou there, the cords
That Romeo bid thee fetch?

35 **Nurse.**   Ay, ay, the cords.
Juliet.
   Ay me! What news? Why dost thou wring thy hands?
Nurse.
   Ah, weraday!° He's dead, he's dead, he's dead!
   We are undone, lady, we are undone!
   Alack the day! He's gone, he's killed, he's dead!
Juliet.
   Can heaven be so envious?
40 **Nurse.**   Romeo can,
   Though heaven cannot. O Romeo, Romeo!
   Who ever would have thought it? Romeo!
Juliet.
   What devil art thou that dost torment me thus?
   This torture should be roared in dismal hell.
45 Hath Romeo slain himself? Say thou but "Ay,"
   And that bare vowel "I" shall poison more
   Than the death-darting eye of cockatrice.°
   I am not I, if there be such an "Ay,"
   Or those eyes' shot that make thee answer "Ay."
50 If he be slain, say "Ay"; or if not, "No."
   Brief sounds determine of my weal or woe.
Nurse.
   I saw the wound, I saw it with mine eyes,
   (God save the mark!)° here on his manly breast.
   A piteous corse,° a bloody piteous corse;
55 Pale, pale as ashes, all bedaubed in blood,
   All in gore-blood. I swounded° at the sight.
Juliet.
   O, break, my heart! Poor bankrout,° break at once!
   To prison, eyes; ne'er look on liberty!
   Vile earth,° to earth resign; end motion here,
60 And thou and Romeo press one heavy bier!
Nurse.
   O Tybalt, Tybalt, the best friend I had!
   O courteous Tybalt! Honest gentleman!
   That ever I should live to see thee dead!

❓ **Staging the Play**
35. *How might the nurse speak this line?*

37. weraday: well-a-day (or alas).

❓ **39.** *The nurse rattles on again—but this time, how does she seem to give the wrong news even as she delays it?*

47. cockatrice: legendary serpent that could kill by a glance.

53. God save the mark!: God forbid!
54. corse: corpse.

56. swounded: swooned (fainted).
57. bankrout: bankrupt.

59. Vile earth: Juliet refers to her own body.
❓ **60.** *This is one of a series of odd scenes in which we cannot share a character's feelings because we know something that the character does not know. What does Juliet think has happened? How does she foreshadow her own death?*

Juliet.
    What storm is this that blows so contrary?
65 Is Romeo slaught'red, and is Tybalt dead?
    My dearest cousin, and my dearer lord?
    Then, dreadful trumpet, sound the general doom!
    For who is living, if those two are gone?
Nurse.
    Tybalt is gone, and Romeo banishèd;
70 Romeo that killed him, he is banishèd.
Juliet.
    O God! Did Romeo's hand shed Tybalt's blood?
Nurse.
    It did, it did! Alas the day, it did!
Juliet.
    O serpent heart, hid with a flow'ring face!
    Did ever dragon keep so fair a cave?
75 Beautiful tyrant! Fiend angelical!
    Dove-feathered raven! Wolvish-ravening lamb!
    Despisèd substance of divinest show!
    Just opposite to what thou justly seem'st—
    A damnèd saint, an honorable villain!
80 O nature, what hadst thou to do in hell
    When thou didst bower the spirit of a fiend
    In mortal paradise of such sweet flesh?
    Was ever book containing such vile matter
    So fairly bound? O, that deceit should dwell
    In such a gorgeous palace!
85 **Nurse.**   There's no trust,
    No faith, no honesty in men; all perjured,
    All forsworn, all naught, all dissemblers.°
    Ah, where's my man? Give me some aqua vitae.°
    These griefs, these woes, these sorrows make me old.
    Shame come to Romeo!
90 **Juliet.**   Blistered be thy tongue
    For such a wish! He was not born to shame.
    Upon his brow shame is ashamed to sit;
    For 'tis a throne where honor may be crowned
    Sole monarch of the universal earth.
95 O, what a beast was I to chide at him!
Nurse.
    Will you speak well of him that killed your cousin?
Juliet.
    Shall I speak ill of him that is my husband?
    Ah, poor my lord, what tongue shall smooth thy name

Staging the Play
70. *Why do you think the nurse waits so long to give Juliet the correct news? Should we feel she is being self-centered here, or is she truly overwhelmed by the news she bears?*

Staging the Play
73. *The news that Romeo has killed Tybalt is terrible for Juliet. Try writing stage directions that will help an actor express her horror.*

85. *A moment ago Juliet thought of Romeo as her "day in night." Now what does she think of him?*
87. dissemblers: liars.
88. aqua vitae (akʹwə vītʹē): brandy (Latin for "water of life").

90. *What does the nurse think about these events? Where does she think the blame lies? Do you see her being selfish here, or is she wholly concerned for Juliet?*

97. *Why does Juliet turn against her nurse here?*

The Tragedy of Romeo and Juliet, Act III, Scene 2   **855**

D Literary Focus

❷ Figurative language. What oxymorons, or pairs of opposites, does Juliet use to express her momentary feeling that Romeo has betrayed her? ["Beautiful tyrant," "Fiend angelical," "Dove-feathered raven," "Wolvish-ravening lamb," "damnèd saint," "honorable villain"] What other character has used this kind of figurative speech? [Romeo, in Act I, Scene 1, ll. 173–178]

E Reading Skills

❷ Expressing an opinion. Do you think the nurse is justified in taking Tybalt's side? Explain. [Possible responses: Yes, because Tybalt is a member of the family whom the nurse serves; no, because she has been a party to the secret wedding between Romeo and Juliet, and she should be loyal to them.]

Responses to Margin Questions

Line 70. It is unlikely that the nurse is merely waiting. She seems truly disturbed. Her rambling, disconnected style of speaking, even when she is not upset, has already been established.

Line 73. Juliet might clench her fists or run her hand through her hair as she speaks.

Line 85. Her entire speech is filled with oxymorons that express her internal conflict. She loves Romeo but feels betrayed.

Line 90. The nurse blames Romeo. Perhaps she is not exactly selfish, but she is incapable of reflection or discrimination. She is angry because Romeo has hurt Juliet; however, the nurse is not perceptive enough to see that Juliet still loves him or that Tybalt was at fault.

Line 97. Perhaps the nurse's attack on Romeo brings Juliet back to her senses. She decides that, whatever Romeo has done, she must be loyal to her husband.

"'Tybalt is dead,
and Romeo—
banishèd.'"

856

When I, thy three-hours wife, have mangled it?
But wherefore, villain, didst thou kill my cousin?
That villain cousin would have killed my husband.
Back, foolish tears, back to your native spring!
Your tributary drops° belong to woe,
Which you, mistaking, offer up to joy.
My husband lives, that Tybalt would have slain;
And Tybalt's dead, that would have slain my husband.
All this is comfort; wherefore weep I then?
Some word there was, worser than Tybalt's death,
That murd'red me. I would forget it fain;°
But O, it presses to my memory
Like damnèd guilty deeds to sinners' minds!
"Tybalt is dead, and Romeo—banishèd."
That "banishèd," that one word "banishèd,"
Hath slain ten thousand Tybalts. Tybalt's death
Was woe enough, if it had ended there;
Or, if sour woe delights in fellowship
And needly will be ranked with° other griefs,
Why followed not, when she said "Tybalt's dead,"
Thy father, or thy mother, nay, or both,
Which modern° lamentation might have moved?°
But with a rearward° following Tybalt's death,
"Romeo is banishèd"—to speak that word
Is father, mother, Tybalt, Romeo, Juliet,
All slain, all dead. "Romeo is banishèd"—
There is no end, no limit, measure, bound,
In that word's death; no words can that woe sound.
Where is my father and my mother, nurse?

Nurse.
Weeping and wailing over Tybalt's corse.
Will you go to them? I will bring you thither.

Juliet.
Wash they his wounds with tears? Mine shall be spent,
When theirs are dry, for Romeo's banishment.
Take up those cords. Poor ropes, you are beguiled,
Both you and I, for Romeo is exiled.
He made you for a highway to my bed;
But I, a maid, die maiden-widowèd.
Come, cords; come, nurse. I'll to my wedding bed;
And death, not Romeo, take my maidenhead!

Nurse.
Hie to your chamber. I'll find Romeo

103. tributary drops: tears poured out in tribute.

109. fain: willingly.

117. ranked with: accompanied by.

120. modern: ordinary. **moved:** provoked.

121. rearward: soldiers at the rear of a troop; here, an additional source of injury and pain after the bad news about Tybalt.

? **124.** *Juliet comprehends what has happened. Why does she fix on the word* banished?

? **Staging the Play**
127. *Juliet pauses before she speaks her last line here. How would she change her tone as she asks the nurse about her father and mother?*

? **137.** *Juliet addresses the rope ladder in this speech. What has she decided to do with the ropes?*

DIRECT TEACHING

A Learners Having Difficulty

Paraphrasing. Read Juliet's speech aloud, line by line, and help students paraphrase her meaning. [Hearing that Romeo is banished is worse than hearing that ten thousand Tybalts had been killed. Hearing that Romeo and I must be separated is as bad as if my parents, Tybalt, Romeo, and I myself were all dead.]

B Reading Skills

Reading Shakespeare's poetry. Ask a student to read Juliet's speech aloud, and have the class note the rhymed couplets.

C Literary Focus

? Turning point. How does Shakespeare use the rope ladder as an ironic symbol that the plot has turned from romance to tragedy? [Possible response: The same ladder that Romeo was supposed to use to climb into Juliet's bedroom on their wedding night is now being considered by Juliet as a means of suicide.]

Responses to Margin Questions

Line 124. Romeo's banishment means one thing to Juliet: They will be separated.

Line 127. Juliet must control her grief and begin to seem aware of other people and their concerns.

Line 137. Juliet has decided to use them to kill herself.

READING SKILLS REVIEW

Dashes. Explain to students that dashes are used to indicate an abrupt halt or reversal in thought or speech, an unfinished statement or question, or an interruption by another character. In a play, actors can use these punctuation marks as clues for interpreting their lines.

Activity. Have students find sections of the play and read these following lines aloud as if the dashes were not there. Then, have them reinsert the dashes and re-read the lines to demonstrate how effectively pauses can be used to add dramatic effect.

- Act III, Scene 2, ll. 112–126
- Act III, Scene 3, ll. 74–78
- Act III, Scene 5, ll. 94–103

The Tragedy of Romeo and Juliet, Act III, Scene 2 **857**

Act III, Scene 3

At Friar Laurence's cell, the friar tells Romeo of the prince's sentence of banishment. Romeo collapses in despair. Death, he says, would be preferable. When the nurse arrives, she reports that Juliet is also distraught. Feeling responsible for her grief, Romeo tries to stab himself. The nurse prevents him, and Friar Laurence offers a plan: Romeo will go to Mantua while the friar works to reconcile the feuding families, reveal the secret marriage, and obtain the Prince's pardon for Romeo, who will then return to Verona. But first Romeo will visit Juliet. However, the friar cautions him that he must be off to Mantua before the watch is set.

DIRECT TEACHING

Ⓐ Literary Focus

❓ **Turning point.** How does Shakespeare use personification to signal the turning of the plot from romance to tragedy? [He personifies the words *affliction* and *calamity,* saying that affliction loves Romeo and calamity has married him.]

Ⓑ Vocabulary Development

Multiple meanings. To help students interpret this line correctly, point out that the word *without* can mean either "lacking" or "outside." Romeo uses the second meaning here: There is no world outside of Verona's walls, that is, away from Juliet.

Response to Margin Question

Line 3. The friar says that affliction desires Romeo and that he is "wedded to calamity."

To comfort you. I wot° well where he is.
140 Hark ye, your Romeo will be here at night.
I'll to him; he is hid at Laurence' cell.
Juliet.
O, find him! Give this ring to my true knight
And bid him come to take his last farewell.

[*Exit with* NURSE.]

139. **wot:** know.

Scene 3. *Friar Laurence's cell.*

Enter FRIAR LAURENCE.

Friar.
Ⓐ Romeo, come forth; come forth, thou fearful man.
Affliction is enamored of thy parts,
And thou art wedded to calamity.

[*Enter* ROMEO.]

Romeo.
Father, what news? What is the prince's doom?
5 What sorrow craves acquaintance at my hand
That I yet know not?
Friar. Too familiar
Is my dear son with such sour company.
I bring thee tidings of the prince's doom.
Romeo.
What less than doomsday° is the prince's doom?
Friar.
10 A gentler judgment vanished° from his lips—
Not body's death, but body's banishment.
Romeo.
Ha, banishment? Be merciful, say "death";
For exile hath more terror in his look,
Much more than death. Do not say "banishment."
Friar.
15 Here from Verona art thou banishèd.
Be patient, for the world is broad and wide.
Romeo.
Ⓑ There is no world without Verona walls,
But purgatory, torture, hell itself.
Hence banishèd is banished from the world,
20 And world's exile is death. Then "banishèd"
Is death mistermed. Calling death "banishèd,"

❓ 3. *When we last saw Romeo, he was speaking of himself as "fortune's fool" (Act III, Scene 1, line 133). Now, in the first lines of this scene, how does the friar remind us again that Romeo seems fated for ill fortune?*

9. **doomsday:** my death.

10. **vanished:** escaped.

READING SKILLS REVIEW

Cause and effect. Remind students that a cause is an event that brings about another event. The resulting event is called an effect. Plots often unfold as a chain of causes and effects, in which each effect then becomes a cause that sets off the next effect. The turning point of a play is an event that causes a chain of increasingly positive or increasingly negative effects. Point out that each cause can have more than one effect, and each effect can have more than one cause.

Activity. As students read the rest of the play, have them complete a cause-and-effect chain that begins with Act III, Scene 1. They can begin like this:

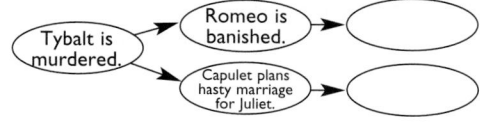

Thou cut'st my head off with a golden ax
And smilest upon the stroke that murders me.

Friar.
O deadly sin! O rude unthankfulness!

25   Thy fault our law calls death; but the kind prince,
Taking thy part, hath rushed aside the law,
And turned that black word "death" to "banishment."
This is dear mercy, and thou see'st it not.

Romeo.
'Tis torture, and not mercy. Heaven is here,

30   Where Juliet lives; and every cat and dog
And little mouse, every unworthy thing,
Live here in heaven and may look on her;
But Romeo may not. More validity,°
More honorable state, more courtship lives

35   In carrion flies than Romeo. They may seize
On the white wonder of dear Juliet's hand
And steal immortal blessing from her lips,
Who, even in pure and vestal modesty,
Still blush, as thinking their own kisses sin;

40   But Romeo may not, he is banishèd.
Flies may do this but I from this must fly;
They are freemen, but I am banishèd.
And sayest thou yet that exile is not death?
Hadst thou no poison mixed, no sharp-ground knife,

45   No sudden mean of death, though ne'er so mean,
But "banishèd" to kill me—"banishèd"?
O friar, the damnèd use that word in hell;
Howling attends it! How hast thou the heart,
Being a divine, a ghostly confessor,

50   A sin-absolver, and my friend professed,
To mangle me with that word "banishèd"?

> ## "'Tis torture, and not mercy."

Friar.
Thou fond° mad man, hear me a little speak.

Romeo.
O, thou wilt speak again of banishment.

Friar.
I'll give thee armor to keep off that word;

55   Adversity's sweet milk, philosophy,
To comfort thee, though thou art banishèd.

? 23. *Romeo and Friar Laurence have just had a* **dialogue**—*the talk between or among characters in a play*—*about the words* banished *and* banishment. *What do these words mean to Romeo? What do they mean to Friar Laurence?*

? 28. *Why is the friar angry at Romeo?*

33. validity: value.

C

D 52. fond: foolish.

E

The Tragedy of Romeo and Juliet, Act III, Scene 3   **859**

DIRECT TEACHING

C Reading Skills
Reading Shakespeare's poetry. Point out how Shakespeare uses a few tricks to make his lines fit the rhythmic pattern of iambic pentameter: Accent marks (`) indicate that a syllable or letter should be pronounced, even though it is usually silent. Apostrophes (') indicate that a syllable or letter has been dropped and should not be pronounced.

D Learners Having Difficulty
Syntax. Have students rearrange the friar's words in the order we would say them today. [You foolish, nutty man, hear me speak a little.]

E Reading Skills
? **Expressing an opinion.** Do you agree with the friar that the pain of life's adversities can be eased through philosophical reflection? Explain. [Responses will vary. Some students may say that philosophical thoughts can distract people from their problems, while others may disagree.]

Responses to Margin Questions
Line 23. For Romeo, banishment from Verona is equivalent to death. For Friar Laurence, Romeo's banishment is "mercy."

Line 28. Romeo ignores the prince's mercy in not sentencing him to death.

DEVELOPING FLUENCY

Paired activity. Have students identify the run-on lines in Romeo's speech (ll. 29–51) and practice reading them so that the meaning flows smoothly from line to line. Then, have one student in each pair read Romeo's entire speech aloud. The other student should listen carefully and summarize the content of the speech, using everyday language. Then partners should reverse roles.

A Literary Focus

? Turning point. Why are the lovers feeling increasingly isolated? [Possible response: They feel that no one can understand the despair they feel about the banishment; even the nurse and the friar, who know about the marriage, can't understand the depth of the lovers' feelings for each other.] **How might this feeling of isolation contribute to the tragedy to come?** [Possible response: Because the lovers feel that no one else can really understand what they are going through, it may seem pointless to confide in friends and family and ask for help.]

Responses to Margin Questions

Line 60. For both the lovers, banishment is as bad as death, for it means they cannot be together. Both "live" only in each other.

Line 62. Romeo is talking about Friar Laurence, who cannot "see" what the banishment will mean.

Line 70. In some ways, the friar's response depends on how Romeo delivers his lines. If Romeo is pitiful, Friar Laurence could be moved, even though Romeo's words are unfair and immature. If Romeo is disdainful, the friar could be angry but be restraining himself. He could also be preparing to chastise Romeo for his melodramatic behavior just as the knock comes at the door.

Line 78. Romeo is lying on the floor, weeping. Friar Laurence keeps dashing between the stricken lover and the door; he is trying to force Romeo to his feet while also shouting at the person who is knocking.

Romeo.
Yet "banishèd"? Hang up philosophy!
Unless philosophy can make a Juliet,
Displant a town, reverse a prince's doom,
60 It helps not, it prevails not. Talk no more.

Friar.
O, then I see that madmen have no ears.

Romeo.
How should they, when that wise men have no eyes?

Friar.
Let me dispute with thee of thy estate.°

Romeo.
Thou canst not speak of that thou dost not feel.
65 Wert thou as young as I, Juliet thy love,
An hour but married, Tybalt murderèd,
Doting like me, and like me banishèd,
Then mightst thou speak, then mightst thou tear thy hair,
And fall upon the ground, as I do now,
70 Taking the measure of an unmade grave.

[*The* NURSE *knocks.*]

Friar.
Arise, one knocks. Good Romeo, hide thyself.

Romeo.
Not I; unless the breath of heartsick groans
Mistlike infold me from the search of eyes.

[*Knock.*]

Friar.
Hark, how they knock! Who's there? Romeo, arise;
75 Thou wilt be taken.—Stay awhile!—Stand up;

[*Knock.*]

Run to my study.—By and by!—God's will,
What simpleness is this.—I come, I come!

[*Knock.*]

Who knocks so hard? Whence come you? What's your will?

[*Enter* NURSE.]

Nurse.
Let me come in, and you shall know my errand.

? 60. *It may seem that Romeo goes on too much. It is important, however, that we get the picture of this "fond mad man" in order to understand the action of the play. None of the other characters can understand Romeo's love. They are more levelheaded (perhaps less lucky in love?). How is Romeo's response to banishment like Juliet's?*

? 62. *Whom is Romeo talking about?*

63. estate: situation.

? Staging the Play
70. *How do you think the friar responds to these harsh words?*

? Staging the Play
78. *There is a great deal of action in this scene while the knocks are heard at the door. What action is the friar engaged in, and what is Romeo doing?*

I come from Lady Juliet.

80   **Friar.**   Welcome then.

  Nurse.

    O holy friar, O, tell me, holy friar,

    Where is my lady's lord, where's Romeo?

  Friar.

    There on the ground, with his own tears made drunk.

  Nurse.

    O, he is even in my mistress' case,°

85   Just in her case! O woeful sympathy!

    Piteous predicament! Even so lies she,

    Blubb'ring and weeping, weeping and blubb'ring.

    Stand up, stand up! Stand, and you be a man.

    For Juliet's sake, for her sake, rise and stand!

90   Why should you fall into so deep an O?°

  Romeo (*rises*). Nurse—

  Nurse.

    Ah sir, ah sir! Death's the end of all.

  Romeo.

    Spakest thou of Juliet? How is it with her?

    Doth not she think me an old murderer,

95   Now I have stained the childhood of our joy

    With blood removed but little from her own?

    Where is she? And how doth she? And what says

    My concealed lady to our canceled love?

  Nurse.

    O, she says nothing, sir, but weeps and weeps;

100   And now falls on her bed, and then starts up,

    And Tybalt calls; and then on Romeo cries,

    And then down falls again.

  Romeo.   As if that name,

    Shot from the deadly level° of a gun,

    Did murder her; as that name's cursèd hand

105   Murdered her kinsman. O, tell me, friar, tell me,

    In what vile part of this anatomy

    Doth my name lodge? Tell me, that I may sack°

    The hateful mansion.

  [*He offers to stab himself, and* NURSE *snatches the dagger away.*]

  Friar.   Hold thy desperate hand.

    Art thou a man? Thy form cries out thou art;

110   Thy tears are womanish, thy wild acts denote

    The unreasonable fury of a beast.

---

84. case: condition.

90. O: fit of moaning ("oh, oh, oh").

? Staging the Play
90. *What action is the nurse engaged in as she speaks these lines?*

103. level: aim.

107. sack: plunder and destroy.

? Staging the Play
108. *Romeo is disarmed without a struggle. He probably stands broken as the friar, in this long speech, gradually reestablishes control over him. It is important to remember that to the people in this play, suicide was a mortal sin, which damned one to hell forever. Where does the friar angrily remind Romeo of this?*

The Tragedy of Romeo and Juliet, Act III, Scene 3   **861**

DIRECT TEACHING

B Reading Skills

? Making comparisons. In what way do Romeo's words echo Juliet's words in Scene 2? [Possible responses: He, too, contemplates suicide; in Juliet's opening soliloquy, she also refers to Romeo's body as a "mansion" (l. 26).]

C Content-Area Connections

Sociology: Ideas About Masculinity and Femininity

Friar Laurence echoes a still-prevalent negative attitude toward "effeminate" behavior in men. His intent is to shame Romeo out of committing suicide. In Act I, Romeo himself blames Juliet's beauty for making him "effeminate" and thus responsible, in part, for Mercutio's death. Point out that since the last decades of the twentieth century, rigid ideas about what is acceptable behavior for males and females have been challenged and are changing.

Responses to Margin Questions

Line 90. The nurse is urging Romeo to stand, probably pulling him up.

Line 108. Friar Laurence says that by committing suicide, Romeo will inflict "damnèd hate" upon himself (l. 118).

READING SKILLS REVIEW

Facts and opinions. Remind students that a fact is a statement that can be proved true or false. An opinion is a statement that expresses a personal belief or feeling, which cannot be proved. Opinions are often signaled by such words as *should, better,* or *worse.*

Activity. Have students re-read ll. 108–145 of Friar Laurence's speech to Romeo. Then, have them make two columns labeled "Fact" and "Opinion" on a sheet of paper. Students should list facts and opinions stated by Friar Laurence regarding Romeo's predicament. Then, ask students which they think Romeo finds more convincing—the facts or the opinions.

The Tragedy of Romeo and Juliet, Act III, Scene 3   **861**

A Content-Area Connections

History: Money Lending
Tell students that a *usurer* is a money-lender who charges high interest rates. In Shakespeare's day the word meant any moneylender who charges interest. In past centuries the Catholic Church condemned usury because it was not considered proper to use money to make more money. Likewise, the friar says, by threatening suicide Romeo is not using his body, mind, and emotions in a proper way.

B Learners Having Difficulty

Summarizing. Read this passage aloud, and help students summarize Friar Laurence's advice to Romeo. [Possible response: Instead of wallowing in self-pity, you should count your blessings and be grateful for your good luck: Juliet is alive, you're alive, the person who wanted to kill you is dead, and the prince has decided to spare your life.]

Response to Margin Question

Line 154. "What, rouse thee, man!" (l. 135) suggests that Romeo is listless. The friar begins shaming Romeo immediately with "Art thou a man?" (l. 109) and continues until he begins the appeal to common sense, "Thy Juliet is alive" (l. 135). Beginning with his instructions "Go get thee to thy love" (l. 146), the friar offers hope that Romeo and Juliet can be reunited.

L   Unseemly woman in a seeming man!
     And ill-beseeming beast in seeming both!
     Thou hast amazed me. By my holy order,
115 I thought thy disposition better tempered.
     Hast thou slain Tybalt? Wilt thou slay thyself?
     And slay thy lady that in thy life lives,
     By doing damnèd hate upon thyself?
     Why rail'st thou on thy birth, the heaven, and earth?
120 Since birth and heaven and earth,° all three do meet
     In thee at once; which thou at once wouldst lose.
     Fie, fie, thou sham'st thy shape, thy love, thy wit,
     Which,° like a usurer, abound'st in all,
     And usest none in that true use indeed
125 Which should bedeck° thy shape, thy love, thy wit.
     Thy noble shape is but a form of wax,
     Digressing from the valor of a man;
     Thy dear love sworn but hollow perjury,
     Killing that love which thou hast vowed to cherish;
130 Thy wit, that ornament to shape and love,
     Misshapen in the conduct° of them both,
     Like powder in a skill-less soldier's flask,
     Is set afire by thine own ignorance,
     And thou dismembered with thine own defense.°
135 What, rouse thee, man! Thy Juliet is alive,
     For whose dear sake thou wast but lately dead.
     There art thou happy.° Tybalt would kill thee,
     But thou slewest Tybalt. There art thou happy.
     The law, that threatened death, becomes thy friend
140 And turns it to exile. There art thou happy.
     A pack of blessings light upon thy back;
     Happiness courts thee in her best array;
     But, like a misbehaved and sullen wench,
     Thou pouts upon thy fortune and thy love.
145 Take heed, take heed, for such die miserable.
     Go get thee to thy love, as was decreed,
     Ascend her chamber, hence and comfort her.
     But look thou stay not till the watch be set,
     For then thou canst not pass to Mantua,
150 Where thou shalt live till we can find a time
     To blaze° your marriage, reconcile your friends,
     Beg pardon of the prince, and call thee back
     With twenty hundred thousand times more joy
     Than thou went'st forth in lamentation.

120. birth and heaven and earth: family origin, soul, and body.

123. Which: who (speaking of Romeo).

125. bedeck: do honor to.

131. conduct: management.

134. And . . . defense: Romeo's own mind (wit), which should protect him, is destroying him.

137. happy: lucky.

151. blaze: announce.

154. *What line in this speech suggests that Romeo has been standing listlessly? Find where the friar first shames Romeo, then appeals to his common sense, then offers him hope.*

CONTENT-AREA CONNECTIONS

Drama: Comic Relief
In her book *An Introduction to Shakespeare*, Marchette Chute makes the following comments about the importance of Mercutio and the nurse as characters in this tragedy: "A lesser writer than Shakespeare might have tried to keep the play to a single note of lyric love. But Shakespeare . . . had no hesitation about putting a couple of cheerful realists into *Romeo and Juliet*. Mercutio and Juliet's nurse do not weaken the tragedy; they enrich it, in the usual astonishing fashion of Shakespeare's comedians. Mercutio is a humorist by intention; he is a subtle and intelligent young man who knows exactly how entertaining he is. . . . The nurse, on the other hand, does not mean to be funny. She feels she is a very sober, sensible, practical woman and she has no idea what actually happens every time she opens her mouth. Shakespeare had no objection to laughter in his tragedies. The two elements combine in real life and they were free to combine in his plays also."

Activity. Ask students to evaluate the facts and opinions expressed by this critic.

155 Go before, nurse. Commend me to thy lady,
And bid her hasten all the house to bed,
Which heavy sorrow makes them apt unto.
Romeo is coming.

Nurse.
O Lord, I could have stayed here all the night
160 To hear good counsel. O, what learning is!
My lord, I'll tell my lady you will come.

Romeo.
Do so, and bid my sweet prepare to chide.

[NURSE *offers to go in and turns again.*]

Nurse.
Here, sir, a ring she bid me give you, sir.
Hie you, make haste, for it grows very late.   [*Exit.*]

Romeo.
165 How well my comfort is revived by this!

Friar.
Go hence; good night; and here stands all your state:°
Either be gone before the watch be set,
Or by the break of day disguised from hence.
Sojourn in Mantua. I'll find out your man,
170 And he shall signify from time to time
Every good hap to you that chances here.
Give me thy hand. 'Tis late. Farewell; good night.

Romeo.
But that a joy past joy calls out on me,
It were a grief so brief to part with thee.
175 Farewell.   [*Exeunt.*]

Scene 4. *A room in Capulet's house.*

Enter old CAPULET, *his wife,* LADY CAPULET, *and* PARIS.

Capulet.
Things have fallen out, sir, so unluckily
That we have had no time to move° our daughter.
Look you, she loved her kinsman Tybalt dearly,
And so did I. Well, we were born to die.
5 'Tis very late; she'll not come down tonight.
I promise you, but for your company,
I would have been abed an hour ago.

155. *The friar turns to the nurse. What are his instructions?*

Staging the Play
161. *The nurse's amazement at what she calls the friar's "learning" often brings a laugh from the audience and breaks the tension. Romeo thus far has said nothing. How do you imagine he shows that the friar's speech has brought him back to life?*

166. state: situation.

175. *In spite of Romeo's and Juliet's anguish, the problem at this point seems to have a simple solution. What plans have been made to resolve the young people's difficulties?*

2. move: persuade (to marry Paris).

7. Dramatic irony *is felt when the audience knows something that the characters onstage do not know. What intense dramatic irony does the audience feel as this scene unfolds? What do we know that the Capulets and Paris are ignorant of?*

Responses to Margin Questions

Line 155. The nurse is to tell Juliet to urge the household to go to bed early, which will enable Romeo to safely join her.

Line 161. Romeo could rush to the nurse, gesturing that she should hurry to Juliet.

Line 175. Friar Laurence is to act as a mediator with the prince and the two sets of parents. He will keep in touch with Romeo by messenger and call him back when all is well.

Summary ⟷ *at grade level*

Act III, Scene 4
Lord Capulet explains to the visiting Paris that it is an inappropriate time to woo Juliet because the girl is extremely distraught over her cousin's murder. However, confident of his daughter's obedience, Capulet promises Paris that Juliet will marry him. The marriage day is set for Thursday—three days hence. Lord Capulet tells his wife to go to Juliet's room to tell her the news and to prepare her for the wedding day.

Response to Margin Question

Line 7. The Capulets and Paris do not know that Juliet is already married to Romeo. Even as this scene unfolds, Romeo is in the house with her.

The Tragedy of Romeo and Juliet, Act III, Scene 4   **863**

A Reading Skills

? Interpreting. How does Lady Capulet interpret the fact that Juliet has shut herself in her room? [Possible responses: She thinks Juliet is overcome with grief over Tybalt; she thinks Juliet is exhausted from crying.]

B Literary Focus

Falling action. The death of Tybalt causes Lord Capulet to make the decision to have Juliet married to Paris as soon as possible. This decision sets the characters more firmly on a tragic course. There will not be time for Friar Laurence to carry out his plans.

C Reading Skills

? Expressing an opinion. Do you think it is inappropriate for Capulet to plan Juliet's wedding so soon after Tybalt's death? [Possible responses: Yes, because not enough time has passed to mourn Tybalt; no, because the wedding could shift the focus from the family's suffering.]

Responses to Margin Questions

Line 19. Capulet is partly motivated by Tybalt's death but also by Paris's social status. His mood is enthusiastic and animated.

Line 32. Lady Capulet may feel that Juliet, distraught, should not marry so soon; she may think that Juliet does not love Paris.

Line 36. For the audience, Romeo and Juliet's happy night is tainted by Capulet's plans.

Paris.
These times of woe afford no times to woo.
Madam, good night. Commend me to your daughter.
Lady Capulet.
10 I will, and know her mind early tomorrow;
Tonight she's mewed up to her heaviness.°
Capulet.
Sir Paris, I will make a desperate tender°
Of my child's love. I think she will be ruled
In all respects by me; nay more, I doubt it not.
15 Wife, go you to her ere you go to bed;
Acquaint her here of my son Paris' love
And bid her (mark you me?) on Wednesday next—
But soft! What day is this?
Paris.   Monday, my lord.
Capulet.
Monday! Ha, ha! Well, Wednesday is too soon.
20 A' Thursday let it be—a' Thursday, tell her,
She shall be married to this noble earl.
Will you be ready? Do you like this haste?
We'll keep no great ado—a friend or two;
For hark you, Tybalt being slain so late,
25 It may be thought we held him carelessly,
Being our kinsman, if we revel much.
Therefore we'll have some half a dozen friends,
And there an end. But what say you to Thursday?
Paris.
My lord, I would that Thursday were tomorrow.
Capulet.
30 Well, get you gone. A' Thursday be it then.
Go you to Juliet ere you go to bed;
Prepare her, wife, against this wedding day.
Farewell, my lord.—Light to my chamber, ho!
Afore me,° it is so very late
35 That we may call it early by and by.
Good night.   [*Exeunt.*]

11. mewed up to her heaviness: shut away because of her great grief.

12. desperate tender: bold offer.

? Staging the Play
19. *In some productions, Capulet is played as a foolish old man. Why might he want to get Juliet married as soon as possible? What do you think his mood is here?*

? Staging the Play
32. *Capulet speaks this line to his wife. In some productions, Lady Capulet expresses uneasiness about her husband's plans here. Why would she be uneasy?*

34. Afore me: indeed.

? 36. *Just as we might feel the situation can be rescued, Shakespeare raises the stakes with this short scene. How does this development increase our tension in the scene that follows, the wedding-night scene?*

> "She shall be married to this noble earl."

Scene 5. *Capulet's orchard.*

Enter ROMEO *and* JULIET *aloft.*

Juliet.

    Wilt thou be gone? It is not yet near day.
    It was the nightingale, and not the lark,
    That pierced the fearful hollow of thine ear.
    Nightly she sings on yond pomegranate tree.
5   Believe me, love, it was the nightingale.

Romeo.

    It was the lark, the herald of the morn;
    No nightingale. Look, love, what envious streaks
    Do lace the severing clouds in yonder east.
    Night's candles are burnt out, and jocund day
10   Stands tiptoe on the misty mountaintops.
    I must be gone and live, or stay and die.

Juliet.

    Yond light is not daylight; I know it, I.
    It is some meteor that the sun exhales°
    To be to thee this night a torchbearer
15   And light thee on thy way to Mantua.
    Therefore stay yet; thou need'st not to be gone.

Romeo.

    Let me be taken, let me be put to death.
    I am content, so thou wilt have it so.
    I'll say yon gray is not the morning's eye,
20   'Tis but the pale reflex° of Cynthia's brow;°
    Nor that is not the lark whose notes do beat
    The vaulty heaven so high above our heads.
    I have more care to stay than will to go.
    Come, death, and welcome! Juliet wills it so.
25   How is't, my soul? Let's talk; it is not day.

Juliet.

    It is, it is! Hie hence, be gone, away!
    It is the lark that sings so out of tune,
    Straining harsh discords and unpleasing sharps.
    Some say the lark makes sweet division;°
30   This doth not so, for she divideth us.
    Some say the lark and loathèd toad change eyes;°
    O, now I would they had changed voices too,

? Staging the Play
Stage direction: *Given the design of Elizabethan theaters, this scene was probably played on the upper stage in Shakespeare's time. Modern directors often place the scene in Juliet's bedroom (with varying degrees of frankness). How would you design the scene for a movie or modern stage production?*

D **? 1.** *Juliet's first words here alert us to the time: It must be near morning, when Romeo must go to Mantua. We hear the song of a lark, which sings at daybreak. The nightingale, on the other hand, sings at night. Why does Juliet insist she hears the nightingale?*

13. exhales: gives off. (It was believed that the sun drew up vapors and ignited them as meteors.)

20. reflex: reflection. **Cynthia's brow:** In Greek mythology, Cynthia is the goddess of the moon.

? 26. *What has Romeo said that makes Juliet suddenly practical and aware of danger?*
29. division: literally, a rapid run of notes, but Juliet is punning on the word's other meaning ("separation").
31. A fable to explain why the lark, which sings so beautifully, has ugly eyes and why the toad, which croaks so harshly, has beautiful ones.

Summary ⬌ *at grade level*

Act III, Scene 5
Romeo and Juliet have spent the night together. The lovers are reluctant to part, but the nurse enters and informs Juliet that her mother is coming. Romeo departs. Lady Capulet enters and tells Juliet of her father's decision, but Juliet refuses to marry Paris. Lord Capulet enters and threatens to disown Juliet if she does not comply. Juliet pleads with her mother to postpone the marriage, but Lady Capulet refuses. The nurse advises Juliet to marry Paris and forget the inferior Romeo. Juliet resolves to visit Friar Laurence for help.

DIRECT TEACHING

D **Reading Skills**
Reading Shakespeare's poetry.
Tell students that this kind of "duet" between parting lovers at dawn is a literary and musical tradition called an *aubade,* or "dawn song."

Response to Margin Questions
Stage direction. Designs will vary. At least by l. 43 or l. 55, Romeo must be on the ground below the balcony.

Line 1. Juliet wants to delay daybreak, when Romeo must leave.

Line 26. When Romeo says, "Let me be taken, let me be put to death" (l. 17), Juliet remembers what will happen to Romeo if he is found in Verona.

CONTENT-AREA CONNECTIONS

Literature: Commentary on Romeo and Juliet's Aubade
Commenting on Romeo and Juliet's aubade, Harold Bloom in *Shakespeare: The Invention of the Human,* writes: "Exquisite in itself, this is also a subtle epitome of the tragedy of this tragedy, for the entire play could be regarded as a dawn song that, alas, is out of phase. . . .

The subtle outrageousness of Shakespeare's drama is that everything is against the lovers: their families and the state, the indifference of nature, the vagaries of time, and the regressive movement of the cosmological contraries of love and strife. Even had Romeo transcended his anger; even if Mercutio and the nurse were not quarrel-

some busybodies, the odds are too great against the triumph of love. That is the aubade's undersong, made explicit in Romeo's great outcry against the contraries: 'More light and light: more dark and dark our woes.'"

"Farewell, farewell! One kiss, and I'll descend."
☆

866

Since arm from arm that voice doth us affray,°

Hunting thee hence with hunt's-up° to the day.

35   O, now be gone! More light and light it grows.

Romeo.

More light and light—more dark and dark our woes.

[*Enter* NURSE.]

Nurse. Madam!

Juliet. Nurse?

Nurse.

Your lady mother is coming to your chamber.

40   The day is broke; be wary, look about.   [*Exit.*]

Juliet.

Then, window, let day in, and let life out.

Romeo.

Farewell, farewell! One kiss, and I'll descend.

[*He goes down.*]

Juliet.

Art thou gone so, love-lord, ay husband-friend?

I must hear from thee every day in the hour,

45   For in a minute there are many days.

O, for this count I shall be much in years

Ere I again behold my Romeo!

Romeo.

Farewell!

I will omit no opportunity

50   That may convey my greetings, love, to thee.

Juliet.

O, think'st thou we shall ever meet again?

Romeo.

I doubt it not; and all these woes shall serve

For sweet discourses in our times to come.

Juliet.

O God, I have an ill-divining soul!

55   Methinks I see thee, now thou art so low,

As one dead in the bottom of a tomb.

Either my eyesight fails, or thou look'st pale.

Romeo.

And trust me, love, in my eye so do you.

Dry° sorrow drinks our blood. Adieu, adieu!   [*Exit.*]

Juliet.

60   O Fortune, Fortune! All men call thee fickle.

affray: frighten.

34. hunt's-up: morning song for hunters.

? Staging the Play
41. *What is Juliet doing as she speaks these lines?*

? Staging the Play
43. *Where is Romeo now, as Juliet asks him to communicate with her?*

? Staging the Play
51. *Remember what the Chorus has told you in the Prologue about what will happen to Romeo and Juliet. How do you feel when you hear Juliet speak this line?*

? 57. *Friar Laurence might have sent Juliet with Romeo into exile in Mantua. We must remember, however, that Juliet is not quite fourteen. At this point in the story, Friar Laurence thinks the situation can be happily resolved. As the lovers part now, where does Juliet foresee Romeo's doom?*

59. Dry: thirsty (sorrow was thought to drain color from the cheeks).

The Tragedy of Romeo and Juliet, Act III, Scene 5   **867**

DIRECT TEACHING

A Literary Focus

? Falling action. How are references to light and darkness used ironically here to suggest the tragedy to come? [Possible responses: The image of the sun rising, usually a sign of hope, becomes a sign of despair because the lovers must separate as the day grows lighter. At this moment they have little hope, and dark despair dominates their outlook for the future.]

B Learners Having Difficulty

Paraphrasing. Have students reread this passage and try to express Juliet's feelings in their own words. [Possible response: Every minute away from you feels like days, so even if we're apart for just a few days, it will feel like years to me.]

C Literary Focus

Foreshadowing. Ironically the next time Juliet will see Romeo is when she awakens in her tomb to find him dead beside her.

Responses to Margin Questions

Line 41. Juliet is opening the window so that Romeo can climb down.

Line 43. Romeo is in the orchard beneath her window.

Line 51. Students may wonder whether the young husband and wife will have no more than one night together before they meet in sorrow at their deaths.

Line 57. Looking at Romeo on the ground below her in the gray light of dawn, Juliet has the eerie sensation that she is looking down on him "in the bottom of a tomb."

CONTENT-AREA CONNECTIONS

Music: Aubade

Among composers who have written songs in the form of an aubade, or dawn song, are John Ireland, Gabriel Fauré, Jules Massenet, and Charles Gounod.

Small-group activity. Have students write lyrics for another aubade that either Romeo or Juliet might deliver. Students with musical abilities can set the lyrics to music or find an appropriate recorded instrumental accompaniment.

A Literary Focus

❓ Personification. How does Juliet address fortune? [She addresses the concept of it as if fortune were a character.]

Responses to Margin Questions

Line 74. Let students express their opinions, but remind them that an actress would consider Lady Capulet's behavior in the entire scene when developing a characterization.

Line 78. Juliet is grieving for Romeo.

Line 82. The passion in Juliet's strong words convinces Lady Capulet that she hates Romeo.

A
    If thou art fickle, what dost thou with him
    That is renowned for faith? Be fickle, Fortune,
    For then I hope thou wilt not keep him long
    But send him back.

[*Enter Juliet's mother,* LADY CAPULET.]

Lady Capulet.
65   Ho, daughter! Are you up?
Juliet.
    Who is't that calls? It is my lady mother.
    Is she not down so late,° or up so early?
    What unaccustomed cause procures her hither?
Lady Capulet.
    Why, how now, Juliet?
Juliet.   Madam, I am not well.
Lady Capulet.
70   Evermore weeping for your cousin's death?
    What, wilt thou wash him from his grave with tears?
    And if thou couldst, thou couldst not make him live.
    Therefore have done. Some grief shows much of love;
    But much of grief shows still some want of wit.
Juliet.
75   Yet let me weep for such a feeling loss.°
Lady Capulet.
    So shall you feel the loss, but not the friend
    Which you weep for.
Juliet.   Feeling so the loss,
    I cannot choose but ever weep the friend.
Lady Capulet.
    Well, girl, thou weep'st not so much for his death
80   As that the villain lives which slaughtered him.
Juliet.
    What villain, madam?
Lady Capulet.   That same villain Romeo.
Juliet (*aside*).
    Villain and he be many miles asunder—
    God pardon him! I do, with all my heart;
    And yet no man like he doth grieve my heart.
Lady Capulet.
85   That is because the traitor murderer lives.
Juliet.
    Ay, madam, from the reach of these my hands.
    Would none but I might venge my cousin's death!

67. down so late: so late getting to bed.

❓ Staging the Play
74. *Actors playing Lady Capulet have interpreted her character in different ways. Some portray her as loving toward Juliet. Others find in her speeches a signal to play her as distant and strong-willed, to contrast with Juliet's helplessness. What do you think Lady Capulet's tone is here, and how would you play the part?*

75. feeling loss: loss so deeply felt.

❓ 78. *All Juliet's lines in this scene have double meanings. Whom is she really grieving for?*

❓ Staging the Play
82. *Juliet's first line here is an* **aside** *that her mother does not hear. In her next lines, how does Juliet convince her mother that she hates Romeo?*

Lady Capulet.
    We will have vengeance for it, fear thou not.
    Then weep no more. I'll send to one in Mantua,
90   Where that same banished runagate° doth live,
    Shall give him such an unaccustomed dram°
    That he shall soon keep Tybalt company;
    And then I hope thou wilt be satisfied.

Juliet.
    Indeed I never shall be satisfied
95   With Romeo till I behold him—dead—
    Is my poor heart so for a kinsman vexed.
    Madam, if you could find out but a man
    To bear a poison, I would temper° it—
    That Romeo should, upon receipt thereof,
100   Soon sleep in quiet. O, how my heart abhors
    To hear him named and cannot come to him,
    To wreak° the love I bore my cousin
    Upon his body that hath slaughtered him!

Lady Capulet.
    Find thou the means, and I'll find such a man.
105   But now I'll tell thee joyful tidings, girl.

Juliet.
    And joy comes well in such a needy time.
    What are they, I beseech your ladyship?

Lady Capulet.
    Well, well, thou hast a careful° father, child;
    One who, to put thee from thy heaviness,
110   Hath sorted out° a sudden day of joy
    That thou expects not nor I looked not for.

Juliet.
    Madam, in happy time!° What day is that?

Lady Capulet.
    Marry, my child, early next Thursday morn
    The gallant, young, and noble gentleman,
115   The County Paris, at Saint Peter's Church,
    Shall happily make thee there a joyful bride.

Juliet.
    Now by Saint Peter's Church, and Peter too,
    He shall not make me there a joyful bride!
    I wonder at this haste, that I must wed
120   Ere he that should be husband comes to woo.
    I pray you tell my lord and father, madam,
    I will not marry yet; and when I do, I swear

---

90. runagate (run′ə·gāt′): fugitive.

91. unaccustomed dram: unexpected drink (of poison).

? **Staging the Play**
93. *This is a hard and fearful threat. How does Juliet reply, and with what hidden emotions does she speak her next words? How does she continue to speak with double meanings?*

? **Staging the Play**
95. *How should lines 95–96 be said to indicate that Juliet intends* dead *to refer to her* heart?

98. temper: mix (she really means "weaken").
102. wreak: avenge (she really means "express").

? **105.** *Has Juliet convinced her mother that she wants Romeo dead?*

? **Staging the Play**
107. *We know what the "tidings" are, but Juliet doesn't. How would she speak these lines?*

108. careful: full of caring (for Juliet).

110. sorted out: selected.

112. in happy time: at a lucky time.

? **Staging the Play**
120. *Juliet becomes sarcastic as she repeats her mother's words. Despite this shocking news, how does Juliet manage to make a reasonable protest to her mother?*

The Tragedy of Romeo and Juliet, Act III, Scene 5   **869**

DIRECT TEACHING

B **Learners Having Difficulty**
Breaking down difficult text.
Read this confusing passage aloud a few times, stopping after each reading to refer to the sidenotes and margin questions until students understand all the double meanings Juliet is using to keep the truth from her mother. After students comprehend the meaning of the passage, ask a volunteer to read it aloud.

C **Learners Having Difficulty**
Paraphrasing. Help students paraphrase this difficult line, composed of many negatives. [Possible response: that neither you nor I expected.]

Responses to Margin Questions
Line 93. Juliet replies with more double meanings that allow her both to placate her mother and to express her love for Romeo. She continues to speak double meanings by defying her mother's emotion and turning the threats against Romeo into their opposite while seeming to endorse punishment for him. She does want Romeo to "sleep in quiet" (l. 100); she does want to come to him when she hears his name (l. 101); she does want to "wreak" her love upon his body (ll. 102–103).

Line 95. Juliet must pause before the word "dead" and must again pause, not fully stop, at the end of l. 95, allowing the audience to hear her meaning of "dead is my poor heart."

Line 105. Clearly Juliet has convinced her mother.

Line 107. Juliet should sound glad, innocent, and unsuspecting.

Line 120. Juliet protests that Paris has not even come to woo her.

A Reading Skills

Reading Shakespeare's poetry.
Explain to students that as the scene develops, Juliet becomes increasingly desperate, and her parents become increasingly angry at her disobedience and seeming ingratitude. Have three students read the roles of Juliet, Capulet, and Lady Capulet to convey how much emotion Shakespeare packs into his poetry here.

B Literary Focus

❓ Extended metaphor. What "tempest," or storm, does Capulet describe in elaborate detail here? [Possible responses: the raging storm of grief Juliet appears to feel over Tybalt's death; the storm of tears Juliet does not seem able to control.]

C Reading Skills

❓ Expressing an opinion. Do you think Capulet is overreacting? **Explain.** [Possible responses: Yes, he is unreasonably furious at Juliet for refusing to accept a husband she barely knows; no, he has tried hard to cheer up Juliet, and she will not obey him.]

Responses to Margin Questions

Line 139. Capulet thinks that Juliet is weeping for Tybalt and that the match he has arranged should cheer her; instead, Juliet weeps for Romeo and is horrified by the match because she is already married.

Line 149. Juliet thanks him for what is "meant love."

                    It shall be Romeo, whom you know I hate,
                    Rather than Paris. These are news indeed!
         (A) Lady Capulet.
    125   Here comes your father. Tell him so yourself,
                    And see how he will take it at your hands.

    [*Enter* CAPULET *and* NURSE.]

    Capulet.
                    When the sun sets the earth doth drizzle dew,
                    But for the sunset of my brother's son
                    It rains downright.
    130   How now? A conduit,° girl? What, still in tears?
                    Evermore showering? In one little body
                    Thou counterfeits a bark,° a sea, a wind:
                    For still thy eyes, which I may call the sea,
                    Do ebb and flow with tears; the bark thy body is,
    135   Sailing in this salt flood; the winds, thy sighs,
                    Who, raging with thy tears and they with them,
                    Without a sudden calm will overset
                    Thy tempest-tossèd body. How now, wife?
                    Have you delivered to her our decree?
         Lady Capulet.
    140   Ay, sir; but she will none, she gives you thanks.
                    I would the fool were married to her grave!
         Capulet.
                    Soft! Take me with you,° take me with you, wife.
                    How? Will she none? Doth she not give us thanks?
                    Is she not proud? Doth she not count her blest,
    145   Unworthy as she is, that we have wrought°
                    So worthy a gentleman to be her bride?
         Juliet.
                    Not proud you have, but thankful that you have.
                    Proud can I never be of what I hate,
                    But thankful even for hate that is meant love.
         Capulet.
    150   How, how, how, how, chopped-logic?° What is this?
                    "Proud"—and "I thank you"—and "I thank you not"—
                        And yet "not proud"? Mistress minion° you,
                        Thank me no thankings, nor proud me no prouds,
                        But fettle° your fine joints 'gainst Thursday next
    155   To go with Paris to Saint Peter's Church,
                    Or I will drag thee on a hurdle thither.

130. conduit (kän′dōō · it): water pipe (Juliet is weeping).

132. counterfeits a bark: imitates a boat.

❓ Staging the Play
139. *Lord Capulet, self-satisfied and certain of his plan, tries to humor and tease the weeping Juliet. Again, what irony do we feel in this scene?*

142. Soft! Take me with you: Wait! Let me understand you.

145. wrought: arranged.

❓ 149. *How does Juliet show that she knows her father loves her even though she hates what he has done for her?*
150. chopped-logic: hair-splitting.
152. minion (min′yən): badly behaved girl.
154. fettle: make ready.

CONTENT-AREA CONNECTIONS

Social Studies: Arranged Marriages
The custom of arranged marriages dates back at least to biblical times and is still practiced in some cultures today. It was practiced by people of all social strata—from peasants to royalty—and sometimes involved even the betrothal of infants.
Small-group activity. Have groups of three students prepare a report on arranged marriages, including information such as the meaning of *betrothal,* the goals of arranged marriages, the role of the matchmaker, the practice of providing a dowry, or bridewealth, and an example of how an arranged marriage resulted in the expansion of a country or empire. Students can collaborate on their research and presentation, with one person researching, one person writing, and one person presenting.

Out, you greensickness carrion! Out, you baggage!
You tallow-face!

Lady Capulet.   Fie, fie! What, are you mad?

Juliet.

Good father, I beseech you on my knees,
160 Hear me with patience but to speak a word.

Capulet.

Hang thee, young baggage! Disobedient wretch!
I tell thee what—get thee to church a' Thursday
Or never after look me in the face.
Speak not, reply not, do not answer me!
165 My fingers itch. Wife, we scarce thought us blest
That God had lent us but this only child;
But now I see this one is one too much,
And that we have a curse in having her.
Out on her, hilding!°

Nurse.   God in heaven bless her!
170 You are to blame, my lord, to rate° her so.

Capulet.

And why, my Lady Wisdom? Hold your tongue,
Good Prudence. Smatter with your gossips,° go!

? **Staging the Play**
158. *What insulting names does Capulet call Juliet? What would Capulet's actions be, as he speaks these vicious words to his only daughter? Whom is Juliet's mother talking to in her next line?*

? **Staging the Play**
160. *In the midst of this tragedy, we have a recognizable domestic scene, a family argument, which might have been played out in any century. What is Juliet doing as she talks to her father here? What does she do during her father's next speech?*

169. hilding: low, contemptible person.
170. rate: berate; scold.

172. Smatter with your gossips: chatter with your gossipy friends.

DIRECT TEACHING

D **Reading Skills**

? **Making predictions.** Do you think this accusation will have any effect on Capulet? Why or why not? [Possible responses: No, because he is so angry with Juliet that he is beyond rational thought; no, because it comes from a servant who is not supposed to accuse her master.]

Responses to Margin Questions

Line 158. Capulet calls Juliet "greensickness carrion" (anemia was called greensickness), "baggage" (a strumpet), and "tallow-face." He may be making threatening gestures or actually pushing her. Lady Capulet is rebuking her husband.

Line 160. Juliet is on her knees, begging him to listen. During Capulet's speech, she again tries to speak, but he silences her: "Speak not, reply not, do not answer me!" As he threatens her, she is probably weeping and cowering.

"Doth she not count her blest, Unworthy as she is, that we have wrought So worthy a gentleman to be her bride?"

871

DIFFERENTIATING INSTRUCTION

Learners Having Difficulty
Have students make two columns on a sheet of paper—one labeled "What Juliet Says" and the other "What Juliet Means." Ask them to quote at least four statements Juliet makes to deceive her mother and then to explain Juliet's concealed meanings. Engage students in a discussion about how Juliet has changed from the innocent, obedient daughter she was in her opening scene in Act I.

A **Reading Skills**

? **Making predictions.** Do you think Capulet's threats will sway Juliet's thinking? Explain. [Possible responses: Yes, she will give in to her father's wishes because she needs a place to live; no, she will not dishonor her marriage vows to Romeo.]

Responses to Margin Questions

Line 188. Lord Capulet thinks Juliet's reasons are that she doesn't love Paris and that she is too young to marry.

Line 197. Capulet will disown Juliet, force her from his house, and never again acknowledge her existence. Juliet then asks her mother to delay the marriage "for a month, a week" and threatens that otherwise, she will kill herself.

GUIDED PRACTICE

Monitoring students' progress. Have students answer these comprehension questions.

Short Answer

1. Why is Tybalt angry in Scene 1? [He is still angry at Romeo for attending the Capulet party uninvited.]

2. What is Romeo's punishment for killing Tybalt? [He is exiled.]

3. What is Juliet's reaction to the news of Tybalt's death? [She has mixed emotions: She is angry with Romeo but also loves him; she grieves for her cousin.]

4. What is Lord Capulet's reaction to Juliet's insistence that she is not ready to marry Paris? [He tells her that she will either marry Paris or be disowned by her family.]

Nurse.
  I speak no treason.

Capulet.   O, God-i-god-en!°

Nurse.
  May not one speak?

Capulet.   Peace, you mumbling fool!
175   Utter your gravity o'er a gossip's bowl,
  For here we need it not.

Lady Capulet.   You are too hot.

Capulet.
  God's bread!° It makes me mad.
  Day, night; hour, tide, time; work, play;
  Alone, in company; still my care hath been
180   To have her matched; and having now provided
  A gentleman of noble parentage,
  Of fair demesnes, youthful, and nobly trained,
  Stuffed, as they say, with honorable parts,
  Proportioned as one's thought would wish a man—
185   And then to have a wretched puling° fool,
  A whining mammet,° in her fortune's tender,°
  To answer "I'll not wed, I cannot love;
  I am too young, I pray you pardon me"!
  But, and you will not wed, I'll pardon you!°
190   Graze where you will, you shall not house with me.
  Look to't, think on't; I do not use to jest.
  Thursday is near; lay hand on heart, advise.°
  And you be mine, I'll give you to my friend;
  And you be not, hang, beg, starve, die in the streets,
195   For, by my soul, I'll ne'er acknowledge thee,
  Nor what is mine shall never do thee good.
  Trust to't. Bethink you. I'll not be forsworn.°   [*Exit.*]

A

Juliet.
  Is there no pity sitting in the clouds
  That sees into the bottom of my grief?
200   O sweet my mother, cast me not away!
  Delay this marriage for a month, a week;
  Or if you do not, make the bridal bed
  In that dim monument where Tybalt lies.

Lady Capulet.
  Talk not to me, for I'll not speak a word.
205   Do as thou wilt, for I have done with thee.   [*Exit.*]

Juliet.
  O God!—O nurse, how shall this be prevented?

---

173. God-i-god-en: Get on with you ("God give you good evening").

177. God's bread: oath on the sacrament of Communion (in the traditional Christian church service).

185. puling (pyool′in): whining.
186. mammet: puppet. **in her fortune's tender:** with all her good fortunes.

? **188.** *What does Lord Capulet think are Juliet's reasons for not wanting to marry Paris?*

189. I'll pardon you: I'll give you permission to go.
192. advise: consider.

197. forsworn: guilty of breaking my vow.

Staging the Play
? **197.** *In most productions there is a moment of stunned silence onstage after Capulet leaves. What exactly will Lord Capulet do if Juliet refuses to marry Paris? In the next speech, how does Juliet appeal to her mother for help?*

FAMILY/COMMUNITY ACTIVITY

Have students imagine that the Capulet family feud is occurring today. Suggest that students inquire as to the kinds of help that would be available in their community for a family such as the Capulets. Students might contact a social worker specializing in family therapy who would be willing to describe the possible ways the Capulets might be helped to resolve their conflict. Students might also describe the Capulet conflict to older family members and ask for their opinions on how to resolve the family's troubles.

My husband is on earth, my faith in heaven.°
How shall that faith return again to earth
Unless that husband send it me from heaven
210   By leaving earth? Comfort me, counsel me.
Alack, alack, that heaven should practice stratagems
Upon so soft a subject as myself!
What say'st thou? Hast thou not a word of joy?
Some comfort, nurse.

Nurse.   Faith, here it is.

215   Romeo is banished; and all the world to nothing°
That he dares ne'er come back to challenge you;
Or if he do, it needs must be by stealth.
Then, since the case so stands as now it doth,
I think it best you married with the county.
220   O, he's a lovely gentleman!
Romeo's a dishclout° to him. An eagle, madam,
Hath not so green, so quick, so fair an eye
As Paris hath. Beshrew° my very heart,
I think you are happy in this second match,
225   For it excels your first; or if it did not,
Your first is dead—or 'twere as good he were
As living here and you no use of him.

Juliet.
Speak'st thou from thy heart?

Nurse.
And from my soul too; else beshrew them both.

230 **Juliet.** Amen!

Nurse. What?

Juliet.
Well, thou hast comforted me marvelous much.
Go in; and tell my lady I am gone,
Having displeased my father, to Laurence' cell,
235   To make confession and to be absolved.

Nurse.
Marry, I will; and this is wisely done.   [*Exit.*]

Juliet.
Ancient damnation!° O most wicked fiend!
Is it more sin to wish me thus forsworn,
Or to dispraise my lord with that same tongue
240   Which she hath praised him with above compare
So many thousand times? Go, counselor!
Thou and my bosom henceforth shall be twain.°
I'll to the friar to know his remedy.
If all else fail, myself have power to die.   [*Exit.*]

The Tragedy of Romeo and Juliet, Act III, Scene 5   **873**

---

207. my faith in heaven: my wedding vow is recorded in heaven.

210. *Romeo and Juliet constantly remind us that they have taken their marriage vows seriously. According to Juliet here, how can these vows be broken?*

B

215. all the world to nothing: it is a safe bet.

221. dishclout: dishcloth; limp and weak.

223. Beshrew: curse.

227. *What is the nurse's "comfort" and advice for Juliet? Which line in this speech suggests that Juliet has reacted with shock and that the nurse must pause? Did you expect such advice from the nurse?*

C

Staging the Play
235. *In most productions the nurse embraces Juliet to comfort her. Now Juliet has made a decision. What do you see Juliet doing as she speaks?*

237. Ancient damnation: Damned old woman.

242. twain: two (thus, separate).

244. *What has Juliet decided about the nurse? We may wonder why Juliet doesn't just tell her parents why she cannot marry Paris. Why do you think she does not take this easy way out?*

B Literary Focus
? Falling action. What reasons does Juliet have for feeling completely desperate and abandoned at this point in the play? [Possible responses: Her lover has been exiled, her father has threatened to disown her if she doesn't marry Paris, her mother has ignored her threats of suicide, and even her nurse, who helped arrange her marriage to Romeo, now seems to betray her by urging her to marry Paris.]

C Reading Skills
? Drawing conclusions. Do you think Juliet is telling the truth about her reason for going to Friar Laurence? Explain. [Possible responses: No, Juliet has a plan and is pretending to be obedient in order to leave the house; yes, Juliet now feels she has no choice but to beg for forgiveness and go along with her parents' plan.]

Responses to Margin Questions
Line 210. The vows can be broken only by death.

Line 227. The nurse's advice is to commit bigamy. Her comfort is that Romeo probably doesn't dare return to Verona and that Paris is a better man anyway. The dash in l. 226 suggests that Juliet has reacted with shock.

Responses will vary. Many students will be shocked that a character they liked can suddenly act with such lack of sensitivity.

Line 235. Juliet's manner could suggest her new self-sufficiency from the nurse. Juliet could also choose to be affectionate with the nurse in order to better deceive her.

Line 244. Juliet thinks the nurse is sinful to counsel bigamy and capriciously change her mind about Romeo; she will no longer confide in the nurse or seek her help. At this point, Juliet feels she can no longer trust her parents.

Response and Analysis

Reading Check

1. Tybalt insults Romeo, and Mercutio challenges Tybalt since Romeo does not. Romeo steps between the two fighting men, blocking Mercutio's line of vision, and Tybalt stabs Mercutio.

2. Romeo kills Tybalt to avenge Mercutio's death and to save his own honor.

3. Juliet threatens to kill herself.

4. The friar hopes to reveal the marriage, reconcile the two families, ask for the prince's pardon, and call Romeo home.

5. Juliet is to marry Paris in three days.

Thinking Critically

6. Possible answer: The killing sets in motion Romeo's banishment and the hatred by the Capulets, two factors that inflame the young couple's sense of desperation. Capulet decides Juliet will marry Paris in three days. Juliet, horrified by the idea of marrying Paris, will seek a solution from the friar. If no remedy can be found, Juliet will take her own life.

7. Responses include:

   Juliet: Scene 2, ll. 45–49, 59–60, 123–124, 135–137; Scene 5, ll. 202–203, 243–244.

   Romeo: Scene 3, ll. 12–14, 17–23, 44–46, 69–70, 107–108.

8. The nurse alienates Juliet by advising her to forget Romeo and marry Paris. This adds to the tragedy that follows because Juliet no longer has support within her own home.

9. Possible answer: In Act III, the death of Mercutio causes Romeo to become vengeful, and he kills Tybalt. He also becomes more ardent and assertive in arguing with Friar Laurence over his banishment; with Juliet,

Response and Analysis

Act III

Reading Check

1. What causes the fatal sword fight between Mercutio and Tybalt in Scene I? How is Mercutio killed?

2. Why does Romeo kill Tybalt?

3. Now the young lovers are in serious trouble. What does Juliet threaten in Scene 2, after hearing of Romeo's banishment?

4. What is the friar's plan to help them in Scene 3?

5. A new **complication** has arisen by the end of Scene 4. What plans have Juliet's parents made for her?

go.
hrw
.com

INTERNET
Projects and Activities
Keyword: LE5 9-11

SKILLS FOCUS

Literary Skills
Analyze characteristics of tragedy, including complication, turning point, and suspense.

Writing Skills
Write a prologue.

Listening and Speaking Skills
Present scenes from the play.

Thinking Critically

6. Romeo's killing of Tybalt is the **turning point** of the play—the point when something happens that turns the action toward either a happy ending (a **comedy**) or an unhappy ending (a **tragedy**). What actions does the killing set in motion, with what possible **tragic** consequences?

7. We already know (from the Prologue, page 787) that the play ends in the deaths of Romeo and Juliet. Their willingness to die comes as no surprise to us, because we have been warned. Point out the instances in this act where each of them mentions this willingness to die if they are separated.

8. How does the nurse offend Juliet in this act and cease to be her ally? How does this development add to the tragedy of the events that follow?

9. Romeo and Juliet are **dynamic characters,** characters who change during the course of the play. De-

scribe how the lovers have changed in this act. What hard lessons have they learned about love?

10. By the end of Act III, we have reached the highest point of suspense. In drama, **suspense** causes us to wonder anxiously, "What will happen next?" Write down the questions you have at the end of Act III.

Extending and Evaluating

11. Does the last scene in this act remind you of encounters between parents and their teenage children that you've seen in movies or on TV shows or that you've read about in novels? Do Juliet and her parents remind you of real-life parents and teenagers today? Explain. Check your Quickwrite notes (page 783) before you answer.

WRITING

Write a Prologue

Did you notice that there is no prologue to Act III? Yet in this act we have some of the strongest action of the play. Write a **prologue** that **summarizes** the main events of the act. (If you want a challenge, try writing it in the form of a sonnet.)

LISTENING AND SPEAKING

Freeze! Speak!

Work in a group to create living pictures of the key action in each scene of Act III. For each scene, choose one character and one of that character's most significant lines. Then, arrange yourself in an appropriate opening position, and freeze. Taking turns with the other members of your group, come to life, say the line, change position, and freeze again. With your group, prepare a short opening and closing statement for the presentation.

he becomes somber in his outlook for the future. Juliet becomes crafty in deceiving her mother; she also becomes defiant toward her parents in refusing to marry Paris. Both lovers learn that their love is plagued by the self-interests of people close to them.

10. Possible responses: Will Juliet have to marry Paris? Will Friar Laurence tell the families the truth about the marriage?

Will Romeo and Juliet see each other alive again?

Extending and Evaluating

11. Answers will vary. Students should see the universality of loving but unreasonable parents and respectful but willful adolescents. Most students will note that parents rarely choose a child's spouse now in the United States.

Vocabulary Development

Word Origins: What's in a Name?

In Act II, Scene 2, Juliet, upset to discover that the handsome young man she has just met is named Montague, speaks these famous lines about the insignificance of a name:

> "What's in a name? That which we call a rose
> By any other word would smell as sweet."

Names, however, *are* significant in Shakespeare's plays. They are often used to suggest something about a person's character or temperament.

PRACTICE

Use a dictionary and the sidenotes for help as you answer the following questions about the names of four characters in *Romeo and Juliet:*

1. Mercutio is named for the chemical element *mercury*, which itself is named for the Roman god Mercury, the messenger of the gods. Which characteristics of both the element and the god match Mercutio's character? What do we mean when we say that someone's temperament is *mercurial*?

2. Benvolio's name comes from the same Latin words as the adjective *benevolent.* What are these Latin words, and what do they mean? How does Benvolio's name match his character?

3. Tybalt is named for a cat that is known for its slyness in the fable "Reynard the Fox." How is Tybalt like the cat he is named for?

4. Paris has the same name as the Trojan prince in Homer's epic the *Iliad,* who persuades Helen to leave her husband and marry him. Although Count Paris never marries Juliet, what does he do in the play that is similar to what the Greek prince does in the epic?

5. If you were renaming these four characters for an updated version of the tragedy, what names would you give them?

SKILLS FOCUS

Vocabulary Skills
Understand word origins.

The Tragedy of Romeo and Juliet, Act III   **875**

Vocabulary Development

Practice
Possible Answers

1. He is quick, volatile, and changeable. Someone who is *mercurial* is quick-tempered, moody, unpredictable; the person could also have the qualities of the god Mercury, who is eloquent, clever, shrewd, and thievish.

2. *Bene* means "well," and *volens* means "wishing"; *benevolent* means "kindly" or "well intentioned." Benvolio is both: he is a friendly type who is not interested in fighting.

3. He is quick to pounce on his victim.

4. He falls in love with someone who is beloved by someone else. In the case of the *Illiad,* Helen is already married when Paris takes her to Troy. Paris falls in love with Juliet *before* she is married; Juliet marries Romeo (unbeknownst to Paris or to Juliet's parents); but Paris still expects to marry her.

5. Mercutio—Silver (for quicksilver); Benvolio—Ben (shortened form); Tybalt—Tom (for tomcat) or Tiger (a king of cats); Paris—Perry (play on the name).

ASSESSING

Assessment
- *Holt Assessment: Literature, Reading, and Vocabulary*

RETEACHING

For a lesson reteaching analyzing dramatic literature, see **Reteaching,** p. 979A. For another selection to teach analyzing dramatic literature, see *The Holt Reader,* Collection 11.

DIFFERENTIATING INSTRUCTION

Learners Having Difficulty
Use the questions and answers on p. 874 in addition to the Reading Check questions to assess students' progress. If students have difficulty recalling answers, have them re-read specific lines from the selection: question 1, ll. 58–88; question 2, ll. 119–126; question 3, ll. 130–137; question 4, ll. 146–158; question 5, ll. 20–29.

Advanced Learners
Have students speculate on the following situation. Suppose Mercutio had killed Tybalt in the sword fight. How might the action of the play have changed? If he had lived, could Mercutio have persuaded Romeo to act differently? Explain why you think the old feud would or would not have erupted again.

Selection Starter

Motivate. Now that students are becoming more familiar with Shakespeare's language, encourage them to paraphrase more often during class discussions. You may want to present the Reading Skills Feature on p. 894 before teaching Act IV.

DIRECT TEACHING

Summary ⇄ at grade level

Act IV, Scene 1

Juliet goes to Friar Laurence's cell and encounters Paris there. Paris speaks of love and their upcoming marriage, but Juliet responds ambiguously. Paris leaves, and Juliet, in great distress, tells the friar that she will commit suicide if he cannot help her. The friar devises a plan to prevent Juliet's marriage to Paris: On the night before the wedding, Juliet will take a drug that induces a deathlike coma for forty-two hours. In the meantime, Friar Laurence will send a message to Romeo, who will return to Verona and wait in the Capulets' burial vault until Juliet awakes. The lovers will then escape to Mantua.

A Reading Skills

Paraphrasing and context clues.
Have students work in small groups to paraphrase Paris's speech. Then, have them answer the margin question for l. 15. Discuss the meaning of the figurative language in l. 8 and the archaic language in ll. 13–14.

Response to Margin Question

Line 15. Lord Capulet thinks that marriage will help Juliet get over her grief for Tybalt.

�֍ ACT IV �֍

Scene 1. *Friar Laurence's cell.*

Enter FRIAR LAURENCE *and* COUNT PARIS.

Friar.
    On Thursday, sir? The time is very short.
Paris.
    My father Capulet will have it so,
    And I am nothing slow to slack his haste.
Friar.
    You say you do not know the lady's mind.
5   Uneven° is the course; I like it not.
Paris.
    Immoderately she weeps for Tybalt's death,
    And therefore have I little talked of love;
    For Venus smiles not in a house of tears.
    Now, sir, her father counts it dangerous
10   That she do give her sorrow so much sway,
    And in his wisdom hastes our marriage
    To stop the inundation of her tears,
    Which, too much minded° by herself alone,
    May be put from her by society.
15   Now do you know the reason of this haste.
Friar (*aside*).
    I would I knew not why it should be slowed,—
    Look, sir, here comes the lady toward my cell.

[*Enter* JULIET.]

Paris.
    Happily met, my lady and my wife!
Juliet.
    That may be, sir, when I may be a wife.
Paris.
20   That "may be" must be, love, on Thursday next.
Juliet.
    What must be shall be.
Friar.   That's a certain text.
Paris.
    Come you to make confession to this father?

5. **Uneven:** irregular or unusual.

13. **minded:** thought about.

? 15. *According to Paris, why is Capulet pushing his daughter to marry so quickly?*

RESOURCES: READING

Differentiating Instruction
- *Holt Reading Solutions*
- *Holt Adapted Reader*
- *Supporting Instruction in Spanish*
- *Audio CD Library, Selections and Summaries in Spanish*

Assessment
- *Holt Online Assessment*

- *One-Stop Planner* CD-ROM with ExamView Test Generator
- *Holt Assessment: Literature, Reading, and Vocabulary*

Media
- *Visual Connections Videocassette Program*
- *Fine Art Transparencies*

Juliet.

To answer that, I should confess to you.

Paris.

Do not deny to him that you love me.

Juliet.

25 I will confess to you that I love him.

Paris.

So will ye, I am sure, that you love me.

Juliet.

If I do so, it will be of more price,

Being spoke behind your back, than to your face.

Paris.

Poor soul, thy face is much abused with tears.

Juliet.

30 The tears have got small victory by that,

For it was bad enough before their spite.°

Paris.

Thou wrong'st it more than tears with that report.

Juliet.

That is no slander, sir, which is a truth;

And what I spake, I spake it to my face.

Paris.

35 Thy face is mine, and thou hast slandered it.

Juliet.

It may be so, for it is not mine own.

Are you at leisure, holy father, now,

Or shall I come to you at evening mass?

Friar.

My leisure serves me, pensive daughter, now.

40 My lord, we must entreat the time alone.

Paris.

God shield° I should disturb devotion!

Juliet, on Thursday early will I rouse ye.

Till then, adieu, and keep this holy kiss. [*Exit.*]

Juliet.

O, shut the door, and when thou hast done so,

45 Come weep with me—past hope, past care, past help!

Friar.

O Juliet, I already know thy grief;

It strains me past the compass of my wits.

I hear thou must, and nothing may prorogue° it,

On Thursday next be married to this county.

? **26.** *In this scene, Juliet's action is to keep up appearances and ward off Paris, who presses his attentions on her. She does this by wittily playing with words. We are fascinated by two things here: what is being done and how it is being done. What double meanings does Juliet intend in the* **dialogue** *with Paris that follows?*

31. spite: injury or damage (to her face).

B

? **Staging the Play**
38. *Juliet must show here that the tension of keeping up this pretense is unbearable. Where do you think she pauses and changes her tone?*

41. God shield: God forbid.

? **45.** *Paris has gone, and Juliet has endured his "holy kiss." What does she now ask Friar Laurence to do?*

48. prorogue (prō · rōg′): postpone.

DIRECT TEACHING

B **Literary Focus**

? **Character traits.** What does this statement reveal about Paris's character? [Possible responses: He is concerned about Juliet; he is observant of her grief.]

Responses to Margin Questions

Line 26. Juliet says that if she "confesses" her love to the friar, rather than to Paris, it will be more valuable ("of more price") because she would have no reason to speak anything but the truth. When Paris laments that tears have "abused" Juliet's face, she says that they could not much damage an already homely face. Paris then accuses her of slandering her face, but she says the truth can't be slander, particularly when spoken openly "to" (that is, about) her face. To Paris's claim "Thy face is mine," Juliet agrees "it is not mine own," by which she may mean both that it is Romeo's and that she is dissembling.

Line 38. Juliet probably changes her tone when she changes the topic of conversation in l. 37.

Line 45. Juliet asks the friar to shut the door, giving them privacy, and to commiserate with her.

A Literary Focus

Falling action. Juliet's sense of desperation about the planned wedding is causing her to consider any plan, no matter how risky, to avoid marriage to Paris. Her desperation locks her into actions that take her deeper and deeper into disaster.

B Reading Skills

Paraphrasing and context clues. Have students express Friar Laurence's speech in their own words. [Possible response: Wait a minute! I have an idea! It's a desperate plan, but then we are pretty desperate people. If you'd really rather kill yourself than marry Paris, maybe you'd be willing to pretend to be dead. If you're brave enough, I'll tell you my plan.]

Responses to Margin Questions

Line 54. Juliet is holding a knife, threatening to kill herself if Friar Laurence has no way to help her escape from marriage to Paris, a marriage that would be immoral, illegal, and disloyal.

Line 62. "Be not so long to speak" (l. 66) indicates that Juliet and the friar have paused.

Line 77. Juliet is agitated, desperate, and courageous. Rather than marry Paris, she would leap from a tower, become a thief, live with serpents, be chained among bears, live nightly in a charnel house, or be buried alive with a corpse.

Juliet.

50 Tell me not, friar, that thou hearest of this,
    Unless thou tell me how I may prevent it.
    If in thy wisdom thou canst give no help,
    Do thou but call my resolution wise
    And with this knife I'll help it presently.
55 God joined my heart and Romeo's, thou our hands;
    And ere this hand, by thee to Romeo's sealed,
    Shall be the label° to another deed,°
    Or my true heart with treacherous revolt
    Turn to another, this shall slay them both.
60 Therefore, out of thy long-experienced time,
    Give me some present counsel; or, behold,
    'Twixt my extremes and me this bloody knife
    Shall play the umpire, arbitrating that
    Which the commission° of thy years and art
65 Could to no issue of true honor bring.
    Be not so long to speak. I long to die
    If what thou speak'st speak not of remedy.

Friar.

    Hold, daughter. I do spy a kind of hope,
    Which craves as desperate an execution
70 As that is desperate which we would prevent.
    If, rather than to marry County Paris,
    Thou hast the strength of will to slay thyself,
    Then is it likely thou wilt undertake
    A thing like death to chide away this shame,
75 That cop'st° with death himself to scape from it;
    And, if thou darest, I'll give thee remedy.

Juliet.

    O, bid me leap, rather than marry Paris,
    From off the battlements of any tower,
    Or walk in thievish ways, or bid me lurk
80 Where serpents are; chain me with roaring bears,
    Or hide me nightly in a charnel house,°
    O'ercovered quite with dead men's rattling bones,
    With reeky° shanks and yellow chapless° skulls;
    Or bid me go into a new-made grave
85 And hide me with a dead man in his shroud—
    Things that, to hear them told, have made me tremble—
    And I will do it without fear or doubt,
    To live an unstained wife to my sweet love.

54. *What is Juliet holding in her hand? What is she threatening to do?*

57. label: seal. **deed:** contract (of marriage).

Staging the Play
62. *The friar has to put up with a good deal of brandishing of knives and daggers from Romeo and Juliet. Now that the nurse is no longer Juliet's ally, the friar has to be the confidant of both Juliet and Romeo. He must listen with patience to their threats of suicide if they cannot be together. What line in Juliet's speech indicates that she has paused and that the friar for a time is silent?*

64. commission: authority.

75. cop'st: negotiates.

Staging the Play
77. *What would Juliet's mood be as she delivers this speech? What is she willing to do rather than marry Paris?*

81. charnel house: house where bones from old graves are kept.

83. reeky: damp, stinking. **chapless:** jawless.

Learners Having Difficulty
Paraphrasing and context clues are introduced in the Reading Skills lesson on p. 894. To prepare students for paraphrasing, review the Vocabulary Development lesson at the end of Act II.

English-Language Learners
These students will find paraphrasing easier if they are allowed to act out scenes of extended dialogue—such as the one between Juliet and Friar Laurence in Scene 1. Assign parts to pairs of students, and have them read their dialogue aloud to each other,

translating it into contemporary English as they go along. Encourage them to act out their translated scenes for the class.

Special Education Students
For lessons designed for special education students, see *Holt Reading Solutions*.

Friar.

Hold, then. Go home, be merry, give consent
90 To marry Paris. Wednesday is tomorrow.
Tomorrow night look that thou lie alone;
Let not the nurse lie with thee in thy chamber.
Take thou this vial, being then in bed,
And this distilling° liquor drink thou off;
95 When presently through all thy veins shall run
A cold and drowsy humor;° for no pulse
Shall keep his native° progress, but surcease;°
No warmth, no breath, shall testify thou livest;
The roses in thy lips and cheeks shall fade
100 To wanny° ashes, thy eyes' windows fall
Like death when he shuts up the day of life;
Each part, deprived of supple government,°
Shall, stiff and stark and cold, appear like death;
And in this borrowed likeness of shrunk death
105 Thou shalt continue two-and-forty hours,
And then awake as from a pleasant sleep.
Now, when the bridegroom in the morning comes
To rouse thee from thy bed, there art thou dead.

89. *Juliet must pay strict attention to the friar's plan, as must the audience. On what day does the friar tell Juliet to take the potion?*

94. distilling: penetrating.

96. humor: fluid.

97. native: natural. **surcease:** stop.

100. wanny: pale.

102. government: control.

106. *This may be the most implausible part of the play, but we have been prepared for it. Where have we seen the friar taking care of his herbs and heard him talk of magical potions before? What will happen to Juliet when she takes the drug?*

"Take thou this vial ..."
☆

879

DIRECT TEACHING

C Literary Focus

❓ Falling action. Do you think Friar Laurence's plan is likely to work, or is it locking the characters deeper into disaster? [Possible responses: Yes, it will work because after Friar Laurence and Romeo awaken Juliet, the two lovers can leave for Mantua; no, they are locking themselves into disaster because there are too many uncontrollable factors, such as Romeo's receiving the friar's message in time and Juliet's responding to the drug exactly as Friar Laurence expects.]

Responses to Margin Questions

Line 89. Juliet is to drink the potion Wednesday night.

Line 106. At the beginning of Act II, Scene 3, the friar was gathering herbs and discussing their powers—both beneficial and dangerous.

When Juliet takes the drug, she will go into a coma and appear to be dead. She will have no pulse or color and will be stiff, but she will awaken in forty-two hours.

Advanced Learners

Enrichment. After students read Act IV through once, have them choose one character who could, at some point, have changed what has happened. They should rewrite the scene from that character's point of view and explain how things would have turned out differently in their version.

Responses to Margin Questions

Line 117. Friar Laurence will send a letter to Romeo so that he can join Friar Laurence in waiting at Juliet's side for her awakening. That same night the couple will depart for Mantua.

Line 122. The friar gives her a vial of the sleeping drug, which she is to take Wednesday night. She will be discovered "dead" the next morning, her wedding day, and will be placed uncovered (that is, not enclosed in a coffin) in the Capulets' large burial vault. In the meantime, a friar will take an explanatory letter to Romeo, who will return to Verona, wait for Juliet to awaken, and then take her back to Mantua.

Line 126. The blessing suggests she needs divine protection and highlights the plan's danger.

Summary ⬌ *at grade level*

Act IV, Scene 2

Lord Capulet is making preparations for the marriage when Juliet enters. She appears contrite and tells him that Friar Laurence has told her to apologize to her father. She does so, saying that she will now obey his wishes and marry Paris. Lord Capulet is relieved and decides to move the wedding up to Wednesday, the very next morning.

Response to Margin Question

Line 1. The happy domestic scene, full of exciting preparations for a celebration, promises new life. The preceding scene, desperate and secretive, was filled with talk of death, conflict, and trouble.

110　Then, as the manner of our country is,
　　In thy best robes uncovered on the bier
　　Thou shalt be borne to that same ancient vault
　　Where all the kindred of the Capulets lie.
　　In the meantime, against° thou shalt awake,
115　Shall Romeo by my letters know our drift;°
　　And hither shall he come; and he and I
　　Will watch thy waking, and that very night
　　Shall Romeo bear thee hence to Mantua.
　　And this shall free thee from this present shame,
　　If no inconstant toy° nor womanish fear
120　Abate thy valor in the acting it.

Juliet.
　　Give me, give me! O, tell not me of fear!

Friar.
　　Hold! Get you gone, be strong and prosperous
　　In this resolve. I'll send a friar with speed
　　To Mantua, with my letters to thy lord.

Juliet.
125　Love give me strength, and strength shall help afford.
　　Farewell, dear father. 　　　　　　[*Exit with* FRIAR.]

Scene 2. *A hall in Capulet's house.*

Enter father CAPULET, LADY CAPULET, NURSE, *and* SERVINGMEN, *two or three.*

Capulet.
　　So many guests invite as here are writ.
　　　　　　　　　　　　　　[*Exit a* SERVINGMAN.]
　　Sirrah, go hire me twenty cunning° cooks.

Servingman. You shall have none ill, sir; for I'll try if they can lick their fingers.

Capulet.
5　　How canst thou try them so?

Servingman. Marry, sir, 'tis an ill cook that cannot lick his own fingers. Therefore he that cannot lick his fingers goes not with me.

Capulet. Go, be gone. 　　　　　　[*Exit* SERVINGMAN.]
10　We shall be much unfurnished° for this time.
　　What, is my daughter gone to Friar Laurence?

Nurse. Ay, forsooth.

---

113. against: before.
114. drift: intentions.

117. *How is Romeo to be told of this plan? When is he to watch Juliet wake and take her to Mantua?*

119. toy: whim.

122. *What does the friar give Juliet as she exits? What exactly is his plan?*

Staging the Play
126. *In some productions the friar holds Juliet back for just a moment and silently blesses her. Why would this make us more anxious about the outcome of his plan?*

Staging the Play
1. *Capulet is sending his servant off to invite guests to Juliet's wedding. How does this comic and busy domestic scene contrast with the previous one?*

2. cunning: skillful.

10. unfurnished: unsupplied (without food).

READING SKILLS REVIEW

Synonyms. An important step in writing a paraphrase is to replace difficult words with simple ones. To do so, students must define unfamiliar words and find appropriate synonyms for them. The synonyms should convey the same shade of meaning as the original word. To find synonyms, students can look words up in a dictionary or a thesaurus.

Activity. Have students use a college dictionary and a thesaurus to find appropriate synonyms for the following words, as they are used on pp. 879–880: *stark* (l. 103), *rouse* (l. 108), *borne* (l. 111), *vault* (l. 111), *kindred* (l. 112), *drift* (l. 114), *hither* (l. 115), *inconstant* (l. 119), *abate* (l. 120), *valor* (l. 120), and *resolve* (l. 123).

Capulet.
    Well, he may chance to do some good on her.
    A peevish self-willed harlotry it is.

[*Enter* JULIET.]

Nurse.
15   See where she comes from shrift with merry look.
Capulet.
    How now, my headstrong? Where have you been
        gadding?
Juliet.
    Where I have learnt me to repent the sin
    Of disobedient opposition
    To you and your behests, and am enjoined
20   By holy Laurence to fall prostrate here
    To beg your pardon. Pardon, I beseech you!
    Henceforward I am ever ruled by you.
Capulet.
    Send for the county. Go tell him of this.
    I'll have this knot knit up tomorrow morning.
Juliet.
25   I met the youthful lord at Laurence' cell
    And gave him what becomèd° love I might,
    Not stepping o'er the bounds of modesty.
Capulet.
    Why, I am glad on't. This is well. Stand up.
    This is as't should be. Let me see the county.
30   Ay, marry, go, I say, and fetch him hither.
    Now, afore God, this reverend holy friar,
    All our whole city is much bound to him.
Juliet.
    Nurse, will you go with me into my closet,°
    To help me sort such needful ornaments
35   As you think fit to furnish me tomorrow?
Lady Capulet.
    No, not till Thursday. There is time enough.
Capulet.
    Go, nurse, go with her. We'll to church tomorrow.
                    [*Exeunt* JULIET *and* NURSE.]
Lady Capulet.
    We shall be short in our provision.
    'Tis now near night.
Capulet.   Tush, I will stir about,
40   And all things shall be well, I warrant thee, wife.

The Tragedy of Romeo and Juliet, Act IV, Scene 2   **881**

? **14.** Harlotry *means a "good-for-nothing," a prostitute. Whom is Capulet referring to as "it"?*

? **15.** *Do you think Juliet really has a "merry look," or is the nurse trying to cover up?*

Ⓐ
? **24.** *Why do you think Capulet pushes the marriage up to Wednesday?*

26. becomèd: proper or becoming.

? **28.** *According to this speech, what has Juliet been doing since she first addressed her father?*

33. closet: private room.

Ⓑ

? **37.** *The wedding has been changed to take place on Wednesday. Lady Capulet tries to change her husband's mind, perhaps in consideration of Juliet, but she is not successful. How will this affect the timing of the friar's plans?*

DIRECT TEACHING

Ⓐ Literary Focus

Falling action. Lord Capulet's haste to have Juliet married increases our feeling of doom and locks the characters further into disaster and a tragic end. Whatever chance Friar Laurence's plan initially had of succeeding is now diminished.

Ⓑ Literary Focus

Dramatic irony. Remind students that we know, but the nurse does not realize, that the clothing to be selected is not for the wedding, but for Juliet's funeral.

Responses to Margin Questions

Line 14. Capulet talks of Juliet, his daughter, as "it," although his tone is no longer enraged. The word *it* might also be a reference to a condition, curse, or disposition from which Capulet thinks Juliet suffers.

Line 15. Juliet could have a merry look, since she now has a plan and expects to be with Romeo soon. However, the nurse may be exaggerating to ease Juliet's encounter with her father.

Line 24. Students may suggest that Lord Capulet shows haste in most of his actions, that Juliet's apology moves him to have a celebration as soon as possible, or that he may fear she will change her mind again.

Line 28. She has been kneeling in a begging position, and he tells her to "Stand up" (l. 28).

Line 37. The new date provides less time to alert Romeo and bring him back to Verona. Juliet will now be buried on Wednesday and awaken in the tomb on Thursday night rather than Friday.

DIFFERENTIATING INSTRUCTION

Learners Having Difficulty
Ask students to monitor their reading strategies by writing questions for each scene as they read Act IV. Demonstrate this for students by writing on the chalkboard questions about character motivation elicited by Scene 1. Examples include "What true feelings does Paris seem to have for Juliet?" "What would Friar Laurence's course of action have been

if Juliet had not insisted on an escape plan?" and "How sincerely does Juliet seem to have taken her wedding vows?" After the conclusion of each scene, invite volunteers to read their questions, and use student notes to generate discussion.

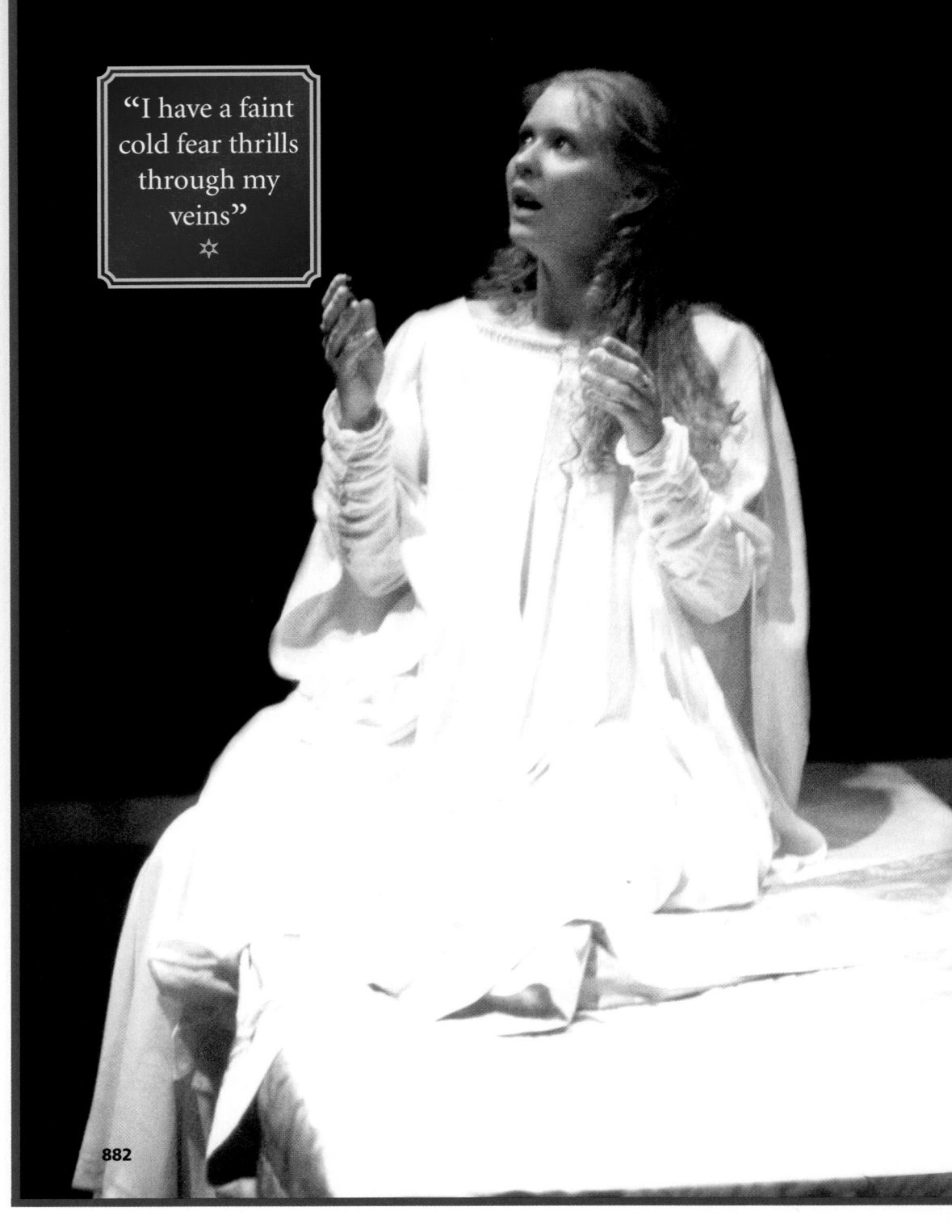

"I have a faint cold fear thrills through my veins"

✧

882

Go thou to Juliet, help to deck up her.
I'll not to bed tonight; let me alone.
I'll play the housewife for this once. What, ho!
They are all forth; well, I will walk myself
45   To County Paris, to prepare up him
Against tomorrow. My heart is wondrous light,
Since this same wayward girl is so reclaimed.

[*Exit with* LADY CAPULET.]

Scene 3. *Juliet's chamber.*

Enter JULIET *and* NURSE.

Juliet.
Ay, those attires are best; but, gentle nurse,
I pray thee leave me to myself tonight;
For I have need of many orisons°
To move the heavens to smile upon my state,
5   Which, well thou knowest, is cross and full of sin.

[*Enter* LADY CAPULET.]

Lady Capulet.
What, are you busy, ho? Need you my help?

Juliet.
No, madam; we have culled such necessaries
As are behoveful° for our state° tomorrow.
So please you, let me now be left alone,
10   And let the nurse this night sit up with you;
For I am sure you have your hands full all
In this so sudden business.

Lady Capulet.   Good night.
Get thee to bed, and rest; for thou hast need.

[*Exeunt* LADY CAPULET *and* NURSE.]

Juliet.
Farewell! God knows when we shall meet again.
15   I have a faint cold fear thrills through my veins
That almost freezes up the heat of life.
I'll call them back again to comfort me.
Nurse!—What should she do here?
My dismal scene I needs must act alone.
20   Come, vial.
What if this mixture do not work at all?
Shall I be married then tomorrow morning?
No, no! This shall forbid it. Lie thou there.

[*Lays down a dagger.*]

❓ 47. *Lord Capulet realizes all the servants are gone. What action is he involved in during this speech? What is his new mood?*

3. orisons (ôr′i·zənz): prayers.

❓ Staging the Play
6. *In some productions, Lady Capulet is played here as loving and gentle with Juliet, perhaps suggesting that she is uneasy about her daughter's change of heart. What emotions should her next speech show?*

8. behoveful: suitable. **state:** ceremonies.

❓ Staging the Play
14. *Here is a fine example of the Shakespearean* **soliloquy,** *where a character who is poised on the edge of action thinks over its pros and cons. What are the fears and doubts that Juliet must consider before taking the potion?*
Juliet is not standing still as she speaks these lines. What do you think she is doing?

The Tragedy of Romeo and Juliet, Act IV, Scene 3   **883**

DIRECT TEACHING

Response to Margin Question
Line 47. Capulet first seeks the servants. He may then prepare to go to Paris's house. He is happy and relieved.

Summary ⬌ *at grade level*

Act IV, Scene 3
The nurse has helped Juliet prepare for her wedding. At Juliet's request, both the nurse and her mother leave her alone for the night. About to take the sleeping potion, Juliet expresses her last-minute doubts in a soliloquy. What if the potion does not work? What if the friar, fearing reprisal for marrying Romeo and Juliet, has actually given her poison? What if she should wake in the tomb before Romeo comes to get her? She especially dreads this last possibility, fearing that she will go mad or that Tybalt's ghost will appear. She recovers her courage and swallows the potion, saying that she drinks to Romeo.

Responses to Margin Questions
Line 6. Most students will probably say that Lady Capulet speaks to Juliet with tenderness, love, and concern.
Line 14. Juliet is afraid the potion will not work. She also momentarily fears that the friar has given her poison because he would be "dishonored" by performing a second, false marriage. She fears awakening in the burial vault before Romeo arrives, knowing the foul air could suffocate her. Worst of all, she fears going mad amid the horrors she would encounter there: skeletons, rotting corpses, and loathsome smells.

Juliet brings the vial to her lips and then puts it away; she finds the dagger and places it by her bed; she may pace her room as she describes her visions.

A Reading Skills

Paraphrasing and context clues.
Have students work in small groups to paraphrase the fears that Juliet expresses here. You might start them off with the following para-phrase of ll. 30–54: "What if I wake up alone in the tomb before Romeo comes to get me? There's not much air in the tomb, so I might die of asphyxiation before Romeo arrives. Or if I live, what if I find the tomb—filled with my ancestors' bones, Tybalt's bloody body, ghosts, bad smells, and awful sounds—so scary it drives me mad, and I kill myself with an ancestor's bone?"

B Content-Area Connections

Culture: Superstitions
❷ Elizabethans tended to be deeply superstitious and believed that ghosts often returned to earth on a specific mission: to warn the living about the future or to avenge their own deaths. Ghosts are dramatically effective and play a prominent role in many of Shakespeare's plays, including *Hamlet, Macbeth,* and *Richard III.* Often the ghosts are visi-ble only to the specific person they are haunting. Why might Juliet fear a visit from Tybalt's ghost? [He might haunt her for betraying her family and loving his murderer.]

Responses to Margin Questions

Line 29. Juliet believes that Friar Laurence is a holy man who always tries to act for the best. But her momentary suspicion in ll. 24–27 suggests that he may be somewhat cowardly: He may fear the censure of the families, both for performing a secret marriage and for seeming to condone bigamy.

Line 54. Allow students who draw illustrations to display their work.

What if it be a poison which the friar
25 Subtly hath ministered to have me dead,
Lest in this marriage he should be dishonored
Because he married me before to Romeo?
I fear it is; and yet methinks it should not,
For he hath still been tried° a holy man.
30 How if, when I am laid into the tomb,
I wake before the time that Romeo
Come to redeem me? There's a fearful point!
Shall I not then be stifled in the vault,
To whose foul mouth no healthsome air breathes in,
35 And there die strangled ere my Romeo comes?
Or, if I live, is it not very like
The horrible conceit of death and night,
Together with the terror of the place—
A As in a vault, an ancient receptacle
40 Where for this many hundred years the bones

> **"Romeo, Romeo, Romeo,
> I drink to thee."**

Of all my buried ancestors are packed;
Where bloody Tybalt, yet but green in earth,°
Lies fest'ring in his shroud; where, as they say,
At some hours in the night spirits resort—
45 Alack, alack, is it not like that I,
So early waking—what with loathsome smells,
And shrieks like mandrakes° torn out of the earth,
That living mortals, hearing them, run mad—
I, if I wake, shall I not be distraught,
50 Environèd with all these hideous fears,
And madly play with my forefathers' joints,
And pluck the mangled Tybalt from his shroud,
And, in this rage, with some great kinsman's bone
As with a club dash out my desp'rate brains?
55 O, look! Methinks I see my cousin's ghost
B Seeking out Romeo, that did spit his body
Upon a rapier's point. Stay, Tybalt, stay!
Romeo, Romeo, Romeo, I drink to thee.

[*She falls upon her bed within the curtains.*]

29. still been tried: always been proved.

❓ **29.** *Audiences always wonder why the friar has not simply told the families of Romeo and Juliet's secret wedding rather than involve them in such a dangerous plan. How does Juliet explain the friar's actions?*

42. green in earth: newly buried.

47. mandrakes: plants resembling the human body, which were said to grow beneath the gallows and to scream when torn up.

❓ **54.** *Draw the mental picture you have of the tomb from Juliet's description of it.*

CONTENT-AREA CONNECTIONS

Science: Botany
The European variety of mandrake, *Mandragora officinarum,* has been used in Mediterranean countries for thousands of years. This poisonous plant was used to make anesthetics for surgery and sleeping potions. It is possible that it might have been an ingredi-ent in the potion that Juliet drinks. (That Shakespeare has Juliet refer to it here, not for its medicinal properties but for its association with the gallows, is uncanny.)

Paired activity. Suggest that students work in pairs to research information on the American variety of mandrake, sometimes called May apple. How is it similar to and different from the European variety?

Scene 4. *A hall in Capulet's house.*

Enter LADY CAPULET *and* NURSE.

Lady Capulet.
    Hold, take these keys and fetch more spices, nurse.
Nurse.
    They call for dates and quinces in the pastry.

[*Enter old* CAPULET.]

Capulet.
    Come, stir, stir, stir! The second cock hath crowed,
    The curfew bell hath rung, 'tis three o'clock.
5   Look to the baked meats, good Angelica;
    Spare not for cost.
Nurse.   Go, you cotquean,° go,
    Get you to bed! Faith, you'll be sick tomorrow
    For this night's watching.
Capulet.
    No, not a whit. What, I have watched ere now
10   All night for lesser cause, and ne'er been sick.
Lady Capulet.
    Ay, you have been a mouse hunt° in your time;
    But I will watch you from such watching now.

                  [*Exeunt* LADY CAPULET *and* NURSE.]

Capulet.
    A jealous hood,° a jealous hood!

[*Enter three or four* FELLOWS *with spits and logs and baskets.*]

                  Now, fellow,
    What is there?
First Fellow.
15   Things for the cook, sir; but I know not what.
Capulet.
    Make haste, make haste.   [*Exit* FIRST FELLOW.]
                  Sirrah, fetch drier logs.
    Call Peter; he will show thee where they are.
Second Fellow.
    I have a head, sir, that will find out logs°
    And never trouble Peter for the matter.
Capulet.
20   Mass,° and well said; a merry whoreson, ha!

---

1. *How does this peaceful domestic scene contrast with what has just happened? What is everyone preparing for?*

5. *Angelica is the nurse's name. How does Lord Capulet treat her now, as opposed to how he treated her in Act III, Scene 5? What humor does the nurse add to this scene?*

6. cotquean (kät′kwēn′): old woman (a man who acts like an old woman).

11. mouse hunt: woman chaser or night prowler.

12. *What is Lady Capulet's tone here?*

13. hood: female.

18. I . . . logs: in other words, "I have a wooden head."

20. Mass: mild oath, "by the Mass."

Act IV, Scene 4

Lord and Lady Capulet, amid much jollity, oversee the wedding preparations. Hearing Count Paris approaching, accompanied by musicians, Lord Capulet sends the nurse to waken Juliet.

DIRECT TEACHING

C Reading Skills

? Connecting with the text. What emotions are generally associated with the day of a family member's wedding? [Possible responses: excitement about the festivities and ceremony; stress due to the responsibilities of planning and coordinating events.]

Responses to Margin Questions

Line 1. The Capulets and their servants are making jokes and busily preparing for the wedding; meanwhile, the bride-to-be lies in her room in a deathlike state, having risked her life to avoid what her family celebrates.

Line 5. Here Lord Capulet calls the nurse "good Angelica" and treats her with affection and courtesy. In Act III, Scene 5, when Juliet announced that she would not marry Paris, Lord Capulet treated the nurse with harshness, disrespect, and anger. In this scene the nurse adds to the humor by fondly making fun of her master.

Line 12. Lady Capulet is teasingly affectionate here, poking fun at her husband about the women he used to chase.

❓ Characteristics of drama: Suspense. Even though we know what the nurse will find when she goes to waken Juliet, we still feel a sense of suspense at this point. **Why?** [Possible responses: We wonder how the nurse will realize that Juliet is "dead," how she will react when she finds out, how she will break the news to the family, and how Juliet's parents and Paris will react.]

Responses to Margin Questions

Line 21. Capulet is probably tasting food, checking wine flasks, and generally getting in everyone's way.
Line 23. The audience knows that Juliet will not be Paris's bride and that the wedding music will give way to a funeral dirge.

Summary ↔ *at grade level*

Act IV, Scene 5

The nurse goes to wake Juliet but, finding her unresponsive, believes that she is dead. She cries out in alarm, and Juliet's parents rush in and lament the death of their daughter. Friar Laurence and Paris enter and are told the bad news. The friar, who knows that Juliet is not really dead, attempts to comfort the others and tells them that they must prepare Juliet for burial in the family tomb. The scene ends with a comic interlude as Peter and the musicians exchange punning jests.

Response to Margin Question

Line 1. In l. 14, the nurse discovers that Juliet is "dead."

Thou shalt be loggerhead.°
　　　　　　　　　[*Exit* SECOND FELLOW, *with the others.*]
　　　　　　　　　Good faith, 'tis day.
The county will be here with music straight,
For so he said he would. (*Play music offstage.*)
　　　　　　　　　I hear him near.
Nurse! Wife! What, ho! What, nurse, I say!

[*Enter* NURSE.]

25　Go waken Juliet; go and trim her up.
　　I'll go and chat with Paris. Hie, make haste,
　　Make haste! The bridegroom he is come already:
　　Make haste, I say.　　　　　　　　　[*Exit.*]

Scene 5. *Juliet's chamber.*

Nurse.
　Mistress! What, mistress! Juliet! Fast,° I warrant her, she.
　Why, lamb! Why, lady! Fie, you slugabed.
　Why, love, I say! Madam; sweetheart! Why, bride!
　What, not a word? You take your pennyworths° now;
5　Sleep for a week; for the next night, I warrant,
　The County Paris hath set up his rest°
　That you shall rest but little. God forgive me!
　Marry, and amen. How sound is she asleep!
　I needs must wake her. Madam, madam, madam!
10　Ay, let the county take you in your bed;
　He'll fright you up, i' faith. Will it not be?

[*Draws aside the curtains.*]

　What, dressed, and in your clothes, and down again?
　I must needs wake you. Lady! Lady! Lady!
　Alas, alas! Help, help! My lady's dead!
15　O weraday that ever I was born!
　Some aqua vitae, ho! My lord! My lady!

[*Enter* LADY CAPULET.]

Lady Capulet.
　What noise is here?
Nurse.　　　　　　　O lamentable day!
Lady Capulet.
　What is the matter?

---

21. **loggerhead:** blockhead.
❓ Staging the Play
21. *Capulet fusses around and has his nose in everything. What actions do you imagine the old man is involved in, in this scene?*

23. *The music is bridal music, for the wedding. What **irony** would the audience sense on hearing this music and knowing what has happened to Juliet?*

1. **Fast:** fast asleep.
❓ Staging the Play
1. *As the nurse speaks to Juliet and to herself, she is busy arranging clothes, opening windows, and doing things around the room. In what line here does she touch Juliet and discover she is cold?*

4. **pennyworths:** small naps.
6. **set up his rest:** become firmly resolved.

CONTENT-AREA CONNECTIONS

Theater: Staging Shakespeare
Writing in *Shakespeare Bulletin,* critic Justin Shaltz praised the staging of this scene in a 1994 production by the Illinois Shakespeare Festival, directed by Patrick O'Gara: "The portrayal of Juliet's liberation from her family and the feud—through her love for Romeo— is the most memorable sequence of the production. When she is found 'dead,' the Capulets lift her from her bed, but, once they do, Juliet stands on her own and dances slowly away from them within a spotlight. The men pantomime carrying her corpse away, her body bound, while Juliet dances across the stage, her spirit free."

Nurse.   Look, look! O heavy day!

Lady Capulet.

    O me, O me! My child, my only life!

20   Revive, look up, or I will die with thee!

    Help, help! Call help.

[*Enter* CAPULET.]

Capulet.

    For shame, bring Juliet forth; her lord is come.

Nurse.

    She's dead, deceased; she's dead, alack the day!

Lady Capulet.

    Alack the day, she's dead, she's dead, she's dead!

B

Capulet.

25   Ha! Let me see her. Out alas! She's cold,

    Her blood is settled, and her joints are stiff;

    Life and these lips have long been separated.

    Death lies on her like an untimely frost

    Upon the sweetest flower of all the field.

Nurse.

    O lamentable day!

30 **Lady Capulet.**   O woeful time!

Capulet.

    Death, that hath ta'en her hence to make me wail,

    Ties up my tongue and will not let me speak.

[*Enter* FRIAR LAURENCE *and* PARIS, *with* MUSICIANS.]

Friar.

    Come, is the bride ready to go to church?

Capulet.

    Ready to go, but never to return.

C

35   O son, the night before thy wedding day

    Hath Death lain with thy wife. There she lies,

    Flower as she was, deflowerèd by him.

    Death is my son-in-law, Death is my heir;

    My daughter he hath wedded. I will die

40   And leave him all. Life, living, all is Death's.

D

Paris.

    Have I thought, love, to see this morning's face,

    And doth it give me such a sight as this?

Lady Capulet.

    Accursed, unhappy, wretched, hateful day!

    Most miserable hour that e'er time saw

? **Staging the Play**

29. *What actions are taking place onstage as the three actors now find Juliet "dead"?*

The Tragedy of Romeo and Juliet, Act IV, Scene 5   **887**

DIRECT TEACHING

B **Reading Skills**

? **Drawing conclusions.** Why does Lady Capulet repeat herself? [Possible responses: She cannot believe what she has heard; she is in shock over the news.]

C **Literary Focus**

? **Dramatic irony.** What do we know about Friar Laurence that the other characters do not? [Friar Laurence knows Juliet is not ready to go to church as a bride because he is the one who gave her the potion; he is just pretending he doesn't know about Juliet's state.]

D **Literary Focus**

? **Figurative language: Personification.** How does Capulet personify death? [Death is personified as a greedy suitor, who has seized Juliet away from Paris, becoming her husband and Capulet's son-in-law.]

Response to Margin Question

Line 29. Lord Capulet is touching Juliet, checking to see if she is really dead. The other actors may be expressing their grief physically by weeping and gesturing, for example.

DIFFERENTIATING INSTRUCTION

Advanced Learners

Enrichment. Share with students the review in Content-Area Connections on p. 886 about the staging of this scene, and have students evaluate the idea of having Juliet's spirit dance while her family believes her to be dead. Invite students interested in dance to choreograph a dance for Juliet's spirit and perform it for their classmates.

A Vocabulary Development

Synonyms. Have students search these speeches to find as many synonyms as they can for the adjective *sad*. ["unhappy," "wretched," "miserable," "woeful," "lamentable," "black"]

B Reading Skills

? Comparing and contrasting. How do these lines contrast with Lord Capulet's earlier threats to dismiss Juliet from his household? [Possible responses: He is filled with grief now rather than anger; he realizes that much of his own happiness was built on his daughter's joy; instead of calling her insulting names, he now calls her "My soul" and "my child."]

Responses to Margin Questions

Line 49. Chief among the lines that indicate Lord Capulet's love for Juliet are ll. 28–29 and 62–64. Lady Capulet's love and grief are evident in ll. 43–48.

Friar Laurence, who could comfort them with the truth, remains silent.

Line 58. Students may suggest extreme grief or a sudden illness. The mourners simply personify death as a villain who has taken Juliet.

Line 64. Because the lines are so repetitive, so exaggerated, and so dependent on apostrophe (addressing things that are not there), they may seem superficial. In addition, the Capulets and Paris concentrate on how cruel death has been to them rather than concentrating on Juliet.

Line 65. Friar Laurence offers the consolation that Juliet is now in heaven: "And all the better is it for the maid" (l. 68). He rebukes the adults for their weeping and lack of faith: "O, in this love, you love your child so ill / That you run mad, seeing that she is well" (ll. 75–76).

---

45 In lasting labor of his pilgrimage!
    But one, poor one, one poor and loving child,
    But one thing to rejoice and solace in,
    And cruel Death hath catched it from my sight.

Nurse.
    O woe! O woeful, woeful, woeful day!
50 Most lamentable day, most woeful day
    That ever ever I did yet behold!
    O day, O day, O day! O hateful day!
    Never was seen so black a day as this.
    O woeful day! O woeful day!

Paris.
55 Beguiled, divorcèd, wrongèd, spited, slain!
    Most detestable Death, by thee beguiled,
    By cruel, cruel thee quite overthrown.
    O love! O life!—not life, but love in death!

Capulet.
    Despised, distressèd, hated, martyred, killed!
60 Uncomfortable time, why cam'st thou now
    To murder, murder our solemnity?
    O child, O child! My soul, and not my child!
    Dead art thou—alack, my child is dead,
    And with my child my joys are burièd!

Friar.
65 Peace, ho, for shame! Confusion's cure lives not
    In these confusions. Heaven and yourself
    Had part in this fair maid—now heaven hath all,
    And all the better is it for the maid.
    Your part in her you could not keep from death,
70 But heaven keeps his part in eternal life.
    The most you sought was her promotion,
    For 'twas your heaven she should be advanced;
    And weep ye now, seeing she is advanced
    Above the clouds, as high as heaven itself?
75 O, in this love, you love your child so ill
    That you run mad, seeing that she is well.°
    She's not well married that lives married long,
    But she's best married that dies married young.
    Dry up your tears and stick your rosemary°
80 On this fair corse, and, as the custom is,
    And in her best array bear her to church;
    For though fond nature° bids us all lament,

? 48. *Here again, as with Juliet's bemoaning Romeo's supposed death in an earlier scene, we have Lord and Lady Capulet and the nurse expressing anguish when we, the audience, know that Juliet is not dead. We listen to them, but we are not moved in the way they are. What words of the Capulets here suggest a loving concern for Juliet that seemed to be missing from earlier scenes? Which character enters and plays dumb about the whole situation?*

? 58. *In your opinion, what might the nurse, Paris, and the Capulets think caused Juliet's death?*

? 64. *These expressions of grief are by now sounding mechanical and repetitive. Shakespeare might have written them this way to prevent grief at a false death from gaining our sympathy. How could these lines of the parents, of the nurse, and of Paris also suggest that the speakers' feelings might not be very deep?*

? 65. *The friar, of course, knows that Juliet is drugged, not dead. His words here suggest that there has been great confusion onstage. What consolation does he offer, and what sharp rebuke does he give the adults?*

76. well: that is, she is in heaven.

79. rosemary: herb that stands for remembrance.

82. fond nature: foolish human nature.

"Alack, my child is dead, And with my child my joys are burièd!"
✧

889

A Literary Focus

Falling action. Although Juliet is not really dead, Capulet's words make the audience feel a growing sense of doom about the play's outcome.

B Literary Focus

? Interactions between characters. What motive might Friar Laurence have in speaking these two lines? [Possible response: to suggest to the family that the loss of their daughter might be punishment for the sin of feuding or for forcing Juliet to marry Paris.]

C English-Language Learners

Musical terms. These students may not recognize the words *re* (pronounced "ray") and *fa* (pronounced "fah"), the second and fourth notes of the European eight-tone scale. Also, the word *crochet* is the word used in British English for a quarter note (in musical notation, a note that is one-quarter in value of a whole note).

Responses to Margin Questions

Line 83. If the Capulets have faith, they must conclude that Juliet is in heaven, happier than she was in her life.

Line 90. Responses may vary. Students might suggest that because Juliet's father thinks of his preparations for the wedding festivities, he might be considered self-centered, although not necessarily selfish, for he is sad and grieving. However, he expresses no guilt.

Line 98. The nurse is referring to the event of Juliet's death.

Yet nature's tears are reason's merriment.
Capulet.
All things that we ordainèd festival
85   Turn from their office to black funeral—
A   Our instruments to melancholy bells,
   Our wedding cheer to a sad burial feast;
   Our solemn hymns to sullen dirges change;
   Our bridal flowers serve for a buried corse;
90   And all things change them to the contrary.
Friar.
   Sir, go you in; and, madam, go with him;
   And go, Sir Paris. Everyone prepare
   To follow this fair corse unto her grave.
B   The heavens do lower° upon you for some ill;
95   Move them no more by crossing their high will.

[*Exeunt, casting rosemary on her and shutting the curtains. The* NURSE *and* MUSICIANS *remain.*]

First Musician.
   Faith, we may put up our pipes and be gone.
Nurse.
   Honest good fellows, ah, put up, put up!
   For well you know this is a pitiful case.   [*Exit.*]
First Musician.
   Ay, by my troth, the case may be amended.

[*Enter* PETER.]

100 **Peter.** Musicians, O, musicians, "Heart's ease," "Heart's ease"! O, and you will have me live, play "Heart's ease."
First Musician. Why "Heart's ease"?
Peter. O, musicians, because my heart itself plays "My heart is full." O, play me some merry dump° to comfort me.
105 **First Musician.** Not a dump we! 'Tis no time to play now.
Peter. You will not then?
First Musician. No.
Peter. I will then give it you soundly.
First Musician. What will you give us?
110 **Peter.** No money, on my faith, but the gleek.° I will give you° the minstrel.
First Musician. Then will I give you the serving-creature.
C **Peter.** Then will I lay the serving-creature's dagger on your pate. I will carry° no crotchets. I'll re you, I'll fa you. Do
115   you note me?

83. *Why does the friar say that reason tells us to be merry about death?*

90. *Does Capulet express any guilt? Is he still self-centered?*

94. lower: frown.

98. *These are the nurse's last lines in the play. True to her character, she jokes as she leaves, though she might do this to cover her grief. The musicians are talking about the cases for their instruments. What "case" is the nurse referring to?*

104. dump: sad tune.

110. gleek: jeer or insult.
111. give you: call you (to be called a minstrel was an insult to a musician).

114. carry: endure.

First Musician. And you re us and fa us, you note us.

Second Musician. Pray you put up your dagger, and put out your wit. Then have at you with my wit!

Peter. I will dry-beat° you with an iron wit, and put up my
120 iron dagger. Answer me like men.
"When griping grief the heart doth wound,
And doleful dumps the mind oppress,
Then music with her silver sound"—
Why "silver sound"? Why "music with her silver sound"?
125 What say you, Simon Catling?°

First Musician. Marry, sir, because silver hath a sweet sound.

Peter. Pretty! What say you, Hugh Rebeck?°

Second Musician. I say "silver sound" because musicians sound for silver.

130 **Peter.** Pretty too! What say you, James Soundpost?°

Third Musician. Faith, I know not what to say.

Peter. O, I cry you mercy,° you are the singer. I will say for you. It is "music with her silver sound" because musicians have no gold for sounding.°
135 "Then music with her silver sound
With speedy help doth lend redress." [*Exit.*]

First Musician. What a pestilent knave is this same!

Second Musician. Hang him, Jack! Come, we'll in here, tarry for the mourners, and stay dinner.

[*Exit with others.*]

---

119. **dry-beat:** beat soundly.

125. **Catling:** lute string.

127. **Rebeck:** fiddle.

130. **Soundpost:** peg on violinlike instrument.

132. **cry you mercy:** beg your pardon.

134. **no gold for sounding:** no money to jingle in their pockets.

? Staging the Play
139. *Peter, who was always bossed about by the nurse, here has grabbed at the chance to boss the musicians, who are a step below him socially. What actions do you imagine during this exchange of insults? (Note that they all want to stay for dinner.) How does this scene provide relief for us and remind us that ordinary life goes on amid tragedy?*

D Reading Skills

? Interpreting. Are the musicians becoming angry with Peter, or are their insults meant in good humor? [Possible responses: The musicians are in good humor, planning on eating the food that was meant for the wedding feast; the musicians are enjoying a battle of wits with Peter.]

Response to Margin Question

Line 139. Peter may be threatening to strike the musicians if they don't play, or he may be giving a mock lecture.

This comic scene momentarily lightens the tragic mood for the audience. By their joking, Peter and the musicians prove that their own lives continue.

GUIDED PRACTICE

Monitoring students' progress. Guide students in answering the following questions.

Short Answer

1. What is the reason for Paris's visit to Friar Laurence in Scene 1? [Paris wants to make wedding arrangements.]

2. What is Friar Laurence's plan to help Juliet with her dilemma? [The friar gives Juliet a potion that will make her appear to be dead, and while she lies in a cemetery vault, he will get a message to Romeo that he should be there when she awakens.]

3. What event is the Capulet household preparing for at the beginning of Scene 2? [the wedding of Juliet to Paris]

4. What are Juliet's fears as she prepares to drink the potion? [that the mixture will not work; that the friar is tricking her; that she will awaken before Romeo finds her; and that the terrors in the tomb will make her go mad]

The film version of *Romeo and Juliet* that students are most likely to be familiar with is Australian director Baz Luhrmann's 1996 production, starring Claire Danes and Leonardo DiCaprio. Set in present-day Florida, this version features a rock music soundtrack, gang members speaking the original Elizabethan dialogue, and the lovers falling into a swimming pool. Invite students who have seen this film to share their responses to it and to compare their responses with those of reviewers at the time the film came out. Students can use the Internet to research movie reviews.

DIRECT TEACHING

A Literary Focus
Identifying and analyzing recurring themes. The fact that more than sixty film versions of *Hamlet* have been made in the last one hundred years is a testament to the ongoing relevance of the themes that Shakespeare addresses in his work. Ask students to identify contemporary films, television shows, or works of literature that share common themes with *Romeo and Juliet* or another of Shakespeare's plays.

B Literary Focus
❓ Analyzing the relevance of setting. In addition to debating the merit of film versions of Shakespeare's play, critics have also debated the merits of producing versions of Shakespeare's plays that are set in contemporary society. How might setting Shakespeare's plays in contemporary society affect how the plays are interpreted? [Possible response: More people might be able to understand the themes if they are presented in familiar language and in a familiar setting; trying to make Shakespeare's plays relevant to contemporary society might obscure the themes that Shakespeare intended to address.]

A CLOSER LOOK
Shakespeare in the Video Store

A Film and television have brought Shakespeare's plays to millions of viewers and confirmed the playwright's position as a world treasure. *Hamlet* has been by far the most popular of his plays, with more than sixty film versions of all or part of the tragedy (as of 2002). The earliest *Hamlet* movie was made in Paris in 1900. This black-and-white silent film had an interesting reversal of the custom of Shakespeare's time, in which boys took women's roles onstage: The role of Hamlet was played by the great Sarah Bernhardt (1844–1923).

For almost a century, film productions of Shakespeare have showcased some of our most distinguished actors: Laurence Olivier, Vanessa Redgrave, Richard Burton, John Gielgud, Katharine Hepburn, Mel Gibson, Glenn Close, Denzel Washington. Between 1978 and 1985, all of Shakespeare's plays were filmed for television. Now Shakespeare is accessible as never before: A performance of one of his plays is as close as your local library or video store.

B Critics have pointed out drawbacks in the performance of these plays on screen. For example, they argue that film controls our perceptions of the plays and deprives us of the tension we feel when seeing the plays live, in a theater. Film and television productions of Shakespearean comedy are at another disadvantage, since the actors can't respond to the feedback of a live audience. Such feedback is unpredictable, but actors say it's critical in comedy.

Laurence Olivier plays the Danish prince in a 1948 film version of Shakespeare's *Hamlet*.

Katharine Hepburn portrays William Shakespeare's Juliet in a 1933 film.

Response and Analysis

Act IV

Reading Check

1. In Scene 1, what does Juliet threaten to do if the friar cannot help her?

2. What is the friar's plan for getting Romeo and Juliet together?

3. In Scene 2, another **complication** comes up. What change does Capulet make in the wedding plans?

4. What is the situation in the Capulet house at the end of Act IV?

Thinking Critically

5. Why is Juliet so willing to trust the friar? Do you think she is wise to follow his advice?

6. One of the pleasures of watching a play is knowing something that a character onstage does not know. Oddly enough, this experience of **dramatic irony** adds **suspense**. We wait anxiously to find out what will happen when the characters discover what we already know. Where do you sense dramatic irony in Scenes 2, 3, and 4?

7. What terrible trials does Juliet face in this act of the **tragedy**? How does she respond to these challenges?

Extending and Evaluating

8. Juliet's parents have plans for their daughter that make it seem impossible for the young couple to stay together. Does Shakespeare present the Capulets as villains? Does he help us see them as complex human beings? Explain your evaluation of these **characters**, using details from the play.

WRITING

Juliet's Thoughts

Write down Juliet's thoughts as you imagine them during this difficult time. (You could write as "I.") Write about her feelings toward her parents, Romeo, her nurse, Paris, and Friar Laurence. Let Juliet describe her feelings about the drug she is about to take and about her horror at being buried alive.

go.
hrw
.com

INTERNET
Projects and
Activities

Keyword: LE5 9-11

The Tragedy of Romeo and Juliet, Act IV   **893**

Literary Skills
Analyze characteristics of tragedy, including complication, turning point, and suspense.

Writing Skills
Write the thoughts of a character.

Response and Analysis

Thinking Critically

5. She is relying on the friar's reputation, holy vows, and affection for Romeo. Students may say Juliet is unwise to trust his abilities as a chemist.

6. Possible answers: *Scene 2*—Lord Capulet is joyful about the good that Friar Laurence has done for Juliet and feels grateful to him when, in fact, the friar has secretly wed Romeo and Juliet and is aiding Juliet in foiling the new wedding plans. *Scene 3*—Lady Capulet urges Juliet to go to bed, unaware that Juliet will not awaken in the morning. *Scene 4*—Everyone is happily preparing for the wedding, but the audience waits in suspense for what will happen when Juliet is found "dead."

7. Juliet must act without Romeo or the nurse, and she goes alone to the friar's cell to see if he can help her avoid the marriage to Paris. Also, she swallows her pride and avoids further confrontation with her parents by apologizing and pretending to agree to the marriage. Although she is afraid the drug could kill her, she risks taking it so that she might be reunited with Romeo.

Extending and Evaluating

8. Although Juliet's parents are unreasonable when she initially refuses to marry Paris, they do love their daughter. Early in the play, for example, Lord Capulet says Juliet should marry a man that she loves when she is ready, and Lady Capulet believes Paris will make a fine husband. When Juliet can't stop grieving, her parents feel that they know what's best for her and arrange the marriage to Paris. Students' feelings about Juliet's parents will vary. Some may not be able to forgive them for the way they treated Juliet in Act III.

Reading Check

1. She threatens to kill herself.

2. He offers Juliet a drug to induce a deathlike coma for forty-two hours. During that time, the friar will send a messenger to Mantua, calling Romeo back to Verona so that he can be with Juliet when she awakens in the burial vault.

3. He changes the wedding from Thursday to Wednesday.

4. Everyone is distraught and grieving over Juliet's apparent death.

Reading Skills

Paraphrasing and Context Clues

This feature focuses on two reading skills that are essential for understanding and appreciating a Shakespeare play: paraphrasing and using context clues. It includes a list of helpful suggestions for students to use when they paraphrase a passage from the play.

Practice

Possible Answers

1. She has been crying so much over Tybalt's death that I haven't talked to her about love. Someone who is grief-stricken doesn't want to think about love.

2. Please say something. I'll just die if you can't help me.

3. You will turn pale, your eyelids will close, and you will appear to be dead.

4. Oh, look! I think I see a vision of my dead cousin Tybalt. He is looking for Romeo because Romeo stabbed him with a rapier. Stop, Tybalt, stop!

ASSESSING

Assessment

■ *Holt Assessment: Literature, Reading, and Vocabulary*

RETEACHING

For a lesson reteaching analyzing dramatic literature, see **Reteaching,** p. 979A. For another selection to teach analyzing dramatic literature, see *The Holt Reader,* Collection 11.

Reading Skills

Paraphrasing and Context Clues

Paraphrasing means restating a text in your own words. A restatement, or paraphrase, simplifies a text, but it doesn't necessarily make it shorter. In fact, a paraphrase might be longer than the original passage, and of course it's never as interesting. Paraphrasing is a good way to check on your understanding of the original text. Here is a speech from Act IV of *Romeo and Juliet* and a paraphrase of the speech:

> **Paris.**
> My father Capulet will have it so,
> And I am nothing slow to slack his haste.
> —Scene I, lines 2–3

> **Paraphrase:** My father-in-law Capulet wants it like that, and I have no desire to slow him down.

A Checklist for Paraphrasing

- Be sure you understand the main idea of the text.
- Look up unfamiliar words in a good dictionary.
- Replace difficult words with simple ones.
- If a word has multiple meanings, be sure to use **context clues** to determine the meaning appropriate to the passage. (Remember: The meaning intended by Shakespeare may now be archaic.)
- Restate figures of speech in your own words, clarifying what's being compared to what.
- Try to reproduce the tone or mood of the text. If the text is satiric, your paraphrase should also be satiric.
- Be sure your paraphrase has accounted for all details in the original.

SKILLS FOCUS

Reading Skills
Paraphrase speeches.

The following speeches are from Act IV. Paraphrase each one. Be sure to compare your paraphrases with those of your classmates. It's almost certain that no two paraphrases will be alike.

1. **Paris** (*speaking about Juliet*).
   Immoderately she weeps for Tybalt's death,
   And therefore have I little talked of love;
   For Venus smiles not in a house of tears.
   —Scene I, lines 6–8

2. **Juliet** (*to the Friar*).
   Be not so long to speak. I long to die
   If what thou speak'st speak not of remedy.
   —Scene I, lines 66–67

3. **Friar Laurence** (*to Juliet*).
   The roses in thy lips and cheeks shall fade
   To wanny ashes, thy eyes' windows fall
   Like death when he shuts up the day of life . . . .
   —Scene I, lines 99–101

4. **Juliet** (*holding the poison*).
   O, look! Methinks I see my cousin's ghost
   Seeking out Romeo, that did spit his body
   Upon a rapier's point. Stay, Tybalt, stay!
   —Scene 3, lines 55–57

DIFFERENTIATING INSTRUCTION

Learners Having Difficulty

Ask students to paraphrase each of the following lines from Act IV. Answers will vary.

1. "Poor soul, thy face is much abused with tears." —Scene 1, l. 29 [Poor thing, your face is all swollen from crying.]

2. "It strains me past the compass of my wits." —Scene 1, l. 47 [It boggles my mind.]

3. "No warmth, no breath, shall testify thou livest." —Scene 1, l. 98 [You will be cold and breathless and appear to be dead.]

4. "What, I have watched ere now / All night for lesser cause, and ne'er been sick." —Scene 4, ll. 9–10 [Hey, I've stayed up all night before for less important things and never gotten sick.]

5. "The heavens do lower upon you for some ill." —Scene 5, l. 94 [God is punishing you for your sins.]

☆ ACT V ☆

Scene 1. *Mantua. A street.*

Enter ROMEO.

Romeo.

If I may trust the flattering truth of sleep,
My dreams presage° some joyful news at hand.
My bosom's lord° sits lightly in his throne,
And all this day an unaccustomed spirit

5   Lifts me above the ground with cheerful thoughts.
I dreamt my lady came and found me dead
(Strange dream that gives a dead man leave to think!)
And breathed such life with kisses in my lips
That I revived and was an emperor.

10   Ah me! How sweet is love itself possessed,
When but love's shadows° are so rich in joy!

[Enter Romeo's man BALTHASAR, *booted from riding.]*

News from Verona! How now, Balthasar?
Dost thou not bring me letters from the friar?
How doth my lady? Is my father well?

15   How fares my Juliet? That I ask again,
For nothing can be ill if she be well.

Balthasar.

Then she is well, and nothing can be ill.
Her body sleeps in Capel's monument,
And her immortal part with angels lives.

20   I saw her laid low in her kindred's vault
And presently took post° to tell it you.
O, pardon me for bringing these ill news,
Since you did leave it for my office,° sir.

Romeo.

Is it e'en so? Then I defy you, stars!

25   Thou knowest my lodging. Get me ink and paper
And hire post horses. I will hence tonight.

Balthasar.

I do beseech you, sir, have patience.
Your looks are pale and wild and do import
Some misadventure.

---

2. presage: foretell.
3. bosom's lord: heart.

11. shadows: dreams.

❓ Staging the Play
16. *Some actors playing Romeo reveal in this line that they suspect bad news. What, meanwhile, would Balthasar be doing?*

21. post: post horse (horse kept at an inn and rented by travelers).
23. office: duty.

❓ Staging the Play
23. *Balthasar must show that he dreads giving his master the tragic news. What do we know that Balthasar does not know?*

❓ Staging the Play
26. *In some productions, actors move away here or hide their faces in their hands. Romeo could address the stars or fate defiantly or tonelessly, to suggest defeat. What would you say is Romeo's tone here?*

❓ **28.** *What does Balthasar suggest Romeo looks like, even though Romeo pretends to be calm?*

Summary ⬌ *at grade level*

Act V, Scene I
Romeo's servant Balthasar arrives in Mantua with news that Juliet is dead. With no message from the friar, Romeo doesn't know the death is a hoax. In despair he buys poison from an apothecary and sets out for Juliet's grave.

DIRECT TEACHING

Ⓐ Literary Focus
Irony and foreshadowing.
Ironically Romeo has a premonition of good news at the moment a messenger arrives to tell him of Juliet's "death." Part of his dream, however, does foreshadow tragic events.

Ⓑ Literary Focus
Characteristics of tragedy.
Rather than mourn Juliet's death, Romeo is planning to be united with her in death. Although he sees this union in death as a triumph over fate, it is, for the audience, the heart of the tragedy.

Responses to Margin Questions

Line 16. Balthasar may be avoiding Romeo's gaze.

Line 23. Juliet is not dead.

Line 26. Some students will favor defiance, based on Romeo's vitality. Others will favor subdued defeat, citing the death of his dreams.

Line 28. Romeo looks "pale and wild," like a man distraught.

RESOURCES: READING

Differentiating Instruction
- *Holt Reading Solutions*
- *Supporting Instruction in Spanish*
- *Audio CD Library, Selections and Summaries in Spanish*

Assessment
- *Holt Assessment: Literature, Reading, and Vocabulary*

- *One-Stop Planner CD-ROM with ExamView Test Generator*
- *Holt Online Assessment*

Media
- *Visual Connections Videocassette Program*
- *Fine Art Transparencies*

A Reading Skills

? Drawing conclusions. Why might the apothecary be willing to sell the illegal poison to Romeo? [The apothecary is in desperate need of money, as Romeo's description of him makes clear.]

B Content-Area Connections

History: Units of Measure
The ducat was a gold coin of considerable value. A fluid dram was equal to one eighth of a fluid ounce. In England the word *dram* came to mean any small drink of alcohol.

Responses to Margin Questions

Line 31. Romeo is hoping for word that he may return to Verona.

Line 34. Romeo sets out to buy poison with which to kill himself. He plunges directly into action.

Line 57. Romeo might be walking toward or looking for the apothecary's house.

Romeo.   Tush, thou art deceived.
30   Leave me and do the thing I bid thee do.
      Hast thou no letters to me from the friar?
Balthasar.
      No, my good lord.
Romeo.   No matter. Get thee gone.
      And hire those horses. I'll be with thee straight.
                                    [*Exit* BALTHASAR.]
      Well, Juliet, I will lie with thee tonight.
35   Let's see for means. O mischief, thou art swift
      To enter in the thoughts of desperate men!
      I do remember an apothecary,
      And hereabouts 'a dwells, which late I noted
      In tattered weeds,° with overwhelming° brows,
40   Culling of simples.° Meager were his looks,
      Sharp misery had worn him to the bones;
      And in his needy shop a tortoise hung,
      An alligator stuffed, and other skins
      Of ill-shaped fishes; and about his shelves
45   A beggarly account° of empty boxes,
      Green earthen pots, bladders, and musty seeds,
      Remnants of packthread, and old cakes of roses
      Were thinly scatterèd, to make up a show.
      Noting this penury,° to myself I said,
50   "And if a man did need a poison now
      Whose sale is present death in Mantua,
      Here lives a caitiff° wretch would sell it him."
      O, this same thought did but forerun my need,
      And this same needy man must sell it me.
55   As I remember, this should be the house.
      Being holiday, the beggar's shop is shut.
      What, ho! Apothecary!

> "O mischief, thou art swift
> To enter in the thoughts
> of desperate men!"

[*Enter* APOTHECARY.]

Apothecary.   Who calls so loud?
Romeo.
      Come hither, man. I see that thou art poor.

---

31. What letter is Romeo waiting for?

Staging the Play
34. This line is spoken in a still, quiet moment. After a pause, what does Romeo immediately set out to do? Does he hesitate at all to consider his course of action, or does he plunge into it?

39. weeds: clothes. **overwhelming:** overhanging.
40. simples: herbs.

45. account: number.

49. penury (pen'yoo·rē): poverty.

52. caitiff (kāt'if): miserable.

Staging the Play
57. What actions do you imagine Romeo is engaged in as he speaks these lines about the apothecary?

DIFFERENTIATING INSTRUCTION

Learners Having Difficulty
Use the Vocabulary Development lesson on figures of speech (pp. 914–915), as well as the sidenotes in your Teacher's Edition, to help students interpret Shakespeare's similes, metaphors, personifications, and puns.

English-Language Learners
To aid comprehension and convey the atmosphere of Act V, have students view the final scene of Zeffirelli's *Romeo and Juliet* or the end of the film *West Side Story*.

Special Education Students
For lessons designed for special education students, see *Holt Reading Solutions*.

60   Hold, there is forty ducats. Let me have
      A dram of poison, such soon-speeding gear°
      As will disperse itself through all the veins
      That the life-weary taker may fall dead,
      And that the trunk° may be discharged of breath
65   As violently as hasty powder fired
      Doth hurry from the fatal cannon's womb.
   Apothecary.
      Such mortal drugs I have; but Mantua's law
      Is death to any he that utters° them.
   Romeo.
      Art thou so bare and full of wretchedness
70   And fear'st to die? Famine is in thy cheeks,
      Need and oppression starveth in thy eyes,
      Contempt and beggary hangs upon thy back:
      The world is not thy friend, nor the world's law;
      The world affords no law to make thee rich;
      Then be not poor, but break it and take this.
   Apothecary.
75   My poverty but not my will consents.
   Romeo.
      I pay thy poverty and not thy will.
   Apothecary.
      Put this in any liquid thing you will
      And drink it off, and if you had the strength
      Of twenty men, it would dispatch you straight.
   Romeo.
80   There is thy gold—worse poison to men's souls,
      Doing more murder in this loathsome world,
      Than these poor compounds that thou mayst not sell.
      I sell thee poison; thou has sold me none.
      Farewell. Buy food and get thyself in flesh.
85   Come, cordial and not poison, go with me
      To Juliet's grave; for there must I use thee.   [*Exeunt.*]

Scene 2. *Friar Laurence's cell.*

Enter FRIAR JOHN.

John.
   Holy Franciscan friar, brother, ho!

[*Enter* FRIAR LAURENCE.]

60. gear: stuff.

63. trunk: body.

67. utters: sells.

? **74.** *What argument does Romeo use to persuade the apothecary to break the law?*

? **Staging the Play**
79. *What actions do you think have taken place before the apothecary gives Romeo instructions for taking the poison?*

? **83.** *What "poison" has Romeo "sold" the apothecary?*

? **85.** *Why does Romeo call the poison a* cordial, *which is a kind of medicine that restores the heartbeat?*

Advanced Learners
These students will be able to appreciate the play's multiple themes and layers of meaning. They may enjoy an extended debate on the Interpretation question 6 (p. 912) about the relative importance of fate and free will as causes of the tragedy.

C **Literary Focus**
Figures of speech: Simile. This simile compares the speed of death by poison to the speed of a fired cannonball. It also continues the imagery of sudden, brief flashes of light that can be destructive.

D **Reading Skills**
? **Expressing an opinion.** Do you agree with Romeo's argument that a poor man is entitled to break the law in order to survive? Explain. [Some students may say that the ends never justify the means. Others may say that desperate people are entitled to use desperate measures to survive.]

Responses to Margin Questions

Line 74. Romeo argues that the "world's law" is not conducive to the man's well-being; he is poor and sickly. If the apothecary defies the law, he will have money and get well.

Line 79. Romeo could have shown the apothecary the coins in his purse; the apothecary could have taken the poison from a shelf.

Line 83. Romeo says that gold is poison to the soul.

Line 85. Romeo's verbal irony is that the poison, because it will reunite him with Juliet, is really a restorative medicine.

Summary ↔ *at grade level*

Act V, Scene 2
Friar Laurence learns that his messenger, Friar John, was unable to deliver to Romeo the letter explaining Juliet's coma. The friar sets off for the Capulet tomb, afraid that Juliet, who is to revive within three hours, will awaken alone.

A **Reading Skills**

? **Making predictions.** Do you think Friar Laurence's adjustments to the plan will work? Explain. [Possible responses: Yes, there is still time for him to greet Juliet when she awakens; no, Romeo may get to the tomb first and kill himself before he realizes that Juliet is not truly dead.]

Responses to Margin Questions

Line 3. The audience might wonder whether Friar John perhaps found Romeo after he left the apothecary.

Line 16. Friar John was quarantined when authorities suspected that he had been exposed to the plague. They would not let the possibly contaminated letter be delivered by another messenger.

Line 29. If Romeo arrives and thinks Juliet is dead, he will kill himself.

Summary ⟷ *at grade level*

Act V, Scene 3

Paris, at the Capulet tomb, sees Romeo and tries to apprehend him. They fight and Paris is killed. Romeo delivers a soliloquy in which he praises Juliet's beauty; he then drinks the poison and dies. The friar arrives, and when Juliet awakens, he tells her that Romeo and Paris are dead. The friar leaves. Left alone, Juliet first attempts to kill herself by kissing Romeo, hoping that poison lingers on his lips. When this fails, she picks up Romeo's dagger and stabs herself. The watch and Paris's boy discover the dead bodies, round up the friar and Balthasar, and summon the Capulets, the Montagues, and the prince. The friar explains what has happened. The prince blames the Montagues and the Capulets for causing their children's deaths, and the repentant families are reconciled.

Laurence.
  This same should be the voice of Friar John.
  Welcome from Mantua. What says Romeo?
  Or, if his mind be writ, give me his letter.
John.
5 Going to find a barefoot brother out,
  One of our order, to associate° me
  Here in this city visiting the sick,
  And finding him, the searchers° of the town,
  Suspecting that we both were in a house
10 Where the infectious pestilence did reign,
  Sealed up the doors, and would not let us forth,
  So that my speed to Mantua there was stayed.
Laurence.
  Who bare my letter, then, to Romeo?
John.
  I could not send it—here it is again—
15 Nor get a messenger to bring it thee,
  So fearful were they of infection.
Laurence.
  Unhappy fortune! By my brotherhood,
  The letter was not nice,° but full of charge,°
  Of dear import; and the neglecting it
20 May do much danger. Friar John, go hence,
  Get me an iron crow and bring it straight
  Unto my cell.
John.   Brother, I'll go and bring it thee. [*Exit.*]
Laurence.
  Now must I to the monument alone.
  Within this three hours will fair Juliet wake.
25 She will beshrew me much that Romeo
A Hath had no notice of these accidents;°
  But I will write again to Mantua,
  And keep her at my cell till Romeo come—
  Poor living corse, closed in a dead man's tomb! [*Exit.*]

Scene 3. *A churchyard; in it, a monument belonging to the Capulets.*

Enter PARIS *and his* PAGE *with flowers and scented water.*

Paris.
  Give me thy torch, boy. Hence, and stand aloof.
  Yet put it out, for I would not be seen.

? **3.** *In the previous scene we learned that Romeo had received no letters from the friar. How would the friar's question immediately put questions in the minds of the audience?*

  6. associate: accompany.

  8. searchers: health officers.

? **16.** *Another accident! Why was the friar's letter never delivered to Romeo?*

18. nice: trivial. **charge:** importance.

26. accidents: happenings.

? **29.** *If we can accept the "accidents" of fate, we have here something like a chase scene. We know, but the friar does not, that Romeo also is on his way to the tomb. Why is it essential that the friar get there first?*

Reading imperative sentences. Remind students that an imperative sentence is one that makes a request or gives a command. The subject of an imperative sentence is always understood to be *you*, although the word *you* does not usually appear in the sentence.

Activity. Have students find six imperative sentences in Paris's speech to his page in ll. 1–9 of Scene 3. Now have students find five imperative sentences in Romeo's orders to Balthasar in ll. 22–39 of Scene 3. Then, ask students how many imperative sentences they can find in Romeo's speech to Paris in ll. 58–67 of Scene 3.

Under yond yew trees lay thee all along,°
Holding the ear close to the hollow ground.

5   So shall no foot upon the churchyard tread
(Being loose, unfirm, with digging up of graves)
But thou shalt hear it. Whistle then to me,
As signal that thou hear'st something approach.
Give me those flowers. Do as I bid thee, go.

       Page (*aside*).

10   I am almost afraid to stand alone
Here in the churchyard; yet I will adventure.°

                                                [*Retires.*]

Paris.

       Sweet flower, with flowers thy bridal bed I strew
            (O woe! thy canopy is dust and stones)
       Which with sweet water nightly I will dew;

15   Or, wanting that, with tears distilled by moans.
       The obsequies° that I for thee will keep
       Nightly shall be to strew thy grave and weep.

[BOY *whistles.*]

       The boy gives warning something doth approach.
       What cursèd foot wanders this way tonight

20   To cross° my obsequies and true love's rite?
       What, with a torch? Muffle° me, night, awhile.

                                                [*Retires.*]

[*Enter* ROMEO *and* BALTHASAR *with a torch, a mattock, and a crowbar of iron.*]

Romeo.

       Give me that mattock and the wrenching iron.
       Hold, take this letter. Early in the morning
       See thou deliver it to my lord and father.

25   Give me the light. Upon thy life I charge thee,
       Whate'er thou hearest or see'st, stand all aloof
       And do not interrupt me in my course.
       Why I descend into this bed of death
       Is partly to behold my lady's face,

30   But chiefly to take thence from her dead finger
       A precious ring—a ring that I must use
       In dear employment.° Therefore hence, be gone.
       But if thou, jealous,° dost return to pry
       In what I farther shall intend to do,

35   By heaven, I will tear thee joint by joint

3. all along: at full length (on the ground).

? **9.** *Paris is a surprise. He adds an interesting complication, as well as some action, to this scene. Why is Paris here?*

? **Staging the Play**
Stage direction: Paris and his page are alone onstage. Whom does the page speak his **aside** *to? Whom does he not want to hear it?*

11. adventure: risk it.

? **Staging the Play**
13. *In Shakespeare's theater we would see a tomb at the rear of the stage. Juliet's body, in its burial gown, would be placed in this tomb, on top of a raised structure. Tybalt's body would lie nearby. What atmosphere must be suggested in this scene? How would lighting be used on a modern stage to create such an atmosphere?*

16. obsequies (äb'si·kwēz'): observances or rituals.
20. cross: interrupt.
21. Muffle: hide.

? **Staging the Play**
22. *Paris enters with flowers and perfumed water, but Romeo enters with iron tools—a mattock, which is something like a hoe, and a crowbar. Like Paris, Romeo and his servant enter at the upper level. What strange excuse does Romeo give his servant for wanting to descend into the tomb alone?*

32. dear employment: important business.
33. jealous: curious.

B **Reading Skills**

? **Speculating.** What do you think Romeo has written in the letter to his father? [Possible response: The letter probably unfolds the whole story of his love for Juliet and their secret marriage and explains why he has decided to kill himself.]

C **Reading Skills**

? **Making inferences.** What does this threat indicate about Romeo's mental state? [Possible responses: He is taking out his anger and frustration on Balthasar and behaving irrationally; he may be rational and consciously trying to relieve Balthasar from any responsibility for his suicide.]

Responses to Margin Questions

Line 9. Paris has come to place flowers on Juliet's bier.

Stage direction. The page addresses his aside to the audience; he does not want Paris to hear it.

Line 13. An eerie, ominous atmosphere should be set. Blue and gray lighting might predominate in a modern staging, and many of the stage areas would be left in shadow to suggest the interior of a tomb.

Line 22. Romeo says he wants to see Juliet's face and take a ring from her finger.

The Tragedy of Romeo and Juliet, Act V, Scene 3   **899**

Learners Having Difficulty
Have students form small groups to review scenes from Act V. Ask two or more students to read the scene—one student to summarize the scene and another student to take notes on the difficulties that arise with comprehension of the text. The group should work together to use the sidenotes to clarify understanding. Have students switch tasks for each scene.

Advanced Learners
Enrichment. Have students work in small groups to create a special edition of *The Verona Times,* focusing on the tragic events that occur in Act V. Have students begin by listing the various features they want to include in their special edition—news reports, obituaries, editorials, cartoons, advice columns, and so on—and then divide the writing among group members. Have

students paste up their final product in newspaper format or use a computer with desktop-publishing software. Distribute copies of the final product.

A Literary Focus

Figurative language: Metaphors.
Help students interpret this extended metaphor: The "detestable maw" and "womb of death" refer to the tomb. "The dearest morsel of the earth" refers to Juliet. The "rotten jaws" refer to the entrance of the tomb. And "more food" refers to Romeo's dead body.

B Reading Skills

Paraphrasing and context clues.
Ask students to paraphrase Paris's speech. [Possible paraphrase: There's that criminal Romeo who murdered Tybalt. He's also responsible for Juliet's death, since it's said she died of grief for her dead cousin. He's probably come here to desecrate the bodies of Tybalt and Juliet. I'll stop the villain. Halt, Montague! Can you still be seeking revenge even though your victims are dead? Come with me, murderer. You are condemned to die.]

Responses to Margin Questions

Line 39. Romeo describes himself as "savage-wild," "fierce," and "inexorable." The images of the hungry tigers and turbulent sea show that he feels dangerous, destructive, and powerful.

Line 48. Romeo is talking to the tomb as he pries it open, promising to feed it his own body.

Line 51. It is supposed that Juliet died of grief over Tybalt's death.

Line 54. Paris may draw his sword as he commands Romeo to stop breaking into the tomb. He is trying to arrest Romeo, who is a "Condemnèd villain" under the prince's order.

Line 67. Romeo is thinking clearly of the consequences of his actions and tries to reason with Paris, wanting to prevent at least one more needless death.

And strew this hungry churchyard with thy limbs.
The time and my intents are savage-wild,
More fierce and more inexorable far
Than empty tigers or the roaring sea.

Balthasar.
40   I will be gone, sir, and not trouble ye.

Romeo.
So shalt thou show me friendship. Take thou that.
Live, and be prosperous; and farewell, good fellow.

Balthasar (*aside*).
For all this same, I'll hide me hereabout.
His looks I fear, and his intents I doubt.   [*Retires.*]

Romeo.
45   **A** Thou detestable maw,° thou womb of death,
Gorged with the dearest morsel of the earth,
Thus I enforce thy rotten jaws to open,
And in despite° I'll cram thee with more food.

[ROMEO *opens the tomb.*]

Paris.
This is that banished haughty Montague
50   That murd'red my love's cousin—with which grief
It is supposed the fair creature died—
And here is come to do some villainous shame
B To the dead bodies. I will apprehend him.
Stop thy unhallowèd toil, vile Montague!
55   Can vengeance be pursued further than death?
Condemnèd villain, I do apprehend thee.
Obey, and go with me; for thou must die.

Romeo.
I must indeed; and therefore came I hither.
Good gentle youth, tempt not a desp'rate man.
60   Fly hence and leave me. Think upon these gone;
Let them affright thee. I beseech thee, youth,
Put not another sin upon my head
By urging me to fury. O, be gone!
By heaven, I love thee better than myself,
65   For I come hither armed against myself.
Stay not, be gone. Live, and hereafter say
A madman's mercy bid thee run away.

Paris.
I do defy thy conjurations°
And apprehend thee for a felon here.

39. *Romeo makes sure his servant will not interrupt him. What do the last three lines tell about his state of mind?*

45. maw: mouth.

48. in despite: to spite you.

Staging the Play
48. *Whom or what is Romeo talking to here? What is he doing? What "food" is he going to feed this "maw"?*

51. *What was believed to be the cause of Juliet's sudden "death"?*

Staging the Play
54. *What does Paris do as he speaks this line?*

67. *Romeo doesn't attempt even to fight Paris. How do his words here show calmness and maturity?*

68. conjurations: solemn orders.

Romeo.

70   Wilt thou provoke me? Then have at thee, boy!

[*They fight.*]

Page.

      O Lord, they fight! I will go call the watch.

                                    [*Exit.* PARIS *falls.*]

Paris.

      O, I am slain! If thou be merciful,

      Open the tomb, lay me with Juliet.   [*Dies.*]

Romeo.

      In faith, I will. Let me peruse this face.

75   Mercutio's kinsman, noble County Paris!

      What said my man when my betossèd soul

      Did not attend° him as we rode? I think

      He told me Paris should have married Juliet.

      Said he not so, or did I dream it so?

80   Or am I mad, hearing him talk of Juliet,

      To think it was so? O, give me thy hand,

      One writ with me in sour misfortune's book!

      I'll bury thee in a triumphant grave.

      A grave? O, no, a lanthorn,° slaught'red youth,

85   For here lies Juliet, and her beauty makes

      This vault a feasting presence full of light.

      Death, lie thou there, by a dead man interred.

[*Lays him in the tomb.*]

      How oft when men are at the point of death

      Have they been merry! Which their keepers° call

90   A lightning before death. O, how may I

      Call this a lightning? O my love, my wife!

      Death, that hath sucked the honey of thy breath,

      Hath had no power yet upon thy beauty.

      Thou art not conquered. Beauty's ensign° yet

95   Is crimson in thy lips and in thy cheeks,

      And death's pale flag is not advancèd there.

      Tybalt, liest thou there in the bloody sheet?

      O, what more favor can I do to thee

      Than with that hand that cut thy youth in twain

100   To sunder his that was thine enemy?

      Forgive me, cousin! Ah, dear Juliet,

      Why art thou yet so fair? Shall I believe

      That unsubstantial Death is amorous,

      And that the lean abhorrèd monster keeps

The Tragedy of Romeo and Juliet, Act V, Scene 3   901

? **70.** *What has Paris done to provoke Romeo?*

? **Staging the Play**
74. *Whatever we thought of Paris before, we understand now that he loved Juliet. What does Romeo do here?*

77. attend: pay attention to.

? **82.** *Remember that Romeo has spoken of himself as "fortune's fool." Why does he see Paris as another victim?*

84. lanthorn: lantern; here, a room with glass walls.

? **Staging the Play**
85. *Romeo, dragging Paris's body across the stage, now sees Juliet. What words indicate that he sees the tomb transformed? Who is the "dead man" in line 87?*

89. keepers: jailers.

94. ensign (en′sīn′)**:** flag (signal).

? **Staging the Play**
97. *Romeo turns to see Tybalt's body. Is he angry at his enemy, or does he ask forgiveness?*

? **102.** *Where in this speech does Romeo see life in Juliet, reminding us that she is not dead?*

CONTENT-AREA CONNECTIONS

Literature: Understanding Shakespeare's Plays

Director and Shakespeare scholar John Barton says the key to understanding Shakespeare's plays is seeing the ever-shifting pattern of antitheses, or contradictions, in the characters' language and thinking. "If you don't . . . play with the antitheses, a great deal of Shakespeare becomes difficult to follow," he claims. "If you do go with it, he's much easier to follow and enjoy."

The progression of light and darkness imagery is one example of the play of contradictions in the tragedy. Sometimes darkness is the friend of lovers; sometimes it foreshadows death and despair. Love is seen as a brief flash of light in the darkness, but daylight is dull and unromantic.

A **Literary Focus**

Climax. With Romeo's suicide, the climax of the play begins. The tragic deaths of the "star-crossed lovers," announced in the Act I prologue and foreshadowed throughout the play, are now occurring.

B **Reading Skills**

? **Identifying cause and effect.** How would the plot have worked out differently if Friar Laurence had arrived at the tomb a half hour earlier? [He could have explained to Romeo that Juliet was not really dead and saved both their lives; he might have saved Paris as well.]

Responses to Margin Questions

Line 108. Romeo embraces Juliet (l. 113), kisses her (l. 114), drinks the poison (l. 119), and dies (l. 120).

Line 120. Students should consider the setting, Romeo's characterization so far, and the punctuation and images in the speech.

Line 130. Friar Laurence must express alarm, fear, and dread.

105 ⌐ Thee here in dark to be his paramour?
         For fear of that I still will stay with thee
         And never from this pallet of dim night
         Depart again. Here, here will I remain
         With worms that are thy chambermaids. O, here
110   Will I set up my everlasting rest
         And shake the yoke of inauspicious stars
         From this world-wearied flesh. Eyes, look your last!
         Arms, take your last embrace! And, lips, O you
         The doors of breath, seal with a righteous kiss
115 **A** A dateless° bargain to engrossing° death!
         Come, bitter conduct;° come, unsavory guide!
         Thou desperate pilot,° now at once run on
         The dashing rocks thy seasick weary bark!
         Here's to my love! (*Drinks.*) O true apothecary!
120   Thy drugs are quick. Thus with a kiss I die.

         [*Falls.*]

         [*Enter* FRIAR LAURENCE, *with lanthorn, crowbar, and spade.*]

Friar.
         Saint Francis be my speed! How oft tonight
         Have my old feet stumbled at graves! Who's there?
Balthasar.
         Here's one, a friend, and one that knows you well.
Friar.
         Bliss be upon you! Tell me, good my friend,
125   What torch is yond that vainly lends his light
         To grubs and eyeless skulls? As I discern,
         It burneth in the Capels' monument.
Balthasar.
         It doth so, holy sir; and there's my master,
         One that you love.
⌐ **Friar.**   Who is it?
 Balthasar.   Romeo.
B **Friar.**
         How long hath he been there?
130 ⌐ **Balthasar.**   Full half an hour.
 Friar.
         Go with me to the vault.
 Balthasar.   I dare not, sir.
         My master knows not but I am gone hence,
         And fearfully did menace me with death
         If I did stay to look on his intents.

? **Staging the Play**
108. *Romeo lies down beside Juliet. What other actions do you see him performing here?*

115. dateless: timeless.
engrossing: all-encompassing.
116. conduct: guide (the poison).
117. desperate pilot: Romeo himself.

? **Staging the Play**
120. *Actors playing Romeo interpret this last speech in different ways: Some play him as if he is in a dream; others as if he is mad; others as if he is in full control of himself; others as if he is desperate and out of his mind with grief, desire, and fear. What clues would direct the way you'd interpret Romeo's feelings as he gives his final* **soliloquy**?

? **Staging the Play**
130. *What feelings must the friar reveal when he hears that Romeo has gotten to the tomb before he has heard of the plan to drug Juliet?*

902 Collection 11 Drama • Synthesizing Sources

CONTENT-AREA CONNECTIONS

Music: *Romeo and Juliet*
Between 1935 and 1936, Russian composer Sergei Prokofiev (1891–1953) wrote a score for a full-length ballet of *Romeo and Juliet*. Although the ballet compresses the play's five acts into four, Prokofiev wrote music for all of the important scenes, with titles such as (Act I) "Romeo," "The Fight," and "The Balcony Scene"; (Act II) "The Nurse";

(Act III) "Farewell Before Parting," "Juliet Alone"; and (Act IV) "Juliet's Death."
Individual activity. Encourage interested students to listen to a recording of Prokofiev's ballet and describe their impressions of how the music portrays the characters and situations. Students interested in dance may wish to choreograph their own dances to the music.

Friar.
135   Stay then; I'll go alone. Fear comes upon me.
       O, much I fear some ill unthrifty° thing.
Balthasar.
       As I did sleep under this yew tree here,
       I dreamt my master and another fought,
       And that my master slew him.
Friar.   Romeo!
140   Alack, alack, what blood is this which stains
       The stony entrance of this sepulcher?
       What mean these masterless and gory swords
       To lie discolored by this place of peace?

       [*Enters the tomb.*]

       Romeo! O, pale! Who else? What, Paris too?
145   And steeped in blood? Ah, what an unkind° hour
       Is guilty of this lamentable chance!
       The lady stirs.

       [JULIET *rises.*]

> "O comfortable friar! Where is my lord?"

Juliet.
       O comfortable° friar! Where is my lord?
       I do remember well where I should be,
150   And there I am. Where is my Romeo?
Friar.
       I hear some noise. Lady, come from that nest
       Of death, contagion, and unnatural sleep.
       A greater power than we can contradict
       Hath thwarted our intents. Come, come away.
155   Thy husband in thy bosom there lies dead;
       And Paris too. Come, I'll dispose of thee
       Among a sisterhood of holy nuns.
       Stay not to question, for the watch is coming.
       Come, go, good Juliet. I dare no longer stay.
Juliet.
160   Go, get thee hence, for I will not away.
                                      [*Exit* FRIAR.]
       What's here? A cup, closed in my truelove's hand?

136. **unthrifty:** unlucky.

141. *Where is the friar as he discovers the bloodstains?*

145. **unkind:** unnatural.

Staging the Play
147. *This short line suggests that the friar rushes to Juliet and waits for her to speak. What must he be feeling?*

148. **comfortable:** comforting.

152. *For the friar this is a terrible moment. What is his reaction to the noise he hears?*

Staging the Play
159. *What plan does the friar propose to Juliet? What is Juliet doing or refusing to do as the friar repeatedly tries to move her?*

Staging the Play
160. *It is hard to believe that after all his concern for these two young lovers, the friar would become a coward at this moment and leave Juliet to harm herself. How must the friar act here to convince us that he is frantic and not very sensible?*

C

C Reading Skills
Paraphrasing and context clues. Ask students to paraphrase the friar's speech. [Possible response: I hear the watch approaching. Juliet, you must leave this burial vault. It is not a place for living beings. Our original intentions have not worked out as planned, but we must accept what has happened. Your beloved Romeo and Paris are dead. I will take you to a convent. You must leave immediately, Juliet. I myself am too frightened to remain here.]

Responses to Margin Questions
Line 141. The friar is at the entrance of the tomb.

Line 147. The friar might feel sad, guilty, fearful, and trapped by circumstances.

Line 152. The friar panics; he wants to leave before he and Juliet are discovered.

Line 159. The friar wants to take Juliet to a convent but Juliet refuses to leave. She may be standing amazed over Romeo or holding and kissing him.

Line 160. To indicate his distraught condition, the friar might dash madly between Juliet and the tomb's entrance and have a frantic edge to his pleading.

The Tragedy of Romeo and Juliet, Act V, Scene 3   **903**

A Literary Focus

Climax. With the death of Juliet, the full climax of the play is realized. The remainder of the play will depict the resolution, in which the loose parts of the plot are all tied up.

B Literary Focus

❓ Analyzing tone. What tone of voice would the chief watchman probably use to make this observation about Juliet? [He would probably sound completely amazed to discover that someone believed to have been dead for two days now appears "bleeding, warm, and newly dead."]

C Literary Focus

Resolution. Everyone but the audience and Friar Laurence is completely puzzled by this mysterious and tragic turn of events. They are crying out for an explanation.

Responses to Margin Questions

Stage direction. Students' responses will vary. However, if Juliet is merely crazed, her suicide becomes a weaker statement of her love for Romeo. The audience is well prepared for Juliet's suicide; her death scene is probably best played as the acting out of a conscious decision to achieve her reunion with Romeo, although an actress may be able to portray her as both calm and mad with love.

Line 184. Friar Laurence is distraught and confused. Until this moment he was still carrying his tools for opening the tomb.

Poison, I see, hath been his timeless° end.
O churl!° Drunk all, and left no friendly drop
To help me after? I will kiss thy lips.
165   Haply some poison yet doth hang on them
To make me die with a restorative.

[*Kisses him.*]

Thy lips are warm!
Chief Watchman (*within*). Lead, boy. Which way?
Juliet.
Yea, noise? Then I'll be brief. O happy° dagger!

[*Snatches Romeo's dagger.*]
170   This is thy sheath; there rust, and let me die.

[*She stabs herself and falls.*]

[*Enter Paris's* BOY *and* WATCH.]

Boy.
This is the place. There, where the torch doth burn.
Chief Watchman.
The ground is bloody. Search about the churchyard.
Go, some of you; whoe'er you find attach.
[*Exeunt some of the* WATCH.]
Pitiful sight! Here lies the county slain;
175   And Juliet bleeding, warm, and newly dead,
Who here hath lain this two days burièd.
Go, tell the prince; run to the Capulets;
Raise up the Montagues; some others search.
[*Exeunt others of the* WATCH.]
We see the ground whereon these woes do lie,
180   But the true ground° of all these piteous woes
We cannot without circumstance° descry.

[*Enter some of the* WATCH, *with Romeo's man* BALTHASAR.]

Second Watchman.
Here's Romeo's man. We found him in the churchyard.
Chief Watchman.
Hold him in safety till the prince come hither.

[*Enter* FRIAR LAURENCE *and another* WATCHMAN.]

Third Watchman.
Here is a friar that trembles, sighs, and weeps.

162. timeless: untimely.
163. churl: rude fellow (spoken teasingly).

169. happy: lucky (to be here when she needs it).

❓ Staging the Play
Stage direction: Do you see Juliet in her last moments as half-crazed? calm and purposeful? something else? Do you think this scene can be played only one way? Can it be played several ways? How would you play the scene?

180. ground: cause.
181. circumstance: details.

❓ 184. How do the watchman's words help us picture the state the friar is in?

CONTENT-AREA CONNECTIONS

History: Plague
Point out to students that scholars believe that Shakespeare wrote many of his sonnets and other poems while theaters in London were temporarily closed due to outbreaks of bubonic plague. Students can research and report on the plague's effect on European civilization during the Middle Ages and the Renaissance or concentrate specifically on the plague in London during Shakespeare's time.

"Drunk all, and left no friendly drop
To help me after?"
✿

905

A Reading Skills

❓ Paraphrasing and context clues. Who does the pronoun *our* refer to? [the prince] What context clues help you make this decision? [Possible responses: the use of the word *person*, which is singular; the convention of royalty to use the plural *we* instead of the singular *I*.]

B Literary Focus

❓ Figures of speech: Simile. What thought does Lady Capulet express through the use of this simile? [that seeing the corpses of the young Romeo and Juliet makes her desire her own death]

Response to Margin Question

Line 193. She suggests that the outcry indicates that something terrible involving Romeo, Juliet, and Paris has taken place in the Capulets' tomb.

185　We took this mattock and this spade from him
　　　As he was coming from this churchyard's side.
Chief Watchman.
　　　A great suspicion! Stay the friar too.

[*Enter the* PRINCE *and* ATTENDANTS.]

A **Prince.**
　　　What misadventure is so early up,
　　　That calls our person from our morning rest?

[*Enter* CAPULET *and his wife,* LADY CAPULET, *with others.*]

Capulet.
190　What should it be, that is so shrieked abroad?
Lady Capulet.
　　　O, the people in the street cry "Romeo,"
　　　Some "Juliet," and some "Paris"; and all run
　　　With open outcry toward our monument.
Prince.
　　　What fear is this which startles in your ears?
Chief Watchman.
195　Sovereign, here lies the County Paris slain;
　　　And Romeo dead; and Juliet, dead before,
　　　Warm and new killed.
Prince.
　　　Search, seek, and know how this foul murder comes.
Chief Watchman.
　　　Here is a friar, and slaughtered Romeo's man,
200　With instruments upon them fit to open
　　　These dead men's tombs.
Capulet.
　　　O heavens! O wife, look how our daughter bleeds!
　　　This dagger hath mista'en, for, lo, his house°
　　　Is empty on the back of Montague,
205　And it missheathèd in my daughter's bosom!
B **Lady Capulet.**
　　　O me, this sight of death is as a bell
　　　That warns° my old age to a sepulcher.

[*Enter* MONTAGUE *and others.*]

Prince.
　　　Come, Montague; for thou art early up
　　　To see thy son and heir more early down.

❓ Staging the Play
193. *As the tomb begins to fill with people, noises and cries are heard offstage. What does Lady Capulet suggest is being "shrieked abroad" in Verona?*

203. house: sheath.

207. warns: summons.

CONTENT-AREA CONNECTIONS

Music: *Romeo and Juliet*
Russian composer Peter Ilich Tchaikovsky (1840–1893) composed a fantasy overture titled *Romeo and Juliet* in 1869. Although an overture is usually the instrumental introduction to an opera, Tchaikovsky's *Romeo and Juliet* is not part of an opera and is performed as an independent work. The title "fantasy" suggests that the work does not literally follow the plot of Shakespeare's play, but is more in the nature of an improvisation shaped by the composer's fancy. **Whole-class activity.** Ask students to try to follow this summary as they listen to Tchaikovsky's overture: After a solemn woodwind introduction describing Friar Laurence, a furious storm of music captures the

Montague.
210   Alas, my liege, my wife is dead tonight!
       Grief of my son's exile hath stopped her breath.
       What further woe conspires against mine age?
Prince.
       Look, and thou shalt see.
Montague.
       O thou untaught! What manners is in this,
215   To press before thy father to a grave?
Prince.
       Seal up the mouth of outrage for a while,
       Till we can clear these ambiguities
       And know their spring, their head, their true descent;
       And then will I be general of your woes°
220   And lead you even to death. Meantime forbear,
       And let mischance be slave to patience.
       Bring forth the parties of suspicion.
Friar.
       I am the greatest, able to do least,
       Yet most suspected, as the time and place
225   Doth make against me, of this direful murder;
       And here I stand, both to impeach and purge°
       Myself condemnèd and myself excused.
Prince.
       Then say at once what thou dost know in this.
Friar.
       I will be brief, for my short date of breath°
230   Is not so long as is a tedious tale.
       Romeo, there dead, was husband to that Juliet;
       And she, there dead, that Romeo's faithful wife.
       I married them; and their stolen marriage day
       Was Tybalt's doomsday, whose untimely death
235   Banished the new-made bridegroom from this city;
       For whom, and not for Tybalt, Juliet pined.
       You, to remove that siege of grief from her,
       Betrothed and would have married her perforce
       To County Paris. Then comes she to me
240   And with wild looks bid me devise some mean
       To rid her from this second marriage,
       Or in my cell there would she kill herself.
       Then gave I her (so tutored by my art)
       A sleeping potion; which so took effect
245   As I intended, for it wrought on her
       The form of death. Meantime I writ to Romeo

? **215.** *Whom is Montague talking to here?*

219. general of your woes: leader of your mourning.

226. impeach and purge: charge and punish.

229. date of breath: term of life.

Staging the Play
230. *All of what the friar says here is known by the audience. In some productions this long* **monologue** *is cut entirely, but it is important for us to imagine the effect the speech has on the Montagues, the Capulets, and the prince. This is the moment when they discover what we've known all along. Where do you think the friar must pause as the families cry out and weep?*

? **237.** *Whom does the friar mean by "you"?*

The Tragedy of Romeo and Juliet, Act V, Scene 3   **907**

DIRECT TEACHING

C **Reading Skills**
Comparing and contrasting. Point out to students that the banishment of Romeo causes both Juliet and Lady Montague great emotional distress. Juliet hopes that the friar's plan will ultimately reunite her with Romeo. However, Lady Montague seems to have had no hope of being reunited with her son. Her grief kills her.

D **Literary Focus**
Resolution. The prince now demands an explanation of how these tragedies came about, and Friar Laurence, the only character still living who knows the whole story, steps forward to explain.

Responses to Margin Questions
Line 215. Montague is speaking to Romeo.

Line 230. Students might suggest the families would cry out when they learn that Romeo and Juliet were married and that Juliet threatened to kill herself, as well as when the friar describes Romeo's and Juliet's deaths.

Line 237. The friar is referring to Lord Capulet.

Capulet-Montague feud. Next comes the love music of Romeo and the response from Juliet, played by the strings. Their love is shattered by the return of the feud music, over which their melodies can at times be heard. The final tragedy, signaled by rumbling kettledrums and a sudden silence, is followed by an epilogue expressing grief over the lovers' death. Some students may wish to create their own fantasy based on *Romeo and Juliet* by combining samples or segments of prerecorded music and adding other sound effects.

A Reading Skills

❷ Evaluating. Is the friar's summary of the plot both brief and accurate? How might you have improved it? [Responses will vary. The summary is hardly brief, but the friar has a complicated story to explain and covers all the main points that the other characters need to know.]

B Literary Focus

❷ Resolution. Do you think the prince will punish Friar Laurence for his involvement in the tragedy? [probably not] Do you think Friar Laurence deserves punishment? Explain. [Possible responses: Yes, because he controlled the fate of Romeo and Juliet and offered misguided advice; no, because he only tried to do what he thought was God's will—he wanted the feuding families to make peace.]

Responses to Margin Questions

Line 261. To answer this question, have students first identify the trials that Romeo and Juliet faced and the characters' reactions to them. Then, have them identify situations in which the adults showed impatience. This question serves as an excellent review of conflict in the play.

Line 269. Friar Laurence says that if the prince decides it was his fault that the plan failed, he accepts responsibility and is willing to die as punishment.

That he should hither come as° this dire night
To help to take her from her borrowed grave,
Being the time the potion's force should cease.
250 But he which bore my letter, Friar John,
Was stayed by accident, and yesternight
Returned my letter back. Then all alone
At the prefixèd hour of her waking
Came I to take her from her kindred's vault,
255 Meaning to keep her closely at my cell
Till I conveniently could send to Romeo.
But when I came, some minute ere the time
Of her awakening, here untimely lay
The noble Paris and true Romeo dead.
260 She wakes; and I entreated her come forth
And bear this work of heaven with patience;
But then a noise did scare me from the tomb,
And she, too desperate, would not go with me,
But, as it seems, did violence on herself.
265 All this I know, and to the marriage
Her nurse is privy;° and if aught in this
Miscarried by my fault, let my old life
Be sacrificed some hour before his time
Unto the rigor of severest law.

Prince.
270 We still° have known thee for a holy man.
Where's Romeo's man? What can he say to this?

Balthasar.
I brought my master news of Juliet's death;
And then in post he came from Mantua
To this same place, to this same monument.
275 This letter he early bid me give his father,
And threat'ned me with death, going in the vault,
If I departed not and left him there.

Prince.
Give me the letter. I will look on it.
Where is the county's page that raised the watch?
280 Sirrah, what made your master in this place?

Boy.
He came with flowers to strew his lady's grave;
And bid me stand aloof, and so I did.
Anon comes one with light to ope the tomb;
And by and by my master drew on him;
285 And then I ran away to call the watch.

247. **as:** on.

❓ 261. *This line expresses the friar's view of life. How would the play have been different if both Romeo and Juliet had been able from the start to bear their trials "with patience"? How does this also apply to the adults in the play?*

266. **to the marriage . . . privy:** Juliet's nurse knows about the marriage.

❓ 269. *Does the friar accept responsibility for his part in the tragedy? What does he say?*

270. **still:** always.

CONTENT-AREA CONNECTIONS

Literature: Theme
To critic Bertrand Evans, this play is about the harm people can unknowingly do to one another, not realizing the chain of tragic events they perpetuate: "More than any other play of Shakespeare's—even more than *Othello,* as a count of pertinent data shows—*Romeo and Juliet* is a tragedy of unawareness. Fate, or Heaven, as the prince calls it, or the 'greater power,' as the friar calls it, working out its purpose without the use of either a human villain or a supernatural agent sent to intervene in mortal affairs, operates through the common human condition of not knowing. Participants in the action, some of them in parts that are minor and seem insignificant, contribute one by one the indispensable stitches which make the pattern, and contribute them not knowing; that is to say, they act when they do not know the truth of the situation in which they act, this truth being known, however, to us who are spectators."

"See what a scourge is laid
upon your hate,
That heaven finds means to kill
your joys with love . . ."

909

Guide the class in answering these comprehension questions.

Short Answer

1. What news does Balthasar bring Romeo at the beginning of Scene 1? [Balthasar tells Romeo that Juliet is dead.]

2. Whom does Romeo visit before leaving Mantua and going to Verona? Why? [He visits an apothecary to buy poison that he can use to kill himself.]

3. What does Juliet find when she awakens? [She sees Friar Laurence who urges her to leave, and she sees the dead bodies of Romeo and Paris.]

4. What is Friar Laurence referring to when he tells Juliet in Scene 3, ll. 153–154, "A greater power than we can contradict / Hath thwarted our intents"? [Friar Laurence is referring to God or fate.]

5. How does Juliet commit suicide? [She stabs herself with Romeo's dagger.]

READING SKILLS REVIEW

Making generalizations. Remind students that a generalization is a statement that applies not just to a specific situation, but to all individuals in similar situations. When students analyze a play's theme, they must think about the general insights about life that the play conveys through its specific characters and events, such as "love conquers time and space."

Activity. Here are two specific lessons the characters in the play might have learned. Have students write a generalization based on the specific lesson. This generalization could be one of the play's themes.

Specific Lesson	Generalization
1. Romeo and Juliet shouldn't have gotten married so quickly after their first meeting.	
2. The Capulets and Montagues should have ended their feud before it destroyed the children.	

The Tragedy of Romeo and Juliet, Act V, Scene 3 **909**

A Literary Focus

? Resolution. What effect do the deaths of Romeo and Juliet have on the feud between their families? [Both Capulet and Montague determine to make peace by honoring each other's child; they are ashamed of the tragic deaths their feud has brought about.]

B Reading Skills

Reading Shakespeare's poetry. The play ends with rhymed speeches by Montague, Capulet, and the prince. Have students analyze the rhyme schemes of the speeches and read them aloud. [Montague's speech ends in a rhymed couplet, and Capulet's response is also a rhymed couplet. The prince's final speech has a rhyme scheme of *ababcc*.]

Responses to Margin Questions

Line 286. The families, perhaps weeping, wait in silence.

Line 295. The prince admits that he should have put a stop to the enmity earlier, before it cost so many lives. He pardoned the families too many times. Most students will feel that Mercutio, Juliet, Paris, and Romeo did not deserve to lose their lives and that the adults, even if they do deserve punishment, have suffered enough with the loss of their children.

Line 304. "Poor sacrifices of our enmity!"

Line 310. Students should answer these questions by first deciding what they feel the different characters represent (holiness and peace, parental authority, irrational self-interest, or simple affection).

Certain colors of light could reinforce the mood of tragedy (perhaps blue, red, or purple), and others could create a sense of transcendence (yellow and gold). The lighting might fade to a single spotlight on the two bodies.

Prince.
This letter doth make good the friar's words,
Their course of love, the tidings of her death;
And here he writes that he did buy a poison
Of a poor pothecary and therewithal
290   Came to this vault to die and lie with Juliet.
Where be these enemies? Capulet, Montague,
See what a scourge is laid upon your hate,
That heaven finds means to kill your joys with love,
And I, for winking at° your discords too,
295   Have lost a brace° of kinsmen. All are punished.

Capulet.
O brother Montague, give me thy hand.
This is my daughter's jointure,° for no more
Can I demand.

Montague.   But I can give thee more;
For I will raise her statue in pure gold,
300   That whiles Verona by that name is known,
There shall no figure at such rate° be set
As that of true and faithful Juliet.

Capulet.
As rich shall Romeo's by his lady's lie—
Poor sacrifices of our enmity!

Prince.
305   A glooming peace this morning with it brings.
     The sun for sorrow will not show his head.
Go hence, to have more talk of these sad things;
     Some shall be pardoned, and some punishèd;
For never was a story of more woe
310   Than this of Juliet and her Romeo. [*Exeunt omnes.*]

> "For never was a story of more woe
> Than this of Juliet and her Romeo."

? Staging the Play
286. *What would the families be doing as the prince now pauses to read the letter?*

294. winking at: closing his eyes to.

295. brace: pair (Mercutio and Paris).

? 295. *We have been repeatedly reminded of the role of fate in this tragedy, but the human characters also admit their responsibility. What does the prince admit? Do you think that some people have been punished too harshly and some not severely enough?*

297. jointure: property passed on to a woman after her husband's death.

301. rate: value.

? Staging the Play
304. *The central focus onstage now is not the families but the bodies of Romeo and Juliet. Over the bodies of their children, the families join hands. What words of Capulet's admit his part in the tragedy?*

? Staging the Play
310. *As the actors solemnly file out, the friar is usually the last to exit. In some productions the fathers leave last. In others the nurse reappears and makes the final exit. What different effects would be produced by having different characters be the last to leave the stage? Which one would you have exit last?*
Finally only the bodies are left onstage. How might lighting be used as the action closes?

CONTENT-AREA CONNECTIONS

Literature: Theme

Whole-class activity. To guide students in making generalizations about the theme of the play, use the Reading Skills Review lesson on p. 909. Then, ask which of the following generalizations, if any, they think best fits the central idea that Shakespeare wanted to convey in *Romeo and Juliet.*

• Love can confer integrity upon two very young people.

• Tragedy can occur when older people's rage is carried over to a new generation.

• Humans are often powerless to make the kind of world they would like to live in.

• Innocence, virtue, and beauty can be quickly and thoughtlessly destroyed.

• A disordered and chaotic world can bring disaster down on those who live in it.

Your Laughter
Pablo Neruda

Take bread away from me, if you wish,
take air away, but
do not take from me your laughter.

5　Do not take away the rose,
the lanceflower that you pluck,
the water that suddenly
bursts forth in your joy,
the sudden wave
of silver born in you.

10　My struggle is harsh and I come back
with eyes tired
at times from having seen
the unchanging earth,
but when your laughter enters
15　it rises to the sky seeking me
and it opens for me all
the doors of life.

My love, in the darkest
hour your laughter
20　opens, and if suddenly
you see my blood staining
the stones of the street,
laugh, because your laughter
will be for my hands
25　like a fresh sword.

Next to the sea in the autumn,
your laughter must raise
its foamy cascade,
and in the spring, love,
30　I want your laughter like
the flower I was waiting for,
the blue flower, the rose
of my echoing country.

Laugh at the night,
35　at the day, at the moon,
laugh at the twisted
streets of the island,
laugh at this clumsy
boy who loves you,
40　but when I open
my eyes and close them,
when my steps go,
when my steps return,
deny me bread, air,
45　light, spring,
but never your laughter
for I would die.

How Do I Love Thee?
Elizabeth Barrett Browning

How do I love thee? Let me count the ways.
I love thee to the depth and breadth and height
My soul can reach, when feeling out of sight
For the ends of Being and ideal Grace.
5　I love thee to the level of everyday's
Most quiet need, by sun and candle light.
I love thee freely, as men strive for Right;
I love thee purely, as they turn from Praise.
I love thee with the passion put to use
10　In my old griefs, and with my childhood's faith.
I love thee with a love I seemed to lose
With my lost saints°—I love thee with the breath,
Smiles, tears, of all my life!—and, if God choose,
I shall but love thee better after death.

---

12. **lost saints:** childhood faith.

Connecting and Comparing Texts

Have students compare the imagery and figures of speech used by Shakespeare's lovers with those used by Neruda's and Browning's speakers. Do these two poets include light and darkness imagery? How do the speakers' attitudes toward death compare with those of Romeo and Juliet? [Possible response: Neruda uses light and darkness imagery in ll. 18–20, 34–35, and 44–45; Browning uses imagery of light in ll. 5–6. All feel that their love is impervious to death.]

Connection

These two poems, written by people who lived in two different centuries and countries, reflect the universal inspiration that love provides.

DIRECT TEACHING

C **Literary Focus**
❓ **Figures of speech: Metaphors.** What metaphors does the speaker use to describe his love's laughter? [He says it is a rose, a lanceflower, a burst of water, and a wave of silver.]

D **Literary Focus**
❓ **Irony.** Why is the speaker's plea for laughter ironic? [Laughter is not the response that a person would expect or consider appropriate in this situation.]

E **Reading Skills**
❓ **Finding the main idea.** What main idea about his love does the speaker want to convey by repeating these images from the first stanza? [Possible response: His love's laughter is more important to him than life itself; he could more easily live without food or air than without her laughter.]

F **Literary Focus**
Sonnet. Point out to students that the Browning poem is an Italian, or Petrarchan, sonnet. It has a slightly different rhyme scheme from the Shakespearean sonnet. Have students analyze the poem's rhyme scheme. [*abbaabba cdcdcd*]

Response and Analysis

Reading Check

1. Balthasar tells Romeo that Juliet has died and is buried in the Capulets' tomb.
2. Romeo buys poison to drink so he can join Juliet in death.
3. The friar's messenger was quarantined because he was thought to have been exposed to the plague.
4. Juliet's apparently dead body
5. Romeo poisons himself. When Juliet awakens to find Romeo dead, she fatally stabs herself.

Thinking Critically

6. Some students may cite when Romeo overhears Juliet declare her love for him or the chance meeting of Tybalt and Mercutio as evidence that fate was to blame. Others may say human actions are more to blame, such as the feud, Lord Capulet's decision to move up the marriage to Paris, or Friar Laurence's decision to have Juliet pretend to be dead.

7. Possible answers: Romeo's soliloquy in Scene 1 (ll. 34–57) conveys his reaction to the news of Juliet's death and his plan for joining her and killing himself. The friar's monologue in Scene 3 (ll. 229–269) summarizes the events of the tragedy. Juliet's last dialogue with the friar in Scene 3 (ll. 148–160) establishes that Juliet will not leave the tomb now that she knows Romeo is dead.

8. Possible answer: Scene 3— Romeo, wrongly believing Juliet dead, fulfills his suicide pledge.

9. The dramatic climax is the double suicide of Romeo and Juliet. Students will likely express horror, anger, and sadness.

10. The two families each love their children. Hatred between the families, however, forces

Response and Analysis

Act V

Reading Check

1. What news does Romeo's servant bring him in Scene 1?
2. Why does Romeo buy the poison?
3. Why doesn't Romeo receive the friar's letter explaining the latest plans?
4. What does Romeo find when he enters the tomb?
5. What finally happens to Romeo and then to Juliet?

Thinking Critically

6. What do you think caused the **tragedy** of Romeo and Juliet? Was it fate or human errors? Draw a web showing all the people or forces that might have been responsible.

Romeo's & Juliet's deaths

7. This act includes examples of **soliloquy** (a long speech in which a character alone onstage expresses thoughts aloud), **monologue** (a long speech that a character delivers to other characters onstage), and **dialogue** (a conversation between two or more characters). Find an example of each, and comment on what it adds to the play.

8. In which scene of this act do you think the **dramatic irony** peaked? Explain why you picked that scene.

9. The **climax** of a play is its most intense moment, when we know how the conflict will end. In a **tragedy** it is a moment when we are overcome by sadness, fear, or regret. The climax of Shakespeare's tragedies comes in the final act. When in this act do you think the climax occurs? What were your feelings at that moment?

10. In Scene 3, look back at the prince's speech about love killing the families' joys. It seems **ironic** that love could kill, so how in this play did love kill joy? In what way is the whole play about the way heaven scourges, or punishes, people for hating? Support your response with details from the text.

11. State the **theme** of the play (its main idea about life) as you see it. Then, compare your statement of theme with your classmates'. How do they vary?

Extending and Evaluating

12. Throughout the eighteenth and nineteenth centuries, *Romeo and Juliet* was often rewritten with a different ending, in which the young lovers live long and happily together. Explain whether you like the ending of the play as it was written or would prefer a happy ending. What changes, if any, would you make in the outcome?

Comparing Texts

Words of Love

The words that Romeo and Juliet speak to each other are words of love. "Your Laughter" and "How Do I Love Thee?" (see the **Connection** on page 911) are about love too. In a brief essay, **compare** and **contrast** these two expressions of love. How does love transform each speaker? How does each speaker say that love conquers death and time? Which poem speaks most powerfully to you? Why?

go.hrw.com

INTERNET
Projects and Activities
Keyword: LE5 9-11

SKILLS FOCUS

Literary Skills
Analyze characteristics of tragedy, including dramatic irony and climax. Analyze soliloquy, monologue, and dialogue.

Writing Skills
Compare a play with a film. Prepare a plan for a modern version of a play. Write an essay analyzing the structure of the play. Write a character analysis.

Listening and Speaking Skills
Prepare an oral report about character types.

Romeo and Juliet to act in secret. The decisions the lovers make to conceal their love lead to their deaths. Ultimately it is the parents who are punished for perpetuating the feud.

11. Throughout the play, Shakespeare stresses that hatred breeds violence and death. Possible theme: Hatred can destroy innocence, virtue, beauty, and even love itself.

Extending and Evaluating

12. Some students may feel that a happy ending would dilute the strength of the play's warning about the effects of hatred. Others may say that a happy ending would give people hope about the power of love in the face of adversity.

Choose from among the following assignments to respond to the play.

WRITING

1. Review It

Look for a film version of *Romeo and Juliet* in your library or a video store. Then, write a short **essay** in which you **compare** one scene of the play with that scene in the film. Which did you find more effective? Why?

▶ Use "Comparing a Play and a Film," pages 926–933, for help with this assignment.

2. The Play Today

As a group, prepare a plan for an updated *Romeo and Juliet* that takes place in the United States. The chart below shows how Arthur Laurents and Stephen Sondheim changed the play to make it into a musical, *West Side Story* (1957). When you finish your rough plan, you might map your scenes. You might even write your own new *Romeo and Juliet*.

Romeo and Juliet	West Side Story
Verona, 1300s	New York, 1950s
Feuding families: Montagues versus Capulets	Gang war: Jets versus Sharks
Lovers: Romeo (Montague); Juliet (Capulet)	Lovers: Tony (Jet); Maria (sister of Shark)
Authority: prince	Authority: New York police officer
Friend/confidant: Benvolio (Romeo's); nurse (Juliet's)	Friend/confidant: Riff (Tony's); Anita (Maria's)
Leaders: Mercutio (Montagues); Tybalt (Capulets)	Leaders: Riff (Jets); Bernardo (Sharks)

3. Tracing the Action

The graphic on page 783 shows the pattern of a typical Shakespearean tragedy. In an **essay, analyze the structure** of *Romeo and Juliet* according to that pattern. Does the play match the structure? You might provide a graphic with your essay summarizing what happens in each act. You might even add illustrations showing the major action in each act.

4. Portrait of Juliet

Write a **character analysis** of Juliet, using the following comment by a critic as the basis of your thesis statement. Be sure to use details from the play to support what the critic says about Juliet and how the world treated her.

> Shakespeare's real miracle . . . was Juliet, transformed from an adolescent arrogantly eager to outdo her elders to an appealing child-woman, barely fourteen, who learns to mix courage with her innocence, yet falls victim to a world that only briefly and unintentionally, but fatally, treats her as a plaything.
>
> —J. A. Bryant, Jr.

LISTENING AND SPEAKING

5. Characters Endure

Prepare an **oral report** for the class in which you tell how the character types presented in *Romeo and Juliet* are found in movies, novels, and TV sitcoms and dramas today. Focus on these types: beautiful girl; handsome boyfriend; socially conscious mother; grumpy father; boyfriend approved by the girl's parents; older confidant; loyal best friend; hot-headed bully; dopey guys who follow the gang leader.

The Tragedy of Romeo and Juliet   **913**

DIFFERENTIATING INSTRUCTION

Learners Having Difficulty

Students who choose the second assignment might enjoy finding a theme song for their updated version of *Romeo and Juliet*. Have them consider various forms of music (rap, rock, country, folk, jazz, classical) before they make their choices. Have each group play the theme song when presenting its plan.

Writing

1. Review It

Encourage students to work in pairs to organize their ideas for comparison and contrast in a chart that uses the following categories: play, movie, most effective, why.

2. The Play Today

Remind students that as they plan their updated version, they need to decide how closely to follow Shakespeare's plot. Students might consider these issues:
- Should a family feud be the basis of the crisis?
- Should fate or self-determination play the larger role?
- How important should friends be to the plot?
- Will the lovers die at the end?

3. Tracing the Action

Encourage students to work in groups, using their notes and any act and scene summaries they have written to help them complete their analysis. Essays must explain whether or not *Romeo and Juliet* matches the typical Shakespearean pattern. Encourage inclusion of graphics; make illustrations of the action optional.

4. Portrait of Juliet

Help students find the main ideas in the thesis statement. [Juliet is transformed from an arrogant adolescent to an appealing young woman; Juliet mixes courage with innocence; Juliet falls victim to a world that treats her as a play-thing.] Then, have the class identify details in the play that support each main idea of the thesis. Allow students who disagree with part of the thesis statement to develop their own statement.

Listening and Speaking

5. Characters Endure

Ask students what is meant by the term *character type*. [A character type is someone who is defined in terms of a specific character trait, a virtue, or a vice.] Point out that a character type does not grow and change or learn from mistakes.

The Tragedy of Romeo and Juliet   **913**

Vocabulary Development

Figures of Speech

Shakespeare's characters use images and figures of speech so rich and so varied that the play, which has lived now for over four hundred years, will probably live as long as English continues to be spoken. As you're focusing on Shakespeare's language, you might try to imitate some of his figures of speech.

Similes. The simplest form of figurative language is the **simile,** a clearly stated comparison between two different things. A simile uses a word such as *like* or *as* or *than* in stating its comparison. For example, Romeo, dejected over Rosaline, says of love, "It pricks like thorn." Romeo's simile suggests that love can cause pain, just as a thorn can.

Metaphors. **Metaphors** omit words such as *like, as,* and *than* and directly equate two different things. When the nurse says of Paris "he's a flower, . . . a very flower," she immediately identifies Paris's good looks with a beautiful blossom. Metaphors may also be **implied.** The prince uses implied metaphors when he angrily accuses the citizens:

"You men, you beasts,
That quench the fire of
    your pernicious rage
With purple fountains
    issuing from your veins!"

The prince compares the anger of the citizens to a fire, and he compares the blood issuing from the wounds to purple water spewing from fountains.

Personification. Personification is a special kind of metaphor, in which something that is not a person is spoken of as if it were human. When Benvolio says that the sun "peered forth the golden window of the East," he is personifying the sun by saying that it peered, as if it had two eyes.

Puns. Shakespeare's audiences loved **puns,** which are plays on the **multiple meanings** of words. (Many jokes today are based on puns. Question: "What has four wheels and flies?" Answer: "A garbage truck." This pun is based on two meanings of the word *flies*.) Many of the puns in *Romeo and Juliet* go over our heads today because jokes go out of fashion very quickly and because some of Shakespeare's wordplay involves words we don't use anymore or involves words whose meanings have changed.

Mercutio is the best punster in the play, though Romeo does pretty well in Act II, when he matches wits with his friend. When Mercutio spies Romeo coming down the street, he says Romeo comes "without his roe." *Roe* can refer to a female deer, so if Romeo is without his roe, he's without his girl. *Roe* also refers to fish eggs, so "without his roe" can mean that Romeo's been gutted (we'd say he's gutless), as a fish is when its eggs have been removed.

If you need help figuring out the examples of figurative language on the next page, go back to the play, and see if the **context** helps you.

SKILLS
FOCUS

**Vocabulary
Skills**
Understand
figures of
speech.

DIFFERENTIATING INSTRUCTION

Learners Having Difficulty

Have students identify and explain the figure of speech used in each of the following passages.

1. Romeo and Mercutio discuss their dreams.

   Romeo.

   Well, what was yours?

   Mercutio.

   That dreamers often lie.

   (Act I, Scene 4, l. 51)

   [*Pun*—Dreamers lie in bed, and dreamers often dream things that are not true.]

2. **Romeo.**

   The brightness of her cheek would shame those stars

   As daylight doth a lamp.

   (Act II, Scene 2, ll. 19–20)

   [*Simile*—Juliet's expression is brighter than starlight, as daylight outshines any lamp.]

3. **Nurse.**

   I think it best you married with the county.

   O, he's a lovely gentleman!

   Romeo's a dishcloth to him.

   (Act III, Scene 5, ll. 219–221)

   [*Metaphor*—Romeo is compared to a dishcloth.]

Similes. For each of the following quotations, identify the similes, and tell what two things are brought together. In what way are the two things alike?

1. Romeo.

O, she doth teach the torches to burn bright!
It seems she hangs upon the cheek of night
As a rich jewel in an Ethiop's ear—
Beauty too rich for use, for earth too dear!
—Act I, Scene 5, lines 44–47

2. Romeo.

Love goes toward love as schoolboys from their books;
But love from love, toward school with heavy looks.
—Act II, Scene 2, lines 157–158

3. Lord Capulet.

Death lies on her like an untimely frost
Upon the sweetest flower of all the field.
—Act IV, Scene 5, lines 28–29

Metaphors. Here are some passages containing metaphors. Pick out each metaphor, and identify the two things that it compares.

1. Romeo (*to Juliet*).

If I profane with my unworthiest hand
This holy shrine, the gentle sin is this:
My lips, two blushing pilgrims, ready stand
To smooth that rough touch with a tender kiss.
—Act I, Scene 5, lines 93–96

2. Romeo (*under Juliet's balcony*).

But soft! What light through yonder window breaks?
It is the East, and Juliet is the sun!
—Act II, Scene 2, lines 2–3

3. Juliet (*to Romeo*).

This bud of love, by summer's ripening breath,
May prove a beauteous flower when next we meet.
—Act II, Scene 2, lines 121–122

Personification. Here are some quotations from *Romeo and Juliet* that contain personifications. In each, what nonhuman thing is spoken of as if it were a person? (Hint: A passage can contain more than one personification.)

1. Capulet.

When well-appareled April on the heel
Of limping winter treads. . . .
—Act I, Scene 2, lines 27–28

2. Chorus.

Now old desire doth in his deathbed lie,
And young affection gapes to be his heir. . . .
—Act II, Chorus, lines 1–2

3. Juliet.

Come, civil night,
Thou sober-suited matron all in black,
And learn me how to lose a winning match. . . .
—Act III, Scene 2, lines 10–12

Puns. Here are two puns from the play. If you can explain the plays on meaning, you'll have caught the jokes.

1. Mercutio (*after he is stabbed*).

Ask for me tomorrow, and you shall find me a grave man.
—Act III, Scene 1, lines 94–95

2. Romeo.

You have dancing shoes
With nimble soles; I have a soul of lead
So stakes me to the ground I cannot move.
—Act I, Scene 4, lines 14–16

Vocabulary Development

Metaphors

1. Juliet (or her hand) is compared to a "holy shrine"; Romeo's lips are two "pilgrims" who want to visit the shrine and make amends for their sins.

2. Juliet, appearing at her window, is compared to the sun rising in the east.

3. Romeo and Juliet's love is compared to a bud that will eventually grow into a flower.

Personification

1. April is a well-dressed person, while winter is someone who limps. April is also personified as stepping on winter's heel.

2. A former love is an old man lying on his deathbed; a new love is a young heir waiting to take his place.

3. Night is an older woman, dressed in black, who can teach Juliet how to play the "game" of love.

Puns

1. To mortally wounded Mercutio, a "grave man" is both a serious man who ponders matters of great importance and a dead man who lies in his grave.

2. The pun involves sole (of a shoe) and soul (of a person). Romeo's "soul of lead" is a heavy spirit that won't let him dance.

Practice

Possible Answers

Similes

1. Juliet, seen at night, is compared to an exotic jeweled earring worn by an Ethiopian. The beauty of both is too great and luxurious for this world.

2. Romeo's relationship with Juliet is compared to schoolboys' attitudes toward books and school. His desire to go to Juliet is the same as the schoolboys' desire to go away from their books. His reluctance to go away from Juliet is the same as the schoolboys' reluctance to go toward school.

3. Since Juliet is so young, her death is compared to an early frost that kills the sweetest flower.

Vocabulary Development

The History of the English Language

The English language has seen many changes since Shakespeare wrote *Romeo and Juliet* more than four hundred years ago. As you learned when reading the play, some of the words Shakespeare uses have different meanings today. For example, *still* now means "yet" instead of "always," and *owe* now means "be in debt" instead of "own; have." Other words found in Shakespeare's plays are considered **archaic:** They are no longer used. Examples are *thence* ("from there"), *sooth* ("truth"), and *wherefore* ("why").

In spite of those and other changes, Shakespeare's English, like ours, is considered Modern English, which began in the late 1400s. If you could travel back to a time before that date, you probably wouldn't be able to understand what anyone was saying. From their armchairs, however, linguists—people who study language—have traced the roots of English far back in time. The paragraphs that follow provide a brief overview of the history of the English language.

Proto-Indo-European

Before 3000 B.C., people living near the Caspian Sea (between the Middle East and Asia) spoke a language we call Proto-Indo-European. (*Proto*– means "first or earliest form," and *Indo*– refers to India.) Over the years, groups of these farmers, herders, and fighters traveled to distant places. In their new lands the Proto-Indo-European they spoke gradually developed into the languages we now call Farsi (or Persian), Hindi, Armenian, Sanskrit, Greek, Russian, Polish, Irish, Italian, French, Spanish, German, Dutch, Swedish, Norwegian—and English. From India to Scandinavia, all these languages have descended from the same Proto-Indo-European roots.

Old English

Much later (from 27 B.C. to A.D. 476), Roman armies conquered most of Europe, North Africa, and the Middle East. Their language, Latin, then influenced the languages of all those lands, including that of the Britons, a Celtic people living in the British Isles. In the fifth century A.D., England was invaded by Anglo-Saxons, who added their Old Germanic tongue to the Celtic of the native Britons. The next invaders to arrive were the Northmen, or Vikings, from Scandinavia, who added Norse to the mix. The language that resulted from all these influences we now call Old English. Like Proto-Indo-European, it was a spoken, or oral, language. Three words from Old English we still use today (among many others) are *horse, night,* and *wife.*

SKILLS FOCUS

Vocabulary Skills
Understand the history of the English language.

Middle English

The last invasion of England was in 1066, by William the Conqueror, from Normandy, in France. For about three hundred years after his conquest, French was spoken by the upper classes and used in the courts and government, while the Catholic clergy spoke and wrote in Latin. The common people—most of the population—continued to speak English, but they were soon borrowing many words from French, thus transforming the language into what is now called Middle English. This is the language of Geoffrey Chaucer's great work, *The Canterbury Tales*. Middle English has many similarities to Modern English, but it is different enough that most people today read Chaucer's poem in a Modern English translation. Three Middle English words (among many others) that were borrowed from French and are used today are *government, justice,* and *literature*.

Modern English

Modern English is generally considered to date from around the time Henry VII was crowned king of England, in 1485. He brought peace to the land and promoted all things English, including the language. Ten years earlier, in 1475, William Caxton had printed the first book in English, which helped to unify and spread the language. After Columbus landed in the New World in 1492, English sailors traveled throughout the Americas and Europe, further spreading the English language and, at the same time, enriching the language with new words. All these influences have given Modern English a vast and international vocabulary. From Spain we get *banana, hammock,* and *tobacco*; from Central America, *chocolate, potato,* and *tomato*; and from the Netherlands, *cruise, knapsack,* and *landscape*—to name a few examples.

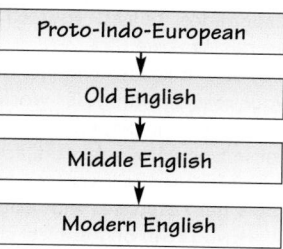

With the spread of science and technology, and especially with the widespread use of the Internet, English is now used worldwide. Still the language continues to pick up new words, such as *software, modem, e-mail*. How much do you think our language is changing? In another four hundred years, do you think people will still be able to read and understand the books we write today?

PRACTICE

Make a list of five words you use every day, and then look up their derivations in a good dictionary. Most dictionaries use abbreviations such as *IE* for "Indo-European," *OE* for "Old English," *ME* for "Middle English," *L* for "Latin," *Fr* for "French," and *Sp* for "Spanish." After you have located the original language for each of your words, share your findings with your classmates. Make a list on the chalkboard of the original languages. Then, from all the words chosen by the class, count the number of words that derive from each language. Do you find many sources for your derivations, or only a few?

Vocabulary Development

Practice

To understand the etymology citation for a word, some students may need to consult the introduction of a dictionary and review the symbols that help to explain a word's origin. For example, the symbol < means "derived from," > means "from which is derived," and * means a word is in an unattested or unverified form, because there is no written form of the language in existence.

Remind students that the etymology of a word is provided in brackets either before or after the definition of the word.

Assessment
■ *Holt Assessment: Literature, Reading, and Vocabulary*

For a lesson reteaching analyzing dramatic literature, see **Reteaching,** p. 979A. For another selection to teach analyzing dramatic literature, see *The Holt Reader,* Collection 11.

Grade-Level Skills

■ **Reading Skills**
Synthesize the content from several sources or works by a single author on a single topic; paraphrase and connect the ideas with related topics in other sources.

Summary 🔲 *at grade level*

"Dear Juliet," a news feature, describes a phenomenon in modern-day Verona, Italy: Hundreds of letters arrive each year addressed to Shakespeare's Juliet, asking for her advice about problems of the lovelorn. These letters are answered by a retired businessman who works for the city of Verona.

"Romeo and Juliet in Bosnia," an op-ed article, describes the tragic deaths of a young couple caught between two warring ethnic and religious groups, Serbs and Muslims, in Sarajevo. When Bosko Brkic, a Serb, and Admira Ismic, a Muslim, tried to escape the conflict, they were shot down by snipers as they crossed a bridge between enemy lines. Each side blamed the other for the couple's deaths. The author uses the fate of these young people to personalize the deadly effects of ethnic and religious hatred.

PRETEACHING

Skills Starter

Motivate. Ask students if they have ever read a story or seen a movie whose characters or conflicts remind them of people or events in real life. Have students discuss the connections they made. Then, tell them that in the works they are about to read, they will make surprising connections between the conflicts of fictional characters and the struggles of real-life people.

Informational Text

LINK TO *THE TRAGEDY OF ROMEO AND JULIET*

Dear Juliet ◆ Romeo and Juliet in Bosnia

Synthesizing Sources: Making Connections

Shakespeare's plays were hits in his own day, four hundred years ago, and they have remained popular ever since because they speak to all kinds of people all over the world. We connect so readily with his plays because they have timeless, universal meaning. That is, they ask the big questions that people everywhere have always wrestled with: Where in the universe do human beings fit in? What do we live for? Why do we love?

Connect and compare. Whenever you read—whether it's a play by Shakespeare, a short story, or a newspaper or Internet article—you look for connections between what you're reading and the world you know. You think about how the subject—a heartache, a family crisis, a societal wrong—**connects** with your own experience. You ask yourself whether the work rings true.

You should also connect and compare your reading with other works you have read. For example, remembering a character in a novel who faces difficulties being with the one she loves, you might **compare** her responses with Juliet's. Each work you read on a subject thus adds to your overall understanding of the topic.

Put it all together. One way to increase your understanding is to **synthesize**—or bring together into a whole—what you have learned from different sources on a topic. To do this, first **paraphrase** the ideas in each source—that is, restate them in your own words. Then, **connect** each source with the others—tell how they are similar and how they are

different. Finally, explain what all the works have added to your understanding of life.

INTERNET
Interactive Reading Model
Keyword: LE5 9-11

SKILLS FOCUS

Reading Skills
Synthesize information from several sources on a single topic.

Vocabulary Development

carnage (kär′nij) *n.*: slaughter; bloodshed.

reminiscing (rem′ə·nis′iŋ) *v.* used as *adj.*: thinking, talking, or writing about one's memories.

relentless (ri·lent′lis) *adj.*: not stopping; persistent; harsh.

mundane (mun′dān′) *adj.*: everyday; commonplace.

compulsory (kəm·pul′sə·rē) *adj.*: required by rule or law.

vulnerable (vul′nər·ə·bəl) *adj.*: affected by a specific influence.

primal (prī′məl) *adj.*: original; primitive.

esteem (ə·stēm′) *n.*: respect.

eradicating (ē·rad′i·kāt′iŋ) *v.* used as *n.*: wiping out; destroying.

dilemma (di·lem′ə) *n.*: difficult choice; serious problem.

Connecting to the Literature

Sometimes a well-known literary work like *Romeo and Juliet* takes on a reality of its own. The following nonfiction articles connect true-life stories with Shakespeare's play. "Dear Juliet" tells of lovelorn individuals who address their letters to Romeo or Juliet, Verona, Italy. "Romeo and Juliet in Bosnia" relates the story of a Bosnian couple who shared the tragic fate of Shakespeare's young lovers.

RESOURCES: READING

Planning
■ *One-Stop Planner* CD-ROM with ExamView Test Generator

Differentiating Instruction
■ *Holt Reading Solutions*
■ *Holt Adapted Reader*
■ *Audio CD Library, Selections and Summaries in Spanish*

■ *Supporting Instruction in Spanish*

Media
■ *Audio CD Library*

Vocabulary
■ *Vocabulary Development*

Assessment
■ *Holt Assessment: Literature, Reading, and Vocabulary*

DEAR JULIET

from *The Wall Street Journal*, November 10, 1992

Lisa Bannon

> *A*ny man that can write may answer a letter.
>
> —William Shakespeare
> from *Romeo and Juliet*, Act II, Scene 4

VERONA, ITALY—Fate bequeathed[1] a strange legacy[2] to this small city in northern Italy.

As the setting for Shakespeare's sixteenth-century tragedy *Romeo and Juliet,* Verona inherited the curiosity of literary scholars, a celebrated theatrical tradition, and several hundred thousand tourists a year.

In the bargain, the city also became the star-crossed lovers' capital of the world.

"We don't know how it started exactly," explains Giulio Tamassia, the bespectacled city spokesman for matters relating to Romeo and Juliet. "But one day in the thirties, these letters started arriving unprompted—addressed to Juliet. At a certain point somebody decided Juliet should write back."

Juliet's Address

What began sixty years ago as an occasional correspondence has grown into an industry. This year more than one thousand letters from the lovelorn will arrive in Verona,

addressed to Shakespeare's tragic heroine. Many of them land on Mr. Tamassia's desk, with no more address than: Juliet, Italy.

"They tend to be sentimental," says Mr. Tamassia, rifling through stacks of musty airmail in the cramped studio that serves as Juliet's headquarters. Inside big pink folders are thousands of sorrowful letters, break-your-heart tales of love and loss. They come from all over—a teenage girl in Guatemala,[3] a businessman in Boston, a high school teacher in London. Some but not many are written by students in Shakespearean language. About two percent of letters received are addressed to Romeo, but Juliet replies.

"Writing the letter itself is really the first step toward solving the problem," says Mr. Tamassia, a fifty-nine-year-old retired businessman who wants it known at the outset that he himself is not Juliet. He is more her correspondence secretary.

"People express feelings in the letters that they would never admit to the person they love. Juliet's story inspires them," he says.

---

1. **bequeathed** (bē·kwēth̸d′) *v.:* handed down or passed on, as in a will.
2. **legacy** (leg′ə·sē) *n.:* gift handed down to someone, as in a will.
3. **Guatemala** (gwät′ə·mä′lə): nation in Central America.

- *One-Stop Planner* CD-ROM with ExamView Test Generator
- *Holt Online Assessment*

Internet
- go.hrw.com (Keyword: LE5 9-11)
- *Elements of Literature Online*

PRETEACHING

Preview Vocabulary

Ask students to choose the Vocabulary word that is close in meaning to the word or phrase underlined in each sentence below.

1. The cost in bloodshed of battle can be enormous. [carnage]
2. In his autobiography the general is telling stories about soldiers in the trenches. [reminiscing]
3. Persistent bombing of enemy territory can lead to surrender. [relentless]
4. Civilians cannot ignore their everyday concerns. [mundane]
5. Should service in the armed forces be required? [compulsory]
6. That city would be defenseless if an air attack occurred. [vulnerable]
7. Hand-to-hand combat can erupt into primitive violence. [primal]
8. Respect for those who defend our country is essential. [esteem]
9. Is wiping out war an impossible goal? [eradicating]
10. Going to war may pose a difficult moral problem. [dilemma]

DIRECT TEACHING

Ⓐ Reading Informational Text

❓ **Synthesizing sources.** Why does the author say that Verona has become "the star-crossed lovers' capital of the world"? [In *Romeo and Juliet,* the two young people are described as "star-crossed lovers," two people whose love seems to be opposed by fate. Today, people who identify with Romeo and Juliet write to Juliet in Verona.]

A Reading Informational Text

? Synthesizing sources. What connections can you make between Hala's situation and Juliet's? [Like Juliet, Hala is in love with a young man whose family is her own family's enemy. She is torn between loyalty to her family and love for the young man.]

A Saudi Version

After much rummaging, he pulls out one of his favorites—describing a modern equivalent of the Montague-Capulet family rivalry.

A ⎡ Hala, an eighteen-year-old Saudi Arabian,[4] wrote in March that she had fallen in love with the only son of her family's mortal enemy.[5] Years ago, in Pakistan,[6] her great-grandfather was responsible for the execution of a man who was using his property for smuggling heroin. From that time on, war was declared between the two families.

Now Hala was in love with a descendant[7] of the executed man. "I am torn between the love for my family, which has made me what I am today, and my love for Omer, the man of my dreams," she wrote.

"Please reply quickly . . . my love, my life and future all depend on your answer." ⎦

---

4. Saudi Arabian: native of Saudi Arabia, a nation in the Middle East.
5. mortal enemy: extremely hostile enemy.
6. Pakistan: Asian nation west of India. The feud described in the letter began in Pakistan, which is a great distance from Saudi Arabia, where the writer of the letter lives.

---

7. descendant (dē·sen′dənt) *n.*: offspring of an ancestor, such as a child, grandchild, or great-grandchild.

This house and balcony in Verona, Italy, are popularly claimed to have been Juliet's.

Romeo and Juliet in Bosnia

OP-ED ARTICLE

from *The New York Times*, May 8, 1994

Bob Herbert

Bosnia and Herzegovina (hert′sə·gō·vē′nə) is a small nation on the Balkan peninsula in eastern Europe. It is newly independent, but its problems are centuries old, since the population has long been divided among three hostile groups: Muslims, Serbs, and Croatians. The divisions are both ethnic and religious, since the Serbs and Croatians are Christians (the Serbs, members of the Eastern Orthodox Church; the Croats, members of the Roman Catholic Church). The area has been plagued by violence, in which warring ethnic groups battle one another. Sarajevo (sar′ə·yä′vō) is the capital of Bosnia and Herzegovina.

If you watch *Frontline* Tuesday night on PBS, you will see the story of two ordinary young people, Bosko Brkic, an Eastern Orthodox Serb, and Admira Ismic, a Muslim, who met at a New Year's Eve party in the mid-1980s, fell in love, tried to pursue the most conventional of dreams, and died together on a hellish bridge in Sarajevo.

The documentary, called "Romeo and Juliet in Sarajevo," achieves its power by focusing our attention on the thoroughly human individuals caught up in a horror that, from afar, can seem abstract and almost unimaginable. It's one thing to hear about the carnage caused by incessant[1] sniper fire and the steady rain of mortar shells on a city; it's something quite different to actually witness a parent desperately groping for meaning while reminiscing about a lost daughter.

For viewers overwhelmed and desensitized by the relentless reports of mass killings and mass rapes, the shock of "Romeo and Juliet in Sarajevo" is that what we see is so real and utterly familiar. We become riveted by the mundane. Bosko and Admira could be a young couple from anywhere, from Queens, or Tokyo, or Barcelona.

We learn that they graduated from high school in June of 1986 and that both were crazy about movies and music. Admira had a cat named Yellow that she loved, and Bosko liked to play practical jokes.

Admira's father, Zijo, speaking amid clouds of cigarette smoke, says, "Well, I knew from the first day about that relationship and I didn't have anything against it. I thought it was good because her guy was so likable, and after a time I started to love him and didn't regard him any differently than Admira."

Admira's grandmother, Sadika Ismic, was

---

1. **incessant** (in·ses′ənt) *adj.:* never stopping; continual.

Vocabulary

carnage (kär′nij) *n.:* slaughter; bloodshed.

reminiscing (rem′ə·nis′iŋ) *v.* used as *adj.:* thinking, talking, or writing about one's memories.

relentless (ri·lent′lis) *adj.:* not stopping; persistent; harsh.

mundane (mun′dān′) *adj.:* everyday; commonplace.

B Reading Informational Text

? Synthesizing sources. How is this opening paragraph similar to the prologue of the play *Romeo and Juliet*? [Both summarize the story in advance; in both, the reader learns that a young couple in love died tragically and that the young lovers came from different backgrounds.]

C Reading Informational Text

? Synthesizing sources. How is the conflict that caused problems for Romeo and Juliet different from the conflict that caused problems for Bosko and Admira? [The conflict in the play is a feud between the lovers' families. The conflict in Bosnia is one between ethnic and religious groups.] **How are the conflicts similar?** [In each case the conflict is between opposing groups to which the lovers belong; in each case, the conflict is beyond the lovers' control.]

DIFFERENTIATING INSTRUCTION

English-Language Learners

Because there are several different kinds of proper nouns in the op-ed article "Romeo and Juliet in Bosnia," work with students to categorize the nouns in order to avoid confusion about which words name people, places, religions, and ethnic groups.

Special Education Students

For lessons designed for English-language learners and special education students, see *Holt Reading Solutions*.

A Content-Area Connections

History: Ethnic Conflict in the Balkans

Though the potential for clashes between ethnic groups in the region goes back hundreds of years, war between Serbs and non-Serbs did not break out until 1992. When Muslims and Croats of the region voted in a referendum for the republic's independence, Serbs opposed the move and fighting erupted.

B Learners Having Difficulty

Paraphrasing. Help students paraphrase this difficult paragraph, which includes four Vocabulary words, as well as abstract nouns such as *civilization, enterprise,* and *tolerance.* [Possible paraphrase: Civilized, peaceful behavior among different kinds of people living together can be easily destroyed by an eruption of ethnic and religious hatred. People's need to feel that their group is powerful and respected can lead them to violate the rights of—and even kill—people who are different from them.]

C Reading Informational Text

❷ Synthesizing sources. How does this scene connect with the tragedy of *Romeo and Juliet*? [Like Juliet, Admira embraces the body of her lover before she herself dies; both sides are equally to blame for the tragic deaths.]

D Reading Skills

❷ Finding the main idea. What main idea does the author express in this article? [Possible response: Ethnic or religious hatred is a cause of violent conflicts in the world, and they always have been.]

---

not so sanguine.[2] "Yes, I did have something against it," she says. "I thought, 'He is Serb, she is a Muslim, and how will it work?'"

For Admira and Bosko, of course, love was the answer to everything. While Bosko was away on compulsory military service soon after high school, Admira wrote: "My dear love, Sarajevo at night is the most beautiful thing in the world. I guess I could live somewhere else but only if I must or if I am forced. Just a little beat of time is left until we are together. After that, absolutely nothing can separate us."

Sarajevo at the time was a cosmopolitan[3] city coming off the triumph of the 1984 Winter Olympics. With a population of Serbs, Croats, Muslims, Jews, and others, the city had become a symbol of ethnic and religious tolerance, a place where people were making a serious attempt to live together in peace.

But civilization is an exceedingly fragile enterprise, and it's especially vulnerable to the primal madness of ethnic and religious hatreds. Simple tolerance is nothing in the face of the relentless, pathetic, and near-universal need to bolster the esteem of the individual and the group by eradicating the rights, and even the existence, of others.

When the madness descended on Sarajevo, Bosko Brkic faced a cruel dilemma. He could not kill Serbs. And he could not go up into the hills and fire back down on his girlfriend's people. Says his mother, Rada: "He was simply a kid who was not for the war."

Bosko and Admira decided to flee Sarajevo. To escape, they had to cross a bridge

---

2. **sanguine** (saŋ'gwin) *adj.:* optimistic; hopeful; cheerful.
3. **cosmopolitan** (käz'mə·päl'ə·tən) *adj.:* worldly; sophisticated.

---

over the Miljacka River in a no man's land[4] between the Serb and Muslim lines. Snipers from both sides overlooked the bridge.

It has not been determined who shot the lovers. They were about two thirds of the way across the bridge when the gunfire erupted. Both sides blame the other. Witnesses said Bosko died instantly. Admira crawled to him. She died a few minutes later. The area in which they were shot was so dangerous that the bodies remained on the bridge, entwined, for six days before being removed.

Only the times and places change. Bosnia today, Rwanda and Burundi[5] tomorrow. Jews versus Arabs, Chinese versus Japanese, blacks versus whites. There are various ostensible reasons for the endless conflicts—ideological[6] differences, border disputes, oil—but dig just a little and you will uncover the ruinous ethnic or religious origins of the clash.

The world stands helpless and sometimes depressed before the madness. Millions upon millions dead, millions more to die. It is not just the curse of our times. It seems to be the curse of all time.

---

4. **no man's land** *n.:* battle zone claimed by both sides in a war but controlled by neither, often where much of the fighting takes place.
5. **Rwanda and Burundi:** African nations that have been the scene of ethnic warfare between the Watusi, or Tutsi, and the Hutu peoples.
6. **ideological** (ī'dē·ə·lä'ji·kəl) *adj.:* based on political, social, or economic beliefs.

Vocabulary
compulsory (kəm·pul'sə·rē) *adj.:* required by rule or law.

vulnerable (vul'nər·ə·bəl) *adj.:* affected by a specific influence.

primal (prī'məl) *adj.:* original; primitive.

esteem (ə·stēm') *n.:* respect.

eradicating (ē·rad'i·kāt'iŋ) *v.* used as *n.:* wiping out; destroying.

dilemma (di·lem'ə) *n.:* difficult choice; serious problem.

DIFFERENTIATING INSTRUCTION

Learners Having Difficulty
To help students synthesize sources, draw a Venn diagram on the chalkboard, and ask students to suggest similarities and differences between the situation and the consequences faced by Romeo and Juliet in the play and those faced by Admira and Bosko in real life.

Write their responses on the Venn diagram. Follow the same process to compare the situation of Hala, the young woman mentioned in "Dear Juliet." Finally, ask students what all three sets of young lovers have in common. [Their love was threatened by a conflict involving groups to which the lovers belonged.]

Analyzing Informational Text

Reading Check

1. As explained in "Dear Juliet," who is Giulio Tamassia, and what does he do?

2. What problem did Hala, the Saudi Arabian girl, write to Juliet about?

3. What difference exists between Admira and Bosko, the couple described in "Romeo and Juliet in Bosnia"?

4. What happened to Admira and Bosko?

 **Test Practice**

1. Which of the following statements *best* expresses the **main idea** of "Dear Juliet"?

   A Many people all over the world fall in love with someone their parents hate.

   B Many people with problems relating to love look to Romeo and Juliet for answers.

   C It is important to answer letters promptly to help people with their problems.

   D Giulio Tamassia helps everyone who writes to him as best he can.

2. In *both* "Romeo and Juliet in Bosnia" and Shakespeare's *Romeo and Juliet* —

   F characters named Romeo and Juliet die

   G innocent lovers die because of a larger conflict

   H the destructiveness and pointlessness of war are described

   J young people are rejected by their families because of a feud

3. What is Bob Herbert's *main* **purpose** in writing "Romeo and Juliet in Bosnia"?

   A To point out parallels between the story of Admira and Bosko and the story of Shakespeare's lovers

   B To show that love can triumph over death

   C To highlight the universal madness of conflicts like the one in Bosnia

   D To show that love is universal

4. Which element in "Dear Juliet" offers the strongest parallel to both *Romeo and Juliet* and "Romeo and Juliet in Bosnia"?

   F The plight Hala describes in her letter

   G Tamassia's sympathy for the letter writers

   H The need of people to write to Juliet

   J The fact that the letters come from all over the world

5. Which statement **synthesizes** themes from *Romeo and Juliet,* "Dear Juliet," and "Romeo and Juliet in Bosnia"?

   A Conflict often destroys love.

   B People in love look to others for help.

   C Loyalty makes love strong.

   D People in love often face difficulties.

Constructed Response

Connect one of these informational pieces to another work you have read or seen—a story about love, for example, or a news report about innocent victims. In a short essay, first **paraphrase** the ideas in each work. Then, discuss their similarities and differences. Finally, **synthesize** what you have learned about life from the two works.

SKILLS FOCUS

Reading Skills
Synthesize information from several sources on a single topic.

Dear Juliet / Romeo and Juliet in Bosnia   **923**

Analyzing Informational Text

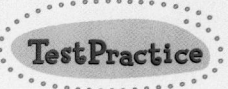 **TestPractice**

Answers and Model Rationales

1. **B** The focus of the news feature is that lovelorn people write letters to Juliet. Only one couple whose families hate one another is cited, so A is incorrect. The idea in C is not stated. The article does not describe Mr. Tamassia's efforts (D).

2. **G** "Romeo and Juliet in Bosnia" describes real people named Bosko and Admira (F); *Romeo and Juliet* does not describe war (H); Admira and Bosko were not rejected by their families (J).

3. **C** The parallels between the stories are only implied (A). The article focuses on the "madness" and universality of "endless conflicts," rather than on the triumph or universality of love, so B and D are wrong.

4. **F** Hala, Juliet, and Admira all fell in love with an "enemy." No one helps the lovers in "Romeo and Juliet in Bosnia" (G). H and J are ideas unique to "Dear Juliet."

5. **A** The idea in A relates to all the lovers. Bosko and Admira did not look to others for help (B), and loyalty to one's family or ethnic or religious group helped none of the lovers (C). "Romeo and Juliet in Bosnia" is concerned with the cruelties of war (D).

Test-Taking Tips

For information on how to answer multiple-choice items, refer students to **Test Smarts**.

Reading Check

1. He is the spokesman for matters relating to Romeo and Juliet in Verona, Italy. He answers letters addressed to Juliet.

2. She fell in love with the son of her family's enemy. She was torn between love for him and loyalty to her family.

3. Admira, a young Muslim woman, and Bosko, a young Serbian man, were lovers in Sarajevo when Muslims and Serbs were at war.

4. They were shot dead by snipers as they crossed a bridge, trying to escape from Sarajevo.

Possible Answers

1. minus sign
2. minus sign
3. minus sign
4. minus sign
5. minus sign
6. minus sign
7. minus sign
8. minus sign
9. minus sign
10. minus sign

Assessment

■ *Holt Assessment: Literature, Reading, and Vocabulary*

For another selection to teach synthesizing sources, see *The Holt Reader*, Part 2.

Vocabulary Development

Denotations and Connotations

Connotations are the emotions and associations that are suggested by a word and that go beyond the word's literal meaning found in a dictionary—its **denotation.** Often connotations show shades of meaning or intensity.

PRACTICE

Use the plus sign (+) or the minus sign (–) to show how each of the following pairs of words compare in intensity. Use the plus sign if the word on the right seems stronger than the numbered Word Bank word on the left. Use the minus sign if the word on the right seems weaker. Use a dictionary for help. Then, discuss your answers with a classmate. You probably won't agree on all of your decisions.

	Word Bank
	carnage
	reminiscing
	relentless
	mundane
	compulsory
	vulnerable
	primal
	esteem
	eradicating
	dilemma

1. carnage ( ) killing
2. reminiscing ( ) remembering
3. relentless ( ) continuing
4. mundane ( ) common
5. compulsory ( ) necessary
6. vulnerable ( ) sensitive
7. primal ( ) first
8. esteem ( ) regard
9. eradicating ( ) erasing
10. dilemma ( ) choice

PEANUTS reprinted by permission of United Feature Syndicate, Inc.

SKILLS FOCUS

Vocabulary Skills
Understand word denotations and connotations.

PLAY

From Balcony to Barrio

Tony and Maria are in love, but they come from different social worlds—Tony is Italian American, and Maria is Puerto Rican. Add to their problems the fact that Tony is the former ringleader of the Jets—a tough street-fighting gang—and Maria's brother, Bernardo, is the leader of the equally fearsome Sharks. If the story line sounds familiar, it should: The musical **West Side Story** takes its cue from *Romeo and Juliet*. This updated spin on Shakespeare's tale of star-crossed lovers is set in New York City in the 1950s.

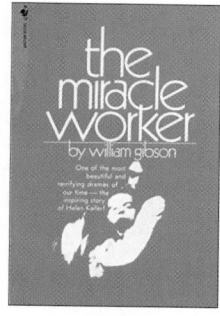

PLAY

Against the Odds

Six-year-old Helen Keller was considered a hopeless case. Blind, hearing impaired, and unable to speak, Helen was an angry prisoner of her own body. A teacher, Annie Sullivan, was asked to help—if help was possible. Slowly but surely the patient instructor taught Helen to "see" with her hands, to learn sign language, and to open herself to a world beyond darkness and silence. William Gibson's play **The Miracle Worker** stands as a classic story of two amazing young women—one a student, the other a teacher.

PLAY

Deep in the Forest

A wedding, an argument, a series of bungling play rehearsals, and misfortunes in love—these four plot elements are woven together in William Shakespeare's comedy **A Midsummer Night's Dream**. This play, which some critics consider Shakespeare's funniest and most imaginative, features characters ranging from fairies and fools to a king and a queen—all of whose paths intersect in surprising ways.

This title is available in the HRW Library.

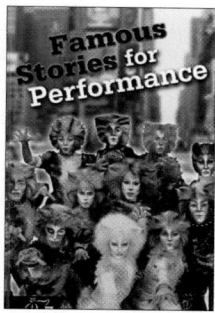

PLAYS

The Play's the Thing

Famous Stories for Performance includes stage plays and teleplays as well as some famous tales adapted for performance with a new dramatic spin. Here you'll find comedy (*Pyramus and Thisby* by William Shakespeare), a tragic true story (*Brian's Song* by William Blinn), and a legend to make the hair on the back of your neck stand up (*The Legend of Sleepy Hollow* by Washington Irving).

This title is available in the HRW Library.

Read On **925**

Read On

For Independent Reading

If students enjoyed the themes and topics explored in this collection, you might recommend these titles for independent reading.

Assessment Options

The following projects can help you evaluate and assess your students' outside reading. Videotapes or audiotapes of completed projects may be included in student portfolios.

- **Design a movie poster.** Tell students to imagine that the play they have read has been made into a movie. Have them design a "Coming Attractions" poster similar to those displayed at movie theaters. The poster should show the major characters, hint at the plot, illustrate or suggest the setting, and perhaps depict a scene.

- **Participate in a radio panel.** Invite students who have read the same play to work in a small group to discuss it. One of the students should be the moderator and prepare questions that panelists can respond to with their opinions. After students have held a practice session, they can tape the discussion as if it were a radio talk show.

- **Make a plaque.** Have students choose a general topic that one of the plays deals with, such as love, friendship, or fear. Then, have them find a quotation from the play that relates to the topic. Students can design a plaque that shows the topic and the quotation, as well as any artistic embellishments they want to add.

DIFFERENTIATING INSTRUCTION

Estimated Word Counts and Reading Levels of Read On Books:

Drama

			Drama		
West Side Story	⬄	26,100	*A Midsummer Night's Dream*	⬆	30,000
The Miracle Worker	⬄	30,900	*Famous Stories for Performance*	⬄	36,400

KEY: ⬆ *above grade level*   ⬄ *at grade level*   ⬇ *below grade level*

Comparing a Play and a Film

Writing Assignment
Write an essay in which you compare a scene from a film with the play from which it was adapted and evaluate the film techniques the director uses.

Now that you've read William Shakespeare's *Romeo and Juliet,* you might feel compelled to go out and rent a video version of it. Since you already know the story's tragic ending, you'd think that you wouldn't be too upset when it's shown. Still, you might find yourself feeling choked up and sad in a way that you weren't when you read the original. Somehow, the filmmakers have affected you in a way the words written on the page didn't. How did they do that?

Prewriting

Choose a Film

Cameras . . . Rolling! Begin by choosing a film that has been adapted from a play. There are many films to choose from. For example, several of Shakespeare's plays have been adapted into films, including *Much Ado About Nothing, Romeo and Juliet,* and *A Midsummer Night's Dream.* You might prefer, instead, a more modern play, such as *The Odd Couple* or *The Glass Menagerie.* You may even find that there is more than one film version of a play that you've enjoyed.

Look for film adaptations of plays in video stores and libraries. If you have trouble finding or choosing a film adaptation, look for movie reviews in newspapers and magazines and on the Internet. Consider asking friends, teachers, or family members to recommend a film adaptation they've enjoyed.

Focus on One Scene

The Scene's the Thing You won't be able to analyze an entire film in a 1,500-word essay, so you'll focus your analysis on one important scene. Find that scene by watching a video of the film. As you watch, take notes on your responses to each scene. Is there a scene that draws a strong emotional reaction from you? Is there a scene that makes you think about your own life or the larger world? After you've watched the film, review your notes. The scene to which you had the strongest reactions will be the best one for you to focus on in your analysis.

SKILLS FOCUS

Writing Skills
Write an essay comparing a scene from a play with its film adaptation.

Compare the Film with the Play

Altered Tales Now, read the same scene in the play and take notes on any differences between the written text of the play and the scene in the film. Filmmakers creating movies based on plays often use

926 Collection 11 Drama • Synthesizing Sources

narrative techniques to make changes to the written play. For example, they may choose to cut dialogue, combine several characters into one, and change the setting of a scene. To analyze the film's narrative techniques, ask yourself the questions in the chart below.

IDENTIFYING NARRATIVE TECHNIQUES IN A FILM

Plot, Characters, and Setting: Did the filmmaker make changes to the characters, plot, or settings? For example, have characters, plot events, or settings been added or eliminated? If so, how do these changes affect the story?

Dialogue: Did the filmmaker cut or add lines of dialogue? Do cuts make the story simpler? Do additions help make ideas from the play clearer?

Theme: Did the filmmaker keep the original theme, or message, of the story? How does a change in theme change the viewer's reaction to the story?

Every Picture Tells a Story In addition to narrative techniques, filmmakers also have various **film techniques,** such as lighting, camera angles and shots, sound, and special effects, with which to tell their stories. These techniques enable the filmmaker to create reactions in viewers that are very different from what readers experience. For example, when you watch a film, you often see close-up shots that show characters' emotions. However, when you read a play, you rely only on word clues to understand the characters' feelings. To analyze the film techniques used in the scene you've chosen, ask yourself the following questions.

IDENTIFYING FILM TECHNIQUES

Camera Shots and Angles: What types of camera shots are used—close-ups, long shots? From what angles does the camera shoot the characters and actions? What effects do the shots and angles create?

Lighting: How is lighting used in the scene? Does the lighting affect the mood of the scene?

Sound: What music or sound effects are present in the scene? How do they affect your reactions to the scene?

Special Effects: What special effects are included that you would not expect to see in a stage production of the play? Are the special effects distracting? Are they helpful to your understanding of the story?

On the next page are some of the notes one viewer took of the examples of narrative and film techniques he found while comparing a scene from Shakespeare's *Romeo and Juliet* to Franco Zeffirelli's 1968 film version of the play. He will use this information as **evidence** in his paper to support his thesis statement.

MODELING AND DEMONSTRATION

Identifying Film Techniques

Play for the class a scene from a film (preferably Franco Zeffirelli's 1968 *Romeo and Juliet,* which is treated in the student sample notes on p. 928), and take some time to discuss the elements listed in the **Identifying Film Techniques** chart. Point out to students that not every question will apply to the scenes they choose—not every scene will have special effects, for example—but that students should be aware of the director's and actors' unique interpretations of the play on which the film is based. After you have modeled answering the questions in the chart, have volunteers demonstrate answering similar questions about the films of their choice.

CORRECTING MISCONCEPTIONS

Students may assume they need only to identify the film's techniques, and they may not take that second step of evaluating or interpreting the techniques. You may want to point out the second item in the "Lighting" section of the chart, which asks about a possible meaning for the lighting. Emphasize to students that they can evaluate the techniques by asking themselves questions such as, *Do the techniques add to or detract from the play's script? Do they combine to make a unique and successful interpretation of the play?*

DIFFERENTIATING INSTRUCTION

Learners Having Difficulty

Students who have difficulty reading a play could be assigned to analyze the difference between two different film versions of a play or between a live performance and a film version of a play. When students see the performances, they may find the analysis less frustrating than if they had to struggle to read the play.

Assessment

- *Holt Assessment: Writing, Listening, and Speaking*
- *One-Stop Planner* CD-ROM with ExamView Test Generator
- *Holt Online Assessment*

Internet

- go.hrw.com (Keyword: LE5 9-11)
- *Elements of Literature Online*

Writing Workshop: Comparing a Play and a Film 927

Write Your Thesis Statement

What Say You? A filmmaker combines narrative and film techniques to create intellectual and emotional responses, known as **aesthetic effects**, in the film's viewers. The **thesis**, or main idea, of your essay identifies the effects created by the techniques.

To write a **thesis statement**, ask yourself, "What response was the filmmaker trying to create?" and "How did the techniques affect me as a viewer?" You'll find the answers to these questions in your notes. The example below shows one student's working thesis statement.

> Franco Zeffirelli uses narrative and film techniques to reduce the final scene to an emotional essence—the two young lovers and their tragic fate.

Organize Your Essay

Getting Your Act Together Your essay really has two parts: the first part compares the narrative techniques of the film with the original play, and the second part analyzes and evaluates the film techniques. To help your readers see how your ideas fit together, organize your essay in these two ways:

- **Point-by-point order:** Discuss the narrative techniques by comparing each narrative technique from the play to the corresponding one from the film.

- **Order of importance:** Discuss the film techniques by evaluating the most important film technique first and the least important one last, or vice versa.

| DO THIS

SKILLS FOCUS

Writing Skills
Establish a thesis statement.
Organize the essay.

PRACTICE & APPLY 1 Compare a film adaptation of a play with the original by analyzing the filmmaker's use of narrative and film techniques. Then, write your thesis statement and organize your ideas.

Writing

Comparing a Play and a Film

A Writer's Framework

Introduction

- Engage your readers immediately with an interesting opening, such as a question, a quote from the play, or a relevant anecdote.
- Identify the original play and the film and their creators.
- Clearly state your thesis.

Body

- Compare the narrative techniques, and organize them in point-by-point order.
- Analyze and evaluate the film techniques, and organize them in order of importance.
- Include specific references to the play and film to support your discussion.

Conclusion

- Remind readers of your thesis by restating it.
- Include a concluding thought or question to leave readers with something to think about.

A Writer's Model

A Rose by Any Other Name

Can Franco Zeffirelli's *Romeo and Juliet* smell quite as sweet as Shakespeare's original play? The 1968 film adaptation remains largely faithful to the original. The unfolding of the tragic love theme in both the play and the film is dramatic and moving. However, Zeffirelli uses narrative and film techniques to reduce the final scene to its emotional essence—the two young lovers and their tragic fate.

The final scene when Romeo and Juliet die serves as a good example of the choices Zeffirelli makes to get to the play's emotional essence. He changes the scene by cutting out plot events and dialogue, and by moving the final setting to a different location. Zeffirelli cuts out the scene at the tomb where Paris arrives, fights with Romeo, and is killed. By cutting the duel, the audience can focus on the tragic events that are about to unfold. Also, at the very end of the play, the entire cast comes onstage, and the Friar explains the tragedy. Zeffirelli moves this gathering to another place and time—the steps of the church on the following morning. The Friar's speech of explanation is cut out entirely, and the Prince bitterly tells the Capulets and Montagues that "all are punished" (V.3.295). The Prince's speech leaves the viewers to consider how the story would have ended if the Capulets and Montagues were not enemies.

(continued)

INTRODUCTION

Introduction of film, play, and creators

Thesis statement

Comparison of narrative techniques

Plot

Setting

Dialogue

A Writer's Model

Students may have trouble finishing their essays with a concluding thought or question that expands upon the restatement of their thesis. You may want to contrast for students the introduction of an essay with its conclusion by pointing out that while an introduction draws a reader into the specific topic of an essay, a conclusion opens up the discussion of the topic once again to the outside world. Show on the chalkboard how an introduction acts as a funnel, going from the general to the specific, while a conclusion acts as a trumpet, going from the specific to the general. To give students practice in developing concluding thoughts and questions, have the class brainstorm for alternative ways to end **A Writer's Model.**

CRITICAL THINKING

Direct students to pay close attention to the ways in which the writer of the model constructs smooth transitions between ideas. Students will benefit from identifying the transitional words and phrases in the essay, but they should also think about how one sentence or paragraph naturally leads to the next. For example, the first sentence of the second paragraph smoothly follows from the preceding sentence not only because of the transitional words "serves as a good example" but also because the sentence mentions one of the techniques hinted at in the thesis. Ask students to find other examples of sentences and paragraphs neatly expanding the sentences and paragraphs that come before.

English-Language Learners

The punctuation of quotations differs greatly from country to country. Before students read **A Writer's Model,** you may want to review with them the standard American English conventions involving punctuating quotations. As students read the model they can identify the rules of punctuation the model's quotations follow.

Advanced Learners

Enrichment. Direct students to cite in the conclusion of their essays a review of the film about which they are writing. Students should look for critical comments about the film's relationship to the play on which it is based and indicate whether they agree or disagree with the reviewer, in either case being sure to give reasons that support their conclusions.

PRACTICE & APPLY 2

Guided and Independent Practice

Spot-check students' outlines to make sure they follow two organizational patterns:

- Their comparison and contrast of the play's and film's narrative techniques should be in point-by-point order.

- Their discussion of the film techniques should be arranged in order of importance.

Students can let ideas for an interesting introduction and conclusion come to them as they write. Then, have students complete **Practice and Apply 2** as independent practice.

(continued)

Discussion of film techniques

Camera shots

Zeffirelli also uses a variety of film techniques to create an emotional response beyond that created by the language of the play. Different camera shots allow the viewer to understand the emotions portrayed in the last scene when Romeo and Juliet die. For example, a long shot from the side provides an overview of the scene. Viewers see Juliet's still form and Romeo's anguished face as he speaks to her. Then, the camera moves to a close-up of Romeo's face as he sobs and drinks the poison. Viewers can experience Romeo's sadness and desperation as they watch him in this shot. Next, viewers see the extreme close-up on Juliet's left hand—the same one Romeo kissed as he died—as the hand stirs with life. Viewers feel hope and anguish at the same time, because even though Juliet is alive, she will soon find that her true love is not. The camera moves back to show Juliet's discovery of Romeo dead by her side. She then stabs herself and rests her head on Romeo's chest. The final close-up shot of the two lovers' faces illustrates the irony of the situation. In life the two could not be together, but in death they can.

Sound and lighting

Music and lighting also play a role in bringing out the emotional aspects of the scene. As Romeo enters this scene, he's shown on horseback approaching the tomb at night as ominous, sad music plays. The quiet of the nighttime graveyard is emphasized when the music fades and only the sound of chirping crickets remains. When Romeo enters the tomb, he sees Juliet in the blue-tinted darkness. A soft white light shines on her alone, giving a false sense of peace. As Romeo kisses her, the music swells in the full orchestral version of their love theme. Music is also played softly as Juliet's hand feels the edge of the stone bier and then her dress, but trumpets interrupt the soft music when Juliet sees Romeo dead. The rest of the scene is shot in a beautiful golden light focused on the two lovers alone, illustrating the purity of their love.

CONCLUSION

Restatement of thesis

Concluding thought

By concentrating on the deaths of Juliet and Romeo, Zeffirelli creates an emotionally wrenching and powerful scene that expresses the heart of Shakespeare's famous tragedy. Zeffirelli's treatment of this ancient tale of love allows the viewer to experience fully the tragedy of these "star-crossed lovers" (Prologue, line 6).

INTERNET

More Writer's Models

Keyword: LE5 9-11

PRACTICE & APPLY 2 Use the framework and Writer's Model to write the first draft of your essay. Be sure to include parenthetical citations whenever you quote lines from the play. For more on **giving credit to sources,** see page 620.

Revising

Revise Your Essay

The Big Picture The revision process is as important as any other phase of the writing process. Some even say it's the *most* important stage. When you revise, you shape both your ideas and how you express them so that they can best achieve their desired effects: strong content, clear organization, and effective style.

PEER REVIEW

As you revise, exchange papers with a classmate. He or she can help ensure that your ideas are organized in two ways: point-by-point and order of importance.

First Reading: Content and Organization Evaluate the content and organization of your essay using the guidelines below as a **think sheet.** First, answer the questions in the left-hand column. If you need help answering them, refer to the tips in the middle column. Then, make the changes suggested by using the revision techniques in the right-hand column.

Rubric: Comparing a Play and a Film

Evaluation Questions	▶ Tips	▶ Revision Techniques
❶ Is the opening engaging? Are the original play, its film version, and their creators introduced in the first paragraph?	▶ **Underline** the engaging opening. **Bracket** the introduction of the subjects.	▶ **Add** a relevant anecdote, an interesting quotation, or an intriguing question. **Add** a sentence introducing the play, film, and their creators.
❷ Does the introduction include a clear thesis statement that identifies the response the filmmaker was trying to create?	▶ **Highlight** the thesis statement. **Circle** the part that identifies the filmmaker's intended response.	▶ **Add** a thesis statement, or **reword** the thesis statement to identify the response the filmmaker intended.
❸ Does evidence support the discussion of each narrative and film technique?	▶ **Put a star** by each example from the play or film.	▶ **Add** evidence, or **elaborate** on existing evidence.
❹ Is the essay well organized so that the reader can easily follow ideas?	▶ **Label** the specific narrative techniques. **Number** the film techniques.	▶ **Rearrange** the narrative techniques so that they are in point-by-point order. **Reorder** the film techniques so that they are arranged in order of importance.
❺ Does the conclusion restate the thesis? Does it contain an interesting concluding thought or question?	▶ **Highlight** the sentence that restates the thesis. **Circle** the concluding thought or question.	▶ **Add** a sentence restating the thesis. If necessary, **add** a concluding thought or summary.

Writing Workshop: Comparing a Play and a Film **931**

DIRECT TEACHING

First Reading: Content and Organization

Remind students that the many elements of their writing are interrelated: if their essays are not organized neatly, they will not be coherent; if their essays are not coherent, they will not be clear or meaningful to a reader. One way students can check the organization and coherence of their essays is to color-code the points in the sections. For example, each comment on narrative techniques could be shaded red, and each statement about film techniques shaded blue. Within the sections, the specific points could be numbered in the same color. Students should find the colors intermixed in the introduction and conclusion but set apart in the body of the essay; the same numbers labeling the thesis and developed in the body should also appear in the conclusion.

DIRECT TEACHING

Elaboration

If students lack sufficient details to support their theses, remind them to look again at the play and the film for details and examples to support their points. If they are having difficulty finding supporting details, have a partner peruse their play and film adaptation and suggest areas where more details can be found.

Second Reading: Style Once you've revised the content and organization of your essay, you can concentrate on its style, or how you've expressed your ideas. One way to improve the style is to use active instead of passive voice. When a writer uses the **active voice,** the subject of the verb performs the action. When a writer uses the **passive voice,** the subject of the verb receives the action. The passive voice takes the attention away from the subject. Look at the following examples.

Passive Voice The tomb **is broken** into by Romeo.
Active Voice Romeo **breaks** into the tomb.

Notice how simple and direct the second sentence is. Follow the guidelines below to make sure your essay uses the active voice.

Style Guidelines

Evaluation Question	▶ Tip	▶ Revision Technique
● Does the essay contain verbs in the active voice?	▶ **Double underline** all *be* verbs (e.g., *be, am, is, are, was, were, been*). Do not underline *be* verbs that express a state of being or that are in quotations.	▶ **Reword** half of the *be* verb sentences so that the subject of the sentence performs the verb.

ANALYZING THE REVISION PROCESS
Study these revisions, and answer the questions that follow.

> The Friar's speech of explanation is cut out entirely, and
>
> *Prince bitterly tells the*
> the~Capulets and Montagues ~~are bitterly told by the Prince~~ that
>
> *The Prince's speech leaves the viewers to*
> "all are punished."~ *consider how the story would have ended if the Capulets and Montagues were not enemies.*

reword

elaborate

Responding to the Revision Process
1. Why do you think the writer revised the first sentence?
2. How does adding the last sentence improve the passage?

SKILLS FOCUS

Writing Skills
Revise for content and style.

PRACTICE & APPLY 3 Revise the content, organization, and style of your essay, using the guidelines in this section. Exchange essays with a peer to get another person's ideas on how you might revise. Reviewing a peer's essay may even give you ideas on how to revise your own.

Responding to the Revision Process

Answers
1. The revision is made to change the passive voice of the sentence to the active voice.
2. The addition provides essential elaboration by specifically identifying the effect of the film's departure from the play's text.

PRACTICE & APPLY 3

Independent Practice
Direct students to make at least three revision passes on their papers, focusing on the following concerns, in order:

- the **Rubric: Comparing a Play and a Film** chart
- active rather than passive voice
- reading the paper aloud and listening for any element that seems out of place or poorly worded

Publishing

Proofread and Publish Your Essay

A Last Look After you've revised your essay, be sure to proofread it. Check for and correct any errors in grammar, usage, and mechanics. Have someone else—a classmate, parent, or friend—proofread your essay, too. Two sets of eyes are always better than one since the other person may catch errors that you missed.

Finally, It's Showtime! Now that you have written, revised, and proofread your essay, it's time for others to read it. Here are some suggestions for publication.

- Watch the film with your family and let them read your essay. Be prepared to discuss your essay and listen to their ideas, thoughts, feelings, and opinions, too.

- With a group of classmates, form a panel discussion about the techniques filmmakers use in their movies. Use your essays as a springboard into the discussion.

- Post your essay to an online movie database or video store. Many invite people to send in comments—both positive and negative—of the videos they discuss or sell.

Reflect on Your Essay

That's a Wrap! After a sporting event, coaches and athletes often review videotapes of the game, match, or race to evaluate individual or team performance. This gives them the opportunity to see what they did well and where they may need improvement before their next outing. You, too, should look back on what you have done. Think about what you've learned in the process of writing this essay. Ask yourself the following questions to improve future writing assignments. The questions will also give you insight on how well you understand media presentations.

- What revisions do you think strengthened your essay the most? Why?

- What additional narrative and film techniques would you have used if you were doing a film adaptation of the same play? Explain each of your answers.

- How did writing this essay help you better understand the choices made by filmmakers?

PRACTICE & APPLY 4 Proofread your essay one last time. Publish your essay by using one of the ideas on this page, or think of your own publishing idea. Finally, write down answers to the reflection questions above.

TIP Careful proofreading will help you make sure that your essay follows the **conventions** of standard American English. For example, you may have listed several different narrative or film techniques in one sentence. Check to make sure that you have used commas correctly between items in a series. For more on **serial commas,** see Commas, 12f, in the Language Handbook.

SKILLS FOCUS

Writing Skills
Proofread, especially for correct use of serial commas.

Proofread and Publish Your Essay

If students choose to publish their essays on the Internet, you need to be aware that the World Wide Web often functions as a public forum and that its content may be unpredictable.

PRACTICE & APPLY 4

Independent Practice
To monitor students' progress, have them write down their publishing idea for you to check. Then, have them complete **Practice and Apply 4** for independent practice.

Motivate. Ask students to think of times during a film, a play, or perhaps in real life that a speaker's words moved them. What was it about the speech that was so affecting and memorable? Discuss with students the techniques and strategies a speaker can use to deliver his or her message effectively.

DIRECT TEACHING

Select a Speech

Take students to explore the school library's audiovisuals section, or arrange with another library to provide you on loan a number of varied tapes of famous persuasive speeches. Students may find it easier to choose a speech to analyze and evaluate if they can listen to it first rather than reading about it and then trying to find it.

If students research historically important speeches on the Internet, you need to be aware that the World Wide Web often functions as a public forum and its content can be unpredictable.

Analyze Content

Lead students to prepare note sheets that list two columns: one side labeled *Arguments* and the other *Rhetorical Devices.* As students watch their chosen speeches, have them make note of the arguments and rhetorical devices the speaker uses, and alert students that speakers often use the same gestures (such as pointing or tapping the podium) when introducing an argument or rhetorical device. After students have completed their notes, have them analyze the types of items in each column (*causation* or *analogy,* for example, in the arguments; *allusion* or *repetition* among the rhetorical devices). Then, lead a class discussion in which students share the devices they found and give their first impressions about their effectiveness.

Analyzing and Evaluating Speeches

Speaking Assignment
Analyze and evaluate a historically significant speech to uncover its impact on an audience.

In *Romeo and Juliet,* Prince Escalus issues a speech to convince the Capulets and Montagues, who "have thrice disturbed the quiet of our streets," to stop their feuding. In history, as in literature, speakers often use the power of persuasion to convince others to take action. In this workshop you'll have the opportunity to look at a **historically significant speech** and determine what made it so persuasive.

Select a Speech

Actions Speak Louder You can find many historically important speeches as written texts, audio recordings, and videotapes at the library, in your history textbook, and on the Internet. Consider what historical events interest you, and do a little research to find what great speeches were given at that point in time. Instead, you may wish to start with an issue that interests you, such as civil rights, space exploration, or freedom of religion, and see what great speeches have been given on either side of those issues. Try to find a speech that you can listen to and watch instead of just read. Great speakers often rely on not only their words, but also their voices, gestures, and body postures to communicate their messages.

Analyze Content

Getting into the Arguments Begin your analysis by viewing the speech you've selected. Pay close attention to the content, the **important points** the speaker wants to make. As you identify these important points, you will probably notice that the speech contains persuasive elements. Keep in mind, though, that a speaker cannot persuade an audience just by stating an opinion. He or she must provide **arguments** that convince listeners to change their minds or take action. Here are some common types of arguments you will find.

INTERNET
Speeches
Keyword: LE5 9-11

SKILLS FOCUS

Listening and Speaking Skills
Analyze a historically significant speech.

- **Causation** shows how a cause-effect relationship supports the speaker's opinion.

- **Analogies** make literal comparisons between things that are generally unlike.

- **Appeals to authority** refer to a trustworthy or knowledgeable authority or expert.

COLLECTION 11 RESOURCES: LISTENING & SPEAKING

Planning
- *One-Stop Planner* CD-ROM with ExamView Test Generator

Differentiating Instruction
- *Workshop Resources: Writing, Listening, and Speaking*
- *Family Involvement Activities in English and Spanish*

- *Supporting Instruction in Spanish*

Listening and Speaking
- *Workshop Resources: Writing, Listening, and Speaking*

Assessment
- *Holt Assessment: Writing, Listening, and Speaking*

- **Emotional appeals** use language to stir feelings of happiness, sadness, or anger in listeners.
- **Logical appeals** speak to the listeners' minds through facts, statistics, anecdotes (brief stories), and examples.

Rhetorical Devices To make their arguments effective and memorable, speakers must master rhetoric, the art of speaking or writing well. Over thousands of years, people who speak effectively have developed **rhetorical devices**—certain ways of using language to make their messages attention-getting, persuasive, and memorable. The following chart lists and defines some rhetorical devices you might find when listening to a speech.

TIP Some speakers use elaborate language to cover up a lack of substance or to mislead listeners. Because of this misuse, some people have negative feelings about the word *rhetoric*.

RHETORICAL DEVICES

Allusion: an indirect reference to literature or an actual person, event, or place

Metaphor: an imaginative comparison between unlike things

Repetition: repeating the same important words or phrases

Diction: word choice that creates specific reactions from the audience

Parallelism: using the same **syntax,** or sentence structure, to point out a similarity in ideas

Analyze Organization

Follow Me Speakers organize their messages according to two different approaches. With the **deductive** approach, they state their thesis first, then deliver their reasons and support. Speakers using this approach start with general ideas, then move to more specific ones. With the **inductive** approach, speakers present reasons and support first, building to a thesis statement. Speakers using the inductive approach usually move their audience from thinking about specific ideas to more general ones. Whichever approach speakers choose, they must make sure that the organization of their ideas is **clear** and **coherent.**

Analyze Delivery

How Are We Feeling Today? In addition to **language,** a speaker's **delivery,** or use of voice and body, often sets the tone and mood of the speech. **Tone** is the speaker's attitude toward the subject and audience. **Mood** is the overall impression the speech makes on the audience. A speaker must choose a tone that is appropriate for the audience and purpose. For instance, a speaker who uses an angry tone when speaking to people who disagree with his opinion might antagonize his listeners, creating a hostile mood. A thoughtful, respectful tone, on the other hand, creates a more positive mood.

SKILLS FOCUS

Listening and Speaking Skills
Analyze rhetorical devices, organization, delivery, tone, and mood.

Learners Having Difficulty

Students may find the terms *deductive* and *inductive* difficult and abstract. Model for students an argument presented both ways by using the following sentences. Providing the sentences in the order in which they are given is the *deductive* approach, while presenting them with the first sentence given last is the *inductive* approach.

1. The school should remove all poison ivy from the baseball field. (thesis)
2. The ivy at the school's baseball field has affected many of the school's players, as well as some spectators. (support)
3. The effects of poison ivy are very unpleasant. (support)
4. Many are hesitant to go near the field. (support)

Ask students to create their own sample arguments they can organize both ways.

- *One-Stop Planner* CD-ROM with ExamView Test Generator

Internet
- go.hrw.com (Keyword: LE5 9-11)
- *Elements of Literature Online*

Speakers often use verbal and nonverbal delivery techniques, like those shown in the following chart, to convey tone and mood, and to get their points across to an audience.

DELIVERY TECHNIQUES

Verbal	Nonverbal
Emphasis is the stress a speaker puts on certain words and phrases. Speakers emphasize key ideas or points in their speeches by saying those words with a little more volume.	**Gestures** are body movements that emphasize emotions or ideas. Good speakers use natural gestures, such as nodding their heads, shrugging their shoulders, or pointing at the audience.
Pauses are small silences in speaking. A good speaker uses pauses to let his or her ideas soak in. Pauses also tell you that what the speaker has just said or is about to say is important.	**Facial expressions** clue listeners in to the speaker's feelings. For example, a smile can suggest warmth and sincerity, while a frown might show that the speaker is angry and wants you to know why.
Enunciation is the clarity with which speakers pronounce their words. Good speakers always want their ideas to be clearly understood. Poor enunciation makes listeners strain, giving them the impression that the speaker does not care about them or the topic.	**Posture** is how the speaker stands. A speaker standing straight and alert suggests confidence in his or her topic, while a slouching speaker suggests that he or she is disinterested and does not truly care about the topic.

A Speaker's Model The following is an excerpt from John F. Kennedy's 1962 "We choose to go to the moon . . . " speech, which helped convince Americans to support the U.S. space exploration program. The annotations in the model's margin identify arguments and rhetorical devices used in the speech. If you're able to listen to or view this speech, pay close attention to Kennedy's use of verbal and nonverbal techniques.

Causation
Emotional appeal

Metaphor and repetition

If . . . history . . . teaches us anything, it is that man, in this quest for knowledge and progress, is determined and cannot be deterred. The exploration of space will go ahead, whether we join in it or not, and it is one of the great adventures of all time, and no nation which expects to be the leader of other nations can expect to stay behind in this race for space.

Those who came before us made certain that this country rode the first waves of the industrial revolution, the first waves of modern invention, and the first waves of nuclear power, and this generation does not intend to founder in the backwash of the coming age of space. We mean to be part of it—we mean to lead it. For the eyes of the world now look into space, to the moon and to the planets beyond, and we have vowed that we shall not see it governed by a hostile flag of conquest, but by a banner of freedom and peace. We have vowed that we shall not see space filled with weapons of mass destruction, but with instruments of knowledge and understanding.

Yet the vows of this Nation can only be fulfilled if we in this Nation are first, and, therefore, we intend to be first. In short, our leadership in science and industry, our hopes for peace and security, our obligations to ourselves as well as others, all require us to make this effort, to solve these mysteries, to solve them for the good of all men, and to become the world's leading space-faring nation.

Emotional appeal
Parallelism

Repetition

Causation
Repetition

Evaluate a Speech

Put It All Together The most important test of a good persuasive speech is your own reaction. A speech should make you think more deeply about a subject and might change your mind or prompt you to take action. Use the following questions to evaluate the effectiveness and quality of a persuasive speech, stating your own **judgments** about it.

EVALUATING PERSUASIVE SPEECHES

Content and Organization	Delivery
What **arguments** and **rhetorical devices** did the speaker use? Was there a variety of arguments and devices?	How did the speaker make good use of **emphasis, enunciation,** and **pauses?** Were his or her **diction** and **syntax** clear?
What **evidence** (facts, statistics, or expert testimony) did the speaker provide to support his or her ideas?	Did the speaker use **facial expressions, gestures,** and **posture** to express tone and mood? If so, describe them.
Were the speaker's main points **clear** and **coherent**—connected to each other and to the main idea? Describe the organizational pattern.	Did the speaker's **overall delivery** capture your attention and help you understand the speech? Explain.

PRACTICE & APPLY 5 Use the information in this workshop to select and analyze a historically significant speech. Then, write a one-paragraph evaluation of the speech's quality and effectiveness. Depending on your access to audio-visual resources, choose one of two options:

- View a recorded speech (on tape or disc, or on the Internet), analyzing the content, organization, and delivery.
- Read the text of a written speech, concentrating on its content and organization. Pay close attention to how the language affects the mood and tone of the speech.

SKILLS FOCUS

Listening and Speaking Skills
Evaluate a historically significant speech.

Listening and Speaking Workshop: Analyzing and Evaluating Speeches **937**

Evaluate a Speech

If students are having trouble identifying and analyzing a speaker's arguments, rhetorical devices, and delivery techniques, play for them a videotaped speech and ask them to respond in their own words to the following questions:

- What does the speaker say to make his or her ideas sound more appealing?
- Does the speaker give support for the ideas? If so, what?
- What surprising connections does the speaker make?
- Does the speaker use any interesting words or phrases?
- What ideas are most important to the speaker, and how can you tell?
- What does the speaker do to make sure his or her words are clear to the audience?

After students have answered the questions and discussed the terms, review with them the questions given in the **Evaluating Persuasive Speeches** chart and point out their similarity to the questions the students have just answered.

PRACTICE & APPLY 5

Guided and Independent Practice

To monitor students' progress, follow these steps:

1. Have students turn in to you the title of the historical speech they plan to analyze and evaluate.
2. Allow class time for students to view their videotapes if they do not have access to a VCR at home.
3. Check students' answers to the first question of the chart on this page.

Then, have students complete **Practice and Apply 5** for independent practice.

SKILLS FOCUS, pp. 938–941

Grade-Level Skills

■ **Literary Skills**
Analyze the characteristics of dramatic literature.

INTRODUCING THE SKILLS REVIEW

Use this review to assess students' grasp of the skills taught in this collection. If necessary, you can use the annotations to guide students in their reading before they answer the questions.

DIRECT TEACHING

Ⓐ Literary Focus
Scene design. Have students identify stage directions in this passage that tell something about the play's scene design. [Possible responses: *crossing to the closet, following after him to the front of the couch, crossing onto bedroom landing, taking her coat from the couch and putting it on the armchair at right.*]

Ⓑ Literary Focus
❓ Dialogue and character traits. What personality differences between Paul and Corie does their dialogue reveal? [Corie is more spontaneous, relaxed, and easygoing. Paul is more restrained and controlled.]

Test Practice

Drama
DIRECTIONS: Read this excerpt from a comedy. Then, read and respond to the questions that follow.

from Barefoot in the Park
Neil Simon

Here's the climactic scene, Act II, Scene 2, of Neil Simon's comedy Barefoot in the Park. *As the scene opens, a young couple—Corie and Paul—have just returned from a late evening with Corie's widowed mother and their colorful next-door neighbor. This neighbor is a gourmet, and he has taken Paul, Corie, and her mother to an unusual restaurant on Staten Island, in New York City. Now he is politely accompanying Corie's mother home to New Jersey. Corie has had a perfectly wonderful evening; Paul has not had a good time at all.*

Corie. What are you so angry about, Paul?
Paul (*crossing to the closet*). I just told you. I felt terrible for your mother. (*He gets the wallet out of his jacket pocket.*)
Corie (*following after him to the front of the couch*). Why? Where is she at this very minute? Alone with probably the most attractive man she's ever met. Don't tell me *that* doesn't beat . . . hair curlers and *The Late Late Show.*
Paul (*crossing onto bedroom landing*). Oh, I can just hear it now. What sparkling conversation. He's probably telling her about a chicken cacciatore he once cooked for the High Lama of Tibet, and she's sitting there shoving pink pills in her mouth.
Corie (*taking her coat from the couch and putting it on the armchair at right*). You can never tell what people talk about when they're alone.
Paul. I don't understand how you can be so unconcerned about this. (*He goes into the bedroom.*)
Corie (*moving to the stairs*). Unconcerned . . . I'm plenty concerned. Do you think I'm going to get one wink of sleep until that phone rings tomorrow? I'm scared to death for my mother. But I'm grateful there's finally the opportunity for something to be scared about . . . (*She moves right, then turns back.*) What I'm really concerned about is you!
Paul (*bursts out of the bedroom, nearly slamming through the door*). Me? Me?
Corie. I'm beginning to wonder if you're capable of *having* a good time.
Paul. Why? Because I like to wear my gloves in the winter?
Corie. No. Because there isn't the least bit of adventure in you. Do you know what you are? You're a Watcher. There are Watchers in this world and there are Do-ers. And the Watchers sit around watching the Do-ers do. Well, tonight you watched and I did.
Paul (*moves down the stairs to* CORIE). Yeah . . . Well, it was harder to watch what you did than it was for you to *do* what I was watching. (*He goes back up the stairs to the landing.*)

SKILLS FOCUS

Pages 938–941 cover
Literary Skills
Understand elements of drama.

READING MINI-LESSON

Reviewing Word-Attack Skills
Activity. Display the following words. Have volunteers read the words and group them by stressed syllable. Is the first syllable or the second syllable said with greater stress?

decent   descent   deserve
formal   forlorn   forage
control   convent   conform
respect   regal   regard

promise   promote   prolong
survive   surprise   surplus

[*First syllable stressed*—decent, formal, forage, convent, regal, promise, surplus. *Second syllable stressed*—descent, deserve, forlorn, control, conform, respect, regard, promote, prolong, survive, surprise.]

Corie. You won't let your hair down for a minute? You couldn't even relax for one night. Boy, Paul, sometimes you act like a . . . a . . . (*She gets her shoes from under the couch.*)

Paul (*stopping on the landing*). What . . . ? A stuffed shirt?

Corie (*drops the shoes on the couch*). I didn't say that.

Paul. That's what you're implying.

Corie (*moves to the right armchair and begins to take off her jewelry*). That's what you're anticipating. I didn't say you're a stuffed shirt. But you are extremely proper and dignified.

Paul. I'm proper and dignified? (*He moves to* CORIE.) When . . . ? When was I proper and dignified? . . .

Corie. Always. You're always dressed right, you always look right, you always say the right things. You're very close to being perfect.

Paul (*hurt to the quick*). That's . . . that's a *rotten* thing to say.

Corie (*moves to* PAUL). I have never seen you without a jacket. I always feel like such a slob compared to you. Before we were married, I was sure you slept with a tie.

Paul. No, no. Just for very *formal* sleeps.

Corie. You can't even walk into a candy store and ask the lady for a Tootsie Roll. (*Playing the scene out, she moves down to right side of the couch.*) You've got to walk up to the counter and point at it and say, "I'll have that thing in the brown-and-white wrapper."

Paul (*moving to the bedroom door*). That's ridiculous.

Corie. And you're not. That's just the trouble. (*She crosses to the foot of the stairs.*) Like Thursday night. You wouldn't

walk barefoot with me in Washington Square Park. Why not?

Paul (*moving to the head of the stairs*). Very simple answer. It was seventeen degrees.

Corie (*moves back to the chair and continues taking down her hair*). Exactly. That's very sensible and logical. Except it isn't any fun.

Paul (*moves down the stairs to the couch*). You know, maybe I *am* too proper and dignified for you. Maybe you would have been happier with someone a little more colorful and flamboyant . . . like the Greek! (*He starts back to the bedroom.*)

Corie. Well, he'd be a lot more laughs than a stuffed shirt.

Paul (*turns back on the landing*). Oh, oh . . . I thought you said I wasn't.

Corie. Well, you are now.

Paul (*reflectively*). I'm not going to listen to this . . . I'm not going to listen . . . (*He starts for the bedroom.*) I've got a case in court in the morning.

Corie (*moves left*). Where are you going?

Paul. To sleep.

Corie. *Now?* How can you sleep now?

Paul (*steps up on the bed and turns back, leaning on the door jamb*). I'm going to close my eyes and count knichis.° Good night!

Corie. You can't go to sleep now. We're having a fight.

Paul. *You* have the fight. When you're through, turn off the lights. (*He turns back into the bedroom.*)

Corie. Ooh, that gets me insane. You can even control your emotions.

Paul (*storms out to the head of the stairs*).

° **knichis** (nē′chĕz) *n. pl.*: unusual appetizer they had eaten with dinner.

C Literary Focus

? Comedy. What techniques does Neil Simon use to make Corie and Paul's argument funny, rather than disturbing? [Possible responses: He uses irony, when Corie accuses Paul of being "very close to being perfect" and Paul, deeply hurt, responds, "That's . . . that's a *rotten* thing to say." He uses exaggeration, when Corie says, "Before we were married, I was sure you slept with a tie."]

D Literary Focus

? Scene design. How does the design of the play's set help reveal Paul's shifting moods and motivations in this scene? [Because the bedroom is located on a landing that is up a flight of stairs, Paul moves up toward the bedroom when he feels like cutting short the argument. He moves back down the stairs when Corie antagonizes him into wanting to make a point in his own defense or to make an accusation against her.]

Activity. Display these sets of words. Have students identify the two words in each set that are homophones. Encourage them to check a dictionary if they are unsure of the pronunciation of any word. Answers are underlined.

1. heir   hair   ere
2. chaste   chased   caste

3. suite   suit   sweet
4. choral   coral   corral
5. pique   pick   peak

Activity. Display these pairs of words. The first word in each pair appears in the second word. Have volunteers tell if the sounds of the first word are also heard in the second word.

1. tile   reptile [yes]
2. line   feline [yes]
3. rile   sterile [no]
4. line   discipline [no]
5. vine   bovine [yes]
6. pine   porcupine [yes]
7. tile   fertile [no]
8. tile   futile [no]

Collection 11: Skills Review

DIRECT TEACHING

A Literary Focus

? Comedy. Corie and Paul are newlyweds. What serious point about newlyweds is Simon making in this comedy? [A husband and a wife often don't understand each other's true personalities very well until they have lived together for a while.] Do you think the play will have a happy ending? Why or why not? [Yes, it will have a happy ending because it is a comedy, and Paul makes it clear that the marriage is founded on love.]

Test-Taking Tips

Remind students to make sure they understand the definitions of literary terms such as *comedy, tragedy, soliloquy, dialogue,* and *scene design* before they answer the questions.

For more instruction on how to answer multiple-choice items, refer students to **Test Smarts.**

Look, I'm just as upset as you are. . . . (*He controls himself.*). But when I get hungry, I eat. And when I get tired, I sleep. You eat and sleep, too. Don't deny it, I've seen you . . .
Corie (*moves right with a grand gesture*). Not in the middle of a crisis.
Paul. What crisis? We're just yelling a little.
Corie. You don't consider this a crisis? Our whole marriage hangs in the balance.
Paul (*sits on the steps*). It does? When did that happen?
Corie. Just now. It's suddenly very clear that you and I have absolutely *nothing* in common.
Paul. Why? Because I won't walk barefoot in the park in winter? . . .
Corie (*seething*). Don't oversimplify this. I'm angry. Can't you see that?
Paul (*brings his hands to his eyes, peers at her through imaginary binoculars, and then looks at his watch*). Corie, it's two-fifteen. If I can fall asleep in about half an hour, I can get about five hours' sleep. I'll call you from court tomorrow, and we can fight over the phone. (*He gets up and moves to the bedroom.*)
Corie. You will *not* go to sleep. You will stay here and fight to save our marriage.
Paul (*in the doorway*). If our marriage hinges on breathing fish balls and poofla-poo pie, it's not worth saving. . . . I am now going to crawl into our tiny little single bed. If you care to join me, we will be sleeping from left to right tonight. (*He goes into the bedroom and slams the door.*)
Corie. You won't discuss it . . . You're

afraid to discuss it . . . I married a coward!! . . . (*She takes a shoe from the couch and throws it at the bedroom door.*)
Paul (*opens the door*). Corie, would you bring in a pail? The closet's dripping.
Corie. Ohh, I hate you! I really, really hate you!
Paul (*storms to the head of the stairs*). Corie, there is one thing I learned in court. Be careful when you're tired and angry. You might say something you will soon regret. I-am-now-tired-and-angry.
Corie. And a coward.
Paul (*comes down the stairs to her at right of the couch*). And I will now say something I will soon regret . . . OK, Corie, maybe you're right. Maybe we have nothing in common. Maybe we rushed into this marriage a little too fast. Maybe Love isn't enough. Maybe two people should have to take more than a blood test. Maybe they should be checked for common sense, understanding, and emotional maturity.
Corie (*that hurt*). All right . . . Why don't you get it passed in the Supreme Court? Only those couples bearing a letter from their psychiatrists proving they're well adjusted will be permitted to be married.
Paul. You're impossible.
Corie. You're unbearable.
Paul. You belong in a nursery school.
Corie. It's a lot more fun than the Home for the Fuddy Duddies.
Paul (*reaches out his hand to her*). All right, Corie, let's not get . . .
Corie. Don't you touch me . . . Don't you touch me . . .

940 Collection 11 Drama • Synthesizing Sources

Using Academic Language

Review of Literary Terms
Ask students to review the collection to find the meanings of the terms listed below. Then, have students show their grasp of the terms by citing passages from the collection that show the meanings of those terms.
Play (p. 752); **Conflict** (pp. 752, 755);

Climax (pp. 752, 783); **Tragedy** (pp. 752, 783); **Tragic Hero** (p. 752); **Tragic Flaw** (p. 752); **Comedy** (pp. 752, 755); **Scene Design** (p. 753); **Dialogue** (p. 754); **Monologue** (p. 754); **Soliloquy** (p. 754); **Stage Directions** (p. 754); **Farce** (p. 755).

Review of Informational Terms
Ask students to use the following terms to explain how to synthesize the content from several sources dealing with a single issue.
Connect (p. 918); **Compare** (p. 918); **Synthesize** (p. 918); **Paraphrase** (p. 918).

940 Collection 11 Drama • Synthesizing Sources

1. Corie is mad at Paul because he —
   A insulted her mother
   B didn't like the restaurant
   C has a court case in the morning
   D doesn't know how to have fun

2. Paul describes Corie's **character** as —
   F impossible
   G charming
   H mature
   J serious

3. Because *Barefoot in the Park* is a **comedy,** you can predict that by the end of the play —
   A Paul and Corie will resolve their differences
   B Paul and Corie will get divorced
   C there will be a funny scene with the neighbor
   D Corie's mother will move in with them

4. If the play were a **tragedy** instead of a comedy, it might end with —
   F Corie's mother getting married
   G the death of Paul and Corie
   H Paul and Corie moving to another apartment
   J Paul's winning his case in court

5. This excerpt from the play consists of —
   A monologues
   B narration
   C dialogue
   D asides

6. Which of the following stage directions tells you something about the **scene design**?
   F *hurt to the quick*
   G *crossing onto bedroom landing*
   H *He controls himself.*
   J *reaches out his hand to her*

7. If this scene were followed by a **soliloquy,** it might be delivered by —
   A Paul telling Corie how he really feels about her
   B Paul and Corie apologizing to each other for getting so angry
   C Corie alone talking about how much she loves Paul
   D Corie's mother telling Paul and Corie what a good time she had

Constructed Response

8. Although the playwright presents a comical argument in this excerpt, what serious topic does he also want the audience to think about? Use evidence from the play excerpt to support your opinion.

Answers and Model Rationales

1. **D** Corie repeatedly states her disappointment with Paul's stuffiness in the scene, beginning with her complaint, "I'm beginning to wonder if you're capable of *having* a good time." There is no mention in the dialogue of Paul insulting Corie's mother or not liking the restaurant, so A and B are incorrect. Paul does have a court case in the morning, but that is not the source of Corie's anger with him, so C is not correct.

2. **F** At the end of the scene, Paul says to Corie, "You're impossible," so F is the correct answer. Paul is angry with Corie; he does not find her delightful (G) in this scene. He also tells Corie that she belongs in a nursery school and implies that she lacks common sense and emotional maturity, so H and J are clearly wrong.

3. **A** By definition, a comedy ends happily, with a satisfying resolution of the central conflict—in this case the argument between and conflicting personalities of Corie and Paul. Only A fits this definition. B describes an unhappy ending. C describes a scene, not a resolution. D does not resolve the play's conflict.

4. **G** By definition, a tragedy ends unhappily. Only G describes an unhappy ending. F, H, and J describe happy endings befitting a comedy.

5. **C** The scene consists of conversation, or dialogue, between Corie and Paul, so C is clearly correct. The scene does not contain monologues, narration, or asides, so A, B, and D are incorrect.

6. **G** Only G tells about the set. The other options describe emotions and actions.

7. **C** In a soliloquy a character is alone onstage, speaking to himself or herself or to the audience. C fits this definition. The other options are examples of dialogue or monologues.

Constructed Response

8. The playwright wants the audience to think about what makes a marriage work. This issue is addressed in Paul's comments about love, such as "Maybe two people should have to take more than a blood test." The line contains humor, but it also addresses a serious issue.

Multiple-Meaning Words

Modeling. Model the thoughts of a good reader answering item 1. Say, "In the passage from the play, the word *rests* is a verb meaning "lies." In D, *rests* has the same meaning. In C, *rests* is used as a noun. In A and B, *rests* is a verb, but it means "sleeps" in A and "depends" in B, not "lies.""

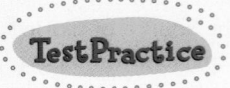

Answers and Model Rationales

1. **D** See rationale above.

2. **H** In the passage, *storms* is a verb meaning "moves angrily" (H). In F and J, *storms* is a noun. In G, it means "attacks."

3. **B** In the passage, *dashes* is a verb meaning "runs" (B). In D, *dashes* is a noun. In A and C, it means "smashes."

4. **F** In the passage and in F, *crushed* means "disappointed" or "hurt." In G, it means "crammed." In H, it means "quelled." In J, it means "broken into tiny pieces."

5. **A** In the passage and in A, *frozen* means "remained immobile; unable to move." In B, *frozen* means "unfriendly." In C, it means "very cold." In D, it means "turned to ice."

6. **G** In the passage and in G, *rings* is a verb that means "makes the sound of a bell." In F, H, and J, *rings* is used as a noun with various meanings.

ASSESSING

Assessment

■ *Holt Assessment: Literature, Reading, and Vocabulary*

Multiple-Meaning Words

DIRECTIONS: Choose the answer in which the underlined word is used in the same way it is used in the passage from *Visitor from Forest Hills*.

1. *"In the bedroom one opened valise containing a young woman's street clothes rests on the floor."*
   A The kindergartner rests after lunch every day.
   B Our success rests on the efforts of everyone on the team.
   C The singer caught his breath during rests in the music.
   D The book rests on the table, opened to her favorite story.

2. *"ROY turns and storms into the bedroom."*
   F Heavy storms are predicted for tonight.
   G The attacking army storms the enemy's camp.
   H Angry at her friend, she storms out of the house.
   J The mayor was faced with storms of criticism.

3. *"He dashes for the bedroom door, not even detouring around the bed. . . . "*
   A The death of the hero dashes the reader's hope for a happy ending.
   B Every morning, Anika dashes out of the house to catch the bus.
   C The ocean current dashes the boats onto the sandbar.
   D Use dashes in a sentence to indicate breaks in thought.

4. *"NORMA is crushed. He looks at her sympathetically."*
   F When Jamal heard the sad news, he was crushed.
   G Passengers on the crowded bus were crushed in the aisle.
   H The rebellion against the dictator was crushed by the troops.
   J We add syrup to crushed ice to make a refreshing summer treat.

5. *"NORMA has frozen in misery by the bedroom door after letting go of the coat."*
   A Frightened by the noise, the children were frozen in their tracks.
   B The countess's frozen manners cast a chill on the party.
   C I lost my right glove, and now my hand is frozen.
   D The children skated happily on the frozen pond.

6. *"The front doorbell rings."*
   F Sarena and Soo Lin exchange friendship rings.
   G The clock in the town hall rings every hour.
   H The clowns perform in all three rings of the circus.
   J You can tell a tree's age by looking at its rings.

SKILLS FOCUS

Vocabulary Skills Understand multiple-meaning words.

Vocabulary Review

Use this activity to assess whether students have retained the collection Vocabulary. Ask students to fill in the blank in each sentence below with a Vocabulary word from the box.

| compulsory | reminiscing | interminable |
| relentless | volatile | |

1. The boring movie was only two hours long, but it seemed _____. [interminable]

2. At our high school, taking gym class is not optional but _____. [compulsory]

3. Matt has a very _____ personality; he is always losing his temper. [volatile]

4. Class reunions are a time for _____ about fun times and old friends. [reminiscing]

5. The pace of the game was _____. Neither team let up for a second. [relentless]

Collection 11: Skills Review
Writing Skills

Collection 11: Skills Review

Writing Skills

Answers

1. B
2. H
3. D
4. H

Test Practice

DIRECTIONS: Read the following paragraph from a draft of a student's essay comparing a film scene with the play on which it is based. Then, read and answer the questions below it.

   (1) While much of the dialogue in the film *The Miracle Worker* is directly from the pages of William Gibson's play, some differences do exist. (2) In the play, Annie tells James Keller that losing her brother, Jimmie, has taught her the importance of never giving up. (3) In the film, this scene is replaced with several in which Annie is haunted by Jimmie's voice in her dreams. (4) In these scenes, film techniques enhance the emotional appeal. (5) Tense and piercing music grows in the background as Annie responds in whispers to Jimmie's desperate cries. (6) The different camera shots also draw an emotional reaction.

1. Which sentence could be added before sentence 2 to provide a clear thesis statement?
   A The film is much better than the play's text because it shows what Annie looks like.
   B The film uses narrative and film techniques to create sympathy for Annie Sullivan.
   C The film follows the play so closely that you can read the words from the play as the actors are saying them.
   D In the film, conversation is not as important as the action, so many dialogue scenes have been cut.

2. What could be added to sentence 2 to make the sentence clearer?
   F an identification of the act and scene
   G a list of characters in the scene
   H an explanation of Jimmie's death
   J the year the film was made

3. Which sentence could be added to elaborate on sentence 4?
   A The scenes include various camera shots and angles.
   B The sound techniques in the film are no more effective than in the script.
   C The scenes foreshadow that Annie will not be a good teacher.
   D The dark lighting in these scenes produces sympathy for Annie.

4. What sentence below could be added to support the point in sentence 6?
   F Annie's complex character makes viewers feel sympathy for her.
   G The audience can't see Jimmie, yet they know that he's crying.
   H The camera zooms in to reveal the tormented features of Annie's face.
   J The light doesn't darken or change when Annie hears Jimmie's voice.

SKILLS FOCUS

Writing Skills
Write an essay comparing a scene from a play with its film adaptation.

Collection 11: Skills Review   **943**

RESOURCES: WRITING

Assessment
- *One-Stop Planner* CD-ROM with ExamView Test Generator
- *Holt Assessment: Writing, Listening, and Speaking*

Internet
- *Holt Online Assessment*
- *Holt Online Essay Scoring*

APPLICATION

Two of a Kind

For homework, have students compare two works on the same theme: two poems, a novel and a film based on the novel, a short story and a painting, a play and a ballet. The two works do not matter, so long as they share the same main idea or basic story. Encourage students to be creative in their choices and to use their analytic skills to come to some interesting and original conclusions. Students should also provide sufficient support for their conclusions by quoting or accurately describing portions of the works. Ask volunteers to give brief oral presentations to the class.

Homework

EXTENSION

Make a Video

Have students work with a small group to select a scene from a play, adapt it for the screen, and create a videotape of it. They will need to write a script that includes directions for the camera as well as for the actors. One group member can act as a director to prepare the actors and consult with the cameraperson about when to shoot, how to focus and move, and when to stop. If possible, have the groups show their videotaped performances to the class.

Collection 12

Consumer and Workplace Documents

About Collection 12

In Collection 12, students will master the following skills:

- **Reading Skills:** Analyze the structure and format of consumer and workplace documents; analyze technical directions; analyze how to cite Internet sources in a *Works Cited* list; and analyze the logic of functional workplace documents.
- **Writing Skills:** Write a business letter; and write the minutes of a meeting.

Minimum Course of Study

Most skills can be taught with a minimum number of selections and features. In the chart to the right, lessons highlighted in green constitute the minimum course of study that provides coverage of the skills taught in Collection 12.

Resource Manager
(pp. 944C–944D)

Lesson and workshop resources are referenced in the Resource Manager on the pages that follow. These resources can be used to reinforce the skills taught in Collection 12, remediate students who are having difficulty, and provide supporting activities for English-language learners.

Scope and Sequence

Selection ▪ Feature	Literary Skills
Introduction: The World of Computer Game Development *by* Flo Ota De Lange *and* Sheri Henderson	
Informational Text: Reading Consumer Documents	
Informational Text: Following Technical Directions	
Informational Text: Citing Internet Sources	
Informational Text: Analyzing Functional Workplace Documents	
Informational Text: Evaluating the Logic of Functional Documents	
Writing Business Letters	
Writing the Minutes of a Meeting	
Skills Review: *Informational Reading Skills*	

Reading Skills	Vocabulary Skills	Writing ■ Grammar and Language ■ Listening and Speaking Skills
• Analyze elements of consumer documents		
• Analyze technical directions		
• Analyze how to cite Internet sources in a *Works Cited* list		
• Analyze the structure and format of functional workplace documents		
• Analyze the logic of functional documents		
		• Write a business letter
		• Write the minutes of a meeting
• Analyze elements of consumer and workplace documents		

Resource Manager

Selection ▪ Feature	Planning	Differentiating Instruction Lesson Plans with ELL Strategies and Practice	Reading Vocabulary
Introduction: The World of Computer Game Development *by* Flo Ota De Lange *and* Sheri Henderson			
Informational Text: Reading Consumer Documents		• Holt Reading Solutions, pp. 374–376	• Holt Reading Solutions
Informational Text: Following Technical Directions		• Holt Reading Solutions, pp. 377–379	• Holt Reading Solutions
Informational Text: Citing Internet Sources		• Holt Reading Solutions, pp. 381–383	• Holt Reading Solutions
Informational Text: Analyzing Functional Workplace Documents		• Holt Reading Solutions, pp. 384–386	• Holt Reading Solutions
Informational Text: Evaluating the Logic of Functional Documents		• Holt Reading Solutions, pp. 387–389	• Holt Reading Solutions
Writing Business Letters	• One-Stop Planner with ExamView Test Generator	• Workshop Resources: Writing, Listening, and Speaking	
Writing the Minutes of a Meeting	• One-Stop Planner with ExamView Test Generator	• Workshop Resources: Writing, Listening, and Speaking	
Skills Review: *Informational Reading Skills*			

The Holt Reader

The Holt Reader is a consumable paperback book which can be used alone or to accompany *Elements of Literature*. It offers guided support throughout the reading process and encourages students to become active readers by circling, underlining, questioning, and jotting down responses as they read. *The Holt Reader* works well for homework, students who have missed class, additional instructional time, reteaching, and remediation.

Holt Reading Solutions (HRS)

Holt Reading Solutions pulls together reading resources in the *Elements of Literature* program to create a powerful tool for intervention and whole-class instruction. *HRS* includes diagnostic assessment tools, lesson plans for English-language learners and special education students, adaptations of selected reading selections, vocabulary and comprehension worksheets, information on phonics and decoding, and additional instruction and practice in remedial reading skills.

Writing ▪ Grammar and Language ▪ Listening and Speaking	Assessment
	• Holt Assessment: Literature, Reading, and Vocabulary
	• Holt Assessment: Literature, Reading, and Vocabulary
	• Holt Assessment: Literature, Reading, and Vocabulary
	• Holt Assessment: Literature, Reading, and Vocabulary
	• Holt Assessment: Literature, Reading, and Vocabulary
• Workshop Resources: Writing, Listening, and Speaking	• Holt Assessment: Writing, Listening, and Speaking • Holt Online Assessment • One-Stop Planner with ExamView Test Generator
• Workshop Resources: Writing, Listening, and Speaking	• Holt Assessment: Writing, Listening, and Speaking • Holt Online Assessment • One-Stop Planner with ExamView Test Generator
	• Holt Assessment: Writing, Listening, and Speaking • One-Stop Planner with ExamView Test Generator

Technology

INTERNET

- go.hrw.com
- Holt Online Assessment
- Holt Online Essay Scoring
- Elements of Literature Online

MEDIA

 • One-Stop Planner with ExamView Test Generator

Transparency		Video	
CD-ROM		Audio CD	

One-Stop Planner with ExamView Test Generator

The *One-Stop Planner* CD-ROM contains electronic versions of print-based teaching resources, clips from the video program, and valuable assessment tools. The *One-Stop Planner* resources are presented in easy-to-follow, point-and-click menu formats. To preview resources or print out worksheets and tests, you simply make a selection and click.

One-Stop Planner CD-ROM

Collection 12

SKILLS FOCUS

Grade-Level Skills

■ **Reading Skills**
Analyze how authors use the structure and format of workplace documents to achieve their purposes.

■ **Reading Skills**
Prepare a bibliography of reference materials using a variety of consumer, workplace, and public documents.

■ **Reading Skills**
Follow technical directions to use technology.

■ **Reading Skills**
Examine functional documents to identify potential reader misunderstandings.

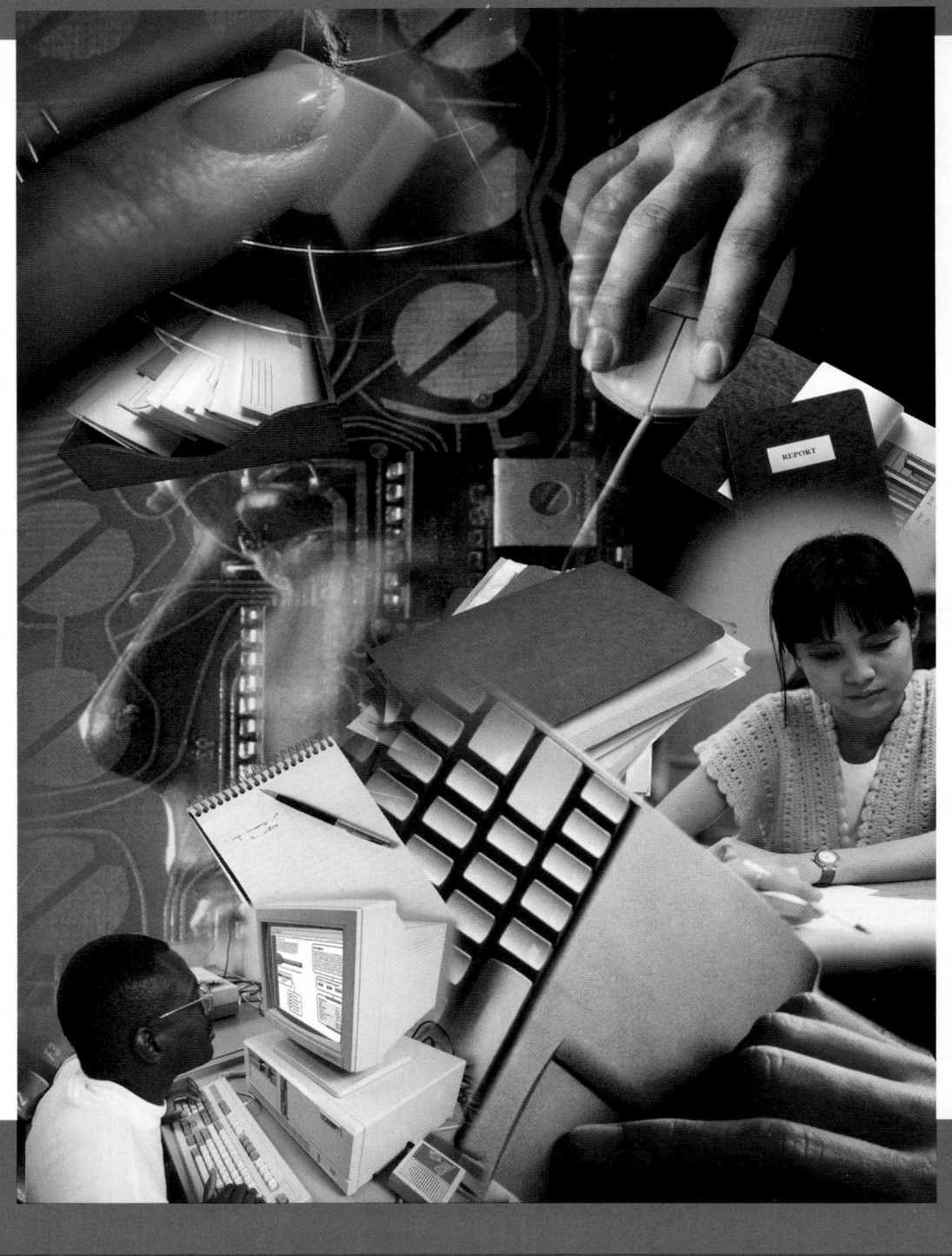

COLLECTION 12 RESOURCES: READING

Planning
■ *One-Stop Planner* CD-ROM with ExamView Test Generator

Differentiating Instruction
■ *Holt Reading Solutions*
■ *Family Involvement Activities in English and Spanish*
■ *Supporting Instruction in Spanish*

Assessment
■ *Holt Assessment: Literature, Reading, and Vocabulary*
■ *One-Stop Planner* CD-ROM with ExamView Test Generator
■ *Holt Online Assessment*

Collection 12

CONSUMER AND WORKPLACE DOCUMENTS

THE WORLD OF COMPUTER GAME DEVELOPMENT

by Flo Ota De Lange *and*
Sheri Henderson

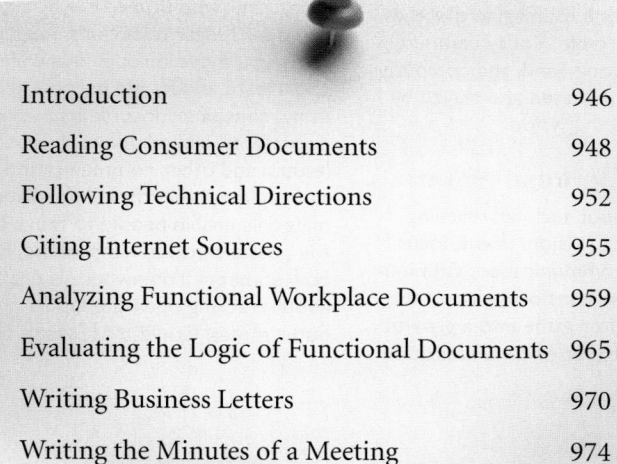

INTERNET

Collection
Resources

Keyword: LE5 9-12

Character • Using Primary and Secondary Sources **945**

INTRODUCING THE COLLECTION

The selections in this collection introduce students to a variety of informational materials related to the world of work. Each of the public, consumer, workplace, and technical documents presented support a single product, a computer game. Students explore how this modern technological commodity requires the support of a host of written materials. Documents are needed to describe the game to consumers, to provide instructions for installation and use, and to define the rights and obligations of both purchasers and the company that produced it.

As students read the selections, they will become familiar with the features and elements of these documents and learn to evaluate them with a critical eye.

The collection culminates with an opportunity for students to create their own workplace documents—a game-related business letter and the minutes of a meeting.

Introduction

The World of Computer Game Development

The only way of discovering the limits of the possible is to venture a little way past them into the impossible.

—Sir Arthur C. Clarke's Second Law

Developing Computer Games

In this collection you'll take a journey into the world of computer game development. Along the way you'll imagine that you're a computer-game-savvy high school student who wants to break into the field. Here's a little background on the subject.

If you have been using computers and playing computer games your entire life, it's easy to think that they've always been around; but in fact they had a beginning. The first video computer game was created in 1962 by Steve Russell, and it was played on a $120,000 computer about the size of a car.

Computer games and computer technology have come a long way in a short time. Not so long ago computers were too huge for anyone to imagine that they could ever be portable. Today computers can be carried in one hand, and computer games are mass marketed and played by people all around the world.

Using Informational Materials

What brought about such far-reaching changes so quickly? Vision, talent, focus, hard work, and communication. Communication? Yes. The transformation of that first video computer game into a growth industry involved a lot of communication

using various **informational materials: consumer documents, public documents, workplace documents, technical documents, business letters,** and more.

It may seem that computer games, with all their excitement, flashy colors, and action, have nothing in common with black-and-white informational materials printed on a page. But if you dig a little deeper, all sorts of connections can be uncovered. (Here's an interesting connection we discovered: Steve Russell based that first computer game on the science fiction writings of E. E. "Doc" Smith. Doc Smith not only wrote great science fiction stories, but he also held a doctorate in chemical engineering. He was the researcher who figured out how to get powdered sugar to stick to doughnuts!)

As you move through this collection, you'll learn about, and become skilled in using, consumer documents, workplace documents, bibliographies, business letters, and other communication tools. Keep in mind that these informational materials enable people to move beyond the possible into the impossible. Right now someone somewhere is dreaming about cracking open the future of computer games. Could that person be you?

INTERNET

More About Consumer and Workplace Documents

Keyword: LE5 9-12

DIFFERENTIATING INSTRUCTION

Learners Having Difficulty

Guide students in understanding the distinctions between different kinds of informational materials (consumer, public, workplace, and technical). Share the following terms and definitions with students:

• *Consumer documents* are company-created materials related to the products and services people buy.

• *Public documents* are materials created and published by public institutions such as government agencies, libraries, and non-profit organizations.

• *Workplace documents* are materials created and used by people on the job.

• *Technical documents* are materials created to help people perform tasks and understand procedures.

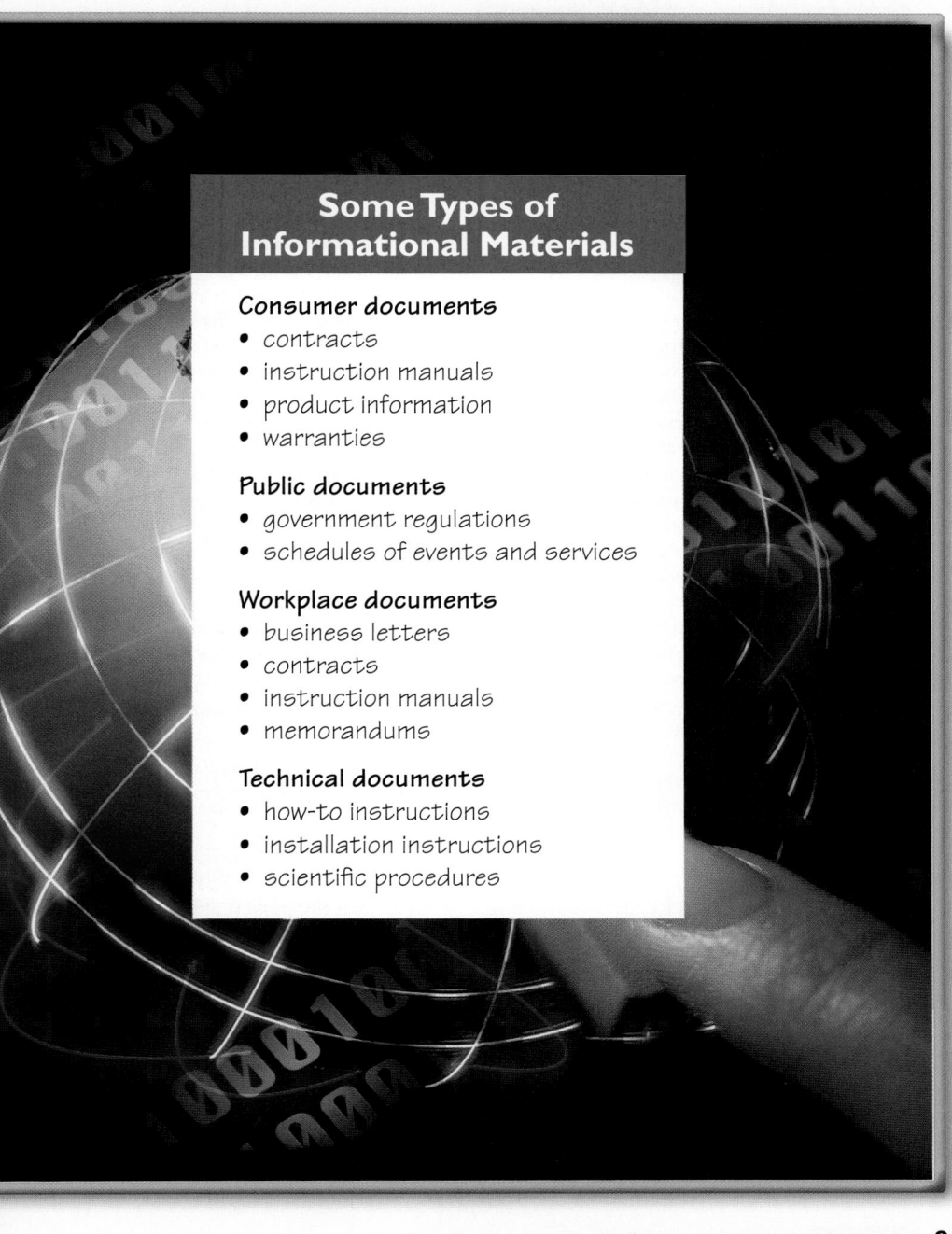

Some Types of Informational Materials

Consumer documents
- contracts
- instruction manuals
- product information
- warranties

Public documents
- government regulations
- schedules of events and services

Workplace documents
- business letters
- contracts
- instruction manuals
- memorandums

Technical documents
- how-to instructions
- installation instructions
- scientific procedures

Focus: Consumer and Workplace Documents

Tell students that, in this collection, as they explore the worlds of consumerism, work, and technology, they will focus on reading skills that they can apply in a practical way right now and in the future.

The collection starts off with examples of consumer materials, such as a warranty and an instruction manual, that students are likely to encounter when they purchase or use any appliance or electronic product.

In the lessons that follow, students will explore different aspects of using the Internet. They will read technical directions, in a FAQ sheet and a step-by-step process, that focus on using a search engine more effectively. They will learn details about how to cite Internet sources in a research report, and they will analyze and evaluate examples of technical documents that are becoming part of everyday life: software licensing agreements, instructions for downloading a game, and directions for installing a wireless Internet system.

Finally, students will review the writing of business letters, a skill that everyone needs to master in order to be a member of today's work world. Students will also learn how to take notes and write the minutes of meetings, a skill they can use now and in the future.

Invite students to review the list of documents and then tell the class about any documents like these that they have used in the past few weeks.

Hand out a variety of documents of each type for students to examine. Have students work together to classify each of the documents.

English-Language Learners
For more instruction on informational materials for English-language learners and special education students, see *Holt Reading Solutions*.

Grade-Level Skills

■ **Reading Skills**
Analyze elements of consumer documents.

Summary ↔ *at grade level*

> The lesson focuses on two documents students may encounter when they purchase a consumer product—a warranty and an instruction manual. In this case, the documents are for a computer game console. Features of the limited warranty include ninety-day coverage for parts and labor, one-year coverage for parts, and instructions for warranty registration. Two elements of the instruction manual are presented: product information that details the technical specifications of the console and safety information that advises readers about possible hazards of using the console.

PRETEACHING

Skills Starter

Motivate. Before reading, ask volunteers to discuss recent electronics purchases. When they open the box, do they immediately install and use the product, or do they stop to examine the consumer documents that accompany the purchase? How do they use these materials? Poll students as to whether they read safety instructions that come with products they buy.

Informational Text

Reading Consumer Documents

Consumer Documents: From the Manufacturer to You

Picture before you an unopened box. In it is the latest and greatest computer game console. Its graphics capabilities will have you thinking real instead of virtual. And the sound chip! Just wait until your friends hear this!

Like most people, you rivet your attention on getting that game console unpacked and loaded. In your hurry to get it out of its box, you let a sheaf of official-looking papers slide to the floor. There they lie, hidden in a scramble of packing litter—the **consumer documents:** the **warranty,** the **product information,** and the **instruction manual.** They are down on the floor in danger of being thrown out when the parental command rescues them: "Puh*leez* clean this mess up."

These consumer documents can make a big difference in how much you enjoy your new game. Before you put them away in a safe place, it's important to read them carefully. To be sure you understand what you are reading, let's take a brief look at the elements and features of consumer documents.

Elements of Consumer Documents

All computer game consoles include certain **elements,** such as a control device, sound and video capability, and a way to load and run the programs. However, you chose the game console in the box in front of you because it offers specific **features** you want, such as a programmable wireless joystick, surround-sound, 3-D video resolution, and DVD. These elements and features combine to make the game fun to play.

The consumer documents that came with the game are also important to your satisfaction. Here are some types of consumer documents and the **elements,** or types of information, that each document provides:

- **product information**—descriptions of what the game console will do
- **contract**—information on the legal uses of the game's software
- **warranty**—details on what happens if the game console does not work as promised and what you must do to receive service
- **instruction manual**—instructions on how to use the game console
- **technical directions**—directions for installation and use

SKILLS FOCUS

Pages 948–950 cover
Reading Skills
Understand elements of consumer documents.

948 Collection 12 Consumer and Workplace Documents

RESOURCES: READING

Differentiating Instruction
■ *Holt Reading Solutions*

Assessment
■ *Holt Assessment: Reading, Literature, and Vocabulary*

Features of Consumer Documents

All electronic equipment comes with these same types of consumer documents, but the documents' features may vary from product to product. For instance, all warranties specify what the manufacturer will do if the product fails, but one company might offer only repair while another will give you a choice of getting your money back. When two products seem nearly identical, the features mentioned in the consumer materials can tip your decision: Does the contract offer technical support that is available 24/7? Is the instruction manual reader friendly?

As you read the following consumer documents, marginal notes will help you identify key elements and features.

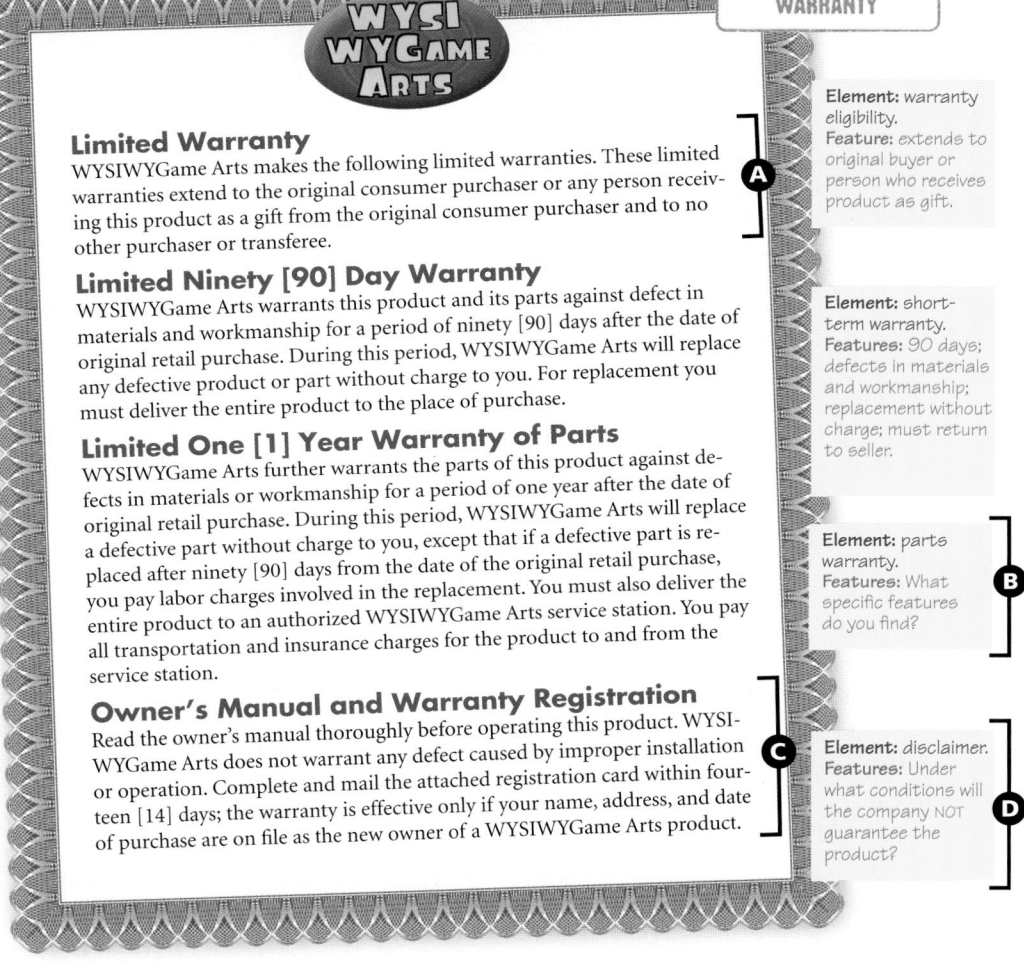

WARRANTY

Limited Warranty

WYSIWYGame Arts makes the following limited warranties. These limited warranties extend to the original consumer purchaser or any person receiving this product as a gift from the original consumer purchaser and to no other purchaser or transferee.

A

Element: warranty eligibility.
Feature: extends to original buyer or person who receives product as gift.

Limited Ninety [90] Day Warranty

WYSIWYGame Arts warrants this product and its parts against defect in materials and workmanship for a period of ninety [90] days after the date of original retail purchase. During this period, WYSIWYGame Arts will replace any defective product or part without charge to you. For replacement you must deliver the entire product to the place of purchase.

Element: short-term warranty.
Features: 90 days; defects in materials and workmanship; replacement without charge; must return to seller.

Limited One [1] Year Warranty of Parts

WYSIWYGame Arts further warrants the parts of this product against defects in materials or workmanship for a period of one year after the date of original retail purchase. During this period, WYSIWYGame Arts will replace a defective part without charge to you, except that if a defective part is replaced after ninety [90] days from the date of the original retail purchase, you pay labor charges involved in the replacement. You must also deliver the entire product to an authorized WYSIWYGame Arts service station. You pay all transportation and insurance charges for the product to and from the service station.

B

Element: parts warranty.
Features: What specific features do you find?

Owner's Manual and Warranty Registration

Read the owner's manual thoroughly before operating this product. WYSIWYGame Arts does not warrant any defect caused by improper installation or operation. Complete and mail the attached registration card within fourteen [14] days; the warranty is effective only if your name, address, and date of purchase are on file as the new owner of a WYSIWYGame Arts product.

C

D

Element: disclaimer.
Features: Under what conditions will the company NOT guarantee the product?

Reading Consumer Documents   **949**

Ⓐ Reading Skills

Identifying features. [Possible response to question: The specifications provide technical information about the game console, such as the type of CPU it has and the amount of memory it contains. Users might draw on this information to assess its capabilities or compare the WYSIWYGame Arts console with competing products.]

Ⓑ Reading Informational Text

❷ Reading consumer documents. A modem and an Ethernet port allow this game console to be connected to computer networks. Why might a game user want to do this? [Possible response: By connecting their console to a network, a game user could use this product to compete against other networked users.]

Ⓒ Reading Skills

Identifying features. [Possible response to question: Choosing a cool, sturdy place that allows the console to receive proper ventilation is the most important thing to do to protect the product.]

Monitoring students' progress
Ask students to give reasons why a consumer might wish to consult an instruction manual or a warranty.

Ⓐ Element: specifications. Features: What kind of information do the specifications provide? Why might you need to know this information?

PRODUCT INFORMATION

CPU	800 MHz
Video Card	250 MHz GPU
Resolution	1920 × 1080 maximum
Memory	128 MB
Storage	Memory Card • Hard Drive
Sound Card	64 Channels
DVD	Yes
Media	12X DVD-ROM 6.2 GB Capacity
Hard Drive	8 GB
Modem	Yes
Ethernet Port	Yes
Controllers	4

WYSI WYGAME ARTS

Ⓑ

INSTRUCTION MANUAL

Ⓒ Element: safety information. Features: What are the most important things you should do to protect the product?

Safety Information

Please follow these important safeguards regarding the use and installation of your game console:

1. When installing your game console, be certain that the unit receives proper ventilation. Vents in the console covering are provided for this purpose. Never block or cover these vents with any objects such as fabric, books, magazines, etc.

2. Do not install your game console in a bookcase or entertainment rack where it cannot receive proper ventilation.

3. Do not place the game console in direct sunlight or near a heat source, such as a radiator or hot-air duct.

4. Do not set the game console on a soft surface, such as a bed, sofa, or rug, since doing so may result in damage to the appliance.

5. Unplug this appliance from the wall outlet, and contact a qualified service person under the following conditions:

  a. The power-supply cord or plug is damaged.

  b. Liquid has been spilled on, or objects have fallen into, the game console.

  c. The game console has been exposed to rain or water.

  d. The game console does not operate normally after you follow the operating instructions.

  e. The game console has been dropped, or the cabinet has been damaged.

  f. The game console exhibits a distinct change in performance.

Do not attempt to service this product yourself. Opening or removing the outside covers may expose you to dangerous voltage or other hazards. All service must be done by qualified service personnel.

950 Collection 12 **Consumer and Workplace Documents**

Advanced Learners
Acceleration. Use the following activity to help advanced learners analyze the way in which clarity of meaning is affected by the patterns of organization.
Activity. Have students comment on the organization of the "Safety Information" page from the instruction manual. Ask, "Is the numerically ordered listing of safety instructions the most effective way to deliver this information to users?" Challenge students to come up with different ways of presenting this information, such as using descriptive headings such as "console placement," "console use," and "electrical dangers" to organize the various points.

Analyzing Informational Text

Reading Check

1. What **features** are offered by the limited ninety-day warranty?

2. What are the differences between the **features** of the ninety-day warranty and the one-year warranty?

3. Where do you look to find out how many sound channels your WYSIWYGame has? What do you find out?

4. If you accidentally dump a can of soda on your game console, what should you do? Where do you find this advice?

Test Practice

1. If you want to tell a friend how powerful your game console is, you would look —
   A in the warranty under "Warranty Registration"
   B in the instruction manual under "Safety Information"
   C in the product information
   D in the warranty under "Limited One [1] Year Warranty of Parts"

2. Items 1–3 under "Safety Information" are intended to protect the unit from —
   F chilling
   G overheating
   H static electricity
   J humidity

3. "Safety Information" and "Limited Warranty" are *similar* in that both address —
   A problems with the product
   B how to operate the product

   C how to buy the product
   D how to set up the product

4. According to the manufacturer's warranty, if you have *not* sent in your owner's registration card and your game console breaks six months after you bought it —
   F WYSIWYGame Arts will pay only for a defective part
   G WYSIWYGame Arts will pay all costs for the repair
   H you will have to pay all costs to an authorized service station; the company will not pay for anything
   J you will have to pay only for transportation and insurance

5. Consumer documents exist to protect —
   A the user
   B the manufacturer
   C both of the above
   D neither of the above

Application

Find the consumer documents that came with a piece of equipment you or someone you know owns. (The equipment might be a cell phone, a pager, a camera, any kitchen appliance, or any piece of electronic equipment.) Read the consumer documents carefully to identify all of the elements and features and to **compare and contrast** them with the WSIWYGame Arts documents.

SKILLS FOCUS

Reading Skills
Analyze elements of consumer documents.

Reading Check

1. The features offered are ninety days of protection against defects in materials and workmanship and replacement without charge.

2. The one-year warranty only covers parts. In addition, the console must be returned to the service station, not the place of purchase.

3. You look in the "Specifications" section. You find that the console has sixty-four channels.

4. You should unplug the console and contact an authorized service provider. The advice is contained in "Safety Information."

Analyzing Informational Text

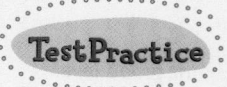

TestPractice

Answers and Model Rationales

1. **C** Facts about product capability are in the "Specifications" section. This information isn't related to safety or warranty, so A, B, and D are incorrect.

2. **G** Items 1–3 relate to ventilation and avoiding heat sources. Lack of ventilation can cause overheating, so G is the best answer.

3. **A** Both documents deal with product problems, so A is the best choice.

4. **H** The document states that without product registration, no warranty exists, so the consumer would have to pay all costs.

5. **C** The warranty protects the user from defects in the product and from hazards, and it protects the manufacturer from being liable for an extended period and from improper use of the product.

Assessment
■ *Holt Assessment: Reading, Literature, and Vocabulary*

For a lesson reteaching comparing consumer documents, see **Reteaching,** p. 979A.

Grade-Level Skills

■ **Reading Skills**
Follow technical directions to use technology.

Summary ⟷ *at grade level*

This lesson presents two different types of informational materials that students can find on the Internet.

The first is a FAQ (frequently asked questions) sheet about Internet search engines. The FAQ uses a question-and-answer format to provide information about using a search engine accurately and efficiently.

The second document provides step-by-step technical directions on how to customize a Web browser so that a search engine's Web site becomes the browser's home page.

PRETEACHING

Skills Starter

Build background. Ask students if they have ever encountered or used an Internet FAQ sheet. Point out that FAQ stands for "frequently asked questions." Explain that these FAQs compile essential information about a subject in a question-and-answer format. Thousands of FAQ sheets are available on the Internet, with topics ranging from software configuration to buying a video camera to snowboarding. FAQs are often compiled by "expert" volunteers—people who have expertise on a topic and want to share their knowledge with others.

Informational Text

Following Technical Directions

Finding Information on the Internet

Before you start to invent the best computer game ever, you might want to learn something about the history of computer game design and development. A good place to start your research, naturally, is on the Internet. There are a lot of computer games out there, so you'll want to make your research as easy as possible.

Your first step is to choose a **search engine**[1] you like and feel comfortable with. When you have found one, it is a good idea to customize your **browser**[2] so that your favorite search engine is your home page. How do you do that? It's easy. You just follow the directions.

---

1. **search engine:** tool that enables you to search World Wide Web pages for a specific topic.
2. **browser:** software program that enables you to access the World Wide Web. Note that a browser is not the same as a search engine.

Reading Technical Directions

Directions for using computers (as well as other scientific, mechanical, and electronic products and activities) are called **technical directions.** You follow technical directions when you read informational materials that tell you how to

- do an experiment in a chemistry lab
- fix a flat on your bicycle for the first time
- program the remote control to access your favorite radio stations
- operate your new microwave oven
- install virus-protection software on your computer

Technical directions may seem complicated and difficult when you first look at them, but if you pay attention and follow each step carefully, they will help you do the things you want to do.

FAQs° About Search Engines

Q: What does a search engine do?
A: A search engine helps you locate information that is available on the World Wide Web.

Q: How does a search engine do this?
A: There are many different search engines, and they all vary somewhat, but each one matches the words of your search request with the keywords in a Web site. It eliminates what doesn't match your request and tells you what does match.

Q: What is an example of a search request?
A: Say you wanted to know about computer games. You would choose a specific search engine, and in the search box you would type, for example, the keyword *computer games*. The search

engine might deliver the first 10 most relevant entries of a possible 2.4 million results.

Q: That's way too many results. How do I narrow my search?
A: You narrow your search by requesting what you specifically want to know about computer games. For example, if you want to know about the most popular computer games, you might phrase your search request in this way: *computer games+most popular.* The search engine might then give you the first 10 most relevant entries of a possible 751,000 results.

Q: That's still too many. How can I narrow my search further?

° **FAQs:** Frequently Asked Questions.

SKILLS FOCUS

Pages 952–954 cover
Reading Skills
Understand technical directions.

RESOURCES: READING

Differentiating Instruction

■ *Holt Reading Solutions*

Assessment

■ *Holt Assessment: Reading, Literature, and Vocabulary*

A: If you want to narrow your search further, on some search engines you can use quotation marks to search for phrases instead of individual words: *"computer games"+"most popular."* A search phrased in this way might return the first 10 most relevant entries of a possible 21,600 results.

Q: There are so many search engines. How do I decide which one to use?
A: The best way is to experiment with some of the most popular search engines. You might ask your computer-savvy friends which ones they use and then put their recommendations on your Favorites or Bookmarks list. Once

you've decided which search engine works best for you, you can make that Web site your home page by customizing your browser.

Q: How do I customize my browser?
A: Customizing your browser involves following technical directions, which are a sequence of steps. First, decide on a search engine, and go to its Web site. Then, find the directions for customizing the browser you are using, and follow them.

Q: Will the directions work with every browser in use today?
A: No, they will work only with the version of the browser they were written for.

Customizing Your Browser

The sample below shows instructions that are typical of those you might find for customizing a browser. They use a made-up search engine called QuickFind. Reading QuickFind's instructions will make you familiar with the process of following **technical directions,** so that when you choose your own favorite search engine—and there are many out there to pick from—you'll have no trouble following the instructions. You will be ready to make your favorite search engine's Web site your home page.

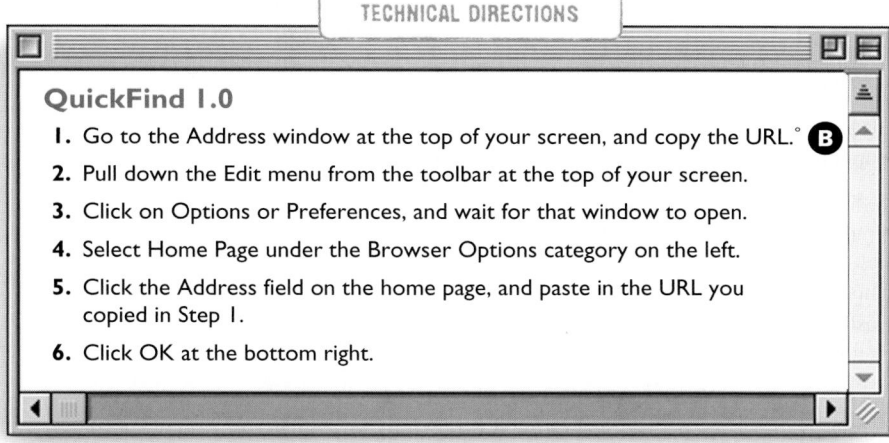

TECHNICAL DIRECTIONS

QuickFind 1.0

1. Go to the Address window at the top of your screen, and copy the URL.° **B**
2. Pull down the Edit menu from the toolbar at the top of your screen.
3. Click on Options or Preferences, and wait for that window to open.
4. Select Home Page under the Browser Options category on the left.
5. Click the Address field on the home page, and paste in the URL you copied in Step 1.
6. Click OK at the bottom right.

° **URL:** uniform resource locator, a site's Internet address.

Whichever search engine you choose, there is one last step to follow: Check your work. Quit your browser, and then open it again. The browser should automatically open to the search engine you've selected. If it doesn't, repeat the process, making sure to follow each step carefully. **C**

Following Technical Directions **953**

Analyzing Informational Text

Reading Check

1. It is used to locate information on the World Wide Web.

2. You might experiment with several; then, select the one that works best for you.

3. Go to the search engine Web site, go to the URL in the Address window, and copy the URL.

4. Check your work by quitting your browser and then seeing if it reopens to the search engine when you restart it.

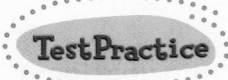
Test Practice

Answers and Model Rationales

1. **C** The FAQ states that *computer games+most popular* is how the keywords should be typed.

2. **G** Question marks, slashes, and parentheses are not mentioned in the FAQ, so F, H, and J are incorrect. The FAQ clearly designates quotation marks for this purpose; G is the correct answer.

3. **D** The technical directions state that going to the Address window is the initial step. One would have to go to the Address window before clicking on the URL (A) or pasting the URL (B). C is referred to in step 3.

4. **J** In QuickFind 1.0, clicking OK is the sixth and last step in customizing a browser; when you click OK, you activate the changes. F, G, and H are previous steps in the process.

5. **B** Looking for the search engine on the Internet every time is not quick, so A is wrong. C and D are means to the end of making the search engine your home page, which allows you quick access to it.

Analyzing Informational Text

Reading Check

1. What does a search engine do?

2. How might you choose a search engine?

3. When using QuickFind, what is your first step in customizing your browser?

4. What is the very last step you should take when customizing any browser?

Test Practice

1. According to "FAQs About Search Engines," which of the following key-words would you use to search for the most popular computer games?
   A mostpopularcomputergames
   B most+popular+computer+games
   C computer games+most popular
   D What are the most popular computer games?

2. According to "FAQs About Search Engines," on some search engines you can narrow a search by enclosing key phrases in —
   F question marks
   G quotation marks
   H slashes
   J parentheses

3. According to the QuickFind 1.0 technical directions for customizing a browser, the first thing you do is —
   A click on the URL
   B paste the URL
   C click on Options
   D go to the Address window

4. According to the QuickFind 1.0 directions for customizing a browser, which of the following steps comes last?
   F Copy the URL in the Address window.
   G Pull down the Edit menu.
   H Click on Address.
   J Click on OK.

5. The *best* way to access your favorite search engine *quickly* is to —
   A look for it on the Internet
   B make it your home page
   C ask your computer-savvy friends
   D follow technical directions

Application

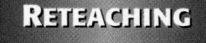

SKILLS FOCUS

Reading Skills
Analyze technical directions.

Find a set of **technical directions** for completing a totally unfamiliar process—something you've never done before. You might try one of the examples listed in the second column on page 952. For a real challenge (and a glimpse of adult life), try completing a 1040EZ income tax form or learning a new trick in your word-processing program, such as creating and using macros. Whatever you set out to do, carefully follow the directions in an **instruction manual.** Report to the class on what you tried to do, how well you did, and how helpful the directions were.

Test-Taking Tips

For instruction on how to answer multiple-choice items, refer students to **Test Smarts.**

ASSESSING

Assessment

■ *Holt Assessment: Reading, Literature, and Vocabulary*

RETEACHING

For another selection to teach following technical directions, see *The Holt Reader,* Part 2.

Informational Text

Citing Internet Sources

You're the Expert

One way to learn more about the computer game industry is to experience the business from the inside. Perhaps your school offers an internship program in which students work at local businesses during the summer.

Since you already own its game console and play its games, your summer internship with WYSIWYGame Arts seems like a wonderful opportunity—the perfect match. You arrive on your first day eager to learn at the side of real experts in the field. Then you are given your first assignment—to write a report.

It turns out that WYSIWYGame Arts considers *you* the real expert in the field of being a teenage consumer. The company wants to know what you like about its products, what you use, and what you want to see improved. Writing about what you like and use will be easy, but writing about what you want improved will be more complicated.

All the gamers you know, including you, want better game graphics. However, if getting better graphics were easy, it would have been done already. So what is really involved? What are the limitations on graphics? What advances have to be made in hardware before software evolves? So many unanswered questions, so little time to do research, but what better place to start researching a fast-moving field like computer games than the Internet?

Documenting Internet Sources

A research report must include an orderly list of *Works Cited* that enables others to find and read the sources you used in your report. Since online information is easily updated (in some cases, daily), citing **Internet sources** requires more information than you may be accustomed to providing in citations of print materials.

You are not, of course, responsible for changes made in a site between the time you make your notation and the time your reader goes there to find the work. You are responsible for giving your reader as much information as you have. In particular, it is crucial that you reproduce the URL (uniform resource locator) —the site's Internet address—exactly so that a reader may access the site.

To see some examples of **citations** for **consumer, public,** and **workplace documents** you might find on the Internet, look at the chart on page 956. (Some of the sites are made up; some are real.) The examples follow the Modern Language Association (MLA) style. If you have any questions about how to document your sources, look for the MLA style book in the library. In preparing a list of sources, the style you follow is less important than choosing one style and sticking to it. Always ask what style your teacher wants you to use.

Pages 955–957 cover
Reading Skills
Understand how to cite Internet sources in a *Works Cited* list.

Citing Internet Sources **955**

SKILLS FOCUS, pp. 955–958

Grade-Level Skills
- **Reading Skills**
Understand how to cite Internet sources in a *Works Cited* list.

Summary   *at grade level*

> Many students who do research on the Internet will find this lesson valuable. It explains the need for a *Works Cited* list as part of a research report, and it contains detailed instructions for compiling such a list of Internet sources. Particularly useful is information about what to include in each citation, a chart of sample *Works Cited* entries, and a series of sample note cards containing information about Internet sources.

PRETEACHING

Skills Starter

Build background. Remind students that a *Works Cited* list should show all the sources consulted and used in writing a research paper. Some students may confuse these citations with footnotes. Explain that footnotes refer to specific instances where a source is cited within a paper, while a *Works Cited* list includes all sources consulted, whether used generally or specifically, in the research paper.

A Reading Informational Text

? Documenting Internet sources. In the first entry, what does the date 7 June 2001 refer to? [It refers to the electronic publication date, or posting date, of this product information.] What does the date 27 July 2001 refer to? [It refers to the date that this source was accessed.]

B English-Language Learners

Abbreviations. You may need to remind these students that FAQ means "frequently asked questions." Often, Web sites will post a list of frequently asked questions and their answers to help guide users.

C Reading Informational Text

? Documenting Internet sources. Suppose that in a research report, you quoted from an e-mail that you had received. Why would you need to cite your source? [to give credit to the author; to help readers evaluate the information] What would you use as the title of the work? [the subject of the e-mail]

General Format for an Online Source

Author's Last Name, Author's First Name (if known). "Title of Work." Title of Web Site or Database. Date of electronic publication. Name of Sponsoring Institution. Date information was accessed <URL>.

Note: If an electronic address, or URL, must be broken at the end of a line, break the address immediately after one of the slash marks. Do not add a hyphen or any other mark of punctuation to indicate the division of an address.

Sample Works Cited Citations for Consumer, Public, and Workplace Documents

Product Information from a Commercial Site

"About the New WYSIWYGame Arts Console." WYSIWYGame Arts Console Page. 7 June 2001. WYSIWYGame Arts 27 July 2001 <http://www.wysiwygame.com/console/index.asp>.

Article from an Online Nonprofit Magazine Dedicated to Protecting Consumers

Sleuthing, I. B. "And the Winner Is—Testing Today's Game Consoles." Digital 25 June 2001. 7 Aug. 2001 <http://www.digital.org/main/article/gamcon/1.html>.

Article from a Reference Database (Encyclopedia)

"Programming Language." Electronic Library Presents: Encyclopedia.com. The Columbia Electronic Encyclopedia, Sixth Ed. 2000. Columbia UP. 15 July 2001 <http://www.encyclopedia.com/articlesnew/10538biblio.html>.

Part of an Online Book Found on a Public-Library Site (Also Available in Print)

Case, Loyd. "Chapter 4—Graphics." Building the Ultimate Game PC. Indianapolis: Macmillan, 2000. netLibrary. 3 Aug. 2001 <http://emedia.netlibrary.com/nlreader/dll?bookid=38549&filename=Page_v.html>.

Copyright Forms from the Library of Congress (Government Office)

United States. Library of Congress. US Copyright Office. Form VA—For a Work of the Visual Arts. Washington: GPO, 1999. 2 Aug. 2001 <http://www.loc.gov/copyright/forms/formva.pdf>.

Information from a Company's FAQ Page

"Resource Code Game Software Developers May Use When Programming for Our Products." ShellGame, Inc. 7 June 2001 <http://www.shellgame.com/corp/faqs/faqslist.html>.

Posting to a Discussion List (Message Board)

GameDawg. "Why More Polygons Mean Awesome Graphics." Online postage. 23 June 2001. Way Kool Net. 16 Aug. 2001 <http://www.waykoolnet.com/mboards/boards.cgi?board=prgm&read=9218>.

Quotation from an E-mail Communication

Nguyen, W. "Re: WYSIWYGame Arts Graphics." E-mail to the author. 21 Aug. 2001.

Learners Having Difficulty
Students may benefit from seeing additional examples of Works Cited citations and note cards. Have volunteers search the Web for examples of consumer, public, and workplace documents and then, as a class, compile note cards and citations for them. You may also wish to turn one of these citations into a diagram, with call outs indicating its various features.

English-Language Learners
Students may find much of the bibliography-related vocabulary and abbreviations challenging. You may wish to pair these students with more fluent English-speakers to review both the sample citations and note cards. Have students make a glossary of any new or difficult terms. They can refer to it now as they read this selection and later when preparing Works Cited lists.

Special Education Students
For lessons designed for special education students, see Holt Reading Solutions.

Using Note Cards

Ready to try a few Internet citations on your own? When you are researching on the Internet, it is a good idea to record your sources on three-by-five-inch cards like the ones below. (Most of these are made-up sources.)

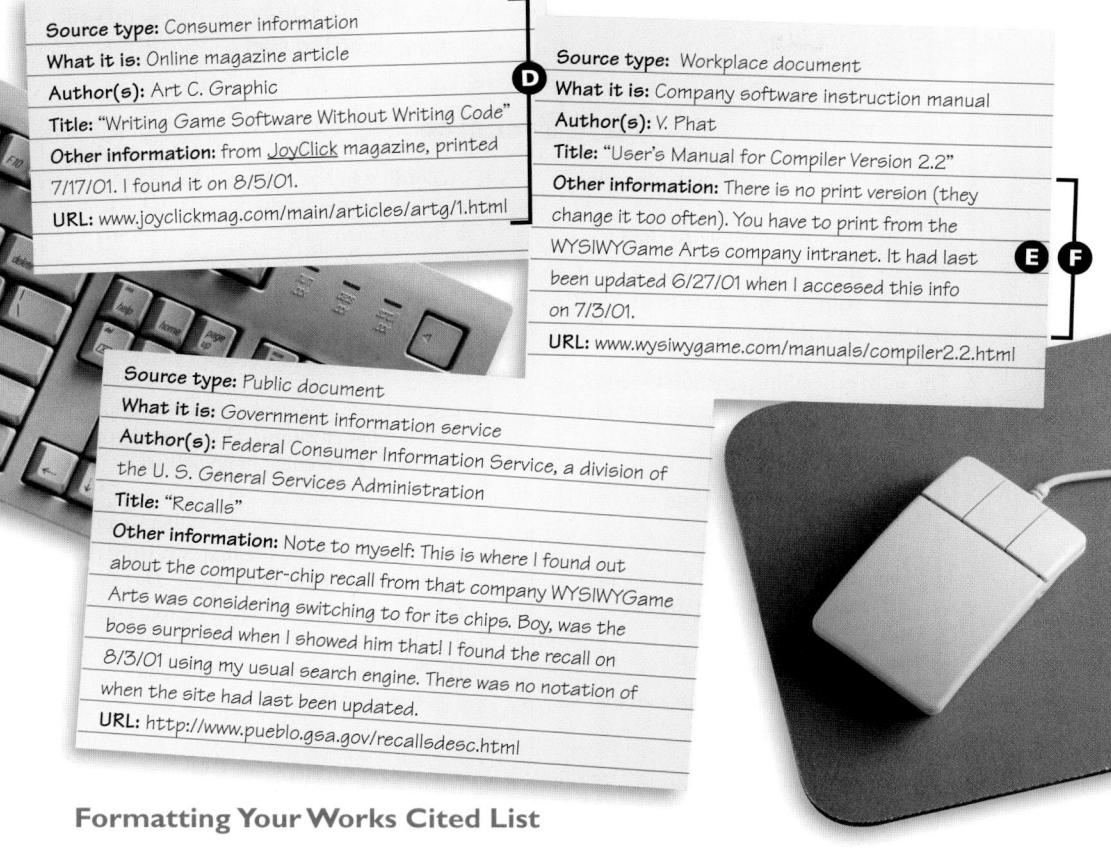

Source type: Consumer information
What it is: Online magazine article
Author(s): Art C. Graphic
Title: "Writing Game Software Without Writing Code"
Other information: from JoyClick magazine, printed 7/17/01. I found it on 8/5/01.
URL: www.joyclickmag.com/main/articles/artg/1.html

Source type: Workplace document
What it is: Company software instruction manual
Author(s): V. Phat
Title: "User's Manual for Compiler Version 2.2"
Other information: There is no print version (they change it too often). You have to print from the WYSIWYGame Arts company intranet. It had last been updated 6/27/01 when I accessed this info on 7/3/01.
URL: www.wysiwygame.com/manuals/compiler2.2.html

Source type: Public document
What it is: Government information service
Author(s): Federal Consumer Information Service, a division of the U. S. General Services Administration
Title: "Recalls"
Other information: Note to myself: This is where I found out about the computer-chip recall from that company WYSIWYGame Arts was considering switching to for its chips. Boy, was the boss surprised when I showed him that! I found the recall on 8/3/01 using my usual search engine. There was no notation of when the site had last been updated.
URL: http://www.pueblo.gsa.gov/recallsdesc.html

Formatting Your Works Cited List

The last step in writing a report is to compile all the sources you have cited in a *Works Cited* list. Follow these formatting steps:

- At the top of the page, center the title *Works Cited*.
- Alphabetize your sources by the author's last name. If no author is listed, alphabetize a source by the first two words in the title, ignoring *A, An,* and *The.*

- If two or more sources are by the same author, use the author's full name in the first entry only. For the other entries, type three dashes in place of the name, followed by a period and the rest of the citation.
- Double-space the list, and begin each entry at the left margin. If an entry runs longer than one line, indent the following lines five spaces.

Citing Internet Sources **957**

Analyzing Informational Text

Reading Check

1. A *Works Cited* list allows others to find, read, and evaluate the sources used in a report.

2. Sites are frequently updated. Sometimes a URL requires much detailed information, and it is vital that the information be exact.

3. Sources should be listed in alphabetical order by the author's last name.

4. Replace author's name with three dashes, period, then the rest of the citation.

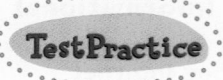

Answers and Model Rationales

1. **D** The text clearly states that the author's name appears (last name first) at the beginning of the citation before the title of the work.

2. **F** The text states that that it is crucial to reproduce the URL accurately. Students can also infer this answer, since readers would need the URL in order to access the information. In addition, with the URL, readers could identify the title and author for themselves (H and J).

3. **D** The format for an online source shows that the author's name appears first, followed by the title of the work and then the title of the Web site, so A, B, and C are incorrect. The sample citations show the URL at the end; D is correct.

4. **J** In the chart on p. 956, which follows MLA style, URLs are cited as in J.

5. **B** As stated on p. 957, citations without an author are alphabetized by the first two words in the title, ignoring *A, An,* or *The.*

Analyzing Informational Text

Reading Check

1. What is the purpose of a *Works Cited* list?

2. List some special problems involved in citing works from Internet sources.

3. In what order should you list your sources in a *Works Cited* list?

4. In a *Works Cited* list, if you have two sources by the same author, how do you list the second source?

Test Practice

1. On a *Works Cited* list an author's name appears —
   A after the title of the work cited
   B last, at the end of the citation
   C first, with the first name first
   D first, with the last name first

2. The most crucial information to reproduce accurately in an Internet citation is the —
   F URL
   G date you accessed the site
   H title of the site
   J author of the site

3. In an Internet citation the URL appears —
   A at the very beginning
   B directly after the author's name
   C directly after the title
   D at the very end

4. According to MLA style, what is the correct way to cite the following URL in a *Works Cited* list?
   F hrw.com
   G www.hrw.com
   H http://www.hrw.com
   J <http://www.hrw.com>.

5. The Web site you wish to use as a source does not list an author. How would you alphabetize the entry in your *Works Cited* list?
   A Use Anonymous as the author's name.
   B Alphabetize by the first two words in the title, ignoring *A, An,* or *The.*
   C Type two dashes and a period, and then alphabetize by the title.
   D Alphabetize by the month you accessed the Web site.

Application

SKILLS FOCUS

Reading Skills
Analyze how to cite Internet sources in a *Works Cited* list.

Now you're ready to search the **Internet** for three more *credible* sources on computer game graphics to use in your report. Remember to gather as much information as you can for your citations, and record that information on a note card for each source.

Then, prepare a *Works Cited* list using your three sources and the three sources shown on the three-by-five-inch note cards on page 957. Follow the MLA style used in the examples on page 956.

958 Collection 12 Consumer and Workplace Documents

Test-Taking Tips

For instruction on how to answer multiple-choice items, refer students to **Test Smarts.**

ASSESSING

Assessment

■ *Holt Assessment: Reading, Literature, and Vocabulary*

RETEACHING

For another selection to teach documenting sources, see *The Holt Reader,* Part 2.

Analyzing Functional Workplace Documents

Workplace Documents for Computer Games

Say you have finished designing your first computer game. What now? Do you want to limit distribution to family and friends, or do you want to make your game more widely available, perhaps as downloadable shareware on the Internet? If it's the latter, then it's time to talk about control structures in cyberspace.

If you put a work you have authored on the World Wide Web, you want to control what happens to it there. In order to do that, you must first establish your ownership of the work by copyrighting it (using that well-known copyright symbol, "©") with the U.S. Copyright Office for a fee.

A **copyright** is an exclusive right granted to you as the author of a work. It gives you the sole right—the *proprietary rights*—to reproduce and distribute that work.

As the owner of the copyright, you may then license others to use the work. You do that by means of a **legal agreement,** or **license,** between you and the user of that software. (This agreement is sometimes called a **shareware license agreement,** or **end user software license.**) The license grants the user of copyrighted software certain rights, but it does not grant any proprietary (or ownership) rights. Those remain with you.

An end user software license, or shareware license agreement, is a kind of **contract.** It is a **functional workplace document** that helps people get things done. In this case, the goal is to inform people how they may, and may not, use your software.

On the next page you'll find an example of a shareware agreement.

SKILLS FOCUS

Pages 959–963 cover **Reading Skills** Analyze the structure and format of functional workplace documents.

Analyzing Functional Workplace Documents 959

Grade-Level Skills

■ **Reading Skills**
Analyze the way authors use the structure and format of workplace documents to achieve their purposes.

Summary *at grade level*

This lesson provides examples of functional workplace documents. The first document is a shareware license agreement for WYSIWYGame Arts. It grants software users certain rights and spells out the limitations the company places upon its product's use. The terms include the fact that the company offers no warranty and accepts no liability. On the next page, the document's features are discussed, as well as elements of structure, format, and sequencing.

The second document is a page from the company's Web site. It allows visitors to learn about the The Show Must Go On game and to download the game software. A variety of structural and formatting features are used to present the information effectively.

PRETEACHING

Skills Starter

Build background. Ask students to share their prior knowledge about software license agreements. Point out that when installing software downloaded from the Internet or purchased in a store, they are usually entering into an agreement with the company or person who has produced the software. Have students familiar with these agreements discuss the process. (When downloading software, the agreement appears as a Web page, which users have to click on to accept. With store-bought software, opening a seal placed over the packaging often implies an acceptance of this agreement.)

A Reading Informational Text

? Workplace documents. How would you paraphrase the information in the opening paragraph? [Possible response: This is an agreement between the company and the user. If you use the company's software, you are agreeing to the company's terms.]

B Reading Informational Text

? Workplace documents. What is the purpose of the number that begins each section header? [Possible response: The numbers aid in separating and identifying the different points that make up the agreement. They do not represent steps in a process, nor do they organize the document's points by order of importance.]

C Reading Informational Text

? Workplace documents. Why are these terms capitalized? [Possible response: They make it easy to see what information will be covered or discussed in each section.]

D Content-Area Connections

Technology: Reverse Engineering Reverse engineering is the process of taking apart a product in order to find out more about how it is constructed or how it functions. The method is often used in manufacturing industries. A car company, for example, might buy an automobile from a competing company and disassemble it to examine its construction and component parts. The information obtained could be used in developing the company's own products.

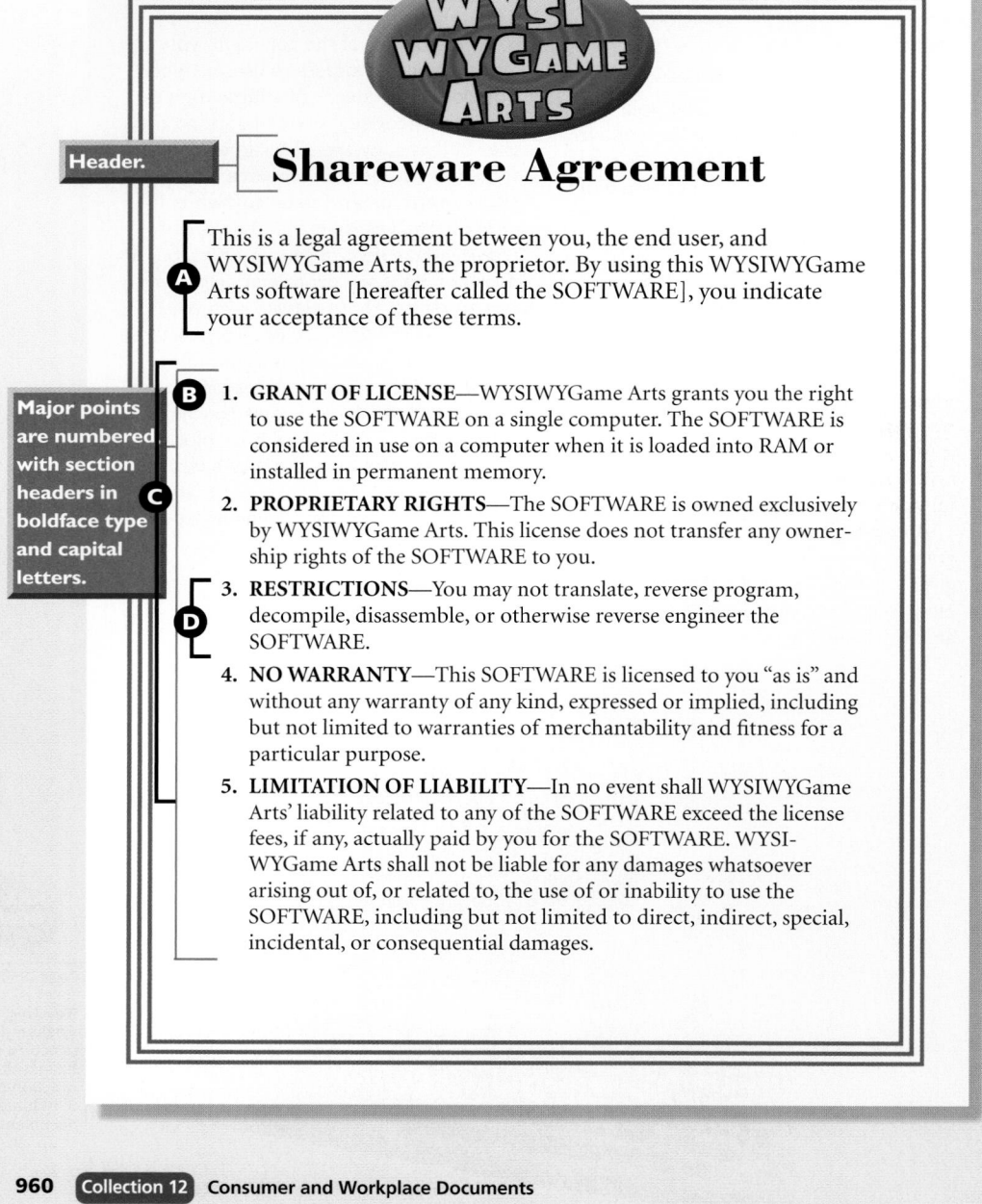

CONTRACT

WYSIWYGame Arts

Header.

Shareware Agreement

A This is a legal agreement between you, the end user, and WYSIWYGame Arts, the proprietor. By using this WYSIWYGame Arts software [hereafter called the SOFTWARE], you indicate your acceptance of these terms.

Major points are numbered with section headers in boldface type and capital letters.

B 1. **GRANT OF LICENSE**—WYSIWYGame Arts grants you the right to use the SOFTWARE on a single computer. The SOFTWARE is considered in use on a computer when it is loaded into RAM or installed in permanent memory.

C 2. **PROPRIETARY RIGHTS**—The SOFTWARE is owned exclusively by WYSIWYGame Arts. This license does not transfer any ownership rights of the SOFTWARE to you.

D 3. **RESTRICTIONS**—You may not translate, reverse program, decompile, disassemble, or otherwise reverse engineer the SOFTWARE.

4. **NO WARRANTY**—This SOFTWARE is licensed to you "as is" and without any warranty of any kind, expressed or implied, including but not limited to warranties of merchantability and fitness for a particular purpose.

5. **LIMITATION OF LIABILITY**—In no event shall WYSIWYGame Arts' liability related to any of the SOFTWARE exceed the license fees, if any, actually paid by you for the SOFTWARE. WYSIWYGame Arts shall not be liable for any damages whatsoever arising out of, or related to, the use of or inability to use the SOFTWARE, including but not limited to direct, indirect, special, incidental, or consequential damages.

960 Collection 12 Consumer and Workplace Documents

DIFFERENTIATING INSTRUCTION

Learners Having Difficulty
You may wish to share a sample document with students and guide them in identifying such features as titles, headers, and sections. Then, discuss formatting elements such as different text styles (bold, italic), and identify graphic elements such as buttons, bullets, icons, and logos. Groups can create a glossary of workplace-document features to reference as they analyze the documents in the collection.

English-Language Learners
Students may have difficulty with the legal language and technical terms contained in the shareware agreement. You may wish to pair these students with more fluent English-speakers to read the document together. Encourage partners to stop after each numerical point to paraphrase the information, omitting legal and technical terms and trying to word them in the language of everyday speech.

Features of the Shareware Agreement

The shareware agreement at the left makes effective use of **structure** and **format** to achieve its purpose. Some of its features are

- a centered **title** (**header**) that clearly states the purpose of the document
- a new **section** for each major topic
- **spacing** between each major section
- **numerical identification** of each major section
- **section headers** in boldface capital letters

The agreement also follows a **logical sequence.** It first states that using the software indicates the user's agreement to the terms, and then it lists those terms. They progress as follows:

1. what the license allows
2. who owns the software
3. restrictions on use of the software
4. warranty (none)
5. liability of the owner (none)

Analyzing Workplace Documents

Let's take a closer look at the structure, format, and sequence of effective functional workplace documents.

Structure

Functional workplace documents are usually divided into sections, each with its own header. Each **section** is often one short paragraph in length, sometimes just one sentence. The **headers** might be titles, subtitles, or numbers. Separating each main idea into its own section makes it easy for the reader to locate information. It also highlights each major point so that the reader will be sure to consider them all.

Format

The **format,** or design, of a document is important to its effectiveness. It focuses the reader's attention on key words, sections, and ideas. Some of the elements involved in designing or creating the format of a functional workplace document are

- **formatting elements**—bold or italic type, margin widths, indentations, and line spacing
- **graphic elements**—drawings, photos, and other artwork
- **design elements**—placement of text and graphic elements on the page, use of white space, and choice of colors

Sequence

The **sequence,** or order, in which ideas are presented can make a big difference to the reader's understanding. Most history books present information in a **chronological sequence;** that is, in the order in which events happened in time. Imagine how difficult it would be if the books had an **alphabetical sequence** by the last names of the participants, as in a bibliography?

A functional workplace document should present its information in a logical sequence. Two examples are

- **Step-by-step sequence**. This type of sequence describes a process and tells what to do first, second, third, and so on. An example is the instructions in "Customizing Your Browser," page 953.
- **Point-by-point sequence**. This type of sequence is based on the relationship of the points to each other. Sometimes the order of the points is not particularly important, as long as each point is stated clearly. An example is the "WYSI-WYGame Arts Shareware Agreement" on page 960.

DIRECT TEACHING

E Learners Having Difficulty

❷ Finding details. You may wish to have students meet in a small group to read this page and to relate its specialized vocabulary terms to the features on the shareware agreement. After students read each point, have them pause to identify the feature, such as title or spacing between each section, on the shareware agreement.

F English-Language Learners

The term *white space* may be confusing to these students. Explain that white space simply means any place on a printed page that does not have text or graphic elements on it. For example, the margins of this page are white space.

Special Education Students
For lessons designed for special education students, see *Holt Reading Solutions.*

Advanced Learners
Enrichment. Use the following activity to encourage students to further explore laws regarding copyrights, licenses, and other legal agreements.

Activity. Encourage pairs of students to review the information presented in the Before You Read section on p. 959. Ask each pair to choose one legal agreement to explore further. For example, students might learn more about obtaining and

enforcing copyrights, or they might explore lawsuits regarding the abuse of copyrights or software licenses. Ask students to compile their data in a fact sheet and share the information with the rest of the class.

A **Reading Informational Text**

? **Workplace documents.**
What words are presented in the largest font sizes on the Web site? Why is this an effective use of font size? [Possible responses: The words in the largest font sizes are the WYSIWYGame Arts logo and the game title—The Show Must Go On. The large font size makes the subject of this Web document immediately clear.] **How else does the document draw attention to the title of the game?** [The words are set in light colors against a dark background.]

B **Reading Informational Text**

? **Workplace documents.** How does the Web site identify "clickable links"? [Possible response: The presence of underlining or text buttons indicates clickable links.]

C **Reading Informational Text**

? **Workplace documents.** Ask students to comment on the structure of the document on p. 962. How are the sections divided? [Possible response: Each section is divided by ample white space, contained within boldly bordered section boxes or a graphic element.]

Analyzing a Web Site

The "WYSIWYGame Arts Shareware Agreement" on page 960 effectively uses a simple structure and format to draw the reader's attention to its features. Now, let's assess the more complicated format of the Web site on which that agreement—and your software—are posted. How has the Webmaster at WYSIWYGame Arts used the structure and format of the Web site to draw the viewer's attention to your game?

WEB SITE

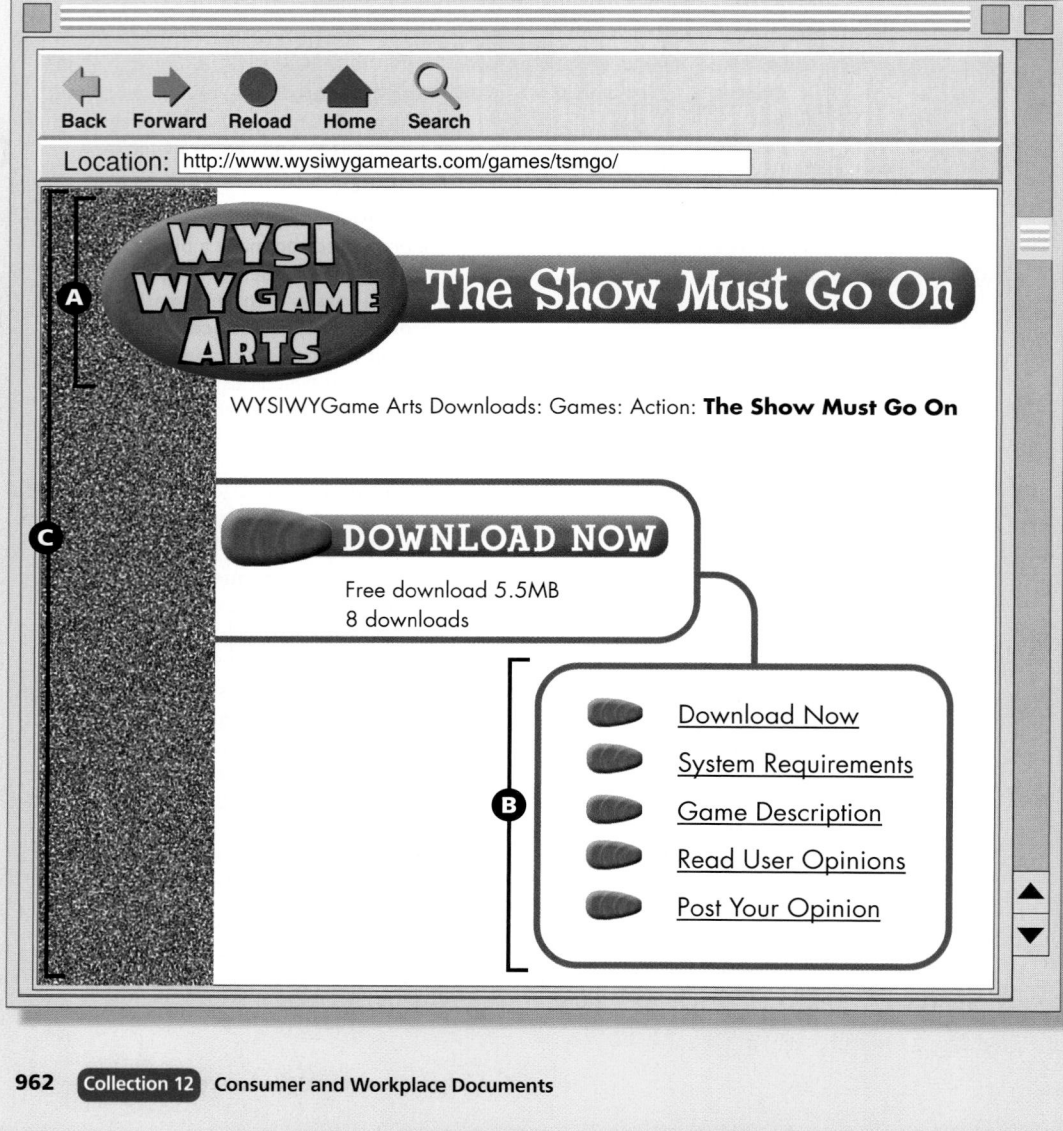

CONTENT-AREA CONNECTIONS

Science: Technology
The licensing agreements that accompany software purchases rarely accompany other consumer products. Automobiles and stereos, for example, do not come with agreements that specify when, where, or how the product may be used. The reason for these agreements is that software, unlike hard goods, can be easily copied and distributed. A single consumer may illegally distribute hundreds or thousands of copies of a product that has cost a software company millions of dollars to develop. According to one industry group, these types of losses to the software industry run well over $10 billion dollars a year. While licensing agreements may not stop consumers from illegally distributing software, they discourage some from doing so and provide a basis for prosecuting offenders if they are caught.

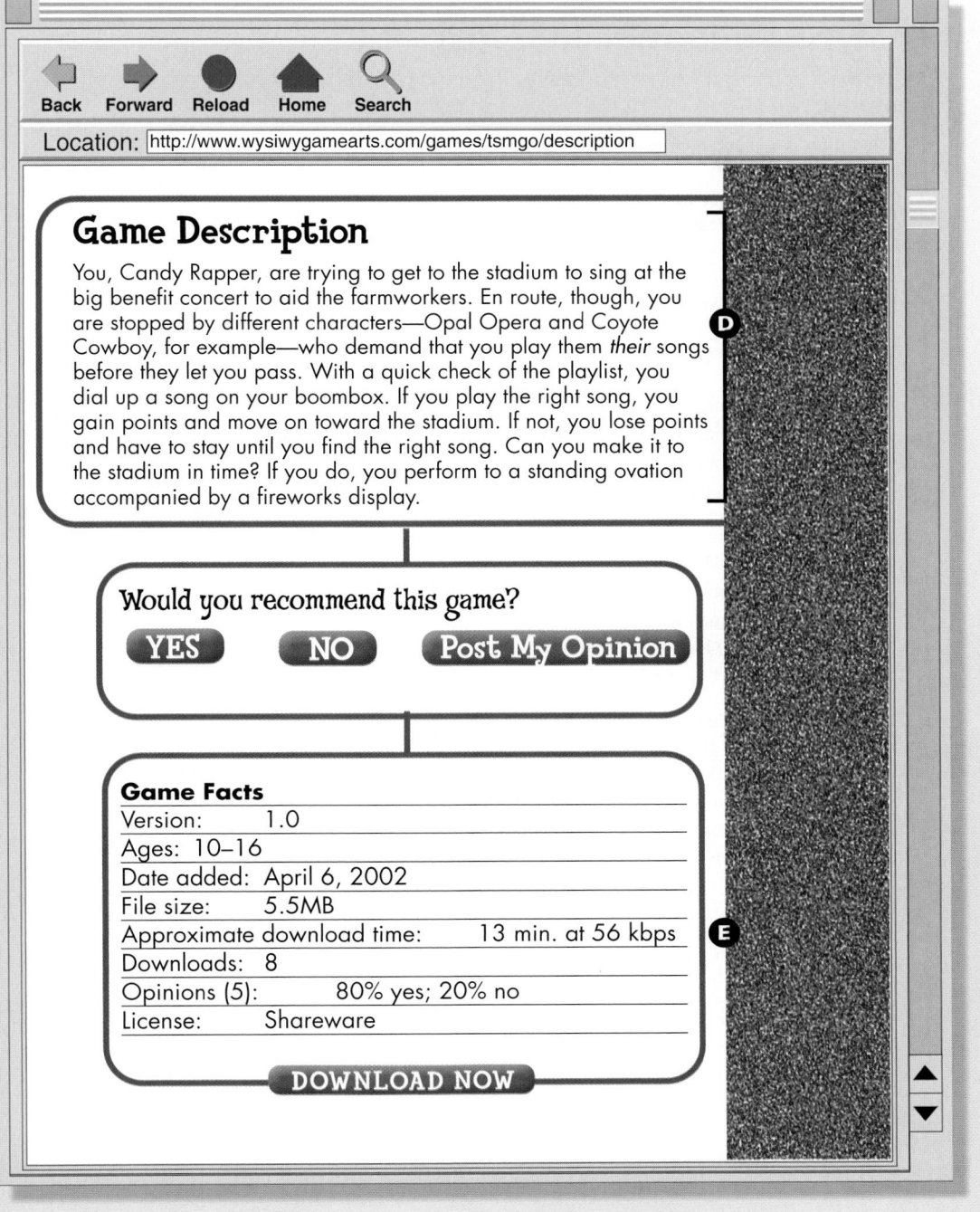

Game Description

You, Candy Rapper, are trying to get to the stadium to sing at the big benefit concert to aid the farmworkers. En route, though, you are stopped by different characters—Opal Opera and Coyote Cowboy, for example—who demand that you play them *their* songs before they let you pass. With a quick check of the playlist, you dial up a song on your boombox. If you play the right song, you gain points and move on toward the stadium. If not, you lose points and have to stay until you find the right song. Can you make it to the stadium in time? If you do, you perform to a standing ovation accompanied by a fireworks display.

Would you recommend this game?

YES   **NO**   **Post My Opinion**

Game Facts

Version:	1.0
Ages:	10–16
Date added:	April 6, 2002
File size:	5.5MB
Approximate download time:	13 min. at 56 kbps
Downloads:	8
Opinions (5):	80% yes; 20% no
License:	Shareware

DOWNLOAD NOW

D Learners Having Difficulty

? Re-reading. How would you summarize the object of the game? You can re-read as necessary to answer the question. [Possible response: The player (Candy Rapper) must overcome difficulties to perform at a big show on time.]

E Reading Informational Text

? Workplace documents. Where can a Web site visitor find out how long it takes to download the software? [This information is contained in the "Game Facts" section.]

GUIDED PRACTICE

Monitoring students' progress. To assess students' understanding of the lesson, ask them to list elements of structure, format, and sequence that are used to organize the information on p. 961. [The information is divided into sections, each with a header. Point-by-point sequence is used. Terms are boldface; there is spacing between sections; there are bulleted and numbered lists.]

FAMILY/COMMUNITY ACTIVITY

Activity. Encourage students to look for licensing agreements that came with software that family members use at home. Suggest that students read these agreements, and then quiz their family members about their familiarity with what they agreed to when they began to use the software. Students might ask the following questions:

• What does the agreement restrict you from doing?
• Can the software be used on more than one computer in the household?
• Who is the owner of the software?
• Is the software company liable if its product damages your computer?

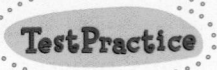

INDEPENDENT PRACTICE

Analyzing Informational Text

Reading Check

1. It allows you to use the software on a single computer.

2. Possible answers: point-by-point sequencing; a centered title; numerical section identification; boldface, capitalized section headers; section spacing

3. The main purpose is to let visitors download The Show Must Go On.

4. Possible answers: icons, oval borders to separate sections, lines to connect sections, text buttons, the company logo

Test Practice

Answers and Model Rationales

1. **B** The section headers are numbered. They are neither colorful nor bulleted nor italicized, so A, C, and D are incorrect.

2. **G** On the Web site the name of the game appears only next to the WYSIWYGame Arts logo.

3. **A** "Download Now" is the one graphic icon that is repeated.

4. **H** All the features listed in F, G, and J are included in the Web site. The page does not use chronological sequencing (H).

5. **D** The only section of the Web site with a bulleted list is the one that identifies the five internal links. The "Game Description" and company name (A, B) do not include lists. "Game Facts" (C) does not use bullets.

6. **G** There is nothing in the "Game Description" about the author, improving the game, or submitting an original game, so F, H, and J can be eliminated.

Analyzing Informational Text

Reading Check

1. What does the shareware agreement allow you to do?

2. List three structural or formatting features of the shareware agreement.

3. What is the main purpose of the Web site?

4. What **graphics** does the Web site use?

Test Practice

1. The **section headers** on the shareware agreement are —
   A boldface and colorful
   B boldface and numbered
   C boldface and bulleted
   D italicized and capitalized

2. On the Web site the name of the computer game is displayed —
   F in a long paragraph
   G next to the company logo
   H under a "Download Now" button
   J next to "Read User Opinions"

3. A repeated **graphic** icon on the Web site draws the reader's attention to —
   A where to download
   B the search button
   C the company logo
   D the game's name

4. The Web site uses *all* of the following elements of **structure** and **format** *except* —
   F bold and colored print
   G graphics and bullets
   H chronological sequence
   J placement of text and graphics on the page

5. The Web site uses the structural element of a bulleted list to —
   A describe the game
   B repeat the company name
   C list game facts
   D identify internal links

6. The main purpose of "Game Description" on the Web site is to help you decide if you want to —
   F find out about the author
   G download the game
   H suggest improvements for the game
   J submit an original game of your own

SKILLS FOCUS

Reading Skills
Analyze the structure and format of functional workplace documents.

Application

Choose three structural, formatting, or graphic features of the Web site (pages 962–963), and describe how each contributes to WYSIWYGame Arts' purpose in creating this site.

Test-Taking Tips

For instruction on how to answer multiple-choice items, refer students to **Test Smarts.**

ASSESSING

Assessment

■ *Holt Assessment: Reading, Literature, and Vocabulary*

RETEACHING

For a lesson reteaching analyzing workplace documents, see **Reteaching,** p. 979A. For another selection to teach analyzing workplace documents, see *The Holt Reader,* Part 2.

Evaluating the Logic of Functional Documents

Using Functional Documents

Functional documents with clear and logical instructions help people get things done. By contrast, documents that are illogically sequenced or missing steps are impossible to use. Such documents offer to get you somewhere, but when you attempt to follow their directions, you end up in Wonderland, thinking, "Off with their heads!"

When you are downloading a software game, putting together your kid sister's new swing set, or following the prompts on an ATM or voice-mail system, you are using functional documents. It may seem odd to think of on-screen or voice prompts as documents, but it makes sense if you remember this: Someone wrote the words and decided on the sequence of the procedures that you see on the ATM screen or hear when you reach a voice-mail system. When instructions are well written, these documents are easy to follow. When they are not well written, they can cause serious misunderstandings.

When a functional document is poorly written, chances are that either a crucial piece of the information you need has been left out or the information is not presented in a logical, step-by-step sequence. Either way you end up scratching your head and thinking, "Huh?"

Missing a Step

Let's say, for example, that you are installing memory chips in a laptop computer that has been designed to let you do this. The first step tells you, in big block letters, to unplug the computer and remove the battery. You follow each of

the next twenty steps flawlessly. The illustrations actually match what you see, and you are confident that you have done everything correctly. The last step tells you to turn the computer on. You take a deep breath, press the On switch, and . . . Nothing. No lights, no whirring, no little *chucka-chucka-chucka* sounds. Finally, you think, "Duh. Plug it in."

We've all been there. The instructions omitted that vital step. As obvious as the step may have seemed to the person who wrote the document, it is still necessary to tell you when it's safe to plug the computer back in, especially after you've been instructed to unplug it. Such a failure in logic creates confusion, and creating confusion is not what a functional document should do.

SKILLS FOCUS

Pages 965–968 cover **Reading Skills** Evaluate the logic of functional documents.

Evaluating the Logic of Functional Documents **965**

RESOURCES: READING

Differentiating Instruction
- *Holt Reading Solutions*

Assessment
- *Holt Assessment: Reading, Literature, and Vocabulary*

Summary 🔄 *at grade level*

In this lesson, students learn to recognize errors in functional documents that are caused by errors in logic. The most common errors are omitting information and placing information in out-of-order sequence. These points are illustrated in two documents that contain step-by-step instructions for completing a process. Each document contains errors that create the potential for confusion—a critical intermediate step is omitted or listed wrongly as the final one.

The first document gives instructions for installing a wireless Internet system. Information in the final step (connecting the wireless system to the cable modem) should have been placed in an earlier step.

The second document presents instructions for downloading and installing a software game. The final step given for the process (downloading decompression software) should have been listed as the first or second step.

PRETEACHING

Skills Starter

Motivate. Ask students if they've ever become frustrated while trying to follow directions for installing software, assembling electronic equipment, or programming video recorders, for example. Call on volunteers to share their most frustrating experiences. Point out that the problem might not have been with their ability to understand, but rather with the document itself. Many of these documents are written unclearly, and sometimes they are simply incorrect.

A **Reading Informational Text**

❓ Using functional documents.
What is the purpose of this functional document? [To instruct users on how to set up a wireless Internet system.]

B **Advanced Learners**

Enrichment. You may wish to ask a volunteer to diagram a wired cable connection and a wireless cable connection on the chalkboard. Other students can use the diagrams as aids in identifying the critical flaws in the document.

C **Reading Informational Text**

❓ Using functional documents.
How are the instructions ordered? [in numerical step-by-step order]

D **Reading Informational Text**

❓ Using functional documents.
Which step instructs the user to plug the modem cable into the wireless system? [step 7]

Steps Out of Order

Logical sequencing requires not only that **all the steps be there** but also that they appear **in the correct order.** If a step is out of order, a great deal of confusion and frustration can result. For example, take a look at the following functional document:

INSTRUCTION MANUAL

Installing Your Wireless Internet Access

1. Your new wireless system will use your existing cable-modem service to access the Internet. Test to see whether the cable connection is working by going to your home page in the usual way. If the connection is working, go on to steps 2–7.

2. Shut down your computer.

3. Unplug the cable modem from your computer.

4. Turn the wireless system on.

5. Restart the computer.

6. Check to see that the wireless system has taken you back to your home page.

7. Plug the cable modem you unplugged from your computer into the wireless system.

Learners Having Difficulty
Encourage students to use their own difficulties with a section of a document as one criterion for critiquing the document's effectiveness. Point out that simplicity and clarity are two standards by which functional documents are measured. Emphasize that part of the reader's job as critic is to identify illogical or unclear aspects of each document.

Encourage them to note each aspect they find difficult to understand.

English-Language Learners
Technical language may hinder students' abilities to effectively evaluate the functional documents presented in this selection. To help students assess the logic of each process presented in the documents, you may wish

to have students work in mixed-ability pairs. A student more fluent with computer-related processes and terms can help clarify the language, making it easier for English-language learners to concentrate on the logic of the instructions.

What's Wrong with This Document?

Hold on here. Put your hand over the paragraphs under this one, and pretend you really are installing wireless Internet access. What confuses you? Critique the sequencing flaw in the document on page 966, "Installing Your Wireless Internet Access." Talk over the sequencing with a partner, and then go on reading below.

What did you decide? Step 7 is clearly out of order. You are now faced with a quandary: You know step 7 should occur sometime after step 3, but should it come between steps 3 and 4, steps 4 and 5, or steps 5 and 6? You have no way of knowing. You are faced with a series of bad choices:

- **Plan A.** Try each of the above choices (the possible places to put step 7) to see if one of them works—but will doing so damage the equipment?

- **Plan B.** Call tech support—but how long until someone answers?

- **Plan C.** Return the product—but will the company take it back?

Let's say you took the risk and used plan A to solve the problem. It worked perfectly once you tried step 7 between steps 3 and 4. Of course, you later found it necessary to go to plan B after all. It is frequently true that a poorly written document will have more than one unclear section. Fortunately, tech support for the product was available twenty-four hours a day and immediately offered a simple solution. (Remember the importance of checking the warranty and the availability of technical support before you buy a product? It paid off here.)

DIRECT TEACHING

E Learners Having Difficulty

Finding sequence. If students are having difficulty evaluating the sequence of steps, you may wish to have partners re-read the text on p. 966 together. Make sure they understand that they are looking for "a sequencing flaw" or a step that is out of order. Say to students, "Suppose you are actually trying to follow these steps in order from 1 to 7. Do you think the new system would work? What is unclear or confusing?" Alert students that anything that seems unclear to them may point to an error in the way the instructions are written.

F English-Language Learners

Informal language. The informal style of the writing in this section may confuse students. You may wish to have a reader who is proficient in English read this page aloud to students who are learning English, so they can hear the conversational style. You may also wish to explain the meanings of two idioms: *Hold on here,* meaning "Pause for a moment," and *It paid off here,* meaning "It proved to be important."

Special Education Students
For lessons designed for special education students, see *Holt Reading Solutions.*

Advanced Learners
Enrichment. Use the following activity to extend students' experience with evaluating functional documents.

Activity. Challenge students to find a functional document that contains errors in sequencing, such as omitted or missing steps. Then, have students revise the documents they have chosen, correcting the error(s) and improving the clarity of the document in any way that they can. Have students share the original and revised documents with partners, who will critique both the originals and the revised works.

Ⓐ Reading Informational Text

❷ Using functional documents.
What function does this element serve? [It provides a concise overview of the five steps in the process described below.]

Ⓑ Reading Informational Text

❷ Using functional documents.
How might step 1c confuse inexperienced computer users? [Possible response: They might not know whether they have specified a folder.]

Ⓒ Reading Informational Text

❷ Using functional documents.
What would happen if the computer user doesn't have decompression software? [Possible response: They probably wouldn't be able to extract the file.]

Ⓓ Reading Informational Text

❷ Using functional documents.
What is odd about this step? [Possible responses: This step concludes the instructions, yet it doesn't tell you what to do with the decompression software; it seems that it has been listed out of order.]

Editing for Logic and Clarity

Let's get back to your newly designed software game. You want the downloading instructions on the WYSIWYGame Arts Web site to be easy and clear for your reader to follow. Below are the instructions provided by the technical-support crew at WYSIWYGame Arts. Critique the logic and clarity of their instructions. Make notations where you think a reader might misunderstand the instructions, and suggest how those misunderstandings might be avoided.

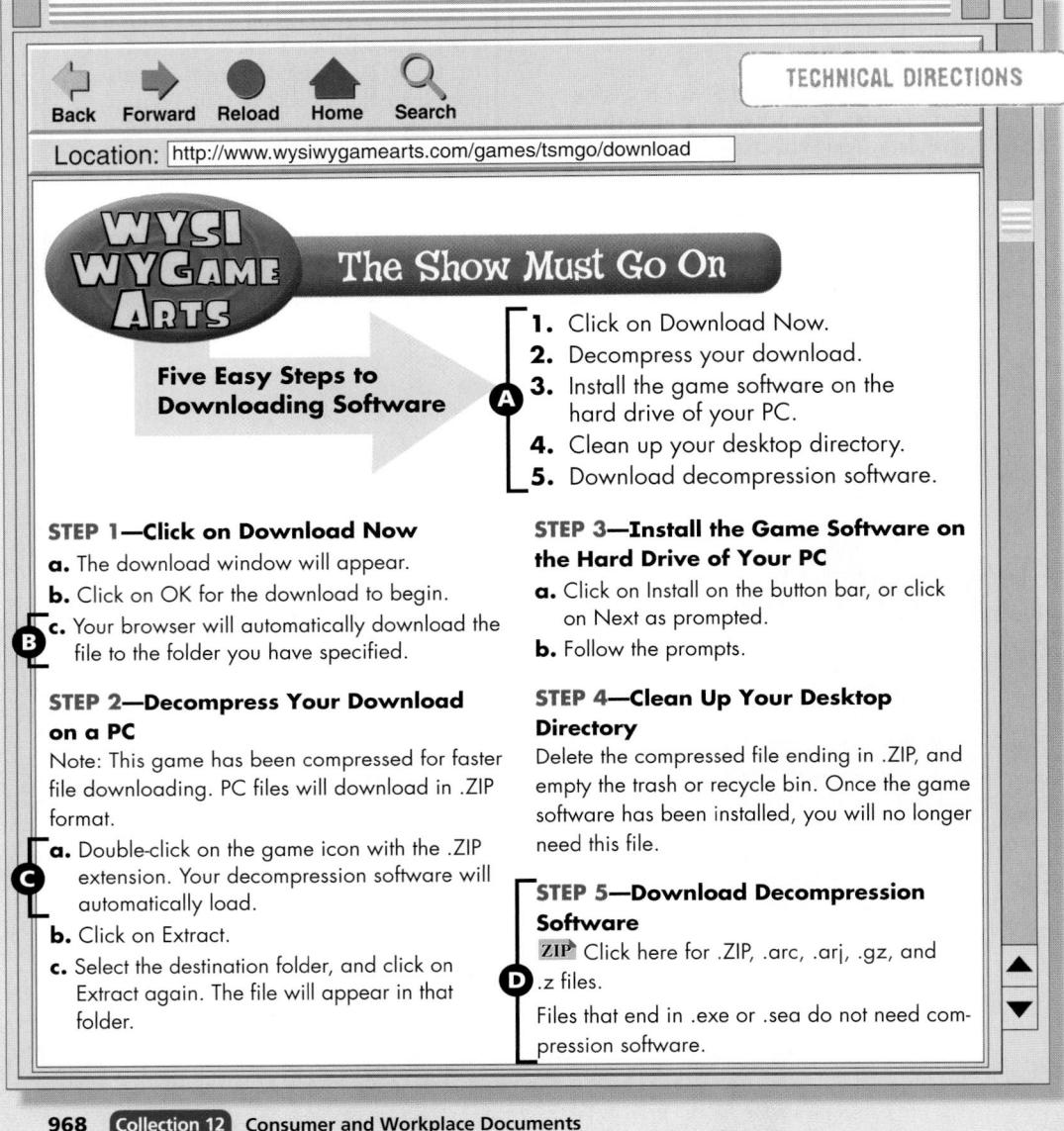

TECHNICAL DIRECTIONS

Location: http://www.wysiwygamearts.com/games/tsmgo/download

WYSIWYGAME ARTS

The Show Must Go On

Five Easy Steps to Downloading Software

1. Click on Download Now.
2. Decompress your download.
3. Install the game software on the hard drive of your PC.
4. Clean up your desktop directory.
5. Download decompression software.

STEP 1—Click on Download Now
a. The download window will appear.
b. Click on OK for the download to begin.
c. Your browser will automatically download the file to the folder you have specified.

STEP 2—Decompress Your Download on a PC
Note: This game has been compressed for faster file downloading. PC files will download in .ZIP format.
a. Double-click on the game icon with the .ZIP extension. Your decompression software will automatically load.
b. Click on Extract.
c. Select the destination folder, and click on Extract again. The file will appear in that folder.

STEP 3—Install the Game Software on the Hard Drive of Your PC
a. Click on Install on the button bar, or click on Next as prompted.
b. Follow the prompts.

STEP 4—Clean Up Your Desktop Directory
Delete the compressed file ending in .ZIP, and empty the trash or recycle bin. Once the game software has been installed, you will no longer need this file.

STEP 5—Download Decompression Software
ZIP Click here for .ZIP, .arc, .arj, .gz, and .z files.
Files that end in .exe or .sea do not need compression software.

DIFFERENTIATING INSTRUCTION

Advanced Learners
Activity. After students have read and critiqued the WYSIWYGame Arts Web site, have them work in groups to create sets of graphics that could accompany and improve the step-by-step text instructions. These graphics should be designed to clear up misunderstandings that they or inexperienced computer users had or might have while reading the instructions. A graphic of a dialogue box to accompany step 2, for example, might help inexperienced users avoid confusion about what selecting a destination folder means. Post completed graphics on a classroom bulletin board. Have students discuss whether these illustrations make the instructions easier to understand.

Analyzing Informational Text

Reading Check

1. Why is a **logical sequence** important in **functional documents**?

2. List two errors often found in the sequencing of poorly written documents.

3. In "Five Easy Steps to Downloading Software," what two main steps do you have to do before you can install the game software on your hard drive?

4. To decompress files on a PC, what format will you download in?

Test Practice

1. In "Five Easy Steps to Downloading Software" (page 968), which step is out of sequence?
   - A "Click on Download Now"
   - B "Decompress Your Download on a PC"
   - C "Install the Game Software on the Hard Drive of Your PC"
   - D "Download Decompression Software"

2. Where *should* the step that is out of sequence be placed?
   - F After step 1
   - G After step 2
   - H After step 3
   - J After step 4

3. The most logical order for giving instructions in any functional document (including "Five Easy Steps to Downloading Software") is —
   - A alphabetical order
   - B order of importance
   - C step-by-step order
   - D spatial order

4. Step 2, "Decompress Your Download on a PC," will probably leave an inexperienced computer user *most* uncertain about which question?
   - F I'm supposed to double-click on *what*?
   - G *What* do I have to do to make the decompression software load?
   - H *How* do I select a destination folder (and what is it)?
   - J Why exactly did I think I wanted this computer game anyway?

5. According to step 4, to clean up your desktop, what should you do once the game software is installed?
   - A Download the .ZIP file.
   - B Delete the compressed .ZIP file.
   - C Decompress the .ZIP file.
   - D Create a new folder.

Application

Write a brief critique of the functional document "Five Easy Steps to Downloading Software" (page 968). Are the procedures presented in a logical sequence? Is the information clear and easily understood? What possible misunderstandings could occur? How could such misunderstandings be prevented? Write your suggestions for changes.

Reading Skills
Analyze the logic of functional documents.

Evaluating the Logic of Functional Documents   969

Test-Taking Tips

For instruction on how to answer multiple-choice items, refer students to **Test Smarts**.

Assessing

Assessment

- *Holt Assessment: Reading, Literature, and Vocabulary*

Reteaching

For a lesson reteaching evaluating functional documents, see **Reteaching**, p. 979A.

Independent Practice

Analyzing Informational Text

Reading Check

1. Functional documents need logical sequence to help people follow instructions.

2. missing steps and out-of-order steps

3. Click on "Download Now" and download decompression software.

4. ZIP format

Test Practice

Answers and Model Rationales

1. **D** Compressed files cannot be decompressed without decompression software, so clearly "Download Decompression Software" should not be the last step.

2. **F** It doesn't matter whether users download the game software or the decompression software first, but it must happen *before* step 2, "Decompress Your Download." For this reason, G, H, and J can be eliminated.

3. **C** A step-by-step sequence is clearly the most logical order to illustrate steps in a process.

4. **H** H is the best answer because a destination folder is presented as an important part of the process, but it is not defined or explained.

5. **B** Step 4 clearly tells users to delete the compressed .ZIP file.

Application

Have students prepare their critiques by charting the document's weaknesses. Categories could include unclear language, poor design, and confusing sequence.

Writing Business Letters

Motivate. Ask students to suggest several occasions for which they might need to write a business letter. [Possible responses: inquiring about a mail-order purchase; applying for a job; requesting information for a research project.] Discuss why letters such as these would differ in form and tone from a personal letter.

Marketing Your Computer Game

So here you are, further down the road of computer game design and development. You've acquired some meaningful hands-on experience, and you're wondering how you can parlay that experience into the next step—whatever that step may be. A new step may seem intimidating, but remember Sir Arthur C. Clarke's second law: "The only way of discovering the limits of the possible is to venture a little way past them into the impossible." Now is the time to get out into the world and make connections.

To market your computer game, you will need to write **business letters**—probably lots of them.

Elements of a Business Letter

When you write a **thank-you letter** to Aunt Cele for your birthday gift (a hand-knit red plaid scarf), you can call the scarf "cool" and use an informal, chatty style. In contrast, the **style** and **tone** of a business letter are **formal**. Focus on these elements whenever you write a business letter:

- **Clarity.** Provide all the information the recipient of the letter needs to know, and say it clearly and briefly.
- **Courtesy.** Even if you're writing a **complaint letter,** be polite. You're asking the recipient to *do* something, and you'll be more successful if you remain courteous.
- **Style.** The **style** of a business letter is **formal.** That means it contains no slang, no contractions, no sentence fragments.

- **Tone.** The recipient of the letter is probably someone you don't know. Be respectful and formal.
- **Vocabulary.** Use appropriate vocabulary, the language you would use in a formal speaking situation. You may need to define terms the recipient of the letter might not know.

Format of a Business Letter

If you want to make a good impression, you can't write letters in just any form. It is important to follow the proper **format** and conventional **style** for a business letter, as shown on pages 971–973.

A business letter has these six parts:
- heading
- inside address
- salutation
- body
- closing
- signature

The example on page 973 uses the **block-style format,** in which all six parts of the letter (heading, inside address, salutation, body, closing, and signature) align at the left margin.

In the **modified-block-style format,** the heading, closing, and signature are indented, as is every paragraph. See the letter on page 972 for an example of the modified block style.

INTERNET

More About
Writing Business
Letters
Keyword: LE5 9-12

SKILLS FOCUS

Pages 970–973
cover
Writing Skills
Write a business
letter.

RESOURCES: WRITING

Planning
- *One-Stop Planner* CD-ROM with ExamView Test Generator

Differentiating Instruction
- *Workshop Resources: Writing, Listening, and Speaking*

Assessment
- *Holt Assessment: Writing, Listening, and Speaking*
- *One-Stop Planner* CD-ROM with ExamView Test Generator

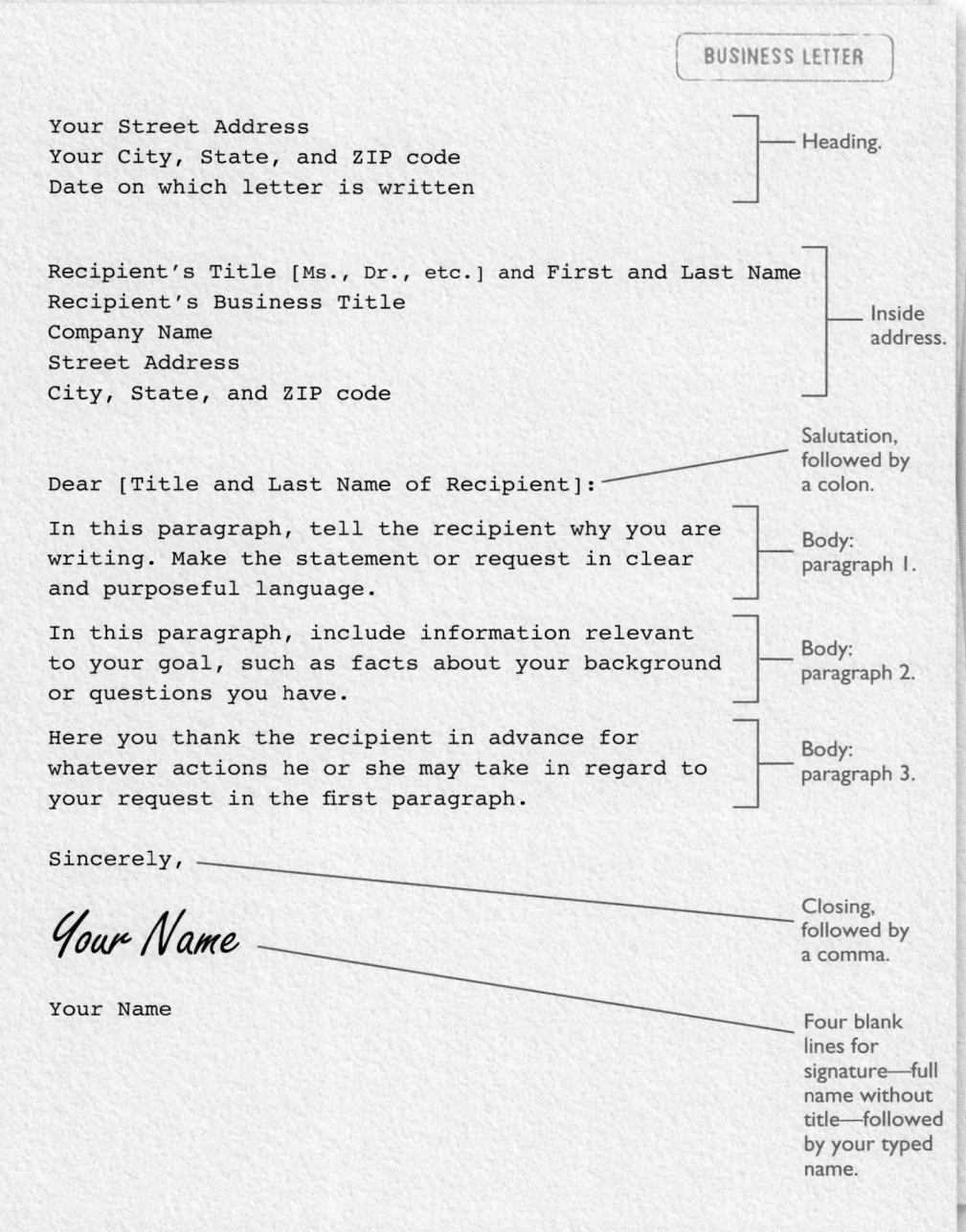

BUSINESS LETTER

Your Street Address
Your City, State, and ZIP code
Date on which letter is written

— Heading.

Recipient's Title [Ms., Dr., etc.] and First and Last Name
Recipient's Business Title
Company Name
Street Address
City, State, and ZIP code

— Inside
address.

Dear [Title and Last Name of Recipient]:

Salutation,
followed by
a colon.

In this paragraph, tell the recipient why you are writing. Make the statement or request in clear and purposeful language.

Body:
paragraph 1.

In this paragraph, include information relevant to your goal, such as facts about your background or questions you have.

Body:
paragraph 2.

Here you thank the recipient in advance for whatever actions he or she may take in regard to your request in the first paragraph.

Body:
paragraph 3.

Sincerely,

Your Name

Closing,
followed by
a comma.

Your Name

Four blank
lines for
signature—full
name without
title—followed
by your typed
name.

**Elements of a
Business Letter**

Discuss each element of a business letter with students: heading, inside address, salutation, body, closing, and signature. Focus on why these elements are important in effective business correspondence, explaining that each plays a role in communicating the main ideas of the letter and in organizing its content.

Business Letter Format

Next, ask students to consider the basic format of this business letter model. Point out that all parts of the letter are set flush with the left margin. Explain that this structured and widely used format allows the reader to skim the letter and easily locate the information he or she needs, such as the writer's name and address.

Analyzing the Model Letter to Mr. S. K. Miyamoto

Invite a volunteer to read the letter to Mr. Miyamoto aloud. You may wish to use the following points to guide class discussion about why the letter is a model of an effective business letter:

- **Clarity.** The writer has carefully organized her thoughts. Each paragraph of the letter is clearly focused on a central idea. The first paragraph comes immediately to the point. In the very first sentence the purpose of the letter is clearly expressed. The second paragraph focuses on the writer's experience, explaining why she wants to attend the conference and why her background makes her a suitable prospect. She tells only that part of her experience that is relevant to her request.

- **Courtesy.** In the final paragraph the writer thanks Mr. Miyamoto for his time and attention. The fact that the letter is brief, organized, and focused also reflects the letter writer's appreciation that Mr. Miyamoto's time is valuable.

- **Style, tone, vocabulary.** Each sentence is complete. No slang is used. The tone is respectful. The style is formal but suited to the persona of a high school student.

Learners Having Difficulty

To make sure students understand the format of a conventional business letter, have them identify the heading, inside address, salutation, body, closing, and signature in the letter to Mr. Miyamoto. If necessary, have them use the model on p. 971 as a guide.

Two Sample Business Letters

Now that you have a sample of the business-letter format, let's look at two actual letters.

BUSINESS LETTER

8 Chimney Rock Way
Suburbanite, CA 98990
April 6, 2002

Mr. S. K. Miyamoto
Conference Project Manager
WYSIWYGame Arts
41311 On Donner Highway
Cybercity, CA 99880

Dear Mr. Miyamoto:

    I am writing to request the chance to attend your upcoming "Making Games Fun Again" conference in May. I see from information provided on the WYSIWYGame Arts Web site that attendance can be arranged through your office.

    I am making this request on account of a lifelong interest in computer games. I am a high school student who has taught myself C++ programming. I have designed several successful computer games, which I am making available as downloadable shareware on my Web site. My Web site has attracted the attention of other gamers.

    Thank you in advance for your time and attention. I hope to have the opportunity to meet you in person.

Sincerely yours,

Judy Realdata

Judy Realdata

Analyzing the Model Letter

Judy Realdata's letter (on page 972) should have a positive effect on Mr. Miyamoto. The **vocabulary** is appropriate—Judy is writing to a business executive. The writer's formal **tone** shows respect and reflects the fact that the writer and the recipient do not know each other.

The letter's **central idea** (in this case, a **request**) is clearly stated in the first paragraph. The **style**—a conventional format, with a standard font and spaces between paragraphs—makes the letter easy to read. Now, let's see what response the letter received.

 **WYSIWYGame Arts**
41311 On Donner Highway
Cybercity, CA 99880

BUSINESS LETTER

April 18, 2002

Ms. Judy Realdata
8 Chimney Rock Way
Suburbanite, CA 98990

Dear Ms. Realdata:

Thank you for your letter of April 6. In regard to your request, WYSIWYGame Arts would like to invite you not only to attend our "Making Games Fun Again" conference in May but also to be the conference's West Coast high school representative.

Please reply in writing by April 30. Once we have your acceptance, we will provide additional information about the conference.

We look forward to hearing from you.

Sincerely,

S. K. Miyamoto

S. K. Miyamoto
Conference Project Manager

PRACTICE

Judy Realdata's carefully prepared letter got an even better response than she'd hoped. Your assignment is to write Judy's reply. Be sure to follow the proper **form** for a business letter and use a **tone** and **style** appropriate to your audience. This assignment gives you practice in writing a business letter, so that you can make business connections that will help you design the best computer game ever.

Analyzing the Response to Ms. Judy Realdata

You may wish to discuss these points with students:

- Mr. Miyamoto's letter is written on the company's letterhead, so that is the heading. He need type in only the date, not his address.
- The first sentence of Mr. Miyamoto's response is courteous and cites the date of Ms. Realdata's letter, in order to avoid any confusion.
- Mr. Miyamoto is direct. He avoids providing information that Ms. Realdata will need only if she accepts his invitation.
- Mr. Miyamoto's positive reply is a clear indication that Ms. Realdata's letter to him has made a good impression.

GUIDED PRACTICE

Monitoring students' progress. Invite students to form small groups to discuss why a business letter can be an important step in helping someone create a good (or bad) first impression. Have students discuss and list the elements of format and style that are recommended for a business letter.

INDEPENDENT PRACTICE

Assign the Practice activity. It will help you assess students' understanding of both the proper form for a business letter and the elements of style, tone, and clarity that are needed to communicate effectively in business.

Skills Starter

Motivate. Invite volunteers to describe business meetings they have attended. For example, they might describe a student council meeting, a band officers' meeting, or a neighborhood action committee meeting. Then, explain that the minutes of a meeting are, in essence, a summary of what occurred at the meeting. Encourage students to tell what they know about taking and reading minutes of such meetings.

Writing the Minutes of a Meeting

Taking Notes at a Meeting

The big day arrives. You are the West Coast high school representative for the WYSIWYGame Arts "Making Games Fun Again" conference. On the first morning you are scheduled to attend a meeting of all the high school representatives from around the country. You are all set to sit back and enjoy yourself. But what's this? You are asked to take **minutes of the meeting,** which is quite a responsibility. Not only that, but you are also asked to go to the business office at the conference center and run off copies of your minutes. Your minutes of the meeting will be distributed to everyone at the conference and sent to a list of interested students from countries all over the world.

Writing a Clear and Logical Summary

Taking notes of what is said in the meeting doesn't seem to be a problem because you take notes in your classes every day. But minutes are different from classroom notes. Both involve listening carefully and noting important information.

When it comes to writing the minutes, however, you'll be writing a **formal report** (no slang or informal language) in complete sentences. In your minutes you'll **summarize** in a sentence or two each speaker's main ideas. You'll report your information **clearly, briefly,** and **accurately,** covering the complete meeting in **chronological order.** You'll also include certain **formal conventions,** such as the names of those who attended and who were unable to attend, the person who chaired (ran) the meeting, and the time that the meeting began and ended.

SKILLS FOCUS

Pages 974–977 cover **Writing Skills** Write the minutes of a meeting.

Formatting Minutes

How do you transform your notes into a presentable form? Lucky for you, your packet of materials for the conference includes a copy of the minutes of last year's meeting. On the following pages you'll see an example of the standard **format** for presenting the minutes of a meeting.

WYSIWYGame Arts
WYSIWYGame Arts Conference 2001
Creating New Graphics!

Meeting of High School Representatives, May 9, 2001

Present:
Laura Lee, Mark Hadley, Pedro Valdez, Samantha Soltano, Abdul Akbar, Jimmy Johnson, Lin Huang, Kim Soo Long, Jerry Gralnik, Renee Letendre, Brian Parke.

Regrets:
Katie Dee.

Call to order:
The meeting was called to order at 9:05 a.m. by Laura Lee, WYSIWYGame Arts Student Coordinator, as chair.

Approval of minutes:
The minutes of the 2001 Meeting of High School Representatives were approved by Mark Hadley, Lin Huang, and Renee Letendre, the only representatives present who had attended that meeting.

Business conducted:
The agenda was approved as submitted by Laura Lee.

The representatives introduced themselves, told where they came from, and said a few words about their experience with computer game design.

The main topic of discussion was high school consumers' complaints about the 3-D Pinball game. Apparently the game appears choppy when played. The ball and flippers do not move smoothly, and the picture in the background is often distorted and fragmented. The game works despite those flaws, and some consumers are not bothered by these problems.

Writing the Minutes of a Meeting   **975**

A Clear and Logical Summary

Point out that in the example the minutes are organized to make them clear and easy to follow and understand. You may wish to discuss the following points:

- The minutes follow chronological order.
- Topics are introduced with bold-face subheads.
- The text is written in complete sentences and uses formal vocabulary.
- Each paragraph focuses on a single subject and is introduced by a topic sentence.
- The writer summarizes the important information, focusing only on the main ideas and important details.
- The meeting opens with the reading of the previous meeting's minutes and closes with the schedule for the next meeting, showing continuity and the next action decided upon.

DIFFERENTIATING INSTRUCTION

English-Language Learners

You may wish to review a few of the subheads, since they may confuse students who are learning English. *Present,* for example, means those who attended or who were present at the meeting. *Regrets* is from the idiom "sent their regrets" and means those who were invited or expected to attend but were unable to. *Call to order* means that the chair announced that the meeting would begin.

A game console was provided, and ten minutes was allotted for those few representatives who had never played 3-D Pinball to see what the game looks like. The consensus of the representatives was that the complaints were justified and had to be addressed.

Laura Lee opened the floor to suggestions for correcting the graphics problems. Kim Soo Long suggested that a new gaming project be started to replace 3-D Pinball completely. Brian Parke said that the company should inspect the hardware—the game console. He believes that the problem lies in the actual game console rather than in the 3-D Pinball software. Jimmy Johnson argued that since other games work well and do not have problems similar to those of 3-D Pinball, the problems must be in the actual game. Pedro Valdez suggested that the group create new graphics for 3-D Pinball and then do thorough tests to ensure that the problems do not reoccur.

Votes taken:
A vote was taken to decide the course of action. The high school representatives voted 9–3 in favor of deleting the current graphics and creating new ones that would be compatible with the game console. It was voted unanimously that another meeting was needed to decide on the new graphics. This meeting is scheduled for May 10, 2001, at 9:00 a.m.

Adjournment:
The current meeting was adjourned at 10:45 a.m.

Minutes prepared by Lin Huang, high school representative

Elements of a Meeting's Minutes

You now know what minutes of a meeting look like. They include the following **elements:**

- the name of the organization and committee, workshop, and so on, that is meeting
- the date of the meeting and the time at which the meeting began
- a list of those present
- a list of those who sent regrets (did not attend)
- a detailed and accurate report of the business of the meeting
- a report of any votes taken and their outcome
- the time of adjournment
- the name of the person writing the minutes

PRACTICE

Choose one of the following activities:

1. Make up minutes for the WYSI-WYGame Arts 2002 "Making Games Fun Again" conference.

2. Take minutes at a meeting of an organization to which you belong.

3. Take minutes at a local council, school-board, or other meeting to which the public is invited.

Whichever activity you choose, be sure to report information clearly, briefly, and accurately. Summarize the important topics that were covered at the meeting, including speakers' main ideas and the outcome of any votes. Write in complete sentences, and follow the standard format for presenting minutes.

GUIDED PRACTICE

Monitoring students' progress. To check students' understanding of the material, ask student pairs to locate and identify in the example of minutes (pp. 975–976) each element listed in the "Elements of a Meeting's Minutes" section. Encourage partners to discuss any questions they have as they complete the activity.

INDEPENDENT PRACTICE

Assign the Practice activity. The activity will help you assess students' ability to summarize the important topics of a meeting and to check their understanding of how to format the minutes of a meeting.

Writing the Minutes of a Meeting   **977**

Collection 12: Skills Review

Reading Skills

SKILLS FOCUS, pp. 978–979

Grade-Level Skills

■ **Reading Skills**
Analyze elements of consumer and workplace documents.

INTRODUCING THE SKILLS REVIEW

Use this review to assess students' grasp of the skills taught in this collection.

Test-Taking Tips

Remind students that when two or more choices are reasonable answers to a question, they should choose the one for which there is the most evidence.

For more information on how to answer multiple-choice items, refer students to **Test Smarts.**

Answers and Model Rationales

1. **B** Information on operating a product is found in the instruction manual. Information about the warranty (C), facts about product capability (D), or the rights and terms between two parties, such as a consumer and a manufacturer (A), would not be of help.

2. **F** The purpose of a warranty is to provide protection to the consumer. Therefore, if the warranty is limited, it means the protection is limited.

3. **A** Mailing the registration card to the manufacturer is the easiest and most common method of providing proof of ownership. B and C do not prove ownership, and D is a different kind of document.

Collection 12: Skills Review

Informational Reading Skills

Consumer and Workplace Documents

DIRECTIONS: Read and respond to the following questions about consumer and workplace documents.

1. Which **consumer document** is *most* likely to help you if you have trouble figuring out how to operate a device?
   - **A** A contract
   - **B** An instruction manual
   - **C** A warranty
   - **D** Product information

2. The **purpose** of a **limited warranty** is to provide —
   - **F** some protection if a product is defective
   - **G** a lifetime provision for repair of a product
   - **H** directions for operating a product
   - **J** a lifetime money-back guarantee of a product

3. For most product **warranties** to be effective, the manufacturer usually requires that the purchaser —
   - **A** mail a registration card to the manufacturer in order to register purchase of the product
   - **B** pay full price, not a reduced price, for the product
   - **C** wait at least thirty days before requesting repairs
   - **D** sign a legal contract with the manufacturer

4. In which of these **consumer documents** are you *most* likely to find out how many phone numbers you can enter in a cell phone's memory?
   - **F** A warranty
   - **G** Product information
   - **H** Safety information
   - **J** A contract

5. What does a **search engine** enable you to do?
   - **A** Design a Web page
   - **B** Send an e-mail message
   - **C** Join an online chat room
   - **D** Locate information that is available on the Web

6. According to MLA style, what is the correct way to cite a URL?
   - **F** Within parentheses
   - **G** Within slash marks
   - **H** Within angled brackets
   - **J** Within dashes

7. In preparing a *Works Cited* list, you should —
   - **A** use cursive handwriting
   - **B** always follow MLA style
   - **C** not be concerned about using a consistent style
   - **D** follow the style that your teacher requests

SKILLS FOCUS

Pages 978–979 cover
Reading Skills
Analyze elements of consumer and workplace documents.

Using Academic Language

Review of Informational Terms

Ask students to review the collection to find the meanings of the terms listed below. Then, have students show their grasp of the skills by citing passages from the collection that show the meanings of those terms.
Consumer Documents (pp. 947, 948); **Warranty** (p. 948); **Product Information** (p. 948); **Instruction Manual** (p. 948);

Elements (p. 948); **Features** (p. 948); **Contract** (p. 948); **Technical Directions** (pp. 948, 952); **Search Engine** (p. 952); **Browser** (p. 952); **Workplace Documents** (pp. 947, 955); **Copyright** (p. 959); **License** (p. 959); **Structure** (p. 961); **Format** (p. 961); **Header** (p. 961); **Section** (p. 961); **Logical Sequence** (pp. 961, 966); **Functional Documents** (pp. 959, 965).

Collection 12: Skills Review

8. In preparing a *Works Cited* list, you should —

F divide a URL only after a period

G divide a URL only after a slash

H divide a URL anywhere in the address as long as you use a hyphen

J not divide a URL at all

9. The **purpose** of a **functional workplace document** is to —

A eliminate some jobs

B increase paperwork

C help people get things done

D lessen people's dependence on computers

10. A **shareware agreement** is a type of —

F software program

G contract

H warranty

J Web browser

11. What type of **sequence** do *most* **functional documents** follow?

A Alphabetical

B Logical

C Spatial

D Chronological

12. Which element is *not* part of the **format,** or **design,** of a document?

F Boldface type

G Drawings

H Color

J Point-by-point sequence

13. A set of **technical directions** is badly flawed if it —

A omits a step

B puts a step in the wrong order

C does either of the above

D does none of the above

14. Which item is *not* necessary to include in the **minutes of a meeting**?

F The names of those present

G The time at which the meeting adjourns

H A record of votes taken

J The kind of refreshments served at the meeting

Constructed Response

15. Think about a product you've purchased or used recently, and write a **business letter** to the manufacturer explaining what you think of it. Be sure to include all six parts of the business-letter format. If you don't know the mailing address of the manufacturer, just make it up.

---

4. G The function of the product information document is to describe what a product can do. The other options serve different functions.

5. D The only function of a search engine is to search the World Wide Web pages for specific topics. It can do none of the other options.

6. H According to MLA style, the correct way to cite a URL is within angled brackets. The other options are incorrect according to MLA.

7. D A *Works Cited* list should always be a clear, orderly list that enables people to easily find the listed sources. While the MLA style is an essential guide (B), it is advised to follow the style requested by your teacher. A and C would probably make the search for sources more difficult.

8. G According to MLA style, if a URL must be divided at the end of a line, it should be divided only after a slash. Periods (F), hyphens (H), or other marks of punctuation are not acceptable.

9. C Functional workplace documents help people get things done by providing the necessary communication. While increased paperwork may be the result (B), it is not the purpose. The idea expressed in C is not addressed in A or D.

10. G A shareware agreement is a legal agreement, or contract, between the author and the user of the software. A warranty (H) details information on how to receive service from a manufacturer of a product. F and J are products.

11. B Logical sequencing requires that *all* the steps appear in correct order so that any possible confusion is eliminated. Because A, C, and D do not provide these requirements as well, B is the option most functional documents follow.

12. J Boldface type (F), drawings (G), and color (H) are all elements of the format. Point-by-point sequence is the order that ideas are presented in and not a format element.

13. C Both omitting a step and putting a step in the wrong order create confusion and frustration for the consumer, so C is the correct answer.

14. J The kinds of refreshments served is not important information. F, G, and H supply important information for the record.

Constructed Response

15. [Accept any reasonable response that is written in the block-style format or modified-block-style format and includes a heading, inside address, salutation, body, closing, and signature.]

Reteaching Lessons

Analyzing Workplace Documents

Objective: To analyze the way authors use the structure and format of workplace documents to achieve their purposes.

Direct Teaching: Share the following information with students.

Workplace documents help people complete tasks quickly and accurately. They are also meant to communicate information clearly and concisely. There are many varieties of such documents, depending on the nature and needs of the user and on the work environment. Examples include step-by-step directions for installing or using electronic or communications equipment, safety instructions, license agreements, warranties, contracts of all kinds, memoranda, reports, and proposals. Using documents properly can save you time and money. For example, when you disregard instructions and proceed by trial and error, you often end up spending far more time on a task than you would if you had read and followed well-designed directions. Also, failing to read legal documents can leave you unaware of your legal rights and responsibilities.

Writers of workplace documents routinely use certain structures and formats to help users easily understand and apply the information in the documents. For instance, these writers often make use of headings and subheadings to let readers know what main topics and subtopics the document addresses. Writers often divide the text into short sections by using spacing, indentation, numbering, or subheads in special typefaces. The best documents present these text sections in a logical order or sequence, often step by step or point by point. Frequently, these types of documents use diagrams and other graphics because they can convey certain types of complex information far more efficiently than just words.

Guided Practice: Analyzing workplace documents. Explain that the writers of workplace documents arrange information logically to suit the content and purpose of the document. Review the types of sequencing often used in workplace documents—step by step and point by point—and discuss the situations in which each type might be used. (For example, step-by-step sequencing might be used for operating instructions; point-by-point sequencing might be used to show the relationship between data contained in a progress report.)

Walk students through the shareware agreement (p. 960). Discuss the structure and format of the agreement; the use of headings and subheadings; the sequence of sections; and how boldface type, caps, indentations, and line spacing are used to make the information easy to follow.

Independent Practice: Analyzing workplace documents. As homework, have students locate documents for installing or operating an electronic device, such as a radio, a DVD player, or a digital camera. (Have functional documents available for students who need them.) Ask individual students to analyze the structure and format of one document and explain how the writer used these features to present information. Encourage students to organize their analysis on a chart like the one below. (Example features are given in the first column of the chart, and sample answers for the first item appear in the second and third columns. Encourage students to identify and list the specific features of their documents, rather than limiting their analysis to the features shown in the chart.) Lead a follow-up discussion for students to compare and contrast similar documents and to evaluate the structural and formatting features.

Feature	Example from Document	Purpose of Feature
headings	centered head at top	announces the purpose of document
subheadings		
step-by-step sequencing		
typeface		
numbered sections		
diagrams		

Analyzing and Elaborating on Ideas

Objective: To analyze and elaborate on ideas presented in primary or secondary sources.

Direct Teaching: Share the following ideas with students.

What would happen if readers never analyzed the material offered in magazines and newspapers? A lot of inaccurate or outdated information would go unchallenged. What if readers never evaluated the opinions of commentators, critics, and columnists? Readers would fail to develop any opinions of their own and would merely parrot the ideas of others. What if readers never bothered to bring their own knowledge and experience to bear on what they read? In that case, there would be a boring sameness to what they read, and little new information or opinions would develop.

Whether you are using informational text as a source for a report or for some other purpose of your own, it's always important to analyze, evaluate, and elaborate on what you read. That means asking questions like: *Who is the author's audience? What does the author want the audience to learn or believe? What are the topic and main ideas? What details support the topic and develop the main ideas? Are the author's facts accurate? Do I agree with what the author proposes or believes? What do I already know about this topic? What more do I want to find out?*

Analyzing, evaluating, and elaborating can be done in any order during the reading process. In fact, the best readers usually begin elaborating on a text as soon as they start reading by making connections between what they already know and what the author is providing.

Guided Practice: Creating a chain of ideas. Have students read the first three paragraphs of "Can Animals Think?" (p. 27). Draw a chain on the chalkboard as follows:

Analyze	+	Evaluate	+	Elaborate

Brainstorm with students for questions they might ask about the opening paragraphs. Work together to decide the category—analyze, evaluate, or elaborate—to which each question belongs. [Possible responses: *Analyze*—Based on the title and opening paragraphs, what does the topic of the article appear to be? For what audience and purpose is the author writing? What facts does he include? What opinions does he offer? *Evaluate*—Does the article make sense so far? Does it suit its intended audience and purpose? Are the facts correct? *Elaborate*—What do I already know about the topic? What personal experience or knowledge can shed light on the topic? What more do I want to know?] Then, have students read the rest of "Can Animals Think?" Ask pairs of students to extend the chain of ideas by answering the questions that the class already developed.

As a group, discuss the question *Can animals think?* Encourage students to refer to their charts during the discussion. Conclude by asking students if they think the author answered the question he posed in his title and how the ideas and experiences of their classmates helped them form their ideas and opinions.

Independent Practice: Evaluating informational text. Divide the class into groups of three, and ask each group to choose for evaluation an article from a magazine or local newspaper. After they have read their article, each group can analyze and evaluate the material presented and decide if the article is a good source of information on its topic. Remind students to elaborate by making connections with their own ideas and experiences as they discuss the merits of the selection. Ask each group to write a short paragraph that states and explains their opinions. Remind students to include specific examples from the text to support their evaluations.

Evaluating Functional Documents

Objective: To evaluate the logic of functional documents.

Direct Teaching: Share the following information with students.

Functional documents that explain a process or give step-by-step instructions (even those provided by a reputable manufacturer or technical expert) are not always flawless. They range in quality from excellent to truly awful. Among the problems that frequently occur are the omission of important steps or the presentation of steps in the wrong order. Mistakes waste users' time and can result in damage to the product. Therefore, it makes sense to read through instructions from start to finish before beginning the process. As you read through the instructions, it is helpful also to visualize the process being described—completing a "dry run" in your mind. If the instructions are for assembling or making something, check the list of materials against the materials you have. Can you anticipate needing something omitted from the list? Pay attention to any diagrams. Think about each step and ask yourself if its place in the overall sequence makes sense. Think about any steps that might be missing. Visualizing the steps in a process will help you spot and solve problems before they happen.

Guided Practice: Evaluating functional documents. Share your own experiences of trying to follow instructions that were badly written and tell what happened as a result. Then, ask students to share similar experiences. Together, discuss what can be learned from such mishaps.

On the chalkboard, write the following instructions for assembling a footrest or provide individual copies of the instructions to the students.

Workstation Footrest Assembly

Materials:
- 1 top piece
- 2 leg pieces
- 4 wooden pegs
- wood glue
- 4 rubber feet

Directions:
1. Put a small amount of glue in the two holes of one leg piece and in the two holes on one end of the top piece.
2. Place this leg piece against the end of the top piece, aligning the holes.
3. Insert one wooden peg in each hole, and tap each peg gently with a small hammer until it is flush with the edge of the leg piece.
4. Use a damp cloth to wipe away any excess glue.
5. Repeat with the second leg.

Have students read through the instructions; then, analyze them together. Guide students to see that although the instructions are straightforward and easy to follow, there is a logical step missing. What is to be done with the four rubber feet mentioned in the materials list? Ask students where the step for inserting these feet into the predrilled holes in the legs should logically be placed. [Students may say that this should be the first step.] Then, talk about how the instructions could be improved. [Students may say that adding a small hammer and damp cloth to the materials list and a diagram of the footrest would be helpful; students may say that the instructions should include descriptions, such as the dimensions, to distinguish the top piece from the two leg pieces.]

Independent Practice: Evaluating instructions for a process. As homework, have students evaluate a set of instructions they have at home for playing or downloading a computer game, assembling a bicycle, or some other step-by-step process. Or provide them with suitable documents from classroom or school resources. Ask students to evaluate the user-friendliness of their instructional documents. Have them consider questions such as:

• Are the steps clear and logically arranged?

• Are any steps missing or out of order?

• What questions or problems might arise for someone using these instructions?

• What could the writer have done to make the instructions more helpful or user-friendly?

Conduct a follow-up discussion in which students point out the strengths and weaknesses of the instructional materials they evaluated. You may want to challenge more advanced or technically confident students to rewrite the flawed instructions to make them clearer and easier to use.

Evaluating an Argument

Objective: To evaluate the credibility of opposing arguments by examining the scope of the evidence and the intentions of the author.

Direct Teaching: Share the following ideas with students.

If you wanted to convince a teacher to let you submit a videotape instead of a written report for a class assignment, would you offer reasons why the school should provide video cameras to all students? Of course you wouldn't. To be convincing, an argument must be supported with evidence that is directly related to the issue at hand. As you read or listen to persuasive material, such as newspaper editorials and political speeches, first identify the writer's or speaker's argument, claim, or generalization—what he or she is trying to prove. Then, pay attention to the facts, examples, or reasons that the writer or speaker uses to support the generalization. Remember that besides provable facts, supporting evidence can come in the form of an anecdote, a story based on personal experience; an opinion from someone the writer or speaker views as an expert; or an analogy or comparison to a similar situation or issue. After you've identified the generalization and the evidence supporting it, decide whether the evidence is both convincing and sufficient. Ask questions such as *Does the evidence relate to the argument? Does the evidence make sense? Is there enough evidence? Does it address all aspects of the issue and anticipate possible counterarguments?*

Guided Practice: Evaluating an argument. Have students read the introduction and first two paragraphs of "Peace Isn't Impossible" (p. 240). On the chalkboard, draw a step chart like the one below, and ask students what the essay is about. [It's about the possibility of achieving a peaceful settlement to the conflict in Northern Ireland.] Then, ask students to identify the specific sentence in which George Mitchell states his generalization on the subject. [Mitchell's claim is stated in the first sentence of the second paragraph.] Write his statement in the chart.

As you continue reading the essay with students, have them identify evidence Mitchell offers to support his claim that reaching peace in Northern Ireland is possible. Add the evidence students cite to the chart. Then, ask students to consider whether Mitchell's evidence is relevant to his claim, if the evidence makes sense, and if he presents enough evidence to make a convincing argument. Guide students in evaluating Mitchell's supporting evidence by helping them to distinguish facts from opinions. Point out that when opinions are offered as evidence, readers should take into account the level of knowledge and expertise of the person offering the opinion. They may, for example, view George Mitchell's opinions on the subject of Northern Ireland as expert, based on the information given about his background in the introduction. Add students' ideas to the chart.

Step 3: Is the evidence sufficient and convincing? Why or why not? [Possible responses: Yes, the evidence, though largely based on Mitchell's opinions, is credible because Mitchell is an experienced negotiator and an expert on the people and issues involved in reaching a settlement; no, although Mitchell is knowledgeable, his evidence is mostly based on his personal opinions and not on hard facts or other objective evidence.]

Step 2: What evidence is given to support the argument? [Possible responses: Most people in Northern Ireland want peace; to give up peacemaking efforts would be to hand a victory to the violent minority at the expense of the majority; without a settlement the violence, fear, and sectarian division will continue indefinitely; Prime Minister Tony Blair is pressing hard for a settlement.]

Step 1: What is the writer's argument or claim? ["I believe a historic opportunity to end centuries of conflict in Northern Ireland still exists."]

Independent Practice: Evaluating an argument. Have pairs of students read an editorial in a local newspaper and complete a step chart to evaluate the credibility of the writer's argument. If more than one pair choose the same editorial, encourage them to compare and discuss their evaluations. When they have finished, ask student pairs to display their charts and share their evaluations with the class.

You may want to ask a group of volunteers to prepare and conduct an in-class debate on a current political or social issue, such as the cost of higher education or violence in schools. The debaters will have to begin by researching the topic and formulating a proposition or affirmative statement about the issue, such as the following statement: *The rising cost of higher education is preventing more and more qualified students from going to college.* One pair of students should speak in favor of the proposition and the other pair against it. After the debate, the class can work together to judge the winning side by evaluating the relative strengths and weaknesses of the pro-and-con arguments.

Comparing Consumer Documents

Objective: To compare and contrast features of consumer documents.

Direct Teaching: Share the following information with students.

Buying an apple is a fairly straightforward purchase. You choose a variety you like, check to make sure the apple isn't bruised or spoiled, and pay for it. Buying a more expensive item, like a power tool or piece of electronic equipment, is a more complicated matter. Here, the variety of features can be bewildering and mistakes can be costly. You need information to help you make a wise choice. One source of information is the manufacturer of the product. Most companies supply printed product information and some sort of purchase agreement, guarantee, or warranty. In addition, they often provide instruction manuals or other technical directions. Studying product information before you make a purchase can help you choose the product that is right for you. For example, the product information for a computer game can tell you if the game's memory requirements are compatible with your computer's capacity. Comparing warranties from two different car dealers might persuade you to purchase a pre-owned car from one dealer instead of the other. Looking at the technical directions for two different cameras might sway you toward the camera that is easier to use or that has clearer instructions. Reading consumer documents—before and after a purchase—can help you to avoid purchasing errors and to get the most value from your new product.

Guided Practice: Comparing consumer documents. Use the following information to review the different types of consumer documents with students.

Product information: physical description of a product (including its components) as well as a description of what a tool, machine, and so on can do; also includes use requirements, such as power, memory (for computer software), size, and capacity.

Contract: information on the legal uses of the product.

Warranty: details on what to do if the product does not work, how it can be serviced, and who is financially responsible for repairs within a specific time span.

Instruction manual: instructions for using the product and its features; usually includes how to troubleshoot common problems.

Technical directions: directions for how to install or assemble the product.

Review the warranty, product information, and safety instructions (pp. 949–950). (If possible, provide students with additional examples of consumer documents from school or classroom purchases.) Analyze the various terms offered in the warranty shown on p. 949, and discuss why there is more than one type of warranty offered. Have students answer the questions in the margin notes (p. 950). [*Product information*—The product information provides the power and memory requirements for the game as well as other technical data. Such information would help consumers know whether the software could be run on their computers. *Safety information*—The most important protections for the product are installing it properly and contacting a qualified service person if problems occur.]

Write the following product information on the chalkboard, or provide individual copies to students.

The Fastax Program
Processor—300 MHz
Installation requirements—16 MB minimum (32 MB optimal)
2X CD-ROM drive (4X optimal)
Video card—minimum 256 colors
Sound card, speakers (to use audio instructions)
Printer—laser (with minimum 1 MB memory) or ink jet

Guide students as they compare and contrast the features of the Fastax program with those of the computer game presented on p. 950. Ask students if the Fastax program could be run on the same computer as the WYGame Arts game and how they know.

Independent Practice: Making product comparisons. As homework, have students compare the features of two products, such as two brands or models of washing machines, watches, or televisions. Have them base their comparisons on information obtained from warranties and instruction manuals and on product information from manufacturers, retailers, or consumer research organizations. Tell students that they may be able to obtain product information from local sources, such as appliance, electronics, and department stores. The Internet may also serve as a source of product information. Encourage students to organize their comparisons in a chart like the one to the right that compares two models of washing machines.

Feature	Model A	Model B
Electrical requirement		
Outside dimension		
Capacity		
Number of cycles		
Amount of water per load		
Average energy use per year		

During a follow-up discussion, have students consider how having the kinds of information they collected for their comparison charts could help them to make wise purchases and to use products properly.

Reteaching Lessons

Analyzing Dramatic Literature

Objective: To analyze the characteristics of tragedy and comedy.

Direct Teaching: Share the following ideas with students.

When you want to watch a movie, but you don't know which to watch, you might ask yourself how you want the movie to make you feel—amused, scared, excited, thoughtful, or inspired? Depending on the effect you desire, you might choose a slapstick comedy, a thriller, an action-adventure, a serious documentary, or a heroic romance. Each type of movie will have certain characteristics designed to produce the expected effect. Like movies, plays have different characteristics, depending on the playwright's purpose or the effect the playwright wishes to have on the audience. Knowing the characteristics of comedies and tragedies won't ruin your enjoyment of them any more than knowing what to expect when you sit down to watch a horror movie. The author of a comedy, for example, wishes to emphasize that characters and societies can overcome obstacles and be restored to happiness and good order. The author of a tragedy, on the other hand, wants to remind us that individuals—even those with great gifts and high standing in society—can make fateful choices that utterly destroy themselves and others. Dramatists have unique ways of revealing the innermost feelings of their characters. These include the soliloquy (a character alone on stage speaks directly to the audience) and the aside (a character turns to the audience or to another character and says something that other characters on stage "cannot" hear).

Guided Practice: Analyzing the characteristics of tragedy. Have students review the characters and plot of *Romeo and Juliet* (p. 783). Point out that the play is a Shakespearean tragedy in which the main character or characters suffer great misfortune, due to both character flaws and the workings of fate or chance. Copy the web below on the chalkboard. (Note that possible examples from *Romeo and Juliet* appear in brackets.) Discuss with students each of the characteristics of tragedy listed in the web. Then, work with them to give examples of each characteristic from *Romeo and Juliet,* or have students copy the web and complete it in pairs or small groups.

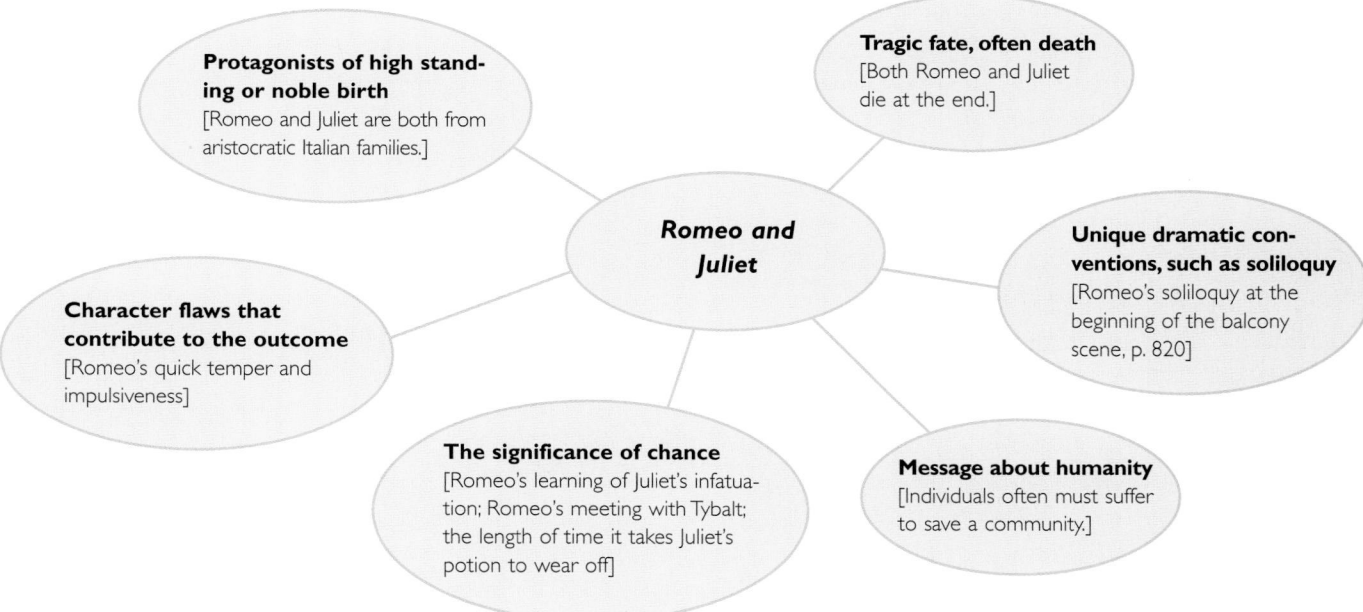

Protagonists of high standing or noble birth
[Romeo and Juliet are both from aristocratic Italian families.]

Tragic fate, often death
[Both Romeo and Juliet die at the end.]

Romeo and Juliet

Character flaws that contribute to the outcome
[Romeo's quick temper and impulsiveness]

Unique dramatic conventions, such as soliloquy
[Romeo's soliloquy at the beginning of the balcony scene, p. 820]

The significance of chance
[Romeo's learning of Juliet's infatuation; Romeo's meeting with Tybalt; the length of time it takes Juliet's potion to wear off]

Message about humanity
[Individuals often must suffer to save a community.]

Independent Practice: Analyzing the characteristics of comedy. Have students complete a similar web for a comedy that they have read, seen, or performed. They may want to analyze *Visitor from Forest Hills* (p. 755). Copy the web below on the chalkboard, or make a copy you can duplicate and distribute to students. (Note that possible examples from *Visitor from Forest Hills* appear in brackets.) Review the elements of comedy with students. Then, have students complete the web as homework.

As an alternative, you might tell advanced students that Shakespeare's story of the ill-fated lovers, *Romeo and Juliet,* has been told and retold over the centuries, using characters with different names and from different cultures and historical eras. These students could work in pairs or small groups to identify a work that borrows from Shakespeare's play and compare it to *Romeo and Juliet,* noting its use of characteristics such as tragic flaws and the role of fate or chance in the outcome.

Students may also want to discuss how the plot of *Romeo and Juliet* could be converted into a comedy. Have them list the characteristics or elements that would have to be changed and how they would change them. Finally, have them write a plot summary of *Romeo and Juliet, The comedy.*

Conflict involves obstacles to love.
[Mimsey locks herself in the bathroom and won't come out for her wedding.]

Characters have traits that create obstacles to their union.
[Norma is emotional, bewildered, and thinks Roy blames her; Roy is excitable and does blame Norma.]

Protagonists can be from any level of society.
[Family is middle class.]

Complications arise that impede resolution.
[Roy goes out on the ledge; a mix-up ensues over the meaning of Mimsey's knocks.]

Visitor from Forest Hills

Unique dramatic conventions, such as an aside
[Norma turns away and tells the audience, "He doesn't believe me. I'll kill myself."]

Happy ending
[Mimsey and Borden get married.]

Questions something we sometimes take for granted
[Do children necessarily "become" their parents?]

Character Traits

Objective: To determine characters' traits by what the characters say about themselves.

Direct Teaching: Share the following ideas with students.

> Think about the characters in a story you have just read. Which ones did you like, and which ones did you dislike? How did you form your opinions about their personalities? If you answer, "By paying attention to what the characters said and did," you would be right. Since writers *want* you to get to know their characters and form opinions about them, they tell you about their traits, or personal qualities, either directly or indirectly. Occasionally, writers will state directly that a character has a certain trait, but more often they will reveal the trait indirectly by having the character act or speak in a particular manner. We can also learn about characters' traits by what other characters say about them, by what they say about themselves when they are telling the story (narration), by their conversation with others (dialogue), and by their thoughts (interior monologues).

Guided Practice: Character-trait chart. Make sure students understand the difference between direct and indirect characterization. If necessary, provide examples of each. Then, have students look at the dialogue between Rainsford and Whitney in "The Most Dangerous Game" (p. 6). Point out Rainsford's speech in the middle of the first column that begins "'Nonsense,' laughed Rainsford." On the chalkboard, draw a chart like the one below. Ask students to read the paragraph and locate the words with which Rainsford reveals his character traits. (Possible answers are given in brackets.) Write students' responses in the chart, and help them to infer Rainsford's character traits from his words. Continue the activity by having students infer the traits revealed by Whitney's speech in the first two paragraphs of the second column, Rainsford's reply (in the third paragraph), and Whitney's response to Rainsford.

Dialogue	Character Trait Implied
[Rainsford: "Luckily, you and I are the hunters."]	[bold, boastful]
[Whitney: "What I felt was a—a mental chill; a sort of sudden dread."]	[honest, fearful]
[Rainsford: "Pure imagination."]	[arrogant, dismissive]
[Whitney: "But sometimes I think sailors have an extra sense.... Evil is a tangible thing.... I'm glad we're getting out of this zone."]	[thoughtful, reflective]

As you discuss the dialogue with students, point out that readers don't have to take the words of a character at face value. As they evaluate what a character says, they should consider anything else they have learned about the character from the story and from their own real-life experience with similar personalities. For example, a character might claim to be honest, but his or her actions in the story might reveal this self-assessment to be untrue.

Independent Practice: Determining character traits.
Have pairs of students choose another story they have read either in their textbook or in another anthology. Ask them to review the story and complete a character-trait chart for the main character. Before students begin, remind them to look for revealing words their characters say both when they are alone or in conversation with other characters. You may want to call students' attention to examples of Rainsford's private speech (p. 18). After completing their charts, ask student pairs to develop a short paragraph, describing their character.

Universal Themes

Objective: To compare works that express a universal theme and provide evidence to support that theme.

Direct Teaching: Share the following ideas with students.

The best writers are interested in exploring issues and questions that concern us all. They are interested, for example, in the causes of war; the nature of love or friendship; and the effects of money, fame, and power. These subjects have universal interest because people of all ages, times, and cultures face similar challenges and have similar desires and limitations. The subject of a work of literature, however, is not its theme. The theme is the particular slant the writer takes on the subject, and it can usually be expressed in a theme statement, which is a generalization that sums up the writer's "take" or message on the subject. For example, the theme of a story on friendship could be summarized in this theme statement: "The greatest threat to friendship is envy." Another writer may offer a similar or different take on the same subject. In order to discover the theme of a literary work, readers must consider all its elements and how they interact. Understanding the conflict and its resolution, however, can be particularly helpful in getting insight into the theme.

Guided Practice: Comparing universal themes. Ask students to read "The Sniper" (pp. 212–215) and "Cranes" (pp. 222–227). On the chalkboard, draw a graphic organizer like the one below. After students have finished reading, discuss with them the common subject that both stories address. (Possible responses appear in brackets.) Guide them as they determine what slant each writer takes on the subject, noting similarities and differences in the writers' approaches. Help students to shape their insights into a statement of a universal theme, which could apply to both stories, and add this theme statement to the chart. Then, have students work together to identify an important difference in the two writers' treatments of this universal theme. Make sure students give specific evidence from the stories with particular emphasis on how each story ends.

Common Subject [the effects of war]

Universal Theme [Possible response: Civil war pits friend against friend and brother against brother, challenging the humanity of everyone involved.]

Difference [Possible response: The main character in "The Sniper" stalks and kills an enemy sniper. At the end, he discovers that the sniper is his own brother. The story emphasizes the tragedy, dehumanization, and waste of war.]

Difference [Possible response: The main character in "Cranes" offers to transport an enemy prisoner who turns out to be a childhood friend. Moved by his memories of their childhood happiness, he allows his prisoner to escape. The ending shows that even during war, individuals can make humane, life-affirming choices.]

Independent Practice: Comparing treatments of a theme. After students have completed their group work, ask them to use the graphic organizer to each write a brief essay, explaining which writer they think is more effective in expressing his message about the effects of civil war. Remind them to consider elements of character, setting, conflict, and resolution in their analysis. The title too may shed light on the theme.

As an alternative, you may want to ask advanced students to choose and compare two other works—from this or another anthology—that share a universal theme. Encourage them to use a graphic organizer to present their ideas.

Literary Devices

Objective: To analyze various literary devices, including figurative language, imagery, allegory, and symbolism.

Direct Teaching: Share the following idea with students.

Anyone can retell a series of events or give a simple description of something they have seen or heard, but what sets talented writers apart is their ability to make experiences and ideas come alive in readers' minds. Amazingly, good writers accomplish this miracle by means of words alone. The words they use, however, are not always ordinary ones; writers make use of a set of literary devices that include figurative comparisons (similes, metaphors, and personification), imagery (vivid words and phrases that fire our senses and imagination), allegory (characters or events used to represent abstract ideas), and symbolism (persons, places, events, or objects that stand for themselves and for something beyond themselves). These devices add richness and detail to a story and help readers make connections with their own experience. They also help readers to visualize events and characters, and to see familiar things in new and different ways. Recognizing these devices is an important part of understanding any text and of enjoying the experience of reading.

Guided Practice: Recognizing literary devices. Explain to students that literary devices such as figures of speech, imagery, allegory, and symbolism are used in both poetry and prose. Have students look up the definitions of these devices in the Handbook of Literary Terms (p. 1019) in the Resource Center. Briefly discuss each term with them, and encourage them, to examine and discuss the examples given.

Have students work in pairs to read "The Seven Ages of Man" (p. 444). After students have read the poem (preferably aloud), draw on the chalkboard a three-column chart like the one below, and fill in the headings in the first column. Ask students to make their own copies of the chart and to fill in the second column with one or more examples of literary devices from Shakespeare's poem. (Possible responses appear in brackets.)

Literary Device	Example	Appeal of the Literary Device
Allegory	[Possible response: The whole poem can be considered an allegory since the concrete actions of individuals are used to represent abstract concepts like youth and old age.]	[Possible response: Shakespeare makes the abstract idea of the stages of human life concrete and understandable by describing them in terms of the actions of individual actors.]
Imagery	[Possible responses: "the infant, / Mewling and puking in the nurses arms"; "the whining schoolboy, with his satchel / And shining morning face."]	[Possible response: calls on readers' own experience of babies, making it possible for them to mentally "hear" the cries and whimpers of infants; helps readers "see" the reluctant child and remember their own school days.]
Metaphor	[Possible response: "All the world's a stage, / And all the men and women merely players."]	[Possible response: helps readers clarify something mysterious or puzzling (the many roles an individual plays in a lifetime) by comparing it to something instantly recognizable—actors on a stage.]
Simile	[Possible responses: "the lover, / Sighing like furnace"; "schoolboy . . . creeping like snail / Unwillingly to school."]	[Possible response: helps readers understand and imagine the power and heat of a lover's passion by visualizing a familiar object.]
Symbolism	[Possible response: The "mewling" and "puking" of the infant symbolizes the infantile qualities that the speaker sees in all men and women.]	[Possible response: makes the difficult conception of imagining the stages of life, particularly one's own life, easier by representing each stage with specific characters and actions.]

After student pairs have filled the second column of their charts, have them share with the class the examples they found. Lead students as they discuss how these devices make Shakespeare's portrait of the stages of human life vivid and convincing. Focus them with questions like the following: How does Shakespeare's language increase the appeal of his poem? How do the literary devices make the poem both more enjoyable and easier to understand? Call attention to the third column of the chart, and have students record their ideas about the appeal of the literary devices.

Independent Practice: Analyzing literary devices. Ask students to choose a favorite poem or short story and make a chart similar to the one shown in the Guided Practice, listing the important literary devices the writer uses. Have students share their charts with partners, taking turns identifying an example of each device from the text and explaining its significance and appeal.

If time allows, students who have analyzed the same story or poem can form groups for an in-depth discussion of the work. Suggest that they compare the examples of literary devices they selected and then discuss how these devices helped them understand and appreciate the work.

Narrator and Tone

Objective: To analyze the way tone and the choice of a narrator affect plot.

Direct Teaching: Share the following with students.

> Imagine that you gave a surprise birthday party for a friend. Because you wanted it to be really special, you invited all of her family and friends and prepared her favorite foods. From your point of view, the party was a big success. The next day at school you were pleased and proud when you told everybody about the party. However, your friend, the guest of honor, was tired and worried on the day of the party. The night before, she had lost her dog and was more interested in finding it than in celebrating her birthday. Would she have remembered the same things about the party that you did, and would she have been as enthusiastic and positive when she described her experience? Probably not. Her account of the party might be completely different than yours. Just as the story of the party would be affected by the person telling it, a writer's choice of narrator influences the events that will be included in a literary work and the tone of the narration.

Guided Practice: Identifying narrator and tone. Remind students that the narrator is the person who tells the story and that tone is the attitude the writer takes toward the subject.

Review with students the differences between omniscient, first-person, and third-person-limited narration, or point of view. Then, help students see how point of view affects plot by asking them to tell the story of the birthday party from the points of view of the host and the guest of honor.

Have students read p. 52 of "A Christmas Memory." On the chalkboard, draw the boxes for point of view and tone from the web below. Ask students to identify the point of view and cite which words from the story led them to make this identification. Fill in this information for the first box on the web. (The responses appear in brackets.) Point out that in first-person narration, all the people and events in the story are seen through the eyes of the narrator and reflect his or her observations, opinions, and interpretations. For example, it is Buddy, the first-person narrator of "A Christmas Memory," who interprets the look in his friend's eyes as "purposeful excitement."

Next, guide students in identifying the tone of the story and the descriptive words and images that convey that tone. Add their responses to the web, and help them see that the warm, almost conspiratorial tone reveals Buddy's feelings toward his friend. She is a source of great happiness to him in an otherwise very unhappy household.

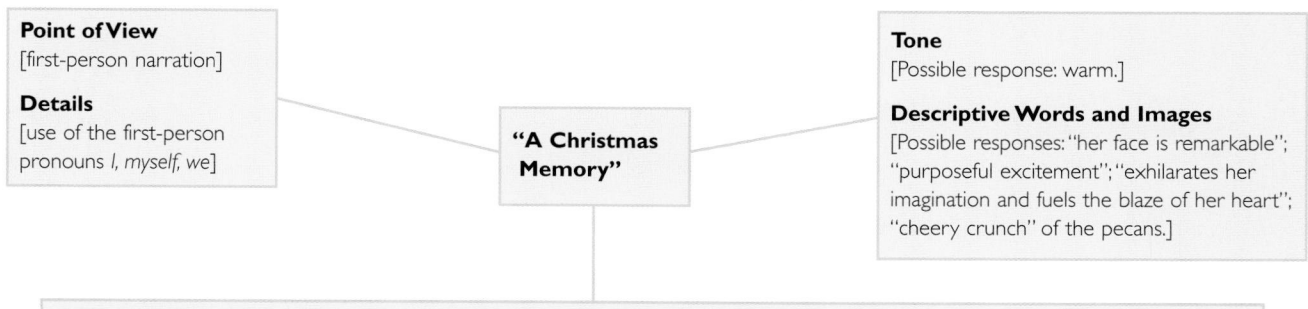

Point of View
[first-person narration]

Details
[use of the first-person pronouns *I, myself, we*]

"A Christmas Memory"

Tone
[Possible response: warm.]

Descriptive Words and Images
[Possible responses: "her face is remarkable"; "purposeful excitement"; "exhilarates her imagination and fuels the blaze of her heart"; "cheery crunch" of the pecans.]

Changes in Tone
[Possible response: At the end of the story, the tone, though still warm and loving, grows sad or bittersweet because the friends are separated and the beloved cousin dies without the narrator ever seeing her again.]

Descriptive Words and Images
[Possible responses: "a miserable succession of bugle-blowing prisons, grim . . . summer camps"; "severing from me an irreplaceable part of myself, letting it loose like a kite on a broken string"; "rather like hearts, a lost pair of kites hurrying toward heaven."]

If time permits, ask students to imagine how the story would differ if it were told by an omniscient, or all-knowing, narrator who is not a participant in the events but knows the thoughts and feelings of all the characters. [The story might reveal the inner life of more than one character, include a wider range of events, and have a more objective or impartial tone.] Discuss also what the story would be like if it were told in the third person by another character, such as one of the shadowy relatives. Such a narrator would not be able to see into the minds and hearts of the other characters. How might the tone of the story differ in this case? How might the events change or be viewed differently?

Tell students that sometimes the tone of a story changes or shifts as the story progresses. A story may begin one way (for example, light and warmhearted, as in "A Christmas Memory") and change later on, depending on how events unfold and the main characters develop. If time allows or students need more guided practice in identifying tone, have them re-read the last column of the story (p. 60). Discuss how the tone has changed and what descriptive words and images signal that change. Continue filling in the web with students' responses.

Independent Practice: Analyzing choice of narrator and tone. If you did not work in class with students on the shift in tone that occurs at the end of the story, have students complete the bottom part of the web at home.

Students may also choose another story they have read and use a web to organize their ideas about its narration and tone. Then, have them draw on the information in their webs to write a short essay explaining how the author's choice of narrator affects the work's tone and plot. Remind students to include specific references to the text in their essay.

Author's Style

Objective: To evaluate the aesthetic qualities of style, including the effect of diction and figurative language on tone and mood.

Direct Teaching: Share the following ideas with students.

Style is the distinctive manner in which writers present their ideas—it's their way with words. Diction, the choice of words, is one way that a writer creates a style. For example, a writer can choose to use a simple, plain word such as *noisy* or a more ornate and fancy one like *tumultuous*. A writer can also choose between words that are formal or informal, modern or old-fashioned, specific or general—to name just a few of the many choices available. Writers can also choose words based on their connotations—that is, on the emotions, images, and ideas associated with them. On p. 502 of "A Sound of Thunder," for instance, Ray Bradbury uses the word *annihilate* rather than *kill* or *destroy*. He probably does so because he is aware that the word *annihilate* is likely to cause readers to think of scenes of utter destruction, such as ruined cities or scorched fields. It is a dramatic word that affects the tone and mood of the entire passage.

Other important components of style include the use of figurative language and vivid imagery, which if fresh and original, give the writing a unique flair or signature.

As you read, pay careful attention to the writer's word choices and think about why the writer chose those particular words. Look to see if certain words create an overall pattern of feeling that pervades the whole work. Ask yourself the following questions:

- **Are most of the words simple or elaborate, formal or slangy, restrained or dramatic?**

- **What is the emotional effect of the words the writer chooses?**

- **Do they create strong visual images?**

- **Does the writer use original and imaginative comparisons that give the work a personal stamp?**

The answers to these questions will help you evaluate the impact of the writer's word choices not only on the tone and mood of the work but also on its theme or message.

Guided Practice: Identifying diction, imagery, and figurative language. Begin with a review of the three main types of figurative language: similes, metaphors, and personification. Explain to students that long, descriptive passages filled with figurative language and evocative diction are typical of Ray Bradbury's writing style. Then, ask students to read the description of the tyrannosaurus on p. 505 of "A Sound of Thunder." Remind them that to a large extent, style is created by a writer's word choices and figurative language. Draw a chart on the chalkboard like the one below, and guide students in finding examples of the style elements in the tyrannosaurus passage. (Possible responses appear in brackets.)

Ornate Language	Vivid Imagery	Figurative Comparisons
["resilient, striding legs"]	["oiled . . . striding legs"]	[metaphor—"watchmaker's claws"]
["reptilian chest"]	["gleam of pebbled skin"]	[metaphor—"lower leg was a piston"]
["sculptured stone"]	["great breathing cage of the upper body"]	[simile—"skin like the mail of a terrible warrior"]
	["pelvic bones crushing aside trees and bushes"]	[simile—"a fence of teeth like daggers"]

Discuss with students how the author's choice of words, images, and figurative comparisons affect the mood and tone of the story and contribute to its overall style. Point out, for example, that Bradbury's description of the tyrannosaurus makes it seem larger than life and enormously powerful, creating an ominous or threatening mood and a tone of awe.

If students have read the entire story, you may want to guide them in contrasting Bradbury's language in the detailed description of the tyrannosaurus with the kinds of words he uses in passages of dialogue. (The latter are simpler and more straightforward.)

Independent Practice: Evaluating author's style. As homework, ask students to select a story by another science fiction writer and write an essay comparing and contrasting the style of its author with that of Ray Bradbury. Tell students to be sure to consider the diction, imagery, and figurative language of each author and how each element contributes to the overall style. For example, students could choose to compare Arthur C. Clarke's style in "Dog Star" (p. 32) with Bradbury's style in "A Sound of Thunder" (p. 498). Students may note in their comparison that Clarke mostly uses spare, exact, straightforward language, such as "my first reaction was one of annoyance" (p. 33), with only the occasional ornate expression, such as "the luminous haze" (p. 35). This diction creates a restrained mood and an objective tone that makes the events of the story seem believable and the main character easy to identify with and to like. Bradbury's style, on the other hand, is more elaborate and imaginative, creating an unsettling, unfamiliar, and less comfortable mood.

Biographical Approach

Objective: To analyze the way a literary work reflects the attitudes and beliefs of its author.

Direct Teaching: Share the following ideas with students.

One way of deepening your understanding of what you read is to recognize the connections that exist between writers' lives and what they write. Good writers draw from their own knowledge, experiences, and interests. Their writing reflects what they understand and believe about the world and the people in it. Biographical factors that can influence a writer's work include cultural or religious background, ethnic or racial heritage, education, work, hobbies, and personal experiences of all kinds. A writer born in Nigeria, for example, would probably write differently about Africa than a person who spent time there as a diplomat or journalist. A writer with scientific training would bring a different perspective and vocabulary to a work of science fiction than a writer without scientific training. Military service, immigration, and loss of a loved one are examples of personal experiences that can have a profound influence on a writer's subject matter and themes. Because these connections between an author's life and work can be so revealing, it is always helpful to find biographical information about an author before reading a literary work and to look for connections during and after your reading.

Guided Practice: Connecting an author's life and work.
Ask students to read or review "Weapons of the Spirit" (p. 375) and the biographical sketch of Albert Einstein that introduces it.

Then, as you read aloud the following passages from the interview with Einstein, have students discuss how each passage reflects what they learned from the introduction about Einstein's heritage, experience, attitudes, and beliefs. (Possible responses appear in brackets.)

- **"Men should continue to fight, but they should fight for things worthwhile, not for imaginary geographical lines, racial prejudices, and private greed draped in the colors of patriotism."**
  [This reflects Einstein's Jewish heritage and thus his disapproval of the politics of Nazi Germany, which he escaped in 1933.]

- **"We must be prepared to make the same heroic sacrifices for the cause of peace that we make ungrudgingly for the cause of war."**
  [This reflects Einstein's commitment to pacifism.]

- **"Nothing that I can do or say will change the structure of the universe."**
  [This reflects Einstein's groundbreaking scientific work, which expanded knowledge of the physical universe.]

Independent Practice: Analyzing biographical influences.
Have students read or review "Dog Star" (p. 33) and the Meet the Writer feature about Arthur C. Clarke (p. 39). If time allows, encourage students to do Internet or library research to find out more about Clarke's life experience, background, and values. Ask students to find details from the story that reflect what they learned about Clarke from their research.

Suggest that students use a chart to organize the connections they see between "Dog Star" and Clarke's life. They can use the chart as a reference during a follow-up group discussion. (Possible details and connections appear in brackets.) Depending on time and students' interest, select other stories written by Clarke. Ask student volunteers to read these stories and record on a chart any connections they see to Clarke's life experience and beliefs. Have them share what they discover in a general discussion of the biographical elements in Clarke's literary work.

Details from "Dog Star"	Connections to Clarke's Life
[main character is an astronomer]	[Clarke's early interest in astronomy; he built a telescope as a boy.]
[the use of outer space for astronomical observation]	[Clarke views himself as someone who predicts the future based on what is happening in the present.]
["It is hardly necessary for me to say I do not believe in the supernatural . . ."; "Yet sometimes I wake now . . . and wish that the dream could have lasted a few seconds longer. . . ."]	[The first passage reflects Clarke's faith in scientific knowledge and rational explanation; the second passage reflects his interest as a writer in human emotion and imagination.]

Resource Center

The Parisian Novels (The Yellow Books), Vincent van Gogh, 1888.

Reading Matters

Why Reading Matters

I read good enough. I mean, most of the time I don't know the answers to the questions that are at the end of the chapter like in my science book or even at the end of stories we read in English, but that's okay, because those questions are hard. Right? Anyway, how are those questions going to help me in real life, you know, when I'm out of school and working?

—Collin, grade 10

Collin takes driver's ed, plays basketball, works at a bagel shop on weekends, and struggles in school. He'd like to make better grades, but because he doesn't read well, he has problems doing his homework and studying for tests. But when you ask (as I did) how he reads, he says, "Good enough." It's good enough for him because he doesn't see the connection between being able to read well and doing well in school and in the job he'll someday have as an adult.

He asks how answering the questions in his social studies, science, and literature books is going to help him in "real life." Well, being able to answer questions in school helps in two ways. First, answering questions is a quick way to show yourself and your teachers what you understand about content. Second, since most of the questions you answer either force you to recall specific information or push you to figure out more complex problems, answering questions can help you become a better thinker. Being a better thinker is helpful in any job.

It all starts with reading. If you can't read the stories and essays in your textbooks or the questions or the tests, then all sorts of negative things begin to happen. That's because no matter where you live, no matter what you do, you are surrounded by print—from textbooks, e-mail messages, and Web pages to how-to instruction manuals and magazines. In a literate society, reading is critical.

The following section is designed to help you with reading. In it you'll find strategies that will help you better comprehend the texts you read. Take some time right now to flip through the pages of this section. You'll see that each lesson is brief—so you can learn a lot in a little bit of time. You can return to this section as often as you need to. Use the strategies suggested here with the selections in this book. Then, try them as you read other texts. The more you think about the topics covered in this section and practice what's suggested here, the better you'll be at reading.

That's important because, after all, *reading matters*.

—Kylene Beers

981

Using Reading Matters

Reading Matters contains practical, easy-to-use lessons and strategies designed to improve students' reading comprehension and reading rate. Think of this section of the text as a handbook that students can use throughout the year—on their own, with a partner, or with the entire class. Like any handbook, Reading Matters can be read in any order, accessed at any point, and referred to frequently.

Some of your students may not need all of the instructions in these lessons, but most will benefit from the reading tips and strategies. Students can apply these strategies to the selections in *Holt Literature and Language Arts* and to any other literary and informational texts they encounter. The lessons teach a set of skills that students can use throughout their lives.

Using Reading Matters with the Student Edition

As you look through Reading Matters, note that each lesson is addressed directly to your students. Students can turn to this section on an as-needed basis. That means you should

- introduce students to Reading Matters early in the school year
- preview the section with students, noting the lesson content, headings, and boxes
- introduce each lesson in class and model each reading strategy
- emphasize that these lessons and strategies can help students with both literary and informational texts
- tell students that to become a proficient reader they must acquire skills that will enable them to read and understand difficult texts on their own

Throughout the year, you might use a particular reading strategy as preteaching instruction for a selection or chapter, or you may choose to target only those students who need remediation. You can also use strategy lessons for reteaching and review.

When the Text Is Tough

Remember the reading you did back in first, second, and third grades? Big print. Short texts. Easy words. Now in high school, however, the texts you read are often filled with small print, long chapters, and complicated plots or topics. Also, you now find yourself reading a variety of material—from your driver's-ed handbook to college applications, from job applications to income-tax forms, from e-mail to e-zines, from classics to comics, from textbooks to checkbooks.

Doing something every day that you find difficult and tedious isn't much fun—and that includes reading. So, this section of this book is designed for you, to show you what to do when the text gets tough. Let's begin by looking at some *reading* matters.

READING UP CLOSE: HOW TO USE THIS SECTION

- **This section is for you.** Turn to it whenever you need to remind yourself about what to do when the text gets tough. Don't wait for your teacher to assign this section for you to read. It's your handbook. Use it.

- **Read the sections that you need.** You don't have to read every word. Skim the headings, and find the information you need.

- **Use this information for help with reading for other classes,** not just for the reading you do in this book.

- **Don't be afraid to re-read the information you find in Reading Matters.** The best readers constantly re-read information.

- **If you need more help, then check the index.** The index will direct you to other pages in this book with information on reading skills and strategies.

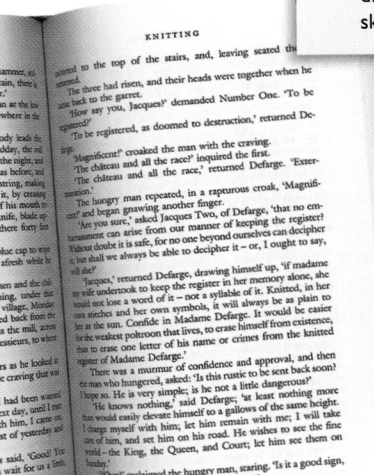

Improving Your Comprehension

Have you seen the reruns of an old weekly television show called *Lost in Space*? Perhaps you saw the more recent movie version of it? If so, you probably remember the robot that constantly tried to warn the young boy, Will Robinson, when danger was near by waving his robot arms and announcing loudly, "Danger approaching, Will Robinson!" Then Will would look up from whatever he was doing, notice whatever evil was moments away, and take action. But until the robot warned him, Will would ignore all warning signs that danger was at hand.

Wouldn't it be nice if something would warn us as we were about to enter a dangerous area when we were reading—a part of the text that we might not understand? Perhaps our own little robots could pop up in books, saying, "Danger, reader! Misunderstandings approaching!" Then we'd know to slow down, pay attention, and carefully study the text we were reading.

Actually those signs do appear, but not as arm-waving robots in the margins of books. Instead, the signs appear in our minds as we are reading. However, unless we are paying attention, we often read on past them, not noticing the warnings they offer. What we need to do is learn to recognize the danger signs so that like Will Robinson, we will know when to look up and take action.

READING UP CLOSE

Looking for the Danger Signs

Study each of the signs to the right, and decide what type of danger each could signify when you read. You might want to copy these signs onto stick-on notes to put on your texts as you read.

1) 2) DEAD END
3) 4) (no U-turn)
5) YIELD 6) (U-turn)
7) (falling rocks) 8) STOP
9) (people working) 10) R×R

Reading Up Close

Have students speculate what the danger signs might signal on the road to understanding a text. Emphasize that there are no right responses.

Possible Responses

1. A fork-in-the-road sign might mark the point in a text where the reader recognizes that the story's plot or the writer's argument takes two or more paths.

2. A dead-end sign might indicate a point at which the reader doesn't understand the text.

3. A winding-road sign might indicate that the reader finds the writer's ideas difficult to follow and that the text requires special attention.

4. The no-U-turn sign might indicate a point in the text where the reader resists the temptation to re-read and continues with the hope of better understanding the text after completing it.

5. A yield sign might indicate a point where the reader has to evaluate and change the predictions that were made earlier in the text.

6. A U-turn sign might indicate a point in the text where the reader has to re-read a passage to improve comprehension.

7. A falling-rocks sign might indicate a part of the text that contains difficult vocabulary words, unfamiliar allusions, or complex ideas.

8. A stop sign might indicate the point where the reader pauses to summarize the text or to note questions or comments.

9. The people-working sign might indicate a point where the reader thinks the writer needs to improve or clarify some aspect of the text.

10. The railroad-crossing sign might indicate a point in the text that requires re-reading and rewording (see p. 987).

Improving Your Comprehension

This lesson contains strategies that students can use to improve their comprehension of both literary and informational texts. You might tell students that the word *comprehension* comes from a Latin root word that means "to catch hold of" or "to seize." (The same root word gives us *apprehend, apprehension, apprehensive,* and *prehensile.*) When students comprehend what they read, they grasp or understand ideas and details. When comprehension fails, the writer's ideas fall out of their grasp.

Using This Lesson

This lesson applies equally to reading both literary and informational texts. If a literary text interests students, they will remain focused and engaged. However, when they are required to read a short story with unappealing characters and a plot that moves slowly, they are much more likely to let their attention wander.

The attention of many students primarily wanders while reading informational texts, such as textbooks and newspaper, magazine, and Internet articles. You might use this lesson before students read the first two informational texts in Chapter 1—"Can Animals Think?" (p. 27) and "Far-out Housekeeping on the ISS" (p. 44). The tips for staying focused work equally well with long, complex narratives, such as the excerpts from the *Odyssey* (p. 649) and *The Tragedy of Romeo and Juliet* (p. 783).

Reading Up Close

Assure students that the Reading Up Close survey is for their enrichment only and their responses will not be graded, so they should answer the questions as honestly as possible.

Note that "When I read" is a broad, general clause encompassing all types of reading. You might ask students to retake the survey with specific kinds of texts in mind, such as novels, poetry, science writing, or history textbooks. They will find that their responses will vary according to the type of text.

Focus on the Tips

Take time in class to explain both of these strategies. Tip 1 shows students how to monitor their reading by pausing to ask themselves questions about the text. Tip 2 encourages them to take notes as they read. Both strategies apply to literary and informational texts.

Danger Sign 1
You can't remember what you read.

This happens to all readers occasionally. You read something, and your attention wanders for a moment, but your eyes don't quit moving from word to word. In a few minutes you realize you are several pages beyond the last point where you can remember thinking about what you were reading. Then you know you need to back up and start over.

Forgetting what you've read is a danger sign only if it happens to you frequently. If you constantly complete a reading assignment but don't remember anything that you've been reading, then you probably are in the habit of letting your mind focus on something else while your eyes are focusing on the words. That's a habit you need to break.

READING UP CLOSE

▶ **Measure Your Attention Quotient**

Take the following survey to see what your attention quotient is. The lower the score, the less attention you pay to what you are reading.

When I read, I . . .

1. **let my mind wander**
   a. most of the time
   b. sometimes
   c. almost never

2. **forget what I'm reading**
   a. most of the time
   b. sometimes
   c. almost never

3. **get confused and stay confused**
   a. most of the time
   b. sometimes
   c. almost never

4. **discover I've turned lots of pages and don't have a clue as to what I've read**
   a. most of the time
   b. sometimes
   c. almost never

5. **rarely finish whatever I'm supposed to be reading**
   a. most of the time
   b. sometimes
   c. almost never

Tips for Staying Focused

1. Don't read from the beginning of the assignment to the end without pausing. Set up **checkpoints** for yourself, either every few pages or every five minutes. At those checkpoints, stop reading and ask yourself some basic questions—"What's happening now? What do I not understand?"

2. As you read, keep paper and pen close by. **Take notes** as you read, in particular jotting down questions you have about what confuses you, interests you, or perhaps even surprises you.

Danger Sign 2
You don't "see" what you are reading.

The ability to **visualize**—or see in your mind—what you are reading is important for comprehension. To understand how visualizing makes a difference, try this quick test. When you get home, turn on a television to a program you enjoy. Then, turn your back to the television set. How long will you keep "watching" the program that way? Probably not long. Why not? Because it would be boring if you couldn't see what was happening. The same is true of reading: If you can't see in your mind what is happening on the page, then you probably will tune out quickly. You can improve your ability to visualize text by practicing the following strategies:

1. **Read a few sentences; then, pause, and describe what is happening on the page.** Forcing yourself to describe the scene will take some time at first, but it will help in the long run.

2. **On a sheet of paper or a stick-on note, make a graphic representation of what is happening as you are reading.** For instance, if two characters are talking, draw two stick figures with arrows pointing between them to show yourself that they are talking.

3. **Discuss a scene or a part of a chapter with a buddy.** Talk about what you "saw" as you were reading.

4. **Read aloud.** If you are having trouble visualizing the text, it might be because you aren't really "hearing" it. Try reading a portion of your text aloud, using good expression and phrasing. As you hear the words, you may find it easier to see the scenes.

READING UP CLOSE

▶ **Visualizing What You Read**

Read the following excerpt from "Blues Ain't No Mockin Bird" by Toni Cade Bambara, and discuss what you "see":

"The puddle had frozen over, and me and Cathy went stompin in it. The twins from next door, Tyrone and Terry, were swingin so high out of sight we forgot we were waitin our turn on the tire. Cathy jumped up and came down hard on her heels and started tap-dancin. And the frozen patch splinterin every which way underneath kinda spooky. 'Looks like a plastic spider web,' she said. 'A sort of weird spider, I guess, with many mental problems.' But really it looked like the crystal paperweight Granny kept in the parlor."

Using This Lesson
The strategies in Danger Sign 2 apply to both literary texts and some informational texts, such as news reports, how-to instructions, and biographical texts.

Use the approach in the Reading Up Close box with short stories, poems, novels, and plays. Have students choose a passage from a selection in the Student Edition. Then, ask volunteers to read aloud the passage that they have chosen and discuss with the class what they "see." You may wish to introduce this strategy with "A Christmas Memory" (p. 51) or with "Marigolds" (p. 119).

Focus on the Tips
Have students practice these strategies in class, working with partners or small groups. After they have completed each of the four steps, have them discuss their reading experience and whether the strategies helped them comprehend the text. Encourage students to use these strategies frequently.

Reading Up Close
Although this lesson uses the word *visualize,* it refers to all kinds of imagery and sensory details, not just to those that appeal to the sense of sight. As students read the passage from "Blues Ain't No Mockin Bird" (or any other literary text), encourage them to note or jot down which details appeal to the senses. [Possible responses: *Sight*—"the puddle had frozen over"; "plastic spider web"; "crystal paperweight." *Sound*—"stompin in it"; "tap-dancin"; "splinterin." *Touch*—"stompin in it"; "came down hard on her heels"; "tap-dancin."]

Using This Lesson

Danger Sign 3 describes a serious problem that students can overcome with a little effort. This lesson suggests five reading strategies that apply to both literary and informational texts. Students may already be familiar with some of these strategies, since they appear in earlier grades of *Holt Literature and Language Arts*.

Using the Think-Aloud Strategy

The **Think-Aloud strategy** will help students remain focused as they read. Although most students will be able to use this strategy easily, some students will have difficulty classifying their comments. (Note that the Reading Up Close box provides an example for each type of comment.) For these students, emphasize that the purpose of the strategy is to help them become active readers who remain engaged with a text and monitor their understanding as they read.

Be sure to model the Think-Aloud strategy in class. You might read a poem or a passage from a difficult text or an informational article, making comments as you read. Modeling should demonstrate two things clearly: the variety in types of comments and the fact that not every sentence or line of text needs a comment.

Reading Up Close

Point out that the Think-Aloud comments for "Cranes" are only a small sample. Students should expect to list many more comments when they apply the strategy to a text. You might ask them to work with a partner to practice the Think-Aloud strategy with a challenging story such as Edgar Allan Poe's "The Cask of Amontillado" (p. 173) or "The Golden Kite, the Silver Wind" (p. 365). The Think-Aloud strategy also works well with complex poems, such as Julia Alvarez's "Exile" (p. 256) or E. E. Cummings's "in Just-" (p. 414).

Danger Sign 3

You constantly answer "I don't know" to questions at the end of reading selections.

If you consistently don't know the answers to questions about what you've been reading, then you probably would benefit from the following strategies:

Think-Aloud. Comprehension problems don't appear only after you *finish* reading. Confusion occurs *as* you read. Therefore, don't wait until you complete your reading assignment to try to understand the text; instead, work on comprehending while reading by becoming an active reader.

Active readers **predict, connect, clarify, question,** and **visualize** as they read. If you don't do those things, then you need to pause while you read to

- make predictions
- make connections
- clarify in your own thoughts what you are reading
- question what you don't understand
- visualize the text and observe key details

Use the Think-Aloud strategy to practice your active-reading skills. Read a selection of text aloud to a partner. As you read, pause to make comments and ask questions. Your partner's job is to tally your comments and classify each according to the list above.

READING UP CLOSE

▶ **One Student's Think-Aloud**

Here's Jamail's Think-Aloud for "Cranes" (p. 222):

<u>Page 222, sixth paragraph:</u> In this part, Sŏngsam suddenly sees a childhood friend he used to know. I also saw a friend of mine the other day, and the last time I had seen him was in first grade. **(Connection)**

<u>Page 222, eleventh paragraph:</u> Sŏngsam says, "I'll take the fellow with me." I bet he plans to find out why Tŏkchae joined the Farmers Communist League. **(Prediction)**

<u>Page 224, thirteenth paragraph:</u> Why does Tŏkchae say his father is ill? **(Question)**

<u>Page 225, fourth paragraph:</u> Oh, now I see. Tŏkchae explains that he didn't escape because he didn't want to leave his sick father. **(Clarification)**

Retelling. While the Think-Aloud strategy keeps you focused as you read, the Retelling strategy helps you after reading. Read the tips for retelling on the next page, and then practice retelling small portions of your reading assignments. You might ask a friend to listen to you retell what you have read, or you might record yourself as you retell a selection.

Retelling Prompts for Fiction

1. State what text you are retelling.
2. Give characters' names, and explain who they are.
3. Sequence the events using words like *first, second, third, then, later, next,* and *last.*
4. Identify the conflict in the story.
5. Explain the resolution of the conflict.
6. Tell what you enjoyed or did not enjoy about the text.

Retelling Prompts for Informational Texts

State what text you are retelling, and identify the **structure** of the text.

- If the structure is a **sequence** (the water cycle), use words like *first, second, third, then, later, afterwards, following that, before,* and *last.*

- If the structure is **comparison and contrast** (the differences between World War I and World War II), use words or phrases such as *by comparison, by contrast, on the other hand, yet, but, however, nevertheless, conversely, then again,* or *in opposition.*

- If showing **cause-and-effect relationships,** use words like *reason, motive, basis,* and *grounds* to discuss **causes,** and use words like *outcome, consequence, result,* and *product* to discuss **effects.**

READING UP CLOSE

▶ **Evaluate Your Retelling**

Listen to your retelling, and ask yourself:

1. Does my retelling make sense?
2. Does it have enough information?
3. Is the information in the correct order?
4. Could a drawing or a diagram help my retelling?
5. If someone listening to my retelling hadn't read the text, what would that person visualize?
6. To improve my next retelling, should I focus on characters, sequence of events, amount of detail, or general conclusions?

Re-reading and Rewording. The best way to improve your comprehension is simply to **re-read.** The first time you read something, you get the basic idea of the text. The next time you read it, you revise your understanding. Try thinking of your first reading as a draft—just like the first draft of an essay. As you revise your essay, you

Using the Retelling Strategy

The **Retelling strategy** helps students to recall specific details and to organize their thoughts as they make an oral summary of a text. This postreading strategy works equally well for literary and informational texts.

In order to introduce this strategy, model retelling a selection so that students recognize the importance of sequencing events and of identifying main ideas. You might retell a short story or an informational text students have just read. Before you begin to retell a selection, ask students to listen for sequencing words (*first, second, then,* or *next*) and words that indicate comparison and contrast or cause and effect.

Not all of your students will need to use this strategy, but those who do will benefit from frequent practice. You might have these students work in pairs or in small groups as they listen to each other retell a selection.

Reading Up Close

Go over the criteria in the Reading Up Close box. Remind students that they can use these criteria to plan their retellings as well as to evaluate them. Ask students to practice the strategy by retelling a longer work such as the short story "The Scarlet Ibis" (p. 343) or a work of nonfiction, such as "Rising Tides" (p. 516). The strategy of retelling would also work well with the excerpts from the *Odyssey* (p. 649) and with the separate acts of *The Tragedy of Romeo and Juliet* (p. 783).

Using the Re-reading and Rewording Strategies

These strategies are useful for all levels of learners.

Re-reading. Tell students that they will find the **Re-reading strategy** especially useful for challenging texts, such as technical instructions, science and history textbooks, and ambiguous stories and poems.

You may wish to model the Re-reading strategy in class by reading aloud a fairly difficult poem that you've never read before. Apply the Think-Aloud strategy from p. 986, emphasizing the questions you have and the points in the text that confuse you. Then, re-read the poem and apply the Think-Aloud strategy a second time to demonstrate that by re-reading you were able to identify parts of the text that puzzled or confused you.

For additional in-class practice, have student apply this strategy to "The Interlopers" (p. 151), "The Cask of Amontillado" (p. 173) or "The Sniper" (p. 212).

Rewording. Students are familiar with the **Rewording strategy** from their work with paraphrasing. Throughout the year, give students practice rewording by occasionally providing them with informational or literary text passages that contain difficult words and complex ideas.

Reading Up Close

Have students discuss the rewording shown in the Reading Up Close box. Point out that Callie used a thesaurus to help her reword the sentences that she did not understand. You may wish to provide a number of additional passages for extra in-class practice or homework.

Using the SWBS Strategy: Summarizing Narrative Text

Students might already be familiar with the **Somebody Wanted But So (SWBS) strategy,** which appears in Grades 6–8 of *Holt Literature and Language Arts.* This is a postreading strategy, a variation on a more detailed summary, that helps students clarify and organize their thinking about a narrative text. Note that the strategy zeroes in on the elements of character, conflict, and point of view.

are improving your writing. As you revise your reading, you are improving your comprehension.

Sometimes, as you re-read, you find some specific sentences or even passages that you just don't understand. When that's the case, you need to spend some time closely studying those sentences. One effective way to tackle tough text is to **reword** it:

1. On a sheet of paper, write the sentences that are confusing you.
2. Leave a few blank lines between each line you write.
3. Then, choose the difficult words, and replace them in the space above.
4. While you wouldn't want to reword every line of a text, this is a powerful way to help you understand key sentences.

READING UP CLOSE

▶ **One Student's Rewording**

After ninth-grader Callie read the article "Romeo and Juliet in Bosnia" (p. 921), she copied a few sentences she didn't understand. After re-reading them, she reworded them, using a thesaurus.

1. "But ~~civilization~~ is an ~~exceedingly fragile enterprise,~~ and it's ~~especially vulnerable to~~ the ~~primal madness~~ of ~~ethnic~~ and religious hatreds."
   (society / a very weak thing, / really in danger of / primitive craziness / racial)

2. "When the madness ~~descended~~ on Sarajevo, Bosko Brkic faced a ~~cruel dilemma.~~"
   (came down / bad problem.)

Summarizing Narrative Text. Understanding a long piece of text is easier if you can summarize chunks of it. If you are reading a **narrative,** or a story, then use a strategy called **Somebody Wanted But So (SWBS)** to help you write a summary of what you are reading. SWBS is a powerful way to think about the characters in a story and note what each did, what conflict each faced, and what the resolution was. As you write an SWBS statement for different characters in the same story, you are forcing yourself to rethink the story from different **points of view.** By analyzing point of view in this way, you get a better understanding of the impact of the author's choice of narrator.

Here are the steps for writing SWBS statements:

1. Write the words *Somebody, Wanted, But,* and *So* across four columns.
2. In the "Somebody" column, write a character's name.

Remind students that an SWBS statement doesn't cover the "whole story" of a narrative text because it omits details and focuses on a single character's conflict. Emphasize that a long or complex narrative may require several SWBS statements.

3. Then, in the "Wanted" column, write what that character wanted to do.

4. Next, in the "But" column, explain what happened that kept the character from doing what he or she wanted.

5. Finally, in the "So" column, explain the eventual outcome.

6. If you're making an SWBS chart for a long story or novel, you'll need to write several statements at different points in the story.

READING UP CLOSE

▶ **One Student's SWBS Chart**

Here is Ben's SWBS chart for "The Scarlet Ibis" (p. 343):

Somebody	Wanted	But	So
Brother	wanted Doodle to be like other kids,	but Doodle's physical problems kept that from happening,	so Brother pushed Doodle too hard and then had to live with guilt when Doodle died.
Doodle	wanted to please Brother,	but he couldn't do all Brother demanded of him,	so he died.

Summarizing Expository Text.

If summarizing the information in **expository,** or informational, texts is difficult, try a strategy called GIST.

Steps for GIST

1. Divide the text you want to summarize into three or four sections.

2. Read the first section.

3. Draw twenty blank lines on a sheet of paper.

4. Write a summary of the first section of text using exactly twenty words—one word for each blank.

5. Read the next section of text. In your next set of twenty blanks, write a new summary statement that combines your first summary with whatever you want to add from this second section of text. It's important to note that even though you've now got two chunks of text to cover, you still have only twenty blanks to fill, not forty.

READING UP CLOSE

▶ **One Student's GIST**

After reading "How Did They Disappear?" (p. 506), Erin wrote the following GIST statements:

GIST 1 (for the first and second paragraphs)
<u>Some</u> <u>scientists</u> <u>believe</u> <u>the</u> <u>earth's</u> <u>rock</u> <u>layers</u> <u>reveal</u> <u>that</u> <u>dinosaurs</u> <u>became</u> <u>extinct</u> <u>after</u> <u>a</u> <u>comet</u> <u>or</u> <u>asteroid</u> <u>struck</u> <u>the</u> <u>earth.</u>

GIST 2 (adding the third paragraph)
<u>Some</u> <u>scientists</u> <u>believe</u> <u>iridium</u> <u>in</u> <u>rock</u> <u>layers</u> <u>indicates</u> <u>a</u> <u>comet</u> <u>or</u> <u>asteroid</u> <u>struck</u> <u>the</u> <u>earth,</u> <u>resulting</u> <u>in</u> <u>the</u> <u>dinosaurs'</u> <u>extinction.</u>

GIST 3 (completing the page)
<u>Some</u> <u>scientists</u> <u>believe</u> <u>a</u> <u>comet</u> <u>or</u> <u>asteroid</u> <u>struck</u> <u>Mexico,</u> <u>and</u> <u>the</u> <u>resulting</u> <u>greenhouse</u> <u>effect</u> <u>caused</u> <u>the</u> <u>extinction</u> <u>of</u> <u>the</u> <u>dinosaurs.</u>

Reading Up Close

Note that the sample SWBS chart (p. 989) provides SWBS statements for the two main characters in the story. For further practice, ask students to use the SWBS strategy with any of the short stories and plays in the Student Edition.

Using the GIST Strategy: Summarizing Expository Text

The **GIST (Generating Interactions between Schemata and Text) strategy** challenges students to generate a summarizing statement that is exactly twenty words long (one word for each blank). Explain to students that applying this strategy is almost like working on a word puzzle. Each statement should summarize the main idea of its section and all preceding sections.

Encourage students to keep trying out different summarizing statements until they find a twenty-word statement that is both reasonable and accurate. Have students compare their statements in pairs or small groups. Point out that this strategy is especially useful for difficult expository texts.

Reading Up Close

Have students compare "How Did They Disappear?" (p. 506) with the GIST statements. Challenge students to suggest improvements or alternative wordings.

Suggest that they apply the GIST strategy on the news feature "An American Story" (p. 262), the newspaper article "Ex-Refugee Is Nominated for Justice Post" (p. 265), or any informational materials texts in the Student Edition. Students might find the strategy especially helpful with the Albert Einstein selections "Weapons of the Spirit" (p. 374), "Letter to President Roosevelt" (p. 376), "On the Abolition of the Threat of War" (p. 378), and "The Arms Race" (p. 379).

Using the Key Words Strategy

The **Key Words strategy** helps students to compare and contrast important elements in literary texts (such as character traits of two different characters) and in informational texts (such as events during two different wars).

Reading Up Close

You might ask students to apply the Key Words strategy to each of the topics in the following selections:

- General Zaroff and Rainsford in "The Most Dangerous Game" (p. 5)
- the characters, events, and themes of "The Sniper" (p. 212) and "Cranes" (p. 222)
- the characters Roy and Norma in *Visitor from Forest Hills* (p. 757)
- comedy and tragedy, as exemplified in *Visitor from Forest Hills* and *The Tragedy of Romeo and Juliet* (p. 787)
- the characters Romeo and Mercutio in *The Tragedy of Romeo and Juliet*

6. Repeat this one or two more times, depending on how much more text you have. When you are finished, you'll have a twenty-word statement that gives you the gist, or overall idea, of what the entire text is about.

Key Words. Sometimes you don't want to write a summary of what you've been reading. Sometimes you just want to jot down some key words to remind yourself about a specific topic. To keep your key words organized, don't forget your ABCs. Fill a page with boxes, as in the example below. You can use your computer to make this page or just grab a pencil and notebook paper. Once your boxes are drawn, all you have to do is decide what information to include.

For instance, Meredith uses her Key Word chart while reading "Thank You, M'am" on page 87. She puts Roger's name in blue at the top of the page and Mrs. Luella Bates Washington Jones's name in red. As Meredith reads the story and thinks of words to describe each character, she puts those key character-description words in the correct box in the correct color. So, she writes "preachy" in red (because she thinks that word describes Mrs. Jones) in the O–P box. She writes "ashamed" in blue (because this word is for Roger) in the A–B box. When completed, the chart could be a starting point for writing a paper that compares and contrasts Roger and Mrs. Jones.

READING UP CLOSE

▶ **Using a Key Word Chart**

Here is Meredith's Key Word chart for "Thank You, M'am." Read the story, and find more key words to describe the two main characters.

Roger   Mrs. Luella Bates Washington Jones

A–B	C–D	E–F	G–H	I–J	K–L
ashamed					

M–N	O–P	Q–R	S–T	U–V–W	X–Y–Z
	preachy				

Improving Your Reading Rate

If your reading concerns are more about getting through the words than figuring out the meaning, then this part of Reading Matters is for you.

If you think you are a slow reader, then reading can seem overwhelming. But you can change your reading rate—the pace at which you read. All you have to do is practice. The point isn't to read so fast that you just rush over words—the I'mgoingtoreadsofastthatallthewordsruntogether approach. Instead, the goal is to find a pace that keeps you moving comfortably through the pages. Why is it important to establish a good reading rate? Let's do a little math to see why your silent reading rate counts.

> **MATH PROBLEM!**
> If you read 40 words per minute (WPM) and there are 400 words on a page, then how long will it take you to read 1 page? 5 pages? 10 pages? How long will it take if you read 80 WPM? 100 WPM? 200 WPM?

As you figure out the problem, you see that it takes 100 minutes to read 10 pages at the slowest pace and only 20 minutes at the fastest pace. See the chart at the right for all the times.

	1 page @400 words/page	5 pages @400 words/page	10 pages @400 words/page
40 WPM	10 minutes	50 minutes	100 minutes
80 WPM	5 minutes	25 minutes	50 minutes
100 WPM	4 minutes	20 minutes	40 minutes
200 WPM	2 minutes	10 minutes	20 minutes

Reading Rate and Homework

Now, assume that with literature homework, science homework, and social studies homework, in one night you have 40 pages to read. If you are reading at 40 WPM, you are spending over *6 hours* just reading the information; but at 100 WPM, you would spend only about 2 hours and 45 minutes. And at 200 WPM, you'd finish in 1 hour and 20 minutes.

READING UP CLOSE

▶ **Tips on Varying Your Reading Rate**

- Increasing your rate doesn't matter if your comprehension goes down.

- Don't rush to read fast if that means understanding less.

- Remember that your rate will vary as your purpose for reading varies. You'll read more slowly when you are studying for a test than when you are skimming a text.

Improving Your Reading Rate

Introduce this lesson at the beginning of the year so that students can track the improvement of their reading rate. Have students complete a base-line reading rate score and retest themselves several times throughout the year.

Point out that reading rates vary according to the reader's purpose. For example, when students are reading to entertain themselves, they will read much more quickly than when they are reading to prepare for an exam.

Reading Rate and Homework

As students move toward high school graduation, they are expected to read a much greater quantity of texts. The math problem and chart (p. 991) should convince students that they will be able to carve more time out of their busy days if they increase their reading rates.

Reading Up Close

Emphasize the importance of the main idea of the Reading Up Close box: Comprehension must not be sacrificed to increase reading speed.

Review with students the following types of reading:

- You **skim** a text when you search for specific information, such as a number, a name, or a place. While skimming you move very quickly through the text without pausing or stopping to understand the details of what you are reading.

- You **scan** a text—read it quickly—when you preview it and look for headers and formatting, graphics, and design elements.

- You do a **close reading** when you need to understand and remember the details of what you are reading. A close reading is appropriate when you are studying for a test, following directions, reading technical information, or analyzing a literary text.

Reading Rate Reminders

Students may be easily convinced that if their reading rate increases, their lives will improve. "But," they might ask, "how can we increase our reading speed?"

With the class, review the five essential steps to faster reading. Explain to students that ridding themselves of bad reading habits takes great effort, but they can improve their reading rates and improve their level of comprehension. Hard work and dedicated practice are necessary but well worth the time and effort.

Figuring Out Your Reading Rate

To determine your silent-reading rate, you'll need three things: a watch or clock with a second hand, a book, and someone who will watch the time for you. Then, follow these steps:

1. Have your friend time you as you begin reading to yourself.
2. Read at your normal rate. Don't speed just because you're being timed.
3. Stop when your friend tells you one minute is up.
4. Count the number of words you read in that minute. Write down that number.
5. Repeat this process several more times, using different passages.
6. Then, add the number of words together, and divide by the number of times you timed yourself. That's your average rate.

> **Example**
>
> 1st minute   180 words
> 2nd minute   215 words
> 3rd minute   190 words
>   585 words ÷ 3 = 195 WPM

Reading Rate Reminders

You can improve your reading rate by using the following strategies:

1. **Make sure you aren't reading just one word at a time with a pause between each word.** Practice phrasing words in your mind as you read. For instance, look at the sample sentence, and pause only where you see the slash marks. One slash (/) means pause a bit. Two slashes (//) mean pause a bit longer.

   > Jack and Jill/ went up the hill/ to fetch a pail of water.// Jack fell down/ and broke his crown/ and Jill came tumbling after.//

   Now, read it again, pausing after each word:

   > Jack/ and/ Jill/ went/ up/ the/ hill/ to/ fetch/ a/ pail/ of/ water.// Jack/ fell/ down/ and/ broke/ his/ crown/ and/ Jill/ came/ tumbling/ after.//

   Hear the difference? Word-at-a-time reading is much slower than phrase reading. If you are reading one word at a time, you'll want to practice reading by phrases. You can hear good phrasing by listening to a book on tape.

2. **Make sure you aren't sounding out each word.** At this point in school, you need to be able to recognize whole words and save the sounding-out strategy for words you haven't seen before. In other words, you ought to be able to read *material* as "material" and not

"ma-ter-i-al," but you might need to move more slowly through *metacognition* so that you read that word as "met-a-cog-ni-tion."

3. **Make sure when you are reading silently that you really are reading silently.** Don't move your lips or read aloud very softly when reading. These habits slow you down. Remember, if you need to slow down (for instance, when the information you are reading is confusing you), then reading aloud to yourself is a smart thing to do. But generally, silent reading means reading silently!

4. **Don't use your finger to point to words as you read.** If you find that you always use your finger to point to words as you read (instead of just occasionally, when you are really concentrating), then you are probably reading one word at a time. Instead, use a bookmark to help yourself stay on the right line, and practice your phrase reading.

5. **As you practice your fluency, remember that the single best way to improve your reading rate is simply to read more!** You won't get better at what you never do. Also, always remember that your rate will vary as your purpose for reading varies. So, time yourself, determine your reading rate, start reading more, and remember these *dos* and *don'ts*. Soon you'll find that reading too slowly isn't a problem anymore.

READING UP CLOSE

▶ Recalculating Your Reading Rate

After putting into practice some of the advice on improving your reading rate provided above, recalculate your average rate. Once again, use the instructions in Figuring Out Your Reading Rate (page 992). This time, however, read one passage from the following material:

1. Page 27: "Can Animals Think?"

2. Page 105: "Helen on Eighty-sixth Street"

3. Page 454: "The Sounds of Poetry"

After you've counted the number of words you read in each passage in one minute, divide by three. The result will be your average rate.

Remember: It's important to slow down your rate when you are confused about what you are reading.

Reading Up Close

Before students complete the Reading Up Close practice on their own, choose a passage from the Student Edition such as "A Warm, Clear Day in Dallas" (p. 580) or President Lyndon B. Johnson's "Address to Congress" (p. 584). Time students as they read the passage and let them figure out their own reading rates. Ask a few simple reading comprehension questions to make sure they have understood the content.

Word Recognition

If you have a student with word recognition problems, have that student study the following word lists. The lists, developed by Dr. Edward Fry, consist of the six hundred most common words in English. Either you or the student can put each word on a flashcard (in sets of a hundred); then you can instruct the student to work through the sets of cards daily until he or she can read each word automatically, with no hesitation. The student should master the first hundred words before moving on to the next hundred.

High Frequency Word List

First Hundred Words

the	he	go	who
a	I	see	an
is	they	then	their
you	one	us	she
to	good	no	new
and	me	him	said
we	about	by	did
that	had	was	boy
in	if	come	three
not	some	get	down
for	up	or	work
at	her	two	put
with	do	man	were
it	when	little	before
on	so	has	just
can	my	them	long
will	very	how	here
are	all	like	other
of	would	our	old
this	any	what	take
your	then	know	cat
as	out	make	again
but	there	which	give
be	from	much	after
have	day	his	many

Second Hundred Words

saw	big	may	fan
home	where	what	five
soon	am	use	read
stand	fall	these	over
box	morning	right	such
upon	live	present	way
first	four	tell	too
came	last	next	shall
girl	color	please	own
house	way	leave	most
find	red	hand	sure
because	friend	more	thing
made	pretty	why	only
could	eat	better	near
book	want	under	than
look	year	while	open
mother	white	should	kind
run	got	never	must
school	play	each	high
people	found	best	bar
night	left	another	both
into	men	seem	end
say	bring	tree	also
think	wish	name	until
back	black	dear	call

Third Hundred Words

ask	hat	off	fire
small	car	sister	ten
yellow	bright	happy	order
show	try	once	part
goes	myself	didn't	early
clean	longer	set	that
buy	those	ground	third
think	hold	dress	same
sleep	full	tell	love
letter	carry	wash	hear
jump	eight	start	yesterday
help	sing	always	eyes
fly	warm	anything	door
don't	sit	around	clothes
fast	dog	close	through
cold	ride	walk	o'clock
today	hot	money	second
does	grow	turn	water
face	cut	might	town
green	seven	hard	took
every	woman	along	hair
brown	funny	fed	now
coat	yes	fine	keep
six	ate	sat	head
gave	stop	hope	food

Fourth Hundred Words

told	time	word	wear
Miss	yet	almost	Mr.
father	true	thought	side
children	above	send	poor
land	still	receive	lost
interest	meet	pay	outside
government	since	nothing	wind
feet	number	need	Mrs.
garden	state	mean	learn
done	matter	late	held
country	line	half	front
different	remember	fight	built
bad	large	enough	family
across	few	feet	begin
yard	hit	during	air
winter	cover	gone	young
table	window	hundred	ago
story	even	week	world
sometimes	city	between	airplane
I'm	together	change	without
tired	sun	being	kill
horse	life	care	ready
something	street	answer	stay
brought	party	course	won't
shoes	suit	against	paper

Fifth Hundred Words

hour	grade	egg	spell
glad	brother	ground	beautiful
follow	remain	afternoon	sick
company	milk	feed	became
believe	several	boat	cry
begin	war	plan	finish
mind	able	question	catch
pass	charge	fish	floor
reach	either	return	stick
month	less	sir	great
point	train	fell	guess
rest	cost	hill	bridge
sent	evening	wood	church
talk	note	add	minute
went	past	ice	tomorrow
bank	room	chair	snow
ship	flew	watch	whom
business	office	alone	women
whole	cow	low	among
short	visit	arm	road
certain	wait	dinner	farm
fair	teacher	hair	cousin
reason	spring	service	bread
summer	picture	class	wrong
fill	bird	quite	age

Sixth Hundred Words

become	herself	demand	aunt
body	idea	however	system
chance	drop	figure	line
act	river	case	cause
die	smile	increase	marry
real	son	enjoy	possible
speak	bat	rather	supply
already	fact	sound	thousand
doctor	sort	eleven	pen
step	king	music	condition
itself	dark	human	perhaps
nine	themselves	court	produce
baby	whose	force	twelve
lady	study	plant	rode
ring	fear	suppose	uncle
wrote	move	law	labor
happen	stood	husband	public
appear	himself	moment	consider
heart	strong	person	thus
swim	knew	result	least
felt	often	continue	power
fourth	toward	price	mark
I'll	wonder	serve	president
kept	twenty	national	voice
well	important	wife	whether

Writer's Handbook

The Writing Process

Good writing doesn't just appear, ready-made, out of nowhere. The writer of an enjoyable piece uses a process to create it. The writing process has four stages, each with several steps. The chart below lists what happens during each stage.

STAGES OF THE WRITING PROCESS	
Prewriting	• Choose your topic. • Identify your purpose and audience. • Generate ideas, and gather information about the topic. • Begin to organize the information. • Draft a sentence that expresses your main point and your perspective on the topic.
Writing a Draft	• Grab your readers' attention in the introduction. • Provide background information. • State and support your main points, and elaborate on them. • Follow a plan of organization. • Wrap up with a conclusion.
Revising	• Evaluate your draft. • Revise the draft's content, organization, and style.
Publishing	• Proofread, or edit, your final draft. • Publish, or share your finished writing with readers. • Reflect on your writing experience.

You can always return to an earlier stage in the process to improve your writing. For example, if in revising you find that you need more information, you can return to prewriting to gather ideas and then draft a new paragraph.

As you progress through the stages of the writing process, make sure you do the following:

● **Keep your ideas focused.** Your writing should be **coherent,** with ideas clearly connected to one another. To keep your writing on track, pin down the specific purpose you want the piece to achieve and establish a coherent thesis. Every idea in a piece must support your thesis or the controlling impression you want to create. Eliminate anything that doesn't fit your distinct perspective or that might detract from a tightly reasoned argument. Your focus should be clear and consistent throughout a piece of writing.

● **Use a consistent tone.** To unify the ideas in a piece of writing, keep your tone consistent. Avoid jumping from a serious, formal tone to a casual or sarcastic tone midway through a piece. Choose your tone by thinking about your specific audience. What tone would they appreciate? Does that tone fit your topic?

● **Plan to publish.** Develop each piece as though it might be published, or shared with an audience. When you proofread, use the following questions to guide you. The numbers in parentheses indicate the sections in the Language Handbook that contain instruction on these topics.

GUIDELINES FOR PROOFREADING

1. Is every sentence complete, not a fragment or run-on? (9a, b)

2. Are punctuation marks used correctly? (12a–r, 13a–j, 14a–o)

3. Are the first letters of sentences and proper nouns and adjectives capitalized? (11a, d)

4. Does each verb agree in number with its subject? (2a) Are verb forms and tenses used correctly? (3a–e)

5. Are subject and object forms of personal pronouns used correctly? (4a–c) Does every pronoun agree with a clear antecedent in number and gender? (4i)

To mark proofreading corrections, use the symbols below.

PROOFREADING SYMBOLS

Symbol	Example	Meaning of Symbol
≡	Fifty-first street	Capitalize a lowercase letter.
/	Jerry's Aunt	Lowercase a capital letter.
∧	the capital of Ohio	Insert a missing word, letter, or punctuation mark.
⌐	beside the river (lake)	Replace a word.
℮	Where's the the key?	Delete a word, letter, or punctuation mark.
∽	thier	Change the order of letters.
¶	¶ "Hi," he smiled.	Begin a new paragraph.

Paragraphs

A **paragraph** is made up of sentences grouped together for a reason—usually to present and support a single idea. Each paragraph in a composition is like a member of a team, working with other paragraphs to develop ideas. Think of a paragraph as a link in a chain connecting ideas.

Paragraphs are used to divide an essay into blocks of separate thoughts or to divide a story into a series of events. Paragraphs signal readers that a new thought or a new speaker is coming. They also allow readers to pause to digest what they've read so far.

Parts of a Body Paragraph

Although some paragraphs—especially in narrative writing—do not have a central focus, most paragraphs do emphasize one **main idea.** Paragraphs like this, often called **body paragraphs,** usually have three major parts: a **topic sentence,** which states the paragraph's main idea; additional **supporting sentences** that elaborate on and support the topic sentence; and (often, but not always) a concluding **clincher sentence.**

The Main Idea and Topic Sentence Together, the sentences in a paragraph make its main idea clear. Many paragraphs express the main idea in a single sentence, called a **topic sentence.**

Although a topic sentence can be placed at any point in the paragraph, it often appears as the first or second sentence. A topic sentence at the beginning of a paragraph helps a reader know what to expect in the rest of the paragraph. The diagram below shows the typical three-part structure of a body paragraph that begins with a topic sentence.

TIP Although many paragraphs you read will not have topic sentences, it's a good idea to use them in your own writing to keep you focused on your main idea and to organize your support.

Typical Body Paragraph Structure

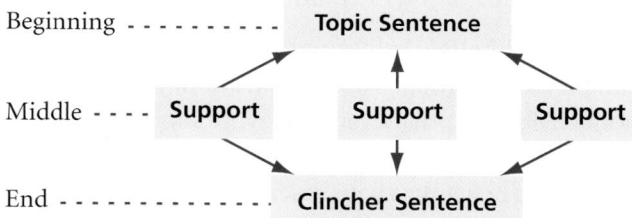

A topic sentence placed at the end of a paragraph can be an effective way to create surprise or summarize ideas. As you read the following paragraph, notice how the writer sews all the details together with a topic sentence at the very end.

In the summer, hosts of big red-and-yellow grasshoppers, with heads shaped like horses, will descend and eat holes in all the softer leaves. Walking sticks fly like boomerangs. Shining brown leaf-shaped palmetto bugs scurry like cockroaches. Spiders like tiny crabs hang in stout webs. The birds snap at small moths and butterflies of every kind. A blue racer, the snake that moves across the cleared land like whiplash, will with one flick destroy the smooth, careful cup of the ant lion in the hot sand. The whole world of the pines and of the rocks hums and glistens and stings with life.

Marjory Stoneman Douglas, *The Everglades: River of Grass*

TIP Supporting sentences don't just provide evidence, but also elaborate on it. Every piece of support must clearly relate to the main idea; you may need to use supporting sentences to explain this connection or simply to explain a piece of evidence to make it more clear.

Supporting Sentences To make your main idea clear and interesting, **elaborate** on it, or develop it in detail. Use supporting sentences to give the types of specific evidence below for the main idea.

Sensory Details **Sensory details** are collected through the senses of sight, hearing, smell, touch, or taste.

Facts and Statistics A **fact** is a statement that can be proved true. A **statistic** is a fact based on numbers, such as "During the Civil War, the South lost about 260,000 soldiers, and the North lost about 360,000." Choose facts and statistics from reliable, unbiased sources.

Examples **Examples** are specific instances or illustrations of a general idea. A cow is an example of an animal.

Other Types of Supporting Evidence Some types of supporting evidence are useful only in certain kinds of writing.

- **Scenarios** are general descriptions of potential events or common situations. They can support ideas in persuasive writing and in cause-and-effect or problem-solution essays.

- **Commonly held beliefs** help support appeals in persuasive pieces. For example, to encourage voter registration, you could note the commonly held belief that everyone's vote should count. You could also grab attention at the beginning of a research report by stating a commonly held belief that your research disproves.

- **Hypotheses** are unproven theories that serve as the basis for investigation. They can support ideas in cause-and-effect papers or in research reports by providing background information or by presenting possible results of events or situations.

- **Definitions** provide support in expository and persuasive pieces by clarifying for readers exactly what a particular term means.

The Clincher Sentence Some paragraphs, especially long ones, end with a **clincher**—a sentence that emphasizes the paragraph's main idea. A clincher pulls together details and signals the end of the paragraph, often using a transition such as *therefore* or *as a result.*

The Makings of a Good Paragraph

A good paragraph has **unity** and **coherence.** Use the following guidelines to give your own writing these two important qualities.

Unity When a paragraph has **unity,** all its sentences work together as a unit to express or support one main idea. Sentences can work as a unit by supporting a main idea that is either stated or implied, or by expressing a related series of actions. Sentences that interrupt the consistent focus of a paragraph destroy its unity.

Coherence A paragraph lacking **coherence** fails to make clear how the ideas it presents fit together. Create coherence by using a clear **order,** or structure, of ideas and by making strong **connections** between ideas.

Order of Ideas How you structure ideas in a paragraph can help your readers follow those ideas. Here are four ways to organize a paragraph:

- Use **chronological order,** relating events in the order they happened, to explain a process, tell a story, or explain a cause-and-effect sequence.

- Use **spatial order,** describing things according to where they are located in relation to one another or to a viewer (for example, moving from nearest to farthest or from left to right), for descriptive writing.

- Use **order of importance,** showing the importance of details in relation to one another, to build up to or down from your most important point. Place that point prominently—first or last.

- Use **logical order,** grouping related ideas together, to **compare and contrast subjects** (explaining how they are alike and different) or to **define a subject.** The paragraph below defines *mummies.*

> A mummy is the preserved body of a human being or an animal, by any means, either deliberate or accidental. Mummies survive from many ancient cultures, some preserved in a wet state, others dry. The bog bodies of northern Europe, such as the 2,000-year-old Lindow Man, found in Cheshire, England, in 1984, belonged to people who had either fallen, or been thrown, into wet, marshy places. The exclusion of oxygen and acidity in the peat of the bog effectively preserved their bodies. Most mummies, though, were preserved by being dried, or desiccated. Many civilizations, including the Egyptian, Chinese, and some South American cultures, tried to achieve this artificially.
>
> Christine El Mahdy, *Mummies, Myth and Magic in Ancient Egypt*

Definition

Specific example

Details

Details
Details

TIP Direct references and transitional words and phrases can make connections *between* paragraphs as well as *within* paragraphs.

Connections Between Ideas Along with putting ideas in an order that makes sense, you create coherence in a paragraph by showing how ideas are connected. You can show connections by using **direct references** and by using **transitional words and phrases.**

● **Direct References** **Direct references** link ideas by referring to a noun or pronoun used earlier in a paragraph. You can make direct references by using a noun or pronoun that refers to a noun used earlier, by repeating a word used earlier, or by using a word or phrase with the same meaning as one used earlier.

● **Transitional Words and Phrases** A **transitional expression**—whether a word, a phrase, or a sentence—shows *how* ideas are connected, often by using a conjunction or preposition. The chart below shows transitions that fit certain types of writing.

TRANSITIONAL WORDS AND PHRASES			
Comparing Ideas	also	another	similarly
	and	moreover	too
Contrasting Ideas	although	in spite of	on the other hand
	however	instead	yet
Showing Cause and Effect	as a result	for	so that
	because	since	thus
	consequently	so	therefore
Showing Chronological Order	after	eventually	meanwhile
	at last	finally	next
	before	first	then
Showing Spatial Order	above	beyond	into
	across	down	next to
	around	here	over
	behind	inside	under
Showing Importance	first	mainly	then
	last	more important	to begin with

PRACTICE & APPLY Draft a paragraph on a topic of your choice. First, identify your main idea. As you write, give your paragraph a clear topic sentence, several types of support for your main idea, and a clincher sentence; unity and coherence, with all ideas creating a controlling impression; and an easy-to-follow structure with clear connections between ideas.

The Writer's Language

Revising to Improve Style

When you revise a draft, be sure to look at your **style**—the way you express your ideas. Consider your **audience** and **purpose,** and examine your draft for **precise language, action verbs, sensory details, appropriate modifiers,** and the **active voice.**

Who and Why   As you re-read your draft, answer these questions:

- **What is my purpose?** Ask yourself *why* you are writing this piece and what you hope it will achieve. Make sure your **tone**—your attitude toward your topic—fits this purpose.

- **Who is my audience? Does my essay speak directly to them?** Consider whether your **level of formality** is appropriate. Avoid making your writing too formal or too informal for your audience.

The Finer Points   When revising, consider your **word choice**—particularly precise language, action verbs, sensory details, and appropriate modifiers. Also, use the **active voice** as much as possible. Read this example:

> I was hungry. I went home after school. Thoughts of eating were starting to come into my mind. I opened the refrigerator door and looked inside. There was nothing good to eat. The loud refrigerator door closed. Then I saw exactly what I wanted to eat—food that had been made for my mother for her birthday. I ate it all and then had to replace it.

   Because it lacks stylistic elements such as precise language and sensory detail, this paragraph fails to create a complete picture.

Precise Language   To paint a clear picture of a subject, use **precise verbs, nouns,** and **adjectives.** For example, the phrase "nothing good to eat" doesn't show what is in the refrigerator. Are there moldy green leftovers? a wilted head of lettuce? Create a vivid picture for readers.

Action Verbs   Avoid overusing dull verbs, such as *be, go, have,* and *do.* To improve the dull sentence "I went home after school," try substituting the more vivid *ran, galloped, dragged,* or *hurried* for the verb *went.* **Action verbs** such as these *show* what happened. When revising, replace dull verbs, especially *be*-verbs, with more-vivid action verbs.

Sensory Details   Words and phrases that appeal to the senses— sight, hearing, taste, touch, and smell—are called **sensory details.** For example, noting the sound of the narrator's growling stomach would help readers experience his hunger.

Appropriate Modifiers **Appropriate modifiers** clearly relate to the correct word. For example, in the paragraph on page 1001, the use of "loud" as an adjective implies that the refrigerator door is loud all by itself. Instead, the adverb "loudly" should modify the verb *closed*. Also, consider whether you really *need* a modifier; a more precise noun or verb is often a better solution, as in the revised sentence, "I slammed the refrigerator door."

Active Voice Use the **active** rather than the **passive voice** whenever possible in your writing. The phrase "food that had been made for my mother" is in the passive voice. The action just "happens" to the subject. To show *who* performed the action, the phrase should be turned around: "food I had made for my mother." To find passive constructions in your writing, first look for *be*-verbs. Then, decide whether the action of the sentence is being done *by* the subject or *to* the subject. If the subject is receiving the action, revise.

Read the following revision of the passage on page 1001. Notice how precise language, action verbs, sensory details, appropriate modifiers, and the active voice make the writing more vivid and entertaining.

A Writer's Model

Action verbs

Precise language and sensory detail

Action verb

Precise language and active voice

My stomach growled, and I galloped home from school—all I could think about was food. I opened the refrigerator door and peeked inside. A wilted head of lettuce stared back at me, along with a mysterious something, squishy and greenish brown in a plastic bag. "Yuck," I thought, hungrier than ever. I slammed the refrigerator door. Suddenly, my mouth watered as I saw just what I wanted to eat on the kitchen counter. The muffins I had made for my mother for a birthday breakfast were irresistible. By the time I thought about what I was doing, I had wolfed down all of them. Now I had to figure out how to replace the birthday treat before my mother got home!

PRACTICE & APPLY Revise the following paragraph to improve its style. Make up details as needed.

A collection of Native American items is on display at a museum in town. They have arrowheads, blankets, and cooking pots. Some of the arrowheads are small, and some are larger. The blankets are colorful, and the cooking pots are interesting. One of the pots can be touched. A lecture is given. The exhibit is unique.

Designing Your Writing

No matter how well-written a document's content might be, if it is sloppy, confusing, or hard to read, it won't make a strong impact on the audience. Some readers may give up trying to read a badly designed document. Others may assume that a writer who is careless about design is also careless about facts. Use the suggestions in this section to get your ideas across clearly.

Page Design

Easy on the Eyes If you want your documents to make a good impression, make sure they are visually appealing and easy to read. You can improve the readability and impact of your papers by using some of the design elements below, whether you create those documents by hand or using a word-processing program.

DESIGN ELEMENTS

Element	Definition	Purpose
Bullets	A *bullet* (•) is an icon used to make information stand out.	Bullets are most often used for lists.
Captions	A *caption* is text printed beneath an illustration.	Captions explain photos, maps, and graphs.
Columns and blocks of text	*Columns* arrange text in two or more separate sections printed side by side. A *block* is a section of text shorter than a page— for example, one story would fill a rectangular block on the front page of the newspaper. Columns and blocks of text are separated from each other by white space.	Columns and blocks make text easier to read.
Headings and subheadings	A *heading* gives readers a general idea of what a section of text, such as a chapter, will be about. A *subheading* is used to indicate subsections of the text.	Headings and subheadings give readers clues about the content and organization of the document.
Leading	*Leading* (rhymes with *heading*) is the amount of white space *between* lines of text. This text is single-spaced.	For school papers, use double-spaced text, which gives your teacher space to comment on your ideas.
Margins	*Margins* are the white space at the top, bottom, and both sides of a page.	Page margins of about one inch create a visual break for readers and make text easier to read.

A Capital Idea Your choice of type can impact a document's readability and attractiveness. You can vary the **case** of type (from the usual mostly **lowercase,** or small type) to add interest to a document and make it easier to navigate.

- **Uppercase,** or all capital, letters attract readers' attention and may be used in headings or titles. Remember that words in uppercase letters can be difficult to read. Use uppercase letters for emphasis, not for large bodies of text.

- **Small caps** are uppercase letters that are reduced in size. Usually they appear in abbreviations of time, such as 9:00 A.M. and A.D. 1500.

Font-astic! A **font** is one complete set of characters (such as letters, numbers, and punctuation marks) of a given size and design. Here are the types of fonts.

Quick! guide

TYPES OF FONTS

Category	Explanation	How They Are Used
decorative, or **script,** fonts	elaborately designed characters that convey a distinct mood or feeling	Decorative fonts are difficult to read and should be used sparingly for an artistic effect.
serif fonts	characters with small strokes (serifs) attached at each end	Because the strokes on serif characters guide the reader's eyes from letter to letter, serif type is often used for large bodies of text.
sans serif fonts	characters formed of neat straight lines, with no serifs at the ends of letters	Sans serif fonts are easy to read and are used for headings, subheadings, callouts, and captions.

Graphics and Visuals

The Big Picture Some information is difficult to communicate in words but easy to communicate visually. Fortunately, advanced publishing software has made creating many kinds of visuals easy. A graphic program may allow you to enter your information and choose the most appropriate type of visual. You can also create nearly any type of graphic by hand.

Choosing the right visual to show a piece of information will help you avoid confusing your readers. Include a **caption** or **title** that explicitly tells readers what they are to see in the visual and why it is there. Use **color** sparingly to emphasize ideas, not as decoration. The following pages explain some useful types of visuals.

● **Charts** show relationships among ideas or data. Two types of charts you are likely to use are flowcharts and pie charts. A **flowchart** uses geometric shapes linked by arrows to show the sequence of events in a process.

EXAMPLE

Writing the First Draft of a Research Paper

Brainstorm possible topics

Choose one topic

Research the topic and take notes

Organize ideas

Write a first draft

A **pie chart** shows the parts of a whole. This type of chart is a circle that is divided into wedges. Each wedge represents a certain percentage of the total. A legend tells what idea or characteristic of the whole is represented by each wedge color.

EXAMPLE

Career Goals of Seniors at Felicity High School

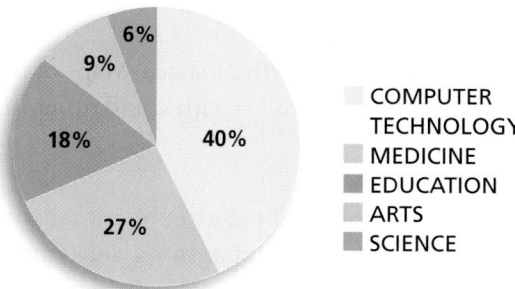

COMPUTER
TECHNOLOGY
MEDICINE
EDUCATION
ARTS
SCIENCE

● **Graphs** use numbers to present facts and figures. There are two types of graphs, both used to show how one thing changes in relation to another. A **bar graph** can be used to compare quantities at a glance, to show trends or changes over time, or to indicate the parts of a whole. Bar graphs, such as the example at the top of the next page, are formed along a vertical and horizontal axis.

EXAMPLE

Number of Students Voting in School Elections by Class

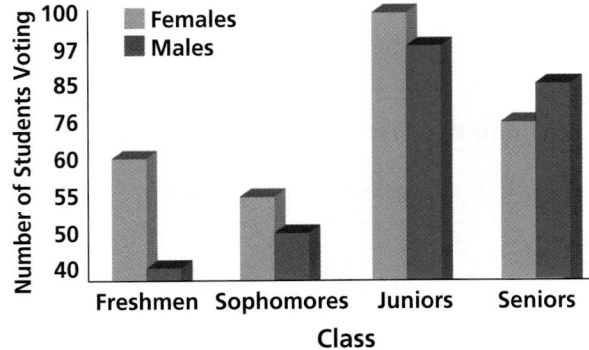

A **line graph** can be used to show changes or trends over time, to compare trends, or to show how two or more variables interact.

EXAMPLE

Number of Students Voting in School Elections

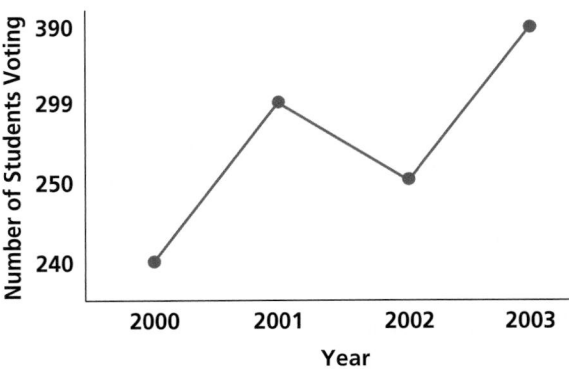

● **Maps** represent part of the earth or space. Maps of the earth may show geographical features, roads, cities, and other important locations.

Other types of visuals you might use to present information include **illustrations** showing your subject, **diagrams** clarifying a process you explain, and **time lines** pinpointing historical events you discuss.

PRACTICE & APPLY Choose the visual you think would most effectively communicate the information below. Then, use the guidelines in this section to create the visual.

Diameters of selected solar system planets in kilometers

Mercury 4,878   Jupiter 142,800
Earth 12,756   Neptune 49,528

Test Smarts

by **Flo Ota De Lange** *and* **Sheri Henderson**

Strategies for Taking Multiple-Choice Tests

Whatever you choose to do in the future, a high school diploma can open doors for you. It is a basic requirement for many, many jobs as well as for getting into college. But to get that diploma, you'll have to pass a lot of tests—pop quizzes in class, midterm exams, finals, your state's standardized tests required for graduation, and the SAT or ACT if you are thinking about college.

Taking tests doesn't have to be the scary nightmare many students make it out to be. With some preparation you'll do just fine. The first thing you have to do, of course, is study. Read all your assignments at least once, and make sure you have mastered the skills being taught.

Even when you know all the material, however, you might not do well on a test if you get nervous or are not familiar with the kinds of questions being asked. This section will give you some strategies that will help you approach your tests with confidence and let your abilities shine through.

Stay Calm

It's test time. You have studied the material, and you know your stuff, but you're still nervous. That's OK. A little nervousness will help you focus, but so will a calm body. Take a few deep breaths—five slow counts in, five slow counts out. Now you're ready to begin the test.

Track Your Time

First, estimate how much time you have for each question. Then, set checkpoints for yourself—how many questions should be completed at a quarter of the time, half of the time, and so on. That way you can **pace yourself** throughout the test. If you're behind, you can speed up. If you're ahead, you can—and should—slow down.

Master the Directions

Read the directions carefully to be sure you know exactly what to do and how to do it. If you are supposed to fill in an oval, fill it in cleanly and carefully. Be careful also to match the number of the question to the number on the answer sheet. Do just what the directions say to do.

Study the Questions

Read each question once, twice, three times—until you are certain you know what the question is asking. Watch out for words like *not* and *except;* they tell you to look for choices that are false, different, or opposite in some way.

Anticipate Answers

Once you are sure you understand the question, **anticipate the answer.** Then, read the choices. If the answer you gave is there, it is probably correct. To be sure, though, check out each choice. If you don't know the answer, eliminate any choices you think are wrong. Then, make an educated—not a wild—guess about the choices that remain. Be careful to **avoid distracters,** answers that are true but don't fit the question.

Don't Give Up

If you are having a hard time with a test, take a deep breath and **keep on going.** On most tests the questions do not get more difficult as you go, and an easier question is probably coming up soon. The last question on a test is worth just as many points as the first, so give it your all—all the way to the end.

Types of Test Questions

You will feel a lot more confident taking a test if you are familiar with the kinds of questions given. The following pages describe and give examples of the different types of multiple-choice questions you'll find on many of your tests. Tips on how to approach the questions are also included.

Reading-Comprehension Questions

Reading-comprehension questions seek to determine not only whether you have gotten the facts straight but also how well you can think critically about what you have read. You have to make accurate **inferences** and **predictions** as well as determine the author's attitude, purpose, and meaning.

The readings and the questions may be long and complicated or short and easy. Pay attention to the purpose of the question, and you will have a good chance of selecting the correct answer.

Following the informational reading below, you will find examples of some of the most common types of reading-comprehension questions.

DIRECTIONS: Read the following selection. Then, choose the best answer for each question that follows.

Dr. Jonas Salk began researching poliomyelitis after World War II, when epidemics of the disease were intensifying. Poliomyelitis, or polio, attacks the nervous system, causing pain and stiffness and often paralysis or even death. Salk worked on developing a vaccine to prevent this incurable disease.

First he studied how polio affects the body. He reasoned that polio is a virus that enters the body through the mouth or nose, eventually reaching the intestines. From there the virus spreads to the central nervous system by means of either blood or nerves. Once the virus enters a nerve cell, it changes how the cell functions. Instead of expelling the virus, the cell reproduces it. The virus then enters the surrounding nerve cells. When enough nerve cells are altered or killed, the nervous system is affected, and paralysis results.

Once Salk knew how the virus spreads through the body, he looked for a substance that would kill it. After lengthy experimentation he discovered that a formaldehyde solution would destroy the virus. He then developed a vaccine using the dead virus. In 1954, the National Foundation for Infantile Paralysis, the current March of Dimes Birth Defects Foundation, gave him the money that enabled him to test the vaccine. After giving the vaccine to nearly two million schoolchildren and testing the results, he proved that the vaccine was both safe and effective.

FACTUAL-RECALL QUESTIONS ask you to do a **close reading** to find **details** or **facts** straight from the selection. Search carefully. The words may not be identical, but the answer will be there.

1. Jonas Salk's purpose in researching polio was to —

 A determine how viruses cause disease

 B study how the human nervous system works

 C cure people who had been paralyzed by polio

 D develop a vaccine to prevent polio

Answer: **D is the correct answer.** The purpose of Salk's research is directly stated at the end of the first paragraph: to develop a vaccine that would prevent people from getting polio. Choices **A** and **B** are both far too broad; Salk wasn't interested in how viruses in general cause disease or in how the human nervous system works. Choice **C** may be tempting, but if you read the article carefully, you know that Salk wasn't searching for a way to cure paralyzed polio victims.

2. All of the following are effects of the polio virus's entering a nerve cell *except* —

   A the cell reproduces the virus

   B the virus leaves the cell and enters the surrounding nerve cells

   C the cell expels the virus

   D the virus changes how the cell functions

Answer: **C is the correct answer.** Notice the word *except* in the question. It makes choices **A, B,** and **D** wrong because they are all clearly described in the second paragraph as effects of the polio virus on a nerve cell.

INFERENCE QUESTIONS ask you to connect **clues.** You read between the lines to make an **educated guess.** An inference question sometimes requires you to apply what you already know.

3. Salk's vaccine had to be tested in two million schoolchildren before —

   A he could develop a formula for the vaccine

   B he could get any money to test the vaccine

   C he could determine how the polio virus spreads

   D it could be approved for general use

Answer: **D is the correct answer** even though it is not directly stated in the text. After Salk's polio vaccine was proved safe and effective on two million schoolchildren, you can infer that the next step (note the word *before*) would be its approval for general use in the population. Choice **A** is incorrect because the vaccine couldn't have been tested if Salk hadn't already developed a formula for the vaccine. **B** is incorrect because the article states directly that the National Foundation for Infantile Paralysis funded the testing of his virus. **C** is incorrect because Salk had to know how the polio virus spreads before he could develop a vaccine.

MAIN-IDEA QUESTIONS ask you to state the selection's **main idea** or **draw a conclusion.**

Sometimes a main-idea question asks you to choose the **best title** for a selection.

4. The main idea of this article is —

   A how Dr. Jonas Salk developed the polio vaccine

   B how a new vaccine is developed

   C how polio affects someone who has the virus

   D how the polio virus spreads

Answer: **A is the correct answer. B** is too broad; the article specifically focuses on Dr. Salk and the polio vaccine. **C** and **D** are incorrect because even though these topics are mentioned in the article, they are not the main focus of the article.

5. Which of the following would make the *best* title for the selection?

   A Dr. Jonas Salk Stalks the Polio Virus

   B How Polio Affects the Nervous System

   C How Viruses Reproduce

   D Testing a New Vaccine

Answer: **A is the correct answer,** the only choice that covers the whole article. **B** covers only part of the article. **C** and **D** are too broad and do not mention polio; also answer **C** is not discussed in the article.

EVALUATION QUESTIONS ask you to use your own knowledge and life experience to give an **opinion** about the selection. Sometimes an evaluation question asks about the writer's purpose or style of writing.

6. The information in this article is probably —

   A unreliable because the writer is not identified

   B unreliable because much of it is opinions, not facts

   C reliable because it gives facts that can be verified in other sources

   D reliable because the writer is an expert on infectious diseases

Answer: **The correct answer is C.** The article's dates and other facts can be verified in other sources. **A** is incorrect because although it's true the writer isn't identified, that doesn't mean the article is unreliable. Encyclopedia articles, for example, often do not identify the writer. **B** is incorrect because the article contains only facts, no opinions. **D** is incorrect because the writer isn't identified.

Vocabulary Questions

Vocabulary questions test your understanding of word meanings, both in and out of context. Some are simple and some are tricky. Read the question carefully.

DIRECTIONS: Read the following auto-biographical excerpt. Then, choose the best answer for each question that follows.

The Chicken

As I was walking down Stanton Street early one Sunday morning, I saw a chicken a few yards ahead of me. I was walking faster than the chicken, so I gradually caught up. By the time we approached Eighteenth Avenue, I was close behind. The chicken turned south on Eighteenth. At the fourth house along, it turned in the walk, hopped up the front steps, and rapped sharply on the metal storm door with its beak. After a moment, the door opened and the chicken went in.

—Linda Elegant
Portland, Oregon
from *I Thought My Father Was God and Other True Tales from the National Story Project*

DEFINITION OR SYNONYM QUESTIONS are the simplest type of vocabulary question. They ask for a definition or synonym of a word. There are no clues to help you. You are expected to know the word's meaning.

7. <u>Gradually</u> means —
   A quickly
   B hurriedly
   C quietly
   D little by little

Answer: **D is the correct answer.**

CONTEXT-CLUE QUESTIONS ask you to define an unfamiliar word. You will find clues to the word's meaning in the **context,** the sentence in which the word appears or the sentences immediately before or after it.

8. What does <u>pullet</u> mean in the following sentence? "This fine specimen was a mature hen, well beyond the <u>pullet</u> stage."
   A old hen
   B young hen
   C rooster
   D roasted chicken

Answer: **B is the correct answer. C** and **D** are incorrect because you know from the context that a pullet is a young hen. **A** is incorrect because the contrasting context clue, *mature,* tells you that a pullet must be young.

MULTIPLE-MEANINGS QUESTIONS ask you to recognize which meaning of a familiar word is being used in a sentence. Then you choose the sentence that uses the word in the same way it is used in the original sentence.

9. "The chicken <u>turned</u> south on Eighteenth."
   A Kerry often <u>turned</u> a pretty phrase when she spoke.
   B Jim <u>turned</u> his jacket inside out.
   C The traffic <u>turned</u> right onto the bridge.
   D The top <u>turned</u> around quickly

Answer: **C is the correct answer.** The chicken isn't speaking, reversing something, or spinning, so you look for an answer using *turned* with the meaning "changed direction," which fits the context.

SENTENCE-COMPLETION OR FILL-IN-THE-BLANK QUESTIONS ask you to choose the appropriate word for the context of the sentence. When these questions have two blanks in an item, the trick is to find the answer that fits both blanks correctly. As a short-cut, first determine which choices contain a word that fits the first blank. Then, consider only those choices when filling in the second blank.

> **10.** "The Chicken" is _____, but it also raises more _____ than it answers.
>
> **A** amusing, anger
>
> **B** sickening, thoughts
>
> **C** funny, questions
>
> **D** autobiographical, pullets

Answer: First, look for choices that will not work in the first blank; you can eliminate those choices immediately. Choice **B** will clearly not work in the first blank: "The Chicken" can be considered amusing, funny, or autobiographical, but it is not sickening. Then, review the remaining choices: **A, C,** and **D.** The only word that works in the second blank is *questions;* the selection does raise more questions than it answers. Therefore, **the correct answer is C.**

ANALOGY QUESTIONS ask you to recognize the relationship between a pair of words and to identify a second pair of words that has the same relationship. An analogy question is written in this form: A : B :: C : D, which can be read as "A is to B as C is to D."

The tricky part of these questions is figuring out the relationship. There are many types of relationships, including the following ones:

- **degree** *(pink : red :: beige : brown)*
- **size** *(hummingbird : ostrich :: house cat : tiger)*
- **part to whole** *(leg : lion :: fin : fish)*
- **cause and effect** *(cold : shiver :: hot : sweat)*
- **synonyms** *(happy : cheery :: sad : glum)*
- **antonyms** *(happy : sad :: nice : mean)*

Once you figure out the relationship between the first pair of words, try expressing it as a sentence—for example, *A leg is a part of a lion.*

Then, pick from the choices the pair of words that has the same relationship—for example, *A fin is a part of a fish.* (For more about analogies, see pages 229 and 576.)

> **11.** Pullet : hen ::
>
> **A** scaffold : building
>
> **B** tree : seed
>
> **C** girl : boy
>
> **D** tadpole : frog

Answer: Try turning the first pair of words into a sentence, as in *A pullet is a young hen.* Now, try each answer out within the same sentence: *A scaffold is a young building. A tree is a young seed. A girl is a young—* Well, you get the idea. **D is the only workable answer.**

Multiple-Choice Writing Questions

Multiple-choice writing questions are designed to test your knowledge of standard written English. To answer them, you will need to know the rules of punctuation, such as when and how to use commas, quotation marks, end marks, italics, and so on. You will also need to know some basic rules of grammar: active versus passive voice, subject-verb agreement, correct verb tense, correct sentence structure, correct diction, parallel construction in sentences and paragraphs, to name a few. Here are some sample questions:

IDENTIFYING-SENTENCE-ERRORS QUESTIONS ask you to look at underlined sections of a sentence and choose the section that includes an error. You are not expected to correct the error.

> **12.** Tara and her sister <u>are planning</u> a twenty-fifth
>   A
> anniversary party for their <u>parents, and</u> they
>   B
> have invited their <u>parents'</u> closest friends and
>   C
> relatives as well as <u>him and I.</u> <u>No error.</u>
>   D   E

Answer: **The correct answer is D** because D contains an error. Instead of the subject pronoun *I*, the sentence should have the object pronoun *me* because *him and me* are direct objects in this sentence.

IMPROVING-SENTENCES QUESTIONS

may ask you to choose the correct version of an underlined section of a sentence:

13. A Magazine Article written in 1949 forecast "Computers of the future may weigh no more than 1.5 tons."

    A In 1949, a magazine article forecast "Computers

    B A magazine article written in 1949 forecast, "Computers

    C A magazine article in 1949 forecast, computers

    D A Magazine Article written in 1949 forecasts "Computers

Answer: **B is the correct answer** because *magazine article* should not be capitalized and because a comma and quotation mark should precede the direct quotation.

14. Irving Fisher professor of economics at Yale University says in 1929, "Stocks have reached what looks like a permanently high plateau."

    A Irving Fisher, professor of economics at Yale University, said in 1929, "Stocks

    B Irving Fisher, professor of economics at Yale University says in 1929, "Stocks

    C Irving Fisher, professor of economics at Yale University, says in 1929, "Stocks

    D Irving Fisher professor of economics at Yale University said in 1929, "Stocks

Answer: **A is the correct answer** because it corrects the two errors in this sentence: It uses commas to set off the appositive *professor of economics at Yale University,* and it changes the verb to the past tense, *said.*

IMPROVING-THE-PARAGRAPH QUESTIONS

are preceded by a paragraph. You may be asked to pick a choice that combines or rewrites portions of sentences. You may be asked to decide which sentences could be added to or removed from the paragraph. You may be asked which sentence could be used to strengthen the argument of the writer. You may be asked to pick a thesis statement for the paragraph. As an example, refer to our paragraph-length selection, "The Chicken," on page 1010. Then, look at the questions below:

15. Which of the sentences would *not* fit well into "The Chicken"?

    A It isn't every day that you meet a chicken out for a morning walk.

    B It is still more unusual to see a chicken knock on a door and go in when the door opens.

    C I thought about knocking on the door myself to ask about the chicken but was afraid the chicken might answer.

    D The numbered streets in my neighborhood go up to Twenty-fifth Street.

Answer: You caught the word *not* in the question, didn't you? **D is the answer;** it is the only sentence that would *not* fit into the paragraph. **A, B,** and **C** would fit because they have the appropriate tone and humor.

16. Which of the following items could be added to "The Chicken" to support the main idea?

    A A chicken can make a good pet.

    B The world is full of unusual and unexpected pleasures.

    C Why did the chicken cross the road?

    D Is this a knock-knock joke?

Answer: Do we even have to say, "**The correct answer is B**"?

Strategies for Taking Writing Tests

➤ Writing a Response to Literature

On tests, you will often be asked to write an essay responding to a literary selection. Your response should demonstrate your understanding of the selection as a whole, including its main ideas and the author's purpose. Follow the steps below to write such a response for a test. The sample responses provided are based on the prompt to the right. ("Thank You M'am" begins on page 87.)

Prompt

Langston Hughes's short story "Thank You M'am" presents two complex characters—the boy, Roger, and the woman, Mrs. Luella Bates Washington Jones. In an essay, analyze one of these characters, drawing a conclusion based on evidence you present from the text.

THINKING IT THROUGH

Writing a Response to Literature

➤ **STEP 1** **Read the prompt carefully, and then read the selection for general understanding.** Get to know the selection's plot, characters, setting, and theme, and consider all parts of the prompt.

I need to take a close look at one of the two characters in this story and draw a conclusion about that person based on details from the story.

➤ **STEP 2** **Choose a topic, and take notes from the piece on your main points.**

I'll write about Mrs. Jones. My main points will have to do with her actions, her words, and her situation. Her actions show some anger but mostly kindness. Her words have an indignant tone but also are basically kind. Her situation is that she is not financially well off, but she still gives Roger food, money, and advice.

➤ **STEP 3** **Generate a thesis for your essay.** To develop a thesis, draw a conclusion based on your main points.

Even though she is angry with Roger for trying to take from her, and she doesn't have much anyway, Mrs. Jones is kinder to him than most people in the same situation would be. My thesis will be: Despite Roger's actions and her own circumstances, Mrs. Jones shows a kindness that will change his life.

➤ **STEP 4** **Support your thesis and main points.** Find details that prove your thesis, and look for relevant subtle or complex ideas in the selection. To elaborate on your evidence, use your own knowledge and experience.

I need to discuss how Mrs. Jones shows trust in Roger despite his attempt to steal her purse and how she hints that her past was not perfect, either. I think she understands that he can be better than his actions if he is shown some kindness.

➤ **STEP 5** **Draft your essay.** Arrange your ideas to show clearly how they relate to each other and to your thesis. Use an objective, serious tone, with precise language and a variety of sentence types. Revise your essay to make sure it shows a thorough understanding of the selection. Then, proofread and correct any errors.

Test Smarts 1013

Writing a Response to Expository Text

When you read and respond to **expository,** or informative, text, you use a different set of skills than for literary texts. If you are asked to write a response to an expository selection on a test, use the steps below. The sample responses provided are based on the prompt to the right. ("Far-out Housekeeping on the ISS" begins on page 44.)

Prompt

In "Far-out Housekeeping on the ISS," what specific purpose is the writer trying to achieve? How do the article's content and organization help achieve this purpose? In an essay, examine the writer's purpose using details from the article.

THINKING IT THROUGH

Writing a Response to Expository Text

▶ **STEP 1** **Read the selection for understanding, and take notes of important points.** Note the main idea and organization of the piece. Use the selection's headings, boldface terms, and graphics to add to your understanding.

The article explains what people on the International Space Station eat, how they contact their families, what happens to waste, and what the astronauts do for fun.

▶ **STEP 2** **Read the prompt, and identify your task and your answer.**

I need to identify the purpose of the article and how the organization and details support that purpose. I think the purpose is to give people who are curious about the space station a look at the everyday activities there and to make the astronauts seem more like regular people and less like movie heroes.

▶ **STEP 3** **Skim the selection looking for support.** Note relevant and interesting evidence that backs up the answer you identified in Step 2.

The article discusses eating, taking out the trash, and having fun. This makes the astronauts seem more like me. Using the astronauts' own words from interviews also makes them seem like regular people.

▶ **STEP 4** **Elaborate on your ideas, and draft a thesis statement.** Make connections to your own knowledge, and consider the meaning of each piece of evidence. Draft a sentence that clearly states your overall impression, or thesis.

I think when you find out you have something in common with someone, it makes it easier to relate to them—that's what this article does, by helping readers imagine themselves doing normal things, but in space. My thesis will be: This article was written to help curious readers imagine themselves as astronauts by showing what everyday life in space is like.

▶ **STEP 5** **Draft your essay.** Choose an arrangement that fits the selection and the prompt. Make that pattern clear to readers by using transitional words and phrases such as *for one thing, also,* and *finally* for logical order or *first, furthermore,* and *most important* for order of importance. Proofread your draft to make sure you use language conventions correctly.

Writing a Biographical Narrative

In a **biographical narrative,** you must present an event from another person's life in such a way that readers can share in the experience. Here are the steps to follow if you are asked to write a biographical narrative for a test. The sample responses below are based on the prompt to the right.

Prompt

Think of a person you know well, and write an essay describing an incident in that person's life that demonstrates an important part of his or her personality or character.

THINKING IT THROUGH · Writing a Biographical Narrative

STEP 1 Carefully read the prompt, and choose a subject. Make sure you address all parts of the prompt.

> The prompt asks me to tell about something that someone I know experienced. I need to pick an experience that shows my subject's personality or character. I'll write about my best friend, Maia, because I've known her since we were little.

STEP 2 Choose an incident to relate, and identify its parts. Outline in sequence the smaller events that make up your chosen experience.

> I'll write about the time when Maia and I were eight and she fell off her bike.
> 1. It was her first time riding without her dad helping.
> 2. I encouraged her to go down a hill on our street.
> 3. She looked nervous but tried it anyway.
> 4. She lost control and landed in the bushes.
> 5. Even though she got scratched, she got back on her bike and rode back home with me. She didn't even seem that upset.

STEP 3 Identify important details about the character, events, and setting. Details should be relevant and specific to bring the incident to life.

> I'll describe the steep hill with the sharp curve at the bottom, Maia's wide eyes and wrinkled forehead before we rode, the path her bike took before landing at the bottom, and her resolve when she got back up.

STEP 4 Draw a conclusion based on the events. Decide why the incident is significant, and plan a thesis statement to guide you as you plan and draft.

> This event is important because it shows how Maia tries things even if she's nervous and how she keeps trying if she doesn't get it right the first time. My thesis will be: Maia showed her bravery and resolve even when she was only an eight-year-old riding a bike.

STEP 5 Use your notes to write a draft of your biographical narrative. Include an introduction to give readers a context for the narrative. Keep your tone consistent, focus on the subject rather than on yourself, and build toward the event's climax. Then, correct any errors in grammar, usage, and mechanics.

Writing an Expository Composition

An **expository composition** provides information about a topic unfamiliar to readers. When you write an expository composition for a test, you must explain ideas clearly and support those ideas with relevant evidence. Follow the steps below. A sample prompt is to the right.

Prompt

Think about a favorite place to visit. Write an essay in which you explain why this place is so important or enjoyable to you.

THINKING IT THROUGH — Writing an Expository Composition

STEP 1 Carefully read the prompt, and choose a topic. Make sure you address all parts of the prompt and choose a topic you know well.

I need to pick out the things that make a place special to me. I'll write about Hastings, the town in the mountains where my grandparents live.

STEP 2 Divide the topic into parts. Outline the main categories of information you will provide about your topic.

I like Hastings because: 1. I get to see lots of relatives when we have family reunions there. 2. It's a beautiful area. 3. I like how remote it is, especially compared with where I live.

STEP 3 Brainstorm details about each part of the topic. Details should answer questions readers will have about the topic and correct any misunderstandings or biases they might have. Try to answer the *5W-How?* questions *(Who? What? Where? When? Why? How?)* with your details.

1. I can go into detail about my favorite relatives and reunion activities.
2. I can explain what makes it beautiful, describing some of the mountain scenery.
3. I can point out how few TV and radio signals you can get, how you can walk for hours without hearing a human sound, and how there's only one tiny grocery store.

STEP 4 Synthesize your ideas to plan a thesis. Draft a thesis statement that explains the point the information about your topic makes.

All of my details show how different Hastings is from where I live. My thesis will be: In Hastings I can see distant relatives, experience the beauty of the mountains, and enjoy being totally alone if I feel like it—all things I could never do at home.

STEP 5 Use your notes to write a draft of your expository composition. Write an attention-getting introduction. Rather than stringing together a lot of obvious facts about your topic, dig deeper and connect these more interesting ideas to your thesis. End with a conclusion that echoes your thesis. Revise to make sure all of your support is relevant. Then, proofread to make sure you have correctly used English-language conventions.

Writing a Persuasive Composition

Writing tests often ask you to write a **persuasive essay** on a given issue. You must decide your opinion or position on the issue, organize your response, write, and proofread—all in a limited amount of time. Use the following strategy to develop a convincing, well-supported essay under pressure. The sample responses provided are based on the prompt to the right.

Prompt

The city council is considering an ordinance banning cycling on all sidewalks. Consider the effects such an ordinance would have, and decide whether you support or oppose the measure. Then, write an essay in which you express and support your opinion on the issue.

THINKING IT THROUGH

Writing a Persuasive Composition

STEP 1 **Read the prompt carefully, and identify your task.** Answer all parts of the prompt.

I need to think about the effects of banning cycling on sidewalks and be able to support my opinion on the issue.

STEP 2 **State your opinion on the topic.**

Based on my experience, I think this ordinance would be a bad idea.

STEP 3 **Plan reasons using the THEMES strategy.** Choose reasons that will address positive or negative effects in some of the following categories: **T**ime, **H**ealth, **E**ducation, **M**oney, **E**nvironment, and **S**afety.

Safety: Banning cycling on sidewalks will force people to ride bikes on often-dangerous city streets.

Health: An effect of banning cycling on sidewalks is that people may choose not to ride bikes at all; less exercise may cause health problems.

Environment: The ban may cause people to drive rather than ride a bike for short errands, adding to air pollution.

STEP 4 **Develop evidence to support each of your reasons.** To elaborate on your evidence, use your own knowledge and experience.

I can discuss the positive effects of bicycling on our community and include personal anecdotes about trying to avoid potholes, parked cars, and reckless drivers while riding my own bike. I can also make an ethical appeal to protect young children who ride bikes to school from harm.

STEP 5 **Draft your essay.** Begin with an attention getter, and state your opinion up front. Arrange reasons in order of importance, and explain how each piece of evidence relates to its reason. End with a call to action, if your position requires readers to act rather than simply to agree with you. Then, find and correct any errors in grammar, usage, and mechanics.

Handbook of Literary Terms

For more information about a topic, turn to the page(s) in this book that are indicated on a separate line at the end of the entry. For example, to learn more about *alliteration,* turn to page 456.

On another line are cross-references to entries in this handbook that provide closely related information. For instance, at the end of *Alliteration* is a cross-reference to *Assonance.*

ALLEGORY **A narrative in which characters and settings stand for abstract ideas or moral qualities.** In addition to the literal meaning of the story, an allegory contains a symbolic, or **allegorical,** meaning. Characters and places in allegories often have names that indicate the abstract ideas they stand for: Justice, Deceit, Vanity. George Orwell's novel *Animal Farm* is a well-known modern allegory.

See pages 341, 364.

ALLITERATION **Repetition of the same or very similar consonant sounds usually at the beginnings of words that are close together in a poem.** In this example the sound "fl" is repeated in line 1, and the "s" sound is repeated in line 2:

> Open here I flung the shutter, when with many a
> flirt and flutter,
> In there stepped a stately Raven of the saintly days
> of yore.
>
> —Edgar Allan Poe, from "The Raven"

See pages 456, 475.
See also *Assonance, Onomatopoeia, Rhyme.*

ALLUSION **Reference to a statement, a person, a place, or an event from literature, history, religion, mythology, politics, sports, science, or pop culture.** In calling one of his stories "The Gift of the Magi" (page 287), O. Henry uses an allusion to the wise men from the East called the Magi, who presented the infant Jesus with the first Christmas gifts.

"I think I'll wait for the next elevator."

Drawing by Chas. Addams; © 1988 The New Yorker Magazine, Inc.

AMBIGUITY **An element of uncertainty in a text, in which something can be interpreted in a number of different ways.** Ambiguity adds a layer of complexity to a story, for it presents us with a variety of possible interpretations, all of which are valid. Edgar Allan Poe's "The Cask of Amontillado" (page 173) is ambiguous because we don't know if we should trust the narrator's claims. **Subtleties,** or fine distinctions in meaning, in a text help create ambiguity. The significance of these subtleties is open to question.

See pages 284–285, 297.

ANALOGY **Comparison made between two things to show how they are alike in some respects.** During the Revolutionary War the writer Thomas Paine drew an analogy between a thief breaking into a house and the king of England interfering in the affairs of the American Colonies (*The Crisis,* No. 1). Similes are a kind of analogy. However, an analogy usually clarifies something, while a simile shows imaginatively how two different things are alike in some unusual way.

See page 308.

Handbook of Literary Terms **1019**

ANECDOTE **Very, very brief story, usually told to make a point.** Historians and other writers of nonfiction often use anecdotes to clarify their texts or to provide human interest.

ASIDE **Words that are spoken by a character in a play to the audience or to another character but that are not supposed to be overheard by the others onstage.** Stage directions usually tell when a speech is an aside. For example, in Shakespeare's *Romeo and Juliet* (page 787), there are two asides in the opening scene. Sampson speaks to Gregory in an aside, and Gregory responds to him in another aside as they pick a fight with the servants of the house of Montague. Sampson and Gregory hear each other's asides, and so do we in the audience, but Montague's servants do not.

See page 754.

ASSONANCE **Repetition of similar vowel sounds that are followed by different consonant sounds, especially in words that are close together in a poem.** The words *base* and *fade* and the words *young* and *love* contain examples of assonance. The lines that follow are especially musical because of assonance:

Seeing the snowman standing all alone
In dusk and cold is more than he can bear.
The small boy weeps to hear the wind prepare
A night of gnashings and enormous moan.

—Richard Wilbur, from "Boy at the Window"

See page 456.
See also *Alliteration, Onomatopoeia, Rhyme.*

AUTHOR The writer of a literary work.

AUTOBIOGRAPHY **An account of the writer's own life.** An example of a book-length autobiography is *When I Was Puerto Rican* by Esmeralda Santiago (see page 543). Judith Ortiz Cofer's "Volar" (page 573) is an example of an autobiographical essay.

See also *Biography.*

BALLAD **Song that tells a story. Folk ballads** are composed by unknown singers and are passed on for generations before they are written down. **Literary ballads,** on the other hand, are poems composed by

known individuals and are written in imitation of the old folk ballads. "Ballad of Birmingham" by Dudley Randall (page 464) is a modern literary ballad. Ballads usually tell sensational stories of tragedy or adventure. They use simple language and a great deal of repetition and usually have regular rhythm and rhyme schemes, which make them easy to memorize.

See page 463.

BIOGRAPHY **An account of a person's life, written or told by another person.** A classic American biography is Carl Sandburg's multivolume life of Abraham Lincoln. Today biographies are written about movie stars, TV personalities, politicians, sports figures, self-made millionaires, even underworld figures. Biographies are among the most popular forms of contemporary literature. On page 184 is an excerpt from Kenneth Silverman's biography of Edgar Allan Poe.

See also *Autobiography.*

BLANK VERSE **Poetry written in unrhymed iambic pentameter.** *Blank* means the poetry is not rhymed. *Iambic pentameter* means that each line contains five iambs, or metrical feet that consist of an unstressed syllable followed by a stressed syllable (˘ ´). Blank verse is the most important poetic form in English epic and dramatic poetry. It is the major verse form used in Shakespeare's plays.

See page 781.
See also *Iambic Pentameter, Meter.*

CHARACTER **Person in a story, poem, or play.** Sometimes, as in George Orwell's novel *Animal Farm*, the characters are animals. In myths the characters are divinities or heroes who have superhuman powers, such as Poseidon and Athena and Odysseus in the *Odyssey* (page 650). Most often a character is an ordinary human being, like Mme. Loisel in Guy de Maupassant's "The Necklace" (page 160).

The process of revealing the personality of a character in a story is called **characterization.** A writer can reveal a character by

1. letting us hear the character speak
2. describing how the character looks and dresses
3. letting us listen to the character's inner thoughts and feelings
4. revealing what other characters in the story think or say about the character

5. showing us what the character does—how he or she acts
6. telling us directly what the character's personality is like: cruel, kind, sneaky, brave, and so on

The first five ways of revealing a character are known as **indirect characterization.** When a writer uses indirect characterization, we have to use our own judgment to decide what a character is like, based on the evidence the writer gives us. But when a writer uses the sixth method, known as **direct characterization,** we don't have to decide for ourselves; we are told directly what the character is like.

Characters can be classified as static or dynamic. A **static character** is one who does not change much in the course of a story. By contrast, a **dynamic character** changes as a result of the story's events.

Characters can also be classified as flat or round. A **flat character** has only one or two traits, and these can be described in a few words. Such a character has no depth, like a piece of cardboard. A **round character,** like a real person, has many different character traits, which sometimes contradict one another.

Static and flat characters often function as **subordinate characters** in a story. This means that they may play important roles in a story but they are not the main actors in the plot.

The fears or conflicts or needs that drive a character are called **motivation.** A character can be motivated by many factors, such as vengeance, fear, greed, love, even boredom.

See pages 84–85, 116–117.

CLIMAX **Moment of great emotional intensity or suspense in a plot.** The major climax in a story or play usually marks the moment when the conflict is decided one way or another.

See pages 2, 783.

COMEDY **In general, a story that ends happily.** The hero or heroine of a comedy is usually an ordinary character who overcomes a series of obstacles that block what he or she wants. Many comedies have a boy-meets-girl plot, in which young lovers must face obstacles to their marrying. At the end of such comedies, the lovers marry, and everyone celebrates, as in Shakespeare's play *A Midsummer Night's Dream.* In structure and characterization, a comedy is the opposite of a **tragedy.**

See pages 752–753, 755.
See also *Comic Relief, Drama, Tragedy.*

COMIC RELIEF **Comic scene or event that breaks up a serious play or narrative.** Comic relief allows writers to lighten the tone of a work and show the humorous side of a dramatic theme. In Shakespeare's tragedy *Romeo and Juliet* (page 787), the nurse and Mercutio provide comic relief.

CONFLICT **Struggle or clash between opposing characters or opposing forces.** In an **external conflict,** a character struggles against an outside force. This outside force might be another character, or society as a whole, or something in nature. "The Most Dangerous Game" by Richard Connell (page 5) is about the external conflict between the evil General Zaroff and the hunter Rainsford. By contrast, an **internal conflict** takes place entirely within a character's own mind. An internal conflict is a struggle between opposing needs or desires or emotions within a single person. In James Hurst's "The Scarlet Ibis" (page 343), the young narrator struggles with an internal conflict—between love for his brother and hatred of his brother's disabilities. Many works, especially longer ones, contain both internal and external conflicts, and an external conflict often leads to internal problems.

See pages 2, 116, 209, 752.

CONNOTATION **All the meanings, associations, or emotions that have come to be attached to some words, in addition to their literal dictionary definitions, or denotations.** For example, *skinny* and *slender* have the same literal definition, or **denotation**—"thin." But their connotations are completely different. If you call someone skinny, you are saying something unflattering. If you call someone slender, you are paying him or her a compliment. The British philosopher Bertrand Russell once gave a classic example of the different connotations of words: "I am firm. You are obstinate. He is a pigheaded fool." Connotations, or the suggestive power of certain words, play an important role in creating **mood** or **tone.**

See pages 260, 436, 540.
See also *Diction, Mood, Tone.*

COUPLET **Two consecutive lines of poetry that rhyme.** Alexander Pope wrote this sarcastic couplet for a dog's collar (Kew is a place in England):

Handbook of Literary Terms **1021**

I am his Highness' dog at Kew;
Pray tell me, Sir, whose dog are you?

—Alexander Pope

Couplets work nicely for humor and satire because the punch line comes so quickly. However, they are most often used to express a completed thought. In Shakespeare's plays an important speech or scene often ends with a couplet.

See pages 422, 781.

DESCRIPTION **Type of writing intended to create a mood or emotion or to re-create a person, a place, a thing, an event, or an experience.** Description is one of the four major techniques used in writing. (The others are **narration, exposition,** and **persuasion.**) Description works by creating images that appeal to the senses of sight, smell, taste, hearing, or touch. Writers use description in all forms of fiction, nonfiction, and poetry.

See also *Imagery*.

DIALECT **Way of speaking that is characteristic of a particular region or a particular group of people.** Dialects may have a distinct vocabulary, pronunciation system, and grammar. In a sense, we all speak dialects; but one dialect usually becomes dominant in a country or culture and becomes accepted as the standard way of speaking. In the United States, for example, the formal language is known as standard English. (This is what you usually hear spoken by TV newscasters on the national channels.)

See page 525.

DIALOGUE **The conversation between characters in a story or play.** Dialogue is an important factor in characterization and in moving the plot forward. Dialogue forms the structure of most plays. The following dialogue is taken from Edgar Allan Poe's "The Cask of Amontillado" (page 173):

"You do not comprehend?" he said.
"Not I," I replied.
"Then you are not of the brotherhood."
"How?"
"You are not of the Masons."

"Yes, yes," I said, "yes, yes."
"You? Impossible! A Mason?"
"A Mason," I replied.
"A sign," he said.
"It is this," I answered, producing a trowel from beneath the folds of my roquelaure.
"You jest," he exclaimed, recoiling a few paces.
"But let us proceed to the amontillado."

DICTION **A writer's or speaker's choice of words.** Diction is an essential element of a writer's **style.** Some writers use simple, down-to-earth, or even slang words *(house, home, digs)*; others use ornate, official-sounding, or even flowery language *(domicile, residence, abode)*. The **connotations** of words are an important aspect of diction.

See pages 436, 496, 525, 541.
See also *Connotation, Tone*.

DRAMA **Story that is written to be acted for an audience.** The action of a drama is usually driven by a character who wants something and takes steps to get it. The elements of a dramatic plot are **exposition, complications, climax,** and **resolution.** The term *drama* is also used to describe a serious play that is neither a **comedy** nor a **tragedy.**

See pages 752–754, 783.
See also *Comedy, Tragedy*.

DRAMATIC MONOLOGUE **A poem in which a speaker addresses one or more silent listeners, often reflecting on a specific problem or situation.** Though the person addressed in a dramatic monologue does not speak, we often can discover something about the listener or listeners—as well as the speaker—by paying close attention to the speaker's words. The speaker in Edgar Lee Masters's dramatic monologue "Lucinda Matlock" is an outspoken old woman who addresses the younger generation from the graveyard in Spoon River:

What is this I hear of sorrow and weariness,
Anger, discontent, and drooping hopes?
Degenerate sons and daughters,
Life is too strong for you—
It takes life to love Life.

See page 84.

EPIC **Long story told in elevated language (usually poetry), which relates the great deeds of a larger-than-life hero who embodies the values of a particular society.** Most epics include elements of myth, legend, folk tale, and history. Their tone is serious and their language is grand. Most epic heroes undertake quests to achieve something of tremendous value to themselves or their people. Often parts of the hero's quest are set in both heaven and hell. Homer's *Iliad* and *Odyssey* (page 650) are the best-known epics in Western civilization. The great epic of ancient Rome is Virgil's *Aeneid,* which, like the *Iliad* and *Odyssey,* is based on events that happened during and immediately after the Trojan War. The great epic of India is the *Mahabharata.* The great epic of Mali in Africa is *Sundiata.* Spain's epic is *El Cid.*

See pages 640–646.

EPITHET **Adjective or descriptive phrase that is regularly used to characterize a person, place, or thing.** We speak of "Honest Abe," for example, and "America the Beautiful."

Homer created so many epithets in his *Iliad* and *Odyssey* that his name is permanently associated with a type of epithet. The **Homeric epithet** in most English translations consists of a compound adjective that is regularly used to modify a particular noun. Three famous examples from the *Odyssey* are "*wine-dark* sea," "*rosy-fingered* dawn," "the *gray-eyed* goddess Athena."

See page 715.

ESSAY **Short piece of nonfiction that examines a single subject from a limited point of view.** Most essays can be categorized as either **personal** or **formal.**

A **personal essay** (sometimes called an **informal essay**) generally reveals a great deal about the writer's personality and tastes. Its tone is often conversational, sometimes even humorous.

A **formal essay** is usually serious, objective, and impersonal in tone. Its purpose is to inform its readers about some topic of interest or to persuade them to accept the writer's views. The statements in a formal essay are supported by facts and logic.

EXPOSITION **Type of writing that explains, gives information, defines, or clarifies an idea.** Exposition is one of the four major techniques used in writing. (The others are **narration, description,** and **persuasion.**) We find exposition in news articles, in histories, in biographies (and even in cookbook recipes). In fact, each entry in this Handbook of Literary Terms is an example of exposition.

Exposition is also the term for that beginning part of a plot that gives information about the characters and their problems or conflicts.

See pages 2, 783.
See also *Plot.*

FABLE **Very brief story in prose or verse that teaches a moral, or a practical lesson about how to get along in life.** The characters in most fables are animals that behave and speak like human beings. Some of the most popular fables are those attributed to Aesop, who scholars believe was a slave in ancient Greece.

See also *Folk Tale, Tall Tale.*

FIGURE OF SPEECH **Word or phrase that describes one thing in terms of another and is not meant to be understood on a literal level.** Most figures of speech, or **figurative language,** involve some sort of imaginative comparison between seemingly unlike things.

Some 250 different types of figures of speech have been identified. The most common are the **simile** ("I wandered lonely as a cloud"), the **metaphor** ("Fame is a bee"), and **personification** ("The wind stood up and gave a shout").

See pages 428–429.
See also *Metaphor, Personification, Simile.*

FLASHBACK **Scene in a movie, play, short story, novel, or narrative poem that interrupts the present action of the plot to flash backward and tell what happened at an earlier time.** That is, a flashback breaks the normal time sequence of events in a narrative, usually to give the readers or viewers some background information that helps them make sense of a story. Much of the *Odyssey* (page 650) is told in the form of a flashback, as Odysseus describes his previous adventures to the Phaeacian court of King Alcinous. Hwang Sunwŏn successfully incorporates flashbacks into his short story "Cranes" (page 222). As Sŏngsam recalls scenes from his childhood, we are transported to the past so that we can fully understand Sŏngsam's present conflict. Flashbacks are extremely common storytelling devices in movies. In fact, the word *flashback* comes from film criticism, and it has spread to the rest of literature.

See pages 3, 32.

FLASH-FORWARD A scene in a movie, play, short story, novel, or narrative poem that interrupts the present action of the plot to shift into the future. Writers may use a flash-forward to create **dramatic irony.** By means of the flash-forward, we know the future, but the story characters do not.

See page 3.

FOIL Character who is used as a contrast to another character. A writer uses a foil to accentuate and clarify the distinct qualities of two characters. The word *foil* is also used for a thin sheet of shiny metal that is placed beneath a gem to intensify its brilliance. A character who is a foil, like the metal behind the gem, sets off or intensifies the qualities of another character. In Shakespeare's *Romeo and Juliet* (page 787), the cynical, sophisticated Mercutio is a foil to the romantic, naive Romeo.

See page 816.

FOLK TALE Story that has no known author and was originally passed on from one generation to another by word of mouth. Unlike myths, which are about gods and heroes, folk tales are usually about ordinary people. Folk tales tend to travel, and you'll often find the same motifs—elements such as characters, images, and story lines—in the tales of different cultures. For example, there are said to be nine hundred versions of the folk tale about Cinderella.

See also *Fable, Tall Tale.*

FORESHADOWING The use of clues to hint at events that will occur later in a plot. Foreshadowing is used to build suspense and, sometimes, anxiety in the reader or viewer. In a drama the gun found in a bureau drawer in Act I is likely to foreshadow violence later in the play. In "The Cask of Amontillado" (page 173), Poe uses foreshadowing skillfully. For example, when Montresor produces a trowel from beneath his cloak, Poe is foreshadowing the means Montresor will use to murder his enemy. When later he begins to build a wall around Fortunato, we remember that trowel.

See pages 3, 4.

FREE VERSE Poetry that does not have a regular meter or rhyme scheme. Poets writing in free verse try to capture the natural rhythms of ordinary speech. To create its music, free verse may use **internal rhyme, alliteration, onomatopoeia, refrain,** and **parallel structure.** For an example of a poem written in free verse, read "Daily" (page 410).

See pages 455–456, 468.
See also *Meter, Rhythm.*

GENRE (zhän′rə) **The category that a work of literature is classified under. Five major genres in literature are nonfiction, fiction, poetry, drama, and myth.** Collections 7, 10, and 11 of this book are organized by genre: by poetry, by epic and myth, and by drama.

See page 244.

HAIKU Japanese verse form consisting of three lines and, usually, seventeen syllables (five in the first line, seven in the second, and five in the third). The writer of a haiku uses association and suggestion to describe a particular moment of discovery or enlightenment. A haiku often presents an image of daily life that relates to a particular season.

See page 418.

HYPERBOLE (hī·pʉr′bə·lē) **Figure of speech that uses exaggeration to express strong emotion or to create a comic effect.** Writers often use hyperbole, also called **overstatement,** to intensify a description or to emphasize the essential nature of something. If you say that a limousine is as long as an ocean liner, you are using hyperbole.

IAMBIC PENTAMETER Line of poetry that contains five iambs. An **iamb** is a metrical foot, or unit of measure, consisting of an unstressed syllable followed by a stressed syllable (˘ ′). *Pentameter* comes from the Greek *penta* (five) and *meter* (measure). Here is one iamb: arĭse′. Here is a line measuring five iambs:

> ˘ ′ ˘ ′ ˘ ′ ˘ ′ ˘
> But soft! What light through yonder window
> ′
> breaks?
>
> —William Shakespeare, from *Romeo and Juliet*

Iambic pentameter is by far the most common verse line in English poetry.

See pages 422, 781.
See also *Blank Verse, Meter.*

IDIOM Expression peculiar to a particular language that means something different from the literal meaning of each word. "It's raining cats and dogs" and "We heard it through the grapevine" are idioms of American English. One of the difficulties of translating a work from another language is translating the idioms.

See page 725.

IMAGERY Language that appeals to the senses. Most images are visual—that is, they create pictures in the reader's mind by appealing to the sense of sight. Images can also appeal to the senses of sound, touch, taste, or smell or even to several senses at once. Imagery is an element in all types of writing, but it is especially important in poetry. The following lines contain images that make us see, hear, and even smell what the speaker experiences as he travels to meet someone he loves.

> Then a mile of warm sea-scented beach;
> Three fields to cross till a farm appears;
> A tap at the pane, the quick sharp scratch
> And blue spurt of a lighted match . . .
>
> —Robert Browning, from "Meeting at Night"

See pages 402–403.
See also *Description*.

INVERSION Reversal of the normal word order of a sentence. The elements of a standard English sentence are subject, verb, and complement, and in most sentences that is the order in which they appear. *(Ray rowed the boat.)* Writers use inversion for emphasis and variety. They may also use it for more technical reasons—to create end rhymes or to accommodate a given meter. In a statement about Ulysses S. Grant and Robert E. Lee, the historian Bruce Catton wrote, "Daring and resourcefulness they had too. . . ." Catton inverts the order of the parts of the sentence so that the important words (*daring* and *resourcefulness*) come first.

IRONY Contrast between expectation and reality—between what is said and what is really meant, between what is expected to happen and what really does happen, or between what appears to be true and what is really true.

In **verbal irony,** a writer or speaker says one thing but really means something completely different. If you call a clumsy basketball player the new Michael Jordan, you are using verbal irony. The murderer in Edgar Allan Poe's "The Cask of Amontillado" (page 173) is using verbal irony when he says to his unsuspecting victim, "Your health is precious."

Situational irony occurs when there is a contrast between what would seem appropriate and what really happens or when there is a contradiction between what we expect to happen and what really does take place.

Dramatic irony occurs when the audience or the reader knows something important that a character in a play or story does not know. In Shakespeare's *Romeo and Juliet* (page 787), we know, but Romeo *does not,* that when he finds Juliet in the tomb, she is drugged, not dead. Thus we feel a terrible sense of dramatic irony as we watch Romeo kill himself upon discovering her body.

See pages 284–285, 286.
See also *Satire, Tone*.

LYRIC POETRY Poetry that does not tell a story but is aimed only at expressing a speaker's emotions or thoughts. Most lyrics are short, and they usually imply, rather than directly state, a single strong emotion. The term *lyric* comes from the Greek. In ancient Greece, lyric poems were recited to the accompaniment of a stringed instrument called a lyre. Today poets still try to make their lyrics "sing," but they rely only on the musical effects they create with words (such as **rhyme, rhythm,** and **onomatopoeia**).

See page 424.
See also *Sonnet*.

METAPHOR Figure of speech that makes a comparison between two unlike things, in which one thing becomes another thing without the use of the word *like, as, than, or resembles.* The poet Robert Burns's famous comparison "O my love is like a red, red rose" is a simile. If he had written, "O my love *is* a red, red rose" or "O my love bursts into bloom," he would have been using a metaphor.

Notice that the comparison in the second metaphor above is implied, or suggested, rather than directly stated, as it is in the first metaphor. An **implied metaphor** does not tell us directly that one thing *is* something else. Instead, it uses words that suggest the nature of the comparison. The phrase "bursts into bloom" implies that the feeling of love is like a budding flower.

An **extended metaphor** is a metaphor that is extended, or developed, over several lines of writing or even throughout an entire poem.

A **dead metaphor** is a metaphor that has been used so often that we no longer realize it is a figure of speech—we simply skip over the metaphorical connection it makes. Examples of dead metaphors are *the roof of the mouth, the eye of the storm, the heart of the matter,* and *the arm of the chair.*

A **mixed metaphor** is the inconsistent mixture of two or more metaphors. Mixed metaphors are a common problem in bad writing, and they are often unintentionally funny. You are using a mixed metaphor if you say, "Put it on the back burner and let it germinate" or "Let's set sail and get this show on the road."

See pages 428–429, 435.
See also *Figure of Speech, Personification, Simile.*

METER **Generally regular pattern of stressed and unstressed syllables in poetry.** When we want to indicate the metrical pattern of a poem, we mark the stressed syllables with the symbol (ˊ) and the unstressed syllables with the symbol (˘). Indicating the metrical pattern of a poem in this way is called **scanning** the poem, or **scansion** (skan′shən). Notice the pattern of stressed and unstressed syllables in the first four lines of this poem:

> Slowly, silently, now the moon
> Walks the night in her silver shoon;
> This way, and that, she peers, and sees
> Silver fruit upon silver trees. . . .
>
> —Walter de la Mare, from "Silver"

See pages 454–455.
See also *Blank Verse, Iambic Pentameter, Rhythm.*

MOOD **A story's atmosphere or the feeling it evokes.** Mood is often created by a story's setting. A story set in a wild forest at night, with wolves howling in the distance, will probably convey a mood of terror, tension, or uneasiness. A story set in a cozy cottage or garden full of sunlight and the chirps of birds will probably create a mood of peace.

See pages 48, 497, 498.
See also *Setting.*

MYTH **Traditional story that is rooted in a particular culture, is basically religious, and usually serves to explain a belief, a ritual, or a mysterious natural phenomenon.** Most myths grew out of religious rituals, and almost all of them involve the influence of gods on human affairs. Every culture has its own mythology. For many centuries the myths of ancient Greece and Rome were very influential in the Western world.

"The Fenris Wolf" (page 728) is a story from Norse mythology, the system of myths developed thousands of years ago by the people of Scandinavia. The myths were part of an oral tradition; the oldest surviving written versions of these ancient tales came from Iceland in the thirteenth century. There are variations in the Norse myths, as there are in the myths of most cultures.

See pages 644, 726–727.

NARRATION **Type of writing or speaking that tells about a series of related events.** Narration is one of the four major techniques used in writing. (The others are **description, exposition,** and **persuasion.**) Narration can be any length, from a brief paragraph to an entire book. It is most often found in short stories, novels, epics, and ballads. But narration is also used in any piece of nonfiction that relates a series of events that tell what happened—such as a biography, an essay, or a news story—and even in a scientific analysis or a report of a business meeting.

See also *Point of View.*

NARRATOR **The voice telling a story.** The choice of a narrator is very important in storytelling. For example, Edgar Allan Poe chose the murderer himself to tell the story "The Cask of Amontillado" (page 173). This choice of a narrator not only increases our sense of horror but also raises many questions, which make us uneasy. For one thing we wonder whether this narrator is telling the truth. We also wonder whom the narrator is talking to as he relates the details of his crime.

See pages 148–149.
See also *Point of View.*

NONFICTION **Prose writing that deals with real people, things, events, and places.** The most popular forms of nonfiction are **biography** and **autobiography.** Other examples include essays, newspaper stories, magazine articles, historical writing, scientific reports, and even personal diaries and letters.

Handbook of Literary Terms

NOVEL **Fictional prose narrative usually consisting of more than fifty thousand words.** In general, the novel uses the same basic literary elements as the short story (**plot, character, setting, theme,** and **point of view**) but develops them more fully. Many novels have several subplots, for instance. Modern writers often do away with one or more of the novel's traditional elements. Some novels today are basically character studies, with only the barest, stripped-down story lines.

ONOMATOPOEIA (än′·ō·mat′·ō·pē′·ə) **Use of a word whose sound imitates or suggests its meaning.** Onomatopoeia is so natural to us that we begin using it instinctively as children. *Crackle, pop, fizz, click, zoom,* and *chirp* are examples of onomatopoeia. Onomatopoeia is an important element in the music of poetry.

> And in the hush of waters was the sound
> Of pebbles, rolling round;
> Forever rolling, with a hollow sound:
>
> And bubbling seaweeds, as the waters go,
> Swish to and fro
> Their long cold tentacles of slimy gray. . . .
>
> —James Stephens, from "The Shell"

See pages 456, 475.
See also *Alliteration, Assonance, Rhyme.*

PARADOX **Statement or situation that seems to be a contradiction but reveals a truth.** Paradoxes in literature are designed to make readers stop and think. They often express aspects of life that are mysterious, surprising, or difficult to describe. When O. Henry, in "The Gift of the Magi" (page 287), refers to the impoverished Della and Jim as "one of the richest couples on earth," he is stating a paradox.

PARALLELISM **Repetition of words, phrases, or sentences that have the same grammatical structure or that state a similar idea.** Parallelism, or **parallel structure,** helps make lines rhythmic and memorable and heightens their emotional effect:

> It was the best of times, it was the worst of times, it was the age of wisdom, it was the age of foolishness, it was the epoch of belief, it was the epoch of incredulity, it was the season of Light, it was the season of Darkness, it was the spring of hope, it was the winter of despair, we had everything before us, we had nothing before us, we were all going direct to Heaven, we were all going direct the other way. . . .
>
> —Charles Dickens, from *A Tale of Two Cities*

See page 363.

PERSONA **Mask or voice assumed by a writer.** Authors often take on other identities in their works. In a short story a writer may assume a persona by using a first-person narrator. When a poet is not the speaker of a poem, the poet is creating a persona.

See pages 172, 472.
See also *Point of View, Speaker.*

PERSONIFICATION **Kind of metaphor in which a nonhuman thing or quality is talked about as if it were human.** Here are a few lines in which poetry itself is personified—that is, it is described as behaving and feeling the way people do:

> This poetry gets bored of being alone,
> it wants to go outdoors to chew on the winds,
> to fill its commas with the keels of rowboats. . . .
>
> —Hugo Margenat, from "Living Poetry"

See pages 429, 450.
See also *Figure of Speech, Metaphor.*

PLOT **Series of related events that make up a story or drama.** Plot is what happens in a story, novel, or play. An outline showing the "bare bones" of a plot would include the story's **basic situation,** or **exposition;** the **conflict,** or problem; the **main events** (including **complications**); the final **climax,** or moment of great emotional intensity or suspense, when we learn what the outcome of the conflict is going to be; and the **resolution,** or denouement.

See pages 2–3, 783.

POETRY Type of rhythmic, compressed language that uses figures of speech and imagery to appeal to the reader's emotions and imagination. The major forms of poetry are the **lyric poem** and **narrative poem.** Two types of narrative poetry are the **epic** and the **ballad.** One popular type of lyric poetry is the **sonnet.** Beyond this, poetry is difficult to define, though many readers feel it is easy to recognize. The poet Wallace Stevens, for example, once described poetry as "a search for the inexplicable."

See also *Ballad, Epic, Lyric Poetry, Sonnet.*

POINT OF VIEW Vantage point from which a writer tells a story. In broad terms there are three possible points of view: omniscient, first person, and third person limited.

In the **omniscient** (or "all-knowing") **point of view,** the person telling the story knows everything there is to know about the characters and their problems. This all-knowing narrator can tell us about the past, the present, and the future of all the characters. He or she can even tell us what the characters are thinking. The narrator can also tell us what is happening in other places. In the omniscient point of view, the narrator is not in the story at all. In fact, the omniscient narrator is like a god telling the story.

In the **first-person point of view,** one of the characters is telling the story, using the pronoun *I.* We get to know this narrator very well, but we can know only what this character knows, and we can observe only what this character observes. All of our information about the events in the story must come from this one character. When a story is told from the first-person point of view, readers often must ask if the narrator is unreliable. An **unreliable narrator** does not always know what is happening in the story, or he or she might be lying or telling us only part of the story.

In the **third-person-limited point of view,** the narrator, who plays no part in the story, zooms in on the thoughts and feelings of just one character. With this point of view, we observe the action through the eyes and with the feelings of this one character.

See pages 148–149, 150, 159, 172.
See also *Narrator, Persona.*

PROTAGONIST Main character in fiction or drama. The protagonist is the character we focus our attention on, the person who sets the plot in motion.

The character or force that blocks the protagonist is the **antagonist.** Most protagonists are rounded, dynamic characters who change in some important way by the end of the story, novel, or play. The antagonist is often but not always the villain in the story. Similarly, the protagonist is often but not always the hero.

See page 116.

PUN Play on the multiple meanings of a word or on two words that sound alike but have different meanings. Most often puns are used for their humorous effects; they are used in jokes all the time. ("What has four wheels and flies?" Answer: "A garbage truck.") Shakespeare was one of the great punsters of all time. The servants in *Romeo and Juliet* (page 787) make crude puns as they clown around at the start of the play. Later, Romeo and his friend Mercutio trade wits in a series of more sophisticated puns. Since word meanings change so quickly, some of Shakespeare's puns are barely understandable to us today, just as puns popular today may be puzzling to people a hundred years from now.

See page 914.

"Does the doctor make mouse calls?"

Drawing by Bernard Schoenbaum; © 1991 The New Yorker Magazine, Inc.

REFRAIN Repeated word, phrase, line, or group of lines. Though refrains are usually associated with songs and poems, they are also used in speeches and other forms of literature. Refrains are most often used to build rhythm, but they may also provide commentary or build suspense.

See page 463.

RHYME **Repetition of accented vowel sounds, and all sounds following them, in words that are close together in a poem.** *Choice* and *voice* are rhymes, as are *tingle* and *jingle*.

End rhymes occur at the ends of lines. In this poem the words *defense/tense, know/go,* and *Spain/Maine* are end rhymes:

Old Mary

My last defense
Is the present tense.
It little hurts me now to know
I shall not go
Cathedral-hunting in Spain
Nor cherrying in Michigan or Maine.

—Gwendolyn Brooks

Internal rhymes occur in the middle of a line. This line has an internal rhyme (*dreary* rhymes with *weary*):

Once upon a midnight dreary, while I pondered, weak and weary

Edgar Allan Poe, from "The Raven"

When two words have some sound in common but do not rhyme exactly, they are called **approximate rhymes** (or **half rhymes, off rhymes,** or **slant rhymes**). In Brooks's poem on this page, the words *now* and *know* are approximate rhymes.

The pattern of end rhymes in a poem is called a **rhyme scheme.** The rhyme scheme of a stanza or a poem is indicated by the use of a different letter of the alphabet for each new rhyme. For example, the rhyme scheme of Brooks's poem is *aabbcc.*

See pages 454, 461.

RHYTHM **Musical quality in language produced by repetition.** Rhythm occurs naturally in all forms of spoken and written language. The most obvious kind of rhythm is produced by **meter,** the regular repetition of stressed and unstressed syllables found in some poetry. But writers can also create rhythm by using rhymes, by repeating words and phrases, and even by repeating whole lines or sentences. This stanza by Walt Whitman is written in free verse and so does not follow a metrical pattern. Yet the lines are rhythmical because of Whitman's repeated use of certain sentence structures, words, and sounds.

Give me the splendid silent sun with all his
  beams full-dazzling,
Give me juicy autumnal fruit ripe and red
  from the orchard,
Give me a field where the unmowed grass grows,
Give me an arbor, give me the trellised grape,
Give me fresh corn and wheat, give me
  serene-moving animals teaching content,
Give me nights perfectly quiet as on high
  plateaus west of the Mississippi, and I
  looking up at the stars. . . .

—Walt Whitman, from "Give Me the
Splendid Silent Sun"

See pages 454–455.
See also *Free Verse, Meter.*

SATIRE **Type of writing that ridicules something—a person, a group of people, humanity at large, an attitude or failing, a social institution—in order to reveal a weakness.** Most satires are an attempt to convince us of a point of view or to persuade us to follow a course of action. They do this by pointing out how the opposite point of view or action is ridiculous or laughable. Satire often involves **exaggeration**—the act of overstating something to make it look worse than it is.

See also *Irony, Tone.*

SCENE DESIGN **Sets, lights, costumes, and props, which bring a play to life onstage. Sets** are the furnishings and scenery that suggest the time and place of the action. **Props** (short for *properties*) are all the objects that the actors use onstage, such as books, telephones, suitcases.

See pages 753–754.

SETTING **The time and place of a story or play.** Most often the setting of a narrative is established early in the story. For example, in the fourth paragraph of "The Cask of Amontillado" (page 173), Edgar Allan Poe tells his readers, "It was about dusk, one evening during the supreme madness of the carnival season. . . ." Setting often contributes to a story's emotional effect. In "The Cask of Amontillado" the descriptions of the gloomy Montresor palace, with its damp catacombs full of bones, help create the story's mood of horror. Setting can also contribute to the conflict in a story, as the harsh environment does in Eugenia W. Collier's "Marigolds" (page 119). Setting can also be used to reveal character, as it does in Truman Capote's "A Christmas Memory" (page 51).

See pages 48–49.

See also *Mood.*

SHORT STORY **Short, concentrated, fictional prose narrative.** Some say Edgar Allan Poe was the first short-story writer. He was also one of the first to attempt to define the short story. He said "unity of effect" is crucial, meaning that a short story ought to concentrate on a single purpose. Short stories are usually built on a plot that consists of these "bare bones": the **basic situation** or **exposition, complications, climax,** and **resolution.** Years ago, most short stories were notable for their strong plots. Today's short-story writers tend to be more interested in character.

SIMILE **Figure of speech that makes a comparison between two unlike things, using a word such as** *like, as, resembles,* **or** *than.* Shakespeare, in one of his famous sonnets, uses a simile with an ironic twist, comparing two things that are *not* alike:

> My mistress' eyes are nothing like the sun

We would expect a love poem to compare the light in a lover's eyes to the bright sun. But instead, Shakespeare puts a twist into a common comparison— in order to make a point about the extravagant similes found in most love poems of his day.

See pages 428, 645–646.

See also *Figure of Speech, Metaphor.*

SOLILOQUY **Long speech in which a character who is onstage alone expresses his or her thoughts aloud.** The soliloquy is a very old dramatic convention, in which the audience is supposedly overhearing the private thoughts of a character. Perhaps the most famous soliloquy is the "To be or not to be" speech in Shakespeare's play *Hamlet.* There are also several soliloquies in *Romeo and Juliet,* including Friar Laurence's soliloquy at the opening of Act II, Scene 3 (pages 827–828); Juliet's at the end of Act IV, Scene 3 (pages 883–884); and Romeo's in Act V, Scene 3 (pages 901–902).

SONNET **Fourteen-line lyric poem that is usually written in iambic pentameter and that has one of several rhyme schemes.** The oldest kind of sonnet is called the **Italian sonnet,** or **Petrarchan sonnet,** after the fourteenth-century Italian poet Petrarch. The first eight lines, or **octet** or **octave,** of the Italian sonnet pose a question or problem about love or some other subject. The concluding six lines, or the **sestet,** are a response to the octet. The octet has the rhyme scheme *abba abba;* the sestet has the rhyme scheme *cde cde.*

Another important sonnet form, widely used by Shakespeare, is called the **Shakespearean sonnet.** It has three four-line units, or **quatrains,** followed by a concluding two-line unit, or **couplet.** The most common rhyme scheme for the Shakespearean sonnet is *abab cdcd efef gg.*

See page 422.

See also *Lyric Poetry.*

SPEAKER **Voice that is talking to us in a poem.** Sometimes the speaker is identical with the poet, but often the speaker and the poet are not the same. The poet may be speaking as a child, a woman, a man, a whole people, an animal, or even an object. For example, the speaker of Maya Angelou's poem "Woman Work" (page 409) is a hard-working woman with several children, who cuts cane and cotton and lives in a hut—not Maya Angelou at all.

See page 472.

See also *Persona.*

STANZA **Group of consecutive lines in a poem that form a single unit.** A stanza in a poem is something like a paragraph in prose: It often expresses a unit of thought. A stanza may consist of any number of lines. The word *stanza* is Italian for "stopping place" or "place to rest." Emily Dickinson's poem "'Hope' is the thing with feathers" (page 435) consists of three four-line stanzas, or **quatrains,** each one expressing a unit of thought.

STYLE **The particular way in which a writer uses language.** Style is created mainly through **diction** (word choice), use of **figurative language,** and sentence patterns. Style can be described as plain, ornate, formal, ironic, conversational, and so on.

See pages 496–497.

SUSPENSE **Uncertainty or anxiety the reader feels about what is going to happen next in a story.** In "The Most Dangerous Game" (page 5) our curiosity is aroused at once when we hear about Ship-Trap Island and sailors' fear of it. When Rainsford lands on that very island and is hunted by the sinister General Zaroff, suspense keeps us on the edge of our seats. We wonder: Will Rainsford be another victim who is hunted down and killed by the evil and weird Zaroff?

See also *Foreshadowing, Plot.*

SYMBOL **Person, place, thing, or event that stands for itself and for something beyond itself as well.** For example, a scale has a real existence as an instrument for measuring weights, but it also is used as a public symbol of justice. Other familiar public symbols are the cross that symbolizes Christianity, the six-pointed star that symbolizes Judaism, the star and crescent that symbolizes Islam, and the bald eagle that symbolizes the United States. These are public symbols that most people know, but in literature, writers sometimes create new, private symbols that can be understood only from their context. One of the great symbols in literature is Herman Melville's great white whale, used as a symbol of the mystery of evil in the novel *Moby-Dick.*

See pages 340–341, 358.

TALL TALE **Exaggerated, far-fetched story that is obviously untrue but is told as though it should be believed.** Most tall tales are humorous. Tall tales are especially popular in the United States. As tall tales are passed on, they often get taller and taller—more and more exaggerated. The tales told about Paul Bunyan, the superheroic logger of the Northern forests, are tall tales.

See also *Fable, Folk Tale.*

THEME **Central idea of a work of literature.** A theme is not the same as a subject. The subject of a work can usually be expressed in a word or two: love, childhood, death. The theme is the idea the writer wishes to reveal *about* that subject. The theme is something that can be expressed in at least one complete sentence. For

example, one theme of Shakespeare's *Romeo and Juliet* (page 787) might be stated in this way: "Love is more powerful than hatred." Theme is not usually stated directly in a work of literature. Most often, the reader has to think about all the elements of the work and use them to make an inference, or educated guess, about what its theme is. Some themes are so commonly found in the literature of all cultures and all ages that they are called **universal themes.** Here are some universal themes found in stories throughout the ages and expressed in the *Odyssey* (page 650): "Heroes must undergo trials and endure losses before they can claim their rightful kindom." "Arrogance and pride can bring destruction." "Love will endure and triumph over evil."

See pages 208–209, 210.

TONE **Attitude a writer takes toward a subject, a character, or the audience.** Tone is conveyed through the writer's choice of words and details. For example, Gary Soto's "The Grandfather" (page 359) is affectionate and nostalgic in tone. James Thurber's "The Princess and the Tin Box" (page 332) is humorous and lightly mocking in tone.

See pages 149, 497.
See also *Connotation, Diction, Irony, Satire.*

TRAGEDY **Play that depicts serious and important events in which the main character comes to an unhappy end.** In a tragedy the main character is usually dignified and courageous. His or her downfall may be caused by a character flaw, or it may result from forces beyond human control. The tragic hero usually wins some self-knowledge and wisdom, even though he or she suffers defeat, perhaps even death.

See pages 752, 783.
See also *Comedy, Drama.*

VOICE **The writer's or speaker's distinctive use of language in a text.** Voice is created by a writer's **tone** and choice of words. Some writers have such a distinctive voice that you can identify their works on the basis of voice alone. The detached, objective tone and simple language in "Old Man at the Bridge" (page 140), for example, make it instantly recognizable as one of Ernest Hemingway's short stories.

See pages 149, 472.

Handbook of Literary Terms   **1031**

Handbook of Reading and Informational Terms

For more information about a topic, turn to the page(s) in this book indicated on a separate line at the end of most entries. To learn more about *Inference,* for example, turn to page 86.

The words in **boldface** are other key terms, with definitions provided in context. On another line there are cross-references to entries in this Handbook that provide closely related information. For instance, *Logic* contains a cross-reference to *Logical Order.*

ARGUMENT **A series of statements in a text designed to convince us of something.** What the writer or speaker wants to prove is called the **claim** (or the **opinion**). An argument might appeal to both our reason and our emotions. An argument in a scientific or historical journal, for instance, would probably present only **logical appeals,** which include sound reasons and factual evidence. An argument in a political text would probably also include **emotional appeals,** which are directed more to our "hearts" than to our minds. Some arguments use **loaded words** (words loaded with emotional connotations) and **anecdotes** (brief, personal stories) that also appeal to our feelings. It is important to be able to recognize emotional appeals used in arguments—and to be aware of how they can trick an audience.

Arguments can be found in editorials, magazine articles, political speeches, professional journals, and primary source material.

See pages 308–309, 516–517, 718.

CAUSE AND EFFECT **A text structure that shows how or why one thing leads to another.** The **cause** is the reason that an action takes place. The **effect** is the result or consequence of the cause. A cause can have more than one effect, and an effect may have several causes. Writers may explain causes only or effects only.

A text may be organized in a cause-effect chain. One cause leads to an effect, which causes another effect, and so on. Notice the cause-effect chain in the following paragraph from "An Arctic Floe of Climate Questions" (page 521):

> But some alarm bells did ring, because there is growing concern that we humans are fouling things up through our burning of gas, oil, and coal, which releases so-called greenhouse gases such as carbon dioxide into the air. These gases, which trap heat, may be causing the world's temperature to steadily creep higher and higher. And an absence of ice at the North Pole seemed like one more ominous sign of impending trouble.

Effect:
Alarm bells rang.

↓

Cause:
Concern was growing about the burning of gas, oil, and coal.

↓

Effect:
They release heat-trapping gases.

↓

Cause/Effect:
World's temperatures climb higher.

↓

Effect:
Ice absent at the North Pole.

Handbook of Reading and Informational Terms **1033**

Writers use the cause-effect pattern in both narrative and informational texts. In most short stories, events in the plot are connected in a cause-effect chain. Some words and phrases that signal the cause-effect pattern are *because, depended on, inspired, produced, resulting in, led to,* and *outcome.* Never assume, either in your reading or in real life, that one event causes another just because it happened before it.

> See pages 364, 498.
> See also *Text Structures.*

CHRONOLOGICAL ORDER **The arrangement of details in time order, that is, in the order in which they occurred.** Chronological order is used in a narrative, which describes a series of events, and in texts that explain the steps in a process.

> See pages 32, 961.
> See also *Text Structures.*

CLAIM **The idea or opinion that a writer tries to prove or defend in an argument.** The claim is stated as a **generalization,** a broad statement or conclusion that covers many situations (or follows from the evidence). The following statements are examples of claims stated as generalizations:

> Edgar Allan Poe died as a result of rabies poisoning. ("Poe's Death is Rewritten as Case of Rabies, Not Telltale Alcohol," page 187)
>
> Everyday acts of heroism are often overlooked. ("Where I Find My Heroes," page 719)

The author of the argument then supports the claim with either logical appeals (reasons backed by factual evidence), emotional appeals, or both.

> See page 308.
> See also *Argument, Generalization.*

COHERENT **Logically integrated, consistent, and understandable.** A text is **coherent** (kō·hir′ənt) when its ideas are arranged in an order that makes sense to the reader. To aid in coherence, writers help readers follow a text by using **transitions,** words and phrases that show how ideas are connected.

Common Transitional Words and Phrases	
Comparing Ideas also, and, too, moreover, similarly, another	**Contrasting Ideas** although, still, yet, but, on the other hand, instead
Showing Cause-Effect for, since, as a result, therefore, so that, because	**Showing Importance** first, last, to begin with, mainly, more important
Showing Location above, across, over, there, inside, behind, next to, through, near	**Showing Time** before, at last, now, when, eventually, at once, finally

COMPARISON/CONTRAST **A method of organizing information by showing similarities and differences among various groups of details.**

> See pages 231, 374, 918.
> See also *Text Structures.*

CONSUMER DOCUMENTS **Informative texts, such as a warranties, contracts, instruction manuals.** Here are some points to keep in mind when you read consumer documents:

1. Try to read the consumer document before you buy the product. Then, you can ask the clerk to explain anything you don't understand.

2. Read all of the pages in whatever language comes most easily to you. (Many documents are printed in two or three languages.) You will often find important information where you least expect it, such as at the end of the document.

3. Read the fine print. *Fine,* here, means "tiny and barely readable." Some fine-print statements in documents are required by law. They are

designed to protect you, the consumer, so the company may not be interested in emphasizing these points.

4. Don't expect the document to be interesting or easy to read. If you don't understand a statement and you can't ask someone at the store that sold you the product, call or write to the company that made it. You should complain to the company if you find its consumer document confusing.

5. Before you sign anything, read everything on the page, and be sure you understand what you're agreeing to. Ask to take the document home, and have your parent or guardian read it. If you are not of legal age, an adult may be responsible for whatever you've signed. Make a copy of any document that you've signed—and keep the copy in a place where you can find it.

See pages 948–950.

CONTEXT CLUES **The words and sentences surrounding a word.** Context clues can sometimes help you guess at the meaning of an unfamiliar word. You will find examples below of three types of context clues. In the examples, the unfamiliar word appears in **boldface.** The context clue is underlined.

Definition: Look for words that define the unfamiliar word, often by giving a synonym or a definition for it.

> Mathilde brought no **dowry** to her marriage—no property or money to give her marriage a good start.

Example: Look for examples that reveal the meaning of the unfamiliar word.

> She wanted **tapestries** on her walls, like those beautiful embroidered hangings that decorated her friend's home.

Contrast: Find words that contrast the unfamiliar word with a word or phrase you already know.

> M. Loisel was **distracted,** but Mathilde was fully involved in the party.

See pages 158, 306.

CREDIBILITY **The believability of a writer's argument.** To evaluate credibility, you first need to determine the author's claim, or opinion. Then you need to look at the **reasons** (statements that explain *why* the author holds the opinion) and the **evidence** (information that supports each reason). To be credible, evidence must be **relevant,** that is, directly related to the argument; **comprehensive,** that is, sufficient to be convincing; and **accurate,** that is, from a source that can be trusted as factually correct or otherwise reliable.

The writer's **intent** should also be considered. If you're reading an opinion essay, for instance, be sure to note any credentials or background information about the writer. Does the writer work for an institution that represents a particular point of view? Has the writer published a book on the same topic? Do emotional appeals and fallacious reasoning reveal a bias even though the writer pretends to be fair to both sides of the argument?

Notice the **tone** of the text. An argument that is based on logical appeals will usually have a serious, sincere tone. An angry or self-righteous tone might make you question the credibility of the argument.

See pages 308–309, 516–517, 579.
See also *Argument.*

DICTIONARY You use a dictionary to find the precise meaning and usage of words. The elements of a typical entry are explained below.

1. **Entry word.** The entry word shows how the word is spelled and divided into syllables. It may also show capitalization and other spellings.

2. **Pronunciation. Phonetic symbols** (such as the *schwa*, ə) and **diacritical marks** (such as the *dieresis*, ä) show how to pronounce the entry word. A key to these symbols and marks usually appears at the bottom of every other page of a dictionary. In this book a pronunciation guide appears at the bottom of every other page of the Glossary (pages 1093–1098).

3. **Part-of-speech label.** This label tells how the entry word is used. When a word can be used as more than one part of speech, definitions are grouped by part of speech. The sample entry shows three definitions of *indulge* as a transitive verb (*vt.*) and one as an intransitive verb (*vi.*).

4. **Other forms.** Sometimes the spellings of plural forms of nouns, principal parts of verbs, and comparative and superlative forms of adjectives and adverbs are shown.

5. **Word origin.** A word's origin, or **etymology** (et′ə·mäl′ə·jē), shows where the word comes from. *Indulge* comes from the Latin *indulgere*, which probably comes from the prefix *in–*, meaning "not," added to the Greek *dolichos*, "long" and the Gothic *tulgus*, "firm."

6. **Examples.** Phrases or sentences show how the entry word is used.

7. **Definitions.** If a word has more than one meaning, the meanings are numbered or lettered.

8. **Special-usage labels.** These labels identify special meanings or special uses of the word. Here, *Archaic* indicates an outdated meaning.

9. **Related word forms.** Other forms of the entry word are listed. Usually these are created by the addition of suffixes.

10. **Synonyms and antonyms. Synonyms** (words similar in meaning) and **antonyms** (words opposite in meaning) may appear at the end of the entry.

A dictionary is available as a book, a CD-ROM, or part of a word-processing program or Web site.

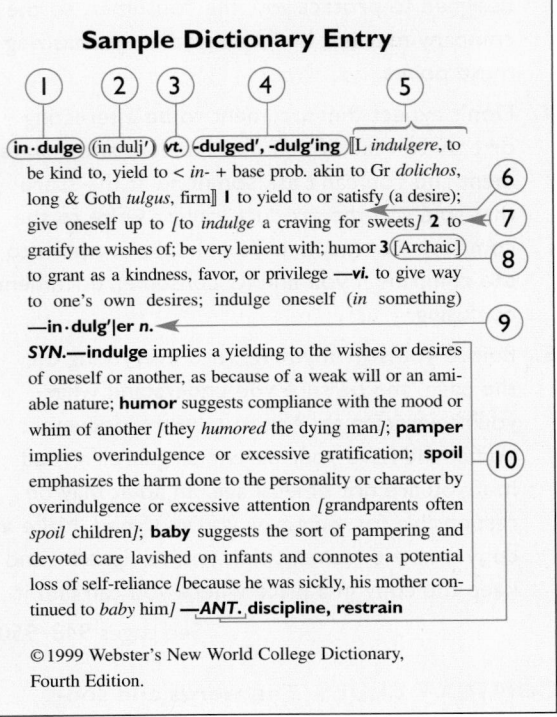

Sample Dictionary Entry

① ② ③ ④ ⑤

in·dulge (in dulj′) *vt.* **-dulged′, -dulg′ing** [L *indulgere*, to be kind to, yield to < *in-* + base prob. akin to Gr *dolichos*, long & Goth *tulgus*, firm] **1** to yield to or satisfy (a desire); give oneself up to [to *indulge* a craving for sweets] **2** to gratify the wishes of; be very lenient with; humor **3** [Archaic] to grant as a kindness, favor, or privilege —*vi.* to give way to one's own desires; indulge oneself (*in* something) —**in·dulg′|er** *n.*

SYN.—indulge implies a yielding to the wishes or desires of oneself or another, as because of a weak will or an amiable nature; **humor** suggests compliance with the mood or whim of another [they *humored* the dying man]; **pamper** implies overindulgence or excessive gratification; **spoil** emphasizes the harm done to the personality or character by overindulgence or excessive attention [grandparents often *spoil* children]; **baby** suggests the sort of pampering and devoted care lavished on infants and connotes a potential loss of self-reliance [because he was sickly, his mother continued to *baby* him] —**ANT.** discipline, restrain

© 1999 Webster's New World College Dictionary, Fourth Edition.

⑥ ⑦ ⑧ ⑨ ⑩

See also *Text Structures*.

EVIDENCE **Specific information or proof that backs up the reasons in an argument. Factual evidence** includes statements that can be proved by direct observation or by checking reliable reference sources. **Statistics** (facts in the form of numbers) and **expert testimony,** statements from people who are recognized as experts or authorities on an issue, may all be considered factual evidence.

In fields where discoveries are constantly being made, such as in astronomy and genetics, facts need to be checked in a recently published source. Remember that a Web site on the Internet may be current, but it may not be reliable. Anybody can post a statement on the Internet. If you suspect that a statement presented as a fact is not true, try to find the same fact in another source.

See pages 183, 308, 516–517.

FALLACIOUS (fə·lā′shəs) **REASONING Faulty reasoning, or mistakes in logical thinking.** (The word *fallacious* comes from a Latin word meaning "deceptive" or "tricky." The word *false* comes from the same root word, as does the word *fallacy*.) Fallacious reasoning leads to false or incorrect conclusions. Here are some types of fallacious reasoning:

1. **Begging the question,** also called **circular reasoning,** assumes the truth of a statement before it has been proved. You appear to be giving a reason to support your opinion, but all you're doing is restating your opinion in different words.

> All students in the ninth grade need to get a laptop computer because it's essential for every ninth grader to have one.

2. **Name calling** uses labels to attack a person who holds an opposing view instead of giving reasons or evidence to atttack the opposing view itself. This fallacy includes criticizing the person's character, situation, or background.

> Why should I listen to someone who doesn't even know who won the World Series?

3. **Stereotyping** gives all members of a group the same (usually undesirable) characteristics. It assumes that everyone (or everything) in that group is alike. (The word *stereotype* comes from the word for a metal plate that was used to print the same image over and over.) Stereotypes are often based on misconceptions about racial, social, religious, gender, or ethnic groups.

> Small towns are boring. Cats are self-centered.

4. **Hasty generalization** is a broad, general statement or conclusion that is made without sufficient evidence to back it up. A hasty generalization is often made on the basis of one or two experiences or observations.

> **Insufficient evidence:** I read about a healthy eighty-eight-year-old woman who smokes a pack of cigarettes every day. My grandfather smokes, too, and he's in great shape physically.
>
> **Hasty generalization:** Smoking does not affect your health.

If any exceptions to the conclusion can be found, the generalization is not true.

5. **Either/or fallacy** assumes that there are only two possible choices or solutions (usually extremes), even though there may be many.

> Either I get a cell phone, or you're never going to know where I am after school.

6. **False cause and effect** occurs when one event is said to be the cause of another event just because the two events happened in sequence. You cannot assume that an event caused whatever happened afterward.

> Her grades improved when she got a job after school.

See page 516.

GENERALIZATION A broad statement that applies to or covers many individuals, experiences, situations, observations, or texts. A **valid generalization** is a type of conclusion that is drawn after considering as many of the facts as possible. Here are some specific facts from "Community Service & You" (page 98) and a generalization based on them. Notice that each fact is one piece of evidence. The generalization then states what the evidence adds up to, drawing

Handbook of Reading and Informational Terms

a conclusion that applies to all members of the group.

> **Specific facts:** Thousands of young people volunteer to tutor children. Others help in massive projects to clean up beaches and rivers. Still others work at soup kitchens, shelters, and playgrounds—all without earning a cent.
>
> **Generalization:** Many young people get involved in voluntary community service.

A generalization jumps from your own specific experiences and observations to a larger, general understanding.

See pages 308, 516.

GRAPHS Graphic depiction of information. **Line graphs** generally show changes in quantity over time. **Bar graphs** usually compare quantities within categories. **Pie graphs,** or **circle graphs,** show proportions by dividing a circle into different-sized sections, like slices of a pie.

How to Read a Graph

1. **Read the title.** The title will tell you the subject and purpose of the graph.

2. **Read the headings and labels.** These will help you determine the type of information presented.

3. **Analyze the details.** Read numbers carefully. Note increases or decreases. Look for the direction or order of events and trends and for relationships.

See pages 1005–1006.

INFERENCE **A guess based on observation and prior experience.** When you make inferences about a literary work, you use evidence from the text as well as from other texts you have read and from your own prior experience. One way to analyze a character, for instance, is to consider what the person says and how he or she interacts with other characters. In the story "Thank You, M'am" (page 87), after the woman is almost mugged, she says to the boy who tried to steal her pocketbook:

> "You ought to be my son. I would teach you right from wrong. Least I can do right now is to wash your face. Are you hungry?"

From these statements, you can infer that the woman is strong and not easily intimidated. You can infer that she is also kind, that she understands why the boy tried to steal from her. Values are important to her, and she is determined to do what she can to help him.

When you're writing about a story or an informational text, you must be sure your inferences are supported by details in the text. **Supported inferences** are based directly on evidence in a text that you can point to and on reasonable prior knowledge. Some interpretation of the evidence is possible, but you cannot ignore or contradict facts that a writer gives you.

See pages 86, 118, 590.

INFORMATIVE TEXTS **Texts that communicate information and data.** When you're reading informative texts, you need to read slowly, looking for main ideas and important details. Slow and careful reading is especially important when you're trying to get meaning from consumer, workplace, and public documents. These documents are often not written by professional writers, so they may be difficult to read.

See also *Consumer Documents, Public Documents, Workplace Documents.*

LOGIC **Correct reasoning.** A logical text presents reasons supported by evidence (facts and examples). A text is illogical when it does not provide reasons backed by evidence. Notice how each sentence in this text, from "A Country Divided" (page 232), gives evidence that supports the sentence that precedes it.

> Through the long years of British rule, the Irish fought for their freedom. They fought with what weapons they had, in rebellions great and small—rebellions that the vast British army always put down. The Irish fought with words as well as weapons. They organized and signed petitions, held massive nonviolent protests, and after Catholics regained the vote in 1829, they lobbied in the English Parliament for their freedom.

See pages 308, 516–517, 718.
See also *Logical Order*.

LOGICAL ORDER **A method of organizing information by putting details into related groupings.** Writers use logical order most often when they want to classify information, that is, to examine a subject and its relationship to other subjects. When you classify, you can divide a subject into its parts (considering global warming in different parts of the world, as in "An Arctic Floe of Climate Questions," page 521). You can define a new term or idea (defining a *polynya* in the same article). Or you can use the comparison-contrast pattern to show similarities and differences among various groups (comparing beneficial and harmful results of global warming, as in "Rising Tides," page 518).

See page 961.
See also *Text Structures*.

MAIN IDEA **The writer's most important point, opinion, or message.** The main idea may be stated directly, or it may be only suggested or implied. If the idea is not stated directly, it's up to you to look at the details and decide on the idea that they all seem to support. Try to restate the writer's main idea in your own words.

In an argument, the main idea (the generalization that the writer is trying to prove) is called the **claim,** or **opinion.**

> **Main idea of an essay:** Every person who tries to help others is a hero (for "Heroes with Solid Feet," page 721).
>
> **Claim of an argument:** The jury system is the best means we have for maintaining justice in a democracy (for "A Defense of the Jury System," page 310).

See page 358.

MAPS **A drawing showing all or part of the earth's surface or of bodies in the sky. Physical maps** illustrate the natural landscape of an area, using shading, lines, and color to show landforms and elevation. **Political maps** show political units, such as states and nations. They usually also show borders and capitals and other major cities. **Special-purpose maps** present specific information, such as the routes of the explorers. The special-purpose map on page 650 shows the route of Odysseus's journey. Use these guidelines to help you read the map on the next page.

How to Read a Map

1. **Determine the focus of the map.** The map's title and labels tell you its focus—its subject and the geographical area it covers.

2. **Study the legend.** The **legend,** or **key,** explains the symbols, lines, colors, and shadings used in the map.

3. **Check directions and distances.** Maps often include a **compass rose,** a diagram that shows north, south, east, and west. If there isn't one, assume that north is at the top, west to the left, and so on. Many maps also include a scale that relates distances on the map to actual distances.

4. **Look at the larger context.** The **absolute location** of any place on earth is given by its **latitude** (the number of degrees north or south of the equator) and its **longitude** (the number of degrees east or west of the **prime meridian,** or 0 degrees longitude). Some maps also include **locator maps,** which show the area depicted in relation to a larger area.

Handbook of Reading and Informational Terms

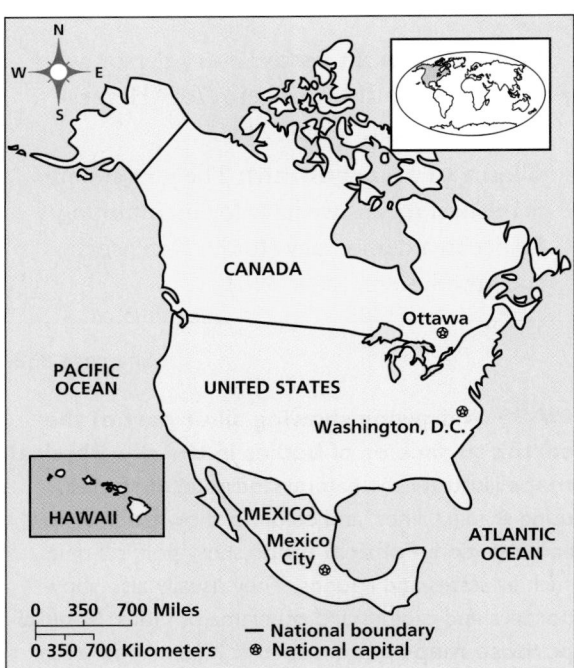

OPINION **A statement of a person's belief, idea, or attitude.** A **fact** is something that can be verified or proved by direct observation or by checking a reliable reference source. An **opinion** cannot be proved to be either true or false—even when it is supported by facts. The following statement is an unsupported opinion:

> William Shakespeare is the greatest writer that the world has ever known.

A **valid opinion** is an opinion that is supported by verifiable facts. In the following example, the verifiable facts are underlined:

> I think that William Shakespeare was a great writer because most of his plays and poems are still read and enjoyed today, four hundred years after they were written.

When you read a persuasive text, remember that statements of opinion can't be proved, but they can and should be supported by facts and logical reasoning.

See pages 261, 579.

ORDER OF IMPORTANCE **A means of organizing information by ranking details in the order of their importance.**

Writers of persuasive texts have to decide whether to give the strongest reason first or to present the weakest reason first and end with the strongest point. Informational texts such as news articles always begin with the most important details because they want to grab the readers' attention immediately. The structure of a news article looks like an upside-down triangle, with the least important details at the bottom.

See pages 386, 393.
See also *Text Structures.*

OUTLINING **A way of organizing information to show relationships among key details in a text.** You can use outlining as a writer and as a reader. Outlining puts main ideas and details in a form that you can review quickly. An **informal outline,** sometimes called a working outline, should have at least three main ideas. You put supporting details under each main idea, like this:

> **Informal Outline**
> I. First main idea
>   A. First detail supporting first main idea
>   B. Second detail supporting first main idea
>   C. Third detail supporting first main idea
> II. Second main idea
>   [etc.]

A **formal outline** is especially useful if you're writing a research paper. You might start with a working outline and then revise it into a formal one. Your teacher may ask you to submit a formal outline with your completed research paper.

Formal outlines use Roman numerals (I, II, III), capital letters (A, B, C) and Arabic numerals (1, 2, 3) to show order, relationship, and relative importance of ideas. The headings in a formal outline should have the same grammatical structure, and you must be consistent in your use of either phrases or sentences. (You can't move back and forth between them.) There should always be at least two divisions under each heading or none at all.

Here is the beginning of a formal outline of "Far-out Housekeeping on the ISS" (page 44):

Formal Outline

I. Setting up housekeeping routines
   A. Discussion with two astronauts about the excitement and routine of living in space
   B. Quotation from Lieutenant Commander Burbank
      1. Space as a hostile environment
      2. Dependence on the Station and on people on the ground
II. Everyday life in space
   A. Different kinds of food
   B. Communicating with home
   C. Recycling and trash

See pages 617–619.

PARAPHRASING Restating each sentence of a text in your own words. Paraphrasing is usually done only for difficult texts. Paraphrasing a text helps you to be certain you understand it. When you paraphrase, you follow the author's sequence of ideas. You carefully reword each line (if it's a poem) or sentence (if it's prose) without changing the author's ideas or leaving anything out. You restate each figure of speech to be sure you understand the basis of the comparison. If sentences are missing words or if the words are wrenched out of the usual order, you rephrase the sentence.

A paraphrase is longer than a **summary,** which is a brief statement of the main ideas in a text. Here are a paraphrase and a summary of a paragraph from "Address to Congress, November 27, 1963" (page 584).

Paraphrase: No speech could honor President Kennedy's memory more than

passing the civil rights bill as soon as possible. He fought to pass this bill and we have talked long enough about it—for more than a hundred years. Now it's time for the next chapter—making equal rights the law.

Summary: Passing the civil rights bill would be the best way to honor President Kennedy's memory.

See pages 374, 894.

PRIMARY SOURCE An original, firsthand account. Primary sources may include an autobiography; an eyewitness testimony; a letter, speech, or literary work; a historical document; or information gathered from firsthand surveys or interviews. For example, Albert Einstein's "Letter to President Roosevelt," (page 376), is a primary source. It's important to use primary sources wherever they are available on a topic, but you need to research widely to make sure that a primary source is not biased.

Be sure to keep track of your primary sources by numbering each source and recording the necessary publishing information. If you quote directly from the primary source, be sure to use quotation marks and to give credit to your source.

See page 578.
See also *Secondary Source.*

PUBLIC DOCUMENTS Informative texts put out by the government or public agencies. Public documents include political platforms, public policy statements, speeches, and debates. These documents inform the public about government policy, laws, municipal codes, records, schedules, and the like.

See pages 584, 947.

RESEARCH QUESTIONS Questions that are focused on a specific subject, which the researcher searches to answer. Such questions are essential tools for focusing your research.

One way to generate research questions is to use a KWL chart as a research guide. (See page 26

Handbook of Reading and Informational Terms

for an example.) This kind of chart is an easy way to organize questions and answers, especially if you know how to set up columns and rows on your computer. In the K column, you note what you already know about the subject. In the W column, you note what you'd like to find out. As you do your research, complete the L column by answering the questions you've asked in the W column.

Research questions can also be generated by brainstorming or by using the *5W-How* questions: *Who? What? When? Where? Why?* and *How?* As you seek primary and secondary source information at libraries and museums, in various electronic media (Internet, films, tapes), and from personal interviews, you will come up with more research questions. Always remember to keep your questions focused on the specific subject you have chosen.

See page 26.

ROOTS, PREFIXES, SUFFIXES

English words are often made up of two or more word parts. These words parts include

- **roots, which carry a word's core meaning**
- **prefixes, added onto the beginning of a word or in front of a word root to form a new word**
- **suffixes, added onto the end of a word or after a word root to form a new word**

Most word roots come from Greek and Latin. Prefixes and suffixes come from Greek, Latin, and Anglo-Saxon.

Greek Roots	Meaning	Examples
–dem– –hydr– –psyche- –syn–, –sym–	people water mind, soul together	de**mo**cracy, epi**dem**ic de**hydr**ate, **hydr**ogen **psych**ic, **psych**ology **syn**thesize, **sym**phony
Latin Roots	**Meaning**	**Examples**
–cog– –dic–, –dict– –juven– –mar– –somn–	think, know say, speak young war sleep	in**cog**nito, re**cog**nize **dict**ion, inter**dict** **juven**ile, re**juven**ate **mar**tial, **mar**tinet **somn**olent, **somn**ambulate
Greek Prefixes	**Meaning**	**Examples**
a– neo–	lacking, without new	**a**moral, **a**typical **neo**classic, **neo**natal
Latin Prefixes	**Meaning**	**Examples**
e–, ef–, ex– retro–	away, from, out back	**ef**face, **ex**punge **retro**active, **retro**spective
Anglo-Saxon/Old English Prefixes	**Meaning**	**Examples**
be– over– mis–	around above badly, not	**be**friend, **be**grime **over**bite, **over**see **mis**hap, **mis**copy

1042 Resource Center   Handbook of Reading and Informational Terms

Greek Suffixes	Meaning	Examples
–logue –ism	speech act, manner	dia**logue**, epi**logue** critic**ism**, ostrac**ism**

Latin Suffixes	Meaning	Examples
–esce –tude	become, grow quality of being	coal**esce**, efferv**esce** apti**tude**, multi**tude**

Anglo-Saxon/Old English Suffixes	Meaning	Examples
–less –ful –en	lacking, without full of, marked by become	aim**less**, rest**less** rest**ful**, wonder**ful** strength**en**, light**en**

SECONDARY SOURCE **A secondhand account written by a writer who did not participate directly in the events he or she interprets, relates, or analyzes.** Secondary sources may include encyclopedias, magazine articles, textbooks, biographies, and technical journals. The news feature "Dear Juliet" (page 919) is an example of a secondary source. A research paper may include both primary and secondary sources.

See page 578.

SPATIAL (spā′shəl) **ORDER** **A means of organizing information by showing where things are located.** (The word *spatial* is related to the word *space*. Spatial order shows where things are located in space.) Spatial order is often used in descriptive writing. Here is an example from "The Most Dangerous Game" (page 5). Phrases showing spatial order are underlined.

> The baying of the hounds drew nearer, then still nearer, nearer, ever nearer. On a ridge Rainsford climbed a tree. Down a watercourse, not a quarter of a mile away, he could see the bush moving.

See pages 386, 393.
See also *Text Structures*.

SYNTHESIZING **Putting all the different sources of information together in a process that gives you a better understanding of the whole subject.** In order to synthesize information, you first gather information about a topic from several sources. Then you find each writer's main ideas. Paraphrasing ideas, restating them in your own words, can help you understand difficult texts. Next you examine the ideas in each source, and you compare and contrast the ideas you've found. To synthesize what you have learned, you draw conclusions about the information you have gathered.

See page 231, 374.
See also *Generalization*.

TEXT STRUCTURES **Any organizational patterns that writers use to make their meaning clear.** In imaginative literature, text structures range from the plot structures in stories and dramas to the sonnet structure in poetry.

In nonfiction and informational texts, the writer's intent or purpose in creating the text determines how the text will be organized. Don't expect writers of informational texts and nonfiction to use the same structure throughout an entire text. Most writers switch from one type of structure to another and may even combine structures. The four basic ways of arranging ideas or details in nonfiction and informational texts are:

Handbook of Reading and Informational Terms (side tab)

1. **Chronological order, time order** or **sequence**—putting events or steps in the order in which they occur. For an example of chronological order, see "A Warm, Clear Day in Dallas" (page 580). Most narrative and historical texts are written in chronological order. Chronological order is also found in writing that explains a process such as technical directions and recipes. This type of chronological order is called **step-by-step order.**

2. **Spatial order**—the order that shows where things are located. This pattern is used in descriptive writing. It is especially useful in helping readers visualize setting. See the first paragraph of "Teaching Chess, and Life" (page 97).

3. **Order of importance**—ranking details from most important to least important or from least important to most important. Writers of persuasive texts in particular have to decide which order makes the strongest impact: putting the strongest reason first and the weaker ones later or saving the strongest reason for last. For an example of a text that uses order of importance, see "Peace Isn't Impossible" (page 240). News articles always begin with the most important details because they want to grab the readers' attention immediately.

4. **Logical order**—classifying details into related groups. One type of logical order is the **comparison and contrast** text structure, which shows similarities and differences among various groups. See a comparison of judges and juries in "A Defense of the Jury System" (page 310).

Other methods used to organize texts include:

- **cause and effect**—showing how events happen as a result of other events. See "Romeo and Juliet in Bosnia" (page 921).
- **problem-solution**—explaining how a problem may be solved. See "Far-out Housekeeping on the ISS" (page 44).
- **question-answer**—asking questions, then giving the answers. See "Can Animals Think?" (page 27).

Recognizing these structures will help you understand the ideas in a text. The following guidelines can help you recognize text structures:

1. Search the text for the main idea. Look for clue words (**transitions**) that signal a specific pattern of organization. Also note colors, special type, headers, numbered lists, and icons that may be used to highlight terms or indicate text structure.

2. Analyze the text for other important ideas. Think about how the ideas connect, and look for an obvious pattern.

3. Remember that a writer might use one organizational pattern throughout a text or combine two or more patterns.

4. Draw a graphic organizer that maps how the text is structured. Some common graphic organizers are a **causal chain** (for the cause-effect text structure), a **flowchart** (showing chronological sequence), and a **Venn diagram** (showing similarities and differences).

See pages 32, 961.
See also *Chronological Order, Logical Order, Order of Importance, Spatial Order.*

WORKPLACE DOCUMENTS Job-related texts, such as job applications, memos, instructional manuals, and employee handbooks. When you read workplace documents, keep these points in mind (in addition to the points about reading consumer documents, cited on pages 1034–1035):

1. Take all the time you need to read and understand the document. Don't let anyone rush you or tell you that a document is unimportant or just a formality.

2. Read technical directions carefully, even if they're just posted on the side of a device you're supposed to operate. Read all of the directions before you start. Ask questions if you're not sure how to proceed. Don't try anything out before you know what will happen next.

3. The employee handbook contains the "rules of the game" at that particular business. It tells you about holidays, work hours, break times, and vacations as well as other important company policies. Read the employee handbook from cover to cover.

See also *Consumer Documents.*

Language Handbook

▌ THE PARTS OF SPEECH

PART OF SPEECH	DEFINITION	EXAMPLES
NOUN	Names person, place, thing, or idea	captain, swimmers, Maria Tallchief, team, Stratford-on-Avon, stories, "The Scarlet Ibis," justice, honesty
PRONOUN	Takes place of one or more nouns or pronouns	
Personal	Refers to one(s) speaking (first person), spoken to (second person), spoken about (third person)	I, me, my, mine, we, us, our, ours you, your, yours he, him, his, she, her, hers, it, its, they, them, their, theirs
Reflexive	Refers to subject and directs action of verb back to subject	myself, ourselves, yourself, yourselves, himself, herself, itself, themselves
Intensive	Refers to and emphasizes noun or another pronoun	(See Reflexive.)
Demonstrative	Refers to specific one(s) of group	this, that, these, those
Interrogative	Introduces question	what, which, who, whom, whose
Relative	Introduces subordinate clause and refers to noun or pronoun outside clause	that, which, who, whom, whose
Indefinite	Refers to one(s) not specifically named	all, any, anyone, both, each, either, everybody, many, none, nothing
ADJECTIVE	Modifies noun or pronoun by telling *what kind, which one, how many,* or *how much*	**an old, flea-bitten** dog, **a Sioux** custom, **that** one, **the twelve red** roses, **more** water
VERB	Shows action or state of being	
Action	Expresses physical or mental activity	paint, jump, write, know, imagine
Linking	Connects subject with word identifying or describing it	appear, be, seem, become, feel, look, smell, sound, taste
Helping (Auxiliary)	Combines with another verb to form a verb phrase	be, have, may, can, shall, will, would
ADVERB	Modifies verb, adjective, or adverb by telling *how, when, where,* or *to what extent*	drives **carefully, quite** dangerous, **shortly afterward,** arrived **there late**
PREPOSITION	Relates noun or pronoun to another word	across, between, into, near, of, on, with, aside from, instead of, next to
CONJUNCTION	Joins words or word groups	
Coordinating	Joins words or word groups used in same way	and, but, for, nor, or, so, yet

(continued)

PART OF SPEECH		DEFINITION	EXAMPLES
	Correlative	A pair of conjunctions that join parallel words or word groups	both . . . and, either . . . or, neither . . . nor, not only . . . but (also)
	Subordinating	Begins subordinate clause and connects it to independent clause	as though, because, if, since, so that, than, when, where, while
INTERJECTION		Expresses emotion	hey, oops, ouch, wow

Determining Parts of Speech

The way a word is used in a sentence determines the word's part of speech.

EXAMPLES
The fine feathers of young birds are called **down.**
　[noun]
She wore a **down** vest. [adjective]
Did the tackle **down** the ball in the end zone?
　[verb]
Her poster fell **down.** [adverb]
My cousin lives **down** the street from my school.
　[preposition]

Let's get a drink of **water.** [noun]
Did you **water** the plants? [verb]
Most **water** sports offer good exercise. [adjective]

He promised us **that** he would meet us after the
　game. [conjunction]
That CD didn't cost much. [adjective]
I never said **that.** [pronoun]

Avoiding Overused Adverbs

The adverbs *really, too, so,* and *very* are often overused. To keep your writing lively, replace those inexact, overused words with more specific adverbs such as *completely, definitely, entirely, especially, extremely, generally, largely, mainly, mostly, particularly, rather,* and *unusually.*

Try It Out

For each of the following sentences, replace the italicized adverb with a more specific adverb.

1. Elie Wiesel's speech was *very* direct.
2. It *really* focused on personal responsibility.
3. People accept injustice *too* easily.
4. One person's actions can be *very* important.
5. The worst part was to be *so* forgotten.

Try It Out
Possible Answers

1. Elie Wiesel's speech was particularly direct.
2. It focused especially on personal responsibility.
3. People accept injustice rather easily.
4. One person's actions can be extremely important.
5. The worst part was to be completely forgotten.

Resources

Grammar and Language

- *Language Handbook Worksheets,* pp. 15–26

2 AGREEMENT

AGREEMENT OF SUBJECT AND VERB

2a. A verb should always agree with its subject in number. Singular subjects take singular verbs. Plural subjects take plural verbs.

SINGULAR	**She searches** for Mme. Forestier's necklace.
PLURAL	**They search** for Mme. Forestier's necklace.
SINGULAR	Miss Lottie's flower **garden was destroyed.**
PLURAL	Miss Lottie's **marigolds were destroyed.**

COMPUTER NOTE Some word-processing programs can identify problems in subject-verb agreement. If you have access to such a program, you can use it to help you search for errors when you are proofreading your writing. If you are not sure whether a problem identified by the word processor is truly an error, look it up in this section of the Language Handbook.

☞ For information about identifying subjects and verbs, see 8b–g.

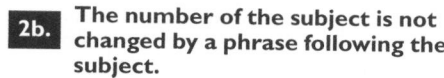

2b. The number of the subject is not changed by a phrase following the subject.

SINGULAR	The **sign** near the glass doors **explains** the theme of the exhibit.
PLURAL	Several **paintings** by Emilio Sánchez **were hanging** in the gallery.
SINGULAR	**Romeo,** together with Benvolio and Mercutio, **goes** to Lord Capulet's party.
PLURAL	The **combs** made of pure tortoise shell **were** expensive.

 For information about kinds of phrases, see 6a–g.

The number of the subject is not changed by a negative construction following the subject.

EXAMPLE
A **human being,** not a tiger nor any other animal, **becomes** the prey hunted by General Zaroff in "The Most Dangerous Game."

2c. The following indefinite pronouns are singular: *anybody, anyone, anything, each, either, everybody, everyone, everything, neither, nobody, no one, nothing, one, somebody, someone, something.*

EXAMPLES
Each of the poems about farm workers **was written** by Gary Soto.
Has anyone else in your study group **read** all of *The Miracle Worker?*

2d. The following indefinite pronouns are plural: *both, few, many, several.*

EXAMPLES
Both of the poems about the San Joaquin Valley **were written** by Gary Soto.
Have many in your study group **read** *The Miracle Worker?*

2e. The indefinite pronouns *all, any, most, none,* and *some* are singular when they refer to singular words and are plural when they refer to plural words.

SINGULAR	**Some** of the show **is** funny.
PLURAL	**Some** of the skits and other acts **are** funny.
SINGULAR	**All** of the house **looks** clean.
PLURAL	**All** of the houses **look** clean.

2f. A *compound subject,* which is two or more subjects that have the same verb, may be singular, plural, or either.

(1) Subjects joined by *and* usually take a plural verb.

EXAMPLE
Both **Leslie Marmon Silko** and **Mari Evans are** poets.

A compound subject that names only one person or thing takes a singular verb.

EXAMPLES
My **pen pal and best friend is** my cousin.
Macaroni and cheese makes a good side dish.

(2) Singular subjects joined by *or* or *nor* take a singular verb.

EXAMPLES
Either the **principal** or the **coach has** to approve it.
Neither **Della** nor **Jim was** disappointed.

(3) When a singular subject and a plural subject are joined by *or* or *nor,* the verb agrees with the subject nearer the verb.

EXAMPLES
Neither the losers nor the **winner was** happy with the outcome of the match.
Neither the winner nor the **losers were** happy with the outcome of the match.

NOTE If such a construction sounds awkward, revise the sentence to give each part of the subject its own verb.

EXAMPLE
The **losers were** not happy with the outcome of the match, and neither **was** the **winner.**

For more information about subjects, see 8b, c, e, and g.

2g. *Don't* and *doesn't* must agree with their subjects.

With the subjects *I* and *you* and with plural subjects, use *don't* (do not).

EXAMPLES
I **don't** know.
You **don't** seem happy.
Some people **don't** care.

With other subjects, use *doesn't* (does not).

EXAMPLES
He **doesn't** drive.
Donna **doesn't** work.
It **doesn't** have one.

Language Handbook **1047**

2h. A collective noun takes a singular verb when the noun refers to the group as a unit and takes a plural verb when the noun refers to the individual parts or members of the group.

A *collective noun* is singular in form but names a group of persons or things.

SINGULAR The class **has** elected its officers. [class = a unit]

PLURAL The class **have** completed their projects on *Romeo and Juliet*. [class = individual students]

Common Collective Nouns

army	club	group	public
assembly	committee	herd	squad
audience	couple	jury	staff
band	crew	majority	swarm
cast	crowd	number	team
chorus	family	pack	troop
class	flock	pair	wildlife

2i. A verb agrees with its subject, not with its predicate nominative.

SINGULAR The main **attraction is** the marching bands.

PLURAL The marching **bands are** the main attraction.

2j. A verb agrees with its subject even when the verb precedes the subject, as in sentences beginning with *here* or *there* and in questions.

SINGULAR Here **is** [*or* here's] my **drawing** of the Cyclops.

PLURAL Here **are** my **drawings** of the Cyclops.

SINGULAR When in the program **does** the **skater perform** her triple axel?

PLURAL When in the program **do** the **fans start** clapping to the music?

NOTE Contractions such as *here's*, *there's*, and *where's* should be used only with subjects that are singular in meaning.

2k. An expression of an amount (a length of time, a statistic, or a fraction, for example) is singular when the amount is thought of as a unit or when it refers to a singular word and is plural when the amount is thought of as many parts or when it refers to a plural word.

SINGULAR **Twenty dollars is** the amount Della receives for her hair. [Twenty dollars is the single amount Della receives.]

PLURAL **Twenty dollars were stuck** together. [Twenty individual dollars were stuck together.]

SINGULAR **Three fourths** of the barrel **is** full. [*Three fourths* refers to *barrel*, a singular word.]

PLURAL **Three fourths** of the barrels **have been** loaded. [*Three fourths* refers to *barrels*, a plural word.]

2l. The title of a creative work (such as a book, song, film, or painting) or the name of an organization, a country, or a city (even if it is plural in form) takes a singular verb.

EXAMPLES
"Marigolds" **is** a story by Eugenia W. Collier.
Friends of the Earth was founded in 1969.
The Netherlands has thousands of canals.

2m. A few nouns, although plural in form, take singular verbs.

EXAMPLE
The **news** of the nominee for the Supreme Court **was** a surprise to many observers.

Some nouns that end in –s take a plural verb even though they refer to a single item.

EXAMPLES
The **scissors need** to be sharpened.
Were these **pants** on sale?
The **pliers are** next to the wrench.

AGREEMENT OF PRONOUN AND ANTECEDENT

A pronoun usually refers to a noun or another pronoun. The word that a pronoun refers to is called its *antecedent*.

2n. A pronoun agrees with its antecedent in number and gender. Singular pronouns refer to singular antecedents. A few personal pronouns indicate gender: feminine, masculine, or neuter. Plural pronouns refer to plural antecedents. No plural pronouns indicate gender.

MASCULINE	he	him	his	himself
FEMININE	she	her	hers	herself
NEUTER	it	it	its	itself

EXAMPLES
Juliet stabs **herself.** [singular, feminine]
General Zaroff thinks that Rainsford has escaped **him.** [singular, masculine]
After eating the Lotus plant, the **men** did not want to return to **their** homeland. [plural]

2o. A singular pronoun is used to refer to *anybody, anyone, anything, each, either, everybody, everyone, everything, neither, nobody, no one, nothing, one, somebody, someone,* or *something.* The gender of any of these pronouns can sometimes be determined by a word in a phrase following the pronoun.

EXAMPLES
Each of the **boys** held some pebbles in **his** hand.
Everyone on the **girls'** tennis team won **her** match.

When the antecedent could be either masculine or feminine, use both the masculine and the feminine pronoun forms connected by *or.*

EXAMPLE
Everybody should choose **his or her** friends carefully.

Avoiding the *His or Her* Construction
When an antecedent could be either masculine or feminine, you can avoid the *his or her* construction by using plural nouns and pronouns. You can also change the possessive *his or her* to an article (*a, an, the*) or eliminate it altogether.

ORIGINAL
A person should choose his or her friends carefully.

REVISED
People should choose **their** friends carefully.
A person should choose **a** friend carefully.
People should choose friends carefully.

Try It Out
Revise each of the following sentences to eliminate the *his or her* construction.

1. Each person had to hide his or her talents.
2. Could anyone take off his or her handicap bag?
3. Everybody had to be equal to his or her neighbor.
4. Did Harrison or the dancer realize his or her fate?
5. Neither he nor she wore his or her handicaps.

2p. A singular pronoun is used to refer to two or more singular antecedents joined by *or* or *nor.*

EXAMPLES
Paula or Janet will present **her** interpretation of Denise Levertov's "The Secret."
Neither **Richard nor Bob** has read **his** report on Ray Bradbury.

If a sentence sounds awkward when the antecedents are of different genders, revise it.

AWKWARD Either Ben or Maya will read his or her report on O. Henry.
REVISED Either **Ben** will read **his** report on O. Henry, or **Maya** will read **hers.**

2q. A plural pronoun is used to refer to two or more antecedents joined by *and.*

EXAMPLES
Romeo and Juliet marry despite the feud between **their** families.
Doodle and his **brother** spent much time with each other; **they** became very close.

2r. The number of a relative pronoun (such as *who, whom, whose, which,* or *that*) depends on the number of its antecedent.

EXAMPLES
Aretha is one **friend who** always **keeps her** word. [*Who* refers to the singular noun *friend.* Therefore, the singular forms *keeps* and *her* are used to agree with *who.*]
Many who volunteer find **their** experiences rewarding. [*Who* refers to the plural pronoun *many.* Therefore, the plural forms *volunteer* and *their* are used to agree with *who.*]

☞ For more about relative pronouns in adjective clauses, see 7d.

Try It Out
Possible Answers
1. People had to hide their talents.
2. Could anyone take off the handicap bag?
3. Everybody had to be equal to everyone else.
4. Did Harrison and the dancer realize their fate?
5. Neither he nor she wore a handicap.

Language Handbook

3 USING VERBS

THE PRINCIPAL PARTS OF VERBS

3a. The four principal parts of a verb are the *base form*, the *present participle*, the *past*, and the *past participle*. These principal parts are used to form all the different verb tenses.

3b. A *regular verb* forms its past and past participle by adding *–d* or *–ed* to the base form.

3c. An *irregular verb* forms its past and past participle in some other way than by adding *–d* or *–ed* to the base form.

COMMON REGULAR VERBS

BASE FORM	PRESENT PARTICIPLE	PAST	PAST PARTICIPLE
ask	(is) asking	asked	(have) asked
attack	(is) attacking	attacked	(have) attacked
raise	(is) raising	raised	(have) raised
plan	(is) planning	planned	(have) planned
try	(is) trying	tried	(have) tried

COMMON IRREGULAR VERBS

BASE FORM	PRESENT PARTICIPLE	PAST	PAST PARTICIPLE
be	(is) being	was, were	(have) been
begin	(is) beginning	began	(have) begun
bring	(is) bringing	brought	(have) brought
burst	(is) bursting	burst	(have) burst
drink	(is) drinking	drank	(have) drunk
drive	(is) driving	drove	(have) driven
eat	(is) eating	ate	(have) eaten
fall	(is) falling	fell	(have) fallen
find	(is) finding	found	(have) found
freeze	(is) freezing	froze	(have) frozen
go	(is) going	went	(have) gone
keep	(is) keeping	kept	(have) kept
lay	(is) laying	laid	(have) laid
lead	(is) leading	led	(have) led
lie	(is) lying	lay	(have) lain
ride	(is) riding	rode	(have) ridden
rise	(is) rising	rose	(have) risen
set	(is) setting	set	(have) set
shake	(is) shaking	shook	(have) shaken
sing	(is) singing	sang	(have) sung
sit	(is) sitting	sat	(have) sat
steal	(is) stealing	stole	(have) stolen
swim	(is) swimming	swam	(have) swum
tear	(is) tearing	tore	(have) torn

NOTE The examples in the chart at the left include *is* and *have* in parentheses to show that helping verbs (forms of *be* and *have*) are used with the present participle and past participle forms.

TIPS FOR SPELLING Drop the final silent *e* in the base form of a verb when adding *–ing* and *–ed* to form the present participle and past participle.

PRESENT PARTICIPLES
share + –ing = shar**ing**
dive + –ing = div**ing**

PAST PARTICIPLES
raise + –ed = rais**ed**
receive + –ed = receiv**ed**

EXCEPTIONS
dye + –ing = dy**eing**
singe + –ing = sing**eing**

 For more about correct spelling when adding suffixes to words, see 15e–j.

NOTE If you are not sure about the principal parts of a verb, look in a dictionary. Entries for irregular verbs give the principal parts. If no principal parts are listed, the verb is a regular verb.

TENSE

3d. The *tense* of a verb indicates the time of the action or the state of being expressed by the verb. Verbs in English have six tenses: *present, past, future, present perfect, past perfect,* and *future perfect.* The tenses are formed from the verb's principal parts.

(1) The *present tense* is used mainly to express an action or a state of being that is occurring now.

EXAMPLES
The car **turns** into the driveway.
They **like** my idea for a science project.

The present tense is also used

- to show a customary or habitual action or state of being
- to express a general truth—something that is always true
- to make historical events seem current (such use is called the *historical present*)
- to discuss a literary work (such use is called the *literary present*)
- to express future time

EXAMPLES
Every November she **bakes** fruitcakes for her friends. [customary action]
The sun **sets** in the west. [general truth]
In 1905, Albert Einstein **proposes** his theory of relativity. [historical present]
Maya Angelou's *I Know Why the Caged Bird Sings* **tells** the story of her childhood. [literary present]
Finals **begin** next week. [future time]

(2) The *past tense* is used to express an action or a state of being that occurred in the past but that is not occurring now.

EXAMPLES
Jim **gave** Della a set of combs.
The children **annoyed** Miss Lottie.

A past action or state of being can also be shown with the verb *used* followed by an infinitive.

EXAMPLE
We **used to live** in Chicago.

(3) The *future tense* (formed with *will* or *shall* and the verb's base form) is used to express an action or a state of being that will occur.

EXAMPLES
I **shall play** the part of Romeo.
They **will arrive** soon.

A future action or state of being can also be shown in other ways.

EXAMPLES
They **are going to win.**
We **leave** for the theater **in an hour.**

(4) The *present perfect tense* (formed with *have* or *has* and the verb's past participle) is used to express an action or a state of being that occurred at some indefinite time in the past.

EXAMPLES
Doodle **has learned** how to walk.
We **have read** the *Odyssey.*

The present perfect tense is also used to express an action or a state of being that began in the past and continues into the present.

EXAMPLE
We **have lived** in the same house for nine years.

(5) The *past perfect tense* (formed with *had* and the verb's past participle) is used to express an action or a state of being that was completed in the past before some other past action or event.

EXAMPLES
Lizabeth regretted what she **had done.** [The doing occurred before the regretting.]
When you called, I **had** already **eaten** supper. [The eating occurred before the calling.]

(6) The *future perfect tense* (formed with *will have* or *shall have* and the verb's past participle) is used to express an action or a state of being that will be completed in the future before some other future occurrence.

EXAMPLES
By the time Mom returns, I **will have done** my chores. [The doing will be completed before the returning.]
He **will have finished** his Hebrew lessons before his bar mitzvah. [The finishing will be completed before the bar mitzvah.]

Each of the six verb tenses has an additional form called the *progressive form.* The progressive form expresses a continuing action or state of being. It consists of the appropriate tense of *be* plus the verb's present participle. For the perfect tenses, the progressive form also includes one or more helping verbs.

Present Progressive	am, are, is giving
Past Progressive	was, were giving
Future Progressive	will (shall) be giving
Present Perfect Progressive	has, have been giving
Past Perfect Progressive	had been giving
Future Perfect Progressive	will (shall) have been giving

Try It Out
Possible Answers

1. Before he went away, they had spent much time together.
2. When they have gathered enough nuts, they go shopping.
3. By the time the moon rises tonight, they will have finished.
4. C
5. He was grateful for all they had shared during the past year.

3e. Do not change needlessly from one tense to another.

INCONSISTENT Jim sold his watch and buys Della a set of combs. [change from past to present tense]

CONSISTENT Jim **sold** his watch and **bought** Della a set of combs. [past tense]

 **Using Appropriate Verb Tenses**

Using different verb tenses is often necessary to show the order of events that occur at different times.

NONSTANDARD I regretted that I chose such a broad topic.

STANDARD I **regretted** that I **had chosen** such a broad topic. [Since the action of choosing was completed before the action of regretting, the verb should be *had chosen*, not *chose*.]

Try It Out

For each of the following sentences, change the verb tenses to show the order of events that occur at different times. If a sentence is correct, write *C*.

1. Before he went away, they spent much time together.
2. When they gathered enough nuts, they go shopping.
3. By the time the moon rises tonight, they will finish.
4. She told ghost stories and was superstitious.
5. He was grateful for all they shared during the past year.

ACTIVE AND PASSIVE VOICE

3f. A verb in the *active voice* expresses an action done by its subject. A verb in the *passive voice* expresses an action received by its subject.

A verb in the passive voice is always a verb phrase that includes a form of *be* and the main verb's past participle.

ACTIVE VOICE Rainsford **surprised** General Zaroff. [The subject, *Rainsford*, performs the action.]

PASSIVE VOICE General Zaroff **was surprised** by Rainsford. [The subject, *General Zaroff*, receives the action.]

ACTIVE VOICE William Gibson **wrote** *The Miracle Worker.*

PASSIVE VOICE *The Miracle Worker* **was written** by William Gibson.

3g. Use the passive voice sparingly.

The passive voice is not any less correct than the active voice, but it is less direct, less forceful, and less concise. As a result, a sentence written in the passive voice can often be wordy and can sound awkward or weak.

AWKWARD PASSIVE Mme. Forestier's necklace was borrowed by Mme. Loisel.

ACTIVE Mme. Loisel **borrowed** Mme. Forestier's necklace.

The passive voice is useful, however, in certain situations:

1. when you do not know the performer of the action

EXAMPLE
The Globe Theater **was built** in 1599.

2. when you do not want to reveal the performer of the action

EXAMPLE
Unfounded accusations **were made** against the candidate.

3. when you want to emphasize the receiver of the action

EXAMPLE
Abraham Lincoln **was elected** president of the United States in 1860.

COMPUTER NOTE
Some software programs can identify and highlight passive-voice verbs. If you use such a program, keep in mind that it can't tell why you used the passive voice. If you did so for one of the reasons listed under 3g above, you may want to leave the verb in the passive voice.

4 USING PRONOUNS

Resources

Grammar and Language

■ *Language Handbook Worksheets,* pp. 42–52

CASE

Case is the form that a noun or pronoun takes to indicate its use in a sentence. In English, there are three cases: *nominative, objective,* and *possessive.* Most personal pronouns have a different form for each case.

NOTE The form of a noun is the same for both the nominative and the objective case. For the possessive case, however, a noun changes its form, usually by adding an apostrophe and an *s* to singular nouns and only an apostrophe to plural nouns.

NOMINATIVE   The **sniper** fired his rifle.
OBJECTIVE   Someone shot the **sniper.**
POSSESSIVE   Who was the **sniper's** enemy?

The Nominative Case

4a. **A subject of a verb is in the nominative case.**

EXAMPLES
She was glad that **they** were elected. [*She* is the subject of *was; they* is the subject of *were elected.*]
Is **Della** or **he** disappointed? [*Della* and *he* are the compound subject of *is.*]

4b. **A predicate nominative is in the nominative case.**

A *predicate nominative* follows a linking verb and explains or identifies the subject of the verb.

EXAMPLES
The woman who borrows the necklace is **she.** [*She* follows *is* and identifies the subject *woman.*]
The main characters are **he** and his **brother** Doodle. [*He* and *brother* follow *are* and identify the subject *characters.*]

NOTE Expressions such as *It's me, That's him,* and *Could it be her?* are informal usage. Avoid such expressions in formal speaking and writing.

The Objective Case

4c. **A direct object of a verb is in the objective case.**

A *direct object* follows an action verb and tells *whom* or *what.*

EXAMPLES
Lizabeth destroyed **them.** [*Them* tells *what* Lizabeth destroyed.]
Friar Laurence helps **her** and **him.** [*Her* and *him* tell *whom* Friar Laurence helps.]

PERSONAL PRONOUNS			
SINGULAR			
	NOMINATIVE	OBJECTIVE	POSSESSIVE
FIRST PERSON	I	me	my, mine
SECOND PERSON	you	you	your, yours
THIRD PERSON	he, she, it	him, her, it	his, her, hers, its
PLURAL			
	NOMINATIVE	OBJECTIVE	POSSESSIVE
FIRST PERSON	we	us	our, ours
SECOND PERSON	you	you	your, yours
THIRD PERSON	they	them	their, theirs

NOTE Notice in the chart at the left that *you* and *it* are the only personal pronouns that have the same form in both the nominative case and the objective case.

For more information on possessive personal pronouns, see 14c.

Try It Out

Possible Answers

1. The girl whom they admired was reading.

2. Do you know boys like the ones of whom he speaks?

3. They talked about the woman whom each of them would marry.

4. The field of carpentry appealed to the boy for whom that kind of work was easy.

5. The other boy of whom Gary Soto wrote said that he would go to school.

4d. An indirect object of a verb is in the objective case.

An *indirect object* comes before a direct object and tells *to whom* or *to what* or *for whom* or *for what*.

EXAMPLES
Buddy gave **her** a kite. [*Her* tells *to whom* Buddy gave a kite.]
Molly made **him** and **me** a tape. [*Him* and *me* tell *for whom* Molly made a tape.]

4e. An object of a preposition is in the objective case.

An *object of a preposition* comes at the end of a phrase that begins with a preposition.

EXAMPLES
Mme. Loisel borrows a necklace from **her.**
This gift is for **him** and **her.**

SPECIAL PRONOUN PROBLEMS

4f. The pronoun *who* (*whoever*) is in the nominative case. The pronoun *whom* (*whomever*) is in the objective case.
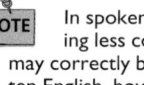

NOMINATIVE | **Who** wrote *Black Boy*? [*Who* is the subject of *wrote*.]
OBJECTIVE | From **whom** did Mme. Loisel borrow the necklace? [*Whom* is the object of the preposition *from*.]

When choosing between *who* and *whom* in a subordinate clause, be sure to base your choice on how the pronoun functions in the subordinate clause.

EXAMPLES
The sniper learned **who** his enemy had been. [*Who* is the predicate nominative identifying the subject *enemy*.]
The sniper learned the identity of the man **whom** he had shot. [*Whom* is the direct object of *had shot*.]

NOTE In spoken English, the use of *whom* is becoming less common. In fact, when speaking, you may correctly begin any question with *who*. In written English, however, you should distinguish between *who* and *whom*.

INFORMAL | **Who** did you see at the mall?
FORMAL | **Whom** did you see at the mall?

INFORMAL | **Who** did you go skating with?
FORMAL | With **whom** did you go skating?

Using *Whom* in Formal Situations
Frequently, *whom* is left out of subordinate clauses.

EXAMPLE
The person [**whom**] I have always admired most is Dr. Margaret Mead. [*Whom* is understood to be the direct object of *admired*.]

Leaving out *whom* in such cases tends to make writing sound more informal. In formal situations, it is generally better to include *whom*.

Try It Out
For each of the following sentences, insert *whom* where appropriate. Make any other changes needed for the sentence to sound correct in a formal situation.

1. The girl they admired was reading.
2. Do you know boys like the ones he speaks of?
3. They talked about the woman each of them would marry.
4. The field of carpentry appealed to the boy that kind of work was easy for.
5. The other boy Gary Soto wrote of said that he would go to school.

4g. An appositive is in the same case as the noun or pronoun to which it refers.
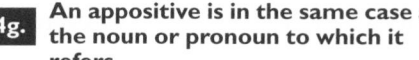

An *appositive* is a noun or pronoun placed next to another noun or pronoun to identify or explain it.

EXAMPLES
In the story, the main characters, **Doodle and he,** are brothers. [The appositive, *Doodle and he,* is in the nominative case because it identifies the subject, *characters*.]
Miss Lottie did not say a word to either of the children, **Lizabeth or him.** [The appositive, *Lizabeth or him,* is in the objective case because it identifies an object of a preposition, *children*.]

Sometimes the pronouns *we* and *us* are used with noun appositives.

EXAMPLES
We cast members have a dress rehearsal tonight. [The pronoun *we* is in the nominative case because it is the subject of *have*.]
The principal praised **us** members of the Ecology Club. [The pronoun *us* is in the objective case because it is the direct object of *praised*.]

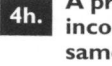 **4h.** A pronoun following *than* or *as* in an incomplete construction is in the same case as it would be if the construction were completed.

Notice how the meaning of each of the following sentences is determined by the pronoun form in the incomplete construction.

EXAMPLES

I wrote you more often than **he** [wrote you].
I wrote you more often than [I wrote] **him.**

Did you help Ada as much as **I** [helped Ada]?
Did you help Ada as much as [you helped] **me**?

Clear Pronoun Reference

 4i. A pronoun should refer clearly to its antecedent.

An **antecedent** is the word a pronoun stands for.

(1) Avoid an **ambiguous reference,** which occurs when a pronoun can refer to any one of two or more antecedents.

AMBIGUOUS	Miss Lottie saw Lizabeth when she was in the garden. [*She* can refer to either Miss Lottie or Lizabeth.]
CLEAR	When **Miss Lottie** was in the garden, **she** saw Lizabeth.
CLEAR	When **Lizabeth** was in the garden, Miss Lottie saw **her.**

(2) Avoid a **general reference,** which occurs when a pronoun refers to a general idea rather than to a specific antecedent.

GENERAL	Rainsford had escaped. This annoyed General Zaroff. [*This* has no specific antecedent.]
CLEAR	That Rainsford had escaped annoyed General Zaroff.

(3) Avoid a **weak reference,** which occurs when a pronoun refers to an implied antecedent.

WEAK	Ralph enjoys writing poetry, but he never shows them to anyone else. [*Them* most likely refers to the unstated plural noun *poems,* but the writer has used the singular noun *poetry* instead.]
CLEAR	Ralph enjoys writing poetry, but he never shows his poems to anyone else.

(4) Avoid using an **indefinite reference,** which occurs when a pronoun (such as *you, it,* or *they*) refers to no particular person or thing.

INDEFINITE	In the owner's manual, they explain how to program the VCR. [*They* has no antecedent.]
CLEAR	The owner's manual explains how to program the VCR.

 NOTE The indefinite use of *it* is acceptable in familiar expressions such as *It is snowing, It seems as though . . . ,* and *It's late.*

5 USING MODIFIERS

WHAT IS A MODIFIER?

A **modifier** is a word or group of words that limits the meaning of another word or group of words. The two kinds of modifiers are *adjectives* and *adverbs*. An **adjective** limits the meaning of a noun or a pronoun. An **adverb** limits the meaning of a verb, an adjective, or another adverb.

Adjective or Adverb?

Although many adverbs end in *–ly,* many others do not. Furthermore, not all words with the *–ly* ending are adverbs. Some adjectives also end in *–ly.* Therefore, you can't tell whether a word is an adjective or adverb simply by looking for the *–ly* ending.

ADVERBS NOT ENDING IN *–LY*	arrive **soon** **not** angry walk **home**	sit **here** run **loose** **very** hot
ADJECTIVES ENDING IN *–LY*	**daily** diet **curly** hair	**holy** place **silly** joke

In addition, some words can be used as either adjectives or adverbs.

ADJECTIVES	ADVERBS
He is an **only** child.	She has **only** one sister.
I have an **early** class.	I get up **early.**
Tina has a **fast** bicycle.	The baby is **fast** asleep.
We caught the **last** bus.	We left **last.**

Resources

Grammar and Language

■ *Language Handbook Worksheets,* pp. 53–62

COMPARISON OF MODIFIERS

5a. The forms of modifiers change to show comparison.

The three degrees of comparison are *positive, comparative,* and *superlative.*

Regular Comparison

(1) Most one-syllable modifiers form the comparative and superlative degrees by adding *–er* and *–est.*

POSITIVE	COMPARATIVE	SUPERLATIVE
deep	deeper	deepest
gentle	gentler	gentlest
careful	more careful	most careful
slowly	more slowly	most slowly
significantly	more significantly	most significantly
fresh	less fresh	least fresh
common	less common	least common

Irregular Comparison

(5) Some modifiers form the comparative and superlative degrees in other ways.

POSITIVE	COMPARATIVE	SUPERLATIVE
bad	worse	worst
good/well	better	best
little	less	least
many/much	more	most

Use of Comparative and Superlative Forms

5b. Use the comparative degree when comparing two things. Use the superlative degree when comparing more than two.

COMPARATIVE   Rainsford was **more resourceful** than Zaroff had expected him to be.

SUPERLATIVE   "The Most Dangerous Game" is one of the **most suspenseful** stories I have ever read.

(2) Some two-syllable modifiers form the comparative and superlative degrees by adding *–er* and *–est.* Other two-syllable modifiers form the comparative and superlative degrees by using *more* and *most.*

(3) Modifiers of more than two syllables form the comparative and superlative degrees by using *more* and *most.*

(4) All modifiers, no matter how many syllables they have, show decreasing degrees of comparison by using *less* and *least.*

Drop the final silent e before adding *–er* or *–est.*

EXAMPLES
strange + –er = strang**er**
noble + –est = nobl**est**

☞ For more information about correct spelling when adding suffixes to words, see 15e–j.

NOTE Do not add *–er, –est, more,* or *most* to irregular comparative and superlative forms. Use *worse,* not *worser* or *more worse,* and *best,* not *bestest.*

☞ For information about using *good* and *well,* see Part 16: Glossary of Usage; for information about using *bad* and *badly,* see Part 16: Glossary of Usage.

5c. Include the word *other* or *else* when comparing one thing with others in the same group.

ILLOGICAL   Ruth is more agile than any member of her gymnastics team. [Ruth is a member of her team. Logically, she cannot be more agile than herself.]

LOGICAL   Ruth is more agile than any **other** member of her gymnastics team.

ILLOGICAL   Carlos ran faster than everyone. [*Everyone* includes Carlos. Logically, he cannot run faster than himself.]

LOGICAL   Carlos ran faster than everyone **else.**

5d. Avoid a *double comparison*—the use of both *–er* and *more* (or *less*) or both *–est* and *most* (or *least*) to modify the same word.

EXAMPLES

William Sydney Porter, **better** [*not* more better] known as O. Henry, wrote "The Gift of the Magi."

This is the **cheapest** [*not* most cheapest] bicycle in the store.

5e. Avoid comparing items that cannot logically be compared.

ILLOGICAL	The average temperature in Dallas is higher than Spokane. [illogical comparison between a temperature and a city]
LOGICAL	The average temperature in Dallas is higher than **the average temperature in** Spokane.
ILLOGICAL	A coral snake's venom is more dangerous than a rattlesnake. [illogical comparison between a snake's venom and a snake]
LOGICAL	A coral snake's venom is more dangerous than a **rattlesnake's** [*or* **rattlesnake's venom**].

State both parts of an incomplete comparison if there is any chance of misunderstanding.

UNCLEAR	I visited her more than Elise.
CLEAR	I visited her more than **I visited** Elise.
CLEAR	I visited her more than Elise **visited her.**

PLACEMENT OF MODIFIERS

5f. Avoid using a *dangling modifier*—a modifying word or word group that does not sensibly modify any word or word group in the same sentence.

DANGLING	Working together, our goal can be attained within a few months.
CLEAR	Working together, we can attain our goal within a few months.
CLEAR	We can attain our goal within a few months by working together.

You may correct a dangling modifier

- by adding a word or words that the dangling modifier can sensibly modify
- by adding a word or words to the dangling modifier
- by rewording the sentence

DANGLING	Peering over the parapet, an armored car was seen. [Who or what was peering over the parapet?]
CLEAR	Peering over the parapet, the **sniper** saw an armored car.
DANGLING	To understand Denise Levertov's poetry, some knowledge of figurative language is necessary. [Who needs to know figurative language?]
CLEAR	To understand Denise Levertov's poetry, the **reader** needs some knowledge of figurative language.
DANGLING	While burying the scarlet ibis, a hymn is sung. [Who or what is burying the scarlet ibis?]
CLEAR	While burying the scarlet ibis, **Doodle** sings a hymn.

 NOTE A sentence may appear to have a dangling modifier when *you* is the understood subject. In such cases, the modifier is not dangling; it modifies the understood subject.

EXAMPLE

To find the correct spelling, [**you**] look up the word in a dictionary.

 For more information about understood subjects, see 8g.

5g. Avoid using a *misplaced modifier*—a modifying word or word group that sounds awkward or unclear because it seems to modify the wrong word or word group.

To correct a misplaced modifier, place the modifier as near as possible to the word or word group you intend it to modify.

MISPLACED	Doodle reveals to his family that he has learned to walk on his sixth birthday. [Does Doodle reveal or does he learn on his sixth birthday?]
CLEAR	**On his sixth birthday,** Doodle reveals to his family that he has learned to walk.
MISPLACED	Born eight weeks ago, we adopted one of the puppies. [Were we or the puppies born eight weeks ago?]
CLEAR	We adopted one of the puppies **born eight weeks ago.**

For more information on phrase and clause modifiers, see 6a–g and 7a–f.

Language Handbook

6 PHRASES

6a. A *phrase* is a group of related words that is used as a single part of speech and that does not contain both a verb and its subject.

EXAMPLES

has been sitting [verb phrase; no subject]
about you and me [prepositional phrase; no subject or verb]

 If a group of words has both a subject and a verb, it is called a clause. For more information about clauses, see 7a–f.

PREPOSITIONAL PHRASES

6b. A *prepositional phrase* begins with a preposition and ends with a noun or pronoun that is called the *object of the preposition*. A prepositional phrase may also contain modifiers of the object of the preposition.

EXAMPLES

The sniper ran **across the street.** [The noun *street* is the object of the preposition *across.*]
In front of him was Fortunato. [The pronoun *him* is the object of the compound preposition *in front of.*]
Kyoko called **to Nancy and me.** [Both *Nancy* and *me* are objects of the preposition *to.*]

(1) A prepositional phrase that modifies a noun or pronoun is called an *adjective phrase.*

An adjective phrase tells *what kind* or *which one.*

EXAMPLES

Lizabeth destroyed Miss Lottie's garden **of marigolds.** [*Of marigolds* modifies the noun *garden,* telling *what kind.*]
All **of them** watched Doodle bury the scarlet ibis. [*Of them* modifies the pronoun *all,* telling *which ones.*]

An adjective phrase usually follows the word it modifies. That word may be the object of another preposition.

EXAMPLE

"Poison" is the title **of a story by Roald Dahl.** [*Of a story* modifies the noun *title. By Roald Dahl* modifies the noun *story,* the object of the preposition *of.*]

More than one adjective phrase may modify the same noun or pronoun.

EXAMPLE

The bottle **of vitamins on the shelf** is almost empty. [*Of vitamins* and *on the shelf* modify the noun *bottle.*]

(2) A prepositional phrase that modifies a verb, an adjective, or an adverb is called an *adverb phrase.*

An adverb phrase tells *when, where, how, why,* or *to what extent.*

EXAMPLES

By his sixth birthday Doodle could walk. [*By his sixth birthday* modifies *could walk,* telling *when.*]
Had a snake crawled **under the sheet**? [*Under the sheet* modifies *had crawled,* telling *where.*]
She answered **with a smile.** [*With a smile* modifies *answered,* telling *how.*]
Everyone remained quiet **because of the snake.** [*Because of the snake* modifies *quiet,* telling *why.*]
Is the water warm enough **for swimming**? [*For swimming* modifies *enough,* telling *to what extent.*]

An adverb phrase may come either before or after the word or word group it modifies.

EXAMPLES

For Christmas, Buddy gave her a kite.
Buddy gave her a kite **for Christmas.**

More than one adverb phrase may modify the same word or group of words.

EXAMPLE

In November she and Buddy bake fruitcakes **for their friends.** [*In November* tells *when* they bake the fruitcakes, and *for their friends* tells *why* they bake them.]

 For more information about placement of modifying phrases, see 5f, g.

VERBALS AND VERBAL PHRASES

A *verbal* is a form of a verb used as a noun, an adjective, or an adverb. A *verbal phrase* consists of a verbal and its modifiers and complements. The three kinds of verbals are *participles, gerunds,* and *infinitives.*

Participles and Participial Phrases

 6c. A *participle* is a verb form that can be used as an adjective. A *participial phrase* consists of a participle and all the words related to the participle.

(1) *Present participles* end in *–ing.*

EXAMPLES
Doodle collapsed in the **pouring** rain. [The present participle *pouring* modifies the noun *rain.*]

Lying quietly in his bed, Harry told Timber about the snake. [The participial phrase *lying quietly in his bed* modifies the noun *Harry.* Both the adverb *quietly* and the adverb phrase *in his bed* modify the present participle *lying.*]

(2) Most *past participles* end in *–d* or *–ed.* Others are irregularly formed.

EXAMPLES
Lizabeth sat in the **ruined** garden and cried. [The past participle *ruined* modifies the noun *garden.*]
The speaker, **known for her strong support of recycling,** was loudly applauded. [The participial phrase *known for her strong support of recycling* modifies the noun *speaker.* The adverb phrase *for her strong support* modifies the past participle *known.* The adjective phrase *of recycling* modifies *support.*]

Do not confuse a participle used as an adjective with a participle used as part of a verb phrase.

ADJECTIVE	Fortunato, **struggling** to free himself, begged Montresor to unchain him.
VERB PHRASE	Fortunato, who **was struggling** to free himself, begged Montresor to unchain him.

 For more information about participles, see 3a–c. For more about the placement of participial phrases, see 5f, g.

Gerunds and Gerund Phrases

 6d. A *gerund* is a verb form ending in *–ing* that is used as a noun. A *gerund phrase* consists of a gerund and all the words related to the gerund.

EXAMPLES
Violently destroying the marigolds was Lizabeth's last act of childhood. [The gerund phrase is the subject of *was.* The adverb *violently* modifies the gerund *destroying,* and *marigolds* is the direct object of *destroying.*]

They enjoy **making fruitcakes together.** [The gerund phrase is the direct object of *enjoy. Fruitcakes* is the direct object of the gerund *making,* and the adverb *together* modifies *making.*]

His job is **giving the customers their menus.** [The gerund phrase is the predicate nominative explaining the subject *job. Customers* is the indirect object and *menus* is the direct object of the gerund *giving.*]

Rainsford escaped from Zaroff by **leaping into the sea.** [The gerund phrase is the object of the preposition *by.* The adverb phrase *into the sea* modifies the gerund *leaping.*]

Do not confuse a gerund with a present participle used as an adjective or as part of a verb phrase.

EXAMPLE
Following the basketball coach's advice, she was **planning** to go on with her **training.** [*Following* is a present participle modifying *she. Planning* is part of the verb phrase *was planning. Training* is a gerund used as the object of the preposition *with.*]

 NOTE When preceding a gerund, a noun or pronoun should be in the possessive form.

EXAMPLES
Pedro's constant practicing improved **his** playing.

Infinitives and Infinitive Phrases

 6e. An *infinitive* is a verb form, usually preceded by *to,* that can be used as a noun, an adjective, or an adverb. An *infinitive phrase* consists of an infinitive and all the words related to the infinitive.

NOUN **To proofread your writing carefully** is important. [The infinitive phrase is the subject of *is. Writing* is the direct object of the infinitive, *to proofread,* and the adverb *carefully* modifies *to proofread.*]
Why did she finally decide **to buy that video?** [The infinitive phrase is the direct object of *decide. Video* is the direct object of the infinitive *to buy.*]
Zaroff's plan was **to hunt Rainsford.** [The infinitive phrase is the predicate nominative identifying the subject *plan. Rainsford* is the direct object of the infinitive *to hunt.*]

ADJECTIVE Friar Laurence's plan **to help Romeo and Juliet** failed. [The infinitive phrase modifies the noun *plan*. *Romeo* and *Juliet* are the direct objects of the infinitive *to help*.]

ADVERB Fortunato was eager **to taste the amontillado.** [The infinitive phrase modifies the adjective *eager*. *Amontillado* is the direct object of the infinitive *to taste*.]

Sometimes the *to* of the infinitive is omitted.

EXAMPLE
You should go [to] get a warmer jacket.

 NOTE Do not confuse an infinitive with a prepositional phrase that begins with *to*.

EXAMPLE
Doodle and he went **to the creek** [prepositional phrase] **to swim.** [infinitive]

6f. An infinitive may have a subject, in which case it forms an *infinitive clause*.

EXAMPLE
Juliet trusted Friar Laurence and asked **him to help her.** [The infinitive clause is the direct object of *asked*. *Him* is the subject of the infinitive *to help*. *Her* is the direct object of *to help*.]

Notice in the example that a pronoun functioning as the subject of an infinitive clause takes the objective form.

Using Verbals and Verbal Phrases
You can use verbals and verbal phrases to clarify relationships between ideas and to make your writing more interesting and concise.

ORIGINAL Coyotes barked near the river. Momaday heard them at dusk.
REVISED Momaday heard coyotes **barking near the river at dusk.** [present participial phrase]

Try It Out ✎
Combine each of the following pairs of sentences by using the predicate of one sentence to form a verbal or verbal phrase that can be placed in the other sentence. Revise your sentence as needed to make it clear and concise.

1. N. Scott Momaday often rode his horse. For him, this activity was "an exercise of the mind."

2. He rode his horse, Pecos, over the hills of New Mexico. Along the way, he imagined that he was traveling with Billy the Kid.
3. Sometimes he and Billy saved a wagon train in trouble. Such a rescue was one of Momaday's favorite adventures.
4. Pecos could outrun the other horses in Jemez. Momaday was proud of his horse's ability.
5. Scents of pine and cedar smoke filled the air. A fresh, cold wind carried them from the canyon.

APPOSITIVES AND APPOSITIVE PHRASES

6g. An *appositive* is a noun or a pronoun placed beside another noun or pronoun to identify it or explain it. An *appositive phrase* consists of an appositive and its modifiers.

EXAMPLES
Kurt Vonnegut wrote the story **"Harrison Bergeron."** [The appositive *"Harrison Bergeron"* identifies the noun *story*.]
In the movie, Anne Bancroft played the role of Annie Sullivan, **Helen's teacher.** [The appositive phrase *Helen's teacher* explains the noun *Annie Sullivan*.]
Odysseus blinded Cyclops, **the one-eyed giant.** [The appositive phrase *the one-eyed giant* explains the noun *Cyclops*.]

An appositive phrase usually follows the noun or pronoun it refers to. For emphasis, however, it may come at the beginning of a sentence.

EXAMPLE
A noble leader of his people, Chief Joseph spoke with quiet dignity.

Appositives and appositive phrases are usually set off by commas. However, if the appositive is closely related to the preceding noun or pronoun, it should not be set off by commas.

EXAMPLES
My brother **Richard** goes to college. [The writer has more than one brother, and the appositive identifies which brother goes to college. Because this information is essential to the meaning of the sentence, it is not set off by commas.]
My brother, **Richard,** goes to college. [The writer has only one brother; therefore, the appositive is not necessary to identify him. Because the information is nonessential, it is set off by commas.]

Try It Out
Possible Answers

1. For N. Scott Momaday, riding his horse was "an exercise of the mind."

2. Riding his horse, Pecos, over the hills of New Mexico, he often imagined that he was traveling with Billy the Kid.

3. Saving a wagon train with Billy was one of Momaday's favorite adventures.

4. Momaday was proud of Pecos's ability to outrun the other horses in Jemez.

5. Scents of pine and cedar smoke, carried from the canyon by a fresh, cold wind, filled the air.

7 CLAUSES

 7a. A *clause* is a group of words that contains a verb and its subject and that is used as part of a sentence.

KINDS OF CLAUSES

 7b. An *independent* (or *main*) *clause* expresses a complete thought and can stand by itself as a sentence.

EXAMPLES

Della gives Jim a watch chain, and **Jim gives Della a set of combs.**

When I wrote my report on William Shakespeare, **I quoted from *Romeo and Juliet, Hamlet,* and *Macbeth.***

7c. A *subordinate* (or *dependent*) *clause* does not express a complete thought and cannot stand alone.

SUBORDINATE CLAUSES

whom you know
because I told him the truth
what the show is about

SENTENCES

Will the player **whom you know** autograph our baseball gloves?

Because I told him the truth, Dad wasn't too angry about the broken window.

Stephanie wants to know **what the show is about.**

 7d. An *adjective clause* is a subordinate clause that modifies a noun or pronoun.

An adjective clause, which always follows the word it modifies, usually begins with a ***relative pronoun,*** such as *who, whom, whose, which,* or *that.* Besides introducing an adjective clause, a relative pronoun has its own function within the clause.

EXAMPLES

In "The Gift of the Magi," Della and Jim, **who are deeply in love,** make sacrifices to buy gifts for each other. [The adjective clause modifies *Della* and *Jim. Who* is the subject of *are.*]

Not all the stories **that Edgar Allan Poe wrote** deal with horror or terror. [The adjective clause modifies *stories. That* is the direct object of *wrote.*]

I read about Sequoyah, **whose invention of a written language aided other Cherokees.** [The adjective clause modifies *Sequoyah. Whose* modifies *invention.*]

A relative pronoun is sometimes left out of an adjective clause.

EXAMPLES

Was *The Miracle Worker* the first play [that] **William Gibson wrote?**

The mechanic [whom] **you recommended** fixed my stepfather's motorcycle.

Occasionally, an adjective clause begins with the ***relative adverb*** *where* or *when.*

EXAMPLES

We visited the town **where Shakespeare was born.**

Summer is the season **when I feel happiest.**

 **Revising for Sentence Variety**

Although short sentences can be effective, it's a good idea to alternate between shorter sentences and longer ones. To change choppy sentences into smoother writing, revise them into adjective clauses that express the same ideas.

CHOPPY Mary Cassatt was an American painter. I enjoy her works. She was an Impressionist.

SMOOTH I enjoy the works of Mary Cassatt, who was an American Impressionist painter.

Try It Out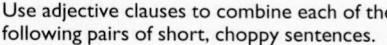

Use adjective clauses to combine each of the following pairs of short, choppy sentences.

1. Many people do not have homes. They wander the cities.
2. Ann appears in this article. She is one of these homeless people.
3. At one time, Ann had lived in a house. It had yellow siding.
4. Now she has only a coat. The coat is dirty and creased.
5. People like Ann need help, not labels. Their lives are hard.

Language Handbook 1061

Try It Out

Possible Answers

1. Many people who do not have homes wander the cities.

2. Ann, who appears in this article, is one of these homeless people.

3. At one time, Ann had lived in a house that had yellow siding.

4. Now she has only a coat that is dirty and creased.

5. People like Ann, whose lives are hard, need help, not labels.

Language Handbook

7e. An *adverb clause* is a subordinate clause that modifies a verb, an adjective, or an adverb.

An adverb clause, which may come before or after the word it modifies, tells *how, when, where, why, to what extent (how much),* or *under what condition.* An adverb clause begins with a **subordinating conjunction,** such as *although, because, if, so that,* or *when.*

EXAMPLES

Because we students did so well in the discussion of *Romeo and Juliet*, our teacher did not assign any homework. [The adverb clause modifies *did assign,* telling *why.*]

I wrote a poem about war **after I read "The Sniper."** [The adverb clause modifies *wrote,* telling *when.*]

If Harry moves, he may disturb the sleeping snake. [The adverb clause modifies *may disturb,* telling *under what condition.*]

His pitching arm is stronger today **than it ever was.** [The adverb clause modifies *stronger,* telling *to what extent.*]

Doodle's brother was able to run faster **than Doodle could.** [The adverb clause modifies *faster,* telling *how much.*]

7f. A *noun clause* is a subordinate clause used as a subject, a predicate nom-inative, a direct object, an indirect object, or an object of a preposition.

The words commonly used to begin noun clauses include *that, what, whether, who,* and *why.*

SUBJECT	**What Odysseus did** was clever.
PREDICATE NOMINATIVE	The captains are **who pick the players for their teams.**
DIRECT OBJECT	The sniper discovered **that his brother was the enemy.**
INDIRECT OBJECT	The clerk should tell **whoever calls** the sale prices.
OBJECT OF PREPOSITION	He knew the price of **whatever they requested.**

The word that introduces a noun clause may or may not have a function within the noun clause.

EXAMPLES

Lizabeth regretted **what she had done.** [*What* is the direct object of *had done.*]

Mme. Loisel learned **that the necklace was fake.** [*That* has no function in the clause.]

Sometimes the word that introduces a noun clause is not stated, but its meaning is understood.

EXAMPLE

His mother said [**that**] **he could go to the concert.**

8 SENTENCE STRUCTURE

SENTENCE OR SENTENCE FRAGMENT?

8a. A *sentence* is a group of words that contains a subject and a verb and that expresses a complete thought.

A sentence should begin with a capital letter and end with a period, a question mark, or an exclamation point. A group of words that either does not contain a subject and verb or does not express a complete thought is called a *sentence fragment.*

FRAGMENT	Romeo banished from Verona?
SENTENCE	Why was Romeo banished from Verona?

FRAGMENT	What a clever plan!
SENTENCE	What a clever plan he had!

FRAGMENT	When the Montagues and the Cap-ulets learned of the deaths of Romeo and Juliet.
SENTENCE	When the Montagues and the Cap-ulets learned of the deaths of Romeo and Juliet, they ended their feud.

COMPUTER NOTE

Many style-checking soft-ware programs can identify sentence fragments. If you have access to such a program, use it to help you evaluate your writing. Then, revise each fragment to make sure that all your sentences express complete thoughts.

SUBJECT AND PREDICATE

8b. A sentence consists of two parts: the subject and the predicate. The *subject* tells *whom* or *what* the sentence is about. The *predicate* tells something about the subject.

In the following examples, all the words labeled *subject* make up the **complete subject,** and all the words labeled *predicate* make up the **complete predicate.**

SUBJECT   PREDICATE
Tybalt | was Juliet's cousin.

      SUBJECT   PREDICATE
Two of Prince Escalus's kinsmen | died.

     SUBJECT   PREDICATE
The setting of the play | is fourteenth-century Italy.

PREDICATE   SUBJECT   PREDICATE
Why did | Juliet | take the sleeping potion?

The Simple Subject

8c. The *simple subject* is the main word or group of words that tells *whom* or *what* the sentence is about.

EXAMPLES
An **excerpt** from Richard Wright's *Black Boy* appears in this book. [The complete subject is *an excerpt from Richard Wright's* Black Boy.]
The talented **Georgia O'Keeffe** is known for her paintings of huge flowers. [The complete subject is *the talented Georgia O'Keeffe.*]

The Simple Predicate

8d. The *simple predicate,* or *verb,* is the main word or group of words that tells something about the subject.

A simple predicate may be a single word or a **verb phrase** (a verb with one or more helping verbs).

EXAMPLES
Montresor **led** Fortunato to the catacombs. [The complete predicate is *led Fortunato to the catacombs.*]
Did Mme. Loisel **find** the necklace? [The complete predicate is *did find the necklace.*]

 NOTE In this book, the term *subject* refers to the simple subject, and the term *verb* refers to the simple predicate unless otherwise indicated.

The Compound Subject and the Compound Verb

8e. A *compound subject* consists of two or more subjects that are joined by a conjunction—usually *and* or *or*—and that have the same verb.

EXAMPLES
Does **Rainsford** or **Zaroff** win the game?
Romeo, Benvolio, and **Mercutio** attend the Capulets' party.

8f. A *compound verb* consists of two or more verbs that are joined by a conjunction—usually *and, but,* or *or*—and that have the same subject.

EXAMPLES
Della **sold** her hair and **bought** Jim a watch chain.
Timber **looked** for the snake but **did** not **find** it.

Finding the Subject of a Sentence

8g. To find the subject of a sentence, ask "Who?" or "What?" before the verb.

EXAMPLE
The price of those videos seems high. [What seems high? The price seems high. *Price* is the subject.]

(1) The subject of a sentence is never in a prepositional phrase.

EXAMPLES
Her **garden** of marigolds was ruined. [What was ruined? *Garden* was ruined. *Marigolds* is the object of the preposition *of.*]
On the rooftop crouched the **sniper.** [Who crouched? *Sniper* crouched. *Rooftop* is the object of the preposition *on.*]

(2) The subject of a sentence expressing a question usually follows the verb or a part of the verb phrase. Turning the question into a statement may help you find the subject.

QUESTION	Did **she** give Buddy a kite?
STATEMENT	**She** did give Buddy a kite.
QUESTION	Is the *Odyssey* an epic?
STATEMENT	The *Odyssey* is an epic.

(3) The word *there* or *here* is never the subject of a sentence.

EXAMPLES
There are your **keys.** [What are there? *Keys* are.]
Here is your **pencil.** [What is here? *Pencil* is.]

(4) The subject of a sentence expressing a command or request is always understood to be *you*, although *you* may not appear in the sentence.

EXAMPLE
[**You**] Listen carefully to his question. [Who is to listen? *You* is understood.]

The subject of a command or request is *you* even when the sentence contains a **noun of direct address,** a word naming the one or ones spoken to.

EXAMPLE
Ellen, [**you**] please read the part of Juliet.

COMPLEMENTS

 8h. A *complement* is a word or group of words that completes the meaning of a verb.

Three kinds of complements are the *subject complement,* the *direct object,* and the *indirect object.*

The Subject Complement

8i. A *subject complement* is a word or word group that completes the meaning of a linking verb and that identifies or modifies the subject.

The two types of subject complements are the *predicate nominative* and the *predicate adjective.*

(1) A ***predicate nominative*** is a noun or pronoun that follows a linking verb and that renames or identifies the subject of the verb.

EXAMPLES
"The Most Dangerous Game" is an exciting **story.** [The noun *story* identifies the subject *"The Most Dangerous Game."*]
The only people in line were **they.** [The pronoun *they* renames the subject *people.*]
The main characters are **Helen Keller** and **Annie Sullivan.** [The nouns *Helen Keller* and *Annie Sullivan* identify the subject *characters.*]

(2) A ***predicate adjective*** is an adjective that follows a linking verb and that modifies the subject of the verb.

EXAMPLES
The necklace was **inexpensive.** [The adjective *inexpensive* modifies the subject *necklace.*]
Miss Lottie looked **sad.** [The adjective *sad* modifies the subject *Miss Lottie.*]
The corn tastes **sweet** and **buttery.** [The adjectives *sweet* and *buttery* modify the subject *corn.*]

The Direct Object and the Indirect Object

 8j. A *direct object* is a noun or pronoun that receives the action of a verb or that shows the result of the action. It tells *whom* or *what* after a transitive verb.

EXAMPLES
The sniper killed his own **brother.** [killed whom? brother]
Although his watch was his most prized possession, Jim sold **it.** [sold what? it]
Shakespeare wrote not only great **plays** but also beautiful **sonnets.** [wrote what? plays and sonnets]

 8k. An *indirect object* is a noun or pronoun that precedes the direct object and that usually tells *to whom* or *for whom* (or *to what* or *for what*) the action of the verb is done.

EXAMPLES
Sheila read the **children** a story by Truman Capote. [read to whom? children]
Frank gave the **Red Cross** a donation. [gave to what? Red Cross]
She made her **neighbors** and other **friends** fruitcakes for Christmas. [made for whom? neighbors and friends]

 NOTE A complement may precede the subject and the verb.

DIRECT OBJECT   What a good **friend** Buddy has!
PREDICATE ADJECTIVE   How **happy** Della and Jim are!

CLASSIFYING SENTENCES ACCORDING TO PURPOSE

 8l. Sentences may be classified as *declarative, imperative, interrogative,* or *exclamatory.*

(1) A ***declarative sentence*** makes a statement. It is followed by a period.

EXAMPLES
One of my favorite stories is "Thank You, M'am."
Jonathan, the CD-ROM you ordered a while back has finally arrived.
It's raining.

(2) An *imperative sentence* makes a request or gives a command. It is usually followed by a period. A very strong command, however, is followed by an exclamation point.

EXAMPLES
Please open your books to page 3. [request]
Be careful of the undertow. [mild command]
Stop! [strong command]

 NOTE In a command or a request, the understood subject is *you.*

(3) An *interrogative sentence* asks a question. It is followed by a question mark.

EXAMPLES
Did Friar Laurence's plan fail?
What did Romeo do when he found Juliet lying there so still and pale?

(4) An *exclamatory sentence* expresses strong feeling. It is followed by an exclamation point.

EXAMPLES
What a mess we're in now!
The battery is dead!

CLASSIFYING SENTENCES ACCORDING TO STRUCTURE

8m. Sentences may be classified as *simple, compound, complex,* or *compound-complex.*

(1) A *simple sentence* has one independent clause and no subordinate clauses.

EXAMPLE
Frankenstein and *Dracula* were both written during the nineteenth century.

(2) A *compound sentence* has two or more independent clauses but no subordinate clauses.

EXAMPLES
Rita wanted to see an adventure film, **but** Carlos preferred a comedy. [two independent clauses joined by a comma and the coordinating conjunction *but*]
Harriet Tubman was a leader of the Underground Railroad; she rescued more than three hundred people. [two independent clauses joined by a semicolon]
Romeo killed Tybalt, Juliet's cousin; **as a result,** Romeo was banished from Verona. [two independent clauses joined by a semicolon and the transitional expression *as a result*]

(3) A *complex sentence* has one independent clause and at least one subordinate clause.

EXAMPLES
Juliet declared her love for Romeo before she spoke to him. [The independent clause is *Juliet declared her love for Romeo.* The subordinate clause is *before she spoke to him.*]
On Shakespeare's gravestone is an inscription that places a curse on anyone who moves his bones. [The independent clause is *on Shakespeare's gravestone is an inscription.* The subordinate clauses are *that places a curse on anyone* and *who moves his bones.*]

(4) A *compound-complex sentence* contains two or more independent clauses and at least one subordinate clause.

EXAMPLE
William Golding received the Nobel Prize in 1983; his best-known novel is *Lord of the Flies,* which he published in 1954. [The independent clauses are *William Golding received the Nobel Prize in 1983* and *his best-known novel is* Lord of the Flies. The subordinate clause is *which he published in 1954.*]

 For more on clauses, see 7a–f.

 TIPS FOR WRITERS

Varying Sentence Structure
Paragraphs in which all the sentences have the same structure can make for monotonous reading. To help keep your readers interested, evaluate your writing to see whether you've used a variety of sentence structures. If you have not, use revising techniques—add, cut, replace, and reorder—to vary the structure of your sentences.

Try It Out
The following paragraph is composed of simple sentences. Revise the paragraph, using a variety of sentence structures.

[1] "The Most Dangerous Game" begins with a conversation about hunting. [2] Rainsford is the protagonist. [3] He and Whitney are on a yacht in the Caribbean. [4] They're near the eerie Ship-Trap Island. [5] Rainsford loves hunting. [6] According to Rainsford, sympathy for the hunted animal is foolish. [7] Later Rainsford falls overboard and swims to the island. [8] He meets General Zaroff at the general's chateau. [9] Zaroff hunts human beings for sport. [10] Soon Rainsford the hunter becomes the hunted.

Try It Out
Possible Answers

"The Most Dangerous Game" begins with a conversation about hunting. Rainsford, the protagonist, and Whitney are on a yacht in the Caribbean, near the eerie Ship-Trap Island. Rainsford loves hunting and says that sympathy for the hunted animal is foolish. Later Rainsford falls overboard and swims to the island, where he meets General Zaroff at the general's chateau. Zaroff hunts human beings for sport, and Rainsford the hunter soon becomes the hunted.

Language Handbook

WRITING COMPLETE SENTENCES

9

SENTENCE FRAGMENTS

9a. Avoid using a *sentence fragment*—a part of a sentence that has been punctuated as if it were a complete sentence.

Here are two ways to correct a sentence fragment:

1. Add words that will make the thought complete.

FRAGMENT	Shortly after his birth, was baptized in a small church in Stratford. [The verb *was baptized* has no subject. Who was baptized?]
SENTENCE	Shortly after his birth, **Shakespeare** was baptized in a small church in Stratford.
FRAGMENT	Odysseus a great hero of the Greeks. [The verb is missing. What about Odysseus?]
SENTENCE	Odysseus **became** a great hero of the Greeks.
FRAGMENT	For the balcony scene in *Romeo and Juliet*. [The subject and the verb are missing. What about the balcony scene?]
SENTENCE	**The actors are preparing** for the balcony scene in *Romeo and Juliet*.

2. Attach the fragment to a sentence that comes before or after it.

EXAMPLE	One of my favorite stories by Edgar Allan Poe is "X-ing a Paragrab." [sentence] A comic tale of a feud between two newspaper editors. [fragment]
REVISED	One of my favorite stories by Edgar Allan Poe is "X-ing a Paragrab," **a comic tale of a feud between two newspaper editors.** [appositive phrase]
EXAMPLE	When she takes off her coat. [fragment] Mme. Loisel discovers that she is no longer wearing the necklace. [sentence]
REVISED	**When she takes off her coat,** Mme. Loisel discovers that she is no longer wearing the necklace. [subordinate clause]

EXAMPLE	Odysseus figured out a way for his men and him. [sentence] To escape from the Cyclops. [fragment]
REVISED	Odysseus figured out a way for his men and him **to escape from the Cyclops.** [infinitive phrase]

 For more information about sentence fragments, see 8a.

RUN-ON SENTENCES

9b. Avoid using a *run-on sentence*—two or more complete sentences that run together as if they were one complete sentence.

There are two kinds of run-on sentences.

● A *fused sentence* has no punctuation between the complete sentences.
● A *comma splice* has only a comma between the complete sentences.

FUSED SENTENCE	Della sold her hair to buy Jim a chain for his watch Jim sold his watch to buy Della combs for her hair.
COMMA SPLICE	Della sold her hair to buy Jim a chain for his watch, Jim sold his watch to buy Della combs for her hair.

Here are five ways to correct a run-on sentence:

1. Make two sentences.

REVISED	Della sold her hair to buy Jim a chain for his watch**.** Jim sold his watch to buy Della combs for her hair.

2. Use a comma and a *coordinating conjunction*—*and, but, or, yet, for, so,* or *nor.*

REVISED	Della sold her hair to buy Jim a chain for his watch**, and** Jim sold his watch to buy Della combs for her hair.

3. Use a semicolon.

REVISED	Della sold her hair to buy Jim a chain for his watch**;** Jim sold his watch to buy Della combs for her hair.

4. Use a semicolon and a *conjunctive adverb,* such as *therefore, instead, meanwhile, still, also,* or *however.* Follow a conjunctive adverb with a comma.

REVISED Della sold her hair to buy Jim a chain for his watch**; however,** Jim sold his watch to buy Della combs for her hair.

5. Change one of the complete thoughts into a subordinate clause.

REVISED Della sold her hair to buy Jim a chain for his watch **while Jim sold his watch to buy Della combs for her hair**.

 For more information about combining sentences, see 10a–e.

COMPUTER NOTE Style-checking software can help you evaluate your writing for the use of clear, complete sentences. Many such programs can identify and highlight sentence fragments. You can also use the "Search" command offered by computer programs to identify sentences in which you've used a comma and a coordinating conjunction—one search for each different conjunction and the comma in front of it. These searches can help you check to make sure that the ideas you've combined in a compound sentence are complete and are closely related and equally important.

 **Identifying Run-on Sentences**

One way to spot run-on sentences is to read your writing aloud. A natural, distinct pause in your speech often means that you need to separate sentences in some way. You can also check for run-ons by identifying subjects and verbs. Checking for clauses will help you find where one complete thought ends and another begins.

RUN-ON The family thought that Doodle would die they built him a coffin.
REVISED **Because** the family thought that Doodle would die, they built him a coffin.
REVISED The family thought that Doodle would die, **so** they built him a coffin.
REVISED The family thought that Doodle would die**; consequently,** they built him a coffin.

Try It Out

Revise each of the following run-on sentences.

1. Doodle and his brother had an active fantasy world, they created stories and imaginary plans.
2. Doodle was afraid of being left behind, he cried when his brother started to leave.
3. Brother taught Doodle to walk Brother was ashamed of Doodle.
4. Doodle didn't think that he could walk after much help and practice, he did.
5. He could walk perhaps he could run.

---

10 WRITING EFFECTIVE SENTENCES

SENTENCE COMBINING

10a. Combine related sentences by taking a key word (or by using another form of the word) from one sentence and inserting it into another.

ORIGINAL Edgar Allan Poe led a short life. His life was tragic.
COMBINED Edgar Allan Poe led a short, **tragic** life.

ORIGINAL Edgar Allan Poe wrote strange stories. He wrote stories of suspense.
COMBINED Edgar Allan Poe wrote strange, **suspenseful** stories.

 When you change the form of a key word, you often need to add an ending that makes the word an adjective or an adverb. Usually this ending is *–ed, –ing,* or *–ly.*

Try It Out
Possible Answers

1. Doodle and his brother had an active fantasy world. They created stories and imaginary plans.
2. Doodle was afraid of being left behind; he cried when his brother started to leave.
3. Brother taught Doodle to walk because Brother was ashamed of Doodle.
4. Although Doodle didn't think that he could walk, after much help and practice, he did.
5. If he could walk, perhaps he could run.

Resources

Grammar and Language

■ *Language Handbook Worksheets,* pp. 102–122

10b. Combine related sentences by taking (or creating) a phrase from one sentence and inserting it into another.

ORIGINAL   *A Fire in My Hands* is a collection of poems. The poems were written by Gary Soto.

COMBINED   *A Fire in My Hands* is a collection of poems **by Gary Soto.** [prepositional phrase]

ORIGINAL   Romeo kills Tybalt. Tybalt is Juliet's cousin.

COMBINED   Romeo kills Tybalt, **Juliet's cousin.** [appositive phrase]

10c. Combine related sentences by using a coordinating conjunction (*and, but, or, or nor*) to make a compound subject, a compound verb, or both.

ORIGINAL   After lunch Doodle went to Horsehead Landing. His brother went, too.

COMBINED   After lunch **Doodle and** his **brother** went to Horsehead Landing. [compound subject]

ORIGINAL   Ernesto Galarza's family immigrated to the United States. They eventually settled in Sacramento, California.

COMBINED   Ernesto Galarza's family **immigrated** to the United States **and** eventually **settled** in Sacramento, California. [compound verb]

Using Compound Subjects and Compound Verbs

When you combine sentences by using compound subjects and compound verbs, make sure that your new subjects and verbs agree in number.

ORIGINAL   Della has little money. Jim also doesn't have much.

COMBINED   **Della and Jim have** little money. [The compound subject *Della and Jim* takes the plural verb *have*.]

Try It Out ✎

Combine each of the following pairs of sentences into one sentence that has a compound subject or a compound verb.

1. Mrs. Johnson's husband moved to Oklahoma. He studied religion.
2. The cotton gin would not hire her. Neither would the lumber mill.
3. She didn't want to become a servant. She saw another possibility.
4. The cotton gin workers walked to her stand and bought lunch. The lumber workers also walked to her stand and bought lunch there.
5. In time, syrup was sold at the store. Canned goods were, too.

10d. Combine related sentences by creating a compound sentence.

You can form a compound sentence by linking two or more independent clauses with a comma and a coordinating conjunction, a semicolon, or a semicolon and a conjunctive adverb.

ORIGINAL   Buddy makes his friend a kite. She makes him one, too.

COMBINED   Buddy makes his friend a kite, **and** she makes him one, too. [comma and coordinating conjunction]

COMBINED   Buddy makes his friend a kite; she makes him one, too. [semicolon]

COMBINED   Buddy makes his friend a kite; **meanwhile,** she makes him one, too. [semicolon and conjunctive adverb]

10e. Combine related sentences by creating a complex sentence.

You can form a complex sentence by joining one independent clause with one or more subordinate clauses (adjective clause, adverb clause, or noun clause).

ORIGINAL   Gwendolyn Brooks often writes about Chicago. She has won a Pulitzer Prize for her poetry.

COMBINED   Gwendolyn Brooks, **who has won a Pulitzer Prize for her poetry,** often writes about Chicago. [adjective clause]

ORIGINAL   Zaroff turned on the light. He saw Rainsford.

COMBINED   **When Zaroff turned on the light,** he saw Rainsford. [adverb clause]

ORIGINAL   The snake in "Poison" is just an illusion on Harry's part. Many readers think this.

COMBINED   Many readers think **that the snake in "Poison" is just an illusion on Harry's part.** [noun clause]

Try It Out

Possible Answers

1. Mrs. Johnson's husband moved to Oklahoma and studied religion.
2. Neither the cotton gin nor the lumber mill would hire her.
3. She didn't want to become a servant and saw another possibility.
4. The cotton gin workers and the lumber workers walked to her stand and bought lunch there.
5. In time, syrup and canned goods were sold at the store.

 For more information about compound and complex sentences, see 8m.

Varying Sentence Structures

TIPS FOR WRITERS

In your writing, try to use a mix of simple, compound, complex, and compound-complex sentences.

EXAMPLE

As the music and the thump of the drums grew louder, the people lined up along the street. [complex] Finally, with a blast of brass, the high school band rounded the corner. [simple] First came the drum major; setting the tempo with her baton, she proudly raised her feet as high as possible. [compound] Behind her, leading the parade of colorful floats, the musicians marched in their bright purple-and-red jackets. [simple sentence]

Try It Out ✎

The following paragraph is composed of simple sentences. Revise the paragraph, using varied sentence structures.

[1] The boy had known hunger before. [2] This hunger was different. [3] It could not be satisfied by just a few bites. [4] It gnawed at his insides and made him weak. [5] His mother got a job. [6] She sent him to the store for groceries. [7] Some boys took his money. [8] She gave him more money and sent him again. [9] Again, the boys took his money. [10] His mother gave him a stick this time and told him to fight.

IMPROVING SENTENCE STYLE

10f. Use the same grammatical form (*parallel structure*) to express equal ideas.

NOT PARALLEL	Buddy and she liked baking fruit-cakes and to fly kites. [gerund phrase paired with infinitive phrase]
PARALLEL	Buddy and she liked **baking fruitcakes** and **flying kites.** [gerund phrase paired with gerund phrase]
PARALLEL	Buddy and she liked **to bake fruitcakes** and **to fly kites.** [infinitive phrase paired with infinitive phrase]

NOT PARALLEL	Harry received help from not only Timber but also from Ganderbai. [noun paired with prepositional phrase]
PARALLEL	Harry received help from not only **Timber** but also **Ganderbai.** [noun paired with noun]
PARALLEL	Harry received help not only **from Timber** but also **from Ganderbai.** [prepositional phrase paired with prepositional phrase]

10g. Avoid using stringy sentences—sentences that have too many independent clauses strung together with coordinating conjunctions like *and* or *but*.

You may revise a stringy sentence in one of two ways.

1. Break the sentence into two or more sentences.
2. Turn some of the independent clauses into subordinate clauses or into phrases.

STRINGY	The fire alarm rang, and everyone started to file out of school, but then our principal came down the hall, and he said that the bell was a mistake, and we went back to our classes.
REVISED	The fire alarm bell rang, and everyone started to file out of school. Then our principal came down the hall to say that the bell was a mistake. We went back to our classes.
REVISED	When the fire alarm bell rang, everyone started to file out of school. Then our principal came down the hall. He said that the bell was a mistake, and we went back to our classes.

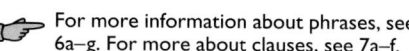 For more information about phrases, see 6a–g. For more about clauses, see 7a–f.

COMPUTER NOTE

Whenever you revise your writing on a computer, you can use functions such as "Copy," "Cut," and "Move" to experiment with your sentences. Try a variety of sentence beginnings and structures. Then, decide which ones work best with the other sentences in a particular paragraph.

Try It Out
Possible Answers

The boy had known hunger before, but this hunger was different. Not to be satisfied by just a few bites, it gnawed at his insides and made him weak. When his mother got a job, she sent him to the store for groceries, but some boys took his money. She gave him more money and sent him again; again, the boys took his money. This time his mother gave him a stick and told him to fight.

10h. Avoid using unnecessary words.

Here are three tips for avoiding wordiness.

1. Don't use more words than you need to use.
2. Don't use difficult words where simple ones will do.
3. Don't repeat yourself unless it's absolutely necessary.

WORDY Fortunato is a wine connoisseur who has much knowledge of and great appreciation for fine wines.

REVISED Fortunato is a connoisseur of fine wines.

WORDY In the event that they were able to find the missing necklace belonging to Mme. Forestier by the last day of the month of February, the Loisels could return the other necklace.

REVISED If they could find Mme. Forestier's necklace by the end of February, the Loisels could return the other necklace.

10i. Use a variety of sentence beginnings.

The basic structure of an English sentence is a subject followed by a verb. The following examples show how you can revise sentences to avoid beginning with the subject every time. Notice that a comma follows the introductory word, phrase, or clause in each revision.

SUBJECT FIRST Della excitedly opened her present.

ADVERB FIRST **Excitedly,** Della opened her present.

SUBJECT FIRST You must study to make good grades.

INFINITIVE PHRASE FIRST **To make good grades,** you must study.

SUBJECT FIRST Romeo fell in love with Juliet as soon as he saw her.

ADVERB CLAUSE FIRST **As soon as Romeo saw Juliet,** he fell in love with her.

11 CAPITALIZATION

11a. Capitalize the first word in every sentence.

EXAMPLES
The two boys in "The Talk" discuss their plans. Stop!

(1) Capitalize the first word of a direct quotation.

EXAMPLE
Maria asked me, "Have you written your report on Gary Soto?"

(2) Traditionally, the first word of a line of poetry is capitalized.

EXAMPLES
Two roads diverged in a wood, and I—
I took the one less traveled by,
And that has made all the difference.
                    —Robert Frost, "The Road Not Taken"

 NOTE Some writers do not follow these practices. When you are quoting, use capital letters exactly as they are used in the source of the quotation.

 For more information about using capital letters in quotations, see pages 13d, e.

11b. Capitalize the first word both in the salutation and in the closing of a letter.

EXAMPLES
To Whom It May Concern:
Dear Ann,   Dear Sir:
Sincerely,   Yours truly,

11c. Capitalize the pronoun *I* and the interjection *O*.

EXAMPLES
Mom says that **I** can go this weekend.
Who says "Romeo can, / Though heaven cannot.
  O Romeo, Romeo"?

11d. Capitalize proper nouns and proper adjectives.

A *common noun* is a general name for a person, a place, a thing, or an idea. A *proper noun* names a particular person, place, thing, or idea. A *proper adjective* is formed from a proper noun.

Proper nouns and proper adjectives are always capitalized. Common nouns are not capitalized unless they begin a sentence, begin a direct quotation, or are part of a title.

COMMON NOUNS	PROPER NOUNS	PROPER ADJECTIVES
poet	Homer	Homeric simile
planet	Mars	Martian landscape

In proper nouns that have more than one word, do *not* capitalize articles (*a, an, the*), prepositions of fewer than five letters (such as *at, for,* and *with*), coordinating conjunctions (*and, but, for, nor, or, so, yet*), or the sign of the infinitive (*to*) unless they are the first word of the proper noun.

EXAMPLES
American Society **f**or the Prevention **o**f Cruelty **t**o Animals
National Campers **a**nd Hikers Association
"Writing **a** Paragraph **t**o Inform"

(1) Capitalize the names of persons and animals.

PERSONS Sandra Cisneros Langston Hughes
ANIMALS Old Yeller Brer Rabbit

(2) Capitalize geographical names.

TYPE OF NAME	EXAMPLES	
Towns and Cities	San Francisco	St. Charles
Counties, Townships, and Parishes	Hayes Township Union Parish	Kane County Manhattan
States and Territories	Florida Guam	North Carolina Northwest Territory
Countries	Canada	United States of America
Continents	Africa	North America
Islands	Long Island	Isle of Palms
Mountains	Rocky Mountains	Mount McKinley
Other Land Forms and Features	Cape Hatteras Kalahari Desert	Niagara Falls Mammoth Cave
Bodies of Water	Pacific Ocean Cross Creek	Gulf of Mexico Blue Springs
Parks	Yellowstone National Park Cleburne State Recreation Area	
Regions	the North New England	the Middle West the Great Plains
Roads, Streets, and Highways	Route 66 Gibbs Drive	Pennsylvania Turnpike Thirty-first Street

For names with more than one word, capitalization may vary. Always check the spelling of such a name with the person whose name it is, or look in a reference source.

EXAMPLES
Kees **v**an Dongen   Henry **V**an Dyke

Abbreviations such as *Ms., Mr., Dr.,* and *Gen.* should always be capitalized.

EXAMPLES
Mr. James Thurber   **Dr.** Mary McLeod Bethune

Capitalize the abbreviations *Jr.* and *Sr.* after a name, and set them off with commas.

EXAMPLE
In 1975, Gen. Daniel James, **Jr.,** became the first African American four-star general in the U.S. Air Force.

 NOTE Words such as *north, west,* and *southeast* are not capitalized when they indicate direction.

EXAMPLES
north of town
traveling **s**outheast

 NOTE In a hyphenated number, the second word begins with a small letter.

EXAMPLE
Thirty-first Street

NOTE Words like *city, river, street,* and *park* are capitalized only when they are part of a name.

EXAMPLES
go to the **p**ark
go to Central Park

across the **r**iver
across the Pecos **R**iver

(3) Capitalize the names of organizations, teams, business firms, institutions, buildings and other structures, and government bodies.

TYPE OF NAME	EXAMPLES
Organizations	United Nations National Basketball Association
Teams	Tampa Bay Buccaneers Minnesota Twins
Business Firms	Quaker Oats Company Aluminum Company of America
Institutions	United States Naval Academy Bethune-Cookman College
Buildings and Other Structures	Apollo Theater Taj Mahal Golden Gate Bridge
Government Bodies	Federal Bureau of Investigation House of Representatives

NOTE Capitalize words such as *democratic* or *republican* only when they refer to a specific political party.

EXAMPLES
The new leaders promised **d**emocratic reforms.
The **D**emocratic candidates for mayor held a rally.

The word *party* in the name of a political party may be capitalized or not.

EXAMPLE
Federalist **P**arty *or* **p**arty

(4) Capitalize the names of historical events and periods, special events, holidays, and other calendar items.

TYPE OF NAME	EXAMPLES
Historical Events and Periods	French Revolution Middle Ages Boston Tea Party Mesozoic Era
Special Events	Interscholastic Debate Tournament Kansas State Fair
Holidays and Calendar Items	Labor Day Saturday December Fourth of July National Book Week

NOTE Do not capitalize the name of a season unless it is being personified or used in the name of a special event.

EXAMPLES
I'm on the committee for the **W**inter Carnival.
Soon **A**utumn will begin painting the leaves in bright colors.

(5) Capitalize the names of ships, trains, aircraft, spacecraft, monuments, awards, planets, and other particular places, things, or events.

TYPE OF NAME	EXAMPLES		
Ships and Trains	*Mayflower* *Silver Meteor*		
Aircraft and Spacecraft	*Spirit of St. Louis* Lockheed **C**-5A **G**alaxy *Pioneer 10* Hubble **S**pace **T**elescope		
Monuments and Memorials	Washington Monument Statue of Liberty Vietnam Veterans Memorial		
Awards	Pulitzer Prize Congressional Medal of Honor Stanley Cup Key Club Achievement Award		
Planets, Stars, and Constellations	Mercury Dog Star Ursa Major Pluto Big Dipper Rigel		

NOTE The word *earth* is not capitalized unless it is used along with the names of other heavenly bodies that are capitalized. The words *sun* and *moon* are not capitalized.

EXAMPLES
The **m**oon is a satellite of the **e**arth.
Venus is closer to Earth than Mars is.

(6) Capitalize the names of nationalities, races, and peoples.

EXAMPLES
Greek   African Americans   Hispanic   Cherokee

(7) Capitalize the brand names of business products but not the common nouns that follow the names.

EXAMPLES
Chevrolet van   Teflon pan

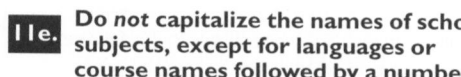 **11e.** Do *not* capitalize the names of school subjects, except for languages or course names followed by a number.

EXAMPLES
algebra   English   Typing I

11f. Capitalize titles.

(1) Capitalize the title of a person when it comes before the person's name.

EXAMPLES
President Clinton   Mr. Vonnegut

TYPE OF TITLE	EXAMPLES
Books	*The Pearl* *I Know Why the Caged Bird Sings*
Periodicals	*The Atlantic Monthly* *Field and Stream*
Poems	"The Road Not Taken" "The Girl Who Loved the Sky"
Stories	"The Cask of Amontillado" "The Most Dangerous Game"
Essays and Speeches	"The Death of a Tree" "Work and What It's Worth"
Plays	*The Miracle Worker* *The Phantom of the Opera*
Historical Documents	Declaration of Independence Emancipation Proclamation
Movies	*Dances with Wolves* *Stand and Deliver*
Radio and Television Programs	*All Things Considered Nova* *Star Trek: The Next Generation*
Works of Art	*American Gothic* *The Thinker*
Musical Compositions	"The Tennessee Waltz" "The Flight of the Bumblebee"
Cartoons	*Calvin and Hobbes* *The Neighborhood*

Usually, do not capitalize a title that is used alone or following a person's name, especially if the title is preceded by *a* or *the*.

EXAMPLE
Cleopatra reigned as the queen of Egypt between 51 and 30 B.C.

When a title is used alone in direct address, it is usually capitalized.

EXAMPLE
I think, Senator, that the issue is critical.

(2) Capitalize words showing family relationship when used with a person's name but *not* when preceded by a possessive.

EXAMPLES
Aunt Clara   my mother
Harold's grandmother

(3) Capitalize the first and last words and all important words in titles of books, periodicals, poems, stories, essays, speeches, plays, historical documents, movies, radio and television programs, works of art, musical compositions, and cartoons.

NOTE Unimportant words in a title are articles (*a, an, the*), prepositions of fewer than five letters (such as *for* and *from*), and co-ordinating conjunctions (*and, but, so, nor, or, yet, for*).

NOTE The words *a, an,* and *the* written before a title are capitalized only when they are part of the official title. The official title of a book is found on the title page. The official title of a newspaper or a periodical is found on the masthead, which is usually on the editorial page.

EXAMPLES
*The Autobiography of
   Malcolm X*
the *Austin American-Statesman*
A Tale of Two Cities

☞ For information about when to use italics for titles, see 13a. For information about when to use quotation marks for titles, see 13j.

Language Handbook

(4) Capitalize the names of religions and their
followers, holy days and celebrations, holy writings,
and specific deities.

TYPE OF NAME	EXAMPLES	
Religions and Followers	Judaism Taoism	Quaker Muslim
Holy Days and Celebrations	Passover Ramadan	Good Friday Lent
Holy Writings	Bible Koran	Upanishads Genesis
Specific Deities	Allah Brahma Zeus	

Some software programs can
identify errors in capitaliza-
tion. However, even the most complete programs may not include all the terms you need.
In addition, the program may be based on rules
that vary from the ones you've been given to
follow. If your software allows it, modify the
capitalization of words already in the program,
and add terms that you use frequently.

12 PUNCTUATION

END MARKS

Sentences

End marks—*periods, question marks, and exclamation
points*—are used to indicate the purpose of a sentence.

☞ For a discussion of how sentences are classified
according to purpose, see 8l. For information
on using quotation marks with end marks,
see 13f.

12a. **A statement (or declarative sentence)
is followed by a period.**

EXAMPLE
Dorothy M. Johnson wrote "A Man Called Horse"

12b. **A question (or interrogative sentence)
is followed by a question mark.**

EXAMPLE
Did Penelope recognize Odysseus

NOTE Be sure to distinguish between a declarative
sentence that contains an indirect question
and an interrogative sentence, which asks a direct
question.

INDIRECT QUESTION	He asked me **what was worrying her.** [declarative]
DIRECT QUESTION	What is worrying her [interrogative]

A direct question may have the same word order as
a declarative sentence. Since it *is* a question, however,
it is followed by a question mark.

EXAMPLES
A cat can see color   The plane was late?

12c. **An exclamation is followed by an
exclamation point.**

EXAMPLE
Wow! What a great play *The Miracle Worker* is!

12d. **A command or request (or imperative sentence) is followed by either a
period or an exclamation point.**

A mild command or an imperative sentence that
makes a request is followed by a period. An imperative
sentence that shows strong feeling is followed by an
exclamation point.

EXAMPLES
Please be quiet. [request]
Turn off your radio. [mild command]
Be quiet! [strong command]

Sometimes a command or request is stated in the
form of a question. Because of its purpose, however,
the sentence is really an imperative sentence and
should be followed by a period or an exclamation
point.

EXAMPLES
Could you please send me twenty-five copies.
Will you stop that!

Abbreviations

12e. An abbreviation is usually followed by a period.

TYPES OF ABBREVIATIONS	EXAMPLES
Personal Names	A. E. Housman Eugenia W. Collier
Organizations and Companies	Assn.　Co.　Inc. Ltd.　Corp.
Titles Used with Names	Mr.　Mrs.　Jr.　Dr.
Times of Day	A.M.　P.M.
Years	B.C. (written after the date) A.D. (written before the date)
Addresses	Ave.　St.　Blvd.　Pkwy.
States	Calif.　Mass.　Tex.　N. Dak.

If a statement ends with an abbreviation, do not use an additional period as an end mark. However, do add a question mark or an exclamation point if the sentence should have one.

EXAMPLES
Mrs. Tavares will be arriving at 3 P.M.
Can you go to meet her at 3 P.M.?

Abbreviations for government agencies and international organizations and some other frequently used abbreviations are written without periods. Abbreviations for most units of measurement are commonly written without periods, especially in science books.

EXAMPLES
CD, VCR, FM, IRS, TV, UFO
cm, kg, lb, ml

 NOTE Include a period with the abbreviation for *inch* (*in.*) so that it will not be confused with *in*, the word.

COMMAS

12f. Use commas to separate items in a series.

EXAMPLES
Odysseus slays Antinous, Eurymachus, and Penelope's other suitors.
We can meet before school, at lunch, or after school.

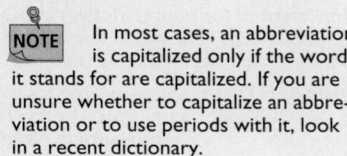 **NOTE** Two-letter state abbreviations without periods are used only when the ZIP Code is included. Each letter of the abbreviation is capitalized, and no comma separates the abbreviation from the ZIP Code.

EXAMPLE
Cincinnati, OH 45233

NOTE In most cases, an abbreviation is capitalized only if the words it stands for are capitalized. If you are unsure whether to capitalize an abbreviation or to use periods with it, look in a recent dictionary.

(1) If all items in a series are joined by *and* or *or*, do not use commas to separate them.

EXAMPLE
The names of the characters in "Poison" are Harry **and** Timber **and** Dr. Ganderbai.

Some words—such as *bread and butter, rod and reel,* and *law and order*—are used in pairs and may be considered one item in a series.

EXAMPLE
My favorite breakfast is milk, **biscuits and gravy**, and fruit.

(2) Independent clauses in a series are generally separated by semicolons. Short independent clauses, however, may be separated by commas.

EXAMPLE
The sky darkened, branches swayed, the cold deepened, and snow fell.

12g. Use commas to separate two or more adjectives preceding a noun.

EXAMPLE
Montresor leads Fortunato to the dark, cold vaults below the palazzo.

When the last adjective in a series is thought of as part of the noun, the comma before the adjective is omitted.

EXAMPLE
The Loisels bought an expensive **diamond necklace**.

12h. Use commas before *and, but, or, nor, for, so,* and *yet* when they join independent clauses.

EXAMPLE
General Zaroff was confident he would kill Rainsford**,** **but** the hunt did not go as he had planned.

You may omit the comma before *and, but, or,* or *nor* if the clauses are very short and there is no chance of misunderstanding.

12i. Use commas to set off nonessential clauses and nonessential participial phrases.

A *nonessential* (or *nonrestrictive*) clause or participial phrase adds information that is not needed to understand the main idea in the sentence.

NONESSENTIAL CLAUSE Langston Hughes**,** **who was a key figure in the Harlem Renaissance,** often used the rhythms of jazz in his poetry.

Omitting the adjective clause in this example would not change the main idea of the sentence: *Langston Hughes often used the rhythms of jazz in his poetry.*

An *essential* (or *restrictive*) clause or phrase provides information that is needed to understand the sentence, and commas are *not* used.

ESSENTIAL PHRASE Actors **missing more than two rehearsals** will be replaced.

Omitting the participial phrase above would affect the meaning of the sentence: The phrase tells *which actors.*

12j. Use commas after certain introductory elements.

(1) Use a comma after a word such as *next, yes,* or *no* as well as after an introductory interjection such as *why, well,* or *oops.*

EXAMPLES
Yes**,** I've read "Salvador Late or Early."
Ah**,** there's nothing like cold water on a hot day!

(2) Use a comma after an introductory participial phrase.

EXAMPLE
Having passed Penelope's last test, Odysseus reclaims his home and his kingdom.

(3) Use a comma after the last of two or more introductory prepositional phrases.

EXAMPLE
Of all of his novels, Charles Dickens liked *David Copperfield* best.

(4) Use a comma after an introductory adverb clause.

EXAMPLE
Until he meets Juliet, Romeo is madly in love with Rosaline.

12k. Use commas to set off elements that interrupt a sentence.

EXAMPLES
Dr. Ganderbai**,** **in fact,** worked very hard.
The storm**,** **the worst this winter,** raged for days.

(1) Appositives and appositive phrases are usually set off by commas.

EXAMPLE
My sister gave me a copy of *Gorilla, My Love,* **Toni Cade Bambara's first collection of stories.**

 NOTE An appositive that tells which one(s) of two or more is a *restrictive appositive* and should not be set off by commas.

EXAMPLE
The television special is about Graham Greene the British writer, not Graham Greene the Canadian actor.

(2) Words used in direct address are set off by commas.

EXAMPLE
Linda**,** please read the part of Juliet.

(3) Parenthetical expressions are set off by commas.

Parenthetical expressions are side remarks that add minor information or that relate ideas to each other.

EXAMPLE
He was not angry and**,** **on the contrary,** was actually glad that you told him about the error.

A contrasting expression introduced by *not* or *yet* is parenthetical and is set off by commas.

EXAMPLE
It is the spirit of the giver**,** **not the cost of the gift,** that counts.

12l. Use commas in certain conventional situations.

(1) Use a comma to separate items in dates and in addresses (except between a two-letter state abbreviation and a ZIP Code).

EXAMPLES
My family moved to Oakland**,** California**,** on Wednesday**,** December 5**,** 1990.
On December 5**,** 1990**,** our address became 25 Peralta Road**,** Oakland**,** CA 94611.

(2) Use a comma after the salutation of a friendly letter and after the closing of any letter.

EXAMPLES
Dear Ms. Chen,   Yours truly,

(3) Use a comma to set off an abbreviation such as *Jr., Sr.,* or *M.D.,* including after the abbreviation unless it ends the sentence.

EXAMPLE
Dr. Martin Luther King, Jr., delivered that speech.

SEMICOLONS

12m. Use a semicolon between independent clauses if they are not joined by *and, but, or, nor, for, so,* or *yet.*

EXAMPLE
I enjoyed reading *The Miracle Worker*; it tells what Helen Keller's youth was like.

12n. Use a semicolon between independent clauses joined by a conjunctive adverb—such as *however, therefore,* and *furthermore*—or a transitional expression—such as *for instance, in fact,* and *that is.*

EXAMPLES
Sherlock Holmes is a fictional character; **however,** many people are convinced that he actually did exist.
My parents are strict; **for example,** I can watch TV only on weekends.

Notice in the two examples above that a comma always follows a conjunctive adverb or a transitional expression that joins independent clauses.

12o. Use a semicolon (rather than a comma) before a coordinating conjunction to join independent clauses that contain commas.

EXAMPLE
Doodle's mother, father, and brother went back inside the house; **but** Doodle remained outside to bury the scarlet ibis.

12p. Use a semicolon between items in a series if the items contain commas.

EXAMPLE
I have postcards from Paris, France; Rome, Italy; Lisbon, Portugal; and London, England.

COLONS

12q. Use a colon to mean "note what follows."

(1) In some cases a colon is used before a list of items, especially after the expressions *the following* and *as follows.*

EXAMPLE
The reading list includes the following titles: "The Gift," "The Sniper," and "The Necklace."

Do not use a colon before a list that follows a verb or a preposition.

INCORRECT   The list of literary terms includes: *conflict, climax,* and *resolution.*
CORRECT   The list of literary terms includes *conflict, climax,* and *resolution.*

INCORRECT   In the past five years, my family has lived in: Texas, Oregon, Ohio, and Florida.
CORRECT   In the past five years, my family has lived in Texas, Oregon, Ohio, and Florida.

(2) Use a colon before a long, formal statement or a long quotation.

EXAMPLE
O. Henry had this to say about Della and Jim: "But in a last word to the wise of these days, let it be said that of all who give gifts, these two were the wisest."

12r. Use a colon in certain conventional situations.

(1) Use a colon between the hour and the minute.
EXAMPLES
9:30 P.M.   8:00 A.M.

(2) Use a colon after the salutation of a business letter.
EXAMPLES
Dear Ms. González: Dear Sir or Madam:
To Whom It May Concern:

(3) Use a colon between chapter and verse in referring to passages from the Bible.
EXAMPLES
Esther 3:5   Exodus 1:6–14

(4) Use a colon between a title and a subtitle.
EXAMPLE
"Shakespeare and His Theater: A Perfect Match"

Language Handbook

13 PUNCTUATION

ITALICS

When writing or typing, indicate italics by underlining. If your composition were to be printed, the typesetter would set the underlined words in italics. For example, if you typed the sentence

Alice Walker wrote The Color Purple.

it would be printed like this:

Alice Walker wrote *The Color Purple.*

COMPUTER NOTE If you use a computer, you can probably set words in italics yourself. Most word-processing software and many printers are capable of producing italic type.

13a. Use underlining (italics) for titles of books, plays, films, periodicals, works of art, recordings, long musical works, television series, trains, ships, aircraft, and spacecraft.

TYPE OF TITLE	EXAMPLES	
Books	*Black Boy*	*Odyssey*
Plays	*The Miracle Worker* *Romeo and Juliet*	
Films	*The Lion King*	*Jurassic Park*
Periodicals	*Seventeen*	*USA Today*

NOTE The articles *a, an,* and *the* written before a title are italicized only when they are part of the official title. The official title of a book appears on the title page. The official title of a newspaper or periodical appears on the masthead, which is usually found on the editorial page.

EXAMPLE
We subscribe to *The Wall Street Journal* and **the** *Austin American-Statesman.*

TYPE OF TITLE	EXAMPLES
Works of Art	*Death of Cleopatra* *Mona Lisa*
Recordings	*Music Box* *Two Worlds, One Heart*
Long Musical Works	*The Magic Flute* *Rhapsody in Blue*
Television Series	*60 Minutes* *The Simpsons*
Trains and Ships	*Orient Express* *U.S.S. Nimitz*
Aircraft and Spacecraft	*Spirit of St. Louis* *Apollo 13*

 For examples of titles that should be placed in quotation marks rather than be italicized, see 13j.

13b. Use underlining (italics) for words, letters, and figures referred to as such and for foreign words not yet a part of English vocabulary.

EXAMPLES
The word *excellent* has two *l*'s.
The *3* on that license plate looks like an *8.*
The *corrido* is a fast-paced ballad.

QUOTATION MARKS

13c. Use quotation marks to enclose a *direct quotation*—a person's exact words.

EXAMPLES
She asked, "How much does the necklace cost?"
"The Loisels pay thirty-six thousand francs," answered Lamont.

Do not use quotation marks for indirect quotations.

DIRECT QUOTATION	Stephanie said, "I'm going to plant some marigolds." [the speaker's exact words]
INDIRECT QUOTATION	Stephanie said that she was going to plant some marigolds. [not the speaker's exact words]

An interrupting expression is not a part of a quotation and should never be inside quotation marks.

EXAMPLE

"Let's fly our kites," Jennifer suggested, "before the breeze dies down."

When two or more sentences by the same speaker are quoted together, use one set of quotation marks.

EXAMPLE

Brennan said, "I'm making a fruitcake. Do you like fruitcake?"

 13d. A direct quotation begins with a capital letter.

EXAMPLES

Mrs. Perez asked, "Who is Mercutio?"
Charles answered, "One of Romeo's friends."
[Although this quotation is not a sentence, it is Charles's complete remark.]

 NOTE If a direct quotation is obviously a fragment of the original quotation, it should begin with a lowercase letter.

EXAMPLE

To Romeo, Juliet is like "a wingèd messenger of heaven."

 13e. When a quoted sentence is divided into two parts by an interrupting expression, the second part begins with a lowercase letter.

EXAMPLE

"I wish," she said, "that we went to the same school."

If the second part of a quotation is a new sentence, a period (not a comma) follows the interrupting expression, and the second part begins with a capital letter.

EXAMPLE

"I requested an interview," the reporter said. "She told me she was too busy."

 13f. When used with quotation marks, other marks of punctuation are placed according to the following rules.

(1) A comma or a period is always placed inside the closing quotation marks.

EXAMPLES

"I haven't seen the film version of *Romeo and Juliet*," remarked Jeannette, "but I understand it's excellent."

(2) A semicolon or a colon is always placed outside the closing quotation marks.

EXAMPLES

My mom's favorite poem is Maya Angelou's "Woman Work"; in fact, I can recite it.
Find examples of the following figures of speech in "I Wandered Lonely as a Cloud": simile, personification, and alliteration.

(3) A question mark or an exclamation point is placed inside the closing quotation marks if the quotation is a question or an exclamation; otherwise, it is placed outside.

EXAMPLES

"Where does Romeo first meet Juliet?" asked Mr. Suarez.
"Help me, please!" she exclaimed.
Which of the characters says "Parting is such sweet sorrow"?
It is *not* an insult to be called a "bookworm"!

 13g. When you write dialogue (a conversation), begin a new paragraph every time the speaker changes.

EXAMPLE

The gait of my friend was unsteady, and the bells upon his cap jingled as he strode.
"The pipe," said he.
"It is farther on," said I; "but observe the white web-work which gleams from these cavern walls."
—Edgar Allan Poe, "The Cask of Amontillado"

 13h. When a quoted passage consists of more than one paragraph, put quotation marks at the beginning of each paragraph and at the end of only the last paragraph.

EXAMPLE

"At nine o'clock this morning," read the news story, "someone entered the Millford Bank by the back entrance, broke through two thick steel doors guarding the bank's vault, and escaped with sixteen bars of gold.
"No arrests have yet been made, but state and local police are confident the case will be solved within a few days.
"FBI agents are due to arrive on the scene later today."

 13i. Use single quotation marks to enclose a quotation within a quotation.

EXAMPLE

"Do you agree with O. Henry that Della and Jim 'were the wisest'?" asked Greg.

13j. Use quotation marks to enclose titles of articles, short stories, essays, poems, songs, individual episodes of TV shows, and chapters and other parts of books and periodicals.

 For examples of titles that should be italicized rather than enclosed in quotation marks, see 13a.

TYPE OF TITLE	EXAMPLES
Articles	"Computers in the Classroom" "Returning from Space"
Short Stories	"Thank You, M'am" "The Princess and the Tin Box"
Essays	"How to Name a Dog" "The Death of a Tree"
Poems	"The Secret" "Fire and Ice" "who are you,little i"
Songs	"Circle of Life" "Lean on Me"
TV Episodes	"Farewell, Friends" "The Surprise Party"
Chapters and Other Parts of Books and Periodicals	"Life in the First Settlements" "The Talk of the Town" "Laughter, the Best Medicine"

 NOTE Neither italics nor quotation marks are used for the titles of major religious texts or for the titles of legal or historical documents.

RELIGIOUS TEXTS
New Testament   Koran   Rig-Veda

LEGAL AND HISTORICAL DOCUMENTS
Declaration of Independence
Code of Hammurabi

EXCEPTION
Names of court cases are usually italicized.

EXAMPLE
Brown v. *Board of Education of Topeka*

Try It Out
Possible Answers

"You know what really bothers me about a lot of stories?" said Kyle.

"What?" inquired Erin.

"I can never—well, not <u>never</u>, but <u>often</u> I can't—figure out if a story is fiction or if it really happened," he explained.

"Yeah," she nodded, "I know what you mean. That reminds me of the story 'A Man Called Horse.' Did it really happen or not?"

"I don't know," he answered. "When I saw the movie, I thought it did, but now I'm not so sure."

Erin added, "It's the same with stories that don't give the narrator's name. I always wonder whether the narrator is the writer or not."

"Yes, and the more I <u>like</u> the story, the more I <u>wonder</u>!" Kyle agreed.

Erin replied, "Hey, let's check the book out again and see if we can find out if Horse was a real person or not."

As they read the notes and comments about the story, Kyle said with surprise, "Wow, it says here that Dorothy Johnson also wrote the story 'The Man Who Shot Liberty Valance'!"

 **TIPS FOR WRITERS**

Using Italics for Emphasis
Occasionally, writers will use italics (underlining) to emphasize a particular word or phrase. This technique can be especially effective in written dialogue. The italic type helps to show how the sentence is spoken by the character. Read the following sentences aloud. Notice that by italicizing different words, the writer can alter the meaning of the sentence.

EXAMPLES
"Are you *certain* that she said to be here at nine o'clock?" asked Suzanne. [Are you certain, not just guessing?]

"Are you certain that *she* said to be here at nine o'clock?" asked Suzanne. [Did she say so, or did someone else?]

"Are you certain that she said to be here at *nine* o'clock?" asked Suzanne. [Did she say nine o'clock, or was it eight?]

Although italicizing (underlining) words for emphasis is a handy technique, it should not be overused, because it can quickly lose its effectiveness.

Try It Out
Revise the following dialogue by adding commas, end marks, quotation marks, and paragraph breaks where necessary. In addition, underline words you think the speakers would emphasize.

[1] You know what really bothers me about a lot of stories? said Kyle. [2] What? inquired Erin. [3] I can never—well, not never, but often I can't—figure out if a story is fiction or if it really happened, he explained. [4] Yeah she nodded I know what you mean. That reminds me of the story A Man Called Horse. Did it really happen or not? [5] I don't know he answered When I saw the movie, I thought it did, but now I'm not so sure. [6] Erin added, It's the same with stories that don't give the narrator's name. [7] I always wonder whether the narrator is the writer or not. [8] Yes, and the more I like the story, the more I wonder! Kyle agreed. [9] Erin replied Hey let's check the book out again and see if we can find out if Horse was a real person or not. [10] As they read the notes and comments about the story, Kyle said with surprise Wow it says here that Dorothy Johnson also wrote the story The Man Who Shot Liberty Valance!

14 PUNCTUATION

APOSTROPHES

Possessive Case

The **possessive case** of a noun or pronoun shows ownership or relationship.

OWNERSHIP   Mme. Forestier's necklace
RELATIONSHIP   Buddy's friend

 14a. To form the possessive case of a singular noun, add an apostrophe and an *s*.

EXAMPLES
Miss Lottie's marigolds   a bus's wheel

NOTE For a proper name ending in *s*, add only an apostrophe if adding *'s* would make the name awkward to pronounce.

EXAMPLES
West Indies' island   Mrs. Saunders' class

 14b. To form the possessive case of a plural noun ending in *s*, add only the apostrophe. To form the possessive case of a plural noun that does not end in *s*, add an apostrophe and an *s*.

EXAMPLES
birds' feathers   Capulets' party
children's shoes   deer's food

Do not use an apostrophe to form the *plural* of a noun. Usually an apostrophe shows ownership or relationship.

PLURAL   Doodle and he are **brothers.**
POSSESSIVE   The **brothers'** relationship is special.

 14c. Possessive personal pronouns—*my, mine, your, yours, his, her, hers, its, our, ours, their,* and *theirs*—do not require an apostrophe.

EXAMPLES
This is **our** plant.
This plant is **ours.**

 14d. Indefinite pronouns—such as *everybody* and *neither*—in the possessive case require an apostrophe and an *s*.

EXAMPLES
nobody's wish   another's viewpoint

 14e. In compound words, names of organizations and businesses, and word groups showing joint possession, only the last word is possessive in form.

EXAMPLES
brother-in-**law's** gift   City **Garage's** tow trucks
United **Fund's** drive   Della and **Jim's** home

 14f. When two or more persons possess something individually, each of their names is possessive in form.

EXAMPLE
Poe's and **Dahl's** stories

Contractions

 14g. Use an apostrophe to show where letters, words, or numerals have been omitted in a contraction.

EXAMPLES
let us . . . . **let's**   you are . . . . . . **you're**
1991 . . . . **'91**   of the clock . . . **o'clock**

Ordinarily, the word *not* is shortened to *–n't* and added to a verb with no change to the verb's spelling.

EXAMPLES
are not . . . . . . **aren't**   has not . . . . . **hasn't**
EXCEPTIONS
will not . . . . . . **won't**   cannot . . . . . .**can't**

Do not confuse contractions with possessive pronouns.

CONTRACTIONS	PRONOUNS
Who's [Who is] at bat?	**Whose** bat is that?
It's [It is] roaring.	Listen to **its** roar.
You're [You are] late.	**Your** friend is late.
There's [There is] a kite.	That kite is **theirs.**
They're [They are] here.	**Their** bus is here.

Resources

Grammar and Language

■ *Language Handbook Worksheets,* pp. 150–158

Plurals

14h. Use an apostrophe and an *s* to form the plurals of all lowercase letters, some capital letters, and some words that are referred to as words.

EXAMPLES
Grandma always tells me to mind my *p*'s and *q*'s.
Those *U*'s look like *V*'s. [Without an apostrophe, the plural of *U* would spell *Us*. An apostrophe and an *s* are used to form the plural of *V* to make the style consistent.]
His *hi*'s are always cheerful. [Without an apostrophe, the plural would spell the word *his*.]

Using Apostrophes
In your reading you may have noticed that some writers do not use apostrophes to form the plurals of numbers, capital letters, symbols, and words used as words.

EXAMPLE
Their music was popular in the **1970s**.

However, using an apostrophe is never wrong. Therefore, it is often best to use the apostrophe.

Try It Out
For each of the following sentences, add an apostrophe wherever it is needed.

1. As in your studies are great, but Bs are good, too.
2. If you use *its*, make sure that they clearly refer to specific words.
3. Try not to include *I*s in the opening paragraph of a business letter.
4. The *10*s in this chart indicate the highest scores.
5. These *his*s should be *theirs*s.

HYPHENS

14i. Use a hyphen to divide a word at the end of a line.

EXAMPLE
"The Most Dangerous Game" is a very suspense-ful story.

When you divide a word at the end of a line, keep in mind the following rules.

(1) Do not divide one-syllable words.

(2) Divide a word only between syllables.
EXAMPLES
fi-an-cé   wor-thy

NOTE If you need to divide a word and are not sure about its syllables, look it up in a current dictionary.

(3) Words with double consonants may usually be divided between those two consonants.
EXAMPLES
rib-bon   man-ners
EXCEPTION
Words that end in double consonants followed by a suffix are divided before the suffix.
fall-ing   will-ing

(4) Usually, a word with a prefix or a suffix may be divided between the prefix or suffix and the base word (or root).
EXAMPLES
pro-gressive   govern-ment

(5) Divide an already hyphenated word only at a hyphen.
EXAMPLES
man-of-war   daughter-in-law

(6) Do not divide a word so that one letter stands alone.

14j. Use a hyphen with compound numbers from *twenty-one* to *ninety-nine* and with fractions used as adjectives.

EXAMPLES
twenty-four chairs
one-half cup [*One-half* is an adjective.]
one half of the money [*Half* is a noun.]

14k. Use a hyphen with the suffix –*elect* and with all prefixes before a proper noun or proper adjective.

EXAMPLES
president-elect   pre-Revolutionary

14l. Hyphenate a compound adjective that precedes the noun it modifies.

EXAMPLES
a well-written book   a world-famous skier

Do not use a hyphen if one of the modifiers is an adverb that ends in –*ly*.

EXAMPLE
a **bitterly cold** day

Try It Out
Answers
1. *A*'s in your studies are great, but *B*'s are good, too.
2. If you use *it's*, make sure that they clearly refer to specific words.
3. Try not to include *I*'s in the opening paragraph of a business letter.
4. The *10*'s in this chart indicate the highest scores.
5. These *his*'s should be *theirs*'s.

NOTE Some compound adjectives are always hyphenated, whether they precede or follow the nouns they modify.

EXAMPLE
an up-to-date dictionary
a dictionary that is up-to-date

If you're not sure whether a compound adjective should be hyphenated, check a recent dictionary.

DASHES

 14m. Use a dash to indicate an abrupt break in thought or speech or an unfinished statement or question.

EXAMPLE
Judy—Ms. Lane, I mean—will be your new coach.

 14n. Use a dash to mean *namely, that is, in other words,* and similar expressions that introduce an explanation.

EXAMPLES
Dr. Ganderbai considered using an anesthetic— ether or chloroform. [namely]
William Sydney Porter—O. Henry—is my favorite writer. [that is]

 NOTE When you type or input your writing on a word processor, you may indicate a dash by using two hyphens. (Do not leave a space before, between, or after the hyphens.) If you are using a computer, you may also find a dash available in your word processing software. When you write by hand, use an unbroken line about as long as two hyphens.

PARENTHESES

14o. Use parentheses to enclose material that is not considered of major importance in a sentence.

EXAMPLES
Richard Wright (1908–1960) wrote *Black Boy.*
Aunt Constance (Mother's aunt and my great-aunt) will meet us at the airport.

Capitalize and use end punctuation for parenthetical matter that stands alone as a sentence. Do not capitalize and use end punctuation for parenthetical matter contained within a sentence.

EXAMPLES
Complete the form. (Please print or type.)
The protagonist (the author did not give him a name) is a sniper.

15 SPELLING

UNDERSTANDING WORD STRUCTURE

Many English words are made up of roots and affixes (prefixes and suffixes). The **root** of a word is the part that carries the word's core meaning. A **prefix** is one or more letters or syllables added to the beginning of a word or word part to create a new word. A **suffix** is one or more letters or syllables added to the end of a word or word part to create a new word. Learning how to spell commonly used word parts and how to combine them can help you spell thousands of words.

COMMONLY USED ROOTS		
ROOTS	**MEANINGS**	**EXAMPLES**
–aud–, –audit–	hear	audible, auditorium
–bene–	well, good	benefit, benevolent
–chron–	time	chronological, synchronize
–cycl–	circle, wheel	cyclone, bicycle
–dem–	people	democracy, epidemic

(continued)

COMMONLY USED ROOTS (continued)

ROOTS	MEANINGS	EXAMPLES
–gen–	birth, kind, origin	generate, generic, generous
–graph–	write, writing	autograph, geography
–hydr–	water	hydrant, hydrate
–log–, –logue–	study, word	logic, mythology, dialogue
–micr–	small	microbe, microscope
–morph–	form	metamorphosis, polymorph
–phil–	like, love	philanthropic, philosophy
–phon–	sound	phonograph, euphony
–port–	carry, bear	export, important
–psych–	mind	psychology, psychosomatic
–verse–, –vert–	turn	reverse, convert
–vid–, –vis–	see	television, evident

COMMONLY USED PREFIXES

PREFIXES	MEANINGS	EXAMPLES
anti–	against, opposing	antipathy, antithesis
bi–	two	bimonthly, bisect
contra–	against	contradict, contrast
de–	away, off, down	defect, desert, decline
dis–	away, off, opposing	dismount, dissent
hemi–	half	hemisphere, hemicycle
hyper–	excessive, over	hyperactive, hypertension
inter–	between, among	intercede, international
mis–	badly, not, wrongly	misfire, misspell
over–	above, excessive	oversee, overdo
post–	after, following	postpone, postscript
re–	back, backward, again	revoke, reflect, reforest
tra–, trans–	across, beyond	traffic, transport
un–	not, reverse of	untrue, unfold

COMMONLY USED SUFFIXES

SUFFIXES	MEANINGS	EXAMPLES
–able	able, likely	capable, changeable
–cy	state, condition	accuracy, normalcy
–er	doer, native of	baker, westerner
–ful	full of, marked by	thankful, masterful
–ic	dealing with, caused by, person or thing showing	classic, choleric, heretic
–ion	action, result, state	union, fusion, dominion
–ish	suggesting, like	smallish, childish
–ist	doer, believer	monopolist, capitalist
–ly	like, characteristic of	friendly, cowardly
–ness	quality, state	softness, shortness
–or	doer, office, action	director, juror, error
–ous	marked by, given to	religious, furious
–tion	action, condition	selection, relation
–tude	quality, state	fortitude, multitude

ie and *ei*

15a. Write *ie* when the sound is long *e*, except after *c*.

EXAMPLES
ach**ie**ve ch**ie**f n**ie**ce c**ei**ling de**cei**t re**cei**ve
EXCEPTIONS
either l**ei**sure n**ei**ther s**ei**ze prot**ei**n

15b. Write *ei* when the sound is not long *e*.

EXAMPLES
for**ei**gn forf**ei**t h**ei**ght h**ei**r r**ei**gn w**ei**gh
EXCEPTIONS
anc**ie**nt consc**ie**nce fr**ie**nd misch**ie**f v**ie**w

–cede, –ceed, and –sede

15c. The only English word ending in *–sede* is *supersede*. The only words ending in *–ceed* are *exceed, proceed,* and *succeed*. Most other words with this sound end in *–cede*.

EXAMPLES
ac**cede** inter**cede** re**cede**
con**cede** pre**cede** se**cede**

Adding Prefixes

15d. When adding a prefix, do not change the spelling of the original word.

EXAMPLES
im + mortal = **im**mortal   mis + step = **mis**step
re + elect = **re**elect   over + run = **over**run

Adding Suffixes

15e. When adding the suffix *–ness* or *–ly*, do not change the spelling of the original word.

EXAMPLES
fair + ness = fair**ness**   sure + ly = sure**ly**
EXCEPTIONS
For most words ending in *y*, change the *y* to *i* before adding *–ness* or *–ly*:
empty—empt**iness**   easy—eas**ily**

However, most one-syllable words ending in *y* follow rule 15e.

EXAMPLES
dry + ness = dry**ness**   sly + ly = sly**ly**

15f. Drop the final silent *e* before a suffix beginning with a vowel.

EXAMPLES
hope + ing = hop**ing**   strange + est = strang**est**
EXCEPTIONS
Keep the final silent *e*

- in words ending in *ce* or *ge* before a suffix that begins with *a* or *o:* knowledg**eable**, outrag**eous**
- in *dye* and in *singe,* before *–ing:* dy**eing**, sing**eing**
- in *mile* before *–age:* mil**eage**

15g. Keep the final silent *e* before a suffix beginning with a consonant.

EXAMPLES
nine + ty = nine**ty**   entire + ly = entire**ly**
EXCEPTIONS
nine + th = nin**th**   awe + ful = aw**ful**
judge + ment = judg**ment**
argue + ment = argu**ment**

15h. For words ending in *y* preceded by a consonant, change the *y* to *i* before any suffix that does not begin with *i*.

EXAMPLES
fifty + eth = fift**ieth**   mystery + ous = myster**ious**

15i. For words ending in *y* preceded by a vowel, simply add the suffix.

EXAMPLES
joy + ful = joy**ful**   boy + hood = boy**hood**
EXCEPTIONS
day + ly = da**ily**   pay + ed = pa**id**
say + ed = sa**id**   lay + ed = la**id**

15j. Double the final consonant before a suffix that begins with a vowel if the word *both* (1) has only one syllable or has the accent on the last syllable *and* (2) ends in a single consonant preceded by a single vowel.

EXAMPLES
drop + ing = dro**pping**
occur + ence = occu**rrence**
strum + ed = stru**mmed**
thin + er = thi**nner**

NOTE The final consonant in some words may or may not be doubled. Both spellings are equally correct.

EXAMPLES
travel + er = trave**ler** *or* trave**ller**
shovel + ed = shove**led** *or* shove**lled**

Forming Plurals of Nouns

15k. To form the plurals of most English nouns, add –*s*.

EXAMPLES
boats   houses   nickels   Lincolns

15l. To form the plurals of other nouns, follow these rules.

(1) For nouns ending in *s, x, z, ch,* or *sh,* add –*es*.

EXAMPLES
glass**es**   box**es**   waltz**es**   beach**es**   Bush**es**

(2) For nouns ending in *y* preceded by a consonant, change the *y* to *i* and add –*es*.

EXAMPLES
arm**ies**   bab**ies**   sk**ies**   myster**ies**
EXCEPTION
For proper nouns, add –*s:* Hard**ys**

(3) For nouns ending in *y* preceded by a vowel, add –*s*.

EXAMPLES
joys   keys   Momadays

(4) For some nouns ending in *f* or *fe,* add –*s*. For others, change the *f* or *fe* to *v* and add –*es*.

EXAMPLES
beliefs   roofs   safes   giraffes
cal**ves**   wi**ves**   lea**ves**   shel**ves**
EXCEPTION
For proper nouns, add –*s:* Radcliffs, Rolfes

(5) For nouns ending in *o* preceded by a vowel, add –*s*.

EXAMPLES
radios   patios   Marios   stereos

(6) For nouns ending in *o* preceded by a consonant, add –*es*.

EXAMPLES
echo**es**   hero**es**   veto**es**   tomato**es**
EXCEPTIONS
For some common nouns ending in *o* preceded by a consonant, especially musical terms, and for proper nouns, add only –*s:* tacos, pianos, Sotos

(7) The plurals of a few nouns are formed in irregular ways.

EXAMPLES
child**ren**   feet   men   teeth   mice

(8) For a few nouns, the singular and the plural forms are the same.

SINGULAR AND PLURAL
deer   Japanese   Navajo   sheep   trout   series

(9) For a compound noun written as one word, form the plural of only the last word of the compound.

EXAMPLES
icebox**es**   blackberr**ies**   business**people**

(10) For a compound noun that is hyphenated or written as separate words, form the plural of the noun that is modified.

EXAMPLES
sisters-in-law   runners-up   music box**es**

(11) For some nouns borrowed from other languages, the plurals are formed as in the original languages.

EXAMPLES
crisis—cris**es**   phenomenon—phenomen**a**

A few nouns borrowed from other languages have two plural forms.

EXAMPLES
appendix—appendi**ces** *or* appendix**es**
formula—formula**s** *or* formula**e**

(12) For numerals, symbols, some capital letters, and words used as words, add an –*s* or both an apostrophe and an –*s*.

EXAMPLES
6—6s *or* 6*'*s   R—Rs *or* R*'*s
&—&s *or* &*'*s   and—ands *or* and*'*s

To prevent confusion, always use an apostrophe and an –*s* to form the plurals of lowercase letters, certain capital letters, and some words used as words.

EXAMPLES
Your ***i'*s** look like ***e'*s.** [Without an apostrophe, the plural of *i* would look like *is*.]
Ramón got all **A*'*s** last semester. [Without an apostrophe, the plural of A would look like *As*.]
Her ***and so'*s** began to get tiresome. [Without the apostrophe, the plural of *so* would look like *sos*.]

COMPUTER NOTE

Spell-checking software can help you proofread your writing. Even the best spelling checkers aren't foolproof, however. Some accept British and archaic spellings, and most do not identify words that are spelled correctly but are used incorrectly (such as *affect* for *effect*). Always double-check your writing to make sure that your spelling is error free.

16 GLOSSARY OF USAGE

The Glossary of Usage is an alphabetical list of words, expressions, and special terms with definitions, explanations, and examples. Some examples have usage labels. *Standard* or *formal* usages are appropriate in serious writing and speaking, such as in compositions and in speeches. *Informal* words and expressions are standard English usages generally appropriate in conversation and in everyday writing such as in personal letters. *Nonstandard* usages do not follow the guidelines of standard English.

---

accept, except   *Accept* is a verb that means "receive." *Except* may be either a verb or a preposition. As a verb, *except* means "leave out." As a preposition, *except* means "excluding."

EXAMPLES
We **accept** your apology.
All children under age three will be **excepted** from the fee. [verb]
Everyone **except** Bob and me has seen the exhibit. [preposition]

advice, advise   *Advice* is a noun meaning "suggestion about what to do." *Advise* is a verb meaning "offer a suggestion; recommend."

EXAMPLES
He gave me some excellent **advice.**
She **advised** me to finish high school.

affect, effect   *Affect* is a verb meaning "influence." As a verb, *effect* means "accomplish." As a noun, *effect* means "result (of an action)."

EXAMPLES
What he said did not **affect** my decision.
The mayor has **effected** many changes during her administration. [verb]
What **effect** will the new factory have on the environment? [noun]

ain't   Avoid using this word in formal speaking and in all writing other than dialogue; it is nonstandard English.

all together, altogether   *All together* means "everyone or everything in the same place." *Altogether* is an adverb meaning "entirely."

EXAMPLES
When we were **all together,** we voted.
He was **altogether** wrong.

a lot   Do not write the expression *a lot* as one word.

EXAMPLE
In addition to short stories, Edgar Allan Poe also wrote **a lot** [*not* alot]of poetry.

among   See **between, among.**

and etc.   The abbreviation for the Latin phrase *et cetera,* meaning "and other things" is *etc.* Thus, do not use *and* with *etc.*

EXAMPLE
My younger sister collects stickers, bottle caps, string, **etc.** [*not* and etc.]

anyways, anywheres   Use these words (and others like them, such as *everywheres, somewheres,* and *nowheres*) without the final *s.*

EXAMPLES
I have to baby-sit tonight **anyway** [*not* anyways].
The Loisels could not find the necklace **anywhere** [*not* anywheres].

as   See **like, as.**

as if   See **like, as if.**

at   Do not use *at* after *where.*

NONSTANDARD   Where was Romeo at?
STANDARD   **Where** was Romeo?

bad, badly   *Bad* is an adjective. *Badly* is an adverb. In standard English, only *bad* should follow a linking verb, such as *feel, look, sound, taste,* or *smell,* or forms of the verb *be.*

EXAMPLE
The fruitcake doesn't taste **bad** [*not* badly].

being as, being that   Use *since* or *because* instead of these expressions.

EXAMPLE
Because [*not* being as] President Clinton admired Maya Angelou's writing, he invited her to write a poem for his inauguration.

beside, besides   *Beside* is a preposition that means "by the side of" or "next to." As a preposition, *besides* means "in addition to" or "other than." As an adverb, *besides* means "moreover."

EXAMPLES
His rifle lay **beside** him.
Who **besides** Timber tried to help? [preposition]
I don't want to go; **besides,** it's snowing. [adverb]

between, among   Use *between* when you are referring to two things at a time, even though they may be part of a group consisting of more than two.

EXAMPLES

There was a feud **between** the Montagues and the Capulets.

The manager could not decide which of the four players to select, because there was not much difference **between** them. [Although there are more than two players, each one is being compared with the others separately.]

Use *among* when referring to a group rather than to separate individuals.

EXAMPLE

We were able to collect only ten dollars **among** the four of us.

bust, busted   Avoid using these words as verbs. Use a form of either *burst* or *break,* depending on the meaning.

EXAMPLES

The balloon **burst** [*not* busted] loudly.

The firefighters **broke** [*not* busted] a window.

consul, council, counsel   *Consul* is a noun meaning "representative of a foreign country." *Council* is a noun meaning "group called together to accomplish a job." As a noun, *counsel* means "advice." As a verb, it means "give advice."

EXAMPLES

The French **consul** outlined his government's plan.

The city **council** will debate the issue.

I'm grateful for your **counsel.** [noun]

Did the doctor **counsel** her to get more rest? [verb]

could of   See **of.**

discover, invent   *Discover* means "be the first to find, see, or learn about something that already exists." *Invent* means "be the first to do or make something."

EXAMPLES

Marguerite Perey **discovered** the element francium.

The zipper was **invented** in 1893.

double negative   A double negative is the use of two negative words when one is enough. Avoid using double negatives.

Common Negative Words			
barely	never	no one	not (–n't)
hardly	no	nowhere	nothing
neither	nobody	none	scarcely

NONSTANDARD	I had not read none of Emily Dickinson's poems.
STANDARD	I **had not read any** of Emily Dickinson's poems.
STANDARD	I **had read none** of Emily Dickinson's poems.

NONSTANDARD	Doodle couldn't hardly walk.
STANDARD	Doodle **could hardly** walk.

double subject   See **he, she, it, they.**

effect   See **affect, effect.**

etc.   See **and etc.**

everywheres   See **anyways, anywheres.**

except   See **accept, except.**

fewer, less   *Fewer* tells "how many"; it is used with plural nouns. *Less* tells "how much"; it is used with singular nouns.

EXAMPLES

There are **fewer** gypsy moths this year than there were last year.

Reading the *Odyssey* took **less** time than we had thought.

good, well   *Good* is an adjective. *Well* may be used as an adjective or an adverb. Never use *good* to modify a verb; instead, use *well* as an adverb meaning "capably" or "satisfactorily."

EXAMPLE

Sandra Cisneros writes **well** [*not* good].

As an adjective, *well* means "healthy" or "satisfactory in appearance or condition."

EXAMPLES

Lying in his bed, Harry did not look **well.**

Friar Laurence thought that all would be **well** with the Montagues and the Capulets.

 NOTE   *Feel good* and *feel well* mean different things. *Feel good* means "feel happy or pleased." *Feel well* means "feel healthy."

EXAMPLES

The news made her feel **good.**

I didn't feel **well,** so I went home.

had ought, hadn't ought   Unlike other verbs, *ought* is not used with *had.*

EXAMPLES

I think Doodle's brother **ought** [*not* had ought] to be more patient; he **ought not** [*not* hadn't ought] to push Doodle so hard.

hardly   See **double negative.**

he, she, it, they   Do not use an unnecessary pronoun after the subject of a verb. This error is called the *double subject.*

| NONSTANDARD | Miss Lottie she likes to grow marigolds. |
| STANDARD | Miss Lottie likes to grow marigolds. |

hisself, theirselves   Do not use these words for *himself* and *themselves.*

EXAMPLE
Romeo unburdens **himself** [*not* hisself] to Friar Laurence.

imply, infer   *Imply* means "suggest indirectly." *Infer* means "interpret" or "draw a conclusion (from a remark or an action)."

EXAMPLES
Doug **implied** that he will vote for me.
From Doug's remark, I **inferred** that he will vote for me.

inside of   See **of.**

invent   See **discover, invent.**

it   See **he, she, it, they.**

its, it's   *Its* is the possessive form of *it. It's* is the contraction of *it is* or *it has.*

EXAMPLES
The bird stopped **its** singing.
It's [it is] an easy problem.
It's [it has] been raining since noon.

kind of, sort of   In formal situations, avoid using these terms to mean *somewhat* or *rather.*

| INFORMAL | Zaroff was kind of surprised to see that Rainsford was still alive. |
| FORMAL | Zaroff was **somewhat** [*or* **rather**] surprised to see that Rainsford was still alive. |

kind of a, sort of a   Avoid using *a* after *kind of* and *sort of* in formal situations.

| INFORMAL | What kind of a snake was it? |
| FORMAL | What **kind of** snake was it? |

kind(s), sort(s), type(s)   Use *this* or *that* with the singular form of each of these nouns. Use *these* or *those* with the plural form.

EXAMPLES
I like **this kind** of jeans better than any of **those** other **kinds.**

lay   See **lie, lay.**

learn, teach   *Learn* means "acquire knowledge." *Teach* means "instruct" or "show how."

EXAMPLES
Doodle **learns** to walk.
His brother **teaches** him to walk.

leave, let   *Leave* means "go away" or "depart from." *Let* means "allow" or "permit." Avoid using *leave* for *let.*

EXAMPLE
Let [*not* leave] her speak if she insists.

less   See **fewer, less.**

let   See **leave, let.**

lie, lay   The verb *lie* means "rest" or "stay, recline, or remain in a certain position." *Lie* never takes an object. Its principal parts are *lie, lying, lay, lain.* The verb *lay* means "put (something) in a place." Its principal parts are *lay, laying, laid, laid. Lay* usually takes an object.

EXAMPLES
Is there a real snake **lying** on Harry's stomach? [no object]
He **laid** her gift on the table. [*Gift* is the object of *laid.*]

like, as   In formal English, use *like* to introduce a prepositional phrase, and use *as* to introduce a subordinate clause.

EXAMPLES
Does Juliet look **like** Rosaline? [The preposition *like* introduces the phrase *like Rosaline.*]
Juliet does **as** Friar Laurence suggests. [The subordinating conjunction *as* introduces the clause *as Friar Laurence suggests.*]

like, as if   In formal situations, *like* should not be used for the compound conjunction *as if* or *as though.*

EXAMPLE
Juliet looks **as though** [*not* like] she is alive.

might of, must of   See **of.**

moral, morale   As an adjective, *moral* means "good; virtuous." As a noun, it means "lesson of conduct." *Morale* is a noun meaning "spirit; mental condition."

EXAMPLES
In Pearl Buck's short story "The Old Demon," Mrs. Wang's **moral** values compel her to help the Japanese pilot. [adjective]
James Thurber's fables end with **morals** quite unlike the ones in traditional fairy tales. [noun]
The employees' **morale** is high.

nowheres   See **anyways, anywheres.**

of   *Of* is a preposition. Do not use *of* in place of *have* after verbs such as *could, should, would, ought (to), might,* and *must.* Also, do not use *had of* for *had.*

NONSTANDARD	You would of enjoyed our production of *The Miracle Worker.*
STANDARD	You **would have** [*or* **would've**] enjoyed our production of *The Miracle Worker.*
NONSTANDARD	If I had of known it was your birthday, I would of given you a card.
STANDARD	If I **had** known it was your birthday, I **would have** given you a card.

Also, do not use *of* after other prepositions such as *inside, off,* or *outside.*

EXAMPLES
The sniper's enemy fell **off** [*not* off of] the roof.
The sleeping Juliet is carried **inside** [*not* inside of] the Capulets' tomb.

off of   See **of.**

ought   See **had ought, hadn't ought.**

ought to of   See **of.**

peace, piece   *Peace* means "calmness; absence of war or strife." *Piece* means "part of something."

EXAMPLES
After the long war, **peace** was welcome.
Do you have a **piece** of paper I can borrow?

principal, principle   As a noun, *principal* means "the head of a school." As an adjective, it means "main or most important." *Principle* is a noun meaning "a rule of conduct" or "a general truth."

EXAMPLES
Ted had a long talk with the **principal.** [noun]
Winning is not our **principal** goal. [adjective]
My friends have high **principles.**
I don't know the **principles** of physics.

rise, raise   The verb *rise* means "go up" or "get up." *Rise* almost never takes an object. Its principal parts are *rise, rising, rose, risen.* The verb *raise* means "cause (something) to rise" or "lift up." *Raise* usually takes an object. Its principal parts are *raise, raising, raised, raised.*

EXAMPLES
Everyone **rose** when the judge entered the room. [no object]
The sniper **raised** his revolver and fired. [*Revolver* is the object of *raised.*]

scarcely   See **double negative.**

set   See **sit, set.**

she   See **he, she, it, they.**

should of   See **of.**

sit, set   The verb *sit* means "rest in an upright, seated position." *Sit* almost never takes an object. Its principal parts are *sit, sitting, sat, sat.* The verb *set* means "put (something) in a place." *Set* usually takes an object. Its principal parts are *set, setting, set, set.*

EXAMPLES
The campers were **sitting** around the fire. [no object]
Ganderbai **set** the bag on a chair. [*Bag* is the object of *set.*]

some, somewhat   In formal situations, do not use *some* to mean "to some extent" or "slightly." Instead, use *somewhat.*

INFORMAL	My spelling has now improved some.
FORMAL	My spelling has now improved **somewhat.**

somewheres   See **anyways, anywheres.**

sort(s)   See **kind(s), sort(s), type(s)** and **kind of a, sort of a.**

sort of   See **kind of, sort of.**

teach   See **learn, teach.**

than, then   *Than* is a conjunction used in comparisons. *Then* is an adverb meaning "at that time" or "next."

EXAMPLES
This box is heavier **than** that one.
Did the sniper know **then** who his enemy was?
First, I read *Romeo and Juliet;* **then,** I watched the film version.

that   See **who, which, that.**

their, there, they're   *Their* is a possessive form of *they.* As an adverb, *there* means "at that place." *There* is also used to begin a sentence. *They're* is the contraction of *they are.*

EXAMPLES
Their daughter, Juliet, was in love with a Montague.
Harry Pope lay **there** quietly.
There is a conflict between Odysseus and the Cyclops.
They're throwing pebbles at Miss Lottie's flowers.

theirs, there's   *Theirs* is a possessive form of the pronoun *they*. *There's* is the contraction of *there is*.

EXAMPLES
Our team was ready to play, and so was **theirs**.
There's a sniper on the rooftop.

theirselves   See **hisself, theirselves.**

them   *Them* should not be used as an adjective. Use *those*.

EXAMPLE
Their unselfish love is symbolized by **those** [*not* them] gifts.

then   See **than, then.**

there   See **their, there, they're.**

there's   See **theirs, there's.**

they   See **he, she, it, they.**

they're   See **their, there, they're.**

this, that, these, those   See **kind(s), sort(s), type(s).**

try and   Use *try to*, not *try and*.

EXAMPLE
Timber and Ganderbai **try to** [*not* try and] keep Harry calm.

type(s)   See **kind(s), sort(s), type(s).**

unless   See **without, unless.**

way, ways   Use *way*, not *ways*, in referring to a distance.

EXAMPLE
Odysseus traveled quite a long **way** [*not* ways] to get back home.

well   See **good, well.**

what   Use *that*, not *what*, to introduce an adjective clause.

EXAMPLE
The poem **that** [*not* what] I wrote about was Naomi Shihab Nye's "Daily."

when, where   Do not use *when* or *where* to begin a definition.

NONSTANDARD	A "bomb" in football is when a backfielder throws a long pass.
STANDARD	A "bomb" in football is a long pass thrown by a backfielder.

Also, do not use *where* for *that*.

EXAMPLE
I read in this book **that** [*not* where] Robert Frost won the Pulitzer Prize four times.

where . . . at   See **at.**

who, which, that   *Who* refers to persons only; *which* refers to things only; *that* may refer to either persons or things.

EXAMPLES
Isn't Walt Whitman the poet **who** [*or* that] wrote
   Leaves of Grass? [person]
They decided to replace Mme. Forestier's necklace,
   which they did not know was fake. [thing]
The necklace **that** the Loisels bought cost thirty-six
   thousand francs. [thing]

who's, whose   *Who's* is the contraction of *who is* or *who has*. *Whose* is the possessive form of *who*.

EXAMPLES
Who's [who is] the narrator of "A Christmas
   Memory"?
Who's [who has] been helping Helen?
Whose autobiography is titled *Black Boy*?

without, unless   Do not use the preposition *without* in place of the conjunction *unless*.

EXAMPLE
I will not be able to sing **unless** [*not* without] my cold gets better.

would of   See **of.**

your, you're   *Your* is a possessive form of *you*. *You're* is the contraction of *you are*.

EXAMPLES
What is **your** opinion of General Zaroff?
You're [you are] my best friend.

Glossary

The glossary that follows is an alphabetical list of words found in the selections in this book. Use this glossary just as you would use a dictionary—to find out the meanings of unfamiliar words. (Some technical, foreign, and more obscure words in this book are not listed here but instead are defined for you in the footnotes that accompany many of the selections.)

Many words in the English language have more than one meaning. This glossary gives the meanings that apply to the words as they are used in the selections in this book. Words closely related in form and meaning are usually listed together in one entry (for instance, *compassion* and *compassionate*), and the definition is given for the first form.

The following abbreviations are used:

adj.	adjective
adv.	adverb
n.	noun
v.	verb

Each word's pronunciation is given in parentheses. A guide to the pronunciation symbols appears at the bottom of this page. For more information about the words in this glossary or for information about words not listed here, consult a dictionary.

A

abhor (ab·hôr′) *v.*: hate.

abolish (ə·bäl′ish) *v.*: put an end to. *Abolition* is the noun form of this word.

abominable (ə·bäm′ə·nə·bəl) *adj.*: extremely unpleasant or disgusting. —**abominably** *adv.*

absorb (ab·sôrb′) *v.*: take in.

acclaim (ə·klām′) *v.*: receive strong approval; applaud.

acquiesce (ak′wē·es′) *v.* (used with *in*): accept; comply with.

admonish (ad·män′ish) *v.*: scold mildly.

admonition (ad′mə·nish′ən) *n.*: scolding; warning.

adorn (ə·dôrn′) *v.*: add beauty to; decorate.

adulation (a′jōō·lā′shən) *n.*: intense or excessive admiration or praise.

adversary (ad′vər·ser′ē) *n.*: enemy; opponent.

adversity (ad·vur′sə·tē) *n.*: hardship; great misfortune.

advocate (ad′və·kāt′) *v.*: support; argue in favor of.

advocate (ad′və·kit) *n.*: supporter.

affluent (af′lōō·ənt) *adj.*: wealthy.

aghast (ə·gast′) *adj.*: terrified; horrified.

agile (aj′əl) *adj.*: moving with ease.

allegiance (ə·lē′jəns) *n.*: loyalty.

aloof (ə·lōōf′) *adj.*: at a distance; unfriendly.

annihilate (ə·nī′ə·lāt′) *v.*: destroy completely; wipe out.

ardor (är′dər) *n.*: passion; enthusiasm.

arid (ar′id) *adj.*: lacking enough water for many types of plants to grow; dry.

ascetic (ə·set′ik) *adj.*: severe; also, self-disciplined.

ascribe (ə·skrīb′) *v.*: assign or attribute something to a cause.

aspire (ə·spīr′) *v.*: seek to gain; desire. —**aspiring** *v.* used as *n.*

astronomer (ə·strän′ə·mər) *n.*: scientist who studies the stars and planets.

austere (ô·stir′) *adj.*: very plain; severe.

avail (ə·vāl′) *v.*: be of use; help.

avert (ə·vurt′) *v.*: turn away. —**averted** *v.* used as *adj.*

awry (ə·rī′) *adv.*: in the wrong manner.

B

balmy (bäm′ē) *adj.*: mild; pleasant.

beckon (bek′ən) *v.*: gesture or signal to request someone to approach or follow.

beguile (bē·gīl′) *v.*: charm; deceive.

---

at, āte, cär; ten, ēve; is, īce; gō, hôrn, look, tōōl; oil, out; up, fur; ə *for unstressed vowels, as* a *in* ago, u *in* focus; ′ *as in* Latin (lat′′n); chin; she; thin; *the*; zh *as in* azure (azh′ər); ŋ *as in* ring (riŋ)

beleaguer (bē·lē′gər) *v.*: surround and attack.
 —**beleaguered** *v.* used as *adj.*

belligerent (bə·lij′ər·ənt) *adj.*: angry and aggressive or
 ready to start a fight.

bigotry (big′ə·trē) *n.*: strong prejudice against a particular group of people.

blight (blīt) *v.*: destroy or prevent growth. —**blighted**
 v. used as *adj.*

bureaucratic (byoor′ə·krat′ik) *adj.*: relating to rigid
 government routine.

C

candor (kan′dər) *n.*: honesty; frankness.

carnage (kär′nij) *n.*: widespread killing; slaughter;
 bloodshed.

cascade (kas·kād′) *n.*: waterfall.

catastrophic (kat′ə·sträf′ik) *adj.*: disastrous.

chronic (krän′ik) *adj.*: frequently occurring.

clarity (klar′ə·tē) *n.*: clearness.

clench (klench) *v.*: tightly close. —**clenched** *v.* used
 as *adj.*

coerce (kō·ʉrs′) *v.*: force.

compulsory (kəm·pul′sə·rē) *adj.*: required by rule
 or law.

conceivable (kən·sēv′ə·bəl) *adj.*: capable of being
 imagined or understood.

condolence (kən·dō′ləns) *n.*: expression of sympathy.

condone (kən·dōn′) *v.*: overlook or excuse an
 offense.

connoisseurship (kän′ə·sʉr′ship) *n.*: expert knowledge.

conscientious (kän′shē·en′shəs) *adj.*: careful and
 thoughtful. —**conscientiously** *adv.*

conspicuous (kən·spik′yoo·əs) *adj.*: obvious; noticeable; notable.

conspiracy (kən·spir′ə·sē) *n.*: secret, often unlawful
 plan carried out by a group.

constitute (kän′stə·toot′) *v.*: make up; form.

contrition (kən·trish′ən) *n.*: deep feelings of guilt and
 repentance.

controversial (kän′trə·vʉr′shəl) *adj.*: stirring up disagreement between groups holding opposing views.

conviction (kən·vik′shən) *n.*: strong belief.

covet (kuv′it) *v.*: long for. —**coveted** *v.* used as *adj.*

D

decrepit (dē·krep′it) *adj.*: falling apart.

default (dē·fôlt′) *n.*: failure to do something.

defer (dē·fʉr′) *v.*: delay; put off.

defiant (dē·fī′ənt) *adj.*: openly and boldly resisting or
 opposing.

deficient (dē·fish′ənt) *adj.*: lacking.

deliberation (di·lib′ər·ā′shən) *n.*: careful thought,
 especially in making a decision.

delirious (di·lir′ē·əs) *adj.*: temporarily confused and
 seeing imaginary things, often because of injury or
 fever.

delirium (di·lir′ē·əm) *n.*: extreme mental disturbance,
 often accompanied by hallucinations (seeing things
 that are not there).

demise (dē·mīz′) *n.*: death; end.

denounce (dē·nʊuns′) *v.*: accuse publicly; condemn.
 —**denouncing** *v.* used as *adj.*

depreciate (dē·prē′shē·āt′) *v.*: make something seem
 less important; lower the value of.

depression (dē·presh′ən) *n.*: major economic downturn. *Depression* also means "sadness."

designate (dez′ig·nāt′) *v.*: point out; indicate.

desolate (des′ə·lāt′) *v.*: produce a feeling of loneliness
 and sadness. —**desolating** *v.* used as *adj.*

despondent (di·spän′dənt) *adj.*: hopeless.
 —**despondently** *adv.*

devious (dē′vē·əs) *adj.*: sneaky; deceptive.

dilapidated (də·lap′ə·dāt′id) *adj.*: in poor condition;
 shabby and neglected; falling apart.

dilemma (di·lem′ə) *n.*: difficult choice; serious
 problem.

dire (dīr) *adj.*: terrible.

disarming (dis·ärm′iŋ) *adj.*: removing or lessening
 suspicions or fears.

disconsolate (dis·kän′sə·lit) *adj.*: causing sadness or
 depression; also, very unhappy.

discreet (di·skrēt′) *adj.*: showing good judgment in
 what one says or does; especially being silent or
 careful.

disdainful (dis·dān′fəl) *adj.*: scornful; regarding someone as beneath you.

disposition (dis′pə·zish′ən) *n.*: usual frame of mind;
 temperament.

distracted (di·strakt′id) *adj.*: unable to concentrate
 on something.

distraught (di·strôt′) *adj.*: deeply troubled, as with
 worry or grief.

divergent (dī·vʉr′jənt) *adj.*: separate; going in different directions.

diverting (də·vʉrt′iŋ) *adj.*: entertaining.

doggedness (dôg′id·nis) *n.*: stubbornness; persistence.

E

eclipse (i·klips′) v.: conceal from view; overshadow.

elation (ē·lā′shən) n.: great joy.

elect (ē·lekt′) v.: choose.

emaciated (ē·mā′shē·āt′id) adj.: extremely thin; wasted away.

embody (em·bäd′ē) v.: convey the impression of; represent.

emulate (em′yo͞o·lāt′) v.: follow the example of; imitate.

endeavor (en·dev′ər) n.: **1.** serious attempt, effort, or undertaking. v.: **2.** try.

enduring (en·do͝or′iŋ) adj.: strong and lasting.

enthrall (en·thrôl′) v.: fascinate.

enunciate (ē·nun′sē·āt′) v.: pronounce; articulate.

equitable (ek′wit·ə·bəl) adj.: fair; just.

eradicate (ē·rad′i·kāt′) v.: wipe out; destroy; eliminate completely; get rid of. —**eradicating** v. used as n.

esteem (ə·stēm′) n.: respect.

exasperation (eg·zas′pər·ā′shən) n.: great annoyance.

exhilarate (eg·zil′ə·rāt′) v.: gladden; excite.

exorbitant (eg·zôr′bi·tənt) adj.: much too high in price or amount.

expendable (ek·spen′də·bəl) adj.: worth sacrificing to gain an objective.

expire (ek·spīr′) v.: die.

exuberant (eg·zo͞o′bər·ənt) adj.: elaborate; extreme; also, high-spirited.

F

fanatic (fə·nat′ik) n.: person whose extreme devotion to a cause is excessive or unreasonable.

fervent (fur′vənt) adj.: passionate.

formidable (fôr′mə·də·bəl) adj.: awe-inspiring by reason of excellence; strikingly impressive; causing fear or dread.

futile (fyo͞ot′'l) adj.: useless; vain.

G

genial (jēn′yəl) adj.: cheerful and friendly.

giddy (gid′ē) adj.: dizzy.

glower (glou′ər) v.: glare; stare angrily.

gurgle (gur′gəl) v.: make a bubbling sound while flowing.

H

hoist (hoist) v.: lift or pull up.

hover (huv′ər) v.: stay suspended over something.

hyperactive (hī′pər·ak′tiv) adj.: abnormally active; very lively.

I

idle (īd′'l) adj.: without aim or purpose. —**idly** adv.

ignorance (ig′nə·rəns) n.: lack of knowledge.

imminent (im′ə·nənt) adj.: near; about to happen.

immolation (im′ə·lā′shən) n.: destruction.

immortal (i·môrt′'l) adj.: lasting or living forever.

impartial (im·pär′shəl) adj.: fair; unbiased.

impend (im·pend′) v.: be about to happen. —**impending** v. used as adj.

implication (im′pli·kā′shən) n.: possible connection or consequence.

impose (im·pōz′) v. (used with upon): take advantage of.

imposing (im·pō′ziŋ) adj.: large and impressive looking.

impoverish (im·päv′ər·ish) v.: make poor. —**impoverished** v. used as adj.

imprudent (im·pro͞od′'nt) adj.: unwise.

impulse (im′puls′) n.: sudden desire to do something.

impunity (im·pyo͞o′ni·tē) n.: freedom from punishment or harm.

inaugurate (in·ô′gyə·rāt′) v.: formally begin.

incantation (in′kan·tā′shən) n.: chant of words or phrases that is meant to produce a magical result.

incessant (in·ses′ənt) adj.: constant; continuous. —**incessantly** adv.

incite (in·sīt′) v.: stir up. —**inciting** v. used as n.

inconsolable (in′kən·sōl′ə·bəl) adj.: unable to be comforted; brokenhearted.

incredulous (in·krej′oo·ləs) adj.: unbelieving; skeptical. —**incredulously** adv.

---

at, āte, cär; ten, ēve; is, īce; gō, hôrn, look, to͞ol; oil, out; up, fur; ə *for unstressed vowels, as* a *in* ago, u *in* focus; ′ *as in* Latin (lat′'n); chin; she; thin; *the*; zh *as in* azure (azh′ər); ŋ *as in* ring (riŋ)

indiscriminate (in'di·skrim'i·nit) *adj.*: careless.

inevitable (in·ev'i·tə·bəl) *adj.*: unavoidable; certain to happen.

infallibility (in·fal'ə·bil'i·tē) *n.*: inability to make a mistake.

infatuated (in·fach'oo·āt'id) *adj.*: carried away by shallow or foolish love.

insensible (in·sen'sə·bəl) *adj.*: not fully conscious or aware.

instigate (in'stə·gāt') *v.*: give rise to. *Instigate* is generally used to mean "urge on to some action, usually negative, or set something in motion."

intangible (in·tan'jə·bəl) *adj.*: cannot be touched or held.

interminable (in·tur'min·nə·bəl) *adj.*: with no end in sight.

intimidate (in·tim'ə·dāt') *v.*: frighten. —**intimidating** *v.* used as *adj.*

intolerance (in·täl'ər·əns) *n.*: prejudice; hostility to other groups.

invariable (in·ver'ē·ə·bəl) *adj.*: always; without changing. —**invariably** *adv.*

invincible (in·vin'sə·bəl) *adj.*: unconquerable.

iridescent (ir'i·des'ənt) *adj.*: rainbowlike; displaying a shifting range of colors.

irrational (i·rash'ə·nəl) *adj.*: not based on reason or logic.

L

labyrinthine (lab'ə·rin'thin) *adj.*: like a maze; complicated.

languor (laŋ'gər) *n.*: weakness; weariness.

lavish (lav'ish) *v.*: give generously.

legislation (lej'is·lā'shən) *n.*: law or body of laws.

linger (liŋ'gər) *v.*: continue to stay; be reluctant to leave.

litany (lit''n·ē) *n.*: repetitive prayer or recitation.

literal (lit'ər·əl) *adj.*: actual. —**literally** *adv.*

luminous (loo'mə·nəs) *adj.*: shining; glowing.

lurk (lurk) *v.*: lie in wait, ready to attack.

M

mainstay (mān'stā') *n.*: principal support.

malicious (mə·lish'əs) *adj.*: showing a desire to harm another; spiteful.

malign (mə·līn') *v.*: falsely accuse of bad conduct; slander. —**maligned** *v.* used as *adj.*

mar (mär) *v.*: damage; spoil.

marauder (mə·rôd'ər) *n.*: person who roams in search of loot, or goods to steal.

meager (mē'gər) *adj.*: thin; small; inadequate.

menace (men'əs) *v.*: threaten. —**menacing** *v.* used as *adj.*

mentorship (men'tər·ship) *n.*: advice or lessons from a mentor, or wise teacher.

misanthropic (mis'ən·thräp'ik) *adj.*: disliking other human beings.

monotony (mə·nät''n·ē) *n.*: lack of variety.

mundane (mun'dān') *adj.*: everyday; commonplace.

N

negotiation (ni·gō'shē·ā'shən) *n.*: discussion aimed at reaching an agreement.

nimble (nim'bəl) *adj.*: quickly moving.

noncommittal (nän'kə·mit''l) *adj.*: not admitting or committing to any particular purpose or point of view.

O

obscure (əb·skyoor') *v.*: conceal; cover up.

obsession (əb·sesh'ən) *n.*: persistent idea or desire that consumes a person's attention.

obstinate (äb'stə·nət) *adj.*: stubborn.

obstruction (əb·struk'shən) *n.*: obstacle; barrier.

odyssey (äd'i·sē) *n.*: extended journey marked by wandering, adventure, and changes of fortune.

omen (ō'mən) *n.*: thing or event believed to be a sign of a future occurrence.

ominous (äm'ə·nəs) *adj.*: threatening.

optimist (äp'tə·mist) *n.*: person who is always hopeful.

P

pandemonium (pan'də·mō'nē·əm) *n.*: great confusion; chaos.

paradox (par'ə·däks') *n.*: something that has or seems to have contradictory qualities.

paraphernalia (par'ə·fər·nāl'yə) *n.*: equipment; gear.

pauper (pô'pər) *n.*: very poor person.

perennial (pə·ren'ē·əl) *adj.*: year-round; continual.

phenomenon (fə·näm′ə·nən) *n.*: extraordinary thing or occurrence.

pious (pī′əs) *adj.*: showing religious devotion.

placid (plas′id) *adj.*: calm; quiet. —**placidly** *adv.*

pliant (plī′ənt) *adj.*: flexible.

poignant (poin′yənt) *adj.*: sharply painful; moving. —**poignantly** *adv.*

polytheism (päl′i·thē·iz′əm) *n.*: belief in more than one god.

portent (pôr′tent) *n.*: thing that warns of events about to occur.

precarious (pri·ker′ē·əs) *adj.*: unsteady; insecure. —**precariously** *adv.*

precipitous (prē·sip′ə·təs) *adj.*: very steep.

preclude (prē·klōōd′) *v.*: make impossible in advance; prevent.

primal (prī′məl) *adj.*: original; primitive.

primeval (prī·mē′vəl) *adj.*: primitive; of the earliest times.

privation (prī·vā′shən) *n.*: hardship; lack of the things needed for a happy, healthy life.

procure (prō·kyoor′) *v.*: get; obtain.

profusion (prō·fyōō′zhən) *n.*: large supply; abundance.

prolong (prō·lôŋ′) *v.*: extend. —**prolonged** *v.* used as *adj.*

prosaic (prō·zā′ik) *adj.*: ordinary.

protracted (prō·trakt′id) *adj.*: extended.

protrude (prō·trōōd′) *v.*: stick out. —**protruding** *v.* used as *adj.*

putrid (pyōō′trid) *adj.*: offensive to the senses; disgusting.

R

radical (rad′i·kəl) *adj.*: extreme; thorough.

rampart (ram′pärt′) *n.*: broad embankment surrounding a castle, fort, or city for defense against attack.

rancor (raŋ′kər) *n.*: bitter hatred; ill will.

ransack (ran′sak′) *v.*: search thoroughly.

ravage (rav′ij) *v.*: destroy violently; ruin.

recede (ri·sēd′) *v.*: become more distant; move back; become less. —**receding** *v.* used as *adj.*

recoil (ri·koil′) *v.*: move backward, as in fear. —**recoiling** *v.* used as *adj.*

reconciliation (rek′ən·sil′ē·ā′shən) *n.*: friendly end to a quarrel.

refuge (ref′yōōj) *n.*: shelter; protection from danger or difficulty.

reiterate (rē·it′ə·rāt′) *v.*: repeat.

relentless (ri·lent′lis) *adj.*: not stopping; persistent; harsh.

reminisce (rem′ə·nis′) *v.*: think, talk, or write about one's memories. —**reminiscing** *v.* used as *adj.*

remit (ri·mit′) *v.*: return payment.

remorse (ri·môrs′) *n.*: deep guilt.

renunciation (ri·nun′sē·ā′shən) *n.*: formal act of giving up something.

reprove (ri·prōōv′) *v.*: disapprove of.

resilient (ri·zil′yənt) *adj.*: able to return to its original shape quickly after being stretched or compressed; elastic.

resolve (ri·zälv′) *n.*: strength of purpose; determination.

restitution (res′tə·tōō′shən) *n.*: compensation; repayment.

retort (ri·tôrt′) *v.*: reply sharply.

retribution (re′trə·byōō′shən) *n.*: punishment.

reunification (rē·yōō′nə·fi′kā′shən) *n.*: joining together of things that had been divided.

revelry (rev′əl·rē) *n.*: merrymaking; festivity.

revoke (ri·vōk′) *v.*: cancel; withdraw.

ruse (rōōz) *n.*: trick.

S

sacrilegious (sak′rə·lij′əs) *adj.*: disrespectful toward religion.

scourge (skʉrj) *n.*: cause of serious trouble or great suffering.

scrutiny (skrōōt′'n·ē) *n.*: close inspection.

serene (sə·rēn′) *adj.*: peaceful; calm.

silhouette (sil′ə·wet′) *n.*: outline. —**silhouetted** *v.* used as *adj.*

singe (sinj) *v.*: slightly burn. —**singed** *v.* used as *adj.*

solace (säl′is) *n.*: comfort; easing of grief.

spectral (spek′trəl) *adj.*: ghostly; unreal.

spurn (spʉrn) *v.*: reject someone or something for being unworthy; scorn.

stellar (stel′ər) *adj.*: of or like a star.

---

at, āte, cär; ten, ēve; is, īce; gō, hôrn, look, tōōl; oil, out; up, fʉr; ə *for unstressed vowels, as* a *in* ago, u *in* focus; ′ *as in* Latin (lat′'n); chin; she; thin; *the*; zh *as in* azure (azh′ər); ŋ *as in* ring (riŋ)

stifle (stī′fəl) v.: smother. —**stifled** v. used as adj.

stupor (stoo′pər) n.: dull, half-conscious state.

subliminal (sub·lim′ə·nəl) adj.: below the level of awareness.

succession (sək·sesh′ən) n.: series.

succor (suk′ər) n.: help given to someone in distress; relief.

suffuse (sə·fyooz′) v.: spread over or through.

sulk (sulk) v.: show resentment and ill-humor.

sullen (sul′ən) adj.: resentful; gloomy. —**sullenly** adv.

superficial (soo′pər·fish′əl) adj.: not deep or thorough; shallow.

supplication (sup′lə·kā′shən) n.: humble plea or request.

surmount (sər·mount′) v.: overcome.

sustain (sə·stān′) v.: support; nourish.

T

terrestrial (tə·res′trē·əl) adj.: earthly; of this world.

tolerance (täl′ər·əns) n.: respect for others who differ from you; freedom from prejudice.

torrent (tôr′ənt) n.: flood; downpour.

transmit (trans·mit′) v.: pass on.

tremulous (trem′yoo·ləs) adj.: trembling; shaking.

truculent (truk′yoo·lənt) adj.: fierce.

tumult (too′mult) n.: commotion; uproar; confusion.

U

unconscious (un·kän′shəs) adj.: not awake and alert.

undaunted (un·dôn′tid) adj.: not discouraged by a difficulty or setback.

undulate (un′jə·lāt′) v.: move in waves. —**undulating** v. used as adj.

unrelenting (un·ri·len′tiŋ) adj.: not letting up or weakening.

unruffled (un·ruf′əld) adj.: calm; not disturbed.

V

vanquish (vaŋ′kwish) v.: defeat.

vehemence (vē′ə·məns) n.: strong feeling or passion.

vexation (vek·sā′shən) n.: disturbance; distress.

vigilant (vij′ə·lənt) adj.: watchful.

virtuous (vʉr′choo·əs) adj.: good and moral; honorable.

vitalize (vīt″l·īz) v.: give life to; energize.

volatile (väl′ə·təl) adj.: explosive; likely to change rapidly.

vulnerable (vul′nər·ə·bəl) adj.: affected by a specific influence.

Spanish Glossary

A

abhor/aborrecer *v.* despreciar; odiar algo en particular.

abolish/abolir *v.* suprimir; eliminar.

abominable/abominable *adj.* espantoso; detestable; horrible.

absorb/absorber *v.* amortiguar; *s.* absorbencia.

acclaim/ovación *v.* aclamar (a un ministro, por ejemplo); ovacionar; aplaudir.

acquiesce/consentir *v.* asentir en; conformarse con; aceptar; acatar.

admonish/amonestar *v.* reprender; advertir; aconsejar.

admonition/amonestación *s.* advertencia; consejo severo; reprensión.

adorn/adornar *v.* embellecer; decorar.

adulation/adulación *s.* alabanza; elogio; aplauso; admiración intensa o excesiva.

adversary/adversario *s.* enemigo; contrincante; antagonista.

adversity/adversidad *s.* infortunio; desgracia; desventura; revés.

advocate/defender *v.* abogar por; recomendar; preconizar.

advocate/defensor *s.* abogado de una causa; *adj.* partidario.

affluent/próspero, a *adj.* acaudalado; rico; opulento.

aghast/espantado, da *adj.* horrorizado; pasmado.

agile/ágil *adj.* ligero; alerta; veloz; que se desplaza con agilidad o ágilmente.

allegiance/lealtad *s.* devoción; sumisión.

aloof/reservado, da *adj.* guardado; cauto; desconfiado.

annihilate/aniquilar *v.* destruir; exterminar.

ardor/ardor *s.* emoción intensa; pasión; entusiasmo.

arid/árido, da *adj.* seco; estéril; improductivo.

ascetic/ascético *adj.* austero; sobrio; disciplinado.

ascribe/atribuir *v.* imputar; hacer cargo.

aspire/aspirar *v.* ambicionar; desear.

   —aspiring/ambicioso *adj.* en potencia.

astronomer/astrónomo *s.* científico que estudia las estrellas y los planetas.

austere/austero *adj.* severo; muy sencillo; puritano.

avail/servir *v.* sacar partido de; valerse de; utilizar.

avert/evitar *v.* alejar; apartar.

awry/descarriado *adj./v.* torcido; salir mal, errado.

B

balmy/agradable *adj.* suave; balsámico; fragrante.

beckon/hacer señas *v.* atraer; llamar la atención; indicar que alguien se acerque.

beguile/seducir *v.* engañar.

beleaguer/sitiar *v.* asediar; cercar.

belligerent/agresivo *adj.* beligerante; combativo.

bigotry/intolerancia *s.* fanatismo; intransigencia; prejuicio intenso hacia un grupo particular de personas.

blight/arruinar *v.* destruir; destrozar; marchitar.

bureaucratic/burocrático *adj.* administrativo; moroso.

C

candor/sinceridad *s.* franqueza; imparcialidad; candidez; ingenuidad.

carnage/matanza *s.* carnicería; hecatombe; destrucción.

cascade/cascada *s.* salto de agua; chorro; torrente.

catastrophic/catastrófico *adj.* calamitoso; trágico, funesto.

chronic/crónico *adj.* empedernido; inexorable, frecuente, asiduo.

clarity/claridad *s.* sinceridad; sencillez; llaneza.

clench/apretar *v.* presionar; remachar un clavo.

coerce/coercer *v.* forzar; obligar.

compulsory/obligatorio *adj.* requerido por una regla o por la ley; forzoso.

conceivable/concebible *adj.* imaginable; que puede ser concebido o comprendido.

condolence/condolencia *s.* acompañar en el sentimiento; dar el pésame por.

condone/condonar *v.* perdonar; permitir que continúe (una ofensa, por ejemplo).

connoisseurship/pericia *s.* conocimiento experto, conocedor.

conscientious/concienzudo *adj.* esmerado; escrupuloso. **—conscientiously/escrupulosamente** *adv.* en forma esmerada y cuidadosa.

conspicuous/visible *adj.* obvio; llamativo; notable; patente; que llama la atención.

conspiracy/conspiración *s.* plan secreto y que suele ser ilegal llevado a cabo por un grupo.

constitute/constituir *v.* realizar; formar; nombrar a un puesto.

contrition/contrición *s.* sentimientos de culpabilidad; arrepentimiento.

controversial/polémico *adj.* que lleva a desacuerdos entre grupos con opiniones contrarias; controvertible.

conviction/convicción *s.* certidumbre; *también* condena; sentencia.

covet/codiciar *v.* ansiar; anhelar; desear con fuerte anhelo. **—coveted/codiciado** *v.* usado como; *adj.* codiciable; algo deseado.

D

decrepit/decrépito *adj.* vetusto; ruinoso.

default/negligencia *s.* omisión; falta; ausencia.

defer/diferir *v.* aplazar; delegar; *también* someter.

defiant/provocativo *adj.* provocador; desafiante; tono de voz retador.

deficient/deficiente *adj.* atrasado; que carece de.

deliberation/deliberación *s.* discusión; lentitud; pensar bien antes de tomar una decisión.

delirious/delirante *adj.* inmoderado; extravagante; que siente confusión o alucina debido a un accidente o una fiebre elevada.

delirium/delirio *s.* disturbio mental intenso que suele conllevar alucinaciones.

demise/fallecimiento *s.* cesión de bienes; transmisión de soberanía.

denounce/denunciar *v.* realizar una acusación pública; condenar.

depreciate/depreciar *v.* disminuir el valor de; menospreciar.

depression/depresión *s.* crisis económica; abatimiento.

designate/designar *v.* nombrar alguien para un puesto; señalar; denominar.

desolating/desolador *adj.* triste; que produce congoja o desamparo.

despondent/desanimado *adj.* sin esperanza; abatido.

devious/sinuoso *adj.* torcido; artificioso; disimulado.

dilapidated/derruido *adj.* desvencijado; muy estropeado; en malas condiciones.

dilemma/dilema *s.* decisión difícil; problema grave; conflicto.

dire/terrible *adj.* espantoso; horrible; medida extrema o necesidad urgente.

disarming/seductor *adj.* que desarma.

disconsolate/desconsolado *adj.* que causa tristeza o depresión; afligido; dolorido.

discreet/discreto *adj.* que demuestra circunspección; prudente en sus decisiones y acciones; silencioso o precavido.

disdainful/desdeñoso *adj.* despectivo; indiferente; altivo.

disposition/disposición *s.* carácter; temperamento; propensión, *también* disposición o determinación testamentaria.

distracted/distraído *adj.* que no se puede concentrar.

distraught/turbado *adj.* azorado; desconcertado; que sufre una gran preocupación.

divergent/divergente *adj.* separado; que sigue direcciones separadas.

diverting/divertido *adj.* que entretiene o divierte.

doggedness/tenacidad *s.* persistencia; obstinación.

E

eclipse/eclipsar *v.* deslucir; oscurecer; privar.

elation/júbilo *s.* gran alegría; regocijo; deleite.

elect/elegir *v.* optar; votar.

emaciated/demacrado *adj.* extremadamente delgado; consumido.

embody/encarnar *v.* personificar; representar; figurar.

emulate/emular *v.* seguir el ejemplo de; imitar; copiar.

endeavor/esfuerzo *s.* intento serio; empeño; tentativa.

enduring/duradero *adj.* perdurable; resistente; paciente.

enthrall/cautivar *v.* fascinar; hechizar; encantar.

enunciate/enunciar *v.* formular un principio; articular sonidos; pronunciar; proclamar.

equitable/justo *adj.* equitativo; imparcial; ecuánime.

eradicate/erradicar *v.* desarraigar plantas; extirpar una mala costumbre; eliminar; arrancar.

esteem/estima *s.* aprecio; consideración.

exasperation/exasperación *s.* irritación; agitación; inquietud.

exhilarate/alegrar *v.* animar; levantar el ánimo; regocijar.

exorbitant/exorbitante *adj.* desorbitado; desmesurado; excesivo.

expendable/prescindible *adj.* innecesario; gastable; que se puede sacrificar por una causa.

expire/expirar *v.* morir; fallecer; caducar; espirar aire.

exuberant/exuberante *adj.* pródigo; excesivo; intenso; abundante.

F

fanatic/fanático *adj./s.* entusiasta; extremista; persona cuya pasión por una causa puede ser excesiva o irrazonable.

fervent/ardiente *adj.* ferviente; vehemente; apasionado.

formidable/formidable *adj.* tremendo; terrible; impresionante; que inspira la admiración de otros; que causa pavor.

futile/vano *adj.* inútil; frívolo; pueril.

G

genial/simpático *adj.* afable; cordial.

giddy/mareado *adj.* vertiginoso; atolondrado; frívolo.

glower/mirar con ira *v.* fijar una mirada furiosa.

gurgle/borbotear *v.* gorjear.

H

hoist/izar *v.* levantar algo pesado; subir una mercancía a un barco.

hover/flotar en el aire *v.* un helicóptero que se cierna; una mariposa que revolotea; rondar alrededor de alguien; esbozar una sonrisa.

hyperactive/hiperactivo *adj.* excesivamente activo; inquieto; revuelto.

I

idle/ocioso *adj.* perezoso, sin objetivo ni meta; desocupado; temor infundado; conversación frívola; capital improductivo; máquina parada.

ignorance/ignorancia *s.* falta de conocimientos; desconocimiento; no saber.

imminent/inminente *adj.* perentorio; urgente; imperioso; cercano

immolation/inmolación *s.* sacrificio; expiación; destrucción.

immortal/inmortal *adj.* que vive para siempre; eterno; indestructible.

impartial/imparcial *adj.* justo; sin prejuicios; razonable.

impend/cernerse *v.* a punto de ocurrir; pender; amenazar.

implication/implicación *s.* conexión o consecuencia posible; complicidad; repercusión.

impose/imponer *v.* instituir condiciones; engañar; aprovecharse de; abusar de.

imposing/imponente *adj.* de apariencia grande e impresionante; grandioso; inmenso.

impoverish/empobrecer *v.* agotar; arruinar; extenuar.

imprudent/imprudente *adj.* irreflexivo; precipitado.

impulse/impulso *s.* deseo repentino; estímulo.

impunity/impunidad *s.* exención; perdón.

inaugurate/inaugurar *v.* introducir; dar posesión de un cargo; descubrir una estatua; abrir.

incantation/conjuro *s.* evocación; sortilegio; hechizo; conjunto de palabras o frases que deben producir un resultado mágico.

incessant/incesante *adj.* constante; continuo; perpetuo.

incite/incitar *v.* fomentar; estimular; provocar; atizar.

inconsolable/inconsolable *v.* desconsolado; apenado; desesperado.

incredulous/incrédulo *adj.* descreído; desconfiado; receloso.

indiscriminate/indistinto *adj.* sin criterio; confuso; indeterminado.

inevitable/inevitable *adj.* necesario; irremediable; fijo.

infallibility/infalibilidad *s.* acierto; perspicacia; agudeza.

infatuated/encaprichado *adj.* persistir por una idea; estar locamente enamorado de una persona.

insensible/insensible *adj.* inconsciente; inerte.

instigate/instigar *v.* llevar o incitar a una acción negativa; fomentar una insurrección.

intangible/intangible *adj.* que no se puede tocar; impalpable; inmaterial; tenue.

interminable/interminable *adj.* sin fin; imperecedero; eterno; perpetuo.

intimidate/intimidar *v.* acobardar; amedrentar; atemorizar; asustar.

intolerance/intolerancia *s.* prejuicio; hostilidad hacia otros grupos; intransigencia; sectarismo.

invariable/invariable *adj.* inmutable; inalterable; sin cambio. **–invariably/invariablemente** *adv.* eternamente; perpetuamente.

invincible/invencible *adj.* que no se puede conquistar; invulnerable; inmune.

iridescent/iridiscente *adj.* irisado; refulgente; parecido a un arco iris.

irrational/irracional *adj.* insensato; absurdo; que no se basa en la razón o la lógica.

L

labyrinthine/laberíntico *adj.* complicado; enredado; embrollado.

languor/languidez *s.* cansancio; fatiga; apatía.

lavish/prodigar *v.* regalar; dar generosamente; agraciar.

legislation/legislación *adj.* ley o conjunto de leyes; código.

linger/quedarse *v.* rezagarse; retrasarse; no querer marcharse.

litany/letanía *s.* discurso; oración o recitación repetitiva.

literal/literal *adj.* actual; en el sentido exacto de la palabra; prosaico. **–literally/literalmente** *adv.* al pie de la letra.

luminous/luminoso *adj.* radiante; resplandeciente; brillante.

lurk/esconderse *v.* estar al acecho; aguardar; rondar.

M

mainstay/fundamento *s.* razón; principio; cimiento.

malicious/malicioso *adj.* pícaro; pérfido; deseoso de hacer el mal.

malign/calumniar *v.* difamar; hablar mal de otro.

mar/estropear *v.* echar a perder; desfigurar; deformar.

marauder/merodeador *s.* delincuente; malandrín; maleante; persona furtiva.

meager/escaso *adj.* insuficiente; parco; pobre; mediocre; flaco.

menace/amenazar *v.* intimidar; inquietar; atemorizar. **–menacing/amenazador** *adj.* inquietante; retador.

mentorship/tutoría *s.* tutela; lecciones o consejos impartidos por un mentor, o persona sagaz.

misanthropic/misantrópico *adj.* sentir antipatía por los seres humanos.

monotony/monotonía *s.* invariabilidad; fastidio; repetición.

mundane/mundano *adj.* frívolo; común; vano.

N

negotiation/negociación *s.* gestión; transacción; contrato; discusión con el fin de llegar a un acuerdo.

nimble/ágil *adj.* vivo; ligero.

noncommittal/evasivo *adj.* ambiguo; precavido; que no compromete a nada.

O

obscure/oscurecer *v.* ocultar; disimular; esconder.

obsession/obsesión *s.* idea o deseo persistente que consume la atención; manía; capricho.

obstinate/obstinado *adj.* terco.

obstruction/obstrucción *s.* dificultad; obstáculo; barrera.

odyssey/odisea *s.* largo viaje en el que abundan las aventuras, los reveses y las peripecias; éxodo.

omen/presagio *s.* augurio; predicción; evento o cosa capaz de predecir un futuro acontecimiento.

ominous/siniestro *adj.* inquietante; adverso.

optimist/optimista *adj.* alegre; confiado; que mantiene vivas las esperanzas.

P

pandemonium/caos *s.* gran confusión; anarquía; jaleo.

paradox/paradoja *s.* concepto que parece disponer de características contradictorias; incongruencia; contrasentido.

paraphernalia/equipo *s.* avíos; trastos; equipaje.

pauper/pobre *s.* persona indigente, mendiga.

perennial/eterno *adj.* continuo; perenne.

phenomenon/fenómeno *s.* entidad o evento extraordinario; prodigio.

pious/piadoso *adj.* devoto; religioso; practicante; creyente.

placid/plácido *adj.* apacible; tranquilo; sosegado.

pliant/flexible *adj.* elástico; maleable; tolerante.

poignant/conmovedor *adj.* patético; triste; melancólico; dolor agudo; mordaz.

polytheism/politeísmo *s.* fe en más de un solo Dios; paganismo.

portent/presagio *s.* augurio; predicción; profecía; presentimiento.

precarious/precario *adj.* inestable; inseguro.

precipitous/empinado *adj.* inclinado; precipitado; pronunicado.

preclude/impedir *v.* imposibilitar; evitar; excluir; frenar; descartar.

primal/primitivo *adj.* original; primordial; fundamental.

primeval/prístino *adj.* inicial; intacto.

privation/privación *s.* estrechez; miseria; carencia de lo necesario para una vida feliz.

procure/proporcionar *v.* obtener; conseguir; lograr.

profusion/profusión *s.* abundancia; prodigalidad; exuberancia; plétora.

prolong/prolongar *v.* extender; amplificar.

prosaic/prosaico *adj.* pedestre; ordinario.

protracted/prolongado *adj.* extendido; amplificado.

protrude/sobresalir *v.* resaltar; despuntar; predominar.

putrid/podrido *adj.* que ofende los sentidos; putrefacto; depravado; repugnante.

R

radical/radical *adj.* fundamental; extremado; soberano.

rampart/muralla *s.* muralla de un castillo; defensa; cerca.

rancor/rencor *s.* odio; resentimiento; aversión.

ransack/saquear *v.* registrar; despojar; rastrear.

ravage/destrozar *v.* asolar; desfigurar; causar estragos; arrasar.

recede/retroceder *v.* retirarse; volverse atrás.

recoil/rechazar *v.* echarse atrás; retroceder; sentir repugnancia por; tener horror.

reconciliation/reconciliación *s.* conciliación; acuerdo amistoso.

refuge/refugio *s.* protección; amparo.

reiterate/reiterar *v.* repetir; insistir; confirmar.

relentless/implacable *adj.* sin cese; persistente; tenaz.

reminisce/recordar *v.* pensar en el pasado; evocar.

remit/remitir *v.* realizar un pago; enviar; expedir; facturar.

remorse/remordimiento *s.* culpabilidad profunda; contrición; arrepentimiento.

renunciation/renuncia *s.* dimisión; sacrificio.

reprove/censurar *v.* condenar; criticar; reprender.

resilient/resistente *adj.* elástico; que puede volver rápidamente a su forma original.

resolve/resolución *s.* decisión; propósito; valor.

restitution/restitución *s.* indemnización; compensación; pago.

retort/réplica *s.* argumento; objeción.

retribution/castigo *s.* sanción; pena; venganza.

reunification/reunificación *s.* unificar lo que se hallaba dividido; reunir; concentrar.

revelry/regocijo *s.* jolgorio; celebración; fiesta.

revoke/revocar *v.* cancelar; anular; disolver.

ruse/ardid *s.* astucia; treta.

S

sacrilegious/sacrílego *adj.* que no respeta la religión; impío; profano.

scourge/plaga *s.* castigo divino; gran sufrimiento; calamidad.

scrutiny/escrutinio *s.* inspección o examinación detallada; investigación.

serene/sereno *adj.* suave; sosegado; tranquilo.

silhouette/silueta *s.* contorno; perfil; trazo.

singe/chamuscar *v.* tostar; quemar ligeramente.

solace/consuelo *s.* alivio; desahogo.

spectral/espectral *adj.* fantasmagórico; ilusorio.

spurn/despreciar *v.* rechazar; menospreciar; desfavorecer; desdeñar.

stellar/estelar *adj.* que trata de las estrellas; papel principal.

stifle/sofocar *v.* ahogar; oprimir.

stupor/estupor *s.* insensibilidad; letargo.

subliminal/subconsciente *adj.* inconsciente; mecánico; instintivo.

succession/sucesión *s.* serie; continuación; proceso; descendencia.

succor/socorro *s.* ayuda; sosiego; auxilio; refuerzo.

suffuse/cubrir *v.* bañar una sala de luz; inundar; difundirse.

sulk/enfurruñarse *v.* poner mala cara; resentir.

sullen/hosco *adj.* ceñudo; resentido; huraño; arisco.

superficial/superficial *adj.* frívolo; que solamente toca la superficie; somero.

supplication/súplica *s.* ruego; demanda humilde; solicitud.

surmount/superar *v.* prevalecer; adelantar; sobrepasar.

sustain/mantener *v.* sostener; conservar; alimentar; nutrir.

T

terrestrial/terrestre *adj.* terrenal; material; físico.

tolerance/tolerancia *s.* respeto por la opinión de los demás; falta de prejuicios; paciencia.

torrent/torrente *s.* arroyo; cascada; llover a cántaros; tumulto.

transmit/transmitir *v.* ceder; traspasar; entregar.

tremulous/trémulo *adj.* tembloroso; estremecido; palpitante.

truculent/feroz *adj.* salvaje; cruel; agresivo.

tumult/tumulto *s.* conmoción; disturbio; alboroto; confusión.

U

unconscious/inconsciente *adj.* sin conocimiento; desvanecido.

undaunted/intrépido *adj.* impávido; que no se deja desalentar o no se descorazona ante dificultades; valeroso; enérgico.

undulate/ondular *v.* hacer ondear; rizar; encrespar.

unrelenting/implacable *adj.* riguroso; que no cede.

unruffled/sereno *adj.* tranquilo; imperturbable; firme; liso.

V

vanquish/vencer *v.* conquistar; dominar sus sentimientos; rendir; imponerse.

vehemence/vehemencia *s.* violencia; fuerte sentimiento o pasión; elocuencia; convicción.

vexation/fastidio *s.* molestia; disturbio; disgusto.

vigilant/vigilante *adj.* alerta; precavido; cuidadoso.

virtuous/virtuoso *adj.* bueno y moral; honorable; honrado.

vitalize/vitalizar *v.* vivificar; animar; rejuvenecer; robustecer.

volatile/volátil *adj.* voluble; inconstante; inestable; explosivo.

vulnerable/vulnerable *adj.* fácil de impresionar; afectado por una influencia particular; sensible; frágil.

Acknowledgments

For permission to reprint copyrighted material, grateful acknowledgment is made to the following sources:

Gillon Aitken Associates Ltd.: "So you want to be an astronaut?" by Richard Knight. Copyright © 2000 by Richard Knight. Originally appeared in *The Times,* London, April 22, 2000.

Arte Público Press: "Volar" from *The Year of Our Revolution* by Judith Ortiz Cofer. Copyright © 1998 by Judith Ortiz Cofer. Published by Arte Público Press–University of Houston, Houston, TX, 1998. "Los Ancianos" from *Borders* by Pat Mora. Copyright © 1986 by Pat Mora. Published by Arte Público Press–University of Houston, Houston, TX. "Legal Alien" and "Extranjera legal" from *Chants* by Pat Mora. Copyright © 1984 by Pat Mora. Published by Arte Público Press–University of Houston, Houston, TX, 1985. "My Father Is a Simple Man" from *The Sadness of Days: Selected and New Poems* by Luis Omar Salinas. Copyright © 1987 by Luis Omar Salinas. Published by Arte Público Press–University of Houston, Houston, TX, 1987.

The Associated Press: "Poe's Death Is Rewritten as Case of Rabies, Not Telltale Alcohol" as it appeared in *The New York Times,* September 15, 1996. Copyright © 1996 by The Associated Press.

Elizabeth Barnett, Literary Executor: "An Ancient Gesture" and "The Courage That My Mother Had" from *Collected Poems of Edna St. Vincent Millay.* Copyright © 1954, 1982 by Norma Millay Ellis. Published by HarperCollins Publishers, Inc. All rights reserved.

R. Michael Benitez: "Rabies Death Theory" by R. Michael Benitez from *The New York Times,* Editorial Desk, September 30, 1996. Copyright © 1996 by R. Michael Benitez.

Susan Bergholz Literary Services, New York: From comments about *Names/Nombres* by Julia Alvarez. Copyright © 1985 by Julia Alvarez. First published in *Nuestro,* March 1985. All rights reserved. From "Alvarez, Julia 1950–" from *Contemporary Authors.* Copyright © 1980 by Julia Alvarez. Published by Gale Research. All rights reserved. "Exile" from *The Other Side/El Otro Lado* by Julia Alvarez. Copyright © 1995 by Julia Alvarez. Published by Plume, a division of Penguin Putnam Inc., and originally in hardcover by Dutton Signet. All rights reserved. "Snow" from *How the García Girls Lost Their Accents* by Julia Alvarez. Published by Plume, a division of Penguin Putnam Inc., and originally in hardcover by Algonquin Books of Chapel Hill. All rights reserved. "Liberty" by Julia Alvarez. Copyright © 1996 by Julia Alvarez. First published in *Writer's Harvest 2,* edited by Ethan Canin, published by Harcourt Brace and Company, 1996. All rights reserved. "Papa Who Wakes Up Tired in the Dark" from *The House on Mango Street* by Sandra Cisneros. Copyright © 1984 by Sandra Cisneros. Published by Vintage Books, a division of Random House, Inc., and in hardcover by Alfred A. Knopf in 1994. All rights reserved. "Salvador Late or Early" from *Woman Hollering Creek* by Sandra Cisneros. Copyright © 1991 by Sandra Cisneros. Published by Vintage Books, a division of Random House, Inc., and originally in hardcover by Random House, Inc. All rights reserved.

Bilingual Press/Editorial Bilingüe, Hispanic Research Center, Arizona State University, Tempe, AZ: "Tiburón" from *Trumpets from the Islands of Their Evictions* by Martín Espada. Copyright © 1987 by Bilingual Review Press.

BOA Editions, Ltd.: "The Gift" from *Rose: Poems* by Li-Young Lee. Copyright © 1986 by Li-Young Lee.

Brandt & Hochman Literary Agents, Inc.: "The Most Dangerous Game" by Richard Connell. Copyright © 1924 by Richard Connell; copyright renewed © 1952 by Louise Fox Connell.

George Braziller, Inc.: "Fork" from *Dismantling the Silence* by Charles Simic. Copyright © 1971 by Charles Simic.

Broadside Press: "Ballad of Birmingham" by Dudley Randall. Published by Third World Press.

Brooks Permissions: "Old Mary" and from "We Real Cool" from *Blacks* by Gwendolyn Brooks. Copyright © 1991 by Gwendolyn Brooks. Published by Third World Press, Chicago.

Carlos Capellan: From "Teaching Chess, and Life" by Carlos Capellan from *The New York Times,* September 3, 2000. Copyright © 2000 by Carlos Capellan.

The Truman Capote Literary Trust: "A Christmas Memory" story from *Breakfast at Tiffany's* by Truman Capote. Copyright © 1956 by Truman Capote.

Abraham Chang: Comment and "Folding Won Tons In" by Abraham Chang. Copyright © 2003 by Abraham Chang.

Chelsea House Publishers: From "A Warm, Clear Day in Dallas" from *World Leaders Past & Present: John F. Kennedy* by Marta Randall. Copyright © 1988 by Chelsea House Publishers, a division of Main Line Book Company.

Judith Ortiz Cofer: From "An Interview with Judith Ortiz Cofer" by Stephanie Gordon from *AWP Chronicle,* October/November 1997 Web site, accessed January 10, 2002, at http://parallel.park.uga.edu/~jcofer/gordoninterview.html.

Eugenia W. Collier: Slightly adapted from "Marigolds" by Eugenia W. Collier from *Negro Digest,* November 1969. Copyright © 1969 by Johnson Publishing Company, Inc. Comment on "Marigolds" by Eugenia W. Collier. Copyright © 1992 by Eugenia W. Collier.

Columbia University Press: From English translation of "Living Poetry" by Hugo Margenat from *Inventing a Word: An Anthology of 20th Century Puerto Rican Poetry* by Julio Marzán. Copyright © 1980 by Columbia University Press.

Don Congdon Associates, Inc.: "A Sound of Thunder" by Ray Bradbury. Copyright © 1952 by the Crowell-Collier Publishing Co.; copyright renewed © 1980 by Ray Bradbury. "The Golden Kite, the Silver Wind" by Ray Bradbury. Copyright © 1953 by Epoch Associates; copyright renewed © 1981 by Ray Bradbury.

Copper Canyon Press: "Country Scene" from *Spring Essence, The Poetry of Hô Xuân Hu'o'ng,* edited and translated by John Balaban. Copyright © 2000 by John Balaban.

Crown Publishers, a division of Random House, Inc.: "On the Abolition of the Threat of War" from *Ideas and Opinions* by Albert Einstein. Copyright © 1954 and renewed © 1982 by Crown Publishers, Inc.

Gary N. Da Silva: Visitor from Forest Hills from *Plaza Suite* by Neil Simon. Copyright © 1969 and renewed © 1997 by Neil Simon. CAUTION: Professionals and amateurs are hereby warned that PLAZA SUITE is fully protected under the Berne Convention and the Universal Copyright Convention and is subject to royalty. All rights, including without limitation professional, amateur, motion picture, television, radio, recitation, lecturing, public reading and foreign translation rights, computer media rights and the right of

Doubleday, a division of Random House, Inc.: Quote by Bill Moyers from *The Power of Myth* by Joseph Campbell and Bill Moyers. Copyright © 1988 by Apostrophe S Productions, Inc., and Bill Moyers and Alfred Van der Marck Editions, Inc. for itself and the estate of Joseph Campbell. "The Road Block" ("Get out of my road") by Miura Chora from *An Introduction to Haiku* by Harold G. Henderson. Copyright © 1958 by Harold G. Henderson.

Dunham Literary as agents for Wendi Kaufman: Adapted from "Helen on 86th Street" by Wendi Kaufman from *The New Yorker*, November 24, 1997. Copyright © 1997 by Wendi Kaufman. Author's comment on "Helen on 86th Street" by Wendi Kaufman. Copyright © 2000 by Wendi Kaufman.

Dutton, a division of Penguin Putnam Inc.: "Can Animals Think?" edited and adapted from *The Parrot's Lament* by Eugene Linden. Copyright © 1999 by Eugene Linden. Originally published in *Time*, 1999.

Anita Endrezze: "The Girl Who Loved the Sky" from *At the Helm of Twilight* by Anita Endrezze. Copyright © 1988 by Anita Endrezze. Published by Broken Moon Press, 1992.

Mari Evans: "If There Be Sorrow" from *I Am a Black Woman* by Mari Evans. Copyright © 1970 by Mari Evans. Published by William Morrow & Co.

Farrar, Straus and Giroux, LLC: From "Survival" from *Going Solo* by Roald Dahl. Copyright © 1986 by Roald Dahl. From "Book 1: A Goddess Intervenes," "Book 5: Sweet Nymph and Open Sea," "Book 9: New Coasts and Poseidon's Son," "Book 10: The Grace of the Witch," "Book 11: A Gathering of Shades," "Book 12: Sea Perils and Defeat," and "Book 16: Father and Son," "Book 17: The Beggar at the Manor," "Book 21: The Test of the Bow," "Book 22: Death in the Great Hall," and "Book 23: The Trunk of the Olive Tree" from *The Odyssey* by Homer, translated by Robert Fitzgerald. Copyright © 1961, 1963 by Robert Fitzgerald; copyright renewed © 1989 by Benedict R. C. Fitzgerald, on behalf of the Fitzgerald children.

The Feminist Press at The City University of New York: "To Da-Duh, In Memoriam" from *Reena and Other Stories* by Paule Marshall. Copyright © 1983 by Paule Marshall.

Florida Classics Library: From *The Everglades: River of Grass* by Marjory Stoneman Douglas. Copyright 1947 by Marjory Stoneman Douglas.

Frances Goldin Literary Agency: "American Hero" from *Ceremonies: Prose and Poetry* by Essex Hemphill. Copyright © 1992 by Essex Hemphill.

GRM Associates, Inc., representing the Ann Elmo Agency: From *Children and the Death of a President: Multi-Disciplinary Studies*, edited by Martha Wolfenstein and Gilbert Kliman. Copyright © 1965 by Gilbert Kliman and Martha Wolfenstein.

Harcourt, Inc.: "The Happy Man's Shirt" from *Italian Folktales, Selected and Retold by Italo Calvino*, translated by George Martin. Copyright © 1956 by Giulio Einaudi editore, s.p.a.; translation copyright © 1980 by Harcourt, Inc. "The Necklace" by Guy de Maupassant from *Adventures in Reading, Laureate Edition*. Copyright © 1963 by Harcourt Brace & Company; copyright renewed © 1991 by Deborah Jean Lodge, Alice Lodge, Jeanne M. Shutes, Jessica Sand, Lydia Winderman, Florence F. Potell, and Mary Rives Bowman. From "Tentative (First Model) Definitions of Poetry" from *The Complete Poems of Carl Sandburg*. Copyright © 1969, 1970 by Lilian Steichen Sandburg, Trustee. "Women" from *Revolutionary Petunias & Other Poems* by Alice Walker. Copyright © 1970 and renewed © 1998 by Alice Walker. "Boy at the Window" from *Things of This World* by Richard Wilbur. Copyright 1952 and renewed © 1980 by Richard Wilbur.

HarperCollins Publishers, Inc.: "The World Is Not a Pleasant Place to Be" from *My House* by Nikki Giovanni. Copyright © 1972 by Nikki Giovanni. "The Cyclops in the Ocean" from *Those Who Ride the Night Winds* by Nikki Giovanni. Copyright © 1983 by Nikki Giovanni. From *Edgar A. Poe: Mournful and Never-Ending Remembrance* by Kenneth Silverman. Copyright © 1991 by Kenneth Silverman.

Joy Harris Literary Agency: "The Sea Call" from *The Odyssey: A Modern Sequel* by Nikos Kazantzakis, translated by Kimon Friar. Copyright © 1958 by Helen Kazantzakis and Kimon Friar; copyright renewed © 1986 by Simon & Schuster.

The Albert Einstein Archives, the Hebrew University of Jerusalem, Israel: From *Einstein on Peace*, edited by Otto Nathan and Heinz Norden. Copyright © 1960 by Otto Nathan.

David Higham Associates Limited: "Beware of the Dog" (slightly abridged) from *Over to You: Ten Stories of Flyers and Flying* by Roald Dahl. Copyright © 1945 by Roald Dahl.

Hill and Wang, a division of Farrar, Straus and Giroux, LLC: "Thank You, M'am" from *Short Stories* by Langston Hughes. Copyright © 1996 by Ramona Bass and Arnold Rampersad.

Henry Holt and Company, LLC: "The Chicken" by Linda Elegant from *I Thought My Father Was God: And Other True Tales From NPR's National Story Project*, edited and introduced by Paul Auster. Copyright © 2001 by Henry Holt and Company, LLC. From "The Figure a Poem Makes" from *Complete Poems of Robert Frost*. Copyright 1930, © 1967 by Henry Holt & Company. "Dust of Snow," "Fire and Ice," and "Once by the Pacific" from *The Poetry of Robert Frost*, edited by Edward Connery Lathem. Copyright 1951, © 1956 by Robert Frost; copyright 1923, 1928, © 1969 by Henry Holt and Company.

Houghton Mifflin Company: "The Fenris Wolf" from *Legends of the North* by Olivia E. Coolidge. Copyright © 1951 and renewed © 1979 by Olivia E. Coolidge. All rights reserved. From *One Belfast Boy* by Patricia McMahon. Copyright © 1999 by Patricia McMahon.

James R. Hurst: "The Scarlet Ibis" by James R. Hurst from *The Atlantic Monthly*, July 1960. Copyright © 1960 by The Atlantic Monthly.

Sharon Ingram: From the diary of Sharon Ingram from *Children of "The Troubles": Our Lives in the Crossfire of Northern Ireland* by Laurel Holliday. Copyright © 1997 by Sharon Ingram. Published by Pocket Books, a division of Simon & Schuster, New York, 1997.

Stephen King: Adapted from "Eyeglasses for the Mind," an interview with Stephen King, by George Christian from *Houston Chronicle*, September 30, 1979. Copyright © 1979 by Houston Chronicle.

Alfred A. Knopf, a division of Random House, Inc.: From *Jurassic Park* by Michael Crichton. Copyright © 1990 by Michael Crichton. "Mother to Son" from *Collected Poems* by Langston Hughes. Copyright © 1994 by the Estate of Langston Hughes.

Juliet S. Kono: "Internment" from *Hilo Rains* by Juliet S. Kono. Copyright © 1988 by Juliet S. Kono.

Li-Young Lee: Untitled essay by Li-Young Lee from *Chinese American Poetry: An Anthology*, edited by L. Ling-chi Wang and Henry Yiheng Zhao. Copyright © 1991 by Li-Young Lee.

Peter H. Lee: "Cranes" by Hwang Sun-won from *Flowers of Fire: Twentieth Century Korean Stories*, edited by Peter H. Lee. Copyright © 1974 by Peter H. Lee.

Little, Brown and Company: From "Mythology of the Norsemen" from *Mythology* by Edith Hamilton. Copyright © 1942 by Edith Hamilton; copyright renewed © 1969 by Dorian Fielding Reid and Doris Fielding Reid.

Liveright Publishing Corporation: "in Just-" from *Complete Poems: 1904-1962* by E. E. Cummings, edited by George J. Firmage. Copyright 1923, 1951, © 1991 by the Trustees for the E. E. Cummings Trust; copyright © 1976 by George James Firmage. From "A Poet's Advice to Students" from *A Miscellany Revised* by E. E. Cummings, edited by George J. Firmage. Copyright © 1955, 1965 by the Trustees for the E. E. Cummings Trust; copyright © 1958, 1965 by George J. Firmage. "Those Winter Sundays" from *Angle of Ascent: New and Selected Poems* by Robert Hayden. Copyright © 1966 by Robert Hayden.

The Literary Trustees of Walter de la Mare and the Society of Authors as their representative: From "Silver" from *The Complete Poems of Walter de la Mare.* Published in the United States in 1970.

Margaret McCrory: "Internment" by Margaret McCrory from *Children of "The Troubles": Our Lives in the Crossfire of Northern Ireland* by Laurel Holliday. Copyright © 1997 by Margaret McCrory. Published by Pocket Books, a division of Simon & Schuster, New York, 1997.

George J. Mitchell c/o Verner, Liipferd, et al.: From "Peace Isn't Impossible" by George J. Mitchell from *Newsweek,* June 30, 1997, page 23. Copyright © 1997 by George J. Mitchell.

New Directions Publishing Corp.: "Your Laughter" from *The Captain's Verses* by Pablo Neruda. Copyright © 1972 by Pablo Neruda and Donald D. Walsh.

The New York Times Company: "An American Story" by Anthony Lewis from *The New York Times,* November 26, 1993. Copyright © 1993 by The New York Times Company. From "In America; Romeo and Juliet in Bosnia" by Bob Herbert from *The New York Times,* May 8, 1994. Copyright © 1994 by The New York Times Company. From "Sunday View; Perfectly Tuned Actors Hit a High Note" by Margo Jefferson from "Arts & Leisure" from *The New York Times,* April 23, 1995. Copyright © 1995 by The New York Times Company. "Rising Tides" by Bob Herbert from *The New York Times,* February 22, 2001. Copyright © 2001 by The New York Times Company. "Heroes with Solid Feet" by Kirk Douglas from *The New York Times,* April 23, 2001. Copyright © 2001 by The New York Times Company.

Newsday, Inc.: "An Arctic Floe of Climate Questions" by Robert Cooke from *Newsday,* April 18, 2001. Copyright © 2001 by Newsday, Inc.

Naomi Shihab Nye: "Daily" from *Hugging the Jukebox* by Naomi Shihab Nye. Copyright © 1982 by Naomi Shihab Nye.

The Orange County Register: From "Ex-Refugee Is Nominated for Justice Post" by Dena Bunis and Anh Do from *The Orange County Register,* Thursday, May 10, 2001. Copyright © 2001 by The Orange County Register.

Pantheon Books, a division of Random House, Inc.: "The Trapper Trapped" from *African Folktales: Traditional Stories of the Black World,* selected and retold by Roger D. Abrahams. Copyright © 1983 by Roger D. Abrahams.

Paramount Pictures: From *Barefoot in the Park* by Neil Simon. Copyright © 1964, 2002 by Paramount Pictures. All rights reserved.

Pearson Education, Inc.: From *Three Genres: The Writing of Poetry, Fiction and Drama,* Seventh Edition, by Stephen Minot. Copyright © 2002 by Prentice Hall, Inc.

People Weekly: From "Feeding Frenzy" by Peter Ames Carlin and Don Sider from *People,* June 2, 1997, pp. 101–102. Copyright © 1997 by People Weekly. All rights reserved.

Perseus Books Publishers, a member of Perseus Books, L.L.C.: "Prologue: How to Eat a Guava" from *When I Was Puerto Rican* by Esmeralda Santiago. Copyright © 1993 by Esmeralda Santiago.

The Peters Fraser & Dunlop Group Limited on behalf of the Estate of Liam O'Flaherty: "The Sniper" from *The Martyr* by Liam O'Flaherty. Copyright © 1933 by Liam O'Flaherty.

Pocket Books, a division of Simon & Schuster, Inc.: From Introduction by Laurel Holliday from *Children of "The Troubles": Our Lives in the Crossfire of Northern Ireland,* edited by Laurel Holliday. Copyright © 1997 by Laurel Holliday.

Burton R. Pollin: "If Only Poe Had Succeeded When He Said Nevermore to Drink" by Burton R. Pollin from *The New York Times,* Editorial Desk, September 23, 1996. Copyright © 1996 by Burton R. Pollin.

Princeton University Press: "Ithaca" from *Collected Poems* by C. P. Cavafy, translated by Edmund Keeley and Philip Sherrard. Copyright © 1992 by Princeton University Press.

Random House, Inc.: "Woman Work" from *And Still I Rise* by Maya Angelou. Copyright © 1978 by Maya Angelou. From "On the Pulse of Morning" from *On the Pulse of Morning* by Maya Angelou. Copyright © 1993 by Maya Angelou. From "Blues Ain't No Mockin Bird" from *Gorilla, My Love* by Toni Cade Bambara. Copyright © 1971 by Toni Cade Bambara.

Pierre Salinger: From Foreword by Pierre Salinger from *Where Were You When President Kennedy Was Shot? Memories and Tributes to a Slain President as Told to Dear Abby.* Foreword copyright © 1993 by Pierre Salinger.

Meredith Anne Schwartz: "Penelope to Ulysses" by Meredith Schwartz from *Dead Center Literary Magazine,* 1992. Copyright © 1992 by Meredith Anne Schwartz. Published by Highland Park High School, Highland Park, New Jersey.

Science@NASA: From "Far-out Housekeeping on the ISS" by Ron Koczor from *Science@NASA* Web site, at http://science.nasa.gov/ headlines/y2000/ast29nov_1.htm. Copyright © 2000 by NASA.

Scovil, Chichak, & Galen: "Dog Star" from *The Nine Billion Names of God: The Best Short Stories of Arthur C. Clarke.* Copyright © 1962 by Galaxy Publishing Corporation.

Scribner, an imprint of Simon & Schuster Adult Publishing Group: "Forgive My Guilt" from *The Collected Poems of Robert P. Tristram Coffin.* Copyright 1946 by Robert P. Tristram Coffin; copyright renewed © 1974 by Richard N. Coffin, Mary Alice Wescott, and Robert P. T. Coffin, Jr. "Old Man at the Bridge" from *The Short Stories of Ernest Hemingway.* Copyright 1938 by Ernest Hemingway; copyright renewed © 1966 by Mary Hemingway.

Scripps Howard Foundation: "Wounded and Trapped" by Ernie Pyle from Scripps Howard wire copy, August 22, 1944. Copyright © 1944 by Scripps Howard Foundation.

Simon & Schuster, Inc.: "The History Behind the Ballad" from *Parting the Waters* by Taylor Branch. Copyright © 1988 by Taylor Branch.

Gloria Steinem: Quote by Alice Walker from "Do You Know This Woman? She Knows You: A Profile of Alice Walker" by Gloria Steinem from *Ms. Magazine,* June 1982. Copyright © 1982 by Ms. Foundation for Education and Communication, Inc.

Oliver Stone: "Where I Find My Heroes" by Oliver Stone from *McCall's Magazine,* November 1992. Copyright © 1992 by Oliver Stone.

Rosemary A. Thurber and The Barbara Hogenson Agency: "The Princess and the Tin Box" from *The Beast in Me and Other Animals* by James Thurber. Copyright © 1948 by James Thurber; copyright renewed © 1976 by Helen Thurber and Rosemary A. Thurber. All rights reserved.

Time Inc.: "Jackie Robinson" by Henry Aaron from *American Legends: From the Time 100.* Copyright © 2001 by Time Inc.

Charles E. Tuttle Co., Inc., Boston, MA and Tokyo, Japan: "The old pond" by Matsuo Bashō, "A morning glory" by Chiyo, and "A dragonfly!" by Kobayashi Issa from *Zen Art for Meditation* by Stewart W. Holmes and Chimoyo Horioka. Copyright in Japan © 1973 by Charles E. Tuttle Co., Inc. All rights reserved.

The University of Georgia Press: Slight adaptation of "American History" from *The Latin Deli: Prose and Poetry* by Judith Ortiz Cofer. Copyright © 1993 by Judith Ortiz Cofer.

The University of North Carolina Press: From "Ain't I a Woman?" by Sojourner Truth, adapted by Erlene Stetson, from *Sojourner Truth: God's Faithful Pilgrim* by Arthur Huff Fauset. Copyright © 1938 by The University of North Carolina Press.

University Press of New England: "The Grandfather" from *A Summer Life* by Gary Soto. Copyright © 1990 by University Press of New England.

Suzanne Vega: Lyrics from "Calypso" from *Solitude Standing* by Suzanne Vega. Copyright © 1978 by Suzanne Vega.

Viking Penguin, a division of Penguin Putnam Inc.: "I May, I Might, I Must" from *The Complete Poems of Marianne Moore*. Copyright © 1959 by Marianne Moore; copyright renewed © 1987 by Lawrence E. Brinn and Louise Crane, Executors of the Estate of Marianne Moore.

The Wall Street Journal: From "Juliet of Verona Gets a Lot of Letters from the Lovelorn" by Lisa Bannon from *The Wall Street Journal*, November 10, 1992. Copyright © 1992 by Dow Jones & Company, Inc. All rights reserved worldwide.

Weekly Reader Corporation: From "Community Service & You" by T. J. Saftner from *Career World*, September 1998. Copyright © 1998 by Weekly Reader Corporation. All rights reserved.

Wesleyan University Press: "The Base Stealer" from *Robert Francis: Collected Poems, 1936–1976*. Copyright © 1960 by Robert Francis. "A Blessing" from *The Branch Will Not Break* by James Wright. Copyright © 1963 by James Wright.

Wiley Publishing, Inc.: Entry for "indulge" and pronunciation key from *Webster's New World™ College Dictionary, Fourth Edition*. Copyright © 1999, 2000 by Wiley Publishing, Inc. All rights reserved.

World Book, Inc.: From "John Fitzgerald Kennedy" by Eric Sevareid from *The World Book Encyclopedia*, vol. 11, pp. 266–268. Copyright © 2001 by World Book, Inc., www.worldbook.com.

Sources Cited

Quote by Brenda Platt from "Is recycling a waste?" by Mark Fearer from *Colorado's Holistic Journal* Web site, accessed January 31, 2002 at http://www.nexuspub.com/july97/recycle.htm.

Quote by Bridie Murphy from *Children of "The Troubles": Our Lives in the Crossfire of Northern Ireland* by Laurel Holliday. Published by Pocket Books, New York, 1997.

Quote by Truman Capote from "The Private World of Truman Capote" (Part I), an interview by Anne Taylor Fleming, from *The New York Times Magazine*, July 9, 1978. Published by The New York Times Company, New York, NY, 1978.

From "What is a mummy?" from *Mummies, Myth and Magic in Ancient Egypt* by Christine El Mahdy. Published by Thames & Hudson Ltd., London, 1989.

Picture Credits

The illustrations and/or photographs on the Contents pages are picked up from pages in the textbook. Credits for those can be found either on the textbook page on which they appear or in the listing below.

Page 5: © John Lund/Stone; **11:** © Julio Larraz; **13:** National Gallery, London/SuperStock; **15:** © Erich Lessing/Art Resource, NY; **21:** © John Lund/Stone; **23:** Brandt & Brandt Literary Agents, Inc.; **27:** © David Hosking/Photo Researchers, Inc.; **29:** © David E. Myers/Stone; **39:** AP Photo/Fiona Hanson; **40:** © Peter Beck/CORBIS/Stock Market; **44:** (top) STS-101 Crew/NASA; (bottom) NASA; **45:** STS-106 Crew/NASA; **53:** © Getty Images; **55:** Photo by: Kirk Eck; **61:** © Nancy Crampton; **65:** (top left) Cover from *The Hobbit*. Copyright © 1966 by J.R.R. Tolkien. Reprinted by permission of Houghton Mifflin Company, HarperCollins in Canada. All rights reserved; (top right) Cover art courtesy Paul Goble; (bottom left) Cover from *Apollo 13* by Jim Lovell and Jeffrey Kluger, reprinted by permission of Houghton Mifflin Company (Boston: Houghton Mifflin, 2000). All rights reserved; (bottom right) From *Woodsong* by Gary Paulsen, cover by Neil Waldman. Copyright © 1991 by Neil Waldman for cover illustration. Used by permission of Penguin Putnam, Inc.; **91:** © Henri Cartier-Bresson/Magnum Photos, Inc.; **97:** Mitsu Yasukawa/New York Daily News; **99:** © James A. Sugar/CORBIS; **101:** © Patty DiRienzo/Silver Image; **113:** Courtesy of Wendi Kaufman, care of Russell and Volkening; **127:** Charles S. Colier; **128:** Corel; **131:** (top left) *A Tree Grows in Brooklyn* by Betty Smith. HarperCollins Publishers; (top right) From *American Dragons: Twenty Five Asian American Voices* by Lawrence Yep. Jacket art by Kam Mak. Used by permission of HarperCollins Publishers; (bottom left) Jacket illustration from *Inside the Walls of Troy* © Joel Peter Johnson. Used by permission of Nancy Bruck; (bottom right) *Black Boy* by Richard Wright. Cover painting © David Diaz. HarperCollins Publishers; **149:** © cartoonbank.com; **164:** © Getty Images; **169:** Brown Brothers; **173:** © RB Studio/CORBIS/Stock Market; (background) © Francisco Hidalgo/Getty Images; **175:** © Mimmo Jodice/CORBIS; **176:** © RB Studio/CORBIS/Stock Market; **178:** © Scala/Art Resource, NY; **179:** © RB Studio/The Stock Market; **180:** © Bettmann/CORBIS; **188:** R. Krubner/H. Armstrong Roberts; **193:** (top left) Cover from *To Kill a Mockingbird* by Harper Lee. Used by permission of Warner Books, Inc.; (top right) Cover from *The Circuit* by Francisco Jimenez, courtesy University of New Mexico Press; (bottom left) *Frankenstein: Or the Modern Prometheus* by Mary Shelley. Cover © HRW, illustration by Cliff Nielsen; (bottom right) From *Chinese Cinderella* by Adeline Yan Mah. Used by permission of Dell Publishing, a division of Random House, Inc.; **212:** © Underwood & Underwood/CORBIS; **215:** © Walshe/Getty Images; **216:** © E. O. Hoppé/Mansell/TimePix; **220:** Roine Magnusson/Image Bank; **233:** © Bettmann/CORBIS; **237:** Corel; **238, 247:** © Getty Images; **248:** Corel; **251:** © Getty Images; **252:** © Theo Westenberger Photography; **253:** © Morton Beebe/CORBIS; **255:** © Tom Bean/CORBIS; **256–258:** (background) Corel; **262:** Richard Tompkins/Gamma Press USA, Inc.; **264:** New York Times; **265:** AP Photo/Ron Edmonds; **269:** (top left) Cover from *Year of Impossible Goodbyes* by Sook Myul Choi (Boston: Houghton Mifflin, 1991). Reprinted by permission of Houghton Mifflin Company. All rights reserved; (top right) *Things Fall Apart* by Chinua Achebe. Cover © HRW, art by Earl Keleny; (bottom left) University of Washington Press; (bottom right) *A Stillness in Appomattox* by Bruce Caton. Cover © HRW, photo by Andrew Yates, design by Will Hornaday; **285:** © cartoonbank.com; **293:** © Bettmann/CORBIS; **294:** Corel; **304:** © Getty Images; **309:** © Getty Images; **311:** Reuters/TimePix; **314–315:** Peter Lindstrom; **316:** © Tom Hollyman/Photo Researchers, Inc.; **317:** © Rob Atkins/Getty Images; **319:** (top left) *Holes* by Louis Sachar. Cover © HRW, art by Sally Vitsky/Artco LLC; (top right) *Fair Is Fair: World Folktales of Justice;* (bottom left) From the book *My World and Welcome To It:* copyright © 1940 by James Thurber. Copyright © renewed 1968 by Helen Thurber and Rosemary A. Thurber. Reprinted by permission arrangement with Rosemary A. Thurber and The Barbara Hogenson Agency. All rights reserved; (bottom right) *Barefoot Heart: Stories of a Migrant Child* by Elva Traviño Hart: © 1999. Cover design by John Wincek: Aerocraft Charter Art Service. Used by permission of Bilingüal Press/Editorial Bilingüe: Arizona State University: Tempe, Ariz.; **338:** David Heald © The Solomon R. Guggenheim Foundation: New York; **343:** © Margarette Mead/Getty Images; **344:** Corel; **348, 351:** © Getty Images; **353:** Corel; **355:** © Giraudon/Art Resource, NY; **359:** © Eric and David Hosking/CORBIS; **360:** © Craig Lovell/CORBIS; **361:** Courtesy of Gary Soto; **365:** ©Walter Bibkow/FPG; **366–367:** © Getty Images; Walter Bibkow/FPG; **369:** © Pete Turner/Image Bank; **370:** © Keren Su/Image Bank; **371, 375:** © Getty Images; **378:** © Getty Images; **380:** © Getty Images; **383:** (top left) *The Little Prince* by Antoine de Saint-Exupéry. Cover illustration © 1943 by Harcourt: renewed 1971 by Consuelo de Saint-Exupéry. Used by permission of Harcourt, Inc.; (top right) *The Chosen* by Chaim Potok. Cover © HRW, illustration by Phillip Dvorak/Chip Caton Represents; (bottom left) *Death Be Not Proud;* (bottom right) From *Living Up the Street* (jacket cover) by Gary Soto: text © 1985 by Gary Soto. Cover art © 1985 by Carmen Lomas Garza. Used by permission of Random House Children's Books, a division of Random House, Inc.; **404–405:** Yva Momatiuk/John Eastcott/Miden Pictures; **406:** Wesleyan University Press; **407:** E. R. Degginger/Photo Researchers, Inc.; **408–409:** © Getty Images; **411:** (top) © Nancy Crampton; (bottom) Photo by Michael Nye; **413:** © Bettmann/CORBIS; **414:** (composite) © Craig Hammell/CORBIS/Stock Market; Mark A. Johnson/The Stock Market; © Getty Images; **415:** © AP Photos; **419:** Photograph © 1982 The Metropolitan Museum of Art; **421:** © Seattle Art Museum/CORBIS; **422:** © Getty Images; **423:** © Douglas Peebles/CORBIS; **425:** © Tim Page/CORBIS; **430:** © Alex Buckingham/Getty Images; **432–433:** Tim Turner/FoodPix; **433:** Copyright © 2001 Eric Chang; **436–437:** © Getty Images; **440:** © Massimo Mastrorillo/CORBIS/Stock Market; **441:** Bridgeman Art Library; **442:** (top) © Guy Gillette/Photo Researchers, Inc.; (bottom) © E. O. Hoppé/CORBIS; **445:** Photograph © 1999 The Metropolitan Museum of Art; **448:** © 2002 Roland L. Freeman; **449:** © Penni Gladstone/CORBIS/Outline; **450–451:** © Marcie Jan Bronstein/nonstock; **452:** © Oscar White/CORBIS; **456:** "Poetry in Motion" poster reprinted by permission of the New York City Transit Authority. All rights reserved; **459–460:** © Getty Images; **462:** © CORBIS;

Illustrations

Maps

Index of Skills

The boldface page numbers indicate an extensive treatment of the topic.

LITERARY SKILLS

Actions, **85**
Allegory, **341, 364,** 372, 394–397, **1019**
Alliteration, **456,** 471, **475,** 478, 492, 843, **1019,** 1024
Allusion, **104,** 114, 453, **1019**
Alter ego, 644
Ambiguity, **284–285, 297,** 305, **1019**
Analysis questions (Interpretations), 24, 41, 63, 94, 114, 129, 157, 170, 181, 217, 228, 253, 259, 266, 295, 305, 318, 356, 362, 372, 407, 412, 416, 421, 427, 431, 434, 439, 443, 446, 449, 453, 460, 462, 467, 471, 474, 478, 514, 539, 546, 575, 607, 687, 713, 731, 774, 816, 843, 874, 893, 912
Anapest, **455**
Antagonist, 116, 1028
Apostrophe, 412
Approximate rhyme, **454,** 456, 462, **1029**
Archetype, **726**
Aside, **754,** 789, 822, 843, 868, 899, **1020**
Assonance, **1020**
Atmosphere, **48.** *See also* Mood.
Audience, 752, 753, 754, 755, 778, 779, 780, 843
Autobiography, 1020, 1026
Ballad, **463,** 467, **1020**
Basic situation, **2,** 1027
Biographical approach, **562–563**
Biography, **1020,** 1026
Blank verse, **781,** 830, **1020**
Catalog poem, **408,** 412
Character, 41, **48,** 63, **84–85,** 114, 140–143, 157, **209,** 217, **220,** 228, 253, 295, 305, 334, 372, 397, 575, 607, **1020–1021**
  actions of, **85**
  appearance and, **84–85**
  comic, 843
  dialogue and, **84, 86,** 94, 143, 816
  dramatic monologue and, **84,** 92, 94, **1022**
  dynamic/static, **117,** 874, 1021
  flat/round, **117,** 1021
  foil, 807, 816, **1024**
  in drama, **752–754, 783,** 843, 893, 941
  interactions, **116–117**
  main, 607, **783**
  motivations of. *See* Motivation.
  other characters' response to, **85**
  private thoughts and, **85**
  soliloquy and. *See* Soliloquy.
  speech and, **84**
  subordinate, **116,** 129, 649, 1021
  traits, 94, **104,** 114, 143, 181, **689,** 713
  types, 755
Character foil, 807, 816, **1024**
Characterization, 41, 142, 170, 266, 305, 362, **1020–1021**
  direct/indirect, **85,** 1021
Chronological order, **3, 32,** 41
Climax, **2,** 752, 774, **783,** 912, 1021, 1027
Comedy, **752–753, 755,** 783, 838, 874, 941, **1021,** 1022
Comic relief, **1021**
  elements, 816
  scenes, 801
Compare and contrast, 546, 731
  characters, 24
  poems, 439, 443
  theme across genres, **244,** 278–279
  themes, **210**
Complication, **2, 753,** 816, 874, 893, 1027
Conflict, **2, 116, 118,** 121, 126, **209, 211,** 372, 539, 575, **590,** 607, 687, **752, 753, 755,** 774, 816, **1021,** 1027
  external, **2, 116, 117, 118,** 129, 142, 217, **649,** 687, **1021**
  internal, **2,** 41, **116, 117, 118,** 129, 142, 217, 228, **1021**
Connotation, **260, 363, 436,** 439, 525, **540, 924, 1021,** 1022
Contradiction, 295, **314,** 318, 794
Contrast, 295, 421, 774
Costumes, **754**
Couplet, 422, **781, 1021–1022,** 1030
Crisis, **783**
Dactyl, **455**
Denotation, **260, 363, 436, 540, 924,** 1021
Denouement, **2, 783,** 1027
Details, **50,** 53, 54, 56, 57, 59, 63, **342,** 345, 350, 352, 354, 356
Dialect, **525,** 539, **1022**
Dialogue, **84, 86,** 94, 143, **754,** 816, 859, 877, 912, **1022**
Diction, 149, 172, **436,** 439, 447, **496, 525,** 539, **541,** 546, 557, **1022**

Direct characterization, **85**
Direct metaphor, **429, 440**
Drama, **752–754,** 938–941, 1022
  aside, **754,** 789, 822, 843, 868, 899
  comedy, **752–753, 755,** 783, 838, 874, 941
  dialogue, **754,** 816, 859, 877, 912, 1022
  modern, **753**
  monologue, 444, 446, **754,** 807, 822, 824, 907, 912
  scene design, **753–754, 778–780,** 820, 843, 941, 1029
  soliloquy, **84, 754,** 820, 822, 827, 838, 853, 883, 902, 912, 941, **1030**
  stage, 753
  stage direction, **754,** 783, 788, 790, 804, 809, 810, 818, 822, 846, 847, 848, 850, 852, 865, 904
  See also Tragedy.
Dramatic irony, **284,** 467, 713, 843, 863, 893, 912, **1025**
Dramatic monologue, **84,** 92, 94, **1022**
Dynamic character, **117,** 874
End rhyme, **454, 461,** 467, **1029**
End-stopped line, in poetry, **432,** 434, **782**
English sonnet, 422, 427
Epic, **640–646,** 1023
Epic simile, **645–646, 688**
Epithet, **715, 1023**
Evaluation questions, 24, 41, 63, 94, 114, 129, 157, 170, 181, 217, 228, 253, 259, 266, 295, 305, 318, 356, 362, 372, 407, 471, 514, 687, 713, 774, 816, 843, 874, 893, 912
Exact rhyme, **454,** 456
Exposition, **2,** 774, **783,** 1023, 1027
Extended metaphor, **435,** 439, **444,** 446
External conflict, **2, 116,** 117, **118,** 129, 142, 217, **649,** 687
Fable, 1023
Falling action, **783**
Farce, **755,** 774
Figures of speech, 59, **130, 357, 428–429,** 434, **440,** 496, 498, 500, 514, **525,** 539, **688,** 820, 843, **914–915,** 1023
  personification, 372, **429, 450,** 453, 460, **914,** 915, **1027**
  pun, **914,** 915, 1023, **1028**
  simile, **130, 255,** 259, **357, 428,** 429, **430,** 431, **432,** 439, 440, 446, 460, 462, 478, 492, 557, 731, **914–915,** 1023, **1030**
  See also Metaphor.

First-person narrator, **84, 148, 172,** 203, **1028**
Flashback, **3, 32, 41,** 228, **1023**
Flash-forward, **3,** 1024
Flat character, **117**
Folk ballad, 463, 1020
Folk tale, **1024**
Foot, poetic, **455**
Foreshadowing, **3, 4,** 24, 41, 687, 816, 843, 853, 854, **1024**
Free verse, **455, 468,** 471, 1024
Generalization, 208
Genres, 208, 266, 279, 1024
  theme across, **244**
Graphic organizers
  character chart, 85, 94, 816
  conflict chart, 117
  image chart, 407, 546
  metaphor chart, 443
  plot diagram, 3
  setting chart, 49
  story map, 24, 157, 259
  theme chart, 209, 210, 244
  tragedy web, 912
  Venn diagram, 24
Haiku, **418, 421, 1024**
Historical setting, 449, **562–563, 564,** 575, **590,** 607
Homeric simile, **645–646, 688,** 713
Hyperbole, 1024
Iamb, **422, 455,** 1024
Iambic pentameter, **422, 781, 1024**
Imagery, **49,** 57, 362, **402–403, 404,** 407, 412, **413,** 416, 418, 421, 431, 434, 446, 471, 491, 498, 514, 541, 546, 653, 731, 802, 820, 827, 843, **1025**
Implied metaphor, **429, 440,** 449, 492
Indirect characterization, **85**
Internal conflict, **2,** 41, **116,** 117, **118,** 129, 142, 217, 228
Internal rhyme, **454,** 1024, **1029**
Inversion, **1025**
Irony, 157, 170, 181, 217, **284–285,** 295, 332–335, 453, 467, 478, 886, 912, **1025**
  dramatic, **284,** 467, 713, 843, 863, 893, 912, **1025**
  situational, **284, 286,** 295, 713, **1025**
  verbal, **284,** 285, 305, 318, **1025**
Italian sonnet, 422, 427, 1030
Lighting, in scene design, **753–754**
Literary ballad, 463, 467, 1020
Literary criticism, 94, 514, 539, 546, 556–557
Lyric poem, **424,** 427, 462, **1025**
Main character, 607
Main events, 94, 295, 575
Main idea, **244,** 261, 266, **358,** 362
  implied, 358
Metaphor, **130, 255,** 259, **428–429, 432,** 435, 439, 443, 446, 462, 471, 474, 492, **914,** 915, 1023, **1025**
  dead, 1025
  direct, **429, 440**

extended, **435, 439, 444,** 446, 1025
implied, **429, 440,** 449, 492, **914,** 1025
mixed, 1025
Meter, **454–455,** 457, 460, **1026,** 1029
  iambic pentameter, **422, 781, 1024**
Monologue, 444, 446, **754,** 807, 822, 824, 907, 912
Mood, **48,** 50, 53, 63, 259, **497, 498,** 514, 539, 557, 1021, **1026**
Moral, 157, 397
Motivation, **116–117,** 118, 121, 123, 125, 126, 129, 143, 181, **220,** 224, 225, 227, 228, **297,** 300, 301, 302, 304, 305, 372, 843, 1021
Myths, 416, **644, 726–727,** 731, **1026**
Narration, **1026**
Narrative poem, 255
Narrator, 41, 143, **148–149,** 202–203, 539, **1026**
  credible, **148**
  first-person, **84, 148, 172,** 203, **1028**
  omniscient, **148, 150,** 157, **1028**
  persona, 148, **172,** 181, **1027**
  third-person-limited point of view, **148–149, 159,** 170, **1028**
  unreliable, **148, 172,** 181
News feature, **261**
News report, **261**
Novel, **1027**
Octave, 422, 1030
Omniscient narrator, **148, 150,** 157, **1028**
Onomatopoeia, **456, 475,** 478, 1024, 1025, **1027**
Paradox, **1027**
Pentameter, 422
Persona, 148, 172, 181, **472,** 474, **1027**
Personification, 372, **429, 450,** 453, 460, **914,** 915, 1023, **1027**
Petrarchan sonnet, 422, 1030
Play, **752.** *See also* Drama.
Plot, **2–3,** 24, 157, **1027**
  basic situation, **2,** 1027
  climax, **2,** 752, 774, **783,** 912, 1021, 1027
  complication, **2, 753,** 816, 874, 893, 1027
  denouement, **2, 783**
  drama and, **752–753, 783**
  exposition, **2,** 774, **783,** 1023, 1027
  resolution, **2,** 687, **783,** 1027
  See also Character, Conflict, Time and sequence.
Poetry, **1028**
  alliteration, **456,** 471, **475,** 478, 492, 843, 1024
  ballad, **463,** 467
  catalog poem, **408,** 412
  comparing, 439, 443
  epic, **640–641, 645–646**
  figures of speech, **428–429,** 492
  free verse, **455, 468,** 471
  haiku, **418,** 421, **1024**
  imagery, **402–403,** 491, **1025**
  lyric poem, **424,** 427, 462

narrative poem, **255**
onomatopoeia, **456, 475,** 478, 1024, 1025, **1027**
  reading a poem, **432,** 434
  rhythm, **454–455,** 457, 463, 467, **468,** 1025, **1029**
  sonnet, 422, 427, 813, 830, **1030**
  sound devices, **454–456**
  See also Meter, Rhyme.
Point of view, **148–149,** 170, 203, **1028**
  first person, **84, 148, 172,** 203, **1028**
  omniscient, **148, 150,** 157, **1028**
  third person limited, **148–149, 159,** 170, **1028**
  See also Narrator.
Props, **754,** 1029
Proscenium stage, 779
Protagonist, **116, 1028**
Pun, **914,** 915, **1028**
Purpose, author's, **244,** 514
Quatrain, 1030
Reading Comprehension (Reading Check), 24, 41, 63, 94, 114, 129, 157, 170, 181, 217, 228, 253, 259, 266, 295, 305, 356, 362, 372, 407, 412, 416, 421, 427, 431, 434, 439, 443, 446, 449, 453, 460, 462, 467, 471, 474, 478, 514, 539, 546, 575, 607, 687, 713, 731, 774, 816, 843, 874, 893, 912
Reading Comprehension (Test Practice), 140–143, 202–203, 278–279, 332–335, 394–397, 490–492, 556–557, 938–941
Refrain, 463, 1024, **1028**
Resolution, **2,** 687, **783,** 1027
Rhapsodes, **645**
Rhyme, **454,** 456, **461,** 463, 843, 1025, **1029**
  approximate, **454,** 456, 462, **1029**
  end, **454, 461,** 467, **1029**
  exact, **454,** 456
  internal, **454,** 1024, **1029**
  rhyme scheme, **454, 461,** 462, 830, **1029**
Rhythm, **454–455,** 457, 463, 467, **468,** 1025, **1029**
Rising action, **783**
Round characters, **117**
Run-on line, in poetry, **432,** 434, **782**
Satire, 774, **1029**
Scanning, of poetry, **455,** 457, 460, 1026
Scene design, **753–754, 778–780,** 820, 843, 941, 1029
Sensory details, **50,** 63
Sentence structure, 471, **475,** 478, 496, 525
Sestet, 422, 1030
Set. *See* Scene design.
Setting, **48–49, 50,** 63, 94, 129, 181, 228, 253, 259, 407, 416, **498,** 514, 575, **1029–1030**
Shakespearean sonnet, 422, 1030
Short story, 1030

Simile, **130, 255,** 259, **357, 428,** 429, **430,** 431, **432,** 439, 440, 446, 460, 462, 478, 492, 557, 731, **914,** 915, 1023, **1030**
Situational irony, **284, 286,** 295, 713, **1025**
Soliloquy, **84, 754,** 820, 822, 827, 838, 853, 883, 902, 912, 941, **1030**
Sonnet, **422,** 427, 813, 830, **1030**
Speaker, 460, 471, **472,** 474, 491, **1030**
Spondee, **455**
Stage. *See Scene design.*
Stage direction, **754,** 783, 788, 790, 804, 809, 810, 818, 822, 846, 847, 848, 850, 852, 865, 904
Staging the Play, 783, 787, 788, 789, 790, 791, 793, 795, 797, 798, 799, 800, 801, 802, 804, 805, 807, 809, 810, 813, 814, 818, 819, 820, 822, 823, 824, 826, 827, 829, 830, 831, 832, 833, 835, 836, 837, 838, 839, 840, 841, 845, 846, 847, 848, 850, 852, 853, 854, 855, 857, 860, 861, 863, 864, 865, 867, 868, 869, 870, 871, 872, 873, 877, 878, 880, 883, 886, 887, 891, 895, 896, 897, 899, 900, 901, 902, 903, 904, 906, 907, 910
Stanza, **1030**
Static character, **117**
Stereotype, 755
Story map. *See Graphic organizers.*
Style, **496–497, 498,** 500, 505, 514, **525,** 539, **541,** 556–557, 1022, 1030–1031
Subject, of literary work, 208
Subordinate character, **116,** 129, 649
Subtlety, 305, 1019
Surprise ending, **150,** 217, 286, 295
Suspense, 607, 874, 893, **1031**
Symbol, 228, 318, **340–341, 342,** 356, **358,** 362, 394–397, 439, 713, **1031**
Tall tale, 1031
Theme, 41, 114, **208–209, 211,** 217, **220,** 228, **245,** 253, **255,** 259, 266, 335, 356, 372, 397, 497, 514, 539, 546, 557, **564,** 575, 912, **1031**
across genres, **208, 244,** 278–279
comparing, **210, 244**
universal, **208, 210,** 1031
Third-person-limited point of view, **148–149, 159,** 170, **1028**
Time and sequence
chronological order, **3, 32,** 41
flashback, **3, 32,** 41, 228, **1023**
flash-forward, **3,** 1024
foreshadowing, **3, 4,** 24, 41, 687, 816, 843, 853, 854, **1024**
Title, 4, 24, 41, **209, 245,** 253, 295, 407, 514, 575, 607
Tone, **48, 149,** 157, 170, 172, 181, 203, 259, 305, 318, 335, 362, 397, 407, 412, **447,** 449, 471, **472,** 474, 492, **497, 541,** 546, 557, 1021, **1031**

Tragedy, **752–753, 783,** 816, 843, 874, 893, 912, 941, 1021, 1022, **1031**
Tragic flaw, **752**
Tragic hero, **752**
Trochee, **455**
Turning point, **783,** 874
Unreliable narrator, **148, 172,** 181
Venn diagram. *See Graphic organizers.*
Verbal irony, **284,** 285, 305, 318, **1025**
Voice, **149, 172,** 181, 202–203, **472,** 474, **1031**

INFORMATIONAL READING SKILLS

Accuracy, 579
Alphabetical sequence, 961
Analogy, 308, **1019**
Analyzing, 30, 47, 76–79, **96,** 99, 100, 102, 191–192, 242–243, 312, 377, 381–382, 523–524, 583, 584, 585, 587, 588–589, 632–635, 724, 744–747, 923, 951, 954, 958, 969
functional workplace documents, **959–964**
sources, **578–579**
Web site, **962**
workplace documents, **961**
Anecdote, 308, 309, 516, **718,** 724, 747, 1020, 1033
Argument, **308–309, 516–517, 718,** 744–747, 1033
claim, **308,** 311, 312, **516,** 518, 521, 522, 523, 524, 724, 1033, **1034,** 1039
credibility, **308–309,** 312, **516–517,** 524, **1035**
evidence, **308,** 311, 312, **516–517,** 518, 522, 524, 1035, **1036**
fallacies, logical, **516, 1037**
generalization, **308,** 310, 516, 520, 1034
intent, author's, **309, 517,** 520, 523, 524, **718,** 724, 747, 1035
logical appeals, **308, 516,** 718, 1033
opposing, **516–517,** 521
tone, author's, 309, 312, **517,** 523, **718,** 724, 747, 1035
See also Emotional appeals.
Attacking the person, 516
Audience, 99, **231,** 374, **578,** 579, 588
Autobiography, 1020, 1026
Begging the question, **1037**
Bias, 579
Bibliography, 96
Biography, **1020,** 1026
Browser, 952, **953**
Business letter, 946, **970–973**
Call to action, 517, 520
Cause and effect, 517, **1033,** 1044
false, 516, **1037**
Chronological sequence, 961, 1034, **1044**
Circular reasoning, 516, 1037
Citing Internet sources, **955–957**

Claim, **308,** 311, 312, **516,** 518, 521, 522, 523, 524, 724, 1033, **1034,** 1039
Compare and contrast, 183, 191, 192, **231, 374,** 517, **918,** 951, 1034, 1044
Computer games, developing, **946**
Conclusions, drawing, 192, 231, 243
Connecting to the Literature, 26, 43, 96, 183, 231, 309, 374, 517, 579, 718, 918
Connections, making, 183, 231, 243, 374, 382, **918**
Consumer documents, 946, 947, **948–950,** 978, **1034–1035**
citing, **955–957**
Contract, 948, 959
Copyright, 959
Credibility, **308–309,** 312, **516–517,** 524, **579, 1035**
Design elements, 961
Either/or fallacy, **1037**
Elaborating, **96,** 98, 102, **579,** 589
Emotional appeals, **308,** 309, 516, 518, 524, **718,** 1033
anecdote, 308, 309, 516, **718,** 724, 747, 1020, 1033
loaded words, 308, 309, 312, 516, 518, **718,** 724, 747, 1033
Essay, 1023
Evaluating, 98, 102, 580, 582, 588, 635
argument, **308–309,** 310, 311, 312, **516–517,** 518, 520, 521, 522, 524, **718,** 724, 744–747
functional documents, **965–969**
sources, **96, 579**
Evidence, 183, 191, **308,** 311, 312, **516–517,** 518, 522, 524, 1035, **1036**
Extending information, 589
Facts, 96, 100, 231, 308, 516, **579,** 582, 589, 747, 1040
Fallacies, logical, **516, 1037**
False cause and effect, 516
5W-How? questions, 26
Format, of documents, **961,** 964
Functional documents, 959, **961, 965,** 969
Generalization, **308,** 310, 520, 1034, **1037–1038**
hasty, 516, **1037**
Graphic elements, 961, 964
Graphic organizers
evaluating-arguments chart, 309, 517, 524
KWL chart, 26
main idea chart, 183
Graphs, **1038**
Hasty generalization, 516, **1037**
Header, 961, 964
Icon, as Web link, 43, 46
Informative texts, **1038**
Instruction manual, 948, 954
Intent, author's, **309, 517,** 520, 523, 524, **718,** 724, 747, 1035. *See also* Purpose.

Word families, **243**
Word origins. *See Derivations.*

READING SKILLS

comparison of a play and a film, 933
of description of a place, 391
persuasion with cause and effect, 741
persuasive essay, 327
research paper, 629
short story, 139
Reformulation, text, 439
Relevant evidence, 322
Repetition, 471, 481
Reply to letter, 973
Report, 102
Request, 973
Research, 731
Research paper, 607, **610–629**
documenting sources for a, 619–620
evaluating and revising, 627–628
evaluating sources for a, 613–614
finding sources for a, 612–613
forming a research question for a, 611
identifying purpose and audience for a, 611–612
integrating quotations for a, 621
organizing information and developing an outline for a, 617–619
peer review of, 627
preparing source cards for a, 614–615
prewriting, 610–621
proofreading, 629
publishing, 629
reflecting on writing, 629
selecting a topic for a, 610
taking notes for a, 615–616
writer's framework, 622
writer's model, 622–626
writing first draft of, 622–626
writing a thesis statement for a, 617
Research question, 611
Research report, 183
Resolution, 133
Resources, 612
Response
to expository text, 1014
to literature, 1013
Revising. See The Writer's Language, 1004
analysis of nonfiction, 199–200
analysis of a poem, 485–486
analysis of a short story, 553–554
autobiographical narrative, 71–72
comparison of media coverage, 275–276
comparison of a play and a film, 931–932
description of a place, 389–390
essay, 268
to improve style, 1001
persuasion with cause and effect, 739–740
persuasive essay, 325–326
research paper, 627–628
short story, 137–138
Rewriting
in another genre, 266
passages with comparisons, 357

sentences, 95, 219, 254, 267, 296
verb tenses, 64
Rhetorical devices, 321, 736
Rhyme, 481
Rhythm, 471, 481
Rising action, 133
Road poem, 318
Scenario, 616, 998
Scene, 356
Scene design, 774, 843
Screenplay, 683
Searching your memory for experiences for autobiographical narrative, 66
Secondary source, 612
Selecting
a news event for comparison of media coverage, 270
a topic for a research paper, 610
Sensory details, 63, 67, 134, 356, 385, 546, 998, 1001
Sensory images, 407
Sentence structure, 478
Sequel, 24, 305
ambiguous, 305
Sequence of events, 66
Sequence of information, 271
Set, 754
Setting, 132, 134, 195, 548, 927
Shifting perspectives, 134
Shifting vantage points, 385
Short story, **132–139**
evaluating and revising, 137–138
finding a story idea for, 132
peer review of, 137
planning, 132–134
prewriting, 132–134
proofreading, 139
publishing, 139
reflecting on writing, 139
writer's framework, 135
writer's model, 135–136
writing first draft of, 135–136
Significance, 66
Significant ideas, 482, 548
Simile, 431, 481, 549
Small caps, 1004
Smooth organization, 322
Sonnet, 874
Sound, 927, 928
Sound devices, 481
Source cards, 614–615
Sources, citing, 322
Spatial organization, 386, 999
Speaker, 480
Special effects, 927
Speech, 181, 183, 228
Stage directions, 754, 774
Stages of the writing process, 995
Statement of argument, 170
Stating your controlling impression for description of a place, 386
Statistic, 998
Story, brief, 114
Story plan, 714

Style, 416, 497, 539, 740, 932, 970, 973, 1001
chart, 539
Stylistic devices, 481, 549
Subheading, 618, 1003
Subjective description, 384
Summarizing, 115, 194, 217, 243, 550, 615, 714, 874, 974, 977
Summarizing-acts graphic, 913
Supporting character, 133
Supporting sentence, 997, 998
Supporting your thesis statement for analysis of a short story, 550
Surprise ending, 157
Symbolism, 549
Symbolic meanings, 362
Synthesizing, 611, 621, 923
Taking notes for a research paper, 615–616
Telephone interview, recording source information for, 615
Television program, recording source information for, 615
Test practice, 81, 145, 205, 281, 337, 399, 493, 559, 637, 749, 943
Test Smarts
biographical narrative, 1015
expository composition, 1016
multiple-choice writing questions, 1011–1012
persuasive composition, 1017
response to expository text, 1014
response to literature, 1013
Text reformulation, 439
Thank-you letter, 970
Theme, 132, 134, 453, 480, 549, 927
Thesis, 272, 617, 928
Thesis statement, 196, 230, 268, 272, 481, 549, 928
Think sheet, 71, 137, 138, 389, 931
Third-person limited point of view, 356
Third-person omniscient narrator, 134
Time line, 191, 1006
Title, 431, 1004
Tone, 296, 384, 453, 480, 486, 617, 970, 1001
formal, 617
Topic sentence, 997
Transitional words and phrases, 276, 1034
Unity, 999
Uppercase, 1003
Vantage points, shifting, 385
Video, recording source information for, 615
Visuals and graphics, 1004
Vivid action verbs, 138
Vocabulary, appropriate, 970, 973
Voice, 181
Web, 612
Web page, 391
Web site, 555, 610
Word choice, 416, 1001

INDEPENDENT READING

Index of Art

Index of Authors and Titles

For permission to reprint copyrighted material, grateful acknowledgment is made to the following sources:

Fitzhenry & Whiteside, Markham, Ontario: From "Romeo and Juliet" from *Northrop Frye on Shakespeare,* edited by Robert Sandler. Copyright © 1986 by Northrop Frye.

The Gale Group: Quote by Ray Bradbury from an interview with David Morgen from *Ray Bradbury* by David Morgen. Copyright © 1986 by Twayne Publishers. All rights reserved. From "Eugenia W. Collier" from *Contemporary Authors,* vol. 49–52, edited by Clare D. Kinsman. Copyright © 1975 by Gale Research Company. All rights reserved.

Modern Language Association: From "The Brevity of Friar Laurence" by Bertrand Evans from *PMLA,* LXV, 1950. Copyright © 1950 by the Modern Language Association of America.

Oxford University Press: From "William Shakespeare" by Philip Edwards from *The Oxford Illustrated History of English Literature,* edited by Pat Rogers. Copyright © 1987 by Oxford University Press.

Shakespeare Bulletin: From a review by Justin Shaltz of the *Romeo and Juliet* production at the Illinois Shakespeare Festival, 1994, from *Shakespeare Bulletin,* vol. 12.4, Fall 1994. Copyright © 1994 by Shakespeare Bulletin.

Simon & Schuster Books for Young Readers, an imprint of Simon & Schuster Children's Publishing Division: From Foreword by Lois Duncan from *Trapped! Cages of Mind and Body,* edited by Lois Duncan. Copyright © 1998 by Lois Duncan.

Stanford University Press: From *Bashō and His Interpreters: Selected Hokku with Commentary* by Makoto Ueda. Copyright © 1992 by the Board of Trustees of the Leland Stanford Junior University. All rights reserved.

Sources Cited
From *An Introduction to Shakespeare* by Marchette Chute. Published by E. P. Dutton and Company, Inc., New York, 1951.

Quote by Julia Alvarez from *Contemporary Literary Criticism,* vol. 93, edited by Brigham Narins, et al. Published by Gale Research, Inc., Detroit, MI, 1996.

Quote by Edmund Wilson from *James Thurber: His Life and Times* by Harrison Kinney. Published by Henry Holt and Company, Inc., New York, 1995.

From *The Letters of Robert Frost to Louis Untermeyer.* Published by Holt, Rinehart and Winston, New York, 1963.

Quote by John Barton from "Speaking Shakespeare" by John Lair from *The New Yorker,* vol. LXXIV, no. 26, September 7, 1998.

From *Shakespeare: The Invention of the Human* by Harold Bloom. Published by Riverhead Books, New York, 1998.

From *Everyday Use* by Alice Walker, edited by Barbara T. Christian. Published by Rutgers University Press, New Brunswick, NJ, 1994.

From *O. Henry: A Biography of William Sydney Porter* by David Stuart. Published by Scarborough House, Chelsea, MI, 1990.

From "Romeo and Juliet" from *Shakespeare's Tragedies* by Phyllis Rackin. Published by Frederick Ungar Publishing Company, New York, 1978.